INGENIX®

2009 ICD-9-CM Expert for Physicians, Volumes 1 & 2

ISBN: 978-1-60151-124-9
Item Number: IPS09
Available: September 2008
Price: $95.95

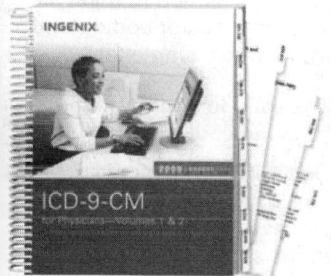

ISBN: 978-1-60151-125-6
Item Number: IPT09
Available: September 2008
Price: $99.95

em Number: 3534
vailable: Now
rice: $169.95

ICD-9-CM Resources That Makes You the Expert.

Why settle for anything less than the best? Our experts add valuable resources and track regulatory and coding changes to bring you a top-notch code reference that meets all your needs. This *Expert* choice helps you comply with HIPAA, stay current with changes and work smarter.

← **Comprehensive integration of coding and reimbursement edits**

← **Designed and edited by staff of experts**

← **Attention to detail creates a premium resource**

Key Features and Benefits

Our experts add valuable resources and track regulatory and coding changes to bring you the *2009 ICD-9-CM Expert for Physicians, Volumes 1 & 2* with critical coding and reimbursement edit alerts on one page. This expert choice helps you to comply with HIPAA, stay current with changes and work smarter.

- **IngenixEdge®—New Format Available!** All the hallmark features of the Expert editions — Plus a set of Exclusive Snap-in tabs featuring detailed new code information by chapter to make training and referencing the code changes a snap.

- **IngenixEdge®—Coding tables.** Simplify coding for complex diagnoses that require additional research and the steps to reduce time spent on code selection for improved accuracy.

- **IngenixEdge®—Valid three-digit code list.** Know at a glance whether a code is valid for claim submission, reducing denied claims due to invalid code usage.

- **IngenixEdge®—Intuitive Color-Coded Symbols and Alerts.** Quickly identify critical coding and reimbursement issues.

- **IngenixEdge®—Email alerts for special reports.** Stay current with the latest regulatory and ICD-9-CM code changes with notification of crucial information posted on our website.

- **IngenixEdge®—V Code Sequencing Restriction Alerts and Additional Digit Required Symbols.**

- **Plus all the features of the** *Professional* **version.**

ngenix | Intelligence for Health Care | Call toll-free 1.800.INGENIX (464.3649), option 1.

0% Money Back Guarantee If our merchandise ever fails to meet your expectations, please contact our Customer Service Department l-free at 1.800.INGENIX (464.3649), option 1, for an immediate response. Software: Credit will be granted for unopened packages only.

so available from your medical bookstore or distributor.

FOBA09

INGENIX®

2009 ICD-9-CM Expert for Hospitals, Volumes 1, 2 & 3

ISBN 978-1-60151-129-4
Item Number: IHS09
Available: September 2008
Price: $99.95

Item Number: 3539
Available: Now
Price: $174.95

SAVE UP TO 20%

with source code FOBAW9

 Visit **www.shopingenix.com** and enter the source code in the lower right-hand corner and save 20%.

 Call toll-free **1.800.INGENIX** (464.3649), option 1 and save 15%.

Dependable ICD-9-CM Coding for Hospitals Starts Here.

Our experts add valuable resources and track regulatory and coding changes to provide a premier code reference that meets your needs. This expert choice is designed to increase coding accuracy and work efficiency by having the code, definitions, illustrations, Medicare code edits—all the critical information on the same page as the code selected.

← **Comprehensive integration of coding and reimbursement edits**

← **Designed and edited by staff of experts**

← **Attention to detail creates the premium resource.**

Key Features and Benefits

The 2009 *ICD-9-CM Expert for Hospitals, Volumes 1, 2 & 3,* is designed to meet all your professional coding needs. Work smarter with our hallmark color coding and intuitive symbols, and integrate coding and reimbursement into a single task.

- **New! IngenixEdge®—Code Changes 2009.** A detailed presentation of all the crucial information concerning the new codes for 2009 featured at the beginning of every chapter for convenient training and quick reference all year.

- **IngenixEdge®—Complete coverage of the MS-DRG system edits.** Exclusive color coding and symbols identify the major Medicare code edits under the new MS-DRG system for diagnoses and procedures.

- **New! IngenixEdge®—Hospital Acquired Condition (HAC) alert.**

- **IngenixEdge®—Present on Admission (POA) Tutorial with Source Documentation Guideline Table.**

- **IngenixEdge®—Email alerts for special reports.** Stay current with the latest regulatory and ICD-9-CM code changes with notification of crucial information posted on our website.

- **IngenixEdge®—Valid three-digit code list.** Know at a glance whether a three-digit code is valid for submitting a claim, improving coding accuracy.

- **IngenixEdge®—Pharmacological listings.** Link drug treatment with disease processes to identify complications and comorbidities that may affect DRG assignment, reducing the potential for "undercoding".

- **IngenixEdge®—Dx/MDC/DRG list.** Perform quick audits by knowing to which DRGs each diagnosis code groups under the MS-DRG system.

- **IngenixEdge®—CC and MCC condition symbol with principal diagnosis exclusions listed right with the code.** Quickly identify complications and comorbidities that affect MS-DRG assignment.

- **IngenixEdge®— MS-DRG Resources.** DRG Mapping Table linking previous CMS-DRG to new MS-DRGs, and complete list of all CC and MCC codes for quick reference.

- **Plus all the features of the *Profession[al]* version.**

Ingenix | Intelligence for Health Care | Call toll-free 1.800.INGENIX (464.3649), option 1.

INGENIX®

Four simple ways to place an order.

Call
1.800.ingenix (464.3649),
option 1. Mention source code
FOBA09 when ordering.

Mail
PO Box 27116
Salt Lake City, UT 84127-0116
With payment and/or
purchase order.

Fax
801.982.4033
With credit card information
and/or purchase order.

Click
www.shopingenix.com
*Save 20% when you order
online today—use source
code FOBAW9.*

ingenix *e*smart
ShopIngenix.com frequent buyer program

GET REWARDS FOR SHOPPING ONLINE!
To find out more, visit www.shopingenix.com

eSmart program available only to Ingenix customers
who are not part of Medallion, Gold Medallion or
Partner Accounts programs. You must be registered
at ShopIngenix.com to have your online purchases
tracked for rewards purposes. Shipping charges and
taxes still apply and cannot be used for rewards.
Offer valid online only.

100% Money Back Guarantee
If our merchandise* ever fails
to meet your expectations,
please contact our Customer
Service Department toll-free at
1.800.ingenix (464.3649), option 1
for an immediate response.

*Software: Credit will be granted for
unopened packages only.

Customer Service Hours
7:00 am - 5:00 pm Mountain Time
9:00 am - 7:00 pm Eastern Time

Shipping and Handling

no. of items	fee
1	$10.95
2-4	$12.95
5-7	$14.95
8-10	$19.95
11+	Call

Order Form

Information

Customer No. _____ Contact No. _____

Source Code _____

Contact Name _____

Title _____ Specialty _____

Company _____

Street Address _____
NO PO BOXES, PLEASE

City _____ State _____ Zip _____

Telephone (____) _____ Fax (____) _____
IN CASE WE HAVE QUESTIONS ABOUT YOUR ORDER

E-mail _____ @ _____
REQUIRED FOR ORDER CONFIRMATION AND SELECT PRODUCT DELIVERY.

Ingenix respects your right to privacy. We will not sell or rent your e-mail address or fax number to anyone outside
Ingenix and its business partners. If you would like to remove your name from Ingenix promotion, please call
1.800.ingenix (464.3649), option 1.

Product

Item No.	Qty	Description	Price	Total

Subtotal _____

UT, VA, TN, OH, CT, IA, MD, MN, NC & NJ residents, please add applicable Sales tax _____

(See chart on the left) Shipping & handling charges _____

All foreign orders, please call for shipping costs

Total _____

Payment

○ Please bill my credit card   ○ MasterCard   ○ VISA   ○ Amex   ○ Discover

Card No. | | | | | | | | | | | | | | | | | | | Expires | |
                                                           MONTH   YEAR

Signature _____

○ Check enclosed, made payable to: Ingenix, Inc.   ○ Please bill my office

Purchase Order No. _____
ATTACH COPY OF PURCHASE ORDER

INGENIX®

Current Procedural
Coding Expert

2009

Notice

The *2009 Current Procedural Coding Expert* is designed to be an accurate and authoritative source of information about the CPT® coding system. Every effort has been made to verify the accuracy of the listings, and all information is believed reliable at the time of publication. Absolute accuracy cannot be guaranteed, however. This publication is made available with the understanding that the publisher is not engaged in rendering legal or other services that require a professional license. If you identify a correction or wish to share information, please email the Ingenix customer service department at customerservice@ingenix.com or fax us at 801.982.4033.

American Medical Association Notice

CPT only © 2008 American Medical Association. All rights reserved.

Fee schedules, relative value units, conversion factors and/or related components are not assigned by the AMA, are not part of CPT, and the AMA is not recommending their use. The AMA does not directly or indirectly practice medicine or dispense medical services. The AMA assumes no liability for data contained or not contained herein.

CPT is a registered trademark of the American Medical Association

Our Commitment to Accuracy

Ingenix is committed to producing accurate and reliable materials.

To report corrections, please visit www.ingenixonline.com/accuracy or email accuracy@ingenix.com. You can also reach customer service by calling 1.800.INGENIX (464.3649), option 1.

For Answers to Coding Questions

Try our new Ingenix Coding Answers—

Validate your coding accuracy and reduce denials. Find answers to those difficult coding procedures in 48 to 72 hours.

Increase your productivity. Access the tool, and submit your questions online 24 hours a day, seven days a week.

Save time and money associated with researching those hard-to-code procedures.

Use existing site content as a research tool. Quickly access previously submitted questions and answers by other users.

Always know where your questions stand during the Q&A process. Access real-time status of pending questions. Email notifications are delivered when a question is answered.

No subscription necessary. Take advantage of the flexible pricing options based on the number of questions you purchase.

For information, please visit www.shopingenix.com or call customer service at 1.800.INGENIX (464.3649), option 1.

Copyright

Copyright © 2008 Ingenix

All rights reserved. No part of this publication may be reproduced or transmitted in any form or by any means electronic or mechanical, including photocopy, recording or storage in a database or retrieval system, without the prior written permission of the publisher.

Made in the USA

ISBN 978-1-60151-196-6

Acknowledgments

Steven Woodward, *Product Manager*
Ralph Wankier, *VP, Product Management*
Lynn Speirs, *Senior Director, Editorial/Desktop Publishing*
Karen Schmidt, BSN, *Technical Director*
Stacy Perry, *Manager, Desktop Publishing*
Lisa Singley, *Project Manager*
Wendy Gabbert, CPC, CPC-H, PCS, FCS *Clinical/Technical Editor*
LaJuana Green RHIA, CCS, *Clinical/Technical Editor*
Karen H. Kachur, RN, CPC, *Clinical/Technical Editor*
Temeka Lewis, MBA, CCS, *Clinical/Technical Editor*
Regina Magnani, RHIT, *Clinical/Technical Editor*
Anita D. Schmidt, RHIT, *Clinical/Technical Editor*
Kate Holden, *Editor*

About the Contributors

Wendy Gabbert, CPC, CPC-H, PCS, FCS

Ms. Gabbert has more than 25 years of experience in the health care field. She has extensive background in CPT/HCPCS and ICD-9-CM coding. She served several years as a coding consultant. Her areas of expertise include physician and hospital CPT coding assessments, chargemaster reviews, and the outpatient prospective payment system (OPPS). She is a member of the American Academy of Professional Coders and American College of Medical Coding Specialists.

Karen H. Kachur, RN, CPC

Ms. Kachur is a clinical/technical editor for Ingenix with expertise in CPT/HCPCS and ICD-9-CM coding, in addition to physician billing, compliance, and fraud and abuse. Prior to joining Ingenix, she worked for many years as a staff RN in a variety of clinical settings, including medicine, surgery, intensive care, and psychiatry. In addition to her clinical background, Ms. Kachur served as assistant director of a hospital utilization management and quality assurance department and has extensive experience as a nurse reviewer for Blue Cross/Blue Shield. She is an active member of the American Academy of Professional Coders and the American College of Medical Coding Specialists.

Temeka Lewis, MBA, CCS

Ms. Lewis is a clinical/technical editor for Ingenix with expertise in hospital inpatient and outpatient coding. Her areas of expertise include ICD-9-CM, CPT, and HCPCS coding. Ms Lewis's past experience includes conducting coding audits and physician education, teaching ICD-9-CM and CPT coding, functioning as a member of a revenue cycle team, maintaining chargemasters, and writing compliance newsletters. Most recently she was responsible for coding and compliance in a specialty hospital. She is an active member of the American Health Information Management Association (AHIMA).

Contents

Introduction

Welcome to Ingenix's *Current Procedural Coding Expert* (formerly *CPT® Expert*), an exciting Medicare coding and reimbursement tool and definitive procedure coding source that combines the work of the Centers for Medicare and Medicaid Services, American Medical Association, and Ingenix experts with the technical components you need for proper reimbursement and coding accuracy.

This new approach to CPT Medicare coding utilizes new, more intuitive ways of communicating the information you need to code claims accurately and efficiently. *Includes* and *Excludes* notes similar to those found in your ICD-9-CM manuals, help determine what services are related to the codes you are reporting. New and expanded icons help you crosswalk the code you are reporting to laboratory and radiology procedures necessary for proper reimbursement. CMS-mandated icons and relative value units (RVUs) help you determine which codes are most appropriate for the service you are reporting. In addition, icons denoting codes that apply to Physician Quality Reporting Initiative (PQRI) quality indicators are included along with their denominators. Add to that additional information identifying age and sex edits, ambulatory surgery center (ASC) and ambulatory payment classification (APC) indicators, and Medicare coverage and payment rule citations and *Current Procedural Coding Expert* provides the best in Medicare procedure reporting.

Current Procedural Coding Expert includes the information needed to submit claims to federal contractors and most commercial payers, and is correct at the time of printing. However, CMS, federal contractors, and commercial payers may change payment rules at any time throughout the year. *Current Procedural Coding Expert* includes codes that will not be published in the AMA's Physicians' Current Procedural Terminology until the following year. Commercial payers will announce changes through monthly news or information posted on their websites. CMS will post changes in policy on its website at http://www.cms.hhs.gov/transmittals. National coverage determinations (NCDs) provide universal and individual contractor guidelines for specific services. The existence of a procedure code does not imply coverage under any given insurance plan.

Current Procedural Coding Expert is based on the AMA's Physicians' Current Procedural Terminology coding system, which is copyrighted and owned by the physician organization. CPT is the nation's official, Health Information Portability and Accountability Act (HIPAA) compliant code set for procedures and services provided by physicians, ASCs, and hospital outpatient services, as well as laboratories, imaging centers, physical therapy clinics, urgent care centers, and others.

GETTING STARTED WITH *CURRENT PROCEDURAL CODING EXPERT*

Current Procedural Coding Expert is an exciting, tool combining the most current material at publication time from the AMA's *CPT 2009*, CMS's online manual system, the Correct Coding Initiative (CCI), CMS fee schedules, official Medicare guidelines for reimbursement and coverage, and Ingenix's own coding expertise.

Note: The AMA releases code changes quarterly. *Current Procedural Coding Expert* contains the most current information from the AMA, including new, changed, and deleted codes that are released on its website for future inclusion in the CPT book. Some of these changes will not appear in the AMA's CPT book until the following year.

Another feature of *Current Procedural Coding Expert* that differs from the official CPT book is the addition to appendix E, "Glossary," of the devices used for cardiovascular monitoring defined by the AMA.

Material is presented in a logical fashion for those billing Medicare, Medicaid, and private payers. The new format, based on customer comments, better addresses what customers tell us they need in a comprehensive Medicare procedure coding guide.

Designed to be easy to use and full of information, this product is an excellent companion to your AMA CPT manual and to Medicare, Ingenix, or other sources.

General Conventions

Sources of information in this book can be determined by color:

Ingenix information derived by our experts is in blue ink.

- Medicare-derived information is in red ink.

- Codes, descriptions, and evaluation and management (E/M) guidelines from the American Medical Association are in black ink.

Icons derived from AMA guidelines or coding conventions are presented as circles. Icons derived from federal guidelines, data, or rules are square.

While CPT codes are presented numerically as in the CPT book, each particular group of CPT codes is organized in a more intuitive fashion for Medicare billing, being grouped by the Medicare rules and regulations that govern payment of these particular procedures and services, as in this example:

99241–99255 Consultations

CMS 100-3,70.1 Consultations with a Beneficiary's Family and Associates

CMS 100-2,15,30 Physician Services

CMS 100-1,5,70 Definition of Physician

CMS 100-4,12,30.6.10 Consultation Services

● **New Codes**

Codes that have been added since the last edition of the book was printed.

▲ **Revised Codes**

Codes that have been revised since the last edition of the book was printed.

Red Color Bar—Not Covered by Medicare

Services and procedures identified by this color bar are never covered benefits under Medicare. Services and procedures that are not covered may be billed directly to the patient at the time of the service.

Yellow Color Bar—Unlisted Procedure

Unlisted CPT codes report procedures that have not been assigned a specific code number. An unlisted code delays payment due to the extra time necessary for review. When using an unlisted procedure code, include a cover letter, documentation of medical necessity, and operative reports as appropriate.

[INCLUDES] Includes notes

Includes notes identify procedures and services that would be bundled in the procedure code. These are derived from AMA, CMS, CCI, and Ingenix coding guidelines. This is not meant to be an all-inclusive list.

[EXCLUDES] Excludes notes

Excludes notes may lead the user away from the procedure or procedures that it is associated with. They may identify services that are not bundled and may be separately reported, or may lead the user to another more appropriate code. These are derived from AMA, CMS CCI, and Ingenix coding guidelines.

Laboratory/Pathology Crosswalk

This icon denotes CPT codes in the laboratory and pathology section of CPT that may be reported separately with the primary CPT code.

Radiology Crosswalk

This icon denotes codes in the radiology section that may be used with the primary CPT code being reported.

[TC] Technical Component Only

Codes with this icon represent only the technical component (staff and equipment costs) of a procedure or service. Do not use either modifier 26 (physician component) or TC (technical component) with these codes.

[26] Professional Component

Only codes with this icon represent the physician's work or professional component of a procedure or service. Do not use either modifier 26 (physician component) or TC (technical component) with these codes.

50 **Bilateral Procedure**
This icon identifies codes that can be reported bilaterally when the same surgeon provides the service for the same patient on the same date. Medicare allows payment for both procedures at 150 percent of the usual amount for one procedure. The modifier does not apply to bilateral procedures inclusive to one code.

80 **Assist-at-Surgery Allowed**
Services noted by this icon are allowed an assist at surgery with a Medicare payment equal to 16 percent of the allowed amount for the global surgery for that procedure. No documentation is required.

80 **Assist-at-Surgery Allowed with Documentation**
Services noted by this icon are allowed an assistant at surgery with a Medicare payment equal to 16 percent of the allowed amount for the global surgery for that procedure. Documentation is required.

+ **Add-on Codes**
This icon identifies procedures reported in addition to the primary procedure. The icon "+" denotes add-on codes. An add-on code is neither a stand-alone code nor subject to multiple procedure rules since it describes work in addition to the primary procedure.

⊘ **Modifier 51 Exempt**
Codes identified by this icon indicate that the procedure should not be reported with modifier 51 (Multiple procedures).

⚑ **Correct Coding Initiative (CCI)**
Current Procedural Coding Expert identifies those codes with a corresponding CCI edit. The CCI edits define correct coding practices that serve as the basis of the national Medicare policy for paying claims. The code noted is the column 1 code within the column 1/column 2 correct coding edits table (formerly called the "comprehensive" code), which indicates the major service/procedure.

☒ **CLIA Waived Test**
This symbol is used to distinguish those laboratory tests that can be performed using test systems that are waived from regulatory oversight established by the Clinical Laboratory Improvement Amendments of 1988 (CLIA). The applicable CPT code for a CLIA waived test may be reported by providers who perform the testing but do not hold a CLIA license.

⊛ **Modifier 63 Exempt**
This icon identifies procedures performed on infants that weigh less than 4 kg. Due to the complexity of performing procedures on infants less than 4 kg, modifier 63 may be added to the surgery codes to inform the payers of the special circumstances involved.

A2–**Z3** **ASC Payment Indicators**
This icon identifies ASC status payment indicators. They indicate how the ASC payment rate was derived and/or how the procedure, item, or service is treated under the revised ASC payment system. For more information about these indicators and how they affect billing, consult Ingenix's *Outpatient Billing Editor*.

A2 Surgical procedure on ASC list in calendar year (CY) 2007; payment based on OPPS relative payment weight.

F4 Corneal tissue acquisition; hepatitis B vaccine; paid at reasonable cost.

G2 Non-office-based surgical procedure added in CY 2008 or later; payment based on outpatient prospective payment system (OPPS) relative payment weight.

H7 Brachytherapy source paid separately when provided integral to a surgical procedure on ASC list; payment contractor-priced.

H8 Device-intensive procedure on ASC list in CY 2007; paid at adjusted rate.

J7 OPPS pass-through device paid separately when provided integral to a surgical procedure on ASC list; payment contractor-priced.

J8 Device-intensive procedure added to ASC list in CY 2008 or later; paid at adjusted rate.

K2 Drugs and biologicals paid separately when provided integral to a surgical procedure on ASC list; payment based on OPPS rate.

K7 Unclassified drugs and biologicals; payment contractor-priced.

L1 Influenza vaccine; pneumococcal vaccine. Packaged item/service; no separate payment made.

L6 New technology intraocular lens (NTIOL); special payment.

N1 Packaged service/item; no separate payment made.

P2 Office-based surgical procedure added to ASC list in CY 2008 or later with Medicare physician fee schedule (MPFS) nonfacility practice expense (PE) RVUs; payment based on OPPS relative payment weight.

P3 Office-based surgical procedure added to ASC list in CY 2008 or later with MPFS nonfacility PE RVUs; payment based on MPFS nonfacility PE RVUs.

R2 Office-based surgical procedure added to ASC list in CY 2008 or later without MPFS nonfacility PE RVUs; payment based on OPPS relative payment weight.

Z2 Radiology service paid separately when provided integral to a surgical procedure on ASC list; payment based on OPPS relative payment weight.

Z3 Radiology service paid separately when provided integral to a surgical procedure on ASC list; payment based on MPFS nonfacility PE RVUs

⊙ **Moderate Sedation**
This icon identifies procedures that include moderate sedation. Moderate sedation codes should not be reported separately with these procedures.

A **Age Edit**
This icon denotes codes intended for use with a specific age group, such as neonate, newborn, pediatric, and adult. Carefully review the code description to ensure the code you report most appropriately reflects the patient's age.

M **Maternity**
This icon identifies procedures that by definition should be used only for maternity patients generally between 12 and 55 years of age.

♀ **Female Only**
This icon identifies procedures that should be reported only for female patients.

♂ **Male Only**
This icon identifies procedures that should be reported only for male patients.

🚑 **Facility RVU**
This icon precedes the facility RVU from CMS's 2009 physician fee schedule (PFS). It can be found under the code description.

⚕ **Nonfacility RVU**
This icon precedes the nonfacility RVU from CMS's 2009 PFS. It can be found under the code description.

Global Days The global period is the time following surgery during which routine care by the physician is considered postoperative and included in the surgical fee. Office visits or other routine care related to the original surgery cannot be separately reported if provided during the global period. Global days are sometimes referred to as "follow-up days," or FUDs. The statuses are:

000 No follow-up care included in this procedure

010 Normal postoperative care is included in this procedure for ten days

090 Normal postoperative care is included in the procedure for 90 days

XXX Follow-up days have not been assigned or are not applicable to the service

CMS: This notation indicates that there is a specific CMS guideline pertaining to this code in the CMS Online Manual System which includes the internet-only manual (IOM) *National Coverage Determinations Manual;* (NCD). These CMS sources present the rules for submitting these services to the federal government or its contractors and are included in the appendix D of this book.

AMA: This indicates discussion of the code in the American Medical Association's *CPT Assistant* newsletter. Use the citation to find the correct issue.

✁ **Drug Not Approved by FDA**
The AMA CPT Editorial Panel is publishing new vaccine product codes prior to Food and Drug Administration approval. This symbol indicates which of these codes are pending FDA approval at press time. Check the Ingenix online website (http://www.ingenixonline.com/content/pn/) or AMA website (http://www.ama-assn.org/ama/pub/category/3113.html) for updates to these codes as they pass through the FDA process.

PQ **Physician Quality Reporting Initiative (PQRI)**
This icon denotes CPT codes that specifically address one or more of the CMS-determined quality measures. See appendix J for a list of denominators that apply to those codes.

A-Y **OPPS Status Indicators (OPSI)**
Status indicators identify how individual CPT codes are paid or not paid under the latest available hospital outpatient prospective payment system (OPPS). The same status indicator is assigned to all the codes within an ambulatory payment classification (APC). Consult your payer or resource to learn which CPT codes fall within various APCs.

A Services not paid under OPPS; paid under fee schedule or other payment system.

B Non-allowed item or service for OPPS

C Inpatient procedure

E Non-allowed item or service

F Corneal tissue acquisition; certain CRNA services and hepatitis B vaccines

G Drug/biological pass-through

H Pass-through device categories, brachytherapy sources, and radiopharmaceutical agents

K Non-pass-through drugs and biologicals, blood, and blood products

L Flu/PPV vaccines

M Service not billable to the FI/MAC

N Items and services packaged into APC rates

P Partial hospitalization service

Q1 STVX-packaged codes

Q2 Packaged codes

Q3 Codes that may be paid through a composite APC

R Blood and blood products

S Significant procedure not subject to multiple procedure discounting

T Significant procedure subject to multiple procedure discounting

U Brachytherapy services

V Clinic or emergency department visit

X Ancillary service

Y Non-implantable DME

For more information about ongoing development of the CPT coding system, consult the AMA website at URL http://www.ama-assn.org/.

Note: All data current as of November 10, 2008

Anatomical Illustrations

BODY PLANES AND MOVEMENTS

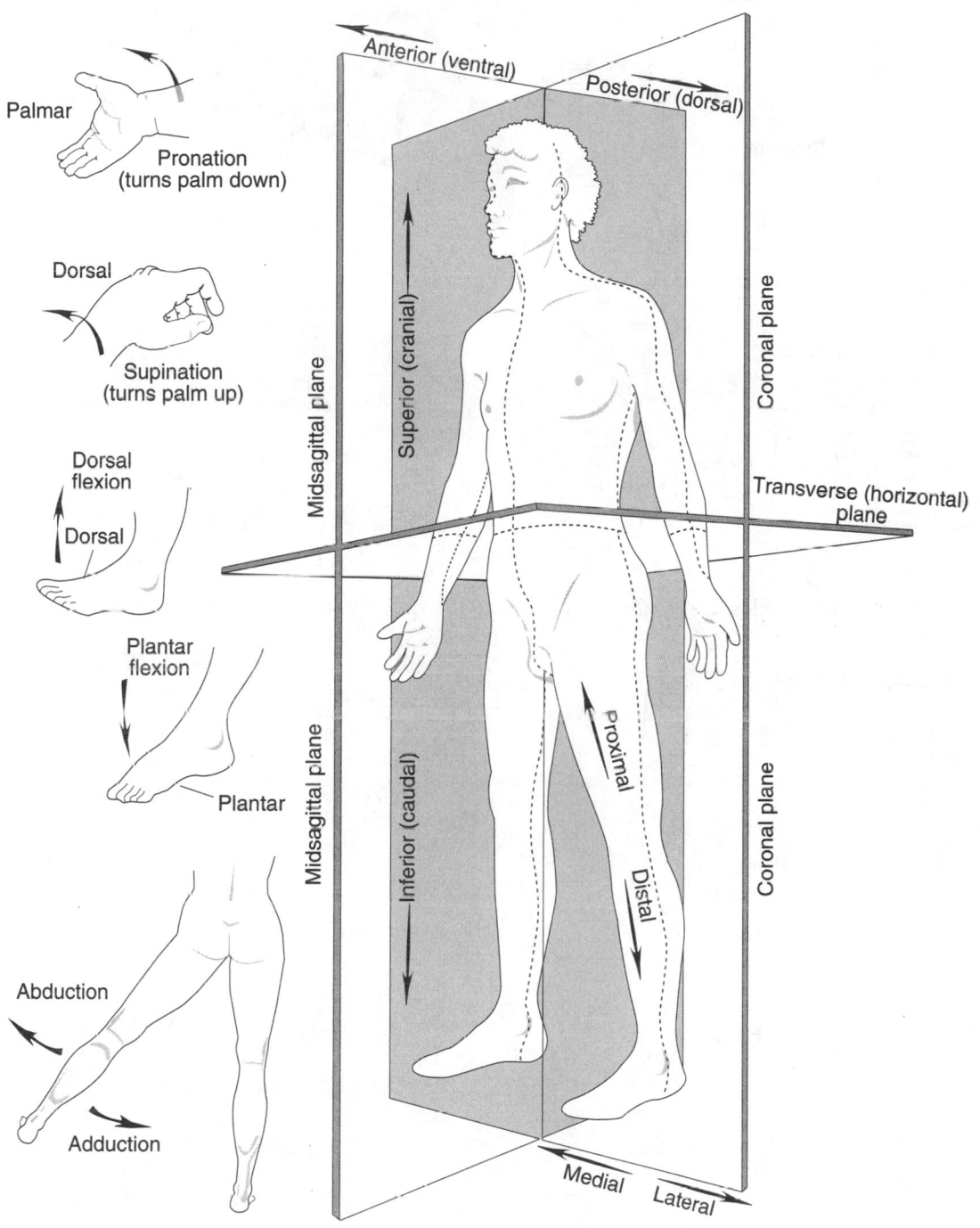

MUSCULOSKELETAL SYSTEM

Anatomical Illustrations

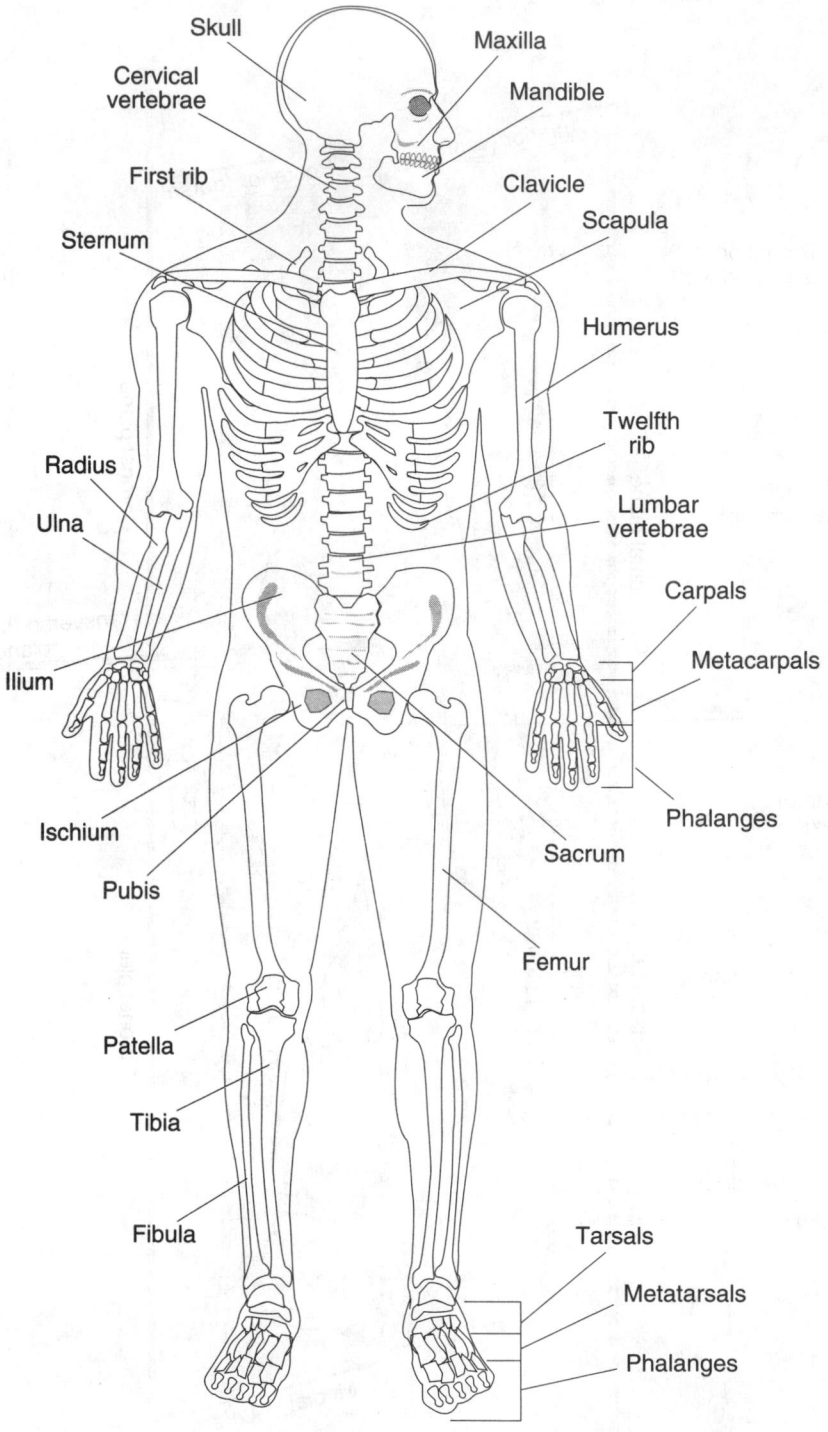

MUSCULOSKELETAL SYSTEM

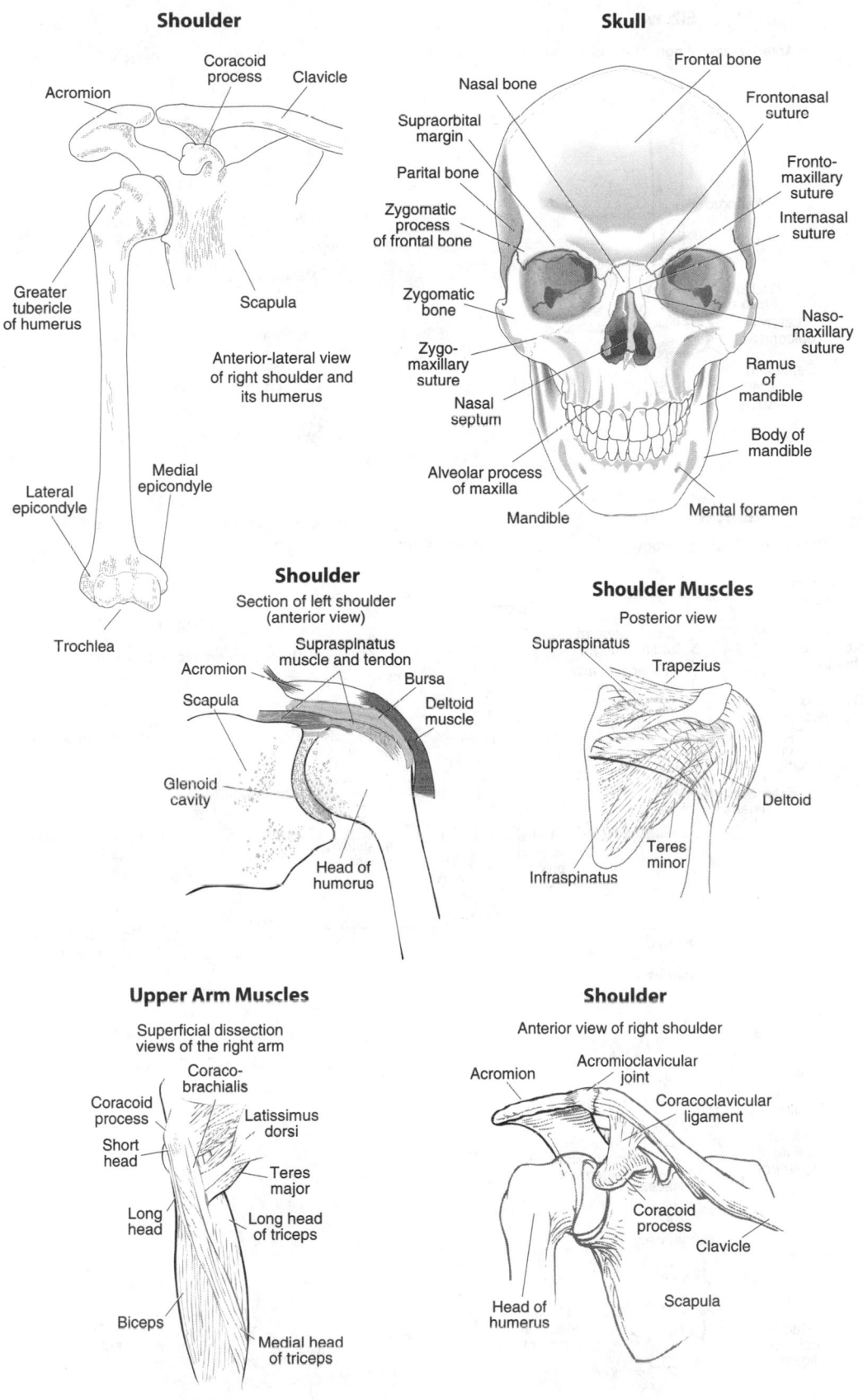

Shoulder

Acromion
Coracoid process
Clavicle

Greater tubericle of humerus

Scapula

Anterior-lateral view of right shoulder and its humerus

Lateral epicondyle

Medial epicondyle

Trochlea

Skull

Nasal bone
Frontal bone
Frontonasal suture
Supraorbital margin
Parital bone
Fronto-maxillary suture
Zygomatic process of frontal bone
Internasal suture
Zygomatic bone
Zygo-maxillary suture
Naso-maxillary suture
Nasal septum
Ramus of mandible
Alveolar process of maxilla
Body of mandible
Mandible
Mental foramen

Shoulder
Section of left shoulder (anterior view)

Acromion
Supraspinatus muscle and tendon
Bursa
Scapula
Deltoid muscle
Glenoid cavity
Head of humerus

Shoulder Muscles
Posterior view

Supraspinatus
Trapezius
Deltoid
Teres minor
Infraspinatus

Upper Arm Muscles
Superficial dissection views of the right arm

Coraco-brachialis
Coracoid process
Latissimus dorsi
Short head
Teres major
Long head
Long head of triceps
Biceps
Medial head of triceps

Shoulder
Anterior view of right shoulder

Acromion
Acromioclavicular joint
Coracoclavicular ligament
Coracoid process
Clavicle
Head of humerus
Scapula

MUSCULOSKELETAL SYSTEM

Elbow

Anterior view of right arm and elbow

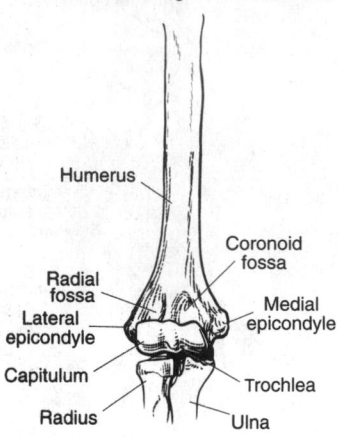

- Humerus
- Coronoid fossa
- Radial fossa
- Medial epicondyle
- Lateral epicondyle
- Capitulum
- Trochlea
- Radius
- Ulna

Elbow

Anterior view of right elbow

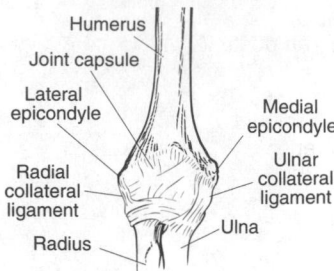

- Humerus
- Joint capsule
- Lateral epicondyle
- Medial epicondyle
- Radial collateral ligament
- Ulnar collateral ligament
- Radius
- Ulna

Lateral view of right elbow joint

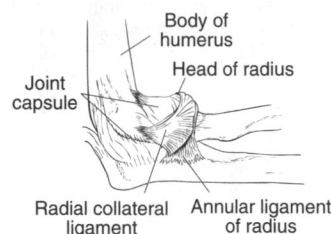

- Body of humerus
- Head of radius
- Joint capsule
- Radial collateral ligament
- Annular ligament of radius

Elbow

Posterior view of right elbow

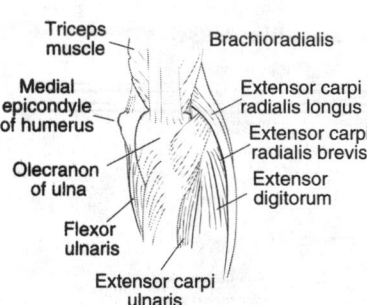

- Triceps muscle
- Brachioradialis
- Medial epicondyle of humerus
- Extensor carpi radialis longus
- Extensor carpi radialis brevis
- Olecranon of ulna
- Extensor digitorum
- Flexor ulnaris
- Extensor carpi ulnaris

Lower Arm

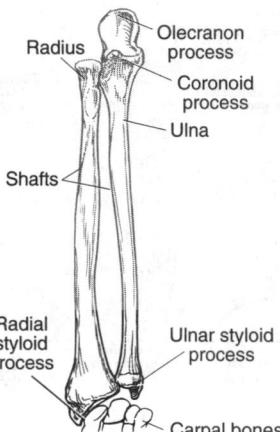

- Radius
- Olecranon process
- Coronoid process
- Ulna
- Shafts
- Radial styloid process
- Ulnar styloid process
- Carpal bones

Finger

Medial schematic of finger joints

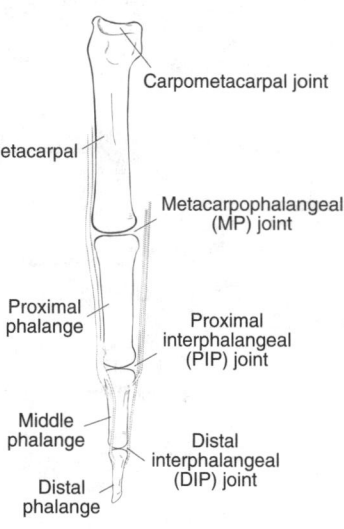

- Carpometacarpal joint
- Metacarpal
- Metacarpophalangeal (MP) joint
- Proximal phalange
- Proximal interphalangeal (PIP) joint
- Middle phalange
- Distal interphalangeal (DIP) joint
- Distal phalange

Hand

Palmar view

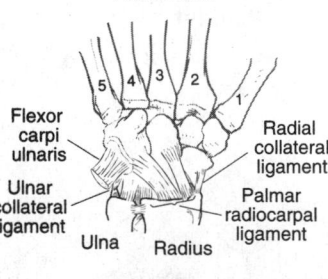

- Flexor carpi ulnaris
- Radial collateral ligament
- Ulnar collateral ligament
- Palmar radiocarpal ligament
- Ulna
- Radius

Dorsal view

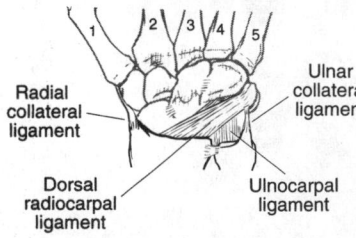

- Radial collateral ligament
- Ulnar collateral ligament
- Dorsal radiocarpal ligament
- Ulnocarpal ligament

Hand

Dorsal view

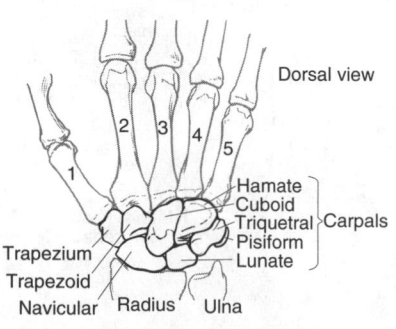

- Hamate
- Cuboid
- Triquetral
- Pisiform
- Lunate
- Carpals
- Trapezium
- Trapezoid
- Navicular
- Radius
- Ulna

MUSCULOSKELETAL SYSTEM

Ankle

Lateral and posterior views of right ankle

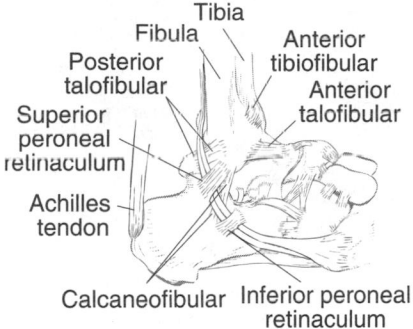

Tibia
Fibula
Anterior tibiofibular
Posterior talofibular
Anterior talofibular
Superior peroneal retinaculum
Achilles tendon
Calcaneofibular
Inferior peroneal retinaculum

Achilles tendon not shown

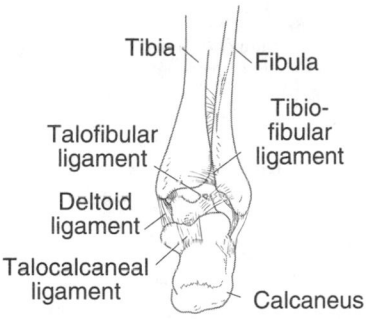

Tibia
Fibula
Talofibular ligament
Tibio-fibular ligament
Deltoid ligament
Talocalcaneal ligament
Calcaneus

Foot

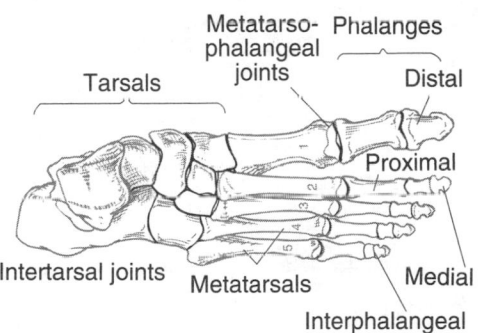

Metatarso-phalangeal joints
Phalanges
Tarsals
Distal
Proximal
Medial
Intertarsal joints
Metatarsals
Interphalangeal

Foot

Select extensors of the foot

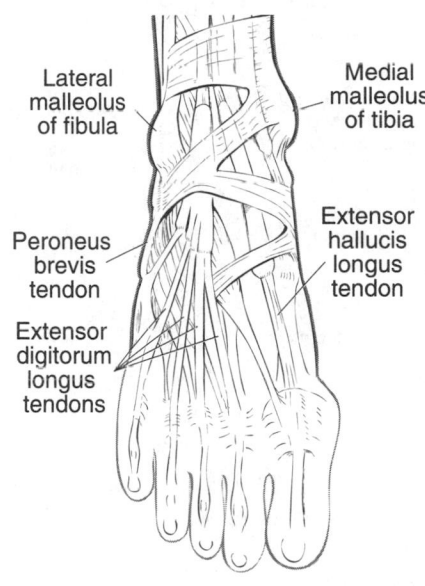

Lateral malleolus of fibula
Medial malleolus of tibia
Peroneus brevis tendon
Extensor hallucis longus tendon
Extensor digitorum longus tendons

Foot

Tarsals, excluding talus and calcaneus (dark), superior view

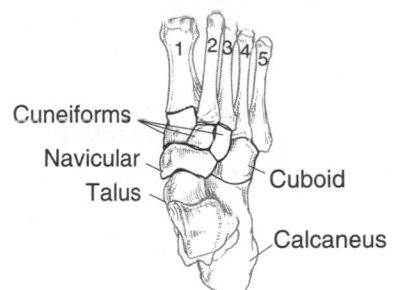

1 2 3 4 5
Cuneiforms
Navicular
Talus
Cuboid
Calcaneus

MUSCULOSKELETAL SYSTEM

Anatomical Illustrations

Leg

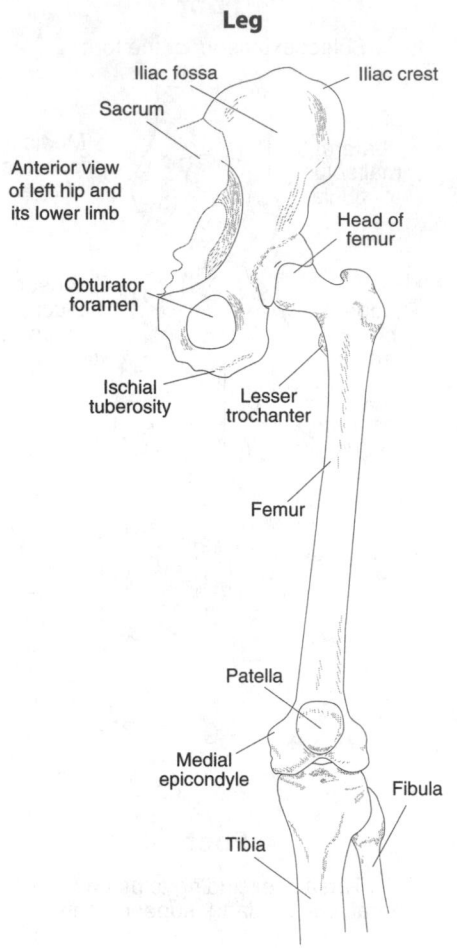

Iliac fossa

Iliac crest

Sacrum

Anterior view
of left hip and
its lower limb

Head of
femur

Obturator
foramen

Ischial
tuberosity

Lesser
trochanter

Femur

Patella

Medial
epicondyle

Fibula

Tibia

Hip

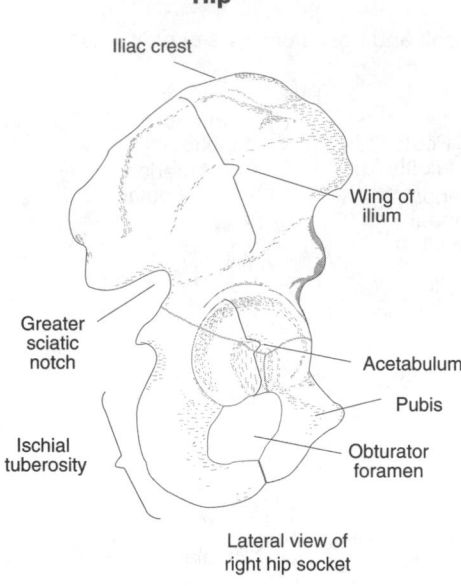

Iliac crest

Wing of
ilium

Greater
sciatic
notch

Acetabulum

Pubis

Ischial
tuberosity

Obturator
foramen

Lateral view of
right hip socket

Knee

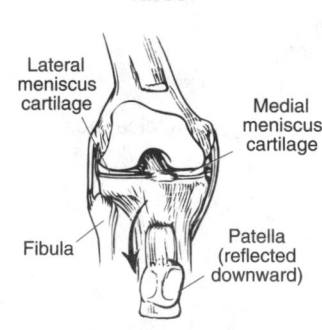

Lateral
meniscus
cartilage

Medial
meniscus
cartilage

Fibula

Patella
(reflected
downward)

Anterior view of right knee

Lower Leg

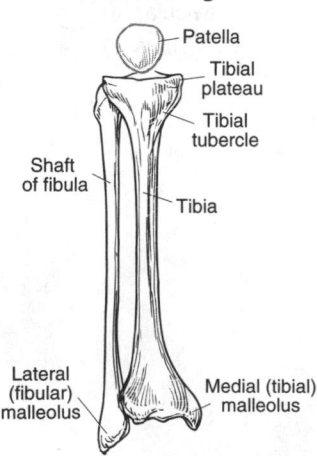

Patella

Tibial
plateau

Tibial
tubercle

Shaft
of fibula

Tibia

Lateral
(fibular)
malleolus

Medial (tibial)
malleolus

Knee

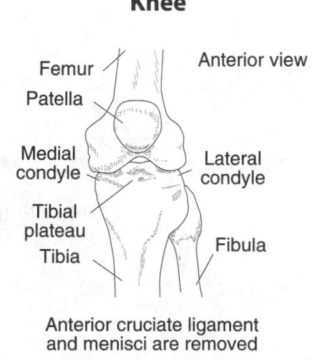

Femur

Anterior view

Patella

Medial
condyle

Lateral
condyle

Tibial
plateau

Tibia

Fibula

Anterior cruciate ligament
and menisci are removed

© 2008 Ingen

RULE OF NINES FOR BURNS

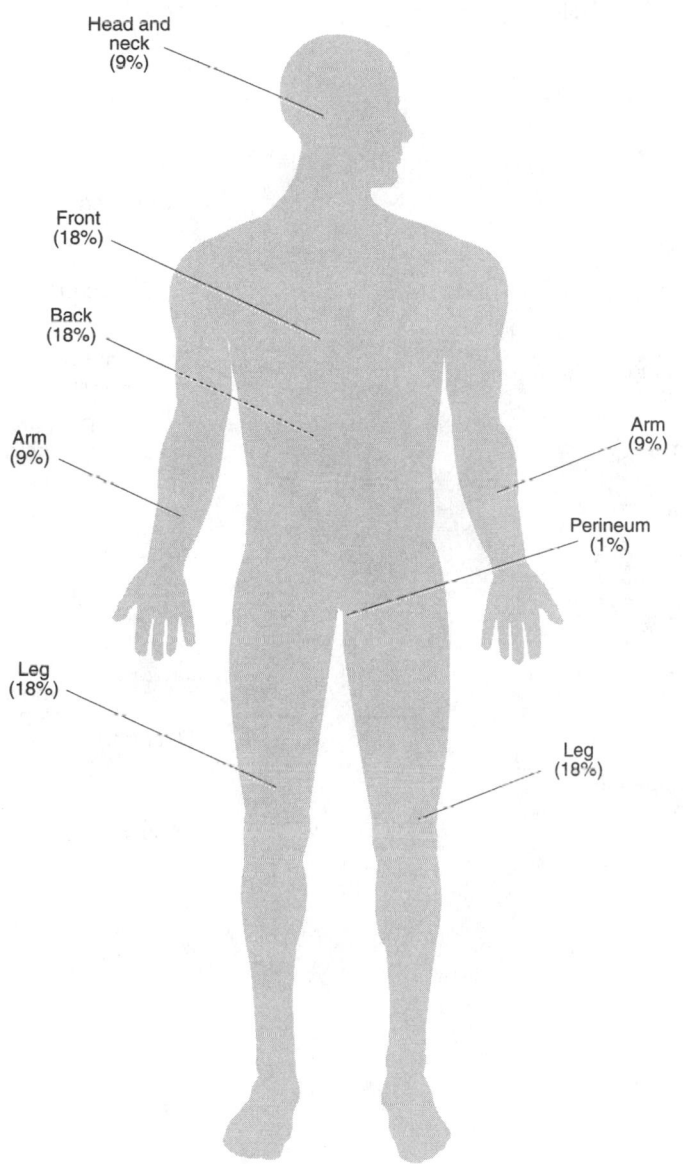

Head and
neck
(9%)

Front
(18%)

Back
(18%)

Arm
(9%)

Arm
(9%)

Perineum
(1%)

Leg
(18%)

Leg
(18%)

First-degree burns involve surface layers only and
tissue destruction is minimal.

Second-degree burns damage deeper epidermal layers
and upper layers of the dermis; damage to sweat glands, hair
follicles, and sebaceous glands may occur.

Third-degree burns include destruction of both epidermis
and dermis and tissue death extends below the hair
follicles and sweat glands.

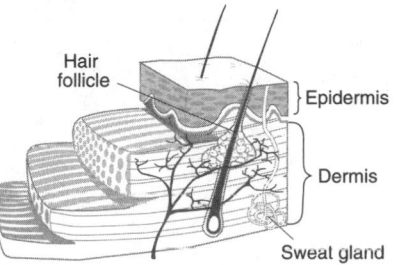

Hair
follicle

Epidermis

Dermis

Sweat gland

DIGESTIVE SYSTEM

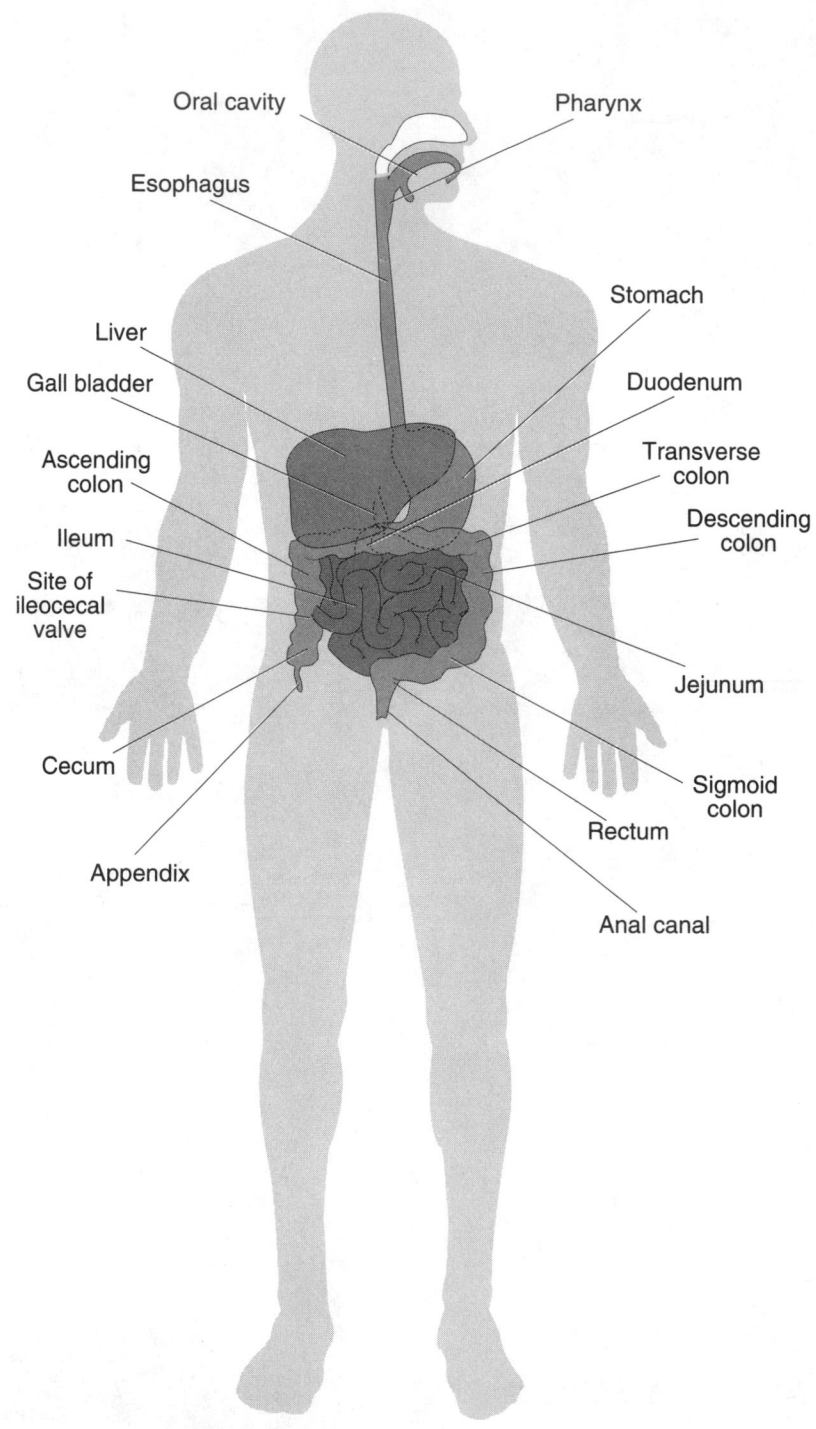

© 2008 Inger

DIGESTIVE SYSTEM

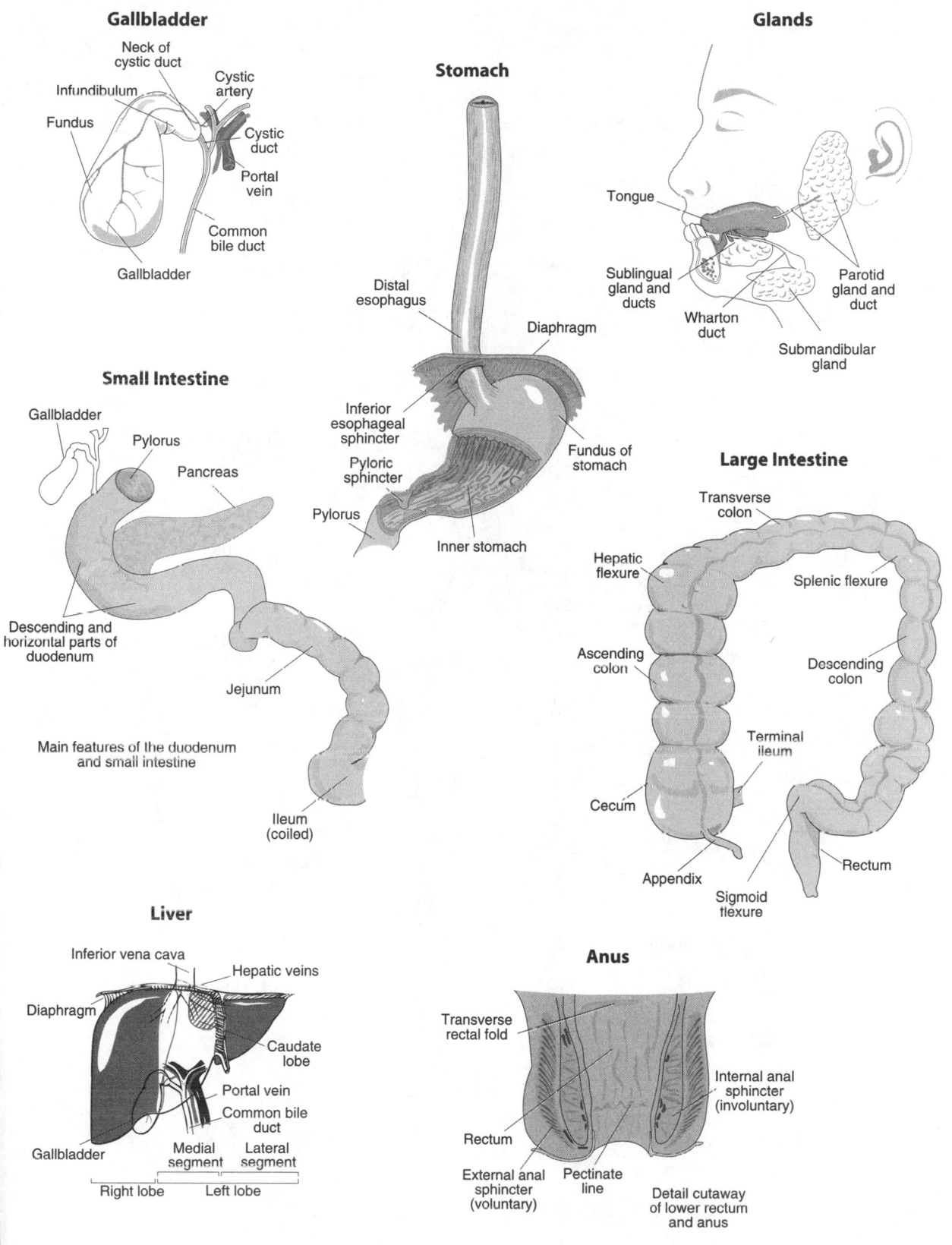

Gallbladder

Neck of cystic duct
Infundibulum
Fundus
Cystic artery
Cystic duct
Portal vein
Common bile duct
Gallbladder

Stomach

Distal esophagus
Diaphragm
Inferior esophageal sphincter
Pyloric sphincter
Pylorus
Fundus of stomach
Inner stomach

Glands

Tongue
Sublingual gland and ducts
Wharton duct
Submandibular gland
Parotid gland and duct

Small Intestine

Gallbladder
Pylorus
Pancreas
Descending and horizontal parts of duodenum
Jejunum
Main features of the duodenum and small intestine
Ileum (coiled)

Large Intestine

Transverse colon
Hepatic flexure
Ascending colon
Cecum
Splenic flexure
Descending colon
Terminal ileum
Appendix
Sigmoid flexure
Rectum

Liver

Inferior vena cava
Hepatic veins
Diaphragm
Caudate lobe
Portal vein
Common bile duct
Gallbladder
Medial segment
Lateral segment
Right lobe
Left lobe

Anus

Transverse rectal fold
Rectum
External anal sphincter (voluntary)
Pectinate line
Internal anal sphincter (involuntary)
Detail cutaway of lower rectum and anus

ARTERIAL SYSTEM

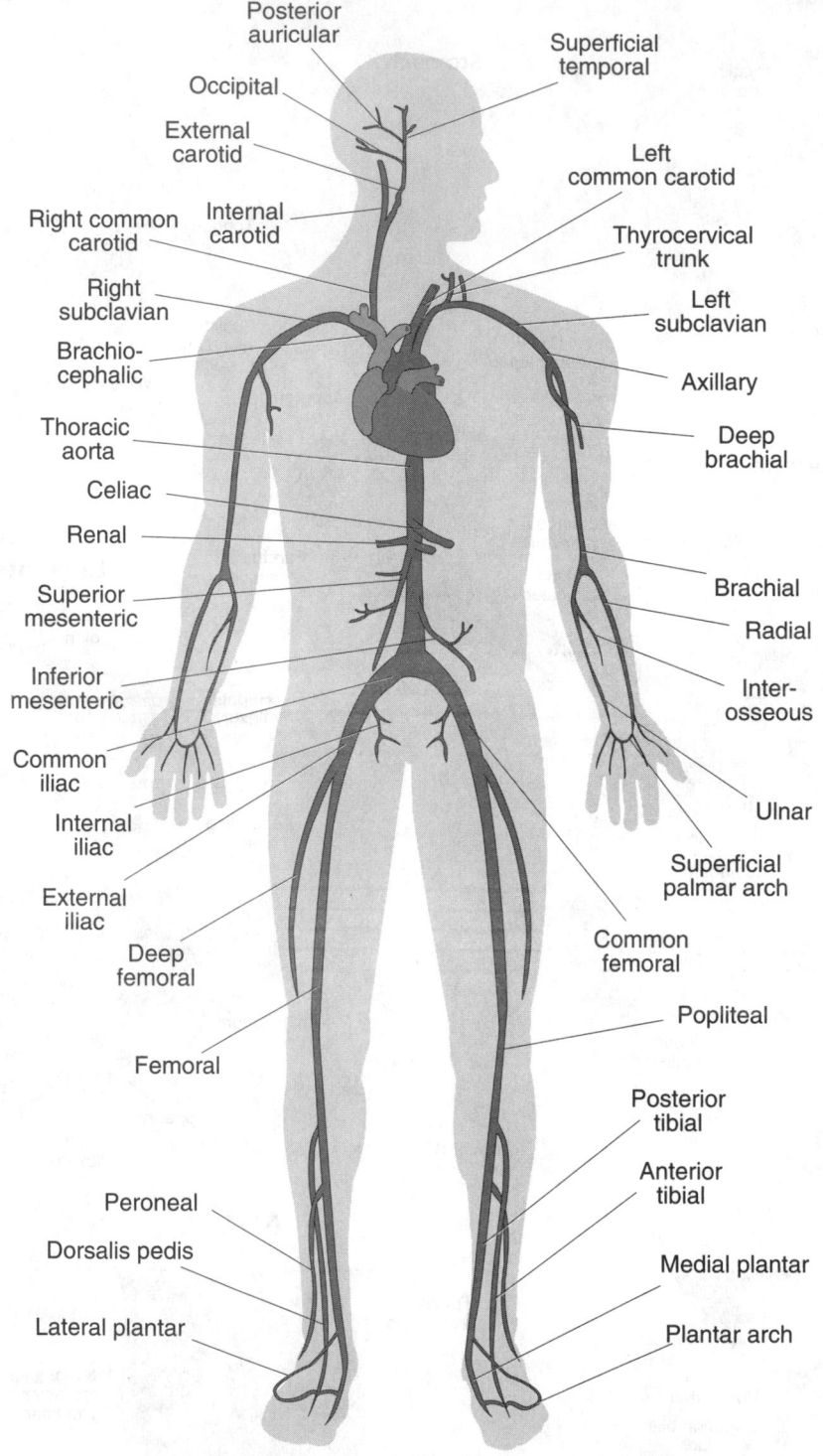

ARTERIAL SYSTEM

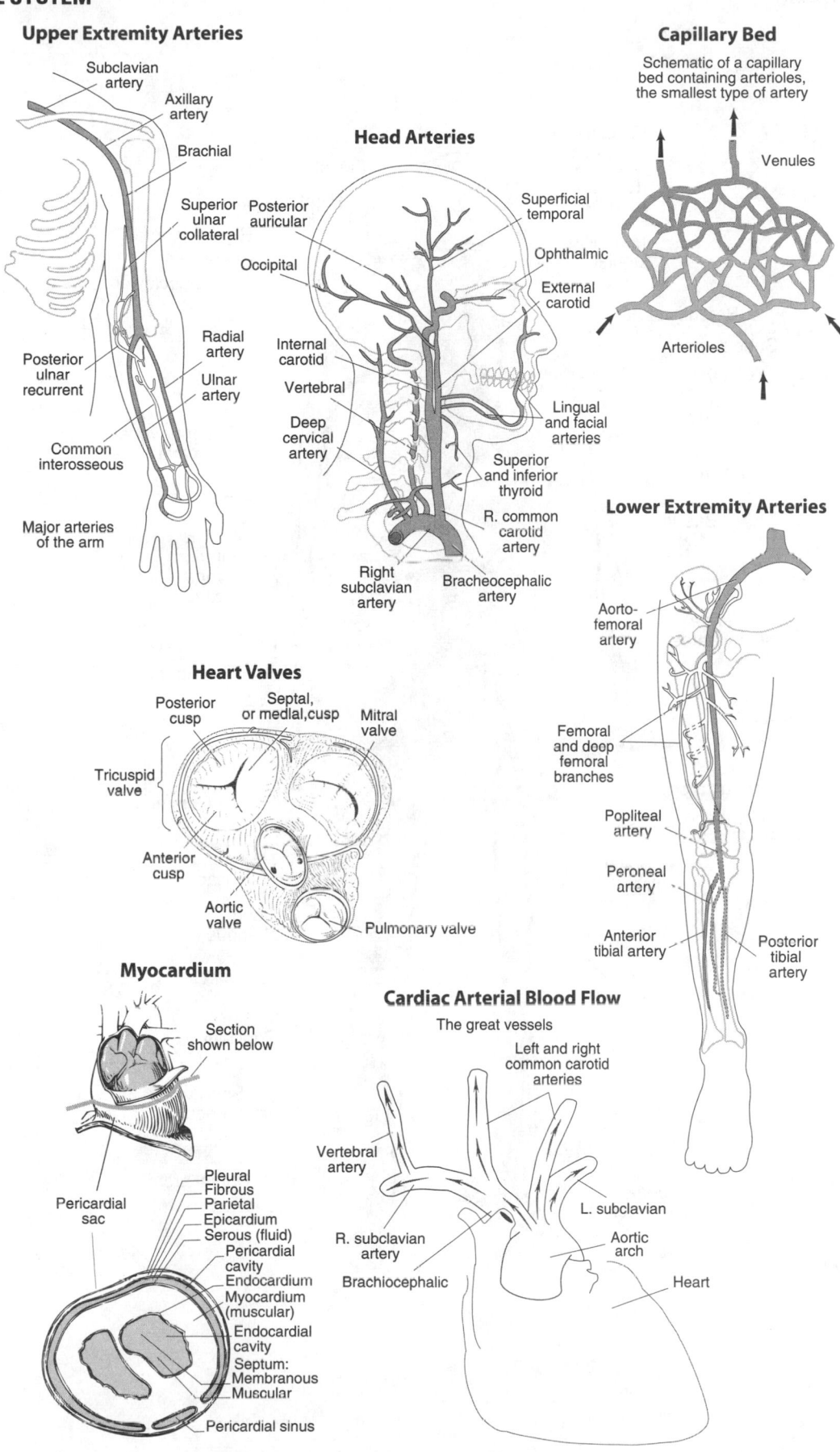

Upper Extremity Arteries

Subclavian artery
Axillary artery
Brachial
Superior ulnar collateral
Posterior ulnar recurrent
Radial artery
Ulnar artery
Common interosseous

Major arteries of the arm

Head Arteries

Posterior auricular
Occipital
Internal carotid
Vertebral
Deep cervical artery

Superficial temporal
Ophthalmic
External carotid
Lingual and facial arteries
Superior and inferior thyroid
R. common carotid artery
Right subclavian artery
Bracheocephalic artery

Capillary Bed

Schematic of a capillary bed containing arterioles, the smallest type of artery

Venules
Arterioles

Lower Extremity Arteries

Aorto-femoral artery
Femoral and deep femoral branches
Popliteal artery
Peroneal artery
Anterior tibial artery
Posterior tibial artery

Heart Valves

Posterior cusp
Septal, or medial, cusp
Mitral valve
Tricuspid valve
Anterior cusp
Aortic valve
Pulmonary valve

Myocardium

Section shown below

Pericardial sac
Pleural
Fibrous
Parietal
Epicardium
Serous (fluid)
Pericardial cavity
Endocardium
Myocardium (muscular)
Endocardial cavity
Septum:
Membranous
Muscular
Pericardial sinus

Cardiac Arterial Blood Flow

The great vessels
Left and right common carotid arteries
Vertebral artery
R. subclavian artery
Brachiocephalic
L. subclavian
Aortic arch
Heart

VENOUS SYSTEM

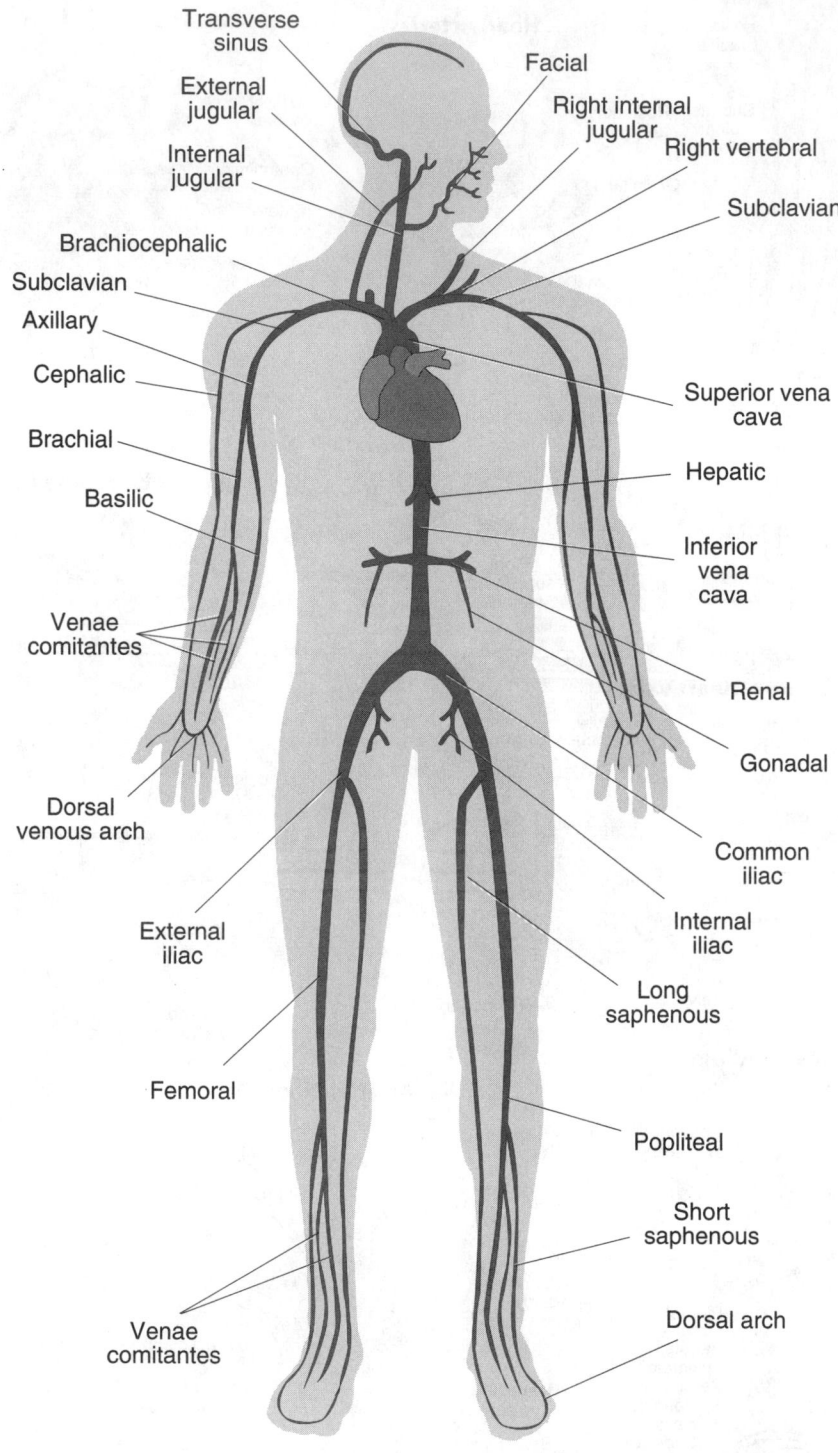

Transverse sinus

Facial

External jugular

Right internal jugular

Internal jugular

Right vertebral

Subclavian

Brachiocephalic

Subclavian

Axillary

Cephalic

Superior vena cava

Brachial

Hepatic

Basilic

Inferior vena cava

Venae comitantes

Renal

Gonadal

Dorsal venous arch

Common iliac

External iliac

Internal iliac

Long saphenous

Femoral

Popliteal

Short saphenous

Venae comitantes

Dorsal arch

VENOUS SYSTEM

Upper Extremity Veins

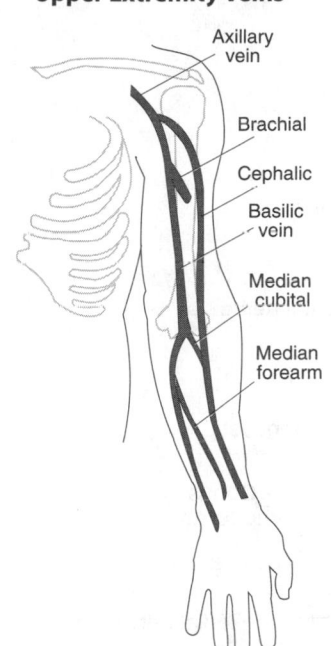

- Axillary vein
- Brachial
- Cephalic
- Basilic vein
- Median cubital
- Median forearm

Venae Comitantes

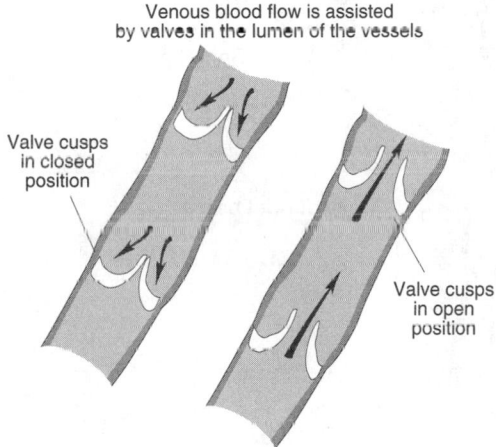

- Artery
- Venae comitantes

Heart Veins

- Superior vena cava vein
- Anterior cardiac veins
- Coronary sinus
- Great cardiac vein
- Small cardiac vein
- Middle cardiac vein

Venous Blood Flow

Venous blood flow is assisted by valves in the lumen of the vessels

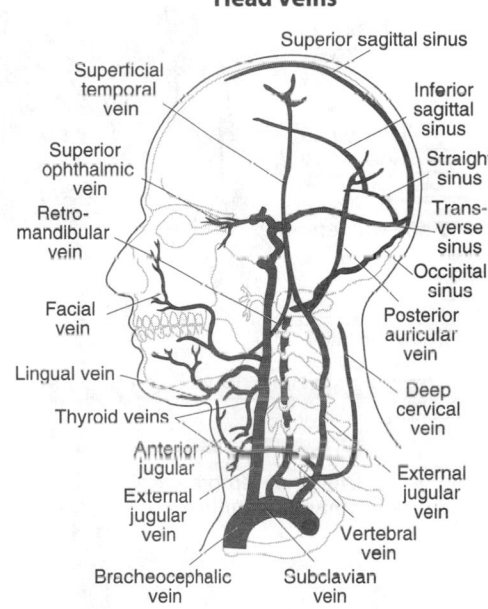

- Valve cusps in closed position
- Valve cusps in open position

Head Veins

- Superior sagittal sinus
- Superficial temporal vein
- Superior ophthalmic vein
- Retro-mandibular vein
- Facial vein
- Lingual vein
- Thyroid veins
- Anterior jugular
- External jugular vein
- Bracheocephalic vein
- Inferior sagittal sinus
- Straight sinus
- Trans-verse sinus
- Occipital sinus
- Posterior auricular vein
- Deep cervical vein
- External jugular vein
- Vertebral vein
- Subclavian vein

Cardiac Venous Blood Flow

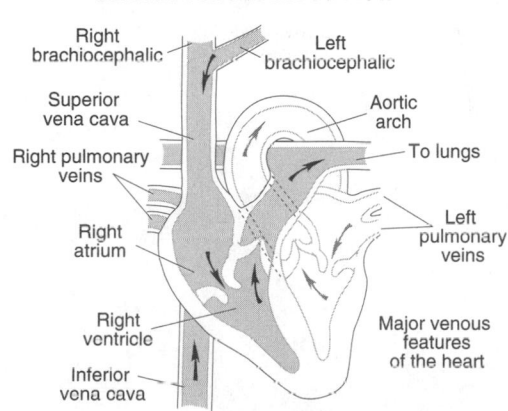

- Right brachiocephalic
- Superior vena cava
- Right pulmonary veins
- Right atrium
- Right ventricle
- Inferior vena cava
- Left brachiocephalic
- Aortic arch
- To lungs
- Left pulmonary veins
- Major venous features of the heart

Abdominal Veins

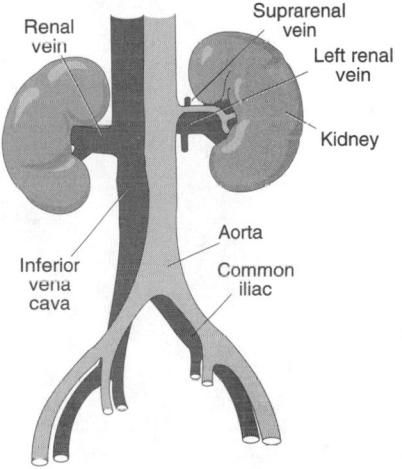

- Renal vein
- Inferior vena cava
- Suprarenal vein
- Left renal vein
- Kidney
- Aorta
- Common iliac

NERVOUS SYSTEM

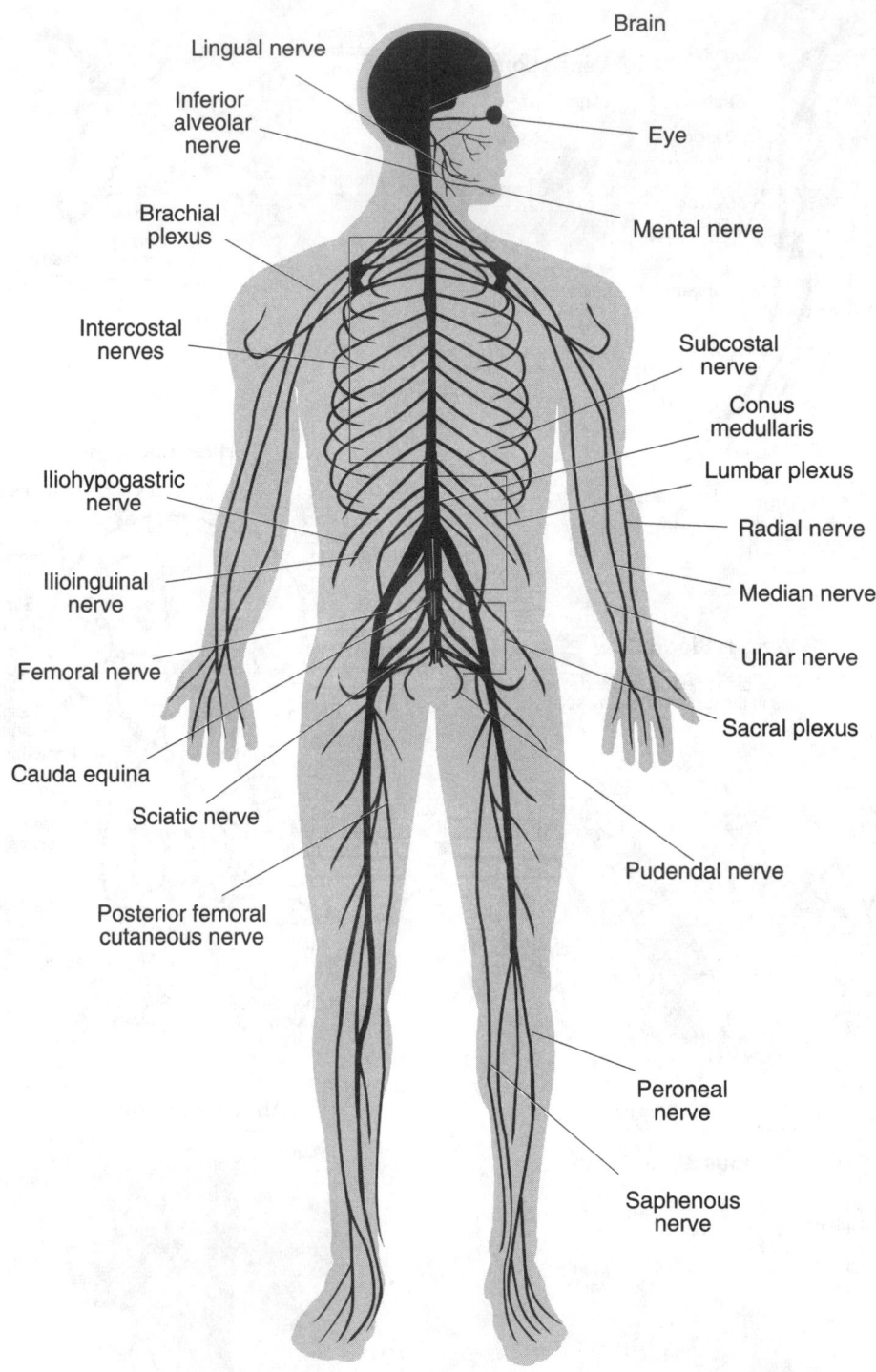

Lingual nerve

Inferior alveolar nerve

Brain

Eye

Mental nerve

Brachial plexus

Intercostal nerves

Subcostal nerve

Conus medullaris

Lumbar plexus

Iliohypogastric nerve

Radial nerve

Median nerve

Ilioinguinal nerve

Femoral nerve

Ulnar nerve

Sacral plexus

Cauda equina

Sciatic nerve

Pudendal nerve

Posterior femoral cutaneous nerve

Peroneal nerve

Saphenous nerve

© 2008 Ingen

NERVOUS SYSTEM

Brain

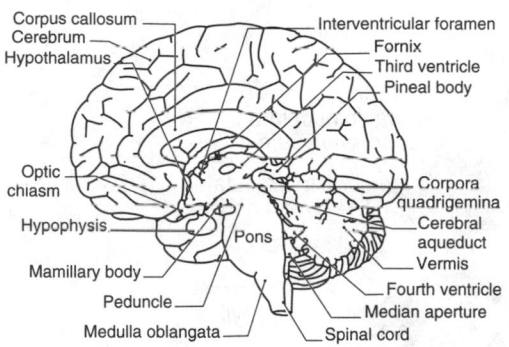

Corpus callosum
Cerebrum
Hypothalamus
Interventricular foramen
Fornix
Third ventricle
Pineal body
Optic chiasm
Corpora quadrigemina
Cerebral aqueduct
Hypophysis
Pons
Vermis
Mamillary body
Fourth ventricle
Peduncle
Median aperture
Medulla oblangata
Spinal cord

Cranial Nerves

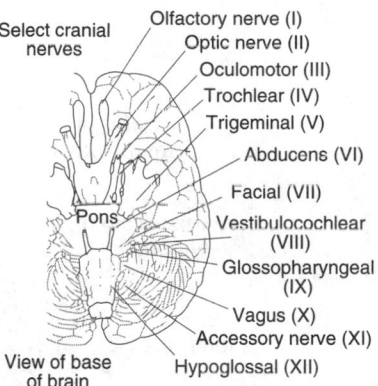

Select cranial nerves
Olfactory nerve (I)
Optic nerve (II)
Oculomotor (III)
Trochlear (IV)
Trigeminal (V)
Abducens (VI)
Facial (VII)
Pons
Vestibulocochlear (VIII)
Glossopharyngeal (IX)
Vagus (X)
Accessory nerve (XI)
View of base of brain
Hypoglossal (XII)

Spinal Cord

Schematic of spinal cord layers

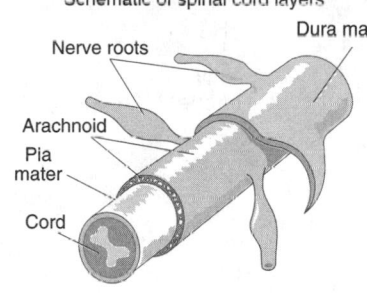

Nerve roots
Dura mater
Arachnoid
Pia mater
Cord

Spinal Column

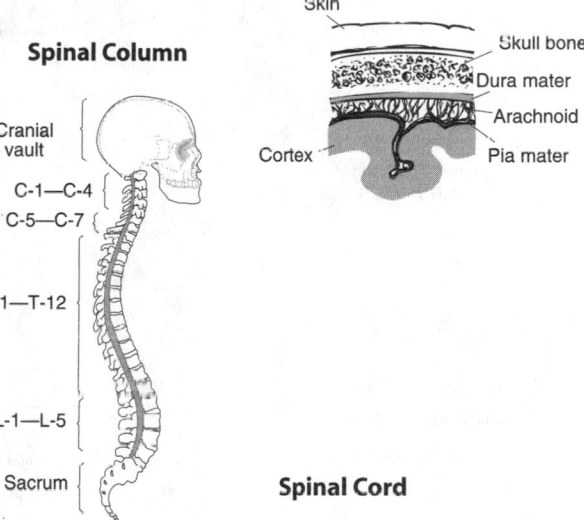

Cranial vault
C-1—C-4
C-5—C-7
T-1—T-12
L-1—L-5
Sacrum

Cranial Layers

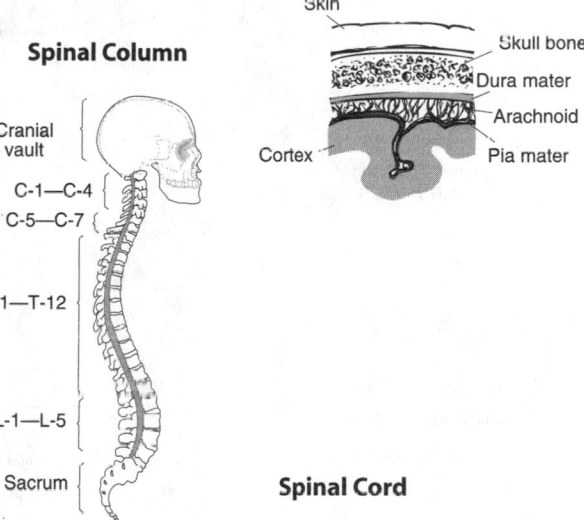

Skin
Skull bone
Dura mater
Arachnoid
Cortex
Pia mater

Spinal Cord

Schematic of spinal cord slice showing simplified sensory tracts and nerve roots

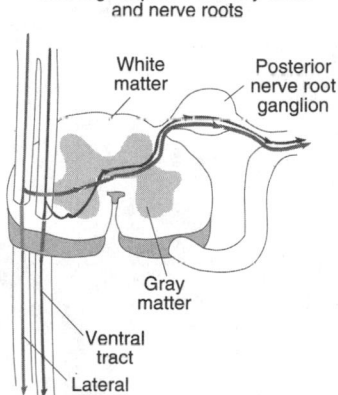

White matter
Posterior nerve root ganglion
Gray matter
Ventral tract
Lateral tract

Spinal Cord

Schematic of spinal cord showing nerve roots

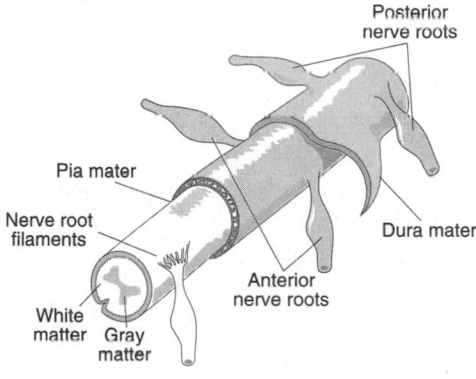

Posterior nerve roots
Pia mater
Nerve root filaments
Dura mater
White matter
Gray matter
Anterior nerve roots

LYMPHATIC SYSTEM

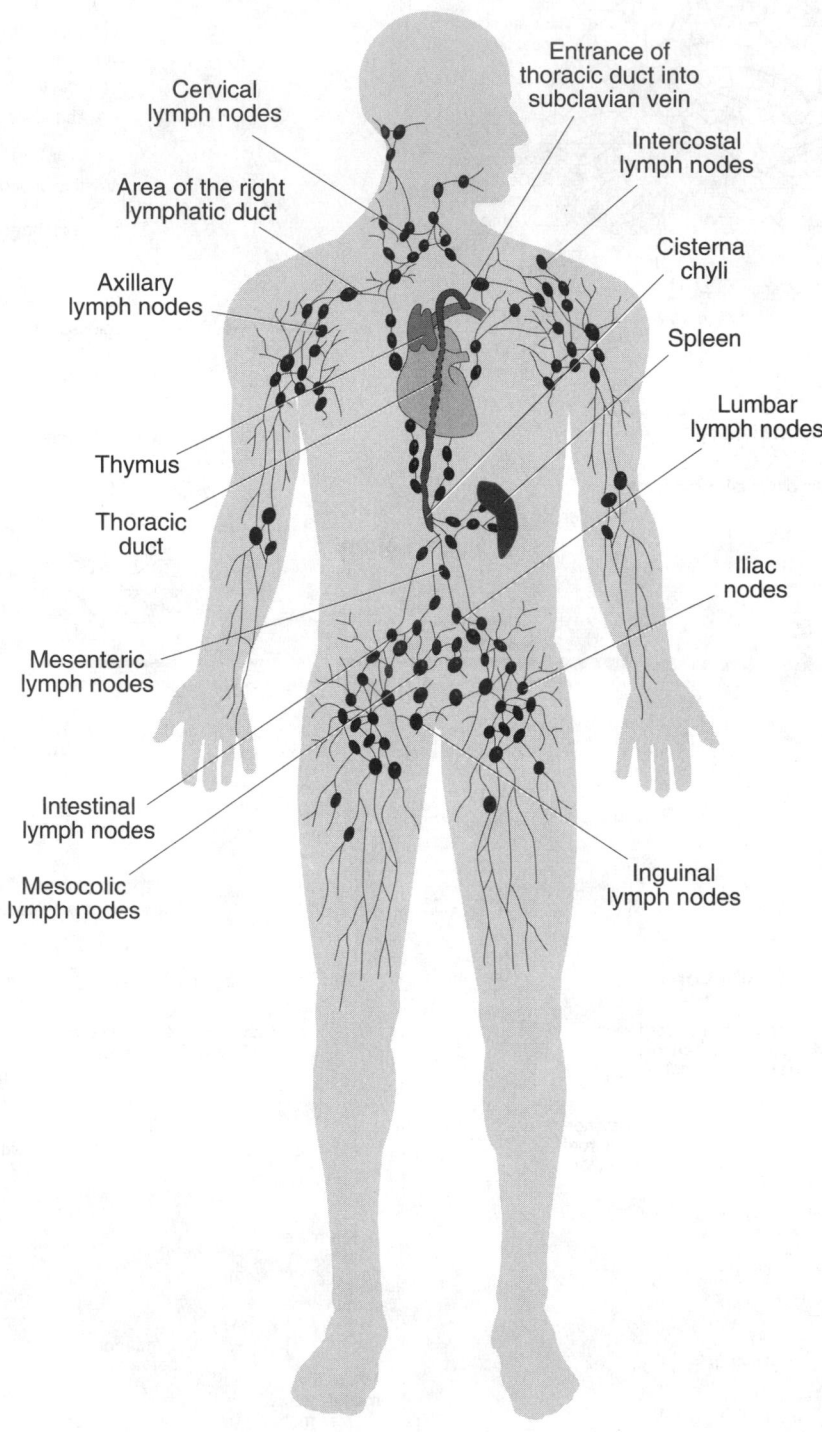

LYMPHATIC SYSTEM

Axillary Lymph Nodes

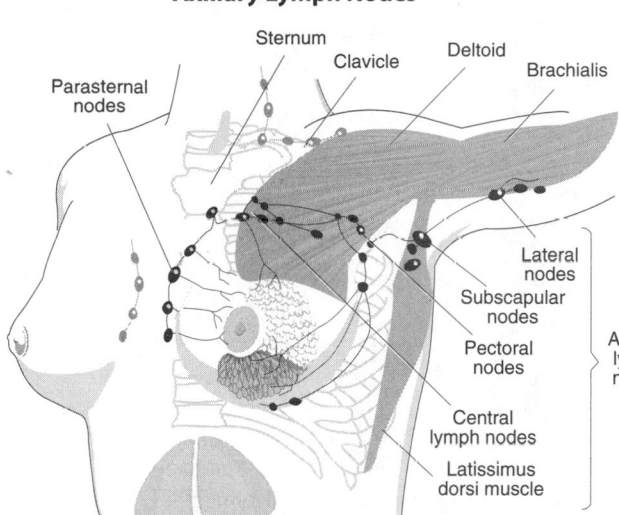

Parasternal nodes
Sternum
Clavicle
Deltoid
Brachialis
Lateral nodes
Subscapular nodes
Pectoral nodes
Axillary lymph nodes
Central lymph nodes
Latissimus dorsi muscle
Rectus abdominis

Lymphatic Capillaries

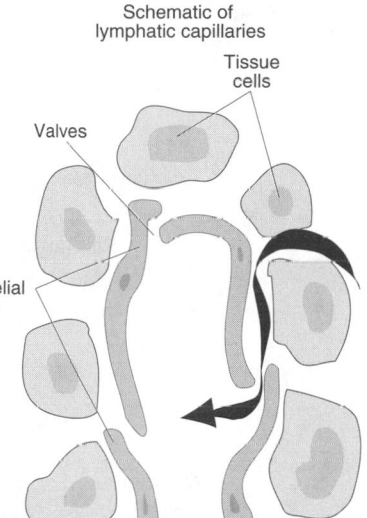

Schematic of lymphatic capillaries
Tissue cells
Valves
Endothelial cells

Fluids and particles can enter the capillary through overlapping valves

Lymphatic Drainage

Lymphatic drainage of the colon follows blood supply

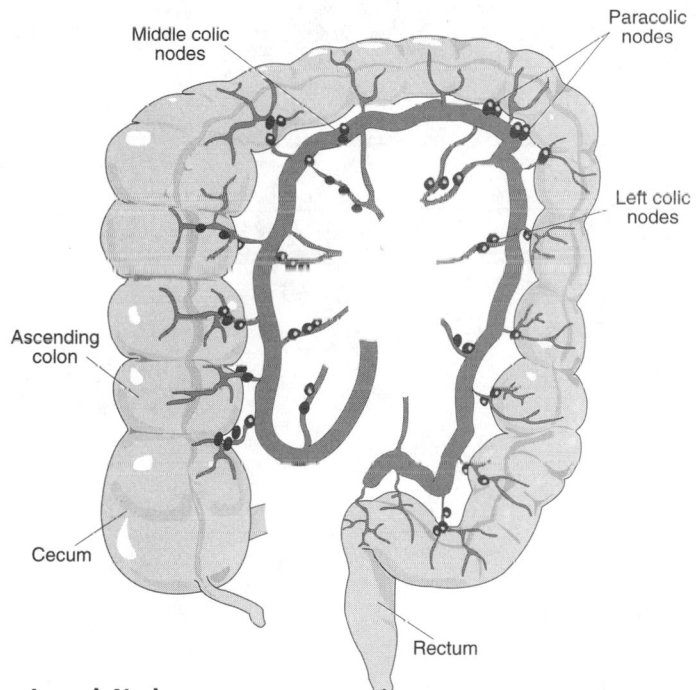

Middle colic nodes
Paracolic nodes
Left colic nodes
Ascending colon
Cecum
Rectum

Lymph Node

Schematic of lymph node

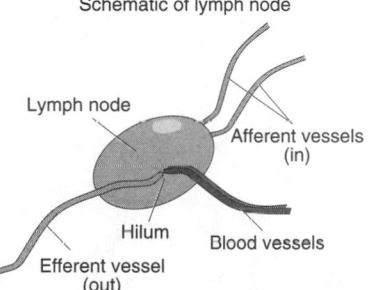

Lymph node
Afferent vessels (in)
Hilum
Blood vessels
Efferent vessel (out)

Neck Lymph Nodes

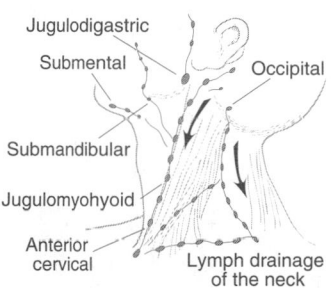

Jugulodigastric
Submental
Occipital
Submandibular
Jugulomyohyoid
Anterior cervical
Lymph drainage of the neck

Anatomical Illustrations

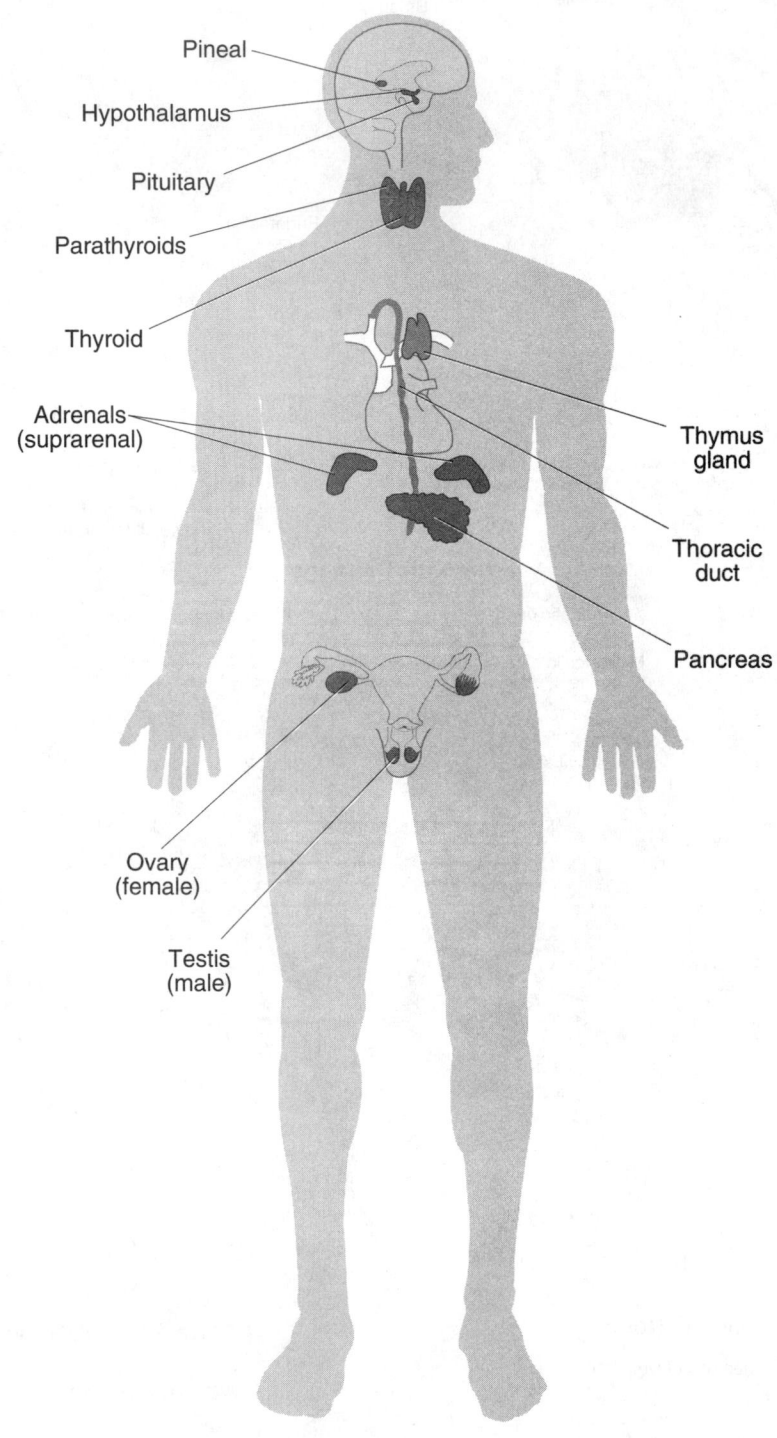

Pineal

Hypothalamus

Pituitary

Parathyroids

Thyroid

Adrenals
(suprarenal)

Thymus
gland

Thoracic
duct

Pancreas

Ovary
(female)

Testis
(male)

© 2008 Inge

ENDOCRINE SYSTEM

Thyroid Glands

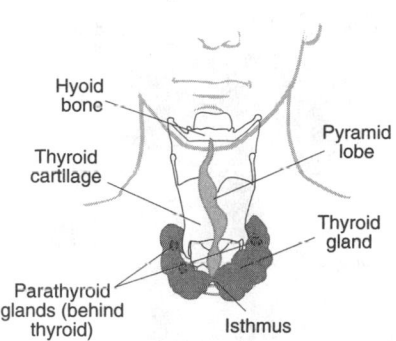

- Hyoid bone
- Thyroid cartilage
- Pyramid lobe
- Thyroid gland
- Parathyroid glands (behind thyroid)
- Isthmus

Pituitary Glands

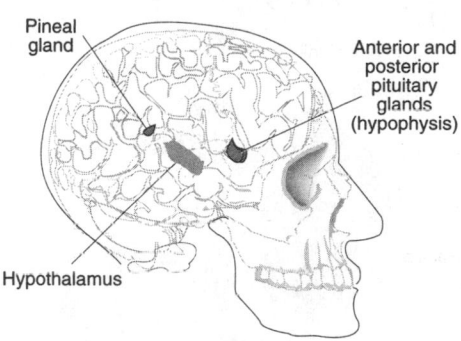

- Pineal gland
- Anterior and posterior pituitary glands (hypophysis)
- Hypothalamus

The pituitary gland and its controller, the hypothalamus, control body growth and stimulate and regulate other glands

Thyroid

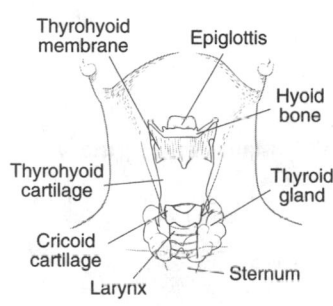

- Thyrohyoid membrane
- Epiglottis
- Hyoid bone
- Thyrohyoid cartilage
- Thyroid gland
- Cricoid cartilage
- Sternum
- Larynx

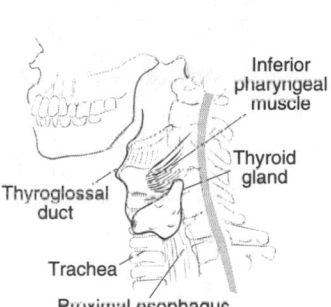

- Inferior pharyngeal muscle
- Thyroid gland
- Thyroglossal duct
- Trachea
- Proximal esophagus

Thyroid

Superior view

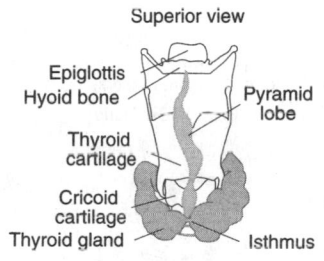

- Epiglottis
- Hyoid bone
- Pyramid lobe
- Thyroid cartilage
- Cricoid cartilage
- Thyroid gland
- Isthmus

Posterior view

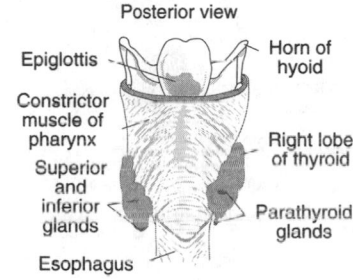

- Epiglottis
- Horn of hyoid
- Constrictor muscle of pharynx
- Superior and inferior glands
- Right lobe of thyroid
- Parathyroid glands
- Esophagus

Placenta

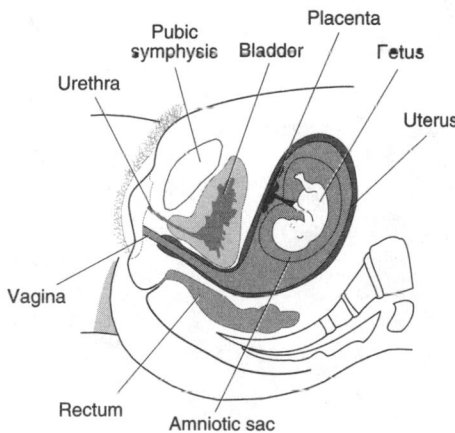

- Pubic symphysis
- Bladder
- Placenta
- Fetus
- Urethra
- Uterus
- Vagina
- Rectum
- Amniotic sac

The placenta is considered part of the endocrine system, secreting chorionic gonadotropin, estrogen, progesterone, and somatomammotropin

GENITOURINARY SYSTEM

Kidney

Cutaway detail of right kidney

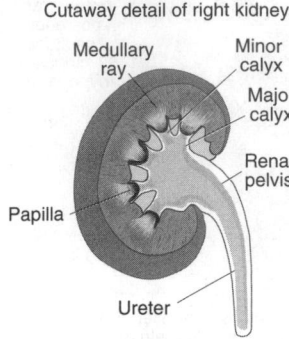

Medullary ray
Minor calyx
Major calyx
Renal pelvis
Papilla
Ureter

Nephron

Schematic of nephron, the tiny filtering mechanism of the kidney

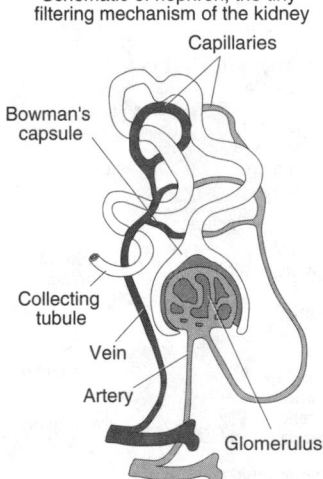

Capillaries
Bowman's capsule
Collecting tubule
Vein
Artery
Glomerulus

Urinary

Posterior view showing location of kidneys and ureters

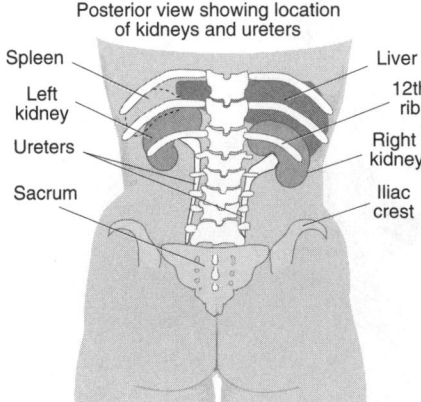

Spleen
Left kidney
Ureters
Sacrum
Liver
12th rib
Right kidney
Iliac crest

Male Urinary

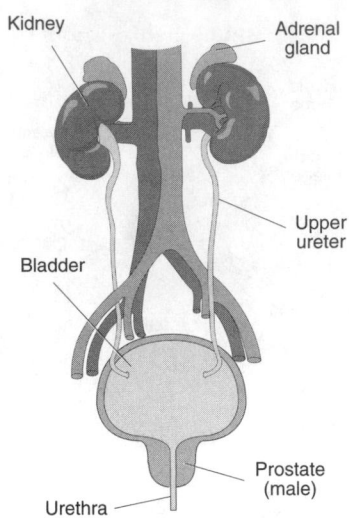

Kidney
Adrenal gland
Upper ureter
Bladder
Prostate (male)
Urethra

Male Genitourinary

Posterior view of male bladder and prostate

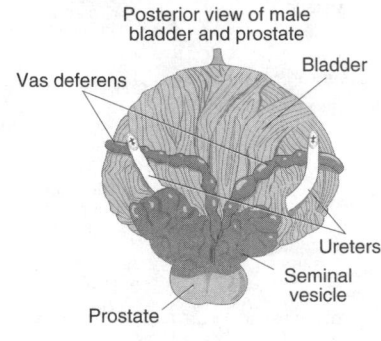

Vas deferens
Bladder
Ureters
Seminal vesicle
Prostate

Male Reproductive

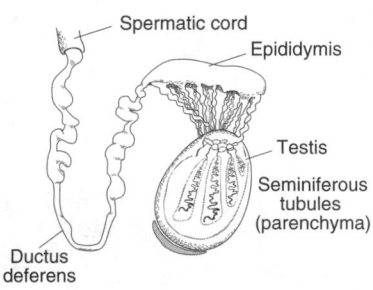

Spermatic cord
Epididymis
Testis
Seminiferous tubules (parenchyma)
Ductus deferens

GENITOURINARY SYSTEM

Female Genitourinary

Sideview schematic of female urogenital system

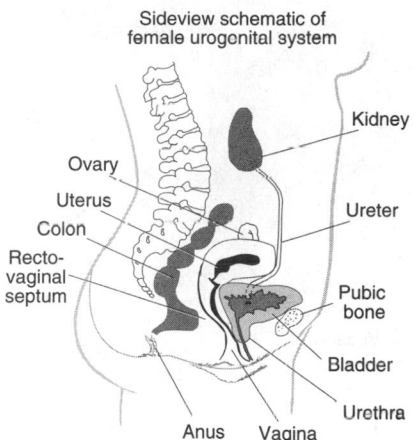

- Kidney
- Ovary
- Uterus
- Colon
- Ureter
- Recto-vaginal septum
- Pubic bone
- Bladder
- Urethra
- Anus
- Vagina

Female Rectoperineal

Lateral schematic showing the female rectoperineal area

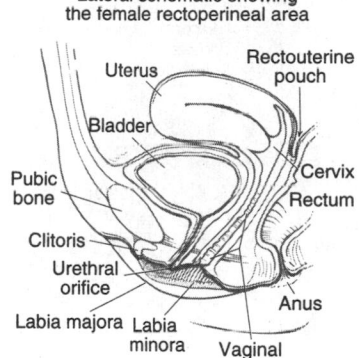

- Uterus
- Rectouterine pouch
- Bladder
- Pubic bone
- Cervix
- Rectum
- Clitoris
- Urethral orifice
- Anus
- Labia majora
- Labia minora
- Vaginal canal

Female Bladder

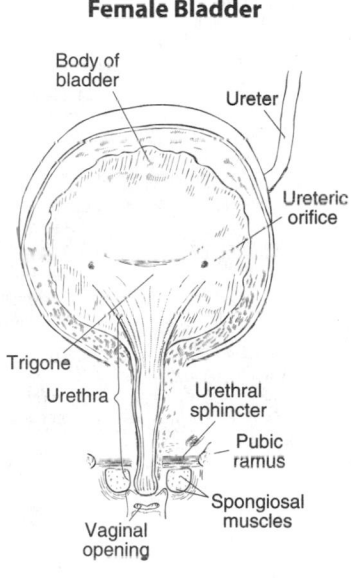

- Body of bladder
- Ureter
- Ureteric orifice
- Trigone
- Urethra
- Urethral sphincter
- Pubic ramus
- Vaginal opening
- Spongiosal muscles

Female Reproductive

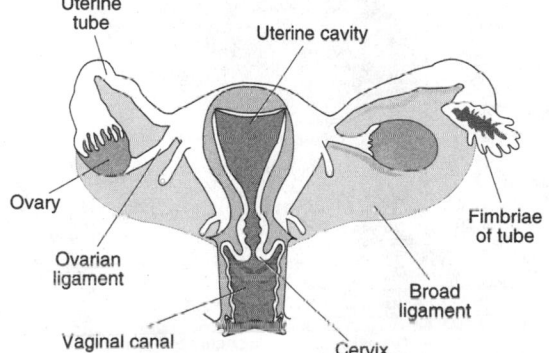

- Uterine tube
- Uterine cavity
- Ovary
- Fimbriae of tube
- Ovarian ligament
- Broad ligament
- Vaginal canal
- Cervix

Female Reproductive

Sideview schematic of female breast

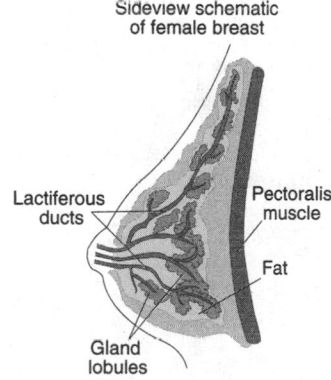

- Lactiferous ducts
- Pectoralis muscle
- Fat
- Gland lobules

RESPIRATORY SYSTEM

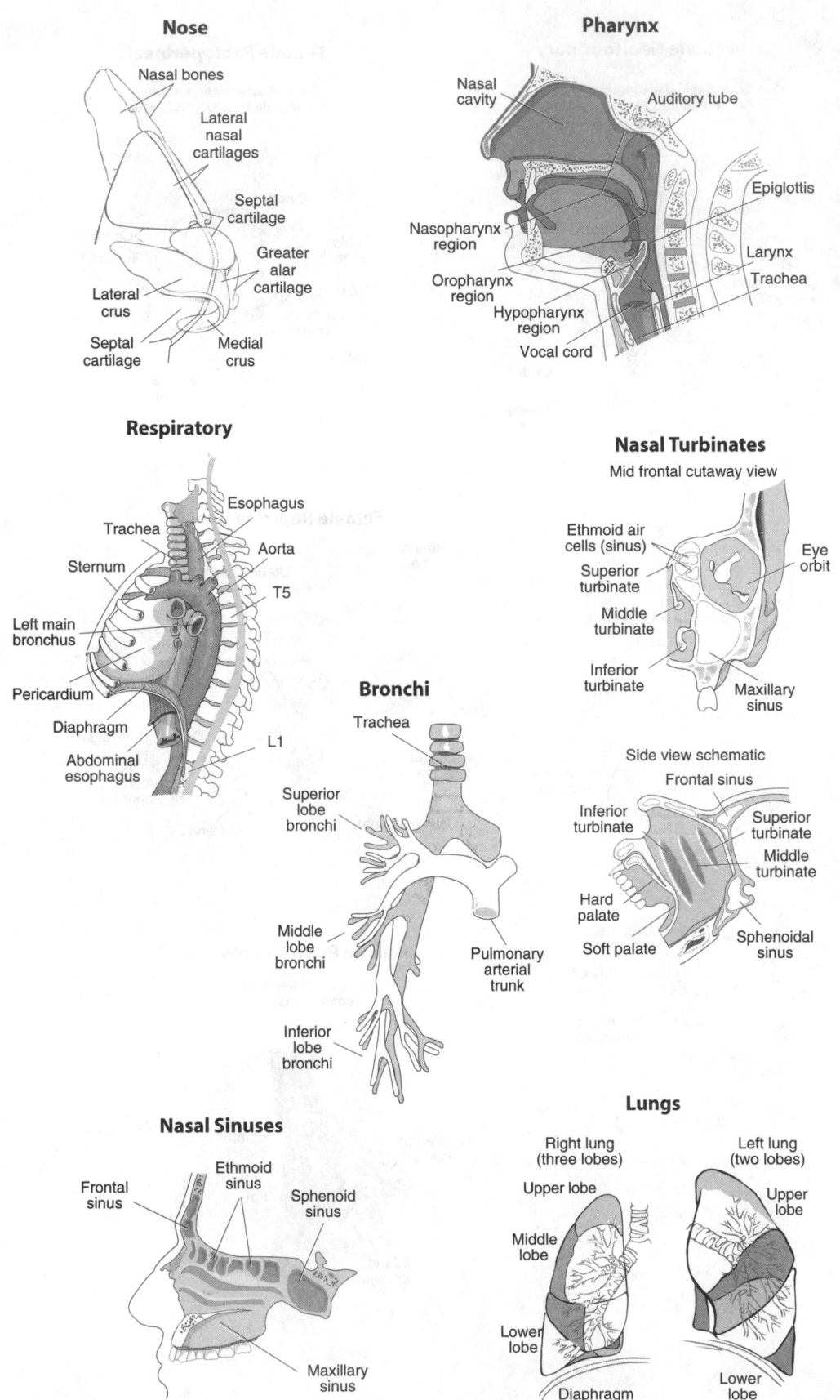

EYE

Eye

Muscles of the right eye

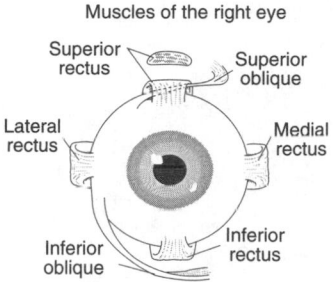

Lacrimal System

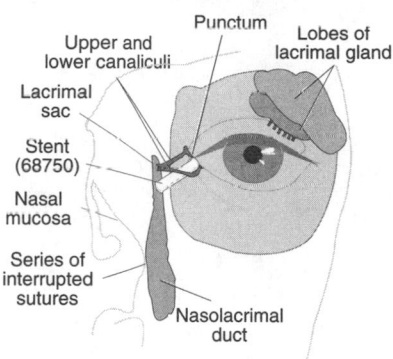

Eye

Anterior and posterior chambers of the eye

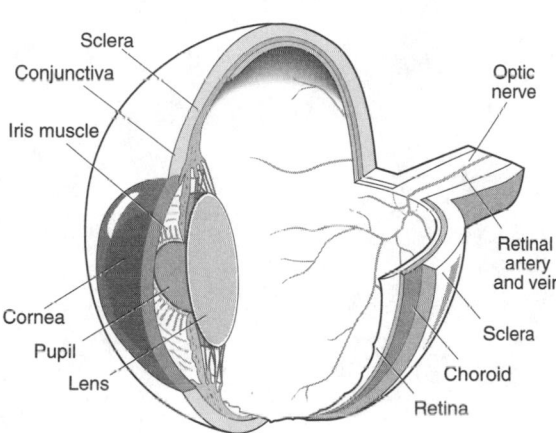

EAR

Ear

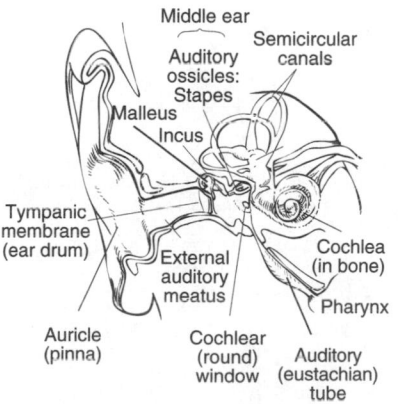

Middle Ear

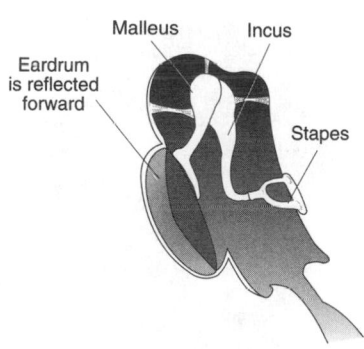

Index — Anesthesia — Anesthesia

© 2008 Ingen

Artery — *continued*
  Femoral — *continued*
    Thromboendarterectomy, 35302, 35371-35372
    Great Vessel Repair, 33770-33781
  Head
    Angiography, 75650
  Hepatic
    Aneurysm, 35121, 35122
  Iliac
    Aneurysm, 35131-35132, 75954
    Angioplasty, 35454
    Atherectomy, 35482, 35492
    Bypass Graft, 35537, 35538, 35563, 35637, 35638, 35663
    Embolectomy, 34151, 34201
    Exposure, 34820, 34833
    Graft, 34900
    Occlusion Device, 34808
    Thrombectomy, 34151, 34201
    Thromboendarterectomy, 35351, 35361, 35363
  Iliofemoral
    Bypass Graft, 35548, 35549, 35565, 35665
    Thromboendarterectomy, 35355, 35363
    X-ray with Contrast, 75630
  Innominate
    Aneurysm, 35021, 35022
    Embolectomy, 34001, 34101
    Thrombectomy, 34001, 34101
    Thromboendarterectomy, 35311
  Leg
    Angiography, 75710, 75716
    Catheterization, 36245-36248
  Mammary
    Angiography, 75756
  Maxillary
    Ligation, 30920
  Mesenteric
    Aneurysm, 35121, 35122
    Bypass Graft, 35331, 35631
    Embolectomy, 34151
    Thrombectomy, 34151
    Thromboendarterectomy, 35341
  Middle Cerebral Artery, Fetal Vascular Studies, 76821
  Neck
    Angiography, 75650
    Ligation, 37615
  Nose
    Incision, 30915, 30920
  Other Angiography, 75774
  Other Artery
    Exploration, 35761
  Pelvic
    Angiography, 75736
    Catheterization, 36245-36248
  Peripheral Arterial Rehabilitation, 93668
  Peroneal
    Bypass Graft, 35566, 35571, 35666, 35671
    Bypass In Situ, 35585, 35587
    Embolectomy, 34203
    Thrombectomy, 34203
    Thromboendarterectomy, 35305-35306
  Popliteal
    Aneurysm, 35151, 35152
    Angioplasty, 35456
    Atherectomy, 35483, 35493
    Bypass Graft, 35551, 35556, 35571, 35623, 35651, 35656, 35671, 35700
    Bypass In Situ, 35583, 35587
    Embolectomy, 34203
    Exploration, 35741
    Thrombectomy, 34203
    Thromboendarterectomy, 35303
  Pulmonary
    Anastomosis, 33606
    Angiography, 75741-75746
    Repair, 33690, 33925-33926

Artery — *continued*
  Radial
    Aneurysm, 35045
    Embolectomy, 34111
    Sympathectomy, 64821
    Thrombectomy, 34111
    Rehabilitation, 93668
  Reimplantation
    Carotid, 35691, 35694, 35695
    Subclavian, 35693-35695
    Vertebral, 35691-35693
    Visceral, 35697
  Renal
    Aneurysm, 35121, 35122
    Angiography, 75722, 75724
    Angioplasty, 35450
    Atherectomy, 35480, 35490
    Bypass Graft, 35536, 35560, 35631, 35636
    Embolectomy, 34151
    Thrombectomy, 34151
    Thromboendarterectomy, 35341
  Repair
    with Other Graft, 35261-35286
    with Vein Graft, 35231-35256
    Aneurysm, 36834, 61697-61708
    Angioplasty, 75962-75968
    Direct, 35201-35226
  Revision
    Hemodialysis Graft or Fistula
      with Thrombectomy, 36833
      without Thrombectomy, 36832
  Spinal
    Angiography, 75705
  Splenic
    Aneurysm, 35111, 35112
    Angioplasty, 35458
    Bypass Graft, 35536, 35636
  Subclavian
    Aneurysm, 35001-35002, 35021-35022
    Angioplasty, 35458
    Bypass Graft, 35506, 35511-35516, 35526, 35606-35616, 35626, 35645
    Embolectomy, 34001-34101
    Thrombectomy, 34001-34101
    Thromboendarterectomy, 35301, 35311
    Transposition, 33889
    Unlisted Services and Procedures, 37799
  Superficial Femoral
    Thromboendarterectomy, 35302
  Superficial Palmar Arch
    Sympathectomy, 64823
  Temporal
    Biopsy, 37609
    Ligation, 37609
  Thoracic
    Catheterization, 36215-36218
    Thrombectomy, 37184-37186
    Hemodialysis Graft or Fistula, 36831
    Other than Hemodialysis Graft or Fistula, 35875, 36870
  Tibial
    Bypass Graft, 35566, 35571, 35623, 35666, 35671
    Bypass In Situ, 35585, 35587
    Embolectomy, 34203
    Thrombectomy, 34203
    Thromboendarterectomy, 35305-35306
  Tibioperoneal
    Angioplasty, 35459, 35470
    Atherectomy, 35485, 35495
  Transcatheter Therapy, 75894, 75896
    with Angiography, 75894
  Transposition
    Carotid, 33889, 35691, 35694, 35695
    Subclavian, 33889, 35693-35695
    Vertebral, 35691, 35693

Artery — *continued*
  Ulnar
    Aneurysm, 35045
    Embolectomy, 34111
    Sympathectomy, 64822
    Thrombectomy, 34111
    Unlisted Services and Procedures, 37799
  Vascular Study
    Extremities, 93922, 93923
  Vertebral
    Aneurysm, 35005, 61698, 61702
    Angiography, 75685
    Bypass Graft, 35508, 35515, 35642, 35645
    Catheterization, 36100
    Decompression, 61597
    Thromboendarterectomy, 35301
  Visceral
    Angioplasty, 35450, 35471
    Atherectomy, 35480, 35490
    Reimplantation, 35697
Artery Catheterization, Pulmonary
  See Catheterization, Pulmonary Artery
Artherectomies, Coronary
  See Artery, Coronary, Atherectomy
Arthrectomy
  Elbow, 24155
Arthrocentesis
  Intermediate Joint, 20605
  Large Joint, 20610
  Small Joint, 20600
Arthrodesis
  Ankle, 27870
    Tibiotalar and Fibulotalar Joints, 29899
  Arthroscopy
    Subtalar Joint, 29907
  Blair, 27870
  Campbell, 27870
  Carpometacarpal Joint
    Hand, 26843, 26844
    Thumb, 26841, 26842
  Cervical Anterior
    with Discectomy, 22554
  Elbow, 24800, 24802
  Finger Joint, 26850-26863
    Interphalangeal, 26860-26863
    Metacarpophalangeal, 26850
  Foot Joint, 28705, 28725, 28740
    with Advancement, 28737
    with Lengthening, 28737
    Pantalar, 28705
    Subtalar, 28725
    Triple, 28715
  Grice, 28725
  Hand Joint, 26843, 26844
  Hip Joint, 27284, 27286
  Intercarpal Joint, 25820
    with Autograft, 25825
    Great Toe, 28755
      with Tendon Transfer, 28760
  Interphalangeal Joint, 26860-26863
    Great Toe, 28755
      with Tendon Transfer, 28760
  Knee, 27580
  Metacarpophalangeal Joint, 26850-26852
    Great Toe, 28750
  Metatarsophalangeal Joint
    Great Toe, 28750
  Pre-Sacral Interbody, 0195T-0196T
  Pubic Symphysis, 27282
  Radioulnar Joint, Distal, 25830
    with Resection of Ulna, 25830
  Sacroiliac Joint, 27280
  Shoulder
    See Shoulder, Arthrodesis
  Shoulder Joint, 23800
    with Autogenous Graft, 23802
  Subtalar Joint, 29907
  Talus
    Pantalar, 28705
    Subtalar, 28725
    Triple, 28715

Arthrodesis — *continued*
  Tarsal Joint, 28730, 28735, 28740
    with Advancement, 28737
    with Lengthening, 28737
  Tarsometatarsal Joint, 28730, 28735, 28740
  Thumb Joint, 26841, 26842
  Tibiofibular Joint, 27871
  Vertebra
    Additional Interspace
      Anterior/Anterolateral Approach, 22585
      Lateral Extracavitary, 22534
      Posterior/Posterolateral and/or Lateral Transverse Process, 22632
    Cervical
      Anterior/Anterolateral Approach, 22548
      Posterior/Posterolateral and/or Lateral Transverse Process, 22590-22600
    Lumbar
      Anterior/Anterolateral Approach, 22558
      Lateral Extracavitary, 22533
      Posterior/Interbody, 22630
      Posterior/Posterolateral and/or Lateral Transverse Process, 22612, 22630
      Presacral Interbody Technique, 0195T-0196T
    Spinal Deformity
      Anterior Approach, 22808-22812
      Posterior Approach, 22800, 22802, 22804
    Spinal Fusion
      Exploration, 22830
    Thoracic
      Anterior/Anterolateral Approach, 22556
      Lateral Extracavitary, 22532
      Posterior/Posterolateral and/or Lateral Traverse Process, 22610
  Vertebrae
    Posterior, 22614
  Wrist, 25800
    with Graft, 25810
    with Sliding Graft, 25805
    Radioulnar Joint, Distal, 25830
Arthrography
  Ankle, 73615
    Injection, 27648
  Elbow, 73085
    Injection, 24220
  Hip, 73525
    Injection, 27093, 27095
  Knee, 73580
    Injection, 27370
  Sacroiliac Joint, 73542
    Injection, 27096
  Shoulder, 73040
    Injection, 23350
  Temporomandibular Joint (TMJ), 70328-70332
    Injection, 21116
  Wrist, 73115
    Injection, 25246
Arthroplasty
  Ankle, 27700-27703
  Bower's, 25332
  Cervical, 0092T, 22856
  Elbow, 24360
    with Implant, 24361, 24362
    Total Replacement, 24363
  Hip, 27132
    Partial Replacement, 27125
    Revision, 27134-27138
    Total Replacement, 27130
  Interphalangeal Joint, 26535, 26536
  Knee, 27437-27443, 27446, 27447
    with Prosthesis, 27438, 27445

Atria — *continued*
   Reconstruction, 33254-33256, 33265-33266
   Surgical, 33265-33266
Atrial Electrogram
   See Cardiology, Diagnostic
   Esophageal Recording, 93615, 93616
Atrial Fibrillation
   See Fibrillation, Atrial
Atrioseptopexy
   See Heart, Repair, Atrial Septum
Atrioseptoplasty
   See Heart, Repair, Atrial Septum
Attachment
   See Fixation
Attendance and Resuscitation Services
   Newborn, 99464
ATTENUVAX, 90705
Atticotomy, 69631, 69635
Audiologic Function Tests
   See Ear, Nose and Throat; Hearing Evaluation
   Acoustic Reflex, 92568
   Acoustic Reflex Decay, 92569
   Audiometry
     Bekesy, 92560, 92561
     Comprehensive, 92557
     Conditioning Play, 92582
     Groups, 92559
     Pure Tone, 92552, 92553
     Select Picture, 92583
     Speech, 92555, 92556
     Visual Reinforcement, 92579
   Central Auditory Function, 92620, 92621
   Diagnostic Analysis
     Auditory Brainstem Implant, 92640
   Electrocochleography, 92584
   Evoked Otoacoustic Emissions, 92587, 92588
   Filtered Speech, 92571
   Lombard Test, 92700
   Loudness Balance, 92562
   Screening, 92551
   Sensorineural Acuity, 92575
   Short Increment Sensitivity Index, 92564
   Staggered Spondaic Word Test, 92572
   Stenger Test, 92565, 92577
   Synthetic Sentence Test, 92576
   Tinnitus Assessment, 92625
   Tone Decay, 92563
Audiometry
   Bekesy, 92560, 92561
   Brainstem Evoked Response, 92585, 92586
   Comprehensive, 92557
   Conditioning Play, 92582
   Groups, 92559
   Pure Tone, 92552, 92553
   Select Picture, 92583
   Speech, 92555, 92556
   Tympanometry, 92567
Auditory Brain Stem Evoked Response, 92585-92586
Auditory Canal
   Decompression, 61591
   External
     Abscess
       Incision and Drainage, 69020
     Atresia, Congenital, 69320
     Biopsy, 69105
     Lesion
       Excision, 69140-69155
     Reconstruction, 69310, 69320
       for Congenital Atresia, 69320
       for Stenosis, 69310
     Removal
       Cerumen, 69210
       Ear Wax, 69210
       Foreign Body, 69200, 69205
   Internal
     Decompression, 69960

Auditory Canal Atresia, External
   See Atresia, Congenital, Auditory Canal, External
Auditory Evoked Otoacoustic Emission, 92587, 92588
Auditory Evoked Potentials, 92585, 92586
Auditory Labyrinth
   See Ear, Inner
Auditory Meatus
   X-ray, 70134
Auditory Tube
   See Eustachian Tube
Augmentation
   Chin, 21120, 21123
   Malar, 21270
   Mandibular Body
     with Bone Graft, 21127
     with Prosthesis, 21125
   Osteoplasty
     Facial Bones, 21208
   Percutaneous
     Spine, 22523-22525
   Vertebral, 22523-22525
Augmentation Mammoplasty
   See Breast, Augmentation
Augmented Histamine Test, 91052
   Gastric Analysis Test, 91052
Aural Rehabilitation Test, 92626-92633
Auricle (Heart)
   See Atria
Auricular Fibrillation
   See Fibrillation, Atrial
Auricular Prosthesis, 21086
Australia Antigen
   Core, 86704
   IgM, 86705
   Surface, 86706
Autograft
   Bone
     Local, 20936
     Morselized, 20937
     Structural, 20938
   Chondrocytes
     Knee, 27412
   Dermal, 15130-15136
   Epidermal, 15110-15111, 15115-15116, 15150-15152, 15155-15157
   Osteochondral
     Knee, 27416
     Talus, 28446
   Skin
     Dermal, 15130-15136
     Epidermal, 15110-15116, 15150-15157
     Harvesting
       for Tissue Culture, 15040
   Spine Surgery
     Local, 20936
     Morselized, 20937
     Structural, 20938
Autologous Blood Transfusion
   See Autotransfusion
Autologous Transplantation
   See Autograft
Automated Lamellar Keratoplasty (ALK), 65710
Autonomic Nervous System Function
   Heart Rate Response, 95921-95923
   Pseudomotor Response, 95921-95923
   Sympathetic Function, 95921-95923
AutoPap, 88152
Autoprothrombin C
   See Thrombokinase
Autoprothrombin I
   See Proconvertin
Autoprothrombin II
   See Christmas Factor
Autoprothrombin III
   See Stuart-Power Factor
Autopsy
   Coroner's Examination, 88045
   Forensic Examination, 88040

Autopsy — *continued*
   Gross and Microscopic
     Examination, 88020-88029
     Infant with Brain, 88028
     Stillborn or Newborn with Brain, 88029
   Gross Examination, 88000-88016
   Organ, 88037
   Regional, 88036
   Unlisted Services and Procedures, 88099
Autotransfusion
   Blood, 86890, 86891
Autotransplant
   See Autograft
Autotransplantation
   Renal, 50380
AVF, 35180-35190, 36815
AV Fistula (Arteriovenous Fistula)
   Cannulization
     Vein, 36815
   Repair
     Abdomen, 35182
       Acquired or Traumatic, 35189
     Head, 35180
       Acquired or Traumatic, 35188
     Lower Extremity, 35184
       Acquired or Traumatic, 35190
     Neck, 35180
       Acquired or Traumatic, 35188
     Thorax, 35182
       Acquired or Traumatic, 35189
     Upper Extremity, 35184
       Acquired or Traumatic, 35190
   Revision
     Hemodialysis Graft or Fistula
       with Thrombectomy, 36833
       without Thrombectomy, 36832
   Thrombectomy
     Dialysis Graft
       without Revision, 36831
A Vitamin, 84590
AV Shunt (Arteriovenous Shunt), 36145, 75790
Avulsion
   Nails, 11730, 11732
   Nerves, 64732-64772
Axilla
   Skin Graft
     Delay of Flap, 15620
     Full Thickness, 15240, 15241
     Pedicle Flap, 15574
     Tissue Transfer, Adjacent, 14040, 14041
Axillary Arteries
   See Artery, Axillary
Axillary Nerve
   Injection
     Anesthetic, 64417
Axis, Dens
   See Odontoid Process
AZH (Assisted Zonal Hatching), 89253

B

Bacillus Calmette Guerin Vaccine
   See BCG Vaccine
Backbench Reconstruction Prior to Implant
   Intestine, 44715-44721
   Kidney, 50323-50329
   Liver, 47143-47147
   Pancreas, 48551-48552
   Wound Exploration, Penetrating, 20102
Backbone
   See Spine
Back/Flank
   Biopsy, 21920, 21925
   Repair
     Hernia, 49540
   Strapping, 29220
   Tumor
     Excision, 21930
     Radical Resection, 21935
   Wound Exploration
     Penetrating, 20102

Bacteria Culture
   Additional Methods, 87077
   Aerobic, 87040-87071
   Anaerobic, 87073-87076
   Blood, 87040
   Feces, 87045, 87046
   Nose, 87070
   Other Source, 87070-87075
   Screening, 87081
   Stool, 87045-87046
   Throat, 87070
   Urine, 87086, 87088
Bacterial Endotoxins, 87176
Bacterial Overgrowth Breath Test, 91065
   Homogenization, Tissue, for Culture, 87176
Bactericidal Titer, Serum, 87197
Bacterium
   Antibody, 86609
BAEP (Brainstem Auditory Evoked Potential), 92585-92586
BAER, 92585-92586
Baker's Cyst, 27345
Baker Tube
   Decompression of Bowel, 44021
Balanoplasty
   See Penis, Repair
Baldy-Webster Operation, 58400
Balkan Grippe
   See Q Fever
Balloon Angioplasty
   See Angioplasty
Balloon Assisted Device
   Aorta, 33967-33974
Balloon, Cardiac Catheter, Insertion, 33967
Banding
   Artery
     Fistula, 37607
     Pulmonary, 33690
Band, Pulmonary Artery
   See Banding, Artery, Pulmonary
Bankart Procedure, 23455
Bank, Blood
   See Blood Banking
B Antibodies, Hepatitis
   See Antibody, Hepatitis B
B Antigens, Hepatitis
   See Hepatitis Antigen, B
Barany Caloric Test, 92533
Barbiturates
   Blood or Urine, 82205
Bardenheuer Operation, 37616
Bariatric Surgery, 43644-43645, 43770-43774, 43842-43848, 43886-43888
Barium, 83015
Barium Enema, 74270, 74280
   Intussusception, 74283
Barker Operation, 28120
Barr Bodies, 88130
Barrel-Stave Procedure, 61559
Barr Procedure, 27690-27692
Barsky's Procedures, 26580
Bartholin's Gland
   Abscess
     Incision and Drainage, 56420
   Cyst
     Repair, 56440
     Excision, 56740
     Marsupialization, 56440
Bartonella
   Antibody, 86611
Bartonella Detection, 87470-87472
Basic Life Services, 99450
Basic Proteins, Myelin
   See Myelin Basic Protein
Basilar Arteries
   See Artery, Basilar
Bassett's Operation, 56630-56640
Batch-Spittler-McFaddin Operation, 27598
Battle's Operation, 44950, 44960

© 2008 Ingen

Bone — *continued*
  X-ray — *continued*
    Osseous Survey, 77074-77077
Bone 4–Carboxyglutamic Protein
  See Osteocalcin
Bone, Carpal
  See Carpal Bone
Bone, Cheek
  See Cheekbone
Bone Conduction Hearing Device, Electromagnetic
  Implantation
    Replacement, 69710
  Removal
    Repair, 69711
Bone Density Study
  Appendicular Skeleton, 77079, 77081
  Axial Skeleton, 77078, 77080
  Ultrasound, 76977
  Vertebral Fracture Assessment, 77082
Bone, Facial
  See Facial Bone
Bone Graft
  Allograft
    Morselized, 20930
    Structural, 20931
  Any Donor Area, 20900-20902
  Augmentation
    Mandibular Body, 21127
  Autograft, 20936
    Morselized, 20937
    Structural, 20938
  Femur, 27170
  Fracture
    Orbit, 21408
  Harvesting, 20900, 20902
  Malar Area, 21210
  Mandible, 21215
  Mandibular Ramus, 21194
  Maxilla, 21210
  Microvascular Anastomosis
    Fibula, 20955
    Iliac Crest, 20956
    Metatarsal Bone, 20957
    Other, 20962
    Rib, 20962
  Nasal Area, 21210
  Nasomaxillary Complex Fracture, 21348
  Open Treatment
    Craniofacial Separation, 21436
  Osteocutaneous Flap, 20969-20973
  Patella, 27599
  Reconstruction
    Mandibular Ramus, 21194
    Midface, 21145-21160
  Skull, 61316
    Excision, 62148
  Spine Surgery
    Allograft
      Morselized, 20930
      Structural, 20931
    Autograft
      Local, 20936
      Morselized, 20937
      Structural, 20938
  Vascular Pedicle, 25430
Bone Healing
  Electrical Stimulation
    Invasive, 20975
    Noninvasive, 20974
  Ultrasound Stimulation, 20979
Bone, Hyoid
  See Hyoid Bone
Bone Infection
  See Osteomyelitis
Bone Marrow
  Aspiration, 38220
  Harvesting, 38230
  Magnetic Resonance Imaging (MRI), 77084
  Needle Biopsy, 38221
  Nuclear Medicine
    Imaging, 78102-78104

Bone Marrow — *continued*
  Smear, 85097
  T-Cell
    Transplantation, 38240, 38241, 38242
  Trocar Biopsy, 38221
Bone, Metatarsal
  See Metatarsal
Bone, Nasal
  See Nasal Bone
Bone, Navicular
  See Navicular
Bone Osseous Survey, 77074-77075
Bone Plate
  Mandible, 21244
Bone, Scan
  See Bone, Nuclear Medicine; Nuclear Medicine
Bone, Semilunar
  See Lunate
Bone, Sesamoid
  See Sesamoid Bone
Bone Spur, 28119
Bone, Tarsal
  See Ankle Bone
Bone, Temporal
  See Temporal, Bone
Bone Wedge Reversal
  Osteotomy, 21122
BOOSTRIX, 90715
Bordetella
  Antibody, 86615
  Antigen Detection
    Direct Fluorescent Antibody, 87265
Borrelia
  Antibody, 86618, 86619
  Antigen, 87475-87477
Borrelia burgdorferi ab, 86618-86619
Borreliosis, Lyme
Borthen Operation, 66165
Bost Fusion
  Arthrodesis, Wrist, 25800-25810
Bosworth Operation, 23550, 23552
Bottle Type Procedure, 55060
Botulinum Toxin
  Chemodenervation
    Extraocular Muscle, 67345
    Facial Muscle, 64612
    Neck Muscle, 64613
Boutonniere Deformity, 26426, 26428
Bowel
  See Intestine(s)
Bower's Arthroplasty, 25332
Bowleg Repair, 27455, 27457
Boxer's Fracture Treatment, 26600-26615
Boyce Operation, 50040, 50045
Boyd Amputation, 27880-27889
Boyd Hip Disarticulation, 27590
Brace
  See Cast
  for Leg Cast, 29358
Brachial Arteries
  See Artery, Brachial
Brachial Plexus
  Decompression, 64713
  Injection
    Anesthetic, 64415, 64416
  Neuroplasty, 64713
  Release, 64713
  Repair
    Suture, 64861
Brachiocephalic Artery
  See Artery, Brachiocephalic
Brachycephaly, 21175
Brachytherapy, 0182T, 77761-77778, 77789
  Dose Plan, 77326-77328
    High Dose Electronic, 0182T
  Remote Afterloading
    1 Channel, 77785
    2-12 Channels, 77786
    Over 12 Channels, 77787
  Unlisted Services and Procedures, 77799

Bradykinin
  Blood or Urine, 82286
Brain
  See Brainstem; Mesencephalon; Skull Base Surgery
  Abscess
    Drainage, 61150, 61151
    Excision, 61514, 61522
    Incision and Drainage, 61320, 61321
  Adhesions
    Lysis, 62161
  Anesthesia, 00210-00218, 00220-00222
  Angiography, 70496
  Biopsy, 61140
    Stereotactic, 61750, 61751
  Catheter
    Irrigation, 62194, 62225
    Replacement, 62160, 62194, 62225
  Catheter Placement
    for Chemotherapy, 0169T
  Cisternography, 70015
  Computer Assisted
    Surgery, 61795
  Cortex
    Magnetic Stimulation, 0160T-0161T
  Craniopharyngioma, 61545
    Excision, 61545
  CT Scan, 0042T, 70450-70470, 70496
  Cyst
    Drainage, 61150, 61151, 62161, 62162
    Excision, 61516, 61524, 62162
  Doppler Transcranial, 93886-93893
  Epileptogenic Focus
    Excision, 61534, 61536
  Excision
    Amygdala, 61566
    Choroid Plexus, 61544
    Hemisphere, 61542-61543
    Hemispherectomy, 61542, 61543
    Hippocampus, 61566
    Other Lobe, 61323, 61539, 61540
    Temporal Lobe, 61537, 61538
  Exploration
    Infratentorial, 61305
    Supratentorial, 61304
  Hematoma
    Drainage, 61154
    Incision and Drainage, 61312-61315
  Implantation
    Chemotherapeutic Agent, 61517
    Electrode, 61850-61875
    Pulse Generator, 61885, 61886
    Receiver, 61885, 61886
    Thermal Perfusion Probe, 0077T
  Incision
    Corpus Callosum, 61541
    Frontal Lobe, 61490
    Mesencephalic Tract, 61480
    Subpial, 61567
  Infusion, 0169T
  Insertion
    Catheter, 61210
    Electrode, 61531, 61533, 61850-61875
    Pulse Generator, 61885, 61886
    Receiver, 61885, 61886
    Reservoir, 61210, 61215
  Lesion
    Aspiration, Stereotactic, 61750, 61751
    Excision, 61534, 61536, 61600-61608, 61615, 61616
  Magnetic Resonance Imaging (MRI), 70551-70555
    Intraoperative, 70557-70559
  Magnetic Stimulation
    Transcranial, 0160T-0161T
  Meningioma
    Excision, 61512, 61519

Brain — *continued*
  Myelography, 70010
  Nuclear Medicine
    Blood Flow, 78610
    Cerebrospinal Fluid, 78630-78650
    Imaging, 78600-78607
      Vascular Flow, 78610
    Shunt Evaluation, 78645
    Positron Emission Tomography (PET), 78608, 78609
  Removal
    Electrode, 61535, 61880
    Foreign Body, 61570, 62163
    Pulse Generator, 61888
    Receiver, 61888
    Shunt, 62256, 62258
  Repair
    Dura, 61618
    Wound, 61571
  Shunt
    Creation, 62180-62192, 62200-62223
    Removal, 62256, 62258
    Replacement, 62160, 62194, 62225-62258
    Reprogramming, 62252
  Skull
    Transcochlear Approach, 61596
    Transcondylar Approach, 61597
    Transpetrosal Approach, 61598
    Transtemporal Approach, 61595
  Skull Base
    Craniofacial Approach, 61580-61585
    Infratemporal Approach, 61590, 61591
    Orbitocranial Zygomatic Approach, 61592
  Stereotactic
    Aspiration, 61750, 61751
    Biopsy, 61750, 61751
    Catheter Placement, 0169T
    Create Lesion, 61720, 61735, 61790, 61791
    Localization for Placement Therapy Fields, 61770
    Radiation Treatment, 77432
    Radiosurgery, 61796-61800, 63620-63621, 77371-77373, 77435
    Surgery, 61795
    Trigeminal Tract, 61791
  Transection
    Subpial, 61567
  Tumor
    Excision, 61510, 61518, 61520, 61521, 61526, 61530, 61545, 62164
  X-ray with Contrast, 70010, 70015
Brain Coverings
  Tumor
    Excision, 61512, 61519
Brain Death
  Determination, 95824
Brainstem (Brain Stem)
  See Brain
  Biopsy, 61575, 61576
  Decompression, 61575, 61576
  Evoked Potentials, 92585, 92586
  Lesion
    Excision, 61575, 61576
Brain Stem Auditory Evoked Potential, 92585-92586
Brain Surface Electrode
  Stimulation, 95961-95962
Brain Tumor, Acoustic Neuroma
  See Brain, Tumor, Excision
Brain Tumor, Craniopharyngioma
  See Craniopharyngioma
Brain Tumor, Meningioma
  See Meningioma
Brain Ventriculography
  See Ventriculography

Branchial Cleft
Cyst
Excision, 42810, 42815
Branchioma
See Branchial Cleft, Cyst
Braun Procedure, 23405-23406
Breast
Ablation
Cryosurgery, 19105
Abscess
Incision and Drainage, 19020
Augmentation, 19324, 19325
Biopsy, 19100-19103
ABBI, 19103
Catheter Placement
for Interstitial Radioelement Application, 19296-19298, 20555, 41019
Cyst
Puncture Aspiration, 19000, 19001
Excision
Biopsy, 19100-19103
Capsules, 19371
Chest Wall Tumor, 19260-19272
Cyst, 19120
Lactiferous Duct Fistula, 19112
Lesion, 19120-19126
by Needle Localization, 19125, 19126
Mastectomy, 19300-19307
Nipple Exploration, 19110
Exploration, 19020
Implants
Insertion, 19340, 19342
Preparation of Moulage, 19396
Removal, 19328, 19330
Supply, 19396
Incision
Capsules, 19370
Injection
Radiologic, 19030
Magnetic Resonance Imaging (MRI), 77058-77059
with Computer-aided Detection, 0159T
Mammoplasty
Augmentation, 19324, 19325
Reduction, 19318
Mastopexy, 19316
Metallic Localization Clip Placement, 19295
Needle Biopsy, 19100
Needle Wire Placement, 19290, 19291
Periprosthetic Capsulectomy, 19371
Periprosthetic Capsulotomy, 19370
Reconstruction, 19357-19369
with Free Flap, 19364
with Latissimus Dorsi Flap, 19361
with Other Techniques, 19366
with Tissue Expander, 19357
with Transverse Rectus Abdominis Myocutaneous (TRAM) Flap, 19367-19369
Augmentation, 19324, 19325
Mammoplasty, 19318-19325
Nipple, 19350-19355
Areola, 19350
Nipple and Areola, 19350
Correction Inverted Nipples, 19355
Revision, 19380
Reduction, 19318
Removal
Capsules, 19371
Modified Radical, 19307
Partial, 19300-19302
Radical, 19305-19306
Simple, Complete, 19303
Subcutaneous, 19304
Repair
Suspension, 19316
Stereotactic Localization, 77031
Ultrasound, 76645

Breast — *continued*
Unlisted Services and Procedures, 19499
X-ray, 77055-77056, 77057
with Computer-aided Detection, 77051-77052
Mammography, 77051-77052
Localization Nodule, 77032
Breathing, Inspiratory Positive–Pressure
See Intermittent Positive Pressure Breathing (IPPB)
Breath Methylated Alkane Contour, 0085T
Breath Odor Alcohol
See Alcohol, Breath
Breath Test
Alcohol, Ethyl, 82075
Heart Transplant Rejection, 0085T
Helicobacter Pylori, 78267, 78268, 83013, 83014
Hydrogen, 91065
Bricker Operation
Intestines Anastomosis, 50820
Brisement Injection, 20550-20551
Bristow Procedure, 23450-23462
Capsulorrhaphy, Anterior, 23450-23462
Brock Operation, 33470-33475
Valvotomy, Pulmonary Valve, 33470-33474
Broken, Nose
See Fracture, Nasal Bone
Bronchi
Aspiration
Catheter, 31720-31725
Endoscopic, 31645-31646
Biopsy
Endoscopic, 31625-31629, 31632, 31633
Brushing
Protected Brushing, 31623
Catheterization
with Bronchial Brush Biopsy, 31717
Insertion
with Intracavitary Radioelement, 31643
Endoscopy
Aspiration, 31645-31646
Biopsy, 31625, 31628, 31629, 31632, 31633
Destruction
Tumor, 31641
Dilation, 31630-31631, 31636-31638
Excision
Lesion, 31640
Exploration, 31622
Foreign Body Removal, 31635
Fracture, 31630
Injection, 31656
Lesion, 31640, 31641
Stenosis, 31641
Tumor, 31640, 31641
Ultrasound, 31620
Exploration
Endoscopic, 31622
Fracture
Endoscopy, 31630
Injection
X-ray, 31656, 31715
Needle Biopsy, 31629, 31633
Reconstruction
Graft Repair, 31770
Stenosis, 31775
Removal
Foreign Body, 31635
Repair
Fistula, 32815
Stenosis
Endoscopic Treatment, 31641
Stent
Placement, 31636-31637
Revision, 31638

Bronchi — *continued*
Tumor
Excision, 31640
Ultrasound, 31620
Unlisted Services and Procedures, 31899
X-ray
with Contrast, 71040, 71060
Bronchial Allergen Challenge
See Bronchial Challenge Test
Bronchial Alveolar Lavage, 31624
Bronchial Brush Biopsy
with Catheterization, 31717
Bronchial Brushings
Protected Brushing, 31623
Bronchial Challenge Test
with Antigens or Gases, 95070
with Chemicals, 95071
See also Allergy Tests
Bronchial Provocation Test
See Allergy Tests, Challenge Test, Bronchial
Bronchoalveolar Lavage, 31624
Broncho–Bronchial Anastomosis, 32486
Bronchography, 71040, 71060
Catheterization
Injection
Transtracheal, 31715
Instillation
Contrast Material
Segmental
Injection, 31656
Bronchoplasty, 32501
Excision Stenosis and Anastomosis, 31775
Graft Repair, 31770
Reconstruction, Bronchi, 32501
Graft Repair, 31770
Stenosis, 31775
Bronchopneumonia, Hiberno–Vernal
See Q Fever
Bronchopulmonary Lavage, 31624
Bronchoscopy
Alveolar Lavage, 31624
Aspiration, 31645, 31646
Biopsy, 31625-31629, 31632, 31633
Brushing, Protected Brushing, 31623
Catheter Placement
Intracavity Radioelement, 31643
Diagnostic, 31622-31624, 31643
Dilation, 31630-31631, 31636-31638
Exploration, 31622
Fracture, 31630
Injection, 31656
Needle Biopsy, 31629, 31633
Removal
Foreign Body, 31635
Tumor, 31640, 31641
Stenosis, 31641
Stent Placement, 31631, 31636-31637
Stent Revision, 31638
Ultrasound, 31620
X-ray Contrast, 31656
Bronchospasm Evaluation, 94060, 94070
Pulmonology, Diagnostic, Spirometry, 94010-94070
Bronkodyl
See Theophylline
Browne's Operation, 54324
Brow Ptosis
Repair, 67900
Brucella, 86000
Antibody, 86622
Bruise
See Hematoma
Brunschwig Operation, 58240
Pelvis, Exenteration, 58240
Brush Biopsy
Bronchi, 31717
Brush Border ab
See Antibody, Heterophile
BSO, 58720

Bucca
See Cheek
Buccal Mucosa
See Mouth, Mucosa
Bulbourethral Gland
Excision, 53250
Bulla
Incision and Drainage
Puncture Aspiration, 10160
Lung
Excision–Plication, 32141
Endoscopic, 32655
BUN, 84520-84545
Bunionectomy
with Implant, 28293
Chevron Procedure, 28296
Concentric Procedure, 28296
Joplin Procedure, 28294
Keller Procedure, 28292
Lapidus Procedure, 28297
Mayo Procedure, 28292
McBride Procedure, 28292
Mitchell, 28296
Reverdin, 28296
Silver Procedure, 28290
Bunion Repair, 28296-28299
with Implant, 28293
Bunionectomy, 28290-28299
Chevron Procedure, 28296
Concentric Procedure, 28296
Joplin Procedure, 28294
Keller Procedure, 28292
Lapidus Procedure, 28297
Mayo Procedure, 28292
McBride Procedure, 28292
Mitchell Procedure, 28296
Reverdin, 28296
Silver Procedure, 28290
Bunnell Procedure, 24301
Burch Operation, 51840-51841
Laparoscopic, 58152
Burgess Amputation
Disarticulation, Ankle, 27889
Burhenne Procedure, 43500
Bile Duct, Removal of Calculus, 43264, 47420, 47425, 47554
Percutaneous, 47630
Burkitt Herpevirus
See Epstein–Barr Virus
Burns
Allograft, 15300-15321, 15330-15336
Anesthesia, 01951-01953
Debridement, 01951-01953, 15002-15003, 15004-15005, 16020-16030
Dressing, 16020-16030
Escharotomy, 16035, 16036
Excision, 01951-01953, 15002, 15004-15005
Initial Treatment, 16000
Tissue Culture Skin Grafts, 15100-15157
Xenograft, 15400-15431
Burr Hole
Anesthesia, 00214
Skull
with Injection, 61120
Biopsy, Brain, 61140
Catheterization, 61210
Drainage
Abscess, 61150, 61151
Cyst, 61150, 61151
Hematoma, 61154, 61156
Exploration
Infratentorial, 61253
Supratentorial, 61250
Implant
Cerebral Thermal Perfusion Probe, 0077T
Neurostimulator Array, 61863-61868
Injection, Contrast Media, 6112
Insertion
Catheter, 61210
Reservoir, 61210

Index

Capsulorrhaphy — Cast

© 2008 Inge

© 2008 Ingen

Collar Bone — *continued*
Dislocation — *continued*
Acromioclavicular Joint
Closed Treatment, 23540, 23545
Open Treatment, 23550, 23552
Sternoclavicular Joint
Closed Treatment, 23520, 23525
Open Treatment, 23530, 23532
Excision
Partial, 23120, 23180
Total, 23125
Fracture
Closed Treatment
with Manipulation, 23505
without Manipulation, 23500
Open Treatment, 23515
Osteotomy, 23480, 23485
Pinning, Wiring, Etc., 23490
Prophylactic Treatment, 23490
Repair Osteotomy, 23480, 23485
Saucerization, 23180
Sequestrectomy, 23170
Tumor
Excision, 23140
with Allograft, 23146
with Autograft, 23145
Radical Resection, 23200
X–ray, 73000
Collateral Ligament
Ankle
Repair, 27695-27698
Interphalangeal Joint, 26545
Knee Joint
Repair, 27409
Knee Repair, 27405
Metacarpophalangeal Joint Repair, 26540-26542
Repair
Ankle, 27695-27698
Collection and Processing
Allogenic Blood
Harvesting of Stem Cells, 38205
Autologous Blood
Harvesting of Stem Cells, 38206
Intraoperative, 86891
Preoperative, 86890
Specimen
Capillary Blood, 36416
Venous Blood, 36415, 36501-36592
Washings
Esophagus, 91000
Stomach, 91055
Colles Fracture, 25600-25609
Colles Fracture Reversed
See Smith Fracture
Collins Syndrome, Treacher
See Treacher–Collins Syndrome
Collis Procedure, 43326
Colon
See Colon–Sigmoid
Biopsy, 44025, 44100, 44322
by Colonoscopy, 45378
Endoscopic, 44389, 45380, 45391-45392
Colostomy, 44320, 44322
Revision, 44340-44346
Colotomy, 44322
Colostomy, 44320
CT Scan
Colonography, 0066T-0067T
Virtual Colonoscopy, 0066T-0067T
Destruction
Lesion, 44393, 45383
Tumor, 44393, 45383
Endoscopy
Biopsy, 44389, 45380, 45391-45392
Destruction
Lesion, 44393
Tumor, 44393, 45383

Colon — *continued*
Endoscopy — *continued*
Dilation, 45386
Exploration, 44388, 45378, 45381, 45386
Hemorrhage, 44391, 45382
Injection
Submucosal, 45381
Placement
Stent, 45387
Removal
Foreign Body, 44390, 45379
Polyp, 44392, 45384, 45385
Tumor, 45384, 45385
Specimen Collection, 45380
Excision
Partial, 44140-44147, 44160
Laparoscopic, 44204-44208
Total, 44150-44156
Laparoscopic, 44210-44212
Exclusion, 44700
Exploration, 44025
Endoscopic, 44388, 45378, 45381, 45386
Hemorrhage
Endoscopic Control, 44391, 45382
Hernia, 44050
Incision
Creation
Stoma, 44320, 44322
Exploration, 44025
Revision
Stoma, 44340-44346
Lavage
Intraoperative, 44701
Lesion
Destruction, 45383
Excision, 44110, 44111
Lysis
Adhesions, 44005
Obstruction, 44025, 44050
Reconstruction
Bladder from, 50810
Removal
Foreign Body, 44025, 44390, 45379
Polyp, 44392
Repair
Diverticula, 44605
Fistula, 44650-44661
Hernia, 44050
Malrotation, 44055
Obstruction, 44050
Ulcer, 44605
Volvulus, 44050
Wound, 44605
Stoma Closure, 44620, 44625
Suture
Diverticula, 44605
Fistula, 44650-44661
Plication, 44680
Stoma, 44620, 44625
Ulcer, 44605
Wound, 44605
Tumor
Ablation, 45339
Destruction, 45383
Ultrasound
Endoscopic, 45391-45392
via Colotomy, 45355
via Stoma, 44388-44397
Virtual, 0066T-0067T
Unlisted Services and Procedures, 44799
X–ray with Contrast
Barium Enema, 74270, 74280
Colonna Procedure, 27120
Acetabulum, Reconstruction, 27120
with Resection, Femoral Head, 27122
Colonography
CT Scan, 0066T-0067T
Colonoscopy
Biopsy, 45380
Collection of Specimen, 45380

Colonoscopy — *continued*
Collection of Specimen — *continued*
via Colotomy, 45355
Destruction
Lesion, 45383
Tumor, 45383
Dilation, 45386
Hemorrhage Control, 45382
Injection, Submucosal, 45381
Placement
Stent, 45387
Removal
Foreign Body, 45379
Polyp, 45384, 45385
Ultrasound, 45391-45392
Tumor, 45384, 45385
via Stoma, 44388-44390
Biopsy, 44393
Destruction
of Lesion, 44393
of Tumor, 44393
Exploration, 44388
Hemorrhage, 44391
Placement
Stent, 44397
Removal
Foreign Body, 44390
Polyp, 44392, 44394
Tumor, 44392, 44394
Virtual, 0066T-0067T
Colon–Sigmoid
See Colon
Biopsy
Endoscopy, 45331
Endoscopy
Ablation
Polyp, 45339
Tumor, 45339
Biopsy, 45331
Dilation, 45340
Exploration, 45330, 45335
Hemorrhage, 45334
Needle Biopsy, 45342
Placement
Stent, 45327, 45345
Removal
Foreign Body, 45332
Polyp, 45333, 45338
Tumor, 45333, 45338
Ultrasound, 45341, 45342
Volvulus, 45337
Exploration
Endoscopy, 45330, 45335
Hemorrhage
Endoscopy, 45334
Needle Biopsy
Endoscopy, 45342
Removal
Foreign Body, 45332
Repair
Volvulus
Endoscopy, 45337
Ultrasound
Endoscopy, 45341, 45342
Colorrhaphy, 44604
Color Vision Examination, 92283
Colostomy, 44320, 45563
Abdominal
Establishment, 50810
Delayed Opening, 44799
Home Visit, 99505
Intestine, Large
with Suture, 44605
Perineal
Establishment, 50810
Revision, 44340
Paracolostomy Hernia, 44345, 44346
Colotomy, 44025
Colpectomy
with Hysterectomy, 58275
with Repair of Enterocele, 58280
Partial, 57106
Total, 57110

Colpoceliocentesis
See Colpocentesis
Colpocentesis, 57020
Colpocleisis, 57120
Colpocleisis Complete
See Vagina, Closure
Colpohysterectomies
See Excision, Uterus, Vaginal
Colpoperineorrhaphy, 57210
Colpopexy, 57280
Extra–peritoneal, 57282
Intraperitoneal, 57283
Laparoscopic, 57425
Colpoplasty
See Repair, Vagina
Colporrhaphy
Anterior, 57240, 57289
with Insertion of Mesh, 57267
with Insertion of Prosthesis, 57267
Anteroposterior, 57260, 57265
with Enterocele Repair, 57265
with Insertion of Mesh, 57267
with Insertion of Prosthesis, 57267
Manchester, 58400
Nonobstetrical, 57200
Posterior, 57250
Colposcopy
Biopsy, 56821, 57421, 57454-57455, 57460
Endometrial, 58110
Cervix, 57421, 57452-57461
Exploration, 57452
Loop Electrode Biopsy, 57460
Loop Electrode Conization, 57461
Perineum, 99170
Vagina, 57420-57421
Vulva, 56820
Biopsy, 56821
Colpotomy
Drainage
Abscess, 57010
Exploration, 57000
Colpo–Urethrocystopexy, 58152, 58267, 58293
Marshall–Marchetti–Krantz procedure, 58152, 58267, 58293
Pereyra Procedure, 58267, 58293
Colprosterone
See Progesterone
Columna Vertebralis
See Spine
Column Chromatography/Mass Spectrometry, 82541-82544
Combined Heart–Lung Transplantation
See Transplantation, Heart–Lung
Combined Right and Left Heart Cardiac Catheterization
See Cardiac Catheterization, Combined Left and Right Heart
Combined Vaccine, 90710
Comedones
Opening or Removal of (Incision and Drainage)
Acne Surgery, 10040
Commando–Type Procedure, 41155
Commissurotomy
Right Ventricular, 33476, 33478
Common Sensory Nerve
Repair, Suture, 64834
Common Truncus
See Truncus, Arteriosus
Communication Device
Non–speech–generating, 92605-92606
Speech–generating, 92607-92609
Community/Work Reintegration
See Physical Medicine/Therapy/Occupational Therapy
Training, 97537
Compatibility Test
Blood, 86920
Electronic, 86923

© 2008 Ingenix

Index

Culdocentesis — Cystectomy

Dual X–ray Absorptiometry (DXA) — *continued*
    Appendicular, 77081
    Axial Skeleton, 77080
    Vertebral Fracture, 77082
Duct, Bile
    See Bile Duct
Duct, Hepatic
    See Hepatic Duct
Duct, Nasolacrimal
    See Nasolacrimal Duct
Ductogram, Mammary
    See Galactogram
Duct, Omphalomesenteric
    See Omphalomesenteric Duct
Duct, Pancreatic
    See Pancreatic Duct
Duct, Salivary
    See Salivary Duct
Duct, Stensen's
    See Parotid Duct
Duct, Thoracic
    See Thoracic Duct
Ductus Arteriosus
    Repair, 33820-33824
Ductus Deferens
    See Vas Deferens
Duhamel Procedure, 45120
Dunn Operation, 28725
Duodenectomy
    Near Total, 48153, 48154
    Total, 48150, 48152
Duodenography, 74260
Duodenotomy, 44010
Duodenum
    Biopsy, 44010
    Exclusion, 48547
    Exploration, 44010
    Incision, 44010
    Removal/Foreign Body, 44010
    X–ray, 74260
Duplex Scan
    See Vascular Studies
    Arterial Studies
        Aorta, 93978, 93979
        Extracranial, 93880, 93882
        Lower Extremity, 93925, 93926
        Penile, 93980, 93981
        Upper Extremity, 93930, 93931
        Visceral, 93975-93979
    Hemodialysis Access, 93990
    Venous Studies
        Extremity, 93970, 93971
        Penile, 93980, 93981
Dupuy–Dutemp Operation, 67971
Dupuytren's Contracture, 26040, 26045
Durand–Nicolas–Favre Disease
    See Lymphogranuloma Venereum
Dust, Angel
    See Phencyclidine
Duvries Operation
    See Tenoplasty
D Vitamin
    See Vitamin, D
Dwyer Procedure, 28300
DXA (Dual Energy X–ray Absorptiometry), 77080-77082
D–Xylose Absorption Test, 84620
Dynamometry
    See Osteotomy, Calcaneus
    Venous Studies
        with Ophthalmoscopy, 92260

E

E1
    See Estrone
E2
    See Estradiol
E3
    See Estriol
E Antigens
    See Hepatitis Antigen, Be
Ear
    Collection of Blood from, 36415, 36416

Ear — *continued*
    Drum, 69420, 69421, 69433, 69436, 69450, 69610, 69620
    See Tympanic Membrane
    External
        Abscess
            Incision and Drainage
                Complicated, 69005
                Simple, 69000
        Biopsy, 69100
        Excision
            Partial, 69110
            Total, 69120
        Hematoma
            Incision and Drainage, 69000, 69005
        Reconstruction, 69300
        Unlisted Services and Procedures, 69399
    Inner
        CT Scan, 70480-70482
        Excision
            Labyrinth, 69905, 69910
        Exploration
            Endolymphatic Sac, 69805, 69806
        Incision
            Labyrinth, 69801, 69802
            Semicircular Canal, 69840
        Insertion
            Cochlear Device, 69930
        Semicircular Canal, 69820
        Unlisted Services and Procedures, 69949
    Middle
        Catheterization, 69405
        CT Scan, 70480-70482
        Exploration, 69440
        Inflation
            with Catheterization, 69400
            without Catheterization, 69401
        Insertion
            Catheter, 69405
        Lesion
            Excision, 69540
        Reconstruction
            Tympanoplasty with Antrotomy or Mastoidectomy, 69635-69637
            Tympanoplasty with Mastoidectomy, 69641-69646
            Tympanoplasty without Mastoidectomy, 69631-69633
        Removal
            Ventilating Tube, 69424
        Repair
            Oval Window, 69666
            Round Window, 69667
        Revision
            Stapes, 69662
        Tumor
            Excision, 69550-69554
        Unlisted Services and Procedures, 69799
    Outer
        CT Scan, 70480-70482
        Skin Graft
            Delay of Flap, 15630
            Full Thickness, 15260, 15261
            Pedicle Flap, 15576
            Split, 15120, 15121
            Tissue Transfer, Adjacent, 14060-14061
Ear Canal
    See Auditory Canal
Ear Cartilage
    Graft
        to Face, 21235
Ear Lobes
    Pierce, 69090
Ear, Nose, and Throat
    See Hearing Aid Services; Otorhinolaryngology

Ear, Nose, and Throat — *continued*
    Audiologic Function Tests
        Acoustic Reflex, 92568
        Acoustic Reflex Decay, 92569
        Audiometry
            Bekesy, 92560, 92561
            Comprehensive, 92557
            Conditioning Play, 92582
            Evoked Response, 92585, 92586
            Groups, 92559
            Pure Tone, 92552, 92553
            Select Picture, 92583
            Speech, 92555, 92556
        Brainstem Evoked Response, 92585, 92586
        Central Auditory Function, 92620-92621
        Ear Protector Evaluation, 92596
        Electrocochleography, 92584
        Filtered Speech, 92571
        Hearing Aid Evaluation, 92590-92595
        Lombard Test, 92700
        Loudness Balance, 92562
        Screening Test, 92551
        Sensorineural Acuity, 92575
        Short Increment Sensitivity Index (SISI), 92564
        Staggered Spondaic Word Test, 92572
        Stenger Test, 92565, 92577
        Synthetic Sentence Test, 92576
        Tone Decay, 92563
        Tympanometry, 92567
    Audiometry
        Evoked Otoacoustic Emissions, 92587, 92588
        Visual Reinforcement, 92579
    Binocular Microscopy, 92504
    Facial Nerve Function Study, 92516
    Hearing Evaluation, 92506
    Language Evaluation, 92506
    Laryngeal Function Study, 92520
    Nasal Function Study, 92512
    Nasopharyngoscopy, 92511
    Speech Evaluation, 92506
    Vestibular Function Tests
        Additional Electrodes, 92547
        Caloric Tests, 92533, 92543
        Nystagmus
            Optokinetic, 92534, 92544
            Positional, 92532, 92542
            Spontaneous, 92531, 92541
        Posturography, 92548
        Torsion Swing Test, 92546
        Tracking Test, 92545
Ear Protector Attenuation, 92596
    See Hearing Aid Services
Ear Wax
    See Cerumen
Ebstein Anomaly Repair, 33468
EBV, 86663-86665
E B Virus
    See Epstein–Barr Virus
ECCE, 66840-66852, 66940
ECG, 3120F, 93000-93024, 93040-93278
ECG, 3120F, 93000-93010
    Signal-Averaged, 93278
    Transmission, 93012-93014
    Wearable, 93224-93227
    Wearable, 93224-93272
        24 Hours, 93228-93272
Echinococcosis, 86171, 93278
ECHO, 76825, 93303-93312, 93314, 93315, 93317-93321, 93350
Echocardiography
    Cardiac, 93320-93350
        Intracardiac, 93662
        Transesophageal, 93318
        Transthoracic, 93303-93317
    Doppler, 93303-93321, 93350, 93662
    Fetal Heart, 76825-76828

Echocardiography — *continued*
    Fetal Heart — *continued*
        Doppler
            Complete, 76827
            Follow–up or Repeat Study, 76828
    for Congenital Anomalies
        Transesophageal, 93315-93317
        Transthoracic, 93303, 93304
    Intracardiac, 93662
    M Mode and Real Time, 99306
    Stress Test, 93350-93351
        with Contrast, 93352
    Transesophageal, 93312-93317
        for Congenital Anomalies, 93315-93317
    Transthoracic, 93303-93317, 93350
        for Congenital Anomalies, 93303, 93304
Echoencephalography, 76506
Echography
    Abdomen, 76700, 76705
    Arm, 76880
    Breast, 76645
    Cardiac, 93303-93317, 93320, 93321, 93350, 93662
        Guidance, 76932
    Chest, 76604
    Extracranial Arteries, 93880, 93882
    Eyes, 76510-76529
    Follow–Up, 76970
    Head, 76536
    Heart
        Radiologic Guidance, 76932
    Hip
        Infant, 76885, 76886
    Intracranial Arteries, 93886-93893
    Intraoperative, 76998
    Kidney
        Transplant, 76776
    Leg, 76880
    Neck, 76536
    Pelvis, 76856, 76857
    Placement Therapy Fields, 76950
    Pregnant Uterus, 76801-76817
    Prostate, 76872-76873
    Retroperitoneal, 76770, 76775
    Scrotum, 76870
    Spine, 76800
    Transrectal, 76872, 76873
    Transvaginal, 76817, 76830
    Unlisted Services and Procedures, 76999
    Vagina, 76817, 76830
Echotomography
    See Echography
ECMO (Extracorporeal Circulation Membrane Oxygenation), 36822
    Isolated with Chemotherapy Perfusion, 36823
ECS
    See Emission Computerized Tomography
ECSF (Erythrocyte Colony Stimulating Factor)
    See Erythropoietin
ECT (Emission Computerized Tomography), 78607
ECT (Electroconvulsive Therapy), 90870
Ectasia
    See Dilation
Ectopic Pregnancy
    See Obstetrical Care
    Abdominal, 59130
    Cervix, 59140
    Interstitial
        Partial Resection Uterus, 59136
        Total Hysterectomy, 59135
    Laparoscopy, 59150
        with Salpingectomy and/or Oophorectomy, 59151
    Tubal, 59121
        with Salpingectomy and/or Oophorectomy, 59120

© 2008 Ingenix

© 2008 Inger

Esophagus — *continued*
Dilation, 43450-43458
    Endoscopic, 43220, 43226, 43248, 43249
    Surgical, 43510
Endoscopy
    Biopsy, 43202
    Dilation, 43220, 43226
    Exploration, 43200
    Hemorrhage, 43227
    Injection, 43201, 43204
    Insertion Stent, 43219
    Needle Biopsy, 43232
    Removal
        Foreign Body, 43215
        Polyp, 43216, 43217, 43228
        Tumor, 43216, 43228
    Ultrasound, 43231, 43232
    Vein Ligation, 43205
Excision
    Diverticula, 43130, 43135
    Partial, 43116-43124
    Total, 43107-43113, 43124
Exploration
    Endoscopy, 43200
Hemorrhage, 43227
Incision, 43020, 43045
    Muscle, 43030
Injection
    Sclerosis Agent, 43204
    Submucosal, 43201
Insertion
    Stent, 43219
    Tamponade, 43460
    Tube, 43510
Intubation with Specimen Collection, 91000
Lesion
    Excision, 43100, 43101
Ligation, 43405
Motility Study, 78258, 91010-91012
Needle Biopsy
    Endoscopy, 43232
Nuclear Medicine
    Imaging (Motility), 78258
    Reflux Study, 78262
Reconstruction, 43300, 43310, 43313
    Creation
        Stoma, 43350-43352
    Esophagostomy, 43350
    Fistula, 43305, 43312, 43314
    Gastrointestinal, 43360, 43361
Removal
    Foreign Bodies, 43020, 43045, 43215, 74235
    Lesion, 43216
    Polyp, 43216, 43217, 43228
Repair, 43300, 43310, 43313
    Esophagogastric Fundoplasty, 43324, 43325
        Laparoscopic, 43280
    Esophagogastrostomy, 43320
    Esophagojejunostomy, 43340, 43341
    Fistula, 43305, 43312, 43314, 43420, 43425
    Muscle, 43330, 43331
    Pre-existing Perforation, 43405
    Varices, 43401
    Wound, 43410, 43415
Stapling Gastroesophageal Junction, 43405
Suture
    Gastroesophageal Junction, 43405
    Wound, 43410, 43415
Ultrasound, 43231, 43232
Unlisted Services and Procedures, 43289, 43499
Vein
    Ligation, 43205, 43400
Video, 74230
X-ray, 74220
ophagus Neoplasm
See Tumor, Esophagus

Esophagus, Varix
See Esophageal Varices
ESR, 85651, 85652
ESRD, 90951-90961, 90967-90970
    Home, 90963-90966
EST, 90870
Established Patient
    Domiciliary or Rest Home Visit, 99334-99337
    Emergency Department Services, 99281-99285
    Home Services, 99347-99350
    Hospital Inpatient Services, 99221-99239
    Hospital Observation Services, 99217-99220
    Initial Inpatient Consultation, 99251-99255
    Office and/or Other Outpatient Consultations, 99241-99245
    Office Visit, 99211-99215
    Online Evaluation and Management Services
        Nonphysician, 98969
        Physician, 99444
    Outpatient Visit, 99211-99215
Establishment
    Colostomy
        Abdominal, 50810
        Perineal, 50810
Estes Operation
    See Ovary, Transposition
Estlander Procedure, 40525, 40527
Estradiol, 82670
    Response, 80415
Estriol
    Blood or Urine, 82677
Estrogen
    Blood or Urine, 82671, 82672
    Receptor, 84233
Estrone
    Blood or Urine, 82679
ESWL, 50590
Ethanediols
    See Ethylene Glycol
Ethanol
    Blood, 82055
    Breath, 82075
    Urine, 82055
Ethchlorvynol
    Blood, 82690
    Urine, 82690
Ethmoid
    Fracture
        with Fixation, 21340
Ethmoidectomy, 31200-31205
    with Nasal
        Sinus Endoscopy, 31254, 31255
    Endoscopic, 31254, 31255
    Skull Base Surgery, 61580, 61581
Ethmoid, Sinus
    See Sinus, Ethmoid
Ethosuccimid
    See Ethosuximide
Ethosuximide, 80168
    Assay, 80168
Ethyl Alcohol (Ethanol)
    Blood, 82055
    Breath, 82075
    Urine, 82055
Ethylene Dichlorides
    See Dichloroethane
Ethylene Glycol, 82693
Ethylmethylsuccimide
    See Ethosuximide
Etiocholanolone, 82696
Etiocholanolone Measurement
    See Etiocholanolone
ETOH, 82055, 82075
EUA, 57410, 92018, 92019, 92502
Euglobulin Lysis, 85360
European Blastomycosis
    See Cryptococcus
Eustachian Tube
    Catheterization, 69405

Eustachian Tube — *continued*
    Inflation
        with Catheterization, 69400
        without Catheterization, 69401
    Myringotomy, 69420
        Anesthesia, 69421
    Insertion
        Catheter, 69405
Eutelegenesis
    See Artificial Insemination
Evacuation
    Cervical Pregnancy, 59140
    Hematoma
        Brain, 61312-61315
        Subungual, 11740
    Hydatidiform Mole, 59870
Evaluation
    Asthma Symptoms, 1005F
    Multiple Molecular Probes, 88384-88386
    Occupation Therapy
        Re-evaluation, 97004
    Physical Therapy
        Re-evaluation, 97002
Evaluation and Management
    Alcohold and/or Substance Abuse, 99408-99409
    Anticoagulant Management, 99363-99364
    Assistive Technology Assessment, 97755
    Athletic Training
        Evaluation, 97005
        Re-evaluation, 97006
    Basic Life and/or Disability Evaluation Services, 99450
    Birthing Center, 99460, 99462-99465
    Care Plan Oversight Services, 99374-99380
        Home Health Agency Care, 99374
        Hospice, 99377
        Nursing Facility, 99379, 99380
    Case Management Services, 99366-99368
    Consultation, 99241-99255
    Critical Care, 99291, 99292
        Interfacility Pediatric Transport, 99466-99467
    Domiciliary or Rest Home, 99324-99337
    Emergency Department, 99281-99288
    Health Behavior
        Assessment, 96150
        Family Intervention, 96154, 96155
        Group Intervention, 96153
        Individual Intervention, 96152
        Re-assessment, 96151
    Home Services, 99341-99350
    Hospital, 99221-99233
    Hospital Discharge, 99238, 99239
    Hospital Services
        Initial, 99221-99233, 99460-99463, 99477
        Intensive Care
            Low Birth Weight, 99478-99480
            Neonate, 99477
        Observation Care, 99217-99220
        Subsequent, 99231, 99462-99463
    Insurance Examination, 99455-99456
    Internet Communication
        Nonphysician, 98969
        Physician, 99444
    Low Birth Weight Infant, 99468-99469, 99478-99480
    Medical
        with Individual Psychotherapy
            Hospital or Residential
            Care, 90817, 90819, 90822, 90824, 90827, 90829

Evaluation and Management — *continued*
    Medical — *continued*
        with Individual Psychotherapy
            Hospital or Residential Care
            — *continued*
                Office or Outpatient, 90805, 90807, 90809
        with Individual Psychotherapy, Interactive
            Office or Outpatient, 90811, 90813, 90815
    Neonatal
        Critical Care, 99468-99469
        Intensive Observation, 99477-99480
    Newborn Care, 99460-99465
    Nursing Facility, 99304-99318
    Observation Care, 99217-99220
    Occupation Therapy Evaluation, 97003
        Re-evaluation, 97004
    Office and Other Outpatient, 99201-99215
    On-line Assessment
        Nonphysician, 98969
        Physician, 99444
    Online Evaluation
        Nonphysician, 98969
        Physician, 99444
    Pediatric
        Critical Care, 99471-99472
        Interfacility Transport, 99466-99467
    Physical Therapy Evaluation, 97001
        Re-evaluation, 97002
    Physician Standby Services, 99360
    Preventive Services, 4000F-4001F, 99381-99429
    Prolonged Services, 99356, 99357
    Psychiatric/Records or Reports, 90885
    Smoking and Tobacco Cessation Counseling, 99406-99407
    Telephone Assessment
        Nonphysician, 98966-98968
        Physician, 99441-99443
    Unlisted Service and Procedures, 99499
    Work-Related and/or Medical Disability Evaluation, 99450
Evaluation Studies, Drug, Preclinical
    See Drug Screen
EVAR (Endovascular Aortic Repair), 34800-34826
Evisceration
    Ocular Contents
        with Implant, 65093
        without Implant, 65091
    Repair
        Abdominal Wall, 49900
    Suture
        Abdominal Wall, 49900
Evisceration, Pelvic
    See Exenteration, Pelvis
E Vitamin
    See Tocopherol
Evocative/Suppression Test, 80400-80440
    Stimulation Panel, 80410
Evoked Potential
    See Audiologic Function Tests
    Auditory Brainstem, 92585, 92586
    Central Motor
        Transcranial Motor Stimulation, 95928-95929
    Somatosensory Testing, 95925-95927
    Visual, CNS, 95930
Ewart Procedure
    Palate, Reconstruction, Lengthening, 42226, 42227
Examination
    Anorectal, 45990
    Involved Joint, 2004F

Excision — Excision

© 2008 Ingeni

Gastrointestinal, Upper —
  continued
  Removal
    Foreign body, 43247
    Lesion, 43250
    Polyp, 43250, 43251
    Tumor, 43250
  Stent Placement, 43256
  Tube Placement
    Endoscopy, 43237, 43238, 43246
  Ultrasound
    Endoscopy, 43237, 43238, 43242, 43259, 76975
Gastrojejunostomy, 43860, 43865
  with Duodenal Exclusion, 48547
  with Partial Gastrectomy, 43632
  with Vagotomy, 43825
  without Vagotomy, 43820
  Revision, 43860
    with Vagotomy, 43865
Gastroplasty
  with Esophagogastric Fundoplasty, 43326
  for Obesity, 43644-43645, 43842-43848
  Restrictive for Obesity, 43842
  Other than Vertical Banded, 43843
Gastrorrhaphy, 43840
Gastroschisis, 49605
Gastrostomy
  with Pancreatic Drain, 48001
  with Pyloroplasty, 43640
  with Vagotomy, 43640
  Closure, 43870
  Laparoscopic
    Permanent, 43832
    Temporary, 43653
  Temporary, 43830
    Laparoscopic, 43653
    Neonatal, 43831
Gastrostomy Tube
  Change of, 43760
  Conversion to Gastro-jejunostomy Tube, 49446
  Directed Placement
    Endoscopic, 43246
  Insertion
    Percutaneous, 43246, 49440
  Percutaneous, 49440
  Replacement, 49450
  Repositioning, 43761
Gastrotomy, 43500, 43501, 43510
GDH, 82965
GE
  Reflux, 78262
Gel Diffusion, 86331
Gene Product
  See Protein
Genioplasty, 21120-21123
  Augmentation, 21120, 21123
  Osteotomy, 21121-21123
Genitalia
  Female
    Anesthesia, 00940-00952
  Male
    Anesthesia, 00920-00938
  Skin Graft
    Delay of Flap, 15620
    Full Thickness, 15240, 15241
    Pedicle Flap, 15574
    Split, 15120, 15121
    Tissue Transfer, Adjacent, 14040, 14041
Genitourinary Sphincter, Artificial
  See Prosthesis, Urethral Sphincter
Genotype Analysis
  by Nucleic Acid
    Infectious Agent
      Hepatitis C Virus, 87902
      HIV-1 Protease/Reverse Transcriptase, 87901
Gentamicin, 80170
  Assay, 80170
Gentiobiase, 82963

Genus: Human Cytomegalovirus Group
  See Cytomegalovirus
GERD
  See Gastroesophageal Reflux Test
German Measles
  See Rubella
Gestational Trophoblastic Tumor
  See Hydatidiform Mole
GGT, 82977
GH, 83003
GHb, 83036
Giardia
  Antigen Detection
    Enzyme Immunoassay, 87329
    Immunofluorescence, 87269
Giardia Lamblia
  Antibody, 86674
Gibbons Stent, 52332
GIF, 84307
GIFT, 58976
Gillies Approach
  Fracture
    Zygomatic Arch, 21356
Gill Operation, 63012
Gingiva
  See Gums
Gingiva, Abscess
  See Abscess
  Fracture
    See Abscess, Gums; Gums
    Zygomatic Arch
      See Abscess, Gums; Gums, Abscess
Gingivectomy, 41820
Gingivoplasty, 41872
Girdlestone Laminectomy
  See Laminectomy
Girdlestone Procedure
  Acetabulum, Reconstruction, 27120, 27122
GI Tract
  See Gastrointestinal Tract
  X–Rays, 74240-74249, 74340, 74360
Glabellar Frown Lines
  Rhytidectomy, 15826
Gland
  See Specific Gland
Gland, Adrenal
  See Adrenal Gland
Gland, Bartholin's
  See Bartholin's Gland
Gland, Bulbourethral
  See Bulbourethral Gland
Gland, Lacrimal
  See Lacrimal Gland
Gland, Mammary
  See Breast
Gland, Parathyroid
  See Parathyroid Gland
Gland, Parotid
  See Parotid Gland
Gland, Pituitary
  See Pituitary Gland
Gland, Salivary
  See Salivary Glands
Gland, Sublingual
  See Sublingual Gland
Gland, Sweat
  See Sweat Glands
Gland, Thymus
  See Thymus Gland
Gland, Thyroid
  See Thyroid Gland
Gla Protein (Bone)
  See Osteocalcin
Glasses
  See Spectacle Services
Glaucoma
  Cryotherapy, 66720
  Cyclophotocoagulation, 66710, 66711
  Diathermy, 66700
  Fistulization of Sclera, 66150
  Provocative Test, 92140

Glaucoma Drainage Implant
  See Aqueous Shunt
GLC, 82486
Glenn Procedure, 33766, 33767
Glenohumeral Joint
  Arthrotomy, 23040
    with Biopsy, 23100
    with Synovectomy, 23105
  Exploration, 23107
  Removal
    Foreign or Loose Body, 23107
Glenoid Fossa
  Reconstruction, 21255
GLN, 82975
Globulin
  Antihuman, 86880-86886
  Immune, 90281-90399
  Sex Hormone Binding, 84270
Globulin, Corticosteroid–Binding, 84449
Globulin, Rh Immune, 90384-90386
Globulin, Thyroxine–Binding, 84442
Glomerular Procoagulant Activity
  See Thromboplastin
Glomus Caroticum
  See Carotid Body
Glossectomies, 41120-41155
Glossectomy, 41120-41155
Glossopexy, 41500
Glossorrhaphy
  See Suture, Tongue
Glucagon, 82943
  Tolerance Panel, 80422, 80424
  Tolerance Test, 82946
Glucose, 80422, 80424, 80430-80435, 95250
  Blood Test, 82947-82950, 82962
  Body Fluid, 82945
  Hormone Panel, 80430
  Interstitial Fluid
    Continuous Monitoring, 95250
  Tolerance Test, 82951, 82952
    with Tolbutamide, 82953
Glucose–6–Phosphate
  Dehydrogenase, 82955, 82960
Glucose Phosphate Isomerase, 84087
Glucose Phosphate Isomerase Measurement, 84087
Glucosidase, 82963
Glucuronide Androstanediol, 82154
Glue
  Cornea Wound, 65286
  Sclera Wound, 65286
Glukagon
  See Glucagon
Glutamate Dehydrogenase, 82965
Glutamate Pyruvate Transaminase, 84460
Glutamic Alanine Transaminase, 84460
Glutamic Aspartic Transaminase, 84450
Glutamic Dehydrogenase, 82965
Glutamine, 82975
Glutamyltransferase, Gamma, 82977
Glutathione, 82978
  Glutathione Reductase, 82979
Glutethimide, 82980
Glycanhydrolase, N–Acetylmuramide
  See Lysozyme
Glycated Hemoglobins
  See Glycohemoglobin
Glycated Protein, 82985
Glycerol, Phosphatidyl
  See Phosphatidylglycerol
Glycerol Phosphoglycerides
  See Phosphatidylglycerol
Glycerophosphatase
  See Alkaline Phophatase
Glycinate, Theophylline Sodium
  See Theophylline
Glycocholic Acid
  See Cholylglycine
Glycohemoglobin, 83036-83037
Glycol, Ethylene
  See Ethylene Glycol

Glycols, Ethylene
  See Ethylene Glycol
Glycosaminoglycan
  See Mucopolysaccharides
GMP (Guanosine Monophosphate), 83008
GMP, Cyclic
  See Guanosine Monophosphate
Goeckerman Treatment
  Photochemotherapy, 96910-96913
Gold
  Assay, 80172
  Blood, 80172
Goldwaite Procedure
  Reconstruction, Patella, for Instability, 27422
Golfer's Elbow, 24357-24359
Gol–Vernet Operation, 50120
Gonadectomy, Female
  See Oophorectomy
Gonadectomy, Male
  See Excision, Testis
Gonadotropin
  Chorionic, 84702, 84703
  FSH, 83001
  ICSH, 83002
  LH, 83002
Gonadotropin Panel, 80426
Goniophotography, 92285
Gonioscopy, 92020
Goniotomy, 65820
Gonococcus
  See Neisseria Gonorrhoeae
Goodenough Harris Drawing Test, 96101-96103
GOTT
  See Transaminase, Glutamic Oxaloacetic
GPUT
  See Galactose–1–Phosphate, uridyl Transferase
Graefe's Operation, 66830
Graft
  See Bone Graft; Bypass Graft
  Anal, 46753
  Aorta, 33840, 33845, 33852, 33860-33877
  Artery
    Coronary, 33503-33505
  Bone
    See Bone Marrow, Transplantation
    Anastomosis, 20969-20973
    Harvesting, 20900, 20902
    Microvascular Anastomosis, 20955-20962
    Osteocutaneous Flap with Microvascular Anastomosis, 20969-20973
    Vascular Pedicle, 25430
  Bone and Skin, 20969-20973
  Cartilage
    Ear to Face, 21235
    Harvesting, 20910, 20912
    See Cartilage Graft
    Rib to Face, 21230
    Three or More Segments
      Two Locations, 35682, 35683
  Composite, 35681-35683
  Conjunctiva, 65782
  Eye
    Amniotic Membrane, 65780
    Conjunctiva, 65782
    Stem Cell, 65781
  Cornea
    with Lesion Excision, 65426
  Corneal Transplant
    in Aphakia, 65750
    in Pseudophakia, 65755
    Lamellar, 65710
    Penetrating, 65730
  Dura
    Spinal Cord, 63710
  Endovascular, 34900
  Facial Nerve Paralysis, 15840-15845

Heart — *continued*
Septal Defect
See Septal Defect
Stimulation and Pacing, 93623
Thrombectomy, 33310-33315
Ventricular Assist Device, 33976
Intracorporeal, 33979
Transplantation, 33935, 33945
Anesthesia, 00580
Tricuspid Valve
See Tricuspid Valve
Tumor
Excision, 33120, 33130
Ultrasound
Radiologic Guidance, 76932
Unlisted Services and Procedures, 33999
Ventriculography
See Ventriculography
Ventriculomyectomy, 33416
Ventriculomyotomy, 33416
Wound
Repair, 33300, 33305
Heart Biopsy
Ultrasound, Radiologic Guidance, 76932
Heartsbreath Test, 0085T
Heart Sounds
Acoustic Recording
with Computer Analysis, 0068T-0070T
Heart Vessels
Angiography
Injection, 93545
Angioplasty
Percutaneous, 92982, 92984
See Angioplasty; Percutaneous Transluminal Angioplasty
Injection
Radiologic, 93545
Insertion
Graft, 33330-33335
Thrombolysis, 92975, 92977
Valvuloplasty
See Valvuloplasty
Percutaneous, 92986-92990
Heat Unstable Haemoglobin
See Hemoglobin, Thermolabile
Heavy Lipoproteins
See Lipoprotein
Heavy Metal, 83015, 83018
Heel
See Calcaneus
Collection of Blood, 36415, 36416
X-ray, 73650
Heel Bone
See Calcaneus
Heel Fracture
See Calcaneus, Fracture
Heel Spur
Excision, 28119
Heine–Medin Disease
See Polio
Heine Operation
See Cyclodialysis
Heinz Bodies, 85441, 85445
Helicobacter Pylori
Antibody, 86677
Antigen Detection
Enzyme Immunoassay, 87338, 87339
Breath Test, 78267, 78268, 83013
Stool, 87338
Urease Activity, 83009, 83013, 83014
Heller Procedure, 32665, 43279, 43330-43331
Helminth
Antibody, 86682
Hemagglutination Inhibition Test, 86280
Hemangioma, 17106-17108
Hemapheresis, 36511-36516
Hematochezia, 82270, 82274

Hematologic Test
See Blood Tests
Hematology
Unlisted Services and Procedures, 85999
Hematoma
Ankle, 27603
Arm, Lower, 25028
Arm, Upper
Incision and Drainage, 23930
Brain
Drainage, 61154, 61156
Evacuation, 61312-61315
Incision and Drainage, 61312-61315
Drain, 61108
Ear, External
Complicated, 69005
Simple, 69000
Elbow
Incision and Drainage, 23930
Epididymis
Incision and Drainage, 54700
Gums
Incision and Drainage, 41800
Hip, 26990
Incision and Drainage
Neck, 21501, 21502
Skin, 10140
Thorax, 21501, 21502
Knee, 27301
Leg, Lower, 27603
Leg, Upper, 27301
Mouth, 41005-41009, 41015-41018
Incision and Drainage, 40800, 40801
Nasal Septum
Incision and Drainage, 30020
Nose
Incision and Drainage, 30000, 30020
Pelvis, 26990
Puncture Aspiration, 10160
Scrotum
Incision and Drainage, 54700
Shoulder
Drainage, 23030
Skin
Incision and Drainage, 10140
Puncture Aspiration, 10160
Subdural, 61108
Subungual
Evacuation, 11740
Testis
Incision and Drainage, 54700
Tongue, 41000-41006, 41015
Vagina
Incision and Drainage, 57022, 57023
Wrist, 25028
Hematopoietic Stem Cell Transplantation
See Stem Cell, Transplantation
Hematopoietin
See Erythropoietin
Hematuria
See Blood, Urine
Hemic System
Unlisted Procedure, 38999
Hemiephyseal Arrest
Elbow, 24470
Hemifacial Microsomia
Reconstruction Mandibular Condyle, 21247
Hemilaminectomy, 63020-63044
Hemilaryngectomy, 31370-31382
Hemipelvectomies
See Amputation, Interperviabdominal
Hemiphalangectomy
Toe, 28160
Hemispherectomy
Partial, 61543
Total, 61542
Hemocytoblast
See Stem Cell
Hemodialysis, 90935, 90937, 99512

Hemodialysis — *continued*
Blood Flow Study, 90940
Duplex Scan of Access, 93990
Hemodynamic Monitoring
Non-invasive Left Ventricular, 0086T
Hemofiltration, 90945, 90947
Hemodialysis, 90935, 90937
Peritoneal Dialysis, 90945, 90947
Hemoglobin
A1C, 83036
Analysis
O2 Affinity, 82820
Antibody
Fecal, 82274
Carboxyhemoglobin, 82375-82376
Chromatography, 83021
Electrophoresis, 83020
Fetal, 83030, 83033, 85460, 85461
Fractionation and Quantitation, 83020
Glyated, 83036
Methemoglobin, 83045, 83050
Non–Automated, 83026
Plasma, 83051
Sulfhemoglobin, 83055, 83060
Thermolabile, 83065, 83068
Transcutaneous
Carboxyhemoglobin, 88740
Methemoglobin, 88741
Urine, 83069
Hemoglobin F
Fetal
Chemical, 83030
Qualitative, 83033
Hemoglobin, Glycosylated, 83036-83037
Hemogram
Added Indices, 85025-85027
Automated, 85025-85027
Manual, 85014, 85018, 85032
Hemolysins, 85475
with Agglutinins, 86940, 86941
Hemolytic Complement
See Complement, Hemolytic
Hemolytic Complement, Total
See Complement, Hemolytic, Total
Hemoperfusion, 90997
Hemophil
See Clotting Factor
Hemophilus Influenza
Antibody, 86684
B Vaccine, 90645-90648, 90720-90721, 90748
Hemorrhage
Abdomen, 49002
Anal
Endoscopic Control, 46614
Bladder
Postoperative, 52214
Chest Cavity
Endoscopic Control, 32654
Colon
Endoscopic Control, 44391, 45382
Colon–Sigmoid
Endoscopic Control, 45334
Esophagus
Endoscopic Control, 43227
Gastrointestinal, Upper
Endoscopic Control, 43255
Intestines, Small
Endoscopic Control, 44366, 44378
Liver
Control, 47350
Lung, 32110
Nasal
Cauterization, 30901-30906
Endoscopic Control, 31238
Nasopharynx, 42970-42972
Nose
Cauterization, 30901-30906
Oropharynx, 42960-42962
Rectum
Endoscopic Control, 45317
Throat, 42960-42962

Hemorrhage — *continued*
Uterus
Postpartum, 59160
Vagina, 57180
Hemorrhoidectomy
Complex, 46260
with Fissurectomy, 46261, 46262
External Complete, 46250
Ligature, 46221
Simple, 46255
with Fissurectomy, 46257, 46258
Whitehead, 46260
Hemorrhoidopexy, 46947
Hemorrhoids
Destruction, 46930
Incision
External, 46083
Injection
Sclerosing Solution, 46500
Ligation, 46945, 46946
Stapling, 46947
Suture, 46945, 46946
Hemosiderin, 83070, 83071
Hemothorax
Thoracostomy, 32551
Heparin, 85520
Clotting Inhibitors, 85300-85305
Neutralization, 85525
Protamine Tolerance Test, 85530
Heparin Cofactor I
See Antithrombin III
Hepatectomy
Extensive, 47122
Left Lobe, 47125
Partial
Donor, 47140-47142
Lobe, 47120
Right Lobe, 47130
Total
Donor, 47133
Hepatic Abscess
See Abscess, Liver
Hepatic Arteries
See Artery, Hepatic
Hepatic Artery Aneurysm
See Artery, Hepatic, Aneurysm
Hepatic Duct
Anastomosis
with Intestines, 47765, 47802
Exploration, 47400
Incision and Drainage, 47400
Nuclear Medicine
Imaging, 78223
Removal
Calculi (Stone), 47400
Repair
with Intestines, 47765, 47802
Unlisted Services and Procedures, 47999
Hepatic Haemorrhage
See Hemorrhage, Liver
Hepaticodochotomy
See Hepaticostomy
Hepaticoenterostomy, 47802
Hepaticostomy, 47400
Hepaticotomy, 47400
Hepatic Portal Vein
See Vein, Hepatic Portal
Hepatic Portoenterostomies
See Hepaticoenterostomy
Hepatic Transplantation
See Liver, Transplantation
Hepatitis A and Hepatitis B, 90636
Hepatitis Antibody
A, 86708, 86709
B core, 86704, 86705
Be, 86707
B Surface, 86706
C, 86803, 86804
Delta Agent, 86692
IgG, 86704, 86708
IgM, 86704, 86705, 86708, 86709
Hepatitis Antigen
B, 87515-87517
Be, 87350
B Surface, 87340, 87341

Hypogastric Plexus — continued
　Injection — continued
　　Neurolytic, 64681
Hypoglossal–Facial Anastomosis
　See Anastomosis, Nerve, Facial to
　　Hypoglossal
Hypoglossal Nerve
　Anastomosis
　　to Facial Nerve, 64868
Hypopharynges
　See Hypopharynx
Hypopharynx
　Biopsy, 42802
Hypophysectomy, 61546, 61548,
　62165
Hypophysis
　See Pituitary Gland
Hypopyrexia
　See Hypothermia
Hypospadias
　Repair, 54300, 54352
　　Complications, 54340-54348
　　First Stage, 54304
　　　Meatal Advancement, 54322
　　　Perineal, 54336
　　　Proximal Penile or Penoscro-
　　　　tal, 54332
　　One Stage
　　　Meatal Advancement, 54322
　　　Perineal, 54336
　　Urethroplasty by
　　　Local Skin Flaps, 54324
　　　Local Skin Flaps and Mobiliza-
　　　　tion of Urethra, 54326
　　　Local Skin Flaps, Skin Graft
　　　　Patch and/or Island
　　　　Flap, 54328
　　Urethroplasty for Second Stage,
　　　54308-54316
　　　Free Skin Graft, 54316
　　Urethroplasty for Third Stage,
　　　54318
Hypotensive Anesthesia, 99135
Hypothermia, 99185, 99186
Hypothermic Anesthesia, 99116
Hypoxia
　Breathing Response, 94450
　High Altitude Simulation Test,
　　94452-94453
Hysterectomy
　Abdominal
　　Radical, 58210
　　Resection of Ovarian Malignancy,
　　　58951, 58953-58954,
　　　58956
　　Supracervical, 58180
　　Total, 58150, 58200
　　　with Colpo–Urethrocystopexy,
　　　　58152
　　　with Omentectomy, 58956
　　　with Partial Vaginectomy,
　　　　58200
　Cesarean
　　with Closure of Vesicouterine
　　　Fistula, 51925
　　After Cesarean Section, 59525
　Removal
　　Lesion, 59100
　Vaginal, 58260-58270, 58290-58294,
　　58550-58554
　　with Colpectomy, 58275, 58280
　　with Colpo–Urethrocystopexy,
　　　58267, 58293
　　See Lysis, Adhesions, Uterus
　　Laparoscopic, 58550
　　Radical, 58285
　　Removal Tubes
　　　Ovaries, 52402, 58262,
　　　　58263, 58291-58292,
　　　　58552-58554
　　　Repair of Enterocele,
　　　　58263, 58292,
　　　　58294
　　Wertheim, 58210
…sterolysis, 58559
…steroplasty, 58540

Hysterorrhaphy, 58520, 59350
Hysterosalpingography, 74740
　Catheterization, 58345
　　Introduction of Contrast, 58340
Hysterosalpingostomy
　See Implantation, Tubouterine
Hysteroscopy
　with Endometrial Ablation, 58563
　with Lysis of Adhesions, 58559
　Ablation
　　Endometrial, 58563
　Diagnostic, 58555
　Lysis
　　Adhesions, 58559
　Placement
　　Fallopian Tube Implants, 58565
　Removal
　　Impacted Foreign Body, 58562
　　Leiomyomata, 58561
　Resection
　　of Intrauterine Septum, 58560
　Surgical with Biopsy, 58558
　Unlisted Services and Procedures,
　　58579
Hysterosonography, 76831
　See Ultrasound
Hysterotomy, 59100
　See Ligation, Uterus
　Induced Abortion
　　with Amniotic Injections, 59852
　　with Vaginal Suppositories,
　　　59857
Hysterotrachelectomy, 57530

I

IA, 36100-36140, 36260
IAB, 33970-33974
IABP, 33970-33974
IAC, 33970-33974
I Angiotensin, 84244
I Antibodies, HTLV, 86687, 86689
IBC, 83550
ICCE, 66920, 66930
Ichthyosis, Sex–Linked, 86592-86593
I Coagulation Factor, 85384-85385
ICSH, 80418, 80426, 83002
Identification
　Oocyte from Follicular Fluid, 89254
　Sentinel Node from Injection, 38792
　Sperm
　　from Aspiration, 89257
　　from Tissue, 89264
IDET (Intradiscal Electrothermal
　Therapy), 0062T-0063T
IDH (Isocitric Dehydrogenase, Blood),
　83570
IG, 82787, 84445, 86023
IgA, Gammaglobulin, 82784
IgD, Gammaglobulin, 82784
IgE
　Allergen Specific, 86003, 86005
　Gammaglobulin, 82785
IgG
　Allergen Specific, 86001
　Gammaglobulin, 82784
IgM, Gammaglobulin, 82784
I Heparin Co–Factor, 85300-85301
II, Coagulation Factor, 85610-85611
II, CranialNerve
　See Optic Nerve
Ileal Conduit
　Visualization, 50690
Ileocolostomy, 44160
Ileoproctostomy, 44150
Ileoscopy, 44380, 44382
　via Stoma, 44383
Ileostomy, 44310, 45136
　Continent (Kock Pouch), 44316
　Laparoscopic, 44186-44187
　Nontube, 44187
　Revision, 44312, 44314
Iliac Arteries
　See Artery, Iliac

Iliac Crest
　Free Osteocutaneous flap with Mi-
　　crovascular Anastomosis,
　　20970
Iliohypogastric Nerve
　Injection
　　Anesthetic, 64425
Ilioinguinal Nerve
　Injection
　　Anesthetic, 64425
Ilium
　Craterization, 27070, 27071
　Cyst, 27065-27067
　Excision, 27070-27071
　Fracture
　　Open Treatment, 27215, 27218
　Saucerization, 27070, 27071
　Tumor, 27065-27067
Ilizarov Procedure
　Application, Bone Fixation Device,
　　20690, 20692
　Monticelli Type, 20692
Imaging
　See Vascular Studies
Imaging, Gamma Camera
　See Nuclear Medicine
Imaging, Magnetic Resonance
　See Magnetic Resonance Imaging
　　(MRI)
Imaging, Ultrasonic
　See Echography
Imbrication
　Diaphragm, 39545
Imidobenzyle
　See Imipramine
IM Injection
　Chemotherapy/Complex Biological,
　　96401-96402
　Diagnostic, Prophylactic, Therapeu-
　　tic, 96372
　Antineoplastic
　　NULL
　　Hormonal, 96402
　　Non-hormonal, 96401
Imipramine
　Assay, 80174
Immune Complex Assay, 86332
Immune Globulin Administration,
　96365-96368, 96372, 96374-
　96375
Immune Globulin E, 82785
Immune Globulins
　Antitoxin
　　Botulinum, 90287
　　Diptheria, 90296
　Botulism, 90288
　Cytomegalovirus, 90291
　Hepatitis B, 90371
　Human, 90281, 90283-90284
　Rabies, 90375, 90376
　Respiratory Syncytial Virus, 90378,
　　90379
　Rho (D), 90384-90386
　Tetanus, 90389
　Unlisted Immune Globulin, 90399
　Vaccinia, 90393
　Varicella–Zoster, 90396
Immune Serum Globulin
　Immunization, 90281, 90283
Immunization
　Active
　　Acellular Pertussis, 90700,
　　　90721-90723
　　BCG, 90585, 90586
　　Cholera, 90725
　　Diphtheria, 90700-90702, 90718-
　　　90723
　　Diphtheria, Tetanus, Pertussis
　　　(DTP), 90701, 90720
　　Diphtheria, Tetanus Toxoids,
　　　Acellular Pertussis, 90700,
　　　90720-90723
　　Diptheria, Tetanus Acellular
　　　Influenza B and Poliovirus In-
　　　activated, Vaccine,
　　　90698

Immunization — continued
　Active — continued
　　Diptheria, Tetanus Acellular —
　　　continued
　　　Pertussis, Haemophilus
　　Hemophilus Influenza B, 90645-
　　　90648, 90720-90721,
　　　90748
　　Hepatitis A, 90632-90636
　　Hepatitis B, 90740-90747, 90748
　　Hepatitis B, Hemophilus Influen-
　　　za B (HIB), 90748
　　Influenza, 90655-90660
　　Influenza B, 90645-90648
　　Japanese Encephalitis, 90735
　　Lyme Disease, 90665
　　Measles, 90705
　　Measles, Mumps, Rubella, 90707
　　Measles, Mumps, Rubella, Varicel-
　　　la Vaccine, 90710
　　Measles, Rubella, 90708
　　Meningococcal Conjugate, 90734
　　Meningococcal Polysaccharide,
　　　90733
　　Mumps, 90704
　　Plague, 90727
　　Pneumococcal, 90732
　　Poliomyelitis, 90713
　　Poliovirus, 90712
　　Rabies, 90675, 90676
　　Rotavirus Vaccine, 90680
　　Rubella, 90706
　　Tetanus and Diphtheria, 90700-
　　　90702, 90718, 90720-
　　　90723
　　Tetanus Diphtheria and Acellular
　　　Pertussis, 90715
　　Tetanus Toxoid, 90703
　　Typhoid, 90690-90693
　　Varicella (Chicken Pox), 90716
　　Yellow Fever, 90717
　Administration
　　Each Additional Vaccine/Toxoid,
　　　90472, 90474
　　with Counseling, 90466,
　　　90468
　　One Vaccine/Toxoid, 90471,
　　　90473
　　with Counseling, 90465,
　　　90467
　Inactive
　　Japanese Encephalitis Virus,
　　　90738
　Passive
　　Hyperimmune Serum Globulin,
　　　90287-90399
　　Immune Serum Globulin, 90281,
　　　90283
　Unlisted Services and Procedures,
　　90749
Immunization Administration
　Each Additional Vaccine/Toxoid,
　　90472, 90474
　　with Counseling, 90466, 90468
　One Vaccine/Toxoid, 90471, 90473
　　with Counseling, 90465, 90467
　Single Vaccine
　　Toxoid, 90471, 90473
　Two or More Vaccines, Each Addition-
　　al
　　Toxoids, 90472, 90474
Immunoassay
　Analyte, 83519, 83520
　　Calprotectin, Fecal, 83993
　Infectious Agent, 86317, 86318,
　　87449-87451, 87809
　Nonantibody, 83516-83519
　Tumor Antigen, 86294, 86316
　　CA 125, 86304
　　CA 15–3, 86300
　　CA 19–9, 86301
Immunoblotting, Western
　HIV, 86689
　Protein, 84181-84182
　Tissue Analysis, 88371-88372

© 2008 Ingen

Kidney — *continued*
Transplantation
Allograft Preparation, 50323-50329
Anesthesia
Donor, 00862
Recipient, 00868
Donor Nephrectomy, 50300-50320, 50547
Graft Implantation, 50360-50365
Implantation of Graft, 50360
Recipient Nephrectomy, 50340, 50365
Reimplantation Kidney, 50380
Removal Transplant Allograft, 50370
Tumor
Ablation
Cryotherapy, 50250, 50593
Ultrasound, 76770-76775, 76776
X-ray with Contrast
Guide Catheter, 74475
Kidney Stone
Removal, Calculi, 50060-50081, 50130, 50561, 50580
Killian Operation, 31020
Sinusotomy, Frontal, 31070-31087
Kinase Creatine
Blood, 82550-82552
Kineplasty
Arm, Lower or Upper, 24940
Kinetic Therapy, 97530
Kininase A, 82164
Kininogen, 85293
Kininogen, High Molecular Weight, 85293
Kleihauer-Betke Test, 85460
Kloramfenikol, 82415
Knee
See Femur; Fibula; Patella; Tibia
Abscess, 27301
Arthrocentesis, 20610
Arthrodesis, 27580
Arthroplasty, 27440-27445, 27447
Revision, 27486, 27487
Arthroscopy
Diagnostic, 29870
Surgical, 29866-29868, 29871-29889
Arthrotomy, 27310, 27330-27335, 27403
Autograft, Osteochondral, Open, 27416
Biopsy, 27323, 27324, 27330, 27331
Synovium, 27330
Bone
Drainage, 27303
Bursa, 27301
Excision, 27340
Cyst
Excision, 27345, 27347
Disarticulation, 27598
Dislocation
Closed Treatment, 27550, 27552, 27560, 27562
Open Treatment, 27556-27558, 27566
Drainage, 27310
Excision
Cartilage, 27332, 27333
Ganglion, 27347
Lesion, 27347
Synovial Lining, 27334, 27335
Exploration, 27310, 27331
Fasciotomy, 27305, 27496-27499
Fracture, 27520, 27524
Arthroscopic Treatment, 29850, 29851
Fusion, 27580
Hematoma, 27301
Incision
Capsule, 27435
Injection
X-ray, 27370
Magnetic Resonance Imaging (MRI), 73721-73723

Knee — *continued*
Manipulation, 27570
Meniscectomy, 27332, 27333
Osteochondral Graft, 27415-27416
Reconstruction, 27437, 27438
with Implantation, 27445
with Prosthesis, 27445
Ligament, 27427-27429
Removal
Foreign Body, 27310, 27331, 27372
Loose Body, 27331
Prosthesis, 27488
Repair
Ligament, 27405-27409
Collateral, 27405
Collateral and Cruciate, 27409
Cruciate, 27407, 27409
Meniscus, 27403
Tendon, 27380, 27381
Replacement, 27447
Retinacular
Release, 27425
Strapping, 29530
Suture
Tendon, 27380, 27381
Transplantation
Chondrocytes, 27412
Meniscus, 29868
Osteochondral
Allograft, 27415, 29867
Autograft, 27412, 29866
Tumor
Excision, 27327-27329, 27365
Unlisted Services and Procedures, 27599
X-ray, 73560-73564
Arthrography, 73580
Bilateral, 73565
X-ray with Contrast
Angiography, 73706
Arthrography, 73580
Kneecap
Excision, 27350
Repair
Instability, 27420-27424
Knee Joint
Arthroplasty, 27446
Knee Prosthesis
See Prosthesis, Knee
Knock-Knee Repair, 27455, 27457
Kocher Operation, 23650-23680
See Clavicle; Scapula; Shoulder, Dislocation, Closed Treatment
Kocher Pylorectomy
Gastrectomy, Partial, 43631
Kock Pouch, 44316
Formation, 50825
Kock Procedure, 44316
KOH
Hair, Nails, Tissue, Examination for Fungi, 87220
Konno Procedure, 33412
Koop Inguinal Orchiopexy, 54640
Kraske Procedure, 45116
Krause Operation
Gasserian Ganglion, Sensory Root, Decompression, 61450
Kroenlein Procedure, 67420
Krukenberg Procedure, 25915
Krupin-Denver Valve
Implant, 66180
Removal, 67120
Revision, 66185
KS, 83586, 83593
KUB, 74241, 74247, 74270, 74420
Kuhlmann Test, 96101-96103
Kuhnt-Szymanowski Procedure, 67917
K-Wire Fixation
Tongue, 41500
Kyphectomy
More than Two Segments, 22819
Up to Two Segments, 22818
Kyphoplasty, 22523-22525

L

Labial Adhesions
Lysis, 56441
Labyrinth
See Ear, Inner
Labyrinthectomy
with Mastoidectomy, 69910
with Skull Base Surgery, 61596
Transcanal, 69905
Labyrinthotomy
with Mastoidectomy, 69802
with Skull Base Surgery, 61596
Inner Ear, 69949
Transcanal
with/without Cryosurgery, 69801
Laceration Repair
See Repair, Laceration, Skin
Lacrimal Duct
Balloon, 68816
Canaliculi
Incision, 68899
Repair, 68700
Dilation, 68816
Exploration, 68810
with Anesthesia, 68811
Canaliculi, 68840
Stent, 68815
Insertion
Stent, 68815
Nasolacrimal Duct Probing, 68816
Removal
Dacryolith, 68530
Foreign Body, 68530
X-ray with Contrast, 70170
Lacrimal Gland
Biopsy, 68510
Close Fistula, 68770
Excision
Partial, 68505
Total, 68500
Fistulization, 68720
Incision and Drainage, 68400
Injection
X-ray, 68850
Nuclear Medicine
Tear Flow, 78660
Removal
Dacryolith, 68530
Foreign Body, 68530
Repair
Fistula, 68770
Tumor
Excision
with Osteotomy, 68550
without Closure, 68540
X-Ray, 70170
Lacrimal Punctum
Closure
by Plug, 68761
by Thermocauterization, Ligation or Laser Surgery, 68760
Dilation, 68801
Incision, 68440
Repair, 68705
Lacrimal Sac
Biopsy, 68525
Excision, 68520
Incision and Drainage, 68420
Lacrimal System
Unlisted Services and Procedures, 68899
Lacryoaptography
Nuclear, 78660
Lactase Deficiency Breath Test, 91065
Lactate, 83605
Lactic Acid, 83605
Lactic Acid Measurement
See Lactate
Lactic Cytochrome Reductase
See Lactic Dehydrogenase
Lactic Dehydrogenase, 83615, 83625
Lactiferous Duct
Excision, 19112
Exploration, 19110
Lactoferrin
Fecal, 83630-83631

Lactogen, Human Placental, 83632
Lactogenic Hormone
See Prolactin
Lactose
Urine, 83633, 83634
Ladd Procedure, 44055
Lagophthalmos
Repair, 67912
Laki Lorand Factor
See Fibrin Stabilizing Factor
L-Alanine
See Aminolevulinic Acid (ALA)
Lamblia Intestinalis
See Giardia Lamblia
Lambrinudi Operation
Arthrodesis, Foot Joints, 28730, 28735, 28740
Lamellar Keratoplasties
See Keratoplasty, Lamellar
Laminaria
Insertion, 59200
Laminectomy, 62351, 63001, 63005-63011, 63015-63044, 63180-63200, 63265-63290, 63600-63655
with Facetectomy, 63045-63048
Decompression
Cervical, 63001, 63015
with Facetectomy and Foraminotomy, 63045, 63048
Laminotomy
Initial
Cervical, 63020
Each Additional Space, 63035
Lumbar, 63030
Reexploration
Cervical, 63040
Each Additional Interspace, 63043
Lumbar, 63042
Each Additional Interspace, 63044
Lumbar, 63005, 63017
with Facetectomy and Foraminotomy, 63046, 63048
Sacral, 63011
Thoracic, 63003, 63016
with Facetectomy and Foraminotomy, 63047, 63048
Excision
Lesion, 63250-63273
Neoplasm, 63275-63290
Lumbar, 22630, 63012
Surgical, 63170-63200
Laminoplasty
Cervical, 63050-63051
Laminotomy
Cervical, One Interspace, 63020
Lumbar, 63042
One Interspace, 63030
Each Additional, 63035
Re-exploration, Cervical, 63040
Landboldt's Operation, 67971, 67973 67975
Lane's Operation, 44150
Langerhans Islands
See Islet Cell
Language Evaluation, 92506
Language Therapy, 92507, 92508
LAP, 83670
Laparoscopic Appendectomy
See Appendectomy, Laparoscopic
Laparoscopic Biopsy of Ovary
See Biopsy, Ovary, Laparoscopic
Laparoscopy
with X-ray, 47560
Abdominal, 49320-49329
Adrenalectomy, 50545
Adrenal Gland
Biopsy, 60650
Excision, 60650
Appendectomy, 44970

Laparoscopy — *continued*
Aspiration, 49322
Biopsy, 47561, 49321
Lymph Nodes, 38570
Bladder
Repair
Sling Procedure, 51992
Urethral Suspension, 51990
Unlisted, 51999
Cecostomy, 44188
Cholangiography, 47560, 47561
Cholecystectomy, 47562-47564
Cholecystoenterostomy, 47570
Closure
Enterostomy, 44227
Colectomy
Partial, 44204-44208, 44213
Total, 44210-44212
Colostomy, 44188
Destruction
Lesion, 58662
Diagnostic, 49320
Drainage
Extraperitoneal Lymphocele, 49323
Ectopic Pregnancy, 59150
with Salpingectomy and/or Oophorectomy, 59151
Electrode
Implantation
Gastric, 0156T, 43647-43648
Removal
Gastric, 0156T, 43648
Replacement
Gastric, 0156T, 43647
Revision
Gastric, 0156T, 43648
Enterectomy, 44202
Enterolysis, 44180
Enterostomy
Closure, 44227
Esophagogastric Fundoplasty, 43280
Esophagomyotomy, 43279
Fimbrioplasty, 58672
Gastric Restrictive Procedures, 43644-43645, 43770-43774
Gastrostomy
Temporary, 43653
Hernia Repair
Epigastric, 49652
Incarcerated or Strangulated, 49653
Incisional, 49654
Incarcerated or Strangulated, 49655
Recurrent, 49656
Incarcerated or Strangulated, 49657
Initial, 49650
Recurrent, 49651
Spigelian, 49652
Incarcerated or Strangulated, 49653
Umbilical, 49652
Incarcerated or Strangulated, 49653
Ventral, 49652
Incarcerated or Strangulated, 49653
Hysterectomy, 58541-58554, 58570-58573
Radical, 58548
Total, 58570-58573
Ileostomy, 44187
Incontinence Repair, 51990, 51992
In Vitro Fertilization, 58976
Retrieve Oocyte, 58970
Transfer Embryo, 58974
Transfer Gamete, 58976
Jejunostomy, 44186-44187
Kidney
Ablation, 50541-50542
Ligation
Veins, Spermatic, 55500

Laparoscopy — *continued*
Liver
Ablation
Tumor, 47370, 47371
Lymphadenectomy, 38571-38572
Lymphatic, 38570-38589
Lysis of Adhesions, 58660
Lysis of Intestinal Adhesions, 44180
Mobilization
Splenic Flexure, 44213
Nephrectomy, 50545-50548
Partial, 50543
Omentopexy, 49326
Orchiectomy, 54690
Orchiopexy, 54692
Ovary
Reimplantation, 59898
Suture, 59898
Oviduct Surgery, 58670, 58671, 58679
Pancreatic Islet Cell Transplantation, 0143T
Pelvis, 49320
Proctectomy, 45395, 45397
with Creation of Colonic Reservoir, 45397
Complete, 45395
Proctopexy, 45400, 45402
Prostatectomy, 55866
Pyloplasty, 50544
Rectum
Resection, 45395-45397
Unlisted, 45499
Removal
Fallopian Tubes, 58661
Leiomyomata, 58545-58546
Ovaries, 58661
Spleen, 38120
Testis, 54690
Resection
Intestines
with Anastomosis, 44202, 44203
Rectum, 45395-45397
Salpingostomy, 58673
Splenectomy, 38120, 38129
Splenic Flexure
Mobilization, 44213
Stomach, 43651-43659
Gastric Bypass, 43644-43645
Gastric Restrictive Procedures, 43770-43774, 43848, 43886-43888
Gastroenterostomy, 43644-43645
Roux-en-Y, 43644
Surgical, 38570-38572, 43651-43653, 44180-44188, 44212, 44213, 44227, 44970, 45395-45402, 47370, 47371, 49321-49323, 49650, 49651, 50541, 50543, 50545, 50945-50948, 51992, 54690, 54692, 55550, 55866, 57425, 58545, 58546, 58552, 58554
with Guided Transhepatic Cholangiography, 47560-47561
Transplantation
Islet Cell, 0143T
Unlisted Services and Procedures, 38129, 38589, 43289, 43659, 44238, 44979, 45499, 47379, 47579, 49329, 49659, 50549, 50949, 51999, 54699, 55559, 58578, 58579, 58679, 59898
Ureterolithotomy, 50945
Ureteroneocystostomy, 50947-50948
Urethral Suspension, 51990
Vaginal Hysterectomy, 58550-58554
Vaginal Suspension, 57425
Vagus Nerves Transection, 43651, 43652
Laparotomy
with Biopsy, 49000

Laparotomy — *continued*
Electrode
Gastric
Implantation, 0157T, 43881
Removal, 0158T, 43882
Replacement, 0157T, 43881
Revision, 0158T, 43882
Exploration, 47015, 49000, 49002, 58960
for Staging, 49220
Hemorrhage Control, 49002
Second Look, 58960
Staging, 58960
Surgical, 44050
Laparotomy, Exploratory
See Abdomen, Exploration
Lapidus Procedure, 28297
Large Bowel
See Anus; Cecum; Rectum
Laroyenne Operation
Vagina, Abscess, Incision and Drainage, 57010
Laryngeal Function Study, 92520
Laryngeal Sensory Testing, 92614-92617
Laryngectomy, 31360-31382
Partial, 31367-31382
Subtotal, 31367, 31368
Total, 31360, 31365
Laryngocele
Removal, 31300
Laryngofissure, 31300
Laryngography, 70373
Laryngopharyngectomy
Excision, Larynx, with Pharynx, 31390, 31395
Laryngopharynx
See Hypopharynx
Laryngoplasty
Burns, 31588
Cricoid Split, 31587
Laryngeal Stenosis, 31582
Laryngeal Web, 31580
Open Reduction of Fracture, 31584
Laryngoscopy
Diagnostic, 31505
Direct, 31515-31571
Exploration, 31505, 31520-31526, 31575
Fiberoptic, 31575-31579
with Stroboscopy, 31579
Indirect, 31505-31513
Newborn, 31520
Operative, 31530-31561
Laryngotomy
Diagnostic, 31320
Partial, 31370-31382
Removal
Tumor, 31300
Total, 31360-31368
Larynx
Aspiration
Endoscopy, 31515
Biopsy
Endoscopy, 31510, 31535, 31536, 31576
Dilation
Endoscopic, 31528, 31529
Electromyography
Needle, 95865
Endoscopy
Direct, 31515-31571
Excision, 31545-31546
Exploration, 31505, 31520-31526, 31575
Fiberoptic, 31575-31579
with Stroboscopy, 31579
Indirect, 31505-31513
Operative, 31530-31561
Excision
with Pharynx, 31390, 31395
Lesion, 31512, 31578
Endoscopic, 31545-31546
Partial, 31367-31382
Total, 31360, 31365

Larynx — *continued*
Exploration
Endoscopic, 31505, 31520-31526, 31575
Fracture
Open Treatment, 31584
Insertion
Obturator, 31527
Nerve
Destruction, 31595
Pharynx
with Pharynx, 31390
Reconstruction
with Pharynx, 31395
Burns, 31588
Cricoid Split, 31587
Other, 31588
Stenosis, 31582
Web, 31580
Removal
Foreign Body
Endoscopic, 31511, 31530, 31531, 31577
Lesion
Endoscopic, 31512, 31545-31546, 31578
Repair
Reinnervation Neuromuscular Pedicle, 31590
Stroboscopy, 31579
Tumor
Excision, 31300
Endoscopic, 31540, 31541
Unlisted Services and Procedures, 31599
Vocal Cord
Injection, 31513, 31570, 31571
X-ray, 70370
with Contrast, 70373
L Ascorbic Acid
See Ascorbic Acid
LASEK, 65760
Laser Surgery
Anal, 46917
Cautery
Esophagus, 43227
Lacrimal Punctum, 68760
Lens
Posterior, 66821
Lesion
Mouth, 40820
Nose, 30117, 30118
Penis, 54057
Skin, 17000-17111, 17260-17286
Prostate, 52647-52649
Spine
Diskectomy, 62287
Tumor
Urethra and Bladder, 52234-52240
Urethra and Bladder, 52214
Laser Treatment, 17000-17286, 96920-96922
See Destruction
Lash Procedure
Tracheoplasty, 31750-31760
LASIK, 65760
L Aspartate 2 Oxoglutarate Aminotransferase
See Transaminase, Glutamic Oxaloacetic
Lateral Epicondylitis
See Tennis Elbow
Latex Fixation, 86403, 86406
LATS, 80438, 80439
Latzko Procedure
Colpocleisis, 57120
LAV
See HIV
LAV-2, 86702-86703
Lavage
Colon, 44701
Lung
Bronchial, 31624
Total, 32997
Peritoneal, 49080

Lesion — *continued*
  Removal
    Larynx, 31512, 31578
  Resection, 52354
  Retina
    Destruction
      Extensive, 67227, 67228
      Localized, 0017T, 67208, 67210
    Radiation by Implantation of Source, 67218
  Sciatic Nerve
    Excision, 64786
  Sclera
    Excision, 66130
  Skin
    Abrasion, 15786, 15787
    Biopsy, 11100, 11101
    Destruction
      Benign, 17000-17250
      Malignant, 17260-17286
        by Photodynamic Therapy, 96567
      Premalignant, 17000-17004
    Excision
      Benign, 11400-11471
      Malignant, 11600-11646
    Injection, 11900, 11901
    Paring or Curettement, 11055-11057
      Benign Hyperkeratotic, 11055-11057
    Shaving, 11300-11313
  Skin Tags
    Removal, 11200, 11201
  Skull
    Excision, 61500, 61600-61608, 61615, 61616
  Spermatic Cord
    Excision, 55520
  Spinal Cord
    Destruction, 62280-62282
    Excision, 63265-63273
  Stomach
    Excision, 43611
  Testis
    Excision, 54512
  Toe
    Excision, 28092
  Tongue
    Excision, 41110-41114
  Uvula
    Destruction, 42145
    Excision, 42104-42107
  Vagina
    Destruction, 57061, 57065
  Vulva
    Destruction
      Extensive, 56515
      Simple, 56501
  Wrist Tendon
    Excision, 25110
Lesion of Sciatic Nerve
  See Sciatic Nerve, Lesion
Leu 2 Antigens
  See CD8
Leucine Aminopeptidase, 83670
Leukapheresis, 36511
Leukemia Lymphoma Virus I, Adult T Cell
  See HTLV-I
Leukemia Lymphoma Virus I Antibodies, Human T Cell
  See Antibody, HTLV-I
Leukemia Lymphoma Virus II Antibodies, Human T Cell
  See Antibody, HTLV-II
Leukemia Virus II, Hairy Cell Associated, Human T Cell
  See HTLV-II
Leukoagglutinins, 86021
Leukocyte
  See White Blood Cell
  Alkaline Phosphatase, 85540
  Antibody, 86021
  Histamine Release Test, 86343

Leukocyte — *continued*
  Phagocytosis, 86344
  Transfusion, 86950
Leukocyte Count, 85032, 85048, 89055
Leukocyte Histamine Release Test, 86343
Levarterenol
  See Noradrenalin
Levator Muscle Rep
  Blepharoptosis, Repair, 67901-67909
LeVeen Shunt
  Insertion, 49425
  Patency Test, 78291
  Revision, 49426
Levulose
  See Fructose
L Glutamine
  See Glutamine
LGV
  Antibody, 86729
LH (Luteinizing Hormone), 80418, 80426, 83002
LHR (Leukocyte Histamine Release Test), 86343
Liberatory Maneuver, 69710
Lidocaine
  Assay, 80176
Lid Suture
  Blepharoptosis, Repair, 67901-67909
Life Support
  Organ Donor, 01990
Lift, Face
  See Face Lift
Ligament
  See Specific Site
  Collateral
    Repair, Knee with Cruciate Ligament, 27409
  Dentate
    Incision, 63180, 63182
    Section, 63180, 63182
  Injection, 20550
  Release
    Coracoacromial, 23415
    Transverse Carpal, 29848
  Repair
    Elbow, 24343-24346
    Knee Joint, 27405-27409
Ligation
  Appendage
    Dermal, 11200
  Artery
    Abdomen, 37617
    Carotid, 37600-37606
    Chest, 37616
    Coronary, 33502
    Coronary Artery, 33502
    Ethmoidal, 30915
    Extremity, 37618
    Fistula, 37607
    Maxillary, 30920
    Neck, 37615
    Temporal, 37609
  Bronchus, 31899
  Esophageal Varices, 43204, 43400
  Fallopian Tube
    Oviduct, 58600-58611, 58670
  Gastroesophageal, 43405
  Hemorrhoids, 46945, 46946
  Oviducts, 59100
  Salivary Duct, 42665
  Shunt
    Aorta
      Pulmonary, 33924
    Peritoneal
      Venous, 49428
  Thoracic Duct, 38380
    Abdominal Approach, 38382
    Thoracic Approach, 38381
  Thyroid Vessels, 37615
  Ureter, 53899
  Vas Deferens, 55450
  Vein
    Clusters, 37785
    Esophagus, 43205, 43244, 43400
    Femoral, 37650

Ligation — *continued*
  Vein — *continued*
    Gastric, 43244
    Iliac, 37660
    Jugular, Internal, 37565
    Perforate, 37760
    Saphenous, 37700-37735, 37780
    Vena Cava, 37620
Ligature Strangulation
  Skin Tags, 11200, 11201
Light Coagulation
  See Photocoagulation
Light Scattering Measurement
  See Nephelometry
Light Therapy, UV
  See Actinotherapy
Limb
  See Extremity
Limited Lymphadenectomy for Staging
  See Lymphadenectomy, Limited, for Staging
Limited Neck Dissection
  with Thyroidectomy, 60252
Limited Resection Mastectomies
  See Breast, Excision, Lesion
Lindholm Operation
  See Tenoplasty
Lingual Bone
  See Hyoid Bone
Lingual Frenectomy
  See Excision, Tongue, Frenum
Lingual Nerve
  Avulsion, 64740
  Incision, 64740
  Transection, 64740
Lingual Tonsil
  See Tonsils, Lingual
Linton Procedure, 37760
Lip
  Biopsy, 40490
  Excision, 40500-40530
    Frenum, 40819
  Incision
    Frenum, 40806
  Reconstruction, 40525, 40527
  Repair, 40650-40654
    Cleft Lip, 40700-40761
    Fistula, 42260
  Unlisted Services and Procedures, 40799
Lipase, 83690
Lip, Cleft
  See Cleft Lip
Lipectomies, Aspiration
  See Liposuction
Lipectomy
  Excision, 15830-15839
  Suction Assisted, 15876-15879
Lipids
  Feces, 82705, 82710
Lipo-Lutin
  See Progesterone
Lipolysis, Aspiration
  See Liposuction
Lipophosphodiesterase I
  See Tissue Typing
Lipoprotein
  (a), 83695
  Blood, 83695, 83700-83721
  LDL, 83700-83701, 83721
  Phospholipase A2, 83698
Lipoprotein, Alpha
  See Lipoprotein
Lipoprotein, Pre-Beta
  See Lipoprotein, Blood
Liposuction, 15876-15879
Lips
  Skin Graft
    Delay of Flap, 15630
    Full Thickness, 15260, 15261
    Pedicle Flap, 15576
    Tissue Transfer, Adjacent, 14060, 14061
Lisfranc Operation
  Amputation, Foot, 28800, 28805

Listeria Monocytogenes
  Antibody, 86723
Lithium
  Assay, 80178
Litholapaxy, 52317, 52318
Lithotripsy
  with Cystourethroscopy, 52353
  See Extracorporeal Shock Wave Therapy
  Bile Duct Calculi (Stone)
    Endoscopy, 43265
  Bladder, 52353
  Kidney, 50590, 52353
  Pancreatic Duct Calculi (Stone)
    Endoscopy, 43265
  Ureter, 52353
  Urethra, 52353
Lithotrity
  See Litholapaxy
Liver
  See Hepatic Duct
  Ablation
    Tumor, 47380-47382
      Laparoscopic, 47370, 47371
  Abscess
    Aspiration, 47015
    Incision and Drainage
      Closed, 47011
      Open, 47010
      Percutaneous, 47011
    Injection, 47015
  Aspiration, 47015
  Biopsy, 47100
    Anesthesia, 00702
  Cyst
    Aspiration, 47015
    Incision and Drainage
      Open, 47010
      Percutaneous, 47011
  Excision
    Extensive, 47122
    Partial, 47120, 47125, 47130, 47140-47142
    Total, 47133
  Injection, 47015
    Radiologic, 47505
    X-ray, 47500
  Lobectomy, 47125, 47130
    Partial, 47120
  Needle Biopsy, 47000, 47001
  Nuclear Medicine
    Function Study, 78220
    Imaging, 78201-78216
    Vascular Flow, 78206
  Repair
    Abscess, 47300
    Cyst, 47300
    Wound, 47350-47362
  Suture
    Wound, 47350-47362
  Transplantation, 47135, 47136
    Allograft preparation, 47143-47147
    Anesthesia, 00796, 01990
  Trisegmentectomy, 47122
  Ultrasound Scan (LUSS), 76705
  Unlisted Services and Procedures, 47379, 47399
Living Activities, Daily, 97535, 97537
LKP, 65710
L-Leucylnaphthylamidase, 83670
Lobectomy
  Brain, 61323, 61537-61540
  Contralateral Subtotal
    Thyroid Gland, 60212, 60225
  Liver, 47120-47130
  Lung, 32480-32482
    Sleeve, 32486
  Parotid Gland, 42410, 42415
  Segmental, 32663
  Sleeve, 32486
  Temporal Lobe, 61537, 61538
  Thyroid Gland
    Partial, 60210, 60212
    Total, 60220, 60225
  Total, 32663

© 2008 Ingeni

Muscle Compartment Syndrome
  Detection, 20950
Muscle Denervation
  See Denervation
Muscle Division
  Scalenus Anticus, 21700, 21705
  Sternocleidomastoid, 21720, 21725
Muscle Flaps, 15731-15738
  Free, 15756
Muscle Grafts, 15841-15845
Muscle, Oculomotor
  See Eye Muscles
Muscles
  Repair
    Extraocular, 65290
Muscle Testing
  Dynamometry, Eye, 92260
  Extraocular Multiple Muscles, 92265
  Manual, 95831-95834
Musculoplasty
  See Muscle, Repair
Musculoskeletal System
  Computer Assisted Surgical Naviga-
    tional Procedure, 0054T-
    0055T, 20985
  Unlisted Services and Procedures,
    20999, 21499, 24999, 25999,
    26989, 27299, 27599, 27899
  Unlisted Services and Procedures,
    Head, 21499
Musculotendinous (Rotator) Cuff
  Repair, 23410, 23412
Mustard Procedure, 33774-33777
  See Repair, Great Arteries, Revision
Mutation Identification, 83914
MVD (Microvascular Decompression),
  61140
MVR, 33430
Myasthenia Gravis
  Tensilon Test, 95857
Myasthenic, Gravis
  See Myasthenia Gravis
Mycobacteria
  Culture, 87116
    Identification, 87118
  Detection, 87550-87562
  Sensitivity Studies, 87190
Mycoplasma
  Antibody, 86738
  Culture, 87109
  Detection, 87580-87582
Mycota
  See Fungus
Myectomy, Anorectal
  See Myomectomy, Anorectal
Myelencephalon
  See Medulla
Myelin Basic Protein
  Cerebrospinal Fluid, 83873
Myelography
  Brain, 70010
  Spine
    Cervical, 72240
    Lumbosacral, 72265
    Thoracic, 72255
    Total, 72270
Myelomeningocele
  Repair, 63704, 63706
  Stereotaxis
    Creation Lesion, 63600
Myelotomy, 63170
Myocardial
  Imaging, 78466, 78468, 78469
  Perfusion Imaging, 78460-78465,
    78478, 78480
  See Nuclear Medicine
  Positron Emission Tomography (PET),
    78459, 78491, 78492
  Repair
    Postinfarction, 33542
Myocutaneous Flaps, 15732-15738,
  15756
**Myofascial Pain Dysfunction Syn-
  drome**
  See Temporomandibular Joint (TMJ)
Myofascial Release, 97140

Myofibroma
  Embolization, 37210
  Removal, 58140, 58545-58546,
    58561
Myoglobin, 83874
Myomectomy
  Anorectal, 45108
  Uterus, 58140-58146, 58545, 58546
Myoplasty
  Extraocular, 65290, 67346
Myotomy
  Esophagus, 43030
  Hyoid, 21685
  Sigmoid Colon
    Intestine, 44799
    Rectum, 45999
Myringoplasty, 69620
Myringostomy, 69420-69421
Myringotomy, 69420, 69421
Myxoid Cyst
  Aspiration/Injection, 20612
  Drainage, 20610
  Wrist
    Excision, 25111-25112

N

Na, 84295
Nabi-HIB, 90371
Naffziger Operation, 61330
Nagel Test, 92283
Nail Bed
  Reconstruction, 11762
  Repair, 11760
Nail Fold
  Excision
    Wedge, 11765
Nail Plate Separation
  See Onychia
Nails
  Avulsion, 11730, 11732
  Biopsy, 11755
  Debridement, 11720, 11721
  Drainage, 10060-10061
  Evacuation
    Hematoma, Subungual, 11740
  Excision, 11750, 11752
    Cyst
      Pilonidal, 11770-11772
  KOH Examination, 87220
  Removal, 11730, 11732, 11750,
    11752
  Trimming, 11719
Narcoanalysis, 90865
Narcosynthesis
  Diagnostic and Therapeutic, 90865
Nasal Abscess, 30000-30020
Nasal Area
  Bone Graft, 21210
Nasal Bleeding
  See Epistaxis
Nasal Bone
  Fracture
    with Manipulation, 21315, 21320
    without Manipulation, 21310
    Closed Treatment, 21310-21320
    Open Treatment, 21325-21335
  X-ray, 70160
Nasal Deformity
  Repair, 40700-40761
Nasal Function Study, 92512
Nasal Polyp
  Excision
    Extensive, 30115
    Simple, 30110
Nasal Prosthesis
  Impression, 21087
Nasal Septum
  Abscess
    Incision and Drainage, 30020
  Fracture
    Closed Treatment, 21337
    Open Treatment, 21336
  Hematoma
    Incision and Drainage, 30020
  Repair, 30630
  Submucous Resection, 30520

Nasal Sinuses
  See Sinus; Sinuses
Nasal Smear
  Eosinophils, 89190
Nasal Turbinate
  Fracture
    Therapeutic, 30930
Nasoethmoid Complex
  Fracture
    Open Treatment, 21338, 21339
    Percutaneous Treatment, 21340
  Reconstruction, 21182-21184
Nasogastric Tube
  Placement, 43752
Nasolacrimal Duct
  Exploration, 68810
    with Anesthesia, 68811
  Insertion
    Stent, 68815
  Probing, 68816
  X-ray
    with Contrast, 70170
Nasomaxillary
  Fracture
    with Bone Grafting, 21348
    Closed Treatment, 21345
    Open Treatment, 21346-21348
Nasopharynges
  See Nasopharynx
Nasopharyngoscopy, 92511
Nasopharynx
  See Pharynx
  Biopsy, 42804, 42806
  Hemorrhage, 42970-42972
  Unlisted Services and Procedures,
    42999
Natriuretic Peptide, 83880
Natural Killer Cells (NK)
  Total Count, 86357
Natural Ostium
  Sinus
    Maxillary, 31000
    Sphenoid, 31002
Navicular
  Arthroplasty
    with Implant, 25443
  Fracture
    with Manipulation, 25624
    Closed Treatment, 25622
    Open Treatment, 25628
  Repair, 25440
Navigation
  Computer Assisted, 20985
NCS (Nerve Conduction Study), 95900-
  95904
Neck
  Angiography, 70498, 70547-70549
  Artery
    Ligation, 37615
  Biopsy, 21550
  Bypass Graft, 35901
  CT Scan, 70490-70492, 70498
  Dissection, Radical
    See Radical Neck Dissection
  Exploration
    Blood Vessels, 35800
    Lymph Nodes, 38542
  Incision and Drainage
    Abscess, 21501, 21502
    Hematoma, 21501, 21502
  Lipectomy, Suction Assisted, 15876
  Magnetic Resonance Angiography
    (MRA), 70547-70549
  Magnetic Resonance Imaging (MRI),
    70540-70543
  Nerve
    Graft, 64885, 64886
  Repair
    with Other Graft, 35261
    with Vein Graft, 35231
    Blood Vessel, 35201
  Rhytidectomy, 15825, 15828
  Skin
    Revision, 15819
  Skin Graft
    Delay of Flap, 15620

Neck — *continued*
  Skin Graft — *continued*
    Full Thickness, 15240, 15241
    Pedicle Flap, 15574
    Split, 15120, 15121
  Surgery, Unlisted, 21899
  Tissue Transfer, Adjacent, 14040,
    14041
  Tumor
    Excision, 21555, 21556
    Excision/Resection, 21557
  Ultrasound Exam, 76536
  Unlisted Services and Procedures,
    21899
  Urinary Bladder
    See Bladder, Neck
  Wound Exploration
    Penetrating, 20100
    X-ray, 70360
Neck, Humerus
  Fracture
    with Shoulder Dislocation
      Closed Treatment, 23680
      Open Treatment, 23675
Neck Muscle
  Division, Scalenus Anticus, 21700,
    21705
    Sternocleidomastoid, 21720-
      21725
Necropsy
  Coroner Examination, 88045
  Forensic Examination, 88040
  Gross and Microscopic Examination,
    88020-88029
  Gross Examination, 88000-88016
  Organ, 88037
  Regional, 88036
  Unlisted Services and Procedures,
    88099
Needle Biopsy
  See Biopsy
  Abdomen Mass, 49180
  Bone, 20220, 20225
  Bone Marrow, 38221
  Breast, 19100
  Colon
    Endoscopy, 45392
  Colon Sigmoid
    Endoscopy, 45342
  CT Scan Guidance, 77012
  Epididymis, 54800
  Esophagus
    Endoscopy, 43232, 43238
  Fluoroscopic Guidance, 77002
  Gastrointestinal, Upper
    Endoscopy, 43238, 43242
  Kidney, 50200
  Liver, 47000, 47001
  Lung, 32405
  Lymph Node, 38505
  Mediastinum, 32405
  Muscle, 20206
  Pancreas, 48102
  Pleura, 32400
  Prostate, 55700
  Retroperitoneal Mass, 49180
  Salivary Gland, 42400
  Spinal Cord, 62269
  Testis, 54500
  Thyroid Gland, 60100
  Transbronchial, 31629, 31633
Needle Localization
  Breast
    with Lesion Excision, 19125,
      19126
    Placement, 19290, 19291
  Magnetic Resonance Guidance,
    77021
Needle Manometer Technique, 20950
Needle Wire
  Introduction
    Trachea, 31730
  Placement
    Breast, 19290, 19291
Neer Procedure, 23470

ORIF — *continued*
  Fracture — *continued*
    Humeral, Humerus
      Anatomical Neck, 23615-23616
      Condylar
        Lateral, 24579
        Medial, 24579
      Epicondylar
        Lateral, 24575
        Medial, 24575
      Proximal, 23615-23616
      Shaft, 24515-24516
      Supracondylar, 24545-24546
        with
          Intercondylar Extension, 24546
      Surgical Neck, 23615-23616
      Transcondylar, 24545-24546
        with
          Intercondylar Extension, 24546
      Tuberosity, 23630
    Hyoid, 21495
    Interphalangeal, 26746
    Knee
      Intercondylar Spine, 27540
      Tuberosity, 27540
    Larynx, Laryngeal, 31584
    LeFort I, 21422-21423
    LeFort II, 21346-21348
    LeFort III, 21432-21436
    Lunate, 25645
    Malar (Area), 21365-21366
      with Malar Tripod, 21365-21366
      with Zygomatic Arch, 21365-21366
    Malleolus
      Lateral, 27792
        with
          Ankle Fracture
            Trimalleolar, 27822-27823
      Medial, 27766
        with
          Ankle Fracture
            Trimalleolar, 27822-27823
    Mandibular, Mandible, 21462, 21470
      Alveolar Ridge, 21445
      Condylar, Condyle, 21465
    Maxillary, Maxilla, 21422-21423
      Alveolar Ridge, 21445
    Metacarpal, 26615
    Metacarpophalangeal, 26715
    Metatarsal, 28485
    Monteggia, 24635
    Nasal Bone, 21330-21335
      with Nasal Septum, 21335
    Nasal Septum, 21335
    Nasoethmoid, 21339
    Nasomaxillary, 21346-21348
    Navicular
      Foot, 28465
      Hand, 25628
    Odontoid, 22318-22319
    Olecranon process, 24685
    Orbit, 21406-21408
    Palate, Palatal, 21422-21423
    Patella, Patellar, 27524
      with
        Patellectomy
          Complete, 27524
          Partial, 27524
        Repair
          Soft Tissue, 27524
    Phalange, Phalangeal
      Foot, 28525
        Great Toe, 28505
      Hand, 26735
        Distal, 26765
    Pisiform, 25645

ORIF — *continued*
  Fracture — *continued*
    Radial, Radius
      and
        Ulnar, Ulna, 25575
      Distal, 25606-25609
        with Fracture
          Ulnar Styloid
      Head, 24665-24666
      Neck, 24665-24666
      or
        Ulnar, Ulna, 25574
      Shaft, 25515, 25525-25526
        with Dislocation
          Distal
            Radio-Ulnar Joint, 25525-25526
        with Repair
          Triangular Cartilage, 25526
    Rib, 21810
    Scaphoid, 25628
    Scapula, Scapular, 23585
    Sesamoid, 28531
    Smith, 25607, 25608-25609
    Sternum, 21825
    Talar, Talus, 28445
    Tarsal
      Calcaneal, 28415
        with Bone Graft, 28420
      Cuboid, 28465
      Cuneiforms, 28465
      Navicular, 28465
      Talus, 28445
    T-Fracture, 27228
    Thigh
      Femur, Femoral
        Condyle
          Lateral, 27514
          Medial, 27514
        Distal, 27514
          Lateral Condyle, 27514
          Medial Condyle, 27514
        Epiphysis, Epiphyseal, 27519
        Head, 27254
          Traumatic, 27254
            with Dislocation
              Hip, 27254
        Intertrochanteric, Intertrochanter, 27244-27245
          with Intermedullary Implant, 27245
        Lateral Condyle, 27514
        Medial Condyle, 27514
        Peritrochanteric, Peritrochanter, 27244-27245
          with Intermedullary Implant, 27245
        Proximal End, 27236
          with Prosthetic Replacement, 27236
        Proximal Neck, 27236
          with Prosthetic Replacement, 27236
        Shaft, 27506-27507
          with Intermedullary Implant, 27245
        Subtrochanteric, Subtrochanter, 27244-27245
        Supracondylar, 27511-27513
          with Intercondylar Extension, 27513
        Transcondylar, 27511-27513
          with Intercondylar Extension, 27513
        Trochanteric, Trochanter
          Greater, 27248
          Intertrochanteric, Intertrochanter, 27244-27245

ORIF — *continued*
  Fracture — *continued*
    Thigh — *continued*
      Femur, Femoral — *continued*
        Trochanteric, Trochanter — *continued*
          Intertrochanteric, Intertrochanter — *continued*
            with Intermedullary Implant, 27245
          Peritrochanteric, Peritrochanter, 27244-27245
            with Intermedullary Implant, 27245
          Subtrochanteric, Subtrochanter, 27244-27245
            with Intermedullary Implant, 27245
    Thumb, 26665
    Tibia and Fibula, 27828
    Tibia, Tibial
      Articular Surface, 27827
        with Fibula, Fibular Fracture, 27828
      Bicondylar, 27536
      Condylar
        Bicondylar, 27536
        Unicondylar, 27535
      Distal, 27826
      Pilon, 27827
        with Fibula, Fibular Fracture, 27828
      Plafond, 27827
        with Fibula, Fibular Fracture, 27828
      Plateau, 27535-27536
      Proximal, 27535-27536
      Shaft, 27758-27759
        with Fibula, Fibular Fracture, 27758-27759
        with Intermedullary Implant, 27759
      Unicondylar, 27535
    Toe, 28525
      Great, 28505
    Trapezium, 25645
    Trapezoid, 25645
    Triquetral, 25645
    Ulna, Ulnar
      and Radial, Radius, 25575
      Monteggia, 24635
      Proximal, 24635, 24685
      Shaft, 25545
      or Radial, Radius, 25574
    Vertebral, 22325-22328
    Zygomatic Arch, 21365-21366
Ormond Disease
  Ureterolysis, 50715
Orogastric Tube
  Placement, 43752
Oropharynx
  Biopsy, 42800
Orthodontic Cephalogram, 70350
Orthomyxoviridae
  Antibody, 86710
  by Immunoassay with Direct Optical Observation, 87804
Orthomyxovirus, 86710, 87804
Orthopantogram, 70355
Orthopedic Cast
  See Cast
Orthopedic Surgery
  Computer Assisted Navigation, 20985
  Stereotaxis
    Computer Assisted, 20985
Orthoptic Training, 92065
Orthoroentgenogram, 77073

Orthosis/Orthotics
  Check-Out, 97762
  Management/Training, 97760
Os Calcis Fracture
  with Manipulation, 28405-28406
  without Manipulation, 28400
  Open Treatment, 28415-28420
  Percutaneous Fixation, 28406
Osmolality
  Blood, 83930
  Urine, 83935
Osseous Survey, 77074-77076
Osseous Tissue
  See Bone
Ossicles
  Excision
    Stapes
      with Footplate Drill Out, 69661
      without Foreign Material, 69660-69661
  Reconstruction
    Ossicular Chain
      Tympanoplasty with Antrotomy or Mastoidotomy, 69636-69637
      Tympanoplasty with Mastoidectomy, 69642, 69644, 69646
      Tympanoplasty without Mastoidectomy, 69632-69633
  Release
    Stapes, 69650
  Replacement
    with Prosthesis, 69633, 69637
OST, 59020
Ostectomy
  Carpal, 25215
  Femur, 27365
  Humerus, 24999
  Metacarpal, 26250-26255
  Metatarsal, 28288
  Phalanges
    Fingers, 26260-26262
  Pressure Ulcer
    Ischial, 15941, 15945
    Sacral, 15933, 15935, 15937
    Trochanter, 15951, 15953, 15958
  Radius, 25999
  Scapula, 23190
  Sternum, 21620
  Ulna, 25999
Osteocalcin, 83937
Osteocartilaginous Exostoses
  Auditory Canal
    Excision, 69140
Osteochondroma
  Auditory Canal
    Excision, 69140
Osteoclasis
  Carpal, 26989
  Clavicle, 23929
  Femur, 27599
  Humerus, 24999
  Metacarpal, 26989
  Metatarsal, 28899
  Patella, 27599
  Radius, 26989
  Scapula, 23929
  Tarsal, 28899
  Thorax, 23929
  Ulna, 26989
Osteocutaneous Flap
  with Microvascular Anastomosis, 20969-20973
Osteoma
  Sinusotomy
    Frontal, 31075
Osteomyelitis
  Excision
    Clavicle, 23180
    Facial, 21026
    Femur, 27360

Index

Pacemaker, Heart — Pathology

Preventive Medicine — *continued*
Respiratory Pattern Recording, 94772
Unlisted Services and Procedures, 99429
Prevnar, 90669
Priapism
Repair
with Shunt, 54420, 54430
Fistulization, 54435
Primidone
Assay, 80188
PRITS (Partial Resection Inferior Turbinates), 30140
PRL
See Prolactin
Proalbumin
See Prealbumin
Probes, DNA
See Nucleic Acid Probe
Probes, Nucleic Acid
See Nucleic Acid Probe
Probing
Nasolacrimal Duct, 68816
Procainamide
Assay, 80190, 80192
Procalcitonin (PCT), 0194T
Procedure, Fontan
See Repair, Heart, Anomaly
Procedure, Maxillofacial
See Maxillofacial Procedures
Process
See anatomic Term (e.g., coracoid, odontoid)
Process, Odontoid
See Odontoid Process
Procidentia
Rectal
Excision, 45130, 45135
Repair, 45900
Procoagulant Activity, Glomerular
See Thromboplastin
Proconvertin, 85230
Proctectasis
See Dilation, Rectum
Proctectomy
Laparoscopic, 45395-45397
with Colectomy/Ileostomy, 44211-44212
Open Approach, 45110-45123
with Colectomy, 45121
with Colectomy/Ileostomy, 44155-44158
Proctocele
See Rectocele
Proctopexy, 45400-45402, 45540-45550
with Sigmoid Excision, 45550
Proctoplasty, 45500, 45505
Proctorrhaphy
Fistula, 45800-45825
Prolapse, 45540-45541
Proctoscopies
See Anoscopy
Proctosigmoidoscopy
Ablation
Polyp or Lesion, 45320
Biopsy, 45305
Destruction
Tumor, 45320
Dilation, 45303
Exploration, 45300
Hemorrhage Control, 45317
Placement
Stent, 45327
Removal
Foreign Body, 45307
Polyp, 45308-45315
Tumor, 45315
Stoma
through Artificial, 45999
Volvulus Repair, 45321
Proctostomy
Closure, 45999
Proctotomy, 45160
Products, Gene
See Protein

Proetz Therapy, 30210
Profibrinolysin, 85420-85421
Progenitor Cell
See Stemm Cell
Progesterone, 84144
Progesterone Receptors, 84234
Progestin Receptors, 84234
Programming
Cardioverter-Defibrillator, 93282-93284, 93287
Loop Recorder, 93285
Pacemaker, 93279-93281, 93286
Proinsulin, 84206
Pro-Insulin C Peptide
See C–Peptide
Projective Test, 96101-96103
Prokallikrein, 85292
Prokallikrein, Plasma, 85292
Prokinogenase, 85292
Prolactin, 80418, 80440, 84146
Prolapse
See procidentia
Prolapse, Rectal
See Procidentia, Rectum
Prolastin
See Alpha–1 Antitrypsin
Prolonged Services
with Direct Patient Contact, 99354-99357
without Direct Patient Contact, 99358, 99359
Physician Standby Services, 99360
PROM, 95851, 95852, 97110, 97530
Pronuclear Stage Tube Transfer (PROST), 58976
Prophylactic Treatment
See Also Preventive Medicine
Antibiotic Documentation, 4042F-4043F, 4045F-4049F
Antimicrobial Documentation, 4041F
Clavicle, 23490
Femoral Neck and Proximal Femur
Nailing, 27187
Pinning, 27187
Wiring, 27187
Femur, 27495
Nailing, 27495
Pinning, 27495
Wiring, 27495
Humerus, 23491
Pinning, Wiring, 24498
Radius, 25490, 25492
Nailing, 25490, 25492
Pinning, 25490, 25492
Plating, 25490, 25492
Wiring, 25490, 25492
Shoulder
Clavicle, 23490
Humerus, 23491
Tibia, 27745
Ulna, 25491, 25492
Nailing, 25491, 25492
Pinning, 25491, 25492
Plating, 25491, 25492
Wiring, 25491, 25492
Venous Thromboembolism (VTE), 4044F
Prophylaxis
Anticoagulant Therapy, 4075F
Deep Vein Thrombosis (DVT), 4070F
Retinal Detachment
Cryotherapy, 67141
Cryotherapy, Diathermy, 67141
Photocoagulation, 67145
Diathermy, 67141
Photocoagulation, 67145
ProQuad, 90710
PROST (Pronuclear Stage Tube Transfer), 58976
Prostaglandin, 84150
Insertion, 59200
Prostanoids
See Prostaglandin

Prostate
Ablation
Cryosurgery, 55873
Abscess
Drainage, 52700
Incision and Drainage, 55720, 55725
Biopsy, 55700, 55705, 55706
Brachytherapy
Needle Insertion, 55875-55876
Coagulation
Laser, 52647
Destruction
Cryosurgery, 55873
Thermotherapy, 53850
Microwave, 53850
Radio Frequency, 53852
Enucleation, Laser, 52649
Excision
Partial, 55801, 55821, 55831
Perineal, 55801-55815
Radical, 55810-55815, 55840-55845
Retropubic, 55831-55845
Suprapubic, 55821
Transurethral, 52402, 52601
Exploration
with Nodes, 55862, 55865
Exposure, 55860
Incision
Exposure, 55860-55865
Transurethral, 52450
Insertion
Catheter, 55875
Needle, 55875
Radioactive Substance, 55860
Needle Biopsy, 55700, 55706
Placement
Catheter, 55875
Dosimeter, 55876
Fiducial Marker, 55876
Interstitial Device, 55876
Needle, 55875
Thermotherapy
Transurethral, 53850
Ultrasound, 76872, 76873
Unlisted Services and Procedures, 54699, 55899
Urinary System, 53899
Urethra
Stent Insertion, 0084T
Transurethral Balloon Dilation
Vaporization
Laser, 52648
Prostatectomy, 52601
Laparoscopic, 55866
Perineal
Partial, 55801
Radical, 55810, 55815
Retropubic
Partial, 55831
Radical, 55840-55845, 55866
Suprapubic
Partial, 55821
Transurethral, 52601
Walsh Modified Radical, 55810
Prostate Specific Antigen
Complexed, 84152
Free, 84154
Total, 84153
Prostatic Abscess
Incision and Drainage, 55720, 55725
Prostatotomy, 55720, 55725
Transurethral, 52700
Prostatotomy, 55720, 55725
Prosthesis
Augmentation
Mandibular Body, 21125
Auricular, 21086
Breast
Insertion, 19340, 19342
Removal, 19328, 19330
Supply, 19396
Check-Out, 97762
See Physical Medicine/Therapy/Occupational Therapy

Prosthesis — *continued*
Cornea, 65770
Endovascular
Thoracic Aorta, 33883-33886
Facial, 21088
Hernia
Mesh, 49568
Hip
Removal, 27090, 27091
Impression and Custom Preparation (by Physician)
Auricular, 21086
Facial, 21088
Mandibular Resection, 21081
Nasal, 21087
Obturator
Definitive, 21080
Interim, 21079
Surgical, 21076
Oral Surgical Splint, 21085
Orbital, 21077
Palatal
Augmentation, 21082
Lift, 21083
Speech Aid, 21084
Intestines, 44700
Knee
Insertion, 27438, 27445
Lens
Insertion, 66982-66985
Manual or Mechanical Technique, 66982-66984
not Associated with Concurrent Cataract Removal, 66985
Mandibular Resection, 21081
Nasal, 21087
Nasal Septum
Insertion, 30220
Obturator, 21076
Definitive, 21080
Interim, 21079
Ocular, 21077, 65770, 66982-66985, 92358
Fitting and Prescription, 92002-92014
Loan, 92358
Prescription, 92002-92014
Orbital, 21077
Orthotic
Check-Out, 97762
Training, 97761
Ossicular Chain
Partial or Total, 69633, 69637
Palatal Augmentation, 21082
Palatal Lift, 21083
Palate, 42280, 42281
Penile
Fitting, 54699, 55899
Insertion, 54400-54405
Removal, 54406, 54410-54417
Repair, 54408
Replacement, 54410, 54411, 54416, 54417
Perineum
Removal, 53442
Skull Plate
Removal, 62142
Replacement, 62143
Spectacle
Fitting, 92352, 92353
Repair, 92371
Speech Aid, 21084
Spinal
Insertion, 22851
Synthetic, 69633, 69637
Temporomandibular Joint
Arthroplasty, 21243
Testicular
Insertion, 54660
Training, 97761
Urethral Sphincter
Insertion, 53444, 53445
Removal, 53446, 53447
Repair, 53449
Replacement, 53448

Index

Reduction — Release

© 2008 Ingeni

Repair — *continued*
  Finger — *continued*
    Volar Plate, 26548
    Web Finger, 26560
  Fistula
    Anorectal, 0170T
    Carotid–Cavernous, 61710
    Coronary, 33500-33501
    Graft-Enteric Fistula, 35870
    Ileoanal Pouch, 46710, 46712
    Mastoid, 69700
    Nasolabial, 42260
    Neurovisceral, 50525-50526
    Oromaxillary, 30580
    Oronasal, 30600
    Rectovaginal, 57308
    Sinus of Valsalva, 33702, 33710
    Ureterovisceral, 50930
  Foot
    Fascia, 28250
    Muscles, 28250
    Tendon, 28200-28226, 28238
  Fracture
    Nasoethmoid, 21340
    Patella, 27524
    Radius, 25526
    Talar Dome, 29892
    Tibial Plafond, 29892
  Gallbladder
    with Gastroenterostomy, 47741
    with Intestines, 47720-47740
    Laceration, 47999
  Great Arteries, 33770-33781
  Great Vessel, 33320-33322
  Hallux Valgus, 28290-28299
  Hammertoe, 28285-28286
  Hamstring, 27097
  Hand
    Cleft Hand, 26580
    Muscles, 26591, 26593
    Tendon
      Extensor, 26410-26416,
        26426, 26428, 26433-
        26437
      Flexor, 26350-26358, 26440
      Profundus, 26370-26373
  Hearing Aid
    Bone Conduction, 69711
  Heart
    Anomaly, 33600-33617
    Aortic Sinus, 33702-33722
    Artificial Heart
      Intracorporeal, 0052T, 0053T
    Atria
      Laparoscopic, 33265-33266
      Open, 33254-33256
    Atrioventricular Canal, 33660,
      33665
      Complete, 33670
    Atrioventricular Valve, 33660,
      33665
    Blood Vessel, 33320-33322
    Cor Triatriatum, 33732
    Fibrillation, 33254, 33255-33256
    Infundibular, 33476, 33478
    Mitral Valve, 33420-33427
    Myocardium, 33542
    Outflow Tract, 33476, 33478
    Post–Infarction, 33542, 33545
    Prosthetic Valve, 33670, 33852,
      33853
    Prosthetic Valve Dysfunction,
      33496
    Pulmonary Artery Shunt, 33924
    Pulmonary Valve, 33470-33474
    Septal Defect, 33545, 33608,
      33610, 33681-33688,
      33692-33697
      Atrial and Ventricular, 33647
      Atrium, 33641
    Sinus of Valsalva, 33702-33722
    Sinus Venosus, 33645
    Tetralogy of Fallot, 33692
    Total Replacement Heart System
      Intracorporeal, 0052T, 0053T
    Tricuspid Valve, 33465

Repair — *continued*
  Heart — *continued*
    Ventricle, 33611, 33612
      Obstruction, 33619
    Ventricular Tunnel, 33722
    Wound, 33300, 33305
  Hepatic Duct
    with Intestines, 47765, 47802
  Hernia
    with Mesh, 49568
    with Spermatic Cord, 54640
    Abdomen, 49565, 49590
      Incisional or Ventral, 49560
    Diaphragmatic, 39520, 39530-
      39531, 39540-39541,
      39560, 39561
    Epigastric
      Incarcerated, 49572
      Reducible, 49570
    Femoral, 49550
      Incarcerated, 49553
      Initial
        Incarcerated, 49553
        Reducible, 49550
      Recurrent, 49555
      Recurrent Incarcerated, 49557
      Reducible Recurrent, 49555
    Hiatus, 39502
    Incisional
      Initial
        Incarcerated, 49566
        Reducible, 49560
      Recurrent
        Reducible, 49565
    Inguinal, 49420
      Initial
        by Laparoscopy, 49650
        Incarcerated, 49496,
          49501, 49507
        Reducible, 49491, 49495,
          49500, 49505
        Strangulated, 49492,
          49496, 49501,
          49507
      Laparoscopy, 49650-49651
      Older Than 50 Weeks,
        Younger than 6 Months,
        49496
      Preterm Older than 50 weeks
        and younger than 6
        months, full term infant
        younger than 6 months,
        49495-49496
      Preterm up to 50 Weeks,
        49491-49492
      Recurrent
        by Laparoscopy, 49651
        Incarcerated, 49521
        Reducible, 49520
        Strangulated, 49521
      Sliding, 49525
    Intestinal, 44025, 44050
    Lumbar, 49540
    Lung, 32800
    Orchiopexy, 54640
    Paracolostomy, 44346
    Parasternal, 49999
    Preterm Infant
      Birth up to 50 Weeks, 49491-
        49492
      Older than 50 weeks, 49495-
        49496
    Reducible
      Initial
        Epigastric, 49570
        Femoral, 49550
        Incisional, 49560
        Inguinal, 49495, 49500,
          49505
        Umbilical, 49580, 49585
        Ventral, 49560
      Recurrent
        Femoral, 49555
        Incisional, 49565
        Inguinal, 49520
        Ventral, 49560

Repair — *continued*
  Hernia — *continued*
    Sliding, 49525
    Spigelian, 49590
    Umbilical, 49580, 49585
      Incarcerated, 49582, 49587
      Reducible, 49580, 49585
    Ventral
      Initial
        Incarcerated, 49561
        Reducible, 49565
  Hip
    Muscle Transfer, 27100-27105,
      27111
    Osteotomy, 27146-27156
    Tendon, 27097
  Humerus, 24420, 24430
    with Graft, 24435
    Osteotomy, 24400, 24410
  Hypoplasia
    Aortic Arch, 33619
  Hypospadias, 54308, 54312, 54316,
    54318, 54322, 54326, 54328,
    54332, 54336, 54340, 54344,
    54348, 54352
  Ileoanal Pouch, 46710-46712
  Ileostomy, 44310, 45136
    Continent (Kock Pouch), 44316
  Interphalangeal Joint
    Volar Plate, 26548
  Intestine
    Large
      Ulcer, 44605
      Wound, 44605
  Intestines
    Enterocele
      Abdominal Approach, 57270
      Vaginal Approach, 57268
    Large
      Closure Enterostomy, 44620-
        44626
      Diverticula, 44605
      Obstruction, 44615
    Intestines, Small
      Closure Enterostomy, 44620-
        44626
      Diverticula, 44602, 44603
      Fistula, 44640-44661
      Hernia, 44050
      Malrotation, 44055
      Obstruction, 44025, 44050
      Ulcer, 44602, 44603
      Wound, 44602, 44603
  Introitus, Vagina, 56800
  Iris, Ciliary Body, 66680
  Jejunum
    Free Transfer with Microvascular
      Anastomosis, 43496
  Kidney
    Fistula, 50520-50526
    Horseshoe, 50540
    Renal Pelvis, 50400, 50405
    Wound, 50500
  Knee
    Cartilage, 27403
    Instability, 27420
    Ligament, 27405-27409
      Collateral, 27405
      Collateral and Cruciate, 27409
      Cruciate, 27407, 27409
    Meniscus, 27403
    Tendons, 27380, 27381
  Laceration, Skin
    Abdomen
      Complex, 13100-13102
      Intermediate, 12031-12037
      Layered, 12031-12037
      Simple, 12001-12007
      Superficial, 12001-12007
    Arm, Arms
      Complex, 13120-13122
      Intermediate, 12031-12037
      Layered, 12031-12037
      Simple, 12001-12007
      Superficial, 12001-12007

Repair — *continued*
  Laceration, Skin — *continued*
    Axilla, Axillae
      Complex, 13131-13133
      Intermediate, 12031-12037
      Layered, 12031-12037
      Simple, 12001-12007
      Superficial, 12001-12007
    Back
      Complex, 13100-13102
      Intermediate, 12031-12037
      Layered, 12031-12037
      Simple, 12001-12007
      Superficial, 12001-12007
    Breast
      Complex, 13100-13102
      Intermediate, 12031-12037
      Layered, 12031-12037
      Simple, 12001-12007
      Superficial, 12001-12007
    Buttock
      Complex, 13100-13102
      Intermediate, 12031-12037
      Layered, 12031-12037
      Simple, 12001-12007
      Superficial, 12001-12007
    Cheek, Cheeks
      Complex, 13131-13133
      Intermediate, 12051-12057
      Layered, 12051-12057
      Simple, 12011-12018
      Superficial, 12011-12018
    Chest
      Complex, 13100-13102
      Intermediate, 12031-12037
      Layered, 12031-12037
      Simple, 12001-12007
      Superficial, 12001-12007
    Chin
      Complex, 13131-13133
      Intermediate, 12051-12057
      Layered, 12051-12057
      Simple, 12011-12018
      Superficial, 12011-12018
    Ear, Ears
      Complex, 13150-13153
      Intermediate, 12051-12057
      Layered, 12051-12057
      2.5 cm or less, 12051
      Simple, 12011-12018
      Superficial, 12011-12018
    External
      Genitalia
        Complex/Intermediate,
          12041-12047
        Layered, 12041-12047
        Simple, 12001-12007
        Superficial, 12041-12047
    Extremity, Extremities
      Complex, 13150-13153
      Complex/Intermediate,
        12031-12037
      Intermediate, 12051-12057
      Layered, 12031-12037
      Simple, 12001-12007
      Superficial, 12001-12007
    Face
      Complex/Intermediate,
        12051-12057
      Layered, 12051-12057
      Simple, 12011-12018
      Superficial, 12011-12018
    Feet
      Complex, 13131-13133
      Intermediate, 12041-12047
      Layered, 12041-12047
      Simple, 12001-12007
      Superficial, 12001-12007
    Finger, Fingers
      Complex, 13131-13133
      Intermediate, 12041-12047
      Layered, 12041-12047
      Simple, 12001-12007
      Superficial, 12001-12007
    Foot
      Complex, 13131-13133

Replacement — Revision

Replacement — *continued*
Neurostimulator — *continued*
Pulse Generator/Receiver — *continued*
Peripheral Nerve, 64590
Spinal, 63685
Ossicles
with Prosthesis, 69633, 69637
Ossicular Replacement, 69633, 69637
Pacemaker, 33206-33208
Catheter, 33210
Electrode, 33210, 33211, 33216, 33217
Pacing Cardioverter–Defibrillator
Leads, 33243, 33244
Pulse Generator Only, 33241
Penile
Prosthesis, 54410, 54411, 54416, 54417
Prosthesis
Skull, 62143
Urethral Sphincter, 53448
Pulmonary Valve, 33475
Pulse Generator
Brain, 61885
Peripheral Nerve, 64590
Spinal Cord, 63685
Pyelostomy Tube, 50398
Receiver
Brain, 61885
Peripheral Nerve, 64590
Spinal Cord, 63685
Skin
Acellular Dermal Matrix, 15170-15176
Skull Plate, 62143
Spinal Cord
Reservoir, 62360
Stent
Ureteral, 50382, 50385, 50387
Strut, 20697
Subcutaneous Port for Gastric Restrictive Procedure, 43888
Tissue Expanders
Skin, 11970
Total Replacement Heart System
Intracorporeal, 0052T-0053T
Total Replacement Hip, 27130-27132
Tricuspid Valve, 33465
Ureter
with Intestines, 50840
Electronic Stimulator, 53899
Uterus
Inverted, 59899
Venous Access Device, 36582, 36583, 36585
Catheter, 36578
Venous Catheter
Central, 36580, 36581, 36584
Replantation, Reimplantation
Adrenal Tissue, 60699
Arm, Upper, 20802
Digit, 20816, 20822
Foot, 20838
Forearm, 20805
Hand, 20808
Scalp, 17999
Thumb, 20824, 20827
Report Preparation
Extended, Medical, 99080
Psychiatric, 90889
Reposition
Toe to Hand, 26551-26556
Repositioning
Canalith, 95992
Central Venous Catheter, Previously Placed, 36597
Electrode
Heart, 33215, 33216, 33217, 33226
Gastrostomy Tube, 43761
Heart
Defibrillator
Leads, 33215, 33216, 33226, 33249

Repositioning — *continued*
Intraocular Lens, 66825
Tricuspid Valve, 33468
Reproductive Tissue
Cryopreserved
Preparation
Thawing, 89354
Storage, 89344
Reprogramming
Shunt
Brain, 62252
Reptilase
Test, 85635
Time, 85670-85675
Resection
Abdomen, 51597
Aortic Valve Stenosis, 33415
Bladder Diverticulum, 52305
Bladder Neck
Transurethral, 52500
Brain Lobe, 61323, 61537-61540
Chest Wall, 19260-19272
Diaphragm, 39560-39561
Endaural, 69905-69910
Humeral Head, 23195
Intestines, Small
Laparoscopic, 44202-44203
Lung, 32503-32504
Mouth
with Tongue Excision, 41153
Myocardium
Aneurysm, 33542
Septal Defect, 33545
Nasal Septum, Submucous, 30520
Nose
Septum, 30520
Ovary, Wedge, 58920
Palate, 42120
Pancoast Tumor, 32503-32504
Phalangeal Head
Toe, 28153
Prostate, Transurethral, 52601
Radical
Abdomen, 51597
Arm, Upper, 24077
Elbow, 24077
with Contracture Release, 24149
Foot, 28046
Humerus, 24150-24151
Radius, 24152-24153
Tumor
Ankle, 27615
Calcaneus or Talus, 27647
Clavicle, 23200
Femur, 27365
Fibula, 27646
Humerus, 23220
with Autograft, 23221
with Prosthetic Replacement, 23222
Knee, 27329, 27365
Leg, Lower, 27615
Leg, Upper, 27329
Metatarsal, 28173
Phalanx, Toe, 28175
Scapula, 23210
Tarsal, 28171
Tibia, 27645
Rhinectomy
Partial, 30150
Total, 30160
Ribs, 19260-19272, 32900
Synovial Membrane
See Synovectomy
Temporal Bone, 69535
Tumor
Fallopian Tube, 58957-58958
Lung, 32503-32504
Ovary, 58957-58958
Peritoneum, 58957-58958
Ulna
Arthrodesis
Radioulnar Joint, 25830
Ureterocele
Ectopic, 52301

Resection — *continued*
Ureterocele — *continued*
Orthotopic, 52300
Vena Cava
with Reconstruction, 37799
Resonance Spectroscopy, Magnetic, 76390
Respiration, Positive–Pressure, 94660
Respiratory Pattern Recording
Preventive
Infant, 94772
Respiratory Syncytial Virus
Antibody, 86756
Antigen Detection
Direct Fluorescent Antibody, 87280
Direct Optical Observation, 87807
Enzyme Immunoassay, 87420
Immune Globulin, 90378-90379
Response, Auditory Evoked, 92585-92586
See Also Audiologic Function Tests
Rest Home Visit
Care Plan Oversight Services, 99339-99340
Established Patient, 99334-99337
New Patient, 99324-99328
Restoration
Ventricular, 33548
Resuscitation
Cardiac Massage via Thoracotomy, 32160
Cardiopulmonary (CPR), 92950
Newborn, 99460-99465
Reticulocyte
Count, 85044-85045
Retina
Examination, Macula/Fundus, Dilated, 2019F-2021F
Communication of Findings for Diabetes Management, 5010F
Incision
Encircling Material, 67115
Lesion
Extensive
Destruction, 67227-67228
Localized
Destruction, 0017T, 67208-67218
Repair
Detachment
with Vitrectomy, 67108, 67112-67113
by Scleral Buckling, 67112
Cryotherapy or Diathermy, 67101
Injection of Air, 67110
Photocoagulation, 67105
Scleral Dissection, 67107
Prophylaxis
Detachment, 67141, 67145
Retinopathy
Destruction
Cryotherapy, Diathermy, 67227, 67229
Photocoagulation, 67228-67229
Preterm Infant, 67229
Retinacular
Knee
Release, 27425
Retinopathy
Destruction/Treatment
Cryotherapy, Diathermy, 67227, 67229
Photocoagulation, 67228-67229
Retinopexy, Pneumatic, 67110
Retraction, Clot
See Clot Retraction
Retrieval
Transcatheter Foreign Body, 37203
Retrocaval Ureter
Ureterolysis, 50725

Retrograde Cholangiopancreatographies, Endoscopic
See Cholangiopancreatography
Retrograde Cystourethrogram
See Urethrocystography, Retrogra
Retrograde Pyelogram
See Urography, Retrograde
Retroperitoneal Area
Abscess
Incision and Drainage
Open, 49060
Percutaneous, 49061
Biopsy, 49010
Cyst
Destruction/Excision, 49203-49205
Endometriomas
Destruction/Excision, 49203-49205
Exploration, 49010
Needle Biopsy
Mass, 49180
Tumor
Destruction
Excision, 49203-49205
Retroperitoneal Fibrosis
Ureterolysis, 50715
Retropubic Prostatectomies
See Prostatectomy, Retropubic
Revascularization
Distal Upper Extremity
with Interval Ligation, 36838
Heart
Arterial Implant, 33999
Myocardial Resection, 33542
Other Tissue Grafts, 20926
Interval Ligation
Distal Upper Extremity, 36838
Penis, 37788
Transmyocardial, 33140-33141
Reverdin Bunionectomy, 28296
Reversal, Vasectomy
See Vasovasorrhaphy
Reverse T3, 84482
Reverse Triiodothyronine, 84482
Revision
See Also Reconstruction
Abdomen
Intraperitoneal Catheter, 4932
Peritoneal-Venous Shunt, 4942
Adjustable Gastric Restrictive Devic
43771
Aorta, 33404
Arthroplasty
Hip, 27125-27138
Spine, 22861-22862
Atrial, 33254-33256
Blepharoplasty, 15820-15823
Breast
Implant, 19380
Bronchial Stent, 31638
Bronchus, 32501
Bypass Graft
Vein Patch, 35685
Cervicoplasty, 15819
Colostomy, 44340
Paracolostomy Hernia, 44345-44346
Cornea
Prosthesis, 65770
Reshaping
Epikeratoplasty, 65767
Keratomileusis, 65760
Keratophakia, 65765
Defibrillator Site
Chest, 33223
Ear, Middle, 69662
Electrode, Stomach, 0156T, 0158T
43648, 43882
External Fixation System, 20693
Eye
Aqueous Shunt, 66185
Gastric Restrictive Device, Adjustable, 43771
Gastric Restrictive Procedure, 4384

© 2008 Ingeni

SAVER (Surgical Anterior Ventricular Endocardial Restoration), 33548
SBFT, 74249
SBRT (Stereotactic Body Radiation Therapy), 77373
Scabies, 87220
Scalenotomy, 21700-21705
Scalenus Anticus
Division, 21700-21705
Scaling
Chemical for Acne, 17360
Scalp
Skin Graft
Delay of Flap, 15610
Full Thickness, 15220-15221
Pedicle Flap, 15572
Split, 15100-15101
Tissue Transfer, Adjacent, 14020-14021
Tumor Resection
Radical, 21015
Scalp Blood Sampling, 59030
Scan
See Also Specific Site; Nuclear Medicine
Abdomen
Computed Tomography, 74150-74175, 75635
Computerized
Ophthalmic, 0187T
CT
See CT Scan
MRI
See Magnetic Resonance Imaging
PET
With Computed Tomography (CT)
Limted, 78814
Skull Base to Mid-thigh, 78815
Whole Body, 78816
Brain, 78608-78609
Heart, 78459
Limited Area, 78811
Myocardial Imaging Perfusion Study, 78491-78492
Skull Base to Mid-Thigh, 78812
Whole Body, 78813
Radionuclide, Brain, 78607
Scanning Radioiosotope
See Nuclear Medicine
Scanogram, 77073
Scaphoid
Fracture
with Manipulation, 25624
Closed Treatment, 25622
Open Treatment, 25628
Scapula
Craterization, 23182
Cyst
Excision, 23140
with Allograft, 23146
with Autograft, 23145
Diaphysectomy, 23182
Excision, 23172, 23190
Partial, 23182
Fracture
Closed Treatment
with Manipulation, 23575
without Manipulation, 23570
Open Treatment, 23585
Ostectomy, 23190
Repair
Fixation, 23400
Scapulopexy, 23400
Saucerization, 23182
Sequestrectomy, 23172
Tumor
Excision, 23140, 23210
with Allograft, 23146
with Autograft, 23145
Radical Resection, 23210
X-ray, 73010
Scapulopexy, 23400
Scarification
Pleural, 32215

Scarification of Pleura
Chemical, 32560
Endoscopic, 32650
SCBE (Single Contrast Barium Enema), 74270
Schanz Operation, 27448
Schauta Operation, 58285
Schede Procedure, 32905-32906
Scheie Procedure, 66155
Schilling Test, 78270-78272
Schlatter Operation, 43620
Schlemm's Canal Dilation, 0176T-0177T
Schlicter Test, 87197
Schocket Procedure, 66180
Schuchard Procedure
Osteotomy
Maxilla, 21206
Schwannoma, Acoustic
See Brain, Tumor, Excision
Sciatic Nerve
Decompression, 64712
Injection
Anesthetic, 64445-64446
Lesion
Excision, 64786
Neuroma
Excision, 64786
Neuroplasty, 64712
Release, 64712
Repair
Suture, 64858
Scintigraphy
See Emission Computerized Tomography
See Nuclear Medicine
Scissoring
Skin Tags, 11200-11201
Sclera
Excision, 66130
Sclerectomy with Punch or Scissors, 66160
Fistulization
for Glaucoma, 0123T
Iridencleisis or Iridotasis, 66165
Sclerectomy with Punch or Scissors with Iridectomy, 66160
Thermocauterization with Iridectomy, 66155
Trabeculectomy ab Externo in Absence of Previous Surgery, 66170
Trephination with Iridectomy, 66150
Incision (Fistulization)
Iridencleisis or Iridotasis, 66165
Sclerectomy with Punch or Scissors with Iridectomy, 66160
Thermocauterization with Iridectomy, 66155
Trabeculectomy ab Externo in Absence of Previous Surgery, 66170
Trephination with Iridectomy, 66150
Lesion
Excision, 66130
Repair
with Glue, 65286
Reinforcement
with Graft, 67255
without Graft, 67250
Staphyloma
with Graft, 66225
without Graft, 66220
Wound (Operative), 66250
Tissue Glue, 65286
Scleral Buckling Operation
Retina, Repair, Detachment, 67107-67112
Scleral Ectasia
Repair, 66220
with Graft, 66225
Sclerectomy, 66160
Sclerotherapy
Venous, 36468-36471

Sclerotomy, 66150-66170
Screening, Drug
Alcohol and/or Substance Abuse, 99408-99409
Chromatography, 82486
Qualitative, 80100-80101
Scribner Cannulation, 36810
Scrotal Varices
Excision, 55530-55540
Scrotoplasty, 55175-55180
Scrotum
Abscess
Incision and Drainage, 54700, 55100
Excision, 55150
Exploration, 55110
Hematoma
Incision and Drainage, 54700
Removal
Foreign Body, 55120
Repair, 55175-55180
Ultrasound, 76870
Unlisted Services and Procedures, 55899
Scrub Typhus, 86000
Second Look Surgery
Carotid Thromboendarterectomy, 35390
Coronary Artery Bypass, 33530
Distal Vessel Bypass, 35700
Valve Procedure, 33530
Section
See Also Decompression
Cesarean
See Cesarean Delivery
Cranial Nerve, 61460
Spinal Access, 63191
Dentate Ligament, 63180-63182
Gasserian Ganglion
Sensory Root, 61450
Medullary Tract, 61470
Mesencephalic Tract, 61480
Nerve Root, 63185-63190
Spinal Accessory Nerve, 63191
Spinal Cord Tract, 63194-63199
Tentorium Cerebelli, 61440
Vestibular Nerve
Transcranial Approach, 69950
Translabyrinthine Approach, 69915
Sedation
Conscious (Moderate), 99143-99150
with Independent Observation, 99143-99145
Seddon–Brookes Procedure, 24320
Sedimentation Rate
Blood Cell
Automated, 85652
Manual, 85651
Segmentectomy
Breast, 19301-19302
Lung, 32484
Selective Cellular Enhancement Technique, 88112
Selenium, 84255
Self Care
See Also Physical Medicine/Therapy/Occupational Therapy
Training, 97535, 98960-98962, 99509
Sella Turcica
CT Scan, 70480-70482
X-ray, 70240
Semen
Cryopreservation
Storage (per year), 89343
Thawing, each aliquot, 89353
Semen Analysis, 89300-89322
with Sperm Isolation, 89260-89261
Sperm Analysis, 89331
Antibodies, 89325
Hyaluronan Binding Test, 0087T
Semenogelase, 84152-84154
Semicircular Canal
Incision
Fenestration, 69820

Semicircular Canal — continued
Incision — continued
Revised, 69840
Semilunar
Bone
See Lunate
Ganglion
See Gasserian Ganglion
Seminal Vesicle
Cyst
Excision, 55680
Excision, 55650
Incision, 55600, 55605
Mullerian Duct
Excision, 55680
Unlisted Services and Procedures, 55899
Seminal Vesicles
Vesiculography, 74440
X-ray with Contrast, 74440
Seminin, 84152-84154
Semiquantitative, 81005
Semont Maneuver, 95992
Sengstaaken Tamponade
Esophagus, 43460
Senning Procedure
Repair, Great Arteries, 33774-33777
Senning Type, 33774-33777
Sensitivity Study
Antibiotic
Agar, 87181
Disc, 87184
Enzyme Detection, 87185
Macrobroth, 87188
MIC, 87186
Microtiter, 87186
MLC, 87187
Mycobacteria, 87190
Antiviral Drugs
HIV–1
Tissue Culture, 87904
Sensorimotor Exam, 92060
Sensor, Transcatheter Placement, 34806
Sensory Nerve
Common
Repair/Suture, 64834
Sensory Testing
Quantitative (QST), Per Extremity
Cooling Stimuli, 0108T
Heat–Pain Stimuli, 0109T
Touch Pressure Stimuli, 0106T
Using Other Stimuli, 0110T
Vibration Stimuli, 0107T
Sentinel Node
Injection Procedure, 38792
SEP (Somatosensory Evoked Potentials), 95925-95927
Separation
Craniofacial
Closed Treatment, 21431
Open Treatment, 21432-21436
Septal Defect
Repair, 33813-33814
Ventricular
Closure
Open, 33675-33688
Percutaneous, 93581
Transmyocardial, 0166T-0167T
Septectomy
Atrial, 33735-33737
Balloon Type, 92992
Blade Method, 92993
Closed, 33735
Submucous Nasal, 30520
Septic Abortion, 59830
Septoplasty, 30520
Septostomy
Atrial, 33735-33737
Balloon Type, 92992
Blade Method, 92993
Septum, Nasal
See Nasal Septum
Sequestrectomy
with Alveolectomy, 41830

© 2008 Ingeni

© 2008 Ingenix

Index

Transferase — Tubed Pedicle Flap

Tubed Pedicle Flap — *continued*
Walking Tube, 15650
Tube, Fallopian
See Fallopian Tube
Tube Placement
Chest, 32551
Endoscopic
Bile Duct, Pancreatic Duct, 43268
Nasobiliary, Nasopancreatic for Drainage, 43267
Gastrostomy Tube, 43246
Nasogastric Tube, 43752
Orogastric Tube, 43752
Tubercle Bacilli
Culture, 87116
Tubercleplasty, Anterior Tibial, 27418
Tuberculin Test, 86580
Tuberculosis
Antigen Response Test, 86480
Culture, 87116
Skin Test, 86580
Tuberculosis Vaccine (BCG), 90585, 90586
Tubes
Endotracheal, 31500
Gastrostomy, 43246, 49440
See Also Gastrostomy Tube
Tudor "Rabbit Ear"
Urethra, Repair
Diverticulum, 53240, 53400, 53405
Fistula, 45820, 45825, 53400, 53405, 53520
Sphincter, 57220
Stricture, 53400, 53405
Urethrocele, 57230
Wound, 53502-53515
Tuffier Vaginal Hysterectomy
See Hysterectomy, Vaginal
TULIP, 52647-52648
Tumor
See Lesion
See Also Craniopharyngioma; Lesion
Abdomen
Destruction
Excision, 49203-49205
Abdominal Wall
Excision, 22900
Acetabulum
Excision, 27076
Ankle, 27615-27619
Arm, Lower, 25075-25077
Arm, Upper, 24075-24077
Back
Flank
Excision, 21930
Radical Resection, 21935
Bile Duct
Destruction, 43272
Extrahepatic, 47711
Intrahepatic, 47712
Bladder, 52234-52240
Excision, 51530, 52355
Brain, 61510
Excision, 61518, 61520, 61521, 61526, 61530, 61545, 62164
Breast
Excision, 19120-19126
Bronchi
Excision, 31640
Calcaneus, 28100-28103
Excision, 27647
Carpal, 25130-25136
Chest Wall
Excision, 19260-19272
Clavicle
Excision, 23140, 23200
with Allograft, 23146
with Autograft, 23145
Coccyx, 49215
Colon
Destruction, 44393, 45383
Cranial Bone
Reconstruction, 21181, 21182

Tumor — *continued*
Destruction
Abdomen, 49203-49205
Chemosurgery, 17311-17315
Urethra, 53220
Ear, Middle
Extended, 69554
Transcanal, 69550
Transmastoid, 69552
Elbow
Excision, 24075-24077
Esophagus
Ablation, 43228
Excision
Femur, 27355-27358
Facial Bones, 21029, 21030, 21034
Fallopian Tube
Resection, 58950, 58952-58956
Femoral, 27355-27358
Excision, 27365
Femur, 27065-27067
Excision, 27365
Fibula, 27635-27638
Excision, 27646
Finger
Excision, 26115-26117
Foot, 28043, 28045, 28046
Forearm
Radical Resection, 25077
Gums
Excision, 41825-41827
Hand, 26115-26117
Heart
Excision, 33120, 33130
Hip, 27047-27049, 27065-27067
Excision, 27075, 27076
Humerus
with Allograft, 23156
with Autograft, 23155
Excision, 23150, 23220-23222, 24110
with Allograft, 23156, 24116
with Autograft, 23155, 24115
Ileum, 27065-27067
Immunoassay for Antigen, 86294, 86316
CA 125, 86304
CA 15-3, 86300
CA 19-9, 86301
Innominate
Excision, 27077
Intestines, Small
Destruction, 44369
Ischial
Excision, 27078, 27079
Kidney
Excision, 52355
Knee
Excision, 27327-27329, 27365
Lacrimal Gland
Excision
with Osteotomy, 68550
Frontal Approach, 68540
Larynx, 31540, 31541
Excision, 31300
Endoscopic, 31540, 31541, 31578
Incision, 31300
Leg, Lower, 27615-27619
Leg, Upper
Excision, 27327-27329
Localization
with Nuclear Medicine, 78800-78803
Mandible, 21040-21045
Maxillary Torus Palatinus, 21032
Mediastinal
Excision, 39220
Mediastinum, 32662
Meningioma
Excision, 61519
Metacarpal, 26200, 26205, 26250, 26255
Metatarsal, 28104-28107
Excision, 28173

Tumor — *continued*
Neck
Excision, 21555, 21556
Radical Resection, 21557
Olecranon Process
with Allograft, 24126
with Autograft, 24125
Excision, 24120
Ovary
Resection, 58950, 58952-58954
Pancreatic Duct
Destruction, 43272
Parotid Gland
Excision, 42410-42426
Pelvis, 27047-27049
Pericardial
Endoscopic, 32661
Excision, 33050
Peritoneum
Resection, 58950-58956
Phalanges
Finger, 26210, 26215, 26260-26262
Toe, 28108
Excision, 28175
Pituitary Gland
Excision, 61546, 61548
Pubis, 27065-27067
Radiation Therapy, 77295
Radius, 25120-25126, 25170
with Allograft, 24126
with Autograft, 24125
Excision, 24120
Rectum
Destruction, 45190, 45320, 46937, 46938
Excision, 0184T, 45160, 45170
Resection
with Cystourethroscopy, 52355
Face, 21015
Scalp, 21015
Retroperitoneal
Destruction
Excision, 49203-49205
Sacrum, 49215
Scapula, 23140
Excision, 23140, 23210
with Allograft, 23146
with Autograft, 23145
Shoulder
Excision, 23075-23077
Skull
Excision, 61500
Soft Tissue
Elbow
Excision, 24075
Finger
Excision, 26115
Forearm
Radical Resection, 25077
Hand
Excision, 26115
Spinal Cord
Excision, 63275-63290
Stomach
Excision, 43610, 43611
Talus, 28100-28103
Excision, 27647
Tarsal, 28104-28107
Excision, 28171
Temporal Bone
Removal, 69970
Testis
Excision, 54530, 54535
Thorax
Excision, 21555, 21556
Radical Resection, 21557
Thyroid
Excision, 60200
Tibia, 27365, 27635-27638
Excision, 27645
Torus Mandibularis, 21031
Trachea
Excision
Cervical, 31785
Thoracic, 31786

Tumor — *continued*
Ulna, 25120-25126, 25170
with Allograft
Excision, 24126
with Autograft
Excision, 24125
Excision, 24120
Ureter
Excision, 52355
Urethra, 52234-52240, 53220
Excision, 52355
Uterus
Excision, 58140, 58145
Vagina
Excision, 57135
Vertebra
Additional Segment
Excision, 22103, 22116
Cervical
Excision, 22100
Lumbar, 22102
Thoracic
Excision, 22101
Wrist, 25075-25077, 25135, 25136
Excision, 25075
Radical Resection, 25077
TUMT (Transurethral Microwave Thermotherapy), 53850
TUNA, 53852
Tunica Vaginalis
Hydrocele
Aspiration, 55000
Excision, 55040, 55041
Repair, 55060
Turbinate
Excision, 30130, 30140
Fracture
Therapeutic, 30930
Injection, 30200
Submucous Resection
Nose
Excision, 30140
Turbinate Mucosa
Ablation, 30801, 30802
Cauterization, 30801, 30802
Turcica, Sella, 70240, 70480-70482
Turnbuckle Jacket, 29020, 29025
Removal, 29715
TURP, 52601, 52630
TVCB (Transvaginal Chorionic Villus Biopsy), 59015
TVH (Total Vaginal Hysterectomy), 58262-58263, 58285, 58291-58292
TVS (Transvaginal Sonography), 76817, 76830
TWINRIX, 90636
Tylectomy, 19120-19126
Tylenol
Urine, 82003
Tympanic Membrane
Create Stoma, 69433, 69436
Incision, 69420, 69421
Reconstruction, 69620
Repair, 69450, 69610
Tympanic Nerve
Excision, 69676
Tympanolysis, 69450
Tympanometry, 92567
Tympanoplasty
with Antrotomy or Mastoidectomy, 69635
with Ossicular Chain Reconstruction, 69636
and Synthetic Prosthesis, 69637
with Mastoidectomy, 69641
with Intact or Reconstructed Wall
without Ossicular Chain Reconstruction, 69643
and Ossicular Chain Reconstruction, 69644
and Ossicular Chain Reconstruction, 69644
without Mastoidectomy, 69631

00100-00126 Anesthesia for Gland, Cleft Lip, Eyelid, ECT, and Ear Procedures

CMS *100-4,12,140.3.2* *Calculation of Anesthesia Time*
CMS *100-4,12,140.2* *Payment for CRNA Services*
CMS *100-4,12,140* *Certified Registered Nurse Anesthetist Services*
CMS *100-4,4,20.6.4* *Modifiers for Discontinued Services*
CMS *100-4,4,20.6* *Modifier Use Under OPPS*
CMS *100-4,4,10.4* *Packaging Rules Under OPPS*
CMS *100-4,12,50* *Anesthesia Services*

00100   **Anesthesia for procedures on salivary glands, including biopsy**   N ▢

    📠 0.00   ✎ 0.00   **Global Days XXX**

AMA: 2008, Apr, 3-4; 2008, Apr, 3-4; 2008, Jan, 10-25; 2008, Apr, 3-4; 2007, Jan, 13-27; 2007, January, 13-27; 2007, Jan, 13-27; 2006, Mar, 15; 2006, Mar, 15; 2006, Feb, 10-15; 2006, Feb, 10-15; 2006, Dec, 10-12; 2006, Dec, 10-12; 2006, Dec, 10-12; 2006, Feb, 9; 2006, March, 16; 2006, December, 10-12; 2006, December, 10-12; 2006, March, 15; 2006, February, 10-15; 2006, March, 16; 2006, Feb, 9; 2006, Dec, 10-12; 2004, Jan, 27; 2004, January, 27; 2004, January, 27; 2004, January, 27; 2004, Jan, 27

00102   **Anesthesia for procedures involving plastic repair of cleft lip**   N ▢

    📠 0.00   ✎ 0.00   **Global Days XXX**

AMA: 2008, Apr, 3-4; 2008, Apr, 3-4; 2008, Apr, 3-4; 2004, Jan, 27; 2004, January, 27; 2004, Jan, 27; 2004, Jan, 27; 2004, Jan, 27

00103   **Anesthesia for reconstructive procedures of eyelid (eg, blepharoplasty, ptosis surgery)**   N ▢

    📠 0.00   ✎ 0.00   **Global Days XXX**

AMA: 2008, Apr, 3-4; 2008, Apr, 3-4; 2008, Apr, 3-4; 2006, Feb, 10-15; 2006, Feb, 10-15; 2006, Feb, 10-15; 2006, Feb, 10-15; 2006, February, 10-15; 2004, Jan, 27; 2004, Jan, 27; 2004, January, 27; 2004, Jan, 27; 2004, Jan, 27

00104   **Anesthesia for electroconvulsive therapy**   N ▢

    📠 0.00   ✎ 0.00   **Global Days XXX**

AMA: 2008, Apr, 3-4; 2008, Apr, 3-4; 2008, Apr, 3-4; 2006, Mar, 15; 2006, Mar, 15; 2006, Feb, 10-15; 2006, Feb, 10-15; 2006, Dec, 10-12; 2006, Dec, 10-12; 2006, Dec, 10-12; 2006, December, 10-12; 2006, December, 10-12; 2006, December, 10-12; 2006, December, 10-12; 2006, March, 15; 2006, February, 10-15; 2006, Dec, 10-12; 2006, Dec, 10-12; 2006, Dec, 10-12; 2006, Dec, 10-12; 2006, Dec, 10-12; 2004, Jan, 27; 2004, January, 27; 2004, Jan, 27

00120   **Anesthesia for procedures on external, middle, and inner ear including biopsy; not otherwise specified**   N ▢

    📠 0.00   ✎ 0.00   **Global Days XXX**

AMA: 2008, Apr, 3-4; 2008, Apr, 3-4; 2008, Apr, 3-4; 2006, Mar, 15; 2006, Mar, 15; 2006, Feb, 10-15; 2006, Feb, 10-15; 2006, Dec, 10-12; 2006, Dec, 10-12; 2006, Dec, 10-12; 2006, December, 10-12; 2006, December, 10-12; 2006, December, 10-12; 2006, December, 10-12; 2006, February, 10-15; 2006, March, 15; 2006, Dec, 10-12; 2006, Dec, 10-12; 2006, Dec, 10-12; 2006, Dec, 10-12; 2006, Dec, 10-12; 2004, Jan, 27; 2004, January, 27; 2004, Jan, 27

00124   **otoscopy**   N ▢

    📠 0.00   ✎ 0.00   **Global Days XXX**

AMA: 2008, Apr, 3-4; 2008, Apr, 3-4; 2008, Apr, 3-4; 2006, Feb, 10-15; 2006, Feb, 10-15; 2006, Mar, 15; 2006, Mar, 15; 2006, Dec, 10-12; 2006, Dec, 10-12; 2006, Dec, 10-12; 2006, December, 10-12; 2006, December, 10-12; 2006, December, 10-12; 2006, December, 10-12; 2006, March, 15; 2006, February, 10-15; 2006, Dec, 10-12; 2006, Dec, 10-12; 2006, Dec, 10-12; 2006, Dec, 10-12; 2006, Dec, 10-12; 2004, Jan, 27; 2004, January, 27; 2004, Jan, 27

00126   **tympanotomy**   N ▢

    📠 0.00   ✎ 0.00   **Global Days XXX**

AMA: 2008, Apr, 3-4; 2008, Apr, 3-4; 2008, Apr, 3-4; 2006, Feb, 10-15; 2006, Feb, 10-15; 2006, Mar, 15; 2006, Mar, 15; 2006, Dec, 10-12; 2006, Dec, 10-12; 2006, Dec, 10-12; 2006, December, 10-12; 2006, December, 10-12; 2006, December, 10-12; 2006, March, 15; 2006, February, 10-15; 2006, Dec, 10-12; 2006, Dec, 10-12; 2006, Dec, 10-12; 2006, Dec, 10-12; 2006, Dec, 10-12; 2004, Jan, 27; 2004, January, 27; 2004, Jan, 27

00140-00148 Anesthesia for Eye Procedures

CMS *100-3,10.1* *Visual Tests Prior to and General Anesthesia During Cataract Surgery*
CMS *100-4,12,140.3.2* *Calculation of Anesthesia Time*
CMS *100-4,12,140* *Certified Registered Nurse Anesthetist Services*
CMS *100-4,4,20.6.4* *Modifiers for Discontinued Services*
CMS *100-4,4,20.6* *Modifier Use Under OPPS*
CMS *100-4,4,10.4* *Packaging Rules Under OPPS*
CMS *100-4,12,50* *Anesthesia Services*

00140   **Anesthesia for procedures on eye; not otherwise specified**   N ▢

    📠 0.00   ✎ 0.00   **Global Days XXX**

AMA: 2008, Apr, 3-4; 2008, Apr, 3-4; 2008, Apr, 3-4; 2006, Mar, 15; 2006, Mar, 15; 2006, Feb, 10-15; 2006, Dec, 10-12; 2006, Feb, 10-15; 2006, Dec, 10-12; 2006, Dec, 10-12; 2006, Dec, 10-12; 2006, Dec, 10-12; 2006, December, 10-12; 2006, December, 10-12; 2006, December, 10-12; 2006, March, 15; 2006, February, 10-15; 2006, Dec, 10-12; 2006, Dec, 10-12; 2004, May, 9; 2004, January, 27; 2004, May, 9; 2004, May, 9; 2004, Jan, 27; 2004, Jan, 27

00142   **lens surgery**   N ▢

    📠 0.00   ✎ 0.00   **Global Days XXX**

AMA: 2008, Apr, 3-4; 2008, Apr, 3-4; 2008, Apr, 3-4; 2006, Mar, 15; 2006, Mar, 15; 2006, Feb, 10-15; 2006, Dec, 10-12; 2006, Feb, 10-15; 2006, Dec, 10-12; 2006, Dec, 10-12; 2006, Dec, 10-12; 2006, Dec, 10-12; 2006, December, 10-12; 2006, December, 10-12; 2006, December, 10-12; 2006, March, 15; 2006, February, 10-15; 2006, Dec, 10-12; 2006, Dec, 10-12; 2004, May, 9; 2004, January, 27; 2004, May, 9; 2004, May, 9; 2004, Jan, 27

00144   **corneal transplant**   N ▢

    📠 0.00   ✎ 0.00   **Global Days XXX**

AMA: 2008, Apr, 3-4; 2008, Apr, 3-4; 2008, Apr, 3-4; 2006, Mar, 15; 2006, Mar, 15; 2006, Feb, 10-15; 2006, Dec, 10-12; 2006, Feb, 10-15; 2006, Dec, 10-12; 2006, Dec, 10-12; 2006, Dec, 10-12; 2006, Dec, 10-12; 2006, December, 10-12; 2006, December, 10-12; 2006, December, 10-12; 2006, March, 15; 2006, February, 10-15; 2006, Dec, 10-12; 2006, Dec, 10-12; 2006, Dec, 10-12; 2006, Dec, 10-12; 2004, May, 9; 2004, January, 27; 2004, May, 9; 2004, May, 9; 2004, Jan, 27; 2004, Jan, 27

00145   **vitreoretinal surgery**   N ▢

    📠 0.00   ✎ 0.00   **Global Days XXX**

AMA: 2008, Apr, 3-4; 2008, Apr, 3-4; 2008, Apr, 3-4; 2006, Feb, 10-15; 2006, Feb, 10-15; 2006, Mar, 15; 2006, Dec, 10-12; 2006, Mar, 15; 2006, Dec, 10-12; 2006, Dec, 10-12; 2006, Dec, 10-12; 2006, Dec, 10-12; 2006, December, 10-12; 2006, December, 10-12; 2006, December, 10-12; 2006, March, 15; 2006, February, 10-15; 2006, Dec, 10-12; 2006, Dec, 10-12; 2006, Dec, 10-12; 2004, Jan, 27; 2004, January, 27; 2004, May, 9; 2004, Jan, 27; 2004, May, 9; 2004, May, 9

● New Code   ▲ Revised Code   ▢ Maternity Edit   ▲ Age Edit   A-Y OPPS Status Indicator   📠 Facility RVU   ✎ Non-Facility RVU
▢ CCI Comprehensive Code   50 Bilateral Procedure   + Add-on Indicator   ◨ Laboratory crosswalk   ◨ Radiology crosswalk

Anesthesia

00147 — 00192

00147 iridectomy N ▣
🔲 0.00 ⚕ 0.00 **Global Days XXX**
AMA: 2008, Apr, 3-4; 2008, Apr, 3-4; 2008, Apr, 3-4; 2006, Mar, 15; 2006, Mar, 15; 2006, Feb, 10-15; 2006, Feb, 10-15; 2006, Dec, 10-12; 2006, Dec, 10-12; 2006, Dec, 10-12; 2006, December, 10-12; 2006, December, 10-12; 2006, December, 10-12; 2006, March, 15; 2006, February, 10-15; 2006, Dec, 10-12; 2006, Dec, 10-12; 2006, Dec, 10-12; 2006, Dec, 10-12; 2004, Jan, 27; 2004, January, 27; 2004, Jan, 27

00148 ophthalmoscopy N ▣
🔲 0.00 ⚕ 0.00 **Global Days XXX**
AMA: 2008, Apr, 3-4; 2008, Apr, 3-4; 2008, Apr, 3-4; 2006, Mar, 15; 2006, Mar, 15; 2006, Feb, 10-15; 2006, Feb, 10-15; 2006, Dec, 10-12; 2006, Dec, 10-12; 2006, Dec, 10-12; 2006, December, 10-12; 2006, December, 10-12; 2006, December, 10-12; 2006, March, 15; 2006, February, 10-15; 2006, Dec, 10-12; 2006, Dec, 10-12; 2006, Dec, 10-12; 2006, Dec, 10-12; 2004, Jan, 27; 2004, January, 27; 2004, Jan, 27

00160-00326 Anesthesia for Face and Head Procedures

CMS *100-4,12,140.3.2* Calculation of Anesthesia Time
CMS *100-4,12,140.2* Payment for CRNA Services
CMS *100-4,12,140* Certified Registered Nurse Anesthetist Services
CMS *100-4,4,20.6* Modifier Use Under OPPS
CMS *100-4,4,10.4* Packaging Rules Under OPPS
CMS *100-4,12,50* Anesthesia Services

00160 Anesthesia for procedures on nose and accessory sinuses; not otherwise specified N ▣
🔲 0.00 ⚕ 0.00 **Global Days XXX**
AMA: 2008, Apr, 3-4; 2008, Apr, 3-4; 2008, Apr, 3-4; 2006, Mar, 15; 2006, Mar, 15; 2006, Feb, 10-15; 2006, Feb, 10-15; 2006, Dec, 10-12; 2006, Dec, 10-12; 2006, Dec, 10-12; 2006, December, 10-12; 2006, December, 10-12; 2006, December, 10-12; 2006, March, 15; 2006, February, 10-15; 2006, Dec, 10-12; 2006, Dec, 10-12; 2006, Dec, 10-12; 2006, Dec, 10-12; 2004, Jan, 27; 2004, January, 27; 2004, Jan, 27

00162 radical surgery N ▣
🔲 0.00 ⚕ 0.00 **Global Days XXX**
AMA: 2008, Apr, 3-4; 2008, Apr, 3-4; 2008, Apr, 3-4; 2006, Mar, 15; 2006, Mar, 15; 2006, Feb, 10-15; 2006, Feb, 10-15; 2006, Dec, 10-12; 2006, Dec, 10-12; 2006, Dec, 10-12; 2006, December, 10-12; 2006, December, 10-12; 2006, December, 10-12; 2006, March, 15; 2006, February, 10-15; 2006, Dec, 10-12; 2006, Dec, 10-12; 2006, Dec, 10-12; 2006, Dec, 10-12; 2004, Jan, 27; 2004, January, 27; 2004, Jan, 27

00164 biopsy, soft tissue N ▣
🔲 0.00 ⚕ 0.00 **Global Days XXX**
AMA: 2008, Apr, 3-4; 2008, Apr, 3-4; 2008, Apr, 3-4; 2006, Feb, 10-15; 2006, Feb, 10-15; 2006, Mar, 15; 2006, Mar, 15; 2006, Dec, 10-12; 2006, Dec, 10-12; 2006, Dec, 10-12; 2006, December, 10-12; 2006, December, 10-12; 2006, December, 10-12; 2006, March, 15; 2006, February, 10-15; 2006, Dec, 10-12; 2006, Dec, 10-12; 2006, Dec, 10-12; 2006, Dec, 10-12; 2004, Jan, 27; 2004, January, 27; 2004, Jan, 27

00170 Anesthesia for intraoral procedures, including biopsy; not otherwise specified N ▣
🔲 0.00 ⚕ 0.00 **Global Days XXX**
AMA: 2008, Apr, 3-4; 2008, Apr, 3-4; 2008, Apr, 3-4; 2006, Mar, 15; 2006, Mar, 15; 2006, Feb, 10-15; 2006, Feb, 10-15; 2006, Dec, 10-12; 2006, Dec, 10-12; 2006, Dec, 10-12; 2006, December, 10-12; 2006, December, 10-12; 2006, December, 10-12; 2006, March, 15; 2006, February, 10-15; 2006, Dec, 10-12; 2006, Dec, 10-12; 2006, Dec, 10-12; 2006, Dec, 10-12; 2004, Jan, 27; 2004, January, 27; 2004, Jan, 27

00172 repair of cleft palate N ▣
🔲 0.00 ⚕ 0.00 **Global Days XXX**
AMA: 2008, Apr, 3-4; 2008, Apr, 3-4; 2008, Apr, 3-4; 2006, Mar, 15; 2006, Mar, 15; 2006, Feb, 10-15; 2006, Feb, 10-15; 2006, Dec, 10-12; 2006, Dec, 10-12; 2006, Dec, 10-12; 2006, December, 10-12; 2006, December, 10-12; 2006, December, 10-12; 2006, March, 15; 2006, February, 10-15; 2006, Dec, 10-12; 2006, Dec, 10-12; 2006, Dec, 10-12; 2006, Dec, 10-12; 2004, Jan, 27; 2004, January, 27; 2004, Jan, 27

00174 excision of retropharyngeal tumor N ▣
🔲 0.00 ⚕ 0.00 **Global Days XXX**
AMA: 2008, Apr, 3-4; 2008, Apr, 3-4; 2008, Apr, 3-4; 2008, Apr, 3-4; 2006, Mar, 15; 2006, Mar, 15; 2006, Feb, 10-15; 2006, Feb, 10-15; 2006, Dec, 10-12; 2006, Dec, 10-12; 2006, Dec, 10-12; 2006, December, 10-12; 2006, December, 10-12; 2006, December, 10-12; 2006, December, 10-12; 2006, February, 10-15; 2006, March, 15; 2006, Dec, 10-12; 2006, Dec, 10-12; 2006, Dec, 10-12; 2006, Dec, 10-12; 2004, Jan, 27; 2004, January, 27; 2004, Jan, 27

00176 radical surgery C ▣
🔲 0.00 ⚕ 0.00 **Global Days XXX**
AMA: 2008, Apr, 3-4; 2008, Apr, 3-4; 2008, Apr, 3-4; 2006, Mar, 15; 2006, Mar, 15; 2006, Feb, 10-15; 2006, Feb, 10-15; 2006, Dec, 10-12; 2006, Dec, 10-12; 2006, Dec, 10-12; 2006, December, 10-12; 2006, December, 10-12; 2006, December, 10-12; 2006, March, 15; 2006, February, 10-15; 2006, Dec, 10-12; 2006, Dec, 10-12; 2006, Dec, 10-12; 2006, Dec, 10-12; 2004, Jan, 27; 2004, January, 27; 2004, Jan, 27

00190 Anesthesia for procedures on facial bones or skull; not otherwise specified N ▣
🔲 0.00 ⚕ 0.00 **Global Days XXX**
AMA: 2008, Apr, 3-4; 2008, Apr, 3-4; 2008, Apr, 3-4; 2006, Mar, 15; 2006, Mar, 15; 2006, Feb, 10-15; 2006, Feb, 10-15; 2006, Dec, 10-12; 2006, Dec, 10-12; 2006, Dec, 10-12; 2006, December, 10-12; 2006, December, 10-12; 2006, December, 10-12; 2006, March, 15; 2006, February, 10-15; 2006, Dec, 10-12; 2006, Dec, 10-12; 2006, Dec, 10-12; 2006, Dec, 10-12; 2004, Jan, 27; 2004, January, 27; 2004, Jan, 27

00192 radical surgery (including prognathism) C ▣
🔲 0.00 ⚕ 0.00 **Global Days XXX**
AMA: 2008, Apr, 3-4; 2008, Apr, 3-4; 2008, Apr, 3-4; 2006, Feb, 10-15; 2006, Feb, 10-15; 2006, Mar, 15; 2006, Mar, 15; 2006, Dec, 10-12; 2006, Dec, 10-12; 2006, Dec, 10-12; 2006, December, 10-12; 2006, December, 10-12; 2006, December, 10-12; 2006, March, 15; 2006, February, 10-15; 2006, Dec, 10-12; 2006, Dec, 10-12; 2006, Dec, 10-12; 2006, Dec, 10-12; 2004, Jan, 27; 2004, January, 27; 2004, Jan, 27

26/ TC Professional/Technical Component Only   80/ 80 Assist-at-Surgery Allowed/With Documentation   Unlisted   Not Covered
AMA: CPT Assistant References   A2- Z3 ASC Payment Indicator   ♂ Male Only   ♀ Female Only   ⊘ Modifier 51 Exempt   PQ PQRI

2   CPT only © 2008 American Medical Association. All Rights Reserved. (Black Ink)   Medicare (Red Ink)   © 2008 Ingenix *(Blue Ink)*

00210   **Anesthesia for intracranial procedures; not otherwise specified**   Ⓝ ▭
     🏥 0.00   ⚕ 0.00   Global Days XXX
     AMA: 2008, Apr, 3-4; 2008, Apr, 3-4; 2008, Apr, 3-4; 2006, Feb, 10-15; 2006, Feb, 10-15; 2006, Mar, 15; 2006, Mar, 15; 2006, Dec, 10-12; 2006, Dec, 10-12; 2006, Dec, 10-12; 2006, December, 10-12; 2006, December, 10-12; 2006, December, 10-12; 2006, December, 10-12; 2006, March, 15; 2006, February, 10-15; 2006, Dec, 10-12; 2006, Dec, 10-12; 2006, Dec, 10-12; 2006, Dec, 10-12; 2006, Dec, 10-12; 2004, Jan, 27; 2004, January, 27; 2004, Jan, 27

● 00211   **craniotomy or craniectomy for evacuation of hematoma**   Ⓒ
     🏥 0.00   ⚕ 0.00   Global Days XXX

00212   **subdural taps**   Ⓝ ▭
     🏥 0.00   ⚕ 0.00   Global Days XXX
     AMA: 2008, Apr, 3-4; 2008, Apr, 3-4; 2008, Apr, 3-4; 2006, Mar, 15; 2006, Mar, 15; 2006, Feb, 10-15; 2006, Feb, 10-15; 2006, Dec, 10-12; 2006, Dec, 10-12; 2006, Dec, 10-12; 2006, December, 10-12; 2006, December, 10-12; 2006, December, 10-12; 2006, December, 10-12; 2006, March, 15; 2006, February, 10-15; 2006, Dec, 10-12; 2006, Dec, 10-12; 2006, Dec, 10-12; 2006, Dec, 10-12; 2006, Dec, 10-12; 2004, Jan, 27; 2004, January, 27; 2004, Jan, 27

00214   **burr holes, including ventriculography**   Ⓒ ▭
     🏥 0.00   ⚕ 0.00   Global Days XXX
     AMA: 2008, Apr, 3-4; 2008, Apr, 3-4; 2008, Apr, 3-4; 2006, Mar, 15; 2006, Mar, 15; 2006, Feb, 10-15; 2006, Feb, 10-15; 2006, Dec, 10-12; 2006, Dec, 10-12; 2006, Dec, 10-12; 2006, December, 10-12; 2006, December, 10-12; 2006, December, 10-12; 2006, December, 10-12; 2006, March, 15; 2006, February, 10-15; 2006, Dec, 10-12; 2006, Dec, 10-12; 2006, Dec, 10-12; 2006, Dec, 10-12; 2006, Dec, 10-12; 2004, Jan, 27; 2004, January, 27; 2004, Jan, 27

00215   **cranioplasty or elevation of depressed skull fracture, extradural (simple or compound)**   Ⓒ ▭
     🏥 0.00   ⚕ 0.00   Global Days XXX
     AMA: 2008, Apr, 3-4; 2008, Apr, 3-4; 2008, Apr, 3-4; 2006, Mar, 15; 2006, Mar, 15; 2006, Feb, 10-15; 2006, Feb, 10-15; 2006, Dec, 10-12; 2006, Dec, 10-12; 2006, Dec, 10-12; 2006, December, 10-12; 2006, December, 10-12; 2006, December, 10-12; 2006, December, 10-12; 2006, March, 15; 2006, February, 10-15; 2006, Dec, 10-12; 2006, Dec, 10-12; 2006, Dec, 10-12; 2006, Dec, 10-12; 2006, Dec, 10-12; 2004, Jan, 27; 2004, January, 27; 2004, Jan, 27

00216   **vascular procedures**   Ⓝ ▭
     🏥 0.00   ⚕ 0.00   Global Days XXX
     AMA: 2008, Apr, 3-4; 2008, Apr, 3-4; 2008, Apr, 3-4; 2006, Feb, 10-15; 2006, Feb, 10-15; 2006, Mar, 15; 2006, Mar, 15; 2006, Dec, 10-12; 2006, Dec, 10-12; 2006, Dec, 10-12; 2006, December, 10-12; 2006, December, 10-12; 2006, December, 10-12; 2006, December, 10-12; 2006, March, 15; 2006, February, 10-15; 2006, Dec, 10-12; 2006, Dec, 10-12; 2006, Dec, 10-12; 2006, Dec, 10-12; 2006, Dec, 10-12; 2004, Jan, 27; 2004, January, 27; 2004, Jan, 27

00218   **procedures in sitting position**   Ⓝ ▭
     🏥 0.00   ⚕ 0.00   Global Days XXX
     AMA: 2008, Apr, 3-4; 2008, Apr, 3-4; 2008, Apr, 3-4; 2006, Feb, 10-15; 2006, Feb, 10-15; 2006, Mar, 15; 2006, Mar, 15; 2006, Dec, 10-12; 2006, Dec, 10-12; 2006, Dec, 10-12; 2006, December, 10-12; 2006, December, 10-12; 2006, December, 10-12; 2006, December, 10-12; 2006, March, 15; 2006, February, 10-15; 2006, Dec, 10-12; 2006, Dec, 10-12; 2006, Dec, 10-12; 2006, Dec, 10-12; 2006, Dec, 10-12; 2004, Jan, 27; 2004, January, 27; 2004, Jan, 27

00220   **cerebrospinal fluid shunting procedures**   Ⓝ ▭
     🏥 0.00   ⚕ 0.00   Global Days XXX
     AMA: 2008, Apr, 3-4; 2008, Apr, 3-4; 2008, Apr, 3-4; 2006, Mar, 15; 2006, Mar, 15; 2006, Feb, 10-15; 2006, Feb, 10-15; 2006, Dec, 10-12; 2006, Dec, 10-12; 2006, Dec, 10-12; 2006, December, 10-12; 2006, December, 10-12; 2006, December, 10-12; 2006, March, 15; 2006, February, 10-15; 2006, Dec, 10-12; 2006, Dec, 10-12; 2006, Dec, 10-12; 2006, Dec, 10-12; 2004, Jan, 27; 2004, January, 27; 2004, Jan, 27

00222   **electrocoagulation of intracranial nerve**   Ⓝ ▭
     🏥 0.00   ⚕ 0.00   Global Days XXX
     AMA: 2008, Apr, 3-4; 2008, Apr, 3-4; 2008, Apr, 3-4; 2006, Mar, 15; 2006, Mar, 15; 2006, Feb, 10-15; 2006, Feb, 10-15; 2006, Dec, 10-12; 2006, Dec, 10-12; 2006, Dec, 10-12; 2006, December, 10-12; 2006, December, 10-12; 2006, December, 10-12; 2006, March, 15; 2006, February, 10-15; 2006, Dec, 10-12; 2006, Dec, 10-12; 2006, Dec, 10-12; 2006, Dec, 10-12; 2006, Dec, 10-12; 2004, Jan, 27; 2004, January, 27; 2004, Jan, 27

00300   **Anesthesia for all procedures on the integumentary system, muscles and nerves of head, neck, and posterior trunk, not otherwise specified**   Ⓝ ▭
     🏥 0.00   ⚕ 0.00   Global Days XXX
     AMA: 2008, Apr, 3-4; 2008, Apr, 3-4; 2008, Apr, 3-4; 2006, Mar, 15; 2006, Mar, 15; 2006, Feb, 10-15; 2006, Feb, 10-15; 2006, Dec, 10-12; 2006, Dec, 10-12; 2006, Dec, 10-12; 2006, December, 10-12; 2006, December, 10-12; 2006, December, 10-12; 2006, December, 10-12; 2006, March, 15; 2006, February, 10-15; 2006, Dec, 10-12; 2006, Dec, 10-12; 2006, Dec, 10-12; 2006, Dec, 10-12; 2006, Dec, 10-12; 2004, Jan, 27; 2004, January, 27; 2004, Jan, 27

00320   **Anesthesia for all procedures on esophagus, thyroid, larynx, trachea and lymphatic system of neck; not otherwise specified, age 1 year or older**   Ⓝ ▭
     🏥 0.00   ⚕ 0.00   Global Days XXX
     AMA: 2008, Apr, 3-4; 2008, Apr, 3-4; 2008, Apr, 3-4; 2006, Mar, 15; 2006, Mar, 15; 2006, Feb, 10-15; 2006, Feb, 10-15; 2006, Dec, 10-12; 2006, Dec, 10-12; 2006, Dec, 10-12; 2006, December, 10-12; 2006, December, 10-12; 2006, December, 10-12; 2006, December, 10-12; 2006, March, 15; 2006, February, 10-15; 2006, Dec, 10-12; 2006, Dec, 10-12; 2006, Dec, 10-12; 2006, Dec, 10-12; 2006, Dec, 10-12; 2004, Jan, 27; 2004, January, 27; 2004, Jan, 27

00322   **needle biopsy of thyroid**   Ⓝ ▭
     EXCLUDES   *cervical spine and spinal cord procedures (00600, 00604, 00670)*
     🏥 0.00   ⚕ 0.00   Global Days XXX
     AMA: 2008, Apr, 3-4; 2008, Apr, 3-4; 2008, Apr, 3-4; 2006, Feb, 10-15; 2006, Feb, 10-15; 2006, Mar, 15; 2006, Mar, 15; 2006, Dec, 10-12; 2006, Dec, 10-12; 2006, Dec, 10-12; 2006, December, 10-12; 2006, December, 10-12; 2006, December, 10-12; 2006, February, 10-15; 2006, March, 15; 2006, Dec, 10-12; 2006, Dec, 10-12; 2006, Dec, 10-12; 2006, Dec, 10-12; 2004, Jan, 27; 2004, January, 27; 2004, Jan, 27

Anesthesia

00326 — 00452

00326 Anesthesia for all procedures on the larynx and trachea in children younger than 1 year of age [A] [N] [▢]

Do not report with (99100)

[▤] 0.00 [✂] 0.00 Global Days XXX

AMA: 2008, Apr, 3-4; 2008, Apr, 3-4; 2008, Apr, 3-4; 2006, Mar, 15; 2006, Mar, 15; 2006, Feb, 10-15; 2006, Feb, 10-15; 2006, Dec, 10-12; 2006, Dec, 10-12; 2006, Dec, 10-12; 2006, December, 10-12; 2006, December, 10-12; 2006, December, 10-12; 2006, February, 10-15; 2006, March, 15; 2006, Dec, 10-12; 2006, Dec, 10-12; 2006, Dec, 10-12; 2006, Dec, 10-12; 2006, Dec, 10-12; 2004, Jan, 27; 2004, January, 27; 2004, Jan, 27

00350-00352 Anesthesia for Neck Vessel Procedures

CMS *100-4,12,140.3.2 Calculation of Anesthesia Time*
CMS *100-4,12,140.2 Payment for CRNA Services*
CMS *100-4,12,140 Certified Registered Nurse Anesthetist Services*
CMS *100-4,4,20.6.4 Modifiers for Discontinued Services*
CMS *100-4,4,20.6 Modifier Use Under OPPS*
CMS *100-4,4,10.4 Packaging Rules Under OPPS*
CMS *100-4,12,50 Anesthesia Services*
EXCLUDES *arteriography (01916)*

00350 Anesthesia for procedures on major vessels of neck; not otherwise specified [N] [▢]

[▤] 0.00 [✂] 0.00 Global Days XXX

AMA: 2008, Apr, 3-4; 2008, Apr, 3-4; 2008, Apr, 3-4; 2006, Mar, 15; 2006, Mar, 15; 2006, Feb, 10-15; 2006, Feb, 10-15; 2006, Dec, 10-12; 2006, Dec, 10-12; 2006, Dec, 10-12; 2006, December, 10-12; 2006, December, 10-12; 2006, December, 10-12; 2006, February, 10-15; 2006, March, 15; 2006, Dec, 10-12; 2006, Dec, 10-12; 2006, Dec, 10-12; 2006, Dec, 10-12; 2006, Dec, 10-12; 2004, Jan, 27; 2004, January, 27; 2004, Jan, 27

00352 simple ligation [N] [▢]

[▤] 0.00 [✂] 0.00 Global Days XXX

AMA: 2008, Apr, 3-4; 2008, Apr, 3-4; 2008, Apr, 3-4; 2006, Feb, 10-15; 2006, Feb, 10-15; 2006, Mar, 15; 2006, Mar, 15; 2006, Dec, 10-12; 2006, Dec, 10-12; 2006, Dec, 10-12; 2006, December, 10-12; 2006, December, 10-12; 2006, December, 10-12; 2006, February, 10-15; 2006, March, 15; 2006, Dec, 10-12; 2006, Dec, 10-12; 2006, Dec, 10-12; 2006, Dec, 10-12; 2006, Dec, 10-12; 2004, Jan, 27; 2004, January, 27; 2004, Jan, 27

00400-00529 Anesthesia for Chest Procedures

CMS *100-4,12,140.3.2 Calculation of Anesthesia Time*
CMS *100-4,12,140.2 Payment for CRNA Services*
CMS *100-4,12,140 Certified Registered Nurse Anesthetist Services*
CMS *100-4,4,20.6.4 Modifiers for Discontinued Services*
CMS *100-4,4,20.6 Modifier Use Under OPPS*
CMS *100-4,4,10.4 Packaging Rules Under OPPS*
CMS *100-4,12,50 Anesthesia Services*

00400 Anesthesia for procedures on the integumentary system on the extremities, anterior trunk and perineum; not otherwise specified [N] [▢]

[▤] 0.00 [✂] 0.00 Global Days XXX

AMA: 2008, Apr, 3-4; 2008, Apr, 3-4; 2008, Apr, 3-4; 2006, Mar, 15; 2006, Mar, 15; 2006, Feb, 10-15; 2006, Feb, 10-15; 2006, Dec, 10-12; 2006, Dec, 10-12; 2006, Dec, 10-12; 2006, December, 10-12; 2006, December, 10-12; 2006, December, 10-12; 2006, February, 10-15; 2006, March, 15; 2006, Dec, 10-12; 2006, Dec, 10-12; 2006, Dec, 10-12; 2006, Dec, 10-12; 2006, Dec, 10-12; 2004, Jan, 27; 2004, January, 27; 2004, Jan, 27

00402 reconstructive procedures on breast (eg, reduction or augmentation mammoplasty, muscle flaps) [N] [▢]

[▤] 0.00 [✂] 0.00 Global Days XXX

AMA: 2008, Apr, 3-4; 2008, Apr, 3-4; 2008, Apr, 3-4; 2006, Feb, 10-15; 2006, Feb, 10-15; 2006, Mar, 15; 2006, Mar, 15; 2006, Dec, 10-12; 2006, Dec, 10-12; 2006, Dec, 10-12; 2006, December, 10-12; 2006, December, 10-12; 2006, December, 10-12; 2006, February, 10-15; 2006, March, 15; 2006, Dec, 10-12; 2006, Dec, 10-12; 2006, Dec, 10-12; 2006, Dec, 10-12; 2006, Dec, 10-12; 2004, Jan, 27; 2004, January, 27; 2004, Jan, 27

00404 radical or modified radical procedures on breast [N] [▢]

[▤] 0.00 [✂] 0.00 Global Days XXX

AMA: 2008, Apr, 3-4; 2008, Apr, 3-4; 2008, Apr, 3-4; 2006, Mar, 15; 2006, Mar, 15; 2006, Feb, 10-15; 2006, Feb, 10-15; 2006, Dec, 10-12; 2006, Dec, 10-12; 2006, Dec, 10-12; 2006, December, 10-12; 2006, December, 10-12; 2006, December, 10-12; 2006, February, 10-15; 2006, March, 15; 2006, Dec, 10-12; 2006, Dec, 10-12; 2006, Dec, 10-12; 2006, Dec, 10-12; 2006, Dec, 10-12; 2004, Jan, 27; 2004, January, 27; 2004, Jan, 27

00406 radical or modified radical procedures on breast with internal mammary node dissection [N] [▢]

[▤] 0.00 [✂] 0.00 Global Days XXX

AMA: 2008, Apr, 3-4; 2008, Apr, 3-4; 2008, Apr, 3-4; 2006, Mar, 15; 2006, Mar, 15; 2006, Feb, 10-15; 2006, Feb, 10-15; 2006, Dec, 10-12; 2006, Dec, 10-12; 2006, Dec, 10-12; 2006, December, 10-12; 2006, December, 10-12; 2006, December, 10-12; 2006, February, 10-15; 2006, March, 15; 2006, Dec, 10-12; 2006, Dec, 10-12; 2006, Dec, 10-12; 2006, Dec, 10-12; 2006, Dec, 10-12; 2004, Jan, 27; 2004, January, 27; 2004, Jan, 27

00410 electrical conversion of arrhythmias [N] [▢]

[▤] 0.00 [✂] 0.00 Global Days XXX

AMA: 2008, Apr, 3-4; 2008, Apr, 3-4; 2008, Apr, 3-4; 2006, Mar, 15; 2006, Mar, 15; 2006, Feb, 10-15; 2006, Feb, 10-15; 2006, Dec, 10-12; 2006, Dec, 10-12; 2006, Dec, 10-12; 2006, December, 10-12; 2006, December, 10-12; 2006, December, 10-12; 2006, February, 10-15; 2006, March, 15; 2006, Dec, 10-12; 2006, Dec, 10-12; 2006, Dec, 10-12; 2006, Dec, 10-12; 2006, Dec, 10-12; 2004, Jan, 27; 2004, January, 27; 2004, Jan, 27

00450 Anesthesia for procedures on clavicle and scapula; not otherwise specified [N] [▢]

[▤] 0.00 [✂] 0.00 Global Days XXX

AMA: 2008, Apr, 3-4; 2008, Apr, 3-4; 2008, Apr, 3-4; 2006, Mar, 15; 2006, Mar, 15; 2006, Feb, 10-15; 2006, Feb, 10-15; 2006, Dec, 10-12; 2006, Dec, 10-12; 2006, Dec, 10-12; 2006, December, 10-12; 2006, December, 10-12; 2006, December, 10-12; 2006, February, 10-15; 2006, March, 15; 2006, Dec, 10-12; 2006, Dec, 10-12; 2006, Dec, 10-12; 2006, Dec, 10-12; 2006, Dec, 10-12; 2004, Jan, 27; 2004, January, 27; 2004, Jan, 27

00452 radical surgery [C] [▢]

[▤] 0.00 [✂] 0.00 Global Days XXX

AMA: 2008, Apr, 3-4; 2008, Apr, 3-4; 2008, Apr, 3-4; 2006, Feb, 10-15; 2006, Feb, 10-15; 2006, Mar, 15; 2006, Mar, 15; 2006, Dec, 10-12; 2006, Dec, 10-12; 2006, Dec, 10-12; 2006, December, 10-12; 2006, December, 10-12; 2006, December, 10-12; 2006, February, 10-15; 2006, March, 15; 2006, Dec, 10-12; 2006, Dec, 10-12; 2006, Dec, 10-12; 2006, Dec, 10-12; 2006, Dec, 10-12; 2004, Jan, 27; 2004, January, 27; 2004, Jan, 27

[26]/[TC] Professional/Technical Component Only   [80]/[80] Assist-at-Surgery Allowed/With Documentation   Unlisted   Not Covered

AMA: CPT Assistant References   [A2]-[Z3] ASC Payment Indicator   ♂ Male Only   ♀ Female Only   ⊘ Modifier 51 Exempt   [PQ] PQRI

4   CPT only © 2008 American Medical Association. All Rights Reserved. (Black Ink)   Medicare (Red Ink)   © 2008 Ingenix (Blue Ink)

00454 biopsy of clavicle ▫ ▫
▫ 0.00 ▫ 0.00 **Global Days XXX**
AMA: 2008, Apr, 3-4; 2008, Apr, 3-4; 2008, Apr, 3-4; 2006, Mar, 15; 2006, Mar, 15; 2006, Feb, 10-15; 2006, Feb, 10-15; 2006, Dec, 10-12; 2006, Dec, 10-12; 2006, Dec, 10-12; 2006, December, 10-12; 2006, December, 10-12; 2006, December, 10-12; 2006, February, 10-15; 2006, March, 15; 2006, Dec, 10-12; 2006, Dec, 10-12; 2006, Dec, 10-12; 2006, Dec, 10-12; 2006, Dec, 10-12; 2004, Jan, 27; 2004, January, 27; 2004, Jan, 27

00470 Anesthesia for partial rib resection; not otherwise specified ▫ ▫
▫ 0.00 ▫ 0.00 **Global Days XXX**
AMA: 2008, Apr, 3-4; 2008, Apr, 3-4; 2008, Apr, 3-4; 2006, Mar, 15; 2006, Mar, 15; 2006, Feb, 10-15; 2006, Feb, 10-15; 2006, Dec, 10-12; 2006, Dec, 10-12; 2006, Dec, 10-12; 2006, December, 10-12; 2006, December, 10-12; 2006, December, 10-12; 2006, February, 10-15; 2006, March, 15; 2006, Dec, 10-12; 2006, Dec, 10-12; 2006, Dec, 10-12; 2006, Dec, 10-12; 2006, Dec, 10-12; 2004, Jan, 27; 2004, January, 27; 2004, Jan, 27

00472 thoracoplasty (any type) ▫ ▫
▫ 0.00 ▫ 0.00 **Global Days XXX**
AMA: 2008, Apr, 3-4; 2008, Apr, 3-4; 2008, Apr, 3-4; 2006, Feb, 10-15; 2006, Feb, 10-15; 2006, Mar, 15; 2006, Mar, 15; 2006, Dec, 10-12; 2006, Dec, 10-12; 2006, Dec, 10-12; 2006, December, 10-12; 2006, December, 10-12; 2006, December, 10-12; 2006, March, 15; 2006, February, 10-15; 2006, Dec, 10-12; 2006, Dec, 10-12; 2006, Dec, 10-12; 2006, Dec, 10-12; 2006, Dec, 10-12; 2004, Jan, 27; 2004, January, 27; 2004, Jan, 27

00474 radical procedures (eg, pectus excavatum) ▫ ▫
▫ 0.00 ▫ 0.00 **Global Days XXX**
AMA: 2008, Apr, 3-4; 2008, Apr, 3-4; 2008, Apr, 3-4; 2006, Mar, 15; 2006, Mar, 15; 2006, Feb, 10-15; 2006, Feb, 10-15; 2006, Dec, 10-12; 2006, Dec, 10-12; 2006, Dec, 10-12; 2006, December, 10-12; 2006, December, 10-12; 2006, December, 10-12; 2006, February, 10-15; 2006, March, 15; 2006, Dec, 10-12; 2006, Dec, 10-12; 2006, Dec, 10-12; 2006, Dec, 10-12; 2006, Dec, 10-12; 2004, Jan, 27; 2004, January, 27; 2004, Jan, 27

00500 Anesthesia for all procedures on esophagus ▫ ▫
▫ 0.00 ▫ 0.00 **Global Days XXX**
AMA: 2008, Apr, 3-4; 2008, Apr, 3-4; 2008, Apr, 3-4; 2006, Mar, 15; 2006, Mar, 15; 2006, Feb, 10-15; 2006, Feb, 10-15; 2006, Dec, 10-12; 2006, Dec, 10-12; 2006, Dec, 10-12; 2006, December, 10-12; 2006, December, 10-12; 2006, December, 10-12; 2006, February, 10-15; 2006, March, 15; 2006, Dec, 10-12; 2006, Dec, 10-12; 2006, Dec, 10-12; 2006, Dec, 10-12; 2006, Dec, 10-12; 2004, Jan, 27; 2004, January, 27; 2004, Jan, 27

00520 Anesthesia for closed chest procedures; (including bronchoscopy) not otherwise specified ▫ ▫
▫ 0.00 ▫ 0.00 **Global Days XXX**
AMA: 2008, Apr, 3-4; 2008, Apr, 3-4; 2008, Apr, 3-4; 2006, Mar, 15; 2006, Mar, 15; 2006, Feb, 10-15; 2006, Feb, 10-15; 2006, Dec, 10-12; 2006, Dec, 10-12; 2006, Dec, 10-12; 2006, December, 10-12; 2006, December, 10-12; 2006, December, 10-12; 2006, February, 10-15; 2006, March, 15; 2006, Dec, 10-12; 2006, Dec, 10-12; 2006, Dec, 10-12; 2006, Dec, 10-12; 2006, Dec, 10-12; 2004, Jan, 27; 2004, January, 27; 2004, Jan, 27

00522 needle biopsy of pleura ▫ ▫
▫ 0.00 ▫ 0.00 **Global Days XXX**
AMA: 2008, Apr, 3-4; 2008, Apr, 3-4; 2008, Apr, 3-4; 2006, Mar, 15; 2006, Mar, 15; 2006, Feb, 10-15; 2006, Feb, 10-15; 2006, Dec, 10-12; 2006, Dec, 10-12; 2006, Dec, 10-12; 2006, December, 10-12; 2006, December, 10-12; 2006, December, 10-12; 2006, February, 10-15; 2006, March, 15; 2006, Dec, 10-12; 2006, Dec, 10-12; 2006, Dec, 10-12; 2006, Dec, 10-12; 2006, Dec, 10-12; 2004, Jan, 27; 2004, January, 27; 2004, Jan, 27

00524 pneumocentesis ▫ ▫
▫ 0.00 ▫ 0.00 **Global Days XXX**
AMA: 2008, Apr, 3-4; 2008, Apr, 3-4; 2008, Apr, 3-4; 2006, Feb, 10-15; 2006, Feb, 10-15; 2006, Mar, 15; 2006, Mar, 15; 2006, Dec, 10-12; 2006, Dec, 10-12; 2006, Dec, 10-12; 2006, December, 10-12; 2006, December, 10-12; 2006, December, 10-12; 2006, February, 10-15; 2006, March, 15; 2006, Dec, 10-12; 2006, Dec, 10-12; 2006, Dec, 10-12; 2006, Dec, 10-12; 2006, Dec, 10-12; 2004, Jan, 27; 2004, January, 27; 2004, Jan, 27

00528 mediastinoscopy and diagnostic thoracoscopy not utilizing one lung ventilation ▫ ▫
EXCLUDES   *transbronchial reconstruction (00539)*

▫ 0.00 ▫ 0.00 **Global Days XXX**
AMA: 2008, Apr, 3-4; 2008, Apr, 3-4; 2008, Apr, 3-4; 2006, Feb, 10-15; 2006, Feb, 10-15; 2006, Mar, 15; 2006, Mar, 15; 2006, Dec, 10-12; 2006, Dec, 10-12; 2006, Dec, 10-12; 2006, December, 10-12; 2006, December, 10-12; 2006, December, 10-12; 2006, February, 10-15; 2006, March, 15; 2006, Dec, 10-12; 2006, Dec, 10-12; 2006, Dec, 10-12; 2006, Dec, 10-12; 2006, Dec, 10-12; 2004, Jan, 27; 2004, January, 27; 2004, Jan, 27

00529 mediastinoscopy and diagnostic thoracoscopy utilizing one lung ventilation ▫ ▫
▫ 0.00 ▫ 0.00 **Global Days XXX**
AMA: 2008, Apr, 3-4; 2008, Apr, 3-4; 2008, Apr, 3-4; 2006, Feb, 10-15; 2006, Feb, 10-15; 2006, Mar, 15; 2006, Dec, 10-12; 2006, Mar, 15; 2006, Dec, 10-12; 2006, Dec, 10-12; 2006, Dec, 10-12; 2006, Dec, 10-12; 2006, December, 10-12; 2006, December, 10-12; 2006, December, 10-12; 2006, February, 10-15; 2006, March, 15; 2006, Dec, 10-12; 2006, Dec, 10-12; 2006, Dec, 10-12; 2004, Jan, 27; 2004, June, 1; 2004, January, 27; 2004, Jan, 27; 2004, Jun, 1; 2004, Jun, 1

00530 Anesthesia for Cardiac Pacemaker Procedure

CMS *100-4,12,140.3.2* Calculation of Anesthesia Time
CMS *100-4,12,140.2* Payment for CRNA Services
CMS *100-4,12,140* Certified Registered Nurse Anesthetist Services
CMS *100-4,4,20.6.4* Modifiers for Discontinued Services
CMS *100-4,4,20.6* Modifier Use Under OPPS
CMS *100-4,4,10.4* Packaging Rules Under OPPS
CMS *100-4,12,50* Anesthesia Services

00530 Anesthesia for permanent transvenous pacemaker insertion ▫ ▫
▫ 0.00 ▫ 0.00 **Global Days XXX**
AMA: 2008, Apr, 3-4; 2008, Apr, 3-4; 2008, Apr, 3-4; 2006, Mar, 15; 2006, Mar, 15; 2006, Feb, 10-15; 2006, Feb, 10-15; 2006, Dec, 10-12; 2006, Dec, 10-12; 2006, Dec, 10-12; 2006, December, 10-12; 2006, December, 10-12; 2006, December, 10-12; 2006, February, 10-15; 2006, March, 15; 2006, Dec, 10-12; 2006, Dec, 10-12; 2006, Dec, 10-12; 2006, Dec, 10-12; 2006, Dec, 10-12; 2004, Jan, 27; 2004, January, 27; 2004, Jan, 27

● New Code   ▲ Revised Code   ▫ Maternity Edit   ▫ Age Edit   ▫-▫ OPPS Status Indicator   ▫ Facility RVU   ▫ Non-Facility RVU
▫ CCI Comprehensive Code   ▫ Bilateral Procedure   + Add-on Indicator   ▫ Laboratory crosswalk   ▫ Radiology crosswalk

Anesthesia

00532 — 00548

00532-00550 Anesthesia for Heart and Lung Procedures

CMS *100-4,12,140.3.2 Calculation of Anesthesia Time*
CMS *100-4,12,140.2 Payment for CRNA Services*
CMS *100-4,12,140 Certified Registered Nurse Anesthetist Services*
CMS *100-4,4,20.6 Modifier Use Under OPPS*
CMS *100-4,4,10.4 Packaging Rules Under OPPS*
CMS *100-4,12,50 Anesthesia Services*

00532   **Anesthesia for access to central venous circulation**   🅽 ▢
    📢 0.00   ⚖ 0.00   **Global Days XXX**
AMA: 2008, Apr, 3-4; 2008, Apr, 3-4; 2008, Apr, 3-4; 2006, Mar, 15; 2006, Mar, 15; 2006, Feb, 10-15; 2006, Feb, 10-15; 2006, Dec, 10-12; 2006, Dec, 10-12; 2006, Dec, 10-12; 2006, December, 10-12; 2006, December, 10-12; 2006, December, 10-12; 2006, December, 10-12; 2006, February, 10-15; 2006, March, 15; 2006, Dec, 10-12; 2006, Dec, 10-12; 2006, Dec, 10-12; 2006, Dec, 10-12; 2006, Dec, 10-12; 2004, Jan, 27; 2004, January, 27; 2004, Jan, 27

00534   **Anesthesia for transvenous insertion or replacement of pacing cardioverter-defibrillator**   🅽 ▢
    EXCLUDES   *transthoracic approach (00560)*
    📢 0.00   ⚖ 0.00   **Global Days XXX**
AMA: 2008, Apr, 3-4; 2008, Apr, 3-4; 2008, Apr, 3-4; 2006, Mar, 15; 2006, Mar, 15; 2006, Feb, 10-15; 2006, Feb, 10-15; 2006, Dec, 10-12; 2006, Dec, 10-12; 2006, Dec, 10-12; 2006, December, 10-12; 2006, December, 10-12; 2006, December, 10-12; 2006, December, 10-12; 2006, February, 10-15; 2006, March, 15; 2006, Dec, 10-12; 2006, Dec, 10-12; 2006, Dec, 10-12; 2006, Dec, 10-12; 2006, Dec, 10-12; 2004, Jan, 27; 2004, January, 27; 2004, Jan, 27

00537   **Anesthesia for cardiac electrophysiologic procedures including radiofrequency ablation**   🅽 ▢
    📢 0.00   ⚖ 0.00   **Global Days XXX**
AMA: 2008, Apr, 3-4; 2008, Apr, 3-4; 2008, Apr, 3-4; 2006, Feb, 10-15; 2006, Feb, 10-15; 2006, Mar, 15; 2006, Mar, 15; 2006, Dec, 10-12; 2006, Dec, 10-12; 2006, Dec, 10-12; 2006, December, 10-12; 2006, December, 10-12; 2006, December, 10-12; 2006, December, 10-12; 2006, February, 10-15; 2006, March, 15; 2006, Dec, 10-12; 2006, Dec, 10-12; 2006, Dec, 10-12; 2006, Dec, 10-12; 2004, Jan, 27; 2004, January, 27; 2004, Jan, 27

00539   **Anesthesia for tracheobronchial reconstruction**   🅽 ▢
    📢 0.00   ⚖ 0.00   **Global Days XXX**
AMA: 2008, Apr, 3-4; 2008, Apr, 3-4; 2008, Apr, 3-4; 2006, Feb, 10-15; 2006, Feb, 10-15; 2006, Mar, 15; 2006, Mar, 15; 2006, Dec, 10-12; 2006, Dec, 10-12; 2006, Dec, 10-12; 2006, December, 10-12; 2006, December, 10-12; 2006, December, 10-12; 2006, March, 15; 2006, February, 10-15; 2006, Dec, 10-12; 2006, Dec, 10-12; 2006, Dec, 10-12; 2006, Dec, 10-12; 2006, Dec, 10-12; 2004, Jan, 27; 2004, January, 27; 2004, Jan, 27

00540   **Anesthesia for thoracotomy procedures involving lungs, pleura, diaphragm, and mediastinum (including surgical thoracoscopy); not otherwise specified**   🅒 ▢
    EXCLUDES   *thoracic spine and spinal cord procedures via anterior transthoracic approach (00625-00626)*
    📢 0.00   ⚖ 0.00   **Global Days XXX**
AMA: 2008, Apr, 3-4; 2008, Apr, 3-4; 2008, Apr, 3-4; 2006, Mar, 15; 2006, Mar, 15; 2006, Feb, 10-15; 2006, Feb, 10-15; 2006, Dec, 10-12; 2006, Dec, 10-12; 2006, Dec, 10-12; 2006, December, 10-12; 2006, December, 10-12; 2006, December, 10-12; 2006, February, 10-15; 2006, March, 15; 2006, Dec, 10-12; 2006, Dec, 10-12; 2006, Dec, 10-12; 2006, Dec, 10-12; 2004, Jan, 27; 2004, January, 27; 2004, Jan, 27

00541   **utilizing one lung ventilation**   🅽 ▢
    EXCLUDES   *thoracic spine and spinal cord procedures via anterior transthoracic approach (00625-00626)*
    📢 0.00   ⚖ 0.00   **Global Days XXX**
AMA: 2008, Apr, 3-4; 2008, Apr, 3-4; 2008, Apr, 3-4; 2006, Mar, 15; 2006, Mar, 15; 2006, Feb, 10-15; 2006, Dec, 10-12; 2006, Feb, 10-15; 2006, Dec, 10-12; 2006, Dec, 10-12; 2006, Dec, 10-12; 2006, Dec, 10-12; 2006, December, 10-12; 2006, December, 10-12; 2006, December, 10-12; 2006, February, 10-15; 2006, March, 15; 2006, Dec, 10-12; 2006, Dec, 10-12; 2004, Jan, 27; 2004, June, 1; 2004, January, 27; 2004, Jan, 27; 2004, Jun, 1; 2004, Jun, 1

00542   **decortication**   🅒 ▢
    📢 0.00   ⚖ 0.00   **Global Days XXX**
AMA: 2008, Apr, 3-4; 2008, Apr, 3-4; 2008, Apr, 3-4; 2006, Feb, 10-15; 2006, Feb, 10-15; 2006, Mar, 15; 2006, Mar, 15; 2006, Dec, 10-12; 2006, Dec, 10-12; 2006, Dec, 10-12; 2006, December, 10-12; 2006, December, 10-12; 2006, December, 10-12; 2006, December, 10-12; 2006, February, 10-15; 2006, March, 15; 2006, Dec, 10-12; 2006, Dec, 10-12; 2006, Dec, 10-12; 2006, Dec, 10-12; 2006, Dec, 10-12; 2004, Jan, 27; 2004, January, 27; 2004, Jan, 27

00546   **pulmonary resection with thoracoplasty**   🅒 ▢
    📢 0.00   ⚖ 0.00   **Global Days XXX**
AMA: 2008, Apr, 3-4; 2008, Apr, 3-4; 2008, Apr, 3-4; 2006, Feb, 10-15; 2006, Feb, 10-15; 2006, Mar, 15; 2006, Mar, 15; 2006, Dec, 10-12; 2006, Dec, 10-12; 2006, Dec, 10-12; 2006, December, 10-12; 2006, December, 10-12; 2006, December, 10-12; 2006, February, 10-15; 2006, March, 15; 2006, Dec, 10-12; 2006, Dec, 10-12; 2006, Dec, 10-12; 2006, Dec, 10-12; 2004, Jan, 27; 2004, January, 27; 2004, Jan, 27

00548   **intrathoracic procedures on the trachea and bronchi**   🅽 ▢
    📢 0.00   ⚖ 0.00   **Global Days XXX**
AMA: 2008, Apr, 3-4; 2008, Apr, 3-4; 2008, Apr, 3-4; 2006, Mar, 15; 2006, Mar, 15; 2006, Feb, 10-15; 2006, Feb, 10-15; 2006, Dec, 10-12; 2006, Dec, 10-12; 2006, Dec, 10-12; 2006, December, 10-12; 2006, December, 10-12; 2006, December, 10-12; 2006, February, 10-15; 2006, March, 15; 2006, Dec, 10-12; 2006, Dec, 10-12; 2006, Dec, 10-12; 2006, Dec, 10-12; 2004, Jan, 27; 2004, January, 27; 2004, Jan, 27

26/ℿ Professional/Technical Component Only   80/ℝ Assist-at-Surgery Allowed/With Documentation   Unlisted   Not Covered
AMA: CPT Assistant References   A2-Z3 ASC Payment Indicator   ♂ Male Only   ♀ Female Only   ⊘ Modifier 51 Exempt   PQ PQRI

6   CPT only © 2008 American Medical Association. All Rights Reserved. (Black Ink)   Medicare (Red Ink)   © 2008 Ingenix (Blue Ink)

00550 Anesthesia for sternal debridement Ⓝ🖥
⚐ 0.00 ⚕ 0.00 **Global Days XXX**
AMA: 2008, Apr, 3-4; 2008, Apr, 3-4; 2008, Apr, 3-4; 2006, Mar, 15; 2006, Mar, 15; 2006, Feb, 10-15; 2006, Feb, 10-15; 2006, Dec, 10-12; 2006, Dec, 10-12; 2006, Dec, 10-12; 2006, December, 10-12; 2006, December, 10-12; 2006, December, 10-12; 2006, February, 10-15; 2006, March, 15; 2006, Dec, 10-12; 2006, Dec, 10-12; 2006, Dec, 10-12; 2006, Dec, 10-12; 2006, Dec, 10-12; 2004, Jan, 27; 2004, January, 27; 2004, Jan, 27

00560-00580 Anesthesia for Open Heart Procedures

CMS *100-3,160.9* *Electroencephalographic (EEG) Monitoring During Open-Heart Surgery*
CMS *100-4,12,140.3.2* *Calculation of Anesthesia Time*
CMS *100-4,12,140.2* *Payment for CRNA Services*
CMS *100-4,12,140* *Certified Registered Nurse Anesthetist Services*
CMS *100-4,12,50* *Anesthesia Services*

00560 Anesthesia for procedures on heart, pericardial sac, and great vessels of chest; without pump oxygenator Ⓒ🖥
⚐ 0.00 ⚕ 0.00 **Global Days XXX**
AMA: 2008, Apr, 3-4; 2008, Apr, 3-4; 2008, Apr, 3-4; 2006, Mar, 15; 2006, Mar, 15; 2006, Feb, 10-15; 2006, Feb, 10-15; 2006, Dec, 10-12; 2006, Dec, 10-12; 2006, Dec, 10-12; 2006, December, 10-12; 2006, December, 10-12; 2006, December, 10-12; 2006, February, 10-15; 2006, March, 15; 2006, Dec, 10-12; 2006, Dec, 10-12; 2006, Dec, 10-12; 2006, Dec, 10-12; 2006, Dec, 10-12; 2004, Jan, 27; 2004, January, 27; 2004, Jan, 27

00561 with pump oxygenator, younger than 1 year of age Ⓐ Ⓒ🖥
Do not report with (99100, 99116, 99135)
⚐ 0.00 ⚕ 0.00 **Global Days XXX**
AMA: 2008, Apr, 3-4; 2008, Apr, 3-4; 2008, Apr, 3-4; 2006, Mar, 15; 2006, Mar, 15; 2006, Feb, 10-15; 2006, Feb, 10-15; 2006, Dec, 10-12; 2006, Dec, 10-12; 2006, Dec, 10-12; 2006, December, 10-12; 2006, December, 10-12; 2006, December, 10-12; 2006, February, 10-15; 2006, March, 15; 2006, Dec, 10-12; 2006, Dec, 10-12; 2006, Dec, 10-12; 2006, Dec, 10-12; 2006, Dec, 10-12; 2004, Jan, 27; 2004, January, 27; 2004, Jan, 27

▲ **00562** with pump oxygenator, age 1 year or older, for all non-coronary bypass procedures (eg, valve procedures) or for re-operation for coronary bypass more than 1 month after original operation Ⓐ Ⓒ🖥
⚐ 0.00 ⚕ 0.00 **Global Days XXX**
AMA: 2008, Apr, 3-4; 2008, Apr, 3-4; 2008, Apr, 3-4; 2006, Mar, 15; 2006, Mar, 15; 2006, Feb, 10-15; 2006, Feb, 10-15; 2006, Dec, 10-12; 2006, Dec, 10-12; 2006, Dec, 10-12; 2006, December, 10-12; 2006, December, 10-12; 2006, December, 10-12; 2006, February, 10-15; 2006, March, 15; 2006, Dec, 10-12; 2006, Dec, 10-12; 2006, Dec, 10-12; 2006, Dec, 10-12; 2006, Dec, 10-12; 2004, Jan, 27; 2004, January, 27; 2004, Jan, 27

00563 with pump oxygenator with hypothermic circulatory arrest Ⓝ🖥
⚐ 0.00 ⚕ 0.00 **Global Days XXX**
AMA: 2008, Apr, 3-4; 2008, Apr, 3-4; 2008, Apr, 3-4; 2006, Feb, 10-15; 2006, Feb, 10-15; 2006, Mar, 15; 2006, Mar, 15; 2006, Dec, 10-12; 2006, Dec, 10-12; 2006, Dec, 10-12; 2006, December, 10-12; 2006, December, 10-12; 2006, December, 10-12; 2006, February, 10-15; 2006, March, 15; 2006, Dec, 10-12; 2006, Dec, 10-12; 2006, Dec, 10-12; 2006, Dec, 10-12; 2006, Dec, 10-12; 2004, Jan, 27; 2004, January, 27; 2004, Jan, 27

▲ **00566** Anesthesia for direct coronary artery bypass grafting; without pump oxygenator Ⓝ🖥
⚐ 0.00 ⚕ 0.00 **Global Days XXX**
AMA: 2008, Apr, 3-4; 2008, Apr, 3-4; 2008, Apr, 3-4; 2006, Mar, 15; 2006, Mar, 15; 2006, Feb, 10-15; 2006, Feb, 10-15; 2006, Dec, 10-12; 2006, Dec, 10-12; 2006, Dec, 10-12; 2006, December, 10-12; 2006, December, 10-12; 2006, December, 10-12; 2006, February, 10-15; 2006, March, 15; 2006, Dec, 10-12; 2006, Dec, 10-12; 2006, Dec, 10-12; 2006, Dec, 10-12; 2006, Dec, 10-12; 2004, Jan, 27; 2004, January, 27; 2004, Jan, 27

● **00567** with pump oxygenator Ⓒ
⚐ 0.00 ⚕ 0.00 **Global Days XXX**

00580 Anesthesia for heart transplant or heart/lung transplant Ⓒ🖥
⚐ 0.00 ⚕ 0.00 **Global Days XXX**
AMA: 2008, Apr, 3-4; 2008, Apr, 3-4; 2006, Mar, 15; 2006, Mar, 15; 2006, Feb, 10-15; 2006, Feb, 10-15; 2006, Dec, 10-12; 2006, Dec, 10-12; 2006, Dec, 10-12; 2006, December, 10-12; 2006, December, 10-12; 2006, December, 10-12; 2006, February, 10-15; 2006, March, 15; 2006, Dec, 10-12; 2006, Dec, 10-12; 2006, Dec, 10-12; 2006, Dec, 10-12; 2006, Dec, 10-12; 2004, Jan, 27; 2004, January, 27; 2004, Jan, 27

00600-00670 Anesthesia for Spinal Procedures

CMS *100-4,12,140.3.2* *Calculation of Anesthesia Time*
CMS *100-4,12,140.2* *Payment for CRNA Services*
CMS *100-4,12,140* *Certified Registered Nurse Anesthetist Services*
CMS *100-4,4,20.6.4* *Modifiers for Discontinued Services*
CMS *100-4,4,20.6* *Modifier Use Under OPPS*
CMS *100-4,4,10.4* *Packaging Rules Under OPPS*
CMS *100-4,12,50* *Anesthesia Services*

00600 Anesthesia for procedures on cervical spine and cord; not otherwise specified Ⓝ🖥
EXCLUDES *percutaneous image-guided spinal cord anesthesia services (01935-01936)*
⚐ 0.00 ⚕ 0.00 **Global Days XXX**
AMA: 2008, Apr, 3-4; 2008, Apr, 3-4; 2008, Apr, 3-4; 2008, Jan, 10-25; 2006, Mar, 15; 2006, Mar, 15; 2006, Feb, 10-15; 2006, Feb, 10-15; 2006, Dec, 10-12; 2006, Dec, 10-12; 2006, Dec, 10-12; 2006, December, 10-12; 2006, December, 10-12; 2006, December, 10-12; 2006, December, 10-12; 2006, February, 10-15; 2006, March, 15; 2006, Dec, 10-12; 2006, Dec, 10 12; 2006, Dec, 10-12; 2006, Dec, 10-12; 2006, Dec, 10-12; 2004, Jan, 27; 2004, January, 27; 2004, Jan, 27

00604 procedures with patient in the sitting position Ⓒ🖥
⚐ 0.00 ⚕ 0.00 **Global Days XXX**
AMA: 2008, Apr, 3-4; 2008, Apr, 3-4; 2008, Apr, 3-4; 2006, Feb, 10-15; 2006, Feb, 10-15; 2006, Mar, 15; 2006, Mar, 15; 2006, Dec, 10-12; 2006, Dec, 10-12; 2006, Dec, 10-12; 2006, December, 10-12; 2006, December, 10-12; 2006, December, 10-12; 2006, March, 15; 2006, February, 10-15; 2006, Dec, 10-12; 2006, Dec, 10-12; 2006, Dec, 10-12; 2006, Dec, 10-12; 2006, Dec, 10-12; 2004, Jan, 27; 2004, January, 27; 2004, Jan, 27

00550 — 00604

● New Code ▲ Revised Code Ⓜ Maternity Edit Ⓐ Age Edit Ⓐ-Ⓨ OPPS Status Indicator ⚐ Facility RVU ⚕ Non-Facility RVU
🖥 CCI Comprehensive Code 50 Bilateral Procedure + Add-on Indicator Ⓝ Laboratory crosswalk Ⓡ Radiology crosswalk

Anesthesia

00620 — 00670

00620 **Anesthesia for procedures on thoracic spine and cord; not otherwise specified** N ▣
 🖩 0.00 ⚕ 0.00 Global Days XXX
 AMA: 2008, Apr, 3-4; 2008, Apr, 3-4; 2008, Jan, 10-25; 2008, Apr, 3-4; 2007, Mar, 9-11; 2007, Mar, 9-11; 2007, March, 9-11; 2006, Mar, 15; 2006, Mar, 15; 2006, Feb, 10-15; 2006, Feb, 10-15; 2006, Dec, 10-12; 2006, Dec, 10-12; 2006, Dec, 10-12; 2006, December, 10-12; 2006, December, 10-12; 2006, December, 10-12; 2006, February, 10-15; 2006, March, 15; 2006, Dec, 10-12; 2006, Dec, 10-12; 2006, Dec, 10-12; 2006, Dec, 10-12; 2004, Jan, 27; 2004, January, 27; 2004, Jan, 27

00622 **thoracolumbar sympathectomy** C ▣
 🖩 0.00 ⚕ 0.00 Global Days XXX
 AMA: 2008, Apr, 3-4; 2008, Apr, 3-4; 2008, Jan, 10-25; 2008, Apr, 3-4; 2007, Mar, 9-11; 2007, Mar, 9-11; 2007, March, 9-11; 2006, Mar, 15; 2006, Mar, 15; 2006, Feb, 10-15; 2006, Feb, 10-15; 2006, Dec, 10-12; 2006, Dec, 10-12; 2006, Dec, 10-12; 2006, December, 10-12; 2006, December, 10-12; 2006, December, 10-12; 2006, December, 10-12; 2006, March, 15; 2006, February, 10-15; 2006, Dec, 10-12; 2006, Dec, 10-12; 2006, Dec, 10-12; 2006, Dec, 10-12; 2004, Jan, 27; 2004, January, 27; 2004, Jan, 27

00625 **Anesthesia for procedures on the thoracic spine and cord, via an anterior transthoracic approach; not utilizing 1 lung ventilation** N
 EXCLUDES *anesthesia services for thoracotomy procedures other than spine (00540-00541)*
 🖩 0.00 ⚕ 0.00 Global Days XXX
 AMA: 2008, Apr, 3-4; 2008, Apr, 3-4; 2008, Apr, 3-4; 2008, Jan, 10-25; 2007, Mar, 9-11; 2007, Mar, 9-11; 2007, March, 9-11; 2006, Dec, 10-12; 2006, Dec, 10-12; 2006, December, 10-12; 2006, December, 10-12; 2006, December, 10-12; 2006, December, 10-12; 2006, Dec, 10-12; 2006, Dec, 10-12; 2006, Dec, 10-12; 2006, Dec, 10-12; 2006, Dec, 10-12; 2006, Dec, 10-12

00626 **utilizing one lung ventilation** N
 EXCLUDES *anesthesia services for thoracotomy procedures other than spine (00540-00541)*
 🖩 0.00 ⚕ 0.00 Global Days XXX
 AMA: 2008, Apr, 3-4; 2008, Apr, 3-4; 2008, Apr, 3-4; 2008, Jan, 10-25; 2007, Mar, 9-11; 2007, Mar, 9-11; 2007, March, 9-11; 2006, Dec, 10-12; 2006, Dec, 10-12; 2006, December, 10-12; 2006, December, 10-12; 2006, December, 10-12; 2006, December, 10-12; 2006, Dec, 10-12; 2006, Dec, 10-12; 2006, Dec, 10-12; 2006, Dec, 10-12; 2006, Dec, 10-12; 2006, Dec, 10-12

00630 **Anesthesia for procedures in lumbar region; not otherwise specified** N ▣
 🖩 0.00 ⚕ 0.00 Global Days XXX
 AMA: 2008, Apr, 3-4; 2008, Apr, 3-4; 2008, Apr, 3-4; 2006, Mar, 15; 2006, Mar, 15; 2006, Feb, 10-15; 2006, Feb, 10-15; 2006, Dec, 10-12; 2006, Dec, 10-12; 2006, Dec, 10-12; 2006, December, 10-12; 2006, December, 10-12; 2006, December, 10-12; 2006, February, 10-15; 2006, March, 15; 2006, Dec, 10-12; 2006, Dec, 10-12; 2006, Dec, 10-12; 2006, Dec, 10-12; 2004, Jan, 27; 2004, January, 27; 2004, Jan, 27

00632 **lumbar sympathectomy** C ▣
 🖩 0.00 ⚕ 0.00 Global Days XXX
 AMA: 2008, Apr, 3-4; 2008, Apr, 3-4; 2008, Apr, 3-4; 2006, Mar, 15; 2006, Mar, 15; 2006, Feb, 10-15; 2006, Feb, 10-15; 2006, Dec, 10-12; 2006, Dec, 10-12; 2006, Dec, 10-12; 2006, December, 10-12; 2006, December, 10-12; 2006, December, 10-12; 2006, February, 10-15; 2006, March, 15; 2006, Dec, 10-12; 2006, Dec, 10-12; 2006, Dec, 10-12; 2006, Dec, 10-12; 2004, Jan, 27; 2004, January, 27; 2004, Jan, 27

00634 **chemonucleolysis** N ▣
 🖩 0.00 ⚕ 0.00 Global Days XXX
 AMA: 2008, Apr, 3-4; 2008, Apr, 3-4; 2008, Apr, 3-4; 2006, Feb, 10-15; 2006, Feb, 10-15; 2006, Mar, 15; 2006, Mar, 15; 2006, Dec, 10-12; 2006, Dec, 10-12; 2006, Dec, 10-12; 2006, December, 10-12; 2006, December, 10-12; 2006, December, 10-12; 2006, February, 10-15; 2006, March, 15; 2006, Dec, 10-12; 2006, Dec, 10-12; 2006, Dec, 10-12; 2006, Dec, 10-12; 2004, Jan, 27; 2004, January, 27; 2004, Jan, 27

00635 **diagnostic or therapeutic lumbar puncture** N ▣
 🖩 0.00 ⚕ 0.00 Global Days XXX
 AMA: 2008, Apr, 3-4; 2008, Apr, 3-4; 2008, Apr, 3-4; 2006, Feb, 10-15; 2006, Feb, 10-15; 2006, Mar, 15; 2006, Mar, 15; 2006, Dec, 10-12; 2006, Dec, 10-12; 2006, Dec, 10-12; 2006, December, 10-12; 2006, December, 10-12; 2006, December, 10-12; 2006, February, 10-15; 2006, March, 15; 2006, Dec, 10-12; 2006, Dec, 10-12; 2006, Dec, 10-12; 2006, Dec, 10-12; 2004, Jan, 27; 2004, January, 27; 2004, Jan, 27

00640 **Anesthesia for manipulation of the spine or for closed procedures on the cervical, thoracic or lumbar spine** N ▣
 🖩 0.00 ⚕ 0.00 Global Days XXX
 AMA: 2008, Apr, 3-4; 2008, Apr, 3-4; 2008, Apr, 3-4; 2006, Mar, 15; 2006, Mar, 15; 2006, Feb, 10-15; 2006, Feb, 10-15; 2006, Dec, 10-12; 2006, Dec, 10-12; 2006, Dec, 10-12; 2006, December, 10-12; 2006, December, 10-12; 2006, December, 10-12; 2006, February, 10-15; 2006, March, 15; 2006, Dec, 10-12; 2006, Dec, 10-12; 2006, Dec, 10-12; 2006, Dec, 10-12; 2004, Jan, 27; 2004, January, 27; 2004, Jan, 27

00670 **Anesthesia for extensive spine and spinal cord procedures (eg, spinal instrumentation or vascular procedures)** C ▣
 🖩 0.00 ⚕ 0.00 Global Days XXX
 AMA: 2008, Apr, 3-4; 2008, Apr, 3-4; 2008, Apr, 3-4; 2006, Mar, 15; 2006, Mar, 15; 2006, Feb, 10-15; 2006, Feb, 10-15; 2006, Dec, 10-12; 2006, Dec, 10-12; 2006, Dec, 10-12; 2006, December, 10-12; 2006, December, 10-12; 2006, December, 10-12; 2006, February, 10-15; 2006, March, 15; 2006, Dec, 10-12; 2006, Dec, 10-12; 2006, Dec, 10-12; 2006, Dec, 10-12; 2004, Jan, 27; 2004, January, 27; 2004, Jan, 27

00700-00882 Anesthesia for Abdominal Procedures

CMS *100-4,12,140.3.2 Calculation of Anesthesia Time*
CMS *100-4,12,140.2 Payment for CRNA Services*
CMS *100-4,12,140 Certified Registered Nurse Anesthetist Services*
CMS *100-4,20.6.4 Modifiers for Discontinued Services*
CMS *100-4,4,20.6 Modifier Use Under OPPS*
CMS *100-4,4,10.4 Packaging Rules Under OPPS*
CMS *100-4,12,50 Anesthesia Services*

00700 **Anesthesia for procedures on upper anterior abdominal wall; not otherwise specified** N

0.00 0.00 Global Days XXX
AMA: 2008, Apr, 3-4; 2008, Apr, 3-4; 2008, Apr, 3-4; 2006, Mar, 15; 2006, Mar, 15; 2006, Feb, 10-15; 2006, Feb, 10-15; 2006, Dec, 10-12; 2006, Dec, 10-12; 2006, Dec, 10-12; 2006, December, 10-12; 2006, December, 10-12; 2006, December, 10-12; 2006, December, 10-12; 2006, February, 10-15; 2006, March, 15; 2006, Dec, 10-12; 2006, Dec, 10-12; 2006, Dec, 10-12; 2006, Dec, 10-12; 2006, Dec, 10-12; 2004, Jan, 27; 2004, January, 27; 2004, Jan, 27

00702 **percutaneous liver biopsy** N

0.00 0.00 Global Days XXX
AMA: 2008, Apr, 3-4; 2008, Apr, 3-4; 2008, Apr, 3-4; 2006, Mar, 15; 2006, Mar, 15; 2006, Feb, 10-15; 2006, Feb, 10-15; 2006, Dec, 10-12; 2006, Dec, 10-12; 2006, Dec, 10-12; 2006, December, 10-12; 2006, December, 10-12; 2006, December, 10-12; 2006, December, 10-12; 2006, February, 10-15; 2006, March, 15; 2006, Dec, 10-12; 2006, Dec, 10-12; 2006, Dec, 10-12; 2006, Dec, 10-12; 2006, Dec, 10-12; 2004, Jan, 27; 2004, January, 27; 2004, Jan, 27

00730 **Anesthesia for procedures on upper posterior abdominal wall** N

0.00 0.00 Global Days XXX
AMA: 2008, Apr, 3-4, 2008, Apr, 3-4; 2008, Apr, 3-4; 2006, Feb, 10-15; 2006, Feb, 10-15; 2006, Mar, 15; 2006, Mar, 15; 2006, Dec, 10-12; 2006, Dec, 10-12; 2006, Dec, 10-12; 2006, December, 10-12; 2006, December, 10-12; 2006, December, 10-12; 2006, December, 10-12; 2006, February, 10-15; 2006, March, 15; 2006, Dec, 10-12; 2006, Dec, 10-12; 2006, Dec, 10-12; 2006, Dec, 10-12; 2006, Dec, 10-12; 2004, Jan, 27; 2004, January, 27; 2004, Jan, 27

00740 **Anesthesia for upper gastrointestinal endoscopic procedures, endoscope introduced proximal to duodenum** N

0.00 0.00 Global Days XXX
AMA: 2008, Apr, 3-4; 2008, Apr, 3-4; 2008, Apr, 3-4; 2006, Feb, 10-15; 2006, Feb, 10-15; 2006, Mar, 15; 2006, Mar, 15; 2006, Dec, 10-12; 2006, Dec, 10-12; 2006, Dec, 10-12; 2006, December, 10-12; 2006, December, 10-12; 2006, December, 10-12; 2006, December, 10-12; 2006, February, 10-15; 2006, March, 15; 2006, Dec, 10-12; 2006, Dec, 10-12; 2006, Dec, 10-12; 2006, Dec, 10-12; 2006, Dec, 10-12; 2004, Jan, 27; 2004, January, 27; 2004, Jan, 27

00750 **Anesthesia for hernia repairs in upper abdomen; not otherwise specified** N

0.00 0.00 Global Days XXX
AMA: 2008, Apr, 3-4; 2008, Apr, 3-4; 2008, Apr, 3-4; 2006, Mar, 15; 2006, Mar, 15; 2006, Feb, 10-15; 2006, Feb, 10-15; 2006, Dec, 10-12; 2006, Dec, 10-12; 2006, Dec, 10-12; 2006, December, 10-12; 2006, December, 10-12; 2006, December, 10-12; 2006, December, 10-12; 2006, February, 10-15; 2006, March, 15; 2006, Dec, 10-12; 2006, Dec, 10-12; 2006, Dec, 10-12; 2006, Dec, 10-12; 2006, Dec, 10-12; 2004, Jan, 27; 2004, January, 27; 2004, Jan, 27

00752 **lumbar and ventral (incisional) hernias and/or wound dehiscence** N

0.00 0.00 Global Days XXX
AMA: 2008, Apr, 3-4; 2008, Apr, 3-4; 2008, Apr, 3-4; 2006, Mar, 15; 2006, Mar, 15; 2006, Feb, 10-15; 2006, Feb, 10-15; 2006, Dec, 10-12; 2006, Dec, 10-12; 2006, Dec, 10-12; 2006, December, 10-12; 2006, December, 10-12; 2006, December, 10-12; 2006, February, 10-15; 2006, March, 15; 2006, Dec, 10-12; 2006, Dec, 10-12; 2006, Dec, 10-12; 2006, Dec, 10-12; 2006, Dec, 10-12; 2004, Jan, 27; 2004, January, 27; 2004, Jan, 27

00754 **omphalocele** N

0.00 0.00 Global Days XXX
AMA: 2008, Apr, 3-4; 2008, Apr, 3-4; 2008, Apr, 3-4; 2006, Mar, 15; 2006, Mar, 15; 2006, Feb, 10-15; 2006, Feb, 10-15; 2006, Dec, 10-12; 2006, Dec, 10-12; 2006, Dec, 10-12; 2006, December, 10-12; 2006, December, 10-12; 2006, December, 10-12; 2006, December, 10-12; 2006, March, 15; 2006, February, 10-15; 2006, Dec, 10-12; 2006, Dec, 10-12; 2006, Dec, 10-12; 2006, Dec, 10-12; 2006, Dec, 10-12; 2004, Jan, 27; 2004, January, 27; 2004, Jan, 27

00756 **transabdominal repair of diaphragmatic hernia** N

0.00 0.00 Global Days XXX
AMA: 2008, Apr, 3-4; 2008, Apr, 3-4; 2008, Apr, 3-4; 2006, Feb, 10-15; 2006, Feb, 10-15; 2006, Mar, 15; 2006, Mar, 15; 2006, Dec, 10-12; 2006, Dec, 10-12; 2006, Dec, 10-12; 2006, December, 10-12; 2006, December, 10-12; 2006, December, 10-12; 2006, February, 10-15; 2006, March, 15; 2006, Dec, 10-12; 2006, Dec, 10-12; 2006, Dec, 10-12; 2006, Dec, 10-12; 2006, Dec, 10-12; 2004, Jan, 27; 2004, January, 27; 2004, Jan, 27

00770 **Anesthesia for all procedures on major abdominal blood vessels** N

0.00 0.00 Global Days XXX
AMA: 2008, Apr, 3-4; 2008, Apr, 3-4; 2008, Apr, 3-4; 2006, Feb, 10-15; 2006, Feb, 10-15; 2006, Mar, 15; 2006, Mar, 15; 2006, Dec, 10-12; 2006, Dec, 10-12; 2006, Dec, 10-12; 2006, December, 10-12; 2006, December, 10-12; 2006, December, 10-12; 2006, February, 10-15; 2006, March, 15; 2006, Dec, 10-12; 2006, Dec, 10-12; 2006, Dec, 10-12; 2006, Dec, 10-12; 2006, Dec, 10-12; 2004, Jan, 27; 2004, January, 27; 2004, Jan, 27

00790 **Anesthesia for intraperitoneal procedures in upper abdomen including laparoscopy; not otherwise specified** N

0.00 0.00 Global Days XXX
AMA: 2008, Apr, 3-4; 2008, Apr, 3-4; 2008, Apr, 3-4; 2006, Mar, 15; 2006, Mar, 15; 2006, Feb, 10-15; 2006, Feb, 10-15; 2006, Dec, 10-12; 2006, Dec, 10-12; 2006, Dec, 10-12; 2006, December, 10-12; 2006, December, 10-12; 2006, December, 10-12; 2006, February, 10-15; 2006, March, 15; 2006, Dec, 10-12; 2006, Dec, 10-12; 2006, Dec, 10-12; 2006, Dec, 10-12; 2006, Dec, 10-12; 2004, Jan, 27; 2004, January, 27; 2004, Jan, 27

00792 **partial hepatectomy or management of liver hemorrhage (excluding liver biopsy)** C

0.00 0.00 Global Days XXX
AMA: 2008, Apr, 3-4; 2008, Apr, 3-4; 2008, Apr, 3-4; 2006, Mar, 15; 2006, Mar, 15; 2006, Feb, 10-15; 2006, Feb, 10-15; 2006, Dec, 10-12; 2006, Dec, 10-12; 2006, Dec, 10-12; 2006, December, 10-12; 2006, December, 10-12; 2006, December, 10-12; 2006, February, 10-15; 2006, March, 15; 2006, Dec, 10-12; 2006, Dec, 10-12; 2006, Dec, 10-12; 2006, Dec, 10-12; 2006, Dec, 10-12; 2004, Jan, 27; 2004, January, 27; 2004, Jan, 27

● New Code   ▲ Revised Code   M Maternity Edit   Age Edit   A-V OPPS Status Indicator   Facility RVU   Non-Facility RVU
CCI Comprehensive Code   50 Bilateral Procedure   + Add-on Indicator   Laboratory crosswalk   Radiology crosswalk

00794   pancreatectomy, partial or total (eg, Whipple procedure)   C ▢

   🕮 0.00   ⚕ 0.00   **Global Days XXX**

AMA: 2008, Apr, 3-4; 2008, Apr, 3-4; 2008, Apr, 3-4; 2006, Mar, 15; 2006, Mar, 15; 2006, Feb, 10-15; 2006, Feb, 10-15; 2006, Dec, 10-12; 2006, Dec, 10-12; 2006, Dec, 10-12; 2006, December, 10-12; 2006, December, 10-12; 2006, December, 10-12; 2006, December, 10-12; 2006, February, 10-15; 2006, March, 15; 2006, Dec, 10-12; 2006, Dec, 10-12; 2006, Dec, 10-12; 2006, Dec, 10-12; 2006, Dec, 10-12; 2004, Jan, 27; 2004, January, 27; 2004, Jan, 27

00796   liver transplant (recipient)   C ▢
   EXCLUDES   *physiological support during liver harvest (01990)*

   🕮 0.00   ⚕ 0.00   **Global Days XXX**

AMA: 2008, Apr, 3-4; 2008, Apr, 3-4; 2008, Apr, 3-4; 2006, Feb, 10-15; 2006, Feb, 10-15; 2006, Mar, 15; 2006, Mar, 15; 2006, Dec, 10-12; 2006, Dec, 10-12; 2006, Dec, 10-12; 2006, December, 10-12; 2006, December, 10-12; 2006, December, 10-12; 2006, December, 10-12; 2006, February, 10-15; 2006, March, 15; 2006, Dec, 10-12; 2006, Dec, 10-12; 2006, Dec, 10-12; 2006, Dec, 10-12; 2006, Dec, 10-12; 2004, Jan, 27; 2004, January, 27; 2004, Jan, 27

00797   gastric restrictive procedure for morbid obesity   N ▢

   🕮 0.00   ⚕ 0.00   **Global Days XXX**

AMA: 2008, Apr, 3-4; 2008, Apr, 3-4; 2008, Apr, 3-4; 2006, Mar, 15; 2006, Mar, 15; 2006, Feb, 10-15; 2006, Feb, 10-15; 2006, Dec, 10-12; 2006, Dec, 10-12; 2006, Dec, 10-12; 2006, December, 10-12; 2006, December, 10-12; 2006, December, 10-12; 2006, December, 10-12; 2006, February, 10-15; 2006, March, 15; 2006, Dec, 10-12; 2006, Dec, 10-12; 2006, Dec, 10-12; 2006, Dec, 10-12; 2006, Dec, 10-12; 2004, Jan, 27; 2004, January, 27; 2004, Jan, 27

00800   Anesthesia for procedures on lower anterior abdominal wall; not otherwise specified   N ▢

   🕮 0.00   ⚕ 0.00   **Global Days XXX**

AMA: 2008, Apr, 3-4; 2008, Apr, 3-4; 2008, Apr, 3-4; 2006, Feb, 10-15; 2006, Feb, 10-15; 2006, Mar, 15; 2006, Mar, 15; 2006, Dec, 10-12; 2006, Dec, 10-12; 2006, Dec, 10-12; 2006, December, 10-12; 2006, December, 10-12; 2006, December, 10-12; 2006, December, 10-12; 2006, February, 10-15; 2006, March, 15; 2006, Dec, 10-12; 2006, Dec, 10-12; 2006, Dec, 10-12; 2006, Dec, 10-12; 2006, Dec, 10-12; 2004, Jan, 27; 2004, January, 27; 2004, Jan, 27

00802   panniculectomy   C ▢

   🕮 0.00   ⚕ 0.00   **Global Days XXX**

AMA: 2008, Apr, 3-4; 2008, Apr, 3-4; 2008, Apr, 3-4; 2006, Mar, 15; 2006, Mar, 15; 2006, Feb, 10-15; 2006, Feb, 10-15; 2006, Dec, 10-12; 2006, Dec, 10-12; 2006, Dec, 10-12; 2006, December, 10-12; 2006, December, 10-12; 2006, December, 10-12; 2006, December, 10-12; 2006, February, 10-15; 2006, March, 15; 2006, Dec, 10-12; 2006, Dec, 10-12; 2006, Dec, 10-12; 2006, Dec, 10-12; 2006, Dec, 10-12; 2004, Jan, 27; 2004, January, 27; 2004, Jan, 27

00810   Anesthesia for lower intestinal endoscopic procedures, endoscope introduced distal to duodenum   N ▢

   🕮 0.00   ⚕ 0.00   **Global Days XXX**

AMA: 2008, Apr, 3-4; 2008, Apr, 3-4; 2008, Apr, 3-4; 2006, Mar, 15; 2006, Mar, 15; 2006, Feb, 10-15; 2006, Feb, 10-15; 2006, Dec, 10-12; 2006, Dec, 10-12; 2006, Dec, 10-12; 2006, December, 10-12; 2006, December, 10-12; 2006, December, 10-12; 2006, December, 10-12; 2006, February, 10-15; 2006, March, 15; 2006, Dec, 10-12; 2006, Dec, 10-12; 2006, Dec, 10-12; 2006, Dec, 10-12; 2006, Dec, 10-12; 2004, Jan, 27; 2004, January, 27; 2004, Jan, 27

00820   Anesthesia for procedures on lower posterior abdominal wall   N ▢

   🕮 0.00   ⚕ 0.00   **Global Days XXX**

AMA: 2008, Apr, 3-4; 2008, Apr, 3-4; 2008, Apr, 3-4; 2006, Feb, 10-15; 2006, Feb, 10-15; 2006, Mar, 15; 2006, Mar, 15; 2006, Dec, 10-12; 2006, Dec, 10-12; 2006, Dec, 10-12; 2006, December, 10-12; 2006, December, 10-12; 2006, December, 10-12; 2006, February, 10-15; 2006, March, 15; 2006, Dec, 10-12; 2006, Dec, 10-12; 2006, Dec, 10-12; 2006, Dec, 10-12; 2006, Dec, 10-12; 2004, Jan, 27; 2004, January, 27; 2004, Jan, 27

00830   Anesthesia for hernia repairs in lower abdomen; not otherwise specified   N ▢
   EXCLUDES   *anesthesia for hernia repairs on infants one year old or younger (00834, 00836)*

   🕮 0.00   ⚕ 0.00   **Global Days XXX**

AMA: 2008, Apr, 3-4; 2008, Apr, 3-4; 2008, Apr, 3-4; 2006, Mar, 15; 2006, Mar, 15; 2006, Feb, 10-15; 2006, Feb, 10-15; 2006, Dec, 10-12; 2006, Dec, 10-12; 2006, Dec, 10-12; 2006, December, 10-12; 2006, December, 10-12; 2006, December, 10-12; 2006, February, 10-15; 2006, March, 15; 2006, Dec, 10-12; 2006, Dec, 10-12; 2006, Dec, 10-12; 2006, Dec, 10-12; 2006, Dec, 10-12; 2004, Jan, 27; 2004, January, 27; 2004, Jan, 27

00832   ventral and incisional hernias   N ▢
   EXCLUDES   *anesthesia for hernia repairs on infants one year old or younger (00834, 00836)*

   🕮 0.00   ⚕ 0.00   **Global Days XXX**

AMA: 2008, Apr, 3-4; 2008, Apr, 3-4; 2008, Apr, 3-4; 2006, Mar, 15; 2006, Mar, 15; 2006, Feb, 10-15; 2006, Feb, 10-15; 2006, Dec, 10-12; 2006, Dec, 10-12; 2006, Dec, 10-12; 2006, December, 10-12; 2006, December, 10-12; 2006, December, 10-12; 2006, March, 15; 2006, February, 10-15; 2006, Dec, 10-12; 2006, Dec, 10-12; 2006, Dec, 10-12; 2006, Dec, 10-12; 2006, Dec, 10-12; 2004, Jan, 27; 2004, January, 27; 2004, Jan, 27

00834   Anesthesia for hernia repairs in the lower abdomen not otherwise specified, younger than 1 year of age   A N ▢

   Do not report with (99100)

   🕮 0.00   ⚕ 0.00   **Global Days XXX**

AMA: 2008, Apr, 3-4; 2008, Apr, 3-4; 2008, Apr, 3-4; 2006, Feb, 10-15; 2006, Feb, 10-15; 2006, Mar, 15; 2006, Mar, 15; 2006, Dec, 10-12; 2006, Dec, 10-12; 2006, Dec, 10-12; 2006, December, 10-12; 2006, December, 10-12; 2006, December, 10-12; 2006, February, 10-15; 2006, March, 15; 2006, Dec, 10-12; 2006, Dec, 10-12; 2006, Dec, 10-12; 2006, Dec, 10-12; 2006, Dec, 10-12; 2004, Jan, 27; 2004, January, 27; 2004, Jan, 27

00836   Anesthesia for hernia repairs in the lower abdomen not otherwise specified, infants younger than 37 weeks gestational age at birth and younger than 50 weeks gestational age at time of surgery   A N ▢

   Do not report with (99100)

   🕮 0.00   ⚕ 0.00   **Global Days XXX**

AMA: 2008, Apr, 3-4; 2008, Apr, 3-4; 2008, Apr, 3-4; 2006, Mar, 15; 2006, Mar, 15; 2006, Feb, 10-15; 2006, Feb, 10-15; 2006, Dec, 10-12; 2006, Dec, 10-12; 2006, Dec, 10-12; 2006, December, 10-12; 2006, December, 10-12; 2006, December, 10-12; 2006, February, 10-15; 2006, March, 15; 2006, Dec, 10-12; 2006, Dec, 10-12; 2006, Dec, 10-12; 2006, Dec, 10-12; 2006, Dec, 10-12; 2004, Jan, 27; 2004, January, 27; 2004, Jan, 27

00840   Anesthesia for intraperitoneal procedures in lower abdomen including laparoscopy; not otherwise specified   Ⓝ▣

💰 0.00 ⚕ 0.00 **Global Days XXX**

AMA: 2008, Apr, 3-4; 2008, Apr, 3-4; 2008, Apr, 3-4; 2006, Mar, 15; 2006, Mar, 15; 2006, Feb, 10-15; 2006, Feb, 10-15; 2006, Dec, 10-12; 2006, Dec, 10-12; 2006, Dec, 10-12; 2006, December, 10-12; 2006, December, 10-12; 2006, December, 10-12; 2006, December, 10-12; 2006, February, 10-15; 2006, March, 15; 2006, Dec, 10-12; 2006, Dec, 10-12; 2006, Dec, 10-12; 2006, Dec, 10-12; 2006, Dec, 10-12; 2004, Jan, 27; 2004, January, 27; 2004, Jan, 27

00842   amniocentesis   Ⓜ♀Ⓝ▣

💰 0.00 ⚕ 0.00 **Global Days XXX**

AMA: 2008, Apr, 3-4; 2008, Apr, 3-4; 2008, Apr, 3-4; 2006, Mar, 15; 2006, Mar, 15; 2006, Feb, 10-15; 2006, Feb, 10-15; 2006, Dec, 10-12; 2006, Dec, 10-12; 2006, Dec, 10-12; 2006, December, 10-12; 2006, December, 10-12; 2006, December, 10-12; 2006, February, 10-15; 2006, March, 15; 2006, Dec, 10-12; 2006, Dec, 10-12; 2006, Dec, 10-12; 2006, Dec, 10-12; 2006, Dec, 10-12; 2004, Jan, 27; 2004, January, 27; 2004, Jan, 27

00844   abdominoperineal resection   Ⓒ▣

💰 0.00 ⚕ 0.00 **Global Days XXX**

AMA: 2008, Apr, 3-4; 2008, Apr, 3-4; 2008, Apr, 3-4; 2006, Mar, 15; 2006, Mar, 15; 2006, Feb, 10-15; 2006, Feb, 10-15; 2006, Dec, 10-12; 2006, Dec, 10-12; 2006, Dec, 10-12; 2006, December, 10-12; 2006, December, 10-12; 2006, December, 10-12; 2006, February, 10-15; 2006, March, 15; 2006, Dec, 10-12; 2006, Dec, 10-12; 2006, Dec, 10-12; 2006, Dec, 10-12; 2006, Dec, 10-12; 2004, Jan, 27; 2004, January, 27; 2004, Jan, 27

00846   radical hysterectomy   ♀Ⓒ▣

💰 0.00 ⚕ 0.00 **Global Days XXX**

AMA: 2008, Apr, 3-4; 2008, Apr, 3-4; 2008, Apr, 3-4; 2006, Mar, 15; 2006, Mar, 15; 2006, Feb, 10-15; 2006, Feb, 10-15; 2006, Dec, 10-12; 2006, Dec, 10-12; 2006, Dec, 10-12; 2006, December, 10-12; 2006, December, 10-12; 2006, December, 10-12; 2006, February, 10-15; 2006, March, 15; 2006, Dec, 10-12; 2006, Dec, 10-12; 2006, Dec, 10-12; 2006, Dec, 10-12; 2006, Dec, 10-12; 2004, Jan, 27; 2004, January, 27; 2004, Jan, 27

00848   pelvic exenteration   Ⓒ▣

💰 0.00 ⚕ 0.00 **Global Days XXX**

AMA: 2008, Apr, 3-4; 2008, Apr, 3-4; 2008, Apr, 3-4; 2006, Mar, 15; 2006, Mar, 15; 2006, Feb, 10-15; 2006, Feb, 10-15; 2006, Dec, 10-12; 2006, Dec, 10-12; 2006, Dec, 10-12; 2006, December, 10-12; 2006, December, 10-12; 2006, December, 10-12; 2006, February, 10-15; 2006, March, 15; 2006, Dec, 10-12; 2006, Dec, 10-12; 2006, Dec, 10-12; 2006, Dec, 10-12; 2006, Dec, 10-12; 2004, Jan, 27; 2004, January, 27; 2004, Jan, 27

00851   tubal ligation/transection   ♀Ⓝ▣

💰 0.00 ⚕ 0.00 **Global Days XXX**

AMA: 2008, Apr, 3-4; 2008, Apr, 3-4; 2008, Apr, 3-4; 2006, Mar, 15; 2006, Mar, 15; 2006, Feb, 10-15; 2006, Feb, 10-15; 2006, Dec, 10-12; 2006, Dec, 10-12; 2006, Dec, 10-12; 2006, December, 10-12; 2006, December, 10-12; 2006, December, 10-12; 2006, February, 10-15; 2006, March, 15; 2006, Dec, 10-12; 2006, Dec, 10-12; 2006, Dec, 10-12; 2006, Dec, 10-12; 2006, Dec, 10-12; 2004, Jan, 27; 2004, January, 27; 2004, Jan, 27

00860   Anesthesia for extraperitoneal procedures in lower abdomen, including urinary tract; not otherwise specified   Ⓝ▣

💰 0.00 ⚕ 0.00 **Global Days XXX**

AMA: 2008, Apr, 3-4; 2008, Apr, 3-4; 2008, Apr, 3-4; 2006, Feb, 10-15; 2006, Feb, 10-15; 2006, Mar, 15; 2006, Mar, 15; 2006, Dec, 10-12; 2006, Dec, 10-12; 2006, Dec, 10-12; 2006, December, 10-12; 2006, December, 10-12; 2006, December, 10-12; 2006, February, 10-15; 2006, March, 15; 2006, Dec, 10-12; 2006, Dec, 10-12; 2006, Dec, 10-12; 2006, Dec, 10-12; 2006, Dec, 10-12; 2004, Jan, 27; 2004, January, 27; 2004, Jan, 27

00862   renal procedures, including upper one-third of ureter, or donor nephrectomy   Ⓝ▣

💰 0.00 ⚕ 0.00 **Global Days XXX**

AMA: 2008, Apr, 3-4; 2008, Apr, 3-4; 2008, Apr, 3-4; 2006, Mar, 15; 2006, Mar, 15; 2006, Feb, 10-15; 2006, Feb, 10-15; 2006, Dec, 10-12; 2006, Dec, 10-12; 2006, Dec, 10-12; 2006, December, 10-12; 2006, December, 10-12; 2006, December, 10-12; 2006, February, 10-15; 2006, March, 15; 2006, Dec, 10-12; 2006, Dec, 10-12; 2006, Dec, 10-12; 2006, Dec, 10-12; 2006, Dec, 10-12; 2004, Jan, 27; 2004, January, 27; 2004, Jan, 27

00864   total cystectomy   Ⓒ▣

💰 0.00 ⚕ 0.00 **Global Days XXX**

AMA: 2008, Apr, 3-4; 2008, Apr, 3-4; 2008, Apr, 3-4; 2006, Mar, 15; 2006, Mar, 15; 2006, Feb, 10-15; 2006, Feb, 10-15; 2006, Dec, 10-12; 2006, Dec, 10-12; 2006, Dec, 10-12; 2006, December, 10-12; 2006, December, 10-12; 2006, December, 10-12; 2006, February, 10-15; 2006, March, 15; 2006, Dec, 10-12; 2006, Dec, 10-12; 2006, Dec, 10-12; 2006, Dec, 10-12; 2006, Dec, 10-12; 2004, Jan, 27; 2004, January, 27; 2004, Jan, 27

00865   radical prostatectomy (suprapubic, retropubic)   ♂Ⓒ▣

💰 0.00 ⚕ 0.00 **Global Days XXX**

AMA: 2008, Apr, 3-4; 2008, Apr, 3-4; 2008, Apr, 3-4; 2006, Mar, 15; 2006, Mar, 15; 2006, Feb, 10-15; 2006, Feb, 10-15; 2006, Dec, 10-12; 2006, Dec, 10-12; 2006, Dec, 10-12; 2006, December, 10-12; 2006, December, 10-12; 2006, December, 10-12; 2006, December, 10-12; 2006, March, 15; 2006, February, 10-15; 2006, Dec, 10-12; 2006, Dec, 10-12; 2006, Dec, 10-12; 2006, Dec, 10-12; 2006, Dec, 10-12; 2004, Jan, 27; 2004, January, 27; 2004, Jan, 27

00866   adrenalectomy   Ⓒ▣

💰 0.00 ⚕ 0.00 **Global Days XXX**

AMA: 2008, Apr, 3-4; 2008, Apr, 3-4; 2008, Apr, 3-4; 2006, Mar, 15; 2006, Mar, 15; 2006, Feb, 10-15; 2006, Feb, 10-15; 2006, Dec, 10-12; 2006, Dec, 10-12; 2006, Dec, 10-12; 2006, December, 10-12; 2006, December, 10-12; 2006, December, 10-12; 2006, February, 10-15; 2006, March, 15; 2006, Dec, 10-12; 2006, Dec, 10-12; 2006, Dec, 10-12; 2006, Dec, 10-12; 2006, Dec, 10-12; 2004, Jan, 27; 2004, January, 27; 2004, Jan, 27

00868   renal transplant (recipient)   Ⓒ▣

EXCLUDES   *anesthesia for donor nephrectomy (00862) harvesting kidney from brain dead patient (01990)*

💰 0.00 ⚕ 0.00 **Global Days XXX**

AMA: 2008, Apr, 3-4; 2008, Apr, 3-4; 2008, Apr, 3-4; 2006, Mar, 15; 2006, Mar, 15; 2006, Feb, 10-15; 2006, Feb, 10-15; 2006, Dec, 10-12; 2006, Dec, 10-12; 2006, Dec, 10-12; 2006, December, 10-12; 2006, December, 10-12; 2006, December, 10-12; 2006, February, 10-15; 2006, March, 15; 2006, Dec, 10-12; 2006, Dec, 10-12; 2006, Dec, 10-12; 2006, Dec, 10-12; 2006, Dec, 10-12; 2004, Jan, 27; 2004, January, 27; 2004, Jan, 27

● New Code   ▲ Revised Code   Ⓜ Maternity Edit   Ⓐ Age Edit   Ⓐ-Ⓨ OPPS Status Indicator   💰 Facility RVU   ⚕ Non-Facility RVU

◗ CCI Comprehensive Code   🔟 Bilateral Procedure   + Add-on Indicator   ◣ Laboratory crosswalk   ✚ Radiology crosswalk

00870   **cystolithotomy**   N 🖵

🎫 0.00   ✂ 0.00   **Global Days XXX**

AMA: 2008, Apr, 3-4; 2008, Apr, 3-4; 2008, Apr, 3-4; 2006, Feb, 10-15; 2006, Feb, 10-15; 2006, Mar, 15; 2006, Mar, 15; 2006, Dec, 10-12; 2006, Dec, 10-12; 2006, Dec, 10-12; 2006, December, 10-12; 2006, December, 10-12; 2006, December, 10-12; 2006, February, 10-15; 2006, March, 15; 2006, Dec, 10-12; 2006, Dec, 10-12; 2006, Dec, 10-12; 2006, Dec, 10-12; 2006, Dec, 10-12; 2004, Jan, 27; 2004, January, 27; 2004, Jan, 27

00872   **Anesthesia for lithotripsy, extracorporeal shock wave; with water bath**   N 🖵

🎫 0.00   ✂ 0.00   **Global Days XXX**

AMA: 2008, Apr, 3-4; 2008, Apr, 3-4; 2008, Apr, 3-4; 2006, Feb, 10-15; 2006, Feb, 10-15; 2006, Mar, 15; 2006, Mar, 15; 2006, Dec, 10-12; 2006, Dec, 10-12; 2006, Dec, 10-12; 2006, December, 10-12; 2006, December, 10-12; 2006, December, 10-12; 2006, February, 10-15; 2006, March, 15; 2006, Dec, 10-12; 2006, Dec, 10-12; 2006, Dec, 10-12; 2006, Dec, 10-12; 2006, Dec, 10-12; 2004, Jan, 27; 2004, January, 27; 2004, Jan, 27

00873   **without water bath**   N 🖵

🎫 0.00   ✂ 0.00   **Global Days XXX**

AMA: 2008, Apr, 3-4; 2008, Apr, 3-4; 2008, Apr, 3-4; 2006, Mar, 15; 2006, Mar, 15; 2006, Feb, 10-15; 2006, Feb, 10-15; 2006, Dec, 10-12; 2006, Dec, 10-12; 2006, Dec, 10-12; 2006, December, 10-12; 2006, December, 10-12; 2006, December, 10-12; 2006, February, 10-15; 2006, March, 15; 2006, Dec, 10-12; 2006, Dec, 10-12; 2006, Dec, 10-12; 2006, Dec, 10-12; 2006, Dec, 10-12; 2004, Jan, 27; 2004, January, 27; 2004, Jan, 27

00880   **Anesthesia for procedures on major lower abdominal vessels; not otherwise specified**   N 🖵

🎫 0.00   ✂ 0.00   **Global Days XXX**

AMA: 2008, Apr, 3-4; 2008, Apr, 3-4; 2008, Apr, 3-4; 2006, Mar, 15; 2006, Mar, 15; 2006, Feb, 10-15; 2006, Feb, 10-15; 2006, Dec, 10-12; 2006, Dec, 10-12; 2006, Dec, 10-12; 2006, December, 10-12; 2006, December, 10-12; 2006, December, 10-12; 2006, February, 10-15; 2006, March, 15; 2006, Dec, 10-12; 2006, Dec, 10-12; 2006, Dec, 10-12; 2006, Dec, 10-12; 2006, Dec, 10-12; 2004, Jan, 27; 2004, January, 27; 2004, Jan, 27

00882   **inferior vena cava ligation**   C 🖵

🎫 0.00   ✂ 0.00   **Global Days XXX**

AMA: 2008, Apr, 3-4; 2008, Apr, 3-4; 2008, Apr, 3-4; 2006, Feb, 10-15; 2006, Feb, 10-15; 2006, Mar, 15; 2006, Mar, 15; 2006, Dec, 10-12; 2006, Dec, 10-12; 2006, Dec, 10-12; 2006, December, 10-12; 2006, December, 10-12; 2006, December, 10-12; 2006, February, 10-15; 2006, March, 15; 2006, Dec, 10-12; 2006, Dec, 10-12; 2006, Dec, 10-12; 2006, Dec, 10-12; 2006, Dec, 10-12; 2004, Jan, 27; 2004, January, 27; 2004, Jan, 27

00902-00952 Anesthesia for Genitourinary Procedures

CMS *100-4,12,140.3.2 Calculation of Anesthesia Time*
CMS *100-4,12,140.2 Payment for CRNA Services*
CMS *100-4,12,140 Certified Registered Nurse Anesthetist Services*
CMS *100-4,4,20.6.4 Modifiers for Discontinued Services*
CMS *100-4,4,20.6 Modifier Use Under OPPS*
CMS *100-4,4,10.4 Packaging Rules Under OPPS*
CMS *100-4,12,50 Anesthesia Services*
EXCLUDES   *perineal procedures on skin, muscles, and nerves (00300, 00400)*

00902   **Anesthesia for; anorectal procedure**   N 🖵

🎫 0.00   ✂ 0.00   **Global Days XXX**

AMA: 2008, Apr, 3-4; 2008, Apr, 3-4; 2008, Apr, 3-4; 2006, Mar, 15; 2006, Mar, 15; 2006, Feb, 10-15; 2006, Feb, 10-15; 2006, Dec, 10-12; 2006, Dec, 10-12; 2006, Dec, 10-12; 2006, December, 10-12; 2006, December, 10-12; 2006, December, 10-12; 2006, February, 10-15; 2006, March, 15; 2006, Dec, 10-12; 2006, Dec, 10-12; 2006, Dec, 10-12; 2006, Dec, 10-12; 2006, Dec, 10-12; 2004, Jan, 27; 2004, January, 27; 2004, Jan, 27

00904   **radical perineal procedure**   C 🖵

🎫 0.00   ✂ 0.00   **Global Days XXX**

AMA: 2008, Apr, 3-4; 2008, Apr, 3-4; 2008, Apr, 3-4; 2006, Mar, 15; 2006, Mar, 15; 2006, Feb, 10-15; 2006, Feb, 10-15; 2006, Dec, 10-12; 2006, Dec, 10-12; 2006, Dec, 10-12; 2006, December, 10-12; 2006, December, 10-12; 2006, December, 10-12; 2006, February, 10-15; 2006, March, 15; 2006, Dec, 10-12; 2006, Dec, 10-12; 2006, Dec, 10-12; 2006, Dec, 10-12; 2006, Dec, 10-12; 2004, Jan, 27; 2004, January, 27; 2004, Jan, 27

00906   **vulvectomy**   ♀ N 🖵

🎫 0.00   ✂ 0.00   **Global Days XXX**

AMA: 2008, Apr, 3-4; 2008, Apr, 3-4; 2008, Apr, 3-4; 2006, Mar, 15; 2006, Mar, 15; 2006, Feb, 10-15; 2006, Feb, 10-15; 2006, Dec, 10-12; 2006, Dec, 10-12; 2006, Dec, 10-12; 2006, December, 10-12; 2006, December, 10-12; 2006, December, 10-12; 2006, February, 10-15; 2006, March, 15; 2006, Dec, 10-12; 2006, Dec, 10-12; 2006, Dec, 10-12; 2006, Dec, 10-12; 2006, Dec, 10-12; 2004, Jan, 27; 2004, January, 27; 2004, Jan, 27

00908   **perineal prostatectomy**   ♂ C 🖵

🎫 0.00   ✂ 0.00   **Global Days XXX**

AMA: 2008, Apr, 3-4; 2008, Apr, 3-4; 2008, Apr, 3-4; 2006, Mar, 15; 2006, Mar, 15; 2006, Feb, 10-15; 2006, Feb, 10-15; 2006, Dec, 10-12; 2006, Dec, 10-12; 2006, Dec, 10-12; 2006, December, 10-12; 2006, December, 10-12; 2006, December, 10-12; 2006, February, 10-15; 2006, March, 15; 2006, Dec, 10-12; 2006, Dec, 10-12; 2006, Dec, 10-12; 2006, Dec, 10-12; 2006, Dec, 10-12; 2004, Jan, 27; 2004, January, 27; 2004, Jan, 27

00910   **Anesthesia for transurethral procedures (including urethrocystoscopy); not otherwise specified**   N 🖵

🎫 0.00   ✂ 0.00   **Global Days XXX**

AMA: 2008, Apr, 3-4; 2008, Apr, 3-4; 2008, Apr, 3-4; 2006, Feb, 10-15; 2006, Feb, 10-15; 2006, Mar, 15; 2006, Mar, 15; 2006, Dec, 10-12; 2006, Dec, 10-12; 2006, Dec, 10-12; 2006, December, 10-12; 2006, December, 10-12; 2006, December, 10-12; 2006, February, 10-15; 2006, March, 15; 2006, Dec, 10-12; 2006, Dec, 10-12; 2006, Dec, 10-12; 2006, Dec, 10-12; 2006, Dec, 10-12; 2004, Jan, 27; 2004, January, 27; 2004, Jan, 27

00912 transurethral resection of bladder tumor(s) N ▢
⚬ 0.00 ⚬ 0.00 Global Days XXX
AMA: 2008, Apr, 3-4; 2008, Apr, 3-4; 2008, Apr, 3-4; 2006, Feb, 10-15; 2006, Feb, 10-15; 2006, Mar, 15; 2006, Mar, 15; 2006, Dec, 10-12; 2006, Dec, 10-12; 2006, Dec, 10-12; 2006, December, 10-12; 2006, December, 10-12; 2006, December, 10-12; 2006, March, 15; 2006, February, 10-15; 2006, Dec, 10-12; 2006, Dec, 10-12; 2006, Dec, 10-12; 2006, Dec, 10-12; 2006, Dec, 10-12; 2004, Jan, 27; 2004, January, 27; 2004, Jan, 27

00914 transurethral resection of prostate ♂ N ▢
⚬ 0.00 ⚬ 0.00 Global Days XXX
AMA: 2008, Apr, 3-4; 2008, Apr, 3-4; 2008, Apr, 3-4; 2006, Mar, 15; 2006, Mar, 15; 2006, Feb, 10-15; 2006, Feb, 10-15, 2006, Dec, 10-12; 2006, Dec, 10-12; 2006, Dec, 10-12; 2006, December, 10-12; 2006, December, 10-12; 2006, December, 10-12; 2006, December, 10-12; 2006, February, 10-15; 2006, March, 15; 2006, Dec, 10-12; 2006, Dec, 10-12; 2006, Dec, 10-12; 2006, Dec, 10-12; 2006, Dec, 10-12; 2004, Jan, 27; 2004, January, 27; 2004, Jan, 27

00916 post-transurethral resection bleeding N ▢
⚬ 0.00 ⚬ 0.00 Global Days XXX
AMA: 2008, Apr, 3-4; 2008, Apr, 3-4; 2008, Apr, 3-4; 2006, Feb, 10-15; 2006, Feb, 10-15; 2006, Mar, 15; 2006, Mar, 15; 2006, Dec, 10-12; 2006, Dec, 10-12; 2006, Dec, 10-12; 2006, December, 10-12; 2006, December, 10-12; 2006, December, 10-12; 2006, February, 10-15; 2006, March, 15; 2006, Dec, 10-12; 2006, Dec, 10-12; 2006, Dec, 10-12; 2006, Dec, 10-12; 2006, Dec, 10-12; 2004, Jan, 27; 2004, January, 27; 2004, Jan, 27

00918 with fragmentation, manipulation and/or removal of ureteral calculus N ▢
⚬ 0.00 ⚬ 0.00 Global Days XXX
AMA: 2008, Apr, 3-4; 2008, Apr, 3-4; 2008, Apr, 3-4; 2006, Mar, 15; 2006, Mar, 15; 2006, Feb, 10-15; 2006, Feb, 10-15; 2006, Dec, 10-12; 2006, Dec, 10-12; 2006, Dec, 10-12; 2006, December, 10-12; 2006, December, 10-12; 2006, December, 10-12; 2006, February, 10-15; 2006, March, 15; 2006, Dec, 10-12; 2006, Dec, 10-12; 2006, Dec, 10-12; 2006, Dec, 10-12; 2006, Dec, 10-12; 2004, Jan, 27; 2004, January, 27; 2004, Jan, 27

00920 Anesthesia for procedures on male genitalia (including open urethral procedures); not otherwise specified ♂ N ▢
⚬ 0.00 ⚬ 0.00 Global Days XXX
AMA: 2008, Apr, 3-4; 2008, Apr, 3-4; 2008, Apr, 3-4; 2006, Mar, 15; 2006, Mar, 15; 2006, Feb, 10-15; 2006, Feb, 10-15; 2006, Dec, 10-12; 2006, Dec, 10-12; 2006, Dec, 10-12; 2006, December, 10-12; 2006, December, 10-12; 2006, December, 10-12; 2006, February, 10-15; 2006, March, 15; 2006, Dec, 10-12; 2006, Dec, 10-12; 2006, Dec, 10-12; 2006, Dec, 10-12; 2006, Dec, 10-12; 2004, Jan, 27; 2004, January, 27; 2004, Jan, 27

00921 vasectomy, unilateral or bilateral ♂ N ▢
⚬ 0.00 ⚬ 0.00 Global Days XXX
AMA: 2008, Apr, 3-4; 2008, Apr, 3-4; 2008, Apr, 3-4; 2006, Feb, 10-15; 2006, Feb, 10-15; 2006, Mar, 15; 2006, Mar, 15; 2006, Dec, 10-12; 2006, Dec, 10-12; 2006, Dec, 10-12; 2006, December, 10-12; 2006, December, 10-12; 2006, December, 10-12; 2006, February, 10-15; 2006, March, 15; 2006, Dec, 10-12; 2006, Dec, 10-12; 2006, Dec, 10-12; 2006, Dec, 10-12; 2006, Dec, 10-12; 2004, Jan, 27; 2004, January, 27; 2004, Jan, 27

00922 seminal vesicles ♂ N ▢
⚬ 0.00 ⚬ 0.00 Global Days XXX
AMA: 2008, Apr, 3-4; 2008, Apr, 3-4; 2008, Apr, 3-4; 2006, Feb, 10-15; 2006, Feb, 10-15; 2006, Mar, 15; 2006, Mar, 15; 2006, Dec, 10-12; 2006, Dec, 10-12; 2006, Dec, 10-12; 2006, December, 10-12; 2006, December, 10-12; 2006, December, 10-12; 2006, February, 10-15; 2006, March, 15; 2006, Dec, 10-12; 2006, Dec, 10-12; 2006, Dec, 10-12; 2006, Dec, 10-12; 2006, Dec, 10-12; 2004, Jan, 27; 2004, January, 27; 2004, Jan, 27

00924 undescended testis, unilateral or bilateral ♂ N ▢
⚬ 0.00 ⚬ 0.00 Global Days XXX
AMA: 2008, Apr, 3-4; 2008, Apr, 3-4; 2008, Apr, 3-4; 2006, Mar, 15; 2006, Mar, 15; 2006, Feb, 10-15; 2006, Feb, 10-15; 2006, Dec, 10-12; 2006, Dec, 10-12; 2006, Dec, 10-12; 2006, December, 10-12; 2006, December, 10-12; 2006, December, 10-12; 2006, February, 10-15; 2006, March, 15; 2006, Dec, 10-12; 2006, Dec, 10-12; 2006, Dec, 10-12; 2006, Dec, 10-12; 2006, Dec, 10-12; 2004, Jan, 27; 2004, January, 27; 2004, Jan, 27

00926 radical orchiectomy, inguinal ♂ N ▢
⚬ 0.00 ⚬ 0.00 Global Days XXX
AMA: 2008, Apr, 3-4; 2008, Apr, 3-4; 2008, Apr, 3-4; 2006, Mar, 15; 2006, Mar, 15; 2006, Feb, 10-15; 2006, Feb, 10-15; 2006, Dec, 10-12; 2006, Dec, 10-12; 2006, Dec, 10-12; 2006, December, 10-12; 2006, December, 10-12; 2006, December, 10-12; 2006, February, 10-15; 2006, March, 15; 2006, Dec, 10-12; 2006, Dec, 10-12; 2006, Dec, 10-12; 2006, Dec, 10-12; 2006, Dec, 10-12; 2004, Jan, 27; 2004, January, 27; 2004, Jan, 27

00928 radical orchiectomy, abdominal ♂ N ▢
⚬ 0.00 ⚬ 0.00 Global Days XXX
AMA: 2008, Apr, 3-4; 2008, Apr, 3-4; 2008, Apr, 3-4; 2006, Mar, 15; 2006, Mar, 15; 2006, Feb, 10-15; 2006, Feb, 10-15; 2006, Dec, 10-12; 2006, Dec, 10-12; 2006, Dec, 10-12; 2006, December, 10-12; 2006, December, 10-12; 2006, December, 10-12; 2006, February, 10-15; 2006, March, 15; 2006, Dec, 10-12; 2006, Dec, 10-12; 2006, Dec, 10-12; 2006, Dec, 10-12; 2006, Dec, 10-12; 2004, Jan, 27; 2004, January, 27; 2004, Jan, 27

00930 orchiopexy, unilateral or bilateral ♂ N ▢
⚬ 0.00 ⚬ 0.00 Global Days XXX
AMA: 2008, Apr, 3-4; 2008, Apr, 3-4; 2008, Apr, 3-4; 2006, Feb, 10-15; 2006, Feb, 10-15; 2006, Mar, 15; 2006, Mar, 15; 2006, Dec, 10-12; 2006, Dec, 10-12; 2006, Dec, 10-12; 2006, December, 10-12; 2006, December, 10-12; 2006, December, 10-12; 2006, February, 10-15; 2006, March, 15; 2006, Dec, 10-12; 2006, Dec, 10-12; 2006, Dec, 10-12; 2006, Dec, 10-12; 2006, Dec, 10-12; 2004, Jan, 27; 2004, January, 27; 2004, Jan, 27

00932 complete amputation of penis ♂ C ▢
⚬ 0.00 ⚬ 0.00 Global Days XXX
AMA: 2008, Apr, 3-4; 2008, Apr, 3-4; 2008, Apr, 3-4; 2006, Mar, 15; 2006, Mar, 15; 2006, Feb, 10-15; 2006, Feb, 10-15; 2006, Dec, 10-12; 2006, Dec, 10-12; 2006, Dec, 10-12; 2006, December, 10-12; 2006, December, 10-12; 2006, December, 10-12; 2006, February, 10-15; 2006, March, 15; 2006, Dec, 10-12; 2006, Dec, 10-12; 2006, Dec, 10-12; 2006, Dec, 10-12; 2006, Dec, 10-12; 2004, Jan, 27; 2004, January, 27; 2004, Jan, 27

● New Code ▲ Revised Code M Maternity Edit A Age Edit A-V OPPS Status Indicator ⚬ Facility RVU ⚬ Non-Facility RVU
▢ CCI Comprehensive Code 50 Bilateral Procedure + Add-on Indicator ▪ Laboratory crosswalk ▪ Radiology crosswalk

00934 radical amputation of penis with bilateral inguinal lymphadenectomy ♂Ⓒ▣

🔢 0.00 🔢 0.00 **Global Days XXX**

AMA: 2008, Apr, 3-4; 2008, Apr, 3-4; 2008, Apr, 3-4; 2006, Mar, 15; 2006, Mar, 15; 2006, Feb, 10-15; 2006, Feb, 10-15; 2006, Dec, 10-12; 2006, Dec, 10-12; 2006, Dec, 10-12; 2006, December, 10-12; 2006, December, 10-12; 2006, December, 10-12; 2006, December, 10-12; 2006, February, 10-15; 2006, March, 15; 2006, Dec, 10-12; 2006, Dec, 10-12; 2006, Dec, 10-12; 2006, Dec, 10-12; 2006, Dec, 10-12; 2004, Jan, 27; 2004, January, 27; 2004, Jan, 27

00936 radical amputation of penis with bilateral inguinal and iliac lymphadenectomy ♂Ⓒ▣

🔢 0.00 🔢 0.00 **Global Days XXX**

AMA: 2008, Apr, 3-4; 2008, Apr, 3-4; 2008, Apr, 3-4; 2006, Mar, 15; 2006, Mar, 15; 2006, Feb, 10-15; 2006, Feb, 10-15; 2006, Dec, 10-12; 2006, Dec, 10-12; 2006, Dec, 10-12; 2006, December, 10-12; 2006, December, 10-12; 2006, December, 10-12; 2006, December, 10-12; 2006, February, 10-15; 2006, March, 15; 2006, Dec, 10-12; 2006, Dec, 10-12; 2006, Dec, 10-12; 2006, Dec, 10-12; 2006, Dec, 10-12; 2004, Jan, 27; 2004, January, 27; 2004, Jan, 27

00938 insertion of penile prosthesis (perineal approach) ♂Ⓝ▣

🔢 0.00 🔢 0.00 **Global Days XXX**

AMA: 2008, Apr, 3-4; 2008, Apr, 3-4; 2008, Apr, 3-4; 2006, Mar, 15; 2006, Mar, 15; 2006, Feb, 10-15; 2006, Feb, 10-15; 2006, Dec, 10-12; 2006, Dec, 10-12; 2006, Dec, 10-12; 2006, December, 10-12; 2006, December, 10-12; 2006, December, 10-12; 2006, December, 10-12; 2006, March, 15; 2006, February, 10-15; 2006, Dec, 10-12; 2006, Dec, 10-12; 2006, Dec, 10-12; 2006, Dec, 10-12; 2006, Dec, 10-12; 2004, Jan, 27; 2004, January, 27; 2004, Jan, 27

00940 Anesthesia for vaginal procedures (including biopsy of labia, vagina, cervix or endometrium); not otherwise specified ♀Ⓝ▣

🔢 0.00 🔢 0.00 **Global Days XXX**

AMA: 2008, Apr, 3-4; 2008, Apr, 3-4; 2008, Apr, 3-4; 2006, Feb, 10-15; 2006, Feb, 10-15; 2006, Mar, 15; 2006, Mar, 15; 2006, Dec, 10-12; 2006, Dec, 10-12; 2006, Dec, 10-12; 2006, December, 10-12; 2006, December, 10-12; 2006, December, 10-12; 2006, February, 10-15; 2006, March, 15; 2006, Dec, 10-12; 2006, Dec, 10-12; 2006, Dec, 10-12; 2006, Dec, 10-12; 2006, Dec, 10-12; 2004, Jan, 27; 2004, January, 27; 2004, Jan, 27

00942 colpotomy, vaginectomy, colporrhaphy, and open urethral procedures ♀Ⓝ▣

🔢 0.00 🔢 0.00 **Global Days XXX**

AMA: 2008, Apr, 3-4; 2008, Apr, 3-4; 2008, Apr, 3-4; 2006, Mar, 15; 2006, Mar, 15; 2006, Feb, 10-15; 2006, Feb, 10-15; 2006, Dec, 10-12; 2006, Dec, 10-12; 2006, Dec, 10-12; 2006, December, 10-12; 2006, December, 10-12; 2006, December, 10-12; 2006, February, 10-15; 2006, March, 15; 2006, Dec, 10-12; 2006, Dec, 10-12; 2006, Dec, 10-12; 2006, Dec, 10-12; 2006, Dec, 10-12; 2004, Jan, 27; 2004, January, 27; 2004, Jan, 27

00944 vaginal hysterectomy ♀Ⓒ▣

🔢 0.00 🔢 0.00 **Global Days XXX**

AMA: 2008, Apr, 3-4; 2008, Apr, 3-4; 2008, Apr, 3-4; 2006, Feb, 10-15; 2006, Feb, 10-15; 2006, Mar, 15; 2006, Mar, 15; 2006, Dec, 10-12; 2006, Dec, 10-12; 2006, Dec, 10-12; 2006, December, 10-12; 2006, December, 10-12; 2006, December, 10-12; 2006, February, 10-15; 2006, March, 15; 2006, Dec, 10-12; 2006, Dec, 10-12; 2006, Dec, 10-12; 2006, Dec, 10-12; 2006, Dec, 10-12; 2004, Jan, 27; 2004, January, 27; 2004, Jan, 27

00948 cervical cerclage ♀Ⓝ▣

🔢 0.00 🔢 0.00 **Global Days XXX**

AMA: 2008, Apr, 3-4; 2008, Apr, 3-4; 2008, Apr, 3-4; 2006, Mar, 15; 2006, Mar, 15; 2006, Feb, 10-15; 2006, Feb, 10-15; 2006, Dec, 10-12; 2006, Dec, 10-12; 2006, Dec, 10-12; 2006, December, 10-12; 2006, December, 10-12; 2006, December, 10-12; 2006, February, 10-15; 2006, March, 15; 2006, Dec, 10-12; 2006, Dec, 10-12; 2006, Dec, 10-12; 2006, Dec, 10-12; 2006, Dec, 10-12; 2004, Jan, 27; 2004, January, 27; 2004, Jan, 27

00950 culdoscopy ♀Ⓝ▣

🔢 0.00 🔢 0.00 **Global Days XXX**

AMA: 2008, Apr, 3-4; 2008, Apr, 3-4; 2008, Apr, 3-4; 2006, Mar, 15; 2006, Mar, 15; 2006, Feb, 10-15; 2006, Feb, 10-15; 2006, Dec, 10-12; 2006, Dec, 10-12; 2006, Dec, 10-12; 2006, December, 10-12; 2006, December, 10-12; 2006, December, 10-12; 2006, February, 10-15; 2006, March, 15; 2006, Dec, 10-12; 2006, Dec, 10-12; 2006, Dec, 10-12; 2006, Dec, 10-12; 2006, Dec, 10-12; 2004, Jan, 27; 2004, January, 27; 2004, Jan, 27

00952 hysteroscopy and/or hysterosalpingography ♀Ⓝ▣

🔢 0.00 🔢 0.00 **Global Days XXX**

AMA: 2008, Apr, 3-4; 2008, Apr, 3-4; 2008, Apr, 3-4; 2006, Feb, 10-15; 2006, Feb, 10-15; 2006, Mar, 15; 2006, Mar, 15; 2006, Dec, 10-12; 2006, Dec, 10-12; 2006, Dec, 10-12; 2006, December, 10-12; 2006, December, 10-12; 2006, December, 10-12; 2006, February, 10-15; 2006, March, 15; 2006, Dec, 10-12; 2006, Dec, 10-12; 2006, Dec, 10-12; 2006, Dec, 10-12; 2006, Dec, 10-12; 2004, Jan, 27; 2004, January, 27; 2004, Jan, 27

01112-01522 Anesthesia for Lower Extremity Procedures

CMS 100-4,12,140.3.2 *Calculation of Anesthesia Time*
CMS 100-4,12,140.2 *Payment for CRNA Services*
CMS 100-4,12,140 *Certified Registered Nurse Anesthetist Services*
CMS 100-4,4,20.6.4 *Modifiers for Discontinued Services*
CMS 100-4,4,20.6 *Modifier Use Under OPPS*
CMS 100-4,4,10.4 *Packaging Rules Under OPPS*
CMS 100-4,12,50 *Anesthesia Services*

01112 Anesthesia for bone marrow aspiration and/or biopsy, anterior or posterior iliac crest Ⓝ▣

🔢 0.00 🔢 0.00 **Global Days XXX**

AMA: 2008, Apr, 3-4; 2008, Apr, 3-4; 2008, Apr, 3-4; 2006, Feb, 10-15; 2006, Feb, 10-15; 2006, Mar, 15; 2006, Mar, 15; 2006, Dec, 10-12; 2006, Dec, 10-12; 2006, Dec, 10-12; 2006, December, 10-12; 2006, December, 10-12; 2006, December, 10-12; 2006, February, 10-15; 2006, March, 15; 2006, Dec, 10-12; 2006, Dec, 10-12; 2006, Dec, 10-12; 2006, Dec, 10-12; 2006, Dec, 10-12; 2004, Jan, 27; 2004, January, 27; 2004, Jan, 27

01120 Anesthesia for procedures on bony pelvis Ⓝ▣

🔢 0.00 🔢 0.00 **Global Days XXX**

AMA: 2008, Apr, 3-4; 2008, Apr, 3-4; 2008, Apr, 3-4; 2006, Mar, 15; 2006, Mar, 15; 2006, Feb, 10-15; 2006, Feb, 10-15; 2006, Dec, 10-12; 2006, Dec, 10-12; 2006, Dec, 10-12; 2006, December, 10-12; 2006, December, 10-12; 2006, December, 10-12; 2006, February, 10-15; 2006, March, 15; 2006, Dec, 10-12; 2006, Dec, 10-12; 2006, Dec, 10-12; 2006, Dec, 10-12; 2006, Dec, 10-12; 2004, Jan, 27; 2004, January, 27; 2004, Jan, 27

01130 Anesthesia for body cast application or revision N ☐
    ✍ 0.00 ✎ 0.00 Global Days XXX
    AMA: 2008, Apr, 3-4; 2008, Apr, 3-4; 2008, Apr, 3-4; 2006, Mar, 15; 2006, Mar, 15; 2006, Feb, 10-15; 2006, Feb, 10-15; 2006, Dec, 10-12; 2006, Dec, 10-12; 2006, Dec, 10-12; 2006, December, 10-12; 2006, December, 10-12; 2006, December, 10-12; 2006, December, 10-12; 2006, February, 10-15; 2006, March, 15; 2006, Dec, 10-12; 2006, Dec, 10-12; 2006, Dec, 10-12; 2006, Dec, 10-12; 2006, Dec, 10-12; 2004, Jan, 27; 2004, January, 27; 2004, Jan, 27

01140 Anesthesia for interpelviabdominal (hindquarter) amputation C ☐
    ✍ 0.00 ✎ 0.00 Global Days XXX
    AMA: 2008, Apr, 3-4; 2008, Apr, 3-4; 2008, Apr, 3-4; 2006, Mar, 15; 2006, Mar, 15; 2006, Feb, 10-15; 2006, Feb, 10-15; 2006, Dec, 10-12; 2006, Dec, 10-12; 2006, Dec, 10-12; 2006, December, 10-12; 2006, December, 10-12; 2006, December, 10-12; 2006, December, 10-12; 2006, February, 10-15; 2006, March, 15; 2006, Dec, 10-12; 2006, Dec, 10-12; 2006, Dec, 10-12; 2006, Dec, 10-12; 2006, Dec, 10-12; 2004, Jan, 27; 2004, January, 27; 2004, Jan, 27

01150 Anesthesia for radical procedures for tumor of pelvis, except hindquarter amputation C ☐
    ✍ 0.00 ✎ 0.00 Global Days XXX
    AMA: 2008, Apr, 3-4; 2008, Apr, 3-4; 2008, Apr, 3-4; 2006, Mar, 15; 2006, Mar, 15; 2006, Feb, 10-15; 2006, Feb, 10-15; 2006, Dec, 10-12; 2006, Dec, 10-12; 2006, Dec, 10-12; 2006, December, 10-12; 2006, December, 10-12; 2006, December, 10-12; 2006, December, 10-12; 2006, February, 10-15; 2006, March, 15; 2006, Dec, 10-12; 2006, Dec, 10-12; 2006, Dec, 10-12; 2006, Dec, 10-12; 2006, Dec, 10-12; 2004, Jan, 27; 2004, January, 27; 2004, Jan, 27

01160 Anesthesia for closed procedures involving symphysis pubis or sacroiliac joint N ☐
    ✍ 0.00 ✎ 0.00 Global Days XXX
    AMA: 2008, Apr, 3-4; 2008, Apr, 3-4; 2008, Apr, 3-4; 2006, Feb, 10-15; 2006, Feb, 10-15; 2006, Mar, 15; 2006, Mar, 15; 2006, Dec, 10-12; 2006, Dec, 10-12; 2006, Dec, 10-12; 2006, December, 10-12; 2006, December, 10-12; 2006, December, 10-12; 2006, December, 10-12; 2006, February, 10-15; 2006, March, 15; 2006, Dec, 10-12; 2006, Dec, 10-12; 2006, Dec, 10-12; 2006, Dec, 10-12; 2006, Dec, 10-12; 2004, Jan, 27; 2004, January, 27; 2004, Jan, 27

01170 Anesthesia for open procedures involving symphysis pubis or sacroiliac joint N ☐
    ✍ 0.00 ✎ 0.00 Global Days XXX
    AMA: 2008, Apr, 3-4; 2008, Apr, 3-4; 2008, Apr, 3-4; 2006, Mar, 15; 2006, Mar, 15; 2006, Feb, 10-15; 2006, Feb, 10-15; 2006, Dec, 10-12; 2006, Dec, 10-12; 2006, Dec, 10-12; 2006, December, 10-12; 2006, December, 10-12; 2006, December, 10-12; 2006, March, 15; 2006, February, 10-15; 2006, Dec, 10-12; 2006, Dec, 10-12; 2006, Dec, 10-12; 2006, Dec, 10-12; 2006, Dec, 10-12; 2004, Jan, 27; 2004, January, 27; 2004, Jan, 27

01173 Anesthesia for open repair of fracture disruption of pelvis or column fracture involving acetabulum N ☐
    ✍ 0.00 ✎ 0.00 Global Days XXX
    AMA: 2008, Apr, 3-4; 2008, Apr, 3-4; 2008, Apr, 3-4; 2006, Mar, 15; 2006, Mar, 15; 2006, Feb, 10-15; 2006, Dec, 10-12; 2006, Feb, 10-15; 2006, Dec, 10-12; 2006, Dec, 10-12; 2006, Dec, 10-12; 2006, Dec, 10-12; 2006, December, 10-12; 2006, December, 10-12; 2006, December, 10-12; 2006, December, 10-12; 2006, February, 10-15; 2006, March, 15; 2006, Dec, 10-12; 2006, Dec, 10-12; 2006, Dec, 10-12; 2004, Jun, 1; 2004, June, 1; 2004, January, 27; 2004, Jun, 1; 2004, Jan, 27; 2004, Jan, 27

01180 Anesthesia for obturator neurectomy; extrapelvic N ☐
    ✍ 0.00 ✎ 0.00 Global Days XXX
    AMA: 2008, Apr, 3-4; 2008, Apr, 3-4; 2008, Apr, 3-4; 2006, Mar, 15; 2006, Mar, 15; 2006, Feb, 10-15; 2006, Feb, 10-15; 2006, Dec, 10-12; 2006, Dec, 10-12; 2006, Dec, 10-12; 2006, December, 10-12; 2006, December, 10-12; 2006, December, 10-12; 2006, December, 10-12; 2006, February, 10-15; 2006, March, 15; 2006, Dec, 10-12; 2006, Dec, 10-12; 2006, Dec, 10-12; 2006, Dec, 10-12; 2006, Dec, 10-12; 2004, Jan, 27; 2004, January, 27; 2004, Jan, 27

01190 intrapelvic N ☐
    ✍ 0.00 ✎ 0.00 Global Days XXX
    AMA: 2008, Apr, 3-4; 2008, Apr, 3-4; 2008, Apr, 3-4; 2006, Mar, 15; 2006, Mar, 15; 2006, Feb, 10-15; 2006, Feb, 10-15; 2006, Dec, 10-12; 2006, Dec, 10-12; 2006, Dec, 10-12; 2006, December, 10-12; 2006, December, 10-12; 2006, December, 10-12; 2006, February, 10-15; 2006, March, 15; 2006, Dec, 10-12; 2006, Dec, 10-12; 2006, Dec, 10-12; 2006, Dec, 10-12; 2006, Dec, 10-12; 2004, Jan, 27; 2004, January, 27; 2004, Jan, 27

01200 Anesthesia for all closed procedures involving hip joint N ☐
    ✍ 0.00 ✎ 0.00 Global Days XXX
    AMA: 2008, Apr, 3-4; 2008, Apr, 3-4; 2008, Apr, 3-4; 2006, Feb, 10-15; 2006, Feb, 10-15; 2006, Mar, 15; 2006, Mar, 15; 2006, Dec, 10-12; 2006, Dec, 10-12; 2006, Dec, 10-12; 2006, December, 10-12; 2006, December, 10-12; 2006, December, 10-12; 2006, December, 10-12; 2006, February, 10-15; 2006, March, 15; 2006, Dec, 10-12; 2006, Dec, 10-12; 2006, Dec, 10-12; 2006, Dec, 10-12; 2006, Dec, 10-12; 2004, Jan, 27; 2004, January, 27; 2004, Jan, 27

01202 Anesthesia for arthroscopic procedures of hip joint N ☐
    ✍ 0.00 ✎ 0.00 Global Days XXX
    AMA: 2008, Apr, 3-4; 2008, Apr, 3-4; 2008, Apr, 3-4; 2006, Mar, 15; 2006, Mar, 15; 2006, Feb, 10-15; 2006, Feb, 10-15; 2006, Dec, 10-12; 2006, Dec, 10-12; 2006, Dec, 10-12; 2006, December, 10-12; 2006, December, 10-12; 2006, December, 10-12; 2006, February, 10-15; 2006, March, 15; 2006, Dec, 10-12; 2006, Dec, 10-12; 2006, Dec, 10-12; 2006, Dec, 10-12; 2006, Dec, 10-12; 2004, Jan, 27; 2004, January, 27; 2004, Jan, 27

01210 Anesthesia for open procedures involving hip joint; not otherwise specified N ☐
    ✍ 0.00 ✎ 0.00 Global Days XXX
    AMA: 2008, Apr, 3-4; 2008, Apr, 3-4; 2008, Apr, 3-4; 2006, Mar, 15; 2006, Mar, 15; 2006, Feb, 10-15; 2006, Feb, 10-15; 2006, Dec, 10-12; 2006, Dec, 10-12; 2006, Dec, 10-12; 2006, December, 10-12; 2006, December, 10-12; 2006, December, 10-12; 2006, February, 10-15; 2006, March, 15; 2006, Dec, 10-12; 2006, Dec, 10-12; 2006, Dec, 10-12; 2006, Dec, 10-12; 2006, Dec, 10-12; 2004, Jan, 27; 2004, January, 27; 2004, Jan, 27

01212 hip disarticulation C ☐
    ✍ 0.00 ✎ 0.00 Global Days XXX
    AMA: 2008, Apr, 3-4; 2008, Apr, 3-4; 2008, Apr, 3-4; 2006, Mar, 15; 2006, Mar, 15; 2006, Feb, 10-15; 2006, Feb, 10-15; 2006, Dec, 10-12; 2006, Dec, 10-12; 2006, Dec, 10-12; 2006, December, 10-12; 2006, December, 10-12; 2006, December, 10-12; 2006, December, 10-12; 2006, February, 10-15; 2006, March, 15; 2006, Dec, 10-12; 2006, Dec, 10-12; 2006, Dec, 10-12; 2006, Dec, 10-12; 2006, Dec, 10-12; 2004, Jan, 27; 2004, January, 27; 2004, Jan, 27

● New Code ▲ Revised Code M Maternity Edit A Age Edit A-Y OPPS Status Indicator ✍ Facility RVU ✎ Non-Facility RVU
☐ CCI Comprehensive Code 50 Bilateral Procedure + Add-on Indicator ☒ Laboratory crosswalk ☒ Radiology crosswalk

01214　total hip arthroplasty 　🅒▢
🔲 0.00　✂ 0.00　**Global Days XXX**
AMA: 2008, Apr, 3-4; 2008, Apr, 3-4; 2008, Apr, 3-4; 2006, Mar, 15; 2006, Mar, 15; 2006, Feb, 10-15; 2006, Feb, 10-15; 2006, Dec, 10-12; 2006, Dec, 10-12; 2006, Dec, 10-12; 2006, December, 10-12; 2006, December, 10-12; 2006, December, 10-12; 2006, February, 10-15; 2006, March, 15; 2006, Dec, 10-12; 2006, Dec, 10-12; 2006, Dec, 10-12; 2006, Dec, 10-12; 2006, Dec, 10-12; 2004, Jan, 27; 2004, January, 27; 2004, Jan, 27

01215　revision of total hip arthroplasty 　🅝▢
🔲 0.00　✂ 0.00　**Global Days XXX**
AMA: 2008, Apr, 3-4; 2008, Apr, 3-4; 2008, Apr, 3-4; 2006, Mar, 15; 2006, Mar, 15; 2006, Feb, 10-15; 2006, Feb, 10-15; 2006, Dec, 10-12; 2006, Dec, 10-12; 2006, Dec, 10-12; 2006, December, 10-12; 2006, December, 10-12; 2006, December, 10-12; 2006, February, 10-15; 2006, March, 15; 2006, Dec, 10-12; 2006, Dec, 10-12; 2006, Dec, 10-12; 2006, Dec, 10-12; 2006, Dec, 10-12; 2004, Jan, 27; 2004, January, 27; 2004, Jan, 27

01220　Anesthesia for all closed procedures involving upper 2/3 of femur 　🅝▢
🔲 0.00　✂ 0.00　**Global Days XXX**
AMA: 2008, Apr, 3-4; 2008, Apr, 3-4; 2008, Apr, 3-4; 2006, Mar, 15; 2006, Mar, 15; 2006, Feb, 10-15; 2006, Feb, 10-15; 2006, Dec, 10-12; 2006, Dec, 10-12; 2006, Dec, 10-12; 2006, December, 10-12; 2006, December, 10-12; 2006, December, 10-12; 2006, February, 10-15; 2006, March, 15; 2006, Dec, 10-12; 2006, Dec, 10-12; 2006, Dec, 10-12; 2006, Dec, 10-12; 2006, Dec, 10-12; 2004, Jan, 27; 2004, January, 27; 2004, Jan, 27

01230　Anesthesia for open procedures involving upper 2/3 of femur; not otherwise specified 　🅝▢
🔲 0.00　✂ 0.00　**Global Days XXX**
AMA: 2008, Apr, 3-4; 2008, Apr, 3-4; 2008, Apr, 3-4; 2006, Mar, 15; 2006, Mar, 15; 2006, Feb, 10-15; 2006, Feb, 10-15; 2006, Dec, 10-12; 2006, Dec, 10-12; 2006, Dec, 10-12; 2006, December, 10-12; 2006, December, 10-12; 2006, December, 10-12; 2006, February, 10-15; 2006, March, 15; 2006, Dec, 10-12; 2006, Dec, 10-12; 2006, Dec, 10-12; 2006, Dec, 10-12; 2006, Dec, 10-12; 2004, Jan, 27; 2004, January, 27; 2004, Jan, 27

01232　amputation 　🅒▢
🔲 0.00　✂ 0.00　**Global Days XXX**
AMA: 2008, Apr, 3-4; 2008, Apr, 3-4; 2008, Apr, 3-4; 2006, Mar, 15; 2006, Mar, 15; 2006, Feb, 10-15; 2006, Feb, 10-15; 2006, Dec, 10-12; 2006, Dec, 10-12; 2006, Dec, 10-12; 2006, December, 10-12; 2006, December, 10-12; 2006, December, 10-12; 2006, February, 10-15; 2006, March, 15; 2006, Dec, 10-12; 2006, Dec, 10-12; 2006, Dec, 10-12; 2006, Dec, 10-12; 2006, Dec, 10-12; 2004, Jan, 27; 2004, January, 27; 2004, Jan, 27

01234　radical resection 　🅒▢
🔲 0.00　✂ 0.00　**Global Days XXX**
AMA: 2008, Apr, 3-4; 2008, Apr, 3-4; 2008, Apr, 3-4; 2006, Mar, 15; 2006, Mar, 15; 2006, Feb, 10-15; 2006, Feb, 10-15; 2006, Dec, 10-12; 2006, Dec, 10-12; 2006, Dec, 10-12; 2006, December, 10-12; 2006, December, 10-12; 2006, December, 10-12; 2006, March, 15; 2006, February, 10-15; 2006, Dec, 10-12; 2006, Dec, 10-12; 2006, Dec, 10-12; 2006, Dec, 10-12; 2006, Dec, 10-12; 2004, Jan, 27; 2004, January, 27; 2004, Jan, 27

01250　Anesthesia for all procedures on nerves, muscles, tendons, fascia, and bursae of upper leg 　🅝▢
🔲 0.00　✂ 0.00　**Global Days XXX**
AMA: 2008, Apr, 3-4; 2008, Apr, 3-4; 2008, Apr, 3-4; 2006, Feb, 10-15; 2006, Feb, 10-15; 2006, Mar, 15; 2006, Mar, 15; 2006, Dec, 10-12; 2006, Dec, 10-12; 2006, Dec, 10-12; 2006, December, 10-12; 2006, December, 10-12; 2006, February, 10-15; 2006, March, 15; 2006, Dec, 10-12; 2006, Dec, 10-12; 2006, Dec, 10-12; 2006, Dec, 10-12; 2004, Jan, 27; 2004, January, 27; 2004, Jan, 27

01260　Anesthesia for all procedures involving veins of upper leg, including exploration 　🅝▢
🔲 0.00　✂ 0.00　**Global Days XXX**
AMA: 2008, Apr, 3-4; 2008, Apr, 3-4; 2008, Apr, 3-4; 2006, Mar, 15; 2006, Mar, 15; 2006, Feb, 10-15; 2006, Feb, 10-15; 2006, Dec, 10-12; 2006, Dec, 10-12; 2006, Dec, 10-12; 2006, December, 10-12; 2006, December, 10-12; 2006, December, 10-12; 2006, February, 10-15; 2006, March, 15; 2006, Dec, 10-12; 2006, Dec, 10-12; 2006, Dec, 10-12; 2006, Dec, 10-12; 2006, Dec, 10-12; 2004, Jan, 27; 2004, January, 27; 2004, Jan, 27

01270　Anesthesia for procedures involving arteries of upper leg, including bypass graft; not otherwise specified 　🅝▢
🔲 0.00　✂ 0.00　**Global Days XXX**
AMA: 2008, Apr, 3-4; 2008, Apr, 3-4; 2008, Apr, 3-4; 2006, Feb, 10-15; 2006, Feb, 10-15; 2006, Mar, 15; 2006, Mar, 15; 2006, Dec, 10-12; 2006, Dec, 10-12; 2006, Dec, 10-12; 2006, December, 10-12; 2006, December, 10-12; 2006, February, 10-15; 2006, March, 15; 2006, Dec, 10-12; 2006, Dec, 10-12; 2006, Dec, 10-12; 2006, Dec, 10-12; 2006, Dec, 10-12; 2004, Jan, 27; 2004, January, 27; 2004, Jan, 27

01272　femoral artery ligation 　🅒▢
🔲 0.00　✂ 0.00　**Global Days XXX**
AMA: 2008, Apr, 3-4; 2008, Apr, 3-4; 2008, Apr, 3-4; 2006, Mar, 15; 2006, Mar, 15; 2006, Feb, 10-15; 2006, Feb, 10-15; 2006, Dec, 10-12; 2006, Dec, 10-12; 2006, Dec, 10-12; 2006, December, 10-12; 2006, December, 10-12; 2006, December, 10-12; 2006, February, 10-15; 2006, March, 15; 2006, Dec, 10-12; 2006, Dec, 10-12; 2006, Dec, 10-12; 2006, Dec, 10-12; 2006, Dec, 10-12; 2004, Jan, 27; 2004, January, 27; 2004, Jan, 27

01274　femoral artery embolectomy 　🅒▢
🔲 0.00　✂ 0.00　**Global Days XXX**
AMA: 2008, Apr, 3-4; 2008, Apr, 3-4; 2008, Apr, 3-4; 2006, Mar, 15; 2006, Mar, 15; 2006, Feb, 10-15; 2006, Feb, 10-15; 2006, Dec, 10-12; 2006, Dec, 10-12; 2006, Dec, 10-12; 2006, December, 10-12; 2006, December, 10-12; 2006, December, 10-12; 2006, February, 10-15; 2006, March, 15; 2006, Dec, 10-12; 2006, Dec, 10-12; 2006, Dec, 10-12; 2006, Dec, 10-12; 2006, Dec, 10-12; 2004, Jan, 27; 2004, January, 27; 2004, Jan, 27

01320　Anesthesia for all procedures on nerves, muscles, tendons, fascia, and bursae of knee and/or popliteal area 　🅝▢
🔲 0.00　✂ 0.00　**Global Days XXX**
AMA: 2008, Apr, 3-4; 2008, Apr, 3-4; 2008, Apr, 3-4; 2006, Mar, 15; 2006, Mar, 15; 2006, Feb, 10-15; 2006, Feb, 10-15; 2006, Dec, 10-12; 2006, Dec, 10-12; 2006, Dec, 10-12; 2006, December, 10-12; 2006, December, 10-12; 2006, December, 10-12; 2006, February, 10-15; 2006, March, 15; 2006, Dec, 10-12; 2006, Dec, 10-12; 2006, Dec, 10-12; 2006, Dec, 10-12; 2006, Dec, 10-12; 2004, Jan, 27; 2004, January, 27; 2004, Jan, 27

01340 Anesthesia for all closed procedures on lower 1/3 of femur Ⓝ ▱

   💲 0.00 ⚭ 0.00 Global Days XXX

AMA: 2008, Apr, 3-4; 2008, Apr, 3-4; 2008, Apr, 3-4; 2006, Feb, 10-15; 2006, Feb, 10-15; 2006, Mar, 15; 2006, Mar, 15; 2006, Dec, 10-12; 2006, Dec, 10-12; 2006, Dec, 10-12; 2006, December, 10-12; 2006, December, 10-12; 2006, December, 10-12; 2006, February, 10-15; 2006, March, 15; 2006, Dec, 10-12; 2006, Dec, 10-12; 2006, Dec, 10-12; 2006, Dec, 10-12; 2006, Dec, 10-12; 2004, Jan, 27; 2004, January, 27; 2004, Jan, 27

01360 Anesthesia for all open procedures on lower 1/3 of femur Ⓝ ▱

   💲 0.00 ⚭ 0.00 Global Days XXX

AMA: 2008, Apr, 3-4; 2008, Apr, 3-4; 2008, Apr, 3-4; 2006, Mar, 15; 2006, Mar, 15; 2006, Feb, 10-15; 2006, Feb, 10-15; 2006, Dec, 10-12; 2006, Dec, 10-12; 2006, Dec, 10-12; 2006, December, 10-12; 2006, December, 10-12; 2006, December, 10-12; 2006, February, 10-15; 2006, March, 15; 2006, Dec, 10-12; 2006, Dec, 10-12; 2006, Dec, 10-12; 2006, Dec, 10-12; 2006, Dec, 10-12; 2004, Jan, 27; 2004, January, 27; 2004, Jan, 27

01380 Anesthesia for all closed procedures on knee joint Ⓝ ▱

   💲 0.00 ⚭ 0.00 Global Days XXX

AMA: 2008, Apr, 3-4; 2008, Apr, 3-4; 2008, Apr, 3-4; 2006, Mar, 15; 2006, Mar, 15; 2006, Feb, 10-15; 2006, Feb, 10-15; 2006, Dec, 10-12; 2006, Dec, 10-12; 2006, Dec, 10-12; 2006, December, 10-12; 2006, December, 10-12; 2006, December, 10-12; 2006, February, 10-15; 2006, March, 15; 2006, Dec, 10-12; 2006, Dec, 10-12; 2006, Dec, 10-12; 2006, Dec, 10-12; 2006, Dec, 10-12; 2004, Jan, 27; 2004, January, 27; 2004, Jan, 27

01382 Anesthesia for diagnostic arthroscopic procedures of knee joint Ⓝ ▱

   💲 0.00 ⚭ 0.00 Global Days XXX

AMA: 2008, Apr, 3-4; 2008, Apr, 3-4; 2008, Apr, 3-4; 2006, Mar, 15; 2006, Mar, 15; 2006, Feb, 10-15; 2006, Feb, 10-15; 2006, Dec, 10-12; 2006, Dec, 10-12; 2006, Dec, 10-12; 2006, December, 10-12; 2006, December, 10-12; 2006, December, 10-12; 2006, February, 10-15; 2006, March, 15; 2006, Dec, 10-12; 2006, Dec, 10-12; 2006, Dec, 10-12; 2006, Dec, 10-12; 2006, Dec, 10-12; 2004, Jan, 27; 2004, January, 27; 2004, Jan, 27

01390 Anesthesia for all closed procedures on upper ends of tibia, fibula, and/or patella Ⓝ ▱

   💲 0.00 ⚭ 0.00 Global Days XXX

AMA: 2008, Apr, 3-4; 2008, Apr, 3-4; 2008, Apr, 3-4; 2006, Mar, 15; 2006, Mar, 15; 2006, Feb, 10-15; 2006, Feb, 10-16; 2006, Dec, 10-12; 2006, Dec, 10-12; 2006, Dec, 10-12; 2006, December, 10-12; 2006, December, 10-12; 2006, December, 10-12; 2006, February, 10-15; 2006, March, 15; 2006, Dec, 10-12; 2006, Dec, 10-12; 2006, Dec, 10-12; 2006, Dec, 10-12; 2006, Dec, 10-12; 2004, Jan, 27; 2004, January, 27; 2004, Jan, 27

01392 Anesthesia for all open procedures on upper ends of tibia, fibula, and/or patella Ⓝ ▱

   💲 0.00 ⚭ 0.00 Global Days XXX

AMA: 2008, Apr, 3-4; 2008, Apr, 3-4; 2008, Apr, 3-4; 2006, Feb, 10-15; 2006, Feb, 10-15; 2006, Mar, 15; 2006, Mar, 15; 2006, Dec, 10-12; 2006, Dec, 10-12; 2006, Dec, 10-12; 2006, December, 10-12; 2006, December, 10-12; 2006, December, 10-12; 2006, March, 15; 2006, February, 10-15; 2006, Dec, 10-12; 2006, Dec, 10-12; 2006, Dec, 10-12; 2006, Dec, 10-12; 2006, Dec, 10-12; 2004, Jan, 27; 2004, January, 27; 2004, Jan, 27

01400 Anesthesia for open or surgical arthroscopic procedures on knee joint; not otherwise specified Ⓝ ▱

   💲 0.00 ⚭ 0.00 Global Days XXX

AMA: 2008, Apr, 3-4; 2008, Apr, 3-4; 2008, Apr, 3-4; 2006, Mar, 15; 2006, Mar, 15; 2006, Feb, 10-15; 2006, Feb, 10-15; 2006, Dec, 10-12; 2006, Dec, 10-12; 2006, Dec, 10-12; 2006, December, 10-12; 2006, December, 10-12; 2006, December, 10-12; 2006, February, 10-15; 2006, March, 15; 2006, Dec, 10-12; 2006, Dec, 10-12; 2006, Dec, 10-12; 2006, Dec, 10-12; 2006, Dec, 10-12; 2004, Jan, 27; 2004, January, 27; 2004, Jan, 27

01402 total knee arthroplasty Ⓒ ▱

   💲 0.00 ⚭ 0.00 Global Days XXX

AMA: 2008, Apr, 3-4; 2008, Apr, 3-4; 2008, Apr, 3-4; 2006, Mar, 15; 2006, Mar, 15; 2006, Feb, 10-15; 2006, Feb, 10-15; 2006, Dec, 10-12; 2006, Dec, 10-12; 2006, Dec, 10-12; 2006, December, 10-12; 2006, December, 10-12; 2006, December, 10-12; 2006, February, 10-15; 2006, March, 15; 2006, Dec, 10-12; 2006, Dec, 10-12; 2006, Dec, 10-12; 2006, Dec, 10-12; 2006, Dec, 10-12; 2004, Jan, 27; 2004, January, 27; 2004, Jan, 27

01404 disarticulation at knee Ⓒ ▱

   💲 0.00 ⚭ 0.00 Global Days XXX

AMA: 2008, Apr, 3-4; 2008, Apr, 3-4; 2008, Apr, 3-4; 2006, Feb, 10-15; 2006, Feb, 10-15; 2006, Mar, 15; 2006, Mar, 15; 2006, Dec, 10-12; 2006, Dec, 10-12; 2006, Dec, 10-12; 2006, December, 10-12; 2006, December, 10-12; 2006, December, 10-12; 2006, February, 10-15; 2006, March, 15; 2006, Dec, 10-12; 2006, Dec, 10-12; 2006, Dec, 10-12; 2006, Dec, 10-12; 2006, Dec, 10-12; 2004, Jan, 27; 2004, January, 27; 2004, Jan, 27

01420 Anesthesia for all cast applications, removal, or repair involving knee joint Ⓝ ▱

   💲 0.00 ⚭ 0.00 Global Days XXX

AMA: 2008, Apr, 3-4; 2008, Apr, 3-4; 2008, Apr, 3-4; 2006, Mar, 15; 2006, Mar, 15; 2006, Feb, 10-15; 2006, Feb, 10-15; 2006, Dec, 10-12; 2006, Dec, 10-12; 2006, Dec, 10-12; 2006, December, 10-12; 2006, December, 10-12; 2006, December, 10-12; 2006, February, 10-15; 2006, March, 15; 2006, Dec, 10-12; 2006, Dec, 10-12; 2006, Dec, 10-12; 2006, Dec, 10-12; 2006, Dec, 10-12; 2004, Jan, 27; 2004, January, 27; 2004, Jan, 27

01430 Anesthesia for procedures on veins of knee and popliteal area; not otherwise specified Ⓝ ▱

   💲 0.00 ⚭ 0.00 Global Days XXX

AMA: 2008, Apr, 3-4; 2008, Apr, 3-4; 2008, Apr, 3-4; 2006, Mar, 15; 2006, Mar, 15; 2006, Feb, 10-15; 2006, Feb, 10-15; 2006, Dec, 10-12; 2006, Dec, 10-12; 2006, Dec, 10-12; 2006, December, 10-12; 2006, December, 10-12; 2006, December, 10-12; 2006, February, 10-15; 2006, March, 15; 2006, Dec, 10-12; 2006, Dec, 10-12; 2006, Dec, 10-12; 2006, Dec, 10-12; 2006, Dec, 10-12; 2004, Jan, 27; 2004, January, 27; 2004, Jan, 27

01432 arteriovenous fistula Ⓝ ▱

   💲 0.00 ⚭ 0.00 Global Days XXX

AMA: 2008, Apr, 3-4; 2008, Apr, 3-4; 2008, Apr, 3-4; 2006, Feb, 10-15; 2006, Feb, 10-15; 2006, Mar, 15; 2006, Mar, 15; 2006, Dec, 10-12; 2006, Dec, 10-12; 2006, Dec, 10-12; 2006, December, 10-12; 2006, December, 10-12; 2006, December, 10-12; 2006, February, 10-15; 2006, March, 15; 2006, Dec, 10-12; 2006, Dec, 10-12; 2006, Dec, 10-12; 2006, Dec, 10-12; 2006, Dec, 10-12; 2004, Jan, 27; 2004, January, 27; 2004, Jan, 27

● New Code   ▲ Revised Code   Ⓜ Maternity Edit   Ⓐ Age Edit   Ⓐ-Ⓨ OPPS Status Indicator   💲 Facility RVU   ⚭ Non-Facility RVU

Ⓒ CCI Comprehensive Code   🔟 Bilateral Procedure   + Add-on Indicator   ▱ Laboratory crosswalk   ▱ Radiology crosswalk

Anesthesia

01440 — 01486

01440   Anesthesia for procedures on arteries of knee and popliteal area; not otherwise specified   N ▫
   🔲 0.00   ⚖ 0.00   **Global Days XXX**
   AMA: 2008, Apr, 3-4; 2008, Apr, 3-4; 2008, Apr, 3-4; 2006, Feb, 10-15; 2006, Feb, 10-15; 2006, Mar, 15; 2006, Mar, 15; 2006, Dec, 10-12; 2006, Dec, 10-12; 2006, Dec, 10-12; 2006, December, 10-12; 2006, December, 10-12; 2006, December, 10-12; 2006, February, 10-15; 2006, March, 15; 2006, Dec, 10-12; 2006, Dec, 10-12; 2006, Dec, 10-12; 2006, Dec, 10-12; 2006, Dec, 10-12; 2004, Jan, 27; 2004, January, 27; 2004, Jan, 27

01442   popliteal thromboendarterectomy, with or without patch graft   C ▫
   🔲 0.00   ⚖ 0.00   **Global Days XXX**
   AMA: 2008, Apr, 3-4; 2008, Apr, 3-4; 2008, Apr, 3-4; 2006, Mar, 15; 2006, Mar, 15; 2006, Feb, 10-15; 2006, Feb, 10-15; 2006, Dec, 10-12; 2006, Dec, 10-12; 2006, Dec, 10-12; 2006, December, 10-12; 2006, December, 10-12; 2006, December, 10-12; 2006, February, 10-15; 2006, March, 15; 2006, Dec, 10-12; 2006, Dec, 10-12; 2006, Dec, 10-12; 2006, Dec, 10-12; 2006, Dec, 10-12; 2004, Jan, 27; 2004, January, 27; 2004, Jan, 27

01444   popliteal excision and graft or repair for occlusion or aneurysm   C ▫
   🔲 0.00   ⚖ 0.00   **Global Days XXX**
   AMA: 2008, Apr, 3-4; 2008, Apr, 3-4; 2008, Apr, 3-4; 2006, Mar, 15; 2006, Mar, 15; 2006, Feb, 10-15; 2006, Feb, 10-15; 2006, Dec, 10-12; 2006, Dec, 10-12; 2006, Dec, 10-12; 2006, December, 10-12; 2006, December, 10-12; 2006, December, 10-12; 2006, February, 10-15; 2006, March, 15; 2006, Dec, 10-12; 2006, Dec, 10-12; 2006, Dec, 10-12; 2006, Dec, 10-12; 2006, Dec, 10-12; 2004, Jan, 27; 2004, January, 27; 2004, Jan, 27

01462   Anesthesia for all closed procedures on lower leg, ankle, and foot   N ▫
   🔲 0.00   ⚖ 0.00   **Global Days XXX**
   AMA: 2008, Apr, 3-4; 2008, Apr, 3-4; 2008, Apr, 3-4; 2006, Mar, 15; 2006, Mar, 15; 2006, Feb, 10-15; 2006, Feb, 10-15; 2006, Dec, 10-12; 2006, Dec, 10-12; 2006, Dec, 10-12; 2006, December, 10-12; 2006, December, 10-12; 2006, December, 10-12; 2006, February, 10-15; 2006, March, 15; 2006, Dec, 10-12; 2006, Dec, 10-12; 2006, Dec, 10-12; 2006, Dec, 10-12; 2006, Dec, 10-12; 2004, Jan, 27; 2004, January, 27; 2004, Jan, 27

01464   Anesthesia for arthroscopic procedures of ankle and/or foot   N ▫
   🔲 0.00   ⚖ 0.00   **Global Days XXX**
   AMA: 2008, Apr, 3-4; 2008, Apr, 3-4; 2008, Apr, 3-4; 2006, Feb, 10-15; 2006, Feb, 10-15; 2006, Mar, 15; 2006, Mar, 15; 2006, Dec, 10-12; 2006, Dec, 10-12; 2006, Dec, 10-12; 2006, December, 10-12; 2006, December, 10-12; 2006, December, 10-12; 2006, February, 10-15; 2006, March, 15; 2006, Dec, 10-12; 2006, Dec, 10-12; 2006, Dec, 10-12; 2006, Dec, 10-12; 2006, Dec, 10-12; 2004, Jan, 27; 2004, January, 27; 2004, Jan, 27

01470   Anesthesia for procedures on nerves, muscles, tendons, and fascia of lower leg, ankle, and foot; not otherwise specified   N ▫
   🔲 0.00   ⚖ 0.00   **Global Days XXX**
   AMA: 2008, Apr, 3-4; 2008, Apr, 3-4; 2008, Apr, 3-4; 2006, Feb, 10-15; 2006, Feb, 10-15; 2006, Mar, 15; 2006, Mar, 15; 2006, Dec, 10-12; 2006, Dec, 10-12; 2006, Dec, 10-12; 2006, December, 10-12; 2006, December, 10-12; 2006, December, 10-12; 2006, February, 10-15; 2006, March, 15; 2006, Dec, 10-12; 2006, Dec, 10-12; 2006, Dec, 10-12; 2006, Dec, 10-12; 2004, Jan, 27; 2004, January, 27; 2004, Jan, 27

01472   repair of ruptured Achilles tendon, with or without graft   N ▫
   🔲 0.00   ⚖ 0.00   **Global Days XXX**
   AMA: 2008, Apr, 3-4; 2008, Apr, 3-4; 2008, Apr, 3-4; 2006, Mar, 15; 2006, Mar, 15; 2006, Feb, 10-15; 2006, Feb, 10-15; 2006, Dec, 10-12; 2006, Dec, 10-12; 2006, Dec, 10-12; 2006, December, 10-12; 2006, December, 10-12; 2006, December, 10-12; 2006, March, 15; 2006, February, 10-15; 2006, Dec, 10-12; 2006, Dec, 10-12; 2006, Dec, 10-12; 2006, Dec, 10-12; 2006, Dec, 10-12; 2004, Jan, 27; 2004, January, 27; 2004, Jan, 27

01474   gastrocnemius recession (eg, Strayer procedure)   N ▫
   🔲 0.00   ⚖ 0.00   **Global Days XXX**
   AMA: 2008, Apr, 3-4; 2008, Apr, 3-4; 2008, Apr, 3-4; 2006, Mar, 15; 2006, Mar, 15; 2006, Feb, 10-15; 2006, Feb, 10-15; 2006, Dec, 10-12; 2006, Dec, 10-12; 2006, Dec, 10-12; 2006, December, 10-12; 2006, December, 10-12; 2006, December, 10-12; 2006, February, 10-15; 2006, March, 15; 2006, Dec, 10-12; 2006, Dec, 10-12; 2006, Dec, 10-12; 2006, Dec, 10-12; 2006, Dec, 10-12; 2004, Jan, 27; 2004, January, 27; 2004, Jan, 27

01480   Anesthesia for open procedures on bones of lower leg, ankle, and foot; not otherwise specified   N ▫
   🔲 0.00   ⚖ 0.00   **Global Days XXX**
   AMA: 2008, Apr, 3-4; 2008, Apr, 3-4; 2008, Apr, 3-4; 2006, Mar, 15; 2006, Mar, 15; 2006, Feb, 10-15; 2006, Feb, 10-15; 2006, Dec, 10-12; 2006, Dec, 10-12; 2006, Dec, 10-12; 2006, December, 10-12; 2006, December, 10-12; 2006, December, 10-12; 2006, February, 10-15; 2006, March, 15; 2006, Dec, 10-12; 2006, Dec, 10-12; 2006, Dec, 10-12; 2006, Dec, 10-12; 2006, Dec, 10-12; 2004, Jan, 27; 2004, January, 27; 2004, Jan, 27

01482   radical resection (including below knee amputation)   N ▫
   🔲 0.00   ⚖ 0.00   **Global Days XXX**
   AMA: 2008, Apr, 3-4; 2008, Apr, 3-4; 2008, Apr, 3-4; 2006, Mar, 15; 2006, Mar, 15; 2006, Feb, 10-15; 2006, Feb, 10-15; 2006, Dec, 10-12; 2006, Dec, 10-12; 2006, Dec, 10-12; 2006, December, 10-12; 2006, December, 10-12; 2006, December, 10-12; 2006, February, 10-15; 2006, March, 15; 2006, Dec, 10-12; 2006, Dec, 10-12; 2006, Dec, 10-12; 2006, Dec, 10-12; 2006, Dec, 10-12; 2004, Jan, 27; 2004, January, 27; 2004, Jan, 27

01484   osteotomy or osteoplasty of tibia and/or fibula   N ▫
   🔲 0.00   ⚖ 0.00   **Global Days XXX**
   AMA: 2008, Apr, 3-4; 2008, Apr, 3-4; 2008, Apr, 3-4; 2006, Feb, 10-15; 2006, Feb, 10-15; 2006, Mar, 15; 2006, Mar, 15; 2006, Dec, 10-12; 2006, Dec, 10-12; 2006, Dec, 10-12; 2006, December, 10-12; 2006, December, 10-12; 2006, December, 10-12; 2006, February, 10-15; 2006, March, 15; 2006, Dec, 10-12; 2006, Dec, 10-12; 2006, Dec, 10-12; 2006, Dec, 10-12; 2006, Dec, 10-12; 2004, Jan, 27; 2004, January, 27; 2004, Jan, 27

01486   total ankle replacement   C ▫
   🔲 0.00   ⚖ 0.00   **Global Days XXX**
   AMA: 2008, Apr, 3-4; 2008, Apr, 3-4; 2008, Apr, 3-4; 2006, Mar, 15; 2006, Mar, 15; 2006, Feb, 10-15; 2006, Feb, 10-15; 2006, Dec, 10-12; 2006, Dec, 10-12; 2006, Dec, 10-12; 2006, December, 10-12; 2006, December, 10-12; 2006, December, 10-12; 2006, February, 10-15; 2006, March, 15; 2006, Dec, 10-12; 2006, Dec, 10-12; 2006, Dec, 10-12; 2006, Dec, 10-12; 2004, Jan, 27; 2004, January, 27; 2004, Jan, 27

26/TC ▫ Professional/Technical Component Only   80/80 ▫ Assist-at-Surgery Allowed/With Documentation   Unlisted   Not Covered
AMA: CPT Assistant References   A2-Z3 ASC Payment Indicator   ♂ Male Only   ♀ Female Only   ⊘ Modifier 51 Exempt   PQRI

18   CPT only © 2008 American Medical Association. All Rights Reserved. (Black Ink)   Medicare (Red Ink)   © 2008 Ingenix (Blue Ink)

01490 Anesthesia for lower leg cast application, removal, or repair ☐N☐
🔲 0.00 ⚖ 0.00 Global Days XXX
AMA: 2008, Apr, 3-4; 2008, Apr, 3-4; 2008, Apr, 3-4; 2006, Mar, 15; 2006, Mar, 15; 2006, Feb, 10-15; 2006, Feb, 10-15; 2006, Dec, 10-12; 2006, Dec, 10-12; 2006, Dec, 10-12; 2006, December, 10-12; 2006, December, 10-12; 2006, December, 10-12; 2006, December, 10-12; 2006, February, 10-15; 2006, March, 15; 2006, Dec, 10-12; 2006, Dec, 10-12; 2006, Dec, 10-12; 2006, Dec, 10-12; 2006, Dec, 10-12; 2004, Jan, 27; 2004, January, 27; 2004, Jan, 27

01500 Anesthesia for procedures on arteries of lower leg, including bypass graft; not otherwise specified ☐N☐
🔲 0.00 ⚖ 0.00 Global Days XXX
AMA: 2008, Apr, 3-4; 2008, Apr, 3-4; 2008, Apr, 3-4; 2006, Mar, 15; 2006, Mar, 15; 2006, Feb, 10-15; 2006, Feb, 10-15; 2006, Dec, 10-12; 2006, Dec, 10-12; 2006, Dec, 10-12; 2006, December, 10-12; 2006, December, 10-12; 2006, December, 10-12; 2006, December, 10-12; 2006, February, 10-15; 2006, March, 15; 2006, Dec, 10-12; 2006, Dec, 10-12; 2006, Dec, 10-12; 2006, Dec, 10-12; 2006, Dec, 10-12; 2004, Jan, 27; 2004, January, 27; 2004, Jan, 27

01502 embolectomy, direct or with catheter ☐C☐
🔲 0.00 ⚖ 0.00 Global Days XXX
AMA: 2008, Apr, 3-4; 2008, Apr, 3-4; 2008, Apr, 3-4; 2006, Feb, 10-15; 2006, Feb, 10-15; 2006, Mar, 15; 2006, Mar, 15; 2006, Dec, 10-12; 2006, Dec, 10-12; 2006, Dec, 10-12; 2006, December, 10-12; 2006, December, 10-12; 2006, December, 10-12; 2006, December, 10-12; 2006, February, 10-15; 2006, March, 15; 2006, Dec, 10-12; 2006, Dec, 10-12; 2006, Dec, 10-12; 2006, Dec, 10-12; 2006, Dec, 10-12; 2004, Jan, 27; 2004, January, 27; 2004, Jan, 27

01520 Anesthesia for procedures on veins of lower leg; not otherwise specified ☐N☐
🔲 0.00 ⚖ 0.00 Global Days XXX
AMA: 2008, Apr, 3-4; 2008, Apr, 3-4; 2008, Apr, 3-4; 2006, Mar, 15; 2006, Mar, 15; 2006, Feb, 10-15; 2006, Feb, 10-15; 2006, Dec, 10-12; 2006, Dec, 10-12; 2006, Dec, 10-12; 2006, December, 10-12; 2006, December, 10-12; 2006, December, 10-12; 2006, December, 10-12; 2006, February, 10-15; 2006, March, 15; 2006, Dec, 10-12; 2006, Dec, 10-12; 2006, Dec, 10-12; 2006, Dec, 10-12; 2006, Dec, 10-12; 2004, Jan, 27; 2004, January, 27; 2004, Jan, 27

01522 venous thrombectomy, direct or with catheter ☐N☐
🔲 0.00 ⚖ 0.00 Global Days XXX
AMA: 2008, Apr, 3-4; 2008, Apr, 3-4; 2008, Apr, 3-4; 2006, Feb, 10-15; 2006, Feb, 10-15; 2006, Mar, 15; 2006, Mar, 15; 2006, Dec, 10-12; 2006, Dec, 10-12; 2006, Dec, 10-12; 2006, December, 10-12; 2006, December, 10-12; 2006, December, 10-12; 2006, December, 10-12; 2006, February, 10-15; 2006, March, 15; 2006, Dec, 10-12; 2006, Dec, 10-12; 2006, Dec, 10-12; 2006, Dec, 10-12; 2006, Dec, 10-12; 2004, Jan, 27; 2004, January, 27; 2004, Jan, 27

01610-01682 Anesthesia for Shoulder Procedures

CMS *100-4,12,140.3.2 Calculation of Anesthesia Time*
CMS *100-4,12,140.2 Payment for CRNA Services*
CMS *100-4,12,140   Certified Registered Nurse Anesthetist Services*
CMS *100-4,12,50   Anesthesia Services*
INCLUDES   acromioclavicular joint
humeral head and neck
shoulder joint
sternoclavicular joint

01610 Anesthesia for all procedures on nerves, muscles, tendons, fascia, and bursae of shoulder and axilla ☐N☐
🔲 0.00 ⚖ 0.00 Global Days XXX
AMA: 2008, Apr, 3-4; 2008, Apr, 3-4; 2006, Mar, 15; 2006, Mar, 15; 2006, Feb, 10-15; 2006, Feb, 10-15; 2006, Dec, 10-12; 2006, Dec, 10-12; 2006, Dec, 10-12; 2006, December, 10-12; 2006, December, 10-12; 2006, December, 10-12; 2006, February, 10-15; 2006, March, 15; 2006, Dec, 10-12; 2006, Dec, 10-12; 2006, Dec, 10-12; 2006, Dec, 10-12; 2006, Dec, 10-12; 2004, Jan, 27; 2004, January, 27; 2004, Jan, 27

01620 Anesthesia for all closed procedures on humeral head and neck, sternoclavicular joint, acromioclavicular joint, and shoulder joint ☐N☐
🔲 0.00 ⚖ 0.00 Global Days XXX
AMA: 2008, Apr, 3-4; 2008, Apr, 3-4; 2008, Apr, 3-4; 2006, Mar, 15; 2006, Mar, 15; 2006, Feb, 10-15; 2006, Feb, 10-15; 2006, Dec, 10-12; 2006, Dec, 10-12; 2006, Dec, 10-12; 2006, December, 10-12; 2006, December, 10-12; 2006, December, 10-12; 2006, February, 10-15; 2006, March, 15; 2006, Dec, 10-12; 2006, Dec, 10-12; 2006, Dec, 10-12; 2006, Dec, 10-12; 2006, Dec, 10-12; 2004, Jan, 27; 2004, January, 27; 2004, Jan, 27

01622 Anesthesia for diagnostic arthroscopic procedures of shoulder joint ☐N☐
🔲 0.00 ⚖ 0.00 Global Days XXX
AMA: 2008, Apr, 3-4; 2008, Apr, 3-4; 2008, Apr, 3-4; 2006, Mar, 15; 2006, Mar, 15; 2006, Feb, 10-15; 2006, Feb, 10-15; 2006, Dec, 10-12; 2006, Dec, 10-12; 2006, Dec, 10-12; 2006, December, 10-12; 2006, December, 10-12; 2006, December, 10-12; 2006, March, 15; 2006, February, 10-15; 2006, Dec, 10-12; 2006, Dec, 10-12; 2006, Dec, 10-12; 2006, Dec, 10-12; 2006, Dec, 10-12; 2004, Jan, 27; 2004, January, 27; 2004, Jan, 27

01630 Anesthesia for open or surgical arthroscopic procedures on humeral head and neck, sternoclavicular joint, acromioclavicular joint, and shoulder joint; not otherwise specified ☐N☐
🔲 0.00 ⚖ 0.00 Global Days XXX
AMA: 2008, Apr, 3-4; 2008, Apr, 3-4; 2008, Apr, 3-4; 2006, Mar, 15; 2006, Mar, 15; 2006, Feb, 10-15; 2006, Feb, 10-15; 2006, Dec, 10-12; 2006, Dec, 10-12; 2006, Dec, 10-12; 2006, December, 10-12; 2006, December, 10-12; 2006, December, 10-12; 2006, March, 15; 2006, February, 10-15; 2006, Dec, 10-12; 2006, Dec, 10-12; 2006, Dec, 10-12; 2006, Dec, 10-12; 2006, Dec, 10-12; 2004, Jan, 27; 2004, January, 27; 2004, Jan, 27

● New Code ▲ Revised Code Ⓜ Maternity Edit Ⓐ Age Edit Ⓐ-Ⓨ OPPS Status Indicator 🔲 Facility RVU ⚖ Non-Facility RVU
☐ CCI Comprehensive Code 🔯 Bilateral Procedure + Add-on Indicator ◼ Laboratory crosswalk ⬛ Radiology crosswalk

01632   radical resection   © ▣

🔢 0.00   ⚕ 0.00   **Global Days XXX**

AMA: 2008, Apr, 3-4; 2008, Apr, 3-4; 2008, Apr, 3-4; 2006, Feb, 10-15; 2006, Feb, 10-15; 2006, Mar, 15; 2006, Mar, 15; 2006, Dec, 10-12; 2006, Dec, 10-12; 2006, Dec, 10-12; 2006, December, 10-12; 2006, December, 10-12; 2006, December, 10-12; 2006, February, 10-15; 2006, March, 15; 2006, Dec, 10-12; 2006, Dec, 10-12; 2006, Dec, 10-12; 2006, Dec, 10-12; 2006, Dec, 10-12; 2004, Jan, 27; 2004, January, 27; 2004, Jan, 27

01634   shoulder disarticulation   © ▣

🔢 0.00   ⚕ 0.00   **Global Days XXX**

AMA: 2008, Apr, 3-4; 2008, Apr, 3-4; 2008, Apr, 3-4; 2006, Feb, 10-15; 2006, Feb, 10-15; 2006, Mar, 15; 2006, Mar, 15; 2006, Dec, 10-12; 2006, Dec, 10-12; 2006, Dec, 10-12; 2006, December, 10-12; 2006, December, 10-12; 2006, December, 10-12; 2006, February, 10-15; 2006, March, 15; 2006, Dec, 10-12; 2006, Dec, 10-12; 2006, Dec, 10-12; 2006, Dec, 10-12; 2006, Dec, 10-12; 2004, Jan, 27; 2004, January, 27; 2004, Jan, 27

01636   interthoracoscapular (forequarter) amputation   © ▣

🔢 0.00   ⚕ 0.00   **Global Days XXX**

AMA: 2008, Apr, 3-4; 2008, Apr, 3-4; 2008, Apr, 3-4; 2006, Mar, 15; 2006, Mar, 15; 2006, Feb, 10-15; 2006, Feb, 10-15; 2006, Dec, 10-12; 2006, Dec, 10-12; 2006, Dec, 10-12; 2006, December, 10-12; 2006, December, 10-12; 2006, December, 10-12; 2006, February, 10-15; 2006, March, 15; 2006, Dec, 10-12; 2006, Dec, 10-12; 2006, Dec, 10-12; 2006, Dec, 10-12; 2006, Dec, 10-12; 2004, Jan, 27; 2004, January, 27; 2004, Jan, 27

01638   total shoulder replacement   © ▣

🔢 0.00   ⚕ 0.00   **Global Days XXX**

AMA: 2008, Apr, 3-4; 2008, Apr, 3-4; 2008, Apr, 3-4; 2006, Mar, 15; 2006, Mar, 15; 2006, Feb, 10-15; 2006, Feb, 10-15; 2006, Dec, 10-12; 2006, Dec, 10-12; 2006, Dec, 10-12; 2006, December, 10-12; 2006, December, 10-12; 2006, December, 10-12; 2006, February, 10-15; 2006, March, 15; 2006, Dec, 10-12; 2006, Dec, 10-12; 2006, Dec, 10-12; 2006, Dec, 10-12; 2006, Dec, 10-12; 2004, Jan, 27; 2004, January, 27; 2004, Jan, 27

01650   Anesthesia for procedures on arteries of shoulder and axilla; not otherwise specified   Ⓝ ▣

🔢 0.00   ⚕ 0.00   **Global Days XXX**

AMA: 2008, Apr, 3-4; 2008, Apr, 3-4; 2008, Apr, 3-4; 2006, Mar, 15; 2006, Mar, 15; 2006, Feb, 10-15; 2006, Feb, 10-15; 2006, Dec, 10-12; 2006, Dec, 10-12; 2006, Dec, 10-12; 2006, December, 10-12; 2006, December, 10-12; 2006, December, 10-12; 2006, February, 10-15; 2006, March, 15; 2006, Dec, 10-12; 2006, Dec, 10-12; 2006, Dec, 10-12; 2006, Dec, 10-12; 2006, Dec, 10-12; 2004, Jan, 27; 2004, January, 27; 2004, Jan, 27

01652   axillary-brachial aneurysm   © ▣

🔢 0.00   ⚕ 0.00   **Global Days XXX**

AMA: 2008, Apr, 3-4; 2008, Apr, 3-4; 2008, Apr, 3-4; 2006, Feb, 10-15; 2006, Feb, 10-15; 2006, Mar, 15; 2006, Mar, 15; 2006, Dec, 10-12; 2006, Dec, 10-12; 2006, Dec, 10-12; 2006, December, 10-12; 2006, December, 10-12; 2006, December, 10-12; 2006, February, 10-15; 2006, March, 15; 2006, Dec, 10-12; 2006, Dec, 10-12; 2006, Dec, 10-12; 2006, Dec, 10-12; 2006, Dec, 10-12; 2004, Jan, 27; 2004, January, 27; 2004, Jan, 27

01654   bypass graft   © ▣

🔢 0.00   ⚕ 0.00   **Global Days XXX**

AMA: 2008, Apr, 3-4; 2008, Apr, 3-4; 2008, Apr, 3-4; 2006, Mar, 15; 2006, Mar, 15; 2006, Feb, 10-15; 2006, Feb, 10-15; 2006, Dec, 10-12; 2006, Dec, 10-12; 2006, Dec, 10-12; 2006, December, 10-12; 2006, December, 10-12; 2006, December, 10-12; 2006, February, 10-15; 2006, March, 15; 2006, Dec, 10-12; 2006, Dec, 10-12; 2006, Dec, 10-12; 2006, Dec, 10-12; 2006, Dec, 10-12; 2004, Jan, 27; 2004, January, 27; 2004, Jan, 27

01656   axillary-femoral bypass graft   © ▣

🔢 0.00   ⚕ 0.00   **Global Days XXX**

AMA: 2008, Apr, 3-4; 2008, Apr, 3-4; 2008, Apr, 3-4; 2006, Feb, 10-15; 2006, Feb, 10-15; 2006, Mar, 15; 2006, Mar, 15; 2006, Dec, 10-12; 2006, Dec, 10-12; 2006, Dec, 10-12; 2006, December, 10-12; 2006, December, 10-12; 2006, December, 10-12; 2006, February, 10-15; 2006, March, 15; 2006, Dec, 10-12; 2006, Dec, 10-12; 2006, Dec, 10-12; 2006, Dec, 10-12; 2006, Dec, 10-12; 2004, Jan, 27; 2004, January, 27; 2004, Jan, 27

01670   Anesthesia for all procedures on veins of shoulder and axilla   Ⓝ ▣

🔢 0.00   ⚕ 0.00   **Global Days XXX**

AMA: 2008, Apr, 3-4; 2008, Apr, 3-4; 2008, Apr, 3-4; 2006, Mar, 15; 2006, Mar, 15; 2006, Feb, 10-15; 2006, Feb, 10-15; 2006, Dec, 10-12; 2006, Dec, 10-12; 2006, Dec, 10-12; 2006, December, 10-12; 2006, December, 10-12; 2006, December, 10-12; 2006, February, 10-15; 2006, March, 15; 2006, Dec, 10-12; 2006, Dec, 10-12; 2006, Dec, 10-12; 2006, Dec, 10-12; 2006, Dec, 10-12; 2004, Jan, 27; 2004, January, 27; 2004, Jan, 27

01680   Anesthesia for shoulder cast application, removal or repair; not otherwise specified   Ⓝ ▣

🔢 0.00   ⚕ 0.00   **Global Days XXX**

AMA: 2008, Apr, 3-4; 2008, Apr, 3-4; 2008, Apr, 3-4; 2006, Mar, 15; 2006, Mar, 15; 2006, Feb, 10-15; 2006, Feb, 10-15; 2006, Dec, 10-12; 2006, Dec, 10-12; 2006, Dec, 10-12; 2006, December, 10-12; 2006, December, 10-12; 2006, December, 10-12; 2006, February, 10-15; 2006, March, 15; 2006, Dec, 10-12; 2006, Dec, 10-12; 2006, Dec, 10-12; 2006, Dec, 10-12; 2006, Dec, 10-12; 2004, Jan, 27; 2004, January, 27; 2004, Jan, 27

01682   shoulder spica   Ⓝ ▣

🔢 0.00   ⚕ 0.00   **Global Days XXX**

AMA: 2008, Apr, 3-4; 2008, Apr, 3-4; 2008, Apr, 3-4; 2006, Feb, 10-15; 2006, Feb, 10-15; 2006, Mar, 15; 2006, Mar, 15; 2006, Dec, 10-12; 2006, Dec, 10-12; 2006, Dec, 10-12; 2006, December, 10-12; 2006, December, 10-12; 2006, December, 10-12; 2006, February, 10-15; 2006, March, 15; 2006, Dec, 10-12; 2006, Dec, 10-12; 2006, Dec, 10-12; 2006, Dec, 10-12; 2006, Dec, 10-12; 2004, Jan, 27; 2004, January, 27; 2004, Jan, 27

01710-01860 Anesthesia for Upper Extremity Procedures

CMS *100-4,12,140.3.2 Calculation of Anesthesia Time*
CMS *100-4,12,140.2 Payment for CRNA Services*
CMS *100-4,12,140 Certified Registered Nurse Anesthetist Services*
CMS *100-4,12,50 Anesthesia Services*

01710 **Anesthesia for procedures on nerves, muscles, tendons, fascia, and bursae of upper arm and elbow; not otherwise specified** N ▣
    📷 0.00   ≷ 0.00 **Global Days XXX**
    AMA: 2008, Apr, 3-4; 2008, Apr, 3-4; 2008, Apr, 3-4; 2006, Mar, 15; 2006, Mar, 15; 2006, Feb, 10-15; 2006, Feb, 10-15; 2006, Dec, 10-12; 2006, Dec, 10-12; 2006, Dec, 10-12; 2006, December, 10-12; 2006, December, 10-12; 2006, December, 10-12; 2006, December, 10-12; 2006, February, 10-15; 2006, March, 15; 2006, Dec, 10-12; 2006, Dec, 10-12; 2006, Dec, 10-12; 2006, Dec, 10-12; 2006, Dec, 10-12; 2004, Jan, 27; 2004, January, 27; 2004, Jan, 27

01712 **tenotomy, elbow to shoulder, open** N ▣
    📷 0.00   ≷ 0.00 **Global Days XXX**
    AMA: 2008, Apr, 3-4; 2008, Apr, 3-4; 2008, Apr, 3-4; 2006, Mar, 15; 2006, Mar, 15; 2006, Feb, 10-15; 2006, Feb, 10-15; 2006, Dec, 10-12; 2006, Dec, 10-12; 2006, Dec, 10-12; 2006, December, 10-12; 2006, December, 10-12; 2006, December, 10-12; 2006, December, 10-12; 2006, February, 10-15; 2006, March, 15; 2006, Dec, 10-12; 2006, Dec, 10-12; 2006, Dec, 10-12; 2006, Dec, 10-12; 2006, Dec, 10-12; 2004, Jan, 27; 2004, January, 27; 2004, Jan, 27

01714 **tenoplasty, elbow to shoulder** N ▣
    📷 0.00   ≷ 0.00 **Global Days XXX**
    AMA: 2000, Apr, 3-4; 2000, Apr, 3-4; 2008, Apr, 3-4; 2000, Mar, 15; 2006, Mar, 15; 2006, Feb, 10-15; 2006, Feb, 10-15; 2006, Dec, 10-12; 2006, Dec, 10-12; 2006, Dec, 10-12; 2006, December, 10-12; 2006, December, 10-12; 2006, December, 10-12; 2006, December, 10-12; 2006, February, 10-15; 2006, March, 15; 2006, Dec, 10-12; 2006, Dec, 10-12; 2006, Dec, 10-12; 2006, Dec, 10-12; 2006, Dec, 10-12; 2004, Jan, 27; 2004, January, 27; 2004, Jan, 27

01716 **tenodesis, rupture of long tendon of biceps** N ▣
    📷 0.00   ≷ 0.00 **Global Days XXX**
    AMA: 2008, Apr, 3-4; 2008, Apr, 3-4; 2008, Apr, 3-4; 2006, Mar, 15; 2006, Mar, 15; 2006, Feb, 10-15; 2006, Feb, 10-15; 2006, Dec, 10-12; 2006, Dec, 10-12; 2006, Dec, 10-12; 2006, December, 10-12; 2006, December, 10-12; 2006, December, 10-12; 2006, December, 10-12; 2006, February, 10-15; 2006, March, 15; 2006, Dec, 10-12; 2006, Dec, 10-12; 2006, Dec, 10-12; 2006, Dec, 10-12; 2000, Dec, 10-12, 2004, Jan, 27, 2004, January, 27, 2004, Jan, 27

01730 **Anesthesia for all closed procedures on humerus and elbow** N ▣
    📷 0.00   ≷ 0.00 **Global Days XXX**
    AMA: 2008, Apr, 3-4; 2008, Apr, 3-4; 2008, Apr, 3-4; 2006, Feb, 10-15; 2006, Feb, 10-15; 2006, Mar, 15; 2006, Mar, 15; 2006, Dec, 10-12; 2006, Dec, 10-12; 2006, Dec, 10-12; 2006, December, 10-12; 2006, December, 10-12; 2006, December, 10-12; 2006, December, 10-12; 2006, March, 15; 2006, February, 10-15; 2006, Dec, 10-12; 2006, Dec, 10-12; 2006, Dec, 10-12; 2006, Dec, 10-12; 2006, Dec, 10-12; 2004, Jan, 27; 2004, January, 27; 2004, Jan, 27

01732 **Anesthesia for diagnostic arthroscopic procedures of elbow joint** N ▣
    📷 0.00   ≷ 0.00 **Global Days XXX**
    AMA: 2008, Apr, 3-4; 2008, Apr, 3-4; 2008, Apr, 3-4; 2006, Mar, 15; 2006, Mar, 15; 2006, Feb, 10-15; 2006, Feb, 10-15; 2006, Dec, 10-12; 2006, Dec, 10-12; 2006, Dec, 10-12; 2006, December, 10-12; 2006, December, 10-12; 2006, December, 10-12; 2006, February, 10-15; 2006, March, 15; 2006, Dec, 10-12; 2006, Dec, 10-12; 2006, Dec, 10-12; 2006, Dec, 10-12; 2006, Dec, 10-12; 2004, Jan, 27; 2004, January, 27; 2004, Jan, 27

01740 **Anesthesia for open or surgical arthroscopic procedures of the elbow; not otherwise specified** N ▣
    📷 0.00   ≷ 0.00 **Global Days XXX**
    AMA: 2008, Apr, 3-4; 2008, Apr, 3-4; 2008, Apr, 3-4; 2006, Mar, 15; 2006, Mar, 15; 2006, Feb, 10-15; 2006, Feb, 10-15; 2006, Dec, 10-12; 2006, Dec, 10-12; 2006, Dec, 10-12; 2006, December, 10-12; 2006, December, 10-12; 2006, December, 10-12; 2006, February, 10-15; 2006, March, 15; 2006, Dec, 10-12; 2006, Dec, 10-12; 2006, Dec, 10-12; 2006, Dec, 10-12; 2006, Dec, 10-12; 2004, Jan, 27; 2004, January, 27; 2004, Jan, 27

01742 **osteotomy of humerus** N ▣
    📷 0.00   ≷ 0.00 **Global Days XXX**
    AMA: 2008, Apr, 3-4; 2008, Apr, 3-4; 2008, Apr, 3-4; 2006, Feb, 10-15; 2006, Feb, 10-15; 2006, Mar, 15; 2006, Mar, 15; 2006, Dec, 10-12; 2006, Dec, 10-12; 2006, Dec, 10-12; 2006, December, 10-12; 2006, December, 10-12; 2006, December, 10-12; 2006, February, 10-15; 2006, March, 15; 2006, Dec, 10-12; 2006, Dec, 10-12; 2006, Dec, 10-12; 2006, Dec, 10-12; 2006, Dec, 10-12; 2004, Jan, 27; 2004, January, 27; 2004, Jan, 27

01744 **repair of nonunion or malunion of humerus** N ▣
    📷 0.00   ≷ 0.00 **Global Days XXX**
    AMA: 2008, Apr, 3-4; 2008, Apr, 3-4; 2008, Apr, 3-4; 2006, Mar, 15; 2006, Mar, 15; 2006, Feb, 10-15; 2006, Feb, 10-15; 2006, Dec, 10-12; 2006, Dec, 10-12; 2006, Dec, 10-12; 2006, December, 10-12; 2006, December, 10-12; 2006, December, 10-12; 2006, February, 10-15; 2006, March, 15; 2006, Dec, 10-12; 2006, Dec, 10-12; 2006, Dec, 10-12; 2006, Dec, 10-12; 2006, Dec, 10-12; 2004, Jan, 27; 2004, January, 27; 2004, Jan, 27

01756 **radical procedures** C ▣
    📷 0.00   ≷ 0.00 **Global Days XXX**
    AMA: 2008, Apr, 3-4; 2008, Apr, 3-4; 2008, Apr, 3-4; 2006, Mar, 15; 2006, Mar, 15; 2006, Feb, 10-15; 2006, Feb, 10-15; 2006, Dec, 10-12; 2006, Dec, 10-12; 2006, Dec, 10-12; 2006, December, 10-12; 2006, December, 10-12; 2006, December, 10-12; 2006, February, 10-15; 2006, March, 15; 2006, Dec, 10-12; 2006, Dec, 10-12; 2006, Dec, 10-12; 2006, Dec, 10-12; 2006, Dec, 10-12; 2004, Jan, 27; 2004, January, 27; 2004, Jan, 27

01758 **excision of cyst or tumor of humerus** N ▣
    📷 0.00   ≷ 0.00 **Global Days XXX**
    AMA: 2008, Apr, 3-4; 2008, Apr, 3-4; 2008, Apr, 3-4; 2006, Mar, 15; 2006, Mar, 15; 2006, Feb, 10-15; 2006, Feb, 10-15; 2006, Dec, 10-12; 2006, Dec, 10-12; 2006, Dec, 10-12; 2006, December, 10-12; 2006, December, 10-12; 2006, December, 10-12; 2006, February, 10-15; 2006, March, 15; 2006, Dec, 10-12; 2006, Dec, 10-12; 2006, Dec, 10-12; 2006, Dec, 10-12; 2006, Dec, 10-12; 2004, Jan, 27; 2004, January, 27; 2004, Jan, 27

Anesthesia

01760 — 01842

01760   total elbow replacement   N ▢
　　　🗨 0.00   ⚖ 0.00   **Global Days XXX**
　　　AMA: 2008, Apr, 3-4; 2008, Apr, 3-4; 2008, Apr, 3-4; 2006, Feb, 10-15; 2006, Feb, 10-15; 2006, Mar, 15; 2006, Mar, 15; 2006, Dec, 10-12; 2006, Dec, 10-12; 2006, Dec, 10-12; 2006, December, 10-12; 2006, December, 10-12; 2006, December, 10-12; 2006, February, 10-15; 2006, March, 15; 2006, Dec, 10-12; 2006, Dec, 10-12; 2006, Dec, 10-12; 2006, Dec, 10-12; 2006, Dec, 10-12; 2004, Jan, 27; 2004, January, 27; 2004, Jan, 27

01770   Anesthesia for procedures on arteries of upper arm and elbow; not otherwise specified   N ▢
　　　🗨 0.00   ⚖ 0.00   **Global Days XXX**
　　　AMA: 2008, Apr, 3-4; 2008, Apr, 3-4; 2008, Apr, 3-4; 2006, Mar, 15; 2006, Mar, 15; 2006, Feb, 10-15; 2006, Feb, 10-15; 2006, Dec, 10-12; 2006, Dec, 10-12; 2006, Dec, 10-12; 2006, December, 10-12; 2006, December, 10-12; 2006, December, 10-12; 2006, March, 15; 2006, February, 10-15; 2006, Dec, 10-12; 2006, Dec, 10-12; 2006, Dec, 10-12; 2006, Dec, 10-12; 2004, Jan, 27; 2004, January, 27; 2004, Jan, 27

01772   embolectomy   N ▢
　　　🗨 0.00   ⚖ 0.00   **Global Days XXX**
　　　AMA: 2008, Apr, 3-4; 2008, Apr, 3-4; 2008, Apr, 3-4; 2006, Mar, 15; 2006, Mar, 15; 2006, Feb, 10-15; 2006, Feb, 10-15; 2006, Dec, 10-12; 2006, Dec, 10-12; 2006, Dec, 10-12; 2006, December, 10-12; 2006, December, 10-12; 2006, December, 10-12; 2006, February, 10-15; 2006, March, 15; 2006, Dec, 10-12; 2006, Dec, 10-12; 2006, Dec, 10-12; 2006, Dec, 10-12; 2004, Jan, 27; 2004, January, 27; 2004, Jan, 27

01780   Anesthesia for procedures on veins of upper arm and elbow; not otherwise specified   N ▢
　　　🗨 0.00   ⚖ 0.00   **Global Days XXX**
　　　AMA: 2008, Apr, 3-4; 2008, Apr, 3-4; 2008, Apr, 3-4; 2006, Feb, 10-15; 2006, Feb, 10-15; 2006, Mar, 15; 2006, Mar, 15; 2006, Dec, 10-12; 2006, Dec, 10-12; 2006, Dec, 10-12; 2006, December, 10-12; 2006, December, 10-12; 2006, December, 10-12; 2006, February, 10-15; 2006, March, 15; 2006, Dec, 10-12; 2006, Dec, 10-12; 2006, Dec, 10-12; 2006, Dec, 10-12; 2004, Jan, 27; 2004, January, 27; 2004, Jan, 27

01782   phleborrhaphy   N ▢
　　　🗨 0.00   ⚖ 0.00   **Global Days XXX**
　　　AMA: 2008, Apr, 3-4; 2008, Apr, 3-4; 2008, Apr, 3-4; 2006, Mar, 15; 2006, Mar, 15; 2006, Feb, 10-15; 2006, Feb, 10-15; 2006, Dec, 10-12; 2006, Dec, 10-12; 2006, Dec, 10-12; 2006, December, 10-12; 2006, December, 10-12; 2006, December, 10-12; 2006, February, 10-15; 2006, March, 15; 2006, Dec, 10-12; 2006, Dec, 10-12; 2006, Dec, 10-12; 2006, Dec, 10-12; 2004, Jan, 27; 2004, January, 27; 2004, Jan, 27

01810   Anesthesia for all procedures on nerves, muscles, tendons, fascia, and bursae of forearm, wrist, and hand   N ▢
　　　🗨 0.00   ⚖ 0.00   **Global Days XXX**
　　　AMA: 2008, Apr, 3-4; 2008, Apr, 3-4; 2008, Apr, 3-4; 2006, Feb, 10-15; 2006, Feb, 10-15; 2006, Mar, 15; 2006, Mar, 15; 2006, Dec, 10-12; 2006, Dec, 10-12; 2006, Dec, 10-12; 2006, December, 10-12; 2006, December, 10-12; 2006, December, 10-12; 2006, February, 10-15; 2006, March, 15; 2006, Dec, 10-12; 2006, Dec, 10-12; 2006, Dec, 10-12; 2006, Dec, 10-12; 2004, Jan, 27; 2004, January, 27; 2004, Jan, 27

01820   Anesthesia for all closed procedures on radius, ulna, wrist, or hand bones   N ▢
　　　🗨 0.00   ⚖ 0.00   **Global Days XXX**
　　　AMA: 2008, Apr, 3-4; 2008, Apr, 3-4; 2008, Apr, 3-4; 2006, Mar, 15; 2006, Mar, 15; 2006, Feb, 10-15; 2006, Feb, 10-15; 2006, Dec, 10-12; 2006, Dec, 10-12; 2006, Dec, 10-12; 2006, December, 10-12; 2006, December, 10-12; 2006, December, 10-12; 2006, March, 15; 2006, February, 10-15; 2006, Dec, 10-12; 2006, Dec, 10-12; 2006, Dec, 10-12; 2006, Dec, 10-12; 2004, Jan, 27; 2004, January, 27; 2004, Jan, 27

01829   Anesthesia for diagnostic arthroscopic procedures on the wrist   N ▢
　　　🗨 0.00   ⚖ 0.00   **Global Days XXX**
　　　AMA: 2008, Apr, 3-4; 2008, Apr, 3-4; 2008, Apr, 3-4; 2006, Mar, 15; 2006, Mar, 15; 2006, Feb, 10-15; 2006, Feb, 10-15; 2006, Dec, 10-12; 2006, Dec, 10-12; 2006, Dec, 10-12; 2006, December, 10-12; 2006, December, 10-12; 2006, December, 10-12; 2006, March, 15; 2006, February, 10-15; 2006, Dec, 10-12; 2006, Dec, 10-12; 2006, Dec, 10-12; 2006, Dec, 10-12; 2004, Jan, 27; 2004, January, 27; 2004, Jan, 27

01830   Anesthesia for open or surgical arthroscopic/endoscopic procedures on distal radius, distal ulna, wrist, or hand joints; not otherwise specified   N ▢
　　　🗨 0.00   ⚖ 0.00   **Global Days XXX**
　　　AMA: 2008, Apr, 3-4; 2008, Apr, 3-4; 2008, Apr, 3-4; 2006, Mar, 15; 2006, Mar, 15; 2006, Feb, 10-15; 2006, Feb, 10-15; 2006, Dec, 10-12; 2006, Dec, 10-12; 2006, Dec, 10-12; 2006, December, 10-12; 2006, December, 10-12; 2006, December, 10-12; 2006, March, 15; 2006, February, 10-15; 2006, Dec, 10-12; 2006, Dec, 10-12; 2006, Dec, 10-12; 2006, Dec, 10-12; 2004, Jan, 27; 2004, January, 27; 2004, Jan, 27

01832   total wrist replacement   N ▢
　　　🗨 0.00   ⚖ 0.00   **Global Days XXX**
　　　AMA: 2008, Apr, 3-4; 2008, Apr, 3-4; 2008, Apr, 3-4; 2006, Feb, 10-15; 2006, Feb, 10-15; 2006, Mar, 15; 2006, Mar, 15; 2006, Dec, 10-12; 2006, Dec, 10-12; 2006, Dec, 10-12; 2006, December, 10-12; 2006, December, 10-12; 2006, December, 10-12; 2006, March, 15; 2006, February, 10-15; 2006, Dec, 10-12; 2006, Dec, 10-12; 2006, Dec, 10-12; 2006, Dec, 10-12; 2004, Jan, 27; 2004, January, 27; 2004, Jan, 27

01840   Anesthesia for procedures on arteries of forearm, wrist, and hand; not otherwise specified   N ▢
　　　🗨 0.00   ⚖ 0.00   **Global Days XXX**
　　　AMA: 2008, Apr, 3-4; 2008, Apr, 3-4; 2008, Apr, 3-4; 2006, Mar, 15; 2006, Mar, 15; 2006, Feb, 10-15; 2006, Feb, 10-15; 2006, Dec, 10-12; 2006, Dec, 10-12; 2006, Dec, 10-12; 2006, December, 10-12; 2006, December, 10-12; 2006, December, 10-12; 2006, March, 15; 2006, February, 10-15; 2006, Dec, 10-12; 2006, Dec, 10-12; 2006, Dec, 10-12; 2006, Dec, 10-12; 2004, Jan, 27; 2004, January, 27; 2004, Jan, 27

01842   embolectomy   N ▢
　　　🗨 0.00   ⚖ 0.00   **Global Days XXX**
　　　AMA: 2008, Apr, 3-4; 2008, Apr, 3-4; 2008, Apr, 3-4; 2006, Feb, 10-15; 2006, Feb, 10-15; 2006, Mar, 15; 2006, Mar, 15; 2006, Dec, 10-12; 2006, Dec, 10-12; 2006, Dec, 10-12; 2006, December, 10-12; 2006, December, 10-12; 2006, December, 10-12; 2006, March, 15; 2006, February, 10-15; 2006, Dec, 10-12; 2006, Dec, 10-12; 2006, Dec, 10-12; 2006, Dec, 10-12; 2004, Jan, 27; 2004, January, 27; 2004, Jan, 27

01844 Anesthesia for vascular shunt, or shunt revision, any type (eg, dialysis) [N] [□]

💷 0.00 ⚕ 0.00 Global Days XXX

AMA: 2008, Apr, 3-4; 2008, Apr, 3-4; 2008, Apr, 3-4; 2006, Mar, 15; 2006, Mar, 15; 2006, Feb, 10-15; 2006, Feb, 10-15; 2006, Dec, 10-12; 2006, Dec, 10-12; 2006, Dec, 10-12; 2006, December, 10-12; 2006, December, 10-12; 2006, December, 10-12; 2006, March, 15; 2006, February, 10-15; 2006, Dec, 10-12; 2006, Dec, 10-12; 2006, Dec, 10-12; 2006, Dec, 10-12; 2006, Dec, 10-12; 2004, Jan, 27; 2004, January, 27; 2004, Jan, 27

01850 Anesthesia for procedures on veins of forearm, wrist, and hand; not otherwise specified [N] [□]

💷 0.00 ⚕ 0.00 Global Days XXX

AMA: 2008, Apr, 3-4; 2008, Apr, 3-4; 2008, Apr, 3-4; 2006, Mar, 15; 2006, Mar, 15; 2006, Feb, 10-15; 2006, Feb, 10-15; 2006, Dec, 10-12; 2006, Dec, 10-12; 2006, Dec, 10-12; 2006, December, 10-12; 2006, December, 10-12; 2006, December, 10-12; 2006, March, 15; 2006, February, 10-15; 2006, Dec, 10-12; 2006, Dec, 10-12; 2006, Dec, 10-12; 2006, Dec, 10-12; 2006, Dec, 10-12; 2004, Jan, 27; 2004, January, 27; 2004, Jan, 27

01852 phleborrhaphy [N] [□]

💷 0.00 ⚕ 0.00 Global Days XXX

AMA: 2008, Apr, 3-4; 2008, Apr, 3-4; 2008, Apr, 3-4; 2006, Feb, 10-15; 2006, Feb, 10-15; 2006, Mar, 15; 2006, Mar, 15; 2006, Dec, 10-12; 2006, Dec, 10-12; 2006, Dec, 10-12; 2006, December, 10-12; 2006, December, 10-12; 2006, December, 10-12; 2006, December, 10-12; 2006, March, 15; 2006, February, 10-15; 2006, Dec, 10-12; 2006, Dec, 10-12; 2006, Dec, 10-12; 2006, Dec, 10-12; 2006, Dec, 10-12; 2004, Jan, 27; 2004, January, 27; 2004, Jan, 27

01860 Anesthesia for forearm, wrist, or hand cast application, removal, or repair [N] [□]

💷 0.00 ⚕ 0.00 Global Days XXX

AMA: 2008, Apr, 3-4; 2008, Apr, 3-4; 2008, Apr, 3-4; 2006, Feb, 10-15; 2006, Feb, 10-15; 2006, Mar, 15; 2006, Mar, 15; 2006, Dec, 10-12; 2006, Dec, 10-12; 2006, Dec, 10-12; 2006, December, 10-12; 2006, December, 10-12; 2006, December, 10-12; 2006, March, 15; 2006, February, 10-15; 2006, Dec, 10-12; 2006, Dec, 10-12; 2006, Dec, 10-12; 2006, Dec, 10-12; 2006, Dec, 10-12; 2004, Jan, 27; 2004, January, 27; 2004, Jan, 27

01916-01936 Anesthesia for Interventional Radiology Procedures

CMS 100-4,12,140.3.2 *Calculation of Anesthesia Time*
CMS 100-4,12,140.2 *Payment for CRNA Services*
CMS 100-4,12,140 *Certified Registered Nurse Anesthetist Services*
CMS 100-4,12,50 *Anesthesia Services*

01916 Anesthesia for diagnostic arteriography/venography [N] [□]

Do not report with (01924-01926, 01930-01933)

💷 0.00 ⚕ 0.00 Global Days XXX

AMA: 2008, Apr, 3-4; 2008, Apr, 3-4; 2008, Apr, 3-4; 2006, Feb, 10-15; 2006, Feb, 10-15; 2006, Mar, 15; 2006, Mar, 15; 2006, Dec, 10-12; 2006, Dec, 10-12; 2006, Dec, 10-12; 2006, December, 10-12; 2006, December, 10-12; 2006, December, 10-12; 2006, March, 15; 2006, February, 10-15; 2006, Dec, 10-12; 2006, Dec, 10-12; 2006, Dec, 10-12; 2006, Dec, 10-12; 2006, Dec, 10-12; 2004, Jan, 27; 2004, January, 27; 2004, Jan, 27

01920 Anesthesia for cardiac catheterization including coronary angiography and ventriculography (not to include Swan-Ganz catheter) [N] [□]

💷 0.00 ⚕ 0.00 Global Days XXX

AMA: 2008, Apr, 3-4; 2008, Apr, 3-4; 2008, Apr, 3-4; 2006, Mar, 15; 2006, Mar, 15; 2006, Feb, 10-15; 2006, Feb, 10-15; 2006, Dec, 10-12; 2006, Dec, 10-12; 2006, Dec, 10-12; 2006, December, 10-12; 2006, December, 10-12; 2006, December, 10-12; 2006, March, 15; 2006, February, 10-15; 2006, Dec, 10-12; 2006, Dec, 10-12; 2006, Dec, 10-12; 2006, Dec, 10-12; 2006, Dec, 10-12; 2004, Jan, 27; 2004, January, 27; 2004, Jan, 27

01922 Anesthesia for non-invasive imaging or radiation therapy [N] [□]

💷 0.00 ⚕ 0.00 Global Days XXX

AMA: 2008, Apr, 3-4; 2008, Apr, 3-4; 2008, Apr, 3-4; 2006, Mar, 15; 2006, Mar, 15; 2006, Feb, 10-15; 2006, Feb, 10-15; 2006, Dec, 10-12; 2006, Dec, 10-12; 2006, Dec, 10-12; 2006, December, 10-12; 2006, December, 10-12; 2006, December, 10-12; 2006, March, 15; 2006, February, 10-15; 2006, Dec, 10-12; 2006, Dec, 10-12; 2006, Dec, 10-12; 2006, Dec, 10-12; 2006, Dec, 10-12; 2004, Jan, 27; 2004, January, 27; 2004, Jan, 27

01924 Anesthesia for therapeutic interventional radiological procedures involving the arterial system; not otherwise specified [N] [□]

💷 0.00 ⚕ 0.00 Global Days XXX

AMA: 2008, Apr, 3-4; 2008, Apr, 3-4; 2008, Apr, 3-4; 2006, Mar, 15; 2006, Mar, 15; 2006, Feb, 10-15; 2006, Feb, 10-15; 2006, Dec, 10-12; 2006, Dec, 10-12; 2006, Dec, 10-12; 2006, December, 10-12; 2006, December, 10-12; 2006, December, 10-12; 2006, March, 15; 2006, February, 10-15; 2006, Dec, 10-12; 2006, Dec, 10-12; 2006, Dec, 10-12; 2006, Dec, 10-12; 2006, Dec, 10-12; 2004, Jan, 27; 2004, January, 27; 2004, Jan, 27

01925 carotid or coronary [N] [□]

💷 0.00 ⚕ 0.00 Global Days XXX

AMA: 2008, Apr, 3-4; 2008, Apr, 3-4; 2008, Apr, 3-4; 2006, Feb, 10-15; 2006, Feb, 10-15; 2006, Mar, 15; 2006, Mar, 15; 2006, Dec, 10-12; 2006, Dec, 10-12; 2006, Dec, 10-12; 2006, December, 10-12; 2006, December, 10-12; 2006, December, 10-12; 2006, March, 15; 2006, February, 10-15; 2006, Dec, 10-12; 2006, Dec, 10-12; 2006, Dec, 10-12; 2006, Dec, 10-12; 2006, Dec, 10-12; 2004, Jan, 27; 2004, January, 27; 2004, Jan, 27

01926 intracranial, intracardiac, or aortic [N] [□]

💷 0.00 ⚕ 0.00 Global Days XXX

AMA: 2008, Apr, 3-4; 2008, Apr, 3-4; 2008, Apr, 3-4; 2006, Mar, 15; 2006, Mar, 15; 2006, Feb, 10-15; 2006, Feb, 10-15; 2006, Dec, 10-12; 2006, Dec, 10-12; 2006, Dec, 10-12; 2006, December, 10-12; 2006, December, 10-12; 2006, December, 10-12; 2006, March, 15; 2006, February, 10-15; 2006, Dec, 10-12; 2006, Dec, 10-12; 2006, Dec, 10-12; 2006, Dec, 10-12; 2006, Dec, 10-12; 2004, Jan, 27; 2004, January, 27; 2004, Jan, 27

01930 Anesthesia for therapeutic interventional radiological procedures involving the venous/lymphatic system (not to include access to the central circulation); not otherwise specified [N] [□]

💷 0.00 ⚕ 0.00 Global Days XXX

AMA: 2008, Apr, 3-4; 2008, Apr, 3-4; 2008, Apr, 3-4; 2006, Mar, 15; 2006, Mar, 15; 2006, Feb, 10-15; 2006, Feb, 10-15; 2006, Dec, 10-12; 2006, Dec, 10-12; 2006, Dec, 10-12; 2006, December, 10-12; 2006, December, 10-12; 2006, December, 10-12; 2006, March, 15; 2006, February, 10-15; 2006, Dec, 10-12; 2006, Dec, 10-12; 2006, Dec, 10-12; 2006, Dec, 10-12; 2006, Dec, 10-12; 2004, Jan, 27; 2004, January, 27; 2004, Jan, 27

● New Code   ▲ Revised Code   [M] Maternity Edit   [A] Age Edit   [A]-[Y] OPPS Status Indicator   💷 Facility RVU   ⚕ Non-Facility RVU

[C] CCI Comprehensive Code   [50] Bilateral Procedure   + Add-on Indicator   [L] Laboratory crosswalk   [R] Radiology crosswalk

01931 intrahepatic or portal circulation (eg, transvenous intrahepatic portosystemic shunt[s] [TIPS]) N ▯

🚑 0.00 ⚕ 0.00 Global Days XXX

AMA: 2008, Apr, 3-4; 2008, Apr, 3-4; 2008, Apr, 3-4; 2006, Mar, 15; 2006, Mar, 15; 2006, Feb, 10-15; 2006, Feb, 10-15; 2006, Dec, 10-12; 2006, Dec, 10-12; 2006, Dec, 10-12; 2006, December, 10-12; 2006, December, 10-12; 2006, December, 10-12; 2006, December, 10-12; 2006, March, 15; 2006, February, 10-15; 2006, Dec, 10-12; 2006, Dec, 10-12; 2006, Dec, 10-12; 2006, Dec, 10-12; 2006, Dec, 10-12; 2004, Jan, 27; 2004, January, 27; 2004, Jan, 27

01932 intrathoracic or jugular N ▯

🚑 0.00 ⚕ 0.00 Global Days XXX

AMA: 2008, Apr, 3-4; 2008, Apr, 3-4; 2008, Apr, 3-4; 2006, Feb, 10-15; 2006, Feb, 10-15; 2006, Mar, 15; 2006, Mar, 15; 2006, Dec, 10-12; 2006, Dec, 10-12; 2006, Dec, 10-12; 2006, December, 10-12; 2006, December, 10-12; 2006, December, 10-12; 2006, December, 10-12; 2006, March, 15; 2006, February, 10-15; 2006, Dec, 10-12; 2006, Dec, 10-12; 2006, Dec, 10-12; 2006, Dec, 10-12; 2006, Dec, 10-12; 2004, Jan, 27; 2004, January, 27; 2004, Jan, 27

01933 intracranial N ▯

🚑 0.00 ⚕ 0.00 Global Days XXX

AMA: 2008, Apr, 3-4; 2008, Apr, 3-4; 2008, Apr, 3-4; 2006, Feb, 10-15; 2006, Feb, 10-15; 2006, Mar, 15; 2006, Mar, 15; 2006, Dec, 10-12; 2006, Dec, 10-12; 2006, Dec, 10-12; 2006, December, 10-12; 2006, December, 10-12; 2006, December, 10-12; 2006, December, 10-12; 2006, March, 15; 2006, February, 10-15; 2006, Dec, 10-12; 2006, Dec, 10-12; 2006, Dec, 10-12; 2006, Dec, 10-12; 2006, Dec, 10-12; 2004, Jan, 27; 2004, January, 27; 2004, Jan, 27

01935 Anesthesia for percutaneous image guided procedures on the spine and spinal cord; diagnostic N

🚑 0.00 ⚕ 0.00 Global Days XXX

AMA: 2008, Apr, 3-4; 2008, Apr, 3-4; 2008, Apr, 3-4

01936 therapeutic N

🚑 0.00 ⚕ 0.00 Global Days XXX

AMA: 2008, Apr, 3-4; 2008, Apr, 3-4; 2008, Apr, 3-4

01951-01953 Anesthesia for Burn Procedures

CMS *100-4,12,140.3.2* Calculation of Anesthesia Time
CMS *100-4,12,140.2* Payment for CRNA Services
CMS *100-4,12,140* Certified Registered Nurse Anesthetist Services
CMS *100-4,12,50* Anesthesia Services
CMS *100-4,3,20.1.2.8* Special Payments for Burn Cases

01951 Anesthesia for second- and third-degree burn excision or debridement with or without skin grafting, any site, for total body surface area (TBSA) treated during anesthesia and surgery; less than 4% total body surface area N ▯

🚑 0.00 ⚕ 0.00 Global Days XXX

AMA: 2008, Apr, 3-4; 2008, Apr, 3-4; 2008, Apr, 3-4; 2006, Feb, 10-15; 2006, Feb, 10-15; 2006, Mar, 15; 2006, Mar, 15; 2006, Dec, 10-12; 2006, Dec, 10-12; 2006, Dec, 10-12; 2006, December, 10-12; 2006, December, 10-12; 2006, December, 10-12; 2006, March, 15; 2006, February, 10-15; 2006, Dec, 10-12; 2006, Dec, 10-12; 2006, Dec, 10-12; 2006, Dec, 10-12; 2006, Dec, 10-12; 2004, Jan, 27; 2004, January, 27; 2004, Jan, 27

01952 between 4% and 9% of total body surface area N ▯

🚑 0.00 ⚕ 0.00 Global Days XXX

AMA: 2008, Apr, 3-4; 2008, Apr, 3-4; 2008, Apr, 3-4; 2006, Mar, 15; 2006, Mar, 15; 2006, Feb, 10-15; 2006, Feb, 10-15; 2006, Dec, 10-12; 2006, Dec, 10-12; 2006, Dec, 10-12; 2006, December, 10-12; 2006, December, 10-12; 2006, December, 10-12; 2006, March, 15; 2006, February, 10-15; 2006, Dec, 10-12; 2006, Dec, 10-12; 2006, Dec, 10-12; 2006, Dec, 10-12; 2006, Dec, 10-12; 2004, Jan, 27; 2004, January, 27; 2004, Jan, 27

+ **01953** each additional 9% total body surface area or part thereof (List separately in addition to code for primary procedure) N ▯

Code first 01952

🚑 0.00 ⚕ 0.00 Global Days XXX

AMA: 2008, Apr, 3-4; 2008, Apr, 3-4; 2008, Apr, 3-4; 2006, Mar, 15; 2006, Mar, 15; 2006, Feb, 10-15; 2006, Feb, 10-15; 2006, Dec, 10-12; 2006, Dec, 10-12; 2006, Dec, 10-12; 2006, December, 10-12; 2006, December, 10-12; 2006, December, 10-12; 2006, March, 15; 2006, February, 10-15; 2006, Dec, 10-12; 2006, Dec, 10-12; 2006, Dec, 10-12; 2006, Dec, 10-12; 2006, Dec, 10-12; 2004, Jan, 27; 2004, January, 27; 2004, Jan, 27

01958-01969 Anesthesia for Obstetric Procedures

CMS *100-4,12,140.3.2* Calculation of Anesthesia Time
CMS *100-4,12,140.2* Payment for CRNA Services
CMS *100-4,12,140* Certified Registered Nurse Anesthetist Services
CMS *100-4,12,50* Anesthesia Services

01958 Anesthesia for external cephalic version procedure M ♀ N ▯

🚑 0.00 ⚕ 0.00 Global Days XXX

AMA: 2008, Apr, 3-4; 2008, Apr, 3-4; 2008, Apr, 3-4; 2006, Feb, 10-15; 2006, Feb, 10-15; 2006, Mar, 15; 2006, Dec, 10-12; 2006, Mar, 15; 2006, Dec, 10-12; 2006, Dec, 10-12; 2006, Dec, 10-12; 2006, Dec, 10-12; 2006, December, 10-12; 2006, December, 10-12; 2006, December, 10-12; 2006, December, 10-12; 2006, March, 15; 2006, February, 10-15; 2006, Dec, 10-12; 2006, Dec, 10-12; 2006, Dec, 10-12; 2004, Jun, 1; 2004, June, 1; 2004, January, 27; 2004, Jun, 1; 2004, Jan, 27; 2004, Jan, 27

01960 Anesthesia for vaginal delivery only M ♀ N ▯

🚑 0.00 ⚕ 0.00 Global Days XXX

AMA: 2008, Apr, 3-4; 2008, Apr, 3-4; 2008, Apr, 3-4; 2006, Mar, 15; 2006, Mar, 15; 2006, Feb, 10-15; 2006, Feb, 10-15; 2006, Dec, 10-12; 2006, Dec, 10-12; 2006, Dec, 10-12; 2006, December, 10-12; 2006, December, 10-12; 2006, December, 10-12; 2006, February, 10-15; 2006, March, 15; 2006, Dec, 10-12; 2006, Dec, 10-12; 2006, Dec, 10-12; 2006, Dec, 10-12; 2006, Dec, 10-12; 2004, Jan, 27; 2004, January, 27; 2004, Jan, 27

01961 Anesthesia for cesarean delivery only M ♀ N ▯

🚑 0.00 ⚕ 0.00 Global Days XXX

AMA: 2008, Apr, 3-4; 2008, Apr, 3-4; 2008, Apr, 3-4; 2006, Mar, 15; 2006, Mar, 15; 2006, Feb, 10-15; 2006, Feb, 10-15; 2006, Dec, 10-12; 2006, Dec, 10-12; 2006, Dec, 10-12; 2006, December, 10-12; 2006, December, 10-12; 2006, December, 10-12; 2006, March, 15; 2006, February, 10-15; 2006, Dec, 10-12; 2006, Dec, 10-12; 2006, Dec, 10-12; 2006, Dec, 10-12; 2006, Dec, 10-12; 2004, Jan, 27; 2004, January, 27; 2004, Jan, 27

01962 Anesthesia for urgent hysterectomy following delivery Ⓜ ♀ Ⓝ ▫

📇 0.00 ⚕ 0.00 **Global Days XXX**
AMA: 2008, Apr, 3-4; 2008, Apr, 3-4; 2008, Apr, 3-4; 2006, Mar, 15; 2006, Mar, 15; 2006, Feb, 10-15; 2006, Feb, 10-15; 2006, Dec, 10-12; 2006, Dec, 10-12; 2006, Dec, 10-12; 2006, December, 10-12; 2006, December, 10-12; 2006, December, 10-12; 2006, March, 15; 2006, February, 10-15; 2006, Dec, 10-12; 2006, Dec, 10-12; 2006, Dec, 10-12; 2006, Dec, 10-12; 2004, Jan, 27; 2004, January, 27; 2004, Jan, 27

01963 Anesthesia for cesarean hysterectomy without any labor analgesia/anesthesia care Ⓜ ♀ Ⓝ ▫

📇 0.00 ⚕ 0.00 **Global Days XXX**
AMA: 2008, Apr, 3-4; 2008, Apr, 3-4; 2008, Apr, 3-4; 2006, Mar, 15; 2006, Mar, 15; 2006, Feb, 10-15; 2006, Feb, 10-15; 2006, Dec, 10-12; 2006, Dec, 10-12; 2006, Dec, 10-12; 2006, December, 10-12; 2006, December, 10-12; 2006, December, 10-12; 2006, December, 10-12; 2006, March, 15; 2006, February, 10-15; 2006, Dec, 10-12; 2006, Dec, 10-12; 2006, Dec, 10-12; 2006, Dec, 10-12; 2004, Jan, 27; 2004, January, 27; 2004, Jan, 27

01965 Anesthesia for incomplete or missed abortion procedures Ⓝ

📇 0.00 ⚕ 0.00 **Global Days XXX**
AMA: 2008, Apr, 3-4; 2008, Apr, 3-4; 2008, Apr, 3-4; 2006, Feb, 10-15; 2006, Feb, 10-15; 2006, Mar, 15; 2006, Mar, 15; 2006, Dec, 10-12; 2006, February, 10-15; 2006, December, 10-12; 2006, December, 10-12; 2006, December, 10-12; 2006, December, 10-12; 2006, March, 15; 2006, Dec, 10-12; 2006, Dec, 10-12; 2006, Dec, 10-12; 2006, Dec, 10-12; 2006, Dec, 10-12; 2006, Dec, 10-12

01966 Anesthesia for induced abortion procedures Ⓝ

📇 0.00 ⚕ 0.00 **Global Days XXX**
AMA: 2008, Apr, 3-4; 2008, Apr, 3-4; 2008, Apr, 3-4; 2006, Mar, 15; 2006, Mar, 15; 2006, Feb, 10-15; 2006, Feb, 10-15; 2006, Dec, 10-12; 2006, February, 10-15; 2006, December, 10-12; 2006, December, 10-12; 2006, December, 10-12; 2006, March, 15; 2006, Dec, 10-12; 2006, Dec, 10-12; 2006, Dec, 10-12; 2006, Dec, 10-12; 2006, Dec, 10-12

01967 Neuraxial labor analgesia/anesthesia for planned vaginal delivery (this includes any repeat subarachnoid needle placement and drug injection and/or any necessary replacement of an epidural catheter during labor) Ⓜ ♀ Ⓝ ▫

📇 0.00 ⚕ 0.00 **Global Days XXX**
AMA: 2008, Apr, 3-4; 2000, Apr, 3-4; 2008, Apr, 3-4; 2006, Mar, 15; 2006, Mar, 15; 2006, Feb, 10-15; 2006, Dec, 10-12; 2006, Feb, 10-15; 2006, Dec, 10-12; 2006, Dec, 10-12; 2006, Dec, 10-12; 2006, Dec, 10-12; 2006, December, 10-12; 2006, December, 10-12; 2006, December, 10-12; 2006, March, 15; 2006, February, 10-15; 2006, Dec, 10-12; 2006, Dec, 10-12; 2006, Dec, 10-12; 2004, Jun, 1; 2004, June, 1; 2004, January, 27; 2004, Jun, 1; 2004, Jan, 27; 2004, Jan, 27

+ 01968 Anesthesia for cesarean delivery following neuraxial labor analgesia/anesthesia (List separately in addition to code for primary procedure performed) Ⓜ ♀ Ⓝ ▫
Code first (01967)
📇 0.00 ⚕ 0.00 **Global Days XXX**
AMA: 2008, Apr, 3-4; 2008, Apr, 3-4; 2008, Apr, 3-4; 2006, Mar, 15; 2006, Mar, 15; 2006, Feb, 10-15; 2006, Feb, 10-15; 2006, Dec, 10-12; 2006, Dec, 10-12; 2006, Dec, 10-12; 2006, December, 10-12; 2006, December, 10-12; 2006, December, 10-12; 2006, December, 10-12; 2006, March, 15; 2006, February, 10-15; 2006, Dec, 10-12; 2006, Dec, 10-12; 2006, Dec, 10-12; 2006, Dec, 10-12; 2004, Jan, 27; 2004, January, 27; 2004, Jan, 27

+ 01969 Anesthesia for cesarean hysterectomy following neuraxial labor analgesia/anesthesia (List separately in addition to code for primary procedure performed) Ⓜ ♀ Ⓝ ▫
Code first (01967)
📇 0.00 ⚕ 0.00 **Global Days XXX**
AMA: 2008, Apr, 3-4; 2008, Apr, 3-4; 2008, Apr, 3-4; 2006, Mar, 15; 2006, Mar, 15; 2006, Feb, 10-15; 2006, Feb, 10-15; 2006, Dec, 10-12; 2006, Dec, 10-12; 2006, Dec, 10-12; 2006, December, 10-12; 2006, December, 10-12; 2006, December, 10-12; 2006, March, 15; 2006, February, 10-15; 2006, Dec, 10-12; 2006, Dec, 10-12; 2006, Dec, 10-12; 2006, Dec, 10-12; 2004, Jan, 27; 2004, January, 27; 2004, Jan, 27

01990-01999 Anesthesia Miscellaneous

CMS 100-4,12,140.3.2 *Calculation of Anesthesia Time*
CMS 100-4,12,140.2 *Payment for CRNA Services*
CMS 100-4,12,140 *Certified Registered Nurse Anesthetist Services*
CMS 100-4,12,50 *Anesthesia Services*

01990 Physiological support for harvesting of organ(s) from brain-dead patient Ⓒ ▫

📇 0.00 ⚕ 0.00 **Global Days XXX**
AMA: 2008, Apr, 3-4; 2008, Apr, 3-4; 2008, Apr, 3-4; 2006, Mar, 15; 2006, Mar, 15; 2006, Feb, 10-15; 2006, Feb, 10-15; 2006, Dec, 10-12; 2006, Dec, 10-12; 2006, Dec, 10-12; 2006, December, 10-12; 2006, December, 10-12; 2006, December, 10-12; 2006, March, 15; 2006, February, 10-15; 2006, Dec, 10-12; 2006, Dec, 10-12; 2006, Dec, 10-12; 2006, Dec, 10-12; 2004, Jan, 27; 2004, January, 27; 2004, Jan, 27

01991 Anesthesia for diagnostic or therapeutic nerve blocks and injections (when block or injection is performed by a different provider); other than the prone position Ⓝ ▫

Do not report with (99143-99150)
EXCLUDES *Bier block for pain management (64999)*
IV or intra-arterial injections (96373-96374)
regional or local anesthesia of arms or legs for surgical procedure

📇 0.00 ⚕ 0.00 **Global Days XXX**
AMA: 2008, Apr, 3-4; 2008, Apr, 3-4; 2008, Apr, 3-4; 2006, Feb, 10-15; 2006, Feb, 10-15; 2006, Mar, 15; 2006, Mar, 15; 2006, Dec, 10-12; 2006, Dec, 10-12; 2006, Dec, 10-12; 2006, December, 10-12; 2006, December, 10-12; 2006, December, 10-12; 2006, December, 10-12; 2006, March, 15; 2006, February, 10-15; 2006, Dec, 10-12; 2006, Dec, 10-12; 2006, Dec, 10-12; 2006, Dec, 10-12; 2004, Jan, 27; 2004, January, 27; 2004, Jan, 27

01992 prone position Ⓝ ▫

Do not report with (99143-99150)
EXCLUDES *Bier block for pain management (64999)*
IV or intra-arterial injections (99143-99150)
pain management via intra-arterial or intravenous therapy (96373-96374)
regional or local anesthesia of arms or legs for surgical procedure

📇 0.00 ⚕ 0.00 **Global Days XXX**
AMA: 2008, Apr, 3-4; 2008, Apr, 3-4; 2008, Apr, 3-4; 2006, Mar, 15; 2006, Mar, 15; 2006, Feb, 10-15; 2006, Feb, 10-15; 2006, Dec, 10-12; 2006, Dec, 10-12; 2006, Dec, 10-12; 2006, December, 10-12; 2006, December, 10-12; 2006, December, 10-12; 2006, December, 10-12; 2006, March, 15; 2006, February, 10-15; 2006, Dec, 10-12; 2006, Dec, 10-12; 2006, Dec, 10-12; 2006, Dec, 10-12; 2004, Jan, 27; 2004, January, 27; 2004, Jan, 27

● New Code ▲ Revised Code Ⓜ Maternity Edit Ⓐ Age Edit Ⓐ-Ⓨ OPPS Status Indicator 📇 Facility RVU ⚕ Non-Facility RVU
▫ CCI Comprehensive Code 50 Bilateral Procedure + Add-on Indicator 🔬 Laboratory crosswalk 📷 Radiology crosswalk

01996 Daily hospital management of epidural or subarachnoid continuous drug administration Ⓝ ▣
[INCLUDES] continuous epidural or subarachnoid drug services performed after insertion of an epidural or subarachnoid catheter

🚗 0.00 🔪 0.00 **Global Days XXX**
AMA: 2008, Apr, 3-4; 2008, Apr, 3-4; 2008, Apr, 3-4; 2006, Mar, 15; 2006, Mar, 15; 2006, Feb, 10-15; 2006, Dec, 10-12; 2006, Feb, 10-15; 2006, Dec, 10-12; 2006, Dec, 10-12; 2006, Dec, 10-12; 2006, Dec, 10-12; 2006, December, 10-12; 2006, December, 10-12; 2006, December, 10-12; 2006, December, 10-12; 2006, March, 15; 2006, February, 10-15; 2006, Dec, 10-12; 2006, Dec, 10-12; 2006, Dec, 10-12; 2004, Jan, 27; 2004, January, 27; 2004, February, 7; 2004, Jan, 27; 2004, Feb, 7; 2004, Feb, 7

01999 Unlisted anesthesia procedure(s) Ⓝ
🚗 0.00 🔪 0.00 **Global Days XXX**
AMA: 2008, Apr, 3-4; 2008, Apr, 3-4; 2008, Jan, 10-25; 2008, Apr, 3-4; 2007, Jan, 13-27; 2007, Jan, 13-27; 2007, January, 13-27; 2006, Mar, 15; 2006, Mar, 15; 2006, Feb, 10-15; 2006, Feb, 10-15; 2006, Dec, 10-12; 2006, Dec, 10-12; 2006, Dec, 10-12; 2006, December, 10-12; 2006, December, 10-12; 2006, December, 10-12; 2006, December, 10-12; 2006, March, 15; 2006, February, 10-15; 2006, Dec, 10-12; 2006, Dec, 10-12; 2006, Dec, 10-12; 2006, Dec, 10-12; 2006, Dec, 10-12; 2004, Jan, 27; 2004, January, 27; 2004, Jan, 27

10021-10022 Fine Needle Aspiration

CMS *100-4,13,80.2* *S&I Multiple Procedure Reduction*
CMS *100-4,13,80.1* *Supervision and Interpretation Codes*
EXCLUDES *percutaneous needle biopsy of:*
abdominal or retroperitoneal mass (49180)
bone (20220, 20225)
bone marrow (38221)
breast (19100)
epididymis (54800)
kidney (50200)
liver (47000-47001)
lung or mediastinum (32405)
lymph node (38505)
muscle (20206)
nucleus pulposus, paravertebral tissue or intervertebral disc (62267)
pancreas (48102)
pleura (32400)
prostate (55700)
salivary gland (42400)
spinal cord (62269)
testis (54500)
thyroid (60100)

10021 **Fine needle aspiration; without imaging guidance** [P2] [T] [60] [▢]
  ◪ *88172-88173*
  ⬚ 1.80 ≳ 3.52 Global Days XXX
  AMA: 2008, Jan, 10-25; 2007, Jan, 13-27; 2007, Jan, 13-27; 2007, Jan, 13-27; 2007, January, 13-27; 2007, Jan, 13-27; 2005, Mar, 11-15; 2005, March, 11-15; 2005, Mar, 11-15; 2005, Mar, 11-15; 2005, Mar, 11-15

10022 **with imaging guidance** [62] [T] [60] [▢]
  ⊞ *76942, 77002, 77012, 77021*
  ◪ *88172-88173*
  ⬚ 1.78 ≳ 3.61 Global Days XXX
  AMA: 2008, Jan, 10-25; 2007, Jun, 10-11; 2007, Jun, 10-11; 2007, June, 10-11

10040-10180 Treatment of Fluid-filled Lesions: Skin and Subcutaneous Tissues

CMS *100-4,12,30*   *Correct Coding Policy*
CMS *100-4,13,80.2* *S&I Multiple Procedure Reduction*
CMS *100-4,13,80.1* *Physician Presence*

10040 **Acne surgery (eg, marsupialization, opening or removal of multiple milia, comedones, cysts, pustules)** [P2] [T] [▢]
  ⬚ 2.19 ≳ 2.50 Global Days 010

10060 **Incision and drainage of abscess (eg, carbuncle, suppurative hidradenitis, cutaneous or subcutaneous abscess, cyst, furuncle, or paronychia); simple or single** [P3] [T] [▢]
  ⬚ 2.35 ≳ 2.72 Global Days 010
  AMA: 2008, Jan, 10-25; 2007, Jan, 13-27; 2007, Jan, 13-27; 2007, Jan, 13-27; 2007, January, 13-27; 2007, Jan, 13-27; 2006, Dec, 14-15; 2006, December, 14-15; 2006, Dec, 14-15; 2006, Dec, 14-15; 2006, Dec, 14-15

10061 **complicated or multiple** [P2] [T] [▢]
  ⬚ 4.18 ≳ 4.67 Global Days 010
  AMA: 2006, Dec, 14-15; 2006, December, 14-15; 2006, Dec, 14-15; 2006, Dec, 14-15; 2006, Dec, 14-15

10080 **Incision and drainage of pilonidal cyst; simple** [P2] [T] [▢]
  ⬚ 2.40 ≳ 4.04 Global Days 010
  AMA: 2007, May, 5-8; 2007, May, 5-8; 2007, May, 5-8; 2006, Dec, 14-15; 2006, Dec, 14-15; 2006, December, 14-15; 2006, Dec, 14-15; 2006, Dec, 14-15

10081 **complicated** [P3] [T] [▢]
  EXCLUDES *excision of pilonidal cyst (11770-11772)*
  ⬚ 4.19 ≳ 6.35 Global Days 010
  AMA: 2007, May, 5-8; 2007, May, 5-8; 2007, May, 5-8; 2006, Dec, 14-15; 2006, Dec, 14-15; 2006, December, 14-15; 2006, Dec, 14-15; 2006, Dec, 14-15

10120 **Incision and removal of foreign body, subcutaneous tissues; simple** [P3] [T] [▢]
  ⬚ 2.30 ≳ 3.33 Global Days 010
  AMA: 2006, Dec, 14-15; 2006, Dec, 14-15; 2006, Dec, 14-15; 2006, Dec, 14-15; 2006, December, 14-15

10121 **complicated** [A2] [T] [▢]
  EXCLUDES *debridement associated with a fracture or dislocation (11010-11012)*
  exploration penetrating wound (20100-20103)
  ⬚ 4.72 ≳ 6.50 Global Days 010
  AMA: 2006, Dec, 14-15; 2006, Dec, 14-15; 2006, Dec, 14-15; 2006, Dec, 14-15; 2006, December, 14-15

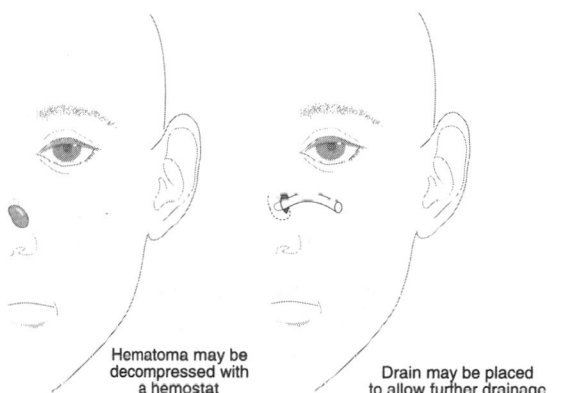

Hematoma may be decompressed with a hemostat

Drain may be placed to allow further drainage

10140 **Incision and drainage of hematoma, seroma or fluid collection** [P3] [T] [▢]
  ⊞ *76942, 77012, 77021*
  ⬚ 3.02 ≳ 3.84 Global Days 010
  AMA: 2008, Jan, 10-25; 2007, Jan, 13-27; 2007, Jan, 13-27; 2007, Jan, 13-27; 2007, Jan, 13-27; 2007, January, 13-27

10160 **Puncture aspiration of abscess, hematoma, bulla, or cyst** [P2] [T] [▢]
  ⊞ *76942, 77012, 77021*
  ⬚ 2.43 ≳ 3.12 Global Days 010

10180 **Incision and drainage, complex, postoperative wound infection** [A2] [T] [▢]
  EXCLUDES *wound dehiscence (12020-12021, 13160)*
  ⬚ 4.48 ≳ 5.79 Global Days 010
  AMA: 2008, Jan, 10-25

● New Code   ▲ Revised Code   Ⓜ Maternity Edit   Ⓐ Age Edit   Ⓐ-Ⓨ OPPS Status Indicator   ⬚ Facility RVU   ≳ Non-Facility RVU
▢ CCI Comprehensive Code   50 Bilateral Procedure   + Add-on Indicator   ◪ Laboratory crosswalk   ⊞ Radiology crosswalk

Integumentary System

11000 — 11057

11000-11012 Removal of Foreign Substances and Infected/Devitalized Tissue

CMS *100-4,12,40.1*   *Global Surgery Package*
CMS *100-4,12,40.2*   *Billing Requirements for Global Surgeries*
EXCLUDES   *burn debridement or treatment (16000-16035)*
         dermabrasions (15780-15783)
         nail debridement (11720-11721)

11000   **Debridement of extensive eczematous or infected skin; up to 10% of body surface**   P3 T ▢
     EXCLUDES   *necrotizing soft tissue infection of:*
         abdominal wall (11005-11006)
         external genitalia and perineum (11004, 11006)
     ⚙ 0.85   ✂ 1.35   **Global Days 000**

+   ▲ **11001**   **each additional 10% of the body surface, or part thereof (List separately in addition to code for primary procedure)**   P3 T
     Code first 11000
     ⚙ 0.43   ✂ 0.57   **Global Days ZZZ**

11004   **Debridement of skin, subcutaneous tissue, muscle and fascia for necrotizing soft tissue infection; external genitalia and perineum**   C ▢
     EXCLUDES   *skin grafts or flaps (14000-14350, 15040-15770)*
     ⚙ 15.03   ✂ 15.03   **Global Days 000**

11005   **abdominal wall, with or without fascial closure**   C 80 ▢
     ⚙ 19.63   ✂ 19.63   **Global Days 000**

11006   **external genitalia, perineum and abdominal wall, with or without fascial closure**   C ▢
     ⚙ 18.72   ✂ 18.72   **Global Days 000**

+   **11008**   **Removal of prosthetic material or mesh, abdominal wall for infection (eg, for chronic or recurrent mesh infection or necrotizing soft tissue infection) (List separately in addition to code for primary procedure)**   C 80
     INCLUDES   debridement:
         associated with an open fracture
         bone
         extensive eczematous or infected skin
         muscle
         skin
         subcutaneous tissue
     EXCLUDES   *insertion of mesh (49568)*
         orchiectomy (54520)
         skin grafts or flaps (14000-14350, 15040-15770)
         testicular transplantation (54680)
     Code first (10180, 11004-11006)
     Do not report with (11000-11001, 11010-11044)
     ⚙ 7.17   ✂ 7.17   **Global Days ZZZ**

11010   **Debridement including removal of foreign material associated with open fracture(s) and/or dislocation(s); skin and subcutaneous tissues**   A2 T ▢
     ⚙ 7.34   ✂ 11.70   **Global Days 010**
     AMA: 2008, Jan, 10-25; 2007, Jan, 13-27; 2007, Jan, 13-27; 2007, Jan, 13-27; 2007, January, 13-27

11011   **skin, subcutaneous tissue, muscle fascia, and muscle**   A2 T ▢
     ⚙ 7.89   ✂ 13.03   **Global Days 000**

11012   **skin, subcutaneous tissue, muscle fascia, muscle, and bone**   A2 T ▢
     ⚙ 11.47   ✂ 17.84   **Global Days 000**
     AMA: 2008, Jan, 10-25; 2007, Jan, 13-2; 2007, Jan, 13-2; 2007, Jan, 13-27; 2007, Jan, 13-27, 2007, January, 13-27

11040-11044 Removal of Infected/Devitalized Tissue

CMS *100-2,15,260*   *Covered ASC Procedures*
CMS *100-4,14,10*   *ASC Procedures*
CMS *100-4,12,40.1*   *Global Surgery Definition*
CMS *100-4,12,40.2*   *Billing Requirements for Global Surgeries*
INCLUDES   active wound care management
         removal of devitalized tissue
EXCLUDES   *burn debridement or treatment (16000-16035)*
         dermabrasions (15780-15783)
         nail debridement (11720-11721)

Do not report with (97597-97602)

11040   **Debridement; skin, partial thickness**   P3 T ▢
     ⚙ 0.73   ✂ 1.18   **Global Days 000**
     AMA: 2008, Jan, 10-25; 2007, Jan, 13-27; 2007, Jan, 13-27; 2007, Jan, 13-27; 2007, January, 13-27; 2005, Jun, 1-4; 2005, Jun, 1-4; 2005, June, 1-4; 2005, June, 9-11; 2005, Jun, 9-11; 2005, Jun, 9-11; 2005, June, 9-11; 2005, June, 9-11

11041   **skin, full thickness**   P3 T ▢
     ⚙ 0.92   ✂ 1.39   **Global Days 000**
     AMA: 2005, Jun, 1-4; 2005, Jun, 1-4; 2005, June, 1-4; 2005, June, 1-4; 2005, June, 1-4

11042   **skin, and subcutaneous tissue**   A2 T ▢
     ⚙ 1.23   ✂ 1.88   **Global Days 000**
     AMA: 2005, Jun, 9-11; 2005, Jun, 9-11; 2005, Jun, 1-4; 2005, Jun, 1-4; 2005, June, 9-11; 2005, June, 9-11; 2005, June, 1-4; 2005, June, 1-4; 2005, June, 9-11; 2005, June, 1-4

11043   **skin, subcutaneous tissue, and muscle**   A2 T ▢
     ⚙ 5.95   ✂ 6.80   **Global Days 010**
     AMA: 2008, Jan, 10-25; 2007, Jan, 13-27; 2007, Jan, 13-27; 2007, Jan, 13-27; 2007, Jan, 13-27; 2007, January, 13-27; 2005, Jun, 1-4; 2005, Jun, 1-4; 2005, Jun, 9-11; 2005, June, 1-4; 2005, June, 9-11; 2005, Jun, 9-11; 2005, June, 9-11; 2005, June, 9-11; 2005, June, 1-4; 2005, June, 1-4

11044   **skin, subcutaneous tissue, muscle, and bone**   A2 T ▢
     ⚙ 8.19   ✂ 9.29   **Global Days 010**
     AMA: 2008, Jan, 10-25; 2007, Jan, 13-27; 2007, Jan, 13-27; 2007, Jan, 13-27; 2007, Jan, 13-27; 2007, January, 13-27; 2005, Jun, 9-11; 2005, Jun, 9-11; 2005, Jun, 1-4; 2005, June, 9-11; 2005, June, 1-4; 2005, Jun, 1-4; 2005, June, 1-4; 2005, June, 1-4; 2005, June, 9-11; 2005, June, 9-11

11055-11057 Excision Benign Hypertrophic Skin Lesions

CMS *100-2,15,290*   *Routine Foot Care*
EXCLUDES   *destruction (17000-17004)*

11055   **Paring or cutting of benign hyperkeratotic lesion (eg, corn or callus); single lesion**   P3 T ▢
     ⚙ 0.61   ✂ 1.21   **Global Days 000**
     AMA: 2008, Jan, 10-25; 2007, Jan, 13-27; 2007, Jan, 13-27; 2007, Jan, 13-27; 2007, Jan, 13-27; 2007, January, 13-27

11056   **2 to 4 lesions**   P3 T ▢
     ⚙ 0.86   ✂ 1.48   **Global Days 000**

11057   **more than 4 lesions**   P2 T ▢
     ⚙ 1.12   ✂ 1.79   **Global Days 000**

26/TC Professional/Technical Component Only   80/80 Assist-at-Surgery Allowed/With Documentation   Unlisted   Not Covered
AMA: CPT Assistant References   A2-Z3 ASC Payment Indicator   ♂ Male Only   ♀ Female Only   ⊘ Modifier 51 Exempt   PQ PQRI

28   CPT only © 2008 American Medical Association. All Rights Reserved. (Black Ink)   Medicare (Red Ink)   © 2008 Ingenix (Blue Ink)

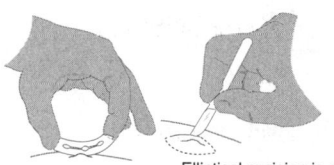

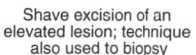

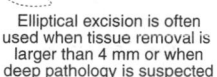

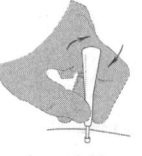

Shave excision of an elevated lesion; technique also used to biopsy

Elliptical excision is often used when tissue removal is larger than 4 mm or when deep pathology is suspected

A punch biopsy cuts a core of tissue as the tool is twisted downward

11100-11101 Surgical Biopsy Skin and Mucous Membranes

CMS *100-4,12,30   Correct Coding Policy*

EXCLUDES *biopsy of:*
        conjunctiva (68100)
        eyelid (67810)

11100   Biopsy of skin, subcutaneous tissue and/or mucous membrane (including simple closure), unless otherwise listed; single lesion 〔P2〕〔T〕〔▭〕
        🔹 **1.24** ✂ **2.55 Global Days 000**
        AMA: 2008, Feb, 1; 2006, Dec, 1-3; 2006, Dec, 1-3; 2006, Dec, 1-3; 2006, Dec, 1-3; 2006, December, 1-3; 2004, Jul, 1; 2004, Jul, 1; 2004, July, 1; 2004, July, 1; 2004, October, 4; 2004, Oct, 4; 2004, Oct, 4; 2004, July, 1; 2004, Oct, 4; 2004, Oct, 4

+   **11101   each separate/additional lesion (List separately in addition to code for primary procedure)** 〔P3〕〔T〕
        Code first 11100
        🔹 **0.64** ✂ **0.83 Global Days ZZZ**
        AMA: 2008, Feb, 1; 2006, Dec, 1-3; 2006, Dec, 1-3; 2006, Dec, 1-3; 2006, Dec, 1-3; 2006, December, 1-3; 2004, Jul, 1; 2004, Jul, 1; 2004, July, 1; 2004, July, 1; 2004, October, 4; 2004, Oct, 4; 2004, Oct, 4; 2004, July, 1; 2004, Oct, 4; 2004, Oct, 4

11200-11201 Skin Tag Removal - All Techniques

CMS *100-4,12,30   Correct Coding Policy*
CMS *100-4,12,40.1   Global Surgery Package Definition*
CMS *100-4,12,40.2   Billing Requirements for Global Surgeries*

INCLUDES chemical destruction
        electrocauterization
        electrosurgical destruction
        ligature strangulation
        removal with or without local anesthesia
        sharp excision or scissoring

EXCLUDES *extensive or complicated secondary wound closure (13160)*

11200   Removal of skin tags, multiple fibrocutaneous tags, any area; up to and including 15 lesions 〔P7〕〔T〕〔▭〕
        🔹 **1.70** ✂ **2.01 Global Days 010**
        AMA: 2008, Jan, 10-25; 2007, Jan, 13-27; 2007, Jan, 13-27; 2007, Jan, 13-27; 2007, Jan, 13-27; 2007, January, 13-27

+   ▲ **11201   each additional 10 lesions, or part thereof (List separately in addition to code for primary procedure)** 〔P3〕〔T〕
        Code first 11200
        🔹 **0.43** ✂ **0.47 Global Days ZZZ**

11300-11313 Skin Lesion Removal: Shaving

CMS *100-4,12,40.2   Global Surgery Billing Requirements*
CMS *100-4,12,40.1   Global Surgery Package Definition*
CMS *100-4,12,50   Local anesthesia*

INCLUDES local anesthesia
        wound cauterization

11300   Shaving of epidermal or dermal lesion, single lesion, trunk, arms or legs; lesion diameter 0.5 cm or less 〔P2〕〔T〕〔80〕〔▭〕
        🔹 **0.76** ✂ **1.67 Global Days 000**
        AMA: 2008, Jan, 10-25; 2008, Feb, 1; 2007, Jan, 13-27; 2007, Jan, 13-27; 2007, Jan, 13-27; 2007, Jan, 13-27; 2007, January, 13-27

11301   lesion diameter 0.6 to 1.0 cm 〔P2〕〔T〕〔80〕〔▭〕
        🔹 **1.29** ✂ **2.29 Global Days 000**
        AMA: 2008, Jan, 10-25; 2008, Feb, 1; 2007, Jan, 13-27; 2007, Jan, 13-27; 2007, Jan, 13-27; 2007, Jan, 13-27; 2007, January, 13-27

11302   lesion diameter 1.1 to 2.0 cm 〔P7〕〔T〕〔80〕〔▭〕
        🔹 **1.60** ✂ **2.74 Global Days 000**
        AMA: 2008, Jan, 10-25; 2008, Feb, 1; 2007, Jan, 13-27; 2007, Jan, 13-27; 2007, Jan, 13-27; 2007, Jan, 13-27; 2007, January, 13-27

11303   lesion diameter over 2.0 cm 〔P2〕〔T〕〔80〕〔▭〕
        🔹 **1.88** ✂ **3.22 Global Days 000**
        AMA: 2008, Jan, 10-25; 2008, Feb, 1; 2007, Jan, 13-27; 2007, Jan, 13-27; 2007, Jan, 13-27; 2007, January, 13-27

11305   Shaving of epidermal or dermal lesion, single lesion, scalp, neck, hands, feet, genitalia; lesion diameter 0.5 cm or less 〔P2〕〔T〕〔80〕〔▭〕
        🔹 **0.97** ✂ **1.73 Global Days 000**
        AMA: 2008, Jan, 10-25, 2008, Feb, 1; 2007, Jan, 13-27; 2007, Jan, 13-27; 2007, Jan, 13-27; 2007, Jan, 13-27; 2007, January, 13-27

11306   lesion diameter 0.6 to 1.0 cm 〔P2〕〔T〕〔80〕〔▭〕
        🔹 **1.46** ✂ **2.38 Global Days 000**
        AMA: 2008, Jan, 10-25; 2008, Feb, 1; 2007, Jan, 13-27; 2007, Jan, 13-27; 2007, Jan, 13-27; 2007, January, 13-27

11307   lesion diameter 1.1 to 2.0 cm 〔P2〕〔T〕〔80〕〔▭〕
        🔹 **1.72** ✂ **2.81 Global Days 000**
        AMA: 2008, Jan, 10-25; 2008, Feb, 1; 2007, Jan, 13-27; 2007, Jan, 13-27; 2007, Jan, 13-27; 2007, January, 13-27

11308   lesion diameter over 2.0 cm 〔P2〕〔T〕〔80〕〔▭〕
        🔹 **2.08** ✂ **3.17 Global Days 000**
        AMA: 2008, Jan, 10-25; 2008, Feb, 1; 2007, Jan, 13-27; 2007, Jan, 13-27; 2007, Jan, 13-27; 2007, January, 13-27

11310   Shaving of epidermal or dermal lesion, single lesion, face, ears, eyelids, nose, lips, mucous membrane; lesion diameter 0.5 cm or less 〔P2〕〔T〕〔80〕〔▭〕
        🔹 **1.10** ✂ **2.08 Global Days 000**
        AMA: 2008, Jan, 10-25; 2008, Feb, 1; 2007, Jan, 13-27; 2007, Jan, 13-27; 2007, Jan, 13-27; 2007, January, 13-27

11311   lesion diameter 0.6 to 1.0 cm 〔P2〕〔T〕〔80〕〔▭〕
        🔹 **1.61** ✂ **2.64 Global Days 000**
        AMA: 2008, Jan, 10-25; 2008, Feb, 1; 2007, Jan, 13-27; 2007, Jan, 13-27; 2007, Jan, 13-27; 2007, January, 13-27

11312   lesion diameter 1.1 to 2.0 cm 〔P2〕〔T〕〔80〕〔▭〕
        🔹 **1.85** ✂ **3.05 Global Days 000**
        AMA: 2008, Jan, 10-25; 2008, Feb, 1; 2007, Jan, 13-27; 2007, Jan, 13-27; 2007, Jan, 13-27; 2007, January, 13-27

The skin is the largest organ of the human body and accounts for about 20 percent of total body weight. It serves mainly as a protective barrier, a temperature regulator, and as a sensory device. The epidermis is outermost and is the thinnest of the skin layers; the major part of the dermis is high in collagen and is notable for its great elasticity and strength; the major blood and nerve network is found in the middermis. Adnexal structures are the hair follicles, sebaceous glands, sweat glands, and the follicles that produce fingernails and toenails. Lesions are small areas of skin disease and may be solitary or multiple

● New Code   ▲ Revised Code   ⓜ Maternity Edit   🄰 Age Edit   〔A-Y〕 OPPS Status Indicator   🔹 Facility RVU   ✂ Non-Facility RVU
▢ CCI Comprehensive Code   〔50〕 Bilateral Procedure   + Add-on Indicator   ▣ Laboratory crosswalk   ▣ Radiology crosswalk

© 2008 Ingenix *(Blue Ink)*   CPT only © 2008 American Medical Association. All Rights Reserved. (Black Ink)   Medicare (Red Ink)   **29**

Integumentary System

11100 — 11312

11313 lesion diameter over 2.0 cm ☐☐☐☐
🔪 2.48 ✂ 3.82 **Global Days 000**
AMA: 2008, Jan, 10-25; 2008, Feb, 1; 2007, Jan, 13-27; 2007, Jan, 13-27; 2007, Jan, 13-27; 2007, Jan, 13-27; 2007, January, 13-27

11400-11446 Skin Lesion Removal: Benign

CMS *100-2,16,120* *Cosmetic Procedures*
CMS *100-4,12,40.1* *Global Surgery Package Definition*
CMS *100-4,12,50* *Local anesthesia*
CMS *100-4,12,40.2* *Billing Requirements br Global Surgeries*

INCLUDES biopsy on same lesion
full thickness removal including margins
local anesthesia
simple, nonlayered closure

EXCLUDES *biopsy of eyelid (67810)*
destruction of eyelid lesion (67850)
excision of chalazion (67800-67808)
excision and reconstruction of eyelid (67961-67975)
eyelid procedures involving more than skin (67800 and subsequent codes)
intermediate or complex closure of defects caused by excision, incision, or trauma
shave removal (11300-11313)

Code also complex closure (13100-13153)
Code also destruction (17000-17250)
Code also intermediate closure (12031-12057)
Code also reconstruction (15002-15261, 15570-15770)

11400 **Excision, benign lesion including margins, except skin tag (unless listed elsewhere), trunk, arms or legs; excised diameter 0.5 cm or less** ☐☐☐
🔪 1.86 ✂ 2.84 **Global Days 010**
AMA: 2008, Jan, 10-25; 2008, Jul, 5-6&15; 2007, Jan, 13-27; 2007, Jan, 13-27; 2007, Jan, 13-27; 2007, Jan, 13-27; 2007, January, 13-27; 2006, Aug, 12-14; 2006, Aug, 12-14; 2006, Aug, 12-14; 2006, August, 12-14; 2006, Aug, 12-14; 2004, Oct, 4; 2004, Oct, 4; 2004, October, 4; 2004, Oct, 4; 2004, Oct, 4

11401 excised diameter 0.6 to 1.0 cm ☐☐☐
🔪 2.48 ✂ 3.50 **Global Days 010**
AMA: 2008, Jul, 5-6&15; 2006, Aug, 12-14; 2006, Aug, 12-14; 2006, Aug, 12-14; 2006, August, 12-14; 2006, Aug, 12-14; 2004, Oct, 4; 2004, October, 4; 2004, Oct, 4; 2004, Oct, 4; 2004, Oct, 4

11402 excised diameter 1.1 to 2.0 cm ☐☐☐
🔪 2.75 ✂ 3.91 **Global Days 010**
AMA: 2008, Jul, 5-6&15; 2006, Aug, 12-14; 2006, Aug, 12-14; 2006, Aug, 12-14; 2006, August, 12-14; 2006, Aug, 12-14; 2004, Oct, 4; 2004, October, 4; 2004, Oct, 4; 2004, Oct, 4; 2004, Oct, 4

11403 excised diameter 2.1 to 3.0 cm ☐☐☐
🔪 3.50 ✂ 4.50 **Global Days 010**
AMA: 2008, Jul, 5-6&15; 2006, Aug, 12-14; 2006, Aug, 12-14; 2006, Aug, 12-14; 2006, August, 12-14; 2006, Aug, 12-14; 2004, Oct, 4; 2004, October, 4; 2004, Oct, 4; 2004, Oct, 4; 2004, Oct, 4

11404 excised diameter 3.1 to 4.0 cm ☐☐☐
🔪 3.90 ✂ 5.13 **Global Days 010**
AMA: 2008, Jul, 5-6&15; 2006, Aug, 12-14; 2006, Aug, 12-14; 2006, Aug, 12-14; 2006, August, 12-14; 2006, Aug, 12-14; 2004, Oct, 4; 2004, October, 4; 2004, Oct, 4; 2004, Oct, 4; 2004, Oct, 4

11406 excised diameter over 4.0 cm ☐☐☐
🔪 5.82 ✂ 7.23 **Global Days 010**
AMA: 2008, Jul, 5-6&15; 2006, Aug, 12-14; 2006, Aug, 12-14; 2006, Aug, 12-14; 2006, August, 12-14; 2006, Aug, 12-14; 2004, Oct, 4; 2004, October, 4; 2004, Oct, 4; 2004, Oct, 4; 2004, Oct, 4

11420 **Excision, benign lesion including margins, except skin tag (unless listed elsewhere), scalp, neck, hands, feet, genitalia; excised diameter 0.5 cm or less** ☐☐☐
🔪 2.02 ✂ 2.88 **Global Days 010**
AMA: 2008, Jul, 5-6&15; 2006, Aug, 12-14; 2006, Aug, 12-14; 2006, Aug, 12-14; 2006, August, 12-14; 2006, Aug, 12-14; 2004, Oct, 4; 2004, October, 4; 2004, Oct, 4; 2004, Oct, 4; 2004, Oct, 4

11421 excised diameter 0.6 to 1.0 cm ☐☐☐
🔪 2.73 ✂ 3.74 **Global Days 010**
AMA: 2008, Jul, 5-6&15; 2006, Aug, 12-14; 2006, Aug, 12-14; 2006, Aug, 12-14; 2006, August, 12-14; 2006, Aug, 12-14; 2004, Oct, 4; 2004, October, 4; 2004, Oct, 4; 2004, Oct, 4; 2004, Oct, 4

11422 excised diameter 1.1 to 2.0 cm ☐☐☐
🔪 3.30 ✂ 4.18 **Global Days 010**
AMA: 2008, Jul, 5-6&15; 2006, Aug, 12-14; 2006, Aug, 12-14; 2006, Aug, 12-14; 2006, August, 12-14; 2006, Aug, 12-14; 2004, Oct, 4; 2004, October, 4; 2004, Oct, 4; 2004, Oct, 4; 2004, Oct, 4

11423 excised diameter 2.1 to 3.0 cm ☐☐☐
🔪 3.85 ✂ 4.87 **Global Days 010**
AMA: 2008, Jul, 5-6&15; 2006, Aug, 12-14; 2006, Aug, 12-14; 2006, Aug, 12-14; 2006, August, 12-14; 2006, Aug, 12-14; 2004, Oct, 4; 2004, October, 4; 2004, Oct, 4; 2004, Oct, 4; 2004, Oct, 4

11424 excised diameter 3.1 to 4.0 cm ☐☐☐
🔪 4.44 ✂ 5.62 **Global Days 010**
AMA: 2008, Jul, 5-6&15; 2006, Aug, 12-14; 2006, Aug, 12-14; 2006, Aug, 12-14; 2006, August, 12-14; 2006, Aug, 12-14; 2004, Oct, 4; 2004, October, 4; 2004, Oct, 4; 2004, Oct, 4; 2004, Oct, 4

11426 excised diameter over 4.0 cm ☐☐☐
🔪 6.79 ✂ 8.07 **Global Days 010**
AMA: 2008, Jul, 5-6&15; 2006, Aug, 12-14; 2006, Aug, 12-14; 2006, Aug, 12-14; 2006, August, 12-14; 2006, Aug, 12-14; 2004, Oct, 4; 2004, October, 4; 2004, Oct, 4; 2004, Oct, 4; 2004, Oct, 4

The physician removes a benign lesion from the external ear, nose, or mucous membranes

Up to 0.5 cm (11440)
3.1 to 4.0 cm (11444)
0.6 to 1.0 cm (11441)
1.1 to 2.0 cm (11442)
2.1 to 3.0 cm (11443)
Larger than 4.0 cm (11446)

11440 **Excision, other benign lesion including margins, except skin tag (unless listed elsewhere), face, ears, eyelids, nose, lips, mucous membrane; excised diameter 0.5 cm or less** ☐☐☐
🔪 2.42 ✂ 3.15 **Global Days 010**
AMA: 2008, Jul, 5-6&15; 2006, Aug, 12-14; 2006, Aug, 12-14; 2006, Aug, 12-14; 2006, August, 12-14; 2006, Aug, 12-14; 2004, Oct, 4; 2004, October, 4; 2004, Oct, 4; 2004, Oct, 4; 2004, Oct, 4

11441 excised diameter 0.6 to 1.0 cm ☐☐☐
🔪 3.18 ✂ 4.00 **Global Days 010**
AMA: 2008, Jul, 5-6&15; 2006, Aug, 12-14; 2006, Aug, 12-14; 2006, Aug, 12-14; 2006, August, 12-14; 2006, Aug, 12-14; 2004, Oct, 4; 2004, October, 4; 2004, Oct, 4; 2004, Oct, 4; 2004, Oct, 4

11442 excised diameter 1.1 to 2.0 cm ☐☐☐
🔪 3.55 ✂ 4.51 **Global Days 010**
AMA: 2008, Jun, 14-15; 2008, Jul, 5-6&15; 2006, Aug, 12-14; 2006, Aug, 12-14; 2006, Aug, 12-14; 2006, August, 12-14; 2006, Aug, 12-14; 2004, Oct, 4; 2004, October, 4; 2004, Oct, 4; 2004, Oct, 4; 2004, Oct, 4

26/16 Professional/Technical Component Only   80/60 Assist-at-Surgery Allowed/With Documentation   Unlisted   Not Covered
AMA: CPT Assistant References   A2-Z3 ASC Payment Indicator   ♂ Male Only   ♀ Female Only   ⊘ Modifier 51 Exempt   PQ PQRI

30   CPT only © 2008 American Medical Association. All Rights Reserved. (Black Ink)   Medicare (Red Ink)   © 2008 Ingenix (Blue Ink)

Integumentary System

11313 — 11442

11443　　excised diameter 2.1 to 3.0 cm　　P3 T ▯
　　　　🔳 4.39　🔾 5.42　Global Days 010
　　　　AMA: 2008, Jul, 5-6&15; 2006, Aug, 12-14; 2006, Aug, 12-14;
　　　　2006, Aug, 12-14; 2006, August, 12-14; 2006, Aug, 12-14; 2004,
　　　　Oct, 4; 2004, October, 4; 2004, Oct, 4; 2004, Oct, 4; 2004, Oct, 4

11444　　excised diameter 3.1 to 4.0 cm　　A2 T ▯
　　　　🔳 5.63　🔾 6.84　Global Days 010
　　　　AMA: 2008, Jul, 5-6&15; 2006, Aug, 12-14; 2006, Aug, 12-14;
　　　　2006, Aug, 12-14; 2006, August, 12-14; 2006, Aug, 12-14; 2004,
　　　　Oct, 4; 2004, October, 4; 2004, Oct, 4; 2004, Oct, 4; 2004, Oct, 4

11446　　excised diameter over 4.0 cm　　A2 T ▯
　　　　🔳 7.96　🔾 9.31　Global Days 010
　　　　AMA: 2008, Jan, 10-25; 2008, Jul, 5-6&15; 2007, Jan, 13-27;
　　　　2007, Jan, 13-27; 2007, January, 13-27; 2006, Aug, 12-14; 2006,
　　　　Aug, 12-14; 2006, Aug, 12-14; 2006, Aug, 12-14; 2006, August,
　　　　12-14; 2004, Oct, 4; 2004, Oct, 4; 2004, Oct, 4; 2004, October, 4;
　　　　2004, Oct, 4

11450-11471 Treatment of Hidradenitis: Excision and Repair

CMS *100-4,12,90.3*　*MD Services in ASCs*
CMS *100-4,14,10*　*General ASC Services*
CMS *100-2,15,260*　*Covered ASC Procedures*
CMS *100-4,4,20.5*　*HCPCS Under OPPS*

Code also closure by skin graft or flap (14000-14350, 15040-15770)

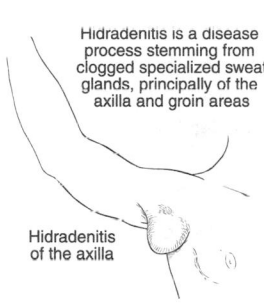
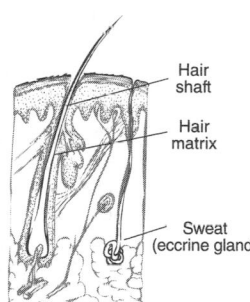

Hidradenitis is a disease process stemming from clogged specialized sweat glands, principally of the axilla and groin areas

Hair shaft

Hair matrix

Sweat (eccrine gland)

Hidradenitis of the axilla

11450　　Excision of skin and subcutaneous tissue for hidradenitis, axillary; with simple or intermediate repair　　A2 T ▯
　　　　🔳 5.82　🔾 8.57　Global Days 090

11451　　with complex repair　　A2 T 80 ▯
　　　　🔳 7.71　🔾 11.23　Global Days 090

11462　　Excision of skin and subcutaneous tissue for hidradenitis, inguinal; with simple or intermediate repair　　A2 T 80 ▯
　　　　🔳 5.60　🔾 8.46　Global Days 090

11463　　with complex repair　　A2 T 80 ▯
　　　　🔳 7.87　🔾 11.55　Global Days 090

11470　　Excision of skin and subcutaneous tissue for hidradenitis, perianal, perineal, or umbilical; with simple or intermediate repair　　A2 T ▯
　　　　🔳 6.63　🔾 9.41　Global Days 090

11471　　with complex repair　　A2 T 80 ▯
　　　　🔳 8.36　🔾 11.85　Global Days 090

11600-11646 Skin Lesion Removal: Malignant

CMS *100-4,12,90.3*　*MD Services in ASCs*
CMS *100-4,14,10*　*General ASC Services*
CMS *100-2,15,260*　*Covered ASC Procedures*
CMS *100-4,4,20.5*　*HCPCS Under OPPS*

INCLUDES　biopsy on same lesion
　　　　excision of additional margin at same operative session
　　　　full thickness removal including margins
　　　　local anesthesia
　　　　simple, nonlayered closure

EXCLUDES　*adjacent tissue transfer at the same time as excision (14000-14300)*
　　　　destruction (17260-17286)
　　　　excision of additional margin at subsequent operative session
　　　　(11600-11646)

Code also intermediate closure (12031-12057)
　　　　reconstruction (15002-15261, 15570-15770)

Code also complex closure (13100-13153)

11600　　Excision, malignant lesion including margins, trunk, arms, or legs; excised diameter 0.5 cm or less　　P3 T ▯
　　　　🔳 2.79　🔾 4.37　Global Days 010
　　　　AMA: 2008, Jan, 10-25; 2008, Feb, 8-9; 2008, Jul, 5-6&15; 2007,
　　　　Jan, 13-27; 2007, Jan, 13-27; 2007, Jan, 13-27; 2007, January,
　　　　13-27; 2007, Jan, 13-27; 2004, Oct, 4; 2004, October, 4; 2004, Oct,
　　　　4; 2004, Oct, 4; 2004, Oct, 4

11601　　excised diameter 0.6 to 1.0 cm　　P3 T ▯
　　　　🔳 3.61　🔾 5.40　Global Days 010
　　　　AMA: 2008, Feb, 8-9; 2008, Jul, 5-6&15; 2007, Jan, 13-27; 2007,
　　　　Jan, 13-27; 2004, Oct, 4; 2004, Oct, 4; 2004, October, 4; 2004,
　　　　Oct, 4; 2004, Oct, 4

11602　　excised diameter 1.1 to 2.0 cm　　P3 T ▯
　　　　🔳 3.97　🔾 5.93　Global Days 010
　　　　AMA: 2008, Feb, 8-9; 2008, Jul, 5-6&15; 2007, Jan, 13-27; 2007,
　　　　Jan, 13-27; 2004, Oct, 4; 2004, Oct, 4; 2004, October, 4; 2004,
　　　　Oct, 4; 2004, Oct, 4

11603　　excised diameter 2.1 to 3.0 cm　　P3 T ▯
　　　　🔳 4.72　🔾 6.74　Global Days 010
　　　　AMA: 2008, Feb, 8-9; 2008, Jul, 5-6&15; 2007, Jan, 13-27; 2007,
　　　　Jan, 13-27; 2004, Oct, 4; 2004, Oct, 4; 2004, October, 4; 2004,
　　　　Oct, 4; 2004, Oct, 4

11604　　excised diameter 3.1 to 4.0 cm　　A2 T ▯
　　　　🔳 5.19　🔾 7.45　Global Days 010
　　　　AMA: 2008, Feb, 8-9; 2008, Jul, 5-6&15; 2007, Jan, 13-27; 2007,
　　　　Jan, 13-27; 2004, Oct, 4; 2004, Oct, 4; 2004, October, 4; 2004,
　　　　Oct, 4; 2004, Oct, 4

11606　　excised diameter over 4.0 cm　　A2 T ▯
　　　　🔳 7.70　🔾 10.50　Global Days 010
　　　　AMA: 2008, Feb, 8-9; 2008, Jul, 5-6&15; 2007, Jan, 13-27; 2007,
　　　　Jan, 13-27; 2004, Oct, 4; 2004, Oct, 4; 2004, October, 4; 2004,
　　　　Oct, 4; 2004, Oct, 4

11620　　Excision, malignant lesion including margins, scalp, neck, hands, feet, genitalia; excised diameter 0.5 cm or less　　P3 T ▯
　　　　🔳 2.83　🔾 4.46　Global Days 010
　　　　AMA: 2008, Feb, 8-9; 2008, Jul, 5-6&15; 2007, Jan, 13-27; 2007,
　　　　Jan, 13-27; 2004, Oct, 4; 2004, Oct, 4; 2004, October, 4; 2004,
　　　　Oct, 4; 2004, Oct, 4

11621　　excised diameter 0.6 to 1.0 cm　　P3 T ▯
　　　　🔳 3.65　🔾 5.45　Global Days 010
　　　　AMA: 2008, Feb, 8-9; 2008, Jul, 5-6&15; 2007, Jan, 13-27; 2007,
　　　　Jan, 13-27; 2004, Oct, 4; 2004, Oct, 4; 2004, October, 4; 2004,
　　　　Oct, 4; 2004, Oct, 4

● New Code　　▲ Revised Code　　Ⅿ Maternity Edit　　🅐 Age Edit　　🅐-🆅 OPPS Status Indicator　　🔳 Facility RVU　　🔾 Non-Facility RVU
▯ CCI Comprehensive Code　　50 Bilateral Procedure　　+ Add-on Indicator　　🅢 Laboratory crosswalk　　🅡 Radiology crosswalk

Integumentary System

11622 — 11772

11622 excised diameter 1.1 to 2.0 cm [P3][T][□]
🔲 4.21 ⚘ 6.17 **Global Days 010**
AMA: 2008, Feb, 8-9; 2008, Jul, 5-6&15; 2007, Jan, 13-27; 2007, Jan, 13-27; 2004, Oct, 4; 2004, Oct, 4; 2004, October, 4; 2004, Oct, 4; 2004, Oct, 4

11623 excised diameter 2.1 to 3.0 cm [P3][T][□]
🔲 5.19 ⚘ 7.21 **Global Days 010**
AMA: 2008, Feb, 8-9; 2008, Jul, 5-6&15; 2007, Jan, 13-27; 2007, Jan, 13-27; 2004, Oct, 4; 2004, Oct, 4; 2004, October, 4; 2004, Oct, 4; 2004, Oct, 4

11624 excised diameter 3.1 to 4.0 cm [A2][T][□]
🔲 5.91 ⚘ 8.12 **Global Days 010**
AMA: 2008, Feb, 8-9; 2008, Jul, 5-6&15; 2007, Jan, 13-27; 2007, Jan, 13-27; 2004, Oct, 4; 2004, Oct, 4; 2004, October, 4; 2004, Oct, 4; 2004, Oct, 4

11626 excised diameter over 4.0 cm [A2][T][□]
🔲 7.43 ⚘ 9.92 **Global Days 010**
AMA: 2008, Feb, 8-9; 2008, Jul, 5-6&15; 2007, Jan, 13-27; 2007, Jan, 13-27; 2004, Oct, 4; 2004, Oct, 4; 2004, October, 4; 2004, Oct, 4; 2004, Oct, 4

11640 Excision, malignant lesion including margins, face, ears, eyelids, nose, lips; excised diameter 0.5 cm or less [P3][T][□]
EXCLUDES eyelid excision involving more than skin (67800 and subsequent codes)
🔲 2.99 ⚘ 4.67 **Global Days 010**
AMA: 2008, Feb, 8-9; 2008, Jul, 5-6&15; 2007, Jan, 13-27; 2007, Jan, 13-27; 2004, Oct, 4; 2004, Oct, 4; 2004, October, 4; 2004, Oct, 4; 2004, Oct, 4

11641 excised diameter 0.6 to 1.0 cm [P3][T][□]
EXCLUDES eyelid excision involving more than skin (67800 and subsequent codes)
🔲 3.91 ⚘ 5.75 **Global Days 010**
AMA: 2008, Feb, 8-9; 2008, Jul, 5-6&15; 2007, Jan, 13-27; 2007, Jan, 13-27; 2004, Oct, 4; 2004, Oct, 4; 2004, October, 4; 2004, Oct, 4; 2004, Oct, 4

11642 excised diameter 1.1 to 2.0 cm [P3][T][□]
EXCLUDES eyelid excision involving more than skin (67800 and subsequent codes)
🔲 4.61 ⚘ 6.63 **Global Days 010**
AMA: 2008, Feb, 8-9; 2008, Jul, 5-6&15; 2007, Jan, 13-27; 2007, Jan, 13-27; 2004, Oct, 4; 2004, Oct, 4; 2004, October, 4; 2004, Oct, 4; 2004, Oct, 4

11643 excised diameter 2.1 to 3.0 cm [P3][T][□]
EXCLUDES eyelid excision involving more than skin (67800 and subsequent codes)
🔲 5.76 ⚘ 7.80 **Global Days 010**
AMA: 2008, Feb, 8-9; 2008, Jul, 5-6&15; 2007, Jan, 13-27; 2007, Jan, 13-27; 2004, Oct, 4; 2004, Oct, 4; 2004, October, 4; 2004, Oct, 4; 2004, Oct, 4

11644 excised diameter 3.1 to 4.0 cm [A2][T][□]
EXCLUDES eyelid excision involving more than skin (67800 and subsequent codes)
🔲 7.19 ⚘ 9.64 **Global Days 010**
AMA: 2008, Feb, 8-9; 2008, Jul, 5-6&15; 2007, Jan, 13-27; 2007, Jan, 13-27; 2004, Oct, 4; 2004, Oct, 4; 2004, October, 4; 2004, Oct, 4; 2004, Oct, 4

11646 excised diameter over 4.0 cm [A2][T][□]
EXCLUDES eyelid excision involving more than skin (67800 and subsequent codes)
🔲 10.14 ⚘ 12.73 **Global Days 010**
AMA: 2008, Jan, 10-25; 2008, Feb, 8-9; 2008, Jul, 5-6&15; 2007, Jan, 13-27; 2007, Jan, 13-27; 2007, Jan, 13-27; 2007, January, 13-27; 2007, Jan, 13-27; 2004, Oct, 4; 2004, October, 4; 2004, Oct, 4; 2004, Oct, 4; 2004, Oct, 4

11719-11765 Nails and Supporting Structures

CMS 100-2,15,290   *Foot Care*
CMS 100-4,4,20.5   *HCPCS Under OPPS*
EXCLUDES   *drainage of paronychia or onychia (10060-10061)*

11719 Trimming of nondystrophic nails, any number [P3][T][□]
🔲 0.24 ⚘ 0.53 **Global Days 000**

11720 Debridement of nail(s) by any method(s); 1 to 5 [P3][T][□]
🔲 0.45 ⚘ 0.78 **Global Days 000**

11721 6 or more [P3][T][□]
🔲 0.77 ⚘ 1.12 **Global Days 000**

11730 Avulsion of nail plate, partial or complete, simple; single [P2][T][□]
🔲 1.56 ⚘ 2.47 **Global Days 000**
AMA: 2008, Jan, 10-25; 2007, Jan, 13-27; 2007, Jan, 13-27; 2007, Jan, 13-27; 2007, Jan, 13-27; 2007, January, 13-27

\+ **11732** each additional nail plate (List separately in addition to code for primary procedure) [P3][T][□]
Code first 11730
🔲 0.81 ⚘ 1.15 **Global Days ZZZ**

11740 Evacuation of subungual hematoma [P2][T][□]
🔲 0.81 ⚘ 1.12 **Global Days 000**

11750 Excision of nail and nail matrix, partial or complete (eg, ingrown or deformed nail), for permanent removal; [P3][T][□]
EXCLUDES   *skin graft (15050)*
🔲 4.44 ⚘ 5.32 **Global Days 010**

11752 with amputation of tuft of distal phalanx [P3][T][□]
🔲 6.65 ⚘ 7.58 **Global Days 010**

11755 Biopsy of nail unit (eg, plate, bed, matrix, hyponychium, proximal and lateral nail folds) (separate procedure) [P3][T][80][□]
🔲 2.21 ⚘ 3.32 **Global Days 000**
AMA: 2008, Jan, 10-25; 2007, Jan, 13-27; 2007, Jan, 13-27; 2007, Jan, 13-27; 2007, January, 13-27; 2007, Jan, 13-27; 2004, Oct, 14; 2004, October, 14; 2004, Oct, 14; 2004, Oct, 14; 2004, Oct, 14

11760 Repair of nail bed [G2][T][□]
🔲 3.33 ⚘ 4.99 **Global Days 010**

11762 Reconstruction of nail bed with graft [P3][T][□]
🔲 5.12 ⚘ 6.71 **Global Days 010**

11765 Wedge excision of skin of nail fold (eg, for ingrown toenail) [P2][T][□]
INCLUDES   Cotting's operation
🔲 1.71 ⚘ 3.17 **Global Days 010**

11770-11772 Treatment Pilonidal Cyst: Excision

CMS 100-4,12,90.3   *MD Services in ASCs*
CMS 100-2,15,260   *Covered ASC Procedures*
CMS 100-4,4,20.5   *HCPCS Under OPPS*
EXCLUDES   *incision of pilonidal cyst (10080-10081)*

11770 Excision of pilonidal cyst or sinus; simple [A2][T][□]
🔲 4.49 ⚘ 6.41 **Global Days 010**

11771 extensive [A2][T][□]
🔲 10.40 ⚘ 13.16 **Global Days 090**

11772 complicated [A2][T][□]
🔲 13.57 ⚘ 15.97 **Global Days 090**

---

[26]/[TC] Professional/Technical Component Only   [80]/[⊞] Assist-at-Surgery Allowed/With Documentation   Unlisted   Not Covered

AMA: CPT Assistant References   [A2]-[Z3] ASC Payment Indicator   ♂ Male Only   ♀ Female Only   ⦸ Modifier 51 Exempt   [PQ] PQRI

32   CPT only © 2008 American Medical Association. All Rights Reserved. (Black Ink)   Medicare (Red Ink)   © 2008 Ingenix (Blue Ink)

11900-11901 Treatment of Lesions: Injection

CMS *100-4,17,20.5.7 Injection Services*
EXCLUDES *injection of veins (36470-36471)*
intralesional chemotherapy (96405-96406)

Do not report for local anesthetic injection performed preoperatively

11900 Injection, intralesional; up to and including 7 lesions [P3] [T] [▭]
    🔹 0.79 ⚒ 1.39 Global Days 000
    AMA: 2008, Jan, 10-25; 2007, Jan, 13-27; 2007, Jan, 13-27; 2007, Jan, 13-27; 2007, Jan, 13-27; 2007, January, 13-27, 2006, Dec, 10-12; 2006, Dec, 10-12; 2006, December, 10-12; 2004, Sep, 12; 2004, Sep, 12; 2004, Sep, 12; 2004, September, 12; 2004, Sep, 12

11901 more than 7 lesions [P2] [T] [▭]
    🔹 1.23 ⚒ 1.76 Global Days 000
    AMA: 2008, Jan, 10-25; 2007, Jan, 13-27; 2007, Jan, 13-27; 2007, Jan, 13-27; 2007, Jan, 13-27; 2007, January, 13-27; 2006, Dec, 10-12; 2006, Dec, 10-12; 2006, December, 10-12; 2004, Sep, 12; 2004, Sep, 12; 2004, Sep, 12; 2004, September, 12; 2004, Sep, 12

11920-11971 Tattoos, Tissue Expanders, and Dermal Fillers

CMS *100-2,16,180 Services Related to Noncovered Procedures*
CMS *100-2,16,120 Cosmetic Procedures*
CMS *100-2,16,10 Exclusions from Coverage*
CMS *100-4,4,20.5 HCPCS Under OPPS*

11920 Tattooing, intradermal introduction of insoluble opaque pigments to correct color defects of skin, including micropigmentation; 6.0 sq cm or less [P3] [T] [80] [▭]
    🔹 2.97 ⚒ 4.54 Global Days 000

11921 6.1 to 20.0 sq cm [P3] [T] [80] [▭]
    🔹 3.50 ⚒ 5.18 Global Days 000

+ ▲ **11922** each additional 20.0 sq cm, or part thereof (List separately in addition to code for primary procedure) [P3] [T] [80]
    Code first 11921
    🔹 0.79 ⚒ 1.52 Global Days ZZZ

11950 Subcutaneous injection of filling material (eg, collagen); 1 cc or less [P1] [T] [AH] [▭]
    🔹 1.30 ⚒ 1.88 Global Days 000

11951 1.1 to 5.0 cc [P3] [T] [80] [▭]
    🔹 1.82 ⚒ 2.52 Global Days 000

11952 5.1 to 10.0 cc [P2] [T] [80] [▭]
    🔹 2.63 ⚒ 3.55 Global Days 000

11954 over 10.0 cc [P2] [T] [80] [▭]
    🔹 2.98 ⚒ 4.08 Global Days 000

11960 Insertion of tissue expander(s) for other than breast, including subsequent expansion [A2] [T] [▭]
    EXCLUDES *breast reconstruction with tissue expander(s) (19357)*
    🔹 22.98 ⚒ 22.98 Global Days 090

11970 Replacement of tissue expander with permanent prosthesis [A2] [T] [▭]
    🔹 15.13 ⚒ 15.13 Global Days 090
    AMA: 2005, Aug, 1-3; 2005, Aug, 1-3; 2005, Aug, 1-3; 2005, Aug, 1-3; 2005, August, 1-3

11971 Removal of tissue expander(s) without insertion of prosthesis [A2] [T] [80] [▭]
    🔹 7.45 ⚒ 11.22 Global Days 090
    AMA: 2008, Jan, 10-25; 2007, Jan, 13-27; 2007, Jan, 13-27; 2007, Jan, 13-27; 2007, January, 13-27; 2007, Jan, 13-27; 2005, Jun, 9-11; 2005, June, 9-11; 2005, Jun, 9-11; 2005, June, 9-11; 2005, June, 9-11

11975-11983 Drug Implantation

CMS *100-2,15,50 Drugs and Biologicals*
CMS *100-2,16,20 General Exclusions*

11975 Insertion, implantable contraceptive capsules ♀ [E]
    🔹 2.17 ⚒ 3.36 Global Days XXX

11976 Removal, implantable contraceptive capsules ♀ [P3] [T] [80] [▭]
    🔹 2.54 ⚒ 3.78 Global Days 000

11977 Removal with reinsertion, implantable contraceptive capsules ♀ [E]
    🔹 4.82 ⚒ 6.08 Global Days XXX

11980 Subcutaneous hormone pellet implantation (implantation of estradiol and/or testosterone pellets beneath the skin) [P2] [X] [▭]
    🔹 2.12 ⚒ 2.67 Global Days 000

11981 Insertion, non-biodegradable drug delivery implant [P2] [X] [80] [▭]
    🔹 2.23 ⚒ 3.45 Global Days XXX
    AMA: 2007, Dec, 10-179

11982 Removal, non-biodegradable drug delivery implant [P2] [X] [80] [▭]
    🔹 2.73 ⚒ 3.98 Global Days XXX

11983 Removal with reinsertion, non-biodegradable drug delivery implant [P2] [X] [80] [▭]
    🔹 4.97 ⚒ 6.14 Global Days XXX

● New Code   ▲ Revised Code   [M] Maternity Edit   [A] Age Edit   [A]-[Y] OPPS Status Indicator   🔹 Facility RVU   ⚒ Non-Facility RVU
[▭] CCI Comprehensive Code   [50] Bilateral Procedure   + Add-on Indicator   [N] Laboratory crosswalk   [R] Radiology crosswalk

Integumentary System

12001 — 12021

12001-12021 Suturing of Superficial Wounds

CMS *100-2,15,260* *Covered ASC Procedures*
CMS *100-4,14,10* *ASC Procedures*
CMS *100-4,4,20.5* *HCPCS Under OPPS*

INCLUDES administration of local anesthesia
cauterization without closure
simple:
  exploration nerves, blood vessels, tendons
  vessel ligation, in wound
simple repair that involves:
  routine debridement and decontamination
  simple one layer closure
  superficial tissues
  sutures, staples, tissue adhesives
  total length of several repairs in same code category

EXCLUDES *adhesive strips only (99201-99499)*
debridement:
  performed separately, no closure (11040-11044)
  that requires:

    comprehensive cleaning

    removal of significant tissue

    removal soft tissue and/or bone, no fracture/dislocation (11040-11044)

    removal soft tissue and/or bone with open fracture/dislocation (11010-11012)
deep tissue repair (12031-13153)
major exploration (20100-20103)
repair nerves, blood vessels, tendons (see appropriate anatomical section)
secondary closure/dehiscense (13160)

12001 **Simple repair of superficial wounds of scalp, neck, axillae, external genitalia, trunk and/or extremities (including hands and feet); 2.5 cm or less** P2 T ▭
  🔪 2.61 ⚖ 3.64 Global Days 010
  AMA: 2008, Jan, 10-25; 2008, Feb, 8-9; 2007, Feb, 10-11; 2007, Feb, 10-11; 2007, Jan, 13-27; 2007, Jan, 13-27; 2007, Jan, 13-27; 2007, Jan, 13-27; 2007, Feb, 10-11; 2007, Feb, 10-11; 2007, January, 13-27; 2007, February, 10-11

12002 **2.6 cm to 7.5 cm** P2 T ▭
  🔪 2.90 ⚖ 3.88 Global Days 010
  AMA: 2008, Jan, 10-25; 2008, Feb, 8-9; 2007, Feb, 10-11; 2007, Feb, 10-11; 2007, Jan, 13-27; 2007, Jan, 13-27; 2007, Jan, 13-27; 2007, Jan, 13-27; 2007, Feb, 10-11; 2007, Feb, 10-11; 2007, January, 13-27; 2007, February, 10-11

12004 **7.6 cm to 12.5 cm** P2 T ▭
  🔪 3.41 ⚖ 4.58 Global Days 010
  AMA: 2008, Jan, 10-25; 2008, Feb, 8-9; 2007, Feb, 10-11; 2007, Feb, 10-11; 2007, Jan, 13-27; 2007, Jan, 13-27; 2007, Jan, 13-27; 2007, Jan, 13-27; 2007, Feb, 10-11; 2007, Feb, 10-11; 2007, January, 13-27; 2007, February, 10-11

12005 **12.6 cm to 20.0 cm** A2 T ▭
  🔪 4.25 ⚖ 5.71 Global Days 010
  AMA: 2008, Jan, 10-25; 2008, Feb, 8-9; 2007, Feb, 10-11; 2007, Feb, 10-11; 2007, Jan, 13-27; 2007, Jan, 13-27; 2007, Jan, 13-27; 2007, Jan, 13-27; 2007, Feb, 10-11; 2007, Feb, 10-11; 2007, January, 13-27; 2007, February, 10-11

12006 **20.1 cm to 30.0 cm** A2 T ▭
  🔪 5.37 ⚖ 7.09 Global Days 010
  AMA: 2008, Jan, 10-25; 2008, Feb, 8-9; 2007, Jan, 13-27; 2007, Jan, 13-27; 2007, Feb, 10-11; 2007, Feb, 10-11; 2007, January, 13-27; 2007, February, 10-11

12007 **over 30.0 cm** A2 T ▭
  🔪 6.16 ⚖ 8.05 Global Days 010
  AMA: 2008, Jan, 10-25; 2008, Feb, 8-9; 2007, Feb, 10-11; 2007, Feb, 10-11; 2007, Jan, 13-27; 2007, Jan, 13-27; 2007, Jan, 13-27; 2007, Jan, 13-27; 2007, Feb, 10-11; 2007, Feb, 10-11; 2007, January, 13-27; 2007, February, 10-11

12011 **Simple repair of superficial wounds of face, ears, eyelids, nose, lips and/or mucous membranes; 2.5 cm or less** P2 T ▭
  🔪 2.70 ⚖ 3.87 Global Days 010
  AMA: 2008, Jan, 10-25; 2008, Feb, 8-9; 2007, Feb, 10-11; 2007, Feb, 10-11; 2007, Jan, 13-27; 2007, Jan, 13-27; 2007, Jan, 13-27; 2007, Jan, 13-27; 2007, Feb, 10-11; 2007, Feb, 10-11; 2007, January, 13-27; 2007, February, 10-11

12013 **2.6 cm to 5.0 cm** P2 T ▭
  🔪 3.08 ⚖ 4.27 Global Days 010
  AMA: 2008, Jan, 10-25; 2008, Feb, 8-9; 2007, Feb, 10-11; 2007, Feb, 10-11; 2007, Jan, 13-27; 2007, Jan, 13-27; 2007, Jan, 13-27; 2007, Jan, 13-27; 2007, Feb, 10-11; 2007, Feb, 10-11; 2007, January, 13-27; 2007, February, 10-11

12014 **5.1 cm to 7.5 cm** P2 T ▭
  🔪 3.71 ⚖ 5.04 Global Days 010
  AMA: 2008, Jan, 10-25; 2008, Feb, 8-9; 2007, Feb, 10-11; 2007, Feb, 10-11; 2007, Jan, 13-27; 2007, Jan, 13-27; 2007, Jan, 13-27; 2007, Jan, 13-27; 2007, Feb, 10-11; 2007, Feb, 10-11; 2007, January, 13-27; 2007, February, 10-11

12015 **7.6 cm to 12.5 cm** G2 T ▭
  🔪 4.65 ⚖ 6.33 Global Days 010
  AMA: 2008, Jan, 10-25; 2008, Feb, 8-9; 2007, Feb, 10-11; 2007, Feb, 10-11; 2007, Jan, 13-27; 2007, Jan, 13-27; 2007, Jan, 13-27; 2007, Jan, 13-27; 2007, Feb, 10-11; 2007, Feb, 10-11; 2007, January, 13-27; 2007, February, 10-11

12016 **12.6 cm to 20.0 cm** A2 T ▭
  🔪 5.68 ⚖ 7.57 Global Days 010
  AMA: 2008, Jan, 10-25; 2008, Feb, 8-9; 2007, Feb, 10-11; 2007, Feb, 10-11; 2007, Jan, 13-27; 2007, Jan, 13-27; 2007, Jan, 13-27; 2007, Jan, 13-27; 2007, Feb, 10-11; 2007, Feb, 10-11; 2007, January, 13-27; 2007, February, 10-11

12017 **20.1 cm to 30.0 cm** A2 T 80 ▭
  🔪 6.77 ⚖ 6.77 Global Days 010
  AMA: 2008, Jan, 10-25; 2008, Feb, 8-9; 2007, Feb, 10-11; 2007, Feb, 10-11; 2007, Jan, 13-27; 2007, Jan, 13-27; 2007, Jan, 13-27; 2007, Jan, 13-27; 2007, Feb, 10-11; 2007, Feb, 10-11; 2007, January, 13-27; 2007, February, 10-11

12018 **over 30.0 cm** A2 T 80 ▭
  🔪 8.41 ⚖ 8.41 Global Days 010
  AMA: 2008, Jan, 10-25; 2008, Feb, 8-9; 2007, Feb, 10-11; 2007, Feb, 10-11; 2007, Jan, 13-27; 2007, Jan, 13-27; 2007, Jan, 13-27; 2007, Jan, 13-27; 2007, Feb, 10-11; 2007, Feb, 10-11; 2007, January, 13-27; 2007, February, 10-11

12020 **Treatment of superficial wound dehiscence; simple closure** A2 T ▭
  EXCLUDES *secondary closure major/complex wound (13160)*
  🔪 4.74 ⚖ 6.62 Global Days 010
  AMA: 2008, Jan, 10-25; 2008, Feb, 8-9; 2007, Feb, 10-11; 2007, Jan, 13-27; 2007, Jan, 13-27; 2007, Jan, 13-27; 2007, Jan, 13-27; 2007, January, 13-27

12021 **with packing** A2 T ▭
  EXCLUDES *secondary closure major/complex wound (13160)*
  🔪 3.45 ⚖ 3.94 Global Days 010
  AMA: 2008, Jan, 10-25; 2008, Feb, 8-9; 2007, Feb, 10-11; 2007, Feb, 10-11; 2007, Jan, 13-27; 2007, Jan, 13-27; 2007, Jan, 13-27; 2007, Jan, 13-27; 2007, January, 13-27

12031-12057 Suturing of Intermediate Wounds

CMS *100-4,12,90.3* *MD Services in ASCs*
CMS *100-4,14,10* *General ASC Services*
CMS *100-4,4,20.5* *HCPCS Under OPPS*

INCLUDES administration of local anesthesia
intermediate repair that involves:
  closure of contaminated single layer wound
  layer closure (e.g., subcutaneous tissue, superficial fascia)
  removal foreign material (e.g. gravel, glass)
  routine debridement and decontamination
simple:
  exploration nerves, blood vessels, tendons in wound
total length of several repairs in same code category

EXCLUDES *debridement*
performed separately, no closure (11040-11044)
  that requires:

    removal soft tissue and/or bone, no fracture/dislocation (11040-11044)

    removal soft tissue/bone due to open fracture/dislocation (11010-11012)
major exploration (20100-20103)
repair nerves, blood vessels, tendons (see appropriate anatomical section)
secondary closure major/complex wound or dehiscense (13160)
wound repair involving more than layer closure

▲ 12031 **Repair, intermediate, wounds of scalp, axillae, trunk and/or extremities (excluding hands and feet); 2.5 cm or less** P2 T ▭
  ⏭ 3.95 ⚕ 5.83 Global Days 010
  AMA: 2008, Jan, 10-25; 2007, Jan, 13-27; 2007, Jan, 13-27; 2007, Feb, 10-11; 2007, Feb, 10-11; 2007, January, 13-27; 2007, February, 10-11

▲ 12032 **2.6 cm to 7.5 cm** P2 T ▭
  ⏭ 4.85 ⚕ 7.50 Global Days 010
  AMA: 2008, Jan, 10-25; 2007, Jan, 13-27; 2007, Jan, 13-27; 2007, Feb, 10-11; 2007, Feb, 10-11; 2007, January, 13-27; 2007, February, 10-11

▲ 12034 **7.6 cm to 12.5 cm** A2 T ▭
  ⏭ 5.08 ⚕ 7.41 Global Days 010
  AMA: 2008, Jan, 10-25; 2007, Jan, 13-27; 2007, Jan, 13-27; 2007, Feb, 10-11; 2007, Feb, 10-11; 2007, January, 13-27; 2007, February, 10-11

▲ 12035 **12.6 cm to 20.0 cm** A2 T ▭
  ⏭ 5.99 ⚕ 9.07 Global Days 010
  AMA: 2008, Jan, 10-25; 2007, Jan, 13-27; 2007, Jan, 13-27; 2007, Feb, 10-11; 2007, Feb, 10-11; 2007, January, 13-27; 2007, February, 10-11

▲ 12036 **20.1 cm to 30.0 cm** A2 T ▭
  ⏭ 6.94 ⚕ 9.98 Global Days 010
  AMA: 2008, Jan, 10-25; 2007, Jan, 13-27; 2007, Jan, 13-27; 2007, Feb, 10-11; 2007, Feb, 10-11; 2007, January, 13-27; 2007, February, 10-11

▲ 12037 **over 30.0 cm** A2 T 80 ▭
  ⏭ 8.09 ⚕ 11.27 Global Days 010
  AMA: 2008, Jan, 10-25; 2007, Jan, 13-27; 2007, Jan, 13-27; 2007, Feb, 10-11; 2007, Feb, 10-11; 2007, January, 13-27; 2007, February, 10-11

▲ 12041 **Repair, intermediate, wounds of neck, hands, feet and/or external genitalia; 2.5 cm or less** P2 T ▭
  ⏭ 4.23 ⚕ 6.11 Global Days 010
  AMA: 2008, Jan, 10-25; 2007, Jan, 13-27; 2007, Jan, 13-27; 2007, Feb, 10-11; 2007, Feb, 10-11; 2007, January, 13-27; 2007, February, 10-11

▲ 12042 **2.6 cm to 7.5 cm** P2 T ▭
  ⏭ 4.93 ⚕ 7.11 Global Days 010
  AMA: 2008, Jan, 10-25; 2007, Jan, 13-27; 2007, Jan, 13-27; 2007, Feb, 10-11; 2007, Feb, 10-11; 2007, January, 13-27; 2007, February, 10-11

▲ 12044 **7.6 cm to 12.5 cm** A2 T ▭
  ⏭ 5.33 ⚕ 8.23 Global Days 010
  AMA: 2008, Jan, 10-25; 2007, Jan, 13-27; 2007, Jan, 13-27; 2007, Feb, 10-11; 2007, Feb, 10-11; 2007, January, 13-27; 2007, February, 10-11

▲ 12045 **12.6 cm to 20.0 cm** A2 T ▭
  ⏭ 6.22 ⚕ 9.15 Global Days 010
  AMA: 2008, Jan, 10-25; 2007, Jan, 13-27; 2007, Jan, 13-27; 2007, Feb, 10-11; 2007, Feb, 10-11; 2007, January, 13-27; 2007, February, 10-11

▲ 12046 **20.1 cm to 30.0 cm** A2 T 80 ▭
  ⏭ 7.35 ⚕ 10.86 Global Days 010
  AMA: 2008, Jan, 10-25; 2007, Jan, 13-27; 2007, Jan, 13-27; 2007, Feb, 10-11; 2007, Feb, 10-11; 2007, January, 13-27; 2007, February, 10-11

▲ 12047 **over 30.0 cm** A2 T 80 ▭
  ⏭ 8.04 ⚕ 11.65 Global Days 010
  AMA: 2008, Jan, 10-25; 2007, Jan, 13-27; 2007, Jan, 13-27; 2007, Feb, 10-11; 2007, Feb, 10-11; 2007, January, 13-27; 2007, February, 10-11

▲ 12051 **Repair, intermediate, wounds of face, ears, eyelids, nose, lips and/or mucous membranes; 2.5 cm or less** P2 T ▭
  ⏭ 4.53 ⚕ 6.57 Global Days 010
  AMA: 2008, Jan, 10-25; 2007, Jan, 13-27; 2007, Jan, 13-27; 2007, Feb, 10-11; 2007, Feb, 10-11; 2007, January, 13-27; 2007, February, 10-11

▲ 12052 **2.6 cm to 5.0 cm** P2 T ▭
  ⏭ 5.30 ⚕ 7.43 Global Days 010
  AMA: 2008, Jan, 10-25; 2008, Jul, 5-6&15; 2007, Jan, 13-27; 2007, Jan, 13-27; 2007, Feb, 10-11; 2007, Feb, 10-11; 2007, January, 13-27; 2007, February, 10-11

▲ 12053 **5.1 cm to 7.5 cm** P2 T ▭
  ⏭ 5.39 ⚕ 8.18 Global Days 010
  AMA: 2008, Jan, 10-25; 2007, Jan, 13-27; 2007, Jan, 13-27; 2007, Feb, 10-11; 2007, Feb, 10-11; 2007, January, 13-27; 2007, February, 10-11

▲ 12054 **7.6 cm to 12.5 cm** A2 T ▭
  ⏭ 5.74 ⚕ 8.67 Global Days 010
  AMA: 2008, Jan, 10-25; 2007, Jan, 13-27; 2007, Jan, 13-27; 2007, Feb, 10-11; 2007, Feb, 10-11; 2007, January, 13-27; 2007, February, 10-11

▲ 12055 **12.6 cm to 20.0 cm** A2 T ▭
  ⏭ 7.02 ⚕ 10.47 Global Days 010
  AMA: 2008, Jan, 10-25; 2007, Jan, 13-27; 2007, Jan, 13-27; 2007, Feb, 10-11; 2007, Feb, 10-11; 2007, January, 13-27; 2007, February, 10-11

▲ 12056 **20.1 cm to 30.0 cm** A2 T 80 ▭
  ⏭ 8.59 ⚕ 12.38 Global Days 010
  AMA: 2008, Jan, 10-25; 2007, Jan, 13-27; 2007, Jan, 13-27; 2007, Feb, 10-11; 2007, Feb, 10-11; 2007, January, 13-27; 2007, February, 10-11

▲ 12057 **over 30.0 cm** A2 T 80 ▭
  ⏭ 9.80 ⚕ 13.80 Global Days 010
  AMA: 2008, Jan, 10-25; 2007, Jan, 13-27; 2007, Jan, 13-27; 2007, Feb, 10-11; 2007, Feb, 10-11; 2007, January, 13-27; 2007, February, 10-11

● New Code   ▲ Revised Code   M Maternity Edit   A Age Edit   A-Y OPPS Status Indicator   ⏭ Facility RVU   ⚕ Non-Facility RVU
▭ CCI Comprehensive Code   50 Bilateral Procedure   + Add-on Indicator   L Laboratory crosswalk   R Radiology crosswalk

Integumentary System

13100 — 13160

13100-13160 Suturing of Complicated Wounds

CMS *100-4,12,90.3*   *MD Services in ASCs*
CMS *100-4,14,10*   *General ASC Services*
CMS *100-4,4,20.5*   *HCPCS Under OPPS*

INCLUDES   creation of defect for repair, such as scar removal
debridement complicated wounds/avulsions
more complicated than layered closure
simple:
     exploration nerves, vessels, tendons in wound
     vessel ligation in wound
total length of several repairs in same code category
undermining, stents, retention sutures

EXCLUDES   *complex/secondary wound closure or dehiscence*
debridement:
     that requires:
     performed separately, no closure (11040-11044)
     soft tissue and/or bone, no fracture/dislocation (11040-11044)
     soft tissue and/or bone due to open fracture/dislocation
       (11010-11012)
     excision:
       benign lesions (11400-11446)
       malignant lesions (11600-11646)
     extensive exploration (20100-20103)
     repair nerves, blood vessels, tendons (see appropriate anatomical
       section)

13100   **Repair, complex, trunk; 1.1 cm to 2.5 cm**   A2 T ▭
     EXCLUDES   *complex repair 1.0 cm or less (12001, 12031)*

     ⊞ **5.92**   ⚖ **7.80**   **Global Days 010**
     AMA: 2008, Jan, 10-25; 2007, Jan, 13-27; 2007, Jan, 13-27; 2007, January, 13-27

13101   **2.6 cm to 7.5 cm**   A2 T ▭
     ⊞ **7.17**   ⚖ **9.83**   **Global Days 010**
     AMA: 2008, Jan, 10-25; 2007, Jan, 13-27; 2007, Jan, 13-27; 2007, January, 13-27

+ **13102**   **each additional 5 cm or less (List separately in addition to code for primary procedure)**   A2 T ▭
     Code first 13101
     ⊞ **1.93**   ⚖ **2.68**   **Global Days ZZZ**
     AMA: 2008, Jan, 10-25; 2007, Jan, 13-27; 2007, Jan, 13-27; 2007, January, 13-27

13120   **Repair, complex, scalp, arms, and/or legs; 1.1 cm to 2.5 cm**   A2 T ▭
     EXCLUDES   *complex repair 1.0 cm or less (12001, 12031)*

     ⊞ **6.18**   ⚖ **8.10**   **Global Days 010**
     AMA: 2008, Jan, 10-25; 2007, Jan, 13-27; 2007, Jan, 13-27; 2007, January, 13-27

13121   **2.6 cm to 7.5 cm**   A2 T ▭
     ⊞ **8.12**   ⚖ **10.87**   **Global Days 010**
     AMA: 2008, Jan, 10-25; 2007, Jan, 13-27; 2007, Jan, 13-27; 2007, January, 13-27

+ **13122**   **each additional 5 cm or less (List separately in addition to code for primary procedure)**   A2 T ▭
     Code first 13121
     ⊞ **2.21**   ⚖ **3.00**   **Global Days ZZZ**
     AMA: 2008, Jan, 10-25; 2007, Jan, 13-27; 2007, Jan, 13-27; 2007, January, 13-27

13131   **Repair, complex, forehead, cheeks, chin, mouth, neck, axillae, genitalia, hands and/or feet; 1.1 cm to 2.5 cm**   A2 T ▭
     EXCLUDES   *complex repair 1.0 cm or less (12001, 12011, 12031, 12041, 12051)*

     ⊞ **6.96**   ⚖ **8.93**   **Global Days 010**
     AMA: 2008, Jan, 10-25; 2007, Jan, 13-27; 2007, Jan, 13-27; 2007, January, 13-27

13132   **2.6 cm to 7.5 cm**   A2 T ▭
     ⊞ **11.69**   ⚖ **14.26**   **Global Days 010**
     AMA: 2008, Jan, 10-25; 2007, Jan, 13-27; 2007, Jan, 13-27; 2007, January, 13-27

+ **13133**   **each additional 5 cm or less (List separately in addition to code for primary procedure)**   A2 T ▭
     Code first 13132
     ⊞ **3.42**   ⚖ **4.23**   **Global Days ZZZ**
     AMA: 2008, Jan, 10-25; 2007, Jan, 13-27; 2007, Jan, 13-27; 2007, January, 13-27

13150   **Repair, complex, eyelids, nose, ears and/or lips; 1.0 cm or less**   A2 T ▭
     ⊞ **6.95**   ⚖ **8.92**   **Global Days 010**
     AMA: 2008, Jan, 10-25; 2007, Jan, 13-27; 2007, Jan, 13-27; 2007, January, 13-27

13151   **1.1 cm to 2.5 cm**   A2 T ▭
     ⊞ **8.06**   ⚖ **10.14**   **Global Days 010**
     AMA: 2008, Jan, 10-25; 2007, Jan, 13-27; 2007, Jan, 13-27; 2007, January, 13-27

13152   **2.6 cm to 7.5 cm**   A2 T ▭
     ⊞ **10.83**   ⚖ **13.96**   **Global Days 010**
     AMA: 2008, Jan, 10-25; 2007, Jan, 13-27; 2007, Jan, 13-27; 2007, January, 13-27

+ **13153**   **each additional 5 cm or less (List separately in addition to code for primary procedure)**   A2 T ▭
     Code first 13152
     ⊞ **3.72**   ⚖ **4.66**   **Global Days ZZZ**
     AMA: 2008, Jan, 10-25; 2007, Jan, 13-27; 2007, Jan, 13-27; 2007, January, 13-27

13160   **Secondary closure of surgical wound or dehiscence, extensive or complicated**   A2 T ▭
     EXCLUDES   *packing or simple secondary wound closure (12020-12021)*

     ⊞ **20.57**   ⚖ **20.57**   **Global Days 090**
     AMA: 2008, Jan, 10-25; 2007, Jan, 13-27; 2007, Jan, 13-27; 2007, January, 13-27

14000-14350 Reposition ContiguousTissue

CMS *100-2,16,120*   *Cosmetic Procedures*
CMS *100-4,12,90.3*   *MD Services in ASCs*
CMS *100-4,14,10*   *Part B ASC Payment*
CMS *100-4,4,20.5*   *HCPCS Under OPPS*

INCLUDES   excision of lesion with repair by adjacent tissue transfer or tissue rearrangement
Z-plasty, W-plasty, VY-plasty, rotation flap, advancement flap, double pedicle flap

EXCLUDES   *full thickness closure of:*
     eyelid (67930-67935, 67961-67975)
     lip (40650-40654)
     skin graft necessary to repair secondary defect (flap defect)

Do not report with (11400-11446, 11600-11646)

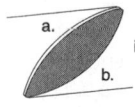

Example of common Z-plasty. Lesion is removed with oval-shaped incision

Two additional incisions (a. and b.) intersect the area

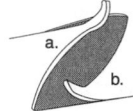

Skin of each incision is reflected back

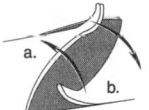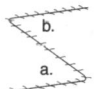

The flaps are then transposed and the repair is closed

An adjacent flap, or other rearrangement flap, is performed to repair a defect of 10 sq cm or less (14000); a larger defect (up to 30 sq cm) is coded 14001

14000   Adjacent tissue transfer or rearrangement, trunk; defect 10 sq cm or less   A2 T ▢

INCLUDES   Burrow's operation

▣ 12.52   ⚕ 15.21   Global Days 090

AMA: 2008, Jan, 10-25; 2008, Jul, 5-6&15; 2007, Jan, 13-27; 2007, Jan, 13-27; 2007, January, 13-27; 2006, Jan, 46-47; 2006, Jan, 46-47; 2006, Dec, 14-15; 2006, December, 14-15; 2006, December, 14-15; 2006, January, 46-47; 2006, Dec, 14-15; 2006, Dec, 14-15; 2006, Dec, 14-15

14001   defect 10.1 sq cm to 30.0 sq cm   A2 T ▢

▣ 16.62   ⚕ 19.78   Global Days 090

AMA: 2008, Jan, 10-25; 2008, Jul, 5-6&15; 2007, Jan, 13-27; 2007, Jan, 13-27; 2007, January, 13-27; 2006, Jan, 46-47; 2006, Jan, 46-47; 2006, Dec, 14-15; 2006, December, 14-15; 2006, December, 14-15; 2006, January, 46-47; 2006, Dec, 14-15; 2006, Dec, 14-15; 2006, Dec, 14-15

14020   Adjacent tissue transfer or rearrangement, scalp, arms and/or legs; defect 10 sq cm or less   A2 T ▢

▣ 14.32   ⚕ 17.12   Global Days 090

AMA: 2008, Jan, 10-25; 2008, Jul, 5-6&15; 2007, Jan, 13-27; 2007, Jan, 13-27; 2007, January, 13-27; 2006, Jan, 46-47; 2006, Jan, 46-47; 2006, Dec, 14-15; 2006, December, 14-15; 2006, December, 14-15; 2006, January, 46-47; 2006, Dec, 14-15; 2006, Dec, 14-15; 2006, Dec, 14-15

14021   defect 10.1 sq cm to 30.0 sq cm   A2 T ▢

▣ 18.49   ⚕ 21.68   Global Days 090

AMA: 2008, Jan, 10-25; 2008, Jul, 5-6&15; 2007, Jan, 13-27; 2007, Jan, 13-27; 2007, January, 13-27; 2006, Jan, 46-47; 2006, Jan, 46-47; 2006, Dec, 14-15; 2006, December, 14-15; 2006, December, 14-15; 2006, January, 46-47; 2006, Dec, 14-15; 2006, Dec, 14-15; 2006, Dec, 14-15

14040   Adjacent tissue transfer or rearrangement, forehead, cheeks, chin, mouth, neck, axillae, genitalia, hands and/or feet; defect 10 sq cm or less   A2 T ▢

INCLUDES   Krimer's palatoplasty

▣ 16.24   ⚕ 18.98   Global Days 090

AMA: 2008, Jan, 10-25; 2008, Jul, 5-6&15; 2007, Jan, 13-27; 2007, Jan, 13-27; 2007, January, 13-27; 2006, Jan, 46-47; 2006, Jan, 46-47; 2006, Dec, 14-15; 2006, December, 14-15; 2006, December, 14-15; 2006, January, 46-47; 2006, Dec, 14-15; 2006, Dec, 14-15; 2006, Dec, 14-15

14041   defect 10.1 sq cm to 30.0 sq cm   A2 T ▢

▣ 20.04   ⚕ 23.60   Global Days 090

AMA: 2008, Jan, 10-25; 2008, Jul, 5-6&15; 2007, Jan, 13-27; 2007, Jan, 13-27; 2007, January, 13-27; 2006, Jan, 46-47; 2006, Jan, 46-47; 2006, Dec, 14-15; 2006, December, 14-15; 2006, December, 14-15; 2006, January, 46-47; 2006, Dec, 14-15; 2006, Dec, 14-15

14060   Adjacent tissue transfer or rearrangement, eyelids, nose, ears and/or lips; defect 10 sq cm or less   A2 T ▢

INCLUDES   Denonvillier's operation

EXCLUDES   *eyelid, full thickness (67961 and subsequent codes)*

▣ 17.15   ⚕ 19.31   Global Days 090

AMA: 2008, Jan, 10-25; 2008, Jul, 5-6&15; 2007, Jan, 13-27; 2007, Jan, 13-27; 2007, January, 13-27; 2006, Jan, 46-47; 2006, Jan, 46-47; 2006, Dec, 14-15; 2006, December, 14-15; 2006, December, 14-15; 2006, January, 46-47; 2006, Dec, 14-15; 2006, Dec, 14-15

14061   defect 10.1 sq cm to 30.0 sq cm   A2 T ▢

EXCLUDES   *eyelid, full thickness (67961 and subsequent codes)*

▣ 21.37   ⚕ 25.28   Global Days 090

AMA: 2008, Jan, 10-25; 2008, Jul, 5-6&15; 2007, Jan, 13-27; 2007, Jan, 13-27; 2007, January, 13-27; 2006, Jan, 46-47; 2006, Jan, 46-47; 2006, Dec, 14-15; 2006, December, 14-15; 2006, December, 14-15; 2006, January, 46-47; 2006, Dec, 14-15; 2006, Dec, 14-15

14300   Adjacent tissue transfer or rearrangement, more than 30 sq cm, unusual or complicated, any area   A2 T ▢

▣ 24.00   ⚕ 27.44   Global Days 090

AMA: 2008, Jan, 10-25; 2008, Jul, 5-6&15; 2007, Jan, 13-27; 2007, Jan, 13-27; 2007, January, 13-27; 2006, Jan, 46-47; 2006, Jan, 46-47; 2006, Dec, 14-15; 2006, December, 14-15; 2006, December, 14-15; 2006, January, 46-47; 2006, Dec, 14-15; 2006, Dec, 14-15

14350   Filleted finger or toe flap, including preparation of recipient site   A2 T 50 ▢

▣ 19.09   ⚕ 19.09   Global Days 090

AMA: 2008, Jan, 10-25, 2008, Jul, 5-6&15; 2007, Jan, 13-27; 2007, Jan, 13-27; 2007, January, 13-27; 2006, Jan, 46-47; 2006, January, 46-47; 2006, Jan, 46-47

Integumentary System

15002 — 15101

15002-15005 Development of Base for Tissue Grafting

CMS *100-4,12,90.3*   *MD Services in ASCs*
CMS *100-4,14,10*   *Part B ASC Payment*
CMS *100-4,3,20.1.2.8 Special Payments for Burn Cases*

INCLUDES   excision of scar or burn eschar or release of scar contracture without graft with application of dressing or other material only
     fixation and anchoring skin graft
     initial wound preparation such as scar or burn eschar removal or release of scar contracture
     routine dressing
     simple tissue debridement
     wound size by percentage of body area for children younger than age 10
     wound size in centimeters for adults age 10 or older

EXCLUDES   *acellular dermal graft (15170-15176)*
     autologous skin graft (15100-15261)
     autologous tissue cultured skin graft (15150-15157)
     excision of:
        benign lesion (11400-11471)
        malignant lesion (11600-11646)
     grafting with skin or skin replacements (15100-15431)
     harvesting of tissue for autologous skin grafts (15040)
     microvascular repair (15756-15758)
     primary procedure such as radical mastectomy, extensive tumor removal, orbitectomy (see appropriate anatomical site)
     repair of donor site with skin grafts or flaps (14000-14350, 15050-15770)
     simple graft application alone
     simple placement of stabilization dressings only
     supply of skin substitute (J7340-J7346)

Code also any immediate:
    allograft skin applications (15300-15336, 15360-15366)
    skin grafting (15050-15261)
    xenogenic dermis application (15400-15421)

15002   **Surgical preparation or creation of recipient site by excision of open wounds, burn eschar, or scar (including subcutaneous tissues), or incisional release of scar contracture, trunk, arms, legs; first 100 sq cm or 1% of body area of infants and children**   A2 T 80
     5.87   8.32 **Global Days 000**
     AMA: 2008, Jan, 10-25; 2008, Mar, 14-15; 2007, Jan, 13-27; 2007, Jan, 13-27; 2007, January, 13-27

+ ▲ **15003**   **each additional 100 sq cm, or part thereof, or each additional 1% of body area of infants and children (List separately in addition to code for primary procedure)**   A2 T 80
     Code first 15002
     1.19   1.81 **Global Days ZZZ**
     AMA: 2008, Jan, 10-25; 2007, Jan, 13-27; 2007, Jan, 13-27; 2007, January, 13-27

15004   **Surgical preparation or creation of recipient site by excision of open wounds, burn eschar, or scar (including subcutaneous tissues), or incisional release of scar contracture, face, scalp, eyelids, mouth, neck, ears, orbits, genitalia, hands, feet and/or multiple digits; first 100 sq cm or 1% of body area of infants and children**   A2 T 80
     7.34   10.10 **Global Days 000**
     AMA: 2008, Jan, 10-25; 2007, Jan, 13-27; 2007, Jan, 13-27; 2007, January, 13-27

+ ▲ **15005**   **each additional 100 sq cm, or part thereof, or each additional 1% of body area of infants and children (List separately in addition to code for primary procedure)**   A2 T 80
     Code first 15004
     2.36   3.05 **Global Days ZZZ**
     AMA: 2008, Jan, 10-25; 2007, Jan, 13-27; 2007, Jan, 13-27; 2007, January, 13-27

15040 Obtain Autograft

CMS *100-4,12,90.3*   *MD Services in ASCs*
CMS *100-4,3,20.1.2.8 Special Payments for Burn Cases*

15040   **Harvest of skin for tissue cultured skin autograft, 100 sq cm or less**   A2 T
     3.29   6.29 **Global Days 000**
     AMA: 2008, Jan, 10-25; 2008, Feb, 3-4; 2007, Jan, 13-27; 2007, Jan, 13-27; 2007, January, 13-27; 2006, Aug, 12-14; 2006, August, 12-14; 2006, Aug, 12-14

15050-15261 Autologous Skin Grafts

CMS *100-4,12,90.3*   *MD Services in ASCs*
CMS *100-4,14,10*   *Part B ASC Payment*
CMS *100-4,3,20.1.2.8 Special Payments for Burn Cases*

INCLUDES   fixation and anchoring skin graft
     routine dressing
     simple tissue debridement
     wound size by percentage of body area for children younger than age 10
     wound size in centimeters for adults age 10 or older (15100-15101)

EXCLUDES   *excision of:*
        benign lesion (11400-11471)
        burn eschar or scar (15002-15005)
        malignant lesion (11600-11646)
     harvesting of tissue for autologous skin graft (15040)
     microvascular repair (15756-15758)
     primary procedures such as radical mastectomy, extensive tumor removal, orbitectomy (see appropriate anatomical site)
     reconstruction of eyelid (67961-67975)
     repair of donor site with skin grafts or flaps (14000-14350, 15050-15431)

15050   **Pinch graft, single or multiple, to cover small ulcer, tip of digit, or other minimal open area (except on face), up to defect size 2 cm diameter**   A2 T ▢
     10.99   13.34 **Global Days 090**
     AMA: 2008, Jan, 10-25; 2007, Jan, 13-27; 2007, Jan, 13-27; 2007, January, 13-27; 2006, Aug, 12-14; 2006, Aug, 12-14; 2006, August, 12-14; 2005, Feb, 10-12; 2005, Feb, 10-12; 2005, February, 10-12

15100   **Split-thickness autograft, trunk, arms, legs; first 100 sq cm or less, or 1% of body area of infants and children (except 15050)**   A2 T ▢
     18.09   21.53 **Global Days 090**
     AMA: 2008, Jan, 10-25; 2008, Feb, 3-4; 2007, Jan, 13-27; 2007, Jan, 13-27; 2007, January, 13-27; 2006, Aug, 12-14; 2006, August, 12-14; 2006, Aug, 12-14

+ **15101**   **each additional 100 sq cm, or each additional 1% of body area of infants and children, or part thereof (List separately in addition to code for primary procedure)**   A2 T
     Code first 15100
     2.91   4.73 **Global Days ZZZ**
     AMA: 2008, Jan, 10-25; 2008, Feb, 3-4; 2007, Jan, 13-27; 2007, Jan, 13-27; 2007, January, 13-27; 2006, Aug, 12-14; 2006, August, 12-14; 2006, Aug, 12-14

15110 Epidermal autograft, trunk, arms, legs; first 100 sq cm or less, or 1% of body area of infants and children ☒☒
  🖩 18.60 ✀ 21.25 Global Days 090
  AMA: 2008, Jan, 10-25; 2008, Feb, 3-4; 2007, Jan, 13-27; 2007, Jan, 13-27; 2007, January, 13-27; 2006, Aug, 12-14; 2006, August, 12-14; 2006, Aug, 12-14

+ **15111** each additional 100 sq cm, or each additional 1% of body area of infants and children, or part thereof (List separately in addition to code for primary procedure) ☒☒
  Code first 15110
  🖩 2.81 ✀ 3.12 Global Days ZZZ
  AMA: 2008, Jan, 10-25; 2008, Feb, 3-4; 2007, Jan, 13-27; 2007, Jan, 13-27; 2007, January, 13-27; 2006, Aug, 12-14; 2006, August, 12-14; 2006, Aug, 12-14

15115 Epidermal autograft, face, scalp, eyelids, mouth, neck, ears, orbits, genitalia, hands, feet, and/or multiple digits; first 100 sq cm or less, or 1% of body area of infants and children ☒☒
  🖩 19.20 ✀ 21.45 Global Days 090
  AMA: 2008, Jan, 10-25; 2008, Feb, 3-4; 2007, Jan, 13-27; 2007, Jan, 13-27; 2007, January, 13-27; 2006, Aug, 12-14; 2006, August, 12-14; 2006, Aug, 12-14

+ **15116** each additional 100 sq cm, or each additional 1% of body area of infants and children, or part thereof (List separately in addition to code for primary procedure) ☒☒
  Code first 15115
  🖩 3.87 ✀ 4.23 Global Days ZZZ
  AMA: 2008, Jan, 10-25; 2008, Feb, 3-4; 2007, Jan, 13-27; 2007, Jan, 13-27; 2007, January, 13-27; 2006, Aug, 12-14; 2006, August, 12 14; 2006, Aug, 12 14

15120 Split-thickness autograft, face, scalp, eyelids, mouth, neck, ears, orbits, genitalia, hands, feet, and/or multiple digits; first 100 sq cm or less, or 1% of body area of infants and children (except 15050) ☒☒☒
  🖩 19.75 ✀ 23.31 Global Days 090
  AMA: 2008, Jan, 10-25; 2008, Feb, 3-4; 2008, Jul, 5-6&15; 2007, Jan, 13-27; 2007, Jan, 13-27; 2007, January, 13-27; 2006, Aug, 12-14; 2006, August, 12-14; 2006, Aug, 12-14

+ **15121** each additional 100 sq cm, or each additional 1% of body area of infants and children, or part thereof (List separately in addition to code for primary procedure) ☒☒
  Code first 15120
  🖩 4.45 ✀ 6.68 Global Days ZZZ
  AMA: 2008, Jan, 10-25; 2008, Feb, 3-4; 2007, Jan, 13-27; 2007, Jan, 13-27; 2007, January, 13-27; 2006, Aug, 12-14; 2006, Aug, 12-14

15130 Dermal autograft, trunk, arms, legs; first 100 sq cm or less, or 1% of body area of infants and children ☒☒
  🖩 14.14 ✀ 16.74 Global Days 090
  AMA: 2008, Jan, 10-25; 2008, Feb, 3-4; 2007, Jan, 13-27; 2007, Jan, 13-27; 2007, January, 13-27; 2006, Aug, 12-14; 2006, August, 12-14; 2006, Aug, 12-14

+ **15131** each additional 100 sq cm, or each additional 1% of body area of infants and children, or part thereof (List separately in addition to code for primary procedure) ☒☒
  Code first 15130
  🖩 2.30 ✀ 2.54 Global Days ZZZ
  AMA: 2008, Jan, 10-25; 2008, Feb, 3-4; 2007, Jan, 13-27; 2007, Jan, 13-27; 2007, January, 13-27; 2006, Aug, 12-14; 2006, August, 12-14; 2006, Aug, 12-14

15135 Dermal autograft, face, scalp, eyelids, mouth, neck, ears, orbits, genitalia, hands, feet, and/or multiple digits; first 100 sq cm or less, or 1% of body area of infants and children ☒☒
  🖩 19.38 ✀ 21.55 Global Days 090
  AMA: 2008, Jan, 10-25; 2008, Feb, 3-4; 2007, Jan, 13-27; 2007, Jan, 13-27; 2007, January, 13-27; 2006, Aug, 12-14; 2006, August, 12-14; 2006, Aug, 12-14

+ **15136** each additional 100 sq cm, or each additional 1% of body area of infants and children, or part thereof (List separately in addition to code for primary procedure) ☒☒
  Code first (15135)
  🖩 2.18 ✀ 2.34 Global Days ZZZ
  AMA: 2008, Jan, 10-25; 2008, Feb, 3-4; 2007, Jan, 13-27; 2007, Jan, 13-27; 2007, January, 13-27; 2006, Aug, 12-14; 2006, August, 12-14; 2006, Aug, 12-14

15150 Tissue cultured epidermal autograft, trunk, arms, legs; first 25 sq cm or less ☒☒
  🖩 16.15 ✀ 17.53 Global Days 090
  AMA: 2008, Jan, 10-25; 2008, Feb, 3-4; 2007, Jan, 13-27; 2007, Jan, 13-27; 2007, January, 13-27; 2006, Aug, 12-14; 2006, August, 12-14; 2006, Aug, 12-14

+ **15151** additional 1 sq cm to 75 sq cm (List separately in addition to code for primary procedure) ☒☒
  Code first 15150
  EXCLUDES grafts over 75 sq cm (15152)
  🖩 3.04 ✀ 3.29 Global Days ZZZ
  AMA: 2008, Jan, 10-25; 2008, Feb, 3-4; 2007, Jan, 13-27; 2007, Jan, 13-27; 2007, January, 13-27; 2006, Aug, 12-14; 2006, August, 12-14; 2006, Aug, 12-14

+ **15152** each additional 100 sq cm, or each additional 1% of body area of infants and children, or part thereof (List separately in addition to code for primary procedure) ☒☒
  Code first 15151
  🖩 4.00 ✀ 4.28 Global Days ZZZ
  AMA: 2008, Jan, 10-25; 2008, Feb, 3-4; 2007, Jan, 13-27; 2007, Jan, 13-27; 2007, January, 13-27; 2006, Aug, 12-14; 2006, August, 12-14; 2006, Aug, 12-14

15155 Tissue cultured epidermal autograft, face, scalp, eyelids, mouth, neck, ears, orbits, genitalia, hands, feet, and/or multiple digits; first 25 sq cm or less ☒☒
  🖩 17.25 ✀ 18.40 Global Days 090
  AMA: 2008, Jan, 10-25; 2008, Feb, 3-4; 2007, Jan, 13-27; 2007, Jan, 13-27; 2007, January, 13-27; 2006, Aug, 12-14; 2006, August, 12-14; 2006, Aug, 12-14

+ **15156** additional 1 sq cm to 75 sq cm (List separately in addition to code for primary procedure) ☒☒
  Code first 15155
  EXCLUDES grafts over 75 sq cm (15157)
  🖩 4.33 ✀ 4.56 Global Days ZZZ
  AMA: 2008, Jan, 10-25; 2008, Feb, 3-4; 2007, Jan, 13-27; 2007, Jan, 13-27; 2007, January, 13-27; 2006, Aug, 12-14; 2006, August, 12-14; 2006, Aug, 12-14

+ **15157** each additional 100 sq cm, or each additional 1% of body area of infants and children, or part thereof (List separately in addition to code for primary procedure) ☒☒
  Code first 15156
  🖩 4.70 ✀ 5.03 Global Days ZZZ
  AMA: 2008, Jan, 10-25; 2008, Feb, 3-4; 2007, Jan, 13-27; 2007, Jan, 13-27; 2007, January, 13-27; 2006, Aug, 12 14; 2006, August, 12-14; 2006, Aug, 12-14

● New Code   ▲ Revised Code   ☒ Maternity Edit   ☒ Age Edit   ☒-☒ OPPS Status Indicator   🖩 Facility RVU   ✀ Non-Facility RVU
☒ CCI Comprehensive Code   ☒ Bilateral Procedure   + Add-on Indicator   ☒ Laboratory crosswalk   ☒ Radiology crosswalk

Integumentary System

15170 — 15300

15170   Acellular dermal replacement, trunk, arms, legs; first 100 sq cm or less, or 1% of body area of infants and children   ⬚ ⬚
   ⬚ 9.25   ⬚ 10.65   Global Days 090
   AMA: 2008, Jan, 10-25; 2008, Feb, 3-4; 2007, Jan, 13-27; 2007, Jan, 13-27; 2007, January, 13-27; 2006, Aug, 12-14; 2006, August, 12-14; 2006, Aug, 12-14

+ **15171**   each additional 100 sq cm, or each additional 1% of body area of infants and children, or part thereof (List separately in addition to code for primary procedure)   ⬚ ⬚
   Code first 15170
   ⬚ 2.30   ⬚ 2.41   Global Days ZZZ
   AMA: 2008, Jan, 10-25; 2008, Feb, 3-4; 2007, Jan, 13-27; 2007, Jan, 13-27; 2007, January, 13-27; 2006, Aug, 12-14; 2006, August, 12-14; 2006, Aug, 12-14

15175   Acellular dermal replacement, face, scalp, eyelids, mouth, neck, ears, orbits, genitalia, hands, feet, and/or multiple digits; first 100 sq cm or less, or 1% of body area of infants and children   ⬚ ⬚
   ⬚ 12.26   ⬚ 13.58   Global Days 090
   AMA: 2008, Jan, 10-25; 2008, Feb, 3-4; 2007, Jan, 13-27; 2007, Jan, 13-27; 2007, January, 13-27; 2006, Aug, 12-14; 2006, August, 12-14; 2006, Aug, 12-14

+ **15176**   each additional 100 sq cm, or each additional 1% of body area of infants and children, or part thereof (List separately in addition to code for primary procedure)   ⬚ ⬚
   Code first 15175
   ⬚ 3.64   ⬚ 3.85   Global Days ZZZ
   AMA: 2008, Jan, 10-25; 2008, Feb, 3-4; 2007, Jan, 13-27; 2007, Jan, 13-27; 2007, January, 13-27; 2006, Aug, 12-14; 2006, August, 12-14; 2006, Aug, 12-14

15200   Full thickness graft, free, including direct closure of donor site, trunk; 20 sq cm or less   ⬚ ⬚ ⬚
   ⬚ 16.50   ⬚ 19.93   Global Days 090
   AMA: 2008, Jan, 10-25; 2008, Feb, 3-4; 2008, Mar, 14-15; 2007, Jan, 13-27; 2007, Jan, 13-27; 2007, January, 13-27; 2006, Aug, 12-14; 2006, August, 12-14; 2006, Aug, 12-14

+ ▲ **15201**   each additional 20 sq cm, or part thereof (List separately in addition to code for primary procedure)   ⬚ ⬚ ⬚
   Code first 15200
   ⬚ 2.08   ⬚ 3.69   Global Days ZZZ
   AMA: 2008, Jan, 10-25; 2008, Feb, 3-4; 2008, Mar, 14-15; 2007, Jan, 13-27; 2007, Jan, 13-27; 2007, January, 13-27; 2006, Aug, 12-14; 2006, August, 12-14; 2006, Aug, 12-14

15220   Full thickness graft, free, including direct closure of donor site, scalp, arms, and/or legs; 20 sq cm or less   ⬚ ⬚ ⬚
   ⬚ 15.59   ⬚ 18.95   Global Days 090
   AMA: 2008, Jan, 10-25; 2008, Feb, 3-4; 2008, Mar, 14-15; 2007, Jan, 13-27; 2007, Jan, 13-27; 2007, January, 13-27; 2006, Aug, 12-14; 2006, August, 12-14; 2006, Aug, 12-14

+ ▲ **15221**   each additional 20 sq cm, or part thereof (List separately in addition to code for primary procedure)   ⬚ ⬚
   Code first 15220
   ⬚ 1.90   ⬚ 3.43   Global Days ZZZ
   AMA: 2008, Jan, 10-25; 2008, Feb, 3-4; 2008, Mar, 14-15; 2007, Jan, 13-27; 2007, Jan, 13-27; 2007, January, 13-27; 2006, Aug, 12-14; 2006, August, 12-14; 2006, Aug, 12-14

15240   Full thickness graft, free, including direct closure of donor site, forehead, cheeks, chin, mouth, neck, axillae, genitalia, hands, and/or feet; 20 sq cm or less   ⬚ ⬚ ⬚
   EXCLUDES   *finger tip graft (15050)*
                 syndactyly repair fingers (26560-26562)
   ⬚ 19.87   ⬚ 22.71   Global Days 090
   AMA: 2008, Jan, 10-25; 2008, Feb, 3-4; 2008, Mar, 14-15; 2007, Jan, 13-27; 2007, Jan, 13-27; 2007, January, 13-27; 2006, Aug, 12-14; 2006, August, 12-14; 2006, Aug, 12-14

+ ▲ **15241**   each additional 20 sq cm, or part thereof (List separately in addition to code for primary procedure)   ⬚ ⬚
   Code first 15240
   ⬚ 2.96   ⬚ 4.59   Global Days ZZZ
   AMA: 2008, Jan, 10-25; 2008, Feb, 3-4; 2008, Mar, 14-15; 2007, Jan, 13-27; 2007, Jan, 13-27; 2007, January, 13-27; 2006, Aug, 12-14; 2006, August, 12-14; 2006, Aug, 12-14

15260   Full thickness graft, free, including direct closure of donor site, nose, ears, eyelids, and/or lips; 20 sq cm or less   ⬚ ⬚ ⬚
   ⬚ 21.43   ⬚ 24.52   Global Days 090
   AMA: 2008, Jan, 10-25; 2008, Feb, 3-4; 2008, Mar, 14-15; 2007, Jan, 13-27; 2007, Jan, 13-27; 2007, January, 13-27; 2006, Aug, 12-14; 2006, August, 12-14; 2006, Aug, 12-14

+ ▲ **15261**   each additional 20 sq cm, or part thereof (List separately in addition to code for primary procedure)   ⬚ ⬚
   Code first 15260
   EXCLUDES   *eyelid reconstruction (67961-67975)*
   ⬚ 3.70   ⬚ 5.33   Global Days ZZZ
   AMA: 2008, Jan, 10-25; 2008, Feb, 3-4; 2008, Mar, 14-15; 2007, Jan, 13-27; 2007, Jan, 13-27; 2007, January, 13-27; 2006, Aug, 12-14; 2006, August, 12-14; 2006, Aug, 12-14

15300-15366 Homografts

CMS *100-4,4,20.5*   *HCPCS Under OPPS*
CMS *100-4,3,20.1.2.8 Special Payments for Burn Cases*
INCLUDES   fixation and anchoring skin graft
   non-autologous human skin graft to repair wound caused by:
      burns
      infection of skin and subcutaneous tissues
      necrosis
      surgical wounds
      traumatic injury
   routine dressing
   simple tissue debridement

EXCLUDES   *autologous tissue cultured skin graft (15150-15157)*
   excision of:
      benign lesion (11400-11471)
      burn eschar or scar (15002-15005)
      malignant lesion (11600-11646)
   harvesting tissue for autologous skin graft (15040)
   microvascular repair (15756-15758)
   primary procedures such as a radical mastectomy, extensive tumor removal, orbitectomy (see appropriate anatomical site)
   repair of donor site with skin grafts or flaps (14000-14350, 15050-15431)

15300   Allograft skin for temporary wound closure, trunk, arms, legs; first 100 sq cm or less, or 1% of body area of infants and children   ⬚ ⬚
   ⬚ 7.38   ⬚ 8.57   Global Days 090
   AMA: 2008, Jan, 10-25; 2007, Jan, 13-27; 2007, Jan, 13-27; 2007, January, 13-27; 2006, Aug, 12-14; 2006, August, 12-14; 2006, Aug, 12-14

+ **15301** each additional 100 sq cm, or each additional 1% of body area of infants and children, or part thereof (List separately in addition to code for primary procedure) A2 T
Code first 15300
1.51 ⚡ 1.63 **Global Days ZZZ**
AMA: 2008, Jan, 10-25; 2007, Jan, 13-27; 2007, Jan, 13-27; 2007, January, 13-27; 2006, Aug, 12-14; 2006, August, 12-14; 2006, Aug, 12-14

15320 Allograft skin for temporary wound closure, face, scalp, eyelids, mouth, neck, ears, orbits, genitalia, hands, feet, and/or multiple digits; first 100 sq cm or less, or 1% of body area of infants and children A2 T
8.36 ⚡ 9.67 **Global Days 090**
AMA: 2008, Jan, 10-25; 2007, Jan, 13-27; 2007, Jan, 13-27; 2007, January, 13-27; 2006, Aug, 12-14; 2006, August, 12-14; 2006, Aug, 12-14

+ **15321** each additional 100 sq cm, or each additional 1% of body area of infants and children, or part thereof (List separately in addition to code for primary procedure) A2 T
Code first 15320
2.27 ⚡ 2.43 **Global Days ZZZ**
AMA: 2008, Jan, 10-25; 2007, Jan, 13-27; 2007, Jan, 13-27; 2007, January, 13-27; 2006, Aug, 12-14; 2006, August, 12-14; 2006, Aug, 12-14

15330 Acellular dermal allograft, trunk, arms, legs; first 100 sq cm or less, or 1% of body area of infants and children A2 T
6.72 ⚡ 7.94 **Global Days 090**
AMA: 2008, Jan, 10-25; 2007, Jan, 13-27; 2007, Jan, 13-27; 2007, January, 13-27; 2006, Aug, 12-14; 2006, August, 12-14; 2006, Aug, 12-14

+ **15331** each additional 100 sq cm, or each additional 1% of body area of infants and children, or part thereof (List separately in addition to code for primary procedure) A2 T
Code first 15330
1.52 ⚡ 1.63 **Global Days ZZZ**
AMA: 2008, Jan, 10-25; 2007, Jan, 13-27; 2007, Jan, 13-27; 2007, January, 13-27; 2006, Aug, 12-14; 2006, August, 12-14; 2006, Aug, 12-14

15335 Acellular dermal allograft, face, scalp, eyelids, mouth, neck, ears, orbits, genitalia, hands, feet, and/or multiple digits; first 100 sq cm or less, or 1% of body area of infants and children A2 T
7.18 ⚡ 8.37 **Global Days 090**
AMA: 2008, Jan, 10-25; 2007, Jan, 13-27; 2007, Jan, 13-27; 2007, January, 13-27; 2006, Aug, 12-14; 2006, August, 12-14; 2006, Aug, 12-14

+ **15336** each additional 100 sq cm, or each additional 1% of body area of infants and children, or part thereof (List separately in addition to code for primary procedure) A2 T
Code first 15335
2.09 ⚡ 2.27 **Global Days ZZZ**
AMA: 2008, Jan, 10-25; 2007, Jan, 13-27; 2007, Jan, 13-27; 2007, January, 13-27; 2006, Aug, 12-14; 2006, August, 12-14; 2006, Aug, 12-14

15340 Tissue cultured allogeneic skin substitute; first 25 sq cm or less 62 T
INCLUDES debridement
surgical creation or preparation of recipient site
Do not report with (11040-11042, 15002-15005)
6.84 ⚡ 7.92 **Global Days 010**
AMA: 2008, Jan, 10-25; 2007, Jan, 13-27; 2007, Jan, 13-27; 2007, January, 13-27; 2006, Aug, 12-14; 2006, August, 12-14; 2006, Aug, 12-14

+ ▲ **15341** each additional 25 sq cm, or part thereof (List separately in addition to code for primary procedure) 62 T
Code first 15340
Do not report with (11040-11042, 15002-15005)
0.72 ⚡ 1.18 **Global Days ZZZ**
AMA: 2008, Jan, 10-25; 2007, Jan, 13-27; 2007, Jan, 13-27; 2007, January, 13-27; 2006, Aug, 12-14; 2006, August, 12-14; 2006, Aug, 12-14

15360 Tissue cultured allogeneic dermal substitute, trunk, arms, legs; first 100 sq cm or less, or 1% of body area of infants and children 62 T
7.70 ⚡ 8.97 **Global Days 090**
AMA: 2008, Jan, 10-25; 2008, Feb, 3-4; 2007, Jan, 13-27; 2007, Jan, 13-27; 2007, January, 13-27; 2006, Aug, 12-14; 2006, August, 12-14; 2006, Aug, 12-14

+ **15361** each additional 100 sq cm, or each additional 1% of body area of infants and children, or part thereof (List separately in addition to code for primary procedure) 62 T
Code first 15360
1.66 ⚡ 1.82 **Global Days ZZZ**
AMA: 2008, Jan, 10-25; 2008, Feb, 3-4; 2007, Jan, 13-27; 2007, Jan, 13-27; 2007, January, 13-27; 2006, Aug, 12-14; 2006, August, 12-14; 2006, Aug, 12-14

15365 Tissue cultured allogeneic dermal substitute, face, scalp, eyelids, mouth, neck, ears, orbits, genitalia, hands, feet, and/or multiple digits; first 100 sq cm or less, or 1% of body area of infants and children 62 T
7.69 ⚡ 8.83 **Global Days 090**
AMA: 2008, Jan, 10-25; 2008, Feb, 3-4; 2007, Jan, 13-27; 2007, Jan, 13-27; 2007, January, 13-27; 2006, Aug, 12-14; 2006, August, 12-14; 2006, Aug, 12-14

+ **15366** each additional 100 sq cm, or each additional 1% of body area of infants and children, or part thereof (List separately in addition to code for primary procedure) 62 T
Code first 15365
2.07 ⚡ 2.24 **Global Days ZZZ**
AMA: 2008, Jan, 10-25; 2007, Jan, 13-27; 2007, Jan, 13-27; 2007, January, 13-27; 2006, Aug, 12-14; 2006, August, 12-14; 2006, Aug, 12-14

15400-15431 Heterografts

CMS *100-4,3,20.1.2.8 Special Payments for Burn Cases*

INCLUDES   fixation and anchoring skin graft
porcine tissue, pig skin, or nonhuman skin replacement
routine dressing
simple tissue debridement
xenograft to repair wound caused by:
  burns
  infection of skin and subcutaneous tissues
  necrosis
  surgical wounds
  traumatic injury

EXCLUDES   *autologous tissue cultured skin graft (15150-15157)*
excision of:
  benign lesion (11400-11471)
  burn eschar or scar (15002-15005)
  malignant lesion (11600-11646)
primary procedures such as a radical mastectomy, extensive tumor
  removal, orbitectomy (see appropriate anatomical site)

Code also supply of graft (J7341, J7343, J7347-J7349)

15400   **Xenograft, skin (dermal), for temporary wound closure, trunk, arms, legs; first 100 sq cm or less, or 1% of body area of infants and children**   A2 T ▢
  🔧 8.87   ⚕ 9.81   **Global Days 090**
  AMA: 2008, Jan, 10-25; 2007, Jan, 13-27; 2007, Jan, 13-27; 2007, January, 13-27; 2006, Aug, 12-14; 2006, Aug, 12-14; 2006, August, 12-14; 2006, January, 2-4,48; 2006, Jan, 2-4,48; 2006, Jan, 2-4,48

+ **15401**   **each additional 100 sq cm, or each additional 1% of body area of infants and children, or part thereof (List separately in addition to code for primary procedure)**   A2 T
  Code first 15400
  🔧 1.50   ⚕ 2.36   **Global Days ZZZ**
  AMA: 2008, Jan, 10-25; 2007, Jan, 13-27; 2007, Jan, 13-27; 2007, January, 13-27; 2006, Jan, 2-4,48; 2006, Jan, 2-4,48; 2006, August, 12-14; 2006, January, 2-4,48; 2006, Aug, 12-14

15420   **Xenograft skin (dermal), for temporary wound closure, face, scalp, eyelids, mouth, neck, ears, orbits, genitalia, hands, feet, and/or multiple digits; first 100 sq cm or less, or 1% of body area of infants and children**   A2 T
  🔧 9.84   ⚕ 11.06   **Global Days 090**
  AMA: 2008, Jan, 10-25; 2007, Jan, 13-27; 2007, Jan, 13-27; 2007, January, 13-27; 2006, Aug, 12-14; 2006, August, 12-14; 2006, Aug, 12-14

+ **15421**   **each additional 100 sq cm, or each additional 1% of body area of infants and children, or part thereof (List separately in addition to code for primary procedure)**   A2 T
  Code first 15420
  🔧 2.24   ⚕ 2.91   **Global Days ZZZ**
  AMA: 2008, Jan, 10-25; 2007, Jan, 13-27; 2007, Jan, 13-27; 2007, January, 13-27; 2006, Aug, 12-14; 2006, August, 12-14; 2006, Aug, 12-14

15430   **Acellular xenograft implant; first 100 sq cm or less, or 1% of body area of infants and children**   A2 T
  INCLUDES   debridement
  surgical creation or preparation of recipient site

  Do not report with (0170T, 11040-11042, 15002-15005)
  🔧 12.58   ⚕ 13.04   **Global Days 090**
  AMA: 2008, Jan, 10-25; 2008, Jun, 3-6; 2007, Jan, 13-27; 2007, Jan, 13-27; 2007, January, 13-27; 2006, Aug, 12-14; 2006, August, 12-14; 2006, Aug, 12-14

+ **15431**   **each additional 100 sq cm, or each additional 1% of body area of infants and children, or part thereof (List separately in addition to code for primary procedure)**   A2 T 80
  Code first 15430
  Do not report with (0170T, 11040-11042, 15002-15005)
  🔧 0.00   ⚕ 0.00   **Global Days ZZZ**
  AMA: 2008, Jan, 10-25; 2008, Jun, 3-6; 2007, Jan, 13-27; 2007, Jan, 13-27; 2007, January, 13-27; 2006, Aug, 12-14; 2006, August, 12-14; 2006, Aug, 12-14

15570-15750 Wound Reconstruction: Skin Flaps

CMS *100-4,4,20.5   HCPCS Under OPPS*
CMS *100-4,3,20.1.2.8 Special Payments for Burn Cases*

INCLUDES   fixation and anchoring skin graft
tube formation for later transfer
xenogenic dermis application
routine dressing
simple tissue debridement

EXCLUDES   *acellular dermal graft (15170-15176)*
adjacent tissue transfer (14000-14300)
application of extensive immobilization apparatus
autologous skin graft (15100-15261)
autologous tissue cultured skin graft (15040)
excision of:
  benign lesion (11400-11471)
  burn eschar or scar (15002-15005)
  malignant lesion (11600-11646)
microvascular repair (15756-15758)
primary procedure such as radical mastectomy, extensive tumor
  removal, orbitectomy (see appropriate anatomical site)
repair of donor site with skin grafts or flaps (14000-14350, 15050-15431)

Pedicle Flap

Defective tissue is identified
And removed
A nearby flap is lifted; a pedicle remains attached to provide an intact blood supply
Pedicle
The flap is rotated and sutured over the defect
The donor site is sutured closed; pedicle remains intact
Pedicle
The pedicle is severed after the graft is established

15570   **Formation of direct or tubed pedicle, with or without transfer; trunk**   A2 T ▢
  🔧 18.10   ⚕ 21.99   **Global Days 090**

15572   **scalp, arms, or legs**   A2 T ▢
  🔧 18.28   ⚕ 21.30   **Global Days 090**

15574 forehead, cheeks, chin, mouth, neck, axillae, genitalia, hands or feet [A2] [T] [⊡]
    📋 19.29   ⚕ 22.45   Global Days 090

15576 eyelids, nose, ears, lips, or intraoral [A2] [T] [⊡]
    📋 16.88   ⚕ 19.89   Global Days 090

15600 **Delay of flap or sectioning of flap (division and inset); at trunk** [A2] [T] [80] [⊡]
    📋 5.04   ⚕ 8.05   Global Days 090

15610 at scalp, arms, or legs [A2] [T] [80] [⊡]
    📋 5.97   ⚕ 8.11   Global Days 090

15620 at forehead, cheeks, chin, neck, axillae, genitalia, hands, or feet [A2] [T] [⊡]
    📋 7.87   ⚕ 10.72   Global Days 090

15630 at eyelids, nose, ears, or lips [A2] [T] [⊡]
    📋 8.59   ⚕ 11.32   Global Days 090

15650 **Transfer, intermediate, of any pedicle flap (eg, abdomen to wrist, Walking tube), any location** [A2] [T] [80] [⊡]
    EXCLUDES   *defatting, revision, or rearranging of transferred pedicle flap or skin graft (13100-14300)*
    📋 9.69   ⚕ 12.64   Global Days 090

15731 **Forehead flap with preservation of vascular pedicle (eg, axial pattern flap, paramedian forehead flap)** [A2] [T] [80]
    EXCLUDES   *muscle, myocutaneous, or fasciocutaneous flap of the head or neck (15732)*
    📋 25.57   ⚕ 28.19   Global Days 090

15732 **Muscle, myocutaneous, or fasciocutaneous flap; head and neck (eg, temporalis, masseter muscle, sternocleidomastoid, levator scapulae)** [A2] [T] [⊡]
    EXCLUDES   *forehead flap with preservation of vascular pedicle (15731)*
    📋 33.36   ⚕ 37.40   Global Days 090

15734 trunk [A2] [T] [90] [⊡] [P0]
    📋 34.41   ⚕ 38.63   Global Days 090

15736 upper extremity [A2] [T] [⊡]
    📋 29.78   ⚕ 34.28   Global Days 090

15738 lower extremity [A2] [T] [80] [⊡] [P0]
    📋 32.43   ⚕ 36.58   Global Days 090
    AMA: 2008, Jan, 10-25; 2007, Jan, 13-27; 2007, Jan, 13-27; 2007, January, 13-27

15740 **Flap; island pedicle** [A2] [T] [⊡]
    📋 21.56   ⚕ 25.06   Global Days 090
    AMA: 2008, Jan, 10-25; 2007, Jan, 13-27; 2007, Jan, 13-27; 2007, January, 13-27; 2004, Mar, 11; 2004, Mar, 11; 2004, Oct, 14; 2004, March, 11; 2004, October, 14; 2004, September, 12; 2004, Oct, 14; 2004, Sep, 12; 2004, Sep, 12

15750 neurovascular pedicle [A2] [T] [80] [⊡]
    📋 23.08   ⚕ 23.08   Global Days 090

15756-15758 Wound Reconstruction: Free Flaps

CMS *104-4,12,30*   Correct Coding Policy
CMS *100-4,3,20.1.2.8*   Special Payments for Burn Cases
INCLUDES   fixation and anchoring skin graft
    operating microscope (69990)
    routine dressing
    simple tissue debridement
EXCLUDES   *acellular dermal graft (15170-15176)*
    adjacent tissue transfer (14000-14300)
    autologous skin graft (15100-15261)
    autologous tissue cultured graft (15040)
    excision of:
        benign lesion (11400-11471)
        burn eschar or scar (15002-15005)
        malignant lesion (11600-11646)
    flaps without addition of a vascular pedicle (15570-15576)
    primary procedure such as radical mastectomy, extensive tumor removal, orbitectomy (see appropriate anatomical section)
    repair of donor site with skin grafts or flaps (14000-14350, 15050-15431)

15756 **Free muscle or myocutaneous flap with microvascular anastomosis** [C] [80] [⊡]
    📋 61.03   ⚕ 61.03   Global Days 090

15757 **Free skin flap with microvascular anastomosis** [C] [80] [⊡]
    📋 60.19   ⚕ 60.19   Global Days 090

15758 **Free fascial flap with microvascular anastomosis** [C] [80] [⊡]
    📋 60.35   ⚕ 60.35   Global Days 090

15760-15770 Grafts Comprised of Multiple Tissue Types

CMS *100-4,4,20.5*   HCPCS Under OPPS
CMS *100-4,3,20.1.2.8*   Special Payments for Burn Cases
INCLUDES   fixation and anchoring skin graft
    routine dressing
    simple tissue debridement
EXCLUDES   *acellular dermal graft (15170-15176)*
    adjacent tissue transfer (14000-14300)
    autologous skin graft (15100-15261)
    excision of:
        benign lesion (11400-11471)
        burn eschar or scar (15002-15005)
        malignant lesion (11600-11646)
    flaps without addition of vascular pedicle (15570-15576)
    microvascular repair (15756-15758)
    primary procedure such as extensive tumor removal (see appropriate anatomical site)
    repair of donor site with skin grafts or flaps (14000-14350, 15050-15431)

15760 **Graft; composite (eg, full thickness of external ear or nasal ala), including primary closure, donor area** [A2] [T] [⊡]
    📋 17.77   ⚕ 20.91   Global Days 090

15770 **derma-fat-fascia** [A2] [T] [80] [⊡]
    📋 16.55   ⚕ 16.55   Global Days 090

15775-15839 Plastic, Reconstructive, and Aesthetic Surgery

CMS *100-2,16,180*   Services Related to Noncovered Procedures
CMS *100-2,16,120*   Cosmetic Procedures
CMS *100-2,16,10*   Exclusions from Coverage
EXCLUDES   *strip transplant (15220)*

Integumentary System

15775 — 15839

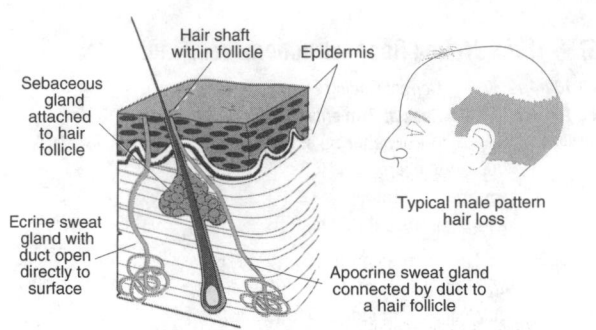

Alopecia means hair loss and the condition is separated into two major categories: that which occurs with associated, visible scalp disease, and that which occurs in the absence of visible disease. Male and female pattern hair loss is of the latter category. Hirsutism is excess hair growth, particularly in women, and is often a sign of a systemic medical syndrome

15775 **Punch graft for hair transplant; 1 to 15 punch grafts** `A2` `T` `80` `□`
    🔪 6.06   ✂ 8.15   Global Days 000

15776   **more than 15 punch grafts** `A2` `T` `80` `□`
    🔪 8.65   ✂ 11.29   Global Days 000

15780 **Dermabrasion; total face (eg, for acne scarring, fine wrinkling, rhytids, general keratosis)** `P3` `T` `80` `□`
    🔪 16.22   ✂ 20.55   Global Days 090
    AMA: 2008, Jan, 10-25; 2007, Jan, 13-27; 2007, Jan, 13-27; 2007, January, 13-27

15781   **segmental, face** `P2` `T` `□`
    🔪 10.66   ✂ 13.16   Global Days 090

15782   **regional, other than face** `P2` `T` `80` `□`
    🔪 10.25   ✂ 13.93   Global Days 090

15783   **superficial, any site (eg, tattoo removal)** `P2` `T` `80` `□`
    🔪 9.23   ✂ 11.97   Global Days 090

15786 **Abrasion; single lesion (eg, keratosis, scar)** `P2` `T` `□`
    🔪 3.46   ✂ 5.86   Global Days 010

+ **15787**   **each additional 4 lesions or less (List separately in addition to code for primary procedure)** `P3` `T`
    Code first 15786
    🔪 0.49   ✂ 1.21   Global Days ZZZ

15788 **Chemical peel, facial; epidermal** `P2` `T` `□`
    🔪 5.86   ✂ 10.42   Global Days 090

15789   **dermal** `P2` `T` `□`
    🔪 10.58   ✂ 13.92   Global Days 090

15792 **Chemical peel, nonfacial; epidermal** `P2` `T` `80` `□`
    🔪 6.45   ✂ 10.26   Global Days 090

15793   **dermal** `P2` `T` `80` `□`
    🔪 8.79   ✂ 11.59   Global Days 090

15819 **Cervicoplasty** `G2` `T` `80` `□`
    🔪 18.53   ✂ 18.53   Global Days 090

15820 **Blepharoplasty, lower eyelid;** `A2` `T` `80` `50` `□`
    🔪 11.92   ✂ 13.16   Global Days 090
    AMA: 2008, Jan, 10-25; 2007, Jan, 13-27; 2007, Jan, 13-27; 2007, January, 13-27; 2005, Feb, 13-16; 2005, Feb, 13-16; 2005, January, 46-47; 2005, Jan, 46-47; 2005, Jan, 46-47; 2005, February, 13-16; 2004, Feb, 11; 2004, Feb, 11; 2004, May, 9; 2004, May, 9; 2004, February, 11; 2004, May, 9

15821   **with extensive herniated fat pad** `A2` `T` `80` `50` `□`
    🔪 12.64   ✂ 14.00   Global Days 090
    AMA: 2005, Feb, 13-16; 2005, Feb, 13-16; 2005, February, 13-16; 2004, Feb, 11; 2004, Feb, 11; 2004, February, 11; 2004, May, 9; 2004, May, 9; 2004, May, 9

15822 **Blepharoplasty, upper eyelid;** `A2` `T` `50` `□`
    🔪 9.15   ✂ 10.33   Global Days 090
    AMA: 2005, Feb, 13-16; 2005, Feb, 13-16; 2005, February, 13-16; 2004, May, 9; 2004, May, 9; 2004, February, 11; 2004, Feb, 11; 2004, Feb, 11

15823   **with excessive skin weighting down lid** `A2` `T` `50` `□`
    🔪 14.99   ✂ 16.28   Global Days 090
    AMA: 2005, Feb, 13-16; 2005, Feb, 13-16; 2005, February, 13-16; 2004, May, 9; 2004, May, 9; 2004, February, 11; 2004, May, 9; 2004, Feb, 11; 2004, Feb, 11

A rhytidectomy is an excision to eliminate wrinkles. This procedure in the forehead region typically involves an incision just inside the scalp line. Skin and underlying tissues are then manipulated to eliminate wrinkles in the forehead

15824 **Rhytidectomy; forehead** `A2` `T` `80` `50` `□`
    EXCLUDES   *repair of brow ptosis (67900)*
    🔪 0.00   ✂ 0.00   Global Days 000

15825   **neck with platysmal tightening (platysmal flap, P-flap)** `A2` `T` `80` `50` `□`
    🔪 0.00   ✂ 0.00   Global Days 000

15826   **glabellar frown lines** `A2` `T` `80` `50` `□`
    🔪 0.00   ✂ 0.00   Global Days 000

15828   **cheek, chin, and neck** `A2` `T` `80` `50` `□`
    🔪 0.00   ✂ 0.00   Global Days 000

15829   **superficial musculoaponeurotic system (SMAS) flap** `A2` `T` `80` `50` `□`
    🔪 0.00   ✂ 0.00   Global Days 000

15830 **Excision, excessive skin and subcutaneous tissue (includes lipectomy); abdomen, infraumbilical panniculectomy** `A2` `T` `80`
    EXCLUDES   *other abdominoplasty (17999)*
    Code also 15847 for abdominoplasty with panniculectomy
    Do not report with (12031-12032, 12034-12037, 13100-13102, 14000-14001, 14300)
    🔪 29.96   ✂ 29.96   Global Days 090

15832   **thigh** `A2` `T` `80` `□`
    🔪 22.58   ✂ 22.58   Global Days 090

15833   **leg** `A2` `T` `80` `□`
    🔪 21.28   ✂ 21.28   Global Days 090

15834   **hip** `A2` `T` `80` `□`
    🔪 21.22   ✂ 21.22   Global Days 090

15835   **buttock** `A2` `T` `80` `□`
    🔪 22.40   ✂ 22.40   Global Days 090

15836   **arm** `A2` `T` `80` `□`
    🔪 18.68   ✂ 18.68   Global Days 090

15837   **forearm or hand** `G2` `T` `80` `□`
    🔪 16.90   ✂ 19.29   Global Days 090

15838   **submental fat pad** `G2` `T` `80` `□`
    🔪 14.42   ✂ 14.42   Global Days 090

15839   **other area** `A2` `T` `80` `□`
    🔪 18.28   ✂ 21.31   Global Days 090

`26`/`TC` Professional/Technical Component Only   `80`/`80` Assist-at-Surgery Allowed/With Documentation   Unlisted   Not Covered

AMA: CPT Assistant References   `A2`-`Z3` ASC Payment Indicator   ♂ Male Only   ♀ Female Only   ⊘ Modifier 51 Exempt   `P0` PQRI

15840-15845 Reanimation of the Paralyzed Face

CMS 100-4,12,40.7   *Bilateral Procedures*
CMS 100-4,12,90.3   *MD Services in ASCs*
CMS 100-2,15,260   *Covered ASC Procedures*
CMS 100-4,4,20.5   *HCPCS Under OPPS*

EXCLUDES   *intravenous fluorescein evaluation of blood flow in graft or flap (15860)*
      nerve:
           decompression (69720, 69725, 69955)
           pedicle transfer (64905, 64907)
           suture (64831-64876, 69740, 69745)

15840   **Graft for facial nerve paralysis; free fascia graft (including obtaining fascia)**   A2 T ▢
      🕮 25.51   ⚕ 25.51   **Global Days 090**

15841   **free muscle graft (including obtaining graft)**   A2 T 80 ▢
      🕮 42.77   ⚕ 42.77   **Global Days 090**

15842   **free muscle flap by microsurgical technique**   G2 T 80 ▢
      INCLUDES   operating microscope (69990)
      🕮 67.85   ⚕ 67.85   **Global Days 090**

15845   **regional muscle transfer**   A2 T 80 ▢
      🕮 23.78   ⚕ 23.78   **Global Days 090**

15847 Removal of Excess Abdominal Tissue Add-on

+   **15847**   **Excision, excessive skin and subcutaneous tissue (includes lipectomy), abdomen (eg, abdominoplasty) (includes umbilical transposition and fascial plication) (List separately in addition to code for primary procedure)**   A2 T 80
      Code first (15830)
      EXCLUDES   *abdominal wall hernia repair (49491-49587)*
             other abdominoplasty (17999)
      🕮 0.00   ⚕ 0.00   **Global Days YYY**

15850-15852 Suture Removal/Dressing Change: Anesthesia Required

CMS 100-4,12,50   *Anesthesia Services*
CMS 100-4,12,40.1   *Global Surgery Package Definition*

15850   **Removal of sutures under anesthesia (other than local), same surgeon**   G2 T
      🕮 1.10   ⚕ 2.26   **Global Days XXX**

15851   **Removal of sutures under anesthesia (other than local), other surgeon**   P3 T ▢
      🕮 1.18   ⚕ 2.31   **Global Days 000**

15852   **Dressing change (for other than burns) under anesthesia (other than local)**   G2 X ▢
      EXCLUDES   *dressing change for burns (16020-16030)*
      🕮 1.24   ⚕ 1.24   **Global Days 000**

15860 Injection for Vascular Flow Determination

15860   **Intravenous injection of agent (eg, fluorescein) to test vascular flow in flap or graft**   G2 X 80 ▢
      🕮 2.94   ⚕ 2.94   **Global Days 000**

15876-15879 Liposuction

CMS 100-4,12,20.4.3   *Payment for Assistant at Surgery*
CMS 100-2,16,180   *Services Related to Noncovered Procedures*
CMS 100-2,16,120   *Cosmetic Procedures*
CMS 100-2,16,10   *Exclusions from Coverage*

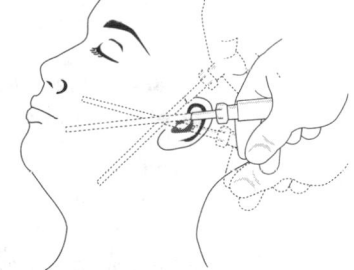

Cannula typically inserted through incision in front of ear

In 15876, a liposuction cannula is inserted through fat deposits creating tunnels and removing excess deposits

15876   **Suction assisted lipectomy; head and neck**   A2 T 80 ▢
      🕮 0.00   ⚕ 0.00   **Global Days 000**

15877   **trunk**   A2 T 80 ▢
      🕮 0.00   ⚕ 0.00   **Global Days 000**
      AMA: 2008, Jan, 10-25; 2007, Jan, 13-27; 2007, Jan, 13-27; 2007, January, 13-27; 2005, Feb, 13-16; 2005, February, 13-16; 2005, Feb, 13-16

15878   **upper extremity**   A2 T 80 50 ▢
      🕮 0.00   ⚕ 0.00   **Global Days 000**

15879   **lower extremity**   A2 T 80 50 ▢
      🕮 0.00   ⚕ 0.00   **Global Days 000**

15920-15999 Treatment of Decubitus Ulcers

CMS 100-3,270.4   *Treatment of Decubitus*
CMS 100-4,12,40.6   *Multiple procedures*
CMS 100-4,12,40.8   *Co-surgery and team surgery*
CMS 100-4,12,20.4.3   *Payment for Assistant at Surgery*

Code also free skin graft to repair ulcer or donor site

15920   **Excision, coccygeal pressure ulcer, with coccygectomy; with primary suture**   A2 T 80 ▢
      🕮 14.80   ⚕ 14.80   **Global Days 090**

15922   **with flap closure**   A2 T 80 ▢
      🕮 18.84   ⚕ 18.84   **Global Days 090**

15931   **Excision, sacral pressure ulcer, with primary suture;**   A2 T ▢
      🕮 16.86   ⚕ 16.86   **Global Days 090**

15933   **with ostectomy**   A2 T 80 ▢
      🕮 20.77   ⚕ 20.77   **Global Days 090**

15934   **Excision, sacral pressure ulcer, with skin flap closure;**   A2 T ▢
      🕮 23.17   ⚕ 23.17   **Global Days 090**

15935   **with ostectomy**   A2 T 80 ▢
      🕮 27.58   ⚕ 27.58   **Global Days 090**

15936   **Excision, sacral pressure ulcer, in preparation for muscle or myocutaneous flap or skin graft closure;**   A2 T ▢
      Code also any defect repair with:
        muscle or myocutaneous flap (15734, 15738)
        split skin graft (15100-15101)
      🕮 22.48   ⚕ 22.48   **Global Days 090**

15937   **with ostectomy**   A2 T ▢
      Code also any defect repair with:
        muscle or myocutaneous flap (15734, 15738)
        split skin graft (15100-15101)
      🕮 26.29   ⚕ 26.29   **Global Days 090**

15940   **Excision, ischial pressure ulcer, with primary suture;**   A2 T ▢
      🕮 17.35   ⚕ 17.35   **Global Days 090**

15941   **with ostectomy (ischiectomy)**   A2 T 80 ▢
      🕮 22.55   ⚕ 22.55   **Global Days 090**

● New Code   ▲ Revised Code   Ⓜ Maternity Edit   Ⓐ Age Edit   A-V OPPS Status Indicator   🕮 Facility RVU   ⚕ Non-Facility RVU
▢ CCI Comprehensive Code   50 Bilateral Procedure   + Add-on Indicator   ▧ Laboratory crosswalk   ▨ Radiology crosswalk

15944 Excision, ischial pressure ulcer, with skin flap
closing; 　　　　A2 T 80 ▭
　　🔧 22.21　 ⚕ 22.21　Global Days 090

15945 with ostectomy 　　　　A2 T 80 ▭
　　🔧 24.68　 ⚕ 24.68　Global Days 090

15946 Excision, ischial pressure ulcer, with ostectomy, in
preparation for muscle or myocutaneous flap or skin graft
closure 　　　　A2 T ▭
　　Code also any defect repair with:
　　　muscle or myocutaneous flap (15734, 15738)
　　　split skin graft (15100-15101)
　　🔧 41.27　 ⚕ 41.27　Global Days 090
　　AMA: 2008, Jan, 10-25; 2007, Jan, 13-27; 2007, Jan, 13-27; 2007,
　　January, 13-27

15950 Excision, trochanteric pressure ulcer, with primary
suture; 　　　　A2 T ▭
　　🔧 14.37　 ⚕ 14.37　Global Days 090

15951 with ostectomy 　　　　A2 T 80 ▭
　　🔧 20.49　 ⚕ 20.49　Global Days 090

15952 Excision, trochanteric pressure ulcer, with skin flap
closure; 　　　　A2 T 80 ▭
　　🔧 21.55　 ⚕ 21.55　Global Days 090

15953 with ostectomy 　　　　A2 T ▭
　　🔧 24.01　 ⚕ 24.01　Global Days 090

15956 Excision, trochanteric pressure ulcer, in preparation for
muscle or myocutaneous flap or skin graft
closure; 　　　　A2 T ▭
　　Code also any defect repair with:
　　　muscle or myocutaneous flap (15734, 15738)
　　　split skin graft (15100-15101)
　　🔧 28.91　 ⚕ 28.91　Global Days 090

15958 with ostectomy 　　　　A2 T ▭
　　Code also any defect repair with:
　　　muscle or myocutaneous flap (15734-15738)
　　　split skin graft (15100-15101)
　　🔧 29.51　 ⚕ 29.51　Global Days 090

15999 Unlisted procedure, excision pressure ulcer 　　T 80
　　🔧 0.00　 ⚕ 0.00　Global Days YYY

16000-16036 Burn Care

CMS *100-4,3,20.1.2.8 Special Payments for Burn Cases*
INCLUDES local care of burn only
EXCLUDES *application of skin grafts (15100-15650)*
evaluation and management services

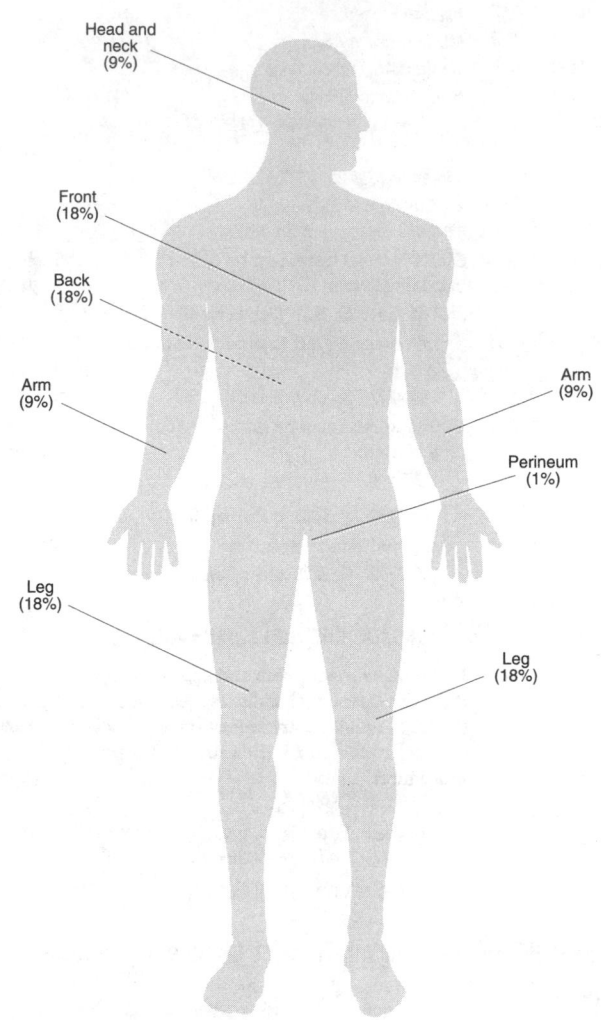

Rule of Nines for Burns

Head and
neck
(9%)

Front
(18%)

Back
(18%)

Arm
(9%)

Arm
(9%)

Perineum
(1%)

Leg
(18%)

Leg
(18%)

16000 Initial treatment, first degree burn, when no more than
local treatment is required 　　　　P3 T ▭
　　🔧 1.21　 ⚕ 1.72　Global Days 000

16020 Dressings and/or debridement of partial-thickness burns,
initial or subsequent; small (less than 5% total body
surface area) 　　　　P3 T ▭
　　INCLUDES wound coverage other than skin graft
　　🔧 1.44　 ⚕ 2.02　Global Days 000

16025 medium (eg, whole face or whole extremity, or 5% to
10% total body surface area) 　　　　A2 T ▭
　　INCLUDES wound coverage other than skin graft
　　🔧 2.95　 ⚕ 3.67　Global Days 000
　　AMA: 2008, Jun, 14-15

16030 large (eg, more than one extremity, or greater than
10% total body surface area) 　　　　A2 T ▭
　　INCLUDES wound coverage other than skin graft
　　🔧 3.36　 ⚕ 4.40　Global Days 000
　　AMA: 2008, Jun, 14-15

16035 Escharotomy; initial incision 　　　　62 T ▭
　　EXCLUDES *debridement or scraping of burn wound
　　　　　　　　(16020-16030)*
　　🔧 5.56　 ⚕ 5.56　Global Days 000

+   16036   **each additional incision (List separately in addition to code for primary procedure)** ☐C
  - **EXCLUDES** *debridement or scraping of burn wound (16020-16030)*
  - Code first 16035
  - 📖 2.22   ♒ 2.22   **Global Days ZZZ**

17000-17004 Destruction Any Method: Premalignant Lesion

CMS *100-3,140.5*   *Laser Procedures*
CMS *100-4,12,40.6*   *Multiple procedures*
CMS *100-2,16,180*   *Services Related to Noncovered Procedures*
CMS *100-2,16,120*   *Cosmetic Procedures*
CMS *100-2,16,10*   *Exclusions from Coverage*
CMS *100-4,4,20.5*   *HCPCS Under OPPS*
EXCLUDES   *cryotherapy acne (17340)*
    destruction of lesion of:
       anus (46900-46917, 46924)
       conjunctiva (68135)
       eyelid (67850)
       penis (54050-54057, 54065)
       vagina (57061, 57065)
       vestibule of mouth (40820)
       vulva (56501, 56515)
    destruction of plantar warts (17110-17111)
    destruction or excision of skin tags (11200-11201)
    localized chemotherapy treatment (99201-99499)
    paring or excision of benign hyperkeratotic lesion (11055-11057)
    shaving skin lesions (11300-11313)

    17000   **Destruction (eg, laser surgery, electrosurgery, cryosurgery, chemosurgery, surgical curettement), premalignant lesions (eg, actinic keratoses); first lesion** P2 T ☐
  - 📖 1.35   ♒ 1.94   **Global Days 010**
  - **AMA:** 2008, Jan, 10-25; 2007, Jan, 13-27; 2007, Jan, 13-27; 2007, Feb, 10-11; 2007, Feb, 10-11; 2007, February, 10-11; 2007, January, 13-27; 2006, May, 16-20; 2006, May, 16-20; 2006, May, 16-20, 2006, April, 11-18; 2006, Apr, 11-18; 2006, Apr, 11-18; 2005, Mar, 11-15; 2005, March, 11-15; 2005, Mar, 11-15

+   17003   **second through 14 lesions, each (List separately in addition to code for first lesion)** P3 T
  - Code first 17000
  - 📖 0.12   ♒ 0.19   **Global Days ZZZ**
  - **AMA:** 2008, Jan, 10-25; 2007, Jan, 13-27; 2007, Jan, 13-27; 2007, Feb, 10-11; 2007, Feb, 10-11; 2007, January, 13-27; 2007, February, 10-11; 2006, May, 16-20; 2006, May, 16-20; 2006, May, 16-20

⊘   17004   **Destruction (eg, laser surgery, electrosurgery, cryosurgery, chemosurgery, surgical curettement), premalignant lesions (eg, actinic keratoses), 15 or more lesions** P3 T ☐
  - Do not report with (17000-17003)
  - 📖 3.40   ♒ 4.35   **Global Days 010**
  - **AMA:** 2008, Jan, 10-25; 2007, Jan, 13-27; 2007, Jan, 13-27; 2007, Feb, 10-11; 2007, Feb, 10-11; 2007, January, 13-27; 2007, February, 10-11

17106-17250 Destruction, Any Method: Vascular Proliferative Lesion

CMS *100-2,16,180*   *Services Related to Noncovered Procedures*
CMS *100-2,16,120*   *Cosmetic Procedures*
CMS *100-2,16,10*   *Exclusions from Coverage*
EXCLUDES   *destruction of lesion of:*
    anus (46900-46917, 46924)
    conjunctiva (68135)
    eyelid (67850)
    penis (54050-54057, 54065)
    vagina (57061, 57065)
    vestibule of mouth (40820)
    vulva (56501, 56515)

    17106   **Destruction of cutaneous vascular proliferative lesions (eg, laser technique); less than 10 sq cm** P2 T ☐
  - 📖 7.07   ♒ 8.59   **Global Days 090**
  - **AMA:** 2008, Jan, 10-25; 2008, Jun, 14-15; 2007, Apr, 11-12; 2007, Apr, 11-12; 2007, April, 11-12

    17107   **10.0 to 50.0 sq cm** P2 T ☐
  - 📖 9.41   ♒ 11.44   **Global Days 090**
  - **AMA:** 2008, Jan, 10-25; 2008, Jun, 14-15; 2007, Apr, 11-12; 2007, Apr, 11-12; 2007, April, 11-12

    17108   **over 50.0 sq cm** P2 T 80 ☐
  - 📖 12.17   ♒ 14.52   **Global Days 090**
  - **AMA:** 2008, Jan, 10-25; 2008, Jun, 14-15; 2007, Apr, 11-12; 2007, Apr, 11-12; 2007, April, 11-12

    17110   **Destruction (eg, laser surgery, electrosurgery, cryosurgery, chemosurgery, surgical curettement), of benign lesions other than skin tags or cutaneous vascular proliferative lesions; up to 14 lesions** P2 T ☐
  - 📖 1.69   ♒ 2.70   **Global Days 010**
  - **AMA:** 2008, Jan, 10-25; 2007, Feb, 10-11; 2007, Feb, 10-11; 2007, Apr, 11-12; 2007, Apr, 11-12; 2007, February, 10-11; 2007, April, 11-12

    17111   **15 or more lesions** P2 T ☐
  - 📖 2.10   ♒ 3.20   **Global Days 010**
  - **AMA:** 2008, Jan, 10-25; 2007, Feb, 10-11; 2007, Feb, 10-11; 2007, Apr, 11-12; 2007, Apr, 11-12; 2007, February, 10-11; 2007, April, 11-12

    17250   **Chemical cauterization of granulation tissue (proud flesh, sinus or fistula)** P3 T ☐
  - Do not report with excision/removal codes for the same lesion
  - 📖 0.93   ♒ 1.84   **Global Days 000**

17260-17286 Destruction, Any Method: Malignant Lesion

CMS *100-3,140.5*   *Laser Procedures*
CMS *100-4,12,30*   *Correct Coding Policy*
EXCLUDES   *destruction of lesion of:*
    anus (46900-46917, 46924)
    conjunctiva (68135)
    eyelid (67850)
    localized chemotherapy treatment (99201-99499)
    penis (54050-54057, 54065)
    shaving skin lesion (11300-11313)
    vestibule of mouth (40820)
    vulva (56501-56515)

    17260   **Destruction, malignant lesion (eg, laser surgery, electrosurgery, cryosurgery, chemosurgery, surgical curettement), trunk, arms or legs; lesion diameter 0.5 cm or less** P3 T ☐
  - 📖 1.68   ♒ 2.34   **Global Days 010**
  - **AMA:** 2006, Apr, 11-18; 2006, Apr, 11-18; 2006, April, 11-18

    17261   **lesion diameter 0.6 to 1.0 cm** P2 T ☐
  - 📖 2.27   ♒ 3.49   **Global Days 010**

Integumentary System

17262 — 17314

17262	lesion diameter 1.1 to 2.0 cm	P2 T ▭
	🔪 2.90 ⚕ 4.25 Global Days 010	
17263	lesion diameter 2.1 to 3.0 cm	P2 T ▭
	🔪 3.21 ⚕ 4.69 Global Days 010	
17264	lesion diameter 3.1 to 4.0 cm	P2 T ▭
	🔪 3.43 ⚕ 5.02 Global Days 010	
17266	lesion diameter over 4.0 cm	P2 T ▭
	🔪 3.99 ⚕ 5.70 Global Days 010	

17270 **Destruction, malignant lesion (eg, laser surgery, electrosurgery, cryosurgery, chemosurgery, surgical curettement), scalp, neck, hands, feet, genitalia; lesion diameter 0.5 cm or less** P2 T ▭
🔪 2.45 ⚕ 3.62 Global Days 010

17271	lesion diameter 0.6 to 1.0 cm	P2 T ▭
	🔪 2.76 ⚕ 4.00 Global Days 010	
17272	lesion diameter 1.1 to 2.0 cm	P2 T ▭
	🔪 3.20 ⚕ 4.58 Global Days 010	
17273	lesion diameter 2.1 to 3.0 cm	P2 T ▭
	🔪 3.61 ⚕ 5.11 Global Days 010	
17274	lesion diameter 3.1 to 4.0 cm	P2 T ▭
	🔪 4.43 ⚕ 6.05 Global Days 010	
17276	lesion diameter over 4.0 cm	P2 T ▭
	🔪 5.34 ⚕ 7.02 Global Days 010	

17280 **Destruction, malignant lesion (eg, laser surgery, electrosurgery, cryosurgery, chemosurgery, surgical curettement), face, ears, eyelids, nose, lips, mucous membrane; lesion diameter 0.5 cm or less** P2 T ▭
🔪 2.23 ⚕ 3.40 Global Days 010

17281	lesion diameter 0.6 to 1.0 cm	P3 T ▭
	🔪 3.11 ⚕ 4.34 Global Days 010	
17282	lesion diameter 1.1 to 2.0 cm	P3 T ▭
	🔪 3.61 ⚕ 5.03 Global Days 010	
17283	lesion diameter 2.1 to 3.0 cm	P2 T ▭
	🔪 4.52 ⚕ 6.08 Global Days 010	
17284	lesion diameter 3.1 to 4.0 cm	P2 T ▭
	🔪 5.39 ⚕ 7.07 Global Days 010	
17286	lesion diameter over 4.0 cm	P2 T ▭
	🔪 7.26 ⚕ 8.96 Global Days 010	

17311-17315 Mohs Surgery

CMS *100-4,12,40.1*   *Global Surgery Package Definition*

INCLUDES the following surgical/pathological services performed by the same physician:
evaluation of skin margins by surgeon
pathology exam on Mohs surgery specimen (88302-88309)
routine frozen section stain (88314)
tumor removal, mapping, preparation, and examination of lesion

Code also any histochemical stain on a frozen section, nonroutine (with modifier 59) (88314)

Code also biopsy if no prior diagnosis determination has been performed (11100-11101)

EXCLUDES *complex repair (13100-13160)*
flaps or grafts (14000-14350, 15050-15770)
frozen section if no prior diagnosis determination has been peformed (88331)
intermediate repair (12031-12057)
simple repair (12001-12021)

17311 **Mohs micrographic technique, including removal of all gross tumor, surgical excision of tissue specimens, mapping, color coding of specimens, microscopic examination of specimens by the surgeon, and histopathologic preparation including routine stain(s) (eg, hematoxylin and eosin, toluidine blue), head, neck, hands, feet, genitalia, or any location with surgery directly involving muscle, cartilage, bone, tendon, major nerves, or vessels; first stage, up to 5 tissue blocks** P2 T
🔪 9.70 ⚕ 17.09 Global Days 000
AMA: 2006, Dec, 1-3; 2006, Dec, 1-3; 2006, Dec, 1-3; 2006, Dec, 1-3; 2006, Dec, 10-12; 2006, Dec, 10-12; 2006, Dec, 1-3; 2006, Dec, 1-3; 2006, Dec, 1-3; 2006, Dec, 1-3; 2006, Dec, 10-12; 2006, Dec, 10-12; 2006, December, 10-12; 2006, December, 1-3; 2006, December, 1-3; 2006, December, 10-12; 2006, December, 1-3; 2006, December, 1-3

+ 17312 **each additional stage after the first stage, up to 5 tissue blocks (List separately in addition to code for primary procedure)** P2 T
🔪 5.16 ⚕ 10.24 Global Days ZZZ
AMA: 2006, Dec, 1-3; 2006, Dec, 1-3; 2006, Dec, 1-3; 2006, Dec, 1-3; 2006, Dec, 1-3; 2006, Dec, 1-3; 2006, Dec, 1-3; 2006, Dec, 1-3; 2006, December, 1-3; 2006, December, 1-3; 2006, December, 1-3; 2006, December, 1-3

17313 **Mohs micrographic technique, including removal of all gross tumor, surgical excision of tissue specimens, mapping, color coding of specimens, microscopic examination of specimens by the surgeon, and histopathologic preparation including routine stain(s) (eg, hematoxylin and eosin, toluidine blue), of the trunk, arms, or legs; first stage, up to 5 tissue blocks** P2 T
🔪 8.71 ⚕ 15.60 Global Days 000
AMA: 2006, Dec, 1-3; 2006, Dec, 1-3; 2006, Dec, 1-3; 2006, Dec, 1-3; 2006, Dec, 10-12; 2006, Dec, 10-12; 2006, Dec, 1-3; 2006, Dec, 1-3; 2006, Dec, 10-12; 2006, Dec, 10-12; 2006, Dec, 1-3; 2006, Dec, 1-3; 2006, December, 10-12; 2006, December, 1-3; 2006, December, 1-3; 2006, December, 1-3; 2006, December, 10-12; 2006, December, 1-3

+ 17314 **each additional stage after the first stage, up to 5 tissue blocks (List separately in addition to code for primary procedure)** P2 T
Code first 17313
🔪 4.79 ⚕ 9.49 Global Days ZZZ
AMA: 2006, Dec, 1-3; 2006, Dec, 1-3; 2006, Dec, 1-3; 2006, Dec, 1-3; 2006, Dec, 1-3; 2006, Dec, 1-3; 2006, Dec, 1-3; 2006, December, 1-3; 2006, December, 1-3; 2006, December, 1-3; 2006, December, 1-3

+   **17315**   Mohs micrographic technique, including removal of all gross tumor, surgical excision of tissue specimens, mapping, color coding of specimens, microscopic examination of specimens by the surgeon, and histopathologic preparation including routine stain(s) (eg, hematoxylin and eosin, toluidine blue), each additional block after the first 5 tissue blocks, any stage (List separately in addition to code for primary procedure)   P3   T

         Code first 17311-17314

         📅 **1.36**   ⚕ **2.04**   **Global Days ZZZ**

         AMA: 2006, Dec, 1-3; 2006, Dec, 1-3; 2006, Dec, 1-3; 2006, Dec, 1-3; 2006, Dec, 1-3; 2006, Dec, 1-3; 2006, Dec, 1-3; 2006, Dec, 1-3; 2006, December, 1-3; 2006, December, 1-3; 2006, December, 1-3; 2006, December, 1-3

17340-17999 Treatment for Active Acne and Permanent Hair Removal

     17340   Cryotherapy (CO2 slush, liquid N2) for acne   P3   T   📷

         📅 **1.18**   ⚕ **1.22**   **Global Days 010**

     17360   Chemical exfoliation for acne (eg, acne paste, acid)   P2   T   📷

         📅 **2.51**   ⚕ **3.26**   **Global Days 010**

     17380   Electrolysis epilation, each 30 minutes   R2   T   80   📷

         EXCLUDES   actinotherapy (96900)

         📅 **0.00**   ⚕ **0.00**   **Global Days 000**

     17999   Unlisted procedure, skin, mucous membrane and subcutaneous tissue   T   80

         📅 **0.00**   ⚕ **0.00**   **Global Days YYY**

         AMA: 2008, Jan, 10-25; 2007, Jan, 13-27; 2007, Jan, 13-27; 2007, January, 13-27; 2005, Jun, 9-11; 2005, June, 9-11; 2005, Jun, 9-11

19000-19030 Treatment of Breast Abscess and Cyst with Injection, Aspiration, Incision

     19000   Puncture aspiration of cyst of breast;   P3   T   📷

         📡 *76942, 77021, 77031, 77032*

         📅 **1.22**   ⚕ **2.85**   **Global Days 000**

         AMA: 2005, Apr, 6-9; 2005, Apr, 6-9; 2005, April, 6-9

+   **19001**   each additional cyst (List separately in addition to code for primary procedure)   P3   T   📷

         Code first 19000

         📡 *76942, 77021, 77031, 77032*

         📅 **0.61**   ⚕ **0.72**   **Global Days ZZZ**

         AMA: 2005, Apr, 6-9; 2005, Apr, 6-8; 2005, April, 6-9

     19020   Mastotomy with exploration or drainage of abscess, deep   A2   T   50   📷

         📅 **7.15**   ⚕ **10.70**   **Global Days 090**

         AMA: 2005, Apr, 6-9; 2005, Apr, 6-9; 2005, April, 6-9

     19030   Injection procedure only for mammary ductogram or galactogram   N1   N   50   📷

         📡 *77053-77054*

         📅 **2.19**   ⚕ **4.36**   **Global Days 000**

         AMA: 2005, Apr, 6-9; 2005, Apr, 6-9; 2005, April, 6-9; 2004, Jul, 7; 2004, July, 7; 2004, Jul, 7

19100-19103 Breast Biopsy

CMS *100-3,220.13*   *Percutaneous Image-guided Breast Biopsy*
CMS *100-4,13,80.2*   *Physician Presence*
CMS *100-4,13,80.1*   *Supervision and Interpretation Codes*
CMS *100-2,15,260*   *Covered ASC Procedures*

INCLUDES   open removal of breast mass without concentration on surgical margins

EXCLUDES   lesion removal without concentration on surgical margins (19110-19126)
         partial mastectomy (19301-19302)
         total mastectomy (19303-19307)

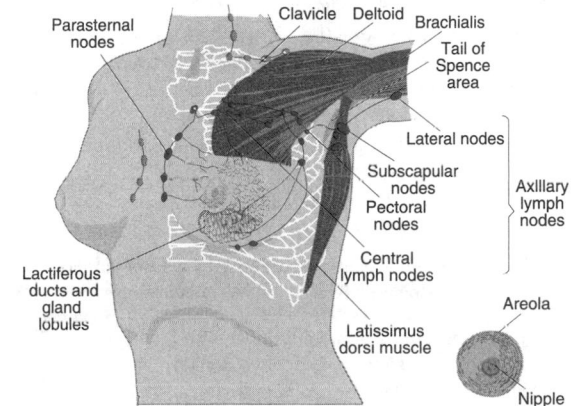

     19100   Biopsy of breast; percutaneous, needle core, not using imaging guidance (separate procedure)   A2   T   50   📷

         EXCLUDES   fine needle aspiration (10021)
                  radiology guided breast biopsy (10022, 19102-19103)

         📅 **1.80**   ⚕ **3.50**   **Global Days 000**

         AMA: 2008, Jan, 10-25; 2007, Jan, 13-27; 2007, Jan, 13-27; 2007, January, 13-27; 2006, Dec, 10-12; 2006, Dec, 10-12; 2006, Dec, 10-12; 2006, December, 10-12; 2006, December, 10-12; 2006, Dec, 10-12; 2005, Apr, 6-9; 2005, April, 6-9; 2005, Apr, 6-9

     19101   open, incisional   A2   T   50   📷

         📅 **5.43**   ⚕ **7.98**   **Global Days 010**

         AMA: 2008, Jan, 10-25; 2007, Jan, 13-27; 2007, Jan, 13-27; 2007, January, 13-27; 2005, Apr, 6-9; 2005, April, 6-9; 2005, Apr, 6-9

     19102   percutaneous, needle core, using imaging guidance   A2   T   50   📷

         EXCLUDES   insertion of percutaneous localization clip if appropriate (19295)

         📡 *76942, 77002, 77012, 77021, 77031-77032*

         📅 **2.87**   ⚕ **5.72**   **Global Days 000**

         AMA: 2008, Jan, 10-25; 2007, Jan, 13-27; 2007, Jan, 13-27; 2007, January, 13-27, 2005, Apr, 6-9; 2005, April, 6-9; 2005, Apr, 6-9

     19103   percutaneous, automated vacuum assisted or rotating biopsy device, using imaging guidance   A2   T   50   📷

         INCLUDES   ABBI biopsy

         EXCLUDES   insertion of percutaneous localization clip if appropriate (19295)

         📡 *76942, 77012, 77021, 77031-77032*

         📅 **5.28**   ⚕ **14.41**   **Global Days 000**

         AMA: 2008, Jan, 10-25; 2007, Jan, 13-27; 2007, Jan, 13-27; 2007, January, 13-27; 2005, Apr, 6-9; 2005, April, 6-9; 2005, Apr, 6-9

● New Code   ▲ Revised Code   Ⓜ Maternity Edit   Ⓐ Age Edit   A-Y OPPS Status Indicator   📅 Facility RVU   ⚕ Non-Facility RVU

🔲 CCI Comprehensive Code   50 Bilateral Procedure   + Add-on Indicator   📡 Laboratory crosswalk   📷 Radiology crosswalk

Integumentary System

19105 — 19300

19105 Treatment of Fibroadenoma: Cryoablation

CMS *100-4,13,80.2* *Physician Presence*
CMS *100-4,13,80.1* *Supervision and Interpretation Codes*
INCLUDES adjacent lesions treated with one cryoprobe
  ultrasound guidance

> **19105** **Ablation, cryosurgical, of fibroadenoma, including ultrasound guidance, each fibroadenoma** 62 T 50
> Do not report with (76940, 76942)
> 5.29 55.21 Global Days 000
> AMA: 2007, Mar, 7-8; 2007, Mar, 7-8; 2007, March, 7-8

19110-19126 Excisional Procedures: Breast

CMS *100-4,12,40.7* *Bilateral Procedures*

> **19110** **Nipple exploration, with or without excision of a solitary lactiferous duct or a papilloma lactiferous duct** A2 T 50
> 8.09 11.12 Global Days 090
> AMA: 2005, Apr, 6-9; 2005, Apr, 6-9; 2005, April, 6-9

> **19112** **Excision of lactiferous duct fistula** A2 T 80 50
> 7.26 10.39 Global Days 090
> AMA: 2005, Apr, 6-9; 2005, Apr, 6-9; 2005, April, 6-9

> **19120** **Excision of cyst, fibroadenoma, or other benign or malignant tumor, aberrant breast tissue, duct lesion, nipple or areolar lesion (except 19300), open, male or female, 1 or more lesions** A2 T 50
> 9.92 11.54 Global Days 090
> AMA: 2008, Jan, 10-25; 2007, Jan, 13-27; 2007, Jan, 13-27; 2007, January, 13-27; 2005, Apr, 13-14; 2005, Apr, 13-14; 2005, April, 6-9; 2005, April, 13-14; 2005, Apr, 6-9; 2005, Apr, 6-9

> **19125** **Excision of breast lesion identified by preoperative placement of radiological marker, open; single lesion** A2 T 50
> 11.00 12.77 Global Days 090
> AMA: 2008, Jan, 10-25; 2007, Jan, 13-27; 2007, Jan, 13-27; 2007, January, 13-27; 2005, Apr, 6-9; 2005, April, 6-9; 2005, Apr, 6-9

> + **19126** **each additional lesion separately identified by a preoperative radiological marker (List separately in addition to code for primary procedure)** A2 T
> Code first 19125
> 4.16 4.16 Global Days ZZZ
> AMA: 2008, Jan, 10-25; 2007, Jan, 13-27; 2007, Jan, 13-27; 2007, January, 13-27; 2005, Apr, 6-9; 2005, April, 6-9; 2005, Apr, 6-9

19260-19272 Excisional Procedures: Chest Wall

CMS *100-4,12,20.4.3* *Payment for Assistant at Surgery*
Do not report with (32100, 32422, 32503-32504, 32551)

> **19260** **Excision of chest wall tumor including ribs** T 80 P0
> 30.32 30.32 Global Days 090
> AMA: 2007, Feb, 4-5; 2007, Feb, 4-5; 2007, February, 4-5; 2005, Apr, 6-9; 2005, April, 6-9; 2005, Apr, 6-9

> **19271** **Excision of chest wall tumor involving ribs, with plastic reconstruction; without mediastinal lymphadenectomy** C 80 P0
> 41.13 41.13 Global Days 090
> AMA: 2007, Feb, 4-5; 2007, Feb, 4-5; 2007, February, 4-5; 2005, Apr, 6-9; 2005, April, 6-9; 2005, Apr, 6-9

> **19272** **with mediastinal lymphadenectomy** C 80 P0
> 45.59 45.59 Global Days 090
> AMA: 2007, Feb, 4-5; 2007, Feb, 4-5; 2007, February, 4-5; 2005, Apr, 6-9; 2005, April, 6-9; 2005, Apr, 6-9

19290-19298 Placement of Localization Markers and Brachytherapy Catheters

CMS *100-4,12,40.7* *Bilateral Procedures*
CMS *100-4,13,80.2* *Physician Presence*
CMS *100-4,13,80.1* *Supervision and Interpretation Codes*

> **19290** **Preoperative placement of needle localization wire, breast;** N1 N 50
> 76942, 77031-77032
> 1.81 4.23 Global Days 000
> AMA: 2005, Apr, 6-9; 2005, Apr, 6-9; 2005, April, 6-9

> + **19291** **each additional lesion (List separately in addition to code for primary procedure)** N1 N 80
> Code first 19290
> 76942, 77031-77032
> 0.90 1.83 Global Days ZZZ
> AMA: 2005, Apr, 6-9; 2005, Apr, 6-9; 2005, April, 6-9

> + **19295** **Image guided placement, metallic localization clip, percutaneous, during breast biopsy (List separately in addition to code for primary procedure)** N1 N 80
> Code first 19102-19103
> 76942, 77031-77032
> 2.36 2.36 Global Days ZZZ
> AMA: 2005, Apr, 6-9; 2005, Apr, 6-9; 2005, April, 6-9

> ▲ **19296** **Placement of radiotherapy afterloading expandable catheter (single or multichannel) into the breast for interstitial radioelement application following partial mastectomy, includes imaging guidance; on date separate from partial mastectomy** A2 T 80 50
> Code also (C1728)
> 5.31 98.48 Global Days 000
> AMA: 2007, Feb, 4-5; 2007, Feb, 4-5; 2007, February, 4-5; 2005, Nov, 14-15; 2005, Nov, 14-15; 2005, November, 14-15; 2005, April, 6-9; 2005, Apr, 6-9; 2005, Apr, 6-9

> + ▲ **19297** **concurrent with partial mastectomy (List separately in addition to code for primary procedure)** A2 T 80
> Code also (C1728)
> Code first 19102-19103 (19301-19302)
> 2.40 2.40 Global Days ZZZ
> AMA: 2007, Feb, 4-5; 2007, Feb, 4-5; 2007, February, 4-5; 2005, Apr, 6-9; 2005, Apr, 6-9; 2005, November, 14-15; 2005, April, 6-9; 2005, Nov, 14-15; 2005, Nov, 14-15

> ⊙ **19298** **Placement of radiotherapy afterloading brachytherapy catheters (multiple tube and button type) into the breast for interstitial radioelement application following (at the time of or subsequent to) partial mastectomy, includes imaging guidance** A2 T 80 50
> Code also brachytherapy catheter (C1728)
> 8.70 33.53 Global Days 000
> AMA: 2007, Feb, 4-5; 2007, Feb, 4-5; 2007, February, 4-5; 2005, Nov, 14-15; 2005, Nov, 14-15; 2005, November, 14-15; 2005, April, 6-9; 2005, Apr, 6-9; 2005, Apr, 6-9

19300-19307 Mastectomies: Partial, Simple, Radical

CMS *100-4,12,40.7* *Bilateral Procedures*
CMS *100-4,12,20.4.3* *Payment for Assistant at Surgery*
EXCLUDES *instantaneous or postponed insertion of prosthesis (19340, 19342)*

> **19300** **Mastectomy for gynecomastia** ♂ A2 T 50
> 9.64 12.30 Global Days 090
> AMA: 2007, Feb, 4-5; 2007, Feb, 4-5; 2007, February, 4-5

19301   Mastectomy, partial (eg, lumpectomy, tylectomy, quadrantectomy, segmentectomy);   A2 T 80 50 P0

    EXCLUDES   *insertion of radiotherapy afterloading balloon or brachytherapy catheters (19296-19298)*

    15.22   15.22   **Global Days 090**

    AMA: 2008, Sep, 5-6; 2007, Feb, 4-5; 2007, Feb, 4-5; 2007, February, 4-5; 2007, Dec, 7-8

19302   with axillary lymphadenectomy   A2 T 80 50 P0

    EXCLUDES   *insertion of radiotherapy afterloading balloon or brachytherapy catheters (19296-19298)*

    22.03   22.03   **Global Days 090**

    AMA: 2008, Jan, 10-25; 2008, Sep, 5-6; 2007, Feb, 4-5; 2007, Feb, 4-5; 2007, February, 4-5; 2007, Dec, 7-8

19303   Mastectomy, simple, complete   A2 T 80 50 P0

    EXCLUDES   *gynecomastia (19300)*

    23.52   23.52   **Global Days 090**

    AMA: 2007, Feb, 4-5; 2007, Feb, 4-5; 2007, February, 4-5

19304   Mastectomy, subcutaneous   A2 T 80 50 P0

    13.78   13.78   **Global Days 090**

    AMA: 2008, Jan, 10-25; 2007, Feb, 4-5; 2007, Feb, 4-5; 2007, February, 4-5; 2007, Dec, 7-8

19305   Mastectomy, radical, including pectoral muscles, axillary lymph nodes   C 80 50 P0

    27.37   27.37   **Global Days 090**

    AMA: 2008, Sep, 5-6; 2007, Feb, 4-5; 2007, Feb, 4-5; 2007, February, 4-5

19306   Mastectomy, radical, including pectoral muscles, axillary and internal mammary lymph nodes (Urban type operation)   C 80 50 P0

    28.71   28.71   **Global Days 090**

    AMA: 2008, Sep, 5-6; 2007, Feb, 4-5; 2007, Feb, 4-5; 2007, February, 4-5

19307   Mastectomy, modified radical, including axillary lymph nodes, with or without pectoralis minor muscle, but excluding pectoralis major muscle   T 80 50 P0

    28.89   28.89   **Global Days 090**

    AMA: 2008, Sep, 5-6; 2007, Feb, 4-5; 2007, Feb, 4-5; 2007, February, 4-5

19316-19499 Plastic, Reconstructive, and Aesthetic Breast Procedures

CMS 100-3,140.2   *Breast Reconstruction Following Mastectomy*
CMS 100-4,12,40.7   *Bilateral Procedures*
CMS 100-2,16,100   *Services Related to Noncovered Procedures*
CMS 100-2,16,120   *Cosmetic Procedures*

19316   Mastopexy   A2 T 80 50 P0

    19.75   19.75   **Global Days 090**

    AMA: 2005, Apr, 6-9; 2005, Apr, 6-9; 2005, April, 6-9

19318   Reduction mammaplasty   ♀ A2 T 80 50 P0

    INCLUDES   Aries-Pitanguy mammaplasty
                 Biesenberger mammaplasty

    29.26   29.26   **Global Days 090**

    AMA: 2008, Jan, 10-25; 2007, Jan, 13-27; 2007, Jan, 13-27; 2007, January, 13-27; 2005, Apr, 6-9; 2005, April, 6-9; 2005, Apr, 6-9

19324   Mammaplasty, augmentation; without prosthetic implant   A2 T 80 50 P0

    12.00   12.00   **Global Days 090**

    AMA: 2005, Apr, 6-9; 2005, Apr, 6-9; 2005, April, 6-9

19325   with prosthetic implant   A2 T 80 50 P0

    Code also (C1789, L8600)

    EXCLUDES   *flap or graft (15100-15650)*

    16.37   16.37   **Global Days 090**

    AMA: 2005, Apr, 6-9; 2005, Apr, 6-9; 2005, April, 6-9

19328   Removal of intact mammary implant   A2 T 50 P0

    12.32   12.32   **Global Days 090**

    AMA: 2005, Apr, 6-9; 2005, Apr, 6-9; 2005, April, 6-9

19330   Removal of mammary implant material   A2 T 50 P0

    15.87   15.87   **Global Days 090**

    AMA: 2008, Jan, 10-25; 2007, Jan, 13-27; 2007, Jan, 13-27; 2007, January, 13-27; 2005, Apr, 6-9; 2005, April, 6-9; 2005, Apr, 6-9

19340   Immediate insertion of breast prosthesis following mastopexy, mastectomy or in reconstruction   A2 T 50

    EXCLUDES   *supply of prosthetic implant (99070, L8030, L8039, L8600)*

    10.37   10.37   **Global Days ZZZ**

    AMA: 2007, Feb, 4-5; 2007, Feb, 4-5; 2007, February, 4-5; 2005, Aug, 1-3; 2005, Aug, 1-3; 2005, August, 1-3; 2005, April, 6-9; 2005, Apr, 6-9; 2005, Apr, 6-9

19342   Delayed insertion of breast prosthesis following mastopexy, mastectomy or in reconstruction   ♀ A2 T 80 50 P0

    Code also (C1789, L8600)

    EXCLUDES   *supply of prosthetic implant (99070, L8030, L8039, L8600)*
                 preparation of moulage for custom breast implant (19396)

    23.33   23.33   **Global Days 090**

    AMA: 2007, Feb, 4-5; 2007, Feb, 4-5; 2007, February, 4-5; 2005, Apr, 6-9; 2005, Apr, 6-9; 2005, August, 1-3; 2005, April, 6-9; 2005, Aug, 1-3; 2005, Aug, 1-3

19350   Nipple/areola reconstruction   A2 T 50 P0

    17.21   21.26   **Global Days 090**

    AMA: 2008, Jan, 10-25; 2007, Jan, 13-27; 2007, Jan, 13-27; 2007, January, 13-27; 2005, Apr, 6-9; 2005, April, 6-9; 2005, Apr, 6-9

19355   Correction of inverted nipples   A2 T 80 50 P0

    14.13   17.55   **Global Days 090**

    AMA: 2005, Apr, 6-9; 2005, Apr, 6-9; 2005, April, 6-9

19357   Breast reconstruction, immediate or delayed, with tissue expander, including subsequent expansion   ♀ A2 T 80 50 P0

    39.15   39.15   **Global Days 090**

    AMA: 2005, Apr, 6-9; 2005, Apr, 6-9; 2005, Aug, 1-3; 2005, Aug, 1-3; 2005, April, 6-9; 2005, August, 1-3

19361   Breast reconstruction with latissimus dorsi flap, without prosthetic implant   ♀ T 80 50 P0

    EXCLUDES   *implant of prosthesis (19340)*

    41.96   41.96   **Global Days 090**

    AMA: 2005, Apr, 6-9; 2005, Apr, 6-9; 2005, Aug, 1-3; 2005, Aug, 1-3; 2005, August, 1-3; 2005, April, 6-9

19364   Breast reconstruction with free flap   C 80 50 P0

    INCLUDES   closure of donor site
                 harvesting of skin graft
                 inset shaping of flap into breast
                 microvascular repair
                 operating microscope (69990)

    72.00   72.00   **Global Days 090**

    AMA: 2005, Aug, 1-3; 2005, Aug, 1-3; 2005, Apr, 6-9; 2005, Apr, 6-9; 2005, April, 6-9; 2005, August, 1-3

Integumentary System

19301 — 19364

● New Code   ▲ Revised Code   M Maternity Edit   A Age Edit   A-Y OPPS Status Indicator   Facility RVU   Non-Facility RVU

□ CCI Comprehensive Code   50 Bilateral Procedure   + Add-on Indicator   Laboratory crosswalk   Radiology crosswalk

Integumentary System

19366 — 19499

19366 **Breast reconstruction with other technique** A2 T 80 50 ▣ P0

> *EXCLUDES* *implant of prosthesis if appropriate (19340, 19342)*
> *operating microscope (69990)*

📇 35.57   ⚅ 35.57   Global Days 090
AMA: 2005, Apr, 6-9; 2005, Apr, 6-9; 2005, April, 6-9

19367 **Breast reconstruction with transverse rectus abdominis myocutaneous flap (TRAM), single pedicle, including closure of donor site;** ♀ C 80 50 ▣ P0

📇 46.59   ⚅ 46.59   Global Days 090
AMA: 2005, Apr, 6-9; 2005, Apr, 6-9; 2005, Aug, 1-3; 2005, Aug, 1-3; 2005, April, 6-9; 2005, August, 1-3

19368 **with microvascular anastomosis (supercharging)** ♀ C 80 50 ▣ P0

> *INCLUDES* operating microscope (69990)

📇 57.91   ⚅ 57.91   Global Days 090
AMA: 2005, Aug, 1-3; 2005, Aug, 1-3; 2005, Apr, 6-9; 2005, Apr, 6-9; 2005, April, 6-9; 2005, August, 1-3

19369 **Breast reconstruction with transverse rectus abdominis myocutaneous flap (TRAM), double pedicle, including closure of donor site** ♀ C 80 50 ▣ P0

📇 52.60   ⚅ 52.60   Global Days 090
AMA: 2005, Aug, 1-3; 2005, Aug, 1-3; 2005, Apr, 6-9; 2005, Apr, 6-9; 2005, April, 6-9; 2005, August, 1-3

19370 **Open periprosthetic capsulotomy, breast** A2 T 50 ▣ P0
📇 17.18   ⚅ 17.18   Global Days 090
AMA: 2005, Apr, 6-9; 2005, Apr, 6-9; 2005, April, 6-9

19371 **Periprosthetic capsulectomy, breast** A2 T 50 ▣ P0
📇 19.86   ⚅ 19.86   Global Days 090
AMA: 2008, Jan, 10-25; 2007, Jan, 13-27; 2007, Jan, 13-27; 2007, January, 13-27; 2005, Apr, 6-9; 2005, April, 6-9; 2005, Apr, 6-9

19380 **Revision of reconstructed breast** A2 T 50 ▣ P0
📇 19.38   ⚅ 19.38   Global Days 090
AMA: 2005, Apr, 6-9; 2005, Apr, 6-9; 2005, April, 6-9

19396 **Preparation of moulage for custom breast implant** G2 T 80 50 ▣
📇 3.45   ⚅ 5.49   Global Days 000
AMA: 2005, Apr, 6-9; 2005, Apr, 6-9; 2005, April, 6-9

19499 **Unlisted procedure, breast** T 80 50
📇 0.00   ⚅ 0.00   Global Days YYY
AMA: 2005, Apr, 6-9; 2005, Apr, 6-9; 2005, April, 6-9

20000-20005 Incisional Treatment Soft Tissue Abscess

20000 Incision of soft tissue abscess (eg, secondary to osteomyelitis); superficial [P2] [T] [▣]
    ☰ 3.97   ℮ 5.12   Global Days 010

20005 deep or complicated [A2] [T] [▣]
    ☰ 6.11   ℮ 7.63   Global Days 010

20100-20103 Exploratory Surgery of Traumatic Wound

INCLUDES   debridement
     extraction of foreign material
     open examination
     tying or coagulation of small vessels

EXCLUDES   *laparotomy (49000-49010)*
     repair of major vessels of:
         abdomen (35221, 35251, 35281)
         chest (35211, 35216, 35241, 35246, 35271, 35276)
         extremity (35206-35207, 35226, 35236, 35256, 35266, 35286)
         neck (35201, 35231, 35261)
     thoracotomy (32100-32160)

20100 Exploration of penetrating wound (separate procedure); neck [T] [80] [50] [▣]
    ☰ 15.22   ℮ 15.22   Global Days 010
    AMA: 2008, Jan, 10-25; 2007, Jan, 13-27; 2007, Jan, 13-27; 2007, January, 13-27; 2006, Sep, 14-16; 2006, September, 14-16; 2006, Sep, 14-16

20101 chest [T] [▣]
    ☰ 5.22   ℮ 9.81   Global Days 010
    AMA: 2008, Jan, 10-25; 2007, Jan, 13-27; 2007, Jan, 13-27; 2007, January, 13-27; 2006, Sep, 14-16; 2006, September, 14-16; 2006, Sep, 14-16

20102 abdomen/flank/back [T] [▣]
    ☰ 6.35   ℮ 11.47   Global Days 010
    AMA: 2008, Jan, 10-25; 2007, Jan, 13-27; 2007, Jan, 13-27; 2007, January, 13-27; 2006, Sep, 14-16; 2006, September, 14-16; 2006, Sep, 14-16

20103 extremity [02] [T] [00] [▣]
    ☰ 9.07   ℮ 14.02   Global Days 010
    AMA: 2008, Jan, 10-25; 2007, Jan, 13-27; 2007, Jan, 13-27; 2007, January, 13-27; 2006, Sep, 14-16; 2006, September, 14-16; 2006, Sep, 14-16

20150 Epiphyseal Bar Resection

EXCLUDES   *bone marrow aspiration (38220)*

20150 Excision of epiphyseal bar, with or without autogenous soft tissue graft obtained through same fascial incision [G2] [T] [80] [50] [▣]
    ☰ 24.76   ℮ 24.76   Global Days 090

20200-20206 Muscle Biopsy

EXCLUDES   *removal of muscle tumor (see appropriate anatomic section)*

20200 Biopsy, muscle; superficial [A2] [T] [▣]
    ☰ 2.42   ℮ 4.77   Global Days 000

20205 deep [A2] [T] [▣]
    ☰ 3.84   ℮ 6.51   Global Days 000

20206 Biopsy, muscle, percutaneous needle [A2] [T] [▣]
    INCLUDES   fluoroscopic guidance (77002)
    EXCLUDES   *fine needle aspiration (10021-10022)*
    ◥ 88172-88173
    ■ 76942, 77012, 77021
    ☰ 1.67   ℮ 6.58   Global Days 000

20220-20225 Percutaneous Bone Biopsy

CMS *100-3,150.3*   *Bone (Mineral) Density Studies*
EXCLUDES   *bone marrow biopsy (38221)*

20220 Biopsy, bone, trocar, or needle; superficial (eg, ilium, sternum, spinous process, ribs) [A2] [T] [▣]
    ■ 77002, 77012, 77021
    ☰ 2.08   ℮ 4.53   Global Days 000

20225 deep (eg, vertebral body, femur) [A2] [T] [▣]
    ■ 77002, 77012, 77021
    ☰ 3.19   ℮ 17.17   Global Days 000

20240-20251 Open Bone Biopsy

CMS *100-3,150.3*   *Bone (Mineral) Density Studies*
EXCLUDES   *sequestrectomy or incision and drainage of bone abscess of:*
     calcaneus (28120)
     carpal bone (25145)
     clavicle (23170)
     humeral head (23174)
     humerus (24134)
     olecranon process (24138)
     radius (24136, 25145)
     scapula (23172)
     skull (61501)
     talus (28120)
     ulna (24138, 24145)

20240 Biopsy, bone, open; superficial (eg, ilium, sternum, spinous process, ribs, trochanter of femur) [A2] [T] [▣]
    ☰ 5.88   ℮ 5.88   Global Days 010
    AMA: 2008, Jan, 10-25; 2007, Jan, 13-27; 2007, Jan, 13-27; 2007, January, 13-27; 2005, Aug, 13-15; 2005, Aug, 13-15; 2005, August, 13-15; 2004, Aug, 11; 2004, Aug, 11; 2004, August, 11

20245 deep (eg, humerus, ischium, femur) [A2] [T] [▣]
    ☰ 16.09   ℮ 16.09   Global Days 010

20250 Biopsy, vertebral body, open; thoracic [A2] [T] [▣]
    ☰ 9.76   ℮ 9.76   Global Days 010

20251 lumbar or cervical [A2] [T] [80] [▣]
    ☰ 10.83   ℮ 10.83   Global Days 010

20500-20501 Injection Fistula/Sinus Tract

CMS *100-4,13,80.2*   *Physician Presence*
CMS *100-4,13,80.1*   *Supervision and Interpretation Codes*
EXCLUDES   *arthrography injection of:*
     ankle (27648)
     elbow (24220)
     hip (27093, 27095)
     knee (27370)
     sacroiliac joint (27096)
     shoulder (23350)
     temporomandibular joint (TMJ) (21116)
     wrist (25246)

20500 Injection of sinus tract; therapeutic (separate procedure) [P3] [T] [▣]
    ■ 76080
    ☰ 2.43   ℮ 2.95   Global Days 010

20501 diagnostic (sinogram) [N1] [N] [▣]
    EXCLUDES   *contrast injection or injections for radiological evaluation of existing gastrostomy, duodenostomy, jejunostomy, gastro-jejunostomy, or cecostomy (or other colonic) tube from percutaneous approach (49465)*
    ■ 76080
    ☰ 1.09   ℮ 3.31   Global Days 000

● New Code   ▲ Revised Code   Ⓜ Maternity Edit   Ⓐ Age Edit   [A]-[Y] OPPS Status Indicator   ☰ Facility RVU   ℮ Non-Facility RVU

□ CCI Comprehensive Code   50 Bilateral Procedure   + Add-on Indicator   ◥ Laboratory crosswalk   ■ Radiology crosswalk

Musculoskeletal System

20520 — 20615

20520-20525 Foreign Body Removal

CMS *100-4,12,30*   *Correct Coding Policy*

20520   Removal of foreign body in muscle or tendon sheath; simple   P3 T ▭

     3.61   4.74   Global Days 010

20525   deep or complicated   A2 T ▭

     6.37   11.59   Global Days 010

20526 Injection for Carpal Tunnel

CMS *100-4,17,20.5.7*   *Injection Services*

20526   Injection, therapeutic (eg, local anesthetic, corticosteroid), carpal tunnel   P3 T 50 ▭

     1.52   1.93   Global Days 000

     AMA: 2008, Jan, 10-25; 2007, Jan, 13-27; 2007, Jan, 13-27; 2007, January, 13-27

20550-20553 Therapeutic Injections: Tendons, Trigger Points

CMS *100-3,150.7*   *Prolotherapy, Joint Sclerotherapy, and Ligamentous Injections with Sclerosing Agents*

CMS *100-4,12,30*   *Correct Coding Policy*

CMS *100-4,13,80.2*   *Physician Presence*

CMS *100-4,13,80.1*   *Supervision and Interpretation Codes*

20550   Injection(s); single tendon sheath, or ligament, aponeurosis (eg, plantar "fascia")   P3 T ▭

     EXCLUDES   *Morton's neuroma injection (64455, 64632)*

     76942, 77002, 77021

     1.11   1.49   Global Days 000

     AMA: 2008, Jan, 10-25; 2007, Jan, 13-27; 2007, Jan, 13-27; 2007, January, 13-27

20551   single tendon origin/insertion   P3 T ▭

     76942, 77002, 77021

     1.13   1.47   Global Days 000

     AMA: 2008, Jan, 10-25; 2007, Jan, 13-27; 2007, Jan, 13-27; 2007, January, 13-27

20552   single or multiple trigger point(s), 1 or 2 muscle(s)   P3 T ▭

     76942, 77002, 77021

     0.95   1.33   Global Days 000

     AMA: 2008, Jan, 10-25; 2007, Jan, 13-27; 2007, Jan, 13-27; 2007, January, 13-27

20553   single or multiple trigger point(s), 3 or more muscle(s)   P3 T ▭

     76942, 77002, 77021

     1.05   1.48   Global Days 000

     AMA: 2008, Jan, 10-25; 2008, Jun, 8-11; 2007, Jan, 13-27; 2007, January, 13-27

20555 Placement of Catheters/Needles for Brachytherapy

20555   Placement of needles or catheters into muscle and/or soft tissue for subsequent interstitial radioelement application (at the time of or subsequent to the procedure)   62 T 80

     EXCLUDES   *interstitial radioelement:*
         application (77776-77787)
         devices placed into the breast (19296-19298)
         placement of needle, catheters, or devices into muscle or soft tissue of the head and neck (41019)
         placement of needles or catheters into pelvic organs or genitalia (55920)
         placement of needles or catheters into prostate (55875)

     76942, 77002, 77012, 77021

     8.76   8.76   Global Days 000

     AMA: 2008, Feb, 8-9; 2008, Jun, 8-11; 2007, Dec, 1-2

20600-20610 Aspiration and/or Injection of Joint

CMS *100-3,150.7*   *Prolotherapy, Joint Sclerotherapy, and Ligamentous Injections with Sclerosing Agents*

CMS *100-3,150.6*   *Vitamin B12 Injections to Strenghen Tendons, Ligaments of Foot*

CMS *100-4,12,30*   *Correct Coding Policy*

CMS *100-4,13,80.2*   *Physician Presence*

CMS *100-4,13,80.1*   *Supervision and Interpretation Codes*

20600   Arthrocentesis, aspiration and/or injection; small joint or bursa (eg, fingers, toes)   P3 T 50 ▭

     76942, 77002, 77012, 77021

     1.06   1.40   Global Days 000

     AMA: 2007, Dec, 10-179

20605   intermediate joint or bursa (eg, temporomandibular, acromioclavicular, wrist, elbow or ankle, olecranon bursa)   P3 T 50 ▭

     76942, 77002, 77012, 77021

     1.10   1.50   Global Days 000

     AMA: 2007, Dec, 10-179

20610   major joint or bursa (eg, shoulder, hip, knee joint, subacromial bursa)   P3 T 50 ▭

     76942, 77002, 77012, 77021

     1.32   1.94   Global Days 000

     AMA: 2008, Jan, 10-25; 2008, Jun, 8-11; 2008, Jul, 9; 2007, Jan, 13-27; 2007, Jan, 13-27; 2007, Dec, 10-179; 2007, January, 13-27; 2006, Apr, 19-20; 2006, Apr, 19-20; 2006, April, 19-20; 2005, Mar, 11-15; 2005, Mar, 11-15; 2005, March, 11-15; 2004, Apr, 15; 2004, Apr, 15; 2004, Nov, 5; 2004, April, 15; 2004, November, 5; 2004, Nov, 5

20612-20615 Aspiration and/or Injection of Cyst

CMS *100-4,12,30*   *Correct Coding Policy*

20612   Aspiration and/or injection of ganglion cyst(s) any location   P3 T ▭

     1.14   1.50   Global Days 000

20615   Aspiration and injection for treatment of bone cyst   P3 T ▭

     4.06   5.43   Global Days 010

20650-20697 Devices Related to External Fixation

CMS *100-4,12,30*   *Correct Coding Policy*

20650   Insertion of wire or pin with application of skeletal traction, including removal (separate procedure)   A2 T ▢
     🖩 4.04   🖎 4.98   **Global Days 010**

20660   Application of cranial tongs, caliper, or stereotactic frame, including removal (separate procedure)   T ▢
     🖩 6.19   🖎 6.55   **Global Days 000**
     AMA: 2008, Jan, 10-25; 2008, Feb, 8-9; 2008, Jul, 10&13; 2007, Jan, 13-27; 2007, Jan, 13-27; 2007, Dec, 1-2; 2007, January, 13-27; 2006, Jan, 46-47; 2006, Jan, 46-47; 2006, Dec, 10-12; 2006, December, 10-12; 2006, December, 10-12; 2006, January, 46-47; 2006, Dec, 10-12; 2006, Dec, 10-12; 2006, Dec, 10-12

20661   Application of halo, including removal; cranial   C ▢
     🖩 11.93   🖎 11.93   **Global Days 090**

20662   pelvic   R2 T 80 ▢
     🖩 12.13   🖎 12.13   **Global Days 090**

20663   femoral   R2 T 80 ▢
     🖩 11.37   🖎 11.37   **Global Days 090**

20664   Application of halo, including removal, cranial, 6 or more pins placed, for thin skull osteology (eg, pediatric patients, hydrocephalus, osteogenesis imperfecta), requiring general anesthesia   C ▢
     🖩 19.48   🖎 19.48   **Global Days 090**

20665   Removal of tongs or halo applied by another physician   62 X 80 ▢
     🖩 2.60   🖎 3.09   **Global Days 010**
     AMA: 2006, Dec, 10-12; 2006, Dec, 10-12; 2006, Dec, 10-12; 2006, Dec, 10-12; 2006, December, 10-12; 2006, December, 10-12

20670   Removal of implant; superficial (eg, buried wire, pin or rod) (separate procedure)   A2 T ▢
     🖩 3.82   🖎 9.78   **Global Days 010**
     AMA: 2008, Jan, 10-25; 2007, Dec, 7-8

20680   deep (eg, buried wire, pin, screw, metal band, nail, rod or plate)   A2 T 80 ▢
     🖩 10.50   🖎 14.73   **Global Days 090**

20690   Application of a uniplane (pins or wires in 1 plane), unilateral, external fixation system   A2 T ▢
     🖩 13.74   🖎 13.74   **Global Days 090**
     AMA: 2008, Jan, 4-5; 2008, Jan, 10-25; 2008, Feb, 8-9; 2007, Jan, 13-27; 2007, Jan, 13-27; 2007, January, 13-27; 2005, Jun, 9-11; 2005, Jun, 9-11; 2005, June, 9-11; 2004, Jan, 27; 2004, Jan, 27; 2004, January, 27

20692   Application of a multiplane (pins or wires in more than 1 plane), unilateral, external fixation system (eg, Ilizarov, Monticelli type)   A2 T 80 ▢
     🖩 25.69   🖎 25.69   **Global Days 090**
     AMA: 2008, Jan, 10-25; 2008, Jan, 4-5; 2008, Feb, 8-9; 2007, Jan, 13-27; 2007, Jan, 13-27; 2007, January, 13-27

20693   Adjustment or revision of external fixation system requiring anesthesia (eg, new pin[s] or wire[s] and/or new ring[s] or bar[s])   A2 T ▢
     🖩 11.78   🖎 11.78   **Global Days 090**
     AMA: 2008, Jan, 10-25; 2007, Jan, 13-27; 2007, Jan, 13-27; 2007, January, 13-27

20694   Removal, under anesthesia, of external fixation system   A2 T ▢
     🖩 8.61   🖎 10.69   **Global Days 090**
     AMA: 2008, Jan, 10-25; 2007, Jan, 13-27; 2007, Jan, 13-27; 2007, January, 13-27

● **20696**   Application of multiplane (pins or wires in more than 1 plane), unilateral, external fixation with stereotactic computer-assisted adjustment (eg, spatial frame), including imaging; initial and subsequent alignment(s), assessment(s), and computation(s) of adjustment schedule(s)   62 T 80
     Do not report with (20692, 20697)
     🖩 28.14   🖎 28.14   **Global Days 090**

⊘   ● **20697**   Application of multiplane (pins or wires in more than 1 plane), unilateral, external fixation with stereotactic computer-assisted adjustment (eg, spatial frame), including imaging; exchange (ie, removal and replacement) of strut, each   62 T 80
     Do not report with (20692, 20696)
     🖩 0.01   🖎 33.09   **Global Days 000**

20802-20838 Reimplantation Procedures

CMS *100-4,12,30*   *Correct Coding Policy*
CMS *100-4,12,40.1*   *Global Surgery Package Definition*

EXCLUDES   *repair of incomplete amputation (see individual repair codes for bone(s), ligament(s), tendon(s), nerve(s), or blood vessel(s))*

20802   Replantation, arm (includes surgical neck of humerus through elbow joint), complete amputation   C 80 50 ▢
     🖩 63.31   🖎 63.31   **Global Days 090**

20805   Replantation, forearm (includes radius and ulna to radial carpal joint), complete amputation   C 80 50 ▢
     🖩 77.65   🖎 77.65   **Global Days 090**

20808   Replantation, hand (includes hand through metacarpophalangeal joints), complete amputation   C 80 50 ▢
     🖩 105.47   🖎 105.47   **Global Days 090**

20816   Replantation, digit, excluding thumb (includes metacarpophalangeal joint to insertion of flexor sublimis tendon), complete amputation   C 80 ▢
     🖩 58.66   🖎 58.66   **Global Days 090**
     AMA: 2008, Jan, 10-25; 2007, Jan, 13-27; 2007, Jan, 13-27; 2007, January, 13-27

20822   Replantation, digit, excluding thumb (includes distal tip to sublimis tendon insertion), complete amputation   67 T 80 ▢
     🖩 49.88   🖎 49.88   **Global Days 090**

20824   Replantation, thumb (includes carpometacarpal joint to MP joint), complete amputation   C 80 50 ▢
     🖩 58.46   🖎 58.46   **Global Days 090**

20827   Replantation, thumb (includes distal tip to MP joint), complete amputation   C 80 50 ▢
     🖩 51.63   🖎 51.63   **Global Days 090**

20838   Replantation, foot, complete amputation   C 80 50 ▢
     🖩 63.06   🖎 63.06   **Global Days 090**

20900-20926 Bone and Tissue Autografts

CMS *100-4,12,30*   *Correct Coding Policy*

EXCLUDES   *acquisition of autogenous bone graft, cartilage, tendon, fascia lata through distinct incision unless included in the code description bone graft procedures on the spine (20930-20938)*

20900   Bone graft, any donor area; minor or small (eg, dowel or button)   A2 T 80 ▢
     🖩 6.98   🖎 10.75   **Global Days 000**
     AMA: 2008, Jan, 10-25; 2007, Jan, 13-27; 2007, Jan, 13-27; 2007, January, 13-27

20902   major or large   A2 T 80 ▢
     🖩 9.63   🖎 9.63   **Global Days 000**
     AMA: 2008, Jan, 10-25; 2007, Jan, 13-27; 2007, Jan, 13-27; 2007, January, 13-27

● New Code   ▲ Revised Code   M Maternity Edit   A Age Edit   A T OPPS Status Indicator   🖩 Facility RVU   🖎 Non-Facility RVU
▢ CCI Comprehensive Code   50 Bilateral Procedure   + Add-on Indicator   ▪ Laboratory crosswalk   ▪ Radiology crosswalk

Musculoskeletal System

20910 — 20979

20910 Cartilage graft; costochondral [A2] [T] [80] [▭]
EXCLUDES *graft with ear cartilage (21235)*
🔧 11.01 ✂ 11.01 Global Days 090

20912 nasal septum [A2] [T] [80] [▭]
EXCLUDES *graft with ear cartilage (21235)*
🔧 12.31 ✂ 12.31 Global Days 090

20920 Fascia lata graft; by stripper [A2] [T] [▭]
🔧 10.40 ✂ 10.40 Global Days 090
AMA: 2005, Jan, 7-13; 2005, Jan, 7-13; 2005, January, 7-13

20922 by incision and area exposure, complex or sheet [A2] [T] [80] [▭]
🔧 12.70 ✂ 15.32 Global Days 090
AMA: 2005, Jan, 7-13; 2005, Jan, 7-13; 2005, January, 7-13

20924 Tendon graft, from a distance (eg, palmaris, toe extensor, plantaris) [A2] [T] [80] [▭]
🔧 12.95 ✂ 12.95 Global Days 090
AMA: 2005, Jan, 7-13; 2005, Jan, 7-13; 2005, January, 7-13

20926 Tissue grafts, other (eg, paratenon, fat, dermis) [A2] [T] [▭]
🔧 11.17 ✂ 11.17 Global Days 090
AMA: 2008, Jan, 10-25; 2007, Jan, 13-27; 2007, Jan, 13-27; 2007, Mar, 9-11; 2007, Mar, 9-11; 2007, January, 13-27; 2007, March, 9-11; 2006, May, 16-20; 2006, May, 16-20; 2006, May, 16-20

20930-20938 Bone Allograft and Autograft of Spine

CMS 100-4,12,40.1 *Global Surgery Package Definition*
EXCLUDES *bone marrow aspiration for grafting (38220)*

+ **20930** Allograft for spine surgery only; morselized (List separately in addition to code for primary procedure) [C]
Code first (0195T-0196T, 22319, 22532-22533, 22548-22558, 22590-22612, 22630, 22800-22812)
🔧 0.00 ✂ 0.00 Global Days XXX
AMA: 2008, Jan, 10-25; 2008, Feb, 8-9; 2007, Jan, 13-27; 2007, Jan, 13-27; 2007, Dec, 1-2; 2007, January, 13-27; 2004, Jan, 27; 2004, January, 27; 2004, Jan, 27

+ **20931** structural (List separately in addition to code for primary procedure) [C] [▭]
Code first (22319, 22532-22533, 22548-22558, 22590-22612, 22630, 22800-22812)
🔧 3.02 ✂ 3.02 Global Days ZZZ
AMA: 2008, Feb, 8-9; 2007, Dec, 1-2; 2005, Feb, 13-16; 2005, Feb, 13-16; 2005, February, 13-16; 2004, Jan, 27; 2004, January, 27; 2004, Jan, 27

+ **20936** Autograft for spine surgery only (includes harvesting the graft); local (eg, ribs, spinous process, or laminar fragments) obtained from same incision (List separately in addition to code for primary procedure) [C]
Code first (0195T-0196T, 22319, 22532-22533, 22548-22558, 22590-22612, 22630, 22800-22812)
🔧 0.00 ✂ 0.00 Global Days XXX
AMA: 2008, Feb, 8-9; 2007, Dec, 1-2; 2004, Jan, 27; 2004, Jan, 27; 2004, January, 27

+ **20937** morselized (through separate skin or fascial incision) (List separately in addition to code for primary procedure) [C] [80] [▭]
Code first (0195T-0196T, 22319, 22532-22533, 22548-22558, 22590-22612, 22630, 22800-22812)
🔧 4.56 ✂ 4.56 Global Days ZZZ
AMA: 2008, Feb, 8-9; 2007, Dec, 1-2; 2004, Jan, 27; 2004, Jan, 27; 2004, January, 27

+ **20938** structural, bicortical or tricortical (through separate skin or fascial incision) (List separately in addition to code for primary procedure) [C] [80] [▭]
Code first (22319, 22532-22533, 22548-22558, 22590-22612, 22630)
🔧 4.97 ✂ 4.97 Global Days ZZZ
AMA: 2008, Feb, 8-9; 2007, Dec, 1-2; 2004, Jan, 27; 2004, Jan, 27; 2004, January, 27

20950 Measurement of Intracompartmental Pressure

CMS 100-4,12,20.4.3 *Payment for Assistant at Surgery*
CMS 100-4,12,30 *Correct Coding Policy*

20950 Monitoring of interstitial fluid pressure (includes insertion of device, eg, wick catheter technique, needle manometer technique) in detection of muscle compartment syndrome [G2] [T] [80] [▭]
🔧 2.36 ✂ 6.14 Global Days 000
AMA: 2008, Jan, 10-25

20955-20973 Bone and Osteocutaneous Grafts

CMS 100-4,12,20.4.3 *Payment for Assistant at Surgery*
CMS 100-4,12,30 *Correct Coding Policy*
INCLUDES *operating microscope (69990)*

20955 Bone graft with microvascular anastomosis; fibula [C] [80] [▭]
🔧 66.17 ✂ 66.17 Global Days 090

20956 iliac crest [C] [80] [▭]
🔧 69.72 ✂ 69.72 Global Days 090

20957 metatarsal [C] [80] [▭]
🔧 66.57 ✂ 66.57 Global Days 090

20962 other than fibula, iliac crest, or metatarsal [C] [80] [▭]
🔧 68.23 ✂ 68.23 Global Days 090

20969 Free osteocutaneous flap with microvascular anastomosis; other than iliac crest, metatarsal, or great toe [C] [80] [▭]
🔧 73.06 ✂ 73.06 Global Days 090

20970 iliac crest [C] [80] [▭]
🔧 74.05 ✂ 74.05 Global Days 090

20972 metatarsal [G2] [T] [80] [▭]
🔧 67.24 ✂ 67.24 Global Days 090

20973 great toe with web space [R2] [T] [80] [▭]
EXCLUDES *wrap-around repair (26551)*
🔧 70.54 ✂ 70.54 Global Days 090

20974-20979 Osteogenic Stimulation

CMS 100-3,150.2 *Osteogenic Stimulation*
CMS 100-4,12,20.4.3 *Payment for Assistant at Surgery*
CMS 100-4,12,30 *Correct Coding Policy*

⊘ **20974** Electrical stimulation to aid bone healing; noninvasive (nonoperative) [A] [▭]
🔧 1.24 ✂ 1.66 Global Days 000
AMA: 2008, Jan, 10-25; 2007, Jan, 13-27; 2007, Jan, 13-27; 2007, January, 13-27

⊘ **20975** invasive (operative) [111] [N] [80] [▭]
🔧 4.68 ✂ 4.68 Global Days 000

20979 Low intensity ultrasound stimulation to aid bone healing, noninvasive (nonoperative) [P3] [X] [▭]
🔧 0.95 ✂ 1.36 Global Days 000
AMA: 2008, Jan, 10-25; 2007, Jan, 13-27; 2007, Jan, 13-27; 2007, January, 13-27

20982-20999 General Musculoskeletal Procedures with Imaging Guidance

CMS *100-4,12,40.7*   *Bilateral Procedures*
CMS *100-4,12,20.4.3*   *Payment for Assistant at Surgery*
CMS *100-4,12,30*   *Correct Coding Policy*

⊙ **20982** **Ablation, bone tumor(s) (eg, osteoid osteoma, metastasis) radiofrequency, percutaneous, including computed tomographic guidance** `62` `T` `50` `□`

Do not report with (77013)

🔲 10.87   ⚖ 94.50 **Global Days 000**

+ ▲ **20985** **Computer-assisted surgical navigational procedure for musculoskeletal procedures, image-less (List separately in addition to code for primary procedure)** `N1` `N` `80`

EXCLUDES *image guidance derived from intraoperative and preoperative obtained images (0054T-0055T)*

Do not report with (61795)

🔲 4.04   ⚖ 4.04 **Global Days ZZZ**
AMA: 2007, Dec, 1-2

~~20986~~ ~~Computer-assisted surgical navigational procedure for musculoskeletal procedures; with image guidance based on intraoperatively obtained images (eg, fluoroscopy, ultrasound) (List separately in addition to code for primary procedure)~~
See 0054T-0055T

~~20987~~ ~~with image guidance based on preoperative images (List separately in addition to code for primary procedure)~~
See 0054T-0055T

20999 **Unlisted procedure, musculoskeletal system, general** `T` `80`

🔲 0.00   ⚖ 0.00 **Global Days YYY**

21010-21070 Procedures of Cranial and Facial Bones

CMS *100-4,12,90.3*   *MD Services in ASCs*
CMS *100-4,12,30*   *Correct Coding Policy*
CMS *100-4,14,10*   *General ASC Services*
CMS *100-4,4,20.5*   *HCPCS Under OPPS*

21010 **Arthrotomy, temporomandibular joint** `A2` `T` `80` `50` `□`

EXCLUDES *excision of foreign body from dentoalveolar site (41805-41806)*
simple abscess and hematoma drainage (20000)

🔲 18.54   ⚖ 18.54 **Global Days 090**

21015 **Radical resection of tumor (eg, malignant neoplasm), soft tissue of face or scalp** `A2` `T` `□`

EXCLUDES *removal of cranial tumor for osteomyelitis (61501)*

🔲 10.85   ⚖ 10.85 **Global Days 090**

21025 **Excision of bone (eg, for osteomyelitis or bone abscess); mandible** `A2` `T` `□`

🔲 19.07   ⚖ 22.30 **Global Days 090**

21026 **facial bone(s)** `A2` `T` `□`

🔲 12.19   ⚖ 14.68 **Global Days 090**

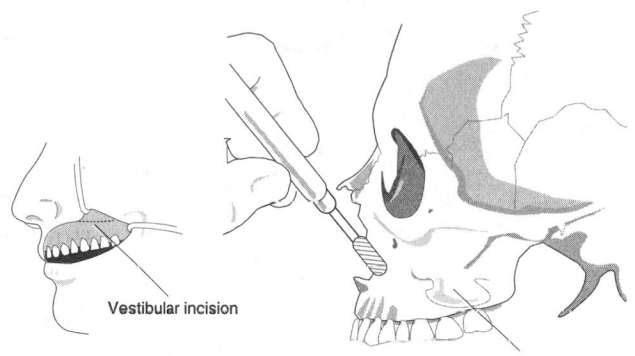

Vestibular incision

Burs, files, and osteotomes used to remove bone   Area of benign bone growth

21029 **Removal by contouring of benign tumor of facial bone (eg, fibrous dysplasia)** `A2` `T` `80` `□`

🔲 15.92   ⚖ 18.74 **Global Days 090**

21030 **Excision of benign tumor or cyst of maxilla or zygoma by enucleation and curettage** `P3` `T` `□`

🔲 10.14   ⚖ 12.29 **Global Days 090**

21031 **Excision of torus mandibularis** `P3` `T` `□`

🔲 7.30   ⚖ 9.49 **Global Days 090**

21032 **Excision of maxillary torus palatinus** `P3` `T` `□`

🔲 7.19   ⚖ 9.61 **Global Days 090**

21034 **Excision of malignant tumor of maxilla or zygoma** `A2` `T` `80` `□`

🔲 29.89   ⚖ 33.50 **Global Days 090**

21040 **Excision of benign tumor or cyst of mandible, by enucleation and/or curettage** `A2` `T` `□`

INCLUDES removal of benign tumor or cyst without osteotomy

EXCLUDES *removal of benign tumor or cyst with osteotomy (21046-21047)*

🔲 10.08   ⚖ 12.39 **Global Days 090**

21044 **Excision of malignant tumor of mandible;** `A2` `T` `80` `□`

🔲 22.31   ⚖ 22.31 **Global Days 090**

21045 **radical resection** `C` `80` `□`

EXCLUDES *bone graft procedure (21215)*

🔲 31.08   ⚖ 31.08 **Global Days 090**

21046 **Excision of benign tumor or cyst of mandible; requiring intra-oral osteotomy (eg, locally aggressive or destructive lesion(s))** `A2` `T` `80` `□`

🔲 27.71   ⚖ 27.71 **Global Days 090**

21047 **requiring extra-oral osteotomy and partial mandibulectomy (eg, locally aggressive or destructive lesion(s))** `A2` `T` `80` `□`

🔲 33.38   ⚖ 33.38 **Global Days 090**

21048 **Excision of benign tumor or cyst of maxilla; requiring intra-oral osteotomy (eg, locally aggressive or destructive lesion(s))** `A2` `T` `80` `□`

🔲 28.03   ⚖ 28.03 **Global Days 090**

21049 **requiring extra-oral osteotomy and partial maxillectomy (eg, locally aggressive or destructive lesion(s))** `T` `80` `□`

🔲 32.13   ⚖ 32.13 **Global Days 090**

21050 **Condylectomy, temporomandibular joint (separate procedure)** `A2` `T` `80` `50` `□`

🔲 22.05   ⚖ 22.05 **Global Days 090**

21060 **Meniscectomy, partial or complete, temporomandibular joint (separate procedure)** `A2` `T` `80` `50` `□`

🔲 20.14   ⚖ 20.14 **Global Days 090**

21070 **Coronoidectomy (separate procedure)** `A2` `T` `80` `50` `□`

🔲 16.43   ⚖ 16.43 **Global Days 090**

● New Code   ▲ Revised Code   🅼 Maternity Edit   △ Age Edit   Ⓐ-Ⓨ OPPS Status Indicator   🔲 Facility RVU   ⚖ Non-Facility RVU
□ CCI Comprehensive Code   50 Bilateral Procedure   + Add-on Indicator   🔲 Laboratory crosswalk   🔲 Radiology crosswalk

Musculoskeletal System

21073 — 21116

21073 Temporomandibular Joint Manipulation with Anesthesia

CMS *100-3,150.1*   *Manipulation*

21073   **Manipulation of temporomandibular joint(s) (TMJ), therapeutic, requiring an anesthesia service (ie, general or monitored anesthesia care)**   P3 T 80 50

     EXCLUDES   *closed treatment of TMJ dislocation (21480, 21485)*

                 manipulation of TMJ without an anesthesia service (97140, 98925-98929, 98943)

     6.09   9.16   Global Days 090

     AMA: 2008, Feb, 8-9; 2007, Dec, 1-2

21076-21089 Medical Impressions for Fabrication Maxillofacial Prosthesis

CMS *100-4,12,30*   *Correct Coding Policy*

INCLUDES   professional services by a physician and not an outside lab

EXCLUDES   *application or removal of caliper or tongs (20660, 20665)*

21076   **Impression and custom preparation; surgical obturator prosthesis**   P3 T 80

     21.72   24.77   Global Days 010

     AMA: 2008, Jan, 10-25; 2007, Jan, 13-27; 2007, Jan, 13-27; 2007, January, 13-27; 2006, Sep, 14-16; 2006, Sep, 14-16; 2006, Dec, 10-12; 2006, December, 10-12; 2006, December, 10-12; 2006, September, 14-16; 2006, Dec, 10-12; 2006, Dec, 10-12; 2006, Dec, 10-12

21077   **orbital prosthesis**   P3 T 80 50

     54.74   60.91   Global Days 090

     AMA: 2006, Sep, 14-16; 2006, Sep, 14-16; 2006, Dec, 10-12; 2006, Dec, 10-12; 2006, Dec, 10-12; 2006, Dec, 10-12; 2006, September, 14-16; 2006, December, 10-12; 2006, December, 10-12

21079   **interim obturator prosthesis**   P3 T

     36.29   41.69   Global Days 090

     AMA: 2006, Sep, 14-16; 2006, Sep, 14-16; 2006, Dec, 10-12; 2006, Dec, 10-12; 2006, Dec, 10-12; 2006, Dec, 10-12; 2006, September, 14-16; 2006, December, 10-12; 2006, December, 10-12

21080   **definitive obturator prosthesis**   P3 T

     40.89   47.41   Global Days 090

     AMA: 2006, Sep, 14-16; 2006, Sep, 14-16; 2006, Dec, 10-12; 2006, Dec, 10-12; 2006, Dec, 10-12; 2006, Dec, 10-12; 2006, September, 14-16; 2006, December, 10-12; 2006, December, 10-12

21081   **mandibular resection prosthesis**   P3 T 80

     37.16   43.20   Global Days 090

     AMA: 2006, Sep, 14-16; 2006, Sep, 14-16; 2006, Dec, 10-12; 2006, Dec, 10-12; 2006, Dec, 10-12; 2006, Dec, 10-12; 2006, September, 14-16; 2006, December, 10-12; 2006, December, 10-12

21082   **palatal augmentation prosthesis**   P3 T 80

     34.49   40.27   Global Days 090

     AMA: 2006, Sep, 14-16; 2006, Sep, 14-16; 2006, Dec, 10-12; 2006, Dec, 10-12; 2006, Dec, 10-12; 2006, Dec, 10-12; 2006, September, 14-16; 2006, December, 10-12; 2006, December, 10-12

21083   **palatal lift prosthesis**   P3 T 80

     31.93   38.23   Global Days 090

     AMA: 2006, Sep, 14-16; 2006, Sep, 14-16; 2006, Dec, 10-12; 2006, Dec, 10-12; 2006, Dec, 10-12; 2006, Dec, 10-12; 2006, September, 14-16; 2006, December, 10-12; 2006, December, 10-12

21084   **speech aid prosthesis**   P3 T 80

     36.20   43.16   Global Days 090

     AMA: 2006, Sep, 14-16; 2006, Sep, 14-16; 2006, Dec, 10-12; 2006, Dec, 10-12; 2006, Dec, 10-12; 2006, Dec, 10-12; 2006, September, 14-16; 2006, December, 10-12; 2006, December, 10-12

21085   **oral surgical splint**   P3 T 80

     14.74   17.60   Global Days 010

     AMA: 2006, Sep, 14-16; 2006, Sep, 14-16; 2006, Dec, 10-12; 2006, Dec, 10-12; 2006, Dec, 10-12; 2006, Dec, 10-12; 2006, September, 14-16; 2006, December, 10-12; 2006, December, 10-12

21086   **auricular prosthesis**   P3 T 80 50

     40.24   44.58   Global Days 090

     AMA: 2006, Sep, 14-16; 2006, Sep, 14-16; 2006, Dec, 10-12; 2006, Dec, 10-12; 2006, Dec, 10-12; 2006, Dec, 10-12; 2006, September, 14-16; 2006, December, 10-12; 2006, December, 10-12

21087   **nasal prosthesis**   P3 T 80

     40.01   44.33   Global Days 090

     AMA: 2006, Sep, 14-16; 2006, Sep, 14-16; 2006, Dec, 10-12; 2006, Dec, 10-12; 2006, Dec, 10-12; 2006, Dec, 10-12; 2006, September, 14-16; 2006, December, 10-12; 2006, December, 10-12

21088   **facial prosthesis**   R2 T 80

     0.00   0.00   Global Days 090

     AMA: 2006, Sep, 14-16; 2006, Sep, 14-16; 2006, Dec, 10-12; 2006, Dec, 10-12; 2006, Dec, 10-12; 2006, Dec, 10-12; 2006, September, 14-16; 2006, December, 10-12; 2006, December, 10-12

21089   **Unlisted maxillofacial prosthetic procedure**   T

     0.00   0.00   Global Days YYY

     AMA: 2008, Jan, 10-25; 2007, Jan, 13-27; 2007, Jan, 13-27; 2007, January, 13-27; 2006, Sep, 14-16; 2006, Sep, 14-16; 2006, Dec, 10-12; 2006, December, 10-12; 2006, December, 10-12; 2006, September, 14-16; 2006, Dec, 10-12; 2006, Dec, 10-12; 2006, Dec, 10-12

21100-21110 Application Fixation Device

CMS *100-4,12,40.1*   *Global Surgery Package Definition*

21100   **Application of halo type appliance for maxillofacial fixation, includes removal (separate procedure)**   A2 T 80

     9.99   17.57   Global Days 090

21110   **Application of interdental fixation device for conditions other than fracture or dislocation, includes removal**   R2 T

     EXCLUDES   *removal of interdental fixation by another doctor (20670-20680)*

     15.86   18.59   Global Days 090

     AMA: 2008, Jan, 10-25; 2007, Jan, 13-27; 2007, Jan, 13-27; 2007, January, 13-27

21116 Injection for TMJ Arthrogram

CMS *100-4,13,80.2*   *Physician Presence*

CMS *100-4,13,80.1*   *Supervision and Interpretation Codes*

     70332

21116   **Injection procedure for temporomandibular joint arthrography**   M1 N

     1.13   3.73   Global Days 000

21120-21299 Repair/Reconstruction Craniofacial Bones

CMS *100-2,16,180*   *Services Related to Noncovered Procedures*

CMS *100-2,16,120*   *Cosmetic Procedures*

CMS *100-2,16,10*   *Exclusions from Coverage*

CMS *100-4,12,40.1*   *Global Surgery Package Definition*

EXCLUDES   *cranioplasty (62116, 62120, 62140-62147)*

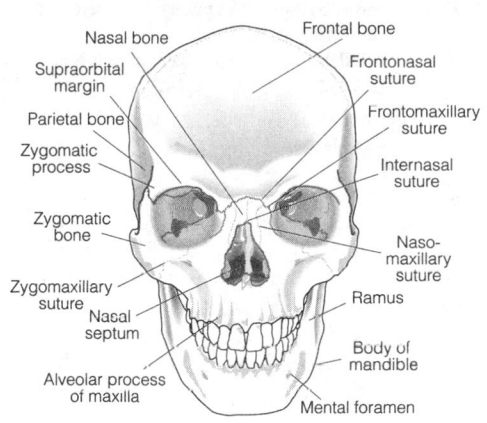

21120   **Genioplasty; augmentation (autograft, allograft, prosthetic material)**   A2 T ▭
    12.45   15.44   Global Days 090

21121   **sliding osteotomy, single piece**   A2 T 80 ▭
    16.51   19.28   Global Days 090

21122   **sliding osteotomies, 2 or more osteotomies (eg, wedge excision or bone wedge reversal for asymmetrical chin)**   A2 T 80 ▭
    18.22   18.22   Global Days 090

21123   **sliding, augmentation with interpositional bone grafts (includes obtaining autografts)**   A2 T 80 ▭
    21.82   21.82   Global Days 090

21125   **Augmentation, mandibular body or angle; prosthetic material**   A2 T 80 ▭
    18.90   75.11   Global Days 090

21127   **with bone graft, onlay or interpositional (includes obtaining autograft)**   A2 T 80 ▭
    22.29   89.61   Global Days 090

21137   **Reduction forehead; contouring only**   G2 T 80 ▭
    18.40   18.40   Global Days 090

21138   **contouring and application of prosthetic material or bone graft (includes obtaining autograft)**   G2 T 80 ▭
    23.01   23.01   Global Days 090

21139   **contouring and setback of anterior frontal sinus wall**   G2 T 80 ▭
    25.54   25.54   Global Days 090

21141   **Reconstruction midface, LeFort I; single piece, segment movement in any direction (eg, for Long Face Syndrome), without bone graft**   C 80 ▭
    34.54   34.54   Global Days 090

21142   **2 pieces, segment movement in any direction, without bone graft**   C 80 ▭
    34.11   34.11   Global Days 090

21143   **3 or more pieces, segment movement in any direction, without bone graft**   C 80 ▭
    35.13   35.13   Global Days 090

21145   **single piece, segment movement in any direction, requiring bone grafts (includes obtaining autografts)**   C 80 ▭
    39.67   39.67   Global Days 090

21146   **2 pieces, segment movement in any direction, requiring bone grafts (includes obtaining autografts) (eg, ungrafted unilateral alveolar cleft)**   C 80 ▭
    42.41   42.41   Global Days 090

21147   **3 or more pieces, segment movement in any direction, requiring bone grafts (includes obtaining autografts) (eg, ungrafted bilateral alveolar cleft or multiple osteotomies)**   C 80 ▭
    43.18   43.18   Global Days 090

21150   **Reconstruction midface, LeFort II; anterior intrusion (eg, Treacher-Collins Syndrome)**   62 T 80 ▭
    43.11   43.11   Global Days 090

21151   **any direction, requiring bone grafts (includes obtaining autografts)**   C 80 ▭
    51.99   51.99   Global Days 090

21154   **Reconstruction midface, LeFort III (extracranial), any type, requiring bone grafts (includes obtaining autografts); without LeFort I**   C 80 ▭
    52.47   52.47   Global Days 090

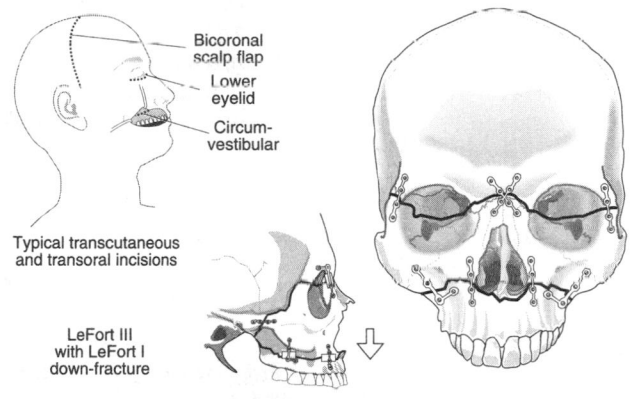

Typical transcutaneous and transoral incisions

LeFort III with LeFort I down-fracture

21155   **with LeFort I**   C 80 ▭
    60.77   60.77   Global Days 090

21159   **Reconstruction midface, LeFort III (extra and intracranial) with forehead advancement (eg, mono bloc), requiring bone grafts (includes obtaining autografts); without LeFort I**   C 80 ▭
    73.52   73.52   Global Days 090

21160   **with LeFort I**   C 80 ▭
    74.13   74.13   Global Days 090

21172   **Reconstruction superior-lateral orbital rim and lower forehead, advancement or alteration, with or without grafts (includes obtaining autografts)**   T 80 ▭
     EXCLUDES   *frontal or parietal craniotomy for craniosynostosis (61556)*
    45.95   45.95   Global Days 090

21175   **Reconstruction, bifrontal, superior-lateral orbital rims and lower forehead, advancement or alteration (eg, plagiocephaly, trigonocephaly, brachycephaly), with or without grafts (includes obtaining autografts)**   T 80 ▭
     EXCLUDES   *bifrontal craniotomy for craniosynostosis (61557)*
    55.69   55.69   Global Days 090

21179   **Reconstruction, entire or majority of forehead and/or supraorbital rims; with grafts (allograft or prosthetic material)**   C 80 ▭
     EXCLUDES   *extensive craniotomy for numerous suture craniosynostosis (61558-61559)*
    38.01   38.01   Global Days 090

21180   **with autograft (includes obtaining grafts)**   C 80 ▭
     EXCLUDES   *extensive craniotomy for numerous suture craniosynostosis (61558-61559)*
    43.44   43.44   Global Days 090

21181   **Reconstruction by contouring of benign tumor of cranial bones (eg, fibrous dysplasia), extracranial**   A2 T 80 ▭
    18.13   18.13   Global Days 090

● New Code   ▲ Revised Code   M Maternity Edit   A Age Edit   A-Y OPPS Status Indicator   Facility RVU   Non-Facility RVU
▭ CCI Comprehensive Code   50 Bilateral Procedure   + Add-on Indicator   Laboratory crosswalk   Radiology crosswalk

Musculoskeletal System

21182 — 21261

21182 Reconstruction of orbital walls, rims, forehead, nasoethmoid complex following intra- and extracranial excision of benign tumor of cranial bone (eg, fibrous dysplasia), with multiple autografts (includes obtaining grafts); total area of bone grafting less than 40 sq cm   C 80
   EXCLUDES   *removal of benign tumor of the skull (61563-61564)*
   52.30   52.30   **Global Days 090**

21183 total area of bone grafting greater than 40 sq cm but less than 80 sq cm   C 80
   EXCLUDES   *removal of benign tumor of the skull (61563-61564)*
   58.97   58.97   **Global Days 090**

21184 total area of bone grafting greater than 80 sq cm   C 80
   EXCLUDES   *removal of benign tumor of the skull (61563-61564)*
   63.33   63.33   **Global Days 090**

21188 Reconstruction midface, osteotomies (other than LeFort type) and bone grafts (includes obtaining autografts)   C 80
   41.41   41.41   **Global Days 090**

21193 Reconstruction of mandibular rami, horizontal, vertical, C, or L osteotomy; without bone graft   C 80
   31.88   31.88   **Global Days 090**
   AMA: 2008, Jan, 10-25; 2007, Jan, 13-27; 2007, Jan, 13-27; 2007, January, 13-27

21194 with bone graft (includes obtaining graft)   C 80
   36.22   36.22   **Global Days 090**

21195 Reconstruction of mandibular rami and/or body, sagittal split; without internal rigid fixation   T 80
   34.01   34.01   **Global Days 090**
   AMA: 2008, Jan, 10-25; 2007, Jan, 13-27; 2007, Jan, 13-27; 2007, January, 13-27

21196 with internal rigid fixation   C 80
   37.16   37.16   **Global Days 090**
   AMA: 2008, Jan, 10-25; 2007, Jan, 13-27; 2007, Jan, 13-27; 2007, January, 13-27

21198 Osteotomy, mandible, segmental;   G2 T 80
   EXCLUDES   *total maxillary osteotomy (21141-21160)*
   29.19   29.19   **Global Days 090**

21199 with genioglossus advancement   G2 T 80
   EXCLUDES   *total maxillary osteotomy (21141-21160)*
   26.34   26.34   **Global Days 090**

21206 Osteotomy, maxilla, segmental (eg, Wassmund or Schuchard)   A2 T 80
   28.72   28.72   **Global Days 090**

21208 Osteoplasty, facial bones; augmentation (autograft, allograft, or prosthetic implant)   A2 T 80
   20.94   42.77   **Global Days 090**

21209 reduction   A2 T 80
   16.15   20.36   **Global Days 090**

21210 Graft, bone; nasal, maxillary or malar areas (includes obtaining graft)   A2 T
   EXCLUDES   *cleft palate treatment (42200-42225)*
   20.98   51.23   **Global Days 090**

21215 mandible (includes obtaining graft)   A2 T
   21.93   87.15   **Global Days 090**

21230 Graft; rib cartilage, autogenous, to face, chin, nose or ear (includes obtaining graft)   A2 T 80
   EXCLUDES   *augmentation graft of the facial bones (21208)*
   19.58   19.58   **Global Days 090**

21235 ear cartilage, autogenous, to nose or ear (includes obtaining graft)   A2 T
   EXCLUDES   *augmentation graft of the facial bones (21208)*
   14.26   18.00   **Global Days 090**
   AMA: 2008, Jan, 10-25; 2007, Mar, 9-11; 2007, Mar, 9-11; 2007, March, 9-11

TMJ syndrome is often related to stress and tooth-grinding; in other cases, arthritis, injury, poorly aligned teeth, or ill-fitting dentures may be the cause

Upper joint space

Lower joint space

Articular disc (meniscus)

Cutaway detail

Condyle

Mandible

Cutaway view of temporomandibular joint (TMJ)

Symptoms include facial pain and chewing problems; TMJ syndrome occurs more frequently in women

21240 Arthroplasty, temporomandibular joint, with or without autograft (includes obtaining graft)   A2 T 80 50
   28.45   28.45   **Global Days 090**

21242 Arthroplasty, temporomandibular joint, with allograft   A2 T 80 50
   25.98   25.98   **Global Days 090**

21243 Arthroplasty, temporomandibular joint, with prosthetic joint replacement   A2 T 80 50
   42.74   42.74   **Global Days 090**

21244 Reconstruction of mandible, extraoral, with transosteal bone plate (eg, mandibular staple bone plate)   A2 T 80
   26.42   26.42   **Global Days 090**
   AMA: 2004, Mar, 7; 2004, Mar, 7; 2004, March, 7

21245 Reconstruction of mandible or maxilla, subperiosteal implant; partial   A2 T 80
   23.26   28.48   **Global Days 090**

21246 complete   A2 T 80
   21.78   21.78   **Global Days 090**

21247 Reconstruction of mandibular condyle with bone and cartilage autografts (includes obtaining grafts) (eg, for hemifacial microsomia)   C 80
   41.44   41.44   **Global Days 090**

21248 Reconstruction of mandible or maxilla, endosteal implant (eg, blade, cylinder); partial   A2 T
   EXCLUDES   *midface reconstruction (21141-21160)*
   22.44   26.93   **Global Days 090**

21249 complete   A2 T 80
   EXCLUDES   *midface reconstruction (21141-21160)*
   31.92   37.44   **Global Days 090**

21255 Reconstruction of zygomatic arch and glenoid fossa with bone and cartilage (includes obtaining autografts)   C 80
   36.76   36.76   **Global Days 090**

21256 Reconstruction of orbit with osteotomies (extracranial) and with bone grafts (includes obtaining autografts) (eg, micro-ophthalmia)   C 80
   29.75   29.75   **Global Days 090**

21260 Periorbital osteotomies for orbital hypertelorism, with bone grafts; extracranial approach   G2 T 80
   33.38   33.38   **Global Days 090**

21261 combined intra- and extracranial approach   T 80
   57.53   57.53   **Global Days 090**

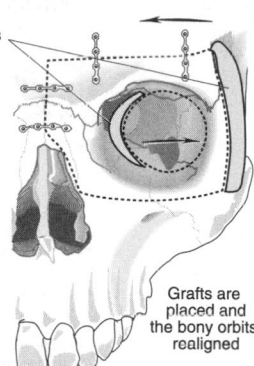

Grafts

In 21263, a frontal craniotomy is performed, the brain retracted, and the orbit approached from inside the skull; frontal bone is advanced and secured

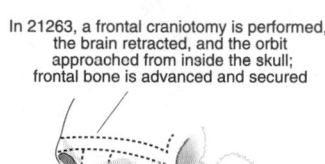

Grafts are placed and the bony orbits realigned

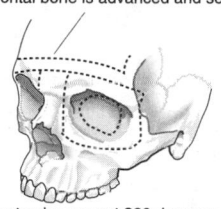

Osteotomies are cut 360 degrees around the orbit; portions of nasal and ethmoid bones are removed

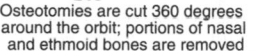

| 21263 | with forehead advancement | T 80 ▢ |
| | 🔹 51.61 ⚲ 51.61 Global Days 090 | |

| 21267 | Orbital repositioning, periorbital osteotomies, unilateral, with bone grafts; extracranial approach | A2 T 80 ▢ |
| | 🔹 39.16 ⚲ 39.16 Global Days 090 | |

| 21268 | combined intra- and extracranial approach | C 80 ▢ |
| | 🔹 49.09 ⚲ 49.09 Global Days 090 | |

21270	Malar augmentation, prosthetic material	A2 T 80 ▢
	EXCLUDES bone graft (21210)	
	🔹 17.69 ⚲ 22.67 Global Days 090	

| 21275 | Secondary revision of orbitocraniofacial reconstruction | A2 T 80 ▢ |
| | 🔹 20.56 ⚲ 20.56 Global Days 090 | |

21280	Medial canthopexy (separate procedure)	A2 T 80 50 ▢
	EXCLUDES reconstruction of canthus (67950)	
	🔹 13.15 ⚲ 13.15 Global Days 090	

| 21282 | Lateral canthopexy | A2 T 50 ▢ |
| | 🔹 8.70 ⚲ 8.70 Global Days 090 | |

| 21295 | Reduction of masseter muscle and bone (eg, for treatment of benign masseteric hypertrophy); extraoral approach | A2 T 80 ▢ |
| | 🔹 4.37 ⚲ 4.37 Global Days 090 | |

| 21296 | intraoral approach | A2 T 80 ▢ |
| | 🔹 10.60 ⚲ 10.60 Global Days 090 | |

| 21299 | Unlisted craniofacial and maxillofacial procedure | T 80 |
| | 🔹 0.00 ⚲ 0.00 Global Days YYY | |

21310-21497 Care of Fractures/Dislocations of the Cranial and Facial Bones

CMS 100-4,12,90.3 *MD Services in ASCs*
CMS 100-4,12,40.1 *Global Surgery Package Definition*
CMS 100-4,14,10 *General ASC Services*
CMS 100-4,4,20.5 *HCPCS Under OPPS*
EXCLUDES *closed treatment of skull fracture (99201-99499)*
           open treatment of skull fracture (62000-62010)

| 21310 | Closed treatment of nasal bone fracture without manipulation | A2 T ▢ |
| | 🔹 0.75 ⚲ 2.63 Global Days 000 | |

| 21315 | Closed treatment of nasal bone fracture; without stabilization | A2 T ▢ |
| | 🔹 3.71 ⚲ 6.43 Global Days 010 | |

| 21320 | with stabilization | A2 T ▢ |
| | 🔹 3.48 ⚲ 6.20 Global Days 010 | |

| 21325 | Open treatment of nasal fracture; uncomplicated | A2 T ▢ |
| | 🔹 11.67 ⚲ 11.67 Global Days 090 | |

| 21330 | complicated, with internal and/or external skeletal fixation | A2 T 80 ▢ |
| | 🔹 14.36 ⚲ 14.36 Global Days 090 | |

| 21335 | with concomitant open treatment of fractured septum | A2 T ▢ |
| | 🔹 18.52 ⚲ 18.52 Global Days 090 | |

| 21336 | Open treatment of nasal septal fracture, with or without stabilization | A2 T 80 ▢ |
| | 🔹 16.00 ⚲ 16.00 Global Days 090 | |

| 21337 | Closed treatment of nasal septal fracture, with or without stabilization | A2 T 80 ▢ |
| | 🔹 7.12 ⚲ 9.64 Global Days 090 | |

| 21338 | Open treatment of nasoethmoid fracture; without external fixation | A2 T 80 ▢ |
| | 🔹 18.41 ⚲ 18.41 Global Days 090 | |

| 21339 | with external fixation | A2 T 80 ▢ |
| | 🔹 20.51 ⚲ 20.51 Global Days 090 | |

| 21340 | Percutaneous treatment of nasoethmoid complex fracture, with splint, wire or headcap fixation, including repair of canthal ligaments and/or the nasolacrimal apparatus | A2 T 80 ▢ |
| | 🔹 20.45 ⚲ 20.45 Global Days 090 | |

| 21343 | Open treatment of depressed frontal sinus fracture | C 80 ▢ |
| | 🔹 29.04 ⚲ 29.04 Global Days 090 | |

| 21344 | Open treatment of complicated (eg, comminuted or involving posterior wall) frontal sinus fracture, via coronal or multiple approaches | C 80 ▢ |
| | 🔹 38.25 ⚲ 38.25 Global Days 090 | |

| 21345 | Closed treatment of nasomaxillary complex fracture (LeFort II type), with interdental wire fixation or fixation of denture or splint | A2 T 80 ▢ |
| | 🔹 16.60 ⚲ 20.06 Global Days 090 | |

| 21346 | Open treatment of nasomaxillary complex fracture (LeFort II type); with wiring and/or local fixation | C ▢ P0 |
| | 🔹 24.06 ⚲ 24.06 Global Days 090 | |

| 21347 | requiring multiple open approaches | C 80 ▢ P0 |
| | 🔹 27.91 ⚲ 27.91 Global Days 090 | |

| 21348 | with bone grafting (includes obtaining graft) | C 80 ▢ P0 |
| | 🔹 29.83 ⚲ 29.83 Global Days 090 | |

| 21355 | Percutaneous treatment of fracture of malar area, including zygomatic arch and malar tripod, with manipulation | A2 T 80 ▢ |
| | 🔹 8.15 ⚲ 10.83 Global Days 010 | |

| 21356 | Open treatment of depressed zygomatic arch fracture (eg, Gillies approach) | A2 T 80 ▢ |
| | 🔹 9.39 ⚲ 12.16 Global Days 010 | |

| 21360 | Open treatment of depressed malar fracture, including zygomatic arch and malar tripod | G2 T 80 ▢ |
| | 🔹 13.38 ⚲ 13.38 Global Days 090 | |

| 21365 | Open treatment of complicated (eg, comminuted or involving cranial nerve foramina) fracture(s) of malar area, including zygomatic arch and malar tripod; with internal fixation and multiple surgical approaches | T 80 ▢ |
| | 🔹 28.05 ⚲ 28.05 Global Days 090 | |

| 21366 | with bone grafting (includes obtaining graft) | C 80 ▢ |
| | 🔹 31.37 ⚲ 31.37 Global Days 090 | |

| 21385 | Open treatment of orbital floor blowout fracture; transantral approach (Caldwell-Luc type operation) | T 80 ▢ |
| | 🔹 18.05 ⚲ 18.05 Global Days 090 | |

21386   periorbital approach   [T] [80] [⬜]
    💰 16.85   🔧 16.85 Global Days 090

21387   combined approach   [T] [80] [⬜]
    💰 18.85   🔧 18.85 Global Days 090

21390   periorbital approach, with alloplastic or other
    implant   [62] [T] [80] [⬜]
    💰 19.42   🔧 19.42 Global Days 090

21395   periorbital approach with bone graft (includes
    obtaining graft)   [C] [80] [⬜]
    💰 24.58   🔧 24.58 Global Days 090

21400   Closed treatment of fracture of orbit, except blowout;
    without manipulation   [A2] [T] [80] [⬜]
    💰 3.60   🔧 4.37 Global Days 090

21401   with manipulation   [A2] [T] [80] [⬜]
    💰 7.40   🔧 11.65 Global Days 090

21406   Open treatment of fracture of orbit, except blowout;
    without implant   [62] [T] [80] [⬜]
    💰 13.64   🔧 13.64 Global Days 090

21407   with implant   [62] [T] [80] [⬜]
    💰 16.17   🔧 16.17 Global Days 090

21408   with bone grafting (includes obtaining graft)   [T] [80] [⬜]
    💰 22.28   🔧 22.28 Global Days 090

21421   Closed treatment of palatal or maxillary fracture (LeFort
    I type), with interdental wire fixation or fixation of
    denture or splint   [A2] [T] [80] [⬜]
    💰 15.45   🔧 18.04 Global Days 090

21422   Open treatment of palatal or maxillary fracture (LeFort
    I type);   [C] [80] [⬜] [P0]
    💰 16.95   🔧 16.95 Global Days 090

21423   complicated (comminuted or involving cranial nerve
    foramina), multiple approaches   [C] [80] [⬜] [P0]
    💰 20.16   🔧 20.16 Global Days 090

21431   Closed treatment of craniofacial separation (LeFort III
    type) using interdental wire fixation of denture or
    splint   [C] [80] [⬜]
    💰 18.43   🔧 18.43 Global Days 090

21432   Open treatment of craniofacial separation (LeFort III
    type); with wiring and/or internal fixation   [C] [80] [⬜] [P0]
    💰 16.84   🔧 16.84 Global Days 090

21433   complicated (eg, comminuted or involving cranial
    nerve foramina), multiple surgical
    approaches   [C] [80] [⬜] [P0]
    💰 43.41   🔧 43.41 Global Days 090

21435   complicated, utilizing internal and/or external fixation
    techniques (eg, head cap, halo device, and/or
    intermaxillary fixation)   [C] [80] [⬜] [P0]
    EXCLUDES   *removal of internal or external fixation (20670)*
    💰 34.18   🔧 34.18 Global Days 090

21436   complicated, multiple surgical approaches, internal
    fixation, with bone grafting (includes obtaining
    graft)   [C] [80] [⬜] [P0]
    💰 50.34   🔧 50.34 Global Days 090

21440   Closed treatment of mandibular or maxillary alveolar
    ridge fracture (separate procedure)   [P3] [T] [80] [⬜]
    💰 10.89   🔧 13.08 Global Days 090

21445   Open treatment of mandibular or maxillary alveolar ridge
    fracture (separate procedure)   [A2] [T] [80] [⬜]
    💰 15.44   🔧 18.63 Global Days 090

21450   Closed treatment of mandibular fracture; without
    manipulation   [A2] [T] [80] [⬜]
    💰 11.39   🔧 13.60 Global Days 090

21451   with manipulation   [A2] [T] [80] [⬜]
    💰 15.37   🔧 18.01 Global Days 090

In 21452, external fixation is necessary

Comminuted fractures

Metal or acrylic bar

Rods and pins placed in drilled holes

21452   Percutaneous treatment of mandibular fracture, with
    external fixation   [A2] [T] [80] [⬜]
    💰 8.24   🔧 14.76 Global Days 090

21453   Closed treatment of mandibular fracture with interdental
    fixation   [A2] [T] [80] [⬜]
    💰 18.54   🔧 20.85 Global Days 090
    AMA: 2008, Jan, 10-25; 2007, Dec, 7-8

21454   Open treatment of mandibular fracture with external
    fixation   [A2] [T] [80] [⬜] [P0]
    💰 13.96   🔧 13.96 Global Days 090

21461   Open treatment of mandibular fracture; without
    interdental fixation   [A2] [T] [⬜] [P0]
    💰 22.91   🔧 47.09 Global Days 090

21462   with interdental fixation   [A2] [T] [80] [⬜] [P0]
    💰 25.43   🔧 50.95 Global Days 090

21465   Open treatment of mandibular condylar
    fracture   [A2] [T] [80] [⬜] [P0]
    💰 23.17   🔧 23.17 Global Days 090

21470   Open treatment of complicated mandibular fracture by
    multiple surgical approaches including internal fixation,
    interdental fixation, and/or wiring of dentures or
    splints   [T] [80] [⬜] [P0]
    💰 30.23   🔧 30.23 Global Days 090
    AMA: 2008, Jan, 10-25; 2007, Jan, 13-27; 2007, Jan, 13-27; 2007,
    January, 13-27

21480   Closed treatment of temporomandibular dislocation;
    initial or subsequent   [A2] [T] [50] [⬜]
    💰 0.85   🔧 2.24 Global Days 000

21485   complicated (eg, recurrent requiring intermaxillary
    fixation or splinting), initial or
    subsequent   [A2] [T] [80] [50] [⬜]
    💰 13.77   🔧 16.09 Global Days 090

21490   Open treatment of temporomandibular
    dislocation   [A2] [T] [80] [50] [⬜]
    EXCLUDES   *interdental wiring (21497)*
    💰 23.64   🔧 23.64 Global Days 090

21495   Open treatment of hyoid fracture   [62] [T] [80] [⬜]
    EXCLUDES   *closed treatment of larynx fracture*
        (99201-99499)
        laryngoplasty with fracture repair (31584)
    💰 16.94   🔧 16.94 Global Days 090

21497   Interdental wiring, for condition other than
    fracture   [A2] [T] [80] [⬜]
    💰 13.92   🔧 16.25 Global Days 090
    AMA: 2008, Jan, 10-25; 2007, Jan, 13-27; 2007, Jan, 13-27; 2007,
    January, 13-27

21499 Unlisted Head Procedures: Musculoskeletal

21499   Unlisted musculoskeletal procedure, head   T 80

EXCLUDES   *unlisted procedures of craniofacial or maxillofacial areas*

🔧 0.00   ✂ 0.00   **Global Days YYY**

21501-21510 Surgical Incision for Drainage: Chest and Soft Tissues of Neck

EXCLUDES   *biopsy of the flank or back (21920-21925)*
simple incision and drainage of abscess or hematoma (10060, 10140)
tumor removal of flank or back (21930-21935)

21501   Incision and drainage, deep abscess or hematoma, soft tissues of neck or thorax;   A2 T

        EXCLUDES   *deep incision and drainage of posterior spine (22010-22015)*

    🔧 7.92   ✂ 10.80   **Global Days 090**

21502   with partial rib ostectomy   A2 T 80

    🔧 13.30   ✂ 13.30   **Global Days 090**

21510   Incision, deep, with opening of bone cortex (eg, for osteomyelitis or bone abscess), thorax   C 80

    🔧 11.75   ✂ 11.75   **Global Days 090**

21550-21632 Resection Areas of Chest and Soft Tissues of Neck

EXCLUDES   *biopsy of bone (20220-20251)*
biopsy of flank or back (21920-21925)
tumor removal of flank or back (21930, 21935)

21550   Biopsy, soft tissue of neck or thorax   G2 T

        EXCLUDES   *soft tissue needle biopsy (20206)*

    🔧 4.01   ✂ 6.32   **Global Days 010**

21555   Excision tumor, soft tissue of neck or thorax; subcutaneous   A2 T

    🔧 8.38   ✂ 10.69   **Global Days 090**

    AMA: 2008, Jan, 10-25; 2007, Jan, 13-27; 2007, Jan, 13-27; 2007, January, 13-27

21556   deep, subfascial, intramuscular   A2 T

    🔧 10.46   ✂ 10.46   **Global Days 090**

21557   Radical resection of tumor (eg, malignant neoplasm), soft tissue of neck or thorax   G2 T 80

    🔧 14.84   ✂ 14.84   **Global Days 090**

21600   Excision of rib, partial   A2 T 80

        EXCLUDES   *extensive debridement (11040-11044)*
                   extensive tumor removal (19260)

    🔧 14.05   ✂ 14.05   **Global Days 090**

21610   Costotransversectomy (separate procedure)   A2 T 80

    🔧 27.67   ✂ 27.67   **Global Days 090**

21615   Excision first and/or cervical rib;   C 80 50

    🔧 17.31   ✂ 17.31   **Global Days 090**

21616   with sympathectomy   C 80 50

    🔧 22.12   ✂ 22.12   **Global Days 090**

21620   Ostectomy of sternum, partial   C 80

    🔧 13.36   ✂ 13.36   **Global Days 090**

21627   Sternal debridement   C 80 P0

        EXCLUDES   *sternotomy closure (21750)*

    🔧 14.04   ✂ 14.04   **Global Days 090**

21630   Radical resection of sternum;   C 80

    🔧 32.71   ✂ 32.71   **Global Days 090**

21632   with mediastinal lymphadenectomy   C 80 P0

    🔧 32.37   ✂ 32.37   **Global Days 090**

21685-21750 Repair/Reconstruction Chest and Soft Tissues Neck

EXCLUDES   *biopsy of flank or back (21920-21925)*
repair of simple wounds (12001-12007)
tumor removal of flank or back (21930, 21935)

21685   Hyoid myotomy and suspension   G2 T 80

    🔧 25.21   ✂ 25.21   **Global Days 090**

    AMA: 2008, Jan, 10-25; 2007, Jan, 13-27; 2007, Jan, 13-27; 2007, January, 13-27; 2004, Aug, 11; 2004, August, 11; 2004, Aug, 11

21700   Division of scalenus anticus; without resection of cervical rib   A2 T 80

    🔧 10.67   ✂ 10.67   **Global Days 090**

21705   with resection of cervical rib   C 80

    🔧 16.70   ✂ 16.70   **Global Days 090**

21720   Division of sternocleidomastoid for torticollis, open operation; without cast application   A2 T 80

        EXCLUDES   *transection of spinal accessory and cervical nerves (63191, 64722)*

    🔧 10.50   ✂ 10.50   **Global Days 090**

21725   with cast application   A2 T 80

        EXCLUDES   *transection of spinal accessory and cervical nerves (63191, 64722)*

    🔧 13.65   ✂ 13.65   **Global Days 090**

21740   Reconstructive repair of pectus excavatum or carinatum; open   C 80 P0

    🔧 28.19   ✂ 28.19   **Global Days 090**

21742   minimally invasive approach (Nuss procedure), without thoracoscopy   T 80

    🔧 0.00   ✂ 0.00   **Global Days 090**

21743   minimally invasive approach (Nuss procedure), with thoracoscopy   T 80

    🔧 0.00   ✂ 0.00   **Global Days 090**

21750   Closure of median sternotomy separation with or without debridement (separate procedure)   C 80 P0

    🔧 18.72   ✂ 18.72   **Global Days 090**

21800-21899 Fracture Care: Ribs and Sternum

21800   Closed treatment of rib fracture, uncomplicated, each   A2 T

    🔧 2.45   ✂ 2.41   **Global Days 090**

21805   Open treatment of rib fracture without fixation, each   A2 T 80 P0

    🔧 6.50   ✂ 6.50   **Global Days 090**

21810   Treatment of rib fracture requiring external fixation (flail chest)   C 80

    🔧 12.76   ✂ 12.76   **Global Days 090**

21820   Closed treatment of sternum fracture   A2 T

    🔧 3.27   ✂ 3.23   **Global Days 090**

21825   Open treatment of sternum fracture with or without skeletal fixation   C 80 P0

        EXCLUDES   *treatment of sternoclavicular dislocation (23520-23532)*

    🔧 14.51   ✂ 14.51   **Global Days 090**

21899   Unlisted procedure, neck or thorax   T 80

    🔧 0.00   ✂ 0.00   **Global Days YYY**

● New Code   ▲ Revised Code   Ⓜ Maternity Edit   ⚠ Age Edit   A-V OPPS Status Indicator   🔧 Facility RVU   ✂ Non-Facility RVU
🖵 CCI Comprehensive Code   50 Bilateral Procedure   + Add-on Indicator   🔬 Laboratory crosswalk   🔲 Radiology crosswalk

© 2008 Ingenix(Blue Ink)   CPT only © 2008 American Medical Association. All Rights Reserved. (Black Ink)   Medicare (Red Ink)   63

21920-21935 Biopsy/Tumor Resection: Soft Tissue of Back and Flank

21920   Biopsy, soft tissue of back or flank; superficial   P3 T ▭
     EXCLUDES   *needle biopsy (20206)*
     🔲 4.00   🔲 6.30   Global Days 010

21925   deep   A2 T ▭
     EXCLUDES   *needle biopsy (20206)*
     🔲 8.52   🔲 10.47   Global Days 090

21930   Excision, tumor, soft tissue of back or flank   A2 T ▭
     🔲 9.44   🔲 11.68   Global Days 090
     AMA: 2008, Jan, 10-25; 2007, Jan, 13-27; 2007, Jan, 13-27; 2007, January, 13-27; 2006, Aug, 12-14; 2006, August, 12-14; 2006, Aug, 12-14

21935   Radical resection of tumor (eg, malignant neoplasm), soft tissue of back or flank   A2 T ▭
     🔲 29.88   🔲 29.88   Global Days 090

22010-22015 Incision for Drainage of Deep Spinal Abscess

EXCLUDES   *incision and drainage of hematoma (10060, 10140)*
     injection:
        chemonucleolysis (62292)
        discography (62290-62291)
        facet joint (64470-64476, 64622-64627)
        myelography (62284)
     needle/trocar biopsy (20220-20225)

22010   Incision and drainage, open, of deep abscess (subfascial), posterior spine; cervical, thoracic, or cervicothoracic   C 80
     🔲 23.00   🔲 23.00   Global Days 090

22015   lumbar, sacral, or lumbosacral   C
     Do not report with (10180, 22010, 22850, 22852)
     🔲 22.87   🔲 22.87   Global Days 090

22100-22103 Partial Resection Vertebral Component

EXCLUDES   *back or flank biopsy (21920-21925)*
     bone biopsy (20220-20251)
     bone grafting procedures (20930-20938)
     injection:
        chemonucleolysis (62292)
        discography (62290-62291)
        facet joint (64470-64476, 64622-64627)
        myelography (62284)
     removal of tumor flank or back (21930)
     soft tissue needle biopsy (20206)

22100   Partial excision of posterior vertebral component (eg, spinous process, lamina or facet) for intrinsic bony lesion, single vertebral segment; cervical   T 80 ▭
     🔲 20.97   🔲 20.97   Global Days 090

22101   thoracic   T 80 ▭
     🔲 20.84   🔲 20.84   Global Days 090

22102   lumbar   62 T 80 ▭
     EXCLUDES   *insertion of posterior spinous process distraction devices (0171T-0172T)*
     🔲 20.75   🔲 20.75   Global Days 090

+ **22103**   each additional segment (List separately in addition to code for primary procedure)   62 T 80 ▭
     Code first 22100-22102
     🔲 3.81   🔲 3.81   Global Days ZZZ

22110-22116 Partial Resection Vertebral Component without Decompression

EXCLUDES   *back or flank biopsy (21920-21925)*
     bone biopsy (20220-20251)
     bone grafting procedures (20930-20938)
     harvest bone graft (20931, 20938)
     injection:
        chemonucleolysis (62292)
        discography (62290-62291)
        facet joint (64470-64476, 64622-64627)
        myelography (62284)
     osteotomy (22210-22226)
     removal of tumor flank or back (21930)
     restoration after vertebral body resection (22585, 63082, or 63086, or 63088, or 63091)
     spinal restoration with graft:
        cervical (20931, or 20938, 22554, 63081)
        lumbar (20931, or 20938, 22558, 63087, or 63090)
        thoracic (20931, or 20938, 22556, 63085, or 63087)
     spinal restoration with prosthesis:
        cervical (20931, or 20938, 22554, 22851, 63081)
        lumbar (20931, or 20938, 22558, 22851, 63087, or 63090)
        thoracic (20931, or 20938, 22556, 22851, 63085, or 63087)
     vertebral corpectomy (63081-63091)

22110   Partial excision of vertebral body, for intrinsic bony lesion, without decompression of spinal cord or nerve root(s), single vertebral segment; cervical   C 80 ▭
     🔲 26.08   🔲 26.08   Global Days 090

22112   thoracic   C 80 ▭
     🔲 25.19   🔲 25.19   Global Days 090

22114   lumbar   C 80 ▭
     🔲 25.87   🔲 25.87   Global Days 090

+ **22116**   each additional vertebral segment (List separately in addition to code for primary procedure)   C 80 ▭
     Code first 22110-22114
     🔲 3.81   🔲 3.81   Global Days ZZZ

22206-22216 Spinal Osteotomy: Posterior/Posterolateral Approach

CMS 100-4,12,40.8   *Co-surgery and team surgery*
EXCLUDES   *decompression of the spinal cord and/or nerve roots (63001-63308)*
     injection:
        chemonucleolysis (62292)
        discography (62290-62292)
        facet joint (64470-64476, 64622-64627)
        myelography (62284)
     repair of vertebral fracture by the anterior approach, see appropriate arthrodesis, bone graft, instrumentation codes, and (63081-63091)

Code also arthrodesis (22590-22632)

Code also bone grafting procedures (20930-20938)

Code also spinal instrumentation (22840-22855)

22206   Osteotomy of spine, posterior or posterolateral approach, 3 columns, 1 vertebral segment (eg, pedicle/vertebral body subtraction); thoracic   C 80
     Do not report with (22207)
     Do not report with the following codes if performed at same level (22210-22226, 22830, 63001-63048, 63055-63066, 63075-63091, 63101-63103)
     🔲 61.87   🔲 61.87   Global Days 090
     AMA: 2008, Feb, 8-9; 2007, Dec, 1-2

22207   lumbar   C 80

Do not report with (22206)

Do not report with the following codes if performed at the same level (22210-22226, 22830, 63001-63048, 63055-63066, 63075-63091, 63101-63103)

61.04   61.04   Global Days 090
AMA: 2008, Feb, 8-9; 2007, Dec, 1-2

+   22208   **each additional vertebral segment (List separately in addition to code for primary procedure)**   C 80

Code first (22206, or 22207)

Do not report with the following codes if performed at the same level (22210-22226, 22830, 63001-63048, 63055-63066, 63075-63091, 63101-63103)

15.72   15.72   Global Days ZZZ
AMA: 2008, Feb, 8-9; 2007, Dec, 1-2

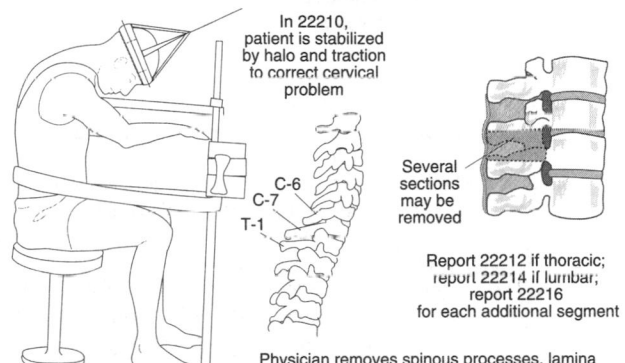

In 22210, patient is stabilized by halo and traction to correct cervical problem

C-6
C-7
T-1

Several sections may be removed

Report 22212 if thoracic;
report 22214 if lumbar;
report 22216 for each additional segment

Physician removes spinous processes, lamina

22210   **Osteotomy of spine, posterior or posterolateral approach, 1 vertebral segment; cervical**   C 80

45.79   45.79   Global Days 090
AMA: 2007, Dec, 1-2

22212   thoracic   C 80

37.68   37.68   Global Days 090
AMA: 2007, Dec, 1-2

22214   lumbar   C 80

37.91   37.91   Global Days 090
AMA: 2007, Dec, 1-2

+   22216   **each additional vertebral segment (List separately in addition to primary procedure)**   C 80

Code first 22210-22214

9.98   9.98   Global Days ZZZ
AMA: 2007, Dec, 1-2

22220-22226 Spinal Osteotomy: Anterior Approach

CMS *100-4,12,40.8   Co-surgery and team surgery*

EXCLUDES   *corpectomy (63081-63091)*
decompression of the spinal cord and/or nerve roots (63001-63308)
injection:
   chemonucleolysis (62292)
   discography (62290-62291)
   facet joint (64470-64476, 64622-64627)
   myelography (62284)
needle/trocar biopsy (20220-20225)
repair of vertebral fracture by the anterior approach, see appropriate arthrodesis, bone graft, instrumentation codes, and (63081-63091)

Code also arthrodesis (22590-22632)
Code also spinal instrumentation (22840-22855)
Code also bone grafting procedures (20930-20938)

22220   **Osteotomy of spine, including discectomy, anterior approach, single vertebral segment; cervical**   C 80

41.28   41.28   Global Days 090

22222   thoracic   T 80

37.44   37.44   Global Days 090

22224   lumbar   C 80

40.58   40.58   Global Days 090

+   22226   **each additional vertebral segment (List separately in addition to code for primary procedure)**   C 80

Code first 22220-22224

9.94   9.94   Global Days ZZZ

22305-22315 Closed Treatment Vertebral Fractures

EXCLUDES   *injection*
   chemonucleolysis (62292)
   discography (62290-62291)
   facet joint (64470-64476, 64622-64627)
   myelography (62284)

22305   **Closed treatment of vertebral process fracture(s)**   A2 T P0

4.32   4.67   Global Days 090

22310   **Closed treatment of vertebral body fracture(s), without manipulation, requiring and including casting or bracing**   A2 T P0

6.71   7.18   Global Days 090
AMA: 2008, Jan, 10-25; 2007, Jan, 13-27; 2007, Jan, 13-27; 2007, January, 13-27; 2006, Jun, 16-17; 2006, June, 16-17; 2006, Jun, 16-17

22315   **Closed treatment of vertebral fracture(s) and/or dislocation(s) requiring casting or bracing, with and including casting and/or bracing, with or without anesthesia, by manipulation or traction**   A2 T P0

EXCLUDES   *spinal manipulation (97140)*

19.24   21.56   Global Days 090

● New Code   ▲ Revised Code   M Maternity Edit   A Age Edit   A-Y OPPS Status Indicator   Facility RVU   Non-Facility RVU
CCI Comprehensive Code   50 Bilateral Procedure   + Add-on Indicator   Laboratory crosswalk   Radiology crosswalk

© 2008 Ingenix *(Blue Ink)*   CPT only © 2008 American Medical Association. All Rights Reserved. (Black Ink)   Medicare (Red Ink)   **65**

Musculoskeletal System

22318 — 22527

22318-22319 Open Treatment Odontoid Fracture: Anterior Approach

EXCLUDES *injection:*
>   *chemonucleolysis (62292)*
>   *discography (62290-62291)*
>   *facet joint (64470-64476, 64622-64627)*
>   *myelography (62284)*
>   *needle/trocar biopsy (20220-20225)*

Code also arthrodesis (22590-22632)
Code also bone grafting procedures (20930-20938)
Code also spinal instrumentation (22840-22855)

22318 Open treatment and/or reduction of odontoid fracture(s) and or dislocation(s) (including os odontoideum), anterior approach, including placement of internal fixation; without grafting `C` `80` `▭` `P0`
>   🔲 41.31 ⚕ 41.31 Global Days 090

22319 with grafting `C` `80` `▭` `P0`
>   🔲 45.46 ⚕ 45.46 Global Days 090

22325-22328 Open Treatment Vertebral Fractures: Posterior Approach

EXCLUDES *corpectomy (63081-63091)*
> *injection:*
>   *chemonucleolysis (62292)*
>   *discography (62290-62291)*
>   *facet joint (64470-64476, 64622-64627)*
>   *myelography (62284)*
> *needle/trocar biopsy (20220-20225)*
> *spine decompression (63001-63091)*
> *vertebral fracture care frontal approach (63081-63091)*

Code also arthrodesis (22548-22632)
Code also bone grafting procedure (20930-20938)
Code also spinal instrumentation (22840-22855)

22325 Open treatment and/or reduction of vertebral fracture(s) and/or dislocation(s), posterior approach, 1 fractured vertebra or dislocated segment; lumbar `C` `80` `▭` `P0`
>   🔲 35.94 ⚕ 35.94 Global Days 090

22326 cervical `C` `80` `▭` `P0`
>   🔲 37.58 ⚕ 37.58 Global Days 090

22327 thoracic `C` `80` `▭` `P0`
>   🔲 37.16 ⚕ 37.16 Global Days 090

+ 22328 each additional fractured vertebra or dislocated segment (List separately in addition to code for primary procedure) `C` `80` `▭`
>   Code first 22325-22327
>   🔲 7.51 ⚕ 7.51 Global Days ZZZ

22505 Spinal Manipulation with Anesthesia

EXCLUDES *manipulation not requiring anesthesia (97140)*

22505 Manipulation of spine requiring anesthesia, any region `A2` `T` `▭`
>   🔲 3.19 ⚕ 3.19 Global Days 010
>   **AMA:** 2008, Jan, 10-25; 2007, Jan, 13-27; 2007, Jan, 13-27; 2007, January, 13-27

22520-22525 Percutaneous Vertebroplasty

EXCLUDES *needle/trocar biopsy (20220-20225)*
> *injection:*
>   *chemonucleolysis (62292)*
>   *discography (62290-62291)*
>   *facet joint (64470-64476, 64622-64627)*
>   *myelography (62284)*

>   🔀 72291-72292

22520 Percutaneous vertebroplasty, 1 vertebral body, unilateral or bilateral injection; thoracic `A2` `T` `▭` `P0`
>   🔲 15.37 ⚕ 58.00 Global Days 010

22521 lumbar `A2` `T` `▭` `P0`
>   🔲 14.48 ⚕ 56.47 Global Days 010

+ 22522 each additional thoracic or lumbar vertebral body (List separately in addition to code for primary procedure) `A2` `T` `▭`
>   Code first 22520-22521
>   🔲 6.79 ⚕ 6.79 Global Days ZZZ

22523 Percutaneous vertebral augmentation, including cavity creation (fracture reduction and bone biopsy included when performed) using mechanical device, 1 vertebral body, unilateral or bilateral cannulation (eg, kyphoplasty); thoracic `62` `T` `P0`
>   🔲 16.07 ⚕ 16.07 Global Days 010

22524 lumbar `62` `T` `P0`
>   🔲 15.38 ⚕ 15.38 Global Days 010

+ 22525 each additional thoracic or lumbar vertebral body (List separately in addition to code for primary procedure) `62` `T`
>   Code first 22523-22524
>   Do not report with augmentation at the same level (22523-22525)
>   🔲 7.21 ⚕ 7.21 Global Days ZZZ

22526-22527 Percutaneous Annuloplasty

EXCLUDES *needle/trocar biopsy (20220-20225)*
> *injection:*
>   *chemonucleolysis (62292)*
>   *discography (62290-62291)*
>   *facet joint (64470-64476, 64622-64627)*
>   *myelography (62284)*
> *procedure performed by other methods (0062T-0063T)*

Do not report with (77002, 77003)

⊙ **22526** Percutaneous intradiscal electrothermal annuloplasty, unilateral or bilateral including fluoroscopic guidance; single level `E`
>   **INCLUDES** contrast injection during fluoroscopic guidance/localization (77003)
>   🔲 9.14 ⚕ 48.80 Global Days 010
>   **AMA:** 2008, Jan, 10-25; 2007, Mar, 7-8; 2007, Mar, 7-8; 2007, March, 7-8

+ ⊙ 22527 one or more additional levels (List separately in addition to code for primary procedure) `E`
>   **INCLUDES** contrast injection during fluoroscopic guidance/localization (77003)
>   🔲 4.18 ⚕ 37.79 Global Days ZZZ
>   **AMA:** 2007, Mar, 7-8; 2007, Mar, 7-8; 2007, March, 7-8

`26`/`TC` Professional/Technical Component Only   `80`/`80` Assist-at-Surgery Allowed/With Documentation   `Unlisted`   `Not Covered`
AMA: CPT Assistant References   `A2`-`Z3` ASC Payment Indicator   ♂ Male Only   ♀ Female Only   ⊘ Modifier 51 Exempt   `P0` PQRI

66   CPT only © 2008 American Medical Association. All Rights Reserved. (Black Ink)   Medicare (Red Ink)   © 2008 Ingenix *(Blue Ink)*

22532-22534 Spinal Fusion: Lateral Extracavitary Approach

CMS 100-3,150.2   Osteogenic Stimulation

EXCLUDES   corpectomy (63101-63103)
exploration of spinal fusion (22830)
fracture care (22305-22328)
injection:
   chemonucleolysis (62292)
   discography (62290-62291)
   facet joint (64470-64476, 64622-64627)
   myelography (62284)
laminectomy (63001-63017)
needle/trocar biopsy (20220-20225)
osteotomy (22206)

Code also bone grafting procedures (20930-20938)

Code also spinal instrumentation (22840-22855)

22532 Arthrodesis, lateral extracavitary technique, including minimal discectomy to prepare interspace (other than for decompression); thoracic   © 80 ▭
   44.57   44.57   Global Days 090

22533 lumbar   © 80 ▭
   41.69   41.69   Global Days 090

+ 22534 thoracic or lumbar, each additional vertebral segment (List separately in addition to code for primary procedure)   © 80 ▭
   Code first 22532-22533
   9.84   9.84   Global Days ZZZ

22548-22632 Spinal Fusion: Anterior and Posterior Approach

CMS 100-3,150.2   Osteogenic Stimulation

EXCLUDES   corpectomy (63081-63091)
exploration of spinal fusion (22830)
fracture care (22305-22328)
injection:
   chemonucleolysis (62292)
   discography (62290-62291)
   facet joint (64470-64476, 64622-64627)
   myelography (62284)
laminectomy (63001-63017)
needle/trocar biopsy (20220-20225)
osteotomy (22206)

Code also bone grafting procedures (20930-20938)

Code also spinal instrumentation (22840-22855)

22548 Arthrodesis, anterior transoral or extraoral technique, clivus-C1-C2 (atlas-axis), with or without excision of odontoid process   © 80 ▭
      EXCLUDES   laminectomy or laminotomy with disc removal (63020-63042)
   47.78   47.78   Global Days 090
   AMA: 2008, Jan, 10-25; 2007, Jan, 13-27; 2007, Jan, 13-27; 2007, January, 13-27

22554 Arthrodesis, anterior interbody technique, including minimal discectomy to prepare interspace (other than for decompression); cervical below C2   © 80 ▭ PQ
   33.26   33.26   Global Days 090
   AMA: 2008, Jan, 10-25; 2007, Jan, 13-27; 2007, Jan, 13-27; 2007, January, 13-27

22556 thoracic   © 80 ▭
   42.58   42.58   Global Days 090
   AMA: 2008, Jan, 10-25; 2007, Jan, 13-27; 2007, Jan, 13-27; 2007, January, 13-27

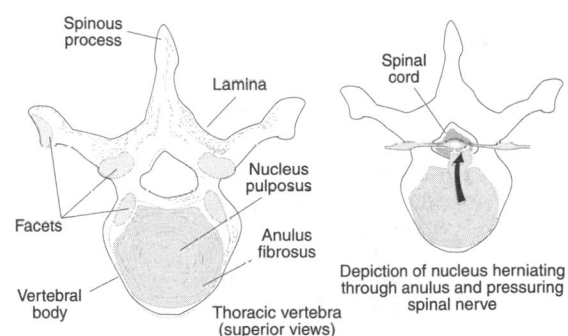

Intervertebral disc displacement and prolapse are major causes of disability among working people. When a disc prolapses, nuclear material bursts through the anulus fibrosus damaging ligaments, nerve roots, and other structures. The herniated matter usually fibroses and shrinks over time

22558 lumbar   © 80 ▭ PQ
   38.85   38.85   Global Days 090
   AMA: 2008, Apr, -11; 2008, Apr, -11; 2008, Apr, -11; 2008, Jan, 10-25; 2007, Jan, 13-27; 2007, January, 13-27; 2007, June, 1-3; 2007, Jan, 13-27; 2007, Jun, 1-3; 2007, Jun, 1-3

+ 22585 each additional interspace (List separately in addition to code for primary procedure)   © 80 ▭
   Code first 22554-22558
   9.12   9.12   Global Days ZZZ
   AMA: 2008, Apr, -11; 2008, Apr, -11; 2008, Apr, -11; 2008, Jan, 10-25; 2007, Jan, 13-27; 2007, January, 13-27; 2007, June, 1-3; 2007, Jan, 13-27; 2007, Jun, 1-3; 2007, Jun, 1-3

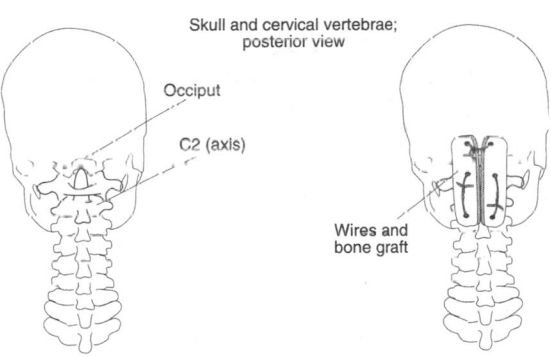

In 22590, the physician fuses skull to C2 (axis) to stabilize cervical vertebrae; anchor holes are drilled in the occiput of the skull

22590 Arthrodesis, posterior technique, craniocervical (occiput-C2)   © 80 ▭
   39.75   39.75   Global Days 090

22595 Arthrodesis, posterior technique, atlas-axis (C1-C2)   © 80 ▭
   37.70   37.70   Global Days 090

22600 Arthrodesis, posterior or posterolateral technique, single level; cervical below C2 segment   © 80 ▭ PQ
   32.31   32.31   Global Days 090

22610 thoracic (with or without lateral transverse technique)   © 80 ▭
   31.84   31.84   Global Days 090

● New Code   ▲ Revised Code   Ⓜ Maternity Edit   Ⓐ Age Edit   A-Y OPPS Status Indicator   Facility RVU   Non-Facility RVU
▭ CCI Comprehensive Code   50 Bilateral Procedure   + Add-on Indicator   Laboratory crosswalk   Radiology crosswalk

22612   **lumbar (with or without lateral transverse technique)** 🔲 T 80 🔲 P0
🔲 41.17   ✂ 41.17 Global Days 090
AMA: 2008, Apr, -11; 2008, Apr, -11; 2008, Jan, 10-25; 2008, Apr, -11; 2008, Jul, 7-8&15; 2007, Jan, 13-27; 2007, Jan, 13-27; 2007, January, 13-27

+ 22614   **each additional vertebral segment (List separately in addition to code for primary procedure)** 🔲 T 80 🔲
Code first 22600-22612
🔲 10.62   ✂ 10.62 Global Days ZZZ

22630   **Arthrodesis, posterior interbody technique, including laminectomy and/or discectomy to prepare interspace (other than for decompression), single interspace; lumbar** 🔲 C 80 🔲 P0
🔲 39.74   ✂ 39.74 Global Days 090
AMA: 2008, Jan, 10-25; 2007, Jan, 13-27; 2007, Jan, 13-27; 2007, January, 13-27

+ 22632   **each additional interspace (List separately in addition to code for primary procedure)** 🔲 C 80 🔲
Code first 22630
🔲 8.64   ✂ 8.64 Global Days ZZZ

22800-22819 Procedures to Correct Anomalous Spinal Vertebrae

Code also bone grafting procedures (20930-20938)

Code also spinal instrumentation (22840-22855)

22800   **Arthrodesis, posterior, for spinal deformity, with or without cast; up to 6 vertebral segments** 🔲 C 80 🔲 P0
🔲 34.98   ✂ 34.98 Global Days 090

22802   **7 to 12 vertebral segments** 🔲 C 80 🔲 P0
🔲 55.66   ✂ 55.66 Global Days 090
AMA: 2008, Jan, 10-25; 2007, Jan, 13-27; 2007, Jan, 13-27; 2007, January, 13-27

22804   **13 or more vertebral segments** 🔲 C 80 🔲 P0
🔲 64.25   ✂ 64.25 Global Days 090

22808   **Arthrodesis, anterior, for spinal deformity, with or without cast; 2 to 3 vertebral segments** 🔲 C 80 🔲
INCLUDES   Smith-Robinson arthrodesis
🔲 47.25   ✂ 47.25 Global Days 090

22810   **4 to 7 vertebral segments** 🔲 C 80 🔲
🔲 52.57   ✂ 52.57 Global Days 090
AMA: 2008, Jan, 10-25; 2007, Jan, 13-27; 2007, Jan, 13-27; 2007, January, 13-27

22812   **8 or more vertebral segments** 🔲 C 80 🔲
🔲 57.43   ✂ 57.43 Global Days 090

22818   **Kyphectomy, circumferential exposure of spine and resection of vertebral segment(s) (including body and posterior elements); single or 2 segments** 🔲 C 80 🔲
EXCLUDES   arthrodesis (22800-22804)
🔲 58.25   ✂ 58.25 Global Days 090

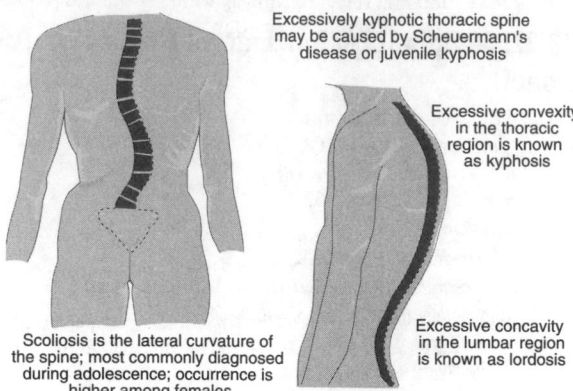

Excessively kyphotic thoracic spine may be caused by Scheuermann's disease or juvenile kyphosis

Excessive convexity in the thoracic region is known as kyphosis

Scoliosis is the lateral curvature of the spine; most commonly diagnosed during adolescence; occurrence is higher among females

Excessive concavity in the lumbar region is known as lordosis

22819   **3 or more segments** 🔲 C 80 🔲
EXCLUDES   arthrodesis (22800-22804)
🔲 67.18   ✂ 67.18 Global Days 090

22830 Surgical Exploration Previous Spinal Fusion

CMS *100-3,150.2   Osteogenic Stimulation*
EXCLUDES   *arthrodesis (22532-22819)*
bone grafting procedures (20930-20938)
spinal decompression (63001-63103)

Code also spinal instrumentation (22840-22855)

22830   **Exploration of spinal fusion** 🔲 C 80 🔲
Do not report with (22850, 22852, 22855)
🔲 20.88   ✂ 20.88 Global Days 090
AMA: 2008, Jan, 10-25; 2007, Jan, 13-27; 2007, Jan, 13-27; 2007, January, 13-27

22840-22855 Spinal Instrumentation: Segmental/Non-segmental

EXCLUDES   *arthrodesis (22532-22534, 22548-22812)*
bone grafting procedures (20930-20938)
exploration of spinal fusion (22830)
fracture treatment (22325-22328)

+ 22840   **Posterior non-segmental instrumentation (eg, Harrington rod technique, pedicle fixation across 1 interspace, atlantoaxial transarticular screw fixation, sublaminar wiring at C1, facet screw fixation) (List separately in addition to code for primary procedure)** 🔲 C 80 🔲
EXCLUDES   *insertion of posterior spinous process distraction devices (0171T-0172T)*
Code first (22100-22102, 22110-22114, 22206-22207, 22210-22214, 22220-22224, 22305-22327, 22532-22533, 22548-22558, 22590-22612, 22630, 22800-22812, 63001-63030, 63040-63042, 63045-63047, 63050-63056, 63064, 63075, 63077, 63081, 63085, 63087, 63090, 63101-63102, 63170-63290, 63300-63307)
🔲 20.76   ✂ 20.76 Global Days ZZZ
AMA: 2008, Jan, 10-25; 2007, Jan, 13-27; 2007, Jan, 13-27; 2007, January, 13-27; 2004, Nov, 11; 2004, November, 11; 2004, Nov, 11

+ **22841** Internal spinal fixation by wiring of spinous processes (List separately in addition to code for primary procedure) ⓒ
  INCLUDES Hibb's fusion

  Code first (22100-22102, 22110-22114, 22206-22207, 22210-22214, 22220-22224, 22305-22327, 22532-22533, 22548-22558, 22590-22612, 22630, 22800-22812, 63001-63030, 63040-63042, 63045-63047, 63050-63056, 63064, 63075, 63077, 63081, 63085, 63087, 63090, 63101-63102, 63170-63290, 63300-63307)

  📠 0.00   ⚖ 0.00 Global Days XXX
  AMA: 2004, Nov, 11; 2004, Nov, 11; 2004, November, 11

+ **22842** Posterior segmental instrumentation (eg, pedicle fixation, dual rods with multiple hooks and sublaminar wires); 3 to 6 vertebral segments (List separately in addition to code for primary procedure) ⓒ 80 ▢

  Code first (22100-22102, 22110-22114, 22206-22207, 22210-22214, 22220-22224, 22305-22327, 22532-22533, 22548-22558, 22590-22612, 22630, 22800-22812, 63001-63030, 63040-63042, 63045-63047, 63050-63056, 63064, 63075, 63077, 63081, 63085, 63087, 63090, 63101-63102, 63170-63290, 63300-63307)

  📠 20.79   ⚖ 20.79 Global Days ZZZ
  AMA: 2004, Nov, 11; 2004, Nov, 11; 2004, November, 11

+ **22843** 7 to 12 vertebral segments (List separately in addition to code for primary procedure) ⓒ 80 ▢

  Code first (22100-22102, 22110-22114, 22206-22207, 22210-22214, 22220-22224, 22305-22327, 22532-22533, 22548-22558, 22590-22612, 22630, 22800-22812, 63001-63030, 63170-63290, 63300-63307)

  📠 22.11   ⚖ 22.11 Global Days ZZZ
  AMA: 2004, Nov, 11; 2004, Nov, 11; 2004, November, 11

+ **22844** 13 or more vertebral segments (List separately in addition to code for primary procedure) ⓒ 80 ▢

  Code first (22100-22102, 22206-22207, 22210-22214, 22210-22214, 22220-22224, 22305-22327, 22532-22533, 22548-22558, 22590-22612, 22630, 22800-22812, 63001-63030, 63040-63042, 63045-63047, 63050-63056, 63064, 63075, 63077, 63081, 63085, 63087, 63090, 63101-63102, 63170-63290, 63300-63307)

  📠 26.99   ⚖ 26.99 Global Days ZZZ
  AMA: 2004, Nov, 11; 2004, Nov, 11; 2004, November, 11

+ **22845** Anterior instrumentation; 2 to 3 vertebral segments (List separately in addition to code for primary procedure) ⓒ 80 ▢
  INCLUDES Dwyer instrumentation technique

  Code first (22100-22102, 22110-22114, 22206-22207, 22210-22214, 22220-22224, 22305-22327, 22532-22533, 22548-22558, 22590-22612, 22630, 22800-22812, 63001-63030, 63040-63042, 63045-63047, 63050-63056, 63064, 63075, 63077, 63081, 63085, 63087, 63090, 63101-63102, 63170-63290, 63300-63307)

  📠 19.92   ⚖ 19.92 Global Days ZZZ
  AMA: 2008, Jan, 10-25; 2007, Jan, 13-27; 2007, Jan, 13-27; 2007, Jun, 1-3; 2007, Jun, 1-3; 2007, January, 13-27; 2007, June, 1-3; 2004, Nov, 11; 2004, Nov, 11; 2004, November, 11

+ **22846** 4 to 7 vertebral segments (List separately in addition to code for primary procedure) ⓒ 80 ▢
  INCLUDES Dwyer instrumentation technique

  Code first (22100-22102, 22110-22114, 22206-22207, 22210-22214, 22220-22224, 22305-22327, 22532-22533, 22548-22558, 22590-22612, 22630, 22800-22812, 63001-63030, 63040-63042, 63045-63047, 63050-63056, 63064, 63075, 63077, 63081, 63085, 63087, 63090, 63101-63102, 63170-63290, 63300-63307)

  📠 20.68   ⚖ 20.68 Global Days ZZZ
  AMA: 2008, Jan, 10-25; 2004, Nov, 11; 2004, Nov, 11; 2004, November, 11

+ **22847** 8 or more vertebral segments (List separately in addition to code for primary procedure) ⓒ 80 ▢
  INCLUDES Dwyer instrumentation technique

  Code first (22100-22102, 22110-22114, 22206-22207, 22210-22214, 22220-22224, 22305-22327, 22532-22533, 22548-22558, 22590-22612, 22630, 22800-22812, 63001-63030, 63040-63042, 63045-63047, 63050-63056, 63064, 63075, 63077, 63081, 63085, 63087, 63090, 63101-63102, 63170-63290, 63300-63307)

  📠 22.73   ⚖ 22.73 Global Days ZZZ
  AMA: 2008, Jan, 10-25; 2004, Nov, 11; 2004, Nov, 11; 2004, November, 11

+ **22848** Pelvic fixation (attachment of caudal end of instrumentation to pelvic bony structures) other than sacrum (List separately in addition to code for primary procedure) ⓒ 80 ▢

  Code first (22100-22102, 22110-22114, 22206-22207, 22210-22214, 22220-22224, 22305-22327, 22532-22533, 22548-22558, 22590-22612, 22630, 22800-22812, 63001-63030, 63040-63042, 63045-63047, 63050-63056, 63064, 63075, 63077, 63081, 63085, 63087, 63090, 63101-63102, 63170-63290, 63300-63307)

  📠 9.83   ⚖ 9.83 Global Days ZZZ
  AMA: 2004, Nov, 11; 2004, Nov, 11; 2004, November, 11

22849 Reinsertion of spinal fixation device ⓒ 80 ▢

  Do not report with removal of instrumentation at the same level (22850, 22852, 22855)

  📠 33.90   ⚖ 33.90 Global Days 090
  AMA: 2004, Nov, 11; 2004, Nov, 11; 2004, November, 11

22850 Removal of posterior nonsegmental instrumentation (eg, Harrington rod) ⓒ 80 ▢
  📠 18.48   ⚖ 18.48 Global Days 090
  AMA: 2004, Nov, 11; 2004, Nov, 11; 2004, November, 11

+ **22851** Application of intervertebral biomechanical device(s) (eg, synthetic cage(s), threaded bone dowel(s), methylmethacrylate) to vertebral defect or interspace (List separately in addition to code for primary procedure) Ⓣ 80 ▢
  EXCLUDES insertion of posterior spinous process distraction devices (0171T-0172T)

  Code first (22100-22102, 22110-22114, 22206-22207, 22210-22214, 22220-22224, 22305-22327, 22532-22533, 22548-22558, 22590-22612, 22630, 22800-22812, 63001-63030, 63040-63042, 63045-63047, 63050-63056, 63064, 63075, 63077, 63081, 63085, 63087, 63090, 63101-63102, 63170-63290, 63300-63307)

  📠 11.07   ⚖ 11.07 Global Days ZZZ
  AMA: 2008, Jan, 10-25; 2007, Jan, 13-27; 2007, Jan, 13-27; 2007, Jun, 1-3; 2007, Jun, 1-3; 2007, June, 1-3; 2007, January, 13-27; 2005, Feb, 13-16; 2005, Feb, 13-16; 2005, February, 13-16; 2005, June, 6-8; 2005, Jun, 6-8; 2005, Jun, 6-8; 2004, Nov, 11; 2004, November, 11; 2004, Nov, 11

22852 Removal of posterior segmental instrumentation ⓒ 80 ▢
  📠 17.65   ⚖ 17.65 Global Days 090
  AMA: 2008, Jan, 10-25; 2007, Jan, 13-27; 2007, Jan, 13-27; 2007, January, 13-27; 2006, May, 16-20; 2006, May, 16-20; 2006, May, 16-20; 2004, Nov, 11; 2004, Nov, 11; 2004, November, 11

22855 Removal of anterior instrumentation ⓒ 80 ▢
  📠 28.78   ⚖ 28.78 Global Days 090
  AMA: 2004, Nov, 11; 2004, Nov, 11; 2004, November, 11

● New Code ▲ Revised Code Ⓜ Maternity Edit Ⓐ Age Edit Ⓐ-Ⓨ OPPS Status Indicator 📠 Facility RVU ⚖ Non-Facility RVU
▢ CCI Comprehensive Code 50 Bilateral Procedure + Add-on Indicator Ⓛ Laboratory crosswalk Ⓡ Radiology crosswalk

© 2008 Ingenix *(Blue Ink)*   CPT only © 2008 American Medical Association. All Rights Reserved. (Black Ink)   Medicare (Red Ink)   69

22856-22899 Artificial Disc Replacement

CMS *100-3,150.10 Lumbar Artificial Disc Replacement (LADR)*
INCLUDES fluoroscopy (76000-76001)
EXCLUDES *spinal decompression (63001-63048)*

● **22856** **Total disc arthroplasty (artificial disc), anterior approach, including discectomy with end plate preparation (includes osteophytectomy for nerve root or spinal cord decompression and microdissection), single interspace, cervical** `C` `80`
   INCLUDES operating microscope (69990)
   same level:
      arthrodesis (22554)
      discectomy (63075)
      instrumentation (22845, 22851)
   EXCLUDES *cervical total disc arthroplasty with additional interspace revision (0092T)*

   🔖 43.15 ⚕ 43.15 Global Days 090

▲ **22857** **Total disc arthroplasty (artificial disc), anterior approach, including discectomy to prepare interspace (other than for decompression), single interspace, lumbar** `C` `80`
   INCLUDES operating microscope (69990)
   same level:
      arthrodesis (22558)
      instrumentation (22845, 22851)
      retroperitoneal exploration (49010)
   EXCLUDES *arthroplasty more than one interspace (0163T)*

   🔖 44.25 ⚕ 44.25 Global Days 090
   AMA: 2007, Jun, 1-3; 2007, Jun, 1-3; 2007, June, 1-3

● **22861** **Revision including replacement of total disc arthroplasty (artificial disc), anterior approach, single interspace; cervical** `C` `80`
   INCLUDES operating microscope (69990)
   EXCLUDES *revision of additional cervical arthroplasty (0098T)*
   same level:
      discectomy (63075)
      instrumentation (22845, 22851)
      removal of artificial disc (22864)

   🔖 52.24 ⚕ 52.24 Global Days 090

▲ **22862** **lumbar** `C` `80`
   INCLUDES same level:
      arthrodesis (22558)
      instrumentation (22845, 22851)
      removal artificial disc (22865)
      retroperitoneal exploration (49010)
   EXCLUDES *arthroplasty revision more than one interspace (0165T)*

   🔖 51.51 ⚕ 51.51 Global Days 090
   AMA: 2007, Jun, 1-3; 2007, Jun, 1-3; 2007, June, 1-3

● **22864** **Removal of total disc arthroplasty (artificial disc), anterior approach, single interspace; cervical** `C` `80`
   INCLUDES operating microscope (69990)
   EXCLUDES *cervical total disc arthroplasty with additional interspace removal (0095T)*

   Do not report with (22861)
   🔖 48.51 ⚕ 48.51 Global Days 090

▲ **22865** **lumbar** `C` `80`
   EXCLUDES *arthroplasty more than one level (0164T)*

   Do not report with (49010)
   🔖 54.95 ⚕ 54.95 Global Days 090
   AMA: 2007, Jun, 1-3; 2007, Jun, 1-3; 2007, June, 1-3

22899 Unlisted procedure, spine `T` `80`
   🔖 0.00 ⚕ 0.00 Global Days YYY
   AMA: 2008, Jan, 10-25; 2007, Jan, 13-27; 2007, Jan, 13-27; 2007, January, 13-27; 2006, May, 16-20; 2006, May, 16-20; 2006, May, 16-20

22900-22999 Musculoskeletal Procedures of Abdomen

22900 Excision, abdominal wall tumor, subfascial (eg, desmoid) `A2` `T` `80` 🔲
   🔖 10.42 ⚕ 10.42 Global Days 090

22999 Unlisted procedure, abdomen, musculoskeletal system `T` `80`
   🔖 0.00 ⚕ 0.00 Global Days YYY

23000-23044 Surgical Incision Shoulder: Drainage, Removal Foreign Body, Release Contracture

23000 Removal of subdeltoid calcareous deposits, open `A2` `T` `80` 🔲
   EXCLUDES *arthroscopic calcium deposit removal (29999)*
   🔖 9.07 ⚕ 13.17 Global Days 090

23020 Capsular contracture release (eg, Sever type procedure) `A2` `T` `80` `50` 🔲
   EXCLUDES *simple incision and drainage (10040-10160)*
   🔖 17.68 ⚕ 17.68 Global Days 090

23030 Incision and drainage, shoulder area; deep abscess or hematoma `A2` `T` 🔲
   🔖 6.57 ⚕ 10.52 Global Days 010

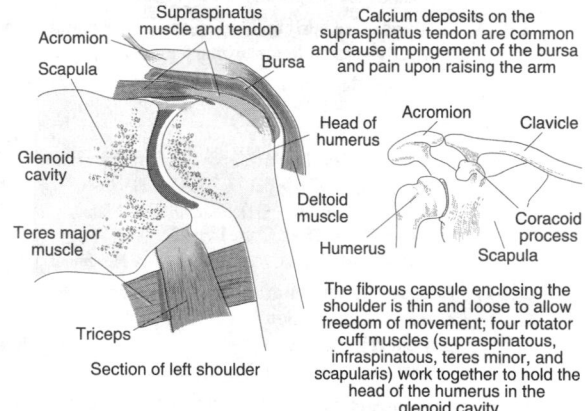

Calcium deposits on the supraspinatus tendon are common and cause impingement of the bursa and pain upon raising the arm

Acromion — Supraspinatus muscle and tendon — Bursa
Scapula
Glenoid cavity
Teres major muscle
Triceps
Section of left shoulder

Head of humerus — Acromion — Clavicle
Deltoid muscle — Coracoid process
Humerus — Scapula

The fibrous capsule enclosing the shoulder is thin and loose to allow freedom of movement; four rotator cuff muscles (supraspinatous, infraspinatous, teres minor, and scapularis) work together to hold the head of the humerus in the glenoid cavity

23031 infected bursa `A2` `T` `50`
   🔖 5.44 ⚕ 9.59 Global Days 010

23035 Incision, bone cortex (eg, osteomyelitis or bone abscess), shoulder area `A2` `T` `80` `50` 🔲
   🔖 17.52 ⚕ 17.52 Global Days 090

23040 Arthrotomy, glenohumeral joint, including exploration, drainage, or removal of foreign body `A2` `T` `80` `50` 🔲
   🔖 18.41 ⚕ 18.41 Global Days 090

23044 Arthrotomy, acromioclavicular, sternoclavicular joint, including exploration, drainage, or removal of foreign body `A2` `T` `50` 🔲
   🔖 14.59 ⚕ 14.59 Global Days 090

23065-23066 Shoulder Biopsy

EXCLUDES *soft tissue needle biopsy (20206)*

23065 Biopsy, soft tissue of shoulder area; superficial `P3` `T` `50` 🔲
   🔖 4.20 ⚕ 5.30 Global Days 010

23066   deep   A2 T 50 ▢
     🔧 8.57   𝄪 12.52   Global Days 090

23075-23222 Resection Areas of Shoulder

23075   Excision, soft tissue tumor, shoulder area;
     subcutaneous   A2 T 50 ▢
     🔧 4.51   𝄪 6.42   Global Days 010

23076   deep, subfascial, or intramuscular   A2 T 50 ▢
     🔧 14.33   𝄪 14.33   Global Days 090

23077   Radical resection of tumor (eg, malignant neoplasm), soft
     tissue of shoulder area   A2 T 80 50 ▢
     🔧 30.39   𝄪 30.39   Global Days 090

23100   Arthrotomy, glenohumeral joint, including
     biopsy   A2 T 80 50 ▢
     🔧 12.41   𝄪 12.41   Global Days 090

23101   Arthrotomy, acromioclavicular joint or sternoclavicular
     joint, including biopsy and/or excision of torn
     cartilage   A2 T 50 ▢
     🔧 11.41   𝄪 11.41   Global Days 090

23105   Arthrotomy; glenohumeral joint, with synovectomy, with
     or without biopsy   A2 T 80 50 ▢
     🔧 16.28   𝄪 16.28   Global Days 090

23106   sternoclavicular joint, with synovectomy, with or
     without biopsy   A2 T 50 ▢
     🔧 12.10   𝄪 12.10   Global Days 090

23107   Arthrotomy, glenohumeral joint, with joint exploration,
     with or without removal of loose or foreign
     body   A2 T 80 50 ▢
     🔧 16.92   𝄪 16.92   Global Days 090

23120   Claviculectomy; partial   A2 T 80 ▢
     INCLUDES   Mumford operation
     EXCLUDES   arthroscopic claviculectomy (29824)
     🔧 14.62   𝄪 14.62   Global Days 090

23125   total   A2 T 80 50 ▢
     🔧 18.01   𝄪 18.01   Global Days 090

23130   Acromioplasty or acromionectomy, partial, with or
     without coracoacromial ligament release   A2 T 50 ▢
     🔧 15.38   𝄪 15.38   Global Days 090
     AMA: 2008, Jan, 10-25; 2007, Jan, 13-27; 2007, Jan, 13-27; 2007,
     January, 13-27

23140   Excision or curettage of bone cyst or benign tumor of
     clavicle or scapula;   A2 T 50 ▢
     🔧 13.08   𝄪 13.08   Global Days 090

23145   with autograft (includes obtaining graft)   A2 T 80 50 ▢
     🔧 17.65   𝄪 17.65   Global Days 090

23146   with allograft   A2 T 80 50 ▢
     🔧 15.35   𝄪 15.35   Global Days 090

23150   Excision or curettage of bone cyst or benign tumor of
     proximal humerus;   A2 T 80 50 ▢
     🔧 16.67   𝄪 16.67   Global Days 090

23155   with autograft (includes obtaining graft)   A2 T 80 50 ▢
     🔧 20.27   𝄪 20.27   Global Days 090

23156   with allograft   A2 T 80 50 ▢
     🔧 17.21   𝄪 17.21   Global Days 090

23170   Sequestrectomy (eg, for osteomyelitis or bone abscess),
     clavicle   A2 T 50 ▢
     🔧 13.50   𝄪 13.50   Global Days 090

23172   Sequestrectomy (eg, for osteomyelitis or bone abscess),
     scapula   A2 T 80 50 ▢
     🔧 13.80   𝄪 13.80   Global Days 090

23174   Sequestrectomy (eg, for osteomyelitis or bone abscess),
     humeral head to surgical neck   A2 T 80 50 ▢
     🔧 19.24   𝄪 19.24   Global Days 090

23180   Partial excision (craterization, saucerization, or
     diaphysectomy) bone (eg, osteomyelitis),
     clavicle   A2 T 50 ▢
     🔧 17.50   𝄪 17.50   Global Days 090

23182   Partial excision (craterization, saucerization, or
     diaphysectomy) bone (eg, osteomyelitis),
     scapula   A2 T 80 50 ▢
     🔧 16.87   𝄪 16.87   Global Days 090

23184   Partial excision (craterization, saucerization, or
     diaphysectomy) bone (eg, osteomyelitis), proximal
     humerus   A2 T 80 50 ▢
     🔧 19.07   𝄪 19.07   Global Days 090

23190   Ostectomy of scapula, partial (eg, superior medial
     angle)   A2 T 80 50 ▢
     🔧 14.18   𝄪 14.18   Global Days 090

23195   Resection, humeral head   A2 T 80 50 ▢
     EXCLUDES   that with replacement with implant (23470)
     🔧 19.28   𝄪 19.28   Global Days 090

23200   Radical resection for tumor; clavicle   C 80 50 ▢
     🔧 22.72   𝄪 22.72   Global Days 090

23210   scapula   C 80 50 ▢
     🔧 23.77   𝄪 23.77   Global Days 090

23220   Radical resection of bone tumor, proximal
     humerus;   C 80 50 ▢
     🔧 27.58   𝄪 27.58   Global Days 090

23221   with autograft (includes obtaining graft)   C 80 50 ▢
     🔧 32.24   𝄪 32.24   Global Days 090

23222   with prosthetic replacement   C 80 50 ▢
     🔧 43.82   𝄪 43.82   Global Days 090

23330-23332 Foreign Body Removal: Shoulder

EXCLUDES   bursal arthrocentesis or needling (20610)
     K-wire or pin insertion (20650)
     K-wire or pin removal (20670, 20680)

23330   Removal of foreign body, shoulder;
     subcutaneous   A2 T 80 50 ▢
     🔧 3.75   𝄪 5.53   Global Days 010

23331   deep (eg, Neer hemiarthroplasty
     removal)   A2 T 80 50 ▢
     🔧 14.98   𝄪 14.98   Global Days 090

23332   complicated (eg, total shoulder)   C 80 50 ▢
     🔧 22.78   𝄪 22.78   Global Days 090
     AMA: 2008, Jan, 10-25; 2007, Jan, 13-27; 2007, Jan, 13-27; 2007,
     January, 13-27

23350 Injection for Shoulder Arthrogram

23350   Injection procedure for shoulder arthrography or
     enhanced CT/MRI shoulder arthrography   N1 N 50 ▢
     EXCLUDES   shoulder biopsy (29805-29826)
     📷 73040, 73201-73202, 73222-73223, 77002
     🔧 1.43   𝄪 3.97   Global Days 000

23395-23491 Repair/Reconstruction of Shoulder

23395   Muscle transfer, any type, shoulder or upper arm;
     single   A2 T 80 ▢
     🔧 33.18   𝄪 33.18   Global Days 090

23397   multiple   A2 T 80 ▢
     🔧 29.75   𝄪 29.75   Global Days 090

23400   Scapulopexy (eg, Sprengels deformity or for
     paralysis)   A2 T 80 50 ▢
     🔧 25.21   𝄪 25.21   Global Days 090

● New Code   ▲ Revised Code   Ⓜ Maternity Edit   Ⓐ Age Edit   A-Y OPPS Status Indicator   🔧 Facility RVU   𝄪 Non-Facility RVU

▢ CCI Comprehensive Code   50 Bilateral Procedure   + Add-on Indicator   ◼ Laboratory crosswalk   📷 Radiology crosswalk

Musculoskeletal System

23405 — 23575

23405   Tenotomy, shoulder area; single tendon   A2 T 80 ▭
   🔁 16.20   ⚖ 16.20   Global Days 090

23406   multiple tendons through same incision   A2 T 80 ▭
   🔁 20.27   ⚖ 20.27   Global Days 090

23410   Repair of ruptured musculotendinous cuff (eg, rotator cuff) open; acute   A2 T 80 50 ▭
   EXCLUDES   arthroscopic repair (29827)
   🔁 21.57   ⚖ 21.57   Global Days 090
   AMA: 2008, Jan, 10-25; 2007, Jan, 13-27; 2007, Jan, 13-27; 2007, January, 13-27

23412   chronic   A2 T 80 50 ▭
   EXCLUDES   arthroscopic repair (29827)
   🔁 22.56   ⚖ 22.56   Global Days 090
   AMA: 2008, Jan, 10-25; 2007, Jan, 13-27; 2007, Jan, 13-27; 2007, January, 13-27

23415   Coracoacromial ligament release, with or without acromioplasty   A2 T 50 ▭
   EXCLUDES   arthroscopic repair (29826)
   🔁 17.94   ⚖ 17.94   Global Days 090

23420   Reconstruction of complete shoulder (rotator) cuff avulsion, chronic (includes acromioplasty)   A2 T 80 50 ▭
   🔁 25.19   ⚖ 25.19   Global Days 090
   AMA: 2008, Jan, 10-25; 2007, Jan, 13-27; 2007, Jan, 13-27; 2007, January, 13-27; 2005, Oct, 23-24; 2005, October, 23-24; 2005, Oct, 23-24

23430   Tenodesis of long tendon of biceps   A2 T 80 50 ▭
   EXCLUDES   arthroscopic biceps tenodesis (29828)
   🔁 19.06   ⚖ 19.06   Global Days 090

23440   Resection or transplantation of long tendon of biceps   A2 T 80 50 ▭
   🔁 19.67   ⚖ 19.67   Global Days 090

23450   Capsulorrhaphy, anterior; Putti-Platt procedure or Magnuson type operation   A2 T 80 50 ▭
   EXCLUDES   arthroscopic thermal capsulorrhaphy (29999)
   🔁 24.69   ⚖ 24.69   Global Days 090

23455   with labral repair (eg, Bankart procedure)   A2 T 80 50 ▭
   EXCLUDES   arthroscopic repair (29806)
   🔁 26.34   ⚖ 26.34   Global Days 090

23460   Capsulorrhaphy, anterior, any type; with bone block   A2 T 80 50 ▭
   INCLUDES   Bristow procedure
   🔁 28.50   ⚖ 28.50   Global Days 090

23462   with coracoid process transfer   A2 T 80 50 ▭
   EXCLUDES   open thermal capsulorrhaphy (23929)
   🔁 27.95   ⚖ 27.95   Global Days 090

23465   Capsulorrhaphy, glenohumeral joint, posterior, with or without bone block   A2 T 80 50 ▭
   EXCLUDES   sternoclavicular and acromioclavicular joint repair (23530, 23550)
   🔁 29.18   ⚖ 29.18   Global Days 090

23466   Capsulorrhaphy, glenohumeral joint, any type multi-directional instability   A2 T 80 50 ▭
   🔁 28.68   ⚖ 28.68   Global Days 090

23470   Arthroplasty, glenohumeral joint; hemiarthroplasty   T 80 50 ▭
   🔁 31.74   ⚖ 31.74   Global Days 090

23472   total shoulder (glenoid and proximal humeral replacement (eg, total shoulder))   C 80 50 ▭
   EXCLUDES   proximal humerus osteotomy (24400)
         removal of total shoulder components (23331-23332)
   🔁 39.29   ⚖ 39.29   Global Days 090
   AMA: 2008, Jan, 10-25; 2007, Jan, 13-27; 2007, Jan, 13-27; 2007, January, 13-27

23480   Osteotomy, clavicle, with or without internal fixation;   A2 T 50 ▭
   🔁 21.20   ⚖ 21.20   Global Days 090

23485   with bone graft for nonunion or malunion (includes obtaining graft and/or necessary fixation)   A2 T 80 50 ▭
   🔁 25.06   ⚖ 25.06   Global Days 090

23490   Prophylactic treatment (nailing, pinning, plating or wiring) with or without methylmethacrylate; clavicle   A2 T 80 50 ▭
   🔁 21.46   ⚖ 21.46   Global Days 090

23491   proximal humerus   A2 T 80 50 ▭
   🔁 26.39   ⚖ 26.39   Global Days 090

23500-23680 Treatment of Shoulder Fracture/Dislocation

23500   Closed treatment of clavicular fracture; without manipulation   A2 T 50 ▭
   🔁 5.09   ⚖ 5.12   Global Days 090

23505   with manipulation   A2 T 50 ▭
   🔁 8.05   ⚖ 8.48   Global Days 090

23515   Open treatment of clavicular fracture, includes internal fixation, when performed   A2 T 80 50 ▭
   🔁 17.87   ⚖ 17.87   Global Days 090
   AMA: 2008, Jan, 4-5

23520   Closed treatment of sternoclavicular dislocation; without manipulation   A2 T 80 50 ▭
   🔁 5.35   ⚖ 5.32   Global Days 090

23525   with manipulation   A2 T 80 50 ▭
   🔁 7.73   ⚖ 8.25   Global Days 090

23530   Open treatment of sternoclavicular dislocation, acute or chronic;   A2 T 80 50 ▭
   🔁 13.76   ⚖ 13.76   Global Days 090

23532   with fascial graft (includes obtaining graft)   A2 T 80 50 ▭
   🔁 15.84   ⚖ 15.84   Global Days 090

23540   Closed treatment of acromioclavicular dislocation; without manipulation   A2 T 50 ▭
   🔁 5.17   ⚖ 5.24   Global Days 090

23545   with manipulation   A2 T 80 50 ▭
   🔁 6.97   ⚖ 7.55   Global Days 090

23550   Open treatment of acromioclavicular dislocation, acute or chronic;   A2 T 80 50 ▭
   🔁 14.60   ⚖ 14.60   Global Days 090

23552   with fascial graft (includes obtaining graft)   A2 T 80 50 ▭
   🔁 16.82   ⚖ 16.82   Global Days 090

23570   Closed treatment of scapular fracture; without manipulation   A2 T 50 ▭
   🔁 5.56   ⚖ 5.49   Global Days 090

23575   with manipulation, with or without skeletal traction (with or without shoulder joint involvement)   A2 T 80 50 ▭
   🔁 8.85   ⚖ 9.37   Global Days 090

▲ 23585 Open treatment of scapular fracture (body, glenoid or acromion) includes internal fixation, when performed A2 T 80 50 ▭
  ⚙ 24.17 ⚕ 24.17 Global Days 090
  AMA: 2008, Jan, 10-25; 2007, Jan, 13-27; 2007, Jan, 13-27; 2007, January, 13-27; 2004, Nov, 10; 2004, November, 10; 2004, Nov, 10

23600 Closed treatment of proximal humeral (surgical or anatomical neck) fracture; without manipulation P2 T 50 ▭
  ⚙ 7.11 ⚕ 7.67 Global Days 090

23605   with manipulation, with or without skeletal traction A2 T 50 ▭
  ⚙ 10.54 ⚕ 11.38 Global Days 090

23615 Open treatment of proximal humeral (surgical or anatomical neck) fracture, includes internal fixation, when performed, includes repair of tuberosity(s), when performed; A2 T 80 50 ▭
  ⚙ 22.21 ⚕ 22.21 Global Days 090
  AMA: 2008, Jan, 4-5

23616   with proximal humeral prosthetic replacement A2 T 80 50 ▭
  ⚙ 33.61 ⚕ 33.61 Global Days 090

23620 Closed treatment of greater humeral tuberosity fracture; without manipulation P2 T 50 ▭
  ⚙ 5.97 ⚕ 6.32 Global Days 090

23625   with manipulation A2 T 50 ▭
  ⚙ 8.68 ⚕ 9.22 Global Days 090

23630 Open treatment of greater humeral tuberosity fracture, includes internal fixation, when performed A2 T 80 50 ▭
  ⚙ 19.03 ⚕ 19.03 Global Days 090

23650 Closed treatment of shoulder dislocation, with manipulation; without anesthesia A2 T 50 ▭
  ⚙ 6.50 ⚕ 7.09 Global Days 090

23655   requiring anesthesia A2 T 50 ▭
  ⚙ 9.53 ⚕ 9.53 Global Days 090

23660 Open treatment of acute shoulder dislocation A2 T 80 50 ▭
  EXCLUDES chronic dislocation repair (23450-23466)
  ⚙ 14.01 ⚕ 14.81 Global Days 090

23665 Closed treatment of shoulder dislocation, with fracture of greater humeral tuberosity, with manipulation A2 T 50 ▭
  ⚙ 9.67 ⚕ 10.25 Global Days 090

23670 Open treatment of shoulder dislocation, with fracture of greater humeral tuberosity, includes internal fixation, when performed A2 T 80 50 ▭
  ⚙ 21.35 ⚕ 21.35 Global Days 090

23675 Closed treatment of shoulder dislocation, with surgical or anatomical neck fracture, with manipulation A2 T 50 ▭
  ⚙ 12.46 ⚕ 13.42 Global Days 090

23680 Open treatment of shoulder dislocation, with surgical or anatomical neck fracture, includes internal fixation, when performed A2 T 80 50 ▭
  ⚙ 23.22 ⚕ 23.22 Global Days 090

23700-23929 Other/Unlisted Shoulder Procedures

23700 Manipulation under anesthesia, shoulder joint, including application of fixation apparatus (dislocation excluded) A2 T ▭
  ⚙ 4.98 ⚕ 4.98 Global Days 010
  AMA: 2008, Jan, 10-25; 2007, Jan, 13-27; 2007, Jan, 13-27; 2007, January, 13-27; 2005, Apr, 13-14; 2005, April, 13-14; 2005, Apr, 13-14

23800 Arthrodesis, glenohumeral joint; A2 T 80 50 ▭
  ⚙ 26.51 ⚕ 26.51 Global Days 090

23802   with autogenous graft (includes obtaining graft) A2 T 80 ▭
  ⚙ 32.14 ⚕ 32.14 Global Days 090

23900 Interthoracoscapular amputation (forequarter) C 80 ▭
  ⚙ 34.40 ⚕ 34.40 Global Days 090

23920 Disarticulation of shoulder; C 80 ▭
  ⚙ 27.83 ⚕ 27.83 Global Days 090

23921   secondary closure or scar revision A2 T ▭
  ⚙ 10.04 ⚕ 10.04 Global Days 090

23929 Unlisted procedure, shoulder T 80
  ⚙ 0.00 ⚕ 0.00 Global Days YYY

23930-24006 Surgical Incision Elbow/Upper Arm: Drainage/Foreign Body Removal/Release of Capsule

EXCLUDES simple incision and drainage procedures (10040-10160)

23930 Incision and drainage, upper arm or elbow area; deep abscess or hematoma A2 T 50 ▭
  ⚙ 5.50 ⚕ 8.72 Global Days 010

23931   bursa A2 T 50 ▭
  ⚙ 3.96 ⚕ 6.79 Global Days 010

23935 Incision, deep, with opening of bone cortex (eg, for osteomyelitis or bone abscess), humerus or elbow A2 T 80 50 ▭
  ⚙ 12.61 ⚕ 12.61 Global Days 090

24000 Arthrotomy, elbow, including exploration, drainage, or removal of foreign body A2 T 80 50 ▭
  ⚙ 11.98 ⚕ 11.98 Global Days 090

24006 Arthrotomy of the elbow, with capsular excision for capsular release (separate procedure) A2 T 80 50 ▭
  ⚙ 18.15 ⚕ 18.15 Global Days 090

24065-24066 Biopsy of Elbow/Upper Arm

24065 Biopsy, soft tissue of upper arm or elbow area; superficial P3 T 50 ▭
  EXCLUDES soft tissue needle biopsy (20206)
  ⚙ 4.17 ⚕ 6.18 Global Days 010

24066   deep (subfascial or intramuscular) A2 T 50 ▭
  EXCLUDES soft tissue needle biopsy (20206)
  ⚙ 10.08 ⚕ 14.48 Global Days 090

24075-24155 Resection Areas of Elbow/Upper Arm

24075 Excision, tumor, soft tissue of upper arm or elbow area; subcutaneous A2 T 50 ▭
  ⚙ 7.86 ⚕ 11.71 Global Days 090

24076   deep (subfascial or intramuscular) A2 T 50 ▭
  ⚙ 12.03 ⚕ 12.03 Global Days 090

24077 Radical resection of tumor (eg, malignant neoplasm), soft tissue of upper arm or elbow area A2 T 50 ▭
  ⚙ 20.85 ⚕ 20.85 Global Days 090

24100 Arthrotomy, elbow; with synovial biopsy only A2 T 80 50 ▭
  ⚙ 10.23 ⚕ 10.23 Global Days 090

24101   with joint exploration, with or without biopsy, with or without removal of loose or foreign body A2 T 80 50 ▭
  ⚙ 12.60 ⚕ 12.60 Global Days 090

24102   with synovectomy A2 T 80 50 ▭
  ⚙ 15.66 ⚕ 15.66 Global Days 090

● New Code   ▲ Revised Code   M Maternity Edit   ⚠ Age Edit   A-V OPPS Status Indicator   ⚙ Facility RVU   ⚕ Non-Facility RVU

▭ CCI Comprehensive Code   50 Bilateral Procedure   + Add-on Indicator   ▣ Laboratory crosswalk   ▣ Radiology crosswalk

24105 Excision, olecranon bursa A2 T 50 🖵
📖 8.43 ⚕ 8.43 Global Days 090

24110 Excision or curettage of bone cyst or benign tumor, humerus; A2 T 50 🖵
📖 14.82 ⚕ 14.82 Global Days 090

24115 with autograft (includes obtaining graft) A2 T 80 50 🖵
📖 18.74 ⚕ 18.74 Global Days 090

24116 with allograft A2 T 80 50 🖵
📖 22.28 ⚕ 22.28 Global Days 090

24120 Excision or curettage of bone cyst or benign tumor of head or neck of radius or olecranon process; A2 T 80 50 🖵
📖 13.25 ⚕ 13.25 Global Days 090

24125 with autograft (includes obtaining graft) A2 T 80 50 🖵
📖 15.24 ⚕ 15.24 Global Days 090

24126 with allograft A2 T 80 50 🖵
📖 16.19 ⚕ 16.19 Global Days 090

24130 Excision, radial head A2 T 50 🖵
EXCLUDES *that with replacement with implant (24366)*
📖 12.79 ⚕ 12.79 Global Days 090

24134 Sequestrectomy (eg, for osteomyelitis or bone abscess), shaft or distal humerus A2 T 80 50 🖵
📖 19.26 ⚕ 19.26 Global Days 090

24136 Sequestrectomy (eg, for osteomyelitis or bone abscess), radial head or neck A2 T 50 🖵
📖 15.25 ⚕ 15.25 Global Days 090

24138 Sequestrectomy (eg, for osteomyelitis or bone abscess), olecranon process A2 T 80 50 🖵
📖 16.80 ⚕ 16.80 Global Days 090

24140 Partial excision (craterization, saucerization, or diaphysectomy) bone (eg, osteomyelitis), humerus A2 T 80 50 🖵
📖 18.33 ⚕ 18.33 Global Days 090

24145 Partial excision (craterization, saucerization, or diaphysectomy) bone (eg, osteomyelitis), radial head or neck A2 T 50 🖵
📖 15.36 ⚕ 15.36 Global Days 090

24147 Partial excision (craterization, saucerization, or diaphysectomy) bone (eg, osteomyelitis), olecranon process A2 T 50 🖵
📖 15.96 ⚕ 15.96 Global Days 090

24149 Radical resection of capsule, soft tissue, and heterotopic bone, elbow, with contracture release (separate procedure) G2 T 80 50 🖵
EXCLUDES *capsular and soft tissue release (24006)*
📖 29.52 ⚕ 29.52 Global Days 090

24150 Radical resection for tumor, shaft or distal humerus; T 80 50 🖵
📖 25.13 ⚕ 25.13 Global Days 090

24151 with autograft (includes obtaining graft) T 80 50 🖵
📖 28.86 ⚕ 28.86 Global Days 090

24152 Radical resection for tumor, radial head or neck; G2 T 80 50 🖵
📖 18.80 ⚕ 18.80 Global Days 090

24153 with autograft (includes obtaining graft) G2 T 80 50 🖵
📖 19.84 ⚕ 19.84 Global Days 090

24155 Resection of elbow joint (arthrectomy) A2 T 80 50 🖵
📖 21.84 ⚕ 21.84 Global Days 090

24160-24201 Removal Implant/Foreign Body from Elbow/Upper Arm

EXCLUDES *bursal or joint arthrocentesis or needling (20605)*
K-wire or pin insertion (20650)
K-wire or pin removal (20670, 20680)

24160 Implant removal; elbow joint A2 T 50 🖵
📖 15.41 ⚕ 15.41 Global Days 090

24164 radial head A2 T 50 🖵
📖 12.58 ⚕ 12.58 Global Days 090

24200 Removal of foreign body, upper arm or elbow area; subcutaneous P3 T 80 50 🖵
📖 3.40 ⚕ 4.84 Global Days 010

24201 deep (subfascial or intramuscular) A2 T 50 🖵
📖 9.19 ⚕ 13.58 Global Days 090

24220 Injection for Elbow Arthrogram

24220 Injection procedure for elbow arthrography N1 N 80 50 🖵
EXCLUDES *injection tennis elbow (20550)*
🔀 73085
📖 1.89 ⚕ 4.36 Global Days 000

24300-24498 Repair/Reconstruction of Elbow/Upper Arm

24300 Manipulation, elbow, under anesthesia G2 T 50 🖵
EXCLUDES *application of external fixation (20690, 20692)*
📖 9.79 ⚕ 9.79 Global Days 090

24301 Muscle or tendon transfer, any type, upper arm or elbow, single (excluding 24320-24331) A2 T 80 🖵
📖 19.30 ⚕ 19.30 Global Days 090

24305 Tendon lengthening, upper arm or elbow, each tendon A2 T 80 🖵
📖 14.69 ⚕ 14.69 Global Days 090

24310 Tenotomy, open, elbow to shoulder, each tendon A2 T 80 🖵
📖 12.03 ⚕ 12.03 Global Days 090

24320 Tenoplasty, with muscle transfer, with or without free graft, elbow to shoulder, single (Seddon-Brookes type procedure) A2 T 80 🖵
📖 19.89 ⚕ 19.89 Global Days 090

24330 Flexor-plasty, elbow (eg, Steindler type advancement); A2 T 80 50 🖵
📖 18.35 ⚕ 18.35 Global Days 090

24331 with extensor advancement A2 T 80 50 🖵
📖 20.30 ⚕ 20.30 Global Days 090

24332 Tenolysis, triceps G2 T 50 🖵
📖 15.34 ⚕ 15.34 Global Days 090

24340 Tenodesis of biceps tendon at elbow (separate procedure) A2 T 80 50 🖵
📖 15.64 ⚕ 15.64 Global Days 090

24341 Repair, tendon or muscle, upper arm or elbow, each tendon or muscle, primary or secondary (excludes rotator cuff) A2 T 80 50 🖵
📖 18.33 ⚕ 18.33 Global Days 090

24342 Reinsertion of ruptured biceps or triceps tendon, distal, with or without tendon graft A2 T 80 50 🖵
📖 20.21 ⚕ 20.21 Global Days 090

24343 Repair lateral collateral ligament, elbow, with local tissue G2 T 80 50 🖵
📖 17.85 ⚕ 17.85 Global Days 090

24344 Reconstruction lateral collateral ligament, elbow, with tendon graft (includes harvesting of graft) [G2] [T] [80] [50] [▭]
  ♻ 27.90   ⚕ 27.90   Global Days 090

24345 Repair medial collateral ligament, elbow, with local tissue [A2] [T] [80] [50] [▭]
  ♻ 17.74   ⚕ 17.74   Global Days 090

24346 Reconstruction medial collateral ligament, elbow, with tendon graft (includes harvesting of graft) [G2] [T] [80] [50] [▭]
  ♻ 27.95   ⚕ 27.95   Global Days 090

24357 Tenotomy, elbow, lateral or medial (eg, epicondylitis, tennis elbow, golfer's elbow); percutaneous [G2] [T] [80] [50]
  Do not report with (29837-29838)
  ♻ 11.17   ⚕ 11.17   Global Days 090
  AMA: 2008, Jan, 4-5

24358   debridement, soft tissue and/or bone, open [G2] [T] [80] [50]
  Do not report with (29837-29838)
  ♻ 13.20   ⚕ 13.20   Global Days 090
  AMA: 2008, Jan, 4-5

24359   debridement, soft tissue and/or bone, open with tendon repair or reattachment [G2] [T] [80] [50]
  Do not report with (29837-29838)
  ♻ 16.64   ⚕ 16.64   Global Days 090
  AMA: 2008, Jan, 4-5

24360 Arthroplasty, elbow; with membrane (eg, fascial) [A8] [T] [80] [50] [▭]
  ♻ 23.21   ⚕ 23.21   Global Days 090

24361   with distal humeral prosthetic replacement [H8] [T] [80] [50] [▭]
  Code also (C1776)
  ♻ 25.99   ⚕ 25.99   Global Days 090

24362   with implant and fascia lata ligament reconstruction [A7] [T] [80] [50] [▭]
  ♻ 27.59   ⚕ 27.59   Global Days 090

24363   with distal humerus and proximal ulnar prosthetic replacement (eg, total elbow) [H8] [T] [80] [50] [▭]
  Code also (C1776)
  ♻ 38.48   ⚕ 38.48   Global Days 090

24365 Arthroplasty, radial head; [A2] [T] [80] [50] [▭]
  ♻ 16.36   ⚕ 16.36   Global Days 090

24366   with implant [H8] [T] [80] [50] [▭]
  Code also implant supply (C1776)
  ♻ 17.53   ⚕ 17.53   Global Days 090

24400 Osteotomy, humerus, with or without internal fixation [A2] [T] [80] [50] [▭]
  ♻ 21.20   ⚕ 21.20   Global Days 090

24410 Multiple osteotomies with realignment on intramedullary rod, humeral shaft (Sofield type procedure) [A2] [T] [80] [50] [▭]
  ♻ 27.13   ⚕ 27.13   Global Days 090

24420 Osteoplasty, humerus (eg, shortening or lengthening) (excluding 64876) [A2] [T] [80] [50] [▭]
  ♻ 25.40   ⚕ 25.40   Global Days 090

24430 Repair of nonunion or malunion, humerus; without graft (eg, compression technique) [A2] [T] [80] [50] [▭]
  ♻ 26.94   ⚕ 26.94   Global Days 090

24435   with iliac or other autograft (includes obtaining graft) [A2] [T] [80] [50] [▭]
  ♻ 27.35   ⚕ 27.35   Global Days 090

24470 Hemiepiphyseal arrest (eg, cubitus varus or valgus, distal humerus) [A2] [T] [80] [50] [▭]
  ♻ 16.15   ⚕ 16.15   Global Days 090

24495 Decompression fasciotomy, forearm, with brachial artery exploration [A2] [T] [80] [50] [▭]
  ♻ 16.70   ⚕ 16.70   Global Days 090

24498 Prophylactic treatment (nailing, pinning, plating or wiring), with or without methylmethacrylate, humeral shaft [A2] [T] [80] [50] [▭]
  ♻ 22.53   ⚕ 22.53   Global Days 090

24500-24685 Treatment of Fracture/Dislocation of Elbow/Upper Arm

24500 Closed treatment of humeral shaft fracture; without manipulation [A2] [T] [50] [▭]
  ♻ 7.58   ⚕ 8.34   Global Days 090

24505   with manipulation, with or without skeletal traction [A2] [T] [50] [▭]
  ♻ 11.18   ⚕ 12.18   Global Days 090

24515 Open treatment of humeral shaft fracture with plate/screws, with or without cerclage [A2] [T] [80] [50] [▭]
  ♻ 22.57   ⚕ 22.57   Global Days 090

24516 Treatment of humeral shaft fracture, with insertion of intramedullary implant, with or without cerclage and/or locking screws [A2] [T] [80] [50] [▭]
  ♻ 22.33   ⚕ 22.33   Global Days 090

24530 Closed treatment of supracondylar or transcondylar humeral fracture, with or without intercondylar extension; without manipulation [A2] [T] [50] [▭]
  ♻ 8.17   ⚕ 8.99   Global Days 090

24535   with manipulation, with or without skin or skeletal traction [A2] [T] [50] [▭]
  ♻ 14.26   ⚕ 15.27   Global Days 090

24538 Percutaneous skeletal fixation of supracondylar or transcondylar humeral fracture, with or without intercondylar extension [A2] [T] [50] [▭]
  ♻ 19.01   ⚕ 19.01   Global Days 090

24545 Open treatment of humeral supracondylar or transcondylar fracture, includes internal fixation, when performed; without intercondylar extension [A2] [T] [80] [50] [▭]
  ♻ 23.38   ⚕ 23.38   Global Days 090

24546   with intercondylar extension [A2] [T] [80] [50] [▭]
  ♻ 27.39   ⚕ 27.39   Global Days 090

24560 Closed treatment of humeral epicondylar fracture, medial or lateral; without manipulation [A2] [T] [50] [▭]
  ♻ 6.67   ⚕ 7.49   Global Days 090

24565   with manipulation [A2] [T] [50] [▭]
  ♻ 11.64   ⚕ 12.54   Global Days 090

24566 Percutaneous skeletal fixation of humeral epicondylar fracture, medial or lateral, with manipulation [A2] [T] [50] [▭]
  ♻ 17.72   ⚕ 17.72   Global Days 090

24575 Open treatment of humeral epicondylar fracture, medial or lateral, includes internal fixation, when performed [A2] [T] [80] [50] [▭]
  ♻ 18.95   ⚕ 18.95   Global Days 090

24576 Closed treatment of humeral condylar fracture, medial or lateral; without manipulation [A2] [T] [50] [▭]
  ♻ 7.10   ⚕ 7.88   Global Days 090

24577   with manipulation [A2] [T] [50] [▭]
  ♻ 12.07   ⚕ 13.04   Global Days 090

24579 Open treatment of humeral condylar fracture, medial or lateral, includes internal fixation, when performed [A2] [T] [80] [50] [▭]
  EXCLUDES   *closed treatment without manipulation (24530, 24560, 24576, 24650, 24670)*
     repair with manipulation (24535, 24565, 24577, 24675)
  ♻ 21.50   ⚕ 21.50   Global Days 090

24582   Percutaneous skeletal fixation of humeral condylar fracture, medial or lateral, with manipulation   A2 T 50 ▢
    🖐 19.78   ✂ 19.78   Global Days 090

24586   Open treatment of periarticular fracture and/or dislocation of the elbow (fracture distal humerus and proximal ulna and/or proximal radius);   A2 T 80 50 ▢
    🖐 28.41   ✂ 28.41   Global Days 090

24587   with implant arthroplasty   A2 T 80 50 ▢
    EXCLUDES   *distal humerus arthroplasty (24361)*
    🖐 28.25   ✂ 28.25   Global Days 090

24600   Treatment of closed elbow dislocation; without anesthesia   A2 T 50 ▢
    🖐 8.03   ✂ 8.79   Global Days 090

24605   requiring anesthesia   A2 T 50 ▢
    🖐 11.48   ✂ 11.48   Global Days 090

24615   Open treatment of acute or chronic elbow dislocation   A2 T 80 50 ▢
    🖐 18.36   ✂ 18.36   Global Days 090

24620   Closed treatment of Monteggia type of fracture dislocation at elbow (fracture proximal end of ulna with dislocation of radial head), with manipulation   A2 T 80 50 ▢
    🖐 13.87   ✂ 13.87   Global Days 090

24635   Open treatment of Monteggia type of fracture dislocation at elbow (fracture proximal end of ulna with dislocation of radial head), includes internal fixation, when performed   A2 T 80 50 ▢
    🖐 19.51   ✂ 19.51   Global Days 090

24640   Closed treatment of radial head subluxation in child, nursemaid elbow, with manipulation   A P3 T 80 50 ▢
    🖐 2.13   ✂ 2.89   Global Days 010

24650   Closed treatment of radial head or neck fracture; without manipulation   P2 T 50 ▢
    🖐 5.51   ✂ 6.08   Global Days 090

24655   with manipulation   A2 T 50 ▢
    🖐 9.69   ✂ 10.54   Global Days 090

24665   Open treatment of radial head or neck fracture, includes internal fixation or radial head excision, when performed;   A2 T 80 50 ▢
    🖐 16.51   ✂ 16.51   Global Days 090

24666   with radial head prosthetic replacement   A2 T 80 50 ▢
    🖐 18.76   ✂ 18.76   Global Days 090

24670   Closed treatment of ulnar fracture, proximal end (eg, olecranon or coronoid process[es]); without manipulation   A2 T 50 ▢
    🖐 6.16   ✂ 6.84   Global Days 090

24675   with manipulation   A2 T 50 ▢
    🖐 10.31   ✂ 11.16   Global Days 090

24685   Open treatment of ulnar fracture, proximal end (eg, olecranon or coronoid process[es]), includes internal fixation, when performed   A2 T 80 50 ▢
    Do not report with (24100-24102)
    🖐 16.62   ✂ 16.62   Global Days 090

24800-24999 Other/Unlisted Elbow/Upper Arm Procedures

24800   Arthrodesis, elbow joint; local   A2 T 80 50 ▢
    🖐 20.32   ✂ 20.32   Global Days 090

24802   with autogenous graft (includes obtaining graft)   A2 T 80 50 ▢
    🖐 25.86   ✂ 25.86   Global Days 090

24900   Amputation, arm through humerus; with primary closure   C 80 50 ▢
    🖐 18.38   ✂ 18.38   Global Days 090

24920   open, circular (guillotine)   C 80 50 ▢
    🖐 18.29   ✂ 18.29   Global Days 090

24925   secondary closure or scar revision   A2 T 80 50 ▢
    🖐 14.16   ✂ 14.16   Global Days 090

24930   re-amputation   C 80 50 ▢
    🖐 19.39   ✂ 19.39   Global Days 090

24931   with implant   C 80 50 ▢
    🖐 21.67   ✂ 21.67   Global Days 090

24935   Stump elongation, upper extremity   T 80 50 ▢
    🖐 26.24   ✂ 26.24   Global Days 090

24940   Cineplasty, upper extremity, complete procedure   C 80 50 ▢
    🖐 0.00   ✂ 0.00   Global Days 090

24999   Unlisted procedure, humerus or elbow   T 80 50
    🖐 0.00   ✂ 0.00   Global Days YYY

25000-25001 Incision Tendon Sheath of Wrist

25000   Incision, extensor tendon sheath, wrist (eg, deQuervains disease)   A2 T 50 ▢
    EXCLUDES   *carpal tunnel release (64721)*
    🖐 8.73   ✂ 8.73   Global Days 090

25001   Incision, flexor tendon sheath, wrist (eg, flexor carpi radialis)   C2 T 50 ▢
    🖐 8.27   ✂ 8.27   Global Days 090

25020-25025 Decompression Fasciotomy Forearm/Wrist

25020   Decompression fasciotomy, forearm and/or wrist, flexor OR extensor compartment; without debridement of nonviable muscle and/or nerve   A2 T 50 ▢
    EXCLUDES   *brachial artery exploration (24495)*
        superficial incision and drainage (10060-10160)
    🖐 14.47   ✂ 14.47   Global Days 090

25023   with debridement of nonviable muscle and/or nerve   A2 T 80 50 ▢
    EXCLUDES   *brachial artery exploration (24495)*
        debridement (11000-11044)
        superficial incision and drainage (10060-10160)
    🖐 27.92   ✂ 27.92   Global Days 090

25024   Decompression fasciotomy, forearm and/or wrist, flexor AND extensor compartment; without debridement of nonviable muscle and/or nerve   A2 T 50 ▢
    🖐 19.49   ✂ 19.49   Global Days 090

25025   with debridement of nonviable muscle and/or nerve   A2 T 80 50 ▢
    🖐 29.96   ✂ 29.96   Global Days 090

25028-25040 Incision for Drainage/Foreign Body Removal

25028   Incision and drainage, forearm and/or wrist; deep abscess or hematoma   A2 T 50 ▢
    🖐 12.88   ✂ 12.88   Global Days 090

25031   bursa   A2 T 80 50 ▢
    🖐 9.48   ✂ 9.48   Global Days 090

25035   Incision, deep, bone cortex, forearm and/or wrist (eg, osteomyelitis or bone abscess)   A2 T 80 50 □
         🔫 16.45   ✄ 16.45 Global Days 090

25040   Arthrotomy, radiocarpal or midcarpal joint, with exploration, drainage, or removal of foreign body   A2 T 80 50 □
         🔫 14.56   ✄ 14.56 Global Days 090

25065-25066 Biopsy Forearm/Wrist

EXCLUDES   soft tissue needle biopsy (20206)

25065   Biopsy, soft tissue of forearm and/or wrist; superficial   P3 T 50 □
         🔫 4.11   ✄ 6.13 Global Days 010

25066   deep (subfascial or intramuscular)   A2 T 50 □
         🔫 9.50   ✄ 9.50 Global Days 090

25075-25240 Resection Areas of Forearm/Wrist

25075   Excision, tumor, soft tissue of forearm and/or wrist area; subcutaneous   A2 T 50 □
         🔫 8.31   ✄ 8.31 Global Days 090

25076   deep (subfascial or intramuscular)   A2 T 50 □
         🔫 11.23   ✄ 11.23 Global Days 090

25077   Radical resection of tumor (eg, malignant neoplasm), soft tissue of forearm and/or wrist area   A2 T 50 □
         🔫 19.08   ✄ 19.08 Global Days 090

25085   Capsulotomy, wrist (eg, contracture)   A2 T 80 50 □
         🔫 11.71   ✄ 11.71 Global Days 090

25100   Arthrotomy, wrist joint; with biopsy   A2 T 80 50 □
         🔫 8.68   ✄ 8.68 Global Days 090

25101   with joint exploration, with or without biopsy, with or without removal of loose or foreign body   A2 T 80 50 □
         🔫 10.25   ✄ 10.25 Global Days 090

25105   with synovectomy   A2 T 80 50 □
         🔫 12.46   ✄ 12.46 Global Days 090

25107   Arthrotomy, distal radioulnar joint including repair of triangular cartilage, complex   A2 T 80 50 □
         🔫 15.44   ✄ 15.44 Global Days 090

25109   Excision of tendon, forearm and/or wrist, flexor or extensor, each   G2 T 50
         🔫 13.22   ✄ 13.22 Global Days 090

25110   Excision, lesion of tendon sheath, forearm and/or wrist   A2 T 50 □
         🔫 9.10   ✄ 9.10 Global Days 090

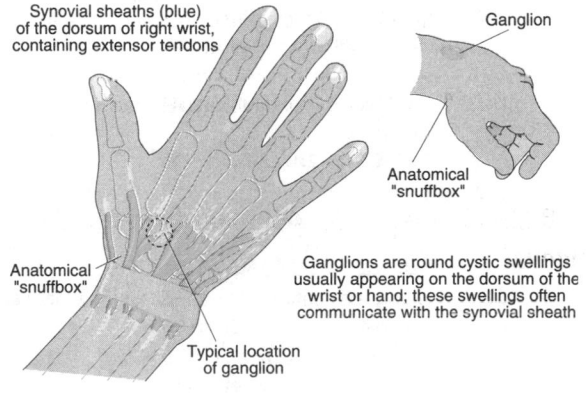

Synovial sheaths (blue) of the dorsum of right wrist, containing extensor tendons

Ganglion

Anatomical "snuffbox"

Anatomical "snuffbox"

Typical location of ganglion

Ganglions are round cystic swellings usually appearing on the dorsum of the wrist or hand; these swellings often communicate with the synovial sheath

25111   Excision of ganglion, wrist (dorsal or volar); primary   A2 T 50 □
         EXCLUDES   excision of ganglion hand or finger (26160)
         🔫 7.89   ✄ 7.89 Global Days 090

25112   recurrent   A2 T 50 □
         EXCLUDES   excision of ganglion hand or finger (26160)
         🔫 9.66   ✄ 9.66 Global Days 090

25115   Radical excision of bursa, synovia of wrist, or forearm tendon sheaths (eg, tenosynovitis, fungus, Tbc, or other granulomas, rheumatoid arthritis); flexors   A2 T 50 □
         EXCLUDES   finger synovectomy (26145)
         🔫 20.36   ✄ 20.36 Global Days 090

25116   extensors, with or without transposition of dorsal retinaculum   A2 T 80 50 □
         EXCLUDES   finger synovectomy (26145)
         🔫 16.49   ✄ 16.49 Global Days 090

25118   Synovectomy, extensor tendon sheath, wrist, single compartment;   A2 T 50 □
         EXCLUDES   finger synovectomy (26145)
         🔫 9.68   ✄ 9.68 Global Days 090

25119   with resection of distal ulna   A2 T 80 50 □
         EXCLUDES   finger synovectomy (26145)
         🔫 12.84   ✄ 12.84 Global Days 090

25120   Excision or curettage of bone cyst or benign tumor of radius or ulna (excluding head or neck of radius and olecranon process);   A2 T 80 50 □
         EXCLUDES   removal of bone cyst or tumor of radial head, neck, or olecranon process (24120-24126)
         🔫 14.09   ✄ 14.09 Global Days 090

25125   with autograft (includes obtaining graft)   A2 T 80 50 □
         🔫 16.36   ✄ 16.36 Global Days 090

25126   with allograft   A2 T 80 50 □
         🔫 16.59   ✄ 16.59 Global Days 090

25130   Excision or curettage of bone cyst or benign tumor of carpal bones;   A2 T 80 50 □
         🔫 11.36   ✄ 11.36 Global Days 090

25135   with autograft (includes obtaining graft)   A2 T 80 50 □
         🔫 14.19   ✄ 14.19 Global Days 090

25136   with allograft   A2 T 80 50 □
         🔫 12.59   ✄ 12.59 Global Days 090

25145   Sequestrectomy (eg, for osteomyelitis or bone abscess), forearm and/or wrist   A2 T 80 50 □
         🔫 14.46   ✄ 14.46 Global Days 090

25150   Partial excision (craterization, saucerization, or diaphysectomy) of bone (eg, for osteomyelitis); ulna   A2 T 50 □
         🔫 14.74   ✄ 14.74 Global Days 090

25151   radius   A2 T 80 50 □
         EXCLUDES   partial removal of radial head, neck, or olecranon process (24145, 24147)
         🔫 16.29   ✄ 16.29 Global Days 090

25170   Radical resection for tumor, radius or ulna   T 80 50 □
         🔫 22.71   ✄ 22.71 Global Days 090

25210   Carpectomy; one bone   A2 T 80 □
         EXCLUDES   carpectomy with insertion of implant (25441-25445)
         🔫 12.45   ✄ 12.45 Global Days 090

25215   all bones of proximal row   A2 T 80 □
         🔫 16.06   ✄ 16.06 Global Days 090

25230   Radial styloidectomy (separate procedure)   A2 T 50 □
         🔫 11.03   ✄ 11.03 Global Days 090

Musculoskeletal System

25240 — 25391

25240 Excision distal ulna partial or complete (eg, Darrach type or matched resection)   A2 T 80 50 ▢
EXCLUDES *acquisition of fascia for interposition (20920, 20922)*
implant replacement (25442)
🔗 11.19   ⚹ 11.19   Global Days 090

25246 Injection for Wrist Arthrogram

EXCLUDES *excision of foreign body (20520)*
K-wire, pin, or rod placement or removal (20650, 20670, 20680)

25246 Injection procedure for wrist arthrography   N1 N 50 ▢
52 73115
🔗 2.08   ⚹ 4.43   Global Days 000

25248-25251 Removal Foreign Body of Wrist

EXCLUDES *excision of superficial foreign body (20520)*
K-wire, pin, or rod placement or removal (20650, 20670, 20680)

25248 Exploration with removal of deep foreign body, forearm or wrist   A2 T 50 ▢
🔗 11.11   ⚹ 11.11   Global Days 090

25250 Removal of wrist prosthesis; (separate procedure)   A2 T 80 50 ▢
🔗 13.26   ⚹ 13.26   Global Days 090

25251 complicated, including total wrist   A2 T 80 ▢
🔗 18.07   ⚹ 18.07   Global Days 090

25259 Manipulation of Wrist with Anesthesia

25259 Manipulation, wrist, under anesthesia   G2 T 50 ▢
EXCLUDES *application of external fixation (20690, 20692)*
🔗 9.81   ⚹ 9.81   Global Days 090
AMA: 2008, Jan, 10-25; 2007, Jan, 13-27; 2007, Jan, 13-27; 2007, January, 13-27; 2005, Jun, 9-11; 2005, Jun, 9-11; 2005, June, 9-11; 2004, Jan, 27; 2004, Jan, 27; 2004, January, 27

25260-25492 Repair/Reconstruction of Forearm/Wrist

25260 Repair, tendon or muscle, flexor, forearm and/or wrist; primary, single, each tendon or muscle   A2 T ▢
🔗 17.26   ⚹ 17.26   Global Days 090

25263 secondary, single, each tendon or muscle   A2 T 80 ▢
🔗 17.23   ⚹ 17.23   Global Days 090

25265 secondary, with free graft (includes obtaining graft), each tendon or muscle   A2 T 80 ▢
🔗 20.47   ⚹ 20.47   Global Days 090

25270 Repair, tendon or muscle, extensor, forearm and/or wrist; primary, single, each tendon or muscle   A2 T 80 ▢
🔗 13.86   ⚹ 13.86   Global Days 090

25272 secondary, single, each tendon or muscle   A2 T 80 ▢
🔗 15.61   ⚹ 15.61   Global Days 090

25274 secondary, with free graft (includes obtaining graft), each tendon or muscle   A2 T 80 ▢
🔗 18.51   ⚹ 18.51   Global Days 090

25275 Repair, tendon sheath, extensor, forearm and/or wrist, with free graft (includes obtaining graft) (eg, for extensor carpi ulnaris subluxation)   A2 T 80 50 ▢
🔗 17.06   ⚹ 17.06   Global Days 090

25280 Lengthening or shortening of flexor or extensor tendon, forearm and/or wrist, single, each tendon   A2 T 80 ▢
🔗 15.80   ⚹ 15.80   Global Days 090

25290 Tenotomy, open, flexor or extensor tendon, forearm and/or wrist, single, each tendon   A2 T ▢
🔗 13.37   ⚹ 13.37   Global Days 090

25295 Tenolysis, flexor or extensor tendon, forearm and/or wrist, single, each tendon   A2 T ▢
🔗 14.71   ⚹ 14.71   Global Days 090
AMA: 2008, Jan, 10-25; 2007, Jan, 13-27; 2007, Jan, 13-27; 2007, January, 13-27

25300 Tenodesis at wrist; flexors of fingers   A2 T 80 50 ▢
🔗 17.36   ⚹ 17.36   Global Days 090

25301 extensors of fingers   A2 T 80 50 ▢
🔗 16.56   ⚹ 16.56   Global Days 090

25310 Tendon transplantation or transfer, flexor or extensor, forearm and/or wrist, single; each tendon   A2 T 80 ▢
🔗 17.12   ⚹ 17.12   Global Days 090
AMA: 2008, Jan, 10-25; 2007, Jan, 13-27; 2007, Jan, 13-27; 2007, January, 13-27; 2005, Jan, 7-13; 2005, January, 7-13; 2005, Jan, 7-13

25312 with tendon graft(s) (includes obtaining graft), each tendon   A2 T 80 ▢
🔗 19.82   ⚹ 19.82   Global Days 090

25315 Flexor origin slide (eg, for cerebral palsy, Volkmann contracture), forearm and/or wrist;   A2 T 80 50 ▢
🔗 21.27   ⚹ 21.27   Global Days 090

25316 with tendon(s) transfer   A2 T 80 50 ▢
🔗 24.57   ⚹ 24.57   Global Days 090

25320 Capsulorrhaphy or reconstruction, wrist, open (eg, capsulodesis, ligament repair, tendon transfer or graft) (includes synovectomy, capsulotomy and open reduction) for carpal instability   A2 T 80 50 ▢
🔗 24.39   ⚹ 24.39   Global Days 090

25332 Arthroplasty, wrist, with or without interposition, with or without external or internal fixation   A2 T 80 50 ▢
EXCLUDES *acquiring fascia for interposition (20920, 20922)*
arthroplasty with prosthesis (25441-25446)
🔗 21.67   ⚹ 21.67   Global Days 090
AMA: 2005, Jan, 7-13; 2005, Jan, 7-13; 2005, January, 7-13

25335 Centralization of wrist on ulna (eg, radial club hand)   A2 T 80 50 ▢
🔗 24.55   ⚹ 24.55   Global Days 090

25337 Reconstruction for stabilization of unstable distal ulna or distal radioulnar joint, secondary by soft tissue stabilization (eg, tendon transfer, tendon graft or weave, or tenodesis) with or without open reduction of distal radioulnar joint   A2 T 50 ▢
EXCLUDES *acquiring fascia lata graft (20920, 20922)*
🔗 22.49   ⚹ 22.49   Global Days 090

25350 Osteotomy, radius; distal third   A2 T 80 50 ▢
🔗 18.89   ⚹ 18.89   Global Days 090

25355 middle or proximal third   A2 T 80 50 ▢
🔗 21.27   ⚹ 21.27   Global Days 090

25360 Osteotomy; ulna   A2 T 80 50 ▢
🔗 18.33   ⚹ 18.33   Global Days 090

25365 radius AND ulna   A2 T 80 50 ▢
🔗 25.02   ⚹ 25.02   Global Days 090

25370 Multiple osteotomies, with realignment on intramedullary rod (Sofield type procedure); radius OR ulna   A2 T 80 50 ▢
🔗 27.25   ⚹ 27.25   Global Days 090

25375 radius AND ulna   A2 T 80 50 ▢
🔗 26.32   ⚹ 26.32   Global Days 090

25390 Osteoplasty, radius OR ulna; shortening   A2 T 80 50 ▢
🔗 21.36   ⚹ 21.36   Global Days 090

25391 lengthening with autograft   A2 T 80 50 ▢
🔗 27.18   ⚹ 27.18   Global Days 090

25392 Osteoplasty, radius AND ulna; shortening (excluding 64876) A2 T 80 50 ▭
🔧 27.54 ✂ 27.54 Global Days 090

25393 lengthening with autograft A2 T 80 50 ▭
🔧 31.08 ✂ 31.08 Global Days 090

25394 Osteoplasty, carpal bone, shortening G2 T 80 50 ▭
🔧 19.87 ✂ 19.87 Global Days 090

25400 Repair of nonunion or malunion, radius OR ulna; without graft (eg, compression technique) A2 T 80 50 ▭
🔧 22.44 ✂ 22.44 Global Days 090

25405 with autograft (includes obtaining graft) A2 T 80 50 ▭
🔧 28.52 ✂ 28.52 Global Days 090

25415 Repair of nonunion or malunion, radius AND ulna; without graft (eg, compression technique) A2 T 80 50 ▭
🔧 26.80 ✂ 26.80 Global Days 090

25420 with autograft (includes obtaining graft) A2 T 80 50 ▭
🔧 31.90 ✂ 31.90 Global Days 090

25425 Repair of defect with autograft; radius OR ulna A2 T 80 50 ▭
🔧 27.54 ✂ 27.54 Global Days 090

25426 radius AND ulna A2 T 80 50 ▭
🔧 28.92 ✂ 28.92 Global Days 090

25430 Insertion of vascular pedicle into carpal bone (eg, Hori procedure) G2 T 50 ▭
INCLUDES Harii procedure
🔧 18.06 ✂ 18.06 Global Days 090

25431 Repair of nonunion of carpal bone (excluding carpal scaphoid (navicular)) (includes obtaining graft and necessary fixation), each bone 02 T 80 50 ▭
🔧 20.17 ✂ 20.17 Global Days 090

25440 Repair of nonunion, scaphoid carpal (navicular) bone, with or without radial styloidectomy (includes obtaining graft and necessary fixation) A2 T 80 50 ▭
🔧 19.96 ✂ 19.96 Global Days 090

25441 Arthroplasty with prosthetic replacement; distal radius H8 T 80 50 ▭
Code also (C1776)
🔧 24.22 ✂ 24.22 Global Days 090
AMA: 2005, Jan, 7-13; 2005, Jan, 7-13; 2005, January, 7-13

25442 distal ulna H8 T 80 50 ▭
Code also (C1776)
🔧 20.56 ✂ 20.56 Global Days 090
AMA: 2005, Jan, 7-13; 2005, Jan, 7-13; 2005, January, 7-13

25443 scaphoid carpal (navicular) A2 T 80 50 ▭
🔧 19.69 ✂ 19.69 Global Days 090
AMA: 2005, Jan, 7-13; 2005, Jan, 7-13; 2005, January, 7-13

25444 lunate A2 T 80 50 ▭
🔧 21.09 ✂ 21.09 Global Days 090
AMA: 2005, Jan, 7-13; 2005, Jan, 7-13; 2005, January, 7-13

25445 trapezium A2 T 50 ▭
🔧 18.48 ✂ 18.48 Global Days 090
AMA: 2005, Jan, 7-13; 2005, Jan, 7-13; 2005, January, 7-13

25446 distal radius and partial or entire carpus (total wrist) H8 T 80 50 ▭
Code also (C1776)
🔧 30.40 ✂ 30.40 Global Days 090
AMA: 2005, Jan, 7-13; 2005, Jan, 7-13; 2005, January, 7-13

25447 Arthroplasty, interposition, intercarpal or carpometacarpal joints A2 T 80 50 ▭
EXCLUDES wrist arthroplasty (25332)
🔧 20.81 ✂ 20.81 Global Days 090
AMA: 2005, Jan, 7-13; 2005, Jan, 7-13; 2005, January, 7-13

25449 Revision of arthroplasty, including removal of implant, wrist joint A2 T 80 50 ▭
🔧 26.65 ✂ 26.65 Global Days 090

25450 Epiphyseal arrest by epiphysiodesis or stapling; distal radius OR ulna A2 T 50 ▭
🔧 15.51 ✂ 15.51 Global Days 090

25455 distal radius AND ulna A2 T 50 ▭
🔧 17.47 ✂ 17.47 Global Days 090

25490 Prophylactic treatment (nailing, pinning, plating or wiring) with or without methylmethacrylate; radius A2 T 80 50 ▭
🔧 19.41 ✂ 19.41 Global Days 090

25491 ulna A2 T 80 50 ▭
🔧 20.52 ✂ 20.52 Global Days 090

25492 radius AND ulna A2 T 80 50 ▭
🔧 24.80 ✂ 24.80 Global Days 090

25500-25695 Treatment of Fracture/Dislocation of Forearm/Wrist

EXCLUDES *external fixation application (20690)*

25500 Closed treatment of radial shaft fracture; without manipulation P2 T 50 ▭
🔧 5.69 ✂ 6.23 Global Days 090

25505 with manipulation A2 T 50 ▭
🔧 11.34 ✂ 12.24 Global Days 090

25515 Open treatment of radial shaft fracture, includes internal fixation, when performed A2 T 80 50 ▭
🔧 17.10 ✂ 17.10 Global Days 090

25520 Closed treatment of radial shaft fracture and closed treatment of dislocation of distal radioulnar joint (Galeazzi fracture/dislocation) A2 T 50 ▭
🔧 12.92 ✂ 13.53 Global Days 090

25525 Open treatment of radial shaft fracture, includes internal fixation, when performed, and closed treatment of distal radioulnar joint dislocation (Galeazzi fracture/dislocation), includes percutaneous skeletal fixation, when performed A2 T 80 50 ▭
🔧 20.74 ✂ 20.74 Global Days 090

25526 Open treatment of radial shaft fracture, includes internal fixation, when performed, and open treatment of distal radioulnar joint dislocation (Galeazzi fracture/dislocation), includes internal fixation, when performed, includes repair of triangular fibrocartilage complex A2 T 80 50 ▭
🔧 25.32 ✂ 25.32 Global Days 090

25530 Closed treatment of ulnar shaft fracture; without manipulation P2 T 50 ▭
🔧 5.44 ✂ 6.04 Global Days 090

25535 with manipulation A2 T 50 ▭
🔧 11.15 ✂ 11.87 Global Days 090

25545 Open treatment of ulnar shaft fracture, includes internal fixation, when performed A2 T 80 50 ▭
🔧 16.02 ✂ 16.02 Global Days 090

25560 Closed treatment of radial and ulnar shaft fractures; without manipulation P2 T 50 ▭
🔧 5.66 ✂ 6.31 Global Days 090

25565 with manipulation A2 T 50 ▭
🔧 11.77 ✂ 12.81 Global Days 090

25574 Open treatment of radial AND ulnar shaft fractures, with internal fixation, when performed; of radius OR ulna A2 T 80 50 ▭
🔧 16.70 ✂ 16.70 Global Days 090

25575 of radius AND ulna A2 T 80 50 ▭
🔧 22.78 ✂ 22.78 Global Days 090

● New Code   ▲ Revised Code   Ⅿ Maternity Edit   ▢ Age Edit   A-Y OPPS Status Indicator   🔧 Facility RVU   ✂ Non-Facility RVU
▭ CCI Comprehensive Code   50 Bilateral Procedure   + Add-on Indicator   ▣ Laboratory crosswalk   ▣ Radiology crosswalk

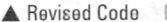

Musculoskeletal System

25600 — 25920

25600	Closed treatment of distal radial fracture (eg, Colles or Smith type) or epiphyseal separation, includes closed treatment of fracture of ulnar styloid, when performed; without manipulation P2 T 50 ▢ P0

Do not report with (25650)

🔪 6.24   ♒ 6.89   Global Days 090

25605	with manipulation A2 T 50 ▢ P0

Do not report with (25650)

🔪 14.24   ♒ 15.02   Global Days 090

25606	Percutaneous skeletal fixation of distal radial fracture or epiphyseal separation A2 T 50 P0

EXCLUDES   *open repair of ulnar styloid fracture (25652)*
percutaneous repair of ulnar styloid fracture (25651)

Do not report with (25650)

🔪 16.74   ♒ 16.74   Global Days 090

25607	Open treatment of distal radial extra-articular fracture or epiphyseal separation, with internal fixation A2 T 80 50 P0

EXCLUDES   *open repair of ulnar styloid fracture (25652)*
percutaneous repair of ulnar styloid fracture (25651)

Do not report with (25650)

🔪 18.08   ♒ 18.08   Global Days 090

25608	Open treatment of distal radial intra-articular fracture or epiphyseal separation; with internal fixation of 2 fragments A2 T 80 50 P0

EXCLUDES   *open repair of ulnar styloid fracture (25652)*
percutaneous repair of ulnar styloid fracture (25651)

Do not report with (25609, 25650)

🔪 20.72   ♒ 20.72   Global Days 090

25609	with internal fixation of 3 or more fragments A2 T 80 50 P0

EXCLUDES   *open repair of ulnar styloid fracture (25652)*
percutaneous repair of ulnar styloid fracture (25651)

Do not report with (25650)

🔪 26.46   ♒ 26.46   Global Days 090

25622	Closed treatment of carpal scaphoid (navicular) fracture; without manipulation P2 T 50 ▢

🔪 6.37   ♒ 7.06   Global Days 090

25624	with manipulation A2 T 80 50 ▢

🔪 10.27   ♒ 11.21   Global Days 090

25628	Open treatment of carpal scaphoid (navicular) fracture, includes internal fixation, when performed A2 T 80 50 ▢

🔪 18.16   ♒ 18.16   Global Days 090

25630	Closed treatment of carpal bone fracture (excluding carpal scaphoid [navicular]); without manipulation, each bone P2 T 50 ▢

🔪 6.56   ♒ 7.24   Global Days 090

25635	with manipulation, each bone A2 T 80 50 ▢

🔪 9.51   ♒ 10.61   Global Days 090

25645	Open treatment of carpal bone fracture (other than carpal scaphoid [navicular]), each bone A2 T 80 50 ▢

🔪 14.37   ♒ 14.37   Global Days 090

25650	Closed treatment of ulnar styloid fracture P2 T 50 ▢

Do not report with (25600, 25605, 25607-25609)

🔪 6.96   ♒ 7.54   Global Days 090

25651	Percutaneous skeletal fixation of ulnar styloid fracture G2 T 80 50 ▢

🔪 11.85   ♒ 11.85   Global Days 090

25652	Open treatment of ulnar styloid fracture G2 T 50 ▢

🔪 15.63   ♒ 15.63   Global Days 090

25660	Closed treatment of radiocarpal or intercarpal dislocation, 1 or more bones, with manipulation A2 T 80 50 ▢

🔪 9.85   ♒ 9.85   Global Days 090

25670	Open treatment of radiocarpal or intercarpal dislocation, 1 or more bones A2 T 80 50 ▢

🔪 15.50   ♒ 15.50   Global Days 090

25671	Percutaneous skeletal fixation of distal radioulnar dislocation A2 T 50 ▢

🔪 13.06   ♒ 13.06   Global Days 090

25675	Closed treatment of distal radioulnar dislocation with manipulation A2 T 80 50 ▢

🔪 9.62   ♒ 10.41   Global Days 090

25676	Open treatment of distal radioulnar dislocation, acute or chronic A2 T 80 50 ▢

🔪 16.06   ♒ 16.06   Global Days 090

25680	Closed treatment of trans-scaphoperilunar type of fracture dislocation, with manipulation A2 T 80 50 ▢

🔪 11.41   ♒ 11.41   Global Days 090

25685	Open treatment of trans-scaphoperilunar type of fracture dislocation A2 T 80 50 ▢

🔪 18.69   ♒ 18.69   Global Days 090

25690	Closed treatment of lunate dislocation, with manipulation A2 T 80 50 ▢

🔪 11.57   ♒ 11.57   Global Days 090

25695	Open treatment of lunate dislocation A2 T 80 50 ▢

🔪 16.10   ♒ 16.10   Global Days 090

25800-25830 Wrist Fusion

25800	Arthrodesis, wrist; complete, without bone graft (includes radiocarpal and/or intercarpal and/or carpometacarpal joints) A2 T 80 50 ▢

🔪 19.05   ♒ 19.05   Global Days 090

25805	with sliding graft A2 T 80 50 ▢

🔪 21.96   ♒ 21.96   Global Days 090

25810	with iliac or other autograft (includes obtaining graft) A2 T 80 50 ▢

🔪 22.12   ♒ 22.12   Global Days 090

25820	limited, without bone graft (eg, intercarpal or radiocarpal) A2 T 80 50 ▢

🔪 15.56   ♒ 15.56   Global Days 090

25825	with autograft (includes obtaining graft) A2 T 80 50 ▢

🔪 19.14   ♒ 19.14   Global Days 090

25830	Arthrodesis, distal radioulnar joint with segmental resection of ulna, with or without bone graft (eg, Sauve-Kapandji procedure) A2 T 80 50 ▢

🔪 23.87   ♒ 23.87   Global Days 090

25900-25931 Amputation Through Forearm/Wrist

25900	Amputation, forearm, through radius and ulna; C 80 50 ▢

🔪 19.04   ♒ 19.04   Global Days 090

25905	open, circular (guillotine) C 80 50 ▢

🔪 18.86   ♒ 18.86   Global Days 090

25907	secondary closure or scar revision A2 T 80 50 ▢

🔪 16.43   ♒ 16.43   Global Days 090

25909	re-amputation C 80 50 ▢

🔪 18.57   ♒ 18.57   Global Days 090

25915	Krukenberg procedure C 80 50 ▢

🔪 32.62   ♒ 32.62   Global Days 090

25920	Disarticulation through wrist; C 80 50 ▢

🔪 17.45   ♒ 17.45   Global Days 090

25922   secondary closure or scar revision   A2 T 80 50
          ⚙ 14.74   ℘ 14.74   Global Days 090

25924   re-amputation   C 80 50
          ⚙ 17.04   ℘ 17.04   Global Days 090

25927   Transmetacarpal amputation;   C 80 50
          ⚙ 19.74   ℘ 19.74   Global Days 090

25929   secondary closure or scar revision   A2 T 80 50
          ⚙ 14.27   ℘ 14.27   Global Days 090

25931   re-amputation   C2 T 50
          ⚙ 17.99   ℘ 17.99   Global Days 090

25999 Unlisted Forearm/Wrist Procedure

25999 Unlisted procedure, forearm or wrist   T 80 50
          ⚙ 0.00   ℘ 0.00   Global Days YYY

26010-26037 Incision for Drainage/Decompression/Foreign Body Removal: Hand/Fingers

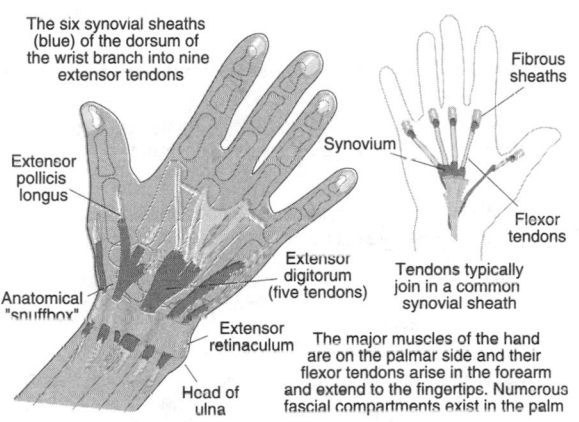

The six synovial sheaths (blue) of the dorsum of the wrist branch into nine extensor tendons

Extensor pollicis longus

Anatomical "snuffbox"

Extensor digitorum (five tendons)

Extensor retinaculum

Head of ulna

Synovium

Fibrous sheaths

Flexor tendons

Tendons typically join in a common synovial sheath

The major muscles of the hand are on the palmar side and their flexor tendons arise in the forearm and extend to the fingertips. Numerous fascial compartments exist in the palm

26010   Drainage of finger abscess; simple   P2 T
         ⚙ 3.29   ℘ 6.14   Global Days 010

26011   complicated (eg, felon)   AL i
         ⚙ 4.62   ℘ 9.39   Global Days 010

26020   Drainage of tendon sheath, digit and/or palm, each   A2 T
         ⚙ 10.65   ℘ 10.65   Global Days 090

26025   Drainage of palmar bursa; single, bursa   A2 T 80
         ⚙ 10.42   ℘ 10.42   Global Days 090

26030   multiple bursa   A2 T 80
         ⚙ 12.32   ℘ 12.32   Global Days 090

26034   Incision, bone cortex, hand or finger (eg, osteomyelitis or bone abscess)   A2 T
         ⚙ 13.36   ℘ 13.36   Global Days 090

26035   Decompression fingers and/or hand, injection injury (eg, grease gun)   C2 T 80
         ⚙ 20.77   ℘ 20.77   Global Days 090

26037   Decompressive fasciotomy, hand (excludes 26035)   T 80
         EXCLUDES   injection injury (26035)
         ⚙ 14.40   ℘ 14.40   Global Days 090

26040-26045 Incision Palmar Fascia

EXCLUDES   fasciectomy (26121, 26123, 26125)

26040   Fasciotomy, palmar (eg, Dupuytren's contracture); percutaneous   A2 T 50
         ⚙ 7.64   ℘ 7.64   Global Days 090

26045   open, partial   A2 T 50
         ⚙ 11.69   ℘ 11.69   Global Days 090

26055-26080 Incision Tendon/Joint of Fingers/Hand

26055   Tendon sheath incision (eg, for trigger finger)   A2 T
         ⚙ 7.30   ℘ 13.71   Global Days 090

26060   Tenotomy, percutaneous, single, each digit   A2 T 80
         EXCLUDES   arthrocentesis (20610)
         ⚙ 6.54   ℘ 6.54   Global Days 090

26070   Arthrotomy, with exploration, drainage, or removal of loose or foreign body; carpometacarpal joint   A2 T 50
         ⚙ 7.43   ℘ 7.43   Global Days 090

26075   metacarpophalangeal joint, each   A2 T 50
         ⚙ 7.88   ℘ 7.88   Global Days 090

26080   interphalangeal joint, each   A2 T
         ⚙ 9.52   ℘ 9.52   Global Days 090

26100-26320 Resection Areas of Fingers and Hand

26100   Arthrotomy with biopsy; carpometacarpal joint, each   A2 T 80 50
         ⚙ 7.99   ℘ 7.99   Global Days 090

26105   metacarpophalangeal joint, each   A2 T 80 50
         ⚙ 8.19   ℘ 8.19   Global Days 090

26110   interphalangeal joint, each   A2 T
         ⚙ 7.85   ℘ 7.85   Global Days 090

26115   Excision, tumor or vascular malformation, soft tissue of hand or finger; subcutaneous   A2 T
         ⚙ 8.90   ℘ 15.08   Global Days 090

26116   deep (subfascial or intramuscular)   A2 T
         ⚙ 11.99   ℘ 11.99   Global Days 090

26117   Radical resection of tumor (eg, malignant neoplasm), soft tissue of hand or finger   A2 T
         ⚙ 16.40   ℘ 16.40   Global Days 090

26121   Fasciectomy, palm only, with or without Z-plasty, other local tissue rearrangement, or skin grafting (includes obtaining graft)   A2 T 50
         EXCLUDES   fasciotomy (26040, 26045)
         ⚙ 15.08   ℘ 15.08   Global Days 090

26123   Fasciectomy, partial palmar with release of single digit including proximal interphalangeal joint, with or without Z-plasty, other local tissue rearrangement, or skin grafting (includes obtaining graft);   A2 T 50
         EXCLUDES   fasciotomy (26040, 26045)
         ⚙ 20.58   ℘ 20.58   Global Days 090

+   26125   each additional digit (List separately in addition to code for primary procedure)   A7 T
         Code first 26123 (26123)
         EXCLUDES   fasciotomy (26040, 26045)
         ⚙ 7.42   ℘ 7.42   Global Days ZZZ

26130   Synovectomy, carpometacarpal joint   A2 T 50
         ⚙ 11.44   ℘ 11.44   Global Days 090

26135   Synovectomy, metacarpophalangeal joint including intrinsic release and extensor hood reconstruction, each digit   A2 T 80
         ⚙ 13.90   ℘ 13.90   Global Days 090

● New Code   ▲ Revised Code   M Maternity Edit   A-Y Age Edit   A-Y OPPS Status Indicator   ⚙ Facility RVU   ℘ Non-Facility RVU
□ CCI Comprehensive Code   50 Bilateral Procedure   + Add-on Indicator   ■ Laboratory crosswalk   ■ Radiology crosswalk

26140 Synovectomy, proximal interphalangeal joint, including extensor reconstruction, each interphalangeal joint ◫ Ⓣ ▭
　📖 12.62　⚕ 12.62　Global Days 090

26145 Synovectomy, tendon sheath, radical (tenosynovectomy), flexor tendon, palm and/or finger, each tendon ◫ Ⓣ ▭
　EXCLUDES　wrist synovectomy (25115-25116)
　📖 12.84　⚕ 12.84　Global Days 090

26160 Excision of lesion of tendon sheath or joint capsule (eg, cyst, mucous cyst, or ganglion), hand or finger ◫ Ⓣ ▭
　EXCLUDES　trigger finger (26055)
　　　　　　wrist ganglion removal (25111-25112)
　📖 7.96　⚕ 13.74　Global Days 090

26170 Excision of tendon, palm, flexor or extensor, single, each tendon ◫ Ⓣ 80 ▭
　Do not report with (26390, 26415)
　📖 10.07　⚕ 10.07　Global Days 090

26180 Excision of tendon, finger, flexor or extensor, each tendon ◫ Ⓣ 80 ▭
　Do not report with (26390, 26415)
　📖 11.02　⚕ 11.02　Global Days 090

26185 Sesamoidectomy, thumb or finger (separate procedure) ◫ Ⓣ 80 50 ▭
　📖 13.13　⚕ 13.13　Global Days 090

26200 Excision or curettage of bone cyst or benign tumor of metacarpal; ◫ Ⓣ 80 ▭
　📖 11.34　⚕ 11.34　Global Days 090

26205 with autograft (includes obtaining graft) ◫ Ⓣ ▭
　📖 15.24　⚕ 15.24　Global Days 090

26210 Excision or curettage of bone cyst or benign tumor of proximal, middle, or distal phalanx of finger; ◫ Ⓣ ▭
　📖 10.97　⚕ 10.97　Global Days 090

26215 with autograft (includes obtaining graft) ◫ Ⓣ ▭
　📖 13.93　⚕ 13.93　Global Days 090

26230 Partial excision (craterization, saucerization, or diaphysectomy) bone (eg, osteomyelitis); metacarpal ◫ Ⓣ 80 ▭
　📖 12.70　⚕ 12.70　Global Days 090

26235 proximal or middle phalanx of finger ◫ Ⓣ 80 ▭
　📖 12.46　⚕ 12.46　Global Days 090

26236 distal phalanx of finger ◫ Ⓣ ▭
　📖 11.03　⚕ 11.03　Global Days 090

26250 Radical resection, metacarpal (eg, tumor); ◫ Ⓣ 80 ▭
　📖 14.70　⚕ 14.70　Global Days 090

26255 with autograft (includes obtaining graft) ◫ Ⓣ 80 ▭
　📖 22.38　⚕ 22.38　Global Days 090

26260 Radical resection, proximal or middle phalanx of finger (eg, tumor); ◫ Ⓣ 80 ▭
　📖 13.77　⚕ 13.77　Global Days 090

26261 with autograft (includes obtaining graft) ◫ Ⓣ 80 ▭
　📖 17.02　⚕ 17.02　Global Days 090

26262 Radical resection, distal phalanx of finger (eg, tumor) ◫ Ⓣ 80 ▭
　📖 11.51　⚕ 11.51　Global Days 090

26320 Removal of implant from finger or hand ◫ Ⓣ ▭
　EXCLUDES　excision of foreign body (20520, 20525)
　📖 8.57　⚕ 8.57　Global Days 090

26340-26548 Repair/Reconstruction of Fingers and Hand

26340 Manipulation, finger joint, under anesthesia, each joint 62 Ⓣ 50 ▭
　EXCLUDES　application of external fixation (20690, 20692)
　📖 7.66　⚕ 7.66　Global Days 090
　AMA: 2008, Jan, 10-25; 2007, Jan, 13-27; 2007, Jan, 13-27; 2007, January, 13-27

26350 Repair or advancement, flexor tendon, not in zone 2 digital flexor tendon sheath (eg, no man's land); primary or secondary without free graft, each tendon ◫ Ⓣ ▭
　📖 17.76　⚕ 17.76　Global Days 090

26352 secondary with free graft (includes obtaining graft), each tendon ◫ Ⓣ 80 ▭
　📖 20.21　⚕ 20.21　Global Days 090

26356 Repair or advancement, flexor tendon, in zone 2 digital flexor tendon sheath (eg, no man's land); primary, without free graft, each tendon ◫ Ⓣ ▭
　📖 26.32　⚕ 26.32　Global Days 090
　AMA: 2008, Jan, 10-25; 2007, Jan, 13-27; 2007, Jan, 13-27; 2007, January, 13-27

26357 secondary, without free graft, each tendon ◫ Ⓣ 80 ▭
　📖 21.74　⚕ 21.74　Global Days 090

26358 secondary, with free graft (includes obtaining graft), each tendon ◫ Ⓣ 80 ▭
　📖 22.98　⚕ 22.98　Global Days 090

26370 Repair or advancement of profundus tendon, with intact superficialis tendon; primary, each tendon ◫ Ⓣ 80 ▭
　📖 19.26　⚕ 19.26　Global Days 090

26372 secondary with free graft (includes obtaining graft), each tendon ◫ Ⓣ 80 ▭
　📖 22.36　⚕ 22.36　Global Days 090

26373 secondary without free graft, each tendon ◫ Ⓣ 80 ▭
　📖 21.22　⚕ 21.22　Global Days 090

26390 Excision flexor tendon, with implantation of synthetic rod for delayed tendon graft, hand or finger, each rod ◫ Ⓣ 80 ▭
　📖 20.88　⚕ 20.88　Global Days 090

26392 Removal of synthetic rod and insertion of flexor tendon graft, hand or finger (includes obtaining graft), each rod ◫ Ⓣ 80 ▭
　📖 24.40　⚕ 24.40　Global Days 090

26410 Repair, extensor tendon, hand, primary or secondary; without free graft, each tendon ◫ Ⓣ ▭
　📖 14.12　⚕ 14.12　Global Days 090

26412 with free graft (includes obtaining graft), each tendon ◫ Ⓣ 80 ▭
　📖 17.17　⚕ 17.17　Global Days 090

26415 Excision of extensor tendon, with implantation of synthetic rod for delayed tendon graft, hand or finger, each rod ◫ Ⓣ 80 ▭
　📖 18.03　⚕ 18.03　Global Days 090

26416 Removal of synthetic rod and insertion of extensor tendon graft (includes obtaining graft), hand or finger, each rod ◫ Ⓣ ▭
　📖 19.22　⚕ 19.22　Global Days 090

26418 Repair, extensor tendon, finger, primary or secondary; without free graft, each tendon ◫ Ⓣ ▭
　📖 14.16　⚕ 14.16　Global Days 090
　AMA: 2008, Jan, 10-25; 2007, Jan, 13-27; 2007, Jan, 13-27; 2007, January, 13-27

26420   with free graft (includes obtaining graft) each tendon   `A2` `T` `80` ▭
🖙 17.86   ⚕ 17.86   Global Days 090

26426   Repair of extensor tendon, central slip, secondary (eg, boutonniere deformity); using local tissue(s), including lateral band(s), each finger   `A2` `T` ▭
🖙 14.40   ⚕ 14.40   Global Days 090

26428   with free graft (includes obtaining graft), each finger   `A2` `T` `80` ▭
🖙 18.76   ⚕ 18.76   Global Days 090

26432   Closed treatment of distal extensor tendon insertion, with or without percutaneous pinning (eg, mallet finger)   `A2` `T` ▭
🖙 12.35   ⚕ 12.35   Global Days 090

26433   Repair of extensor tendon, distal insertion, primary or secondary; without graft (eg, mallet finger)   `A2` `T` ▭
EXCLUDES   *trigger finger (26055)*
🖙 13.26   ⚕ 13.26   Global Days 090

26434   with free graft (includes obtaining graft)   `A2` `T` `80` ▭
EXCLUDES   *trigger finger (26055)*
🖙 15.93   ⚕ 15.93   Global Days 090

26437   Realignment of extensor tendon, hand, each tendon   `A2` `T` ▭
🖙 15.52   ⚕ 15.52   Global Days 090

26440   Tenolysis, flexor tendon; palm OR finger, each tendon   `A2` `T` ▭
🖙 15.55   ⚕ 15.55   Global Days 090
AMA: 2008, Jan, 10-25; 2007, Jan, 13-27; 2007, Jan, 13-27; 2007, January, 13-27

26442   palm AND finger, each tendon   `A2` `T` ▭
🖙 23.56   ⚕ 23.56   Global Days 090

26445   Tenolysis, extensor tendon, hand OR finger, each tendon   `A2` `T` ▭
🖙 14.42   ⚕ 14.42   Global Days 090
AMA: 2008, Jan, 10-25; 2007, Jan, 13-27; 2007, Jan, 13-27; 2007, January, 13-27

26449   Tenolysis, complex, extensor tendon, finger, including forearm, each tendon   `A2` `T` `80` ▭
🖙 18.94   ⚕ 18.94   Global Days 090

26450   Tenotomy, flexor, palm, open, each tendon   `A2` `T` `80` ▭
🖙 10.02   ⚕ 10.02   Global Days 090

26455   Tenotomy, flexor, finger, open, each tendon   `A2` `T` `80` ▭
🖙 9.95   ⚕ 9.95   Global Days 090

26460   Tenotomy, extensor, hand or finger, open, each tendon   `A2` `T` ▭
🖙 9.67   ⚕ 9.67   Global Days 090

26471   Tenodesis; of proximal interphalangeal joint, each joint   `A2` `T` `80` ▭
🖙 15.29   ⚕ 15.29   Global Days 090

26474   of distal joint, each joint   `A2` `T` `80` ▭
🖙 14.64   ⚕ 14.64   Global Days 090

26476   Lengthening of tendon, extensor, hand or finger, each tendon   `A2` `T` ▭
🖙 14.27   ⚕ 14.27   Global Days 090

26477   Shortening of tendon, extensor, hand or finger, each tendon   `A2` `T` ▭
🖙 14.40   ⚕ 14.40   Global Days 090

26478   Lengthening of tendon, flexor, hand or finger, each tendon   `A2` `T` `80` ▭
🖙 15.64   ⚕ 15.64   Global Days 090

26479   Shortening of tendon, flexor, hand or finger, each tendon   `A2` `T` `80` ▭
🖙 15.48   ⚕ 15.48   Global Days 090

26480   Transfer or transplant of tendon, carpometacarpal area or dorsum of hand; without free graft, each tendon   `A2` `T` `80` ▭
🖙 18.80   ⚕ 18.80   Global Days 090
AMA: 2005, Jan, 7-13; 2005, Jan, 7-13, 2005, January, 7-13

26483   with free tendon graft (includes obtaining graft), each tendon   `A2` `T` `80` ▭
🖙 21.26   ⚕ 21.26   Global Days 090

26485   Transfer or transplant of tendon, palmar; without free tendon graft, each tendon   `A2` `T` `80` ▭
🖙 20.35   ⚕ 20.35   Global Days 090

26489   with free tendon graft (includes obtaining graft), each tendon   `A2` `T` `80` ▭
🖙 22.00   ⚕ 22.00   Global Days 090

26490   Opponensplasty; superficialis tendon transfer type, each tendon   `A2` `T` `80` ▭
EXCLUDES   *thumb fusion (26820)*
🖙 19.69   ⚕ 19.69   Global Days 090

26492   tendon transfer with graft (includes obtaining graft), each tendon   `A2` `T` `80` ▭
EXCLUDES   *thumb fusion (26820)*
🖙 21.96   ⚕ 21.96   Global Days 090

26494   hypothenar muscle transfer   `A2` `T` `80` ▭
EXCLUDES   *thumb fusion (26820)*
🖙 19.95   ⚕ 19.95   Global Days 090

26496   other methods   `A2` `T` `80` ▭
EXCLUDES   *thumb fusion (26820)*
🖙 21.66   ⚕ 21.66   Global Days 090

26497   Transfer of tendon to restore intrinsic function; ring and small finger   `A2` `T` `80` ▭
🖙 21.66   ⚕ 21.66   Global Days 090

26498   all 4 fingers   `A2` `T` `80` ▭
🖙 29.01   ⚕ 29.01   Global Days 090

26499   Correction claw finger, other methods   `A2` `T` `80` ▭
🖙 20.70   ⚕ 20.70   Global Days 090

26500   Reconstruction of tendon pulley, each tendon; with local tissues (separate procedure)   `A2` `T` `80` ▭
🖙 15.61   ⚕ 15.61   Global Days 090

26502   with tendon or fascial graft (includes obtaining graft) (separate procedure)   `A2` `T` `80` ▭
🖙 17.66   ⚕ 17.66   Global Days 090

26508   Release of thenar muscle(s) (eg, thumb contracture)   `A0` `T` `80` ▭
🖙 15.72   ⚕ 15.72   Global Days 090

26510   Cross intrinsic transfer, each tendon   `A2` `T` `80` ▭
🖙 14.86   ⚕ 14.86   Global Days 090

26516   Capsulodesis, metacarpophalangeal joint; single digit   `A2` `T` `80` ▭
🖙 17.60   ⚕ 17.60   Global Days 090

26517   2 digits   `A2` `T` `80` ▭
🖙 20.76   ⚕ 20.76   Global Days 090

26518   3 or 4 digits   `A2` `T` `80` ▭
🖙 20.93   ⚕ 20.93   Global Days 090

26520   Capsulectomy or capsulotomy; metacarpophalangeal joint, each joint   `A2` `T` ▭
EXCLUDES   *carpometacarpal joint arthroplasty (25447)*
🖙 16.26   ⚕ 16.26   Global Days 090

26525   interphalangeal joint, each joint   `A2` `T` ▭
EXCLUDES   *carpometacarpal joint arthroplasty (25447)*
🖙 16.33   ⚕ 16.33   Global Days 090
AMA: 2008, Jan, 10-25; 2007, Jan, 13-27; 2007, Jan, 13-27; 2007, January, 13-27

● New Code   ▲ Revised Code   Ⓜ Maternity Edit   🅰 Age Edit   🄰 🅅 OPPS Status Indicator   🖙 Facility RVU   ⚕ Non-Facility RVU

▭ CCI Comprehensive Code   🔟 Bilateral Procedure   + Add-on Indicator   ◣ Laboratory crosswalk   ◪ Radiology crosswalk

26530 Arthroplasty, metacarpophalangeal joint; each joint A2 T 80 ▭
EXCLUDES *carpometacarpal joint arthroplasty (25447)*
🔗 13.48 ⚕ 13.48 Global Days 090

26531 with prosthetic implant, each joint A2 T 80 ▭
EXCLUDES *carpometacarpal joint arthroplasty (25447)*
🔗 15.68 ⚕ 15.68 Global Days 090

26535 Arthroplasty, interphalangeal joint; each joint A2 T ▭
EXCLUDES *carpometacarpal joint arthroplasty (25447)*
🔗 10.08 ⚕ 10.08 Global Days 090

26536 with prosthetic implant, each joint A2 T 80 ▭
EXCLUDES *carpometacarpal joint arthroplasty (25447)*
🔗 16.75 ⚕ 16.75 Global Days 090

26540 Repair of collateral ligament, metacarpophalangeal or interphalangeal joint A2 T 80 ▭
🔗 16.51 ⚕ 16.51 Global Days 090

26541 Reconstruction, collateral ligament, metacarpophalangeal joint, single; with tendon or fascial graft (includes obtaining graft) A2 T 80 ▭
🔗 20.20 ⚕ 20.20 Global Days 090

26542 with local tissue (eg, adductor advancement) A2 T 80 ▭
🔗 17.07 ⚕ 17.07 Global Days 090

26545 Reconstruction, collateral ligament, interphalangeal joint, single, including graft, each joint A2 T 80 ▭
🔗 17.38 ⚕ 17.38 Global Days 090

26546 Repair non-union, metacarpal or phalanx (includes obtaining bone graft with or without external or internal fixation) A2 T 80 50 ▭
🔗 24.39 ⚕ 24.39 Global Days 090

26548 Repair and reconstruction, finger, volar plate, interphalangeal joint A2 T 80 ▭
🔗 19.15 ⚕ 19.15 Global Days 090

26550-26556 Reconstruction Procedures with Finger and Toe Transplants

26550 Pollicization of a digit A2 T 80 ▭
🔗 37.71 ⚕ 37.71 Global Days 090

26551 Transfer, toe-to-hand with microvascular anastomosis; great toe wrap-around with bone graft C 80 ▭
EXCLUDES *big toe with web space (20973)*
INCLUDES operating microscope (69990)
🔗 83.01 ⚕ 83.01 Global Days 090

26553 other than great toe, single C 80 ▭
INCLUDES operating microscope (69990)
🔗 71.04 ⚕ 71.04 Global Days 090

26554 other than great toe, double C 80 ▭
INCLUDES operating microscope (69990)
🔗 95.07 ⚕ 95.07 Global Days 090

26555 Transfer, finger to another position without microvascular anastomosis A2 T 80 ▭
🔗 34.75 ⚕ 34.75 Global Days 090

26556 Transfer, free toe joint, with microvascular anastomosis C 80 ▭
INCLUDES operating microscope (69990)
EXCLUDES *big toe to hand transfer (20973)*
🔗 73.42 ⚕ 73.42 Global Days 090

26560-26596 Repair of Other Deformities of the Fingers/Hand

26560 Repair of syndactyly (web finger) each web space; with skin flaps A2 T 80 ▭
🔗 14.22 ⚕ 14.22 Global Days 090

26561 with skin flaps and grafts A2 T 80 ▭
🔗 22.82 ⚕ 22.82 Global Days 090

26562 complex (eg, involving bone, nails) A2 T 80 ▭
🔗 33.26 ⚕ 33.26 Global Days 090

26565 Osteotomy; metacarpal, each A2 T 80 ▭
🔗 16.91 ⚕ 16.91 Global Days 090

26567 phalanx of finger, each A2 T 80 ▭
🔗 17.09 ⚕ 17.09 Global Days 090

26568 Osteoplasty, lengthening, metacarpal or phalanx A2 T 80 ▭
🔗 22.54 ⚕ 22.54 Global Days 090

26580 Repair cleft hand A2 T 80 ▭
INCLUDES Barsky's procedure
🔗 35.29 ⚕ 35.29 Global Days 090

26587 Reconstruction of polydactylous digit, soft tissue and bone A2 T 80 ▭
EXCLUDES *soft tissue removal only (11200)*
🔗 24.14 ⚕ 24.14 Global Days 090
AMA: 2008, Jan, 10-25; 2007, Jan, 13-27; 2007, Jan, 13-27; 2007, January, 13-27; 2004, May, 16; 2004, May, 16; 2004, May, 16

26590 Repair macrodactylia, each digit A2 T 80 ▭
🔗 32.35 ⚕ 32.35 Global Days 090
AMA: 2008, Jan, 10-25; 2007, Jan, 13-27; 2007, Jan, 13-27; 2007, January, 13-27; 2004, May, 16; 2004, May, 16; 2004, May, 16

26591 Repair, intrinsic muscles of hand, each muscle A2 T 80 ▭
🔗 10.83 ⚕ 10.83 Global Days 090
AMA: 2008, Jan, 10-25; 2007, Jan, 13-27; 2007, Jan, 13-27; 2007, January, 13-27

26593 Release, intrinsic muscles of hand, each muscle A2 T ▭
🔗 14.82 ⚕ 14.82 Global Days 090

26596 Excision of constricting ring of finger, with multiple Z-plasties A2 T 80 ▭
EXCLUDES *release of scar contracture or treatment with graft (11041-11042, 14040-14041, 15120, 15240)*
🔗 18.52 ⚕ 18.52 Global Days 090

26600-26785 Treatment of Fracture/Dislocation of Fingers and Hand

26600 Closed treatment of metacarpal fracture, single; without manipulation, each bone P2 T ▭
🔗 6.06 ⚕ 6.55 Global Days 090

26605 with manipulation, each bone A2 T ▭
🔗 6.96 ⚕ 7.61 Global Days 090

26607 Closed treatment of metacarpal fracture, with manipulation, with external fixation, each bone A2 T 80 ▭
🔗 10.97 ⚕ 10.97 Global Days 090

26608 Percutaneous skeletal fixation of metacarpal fracture, each bone A2 T 80 ▭
🔗 11.86 ⚕ 11.86 Global Days 090

26615 Open treatment of metacarpal fracture, single, includes internal fixation, when performed, each bone A2 T ▭
🔗 13.70 ⚕ 13.70 Global Days 090

26641 Closed treatment of carpometacarpal dislocation, thumb, with manipulation ☐P2☐T☐50☐
🔹 7.95 ⚖ 8.68 Global Days 090

26645 Closed treatment of carpometacarpal fracture dislocation, thumb (Bennett fracture), with manipulation ☐A2☐T☐50☐
🔹 9.24 ⚖ 9.99 Global Days 090

26650 Percutaneous skeletal fixation of carpometacarpal fracture dislocation, thumb (Bennett fracture), with manipulation ☐A2☐T☐
🔹 11.89 ⚖ 11.89 Global Days 090

26665 Open treatment of carpometacarpal fracture dislocation, thumb (Bennett fracture), includes internal fixation, when performed ☐A2☐T☐
🔹 15.19 ⚖ 15.19 Global Days 090

26670 Closed treatment of carpometacarpal dislocation, other than thumb, with manipulation, each joint; without anesthesia ☐P2☐T☐80☐
🔹 7.10 ⚖ 7.85 Global Days 090

26675 requiring anesthesia ☐A2☐T☐80☐
🔹 9.90 ⚖ 10.68 Global Days 090

26676 Percutaneous skeletal fixation of carpometacarpal dislocation, other than thumb, with manipulation, each joint ☐A2☐T☐
🔹 12.43 ⚖ 12.43 Global Days 090

26685 Open treatment of carpometacarpal dislocation, other than thumb; includes internal fixation, when performed, each joint ☐A2☐T☐
🔹 14.13 ⚖ 14.13 Global Days 090

26686 complex, multiple, or delayed reduction ☐A2☐T☐80☐
🔹 15.67 ⚖ 15.67 Global Days 090

26700 Closed treatment of metacarpophalangeal dislocation, single, with manipulation; without anesthesia ☐P2☐T☐
🔹 6.98 ⚖ 7.48 Global Days 090

26705 requiring anesthesia ☐A2☐T☐80☐
🔹 9.01 ⚖ 9.78 Global Days 090

26706 Percutaneous skeletal fixation of metacarpophalangeal dislocation, single, with manipulation ☐A2☐T☐
🔹 10.78 ⚖ 10.78 Global Days 090

26715 Open treatment of metacarpophalangeal dislocation, single, includes internal fixation, when performed ☐A2☐T☐80☐
🔹 13.74 ⚖ 13.74 Global Days 090

26720 Closed treatment of phalangeal shaft fracture, proximal or middle phalanx, finger or thumb; without manipulation, each ☐P2☐T☐
🔹 4.17 ⚖ 4.55 Global Days 090

26725 with manipulation, with or without skin or skeletal traction, each ☐P2☐T☐
🔹 7.36 ⚖ 8.17 Global Days 090

26727 Percutaneous skeletal fixation of unstable phalangeal shaft fracture, proximal or middle phalanx, finger or thumb, with manipulation, each ☐A2☐T☐
🔹 11.65 ⚖ 11.65 Global Days 090

26735 Open treatment of phalangeal shaft fracture, proximal or middle phalanx, finger or thumb, includes internal fixation, when performed, each ☐A2☐T☐
🔹 14.31 ⚖ 14.31 Global Days 090

26740 Closed treatment of articular fracture, involving metacarpophalangeal or interphalangeal joint; without manipulation, each ☐P2☐T☐
🔹 4.99 ⚖ 5.31 Global Days 090

26742 with manipulation, each ☐A2☐T☐
🔹 8.16 ⚖ 8.95 Global Days 090

26746 Open treatment of articular fracture, involving metacarpophalangeal or interphalangeal joint, includes internal fixation, when performed, each ☐A2☐T☐
🔹 17.43 ⚖ 17.43 Global Days 090

26750 Closed treatment of distal phalangeal fracture, finger or thumb; without manipulation, each ☐P2☐T☐
🔹 4.14 ⚖ 4.25 Global Days 090

26755 with manipulation, each ☐G2☐T☐
🔹 6.54 ⚖ 7.48 Global Days 090

26756 Percutaneous skeletal fixation of distal phalangeal fracture, finger or thumb, each ☐A2☐T☐80☐
🔹 10.26 ⚖ 10.26 Global Days 090

26765 Open treatment of distal phalangeal fracture, finger or thumb, includes internal fixation, when performed, each ☐A2☐T☐
🔹 11.60 ⚖ 11.60 Global Days 090

26770 Closed treatment of interphalangeal joint dislocation, single, with manipulation; without anesthesia ☐G2☐T☐
🔹 5.81 ⚖ 6.34 Global Days 090

26775 requiring anesthesia ☐P3☐T☐
🔹 8.20 ⚖ 9.10 Global Days 090

26776 Percutaneous skeletal fixation of interphalangeal joint dislocation, single, with manipulation ☐A2☐T☐
🔹 10.92 ⚖ 10.92 Global Days 090

26785 Open treatment of interphalangeal joint dislocation, includes internal fixation, when performed, single ☐A2☐T☐
🔹 12.64 ⚖ 12.64 Global Days 090

26820-26863 Fusion of Joint(s) of Fingers or Hand

26820 Fusion in opposition, thumb, with autogenous graft (includes obtaining graft) ☐A2☐T☐80☐
🔹 19.76 ⚖ 19.76 Global Days 090

26841 Arthrodesis, carpometacarpal joint, thumb, with or without internal fixation; ☐A2☐T☐80☐
🔹 18.29 ⚖ 18.29 Global Days 090

26842 with autograft (includes obtaining graft) ☐A2☐T☐80☐
🔹 19.88 ⚖ 19.88 Global Days 090

26843 Arthrodesis, carpometacarpal joint, digit, other than thumb, each; ☐A2☐T☐80☐
🔹 18.38 ⚖ 18.38 Global Days 090
AMA: 2008, Jan, 10-25; 2007, Jan, 13-27; 2007, Jan, 13-27; 2007, January, 13-27

26844 with autograft (includes obtaining graft) ☐A2☐T☐80☐
🔹 20.52 ⚖ 20.52 Global Days 090

26850 Arthrodesis, metacarpophalangeal joint, with or without internal fixation; ☐A2☐T☐80☐
🔹 17.41 ⚖ 17.41 Global Days 090

26852 with autograft (includes obtaining graft) ☐A2☐T☐80☐
🔹 19.96 ⚖ 19.96 Global Days 090

26860 Arthrodesis, interphalangeal joint, with or without internal fixation; ☐A2☐T☐
🔹 13.93 ⚖ 13.93 Global Days 090

+ **26861** each additional interphalangeal joint (List separately in addition to code for primary procedure) ☐A2☐T☐
Code first 26860
🔹 2.80 ⚖ 2.80 Global Days ZZZ

26862 with autograft (includes obtaining graft) ☐A2☐T☐80☐
🔹 18.15 ⚖ 18.15 Global Days 090

+ **26863** with autograft (includes obtaining graft), each additional joint (List separately in addition to code for primary procedure) ☐A2☐T☐80☐
Code first 26862
🔹 6.23 ⚖ 6.23 Global Days ZZZ

Musculoskeletal System

26910 — 27066

26910-26952 Amputation Finger/Hand

26910 Amputation, metacarpal, with finger or thumb (ray amputation), single, with or without interosseous transfer   A2 T ▣
> **EXCLUDES** *repositioning (26550, 26555)*
> *transmetacarpal amputation of hand (25927)*
>
> 🔪 17.89   ✂ 17.89   Global Days 090

26951 Amputation, finger or thumb, primary or secondary, any joint or phalanx, single, including neurectomies; with direct closure   A2 T ▣
> **EXCLUDES** *repair necessitating flaps or grafts (15050-15758)*
> *transmetacarpal amputation of hand (25927)*
>
> 🔪 15.37   ✂ 15.37   Global Days 090

26952 with local advancement flaps (V-Y, hood)   A2 T ▣
> **EXCLUDES** *repair necessitating flaps or grafts (15050-15758)*
> *transmetacarpal amputation of hand (25927)*
>
> 🔪 16.18   ✂ 16.18   Global Days 090

26989 Unlisted Procedure of Finger/Hand

26989 Unlisted procedure, hands or fingers   T
> 🔪 0.00   ✂ 0.00   Global Days YYY

26990-26992 Incision for Drainage of Pelvis or Hip

EXCLUDES *simple incision and drainage procedures (10040-10160)*

26990 Incision and drainage, pelvis or hip joint area; deep abscess or hematoma   A2 T ▣
> 🔪 15.64   ✂ 15.64   Global Days 090

26991 infected bursa   A2 T 80 ▣
> 🔪 13.23   ✂ 17.41   Global Days 090

26992 Incision, bone cortex, pelvis and/or hip joint (eg, osteomyelitis or bone abscess)   C 80 ▣
> 🔪 24.73   ✂ 24.73   Global Days 090
> **AMA:** 2008, Jan, 10-25; 2007, Jan, 13-27; 2007, Jan, 13-27; 2007, January, 13-27

27000-27006 Tenotomy Procedures of Hip

27000 Tenotomy, adductor of hip, percutaneous (separate procedure)   A2 T 50 ▣
> 🔪 11.39   ✂ 11.39   Global Days 090

27001 Tenotomy, adductor of hip, open   A2 T 80 50 ▣
> 🔪 13.83   ✂ 13.83   Global Days 090

27003 Tenotomy, adductor, subcutaneous, open, with obturator neurectomy   A2 T 80 50 ▣
> 🔪 14.78   ✂ 14.78   Global Days 090

27005 Tenotomy, hip flexor(s), open (separate procedure)   C 80 50 ▣
> 🔪 18.77   ✂ 18.77   Global Days 090

27006 Tenotomy, abductors and/or extensor(s) of hip, open (separate procedure)   T 80 50 ▣
> 🔪 18.95   ✂ 18.95   Global Days 090

27025-27036 Surgical Incision of Hip

CMS   *Induced Lesions of Nerve Tracts*

27025 Fasciotomy, hip or thigh, any type   C 80 50 ▣
> 🔪 22.88   ✂ 22.88   Global Days 090

● **27027** Decompression fasciotomy(ies), pelvic (buttock) compartment(s) (eg, gluteus medius-minimus, gluteus maximus, iliopsoas, and/or tensor fascia lata muscle), unilateral   T 80 50
> 🔪 22.36   ✂ 22.36   Global Days 090

27030 Arthrotomy, hip, with drainage (eg, infection)   C 80 50 ▣
> 🔪 24.51   ✂ 24.51   Global Days 090

27033 Arthrotomy, hip, including exploration or removal of loose or foreign body   A2 T 80 50 ▣
> 🔪 25.37   ✂ 25.37   Global Days 090

27035 Denervation, hip joint, intrapelvic or extrapelvic intra-articular branches of sciatic, femoral, or obturator nerves   A2 T 80 50 ▣
> **EXCLUDES** *transection of obturator nerve (64763, 64766)*
>
> 🔪 28.23   ✂ 28.23   Global Days 090

27036 Capsulectomy or capsulotomy, hip, with or without excision of heterotopic bone, with release of hip flexor muscles (ie, gluteus medius, gluteus minimus, tensor fascia latae, rectus femoris, sartorius, iliopsoas)   C 80 50 ▣
> 🔪 25.90   ✂ 25.90   Global Days 090

27040-27041 Biopsy of Hip/Pelvis

EXCLUDES *soft tissue needle biopsy (20206)*

27040 Biopsy, soft tissue of pelvis and hip area; superficial   A2 T 50 ▣
> 🔪 5.14   ✂ 8.41   Global Days 010

27041 deep, subfascial or intramuscular   A2 T 50 ▣
> 🔪 17.63   ✂ 17.63   Global Days 090

27047-27080 Resection Areas of Hip and Pelvis

27047 Excision, tumor, pelvis and hip area; subcutaneous tissue   A2 T 50 ▣
> 🔪 13.16   ✂ 15.59   Global Days 090

27048 deep, subfascial, intramuscular   A2 T 80 50 ▣
> 🔪 12.09   ✂ 12.09   Global Days 090

27049 Radical resection of tumor, soft tissue of pelvis and hip area (eg, malignant neoplasm)   A2 T 80 50 ▣
> 🔪 25.67   ✂ 25.67   Global Days 090

27050 Arthrotomy, with biopsy; sacroiliac joint   A2 T 80 50 ▣
> 🔪 8.82   ✂ 8.82   Global Days 090

27052 hip joint   A2 T 80 50 ▣
> 🔪 14.12   ✂ 14.12   Global Days 090

27054 Arthrotomy with synovectomy, hip joint   C 80 50 ▣
> 🔪 17.39   ✂ 17.39   Global Days 090

● **27057** Decompression fasciotomy(ies), pelvic (buttock) compartment(s) (eg, gluteus medius-minimus, gluteus maximus, iliopsoas, and/or tensor fascia lata muscle) with debridement of nonviable muscle, unilateral   T 80 50
> 🔪 24.61   ✂ 24.61   Global Days 090

27060 Excision; ischial bursa   A2 T 50 ▣
> 🔪 10.90   ✂ 10.90   Global Days 090

27062 trochanteric bursa or calcification   A2 T 50 ▣
> **EXCLUDES** *arthrocentesis (20610)*
>
> 🔪 11.42   ✂ 11.42   Global Days 090

27065 Excision of bone cyst or benign tumor; superficial (wing of ilium, symphysis pubis, or greater trochanter of femur) with or without autograft   A2 T 80 50 ▣
> 🔪 12.73   ✂ 12.73   Global Days 090

27066 deep, with or without autograft   A2 T 80 50 ▣
> 🔪 20.75   ✂ 20.75   Global Days 090

| 27067 | with autograft requiring separate incision | A2 T 80 50 ▭ |

📁 26.18   ⚖ 26.18   Global Days 090

27070   Partial excision (craterization, saucerization) (eg, osteomyelitis or bone abscess); superficial (eg, wing of ilium, symphysis pubis, or greater trochanter of femur)   C 80 50 ▭

📁 21.69   ⚖ 21.69   Global Days 090

27071   deep (subfascial or intramuscular)   C 80 50 ▭

📁 23.30   ⚖ 23.30   Global Days 090

27075   Radical resection of tumor or infection; wing of ilium, 1 pubic or ischial ramus or symphysis pubis   C 80 ▭

📁 60.24   ⚖ 60.24   Global Days 090

27076   ilium, including acetabulum, both pubic rami, or ischium and acetabulum   C 80 ▭

📁 41.50   ⚖ 41.50   Global Days 090

27077   innominate bone, total   C 80 ▭

📁 69.49   ⚖ 69.49   Global Days 090

27078   ischial tuberosity and greater trochanter of femur   C 80 ▭

📁 26.19   ⚖ 26.19   Global Days 090

27079   ischial tuberosity and greater trochanter of femur, with skin flaps   C 80 ▭

📁 25.00   ⚖ 25.00   Global Days 090

27080   Coccygectomy, primary   A2 T 80 ▭

EXCLUDES   excision of pressure ulcer (15920, 15922, 15931-15958)

📁 12.53   ⚖ 12.53   Global Days 090

27086-27091 Removal Foreign Body or Hip Prosthetic

27086   Removal of foreign body, pelvis or hip; subcutaneous tissue   A2 T 80 50 ▭

📁 3.75   ⚖ 6.05   Global Days 010

27087   deep (subfascial or intramuscular)   A2 T 80 50 ▭

📁 16.18   ⚖ 16.18   Global Days 090

27090   Removal of hip prosthesis; (separate procedure)   C 80 50 ▭

📁 21.48   ⚖ 21.48   Global Days 090

27091   complicated, including total hip prosthesis, methylmethacrylate with or without insertion of spacer   C 80 50 ▭

📁 41.64   ⚖ 41.64   Global Days 090

27093-27096 Injection for Arthrogram Hip/Sacroiliac Joint

27093   Injection procedure for hip arthrography; without anesthesia   N1 N 50 ▭

📷 73525

📁 1.93   ⚖ 4.90   Global Days 000

27095   with anesthesia   N1 N 50 ▭

📷 73525

📁 2.20   ⚖ 5.91   Global Days 000

27096   Injection procedure for sacroiliac joint, arthrography and/or anesthetic/steroid   B 50 ▭

INCLUDES   verification of position

📷 73542, 77003

📁 1.83   ⚖ 4.48   Global Days 000

AMA: 2008, Jan, 10-25; 2008, Jul, 9; 2007, Jan, 13-27; 2007, Jan, 13-27; 2007, January, 13-27; 2004, Apr, 15; 2004, April, 15; 2004, Apr, 15

27097-27187 Revision/Reconstruction Hip and Pelvis

27097   Release or recession, hamstring, proximal   A2 T 80 50 ▭

📁 17.13   ⚖ 17.13   Global Days 090

27098   Transfer, adductor to ischium   A2 T 80 50 ▭

📁 15.81   ⚖ 15.81   Global Days 090

27100   Transfer external oblique muscle to greater trochanter including fascial or tendon extension (graft)   A2 T 80 50 ▭

INCLUDES   Eggers procedure

📁 21.10   ⚖ 21.10   Global Days 090

27105   Transfer paraspinal muscle to hip (includes fascial or tendon extension graft)   A2 T 80 50 ▭

📁 22.02   ⚖ 22.02   Global Days 090

27110   Transfer iliopsoas; to greater trochanter of femur   A2 T 80 50 ▭

📁 24.68   ⚖ 24.68   Global Days 090

27111   to femoral neck   A2 T 80 50 ▭

📁 22.01   ⚖ 22.01   Global Days 090

27120   Acetabuloplasty; (eg, Whitman, Colonna, Haygroves, or cup type)   C 80 50 ▭

📁 33.51   ⚖ 33.51   Global Days 090

27122   resection, femoral head (eg, Girdlestone procedure)   C 80 50 ▭

📁 28.69   ⚖ 28.69   Global Days 090

27125   Hemiarthroplasty, hip, partial (eg, femoral stem prosthesis, bipolar arthroplasty)   C 80 50 ▭ P0

EXCLUDES   total joint following hip fracture (27236)

📁 29.17   ⚖ 29.17   Global Days 090

AMA: 2008, Jan, 10-25; 2007, Jan, 13-27; 2007, Jan, 13-27; 2007, January, 13-27

27130   Arthroplasty, acetabular and proximal femoral prosthetic replacement (total hip arthroplasty), with or without autograft or allograft   C 80 50 ▭ P0

📁 37.70   ⚖ 37.70   Global Days 090

AMA: 2007, Jan, 1-5; 2007, Jan, 1-5; 2007, January, 1-5

27132   Conversion of previous hip surgery to total hip arthroplasty, with or without autograft or allograft   C 80 50 ▭ P0

📁 44.04   ⚖ 44.04   Global Days 090

27134   Revision of total hip arthroplasty; both components, with or without autograft or allograft   C 80 50 ▭ P0

📁 51.18   ⚖ 51.18   Global Days 090

27137   acetabular component only, with or without autograft or allograft   C 80 50 ▭ P0

📁 38.97   ⚖ 38.97   Global Days 090

27138   femoral component only, with or without allograft   C 80 50 ▭ P0

📁 40.57   ⚖ 40.57   Global Days 090

27140   Osteotomy and transfer of greater trochanter of femur (separate procedure)   C 80 50 ▭

📁 23.28   ⚖ 23.28   Global Days 090

27146   Osteotomy, iliac, acetabular or innominate bone;   C 80 50 ▭

INCLUDES   Salter osteotomy

📁 32.83   ⚖ 32.83   Global Days 090

AMA: 2008, Jan, 10-25; 2007, Jan, 13-27; 2007, Jan, 13-27; 2007, January, 13-27

27147   with open reduction of hip   C 80 50 ▭

INCLUDES   Pemberton osteotomy

📁 38.30   ⚖ 38.30   Global Days 090

27151   with femoral osteotomy   C 80 50 ▭

📁 39.96   ⚖ 39.96   Global Days 090

● New Code   ▲ Revised Code   M Maternity Edit   A Age Edit   A-Y OPPS Status Indicator   📁 Facility RVU   ⚖ Non-Facility RVU

▭ CCI Comprehensive Code   50 Bilateral Procedure   + Add-on Indicator   N Laboratory crosswalk   📷 Radiology crosswalk

Musculoskeletal System

27156 — 27244

27156   with femoral osteotomy and with open reduction of hip   C 80 50 ▣
   INCLUDES   Chiari osteotomy
   ⚕ 44.70   ✂ 44.70   Global Days 090

27158   Osteotomy, pelvis, bilateral (eg, congenital malformation)   C 80 ▣
   ⚕ 35.85   ✂ 35.85   Global Days 090

27161   Osteotomy, femoral neck (separate procedure)   C 80 50 ▣
   ⚕ 31.78   ✂ 31.78   Global Days 090

27165   Osteotomy, intertrochanteric or subtrochanteric including internal or external fixation and/or cast   C 80 50 ▣
   ⚕ 35.44   ✂ 35.44   Global Days 090

27170   Bone graft, femoral head, neck, intertrochanteric or subtrochanteric area (includes obtaining bone graft)   C 80 50 ▣
   ⚕ 30.74   ✂ 30.74   Global Days 090

27175   Treatment of slipped femoral epiphysis; by traction, without reduction   C 80 50 ▣
   ⚕ 17.05   ✂ 17.05   Global Days 090

27176   by single or multiple pinning, in situ   C 80 50 ▣
   ⚕ 23.64   ✂ 23.64   Global Days 090

27177   Open treatment of slipped femoral epiphysis; single or multiple pinning or bone graft (includes obtaining graft)   C 80 50 ▣
   ⚕ 28.81   ✂ 28.81   Global Days 090

27178   closed manipulation with single or multiple pinning   C 80 50 ▣
   ⚕ 23.35   ✂ 23.35   Global Days 090

27179   osteoplasty of femoral neck (Heyman type procedure)   C 80 50 ▣
   ⚕ 25.16   ✂ 25.16   Global Days 090

27181   osteotomy and internal fixation   C 80 50 ▣
   ⚕ 27.70   ✂ 27.70   Global Days 090

27185   Epiphyseal arrest by epiphysiodesis or stapling, greater trochanter of femur   C 50 ▣
   ⚕ 18.05   ✂ 18.05   Global Days 090

27187   Prophylactic treatment (nailing, pinning, plating or wiring) with or without methylmethacrylate, femoral neck and proximal femur   C 80 50 ▣
   ⚕ 25.82   ✂ 25.82   Global Days 090

27193-27269 Treatment of Fracture/Dislocation Hip /Pelvis

27193   Closed treatment of pelvic ring fracture, dislocation, diastasis or subluxation; without manipulation   A2 T ▣
   ⚕ 11.87   ✂ 11.77   Global Days 090

27194   with manipulation, requiring more than local anesthesia   A2 T 80 ▣
   ⚕ 18.40   ✂ 18.40   Global Days 090

27200   Closed treatment of coccygeal fracture   P2 T ▣
   ⚕ 4.34   ✂ 4.25   Global Days 090

27202   Open treatment of coccygeal fracture   A2 T 80 ▣
   ⚕ 16.24   ✂ 16.24   Global Days 090

▲ 27215   Open treatment of iliac spine(s), tuberosity avulsion, or iliac wing fracture(s), unilateral, for pelvic bone fracture patterns that do not disrupt the pelvic ring, includes internal fixation, when performed   E ▣
   ⚕ 19.14   ✂ 19.14   Global Days 090

▲ 27216   Percutaneous skeletal fixation of posterior pelvic bone fracture and/or dislocation, for fracture patterns that disrupt the pelvic ring, unilateral (includes ipsilateral ilium, sacroiliac joint and/or sacrum)   E ▣
   ⚕ 27.90   ✂ 27.90   Global Days 090

▲ 27217   Open treatment of anterior pelvic bone fracture and/or dislocation for fracture patterns that disrupt the pelvic ring, unilateral, includes internal fixation, when performed (includes pubic symphysis and/or ipsilateral superior/inferior rami)   E ▣
   ⚕ 26.38   ✂ 26.38   Global Days 090

▲ 27218   Open treatment of posterior pelvic bone fracture and/or dislocation, for fracture patterns that disrupt the pelvic ring, unilateral, includes internal fixation, when performed (includes ipsilateral ilium, sacroiliac joint and/or sacrum)   E ▣
   ⚕ 36.10   ✂ 36.10   Global Days 090

27220   Closed treatment of acetabulum (hip socket) fracture(s); without manipulation   B2 T 50 ▣
   ⚕ 13.17   ✂ 13.26   Global Days 090

27222   with manipulation, with or without skeletal traction   C 50 ▣
   ⚕ 25.26   ✂ 25.26   Global Days 090

27226   Open treatment of posterior or anterior acetabular wall fracture, with internal fixation   C 80 50 ▣
   ⚕ 26.93   ✂ 26.93   Global Days 090

27227   Open treatment of acetabular fracture(s) involving anterior or posterior (1) column, or a fracture running transversely across the acetabulum, with internal fixation   C 80 50 ▣
   ⚕ 43.64   ✂ 43.64   Global Days 090

27228   Open treatment of acetabular fracture(s) involving anterior and posterior (2) columns, includes T-fracture and both column fracture with complete articular detachment, or single column or transverse fracture with associated acetabular wall fracture, with internal fixation   C 80 50 ▣
   ⚕ 49.99   ✂ 49.99   Global Days 090

27230   Closed treatment of femoral fracture, proximal end, neck; without manipulation   A2 T 50 ▣ P0
   ⚕ 11.65   ✂ 11.80   Global Days 090

27232   with manipulation, with or without skeletal traction   C 50 ▣ P0
   ⚕ 20.10   ✂ 20.10   Global Days 090

27235   Percutaneous skeletal fixation of femoral fracture, proximal end, neck   T 50 ▣ P0
   ⚕ 23.59   ✂ 23.59   Global Days 090

27236   Open treatment of femoral fracture, proximal end, neck, internal fixation or prosthetic replacement   C 80 50 ▣ P0
   ⚕ 30.85   ✂ 30.85   Global Days 090
   AMA: 2008, Jan, 10-25; 2007, Jan, 13-27; 2007, Jan, 13-27; 2007, Jan, 1-5; 2007, Jan, 1-5; 2007, January, 1-5; 2007, January, 13-27

27238   Closed treatment of intertrochanteric, peritrochanteric, or subtrochanteric femoral fracture; without manipulation   A2 T 50 ▣ P0
   ⚕ 11.40   ✂ 11.40   Global Days 090

27240   with manipulation, with or without skin or skeletal traction   C 50 ▣ P0
   ⚕ 24.66   ✂ 24.66   Global Days 090

27244   Treatment of intertrochanteric, peritrochanteric, or subtrochanteric femoral fracture; with plate/screw type implant, with or without cerclage   C 80 50 ▣ P0
   ⚕ 31.73   ✂ 31.73   Global Days 090

27245 with intramedullary implant, with or without interlocking screws and/or cerclage `C` `80` `50` `▢` `P0`
🔹 33.11 ≷ 33.11 Global Days 090

27246 Closed treatment of greater trochanteric fracture, without manipulation `A2` `T` `50` `▢` `P0`
🔹 9.69 ≷ 9.67 Global Days 090

27248 Open treatment of greater trochanteric fracture, includes internal fixation, when performed `C` `80` `50` `▢` `P0`
🔹 19.51 ≷ 19.51 Global Days 090

27250 Closed treatment of hip dislocation, traumatic; without anesthesia `A2` `T` `50` `▢`
🔹 6.16 ≷ 6.16 Global Days 000

27252 requiring anesthesia `A2` `T` `50` `▢`
🔹 19.46 ≷ 19.46 Global Days 090

27253 Open treatment of hip dislocation, traumatic, without internal fixation `C` `80` `50` `▢`
🔹 24.53 ≷ 24.53 Global Days 090

27254 Open treatment of hip dislocation, traumatic, with acetabular wall and femoral head fracture, with or without internal or external fixation `C` `80` `50` `▢`
EXCLUDES *acetabular fracture treatment (27226-27227)*
🔹 33.21 ≷ 33.21 Global Days 090

27256 Treatment of spontaneous hip dislocation (developmental, including congenital or pathological), by abduction, splint or traction; without anesthesia, without manipulation `G2` `T` `80` `50` `▢`
🔹 6.29 ≷ 7.41 Global Days 010

27257 with manipulation, requiring anesthesia `A2` `T` `80` `50` `▢`
🔹 8.66 ≷ 8.66 Global Days 010

27258 Open treatment of spontaneous hip dislocation (developmental, including congenital or pathological), replacement of femoral head in acetabulum (including tenotomy, etc); `C` `80` `50` `▢`
INCLUDES Lorenz's operation
🔹 28.77 ≷ 28.77 Global Days 090

27259 with femoral shaft shortening `C` `80` `50` `▢`
🔹 40.37 ≷ 40.37 Global Days 090

27265 Closed treatment of post hip arthroplasty dislocation; without anesthesia `A2` `T` `50` `▢`
🔹 9.83 ≷ 9.83 Global Days 090

27266 requiring regional or general anesthesia `A2` `T` `50` `▢`
🔹 14.80 ≷ 14.80 Global Days 090

27267 Closed treatment of femoral fracture, proximal end, head; without manipulation `G2` `T` `80` `50`
🔹 10.55 ≷ 10.55 Global Days 090
AMA: 2008, Jan, 4-5

27268 with manipulation `C` `80` `50`
🔹 13.09 ≷ 13.09 Global Days 090
AMA: 2008, Jan, 4-5

27269 Open treatment of femoral fracture, proximal end, head, includes internal fixation, when performed `C` `80` `50`
Do not report with (27033, 27253)
🔹 31.57 ≷ 31.57 Global Days 090
AMA: 2008, Jan, 4-5

27275 Hip Manipulation with Anesthesia

27275 Manipulation, hip joint, requiring general anesthesia `A2` `T` `▢`
🔹 4.59 ≷ 4.59 Global Days 010

27280-27286 Arthrodesis of Hip and Pelvis

27280 Arthrodesis, sacroiliac joint (including obtaining graft) `C` `80` `50` `▢`
🔹 26.65 ≷ 26.65 Global Days 090

27282 Arthrodesis, symphysis pubis (including obtaining graft) `C` `80` `▢`
🔹 20.84 ≷ 20.84 Global Days 090

27284 Arthrodesis, hip joint (including obtaining graft); `C` `80` `50` `▢`
🔹 40.57 ≷ 40.57 Global Days 090

27286 with subtrochanteric osteotomy `C` `80` `50` `▢`
🔹 42.53 ≷ 42.53 Global Days 090

27290-27299 Amputations and Unlisted Procedures of Hip and Pelvis

27290 Interpelviabdominal amputation (hindquarter amputation) `C` `80` `▢`
INCLUDES Pean's amputation
🔹 40.76 ≷ 40.76 Global Days 090

27295 Disarticulation of hip `C` `80` `▢`
🔹 32.98 ≷ 32.98 Global Days 090

27299 Unlisted procedure, pelvis or hip joint `T` `80` `50`
🔹 0.00 ≷ 0.00 Global Days YYY
AMA: 2008, Jan, 10-25; 2007, Jan, 13-27; 2007, Jan, 13-27; 2007, January, 13-27; 2005, Dec, 9-11; 2005, December, 9-11; 2005, Dec, 9-11

27301-27303 Incision for Drainage Femur or Knee

INCLUDES superficial incision and drainage (10040-10160)

27301 Incision and drainage, deep abscess, bursa, or hematoma, thigh or knee region `A2` `T` `50` `▢`
🔹 12.59 ≷ 16.43 Global Days 090

27303 Incision, deep, with opening of bone cortex, femur or knee (eg, osteomyelitis or bone abscess) `C` `80` `50` `▢`
🔹 16.34 ≷ 16.34 Global Days 090

27305-27310 Other Incisional Procedures Femur and Knee

EXCLUDES *superficial incision and drainage (10040-10160)*

27305 Fasciotomy, iliotibial (tenotomy), open `A2` `T` `80` `50` `▢`
EXCLUDES *Ober-Yount (gluteal-iliotibial) fasciotomy (27025)*
🔹 11.90 ≷ 11.90 Global Days 090

27306 Tenotomy, percutaneous, adductor or hamstring; single tendon (separate procedure) `A2` `T` `80` `50` `▢`
🔹 9.64 ≷ 9.64 Global Days 090

27307 multiple tendons `A2` `T` `80` `50` `▢`
🔹 11.87 ≷ 11.87 Global Days 090

27310 Arthrotomy, knee, with exploration, drainage, or removal of foreign body (eg, infection) `A2` `T` `80` `50` `▢`
🔹 18.63 ≷ 18.63 Global Days 090

27323-27324 Biopsy Femur or Knee

EXCLUDES *soft tissue needle biopsy (20206)*

27323 Biopsy, soft tissue of thigh or knee area; superficial `A2` `T` `50` `▢`
🔹 4.49 ≷ 6.55 Global Days 010

● New Code ▲ Revised Code ⓂMaternity Edit 🄰 Age Edit Ⓐ-Ⓨ OPPS Status Indicator 🔹 Facility RVU ≷ Non-Facility RVU ▢ CCI Comprehensive Code `50` Bilateral Procedure + Add-on Indicator 🅽 Laboratory crosswalk 🆁 Radiology crosswalk

© 2008 Ingenix *(Blue Ink)* CPT only © 2008 American Medical Association. All Rights Reserved. (Black Ink) Medicare (Red Ink) 89

Musculoskeletal System

27324 — 27396

27324   deep (subfascial or intramuscular)   A2 T 50 ▭
   📋 9.67   ⚕ 9.67   Global Days 090
   AMA: 2006, Mar, 6-9; 2006, Mar, 6-9; 2006, March, 6-9

27325-27365 Resection Areas of Femur or Knee

27325   Neurectomy, hamstring muscle   A2 T 80 50
   📋 13.42   ⚕ 13.42   Global Days 090

27326   Neurectomy, popliteal (gastrocnemius)   A2 T 80 50
   📋 12.40   ⚕ 12.40   Global Days 090

27327   Excision, tumor, thigh or knee area;
   subcutaneous   A2 T 50 ▭
   📋 8.82   ⚕ 11.18   Global Days 090

27328   deep, subfascial, or intramuscular   A2 T 50 ▭
   📋 10.67   ⚕ 10.67   Global Days 090

27329   Radical resection of tumor (eg, malignant neoplasm), soft
   tissue of thigh or knee area   A2 T 80 50 ▭
   📋 26.67   ⚕ 26.67   Global Days 090

27330   Arthrotomy, knee; with synovial biopsy only   A2 T 50 ▭
   📋 10.16   ⚕ 10.16   Global Days 090

27331   including joint exploration, biopsy, or removal of loose
   or foreign bodies   A2 T 80 50 ▭
   📋 12.01   ⚕ 12.01   Global Days 090

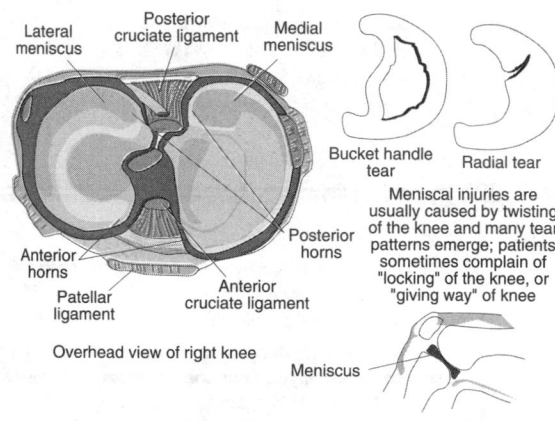

Lateral meniscus · Posterior cruciate ligament · Medial meniscus

Bucket handle tear · Radial tear

Meniscal injuries are usually caused by twisting of the knee and many tear patterns emerge; patients sometimes complain of "locking" of the knee, or "giving way" of knee

Posterior horns · Anterior horns · Patellar ligament · Anterior cruciate ligament

Overhead view of right knee · Meniscus

27332   Arthrotomy, with excision of semilunar cartilage
   (meniscectomy) knee; medial OR lateral   A2 T 80 50 ▭
   📋 16.32   ⚕ 16.32   Global Days 090

27333   medial AND lateral   A2 T 80 50 ▭
   📋 14.77   ⚕ 14.77   Global Days 090

27334   Arthrotomy, with synovectomy, knee; anterior OR
   posterior   A2 T 80 50 ▭
   📋 17.37   ⚕ 17.37   Global Days 090

27335   anterior AND posterior including popliteal
   area   A2 T 80 50 ▭
   📋 19.67   ⚕ 19.67   Global Days 090

27340   Excision, prepatellar bursa   A2 T 50 ▭
   📋 9.17   ⚕ 9.17   Global Days 090

27345   Excision of synovial cyst of popliteal space (eg, Baker's
   cyst)   A2 T 80 50 ▭
   📋 12.15   ⚕ 12.15   Global Days 090

27347   Excision of lesion of meniscus or capsule (eg, cyst,
   ganglion), knee   A2 T 80 50 ▭
   📋 13.00   ⚕ 13.00   Global Days 090

27350   Patellectomy or hemipatellectomy   A2 T 80 50 ▭
   📋 16.59   ⚕ 16.59   Global Days 090

27355   Excision or curettage of bone cyst or benign tumor of
   femur;   A2 T 80 50 ▭
   📋 15.38   ⚕ 15.38   Global Days 090

27356   with allograft   A2 T 80 50 ▭
   📋 18.88   ⚕ 18.88   Global Days 090

27357   with autograft (includes obtaining graft)   A2 T 80 50 ▭
   📋 20.98   ⚕ 20.98   Global Days 090
   AMA: 2008, Jan, 10-25; 2007, Jan, 13-27; 2007, Jan, 13-27; 2007,
   January, 13-27

+ 27358   with internal fixation (List in addition to code for
   primary procedure)   A2 T 80 ▭
   Code first 27355-27357
   📋 7.69   ⚕ 7.69   Global Days ZZZ

27360   Partial excision (craterization, saucerization, or
   diaphysectomy) bone, femur, proximal tibia and/or fibula
   (eg, osteomyelitis or bone abscess)   A2 T 80 50 ▭
   📋 21.77   ⚕ 21.77   Global Days 090

27365   Radical resection of tumor, bone, femur or
   knee   C 80 50 ▭
   EXCLUDES   soft tissue tumor excision (27329)
   📋 31.78   ⚕ 31.78   Global Days 090

27370 Injection for Arthrogram of Knee

27370   Injection procedure for knee arthrography   N1 N 50 ▭
   ▣ 73580
   📋 1.40   ⚕ 4.18   Global Days 000

27372 Foreign Body Removal Femur or Knee

27372   Removal of foreign body, deep, thigh region or knee
   area   A2 T 80 50 ▭
   EXCLUDES   arthroscopic procedures (29870-29887)
             knee prosthesis (27488)
   📋 10.24   ⚕ 14.73   Global Days 090

27380-27499 Repair/Reconstruction of Femur or Knee

27380   Suture of infrapatellar tendon; primary   A2 T 80 50 ▭
   📋 15.04   ⚕ 15.04   Global Days 090

27381   secondary reconstruction, including fascial or tendon
   graft   A2 T 80 50 ▭
   📋 20.56   ⚕ 20.56   Global Days 090

27385   Suture of quadriceps or hamstring muscle rupture;
   primary   A2 T 80 50 ▭
   📋 16.12   ⚕ 16.12   Global Days 090

27386   secondary reconstruction, including fascial or tendon
   graft   A2 T 80 50 ▭
   📋 21.32   ⚕ 21.32   Global Days 090

27390   Tenotomy, open, hamstring, knee to hip; single
   tendon   A2 T 80 ▭
   📋 11.15   ⚕ 11.15   Global Days 090

27391   multiple tendons, one leg   A2 T 80 ▭
   📋 14.55   ⚕ 14.55   Global Days 090

27392   multiple tendons, bilateral   A2 T 80 ▭
   📋 17.96   ⚕ 17.96   Global Days 090

27393   Lengthening of hamstring tendon; single
   tendon   A2 T 80 ▭
   📋 12.90   ⚕ 12.90   Global Days 090

27394   multiple tendons, one leg   A2 T 80 ▭
   📋 16.70   ⚕ 16.70   Global Days 090

27395   multiple tendons, bilateral   A2 T 80 ▭
   📋 22.65   ⚕ 22.65   Global Days 090

▲ 27396   Transplant or transfer (with muscle redirection or
   rerouting), thigh (eg, extensor to flexor); single
   tendon   A2 T 80 ▭
   📋 15.68   ⚕ 15.68   Global Days 090

▲ 27397   multiple tendons   A2 T 80 ▣
    🚗 23.06   ≳ 23.06   Global Days 090

27400   **Transfer, tendon or muscle, hamstrings to femur (eg, Egger's type procedure)**   A2 T 80 50 ▣
    🚗 17.41   ≳ 17.41   Global Days 090

27403   **Arthrotomy with meniscus repair, knee**   A2 T 80 50 ▣
    EXCLUDES   *arthroscopic treatment (29882)*
    🚗 16.43   ≳ 16.43   Global Days 090

27405   **Repair, primary, torn ligament and/or capsule, knee; collateral**   A2 T 80 50 ▣
    🚗 17.31   ≳ 17.31   Global Days 090

27407   **cruciate**   A2 T 80 50 ▣
    EXCLUDES   *reconstruction (27427)*
    🚗 19.80   ≳ 19.80   Global Days 090

27409   **collateral and cruciate ligaments**   A2 T 80 50 ▣
    EXCLUDES   *reconstruction (27427-27429)*
    🚗 24.91   ≳ 24.91   Global Days 090

27412   **Autologous chondrocyte implantation, knee**   T 80 50 ▣
    INCLUDES   knee arthrotomy (27331)
          manipulation of knee joint (27570)
          tissue graft (20926)
    EXCLUDES   *obtaining chondrocytes (29870)*
    🚗 43.32   ≳ 43.32   Global Days 090

27415   **Osteochondral allograft, knee, open**   T 80 50 ▣
    EXCLUDES   *arthroscopic procedure (29867)*
    Do not report with (27416)
    🚗 36.50   ≳ 36.50   Global Days 090

27416   **Osteochondral autograft(s), knee, open (eg, mosaicplasty) (includes harvesting of autograft[s])**   G2 T 80 50
    EXCLUDES   *surgical arthroscopy of the knee with*
          osteochondral autograft(s) (29866)
    Do not report with the following procedures in the same compartment (29874, 29877, 29879, 29885-29887)
    Do not report with the following procedures performed at the same surgical session (27415, 29870-29871, 29875, 29884)
    🚗 24.99   ≳ 24.99   Global Days 090
    AMA: 2008, Jan, 4-5

27418   **Anterior tibial tubercleplasty (eg, Maquet type procedure)**   A2 T 80 50 ▣
    🚗 21.47   ≳ 21.47   Global Days 090

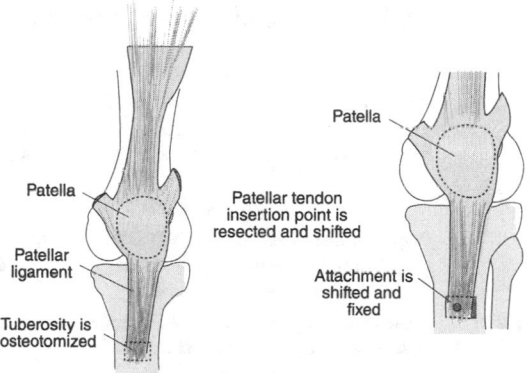

Patella

Patellar tendon insertion point is resected and shifted

Patella

Patellar ligament

Attachment is shifted and fixed

Tuberosity is osteotomized

27420   **Reconstruction of dislocating patella; (eg, Hauser type procedure)**   A2 T 80 50 ▣
    🚗 19.23   ≳ 19.23   Global Days 090

27422   **with extensor realignment and/or muscle advancement or release (eg, Campbell, Goldwaite type procedure)**   A2 T 80 50 ▣
    🚗 19.15   ≳ 19.15   Global Days 090

27424   **with patellectomy**   A2 T 80 50 ▣
    🚗 19.20   ≳ 19.20   Global Days 090

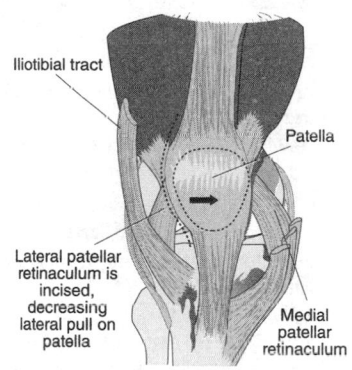

Iliotibial tract

Patella

Lateral patellar retinaculum is incised, decreasing lateral pull on patella

Medial patellar retinaculum

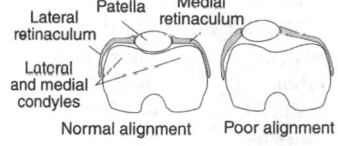

Lateral retinaculum   Patella   Medial retinaculum

Lateral and medial condyles

Normal alignment   Poor alignment

27425   **Lateral retinacular release, open**   A2 T 50 ▣
    EXCLUDES   *arthroscopic release (29873)*
    🚗 11.15   ≳ 11.15   Global Days 090
    AMA: 2008, Jan, 10-25; 2007, Jan, 13-27; 2007, Jan, 13-27; 2007, January, 13-27

27427   **Ligamentous reconstruction (augmentation), knee; extra-articular**   A2 T 00 50 ▣
    EXCLUDES   *primary repair of ligament(s) (27405, 27407, 27409)*
    🚗 18.43   ≳ 18.43   Global Days 090

27428   **intra-articular (open)**   A2 T 80 50 ▣
    EXCLUDES   *primary repair of ligament(s) (27405, 27407, 27409)*
    🚗 28.37   ≳ 28.37   Global Days 090

27429   **intra-articular (open) and extra-articular**   A2 T 80 50 ▣
    EXCLUDES   *primary repair of ligament(s) (27405, 27407, 27409)*
    🚗 31.77   ≳ 31.77   Global Days 090

27430   **Quadricepsplasty (eg, Bennett or Thompson type)**   A2 T 80 50 ▣
    🚗 19.03   ≳ 19.03   Global Days 090

27435   **Capsulotomy, posterior capsular release, knee**   A2 T 80 50 ▣
    🚗 20.37   ≳ 20.37   Global Days 090

27437   **Arthroplasty, patella; without prosthesis**   A2 T 50 ▣
    🚗 16.91   ≳ 16.91   Global Days 090

27438   **with prosthesis**   A2 T 80 50 ▣
    🚗 21.70   ≳ 21.70   Global Days 090

27440   **Arthroplasty, knee, tibial plateau;**   G2 T 80 50 ▣ P0
    🚗 19.83   ≳ 19.83   Global Days 090

27441   **with debridement and partial synovectomy**   A2 T 80 50 ▣ P0
    🚗 20.48   ≳ 20.48   Global Days 090

Musculoskeletal System

27442 — 27509

27442 Arthroplasty, femoral condyles or tibial plateau(s), knee; `A2` `T` `80` `50` `▭` `P0`
🔪 22.50 ⚕ 22.50 Global Days 090

27443 with debridement and partial synovectomy `A2` `T` `80` `50` `▭` `P0`
🔪 21.05 ⚕ 21.05 Global Days 090

27445 Arthroplasty, knee, hinge prosthesis (eg, Walldius type) `C` `80` `50` `▭` `P0`
EXCLUDES *removal knee prosthesis (27488)*
revision knee arthroplasty (27487)
🔪 32.86 ⚕ 32.86 Global Days 090

27446 Arthroplasty, knee, condyle and plateau; medial OR lateral compartment `J8` `T` `80` `50` `▭` `P0`
EXCLUDES *removal knee prosthesis (27488)*
revision knee arthroplasty (27487)

Code also (C1776)
🔪 29.16 ⚕ 29.16 Global Days 090

27447 medial AND lateral compartments with or without patella resurfacing (total knee arthroplasty) `C` `80` `50` `▭` `P0`
EXCLUDES *removal knee prosthesis (27488)*
revision knee arthroplasty (27487)

🔪 40.38 ⚕ 40.38 Global Days 090
AMA: 2007, Jan, 1-5; 2007, Jan, 1-5; 2007, January, 1-5; 2005, Mar, 11-15; 2005, March, 11-15; 2005, Mar, 11-15

27448 Osteotomy, femur, shaft or supracondylar; without fixation `C` `80` `50` `▭`
🔪 21.21 ⚕ 21.21 Global Days 090

27450 with fixation `C` `80` `50` `▭`
🔪 26.44 ⚕ 26.44 Global Days 090

27454 Osteotomy, multiple, with realignment on intramedullary rod, femoral shaft (eg, Sofield type procedure) `C` `80` `50` `▭`
🔪 33.39 ⚕ 33.39 Global Days 090

27455 Osteotomy, proximal tibia, including fibular excision or osteotomy (includes correction of genu varus [bowleg] or genu valgus [knock-knee]); before epiphyseal closure `C` `80` `50` `▭`
🔪 24.43 ⚕ 24.43 Global Days 090

27457 after epiphyseal closure `C` `80` `50` `▭`
🔪 25.18 ⚕ 25.18 Global Days 090

27465 Osteoplasty, femur; shortening (excluding 64876) `C` `80` `50` `▭`
🔪 31.56 ⚕ 31.56 Global Days 090

27466 lengthening `C` `80` `50` `▭`
🔪 30.74 ⚕ 30.74 Global Days 090

27468 combined, lengthening and shortening with femoral segment transfer `C` `80` `50` `▭`
🔪 34.88 ⚕ 34.88 Global Days 090

27470 Repair, nonunion or malunion, femur, distal to head and neck; without graft (eg, compression technique) `C` `80` `50` `▭`
🔪 30.66 ⚕ 30.66 Global Days 090

27472 with iliac or other autogenous bone graft (includes obtaining graft) `C` `80` `50` `▭`
🔪 33.17 ⚕ 33.17 Global Days 090

27475 Arrest, epiphyseal, any method (eg, epiphysiodesis); distal femur `T` `50` `▭`
🔪 16.78 ⚕ 16.78 Global Days 090

27477 tibia and fibula, proximal `C` `50` `▭`
🔪 18.89 ⚕ 18.89 Global Days 090

27479 combined distal femur, proximal tibia and fibula `T` `80` `50` `▭`
🔪 24.52 ⚕ 24.52 Global Days 090

27485 Arrest, hemiepiphyseal, distal femur or proximal tibia or fibula (eg, genu varus or valgus) `C` `50` `▭`
🔪 17.22 ⚕ 17.22 Global Days 090

27486 Revision of total knee arthroplasty, with or without allograft; 1 component `C` `80` `50` `▭`
🔪 36.80 ⚕ 36.80 Global Days 090

27487 femoral and entire tibial component `C` `80` `50` `▭`
🔪 46.49 ⚕ 46.49 Global Days 090

27488 Removal of prosthesis, including total knee prosthesis, methylmethacrylate with or without insertion of spacer, knee `C` `80` `50` `▭`
🔪 31.09 ⚕ 31.09 Global Days 090

27495 Prophylactic treatment (nailing, pinning, plating, or wiring) with or without methylmethacrylate, femur `C` `80` `50` `▭`
🔪 29.49 ⚕ 29.49 Global Days 090

27496 Decompression fasciotomy, thigh and/or knee, 1 compartment (flexor or extensor or adductor); `A2` `T` `50`
🔪 12.78 ⚕ 12.78 Global Days 090

27497 with debridement of nonviable muscle and/or nerve `A2` `T` `80` `50`
🔪 13.91 ⚕ 13.91 Global Days 090

27498 Decompression fasciotomy, thigh and/or knee, multiple compartments; `A2` `T` `80` `50` `▭`
🔪 15.16 ⚕ 15.16 Global Days 090

27499 with debridement of nonviable muscle and/or nerve `A2` `T` `80` `50` `▭`
🔪 16.85 ⚕ 16.85 Global Days 090

27500-27566 Treatment of Fracture/Dislocation of Femur/Knee

27500 Closed treatment of femoral shaft fracture, without manipulation `A2` `T` `50`
🔪 12.02 ⚕ 12.88 Global Days 090

27501 Closed treatment of supracondylar or transcondylar femoral fracture with or without intercondylar extension, without manipulation `A2` `T` `80` `50`
🔪 12.50 ⚕ 12.67 Global Days 090

27502 Closed treatment of femoral shaft fracture, with manipulation, with or without skin or skeletal traction `A2` `T` `50` `▭`
🔪 20.29 ⚕ 20.29 Global Days 090

27503 Closed treatment of supracondylar or transcondylar femoral fracture with or without intercondylar extension, with manipulation, with or without skin or skeletal traction `A2` `T` `80` `50` `▭`
🔪 20.66 ⚕ 20.66 Global Days 090

27506 Open treatment of femoral shaft fracture, with or without external fixation, with insertion of intramedullary implant, with or without cerclage and/or locking screws `C` `80` `50` `▭`
🔪 34.55 ⚕ 34.55 Global Days 090

27507 Open treatment of femoral shaft fracture with plate/screws, with or without cerclage `C` `80` `50` `▭`
🔪 25.66 ⚕ 25.66 Global Days 090

27508 Closed treatment of femoral fracture, distal end, medial or lateral condyle, without manipulation `A2` `T` `50` `▭`
🔪 12.27 ⚕ 12.97 Global Days 090

27509 Percutaneous skeletal fixation of femoral fracture, distal end, medial or lateral condyle, or supracondylar or transcondylar, with or without intercondylar extension, or distal femoral epiphyseal separation `A2` `T` `80` `50` `▭`
🔪 16.38 ⚕ 16.38 Global Days 090

`26`/`TC` Professional/Technical Component Only   `80`/`60` Assist-at-Surgery Allowed/With Documentation   Unlisted   Not Covered
AMA: CPT Assistant References   `A2`-`Z3` ASC Payment Indicator   ♂ Male Only   ♀ Female Only   ⊘ Modifier 51 Exempt   `P0` PQRI

92   CPT only © 2008 American Medical Association. All Rights Reserved. (Black Ink)   Medicare (Red Ink)   © 2008 Ingenix (*Blue Ink*)

27510   Closed treatment of femoral fracture, distal end, medial or lateral condyle, with manipulation   A2 T 50
    17.91   17.91   Global Days 090

27511   Open treatment of femoral supracondylar or transcondylar fracture without intercondylar extension, includes internal fixation, when performed   C 80 50
    26.53   26.53   Global Days 090

27513   Open treatment of femoral supracondylar or transcondylar fracture with intercondylar extension, includes internal fixation, when performed   C 80 50
    33.42   33.42   Global Days 090

27514   Open treatment of femoral fracture, distal end, medial or lateral condyle, includes internal fixation, when performed   C 80 50
    27.02   27.02   Global Days 090

27516   Closed treatment of distal femoral epiphyseal separation; without manipulation   A2 T 50
    11.44   12.10   Global Days 090

27517   with manipulation, with or without skin or skeletal traction   A2 T 80 50
    17.10   17.10   Global Days 090

27519   Open treatment of distal femoral epiphyseal separation, includes internal fixation, when performed   C 80 50
    24.38   24.38   Global Days 090

27520   Closed treatment of patellar fracture, without manipulation   A2 T 50
    6.91   7.61   Global Days 090

27524   Open treatment of patellar fracture, with internal fixation and/or partial or complete patellectomy and soft tissue repair   T 80 50
    19.43   19.43   Global Days 090

27530   Closed treatment of tibial fracture, proximal (plateau); without manipulation   A2 T 50
   EXCLUDES   arthroscopic repair (29855-29856)
    8.94   9.58   Global Days 090

27532   with or without manipulation, with skeletal traction   A2 T 50
   EXCLUDES   arthroscopic repair (29855-29856)
    14.63   15.42   Global Days 090

27535   Open treatment of tibial fracture, proximal (plateau); unicondylar, includes internal fixation, when performed   C 80 50
   EXCLUDES   arthroscopic repair (29855-29856)
    23.64   23.64   Global Days 090

27536   bicondylar, with or without internal fixation   C 80 50
   EXCLUDES   arthroscopic repair (29855-29856)
    30.80   30.80   Global Days 090

27538   Closed treatment of intercondylar spine(s) and/or tuberosity fracture(s) of knee, with or without manipulation   A2 T 80 50
   EXCLUDES   arthroscopic repair (29850-29851)
    10.80   11.49   Global Days 090

27540   Open treatment of intercondylar spine(s) and/or tuberosity fracture(s) of the knee, includes internal fixation, when performed   C 80 50
    21.60   21.60   Global Days 090

27550   Closed treatment of knee dislocation; without anesthesia   A2 T 80 50
    11.31   12.11   Global Days 090

27552   requiring anesthesia   A2 T 80 50
    15.82   15.82   Global Days 090

27556   Open treatment of knee dislocation, includes internal fixation, when performed; without primary ligamentous repair or augmentation/reconstruction   C 80 50
    23.97   23.97   Global Days 090

27557   with primary ligamentous repair   C 80 50
    28.68   28.68   Global Days 090

27558   with primary ligamentous repair, with augmentation/reconstruction   C 80 50
    32.10   32.10   Global Days 090

27560   Closed treatment of patellar dislocation; without anesthesia   A2 T 50
   EXCLUDES   recurrent dislocation (27420-27424)
    8.01   8.81   Global Days 090

27562   requiring anesthesia   A2 T 80 50
   EXCLUDES   recurrent dislocation (27420-27424)
    11.65   11.65   Global Days 090

27566   Open treatment of patellar dislocation, with or without partial or total patellectomy   A2 T 80 50
   EXCLUDES   recurrent dislocation (27420-27424)
    23.16   23.16   Global Days 090

27570 Knee Manipulation with Anesthesia

27570   Manipulation of knee joint under general anesthesia (includes application of traction or other fixation devices)   A2 T
    3.74   3.74   Global Days 010

27580 Knee Arthrodesis

27580   Arthrodesis, knee, any technique   C 80 50
   INCLUDES   Albert's operation
    37.53   37.53   Global Days 090

27590-27599 Amputations at Femur or Knee

27590   Amputation, thigh, through femur, any level;   C 80 50
    21.42   21.42   Global Days 090

27591   immediate fitting technique including first cast   C 80 50
    23.76   23.76   Global Days 090

27592   open, circular (guillotine)   C 80 50
    18.16   18.16   Global Days 090

27594   secondary closure or scar revision   A2 T 50
    13.12   13.12   Global Days 090

27596   re-amputation   C 50
    19.04   19.04   Global Days 090

27598   Disarticulation at knee   C 80 50
   INCLUDES   Batch-Spittler-McFaddin operation
           Callandar knee disarticulation
           Gritti amputation
    19.37   19.37   Global Days 090

27599   Unlisted procedure, femur or knee   T 80 50
    0.00   0.00   Global Days YYY
   AMA: 2008, Jan, 4-5; 2008, Mar, 14-15

27600-27602 Decompression Fasciotomy of Leg

EXCLUDES   fasciotomy with debridement (27892-27894)
          simple incision and drainage (10140-10160)

27600   Decompression fasciotomy, leg; anterior and/or lateral compartments only   A2 T 50
    10.90   10.90   Global Days 090

27601   posterior compartment(s) only   A2 T 50
    11.27   11.27   Global Days 090

● New Code   ▲ Revised Code   M Maternity Edit   A Age Edit   A-Y OPPS Status Indicator   Facility RVU   Non-Facility RVU

CCI Comprehensive Code   50 Bilateral Procedure   + Add-on Indicator   Laboratory crosswalk   Radiology crosswalk

Musculoskeletal System

27602 — 27687

27602	anterior and/or lateral, and posterior compartment(s) [A2] [T] [80] [50] ▣

🔁 13.38   ⚒ 13.38   Global Days 090

27603-27612 Incisional Procedures Lower Leg and Ankle

27603   Incision and drainage, leg or ankle; deep abscess or hematoma [A2] [T] [50] ▣

🔁 9.86   ⚒ 12.99   Global Days 090

27604   infected bursa [A2] [T] [80] [50] ▣

🔁 8.70   ⚒ 11.41   Global Days 090

27605   Tenotomy, percutaneous, Achilles tendon (separate procedure); local anesthesia [A2] [T] [80] [50] ▣

🔁 5.21   ⚒ 9.05   Global Days 010

27606   general anesthesia [A2] [T] [50] ▣

🔁 7.69   ⚒ 7.69   Global Days 010

27607   Incision (eg, osteomyelitis or bone abscess), leg or ankle [A2] [T] [50] ▣

🔁 15.80   ⚒ 15.80   Global Days 090

27610   Arthrotomy, ankle, including exploration, drainage, or removal of foreign body [A2] [T] [50] ▣

🔁 16.87   ⚒ 16.87   Global Days 090

27612   Arthrotomy, posterior capsular release, ankle, with or without Achilles tendon lengthening [A2] [T] [80] [50] ▣

EXCLUDES   *lengthening or shortening tendon (27685)*

🔁 14.69   ⚒ 14.69   Global Days 090

27613-27614 Biopsy Lower Leg and Ankle

EXCLUDES   *needle biopsy (20206)*

27613   Biopsy, soft tissue of leg or ankle area; superficial [P3] [T] [50] ▣

🔁 4.21   ⚒ 6.14   Global Days 010

27614   deep (subfascial or intramuscular) [A2] [T] [50] ▣

🔁 10.53   ⚒ 13.95   Global Days 090

27615-27647 Resection Areas Lower Leg or Ankle

27615   Radical resection of tumor (eg, malignant neoplasm), soft tissue of leg or ankle area [A2] [T] [80] [50] ▣

🔁 22.70   ⚒ 22.70   Global Days 090

27618   Excision, tumor, leg or ankle area; subcutaneous tissue [A2] [T] [50] ▣

🔁 9.76   ⚒ 12.19   Global Days 090

27619   deep (subfascial or intramuscular) [A2] [T] [50] ▣

🔁 15.18   ⚒ 19.48   Global Days 090

27620   Arthrotomy, ankle, with joint exploration, with or without biopsy, with or without removal of loose or foreign body [A2] [T] [80] [50] ▣

🔁 11.86   ⚒ 11.86   Global Days 090

27625   Arthrotomy, with synovectomy, ankle; [A2] [T] [80] [50] ▣

🔁 15.36   ⚒ 15.36   Global Days 090

27626   including tenosynovectomy [A2] [T] [80] [50] ▣

🔁 16.62   ⚒ 16.62   Global Days 090

27630   Excision of lesion of tendon sheath or capsule (eg, cyst or ganglion), leg and/or ankle [A2] [T] [50] ▣

🔁 9.53   ⚒ 13.33   Global Days 090

27635   Excision or curettage of bone cyst or benign tumor, tibia or fibula; [A2] [T] [50] ▣

🔁 15.28   ⚒ 15.28   Global Days 090

27637   with autograft (includes obtaining graft) [A2] [T] [80] [50] ▣

🔁 19.38   ⚒ 19.38   Global Days 090

27638   with allograft [A2] [T] [80] [50] ▣

🔁 20.24   ⚒ 20.24   Global Days 090

27640   Partial excision (craterization, saucerization, or diaphysectomy) bone (eg, osteomyelitis or exostosis); tibia [A2] [T] [50] ▣

🔁 22.37   ⚒ 22.37   Global Days 090

27641   fibula [A2] [T] [50] ▣

🔁 17.91   ⚒ 17.91   Global Days 090

27645   Radical resection of tumor, bone; tibia [C] [80] [50] ▣

🔁 27.18   ⚒ 27.18   Global Days 090

27646   fibula [C] [80] [50] ▣

🔁 24.01   ⚒ 24.01   Global Days 090

27647   talus or calcaneus [A2] [T] [80] [50] ▣

🔁 21.22   ⚒ 21.22   Global Days 090

27648 Injection for Ankle Arthrogram

EXCLUDES   *arthroscopy (29894-29898)*

27648   Injection procedure for ankle arthrography [N1] [N] [80] [50] ▣

⇄ *73615*

🔁 1.39   ⚒ 4.03   Global Days 000

27650-27745 Repair/Reconstruction Lower Leg/Ankle

27650   Repair, primary, open or percutaneous, ruptured Achilles tendon; [A2] [T] [80] [50] ▣

🔁 17.49   ⚒ 17.49   Global Days 090

27652   with graft (includes obtaining graft) [A2] [T] [50] ▣

🔁 19.25   ⚒ 19.25   Global Days 090

27654   Repair, secondary, Achilles tendon, with or without graft [A2] [T] [80] [50] ▣

🔁 18.76   ⚒ 18.76   Global Days 090

27656   Repair, fascial defect of leg [A2] [T] [80] [50] ▣

🔁 9.00   ⚒ 13.39   Global Days 090

27658   Repair, flexor tendon, leg; primary, without graft, each tendon [A2] [T] [80] ▣

🔁 9.88   ⚒ 9.88   Global Days 090

27659   secondary, with or without graft, each tendon [A2] [T] [80] ▣

🔁 13.00   ⚒ 13.00   Global Days 090

27664   Repair, extensor tendon, leg; primary, without graft, each tendon [A2] [T] [80] ▣

🔁 9.42   ⚒ 9.42   Global Days 090

27665   secondary, with or without graft, each tendon [A2] [T] [80] ▣

🔁 10.80   ⚒ 10.80   Global Days 090

27675   Repair, dislocating peroneal tendons; without fibular osteotomy [A2] [T] [80] [50] ▣

🔁 13.25   ⚒ 13.25   Global Days 090

27676   with fibular osteotomy [A2] [T] [80] [50] ▣

🔁 16.09   ⚒ 16.09   Global Days 090

27680   Tenolysis, flexor or extensor tendon, leg and/or ankle; single, each tendon [A2] [T] ▣

🔁 11.21   ⚒ 11.21   Global Days 090

27681   multiple tendons (through separate incision(s)) [A2] [T] ▣

🔁 13.37   ⚒ 13.37   Global Days 090

27685   Lengthening or shortening of tendon, leg or ankle; single tendon (separate procedure) [A2] [T] [80] ▣

🔁 12.35   ⚒ 15.85   Global Days 090

27686   multiple tendons (through same incision), each [A2] [T] ▣

🔁 14.59   ⚒ 14.59   Global Days 090

27687   Gastrocnemius recession (eg, Strayer procedure) [A2] [T] [80] [50] ▣

🔁 12.00   ⚒ 12.00   Global Days 090

---

[26]/[TC] Professional/Technical Component Only   [80]/[80] Assist-at-Surgery Allowed/With Documentation   Unlisted   Not Covered

AMA: CPT Assistant References   [A2]-[Z3] ASC Payment Indicator   ♂ Male Only   ♀ Female Only   ⊘ Modifier 51 Exempt   [PQ] PQRI

94   CPT only © 2008 American Medical Association. All Rights Reserved. (Black Ink)   Medicare (Red Ink)   © 2008 Ingenix (*Blue Ink*)

27690   Transfer or transplant of single tendon (with muscle redirection or rerouting); superficial (eg, anterior tibial extensors into midfoot)   A2 T 80 50 ▢
    INCLUDES   toe extensors considered a single tendon with transplant into midfoot

    🖪 16.51   ⚕ 16.51   Global Days 090

27691   deep (eg, anterior tibial or posterior tibial through interosseous space, flexor digitorum longus, flexor hallucis longus, or peroneal tendon to midfoot or hindfoot)   A2 T 80 50 ▢
    INCLUDES   Barr procedure
        toe extensors considered a single tendon with transplant into midfoot

    🖪 19.40   ⚕ 19.40   Global Days 090

+   27692   each additional tendon (List separately in addition to code for primary procedure)   A2 T 80
    INCLUDES   toe extensors considered a single tendon with transplant into midfoot

    Code first 27690-27691
    🖪 2.98   ⚕ 2.98   Global Days ZZZ

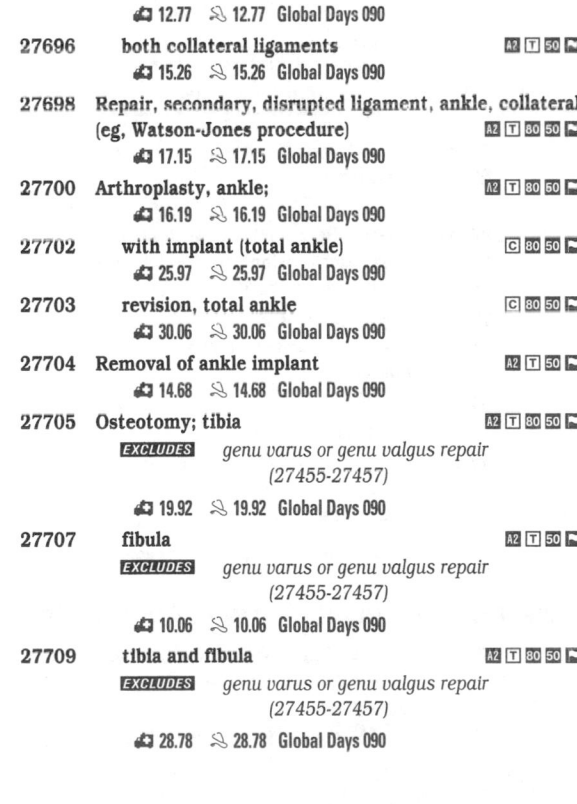

Lateral view of right ankle showing components of the collateral ligament

The components of the collateral ligament are often affected in sprained ankle type of injuries. Code 27695 reports first time repair of a disrupted collateral ligament. Report 27696 for repair to more than one collateral ligament.

27695   Repair, primary, disrupted ligament, ankle; collateral   A2 T 50 ▢
    🖪 12.77   ⚕ 12.77   Global Days 090

27696   both collateral ligaments   A2 T 50 ▢
    🖪 15.26   ⚕ 15.26   Global Days 090

27698   Repair, secondary, disrupted ligament, ankle, collateral (eg, Watson-Jones procedure)   A2 T 80 50 ▢
    🖪 17.15   ⚕ 17.15   Global Days 090

27700   Arthroplasty, ankle;   A2 T 80 50 ▢
    🖪 16.19   ⚕ 16.19   Global Days 090

27702   with implant (total ankle)   C 80 50 ▢
    🖪 25.97   ⚕ 25.97   Global Days 090

27703   revision, total ankle   C 80 50 ▢
    🖪 30.06   ⚕ 30.06   Global Days 090

27704   Removal of ankle implant   A2 T 50 ▢
    🖪 14.68   ⚕ 14.68   Global Days 090

27705   Osteotomy; tibia   A2 T 80 50 ▢
    EXCLUDES   genu varus or genu valgus repair (27455-27457)

    🖪 19.92   ⚕ 19.92   Global Days 090

27707   fibula   A2 T 50 ▢
    EXCLUDES   genu varus or genu valgus repair (27455-27457)

    🖪 10.06   ⚕ 10.06   Global Days 090

27709   tibia and fibula   A2 T 80 50 ▢
    EXCLUDES   genu varus or genu valgus repair (27455-27457)

    🖪 28.78   ⚕ 28.78   Global Days 090

27712   multiple, with realignment on intramedullary rod (eg, Sofield type procedure)   C 80 50 ▢
    EXCLUDES   genu varus or genu valgus repair (27455-27457)

    🖪 28.37   ⚕ 28.37   Global Days 090

27715   Osteoplasty, tibia and fibula, lengthening or shortening   C 80 50 ▢
    INCLUDES   Anderson tibial lengthening

    🖪 27.73   ⚕ 27.73   Global Days 090

27720   Repair of nonunion or malunion, tibia; without graft, (eg, compression technique)   T 80 50 ▢
    🖪 22.79   ⚕ 22.79   Global Days 090

27722   with sliding graft   T 80 50 ▢
    🖪 22.74   ⚕ 22.74   Global Days 090

27724   with iliac or other autograft (includes obtaining graft)   C 80 50 ▢
    🖪 33.54   ⚕ 33.54   Global Days 090

27725   by synostosis, with fibula, any method   C 80 50 ▢
    🖪 31.12   ⚕ 31.12   Global Days 090

27726   Repair of fibula nonunion and/or malunion with internal fixation   62 T 50
    Do not report with (27707)
    🖪 23.50   ⚕ 23.50   Global Days 090
    AMA: 2008, Jan, 4-5

27727   Repair of congenital pseudarthrosis, tibia   C 80 50 ▢
    🖪 25.34   ⚕ 25.34   Global Days 090

27730   Arrest, epiphyseal (epiphysiodesis), open; distal tibia   A2 T 50 ▢
    🖪 15.29   ⚕ 15.29   Global Days 090

27732   distal fibula   A2 T 50 ▢
    🖪 10.25   ⚕ 10.25   Global Days 090

27734   distal tibia and fibula   A2 T 50 ▢
    🖪 15.44   ⚕ 15.44   Global Days 090

27740   Arrest, epiphyseal (epiphysiodesis), any method, combined, proximal and distal tibia and fibula;   A2 T 80 50 ▢
    EXCLUDES   epiphyseal arrest of proximal tibia and fibula (27477)

    🖪 17.18   ⚕ 17.18   Global Days 090

27742   and distal femur   A2 T 80 50 ▢
    EXCLUDES   epiphyseal arrest of proximal tibia and fibula (27477)

    🖪 18.12   ⚕ 18.12   Global Days 090

27745   Prophylactic treatment (nailing, pinning, plating or wiring) with or without methylmethacrylate, tibia   A2 T 80 50 ▢
    🖪 19.55   ⚕ 19.55   Global Days 090

27750-27848 Treatment of Fracture/Dislocation Lower Leg/Ankle

27750   Closed treatment of tibial shaft fracture (with or without fibular fracture); without manipulation   A2 T 50 ▢
    🖪 7.58   ⚕ 8.24   Global Days 090
    AMA: 2008, Jan, 10-25; 2007, Jan, 13-27; 2007, Jan, 13-27; 2007, January, 13-27

27752   with manipulation, with or without skeletal traction   A2 T 50 ▢
    🖪 12.47   ⚕ 13.33   Global Days 090

27756   Percutaneous skeletal fixation of tibial shaft fracture (with or without fibular fracture) (eg, pins or screws)   A2 T 80 50 ▢
    🖪 14.49   ⚕ 14.49   Global Days 090

● New Code   ▲ Revised Code   Ⓜ Maternity Edit   🄰 Age Edit   Ⓐ-Ⓨ OPPS Status Indicator   🖪 Facility RVU   ⚕ Non-Facility RVU
▢ CCI Comprehensive Code   50 Bilateral Procedure   + Add-on Indicator   🅽 Laboratory crosswalk   🅡 Radiology crosswalk

Musculoskeletal System

27758 — 27860

27758 Open treatment of tibial shaft fracture (with or without fibular fracture), with plate/screws, with or without cerclage   A2 T 80 50 ▢ P0
   🔲 22.96   ⚕ 22.96   Global Days 090
   AMA: 2008, Jan, 10-25; 2007, Jan, 13-27; 2007, Jan, 13-27; 2007, January, 13-27

27759 Treatment of tibial shaft fracture (with or without fibular fracture) by intramedullary implant, with or without interlocking screws and/or cerclage   A2 T 80 50 ▢ P0
   🔲 26.05   ⚕ 26.05   Global Days 090

27760 Closed treatment of medial malleolus fracture; without manipulation   A2 T 50 ▢
   🔲 7.21   ⚕ 7.92   Global Days 090

27762   with manipulation, with or without skin or skeletal traction   A2 T 50 ▢
   🔲 11.04   ⚕ 11.91   Global Days 090

27766 Open treatment of medial malleolus fracture, includes internal fixation, when performed   A2 T 50 ▢ P0
   🔲 15.66   ⚕ 15.66   Global Days 090

27767 Closed treatment of posterior malleolus fracture; without manipulation   62 T 50

   Do not report with (27808-27823)
   🔲 6.29   ⚕ 6.26   Global Days 090

27768   with manipulation   62 T 50

   Do not report with (27808-27823)
   🔲 10.20   ⚕ 10.20   Global Days 090

27769 Open treatment of posterior malleolus fracture, includes internal fixation, when performed   62 T 50

   Do not report with (27808-27823)
   🔲 17.79   ⚕ 17.79   Global Days 090

27780 Closed treatment of proximal fibula or shaft fracture; without manipulation   A2 T 50 ▢
   🔲 6.43   ⚕ 7.08   Global Days 090

27781   with manipulation   A2 T 50 ▢
   🔲 9.64   ⚕ 10.31   Global Days 090

27784 Open treatment of proximal fibula or shaft fracture, includes internal fixation, when performed   A2 T 50 ▢
   🔲 17.63   ⚕ 17.63   Global Days 090
   AMA: 2008, Jan, 10-25; 2007, Jan, 13-27; 2007, Jan, 13-27; 2007, January, 13-27

27786 Closed treatment of distal fibular fracture (lateral malleolus); without manipulation   A2 T 50 ▢
   🔲 6.78   ⚕ 7.51   Global Days 090

27788   with manipulation   A2 T 50 ▢
   🔲 9.62   ⚕ 10.40   Global Days 090

27792 Open treatment of distal fibular fracture (lateral malleolus), includes internal fixation, when performed   A2 T 50 ▢ P0
   EXCLUDES   repair of tibia and fibula shaft fracture (27750-27759)
   🔲 17.85   ⚕ 17.85   Global Days 090

27808 Closed treatment of bimalleolar ankle fracture (eg, lateral and medial malleoli, or lateral and posterior malleoli or medial and posterior malleoli); without manipulation   A2 T 50 ▢
   🔲 7.07   ⚕ 7.85   Global Days 090

27810   with manipulation   A2 T 50 ▢
   🔲 10.76   ⚕ 11.65   Global Days 090

27814 Open treatment of bimalleolar ankle fracture (eg, lateral and medial malleoli, or lateral and posterior malleoli, or medial and posterior malleoli), includes internal fixation, when performed   A2 T 80 50 ▢ P0
   🔲 20.06   ⚕ 20.06   Global Days 090

27816 Closed treatment of trimalleolar ankle fracture; without manipulation   A2 T 50 ▢
   🔲 6.71   ⚕ 7.43   Global Days 090

27818   with manipulation   A2 T 50 ▢
   🔲 10.99   ⚕ 12.00   Global Days 090

27822 Open treatment of trimalleolar ankle fracture, includes internal fixation, when performed, medial and/or lateral malleolus; without fixation of posterior lip   A2 T 80 50 ▢
   🔲 21.93   ⚕ 21.93   Global Days 090

27823   with fixation of posterior lip   A2 T 80 50 ▢
   🔲 25.01   ⚕ 25.01   Global Days 090

27824 Closed treatment of fracture of weight bearing articular portion of distal tibia (eg, pilon or tibial plafond), with or without anesthesia; without manipulation   A2 T 50 ▢
   🔲 7.20   ⚕ 7.47   Global Days 090

27825   with skeletal traction and/or requiring manipulation   A2 T 80 50 ▢
   🔲 12.64   ⚕ 13.70   Global Days 090

27826 Open treatment of fracture of weight bearing articular surface/portion of distal tibia (eg, pilon or tibial plafond), with internal fixation, when performed; of fibula only   A2 T 80 50 ▢
   🔲 20.91   ⚕ 20.91   Global Days 090

27827   of tibia only   A2 T 80 50 ▢
   🔲 28.05   ⚕ 28.05   Global Days 090

27828   of both tibia and fibula   A2 T 80 50 ▢
   🔲 33.51   ⚕ 33.51   Global Days 090

27829 Open treatment of distal tibiofibular joint (syndesmosis) disruption, includes internal fixation, when performed   A2 T 80 50 ▢
   🔲 16.63   ⚕ 16.63   Global Days 090

27830 Closed treatment of proximal tibiofibular joint dislocation; without anesthesia   A2 T 80 50 ▢
   🔲 8.16   ⚕ 8.69   Global Days 090

27831   requiring anesthesia   A2 T 80 50 ▢
   🔲 9.54   ⚕ 9.54   Global Days 090

27832 Open treatment of proximal tibiofibular joint dislocation, includes internal fixation, when performed, or with excision of proximal fibula   A2 T 80 50 ▢
   🔲 17.90   ⚕ 17.90   Global Days 090

27840 Closed treatment of ankle dislocation; without anesthesia   A2 T 50 ▢
   🔲 8.72   ⚕ 8.72   Global Days 090

27842   requiring anesthesia, with or without percutaneous skeletal fixation   A2 T 50 ▢
   🔲 12.33   ⚕ 12.33   Global Days 090

27846 Open treatment of ankle dislocation, with or without percutaneous skeletal fixation; without repair or internal fixation   A2 T 80 50 ▢
   EXCLUDES   arthroscopy (29894-29898)
   🔲 19.12   ⚕ 19.12   Global Days 090

27848   with repair or internal or external fixation   A2 T 80 50 ▢
   EXCLUDES   arthroscopy (29894-29898)
   🔲 21.65   ⚕ 21.65   Global Days 090

27860 Ankle Manipulation with Anesthesia

27860 Manipulation of ankle under general anesthesia (includes application of traction or other fixation apparatus)   A2 T 80 ▢
   🔲 4.61   ⚕ 4.61   Global Days 010

27870-27871 Arthrodesis Lower Leg/Ankle

27870 Arthrodesis, ankle, open A2 T 80 50 ▢
  EXCLUDES *arthroscopic arthrodesis of ankle (29899)*
  ⚙ 27.27 ⚕ 27.27 Global Days 090

27871 Arthrodesis, tibiofibular joint, proximal or distal A2 T 80 50 ▢
  ⚙ 17.92 ⚕ 17.92 Global Days 090

27880-27889 Amputations of Lower Leg/Ankle

27880 Amputation, leg, through tibia and fibula; C 80 50 ▢
  INCLUDES Burgess amputation
  ⚙ 23.98 ⚕ 23.98 Global Days 090

27881 with immediate fitting technique including application of first cast C 80 50 ▢
  ⚙ 23.23 ⚕ 23.23 Global Days 090

27882 open, circular (guillotine) C 80 50 ▢
  ⚙ 16.33 ⚕ 16.33 Global Days 090

27884 secondary closure or scar revision A2 T 50 ▢
  ⚙ 15.19 ⚕ 15.19 Global Days 090

27886 re-amputation C 50 ▢
  ⚙ 17.33 ⚕ 17.33 Global Days 090

27888 Amputation, ankle, through malleoli of tibia and fibula (eg, Syme, Pirogoff type procedures), with plastic closure and resection of nerves C 80 50 ▢
  ⚙ 18.34 ⚕ 18.34 Global Days 090

27889 Ankle disarticulation A2 T 50 ▢
  ⚙ 17.90 ⚕ 17.90 Global Days 090

27892-27899 Decompression Fasciotomy Lower Leg

EXCLUDES *decompression fasciotomy without debridement (27601)*

27892 Decompression fasciotomy, leg; anterior and/or lateral compartments only, with debridement of nonviable muscle and/or nerve A2 T A0 50 ▢
  ⚙ 14.05 ⚕ 14.05 Global Days 090

27893 posterior compartment(s) only, with debridement of nonviable muscle and/or nerve A2 T A0 50 ▢
  ⚙ 14.22 ⚕ 14.22 Global Days 090

27894 anterior and/or lateral, and posterior compartment(s), with debridement of nonviable muscle and/or nerve A2 T 80 50 ▢
  ⚙ 21.82 ⚕ 21.82 Global Days 090

27899 Unlisted procedure, leg or ankle T 80 50
  ⚙ 0.00 ⚕ 0.00 Global Days YYY
  AMA: 2008, Jan, 10-25; 2007, Jan, 13-27; 2007, Jan, 13-27; 2007, January, 13-27

28001-28008 Surgical Incision Foot/Toe

EXCLUDES *simple incision and drainage (10140-10160)*

28001 Incision and drainage, bursa, foot P3 T ▢
  ⚙ 4.76 ⚕ 6.74 Global Days 010

28002 Incision and drainage below fascia, with or without tendon sheath involvement, foot; single bursal space A2 T ▢
  ⚙ 10.01 ⚕ 12.56 Global Days 010

28003 multiple areas A2 T ▢
  ⚙ 14.82 ⚕ 17.40 Global Days 090

28005 Incision, bone cortex (eg, osteomyelitis or bone abscess), foot A2 T ▢
  ⚙ 16.13 ⚕ 16.13 Global Days 090

28008 Fasciotomy, foot and/or toe A2 T 50 ▢
  EXCLUDES *plantar fascia division (28250)*
  plantar fasciectomy (28060, 28062)
  ⚙ 8.06 ⚕ 10.66 Global Days 090

28010-28011 Tenotomy/Toe

EXCLUDES *open tenotomy (28230-28234)*
  simple incision and drainage (10140-10160)

28010 Tenotomy, percutaneous, toe; single tendon P3 T ▢
  ⚙ 5.57 ⚕ 5.94 Global Days 090

28011 multiple tendons A2 T ▢
  ⚙ 7.88 ⚕ 8.44 Global Days 090

28020-28024 Arthrotomy Foot/Toe

EXCLUDES *simple incision and drainage (10140-10160)*

28020 Arthrotomy, including exploration, drainage, or removal of loose or foreign body; intertarsal or tarsometatarsal joint A2 T ▢
  ⚙ 9.48 ⚕ 12.67 Global Days 090

28022 metatarsophalangeal joint A2 T ▢
  ⚙ 8.76 ⚕ 11.68 Global Days 090

28024 interphalangeal joint A2 T ▢
  ⚙ 8.30 ⚕ 11.10 Global Days 090

28035 Tarsal Tunnel Release

EXCLUDES *other nerve decompression (64722)*
  other neuroplasty (64704)

28035 Release, tarsal tunnel (posterior tibial nerve decompression) A2 T ▢
  ⚙ 9.56 ⚕ 12.74 Global Days 090

28043-28175 Resection Area of Foot/Toe

28043 Excision, tumor, foot; subcutaneous tissue A2 T 50 ▢
  ⚙ 6.85 ⚕ 8.49 Global Days 090

28045 deep, subfascial, intramuscular A2 T 80 50 ▢
  ⚙ 8.72 ⚕ 11.90 Global Days 090

28046 Radical resection of tumor (eg, malignant neoplasm), soft tissue of foot A2 T 50 ▢
  ⚙ 17.85 ⚕ 21.73 Global Days 090

28050 Arthrotomy with biopsy; intertarsal or tarsometatarsal joint A2 T 50 ▢
  ⚙ 8.24 ⚕ 11.19 Global Days 090

28052 metatarsophalangeal joint A2 T 50 ▢
  ⚙ 7.49 ⚕ 10.31 Global Days 090

28054 interphalangeal joint A2 T 80 50 ▢
  ⚙ 6.82 ⚕ 9.67 Global Days 090

28055 Neurectomy, intrinsic musculature of foot A2 T A0
  ⚙ 10.47 ⚕ 10.47 Global Days 090

28060 Fasciectomy, plantar fascia; partial (separate procedure) A2 T 50 ▢
  EXCLUDES *plantar fasciotomy (28008, 28250)*
  ⚙ 9.60 ⚕ 12.56 Global Days 090
  AMA: 2008, Mar, 14-15

28062 radical (separate procedure) A2 T ▢
  EXCLUDES *plantar fasciotomy (28008, 28250)*
  ⚙ 11.26 ⚕ 14.78 Global Days 090

28070 Synovectomy; intertarsal or tarsometatarsal joint, each A2 T ▢
  ⚙ 9.41 ⚕ 12.47 Global Days 090

28072 metatarsophalangeal joint, each A2 T ▢
  ⚙ 9.10 ⚕ 12.28 Global Days 090

● New Code ▲ Revised Code M Maternity Edit A Age Edit [A]-[Y] UPPS Status Indicator ⚙ Facility RVU ⚕ Non-Facility RVU
▢ CCI Comprehensive Code 50 Bilateral Procedure + Add-on Indicator N Laboratory crosswalk ▣ Radiology crosswalk

Musculoskeletal System

28080 — 28193

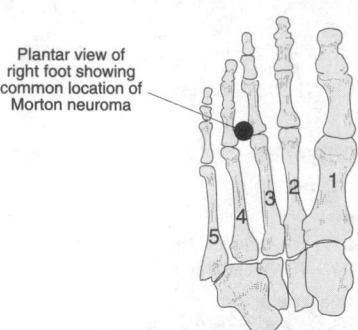

Plantar view of right foot showing common location of Morton neuroma

Morton neuroma is a chronic inflammation or irritation of the nerves in the web space between the heads of the metatarsals and phalanges

28080 Excision, interdigital (Morton) neuroma, single, each 　A2 T 80 🔲
9.12 　11.98 Global Days 090

28086 Synovectomy, tendon sheath, foot; flexor 　A2 T 80 50 🔲
9.52 　13.19 Global Days 090

28088 extensor 　A2 T 80 50 🔲
7.92 　11.18 Global Days 090

28090 Excision of lesion, tendon, tendon sheath, or capsule (including synovectomy) (eg, cyst or ganglion); foot 　A2 T 50 🔲
8.27 　11.28 Global Days 090

28092 toe(s), each 　A2 T 🔲
7.25 　10.17 Global Days 090

28100 Excision or curettage of bone cyst or benign tumor, talus or calcaneus; 　A2 T 80 50 🔲
10.76 　14.57 Global Days 090

28102 with iliac or other autograft (includes obtaining graft) 　A2 T 80 50 🔲
14.69 　14.69 Global Days 090

28103 with allograft 　A2 T 80 50 🔲
11.86 　11.86 Global Days 090

28104 Excision or curettage of bone cyst or benign tumor, tarsal or metatarsal, except talus or calcaneus; 　A2 T 80 🔲
9.41 　12.50 Global Days 090

28106 with iliac or other autograft (includes obtaining graft) 　A2 T 80 🔲
12.53 　12.53 Global Days 090

28107 with allograft 　A2 T 80 🔲
10.26 　13.86 Global Days 090

28108 Excision or curettage of bone cyst or benign tumor, phalanges of foot 　A2 T 🔲
EXCLUDES　hallux valgus (28290)
7.75 　10.50 Global Days 090

28110 Ostectomy, partial excision, fifth metatarsal head (bunionette) (separate procedure) 　A2 T 50 🔲
7.74 　11.02 Global Days 090
AMA: 2008, Jan, 10-25; 2007, Jan, 13-27; 2007, Jan, 13-27; 2007, January, 13-27

28111 Ostectomy, complete excision; first metatarsal head 　A2 T 50 🔲
9.06 　12.56 Global Days 090

28112 other metatarsal head (second, third or fourth) 　A2 T 50 🔲
8.47 　11.88 Global Days 090

28113 fifth metatarsal head 　A2 T 80 50 🔲
11.01 　14.17 Global Days 090

28114 all metatarsal heads, with partial proximal phalangectomy, excluding first metatarsal (eg, Clayton type procedure) 　A2 T 80 50 🔲
21.36 　25.85 Global Days 090

28116 Ostectomy, excision of tarsal coalition 　A2 T 50 🔲
15.16 　18.48 Global Days 090

28118 Ostectomy, calcaneus; 　A2 T 80 50 🔲
11.01 　14.34 Global Days 090

28119 for spur, with or without plantar fascial release 　A2 T 50 🔲
9.72 　12.76 Global Days 090

28120 Partial excision (craterization, saucerization, sequestrectomy, or diaphysectomy) bone (eg, osteomyelitis or bossing); talus or calcaneus 　A2 T 50 🔲
INCLUDES　Barker operation
10.47 　14.16 Global Days 090

28122 tarsal or metatarsal bone, except talus or calcaneus 　A2 T 80 50 🔲
EXCLUDES　hallux rigidus cheilectomy (28289)
partial removal of talus or calcaneus (28120)
13.43 　16.49 Global Days 090

28124 phalanx of toe 　P3 T 50 🔲
8.95 　11.67 Global Days 090

28126 Resection, partial or complete, phalangeal base, each toe 　A2 T 🔲
6.73 　9.42 Global Days 090

28130 Talectomy (astragalectomy) 　A2 T 80 50 🔲
INCLUDES　Whitman astragalectomy
EXCLUDES　calcanectomy (28118)
16.71 　16.71 Global Days 090

28140 Metatarsectomy 　A2 T 🔲
12.23 　15.52 Global Days 090

28150 Phalangectomy, toe, each toe 　A2 T 🔲
7.69 　10.51 Global Days 090

28153 Resection, condyle(s), distal end of phalanx, each toe 　A2 T 🔲
6.99 　9.79 Global Days 090

28160 Hemiphalangectomy or interphalangeal joint excision, toe, proximal end of phalanx, each 　A2 T 🔲
7.29 　10.05 Global Days 090

28171 Radical resection of tumor, bone; tarsal (except talus or calcaneus) 　A2 T 80 🔲
EXCLUDES　talus or calcaneus resection (27647)
16.40 　16.40 Global Days 090

28173 metatarsal 　A2 T 🔲
EXCLUDES　talus or calcaneus resection (27647)
14.93 　18.50 Global Days 090

28175 phalanx of toe 　A2 T 🔲
EXCLUDES　talus or calcaneus resection (27647)
10.51 　13.54 Global Days 090

28190-28193 Foreign Body Removal: Foot

28190 Removal of foreign body, foot; subcutaneous 　P3 T 50 🔲
3.56 　5.98 Global Days 010

28192 deep 　A2 T 50 🔲
8.56 　11.55 Global Days 090

28193 complicated 　A2 T 50 🔲
10.18 　13.26 Global Days 090

28200-28360 Repair/Reconstruction of Foot/Toe

28200 Repair, tendon, flexor, foot; primary or secondary, without free graft, each tendon `A2` `T` `□`
  🔶 8.54 ⚲ 11.55 Global Days 090

28202 secondary with free graft, each tendon (includes obtaining graft) `A2` `T` `80` `□`
  🔶 11.94 ⚲ 15.39 Global Days 090

28208 Repair, tendon, extensor, foot; primary or secondary, each tendon `A2` `T` `□`
  🔶 8.20 ⚲ 11.12 Global Days 090

28210 secondary with free graft, each tendon (includes obtaining graft) `A2` `T` `80` `□`
  🔶 11.14 ⚲ 14.33 Global Days 090

28220 Tenolysis, flexor, foot; single tendon `P3` `T` `□`
  🔶 8.27 ⚲ 10.98 Global Days 090

28222 multiple tendons `A2` `T` `□`
  🔶 9.85 ⚲ 12.70 Global Days 090

28225 Tenolysis, extensor, foot; single tendon `A2` `T` `□`
  🔶 6.85 ⚲ 9.53 Global Days 090

28226 multiple tendons `A2` `T` `□`
  🔶 8.55 ⚲ 11.46 Global Days 090

28230 Tenotomy, open, tendon flexor; foot, single or multiple tendon(s) (separate procedure) `P3` `T` `□`
  🔶 7.87 ⚲ 10.55 Global Days 090

28232 toe, single tendon (separate procedure) `P3` `T` `□`
  🔶 6.68 ⚲ 9.34 Global Days 090

28234 Tenotomy, open, extensor, foot or toe, each tendon `A2` `T` `□`
  EXCLUDES tendon transfer (27690-27691)
  🔶 6.99 ⚲ 9.68 Global Days 090

28238 Reconstruction (advancement), posterior tibial tendon with excision of accessory tarsal navicular bone (eg, Kidner type procedure) `A2` `T` `80` `50` `□`
  EXCLUDES extensor hallucis longus transfer with big toe fusion (28760)
       Jones procedure (28760)
       subcutaneous tenotomy (28010-28011)
       transfer or transplant of tendon with muscle redirection or rerouting (27690-27692)
  🔶 13.42 ⚲ 16.90 Global Days 090

28240 Tenotomy, lengthening, or release, abductor hallucis muscle `A2` `T` `50` `□`
  🔶 8.08 ⚲ 10.86 Global Days 090

28250 Division of plantar fascia and muscle (eg, Steindler stripping) (separate procedure) `A2` `T` `80` `50` `□`
  🔶 10.74 ⚲ 13.84 Global Days 090

28260 Capsulotomy, midfoot; medial release only (separate procedure) `A2` `T` `80` `50` `□`
  🔶 13.89 ⚲ 16.96 Global Days 090

28261 with tendon lengthening `A2` `T` `80` `50` `□`
  🔶 21.09 ⚲ 24.56 Global Days 090

28262 extensive, including posterior talotibial capsulotomy and tendon(s) lengthening (eg, resistant clubfoot deformity) `A2` `T` `80` `50` `□`
  🔶 29.70 ⚲ 34.48 Global Days 090

28264 Capsulotomy, midtarsal (eg, Heyman type procedure) `A2` `T` `80` `50` `□`
  🔶 18.64 ⚲ 22.02 Global Days 090

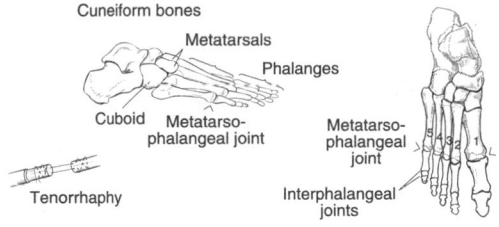

Tarsals, metatarsals, and phalanges

The metatarsophalangeal joint capsule is incised (capsulotomy)

28270 Capsulotomy; metatarsophalangeal joint, with or without tenorrhaphy, each joint (separate procedure) `A2` `T` `50` `□`
  🔶 8.94 ⚲ 11.74 Global Days 090

28272 interphalangeal joint, each joint (separate procedure) `P3` `T` `50` `□`
  🔶 6.96 ⚲ 9.58 Global Days 090
  AMA: 2008, Jan, 10-25; 2007, Jan, 13-27; 2007, Jan, 13-27; 2007, January, 13-27

28280 Syndactylization, toes (eg, webbing or Kelikian type procedure) `A2` `T` `80` `50` `□`
  🔶 9.74 ⚲ 12.90 Global Days 090

28285 Correction, hammertoe (eg, interphalangeal fusion, partial or total phalangectomy) `A2` `T` `50` `□`
  🔶 8.58 ⚲ 11.37 Global Days 090
  AMA: 2008, Jan, 10-25; 2007, Jan, 13-27; 2007, Jan, 13-27; 2007, January, 13-27; 2006, May, 16-20; 2006, May, 16-20; 2006, May, 16-20

28286 Correction, cock-up fifth toe, with plastic skin closure (eg, Ruiz-Mora type procedure) `A2` `T` `□`
  🔶 8.24 ⚲ 11.11 Global Days 090

28288 Ostectomy, partial, exostectomy or condylectomy, metatarsal head, each metatarsal head `A2` `T` `□`
  🔶 11.14 ⚲ 14.21 Global Days 090

28289 Hallux rigidus correction with cheilectomy, debridement and capsular release of the first metatarsophalangeal joint `A2` `T` `80` `50` `□`
  🔶 14.54 ⚲ 18.03 Global Days 090

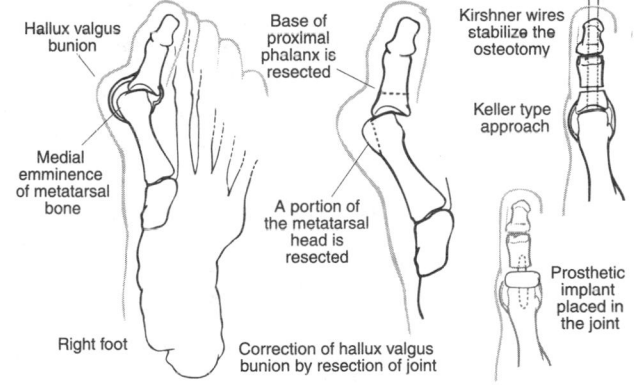

Correction of hallux valgus bunion by resection of joint

28290 Correction, hallux valgus (bunion), with or without sesamoidectomy; simple exostectomy (eg, Silver type procedure) `A2` `T` `50` `□`
  🔶 10.66 ⚲ 14.07 Global Days 090
  AMA: 2008, Jan, 10-25; 2007, Jan, 28-31; 2007, Jan, 28-31; 2007, January, 28-31

Musculoskeletal System

28200 — 28290

Musculoskeletal System

28292 — 28445

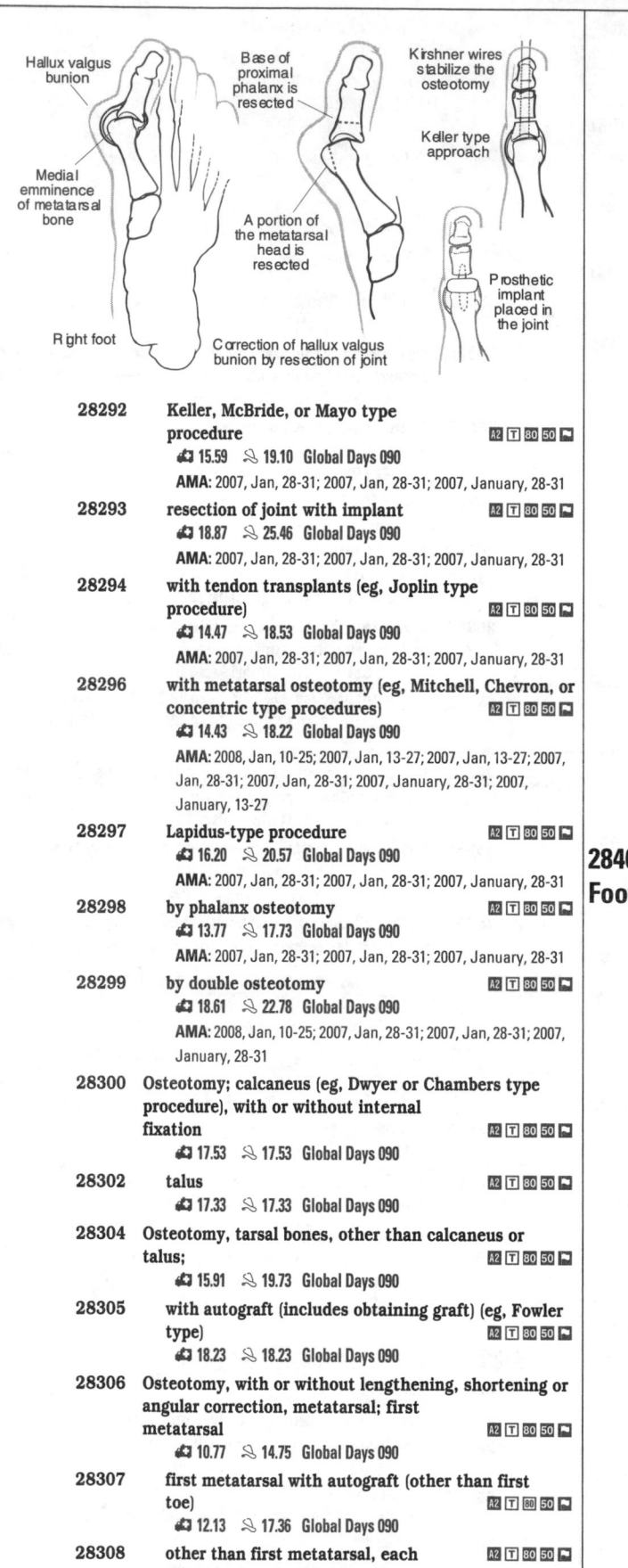

Hallux valgus bunion

Base of proximal phalanx is resected

Kirshner wires stabilize the osteotomy

Keller type approach

Medial emminence of metatarsal bone

A portion of the metatarsal head is resected

Prosthetic implant placed in the joint

Right foot

Correction of hallux valgus bunion by resection of joint

28292   Keller, McBride, or Mayo type procedure   A2 T 80 50 □
   15.59   19.10   Global Days 090
   AMA: 2007, Jan, 28-31; 2007, Jan, 28-31; 2007, January, 28-31

28293   resection of joint with implant   A2 T 80 50 □
   18.87   25.46   Global Days 090
   AMA: 2007, Jan, 28-31; 2007, Jan, 28-31; 2007, January, 28-31

28294   with tendon transplants (eg, Joplin type procedure)   A2 T 80 50 □
   14.47   18.53   Global Days 090
   AMA: 2007, Jan, 28-31; 2007, Jan, 28-31; 2007, January, 28-31

28296   with metatarsal osteotomy (eg, Mitchell, Chevron, or concentric type procedures)   A2 T 80 50 □
   14.43   18.22   Global Days 090
   AMA: 2008, Jan, 10-25; 2007, Jan, 13-27; 2007, Jan, 13-27; 2007, Jan, 28-31; 2007, Jan, 28-31; 2007, January, 28-31; 2007, January, 13-27

28297   Lapidus-type procedure   A2 T 80 50 □
   16.20   20.57   Global Days 090
   AMA: 2007, Jan, 28-31; 2007, Jan, 28-31; 2007, January, 28-31

28298   by phalanx osteotomy   A2 T 80 50 □
   13.77   17.73   Global Days 090
   AMA: 2007, Jan, 28-31; 2007, Jan, 28-31; 2007, January, 28-31

28299   by double osteotomy   A2 T 80 50 □
   18.61   22.78   Global Days 090
   AMA: 2008, Jan, 10-25; 2007, Jan, 28-31; 2007, Jan, 28-31; 2007, January, 28-31

28300   Osteotomy; calcaneus (eg, Dwyer or Chambers type procedure), with or without internal fixation   A2 T 80 50 □
   17.53   17.53   Global Days 090

28302   talus   A2 T 80 50 □
   17.33   17.33   Global Days 090

28304   Osteotomy, tarsal bones, other than calcaneus or talus;   A2 T 80 50 □
   15.91   19.73   Global Days 090

28305   with autograft (includes obtaining graft) (eg, Fowler type)   A2 T 80 50 □
   18.23   18.23   Global Days 090

28306   Osteotomy, with or without lengthening, shortening or angular correction, metatarsal; first metatarsal   A2 T 80 50 □
   10.77   14.75   Global Days 090

28307   first metatarsal with autograft (other than first toe)   A2 T 80 50 □
   12.13   17.36   Global Days 090

28308   other than first metatarsal, each   A2 T 80 50 □
   9.85   13.34   Global Days 090

28309   multiple (eg, Swanson type cavus foot procedure)   A2 T 80 50 □
   23.64   23.64   Global Days 090

28310   Osteotomy, shortening, angular or rotational correction; proximal phalanx, first toe (separate procedure)   A2 T □
   9.61   13.14   Global Days 090

28312   other phalanges, any toe   A2 T □
   8.57   12.03   Global Days 090

28313   Reconstruction, angular deformity of toe, soft tissue procedures only (eg, overlapping second toe, fifth toe, curly toes)   A2 T □
   9.82   12.66   Global Days 090

28315   Sesamoidectomy, first toe (separate procedure)   A2 T 50 □
   8.75   11.61   Global Days 090

28320   Repair, nonunion or malunion; tarsal bones   A2 T 80 □
   16.57   16.57   Global Days 090

28322   metatarsal, with or without bone graft (includes obtaining graft)   A2 T 80 □
   15.28   19.19   Global Days 090

28340   Reconstruction, toe, macrodactyly; soft tissue resection   A2 T □
   11.86   15.23   Global Days 090

28341   requiring bone resection   A2 T □
   14.04   17.56   Global Days 090

28344   Reconstruction, toe(s); polydactyly   A2 T □
   8.30   11.65   Global Days 090

28345   syndactyly, with or without skin graft(s), each web   A2 T 80 □
   10.89   14.12   Global Days 090

28360   Reconstruction, cleft foot   T 80 □
   25.53   25.53   Global Days 090

28400-28675 Treatment of Fracture/Dislocation of Foot/Toe

28400   Closed treatment of calcaneal fracture; without manipulation   A2 T 50 □
   5.49   5.96   Global Days 090

28405   with manipulation   A2 T 80 50 □
   INCLUDES   Bohler reduction
   9.20   9.79   Global Days 090

28406   Percutaneous skeletal fixation of calcaneal fracture, with manipulation   A2 T 80 50 □
   13.48   13.48   Global Days 090

28415   Open treatment of calcaneal fracture, includes internal fixation, when performed;   A2 T 80 50 □
   29.72   29.72   Global Days 090

28420   with primary iliac or other autogenous bone graft (includes obtaining graft)   A2 T 80 50 □
   31.29   31.29   Global Days 090

28430   Closed treatment of talus fracture; without manipulation   P2 T 50 □
   4.98   5.57   Global Days 090

28435   with manipulation   A2 T 80 50 □
   7.35   7.91   Global Days 090

28436   Percutaneous skeletal fixation of talus fracture, with manipulation   A2 T 50 □
   10.78   10.78   Global Days 090

28445   Open treatment of talus fracture, includes internal fixation, when performed   A2 T 80 50 □
   28.05   28.05   Global Days 090

28446   Open osteochondral autograft, talus (includes obtaining graft[s])   `G2` `T` `80` `50`

> EXCLUDES   *arthroscopically aided osteochondral talus graft (29892)*
> *open osteochondral allograft or repairs with industrial grafts (28899)*

> Do not report with (27705-27707)

   🔶 30.60   🔸 30.60   Global Days 090
   AMA: 2008, Jan, 4-5

28450   Treatment of tarsal bone fracture (except talus and calcaneus); without manipulation, each   `P2` `T` `🔲`

   🔶 4.63   🔸 5.15   Global Days 090
   AMA: 2008, Jan, 10-25; 2007, Jan, 13-27; 2007, Jan, 13-27; 2007, January, 13-27

28455   with manipulation, each   `P2` `T` `80` `🔲`

   🔶 6.71   🔸 7.17   Global Days 090

28456   Percutaneous skeletal fixation of tarsal bone fracture (except talus and calcaneus), with manipulation, each   `A2` `T` `🔲`

   🔶 6.89   🔸 6.89   Global Days 090

28465   Open treatment of tarsal bone fracture (except talus and calcaneus), includes internal fixation, when performed, each   `A2` `T` `🔲`

   🔶 15.83   🔸 15.83   Global Days 090

28470   Closed treatment of metatarsal fracture; without manipulation, each   `P2` `T` `🔲`

   🔶 4.66   🔸 5.15   Global Days 090

28475   with manipulation, each   `P2` `T` `🔲`

   🔶 6.08   🔸 6.56   Global Days 090

28476   Percutaneous skeletal fixation of metatarsal fracture, with manipulation, each   `A2` `T` `80` `🔲`

   🔶 8.53   🔸 8.53   Global Days 090

28485   Open treatment of metatarsal fracture, includes internal fixation, when performed, each   `A2` `T` `🔲`

   🔶 13.62   🔸 13.62   Global Days 090

28490   Closed treatment of fracture great toe, phalanx or phalanges; without manipulation   `P2` `T` `🔲`

   🔶 2.90   🔸 3.30   Global Days 090

28495   with manipulation   `P2` `T` `🔲`

   🔶 3.72   🔸 4.18   Global Days 090

28496   Percutaneous skeletal fixation of fracture great toe, phalanx or phalanges, with manipulation   `A2` `T` `🔲`

   🔶 5.72   🔸 10.11   Global Days 090

28505   Open treatment of fracture, great toe, phalanx or phalanges, includes internal fixation, when performed   `A2` `T` `🔲`

   🔶 12.44   🔸 16.12   Global Days 090

28510   Closed treatment of fracture, phalanx or phalanges, other than great toe; without manipulation, each   `P3` `T` `🔲`

   🔶 2.82   🔸 2.87   Global Days 090

28515   with manipulation, each   `P2` `T` `🔲`

   🔶 3.49   🔸 3.78   Global Days 090

28525   Open treatment of fracture, phalanx or phalanges, other than great toe, includes internal fixation, when performed, each   `A2` `T` `80` `🔲`

   🔶 9.91   🔸 13.58   Global Days 090

28530   Closed treatment of sesamoid fracture   `P3` `T` `80` `🔲`

   🔶 2.57   🔸 2.77   Global Days 090

28531   Open treatment of sesamoid fracture, with or without internal fixation   `A2` `T` `🔲`

   🔶 4.95   🔸 8.94   Global Days 090

28540   Closed treatment of tarsal bone dislocation, other than talotarsal; without anesthesia   `P2` `T` `80` `🔲`

   🔶 4.61   🔸 4.92   Global Days 090

28545   requiring anesthesia   `A2` `T` `80` `🔲`

   🔶 5.61   🔸 6.07   Global Days 090

28546   Percutaneous skeletal fixation of tarsal bone dislocation, other than talotarsal, with manipulation   `A2` `T` `80` `🔲`

   🔶 7.58   🔸 11.39   Global Days 090

28555   Open treatment of tarsal bone dislocation, includes internal fixation, when performed   `A2` `T` `80` `🔲`

   🔶 16.82   🔸 21.19   Global Days 090

28570   Closed treatment of talotarsal joint dislocation; without anesthesia   `P3` `T` `80` `🔲`

   🔶 3.84   🔸 4.25   Global Days 090

28575   requiring anesthesia   `A2` `T` `80` `🔲`

   🔶 7.67   🔸 8.18   Global Days 090

28576   Percutaneous skeletal fixation of talotarsal joint dislocation, with manipulation   `A2` `T` `80` `🔲`

   🔶 9.01   🔸 9.01   Global Days 090

28585   Open treatment of talotarsal joint dislocation, includes internal fixation, when performed   `A2` `T` `80` `🔲`

   🔶 18.94   🔸 22.65   Global Days 090

28600   Closed treatment of tarsometatarsal joint dislocation; without anesthesia   `P2` `T` `80` `🔲`

   🔶 4.63   🔸 5.13   Global Days 090

28605   requiring anesthesia   `A2` `T` `80` `🔲`

   🔶 6.23   🔸 6.65   Global Days 090

28606   Percutaneous skeletal fixation of tarsometatarsal joint dislocation, with manipulation   `A2` `T` `🔲`

   🔶 9.99   🔸 9.99   Global Days 090

28615   Open treatment of tarsometatarsal joint dislocation, includes internal fixation, when performed   `A2` `T` `80` `🔲`

   🔶 19.90   🔸 19.90   Global Days 090

28630   Closed treatment of metatarsophalangeal joint dislocation; without anesthesia   `P2` `T` `80` `🔲`

   🔶 2.85   🔸 3.66   Global Days 010

28635   requiring anesthesia   `A2` `T` `80` `🔲`

   🔶 3.57   🔸 4.38   Global Days 010

28636   Percutaneous skeletal fixation of metatarsophalangeal joint dislocation, with manipulation   `A2` `T` `🔲`

   🔶 5.31   🔸 7.22   Global Days 010

28645   Open treatment of metatarsophalangeal joint dislocation, includes internal fixation, when performed   `A2` `T` `🔲`

   🔶 12.15   🔸 15.27   Global Days 090

28660   Closed treatment of interphalangeal joint dislocation; without anesthesia   `P3` `T` `🔲`

   🔶 2.17   🔸 2.66   Global Days 010

28665   requiring anesthesia   `A2` `T` `80` `🔲`

   🔶 3.55   🔸 3.91   Global Days 010

28666   Percutaneous skeletal fixation of interphalangeal joint dislocation, with manipulation   `A2` `T` `🔲`

   🔶 5.09   🔸 5.09   Global Days 010

28675   Open treatment of interphalangeal joint dislocation, includes internal fixation, when performed   `A2` `T` `🔲`

   🔶 10.14   🔸 13.88   Global Days 090

28705-28760 Arthrodesis of Foot/Toe

28705   Arthrodesis; pantalar   `A2` `T` `80` `🔲`

   🔶 34.55   🔸 34.55   Global Days 090

28715   triple   `A2` `T` `80` `🔲`

   🔶 25.54   🔸 25.54   Global Days 090

28725   subtalar   `A2` `T` `80` `🔲`

> INCLUDES   Dunn arthrodesis
> Grice arthrosis

   🔶 21.05   🔸 21.05   Global Days 090

Musculoskeletal System

28730 — 29130

28730 Arthrodesis, midtarsal or tarsometatarsal, multiple or transverse;   A2 T 80 ☐
INCLUDES   Lambrinudi arthrodesis
🔖 21.94   ≿ 21.94   Global Days 090

28735 with osteotomy (eg, flatfoot correction)   A2 T 80 ☐
🔖 21.00   ≿ 21.00   Global Days 090

28737 Arthrodesis, with tendon lengthening and advancement, midtarsal, tarsal navicular-cuneiform (eg, Miller type procedure)   A2 T 80 ☐
🔖 18.61   ≿ 18.61   Global Days 090

28740 Arthrodesis, midtarsal or tarsometatarsal, single joint   A2 T 80 ☐
🔖 16.43   ≿ 21.05   Global Days 090

28750 Arthrodesis, great toe; metatarsophalangeal joint   A2 T 80 50 ☐
🔖 15.63   ≿ 20.48   Global Days 090

28755 interphalangeal joint   A2 T 50 ☐
🔖 8.89   ≿ 12.32   Global Days 090

28760 Arthrodesis, with extensor hallucis longus transfer to first metatarsal neck, great toe, interphalangeal joint (eg, Jones type procedure)   A2 T 80 50 ☐
EXCLUDES   hammer toe repair or interphalangeal fusion (28285)
🔖 15.38   ≿ 19.36   Global Days 090

28800-28825 Amputation Foot/Toe

28800 Amputation, foot; midtarsal (eg, Chopart type procedure)   C 80 50 ☐
🔖 15.02   ≿ 15.02   Global Days 090

28805 transmetatarsal   C 80 50 ☐
🔖 19.65   ≿ 19.65   Global Days 090

28810 Amputation, metatarsal, with toe, single   A2 T 80 ☐
EXCLUDES   removal of tuft of distal phalanx (11752)
🔖 11.56   ≿ 11.56   Global Days 090

28820 Amputation, toe; metatarsophalangeal joint   A2 T ☐
EXCLUDES   removal of tuft of distal phalanx (11752)
🔖 9.10   ≿ 13.01   Global Days 090

28825 interphalangeal joint   A2 T ☐
EXCLUDES   removal of tuft of distal phalanx
🔖 10.30   ≿ 14.04   Global Days 090

28890-28899 Other/Unlisted Procedures Foot/Toe

28890 Extracorporeal shock wave, high energy, performed by a physician, requiring anesthesia other than local, including ultrasound guidance, involving the plantar fascia   P3 T 50
EXCLUDES   extracorporeal shock wave therapy of musculoskeletal system not otherwise specified (0019T, 0101T, 0102T)
🔖 5.93   ≿ 8.56   Global Days 090
AMA: 2008, Jan, 10-25; 2007, Jan, 13-27; 2007, Jan, 13-27; 2007, January, 13-27; 2006, Mar, 1-5; 2006, Mar, 1-5; 2006, March, 1-5; 2005, Dec, 9-11; 2005, Dec, 9-11; 2005, December, 9-11

28899 Unlisted procedure, foot or toes   T 80
🔖 0.00   ≿ 0.00   Global Days YYY
AMA: 2008, Jan, 4-5

29000-29086 Casting: Arm/Shoulder/Torso

CMS *100-2,15,100*   *Surgical Dressings, Splints, Casts, and Devices for Reductions of Fractures/Dislocations*
CMS *100-4,4,240*   *Inpatient Part B Hospital Services Paid Under OPPS*
EXCLUDES   *cast or splint material (99070, Q4001-Q4051)*
orthotic supervision and training (97760-97762)

29000 Application of halo type body cast (see 20661-20663 for insertion)   G2 S 80 ☐
🔖 4.42   ≿ 6.64   Global Days 000

29010 Application of Risser jacket, localizer, body; only   P2 S 80 ☐
🔖 4.10   ≿ 6.08   Global Days 000

29015 including head   P2 S 80 ☐
🔖 4.14   ≿ 5.85   Global Days 000

29020 Application of turnbuckle jacket, body; only   G2 S 80 ☐
🔖 3.73   ≿ 5.60   Global Days 000

29025 including head   P2 S 80 ☐
🔖 4.58   ≿ 6.40   Global Days 000

29035 Application of body cast, shoulder to hips;   P2 S 80 ☐
🔖 3.60   ≿ 5.88   Global Days 000

29040 including head, Minerva type   G2 S 80 ☐
🔖 4.04   ≿ 5.71   Global Days 000

29044 including one thigh   P2 S 80 ☐
🔖 4.20   ≿ 6.39   Global Days 000

29046 including both thighs   G2 S 80 ☐
🔖 4.82   ≿ 6.99   Global Days 000

29049 Application, cast; figure-of-eight   P3 S 80 ☐
🔖 1.57   ≿ 2.12   Global Days 000
AMA: 2007, Feb, 8-9; 2007, Feb, 8-9; 2007, February, 8-9

29055 shoulder spica   P2 S 80 ☐
🔖 3.47   ≿ 5.07   Global Days 000

29058 plaster Velpeau   P2 S 80 ☐
🔖 2.14   ≿ 2.74   Global Days 000

29065 shoulder to hand (long arm)   P3 S 50 ☐
🔖 1.74   ≿ 2.31   Global Days 000

29075 elbow to finger (short arm)   P3 S 50 ☐
🔖 1.57   ≿ 2.14   Global Days 000

29085 hand and lower forearm (gauntlet)   P2 S 50 ☐
🔖 1.69   ≿ 2.28   Global Days 000
AMA: 2008, Jan, 10-25; 2007, Jan, 13-27; 2007, Jan, 13-27; 2007, January, 13-27

29086 finger (eg, contracture)   P3 S 50 ☐
🔖 1.23   ≿ 1.73   Global Days 000

29105-29280 Splinting and Strapping: Torso/Upper Extremities

CMS *100-2,15,100*   *Surgical Dressings, Splints, Casts, and Devices for Reductions of Fractures/Dislocations*
CMS *100-4,4,240*   *Inpatient Part B Hospital Services Paid Under OPPS*
EXCLUDES   *orthotic supervision and training (97760-97762)*

29105 Application of long arm splint (shoulder to hand)   P3 S 50 ☐
🔖 1.52   ≿ 2.11   Global Days 000

29125 Application of short arm splint (forearm to hand); static   P3 S 50 ☐
🔖 1.08   ≿ 1.63   Global Days 000

29126 dynamic   P3 S 50 ☐
🔖 1.32   ≿ 1.87   Global Days 000

29130 Application of finger splint; static   P3 S 50 ☐
🔖 0.75   ≿ 1.00   Global Days 000

29131	dynamic	P3 S 50
	0.83 1.22 Global Days 000	
29200	Strapping; thorax	P3 S
	1.03 1.31 Global Days 000	
29220	low back	P3 S
	1.07 1.35 Global Days 000	
29240	shoulder (eg, Velpeau)	P3 S
	1.15 1.47 Global Days 000	
29260	elbow or wrist	P3 S 50
	0.95 1.27 Global Days 000	
29280	hand or finger	P3 S 50
	0.89 1.22 Global Days 000	

29305-29450 Casting: Legs

CMS *100-2,15,100*   *Surgical Dressings, Splints, Casts, and Devices for Reductions of Fractures/Dislocations*

CMS *100-4,4,240*   *Inpatient Part B Hospital Services Paid Under OPPS*

EXCLUDES   *cast or splint supplies (99070, Q4001-Q4051)*

orthotic supervision and training (97760-97762)

29305	Application of hip spica cast; one leg	P2 S 80
	EXCLUDES *hip spica cast thighs only (29046)*	
	4.05 5.73 Global Days 000	
29325	one and one-half spica or both legs	P2 S 80
	EXCLUDES *hip spica cast thighs only (29046)*	
	4.58 6.38 Global Days 000	
29345	Application of long leg cast (thigh to toes);	P3 S 50
	2.63 3.33 Global Days 000	
29355	walker or ambulatory type	P3 S 50
	2.80 3.45 Global Days 000	
29358	Application of long leg cast brace	P3 S 50
	2.68 3.74 Global Days 000	
29365	Application of cylinder cast (thigh to ankle)	P3 S 50
	2.28 2.98 Global Days 000	
29405	Application of short leg cast (below knee to toes);	P3 S 50
	1.67 2.19 Global Days 000	
29425	walking or ambulatory type	P3 S 50
	1.84 2.37 Global Days 000	
29435	Application of patellar tendon bearing (PTB) cast	P3 S 50
	2.23 2.91 Global Days 000	
29440	Adding walker to previously applied cast	P3 S 50
	0.91 1.30 Global Days 000	
29445	Application of rigid total contact leg cast	P3 S 50
	2.96 3.66 Global Days 000	
29450	Application of clubfoot cast with molding or manipulation, long or short leg	P2 S 50
	3.28 3.86 Global Days 000	

29505-29590 Splinting and Strapping Ankle/Foot/Leg/Toes

CMS *100-2,15,100*   *Surgical Dressings, Splints, Casts, and Devices for Reductions of Fractures/Dislocations*

CMS *100-4,4,240*   *Inpatient Part B Hospital Services Paid Under OPPS*

EXCLUDES   *orthotic supervision and training (97760-97762)*

29505	Application of long leg splint (thigh to ankle or toes)	P3 S 50
	1.22 1.85 Global Days 000	
29515	Application of short leg splint (calf to foot)	P3 S 50
	1.28 1.74 Global Days 000	

29520	Strapping; hip	P3 S 80
	0.94 1.23 Global Days 000	
29530	knee	P3 S
	0.97 1.29 Global Days 000	
29540	ankle and/or foot	P3 S
	0.87 1.07 Global Days 000	
29550	toes	P3 S
	0.82 1.04 Global Days 000	
29580	Unna boot	P3 S 50
	0.96 1.31 Global Days 000	
	AMA: 2008, Jan, 10-25; 2007, Jan, 13-27; 2007, Jan, 13-27; 2007, January, 13-27	
29590	Denis-Browne splint strapping	P3 S
	1.12 1.41 Global Days 000	

29700-29799 Casting Services Other Than Application

INCLUDES   casts applied by treating physician

29700	Removal or bivalving; gauntlet, boot or body cast	P3 S
	0.92 1.58 Global Days 000	
29705	full arm or full leg cast	P3 S 50
	1.27 1.68 Global Days 000	
29710	shoulder or hip spica, Minerva, or Risser jacket, etc.	P3 S 80 50
	2.17 2.93 Global Days 000	
29715	turnbuckle jacket	P2 S 80
	1.47 2.21 Global Days 000	
29720	Repair of spica, body cast or jacket	P3 S
	1.17 1.96 Global Days 000	
29730	Windowing of cast	P3 S
	1.22 1.63 Global Days 000	
29740	Wedging of cast (except clubfoot casts)	P3 S
	1.78 2.34 Global Days 000	
29750	Wedging of clubfoot cast	P3 S 80 50
	2.04 2.56 Global Days 000	
29799	Unlisted procedure, casting or strapping	S 80
	0.00 0.00 Global Days YYY	

29800-29999 Arthroscopic Musculoskeletal Procedures

INCLUDES   diagnostic arthroscopy with surgical arthroscopy

29800	Arthroscopy, temporomandibular joint, diagnostic, with or without synovial biopsy (separate procedure)	A2 T 80 50
	13.21 13.21 Global Days 090	
29804	Arthroscopy, temporomandibular joint, surgical	A2 T 80 50
	EXCLUDES *open surgery (21010)*	
	16.45 16.45 Global Days 090	
29805	Arthroscopy, shoulder, diagnostic, with or without synovial biopsy (separate procedure)	A2 T 50
	EXCLUDES *open surgery (23065-23066, 23100-23101)*	
	12.00 12.00 Global Days 090	
29806	Arthroscopy, shoulder, surgical; capsulorrhaphy	A2 T 50
	EXCLUDES *capsulorrhaphy (29999)*	
	open surgery (23450-23466)	
	27.54 27.54 Global Days 090	
29807	repair of SLAP lesion	A2 T 50
	26.82 26.82 Global Days 090	

Musculoskeletal System

29819 — 29863

29819 with removal of loose body or foreign body ⒶⓉ50▣
EXCLUDES *open surgery (23040-23044, 23107)*
🔧 15.06 ⚕ 15.06 Global Days 090

29820 synovectomy, partial ⒶⓉ80 50▣
EXCLUDES *open surgery (23105)*
🔧 13.90 ⚕ 13.90 Global Days 090

29821 synovectomy, complete ⒶⓉ80 50▣
EXCLUDES *open surgery (23105)*
🔧 15.18 ⚕ 15.18 Global Days 090

29822 debridement, limited ⒶⓉ80 50▣
EXCLUDES *open surgery (see specific shoulder section)*
🔧 14.74 ⚕ 14.74 Global Days 090

29823 debridement, extensive ⒶⓉ80 50▣
EXCLUDES *open surgery (see specific shoulder section)*
🔧 16.13 ⚕ 16.13 Global Days 090

29824 distal claviculectomy including distal articular surface (Mumford procedure) ⒶⓉ80 50▣
INCLUDES Mumford procedure
EXCLUDES *open surgery (23120)*
🔧 17.16 ⚕ 17.16 Global Days 090

29825 with lysis and resection of adhesions, with or without manipulation ⒶⓉ80 50▣
EXCLUDES *open surgery (see specific shoulder section)*
🔧 15.04 ⚕ 15.04 Global Days 090

29826 decompression of subacromial space with partial acromioplasty, with or without coracoacromial release ⒶⓉ80 50▣
EXCLUDES *open surgery (23130, 23415)*
🔧 17.27 ⚕ 17.27 Global Days 090

29827 with rotator cuff repair ⒶⓉ80 50▣
EXCLUDES *distal clavicle excision (29824)*
open surgery (23412)
subacromial decompression (29826)
🔧 28.27 ⚕ 28.27 Global Days 090
AMA: 2008, Mar, 14-15

29828 biceps tenodesis 62 Ⓣ80 50
EXCLUDES *tenodesis of long tendon of biceps (23430)*

Do not report with (29805, 29820, 29822)
🔧 23.63 ⚕ 23.63 Global Days 090
AMA: 2008, Feb, 8-9

29830 Arthroscopy, elbow, diagnostic, with or without synovial biopsy (separate procedure) ⒶⓉ50▣
🔧 11.58 ⚕ 11.58 Global Days 090

29834 Arthroscopy, elbow, surgical; with removal of loose body or foreign body ⒶⓉ80 50▣
🔧 12.62 ⚕ 12.62 Global Days 090

29835 synovectomy, partial ⒶⓉ80 50▣
🔧 12.96 ⚕ 12.96 Global Days 090

29836 synovectomy, complete ⒶⓉ80 50▣
🔧 14.87 ⚕ 14.87 Global Days 090

29837 debridement, limited ⒶⓉ80 50▣
🔧 13.59 ⚕ 13.59 Global Days 090

29838 debridement, extensive ⒶⓉ80 50▣
🔧 15.18 ⚕ 15.18 Global Days 090

29840 Arthroscopy, wrist, diagnostic, with or without synovial biopsy (separate procedure) ⒶⓉ80 50▣
🔧 11.31 ⚕ 11.31 Global Days 090

29843 Arthroscopy, wrist, surgical; for infection, lavage and drainage ⒶⓉ80 50▣
🔧 12.16 ⚕ 12.16 Global Days 090

29844 synovectomy, partial ⒶⓉ80 50▣
🔧 12.66 ⚕ 12.66 Global Days 090

29845 synovectomy, complete ⒶⓉ80 50▣
🔧 14.39 ⚕ 14.39 Global Days 090
AMA: 2008, Jan, 10-25; 2007, Jan, 13-27; 2007, Jan, 13-27; 2007, January, 13-27

29846 excision and/or repair of triangular fibrocartilage and/or joint debridement ⒶⓉ80 50▣
🔧 13.31 ⚕ 13.31 Global Days 090
AMA: 2008, Jan, 10-25; 2007, Jan, 13-27; 2007, Jan, 13-27; 2007, January, 13-27

29847 internal fixation for fracture or instability ⒶⓉ80 50▣
🔧 13.81 ⚕ 13.81 Global Days 090

29848 Endoscopy, wrist, surgical, with release of transverse carpal ligament ⒶⓉ50▣
EXCLUDES *open surgery (64721)*
🔧 12.54 ⚕ 12.54 Global Days 090

29850 Arthroscopically aided treatment of intercondylar spine(s) and/or tuberosity fracture(s) of the knee, with or without manipulation; without internal or external fixation (includes arthroscopy) ⒶⓉ80 50▣
🔧 14.67 ⚕ 14.67 Global Days 090

29851 with internal or external fixation (includes arthroscopy) ⒶⓉ80 50▣
EXCLUDES *bone graft (20900, 20902)*
🔧 24.28 ⚕ 24.28 Global Days 090

29855 Arthroscopically aided treatment of tibial fracture, proximal (plateau); unicondylar, includes internal fixation, when performed (includes arthroscopy) ⒶⓉ80 50▣
🔧 20.29 ⚕ 20.29 Global Days 090

29856 bicondylar, includes internal fixation, when performed (includes arthroscopy) ⒶⓉ80 50▣
EXCLUDES *bone graft (20900, 20902)*
🔧 25.98 ⚕ 25.98 Global Days 090

29860 Arthroscopy, hip, diagnostic with or without synovial biopsy (separate procedure) ⒶⓉ80 50▣
🔧 16.65 ⚕ 16.65 Global Days 090

29861 Arthroscopy, hip, surgical; with removal of loose body or foreign body ⒶⓉ80 50▣
🔧 18.50 ⚕ 18.50 Global Days 090

29862 with debridement/shaving of articular cartilage (chondroplasty), abrasion arthroplasty, and/or resection of labrum ⒶⓉ80 50▣
🔧 20.61 ⚕ 20.61 Global Days 090

29863 with synovectomy ⒶⓉ80 50▣
🔧 20.33 ⚕ 20.33 Global Days 090

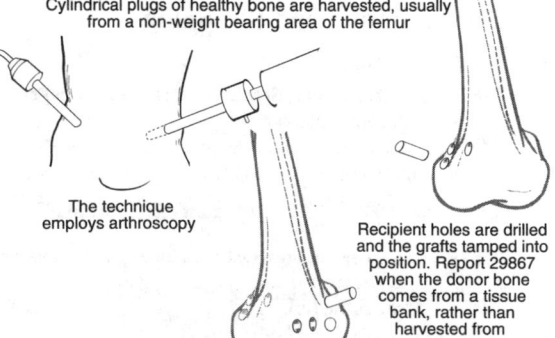

Cylindrical plugs of healthy bone are harvested, usually from a non-weight bearing area of the femur

The technique employs arthroscopy

Recipient holes are drilled and the grafts tamped into position. Report 29867 when the donor bone comes from a tissue bank, rather than harvested from the patient

---

29866   Arthroscopy, knee, surgical; osteochondral autograft(s) (eg, mosaicplasty) (includes harvesting of the autograft[s])　62 T 80 50 ▢

     EXCLUDES   *open osteochondral autograft of the knee (27416)*

     Do not report with procedure performed in the same compartment (29874, 29877, 29879, 29885-29887)

     Do not report with procedure performed at the same surgical session (29870, 29871, 29875, 29884)

     🔷 26.98   ✂ 26.98   Global Days 090

29867   osteochondral allograft (eg, mosaicplasty)　T 80 50 ▢

     Do not report with procedures performed in the same compartment (29874, 29877, 29879, 29885-29887)

     Do not report with procedures performed at the same surgical session (27415, 27570, 29870-29871, 29875, 29884)

     🔷 32.66   ✂ 32.66   Global Days 090

29868   meniscal transplantation (includes arthrotomy for meniscal insertion), medial or lateral　T 80 50 ▢

     Do not report with procedure performed in same compartment (29874, 29877, 29881-29882)

     Do not report with procedures performed at same surgical session (29870-29871, 29875, 29880, 29883-29884)

     🔷 43.90   ✂ 43.90   Global Days 090

29870   Arthroscopy, knee, diagnostic, with or without synovial biopsy (separate procedure)　A2 T 50 ▢

     EXCLUDES   *open procedure (27412)*

     🔷 10.40   ✂ 10.40   Global Days 090
     AMA: 2007, Dec, 10-179

29871   for infection, lavage and drainage　A2 T 50 ▢

     EXCLUDES   *osteochondral graft (27412, 27415, 29866-29867)*

     🔷 13.10   ✂ 13.10   Global Days 090
     AMA: 2007, Dec, 10-179

29873   with lateral release　A2 T 50 ▢

     EXCLUDES   *open procedure (27425)*

     🔷 13.05   ✂ 13.05   Global Days 090
     AMA: 2007, Dec, 10-179

29874   for removal of loose body or foreign body (eg, osteochondritis dissecans fragmentation, chondral fragmentation)　A2 T 80 50 ▢

     🔷 13.71   ✂ 13.71   Global Days 090
     AMA: 2007, Dec, 10-179

29875   synovectomy, limited (eg, plica or shelf resection) (separate procedure)　A2 T 80 50 ▢

     🔷 12.67   ✂ 12.67   Global Days 090
     AMA: 2007, Dec, 10-179

29876   synovectomy, major, 2 or more compartments (eg, medial or lateral)　A2 T 50 ▢

     🔷 16.63   ✂ 16.63   Global Days 090
     AMA: 2007, Dec, 10-179

29877   debridement/shaving of articular cartilage (chondroplasty)　A2 T 80 50 ▢

     🔷 15.73   ✂ 15.73   Global Days 090
     AMA: 2008, Jan, 10-25; 2007, Jan, 13-27; 2007, Jan, 13-27; 2007, Dec, 10-179; 2007, January, 13-27; 2005, Apr, 13-14; 2005, April, 13-14; 2005, Apr, 13-14

29879   abrasion arthroplasty (includes chondroplasty where necessary) or multiple drilling or microfracture　A2 T 80 50 ▢

     🔷 16.84   ✂ 16.84   Global Days 090
     AMA: 2007, Dec, 10-179

29880   with meniscectomy (medial AND lateral, including any meniscal shaving)　A2 T 80 50 ▢

     🔷 17.59   ✂ 17.59   Global Days 090
     AMA: 2007, Dec, 10-179

29881   with meniscectomy (medial OR lateral, including any meniscal shaving)　A2 T 80 50 ▢

     🔷 16.38   ✂ 16.38   Global Days 090
     AMA: 2008, Jan, 10-25; 2007, Jan, 13-27; 2007, Jan, 13-27; 2007, Dec, 10-179; 2007, January, 13-27; 2005, Apr, 13-14; 2005, April, 13-14; 2005, Apr, 13-14

29882   with meniscus repair (medial OR lateral)　A2 T 50 ▢

     EXCLUDES   *meniscus transplant (29868)*

     🔷 17.76   ✂ 17.76   Global Days 090
     AMA: 2008, Jan, 10-25; 2007, Jan, 13-27; 2007, Jan, 13-27; 2007, Dec, 10-179; 2007, January, 13-27; 2004, Sep, 12; 2004, September, 12; 2004, Sep, 12

29883   with meniscus repair (medial AND lateral)　A2 T 80 50 ▢

     EXCLUDES   *meniscus transplant (29868)*

     🔷 21.72   ✂ 21.72   Global Days 090
     AMA: 2008, Jan, 10-25; 2007, Jan, 13-27; 2007, Jan, 13-27; 2007, Dec, 10-179; 2007, January, 13-27; 2004, Sep, 12; 2004, September, 12; 2004, Sep, 12

29884   with lysis of adhesions, with or without manipulation (separate procedure)　A2 T 80 50 ▢

     🔷 15.68   ✂ 15.68   Global Days 090
     AMA: 2007, Dec, 10-179

29885   drilling for osteochondritis dissecans with bone grafting, with or without internal fixation (including debridement of base of lesion)　A2 T 80 50 ▢

     🔷 19.04   ✂ 19.04   Global Days 090
     AMA: 2007, Dec, 10-179

29886   drilling for intact osteochondritis dissecans lesion　A2 T 50 ▢

     🔷 16.04   ✂ 16.04   Global Days 090
     AMA: 2007, Dec, 10-179

29887   drilling for intact osteochondritis dissecans lesion with internal fixation　A2 T 80 50 ▢

     🔷 18.93   ✂ 18.93   Global Days 090
     AMA: 2007, Dec, 10-179

29888   Arthroscopically aided anterior cruciate ligament repair/augmentation or reconstruction　A2 T 80 50 ▢

     Do not report with ligamentous reconstruction (27427-27429)

     🔷 25.79   ✂ 25.79   Global Days 090
     AMA: 2008, Jan, 10-25; 2007, Jan, 13-27; 2007, Jan, 13-27; 2007, January, 13-27; 2007, Dec, 10-179

29889   Arthroscopically aided posterior cruciate ligament repair/augmentation or reconstruction　A2 T 80 50 ▢

     Do not report with ligamentous reconstruction (27427-27429)

     🔷 31.45   ✂ 31.45   Global Days 090
     AMA: 2008, Jan, 10-25; 2007, Jan, 13-27; 2007, Jan, 13-27; 2007, January, 13-27; 2007, Dec, 10-179

29891   Arthroscopy, ankle, surgical, excision of osteochondral defect of talus and/or tibia, including drilling of the defect　A2 T 80 50 ▢

     🔷 17.82   ✂ 17.82   Global Days 090

29892   Arthroscopically aided repair of large osteochondritis dissecans lesion, talar dome fracture, or tibial plafond fracture, with or without internal fixation (includes arthroscopy)　A2 T 80 50 ▢

     🔷 18.21   ✂ 18.21   Global Days 090

Musculoskeletal System

29893 — 29999

29893 Endoscopic plantar fasciotomy   A2 T 50 ▭
  📷 11.12   ⚮ 14.69   Global Days 090

29894 Arthroscopy, ankle (tibiotalar and fibulotalar joints), surgical; with removal of loose body or foreign body   A2 T 80 50 ▭
  📷 13.41   ⚮ 13.41   Global Days 090

29895   synovectomy, partial   A2 T 80 50 ▭
  📷 12.97   ⚮ 12.97   Global Days 090

29897   debridement, limited   A2 T 80 50 ▭
  📷 13.59   ⚮ 13.59   Global Days 090

29898   debridement, extensive   A2 T 80 50 ▭
  📷 15.18   ⚮ 15.18   Global Days 090

29899   with ankle arthrodesis   A2 T 80 50 ▭
  EXCLUDES   open procedure (27870)

  📷 27.34   ⚮ 27.34   Global Days 090

29900 Arthroscopy, metacarpophalangeal joint, diagnostic, includes synovial biopsy   A2 T 80 50 ▭
  Do not report with (29901-29902)
  📷 11.65   ⚮ 11.65   Global Days 090

29901 Arthroscopy, metacarpophalangeal joint, surgical; with debridement   A2 T 80 50 ▭
  📷 12.78   ⚮ 12.78   Global Days 090

29902   with reduction of displaced ulnar collateral ligament (eg, Stenar lesion)   A2 T 80 50 ▭
  📷 13.66   ⚮ 13.66   Global Days 090

29904 Arthroscopy, subtalar joint, surgical; with removal of loose body or foreign body   G2 T 80 50
  📷 15.83   ⚮ 15.83   Global Days 090

29905   with synovectomy   G2 T 80 50
  📷 17.03   ⚮ 17.03   Global Days 090

29906   with debridement   G2 T 80 50
  📷 17.94   ⚮ 17.94   Global Days 090

29907   with subtalar arthrodesis   G2 T 80 50
  📷 22.05   ⚮ 22.05   Global Days 090

29999 Unlisted procedure, arthroscopy   T 80 50 ▭
  📷 0.00   ⚮ 0.00   Global Days YYY
  AMA: 2008, Jan, 10-25; 2007, Jan, 13-27; 2007, Jan, 13-27; 2007, January, 13-27; 2004, Sep, 12; 2004, September, 12; 2004, Sep, 12

26/TC Professional/Technical Component Only   80/80 Assist-at-Surgery Allowed/With Documentation   Unlisted   Not Covered
AMA: CPT Assistant References   A2-Z3 ASC Payment Indicator   ♂ Male Only   ♀ Female Only   ⊘ Modifier 51 Exempt   PQ PQRI
106   CPT only © 2008 American Medical Association. All Rights Reserved. (Black Ink)   **Medicare** (Red Ink)   © 2008 **Ingenix** *(Blue Ink)*

30000-30115 I&D, Biopsy, Excision Procedures of the Nose

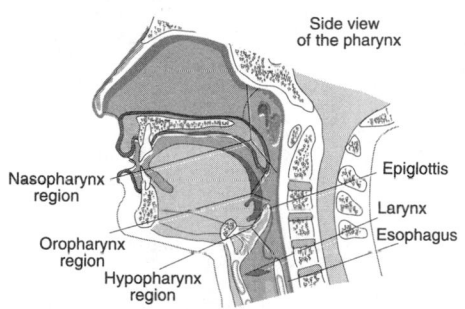

Side view of the pharynx

Nasopharynx region
Oropharynx region
Hypopharynx region
Epiglottis
Larynx
Esophagus

The nasopharynx is the membranous passage above the level of the soft palate; the oropharynx is the region between the soft palate and the upper edge of the epiglottis; the hypopharynx is the region of the epiglottis to the juncture of the larynx and esophagus; the three regions are collectively known as the pharynx

30000 Drainage abscess or hematoma, nasal, internal approach `P2` `T` `00` `□`
> **EXCLUDES** *incision and drainage (10060, 10140)*
>
> 🔧 2.95 ✎ 5.61 Global Days 010
> **AMA:** 2005, May, 13-14; 2005, May, 13-14; 2005, May, 13-14

30020 Drainage abscess or hematoma, nasal septum `P2` `T` `□`
> **EXCLUDES** *lateral rhinotomy incision (30118, 30320)*
>
> 🔧 2.97 ✎ 5.43 Global Days 010

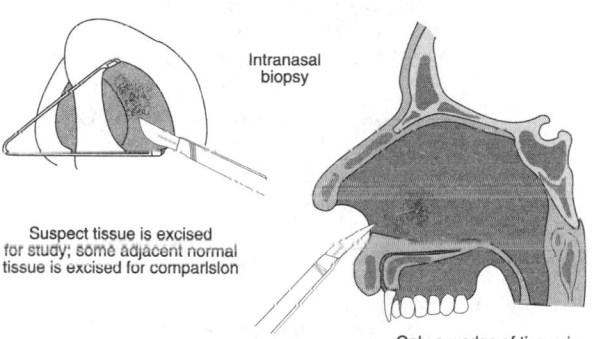

Intranasal biopsy

Suspect tissue is excised for study; some adjacent normal tissue is excised for comparision

Only a wedge of tissue is removed for larger lesions

30100 Biopsy, intranasal `P3` `T` `□`
> **EXCLUDES** *superficial biopsy of nose (11100-11101)*
>
> 🔧 1.79 ✎ 3.41 Global Days 000

30110 Excision, nasal polyp(s), simple `P3` `T` `50` `□`
> 🔧 3.29 ✎ 5.50 Global Days 010

30115 Excision, nasal polyp(s), extensive `A2` `T` `50` `□`
> 🔧 10.72 ✎ 10.72 Global Days 090

30117-30118 Destruction Procedures Nose

CMS *100-3,140.5*   *Laser Procedures*

30117 Excision or destruction (eg, laser), intranasal lesion; internal approach `A2` `T` `□`
> 🔧 8.29 ✎ 20.12 Global Days 090

30118 external approach (lateral rhinotomy) `A2` `T` `□`
> 🔧 19.37 ✎ 19.37 Global Days 090

30120-30140 Excision Procedures Nose, Turbinate

30120 Excision or surgical planing of skin of nose for rhinophyma `A2` `T` `□`
> 🔧 11.30 ✎ 12.90 Global Days 090
> **AMA:** 2008, Jan, 10-25; 2007, May, 9-11; 2007, May, 9-11; 2007, May, 9-11

30124 Excision dermoid cyst, nose; simple, skin, subcutaneous `R2` `T` `□`
> 🔧 6.78 ✎ 6.78 Global Days 090

30125 complex, under bone or cartilage `A2` `T` `80` `□`
> 🔧 15.45 ✎ 15.45 Global Days 090

30130 Excision inferior turbinate, partial or complete, any method `A2` `I` `50` `□`
> **EXCLUDES** *excision middle/superior turbinate(s) (30999)*
>
> Do not report with (30801, 30802, 30930)
>
> 🔧 9.34 ✎ 9.34 Global Days 090
> **AMA:** 2008, Jan, 10-25; 2007, Jan, 13-27; 2007, Jan, 13-27; 2007, January, 13-27

30140 Submucous resection inferior turbinate, partial or complete, any method `A2` `T` `50` `□`
> **EXCLUDES** *endoscopic resection of concha bullosa of middle turbinate (31240)*
> *reduction of turbinates, report 30140-52 (30140)*
> *submucous resection:*
> *nasal septum (30520)*
> *superior or middle turbinate (30999)*
>
> Do not report with (30801, 30802, 30930)
>
> 🔧 10.67 ✎ 10.67 Global Days 090
> **AMA:** 2008, Jan, 10-25; 2008, Mar, 14-15; 2007, Jan, 13-27; 2007, Jan, 13-27; 2007, January, 13-27; 2004, Dec, 18; 2004, December, 18; 2004, Dec, 18

30150-30160 Surgical Removal: Nose

> **EXCLUDES** *reconstruction and/or closure (primary or delayed primary intention) (13150-13160, 14060-14300, 15120, 15121, 15260, 15261, 15760, 20900-20912)*

30150 Rhinectomy; partial `A2` `T` `□`
> 🔧 19.88 ✎ 19.88 Global Days 090

30160 total `A2` `T` `80` `□`
> 🔧 19.96 ✎ 19.96 Global Days 090

30200-30320 Turbinate Injection, Removal Foreign Substance in the Nose

30200 Injection into turbinate(s), therapeutic `P3` `T` `□`
> 🔧 1.53 ✎ 2.73 Global Days 000
> **AMA:** 2008, Jan, 10-25; 2007, Jan, 13-27; 2007, Jan, 13-27; 2007, January, 13-27; 2004, Dec, 19; 2004, December, 19; 2004, Dec, 19

30210 Displacement therapy (Proetz type) `P3` `T` `□`
> 🔧 2.48 ✎ 3.59 Global Days 010

30220 Insertion, nasal septal prosthesis (button) `A2` `T` `□`
> 🔧 3.15 ✎ 7.05 Global Days 010

30300 Removal foreign body, intranasal; office type procedure `P2` `X` `□`
> 🔧 3.01 ✎ 5.47 Global Days 010

30310 requiring general anesthesia `A2` `T` `80` `□`
> 🔧 5.09 ✎ 5.09 Global Days 010

30320 by lateral rhinotomy `A2` `T` `80` `□`
> 🔧 11.24 ✎ 11.24 Global Days 090

Respiratory System

30400-30630 Reconstruction or Repair of Nose

EXCLUDES   bone/tissue grafts (20900-20926, 21210)

30400   Rhinoplasty, primary; lateral and alar cartilages and/or elevation of nasal tip   A2 T 60 ▣

       INCLUDES   Carpue's operation

       EXCLUDES   reconstruction of columella (13150-13153)

       🔲 25.94   ⚕ 25.94   Global Days 090

30410   complete, external parts including bony pyramid, lateral and alar cartilages, and/or elevation of nasal tip   A2 T 80 ▣

       🔲 30.81   ⚕ 30.81   Global Days 090

30420   including major septal repair   A2 T ▣

       🔲 34.58   ⚕ 34.58   Global Days 090

30430   Rhinoplasty, secondary; minor revision (small amount of nasal tip work)   A2 T 80 ▣

       🔲 22.64   ⚕ 22.64   Global Days 090

30435   intermediate revision (bony work with osteotomies)   A2 T 80 ▣

       🔲 29.95   ⚕ 29.95   Global Days 090

30450   major revision (nasal tip work and osteotomies)   A2 T 80 ▣

       🔲 39.89   ⚕ 39.89   Global Days 090

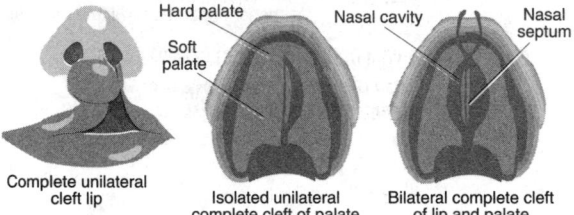

Cleft lip and cleft palate are described according to length of cleft and whether bilateral or unilateral

Hard palate | Nasal cavity | Nasal septum
Soft palate

Complete unilateral cleft lip   Isolated unilateral complete cleft of palate   Bilateral complete cleft of lip and palate

Cleft lip with or without cleft palate is a common birth defect and is seen once or twice per 1000 live births; the condition is twice as common among boys than girls; isolated cleft palate is distinct from cleft lip with or without cleft palate and occurs about once in 2000 births; the condition is more common among girls than boys

30460   Rhinoplasty for nasal deformity secondary to congenital cleft lip and/or palate, including columellar lengthening; tip only   A2 T 80 ▣

       🔲 19.33   ⚕ 19.33   Global Days 090

30462   tip, septum, osteotomies   A2 T 80 ▣

       🔲 39.04   ⚕ 39.04   Global Days 090

30465   Repair of nasal vestibular stenosis (eg, spreader grafting, lateral nasal wall reconstruction)   A2 T 60 ▣

       🔲 24.67   ⚕ 24.67   Global Days 090

30520   Septoplasty or submucous resection, with or without cartilage scoring, contouring or replacement with graft   A2 T ▣

       EXCLUDES   turbinate resection (30140)

       🔲 15.03   ⚕ 15.03   Global Days 090

       AMA: 2008, Jan, 10-25; 2007, Jan, 13-27; 2007, Jan, 13-27; 2007, January, 13-27

30540   Repair choanal atresia; intranasal   A2 T 80 ⊛ ▣

       🔲 16.83   ⚕ 16.83   Global Days 090

30545   transpalatine   A2 T 80 ⊛ ▣

       🔲 24.59   ⚕ 24.59   Global Days 090

30560   Lysis intranasal synechia   A2 T ▣

       🔲 3.43   ⚕ 6.48   Global Days 010

30580   Repair fistula; oromaxillary (combine with 31030 if antrotomy is included)   A2 T ▣

       🔲 12.75   ⚕ 15.79   Global Days 090

30600   oronasal   A2 T 80 ▣

       🔲 11.28   ⚕ 14.49   Global Days 090

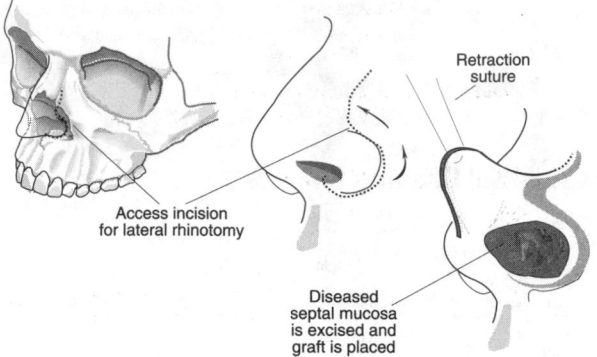

Retraction suture

Access incision for lateral rhinotomy

Diseased septal mucosa is excised and graft is placed

30620   Septal or other intranasal dermatoplasty (does not include obtaining graft)   A2 T ▣

       🔲 15.37   ⚕ 15.37   Global Days 090

30630   Repair nasal septal perforations   A2 T 80 ▣

       🔲 15.62   ⚕ 15.62   Global Days 090

30801-30802 Turbinate Destruction

EXCLUDES   cautery to stop nasal bleeding (30901-30906)

Do not report with (30130, 30140)

30801   Cautery and/or ablation, mucosa of inferior turbinates, unilateral or bilateral, any method; superficial   A2 T ▣

       EXCLUDES   cautery/ablation middle/superior turbinates (30999)

       🔲 3.28   ⚕ 5.45   Global Days 010

30802   intramural   A2 T ▣

       🔲 4.69   ⚕ 7.06   Global Days 010

       AMA: 2008, Mar, 14-15

30901-30999 Control Nose Bleed

30901   Control nasal hemorrhage, anterior, simple (limited cautery and/or packing) any method   P2 T 50 ▣

       🔲 1.64   ⚕ 2.61   Global Days 000

30903   Control nasal hemorrhage, anterior, complex (extensive cautery and/or packing) any method   A2 T 50 ▣

       🔲 2.13   ⚕ 4.76   Global Days 000

30905   Control nasal hemorrhage, posterior, with posterior nasal packs and/or cautery, any method; initial   A2 T ▣

       🔲 2.74   ⚕ 5.93   Global Days 000

30906   subsequent   A2 T ▣

       🔲 3.57   ⚕ 6.82   Global Days 000

30915   Ligation arteries; ethmoidal   A2 T ▣

       EXCLUDES   external carotid artery (37600)

       🔲 14.51   ⚕ 14.51   Global Days 090

30920   internal maxillary artery, transantral   A2 T ▣

       EXCLUDES   external carotid artery (37600)

       🔲 20.88   ⚕ 20.88   Global Days 090

30400 — 30920

| 30930 | Fracture nasal inferior turbinate(s), therapeutic | A2 T 50 ▣ |

> **EXCLUDES**   *fracture of superior or middle turbinate(s) (30999)*

Do not report with (30130, 30140)

🔧 3.04   ✂ 3.04   Global Days 010

AMA: 2008, Jan, 10-25; 2007, Jan, 13-27; 2007, Jan, 13-27; 2007, January, 13-27; 2004, Dec, 18; 2004, December, 18; 2004, Dec, 18

| 30999 | Unlisted procedure, nose | T 80 |

🔧 0.00   ✂ 0.00   Global Days YYY

31000-31230 Opening Sinuses

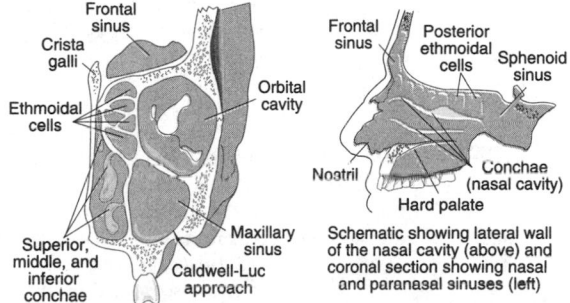

Crista galli, Frontal sinus, Ethmoidal cells, Orbital cavity, Maxillary sinus, Caldwell-Luc approach, Superior, middle, and inferior conchae

Frontal sinus, Posterior ethmoidal cells, Sphenoid sinus, Nostril, Conchae (nasal cavity), Hard palate

Schematic showing lateral wall of the nasal cavity (above) and coronal section showing nasal and paranasal sinuses (left)

The nasal sinuses are air filled cavities in the cranial bones that bear their names; all are lined with mucous membrane continuous with the nasal cavity and all drain fluids into the nasal cavity. The ethmoid cells vary in size and number and feature very thin septa, or walls. The maxillary sinuses are the largest and are the most frequently infected.

| 31000 | Lavage by cannulation; maxillary sinus (antrum puncture or natural ostium) | P3 T 50 ▣ |

🔧 2.62   ✂ 4.35   Global Days 010

| 31002 | sphenoid sinus | R2 T 80 50 ▣ |

🔧 5.00   ✂ 5.00   Global Days 010

| 31020 | Sinusotomy, maxillary (antrotomy); intranasal | A2 V 50 ▣ |

🔧 8.72   ✂ 11.80   Global Days 090

| 31030 | radical (Caldwell-Luc) without removal of antrochoanal polyps | A2 V 50 ▣ |

🔧 13.12   ✂ 17.25   Global Days 090

| 31032 | radical (Caldwell-Luc) with removal of antrochoanal polyps | A2 V 50 ▣ |

🔧 14.31   ✂ 14.31   Global Days 090

| 31040 | Pterygomaxillary fossa surgery, any approach | R2 T ▣ |

> **EXCLUDES**   *transantral ligation internal maxillary artery (30920)*

🔧 18.88   ✂ 18.88   Global Days 090

| 31050 | Sinusotomy, sphenoid, with or without biopsy; | A2 T 50 ▣ |

🔧 12.35   ✂ 12.35   Global Days 090

| 31051 | with mucosal stripping or removal of polyp(s) | A2 T 50 ▣ |

🔧 16.13   ✂ 16.13   Global Days 090

| 31070 | Sinusotomy frontal; external, simple (trephine operation) | A2 T 50 ▣ |

> **INCLUDES**   Killian operation

> **EXCLUDES**   *intranasal frontal sinusotomy (31276)*

🔧 10.83   ✂ 10.83   Global Days 090

| 31075 | transorbital, unilateral (for mucocele or osteoma, Lynch type) | A2 T 80 50 ▣ |

🔧 19.69   ✂ 19.69   Global Days 090

| 31080 | obliterative without osteoplastic flap, brow incision (includes ablation) | A2 T 80 50 ▣ |

> **INCLUDES**   Ridell sinusotomy

🔧 25.52   ✂ 25.52   Global Days 090

| 31081 | obliterative, without osteoplastic flap, coronal incision (includes ablation) | A2 T 80 50 ▣ |

🔧 31.51   ✂ 31.51   Global Days 090

| 31084 | obliterative, with osteoplastic flap, brow incision | A2 T 80 50 ▣ |

🔧 29.72   ✂ 29.72   Global Days 090

| 31085 | obliterative, with osteoplastic flap, coronal incision | A2 T 80 50 ▣ |

🔧 31.59   ✂ 31.59   Global Days 090

| 31086 | nonobliterative, with osteoplastic flap, brow incision | A2 T 80 50 ▣ |

🔧 28.11   ✂ 28.11   Global Days 090

| 31087 | nonobliterative, with osteoplastic flap, coronal incision | A2 T 80 50 ▣ |

🔧 27.98   ✂ 27.98   Global Days 090

| 31090 | Sinusotomy, unilateral, 3 or more paranasal sinuses (frontal, maxillary, ethmoid, sphenoid) | A2 T 50 ▣ |

🔧 25.03   ✂ 25.03   Global Days 090

| 31200 | Ethmoidectomy; intranasal, anterior | A2 T 50 ▣ |

🔧 13.26   ✂ 13.26   Global Days 090

| 31201 | intranasal, total | A2 T 50 ▣ |

🔧 18.39   ✂ 18.39   Global Days 090

| 31205 | extranasal, total | A2 T 80 50 ▣ |

🔧 21.47   ✂ 21.47   Global Days 090

| 31225 | Maxillectomy; without orbital exenteration | C 80 50 ▣ |

🔧 46.30   ✂ 46.30   Global Days 090

| 31230 | with orbital exenteration (en bloc) | C 80 50 ▣ |

> **EXCLUDES**   *orbital exenteration without maxillectomy (65110-65114)*
> *skin grafts (15120-15121)*

🔧 51.90   ✂ 51.90   Global Days 090

31231-31235 Nasal Endoscopy, Diagnostic

CMS 100-3,100.2   *Endoscopy*
CMS 100-4,12,40.6   *Multiple procedures*
INCLUDES   complete sinus exam (e.g., nasal cavity, turbinates, sphenoethmoidal recess)

| 31231 | Nasal endoscopy, diagnostic, unilateral or bilateral (separate procedure) | P2 T ▣ |

🔧 2.00   ✂ 4.69   Global Days 000

| 31233 | Nasal/sinus endoscopy, diagnostic with maxillary sinusoscopy (via inferior meatus or canine fossa puncture) | A2 T 50 ▣ |

🔧 3.62   ✂ 6.63   Global Days 000

| 31235 | Nasal/sinus endoscopy, diagnostic with sphenoid sinusoscopy (via puncture of sphenoidal face or cannulation of ostium) | A2 T 50 ▣ |

🔧 4.33   ✂ 7.63   Global Days 000

● New Code   ▲ Revised Code   M Maternity Edit   A Age Edit   A-V OPPS Status Indicator   🔧 Facility RVU   ✂ Non-Facility RVU

□ CCI Comprehensive Code   50 Bilateral Procedure   + Add-on Indicator   ▣ Laboratory crosswalk   ▣ Radiology crosswalk

31237-31240 Nasal Endoscopy, Surgical

CMS *100-3,100.2* *Endoscopy*
INCLUDES diagnostic nasal/sinus endoscopy
sinusotomy, when applicable

EXCLUDES *endoscopic frontal sinus exploration, osteomeatal complex (OMC) resection and/or anterior ethmoidectomy, with antrostomy, with/without polyp removal, report all: (31254, 31256, 31276)*
endoscopic frontal sinus exploration, osteomeatal complex (OMC) resection and/or anterior ethmoidectomy, with/without polyp removal, report both: (31254, 31276)
endoscopic frontal sinus exploration, osteomeatal complex (OMC) resection, antrostomy, removal of antral mucosal disease and/or anterior ethmoidectomy, with/without polyp removal, report all: (31254, 31267, 31276)
endoscopic osteomeatal complex (OMC) resection with antrostomy and/or anterior ethmoidectomy, with/without polyp removal, report both: (31254, 31256)
endoscopic osteomeatal complex (OMC) resection with antrostomy, removal of antral mucosal disease, and/or anterior ethmoidectomy, with/without polyp removal, report both: (31254, 31267)

31237 **Nasal/sinus endoscopy, surgical; with biopsy, polypectomy or debridement (separate procedure)** A2 T 50
4.82 8.22 Global Days 000
AMA: 2008, Jan, 10-25; 2007, Jan, 13-27; 2007, Jan, 13-27; 2007, January, 13-27

31238 **with control of nasal hemorrhage** A2 T 80 50
5.22 8.46 Global Days 000

31239 **with dacryocystorhinostomy** A2 T 80 50
16.85 16.85 Global Days 010

31240 **with concha bullosa resection** A2 T 80 50
4.28 4.28 Global Days 000

31254-31255 Nasal Endoscopy with Ethmoid Removal

CMS *100-3,100.2* *Endoscopy*
CMS *100-4,12,40.6* *Multiple procedures*
INCLUDES diagnostic nasal/sinus endoscopy
sinusotomy, when applicable

31254 **Nasal/sinus endoscopy, surgical; with ethmoidectomy, partial (anterior)** A2 T 50
EXCLUDES *endoscopic exploration frontal sinus, resection osteomeatal complex (OMC), antrostomy, and/or anterior ethmoidectomy, with/without polyp removal, report all: (31254, 31256, 31276)*
endoscopic exploration frontal sinus, resection osteomeatal complex (OMC), antrostomy, removal of antral mucosal disease and/or anterior ethmoidectomy, with/without polyp removal, report all: (31254, 31267, 31276)
endoscopic frontal sinus exploration, osteomeatal complex (OMC) resection and/or anterior ethmoidectomy, with/without polyp removal, report both: (31254, 31276)
endoscopic resection osteomeatal complex (OMC) and antrostomy, removal antral mucosal disease, and/or anterior ethmoidectomy, with/without polyp removal, report both: (31254, 31267)
endoscopic resection osteomeatal complex (OMC), antrostomy, and/or anterior ethmoidectomy, with/without polyp removal, report both: (31254, 31256)

7.34 7.34 Global Days 000
AMA: 2008, Jan, 10-25; 2007, Jan, 13-27; 2007, Jan, 13-27; 2007, January, 13-27

31255   **with ethmoidectomy, total (anterior and posterior)**   A2 T 50 ▣

EXCLUDES endoscopic anterior and posterior ethmoidectomy (APE), antrostomy, removal disease of antral mucosa, with/without polyp removal, report both: (31255, 31267)
endoscopic anterior and posterior ethmoidectomy (APE), antrostomy, with/without polyp removal, report both: (31255, 31256)
endoscopic anterior and posterior ethmoidectomy and sphenoidotomy (APS), antrostomy, and removal of diseased antral mucosa, with/without polyp removal, report 31255 and 31267 with: (31287, or 31288)
endoscopic anterior and posterior ethmoidectomy and sphenoidotomy (APS), antrostomy, with/without polyp removal, report 31255 and 31256 with: (31287, or 31288)
endoscopic anterior and posterior ethmoidectomy and sphenoidotomy (APS), with/without polyp removal, report 31255 with: (31287, or 31288)
endoscopic frontal sinus exploration, anterior and posterior ethmoidectomy and sphenoidotomy (APS), antrostomy, removal diseased antral mucosa, with/without polyp removal, report 31255, 31267, and 31276 with: (31287, or 31288)
endoscopic frontal sinus exploration, anterior and posterior ethmoidectomy and sphenoidotomy (APS), antrostomy, with/without polyp removal, report 31255, 31256, and 31276 with: (31287, or 31288)
endoscopic frontal sinus exploration, anterior and posterior ethmoidectomy and sphenoidotomy (APS), with/without polyp removal, report 31255 and 31276 with: (31287, or 31288)
endoscopic frontal sinus exploration, anterior and posterior ethmoidectomy (APE), antrostomy, removal diseased antral mucosa, with/without polyp removal, report all: (31255, 31267, 31276)
endoscopic frontal sinus exploration, anterior and posterior ethmoidectomy (APE), antrostomy, with/without polyp removal, report all: (31255, 31256, 31276)
endoscopic frontal sinus exploration, anterior and posterior ethmoidectomy (APE), with/without polyp removal, report both: (31255, 31276)

⚒ 10.86   ⚒ 10.86   Global Days 000
AMA: 2008, Jan, 10-25; 2007, Jan, 13-27; 2007, Jan, 13-27; 2007, January, 13-27

31256-31267 Nasal Endoscopy with Maxillary Procedures

CMS 100-3,100.2   *Endoscopy*
CMS 100-4,12,40.6   *Multiple procedures*
INCLUDES   diagnostic nasal/sinus endoscopy
sinusotomy, when applicable

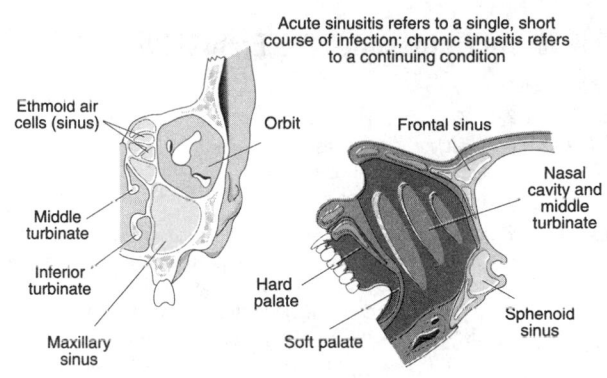

Acute sinusitis refers to a single, short course of infection; chronic sinusitis refers to a continuing condition

31256   **Nasal/sinus endoscopy, surgical, with maxillary antrostomy;**   A2 T 50 ▣

EXCLUDES endoscopic anterior and posterior ethmoidectomy and sphenoidotomy (APS), antrostomy, with/without polyp removal, report 31255 and 31256 with: (31287, or 31288)
endoscopic anterior and posterior ethmoidectomy and sphenoidotomy (APS), frontal sinus exploration, and antrostomy, with/without polyp removal, report 31255, 31256 and 31276 with: (31287, or 31288)
endoscopic anterior and posterior ethmoidectomy (APE), antrostomy, with/without polyp removal, report both: (31255, 31256)
endoscopic anterior and posterior ethmoidectomy (APE), frontal sinus exploration, antrostomy, with/without polyp removal, report all: (31255, 31256, 31276)

⚒ 5.32   ⚒ 5.32   Global Days 000

31267   **with removal of tissue from maxillary sinus**   A2 T 50 ▣

EXCLUDES endoscopic anterior and posterior ethmoidectomy and sphenoidotomy (APS), antrostomy, and removal of diseased antral mucosal, with/without polyp removal, report 31255, 31267 with: (31287, or 31288)
endoscopic anterior and posterior ethmoidectomy and sphenoidotomy (APS), frontal sinus exploration, antrostomy, and removal of diseased antral mucosa, with/without polyp removal, report 31255, 31267 and 31276 with: (31287, or 31288)
endoscopic anterior and posterior ethmoidectomy (APE), antrostomy, removal of antral mucosal disease, with/without polyp removal, report both: (31255, 31267)
endoscopic anterior and posterior ethmoidectomy (APE), frontal sinus exploration, antrostomy and removal of antral mucosal disease, with/without polyp removal, report all: (31255, 31267, 31276)

⚒ 8.57   ⚒ 8.57   Global Days 000
AMA: 2008, Jan, 10-25; 2007, Jan, 13-27; 2007, Jan, 13-27; 2007, January, 13-27

● New Code   ▲ Revised Code   ᴹ Maternity Edit   ◭ Age Edit   Ⓐ-Ⓨ OPPS Status Indicator   ⚒ Facility RVU   ⚒ Non-Facility RVU
▣ CCI Comprehensive Code   50 Bilateral Procedure   + Add-on Indicator   ◪ Laboratory crosswalk   ⊞ Radiology crosswalk

© 2008 Ingenix *(Blue Ink)*   CPT only © 2008 American Medical Association. All Rights Reserved. (Black Ink)   Medicare (Red Ink)   **111**

Respiratory System

31276 Nasal Endoscopy with Frontal Sinus Examination

CMS 100-3,100.2   *Endoscopy*
CMS 100-4,12,40.6   *Multiple procedures*
INCLUDES   diagnostic nasal/sinus endoscopy
      sinusotomy, when applicable

EXCLUDES   *endoscopic anterior and posterior ethmoidectomy and sphenoidotomy (APS), frontal sinus exploration, with/without polyp removal, report: 31255 and 31276 and (31287, or 31288)*
endoscopic anterior and posterior ethmoidectomy and sphenoidotomy (APS), with frontal sinus exploration, antrostomy and removal of antral mucosal disease, with/without polyp removal, report: 31255 and 31267 and 31276 and (31287, or 31288)
endoscopic anterior and posterior ethmoidectomy and sphenoidotomy (APS), with/without polyp removal, with frontal sinus exploration and antrostomy report: 31255 and 31256 and 31276 and (31287, or 31288)
endoscopic anterior and posterior ethmoidectomy (APE), frontal sinus exploration, with/without polyp removal, report both: (31255, 31276)
unilateral endoscopy two or more sinuses (31231-31235)

31276   **Nasal/sinus endoscopy, surgical with frontal sinus exploration, with or without removal of tissue from frontal sinus**   A2 T 50 ▢
   📅 13.69   ⚕ 13.69   Global Days 000

31287-31288 Nasal Endoscopy with Sphenoid Procedures

CMS 100-3,100.2   *Endoscopy*
CMS 100-4,12,40.6   *Multiple procedures*

31287   **Nasal/sinus endoscopy, surgical, with sphenoidotomy;**   A2 T 80 50 ▢
   📅 6.25   ⚕ 6.25   Global Days 000

31288   **with removal of tissue from the sphenoid sinus**   A2 T 80 50 ▢
   📅 7.25   ⚕ 7.25   Global Days 000

31290-31299 Nasal Endoscopy with Repair and Decompression

CMS 100-3,100.2   *Endoscopy*
CMS 100-4,12,40.6   *Multiple procedures*
INCLUDES   diagnostic nasal/sinus endoscopy
      sinusotomy, when applicable

31290   **Nasal/sinus endoscopy, surgical, with repair of cerebrospinal fluid leak; ethmoid region**   C 80 50 ▢
   📅 30.02   ⚕ 30.02   Global Days 010

31291   **sphenoid region**   C 80 50 ▢
   📅 31.71   ⚕ 31.71   Global Days 010

31292   **Nasal/sinus endoscopy, surgical; with medial or inferior orbital wall decompression**   T 80 50 ▢
   📅 25.98   ⚕ 25.98   Global Days 010

31293   **with medial orbital wall and inferior orbital wall decompression**   T 80 50 ▢
   📅 28.29   ⚕ 28.29   Global Days 010

31294   **with optic nerve decompression**   T 80 50 ▢
   📅 32.50   ⚕ 32.50   Global Days 010

31299   **Unlisted procedure, accessory sinuses**   T 80
   EXCLUDES   *hypophysectomy (61546, 61548)*
   📅 0.00   ⚕ 0.00   Global Days YYY

31300-31502 Procedures of the Larynx

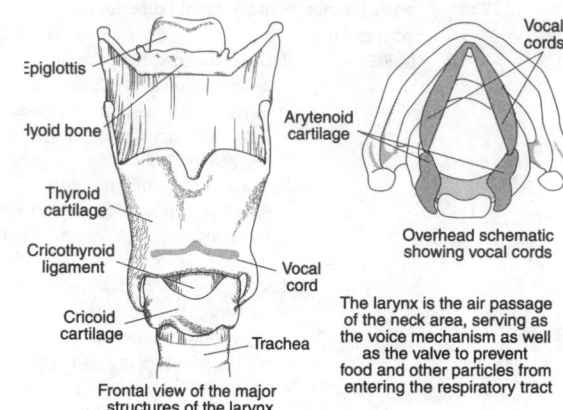

Epiglottis
Hyoid bone
Thyroid cartilage
Cricothyroid ligament
Cricoid cartilage
Vocal cord
Trachea
Frontal view of the major structures of the larynx

Vocal cords
Arytenoid cartilage
Overhead schematic showing vocal cords

The larynx is the air passage of the neck area, serving as the voice mechanism as well as the valve to prevent food and other particles from entering the respiratory tract

31300   **Laryngotomy (thyrotomy, laryngofissure); with removal of tumor or laryngocele, cordectomy**   A2 T 80 ▢
   📅 31.77   ⚕ 31.77   Global Days 090

31320   **diagnostic**   A2 T 80 ▢
   📅 16.14   ⚕ 16.14   Global Days 090

31360   **Laryngectomy; total, without radical neck dissection**   C 80 ▢ P0
   📅 50.55   ⚕ 50.55   Global Days 090

31365   **total, with radical neck dissection**   C 80 ▢ P0
   📅 63.35   ⚕ 63.35   Global Days 090
   AMA: 2008, Jan, 10-25; 2007, Jan, 13-27; 2007, Jan, 13-27; 2007, January, 13-27

31367   **subtotal supraglottic, without radical neck dissection**   C 80 ▢ P0
   📅 54.74   ⚕ 54.74   Global Days 090

31368   **subtotal supraglottic, with radical neck dissection**   C 80 ▢ P0
   📅 61.23   ⚕ 61.23   Global Days 090

31370   **Partial laryngectomy (hemilaryngectomy); horizontal**   C 80 ▢ P0
   📅 51.52   ⚕ 51.52   Global Days 090

31375   **laterovertical**   C 80 ▢ P0
   📅 48.72   ⚕ 48.72   Global Days 090

31380   **anterovertical**   C 80 ▢ P0
   📅 48.05   ⚕ 48.05   Global Days 090

31382   **antero-latero-vertical**   C 80 ▢ P0
   📅 52.56   ⚕ 52.56   Global Days 090

31390   **Pharyngolaryngectomy, with radical neck dissection; without reconstruction**   C 80 ▢ P0
   📅 70.60   ⚕ 70.60   Global Days 090

31395   **with reconstruction**   C 80 ▢ P0
   📅 74.95   ⚕ 74.95   Global Days 090

31400   **Arytenoidectomy or arytenoidopexy, external approach**   A2 T 80 ▢
   EXCLUDES   *endoscopic arytenoidectomy (31560)*
   📅 25.23   ⚕ 25.23   Global Days 090

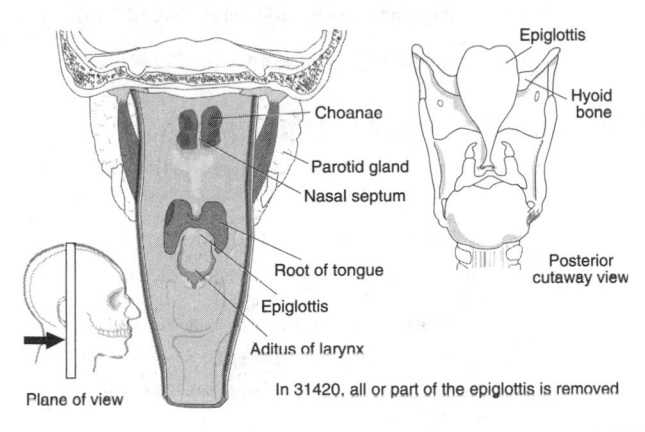

Choanae

Epiglottis

Hyoid bone

Parotid gland

Nasal septum

Root of tongue

Epiglottis

Aditus of larynx

Posterior cutaway view

Plane of view

In 31420, all or part of the epiglottis is removed

31420 Epiglottidectomy [A2] [T] [80] ▭
  ⛏ 21.20 ⚕ 21.20 Global Days 090

⊘ **31500** Intubation, endotracheal, emergency procedure [G2] [S] ▭
  EXCLUDES injection of contrast for segmental bronchography (31656)
  ⛏ 2.96 ⚕ 2.96 Global Days 000
  AMA: 2007, Apr, 3-6; 2007, Apr, 3-6; 2007, April, 3-6; 2007, Jul, 1-4; 2006, May, 1-9; 2006, May, 1-9; 2006, May, 1-9; 2004, Aug, 7; 2004, Aug, 7; 2004, August, 7

31502 Tracheotomy tube change prior to establishment of fistula tract [G2] [S] ▭
  ⛏ 0.94 ⚕ 0.94 Global Days 000

31505-31541 Endoscopy of the Larynx

CMS 100-3,100.2 *Endoscopy*
CMS 100-4,12,40.6 *Multiple procedures*

31505 Laryngoscopy, indirect; diagnostic (separate procedure) [P2] [T] ▭
  ⛏ 1.26 ⚕ 2.08 Global Days 000

31510 with biopsy [A2] [T] [80] ▭
  ⛏ 3.18 ⚕ 5.32 Global Days 000

31511 with removal of foreign body [A2] [T] ▭
  ⛏ 3.42 ⚕ 5.34 Global Days 000

31512 with removal of lesion [A2] [T] [80] ▭
  ⛏ 3.43 ⚕ 5.27 Global Days 000

31513 with vocal cord injection [A2] [T] [80] ▭
  ⛏ 3.49 ⚕ 3.49 Global Days 000

31515 Laryngoscopy direct, with or without tracheoscopy; for aspiration [A2] [T] ▭
  ⛏ 2.90 ⚕ 5.25 Global Days 000

31520 diagnostic, newborn [A] [G2] [T] [80] ⊛ ▭
  ⛏ 4.06 ⚕ 4.06 Global Days 000

31525 diagnostic, except newborn [A2] [T] ▭
  ⛏ 4.22 ⚕ 6.33 Global Days 000

31526 diagnostic, with operating microscope or telescope [A2] [T] ▭
  INCLUDES operating microscope (69990)
  ⛏ 4.19 ⚕ 4.19 Global Days 000

31527 with insertion of obturator [A2] [T] [80] ▭
  ⛏ 5.12 ⚕ 5.12 Global Days 000

31528 with dilation, initial [A2] [T] [80] ▭
  ⛏ 3.82 ⚕ 3.82 Global Days 000

31529 with dilation, subsequent [A2] [T] [80] ▭
  ⛏ 4.31 ⚕ 4.31 Global Days 000

31530 Laryngoscopy, direct, operative, with foreign body removal; [A2] [T] ▭
  ⛏ 5.28 ⚕ 5.28 Global Days 000

31531 with operating microscope or telescope [A2] [T] [80] ▭
  INCLUDES operating microscope (69990)
  ⛏ 5.68 ⚕ 5.68 Global Days 000

31535 Laryngoscopy, direct, operative, with biopsy; [A2] [T] ▭
  ⛏ 5.05 ⚕ 5.05 Global Days 000

31536 with operating microscope or telescope [A2] [T] ▭
  INCLUDES operating microscope (69990)
  ⛏ 5.64 ⚕ 5.64 Global Days 000

31540 Laryngoscopy, direct, operative, with excision of tumor and/or stripping of vocal cords or epiglottis; [A2] [T] ▭
  ⛏ 6.48 ⚕ 6.48 Global Days 000

31541 with operating microscope or telescope [A2] [T] ▭
  INCLUDES operating microscope (69990)
  ⛏ 7.09 ⚕ 7.09 Global Days 000

31545-31546 Endoscopy of Larynx with Reconstruction

INCLUDES operating microscope (69990)
EXCLUDES *vocal cord reconstruction with allograft (31599)*

Do not report with (31540, 31541, 69990)

31545 Laryngoscopy, direct, operative, with operating microscope or telescope, with submucosal removal of non-neoplastic lesion(s) of vocal cord; reconstruction with local tissue flap(s) [A2] [T] [50] ▭
  ⛏ 9.55 ⚕ 9.55 Global Days 000

31546 reconstruction with graft(s) (includes obtaining autograft) [A2] [T] [50] ▭
  Do not report with (20926)
  ⛏ 14.62 ⚕ 14.62 Global Days 000
  AMA: 2008, Jan, 10-25; 2007, Jan, 13-27; 2007, Jan, 13-27; 2007, January, 13-27; 2006, May, 16-20; 2006, May, 16-20; 2006, May, 16-20

31560-31571 Endoscopy of Larynx with Arytenoid Removal, Vocal Cord Injection

CMS 100-3,100.2 *Endoscopy*
CMS 100-4,12,40.6 *Multiple procedures*

31560 Laryngoscopy, direct, operative, with arytenoidectomy; [A2] [T] [80] ▭
  ⛏ 8.39 ⚕ 8.39 Global Days 000

31561 with operating microscope or telescope [A2] [T] [80] ▭
  INCLUDES operating microscope (69990)
  ⛏ 9.20 ⚕ 9.20 Global Days 000

31570 Laryngoscopy, direct, with injection into vocal cord(s), therapeutic; [A2] [T] ▭
  ⛏ 6.07 ⚕ 8.82 Global Days 000

31571 with operating microscope or telescope [A2] [T] ▭
  INCLUDES operating microscope (69990)
  ⛏ 6.69 ⚕ 6.69 Global Days 000

31575-31579 Endoscopy of Larynx, Flexible Fiberoptic

EXCLUDES *evaluation by flexible fiberoptic endoscope:*
  sensory assessment (92614-92615)
  swallowing (92612-92613)
  swallowing and sensory assessment (92616-92617)
  flexible fiberoptic endoscopic examination/testing by cine or video recording (92612-92617)

31575 Laryngoscopy, flexible fiberoptic; diagnostic [P3] [T] ▭
  ⛏ 2.00 ⚕ 2.93 Global Days 000

31576 with biopsy [A2] [T] ▭
  ⛏ 3.25 ⚕ 5.68 Global Days 000

● New Code ▲ Revised Code [M] Maternity Edit [A] Age Edit [A-V] OPPS Status Indicator ⛏ Facility RVU ⚕ Non-Facility RVU
▭ CCI Comprehensive Code [50] Bilateral Procedure + Add-on Indicator ◼ Laboratory crosswalk ☒ Radiology crosswalk

© 2008 Ingenix *(Blue Ink)*   CPT only © 2008 American Medical Association. All Rights Reserved. (Black Ink)   Medicare (Red Ink)   113

31420 — 31576

Respiratory System

31577 — 31625

31577	**with removal of foreign body**	A2 T 80 ▣
	📷 3.96 ⚕ 6.15 Global Days 000	
31578	**with removal of lesion**	A2 T 80 ▣
	📷 4.50 ⚕ 7.14 Global Days 000	
31579	**Laryngoscopy, flexible or rigid fiberoptic, with stroboscopy**	P3 T ▣
	📷 3.71 ⚕ 5.54 Global Days 000	

31580-31599 Larynx Reconstruction

31580	**Laryngoplasty; for laryngeal web, 2 stage, with keel insertion and removal**	A2 T 80 ▣
	📷 30.29 ⚕ 30.29 Global Days 090	
31582	**for laryngeal stenosis, with graft or core mold, including tracheotomy**	A2 T ▣
	📷 48.22 ⚕ 48.22 Global Days 090	
31584	**with open reduction of fracture**	C 80 ▣
	📷 38.68 ⚕ 38.68 Global Days 090	
31587	**Laryngoplasty, cricoid split**	C 80 ▣
	📷 25.21 ⚕ 25.21 Global Days 090	
31588	**Laryngoplasty, not otherwise specified (eg, for burns, reconstruction after partial laryngectomy)**	A2 T 80 ▣
	📷 28.61 ⚕ 28.61 Global Days 090	
	AMA: 2008, Jan, 10-25; 2007, Jan, 13-27; 2007, Jan, 13-27; 2007, January, 13-27; 2004, Aug, 11; 2004, August, 11; 2004, Aug, 11	
31590	**Laryngeal reinnervation by neuromuscular pedicle**	A2 T 80 ▣
	📷 22.40 ⚕ 22.40 Global Days 090	

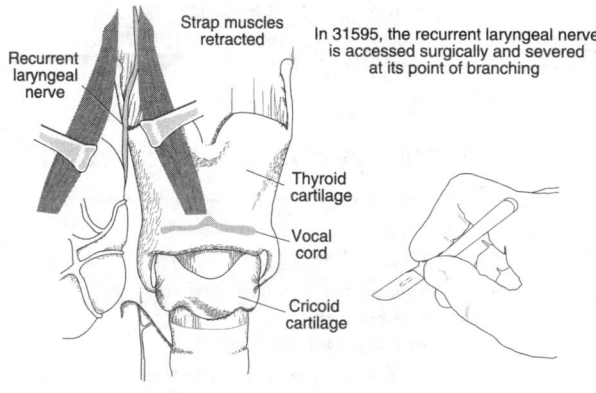

Strap muscles retracted

Recurrent laryngeal nerve

In 31595, the recurrent laryngeal nerve is accessed surgically and severed at its point of branching

Thyroid cartilage

Vocal cord

Cricoid cartilage

31595	**Section recurrent laryngeal nerve, therapeutic (separate procedure), unilateral**	T 80 ▣
	📷 19.34 ⚕ 19.34 Global Days 090	
31599	**Unlisted procedure, larynx**	T 80
	📷 0.00 ⚕ 0.00 Global Days YYY	

31600-31610 Stoma Creation: Trachea

EXCLUDES *aspiration of trachea, direct vision (31515)*
endotracheal intubation (31500)

31600	**Tracheostomy, planned (separate procedure);**	T ▣
	📷 10.59 ⚕ 10.59 Global Days 000	
31601	**younger than 2 years**	A T 80 ▣
	📷 6.96 ⚕ 6.96 Global Days 000	
31603	**Tracheostomy, emergency procedure; transtracheal**	A2 T ▣
	📷 5.97 ⚕ 5.97 Global Days 000	
31605	**cricothyroid membrane**	G2 T ▣
	📷 4.93 ⚕ 4.93 Global Days 000	

31610	**Tracheostomy, fenestration procedure with skin flaps**	T ▣
	📷 18.02 ⚕ 18.02 Global Days 090	

31611-31614 Procedures of the Trachea

31611	**Construction of tracheoesophageal fistula and subsequent insertion of an alaryngeal speech prosthesis (eg, voice button, Blom-Singer prosthesis)**	A2 T 80 ▣
	📷 13.47 ⚕ 13.47 Global Days 090	
31612	**Tracheal puncture, percutaneous with transtracheal aspiration and/or injection**	A2 T 80 ▣
	EXCLUDES *tracheal aspiration under direct vision (31515)*	
	📷 1.28 ⚕ 2.06 Global Days 000	
31613	**Tracheostoma revision; simple, without flap rotation**	A2 T ▣
	📷 11.16 ⚕ 11.16 Global Days 090	
31614	**complex, with flap rotation**	A2 T ▣
	📷 18.47 ⚕ 18.47 Global Days 090	

31615 Endoscopy Through Tracheostomy

INCLUDES diagnostic bronchoscopy

⊙	31615	**Tracheobronchoscopy through established tracheostomy incision**	A2 T ▣
		📷 3.36 ⚕ 4.68 Global Days 000	

31620 Endobronchial Ultrasound (EBUS)

+ ⊙	31620	**Endobronchial ultrasound (EBUS) during bronchoscopic diagnostic or therapeutic intervention(s) (List separately in addition to code for primary procedure[s])**	N1 N
		Code first (31622-31646)	
		📷 1.91 ⚕ 7.30 Global Days ZZZ	
		AMA: 2005, Aug, 4-6; 2005, Aug, 4-6; 2005, August, 4-6	

31622-31656 Endoscopy of Lung

INCLUDES diagnostic bronchoscopy with surgical bronchoscopy procedures
fluoroscopic guidance for codes 31622-31646

⊙	31622	**Bronchoscopy, rigid or flexible, with or without fluoroscopic guidance; diagnostic, with or without cell washing (separate procedure)**	A2 T ▣
		📷 3.92 ⚕ 8.21 Global Days 000	
		AMA: 2008, Jan, 10-25; 2007, Jan, 13-27; 2007, Jan, 13-27; 2007, January, 13-27; 2005, Aug, 4-6; 2005, August, 4-6; 2005, Aug, 4-6; 2004, Sep, 8; 2004, September, 8; 2004, September, 12; 2004, Sep, 8; 2004, Sep, 12; 2004, Sep, 12	
⊙	31623	**with brushing or protected brushings**	A2 T ▣
		📷 3.95 ⚕ 8.97 Global Days 000	
		AMA: 2008, Jan, 10-25; 2008, May, 9-11; 2007, Jan, 13-27; 2007, Jan, 13-27; 2007, January, 13-27; 2005, Aug, 4-6; 2005, Aug, 4-6; 2005, August, 4-6; 2004, Sep, 8; 2004, Sep, 8; 2004, September, 8	
⊙	31624	**with bronchial alveolar lavage**	A2 T ▣
		📷 3.96 ⚕ 8.34 Global Days 000	
		AMA: 2008, Jan, 10-25; 2008, May, 9-11; 2007, Jan, 13-27; 2007, Jan, 13-27; 2007, January, 13-27; 2005, Aug, 4-6; 2005, Aug, 4-6; 2005, August, 4-6; 2004, Sep, 8; 2004, Sep, 8; 2004, September, 8	
⊙	31625	**with bronchial or endobronchial biopsy(s), single or multiple sites**	A2 T ▣
		📷 4.62 ⚕ 9.00 Global Days 000	
		AMA: 2008, Jan, 10-25; 2007, Jan, 13-27; 2007, Jan, 13-27; 2007, January, 13-27; 2005, Aug, 4-6; 2005, August, 4-6; 2005, Aug, 4-6; 2004, Sep, 8; 2004, June, 11; 2004, September, 8; 2004, Sep, 8; 2004, Jun, 11; 2004, Jun, 11	

⊙ **31628** **with transbronchial lung biopsy(s), single lobe** A2 T
> INCLUDES all biopsies taken from lobe
> EXCLUDES *transbronchial biopsies by needle aspiration (31629, 31633)*
> *transbronchial biopsies of additional lobe(s) (31632)*

⚡ 5.15 ☌ 10.80 Global Days 000

AMA: 2008, Jan, 10-25; 2008, May, 9-11; 2007, Jan, 13-27; 2007, Jan, 13-27; 2007, January, 13-27; 2005, Aug, 4-6; 2005, Aug, 4-6; 2005, August, 4-6; 2004, Sep, 8; 2004, Sep, 8; 2004, September, 8

⊙ **31629** **with transbronchial needle aspiration biopsy(s), trachea, main stem and/or lobar bronchus(i)** A2 T
> INCLUDES all biopsies from same lobe
> EXCLUDES *transbronchial biopsies of lung (31628, 31632)*
> *transbronchial needle biopsies of another lobe(s) (31633)*

⚡ 5.50 ☌ 16.51 Global Days 000

AMA: 2008, Jan, 10-25; 2007, Jan, 13-27; 2007, Jan, 13-27; 2007, January, 13-27; 2005, Aug, 4-6; 2005, Aug, 4-6; 2005, August, 4-6; 2004, Jul, 13; 2004, Jul, 13; 2004, July, 13; 2004, May, 15; 2004, September, 8; 2004, May, 15; 2004, May, 15; 2004, Sep, 8; 2004, Sep, 8

31630 **with tracheal/bronchial dilation or closed reduction of fracture** A2 T
⚡ 5.55 ☌ 5.55 Global Days 000

AMA: 2005, Aug, 4-6; 2005, Aug, 4-6; 2005, August, 4-6

31631 **with placement of tracheal stent(s) (includes tracheal/bronchial dilation as required)** A2 T
> EXCLUDES *bronchial stent placement (31636-31637)*
> *revision bronchial or tracheal stent (31638)*

⚡ 6.25 ☌ 6.25 Global Days 000

AMA: 2005, Aug, 4-6; 2005, Aug, 4-6; 2005, August, 4-6

+ **31632** **with transbronchial lung biopsy(s), each additional lobe (List separately in addition to code for primary procedure)** G2 T
> INCLUDES all biopsies of additional lobe of lung

Code first (31628)
⚡ 1.47 ☌ 2.04 Global Days ZZZ

AMA: 2005, Aug, 4-6; 2005, Aug, 4-6; 2005, August, 4-6; 2004, Sep, 8; 2004, September, 8; 2004, Sep, 8

+ **31633** **with transbronchial needle aspiration biopsy(s), each additional lobe (List separately in addition to code for primary procedure)** G2 T
> INCLUDES all needle biopsies from another lobe or from trachea

Code first 31629
⚡ 1.82 ☌ 2.44 Global Days ZZZ

AMA: 2008, Jan, 10-25; 2007, Jan, 13-27; 2007, Jan, 13-27; 2007, January, 13-27; 2005, Aug, 4-6; 2005, Aug, 4-6; 2005, August, 4-6; 2004, May, 15; 2004, May, 15; 2004, September, 8; 2004, May, 15; 2004, July, 13; 2004, Jul, 13; 2004, Jul, 13; 2004, Sep, 8; 2004, Sep, 8

⊙ **31635** **with removal of foreign body** A2 T
⚡ 5.14 ☌ 9.26 Global Days 000

AMA: 2008, Jan, 10-25; 2007, Jan, 13-27; 2007, Jan, 13-27; 2007, January, 13-27; 2005, Aug, 4-6; 2005, August, 4-6; 2005, Aug, 4-6

31636 **with placement of bronchial stent(s) (includes tracheal/bronchial dilation as required), initial bronchus** A2 T
⚡ 6.10 ☌ 6.10 Global Days 000

AMA: 2005, Aug, 4-6; 2005, Aug, 4-6; 2005, August, 4-6

+ **31637** **each additional major bronchus stented (List separately in addition to code for primary procedure)** A2 T
Code first 31636
⚡ 2.17 ☌ 2.17 Global Days ZZZ

AMA: 2005, Aug, 4-6; 2005, Aug, 4-6; 2005, August, 4-6

31638 **with revision of tracheal or bronchial stent inserted at previous session (includes tracheal/bronchial dilation as required)** A2 T
⚡ 6.80 ☌ 6.80 Global Days 000

AMA: 2005, Aug, 4-6; 2005, Aug, 4-6; 2005, August, 4-6

31640 **with excision of tumor** A2
⚡ 7.12 ☌ 7.12 Global Days 000

AMA: 2005, Aug, 4-6; 2005, Aug, 4-6; 2005, August, 4-6

31641 **Bronchoscopy (rigid or flexible); with destruction of tumor or relief of stenosis by any method other than excision (eg, laser therapy, cryotherapy)** A2 T
> Code also any photodynamic therapy via bronchoscopy (96570-96571)

⚡ 7.00 ☌ 7.00 Global Days 000

AMA: 2005, Aug, 4-6; 2005, Aug, 4-6; 2005, August, 4-6

31643 **with placement of catheter(s) for intracavitary radioelement application** A2 T
> Code also if appropriate (77761-77763, 77785-77787)

⚡ 4.79 ☌ 4.79 Global Days 000

AMA: 2005, Aug, 4-6; 2005, Aug, 4-6; 2005, August, 4-6

⊙ **31645** **with therapeutic aspiration of tracheobronchial tree, initial (eg, drainage of lung abscess)** A2 T
> EXCLUDES *bedside aspiration of trachea, bronchi (31725)*

⚡ 4.34 ☌ 8.06 Global Days 000

AMA: 2005, Aug, 4-6; 2005, Aug, 4-6; 2005, August, 4-6

⊙ **31646** **with therapeutic aspiration of tracheobronchial tree, subsequent** A2 T
> EXCLUDES *bedside aspiration of trachea, bronchi (31725)*

⚡ 3.76 ☌ 7.32 Global Days 000

AMA: 2005, Aug, 4-6; 2005, Aug, 4-6; 2005, August, 4-6

⊙ **31656** **with injection of contrast material for segmental bronchography (fiberscope only)** A2 T 80
⚡ 71040, 71060
⚡ 3.06 ☌ 8.37 Global Days 000

31715-31899 Respiratory Procedures
> EXCLUDES *endotracheal intubation (31500)*
> *tracheal aspiration under direct vision (31515)*

31715 **Transtracheal injection for bronchography** N1 N 80 50
> EXCLUDES *prolonged services (99354-99360)*

⚡ 71040, 71060
⚡ 1.51 ☌ 1.51 Global Days 000

31717 **Catheterization with bronchial brush biopsy** A2 T
⚡ 3.00 ☌ 7.86 Global Days 000

AMA: 2008, Jan, 10-25; 2007, Jan, 13-27; 2007, Jan, 13-27; 2007, January, 13-27

31720 **Catheter aspiration (separate procedure); nasotracheal** A2 S
⚡ 1.42 ☌ 1.42 Global Days 000

⊙ **31725** **tracheobronchial with fiberscope, bedside** C
⚡ 2.56 ☌ 2.56 Global Days 000

31730 **Transtracheal (percutaneous) introduction of needle wire dilator/stent or indwelling tube for oxygen therapy** A2 T
⚡ 3.92 ☌ 22.32 Global Days 000

31750 **Tracheoplasty; cervical** A2 T 80
⚡ 33.80 ☌ 33.80 Global Days 090

Respiratory System

31755 — 32320

31755	tracheopharyngeal fistulization, each stage	A2 T 80	
	42.84 42.84 Global Days 090		
31760	intrathoracic	C 80 P0	
	37.07 37.07 Global Days 090		
31766	Carinal reconstruction	C 80 P0	
	48.61 48.61 Global Days 090		
31770	Bronchoplasty; graft repair	C 80 P0	
	EXCLUDES bronchoplasty done with lobectomy (32501)		
	35.84 35.84 Global Days 090		
31775	excision stenosis and anastomosis	C 80 P0	
	EXCLUDES bronchoplasty done with lobectomy (32501)		
	37.08 37.08 Global Days 090		
31780	Excision tracheal stenosis and anastomosis; cervical	C 80	
	31.06 31.06 Global Days 090		
31781	cervicothoracic	C 80	
	37.73 37.73 Global Days 090		
31785	Excision of tracheal tumor or carcinoma; cervical	T 80	
	28.46 28.46 Global Days 090		
31786	thoracic	C 80 P0	
	39.96 39.96 Global Days 090		
31800	Suture of tracheal wound or injury; cervical	C 80	
	17.78 17.78 Global Days 090		
31805	intrathoracic	C 80 P0	
	22.03 22.03 Global Days 090		
31820	Surgical closure tracheostomy or fistula; without plastic repair	A2 T 80	
	EXCLUDES tracheoesophageal fistula repair (43305, 43312)		
	8.37 10.78 Global Days 090		
31825	with plastic repair	A2 T 80	
	EXCLUDES tracheoesophageal fistula repair (43305, 43312)		
	12.33 15.08 Global Days 090		

Thyroid cartilage

Cricoid cartilage

1st ring

2nd ring

3rd ring

Tracheostomies typically enter at the second, third, or fourth ring

Any of a wide variety of scar revision techniques may be employed. A Z-plasty may be used to lengthen or irregularize the scar line. Revision also serves to neutralize contractures that occur along the scar line

Example of a common Z-plasty where flaps are rotated to break scar line

A tracheostomy closure scar is revised, usually to make the scar less noticeable (31830)

31830	Revision of tracheostomy scar	A2 T 80	
	8.69 10.88 Global Days 090		
31899	Unlisted procedure, trachea, bronchi	T 80	
	0.00 0.00 Global Days YYY		

32035-32036 Procedures for Empyema

32035	Thoracostomy; with rib resection for empyema	C 80 P0	
	18.66 18.66 Global Days 090		
32036	with open flap drainage for empyema	C 80 P0	
	20.26 20.26 Global Days 090		

32095-32160 Open Procedures: Chest

INCLUDES   exploration of penetrating wound of chest

EXCLUDES   lung resection (32480-32504)

32095	Thoracotomy, limited, for biopsy of lung or pleura	C 80 P0	
	EXCLUDES Exploration without thoracotomy of wound due to penetrating trauma (20102)		
	16.64 16.64 Global Days 090		
32100	Thoracotomy, major; with exploration and biopsy	C 80 P0	
	Do not report with (19260, 19271-19272, 32503-32504)		
	25.83 25.83 Global Days 090		
	AMA: 2007, Mar, 1-3; 2007, Mar, 1-3; 2007, March, 1-3		
32110	with control of traumatic hemorrhage and/or repair of lung tear	C 80 P0	
	38.86 38.86 Global Days 090		
32120	for postoperative complications	C 80 P0	
	23.03 23.03 Global Days 090		
32124	with open intrapleural pneumonolysis	C 80 P0	
	24.54 24.54 Global Days 090		
32140	with cyst(s) removal, with or without a pleural procedure	C 80 P0	
	26.23 26.23 Global Days 090		
32141	with excision-plication of bullae, with or without any pleural procedure	C 80 P0	
	EXCLUDES lung volume reduction (32491)		
	39.27 39.27 Global Days 090		
32150	with removal of intrapleural foreign body or fibrin deposit	C 80 P0	
	26.44 26.44 Global Days 090		
32151	with removal of intrapulmonary foreign body	C 80	
	27.04 27.04 Global Days 090		
32160	with cardiac massage	C 80	
	20.22 20.22 Global Days 090		

32200-32320 Open Procedures: Lung

32200	Pneumonostomy; with open drainage of abscess or cyst	C 80 P0	
	75989		
	29.64 29.64 Global Days 090		
32201	with percutaneous drainage of abscess or cyst	T	
	75989		
	5.73 24.27 Global Days 000		
32215	Pleural scarification for repeat pneumothorax	C 80 P0	
	21.32 21.32 Global Days 090		
32220	Decortication, pulmonary (separate procedure); total	C 80 P0	
	42.67 42.67 Global Days 090		
32225	partial	C 80 P0	
	26.49 26.49 Global Days 090		
32310	Pleurectomy, parietal (separate procedure)	C 80 P0	
	24.47 24.47 Global Days 090		
32320	Decortication and parietal pleurectomy	C 80 P0	
	42.73 42.73 Global Days 090		

32400-32405 Lung Biopsy

EXCLUDES *fine needle aspiration biopsy (10021, 10022)*

32400 Biopsy, pleura; percutaneous needle A2 T ▭

     ⌧ *76942, 77002, 77012, 77021*

     ⬙ *88172-88173*

     🔗 2.46   ⚒ 4.03   Global Days 000

32402 open C 80 ▭ P0

     🔗 14.98   ⚒ 14.98   Global Days 090

32405 Biopsy, lung or mediastinum, percutaneous needle A2 T ▭

     ⌧ *76942, 77002, 77012, 77021*

     ⬙ *88172-88173*

     🔗 2.77   ⚒ 2.78   Global Days 000

     AMA: 2008, Jan, 10-25; 2007, Jan, 13-27; 2007, Jan, 13-27; 2007, January, 13-27

32420-32422 Needle Insertion: Chest

32420 Pneumocentesis, puncture of lung for aspiration A2 T ▭

     🔗 3.06   ⚒ 3.06   Global Days 000

32421 Thoracentesis, puncture of pleural cavity for aspiration, initial or subsequent A2 T 50

     EXCLUDES *total lung lavage (32997)*

     ⌧ *76942, 77002, 77012*

     🔗 2.12   ⚒ 4.19   Global Days 000

32422 Thoracentesis with insertion of tube, includes water seal (eg, for pneumothorax), when performed (separate procedure) G2 T 50

     Do not report with (19260, 19271-19272, 32503-32504)

     ⌧ *76942, 77002, 77012*

     🔗 3.40   ⚒ 5.29   Global Days 000

32440-32501 Lung Resection

Code also resection of chest wall tumor, as appropriate, (19260-19272)

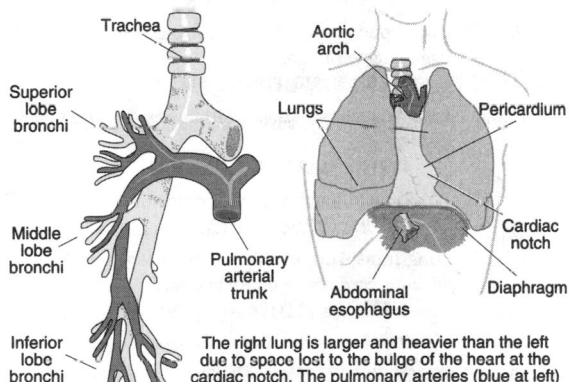

Trachea

Aortic arch

Superior lobe bronchi

Lungs

Pericardium

Middle lobe bronchi

Pulmonary arterial trunk

Cardiac notch

Abdominal esophagus

Diaphragm

Inferior lobe bronchi

The right lung is larger and heavier than the left due to space lost to the bulge of the heart at the cardiac notch. The pulmonary arteries (blue at left) deliver venous blood to the lungs where it is oxygenated and converted into arterial blood

32440 Removal of lung, total pneumonectomy; C 80 ▭ P0

     🔗 42.78   ⚒ 42.78   Global Days 090

32442 with resection of segment of trachea followed by broncho-tracheal anastomosis (sleeve pneumonectomy) C 80 ▭ P0

     🔗 78.41   ⚒ 78.41   Global Days 090

32445 extrapleural C 80 ▭ P0

     EXCLUDES *empyemectomy with extrapleural pneumonectomy (32540)*

     🔗 88.89   ⚒ 88.89   Global Days 090

32480 Removal of lung, other than total pneumonectomy; single lobe (lobectomy) C 80 ▭ P0

     EXCLUDES *lung removal with bronchoplasty (32501)*

     Code also (32320)

     🔗 40.38   ⚒ 40.38   Global Days 090

32482 2 lobes (bilobectomy) C 80 ▭ P0

     EXCLUDES *lung removal with bronchoplasty (32501)*

     Code also (32320)

     🔗 43.05   ⚒ 43.05   Global Days 090

     AMA: 2008, Jan, 10-25; 2007, Jan, 28-31; 2007, Jan, 28-31; 2007, January, 28-31

32484 single segment (segmentectomy) C 80 ▭ P0

     EXCLUDES *lung removal with bronchoplasty (32501)*

     Code also (32320)

     🔗 38.83   ⚒ 38.83   Global Days 090

32486 with circumferential resection of segment of bronchus followed by broncho-bronchial anastomosis (sleeve lobectomy) C 80 ▭ P0

     Code also (32320)

     🔗 61.47   ⚒ 61.47   Global Days 090

32488 all remaining lung following previous removal of a portion of lung (completion pneumonectomy) C 80 ▭ P0

     Code also (32320)

     🔗 62.37   ⚒ 62.37   Global Days 090

32491 excision-plication of emphysematous lung(s) (bullous or non-bullous) for lung volume reduction, sternal split or transthoracic approach, with or without any pleural procedure C 80 50 ▭ P0

     🔗 39.94   ⚒ 39.94   Global Days 090

32500 wedge resection, single or multiple C 80 ▭ PU

     🔗 39.00   ⚒ 39.00   Global Days 090

+ 32501 Resection and repair of portion of bronchus (bronchoplasty) when performed at time of lobectomy or segmentectomy (List separately in addition to code for primary procedure) C 80 PU

     Code first 32480-32484

     🔗 6.83   ⚒ 6.83   Global Days ZZZ

32503-32504 Excision of Lung Neoplasm

EXCLUDES *lung resection performed in conjunction with chest wall resection*

Do not report with (19260, 19271-19272, 32100, 32422, 32551)

32503 Resection of apical lung tumor (eg, Pancoast tumor), including chest wall resection, rib(s) resection(s), neurovascular dissection, when performed; without chest wall reconstruction(s) C 80

     🔗 49.32   ⚒ 49.32   Global Days 090

32504 with chest wall reconstruction C 80

     🔗 56.67   ⚒ 56.67   Global Days 090

32540 Removal of Empyema

32540 Extrapleural enucleation of empyema (empyemectomy) C 80 ▭ P0

     EXCLUDES *lung removal code when empyemectomy is performed with lobectomy (see appropriate lung removal code)*

     Code also appropriate removal of lung code when done with lobectomy (32480-32488)

     🔗 44.17   ⚒ 44.17   Global Days 090

32400 — 32540

● New Code   ▲ Revised Code   M Maternity Edit   A Age Edit   A-Y OPPS Status Indicator   🔗 Facility RVU   ⚒ Non-Facility RVU

▭ CCI Comprehensive Code   50 Bilateral Procedure   + Add-on Indicator   ⬙ Laboratory crosswalk   ⌧ Radiology crosswalk

Respiratory System

32550 — 32856

32550-32560 Chest Tube

⊙ **32550** Insertion of indwelling tunneled pleural catheter with cuff [62] [T]

Code also drainage catheter (C1729)

Do not report with (32421-32422)

▸◂ 75989

🔁 6.23 ✂ 20.73 Global Days 000

⊙ **32551** Tube thoracostomy, includes water seal (eg, for abscess, hemothorax, empyema), when performed (separate procedure) [T] [50]

Do not report with (19260, 19271-19272, 32503-32504)

▸◂ 75989

🔁 4.85 ✂ 4.85 Global Days 000

32560 Chemical pleurodesis (eg, for recurrent or persistent pneumothorax) [T]

🔁 3.07 ✂ 7.78 Global Days 000

32601-32820 Endoscopy of Chest, Repair, Reconstruction

CMS 100-3,100.2   *Endoscopy*
CMS 100-4,12,40.6   *Multiple procedures*
[INCLUDES]   diagnostic thoracoscopy in surgical thorascopy

32601 Thoracoscopy, diagnostic (separate procedure); lungs and pleural space, without biopsy [T] [80] 🔲 [PQ]

🔁 8.50 ✂ 8.50 Global Days 000

32602 lungs and pleural space, with biopsy [T] [80] 🔲 [PQ]

🔁 9.22 ✂ 9.22 Global Days 000

32603 pericardial sac, without biopsy [T] [80] 🔲 [PQ]

🔁 11.95 ✂ 11.95 Global Days 000

32604 pericardial sac, with biopsy [T] [80] 🔲 [PQ]

🔁 13.41 ✂ 13.41 Global Days 000

32605 mediastinal space, without biopsy [T] [80] 🔲 [PQ]

🔁 10.59 ✂ 10.59 Global Days 000

32606 mediastinal space, with biopsy [T] [80] 🔲 [PQ]

🔁 12.82 ✂ 12.82 Global Days 000

32650 Thoracoscopy, surgical; with pleurodesis (eg, mechanical or chemical) [C] [80] 🔲 [PQ]

🔁 18.16 ✂ 18.16 Global Days 090

32651 with partial pulmonary decortication [C] [80] 🔲 [PQ]

🔁 28.44 ✂ 28.44 Global Days 090

32652 with total pulmonary decortication, including intrapleural pneumonolysis [C] [80] 🔲 [PQ]

🔁 43.14 ✂ 43.14 Global Days 090

32653 with removal of intrapleural foreign body or fibrin deposit [C] [80] 🔲 [PQ]

🔁 27.59 ✂ 27.59 Global Days 090

32654 with control of traumatic hemorrhage [C] [80] 🔲 [PQ]

🔁 30.33 ✂ 30.33 Global Days 090

32655 with excision-plication of bullae, including any pleural procedure [C] [80] 🔲 [PQ]

🔁 25.25 ✂ 25.25 Global Days 090

AMA: 2008, Jan, 10-25; 2007, Jan, 13-27; 2007, Jan, 13-27; 2007, January, 13-27; 2005, Aug, 13-15; 2005, August, 13-15; 2005, Aug, 13-15

32656 with parietal pleurectomy [C] [80] 🔲 [PQ]

🔁 21.74 ✂ 21.74 Global Days 090

32657 with wedge resection of lung, single or multiple [C] [80] 🔲 [PQ]

🔁 21.49 ✂ 21.49 Global Days 090

32658 with removal of clot or foreign body from pericardial sac [C] [80] 🔲 [PQ]

🔁 19.60 ✂ 19.60 Global Days 090

32659 with creation of pericardial window or partial resection of pericardial sac for drainage [C] [80] 🔲 [PQ]

🔁 19.88 ✂ 19.88 Global Days 090

32660 with total pericardiectomy [C] [80] 🔲 [PQ]

🔁 27.98 ✂ 27.98 Global Days 090

32661 with excision of pericardial cyst, tumor, or mass [C] [80] 🔲 [PQ]

🔁 21.90 ✂ 21.90 Global Days 090

32662 with excision of mediastinal cyst, tumor, or mass [C] [80] 🔲 [PQ]

🔁 24.52 ✂ 24.52 Global Days 090

AMA: 2007, Dec, 10-179

32663 with lobectomy, total or segmental [C] [80] 🔲 [PQ]

🔁 37.52 ✂ 37.52 Global Days 090

32664 with thoracic sympathectomy [C] [80] [50] 🔲 [PQ]

🔁 23.38 ✂ 23.38 Global Days 090

AMA: 2008, Jan, 10-25; 2007, Jan, 13-27; 2007, Jan, 13-27; 2007, January, 13-27

32665 with esophagomyotomy (Heller type) [C] [80] 🔲 [PQ]

🔁 32.41 ✂ 32.41 Global Days 090

32800 Repair lung hernia through chest wall [C] [80] 🔲 [PQ]

🔁 24.96 ✂ 24.96 Global Days 090

32810 Closure of chest wall following open flap drainage for empyema (Clagett type procedure) [C] [80] 🔲 [PQ]

🔁 24.16 ✂ 24.16 Global Days 090

32815 Open closure of major bronchial fistula [C] [80] 🔲 [PQ]

🔁 70.59 ✂ 70.59 Global Days 090

32820 Major reconstruction, chest wall (posttraumatic) [C] [80] 🔲

🔁 35.87 ✂ 35.87 Global Days 090

32850-32856 Lung Transplant Procedures

[INCLUDES]   harvesting donor lung(s), cold preservation, preparation of donor lung(s), transplantation into recipient

[EXCLUDES]   *repairs or resection of donor lung(s) (32491, 32500, 35216, 35276)*

32850 Donor pneumonectomy(s) (including cold preservation), from cadaver donor [C] 🔲

🔁 0.00 ✂ 0.00 Global Days XXX

32851 Lung transplant, single; without cardiopulmonary bypass [C] [80] 🔲

🔁 69.64 ✂ 69.64 Global Days 090

32852 with cardiopulmonary bypass [C] [80] 🔲

🔁 77.05 ✂ 77.05 Global Days 090

32853 Lung transplant, double (bilateral sequential or en bloc); without cardiopulmonary bypass [C] [80] 🔲

🔁 83.33 ✂ 83.33 Global Days 090

32854 with cardiopulmonary bypass [C] [80] 🔲

🔁 90.60 ✂ 90.60 Global Days 090

32855 Backbench standard preparation of cadaver donor lung allograft prior to transplantation, including dissection of allograft from surrounding soft tissues to prepare pulmonary venous/atrial cuff, pulmonary artery, and bronchus; unilateral [C] [80] 🔲

🔁 0.00 ✂ 0.00 Global Days XXX

32856 bilateral [C] [80] 🔲

🔁 0.00 ✂ 0.00 Global Days XXX

[26]/[TC] Professional/Technical Component Only   [80]/[80] Assist-at-Surgery Allowed/With Documentation   Unlisted   Not Covered

AMA: CPT Assistant References   [A2]-[Z3] ASC Payment Indicator   ♂ Male Only   ♀ Female Only   ⊘ Modifier 51 Exempt   [PQ] PQRI

118   CPT only © 2008 American Medical Association. All Rights Reserved. (Black Ink)   Medicare (Red Ink)   © 2008 Ingenix (Blue Ink)

32900-32997 Chest and Respiratory Procedures

CMS 100-4,12,40.6   *Multiple procedures*

32900   **Resection of ribs, extrapleural, all stages**   C 80 ▭ PQ
　　　　🖩 36.70   ⚖ 36.70   Global Days 090

32905   **Thoracoplasty, Schede type or extrapleural (all stages);**   C 80 ▭ PQ
　　　　🖩 36.29   ⚖ 36.29   Global Days 090

32906   **with closure of bronchopleural fistula**   C 80 ▭ PQ
　　　　EXCLUDES   *open closure of bronchial fistula (32815)*
　　　　　　　　resection first rib for thoracic compression (21615, 21616)
　　　　🖩 45.08   ⚖ 45.08   Global Days 090

32940   **Pneumonolysis, extraperiosteal, including filling or packing procedures**   C 80 ▭ PQ
　　　　🖩 33.25   ⚖ 33.25   Global Days 090

32960   **Pneumothorax, therapeutic, intrapleural injection of air**   62 T ▭
　　　　🖩 2.72   ⚖ 3.70   Global Days 000

32997   **Total lung lavage (unilateral)**   C ▭
　　　　EXCLUDES   *broncho-alveolar lavage by bronchoscopy (31624)*
　　　　🖩 9.72   ⚖ 9.72   Global Days 000

32998-32999 Destruction of Lung Neoplasm

32998   **Ablation therapy for reduction or eradication of 1 or more pulmonary tumor(s) including pleura or chest wall when involved by tumor extension, percutaneous, radiofrequency, unilateral**   62 T 80
　　　　▧ *76940, 77013, 77022*
　　　　🖩 8.39   ⚖ 74.25   Global Days 000

32999   **Unlisted procedure, lungs and pleura**   T
　　　　🖩 0.00   ⚖ 0.00   Global Days YYY
　　　　AMA: 2008, Jan, 10-25; 2008, Jul, 10&13; 2007, Jan, 13-27; 2007, Jan, 13-27; 2007, January, 13-27

Cardiovascular System

33010 — 33211

33010-33050 Procedures of the Pericardial Sac

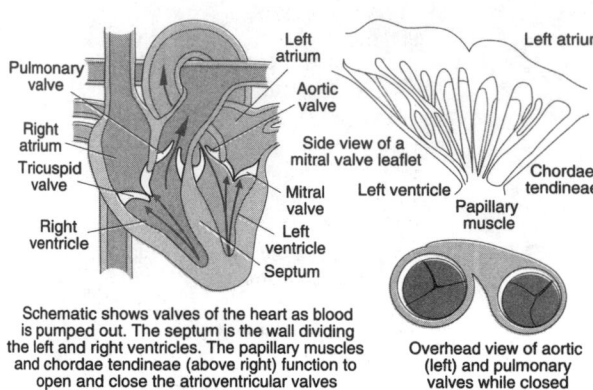

Schematic shows valves of the heart as blood is pumped out. The septum is the wall dividing the left and right ventricles. The papillary muscles and chordae tendineae (above right) function to open and close the atrioventricular valves

Overhead view of aortic (left) and pulmonary valves while closed

⊙ **33010** **Pericardiocentesis; initial**   A2 T ▫
 ⊠ 76930
 🔗 3.38   ⚕ 3.38   Global Days 000

⊙ **33011** **subsequent**   A2 T 80 ▫
 ⊠ 76930
 🔗 3.31   ⚕ 3.31   Global Days 000

33015 **Tube pericardiostomy**   C ▫
 🔗 14.38   ⚕ 14.38   Global Days 090

33020 **Pericardiotomy for removal of clot or foreign body (primary procedure)**   C 80 ▫ PQ
 🔗 23.46   ⚕ 23.46   Global Days 090

33025 **Creation of pericardial window or partial resection for drainage**   C 80 ▫ PQ
 🔗 21.71   ⚕ 21.71   Global Days 090

33030 **Pericardiectomy, subtotal or complete; without cardiopulmonary bypass**   C 80 ▫ PQ
 INCLUDES   Delorme pericardiectomy
 🔗 34.72   ⚕ 34.72   Global Days 090

33031 **with cardiopulmonary bypass**   C 80 ▫ PQ
 🔗 38.75   ⚕ 38.75   Global Days 090

33050 **Excision of pericardial cyst or tumor**   C 80 ▫ PQ
 🔗 26.83   ⚕ 26.83   Global Days 090

33120-33130 Neoplasms of Heart

33120 **Excision of intracardiac tumor, resection with cardiopulmonary bypass**   C 80 ▫ PQ
 🔗 42.47   ⚕ 42.47   Global Days 090
 AMA: 2007, Mar, 1-3; 2007, Mar, 1-3; 2007, March, 1-3

33130 **Resection of external cardiac tumor**   C 80 ▫ PQ
 🔗 37.32   ⚕ 37.32   Global Days 090
 AMA: 2007, Mar, 1-3; 2007, Mar, 1-3; 2007, March, 1-3

33140-33141 Transmyocardial Revascularization

CMS *100-3,20.6*   *Transmyocardial Revascularization (TMR) for Severe Angina*

33140 **Transmyocardial laser revascularization, by thoracotomy; (separate procedure)**   C 80 ▫ PQ
 🔗 42.38   ⚕ 42.38   Global Days 090
 AMA: 2008, Jan, 10-25; 2007, Jan, 13-27; 2007, Jan, 13-27; 2007, January, 13-27

+ **33141** **performed at the time of other open cardiac procedure(s) (List separately in addition to code for primary procedure)**   C 80 PQ
 Code first 33400-33496, 33510-33536, 33542
 🔗 4.26   ⚕ 4.26   Global Days ZZZ

33202-33249 Pacemakers/Implantable Defibrillators

CMS *100-3,20.4*   *Implantable Automatic Defibrillators*
CMS *100-3,20.8.2*   *Self-contained Pacemaker Monitors*
CMS *100-3,20.8.1.1*   *Transtelephonic Monitoring of Cardiac Pacemakers*
CMS *100-3,20.8.1*   *Cardiac Pacemaker Evaluation Services*
CMS *100-3,20.8*   *Cardiac Pacemakers*
EXCLUDES   *electronic analysis of internal pacemaker (93279-93280, 93288, 93293-93294)*

33202 **Insertion of epicardial electrode(s); open incision (eg, thoracotomy, median sternotomy, subxiphoid approach)**   C PQ
 ⊠ 71090
 Code also insertion of pulse generator by same physician/same surgical session (33212-33213)
 🔗 21.17   ⚕ 21.17   Global Days 090

33203 **endoscopic approach (eg, thoracoscopy, pericardioscopy)**   C PQ
 ⊠ 71090
 Code also insertion of pulse generator by same physician/same surgical session (33212-33213)
 🔗 22.18   ⚕ 22.18   Global Days 090

⊙ **33206** **Insertion or replacement of permanent pacemaker with transvenous electrode(s); atrial**   J8 T ▫ PQ
 ⊠ 71090
 INCLUDES   pulse generator insertion/electrode placement
 Code also (C1779, C1785, C1786, C1898, C2619, C2620, C2621)
 🔗 12.80   ⚕ 12.80   Global Days 090
 AMA: 2008, Jun, 14-15

⊙ **33207** **ventricular**   J8 T ▫ PQ
 INCLUDES   pulse generator insertion/electrode placement
 Code also (C1779, C1785, C1786, C1898, C2619, C2620, C2621)
 ⊠ 71090
 🔗 13.71   ⚕ 13.71   Global Days 090
 AMA: 2008, Jun, 14-15

⊙ **33208** **atrial and ventricular**   J8 T ▫ PQ
 INCLUDES   pulse generator insertion/electrode placement
 Code also (C1779, C1785, C1898, C2619, C2621)
 ⊠ 71090
 🔗 14.75   ⚕ 14.75   Global Days 090
 AMA: 2008, Jan, 10-25; 2008, Jun, 14-15; 2007, Jan, 13-27; 2007, Jan, 13-27; 2007, January, 13-27

⊙ **33210** **Insertion or replacement of temporary transvenous single chamber cardiac electrode or pacemaker catheter (separate procedure)**   62 T ▫
 ⊠ 71090
 🔗 5.06   ⚕ 5.06   Global Days 000
 AMA: 2007, Mar, 1-3; 2007, Mar, 1-3; 2007, March, 1-3

⊙ **33211** **Insertion or replacement of temporary transvenous dual chamber pacing electrodes (separate procedure)**   62 T ▫
 Code also (C1779, C1898)
 ⊠ 71090
 🔗 5.09   ⚕ 5.09   Global Days 000
 AMA: 2007, Mar, 1-3; 2007, Mar, 1-3; 2007, March, 1-3

⊙ 33212 **Insertion or replacement of pacemaker pulse generator only; single chamber, atrial or ventricular** H8 T 🖵 P0
Code also placement of epicardial leads by same physician/same surgical session (33202-33203)
Code also (C1786, C2620, C2621)
🔀 *71090*
🔢 9.58 ⚲ 9.58 Global Days 090
AMA: 2008, Jan, 10-25; 2008, Jun, 14-15; 2007, Jan, 13-27; 2007, Jan, 13-27; 2007, January, 13-27; 2004, May, 15; 2004, May, 15; 2004, May, 15

⊙ 33213 **dual chamber** H8 T 🖵 P0
Code also placement of epicardial leads by same physician/same surgical session (33202-33203)
Code also (C1785, C2619, C2621)
🔀 *71090*
🔢 10.92 ⚲ 10.92 Global Days 090
AMA: 2008, Jan, 10-25; 2008, Jun, 14-15; 2007, Jan, 13-27; 2007, Jan, 13-27; 2007, January, 13-27

⊙ 33214 **Upgrade of implanted pacemaker system, conversion of single chamber system to dual chamber system (includes removal of previously placed pulse generator, testing of existing lead, insertion of new lead, insertion of new pulse generator)** J8 T 00 🖵 P0
Code also placement of epicardial leads by same physician/same surgical session when appropriate (33202-33203)
Code also (C1779, C1785, C1898, C2619, C2621)
Do not report with (33216-33217)
🔀 *71090*
🔢 13.55 ⚲ 13.55 Global Days 090
AMA: 2008, Jun, 14-15

33215 **Repositioning of previously implanted transvenous pacemaker or pacing cardioverter-defibrillator (right atrial or right ventricular) electrode** G2 T 🖵 P0
🔀 *71090*
🔢 8.66 ⚲ 8.66 Global Days 090

⊙ 33216 **Insertion of a transvenous electrode; single chamber (1 electrode) permanent pacemaker or single chamber pacing cardioverter-defibrillator** G2 T 🖵 P0
Code also (C1777, C1779, C1895, C1896, C1898, C1899)
Do not report with (33214)
🔀 *71090*
🔢 10.64 ⚲ 10.64 Global Days 090
AMA: 2008, Jan, 10-25; 2007, Jan, 13-27; 2007, Jan, 13-27; 2007, January, 13-27

⊙ 33217 **dual chamber (2 electrodes) permanent pacemaker or dual chamber pacing cardioverter-defibrillator** G2 T 🖵 P0
Code also (C1777, C1779, C1895, C1896, C1898, C1899)
Do not report with (33214)
🔀 *71090*
🔢 10.56 ⚲ 10.56 Global Days 090
AMA: 2008, Jan, 10-25; 2007, Jan, 13-27; 2007, Jan, 13-27; 2007, January, 13-27

⊙ 33218 **Repair of single transvenous electrode for a single chamber, permanent pacemaker or single chamber pacing cardioverter-defibrillator** G2 T 🖵 P0
Code also insertion of pulse generator replacement when appropriate (33212, or 33213)
🔀 *71090*
🔢 11.00 ⚲ 11.00 Global Days 090
AMA: 2008, Jan, 10-25; 2007, Jan, 13-27; 2007, Jan, 13-27; 2007, January, 13-27; 2005, Jan, 46-47; 2005, January, 46-47; 2005, Jan, 46-47

⊙ 33220 **Repair of 2 transvenous electrodes for a dual chamber permanent pacemaker or dual chamber pacing cardioverter-defibrillator** G2 T 🖵 P0
Code also pulse generator replacement when appropriate (33212, or 33213)
🔀 *71090*
🔢 11.10 ⚲ 11.10 Global Days 090
AMA: 2008, Jun, 14-15

⊙ 33222 **Revision or relocation of skin pocket for pacemaker** A2 T 🖵 P0
🔀 *71090*
🔢 9.72 ⚲ 9.72 Global Days 090
AMA: 2008, Jun, 14-15

⊙ 33223 **Revision of skin pocket for single or dual chamber pacing cardioverter-defibrillator** A2 T 80 🖵 P0
🔀 *71090*
🔢 11.74 ⚲ 11.74 Global Days 090
AMA: 2008, Jun, 14-15

33224 **Insertion of pacing electrode, cardiac venous system, for left ventricular pacing, with attachment to previously placed pacemaker or pacing cardioverter-defibrillator pulse generator (including revision of pocket, removal, insertion, and/or replacement of generator)** J8 T 🖵 P0
Code also placement of epicardial electrode when appropriate (33202-33203)
Code also (C1900)
🔀 *71090*
🔢 14.31 ⚲ 14.31 Global Days 000
AMA: 2007, Dec, 10-179

+ 33225 **Insertion of pacing electrode, cardiac venous system, for left ventricular pacing, at time of insertion of pacing cardioverter-defibrillator or pacemaker pulse generator (including upgrade to dual chamber system) (List separately in addition to code for primary procedure)** J8 T 🖵 P0
Code also 33206-33208, 33212-33214, 33216-33217, 33222, 33233-33235, 33240, 33249 (33206-33208, 33212-33214, 33216-33217, 33222, 33233-33235, 33240, 33249, C1900)
🔀 *71090*
🔢 12.89 ⚲ 12.89 Global Days ZZZ
AMA: 2007, Dec, 10-179

33226 **Repositioning of previously implanted cardiac venous system (left ventricular) electrode (including removal, insertion and/or replacement of generator)** G2 T 🖵 P0
🔀 *71090*
🔢 13.85 ⚲ 13.85 Global Days 000

⊙ 33233 **Removal of permanent pacemaker pulse generator** A2 T 🖵 P0
🔀 *71090*
🔢 6.78 ⚲ 6.78 Global Days 090
AMA: 2008, Jan, 10-25; 2007, Jan, 13-27; 2007, Jan, 13-27; 2007, January, 13-27; 2004, May, 15; 2004, May, 15; 2004, May, 15

⊙ 33234 **Removal of transvenous pacemaker electrode(s); single lead system, atrial or ventricular** G2 T 🖵 P0
🔀 *71090*
🔢 13.75 ⚲ 13.75 Global Days 090

⊙ 33235 **dual lead system** G2 T 🖵 P0
🔀 *71090*
🔢 17.78 ⚲ 17.78 Global Days 090

● New Code ▲ Revised Code Ⓜ Maternity Edit 🅰 Age Edit 🅰-🆅 OPPS Status Indicator 🔢 Facility RVU ⚲ Non-Facility RVU
🖵 CCI Comprehensive Code 50 Bilateral Procedure + Add-on Indicator 🅽 Laboratory crosswalk 🔀 Radiology crosswalk

33236 Removal of permanent epicardial pacemaker and electrodes by thoracotomy; single lead system, atrial or ventricular ☐ 26 80 ☐ P0

EXCLUDES *removal of pacing cardioverter-defibrillator electrode(s) by thoracotomy (33243) removal of transvenous pacemaker electrodes, single or dual lead system (33234, 33235)*

⬛ 71090

📋 21.24 ✂ 21.24 Global Days 090

33237 dual lead system ☐ 26 80 ☐ P0

EXCLUDES *removal of pacing cardioverter-defibrillator electrode(s) by thoracotomy (33243) removal of transvenous pacemaker electrodes, single or dual lead system (33234, 33235)*

⬛ 71090

📋 23.38 ✂ 23.38 Global Days 090

33238 Removal of permanent transvenous electrode(s) by thoracotomy ☐ 26 80 ☐ P0

EXCLUDES *removal of pacing cardioverter-defibrillator electrode(s) by thoracotomy (33243) removal of transvenous pacemaker electrodes, single or dual lead system (33234, 33235)*

⬛ 71090

📋 25.32 ✂ 25.32 Global Days 090

⊙ **33240** Insertion of single or dual chamber pacing cardioverter-defibrillator pulse generator J8 T ☐ P0

Code also cardioverter-defibrillator (C1721-C1722, C1882)

⬛ 71090

Code also placement of epicardial leads by same physican/same surgical session (33202-33203)

📋 13.10 ✂ 13.10 Global Days 090

AMA: 2008, Jan, 10-25; 2008, Jun, 14-15; 2007, Jan, 13-27; 2007, Jan, 13-27; 2007, January, 13-27; 2004, Apr, 6; 2004, April, 6; 2004, Apr, 6

⊙ **33241** Subcutaneous removal of single or dual chamber pacing cardioverter-defibrillator pulse generator 62 T 80 ☐ P0

⬛ 71090

EXCLUDES *repair cardioverter-defibrillator generator and/or leads (33218, 33220)*

Code also removal with reinsertion of pacing cardioverter-defibrillator system; report with (33243, or 33244, 33249)

Code also electrode removal if applicable (33243-33244)

📋 6.40 ✂ 6.40 Global Days 090

AMA: 2004, May, 15; 2004, May, 15; 2004, May, 15

33243 Removal of single or dual chamber pacing cardioverter-defibrillator electrode(s); by thoracotomy ☐ 80 ☐ P0

Code also subcutaneous removal pulse generator (33241)

⬛ 71090

📋 36.94 ✂ 36.94 Global Days 090

⊙ **33244** by transvenous extraction T ☐ P0

⬛ 71090

Code also subcutaneous removal pulse generator (33241)

📋 24.16 ✂ 24.16 Global Days 090

⊙ **33249** Insertion or repositioning of electrode lead(s) for single or dual chamber pacing cardioverter-defibrillator and insertion of pulse generator J8 T ☐ P0

EXCLUDES *ICD lead insertion without thoracotomy (33216)*

Code also cardio-defibrillator (C1721-C1722, C1882)

Code also removal/reinsertion pacing cardioverter-defibrillator system; report (33241, 33243, or 33244, 33249)

⬛ 71090

📋 25.47 ✂ 25.47 Global Days 090

AMA: 2008, May, 9-11; 2008, Jun, 14-15; 2004, Apr, 6; 2004, Apr, 6; 2004, April, 6

33250-33251 Surgical Ablation Arrhythmogenic Foci, Supraventricular

INCLUDES procedures using cryotherapy, laser, microwave, radiofrequency, and ultrasound

33250 Operative ablation of supraventricular arrhythmogenic focus or pathway (eg, Wolff-Parkinson-White, atrioventricular node re-entry), tract(s) and/or focus (foci); without cardiopulmonary bypass ☐ 80 ☐ P0

EXCLUDES *pacing and mapping during surgery by other provider (93631)*

📋 39.86 ✂ 39.86 Global Days 090

33251 with cardiopulmonary bypass ☐ 80 ☐ P0

📋 44.19 ✂ 44.19 Global Days 090

33254-33256 Surgical Ablation Arrhythmogenic Foci, Atrial (e.g., Maze)

INCLUDES excision or isolation of the left atrial appendage procedures using cryotherapy, laser, microwave, radiofrequency, and ultrasound

Do not report with (32100, 32551, 33120, 33130, 33210-33211, 33400-33507, 33510-33523, 33533-33548, 33600-33853, 33860-33864, 33910-33920)

33254 Operative tissue ablation and reconstruction of atria, limited (eg, modified maze procedure) ☐ 80 P0

📋 37.31 ✂ 37.31 Global Days 090

AMA: 2007, Mar, 1-3; 2007, Mar, 1-3; 2007, March, 1-3

33255 Operative tissue ablation and reconstruction of atria, extensive (eg, maze procedure); without cardiopulmonary bypass ☐ 80 P0

📋 45.59 ✂ 45.59 Global Days 090

AMA: 2007, Mar, 1-3; 2007, Mar, 1-3; 2007, March, 1-3

33256 with cardiopulmonary bypass ☐ 80 P0

📋 54.45 ✂ 54.45 Global Days 090

AMA: 2007, Mar, 1-3; 2007, Mar, 1-3; 2007, March, 1-3

33257-33259 Surgical Ablation Arrhythmogenic Foci, Atrial, with Other Heart Procedure(s)

Do not report with (32551, 33210-33211, 33254-33256, 33265-33266)

+ **33257** Operative tissue ablation and reconstruction of atria, performed at the time of other cardiac procedure(s), limited (eg, modified maze procedure) (List separately in addition to code for primary procedure) ☐ 80

Code first (33120-33130, 33250-33251, 33261, 33300-33335, 33400-33496, 33500-33507, 33510-33516, 33533-33548, 33600-33619, 33641-33697, 33702-33732, 33735-33767, 33770-33814, 33840-33877, 33910-33922, 33925-33926, 33935, 33945, 33975-33980)

📋 15.57 ✂ 15.57 Global Days ZZZ

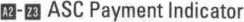

+ 33258 Operative tissue ablation and reconstruction of atria, performed at the time of other cardiac procedure(s), extensive (eg, maze procedure), without cardiopulmonary bypass (List separately in addition to code for primary procedure) [C] [80]

Code first (33130, 33250, 33300, 33310, 33320-33321, 33330, 33332, 33401, 33414-33417, 33420, 33470-33472, 33501-33503, 33510-33516, 33533-33536, 33690, 33735, 33737, 33800-33813, 33840-33852, 33915, 33925)

⚕ 17.61 ⚕ 17.61 Global Days ZZZ

+ 33259 Operative tissue ablation and reconstruction of atria, performed at the time of other cardiac procedure(s), extensive (eg, maze procedure), with cardiopulmonary bypass (List separately in addition to code for primary procedure) [C] [80]

Code first (33120, 33251, 33261, 33305, 33315, 33322, 33335, 33400, 33403-33413, 33422-33468, 33474-33478, 33496, 33500, 33504-33507, 33510-33516, 33533-33548, 33600-33688, 33692-33722, 33730, 33732, 33736, 33750-33767, 33770-33781, 33786-33788, 33814, 33853, 33860-33877, 33910, 33916-33922, 33926, 33935, 33945, 33975-33980)

⚕ 23.10 ⚕ 23.10 Global Days ZZZ

33261 Surgical Ablation Arrhythmogenic Foci, Ventricular

33261 Operative ablation of ventricular arrhythmogenic focus with cardiopulmonary bypass [C] [80] [◻] [P0]

⚕ 43.93 ⚕ 43.93 Global Days 090

33265-33266 Surgical Ablation Arrhythmogenic Foci, Endoscopic

Do not report with (32551, 33210-33211)

33265 Endoscopy, surgical; operative tissue ablation and reconstruction of atria, limited (eg, modified maze procedure), without cardiopulmonary bypass [C] [80]

⚕ 37.23 ⚕ 37.23 Global Days 090

AMA: 2007, Mar, 1-3; 2007, Mar, 1-3; 2007, March, 1-3

33266 operative tissue ablation and reconstruction of atria, extensive (eg, maze procedure), without cardiopulmonary bypass [C] [80]

⚕ 51.15 ⚕ 51.15 Global Days 090

AMA: 2007, Mar, 1-3; 2007, Mar, 1-3; 2007, March, 1-3

33282-33284 Implantable Loop Recorder

CMS 100-3,20.15 *Electrocardiographic Services*

33282 Implantation of patient-activated cardiac event recorder [J8] [S] [◻]

INCLUDES   initial programming of device

EXCLUDES   *subsequent electronic analysis and/or reprogramming of device (93285, 93291, 93298)*

Code also (C1764)

⚕ 9.08 ⚕ 9.08 Global Days 090

AMA: 2008, Jun, 14-15

33284 Removal of an implantable, patient-activated cardiac event recorder [62] [T] [◻]

⚕ 6.54 ⚕ 6.54 Global Days 090

33300-33315 Procedures for Injury of the Heart

33300 Repair of cardiac wound; without bypass [C] [80] [◻] [P0]

⚕ 62.14 ⚕ 62.14 Global Days 090

33305 with cardiopulmonary bypass [C] [80] [◻] [P0]

⚕ 103.23 ⚕ 103.23 Global Days 090

33310 Cardiotomy, exploratory (includes removal of foreign body, atrial or ventricular thrombus); without bypass [C] [80] [◻] [P0]

Do not report with other cardiac procedures unless separate incision into heart is necessary in order to remove thrombus

⚕ 31.81 ⚕ 31.81 Global Days 090

33315 with cardiopulmonary bypass [C] [80] [◻] [P0]

Code also excision of thrombus with cardiopulmonary bypass as appropriate if separate incision is required (33120, 33130, 33420-33430, 33460-33468, 33496, 33542, 33545, 33641-33647, 33670, 33681, 33975-33980)

Do not report with other cardiac procedures unless separate incision into heart is necessary in order to remove thrombus; in this case, append modifier 59

⚕ 40.44 ⚕ 40.44 Global Days 090

33320-33335 Procedures for Injury of the Aorta/Great Vessels

33320 Suture repair of aorta or great vessels; without shunt or cardiopulmonary bypass [C] [80] [◻] [P0]

⚕ 28.75 ⚕ 28.75 Global Days 090

33321 with shunt bypass [C] [80] [◻] [P0]

⚕ 32.61 ⚕ 32.61 Global Days 090

33322 with cardiopulmonary bypass [C] [80] [◻] [P0]

⚕ 37.69 ⚕ 37.69 Global Days 090

33330 Insertion of graft, aorta or great vessels; without shunt, or cardiopulmonary bypass [C] [80] [◻]

⚕ 38.01 ⚕ 38.01 Global Days 090

33332 with shunt bypass [C] [80] [◻] [P0]

⚕ 38.05 ⚕ 38.05 Global Days 090

33335 with cardiopulmonary bypass [C] [00] [◻] [P0]

⚕ 51.44 ⚕ 51.44 Global Days 090

33400-33415 Aortic Valve Procedures

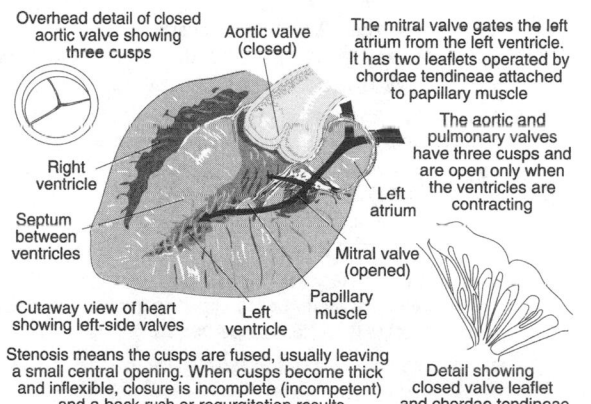

Overhead detail of closed aortic valve showing three cusps

Aortic valve (closed)

The mitral valve gates the left atrium from the left ventricle. It has two leaflets operated by chordae tendineae attached to papillary muscle

The aortic and pulmonary valves have three cusps and are open only when the ventricles are contracting

Right ventricle

Septum between ventricles

Left atrium

Mitral valve (opened)

Papillary muscle

Cutaway view of heart showing left-side valves

Left ventricle

Detail showing closed valve leaflet and chordae tendineae

Stenosis means the cusps are fused, usually leaving a small central opening. When cusps become thick and inflexible, closure is incomplete (incompetent) and a back-rush or regurgitation results

33400 Valvuloplasty, aortic valve; open, with cardiopulmonary bypass [C] [80] [◻] [P0]

⚕ 61.62 ⚕ 61.62 Global Days 090

AMA: 2007, Mar, 1-3; 2007, Mar, 1-3; 2007, March, 1-3; 2005, Feb, 13-16; 2005, February, 13-16; 2005, Feb, 13-16

33258 — 33400

Cardiovascular System

33401 — 33464

33401   open, with inflow occlusion   C 80 ⊛ ▭ P0
▱ 41.06   ⚬ 41.06   **Global Days 090**
AMA: 2007, Mar, 1-3; 2007, Mar, 1-3; 2007, March, 1-3; 2005, Feb, 13-16; 2005, February, 13-16; 2005, Feb, 13-16

33403   using transventricular dilation, with cardiopulmonary bypass   C 80 ⊛ ▭ P0
▱ 41.24   ⚬ 41.24   **Global Days 090**
AMA: 2007, Mar, 1-3; 2007, Mar, 1-3; 2007, March, 1-3; 2005, Feb, 13-16; 2005, February, 13-16; 2005, Feb, 13-16

33404   Construction of apical-aortic conduit   C 80 ▭ P0
▱ 48.89   ⚬ 48.89   **Global Days 090**
AMA: 2008, Jan, 10-25; 2007, Jan, 13-27; 2007, Jan, 13-27; 2007, Mar, 1-3; 2007, March, 1-3; 2007, January, 13-27; 2007, Mar, 1-3; 2005, Feb, 13-16; 2005, February, 13-16; 2005, Feb, 13-16; 2004, Jan, 28; 2004, January, 28; 2004, Jan, 28

33405   Replacement, aortic valve, with cardiopulmonary bypass; with prosthetic valve other than homograft or stentless valve   C 80 ▭ P0
    EXCLUDES   *valvotomy of aortic valve:*
       with cardiopulmonary bypass (33403)
       with inflow occlusion (33401)
▱ 63.27   ⚬ 63.27   **Global Days 090**
AMA: 2007, Mar, 1-3; 2007, Mar, 1-3; 2007, March, 1-3; 2005, Feb, 13-16; 2005, February, 13-16; 2005, Feb, 13-16

33406   with allograft valve (freehand)   C 80 ▭ P0
    EXCLUDES   *valvotomy of aortic valve:*
       with cardiopulmonary bypass (33403)
       with inflow occlusion (33401)
▱ 77.68   ⚬ 77.68   **Global Days 090**
AMA: 2007, Mar, 1-3; 2007, Mar, 1-3; 2007, March, 1-3; 2005, Feb, 13-16; 2005, February, 13-16; 2005, Feb, 13-16

33410   with stentless tissue valve   C 80 ▭ P0
▱ 68.51   ⚬ 68.51   **Global Days 090**
AMA: 2007, Mar, 1-3; 2007, Mar, 1-3; 2007, March, 1-3; 2005, Feb, 13-16; 2005, February, 13-16; 2005, Feb, 13-16

33411   Replacement, aortic valve; with aortic annulus enlargement, noncoronary cusp   C 80 ▭ P0
▱ 89.23   ⚬ 89.23   **Global Days 090**
AMA: 2007, Mar, 1-3; 2007, Mar, 1-3; 2007, March, 1-3; 2005, Feb, 13-16; 2005, February, 13-16; 2005, Feb, 13-16

33412   with transventricular aortic annulus enlargement (Konno procedure)   C 80 ▭
▱ 68.51   ⚬ 68.51   **Global Days 090**
AMA: 2007, Mar, 1-3; 2007, Mar, 1-3; 2007, March, 1-3; 2005, Feb, 13-16; 2005, February, 13-16; 2005, Feb, 13-16

33413   by translocation of autologous pulmonary valve with allograft replacement of pulmonary valve (Ross procedure)   C 80 ▭ P0
▱ 88.35   ⚬ 88.35   **Global Days 090**
AMA: 2007, Mar, 1-3; 2007, Mar, 1-3; 2007, March, 1-3; 2005, Feb, 13-16; 2005, February, 13-16; 2005, Feb, 13-16

33414   Repair of left ventricular outflow tract obstruction by patch enlargement of the outflow tract   C 80 ▭
▱ 59.13   ⚬ 59.13   **Global Days 090**
AMA: 2007, Mar, 1-3; 2007, Mar, 1-3; 2007, March, 1-3; 2005, Feb, 13-16; 2005, February, 13-16; 2005, Feb, 13-16

33415   Resection or incision of subvalvular tissue for discrete subvalvular aortic stenosis   C 80 ▭
▱ 54.76   ⚬ 54.76   **Global Days 090**
AMA: 2007, Mar, 1-3; 2007, Mar, 1-3; 2007, March, 1-3; 2005, Feb, 13-16; 2005, February, 13-16; 2005, Feb, 13-16

33416 Ventriculectomy

CMS *100-3,20.26*   *Partial Ventriculectomy*

33416   Ventriculomyotomy (-myectomy) for idiopathic hypertrophic subaortic stenosis (eg, asymmetric septal hypertrophy)   C 80 ▭ P0
▱ 55.16   ⚬ 55.16   **Global Days 090**
AMA: 2007, Mar, 1-3; 2007, Mar, 1-3; 2007, March, 1-3; 2005, Feb, 13-16; 2005, February, 13-16; 2005, Feb, 13-16

33417 Repair of Supravalvular Stenosis by Aortoplasty

33417   Aortoplasty (gusset) for supravalvular stenosis   C 80 ▭
▱ 46.11   ⚬ 46.11   **Global Days 090**
AMA: 2007, Mar, 1-3; 2007, Mar, 1-3; 2007, March, 1-3; 2005, Feb, 13-16; 2005, February, 13-16; 2005, Feb, 13-16

33420-33468 Mitral and Tricuspid Valve Procedures

INCLUDES   procedures on mitral and tricuspid valves

Code also removal of thrombus through a separate heart incision if applicable (33310, 33315)

33420   Valvotomy, mitral valve; closed heart   C ▭
▱ 36.89   ⚬ 36.89   **Global Days 090**
AMA: 2007, Mar, 1-3; 2007, Mar, 1-3; 2007, March, 1-3; 2005, Feb, 13-16; 2005, February, 13-16; 2005, Feb, 13-16

33422   open heart, with cardiopulmonary bypass   C 80 ▭ P0
▱ 46.23   ⚬ 46.23   **Global Days 090**
AMA: 2007, Mar, 1-3; 2007, Mar, 1-3; 2007, March, 1-3; 2005, Feb, 13-16; 2005, February, 13-16; 2005, Feb, 13-16

33425   Valvuloplasty, mitral valve, with cardiopulmonary bypass;   C 80 ▭ P0
▱ 71.32   ⚬ 71.32   **Global Days 090**
AMA: 2008, Jan, 10-25; 2007, Jan, 13-27; 2007, Jan, 13-27; 2007, Mar, 1-3; 2007, Mar, 1-3; 2007, January, 13-27; 2007, March, 1-3; 2005, Feb, 13-16; 2005, Feb, 13-16; 2005, February, 13-16

33426   with prosthetic ring   C 80 ▭ P0
▱ 65.19   ⚬ 65.19   **Global Days 090**
AMA: 2007, Mar, 1-3; 2007, Mar, 1-3; 2007, March, 1-3; 2005, Feb, 13-16; 2005, February, 13-16; 2005, Feb, 13-16

33427   radical reconstruction, with or without ring   C 80 ▭ P0
▱ 68.31   ⚬ 68.31   **Global Days 090**
AMA: 2007, Mar, 1-3; 2007, Mar, 1-3; 2007, March, 1-3; 2005, Feb, 13-16; 2005, February, 13-16; 2005, Feb, 13-16

33430   Replacement, mitral valve, with cardiopulmonary bypass   C 80 ▭ P0
▱ 75.16   ⚬ 75.16   **Global Days 090**
AMA: 2007, Mar, 1-3; 2007, Mar, 1-3; 2007, March, 1-3; 2005, Feb, 13-16; 2005, February, 13-16; 2005, Feb, 13-16

33460   Valvectomy, tricuspid valve, with cardiopulmonary bypass   C 80 ▭ P0
▱ 63.40   ⚬ 63.40   **Global Days 090**
AMA: 2007, Mar, 1-3; 2007, Mar, 1-3; 2007, March, 1-3; 2005, Feb, 13-16; 2005, February, 13-16; 2005, Feb, 13-16

33463   Valvuloplasty, tricuspid valve; without ring insertion   C 80 ▭ P0
▱ 79.94   ⚬ 79.94   **Global Days 090**
AMA: 2007, Mar, 1-3; 2007, Mar, 1-3; 2007, March, 1-3; 2005, Feb, 13-16; 2005, February, 13-16; 2005, Feb, 13-16

33464   with ring insertion   C 80 ▭ P0
▱ 64.76   ⚬ 64.76   **Global Days 090**
AMA: 2007, Mar, 1-3; 2007, Mar, 1-3; 2007, March, 1-3; 2005, Feb, 13-16; 2005, February, 13-16; 2005, Feb, 13-16

33465 Replacement, tricuspid valve, with cardiopulmonary bypass C 80 ▣ P0
  🗲 72.39 ⚕ 72.39 Global Days 090
  AMA: 2007, Mar, 1-3; 2007, Mar, 1-3; 2007, March, 1-3; 2005, Feb, 13-16; 2005, February, 13-16; 2005, Feb, 13-16

33468 Tricuspid valve repositioning and plication for Ebstein anomaly C 80 ▣
  🗲 51.41 ⚕ 51.41 Global Days 090
  AMA: 2007, Mar, 1-3; 2007, Mar, 1-3; 2007, March, 1-3; 2005, Feb, 13-16; 2005, February, 13-16; 2005, Feb, 13-16

33470-33474 Pulmonary Valvotomy

INCLUDES Brock's operation

Code also the concurrent ligation/takedown of a systemic-to-pulmonary artery shunt (33924)

33470 Valvotomy, pulmonary valve, closed heart; transventricular C 80 ⊚ ▣
  🗲 31.95 ⚕ 31.95 Global Days 090
  AMA: 2007, Mar, 1-3; 2007, Mar, 1-3; 2007, March, 1-3; 2005, Feb, 13-16; 2005, February, 13-16; 2005, Feb, 13-16

33471 via pulmonary artery C 80 ▣
  EXCLUDES percutaneous valvuloplasty of pulmonary valve (92990)
  🗲 36.39 ⚕ 36.39 Global Days 090
  AMA: 2007, Mar, 1-3; 2007, Mar, 1-3; 2007, March, 1-3; 2005, Feb, 13-16; 2005, February, 13-16; 2005, Feb, 13-16

33472 Valvotomy, pulmonary valve, open heart; with inflow occlusion C 80 ⊚ ▣
  🗲 36.79 ⚕ 36.79 Global Days 090
  AMA: 2007, Mar, 1-3; 2007, Mar, 1-3; 2007, March, 1-3; 2005, Feb, 13-16; 2005, February, 13-16; 2005, Feb, 13-16

33474 with cardiopulmonary bypass C 00 ▣
  🗲 55.67 ⚕ 55.67 Global Days 090
  AMA: 2007, Mar, 1-3; 2007, Mar, 1-3; 2007, March, 1-3; 2005, Feb, 13-16; 2005, February, 13-16; 2005, Feb, 13-16

33475-33478 Other Procedures Pulmonary Valve

33475 Replacement, pulmonary valve C 80 ▣ P0
  EXCLUDES concurrent ligation/takedown of a systemic-to-pulmonary artery shunt (33924)
  🗲 63.16 ⚕ 63.16 Global Days 090
  AMA: 2007, Mar, 1-3; 2007, Mar, 1-3; 2007, March, 1-3; 2005, Feb, 13-16; 2005, February, 13-16; 2005, Feb, 13-16

33476 Right ventricular resection for infundibular stenosis, with or without commissurotomy C 80 ▣
  INCLUDES Brock's operation
  🗲 39.75 ⚕ 39.75 Global Days 090
  AMA: 2007, Mar, 1-3; 2007, Mar, 1-3; 2007, March, 1-3; 2005, Feb, 13-16; 2005, February, 13-16; 2005, Feb, 13-16

33478 Outflow tract augmentation (gusset), with or without commissurotomy or infundibular resection C 80 ▣
  Code also 33768 for cavopulmonary anastomosis to a second superior vena cava
  🗲 43.19 ⚕ 43.19 Global Days 090
  AMA: 2007, Mar, 1-3; 2007, Mar, 1-3; 2007, March, 1-3; 2005, Feb, 13-16; 2005, February, 13-16; 2005, Feb, 13-16

33496 Prosthetic Valve Repair

Code also reoperation if performed (33530)

Code also separate incision into heart to remove thrombus if applicable; append modifier 59 to (33315)

33496 Repair of non-structural prosthetic valve dysfunction with cardiopulmonary bypass (separate procedure) C 80 ▣ P0
  🗲 46.18 ⚕ 46.18 Global Days 090
  AMA: 2007, Mar, 1-3; 2007, Mar, 1-3; 2007, March, 1-3; 2005, Feb, 13-16; 2005, February, 13-16; 2005, Feb, 13-16

33500-33507 Repair Aberrant Coronary Artery Anatomy

INCLUDES angioplasty and/or endarterectomy

33500 Repair of coronary arteriovenous or arteriocardiac chamber fistula; with cardiopulmonary bypass C 80 ▣
  🗲 43.33 ⚕ 43.33 Global Days 090
  AMA: 2007, Mar, 1-3; 2007, Mar, 1-3; 2007, March, 1-3

33501 without cardiopulmonary bypass C 80 ▣
  🗲 29.81 ⚕ 29.81 Global Days 090
  AMA: 2007, Mar, 1-3; 2007, Mar, 1-3; 2007, March, 1-3

33502 Repair of anomalous coronary artery from pulmonary artery origin; by ligation C 80 ⊚ ▣
  🗲 34.72 ⚕ 34.72 Global Days 090
  AMA: 2007, Mar, 1-3; 2007, Mar, 1-3; 2007, March, 1-3

33503 by graft, without cardiopulmonary bypass C 80 ⊚ ▣
  🗲 36.75 ⚕ 36.75 Global Days 090
  AMA: 2007, Mar, 1-3; 2007, Mar, 1-3; 2007, March, 1-3

33504 by graft, with cardiopulmonary bypass C 80 ▣
  🗲 39.61 ⚕ 39.61 Global Days 090
  AMA: 2007, Mar, 1-3; 2007, Mar, 1-3; 2007, March, 1-3

33505 with construction of intrapulmonary artery tunnel (Takeuchi procedure) C 80 ⊚ ▣
  🗲 53.61 ⚕ 53.61 Global Days 090
  AMA: 2007, Mar, 1-3; 2007, Mar, 1-3; 2007, March, 1-3

33506 by translocation from pulmonary artery to aorta C 80 ⊚ ▣
  🗲 56.40 ⚕ 56.40 Global Days 090
  AMA: 2007, Mar, 1-3; 2007, Mar, 1-3; 2007, March, 1-3

33507 Repair of anomalous (eg, intramural) aortic origin of coronary artery by unroofing or translocation C 80
  🗲 47.76 ⚕ 47.76 Global Days 090
  AMA: 2007, Mar, 1-3; 2007, Mar, 1-3; 2007, March, 1-3

33508 Endoscopic Harvesting of Venous Graft

+ **33508** Endoscopy, surgical, including video-assisted harvest of vein(s) for coronary artery bypass procedure (List separately in addition to code for primary procedure) N1 N 80 ▣
  EXCLUDES harvesting of vein of upper extremity (35500)
  Code first 33510-33523
  🗲 0.45 ⚕ 0.45 Global Days ZZZ

● New Code   ▲ Revised Code   ▣ Maternity Edit   🅐 Age Edit   A-Y OPPS Status Indicator   🗲 Facility RVU   ⚕ Non-Facility RVU
▣ CCI Comprehensive Code   50 Bilateral Procedure   + Add-on Indicator   ◪ Laboratory crosswalk   ◪ Radiology crosswalk

Cardiovascular System

33510 — 33530

33510-33516 Coronary Artery Bypass: Venous Grafts

INCLUDES harvesting of saphenous vein grafts
venous grafting only

EXCLUDES *arterial grafting only (33533-33536)*
combined arterial-venous grafts; 33517-33523 and (33533-33535)
harvesting of vein graft:
   of femoropopliteal vein (35572)
   of upper extremity vein (35500)
   performed by surgical assistant

33510 **Coronary artery bypass, vein only; single coronary venous graft** C 80 ⬛ P0
   🔪 53.77 ✂ 53.77 Global Days 090
   AMA: 2008, Jan, 10-25; 2007, Jan, 7-10; 2007, Jan, 7-10; 2007, Jan, 13-27; 2007, Jan, 13-27; 2007, Mar, 1-3; 2007, January, 13-27; 2007, March, 1-3; 2007, January, 7-10; 2007, Mar, 1-3; 2005, Feb, 13-16; 2005, February, 13-16; 2005, Feb, 13-16

33511 **2 coronary venous grafts** C 80 ⬛ P0
   🔪 58.60 ✂ 58.60 Global Days 090
   AMA: 2007, Jan, 7-10; 2007, Jan, 7-10; 2007, Mar, 1-3; 2007, Mar, 1-3; 2007, January, 7-10; 2007, March, 1-3; 2005, Feb, 13-16; 2005, Feb, 13-16; 2005, February, 13-16

33512 **3 coronary venous grafts** C 80 ⬛ P0
   🔪 65.83 ✂ 65.83 Global Days 090
   AMA: 2007, Jan, 7-10; 2007, Jan, 7-10; 2007, Mar, 1-3; 2007, Mar, 1-3; 2007, January, 7-10; 2007, March, 1-3; 2005, Feb, 13-16; 2005, Feb, 13-16; 2005, February, 13-16

33513 **4 coronary venous grafts** C 80 ⬛ P0
   🔪 67.27 ✂ 67.27 Global Days 090
   AMA: 2007, Jan, 7-10; 2007, Jan, 7-10; 2007, Mar, 1-3; 2007, Mar, 1-3; 2007, January, 7-10; 2007, March, 1-3; 2005, Feb, 13-16; 2005, Feb, 13-16; 2005, February, 13-16

33514 **five coronary venous grafts** C 80 ⬛ P0
   🔪 71.16 ✂ 71.16 Global Days 090
   AMA: 2007, Jan, 7-10; 2007, Jan, 7-10; 2007, Mar, 1-3; 2007, Mar, 1-3; 2007, January, 7-10; 2007, March, 1-3; 2005, Feb, 13-16; 2005, Feb, 13-16; 2005, February, 13-16

33516 **6 or more coronary venous grafts** C 80 ⬛ P0
   🔪 74.05 ✂ 74.05 Global Days 090
   AMA: 2007, Jan, 7-10; 2007, Jan, 7-10; 2007, Mar, 1-3; 2007, Mar, 1-3; 2007, January, 7-10; 2007, March, 1-3; 2005, Feb, 13-16; 2005, Feb, 13-16; 2005, February, 13-16

33517-33523 Coronary Artery Bypass: Venous AND Arterial Grafts

INCLUDES harvesting of saphenous vein grafts

EXCLUDES *harvesting of artery from upper extremity (35600)*
harvesting of femoropopliteal vein graft (35572)
harvesting of vein of upper extremity (35500)
harvesting of venous or arterial graft by surgical assistant

Code also appropriate code from (33533-33536)

+ **33517** **Coronary artery bypass, using venous graft(s) and arterial graft(s); single vein graft (List separately in addition to code for primary procedure)** C 80 ⬛ P0
   🔪 5.10 ✂ 5.10 Global Days ZZZ
   AMA: 2007, Jan, 7-10; 2007, Jan, 7-10; 2007, Mar, 1-3; 2007, Mar, 1-3; 2007, January, 7-10; 2007, March, 1-3; 2005, Feb, 13-16; 2005, Feb, 13-16; 2005, February, 13-16

+ **33518** **2 venous grafts (List separately in addition to code for primary procedure)** C 80 ⬛ P0
   🔪 11.00 ✂ 11.00 Global Days ZZZ
   AMA: 2007, Jan, 7-10; 2007, Jan, 7-10; 2007, Mar, 1-3; 2007, Mar, 1-3; 2007, January, 7-10; 2007, March, 1-3; 2005, Feb, 13-16; 2005, Feb, 13-16; 2005, February, 13-16

+ **33519** **3 venous grafts (List separately in addition to code for primary procedure)** C 80 ⬛ P0
   🔪 14.70 ✂ 14.70 Global Days ZZZ
   AMA: 2007, Jan, 7-10; 2007, Jan, 7-10; 2007, Mar, 1-3; 2007, Mar, 1-3; 2007, January, 7-10; 2007, March, 1-3; 2005, Feb, 13-16; 2005, Feb, 13-16; 2005, February, 13-16

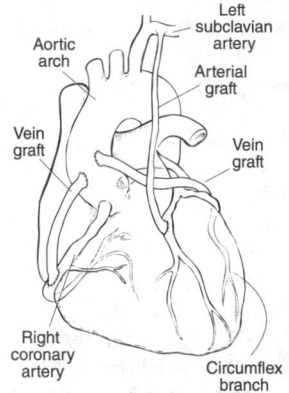

Left subclavian artery
Aortic arch
Arterial graft
Vein graft
Vein graft
Right coronary artery
Circumflex branch

33521: four vein grafts
33522: five vein grafts
33523: six or more

The left internal thoracic (or mammary) artery is the most commonly used arterial graft. Arising from the subclavian artery, each side descends just behind the rib cartilage. The artery is left intact at the subclavian end and anastomosed to the coronary just beyond the occlusion. These codes are not reported alone; code the arterial preparation separately

+ **33521** **4 venous grafts (List separately in addition to code for primary procedure)** C 80 ⬛ P0
   🔪 17.83 ✂ 17.83 Global Days ZZZ
   AMA: 2007, Jan, 7-10; 2007, Jan, 7-10; 2007, Mar, 1-3; 2007, Mar, 1-3; 2007, January, 7-10; 2007, March, 1-3; 2005, Feb, 13-16; 2005, Feb, 13-16; 2005, February, 13-16

+ **33522** **five venous grafts (List separately in addition to code for primary procedure)** C 80 ⬛ P0
   🔪 20.36 ✂ 20.36 Global Days ZZZ
   AMA: 2007, Jan, 7-10; 2007, Jan, 7-10; 2007, Mar, 1-3; 2007, Mar, 1-3; 2007, January, 7-10; 2007, March, 1-3; 2005, Feb, 13-16; 2005, Feb, 13-16; 2005, February, 13-16

+ **33523** **6 or more venous grafts (List separately in addition to code for primary procedure)** C 80 ⬛ P0
   🔪 23.27 ✂ 23.27 Global Days ZZZ
   AMA: 2007, Jan, 7-10; 2007, Jan, 7-10; 2007, Mar, 1-3; 2007, Mar, 1-3; 2007, January, 7-10; 2007, March, 1-3; 2005, Feb, 13-16; 2005, Feb, 13-16; 2005, February, 13-16

33530 Reoperative Coronary Artery Bypass Graft or Valve Procedure

+ **33530** **Reoperation, coronary artery bypass procedure or valve procedure, more than 1 month after original operation (List separately in addition to code for primary procedure)** C 80 ⬛ P0
   Code first (33400-33496, 33510-33536, 33863)
   🔪 13.97 ✂ 13.97 Global Days ZZZ
   AMA: 2008, Jan, 10-25; 2007, Jan, 7-10; 2007, Jan, 7-10; 2007, Jan, 13-27; 2007, Jan, 13-27; 2007, January, 13-27; 2007, January, 7-10; 2005, Feb, 13-16; 2005, Feb, 13-16; 2005, February, 13-16

33533-33536 Coronary Artery Bypass: Arterial Grafts

INCLUDES harvesting of arterial graft excluding upper extremity (e.g., epigastric, internal mammary, gastroepiploic and others)

EXCLUDES harvesting of arterial/venous grafts:
of femoropopliteal vein (35572)
of upper extremity vein or artery (35500, 35600)
performed by surgical assistant
venous grafts only (33510-33516)

Code also appropriate code from 33517-33523 to report combined arterial-venous grafts

33533 Coronary artery bypass, using arterial graft(s); single arterial graft C 80 ▱ P0
　🗐 52.46　🔦 52.46　Global Days 090
AMA: 2007, Jan, 7-10; 2007, Jan, 7-10; 2007, Mar, 1-3; 2007, March, 1-3; 2007, January, 7-10; 2007, Mar, 1-3; 2005, Mar, 11-15; 2005, February, 13-16; 2005, March, 11-15; 2005, Mar, 11-15; 2005, Feb, 13-16; 2005, Feb, 13-16

33534 2 coronary arterial grafts C 80 ▱ P0
　🗐 60.78　🔦 60.78　Global Days 090
AMA: 2007, Jan, 7-10; 2007, Jan, 7-10; 2007, Mar, 1-3; 2007, Mar, 1-3; 2007, January, 7-10; 2007, March, 1-3; 2005, Feb, 13-16; 2005, Feb, 13-16; 2005, February, 13-16

33535 3 coronary arterial grafts C 80 ▱ P0
　🗐 67.41　🔦 67.41　Global Days 090
AMA: 2007, Jan, 7-10; 2007, Jan, 7-10; 2007, Mar, 1-3; 2007, Mar, 1-3; 2007, January, 7-10; 2007, March, 1-3; 2005, Feb, 13-16; 2005, Feb, 13-16; 2005, February, 13-16

33536 4 or more coronary arterial grafts C 80 ▱ P0
　🗐 72.23　🔦 72.23　Global Days 090
AMA: 2007, Jan, 7-10; 2007, Jan, 7-10; 2007, Mar, 1-3; 2007, Mar, 1-3; 2007, January, 7-10; 2007, March, 1-3; 2005, Feb, 13-16; 2005, Feb, 13-16; 2005, February, 13-16

33542-33548 Ventricular Reconstruction

CMS 100-3,20.26　Partial Ventriculectomy

33542 Myocardial resection (eg, ventricular aneurysmectomy) C 80 ▱ P0
Code also separate incision in heart to remove thrombus
　🗐 69.28　🔦 69.28　Global Days 090
AMA: 2007, Mar, 1-3; 2007, Mar, 1-3; 2007, March, 1-3

33545 Repair of postinfarction ventricular septal defect, with or without myocardial resection C 80 ▱ P0
Code also separate incision in heart to remove thrombus
　🗐 81.75　🔦 81.75　Global Days 090
AMA: 2007, Mar, 1-3; 2007, Mar, 1-3; 2007, March, 1-3

33548 Surgical ventricular restoration procedure, includes prosthetic patch, when performed (eg, ventricular remodeling, SVR, SAVER, Dor procedures) C 80 P0
Do not report with (33210-33211, 33251, 33310, 33315)
EXCLUDES Batista procedure or pachopexy (33999)
　🗐 80.40　🔦 80.40　Global Days 090
AMA: 2008, Jan, 10-25; 2007, Jan, 13-27; 2007, Jan, 13-27; 2007, Mar, 1-3; 2007, January, 13-27; 2007, Mar, 1-3; 2007, March, 1-3; 2006, Dec, 10-12; 2006, Dec, 10-12; 2006, Dec, 10-12; 2006, Dec, 10-12; 2006, Dec, 10-12; 2006, Dec, 10-12; 2006, December, 10-12; 2006, December, 10-12; 2006, December, 10-12; 2006, December, 10-12; 2006, December, 10-12; 2006, December, 10-12; 2006, Dec, 10-12; 2006, Dec, 10-12; 2006, Dec, 10-12; 2006, Dec, 10-12; 2006, Dec, 10-12; 2006, Dec, 10-12; 2006, Dec, 10-12

33572 Endarterectomy with CABG (LAD, RCA, Cx)

+ **33572** Coronary endarterectomy, open, any method, of left anterior descending, circumflex, or right coronary artery performed in conjunction with coronary artery bypass graft procedure, each vessel (List separately in addition to primary procedure) C 80 ▱ P0
Code first (33510-33516, 33533-33536)
　🗐 6.53　🔦 6.53　Global Days ZZZ

33600-33619 Repair Aberrant Heart Anatomy

Code also the concurrent ligation/takedown of a systemic-to-pulmonary artery shunt (33924)

33600 Closure of atrioventricular valve (mitral or tricuspid) by suture or patch C 80 ▱
　🗐 47.07　🔦 47.07　Global Days 090
AMA: 2007, Mar, 1-3; 2007, Mar, 1-3; 2007, March, 1-3

33602 Closure of semilunar valve (aortic or pulmonary) by suture or patch C 80 ▱
　🗐 44.70　🔦 44.70　Global Days 090
AMA: 2007, Mar, 1-3; 2007, Mar, 1-3; 2007, March, 1-3

33606 Anastomosis of pulmonary artery to aorta (Damus-Kaye-Stansel procedure) C 80 ▱
　🗐 48.79　🔦 48.79　Global Days 090
AMA: 2007, Mar, 1-3; 2007, Mar, 1-3; 2007, March, 1-3

33608 Repair of complex cardiac anomaly other than pulmonary atresia with ventricular septal defect by construction or replacement of conduit from right or left ventricle to pulmonary artery C 80 ▱
EXCLUDES unifocalization of arborization anomalies of pulmonary artery (33925, 33926)
　🗐 50.18　🔦 50.18　Global Days 090
AMA: 2007, Mar, 1-3; 2007, Mar, 1-3; 2007, March, 1-3

33610 Repair of complex cardiac anomalies (eg, single ventricle with subaortic obstruction) by surgical enlargement of ventricular septal defect C 80 ⊛ ▱
　🗐 48.93　🔦 48.93　Global Days 090
AMA: 2007, Mar, 1-3; 2007, Mar, 1-3; 2007, March, 1-3

33611 Repair of double outlet right ventricle with intraventricular tunnel repair; C 80 ⊛ ▱
　🗐 53.54　🔦 53.54　Global Days 090
AMA: 2007, Mar, 1-3; 2007, Mar, 1-3; 2007, March, 1-3

33612 with repair of right ventricular outflow tract obstruction C 80 ▱
　🗐 55.55　🔦 55.55　Global Days 090
AMA: 2007, Mar, 1-3; 2007, Mar, 1-3; 2007, March, 1-3

33615 Repair of complex cardiac anomalies (eg, tricuspid atresia) by closure of atrial septal defect and anastomosis of atria or vena cava to pulmonary artery (simple Fontan procedure) C 80 ▱
　🗐 55.07　🔦 55.07　Global Days 090
AMA: 2007, Mar, 1-3; 2007, Mar, 1-3; 2007, March, 1-3

33617 Repair of complex cardiac anomalies (eg, single ventricle) by modified Fontan procedure C 80 ▱
Code also 33768 for cavopulmonary anastomosis to a second superior vena cava
　🗐 59.40　🔦 59.40　Global Days 090
AMA: 2007, Mar, 1-3; 2007, Mar, 1-3; 2007, March, 1-3

33619 Repair of single ventricle with aortic outflow obstruction and aortic arch hypoplasia (hypoplastic left heart syndrome) (eg, Norwood procedure) C 80 ⊛ ▱
　🗐 72.60　🔦 72.60　Global Days 090
AMA: 2007, Mar, 1-3; 2007, Mar, 1-3; 2007, March, 1-3

● New Code　▲ Revised Code　Ⓜ Maternity Edit　Ⓐ Age Edit　Ⓐ-Ⓨ OPPS Status Indicator　🗐 Facility RVU　🔦 Non-Facility RVU
▱ CCI Comprehensive Code　50 Bilateral Procedure　+ Add-on Indicator　🔬 Laboratory crosswalk　📷 Radiology crosswalk

33641-33645 Closure of Defect: Atrium

33641 Repair atrial septal defect, secundum, with cardiopulmonary bypass, with or without patch C 80 ▣
🔲 43.88 ⚕ 43.88 Global Days 090
AMA: 2007, Mar, 1-3; 2007, Mar, 1-3; 2007, March, 1-3

33645 Direct or patch closure, sinus venosus, with or without anomalous pulmonary venous drainage C 80 ▣
Do not report with (33724, 33726)
🔲 43.45 ⚕ 43.45 Global Days 090
AMA: 2007, Mar, 1-3; 2007, Mar, 1-3; 2007, March, 1-3

33647 Closure of Septal Defect: Atrial AND Ventricular

33647 Repair of atrial septal defect and ventricular septal defect, with direct or patch closure C 80 🚫 ▣
EXCLUDES   tricuspid atresia repair procedures (33615)
🔲 46.00 ⚕ 46.00 Global Days 090
AMA: 2007, Mar, 1-3; 2007, Mar, 1-3; 2007, March, 1-3

33660-33670 Closure of Defect: Atrioventricular Canal

33660 Repair of incomplete or partial atrioventricular canal (ostium primum atrial septal defect), with or without atrioventricular valve repair C 80 ▣
🔲 48.49 ⚕ 48.49 Global Days 090
AMA: 2007, Mar, 1-3; 2007, Mar, 1-3; 2007, March, 1-3

33665 Repair of intermediate or transitional atrioventricular canal, with or without atrioventricular valve repair C 80 ▣
🔲 52.18 ⚕ 52.18 Global Days 090
AMA: 2007, Mar, 1-3; 2007, Mar, 1-3; 2007, March, 1-3

33670 Repair of complete atrioventricular canal, with or without prosthetic valve C 80 🚫 ▣
🔲 54.41 ⚕ 54.41 Global Days 090
AMA: 2007, Mar, 1-3; 2007, Mar, 1-3; 2007, March, 1-3

33675-33677 Closure of Multiple Septal Defects: Ventricle

EXCLUDES   percutaneous closure (93581)
transmyocardial closure ventricular septal defect (0166T, 0167T)
Do not report with (32100, 32422, 32551, 33210, 33681, 33684, 33688)

33675 Closure of multiple ventricular septal defects; C 80
🔲 54.42 ⚕ 54.42 Global Days 090
AMA: 2007, Mar, 1-3; 2007, Mar, 1-3; 2007, March, 1-3

33676 with pulmonary valvotomy or infundibular resection (acyanotic) C 80
🔲 56.75 ⚕ 56.75 Global Days 090
AMA: 2007, Mar, 1-3; 2007, Mar, 1-3; 2007, March, 1-3

33677 with removal of pulmonary artery band, with or without gusset C 80
🔲 58.99 ⚕ 58.99 Global Days 090
AMA: 2007, Mar, 1-3; 2007, Mar, 1-3; 2007, March, 1-3

33681-33688 Closure of Septal Defect: Ventricle

EXCLUDES   repair of pulmonary vein that requires creating an atrial septal defect (33724)

33681 Closure of single ventricular septal defect, with or without patch; C 80 ▣
🔲 50.32 ⚕ 50.32 Global Days 090
AMA: 2007, Mar, 1-3; 2007, Mar, 1-3; 2007, March, 1-3

33684 with pulmonary valvotomy or infundibular resection (acyanotic) C 80 ▣
Code also concurrent ligation/takedown of a systemic-to-pulmonary artery shunt if performed (33924)
🔲 50.94 ⚕ 50.94 Global Days 090
AMA: 2007, Mar, 1-3; 2007, Mar, 1-3; 2007, March, 1-3

33688 with removal of pulmonary artery band, with or without gusset C 80 ▣
Code also the concurrent ligation/takedown of a systemic-to-pulmonary artery shunt if performed (33924)
🔲 51.58 ⚕ 51.58 Global Days 090
AMA: 2007, Mar, 1-3; 2007, Mar, 1-3; 2007, March, 1-3

33690 Reduce Pulmonary Overcirculation in Septal Defects

33690 Banding of pulmonary artery C 80 🚫 ▣
🔲 31.43 ⚕ 31.43 Global Days 090
AMA: 2007, Mar, 1-3; 2007, Mar, 1-3; 2007, March, 1-3

33692-33697 Repair of Defects of Tetralogy of Fallot

Code also the concurrent ligation/takedown of a systemic-to-pulmonary artery shunt (33924)

33692 Complete repair tetralogy of Fallot without pulmonary atresia; C 80 ▣
🔲 48.64 ⚕ 48.64 Global Days 090
AMA: 2007, Mar, 1-3; 2007, Mar, 1-3; 2007, March, 1-3

33694 with transannular patch C 80 🚫 ▣
🔲 54.82 ⚕ 54.82 Global Days 090
AMA: 2007, Mar, 1-3; 2007, Mar, 1-3; 2007, March, 1-3

33697 Complete repair tetralogy of Fallot with pulmonary atresia including construction of conduit from right ventricle to pulmonary artery and closure of ventricular septal defect C 80 ▣
🔲 58.55 ⚕ 58.55 Global Days 090
AMA: 2007, Mar, 1-3; 2007, Mar, 1-3; 2007, March, 1-3

33702-33722 Repair Anomalies Sinus of Valsalva

33702 Repair sinus of Valsalva fistula, with cardiopulmonary bypass; C 80 ▣
🔲 42.10 ⚕ 42.10 Global Days 090
AMA: 2007, Mar, 1-3; 2007, Mar, 1-3; 2007, March, 1-3

33710 with repair of ventricular septal defect C 80 ▣
🔲 51.04 ⚕ 51.04 Global Days 090
AMA: 2007, Mar, 1-3; 2007, Mar, 1-3; 2007, March, 1-3

33720 Repair sinus of Valsalva aneurysm, with cardiopulmonary bypass C 80 ▣
🔲 42.71 ⚕ 42.71 Global Days 090
AMA: 2007, Mar, 1-3; 2007, Mar, 1-3; 2007, March, 1-3

33722 Closure of aortico-left ventricular tunnel C 80 ▣
🔲 41.62 ⚕ 41.62 Global Days 090
AMA: 2007, Mar, 1-3; 2007, Mar, 1-3; 2007, March, 1-3

33724-33732 Repair Aberrant Pulmonary Venous Connection

33724 Repair of isolated partial anomalous pulmonary venous return (eg, Scimitar Syndrome) C 80
Do not report with (32551, 33210-33211)
🔲 43.38 ⚕ 43.38 Global Days 090
AMA: 2007, Mar, 1-3; 2007, Mar, 1-3; 2007, March, 1-3

33726 Repair of pulmonary venous stenosis   ⒸⓈ⓪
Do not report with (32551, 33210-33211)
   ⊞ 56.57   ⚘ 56.57   **Global Days 090**
   AMA: 2007, Mar, 1-3; 2007, Mar, 1-3; 2007, March, 1-3

33730 Complete repair of anomalous pulmonary venous return (supracardiac, intracardiac, or infracardiac types)   ⒸⓈ⓪▭
   EXCLUDES   partial anomalous pulmonary venous return (33724)
                repair of pulmonary venous stenosis (33726)
   ⊞ 53.96   ⚘ 53.96   **Global Days 090**
   AMA: 2007, Mar, 1-3; 2007, Mar, 1-3; 2007, March, 1-3

33732 Repair of cor triatriatum or supravalvular mitral ring by resection of left atrial membrane   ⒸⓈ⓪▭
   ⊞ 44.92   ⚘ 44.92   **Global Days 090**
   AMA: 2007, Mar, 1-3; 2007, Mar, 1-3; 2007, March, 1-3

33735-33737 Creation of Atrial Septal Defect

Code also the concurrent ligation/takedown of a systemic-to-pulmonary artery shunt (33924)

33735 Atrial septectomy or septostomy; closed heart (Blalock-Hanlon type operation)   ⒸⓈ⓪▭
   ⊞ 33.92   ⚘ 33.92   **Global Days 090**
   AMA: 2007, Mar, 1-3; 2007, Mar, 1-3; 2007, March, 1-3

33736 open heart with cardiopulmonary bypass   ⒸⓈ⓪▭
   ⊞ 38.15   ⚘ 38.15   **Global Days 090**
   AMA: 2007, Mar, 1-3; 2007, Mar, 1-3; 2007, March, 1-3

33737 open heart, with inflow occlusion   ⒸⓈ▭
   EXCLUDES   atrial septectomy/septostomy:
                blade method (92993)
                transvenous balloon method (92992)
   ⊞ 35.71   ⚘ 35.71   **Global Days 090**
   AMA: 2007, Mar, 1-3; 2007, Mar, 1-3; 2007, March, 1-3

33750-33767 Systemic Vessel to Pulmonary Artery Shunts

Code also the concurrent ligation/takedown of a systemic-to-pulmonary artery shunt (33924)

33750 Shunt; subclavian to pulmonary artery (Blalock-Taussig type operation)   ⒸⓈ⓪▭
   ⊞ 35.29   ⚘ 35.29   **Global Days 090**
   AMA: 2007, Mar, 1-3; 2007, Mar, 1-3; 2007, March, 1-3

33755 ascending aorta to pulmonary artery (Waterston type operation)   ⒸⓈ⓪▭
   ⊞ 35.50   ⚘ 35.50   **Global Days 090**
   AMA: 2007, Mar, 1-3; 2007, Mar, 1-3; 2007, March, 1-3

33762 descending aorta to pulmonary artery (Potts-Smith type operation)   ⒸⓈ⓪▭
   ⊞ 35.40   ⚘ 35.40   **Global Days 090**
   AMA: 2007, Mar, 1-3; 2007, Mar, 1-3; 2007, March, 1-3

33764 central, with prosthetic graft   ⒸⓈ▭
   ⊞ 34.84   ⚘ 34.84   **Global Days 090**
   AMA: 2007, Mar, 1-3; 2007, Mar, 1-3; 2007, March, 1-3

33766 superior vena cava to pulmonary artery for flow to one lung (classical Glenn procedure)   ⒸⓈ▭
   ⊞ 38.54   ⚘ 38.54   **Global Days 090**
   AMA: 2007, Mar, 1-3; 2007, Mar, 1-3; 2007, March, 1-3

33767 superior vena cava to pulmonary artery for flow to both lungs (bidirectional Glenn procedure)   ⒸⓈ▭
   ⊞ 38.95   ⚘ 38.95   **Global Days 090**
   AMA: 2007, Mar, 1-3; 2007, Mar, 1-3; 2007, March, 1-3

33768 Cavopulmonary Anastomosis to Decrease Volume Load

Do not report with (32551, 33210-33211)

+ **33768** Anastomosis, cavopulmonary, second superior vena cava (List separately in addition to primary procedure)   ⒸⓈ
   Code first (33478, 33617, 33767)
   ⊞ 11.87   ⚘ 11.87   **Global Days ZZZ**
   AMA: 2007, Mar, 1-3; 2007, Mar, 1-3; 2007, March, 1-3

33770-33781 Repair Aberrant Anatomy: Transposition Great Vessels

Code also the concurrent ligation/takedown of a systemic-to-pulmonary artery shunt (33924)

33770 Repair of transposition of the great arteries with ventricular septal defect and subpulmonary stenosis; without surgical enlargement of ventricular septal defect   ⒸⓈⓄ▭
   ⊞ 59.17   ⚘ 59.17   **Global Days 090**
   AMA: 2007, Mar, 1-3; 2007, Mar, 1-3; 2007, March, 1-3

33771 with surgical enlargement of ventricular septal defect   ⒸⓈ▭
   ⊞ 60.56   ⚘ 60.56   **Global Days 090**
   AMA: 2007, Mar, 1-3; 2007, Mar, 1-3; 2007, March, 1-3

33774 Repair of transposition of the great arteries, atrial baffle procedure (eg, Mustard or Senning type) with cardiopulmonary bypass;   ⒸⓈ▭
   ⊞ 49.93   ⚘ 49.93   **Global Days 090**
   AMA: 2007, Mar, 1-3; 2007, Mar, 1-3; 2007, March, 1-3

33775 with removal of pulmonary band   ⒸⓈ▭
   ⊞ 51.94   ⚘ 51.94   **Global Days 090**
   AMA: 2007, Mar, 1-3; 2007, Mar, 1-3; 2007, March, 1-3

33776 with closure of ventricular septal defect   ⒸⓈ▭
   ⊞ 54.60   ⚘ 54.60   **Global Days 090**
   AMA: 2007, Mar, 1-3; 2007, Mar, 1-3; 2007, March, 1-3

33777 with repair of subpulmonic obstruction   ⒸⓈ▭
   ⊞ 53.64   ⚘ 53.64   **Global Days 090**
   AMA: 2007, Mar, 1-3; 2007, Mar, 1-3; 2007, March, 1-3

33778 Repair of transposition of the great arteries, aortic pulmonary artery reconstruction (eg, Jatene type);   ⒸⓈⓄ▭
   ⊞ 65.69   ⚘ 65.69   **Global Days 090**
   AMA: 2007, Mar, 1-3; 2007, Mar, 1-3; 2007, March, 1-3

33779 with removal of pulmonary band   ⒸⓈ▭
   ⊞ 61.95   ⚘ 61.95   **Global Days 090**
   AMA: 2007, Mar, 1-3; 2007, Mar, 1-3; 2007, March, 1-3

33780 with closure of ventricular septal defect   ⒸⓈ▭
   ⊞ 64.65   ⚘ 64.65   **Global Days 090**
   AMA: 2007, Mar, 1-3; 2007, Mar, 1-3; 2007, March, 1-3

33781 with repair of subpulmonic obstruction   ⒸⓈ▭
   ⊞ 64.32   ⚘ 64.32   **Global Days 090**
   AMA: 2007, Mar, 1-3; 2007, Mar, 1-3; 2007, March, 1-3

33786-33788 Repair Aberrant Anatomy: Truncus Arteriosus

33786 Total repair, truncus arteriosus (Rastelli type operation)   ⒸⓈⓄ▭
   Code also the concurrent ligation/takedown of a systemic-to-pulmonary artery shunt (33924)
   ⊞ 63.22   ⚘ 63.22   **Global Days 090**
   AMA: 2007, Mar, 1-3; 2007, Mar, 1-3; 2007, March, 1-3

● New Code   ▲ Revised Code   Ⓜ Maternity Edit   Ⓐ Age Edit   Ⓐ-Ⓨ OPPS Status Indicator   ⊞ Facility RVU   ⚘ Non-Facility RVU
▭ CCI Comprehensive Code   ⑤⓪ Bilateral Procedure   + Add-on Indicator   ◧ Laboratory crosswalk   ◪ Radiology crosswalk

© 2008 Ingenix(*Blue Ink*)   CPT only © 2008 American Medical Association. All Rights Reserved. (Black Ink)   Medicare (Red Ink)   **129**

Cardiovascular System

33788 — 33875

33788 Reimplantation of an anomalous pulmonary artery   C 80 ▢

     EXCLUDES   *pulmonary artery banding (33690)*

     🔁 42.77   ✂ 42.77   Global Days 090

     AMA: 2007, Mar, 1-3; 2007, Mar, 1-3; 2007, March, 1-3

33800-33853 Repair Aberrant Anatomy: Aorta

33800 Aortic suspension (aortopexy) for tracheal decompression (eg, for tracheomalacia) (separate procedure)   C 80 ▢

     🔁 26.80   ✂ 26.80   Global Days 090

     AMA: 2007, Mar, 1-3; 2007, Mar, 1-3; 2007, March, 1-3

33802 Division of aberrant vessel (vascular ring);   C 80 ▢

     🔁 28.71   ✂ 28.71   Global Days 090

     AMA: 2007, Mar, 1-3; 2007, Mar, 1-3; 2007, March, 1-3

33803   with reanastomosis   C 80 ▢

     🔁 31.46   ✂ 31.46   Global Days 090

     AMA: 2007, Mar, 1-3; 2007, Mar, 1-3; 2007, March, 1-3

33813 Obliteration of aortopulmonary septal defect; without cardiopulmonary bypass   C 80 ▢

     🔁 35.58   ✂ 35.58   Global Days 090

     AMA: 2007, Mar, 1-3; 2007, Mar, 1-3; 2007, March, 1-3

33814   with cardiopulmonary bypass   C 80 ▢

     🔁 41.93   ✂ 41.93   Global Days 090

     AMA: 2007, Mar, 1-3; 2007, Mar, 1-3; 2007, March, 1-3

33820 Repair of patent ductus arteriosus; by ligation   C 80 ▢

     🔁 26.82   ✂ 26.82   Global Days 090

     AMA: 2007, Mar, 1-3; 2007, Mar, 1-3; 2007, March, 1-3

33822   by division, younger than 18 years   A C 80 ▢

     🔁 28.54   ✂ 28.54   Global Days 090

     AMA: 2007, Mar, 1-3; 2007, Mar, 1-3; 2007, March, 1-3

33824   by division, 18 years and older   C 80 ▢

     🔁 32.22   ✂ 32.22   Global Days 090

     AMA: 2007, Mar, 1-3; 2007, Mar, 1-3; 2007, March, 1-3

33840 Excision of coarctation of aorta, with or without associated patent ductus arteriosus; with direct anastomosis   C 80 ▢

     🔁 32.29   ✂ 32.29   Global Days 090

     AMA: 2007, Mar, 1-3; 2007, Mar, 1-3; 2007, March, 1-3

33845   with graft   C 80 ▢

     🔁 37.56   ✂ 37.56   Global Days 090

     AMA: 2007, Mar, 1-3; 2007, Mar, 1-3; 2007, March, 1-3

33851   repair using either left subclavian artery or prosthetic material as gusset for enlargement   C 80 ▢

     🔁 34.57   ✂ 34.57   Global Days 090

     AMA: 2007, Mar, 1-3; 2007, Mar, 1-3; 2007, March, 1-3

33852 Repair of hypoplastic or interrupted aortic arch using autogenous or prosthetic material; without cardiopulmonary bypass   C 80 ▢

     EXCLUDES   *hypoplastic left heart syndrome repair by excision of coarctation of aorta (33619)*

     🔁 37.11   ✂ 37.11   Global Days 090

     AMA: 2007, Mar, 1-3; 2007, Mar, 1-3; 2007, March, 1-3

Aortic valve   Left coronary artery   Left, right atria   Basal

Descending branch (anterior ventricular)

Right coronary artery   Descending branch (posterior interventricular)   Apical

Posterior wall   Intraventricular septum divides left and right ventricles

Coronary arterial branching patterns may vary widely; dead heart tissue, usually caused by arterial occlusion, is called a myocardial infarct and about 1.5 million cases are reported annually. Inadequate blood supply can lead to "angina pectoris," or chest pain

Interior heart schematic to locate a myocardial infarction; walls of the left ventrical are much thicker and more than half of MI occurrences will see some degree of transient impairment to the left ventricle

33853   with cardiopulmonary bypass   C 80 ▢

     EXCLUDES   *hypoplastic left heart syndrome repair by excision of coarctation of aorta (33619)*

     🔁 51.72   ✂ 51.72   Global Days 090

     AMA: 2007, Mar, 1-3; 2007, Mar, 1-3; 2007, March, 1-3

33860-33877 Aortic Graft Procedures

33860 Ascending aorta graft, with cardiopulmonary bypass, with or without valve suspension;   C 80 ▢

     Code also concurrent aortic valve replacement (33405, or 33406)

     🔁 85.63   ✂ 85.63   Global Days 090

     AMA: 2007, Mar, 1-3; 2007, Mar, 1-3; 2007, March, 1-3

33861   with coronary reconstruction   C 80 ▢

     Code also concurrent aortic valve replacement (33405, or 33406)

     🔁 67.39   ✂ 67.39   Global Days 090

     AMA: 2007, Mar, 1-3; 2007, Mar, 1-3; 2007, March, 1-3

33863   with aortic root replacement using composite prosthesis and coronary reconstruction   C 80 ▢

     🔁 85.85   ✂ 85.85   Global Days 090

     AMA: 2007, Mar, 1-3; 2007, Mar, 1-3; 2007, March, 1-3; 2005, Feb, 13-16; 2005, February, 13-16; 2005, Feb, 13-16

33864 Ascending aorta graft, with cardiopulmonary bypass with valve suspension, with coronary reconstruction and valve-sparing aortic annulus remodeling (eg, David Procedure, Yacoub Procedure)   C 80

     Do not report with (32551, 33210-33211, 33400, 33860-33863)

     🔁 88.23   ✂ 88.23   Global Days 090

33870 Transverse arch graft, with cardiopulmonary bypass   C 80 ▢

     🔁 70.33   ✂ 70.33   Global Days 090

33875 Descending thoracic aorta graft, with or without bypass   C 80 ▢

     🔁 54.50   ✂ 54.50   Global Days 090

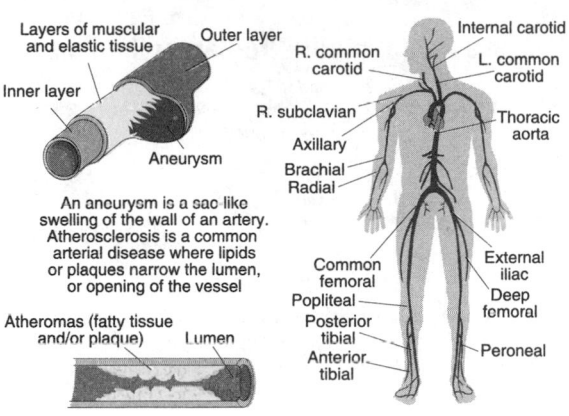

An aneurysm is a sac-like swelling of the wall of an artery. Atherosclerosis is a common arterial disease where lipids or plaques narrow the lumen, or opening of the vessel

33877   Repair of thoracoabdominal aortic aneurysm with graft, with or without cardiopulmonary bypass C 80 ▢ P0
🔁 95.87 ⚖ 95.87 Global Days 090

33880-33891 Endovascular Repair Aortic Aneurysm: Thoracic

INCLUDES   balloon angioplasty
introduction, manipulation, placement, and deployment of the device

EXCLUDES   *additional interventional procedures provided during the endovascular repair*
carotid-carotid bypass (33891)
guidewire and catheter insertion (36140, 36200-36218)
open exposure of artery/subsequent closure (34812, 34820, 34833, 34834)
study, interpretation, and report of implanted wireless pressure sensor in an aneurysmal sac (93982)
subclavian to carotid artery transposition (33889)
substantial artery repair/replacement (35226, 35286)
transcatheter insertion of wireless physiologic sensor in an aneurysmal sac (34806)

33880   Endovascular repair of descending thoracic aorta (eg, aneurysm, pseudoaneurysm, dissection, penetrating ulcer, intramural hematoma, or traumatic disruption); involving coverage of left subclavian artery origin, initial endoprosthesis plus descending thoracic aortic extension(s), if required, to level of celiac artery origin C 80 P0
INCLUDES   placement of distal extensions
EXCLUDES   *proximal extensions*
📺 75956
🔁 49.55 ⚖ 49.55 Global Days 090
AMA: 2006, May, 10-11; 2006, May, 10-11; 2006, May, 10-11

33881   not involving coverage of left subclavian artery origin, initial endoprosthesis plus descending thoracic aortic extension(s), if required, to level of celiac artery origin C 80 P0
INCLUDES   placement of distal extensions in distal thoracic aorta
EXCLUDES   *proximal extensions*
📺 75957
🔁 42.53 ⚖ 42.53 Global Days 090
AMA: 2006, May, 10-11; 2006, May, 10-11; 2006, May, 10-11

33883   Placement of proximal extension prosthesis for endovascular repair of descending thoracic aorta (eg, aneurysm, pseudoaneurysm, dissection, penetrating ulcer, intramural hematoma, or traumatic disruption); initial extension C 80 P0
📺 75958
🔁 31.21 ⚖ 31.21 Global Days 090
AMA: 2006, May, 10-11; 2006, May, 10-11; 2006, May, 10-11

+ **33884**   each additional proximal extension (List separately in addition to code for primary procedure) C 80
Code first 33883
📺 75958
🔁 11.43 ⚖ 11.43 Global Days ZZZ
AMA: 2006, May, 10-11; 2006, May, 10-11; 2006, May, 10-11

33886   Placement of distal extension prosthesis(s) delayed after endovascular repair of descending thoracic aorta C 80 P0
INCLUDES   all modules deployed
Do not report with (33880, 33881)
📺 75959
🔁 26.81 ⚖ 26.81 Global Days 090
AMA: 2006, May, 10-11; 2006, May, 10-11; 2006, May, 10-11

33889   Open subclavian to carotid artery transposition performed in conjunction with endovascular repair of descending thoracic aorta, by neck incision, unilateral C 80 50
Do not report with (35694)
🔁 22.61 ⚖ 22.61 Global Days 000
AMA: 2006, May, 10-11; 2006, May, 10-11; 2006, May, 10-11

33891   Bypass graft, with other than vein, transcervical retropharyngeal carotid-carotid, performed in conjunction with endovascular repair of descending thoracic aorta, by neck incision C 80 50 P0
Do not report with (35509, 35601)
🔁 28.28 ⚖ 28.28 Global Days 000
AMA: 2006, May, 10-11; 2006, May, 10-11; 2006, May, 10-11

33910-33926 Surgical Procedures of Pulmonary Artery

CMS 100-3,240.6   *Transvenous (Catheter) Pulmonary Embolectomy*

33910   Pulmonary artery embolectomy, with cardiopulmonary bypass C 80 ▢
🔁 45.49 ⚖ 45.49 Global Days 090
AMA: 2007, Mar, 1-3; 2007, Mar, 1-3; 2007, March, 1-3

33915   without cardiopulmonary bypass C 80 ▢
🔁 35.84 ⚖ 35.84 Global Days 090
AMA: 2007, Mar, 1-3; 2007, Mar, 1-3; 2007, March, 1-3

33916   Pulmonary endarterectomy, with or without embolectomy, with cardiopulmonary bypass C 80 ▢
🔁 45.58 ⚖ 45.58 Global Days 090
AMA: 2007, Mar, 1-3; 2007, Mar, 1-3; 2007, March, 1-3

33917   Repair of pulmonary artery stenosis by reconstruction with patch or graft C 80 ▢
🔁 41.39 ⚖ 41.39 Global Days 090
AMA: 2007, Mar, 1-3; 2007, Mar, 1-3; 2007, March, 1-3

33920   Repair of pulmonary atresia with ventricular septal defect, by construction or replacement of conduit from right or left ventricle to pulmonary artery C 80 ▢
Code also the concurrent ligation/takedown of a systemic-to-pulmonary artery shunt (33924)
EXCLUDES   *repair of complicated cardiac anomalies by creating/replacing conduit from ventricle to pulmonary artery (33608)*
🔁 49.89 ⚖ 49.89 Global Days 090
AMA: 2007, Mar, 1-3; 2007, Mar, 1-3; 2007, March, 1-3

● New Code   ▲ Revised Code   Ⓜ Maternity Edit   🅰 Age Edit   Ⓐ Ⓥ OPPS Status Indicator   🔁 Facility RVU   ⚖ Non-Facility RVU
▢ CCI Comprehensive Code   50 Bilateral Procedure   + Add-on Indicator   Ⓝ Laboratory crosswalk   📺 Radiology crosswalk

© 2008 Ingenix *(Blue Ink)*   CPT only © 2008 American Medical Association. All Rights Reserved. (Black Ink)   Medicare (Red Ink)   **131**

Cardiovascular System

33922 — 33979

33922 **Transection of pulmonary artery with cardiopulmonary bypass** ⒸⓈⓄ
Code also the concurrent ligation/takedown of a systemic-to-pulmonary artery shunt (33924)
🔗 37.68 ⚕ 37.68 Global Days 090

+ **33924** **Ligation and takedown of a systemic-to-pulmonary artery shunt, performed in conjunction with a congenital heart procedure (List separately in addition to code for primary procedure)** ⒸⓈⓄ
Code first (33470-33475, 33600-33619, 33684-33688, 33692-33697, 33735-33767, 33770-33781, 33786, 33920-33922)
🔗 8.01 ⚕ 8.01 Global Days ZZZ

33925 **Repair of pulmonary artery arborization anomalies by unifocalization; without cardiopulmonary bypass** ⒸⓈⓄ
Do not report with (33697)
🔗 48.68 ⚕ 48.68 Global Days 090

33926 **with cardiopulmonary bypass** ⒸⓈⓄ
Do not report with (33697)
🔗 64.72 ⚕ 64.72 Global Days 090

33930-33945 Heart and Heart-Lung Transplants

CMS 100-4,3,90.2 *Heart Transplants*
CMS 100-4,3,90.2.1 *Artificial Hearts and Related Devices*
INCLUDES backbench work to prepare the donor heart and/or lungs for transplantation (33933, 33944)
harvesting of donor organs with cold preservation (33930, 33940)
transplantation of heart and/or lungs into recipient (33935, 33945)
EXCLUDES *implantation/repair/replacement of artificial heart or components (0051T-0053T)*
procedures performed on donor heart (33300, 33310, 33320, 33400, 33463, 33464, 33510, 33641, 35216, 35276, 35685)

33930 **Donor cardiectomy-pneumonectomy (including cold preservation)** ⒸⓄ
🔗 0.00 ⚕ 0.00 Global Days XXX

33933 **Backbench standard preparation of cadaver donor heart/lung allograft prior to transplantation, including dissection of allograft from surrounding soft tissues to prepare aorta, superior vena cava, inferior vena cava, and trachea for implantation** ⒸⓈⓄ
🔗 0.00 ⚕ 0.00 Global Days XXX

33935 **Heart-lung transplant with recipient cardiectomy-pneumonectomy** ⒸⓈⓄ
🔗 95.78 ⚕ 95.78 Global Days 090

33940 **Donor cardiectomy (including cold preservation)** ⒸⓄ
🔗 0.00 ⚕ 0.00 Global Days XXX
AMA: 2005, Apr, 10-12; 2005, Apr, 10-12; 2005, April, 10-12

33944 **Backbench standard preparation of cadaver donor heart allograft prior to transplantation, including dissection of allograft from surrounding soft tissues to prepare aorta, superior vena cava, inferior vena cava, pulmonary artery, and left atrium for implantation** ⒸⓈⓄ
🔗 0.00 ⚕ 0.00 Global Days XXX

33945 **Heart transplant, with or without recipient cardiectomy** ⒸⓈⓄ
🔗 125.31 ⚕ 125.31 Global Days 090

33960-33999 Mechanical Circulatory Support

CMS 100-4,3,90.2.1 *Artificial Hearts and Related Devices*
EXCLUDES *implantation or removal of extracorporeal ventricular assist device via percutaneous approach (0048T, 0050T)*

33960 **Prolonged extracorporeal circulation for cardiopulmonary insufficiency; initial 24 hours** ⒸⓈⓄ
EXCLUDES *cannula insertion for prolonged extracorporeal circulation (36822)*
🔗 27.77 ⚕ 27.77 Global Days 000

+ **33961** **each additional 24 hours (List separately in addition to code for primary procedure)** ⒸⓈ
EXCLUDES *cannula insertion for prolonged extracorporeal circulation (36822)*
Code first 33960
🔗 15.27 ⚕ 15.27 Global Days ZZZ

33967 **Insertion of intra-aortic balloon assist device, percutaneous** ⒸⓈⓄ
🔗 7.50 ⚕ 7.50 Global Days 000

33968 **Removal of intra-aortic balloon assist device, percutaneous** Ⓒ
🔗 0.97 ⚕ 0.97 Global Days 000
AMA: 2008, Jan, 10-25; 2007, Jan, 13-27; 2007, Jan, 13-27; 2007, January, 13-27

33970 **Insertion of intra-aortic balloon assist device through the femoral artery, open approach** ⒸⓈⓄ
EXCLUDES *percutaneous insertion of intra-aortic balloon assist device (33967)*
🔗 10.18 ⚕ 10.18 Global Days 000

33971 **Removal of intra-aortic balloon assist device including repair of femoral artery, with or without graft** Ⓒ
🔗 19.47 ⚕ 19.47 Global Days 090

33973 **Insertion of intra-aortic balloon assist device through the ascending aorta** ⒸⓈⓄ
🔗 14.86 ⚕ 14.86 Global Days 000

33974 **Removal of intra-aortic balloon assist device from the ascending aorta, including repair of the ascending aorta, with or without graft** Ⓒ
🔗 24.86 ⚕ 24.86 Global Days 090

33975 **Insertion of ventricular assist device; extracorporeal, single ventricle** ⒸⓈⓄ
Code also removal atrial/ventricular thrombi through a separate incision
🔗 30.88 ⚕ 30.88 Global Days XXX
AMA: 2008, Jan, 10-25; 2007, Jan, 13-27; 2007, Jan, 13-27; 2007, January, 13-27; 2004, Jan, 28; 2004, January, 28; 2004, Jan, 28

33976 **extracorporeal, biventricular** ⒸⓈⓄ
Code also removal atrial/ventricular thrombi through a separate incision
🔗 34.27 ⚕ 34.27 Global Days XXX

33977 **Removal of ventricular assist device; extracorporeal, single ventricle** ⒸⓈⓄ
Code also removal atrial/ventricular thrombi through a separate incision
🔗 33.09 ⚕ 33.09 Global Days 090

33978 **extracorporeal, biventricular** ⒸⓈⓄ
Code also removal atrial/ventricular thrombi through a separate incision
🔗 36.50 ⚕ 36.50 Global Days 090

33979 **Insertion of ventricular assist device, implantable intracorporeal, single ventricle** ⒸⓈⓄ
Code also removal atrial/ventricular thrombi through a separate incision
🔗 67.80 ⚕ 67.80 Global Days XXX

33980 Removal of ventricular assist device, implantable intracorporeal, single ventricle   Ⓒ 80 ▢

    Code also removal atrial/ventricular thrombi through a separate incision

    ⚡ 99.15   ⚘ 99.15   Global Days 090

33999 Unlisted procedure, cardiac surgery   Ⓣ 80

    ⚡ 0.00   ⚘ 0.00   Global Days YYY

    AMA: 2008, Jan, 10-25; 2007, Jan, 13-27; 2007, Jan, 13-27; 2007, Mar, 1-3; 2007, Mar, 1-3; 2007, January, 13-27; 2007, March, 1-3; 2004, Jun, 7; 2004, Jun, 7; 2004, June, 7

34001-34530 Surgical Revascularization: Veins and Arteries

INCLUDES   repair of blood vessel
            surgeon's component of operative arteriogram

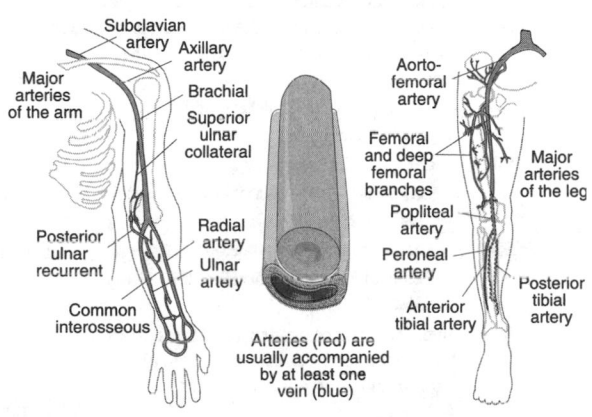

Arteries (red) are usually accompanied by at least one vein (blue)

34001 Embolectomy or thrombectomy, with or without catheter; carotid, subclavian or innominate artery, by neck incision   Ⓒ 80 50 ▢

    ⚡ 26.47   ⚘ 26.47   Global Days 090

34051 innominate, subclavian artery, by thoracic incision   Ⓛ 80 50 ▢ P0

    ⚡ 26.68   ⚘ 26.68   Global Days 090

34101 axillary, brachial, innominate, subclavian artery, by arm incision   Ⓣ 80 50 ▢

    ⚡ 16.94   ⚘ 16.94   Global Days 090

34111 radial or ulnar artery, by arm incision   Ⓣ 80 50 ▢

    ⚡ 16.93   ⚘ 16.93   Global Days 090

34151 renal, celiac, mesentery, aortoiliac artery, by abdominal incision   Ⓒ 80 50 ▢

    ⚡ 39.29   ⚘ 39.29   Global Days 090

34201 femoropopliteal, aortoiliac artery, by leg incision   Ⓣ 80 50 ▢

    ⚡ 27.32   ⚘ 27.32   Global Days 090

34203 popliteal-tibio-peroneal artery, by leg incision   Ⓣ 80 50 ▢

    ⚡ 27.12   ⚘ 27.12   Global Days 090

34401 Thrombectomy, direct or with catheter; vena cava, iliac vein, by abdominal incision   Ⓒ 80 50 ▢

    ⚡ 40.34   ⚘ 40.34   Global Days 090

34421 vena cava, iliac, femoropopliteal vein, by leg incision   Ⓣ 80 50 ▢

    ⚡ 20.47   ⚘ 20.47   Global Days 090

34451 vena cava, iliac, femoropopliteal vein, by abdominal and leg incision   Ⓒ 80 50 ▢

    ⚡ 42.43   ⚘ 42.43   Global Days 090

34471 subclavian vein, by neck incision   Ⓣ 50 ▢

    ⚡ 29.19   ⚘ 29.19   Global Days 090

34490 axillary and subclavian vein, by arm incision   62 Ⓣ 50 ▢

    ⚡ 17.03   ⚘ 17.03   Global Days 090

34501 Valvuloplasty, femoral vein   Ⓣ 80 50 ▢

    ⚡ 26.46   ⚘ 26.46   Global Days 090

34502 Reconstruction of vena cava, any method   Ⓒ 80 ▢

    ⚡ 42.76   ⚘ 42.76   Global Days 090

34510 Venous valve transposition, any vein donor   Ⓣ 80 50 ▢

    ⚡ 29.92   ⚘ 29.92   Global Days 090

34520 Cross-over vein graft to venous system   Ⓣ 80 50 ▢

    ⚡ 28.75   ⚘ 28.75   Global Days 090

34530 Saphenopopliteal vein anastomosis   Ⓣ 80 50 ▢

    ⚡ 26.89   ⚘ 26.89   Global Days 090

34800-34834 Endovascular Stent Grafting for Abdominal Aneurysms

CMS *100-3,20.23*   *Fabric Wrapping of Abdominal Aneurysms*

INCLUDES   balloon angioplasty
            introduction, manipulation, placement, and deployment
            open exposure of artery/subsequent closure
            thromboendarterectomy at site of aneurysm

EXCLUDES   *additional interventional procedures*
            guidewire and catheter insertion (36140, 36200, 36245-36248)
            substantial artery repair/replacement (35226, 35286)

    🔀 *75952, 75953*

34800 Endovascular repair of infrarenal abdominal aortic aneurysm or dissection; using aorto-aortic tube prosthesis   Ⓒ 00 ▢ P0

    Code also open arterial exposure as appropriate (34812, 34820, 34833, 34834)

    🔀 *75952*

    ⚡ 32.13   ⚘ 32.13   Global Days 090

    AMA: 2008, Jan, 10-25; 2007, Jan, 13-27; 2007, Jan, 13-27; 2007, January, 13-27; 2006, Apr, 11-18; 2006, April, 11-18; 2006, Apr, 11-18; 2005, Jun, 6-8; 2005, June, 6-8; 2005, Jun, 6-8, 2004, Dec, 18; 2004, December, 18; 2004, Dec, 18

34802 using modular bifurcated prosthesis (one docking limb)   Ⓒ 00 ▢ P0

    Code also open arterial exposure as appropriate (34812, 34820, 34833, 34834)

    🔀 *75952*

    ⚡ 34.96   ⚘ 34.96   Global Days 090

    AMA: 2008, Jan, 10-25; 2007, Jan, 13-27; 2007, Jan, 13-27; 2007, January, 13-27; 2006, Apr, 11-18; 2006, April, 11-18; 2006, Apr, 11-18; 2005, Jun, 6-8; 2005, June, 6-8; 2005, Jun, 6-8, 2004, Dec, 18; 2004, December, 18; 2004, Dec, 18

34803 using modular bifurcated prosthesis (2 docking limbs)   Ⓒ 80 ▢ P0

    EXCLUDES   *use of prosthesis for associated visceral vessels (0078T, 0079T)*

    Code also open arterial exposure as appropriate (34812, 34820, 34833, 34834)

    🔀 *75952*

    ⚡ 35.64   ⚘ 35.64   Global Days 090

    AMA: 2006, Apr, 11-18; 2006, Apr, 11-18; 2006, April, 11-18; 2005, Jun, 6-8; 2005, June, 6-8; 2005, Jun, 6-8

34804 using unibody bifurcated prosthesis   Ⓒ 80 ▢ P0

    Code also open arterial exposure as appropriate (34812, 34820, 34833, 34834)

    🔀 *75952*

    ⚡ 34.93   ⚘ 34.93   Global Days 090

    AMA: 2006, Apr, 11-18; 2006, Apr, 11-18; 2006, April, 11-18; 2005, Jun, 6-8; 2005, June, 6-8; 2005, Jun, 6-8

● New Code   ▲ Revised Code   Ⓜ Maternity Edit   Ⓐ Age Edit   Ⓐ-Ⓣ OPPS Status Indicator   ⚡ Facility RVU   ⚘ Non-Facility RVU

▢ CCI Comprehensive Code   50 Bilateral Procedure   + Add-on Indicator   🔬 Laboratory crosswalk   🔀 Radiology crosswalk

Cardiovascular System

34805 — 34900

34805 using aorto-uniiliac or aorto-unifemoral
prosthesis C 80 ▣ P0
Code also open arterial exposure as appropriate (34812,
34820, 34833, 34834)
▨ 75952
⚙ 32.75 ⚒ 32.75 **Global Days 090**
AMA: 2008, Jan, 10-25; 2007, Jan, 13-27; 2007, Jan, 13-27; 2007,
January, 13-27; 2006, Apr, 11-18; 2006, April, 11-18; 2006, Apr,
11-18; 2005, Jun, 6-8; 2005, Jun, 6-8; 2005, June, 6-8; 2004, Jun,
7; 2004, December, 18; 2004, December, 18; 2004, June, 7; 2004,
Jun, 7; 2004, Dec, 18; 2004, Dec, 18; 2004, Dec, 18; 2004, Dec,
18

+ ▲ **34806** Transcatheter placement of wireless physiologic sensor
in aneurysmal sac during endovascular repair, including
radiological supervision and interpretation, instrument
calibration, and collection of pressure data (List
separately in addition to code for primary
procedure) C 80
Code first (33880-33881, 33886, 34800-34805, 34825, 34900)
Code also open arterial exposure as appropriate (34812,
34820, 34833-34834)
Do not report with (93982)
⚙ 3.00 ⚒ 3.00 **Global Days ZZZ**

+ **34808** Endovascular placement of iliac artery occlusion device
(List separately in addition to code for primary
procedure) C 80 ▣
Code first 34800, 34805, 34813, 34825, 34826
Code also open arterial exposure as appropriate (34812,
34820, 34833-34834)
▨ 75952
⚙ 5.90 ⚒ 5.90 **Global Days ZZZ**
AMA: 2005, Jun, 6-8; 2005, Jun, 6-8; 2005, June, 6-8

34812 Open femoral artery exposure for delivery of endovascular
prosthesis, by groin incision, unilateral C 80 50 ▣
Code also as appropriate (34800-34808)
⚙ 9.83 ⚒ 9.83 **Global Days 000**
AMA: 2008, Jan, 10-25; 2007, Jan, 13-27; 2007, Jan, 13-27; 2007,
January, 13-27; 2006, May, 10-11; 2006, May, 10-11; 2006, May,
10-11; 2005, Jun, 6-8; 2005, June, 6-8; 2005, Jun, 6-8; 2004, Mar,
10; 2004, March, 10; 2004, Mar, 10

+ **34813** Placement of femoral-femoral prosthetic graft during
endovascular aortic aneurysm repair (List separately in
addition to code for primary procedure) C 80 ▣
EXCLUDES grafting of femoral artery (35521, 35533,
35539, 35540, 35551-35558, 35566,
35621, 35646, 35651-35661, 35666,
35700)
Code first 34812
⚙ 6.78 ⚒ 6.78 **Global Days ZZZ**
AMA: 2005, Jun, 6-8; 2005, Jun, 6-8; 2005, June, 6-8

34820 Open iliac artery exposure for delivery of endovascular
prosthesis or iliac occlusion during endovascular therapy,
by abdominal or retroperitoneal incision,
unilateral C 80 50 ▣
Code also endovascular repair of abdominal aorta
aneurysm as appropriate (34800-34808)
⚙ 14.05 ⚒ 14.05 **Global Days 000**
AMA: 2008, Jan, 10-25; 2007, Jan, 13-27; 2007, Jan, 13-27; 2007,
January, 13-27; 2006, May, 10-11; 2006, May, 10-11; 2006, May,
10-11; 2005, Jun, 6-8; 2005, June, 6-8; 2005, Jun, 6-8; 2004, Aug,
10; 2004, August, 10; 2004, Aug, 10

34825 Placement of proximal or distal extension prosthesis for
endovascular repair of infrarenal abdominal aortic or iliac
aneurysm, false aneurysm, or dissection; initial
vessel C 80 ▣ P0
Code also endovascular repair of abdominal aorta or iliac
aneurysm as appropriate (34800-34808, 34900)
▨ 75953
⚙ 19.58 ⚒ 19.58 **Global Days 090**
AMA: 2005, Jun, 6-8; 2005, Jun, 6-8; 2005, June, 6-8

+ **34826** each additional vessel (List separately in addition to
code for primary procedure) C 80 ▣
▨ 75953
Code also endovascular repair of abdominal aorta or iliac
aneurysm as appropriate (34800-34808, 34900)
Code first 34825
⚙ 5.81 ⚒ 5.81 **Global Days ZZZ**
AMA: 2005, Jun, 6-8; 2005, Jun, 6-8; 2005, June, 6-8

34830 Open repair of infrarenal aortic aneurysm or dissection,
plus repair of associated arterial trauma, following
unsuccessful endovascular repair; tube
prosthesis C 80 ▣ P0
⚙ 51.52 ⚒ 51.52 **Global Days 090**
AMA: 2008, Oct, 10-11

34831 aorto-bi-iliac prosthesis C 80 ▣ P0
⚙ 54.60 ⚒ 54.60 **Global Days 090**
AMA: 2008, Oct, 10-11

34832 aorto-bifemoral prosthesis C 80 ▣ P0
⚙ 55.34 ⚒ 55.34 **Global Days 090**
AMA: 2008, Oct, 10-11

34833 Open iliac artery exposure with creation of conduit for
delivery of aortic or iliac endovascular prosthesis, by
abdominal or retroperitoneal incision,
unilateral C 80 50 ▣
Do not report with (34820)
⚙ 17.43 ⚒ 17.43 **Global Days 000**
AMA: 2008, Jan, 10-25; 2007, Jan, 13-27; 2007, Jan, 13-27; 2007,
January, 13-27; 2006, May, 10-11; 2006, May, 10-11; 2006, May,
10-11; 2004, Aug, 10; 2004, Aug, 10; 2004, August, 10

34834 Open brachial artery exposure to assist in the deployment
of aortic or iliac endovascular prosthesis by arm incision,
unilateral C 80 50 ▣
⚙ 7.90 ⚒ 7.90 **Global Days 000**
AMA: 2006, May, 10-11; 2006, May, 10-11; 2006, May, 10-11

34900 Endovascular Stent Grafting Iliac Artery

INCLUDES balloon angioplasty
introduction, manipulation, placement, and deployment
EXCLUDES insertion guidewires, catheters (36200, 36215-36218)
open exposure femoral or iliac artery (34812, 34820)
other concurrent interventional procedures
placement extension prosthesis (34825)
substantial artery repair/replacemt (35206-35286)

▨ 75954

34900 Endovascular graft placement for repair of iliac artery
(eg, aneurysm, pseudoaneurysm, arteriovenous
malformation, trauma) C 80 50 ▣ P0
⚙ 25.53 ⚒ 25.53 **Global Days 090**
AMA: 2006, Apr, 11-18; 2006, Apr, 11-18; 2006, April, 11-18

35001-35152 Repair Aneurysm, False Aneurysm, Related Arterial Disease

INCLUDES   endarterectomy procedures

EXCLUDES   *endovascular repairs of:*
     abdominal aortic aneurysm (34800-34826)
     aneurysm of iliac artery (34900)
     thoracic aortic aneurysm (33880)
   intracranial aneurysms (61697-61710)
   open repairs thoracic aortic aneurysm (33860-33875)
   repairs related to occlusive disease only (35201-35286)

35001   Direct repair of aneurysm, pseudoaneurysm, or excision (partial or total) and graft insertion, with or without patch graft; for aneurysm and associated occlusive disease, carotid, subclavian artery, by neck incision   C 80 50 ▭
     ♥ 31.95   ⚕ 31.95   Global Days 090

35002   for ruptured aneurysm, carotid, subclavian artery, by neck incision   C 80 50 ▭
     ♥ 33.74   ⚕ 33.74   Global Days 090

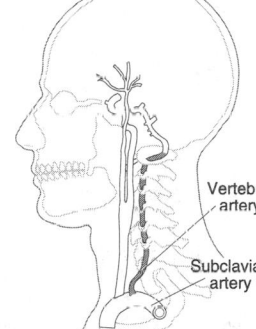

An incision is made in the back of the neck to directly approach an aneurysm or false aneurysm of the vertebral artery. The artery is either repaired directly or excised with a graft.

Graft repair — Vertebral artery — Subclavian artery

35005   for aneurysm, pseudoaneurysm, and associated occlusive disease, vertebral artery   C 80 50 ▭
     ♥ 29.08   ⚕ 29.08   Global Days 090

35011   for aneurysm and associated occlusive disease, axillary-brachial artery, by arm incision   T 80 50 ▭
     ♥ 28.06   ⚕ 28.06   Global Days 090

35013   for ruptured aneurysm, axillary-brachial artery, by arm incision   C 80 50 ▭
     ♥ 34.79   ⚕ 34.79   Global Days 090

35021   for aneurysm, pseudoaneurysm, and associated occlusive disease, innominate, subclavian artery, by thoracic incision   C 80 50 ▭ P0
     ♥ 34.08   ⚕ 34.08   Global Days 090

35022   for ruptured aneurysm, innominate, subclavian artery, by thoracic incision   C 80 50 ▭
     ♥ 38.49   ⚕ 38.49   Global Days 090

35045   for aneurysm, pseudoaneurysm, and associated occlusive disease, radial or ulnar artery   C 80 50 ▭
     ♥ 27.28   ⚕ 27.28   Global Days 090

35081   for aneurysm, pseudoaneurysm, and associated occlusive disease, abdominal aorta   C 80 ▭ P0
     ♥ 48.74   ⚕ 48.74   Global Days 090
     AMA: 2008, Jan, 10-25; 2007, Jan, 13-27; 2007, Jan, 13-27; 2007, January, 13-27; 2005, Jun, 6-8; 2005, June, 6-8; 2005, Jun, 6-8

35082   for ruptured aneurysm, abdominal aorta   C 80 ▭
     ♥ 61.35   ⚕ 61.35   Global Days 090

35091   for aneurysm, pseudoaneurysm, and associated occlusive disease, abdominal aorta involving visceral vessels (mesenteric, celiac, renal)   C 80 50 ▭ P0
     ♥ 51.86   ⚕ 51.86   Global Days 090

35092   for ruptured aneurysm, abdominal aorta involving visceral vessels (mesenteric, celiac, renal)   C 80 50 ▭
     ♥ 73.23   ⚕ 73.23   Global Days 090

35102   for aneurysm, pseudoaneurysm, and associated occlusive disease, abdominal aorta involving iliac vessels (common, hypogastric, external)   C 80 50 ▭ P0
     ♥ 52.92   ⚕ 52.92   Global Days 090
     AMA: 2005, Jun, 6-8; 2005, Jun, 6-8; 2005, June, 6-8

35103   for ruptured aneurysm, abdominal aorta involving iliac vessels (common, hypogastric, external)   C 80 50 ▭
     ♥ 63.44   ⚕ 63.44   Global Days 090

35111   for aneurysm, pseudoaneurysm, and associated occlusive disease, splenic artery   C 80 50 ▭
     ♥ 39.07   ⚕ 39.07   Global Days 090

35112   for ruptured aneurysm, splenic artery   C 80 50 ▭
     ♥ 47.81   ⚕ 47.81   Global Days 090

35121   for aneurysm, pseudoaneurysm, and associated occlusive disease, hepatic, celiac, renal, or mesenteric artery   C 80 50 ▭
     ♥ 46.44   ⚕ 46.44   Global Days 090

35122   for ruptured aneurysm, hepatic, celiac, renal, or mesenteric artery   C 80 50 ▭
     ♥ 55.46   ⚕ 55.46   Global Days 090

35131   for aneurysm, pseudoaneurysm, and associated occlusive disease, iliac artery (common, hypogastric, external)   C 80 50 ▭ P0
     ♥ 39.66   ⚕ 39.66   Global Days 090

35132   for ruptured aneurysm, iliac artery (common, hypogastric, external)   C 80 50 ▭
     ♥ 47.82   ⚕ 47.82   Global Days 090

35141   for aneurysm, pseudoaneurysm, and associated occlusive disease, common femoral artery (profunda femoris, superficial femoral)   C 80 50 ▭ P0
     ♥ 31.42   ⚕ 31.42   Global Days 090

35142   for ruptured aneurysm, common femoral artery (profunda femoris, superficial femoral)   C 80 50 ▭
     ♥ 37.55   ⚕ 37.55   Global Days 090

35151   for aneurysm, pseudoaneurysm, and associated occlusive disease, popliteal artery   C 80 50 ▭ P0
     ♥ 35.42   ⚕ 35.42   Global Days 090

35152   for ruptured aneurysm, popliteal artery   C 80 50 ▭
     ♥ 41.08   ⚕ 41.08   Global Days 090

35180-35190 Repair Arteriovenous Malformations

35180   Repair, congenital arteriovenous fistula; head and neck   T 80 ▭
     ♥ 23.18   ⚕ 23.18   Global Days 090

35182   thorax and abdomen   C 80 ▭
     ♥ 48.35   ⚕ 48.35   Global Days 090

35184   extremities   T 80 ▭
     ♥ 28.47   ⚕ 28.47   Global Days 090

35188   Repair, acquired or traumatic arteriovenous fistula; head and neck   A2 T 80 ▭
     ♥ 23.90   ⚕ 23.90   Global Days 090

35189   thorax and abdomen   C 80 ▭
     ♥ 44.59   ⚕ 44.59   Global Days 090

35190   extremities   T 80 ▭
     ♥ 20.84   ⚕ 20.84   Global Days 090

● New Code   ▲ Revised Code   M Maternity Edit   ■ Age Edit   A Y OPPS Status Indicator   ♥ Facility RVU   ⚕ Non-Facility RVU
▭ CCI Comprehensive Code   50 Bilateral Procedure   + Add-on Indicator   ▣ Laboratory crosswalk   ▣ Radiology crosswalk

Cardiovascular System

35201 — 35306

35201-35286 Surgical Repair Artery or Vein

EXCLUDES *arteriovenous fistula repair (35180-35190)*

Do not report with a primary open vascular procedure.

35201   **Repair blood vessel, direct; neck**   T 80 50 🔲
       🔧 26.17   ⚕ 26.17   Global Days 090

35206   **upper extremity**   T 80 50 🔲
       🔧 21.37   ⚕ 21.37   Global Days 090
       AMA: 2004, Oct, 6; 2004, Oct, 6; 2004, October, 6

35207   **hand, finger**   A2 T 50 🔲
       🔧 19.29   ⚕ 19.29   Global Days 090

35211   **intrathoracic, with bypass**   C 80 50 🔲 PQ
       🔧 37.93   ⚕ 37.93   Global Days 090

35216   **intrathoracic, without bypass**   C 80 50 🔲 PQ
       🔧 52.15   ⚕ 52.15   Global Days 090
       AMA: 2005, Apr, 10-12; 2005, Apr, 10-12; 2005, April, 10-12

35221   **intra-abdominal**   C 80 50 🔲
       🔧 39.06   ⚕ 39.06   Global Days 090

35226   **lower extremity**   T 80 50 🔲
       🔧 23.58   ⚕ 23.58   Global Days 090
       AMA: 2006, May, 10-11; 2006, May, 10-11; 2006, May, 10-11

35231   **Repair blood vessel with vein graft; neck**   T 80 50 🔲
       🔧 32.80   ⚕ 32.80   Global Days 090

35236   **upper extremity**   T 80 50 🔲
       🔧 27.35   ⚕ 27.35   Global Days 090
       AMA: 2004, Oct, 6; 2004, Oct, 6; 2004, October, 6

35241   **intrathoracic, with bypass**   C 80 50 🔲 PQ
       🔧 39.68   ⚕ 39.68   Global Days 090

35246   **intrathoracic, without bypass**   C 80 50 🔲 PQ
       🔧 43.14   ⚕ 43.14   Global Days 090

35251   **intra-abdominal**   C 80 50 🔲
       🔧 46.48   ⚕ 46.48   Global Days 090

35256   **lower extremity**   T 80 50 🔲
       🔧 28.78   ⚕ 28.78   Global Days 090

35261   **Repair blood vessel with graft other than vein; neck**   T 80 50 🔲
       Code also (C1768, L8670)
       🔧 29.08   ⚕ 29.08   Global Days 090

35266   **upper extremity**   T 80 50 🔲
       Code also (C1768, L8670)
       🔧 24.08   ⚕ 24.08   Global Days 090
       AMA: 2004, Oct, 6; 2004, Oct, 6; 2004, October, 6

35271   **intrathoracic, with bypass**   C 80 50 🔲 PQ
       🔧 37.86   ⚕ 37.86   Global Days 090

35276   **intrathoracic, without bypass**   C 80 50 🔲 PQ
       🔧 39.80   ⚕ 39.80   Global Days 090

35281   **intra-abdominal**   C 80 50 🔲
       🔧 44.43   ⚕ 44.43   Global Days 090

35286   **lower extremity**   T 80 50 🔲
       Code also (C1768, L8670)
       🔧 26.39   ⚕ 26.39   Global Days 090
       AMA: 2006, May, 10-11; 2006, May, 10-11; 2006, May, 10-11

35301-35390 Surgical Thromboendarterectomy Peripheral and Visceral Arteries

CMS *100-3,160.8*   *Electroencephalographic Monitoring During Cerebral Vasculature Surgery*

CMS *100-3,20.1*   *Vertebral Artery Surgery*

INCLUDES   obtaining saphenous or arm vein for graft thrombectomy/embolectomy

EXCLUDES   *coronary artery bypass procedures (33510-33536, 33572)*
thromboendarterectomy for vascular occlusion on a different vessel during the same session

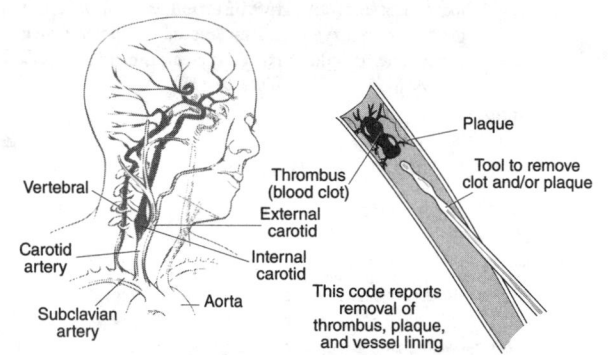

Vertebral   Carotid artery   Subclavian artery   Aorta   Thrombus (blood clot)   External carotid   Internal carotid   Plaque   Tool to remove clot and/or plaque

This code reports removal of thrombus, plaque, and vessel lining

Patch graft may be applied following removal of clot

35301   **Thromboendarterectomy, including patch graft, if performed; carotid, vertebral, subclavian, by neck incision**   C 80 50 🔲 PQ
       🔧 29.61   ⚕ 29.61   Global Days 090
       AMA: 2007, Jan, 7-10; 2007, Jan, 7-10; 2007, January, 7-10

35302   **superficial femoral artery**   C 80 50
       Do not report with (35483, 35500)
       🔧 31.53   ⚕ 31.53   Global Days 090
       AMA: 2007, Jan, 7-10; 2007, Jan, 7-10; 2007, May, 9-11; 2007, May, 9-11; 2007, January, 7-10; 2007, May, 9-11

35303   **popliteal artery**   C 80 50
       Do not report with (35483, 35500)
       🔧 34.69   ⚕ 34.69   Global Days 090
       AMA: 2007, Jan, 7-10; 2007, Jan, 7-10; 2007, May, 9-11; 2007, May, 9-11; 2007, January, 7-10; 2007, May, 9-11

35304   **tibioperoneal trunk artery**   C 80 50
       Do not report with (35485, 35500)
       🔧 36.08   ⚕ 36.08   Global Days 090
       AMA: 2007, Jan, 7-10; 2007, Jan, 7-10; 2007, May, 9-11; 2007, May, 9-11; 2007, January, 7-10; 2007, May, 9-11

35305   **tibial or peroneal artery, initial vessel**   C 80 50
       Do not report with (35485, 35500)
       🔧 34.65   ⚕ 34.65   Global Days 090
       AMA: 2008, Jan, 10-25; 2007, Jan, 7-10; 2007, Jan, 7-10; 2007, May, 9-11; 2007, May, 9-11; 2007, January, 7-10; 2007, May, 9-11

+ **35306**   **each additional tibial or peroneal artery (List separately in addition to code for primary procedure)**   C 80
       Code first (35305)
       Do not report with (35485, 35500)
       🔧 13.00   ⚕ 13.00   Global Days ZZZ
       AMA: 2007, Jan, 7-10; 2007, Jan, 7-10; 2007, May, 9-11; 2007, May, 9-11; 2007, January, 7-10; 2007, May, 9-11

	35311	subclavian, innominate, by thoracic incision	C 80 50 ▣ P0
		🏥 42.30 🔬 42.30 Global Days 090	
	35321	axillary-brachial	T 80 50 ▣
		🏥 25.17 🔬 25.17 Global Days 090	
	35331	abdominal aorta	C 80 50 ▣
		🏥 41.59 🔬 41.59 Global Days 090	
	35341	mesenteric, celiac, or renal	C 80 50 ▣
		🏥 39.20 🔬 39.20 Global Days 090	
	35351	iliac	C 80 50 ▣
		🏥 36.38 🔬 36.38 Global Days 090	
	35355	iliofemoral	C 80 50 ▣
		🏥 29.53 🔬 29.53 Global Days 090	
	35361	combined aortoiliac	C 80 50 ▣
		🏥 44.79 🔬 44.79 Global Days 090	
	35363	combined aortoiliofemoral	C 80 50 ▣
		🏥 48.72 🔬 48.72 Global Days 090	
	35371	common femoral	C 80 50 ▣
		🏥 23.29 🔬 23.29 Global Days 090	
		AMA: 2007, Jan, 7-10; 2007, Jan, 7-10; 2007, January, 7-10	
	35372	deep (profunda) femoral	C 80 50 ▣
		🏥 27.97 🔬 27.97 Global Days 090	
		AMA: 2007, Jan, 7-10; 2007, Jan, 7-10; 2007, January, 7-10	
+	35390	Reoperation, carotid, thromboendarterectomy, more than 1 month after original operation (List separately in addition to code for primary procedure)	C 80 ▣
		Code first 35301	
		🏥 4.58 🔬 4.58 Global Days ZZZ	

35400 Endoscopic Visualization of Vessels

+	35400	Angioscopy (non-coronary vessels or grafts) during therapeutic intervention (List separately in addition to code for primary procedure)	C 80 ▣
		Code first the therapeutic intervention	
		🏥 4.33 🔬 4.33 Global Days ZZZ	

35450-35460 Transluminal Angioplasty: Open

📻 75962-75968, 75978

	35450	Transluminal balloon angioplasty, open; renal or other visceral artery	C 80 50 ▣
		🏥 14.59 🔬 14.59 Global Days 000	
	35452	aortic	C 80 50 ▣
		🏥 10.15 🔬 10.15 Global Days 000	
		AMA: 2005, Jun, 6-8; 2005, Jun, 6-8; 2005, June, 6-8	
	35454	iliac	C 80 50 ▣
		🏥 8.92 🔬 8.92 Global Days 000	
		AMA: 2005, Jun, 6-8; 2005, Jun, 6-8; 2005, June, 6-8	
	35456	femoral-popliteal	C 80 50 ▣
		🏥 10.79 🔬 10.79 Global Days 000	
	35458	brachiocephalic trunk or branches, each vessel	T 80 50 ▣
		Code also (C1725, C1874, C1876, C1885, C2625)	
		🏥 13.82 🔬 13.82 Global Days 000	
		AMA: 2008, Jan, 10-25; 2007, Jan, 13-27; 2007, Jan, 13-27; 2007, January, 13-27	
	35459	tibioperoneal trunk and branches	T 80 50 ▣
		Code also (C1725, C1874, C1876, C1885, C2625)	
		🏥 12.71 🔬 12.71 Global Days 000	
	35460	venous	T 50 ▣
		Code also (C1725, C1874, C1876, C1885, C2625)	
		🏥 8.83 🔬 8.83 Global Days 000	

35470-35476 Transluminal Angioplasty: Percutaneous

CMS 100-3,20.7   *Percutaneous Transluminal Angioplasty (PTA)*

🚫 EXCLUDES   *catheter placement*

📻 75978

⊙	35470	Transluminal balloon angioplasty, percutaneous; tibioperoneal trunk or branches, each vessel	T 50 ▣
		Code also (C1725, C1874, C1876, C1885, C2625)	
		🏥 12.84 🔬 76.20 Global Days 000	

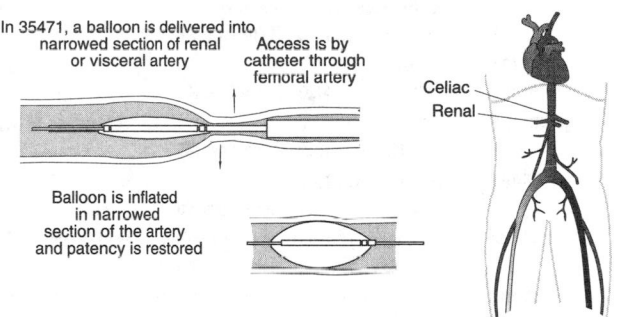

In 35471, a balloon is delivered into narrowed section of renal or visceral artery

Access is by catheter through femoral artery

Celiac
Renal

Balloon is inflated in narrowed section of the artery and patency is restored

A balloon angioplasty is performed on the renal or visceral artery in a percutaneous procedure

⊙	35471	renal or visceral artery	T 50 ▣
		Code also (C1725, C1874, C1876, C1885, C2625)	
		🏥 15.30 🔬 83.71 Global Days 000	
⊙	35472	aortic	T 80 50 ▣
		Code also (C1725, C1874, C1876, C1885, C2625)	
		🏥 10.27 🔬 58.10 Global Days 000	
		AMA: 2005, Jun, 6-8; 2005, Jun, 6-8; 2005, June, 6-8	
⊙	35473	iliac	62 T 50 ▣
		Code also (C1725, C1874, C1876, C1885, C2625)	
		🏥 9.09 🔬 55.47 Global Days 000	
		AMA: 2007, Dec, 10-179	
⊙	35474	femoral-popliteal	T 50 ▣
		Code also (C1725, C1874, C1876, C1885, C2625)	
		🏥 10.97 🔬 73.96 Global Days 000	
		AMA: 2008, Jan, 10-25; 2007, Jan, 13-27; 2007, Jan, 13-27; 2007, Dec, 10-179; 2007, January, 13-27; 2006, Aug, 12-14; 2006, August, 12-14; 2006, Aug, 12-14	
⊙	35475	brachiocephalic trunk or branches, each vessel	T 50 ▣
		Code also (C1725, C1874, C1876, C1885, C2625)	
		🏥 13.70 🔬 59.81 Global Days 000	
		AMA: 2008, Sep, 10▢-11	
⊙	35476	venous	62 T 50 ▣
		Code also (C1725, C1874, C1876, C1885, C2625)	
		🏥 8.73 🔬 45.14 Global Days 000	

35480-35485 Transluminal Atherectomy via Cutdown

📻 75992-75996

	35480	Transluminal peripheral atherectomy, open; renal or other visceral artery	C 80 ▣
		🏥 15.80 🔬 15.80 Global Days 000	
	35481	aortic	C 80 ▣ P0
		🏥 11.46 🔬 11.46 Global Days 000	
	35482	iliac	C 80 ▣
		🏥 9.99 🔬 9.99 Global Days 000	
	35483	femoral-popliteal	C 80 ▣
		🏥 12.08 🔬 12.08 Global Days 000	

| ● New Code | ▲ Revised Code | Ⓜ Maternity Edit | Ⓐ Age Edit | Ⓐ Ⓨ OPPS Status Indicator | 🏥 Facility RVU |
| 🔲 CCI Comprehensive Code | 50 Bilateral Procedure | + Add-on Indicator | 🔬 Non-Facility RVU | ▣ Laboratory crosswalk | 📻 Radiology crosswalk |

Cardiovascular System

35484 — 35538

35484	brachiocephalic trunk or branches, each vessel	T 80 ▭
	⏩ 14.99 ⚕ 14.99 Global Days 000	
35485	tibioperoneal trunk and branches	T 80 ▭
	⏩ 14.01 ⚕ 14.01 Global Days 000	

35490-35495 Transluminal Atherectomy, Percutaneous

EXCLUDES catheter placement

⊠ 75992-75996

35490	Transluminal peripheral atherectomy, percutaneous; renal or other visceral artery	T ▭
	⏩ 17.06 ⚕ 17.06 Global Days 000	
35491	aortic	T 80 ▭
	⏩ 11.53 ⚕ 11.53 Global Days 000	
35492	iliac	62 T ▭
	⏩ 10.38 ⚕ 10.38 Global Days 000	
35493	femoral-popliteal	T ▭
	⏩ 12.66 ⚕ 12.66 Global Days 000	
35494	brachiocephalic trunk or branches, each vessel	T ▭
	⏩ 16.01 ⚕ 16.01 Global Days 000	
35495	tibioperoneal trunk and branches	T 80 ▭
	⏩ 14.68 ⚕ 14.68 Global Days 000	
	AMA: 2008, Jan, 10-25; 2007, Jul, 12-13	

35500 Obtain Arm Vein for Graft

EXCLUDES endoscopic harvest (33508)
harvesting of multiple vein segments (35682, 35683)

+ **35500** Harvest of upper extremity vein, 1 segment, for lower extremity or coronary artery bypass procedure (List separately in addition to code for primary procedure) T 80 ▭
Code first (33510-33536, 35556, 35566, 35571, 35583-35587)
⏩ 9.17 ⚕ 9.17 Global Days ZZZ
AMA: 2007, Jan, 7-10; 2007, Jan, 7-10; 2007, January, 7-10; 2004, Oct, 6; 2004, October, 6; 2004, Oct, 6

35501-35571 Arterial Bypass Using Vein Grafts

CMS 100-3,20.2 *Extracranial-intracranial (EC-IC) Arterial Bypass Surgery*
CMS 100-3,160.8 *Electroencephalographic Monitoring During Cerebral Vasculature Surgery*
CMS 100-3,20.1 *Vertebral Artery Surgery*
INCLUDES harvesting of saphenous vein grafts
EXCLUDES harvesting of multiple vein segments (35682, 35683)
harvesting of vein graft, upper extremity or femoropopliteal (35500, 35572)
treatment of different sites with different bypass procedures during the same operative session

35501	Bypass graft, with vein; common carotid-ipsilateral internal carotid	C 80 50 ▭
	⏩ 44.15 ⚕ 44.15 Global Days 090	
	AMA: 2007, Jan, 7-10; 2007, Jan, 7-10; 2007, January, 7-10	
35506	carotid-subclavian or subclavian-carotid	C 80 50 ▭
	⏩ 37.35 ⚕ 37.35 Global Days 090	
	AMA: 2007, Jan, 7-10; 2007, Jan, 7-10; 2007, January, 7-10; 2004, Oct, 6; 2004, October, 6; 2004, Oct, 6	
35508	carotid-vertebral	C 80 50 ▭
	INCLUDES endoscopic procedure	
	⏩ 38.53 ⚕ 38.53 Global Days 090	
35509	carotid-contralateral carotid	C 80 50 ▭
	⏩ 42.43 ⚕ 42.43 Global Days 090	
	AMA: 2008, Jan, 10-25; 2007, Jan, 7-10; 2007, Jan, 7-10; 2007, May, 9-11; 2007, May, 9-11; 2007, January, 7-10; 2007, May, 9-11; 2006, May, 10-11; 2006, May, 10-11; 2006, May, 10-11	

35510	carotid-brachial	C 80 50 ▭
	⏩ 35.20 ⚕ 35.20 Global Days 090	
	AMA: 2008, Jan, 10-25; 2004, Oct, 6; 2004, Oct, 6; 2004, October, 6	
35511	subclavian-subclavian	C 80 50 ▭
	⏩ 33.43 ⚕ 33.43 Global Days 090	
	AMA: 2004, Oct, 6; 2004, Oct, 6; 2004, October, 6	
35512	subclavian-brachial	C 80 50 ▭
	⏩ 34.33 ⚕ 34.33 Global Days 090	
	AMA: 2004, Oct, 6; 2004, Oct, 6; 2004, October, 6	
35515	subclavian-vertebral	C 80 50 ▭
	⏩ 37.21 ⚕ 37.21 Global Days 090	
35516	subclavian-axillary	C 80 50 ▭
	⏩ 34.00 ⚕ 34.00 Global Days 090	
35518	axillary-axillary	C 80 50 ▭
	⏩ 34.05 ⚕ 34.05 Global Days 090	
	AMA: 2004, Oct, 6; 2004, Oct, 6; 2004, October, 6	
35521	axillary-femoral	C 80 50 ▭
	EXCLUDES synthetic graft (35621)	
	⏩ 35.80 ⚕ 35.80 Global Days 090	
	AMA: 2004, Oct, 6; 2004, Oct, 6; 2004, October, 6	
35522	axillary-brachial	C 80 50 ▭
	⏩ 33.56 ⚕ 33.56 Global Days 090	
	AMA: 2004, Oct, 6; 2004, Oct, 6; 2004, October, 6	
35523	brachial-ulnar or -radial	C 80 50
	EXCLUDES bypass graft performed with synthetic conduit (37799)	
	Do not report with (35206, 35500, 35525, 36838)	
	⏩ 35.51 ⚕ 35.51 Global Days 090	
35525	brachial-brachial	C 80 50 ▭
	⏩ 31.54 ⚕ 31.54 Global Days 090	
	AMA: 2004, Oct, 6; 2004, Oct, 6; 2004, October, 6	
35526	aortosubclavian or carotid	C 80 50 ▭ P0
	EXCLUDES synthetic graft (35626)	
	⏩ 46.72 ⚕ 46.72 Global Days 090	
35531	aortoceliac or aortomesenteric	C 80 50 ▭
	⏩ 57.21 ⚕ 57.21 Global Days 090	
35533	axillary-femoral-femoral	C 80 50 ▭
	EXCLUDES synthetic graft (35654)	
	⏩ 44.25 ⚕ 44.25 Global Days 090	
● 35535	hepatorenal	C 80 50
	Do not report with (35221, 35251, 35281, 35500, 35536, 35560, 35631, 35636)	
	⏩ 56.81 ⚕ 56.81 Global Days 090	
35536	splenorenal	C 80 50 ▭
	⏩ 49.38 ⚕ 49.38 Global Days 090	
	AMA: 2008, Jan, 10-25; 2007, Jan, 13-27; 2007, Jan, 13-27; 2007, January, 13-27	
35537	aortoiliac	C 80
	EXCLUDES synthetic graft (35637)	
	Do not report with (35538)	
	⏩ 61.24 ⚕ 61.24 Global Days 090	
	AMA: 2007, Jan, 7-10; 2007, Jan, 7-10; 2007, January, 7-10	
35538	aortobi-iliac	C 80
	Do not report with (35537)	
	EXCLUDES synthetic graft (35638)	
	⏩ 68.73 ⚕ 68.73 Global Days 090	
	AMA: 2007, Jan, 7-10; 2007, Jan, 7-10; 2007, January, 7-10	

35539   **aortofemoral**   C 80 50
> EXCLUDES   *synthetic graft (35647)*

Do not report with (35540)

🔧 63.75   ✂ 63.75   **Global Days 090**
AMA: 2007, Jan, 7-10; 2007, Jan, 7-10; 2007, January, 7-10

35540   **aortobifemoral**   C 50

Do not report with (35539)
> EXCLUDES   *synthetic graft (35646)*

🔧 71.42   ✂ 71.42   **Global Days 090**
AMA: 2007, Jan, 7-10; 2007, Jan, 7-10; 2007, January, 7-10

35548   **aortoiliofemoral, unilateral**   C 80
> EXCLUDES   *synthetic graft (37799)*

🔧 33.96   ✂ 33.96   **Global Days 090**

35549   **aortoiliofemoral, bilateral**   C 80
> EXCLUDES   *synthetic graft (37799)*

🔧 36.93   ✂ 36.93   **Global Days 090**

35551   **aortofemoral-popliteal**   C 80 50
🔧 42.08   ✂ 42.08   **Global Days 090**

35556   **femoral-popliteal**   C 80 50
🔧 38.95   ✂ 38.95   **Global Days 090**
AMA: 2007, Jan, 7-10; 2007, Jan, 7-10; 2007, January, 7-10

35558   **femoral-femoral**   C 80 50
🔧 34.59   ✂ 34.59   **Global Days 090**

35560   **aortorenal**   C 80 50
🔧 50.44   ✂ 50.44   **Global Days 090**
AMA: 2008, Jan, 10-25; 2007, Jan, 13-27; 2007, Jan, 13-27; 2007, January, 13-27

35563   **ilioiliac**   C 80 50
🔧 38.62   ✂ 38.62   **Global Days 090**

35565   **iliofemoral**   C 80 50
🔧 37.38   ✂ 37.38   **Global Days 090**
AMA: 2004, Oct, 6; 2004, Oct, 6; 2004, October, 6

35566   **femoral-anterior tibial, posterior tibial, peroneal artery or other distal vessels**   C 80 50
🔧 46.77   ✂ 46.77   **Global Days 090**
AMA: 2007, Jan, 7-10; 2007, Jan, 7-10; 2007, January, 7-10

● 35570   **tibial tibial, peroneal tibial, or tibial/peroneal trunk-tibial**   C 80 50

Do not report with (35256, 35286)

🔧 43.86   ✂ 43.86   **Global Days 090**

35571   **popliteal-tibial, -peroneal artery or other distal vessels**   C 80 50
🔧 37.95   ✂ 37.95   **Global Days 090**
AMA: 2007, Jan, 7-10; 2007, Jan, 7-10; 2007, January, 7-10

35572 Obtain Femoropopliteal Vein for Graft

+   35572   **Harvest of femoropopliteal vein, 1 segment, for vascular reconstruction procedure (eg, aortic, vena caval, coronary, peripheral artery) (List separately in addition to code for primary procedure)**   M N 80
> Code first (33510-33523, 33533-33536, 34502, 34520, 35001, 35002, 35011-35022, 35102-35103, 35121-35152, 35231-35256, 35501-35587, 35879-35907)

🔧 9.93   ✂ 9.93   **Global Days ZZZ**
AMA: 2008, Jan, 10-25; 2007, Jan, 28-31; 2007, Jan, 28-31; 2007, January, 28-31

35583-35587 Lower Extremity Revascularization: In-situ Vein Bypass

> INCLUDES   harvesting of saphenous vein grafts
> EXCLUDES   *harvesting of multiple vein segments (35682, 35683)*
> *harvesting of vein graft, upper extremity or femoropopliteal (35500, 35572)*

35583   **In-situ vein bypass; femoral-popliteal**   C 80 50
> Code also concurrent aortobifemoral bypass (synthetic) (35646)
> Code also concurrent aortofemoral bypass (synthetic) (35647)
> Code also concurrent aortobifemoral bypass (vein) (35539)

🔧 40.21   ✂ 40.21   **Global Days 090**
AMA: 2007, Jan, 7-10; 2007, Jan, 7-10; 2007, January, 7-10

35585   **femoral-anterior tibial, posterior tibial, or peroneal artery**   C 80 50
🔧 47.19   ✂ 47.19   **Global Days 090**
AMA: 2007, Jan, 7-10; 2007, Jan, 7-10; 2007, January, 7-10

35587   **popliteal-tibial, peroneal**   C 80 50
🔧 39.13   ✂ 39.13   **Global Days 090**
AMA: 2007, Jan, 7-10; 2007, Jan, 7-10; 2007, January, 7-10

35600 Obtain Arm Artery for Coronary Bypass

> EXCLUDES   *arterial reimplantation (35691-35695)*
> *transposition of arteries (35691-35695)*

+   35600   **Harvest of upper extremity artery, 1 segment, for coronary artery bypass procedure (List separately in addition to code for primary procedure)**   C 80
> Code first (33533-33536)

🔧 7.31   ✂ 7.31   **Global Days ZZZ**
AMA: 2008, Jan, 10-25

35601-35671 Arterial Bypass with Synthetic Grafts

CMS 100-3,20.2   *Extracranial-intracranial (EC-IC) Arterial Bypass Surgery*
CMS 100-3,160.8   *Electroencephalographic Monitoring During Cerebral Vasculature Surgery*
CMS 100-3,20.1   *Vertebral Artery Surgery*
> EXCLUDES   *transposition and/or reimplantation of arteries (35691-35695)*

35601   **Bypass graft, with other than vein; common carotid-ipsilateral internal carotid**   C 80 50 PO
> EXCLUDES   *open transcervical common carotid-common carotid bypass with endovascular repair of descending thoracic aorta (33891)*

🔧 40.78   ✂ 40.78   **Global Days 090**
AMA: 2007, Jan, 7-10; 2007, Jan, 7-10; 2007, January, 7-10; 2006, May, 10-11; 2006, May, 10-11; 2006, May, 10-11

35606   **carotid-subclavian**   C 80 50 PO
> EXCLUDES   *open subclavian to carotid artery transposition performed with endovascular thoracic aneurysm repair via neck incision (33889)*

🔧 33.08   ✂ 33.08   **Global Days 090**

35612   **subclavian-subclavian**   C 80 50 PO
🔧 25.90   ✂ 25.90   **Global Days 090**

35616   **subclavian-axillary**   C 80 50 PO
🔧 31.53   ✂ 31.53   **Global Days 090**

35621   **axillary-femoral**   C 80 50 PO
🔧 31.38   ✂ 31.38   **Global Days 090**
AMA: 2007, Jan, 7-10; 2007, Jan, 7-10; 2007, January, 7-10

35623   **axillary-popliteal or -tibial**   C 80 50 PO
🔧 38.47   ✂ 38.47   **Global Days 090**

● New Code   ▲ Revised Code   M Maternity Edit   A Age Edit   A-Y OPPS Status Indicator   🔧 Facility RVU   ✂ Non-Facility RVU
C CCI Comprehensive Code   50 Bilateral Procedure   + Add-on Indicator   N Laboratory crosswalk   R Radiology crosswalk

35626 — 35686

Cardiovascular System

35626   aortosubclavian or carotid   [C] [80] [50] [☐] [PQ]
         ⊞ 44.22   ⚲ 44.22   Global Days 090

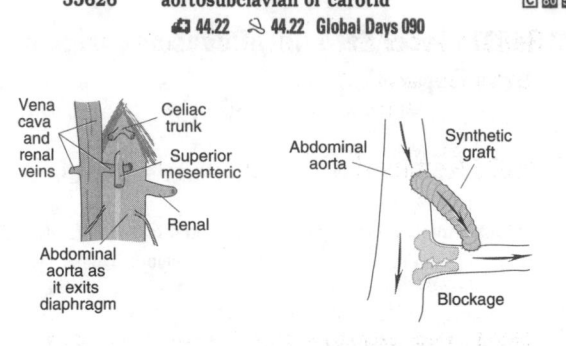

In 35631, a bypass graft of material other than vein is surgically installed from the aorta to the celiac, mesenteric, or renal arteries. The graft is typically placed in an end-to-side fashion on both the aorta and the recipient vessel downstream from the blockage

35631   aortoceliac, aortomesenteric, aortorenal [C] [80] [50] [☐] [PQ]
         ⊞ 52.70   ⚲ 52.70   Global Days 090

● 35632 ilio-celiac   [C] [80] [50]
         Do not report with (35221, 35251, 35281, 35531, 35631)
         ⊞ 53.94   ⚲ 53.94   Global Days 090

● 35633 ilio-mesenteric   [C] [80] [50]
         Do not report with (35221, 35251, 35281, 35531, 35631)
         ⊞ 58.25   ⚲ 58.25   Global Days 090

● 35634 iliorenal   [C] [80] [50]
         Do not report with (35221, 35251, 35281, 35536, 35560, 35631)
         ⊞ 52.79   ⚲ 52.79   Global Days 090

35636   splenorenal (splenic to renal arterial
         anastomosis)   [C] [80] [50] [☐] [PQ]
         ⊞ 46.69   ⚲ 46.69   Global Days 090

35637   aortoiliac   [C] [80] [PQ]
         Do not report with (35638, 35646)
         ⊞ 48.36   ⚲ 48.36   Global Days 090
         AMA: 2008, Jan, 10-25; 2007, Jan, 7-10; 2007, Jan, 7-10; 2007, January, 7-10

35638   aortobi-iliac   [C] [80] [PQ]
         EXCLUDES   open placement of aorto-bi-iliac prosthesis
                    after a failed endovascular repair
                    (34831)
         Do not report with (35637, 35646)
         ⊞ 49.41   ⚲ 49.41   Global Days 090
         AMA: 2008, Jan, 10-25; 2007, Jan, 7-10; 2007, Jan, 7-10; 2007, January, 7-10

35642   carotid-vertebral   [C] [80] [50] [☐] [PQ]
         ⊞ 29.17   ⚲ 29.17   Global Days 090

35645   subclavian-vertebral   [C] [80] [50] [☐] [PQ]
         ⊞ 27.75   ⚲ 27.75   Global Days 090

35646   aortobifemoral   [C] [80] [☐] [PQ]
         EXCLUDES   open placement of aortobifemoral prostheses
                    after a failed endovascular repair
                    (34832)
                    bypass graft using vein graft (35540)
         ⊞ 48.79   ⚲ 48.79   Global Days 090
         AMA: 2007, Jan, 7-10; 2007, Jan, 7-10; 2007, January, 7-10

35647   aortofemoral   [C] [80] [50] [☐] [PQ]
         EXCLUDES   bypass graft using vein graft (35539)
         ⊞ 44.16   ⚲ 44.16   Global Days 090
         AMA: 2007, Jan, 7-10; 2007, Jan, 7-10; 2007, January, 7-10

35650   axillary-axillary   [C] [80] [50] [☐] [PQ]
         ⊞ 30.20   ⚲ 30.20   Global Days 090

35651   aortofemoral-popliteal   [C] [80] [50] [☐] [PQ]
         ⊞ 39.05   ⚲ 39.05   Global Days 090

35654   axillary-femoral-femoral   [C] [80] [☐] [PQ]
         ⊞ 38.98   ⚲ 38.98   Global Days 090
         AMA: 2007, Jan, 7-10; 2007, Jan, 7-10; 2007, January, 7-10

35656   femoral-popliteal   [C] [80] [50] [☐] [PQ]
         ⊞ 30.73   ⚲ 30.73   Global Days 090

35661   femoral-femoral   [C] [80] [50] [☐] [PQ]
         ⊞ 30.74   ⚲ 30.74   Global Days 090
         AMA: 2007, Jan, 7-10; 2007, Jan, 7-10; 2007, January, 7-10

35663   ilioiliac   [C] [80] [50] [☐] [PQ]
         ⊞ 35.62   ⚲ 35.62   Global Days 090

35665   iliofemoral   [C] [80] [50] [☐] [PQ]
         ⊞ 33.40   ⚲ 33.40   Global Days 090
         AMA: 2007, Jan, 7-10; 2007, Jan, 7-10; 2007, January, 7-10

35666   femoral-anterior tibial, posterior tibial, or peroneal
         artery   [C] [80] [50] [☐] [PQ]
         ⊞ 36.00   ⚲ 36.00   Global Days 090

35671   popliteal-tibial or -peroneal artery   [C] [80] [50] [☐] [PQ]
         ⊞ 31.72   ⚲ 31.72   Global Days 090

35681-35686 Arterial Bypass Using Combination Synthetic and Donor Graft

+ 35681 Bypass graft; composite, prosthetic and vein (List
         separately in addition to code for primary
         procedure)   [C] [80] [☐]
         Do not report with (35682, 35683)
         ⊞ 2.29   ⚲ 2.29   Global Days ZZZ
         AMA: 2008, Jan, 10-25; 2007, Jan, 13-27; 2007, Jan, 13-27; 2007, January, 13-27

+ 35682 autogenous composite, 2 segments of veins from 2
         locations (List separately in addition to code for
         primary procedure)   [C] [80] [☐]
         Code first (35556, 35566, 35571, 35583-35587)
         Do not report with (35681, 35683)
         ⊞ 10.22   ⚲ 10.22   Global Days ZZZ
         AMA: 2008, Jan, 10-25; 2007, Jan, 13-27; 2007, Jan, 13-27; 2007, January, 13-27

+ 35683 autogenous composite, 3 or more segments of vein
         from 2 or more locations (List separately in addition
         to code for primary procedure)   [C] [80] [☐]
         Code first (35556, 35566, 35571, 35583-35587)
         Do not report with (35681, 35682)
         ⊞ 12.05   ⚲ 12.05   Global Days ZZZ
         AMA: 2008, Jan, 10-25; 2007, Jan, 13-27; 2007, Jan, 13-27; 2007, January, 13-27

+ 35685 Placement of vein patch or cuff at distal anastomosis of
         bypass graft, synthetic conduit (List separately in
         addition to code for primary procedure)   [T] [80] [☐]
         EXCLUDES   composite grafts (35681-35683)
         Code first (35656, 35666, or 35671)
         ⊞ 5.74   ⚲ 5.74   Global Days ZZZ

+ 35686 Creation of distal arteriovenous fistula during lower
         extremity bypass surgery (non-hemodialysis) (List
         separately in addition to code for primary
         procedure)   [T] [80] [☐]
         EXCLUDES   composite grafts (35681-35683)
         Code first (35556, 35566, 35571, 35583-35587, 35623, 35656, 35666, 35671)
         ⊞ 4.80   ⚲ 4.80   Global Days ZZZ

35691-35697 Arterial Translocation

CMS *100-3,20.2*   *Extracranial-intracranial (EC-IC) Arterial Bypass Surgery*
CMS *100-3,160.8*   *Electroencephalographic Monitoring During Cerebral Vasculature Surgery*
CMS *100-3,20.1*   *Vertebral Artery Surgery*

35691   **Transposition and/or reimplantation; vertebral to carotid artery**   C 80 50
    28.00   28.00   Global Days 090

35693   **vertebral to subclavian artery**   C 80 50
    24.82   24.82   Global Days 090

35694   **subclavian to carotid artery**   C 80 50
    EXCLUDES   *subclavian to carotid artery transposition procedure (open) with concurrent repair of descending thoracic aorta (endovascular) (33889)*
    28.95   28.95   Global Days 090

35695   **carotid to subclavian artery**   C 80 50
    30.13   30.13   Global Days 090

+   35697   **Reimplantation, visceral artery to infrarenal aortic prosthesis, each artery (List separately in addition to code for primary procedure)**   C 80
    Do not report with (33877)
    4.27   4.27   Global Days ZZZ

35700 Reoperative Bypass Lower Extremities

+   35700   **Reoperation, femoral-popliteal or femoral (popliteal)-anterior tibial, posterior tibial, peroneal artery, or other distal vessels, more than 1 month after original operation (List separately in addition to code for primary procedure)**   C 80
    Code first (35556, 35566, 35571, 35583, 35585, 35587, 35656, 35666, 35671)
    4.40   4.40   Global Days ZZZ

35701-35761 Arterial Exploration without Repair

35701   **Exploration (not followed by surgical repair), with or without lysis of artery; carotid artery**   C 80 50
    14.93   14.93   Global Days 090

35721   **femoral artery**   C 80 50
    12.71   12.71   Global Days 090

35741   **popliteal artery**   C 80 50
    13.91   13.91   Global Days 090

35761   **other vessels**   62 T 80 50
    10.26   10.26   Global Days 090

35800-35860 Arterial Exploration for Postoperative Complication

INCLUDES   *return to the operating room for postoperative hemorrhage*

35800   **Exploration for postoperative hemorrhage, thrombosis or infection; neck**   C 80
    13.18   13.18   Global Days 090

35820   **chest**   C 80 P0
    50.96   50.96   Global Days 090

35840   **abdomen**   C 80
    17.25   17.25   Global Days 090

35860   **extremity**   T 80
    11.13   11.13   Global Days 090

35870 Repair Secondary Aortoenteric Fistula

35870   **Repair of graft-enteric fistula**   C 80
    36.13   36.13   Global Days 090

35875-35876 Removal of Thrombus from Graft

EXCLUDES   *thrombectomy dialysis fistula or graft (36831, 36833)*
    thrombectomy with blood vessel repair, lower extremity, vein graft (35256)
    thrombectomy with blood vessel repair, lower extremity, with/without patch angioplasty (35226)

35875   **Thrombectomy of arterial or venous graft (other than hemodialysis graft or fistula);**   A2 T
    16.67   16.67   Global Days 090
    AMA: 2008, Jan, 10-25; 2007, Jan, 13-27; 2007, Jan, 13-27; 2007, January, 13-27

35876   **with revision of arterial or venous graft**   A2 T 80
    26.73   26.73   Global Days 090

35879-35884 Revision Lower Extremity Bypass Graft

EXCLUDES   *removal of infected graft (35901-35907)*
    revascularization following removal of infected graft(s)

35879   **Revision, lower extremity arterial bypass, without thrombectomy, open; with vein patch angioplasty**   T A0 K0
    26.14   26.14   Global Days 090
    AMA: 2007, Jan, 7-10; 2007, Jan, 7-10; 2007, January, 7-10

35881   **with segmental vein interposition**   T 80 50
    EXCLUDES   *revision of femoral anastomosis of synthetic arterial bypass graft (35883-35884)*
    29.07   29.07   Global Days 090
    AMA: 2007, Jan, 7-10; 2007, Jan, 7-10; 2007, January, 7-10

35883   **Revision, femoral anastomosis of synthetic arterial bypass graft in groin, open; with nonautogenous patch graft (eg, Dacron, ePTFE, bovine pericardium)**   T 80 50
    Do not report with (35700, 35875-35876, 35884)
    33.95   33.95   Global Days 090
    AMA: 2008, Jan, 10-25; 2007, Jan, 7-10; 2007, Jan, 7-10; 2007, January, 7-10

35884   **with autogenous vein patch graft**   T 80 50
    Do not report with (35700, 35875-35876, 35883)
    35.82   35.82   Global Days 090
    AMA: 2008, Jan, 10-25; 2007, Jan, 7-10; 2007, Jan, 7-10; 2007, January, 7-10

35901-35907 Removal of Infected Graft

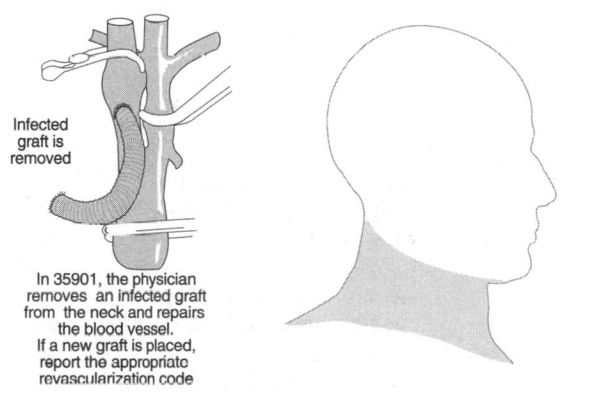

Infected graft is removed

In 35901, the physician removes an infected graft from the neck and repairs the blood vessel. If a new graft is placed, report the appropriate revascularization code

---

● New Code   ▲ Revised Code   M Maternity Edit   A Age Edit   A-Y OPPS Status Indicator   Facility RVU   Non-Facility RVU
CCI Comprehensive Code   50 Bilateral Procedure   + Add-on Indicator   Laboratory crosswalk   Radiology crosswalk

© 2008 Ingenix *(Blue Ink)*   CPT only © 2008 American Medical Association. All Rights Reserved. (Black Ink)   Medicare (Red Ink)   141

Cardiovascular System

35901 — 36216

35901	Excision of infected graft; neck	C 80 🔲
	🔧 13.99　⚕ 13.99　Global Days 090	
35903	extremity	T 80 🔲
	🔧 15.82　⚕ 15.82　Global Days 090	
35905	thorax	C 80 🔲
	🔧 49.26　⚕ 49.26　Global Days 090	
35907	abdomen	C 80 🔲
	🔧 54.27　⚕ 54.27　Global Days 090	

36000 Intravenous Access Established

INCLUDES　venous access for phlebotomy, prophylactic intravenous access, infusion therapy, chemotherapy, hydration, transfusion, drug administration, etc. which is included in the work value of the primary procedure

36000　Introduction of needle or intracatheter, vein　N1 N 50 🔲
　　　🔧 0.26　⚕ 0.67　Global Days XXX
　　　AMA: 2008, Jan, 10-25; 2007, Jan, 13-27; 2007, Jan, 13-27; 2007, Feb, 10-11; 2007, Feb, 10-11; 2007, January, 13-27; 2007, Jul, 1-4; 2007, February, 10-11; 2006, May, 1-9; 2006, May, 1-9; 2006, May, 1-9

36002 Injection Treatment of Pseudoaneurysm

INCLUDES　insertion of needle or catheter, local anesthesia, injection of contrast, power injections

EXCLUDES　compression repair pseudoaneurysm, ultrasound guided (76936)
　　　medications, contrast material, catheters

36002　Injection procedures (eg, thrombin) for percutaneous treatment of extremity pseudoaneurysm　G2 S 50 🔲
　　　🔗 76942, 77002, 77012, 77021
　　　🔧 3.06　⚕ 4.56　Global Days 000

36005-36015 Insertion Needle or Intracatheter: Venous

INCLUDES　insertion of needle/catheter, local anesthesia, injection of contrast, power injections

EXCLUDES　medications, contrast materials, catheters

Code also catheterization of second order vessels (or higher) supplied by the same first order branch, same vascular family

Code also each vascular family (e.g., bilateral procedures are separate vascular families)

36005　Injection procedure for extremity venography (including introduction of needle or intracatheter)　N1 N 80 50 🔲
　　　🔗 75820, 75822
　　　🔧 1.37　⚕ 9.06　Global Days 000

36010　Introduction of catheter, superior or inferior vena cava　N1 N 50 🔲
　　　🔧 3.47　⚕ 15.68　Global Days XXX
　　　AMA: 2008, Jan, 10-25; 2008, Oct, 10-11; 2007, Jan, 13-27; 2007, Jan, 13-27; 2007, January, 13-27; 2004, Dec, 6; 2004, December, 6; 2004, Dec, 6

36011　Selective catheter placement, venous system; first order branch (eg, renal vein, jugular vein)　N1 N 50 🔲
　　　🔧 4.49　⚕ 24.81　Global Days XXX
　　　AMA: 2004, Dec, 6; 2004, Dec, 6; 2004, December, 6

36012　second order, or more selective, branch (eg, left adrenal vein, petrosal sinus)　N1 N 50 🔲
　　　🔧 5.04　⚕ 23.32　Global Days XXX
　　　AMA: 2004, Dec, 6; 2004, Dec, 6; 2004, December, 6

36013　Introduction of catheter, right heart or main pulmonary artery　N1 N 🔲
　　　🔧 3.65　⚕ 21.56　Global Days XXX
　　　AMA: 2008, Oct, 10-11

36014　Selective catheter placement, left or right pulmonary artery　N1 N 50 🔲
　　　🔧 4.38　⚕ 22.47　Global Days XXX

36015　Selective catheter placement, segmental or subsegmental pulmonary artery　N1 N 50 🔲
　　　EXCLUDES　placement of Swan Ganz/other flow directed catheter for monitoring (93503)
　　　selective blood sampling, specific organs (36500)
　　　🔧 5.06　⚕ 24.64　Global Days XXX

36100-36248 Insertion Needle or Intracatheter: Arterial

INCLUDES　introduction of the catheter and catheterization of all lesser order vessels used for the approach
　　　local anesthesia, placement of catheter/needle, injection of contrast, power injections

EXCLUDES　angioplasty (35470-35475)
　　　injection procedures for cardiac catheterizations (93541-93545)
　　　medications, contrast, catheters
　　　transcatheter procedures (37200-37208, 61624, 61626)

Code also catheterization of second and third order vessels supplied by the same first order branch, same vascular family (36218, 36248)

　　　🔗 75600-75790

36100　Introduction of needle or intracatheter, carotid or vertebral artery　N1 N 50 🔲
　　　🔧 4.46　⚕ 14.33　Global Days XXX

36120　Introduction of needle or intracatheter; retrograde brachial artery　N1 N 🔲
　　　🔧 2.80　⚕ 11.83　Global Days XXX

36140　extremity artery　N1 N 🔲
　　　🔧 2.89　⚕ 13.07　Global Days XXX
　　　AMA: 2007, Jul, 1-4; 2007, Dec, 10-179; 2006, May, 1-9; 2006, May, 1-9; 2006, May, 10-11; 2006, May, 10-11; 2006, May, 10-11; 2006, May, 1-9

36145　arteriovenous shunt created for dialysis (cannula, fistula, or graft)　N1 N 🔲
　　　EXCLUDES　arteriovenous (AV) cannula placement (36810-36821)
　　　🔧 2.81　⚕ 12.93　Global Days XXX
　　　AMA: 2007, Dec, 10-179

36160　Introduction of needle or intracatheter, aortic, translumbar　N1 N 🔲
　　　🔧 3.78　⚕ 14.41　Global Days XXX
　　　AMA: 2007, Dec, 10-179

36200　Introduction of catheter, aorta　N1 N 50 🔲
　　　🔧 4.32　⚕ 17.48　Global Days XXX
　　　AMA: 2008, Apr, -11; 2008, Apr, -11; 2008, Apr, -11; 2007, Dec, 10-179; 2006, May, 10-11; 2006, May, 10-11; 2006, May, 10-11

36215　Selective catheter placement, arterial system; each first order thoracic or brachiocephalic branch, within a vascular family　N1 N 🔲
　　　EXCLUDES　placement of catheter for coronary angiography (93508)
　　　🔧 6.82　⚕ 30.74　Global Days XXX
　　　AMA: 2008, Jan, 10-25; 2007, Jan, 13-27; 2007, Jan, 13-27; 2007, Dec, 10-179; 2007, January, 13-27; 2006, May, 10-11; 2006, May, 10-11; 2006, May, 10-11

36216　initial second order thoracic or brachiocephalic branch, within a vascular family　N1 N 🔲
　　　🔧 7.69　⚕ 33.60　Global Days XXX
　　　AMA: 2007, Dec, 10-179; 2006, May, 10-11; 2006, May, 10-11; 2006, May, 10-11

36217   initial third order or more selective thoracic or brachiocephalic branch, within a vascular family   Ⓜ Ⓝ 🔲

   🔁 9.23   ⚖ 54.73   Global Days XXX

   AMA: 2007, Dec, 10-179; 2006, May, 10-11; 2006, May, 10-11; 2006, May, 10-11

+ 36218   additional second order, third order, and beyond, thoracic or brachiocephalic branch, within a vascular family (List in addition to code for initial second or third order vessel as appropriate)   Ⓜ Ⓝ 🔲

   Code first (36216, 36217)

   🔁 1.47   ⚖ 5.16   Global Days ZZZ

   AMA: 2007, Dec, 10-179; 2006, May, 10-11; 2006, May, 10-11; 2006, May, 10-11

36245   Selective catheter placement, arterial system; each first order abdominal, pelvic, or lower extremity artery branch, within a vascular family   Ⓝ Ⓝ 50 🔲

   🔁 7.04   ⚖ 33.91   Global Days XXX

   AMA: 2008, Jan, 10-25; 2007, Jan, 13-27; 2007, Jan, 13-27; 2007, Jan, 7-10; 2007, Jan, 7-10; 2007, January, 7-10; 2007, January, 13-27; 2007, Dec, 10-179

36246   initial second order abdominal, pelvic, or lower extremity artery branch, within a vascular family   Ⓝ Ⓝ 50 🔲

   🔁 7.69   ⚖ 33.34   Global Days XXX

   AMA: 2008, Jan, 10-25; 2007, Jan, 13-27; 2007, Jan, 13-27; 2007, Jan, 7-10; 2007, Jan, 7-10, 2007, January, 7-10, 2007, January, 13-27; 2007, Dec, 10-179

36247   initial third order or more selective abdominal, pelvic, or lower extremity artery branch, within a vascular family   Ⓝ Ⓝ 50 🔲

   🔁 9.16   ⚖ 52.31   Global Days XXX

   AMA: 2008, Jan, 10-25; 2007, Jan, 13-27; 2007, Jan, 13-27; 2007, Jan, 7-10; 2007, Jan, 7-10; 2007, January, 13-27; 2007, January, 7-10; 2007, Dec, 10-179

+ 36248   additional second order, third order, and beyond, abdominal, pelvic, or lower extremity artery branch, within a vascular family (List in addition to code for initial second or third order vessel as appropriate)   Ⓝ Ⓝ 🔲

   Code first (36246, 36247)

   🔁 1.47   ⚖ 4.44   Global Days ZZZ

   AMA: 2008, Jan, 10-25; 2007, Jan, 13-27; 2007, Jan, 13-27; 2007, Jan, 7-10; 2007, Jan, 7-10; 2007, January, 7-10; 2007, January, 13-27

36260-36299 Implanted Infusion Pumps: Intra-arterial

CMS 100-3,280.14   *Infusion Pumps*

36260   Insertion of implantable intra-arterial infusion pump (eg, for chemotherapy of liver)   A2 Ⓣ 🔲

   Code also (C1772, C1891, C2626)

   🔁 15.89   ⚖ 15.89   Global Days 090

36261   Revision of implanted intra-arterial infusion pump   A2 Ⓣ 80 🔲

   🔁 9.66   ⚖ 9.66   Global Days 090

36262   Removal of implanted intra-arterial infusion pump   A2 Ⓣ 🔲

   🔁 7.36   ⚖ 7.36   Global Days 090

36299   Unlisted procedure, vascular injection   Ⓝ 80

   🔁 0.00   ⚖ 0.00   Global Days YYY

36400-36425 Specimen Collection: Phlebotomy

EXCLUDES   collection of specimen from:
   a completely implantable device (36591)
   an established catheter (36592)

36400   Venipuncture, younger than age 3 years, necessitating physician's skill, not to be used for routine venipuncture; femoral or jugular vein   Ⓐ Ⓜ Ⓝ 🔲

   🔁 0.49   ⚖ 0.69   Global Days XXX

   AMA: 2007, Jul, 1-4; 2006, May, 1-9; 2006, May, 1-9; 2006, May, 1-9

36405   scalp vein   Ⓐ Ⓜ Ⓝ 🔲

   🔁 0.43   ⚖ 0.63   Global Days XXX

   AMA: 2007, Jul, 1-4; 2006, May, 1-9; 2006, May, 1-9; 2006, May, 1-9

36406   other vein   Ⓐ Ⓜ Ⓝ 🔲

   🔁 0.25   ⚖ 0.45   Global Days XXX

   AMA: 2007, Jul, 1-4; 2006, May, 1-9; 2006, May, 1-9; 2006, May, 1-9

36410   Venipuncture, age 3 years or older, necessitating physician's skill (separate procedure), for diagnostic or therapeutic purposes (not to be used for routine venipuncture)   Ⓜ Ⓝ 🔲

   🔁 0.24   ⚖ 0.50   Global Days XXX

   AMA: 2008, Jan, 10-25; 2007, Jan, 13-27; 2007, Jan, 13-27; 2007, Feb, 10-11, 2007, Feb, 10-11; 2007, January, 13-27; 2007, February, 10-11; 2007, Jul, 1-4

36415   Collection of venous blood by venipuncture   Ⓐ ⊕

   🔁 0.00   ⚖ 0.00   Global Days XXX

   AMA: 2008, Apr, -9; 2008, Apr, -9; 2008, Apr, -9; 2008, Jan, 10-25; 2007, Jan, 13-27; 2007, January, 13-27; 2007, Jul, 1-4; 2007, February, 10-11; 2007, Jan, 13-27; 2007, Feb, 10-11; 2007, Feb, 10-11

36416   Collection of capillary blood specimen (eg, finger, heel, ear stick)   Ⓜ Ⓝ

   🔁 0.00   ⚖ 0.00   Global Days XXX

   AMA: 2008, Apr, -9; 2008, Apr, -9; 2008, Apr, -9

36420   Venipuncture, cutdown; younger than age 1 year   Ⓐ 62 Ⓧ 80 ⊕ 🔲

   🔁 1.33   ⚖ 1.33   Global Days XXX

   AMA: 2007, Jul, 1-4; 2006, May, 1-9; 2006, May, 1-9; 2006, May, 1-9

36425   age 1 or over   R2 Ⓧ 🔲

   🔁 1.05   ⚖ 1.05   Global Days XXX

36430-36460 Transfusions

CMS 100-3,110.8   *Blood Platelet Transfusions*
CMS 100-2,1,10   *Inpatient Hospital Services Covered Under Part A*
CMS 100-1,3,20.5.2   *Part B Blood Deductible*
CMS 100-1,3,20.5   *Blood Deductibles*
CMS 100-4,3,40.2.2   *Beneficiary Charges for Part A Services*
CMS 100-3,110.7   *Blood Transfusions*
CMS 100-3,110.5   *Granulocyte Transfulsions*
CMS 100-3,110.16   *Nonselective (Random) Transfusions and Living-Related Donor Specific Transfusions (DST) in Kidney Transplantation*

36430   Transfusion, blood or blood components   P3 Ⓢ 🔲

   🔁 1.00   ⚖ 1.00   Global Days XXX

   AMA: 2008, Jan, 10-25; 2007, Jan, 13-27; 2007, Jan, 13-27; 2007, Jul, 1-4; 2007, January, 13-27; 2006, May, 1-9; 2006, May, 1-9; 2006, May, 1-9

36440   Push transfusion, blood, 2 years or younger   Ⓐ R2 Ⓢ 80 🔲

   🔁 1.41   ⚖ 1.41   Global Days XXX

   AMA: 2007, Jul, 1-4; 2006, May, 1-9; 2006, May, 1-9; 2006, May, 1-9

● New Code   ▲ Revised Code   Ⓜ Maternity Edit   Ⓐ Age Edit   Ⓐ Ⓥ OPPS Status Indicator   🔁 Facility RVU   ⚖ Non-Facility RVU

🔲 CCI Comprehensive Code   50 Bilateral Procedure   + Add-on Indicator   Ⓢ Laboratory crosswalk   Ⓧ Radiology crosswalk

Cardiovascular System

36450 — 36522

36450 Exchange transfusion, blood; newborn A 62 S 80 ⊗ ▭
    3.24 3.24 Global Days XXX

36455   other than newborn 62 S ▭
    3.51 3.51 Global Days XXX

36460 Transfusion, intrauterine, fetal A ♀ S 80 ⊗ ▭
    76941
    9.29 9.29 Global Days XXX

36468-36479 Destruction of Veins

CMS *100-2,16,180* *Services Related to Noncovered Procedures*
CMS *100-2,16,120* *Cosmetic Procedures*
CMS *100-2,16,10* *Exclusions from Coverage*

36468 Single or multiple injections of sclerosing solutions, spider veins (telangiectasia); limb or trunk R2 T 80 ▭
    0.00 0.00 Global Days 000

36469   face R2 T 80 ▭
    0.00 0.00 Global Days 000

36470 Injection of sclerosing solution; single vein P2 T 50 ▭
    1.88 3.64 Global Days 010

36471   multiple veins, same leg P2 T 50 ▭
    2.65 4.50 Global Days 010

36475 Endovenous ablation therapy of incompetent vein, extremity, inclusive of all imaging guidance and monitoring, percutaneous, radiofrequency; first vein treated R2 T 50 ▭

Do not report with (36000-36005, 36410, 36425, 36478-36479, 37204, 75894, 76000-76001, 76937, 76942, 76998, 77022, 93970-93971)
    9.29 47.10 Global Days 000

\+ **36476**   second and subsequent veins treated in a single extremity, each through separate access sites (List separately in addition to code for primary procedure) A2 T 50

Code first (36475)

Do not report with (36000-36005, 36410, 36425, 36478-36479, 37204, 75894, 76000-76001, 76937, 76942, 76998, 77022, 93970-93971)
    4.54 10.13 Global Days ZZZ

36478 Endovenous ablation therapy of incompetent vein, extremity, inclusive of all imaging guidance and monitoring, percutaneous, laser; first vein treated A2 T 50 ▭

Do not report with (36000-36005, 36410, 36425, 36475-36476, 37204, 75894, 76000-76001, 76937, 76942, 76998, 77022, 93970-93971)
    9.38 38.83 Global Days 000

\+ **36479**   second and subsequent veins treated in a single extremity, each through separate access sites (List separately in addition to code for primary procedure) A2 T 50

Code first (36478)

Do not report with (36000-36005, 36410, 36425, 36475-36476, 37204, 75894, 76000-76001, 76937, 76942, 76998, 77022, 93970-93971)
    4.57 10.65 Global Days ZZZ

36481-36510 Other Venous Catheterization Procedures

EXCLUDES *collection of a specimen from:*
   a completely implantable device (36591)
   an established catheter (36592)

36481 Percutaneous portal vein catheterization by any method NI N ▭
    75885, 75887
    11.36 11.36 Global Days 000
    AMA: 2008, Jan, 10-25; 2007, Jan, 13-27; 2007, Jan, 13-27; 2007, January, 13-27; 2006, Apr, 11-18; 2006, April, 11-18; 2006, Apr, 11-18

36500 Venous catheterization for selective organ blood sampling NI N ▭
    EXCLUDES *inferior or superior vena cava catheterization (36010)*
    75893
    5.03 5.03 Global Days 000

36510 Catheterization of umbilical vein for diagnosis or therapy, newborn A NI N 80 ⊗ ▭
    EXCLUDES *collection of a specimen from:*
      capillary blood (36416)
      venipuncture (36415)
    1.57 2.92 Global Days 000
    AMA: 2007, Jul, 1-4; 2006, May, 1-9; 2006, May, 1-9; 2006, May, 1-9; 2004, Aug, 7; 2004, August, 7; 2004, Aug, 7

36511-36516 Apheresis

CMS *100-3,110.14* *Apheresis (Therapeutic Pheresis)*
CMS *100-1,3,20.5.2* *Part B Blood Deductible*
EXCLUDES *collection of a specimen from:*
   a completely implantable device (36591)
   an established catheter (36592)

36511 Therapeutic apheresis; for white blood cells 62 S ▭
    2.44 2.44 Global Days 000

36512   for red blood cells 62 S ▭
    2.48 2.48 Global Days 000

36513   for platelets 62 S ▭
    2.59 2.59 Global Days 000

36514   for plasma pheresis 62 S ▭
    2.42 13.73 Global Days 000

36515   with extracorporeal immunoadsorption and plasma reinfusion P2 S ▭
    2.37 51.17 Global Days 000

36516   with extracorporeal selective adsorption or selective filtration and plasma reinfusion P2 S ▭
    1.71 57.93 Global Days 000

36522 Extracorporeal Photopheresis

CMS *100-3,110.4* *Extracorporeal Photopheresis*

36522 Photopheresis, extracorporeal 62 S ▭
    2.77 36.15 Global Days 000

36555-36571 Placement of Implantable Venous Access Device

INCLUDES devices that are inserted via cutdown or percutaneous access, either centrally (e.g., femoral, jugular, subclavian veins, or vena cava) or peripherally (e.g., basilic or cephalic)
devices that terminate in the brachiocephalic (innominate), iliac, or subclavian veins, vena cava, or right atrium

EXCLUDES *maintenance/refilling of implantable pump/reservoir (96522)*

🔀 *76937, 77001*

⊙ **36555** Insertion of non-tunneled centrally inserted central venous catheter; younger than 5 years of age Ⓐ Ⓐ2 Ⓣ ▭
　　　　EXCLUDES *that by peripheral insertion (36568)*

　　　　🚑 3.46 ⚕ 7.28 Global Days 000
　　　　AMA: 2008, Jun, 8-11; 2007, Jul, 1-4; 2006, May, 1-9; 2006, May, 1-9; 2006, May, 1-9; 2004, Jun, 10; 2004, Jun, 10; 2004, December, 6; 2004, June, 10; 2004, Dec, 6; 2004, Dec, 6

　36556 age 5 years or older Ⓐ Ⓐ2 Ⓣ ▭
　　　　EXCLUDES *that by peripheral insertion (36569)*

　　　　🚑 3.31 ⚕ 6.24 Global Days 000
　　　　AMA: 2008, Jun, 8-11; 2004, Dec, 6; 2004, Dec, 6; 2004, Jun, 10; 2004, Jun, 10; 2004, June, 10; 2004, December, 6

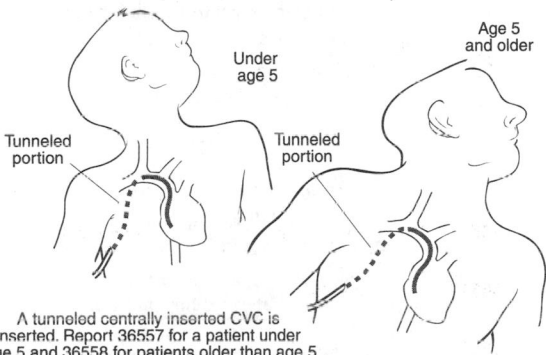

Under age 5

Age 5 and older

Tunneled portion

Tunneled portion

A tunneled centrally inserted CVC is inserted. Report 36557 for a patient under age 5 and 36558 for patients older than age 5

⊙ **36557** Insertion of tunneled centrally inserted central venous catheter, without subcutaneous port or pump; younger than 5 years of age Ⓐ Ⓐ2 Ⓣ 80 50 ▭
　　　　Code also (C1750, C1751, C1752)
　　　　🚑 8.24 ⚕ 22.45 Global Days 010
　　　　AMA: 2008, Jun, 8-11; 2004, Dec, 6; 2004, Dec, 6; 2004, Jun, 10; 2004, Jun, 10; 2004, June, 10; 2004, December, 6

⊙ **36558** age 5 years or older Ⓐ Ⓐ2 Ⓣ 80 50 ▭
　　　　EXCLUDES *that by peripheral insertion (36571)*

　　　　Code also (C1750, C1751, C1752)
　　　　🚑 7.89 ⚕ 21.73 Global Days 010
　　　　AMA: 2008, Jun, 8-11; 2004, Dec, 6; 2004, Dec, 6; 2004, Jun, 10; 2004, Jun, 10; 2004, June, 10; 2004, December, 6

⊙ **36560** Insertion of tunneled centrally inserted central venous access device, with subcutaneous port; younger than 5 years of age Ⓐ Ⓐ2 Ⓣ 80 50 ▭
　　　　EXCLUDES *that by peripheral insertion (36570)*

　　　　Code also (C1751, C1788)
　　　　🚑 9.71 ⚕ 30.76 Global Days 010
　　　　AMA: 2008, Jun, 8-11; 2004, Jun, 10; 2004, Jun, 10; 2004, Dec, 6; 2004, Dec, 6; 2004, June, 10; 2004, December, 6

⊙ **36561** age 5 years or older Ⓐ Ⓐ2 Ⓣ 80 50 ▭
　　　　EXCLUDES *that by peripheral insertion (36571)*

　　　　Code also (C1751, C1788)
　　　　🚑 9.40 ⚕ 30.44 Global Days 010
　　　　AMA: 2008, Jun, 8-11; 2004, Dec, 6; 2004, Dec, 6; 2004, Jun, 10; 2004, Jun, 10; 2004, June, 10; 2004, December, 6

⊙ **36563** Insertion of tunneled centrally inserted central venous access device with subcutaneous pump Ⓐ2 Ⓣ 80 ▭
　　　　Code also (C1772, C1891, C2626)
　　　　🚑 9.84 ⚕ 30.86 Global Days 010
　　　　AMA: 2008, Jun, 8-11; 2004, Jun, 10; 2004, Jun, 10; 2004, Dec, 6; 2004, Dec, 6; 2004, June, 10; 2004, December, 6

⊙ **36565** Insertion of tunneled centrally inserted central venous access device, requiring 2 catheters via 2 separate venous access sites; without subcutaneous port or pump (eg, Tesio type catheter) Ⓐ2 Ⓣ 80 50 ▭
　　　　Code also (C1750, C1751, C1752)
　　　　🚑 9.26 ⚕ 25.77 Global Days 010
　　　　AMA: 2008, Jun, 8-11; 2004, Jun, 10; 2004, Jun, 10; 2004, Dec, 6; 2004, Dec, 6; 2004, June, 10; 2004, December, 6

⊙ **36566** with subcutaneous port(s) Ⓐ2 Ⓣ 80 50 ▭
　　　　Code also (C1881)
　　　　🚑 9.90 ⚕ 95.74 Global Days 010
　　　　AMA: 2008, Jun, 8-11; 2004, Dec, 6; 2004, Dec, 6; 2004, Jun, 10; 2004, Jun, 10; 2004, June, 10; 2004, December, 6

⊙ **36568** Insertion of peripherally inserted central venous catheter (PICC), without subcutaneous port or pump; younger than 5 years of age Ⓐ Ⓐ2 Ⓣ ▭
　　　　EXCLUDES *centrally inserted placement (36555)*

　　　　🚑 2.67 ⚕ 8.27 Global Days 000
　　　　AMA: 2008, Jan, 10-25; 2008, Jun, 8-11; 2007, Jan, 13-27; 2007, Jan, 13-27; 2007, January, 13-27; 2005, May, 13-14; 2005, May, 13-14; 2005, May, 13-14; 2004, Dec, 6; 2004, Dec, 6; 2004, December, 6; 2004, October, 14; 2004, June, 10; 2004, Jun, 10; 2004, Jun, 10; 2004, Oct, 14; 2004, Oct, 14

　36569 age 5 years or older Ⓐ Ⓐ2 Ⓣ ▭
　　　　EXCLUDES *centrally inserted placement (36556)*

　　　　🚑 2.70 ⚕ 7.22 Global Days 000
　　　　AMA: 2008, Jan, 10-25; 2008, Jun, 8-11; 2007, Jan, 13-27; 2007, Jan, 13-27; 2007, January, 13-27; 2005, May, 13-14; 2005, May, 13-14; 2005, May, 13-14; 2004, Jun, 10; 2004, Jun, 10; 2004, October, 14; 2004, December, 6; 2004, June, 10; 2004, Oct, 14; 2004, Oct, 14; 2004, Dec, 6; 2004, Dec, 6

⊙ **36570** Insertion of peripherally inserted central venous access device, with subcutaneous port; younger than 5 years of age Ⓐ Ⓐ2 Ⓣ 80 50 ▭
　　　　EXCLUDES *centrally inserted placement (36560)*

　　　　Code also (C1751, C1788)
　　　　🚑 8.70 ⚕ 31.28 Global Days 010
　　　　AMA: 2008, Jun, 8-11; 2004, Dec, 6; 2004, Dec, 6; 2004, Jun, 10; 2004, Jun, 10; 2004, June, 10; 2004, December, 6

⊙ **36571** age 5 years or older Ⓐ Ⓐ2 Ⓣ 80 50 ▭
　　　　EXCLUDES *centrally inserted placement (36561)*

　　　　Code also (C1751, C1788)
　　　　🚑 8.46 ⚕ 32.44 Global Days 010
　　　　AMA: 2008, Jun, 8-11; 2004, Jun, 10; 2004, Jun, 10; 2004, Dec, 6; 2004, Dec, 6; 2004, June, 10; 2004, December, 6

● New Code　　▲ Revised Code　　Ⓜ Maternity Edit　　Ⓐ Age Edit　　Ⓐ-Ⓨ OPPS Status Indicator　　🚑 Facility RVU　　⚕ Non-Facility RVU
▣ CCI Comprehensive Code　　50 Bilateral Procedure　　+ Add-on Indicator　　▨ Laboratory crosswalk　　🔀 Radiology crosswalk

Cardiovascular System

36575 — 36595

36575-36590 Repair, Removal, and Replacement Implantable Venous Access Device

INCLUDES   complete removal/all components (36589-36590)
complete replacement (replace all components/same access site) (36580-36585)
partial replacement (catheter only) (36578)
repair of the device without replacing any parts (36575-36576)

EXCLUDES   *mechanical removal obstructive material, pericatheter/intraluminal (36595, 36596)*

36575   **Repair of tunneled or non-tunneled central venous access catheter, without subcutaneous port or pump, central or peripheral insertion site**   A2 T 80 ▣
    🔧 1.12 ⚖ 4.33 **Global Days 000**
    AMA: 2008, Jun, 8-11; 2004, Jun, 10; 2004, Jun, 10; 2004, Dec, 6; 2004, Dec, 6; 2004, June, 10; 2004, December, 6

⊙ **36576**   **Repair of central venous access device, with subcutaneous port or pump, central or peripheral insertion site**   A2 T 80 ▣
    🔧 5.08 ⚖ 9.55 **Global Days 010**
    AMA: 2008, Jun, 8-11; 2004, Jun, 10; 2004, Jun, 10; 2004, Dec, 6; 2004, Dec, 6; 2004, June, 10; 2004, December, 6

⊙ **36578**   **Replacement, catheter only, of central venous access device, with subcutaneous port or pump, central or peripheral insertion site**   A2 T 80 ▣
    Code also hemodialysis catheter (C1752)
    Code also implantable dialysis access system (C1881)
    Code also infusion catheter (C1751)
    🔧 5.81 ⚖ 13.34 **Global Days 010**
    AMA: 2008, Jun, 8-11; 2004, Dec, 6; 2004, Dec, 6; 2004, Jun, 10; 2004, Jun, 10; 2004, June, 10; 2004, December, 6

36580   **Replacement, complete, of a non-tunneled centrally inserted central venous catheter, without subcutaneous port or pump, through same venous access**   A2 T ▣
    🔧 1.96 ⚖ 6.21 **Global Days 000**
    AMA: 2008, Jun, 8-11; 2004, Jun, 10; 2004, Jun, 10; 2004, Dec, 6; 2004, Dec, 6; 2004, June, 10; 2004, December, 6

⊙ **36581**   **Replacement, complete, of a tunneled centrally inserted central venous catheter, without subcutaneous port or pump, through same venous access**   A2 T 80 ▣
    Code also (C1750, C1751, C1752)
    🔧 5.50 ⚖ 20.12 **Global Days 010**
    AMA: 2008, Jun, 8-11; 2004, Jun, 10; 2004, Jun, 10; 2004, Dec, 6; 2004, Dec, 6; 2004, June, 10; 2004, December, 6

⊙ **36582**   **Replacement, complete, of a tunneled centrally inserted central venous access device, with subcutaneous port, through same venous access**   A2 T 80 ▣
    Code also (C1751, C1788, C1881)
    🔧 8.04 ⚖ 28.04 **Global Days 010**
    AMA: 2008, Jun, 8-11; 2004, Jun, 10; 2004, Jun, 10; 2004, Dec, 6; 2004, Dec, 6; 2004, June, 10; 2004, December, 6

⊙ **36583**   **Replacement, complete, of a tunneled centrally inserted central venous access device, with subcutaneous pump, through same venous access**   A2 T 80 ▣
    Code also (C1772, C1891, C2626)
    🔧 8.05 ⚖ 28.05 **Global Days 010**
    AMA: 2008, Jun, 8-11; 2004, Jun, 10; 2004, Jun, 10; 2004, Dec, 6; 2004, Dec, 6; 2004, June, 10; 2004, December, 6

36584   **Replacement, complete, of a peripherally inserted central venous catheter (PICC), without subcutaneous port or pump, through same venous access**   A2 T ▣
    🔧 2.02 ⚖ 6.12 **Global Days 000**
    AMA: 2008, Jun, 8-11; 2004, Jun, 10; 2004, Jun, 10; 2004, Dec, 6; 2004, Dec, 6; 2004, June, 10; 2004, December, 6

⊙ **36585**   **Replacement, complete, of a peripherally inserted central venous access device, with subcutaneous port, through same venous access**   A2 T 80 ▣
    Code also (C1751, C1788)
    🔧 7.56 ⚖ 28.80 **Global Days 010**
    AMA: 2008, Jun, 8-11; 2004, Jun, 10; 2004, Jun, 10; 2004, Dec, 6; 2004, Dec, 6; 2004, June, 10; 2004, December, 6

36589   **Removal of tunneled central venous catheter, without subcutaneous port or pump**   A2 T 80 50 ▣
    EXCLUDES *non-tunneled central venous catheter removal; report appropriate E/M code*
    🔧 3.82 ⚖ 4.50 **Global Days 010**
    AMA: 2008, Jun, 8-11; 2004, Jun, 10; 2004, Jun, 10; 2004, Dec, 6; 2004, Dec, 6; 2004, June, 10; 2004, December, 6

⊙ **36590**   **Removal of tunneled central venous access device, with subcutaneous port or pump, central or peripheral insertion**   A2 T 80 ▣
    Do not report with non-tunneled central venous catheter removal; report appropriate E/M code
    🔧 5.44 ⚖ 7.34 **Global Days 010**
    AMA: 2008, Jun, 8-11; 2004, Jun, 10; 2004, Jun, 10; 2004, Dec, 6; 2004, Dec, 6; 2004, June, 10; 2004, December, 6

36591-36592 Obtain Blood Specimen from Implanted Device or Catheter

36591   **Collection of blood specimen from a completely implantable venous access device**   N1 Q1 80
    EXCLUDES *collection of:*
        capillary blood specimen (36416)
        venous blood specimen by venipuncture (36415)
    Do not report with any other service
    🔧 0.61 ⚖ 0.61 **Global Days XXX**
    AMA: 2008, Apr, -9; 2008, Apr, -9; 2008, Apr, -9

36592   **Collection of blood specimen using established central or peripheral catheter, venous, not otherwise specified**   N1 Q1 80
    EXCLUDES *collection of blood from an established arterial catheter (37799)*
    Do not report with any other service
    🔧 0.67 ⚖ 0.67 **Global Days XXX**
    AMA: 2008, Apr, -9; 2008, Apr, -9; 2008, Apr, -9

36593-36596 Restore Patency of Occluded Catheter or Device

EXCLUDES *venous catheterization (36010-36012)*

36593   **Declotting by thrombolytic agent of implanted vascular access device or catheter**   P3 T 80
    🔧 1.08 ⚖ 1.08 **Global Days XXX**
    AMA: 2008, Apr, -9; 2008, Apr, -9; 2008, Apr, -9

36595   **Mechanical removal of pericatheter obstructive material (eg, fibrin sheath) from central venous device via separate venous access**   62 T ▣
    EXCLUDES *venous catheterization (36010-36012)*
    Do not report with (36593)
    🔗 *75901*
    🔧 5.31 ⚖ 16.25 **Global Days 000**
    AMA: 2004, Jun, 10; 2004, Jun, 10; 2004, Dec, 6; 2004, Dec, 6; 2004, June, 10; 2004, December, 6

36596 Mechanical removal of intraluminal (intracatheter) obstructive material from central venous device through device lumen 〇2 T ▭
EXCLUDES *venous catheterization (36010-36012)*

Do not report with (36593)
⇌ *75902*
⟐ 1.26 ⚒ 3.65 Global Days 000
AMA: 2004, Dec, 6; 2004, Dec, 6; 2004, Jun, 10; 2004, Jun, 10; 2004, June, 10; 2004, December, 6

36597-36598 Repositioning or Assessment of In Situ Venous Access Device

36597 Repositioning of previously placed central venous catheter under fluoroscopic guidance 〇2 T ▭
⇌ *76000*
⟐ 1.77 ⚒ 3.43 Global Days 000
AMA: 2004, Jun, 10; 2004, Jun, 10; 2004, Dec, 6; 2004, Dec, 6; 2004, December, 6; 2004, June, 10

36598 Contrast injection(s) for radiologic evaluation of existing central venous access device, including fluoroscopy, image documentation and report P3 T 〇0 50
EXCLUDES *complete venography studies (75820, 75825, 75827)*

Do not report with (36595-36596, 76000)
⟐ 1.67 ⚒ 3.08 Global Days 000

36600-36660 Insertion Needle or Catheter: Artery

36600 Arterial puncture, withdrawal of blood for diagnosis N1 〇1 ▭
Do not report with critical care services
⟐ 0.42 ⚒ 0.82 Global Days XXX
AMA: 2007, Feb, 10-11; 2007, Feb, 10-11; 2007, February, 10-11; 2007, Jul, 1-4; 2006, May, 1-9; 2006, May, 1-9; 2006, May, 1-9; 2005, Jul, 11-12; 2005, Jul, 11-12; 2005, July, 11-12

⊘ 36620 Arterial catheterization or cannulation for sampling, monitoring or transfusion (separate procedure); percutaneous N1 N ▭
⟐ 1.39 ⚒ 1.39 Global Days 000
AMA: 2007, Jul, 1-4; 2006, May, 1-9; 2006, May, 1-9; 2006, May, 1-9

36625 cutdown N1 N ▭
⟐ 2.93 ⚒ 2.93 Global Days 000

36640 Arterial catheterization for prolonged infusion therapy (chemotherapy), cutdown A2 T ▭
EXCLUDES *intraarterial chemotherapy (96420-96425) transcatheter embolization (75894)*

Code also (C1751)
⟐ 3.27 ⚒ 3.27 Global Days 000

36660 Catheterization, umbilical artery, newborn, for diagnosis or therapy A C 〇0 @ ▭
⟐ 1.85 ⚒ 1.85 Global Days 000
AMA: 2007, Jul, 1-4; 2006, May, 1-9; 2006, May, 1-9; 2006, May, 1-9

36680 Percutaneous Placement of Catheter/Needle into Bone Marrow Cavity

36680 Placement of needle for intraosseous infusion 〇2 T 〇0 ▭
⟐ 1.63 ⚒ 1.63 Global Days 000

36800-36821 Vascular Access for Hemodialysis

36800 Insertion of cannula for hemodialysis, other purpose (separate procedure); vein to vein A2 T ▭
Code also (C1750, C1752)
⟐ 4.30 ⚒ 4.30 Global Days 000

36810 arteriovenous, external (Scribner type) A2 T ▭
Code also (C1750, C1752)
⟐ 5.78 ⚒ 5.78 Global Days 000

36815 arteriovenous, external revision, or closure A2 T ▭
Code also (C1750, C1752)
⟐ 4.10 ⚒ 4.10 Global Days 000

36818 Arteriovenous anastomosis, open; by upper arm cephalic vein transposition A2 T 80 ▭
⟐ 18.75 ⚒ 18.75 Global Days 090
AMA: 2005, Jul, 9-10; 2005, Jul, 9-10; 2005, July, 9-10

36819 by upper arm basilic vein transposition A2 T 80 ▭
⟐ 21.98 ⚒ 21.98 Global Days 090
AMA: 2005, Jul, 9-10; 2005, Jul, 9-10; 2005, July, 9-10

36820 by forearm vein transposition A2 T 80 50 ▭
⟐ 22.05 ⚒ 22.05 Global Days 090
AMA: 2005, Jul, 9-10; 2005, Jul, 9-10; 2005, July, 9-10

36821 direct, any site (eg, Cimino type) (separate procedure) A2 T 80 ▭
⟐ 18.19 ⚒ 18.19 Global Days 090
AMA: 2005, Jul, 9-10; 2005, Jul, 9-10; 2005, July, 9-10

36822-36823 Vascular Access for Extracorporeal Circulation

EXCLUDES *maintenance for prolonged extracorporeal circulation (33960, 33961)*

36822 Insertion of cannula(s) for prolonged extracorporeal circulation for cardiopulmonary insufficiency (ECMO) (separate procedure) C ▭
EXCLUDES *maintenance for prolonged circulation (33960, 33961)*

⟐ 10.29 ⚒ 10.29 Global Days 090
AMA: 2008, Jan, 10-25; 2007, Jan, 13-27; 2007, Jan, 13-27; 2007, January, 13-27

36823 Insertion of arterial and venous cannula(s) for isolated extracorporeal circulation including regional chemotherapy perfusion to an extremity, with or without hyperthermia, with removal of cannula(s) and repair of arteriotomy and venotomy sites C ▭
INCLUDES chemotherapy perfusion

Do not report with (96409-96425)
⟐ 35.02 ⚒ 35.02 Global Days 090

36825-36835 Permanent Vascular Access Procedures

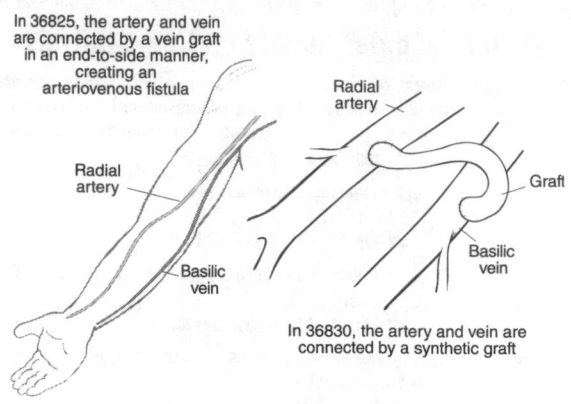

In 36825, the artery and vein are connected by a vein graft in an end-to-side manner, creating an arteriovenous fistula

Radial artery

Radial artery

Radial artery

Graft

Basilic vein

Basilic vein

In 36830, the artery and vein are connected by a synthetic graft

36825   Creation of arteriovenous fistula by other than direct arteriovenous anastomosis (separate procedure); autogenous graft   A2 T 80 ▭
    EXCLUDES   direct arteriovenous (AV) anastomosis (36821)
    🔲 15.91   ✂ 15.91   Global Days 090
    AMA: 2005, Jul, 9-10; 2005, Jul, 9-10; 2005, July, 9-10

36830   nonautogenous graft (eg, biological collagen, thermoplastic graft)   A2 T 80 ▭ PQ
    EXCLUDES   direct arteriovenous (AV) anastomosis (36821)
    🔲 18.22   ✂ 18.22   Global Days 090
    AMA: 2005, Jul, 9-10; 2005, Jul, 9-10; 2005, July, 9-10

36831   Thrombectomy, open, arteriovenous fistula without revision, autogenous or nonautogenous dialysis graft (separate procedure)   A2 T 80 ▭
    🔲 12.57   ✂ 12.57   Global Days 090
    AMA: 2008, Jan, 10-25; 2007, Jan, 13-27; 2007, Jan, 13-27; 2007, January, 13-27

36832   Revision, open, arteriovenous fistula; without thrombectomy, autogenous or nonautogenous dialysis graft (separate procedure)   A2 T 80 ▭
    🔲 16.06   ✂ 16.06   Global Days 090
    AMA: 2008, Jan, 10-25; 2007, Jan, 13-27; 2007, Jan, 13-27; 2007, January, 13-27

36833   with thrombectomy, autogenous or nonautogenous dialysis graft (separate procedure)   A2 T 80 ▭
    🔲 18.15   ✂ 18.15   Global Days 090
    AMA: 2008, Jan, 10-25; 2007, Jan, 13-27; 2007, Jan, 13-27; 2007, January, 13-27

36834   Plastic repair of arteriovenous aneurysm (separate procedure)   A2 T 80 ▭
    🔲 16.98   ✂ 16.98   Global Days 090

36835   Insertion of Thomas shunt (separate procedure)   A2 T ▭
    Code also (C1750, C1752)
    🔲 12.56   ✂ 12.56   Global Days 090

36838 DRIL Procedure for Ischemic Steal Syndrome

INCLUDES   banding/ligation angioacess arteriovenous (AV) fistula
          ligation artery of extremity
          open revision arteriovenous (AV) fistula
          subclavian-brachial or axilary-brachial bypass grafts

Do not report with (35512, 35522-35523, 36832, 37607, 37618)

36838   Distal revascularization and interval ligation (DRIL), upper extremity hemodialysis access (steal syndrome)   T 80 50 ▭
    🔲 32.45   ✂ 32.45   Global Days 090

36860-36870 Restore Patency of Occluded Cannula or Arteriovenous Fistula

36860   External cannula declotting (separate procedure); without balloon catheter   A2 T ▭
    🔀 76000
    🔲 2.80   ✂ 5.09   Global Days 000

36861   with balloon catheter   A2 T ▭
    🔀 76000
    Code also (C1757)
    🔲 4.12   ✂ 4.12   Global Days 000

⊙ 36870   Thrombectomy, percutaneous, arteriovenous fistula, autogenous or nonautogenous graft (includes mechanical thrombus extraction and intra-graft thrombolysis)   A2 T 50 ▭
    🔀 75790
    INCLUDES   declotting using thrombolytics
    EXCLUDES   catheterization for arteriovenous (AV) shunt (36145)

    Do not report with (36593)
    🔲 8.40   ✂ 49.08   Global Days 090

37140-37181 Open Decompression of Portal Circulation

EXCLUDES   peritoneal-venous shunt (49425)

37140   Venous anastomosis, open; portocaval   C ▭
    🔲 36.62   ✂ 36.62   Global Days 090

37145   renoportal   C 80 ▭
    🔲 39.90   ✂ 39.90   Global Days 090

37160   caval-mesenteric   C 80 ▭
    🔲 34.68   ✂ 34.68   Global Days 090

37180   splenorenal, proximal   C 80 ▭
    🔲 38.91   ✂ 38.91   Global Days 090

37181   splenorenal, distal (selective decompression of esophagogastric varices, any technique)   C 80 ▭
    EXCLUDES   percutaneous procedure (37182)
    🔲 41.99   ✂ 41.99   Global Days 090

37182-37183 Transvenous Decompression of Portal Circulation

Do not report with (75885, 75887)

37182   Insertion of transvenous intrahepatic portosystemic shunt(s) (TIPS) (includes venous access, hepatic and portal vein catheterization, portography with hemodynamic evaluation, intrahepatic tract formation/dilatation, stent placement and all associated imaging guidance and documentation)   C 80 ▭
    EXCLUDES   open procedure (37140)
    🔲 24.78   ✂ 24.78   Global Days 000
    AMA: 2008, Jan, 10-25; 2007, Jan, 13-27; 2007, Jan, 13-27; 2007, January, 13-27

37183   Revision of transvenous intrahepatic portosystemic shunt(s) (TIPS) (includes venous access, hepatic and portal vein catheterization, portography with hemodynamic evaluation, intrahepatic tract recanulization/dilatation, stent placement and all associated imaging guidance and documentation)   T 80 ▭
    EXCLUDES   arteriovenous (AV) aneurysm repair (36834)
    🔲 11.78   ✂ 11.78   Global Days 000
    AMA: 2008, Jan, 10-25; 2007, Jan, 13-27; 2007, Jan, 13-27; 2007, January, 13-27

26/TC Professional/Technical Component Only   80/80 Assist-at-Surgery Allowed/With Documentation   Unlisted   Not Covered
AMA: CPT Assistant References   A2-Z3 ASC Payment Indicator   ♂ Male Only   ♀ Female Only   ⊘ Modifier 51 Exempt   PQ PQRI

148   CPT only © 2008 American Medical Association. All Rights Reserved. (Black Ink)   Medicare (Red Ink)   © 2008 Ingenix (Blue Ink)

37184-37188 Removal of Thrombus from Vessel: Percutaneous

INCLUDES
fluoroscopic guidance
injection(s) of thrombolytics during the procedure
postprocedure evaluation
pretreatment planning

EXCLUDES
continuous infusion of thrombolytics prior to and after the procedure (37201, 75896, 75898)
diagnostic studies
mechanical thrombectomy, coronary (92973)
other interventions performed percutaneously (e.g., balloon angioplasty)
percutaneous thrombectomy of an arteriovenous fistula (36870)
placement of catheters
radiological supervision/interpretation

⊙ 37184 **Primary percutaneous transluminal mechanical thrombectomy, noncoronary, arterial or arterial bypass graft, including fluoroscopic guidance and intraprocedural pharmacological thrombolytic injection(s); initial vessel** 62 T 50

EXCLUDES
mechanical thrombectomy of another vascular family, separate access site, append modifier 51 to code, as appropriate secondary mechanical thrombectomy for treating of embolus/thrombus complicating another percutaneous intervention (37186)

Code also (C1757)
Do not report with (76000-76001, 96374, 99143-99150)
♨ 12.69 ⚖ 64.60 Global Days 000

+ ⊙ 37185 **second and all subsequent vessel(s) within the same vascular family (List separately in addition to code for primary mechanical thrombectomy procedure)** 62 T

INCLUDES
treatment of second and all succeeding vessel(s) in same vascular family

EXCLUDES
intravenous drug injections administered subsequent to an initial service mechanical thrombectomy for embolus/thrombus complicating another percutaneous interventional procedure (37186)
mechanical thrombectomy of another vascular family/separate access site, append modifier 51 to code as appropriate

Code first (37184)
Do not report with (76000-76001, 96375)
♨ 4.67 ⚖ 21.36 Global Days ZZZ

+ ⊙ 37186 **Secondary percutaneous transluminal thrombectomy (eg, nonprimary mechanical, snare basket, suction technique), noncoronary, arterial or arterial bypass graft, including fluoroscopic guidance and intraprocedural pharmacological thrombolytic injections, provided in conjunction with another percutaneous intervention other than primary mechanical thrombectomy (List separately in addition to code for primary procedure)** 62 T

INCLUDES
removal of small emboli/thrombi prior to or after another percutaneous procedure

Do not report with (76000-76001, 96375)
Code first primary procedure
♨ 7.18 ⚖ 43.54 Global Days ZZZ
AMA: 2008, May, 9-11

⊙ 37187 **Percutaneous transluminal mechanical thrombectomy, vein(s), including intraprocedural pharmacological thrombolytic injections and fluoroscopic guidance** 62 T 50

INCLUDES
secondary or subsequent intravenous injection after another initial service

Do not report with (76000-76001, 96375)
Code also (C1757)
♨ 11.79 ⚖ 61.90 Global Days 000

⊙ 37188 **Percutaneous transluminal mechanical thrombectomy, vein(s), including intraprocedural pharmacological thrombolytic injections and fluoroscopic guidance, repeat treatment on subsequent day during course of thrombolytic therapy** 62 T 50

Code also (C1757)
Do not report with (76000-76001, 96375)
♨ 8.54 ⚖ 52.60 Global Days 000

37195-37203 Miscellaneous Transcatheter Procedures: Infusions, Biopsy, Foreign Body Removal

37195 **Thrombolysis, cerebral, by intravenous infusion** T 80 ▣
♨ 0.00 ⚖ 0.00 Global Days XXX

37200 **Transcatheter biopsy** 62 T ▣
▣ 75970
♨ 6.58 ⚖ 6.58 Global Days 000

37201 **Transcatheter therapy, infusion for thrombolysis other than coronary** T ▣

EXCLUDES
thrombolysis of coronary vessels (92975-92977)

▣ 75896
♨ 7.80 ⚖ 7.80 Global Days 000
AMA: 2008, Jan, 10-25; 2007, Jan, 13-27; 2007, Jan, 13-27; 2007, January, 13-27

37202 **Transcatheter therapy, infusion other than for thrombolysis, any type (eg, spasmolytic, vasoconstrictive)** T ▣

EXCLUDES
thrombolysis of coronary vessels (92975-92977)

▣ 75896
♨ 9.40 ⚖ 9.40 Global Days 000
AMA: 2008, Jan, 10-25; 2007, Jan, 13-27; 2007, Jan, 13-27; 2007, January, 13-27

⊙ 37203 **Transcatheter retrieval, percutaneous, of intravascular foreign body (eg, fractured venous or arterial catheter)** 62 T ▣
▣ 75961
♨ 7.48 ⚖ 35.81 Global Days 000
AMA: 2008, Oct, 10-11

● New Code ▲ Revised Code ▣ Maternity Edit ▣ Age Edit A-Y OPPS Status Indicator ♨ Facility RVU ⚖ Non-Facility RVU
▣ CCI Comprehensive Code 50 Bilateral Procedure + Add-on Indicator ▣ Laboratory crosswalk ▣ Radiology crosswalk

Cardiovascular System

37204 — 37251

37204 Therapeutic Embolization (Except UFE)

CMS *100-3,20.28*   *Therapeutic Embolization*

INCLUDES Ob/Gyn procedures except uterine fibroid embolization

EXCLUDES *embolization/uterine fibroids (37210)*
transcatheter occlusion or embolization for treatment of a tumor,
vascular malformation, or hemorrhage (61624, 61626)

☒ *75894*

37204 **Transcatheter occlusion or embolization (eg, for tumor destruction, to achieve hemostasis, to occlude a vascular malformation), percutaneous, any method, non-central nervous system, non-head or neck** T ▢
📖 26.27 ⚕ 26.27 Global Days 000
AMA: 2008, Jan, 10-25; 2008, Feb, 5-6; 2007, Jan, 13-27; 2007, Jan, 13-27; 2007, Jan, 7-10; 2007, Jan, 7-10; 2007, January, 13-27; 2007, January, 7-10

37205-37208 Insertion Intravascular Stent

EXCLUDES *placement stent(s):*
extracranial vertebral or intrathoracic carotid artery (0075T, 0076T)
intracoronary (92980, 92981)
intracranial (61635)
intravascular cervical carotid artery (37215-37216)
selective catheter placement (36215-36248)

☒ *75960*

37205 **Transcatheter placement of an intravascular stent(s) (except coronary, carotid, and vertebral vessel), percutaneous; initial vessel** T 80 ▢
Code also (C1874, C1875, C1876, C1877, C2617, C2625)
📖 12.33 ⚕ 88.83 Global Days 000
AMA: 2005, Jun, 6-8; 2005, Jun, 6-8; 2005, June, 6-8

+ 37206 **each additional vessel (List separately in addition to code for primary procedure)** T 80 ▢
Code first (37205)
Code also (C1874, C1875, C1876, C1877, C2617, C2625)
📖 6.01 ⚕ 53.07 Global Days ZZZ
AMA: 2005, Jun, 6-8; 2005, Jun, 6-8; 2005, June, 6-8

37207 **Transcatheter placement of an intravascular stent(s) (non-coronary vessel), open; initial vessel** T 80 50 ▢
Code also (C1874, C1875, C1876, C1877, C2617, C2625)
📖 12.14 ⚕ 12.14 Global Days 000
AMA: 2005, Jun, 6-8; 2005, Jun, 6-8; 2005, June, 6-8

+ 37208 **each additional vessel (List separately in addition to code for primary procedure)** T 80
Code first (37207)
Code also (C1874, C1875, C1876, C1877, C2625)
📖 5.88 ⚕ 5.88 Global Days ZZZ
AMA: 2005, Jun, 6-8; 2005, Jun, 6-8; 2005, June, 6-8

37209 Replace Intravascular Catheter

☒ *75900*

37209 **Exchange of a previously placed intravascular catheter during thrombolytic therapy** T ▢
Code also hemodialysis catheter (C1750, C1752)
Code also infusion catheter (C1751)
📖 3.23 ⚕ 3.23 Global Days 000

37210 Therapeutic Embolization, Uterine Fibroid

CMS *100-3,20.28*   *Therapeutic Embolization*

INCLUDES access and imaging
angiography follow-up evaluation
transcatheter therapy, radiological supervision and interpretation
vascular access procedures

EXCLUDES *Ob/Gyn procedures other than UFE*
transcatheter embolization for conditions other than CNS/head or neck (37204)

Do not report with (36200, 36245-36248, 37204, 75894, 75898)

⊙ 37210 **Uterine fibroid embolization (UFE, embolization of the uterine arteries to treat uterine fibroids, leiomyomata), percutaneous approach inclusive of vascular access, vessel selection, embolization, and all radiological supervision and interpretation, intraprocedural roadmapping, and imaging guidance necessary to complete the procedure** T
📖 15.57 ⚕ 94.23 Global Days 000
AMA: 2008, Jan, 10-25; 2008, Feb, 5-6; 2007, Jan, 7-10; 2007, Jan, 7-10; 2007, January, 7-10

37215-37216 Stenting of Carotid Artery with/without Insertion Distal Embolic Protection Device

INCLUDES carotid stenting, if required
ipsilateral selective carotid catheterization
diagnostic imaging/supervision and interpretation

EXCLUDES *carotid catheterization and imaging, if carotid stenting not required*
percutaneous placement intravascular stents besides coronary, carotid, vertebral (37205, 37206)
transcatheter placement extracranial vertebral or intrathoracic carotid artery stents (0075T, 0076T)

Do not report with (75671, 75680)

⊙ 37215 **Transcatheter placement of intravascular stent(s), cervical carotid artery, percutaneous; with distal embolic protection** C 80 ▢
📖 30.54 ⚕ 30.54 Global Days 090
AMA: 2005, May, 7-12; 2005, May, 7-12; 2005, May, 7-12

⊙ 37216 **without distal embolic protection** E ▢
📖 28.01 ⚕ 28.01 Global Days 090
AMA: 2005, May, 7-12; 2005, May, 7-12; 2005, May, 7-12

37250-37251 Intravascular Ultrasound: Noncoronary

CMS *100-3,220.5*   *Ultrasound Diagnostic Procedures*

INCLUDES manipulation and repositioning of the transducer prior to and after therapeutic interventional procedures

EXCLUDES *selective catheter placement for access (36215-36248)*
transcatheter procedures (37200-37208, 61624, 61626)

☒ *75945, 75946*

+ 37250 **Intravascular ultrasound (non-coronary vessel) during diagnostic evaluation and/or therapeutic intervention; initial vessel (List separately in addition to code for primary procedure)** N1 N 80 ▢
📖 3.09 ⚕ 3.09 Global Days ZZZ

+ 37251 **each additional vessel (List separately in addition to code for primary procedure)** N1 N 80
Code first (37250)
📖 2.31 ⚕ 2.31 Global Days ZZZ

37500-37501 Vascular Endoscopic Procedures

INCLUDES diagnostic endoscopy

EXCLUDES open procedure (37760)

37500 Vascular endoscopy, surgical, with ligation of perforator veins, subfascial (SEPS)   A2 T 50 ▭
🔧 18.94   ✂ 18.94   Global Days 090
AMA: 2004, Aug, 5; 2004, Aug, 5; 2004, August, 5

37501 Unlisted vascular endoscopy procedure   T 50
🔧 0.00   ✂ 0.00   Global Days YYY

37565-37606 Ligation Procedures: Jugular Vein, Carotid Arteries

CMS 100-3,160.8   Electroencephalographic Monitoring During Cerebral Vasculature Surgery

EXCLUDES arterial balloon occlusion, endovascular, temporary (61623)
for treatment intracranial aneurysm (61703)
suture of arteries and veins (35201-35286)
transcatheter arterial embolization/occlusion, permanent (61624, 61626)

37565 Ligation, internal jugular vein   T 80 ▭
🔧 18.74   ✂ 18.74   Global Days 090

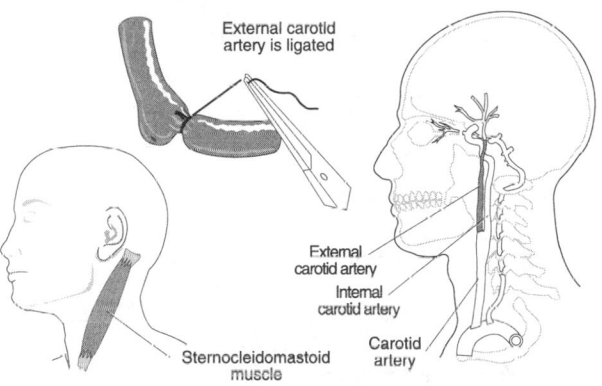

External carotid artery is ligated

External carotid artery
Internal carotid artery
Carotid artery
Sternocleidomastoid muscle

37600 Ligation; external carotid artery   T 80 ▭
🔧 19.18   ✂ 19.18   Global Days 090

37605 internal or common carotid artery   T 80 ▭
🔧 22.07   ✂ 22.07   Global Days 090

37606 internal or common carotid artery, with gradual occlusion, as with Selverstone or Crutchfield clamp   T 80 ▭
🔧 14.38   ✂ 14.38   Global Days 090

37607-37609 Ligation Hemodialysis Angioaccess or Temporal Artery

EXCLUDES suture of arteries and veins (35201-35286)

37607 Ligation or banding of angioaccess arteriovenous fistula   A2 T ▭
🔧 10.26   ✂ 10.26   Global Days 090

37609 Ligation or biopsy, temporal artery   A2 T 50 ▭
🔧 5.27   ✂ 7.65   Global Days 010

37615-37618 Arterial Ligation, Major Vessel, for Injury/Rupture

EXCLUDES suture of arteries and veins (35201-35286)

37615 Ligation, major artery (eg, post-traumatic, rupture); neck   T 80 ▭
INCLUDES Touroff ligation
🔧 12.59   ✂ 12.59   Global Days 090

37616 chest   C 80 ▭ P0
INCLUDES Bardenheurer operation
🔧 29.51   ✂ 29.51   Global Days 090

37617 abdomen   C 80 ▭
🔧 35.17   ✂ 35.17   Global Days 090

37618 extremity   C 80 ▭
🔧 10.11   ✂ 10.11   Global Days 090

37620 Ligation, Any Method, Inferior Vena Cava

EXCLUDES suture of arteries and veins (35201-35286)

🔁 75940

37620 Interruption, partial or complete, of inferior vena cava by suture, ligation, plication, clip, extravascular, intravascular (umbrella device)   T ▭
🔁 75940
🔧 18.18   ✂ 18.18   Global Days 090
AMA: 2008, Jan, 10-25; 2008, Oct, 10-11; 2007, Jan, 13-27; 2007, Jan, 13-27; 2007, January, 13-27

37650-37660 Venous Ligation, Femoral and Common Iliac

EXCLUDES suture of arteries and veins (35201-35286)

37650 Ligation of femoral vein   A2 T 50 ▭
🔧 13.83   ✂ 13.83   Global Days 090

37660 Ligation of common iliac vein   C 80 ▭
🔧 32.83   ✂ 32.83   Global Days 090

37700-37785 Treatment of Varicose Veins of Legs

EXCLUDES suture of arteries and veins (35201-35286)

37700 Ligation and division of long saphenous vein at saphenofemoral junction, or distal interruptions   A2 T 50 ▭
INCLUDES Babcock operation
Do not report with (37718, 37722)
🔧 6.81   ✂ 6.81   Global Days 090
AMA: 2008, Jan, 10-25; 2007, Jan, 13-27; 2007, Jan, 13-27; 2007, January, 13-27; 2004, Aug, 5; 2004, August, 5; 2004, Aug, 5

37718 Ligation, division, and stripping, short saphenous vein   A2 T 50
Do not report with (37735, 37780)
🔧 10.95   ✂ 10.95   Global Days 090

37722 Ligation, division, and stripping, long (greater) saphenous veins from saphenofemoral junction to knee or below   A2 T 50
EXCLUDES ligation/division/stripping short saphenous vein (37718)
Do not report with (37700, 37735)
🔧 12.90   ✂ 12.90   Global Days 090

Hemic/Lymphatic

37735 — 38220

37735 Ligation and division and complete stripping of long or short saphenous veins with radical excision of ulcer and skin graft and/or interruption of communicating veins of lower leg, with excision of deep fascia A2 T 50 ▭

Do not report with (37700, 37718, 37722, 37780)

🔧 17.27 ⚕ 17.27 Global Days 090

AMA: 2004, Aug, 5; 2004, Aug, 5; 2004, August, 5

37760 Ligation of perforator veins, subfascial, radical (Linton type), with or without skin graft, open A2 T ▭

EXCLUDES *endoscopic vascular procedure (37500)*

🔧 17.00 ⚕ 17.00 Global Days 090

AMA: 2004, Aug, 5; 2004, Aug, 5; 2004, August, 5

37765 Stab phlebectomy of varicose veins, 1 extremity; 10-20 stab incisions R2 T 50 ▭

EXCLUDES *fewer than 10 incisions (37799)*

🔧 12.04 ⚕ 12.04 Global Days 090

AMA: 2004, Aug, 5; 2004, Aug, 5; 2004, August, 5

37766 more than 20 incisions R2 T 50 ▭

EXCLUDES *fewer than 10 incisions (37799)*

🔧 14.60 ⚕ 14.60 Global Days 090

AMA: 2004, Aug, 5; 2004, Aug, 5; 2004, August, 5

37780 Ligation and division of short saphenous vein at saphenopopliteal junction (separate procedure) A2 T 50 ▭

🔧 7.02 ⚕ 7.02 Global Days 090

AMA: 2008, Jan, 10-25; 2007, Jan, 13-27; 2007, Jan, 13-27; 2007, January, 13-27

37785 Ligation, division, and/or excision of varicose vein cluster(s), 1 leg A2 T 50 ▭

🔧 7.04 ⚕ 9.37 Global Days 090

AMA: 2004, Aug, 5; 2004, Aug, 5; 2004, August, 5

37788-37799 Treatment of Vascular Disease of the Penis

37788 Penile revascularization, artery, with or without vein graft ♂ C 80 ▭

🔧 37.38 ⚕ 37.38 Global Days 090

37790 Penile venous occlusive procedure ♂ A2 T 80 ▭

🔧 13.48 ⚕ 13.48 Global Days 090

37799 Unlisted procedure, vascular surgery T 80

🔧 0.00 ⚕ 0.00 Global Days YYY

AMA: 2008, Jan, 10-25; 2007, Jan, 13-27; 2007, Jan, 13-27; 2007, January, 13-27; 2004, Oct, 6; 2004, Oct, 6; 2004, August, 5; 2004, October, 6; 2004, Aug, 5; 2004, Aug, 5

38100-38200 Splenic Procedures

38100 Splenectomy; total (separate procedure) C 80 ▭ PQ

🔧 28.32 ⚕ 28.32 Global Days 090

38101 partial (separate procedure) C 80 ▭ PQ

🔧 28.51 ⚕ 28.51 Global Days 090

+ **38102** total, en bloc for extensive disease, in conjunction with other procedure (List in addition to code for primary procedure) C 80 ▭

Code first primary procedure

🔧 6.83 ⚕ 6.83 Global Days ZZZ

38115 Repair of ruptured spleen (splenorrhaphy) with or without partial splenectomy C 80 ▭ PQ

🔧 31.48 ⚕ 31.48 Global Days 090

38120 Laparoscopy, surgical, splenectomy T 80 ▭ PQ

INCLUDES diagnostic laparoscopy

🔧 26.43 ⚕ 26.43 Global Days 090

38129 Unlisted laparoscopy procedure, spleen T 80

🔧 0.00 ⚕ 0.00 Global Days YYY

38200 Injection procedure for splenoportography N1 N 80 ▭

🔗 75810

🔧 3.76 ⚕ 3.76 Global Days 000

38204-38215 Hematopoietic Stem Cell Procedures

CMS *100-3,110.8.1* *Stem Cell Transplantation*

INCLUDES preservation, preparation, purification before transplant or reinfusion

bone marrow

stem cells

reporting each code no more than once per day

Do not report with flow cytometry (88182, 88184-88189)

38204 Management of recipient hematopoietic progenitor cell donor search and cell acquisition N1 N

🔧 2.73 ⚕ 2.73 Global Days XXX

38205 Blood-derived hematopoietic progenitor cell harvesting for transplantation, per collection; allogenic G2 S 80 ▭

🔧 2.17 ⚕ 2.17 Global Days 000

38206 autologous G2 S 80 ▭

🔧 2.17 ⚕ 2.17 Global Days 000

38207 Transplant preparation of hematopoietic progenitor cells; cryopreservation and storage S

🔗 88240

🔧 1.34 ⚕ 1.34 Global Days XXX

38208 thawing of previously frozen harvest, without washing S

🔗 88241

🔧 0.86 ⚕ 0.86 Global Days XXX

38209 thawing of previously frozen harvest, with washing S

🔧 0.37 ⚕ 0.37 Global Days XXX

38210 specific cell depletion within harvest, T-cell depletion S

🔧 2.38 ⚕ 2.38 Global Days XXX

38211 tumor cell depletion S

🔧 2.15 ⚕ 2.15 Global Days XXX

38212 red blood cell removal S

🔧 1.43 ⚕ 1.43 Global Days XXX

38213 platelet depletion S

🔧 0.37 ⚕ 0.37 Global Days XXX

38214 plasma (volume) depletion S

🔧 1.22 ⚕ 1.22 Global Days XXX

38215 cell concentration in plasma, mononuclear, or buffy coat layer S

🔧 1.43 ⚕ 1.43 Global Days XXX

38220-38242 Bone Marrow Procedures

CMS *100-3,110.8.1* *Stem Cell Transplantation*
CMS *100-1,5,90.2* *Laboratory Defined*
CMS *100-2,15,80.1* *Payment for Clinical Laboratory Services*
CMS *100-2,15,80* *Physician Supervision Requirements for Diagnostic Tests*
CMS *100-4,32,90* *Billing for Stem Cell Transplantation*
CMS *100-4,3,90.3.3* *Billing for Stem Cell Transplantation*
CMS *100-4,3,90.3.1* *Allogeneic Stem Cell Transplantation*
CMS *100-4,3,90.3* *Stem Cell Transplantation*

EXCLUDES *modification, treatment, processing of bone marrow/blood-derived stem cell specimens for transplantation (38210-38213)*

38220 Bone marrow; aspiration only P3 T 80 50 ▭

🔧 1.63 ⚕ 4.08 Global Days XXX

AMA: 2008, Jan, 10-25; 2007, Jan, 13-27; 2007, Jan, 13-27; 2007, Jun, 10-11; 2007, Jun, 10-11; 2007, January, 13-27; 2007, June, 10-11; 2004, Jan, 26; 2004, Jan, 26; 2004, January, 26

38221　biopsy, needle or trocar　P3 T 80 50 ▣
　　　🔌 88305
　　　💠 2.07　🔨 4.53　Global Days XXX

38230　Bone marrow harvesting for transplantation　G2 S 80 ▣
　　　EXCLUDES　allogenic blood-derived hematopoietic
　　　　　　progenitor cell harvesting for transplant
　　　　　　(38205)
　　　　　　autologous blood-derived hematopoietic
　　　　　　progenitor cell harvesting for transplant
　　　　　　(38206)

　　　🔌 86812-86822, 88240-88241
　　　💠 8.43　🔨 8.43　Global Days 010

38240　Bone marrow or blood-derived peripheral stem cell
　　　transplantation; allogenic　S 80 ▣
　　　🔌 86812-86822, 88240 88241
　　　💠 3.36　🔨 3.36　Global Days XXX

38241　autologous　G2 S 80 ▣
　　　🔌 86812-86822, 88240-88241
　　　💠 3.38　🔨 3.38　Global Days XXX

38242　allogeneic donor lymphocyte infusions　R2 S 80 ▣
　　　🔌 86812-86822, 88240-88241
　　　💠 2.56　🔨 2.56　Global Days 000

38300-38382 Incision Lymphatic Vessels

38300　Drainage of lymph node abscess or lymphadenitis;
　　　simple　A2 T ▣
　　　💠 4.59　🔨 6.78　Global Days 010

38305　extensive　A2 T ▣
　　　💠 11.71　🔨 11.71　Global Days 090

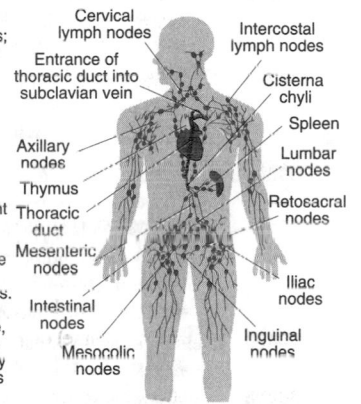

Cancers of the lymphatic system are called lymphomas; they are more common after age 50 and occur most frequently in the groin (inguinal), neck (cervical), and armpit (axillary) nodes.

About 14 percent of malignant lymphomas are Hodgkin's disease, a form of cancer distinguished by the presence of unique, large, R-S cells; incidence peaks in the late 20s. Because the malignant lymphomas occur early in life, they account for more years of potential life lost than many of the more common cancers.

Cervical lymph nodes
Intercostal lymph nodes
Entrance of thoracic duct into subclavian vein
Cisterna chyli
Spleen
Axillary nodes
Lumbar nodes
Thymus
Thoracic duct
Retosacral nodes
Mesenteric nodes
Iliac nodes
Intestinal nodes
Inguinal nodes
Mesocolic nodes

38308　Lymphangiotomy or other operations on lymphatic
　　　channels　A2 T 80 ▣
　　　💠 11.23　🔨 11.23　Global Days 090

38380　Suture and/or ligation of thoracic duct; cervical
　　　approach　C 80 ▣
　　　💠 14.36　🔨 14.36　Global Days 090

38381　thoracic approach　C 80 ▣ P0
　　　💠 21.63　🔨 21.63　Global Days 090

38382　abdominal approach　C 80 ▣
　　　💠 17.44　🔨 17.44　Global Days 090

38500-38555 Biopsy/Excision Lymphatic Vessels

CMS 100-4,12,30　　Correct Coding Policy
EXCLUDES　injection for sentinel node identification (38792)
　　　percutaneous needle biopsy retroperitoneal mass (49180)

38500　Biopsy or excision of lymph node(s); open,
　　　superficial　A2 T 50 ▣
　　　Do not report with (38700-38780)
　　　💠 6.33　🔨 7.99　Global Days 010
　　　AMA: 2008, Jan, 10-25; 2008, Sep, 5-6; 2007, Jan, 13-27; 2007,
　　　Jan, 13-27; 2007, Dec, 7-8; 2007, January, 13-27; 2005, Oct,
　　　23-24; 2005, October, 23-24; 2005, Oct, 23-24

38505　by needle, superficial (eg, cervical, inguinal,
　　　axillary)　A2 T 50 ▣
　　　EXCLUDES　fine needle aspiration (10021-10022)

　　　📷 76942, 77012, 77021
　　　🔌 88172, 88173
　　　💠 2.00　🔨 3.33　Global Days 000

38510　open, deep cervical node(s)　A2 T 50 ▣
　　　💠 10.69　🔨 12.89　Global Days 010
　　　AMA: 2008, Jan, 10-25; 2007, Jan, 13-27; 2007, Jan, 13-27; 2007,
　　　January, 13-27

38520　open, deep cervical node(s) with excision scalene fat
　　　pad　A2 T 50 ▣
　　　💠 11.72　🔨 11.72　Global Days 090
　　　AMA: 2008, Jan, 10-25; 2007, Jan, 13-27, 2007, Jan, 13-27; 2007,
　　　January, 13-27

38525　open, deep axillary node(s)　A2 T 50 ▣
　　　💠 10.63　🔨 10.63　Global Days 090
　　　AMA: 2008, Jan, 10-25; 2008, Sep, 5-6; 2007, Jan, 13-27; 2007,
　　　Jan, 13-27; 2007, Dec, 7-8; 2007, January, 13-27; 2005, Oct,
　　　23-24; 2005, October, 23-24; 2005, Oct, 23-24

38530　open, internal mammary node(s)　A2 T 80 50 ▣
　　　EXCLUDES　fine needle aspiration (10022)
　　　Do not report with (38720-38746)
　　　💠 13.70　🔨 13.70　Global Days 090
　　　AMA: 2008, Sep, 5-6

38542　Dissection, deep jugular node(s)　▢ T ▢ ▢ ▣
　　　EXCLUDES　complete cervical lymphadenectomy (38720)
　　　💠 12.94　🔨 12.94　Global Days 090

38550　Excision of cystic hygroma, axillary or cervical; without
　　　deep neurovascular dissection　A2 T 80 ▣
　　　💠 12.10　🔨 12.10　Global Days 090

38555　with deep neurovascular dissection　A2 T 80 ▣
　　　💠 25.13　🔨 25.13　Global Days 090

38562-38564 Limited Lymphadenectomy: Staging

38562　Limited lymphadenectomy for staging (separate
　　　procedure); pelvic and para-aortic　C 80 ▣
　　　EXCLUDES　with prostatectomy (55812, 55842)
　　　　　　with radioactive substance inserted into
　　　　　　prostate (55862)

　　　💠 18.04　🔨 18.04　Global Days 090
　　　AMA: 2008, Jan, 10-25; 2007, Jan, 13-27; 2007, Jan, 13-27; 2007,
　　　January, 13-27

38564　retroperitoneal (aortic and/or splenic)　C 80 ▣
　　　💠 17.93　🔨 17.93　Global Days 090

● New Code　▲ Revised Code　Ⓜ Maternity Edit　Ⓐ Age Edit　A-Y OPPS Status Indicator　💠 Facility RVU　🔨 Non-Facility RVU
☐ CCI Comprehensive Code　50 Bilateral Procedure　+ Add-on Indicator　🔌 Laboratory crosswalk　📷 Radiology crosswalk

Mediastinum

38570-38589 Laparoscopic Lymph Node Procedures

INCLUDES   diagnostic laparoscopy

EXCLUDES   *laparoscopy with draining of lymphocele to peritoneal cavity (49323)*

38570   Laparoscopy, surgical; with retroperitoneal lymph node sampling (biopsy), single or multiple   [A2] [T] [80] [⬛]
14.64   14.64   Global Days 010

38571   with bilateral total pelvic lymphadenectomy   [A2] [T] [80] [⬛] [PQ]
22.82   22.82   Global Days 010

38572   with bilateral total pelvic lymphadenectomy and peri-aortic lymph node sampling (biopsy), single or multiple   [A2] [T] [80] [⬛] [PQ]
25.26   25.26   Global Days 010

38589   Unlisted laparoscopy procedure, lymphatic system   [T] [80] [50]
0.00   0.00   Global Days YYY

38700-38780 Lymphadenectomy Procedures

INCLUDES   lymph node biopsy/excision

EXCLUDES   *limited lymphadenectomy*
pelvic (38562)
retroperitoneal (38564)

Do not report with (38500)

38700   Suprahyoid lymphadenectomy   [62] [T] [80] [⬛] [PQ]
20.03   20.03   Global Days 090

38720   Cervical lymphadenectomy (complete)   [T] [80] [50] [⬛] [PQ]
33.25   33.25   Global Days 090
AMA: 2008, Jan, 10-25; 2007, Jan, 13-27; 2007, Jan, 13-27; 2007, January, 13-27

38724   Cervical lymphadenectomy (modified radical neck dissection)   [C] [80] [50] [⬛] [PQ]
36.05   36.05   Global Days 090
AMA: 2008, Jan, 10-25; 2007, Jan, 13-27; 2007, Jan, 13-27; 2007, January, 13-27

38740   Axillary lymphadenectomy; superficial   [A2] [T] [80] [50] [⬛] [PQ]
17.01   17.01   Global Days 090

38745   complete   [A2] [T] [80] [50] [⬛] [PQ]
21.66   21.66   Global Days 090

+   38746   Thoracic lymphadenectomy, regional, including mediastinal and peritracheal nodes (List separately in addition to code for primary procedure)   [C] [80] [⬛] [PQ]
Code first primary procedure
7.17   7.17   Global Days ZZZ

+   38747   Abdominal lymphadenectomy, regional, including celiac, gastric, portal, peripancreatic, with or without para-aortic and vena caval nodes (List separately in addition to code for primary procedure)   [C] [80] [⬛] [PQ]
Code first primary procedure
6.96   6.96   Global Days ZZZ

38760   Inguinofemoral lymphadenectomy, superficial, including Cloquets node (separate procedure)   [A2] [T] [80] [50] [⬛] [PQ]
21.37   21.37   Global Days 090

38765   Inguinofemoral lymphadenectomy, superficial, in continuity with pelvic lymphadenectomy, including external iliac, hypogastric, and obturator nodes (separate procedure)   [C] [80] [50] [⬛] [PQ]
INCLUDES   lymph node biopsy/excision
EXCLUDES   *limited lymphadenectomy*
pelvic (38562)
retroperitoneal (38564)
33.14   33.14   Global Days 090

38770   Pelvic lymphadenectomy, including external iliac, hypogastric, and obturator nodes (separate procedure)   [C] [80] [50] [⬛] [PQ]
INCLUDES   lymph node biopsy/excision
EXCLUDES   *limited lymphadenectomy*
pelvic (38562)
retroperitoneal (38564)
22.16   22.16   Global Days 090

38780   Retroperitoneal transabdominal lymphadenectomy, extensive, including pelvic, aortic, and renal nodes (separate procedure)   [C] [80] [⬛] [PQ]
INCLUDES   lymph node biopsy/excision
EXCLUDES   *limited lymphadenectomy*
pelvic (38562)
retroperitoneal (38564)
27.95   27.95   Global Days 090

38790-38999 Cannulation/Injection/Other Procedures

38790   Injection procedure; lymphangiography   [N1] [N] [50] [⬛]
🔗 75801-75807
2.18   2.18   Global Days 000

38792   for identification of sentinel node   [N1] [01] [50] [⬛]
EXCLUDES   *sentinel node excision (38500-38542)*
🔗 78195
1.06   1.06   Global Days 000
AMA: 2008, Jan, 10-25; 2008, Sep, 5-6; 2007, Dec, 7-8

38794   Cannulation, thoracic duct   [N1] [N] [80] [⬛]
8.23   8.23   Global Days 090

38999   Unlisted procedure, hemic or lymphatic system   [S]
0.00   0.00   Global Days YYY
AMA: 2008, Jan, 10-25; 2007, Jan, 13-27; 2007, Jan, 13-27; 2007, January, 13-27

39000-39499 Surgical Procedures: Mediastinum

39000   Mediastinotomy with exploration, drainage, removal of foreign body, or biopsy; cervical approach   [C] [80] [⬛] [PQ]
12.93   12.93   Global Days 090

39010   transthoracic approach, including either transthoracic or median sternotomy   [C] [80] [⬛] [PQ]
21.51   21.51   Global Days 090

39200   Excision of mediastinal cyst   [C] [80] [⬛] [PQ]
23.85   23.85   Global Days 090

39220   Excision of mediastinal tumor   [C] [80] [⬛] [PQ]
EXCLUDES   *thymectomy (60520)*
thyroidectomy, substernal (60270)
30.66   30.66   Global Days 090

39400   Mediastinoscopy, with or without biopsy   [T] [⬛]
13.28   13.28   Global Days 010

39499   Unlisted procedure, mediastinum   [C] [80]
0.00   0.00   Global Days YYY

39501-39599 Surgical Procedures: Diaphragm

EXCLUDES   *transabdominal repair of diaphragmatic hernia (43324-43325)*

39501   Repair, laceration of diaphragm, any approach   [C] [80] [⬛] [PQ]
21.83   21.83   Global Days 090

38570 — 39501

---

[26][TC] Professional/Technical Component Only   [80]/[80] Assist-at-Surgery Allowed/With Documentation   Unlisted   Not Covered

AMA: CPT Assistant References   [A2]-[Z3] ASC Payment Indicator   ♂ Male Only   ♀ Female Only   ⊘ Modifier 51 Exempt   [PQ] PQRI

154   CPT only © 2008 American Medical Association. All Rights Reserved. (Black Ink)   Medicare (Red Ink)   © 2008 Ingenix (Blue Ink)

39502   Repair, paraesophageal hiatus hernia, transabdominal, with or without fundoplasty, vagotomy, and/or pyloroplasty, except neonatal   C 80 ▢ P0

    EXCLUDES   *diaphragmatic hernia repair via transabdominal approach (43324-43325)*

    🚲 26.19   🔾 26.19   Global Days 090

    AMA: 2008, Jun, 3-6

39599   Unlisted procedure, diaphragm   C 80

    🚲 0.00   🔾 0.00   Global Days YYY

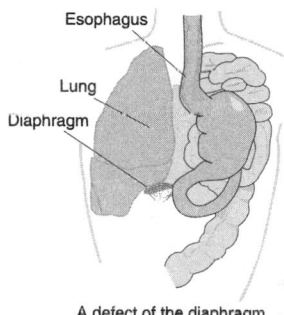

Esophagus

Lung

Diaphragm

A defect of the diaphragm can allow abdominal contents to herniate into the thoracic cavity

Code 39503 reports the repair of a diaphragmatic hernia in a neonate. The nature of the repair may necessitate the creation of a ventral hernia (an opening in the anterior abdomen to accommodate the viscera). A chest tube may or may not be required

The code is reserved for procedures on neonates

39503   Repair, neonatal diaphragmatic hernia, with or without chest tube insertion and with or without creation of ventral hernia   A C 80 ⊛ ▢ P0

    🚲 151.87   🔾 151.87   Global Days 090

    AMA: 2008, Jun, 3-6

39520   Repair, diaphragmatic hernia (esophageal hiatal); transthoracic   C 80 ▢ P0

    EXCLUDES   *diaphragmatic hernia repair via transabdominal approach (43324-43325)*

    🚲 26.20   🔾 26.20   Global Days 090

    AMA: 2008, Jun, 3-6

39530   combined, thoracoabdominal   C 80 ▢ P0

    EXCLUDES   *diaphragmatic hernia repair via transabdominal approach (43324-43325)*

    🚲 25.06   🔾 25.06   Global Days 090

    AMA: 2008, Jun, 3-6

39531   combined, thoracoabdominal, with dilation of stricture (with or without gastroplasty)   C 90 ▢ P0

    EXCLUDES   *diaphragmatic hernia repair via transabdominal approach (43324-43325)*

    🚲 26.18   🔾 26.18   Global Days 090

    AMA: 2008, Jun, 3-6

39540   Repair, diaphragmatic hernia (other than neonatal), traumatic; acute   C 80 ▢ P0

    🚲 22.29   🔾 22.29   Global Days 090

    AMA: 2008, Jun, 3-6

39541   chronic   C 80 ▢ P0

    🚲 24.04   🔾 24.04   Global Days 090

    AMA: 2008, Jun, 3-6

39545   Imbrication of diaphragm for eventration, transthoracic or transabdominal, paralytic or nonparalytic   C 80 ▢ P0

    🚲 23.69   🔾 23.69   Global Days 090

39560   Resection, diaphragm; with simple repair (eg, primary suture)   C 80 ▢ P0

    🚲 20.45   🔾 20.45   Global Days 090

39561   with complex repair (eg, prosthetic material, local muscle flap)   C 80 ▢ P0

    🚲 31.81   🔾 31.81   Global Days 090

● New Code   ▲ Revised Code   Ⓜ Maternity Edit   Ⓐ Age Edit   Ⓐ-Ⓨ OPPS Status Indicator   🚲 Facility RVU   🔾 Non-Facility RVU

▢ CCI Comprehensive Code   50 Bilateral Procedure   + Add-on Indicator   ▣ Laboratory crosswalk   ▣ Radiology crosswalk

40490-40799 Resection and Repair Procedures of the Lips

EXCLUDES *procedures on the skin of lips (10040-17999)*

40490 Biopsy of lip   P3 T ▭
   🗋 1.89   ⚒ 3.24   **Global Days 000**

40500 Vermilionectomy (lip shave), with mucosal advancement   A2 T ▭
   🗋 9.09   ⚒ 12.31   **Global Days 090**

40510 Excision of lip; transverse wedge excision with primary closure   A2 T ▭
   EXCLUDES *excision of mucous lesions (40810-40816)*
   🗋 9.03   ⚒ 11.96   **Global Days 090**

40520 V-excision with primary direct linear closure   A2 T ▭
   EXCLUDES *excision of mucous lesions (40810-40816)*
   🗋 9.14   ⚒ 12.30   **Global Days 090**

40525 full thickness, reconstruction with local flap (eg, Estlander or fan)   A2 T ▭
   🗋 14.21   ⚒ 14.21   **Global Days 090**

40527 full thickness, reconstruction with cross lip flap (Abbe-Estlander)   A2 T 80 ▭
   EXCLUDES *cleft lip repair with cross lip pedicle flap (40761)*
   🗋 16.77   ⚒ 16.77   **Global Days 090**

40530 Resection of lip, more than 1/4, without reconstruction   A2 T ▭
   EXCLUDES *reconstruction (13131-13153)*
   🗋 10.35   ⚒ 13.56   **Global Days 090**

40650 Repair lip, full thickness; vermilion only   A2 T 80 ▭
   🗋 7.27   ⚒ 10.20   **Global Days 090**
   AMA: 2008, Jan, 10-25; 2007, Jan, 13-27; 2007, Jan, 13-27; 2007, January, 13-27

40652 up to half vertical height   A2 T 80 ▭
   🗋 8.89   ⚒ 12.03   **Global Days 090**
   AMA: 2008, Jan, 10-25; 2007, Jan, 13-27; 2007, Jan, 13-27; 2007, January, 13-27

40654 over 1/2 vertical height, or complex   A2 T ▭
   🗋 10.78   ⚒ 14.18   **Global Days 090**

40700 Plastic repair of cleft lip/nasal deformity; primary, partial or complete, unilateral   A2 T 80 ▭
   EXCLUDES *cleft lip repair with cross lip pedicle flap (Abbe-Estlander type) (40761)*
   rhinoplasty for nasal deformity secondary to congenital cleft lip (30460, 30462)
   🗋 23.61   ⚒ 23.61   **Global Days 090**

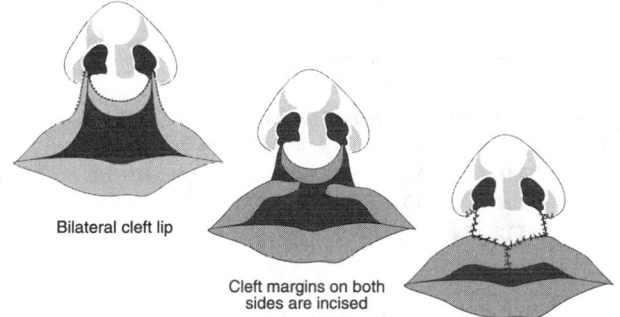

Bilateral cleft lip

Cleft margins on both sides are incised

Margins are closed, correcting cleft

40701 primary bilateral, 1 stage procedure   A2 T 80 ▭
   EXCLUDES *cleft lip repair with cross lip pedicle flap (Abbe-Estlander type) (40761)*
   rhinoplasty for nasal deformity secondary to congenital cleft lip (30460, 30462)
   🗋 29.47   ⚒ 29.47   **Global Days 090**

40702 primary bilateral, 1 of 2 stages   R2 T 80 ▭
   EXCLUDES *cleft lip repair with cross lip pedicle flap (Abbe-Estlander type) (40761)*
   rhinoplasty for nasal deformity secondary to congenital cleft lip (30460, 30462)
   🗋 22.83   ⚒ 22.83   **Global Days 090**

40720 secondary, by recreation of defect and reclosure   A2 T 80 50 ▭
   EXCLUDES *cleft lip repair with cross lip pedicle flap (Abbe-Estlander type) (40761)*
   rhinoplasty for nasal deformity secondary to congenital cleft lip (30460, 30462)
   🗋 25.35   ⚒ 25.35   **Global Days 090**

40761 with cross lip pedicle flap (Abbe-Estlander type), including sectioning and inserting of pedicle   A2 T ▭
   EXCLUDES *cleft palate repair (42200-42225)*
   other reconstructive procedures (14060, 14061, 15120-15261, 15574, 15576, 15630)
   🗋 27.45   ⚒ 27.45   **Global Days 090**

40799 Unlisted procedure, lips   T 80
   🗋 0.00   ⚒ 0.00   **Global Days YYY**

40800-40819 Incision and Resection of Buccal Cavity

INCLUDES mucosal/submucosal tissue of lips/cheeks
oral cavity outside the dentoalveolar structures

40800 Drainage of abscess, cyst, hematoma, vestibule of mouth; simple   P2 T ▭
   🗋 3.18   ⚒ 4.92   **Global Days 010**

40801 complicated   A2 T ▭
   🗋 5.55   ⚒ 7.58   **Global Days 010**

40804 Removal of embedded foreign body, vestibule of mouth; simple   P2 X 60 ▭
   🗋 3.21   ⚒ 5.01   **Global Days 010**

40805 complicated   P3 T 80 ▭
   🗋 5.75   ⚒ 7.94   **Global Days 010**

40806 Incision of labial frenum (frenotomy)   P3 T 80 ▭
   🗋 0.86   ⚒ 2.60   **Global Days 000**

40808 Biopsy, vestibule of mouth   P3 T ▭
   🗋 2.67   ⚒ 4.42   **Global Days 010**

40810 Excision of lesion of mucosa and submucosa, vestibule of mouth; without repair   P3 T ▭
   🗋 3.17   ⚒ 4.92   **Global Days 010**

40812 with simple repair   P3 T ▭
   🗋 4.95   ⚒ 6.95   **Global Days 010**

40814 with complex repair   A2 T ▭
   🗋 7.64   ⚒ 9.36   **Global Days 090**

40816 complex, with excision of underlying muscle   A2 T ▭
   🗋 7.98   ⚒ 9.85   **Global Days 090**

40818 Excision of mucosa of vestibule of mouth as donor graft   A2 T 80 ▭
   🗋 6.79   ⚒ 8.62   **Global Days 090**

40819 Excision of frenum, labial or buccal (frenumectomy, frenulectomy, frenectomy)   A2 T 80 ▭
   🗋 5.86   ⚒ 7.44   **Global Days 090**

● New Code   ▲ Revised Code   M Maternity Edit   A Age Edit   A-Y OPPS Status Indicator   🗋 Facility RVU   ⚒ Non-Facility RVU
▭ CCI Comprehensive Code   50 Bilateral Procedure   + Add-on Indicator   ◣ Laboratory crosswalk   ◳ Radiology crosswalk

40820 Destruction of Lesion of Buccal Cavity

CMS *100-3,140.5*   *Laser Procedures*

INCLUDES mucosal/submucosal tissue of lips/cheeks
oral cavity outside the dentoalveolar structures

40820 Destruction of lesion or scar of vestibule of mouth by physical methods (eg, laser, thermal, cryo, chemical) P3 T ▭
  ⟷ 4.26 ⚕ 6.40 Global Days 010

40830-40899 Repair Procedures of the Buccal Cavity

INCLUDES mucosal/submucosal tissue of lips/cheeks
oral cavity outside the dentoalveolar structures

EXCLUDES *skin grafts (15002-15630)*

40830 Closure of laceration, vestibule of mouth; 2.5 cm or less G2 T 80 ▭
  ⟷ 3.99 ⚕ 5.92 Global Days 010

40831 over 2.5 cm or complex A2 T 80 ▭
  ⟷ 5.62 ⚕ 7.87 Global Days 010

40840 Vestibuloplasty; anterior A2 T 80 ▭
  ⟷ 16.24 ⚕ 20.24 Global Days 090

40842 posterior, unilateral A2 T 80 ▭
  ⟷ 15.90 ⚕ 19.93 Global Days 090

40843 posterior, bilateral A2 T 80 ▭
  ⟷ 20.64 ⚕ 25.99 Global Days 090

40844 entire arch A2 T 80 ▭
  ⟷ 28.90 ⚕ 34.53 Global Days 090

40845 complex (including ridge extension, muscle repositioning) A2 T 80 ▭
  ⟷ 32.29 ⚕ 37.50 Global Days 090

40899 Unlisted procedure, vestibule of mouth T 80
  ⟷ 0.00 ⚕ 0.00 Global Days YYY

41000-41018 Surgical Incision of Floor of Mouth or Tongue

EXCLUDES *frenoplasty (41520)*

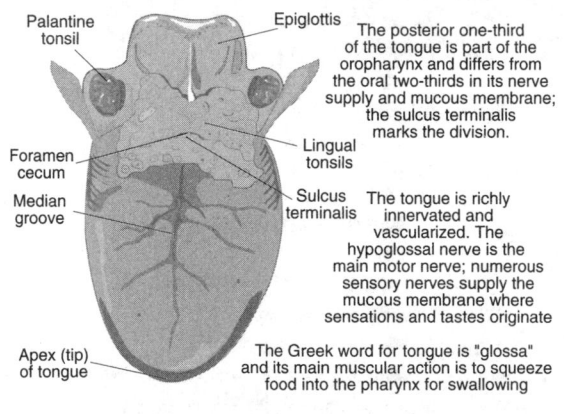

Palantine tonsil
Epiglottis
The posterior one-third of the tongue is part of the oropharynx and differs from the oral two-thirds in its nerve supply and mucous membrane; the sulcus terminalis marks the division.
Foramen cecum
Lingual tonsils
Median groove
Sulcus terminalis
The tongue is richly innervated and vascularized. The hypoglossal nerve is the main motor nerve; numerous sensory nerves supply the mucous membrane where sensations and tastes originate
Apex (tip) of tongue
The Greek word for tongue is "glossa" and its main muscular action is to squeeze food into the pharynx for swallowing

41000 Intraoral incision and drainage of abscess, cyst, or hematoma of tongue or floor of mouth; lingual P3 T ▭
  ⟷ 2.80 ⚕ 3.92 Global Days 010

41005 sublingual, superficial A2 T 80 ▭
  ⟷ 3.19 ⚕ 5.49 Global Days 010

41006 sublingual, deep, supramylohyoid A2 T 80 ▭
  ⟷ 6.56 ⚕ 8.86 Global Days 090

41007 submental space A2 T 80 ▭
  ⟷ 6.36 ⚕ 8.87 Global Days 090

41008 submandibular space A2 T 80 ▭
  ⟷ 6.82 ⚕ 9.16 Global Days 090

41009 masticator space A2 T 80 ▭
  ⟷ 7.41 ⚕ 9.74 Global Days 090

41010 Incision of lingual frenum (frenotomy) A2 T 80 ▭
  ⟷ 2.73 ⚕ 4.92 Global Days 010

41015 Extraoral incision and drainage of abscess, cyst, or hematoma of floor of mouth; sublingual A2 T 80 ▭
  ⟷ 8.48 ⚕ 10.46 Global Days 090

41016 submental A2 T 80 ▭
  ⟷ 8.82 ⚕ 10.76 Global Days 090

41017 submandibular A2 T 80 ▭
  ⟷ 8.86 ⚕ 10.84 Global Days 090

41018 masticator space A2 T 80 ▭
  ⟷ 10.38 ⚕ 12.44 Global Days 090

41019 Placement of Devices for Brachytherapy

41019 Placement of needles, catheters, or other device(s) into the head and/or neck region (percutaneous, transoral, or transnasal) for subsequent interstitial radioelement application G2 T 80
  EXCLUDES *application of interstitial radioelements (77776-77787)*
  intracranial brachytherapy radiation sources with stereotactic insertion (61770)
  ⚡ *76942, 77002, 77012, 77021*
  ⟷ 12.96 ⚕ 12.96 Global Days 000

41100-41599 Resection and Repair of the Tongue

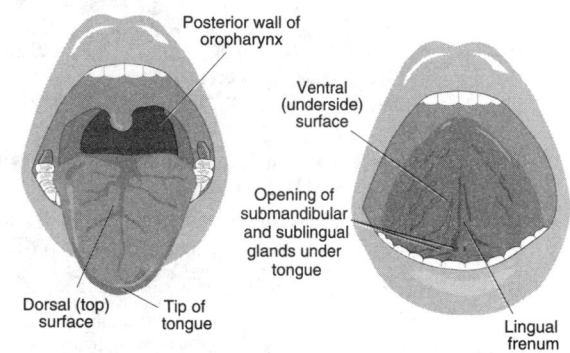

Posterior wall of oropharynx
Ventral (underside) surface
Opening of submandibular and sublingual glands under tongue
Dorsal (top) surface
Tip of tongue
Lingual frenum

Anterior (front) two-thirds of tongue comprises most of easily visible portions; the base, or root, comprises the remainder of tongue

41100 Biopsy of tongue; anterior 2/3 P3 T ▭
  ⟷ 2.79 ⚕ 4.15 Global Days 010

41105 posterior one-third P3 T ▭
  ⟷ 2.82 ⚕ 4.15 Global Days 010

41108 Biopsy of floor of mouth P3 T ▭
  ⟷ 2.27 ⚕ 3.56 Global Days 010

41110 Excision of lesion of tongue without closure P3 T ▭
  ⟷ 3.31 ⚕ 5.12 Global Days 010

41112 Excision of lesion of tongue with closure; anterior 2/3 A2 T ▭
  ⟷ 6.30 ⚕ 8.10 Global Days 090

41113 posterior one-third A2 T ▭
  ⟷ 7.01 ⚕ 8.89 Global Days 090

41114   with local tongue flap   `A2` `T` `80` `▭`
Code also excision lesion of tongue with closure anterior/posterior two-thirds (41112, 41113)
🔧 16.22   ✂ 16.22   Global Days 090

41115   Excision of lingual frenum (frenectomy)   `P3` `T` `80` `▭`
🔧 3.75   ✂ 5.97   Global Days 010

41116   Excision, lesion of floor of mouth   `A2` `T` `▭`
🔧 5.51   ✂ 7.92   Global Days 090

41120   Glossectomy; less than 1/2 tongue   `A2` `T` `80` `▭`
🔧 26.36   ✂ 26.36   Global Days 090

41130   hemiglossectomy   `C` `80` `▭` `P0`
🔧 32.50   ✂ 32.50   Global Days 090

41135   partial, with unilateral radical neck dissection   `C` `80` `▭` `P0`
🔧 54.27   ✂ 54.27   Global Days 090

41140   complete or total, with or without tracheostomy, without radical neck dissection   `C` `80` `▭` `P0`
    INCLUDES   Regnolli's excision
🔧 55.94   ✂ 55.94   Global Days 090

41145   complete or total, with or without tracheostomy, with unilateral radical neck dissection   `C` `80` `▭` `P0`
🔧 69.94   ✂ 69.94   Global Days 090

41150   composite procedure with resection floor of mouth and mandibular resection, without radical neck dissection   `C` `80` `▭` `P0`
🔧 55.29   ✂ 55.29   Global Days 090

41153   composite procedure with resection floor of mouth, with suprahyoid neck dissection   `C` `80` `▭` `P0`
🔧 59.91   ✂ 59.91   Global Days 090

41155   composite procedure with resection floor of mouth, mandibular resection, and radical neck dissection (Commando type)   `C` `80` `▭` `P0`
🔧 74.41   ✂ 74.41   Global Days 090
AMA: 2008, Jan, 10-25; 2007, Jan, 13-27; 2007, Jan, 13-27; 2007, January, 13-27

41250   Repair of laceration 2.5 cm or less; floor of mouth and/or anterior 2/3 of tongue   `A2` `T` `80` `▭`
🔧 3.58   ✂ 5.58   Global Days 010

41251   posterior one-third of tongue   `A2` `T` `80` `▭`
🔧 4.17   ✂ 5.78   Global Days 010

41252   Repair of laceration of tongue, floor of mouth, over 2.6 cm or complex   `A2` `T` `80` `▭`
🔧 5.40   ✂ 7.58   Global Days 010

41500   Fixation of tongue, mechanical, other than suture (eg, K-wire)   `A2` `T` `80` `▭`
🔧 11.16   ✂ 11.16   Global Days 090

41510   Suture of tongue to lip for micrognathia (Douglas type procedure)   `A2` `T` `80` `▭`
🔧 10.22   ✂ 10.22   Global Days 090

● 41512   Tongue base suspension, permanent suture technique   `T` `80`
    EXCLUDES   mechanical fixation of tongue, other than suture (41500)
        suture tongue to lip for micrognathia (41510)
🔧 15.66   ✂ 15.66   Global Days 090

41520   Frenoplasty (surgical revision of frenum, eg, with Z-plasty)   `A2` `T` `80` `▭`
    EXCLUDES   frenotomy (40806, 41010)
🔧 6.38   ✂ 8.47   Global Days 090

● 41530   Submucosal ablation of the tongue base, radiofrequency,1 or more sites, per session   `G2` `T` `80`
🔧 10.26   ✂ 77.81   Global Days 010

41599   Unlisted procedure, tongue, floor of mouth   `T` `80`
🔧 0.00   ✂ 0.00   Global Days YYY
AMA: 2008, Jan, 10-25; 2007, Jan, 13-27; 2007, Jan, 13-27; 2007, January, 13-27

41800-41899 Procedures of the Teeth and Supporting Structures

CMS 100-2,15,150   *Dental Services*

41800   Drainage of abscess, cyst, hematoma from dentoalveolar structures   `A2` `T` `▭`
🔧 3.22   ✂ 5.53   Global Days 010

41805   Removal of embedded foreign body from dentoalveolar structures; soft tissues   `P3` `T` `80` `▭`
🔧 4.09   ✂ 5.71   Global Days 010

41806   bone   `P3` `T` `80` `▭`
🔧 6.42   ✂ 8.40   Global Days 010

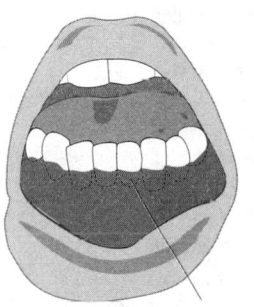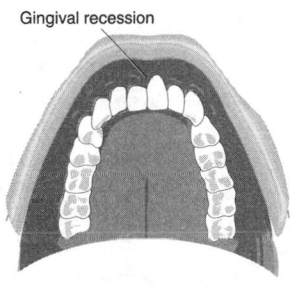

Gingival recession

Excessive mucosal growth

Gingivitis is an inflammatory response to bacteria on the teeth; it is characterized by tender, red, swollen gums and can lead to gingival recession

41820   Gingivectomy, excision gingiva, each quadrant   `R2` `T` `80` `▭`
🔧 0.00   ✂ 0.00   Global Days 000

41821   Operculectomy, excision pericoronal tissues   `G2` `T` `80` `▭`
🔧 0.00   ✂ 0.00   Global Days 000

41822   Excision of fibrous tuberosities, dentoalveolar structures   `P3` `T` `80` `▭`
🔧 4.47   ✂ 7.05   Global Days 010

41823   Excision of osseous tuberosities, dentoalveolar structures   `P3` `T` `80` `▭`
🔧 8.05   ✂ 10.50   Global Days 090

41825   Excision of lesion or tumor (except listed above), dentoalveolar structures; without repair   `R3` `T` `▭`
    EXCLUDES   lesion destruction nonexcisional (41850)
🔧 3.18   ✂ 5.02   Global Days 010

41826   with simple repair   `P3` `T`
    EXCLUDES   lesion destruction nonexcisional (41850)
🔧 5.14   ✂ 7.08   Global Days 010

41827   with complex repair   `A2` `T` `▭`
    EXCLUDES   lesion destruction nonexcisional (41850)
🔧 7.59   ✂ 10.47   Global Days 090

41828   Excision of hyperplastic alveolar mucosa, each quadrant (specify)   `P3` `T` `80` `▭`
🔧 5.56   ✂ 7.55   Global Days 010

41830   Alveolectomy, including curettage of osteitis or sequestrectomy   `P3` `T` `80` `▭`
🔧 7.07   ✂ 9.50   Global Days 010

41850   Destruction of lesion (except excision), dentoalveolar structures   `R2` `T` `80` `▭`
🔧 0.00   ✂ 0.00   Global Days 000

● New Code   ▲ Revised Code   `M` Maternity Edit   `A` Age Edit   `A-Y` OPPS Status Indicator   🔧 Facility RVU   ✂ Non-Facility RVU
`▭` CCI Comprehensive Code   `50` Bilateral Procedure   + Add-on Indicator   `N` Laboratory crosswalk   `R` Radiology crosswalk

Digestive

41870 — 42409

41870   Periodontal mucosal grafting   G2 T 80 🖵
   🔪 0.00   ⚘ 0.00   **Global Days** 000

41872   Gingivoplasty, each quadrant (specify)   P3 T 80 🖵
   🔪 6.54   ⚘ 8.88   **Global Days** 090

41874   Alveoloplasty, each quadrant (specify)   P3 80 🖵
   EXCLUDES   *fracture reduction (21421-21490)*
            laceration closure (40830, 40831)
            maxilla osteotomy, segmental (21206)

   🔪 6.47   ⚘ 9.06   **Global Days** 090

41899   Unlisted procedure, dentoalveolar structures   T 80
   🔪 0.00   ⚘ 0.00   **Global Days** YYY

42000-42299 Procedures of the Palate and Uvula

42000   Drainage of abscess of palate, uvula   A2 T 80 🖵
   🔪 2.60   ⚘ 3.87   **Global Days** 010

42100   Biopsy of palate, uvula   P3 T 🖵
   🔪 2.76   ⚘ 3.68   **Global Days** 010

42104   Excision, lesion of palate, uvula; without
       closure   P3 T 🖵
   🔪 3.47   ⚘ 5.12   **Global Days** 010

42106   with simple primary closure   P3 T 🖵
   🔪 4.56   ⚘ 6.51   **Global Days** 010

42107   with local flap closure   A2 T 🖵
   EXCLUDES   *mucosal graft (40818)*
            skin graft (14040-14300)

   🔪 8.76   ⚘ 11.30   **Global Days** 090

42120   Resection of palate or extensive resection of
       lesion   A2 T 80 🖵
   EXCLUDES   *reconstruction of palate with extraoral tissue*
            (14040-14300, 15050, 15120, 15240,
            15576)

   🔪 24.42   ⚘ 24.42   **Global Days** 090

42140   Uvulectomy, excision of uvula   A2 T 🖵
   🔪 3.89   ⚘ 6.10   **Global Days** 090

42145   Palatopharyngoplasty (eg, uvulopalatopharyngoplasty,
       uvulopharyngoplasty)   A2 T 🖵
   EXCLUDES   *removal of exostosis of the bony palate*
            (21031, 21032)

   🔪 17.83   ⚘ 17.83   **Global Days** 090
   AMA: 2008, Jan, 10-25; 2007, Jan, 13-27; 2007, Jan, 13-27; 2007,
   January, 13-27; 2005, Jan, 46-47; 2005, Jan, 46-47; 2005,
   January, 46-47; 2004, Dec, 19; 2004, Dec, 19; 2004, December,
   19

42160   Destruction of lesion, palate or uvula (thermal, cryo or
       chemical)   P3 T 80 🖵
   🔪 3.87   ⚘ 5.91   **Global Days** 010

42180   Repair, laceration of palate; up to 2 cm   A2 T 80 🖵
   🔪 4.69   ⚘ 6.01   **Global Days** 010

42182   over 2 cm or complex   A2 T 80 🖵
   🔪 6.87   ⚘ 8.26   **Global Days** 010

42200   Palatoplasty for cleft palate, soft and/or hard palate
       only   A2 T 80 🖵
   🔪 22.75   ⚘ 22.75   **Global Days** 090

42205   Palatoplasty for cleft palate, with closure of alveolar
       ridge; soft tissue only   A2 T 80 🖵
   🔪 24.32   ⚘ 24.32   **Global Days** 090

42210   with bone graft to alveolar ridge (includes obtaining
       graft)   A2 T 80 🖵
   🔪 27.58   ⚘ 27.58   **Global Days** 090

42215   Palatoplasty for cleft palate; major revision   A2 T 80 🖵
   🔪 18.07   ⚘ 18.07   **Global Days** 090

42220   secondary lengthening procedure   A2 T 80 🖵
   🔪 13.94   ⚘ 13.94   **Global Days** 090

42225   attachment pharyngeal flap   T 80 🖵
   🔪 23.87   ⚘ 23.87   **Global Days** 090
   AMA: 2008, Jan, 10-25; 2007, Jan, 13-27; 2007, Jan, 13-27; 2007,
   January, 13-27

42226   Lengthening of palate, and pharyngeal flap   A2 T 80 🖵
   🔪 23.75   ⚘ 23.75   **Global Days** 090

42227   Lengthening of palate, with island flap   T 80 🖵
   🔪 23.09   ⚘ 23.09   **Global Days** 090

42235   Repair of anterior palate, including vomer
       flap   A2 T 80 🖵
   EXCLUDES   *oronasal fistula repair (30600)*

   🔪 18.83   ⚘ 18.83   **Global Days** 090

42260   Repair of nasolabial fistula   A2 T 80 🖵
   EXCLUDES   *cleft lip repair (40700-40761)*

   🔪 17.65   ⚘ 21.13   **Global Days** 090

42280   Maxillary impression for palatal prosthesis   P3 T 80 🖵
   🔪 2.68   ⚘ 3.91   **Global Days** 010

42281   Insertion of pin-retained palatal prosthesis   G2 T 80 🖵
   🔪 3.87   ⚘ 5.03   **Global Days** 010

42299   Unlisted procedure, palate, uvula   T 80
   🔪 0.00   ⚘ 0.00   **Global Days** YYY
   AMA: 2008, Jan, 10-25; 2007, Jan, 13-27; 2007, Jan, 13-27; 2007,
   January, 13-27; 2005, Jan, 46-47; 2005, January, 46-47; 2005,
   Jan, 46-47; 2004, Dec, 19; 2004, December, 19; 2004, December,
   19; 2004, Dec, 19; 2004, Dec, 19; 2004, Dec, 19

42300-42699 Procedures of the Salivary Ducts and Glands

42300   Drainage of abscess; parotid, simple   A2 T 🖵
   🔪 3.87   ⚘ 5.14   **Global Days** 010

42305   parotid, complicated   A2 T 80 🖵
   🔪 11.05   ⚘ 11.05   **Global Days** 090

42310   Drainage of abscess; submaxillary or sublingual,
       intraoral   A2 T 80 🖵
   🔪 3.16   ⚘ 4.00   **Global Days** 010

42320   submaxillary, external   A2 T 80 🖵
   🔪 4.54   ⚘ 6.19   **Global Days** 010

42330   Sialolithotomy; submandibular (submaxillary), sublingual
       or parotid, uncomplicated, intraoral   P3 T 🖵
   🔪 4.21   ⚘ 5.76   **Global Days** 010

42335   submandibular (submaxillary), complicated,
       intraoral   P3 T 🖵
   🔪 6.60   ⚘ 9.18   **Global Days** 090

42340   parotid, extraoral or complicated intraoral   A2 T 80 🖵
   🔪 8.69   ⚘ 11.55   **Global Days** 090

42400   Biopsy of salivary gland; needle   P3 T 🖵
   EXCLUDES   *fine needle aspiration (10021, 10022)*

   ⬛   *76942, 77002, 77012, 77021*
   ◣   *88172, 88173*
   🔪 1.51   ⚘ 2.72   **Global Days** 000

42405   incisional   A2 T 🖵
   ⬛   *76942, 77002, 77012, 77021*
   🔪 5.87   ⚘ 7.59   **Global Days** 010

42408   Excision of sublingual salivary cyst (ranula)   A2 T 80 🖵
   🔪 8.44   ⚘ 11.32   **Global Days** 090

42409   Marsupialization of sublingual salivary cyst
       (ranula)   A2 T 80 🖵
   🔪 5.72   ⚘ 8.18   **Global Days** 090

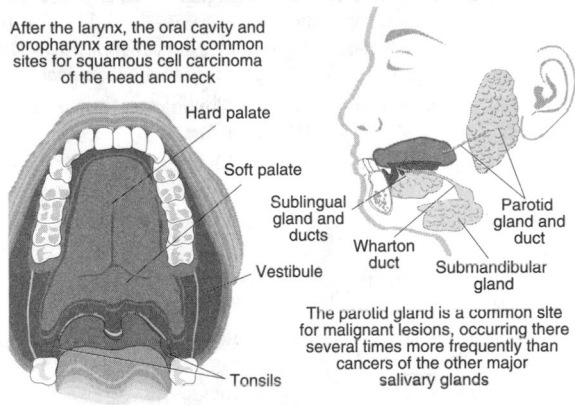

After the larynx, the oral cavity and oropharynx are the most common sites for squamous cell carcinoma of the head and neck

Hard palate

Soft palate

Sublingual gland and ducts

Parotid gland and duct

Wharton duct

Submandibular gland

Vestibule

Tonsils

The parotid gland is a common site for malignant lesions, occurring there several times more frequently than cancers of the other major salivary glands

42410 Excision of parotid tumor or parotid gland; lateral lobe, without nerve dissection A2 T 80 ▭
EXCLUDES *facial nerve suture or graft (64864, 64865, 69740, 69745)*

🔧 16.07 ⚕ 16.07 Global Days 090

42415 lateral lobe, with dissection and preservation of facial nerve A2 T 80 ▭
EXCLUDES *facial nerve suture or graft (64864, 64865, 69740, 69745)*

🔧 28.92 ⚕ 28.92 Global Days 090

42420 total, with dissection and preservation of facial nerve A2 T 80 ▭
EXCLUDES *facial nerve suture or graft (64864, 64865, 69740, 69745)*

🔧 33.15 ⚕ 33.15 Global Days 090

42425 total, en bloc removal with sacrifice of facial nerve A2 T 80 ▭
EXCLUDES *facial nerve suture or graft (64864, 64865, 69740, 69745)*

🔧 21.82 ⚕ 21.82 Global Days 090

42426 total, with unilateral radical neck dissection C 80 ▭
EXCLUDES *facial nerve suture or graft (64864, 64865, 69740, 69745)*

🔧 35.48 ⚕ 35.48 Global Days 090

42440 Excision of submandibular (submaxillary) gland A2 T 80 ▭

🔧 12.06 ⚕ 12.06 Global Days 090

42450 Excision of sublingual gland A2 T 80 ▭

🔧 9.18 ⚕ 11.30 Global Days 090

42500 Plastic repair of salivary duct, sialodochoplasty; primary or simple A2 T 80 ▭

🔧 8.74 ⚕ 10.78 Global Days 090

42505 secondary or complicated A2 T ▭

🔧 11.69 ⚕ 13.99 Global Days 090

42507 Parotid duct diversion, bilateral (Wilke type procedure); A2 T 80 ▭

🔧 13.11 ⚕ 13.11 Global Days 090

42508 with excision of one submandibular gland A2 T 80 ▭

🔧 18.76 ⚕ 18.76 Global Days 090

42509 with excision of both submandibular glands A2 T 80 ▭

🔧 21.38 ⚕ 21.38 Global Days 090

42510 with ligation of both submandibular (Wharton's) ducts A2 T 80 ▭

🔧 16.16 ⚕ 16.16 Global Days 090

42550 Injection procedure for sialography N N ▭
✖ *70390*

🔧 1.79 ⚕ 3.84 Global Days 000

42600 Closure salivary fistula A2 T 60 ▭

🔧 9.10 ⚕ 12.11 Global Days 090

42650 Dilation salivary duct P3 T ▭

🔧 1.52 ⚕ 2.07 Global Days 000

42660 Dilation and catheterization of salivary duct, with or without injection P3 T 60 ▭

🔧 2.02 ⚕ 2.66 Global Days 000

42665 Ligation salivary duct, intraoral A2 T 80 ▭

🔧 5.29 ⚕ 7.65 Global Days 090

42699 Unlisted procedure, salivary glands or ducts T 80 ▭

🔧 0.00 ⚕ 0.00 Global Days YYY

42700-42999 Procedures of the Adenoids/Throat/Tonsils

42700 Incision and drainage abscess; peritonsillar A2 T ▭

🔧 3.45 ⚕ 4.65 Global Days 010

42720 retropharyngeal or parapharyngeal, intraoral approach A2 T 80 ▭

🔧 10.22 ⚕ 11.60 Global Days 010

42725 retropharyngeal or parapharyngeal, external approach A2 T 80 ▭

🔧 20.86 ⚕ 20.86 Global Days 090

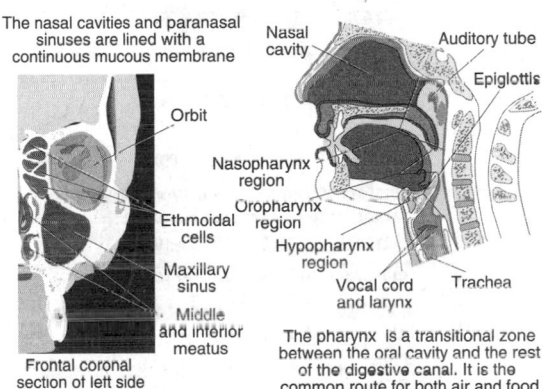

The nasal cavities and paranasal sinuses are lined with a continuous mucous membrane

Nasal cavity

Auditory tube

Epiglottis

Orbit

Nasopharynx region

Oropharynx region

Ethmoidal cells

Hypopharynx region

Maxillary sinus

Vocal cord and larynx

Trachea

Middle and inferior meatus

Frontal coronal section of left side of skull showing sinuses

The pharynx is a transitional zone between the oral cavity and the rest of the digestive canal. It is the common route for both air and food

42800 Biopsy; oropharynx P3 T ▭
EXCLUDES *laryngoscopy with biopsy (31510, 31535, 31536)*

🔧 2.85 ⚕ 3.90 Global Days 010

42802 hypopharynx A2 T ▭
EXCLUDES *laryngoscopy with biopsy (31510, 31535, 31536)*

🔧 3.46 ⚕ 5.94 Global Days 010

42804 nasopharynx, visible lesion, simple A2 T ▭
EXCLUDES *laryngoscopy with biopsy (31510, 31535, 31536)*

🔧 2.93 ⚕ 4.96 Global Days 010

42806 nasopharynx, survey for unknown primary lesion A2 T ▭
EXCLUDES *laryngoscopy with biopsy (31510, 31535, 31536)*

🔧 3.44 ⚕ 5.60 Global Days 010

42808 Excision or destruction of lesion of pharynx, any method A2 T ▭

🔧 4.23 ⚕ 5.70 Global Days 010

42410 — 42808

Digestive

42809 — 42971

42809 Removal of foreign body from pharynx ☒ Ⓧ ▭
   🔁 3.32   ⚕ 4.25   Global Days 010

42810 Excision branchial cleft cyst or vestige, confined to skin and subcutaneous tissues ⒜② Ⓣ ⑧ ▭
   🔁 7.25   ⚕ 9.59   Global Days 090

42815 Excision branchial cleft cyst, vestige, or fistula, extending beneath subcutaneous tissues and/or into pharynx ⒜② Ⓣ ⑧ ▭
   🔁 14.20   ⚕ 14.20   Global Days 090

42820 Tonsillectomy and adenoidectomy; younger than age 12 Ⓐ ⒜② Ⓣ ⑧ ▭
   🔁 7.49   ⚕ 7.49   Global Days 090
   AMA: 2008, Jan, 10-25; 2008, Mar, 14-15; 2008, May, 9-11; 2007, Jan, 13-27; 2007, Jan, 13-27; 2007, January, 13-27

42821 age 12 or over Ⓐ ⒜② Ⓣ ⑧ ▭
   🔁 7.83   ⚕ 7.83   Global Days 090
   AMA: 2008, Mar, 14-15; 2008, May, 9-11

42825 Tonsillectomy, primary or secondary; younger than age 12 Ⓐ ⒜② Ⓣ ⑧ ▭
   🔁 6.70   ⚕ 6.70   Global Days 090
   AMA: 2008, Mar, 14-15

42826 age 12 or over Ⓐ ⒜② Ⓣ ▭
   🔁 6.48   ⚕ 6.48   Global Days 090
   AMA: 2008, Mar, 14-15

42830 Adenoidectomy, primary; younger than age 12 Ⓐ ⒜② Ⓣ ⑧ ▭
   🔁 5.28   ⚕ 5.28   Global Days 090

42831 age 12 or over Ⓐ ⒜② Ⓣ ⑧ ▭
   🔁 5.70   ⚕ 5.70   Global Days 090

42835 Adenoidectomy, secondary; younger than age 12 Ⓐ ⒜② Ⓣ ⑧ ▭
   🔁 4.77   ⚕ 4.77   Global Days 090

42836 age 12 or over Ⓐ ⒜② Ⓣ ⑧ ▭
   🔁 6.22   ⚕ 6.22   Global Days 090

42842 Radical resection of tonsil, tonsillar pillars, and/or retromolar trigone; without closure Ⓣ ⑧ ▭
   🔁 24.59   ⚕ 24.59   Global Days 090

42844 closure with local flap (eg, tongue, buccal) Ⓣ ⑧ ▭
   🔁 34.61   ⚕ 34.61   Global Days 090

42845 closure with other flap Ⓒ ⑧ ▭
   Code also closure with other flap(s)
   Code also radical neck dissection when combined (38720)
   🔁 56.59   ⚕ 56.59   Global Days 090

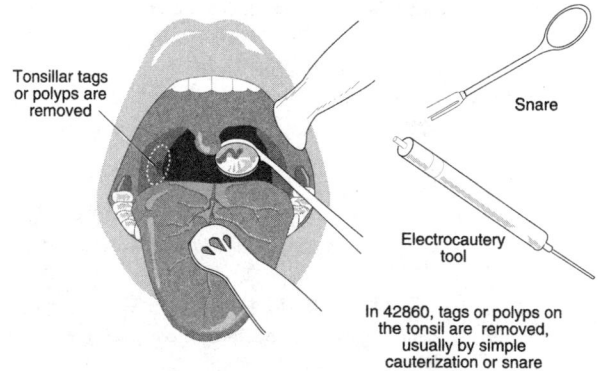

Tonsillar tags or polyps are removed

Snare

Electrocautery tool

In 42860, tags or polyps on the tonsil are removed, usually by simple cauterization or snare

42860 Excision of tonsil tags ⒜② Ⓣ ⑧ ▭
   🔁 4.78   ⚕ 4.78   Global Days 090

42870 Excision or destruction lingual tonsil, any method (separate procedure) ⒜② Ⓣ ⑧ ▭
   EXCLUDES   *nasopharynx resection (juvenile angiofibroma) by transzygomatic/bicoronal approach (61586, 61600)*
   🔁 14.55   ⚕ 14.55   Global Days 090

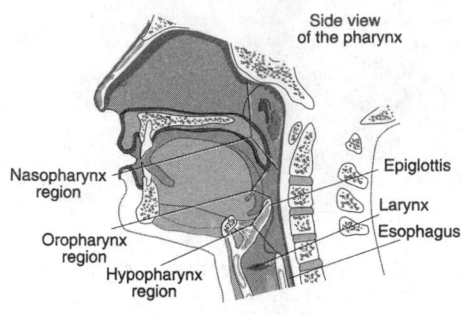

Side view of the pharynx

Nasopharynx region

Oropharynx region

Hypopharynx region

Epiglottis

Larynx

Esophagus

The nasopharynx is the membranous passage above the level of the soft palate; the oropharynx is the region between the soft palate and the upper edge of the epiglottis; the hypopharynx is the region of the epiglottis to the juncture of the larynx and esophagus; the three regions are collectively known as the pharynx

42890 Limited pharyngectomy ⒜② Ⓣ ⑧ ▭
   Code also radical neck dissection when combined (38720)
   🔁 35.15   ⚕ 35.15   Global Days 090

42892 Resection of lateral pharyngeal wall or pyriform sinus, direct closure by advancement of lateral and posterior pharyngeal walls ⒜② Ⓣ ⑧ ▭
   Code also radical neck dissection when combined (38720)
   🔁 46.06   ⚕ 46.06   Global Days 090

42894 Resection of pharyngeal wall requiring closure with myocutaneous flap Ⓒ ⑧ ▭
   EXCLUDES   *limited pharyngectomy with radical neck dissection (38720, 42890)*
   Code also radical neck dissection when combined (38720)
   🔁 59.08   ⚕ 59.08   Global Days 090
   AMA: 2008, Jan, 10-25

42900 Suture pharynx for wound or injury ⒜② Ⓣ ⑧ ▭
   🔁 8.96   ⚕ 8.96   Global Days 010

42950 Pharyngoplasty (plastic or reconstructive operation on pharynx) ⒜② Ⓣ ⑧ ▭
   EXCLUDES   *pharyngeal flap (42225)*
   🔁 20.16   ⚕ 20.16   Global Days 090

42953 Pharyngoesophageal repair Ⓒ ⑧ ▭
   Code also closure using myocutaneous or other flap
   🔁 24.81   ⚕ 24.81   Global Days 090

42955 Pharyngostomy (fistulization of pharynx, external for feeding) ⒜② Ⓣ ⑧ ▭
   🔁 19.02   ⚕ 19.02   Global Days 090

42960 Control oropharyngeal hemorrhage, primary or secondary (eg, post-tonsillectomy); simple ⒜② Ⓣ ⑧ ▭
   🔁 4.35   ⚕ 4.35   Global Days 010

42961 complicated, requiring hospitalization Ⓒ ⑧ ▭
   🔁 10.79   ⚕ 10.79   Global Days 090

42962 with secondary surgical intervention ⒜② Ⓣ
   🔁 13.37   ⚕ 13.37   Global Days 090

42970 Control of nasopharyngeal hemorrhage, primary or secondary (eg, postadenoidectomy); simple, with posterior nasal packs, with or without anterior packs and/or cautery ☒ Ⓣ ▭
   🔁 9.98   ⚕ 9.98   Global Days 090

42971 complicated, requiring hospitalization Ⓒ ⑧ ▭
   🔁 11.78   ⚕ 11.78   Global Days 090

42972 　with secondary surgical intervention 　A2 T 80 ▢
　　　🔧 13.25 　⚕ 13.25 　Global Days 090

42999 　Unlisted procedure, pharynx, adenoids, or tonsils 　T 80
　　　🔧 0.00 　⚕ 0.00 　Global Days YYY

43020-43135 Incision/Resection of Esophagus

EXCLUDES 　*gastrointestinal reconstruction for previous esophagectomy (43360, 43361)*
　gastrotomy with intraluminal tube insertion (43510)

43020 　Esophagotomy, cervical approach, with removal of foreign body 　T 80 ▢ P0
　　EXCLUDES 　*laparotomy with esophageal intubation (43510)*
　　　🔧 13.69 　⚕ 13.69 　Global Days 090

43030 　Cricopharyngeal myotomy 　G2 T 80 ▢ P0
　　EXCLUDES 　*laparotomy with esophageal intubation (43510)*
　　　🔧 13.51 　⚕ 13.51 　Global Days 090

43045 　Esophagotomy, thoracic approach, with removal of foreign body 　C 80 ▢ P0
　　EXCLUDES 　*laparotomy with esophageal intubation (43510)*
　　　🔧 34.53 　⚕ 34.53 　Global Days 090

43100 　Excision of lesion, esophagus, with primary repair; cervical approach 　C 80 ▢ PU
　　EXCLUDES 　*wide excision of malignant lesion of cervical esophagus with total laryngectomy with radical neck dissection (31365, 43107, 43116, 43124)*
　　　wide excision of malignant lesion of cervical esophagus, with total laryngectomy without radical neck dissection (31360, 43107, 43116, 43124)
　　　🔧 16.18 　⚕ 16.18 　Global Days 090

43101 　thoracic or abdominal approach 　C 80 ▢ P0
　　EXCLUDES 　*wide excision of malignant lesion of cervical esophagus with total laryngectomy with radical neck dissection (31365, 43107, 43116, 43124)*
　　　wide excision of malignant lesion of cervical esophagus, with total laryngectomy without radical neck dissection (31360, 43107, 43116, 43124)
　　　🔧 27.07 　⚕ 27.07 　Global Days 090

43107 　Total or near total esophagectomy, without thoracotomy; with pharyngogastrostomy or cervical esophagogastrostomy, with or without pyloroplasty (transhiatal) 　C 80 ▢ P0
　　　🔧 66.75 　⚕ 66.75 　Global Days 090

43108 　with colon interposition or small intestine reconstruction, including intestine mobilization, preparation and anastomosis(es) 　C 80 ▢ P0
　　　🔧 110.69 　⚕ 110.69 　Global Days 090

43112 　Total or near total esophagectomy, with thoracotomy; with pharyngogastrostomy or cervical esophagogastrostomy, with or without pyloroplasty 　C 80 ▢ P0
　　　🔧 71.41 　⚕ 71.41 　Global Days 090

43113 　with colon interposition or small intestine reconstruction, including intestine mobilization, preparation, and anastomosis(es) 　C 80 ▢ P0
　　　🔧 110.77 　⚕ 110.77 　Global Days 090

43116 　Partial esophagectomy, cervical, with free intestinal graft, including microvascular anastomosis, obtaining the graft and intestinal reconstruction 　C 80 ▢ P0
　　EXCLUDES 　*free jejunal graft with microvascular anastomosis done by a different physician (43496)*
　　Code also modifier 52 if intestinal or free jejunal graft with microvascular anastomosis is done by another physician
　　INCLUDES 　operating microscope (69990)
　　　🔧 125.31 　⚕ 125.31 　Global Days 090

43117 　Partial esophagectomy, distal 2/3, with thoracotomy and separate abdominal incision, with or without proximal gastrectomy; with thoracic esophagogastrostomy, with or without pyloroplasty (Ivor Lewis) 　C 80 ▢ P0
　　EXCLUDES 　*esophagogastrectomy (lower third) and vagotomy (43122)*
　　　total esophagectomy with gastropharyngostomy (43107, 43124)
　　　🔧 65.27 　⚕ 65.27 　Global Days 090

43118 　with colon interposition or small intestine reconstruction, including intestine mobilization, preparation, and anastomosis(es) 　C 80 ▢ P0
　　EXCLUDES 　*esophagogastrectomy (lower third) and vagotomy (43122)*
　　　total esophagectomy with gastropharyngostomy (43107, 43124)
　　　🔧 91.39 　⚕ 91.39 　Global Days 090

43121 　Partial esophagectomy, distal 2/3, with thoracotomy only, with or without proximal gastrectomy, with thoracic esophagogastrostomy, with or without pyloroplasty 　C 80 ▢ P0
　　　🔧 72.85 　⚕ 72.85 　Global Days 090

43122 　Partial esophagectomy, thoracoabdominal or abdominal approach, with or without proximal gastrectomy; with esophagogastrostomy, with or without pyloroplasty 　C 80 ▢ P0
　　　🔧 66.06 　⚕ 66.06 　Global Days 090

43123 　with colon interposition or small intestine reconstruction, including intestine mobilization, preparation, and anastomosis(es) 　C 80 ▢ P0
　　　🔧 111.30 　⚕ 111.30 　Global Days 090

43124 　Total or partial esophagectomy, without reconstruction (any approach), with cervical esophagostomy 　C 80 ▢ P0
　　　🔧 95.23 　⚕ 95.23 　Global Days 090

43130 　Diverticulectomy of hypopharynx or esophagus, with or without myotomy; cervical approach 　T 80 ▢ P0
　　　🔧 20.48 　⚕ 20.48 　Global Days 090

43135 　thoracic approach 　C 80 ▢ P0
　　　🔧 38.30 　⚕ 38.30 　Global Days 090

43200-43259 Endoscopic Procedures: Upper GI

CMS *100-3,100.2* 　*Endoscopy*
INCLUDES 　diagnostic endoscopy with surgical endoscopy

Code also appropriate endoscopy of each anatomic site examined

⊙ 　**43200** 　Esophagoscopy, rigid or flexible; diagnostic, with or without collection of specimen(s) by brushing or washing (separate procedure) 　A2 T ▢ P0
　　　🔧 2.74 　⚕ 5.49 　Global Days 000
　　AMA: 2008, Jan, 10-25; 2008, Oct, 6-7; 2007, Jan, 13-27; 2007, Jan, 13-27; 2007, January, 13-27

● New Code 　▲ Revised Code 　Ⓜ Maternity Edit 　Ⓐ Age Edit 　A-Y OPPS Status Indicator 　🔧 Facility RVU 　⚕ Non-Facility RVU
▢ CCI Comprehensive Code 　50 Bilateral Procedure 　+ Add-on Indicator 　Ⓝ Laboratory crosswalk 　Ⓡ Radiology crosswalk

© 2008 Ingenix *(Blue Ink)* 　CPT only © 2008 American Medical Association. All Rights Reserved. *(Black Ink)* 　Medicare *(Red Ink)* 　163

Digestive

43201 — 43241

⊙ 43201   with directed submucosal injection(s), any substance   A2 T 🖵 P0

    EXCLUDES   *injection sclerosis of esophageal varices (43204)*

    🔗 3.44   ✂ 7.54   Global Days 000
    AMA: 2008, Oct, 6-7

⊙ 43202   with biopsy, single or multiple   A2 T 🖵 P0
    🔗 3.04   ✂ 7.21   Global Days 000
    AMA: 2008, Oct, 6-7

⊙ 43204   with injection sclerosis of esophageal varices   A2 T 🖵
    🔗 5.99   ✂ 5.99   Global Days 000
    AMA: 2008, Oct, 6-7

⊙ 43205   with band ligation of esophageal varices   A2 T 80 🖵
    🔗 6.00   ✂ 6.00   Global Days 000
    AMA: 2008, Oct, 6-7

⊙ 43215   with removal of foreign body   A2 T 🖵
    📷 74235
    🔗 4.11   ✂ 4.11   Global Days 000
    AMA: 2008, Oct, 6-7

⊙ 43216   with removal of tumor(s), polyp(s), or other lesion(s) by hot biopsy forceps or bipolar cautery   A2 T 80 🖵 P0
    🔗 3.83   ✂ 5.13   Global Days 000
    AMA: 2008, Oct, 6-7

⊙ 43217   with removal of tumor(s), polyp(s), or other lesion(s) by snare technique   A2 T 🖵 P0
    🔗 4.52   ✂ 9.67   Global Days 000
    AMA: 2008, Oct, 6-7

⊙ 43219   with insertion of plastic tube or stent   A2 T 🖵
    🔗 4.57   ✂ 4.57   Global Days 000
    AMA: 2008, Oct, 6-7

⊙ 43220   with balloon dilation (less than 30 mm diameter)   A2 T 🖵

    EXCLUDES   *dilation of esophagus with balloon 30mm diameter or larger (43458)*
       dilation of esophagus without visualization (43450-43453)
       fiberoptic esophagogastroscopy:
         diagnostic (43200, 43235)
         with biopsy or collection of specimen (43200, 43202, 43235, 43239)
         with removal of foreign body (43215, 43247)
         with removal of polyps(s) (43217, 43251)

    📷 74360
    🔗 3.38   ✂ 3.38   Global Days 000
    AMA: 2008, Jan, 10-25; 2008, Oct, 6-7; 2007, Jan, 13-27; 2007, Jan, 13-27; 2007, January, 13-27; 2005, May, 3-6; 2005, May, 3-6; 2005, May, 3-6

⊙ 43226   with insertion of guide wire followed by dilation over guide wire   A2 T 🖵
    📷 74360
    🔗 3.77   ✂ 3.77   Global Days 000
    AMA: 2008, Oct, 6-7

⊙ 43227   with control of bleeding (eg, injection, bipolar cautery, unipolar cautery, laser, heater probe, stapler, plasma coagulator)   A2 T 🖵
    🔗 5.61   ✂ 5.61   Global Days 000
    AMA: 2008, Oct, 6-7

⊙ 43228   with ablation of tumor(s), polyp(s), or other lesion(s), not amenable to removal by hot biopsy forceps, bipolar cautery or snare technique   A2 T 🖵 P0
    Code also esophagoscopic photodynamic therapy if performed (96570, 96571)
    🔗 6.00   ✂ 6.00   Global Days 000
    AMA: 2008, Oct, 6-7

⊙ 43231   with endoscopic ultrasound examination   A2 T 80 🖵
    Do not report with (76975)
    🔗 5.09   ✂ 5.09   Global Days 000
    AMA: 2008, Oct, 6-7; 2004, May, 6; 2004, May, 6; 2004, May, 6

⊙ 43232   with transendoscopic ultrasound-guided intramural or transmural fine needle aspiration/biopsy(s)   A2 T 80 🖵
    Do not report with (76942, 76975)
    📷 88172-88173
    🔗 7.02   ✂ 7.02   Global Days 000
    AMA: 2008, Jan, 10-25; 2008, Oct, 6-7; 2007, Jan, 13-27; 2007, Jan, 13-27; 2007, January, 13-27; 2004, May, 6; 2004, May, 6; 2004, March, 11; 2004, May, 6; 2004, Mar, 11; 2004, Mar, 11

⊙ 43234   **Upper gastrointestinal endoscopy, simple primary examination (eg, with small diameter flexible endoscope) (separate procedure)**   A2 T 🖵 P0
    🔗 3.18   ✂ 7.16   Global Days 000
    AMA: 2008, Jan, 10-25; 2007, May, 9-11; 2007, May, 9-11; 2007, May, 9-11

⊙ 43235   **Upper gastrointestinal endoscopy including esophagus, stomach, and either the duodenum and/or jejunum as appropriate; diagnostic, with or without collection of specimen(s) by brushing or washing (separate procedure)**   A2 T 🖵 P0
    🔗 3.88   ✂ 7.74   Global Days 000
    AMA: 2008, Jan, 10-25; 2008, Oct, 6-7; 2007, Jan, 13-27; 2007, Jan, 13-27; 2007, January, 13-27

⊙ 43236   with directed submucosal injection(s), any substance   A2 T 🖵 P0
    EXCLUDES   *injection sclerosis of varices, esophageal/gastric (43243)*
    🔗 4.71   ✂ 9.63   Global Days 000
    AMA: 2008, Oct, 6-7

⊙ 43237   with endoscopic ultrasound examination limited to the esophagus   A2 T 80 🖵
    Do not report with (76942, 76975)
    🔗 6.46   ✂ 6.46   Global Days 000
    AMA: 2008, Oct, 6-7; 2004, May, 6; 2004, May, 6; 2004, May, 6

⊙ 43238   with transendoscopic ultrasound-guided intramural or transmural fine needle aspiration/biopsy(s), esophagus (includes endoscopic ultrasound examination limited to the esophagus)   A2 T 80 🖵
    Do not report with (76942, 76975)
    🔗 7.97   ✂ 7.97   Global Days 000
    AMA: 2008, Oct, 6-7; 2004, May, 6; 2004, May, 6; 2004, May, 6

⊙ 43239   with biopsy, single or multiple   A2 T 🖵 P0
    🔗 4.59   ✂ 8.96   Global Days 000
    AMA: 2008, Jan, 10-25; 2008, Oct, 6-7; 2007, Jan, 13-27; 2007, Jan, 13-27; 2007, January, 13-27; 2005, Mar, 11-15; 2005, Mar, 11-15; 2005, March, 11-15; 2004, Jan, 26; 2004, Jan, 26; 2004, January, 26

⊙ 43240   with transmural drainage of pseudocyst   A2 T 🖵
    🔗 10.69   ✂ 10.69   Global Days 000
    AMA: 2008, Oct, 6-7

⊙ 43241   with transendoscopic intraluminal tube or catheter placement   A2 T 🖵
    🔗 4.17   ✂ 4.17   Global Days 000
    AMA: 2008, Oct, 6-7

⊙ **43242** with transendoscopic ultrasound-guided intramural or transmural fine needle aspiration/biopsy(s) (includes endoscopic ultrasound examination of the esophagus, stomach, and either the duodenum and/or jejunum as appropriate) [A2] [T] [80] [▢]

> *EXCLUDES* *fine needle biopsy/aspiration, transendoscopic, of only the esophagus (43238)*

Do not report with (76942, 76975)

> ▨ *88172-88173*

⌖ 11.38   ⌖ 11.38   Global Days 000
AMA: 2008, Oct, 6-7; 2004, May, 6; 2004, May, 6; 2004, May, 6

⊙ **43243** with injection sclerosis of esophageal and/or gastric varices [A2] [T] [▢]

⌖ 7.17   ⌖ 7.17   Global Days 000
AMA: 2008, Oct, 6-7

⊙ **43244** with band ligation of esophageal and/or gastric varices [A2] [T] [80] [▢]

⌖ 7.95   ⌖ 7.95   Global Days 000
AMA: 2008, Oct, 6-7

⊙ **43245** with dilation of gastric outlet for obstruction (eg, balloon, guide wire, bougie) [A2] [T] [▢]

Do not report with (43256)

⌖ 5.02   ⌖ 5.02   Global Days 000
AMA: 2008, Jan, 10-25; 2008, Oct, 6-7; 2007, Jan, 13-27; 2007, Jan, 13-27; 2007, January, 13-27; 2004, Jan, 26; 2004, January, 26, 2004, Jan, 26

⊙ **43246** with directed placement of percutaneous gastrostomy tube [A2] [T] [80] [▢]

> *EXCLUDES* *percutaneous insertion of gastrostomy tube, nonendoscopic (49440)*

⌖ 6.72   ⌖ 6.72   Global Days 000
AMA: 2008, Jan, 10-25; 2008, Oct, 6-7; 2007, Jan, 13-27; 2007, Jan, 13-27; 2007, January, 13-27

⊙ **43247** with removal of foreign body [A2] [T] [▢]

> ▨ *74235*

⌖ 5.37   ⌖ 5.37   Global Days 000
AMA: 2008, Jan, 10-25; 2008, Oct, 6-7; 2007, Dec, 7-8

⊙ **43248** with insertion of guide wire followed by dilation of esophagus over guide wire [A2] [T] [▢]

⌖ 5.07   ⌖ 5.07   Global Days 000
AMA: 2008, Jan, 10-25; 2008, Oct, 6-7; 2007, Jan, 13-27; 2007, Jan, 13-27; 2007, January, 13-27

⊙ **43249** with balloon dilation of esophagus (less than 30 mm diameter) [A2] [T] [▢]

⌖ 4.67   ⌖ 4.67   Global Days 000
AMA: 2008, Oct, 6-7; 2005, May, 3-6; 2005, May, 3-6; 2005, May, 3-6

⊙ **43250** with removal of tumor(s), polyp(s), or other lesion(s) by hot biopsy forceps or bipolar cautery [A2] [T] [▢] [P0]

⌖ 5.02   ⌖ 5.02   Global Days 000
AMA: 2008, Jan, 10-25; 2008, Oct, 6-7; 2007, Jan, 13-27; 2007, January, 13-27

⊙ **43251** with removal of tumor(s), polyp(s), or other lesion(s) by snare technique [A2] [T] [▢] [P0]

⌖ 5.84   ⌖ 5.84   Global Days 000
AMA: 2008, Oct, 6-7; 2004, Oct, 12; 2004, Oct, 12; 2004, October, 12

⊙ **43255** with control of bleeding, any method [A2] [T] [▢]

⌖ 7.59   ⌖ 7.59   Global Days 000
AMA: 2008, Oct, 6-7

⊙ **43256** with transendoscopic stent placement (includes predilation) [A2] [T] [▢]

Code also (C1874, C1875, C1876, C1877, C2617, C2625)

⌖ 6.82   ⌖ 6.82   Global Days 000
AMA: 2008, Oct, 6-7

⊙ **43257** with delivery of thermal energy to the muscle of lower esophageal sphincter and/or gastric cardia, for treatment of gastroesophageal reflux disease [A2] [T] [▢]

⌖ 8.36   ⌖ 8.36   Global Days 000
AMA: 2008, Oct, 6-7; 2005, May, 3-6; 2005, May, 3-6; 2005, May, 3-6

⊙ **43258** with ablation of tumor(s), polyp(s), or other lesion(s) not amenable to removal by hot biopsy forceps, bipolar cautery or snare technique [A2] [T] [▢] [P0]

> *EXCLUDES* *esophagoscopy with injection sclerosis of esophageal varices (43204)*
> *upper gastrointestinal endoscopy with injection sclerosis of esophageal varices (43243)*

⌖ 7.15   ⌖ 7.15   Global Days 000
AMA: 2008, Oct, 6-7

⊙ **43259** with endoscopic ultrasound examination, including the esophagus, stomach, and either the duodenum and/or jejunum as appropriate [A2] [T] [80] [▢]

Do not report with (76975)

⌖ 8.14   ⌖ 8.14   Global Days 000
AMA: 2008, Oct, 6-7; 2004, May, 6; 2004, May, 6; 2004, May, 6

43260-43273 Endoscopic Procedures: ERCP

> *INCLUDES* diagnostic endoscopy with surgical endoscopy

Code also appropriate endoscopy of each anatomic site examined.

⊙ **43260** Endoscopic retrograde cholangiopancreatography (ERCP); diagnostic, with or without collection of specimen(s) by brushing or washing (separate procedure) [A2] [T] [▢]

> ▨ *74328-74330*

⌖ 9.33   ⌖ 9.33   Global Days 000
AMA: 2008, May, 9-11; 2004, Oct, 12; 2004, Oct, 12; 2004, October, 12

⊙ **43261** with biopsy, single or multiple [A2] [T] [▢]

> ▨ *74328-74330*

⌖ 9.81   ⌖ 9.81   Global Days 000

⊙ **43262** with sphincterotomy/papillotomy [A2] [T] [▢]

> ▨ *74328-74330*

⌖ 11.52   ⌖ 11.52   Global Days 000
AMA: 2004, Oct, 12; 2004, Oct, 12; 2004, October, 12

⊙ **43263** with pressure measurement of sphincter of Oddi (pancreatic duct or common bile duct) [A2] [T] [▢]

> ▨ *74328-74330*

⌖ 11.40   ⌖ 11.40   Global Days 000
AMA: 2004, Oct, 12; 2004, Oct, 12; 2004, October, 12

⊙ **43264** with endoscopic retrograde removal of calculus/calculi from biliary and/or pancreatic ducts [A2] [T] [▢]

Code also sphincterotomy, when performed (43262)

> ▨ *74328-74330*

⌖ 13.83   ⌖ 13.83   Global Days 000
AMA: 2007, Dec, 10-179

⊙ **43265** with endoscopic retrograde destruction, lithotripsy of calculus/calculi, any method [A2] [T] [▢]

Code also sphincterotomy, when performed (43262)

> ▨ *74328-74330*

⌖ 15.52   ⌖ 15.52   Global Days 000

⊙ **43267** with endoscopic retrograde insertion of nasobiliary or nasopancreatic drainage tube [A2] [T] [▢]

Code also sphincterotomy, when performed (43262)

> ▨ *74328-74330*

⌖ 11.47   ⌖ 11.47   Global Days 000

● New Code   ▲ Revised Code   Ⓜ Maternity Edit   Ⓐ Age Edit   Ⓐ-Ⓥ OPPS Status Indicator   ⌖ Facility RVU   ⌖ Non-Facility RVU
▢ CCI Comprehensive Code   50 Bilateral Procedure   + Add-on Indicator   ▨ Laboratory crosswalk   ▨ Radiology crosswalk

© 2008 Ingenix *(Blue Ink)*   CPT only © 2008 American Medical Association. All Rights Reserved. (Black Ink)   Medicare (Red Ink)   165

Digestive

43268 — 43341

⊙ **43268** with endoscopic retrograde insertion of tube or stent into bile or pancreatic duct A2 T ▢
Code also sphincterotomy, when performed (43262)
⊡ 74328-74330
🔊 11.66 ⚕ 11.66 Global Days 000
AMA: 2008, Jan, 10-25; 2007, Jan, 13-27; 2007, Jan, 13-27; 2007, January, 13-27; 2004, Oct, 12; 2004, Oct, 12; 2004, September, 13; 2004, October, 12; 2004, Sep, 13; 2004, Sep, 13

⊙ **43269** with endoscopic retrograde removal of foreign body and/or change of tube or stent A2 T ▢
Code also sphincterotomy, when performed (43262)
⊡ 74328-74330
🔊 12.77 ⚕ 12.77 Global Days 000

⊙ **43271** with endoscopic retrograde balloon dilation of ampulla, biliary and/or pancreatic duct(s) A2 T ▢
Code also sphincterotomy, when performed (43262)
⊡ 74328-74330
🔊 11.51 ⚕ 11.51 Global Days 000

⊙ **43272** with ablation of tumor(s), polyp(s), or other lesion(s) not amenable to removal by hot biopsy forceps, bipolar cautery or snare technique A2 T 80 ▢
⊡ 74328-74330
🔊 11.49 ⚕ 11.49 Global Days 000

+ ⊙ ● **43273** Endoscopic cannulation of papilla with direct visualization of common bile duct(s) and/or pancreatic duct(s) (List separately in addition to code(s) for primary procedure) C2 T 80
Code first (43260-43261, 43263-43265, 43267-43272)
🔊 3.48 ⚕ 3.48 Global Days ZZZ

43279-43289 Laparoscopic Procedures of Esophagus

● **43279** Laparoscopy, surgical, esophagomyotomy (Heller type), with fundoplasty, when performed C 80
INCLUDES diagnostic laparoscopy with surgical laparoscopy
EXCLUDES esophagomyotomy, open method (43330-43331)
Do not report with (43280)
🔊 32.69 ⚕ 32.69 Global Days 090

43280 Laparoscopy, surgical, esophagogastric fundoplasty (eg, Nissen, Toupet procedures) T 80 ▢ P0
INCLUDES diagnostic laparoscopy with surgical laparoscopy
EXCLUDES esophagogastric fundoplasty, open method (43324)
Do not report with (43279)
🔊 27.32 ⚕ 27.32 Global Days 090

43289 Unlisted laparoscopy procedure, esophagus T 80 50
🔊 0.00 ⚕ 0.00 Global Days YYY

43300-43425 Open Esophageal Repair Procedures

Proximal esophagus
Intestinal esophagus
Diaphragm
Stomach
Thyroid cartilage
Cricoid cartilage
Trachea
Esophagus

Sections of stomach or bowel are commonly used to repair a resected portion of the esophagus

The esophagus is a muscular tube that delivers food from the oral cavity to the stomach. It spans the cervical, thoracic, and abdominal regions and numerous surgical approaches may be used

43300 Esophagoplasty (plastic repair or reconstruction), cervical approach; without repair of tracheoesophageal fistula C 80 ▢ P0
🔊 16.14 ⚕ 16.14 Global Days 090

43305 with repair of tracheoesophageal fistula C 80 ▢ P0
🔊 28.72 ⚕ 28.72 Global Days 090

43310 Esophagoplasty (plastic repair or reconstruction), thoracic approach; without repair of tracheoesophageal fistula C 80 ▢ P0
🔊 40.52 ⚕ 40.52 Global Days 090

43312 with repair of tracheoesophageal fistula C 80 ▢ P0
🔊 44.74 ⚕ 44.74 Global Days 090

43313 Esophagoplasty for congenital defect (plastic repair or reconstruction), thoracic approach; without repair of congenital tracheoesophageal fistula C 80 ⊙ ▢ P0
🔊 70.86 ⚕ 70.86 Global Days 090

43314 with repair of congenital tracheoesophageal fistula C 80 ⊙ ▢ P0
🔊 81.42 ⚕ 81.42 Global Days 090

43320 Esophagogastrostomy (cardioplasty), with or without vagotomy and pyloroplasty, transabdominal or transthoracic approach C 80 ▢ P0
🔊 35.45 ⚕ 35.45 Global Days 090

43324 Esophagogastric fundoplasty (eg, Nissen, Belsey IV, Hill procedures) C 80 ▢ P0
EXCLUDES laparoscopic approach (43280)
🔊 34.40 ⚕ 34.40 Global Days 090
AMA: 2008, Jan, 10-25; 2007, Jan, 13-27; 2007, Jan, 13-27; 2007, January, 13-27; 2005, May, 3-6; 2005, May, 3-6; 2005, May, 3-6

43325 Esophagogastric fundoplasty; with fundic patch (Thal-Nissen procedure) C 80 ▢ P0
EXCLUDES myotomy, cricopharyngeal (43030)
🔊 33.82 ⚕ 33.82 Global Days 090

43326 with gastroplasty (eg, Collis) C 80 ▢ P0
🔊 34.56 ⚕ 34.56 Global Days 090

43330 Esophagomyotomy (Heller type); abdominal approach C 80 ▢ P0
EXCLUDES esophagomyotomy, laparoscopic method (43279)
🔊 33.20 ⚕ 33.20 Global Days 090

43331 thoracic approach C 80 ▢ P0
EXCLUDES thoracoscopy with esophagomyotomy (32665)
🔊 36.05 ⚕ 36.05 Global Days 090

43340 Esophagojejunostomy (without total gastrectomy); abdominal approach C 80 ▢ P0
🔊 34.38 ⚕ 34.38 Global Days 090

43341 thoracic approach C 80 ▢ P0
🔊 37.96 ⚕ 37.96 Global Days 090

43350 Esophagostomy, fistulization of esophagus, external; abdominal approach   C 80 □ P0
   🔁 29.12   🔍 29.12   Global Days 090

43351 thoracic approach   C 80 □ P0
   🔁 34.48   🔍 34.48   Global Days 090

43352 cervical approach   C 80 □ P0
   🔁 28.22   🔍 28.22   Global Days 090

43360 Gastrointestinal reconstruction for previous esophagectomy, for obstructing esophageal lesion or fistula, or for previous esophageal exclusion; with stomach, with or without pyloroplasty   C 80 □ P0
   🔁 60.55   🔍 60.55   Global Days 090

43361 with colon interposition or small intestine reconstruction, including intestine mobilization, preparation, and anastomosis(es)   C 80 □ P0
   🔁 67.26   🔍 67.26   Global Days 090

43400 Ligation, direct, esophageal varices   C 80 □ P0
   🔁 41.24   🔍 41.24   Global Days 090

43401 Transection of esophagus with repair, for esophageal varices   C 80 □ P0
   🔁 39.33   🔍 39.33   Global Days 090

43405 Ligation or stapling at gastroesophageal junction for pre-existing esophageal perforation   C 80 □ P0
   🔁 38.10   🔍 38.10   Global Days 090

43410 Suture of esophageal wound or injury; cervical approach   C 80 □ P0
   🔁 26.02   🔍 26.02   Global Days 090

43415 transthoracic or transabdominal approach   C 80 □ P0
   🔁 44.48   🔍 44.48   Global Days 090

43420 Closure of esophagostomy or fistula; cervical approach   T 80 □ P0
   🔁 25.93   🔍 25.93   Global Days 090

43425 transthoracic or transabdominal approach   C 80 □ P0
   EXCLUDES   *esophageal hiatal hernia repair (39520-39531)*
   🔁 39.07   🔍 39.07   Global Days 090

43450-43458 Esophageal Dilation

43450 Dilation of esophagus, by unguided sound or bougie, single or multiple passes   A2 T □
   ☒ *74220, 74360*
   🔁 2.37   🔍 4.11   Global Days 000
   AMA: 2008, Jan, 10-25; 2007, Jan, 13-27; 2007, Jan, 13-27; 2007, January, 13-27

⊙ **43453** Dilation of esophagus, over guide wire   A2 T □
   EXCLUDES   *dilation performed with direct visualization (43220)*
               esophagus dilation performed by dilator or balloon (43220, 43458, 74360)
   ☒ *74220, 74360*
   🔁 2.57   🔍 7.70   Global Days 000
   AMA: 2008, Jan, 10-25; 2007, Jan, 13-27; 2007, Jan, 13-27; 2007, January, 13-27

⊙ **43456** Dilation of esophagus, by balloon or dilator, retrograde   A2 T □
   ☒ *74220, 74360*
   🔁 4.15   🔍 15.58   Global Days 000
   AMA: 2005, May, 3-6; 2005, May, 3-6; 2005, May, 3-6

⊙ **43458** Dilation of esophagus with balloon (30 mm diameter or larger) for achalasia   A2 T □
   EXCLUDES   *balloon dilation less than 30 mm diameter (43220)*
   ☒ *74220, 74360*
   🔁 4.85   🔍 10.03   Global Days 000
   AMA: 2008, Jan, 10-25; 2008, Oct, 6-7; 2007, Jan, 13-27; 2007, Jan, 13-27; 2007, January, 13-27; 2005, May, 3-6; 2005, May, 3-6; 2005, May, 3-6

43460-43499 Other and Unlisted Esophageal Procedures

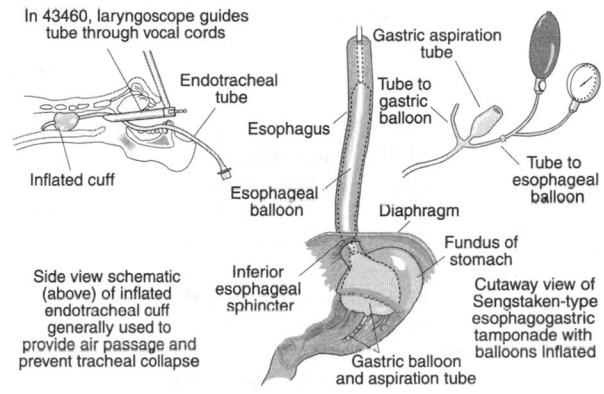

In 43460, laryngoscope guides tube through vocal cords — Endotracheal tube — Esophagus — Inflated cuff — Esophageal balloon — Side view schematic (above) of inflated endotracheal cuff generally used to provide air passage and prevent tracheal collapse — Gastric aspiration tube — Tube to gastric balloon — Tube to esophageal balloon — Diaphragm — Inferior esophageal sphincter — Fundus of stomach — Cutaway view of Sengstaken-type esophagogastric tamponade with balloons inflated — Gastric balloon and aspiration tube

43460 Esophagogastric tamponade, with balloon (Sengstaken type)   C □
   EXCLUDES   *removal of foreign body of the esophagus with balloon catheter (43215, 43247, 74235)*
   🔁 5.89   🔍 5.89   Global Days 000

43496 Free jejunum transfer with microvascular anastomosis   C 80 □ P0
   INCLUDES   operating microscope (69990)
   🔁 0.00   🔍 0.00   Global Days 090

43499 Unlisted procedure, esophagus   T
   🔁 0.00   🔍 0.00   Global Days YYY
   AMA: 2008, Jan, 10-25; 2007, May, 9-11; 2007, May, 9-11; 2007, May, 9-11

43500-43641 Open Gastric Incisional and Resection Procedures

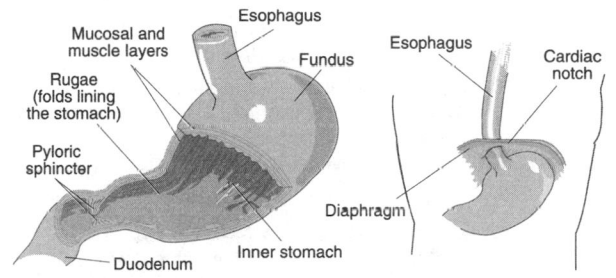

Esophagus — Mucosal and muscle layers — Rugae (folds lining the stomach) — Pyloric sphincter — Duodenum — Fundus — Inner stomach — Diaphragm — Esophagus — Cardiac notch

The stomach is a highly distensible organ that serves as a reservoir to mix food and break it down with digestive juices. The esophagus pierces the diaphragm at the cardiac notch, where the stomach begins. The pyloric sphincter marks the inferior border of the stomach. The vagal nerve trunks run down the front and back of the esophagus and serve the stomach by controlling secretion of digestive acids.

● New Code   ▲ Revised Code   M Maternity Edit   A Age Edit   A-Y OPPS Status Indicator   🔁 Facility RVU   🔍 Non-Facility RVU
□ CCI Comprehensive Code   50 Bilateral Procedure   + Add-on Indicator   ☒ Laboratory crosswalk   ☒ Radiology crosswalk

© 2008 Ingenix *(Blue Ink)*   CPT only © 2008 American Medical Association. All Rights Reserved. (Black Ink)   Medicare (Red Ink)   167

Digestive

43500 — 43648

43500 Gastrotomy; with exploration or foreign body removal [C][80][▣][P0]
   ⏷ 19.48 ⚕ 19.48 Global Days 090

43501 with suture repair of bleeding ulcer [C][80][▣][P0]
   ⏷ 33.54 ⚕ 33.54 Global Days 090

43502 with suture repair of pre-existing esophagogastric laceration (eg, Mallory-Weiss) [C][80][▣][P0]
   ⏷ 38.01 ⚕ 38.01 Global Days 090

43510 with esophageal dilation and insertion of permanent intraluminal tube (eg, Celestin or Mousseaux-Barbin) [T][80][▣][P0]
   ⏷ 24.00 ⚕ 24.00 Global Days 090

43520 Pyloromyotomy, cutting of pyloric muscle (Fredet-Ramstedt type operation) [C][80][♂][▣][P0]
   ⏷ 17.65 ⚕ 17.65 Global Days 090

43600 Biopsy of stomach; by capsule, tube, peroral (1 or more specimens) [A2][T][▣][P0]
   ⏷ 2.85 ⚕ 2.85 Global Days 000

43605 by laparotomy [C][80][▣][P0]
   ⏷ 20.69 ⚕ 20.69 Global Days 090

43610 Excision, local; ulcer or benign tumor of stomach [C][80][▣][P0]
   ⏷ 24.46 ⚕ 24.46 Global Days 090

43611 malignant tumor of stomach [C][80][▣][P0]
   ⏷ 30.42 ⚕ 30.42 Global Days 090

43620 Gastrectomy, total; with esophagoenterostomy [C][80][▣][P0]
   ⏷ 49.59 ⚕ 49.59 Global Days 090

43621 with Roux-en-Y reconstruction [C][80][▣][P0]
   ⏷ 56.28 ⚕ 56.28 Global Days 090

43622 with formation of intestinal pouch, any type [C][80][▣][P0]
   ⏷ 57.18 ⚕ 57.18 Global Days 090

43631 Gastrectomy, partial, distal; with gastroduodenostomy [C][80][▣][P0]
   INCLUDES Billroth operation
   ⏷ 36.41 ⚕ 36.41 Global Days 090

43632 with gastrojejunostomy [C][80][▣][P0]
   INCLUDES Polya anastomosis
   ⏷ 49.19 ⚕ 49.19 Global Days 090

43633 with Roux-en-Y reconstruction [C][80][▣][P0]
   ⏷ 46.89 ⚕ 46.89 Global Days 090

43634 with formation of intestinal pouch [C][80][▣][P0]
   ⏷ 51.77 ⚕ 51.77 Global Days 090

+ **43635** Vagotomy when performed with partial distal gastrectomy (List separately in addition to code[s] for primary procedure) [C][80][▣]
   Code first as appropriate (43631-43634)
   ⏷ 2.92 ⚕ 2.92 Global Days ZZZ

43640 Vagotomy including pyloroplasty, with or without gastrostomy; truncal or selective [C][80][▣][P0]
   EXCLUDES pyloroplasty (43800)
      vagotomy (64752-64760)
   ⏷ 29.23 ⚕ 29.23 Global Days 090

43641 parietal cell (highly selective) [C][80][▣][P0]
   EXCLUDES upper gastrointestinal endoscopy (43234-43259)
   ⏷ 29.47 ⚕ 29.47 Global Days 090

43644-43645 Laparoscopic Gastric Bypass with Small Bowel Resection

CMS 100-3,100.8 *Intestinal Bypass Surgery*
CMS 100-3,40.5 *Treatment of Obesity*
CMS 100-3,100.1 *Bariatric Surgery for Treatment of Morbid Obesity*
INCLUDES diagnostic laparoscopy
EXCLUDES *endoscopy, upper gastrointestinal, (esophagus/stomach/duodenum/jejunum) (43235-43259)*

43644 Laparoscopy, surgical, gastric restrictive procedure; with gastric bypass and Roux-en-Y gastroenterostomy (roux limb 150 cm or less) [C][80][▣][P0]
   EXCLUDES *open method (43846)*
      roux limb greater than 150 cm (43645)

   Do not report with (43846, 49320)
   ⏷ 43.19 ⚕ 43.19 Global Days 090
   AMA: 2005, May, 3-6; 2005, May, 3-6; 2005, May, 3-6

43645 with gastric bypass and small intestine reconstruction to limit absorption [C][80][▣][P0]
   Do not report with (43847, 49320)
   ⏷ 46.26 ⚕ 46.26 Global Days 090
   AMA: 2005, May, 3-6; 2005, May, 3-6; 2005, May, 3-6

43647-43659 Other and Unlisted Laparoscopic Gastric Procedures

INCLUDES diagnostic laparoscopy
EXCLUDES *endoscopy, upper gastrointestinal, (esophagus/stomach/duodenum/jejunum) (43235-43259)*

43647 Laparoscopy, surgical; implantation or replacement of gastric neurostimulator electrodes, antrum [S][80]
   EXCLUDES *electronic analysis/programming gastric neurostimulator pulse generator (95980-95982)*
      electronic analysis/programming/reprogramming gastric neurostimulator pulse generator, lesser curvature (morbid obesity) (95980-95982)
      implantation or replacement of gastric stimulation electrodes, lesser curvature, performed laparoscopically (0155T)
      insertion/replacement gastric neurostimulator pulse generator (64590)
      open method (43881)

   Code also neurostimulator lead (C1778, C1897)
   ⏷ 0.00 ⚕ 0.00 Global Days YYY
   AMA: 2008, Jan, 8-9; 2007, Mar, 4-5; 2007, Mar, 4-5; 2007, March, 4-5

43648 revision or removal of gastric neurostimulator electrodes, antrum [T][80]
   EXCLUDES *electronic analysis/programming gastric neurostimulator pulse generator (95980-95982)*
      open method (43882)
      revision or removal of gastric stimulation electrodes, lesser curvature, performed laparoscopically (0156T)
      revision/removal gastric neurostimulator pulse generator (64595)

   ⏷ 0.00 ⚕ 0.00 Global Days YYY
   AMA: 2007, Mar, 4-5; 2007, Mar, 4-5; 2007, March, 4-5

43651   Laparoscopy, surgical; transection of vagus nerves, truncal   T 80 ▢ P0
    🔧 16.28   ✂ 16.28   Global Days 090

43652   transection of vagus nerves, selective or highly selective   T 80 ▢ P0
    🔧 19.05   ✂ 19.05   Global Days 090

43653   gastrostomy, without construction of gastric tube (eg, Stamm procedure) (separate procedure)   A2 T 80 ▢ P0
    🔧 13.86   ✂ 13.86   Global Days 090

43659   Unlisted laparoscopy procedure, stomach   T 80 50
    🔧 0.00   ✂ 0.00   Global Days YYY
    AMA: 2008, Jan, 10-25; 2007, Jan, 13-27; 2007, Jan, 13-27; 2007, January, 13-27; 2007, Dec, 10-179; 2006, Jun, 16-17; 2006, Jun, 16-17; 2006, April, 19-20; 2006, June, 16-17; 2006, Apr, 19-20; 2006, Apr, 19 20

43752-43761 Nonsurgical Gastric Tube Procedures

CMS 100-4,20,100.2.2 *Medical Necessity for Parenteral and Enteral Nutrition Therapy*
CMS 100-4,20,50.3   *Payment for Replacement of Parenteral and Enteral Pumps*

43752   Naso- or oro-gastric tube placement, requiring physician's skill and fluoroscopic guidance (includes fluoroscopy, image documentation and report)   X ▢
    EXCLUDES   *percutaneous insertion of gastrostomy tube (43246, 49440)*
      placement of enteric tube (44500, 74340)

    Do not report with (99291-99292, 99468-99469, 99471-99472, 99478-99479)
    🔧 1.11   ✂ 1.11   Global Days 000
    AMA: 2008, Jan, 10-25; 2007, Jan, 13-27; 2007, Jan, 13-27; 2007, Feb, 10-11; 2007, Feb, 10-11; 2007, January, 13-27; 2007, Jul, 1-4; 2007, February, 10-11; 2006, May, 1-9; 2006, May, 1-9; 2006, May, 1-9

43760   Change of gastrostomy tube, percutaneous, without imaging or endoscopic guidance   A2 T ▢
    EXCLUDES   *fluoroscopically guided gastrostomy replacement (49450)*
      gastrostomy tube, placed endoscopically (43246)

    🔧 1.36   ✂ 8.66   Global Days 000
    AMA: 2008, Apr, -11; 2008, Apr, -11; 2008, Apr, -11

43761   Repositioning of the gastric feeding tube, through the duodenum for enteric nutrition   A2 T ▢
    EXCLUDES   *gastrostomy tube converted endoscopically to jejunostomy tube (44373)*
      introduction of long gastrointestinal tube into the duodenum (44500)

    Do not report with (44500, 49446)
    📷 76000
    🔧 2.89   ✂ 3.27   Global Days 000
    AMA: 2008, Jun, 8-11

43770-43774 Laparoscopic Bariatric Procedures

CMS 100-3,100.1   *Bariatric Surgery for Treatment of Morbid Obesity*
INCLUDES   diagnostic laparoscopy
    stomach/duodenum/jejunum/ileum
    subsequent band adjustments (change of the gastric band component diameter by injection/aspiration of fluid through the subcutaneous port component) during the postoperative period

43770   Laparoscopy, surgical, gastric restrictive procedure; placement of adjustable gastric restrictive device (eg, gastric band and subcutaneous port components)   C 80 P0
    Code also modifier 52 for placement of individual component
    🔧 27.76   ✂ 27.76   Global Days 090
    AMA: 2008, Jan, 10-25; 2007, Jan, 13-27; 2007, Jan, 13-27; 2007, January, 13-27; 2006, Apr, 19-20; 2006, Apr, 19-20; 2006, April, 19-20; 2006, April, 1-7; 2006, Apr, 1-7; 2006, Apr, 1-7

43771   revision of adjustable gastric restrictive device component only   C 80 P0
    🔧 31.67   ✂ 31.67   Global Days 090
    AMA: 2006, Apr, 1-7; 2006, Apr, 1-7; 2006, April, 1-7

43772   removal of adjustable gastric restrictive device component only   C 80 P0
    🔧 23.95   ✂ 23.95   Global Days 090
    AMA: 2006, Apr, 1-7; 2006, Apr, 1-7; 2006, April, 1-7

43773   removal and replacement of adjustable gastric restrictive device component only   C 80 P0
    Do not report with (43772)
    🔧 31.70   ✂ 31.70   Global Days 090
    AMA: 2006, Apr, 1-7; 2006, Apr, 1-7; 2006, April, 1-7

43774   removal of adjustable gastric restrictive device and subcutaneous port components   C 80 P0
    EXCLUDES   *removal/replacement of subcutaneous port components and gastric band (43659)*
    🔧 23.95   ✂ 23.95   Global Days 090
    AMA: 2008, Jan, 10-25; 2007, Jan, 13-27; 2007, Jan, 13-27; 2007, January, 13-27; 2006, Apr, 19-20; 2006, Apr, 19-20; 2006, Apr, 1 7; 2006, April, 10 20; 2006, April, 1 7; 2006, June, 16-17; 2006, Apr, 1-7; 2006, Jun, 16-17; 2006, Jun, 16-17

43800-43840 Open Gastric Incisional/Repair/Resection Procedures

43800   Pyloroplasty   C 80 ▢ P0
    EXCLUDES   *vagotomy with pyloroplasty (43640)*
    🔧 23.21   ✂ 23.21   Global Days 090

43810   Gastroduodenostomy   C 80 ▢ P0
    🔧 25.14   ✂ 25.14   Global Days 090

43820   Gastrojejunostomy; without vagotomy   C 80 ▢ P0
    🔧 32.39   ✂ 32.39   Global Days 090

43825   with vagotomy, any type   C 80 ▢ P0
    🔧 32.36   ✂ 32.36   Global Days 090

43830   Gastrostomy, open; without construction of gastric tube (eg, Stamm procedure) (separate procedure)   T 80 ▢ P0
    🔧 17.21   ✂ 17.21   Global Days 090

43831   neonatal, for feeding   A T 80 ☺ ▢ P0
    EXCLUDES   *change of gastrostomy tube (43760)*
    🔧 14.40   ✂ 14.40   Global Days 090

43832   with construction of gastric tube (eg, Janeway procedure)   C 80 ◰ P0

> EXCLUDES   *endoscopic placement of percutaneous gastrostomy tube (43246)*

🔗 26.49   ⚕ 26.49   Global Days 090

43840   Gastrorrhaphy, suture of perforated duodenal or gastric ulcer, wound, or injury   C 80 ◰ P0
🔗 32.85   ⚕ 32.85   Global Days 090

43842-43848 Open Bariatric Procedures for Morbid Obesity

CMS *100-3,100.8*   *Intestinal Bypass Surgery*
CMS *100-3,40.5*   *Treatment of Obesity*
CMS *100-3,100.1*   *Bariatric Surgery for Treatment of Morbid Obesity*

43842   Gastric restrictive procedure, without gastric bypass, for morbid obesity; vertical-banded gastroplasty   E ◰ P0
🔗 32.16   ⚕ 32.16   Global Days 090

43843   other than vertical-banded gastroplasty   C 80 ◰ P0
🔗 31.54   ⚕ 31.54   Global Days 090

43845   Gastric restrictive procedure with partial gastrectomy, pylorus-preserving duodenoileostomy and ileoileostomy (50 to 100 cm common channel) to limit absorption (biliopancreatic diversion with duodenal switch)   C 80 ◰ P0

> Do not report with (43633, 43847, 44130, 49000)

🔗 48.90   ⚕ 48.90   Global Days 090
AMA: 2005, May, 3-6; 2005, May, 3-6; 2005, May, 3-6

43846   Gastric restrictive procedure, with gastric bypass for morbid obesity; with short limb (150 cm or less) Roux-en-Y gastroenterostomy   C 80 ◰ P0

> EXCLUDES   *gastric bypass with Roux-en-Y gastroenterostomy performed laparoscopically (43644)*
> *more than 150 cm (43847)*

🔗 40.68   ⚕ 40.68   Global Days 090
AMA: 2005, May, 3-6; 2005, May, 3-6; 2005, May, 3-6

43847   with small intestine reconstruction to limit absorption   C 80 ◰ P0
🔗 44.46   ⚕ 44.46   Global Days 090

43848   Revision, open, of gastric restrictive procedure for morbid obesity, other than adjustable gastric restrictive device (separate procedure)   C 80 ◰ P0

> EXCLUDES   *procedures for adjustable gastric restrictive devices (43770-43774, 43886-43888)*

🔗 48.26   ⚕ 48.26   Global Days 090
AMA: 2006, Apr, 1-7; 2006, Apr, 1-7; 2006, April, 1-7

43850-43882 Open Gastric Procedures: Closure/Implantation/Replacement/Revision

43850   Revision of gastroduodenal anastomosis (gastroduodenostomy) with reconstruction; without vagotomy   C 80 ◰ P0
🔗 40.42   ⚕ 40.42   Global Days 090

43855   with vagotomy   C 80 ◰ P0
🔗 42.26   ⚕ 42.26   Global Days 090

43860   Revision of gastrojejunal anastomosis (gastrojejunostomy) with reconstruction, with or without partial gastrectomy or intestine resection; without vagotomy   C 80 ◰ P0
🔗 41.04   ⚕ 41.04   Global Days 090

43865   with vagotomy   C 80 ◰ P0
🔗 42.71   ⚕ 42.71   Global Days 090

43870   Closure of gastrostomy, surgical   A2 T 80 ◰ P0
🔗 17.55   ⚕ 17.55   Global Days 090

43880   Closure of gastrocolic fistula   C 80 ◰ P0
🔗 40.11   ⚕ 40.11   Global Days 090

43881   Implantation or replacement of gastric neurostimulator electrodes, antrum, open   C 80

> EXCLUDES   *electronic analysis/programming/reprogramming gastric neurostimulator pulse generator, lesser curvature (morbid obesity) (95980-95982)*
> *gastric neurostimulator pulse generator programming/electronic analysis (95999)*
> *implantation/replacement performed laparoscopically (43647)*
> *insertion/replacement gastric neurostimulator pulse generator (64590)*
> *laparotomy with implantation, replacement, revision, or removal of gastric stimulation electrodes, lesser curvature (0157T, 0158T)*

🔗 0.00   ⚕ 0.00   Global Days YYY
AMA: 2007, Mar, 4-5; 2007, Mar, 4-5; 2007, March, 4-5

43882   Revision or removal of gastric neurostimulator electrodes, antrum, open   C 80

> EXCLUDES   *electronic analysis and programming (95980-95982)*
> *insertion of gastric neurostimulator pulse generator (64590)*
> *laparotomy with implantation, replacement, revision, or removal of gastric stimulation electrodes, lesser curvature (0157T, 0158T)*
> *revision/removal gastric neurostimulator pulse generator (64595)*
> *revision/removal performed laparoscopically (43648)*

🔗 0.00   ⚕ 0.00   Global Days YYY
AMA: 2007, Mar, 4-5; 2007, Mar, 4-5; 2007, March, 4-5

43886-43999 Bariatric Procedures: Removal/Replacement/Revision Port Components

CMS *100-3,40.5*   *Treatment of Obesity*
CMS *100-3,100.1*   *Bariatric Surgery for Treatment of Morbid Obesity*

43886   Gastric restrictive procedure, open; revision of subcutaneous port component only   G2 T 80 P0
🔗 8.19   ⚕ 8.19   Global Days 090
AMA: 2006, Apr, 1-7; 2006, Apr, 1-7; 2006, April, 1-7

43887   removal of subcutaneous port component only   G2 T 80 P0

> EXCLUDES   *gastric band and subcutaneous port components:*
> *removal and replacement (43659)*
> *removal performed laparascopically (43774)*

🔗 7.78   ⚕ 7.78   Global Days 090
AMA: 2006, Apr, 1-7; 2006, Apr, 1-7; 2006, April, 1-7

43888   removal and replacement of subcutaneous port component only   G2 T 80 P0

> EXCLUDES   *gastric band and subcutaneous port components:*
> *removal and replacement (43659)*
> *removal performed laparascopically (43774)*

> Do not report with (43774, 43887)

🔗 10.97   ⚕ 10.97   Global Days 090
AMA: 2006, Apr, 1-7; 2006, Apr, 1-7; 2006, April, 1-7

43999   Unlisted procedure, stomach   T 80
         🖚 0.00   ≋ 0.00 Global Days YYY

44005-44130 Incisional and Resection Procedures of Bowel

44005   Enterolysis (freeing of intestinal adhesion) (separate procedure)   C 80 ▢ P0
         EXCLUDES enterolysis performed laparoscopically (44180)

         Do not report with (45136)
         🖚 27.38   ≋ 27.38 Global Days 090
         AMA: 2008, Jan, 10-25; 2007, Jan, 13-27; 2007, Jan, 13-27; 2007, January, 13-27

44010   Duodenotomy, for exploration, biopsy(s), or foreign body removal   C 80 ▢ P0
         🖚 21.52   ≋ 21.52 Global Days 090

+ 44015   Tube or needle catheter jejunostomy for enteral alimentation, intraoperative, any method (List separately in addition to primary procedure)   C 80 ▢
         Code first the primary procedure
         🖚 3.75   ≋ 3.75 Global Days ZZZ
         AMA: 2008, Jan, 10-25; 2007, Jan, 13-27; 2007, Jan, 13-27; 2007, January, 13-27

44020   Enterotomy, small intestine, other than duodenum; for exploration, biopsy(s), or foreign body removal   C 80 ▢ P0
         🖚 24.19   ≋ 24.19 Global Days 090

Anterior abdominal skin
Baker-type tube
Depicted at left is a tube threaded through intestine for decompression
Peritoneum
Bowel lumen
Note that the bowel is sutured to the abdominal wall

In 44021, a select portion of intestine is surgically approached and incised. A tube is inserted into the bowel lumen and threaded distally, often to a point of obstruction. The tube is used to decompress the bowel segment it passes through, often during or immediately following surgery for bowel obstruction

44021   for decompression (eg, Baker tube)   C 80 ▢ P0
         🖚 24.47   ≋ 24.47 Global Days 090

44025   Colotomy, for exploration, biopsy(s), or foreign body removal   C 80 ▢ P0
         INCLUDES Amussat's operation
         EXCLUDES intestine exteriorization (Mikulicz resection with crushing of spur) (44602-44605)
         🖚 24.63   ≋ 24.63 Global Days 090

44050   Reduction of volvulus, intussusception, internal hernia, by laparotomy   C 80 ▢ P0
         🖚 23.34   ≋ 23.34 Global Days 090

44055   Correction of malrotation by lysis of duodenal bands and/or reduction of midgut volvulus (eg, Ladd procedure)   C 80 ⊛ ▢ P0
         🖚 37.34   ≋ 37.34 Global Days 090

44100   Biopsy of intestine by capsule, tube, peroral (1 or more specimens)   A2 T ▢ P0
         🖚 3.08   ≋ 3.08 Global Days 000

44110   Excision of 1 or more lesions of small or large intestine not requiring anastomosis, exteriorization, or fistulization; single enterotomy   C 80 ▢ P0
         🖚 21.08   ≋ 21.08 Global Days 090

44111   multiple enterotomies   C 80 ▢ P0
         🖚 24.56   ≋ 24.56 Global Days 090

44120   Enterectomy, resection of small intestine; single resection and anastomosis   C 80 ▢ P0
         Do not report with (45136)
         🖚 30.39   ≋ 30.39 Global Days 090
         AMA: 2004, Mar, 1; 2004, Mar, 1; 2004, March, 1

+ 44121   each additional resection and anastomosis (List separately in addition to code for primary procedure)   C 80 ▢
         Code first single resection of small intestine (44120)
         🖚 6.30   ≋ 6.30 Global Days ZZZ

44125   with enterostomy   C 80 ▢ P0
         🖚 29.54   ≋ 29.54 Global Days 090

44126   Enterectomy, resection of small intestine for congenital atresia, single resection and anastomosis of proximal segment of intestine; without tapering   C 80 ⊛ ▢ P0
         🖚 60.98   ≋ 60.98 Global Days 090

44127   with tapering   C 80 ⊛ ▢ P0
         🖚 71.10   ≋ 71.10 Global Days 090

+ 44128   each additional resection and anastomosis (List separately in addition to code for primary procedure)   C 80 ⊛ ▢
         Code first single resection of small intestine (44126, 44127)
         🖚 6.34   ≋ 6.34 Global Days ZZZ

44130   Enteroenterostomy, anastomosis of intestine, with or without cutaneous enterostomy (separate procedure)   C 80 ▢ P0
         🖚 31.66   ≋ 31.66 Global Days 090

44132-44137 Intestine Transplant Procedures

CMS 100-3,260.5   *Intestinal and Multi-Visceral Transplantation*
CMS 100-4,3,90.6   *Intestinal and Multi-Visceral Transplants*

44132   Donor enterectomy (including cold preservation), open; from cadaver donor   C 80 M2 I0
         INCLUDES graft:
                       cold preservation
                       harvest
         🖚 0.00   ≋ 0.00 Global Days XXX

44133   partial, from living donor   C 80 ▢ P0
         INCLUDES donor care
                       graft:
                       cold preservation
                       harvest
         EXCLUDES preparation/reconstruction of backbench intestinal graft (44715, 44720, 44721)
         🖚 0.00   ≋ 0.00 Global Days XXX

44135   Intestinal allotransplantation; from cadaver donor   C 80 ▢ P0
         INCLUDES allograft transplantation
                       recipient care
         🖚 0.00   ≋ 0.00 Global Days XXX

44136   from living donor   C 80 ▢ P0
         INCLUDES allograft transplantation
                       recipient care
         🖚 0.00   ≋ 0.00 Global Days XXX

● New Code   ▲ Revised Code   Ⓜ Maternity Edit   Ⓐ Age Edit   A-Y OPPS Status Indicator   🖚 Facility RVU   ≋ Non-Facility RVU
▢ CCI Comprehensive Code   50 Bilateral Procedure   + Add-on Indicator   ▨ Laboratory crosswalk   ▨ Radiology crosswalk

44137 — 44206

44137 Removal of transplanted intestinal allograft, complete C 80 ⬚
  EXCLUDES *partial removal of transplant allograft (44120, 44121, 44140)*
  ⬚ 0.00 ⬚ 0.00 Global Days XXX

44139-44160 Colon Resection Procedures

+ 44139 Mobilization (take-down) of splenic flexure performed in conjunction with partial colectomy (List separately in addition to primary procedure) C 80 ⬚
  Code first partial colectomy (44140-44147)
  ⬚ 3.15 ⬚ 3.15 Global Days ZZZ
  AMA: 2006, Apr, 1-7; 2006, Apr, 1-7; 2006, April, 1-7

44140 Colectomy, partial; with anastomosis C 80 ⬚ PQ
  EXCLUDES *partial colectomy with anastomosis performed laparoscopically (44204)*
  ⬚ 33.67 ⬚ 33.67 Global Days 090

44141 with skin level cecostomy or colostomy C 80 ⬚ PQ
  ⬚ 44.00 ⬚ 44.00 Global Days 090

44143 with end colostomy and closure of distal segment (Hartmann type procedure) C 80 ⬚ PQ
  EXCLUDES *laparoscopic method (44206)*
  ⬚ 41.40 ⬚ 41.40 Global Days 090

44144 with resection, with colostomy or ileostomy and creation of mucofistula C 80 ⬚ PQ
  ⬚ 43.35 ⬚ 43.35 Global Days 090

44145 with coloproctostomy (low pelvic anastomosis) C 80 ⬚ PQ
  EXCLUDES *laparoscopic method (44207)*
  ⬚ 41.92 ⬚ 41.92 Global Days 090

44146 with coloproctostomy (low pelvic anastomosis), with colostomy C 80 ⬚ PQ
  EXCLUDES *laparoscopic method (44208)*
  ⬚ 52.20 ⬚ 52.20 Global Days 090

44147 abdominal and transanal approach C 80 ⬚ PQ
  ⬚ 46.83 ⬚ 46.83 Global Days 090

44150 Colectomy, total, abdominal, without proctectomy; with ileostomy or ileoproctostomy C 80 ⬚ PQ
  INCLUDES Lane's operation
  EXCLUDES *laparoscopic method (44210)*
  ⬚ 45.81 ⬚ 45.81 Global Days 090

44151 with continent ileostomy C 80 ⬚ PQ
  ⬚ 52.37 ⬚ 52.37 Global Days 090

44155 Colectomy, total, abdominal, with proctectomy; with ileostomy C 80 ⬚ PQ
  INCLUDES Miles' colectomy
  EXCLUDES *laparoscopic method (44212)*
  ⬚ 51.26 ⬚ 51.26 Global Days 090

44156 with continent ileostomy C 80 ⬚ PQ
  ⬚ 56.46 ⬚ 56.46 Global Days 090

44157 with ileoanal anastomosis, includes loop ileostomy, and rectal mucosectomy, when performed C 80 PQ
  ⬚ 53.68 ⬚ 53.68 Global Days 090

44158 with ileoanal anastomosis, creation of ileal reservoir (S or J), includes loop ileostomy, and rectal mucosectomy, when performed C 80 PQ
  EXCLUDES *laparoscopic method (44211)*
  ⬚ 55.03 ⬚ 55.03 Global Days 090

44160 Colectomy, partial, with removal of terminal ileum with ileocolostomy C 80 ⬚ PQ
  EXCLUDES *laparoscopic method (44205)*
  ⬚ 30.98 ⬚ 30.98 Global Days 090

44180 Laparoscopic Enterolysis

INCLUDES diagnostic laparoscopy when performed with a surgical laparoscopy

44180 Laparoscopy, surgical, enterolysis (freeing of intestinal adhesion) (separate procedure) T 80 PQ
  EXCLUDES *laparoscopic salpingolysis / ovariolysis (58660)*
  ⬚ 23.14 ⬚ 23.14 Global Days 090
  AMA: 2006, Apr, 1-7; 2006, Apr, 1-7; 2006, April, 1-7

44186-44238 Laparoscopic Enterostomy Procedures

INCLUDES diagnostic laparoscopy when performed with a surgical laparoscopy

44186 Laparoscopy, surgical; jejunostomy (eg, for decompression or feeding) T 80 PQ
  ⬚ 16.32 ⬚ 16.32 Global Days 090
  AMA: 2006, Apr, 1-7; 2006, Apr, 1-7; 2006, April, 1-7

44187 ileostomy or jejunostomy, non-tube C 80 PQ
  EXCLUDES *open method (44310)*
  ⬚ 27.45 ⬚ 27.45 Global Days 090
  AMA: 2006, Apr, 1-7; 2006, Apr, 1-7; 2006, April, 1-7

44188 Laparoscopy, surgical, colostomy or skin level cecostomy C 80 PQ
  EXCLUDES *open method (44320)*
  Do not report with (44970)
  ⬚ 30.39 ⬚ 30.39 Global Days 090
  AMA: 2008, Jan, 10-25; 2007, Jan, 13-27; 2007, Jan, 13-27; 2007, January, 13-27; 2006, Apr, 19-20; 2006, Apr, 19-20; 2006, April, 1-7; 2006, April, 19-20; 2006, Apr, 1-7; 2006, Apr, 1-7

44202 Laparoscopy, surgical; enterectomy, resection of small intestine, single resection and anastomosis C 80 ⬚ PQ
  EXCLUDES *open method (44120)*
  ⬚ 34.86 ⬚ 34.86 Global Days 090
  AMA: 2006, Apr, 1-7; 2006, Apr, 1-7; 2006, April, 1-7; 2005, Dec, 9-11; 2005, December, 9-11; 2005, Dec, 9-11

+ 44203 each additional small intestine resection and anastomosis (List separately in addition to code for primary procedure) C 80 ⬚
  EXCLUDES *open method (44121)*
  Code first single resection of small intestine (44202)
  ⬚ 6.27 ⬚ 6.27 Global Days ZZZ

44204 colectomy, partial, with anastomosis C 80 ⬚ PQ
  EXCLUDES *open method (44140)*
  ⬚ 38.89 ⬚ 38.89 Global Days 090
  AMA: 2008, Jan, 10-25; 2007, Jan, 13-27; 2007, Jan, 13-27; 2007, January, 13-27; 2006, Apr, 19-20; 2006, Apr, 19-20; 2006, April, 1-7; 2006, April, 19-20; 2006, Apr, 1-7; 2006, Apr, 1-7

44205 colectomy, partial, with removal of terminal ileum with ileocolostomy C 80 ⬚ PQ
  EXCLUDES *open method (44160)*
  ⬚ 33.97 ⬚ 33.97 Global Days 090
  AMA: 2006, Apr, 1-7; 2006, Apr, 1-7; 2006, April, 1-7

44206 colectomy, partial, with end colostomy and closure of distal segment (Hartmann type procedure) T 80 ⬚ PQ
  EXCLUDES *open method (44143)*
  ⬚ 44.11 ⬚ 44.11 Global Days 090
  AMA: 2006, Apr, 1-7; 2006, Apr, 1-7; 2006, April, 1-7

44207   colectomy, partial, with anastomosis, with coloproctostomy (low pelvic anastomosis) ⊤ 80 ☐ P0
    EXCLUDES   *open method (44145)*

    🔟 46.33   ⚕ 46.33   Global Days 090
    AMA: 2006, Apr, 1-7; 2006, Apr, 1-7; 2006, April, 1-7

44208   colectomy, partial, with anastomosis, with coloproctostomy (low pelvic anastomosis) with colostomy ⊤ 80 ☐ P0
    EXCLUDES   *open method (44146)*

    🔟 50.36   ⚕ 50.36   Global Days 090
    AMA: 2006, Apr, 1-7; 2006, Apr, 1-7; 2006, April, 1-7

44210   colectomy, total, abdominal, without proctectomy, with ileostomy or ileoproctostomy C 80 ☐ P0
    EXCLUDES   *open method (44150)*

    🔟 45.01   ⚕ 45.01   Global Days 090

44211   colectomy, total, abdominal, with proctectomy, with ileoanal anastomosis, creation of ileal reservoir (S or J), with loop ileostomy, includes rectal mucosectomy, when performed C 80 ☐ P0
    EXCLUDES   *open method (44157, 44158)*

    🔟 55.24   ⚕ 55.24   Global Days 090

44212   colectomy, total, abdominal, with proctectomy, with ileostomy C 80 ☐ P0
    EXCLUDES   *open method (44155)*

    🔟 51.78   ⚕ 51.78   Global Days 090

+ 44213   Laparoscopy, surgical, mobilization (take-down) of splenic flexure performed in conjunction with partial colectomy (List separately in addition to primary procedure) ⊤ 80
    EXCLUDES   *open method (44139)*

    Code first partial colectomy (44204-44208)
    🔟 4.94   ⚕ 4.94   Global Days ZZZ
    AMA: 2008, Jan, 10-25; 2007, Jan, 13-27; 2007, Jan, 13-27; 2007, January, 13-27; 2006, Apr, 1-7; 2006, Apr, 1-7; 2006, April, 1-7; 2006, April, 19-20; 2006, Apr, 19-20; 2006, Apr, 19-20

44227   Laparoscopy, surgical, closure of enterostomy, large or small intestine, with resection and anastomosis C 80 P0
    EXCLUDES   *open method (44625, 44626)*

    🔟 42.11   ⚕ 42.11   Global Days 090
    AMA: 2006, Apr, 1-7; 2006, Apr, 1-7; 2006, April, 1-7

44238   Unlisted laparoscopy procedure, intestine (except rectum) ⊤ 80 50 ☐
    🔟 0.00   ⚕ 0.00   Global Days YYY

44300-44346 Open Enterostomy Procedures

44300   Placement, enterostomy or cecostomy, tube open (eg, for feeding or decompression) (separate procedure) C 80 ☐ P0
    EXCLUDES   *other colonic tube(s) placed percutaneously with fluoroscopic imaging guidance (49441-49442)*

    🔟 20.95   ⚕ 20.95   Global Days 090
    AMA: 2008, Jan, 10-25; 2007, Jan, 13-27; 2007, Jan, 13-27; 2007, January, 13-27

44310   Ileostomy or jejunostomy, non-tube C 80 ☐ P0
    EXCLUDES   *laparoscopic method (44187)*

    Do not report with (44144, 44150-44151, 44155, 45113, 45119, 45136)
    🔟 26.18   ⚕ 26.18   Global Days 090
    AMA: 2008, Jan, 10-25; 2007, Jan, 13-27; 2007, Jan, 13-27; 2007, January, 13-27; 2006, Apr, 1-7; 2006, April, 1-7; 2006, Apr, 1-7

44312   Revision of ileostomy; simple (release of superficial scar) (separate procedure) A2 ⊤ 80 ☐ P0
    🔟 14.84   ⚕ 14.84   Global Days 090

44314   complicated (reconstruction in-depth) (separate procedure) C 80 ☐ P0
    🔟 25.30   ⚕ 25.30   Global Days 090

44316   Continent ileostomy (Kock procedure) (separate procedure) C 80 ☐ P0
    EXCLUDES   *fiberoptic evaluation (44385)*

    🔟 34.61   ⚕ 34.61   Global Days 090

44320   Colostomy or skin level cecostomy; C 80 ☐ P0
    EXCLUDES   *laparoscopic method (44188)*

    Do not report with (44141, 44144, 44146, 44605, 45110, 45119, 45126, 45563, 45805, 45825, 50810, 51597, 57307, 58240)
    🔟 29.86   ⚕ 29.86   Global Days 090
    AMA: 2006, Apr, 1-7; 2006, Apr, 1-7; 2006, April, 1-7

44322   with multiple biopsies (eg, for congenital megacolon) (separate procedure) C 80 ☐ P0
    🔟 23.72   ⚕ 23.72   Global Days 090

44340   Revision of colostomy; simple (release of superficial scar) (separate procedure) A2 ⊤ ☐ P0
    🔟 14.96   ⚕ 14.96   Global Days 090

44345   complicated (reconstruction in-depth) (separate procedure) C 80 ☐ P0
    🔟 26.14   ⚕ 26.14   Global Days 090

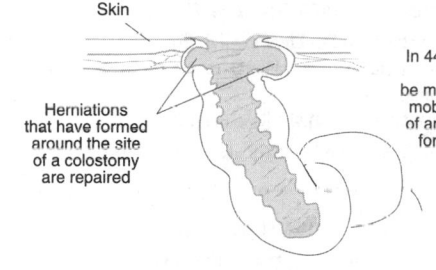

Skin

Herniations that have formed around the site of a colostomy are repaired

In 44346, the site of the colostomy may be moved. The bowel is mobilized and trimmed of any herniations. The former site is closed

The colon is mobilized, trimmed if necessary, and a new stoma is often created

44346   with repair of paracolostomy hernia (separate procedure) C 80 ☐ P0
    🔟 29.31   ⚕ 29.31   Global Days 090

44360-44386 Endoscopy of Small Intestine

CMS *100-3,100.2   Endoscopy*
INCLUDES   diagnostic endoscopy performed with a surgical endoscopy
EXCLUDES   *endoscopy, upper gastrointestinal (43234-43258)*

⊙ 44360   Small intestinal endoscopy, enteroscopy beyond second portion of duodenum, not including ileum; diagnostic, with or without collection of specimen(s) by brushing or washing (separate procedure) A2 ⊤ ☐
    🔟 4.22   ⚕ 4.22   Global Days 000

⊙ 44361   with biopsy, single or multiple A2 ⊤ ☐
    🔟 4.65   ⚕ 4.65   Global Days 000

⊙ 44363   with removal of foreign body A2 ⊤ 80 ☐
    🔟 5.51   ⚕ 5.51   Global Days 000

⊙ 44364   with removal of tumor(s), polyp(s), or other lesion(s) by snare technique A2 ⊤ 80 ☐
    🔟 5.93   ⚕ 5.93   Global Days 000

⊙ 44365   with removal of tumor(s), polyp(s), or other lesion(s) by hot biopsy forceps or bipolar cautery A2 ⊤ 80 ☐
    🔟 5.28   ⚕ 5.28   Global Days 000

Digestive

44366 — 44615

⊙ 📠   44366   with control of bleeding (eg, injection, bipolar cautery, unipolar cautery, laser, heater probe, stapler, plasma coagulator)   A2 T 🖵
    📠 6.99   ⚕ 6.99   Global Days 000

⊙   44369   with ablation of tumor(s), polyp(s), or other lesion(s) not amenable to removal by hot biopsy forceps, bipolar cautery or snare technique   A2 T 80 🖵
    📠 7.14   ⚕ 7.14   Global Days 000

⊙   44370   with transendoscopic stent placement (includes predilation)   A2 T 80 🖵
    Code also (C1874, C1875, C1876, C1877, C2617, C2625)
    📠 7.70   ⚕ 7.70   Global Days 000

⊙   44372   with placement of percutaneous jejunostomy tube   A2 T 🖵
    📠 6.81   ⚕ 6.81   Global Days 000

⊙   44373   with conversion of percutaneous gastrostomy tube to percutaneous jejunostomy tube   A2 T 🖵
    EXCLUDES   *jejunostomy, fiberoptic, through stoma (43235)*
    📠 5.51   ⚕ 5.51   Global Days 000

⊙   44376   Small intestinal endoscopy, enteroscopy beyond second portion of duodenum, including ileum; diagnostic, with or without collection of specimen(s) by brushing or washing (separate procedure)   A2 T 80 🖵
    📠 8.15   ⚕ 8.15   Global Days 000

⊙   44377   with biopsy, single or multiple   A2 T 80 🖵
    📠 8.63   ⚕ 8.63   Global Days 000

⊙   44378   with control of bleeding (eg, injection, bipolar cautery, unipolar cautery, laser, heater probe, stapler, plasma coagulator)   A2 T 80 🖵
    📠 11.07   ⚕ 11.07   Global Days 000

⊙   44379   with transendoscopic stent placement (includes predilation)   A2 T 80 🖵
    Code also (C1874, C1875, C1876, C1877, C2617, C2625)
    📠 11.76   ⚕ 11.76   Global Days 000

⊙   44380   Ileoscopy, through stoma; diagnostic, with or without collection of specimen(s) by brushing or washing (separate procedure)   A2 T 🖵
    📠 1.84   ⚕ 1.84   Global Days 000

⊙   44382   with biopsy, single or multiple   A2 T 🖵
    📠 2.22   ⚕ 2.22   Global Days 000

⊙   44383   with transendoscopic stent placement (includes predilation)   A2 T 🖵
    Code also (C1874, C1875, C1876, C1877, C2617, C2625)
    📠 4.74   ⚕ 4.74   Global Days 000

⊙   44385   Endoscopic evaluation of small intestinal (abdominal or pelvic) pouch; diagnostic, with or without collection of specimen(s) by brushing or washing (separate procedure)   A2 T 🖵
    📠 2.83   ⚕ 6.37   Global Days 000

⊙   44386   with biopsy, single or multiple   A2 T 80 🖵
    📠 3.33   ⚕ 8.86   Global Days 000

44388-44397 Colonoscopy Via Stoma

CMS *100-3,100.2*   *Endoscopy*
INCLUDES   diagnostic endoscopy when performed with a surgical endoscopy
EXCLUDES   *endoscopy, upper gastrointestinal (43234-43258)*

⊙   44388   Colonoscopy through stoma; diagnostic, with or without collection of specimen(s) by brushing or washing (separate procedure)   A2 T 🖵
    📠 4.42   ⚕ 8.84   Global Days 000
    AMA: 2008, Jan, 10-25

⊙   44389   with biopsy, single or multiple   A2 T 🖵
    📠 4.93   ⚕ 10.26   Global Days 000

⊙   44390   with removal of foreign body   A2 T 80 🖵
    📠 5.91   ⚕ 11.85   Global Days 000

⊙   44391   with control of bleeding (eg, injection, bipolar cautery, unipolar cautery, laser, heater probe, stapler, plasma coagulator)   A2 T 80 🖵
    📠 6.73   ⚕ 13.27   Global Days 000

⊙   44392   with removal of tumor(s), polyp(s), or other lesion(s) by hot biopsy forceps or bipolar cautery   A2 T 🖵
    📠 5.82   ⚕ 11.13   Global Days 000

Cancer of the colon and rectum is a major cause of mortality in the U.S. with about 140,000 new cases identified annually; peak incidence is about 70 years of age; rectal cancer is more common among men, colon cancer among women

⊙   44393   with ablation of tumor(s), polyp(s), or other lesion(s) not amenable to removal by hot biopsy forceps, bipolar cautery or snare technique   A2 T 🖵
    📠 7.41   ⚕ 12.94   Global Days 000

⊙   44394   with removal of tumor(s), polyp(s), or other lesion(s) by snare technique   A2 T 🖵
    EXCLUDES   *colonoscopy/rectum (45330-45385)*
    📠 6.86   ⚕ 13.02   Global Days 000

⊙   44397   with transendoscopic stent placement (includes predilation)   A2 T 🖵
    Code also (C1874, C1875-C1877, C2617, C2625)
    📠 7.40   ⚕ 7.40   Global Days 000

44500 Gastrointestinal Intubation

⊘ ⊙   44500   Introduction of long gastrointestinal tube (eg, Miller-Abbott) (separate procedure)   B2 T 80 🖵
    EXCLUDES   *placement of oro- or naso-gastric tube (43752)*
    📷 *74340*
    📠 0.70   ⚕ 0.70   Global Days 000

44602-44680 Open Repair Procedures of Intestines

   44602   Suture of small intestine (enterorrhaphy) for perforated ulcer, diverticulum, wound, injury or rupture; single perforation   C 80 🖵 PQ
    📠 34.32   ⚕ 34.32   Global Days 090

   44603   multiple perforations   C 80 🖵 PQ
    📠 39.34   ⚕ 39.34   Global Days 090

   44604   Suture of large intestine (colorrhaphy) for perforated ulcer, diverticulum, wound, injury or rupture (single or multiple perforations); without colostomy   C 80 🖵 PQ
    📠 26.57   ⚕ 26.57   Global Days 090

   44605   with colostomy   C 80 🖵 PQ
    📠 32.74   ⚕ 32.74   Global Days 090

   44615   Intestinal stricturoplasty (enterotomy and enterorrhaphy) with or without dilation, for intestinal obstruction   C 80 🖵 PQ
    📠 26.97   ⚕ 26.97   Global Days 090

| 44620 | Closure of enterostomy, large or small intestine; | C 80 ▢ P0 |
| | 🔩 21.49   ⚖ 21.49 Global Days 090 | |

44625	with resection and anastomosis other than colorectal	C 80 ▢ P0
	EXCLUDES laparoscopic method (44227)	
	🔩 25.47 ⚖ 25.47 Global Days 090	

44626	with resection and colorectal anastomosis (eg, closure of Hartmann type procedure)	C 80 ▢ P0
	EXCLUDES laparoscopic method (44227)	
	🔩 40.59 ⚖ 40.59 Global Days 090	

| 44640 | Closure of intestinal cutaneous fistula | C 80 ▢ P0 |
| | 🔩 35.39   ⚖ 35.39 Global Days 090 | |

| 44650 | Closure of enteroenteric or enterocolic fistula | C 80 ▢ P0 |
| | 🔩 36.82   ⚖ 36.82 Global Days 090 | |

44660	Closure of enterovesical fistula; without intestinal or bladder resection	C 80 ▢ P0
	EXCLUDES closure of fistula	
	gastrocolic (43880)	
	rectovesical (45800, 45805)	
	renocolic (50525, 50526)	
	🔩 35.49 ⚖ 35.49 Global Days 090	

44661	with intestine and/or bladder resection	C 80 ▢ P0
	EXCLUDES closure of fistula	
	gastrocolic (43880)	
	rectovesical (45800, 45805)	
	renocolic (50525, 50526)	
	🔩 39.90 ⚖ 39.90 Global Days 090	

44680	Intestinal plication (separate procedure)	C 80 ▢ P0
	INCLUDES Noble intestinal plication	
	🔩 26.62 ⚖ 26.62 Global Days 090	

44700-44701 Other Intestinal Procedures

44700	Exclusion of small intestine from pelvis by mesh or other prosthesis, or native tissue (eg, bladder or omentum)	C 80 ▢ P0
	EXCLUDES therapeutic radiation clinical treatment (77261-77799)	
	🔩 25.74 ⚖ 25.74 Global Days 090	

+ 44701	Intraoperative colonic lavage (List separately in addition to code for primary procedure)	NI N 80 ▢
	Code first as appropriate (44140, 44145, 44150, 44604)	
	Do not report with (44300, 44950-44960)	
	🔩 4.35 ⚖ 4.35 Global Days ZZZ	

44715-44799 Backbench Transplant Procedures

CMS 100-3,260.5   *Intestinal and Multi-Visceral Transplantation*
CMS 100-4,3,90.6   *Intestinal and Multi-Visceral Transplants*

44715	Backbench standard preparation of cadaver or living donor intestine allograft prior to transplantation, including mobilization and fashioning of the superior mesenteric artery and vein	C 80 ▢
	INCLUDES mobilization/fashioning of superior mesenteric vein/artery	
	🔩 0.00 ⚖ 0.00 Global Days XXX	

| 44720 | Backbench reconstruction of cadaver or living donor intestine allograft prior to transplantation; venous anastomosis, each | C 80 ▢ |
| | 🔩 7.06   ⚖ 7.06 Global Days XXX | |

44721	arterial anastomosis, each	C 80 ▢
	🔩 10.05 ⚖ 10.05 Global Days XXX	
	AMA: 2005, Apr, 10-12; 2005, Apr, 10-12; 2005, April, 10-12	

44799	Unlisted procedure, intestine	T ▢
	🔩 0.00 ⚖ 0.00 Global Days YYY	
	AMA: 2008, Jan, 10-25; 2008, May, 9-11; 2007, Jan, 13-27; 2007, Jan, 13-27; 2007, January, 13-27	

44800-44899 Meckel's Diverticulum and Mesentery Procedures

| 44800 | Excision of Meckel's diverticulum (diverticulectomy) or omphalomesenteric duct | C 80 ▢ P0 |
| | 🔩 18.99   ⚖ 18.99 Global Days 090 | |

44820	Excision of lesion of mesentery (separate procedure)	C 80 ▢ P0
	EXCLUDES resection of intestine (44120-44128, 44140-44160)	
	🔩 20.95 ⚖ 20.95 Global Days 090	

44850	Suture of mesentery (separate procedure)	C 80 ▢ P0
	EXCLUDES internal hernia repair/reduction (44050)	
	🔩 18.48 ⚖ 18.48 Global Days 090	

| 44899 | Unlisted procedure, Meckel's diverticulum and the mesentery | C 80 |
| | 🔩 0.00   ⚖ 0.00 Global Days YYY | |

44900-44979 Open and Endoscopic Appendix Procedures

| 44900 | Incision and drainage of appendiceal abscess; open | C 80 ▢ P0 |
| | 🔩 18.90   ⚖ 18.90 Global Days 090 | |

☉ 44901	percutaneous	T ▢
	📷 75989	
	🔩 4.83 ⚖ 25.44 Global Days 000	

Failure to treat appendicitis can lead to peritonitis

Ascending colon

Ileum

Cecum

Free tenia

Appendix and appendicular artery

Mesoappendix

Appendicitis, the inflammation and infection of the appendix, is most prevalent between the ages of 15 and 24

Peritonitis is the inflammation of the lining of the abdominal cavity

44950	Appendectomy;	C 80 ▢ P0
	INCLUDES Battle's operation	
	🔩 16.07 ⚖ 16.07 Global Days 090	

+ 44955	when done for indicated purpose at time of other major procedure (not as separate procedure) (List separately in addition to code for primary procedure)	C 80 ▢
	Code first primary procedure	
	🔩 2.19 ⚖ 2.19 Global Days ZZZ	

● New Code   ▲ Revised Code   M Maternity Edit   A Age Edit   A-T OPPS Status Indicator   🔩 Facility RVU   ⚖ Non-Facility RVU

▢ CCI Comprehensive Code   50 Bilateral Procedure   + Add-on Indicator   S Laboratory crosswalk   📷 Radiology crosswalk

44960 for ruptured appendix with abscess or generalized peritonitis ⬚C⬚80⬚⬚P0

INCLUDES   Battle's operation

🔲 21.59   ⚕ 21.59   Global Days 090

44970 Laparoscopy, surgical, appendectomy ⬚T⬚80⬚⬚P0

INCLUDES   diagnostic laparoscopy

🔲 14.76   ⚕ 14.76   Global Days 090

AMA: 2008, Jan, 10-25; 2007, Jan, 13-27; 2007, Jan, 13-27; 2007, January, 13-27; 2006, Apr, 1-7; 2006, Apr, 1-7; 2006, April, 1-7; 2006, April, 19-20; 2006, Apr, 19-20; 2006, Apr, 19-20

44979 Unlisted laparoscopy procedure, appendix ⬚T⬚80⬚50

🔲 0.00   ⚕ 0.00   Global Days YYY

45000-45190 Open and Transrectal Procedures of Rectum

45000 Transrectal drainage of pelvic abscess ⬚A2⬚T⬚⬚P0

🔲 10.23   ⚕ 10.23   Global Days 090

45005 Incision and drainage of submucosal abscess, rectum ⬚A2⬚T⬚

🔲 3.83   ⚕ 6.19   Global Days 010

45020 Incision and drainage of deep supralevator, pelvirectal, or retrorectal abscess ⬚A2⬚T⬚⬚P0

EXCLUDES   incision and drainage of perianal, ischiorectal, intramural abscess (46050, 46060)

🔲 13.30   ⚕ 13.30   Global Days 090

45100 Biopsy of anorectal wall, anal approach (eg, congenital megacolon) ⬚A2⬚T⬚⬚P0

EXCLUDES   biopsy performed endoscopically (45305)

🔲 7.14   ⚕ 7.14   Global Days 090

45108 Anorectal myomectomy ⬚A2⬚T⬚⬚P0

🔲 8.70   ⚕ 8.70   Global Days 090

45110 Proctectomy; complete, combined abdominoperineal, with colostomy ⬚C⬚80⬚⬚P0

EXCLUDES   laparoscopic method (45395)

🔲 46.27   ⚕ 46.27   Global Days 090

45111 partial resection of rectum, transabdominal approach ⬚C⬚80⬚⬚P0

INCLUDES   Luschka proctectomy

🔲 27.21   ⚕ 27.21   Global Days 090

45112 Proctectomy, combined abdominoperineal, pull-through procedure (eg, colo-anal anastomosis) ⬚C⬚80⬚⬚P0

EXCLUDES   proctectomy for colo-anal anastomosis with creation of colonic pouch or reservoir (45119)

🔲 47.65   ⚕ 47.65   Global Days 090

45113 Proctectomy, partial, with rectal mucosectomy, ileoanal anastomosis, creation of ileal reservoir (S or J), with or without loop ileostomy ⬚C⬚80⬚⬚P0

🔲 48.87   ⚕ 48.87   Global Days 090

45114 Proctectomy, partial, with anastomosis; abdominal and transsacral approach ⬚C⬚80⬚⬚P0

🔲 44.68   ⚕ 44.68   Global Days 090

45116 transsacral approach only (Kraske type) ⬚C⬚80⬚⬚P0

🔲 40.10   ⚕ 40.10   Global Days 090

45119 Proctectomy, combined abdominoperineal pull-through procedure (eg, colo-anal anastomosis), with creation of colonic reservoir (eg, J-pouch), with diverting enterostomy when performed ⬚C⬚80⬚⬚P0

EXCLUDES   laparoscopic method (45397)

🔲 48.89   ⚕ 48.89   Global Days 090

AMA: 2006, Apr, 1-7; 2006, Apr, 1-7; 2006, April, 1-7

45120 Proctectomy, complete (for congenital megacolon), abdominal and perineal approach; with pull-through procedure and anastomosis (eg, Swenson, Duhamel, or Soave type operation) ⬚C⬚80⬚⬚P0

🔲 39.15   ⚕ 39.15   Global Days 090

45121 with subtotal or total colectomy, with multiple biopsies ⬚C⬚80⬚⬚P0

🔲 42.86   ⚕ 42.86   Global Days 090

45123 Proctectomy, partial, without anastomosis, perineal approach ⬚C⬚80⬚⬚P0

🔲 27.70   ⚕ 27.70   Global Days 090

45126 Pelvic exenteration for colorectal malignancy, with proctectomy (with or without colostomy), with removal of bladder and ureteral transplantations, and/or hysterectomy, or cervicectomy, with or without removal of tube(s), with or without removal of ovary(s), or any combination thereof ⬚C⬚80⬚⬚P0

🔲 72.05   ⚕ 72.05   Global Days 090

45130 Excision of rectal procidentia, with anastomosis; perineal approach ⬚C⬚80⬚⬚P0

INCLUDES   Altemeier procedure

🔲 27.08   ⚕ 27.08   Global Days 090

45135 abdominal and perineal approach ⬚C⬚80⬚⬚P0

INCLUDES   Altemeier procedure

🔲 33.22   ⚕ 33.22   Global Days 090

45136 Excision of ileoanal reservoir with ileostomy ⬚C⬚80⬚⬚P0

Do not report with (44005, 44120, 44310)

🔲 45.85   ⚕ 45.85   Global Days 090

45150 Division of stricture of rectum ⬚A2⬚T⬚80⬚⬚P0

🔲 9.88   ⚕ 9.88   Global Days 090

45160 Excision of rectal tumor by proctotomy, transsacral or transcoccygeal approach ⬚A2⬚T⬚80⬚⬚P0

🔲 24.67   ⚕ 24.67   Global Days 090

AMA: 2008, Jan, 6-7

45170 Excision of rectal tumor, transanal approach ⬚A2⬚T⬚80⬚⬚P0

EXCLUDES   excision of rectal tumor, transanal endoscopic microsurgical method (0184T)

🔲 19.30   ⚕ 19.30   Global Days 090

AMA: 2008, Jan, 6-7

45190 Destruction of rectal tumor (eg, electrodesiccation, electrosurgery, laser ablation, laser resection, cryosurgery) transanal approach ⬚A2⬚T⬚⬚P0

🔲 16.79   ⚕ 16.79   Global Days 090

AMA: 2006, Dec, 10-12; 2006, Dec, 10-12; 2006, Dec, 10-12; 2006, Dec, 10-12; 2006, December, 10-12; 2006, December, 10-12

45300-45327 Rigid Proctosigmoidoscopy Procedures

CMS 100-3, 100.2   Endoscopy

INCLUDES   exam of:
  rectum
  sigmoid colon

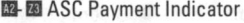

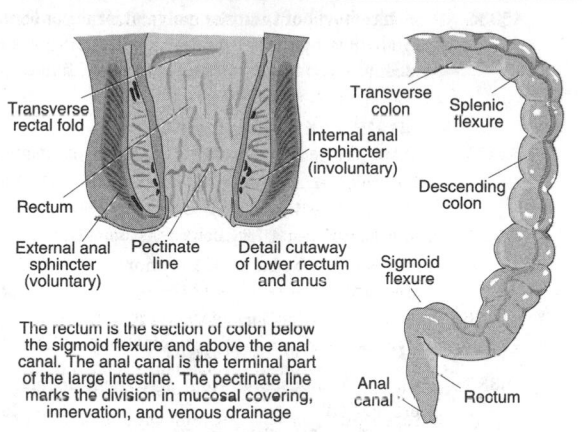

Transverse rectal fold

Rectum

External anal sphincter (voluntary)

Pectinate line

Detail cutaway of lower rectum and anus

Internal anal sphincter (involuntary)

Transverse colon

Splenic flexure

Descending colon

Sigmoid flexure

Anal canal

Rectum

The rectum is the section of colon below the sigmoid flexure and above the anal canal. The anal canal is the terminal part of the large intestine. The pectinate line marks the division in mucosal covering, innervation, and venous drainage

45300 Proctosigmoidoscopy, rigid; diagnostic, with or without collection of specimen(s) by brushing or washing (separate procedure) P3 T ▢
🔷 1.26 ⚲ 2.68 **Global Days** 000
AMA: 2008, Jan, 6-7; 2006, Apr, 1-7; 2006, Apr, 1-7; 2006, April, 1-7

⊙ **45303** with dilation (eg, balloon, guide wire, bougie) P2 T ▢
🔶 74360
🔷 2.14 ⚲ 20.77 **Global Days** 000
AMA: 2008, Jan, 6-7; 2006, Apr, 1-7; 2006, Apr, 1-7; 2006, April, 1-7

⊙ **45305** with biopsy, single or multiple A2 T ▢
🔷 1.95 ⚲ 4.38 **Global Days** 000
AMA: 2008, Jan, 6-7; 2006, Apr, 1-7; 2006, Apr, 1-7; 2006, April, 1-7

⊙ **45307** with removal of foreign body A2 T 80 ▢
🔷 2.45 ⚲ 4.87 **Global Days** 000
AMA: 2008, Jan, 6-7; 2006, Apr, 1-7; 2006, Apr, 1-7; 2006, April, 1-7

⊙ **45308** with removal of single tumor, polyp, or other lesion by hot biopsy forceps or bipolar cautery A2 T ▢
🔷 2.08 ⚲ 4.46 **Global Days** 000
AMA: 2008, Jan, 6-7; 2006, Apr, 1-7; 2006, Apr, 1-7; 2006, April, 1-7

⊙ **45309** with removal of single tumor, polyp, or other lesion by snare technique A2 T ▢
🔷 2.46 ⚲ 5.06 **Global Days** 000
AMA: 2008, Jan, 6-7; 2006, Apr, 1-7; 2006, Apr, 1-7; 2006, April, 1-7

⊙ **45315** with removal of multiple tumors, polyps, or other lesions by hot biopsy forceps, bipolar cautery or snare technique A2 T ▢
🔷 2.76 ⚲ 5.42 **Global Days** 000
AMA: 2008, Jan, 6-7; 2006, Apr, 1-7; 2006, Apr, 1-7; 2006, April, 1-7

⊙ **45317** with control of bleeding (eg, injection, bipolar cautery, unipolar cautery, laser, heater probe, stapler, plasma coagulator) A2 T ▢
🔷 2.90 ⚲ 5.24 **Global Days** 000
AMA: 2000, Jan, 6-7; 2000, Apr, 1-7; 2000, Apr, 1-7; 2000, April, 1-7

⊙ **45320** with ablation of tumor(s), polyp(s), or other lesion(s) not amenable to removal by hot biopsy forceps, bipolar cautery or snare technique (eg, laser) A2 T ▢
🔷 2.77 ⚲ 5.28 **Global Days** 000
AMA: 2008, Jan, 6-7; 2006, Apr, 1-7; 2006, Apr, 1-7; 2006, April, 1-7

⊙ **45321** with decompression of volvulus A2 T ▢
🔷 2.67 ⚲ 2.67 **Global Days** 000
AMA: 2008, Jan, 6-7; 2006, Apr, 1-7; 2006, Apr, 1-7; 2006, April, 1-7

⊙ **45327** with transendoscopic stent placement (includes predilation) A2 T ▢
Code also (C1874, C1875, C1876, C1877, C2617, C2625)
🔷 3.12 ⚲ 3.12 **Global Days** 000
AMA: 2008, Jan, 6-7; 2006, Apr, 1-7; 2006, Apr, 1-7; 2006, April, 1-7

45330-45345 Flexible Sigmoidoscopy Procedures

CMS *100-3,100.2* *Endoscopy*
[INCLUDES] exam of:
entire rectum
entire sigmoid colon
portion of descending colon (may include)

45330 Sigmoidoscopy, flexible; diagnostic, with or without collection of specimen(s) by brushing or washing (separate procedure) P3 T ▢
🔷 1.64 ⚲ 3.47 **Global Days** 000
AMA: 2008, Jan, 10-25; 2007, May, 9-11; 2007, May, 9-11; 2007, May, 9-11; 2005, May, 3-6; 2005, May, 3-6; 2005, May, 3-6

45331 with biopsy, single or multiple A2 T ▢
🔷 1.99 ⚲ 4.41 **Global Days** 000
AMA: 2008, Jan, 10-25; 2007, Jan, 28-31; 2007, Jan, 28-31; 2007, January, 28-31

⊙ **45332** with removal of foreign body A2 T ▢
🔷 2.92 ⚲ 7.25 **Global Days** 000

⊙ **45333** with removal of tumor(s), polyp(s), or other lesion(s) by hot biopsy forceps or bipolar cautery A2 T ▢
🔷 2.90 ⚲ 7.29 **Global Days** 000

⊙ **45334** with control of bleeding (eg, injection, bipolar cautery, unipolar cautery, laser, heater probe, stapler, plasma coagulator) A2 T ▢
🔷 4.39 ⚲ 4.39 **Global Days** 000
AMA: 2008, Jan, 10-25; 2007, Jan, 28-31; 2007, Jan, 28-31; 2007, January, 28-31

⊙ **45335** with directed submucosal injection(s), any substance A2 T ▢
🔷 2.42 ⚲ 6.23 **Global Days** 000
AMA: 2008, Jan, 10-25; 2007, Jan, 13-27; 2007, Jan, 13-27; 2007, January, 13-27

⊙ **45337** with decompression of volvulus, any method A2 T ▢
🔷 3.77 ⚲ 3.77 **Global Days** 000

⊙ **45338** with removal of tumor(s), polyp(s), or other lesion(s) by snare technique A2 T ▢
🔷 3.77 ⚲ 8.14 **Global Days** 000

⊙ **45339** with ablation of tumor(s), polyp(s), or other lesion(s) not amenable to removal by hot biopsy forceps, bipolar cautery or snare technique A2 ▢
🔷 4.99 ⚲ 8.46 **Global Days** 000

⊙ **45340** with dilation by balloon, 1 or more strictures A2 T ▢
Do not report with (45345)
🔷 3.05 ⚲ 11.10 **Global Days** 000

⊙ **45341** with endoscopic ultrasound examination A2 T ▢
Do not report with (76942, 76975)
🔷 4.19 ⚲ 4.19 **Global Days** 000
AMA: 2005, May, 3-6; 2005, May, 3-6; 2005, May, 3-6

45300 — 45341

45342 — 45505

⊙ 45342 with transendoscopic ultrasound guided intramural or transmural fine needle aspiration/biopsy(s) A2 T ▭
EXCLUDES transrectal ultrasound with rigid probe device (76872)

Do not report with (76942, 76975)
◣ 88172-88173
⚕ 6.41 ⚕ 6.41 Global Days 000
AMA: 2005, May, 3-6; 2005, May, 3-6; 2005, May, 3-6

⊙ 45345 with transendoscopic stent placement (includes predilation) A2 T ▭
Code also (C1874, C1875, C1876, C1877, C2617, C2625)
⚕ 4.66 ⚕ 4.66 Global Days 000

45355-45392 Flexible and Rigid Colonoscopy Procedures

CMS 100-3,100.2 *Endoscopy*
INCLUDES exam of:
entire colon (rectum to cecum)
terminal ileum (may include)

⊙ 45355 Colonoscopy, rigid or flexible, transabdominal via colotomy, single or multiple A2 T ▭
EXCLUDES colonoscopy, fiberoptic, past 25cm to splenic flexure (45330-45345)
⚕ 5.39 ⚕ 5.39 Global Days 000

⊙ 45378 Colonoscopy, flexible, proximal to splenic flexure; diagnostic, with or without collection of specimen(s) by brushing or washing, with or without colon decompression (separate procedure) A2 T ▭
⚕ 5.77 ⚕ 10.23 Global Days 000
AMA: 2005, Mar, 11-15; 2005, Mar, 11-15; 2005, May, 3-6; 2005, May, 3-6; 2005, March, 11-15; 2005, May, 3-6; 2004, Jan, 4; 2004, Jan, 4; 2004, January, 4

⊙ 45379 with removal of foreign body A2 T ▭
⚕ 7.23 ⚕ 12.99 Global Days 000

⊙ 45380 with biopsy, single or multiple A2 T ▭
⚕ 6.95 ⚕ 12.28 Global Days 000
AMA: 2008, Jan, 10-25; 2007, Jan, 13-27; 2007, Jan, 13-27; 2007, January, 13-27; 2004, Jul, 15; 2004, Jul, 15; 2004, January, 4; 2004, July, 15; 2004, Jan, 4; 2004, Jan, 4

⊙ 45381 with directed submucosal injection(s), any substance A2 T ▭
⚕ 6.57 ⚕ 11.94 Global Days 000
AMA: 2008, Jan, 10-25; 2007, Jan, 13-27; 2007, Jan, 13-27; 2007, January, 13-27; 2004, Jan, 4; 2004, January, 4; 2004, Jan, 4

⊙ 45382 with control of bleeding (eg, injection, bipolar cautery, unipolar cautery, laser, heater probe, stapler, plasma coagulator) A2 T ▭
⚕ 8.87 ⚕ 16.17 Global Days 000
AMA: 2004, Jan, 4; 2004, Jan, 4; 2004, January, 4

⊙ 45383 with ablation of tumor(s), polyp(s), or other lesion(s) not amenable to removal by hot biopsy forceps, bipolar cautery or snare technique A2 T ▭
⚕ 8.94 ⚕ 14.63 Global Days 000
AMA: 2004, Jan, 4; 2004, Jan, 4; 2004, January, 4

⊙ 45384 with removal of tumor(s), polyp(s), or other lesion(s) by hot biopsy forceps or bipolar cautery A2 T ▭
⚕ 7.22 ⚕ 12.07 Global Days 000
AMA: 2008, Jan, 10-25; 2007, Jan, 13-27; 2007, Jan, 13-27; 2007, January, 13-27; 2004, Jul, 15; 2004, Jul, 15; 2004, January, 4; 2004, July, 15; 2004, Jan, 4; 2004, Jan, 4

⊙ 45385 with removal of tumor(s), polyp(s), or other lesion(s) by snare technique A2 T ▭
EXCLUDES endoscopy, small intestine/stomal (44360-44393)
⚕ 8.25 ⚕ 13.85 Global Days 000
AMA: 2008, Jan, 10-25; 2007, Jan, 13-27; 2007, Jan, 13-27; 2007, January, 13-27; 2005, Mar, 11-15; 2005, March, 11-15; 2005, Mar, 11-15; 2004, Jul, 15; 2004, January, 4; 2004, July, 15; 2004, Jul, 15; 2004, Jan, 4; 2004, Jan, 4

⊙ 45386 with dilation by balloon, 1 or more strictures A2 T ▭
Do not report with (45387)
⚕ 7.10 ⚕ 17.07 Global Days 000

⊙ 45387 with transendoscopic stent placement (includes predilation) A2 T ▭
⚕ 9.25 ⚕ 9.25 Global Days 000

⊙ 45391 with endoscopic ultrasound examination A2 T ▭
Do not report with (45330, 45341-45342, 45378, 76872)
⚕ 7.99 ⚕ 7.99 Global Days 000
AMA: 2005, May, 3-6; 2005, May, 3-6; 2005, May, 3-6

⊙ 45392 with transendoscopic ultrasound guided intramural or transmural fine needle aspiration/biopsy(s) A2 T ▭
Do not report with (45330, 45341-45342, 45378, 76872)
⚕ 10.07 ⚕ 10.07 Global Days 000
AMA: 2005, May, 3-6; 2005, May, 3-6; 2005, May, 3-6

45395-45499 Laparoscopic Procedures of Rectum

INCLUDES diagnostic laparoscopy

45395 Laparoscopy, surgical; proctectomy, complete, combined abdominoperineal, with colostomy C 80 P0
EXCLUDES open method (45110)
⚕ 50.02 ⚕ 50.02 Global Days 090
AMA: 2006, Apr, 1-7; 2006, Apr, 1-7; 2006, April, 1-7

45397 proctectomy, combined abdominoperineal pull-through procedure (eg, colo-anal anastomosis), with creation of colonic reservoir (eg, J-pouch), with diverting enterostomy, when performed C 80 P0
EXCLUDES open method (45119)
⚕ 54.08 ⚕ 54.08 Global Days 090
AMA: 2008, Jan, 10-25; 2007, Jan, 13-27; 2007, Jan, 13-27; 2007, January, 13-27; 2006, Apr, 19-20; 2006, Apr, 19-20; 2006, April, 1-7; 2006, April, 19-20; 2006, Apr, 1-7; 2006, Apr, 1-7

45400 proctopexy (for prolapse) C 80 P0
EXCLUDES open method (45540, 45541)
⚕ 28.84 ⚕ 28.84 Global Days 090
AMA: 2006, Apr, 1-7; 2006, Apr, 1-7; 2006, April, 1-7

45402 proctopexy (for prolapse), with sigmoid resection C 80 P0
EXCLUDES open method (45550)
⚕ 38.60 ⚕ 38.60 Global Days 090
AMA: 2006, Apr, 1-7; 2006, Apr, 1-7; 2006, April, 1-7

45499 Unlisted laparoscopy procedure, rectum T 80
⚕ 0.00 ⚕ 0.00 Global Days YYY

45500-45825 Open Repairs of Rectum

45500 Proctoplasty; for stenosis A2 T 80 ▭ P0
⚕ 12.66 ⚕ 12.66 Global Days 090

45505 for prolapse of mucous membrane A2 T ▭ P0
⚕ 13.90 ⚕ 13.90 Global Days 090

Digestive

45520 Perirectal injection of sclerosing solution for prolapse P2 T 📠 P0
  📠 0.98 ≷ 3.12 Global Days 000
  AMA: 2008, Jan, 10-25; 2007, Jan, 13-27; 2007, Jan, 13-27; 2007, January, 13-27

45540 Proctopexy (eg, for prolapse); abdominal approach C 80 📠 P0
  EXCLUDES *laparoscopic method (45400)*
  📠 26.60 ≷ 26.60 Global Days 090

45541 perineal approach T 80 📠 P0
  📠 22.86 ≷ 22.86 Global Days 090

45550 with sigmoid resection, abdominal approach C 80 📠 P0
  INCLUDES Frickman proctopexy
  EXCLUDES *laparoscopic method (45402)*
  📠 36.61 ≷ 36.61 Global Days 090

45560 Repair of rectocele (separate procedure) A2 T 80 📠 P0
  EXCLUDES *posterior colporrhaphy with rectocele repair (57250)*
  📠 18.07 ≷ 18.07 Global Days 090

45562 Exploration, repair, and presacral drainage for rectal injury; C 80 📠 P0
  📠 27.73 ≷ 27.73 Global Days 090

45563 with colostomy C 80 📠 P0
  INCLUDES Maydl colostomy
  📠 40.30 ≷ 40.30 Global Days 090

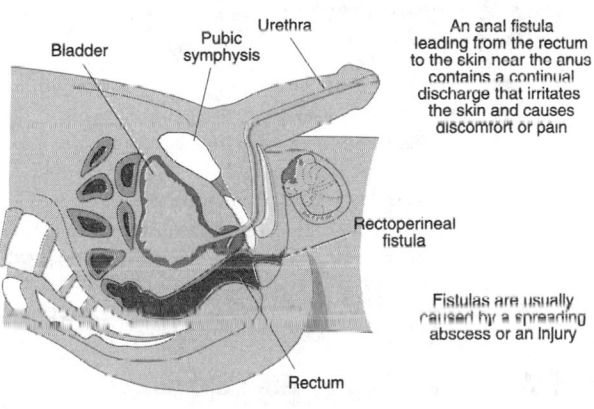

Bladder · Pubic symphysis · Urethra

An anal fistula leading from the rectum to the skin near the anus contains a continual discharge that irritates the skin and causes discomfort or pain

Rectoperineal fistula

Fistulas are usually caused by a spreading abscess or an injury

Rectum

45800 Closure of rectovesical fistula; C 80 📠 P0
  📠 31.07 ≷ 31.07 Global Days 090

45805 with colostomy C 80 📠 P0
  📠 35.07 ≷ 35.07 Global Days 090

45820 Closure of rectourethral fistula; C 80 📠 P0
  EXCLUDES *closure of fistula, rectovaginal (57300-57308)*
  📠 30.76 ≷ 30.76 Global Days 090

45825 with colostomy C 80 📠 P0
  EXCLUDES *closure of fistula, rectovaginal (57300-57308)*
  📠 37.17 ≷ 37.17 Global Days 090

45900-45999 Closed Procedures of Rectum With Anesthesia

45900 Reduction of procidentia (separate procedure) under anesthesia A2 T 80 📠
  📠 4.90 ≷ 4.90 Global Days 010

45905 Dilation of anal sphincter (separate procedure) under anesthesia other than local A2 T 📠
  📠 4.17 ≷ 4.17 Global Days 010

45910 Dilation of rectal stricture (separate procedure) under anesthesia other than local A2 T 📠
  📠 4.93 ≷ 4.93 Global Days 010

45915 Removal of fecal impaction or foreign body (separate procedure) under anesthesia A2 T 📠
  📠 5.51 ≷ 7.66 Global Days 010
  AMA: 2008, Jan, 10-25; 2007, Jan, 13-27; 2007, Jan, 13-27; 2007, January, 13-27; 2006, Jun, 16-17; 2006, June, 16-17; 2006, Jun, 16-17

45990 Anorectal exam, surgical, requiring anesthesia (general, spinal, or epidural), diagnostic A2 T 80
  INCLUDES diagnostic
    anoscopy
    proctoscopy, rigid
    exam
      pelvic (when performed)
      perineal, external
      rectal, digital

  Do not report with (45300-45327, 46600, 57410, 99170)
  📠 2.74 ≷ 2.74 Global Days 000
  AMA: 2008, Jan, 10-25; 2007, Jan, 13-27; 2007, Jan, 13-27; 2007, January, 13-27; 2006, Apr, 1-7; 2006, Apr, 1-7; 2006, May, 16-20; 2006, April, 1-7; 2006, May, 16-20; 2006, May, 16-20

45999 Unlisted procedure, rectum T 80
  📠 0.00 ≷ 0.00 Global Days YYY
  AMA: 2006, Apr, 1-7; 2006, Apr, 1-7; 2006, April, 1-7

46020-46083 Surgical Incision of Anus

EXCLUDES *fistulotomy, subcutaneous (46270)*

46020 Placement of seton A2 T 📠
  Do not report with (46060, 46280, 46600)
  📠 5.45 ≷ 6.21 Global Days 010

46030 Removal of anal seton, other marker A2 T 80 📠
  📠 2.17 ≷ 3.12 Global Days 010

46040 Incision and drainage of ischiorectal and/or perirectal abscess (separate procedure) A2 T 📠
  📠 9.79 ≷ 12.13 Global Days 090

46045 Incision and drainage of intramural, intramuscular, or submucosal abscess, transanal, under anesthesia A2 T 📠
  📠 10.04 ≷ 10.04 Global Days 090

46050 Incision and drainage, perianal abscess, superficial A2 T 📠
  EXCLUDES *incision and drainage abscess*
    ischiorectal/intramural (46060)
    supralevator/pelvirectal/retrorectal (45020)
  📠 2.29 ≷ 4.33 Global Days 010

46060 Incision and drainage of ischiorectal or intramural abscess, with fistulectomy or fistulotomy, submuscular, with or without placement of seton A2 T 📠
  EXCLUDES *incision and drainage abscess*
    supralevator/pelvirectal/retrorectal (45020)
  Do not report with (46020)
  📠 11.08 ≷ 11.08 Global Days 090

46070 Incision, anal septum (infant) A G2 T 80 ⊛ 📠
  EXCLUDES *anoplasty (46700-46705)*
  📠 5.67 ≷ 5.67 Global Days 090

46080 Sphincterotomy, anal, division of sphincter (separate procedure) A2 T 📠
  📠 3.95 ≷ 5.68 Global Days 010

45520 — 46080

Digestive

46083 — 46600

46083   Incision of thrombosed hemorrhoid, external   P2 T ▭
    🔁 2.64   ✂ 4.28   **Global Days** 010
    AMA: 2008, Jan, 10-25; 2007, Jan, 13-27; 2007, Jan, 13-27; 2007, January, 13-27

46200-46220 Resection of Anus

46200   Fissurectomy, with or without sphincterotomy   A2 T ▭
    🔁 7.38   ✂ 9.50   **Global Days** 090

46210   Cryptectomy; single   A2 T 80 ▭
    🔁 6.21   ✂ 8.71   **Global Days** 090

46211   multiple (separate procedure)   A2 T 80 ▭
    🔁 9.05   ✂ 11.80   **Global Days** 090

46220   Papillectomy or excision of single tag, anus (separate procedure)   A2 T ▭
    🔁 2.83   ✂ 4.57   **Global Days** 010

46221-46262 Hemorrhoidectomies

EXCLUDES   *other hemorrhoid procedures:*
     destruction (46930)
     hemorrhoidopexy (46947)
     injection sclerosing solution (46500)
     ligation (46945-46946)

46221   Hemorrhoidectomy, by simple ligature (eg, rubber band)   P3 T ▭
    🔁 4.48   ✂ 5.98   **Global Days** 010

46230   Excision of external hemorrhoid tags and/or multiple papillae   A2 T ▭
    🔁 4.24   ✂ 6.28   **Global Days** 010

46250   Hemorrhoidectomy, external, complete   A2 T ▭
    🔁 7.47   ✂ 10.45   **Global Days** 090

46255   Hemorrhoidectomy, internal and external, simple;   A2 T ▭
    🔁 8.51   ✂ 11.67   **Global Days** 090

46257   with fissurectomy   A2 T ▭
    🔁 9.94   ✂ 9.94   **Global Days** 090

46258   with fistulectomy, with or without fissurectomy   A2 T 80 ▭
    🔁 10.86   ✂ 10.86   **Global Days** 090

46260   Hemorrhoidectomy, internal and external, complex or extensive;   A2 T ▭
    INCLUDES   Whitehead hemorrhoidectomy
    🔁 11.30   ✂ 11.30   **Global Days** 090

46261   with fissurectomy   A2 T ▭
    🔁 12.61   ✂ 12.61   **Global Days** 090

46262   with fistulectomy, with or without fissurectomy   A2 T ▭
    EXCLUDES   *other hemorrhoid procedures:*
      hemorrhoidopexy (46947)
      injection sclerosing solution (46500)
      ligation (46945-46946)
      thermal energy destruction (46930)
    🔁 13.17   ✂ 13.17   **Global Days** 090
    AMA: 2005, May, 3-6; 2005, May, 3-6; 2005, May, 3-6

46270-46288 Resection of Anal Fistula

46270   Surgical treatment of anal fistula (fistulectomy/fistulotomy); subcutaneous   A2 T ▭
    🔁 8.93   ✂ 11.27   **Global Days** 090

46275   submuscular   A2 T ▭
    🔁 9.58   ✂ 11.94   **Global Days** 090

46280   complex or multiple, with or without placement of seton   A2 T ▭
    Do not report with (46020)
    🔁 10.99   ✂ 10.99   **Global Days** 090

46285   second stage   A2 T ▭
    🔁 9.43   ✂ 11.58   **Global Days** 090

46288   Closure of anal fistula with rectal advancement flap   A2 T ▭
    🔁 12.99   ✂ 12.99   **Global Days** 090

46320-46500 Other Hemorrhoid Procedures

46320   Enucleation or excision of external thrombotic hemorrhoid   P3 T ▭
    🔁 2.69   ✂ 4.13   **Global Days** 010

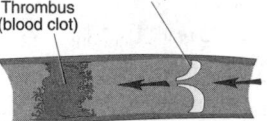

Varicose veins commonly develop in the lower legs, particularly in the elderly, when impaired valves cause the vessels to swell and become inflamed; the risk of clot formation increases with inflamed veins; thrombophlebitis is the inflammation which may result in blood clots in veins

Rectum

Valve cusps become incompetent in the varicose vein causing blood to pool

Anal sphincter   Internal hemorrhoid   External hemorrhoid

Thrombus (blood clot)

Varicose veins and hemorrhoids (varicose rectal veins) are often associated; internal hemorrhoids (also called piles) are varicosities of the tributaries of the superior rectal veins and are covered by mucous membranes; external hemorrhoids are of the inferior rectal veins and are covered by skin

46500   Injection of sclerosing solution, hemorrhoids   P3 T ▭
    EXCLUDES   *other hemorrhoid procedures:*
      excision (46250-46262)
      hemorrhoidopexy (46947)
      ligation (46945-46946)
      thermal energy destruction (46930)
    🔁 3.04   ✂ 5.01   **Global Days** 010
    AMA: 2005, May, 3-6; 2005, May, 3-6; 2005, May, 3-6

46505 Chemodenervation Anal Sphincter

46505   Chemodenervation of internal anal sphincter   G2 T 50
    EXCLUDES   *chemodenervation of*
      extremity/trunk muscles (64614)
      muscles/facial nerve (64612)
      neck muscles (64613)
      other peripheral nerve/branch (64640)
    Code also drug(s)/substance(s) given
    🔁 5.50   ✂ 6.50   **Global Days** 010
    AMA: 2006, Apr, 1-7; 2006, Apr, 1-7; 2006, April, 1-7

46600-46615 Anoscopic Procedures

CMS *100-3,100.2*   *Endoscopy*

46600   Anoscopy; diagnostic, with or without collection of specimen(s) by brushing or washing (separate procedure)   P2 X ▭
    Do not report with (46020)
    🔁 0.97   ✂ 2.01   **Global Days** 000
    AMA: 2006, Apr, 1-7; 2006, Apr, 1-7; 2006, April, 1-7

46604 with dilation (eg, balloon, guide wire, bougie) [P2] [T] [⊡]
INCLUDES diagnostic anosocpy (46600)
📠 1.69   ⚥ 12.48 Global Days 000

46606 with biopsy, single or multiple [P3] [T] [⊡]
INCLUDES diagnostic anoscopy (46600)
📠 1.85   ⚥ 5.13 Global Days 000

46608 with removal of foreign body [A2] [T] [80] [⊡]
INCLUDES diagnostic anoscopy (46600)
📠 2.06   ⚥ 5.32 Global Days 000

46610 with removal of single tumor, polyp, or other lesion by hot biopsy forceps or bipolar cautery [A2] [T] [⊡]
INCLUDES diagnostic anoscopy (46600)
📠 2.04   ⚥ 5.26 Global Days 000

46611 with removal of single tumor, polyp, or other lesion by snare technique [A2] [T] [80] [⊡]
INCLUDES diagnostic anoscopy (46600)
📠 2.12   ⚥ 4.17 Global Days 000

46612 with removal of multiple tumors, polyps, or other lesions by hot biopsy forceps, bipolar cautery or snare technique [A2] [T] [80] [⊡]
INCLUDES diagnostic anoscopy (46600)
📠 2.53   ⚥ 6.34 Global Days 000

46614 with control of bleeding (eg, injection, bipolar cautery, unipolar cautery, laser, heater probe, stapler, plasma coagulator) [P3] [T] [⊡]
INCLUDES diagnostic anoscopy (46600)
📠 1.81   ⚥ 3.22 Global Days 000

46615 with ablation of tumor(s), polyp(s), or other lesion(s) not amenable to removal by hot biopsy forceps, bipolar cautery or snare technique [A2] [T] [80] [⊡]
INCLUDES diagnostic anoscopy (46600)
📠 2.59   ⚥ 3.74 Global Days 000

46700-46762 Open Repairs of Anus

46700 Anoplasty, plastic operation for stricture; adult [A2] [T] [⊡]
📠 15.63   ⚥ 15.63 Global Days 090

46705 infant [C] [80] [63] [⊡]
EXCLUDES anal septum incision (46070)
📠 12.95   ⚥ 12.95 Global Days 090

46706 Repair of anal fistula with fibrin glue [A2] [T] [⊡]
📠 4.15   ⚥ 4.15 Global Days 010

46710 Repair of ileoanal pouch fistula/sinus (eg, perineal or vaginal), pouch advancement; transperineal approach [C] [80]
📠 26.53   ⚥ 26.53 Global Days 090
AMA: 2006, Apr, 1-7; 2006, Apr, 1-7; 2006, April, 1-7

46712 combined transperineal and transabdominal approach [C] [80]
📠 54.39   ⚥ 54.39 Global Days 090
AMA: 2006, Apr, 1-7; 2006, Apr, 1-7; 2006, April, 1-7

46715 Repair of low imperforate anus; with anoperineal fistula (cut-back procedure) [C] [80] [63] [⊡] [P0]
📠 12.00   ⚥ 12.00 Global Days 090

46716 with transposition of anoperineal or anovestibular fistula [C] [80] [63] [⊡] [P0]
📠 31.12   ⚥ 31.12 Global Days 090

46730 Repair of high imperforate anus without fistula; perineal or sacroperineal approach [C] [80] [63] [⊡] [P0]
📠 47.06   ⚥ 47.06 Global Days 090

46735 combined transabdominal and sacroperineal approaches [C] [80] [63] [⊡] [P0]
📠 55.06   ⚥ 55.06 Global Days 090

46740 Repair of high imperforate anus with rectourethral or rectovaginal fistula; perineal or sacroperineal approach [C] [80] [63] [⊡] [P0]
📠 50.40   ⚥ 50.40 Global Days 090

46742 combined transabdominal and sacroperineal approaches [C] [80] [63] [⊡] [P0]
📠 59.68   ⚥ 59.68 Global Days 090

46744 Repair of cloacal anomaly by anorectovaginoplasty and urethroplasty, sacroperineal approach ♀ [C] [80] [63] [⊡] [P0]
📠 85.71   ⚥ 85.71 Global Days 090

46746 Repair of cloacal anomaly by anorectovaginoplasty and urethroplasty, combined abdominal and sacroperineal approach; ♀ [C] [80] [⊡] [P0]
📠 99.18   ⚥ 99.18 Global Days 090

46748 with vaginal lengthening by intestinal graft or pedicle flaps ♀ [C] [80] [⊡] [P0]
📠 101.96   ⚥ 101.96 Global Days 090

46750 Sphincteroplasty, anal, for incontinence or prolapse; adult [A2] [T] [80] [⊡] [P0]
📠 18.88   ⚥ 18.88 Global Days 090

46751 child [A] [C] [80] [⊡] [P0]
📠 15.71   ⚥ 15.71 Global Days 090

46753 Graft (Thiersch operation) for rectal incontinence and/or prolapse [A2] [T] [⊡] [P0]
📠 14.30   ⚥ 14.30 Global Days 090

46754 Removal of Thiersch wire or suture, anal canal [A2] [T] [80] [⊡] [P0]
📠 5.21   ⚥ 6.76 Global Days 010

46760 Sphincteroplasty, anal, for incontinence, adult; muscle transplant [A2] [T] [80] [⊡] [P0]
📠 26.72   ⚥ 26.72 Global Days 090

46761 levator muscle imbrication (Park posterior anal repair) [A2] [T] [80] [⊡] [P0]
📠 23.12   ⚥ 23.12 Global Days 090

46762 implantation artificial sphincter [A2] [T] [80] [⊡] [P0]
📠 22.74   ⚥ 22.74 Global Days 090

46900-46924 Destruction of Anal Lesions

46900 Destruction of lesion(s), anus (eg, condyloma, papilloma, molluscum contagiosum, herpetic vesicle), simple; chemical [P2] [T] [⊡]
📠 3.41   ⚥ 5.48 Global Days 010

46910 electrodesiccation [P3] [T] [⊡]
📠 3.27   ⚥ 5.72 Global Days 010

46916 cryosurgery [P2] [T] [⊡]
📠 3.57   ⚥ 5.64 Global Days 010

46917 laser surgery [A2] [T] [⊡]
📠 3.30   ⚥ 10.88 Global Days 010

46922 surgical excision [A2] [T] [⊡]
📠 3.28   ⚥ 5.97 Global Days 010

46924 Destruction of lesion(s), anus (eg, condyloma, papilloma, molluscum contagiosum, herpetic vesicle), extensive (eg, laser surgery, electrosurgery, cryosurgery, chemosurgery) [A2] [T] [⊡]
📠 4.66   ⚥ 12.33 Global Days 010

● New Code   ▲ Revised Code   M Maternity Edit   🅐 Age Edit   🅐-🆅 OPPS Status Indicator   📠 Facility RVU   ⚥ Non-Facility RVU
⊡ CCI Comprehensive Code   🔟 Bilateral Procedure   + Add-on Indicator   ▪Laboratory crosswalk   ▪Radiology crosswalk

Digestive

46930 — 47100

46930 Destruction of Internal Hemorrhoids: Thermal Energy

● 46930 Destruction of internal hemorrhoid(s) by thermal energy (eg, infrared coagulation, cautery, radiofrequency)   P3 T 80

EXCLUDES *other hemorrhoid procedures:*
cryosurgery destruction (46999)
destruction with heat (46930)
excision (46250-46262, 46320)
hemorrhoidopexy (46947)
incision (46083)
injection sclerosing solution (46500)
ligation (46221, 46945-46946)

🔗 3.81   ✂ 5.26   **Global Days 090**

46934-46999 Other and Unlisted Anal Procedures

~~46934~~   ~~Destruction of hemorrhoids, any method; internal~~
See 46930, 46999

~~46935~~   ~~external~~

~~46936~~   ~~internal and external~~

46937   Cryosurgery of rectal tumor; benign   A2 T 80
🔗 4.32   ✂ 6.11   **Global Days 010**

46938   malignant   A2 T 80
🔗 8.93   ✂ 10.78   **Global Days 090**

46940   Curettage or cautery of anal fissure, including dilation of anal sphincter (separate procedure); initial   P3 T
🔗 3.64   ✂ 5.18   **Global Days 010**

46942   subsequent   P3 T 80
🔗 3.23   ✂ 4.79   **Global Days 010**

46945   Ligation of internal hemorrhoids; single procedure   P3 T
EXCLUDES *other hemorrhoid procedures:*
destruction (46930)
excision (46250-46262)
injection sclerosing solution (46500)

🔗 5.14   ✂ 6.66   **Global Days 090**

46946   multiple procedures   A2 T
EXCLUDES *other hemorrhoid procedures:*
destruction (46930)
excision (46250-46262)
injection sclerosing solution (46500)

🔗 5.45   ✂ 7.23   **Global Days 090**

46947   Hemorrhoidopexy (eg, for prolapsing internal hemorrhoids) by stapling   A2 T
EXCLUDES *other hemorrhoid procedures:*
destruction (46930)
excision (46250-46262)
injection sclerosing solution (46500)

🔗 9.30   ✂ 9.30   **Global Days 090**
AMA: 2008, Jan, 10-25; 2007, Jan, 13-27; 2007, Jan, 13-27; 2007, January, 13-27; 2005, May, 13-14; 2005, May, 13-14; 2005, May, 13-14; 2005, May, 3-6; 2005, May, 3-6; 2005, May, 3-6

46999   Unlisted procedure, anus   T 80
🔗 0.00   ✂ 0.00   **Global Days YYY**

47000-47001 Needle Biopsy of Liver

EXCLUDES *fine needle aspiration (10021, 10022)*

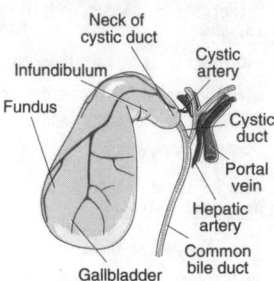

The liver is divided into four lobes for descriptive purposes, although the left and right halves are functionally separate, each receiving its own arterial supply and venous drainage. The liver is the largest gland in the body and serves many metabolic purposes including secretion of bile. The gallbladder is located on the visceral side of the quadrate lobe and stores bile between active phases of digestion; positions of the sac and its structures vary

47000   Biopsy of liver, needle; percutaneous   A2 T
📷 88172-88173
📊 76942, 77002, 77012, 77021
🔗 2.75   ✂ 8.50   **Global Days 000**
AMA: 2008, Jan, 10-25; 2007, Jun, 10-11; 2007, Jun, 10-11; 2007, June, 10-11

+ 47001   when done for indicated purpose at time of other major procedure (List separately in addition to code for primary procedure)   N1 N
Code first primary procedure
📊 76942, 77002
📷 88172-88173
🔗 2.70   ✂ 2.70   **Global Days ZZZ**
AMA: 2008, Jan, 10-25; 2007, Jun, 10-11; 2007, Jun, 10-11; 2007, June, 10-11

47010-47130 Open Incisional and Resection Procedures of Liver

47010   Hepatotomy; for open drainage of abscess or cyst, 1 or 2 stages   C 80 PQ
🔗 29.62   ✂ 29.62   **Global Days 090**

⊙ 47011   for percutaneous drainage of abscess or cyst, 1 or 2 stages   T
📊 75989
🔗 5.32   ✂ 5.32   **Global Days 000**

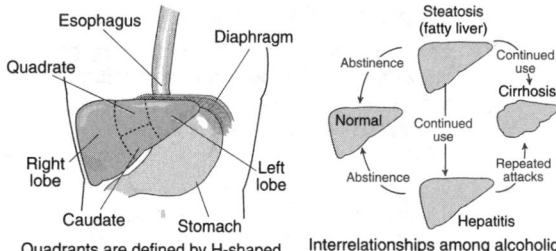

Quadrants are defined by H-shaped grooves on the visceral side

Interrelationships among alcoholic steatosis, hepatitis, and cirrhosis

The liver is the largest gland in the body and serves many metabolic purposes including secretion of bile. Chronic alcohol use leads to three similar forms of alcoholic liver disease: steatosis (fatty liver), hepatitis, and cirrhosis. The conditions have many overlapping features and each may occur without involvement of alcohol. Alcoholic cirrhosis accounts for about 60 percent of all cirrhosis cases and the risk appears to rise with the amount of alcohol consumed daily. The liver tends to shrink and become fibrotic

47015   Laparotomy, with aspiration and/or injection of hepatic parasitic (eg, amoebic or echinococcal) cyst(s) or abscess(es)   C 80
🔗 28.14   ✂ 28.14   **Global Days 090**

47100   Biopsy of liver, wedge   C 80 PQ
🔗 20.69   ✂ 20.69   **Global Days 090**

47120   Hepatectomy, resection of liver; partial
        lobectomy   C 80 ▭ P0
        ⚚ 58.30   ⚘ 58.30 Global Days 090
        AMA: 2008, Jan, 10-25; 2007, Jan, 13-27; 2007, Jan, 13-27; 2007,
        January, 13-27

47122   trisegmentectomy   C 80 ▭ P0
            ⚚ 86.82   ⚘ 86.82 Global Days 090

47125   total left lobectomy   C 80 ▭ P0
            ⚚ 77.77   ⚘ 77.77 Global Days 090

47130   total right lobectomy   C 80 ▭ P0
            ⚚ 83.62   ⚘ 83.62 Global Days 090

47133-47147 Liver Transplant Procedures

CMS 100-4,3,90.4.2   *Billing for Liver Transplant and Acquisition Services*
CMS 100-4,3,90.4.1   *Standard Liver Acquisition Charge*
CMS 100-4,3,90.4   *Liver Transplants*
CMS 100-3,260.2   *Pediatric Liver Transplantation*
CMS 100-3,260.1   *Adult Liver Transplantation*
CMS 100-4,3,90.6   *Intestinal and Multi-Visceral Transplants*

47133   Donor hepatectomy (including cold preservation), from
        cadaver donor   C ▭ P0
        [INCLUDES]   graft:
                        cold preservation
                        harvest

        ⚚ 0.00   ⚘ 0.00 Global Days XXX

47135   Liver allotransplantation; orthotopic, partial or whole,
        from cadaver or living donor, any age   C 80 ▭ P0
        [INCLUDES]   partial/whole recipient hepatectomy
                     partial/whole transplant of allograft
                     recipient care

        ⚚ 122.99   ⚘ 122.99 Global Days 090

47136   heterotopic, partial or whole, from cadaver or living
        donor, any age   C 80 ▭ P0
        [INCLUDES]   partial/whole recipient hepatectomy
                     partial/whole transplant of allograft
                     recipient care

        ⚚ 104.89   ⚘ 104.89 Global Days 090

47140   Donor hepatectomy (including cold preservation), from
        living donor; left lateral segment only (segments II and
        III)   C 80 ▭ P0
        [INCLUDES]   donor care
                     graft:
                        cold preservation
                        harvest

        ⚚ 86.92   ⚘ 86.92 Global Days 090

47141   total left lobectomy (segments II, III and
        IV)   C 80 ▭ P0
        [INCLUDES]   donor care
                     graft:
                        cold preservation
                        harvest

        ⚚ 103.09   ⚘ 103.09 Global Days 090

47142   total right lobectomy (segments V, VI, VII and
        VIII)   C 80 ▭ P0
        [INCLUDES]   donor care
                     graft:
                        cold preservation
                        harvest

        ⚚ 113.30   ⚘ 113.30 Global Days 090

47143   Backbench standard preparation of cadaver donor whole
        liver graft prior to allotransplantation, including
        cholecystectomy, if necessary, and dissection and
        removal of surrounding soft tissues to prepare the vena
        cava, portal vein, hepatic artery, and common bile duct
        for implantation; without trisegment or lobe
        split   C 80 ▭
        Do not report with (47120-47125, 47600, 47610)
        ⚚ 0.00   ⚘ 0.00 Global Days XXX
        AMA: 2005, Apr, 10-12; 2005, Apr, 10-12; 2005, April, 10-12

47144   with trisegment split of whole liver graft into 2 partial
        liver grafts (ie, left lateral segment [segments II and
        III] and right trisegment [segments I and IV through
        VIII])   C 00 ▭
        Do not report with (47120-47125, 47600, 47610)
        ⚚ 0.00   ⚘ 0.00 Global Days 090

47145   with lobe split of whole liver graft into 2 partial liver
        grafts (ie, left lobe [segments II, III, and IV] and right
        lobe [segments I and V through VIII])   C 80 ▭
        Do not report with (47120-47125, 47600, 47610)
        ⚚ 0.00   ⚘ 0.00 Global Days XXX

47146   Backbench reconstruction of cadaver or living donor liver
        graft prior to allotransplantation; venous anastomosis,
        each   C 80 ▭
        Do not report with (47120-47125, 47600, 47610)
        ⚚ 8.57   ⚘ 8.57 Global Days XXX

47147   arterial anastomosis, each   C 80 ▭
        Do not report with (47120-47125, 47600, 47610)
        ⚚ 10.00   ⚘ 10.00 Global Days XXX

47300-47362 Open Repair of Liver

47300   Marsupialization of cyst or abscess of liver   C 80 ▭ P0
        ⚚ 27.75   ⚘ 27.75 Global Days 090

47350   Management of liver hemorrhage; simple suture of liver
        wound or injury   C 80 ▭ P0
        ⚚ 34.10   ⚘ 34.10 Global Days 090

47360   complex suture of liver wound or injury, with or
            without hepatic artery ligation   C 80 ▭ P0
        ⚚ 46.34   ⚘ 46.34 Global Days 090

47361   exploration of hepatic wound, extensive debridement,
            coagulation and/or suture, with or without packing
            of liver   C 80 ▭ P0
        ⚚ 76.26   ⚘ 76.26 Global Days 090

47362   re-exploration of hepatic wound for removal of
            packing   C 80 ▭ P0
        ⚚ 35.32   ⚘ 35.32 Global Days 090

47370-47379 Laparoscopic Ablation Liver Tumors

47370   Laparoscopy, surgical, ablation of 1 or more liver
        tumor(s); radiofrequency   T 80 ▭ P0
        [INCLUDES]   diagnostic laparoscopy

        ▨ 76940
        ⚚ 31.24   ⚘ 31.24 Global Days 090

47371   cryosurgical   T 80 ▭ P0
        [INCLUDES]   diagnostic laparoscopy

        ▨ 76940
        ⚚ 31.83   ⚘ 31.83 Global Days 090

47379   Unlisted laparoscopic procedure, liver   T 80
        ⚚ 0.00   ⚘ 0.00 Global Days YYY
        AMA: 2008, Jan, 10-25; 2007, Jan, 13-27; 2007, Jan, 13-27; 2007,
        Dec, 10-179; 2007, January, 13-27; 2006, Aug, 12-14; 2006,
        August, 12-14; 2006, Aug, 12-14

● New Code	▲ Revised Code	▥ Maternity Edit	▨ Age Edit	Ⓐ-Ⓨ OPPS Status Indicator	⚚ Facility RVU	⚘ Non-Facility RVU
▭ CCI Comprehensive Code	50 Bilateral Procedure	+ Add-on Indicator	▨ Laboratory crosswalk	▨ Radiology crosswalk		

47380-47399 Open and Percutaneous Ablation of Liver Tumors

47380 Ablation, open, of 1 or more liver tumor(s); radiofrequency   C 80 ▢ P0
- 76940
- 36.48   36.48   Global Days 090

47381 cryosurgical   C 80 ▢ P0
- 76940
- 37.17   37.17   Global Days 090

47382 Ablation, 1 or more liver tumor(s), percutaneous, radiofrequency   G2 T ▢ P0
- 76940, 77013, 77022
- 22.79   22.79   Global Days 010

47399 Unlisted procedure, liver   T
- 0.00   0.00   Global Days YYY

47400-47490 Surgical Incision Biliary Tract

47400 Hepaticotomy or hepaticostomy with exploration, drainage, or removal of calculus   C 80 ▢ P0
- 52.60   52.60   Global Days 090

47420 Choledochotomy or choledochostomy with exploration, drainage, or removal of calculus, with or without cholecystotomy; without transduodenal sphincterotomy or sphincteroplasty   C 80 ▢ P0
- 33.42   33.42   Global Days 090

47425 with transduodenal sphincterotomy or sphincteroplasty   C 80 ▢ P0
- 33.74   33.74   Global Days 090

47460 Transduodenal sphincterotomy or sphincteroplasty, with or without transduodenal extraction of calculus (separate procedure)   C 80 ▢ P0
- 31.78   31.78   Global Days 090

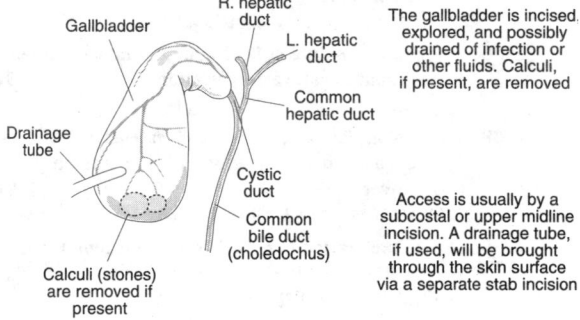

Gallbladder — R. hepatic duct — L. hepatic duct — Common hepatic duct — Drainage tube — Cystic duct — Common bile duct (choledochus) — Calculi (stones) are removed if present

The gallbladder is incised, explored, and possibly drained of infection or other fluids. Calculi, if present, are removed

Access is usually by a subcostal or upper midline incision. A drainage tube, if used, will be brought through the skin surface via a separate stab incision

47480 Cholecystotomy or cholecystostomy with exploration, drainage, or removal of calculus (separate procedure)   C 80 ▢ P0
- 21.15   21.15   Global Days 090

47490 Percutaneous cholecystostomy   T ▢ P0
- 75989
- 14.07   14.07   Global Days 090

47500-47530 Injection/Insertion Procedures of Biliary Tract

47500 Injection procedure for percutaneous transhepatic cholangiography   N1 N ▢ P0
- 74320
- 2.83   2.83   Global Days 000

47505 Injection procedure for cholangiography through an existing catheter (eg, percutaneous transhepatic or T-tube)   N1 N 80 ▢ P0
- 74305
- 1.09   1.09   Global Days 000

47510 Introduction of percutaneous transhepatic catheter for biliary drainage   A2 T ▢ P0
- 75980
- 13.34   13.34   Global Days 090

47511 Introduction of percutaneous transhepatic stent for internal and external biliary drainage   A2 T 50 ▢ P0
- 75982
- 16.76   16.76   Global Days 090

47525 Change of percutaneous biliary drainage catheter   A2 T 50 ▢ P0
- Code also (C1729)
- 75984
- 3.54   15.71   Global Days 010

47530 Revision and/or reinsertion of transhepatic tube   A2 T ▢ P0
- 75984
- 10.03   37.78   Global Days 090

47550-47556 Endoscopic Procedures of the Biliary Tract

CMS 100-3,100.2   *Endoscopy*

+ 47550 Biliary endoscopy, intraoperative (choledochoscopy) (List separately in addition to code for primary procedure)   C 80
- Code first primary procedure
- 4.32   4.32   Global Days ZZZ

47552 Biliary endoscopy, percutaneous via T-tube or other tract; diagnostic, with or without collection of specimen(s) by brushing and/or washing (separate procedure)   A2 T ▢
- 9.12   9.12   Global Days 000

47553 with biopsy, single or multiple   A2 T ▢
- INCLUDES   diagnostic endoscopy
- 9.10   9.10   Global Days 000

47554 with removal of calculus/calculi   A2 T ▢
- INCLUDES   diagnostic endoscopy
- 13.47   13.47   Global Days 000

47555 with dilation of biliary duct stricture(s) without stent   A2 T ▢
- INCLUDES   diagnostic endoscopy
- 10.92   10.92   Global Days 000

47556 with dilation of biliary duct stricture(s) with stent   A2 T ▢
- INCLUDES   diagnostic endoscopy
- EXCLUDES   *endoscopic retrograde cholangiopancreatography (ERCP) (43260-43272, 74363)*
- 74363, 75982
- 12.35   12.35   Global Days 000

47560-47579 Laparoscopic Gallbladder Procedures

CMS 100-3,100.13   *Laparoscopic Cholecystectomy*

INCLUDES   diagnostic laparoscopy

47560 Laparoscopy, surgical; with guided transhepatic cholangiography, without biopsy   A2 T 80 ▢ P0
- 6.98   6.98   Global Days 000

| 47561 | with guided transhepatic cholangiography with biopsy | A2 T 80 🖵 P0 |

🔢 7.56 ✂ 7.56 Global Days 000

| 47562 | cholecystectomy | G2 T 80 🖵 P0 |

🔢 18.41 ✂ 18.41 Global Days 090
AMA: 2007, Dec, 10-179

| 47563 | cholecystectomy with cholangiography | G2 T 80 🖵 P0 |

🔢 18.87 ✂ 18.87 Global Days 090
AMA: 2008, Jan, 10-25; 2007, Jan, 13-27; 2007, Jan, 13-27; 2007, January, 13-27; 2007, Dec, 10-179

| 47564 | cholecystectomy with exploration of common duct | G2 T 80 🖵 P0 |

🔢 21.82 ✂ 21.82 Global Days 090
AMA: 2007, Dec, 10-179

| 47570 | cholecystoenterostomy | C 80 🖵 P0 |

🔢 19.47 ✂ 19.47 Global Days 090

| 47579 | Unlisted laparoscopy procedure, biliary tract | T 80 50 |

🔢 0.00 ✂ 0.00 Global Days YYY

47600-47620 Open Gallbladder Procedures

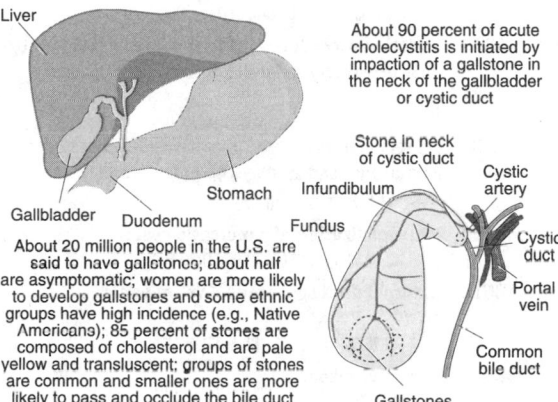

Liver

About 90 percent of acute cholecystitis is initiated by impaction of a gallstone in the neck of the gallbladder or cystic duct

Stone in neck of cystic duct

Cystic artery

Infundibulum

Stomach

Gallbladder   Duodenum

Fundus

Cystic duct

Portal vein

Common bile duct

About 20 million people in the U.S. are said to have gallstones; about half are asymptomatic; women are more likely to develop gallstones and some ethnic groups have high incidence (e.g., Native Americans); 85 percent of stones are composed of cholesterol and are pale yellow and translucent; groups of stones are common and smaller ones are more likely to pass and occlude the bile duct

Gallstones

| 47600 | Cholecystectomy; | C 80 🖵 P0 |

EXCLUDES   *laparoscopic method (47562)*

🔢 26.29 ✂ 26.29 Global Days 090

| 47605 | with cholangiography | C 80 🖵 P0 |

EXCLUDES   *laparoscopic method (47564)*

🔢 24.43 ✂ 24.43 Global Days 090
AMA: 2008, Jan, 10-25; 2007, Jan, 13-27; 2007, Jan, 13-27, 2007, January, 13-27

| 47610 | Cholecystectomy with exploration of common duct; | C 80 🖵 P0 |

Code also biliary endoscopy when performed in conjunction with cholecystectomy with exploration of common duct (47550)

🔢 31.31 ✂ 31.31 Global Days 090
AMA: 2008, Jan, 10-25; 2007, Jan, 13-27; 2007, Jan, 13-27, 2007, January, 13-27

| 47612 | with choledochoenterostomy | C 80 🖵 P0 |

🔢 31.62 ✂ 31.62 Global Days 090

| 47620 | with transduodenal sphincterotomy or sphincteroplasty, with or without cholangiography | C 80 🖵 P0 |

🔢 34.34 ✂ 34.34 Global Days 090

47630-47999 Open Resection and Repair of Biliary Tract

| 47630 | Biliary duct stone extraction, percutaneous via T-tube tract, basket, or snare (eg, Burhenne technique) | A2 T 🖵 P0 |

📷 74327
🔢 15.24 ✂ 15.24 Global Days 090
AMA: 2008, Jan, 10-25; 2007, Jan, 13-27; 2007, Jan, 13-27; 2007, January, 13-27

| 47700 | Exploration for congenital atresia of bile ducts, without repair, with or without liver biopsy, with or without cholangiography | C 80 63 🖵 P0 |

🔢 26.08 ✂ 26.08 Global Days 090

| 47701 | Portoenterostomy (eg, Kasai procedure) | C 80 63 🖵 P0 |

🔢 44.90 ✂ 44.90 Global Days 090

| 47711 | Excision of bile duct tumor, with or without primary repair of bile duct; extrahepatic | C 80 🖵 P0 |

🔢 38.86 ✂ 38.86 Global Days 090

| 47712 | intrahepatic | C 80 🖵 P0 |

EXCLUDES   *anastomosis (47760-47800)*

🔢 49.76 ✂ 49.76 Global Days 090

| 47715 | Excision of choledochal cyst | C 80 🖵 P0 |

🔢 32.64 ✂ 32.64 Global Days 090

| 47720 | Cholecystoenterostomy; direct | C 80 🖵 P0 |

EXCLUDES   *laparoscopic method (47570)*

🔢 28.19 ✂ 28.19 Global Days 090

| 47721 | with gastroenterostomy | C 80 🖵 P0 |

🔢 33.27 ✂ 33.27 Global Days 090

| 47740 | Roux-en-Y | C 80 🖵 P0 |

🔢 32.14 ✂ 32.14 Global Days 090

| 47741 | Roux-en-Y with gastroenterostomy | C 80 🖵 P0 |

🔢 36.44 ✂ 36.44 Global Days 090

| 47760 | Anastomosis, of extrahepatic biliary ducts and gastrointestinal tract | C 80 🖵 P0 |

🔢 54.55 ✂ 54.55 Global Days 090

| 47765 | Anastomosis, of intrahepatic ducts and gastrointestinal tract | C 80 🖵 P0 |

INCLUDES   Longmire anastomosis

🔢 71.56 ✂ 71.56 Global Days 090

| 47780 | Anastomosis, Roux-en-Y, of extrahepatic biliary ducts and gastrointestinal tract | C 80 🖵 P0 |

🔢 59.56 ✂ 59.56 Global Days 090

| 47785 | Anastomosis, Roux-en-Y, of intrahepatic biliary ducts and gastrointestinal tract | C 80 🖵 P0 |

🔢 77.47 ✂ 77.47 Global Days 090

| 47800 | Reconstruction, plastic, of extrahepatic biliary ducts with end-to-end anastomosis | C 80 🖵 P0 |

🔢 39.24 ✂ 39.24 Global Days 090

| 47801 | Placement of choledochal stent | C 80 🖵 P0 |

🔢 27.43 ✂ 27.43 Global Days 090

| 47802 | U-tube hepaticoenterostomy | C 80 🖵 P0 |

🔢 37.64 ✂ 37.64 Global Days 090

| 47900 | Suture of extrahepatic biliary duct for pre-existing injury (separate procedure) | C 80 🖵 P0 |

🔢 33.95 ✂ 33.95 Global Days 090

| 47999 | Unlisted procedure, biliary tract | T |

🔢 0.00 ✂ 0.00 Global Days YYY

47561 — 47999

● New Code   ▲ Revised Code   Ⓜ Maternity Edit   Ⓐ Age Edit   A-Y OPPS Status Indicator   🔢 Facility RVU   ✂ Non-Facility RVU
🖵 CCI Comprehensive Code   50 Bilateral Procedure   + Add-on Indicator   ◼ Laboratory crosswalk   📷 Radiology crosswalk

Digestive

48000-48548 Open Procedures of the Pancreas

EXCLUDES   *peroral pancreatic procedures performed endoscopically (43260-43272)*

48000   Placement of drains, peripancreatic, for acute pancreatitis;   C 80 ▭ P0
     📖 46.98   ⚕ 46.98   Global Days 090

48001   with cholecystostomy, gastrostomy, and jejunostomy   C 80 ▭ P0
     📖 57.88   ⚕ 57.88   Global Days 090

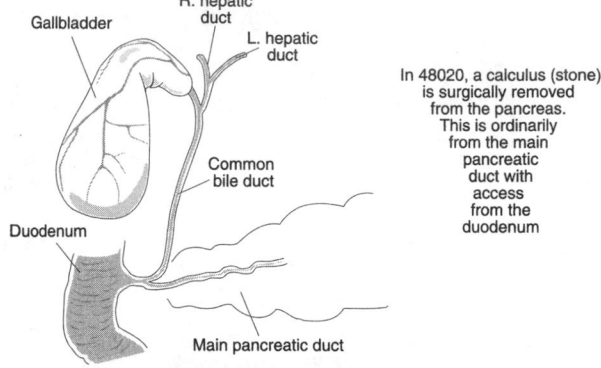

In 48020, a calculus (stone) is surgically removed from the pancreas. This is ordinarily from the main pancreatic duct with access from the duodenum

48020   Removal of pancreatic calculus   C 80 ▭ P0
     📖 28.98   ⚕ 28.98   Global Days 090

48100   Biopsy of pancreas, open (eg, fine needle aspiration, needle core biopsy, wedge biopsy)   C 80 ▭ P0
     📖 22.00   ⚕ 22.00   Global Days 090

48102   Biopsy of pancreas, percutaneous needle   A2 T ▭ P0
    EXCLUDES   *aspiration, fine needle (10022)*
     🔀 76942, 77002, 77012, 77021
     🔀 88172, 88173
     📖 7.02   ⚕ 14.24   Global Days 010

48105   Resection or debridement of pancreas and peripancreatic tissue for acute necrotizing pancreatitis   C 80 P0
     📖 71.26   ⚕ 71.26   Global Days 090

48120   Excision of lesion of pancreas (eg, cyst, adenoma)   C 80 ▭ P0
     📖 27.50   ⚕ 27.50   Global Days 090

48140   Pancreatectomy, distal subtotal, with or without splenectomy; without pancreaticojejunostomy   C 80 ▭ P0
     📖 38.95   ⚕ 38.95   Global Days 090

48145   with pancreaticojejunostomy   C 80 ▭ P0
     📖 40.46   ⚕ 40.46   Global Days 090

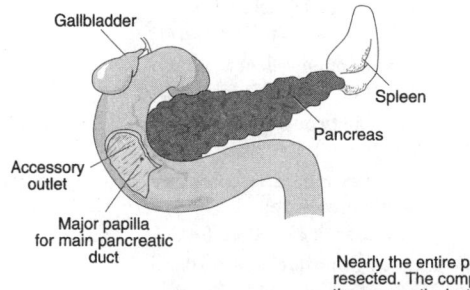

Nearly the entire pancreas is resected. The complex where the pancreatic ducts enter the duodenum is preserved (48146).

48146   Pancreatectomy, distal, near-total with preservation of duodenum (Child-type procedure)   C 80 ▭ P0
     📖 46.14   ⚕ 46.14   Global Days 090

48148   Excision of ampulla of Vater   C 80 ▭ P0
     📖 30.63   ⚕ 30.63   Global Days 090

48150   Pancreatectomy, proximal subtotal with total duodenectomy, partial gastrectomy, choledochoenterostomy and gastrojejunostomy (Whipple-type procedure); with pancreatojejunostomy   C 80 ▭ P0
     📖 78.01   ⚕ 78.01   Global Days 090

48152   without pancreatojejunostomy   C 80 ▭ P0
     📖 72.12   ⚕ 72.12   Global Days 090

48153   Pancreatectomy, proximal subtotal with near-total duodenectomy, choledochoenterostomy and duodenojejunostomy (pylorus-sparing, Whipple-type procedure); with pancreatojejunostomy   C 80 ▭ P0
     📖 77.90   ⚕ 77.90   Global Days 090

48154   without pancreatojejunostomy   C 80 ▭ P0
     📖 72.31   ⚕ 72.31   Global Days 090

48155   Pancreatectomy, total   C 80 ▭ P0
     📖 44.72   ⚕ 44.72   Global Days 090

48160   Pancreatectomy, total or subtotal, with autologous transplantation of pancreas or pancreatic islet cells   E P0
     📖 0.00   ⚕ 0.00   Global Days XXX

+   48400   Injection procedure for intraoperative pancreatography (List separately in addition to code for primary procedure)   C 80 ▭
     Code first primary procedure
     🔀 74300-74305
     📖 2.81   ⚕ 2.81   Global Days ZZZ
     AMA: 2007, Dec, 10-179

48500   Marsupialization of pancreatic cyst   C 80 ▭ P0
     📖 28.02   ⚕ 28.02   Global Days 090

48510   External drainage, pseudocyst of pancreas; open   C 80 ▭ P0
     📖 26.58   ⚕ 26.58   Global Days 090

⊙   48511   percutaneous   T ▭ P0
     🔀 75989
     📖 5.76   ⚕ 24.66   Global Days 000

48520   Internal anastomosis of pancreatic cyst to gastrointestinal tract; direct   C 80 ▭ P0
     📖 27.18   ⚕ 27.18   Global Days 090

48540   Roux-en-Y   C 80 ▭ P0
     📖 32.53   ⚕ 32.53   Global Days 090

48545   Pancreatorrhaphy for injury   C 80 ▭ P0
     📖 32.85   ⚕ 32.85   Global Days 090

48547   Duodenal exclusion with gastrojejunostomy for pancreatic injury   C 80 ▭ P0
     📖 44.37   ⚕ 44.37   Global Days 090

48548   Pancreaticojejunostomy, side-to-side anastomosis (Puestow-type operation)   C 80 P0
     📖 41.59   ⚕ 41.59   Global Days 090

48550-48999 Pancreas Transplant Procedures

CMS *100-4,3,90.5*   *Pancreas Transplants with Kidney Transplants*
CMS *100-3,260.3*   *Pancreas Transplants*

48550   Donor pancreatectomy (including cold preservation), with or without duodenal segment for transplantation   E ▭ P0
    INCLUDES   graft:
         cold preservation
         harvest (with or without duodenal segment)
     📖 0.00   ⚕ 0.00   Global Days XXX
     AMA: 2005, Apr, 10-12; 2005, Apr, 10-12; 2005, April, 10-12

48000 — 48550

48551 Backbench standard preparation of cadaver donor pancreas allograft prior to transplantation, including dissection of allograft from surrounding soft tissues, splenectomy, duodenotomy, ligation of bile duct, ligation of mesenteric vessels, and Y-graft arterial anastomoses from iliac artery to superior mesenteric artery and to splenic artery   C 80 ▢

> Do not report with (35531, 35563, 35685, 38100-38102, 44010, 44820, 44850, 47460, 47505-47525, 47550-47556, 48100-48120, 48545)

> 🔾 0.00   🔾 0.00   Global Days XXX

48552 Backbench reconstruction of cadaver donor pancreas allograft prior to transplantation, venous anastomosis, each   C 80 ▢

> Do not report with (35531, 35563, 35685, 38100-38102, 44010, 44820, 44850, 47460, 47505-47525, 47550-47556, 48100-48120, 48545)

> 🔾 5.90   🔾 5.90   Global Days XXX

48554 Transplantation of pancreatic allograft   C 80 ▢ P0
> **INCLUDES** allograft transplant recipient care

> 🔾 61.61   🔾 61.61   Global Days 090

48556 Removal of transplanted pancreatic allograft   C 80 ▢ P0
> 🔾 30.69   🔾 30.69   Global Days 090

48999 Unlisted procedure, pancreas   T 80
> 🔾 0.00   🔾 0.00   Global Days YYY
> AMA: 2007, Dec, 10-179

49000-49081 Exploratory and Drainage Procedures: Abdomen/Peritoneum

49000 Exploratory laparotomy, exploratory celiotomy with or without biopsy(s) (separate procedure)   C 80 ▢ P0
> **EXCLUDES** exploration of penetrating wound without laparotomy (20102)

> 🔾 19.37   🔾 19.37   Global Days 090
> AMA: 2008, Jan, 10-25; 2007, Jan, 13-27; 2007, Jan, 13-27; 2007, January, 13-27; 2006, Apr, 11-18; 2006, April, 11-18; 2006, Apr, 11-18

49002 Reopening of recent laparotomy   C 80 ▢ P0
> **EXCLUDES** hepatic wound re-exploration for packing removal (47362)

> 🔾 25.18   🔾 25.18   Global Days 090
> AMA: 2006, Apr, 11-18; 2006, Apr, 11-18; 2006, April, 11-10

49010 Exploration, retroperitoneal area with or without biopsy(s) (separate procedure)   C 80 ▢ P0
> **EXCLUDES** exploration of penetrating wound without laparotomy (20102)

> 🔾 23.87   🔾 23.87   Global Days 090
> AMA: 2007, Jun, 1-3; 2007, Jun, 1-3; 2007, June, 1-3; 2005, Jun, 6-8; 2005, June, 6-8; 2005, Jun, 6-8

49020 Drainage of peritoneal abscess or localized peritonitis, exclusive of appendiceal abscess; open   C 80 ▢ P0
> **EXCLUDES** appendiceal abscess (44900)

> 🔾 39.61   🔾 39.61   Global Days 090

⊙ **49021** percutaneous   T ▢
> ⊠ 75989
> 🔾 4.86   🔾 23.56   Global Days 000

49040 Drainage of subdiaphragmatic or subphrenic abscess; open   C 80 ▢ P0
> 🔾 24.80   🔾 24.80   Global Days 090

⊙ **49041** percutaneous   T ▢
> ⊠ 75989
> 🔾 5.75   🔾 24.06   Global Days 000

49060 Drainage of retroperitoneal abscess; open   C ▢ P0
> **EXCLUDES** drainage performed laparoscopically (49323)

> 🔾 27.71   🔾 27.71   Global Days 090
> AMA: 2008, Jan, 10-25; 2007, Jan, 13-27; 2007, Jan, 13-27; 2007, January, 13-27

⊙ **49061** percutaneous   T ▢
> **EXCLUDES** drainage performed laparoscopically (49323)

> ⊠ 75989
> 🔾 5.32   🔾 23.64   Global Days 000
> AMA: 2008, Jan, 10-25; 2007, Jan, 13-27; 2007, Jan, 13 27; 2007, January, 13-27

49062 Drainage of extraperitoneal lymphocele to peritoneal cavity, open   C 80 ▢
> 🔾 18.91   🔾 18.91   Global Days 090
> AMA: 2008, Jan, 10-25; 2007, Jan, 13-27; 2007, Jan, 13-27; 2007, January, 13-27

49080 Peritoneocentesis, abdominal paracentesis, or peritoneal lavage (diagnostic or therapeutic); initial   A2 T ▢
> ⊠ 76942, 77012
> 🔾 1.94   🔾 4.48   Global Days 000

49081 subsequent   A2 T ▢
> ⊠ 76942, 77012
> 🔾 1.83   🔾 4.19   Global Days 000

49180 Biopsy of Mass: Abdomen/Retroperitoneum

49180 Biopsy, abdominal or retroperitoneal mass, percutaneous needle   A2 T ▢ P0
> **EXCLUDES** aspiration, fine needle (10021, 10022)
> lysis of intestinal adhesions (44005)

> ⊠ 76942, 77002, 77012, 77021
> ⊠ 88172, 88173
> 🔾 2.49   🔾 4.50   Global Days 000

49203-49205 Open Destruction or Excision: Abdominal Tumors

EXCLUDES cryoablation of renal tumor (50250, 50593)
lysis of intestinal adhesions (44005)
primary, recurrent ovarian, uterine, or tubal resection (58957-58958)

Code also colectomy (44140)

Code also small bowel resection (44120)

Code also total nephrectomy (50220, or 50240)

Code also vena caval resection with reconstruction (37799)

Do not report with (38770, 38780, 49000, 49010, 49215, 50010, 50205, 50225, 50236, 50250, 50290, 58900-58960)

49203 Excision or destruction, open, intra-abdominal tumors, cysts or endometriomas, 1 or more peritoneal, mesenteric, or retroperitoneal primary or secondary tumors; largest tumor 5 cm diameter or less   C 80
> 🔾 30.30   🔾 30.30   Global Days 090

49204 largest tumor 5.1-10.0 cm diameter   C 80
> 🔾 38.70   🔾 38.70   Global Days 090

49205 largest tumor greater than 10.0 cm diameter   C 80
> 🔾 44.32   🔾 44.32   Global Days 090

49215 Resection Presacral/Sacrococcygeal Tumor

49215 Excision of presacral or sacrococcygeal tumor   C 80 63 ▢ P0
> 🔾 55.61   🔾 55.61   Global Days 090

● New Code   ▲ Revised Code   M Maternity Edit   Age Edit   A-Y OPPS Status Indicator   🔾 Facility RVU   🔾 Non-Facility RVU

▢ CCI Comprehensive Code   50 Bilateral Procedure   + Add-on Indicator   ⊠ Laboratory crosswalk   ⊠ Radiology crosswalk

49220 — 49428

49220-49255 Other Open Abdominal Procedures

EXCLUDES   *lysis of intestinal adhesions (44005)*

49220   Staging laparotomy for Hodgkins disease or lymphoma (includes splenectomy, needle or open biopsies of both liver lobes, possibly also removal of abdominal nodes, abdominal node and/or bone marrow biopsies, ovarian repositioning)   C 80 ▪ P0
         💰 24.20   ⚕ 24.20   Global Days 090

49250   Umbilectomy, omphalectomy, excision of umbilicus (separate procedure)   A2 T ▪ P0
         💰 14.45   ⚕ 14.45   Global Days 090

49255   Omentectomy, epiploectomy, resection of omentum (separate procedure)   C 80 ▪ P0
         💰 19.60   ⚕ 19.60   Global Days 090

49320-49329 Laparoscopic Procedures of the Abdomen/Peritoneum/Omentum

INCLUDES   diagnostic laparoscopy

EXCLUDES   *fulguration/excision of lesions of ovary/pelvic viscera/peritoneal surface, performed laparoscopically (58662)*

49320   Laparoscopy, abdomen, peritoneum, and omentum, diagnostic, with or without collection of specimen(s) by brushing or washing (separate procedure)   A2 T 80 ▪ P0
         💰 8.29   ⚕ 8.29   Global Days 010
         AMA: 2008, Jan, 10-25; 2007, Jan, 13-27; 2007, Jan, 13-27; 2007, Mar, 4-5; 2007, March, 4-5; 2007, January, 13-27; 2007, Mar, 4-5; 2006, Apr, 11-18; 2006, April, 19-20; 2006, April, 11-18; 2006, Apr, 11-18; 2006, Apr, 19-20; 2006, Apr, 19-20

49321   Laparoscopy, surgical; with biopsy (single or multiple)   A2 T 80 ▪ P0
         💰 8.73   ⚕ 8.73   Global Days 010

49322   with aspiration of cavity or cyst (eg, ovarian cyst) (single or multiple)   A2 T 80 ▪ P0
         💰 9.47   ⚕ 9.47   Global Days 010

49323   with drainage of lymphocele to peritoneal cavity   T 80 ▪ P0
         EXCLUDES   *retroperitoneal abscess drainage:*
                       open (49060)
                       percutaneous (49061)
         💰 16.08   ⚕ 16.08   Global Days 090
         AMA: 2008, Jan, 10-25; 2007, Jan, 13-27; 2007, Jan, 13-27; 2007, January, 13-27

49324   with insertion of intraperitoneal cannula or catheter, permanent   G2 T 80
         EXCLUDES   *open approach (49421)*

         Code also insertion of subcutaneous extension to intraperitoneal cannula with remote chest exit site, when appropriate (49435)
         💰 9.85   ⚕ 9.85   Global Days 010

49325   with revision of previously placed intraperitoneal cannula or catheter, with removal of intraluminal obstructive material if performed   G2 T 80
         💰 10.60   ⚕ 10.60   Global Days 010

+ 49326   with omentopexy (omental tacking procedure) (List separately in addition to code for primary procedure)   G2 T 80
         Code first laparoscopy with permanent intraperitoneal cannula or catheter insertion or revision of previously placed catheter/cannula (49324, 49325)
         💰 4.89   ⚕ 4.89   Global Days ZZZ

49329   Unlisted laparoscopy procedure, abdomen, peritoneum and omentum   T 80 50
         💰 0.00   ⚕ 0.00   Global Days YYY
         AMA: 2008, Jan, 10-25; 2007, Jan, 13-27; 2007, Jan, 13-27; 2007, January, 13-27

49400-49436 Peritoneal Procedures: Insertion/Modifications/Removal

49400   Injection of air or contrast into peritoneal cavity (separate procedure)   M N ▪
         Code also (49446)
         💰 2.71   ⚕ 4.70   Global Days 000

49402   Removal of peritoneal foreign body from peritoneal cavity   A2 T
         EXCLUDES   *enterolysis (44005)*
         💰 21.35   ⚕ 21.35   Global Days 090

49419   Insertion of intraperitoneal cannula or catheter, with subcutaneous reservoir, permanent (ie, totally implantable)   A2 T ▪
         EXCLUDES   *removal of catheter/cannula (49422)*
         Code also (C1788)
         💰 11.42   ⚕ 11.42   Global Days 090

49420   Insertion of intraperitoneal cannula or catheter for drainage or dialysis; temporary   A2 T ▪
         💰 3.61   ⚕ 3.61   Global Days 000

49421   permanent   A2 T ▪
         EXCLUDES   *laparoscopic approach (49324)*
         Code also insertion of subcutaneous extension to intraperitoneal cannula with remote chest exit site, when appropriate (49435)
         💰 9.81   ⚕ 9.81   Global Days 090
         AMA: 2008, Jan, 10-25; 2007, Jan, 13-27; 2007, Jan, 13-27; 2007, January, 13-27; 2006, May, 16-20; 2006, May, 16-20; 2006, May, 16-20

49422   Removal of permanent intraperitoneal cannula or catheter   A2 T ▪
         EXCLUDES   *removal temporary catheter or cannula (99201-99499)*
         💰 9.86   ⚕ 9.86   Global Days 010

49423   Exchange of previously placed abscess or cyst drainage catheter under radiological guidance (separate procedure)   G2 T 80 ▪
         Code also drainage catheter (C1729)
         🔁 75984
         💰 2.15   ⚕ 14.90   Global Days 000

49424   Contrast injection for assessment of abscess or cyst via previously placed drainage catheter or tube (separate procedure)   M N 80 ▪
         🔁 76080
         💰 1.12   ⚕ 4.05   Global Days 000
         AMA: 2008, Jan, 10-25; 2007, Jan, 13-27; 2007, Jan, 13-27; 2007, January, 13-27

49425   Insertion of peritoneal-venous shunt   C 80 ▪
         💰 19.23   ⚕ 19.23   Global Days 090

49426   Revision of peritoneal-venous shunt   A2 T ▪
         EXCLUDES   *shunt patency test (78291)*
         💰 16.37   ⚕ 16.37   Global Days 090

49427   Injection procedure (eg, contrast media) for evaluation of previously placed peritoneal-venous shunt   M N 80 ▪
         🔁 75809, 78291
         💰 1.30   ⚕ 1.30   Global Days 000

49428   Ligation of peritoneal-venous shunt   C ▪
         💰 11.00   ⚕ 11.00   Global Days 010

26/TC Professional/Technical Component Only   80/80 Assist-at-Surgery Allowed/With Documentation   Unlisted   Not Covered
AMA: CPT Assistant References   A2-T3 ASC Payment Indicator   ♂ Male Only   ♀ Female Only   ⃠ Modifier 51 Exempt   P0 PQRI

188   CPT only © 2008 American Medical Association. All Rights Reserved. (Black Ink)   Medicare (Red Ink)   © 2008 Ingenix *(Blue Ink)*

49429   Removal of peritoneal-venous shunt   62 T ▭
     🔗 11.67   ≷ 11.67   Global Days 010

+   49435   Insertion of subcutaneous extension to intraperitoneal cannula or catheter with remote chest exit site (List separately in addition to code for primary procedure)   T 80
     Code first permanent insertion of intraperitoneal catheter/cannula (49324, 49421)
     🔗 3.13   ≷ 3.13   Global Days ZZZ

49436   Delayed creation of exit site from embedded subcutaneous segment of intraperitoneal cannula or catheter   T 80
     🔗 4.58   ≷ 4.58   Global Days 010

49440-49442 Insertion of Percutaneous Gastrointestinal Tube

Do not report with (43752)

⊙   49440   Insertion of gastrostomy tube, percutaneous, under fluoroscopic guidance including contrast injection(s), image documentation and report   62 T 80
     EXCLUDES   *gastrostomy tube to gastrojejunostomy tube when gastrostomy first placed, report 49440 and (49446)*
     🔗 6.58   ≷ 29.09   Global Days 010
     AMA: 2008, Jan, 8-9; 2008, Jun, 8-11; 2007, Dec, 10-179

⊙   49441   Insertion of duodenostomy or jejunostomy tube, percutaneous, under fluoroscopic guidance including contrast injection(s), image documentation and report   62 T 80
     EXCLUDES   *gastrostrostomy tube to gastrojejunostomy tube conversion (49446)*
     🔗 7.18   ≷ 31.50   Global Days 010
     AMA: 2008, Jan, 8-9; 2008, Jun, 8-11; 2007, Dec, 10-179

⊙   49442   Insertion of cecostomy or other colonic tube, percutaneous, under fluoroscopic guidance including contrast injection(s), image documentation and report   T 80
     🔗 5.93   ≷ 28.23   Global Days 010
     AMA: 2008, Jan, 8-9; 2008, Jun, 8-11; 2007, Dec, 10-179

49446 Percutaneous Conversion: Gastrostomy to Gastro-jejunostomy Tube

⊙   49446   Conversion of gastrostomy tube to gastro-jejunostomy tube, percutaneous, under fluoroscopic guidance including contrast injection(s), image documentation and report   67 T 80
     EXCLUDES   *Gastrostomy tube to gastrojejunostomy tube conversion when gastrostomy tube first placed, report 49446 and (49440)*
     🔗 4.77   ≷ 26.36   Global Days 000
     AMA: 2008, Jun, 8-11; 2007, Dec, 10-179

49450-49452 Replacement Gastrointestinal Tube

EXCLUDES   *placement of new tube whether gastrostomy, jejunostomy, duodenostomy, gastro-jejunostomy, or cecostomy at different percutaneous site (49440-49442)*

49450   Replacement of gastrostomy or cecostomy (or other colonic) tube, percutaneous, under fluoroscopic guidance including contrast injection(s), image documentation and report   62 T 80
     🔗 1.91   ≷ 19.71   Global Days 000
     AMA: 2008, Jun, 8-11

49451   Replacement of duodenostomy or jejunostomy tube, percutaneous, under fluoroscopic guidance including contrast injection(s), image documentation and report   62 T 80
     🔗 2.66   ≷ 18.77   Global Days 000
     AMA: 2008, Jan, 8-9; 2008, Jun, 8-11; 2007, Dec, 10-179

49452   Replacement of gastro-jejunostomy tube, percutaneous, under fluoroscopic guidance including contrast injection(s), image documentation and report   62 T 80
     🔗 4.15   ≷ 23.65   Global Days 000
     AMA: 2008, Jun, 8-11

49460-49465 Removal of Obstruction/Injection for Contrast Through Gastrointestinal Tube

49460   Mechanical removal of obstructive material from gastrostomy, duodenostomy, jejunostomy, gastro-jejunostomy, or cecostomy (or other colonic) tube, any method, under fluoroscopic guidance including contrast injection(s), if performed, image documentation and report   62 T 80
     Do not report with (49450-49452, 49465)
     🔗 1.36   ≷ 21.60   Global Days 000
     AMA: 2008, Jun, 8-11

49465   Contrast injection(s) for radiological evaluation of existing gastrostomy, duodenostomy, jejunostomy, gastro-jejunostomy, or cecostomy (or other colonic) tube, from a percutaneous approach including image documentation and report   N1 91 80
     Do not report with (49450-49460)
     🔗 0.89   ≷ 4.52   Global Days 000
     AMA: 2008, Jun, 8-11

49491-49492 Inguinal Hernia Repair on Premature Infant

INCLUDES   hernia repairs done on preterm infants younger than or equal to 50 weeks postconception age but younger than 6 months of age since birth
     initial repair: no previous repair required
     mesh or other prosthesis

EXCLUDES   *abdominal wall debridement (11042, 11043)*
     intra-abdominal hernia repair/reduction (44050)

Code also repair or excision of testicle(s), intestine, ovaries if performed (44120, 54520, 58940)

49491   Repair, initial inguinal hernia, preterm infant (younger than 37 weeks gestation at birth), performed from birth up to 50 weeks postconception age, with or without hydrocelectomy; reducible   A T 80 50 ⊛ ▭
     🔗 19.28   ≷ 19.28   Global Days 090
     AMA: 2008, Jan, 10-25; 2008, Jun, 3-6; 2004, Mar, 1; 2004, Mar, 1; 2004, March, 1

49492   incarcerated or strangulated   A T 80 50 ⊛ ▭
     🔗 23.58   ≷ 23.58   Global Days 090
     AMA: 2008, Jun, 3-6; 2004, Mar, 1; 2004, Mar, 1; 2004, March, 1

Digestive

49495-49557 Hernia Repair: Femoral/Inguinal /Lumbar

INCLUDES   initial repair: no previous repair required
            mesh or other prosthesis
            recurrent repair: required previous repair(s)

EXCLUDES   *abdominal wall debridement (11042, 11043)*
            intra-abdominal hernia repair/reduction (44050)

Code also repair or excision of testicle(s), intestine, ovaries if performed (44120, 54520, 58940)

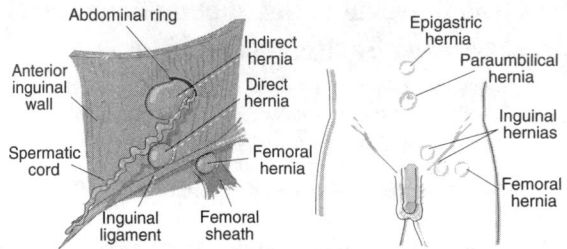

A hernia is a protrusion, usually through an abdominal wall containment. Often, hernias are congenital. Groin hernias are common among both sexes and all age groups. In males, indirect hernias are often associated with incomplete closure of the path the testicle takes as it descends just prior to birth (the processus vaginalis). Direct hernias simply protrude through the wall. Femoral hernias occur below the inguinal ligament. Strangulation and necrosis of the protruding bowel section can occur. Umbilical hernias are often linked to incomplete closure of the umbilicus.

49495   **Repair, initial inguinal hernia, full term infant younger than age 6 months, or preterm infant older than 50 weeks postconception age and younger than age 6 months at the time of surgery, with or without hydrocelectomy; reducible**   A A2 T 80 50 ⊗ ▢

INCLUDES   hernia repairs done on preterm infants older than 50 weeks postconception age and younger than 6 months

⏢ 9.82   ⚲ 9.82   **Global Days 090**
AMA: 2008, Jan, 10-25; 2008, Jun, 3-6; 2007, Jan, 13-27; 2007, Jan, 13-27; 2007, January, 13-27; 2004, May, 14; 2004, May, 14; 2004, Jan, 27; 2004, Jan, 27; 2004, May, 14; 2004, March, 1; 2004, January, 27; 2004, March, 10; 2004, Mar, 10; 2004, Mar, 10; 2004, Mar, 1; 2004, Mar, 1

49496   **incarcerated or strangulated**   A A2 T 80 50 ⊗ ▢

INCLUDES   hernia repairs done on preterm infants older than 50 weeks postconception age and younger than 6 months

⏢ 14.88   ⚲ 14.88   **Global Days 090**
AMA: 2008, Jan, 10-25; 2008, Jun, 3-6; 2007, Jan, 13-27; 2007, Jan, 13-27; 2007, January, 13-27; 2004, Mar, 1; 2004, Mar, 1; 2004, May, 14; 2004, May, 14; 2004, May, 14; 2004, January, 27; 2004, March, 1; 2004, March, 10; 2004, Mar, 10; 2004, Mar, 10; 2004, Jan, 27; 2004, Jan, 27

49500   **Repair initial inguinal hernia, age 6 months to younger than 5 years, with or without hydrocelectomy; reducible**   A A2 T 80 50 ▢

INCLUDES   repairs performed on patients 6 months to younger than 5 years old

⏢ 9.77   ⚲ 9.77   **Global Days 090**
AMA: 2008, Jan, 10-25; 2008, Jun, 3-6; 2007, Jan, 13-27; 2007, Jan, 13-27; 2007, January, 13-27; 2004, Mar, 10; 2004, Mar, 10; 2004, Jan, 27; 2004, January, 27; 2004, March, 1; 2004, March, 10; 2004, Jan, 27; 2004, Mar, 1; 2004, Mar, 1

49501   **incarcerated or strangulated**   A A2 T 80 50 ▢

INCLUDES   repairs performed on patients 6 months to younger than 5 years old

⏢ 14.79   ⚲ 14.79   **Global Days 090**
AMA: 2008, Jan, 10-25; 2008, Jun, 3-6; 2007, Jan, 13-27; 2007, Jan, 13-27; 2007, January, 13-27; 2004, Jan, 27; 2004, Jan, 27; 2004, Mar, 10; 2004, March, 1; 2004, January, 27; 2004, March, 10; 2004, Mar, 10; 2004, Mar, 1; 2004, Mar, 1

49505   **Repair initial inguinal hernia, age 5 years or older; reducible**   A2 T 80 50 ▢

INCLUDES   MacEwen hernia repair

Code also when performed:
   excision of hydrocele (55040)
   excision of spermatocele (54840)
   simple orchiectomy (54520)
⏢ 12.84   ⚲ 12.84   **Global Days 090**
AMA: 2008, Jan, 10-25; 2008, Jun, 3-6; 2007, Jan, 13-27; 2007, Jan, 13-27; 2007, January, 13-27; 2004, Jan, 27; 2004, Jan, 27; 2004, Mar, 10; 2004, March, 10; 2004, March, 1; 2004, January, 27; 2004, Mar, 10; 2004, Mar, 1; 2004, Mar, 1

49507   **incarcerated or strangulated**   A A2 T 80 50 ▢

Code also when performed:
   excision of hydrocele (55040)
   excision of spermatocele (54840)
   simple orchiectomy (54520)
⏢ 15.80   ⚲ 15.80   **Global Days 090**
AMA: 2008, Jan, 10-25; 2008, Jun, 3-6; 2007, Jan, 13-27; 2007, Jan, 13-27; 2007, January, 13-27; 2004, Jan, 27; 2004, Jan, 27; 2004, Mar, 10; 2004, March, 1; 2004, January, 27; 2004, March, 10; 2004, Mar, 10; 2004, Mar, 1; 2004, Mar, 1

49520   **Repair recurrent inguinal hernia, any age; reducible**   A2 T 80 50 ▢

⏢ 15.69   ⚲ 15.69   **Global Days 090**
AMA: 2008, Jan, 10-25; 2008, Jun, 3-6; 2007, Jan, 13-27; 2007, Jan, 13-27; 2007, January, 13-27; 2004, Mar, 10; 2004, Mar, 10; 2004, Jan, 27; 2004, March, 1; 2004, January, 27; 2004, March, 10; 2004, Jan, 27; 2004, Mar, 1; 2004, Mar, 1

49521   **incarcerated or strangulated**   A2 T 80 50 ▢

⏢ 19.14   ⚲ 19.14   **Global Days 090**
AMA: 2008, Jan, 10-25; 2008, Jun, 3-6; 2007, Jan, 13-27; 2007, Jan, 13-27; 2007, January, 13-27; 2004, Mar, 1; 2004, Mar, 1; 2004, Jan, 27; 2004, March, 1; 2004, January, 27; 2004, March, 10; 2004, Jan, 27; 2004, Mar, 10; 2004, Mar, 10

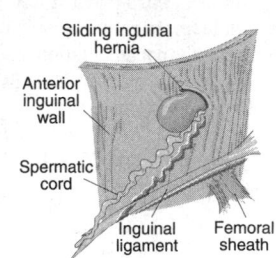

Patient may be of either sex and of any age

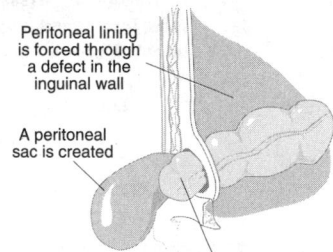

In 49525, a sliding inguinal hernia (depicted above, right) is repaired in a patient of any age

49495 — 49521

49525   **Repair inguinal hernia, sliding, any age**   A2 T 80 50 🔲

     EXCLUDES   *inguinal hernia repair, incarcerated/strangulated (49496, 49501, 49507, 49521)*

     🚗 14.18   ✂ 14.18   Global Days 090

     AMA: 2008, Jan, 10-25; 2008, Jun, 3-6; 2007, Jan, 13-27; 2007, Jan, 13-27; 2007, January, 13-27; 2004, Mar, 10; 2004, Mar, 10; 2004, Jan, 27; 2004, March, 1; 2004, January, 27; 2004, March, 10; 2004, Jan, 27; 2004, Mar, 1; 2004, Mar, 1

49540   **Repair lumbar hernia**   A2 T 80 50 🔲

     🚗 16.78   ✂ 16.78   Global Days 090

     AMA: 2008, Jun, 3-6; 2004, Mar, 1; 2004, Mar, 1; 2004, March, 1

49550   **Repair initial femoral hernia, any age; reducible**   A2 T 80 50 🔲

     🚗 14.25   ✂ 14.25   Global Days 090

     AMA: 2008, Jun, 3-6; 2004, Mar, 1; 2004, Mar, 1; 2004, March, 1

49553   **incarcerated or strangulated**   A2 T 80 50 🔲

     🚗 15.59   ✂ 15.59   Global Days 090

     AMA: 2008, Jun, 3-6; 2004, Mar, 1; 2004, Mar, 1; 2004, March, 1

49555   **Repair recurrent femoral hernia; reducible**   A2 T 80 50 🔲

     🚗 14.84   ✂ 14.84   Global Days 090

     AMA: 2008, Jun, 3-6; 2004, Mar, 1; 2004, Mar, 1; 2004, March, 1

49557   **incarcerated or strangulated**   A2 T 80 50 🔲

     🚗 18.02   ✂ 18.02   Global Days 090

     AMA: 2008, Jun, 3-6; 2004, Mar, 1; 2004, Mar, 1; 2004, March, 1

49560-49568 Hernia Repair: Incisional/Ventral

INCLUDES   initial repair: no previous repair required
     recurrent repair: required previous repair(s)

EXCLUDES   *abdominal wall debridement (11042, 11043)*
     intra-abdominal hernia repair/reduction (44050)

Code also repair or excision of testicle(s), intestine, ovaries if performed (44120, 54520, 58940)

49560   **Repair initial incisional or ventral hernia; reducible**   A2 T 80 50 🔲 P0

     Code also implantation of mesh or other prosthesis if performed (49568)

     🚗 18.43   ✂ 18.43   Global Days 090

     AMA: 2008, Jun, 3-6; 2004, Mar, 1; 2004, Mar, 1; 2004, March, 1

49561   **incarcerated or strangulated**   A2 T 80 50 🔲 P0

     Code also implantation of mesh or other prosthesis if performed (49568)

     🚗 23.23   ✂ 23.23   Global Days 090

     AMA: 2008, Jun, 3-6; 2004, Mar, 1; 2004, Mar, 1; 2004, March, 1

49565   **Repair recurrent incisional or ventral hernia; reducible**   A2 T 80 50 🔲 P0

     Code also implantation of mesh or other prosthesis if performed (49568)

     🚗 19.09   ✂ 19.09   Global Days 090

     AMA: 2008, Jun, 3-6; 2004, Mar, 1; 2004, Mar, 1; 2004, March, 1

49566   **incarcerated or strangulated**   A2 T 80 50 🔲 P0

     Code also implantation of mesh or other prosthesis if performed (49568)

     🚗 23.47   ✂ 23.47   Global Days 090

     AMA: 2008, Jun, 3-6; 2004, Mar, 1; 2004, Mar, 1; 2004, March, 1

+ ▲ **49568**   **Implantation of mesh or other prosthesis for open incisional or ventral hernia repair or mesh for closure of debridement for necrotizing soft tissue infection (List separately in addition to code for the incisional or ventral hernia repair)**   A2 T 80 🔲 P0

     Code first hernia repair, incisional/ventral (49560-49566)

     🚗 6.94   ✂ 6.94   Global Days ZZZ

     AMA: 2008, Jan, 10-25; 2008, Jun, 3-6; 2007, Jan, 13-27; 2007, Jan, 13-27; 2007, January, 13-27; 2005, Nov, 14-15; 2005, Nov, 14-15; 2005, November, 14-15; 2004, Mar, 1; 2004, Mar, 1; 2004, March, 1

49570-49590 Hernia Repair: Epigastric/Lateral Ventral/Umbilical

INCLUDES   mesh or other prosthesis

EXCLUDES   *abdominal wall debridement (11042, 11043)*
     intra-abdominal hernia repair/reduction (44050)

Code also repair or excision of testicle(s), intestine, ovaries if performed (44120, 54520, 58940)

49570   **Repair epigastric hernia (eg, preperitoneal fat); reducible (separate procedure)**   A2 T 80 50 🔲 P0

     🚗 10.09   ✂ 10.09   Global Days 090

     AMA: 2008, Jun, 3-6; 2004, Mar, 1; 2004, Mar, 1; 2004, March, 1

49572   **incarcerated or strangulated**   A2 T 80 50 🔲

     🚗 12.48   ✂ 12.48   Global Days 090

     AMA: 2008, Jun, 3-6; 2004, Mar, 1; 2004, Mar, 1; 2004, March, 1

49580   **Repair umbilical hernia, younger than age 5 years; reducible**   A A2 T 80 🔲

     🚗 7.85   ✂ 7.85   Global Days 090

     AMA: 2008, Jun, 3-6; 2004, Mar, 1; 2004, Mar, 1; 2004, March, 1

49582   **incarcerated or strangulated**   A A2 T 80 🔲

     🚗 11.67   ✂ 11.67   Global Days 090

     AMA: 2008, Jun, 3-6; 2004, Mar, 1; 2004, Mar, 1; 2004, March, 1

49585   **Repair umbilical hernia, age 5 years or older; reducible**   A A2 T 80 🔲

     INCLUDES   Mayo hernia repair

     🚗 10.85   ✂ 10.85   Global Days 090

     AMA: 2008, Jun, 3-6; 2004, Mar, 1; 2004, Mar, 1; 2004, March, 1

49587   **incarcerated or strangulated**   A A2 T 80 🔲

     🚗 12.86   ✂ 12.86   Global Days 090

     AMA: 2008, Jun, 3-6; 2004, Mar, 1; 2004, Mar, 1; 2004, March, 1

49590   **Repair spigelian hernia**   A2 T 80 50 🔲

     🚗 14.13   ✂ 14.13   Global Days 090

     AMA: 2008, Jun, 3-6; 2004, Mar, 1; 2004, Mar, 1; 2004, March, 1

● New Code   ▲ Revised Code   M Maternity Edit   A Age Edit   A-Y OPPS Status Indicator   🚗 Facility RVU   ✂ Non-Facility RVU

🔲 CCI Comprehensive Code   50 Bilateral Procedure   + Add-on Indicator   ◼ Laboratory crosswalk   ◼ Radiology crosswalk

Digestive

49600 — 49999

49600-49611 Repair Birth Defect Abdominal Wall: Omphalocele/Gastroschisis

INCLUDES mesh or other prosthesis

EXCLUDES abdominal wall debridement (11042, 11043)
intra-abdominal hernia repair/reduction (44050)
repair of:
diaphragmatic or hiatal hernia (39502-39541)
omentum (49999)

49600 Repair of small omphalocele, with primary closure A2 T 80 ♂ ▭
🗁 18.19 ⚕ 18.19 Global Days 090
AMA: 2008, Jun, 3-6; 2004, Mar, 1; 2004, Mar, 1; 2004, March, 1

49605 Repair of large omphalocele or gastroschisis; with or without prosthesis C 80 ♂ ▭
🗁 125.57 ⚕ 125.57 Global Days 090
AMA: 2008, Jun, 3-6; 2004, Mar, 1; 2004, Mar, 1; 2004, March, 1

49606 with removal of prosthesis, final reduction and closure, in operating room C 80 ♂ ▭
🗁 28.56 ⚕ 28.56 Global Days 090
AMA: 2008, Jun, 3-6; 2004, Mar, 1; 2004, Mar, 1; 2004, March, 1

49610 Repair of omphalocele (Gross type operation); first stage C 80 ♂ ▭
🗁 16.86 ⚕ 16.86 Global Days 090
AMA: 2008, Jun, 3-6; 2004, Mar, 1; 2004, Mar, 1; 2004, March, 1

49611 second stage C 80 ♂ ▭
🗁 15.14 ⚕ 15.14 Global Days 090
AMA: 2008, Jan, 10-25; 2008, Jun, 3-6; 2004, Mar, 1; 2004, Mar, 1; 2004, March, 1

49650-49659 Laparoscopic Hernia Repair

INCLUDES diagnostic laparoscopy

49650 Laparoscopy, surgical; repair initial inguinal hernia A2 T 80 50 ▭
🗁 10.60 ⚕ 10.60 Global Days 090
AMA: 2008, Jun, 3-6; 2004, Mar, 1; 2004, Mar, 1; 2004, March, 1

49651 repair recurrent inguinal hernia A2 T 80 50 ▭
🗁 13.68 ⚕ 13.68 Global Days 090
AMA: 2008, Jun, 3-6; 2004, Mar, 1; 2004, Mar, 1; 2004, March, 1

● 49652 Laparoscopy, surgical, repair, ventral, umbilical, spigelian or epigastric hernia (includes mesh insertion, when performed); reducible 62 T 80 50
Do not report with (44180, 49568)
🗁 19.87 ⚕ 19.87 Global Days 090

● 49653 incarcerated or strangulated 62 T 80 50
Do not report with (44180, 49568)
🗁 24.80 ⚕ 24.80 Global Days 090

● 49654 Laparoscopy, surgical, repair, incisional hernia (includes mesh insertion, when performed); reducible 62 T 80 50
Do not report with (44180, 49568)
🗁 22.80 ⚕ 22.80 Global Days 090

● 49655 incarcerated or strangulated 62 T 80 50
Do not report with (44180, 49568)
🗁 27.45 ⚕ 27.45 Global Days 090

● 49656 Laparoscopy, surgical, repair, recurrent incisional hernia (includes mesh insertion, when performed); reducible 62 T 80 50
Do not report with (44180, 49568)
🗁 22.89 ⚕ 22.89 Global Days 090

● 49657 incarcerated or strangulated 62 T 80 50
Do not report with (44180, 49568)
🗁 33.05 ⚕ 33.05 Global Days 090

49659 Unlisted laparoscopy procedure, hernioplasty, herniorrhaphy, herniotomy T 80 50
🗁 0.00 ⚕ 0.00 Global Days YYY
AMA: 2008, Jan, 10-25; 2008, Jun, 3-6; 2007, Jan, 13-27; 2007, Jan, 13-27; 2007, January, 13-27; 2005, Nov, 14-15; 2005, November, 14-15; 2005, Nov, 14-15

49900 Surgical Repair Abdominal Wall

EXCLUDES abdominal wall debridement (11042, 11043)
suture of ruptured diaphragm (39540, 39541)

49900 Suture, secondary, of abdominal wall for evisceration or dehiscence C 80 ▭
🗁 20.29 ⚕ 20.29 Global Days 090

49904-49999 Harvesting of Omental Flap

49904 Omental flap, extra-abdominal (eg, for reconstruction of sternal and chest wall defects) C ▭
INCLUDES harvest and transfer
EXCLUDES omental flap harvest by second surgeon: both surgeons code 49904 with modifier 62
🗁 37.73 ⚕ 37.73 Global Days 090

+ 49905 Omental flap, intra-abdominal (List separately in addition to code for primary procedure) C 80 ▭
Code first primary procedure
Do not report with (44700)
🗁 9.23 ⚕ 9.23 Global Days ZZZ
AMA: 2008, Jan, 10-25; 2007, Jan, 13-27; 2007, Jan, 13-27; 2007, January, 13-27

49906 Free omental flap with microvascular anastomosis C ▭
INCLUDES operating microscope (69990)
🗁 0.00 ⚕ 0.00 Global Days 090

49999 Unlisted procedure, abdomen, peritoneum and omentum T
🗁 0.00 ⚕ 0.00 Global Days YYY
AMA: 2008, Jun, 3-6; 2006, May, 16-20; 2006, May, 16-20; 2006, May, 16-20

50010-50045 Kidney Procedures for Exploration or Drainage

EXCLUDES retroperitoneal
    abscess drainage (49060)
    exploration (49010)
    tumor/cyst excision (49203-49205)

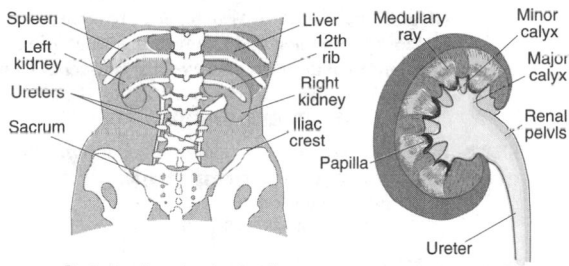

Posterior view showing location of kidneys and ureters

Cutaway view of right kidney showing internal structures

The kidneys remove waste products of protein metabolism and other excess materials and fluids from the blood. Variations in kidney anatomy are fairly common, though abnormalities can complicate procedures. "Pyelo" refers to the renal pelvis, an important access site to the inner kidney. Each kidney is imbedded in a mass of peritoneal fat that helps to enclose and position it

50010 **Renal exploration, not necessitating other specific procedures** ◯ 00 ▭
    EXCLUDES Laparoscopic ablation of mass lesions of kidney (50542)
    ⚷ 19.65   ✂ 19.65   Global Days 090

50020 **Drainage of perirenal or renal abscess; open** T ▭ P0
    ⚷ 28.02   ✂ 28.02   Global Days 090

⊙ **50021** **percutaneous** T ▭
    ▦ 75989
    ⚷ 4.85   ✂ 24.79   Global Days 000

50040 **Nephrostomy, nephrotomy with drainage** C ▭
    ⚷ 26.34   ✂ 26.34   Global Days 090

50045 **Nephrotomy, with exploration** C 80 ▭
    EXCLUDES renal endoscopy through nephrotomy (50570-50580)
    ⚷ 26.66   ✂ 26.66   Global Days 090

50060-50081 Treatment of Kidney Stones

CMS 100-3,230.1   *Treatment of Kidney Stones*
EXCLUDES retroperitoneal
    abscess drainage (49060)
    exploration (49010)
    tumor/cyst excision (49203-49205)

50060 **Nephrolithotomy; removal of calculus** C 80 ▭
    ⚷ 32.77   ✂ 32.77   Global Days 090

50065 **secondary surgical operation for calculus** C 80 ▭
    ⚷ 34.49   ✂ 34.49   Global Days 090

50070 **complicated by congenital kidney abnormality** C 80 ▭
    ⚷ 34.25   ✂ 34.25   Global Days 090

50075 **removal of large staghorn calculus filling renal pelvis and calyces (including anatrophic pyelolithotomy)** C 80 ▭
    ⚷ 42.11   ✂ 42.11   Global Days 090

50080 **Percutaneous nephrostolithotomy or pyelostolithotomy, with or without dilation, endoscopy, lithotripsy, stenting, or basket extraction; up to 2 cm** T 50 ▭
    EXCLUDES nephrostomy without nephrostolithotomy (50040, 50395, 52334)
    ⚷ 25.04   ✂ 25.04   Global Days 090

50081 **over 2 cm** T 80 50 ▭
    EXCLUDES nephrostomy without nephrostolithotomy (50040, 50395, 52334)
    ▦ 76000, 76001
    ⚷ 36.77   ✂ 36.77   Global Days 090

50100 Repair of Anomalous Vessels of the Kidney

EXCLUDES retroperitoneal:
    abscess drainage (49060)
    exploration (49010)
    tumor/cyst excision (49203-49205)

50100 **Transection or repositioning of aberrant renal vessels (separate procedure)** C 80 ▭
    ⚷ 27.09   ✂ 27.09   Global Days 090

50120-50135 Procedures of Renal Pelvis

EXCLUDES retroperitoneal:
    abscess drainage (49060)
    exploration (49010)
    tumor/cyst excision (49203-49205)

50120 **Pyelotomy; with exploration** C 80 50 ▭
    INCLUDES Gol-Vernet pyelotomy
    EXCLUDES renal endoscopy through pyelotomy (50570-50580)
    ⚷ 27.16   ✂ 27.16   Global Days 090

50125 **with drainage, pyelostomy** C 80 50 ▭
    ⚷ 28.14   ✂ 28.14   Global Days 090

50130 **with removal of calculus (pyelolithotomy, pelviolithotomy, including coagulum pyelolithotomy)** C 80 50 ▭
    ⚷ 29.69   ✂ 29.69   Global Days 090

50135 **complicated (eg, secondary operation, congenital kidney abnormality)** C 80 50 ▭
    ⚷ 32.15   ✂ 32.15   Global Days 090

50200-50205 Biopsy of Kidney

CMS 100-3,190.4   *Electron Microscope*
EXCLUDES laparoscopic renal mass lesion ablation (50542)
    retroperitoneal tumor/cyst excision (49203-49205)

50200 **Renal biopsy; percutaneous, by trocar or needle** A2 T 50 ▭
    EXCLUDES evaluation of fine needle aspirate (88172, 88173)
    fine needle aspiration (10022)
    ▦ 76942, 77002, 77012, 77021
    ⚷ 4.06   ✂ 4.06   Global Days 000

50205 **by surgical exposure of kidney** C 80 50 ▭
    ⚷ 10.03   ✂ 10.03   Global Days 000

50220-50240 Nephrectomy Procedures

EXCLUDES retroperitoneal tumor/cyst excision (49203-49205)

50220 **Nephrectomy, including partial ureterectomy, any open approach including rib resection;** C 80 50 ▭ P0
    ⚷ 29.27   ✂ 29.27   Global Days 090

50225 **complicated because of previous surgery on same kidney** C 80 50 ▭ P0
    ⚷ 33.88   ✂ 33.88   Global Days 090

● New Code   ▲ Revised Code   M Maternity Edit   A Age Edit   A-Y OPPS Status Indicator   ⚷ Facility RVU   ✂ Non-Facility RVU
▭ CCI Comprehensive Code   50 Bilateral Procedure   + Add-on Indicator   ▨ Laboratory crosswalk   ▦ Radiology crosswalk

50230 radical, with regional lymphadenectomy and/or vena caval thrombectomy [C] [80] [50] [⊡] [P0]
    EXCLUDES *vena caval resection with reconstruction (37799)*

    🔁 36.71   ⚕ 36.71   Global Days 090

50234 Nephrectomy with total ureterectomy and bladder cuff; through same incision [C] [80] [⊡] [P0]
    🔁 37.28   ⚕ 37.28   Global Days 090

50236 through separate incision [C] [80] [⊡] [P0]
    🔁 42.19   ⚕ 42.19   Global Days 090

50240 Nephrectomy, partial [C] [80] [⊡] [P0]
    EXCLUDES *laparoscopic partial nephrectomy (50543)*

    🔁 37.88   ⚕ 37.88   Global Days 090
    AMA: 2005, Apr, 10-12; 2005, Apr, 10-12; 2005, April, 10-12

50250-50290 Open Removal Kidney Lesions

50250 Ablation, open, 1 or more renal mass lesion(s), cryosurgical, including intraoperative ultrasound, if performed [C] [80]
    open destruction or excision intra-abdominal tumors (49203-49205)

    EXCLUDES *cryoablation of renal tumors (50593)*
    laparoscopic renal mass lesion ablation (50542)

    🔁 35.14   ⚕ 35.14   Global Days 090
    AMA: 2008, Jan, 10-25; 2007, Jan, 13-27; 2007, Jan, 13-27; 2007, January, 13-27; 2006, May, 16-20; 2006, May, 16-20; 2006, May, 16-20

50280 Excision or unroofing of cyst(s) of kidney [C] [80] [⊡]
    EXCLUDES *renal cyst laparoscopic ablation (50541)*

    🔁 27.04   ⚕ 27.04   Global Days 090

50290 Excision of perinephric cyst [C] [80] [⊡]
    open destruction or excision intra-abdominal tumors (49203-49205)

    🔁 25.04   ⚕ 25.04   Global Days 090

50300-50380 Kidney Transplant Procedures

CMS *100-3,260.7*   *Lymphocyte Immune Globulin, Anti-Thymocyte Globulin (Equine)*
CMS *100-3,190.1*   *Histocompatibility Testing*
CMS *100-3,110.16*   *Nonselective (Random) Transfusions and Living-Related Donor Specific Transfusions (DST) in Kidney Transplantation*
CMS *100-3,20.3*   *Thoracic Duct Drainage (TDD) in Renal Transplants*
CMS *100-4,3,90.1.2*   *Billing for Kidney Transplant and Acquisition Services*
CMS *100-4,3,90.1.1*   *Standard Kidney Acquisition Charge*
CMS *100-4,3,90.1*   *Kidney Transplant - General*
    lymphocele drainage to peritoneal cavity performed laparoscopically (49323)

50300 Donor nephrectomy (including cold preservation); from cadaver donor, unilateral or bilateral [C] [⊡] [P0]
    INCLUDES graft:
        cold preservation
        harvesting

    🔁 0.00   ⚕ 0.00   Global Days XXX
    AMA: 2005, Apr, 10-12; 2005, Apr, 10-12; 2005, April, 10-12

50320 open, from living donor [C] [80] [50] [⊡] [P0]
    INCLUDES donor care
    graft:
        cold preservation
        harvesting

    EXCLUDES *donor nephrectomy performed laparoscopically (50547)*

    🔁 37.09   ⚕ 37.09   Global Days 090

50323 Backbench standard preparation of cadaver donor renal allograft prior to transplantation, including dissection and removal of perinephric fat, diaphragmatic and retroperitoneal attachments, excision of adrenal gland, and preparation of ureter(s), renal vein(s), and renal artery(s), ligating branches, as necessary [C] [80] [⊡]
    Do not report with (60540, 60545)

    🔁 0.00   ⚕ 0.00   Global Days XXX
    AMA: 2005, Apr, 10-12; 2005, Apr, 10-12; 2005, April, 10-12

50325 Backbench standard preparation of living donor renal allograft (open or laparoscopic) prior to transplantation, including dissection and removal of perinephric fat and preparation of ureter(s), renal vein(s), and renal artery(s), ligating branches, as necessary [C] [80] [⊡]
    🔁 0.00   ⚕ 0.00   Global Days XXX

50327 Backbench reconstruction of cadaver or living donor renal allograft prior to transplantation; venous anastomosis, each [C] [80] [⊡]
    🔁 5.52   ⚕ 5.52   Global Days XXX

50328 arterial anastomosis, each [C] [80] [⊡]
    🔁 4.85   ⚕ 4.85   Global Days XXX

50329 ureteral anastomosis, each [C] [80] [⊡]
    🔁 4.79   ⚕ 4.79   Global Days XXX

50340 Recipient nephrectomy (separate procedure) [C] [80] [50] [⊡] [P0]
    🔁 22.93   ⚕ 22.93   Global Days 090

50360 Renal allotransplantation, implantation of graft; without recipient nephrectomy [C] [80] [⊡] [P0]
    INCLUDES allograft transplantation recipient care

    🔁 62.61   ⚕ 62.61   Global Days 090

50365 with recipient nephrectomy [C] [80] [50] [⊡] [P0]
    INCLUDES allograft transplantation recipient care

    🔁 70.57   ⚕ 70.57   Global Days 090
    AMA: 2005, Apr, 10-12; 2005, Apr, 10-12; 2005, April, 10-12

50370 Removal of transplanted renal allograft [C] [80] [⊡] [P0]
    🔁 29.24   ⚕ 29.24   Global Days 090

50380 Renal autotransplantation, reimplantation of kidney [C] [80] [⊡] [P0]
    INCLUDES reimplantation of autograft

    Code also nephrolithotomy (50060-50075)
    Code also partial nephrectomy (50240, 50543)
    🔁 49.39   ⚕ 49.39   Global Days 090
    AMA: 2005, Apr, 10-12; 2005, Apr, 10-12; 2005, April, 10-12

50382-50386 Removal With/Without Replacement Internal Ureteral Stent

INCLUDES radiological supervision and interpretation

⊙   **50382** Removal (via snare/capture) and replacement of internally dwelling ureteral stent via percutaneous approach, including radiological supervision and interpretation [62] [T] [50]
    Do not report with (50395)

    EXCLUDES *removal and replacement of an internally dwelling ureteral stent using a transurethral approach (50385)*

    🔁 8.03   ⚕ 34.91   Global Days 000
    AMA: 2008, Oct, 8-9; 2006, Sep, 1-4; 2006, Sep, 1-4; 2006, September, 1-4

⊙ **50384** Removal (via snare/capture) of internally dwelling ureteral stent via percutaneous approach, including radiological supervision and interpretation ⬚62⬚ ⬚T⬚ ⬚50⬚

     Do not report with (50395)

     EXCLUDES   *removal of an internally dwelling ureteral stent using a transurethral approach (50386)*

     🔧 7.31   ✂ 30.03   Global Days 000

     AMA: 2008, Oct, 8-9; 2006, Sep, 1-4; 2006, Sep, 1-4; 2006, September, 1-4

⊙ **50385** Removal (via snare/capture) and replacement of internally dwelling ureteral stent via transurethral approach, without use of cystoscopy, including radiological supervision and interpretation ⬚62⬚ ⬚T⬚ ⬚80⬚ ⬚50⬚

     🔧 6.86   ✂ 34.15   Global Days 000

     AMA: 2008, Oct, 8-9

⊙ **50386** Removal (via snare/capture) of internally dwelling ureteral stent via transurethral approach, without use of cystoscopy, including radiological supervision and interpretation ⬚62⬚ ⬚T⬚ ⬚80⬚ ⬚50⬚

     🔧 5.18   ✂ 22.14   Global Days 000

     AMA: 2008, Oct, 8-9

50387 Remove/Replace Accessible Ureteral Stent

CMS 100-4,4,61.2   *Requirements for Specific Procedures to be Repoted With Device Codes*

EXCLUDES   *removal and replacement of ureterostomy tube or externally accessible ureteral stent via ileal conduit (50688)*

removal without replacement of externally accessible ureteral stent without fluoroscopic guidance (99201-99499)

⊙ **50387** Removal and replacement of externally accessible transnephric ureteral stent (eg, external/internal stent) requiring fluoroscopic guidance, including radiological supervision and interpretation ⬚62⬚ ⬚T⬚ ⬚80⬚ ⬚50⬚

     Code also (C1875, C1877, C2617, C2625)

     🔧 2.91   ✂ 16.15   Global Days 000

     AMA: 2006, Sep, 1-4; 2006, Sep, 1-4; 2006, September, 1-4

50389-50398 Percutaneous and Injection Procedures With/Without Indwelling Tube/Catheter Access

50389 Removal of nephrostomy tube, requiring fluoroscopic guidance (eg, with concurrent indwelling ureteral stent) ⬚62⬚ ⬚T⬚ ⬚50⬚

     EXCLUDES   *nephrostomy tube removal without fluoroscopic guidance (99201-99499)*

     🔧 1.60   ✂ 9.37   Global Days 000

     AMA: 2006, Sep, 1-4; 2006, Sep, 1-4; 2006, September, 1-4

50390 Aspiration and/or injection of renal cyst or pelvis by needle, percutaneous ⬚A2⬚ ⬚T⬚ ⬚50⬚ 🗗

     ⬚⬚ *74425, 74470, 76942, 77002, 77012, 77021*

     ⬚⬚ *88172-88173*

     🔧 2.83   ✂ 2.83   Global Days 000

     AMA: 2008, Oct, 8-9; 2005, Oct, 18-22; 2005, Oct, 18-22; 2005, October, 18-22

50391 Instillation(s) of therapeutic agent into renal pelvis and/or ureter through established nephrostomy, pyelostomy or ureterostomy tube (eg, anticarcinogenic or antifungal agent) ⬚P2⬚ ⬚T⬚ 🗗

     🔧 2.89   ✂ 3.64   Global Days 000

     AMA: 2005, Oct, 18-22; 2005, Oct, 18-22; 2005, October, 18-22

50392 Introduction of intracatheter or catheter into renal pelvis for drainage and/or injection, percutaneous ⬚A2⬚ ⬚T⬚ ⬚50⬚ 🗗

     ⬚⬚ *74475, 76942, 77012*

     🔧 5.19   ✂ 5.19   Global Days 000

     AMA: 2008, Oct, 8-9; 2005, Oct, 18-22; 2005, Oct, 18-22; 2005, October, 18-22

50393 Introduction of ureteral catheter or stent into ureter through renal pelvis for drainage and/or injection, percutaneous ⬚A2⬚ ⬚T⬚ ⬚50⬚ 🗗

     ⬚⬚ *74480, 76942, 77002, 77012*

     🔧 6.33   ✂ 6.33   Global Days 000

     AMA: 2005, Oct, 18-22; 2005, Oct, 18-22; 2005, October, 18-22

50394 Injection procedure for pyelography (as nephrostogram, pyelostogram, antegrade pyeloureterograms) through nephrostomy or pyelostomy tube, or indwelling ureteral catheter ⬚N1⬚ ⬚N⬚ ⬚50⬚

     ⬚⬚ *74425*

     🔧 1.43   ✂ 2.90   Global Days 000

     AMA: 2005, Oct, 18-22; 2005, Oct, 18-22; 2005, October, 18-22

50395 Introduction of guide into renal pelvis and/or ureter with dilation to establish nephrostomy tract, percutaneous ⬚A2⬚ ⬚T⬚ ⬚50⬚ 🗗

     EXCLUDES   *percutaneous nephrostolithotomy (50080, 50081)*

           renal endoscopy (50551-50561)

           retrograde percutaneous nephrostomy (52334)

     ⬚⬚ *74475, 74480, 74485*

     🔧 5.23   ✂ 5.23   Global Days 000

     AMA: 2006, Sep, 1-4; 2006, Sep, 1-4; 2006, September, 1-4; 2005, Oct, 18-22; 2005, October, 18-22; 2005, Oct, 18-22

50396 Manometric studies through nephrostomy or pyelostomy tube, or indwelling ureteral catheter ⬚A2⬚ ⬚T⬚ ⬚80⬚ ⬚50⬚ 🗗

     ⬚⬚ *74425, 74475, 74480*

     🔧 3.38   ✂ 3.38   Global Days 000

50398 Change of nephrostomy or pyelostomy tube ⬚A2⬚ ⬚T⬚ ⬚50⬚ 🗗

     Code also (C1729)

     ⬚⬚ *75984*

     🔧 2.15   ✂ 14.49   Global Days 000

     AMA: 2005, Oct, 18-22; 2005, Oct, 18-22; 2005, October, 18-22

50400-50540 Open Surgical Procedures of Kidney

50400 Pyeloplasty (Foley Y-pyeloplasty), plastic operation on renal pelvis, with or without plastic operation on ureter, nephropexy, nephrostomy, pyelostomy, or ureteral splinting; simple ⬚C⬚ ⬚80⬚ 🗗

     EXCLUDES   *laparoscopic pyeloplasty (50544)*

     🔧 33.09   ✂ 33.09   Global Days 090

50405 complicated (congenital kidney abnormality, secondary pyeloplasty, solitary kidney, calycoplasty) ⬚C⬚ ⬚80⬚ 🗗

     EXCLUDES   *laparoscopic pyeloplasty (50544)*

     🔧 40.18   ✂ 40.18   Global Days 090

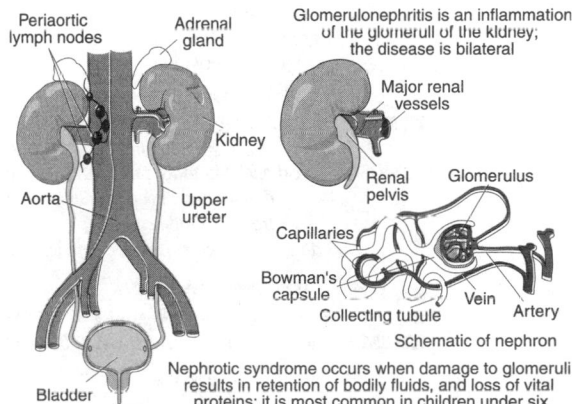

Glomerulonephritis is an inflammation of the glomeruli of the kidney; the disease is bilateral

Periaortic lymph nodes — Adrenal gland — Kidney — Aorta — Upper ureter — Bladder

Major renal vessels — Renal pelvis — Glomerulus — Capillaries — Bowman's capsule — Vein — Artery — Collecting tubule — Schematic of nephron

Nephrotic syndrome occurs when damage to glomeruli results in retention of bodily fluids, and loss of vital proteins; it is most common in children under six

● New Code   ▲ Revised Code   ⬚M⬚ Maternity Edit   ⬚A⬚ Age Edit   ⬚A⬚-⬚T⬚ OPPS Status Indicator   🔧 Facility RVU   ✂ Non-Facility RVU

🗗 CCI Comprehensive Code   ⬚50⬚ Bilateral Procedure   + Add-on Indicator   ⬚⬚ Laboratory crosswalk   ⬚⬚ Radiology crosswalk

    195

Urinary System

50500 — 50580

50500 Nephrorrhaphy, suture of kidney wound or injury C 80 □
 🖘 32.25 ⚕ 32.25 Global Days 090

50520 Closure of nephrocutaneous or pyelocutaneous fistula C 80 □
 🖘 29.76 ⚕ 29.76 Global Days 090

50525 Closure of nephrovisceral fistula (eg, renocolic), including visceral repair; abdominal approach C 80 □
 🖘 37.17 ⚕ 37.17 Global Days 090

50526 thoracic approach C 80 □
 🖘 38.91 ⚕ 38.91 Global Days 090

50540 Symphysiotomy for horseshoe kidney with or without pyeloplasty and/or other plastic procedure, unilateral or bilateral (1 operation) C 80 □
 🖘 32.41 ⚕ 32.41 Global Days 090

50541-50549 Laparoscopic Surgical Procedures of the Kidney

INCLUDES diagnostic laparoscopy

EXCLUDES *laparoscopic drainage of lymphocele to peritoneal cavity (49323)*

50541 Laparoscopy, surgical; ablation of renal cysts T 80 □
 🖘 26.43 ⚕ 26.43 Global Days 090

50542 ablation of renal mass lesion(s) T 80 □
 EXCLUDES *cryosurgical open ablation of renal mass lesion(s) (50250)*
 nephrectomy, open approach (50220-50240)
 🖘 33.52 ⚕ 33.52 Global Days 090
 AMA: 2008, Jan, 10-25; 2007, Jan, 13-27; 2007, Jan, 13-27; 2007, January, 13-27; 2004, Aug, 12; 2004, August, 12; 2004, Aug, 12

50543 partial nephrectomy T 80 □ PQ
 EXCLUDES *partial nephrectomy, open approach (50240)*
 🖘 42.78 ⚕ 42.78 Global Days 090

50544 pyeloplasty T 80 □
 🖘 36.07 ⚕ 36.07 Global Days 090

50545 radical nephrectomy (includes removal of Gerota's fascia and surrounding fatty tissue, removal of regional lymph nodes, and adrenalectomy) C 80 50 □ PQ
 EXCLUDES *radical nephrectomy, open approach (50230)*
 🖘 38.72 ⚕ 38.72 Global Days 090

50546 nephrectomy, including partial ureterectomy C 80 50 □ PQ
 🖘 34.36 ⚕ 34.36 Global Days 090

50547 donor nephrectomy (including cold preservation), from living donor C 80 50 □ PQ
 INCLUDES donor care
 graft:
 cold preservation
 harvesting
 EXCLUDES *backbench reconstruction renal allograft prior to transplantation (50327-50329)*
 backbench standard preparation of living donor renal allograft prior to transplantation (50325)
 donor nephrectomy, open approach (50320)
 🖘 41.54 ⚕ 41.54 Global Days 090

50548 nephrectomy with total ureterectomy C 80 □ PQ
 EXCLUDES *nephrectomy, open approach (50234, 50236)*
 🖘 39.04 ⚕ 39.04 Global Days 090

50549 Unlisted laparoscopy procedure, renal T 80 50
 🖘 0.00 ⚕ 0.00 Global Days YYY
 AMA: 2008, Jan, 10-25; 2007, Jan, 13-27; 2007, Jan, 13-27; 2007, January, 13-27

50551-50562 Endoscopic Procedures of Kidney via Established Nephrostomy/Pyelostomy Access

EXCLUDES *materials and supplies (99070)*

50551 Renal endoscopy through established nephrostomy or pyelostomy, with or without irrigation, instillation, or ureteropyelography, exclusive of radiologic service; A2 T 80 50 □
 🖘 8.61 ⚕ 10.58 Global Days 000

50553 with ureteral catheterization, with or without dilation of ureter A2 T 50 □
 🖘 9.08 ⚕ 11.03 Global Days 000

50555 with biopsy A2 T 80 50 □
 🖘 9.95 ⚕ 12.04 Global Days 000

50557 with fulguration and/or incision, with or without biopsy A2 T 80 50 □
 🖘 10.11 ⚕ 12.29 Global Days 000

50561 with removal of foreign body or calculus A2 T 80 50 □
 🖘 11.55 ⚕ 13.94 Global Days 000

50562 with resection of tumor C2 T 80 □
 🖘 16.99 ⚕ 16.99 Global Days 090

50570-50580 Endoscopic Procedures of Kidney via Nephrotomy/Pyelotomy Access

EXCLUDES *materials and supplies (99070)*
 nephrotomy (50045)
 pyelotomy (50120)

50570 Renal endoscopy through nephrotomy or pyelotomy, with or without irrigation, instillation, or ureteropyelography, exclusive of radiologic service; C2 T 80 50 □
 🖘 14.42 ⚕ 14.42 Global Days 000

50572 with ureteral catheterization, with or without dilation of ureter C2 T 80 50 □
 🖘 15.73 ⚕ 15.73 Global Days 000

50574 with biopsy C2 T 80 50 □
 🖘 16.57 ⚕ 16.57 Global Days 000

50575 with endopyelotomy (includes cystoscopy, ureteroscopy, dilation of ureter and ureteral pelvic junction, incision of ureteral pelvic junction and insertion of endopyelotomy stent) C2 T 50 □
 🖘 20.96 ⚕ 20.96 Global Days 000
 AMA: 2008, Jan, 10-25; 2007, Jan, 13-27; 2007, Jan, 13-27; 2007, January, 13-27

50576 with fulguration and/or incision, with or without biopsy C2 T 80 50 □
 🖘 16.55 ⚕ 16.55 Global Days 000

50580 with removal of foreign body or calculus C2 T 80 50 □
 🖘 17.72 ⚕ 17.72 Global Days 000

50590-50593 Noninvasive and Minimally Invasive Procedures of the Kidney

CMS *100-3,230.1* *Treatment of Kidney Stones*

26/TC Professional/Technical Component Only   80/80 Assist-at-Surgery Allowed/With Documentation   Unlisted   Not Covered
AMA: CPT Assistant References   A2-A3 ASC Payment Indicator   ♂ Male Only   ♀ Female Only   ⊘ Modifier 51 Exempt   PQ PQRI

196   CPT only © 2008 American Medical Association. All Rights Reserved. (Black Ink)   Medicare (Red Ink)   © 2008 Ingenix (Blue Ink)

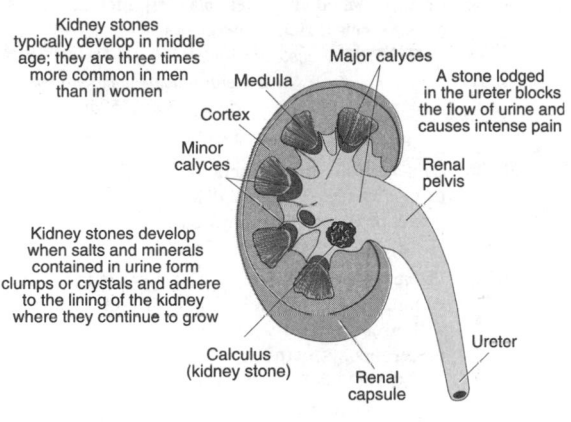

Kidney stones typically develop in middle age; they are three times more common in men than in women

Major calyces

Medulla

Cortex

Minor calyces

A stone lodged in the ureter blocks the flow of urine and causes intense pain

Renal pelvis

Kidney stones develop when salts and minerals contained in urine form clumps or crystals and adhere to the lining of the kidney where they continue to grow

Ureter

Calculus (kidney stone)

Renal capsule

50590   Lithotripsy, extracorporeal shock wave   02 T 50 🔲
   🔹 16.14   🔸 26.27   **Global Days 090**
   AMA: 2008, Jan, 10-25; 2007, Jan, 13-27; 2007, Jan, 13-27; 2007, January, 13-27

⊙ **50592   Ablation, 1 or more renal tumor(s), percutaneous, unilateral, radiofrequency**   02 T 50
   🔲 76940, 77013, 77022
   🔹 10.44   🔸 99.02   **Global Days 010**

⊙ **50593   Ablation, renal tumor(s), unilateral, percutaneous, cryotherapy**   T 80
   🔲 76940, 77013, 77022
   🔹 13.25   🔸 127.81   **Global Days 010**

50600-50940 Open and Injection Procedures of Ureter

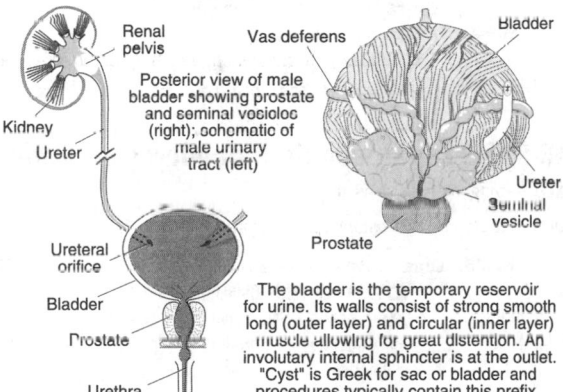

Renal pelvis

Vas deferens

Bladder

Kidney

Ureter

Posterior view of male bladder showing prostate and seminal vesicles (right); schematic of male urinary tract (left)

Ureter

Seminal vesicle

Prostate

Ureteral orifice

Bladder

Prostate

Urethra

The bladder is the temporary reservoir for urine. Its walls consist of strong smooth long (outer layer) and circular (inner layer) muscle allowing for great distention. An involutary internal sphincter is at the outlet. "Cyst" is Greek for sac or bladder and procedures typically contain this prefix

50600   Ureterotomy with exploration or drainage (separate procedure)   C 80 50 🔲
   EXCLUDES   *ureteral endoscopy through ureterotomy (50970-50980)*
   🔹 26.82   🔸 26.82   **Global Days 090**

50605   Ureterotomy for insertion of indwelling stent, all types   C 80 50 🔲
   🔹 25.95   🔸 25.95   **Global Days 090**

50610   Ureterolithotomy; upper 1/3 of ureter   C 80 50 🔲
   EXCLUDES   *cystotomy with calculus basket extraction of ureteral calculus (51065)*
      transvesical ureterolithotomy (51060)
      ureteral calculus manipulation/extraction performed endoscopically (50080, 50081, 50561, 50961, 50980, 52320-52330, 52352, 52353)
      ureterolithotomy performed laparoscopically (50945)
   🔹 27.47   🔸 27.47   **Global Days 090**

50620   middle one-third of ureter   C 80 50 🔲
   EXCLUDES   *cystotomy with calculus basket extraction of ureteral calculus (51065)*
      transvesical ureterolithotomy (51060)
      ureteral calculus manipulation/extraction performed endoscopically (50080, 50081, 50561, 50961, 50980, 52320-52330, 52352, 52353)
      ureterolithotomy performed laparoscopically (50945)
   🔹 25.96   🔸 25.96   **Global Days 090**

50630   lower one-third of ureter   C 80 50 🔲
   EXCLUDES   *cystotomy with calculus basket extraction of ureteral calculus (51065)*
      transvesical ureterolithotomy (51060)
      ureteral calculus manipulation/extraction performed endoscopically (50080, 50081, 50561, 50961, 50980, 52320-52330, 52352, 52353)
      ureterolithotomy performed laparoscopically (50945)
   🔹 25.32   🔸 25.32   **Global Days 090**

50650   Ureterectomy, with bladder cuff (separate procedure)   C 80 🔲
   EXCLUDES   *ureterocele (51535, 52300)*
   🔹 29.60   🔸 29.60   **Global Days 090**

50660   Ureterectomy, total, ectopic ureter, combination abdominal, vaginal and/or perineal approach   C 80 🔲
   EXCLUDES   *ureterocele (51535, 52300)*
   🔹 32.73   🔸 32.73   **Global Days 090**

50684   Injection procedure for ureterography or ureteropyelography through ureterostomy or indwelling ureteral catheter   N1 N 50 🔲
   🔲 74425
   🔹 1.42   🔸 5.00   **Global Days 000**

50686   Manometric studies through ureterostomy or indwelling ureteral catheter   R2 T 80 🔲
   🔹 2.60   🔸 2.60   **Global Days 000**

50688   Change of ureterostomy tube or externally accessible ureteral stent via ileal conduit   A2 Y 🔲
   Code also (C1729, C1758, C2617, C2625)
   🔲 75984
   🔹 2.26   🔸 2.26   **Global Days 010**

50690   Injection procedure for visualization of ileal conduit and/or ureteropyelography, exclusive of radiologic service   N1 N 🔲
   🔲 74425
   🔹 2.00   🔸 2.81   **Global Days 000**

50700   Ureteroplasty, plastic operation on ureter (eg, stricture)   C 80 🔲
   🔹 26.57   🔸 26.57   **Global Days 090**

50715   Ureterolysis, with or without repositioning of ureter for retroperitoneal fibrosis   C 80 50 🔲 P0
   🔹 31.57   🔸 31.57   **Global Days 090**

● New Code   ▲ Revised Code   Ⓜ Maternity Edit   Ⓐ Age Edit   A-Y OPPS Status Indicator   🔹 Facility RVU   🔸 Non-Facility RVU
🔲 CCI Comprehensive Code   50 Bilateral Procedure   + Add-on Indicator   🔲 Laboratory crosswalk   🔲 Radiology crosswalk

© 2008 Ingenix *(Blue Ink)*   CPT only © 2008 American Medical Association. All Rights Reserved. (Black Ink)   Medicare (Red Ink)   197

50722 Ureterolysis for ovarian vein syndrome ♀ C 80 ▭ P0
🔄 27.48 ⚖ 27.48 Global Days 090

50725 Ureterolysis for retrocaval ureter, with reanastomosis of upper urinary tract or vena cava C 80 ▭ P0
🔄 31.23 ⚖ 31.23 Global Days 090

50727 Revision of urinary-cutaneous anastomosis (any type urostomy); T 80 ▭ P0
🔄 14.33 ⚖ 14.33 Global Days 090

50728 with repair of fascial defect and hernia C 80 ▭ P0
🔄 19.77 ⚖ 19.77 Global Days 090

50740 Ureteropyelostomy, anastomosis of ureter and renal pelvis C 80 ▭
🔄 30.88 ⚖ 30.88 Global Days 090

50750 Ureterocalycostomy, anastomosis of ureter to renal calyx C 80 ▭
🔄 33.30 ⚖ 33.30 Global Days 090

50760 Ureteroureterostomy C 80 ▭ P0
🔄 31.14 ⚖ 31.14 Global Days 090

50770 Transureteroureterostomy, anastomosis of ureter to contralateral ureter C 80 ▭ P0
🔄 32.26 ⚖ 32.26 Global Days 090

50780 Ureteroneocystostomy; anastomosis of single ureter to bladder C 80 50 ▭ P0
INCLUDES minor procedures to prevent vesicoureteral reflux
EXCLUDES cystourethroplasty with ureteroneocystostomy (51820)
🔄 31.22 ⚖ 31.22 Global Days 090

50782 anastomosis of duplicated ureter to bladder C 80 50 ▭ P0
INCLUDES minor procedures to prevent vesicoureteral reflux
🔄 30.69 ⚖ 30.69 Global Days 090

50783 with extensive ureteral tailoring C 80 50 ▭ P0
INCLUDES minor procedures to prevent vesicoureteral reflux
🔄 31.93 ⚖ 31.93 Global Days 090

50785 with vesico-psoas hitch or bladder flap C 80 50 ▭ P0
INCLUDES minor procedures to prevent vesicoureteral reflux
🔄 34.57 ⚖ 34.57 Global Days 090

50800 Ureteroenterostomy, direct anastomosis of ureter to intestine C 80 50 ▭ P0
EXCLUDES cystectomy with ureterosigmoidostomy / ureteroileal conduit (51580-51595)
🔄 26.30 ⚖ 26.30 Global Days 090

50810 Ureterosigmoidostomy, with creation of sigmoid bladder and establishment of abdominal or perineal colostomy, including intestine anastomosis C 80 ▭ P0
EXCLUDES cystectomy with ureterosigmoidostomy / ureteroileal conduit (51580-51595)
🔄 34.81 ⚖ 34.81 Global Days 090

50815 Ureterocolon conduit, including intestine anastomosis C 80 50 ▭ P0
EXCLUDES cystectomy with ureterosigmoidostomy / ureteroileal conduit (51580-51595)
🔄 35.05 ⚖ 35.05 Global Days 090

50820 Ureteroileal conduit (ileal bladder), including intestine anastomosis (Bricker operation) C 80 50 ▭ P0
EXCLUDES cystectomy with ureterosigmoidostomy / ureteroileal conduit (51580-51595)
🔄 37.40 ⚖ 37.40 Global Days 090

50825 Continent diversion, including intestine anastomosis using any segment of small and/or large intestine (Kock pouch or Camey enterocystoplasty) C 80 ▭
🔄 47.35 ⚖ 47.35 Global Days 090

50830 Urinary undiversion (eg, taking down of ureteroileal conduit, ureterosigmoidostomy or ureteroenterostomy with ureteroureterostomy or ureteroneocystostomy) C 80 ▭
🔄 51.43 ⚖ 51.43 Global Days 090

50840 Replacement of all or part of ureter by intestine segment, including intestine anastomosis C 80 50 ▭
🔄 35.25 ⚖ 35.25 Global Days 090

50845 Cutaneous appendico-vesicostomy C 80 ▭
INCLUDES Mitrofanoff operation
🔄 35.79 ⚖ 35.79 Global Days 090

50860 Ureterostomy, transplantation of ureter to skin C 80 50 ▭
🔄 27.14 ⚖ 27.14 Global Days 090

50900 Ureterorrhaphy, suture of ureter (separate procedure) C 80 ▭
🔄 23.88 ⚖ 23.88 Global Days 090

50920 Closure of ureterocutaneous fistula C 80 ▭
🔄 25.19 ⚖ 25.19 Global Days 090

50930 Closure of ureterovisceral fistula (including visceral repair) C 80 ▭
🔄 30.48 ⚖ 30.48 Global Days 090

50940 Deligation of ureter C 80 50 ▭
EXCLUDES ureteroplasty / ureterolysis (50700-50860)
🔄 25.42 ⚖ 25.42 Global Days 090

50945-50949 Laparoscopic Procedures of Ureter

INCLUDES diagnostic laparoscopy

EXCLUDES ureteroneocystostomy, open approach (50780-50785)

50945 Laparoscopy, surgical; ureterolithotomy T 80 50
🔄 28.19 ⚖ 28.19 Global Days 090
AMA: 2008, Jan, 10-25; 2007, Jan, 13-27; 2007, Jan, 13-27; 2007, January, 13-27; 2006, Sep, 14-16; 2006, September, 14-16; 2006, Sep, 14-16

50947 ureteroneocystostomy with cystoscopy and ureteral stent placement A2 T 80 50 ▭ P0
🔄 40.04 ⚖ 40.04 Global Days 090

50948 ureteroneocystostomy without cystoscopy and ureteral stent placement A2 T 80 50 ▭ P0
🔄 37.07 ⚖ 37.07 Global Days 090

50949 Unlisted laparoscopy procedure, ureter T 80 50
🔄 0.00 ⚖ 0.00 Global Days YYY

50951-50961 Endoscopic Procedures of Ureter via Established Ureterostomy Access

50951 Ureteral endoscopy through established ureterostomy, with or without irrigation, instillation, or ureteropyelography, exclusive of radiologic service; A2 T 80 50 ▭
🔄 8.98 ⚖ 11.05 Global Days 000
AMA: 2008, Jan, 10-25; 2007, Mar, 9-11; 2007, Mar, 9-11; 2007, March, 9-11

50953   with ureteral catheterization, with or without dilation of ureter   A2 T 80 50 ▢
   🔁 9.88   ✄ 11.66   Global Days 000
   AMA: 2007, Mar, 9-11; 2007, Mar, 9-11; 2007, March, 9-11

50955   with biopsy   A2 T 80 50 ▢
   🔁 10.68   ✄ 12.90   Global Days 000
   AMA: 2007, Mar, 9-11; 2007, Mar, 9-11; 2007, March, 9-11

50957   with fulguration and/or incision, with or without biopsy   A2 T 80 50 ▢
   🔁 10.36   ✄ 12.55   Global Days 000
   AMA: 2007, Mar, 9-11; 2007, Mar, 9-11; 2007, March, 9-11

50961   with removal of foreign body or calculus   A2 T 80 50 ▢
   🔁 9.27   ✄ 11.32   Global Days 000
   AMA: 2008, Jan, 10-25; 2007, Mar, 9-11; 2007, Mar, 9-11; 2007, Apr, 11-12; 2007, Apr, 11-12; 2007, March, 9-11; 2007, April, 11-12

50970-50980 Endoscopic Procedures of Ureter via Ureterotomy

EXCLUDES   *ureterotomy (50600)*

50970   Ureteral endoscopy through ureterotomy, with or without irrigation, instillation, or ureteropyelography, exclusive of radiologic service;   A2 T 80 50 ▢
   🔁 10.88   ✄ 10.88   Global Days 000

50972   with ureteral catheterization, with or without dilation of ureter   A2 T 80 50 ▢
   🔁 10.47   ✄ 10.47   Global Days 000

50974   with biopsy   A2 T 80 50 ▢
   🔁 13.86   ✄ 13.86   Global Days 000

50976   with fulguration and/or incision, with or without biopsy   A2 T 80 50 ▢
   🔁 13.88   ✄ 13.88   Global Days 000

50980   with removal of foreign body or calculus   A2 T 80 50 ▢
   🔁 10.44   ✄ 10.44   Global Days 000

51020-51080 Open Incisional Procedures of Bladder

51020   Cystotomy or cystostomy; with fulguration and/or insertion of radioactive material   A2 T 80 ▢
   🔁 13.25   ✄ 13.25   Global Days 090

51030   with cryosurgical destruction of intravesical lesion   A2 T 80 ▢
   🔁 13.16   ✄ 13.16   Global Days 090

51040   Cystostomy, cystotomy with drainage   A2 T 80 ▢
   🔁 8.29   ✄ 8.29   Global Days 090

51045   Cystotomy, with insertion of ureteral catheter or stent (separate procedure)   A2 T 80 ▢
   🔁 13.22   ✄ 13.22   Global Days 090

51050   Cystolithotomy, cystotomy with removal of calculus, without vesical neck resection   A2 T 80 ▢
   🔁 13.45   ✄ 13.45   Global Days 090

51060   Transvesical ureterolithotomy   C 80 ▢
   🔁 16.57   ✄ 16.57   Global Days 090

51065   Cystotomy, with calculus basket extraction and/or ultrasonic or electrohydraulic fragmentation of ureteral calculus   A2 T 80 ▢
   🔁 16.46   ✄ 16.46   Global Days 090

51080   Drainage of perivesical or prevesical space abscess   A2 T 80 ▢
   🔁 11.53   ✄ 11.53   Global Days 090

51100-51102 Bladder Aspiration Procedures

📹 *76942, 77002, 77012*

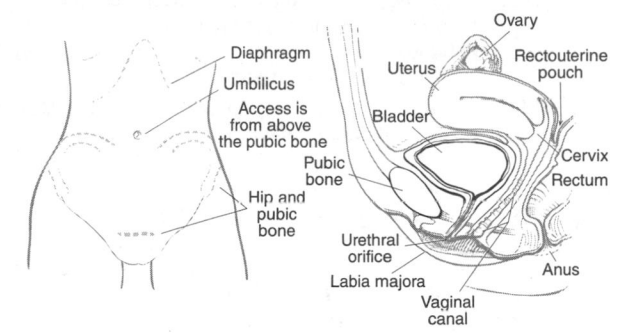

Labels: Diaphragm, Umbilicus, Access is from above the pubic bone, Pubic bone, Hip and pubic bone, Urethral orifice, Labia majora, Vaginal canal, Ovary, Uterus, Rectouterine pouch, Bladder, Cervix, Rectum, Anus

51100   Aspiration of bladder; by needle   P3 T
   🔁 1.11   ✄ 1.72   Global Days 000
   AMA: 2008, Jun, 8-11

51101   by trocar or intracatheter   P2 T
   🔁 1.50   ✄ 3.53   Global Days 000
   AMA: 2008, Jun, 8-11

51102   with insertion of suprapubic catheter   A2 T
   🔁 4.36   ✄ 6.70   Global Days 000
   AMA: 2008, Jun, 8-11; 2007, Dec, 10-179

51500-51597 Open Excisional Procedures of Bladder

51500   Excision of urachal cyst or sinus, with or without umbilical hernia repair   A2 T 80 ▢
   🔁 17.83   ✄ 17.83   Global Days 090

51520   Cystotomy; for simple excision of vesical neck (separate procedure)   A2 T 80 ▢
   🔁 16.71   ✄ 16.71   Global Days 090

51525   for excision of bladder diverticulum, single or multiple (separate procedure)   C 80 ▢
   EXCLUDES   *transurethral resection (52305)*
   🔁 24.56   ✄ 24.56   Global Days 090

51530   for excision of bladder tumor   C 80 ▢
   EXCLUDES   *transurethral resection (52234-52240)*
   🔁 21.94   ✄ 21.94   Global Days 090

51535   Cystotomy for excision, incision, or repair of ureterocele   T 80 50 ▢
   EXCLUDES   *transurethral excision (52300)*
   🔁 22.34   ✄ 22.34   Global Days 090

51550   Cystectomy, partial; simple   C 80 ▢ P0
   🔁 27.07   ✄ 27.07   Global Days 090

51555   complicated (eg, postradiation, previous surgery, difficult location)   C 80 ▢ P0
   🔁 35.98   ✄ 35.98   Global Days 090

51565   Cystectomy, partial, with reimplantation of ureter(s) into bladder (ureteroneocystostomy)   C 80 ▢ P0
   🔁 36.75   ✄ 36.75   Global Days 090

51570   Cystectomy, complete; (separate procedure)   C 80 ▢ P0
   🔁 41.91   ✄ 41.91   Global Days 090

51575   with bilateral pelvic lymphadenectomy, including external iliac, hypogastric, and obturator nodes   C 80 ▢ P0
   🔁 52.41   ✄ 52.41   Global Days 090

51580   Cystectomy, complete, with ureterosigmoidostomy or ureterocutaneous transplantations;   C 80 ▢ P0
   🔁 54.62   ✄ 54.62   Global Days 090

51585   with bilateral pelvic lymphadenectomy, including external iliac, hypogastric, and obturator nodes   C 80 ▢ P0
   🔁 60.83   ✄ 60.83   Global Days 090

● New Code   ▲ Revised Code   M Maternity Edit   A Age Edit   A/Y OPPS Status Indicator   🔁 Facility RVU   ✄ Non-Facility RVU
▢ CCI Comprehensive Code   50 Bilateral Procedure   + Add-on Indicator   ◣ Laboratory crosswalk   📹 Radiology crosswalk

51590 Cystectomy, complete, with ureteroileal conduit or sigmoid bladder, including intestine anastomosis; C 80 ▢ P0
  ⊞ 55.41 ⚲ 55.41 Global Days 090

51595 with bilateral pelvic lymphadenectomy, including external iliac, hypogastric, and obturator nodes C 80 ▢ P0
  ⊞ 62.98 ⚲ 62.98 Global Days 090

51596 Cystectomy, complete, with continent diversion, any open technique, using any segment of small and/or large intestine to construct neobladder C 80 ▢ P0
  ⊞ 67.70 ⚲ 67.70 Global Days 090

51597 Pelvic exenteration, complete, for vesical, prostatic or urethral malignancy, with removal of bladder and ureteral transplantations, with or without hysterectomy and/or abdominoperineal resection of rectum and colon and colostomy, or any combination thereof C 80 ▢ P0

  EXCLUDES *pelvic exenteration for gynecologic malignancy (58240)*

  ⊞ 65.33 ⚲ 65.33 Global Days 090

51600-51720 Injection/Insertion/Instillation Procedures of Bladder

51600 Injection procedure for cystography or voiding urethrocystography N1 N ▢
  ⊠ *74430, 74455*
  ⊞ 1.28 ⚲ 5.38 Global Days 000

51605 Injection procedure and placement of chain for contrast and/or chain urethrocystography N1 N ▢
  ⊠ *74430*
  ⊞ 1.10 ⚲ 1.10 Global Days 000

51610 Injection procedure for retrograde urethrocystography N1 N ▢
  ⊠ *74450*
  ⊞ 1.82 ⚲ 3.13 Global Days 000

51700 Bladder irrigation, simple, lavage and/or instillation P3 T ▢
  ⊞ 1.28 ⚲ 2.46 Global Days 000

51701 Insertion of non-indwelling bladder catheter (eg, straight catheterization for residual urine) P2 X ▢

  Do not report with insertion of catheter as an inclusive component of another procedure

  ⊞ 0.78 ⚲ 1.71 Global Days 000
  AMA: 2008, Jan, 10-25; 2007, Jan, 28-31; 2007, Jan, 28-31; 2007, Jul, 1-4; 2007, January, 28-31; 2006, May, 1-9; 2006, May, 1-9; 2006, May, 1-9

51702 Insertion of temporary indwelling bladder catheter; simple (eg, Foley) P2 X ▢

  Do not report with insertion of catheter as an inclusive component of another procedure

  ⊞ 0.86 ⚲ 2.20 Global Days 000
  AMA: 2008, Jan, 10-25; 2007, Jan, 13-27; 2007, Jan, 13-27; 2007, Jan, 28-31; 2007, January, 13-27; 2007, Jul, 1-4; 2007, January, 28-31; 2007, Jan, 28-31; 2006, May, 1-9; 2006, May, 1-9; 2006, May, 1-9; 2004, Jul, 7; 2004, July, 7; 2004, Jul, 7

51703 complicated (eg, altered anatomy, fractured catheter/balloon) P2 T ▢
  ⊞ 2.35 ⚲ 3.97 Global Days 000
  AMA: 2007, Jan, 28-31; 2007, Jan, 28-31; 2007, January, 28-31

51705 Change of cystostomy tube; simple P2 T ▢
  ⊞ 1.91 ⚲ 3.19 Global Days 010
  AMA: 2008, Jan, 10-25; 2007, Jan, 28-31; 2007, Jan, 28-31; 2007, January, 28-31; 2007, Dec, 10-179

51710 complicated A2 T ▢
  Code also (C2627)
  ⊠ *75984*
  ⊞ 2.72 ⚲ 4.50 Global Days 010
  AMA: 2007, Dec, 10-179

51715 Endoscopic injection of implant material into the submucosal tissues of the urethra and/or bladder neck A2 T 80 ▢
  Code also (L8603, L8606)
  ⊞ 5.74 ⚲ 8.35 Global Days 000

51720 Bladder instillation of anticarcinogenic agent (including retention time) P3 T ▢
  ⊞ 2.41 ⚲ 3.32 Global Days 000
  AMA: 2008, Jan, 10-25; 2007, Jan, 13-27; 2007, Jan, 13-27; 2007, January, 13-27

51725-51798 Uroflowmetric Evaluations

CMS *100-3,230.2*   *Uroflowmetric Evaluations*

51725 Simple cystometrogram (CMG) (eg, spinal manometer) P2 T 80 ▢
  ⊞ 6.21 ⚲ 6.21 Global Days 000

51726 Complex cystometrogram (eg, calibrated electronic equipment) A2 T ▢
  ⊞ 9.02 ⚲ 9.02 Global Days 000

51736 Simple uroflowmetry (UFR) (eg, stop-watch flow rate, mechanical uroflowmeter) P3 T 80 ▢
  ⊞ 1.52 ⚲ 1.52 Global Days 000

51741 Complex uroflowmetry (eg, calibrated electronic equipment) P3 T ▢
  ⊞ 2.41 ⚲ 2.41 Global Days 000

51772 Urethral pressure profile studies (UPP) (urethral closure pressure profile), any technique A2 T 80 ▢
  INCLUDES Keitzer test
  ⊞ 6.96 ⚲ 6.96 Global Days 000
  AMA: 2008, Jan, 10-25; 2007, Jan, 13-27; 2007, Jan, 13-27; 2007, January, 13-27; 2005, Nov, 14-15; 2005, November, 14-15; 2005, Nov, 14-15

51784 Electromyography studies (EMG) of anal or urethral sphincter, other than needle, any technique P2 T ▢
  ⊞ 5.70 ⚲ 5.70 Global Days 000

51785 Needle electromyography studies (EMG) of anal or urethral sphincter, any technique A2 T 80 ▢
  ⊞ 6.18 ⚲ 6.18 Global Days 000
  AMA: 2008, Jan, 10-25; 2007, Jan, 13-27; 2007, Jan, 13-27; 2007, January, 13-27; 2004, Jul, 13; 2004, July, 13; 2004, Jul, 13

51792 Stimulus evoked response (eg, measurement of bulbocavernosus reflex latency time) P2 T 80 ▢
  ⊞ 6.50 ⚲ 6.50 Global Days 000

51795 Voiding pressure studies (VP); bladder voiding pressure, any technique P2 T 80 ▢
  ⊞ 8.52 ⚲ 8.52 Global Days 000
  AMA: 2008, Jan, 10-25; 2007, Jan, 13-27; 2007, Jan, 13-27; 2007, January, 13-27

+ 51797 intra-abdominal voiding pressure (AP) (rectal, gastric, intraperitoneal) (List separately in addition to code for primary procedure) P2 T 80 ▢
  Code first (51795)
  ⊞ 4.23 ⚲ 4.23 Global Days ZZZ
  AMA: 2008, Jan, 10-25; 2007, Jan, 13-27; 2007, Jan, 13-27; 2007, January, 13-27

51798 Measurement of post-voiding residual urine and/or bladder capacity by ultrasound, non-imaging P3 X 80 ▢
  ⊞ 0.60 ⚲ 0.60 Global Days XXX
  AMA: 2005, Dec, 3-6; 2005, Dec, 3-6; 2005, December, 3-6

51800-51980 Open Repairs Urinary System

51800 Cystoplasty or cystourethroplasty, plastic operation on bladder and/or vesical neck (anterior Y-plasty, vesical fundus resection), any procedure, with or without wedge resection of posterior vesical neck `C` `80` `□` `P0`
🗎 29.88 ⚕ 29.88 Global Days 090

51820 Cystourethroplasty with unilateral or bilateral ureteroneocystostomy `C` `80` `□` `P0`
🗎 30.57 ⚕ 30.57 Global Days 090

51840 Anterior vesicourethropexy, or urethropexy (eg, Marshall-Marchetti-Krantz, Burch); simple `C` `80` `□`
EXCLUDES Pereyra type urethropexy (57289)
🗎 18.27 ⚕ 18.27 Global Days 090
AMA: 2008, Jan, 10-25; 2007, Jan, 13-27; 2007, Jan, 13-27; 2007, January, 13-27; 2006, May, 16-20; 2006, May, 16-20; 2006, May, 16-20

51841 complicated (eg, secondary repair) `C` `80` `□`
EXCLUDES Pereyra type urethropexy (57289)
🗎 21.67 ⚕ 21.67 Global Days 090

51845 Abdomino-vaginal vesical neck suspension, with or without endoscopic control (eg, Stamey, Raz, modified Pereyra) ♀ `T` `80` `□`
🗎 16.60 ⚕ 16.60 Global Days 090

51860 Cystorrhaphy, suture of bladder wound, injury or rupture; simple `T` `80` `□`
🗎 20.35 ⚕ 20.35 Global Days 090

51865 complicated `C` `80` `□`
🗎 25.14 ⚕ 25.14 Global Days 090

51880 Closure of cystostomy (separate procedure) `A2` `T` `80` `□`
🗎 13.20 ⚕ 13.20 Global Days 090

51900 Closure of vesicovaginal fistula, abdominal approach ♀ `C` `80` `□` `P0`
EXCLUDES vesicovaginal fistula closure, vaginal approach (57320-57330)
🗎 23.34 ⚕ 23.34 Global Days 090

51920 Closure of vesicouterine fistula; ♀ `C` `80` `□` `P0`
EXCLUDES enterovesical fistula closure (44660, 44661)
rectovesical fistula closure (45800-45805)
🗎 21.60 ⚕ 21.60 Global Days 090

51925 with hysterectomy ♀ `C` `80` `□` `P0`
EXCLUDES enterovesical fistula closure (44660, 44661)
rectovesical fistula closure (45800-45805)
🗎 28.32 ⚕ 28.32 Global Days 090

51940 Closure, exstrophy of bladder `C` `80` `□`
EXCLUDES epispadias reconstruction with exstropy of bladder (54390)
🗎 46.00 ⚕ 46.00 Global Days 090

51960 Enterocystoplasty, including intestinal anastomosis `C` `80` `□` `P0`
🗎 39.67 ⚕ 39.67 Global Days 090

51980 Cutaneous vesicostomy `C` `80` `□`
🗎 20.34 ⚕ 20.34 Global Days 090

51990-51999 Laparoscopic Procedures of Urinary System

INCLUDES diagnostic laparoscopy

51990 Laparoscopy, surgical; urethral suspension for stress incontinence `T` `80` `□`
🗎 21.06 ⚕ 21.06 Global Days 090

51992 sling operation for stress incontinence (eg, fascia or synthetic) ♀ `A2` `T` `80` `□`
EXCLUDES removal/revision of sling for stress incontinence (57287)
sling operation for stress incontinence, open approach (57288)
🗎 22.93 ⚕ 22.93 Global Days 090

51999 Unlisted laparoscopy procedure, bladder `T` `80`
🗎 0.00 ⚕ 0.00 Global Days YYY

52000-52318 Endoscopic Procedures via Urethra: Bladder and Urethra

52000 Cystourethroscopy (separate procedure) `A2` `T` `□`
🗎 3.60 ⚕ 5.96 Global Days 000
AMA: 2008, Jan, 10-25; 2007, Jan, 13-27; 2007, Jan, 13-27; 2007, January, 13-27; 2005, Oct, 23-24; 2005, Oct, 23-24; 2005, Mar, 11-15; 2005, March, 11-15; 2005, October, 23-24; 2005, Mar, 11-15; 2004, Sep, 11; 2004, September, 11; 2004, Sep, 11

52001 Cystourethroscopy with irrigation and evacuation of multiple obstructing clots `A2` `T` `□`
Do not report with (52000)
🗎 8.37 ⚕ 11.00 Global Days 000

52005 Cystourethroscopy, with ureteral catheterization, with or without irrigation, instillation, or ureteropyelography, exclusive of radiologic service; `A2` `T` `□`
INCLUDES Howard test
🗎 3.85 ⚕ 8.22 Global Days 000
AMA: 2008, Jan, 10-25; 2007, Jan, 13-27; 2007, Jan, 13-27; 2007, January, 13-27

52007 with brush biopsy of ureter and/or renal pelvis `A2` `T` `50` `□`
🗎 4.82 ⚕ 15.36 Global Days 000

52010 Cystourethroscopy, with ejaculatory duct catheterization, with or without irrigation, instillation, or duct radiography, exclusive of radiologic service ♂ `A2` `T` `□`
📷 74440
🗎 4.67 ⚕ 11.45 Global Days 000

52204 Cystourethroscopy, with biopsy(s) `A2` `T` `□`
🗎 4.08 ⚕ 12.58 Global Days 000
AMA: 2008, Jan, 10-25; 2007, Jan, 13-27; 2007, Jan, 13-27; 2007, January, 13-27

52214 Cystourethroscopy, with fulguration (including cryosurgery or laser surgery) of trigone, bladder neck, prostatic fossa, urethra, or periurethral glands `A2` `T` `□`
🗎 6.32 ⚕ 16.54 Global Days 000

52224 Cystourethroscopy, with fulguration (including cryosurgery or laser surgery) or treatment of MINOR (less than 0.5 cm) lesion(s) with or without biopsy `A2` `T` `□`
🗎 4.93 ⚕ 23.58 Global Days 000
AMA: 2008, Jan, 10-25; 2007, Dec, 7-8

52234 Cystourethroscopy, with fulguration (including cryosurgery or laser surgery) and/or resection of; SMALL bladder tumor(s) (0.5 up to 2.0 cm) `A2` `T` `□`
EXCLUDES bladder tumor excision through cystotomy (51530)
🗎 7.19 ⚕ 7.19 Global Days 000
AMA: 2008, Jan, 10-25; 2007, Jan, 13-27; 2007, Jan, 13-27; 2007, January, 13-27; 2007, Dec, 7-8

52235 MEDIUM bladder tumor(s) (2.0 to 5.0 cm) `A2` `T` `□`
EXCLUDES bladder tumor excision through cystotomy (51530)
🗎 8.43 ⚕ 8.43 Global Days 000

● New Code ▲ Revised Code ⊞ Maternity Edit ⬛ Age Edit `A-Y` OPPS Status Indicator 🗎 Facility RVU ⚕ Non-Facility RVU
□ CCI Comprehensive Code `50` Bilateral Procedure + Add-on Indicator ◪ Laboratory crosswalk 📷 Radiology crosswalk

© 2008 Ingenix *(Blue Ink)* CPT only © 2008 American Medical Association. All Rights Reserved. *(Black Ink)* Medicare *(Red Ink)* 201

Urinary System

52240 — 52330

52240 LARGE bladder tumor(s) [A2][T][□]
> EXCLUDES bladder tumor excision through cystotomy (51530)
>
> 📷 14.74 ✂ 14.74 Global Days 000

52250 Cystourethroscopy with insertion of radioactive substance, with or without biopsy or fulguration [A2][T][□]
> 📷 7.06 ✂ 7.06 Global Days 000

52260 Cystourethroscopy, with dilation of bladder for interstitial cystitis; general or conduction (spinal) anesthesia [A2][T][□]
> 📷 6.09 ✂ 6.09 Global Days 000
> AMA: 2008, Jan, 10-25; 2007, Jan, 13-27; 2007, Jan, 13-27; 2007, January, 13-27; 2005, Oct, 23-24; 2005, October, 23-24; 2005, Oct, 23-24

52265 local anesthesia [P2][T][□]
> 📷 4.59 ✂ 12.05 Global Days 000

52270 Cystourethroscopy, with internal urethrotomy; female ♀ [A2][T][□]
> 📷 5.30 ✂ 11.63 Global Days 000

52275 male ♂ [A2][T][□]
> 📷 7.26 ✂ 15.91 Global Days 000

52276 Cystourethroscopy with direct vision internal urethrotomy [A2][T][□]
> 📷 7.75 ✂ 7.75 Global Days 000

52277 Cystourethroscopy, with resection of external sphincter (sphincterotomy) [A2][T][80][□]
> 📷 9.47 ✂ 9.47 Global Days 000

52281 Cystourethroscopy, with calibration and/or dilation of urethral stricture or stenosis, with or without meatotomy, with or without injection procedure for cystography, male or female [A2][T][□]
> 📷 4.49 ✂ 8.75 Global Days 000
> AMA: 2008, Jan, 10-25; 2007, Jun, 10-11; 2007, Jun, 10-11; 2007, June, 10-11

52282 Cystourethroscopy, with insertion of urethral stent [A2][T][□]
> 📷 9.77 ✂ 9.77 Global Days 000

52283 Cystourethroscopy, with steroid injection into stricture [A2][T][□]
> 📷 5.83 ✂ 8.09 Global Days 000

52285 Cystourethroscopy for treatment of the female urethral syndrome with any or all of the following: urethral meatotomy, urethral dilation, internal urethrotomy, lysis of urethrovaginal septal fibrosis, lateral incisions of the bladder neck, and fulguration of polyp(s) of urethra, bladder neck, and/or trigone ♀ [A2][T][□]
> 📷 5.65 ✂ 8.15 Global Days 000

52290 Cystourethroscopy; with ureteral meatotomy, unilateral or bilateral [A2][T][□]
> 📷 7.13 ✂ 7.13 Global Days 000

52300 with resection or fulguration of orthotopic ureterocele(s), unilateral or bilateral [A2][T][80][□]
> 📷 8.19 ✂ 8.19 Global Days 000

52301 with resection or fulguration of ectopic ureterocele(s), unilateral or bilateral [A2][T][80][□]
> 📷 8.63 ✂ 8.63 Global Days 000

Diverticulum of bladder
Bladder
Rectum
Pubic bone
Urethra
Diverticula are pouches that push out through the wall of an organ; bladder diverticula may be acquired or congenital and may cause urinary incontinence or increased urgency to urinate
This condition is most common in older men

52305 with incision or resection of orifice of bladder diverticulum, single or multiple [A2][T][□]
> 📷 8.14 ✂ 8.14 Global Days 000

52310 Cystourethroscopy, with removal of foreign body, calculus, or ureteral stent from urethra or bladder (separate procedure); simple [A2][T][□]
> 📷 4.41 ✂ 7.22 Global Days 000

52315 complicated [A2][T][□]
> 📷 8.02 ✂ 12.78 Global Days 000

52317 Litholapaxy: crushing or fragmentation of calculus by any means in bladder and removal of fragments; simple or small (less than 2.5 cm) [A2][T][□]
> 📷 10.18 ✂ 27.21 Global Days 000

52318 complicated or large (over 2.5 cm) [A2][T][□]
> 📷 13.87 ✂ 13.87 Global Days 000

52320-52355 Endoscopic Procedures via Urethra: Renal Pelvis and Ureter

> INCLUDES diagnostic cystourethroscopy with therapeutic cystourethroscopy insertion/removal of temporary ureteral catheter
>
> EXCLUDES diagnostic cystourethroscopy only (52000)
> self-retaining/indwelling ureteral stent removal by cystourethroscope (52310, 52315)

Code also the insertion of an indwelling stent performed in addition to other procedures within this section (52332)

Do not report with (52005)

52320 Cystourethroscopy (including ureteral catheterization); with removal of ureteral calculus [A2][T][50][□]
> Do not report with (52000)
> 📷 7.20 ✂ 7.20 Global Days 000
> AMA: 2008, Jan, 10-25; 2007, Jan, 13-27; 2007, Jan, 13-27; 2007, January, 13-27

52325 with fragmentation of ureteral calculus (eg, ultrasonic or electro-hydraulic technique) [A2][T][50][□]
> Do not report with (52000)
> 📷 9.37 ✂ 9.37 Global Days 000
> AMA: 2007, Dec, 10-179

52327 with subureteric injection of implant material [A2][T][50][□]
> Do not report with (52000)
> 📷 7.67 ✂ 15.19 Global Days 000

52330 with manipulation, without removal of ureteral calculus [A2][T][50][□]
> Do not report with (52000)
> 📷 7.71 ✂ 22.13 Global Days 000
> AMA: 2008, Jan, 10-25; 2007, Jan, 13-27; 2007, Jan, 13-27; 2007, January, 13-27

52332   Cystourethroscopy, with insertion of indwelling ureteral stent (eg, Gibbons or double-J type)   A2 T 50 ▣

     Do not report with (52000)

     ✚ 4.54   ✂ 13.69   Global Days 000
     AMA: 2008, Jan, 10-25; 2007, Jan, 13-27; 2007, Jan, 13-27; 2007, January, 13-27; 2005, Oct, 18-22; 2005, October, 18-22; 2005, Oct, 18-22

52334   Cystourethroscopy with insertion of ureteral guide wire through kidney to establish a percutaneous nephrostomy, retrograde   A2 T 50 ▣

     EXCLUDES   cystourethroscopy with incision/fulguration/resection of congenital posterior urethral valves/obstructive hypertrophic mucosal folds (52400)
         cystourethroscopy with pyeloscopy and/or ureteroscopy (52351-52355)
         nephrostomy tract establishment only (50395)
         percutaneous nephrostolithotomy (50080, 50081)

     Do not report with (52000)

     ✚ 7.49   ✂ 7.49   Global Days 000

52341   Cystourethroscopy; with treatment of ureteral stricture (eg, balloon dilation, laser, electrocautery, and incision)   A2 T 50 ▣

     INCLUDES   diagnostic cystourethroscopy with ureteroscopy/pyeloscopy

     Do not report with (52000, 52341)

     ✚ 8.53   ✂ 8.53   Global Days 000

52342   with treatment of ureteropelvic junction stricture (eg, balloon dilation, laser, electrocautery, and incision)   A2 T 50 ▣

     INCLUDES   diagnostic cystourethroscopy with ureteroscopy/pyeloscopy

     Do not report with (52000, 52351)

     ✚ 9.27   ✂ 9.27   Global Days 000
     AMA: 2008, Jan, 10-25; 2007, Jan, 13-27; 2007, Jan, 13-27; 2007, January, 13-27

52343   with treatment of intra-renal stricture (eg, balloon dilation, laser, electrocautery, and incision)   A2 T 50 ▣

     INCLUDES   diagnostic cystourethroscopy with ureteroscopy/pyeloscopy

     Do not report with (52000, 52351)

     ✚ 10.31   ✂ 10.31   Global Days 000

52344   Cystourethroscopy with ureteroscopy; with treatment of ureteral stricture (eg, balloon dilation, laser, electrocautery, and incision)   A2 T 50 ▣

     INCLUDES   diagnostic cystourethroscopy with ureteroscopy/pyeloscopy

     Do not report with (52351)

     ✚ 11.18   ✂ 11.18   Global Days 000

52345   with treatment of ureteropelvic junction stricture (eg, balloon dilation, laser, electrocautery, and incision)   A2 T 80 ▣

     INCLUDES   diagnostic cystourethroscopy with ureteroscopy/pyeloscopy

     Do not report with (52351)

     ✚ 11.92   ✂ 11.92   Global Days 000

52346   with treatment of intra-renal stricture (eg, balloon dilation, laser, electrocautery, and incision)   A2 T 80 ▣

     INCLUDES   diagnostic cystourethroscopy with ureteroscopy/pyeloscopy

     EXCLUDES   cystourethroscopy with transurethral resection or incision of ejaculatory ducts (52402)

     Do not report with (52351)

     ✚ 13.45   ✂ 13.45   Global Days 000

52351   Cystourethroscopy, with ureteroscopy and/or pyeloscopy; diagnostic   A2 T

     Do not report with (52341-52346, 52352-52355)

     ▣ 74485

     ✚ 9.16   ✂ 9.16   Global Days 000

52352   with removal or manipulation of calculus (ureteral catheterization is included)   A2 T 50 ▣

     INCLUDES   diagnostic cystourethroscopy with ureteroscopy/pyeloscopy

     Do not report with (52351)

     ✚ 10.76   ✂ 10.76   Global Days 000
     AMA: 2008, Jan, 10-25; 2007, Jun, 10-11; 2007, Jun, 10-11; 2007, June, 10-11

52353   with lithotripsy (ureteral catheterization is included)   A2 T 50 ▣

     INCLUDES   diagnostic cystourethroscopy with ureteroscopy/pyeloscopy

     Do not report with (52351)

     ✚ 12.38   ✂ 12.38   Global Days 000
     AMA: 2007, Dec, 10-179

52354   with biopsy and/or fulguration of ureteral or renal pelvic lesion   A2 T 50 ▣

     INCLUDES   diagnostic cystourethroscopy with ureteroscopy/pyeloscopy

     Do not report with (52351)

     ✚ 11.44   ✂ 11.44   Global Days 000

52355   with resection of ureteral or renal pelvic tumor   A2 T 50 ▣

     INCLUDES   diagnostic cystourethroscopy with ureteroscopy/pyeloscopy

     Do not report with (52351)

     ✚ 13.64   ✂ 13.64   Global Days 000

52400-52700 Endoscopic Procedures via Urethra: Prostate and Vesical Neck

52400   Cystourethroscopy with incision, fulguration, or resection of congenital posterior urethral valves, or congenital obstructive hypertrophic mucosal folds   A2 T ▣
     ✚ 14.03   ✂ 14.03   Global Days 090

52402   Cystourethroscopy with transurethral resection or incision of ejaculatory ducts   ♂ A2 T 80 ▣
     ✚ 7.86   ✂ 7.86   Global Days 000

52450   Transurethral incision of prostate   ♂ A2 T ▣ N0
     ✚ 13.36   ✂ 13.36   Global Days 090
     AMA: 2008, Jan, 10-25; 2007, Jan, 13-27; 2007, Jan, 13-27; 2007, January, 13-27; 2005, Jul, 13-16; 2005, July, 13-16; 2005, Jul, 13-16

52500   Transurethral resection of bladder neck (separate procedure)   A2 T
     ✚ 13.97   ✂ 13.97   Global Days 090
     AMA: 2008, Jan, 10-25; 2007, Jan, 13-27; 2007, Jan, 13-27; 2007, January, 13-27; 2005, Jul, 13-16; 2005, Jul, 13-16; 2005, July, 13-16; 2004, Jan, 27; 2004, Jan, 27; 2004, January, 27

● New Code   ▲ Revised Code   M Maternity Edit   A Age Edit   A-Y OPPS Status Indicator   ✚ Facility RVU   ✂ Non-Facility RVU
▢ CCI Comprehensive Code   50 Bilateral Procedure   + Add-on Indicator   ▣ Laboratory crosswalk   ▣ Radiology crosswalk

52601 Transurethral electrosurgical resection of prostate, including control of postoperative bleeding, complete (vasectomy, meatotomy, cystourethroscopy, urethral calibration and/or dilation, and internal urethrotomy are included) ♂ A2 T ▭ P0

    EXCLUDES   *excision of prostate (55801-55845)*

    🔁 23.63   ✂ 23.63   **Global Days 090**

~~**52606**~~ ~~Transurethral fulguration for postoperative bleeding occurring after the usual follow-up time~~
See 52214

~~**52612**~~ ~~Transurethral resection of prostate; first stage of two-stage resection (partial resection)~~
See 52601

~~**52614**~~   ~~second stage of two-stage resection (resection completed)~~
See 52601

~~**52620**~~ ~~Transurethral resection; of residual obstructive tissue after 90 days postoperative~~
See 52630

▲ **52630** Transurethral resection; residual or regrowth of obstructive prostate tissue including control of postoperative bleeding, complete (vasectomy, meatotomy, cystourethroscopy, urethral calibration and/or dilation, and internal urethrotomy are included) ♂ A2 T ▭ P0

    EXCLUDES   *excision of prostate (55801-55845)*

    🔁 12.68   ✂ 12.68   **Global Days 090**

52640   of postoperative bladder neck contracture ♂ A2 T ▭

    EXCLUDES   *excision of prostate (55801-55845)*

    🔁 8.71   ✂ 8.71   **Global Days 090**

52647 Laser coagulation of prostate, including control of postoperative bleeding, complete (vasectomy, meatotomy, cystourethroscopy, urethral calibration and/or dilation, and internal urethrotomy are included if performed) ♂ A2 T ▭ P0

    🔁 18.45   ✂ 61.60   **Global Days 090**

    AMA: 2008, Jan, 10-25; 2007, Jan, 13-27; 2007, Jan, 13-27; 2007, January, 13-27; 2006, Dec, 10-12; 2006, Dec, 10-12; 2006, Dec, 10-12; 2006, Dec, 10-12; 2006, December, 10-12; 2006, December, 10-12; 2006, December, 10-12; 2006, December, 10-12; 2006, Dec, 10-12; 2006, Dec, 10-12; 2006, Dec, 10-12; 2006, Dec, 10-12

52648 Laser vaporization of prostate, including control of postoperative bleeding, complete (vasectomy, meatotomy, cystourethroscopy, urethral calibration and/or dilation, internal urethrotomy and transurethral resection of prostate are included if performed) ♂ A2 T ▭ P0

    🔁 19.69   ✂ 62.92   **Global Days 090**

    AMA: 2008, Jan, 10-25; 2007, Jan, 13-27; 2007, Jan, 13-27; 2007, January, 13-27; 2006, Dec, 10-12; 2006, Dec, 10-12; 2006, Dec, 10-12; 2006, Dec, 10-12; 2006, Dec, 10-12; 2006, December, 10-12; 2006, December, 10-12; 2006, December, 10-12; 2006, December, 10-12; 2006, Dec, 10-12; 2006, Dec, 10-12; 2006, Dec, 10-12; 2005, Jul, 13-16; 2005, Jul, 13-16; 2005, July, 13-16

52649 Laser enucleation of the prostate with morcellation, including control of postoperative bleeding, complete (vasectomy, meatotomy, cystourethroscopy, urethral calibration and/or dilation, internal urethrotomy and transurethral resection of prostate are included if performed) ♂ T 80

    Do not report with (52000, 52276, 52281, 52601, 52647-52648, 53020, 55250)

    🔁 28.14   ✂ 28.14   **Global Days 090**

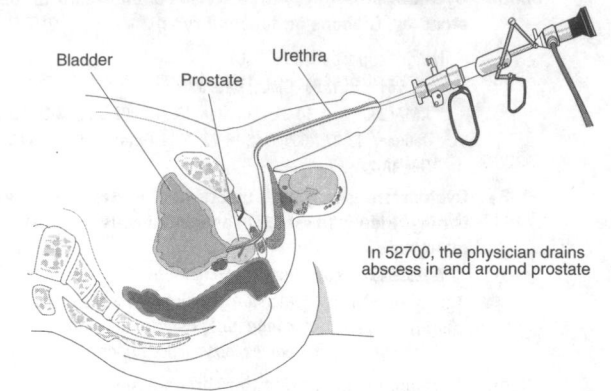

Bladder   Prostate   Urethra

In 52700, the physician drains abscess in and around prostate

52700 Transurethral drainage of prostatic abscess ♂ A2 T 80 ▭

    EXCLUDES   *litholapaxy (52317, 52318)*

    🔁 12.38   ✂ 12.38   **Global Days 090**

53000-53520 Open Surgical Procedures of Urethra

EXCLUDES   *endoscopic procedures; cystoscopy, urethroscopy, cystourethroscopy (52000-52700)*
hypospadias repair (54300-54352)
urethrocystography injection procedure (51600-51610)

53000 Urethrotomy or urethrostomy, external (separate procedure); pendulous urethra   A2 T ▭

    EXCLUDES   *endoscopic procedures; cystoscopy, urethroscopy, cystourethroscopy (52000-52700)*
    urethrocystography injection procedure (51600-51610)

    🔁 4.24   ✂ 4.24   **Global Days 010**

53010   perineal urethra, external   A2 T ▭

    EXCLUDES   *endoscopic procedures; cystoscopy, urethroscopy, cystourethroscopy (52000-52700)*
    urethrocystography injection procedure (51600-51610)

    🔁 8.29   ✂ 8.29   **Global Days 090**

53020 Meatotomy, cutting of meatus (separate procedure); except infant   A2 T ▭

    🔁 2.82   ✂ 2.82   **Global Days 000**

53025   infant   A R2 T 80 ⊘ ▭

    🔁 1.85   ✂ 1.85   **Global Days 000**

53040 Drainage of deep periurethral abscess   A2 T 80 ▭

    EXCLUDES   *incision and drainage of subcutaneous abscess (10060, 10061)*

    🔁 11.20   ✂ 11.20   **Global Days 090**

53060 Drainage of Skene's gland abscess or cyst   ♀ P3 T ▭

    🔁 4.40   ✂ 4.96   **Global Days 010**

53080 Drainage of perineal urinary extravasation; uncomplicated (separate procedure)   A2 T ▭

    🔁 12.43   ✂ 12.43   **Global Days 090**

53085   complicated   R2 T 80 ▭

    🔁 17.64   ✂ 17.64   **Global Days 090**

53200 Biopsy of urethra   A2 T ▭

    🔁 4.06   ✂ 4.45   **Global Days 000**

53210 Urethrectomy, total, including cystostomy; female   ♀ A2 T 80 ▭

    🔁 22.01   ✂ 22.01   **Global Days 090**

53215   male   ♂ A2 T 80 ▭

    🔁 26.74   ✂ 26.74   **Global Days 090**

26/TC Professional/Technical Component Only   80/80 Assist-at-Surgery Allowed/With Documentation   Unlisted   Not Covered

AMA: CPT Assistant References   R2-Z0 ASC Payment Indicator   ♂ Male Only   ♀ Female Only   ⊘ Modifier 51 Exempt   P0 PQRI

53220 Excision or fulguration of carcinoma of urethra A2 T 80 ▱
 ⚙ 12.85 ✂ 12.85 Global Days 090

53230 Excision of urethral diverticulum (separate procedure); female ♀ A2 T 80 ▱
 ⚙ 17.15 ✂ 17.15 Global Days 090

53235 male ♂ A2 T 80 ▱
 ⚙ 18.23 ✂ 18.23 Global Days 090

53240 Marsupialization of urethral diverticulum, male or female A2 T ▱
 ⚙ 12.26 ✂ 12.26 Global Days 090

53250 Excision of bulbourethral gland (Cowper's gland) ♂ A2 T ▱
 ⚙ 11.38 ✂ 11.38 Global Days 090

53260 Excision or fulguration; urethral polyp(s), distal urethra A2 T ▱
 EXCLUDES endoscopic method (52214, 52224)
 ⚙ 5.02 ✂ 5.67 Global Days 010

53265 urethral caruncle A2 T ▱
 EXCLUDES endoscopic method (52214, 52224)
 ⚙ 5.27 ✂ 6.29 Global Days 010

53270 Skene's glands ♀ A2 T ▱
 EXCLUDES endoscopic method (52214, 52224)
 ⚙ 5.18 ✂ 5.79 Global Days 010

53275 urethral prolapse ♀ A2 T ▱
 EXCLUDES endoscopic method (52214, 52224)
 ⚙ 7.60 ✂ 7.60 Global Days 010

53400 Urethroplasty; first stage, for fistula, diverticulum, or stricture (eg, Johannsen type) A2 T 80 ▱
 EXCLUDES hypospadias repair (54300-54352)
 ⚙ 22.91 ✂ 22.91 Global Days 090

53405 second stage (formation of urethra), including urinary diversion A2 T 80 ▱
 EXCLUDES hypospadias repair (54300-54352)
 ⚙ 25.24 ✂ 25.24 Global Days 090

53410 Urethroplasty, 1-stage reconstruction of male anterior urethra ♂ A2 T 80 ▱
 EXCLUDES hypospadias repair (54300-54352)
 ⚙ 28.14 ✂ 28.14 Global Days 090

53415 Urethroplasty, transpubic or perineal, one stage, for reconstruction or repair of prostatic or membranous urethra ♂ C 80 ▱
 ⚙ 32.46 ✂ 32.46 Global Days 090

53420 Urethroplasty, 2-stage reconstruction or repair of prostatic or membranous urethra; first stage ♂ A4 I ▱
 ⚙ 23.05 ✂ 23.05 Global Days 090

53425 second stage ♂ A2 T 80 ▱
 ⚙ 27.11 ✂ 27.11 Global Days 090

53430 Urethroplasty, reconstruction of female urethra ♀ A2 T 80 ▱
 ⚙ 27.04 ✂ 27.04 Global Days 090

53431 Urethroplasty with tubularization of posterior urethra and/or lower bladder for incontinence (eg, Tenago, Leadbetter procedure) A2 T 80 ▱
 ⚙ 33.18 ✂ 33.18 Global Days 090

53440 Sling operation for correction of male urinary incontinence (eg, fascia or synthetic) ♂ H8 S 80 ▱
 Code also (C1762, C1763, C1771, C1781, C2631)
 ⚙ 25.09 ✂ 25.09 Global Days 090

53442 Removal or revision of sling for male urinary incontinence (eg, fascia or synthetic) ♂ A2 T 80 ▱
 ⚙ 22.09 ✂ 22.09 Global Days 090

53444 Insertion of tandem cuff (dual cuff) H8 S 80 ▱
 Code also (C1815)
 ⚙ 22.84 ✂ 22.84 Global Days 090

53445 Insertion of inflatable urethral/bladder neck sphincter, including placement of pump, reservoir, and cuff H8 S 80 ▱
 Code also (C1815)
 ⚙ 25.21 ✂ 25.21 Global Days 090

53446 Removal of inflatable urethral/bladder neck sphincter, including pump, reservoir, and cuff A2 T 80 ▱
 ⚙ 18.43 ✂ 18.43 Global Days 090

53447 Removal and replacement of inflatable urethral/bladder neck sphincter including pump, reservoir, and cuff at the same operative session H8 S 80 ▱
 Code also (C1815)
 ⚙ 23.32 ✂ 23.32 Global Days 090

53448 Removal and replacement of inflatable urethral/bladder neck sphincter including pump, reservoir, and cuff through an infected field at the same operative session including irrigation and debridement of infected tissue C 80 ▱
 Do not report with (11040-11043)
 ⚙ 36.84 ✂ 36.84 Global Days 090

53449 Repair of inflatable urethral/bladder neck sphincter, including pump, reservoir, and cuff A2 T 80 ▱
 ⚙ 17.52 ✂ 17.52 Global Days 090

53450 Urethromeatoplasty, with mucosal advancement A2 T ▱
 EXCLUDES meatotomy (53020, 53025)
 ⚙ 11.65 ✂ 11.65 Global Days 090

53460 Urethromeatoplasty, with partial excision of distal urethral segment (Richardson type procedure) A2 T 80 ▱
 ⚙ 13.09 ✂ 13.09 Global Days 090

53500 Urethrolysis, transvaginal, secondary, open, including cystourethroscopy (eg, postsurgical obstruction, scarring) ♀ T 80 ▱
 EXCLUDES retropubic approach (53899)
 Do not report with (52000)
 ⚙ 21.07 ✂ 21.07 Global Days 090
 AMA: 2004, Sep, 11; 2004, Sep, 11; 2004, September, 11

53502 Urethrorrhaphy, suture of urethral wound or injury, female ♀ A2 T ▱
 ⚙ 13.87 ✂ 13.87 Global Days 090

53505 Urethrorrhaphy, suture of urethral wound or injury; penile ♂ A2 T 80 ▱
 ⚙ 13.91 ✂ 13.91 Global Days 090

53510 perineal A2 T 80 ▱
 ⚙ 18.11 ✂ 18.11 Global Days 090

53515 prostatomembranous ♂ A2 T 80 ▱
 ⚙ 22.87 ✂ 22.87 Global Days 090

53520 Closure of urethrostomy or urethrocutaneous fistula, male (separate procedure) ♂ A2 T ▱
 EXCLUDES closure of fistula:
  urethrorectal (45820, 45825)
  urethrovaginal (57310)
 ⚙ 15.88 ✂ 15.88 Global Days 090

● New Code ▲ Revised Code M Maternity Edit Age Edit A-V OPPS Status Indicator ⚙ Facility RVU ✂ Non-Facility RVU
▱ CCI Comprehensive Code 50 Bilateral Procedure + Add-on Indicator Laboratory crosswalk Radiology crosswalk

Urinary System

53600-53665 Urethral Dilation

EXCLUDES *endoscopic procedures; cystoscopy, urethroscopy, cystourethroscopy*
(52000-52700)
urethral catheterization (51701-51703)
urethrocystography injection procedure (51600-51610)

74485

53600 Dilation of urethral stricture by passage of sound or
urethral dilator, male; initial   ♂ P3 T ▭
🔄 1.87 ⚲ 2.47 Global Days 000

53601   subsequent   ♂ P2 T ▭
🔄 1.56 ⚲ 2.40 Global Days 000

53605 Dilation of urethral stricture or vesical neck by passage
of sound or urethral dilator, male, general or conduction
(spinal) anesthesia   ♂ A2 T ▭
EXCLUDES   *procedure performed under local anesthesia*
(53600-53601, 53620-53621)
🔄 1.88 ⚲ 1.88 Global Days 000

53620 Dilation of urethral stricture by passage of filiform and
follower, male; initial   ♂ P3 T ▭
🔄 2.54 ⚲ 3.53 Global Days 000

53621   subsequent   ♂ P3 T ▭
🔄 2.11 ⚲ 3.34 Global Days 000

53660 Dilation of female urethra including suppository and/or
instillation; initial   ♀ P2 T ▭
🔄 1.19 ⚲ 2.08 Global Days 000

53661   subsequent   ♀ P2 T ▭
🔄 1.17 ⚲ 2.07 Global Days 000

53665 Dilation of female urethra, general or conduction (spinal)
anesthesia   ♀ A2 T ▭
EXCLUDES   *procedure performed under local anesthesia*
(53660-53661)

74485
🔄 1.10 ⚲ 1.10 Global Days 000

53850-53899 Endoscopic Procedures via Urethra: Prostate

EXCLUDES *endoscopic procedures; cystoscopy, urethroscopy, cystourethroscopy*
(52000-52700)
urethrocystography injection procedure (51600-51610)

53850 Transurethral destruction of prostate tissue; by
microwave thermotherapy   ♂ P2 T ▭
▧ *81020*
🔄 16.28 ⚲ 70.72 Global Days 090

53852   by radiofrequency thermotherapy   ♂ P2 T ▭
▧ *81020*
🔄 17.72 ⚲ 68.06 Global Days 090

~~**53853**~~   ~~by water-induced thermotherapy~~
See 55899

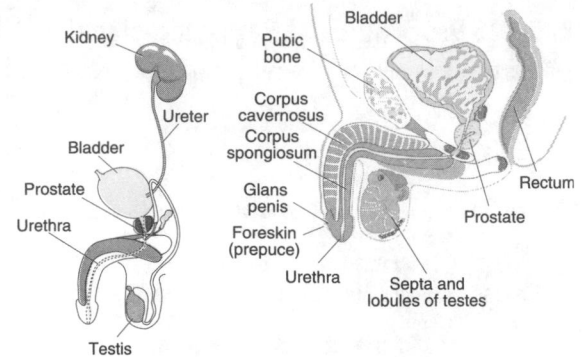

53899 Unlisted procedure, urinary system   T 80
▧ *81020*
🔄 0.00 ⚲ 0.00 Global Days YYY
AMA: 2008, Jan, 10-25; 2007, Jan, 13-27; 2007, Jan, 13-27; 2007,
January, 13-27; 2006, Feb, 16-18; 2006, February, 16-18; 2006,
Feb, 16-18; 2005, Oct, 18-22; 2005, Oct, 18-22; 2005, Oct, 23-24;
2005, Oct, 23-24; 2005, October, 23-24; 2005, October, 18-22;
2004, Aug, 12; 2004, Aug, 12; 2004, September, 11; 2004, August,
12; 2004, Sep, 11; 2004, Sep, 11

54000-54015 Procedures of Penis: Incisional

EXCLUDES *debridement of abdominal perineal gangrene (11004-11006)*

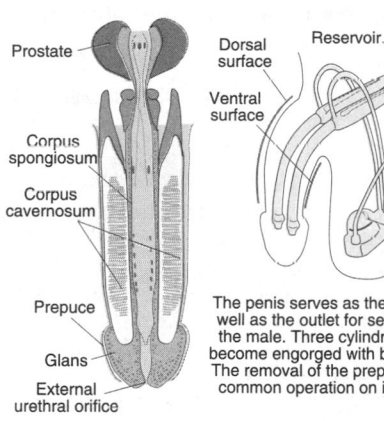

Prostate · Dorsal surface · Reservoir · Ventral surface · Corpus spongiosum · Corpus cavernosum · Prepuce · Glans · External urethral orifice · Pump in scrotum

An implanted, inflatable penile prosthesis (left); schematic of the main features of the penis (far left)

The penis serves as the organ of copulation as well as the outlet for seminal fluid and urine in the male. Three cylindrical bodies, or corpora, become engorged with blood to form an erection. The removal of the prepuce by circumcision is a common operation on infant and young males.

54000 Slitting of prepuce, dorsal or lateral (separate procedure); newborn ♂ A A2 T 80 ☺ ▭
 ▱ 3.05 ⚷ 4.45 Global Days 010

54001 except newborn ♂ A2 T ▭
 ▱ 3.93 ⚷ 5.47 Global Days 010

54015 Incision and drainage of penis, deep ♂ A6 T 00 ▭
 EXCLUDES *abscess, skin/subcutaneous (10060-10160)*
 ▱ 8.88 ⚷ 8.88 Global Days 010

54050-54065 Destruction of Penis Lesions: Multiple Methods

CMS 100-3,140.5 *Laser Procedures*
EXCLUDES *excision/destruction other lesions (11420-11426, 11620-11626, 17000-17250, 17270-17276)*

54050 Destruction of lesion(s), penis (eg, condyloma, papilloma, molluscum contagiosum, herpetic vesicle), simple; chemical ♂ P2 T ▭
 ▱ 2.67 ⚷ 3.35 Global Days 010

54055 electrodesiccation ♂ P3 T ▭
 ▱ 2.46 ⚷ 3.20 Global Days 010

54056 cryosurgery ♂ P2 T ▭
 ▱ 2.75 ⚷ 3.49 Global Days 010

54057 laser surgery ♂ A2 T ▭
 ▱ 2.59 ⚷ 3.85 Global Days 010

54060 surgical excision ♂ A2 T ▭
 ▱ 3.61 ⚷ 5.20 Global Days 010

54065 Destruction of lesion(s), penis (eg, condyloma, papilloma, molluscum contagiosum, herpetic vesicle), extensive (eg, laser surgery, electrosurgery, cryosurgery, chemosurgery) ♂ A7 T ▭
 ▱ 4.40 ⚷ 5.69 Global Days 010

54100-54115 Procedures of Penis: Excisional

54100 Biopsy of penis; (separate procedure) ♂ A2 T ▭
 ▱ 3.27 ⚷ 5.22 Global Days 000

54105 deep structures ♂ A2 T ▭
 ▱ 6.16 ⚷ 7.88 Global Days 010

54110 Excision of penile plaque (Peyronie disease); ♂ A2 T 80 ▭
 ▱ 17.84 ⚷ 17.84 Global Days 090

54111 with graft to 5 cm in length ♂ A2 T 80 ▭
 ▱ 23.06 ⚷ 23.06 Global Days 090
 AMA: 2008, Jan, 10-25; 2007, Jan, 13-27; 2007, Jan, 13-27; 2007, January, 13-27

54112 with graft greater than 5 cm in length ♂ A2 T 80 ▭
 ▱ 27.06 ⚷ 27.06 Global Days 090

54115 Removal foreign body from deep penile tissue (eg, plastic implant) ♂ A2 T 80 ▭
 ▱ 11.99 ⚷ 12.83 Global Days 090

54120-54135 Amputation of Penis

EXCLUDES *lymphadenectomy (separate procedure) (38760-38770)*

54120 Amputation of penis; partial ♂ A2 T 80 ▭
 ▱ 18.03 ⚷ 18.03 Global Days 090

54125 complete ♂ C 80 ▭
 ▱ 23.26 ⚷ 23.26 Global Days 090

54130 Amputation of penis, radical; with bilateral inguinofemoral lymphadenectomy ♂ C 80 ▭
 ▱ 34.46 ⚷ 34.46 Global Days 090

54135 in continuity with bilateral pelvic lymphadenectomy, including external iliac, hypogastric and obturator nodes ♂ C 80 ▭
 ▱ 43.72 ⚷ 43.72 Global Days 090

54150-54164 Circumcision Procedures

54150 Circumcision, using clamp or other device with regional dorsal penile or ring block ♂ A A2 T 80 ☺ ▭
 Code also modifier 52 when performed without dorsal penile or ring block
 ▱ 2.81 ⚷ 4.79 Global Days 000
 AMA: 2008, Jan, 10-25; 2007, Jan, 13-27; 2007, Jan, 13-27; 2007, May, 9-11; 2007, May, 9-11; 2007, January, 13-27; 2007, May, 9-11; 2007, Jul, 5

54160 Circumcision, surgical excision other than clamp, device, or dorsal slit; neonate (28 days of age or less) ♂ A A2 T ☺ ▭
 ▱ 4.16 ⚷ 6.63 Global Days 010
 AMA: 2008, Jan, 10-25; 2007, Jan, 13-27; 2007, Jan, 13-27; 2007, May, 9-11; 2007, May, 9-11; 2007, January, 13-27; 2007, May, 9-11; 2007, Jul, 5

54161 older than 28 days of age ♂ A2 T ▭
 ▱ 5.64 ⚷ 5.64 Global Days 010
 AMA: 2008, Jan, 10-25; 2007, Jan, 13-27; 2007, Jan, 13-27; 2007, May, 9-11; 2007, May, 9-11; 2007, January, 13-27; 2007, May, 9-11; 2007, Jul, 5

54162 Lysis or excision of penile post-circumcision adhesions ♂ A2 T ▭
 ▱ 5.60 ⚷ 7.68 Global Days 010

54163 Repair incomplete circumcision ♂ A2 T ▭
 ▱ 6.20 ⚷ 6.20 Global Days 010

54164 Frenulotomy of penis ♂ A2 T ▭
 Do not report with (54150, 54160-54163)
 ▱ 5.46 ⚷ 5.46 Global Days 010

54200-54250 Evaluation and Treatment of Erectile Abnormalities

54200 Injection procedure for Peyronie disease; ♂ P3 T ▭
 ▱ 2.40 ⚷ 3.13 Global Days 010

54205 with surgical exposure of plaque ♂ A2 T 80 ▭
 ▱ 15.32 ⚷ 15.32 Global Days 090

54220 Irrigation of corpora cavernosa for priapism ♂ A2 T ▭
 ▱ 3.88 ⚷ 6.06 Global Days 000

● New Code ▲ Revised Code ▥ Maternity Edit ⒜ Age Edit A-Y OPPS Status Indicator ▱ Facility RVU ⚷ Non-Facility RVU
▭ CCI Comprehensive Code 80 Bilateral Procedure + Add-on Indicator ◣ Laboratory crosswalk ▤ Radiology crosswalk

© 2008 Ingenix *(Blue Ink)*   CPT only © 2008 American Medical Association. All Rights Reserved. (Black Ink)   Medicare (Red Ink)   **207**

54000 — 54220

54230 Injection procedure for corpora cavernosography ♂ ⬛Ⓝ▢
　　📷 74445
　　🔲 2.30　🔲 2.79　Global Days 000

54231 Dynamic cavernosometry, including intracavernosal injection of vasoactive drugs (eg, papaverine, phentolamine) ♂ P3 Ⓣ▢
　　🔲 3.40　🔲 4.05　Global Days 000

54235 Injection of corpora cavernosa with pharmacologic agent(s) (eg, papaverine, phentolamine) ♂ P3 Ⓣ▢
　　🔲 2.11　🔲 2.58　Global Days 000
　　AMA: 2008, Jan, 10-25; 2007, Jan, 13-27; 2007, Jan, 13-27; 2007, January, 13-27

54240 Penile plethysmography ♂ P3 Ⓣ 80 ▢
　　🔲 2.93　🔲 2.93　Global Days 000

54250 Nocturnal penile tumescence and/or rigidity test ♂ P3 Ⓣ 80 ▢
　　🔲 3.63　🔲 3.63　Global Days 000

54300-54390 Hypospadias Repair and Related Procedures

EXCLUDES other urethroplasties (53400-53430)
revascularization of penis (37788)

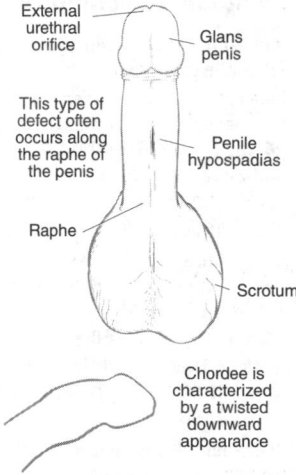

External urethral orifice
Glans penis
This type of defect often occurs along the raphe of the penis
Penile hypospadias
Raphe
Scrotum
Chordee is characterized by a twisted downward appearance

Plastic repair is performed on the penis. Report 54300 to straighten chordee and 54304 to otherwise address chordee and or hypospadias repair

54300 Plastic operation of penis for straightening of chordee (eg, hypospadias), with or without mobilization of urethra ♂ A2 Ⓣ 80 ▢
　　🔲 18.60　🔲 18.60　Global Days 090

54304 Plastic operation on penis for correction of chordee or for first stage hypospadias repair with or without transplantation of prepuce and/or skin flaps ♂ A2 Ⓣ 80 ▢
　　🔲 21.78　🔲 21.78　Global Days 090

54308 Urethroplasty for second stage hypospadias repair (including urinary diversion); less than 3 cm ♂ A2 Ⓣ 80 ▢
　　🔲 20.74　🔲 20.74　Global Days 090

54312 　greater than 3 cm ♂ A2 Ⓣ 80 ▢
　　🔲 24.06　🔲 24.06　Global Days 090

54316 Urethroplasty for second stage hypospadias repair (including urinary diversion) with free skin graft obtained from site other than genitalia ♂ A2 Ⓣ 80 ▢
　　🔲 29.00　🔲 29.00　Global Days 090

54318 Urethroplasty for third stage hypospadias repair to release penis from scrotum (eg, third stage Cecil repair) ♂ A2 Ⓣ 80 ▢
　　🔲 21.09　🔲 21.09　Global Days 090

54322 1 stage distal hypospadias repair (with or without chordee or circumcision); with simple meatal advancement (eg, Magpi, V-flap) ♂ A2 Ⓣ 80 ▢
　　🔲 22.68　🔲 22.68　Global Days 090

54324 　with urethroplasty by local skin flaps (eg, flip-flap, prepucial flap) ♂ A2 Ⓣ 80 ▢
　　INCLUDES Browne's operation
　　🔲 28.18　🔲 28.18　Global Days 090

54326 　with urethroplasty by local skin flaps and mobilization of urethra ♂ A2 Ⓣ 80 ▢
　　🔲 26.48　🔲 26.48　Global Days 090

54328 1 stage distal hypospadias repair (with or without chordee or circumcision); with extensive dissection to correct chordee and urethroplasty with local skin flaps, skin graft patch, and/or island flap ♂ A2 Ⓣ 80 ▢
　　EXCLUDES urethroplasty/straightening of chordee (54308)
　　🔲 26.82　🔲 26.82　Global Days 090
　　AMA: 2008, Jan, 10-25; 2007, Jan, 13-27; 2007, Jan, 13-27; 2007, January, 13-27; 2004, Oct, 14; 2004, October, 14; 2004, Oct, 14

54332 1 stage proximal penile or penoscrotal hypospadias repair requiring extensive dissection to correct chordee and urethroplasty by use of skin graft tube and/or island flap ♂ Ⓣ 80 ▢
　　🔲 29.37　🔲 29.37　Global Days 090
　　AMA: 2008, Jan, 10-25; 2007, Jan, 13-27; 2007, Jan, 13-27; 2007, January, 13-27; 2004, Sep, 12; 2004, Sep, 12; 2004, September, 12; 2004, March, 11; 2004, Mar, 11; 2004, Mar, 11

54336 1 stage perineal hypospadias repair requiring extensive dissection to correct chordee and urethroplasty by use of skin graft tube and/or island flap ♂ Ⓣ 80 ▢
　　🔲 33.58　🔲 33.58　Global Days 090
　　AMA: 2008, Jan, 10-25; 2007, Jan, 13-27; 2007, Jan, 13-27; 2007, January, 13-27; 2004, Oct, 14; 2004, October, 14; 2004, Oct, 14

54340 Repair of hypospadias complications (ie, fistula, stricture, diverticula); by closure, incision, or excision, simple ♂ A2 Ⓣ 80 ▢
　　🔲 16.14　🔲 16.14　Global Days 090

54344 　requiring mobilization of skin flaps and urethroplasty with flap or patch graft ♂ A2 Ⓣ 80 ▢
　　🔲 27.96　🔲 27.96　Global Days 090

54348 　requiring extensive dissection and urethroplasty with flap, patch or tubed graft (includes urinary diversion) ♂ A2 Ⓣ 80 ▢
　　🔲 29.54　🔲 29.54　Global Days 090

54352 Repair of hypospadias cripple requiring extensive dissection and excision of previously constructed structures including re-release of chordee and reconstruction of urethra and penis by use of local skin as grafts and island flaps and skin brought in as flaps or grafts ♂ A2 Ⓣ 80 ▢
　　🔲 41.81　🔲 41.81　Global Days 090

54360 Plastic operation on penis to correct angulation ♂ A2 Ⓣ 80 ▢
　　🔲 20.90　🔲 20.90　Global Days 090

54380 Plastic operation on penis for epispadias distal to external sphincter; ♂ A2 Ⓣ 80 ▢
　　INCLUDES Lowsley's operation
　　🔲 23.16　🔲 23.16　Global Days 090

54385 　with incontinence ♂ A2 Ⓣ 80 ▢
　　🔲 27.92　🔲 27.92　Global Days 090

54390   with exstrophy of bladder   ♂ C 80 ▢
              🚑 34.00   ⚕ 34.00   Global Days 090

54400-54417 Procedures to Treat Impotence

CMS 100-3,230.4   *Diagnosis and Treatment of Impotence*
EXCLUDES   *other urethroplasties (53400-53430)*
             revascularization of penis (37788)

54400   Insertion of penile prosthesis; non-inflatable
              (semi-rigid)   ♂ H8 S ▢
              EXCLUDES   *replacement/removal penile prosthesis*
                           (54415, 54416)

              Code also (C2622)
              🚑 15.32   ⚕ 15.32   Global Days 090

54401   inflatable (self-contained)   ♂ H8 S ▢ P0
              EXCLUDES   *replacement/removal penile prosthesis*
                           (54415, 54416)

              Code also (C1813)
              🚑 18.74   ⚕ 18.74   Global Days 090

54405   Insertion of multi-component, inflatable penile
              prosthesis, including placement of pump, cylinders, and
              reservoir   ♂ H8 S 80 ▢ P0
              Code also (C1813)
              🚑 23.27   ⚕ 23.27   Global Days 090

54406   Removal of all components of a multi-component,
              inflatable penile prosthesis without replacement of
              prosthesis   ♂ A2 T 80 ▢ P0
              🚑 20.98   ⚕ 20.98   Global Days 090

54408   Repair of component(s) of a multi-component, inflatable
              penile prosthesis   ♂ A2 T 80 ▢ P0
              🚑 22.58   ⚕ 22.58   Global Days 090

54410   Removal and replacement of all component(s) of a
              multi-component, inflatable penile prosthesis at the same
              operative session   ♂ H8 S 80 ▢ P0
              Code also (C1813)
              🚑 24.82   ⚕ 24.82   Global Days 090

54411   Removal and replacement of all components of a
              multi-component inflatable penile prosthesis through an
              infected field at the same operative session, including
              irrigation and debridement of infected tissue   ♂ C 80 ▢
              Do not report with (11040-11043)
              🚑 29.30   ⚕ 29.30   Global Days 090

54415   Removal of non-inflatable (semi-rigid) or inflatable
              (self-contained) penile prosthesis, without replacement
              of prosthesis   ♂ A2 T 80 ▢ P0
              🚑 15.07   ⚕ 15.07   Global Days 090

54416   Removal and replacement of non-inflatable (semi-rigid)
              or inflatable (self-contained) penile prosthesis at the same
              operative session   ♂ H8 S 80 ▢ P0
              Code also (C1813, C2622)
              🚑 20.19   ⚕ 20.19   Global Days 090

54417   Removal and replacement of non-inflatable (semi-rigid)
              or inflatable (self-contained) penile prosthesis through
              an infected field at the same operative session, including
              irrigation and debridement of infected tissue   ♂ C 80 ▢
              Do not report with (11040-11043)
              🚑 25.71   ⚕ 25.71   Global Days 090

54420-54450 Other Procedures of the Penis

EXCLUDES   *other urethroplasties (53400-53430)*
             revascularization of penis (37788)

54420   Corpora cavernosa-saphenous vein shunt (priapism
              operation), unilateral or bilateral   ♂ A2 T 80 ▢
              🚑 20.33   ⚕ 20.33   Global Days 090

54430   Corpora cavernosa-corpus spongiosum shunt (priapism
              operation), unilateral or bilateral   ♂ C 80 ▢
              🚑 18.42   ⚕ 18.42   Global Days 090

54435   Corpora cavernosa-glans penis fistulization (eg, biopsy
              needle, Winter procedure, rongeur, or punch) for
              priapism   ♂ A2 T ▢
              🚑 11.92   ⚕ 11.92   Global Days 090

54440   Plastic operation of penis for injury   ♂ A2 T 80 ▢
              🚑 0.00   ⚕ 0.00   Global Days 090

54450   Foreskin manipulation including lysis of preputial
              adhesions and stretching   ♂ A2 T ▢
              🚑 1.70   ⚕ 2.10   Global Days 000

54500-54560 Testicular Procedures: Incisional

EXCLUDES   *debridement of abdominal perineal gangrene (11004-11006)*

54500   Biopsy of testis, needle (separate
              procedure)   ♂ A2 T 80 50 ▢
              EXCLUDES   *fine needle aspiration (10021, 10022)*

              ◤   *88172, 88173*
              🚑 2.18   ⚕ 2.18   Global Days 000

54505   Biopsy of testis, incisional (separate
              procedure)   ♂ A2 T 80 50 ▢
              Code also vasotomy for vasogram, seminal vesiculogram,
              epididymogram when combined (55300)
              🚑 6.12   ⚕ 6.12   Global Days 010

54512   Excision of extraparenchymal lesion of
              testis   ♂ A2 T 50 ▢
              🚑 15.35   ⚕ 15.35   Global Days 090
              AMA: 2008, Jan, 10-25; 2007, Jan, 13-27; 2007, Jan, 13-27; 2007,
              January, 13-27; 2005, Aug, 13-15; 2005, August, 13-15; 2005,
              Aug, 13-15

54520   Orchiectomy, simple (including subcapsular), with or
              without testicular prosthesis, scrotal or inguinal
              approach   ♂ A2 T 50 ▢
              INCLUDES   Huggins' orchiectomy
              EXCLUDES   *lymphadenectomy, radical retroperitoneal*
                           (38780)
              Code also hernia repair if performed (49505, 49507)
              🚑 9.34   ⚕ 9.34   Global Days 090
              AMA: 2004, Mar, 1; 2004, Mar, 1; 2004, March, 1

54522   Orchiectomy, partial   ♂ A2 T 80 50 ▢
              EXCLUDES   *lymphadenectomy, radical retroperitoneal*
                           (38780)
              🚑 16.71   ⚕ 16.71   Global Days 090

54530   Orchiectomy, radical, for tumor; inguinal
              approach   ♂ A2 T 80 50 ▢
              EXCLUDES   *lymphadenectomy, radical retroperitoneal*
                           (38780)
              🚑 14.53   ⚕ 14.53   Global Days 090

54535   with abdominal exploration   ♂ T 80 50 ▢
              EXCLUDES   *lymphadenectomy, radical retroperitoneal*
                           (38780)
              🚑 21.07   ⚕ 21.07   Global Days 090

● New Code   ▲ Revised Code   M Maternity Edit   A Age Edit   A-Y OPPS Status Indicator   🚑 Facility RVU   ⚕ Non-Facility RVU
▢ CCI Comprehensive Code   50 Bilateral Procedure   + Add-on Indicator   ◤ Laboratory crosswalk   ◨ Radiology crosswalk

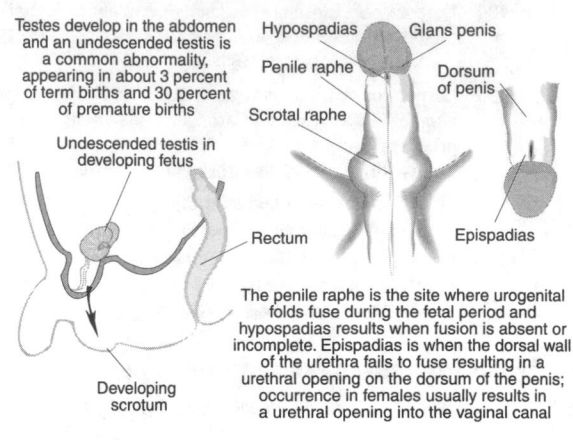

Testes develop in the abdomen and an undescended testis is a common abnormality, appearing in about 3 percent of term births and 30 percent of premature births

Hypospadias Glans penis

Penile raphe

Dorsum of penis

Scrotal raphe

Undescended testis in developing fetus

Rectum

Epispadias

Developing scrotum

The penile raphe is the site where urogenital folds fuse during the fetal period and hypospadias results when fusion is absent or incomplete. Epispadias is when the dorsal wall of the urethra fails to fuse resulting in a urethral opening on the dorsum of the penis; occurrence in females usually results in a urethral opening into the vaginal canal

54550   **Exploration for undescended testis (inguinal or scrotal area)** ♂ A2 T 80 50 ▣

    13.99   13.99   Global Days 090

    AMA: 2007, Jul, 5

54560   **Exploration for undescended testis with abdominal exploration** ♂ G2 T 80 50 ▣

    19.09   19.09   Global Days 090

    AMA: 2007, Jul, 5

54600-54699 Open and Laparoscopic Testicular Procedures

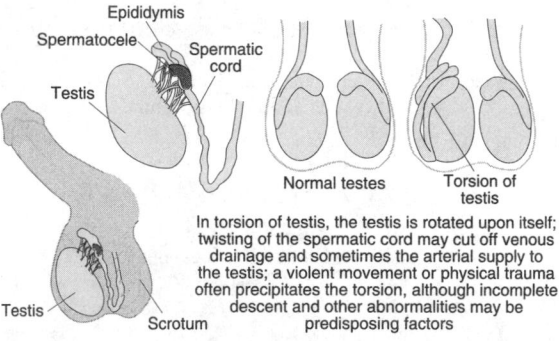

Epididymis

Spermatocele

Spermatic cord

Testis

Normal testes

Torsion of testis

Testis

Scrotum

In torsion of testis, the testis is rotated upon itself; twisting of the spermatic cord may cut off venous drainage and sometimes the arterial supply to the testis; a violent movement or physical trauma often precipitates the torsion, although incomplete descent and other abnormalities may be predisposing factors

A spermatocele is a cystic accumulation of semen, usually in the spermatic cord or at the head of the epididymis

54600   **Reduction of torsion of testis, surgical, with or without fixation of contralateral testis** ♂ A2 T 50 ▣

    12.93   12.93   Global Days 090

    AMA: 2008, Jan, 10-25; 2007, Jan, 13-27; 2007, Jan, 13-27; 2007, January, 13-27; 2005, Aug, 13-15; 2005, August, 13-15; 2005, Aug, 13-15

54620   **Fixation of contralateral testis (separate procedure)** ♂ A2 T 50 ▣

    8.69   8.69   Global Days 010

54640   **Orchiopexy, inguinal approach, with or without hernia repair** ♂ A2 T 80 50 ▣

    INCLUDES   Bevan's operation
              Koop inguinal orchiopexy
              Prentice orchiopexy

    EXCLUDES   *repair inguinal hernia with inguinal orchiopexy (49495-49525)*

    13.32   13.32   Global Days 090

    AMA: 2008, Jan, 10-25; 2008, Jun, 3-6; 2007, Jan, 13-27; 2007, Jan, 13-27; 2007, January, 13-27; 2004, Mar, 10; 2004, Mar, 10; 2004, March, 10; 2004, January, 27; 2004, Jan, 27; 2004, Jan, 27

54650   **Orchiopexy, abdominal approach, for intra-abdominal testis (eg, Fowler-Stephens)** ♂ C 80 50 ▣

    EXCLUDES   *laparoscopic orchiopexy (54692)*

    20.45   20.45   Global Days 090

54660   **Insertion of testicular prosthesis (separate procedure)** ♂ A2 T 80 50 ▣

    10.16   10.16   Global Days 090

54670   **Suture or repair of testicular injury** ♂ A2 T 80 50 ▣

    11.56   11.56   Global Days 090

54680   **Transplantation of testis(es) to thigh (because of scrotal destruction)** ♂ A2 T 80 50 ▣

    22.53   22.53   Global Days 090

54690   **Laparoscopy, surgical; orchiectomy** ♂ A2 T 80 50 ▣

    INCLUDES   diagnostic laparoscopy

    18.21   18.21   Global Days 090

54692   **orchiopexy for intra-abdominal testis** ♂ G2 T 50 ▣

    INCLUDES   diagnostic laparoscopy

    22.31   22.31   Global Days 090

54699   Unlisted laparoscopy procedure, testis   T 80 50

    0.00   0.00   Global Days YYY

54700-54901 Open Procedures of the Epididymis

54700   **Incision and drainage of epididymis, testis and/or scrotal space (eg, abscess or hematoma)** ♂ A2 T ▣

    EXCLUDES   *debridement of genitalia for necrotizing soft tissue infection (11004-11006)*

    6.04   6.04   Global Days 010

54800   **Biopsy of epididymis, needle** ♂ A2 T 80 ▣

    EXCLUDES   *fine needle aspiration (10021, 10022)*

    ◼   88172, 88173

    3.83   3.83   Global Days 000

    AMA: 2007, Jul, 5

54830   **Excision of local lesion of epididymis** ♂ A2 T 80 ▣

    10.52   10.52   Global Days 090

54840   **Excision of spermatocele, with or without epididymectomy** ♂ A2 T ▣

    9.24   9.24   Global Days 090

54860   **Epididymectomy; unilateral** ♂ A2 T ▣

    11.92   11.92   Global Days 090

54861   **bilateral** ♂ A2 T 80 ▣

    16.12   16.12   Global Days 090

54865   **Exploration of epididymis, with or without biopsy** ♂ A2 T 80

    10.16   10.16   Global Days 090

    AMA: 2007, Jul, 5

54900   **Epididymovasostomy, anastomosis of epididymis to vas deferens; unilateral** ♂ A2 T 80 ▣

    EXCLUDES   *operating microscope (69990)*

    21.62   21.62   Global Days 090

    AMA: 2008, Jan, 10-25; 2007, Jan, 13-27; 2007, Jan, 13-27; 2007, January, 13-27; 2004, Jun, 11; 2004, June, 11; 2004, Jun, 11

54901   **bilateral** ♂ A2 T 80 ▣

    EXCLUDES   *operating microscope (69990)*

    30.99   30.99   Global Days 090

    AMA: 2008, Jan, 10-25; 2007, Jan, 13-27; 2007, Jan, 13-27; 2007, January, 13-27; 2004, Jun, 11; 2004, June, 11; 2004, Jun, 11

55000-55180 Procedures of the Tunica Vaginalis and Scrotum

26/TC Professional/Technical Component Only   80/80 Assist-at-Surgery Allowed/With Documentation   Unlisted   Not Covered

AMA: CPT Assistant References   A2-Z3 ASC Payment Indicator   ♂ Male Only   ♀ Female Only   ⊘ Modifier 51 Exempt   PQ PQRI

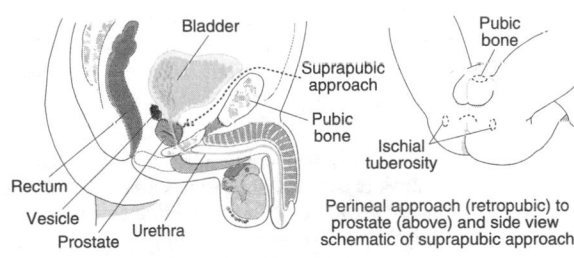

The tunica vaginalis is a closed sac within the scrotum and is the lower remnant of the path taken by the testis as it descends from the abdomen just prior to birth. The presence of fluid in this pathway is called a hydrocele. The testes, or testicles, are the male reproductive organs. Each produces sperm and male sex hormones

55000 Puncture aspiration of hydrocele, tunica vaginalis, with or without injection of medication ♂ P3 T ▯
🔧 2.42 ⚕ 3.46 Global Days 000

55040 Excision of hydrocele; unilateral ♂ A2 T ▯
EXCLUDES repair of hernia with hydrocelectomy (49495-49501)
🔧 9.62 ⚕ 9.62 Global Days 090
AMA: 2008, Jun, 3-6

55041 bilateral ♂ A2 T ▯
EXCLUDES repair of hernia with hydrocelectomy (49495-49501)
🔧 14.45 ⚕ 14.45 Global Days 090

55060 Repair of tunica vaginalis hydrocele (Bottle type) ♂ A2 T 80 50 ▯
🔧 10.75 ⚕ 10.75 Global Days 090

55100 Drainage of scrotal wall abscess ♂ A2 T ▯
EXCLUDES debridement of genitalia for necrotizing soft tissue infection (11004-11006) incision and drainage of scrotal space (54700)
🔧 4.56 ⚕ 6.11 Global Days 010

55110 Scrotal exploration ♂ A2 T ▯
🔧 10.92 ⚕ 10.92 Global Days 090

55120 Removal of foreign body in scrotum ♂ A2 T 80 ▯
🔧 10.02 ⚕ 10.02 Global Days 090

55150 Resection of scrotum ♂ A2 T 80 ▯
EXCLUDES lesion excision of skin of scrotum (11420-11426, 11620-11626)
🔧 13.84 ⚕ 13.84 Global Days 090

55175 Scrotoplasty; simple ♂ A2 T 80 ▯
🔧 10.27 ⚕ 10.27 Global Days 090

55180 complicated ♂ A2 T 80 ▯
🔧 19.58 ⚕ 19.58 Global Days 090

55200-55680 Procedures of Other Male Genital Ducts and Glands

55200 Vasotomy, cannulization with or without incision of vas, unilateral or bilateral (separate procedure) ♂ A2 T 80 ▯
🔧 7.88 ⚕ 13.91 Global Days 090

55250 Vasectomy, unilateral or bilateral (separate procedure), including postoperative semen examination(s) ♂ A2 T ▯
🔧 6.46 ⚕ 12.27 Global Days 090
AMA: 2008, Jan, 10-25; 2007, Jan, 13-27; 2007, Jan, 13-27; 2007, January, 13-27

55300 Vasotomy for vasograms, seminal vesiculograms, or epididymograms, unilateral or bilateral ♂ M N 80 ▯
Code also biopsy of testis when combined (54505)
📷 74440
🔧 5.20 ⚕ 5.20 Global Days 000

55400 Vasovasostomy, vasovasorrhaphy ♂ A2 T 80 50 ▯
EXCLUDES operating microscope (69990)
🔧 14.46 ⚕ 14.46 Global Days 090
AMA: 2008, Jan, 10-25; 2007, Jan, 13-27; 2007, Jan, 13-27; 2007, January, 13-27; 2004, Jun, 10; 2004, June, 10; 2004, Jun, 10

55450 Ligation (percutaneous) of vas deferens, unilateral or bilateral (separate procedure) ♂ P3 T 80 ▯
🔧 7.28 ⚕ 10.85 Global Days 010

55500 Excision of hydrocele of spermatic cord, unilateral (separate procedure) ♂ A2 T 80 ▯
🔧 10.69 ⚕ 10.69 Global Days 090

55520 Excision of lesion of spermatic cord (separate procedure) ♂ A2 T 80 ▯
🔧 11.05 ⚕ 11.05 Global Days 090
AMA: 2008, Jan, 10-25; 2007, Jan, 13-27; 2007, Jan, 13-27; 2007, January, 13-27

55530 Excision of varicocele or ligation of spermatic veins for varicocele; (separate procedure) ♂ A2 T 50 ▯
🔧 10.09 ⚕ 10.09 Global Days 090

55535 abdominal approach ♂ A2 T 80 50 ▯
🔧 12.17 ⚕ 12.17 Global Days 090

55540 with hernia repair ♂ A2 T 50 ▯
🔧 13.40 ⚕ 13.40 Global Days 090

55550 Laparoscopy, surgical, with ligation of spermatic veins for varicocele ♂ A2 T 80 50 ▯
INCLUDES diagnostic laparoscopy
🔧 12.08 ⚕ 12.08 Global Days 090

55559 Unlisted laparoscopy procedure, spermatic cord T 80 50
🔧 0.00 ⚕ 0.00 Global Days YYY

55600 Vesiculotomy; ♂ A2 T 80 50 ▯
🔧 12.20 ⚕ 12.20 Global Days 090

55605 complicated ♂ C 80 50 ▯
🔧 14.37 ⚕ 14.37 Global Days 090

55650 Vesiculectomy, any approach ♂ C 80 50 ▯
🔧 20.45 ⚕ 20.45 Global Days 090

55680 Excision of Mullerian duct cyst ♂ A2 T 80 ▯
EXCLUDES injection procedure (52010, 55300)
🔧 9.70 ⚕ 9.70 Global Days 090

55700-55725 Procedures of Prostate: Incisional

The walnut-sized prostate gland secretes a thin, milky fluid that mixes with spermatic fluids during ejaculation; its secretion constitutes about one-third of the volume of seminal fluid. The prostate is palpable via the rectum. Some procedures are via the urethra, which can be dilated to accommodate instruments. The seminal vesicles may also be palpated via the rectum. Each is a long, coiled tube which secretes a thick fluid that mixes with sperm as it passes along the ejaculatory ducts. The ejaculatory ducts are the union of the seminal vesicles and the sperm-carrying ductus deferens

● New Code ▲ Revised Code Ⓜ Maternity Edit Ⓐ Age Edit A-T OPPS Status Indicator 🔧 Facility RVU ⚕ Non-Facility RVU
▯ CCI Comprehensive Code 50 Bilateral Procedure + Add-on Indicator 📷 Laboratory crosswalk 📷 Radiology crosswalk

© 2008 Ingenix *(Blue Ink)* CPT only © 2008 American Medical Association. All Rights Reserved. (Black Ink) Medicare (Red Ink) **211**

Male Genital System

55700 — 55899

55700 Biopsy, prostate; needle or punch, single or multiple, any approach ♂ A2 T ▣

    EXCLUDES   *fine needle aspiration (10021, 10022)*

               needle biopsy of prostate, saturation sampling
               for prostate mapping (55706)

        ◪ *88172, 88173*

        ◪ *76942*

        ⚕ 3.91 ⚕ 6.55 Global Days 000
        AMA: 2006, Apr, 11-18; 2006, Apr, 11-18; 2006, April, 11-18

55705 incisional, any approach ♂ A2 T ▣

        ⚕ 7.73 ⚕ 7.73 Global Days 010

● **55706** Biopsies, prostate, needle, transperineal, stereotactic template guided saturation sampling, including imaging guidance ♂ 02 T 80

    Do not report with (55700)

        ⚕ 10.93 ⚕ 10.93 Global Days 010

55720 Prostatotomy, external drainage of prostatic abscess, any approach; simple ♂ A2 T 80 ▣

    EXCLUDES   *drainage of prostatic abscess, transurethral (52700)*

        ⚕ 13.37 ⚕ 13.37 Global Days 090

55725 complicated ♂ A2 T 80 ▣

    EXCLUDES   *drainage of prostatic abscess, transurethral (52700)*

        ⚕ 16.80 ⚕ 16.80 Global Days 090

55801-55845 Open Prostatectomy

EXCLUDES   *node dissection, independent (38770-38780)*

    pelvic limited lymphadenectomy for staging (separate procedure) (38562)

    transurethral prostate
        destruction (53850-53852)
        resection (52601-52640)

55801 Prostatectomy, perineal, subtotal (including control of postoperative bleeding, vasectomy, meatotomy, urethral calibration and/or dilation, and internal urethrotomy) ♂ C 80 ▣ P0

        ⚕ 31.21 ⚕ 31.21 Global Days 090

55810 Prostatectomy, perineal radical; ♂ C 80 ▣ P0

    INCLUDES   Walsh modified radical prostatectomy

        ⚕ 37.74 ⚕ 37.74 Global Days 090

55812 with lymph node biopsy(s) (limited pelvic lymphadenectomy) ♂ C 80 ▣ P0

        ⚕ 46.41 ⚕ 46.41 Global Days 090

55815 with bilateral pelvic lymphadenectomy, including external iliac, hypogastric and obturator nodes ♂ C 80 ▣ P0

    EXCLUDES   *perineal radical prostatectomy when performed on a separate day from bilateral pelvic lymphadenectomy (38770, 55810)*

        ⚕ 50.88 ⚕ 50.88 Global Days 090

55821 Prostatectomy (including control of postoperative bleeding, vasectomy, meatotomy, urethral calibration and/or dilation, and internal urethrotomy); suprapubic, subtotal, 1 or 2 stages ♂ C 80 ▣ P0

        ⚕ 25.09 ⚕ 25.09 Global Days 090

55831 retropubic, subtotal ♂ C 80 ▣ P0

        ⚕ 27.19 ⚕ 27.19 Global Days 090

55840 Prostatectomy, retropubic radical, with or without nerve sparing; ♂ C 80 ▣ P0

    EXCLUDES   *prostatectomy, radical retropubic, performed laparoscopically (55866)*

        ⚕ 38.51 ⚕ 38.51 Global Days 090

55842 with lymph node biopsy(s) (limited pelvic lymphadenectomy) ♂ C 80 ▣ P0

        ⚕ 41.27 ⚕ 41.27 Global Days 090

55845 with bilateral pelvic lymphadenectomy, including external iliac, hypogastric, and obturator nodes ♂ C 80 ▣ P0

    EXCLUDES   *radical retropubic prostatectomy when performed on a separate day from bilateral pelvic lymphadenectomy (38770, 55840)*

        ⚕ 47.22 ⚕ 47.22 Global Days 090

55860-55865 Prostate Exposure for Radiation Source Application

55860 Exposure of prostate, any approach, for insertion of radioactive substance; ♂ 02 T ▣

    ◪ *77776-77778*

        ⚕ 25.17 ⚕ 25.17 Global Days 090

55862 with lymph node biopsy(s) (limited pelvic lymphadenectomy) ♂ C 80 ▣

        ⚕ 31.87 ⚕ 31.87 Global Days 090

55865 with bilateral pelvic lymphadenectomy, including external iliac, hypogastric and obturator nodes ♂ C 80 ▣

        ⚕ 38.55 ⚕ 38.55 Global Days 090

55866 Laparoscopic Prostatectomy

55866 Laparoscopy, surgical prostatectomy, retropubic radical, including nerve sparing ♂ C 80 ▣ P0

    INCLUDES   diagnostic laparoscopy

    EXCLUDES   *open method (55840)*

        ⚕ 50.18 ⚕ 50.18 Global Days 090

55870-55899 Miscellaneous Prostate Procedures

55870 Electroejaculation ♂ P3 T ▣

    EXCLUDES   *artificial insemination (58321-58322)*

        ⚕ 4.15 ⚕ 5.02 Global Days 000

55873 Cryosurgical ablation of the prostate (includes ultrasonic guidance for interstitial cryosurgical probe placement) ♂ H8 T ▣

    Code also (C2618)

        ⚕ 32.83 ⚕ 32.83 Global Days 090
        AMA: 2006, Apr, 11-18; 2006, Apr, 11-18; 2006, April, 11-18

55875 Transperineal placement of needles or catheters into prostate for interstitial radioelement application, with or without cystoscopy A2 03 80

    EXCLUDES   *the placement of needles or catheters into the pelvic organs and/or genitalia (except for the prostate) for interstitial radioelement application (55920)*

    ◪ *76965, 77776-77787*

        ⚕ 21.85 ⚕ 21.85 Global Days 090
        AMA: 2008, Jun, 8-11; 2007, Mar, 7-8; 2007, Mar, 7-8; 2007, May, 1-2; 2007, May, 1-2; 2007, March, 7-8; 2007, May, 1-2

55876 Placement of interstitial device(s) for radiation therapy guidance (eg, fiducial markers, dosimeter), prostate (via needle, any approach), single or multiple ♂ P3 X

    Code also supply of device

    ◪ *76942, 77002, 77012, 77021*

        ⚕ 3.11 ⚕ 4.10 Global Days 000
        AMA: 2007, May, 1-2; 2007, May, 1-2; 2007, May, 1-2

55899 Unlisted procedure, male genital system ♂ T

        ⚕ 0.00 ⚕ 0.00 Global Days YYY
        AMA: 2007, May, 1-2; 2007, May, 1-2; 2007, May, 1-2

26/16 Professional/Technical Component Only   80/80 Assist-at-Surgery Allowed/With Documentation   Unlisted   Not Covered

AMA: CPT Assistant References   A2-Z3 ASC Payment Indicator   ♂ Male Only   ♀ Female Only   ⊘ Modifier 51 Exempt   P0 PQRI

55920 Insertion Brachytherapy Catheters/Needles Pelvis/Genitalia, Male/Female

EXCLUDES *insertion of Heyman capsules for purposes of brachytherapy (58346)*
insertion of vaginal ovoids and/or uterine tandems for purposes of brachytherapy (57155)
placement of catheters or needles, prostate (55875)

55920 **Placement of needles or catheters into pelvic organs and/or genitalia (except prostate) for subsequent interstitial radioelement application** 62 T 80

> **EXCLUDES** *insertion of Heyman capsules for purposes of brachytherapy (58346)*
> *insertion of vaginal ovoids and/or uterine tandems for purposes of brachytherapy (57155)*
> *placement of catheters or needles, prostate (55875)*

🔲 12.31   ⚌ 12.31   Global Days 000

55970-55980 Transsexual Surgery

CMS 100-3,140.3   *Transexual Surgery*
CMS 100-2,16,180   *Services Related to Noncovered Procedures*

55970 **Intersex surgery; male to female**   E
🔲 0.00   ⚌ 0.00   Global Days XXX

55980 **female to male**   ♀ E
🔲 0.00   ⚌ 0.00   Global Days XXX

56405-56420 Incision and Drainage of Abscess

EXCLUDES *incision and drainage Skene's gland cyst/abscess (53060)*
incision and drainage subcutaneous abscess/cyst/furuncle (10040, 10060, 10061)

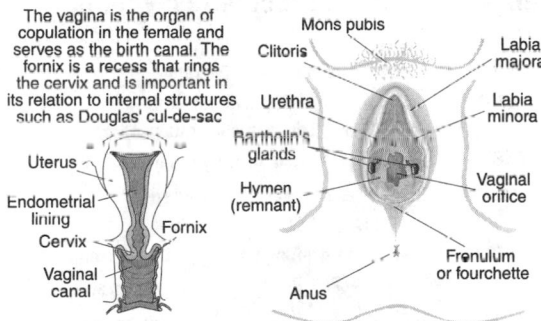

The vagina is the organ of copulation in the female and serves as the birth canal. The fornix is a recess that rings the cervix and is important in its relation to internal structures such as Douglas' cul-de-sac

Mons pubis · Clitoris · Labia majora · Urethra · Labia minora · Bartholin's glands · Hymen (remnant) · Vaginal orifice · Vaginal canal · Anus · Frenulum or fourchette · Uterus · Endometrial lining · Cervix · Fornix · Vaginal canal

The external female genital region is collectively known as the vulva, or sometimes, the pudendum. A Bartholin's gland is located on either side of the orifice. The perineum is the space between the anus and the vagina, but is often generally defined as the entire pelvic floor and its related structures. Introitus is a general term for the vaginal entrance.

56405 **Incision and drainage of vulva or perineal abscess**   ♀ P3 T 🔲
🔲 2.79   ⚌ 2.85   Global Days 010

56420 **Incision and drainage of Bartholin's gland abscess**   ♀ P2 T 🔲
🔲 2.42   ⚌ 3.28   Global Days 010

56440-56442 Other Female Genital Incisional Procedures

EXCLUDES *incision and drainage subcutaneous abscess/cyst/furuncle (10040, 10060, 10061)*

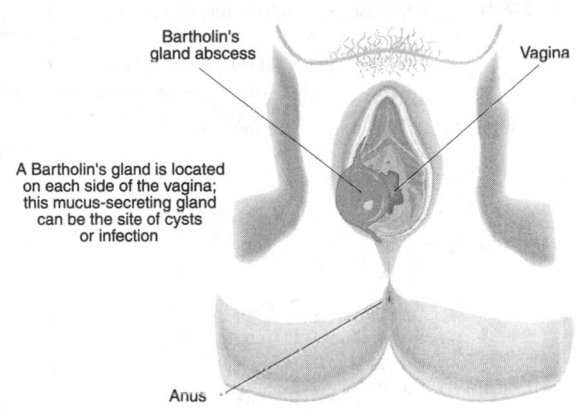

Bartholin's gland abscess · Vagina · Anus

A Bartholin's gland is located on each side of the vagina; this mucus-secreting gland can be the site of cysts or infection

56440 **Marsupialization of Bartholin's gland cyst**   ♀ A2 T 🔲
🔲 4.83   ⚌ 4.83   Global Days 010

56441 **Lysis of labial adhesions**   ♀ A2 T 80 🔲
🔲 3.73   ⚌ 3.94   Global Days 010

56442 **Hymenotomy, simple incision**   ♀ A2 T 80
🔲 1.29   ⚌ 1.29   Global Days 000

56501-56515 Destruction of Vulvar Lesions, Any Method

CMS 100-3,140.5   *Laser Procedures*
EXCLUDES *excision/fulguration/destruction*
Skene's glands (53270)
urethral caruncle (53265)

56501 **Destruction of lesion(s), vulva; simple (eg, laser surgery, electrosurgery, cryosurgery, chemosurgery)**   ♀ P3 T 🔲
🔲 2.97   ⚌ 3.41   Global Days 010
AMA: 2006, Apr, 11-18; 2006, Apr, 11-18; 2006, April, 11-18

56515 **extensive (eg, laser surgery, electrosurgery, cryosurgery, chemosurgery)**   ♀ A2 T 🔲
🔲 5.16   ⚌ 5.82   Global Days 010

56605-56606 Vulvar and Perineal Biopsies

EXCLUDES *excision local lesion (11420-11426, 11620-11626)*

56605 **Biopsy of vulva or perineum (separate procedure); one lesion**   ♀ P3 T 🔲
🔲 1.62   ⚌ 2.20   Global Days 000
AMA: 2008, Jun, 3-6

+ **56606** **each separate additional lesion (List separately in addition to code for primary procedure)**   ♀ P3 T 🔲
Code first (56605)
🔲 0.80   ⚌ 1.02   Global Days ZZZ

56620-56640 Vulvectomy Procedures

INCLUDES removal of:
greater than 80% of the vulvar area - complete procedure
less than 80% of the vulvar area - partial procedure
skin and deep subcutaneous tissue - radical procedure
skin and superficial subcutaneous tissues - simple procedure

EXCLUDES *skin graft (15004-15005, 15120, 15121, 15240, 15241)*

56620 **Vulvectomy simple; partial**   ♀ A2 T 80 🔲
🔲 12.99   ⚌ 12.99   Global Days 090

56625 **complete**   ♀ A2 T 80 🔲
🔲 15.60   ⚌ 15.60   Global Days 090

56630 **Vulvectomy, radical, partial;**   ♀ C 80 🔲 P0
🔲 22.80   ⚌ 22.80   Global Days 090

● New Code   ▲ Revised Code   ▥ Maternity Edit   ⬛ Age Edit   A-Y OPPS Status Indicator   🔲 Facility RVU   ⚌ Non-Facility RVU
🔲 CCI Comprehensive Code   50 Bilateral Procedure   + Add-on Indicator   ▣ Laboratory crosswalk   ▣ Radiology crosswalk

56631   with unilateral inguinofemoral lymphadenectomy   ♀ C 80 ◻ P0
   [INCLUDES]   Bassett's operation

   🔧 29.03   ✂ 29.03   Global Days 090

56632   with bilateral inguinofemoral lymphadenectomy   ♀ C 80 ◻ P0
   [INCLUDES]   Bassett's operation

   🔧 33.66   ✂ 33.66   Global Days 090

56633   Vulvectomy, radical, complete;   ♀ C 80 ◻ P0
   [INCLUDES]   Bassett's operation

   🔧 29.75   ✂ 29.75   Global Days 090

56634   with unilateral inguinofemoral lymphadenectomy   ♀ C 80 ◻ P0
   [INCLUDES]   Bassett's operation

   🔧 31.46   ✂ 31.46   Global Days 090

56637   with bilateral inguinofemoral lymphadenectomy   ♀ C 80 ◻ P0
   [INCLUDES]   Bassett's operation

   🔧 37.19   ✂ 37.19   Global Days 090

56640   Vulvectomy, radical, complete, with inguinofemoral, iliac, and pelvic lymphadenectomy   ♀ C 80 50 ◻ P0
   [INCLUDES]   Bassett's operation
   [EXCLUDES]   *lymphadenectomy (38760-38780)*

   🔧 37.18   ✂ 37.18   Global Days 090

56700-56740 Other Excisional Procedures: External Female Genitalia

56700   Partial hymenectomy or revision of hymenal ring   ♀ A2 T 80 ◻

   🔧 4.88   ✂ 4.88   Global Days 010

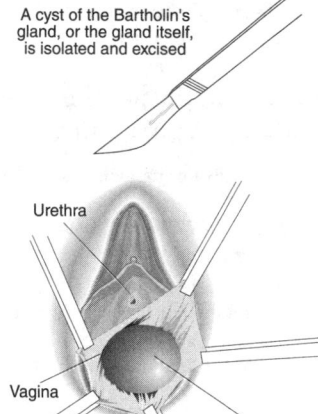

A cyst of the Bartholin's gland, or the gland itself, is isolated and excised

Urethra

Vagina

Bartholin's gland cyst

Anus

The operative site is closed with layered sutures

56740   Excision of Bartholin's gland or cyst   ♀ A2 T ◻
   [EXCLUDES]   *excision/fulguration/marsupialization*
     Skene's glands (53270)
     urethral carcinoma (53220)
     urethral caruncle (53265)
     urethral diverticulum (53230, 53240)

   🔧 7.82   ✂ 7.82   Global Days 010

56800-56810 Repair/Reconstruction External Female Genitalia

[EXCLUDES]   *repair of urethra for mucosal prolapse (53275)*

56800   Plastic repair of introitus   ♀ A2 T 80 ◻
   [INCLUDES]   Emmet's operation

   🔧 6.43   ✂ 6.43   Global Days 010

56805   Clitoroplasty for intersex state   ♀ G2 T 80 ◻

   🔧 30.29   ✂ 30.29   Global Days 090

56810   Perineoplasty, repair of perineum, nonobstetrical (separate procedure)   ♀ A2 T 80 ◻
   [INCLUDES]   Emmet's operation
   [EXCLUDES]   *genitalia wound repair (12001-12007,*
     12041-12047, 13131-13133)
     introitus plastic repair (56800)
     sphincteroplasty, anal (46750, 46751)
     vaginal/perineum recent injury repair,
     nonobstetrical (57210)
     vulva/perineum
     episiorrhaphy/episioperineorrhaphy for
     recent injury, nonobstetrical (57210)

   🔧 6.91   ✂ 6.91   Global Days 010

56820-56821 Vulvar Colposcopy with/without Biopsy

[EXCLUDES]   *colposcopic procedures and/or examinations:*
   cervix (57452-57461)
   vagina (57420, 57421)

56820   Colposcopy of the vulva;   ♀ P3 T ◻
   🔧 2.26   ✂ 2.92   Global Days 000

56821   with biopsy(s)   ♀ P2 T ◻
   🔧 3.07   ✂ 3.91   Global Days 000

57000-57023 Incisional Procedures: Vagina

57000   Colpotomy; with exploration   ♀ A2 T 80 ◻
   🔧 5.02   ✂ 5.02   Global Days 010

57010   with drainage of pelvic abscess   ♀ A2 T 80 ◻
   [INCLUDES]   Laroyenne operation

   🔧 11.29   ✂ 11.29   Global Days 090

57020   Colpocentesis (separate procedure)   ♀ A2 T 80 ◻
   🔧 2.18   ✂ 2.50   Global Days 000

57022   Incision and drainage of vaginal hematoma; obstetrical/postpartum   ♀ G2 T 80 ◻
   🔧 4.37   ✂ 4.37   Global Days 010

57023   non-obstetrical (eg, post-trauma, spontaneous bleeding)   ♀ A2 T 80 ◻
   🔧 8.22   ✂ 8.22   Global Days 010

57061-57065 Destruction of Vaginal Lesions, Any Method

CMS *100-3,140.5*   *Laser Procedures*

57061   Destruction of vaginal lesion(s); simple (eg, laser surgery, electrosurgery, cryosurgery, chemosurgery)   ♀ P3 T ◻
   🔧 2.54   ✂ 2.97   Global Days 010
   AMA: 2008, Jan, 10-25; 2007, Jan, 13-27; 2007, Jan, 13-27; 2007, January, 13-27

57065   extensive (eg, laser surgery, electrosurgery, cryosurgery, chemosurgery)   ♀ A2 T ◻
   🔧 4.50   ✂ 5.05   Global Days 010
   AMA: 2008, Jan, 10-25; 2007, Jan, 13-27; 2007, Jan, 13-27; 2007, January, 13-27

57100-57135 Excisional Procedures: Vagina

57100   Biopsy of vaginal mucosa; simple (separate procedure)   ♀ P3 T 🖵
     🖀 1.75   ⚒ 2.33   Global Days 000

57105   extensive, requiring suture (including cysts)   ♀ A2 T 🖵
     🖀 3.28   ⚒ 3.56   Global Days 010

57106   Vaginectomy, partial removal of vaginal wall;   ♀ T 80 🖵
     🖀 12.43   ⚒ 12.43   Global Days 090

57107   with removal of paravaginal tissue (radical vaginectomy)   ♀ T 80 🖵
     🖀 36.95   ⚒ 36.95   Global Days 090

57109   with removal of paravaginal tissue (radical vaginectomy) with bilateral total pelvic lymphadenectomy and para-aortic lymph node sampling (biopsy)   ♀ T 80 🖵
     🖀 42.27   ⚒ 42.27   Global Days 090

57110   Vaginectomy, complete removal of vaginal wall;   ♀ C 80 🖵
     🖀 23.79   ⚒ 23.79   Global Days 090

57111   with removal of paravaginal tissue (radical vaginectomy)   ♀ C 80 🖵
     🖀 42.70   ⚒ 42.70   Global Days 090

57112   with removal of paravaginal tissue (radical vaginectomy) with bilateral total pelvic lymphadenectomy and para-aortic lymph node sampling (biopsy)   ♀ C 80 🖵
     🖀 45.23   ⚒ 45.23   Global Days 090

57120   Colpocleisis (Le Fort type)   ♀ T 80 🖵
     🖀 13.47   ⚒ 13.47   Global Days 090

57130   Excision of vaginal septum   ♀ A2 T 80 🖵
     🖀 4.25   ⚒ 4.76   Global Days 010

57135   Excision of vaginal cyst or tumor   ♀ A2 T 🖵
     🖀 4.58   ⚒ 5.10   Global Days 010

57150-57180 Irrigation/Insertion/Introduction Vaginal Medication or Supply

57150   Irrigation of vagina and/or application of medicament for treatment of bacterial, parasitic, or fungoid disease   ♀ P3 T 🖵
     🖀 0.80   ⚒ 1.34   Global Days 000

57155   Insertion of uterine tandems and/or vaginal ovoids for clinical brachytherapy   ♀ A2 T 🖵

     EXCLUDES   *the placement of needles or catheters into the pelvic organs and/or genitalia (except for the prostate) for interstitial radioelement application (55920)*

     ⊞ *77761-77763, 77785-77787*
     🖀 11.06   ⚒ 11.06   Global Days 090

57160   Fitting and insertion of pessary or other intravaginal support device   ♀ P3 T 🖵
     🖀 1.28   ⚒ 2.03   Global Days 000
     AMA: 2008, Jan, 10-26; 2007, Jan, 13-27; 2007, Jan, 13-27; 2007, January, 13-27

57170   Diaphragm or cervical cap fitting with instructions   ♀ P2 T 80 🖵
     🖀 1.30   ⚒ 1.83   Global Days 000

57180   Introduction of any hemostatic agent or pack for spontaneous or traumatic nonobstetrical vaginal hemorrhage (separate procedure)   ♀ A2 T 🖵
     🖀 2.82   ⚒ 3.73   Global Days 010

57200-57335 Vaginal Repair and Reconstruction

CMS *100-3,230.10*   Incontinence Control Devices
EXCLUDES   *Marshall-Marchetti-Kranz type urethral suspension, abdominal approach (51840, 51841)*
urethral suspension performed laparoscopically (51990)

57200   Colporrhaphy, suture of injury of vagina (nonobstetrical)   ♀ A2 T 80 🖵
     🖀 7.78   ⚒ 7.78   Global Days 090

57210   Colpoperineorrhaphy, suture of injury of vagina and/or perineum (nonobstetrical)   ♀ A2 T 80 🖵
     🖀 9.66   ⚒ 9.66   Global Days 090

57220   Plastic operation on urethral sphincter, vaginal approach (eg, Kelly urethral plication)   ♀ A2 T 80 🖵
     🖀 8.39   ⚒ 8.39   Global Days 090

57230   Plastic repair of urethrocele   ♀ A2 T 80 🖵
     🖀 10.46   ⚒ 10.46   Global Days 090

57240   Anterior colporrhaphy, repair of cystocele with or without repair of urethrocele   ♀ A2 T 80 🖵
     🖀 17.29   ⚒ 17.29   Global Days 090

57250   Posterior colporrhaphy, repair of rectocele with or without perineorrhaphy   ♀ A2 T 80 🖵

     EXCLUDES   *rectocele repair (separate procedure) without posterior colporrhaphy (45560)*

     🖀 16.92   ⚒ 16.92   Global Days 090

57260   Combined anteroposterior colporrhaphy;   ♀ A2 T 80 🖵
     🖀 21.14   ⚒ 21.14   Global Days 090

57265   with enterocele repair   ♀ A2 T 80 🖵
     🖀 23.70   ⚒ 23.70   Global Days 090

+ **57267**   Insertion of mesh or other prosthesis for repair of pelvic floor defect, each site (anterior, posterior compartment), vaginal approach (List separately in addition to code for primary procedure)   ♀ A2 T 80
     Code first (45560, 57240-57265, 57285)
     🖀 7.23   ⚒ 7.23   Global Days ZZZ
     AMA: 2008, Jan, 10-25; 2007, Jan, 13-27; 2007, Jan, 13-27; 2007, January, 13-27; 2005, Jul, 13-16; 2005, July, 13-16; 2005, Jul, 13-16

57268   Repair of enterocele, vaginal approach (separate procedure)   ♀ A2 T 80 🖵
     🖀 12.65   ⚒ 12.65   Global Days 090

57270   Repair of enterocele, abdominal approach (separate procedure)   ♀ C 80 🖵
     🖀 21.03   ⚒ 21.03   Global Days 090

57280   Colpopexy, abdominal approach   ♀ C 80 🖵
     🖀 25.56   ⚒ 25.56   Global Days 090

57282   Colpopexy, vaginal; extra-peritoneal approach (sacrospinous, iliococcygeus)   ♀ T 80 🖵
     🖀 13.48   ⚒ 13.48   Global Days 090

57283   intra-peritoneal approach (uterosacral, levator myorrhaphy)   ♀ T 80 🖵
     🖀 18.07   ⚒ 18.07   Global Days 090

57284   Paravaginal defect repair (including repair of cystocele, if performed); open abdominal approach   ♀ T 80 🖵
     Do not report with (51840-51841, 51990, 57240, 57260-57265, 58152, 58267)
     🖀 22.14   ⚒ 22.14   Global Days 090
     AMA: 2008, Jan, 10-25; 2007, Jan, 13-27; 2007, Jan, 13-27; 2007, January, 13-27; 2005, Jul, 13-16; 2005, July, 13-16; 2005, Jul, 13-16

57285   vaginal approach   ♀ T 80
     Do not report with (51990, 57240, 57260-57265, 58267)
     🖀 17.51   ⚒ 17.51   Global Days 090

● New Code   ▲ Revised Code   🄼 Maternity Edit   Age Edit   A- V OPPS Status Indicator   🖀 Facility RVU   ⚒ Non-Facility RVU
🖵 CCI Comprehensive Code   50 Bilateral Procedure   + Add-on Indicator   ⬛ Laboratory crosswalk   ⬛ Radiology crosswalk

Female Genital System

57287 — 57454

57287 Removal or revision of sling for stress incontinence (eg, fascia or synthetic) ♀ 62 T 80 ▭
    🔪 18.53   ✂ 18.53   Global Days 090
    AMA: 2008, Jan, 10-25

57288 Sling operation for stress incontinence (eg, fascia or synthetic) ♀ A2 T 80 ▭
    INCLUDES Millin-Read operation
    EXCLUDES sling operation for stress incontinence performed laparoscopically (51992)
    Code also (C1762, C1763, C1771, C1781, C2631)
    🔪 19.53   ✂ 19.53   Global Days 090
    AMA: 2008, Jan, 10-25; 2007, Jan, 13-27; 2007, Jan, 13-27; 2007, January, 13-27

57289 Pereyra procedure, including anterior colporrhaphy ♀ A2 T 80 ▭
    🔪 20.53   ✂ 20.53   Global Days 090

57291 Construction of artificial vagina; without graft ♀ A2 T 80 ▭
    INCLUDES McIndoe vaginal construction
    🔪 14.29   ✂ 14.29   Global Days 090

57292 with graft ♀ T 80 ▭
    🔪 21.92   ✂ 21.92   Global Days 090

57295 Revision (including removal) of prosthetic vaginal graft; vaginal approach ♀ T 80
    🔪 13.03   ✂ 13.03   Global Days 090

57296 open abdominal approach ♀ C 80
    🔪 25.02   ✂ 25.02   Global Days 090

57300 Closure of rectovaginal fistula; vaginal or transanal approach ♀ A2 T 80 ▭
    🔪 13.96   ✂ 13.96   Global Days 090

57305 abdominal approach ♀ C 80 ▭
    🔪 23.40   ✂ 23.40   Global Days 090

57307 abdominal approach, with concomitant colostomy ♀ C 80 ▭
    🔪 26.21   ✂ 26.21   Global Days 090

57308 transperineal approach, with perineal body reconstruction, with or without levator plication ♀ C 80 ▭
    🔪 16.69   ✂ 16.69   Global Days 090

57310 Closure of urethrovaginal fistula; ♀ T 80 ▭
    🔪 12.95   ✂ 12.95   Global Days 090

57311 with bulbocavernosus transplant ♀ C 80 ▭
    🔪 14.79   ✂ 14.79   Global Days 090

57320 Closure of vesicovaginal fistula; vaginal approach ♀ 62 T 80 ▭
    EXCLUDES cystostomy, concomitant (51020-51040, 51101-51102)
    🔪 14.75   ✂ 14.75   Global Days 090

57330 transvesical and vaginal approach ♀ T 80 ▭
    EXCLUDES vesicovaginal fistula closure, abdominal approach (51900)
    🔪 20.96   ✂ 20.96   Global Days 090

57335 Vaginoplasty for intersex state ♀ T 80 ▭
    🔪 30.67   ✂ 30.67   Global Days 090

57400-57415 Treatment of Vaginal Disorders Under Anesthesia

▲ **57400** Dilation of vagina under anesthesia (other than local) ♀ A2 T 80 ▭
    🔪 3.60   ✂ 3.60   Global Days 000

▲ **57410** Pelvic examination under anesthesia (other than local) ♀ A2 T ▭
    🔪 2.82   ✂ 2.82   Global Days 000
    AMA: 2006, Apr, 1-7; 2006, Apr, 1-7; 2006, April, 1-7

▲ **57415** Removal of impacted vaginal foreign body (separate procedure) under anesthesia (other than local) ♀ A2 T 80 ▭
    EXCLUDES removal of impacted vaginal foreign body without anesthesia (99201-99499)
    🔪 4.20   ✂ 4.20   Global Days 010

57420-57425 Endoscopic Vaginal Procedures

57420 Colposcopy of the entire vagina, with cervix if present; ♀ P3 T ▭
    EXCLUDES colposcopic procedures and/or examinations cervix (57452-57461)
        vulva (56820-56821)
        colposcopy of cervix and upper adjacent vagina (57452)
        endometrial sampling (biopsy) performed at the same time as colposcopy (58110)
    🔪 2.40   ✂ 3.07   Global Days 000

57421 with biopsy(s) of vagina/cervix ♀ P3 T ▭
    EXCLUDES colposcopic procedures and/or examinations cervix (57452-57461)
        vulva (56820-56821)
        colposcopy of cervix and upper adjacent vagina (57452)
        endometrial sampling (biopsy) performed at the same time as colposcopy (58110)
    🔪 3.28   ✂ 4.14   Global Days 000
    AMA: 2008, Jan, 10-25; 2007, Jan, 13-27; 2007, Jan, 13-27; 2007, January, 13-27; 2006, Jun, 16-17; 2006, June, 16-17; 2006, Jun, 16-17

57423 Paravaginal defect repair (including repair of cystocele, if performed), laparoscopic approach ♀ T 80
    Do not report with (49320, 51840-51841, 51990, 57240, 57260, 58152, 58267)
    🔪 24.46   ✂ 24.46   Global Days 090

57425 Laparoscopy, surgical, colpopexy (suspension of vaginal apex) ♀ T 80 ▭
    🔪 25.80   ✂ 25.80   Global Days 090

57452-57461 Endoscopic Cervical Procedures

EXCLUDES cervicography

57452 Colposcopy of the cervix including upper/adjacent vagina; ♀ P3 T ▭
    EXCLUDES colposcopic procedures and/or examinations vagina (57420, 57421)
        vulva (56820, 56821)
        endometrial sampling (biopsy) performed at the same time as colposcopy (58110)
    Do not report with (57454-57461)
    🔪 2.44   ✂ 2.89   Global Days 000

57454 with biopsy(s) of the cervix and endocervical curettage ♀ P3 T ▭
    EXCLUDES colposcopic procedures and/or examinations vagina (57420, 57421)
        vulva (56820, 56821)
        endometrial sampling (biopsy) performed at the same time as colposcopy (58110)
    🔪 3.64   ✂ 4.09   Global Days 000

26/TC Professional/Technical Component Only   80/80 Assist-at-Surgery Allowed/With Documentation   Unlisted   Not Covered
AMA: CPT Assistant References   A2-Z3 ASC Payment Indicator   ♂ Male Only   ♀ Female Only   ⊘ Modifier-51 Exempt   P0 PQRI

57455　　with biopsy(s) of the cervix　　　♀ P3 T 🔲
　　　　　EXCLUDES　colposcopic procedures and / or examinations
　　　　　　　　　vagina (57420, 57421)
　　　　　　　　　vulva (56820, 56821)
　　　　　　　　　endometrial sampling (biopsy) performed at
　　　　　　　　　　the same time as colposcopy (58110)
　　　　　🗍 2.97　⚕ 3.80　Global Days 000

57456　　with endocervical curettage　　　♀ P3 T 🔲
　　　　　EXCLUDES　colposcopic procedures and / or examinations
　　　　　　　　　vagina (57420, 57421)
　　　　　　　　　vulva (56820, 56821)
　　　　　　　　　endometrial sampling (biopsy) performed at
　　　　　　　　　　the same time as colposcopy (58110)

　　　Do not report with (57461)
　　　　　🗍 2.77　⚕ 3.59　Global Days 000
　　　　　AMA: 2008, Jan, 10-25; 2007, Jan, 13-27; 2007, Jan, 13-27; 2007,
　　　　　January, 13-27

57460　　with loop electrode biopsy(s) of the cervix　♀ P3 T 🔲
　　　　　EXCLUDES　colposcopic procedures and / or examinations
　　　　　　　　　vagina (57420, 57421)
　　　　　　　　　vulva (56820, 56821)
　　　　　　　　　endometrial sampling (biopsy) performed at
　　　　　　　　　　the same time as colposcopy (58110)
　　　　　🗍 4.37　⚕ 7.84　Global Days 000
　　　　　AMA: 2008, Jan, 10-25, 2007, Jan, 13-27, 2007, Jan, 13-27; 2007,
　　　　　January, 13-27; 2005, Jul, 13-16; 2005, July, 13-16; 2005, Jul,
　　　　　13-16

57461　　with loop electrode conization of the
　　　　　cervix　　　　　　　　　　♀ P3 T 🔲
　　　　　EXCLUDES　colposcopic procedures and / or examinations
　　　　　　　　　vagina (57420, 57421)
　　　　　　　　　vulva (56820, 56821)
　　　　　　　　　endometrial sampling (biopsy) performed at
　　　　　　　　　　the same time as colposcopy (58110)

　　　Do not report with (57456)
　　　　　🗍 5.05　⚕ 8.80　Global Days 000
　　　　　AMA: 2008, Jan, 10-25; 2007, Jan, 13-27; 2007, Jan, 13-27; 2007,
　　　　　January, 13-27; 2006, Dec, 14-15; 2006, Dec, 14-15; 2006,
　　　　　December, 14-15; 2006, December, 14-15; 2006, Dec, 14-15;
　　　　　2006, Dec, 14-15

57500-57556 Cervical Procedures: Multiple Techniques

EXCLUDES　destrictopm / excision of endometriomas, open method (49203-49205,
　　　　　58957-58958)
　　　　　radical surgical procedures (58200-58240)

57500　Biopsy of cervix, single or multiple, or local excision of
　　　　　lesion, with or without fulguration (separate
　　　　　procedure)　　　　　　　　　　♀ P3 T 🔲
　　　　　🗍 1.97　⚕ 3.46　Global Days 000

57505　Endocervical curettage (not done as part of a dilation
　　　　　and curettage)　　　　　　　　♀ P3 T 🔲
　　　　　🗍 2.38　⚕ 2.66　Global Days 010
　　　　　AMA: 2008, Jan, 10-25; 2007, Jan, 13-27; 2007, Jan, 13-27; 2007,
　　　　　January, 13-27; 2005, Jul, 13-16; 2005, July, 13-16; 2005, Jul,
　　　　　13-16

57510　Cautery of cervix; electro or thermal　♀ P3 T 🔲
　　　　　🗍 3.08　⚕ 3.51　Global Days 010

57511　cryocautery, initial or repeat　　♀ P7 T 🔲
　　　　　🗍 3.46　⚕ 3.82　Global Days 010

57513　laser ablation　　　　　　　♀ A2 T 🔲
　　　　　🗍 3.48　⚕ 3.77　Global Days 010

57520　Conization of cervix, with or without fulguration, with
　　　　　or without dilation and curettage, with or without repair;
　　　　　cold knife or laser　　　　　　　♀ A2 T 🔲
　　　　　EXCLUDES　dilation and curettage, diagnostic / therapeutic,
　　　　　　　　　nonobstetrical (58120)
　　　　　🗍 7.19　⚕ 8.09　Global Days 090

57522　loop electrode excision　　　　♀ A2 T 🔲
　　　　　🗍 6.37　⚕ 6.92　Global Days 090
　　　　　AMA: 2008, Jan, 10-25; 2007, Jan, 13-27; 2007, Jan, 13-27; 2007,
　　　　　January, 13-27

57530　Trachelectomy (cervicectomy), amputation of cervix
　　　　　(separate procedure)　　　　　　♀ A2 T 80 🔲
　　　　　🗍 9.03　⚕ 9.03　Global Days 090

57531　Radical trachelectomy, with bilateral total pelvic
　　　　　lymphadenecctomy and para-aortic lymph nodc sampling
　　　　　biopsy, with or without removal of tube(s), with or
　　　　　without removal of ovary(s)　　　　♀ C 80 🔲
　　　　　🗍 44.87　⚕ 44.87　Global Days 090

57540　Excision of cervical stump, abdominal
　　　　　approach;　　　　　　　　　　♀ C 80 🔲
　　　　　🗍 20.54　⚕ 20.54　Global Days 090

57545　with pelvic floor repair　　　　♀ C 80 🔲
　　　　　🗍 21.65　⚕ 21.65　Global Days 090

57550　Excision of cervical stump, vaginal
　　　　　approach;　　　　　　　　　　♀ A2 T 80 🔲
　　　　　🗍 10.67　⚕ 10.67　Global Days 090

57555　with anterior and / or posterior repair　♀ T 80 🔲
　　　　　🗍 15.78　⚕ 15.78　Global Days 090

57556　with repair of enterocele　　　♀ A2 T 80 🔲
　　　　　EXCLUDES　insertion of hemostatic agent / pack for
　　　　　　　　　spontaneous / traumatic nonobstetrical
　　　　　　　　　vaginal hemorrhage (57180)
　　　　　　　　　intrauterine device insertion (58300)
　　　　　🗍 15.03　⚕ 15.03　Global Days 090

57558-57800 Cervical Procedures: Dilation, Suturing, or Instrumentation

EXCLUDES　destruction / excision of endometriomas, open method (49203-49205,
　　　　　58957-58958)

57558　Dilation and curettage of cervical stump　♀ A2 T
　　　　　EXCLUDES　radical surgical procedures (58200-58240)
　　　　　🗍 2.98　⚕ 3.29　Global Days 010

57700　Cerclage of uterine cervix, nonobstetrical　♀ A2 T 80 🔲
　　　　　INCLUDES　McDonald cerclage
　　　　　　　　　Shirodker operation
　　　　　🗍 8.00　⚕ 8.00　Global Days 090

57720　Trachelorrhaphy, plastic repair of uterine cervix, vaginal
　　　　　approach　　　　　　　　　　♀ A2 T 80 🔲
　　　　　INCLUDES　Emmet operation
　　　　　🗍 8.03　⚕ 8.03　Global Days 090

57800　Dilation of cervical canal, instrumental (separate
　　　　　procedure)　　　　　　　　　　♀ P3 T 🔲
　　　　　🗍 1.29　⚕ 1.59　Global Days 000

● New Code　▲ Revised Code　🅼 Maternity Edit　🅐 Age Edit　🄰-🅈 OPPS Status Indicator　🗍 Facility RVU　⚕ Non-Facility RVU
🔲 CCI Comprehensive Code　50 Bilateral Procedure　+ Add-on Indicator　🔳 Laboratory crosswalk　🔲 Radiology crosswalk

58100-58120 Procedures Involving the Endometrium

CMS *100-3,230.6*   *Vabra Aspirator*

58100   Endometrial sampling (biopsy) with or without endocervical sampling (biopsy), without cervical dilation, any method (separate procedure)   ♀ P3 T 🔲

> **EXCLUDES**   *endocervical curettage only (57505)*
> *endometrial sampling (biopsy) performed in*
> *conjunction with colposcopy (58110)*

📖 2.34   ⚕ 2.91   **Global Days 000**

+   **58110**   Endometrial sampling (biopsy) performed in conjunction with colposcopy (List separately in addition to code for primary procedure)   ♀ N1 N 80

> Code first colposcopy (57420-57421, 57452-57461)

📖 1.11   ⚕ 1.30   **Global Days ZZZ**

AMA: 2006, Jun, 16-17; 2006, Jun, 16-17; 2006, June, 16-17

58120   Dilation and curettage, diagnostic and/or therapeutic (nonobstetrical)   ♀ A2 T 🔲

> **EXCLUDES**   *postpartum hemorrhage (59160)*

📖 5.68   ⚕ 6.56   **Global Days 010**

AMA: 2008, Jan, 10-25; 2007, Jan, 13-27; 2007, Jan, 13-27; 2007, January, 13-27

58140-58146 Myomectomy Procedures

58140   Myomectomy, excision of fibroid tumor(s) of uterus, 1 to 4 intramural myoma(s) with total weight of 250 g or less and/or removal of surface myomas; abdominal approach   ♀ C 80 🔲

📖 24.10   ⚕ 24.10   **Global Days 090**

AMA: 2008, Jan, 10-25; 2007, Jan, 13-27; 2007, Jan, 13-27; 2007, January, 13-27

58145   vaginal approach   ♀ A2 T 80 🔲

📖 14.26   ⚕ 14.26   **Global Days 090**

58146   Myomectomy, excision of fibroid tumor(s) of uterus, 5 or more intramural myomas and/or intramural myomas with total weight greater than 250 g, abdominal approach   ♀ C 80 🔲

> Do not report with (58140-58145, 58150-58240)

📖 30.70   ⚕ 30.70   **Global Days 090**

AMA: 2008, Jan, 10-25; 2007, Jan, 13-27; 2007, Jan, 13-27; 2007, January, 13-27

58150-58294 Abdominal and Vaginal Hysterectomies

CMS *100-3,230.3*   *Sterilization*

EXCLUDES   *destruction/excision of endometriomas, open method (49203-49205, 58957-58958)*

58150   Total abdominal hysterectomy (corpus and cervix), with or without removal of tube(s), with or without removal of ovary(s);   ♀ C 80 🔲 PQ

📖 26.07   ⚕ 26.07   **Global Days 090**

AMA: 2008, Jan, 10-25; 2007, Jan, 13-27; 2007, Jan, 13-27; 2007, January, 13-27

58152   with colpo-urethrocystopexy (eg, Marshall-Marchetti-Krantz, Burch)   ♀ C 80 🔲 PQ

> **EXCLUDES**   *urethrocystopexy without hysterectomy*
> *(51840, 51841)*

📖 32.96   ⚕ 32.96   **Global Days 090**

58180   Supracervical abdominal hysterectomy (subtotal hysterectomy), with or without removal of tube(s), with or without removal of ovary(s)   ♀ C 80 🔲 PQ

📖 24.99   ⚕ 24.99   **Global Days 090**

58200   Total abdominal hysterectomy, including partial vaginectomy, with para-aortic and pelvic lymph node sampling, with or without removal of tube(s), with or without removal of ovary(s)   ♀ C 80 🔲 PQ

📖 34.50   ⚕ 34.50   **Global Days 090**

58210   Radical abdominal hysterectomy, with bilateral total pelvic lymphadenectomy and para-aortic lymph node sampling (biopsy), with or without removal of tube(s), with or without removal of ovary(s)   ♀ C 80 🔲 PQ

> **INCLUDES**   Wertheim hysterectomy

> **EXCLUDES**   *hysterectomy, radical, with transposition of*
> *ovary(s) (58825)*

📖 45.95   ⚕ 45.95   **Global Days 090**

58240   Pelvic exenteration for gynecologic malignancy, with total abdominal hysterectomy or cervicectomy, with or without removal of tube(s), with or without removal of ovary(s), with removal of bladder and ureteral transplantations, and/or abdominoperineal resection of rectum and colon and colostomy, or any combination thereof   ♀ C 80 🔲 PQ

> **EXCLUDES**   *pelvic exenteration for male genital*
> *malignancy or lower urinary tract*
> *(51597)*

📖 71.86   ⚕ 71.86   **Global Days 090**

58260   Vaginal hysterectomy, for uterus 250 g or less;   ♀ T 80 🔲 PQ

📖 21.79   ⚕ 21.79   **Global Days 090**

58262   with removal of tube(s), and/or ovary(s)   ♀ T 80 🔲 PQ

📖 24.36   ⚕ 24.36   **Global Days 090**

58263   with removal of tube(s), and/or ovary(s), with repair of enterocele   ♀ T 80 🔲 PQ

> Do not report with (57283)

📖 26.25   ⚕ 26.25   **Global Days 090**

58267   with colpo-urethrocystopexy (Marshall-Marchetti-Krantz type, Pereyra type) with or without endoscopic control   ♀ C 80 🔲 PQ

📖 27.89   ⚕ 27.89   **Global Days 090**

58270   with repair of enterocele   ♀ T 80 🔲 PQ

> **EXCLUDES**   *vaginal hysterectomy with repair of enterocele*
> *and removal of tubes and/or ovaries*
> *(58263)*

📖 23.36   ⚕ 23.36   **Global Days 090**

58275   Vaginal hysterectomy, with total or partial vaginectomy;   ♀ C 80 🔲 PQ

📖 25.99   ⚕ 25.99   **Global Days 090**

58280   with repair of enterocele   ♀ C 80 🔲 PQ

📖 27.81   ⚕ 27.81   **Global Days 090**

58285   Vaginal hysterectomy, radical (Schauta type operation)   ♀ C 80 🔲 PQ

📖 34.92   ⚕ 34.92   **Global Days 090**

58290   Vaginal hysterectomy, for uterus greater than 250 g;   ♀ T 80 🔲 PQ

📖 30.55   ⚕ 30.55   **Global Days 090**

58291   with removal of tube(s) and/or ovary(s)   ♀ T 80 🔲 PQ

📖 33.21   ⚕ 33.21   **Global Days 090**

58292   with removal of tube(s) and/or ovary(s), with repair of enterocele   ♀ T 80 🔲 PQ

📖 35.00   ⚕ 35.00   **Global Days 090**

58293   with colpo-urethrocystopexy (Marshall-Marchetti-Krantz type, Pereyra type) with or without endoscopic control   ♀ C 80 🔲 PQ

📖 36.34   ⚕ 36.34   **Global Days 090**

58294   with repair of enterocele   ♀ T 80 🔲 PQ

📖 32.26   ⚕ 32.26   **Global Days 090**

58300-58323 Contraception and Reproduction Procedures

58300 Insertion of intrauterine device (IUD) ♀ E
> **EXCLUDES** *insertion and/or removal of implantable contraceptive capsules (11975-11977)*
>
> ⚕ 1.48 ⚕ 2.07 Global Days XXX
>
> **AMA:** 2008, Jan, 10-25; 2007, Jan, 13-27; 2007, Jan, 13-27; 2007, January, 13-27

58301 Removal of intrauterine device (IUD) ♀ P3 T 80 ▢
> **EXCLUDES** *insertion and/or removal of implantable contraceptive capsules (11975-11977)*
>
> ⚕ 1.82 ⚕ 2.54 Global Days 000
>
> **AMA:** 2008, Jan, 10-25; 2007, Jan, 13-27; 2007, Jan, 13-27; 2007, January, 13-27

58321 Artificial insemination; intra-cervical ♀ P3 T 80 ▢
> ⚕ 1.33 ⚕ 2.07 Global Days 000

58322 intra-uterine ♀ P3 T 80 ▢
> ⚕ 1.58 ⚕ 2.31 Global Days 000

58323 Sperm washing for artificial insemination ♀ P3 T 80 ▢
> ⚕ 0.34 ⚕ 0.51 Global Days 000

58340-58350 Fallopian Tube Patency and Brachytherapy Procedures

58340 Catheterization and introduction of saline or contrast material for saline infusion sonohysterography (SIS) or hysterosalpingography ♀ M N ▢
> ⚕ 74740, 76831
>
> ⚕ 1.57 ⚕ 3.36 Global Days 000

58345 Transcervical introduction of fallopian tube catheter for diagnosis and/or re-establishing patency (any method), with or without hysterosalpingography ♀ P2 T 80 50 ▢
> ⚕ 74742
>
> ⚕ 7.32 ⚕ 7.32 Global Days 010

58346 Insertion of Heyman capsules for clinical brachytherapy ♀ A2 T ▢
> **EXCLUDES** *the placement of needles or catheters into the pelvic organs and/or genitalia (except for the prostate) for interstitial radioelement application (55920)*
>
> ⚕ 77761-77763, 77785-77787
>
> ⚕ 11.92 ⚕ 11.92 Global Days 090

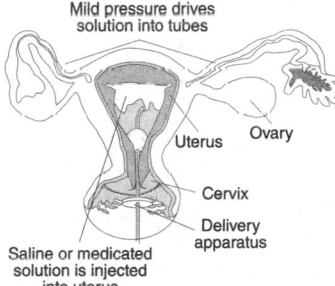

Mild pressure drives solution into tubes

Ovary

Uterus

Cervix

Delivery apparatus

Saline or medicated solution is injected into uterus

58350 Chromotubation of oviduct, including materials ♀ A2 T ▢
> **EXCLUDES** *materials and supplies provided by the physician (99070)*
>
> ⚕ 2.05 ⚕ 2.53 Global Days 010
>
> **AMA:** 2008, Jan, 10-25; 2007, Jan, 13-27; 2007, Jan, 13-27; 2007, January, 13-27

58353-58356 Ablation of Endometrium

58353 Endometrial ablation, thermal, without hysteroscopic guidance ♀ A2 T ▢
> **EXCLUDES** *endometrial ablation performed hysteroscopically (58563)*
>
> ⚕ 5.84 ⚕ 29.75 Global Days 010
>
> **AMA:** 2008, Jan, 10-25; 2007, Jan, 13-27; 2007, Jan, 13-27; 2007, January, 13-27

58356 Endometrial cryoablation with ultrasonic guidance, including endometrial curettage, when performed ♀ P2 T 80 ▢
> Code also (C2618)
>
> Do not report with (58100, 58120, 58340, 76700, 76856)
>
> ⚕ 9.34 ⚕ 54.53 Global Days 010

58400-58540 Uterine Repairs: Vaginal and Abdominal

58400 Uterine suspension, with or without shortening of round ligaments, with or without shortening of sacrouterine ligaments; (separate procedure) ♀ C 80 ▢
> **INCLUDES** Alexander's operation
> Baldy-Webster operation
> Manchester colporrhaphy
>
> **EXCLUDES** *anastomosis of tubes to uterus (58752)*
>
> ⚕ 11.78 ⚕ 11.78 Global Days 090

58410 with presacral sympathectomy ♀ C 80 ▢
> **INCLUDES** Alexander's operation
>
> **EXCLUDES** *anastomosis of tubes to uterus (58752)*
>
> ⚕ 21.11 ⚕ 21.11 Global Days 090
>
> **AMA:** 2008, Jan, 10-25; 2007, Mar, 9-11; 2007, Mar, 9-11; 2007, March, 9-11

58520 Hysterorrhaphy, repair of ruptured uterus (nonobstetrical) ♀ C 80 ▢
> ⚕ 20.63 ⚕ 20.63 Global Days 090

58540 Hysteroplasty, repair of uterine anomaly (Strassman type) ♀ C 80 ▢
> **INCLUDES** Strassman type
>
> **EXCLUDES** *vesicouterine fistula closure (51920)*
>
> ⚕ 23.98 ⚕ 23.98 Global Days 090

58541-58579 Endoscopic Procedures of the Uterus

INCLUDES diagnostic laparoscopy

EXCLUDES *diagnostic hysteroscopy (58555)*

58541 Laparoscopy, surgical, supracervical hysterectomy, for uterus 250 g or less; ♀ T 80
> Do not report with (49320, 57000, 57180, 57410, 58140-58146, 58545-58546, 58561, 58661, 58670-58671)
>
> ⚕ 22.62 ⚕ 22.62 Global Days 090

58542 with removal of tube(s) and/or ovary(s) ♀ T 80
> Do not report with (49320, 57000, 57180, 57410, 58140-58146, 58545-58546, 58561, 58661, 58670-58671)
>
> ⚕ 25.06 ⚕ 25.06 Global Days 090

58543 Laparoscopy, surgical, supracervical hysterectomy, for uterus greater than 250 g; ♀ T 80
> Do not report with (49320, 57000, 57180, 57410, 58140-58146, 58545-58546, 58561, 58661, 58670-58671)
>
> ⚕ 25.48 ⚕ 25.48 Global Days 090

● New Code　▲ Revised Code　Ⓜ Maternity Edit　Ⓐ Age Edit　Ⓐ-Ⓥ OPPS Status Indicator　⚕ Facility RVU　⚕ Non-Facility RVU
□ CCI Comprehensive Code　50 Bilateral Procedure　+ Add-on Indicator　◣ Laboratory crosswalk　▣ Radiology crosswalk

Female Genital System

58544 — 58600

58544　with removal of tube(s) and/or ovary(s)　♀ T 80

Do not report with (49320, 57000, 57180, 57410, 58140-58146, 58545-58546, 58561, 58661, 58670-58671)

27.54　27.54　Global Days 090

58545　Laparoscopy, surgical, myomectomy, excision; 1 to 4 intramural myomas with total weight of 250 g or less and/or removal of surface myomas　♀ A2 T 80

23.62　23.62　Global Days 090

58546　5 or more intramural myomas and/or intramural myomas with total weight greater than 250 g　♀ A2 T 80

29.95　29.95　Global Days 090

AMA: 2008, Jan, 10-25; 2007, Jan, 13-27; 2007, Jan, 13-27; 2007, January, 13-27; 2004, Jan, 26; 2004, January, 26; 2004, Jan, 26

58548　Laparoscopy, surgical, with radical hysterectomy, with bilateral total pelvic lymphadenectomy and para-aortic lymph node sampling (biopsy), with removal of tube(s) and ovary(s), if performed　♀ C 80

Do not report with (38570-38572, 58210, 58285, 58550-58554)

46.67　46.67　Global Days 090

58550　Laparoscopy, surgical, with vaginal hysterectomy, for uterus 250 g or less;　♀ A2 T 80

Do not report with (49320, 57000, 57180, 57410, 58140-58146, 58545-58546, 58561, 58661, 58670-58671)

23.32　23.32　Global Days 090

58552　with removal of tube(s) and/or ovary(s)　♀ 62 T 80

Do not report with (49320, 57000, 57180, 57410, 58140-58146, 58545-58546, 58561, 58661, 58670-58671)

25.67　25.67　Global Days 090

58553　Laparoscopy, surgical, with vaginal hysterectomy, for uterus greater than 250 g;　♀ T 80

Do not report with (49320, 57000, 57180, 57410, 58140-58146, 58545-58546, 58561, 58661, 58670-58671)

30.10　30.10　Global Days 090

58554　with removal of tube(s) and/or ovary(s)　♀ T 80

Do not report with (49320, 57000, 57180, 57410, 58140-58146, 58545-58546, 58561, 58661, 58670-58671)

34.37　34.37　Global Days 090

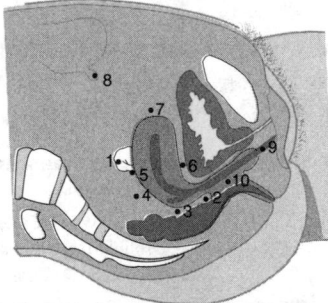

Some common sites of endometriosis, in descending order of frequency:
(1) ovary,
(2) cul de sac,
(3) uterosacral ligaments,
(4) broad ligaments,
(5) fallopian tube,
(6) uterovesical fold,
(7) round ligament,
(8) vermiform appendix,
(9) vagina,
(10) rectovaginal septum

Endometriosis is a benign condition in which endometrial matter is present outside of the endometrial cavity; it is estimated that 15 percent of women have some degree of the disease; occurrence is most common in the ovaries and about 60 percent of patients will have ovarian involvement, many with cyst development

58555　Hysteroscopy, diagnostic (separate procedure)　♀ A2 T 80

5.08　6.36　Global Days 000

58558　Hysteroscopy, surgical; with sampling (biopsy) of endometrium and/or polypectomy, with or without D & C　♀ A2 T

7.16　8.60　Global Days 000

AMA: 2008, Jan, 10-25; 2007, Jan, 13-27; 2007, Jan, 13-27; 2007, January, 13-27

58559　with lysis of intrauterine adhesions (any method)　♀ A2 T

9.21　9.21　Global Days 000

58560　with division or resection of intrauterine septum (any method)　♀ A2 T 80

10.41　10.41　Global Days 000

58561　with removal of leiomyomata　♀ A2 T 80

14.74　14.74　Global Days 000

58562　with removal of impacted foreign body　♀ A2 T

7.81　9.10　Global Days 000

AMA: 2008, Jan, 10-25

58563　with endometrial ablation (eg, endometrial resection, electrosurgical ablation, thermoablation)　♀ A2 T 80

9.21　48.44　Global Days 000

AMA: 2008, Jan, 10-25; 2007, Jan, 13-27; 2007, Jan, 13-27; 2007, January, 13-27

58565　with bilateral fallopian tube cannulation to induce occlusion by placement of permanent implants　♀ A2 T

Do not report with (57800, 58555)

11.84　51.64　Global Days 090

58570　Laparoscopy, surgical, with total hysterectomy, for uterus 250 g or less;　♀ T 80

Do not report with (49320, 57000, 57180, 57410, 58140-58146, 58150, 58545, 58546, 58561, 58661, 58670, 58671)

24.29　24.29　Global Days 090

58571　with removal of tube(s) and/or ovary(s)　T 80

Do not report with (49320, 57100, 57180, 57410, 58140-58146, 58150, 58545, 58546, 58561, 58661, 58670, 58671)

26.62　26.62　Global Days 090

58572　Laparoscopy, surgical, with total hysterectomy, for uterus greater than 250 g;　♀ 80

Do not report with (49320, 57000, 57180, 57410, 58140-58146, 58150, 58545, 58546, 58561, 58661, 58670, 58671)

30.21　30.21　Global Days 090

58573　with removal of tube(s) and/or ovary(s)　♀ T 80

Do not report with (49320, 57000, 57180, 57410, 58140-58146, 58150, 58545, 58546, 58561, 58661, 58670, 58671)

34.08　34.08　Global Days 090

58578　Unlisted laparoscopy procedure, uterus　T 80 50

0.00　0.00　Global Days YYY

AMA: 2008, Jan, 10-25; 2007, Mar, 9-11; 2007, Mar, 9-11; 2007, March, 9-11

58579　Unlisted hysteroscopy procedure, uterus　T 80 50

0.00　0.00　Global Days YYY

58600-58615 Sterilization by Tubal Interruption

CMS 100-3,230.3　*Sterilization*

EXCLUDES　(49203-49205, 58957-58958)

58600　Ligation or transection of fallopian tube(s), abdominal or vaginal approach, unilateral or bilateral　♀ 62 T 80

INCLUDES　Madlener operation

9.56　9.56　Global Days 090

58605 Ligation or transection of fallopian tube(s), abdominal or vaginal approach, postpartum, unilateral or bilateral, during same hospitalization (separate procedure) ♀Ⓒ80▢

EXCLUDES *laparoscopic methods (58670, 58671)*

⚏ 8.69 ⚖ 8.69 Global Days 090

+ **58611** Ligation or transection of fallopian tube(s) when done at the time of cesarean delivery or intra-abdominal surgery (not a separate procedure) (List separately in addition to code for primary procedure) ♀Ⓒ80▢

Code first primary procedure

⚏ 2.09 ⚖ 2.09 Global Days ZZZ

58615 Occlusion of fallopian tube(s) by device (eg, band, clip, Falope ring) vaginal or suprapubic approach ♀Ⓐ2ⓉⒺ80▢

EXCLUDES *laparoscopic method (58671)*
lysis of adnexal adhesions (58740)

⚏ 6.58 ⚖ 6.58 Global Days 010

58660-58679 Endoscopic Procedures Fallopian Tubes and/or Ovaries

CMS *100-3,230.3* *Sterilization*

INCLUDES diagnostic laparoscopy

EXCLUDES *laparoscopy with biopsy of fallopian tube or ovary (49321)*
laparoscopy with ovarian cyst aspiration (49322)

58660 Laparoscopy, surgical; with lysis of adhesions (salpingolysis, ovariolysis) (separate procedure) ♀Ⓐ2Ⓣ80▢

⚏ 17.78 ⚖ 17.78 Global Days 090

AMA: 2008, Jan, 10-25; 2007, Jan, 13-27; 2007, Jan, 13-27; 2007, January, 13-27

58661 with removal of adnexal structures (partial or total oophorectomy and/or salpingectomy) ♀Ⓐ2Ⓣ80▢

⚏ 17.08 ⚖ 17.08 Global Days 010

AMA: 2008, Jan, 10-25; 2007, Jan, 13-27; 2007, Jan, 13-27; 2007, January, 13-27

58662 with fulguration or excision of lesions of the ovary, pelvic viscera, or peritoneal surface by any method ♀Ⓐ2Ⓣ80▢

⚏ 18.68 ⚖ 18.68 Global Days 090

58670 with fulguration of oviducts (with or without transection) ♀Ⓐ2Ⓣ▢

⚏ 9.63 ⚖ 9.63 Global Days 090

58671 with occlusion of oviducts by device (eg, band, clip, or Falope ring) ♀Ⓐ2Ⓣ▢

⚏ 9.63 ⚖ 9.63 Global Days 090

58672 with fimbrioplasty ♀Ⓐ2Ⓣ80Ⓔ0▢

⚏ 19.69 ⚖ 19.69 Global Days 090

58673 with salpingostomy (salpingoneostomy) ♀Ⓐ2Ⓣ80Ⓔ0▢

⚏ 21.40 ⚖ 21.40 Global Days 090

AMA: 2008, Jan, 10-25; 2007, Jan, 13-27; 2007, Jan, 13-27; 2007, January, 13-27

58679 Unlisted laparoscopy procedure, oviduct, ovary Ⓣ80Ⓔ0

⚏ 0.00 ⚖ 0.00 Global Days YYY

58700-58770 Open Procedures of Fallopian Tubes, with/without Ovaries

EXCLUDES *destruction/excision of endometriomas, open method (49203-49205, 58957-58958)*

58700 Salpingectomy, complete or partial, unilateral or bilateral (separate procedure) ♀Ⓒ80▢

⚏ 20.11 ⚖ 20.11 Global Days 090

58720 Salpingo-oophorectomy, complete or partial, unilateral or bilateral (separate procedure) ♀Ⓒ80▢

⚏ 18.89 ⚖ 18.89 Global Days 090

AMA: 2008, Jan, 10-25; 2007, Jan, 13-27; 2007, Jan, 13-27; 2007, January, 13-27; 2006, May, 16-20; 2006, May, 16-20; 2006, May, 16-20

58740 Lysis of adhesions (salpingolysis, ovariolysis) ♀Ⓒ80▢

EXCLUDES *excision/fulguration of lesions performed laparoscopically (58662)*
laparoscopic method (58660)

⚏ 23.04 ⚖ 23.04 Global Days 090

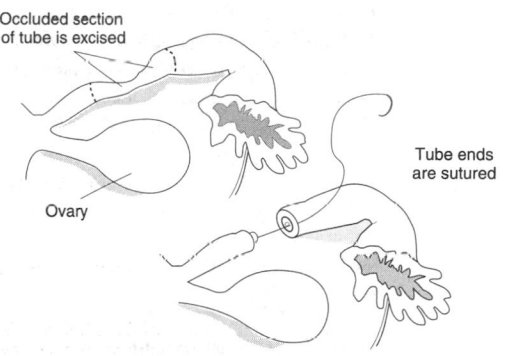

Occluded section of tube is excised

Ovary

Tube ends are sutured

58750 Tubotubal anastomosis ♀Ⓒ80▢

⚏ 24.00 ⚖ 24.00 Global Days 090

58752 Tubouterine implantation ♀Ⓒ80▢

⚏ 24.16 ⚖ 24.16 Global Days 090

58760 Fimbrioplasty ♀Ⓒ80Ⓔ0▢

EXCLUDES *laparoscopic method (58672)*

⚏ 21.77 ⚖ 21.77 Global Days 090

58770 Salpingostomy (salpingoneostomy) ♀Ⓣ80Ⓔ0▢

EXCLUDES *laparoscopic method (58673)*

⚏ 22.28 ⚖ 22.28 Global Days 090

58800-58925 Open Procedures: Ovary

CMS *100-3,230.3* *Sterilization*

EXCLUDES *destruction/excision of endometriomas, open method (49203-49205, 58957-58958)*

58800 Drainage of ovarian cyst(s), unilateral or bilateral (separate procedure); vaginal approach ♀ⒶⓉ▢

⚏ 7.80 ⚖ 8.37 Global Days 090

58805 abdominal approach ♀Ⓐ2Ⓣ80▢

⚏ 10.63 ⚖ 10.63 Global Days 090

58820 Drainage of ovarian abscess; vaginal approach, open ♀Ⓐ2Ⓣ80▢

⚏ 8.21 ⚖ 8.21 Global Days 090

58822 abdominal approach ♀Ⓒ80▢

⚏ 18.51 ⚖ 18.51 Global Days 090

⊙ **58823** Drainage of pelvic abscess, transvaginal or transrectal approach, percutaneous (eg, ovarian, pericolic) ♀Ⓣ▢

⚭ 75989

⚏ 4.86 ⚖ 23.85 Global Days 000

58825 Transposition, ovary(s) ♀Ⓒ80▢

⚏ 18.35 ⚖ 18.35 Global Days 090

58900 Biopsy of ovary, unilateral or bilateral (separate procedure) ♀Ⓐ2Ⓣ80▢

EXCLUDES *laparoscopy with biopsy of fallopian tube or ovary (49321)*

⚏ 10.84 ⚖ 10.84 Global Days 090

● New Code ▲ Revised Code ⬚ Maternity Edit Ⓐ Age Edit ⒶⓎ OPPS Status Indicator ⚏ Facility RVU ⚖ Non-Facility RVU

▢ CCI Comprehensive Code Ⓔ0 Bilateral Procedure + Add-on Indicator ◼ Laboratory crosswalk ⚭ Radiology crosswalk

58920   Wedge resection or bisection of ovary, unilateral or bilateral   ♀ T 80 ▢
   ♻ 18.51   ⚒ 18.51   Global Days 090

58925   Ovarian cystectomy, unilateral or bilateral   ♀ T 80 ▢
   ♻ 19.27   ⚒ 19.27   Global Days 090

58940-58960 Removal Ovary(s) with/without Multiple Procedures for Malignancy

EXCLUDES   *destruction/excision of endometriomas, open method (49203-49205, 58957-58958)*

58940   Oophorectomy, partial or total, unilateral or bilateral;   ♀ C 80 ▢
   EXCLUDES   *oophorectomy with concomitant debulking for ovarian malignancy (58952)*
   ♻ 13.18   ⚒ 13.18   Global Days 090
   AMA: 2004, Mar, 1; 2004, Mar, 1; 2004, March, 1

58943   for ovarian, tubal or primary peritoneal malignancy, with para-aortic and pelvic lymph node biopsies, peritoneal washings, peritoneal biopsies, diaphragmatic assessments, with or without salpingectomy(s), with or without omentectomy   ♀ C 80 ▢
   ♻ 29.47   ⚒ 29.47   Global Days 090

58950   Resection (initial) of ovarian, tubal or primary peritoneal malignancy with bilateral salpingo-oophorectomy and omentectomy;   ♀ C 80 ▢
   ♻ 28.08   ⚒ 28.08   Global Days 090

58951   with total abdominal hysterectomy, pelvic and limited para-aortic lymphadenectomy   ♀ C 80 ▢ P0
   EXCLUDES   *resection/tumor debulking of recurrent ovarian/tubal/primary peritoneal/uterine malignancy (58957, 58958)*
   ♻ 36.21   ⚒ 36.21   Global Days 090
   AMA: 2008, Jan, 10-25; 2007, Jan, 13-27; 2007, Jan, 13-27; 2007, January, 13-27

58952   with radical dissection for debulking (ie, radical excision or destruction, intra-abdominal or retroperitoneal tumors)   ♀ C 80 ▢
   EXCLUDES   *resection/tumor debulking of recurrent ovarian/tubal/primary peritoneal/uterine malignancy (58957, 58958)*
   ♻ 40.86   ⚒ 40.86   Global Days 090
   AMA: 2008, Jan, 10-25; 2007, Jan, 13-27; 2007, Jan, 13-27; 2007, January, 13-27

58953   Bilateral salpingo-oophorectomy with omentectomy, total abdominal hysterectomy and radical dissection for debulking;   ♀ C 80 ▢ P0
   ♻ 50.71   ⚒ 50.71   Global Days 090

58954   with pelvic lymphadenectomy and limited para-aortic lymphadenectomy   ♀ C 80 ▢ P0
   ♻ 55.05   ⚒ 55.05   Global Days 090

58956   Bilateral salpingo-oophorectomy with total omentectomy, total abdominal hysterectomy for malignancy   ♀ C 80 ▢ P0
   Do not report with (49255, 58150, 58180, 58262-58263, 58550, 58661, 58700, 58720, 58900, 58925, 58940, 58957-58958)
   ♻ 36.00   ⚒ 36.00   Global Days 090

58957   Resection (tumor debulking) of recurrent ovarian, tubal, primary peritoneal, uterine malignancy (intra-abdominal, retroperitoneal tumors), with omentectomy, if performed;   ♀ C 80
   Do not report with (38770, 38780, 44005, 49000, 49203-49215, 49255, 58900-58960)
   ♻ 39.03   ⚒ 39.03   Global Days 090

58958   with pelvic lymphadenectomy and limited para-aortic lymphadenectomy   ♀ C 80
   Do not report with (38770, 38780, 44005, 49000, 49203-49215, 49255, 58900-58960)
   ♻ 43.38   ⚒ 43.38   Global Days 090

58960   Laparotomy, for staging or restaging of ovarian, tubal, or primary peritoneal malignancy (second look), with or without omentectomy, peritoneal washing, biopsy of abdominal and pelvic peritoneum, diaphragmatic assessment with pelvic and limited para-aortic lymphadenectomy   ♀ C 80 ▢
   Do not report with (58957, 58958)
   ♻ 24.28   ⚒ 24.28   Global Days 090

58970-58976 Procedural Components: In Vitro Fertilization

58970   Follicle puncture for oocyte retrieval, any method   ♀ A2 T 80 ▢
   🔗 76948
   ♻ 5.32   ⚒ 5.95   Global Days 000
   AMA: 2004, Apr, 1; 2004, Apr, 1; 2004, April, 1

58974   Embryo transfer, intrauterine   M ♀ A2 T 80 ▢
   ♻ 0.00   ⚒ 0.00   Global Days 000
   AMA: 2004, Apr, 1; 2004, Apr, 1; 2004, April, 1

58976   Gamete, zygote, or embryo intrafallopian transfer, any method   M ♀ A2 T 80 ▢
   EXCLUDES   *adnexal procedures performed laparoscopically (58660-58673)*
   ♻ 5.97   ⚒ 6.80   Global Days 000
   AMA: 2004, Apr, 1; 2004, Apr, 1; 2004, April, 1

58999 Unlisted Female Genital Procedure; Not Pregnancy-related

58999   Unlisted procedure, female genital system (nonobstetrical)   ♀ T
   ♻ 0.00   ⚒ 0.00   Global Days YYY

59000-59001 Aspiration of Amniotic Fluid

CMS *100-3,220.5*   *Ultrasound Diagnostic Procedures*

59000   Amniocentesis; diagnostic   M ♀ A3 T ▢
   🔗 76946
   ♻ 2.20   ⚒ 3.44   Global Days 000
   AMA: 2004, May, 1; 2004, May, 1; 2004, May, 1

59001   therapeutic amniotic fluid reduction (includes ultrasound guidance)   M ♀ A2 T ▢
   ♻ 5.03   ⚒ 5.03   Global Days 000

59012-59076 Fetal Testing and Treatment

EXCLUDES   *newborn circumcision (54150, 54160)*
   unlisted fetal invasive procedures (59897)

59012   Cordocentesis (intrauterine), any method   M ♀ A2 T 80 ▢
   🔗 76941
   ♻ 5.55   ⚒ 5.55   Global Days 000

59015   Chorionic villus sampling, any method   Ⓜ ♀P3 T 80 ▢
        ⊠ 76945
        🔲 3.61   ⚲ 4.20 Global Days 000

59020   Fetal contraction stress test   Ⓜ ♀P3 T 80 ▢
        🔲 1.91   ⚲ 1.91 Global Days 000

59025   Fetal non-stress test   Ⓜ ♀P3 T 80 ▢
        🔲 1.26   ⚲ 1.26 Global Days 000
        AMA: 2008, Jan, 10-25; 2007, Jan, 13-27; 2007, Jan, 13-27; 2007,
        January, 13-27; 2004, Nov, 10; 2004, November, 10; 2004, Nov,
        10

59030   Fetal scalp blood sampling   Ⓜ ♀ T 80 ▢
        🔲 3.09   ⚲ 3.09 Global Days 000

59050   Fetal monitoring during labor by consulting physician
        (ie, non-attending physician) with written report;
        supervision and interpretation   Ⓜ ♀M 00 ▢
        🔲 1.38   ⚲ 1.38 Global Days XXX

59051   interpretation only   Ⓜ ♀B 80 ▢
        🔲 1.14   ⚲ 1.14 Global Days XXX

59070   Transabdominal amnioinfusion, including ultrasound
        guidance   Ⓜ ♀62 T 80 ▢
        🔲 7.63   ⚲ 10.32 Global Days 000
        AMA: 2008, Jan, 10-25; 2007, Jan, 13-27; 2007, Jan, 13-27; 2007,
        January, 13-27; 2004, Jun, 11; 2004, Jun, 11; 2004, May, 1; 2004,
        June, 11; 2004, May, 1; 2004, May, 1

59072   Fetal umbilical cord occlusion, including ultrasound
        guidance   Ⓜ ♀62 i ▢
        🔲 12.46   ⚲ 12.46 Global Days 000
        AMA: 2008, Jan, 10-25; 2007, Jan, 13-27; 2007, Jan, 13-27; 2007,
        January, 13-27; 2004, May, 1; 2004, May, 1; 2004, May, 1; 2004,
        June, 11; 2004, Jun, 11; 2004, Jun, 11

59074   Fetal fluid drainage (eg, vesicocentesis, thoracocentesis,
        paracentesis), including ultrasound
        guidance   Ⓜ ♀ T 80 ▢
        🔲 7.56   ⚲ 9.78 Global Days 000
        AMA: 2008, Jan, 10-25; 2007, Jan, 13-27; 2007, Jan, 13-27; 2007,
        January, 13-27; 2004, Jun, 11; 2004, Jun, 11; 2004, Dec, 19; 2004,
        May, 1; 2004, December, 19; 2004, June, 19; 2004, Dec, 19; 2004,
        May, 1; 2004, May, 1

59076   Fetal shunt placement, including ultrasound
        guidance   Ⓜ ♀P2 T 00 ▢
        🔲 12.18   ⚲ 12.18 Global Days 000
        AMA: 2008, Jan, 10-25; 2007, Jan, 13-27; 2007, Jan, 13-27; 2007,
        January, 13-27; 2004, May, 1; 2004, May, 1; 2004, Dec, 19; 2004,
        May, 1; 2004, December, 19; 2004, June, 11; 2004, Dec, 19; 2004,
        Jun, 11, 2004, Jun, 11

59100-59151 Tubal Pregnancy/Hysterotomy Procedures

CMS 100-3,230.3   *Sterilization*

59100   Hysterotomy, abdominal (eg, for hydatidiform mole,
        abortion)   Ⓜ ♀62 T 80 ▢
        Code also ligation of fallopian tubes when performed at
        the same time as hysterotomy (58611)
        🔲 22.09   ⚲ 22.09 Global Days 090

59120   Surgical treatment of ectopic pregnancy; tubal or ovarian,
        requiring salpingectomy and/or oophorectomy, abdominal
        or vaginal approach   Ⓜ ♀C 80 ▢
        🔲 21.08   ⚲ 21.08 Global Days 090

59121   tubal or ovarian, without salpingectomy and/or
        oophorectomy   Ⓜ ♀C 80 ▢
        🔲 21.19   ⚲ 21.19 Global Days 090

59130   abdominal pregnancy   Ⓜ ♀C 80 ▢
        🔲 24.77   ⚲ 24.77 Global Days 090

59135   interstitial, uterine pregnancy requiring total
        hysterectomy   Ⓜ ♀C 80 ▢
        🔲 25.05   ⚲ 25.05 Global Days 090

59136   interstitial, uterine pregnancy with partial resection
        of uterus   Ⓜ ♀C 80 ▢
        🔲 23.41   ⚲ 23.41 Global Days 090

59140   cervical, with evacuation   Ⓜ ♀C 80 ▢
        🔲 10.47   ⚲ 10.47 Global Days 090

59150   Laparoscopic treatment of ectopic pregnancy; without
        salpingectomy and/or oophorectomy   Ⓜ ♀62 T 80 ▢
        🔲 20.54   ⚲ 20.54 Global Days 090

Ectopic pregnancies are reported by site where abnormal attachment occurs; more than 95 percent occur in the fallopian tube

Ectopic pregnancy in tube

Abdominal pregnancy

Site of interstitial pregnancy

Cervix and cervical canal

Ectopic pregnancy in cervix

Ovarian pregnancy

Uterus

Broad ligament (mesometric)

Half of all ectopic pregnancies resolve spontaneously without rupture but surgical intervention is usually necessary for the remainder; rarely, an abdominal or mesometric pregnancy may continue until a viable fetus is delivered through an abdominal incision

59151   with salpingectomy and/or
        oophorectomy   Ⓜ ♀62 T 80 ▢
        🔲 20.07   ⚲ 20.07 Global Days 090

59160-59200 Procedures of Uterus Prior To/After Delivery

59160   Curettage, postpartum   Ⓜ ♀A2 T 80 ▢
        🔲 4.83   ⚲ 5.71 Global Days 010
        AMA: 2008, Jan, 10-25; 2007, Jan, 13-27; 2007, Jan, 13-27; 2007,
        January, 13-27

59200   Insertion of cervical dilator (eg, laminaria, prostaglandin)
        (separate procedure)   Ⓜ ♀P3 T ▢
        EXCLUDES   *fetal transfusion, intrauterine (36460)*
                       hypertonic solution/prostaglandin introduction
                       for labor initiation (59850-59857)
        🔲 1.23   ⚲ 1.98 Global Days 000
        AMA: 2005, Jul, 13-16; 2005, Jul, 13-16; 2005, July, 13-16

59300-59350 Postpartum Vaginal/Cervical/Uterine Repairs

EXCLUDES   *Nonpregnancy-related cerclage (57700)*

59300   Episiotomy or vaginal repair, by other than attending
        physician   Ⓜ ♀P3 T 80 ▢
        EXCLUDES   *tracheloplasty (57700)*
        🔲 3.97   ⚲ 5.14 Global Days 000

59320   Cerclage of cervix, during pregnancy;
        vaginal   Ⓜ ♀A2 T 80 ▢
        🔲 4.16   ⚲ 4.16 Global Days 000
        AMA: 2008, Jan, 10-25; 2007, Jan, 13-27; 2007, Jan, 13-27; 2007,
        Feb, 10-11; 2007, January, 13-27; 2007, Feb, 10-11; 2007,
        February, 10-11; 2006, Dec, 10-12; 2006, Dec, 10-12; 2006, Dec,
        10-12; 2006, December, 10-12; 2006, December, 10-12; 2006,
        December, 10-12; 2006, December, 10-12; 2006, Dec, 10-12;
        2006, Dec, 10-12; 2006, Dec, 10-12; 2006, Dec, 10-12; 2006, Dec,
        10-12

● New Code   ▲ Revised Code   Ⓜ Maternity Edit   Ⓐ Age Edit   A Y OPPS Status Indicator   🔲 Facility RVU   ⚲ Non-Facility RVU
▢ CCI Comprehensive Code   50 Bilateral Procedure   + Add-on Indicator   Laboratory crosswalk   Radiology crosswalk

© 2008 Ingenix *(Blue Ink)*   CPT only © 2008 American Medical Association. All Rights Reserved. (Black Ink)   Medicare (Red Ink)   **223**

Maternity Care/Delivery

59325 — 59414

59325 abdominal Ⓜ ♀ Ⓒ Ⓜ 🖳
  🔳 6.54 ⚖ 6.54 Global Days 000
  AMA: 2008, Jan, 10-25; 2007, Jan, 13-27; 2007, Jan, 13-27; 2007, Feb, 10-11; 2007, January, 13-27; 2007, Feb, 10-11; 2007, February, 10-11; 2006, Dec, 10-12; 2006, Dec, 10-12; 2006, December, 10-12; 2006, December, 10-12; 2006, December, 10-12; 2006, December, 10-12; 2006, Dec, 10-12; 2006, Dec, 10-12; 2006, Dec, 10-12; 2006, Dec, 10-12; 2006, Dec, 10-12

59350 Hysterorrhaphy of ruptured uterus Ⓜ ♀ Ⓒ Ⓜ 🖳
  🔳 7.57 ⚖ 7.57 Global Days 000

59400-59410 Vaginal Delivery: Comprehensive and Component Services

CMS 100-2,15,180 *Nurse-Midwife (CNM) Services*
CMS 100-2,15,20.1 *Physician Expense for Surgery, Childbirth, and Treatment for Infertility*

[INCLUDES] admission history
  admission to hospital
  management of uncomplicated labor
  physical exam
  vaginal delivery with or without episiotomy or forceps

[EXCLUDES] *medical complications of pregnancy:*
    cardiac problems
    diabetes
    hyperemesis
    hypertension
    neurological problems
    premature rupture of membranes
    pre-term labor
    toxemia
  medical problems complicating labor and delivery
  newborn circumcision (54150, 54160)
  surgical complications of pregnancy:
    appendectomy
    Bartholin cyst
    hernia
    ovarian cyst

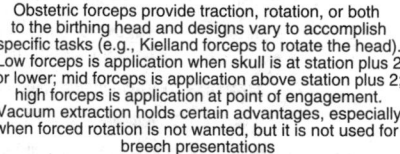

Breech presentation (left) and Simpson forceps delivery of aftercoming head (right)

Vacuum extractor attached to posterior fontanelle to flex head downward (below left)

Obstetric forceps provide traction, rotation, or both to the birthing head and designs vary to accomplish specific tasks (e.g., Kielland forceps to rotate the head). Low forceps is application when skull is at station plus 2 or lower; mid forceps is application above station plus 2; high forceps is application at point of engagement. Vacuum extraction holds certain advantages, especially when forced rotation is not wanted, but it is not used for breech presentations

59400 Routine obstetric care including antepartum care, vaginal delivery (with or without episiotomy, and/or forceps) and postpartum care Ⓜ ♀ Ⓑ 🖳
  [INCLUDES] biweekly visits to 36 weeks gestation
    fetal heart tones
    hospital/office visits following cesarean section or vaginal delivery
    initial/subsequent history
    monthly visits up to 28 weeks gestation
    physical exams
    recording of weight/blood pressures
    routine chemical urinalysis
    weekly visits until delivery
  🔳 47.01 ⚖ 47.01 Global Days MMM
  AMA: 2008, Jan, 10-25; 2007, Jan, 13-27; 2007, Jan, 13-27; 2007, January, 13-27

59409 Vaginal delivery only (with or without episiotomy and/or forceps); Ⓜ ♀ Ⓣ Ⓜ 🖳
  🔳 20.99 ⚖ 20.99 Global Days MMM
  AMA: 2008, Jan, 10-25; 2007, Jan, 13-27; 2007, Jan, 13-27; 2007, January, 13-27; 2007, Dec, 10-179

59410 including postpartum care Ⓜ ♀ Ⓑ 🖳
  [INCLUDES] hospital/office visits following cesarean section or vaginal delivery
  🔳 24.30 ⚖ 24.30 Global Days MMM
  AMA: 2006, Dec, 1-3; 2006, Dec, 1-3; 2006, Dec, 1-3; 2006, Dec, 1-3; 2006, Dec, 1-3; 2006, Dec, 1-3; 2006, December, 1-3; 2006, December, 1-3; 2006, December, 1-3; 2006, December, 1-3; 2006, Dec, 1-3; 2006, Dec, 1-3; 2004, Jul, 1; 2004, July, 1; 2004, Jul, 1

59412-59414 Other Maternity Services

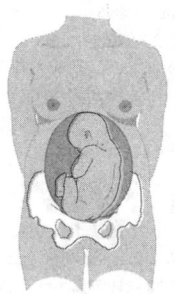

Shoulder presentation

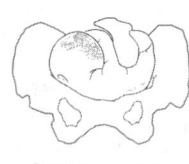

"Footling"

Complete breech presentation at term

Malposition and malpresentation occur when the fetus is in any presentation other than vertex; breech is most common at about 3 percent of deliveries; prematurity is a major predisposing factor

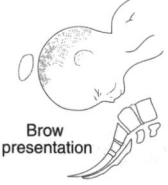

Brow presentation

59412 External cephalic version, with or without tocolysis Ⓜ ♀ Ⓖ Ⓣ Ⓜ 🖳
  Code also delivery code(s)
  🔳 2.81 ⚖ 2.81 Global Days MMM

59414 Delivery of placenta (separate procedure) Ⓜ ♀ Ⓖ Ⓣ Ⓜ 🖳
  🔳 2.50 ⚖ 2.50 Global Days MMM
  AMA: 2008, Jan, 10-25; 2007, Jan, 13-27; 2007, Jan, 13-27; 2007, January, 13-27

59425-59430 Prenatal and Postpartum Visits

CMS *100-2,15,180*   *Nurse-Midwife (CNM) Services*
CMS *100-2,15,20.1*   *Physician Expense for Surgery, Childbirth, and Treatment for Infertility*

INCLUDES   physician providing all or a portion of antepartum/postpartum care, but no delivery due to

    referral to another physician for delivery

    termination of pregnancy by abortion

EXCLUDES   *antepartum care, 1-3 visits (99201-99499)*
newborn circumcision (54150, 54160)
medical complications of pregnancy:

    cardiac problems
    diabetes
    neurological problems
    hyperemesis
    hypertension
    premature rupture of membranes
    pre-term labor
    toxemia

surgical complications of pregnancy:

    appendectomy
    Bartholin cyst
    hernia
    ovarian cyst

59425   **Antepartum care only; 4-6 visits**   M ♀ Ⓥ Ⓦ ▱

    INCLUDES   biweekly visits to 36 weeks gestation
      fetal heart tones
      initial/subsequent history
      monthly visits up to 28 weeks gestation
      physical exams
      recording of weight/blood pressures
      routine chemical urinalysis
      weekly visits until delivery

    🗐 **9.18**   ⚖ **11.65**   **Global Days MMM**
    AMA: 2008, Jan, 10-25; 2007, Jan, 13-27; 2007, Jan, 13-27; 2007, January, 13-27

59426   **7 or more visits**   M ♀ Ⓑ Ⓐ ▱

    INCLUDES   biweekly visits to 36 weeks gestation
      fetal heart tones
      initial/subsequent history
      monthly visits up to 28 weeks gestation
      physical exams
      recording of weight/blood pressures
      routine chemical urinalysis
      weekly visits until delivery

    🗐 **16.23**   ⚖ **20.83**   **Global Days MMM**
    AMA: 2008, Jan, 10-25; 2007, Jan, 13-27; 2007, Jan, 13-27; 2007, January, 13-27

59430   **Postpartum care only (separate procedure)**   M ♀ Ⓑ ▱

    INCLUDES   hospital/office visits following cesarean
      section or vaginal delivery

    🗐 **3.42**   ⚖ **3.77**   **Global Days MMM**
    AMA: 2008, Jan, 10-25; 2007, Jan, 13-27; 2007, Jan, 13-27; 2007, January, 13-27

59510-59525 Cesarean Section Delivery: Comprehensive and Components of Care

INCLUDES   classic cesarean section
    low cervical cesarean section

EXCLUDES   *infant standby attendance (99360)*
medical complications of pregnancy:

    cardiac problems
    diabetes
    hyperemesis
    hypertension
    neurological problems
    premature rupture of membranes
    pre-term labor
    toxemia

newborn circumcision (54150, 54160)

surgical complications of pregnancy:

    appendectomy
    Bartholin cyst
    hernia
    ovarian cyst

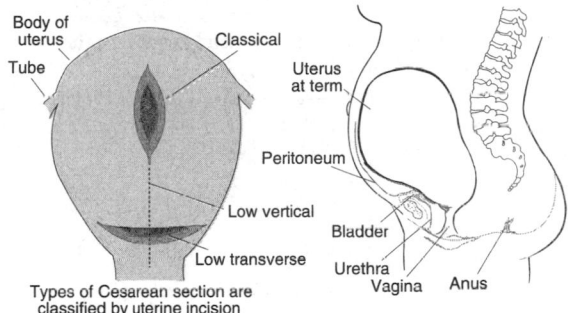

Body of uterus   Classical
Tube
Uterus at term
Peritoneum
Low vertical
Bladder
Low transverse
Urethra   Vagina   Anus

Types of Cesarean section are classified by uterine incision

Cesarean section is delivery through incisions in the anterior abdominal and uterine walls and is indicated for numerous conditions in both the fetus and the mother. Although other approaches may be warranted, low transverse is preferred to decrease chance of uterine rupture during future pregnancies

59510   **Routine obstetric care including antepartum care, cesarean delivery, and postpartum care**   M ♀ Ⓑ ▱

    INCLUDES   admission history
      admission to hospital
      biweekly visits to 36 weeks gestation
      cesarean delivery
      fetal heart tones
      hospital/office visits following cesarean section
      initial/subsequent history
      management of uncomplicated labor
      monthly visits up to 28 weeks gestation
      physical exam
      recording of weight/blood pressures
      routine chemical urinalysis
      weekly visits until delivery

    EXCLUDES   *medical problems complicating labor and delivery*

    🗐 **53.24**   ⚖ **53.24**   **Global Days MMM**
    AMA: 2008, Jan, 10-25; 2007, Jan, 13-27; 2007, Jan, 13-27; 2007, January, 13-27

● New Code   ▲ Revised Code   M Maternity Edit   ⚠ Age Edit   Ⓐ Ⓥ OPPS Status Indicator   🗐 Facility RVU   ⚖ Non-Facility RVU
▱ CCI Comprehensive Code   50 Bilateral Procedure   + Add-on Indicator   ◨ Laboratory crosswalk   ◨ Radiology crosswalk

© 2008 Ingenix *(Blue Ink)*   CPT only © 2008 American Medical Association. All Rights Reserved. (Black Ink)   Medicare (Red Ink)   **225**

59514   Cesarean delivery only;   Ⓜ♀ⒸⒽ🖵

    INCLUDES admission history
          admission to hospital
          cesarean delivery
          management of uncomplicated labor
          physical exam

    EXCLUDES *medical problems complicating labor and delivery*

    💰 24.85   ✄ 24.85 **Global Days MMM**
    AMA: 2008, Jan, 10-25; 2007, Jan, 13-27; 2007, Jan, 13-27; 2007, January, 13-27

59515   including postpartum care   Ⓜ♀Ⓑ🖵

    INCLUDES admission history
          admission to hospital
          cesarean delivery
          hospital/office visits following cesarean section or vaginal delivery
          management of uncomplicated labor
          physical exam

    EXCLUDES *medical problems complicating labor and delivery*

    💰 29.23   ✄ 29.23 **Global Days MMM**

+ **59525   Subtotal or total hysterectomy after cesarean delivery (List separately in addition to code for primary procedure)**   Ⓜ♀ⒸⒽ🖵

    Code first cesarean delivery (59510, 59514, 59515, 59620, 59622)
    💰 13.20   ✄ 13.20 **Global Days ZZZ**

59610-59614 Vaginal Delivery After Prior Cesarean Section: Comprehensive and Components of Care

CMS *100-2,15,180*   *Nurse-Midwife (CNM) Services*
CMS *100-2,15,20.1*   *Physician Expense for Surgery, Childbirth, and Treatment for Infertility*

INCLUDES admission history
      admission to hospital
      management of uncomplicated labor
      patients with previous cesarean delivery who present with the expectation of a vaginal delivery
      physical exam
      successful vaginal delivery after previous cesarean delivery (VBAC)
      vaginal delivery with or without episiotomy or forceps

EXCLUDES *elective cesarean delivery (59510, 59514, 59515)*
      medical complications of pregnancy:
        cardiac problems
        diabetes
        hyperemesis
        hypertension
        neurological problems
        premature rupture of membranes
        pre-term labor
        toxemia
      medical problems complicating labor and delivery
      newborn circumcision (54150, 54160)
      surgical complications of pregnancy:
        appendectomy
        Bartholin cyst
        hernia
        ovarian cyst

59610   Routine obstetric care including antepartum care, vaginal delivery (with or without episiotomy, and/or forceps) and postpartum care, after previous cesarean delivery   Ⓜ♀Ⓑ🖵

    INCLUDES biweekly visits to 36 weeks gestation
          fetal heart tones
          hospital/office visits following cesarean section or vaginal delivery
          initial/subsequent history
          monthly visits up to 28 weeks gestation
          physical exams
          recording of weight/blood pressures
          routine chemical urinalysis
          weekly visits until delivery

    💰 49.53   ✄ 49.53 **Global Days MMM**

59612   Vaginal delivery only, after previous cesarean delivery (with or without episiotomy and/or forceps);   Ⓜ♀Ⓣ🖵

    💰 23.51   ✄ 23.51 **Global Days MMM**

59614   including postpartum care   Ⓜ♀Ⓑ🖵

    INCLUDES hospital/office visits following cesarean section or vaginal delivery

    💰 26.30   ✄ 26.30 **Global Days MMM**

59618-59622 Cesarean Section After Attempted Vaginal Birth/Prior C-Section

INCLUDES
admission history
admission to hospital
cesarean delivery
cesarean delivery following an unsuccessful vaginal delivery attempt after previous cesarean delivery
management of uncomplicated labor
patients with previous cesarean delivery who present with the expectation of a vaginal delivery
physical exam

EXCLUDES
elective cesarean delivery (59510, 59514, 59515)
medical complications of pregnancy:
  cardiac problems
  diabetes
  hyperemesis
  hypertension
  neurological problems
  premature rupture of membranes
  pre-term labor
  toxemia
medical problems complicating labor and delivery
newborn circumcision (54150, 54160)
surgical complications of pregnancy:
  appendectomy
  Bartholin cyst
  hernia
  ovarian cyst

59618 **Routine obstetric care including antepartum care, cesarean delivery, and postpartum care, following attempted vaginal delivery after previous cesarean delivery**   M ♀ B 80 ▭
INCLUDES   biweekly visits to 36 weeks gestation
fetal heart tones
hospital/office visits following cesarean section or vaginal delivery
initial/subsequent history
monthly visits up to 28 weeks gestation
physical exams
recording of weight/blood pressures
routine chemical urinalysis
weekly visits until delivery

🔾 55.72 ⚖ 55.72 Global Days MMM

59620 **Cesarean delivery only, following attempted vaginal delivery after previous cesarean delivery;**   M ♀ C 80 ▭
🔾 27.28 ⚖ 27.28 Global Days MMM

59622   **including postpartum care**   M ♀ R m ▭
INCLUDES   hospital/office visits following cesarean section or vaginal delivery
🔾 31.70 ⚖ 31.70 Global Days MMM

59812-59830 Treatment of Miscarriage

EXCLUDES
medical treatment of spontaneous complete abortion, any trimester (99201-99233)

59812 **Treatment of incomplete abortion, any trimester, completed surgically**   M ♀ A2 T ▭
INCLUDES   surgical treatment of spontaneous abortion
🔾 7.79 ⚖ 8.34 Global Days 090

59820 **Treatment of missed abortion, completed surgically; first trimester**   M ♀ A2 T ▭
🔾 9.15 ⚖ 9.82 Global Days 090

59821   **second trimester**   M ♀ A2 T 80 ▭
🔾 9.31 ⚖ 10.02 Global Days 090

59830 **Treatment of septic abortion, completed surgically**   M ♀ C 80 ▭
🔾 11.60 ⚖ 11.60 Global Days 090

59840-59866 Elective Abortions

CMS 100-4,3,100.1 *Billing for Abortion Services*
CMS 100-3,140.1 *Abortion*

59840 **Induced abortion, by dilation and curettage**   M ♀ A2 T 80 ▭
🔾 5.62 ⚖ 5.80 Global Days 010
AMA: 2008, Jan, 10-25; 2007, Jan, 13-27; 2007, Jan, 13-27; 2007, January, 13-27

59841 **Induced abortion, by dilation and evacuation**   M ♀ A2 T 80 ▭
🔾 9.53 ⚖ 10.08 Global Days 010

59850 **Induced abortion, by one or more intra-amniotic injections (amniocentesis-injections), including hospital admission and visits, delivery of fetus and secundines;**   M ♀ C 80 ▭
EXCLUDES   *cervical dilator insertion (59200)*
🔾 10.38 ⚖ 10.38 Global Days 090

59851   **with dilation and curettage and/or evacuation**   M ♀ C 80 ▭
EXCLUDES   *cervical dilator insertion (59200)*
🔾 10.65 ⚖ 10.65 Global Days 090

59852   **with hysterotomy (failed intra-amniotic injection)**   M ♀ C 80 ▭
EXCLUDES   *cervical dilator insertion (59200)*
🔾 14.96 ⚖ 14.96 Global Days 090

59855 **Induced abortion, by one or more vaginal suppositories (eg, prostaglandin) with or without cervical dilation (eg, laminaria), including hospital admission and visits, delivery of fetus and secundines;**   M ♀ C 80 ▭
🔾 11.10 ⚖ 11.10 Global Days 090

59856   **with dilation and curettage and/or evacuation**   M ♀ C 80 ▭
🔾 13.13 ⚖ 13.13 Global Days 090

59857   **with hysterotomy (failed medical evacuation)**   M ♀ C 80 ▭
🔾 15.67 ⚖ 15.67 Global Days 090

59866 **Multifetal pregnancy reduction(s) (MPR)**   M ♀ A2 T 80 ▭
🔾 6.48 ⚖ 6.48 Global Days 000

59870-59899 Miscellaneous Obstetrical Procedures

59870 **Uterine evacuation and curettage for hydatidiform mole**   M ♀ A2 T 80 ▭
🔾 12.45 ⚖ 12.45 Global Days 090
AMA: 2008, Jan, 10-25; 2007, Jan, 13-27; 2007, Jan, 13-27; 2007, January, 13-27

59871 **Removal of cerclage suture under anesthesia (other than local)**   M ♀ A2 T 80 ▭
🔾 3.63 ⚖ 3.63 Global Days 000
AMA: 2007, Feb, 10-11; 2007, Feb, 10-11; 2007, February, 10-11; 2006, Dec, 10-12; 2006, Dec, 10-12; 2006, Dec, 10-12; 2006, Dec, 10-12; 2006, December, 10-12; 2006, December, 10-12; 2006, December, 10-12; 2006, December, 10-12; 2006, Dec, 10-12; 2006, Dec, 10-12; 2006, Dec, 10-12; 2006, Dec, 10-12

59897 **Unlisted fetal invasive procedure, including ultrasound guidance**   T ▭
🔾 0.00 ⚖ 0.00 Global Days YYY
AMA: 2005, Jul, 13-16; 2005, Jul, 13-16; 2005, July, 13-16; 2004, May, 1; 2004, May, 1; 2004, May, 1

● New Code ▲ Revised Code M Maternity Edit A Age Edit A-T OPPS Status Indicator 🔾 Facility RVU ⚖ Non-Facility RVU
▭ CCI Comprehensive Code 50 Bilateral Procedure + Add-on Indicator N Laboratory crosswalk R Radiology crosswalk

Endocrine System

59898 — 60505

59898	Unlisted laparoscopy procedure, maternity care and delivery ⬛ ♀ Ⓣ 80 50
	🔲 0.00 ⚖ 0.00 Global Days YYY
59899	Unlisted procedure, maternity care and delivery ⬛ ♀ Ⓣ 80
	🔲 0.00 ⚖ 0.00 Global Days YYY
	AMA: 2008, Jan, 10-25; 2007, Jan, 13-27; 2007, Jan, 13-27; 2007, January, 13-27; 2004, May, 1; 2004, May, 1; 2004, May, 1

60000 I&D of Infected Thyroglossal Cyst

60000	Incision and drainage of thyroglossal duct cyst, infected A2 Ⓣ 80 🔲
	🔲 3.71 ⚖ 4.06 Global Days 010

60100 Core Needle Biopsy: Thyroid

EXCLUDES *fine needle aspiration (10021-10022)*

60100	Biopsy thyroid, percutaneous core needle P3 Ⓣ 🔲
	🔲 76942, 77002, 77012, 77021
	🔲 88172-88173
	🔲 2.22 ⚖ 3.03 Global Days 000
	AMA: 2008, Jan, 10-25; 2008, Jun, 8-11; 2007, Jun, 10-11; 2007, Jun, 10-11; 2007, June, 10-11

60200 Surgical Removal Thyroid Cyst or Mass; Division of Isthmus

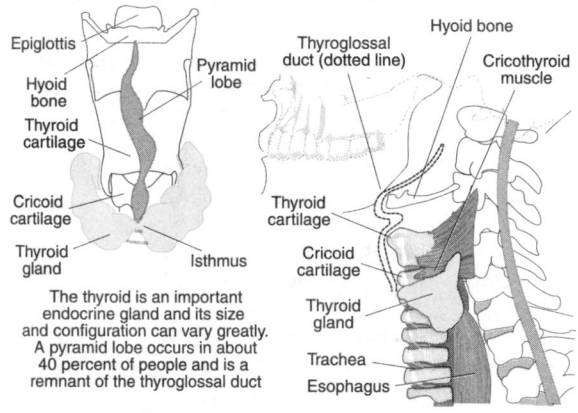

The thyroid is an important endocrine gland and its size and configuration can vary greatly. A pyramid lobe occurs in about 40 percent of people and is a remnant of the thyroglossal duct

60200	Excision of cyst or adenoma of thyroid, or transection of isthmus A2 Ⓣ 80 🔲 P0
	🔲 16.67 ⚖ 16.67 Global Days 090

60210-60225 Subtotal Thyroidectomy

CMS *100-4,12,40.7*

Bilateral Procedures

60210	Partial thyroid lobectomy, unilateral; with or without isthmusectomy Ⓣ 80 🔲 P0
	🔲 17.87 ⚖ 17.87 Global Days 090
60212	with contralateral subtotal lobectomy, including isthmusectomy Ⓣ 80 🔲 P0
	🔲 25.72 ⚖ 25.72 Global Days 090
60220	Total thyroid lobectomy, unilateral; with or without isthmusectomy Ⓣ 80 🔲 P0
	🔲 19.58 ⚖ 19.58 Global Days 090
60225	with contralateral subtotal lobectomy, including isthmusectomy Ⓣ 80 🔲 P0
	🔲 23.55 ⚖ 23.55 Global Days 090

60240-60271 Complete Thyroidectomy Procedures

60240	Thyroidectomy, total or complete Ⓣ 80 🔲 P0
	EXCLUDES *subtotal or partial thyroidectomy (60271)*
	🔲 24.97 ⚖ 24.97 Global Days 090
60252	Thyroidectomy, total or subtotal for malignancy; with limited neck dissection Ⓣ 80 🔲 P0
	🔲 33.65 ⚖ 33.65 Global Days 090
	AMA: 2008, Jan, 10-25; 2007, Jan, 13-27; 2007, Jan, 13-27; 2007, January, 13-27
60254	with radical neck dissection C 80 🔲 P0
	🔲 43.25 ⚖ 43.25 Global Days 090
	AMA: 2008, Jan, 10-25; 2007, Jan, 13-27; 2007, Jan, 13-27; 2007, January, 13-27
60260	Thyroidectomy, removal of all remaining thyroid tissue following previous removal of a portion of thyroid Ⓣ 80 50 🔲 P0
	🔲 28.11 ⚖ 28.11 Global Days 090
60270	Thyroidectomy, including substernal thyroid; sternal split or transthoracic approach C 80 🔲 P0
	🔲 35.38 ⚖ 35.38 Global Days 090
60271	cervical approach Ⓣ 80 🔲 P0
	🔲 27.12 ⚖ 27.12 Global Days 090

60280-60300 Treatment of Cyst/Sinus of Thyroid

60280	Excision of thyroglossal duct cyst or sinus; A2 Ⓣ 80 🔲 P0
	🔲 11.18 ⚖ 11.18 Global Days 090
60281	recurrent A2 Ⓣ 80 🔲 P0
	🔲 14.92 ⚖ 14.92 Global Days 090
60300	Aspiration and/or injection, thyroid cyst P3 Ⓣ
	EXCLUDES *fine needle aspiration (10021-10022)*
	🔲 76942, 77012
	🔲 1.37 ⚖ 2.84 Global Days 000

60500-60512 Parathyroid Procedures

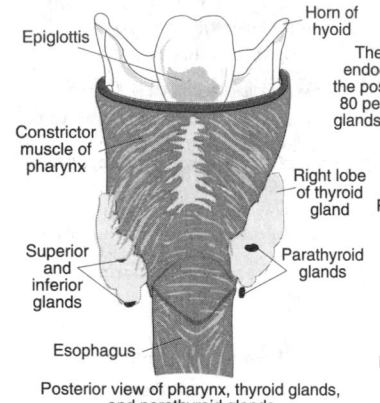

The parathyroid glands are endocrine nodes hidden along the posterior of the thyroid; about 80 percent of people have four glands, two on each thyroid lobe

Parathyroid glands regulate serum calcium levels and all of the glands are not usually removed since substitute therapy is difficult. During any thyroidectomy great care is taken to not disturb the parathyroids; during parathyroidectomy, usually only affected glands are removed

Posterior view of pharynx, thyroid glands, and parathyroid glands

60500	Parathyroidectomy or exploration of parathyroid(s); Ⓣ 80 🔲 P0
	🔲 25.92 ⚖ 25.92 Global Days 090
60502	re-exploration Ⓣ 80 🔲 P0
	🔲 32.54 ⚖ 32.54 Global Days 090
60505	with mediastinal exploration, sternal split or transthoracic approach C 80 🔲 P0
	🔲 35.70 ⚖ 35.70 Global Days 090

+   60512   **Parathyroid autotransplantation (List separately in addition to code for primary procedure)**   T 80
       Code first 60212, 60225, 60240, 60252, 60254, 60260, 60270-60271, 60500, 60502, 60505
       🖪 6.35   ⚕ 6.35   Global Days ZZZ

60520-60522 Thymus Procedures

   60520   **Thymectomy, partial or total; transcervical approach (separate procedure)**   T 80 ▣ P0
       🖪 26.75   ⚕ 26.75   Global Days 090

   60521   **sternal split or transthoracic approach, without radical mediastinal dissection (separate procedure)**   C 80 ▣ P0
       🖪 30.82   ⚕ 30.82   Global Days 090
       AMA: 2007, Dec, 10-179

   60522   **sternal split or transthoracic approach, with radical mediastinal dissection (separate procedure)**   C 80 ▣ P0
       🖪 37.12   ⚕ 37.12   Global Days 090

60540-60545 Adrenal Gland Procedures

EXCLUDES   *laparoscopic approach (60650)*
       removal of remote or disseminated pheochromocytoma (49203-49205)

Do not report with (50323)

   60540   **Adrenalectomy, partial or complete, or exploration of adrenal gland with or without biopsy, transabdominal, lumbar or dorsal (separate procedure);**   C 80 50 ▣ P0
       🖪 28.03   ⚕ 28.03   Global Days 090

   60545   **with excision of adjacent retroperitoneal tumor**   C 80 ▣ P0
       🖪 31.91   ⚕ 31.91   Global Days 090

60600-60605 Carotid Body Procedures

CMS *100-3,20.18*   *Carotid Body Resection/Carotid Body Denervation*

   60600   **Excision of carotid body tumor; without excision of carotid artery**   C 80 ▣ P0
       🖪 36.99   ⚕ 36.99   Global Days 090

   60605   **with excision of carotid artery**   C 80 ▣ P0
       🖪 46.43   ⚕ 46.43   Global Days 090

60650-60699 Laparoscopic and Unlisted Procedures

INCLUDES   diagnostic laparoscopy

   60650   **Laparoscopy, surgical, with adrenalectomy, partial or complete, or exploration of adrenal gland with or without biopsy, transabdominal, lumbar or dorsal**   C 80 50 ▣ P0
       🖪 31.32   ⚕ 31.32   Global Days 090

   60659   **Unlisted laparoscopy procedure, endocrine system**   T 80 50
       🖪 0.00   ⚕ 0.00   Global Days YYY

   60699   **Unlisted procedure, endocrine system**   T 80
       🖪 0.00   ⚕ 0.00   Global Days YYY
       AMA: 2008, Jan, 10-25; 2007, Jan, 13-27; 2007, Jan, 13-27; 2007, January, 13-27; 2007, Dec, 10-179

● New Code   ▲ Revised Code   M Maternity Edit   A Age Edit   A-V OPPS Status Indicator   🖪 Facility RVU   ⚕ Non-Facility RVU
▣ CCI Comprehensive Code   50 Bilateral Procedure   + Add-on Indicator   ◤ Laboratory crosswalk   🔲 Radiology crosswalk

61000-61253 Transcranial Access via Puncture, Burr Hole, Twist Hole, or Trephine

EXCLUDES injection for:
pneumoencephalography (61055)
ventriculography (61026, 61120)
cerebral angiography (36100-36218)

61000 Subdural tap through fontanelle, or suture, infant, unilateral or bilateral; initial [A] [R2] [T] ▣

EXCLUDES injection for:
ventriculography (61026, 61120)
pneumoencephalography (61055)
cerebral angiography (36100-36218)

⚕ 2.84 ⚕ 2.84 Global Days 000

61001 subsequent taps [A] [R2] [T] ▣
⚕ 2.79 ⚕ 2.79 Global Days 000

61020 Ventricular puncture through previous burr hole, fontanelle, suture, or implanted ventricular catheter/reservoir; without injection [A2] [T] ▣
⚕ 3.38 ⚕ 3.38 Global Days 000

61026 with injection of medication or other substance for diagnosis or treatment [A2] [T] ▣

EXCLUDES injection for:

⚕ 3.37 ⚕ 3.37 Global Days 000

61050 Cisternal or lateral cervical (C1-C2) puncture; without injection (separate procedure) [A2] [T] [80] ▣
⚕ 2.82 ⚕ 2.82 Global Days 000

61055 with injection of medication or other substance for diagnosis or treatment (eg, C1-C2) [A2] [T] ▣

EXCLUDES radiology procedures

⚕ 3.64 ⚕ 3.64 Global Days 000

61070 Puncture of shunt tubing or reservoir for aspiration or injection procedure [A2] [T] ▣
✖ 75809
⚕ 2.14 ⚕ 2.14 Global Days 000
AMA: 2008, Jul, 10&13; 2008, Sep, 10-11

61105 Twist drill hole for subdural or ventricular puncture [C] [80] ▣
⚕ 11.17 ⚕ 11.17 Global Days 090

⊘ **61107** Twist drill hole(s) for subdural, intracerebral, or ventricular puncture; for implanting ventricular catheter, pressure recording device, or other intracerebral monitoring device [C] ▣

EXCLUDES intracranial neuroendoscopic ventricular catheter insertion or reinsertion (62160)
twist drill or burr hole for thermal perfusion probe (0077T)

⚕ 8.37 ⚕ 8.37 Global Days 000
AMA: 2007, Jun, 10-11; 2007, Jun, 10-11; 2007, June, 10-11; 2005, May, 7-12; 2005, May, 7-12; 2005, May, 7-12

61108 for evacuation and/or drainage of subdural hematoma [C] ▣
⚕ 22.18 ⚕ 22.18 Global Days 090

61120 Burr hole(s) for ventricular puncture (including injection of gas, contrast media, dye, or radioactive material) [C] [80] ▣
⚕ 18.16 ⚕ 18.16 Global Days 090

61140 Burr hole(s) or trephine; with biopsy of brain or intracranial lesion [C] [80] ▣
⚕ 31.65 ⚕ 31.65 Global Days 090

61150 with drainage of brain abscess or cyst [C] ▣
⚕ 33.83 ⚕ 33.83 Global Days 090

61151 with subsequent tapping (aspiration) of intracranial abscess or cyst [C] ▣
⚕ 24.46 ⚕ 24.46 Global Days 090

61154 Burr hole(s) with evacuation and/or drainage of hematoma, extradural or subdural [C] [80] [50] ▣ [P0]
⚕ 31.74 ⚕ 31.74 Global Days 090

61156 Burr hole(s); with aspiration of hematoma or cyst, intracerebral [C] [80] ▣
⚕ 31.64 ⚕ 31.64 Global Days 090

61210 for implanting ventricular catheter, reservoir, EEG electrode(s), pressure recording device, or other cerebral monitoring device (separate procedure) [C] ▣

EXCLUDES intracranial neuroendoscopic ventricular insertion (62160)

⚕ 9.77 ⚕ 9.77 Global Days 000
AMA: 2008, May, 9-11; 2008, Jul, 4; 2007, Jun, 10-11; 2007, Jun, 10-11; 2007, June, 10-11

61215 Insertion of subcutaneous reservoir, pump or continuous infusion system for connection to ventricular catheter [A2] [T] ▣

EXCLUDES chemotherapy (96450)
refilling and maintenance of implantable infusion pump (95990)

⚕ 12.09 ⚕ 12.09 Global Days 090

61250 Burr hole(s) or trephine, supratentorial, exploratory, not followed by other surgery [C] [80] [50] ▣
⚕ 21.35 ⚕ 21.35 Global Days 090

61253 Burr hole(s) or trephine, infratentorial, unilateral or bilateral [C] [80] ▣

EXCLUDES burr hole or trephine followed by craniotomy at same operative session (61304-61321)

⚕ 23.36 ⚕ 23.36 Global Days 090
AMA: 2008, Jan, 10-25; 2007, Jan, 13-27; 2007, Jan, 13-27; 2007, January, 13-27

61304-61323 Craniectomy/Craniotomy: By Indication/Specific Area of Brain

EXCLUDES injection for:
cerebral angiography (36100-36218)
pneumoencephalography (61055)
ventriculography (61026, 61120)

61304 Craniectomy or craniotomy, exploratory; supratentorial [C] [80] ▣
⚕ 41.77 ⚕ 41.77 Global Days 090

61305 infratentorial (posterior fossa) [C] [80] ▣
⚕ 50.13 ⚕ 50.13 Global Days 090

61312 Craniectomy or craniotomy for evacuation of hematoma, supratentorial; extradural or subdural [C] [80] ▣ [P0]
⚕ 52.01 ⚕ 52.01 Global Days 090

61313 intracerebral [C] [80] ▣ [P0]
⚕ 49.85 ⚕ 49.85 Global Days 090

61314 Craniectomy or craniotomy for evacuation of hematoma, infratentorial; extradural or subdural [C] [80] ▣
⚕ 46.24 ⚕ 46.24 Global Days 090

61315 intracerebellar [C] [80] ▣ [P0]
⚕ 52.64 ⚕ 52.64 Global Days 090

+ **61316** Incision and subcutaneous placement of cranial bone graft (List separately in addition to code for primary procedure) [C] ▣
Code first (61304, 61312-61313, 61322-61323, 61340, 61570-61571, 61680-61705)
⚕ 2.30 ⚕ 2.30 Global Days ZZZ

61320 Craniectomy or craniotomy, drainage of intracranial abscess; supratentorial `C` `80` `□`
    📖 48.68   🔧 48.68   Global Days 090

61321   infratentorial `C` `80` `□`
    📖 53.31   🔧 53.31   Global Days 090

61322 Craniectomy or craniotomy, decompressive, with or without duraplasty, for treatment of intracranial hypertension, without evacuation of associated intraparenchymal hematoma; without lobectomy `C` `80` `□`
    Do not report with (61313)
    EXCLUDES   *subtemporal decompression (61340)*
    📖 59.08   🔧 59.08   Global Days 090

61323   with lobectomy `C` `□`
    EXCLUDES   *subtemporal decompression (61340)*
    Do not report with (61313)
    📖 60.19   🔧 60.19   Global Days 090

61330-61530 Craniectomy/Craniotomy/Decompression Brain By Surgical Approach/Specific Area of Brain

EXCLUDES   *injection for:*
    cerebral angiography (36100-36218)
    pneumoencephalography (61055)
    ventriculography (61026, 61120)

61330 Decompression of orbit only, transcranial approach `62` `T` `80` `50` `□`
    INCLUDES   Naffziger operation
    📖 40.21   🔧 40.21   Global Days 090

61332 Exploration of orbit (transcranial approach); with biopsy `C` `80` `□`
    📖 47.30   🔧 47.30   Global Days 090

61333   with removal of lesion `C` `80` `□`
    📖 47.47   🔧 47.47   Global Days 090

61334   with removal of foreign body `62` `T` `80` `□`
    📖 30.54   🔧 30.54   Global Days 090

61340 Subtemporal cranial decompression (pseudotumor cerebri, slit ventricle syndrome) `C` `80` `50` `□`
    EXCLUDES   *decompression craniotomy or craniectomy for intracranial hypertension, without hematoma removal (61322-61323)*
    📖 36.23   🔧 36.23   Global Days 090

61343 Craniectomy, suboccipital with cervical laminectomy for decompression of medulla and spinal cord, with or without dural graft (eg, Arnold-Chiari malformation) `C` `80` `□`
    📖 56.02   🔧 56.02   Global Days 090

61345 Other cranial decompression, posterior fossa `C` `80` `□`
    EXCLUDES   *Kroenlein procedure (67445)*
         orbital decompression using a lateral wall approach (67445)
    📖 51.84   🔧 51.84   Global Days 090

61440 Craniotomy for section of tentorium cerebelli (separate procedure) `C` `80` `□`
    📖 50.75   🔧 50.75   Global Days 090

61450 Craniectomy, subtemporal, for section, compression, or decompression of sensory root of gasserian ganglion `C` `80` `□`
    INCLUDES   Frazier-Spiller procedure
         Hartley-Krause
         Krause decompression
         Taarnhoj procedure
    📖 47.82   🔧 47.82   Global Days 090

61458 Craniectomy, suboccipital; for exploration or decompression of cranial nerves `C` `80` `□`
    INCLUDES   Jannetta decompression
    📖 51.28   🔧 51.28   Global Days 090

61460   for section of one or more cranial nerves `C` `80` `□`
    📖 51.61   🔧 51.61   Global Days 090

61470   for medullary tractotomy `C` `80` `□`
    📖 48.00   🔧 48.00   Global Days 090

61480   for mesencephalic tractotomy or pedunculotomy `C` `80` `□`
    📖 46.95   🔧 46.95   Global Days 090

61490 Craniotomy for lobotomy, including cingulotomy `C` `80` `50` `□`
    📖 48.62   🔧 48.62   Global Days 090

61500 Craniectomy; with excision of tumor or other bone lesion of skull `C` `80` `□`
    📖 34.12   🔧 34.12   Global Days 090

61501   for osteomyelitis `C` `80` `□`
    📖 29.15   🔧 29.15   Global Days 090

61510 Craniectomy, trephination, bone flap craniotomy; for excision of brain tumor, supratentorial, except meningioma `C` `80` `□` `P0`
    📖 55.24   🔧 55.24   Global Days 090

61512   for excision of meningioma, supratentorial `C` `80` `□` `P0`
    📖 65.33   🔧 65.33   Global Days 090

61514   for excision of brain abscess, supratentorial `C` `80` `□`
    📖 48.43   🔧 48.43   Global Days 090

61516   for excision or fenestration of cyst, supratentorial `C` `80` `□`
    EXCLUDES   *craniopharyngioma (61545)*
         pituitary tumor removal (61546, 61548)
    📖 47.24   🔧 47.24   Global Days 090

+ **61517** Implantation of brain intracavitary chemotherapy agent (List separately in addition to code for primary procedure) `C` `□`
    intracavity radioelement source or ribbon implantation (77785-77787)
    Code first (61510, 61518)
    📖 2.30   🔧 2.30   Global Days ZZZ

61518 Craniectomy for excision of brain tumor, infratentorial or posterior fossa; except meningioma, cerebellopontine angle tumor, or midline tumor at base of skull `C` `80` `□` `P0`
    📖 70.26   🔧 70.26   Global Days 090

61519   meningioma `C` `80` `□`
    📖 75.73   🔧 75.73   Global Days 090

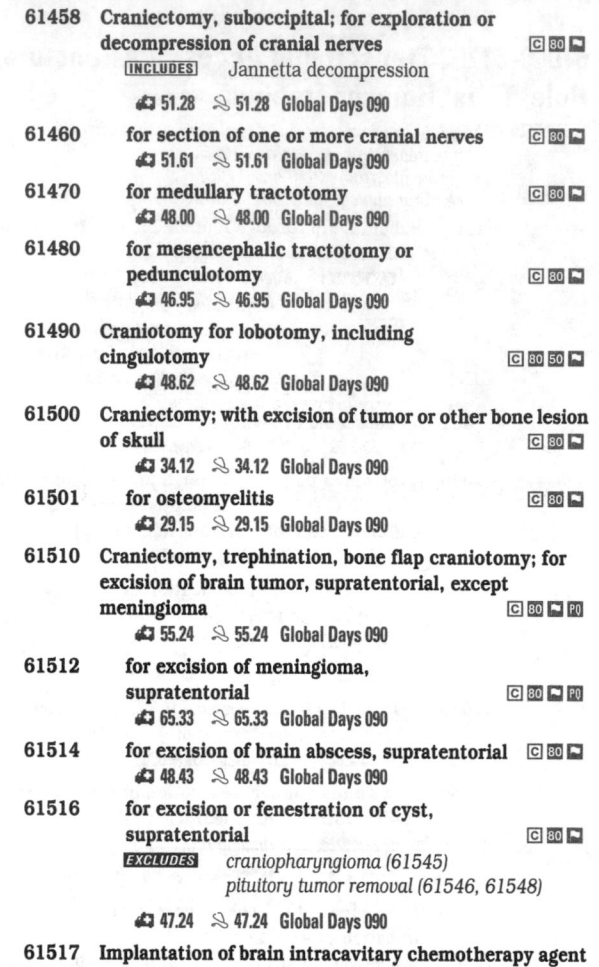

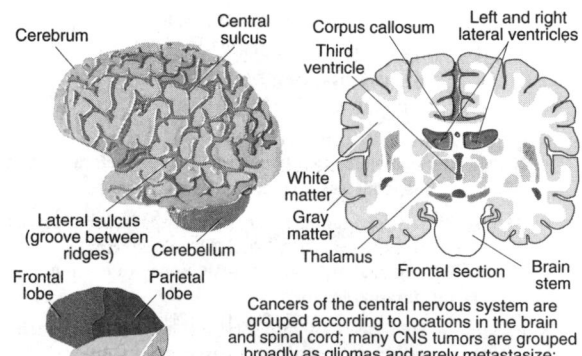

Cancers of the central nervous system are grouped according to locations in the brain and spinal cord; many CNS tumors are grouped broadly as gliomas and rarely metastasize; secondary tumors are ones that have metastasized to the CNS and are often encountered with melanomas and lung cancers

`26` `TC` Professional/Technical Component Only	`80` `/80` Assist-at-Surgery Allowed/With Documentation Unlisted Not Covered
AMA: CPT Assistant References `A2` `Z3` ASC Payment Indicator ♂ Male Only ♀ Female Only ⊘ Modifier 51 Exempt `P0` PQRI	

232   CPT only © 2008 American Medical Association. All Rights Reserved. (Black Ink)   Medicare (Red Ink)   © 2008 Ingenix (*Blue Ink*)

61520　　cerebellopontine angle tumor　　Ⓒ 80 ▢ P0
　　　　🔹 96.01　 🔍 96.01　Global Days 090

61521　　midline tumor at base of skull　　Ⓒ 80 ▢
　　　　🔹 81.36　 🔍 81.36　Global Days 090

61522　Craniectomy, infratentorial or posterior fossa; for
　　　excision of brain abscess　　Ⓒ 80 ▢
　　　　🔹 55.76　 🔍 55.76　Global Days 090

61524　　for excision or fenestration of cyst　　Ⓒ 80 ▢
　　　　🔹 52.63　 🔍 52.63　Global Days 090

61526　Craniectomy, bone flap craniotomy, transtemporal
　　　(mastoid) for excision of cerebellopontine angle
　　　tumor;　　Ⓒ ▢ P0
　　　　🔹 86.13　 🔍 86.13　Global Days 090

61530　　combined with middle/posterior fossa
　　　　craniotomy/craniectomy　　Ⓒ ▢ P0
　　　　🔹 73.21　 🔍 73.21　Global Days 090

61531-61545 Procedures for Seizures/Implanted Electrodes/Choroid Plexus/Craniopharyngioma

CMS *100-3,160.5*　　*Stereotaxic Depth Electrode Implantation*

EXCLUDES　*craniotomy for:*
　　multiple subpial transections during procedure (61567)
　　selective amygdalohippocampectomy (61566)
　injection for:
　　cerebral angiography (36100-36218)
　　pneumoencephalography (61055)
　　ventriculography (61026, 61120)

61531　Subdural implantation of strip electrodes through one
　　　or more burr or trephine hole(s) for long-term seizure
　　　monitoring　　Ⓒ 80 ▢
　　　　EXCLUDES　*craniotomy for intracranial arteriovenous*
　　　　　malformation removal (61680-61692)
　　　　　stereotactic insertion of electrodes (61760)
　　　　🔹 30.40　 🔍 30.40　Global Days 090

61533　Craniotomy with elevation of bone flap; for subdural
　　　implantation of an electrode array, for long-term seizure
　　　monitoring　　Ⓒ 00 ▢
　　　　EXCLUDES　*continuous EEG observation (95950-95954)*
　　　　🔹 38.48　 🔍 38.48　Global Days 090

61534　　for excision of epileptogenic focus without
　　　　electrocorticography during surgery　　Ⓒ 80 ▢
　　　　🔹 41.43　 🔍 41.43　Global Days 090

61535　　for removal of epidural or subdural electrode array,
　　　　without excision of cerebral tissue (separate
　　　　procedure)　　Ⓒ 80 ▢
　　　　🔹 24.73　 🔍 24.73　Global Days 090

61536　　for excision of cerebral epileptogenic focus, with
　　　　electrocorticography during surgery (includes removal
　　　　of electrode array)　　Ⓒ 80 ▢
　　　　🔹 66.21　 🔍 66.21　Global Days 090

61537　　for lobectomy, temporal lobe, without
　　　　electrocorticography during surgery　　Ⓒ 80 ▢
　　　　🔹 60.45　 🔍 60.45　Global Days 090

61538　　for lobectomy, temporal lobe, with
　　　　electrocorticography during surgery　　Ⓒ 80 ▢
　　　　🔹 64.64　 🔍 64.64　Global Days 090

61539　　for lobectomy, other than temporal lobe, partial or
　　　　total, with electrocorticography during
　　　　surgery　　Ⓒ 80 ▢
　　　　🔹 59.93　 🔍 59.93　Global Days 090

61540　　for lobectomy, other than temporal lobe, partial or
　　　　total, without electrocorticography during
　　　　surgery　　Ⓒ 80 ▢
　　　　🔹 56.40　 🔍 56.40　Global Days 090

61541　　for transection of corpus callosum　　Ⓒ 80 ▢
　　　　🔹 53.68　 🔍 53.68　Global Days 090

61542　　for total hemispherectomy　　Ⓒ 80 ▢
　　　　🔹 58.53　 🔍 58.53　Global Days 090

61543　　for partial or subtotal (functional)
　　　　hemispherectomy　　Ⓒ 80 ▢
　　　　🔹 54.69　 🔍 54.69　Global Days 090

61544　　for excision or coagulation of choroid plexus　　Ⓒ 80 ▢
　　　　🔹 45.02　 🔍 45.02　Global Days 090

61545　　for excision of craniopharyngioma　　Ⓒ 80 ▢
　　　　🔹 80.40　 🔍 80.40　Global Days 090

61546-61548 Removal Pituitary Gland/Tumor

EXCLUDES　*injection for:*
　　cerebral angiography (36100-36218)
　　pneumoencephalography (61055)
　　ventriculography (61026, 61120)

61546　Craniotomy for hypophysectomy or excision of pituitary
　　　tumor, intracranial approach　　Ⓒ 80 ▢
　　　　🔹 58.26　 🔍 58.26　Global Days 090

61548　Hypophysectomy or excision of pituitary tumor,
　　　transnasal or transseptal approach,
　　　nonstereotactic　　Ⓒ 80 ▢ P0
　　　　INCLUDES　operating microscope (69990)
　　　　🔹 38.94　 🔍 38.94　Global Days 090

61550-61559 Craniosynostosis Procedures

EXCLUDES　*injection for:*
　　cerebral angiography (36100-36218)
　　pneumoencephalography (61055)
　　ventriculography (61026, 61120)
　orbital hypertelorism reconstruction (21260-21263)
　reconstruction (21172-21180)

61550　Craniectomy for craniosynostosis; single cranial
　　　suture　　Ⓒ 80 ▢
　　　　🔹 25.11　 🔍 25.11　Global Days 090

61552　　multiple cranial sutures　　Ⓒ 00 ▢
　　　　🔹 32.91　 🔍 32.91　Global Days 090

61556　Craniotomy for craniosynostosis; frontal or parietal bone
　　　flap　　Ⓒ 80 ▢
　　　　🔹 41.28　 🔍 41.28　Global Days 090

61557　　bifrontal bone flap　　Ⓒ 80 ▢
　　　　🔹 42.83　 🔍 42.83　Global Days 090

61558　Extensive craniectomy for multiple cranial suture
　　　craniosynostosis (eg, cloverleaf skull); not requiring bone
　　　grafts　　Ⓒ 80 ▢
　　　　🔹 42.57　 🔍 42.57　Global Days 090

61559　　recontouring with multiple osteotomies and bone
　　　　autografts (eg, barrel-stave procedure) (includes
　　　　obtaining grafts)　　Ⓒ 80 ▢
　　　　🔹 61.34　 🔍 61.34　Global Days 090

61563-61564 Removal Cranial Bone Tumor With/Without Optic Nerve Decompression

EXCLUDES　*injection for:*
　　cerebral angiography (36100-36218)
　　pneumoencephalography (61055)
　　ventriculography (61026, 61120)
　reconstruction (21181-21183)

61563　Excision, intra and extracranial, benign tumor of cranial
　　　bone (eg, fibrous dysplasia); without optic nerve
　　　decompression　　Ⓒ 80 ▢
　　　　🔹 48.75　 🔍 48.75　Global Days 090

● New Code　　▲ Revised Code　　Ⓜ Maternity Edit　　Ⓐ Age Edit　　Ⓐ-Ⓨ OPPS Status Indicator　　🔹 Facility RVU　　🔍 Non-Facility RVU
Ⓒ CCI Comprehensive Code　　50 Bilateral Procedure　　+ Add-on Indicator　　◼ Laboratory crosswalk　　◼ Radiology crosswalk

Nervous System

61564 — 61598

61564   with optic nerve decompression   C 80 ▭
         61.81   61.81   Global Days 090

61566-61567 Craniotomy for Seizures

EXCLUDES   injection for:
       cerebral angiography (36100-36218)
       pneumoencephalography (61055)
       ventriculography (61026, 61120)

61566   Craniotomy with elevation of bone flap; for selective
       amygdalohippocampectomy   C 80 ▭
       56.66   56.66   Global Days 090

61567   for multiple subpial transections, with
       electrocorticography during surgery   C 80 ▭
       63.32   63.32   Global Days 090

61570-61571 Removal of Foreign Body from Brain

EXCLUDES   injection for:
       cerebral angiography (36100-36218)
       pneumoencephalography (61055)
       ventriculography (61026, 61120)
     sequestrectomy for osteomyelitis (61501)

61570   Craniectomy or craniotomy; with excision of foreign body
       from brain   C 80 ▭
       46.42   46.42   Global Days 090

61571   with treatment of penetrating wound of
       brain   C 80 ▭
       50.56   50.56   Global Days 090

61575-61576 Transoral Approach Posterior Cranial Fossa/Upper Cervical Cord

EXCLUDES   arthrodesis (22548)
     injection for:
       cerebral angiography (36100-36218)
       pneumoencephalography (61055)
       ventriculography (61026, 61120)

61575   Transoral approach to skull base, brain stem or upper
       spinal cord for biopsy, decompression or excision of
       lesion;   C 80 ▭
       59.31   59.31   Global Days 090

61576   requiring splitting of tongue and/or mandible
       (including tracheostomy)   C 80 ▭
       93.90   93.90   Global Days 090

61580-61598 Surgical Approach: Cranial Fossae

EXCLUDES   definitive surgery (61600-61616)
     injection for:
       cerebral angiography (36100-36218)
       pneumoencephalography (61055)
       ventriculography (61026, 61120)
     primary closure (15732, 15756-15758)
     repair and/or reconstruction (61618-61619)

61580   Craniofacial approach to anterior cranial fossa;
       extradural, including lateral rhinotomy, ethmoidectomy,
       sphenoidectomy, without maxillectomy or orbital
       exenteration   C 50 ▭
       61.64   61.64   Global Days 090

61581   extradural, including lateral rhinotomy, orbital
       exenteration, ethmoidectomy, sphenoidectomy and/or
       maxillectomy   C 50 ▭
       69.24   69.24   Global Days 090

61582   extradural, including unilateral or bifrontal
       craniotomy, elevation of frontal lobe(s), osteotomy of
       base of anterior cranial fossa   C 80 ▭
       72.11   72.11   Global Days 090

61583   intradural, including unilateral or bifrontal
       craniotomy, elevation or resection of frontal lobe,
       osteotomy of base of anterior cranial fossa   C 80 ▭
       73.53   73.53   Global Days 090

61584   Orbitocranial approach to anterior cranial fossa,
       extradural, including supraorbital ridge osteotomy and
       elevation of frontal and/or temporal lobe(s); without
       orbital exenteration   C 80 50 ▭
       71.35   71.35   Global Days 090

61585   with orbital exenteration   C 80 50 ▭
       75.06   75.06   Global Days 090

61586   Bicoronal, transzygomatic and/or LeFort I osteotomy
       approach to anterior cranial fossa with or without internal
       fixation, without bone graft   C 80 ▭
       53.88   53.88   Global Days 090

61590   Infratemporal pre-auricular approach to middle cranial
       fossa (parapharyngeal space, infratemporal and midline
       skull base, nasopharynx), with or without disarticulation
       of the mandible, including parotidectomy, craniotomy,
       decompression and/or mobilization of the facial nerve
       and/or petrous carotid artery   C 80 50 ▭
       78.77   78.77   Global Days 090

61591   Infratemporal post-auricular approach to middle cranial
       fossa (internal auditory meatus, petrous apex, tentorium,
       cavernous sinus, parasellar area, infratemporal fossa)
       including mastoidectomy, resection of sigmoid sinus,
       with or without decompression and/or mobilization of
       contents of auditory canal or petrous carotid
       artery   C 80 50 ▭ P0
       79.43   79.43   Global Days 090

61592   Orbitocranial zygomatic approach to middle cranial fossa
       (cavernous sinus and carotid artery, clivus, basilar artery
       or petrous apex) including osteotomy of zygoma,
       craniotomy, extra- or intradural elevation of temporal
       lobe   C 80 50 ▭
       80.59   80.59   Global Days 090

61595   Transtemporal approach to posterior cranial fossa, jugular
       foramen or midline skull base, including mastoidectomy,
       decompression of sigmoid sinus and/or facial nerve, with
       or without mobilization   C 50 ▭ P0
       59.60   59.60   Global Days 090

61596   Transcochlear approach to posterior cranial fossa, jugular
       foramen or midline skull base, including labyrinthectomy,
       decompression, with or without mobilization of facial
       nerve and/or petrous carotid artery   C 80 50 ▭ P0
       65.18   65.18   Global Days 090

61597   Transcondylar (far lateral) approach to posterior cranial
       fossa, jugular foramen or midline skull base, including
       occipital condylectomy, mastoidectomy, resection of
       C1-C3 vertebral body(s), decompression of vertebral
       artery, with or without mobilization   C 80 50 ▭
       72.96   72.96   Global Days 090

61598   Transpetrosal approach to posterior cranial fossa, clivus
       or foramen magnum, including ligation of superior
       petrosal sinus and/or sigmoid sinus   C 80 ▭ P0
       64.02   64.02   Global Days 090

61600-61616 Definitive Procedures: Cranial Fossae

EXCLUDES   *injection for:*
    cerebral angiography (36100-36218)
    pneumoencephalography (61055)
    ventriculography (61026, 61120)
  primary closure (15732, 15756-15758)
  repair and/or reconstruction (61618-61619)
  surgical approach (61580-61598)

61600 Resection or excision of neoplastic, vascular or infectious lesion of base of anterior cranial fossa; extradural   C 80 🔲
    🔧 53.74   ✂ 53.74   Global Days 090

61601 intradural, including dural repair, with or without graft   C 80 🔲
    🔧 59.52   ✂ 59.52   Global Days 090

61605 Resection or excision of neoplastic, vascular or infectious lesion of infratemporal fossa, parapharyngeal space, petrous apex; extradural   C 80 🔲
    🔧 55.90   ✂ 55.90   Global Days 090

61606 intradural, including dural repair, with or without graft   C 80 🔲 P0
    🔧 76.48   ✂ 76.48   Global Days 090

61607 Resection or excision of neoplastic, vascular or infectious lesion of parasellar area, cavernous sinus, clivus or midline skull base; extradural   C 80 🔲
    🔧 70.45   ✂ 70.45   Global Days 090

61608 intradural, including dural repair, with or without graft   C 80 🔲
    🔧 82.84   ✂ 82.84   Global Days 090

+ **61609** Transection or ligation, carotid artery in cavernous sinus; without repair (List separately in addition to code for primary procedure)   C 80 🔲
    Code first (61605-61608)
    🔧 16.14   ✂ 16.14   Global Days ZZZ

+ **61610** with repair by anastomosis or graft (List separately in addition to code for primary procedure)   C 80 🔲
    Code first (61605-61608)
    🔧 49.42   ✂ 49.42   Global Days ZZZ

+ **61611** Transection or ligation, carotid artery in petrous canal; without repair (List separately in addition to code for primary procedure)   C 80 🔲
    Code first (61605-61608)
    🔧 12.46   ✂ 12.46   Global Days ZZZ

+ **61612** with repair by anastomosis or graft (List separately in addition to code for primary procedure)   C 80 🔲
    Code first (61605-61608)
    🔧 43.09   ✂ 43.09   Global Days ZZZ

61613 Obliteration of carotid aneurysm, arteriovenous malformation, or carotid-cavernous fistula by dissection within cavernous sinus   C 80 50 🔲
    🔧 79.87   ✂ 79.87   Global Days 090

61615 Resection or excision of neoplastic, vascular or infectious lesion of base of posterior cranial fossa, jugular foramen, foramen magnum, or C1-C3 vertebral bodies; extradural   C 80 🔲
    🔧 62.54   ✂ 62.54   Global Days 090

61616 intradural, including dural repair, with or without graft   C 80 🔲 P0
    🔧 82.77   ✂ 82.77   Global Days 090

61618-61619 Reconstruction Post-Surgical Cranial Fossae Defects

EXCLUDES   *definitive surgery (61600-61616)*
  injection for:
    cerebral angiography (36100-36218)
    pneumoencephalography (61055)
    ventriculography (61026, 61120)
  primary closure (15732, 15756-15758)
  surgical approach (61580-61598)

61618 Secondary repair of dura for cerebrospinal fluid leak, anterior, middle or posterior cranial fossa following surgery of the skull base; by free tissue graft (eg, pericranium, fascia, tensor fascia lata, adipose tissue, homologous or synthetic grafts)   C 80 🔲 P0
    🔧 32.85   ✂ 32.85   Global Days 090
    AMA: 2008, Jan, 10-25; 2007, Jan, 13-27; 2007, Jan, 13-27; 2007, January, 13-27

61619 by local or regionalized vascularized pedicle flap or myocutaneous flap (including galea, temporalis, frontalis or occipitalis muscle)   C 80 🔲 P0
    🔧 37.76   ✂ 37.76   Global Days 090
    AMA: 2008, Jan, 10-25; 2007, Jan, 13-27; 2007, Jan, 13-27; 2007, January, 13-27

61623-61642 Neurovascular Interventional Procedures

CMS *100-3,20.28*   *Therapeutic Embolization*
CMS *100-4,4,61.2*   *Requirements for Specific Procedures to be Repoted With Device Codes*
CMS *100-4,4,61.1*   *Hospital Requirement for Device Codes on OPPS Claims*
CMS *100-2,16,180*   *Services Related to Noncovered Procedures*
CMS *100-2,16,10*   *Exclusions from Coverage*

61623 Endovascular temporary balloon arterial occlusion, head or neck (extracranial/intracranial) including selective catheterization of vessel to be occluded, positioning and inflation of occlusion balloon, concomitant neurological monitoring, and radiologic supervision and interpretation of all angiography required for balloon occlusion and to exclude vascular injury post occlusion   T 🔲
    Code also (C2628)
    🔧 15.00   ✂ 15.00   Global Days 000
    AMA: 2006, Dec, 4-7; 2006, Dec, 4-7; 2006, Dec, 4-7; 2006, Dec, 4-7; 2006, Dec, 4-7; 2006, Dec, 4-7; 2006, Dec, 4-7; 2006, Dec, 4-7; 2006, December, 4-7; 2006, December, 4-7; 2006, December, 4-7; 2006, December, 4-7

61624 Transcatheter permanent occlusion or embolization (eg, for tumor destruction, to achieve hemostasis, to occlude a vascular malformation), percutaneous, any method; central nervous system (intracranial, spinal cord)   C 🔲
    EXCLUDES   *transcatheter occlusion or embolization other than head or neck (37204)*
    📷 *75894*
    🔧 29.81   ✂ 29.81   Global Days 000
    AMA: 2008, Jan, 10-25; 2007, Jan, 13-27; 2007, Jan, 13-27; 2007, January, 13-27; 2006, Dec, 4-7; 2006, Dec, 4-7; 2006, Dec, 4-7; 2006, Dec, 4-7; 2006, December, 4-7; 2006, December, 4-7; 2006, December, 4-7; 2006, December, 4-7; 2006, Dec, 4-7; 2006, Dec, 4-7; 2006, Dec, 4-7; 2006, Dec, 4-7

61600 — 61624

Nervous System

61626 — 61697

61626   **non-central nervous system, head or neck (extracranial, brachiocephalic branch)** 🅣 ▣
> *EXCLUDES*   *transcatheter occlusion or embolization other than head or neck (37204)*

Code also (C1769, C1887, C2628)
🔁 *75894*
💰 24.17   ⚕ 24.17   **Global Days 000**
AMA: 2006, Dec, 4-7; 2006, Dec, 4-7; 2006, Dec, 4-7; 2006, Dec, 4-7; 2006, Dec, 4-7; 2006, Dec, 4-7; 2006, Dec, 4-7; 2006, Dec, 4-7; 2006, December, 4-7; 2006, December, 4-7; 2006, December, 4-7; 2006, December, 4-7

61630   **Balloon angioplasty, intracranial (eg, atherosclerotic stenosis), percutaneous** 🅒 🞐
> *INCLUDES*   diagnostic arteriogram if stent or angioplasty is necessary
> radiology services for arteriography of target vascular family
> selective catheterization of the target vascular family
>
> *EXCLUDES*   *diagnostic arteriogram if stent or angioplasty is not necessary (use applicable code for selective catheterization and radiology services)*

💰 33.90   ⚕ 33.90   **Global Days XXX**
AMA: 2006, Dec, 4-7; 2006, Dec, 4-7; 2006, Dec, 4-7; 2006, Dec, 4-7; 2006, Dec, 4-7; 2006, Dec, 4-7; 2006, Dec, 4-7; 2006, Dec, 4-7; 2006, December, 4-7; 2006, December, 4-7; 2006, December, 4-7; 2006, December, 4-7

61635   **Transcatheter placement of intravascular stent(s), intracranial (eg, atherosclerotic stenosis), including balloon angioplasty, if performed** 🅒 🞐
> *INCLUDES*   diagnostic arteriogram if stent or angioplasty is necessary
> radiology services for arteriography of target vascular family
> selective catheterization of the target vascular family
>
> *EXCLUDES*   *diagnostic arteriogram if stent or angioplasty is not necessary (use applicable code for selective catheterization and radiology services)*

💰 37.12   ⚕ 37.12   **Global Days XXX**
AMA: 2006, Dec, 4-7; 2006, Dec, 4-7; 2006, Dec, 4-7; 2006, Dec, 4-7; 2006, Dec, 4-7; 2006, Dec, 4-7; 2006, Dec, 4-7; 2006, Dec, 4-7; 2006, December, 4-7; 2006, December, 4-7; 2006, December, 4-7; 2006, December, 4-7

61640   **Balloon dilatation of intracranial vasospasm, percutaneous; initial vessel** 🅔
> *INCLUDES*   angiography after dilation of vessel
> fluoroscopic guidance
> injection of contrast material
> roadmapping
> selective catheterization of target vessel
> vessel analysis

💰 17.16   ⚕ 17.16   **Global Days 000**
AMA: 2006, Dec, 4-7; 2006, Dec, 4-7; 2006, Dec, 4-7; 2006, Dec, 4-7; 2006, Dec, 4-7; 2006, Dec, 4-7; 2006, Dec, 4-7; 2006, Dec, 4-7; 2006, December, 4-7; 2006, December, 4-7; 2006, December, 4-7; 2006, December, 4-7

+   **61641**   **each additional vessel in same vascular family (List separately in addition to code for primary procedure)** 🅔
> *INCLUDES*   angiography after dilation of vessel
> fluoroscopic guidance
> injection of contrast material
> roadmapping
> selective catheterization of target vessel
> vessel analysis

Code first (61640)
💰 6.03   ⚕ 6.03   **Global Days ZZZ**
AMA: 2006, Dec, 4-7; 2006, Dec, 4-7; 2006, Dec, 4-7; 2006, Dec, 4-7; 2006, Dec, 4-7; 2006, Dec, 4-7; 2006, Dec, 4-7; 2006, Dec, 4-7; 2006, December, 4-7; 2006, December, 4-7; 2006, December, 4-7; 2006, December, 4-7

+   **61642**   **each additional vessel in different vascular family (List separately in addition to code for primary procedure)** 🅔
> *INCLUDES*   angiography after dilation of vessel
> injection of contrast material
> fluoroscopic guidance
> roadmapping
> selective catheterization of target vessel
> vessel analysis

Code first (61640)
💰 12.06   ⚕ 12.06   **Global Days ZZZ**
AMA: 2006, Dec, 4-7; 2006, Dec, 4-7; 2006, Dec, 4-7; 2006, Dec, 4-7; 2006, Dec, 4-7; 2006, Dec, 4-7; 2006, Dec, 4-7; 2006, Dec, 4-7; 2006, December, 4-7; 2006, December, 4-7; 2006, December, 4-7; 2006, December, 4-7

61680-61692 Surgical Treatment of Arteriovenous Malformation of the Brain

CMS *100-4,12,30*   *Correct Coding Policy*
INCLUDES   craniotomy

61680   **Surgery of intracranial arteriovenous malformation; supratentorial, simple** 🅒 🞐 ▣
💰 57.78   ⚕ 57.78   **Global Days 090**

61682   **supratentorial, complex** 🅒 🞐 ▣
💰 108.87   ⚕ 108.87   **Global Days 090**

61684   **infratentorial, simple** 🅒 🞐 ▣
💰 72.39   ⚕ 72.39   **Global Days 090**

61686   **infratentorial, complex** 🅒 🞐 ▣
💰 116.46   ⚕ 116.46   **Global Days 090**

61690   **dural, simple** 🅒 🞐 ▣
💰 54.77   ⚕ 54.77   **Global Days 090**

61692   **dural, complex** 🅒 🞐 ▣
💰 94.04   ⚕ 94.04   **Global Days 090**

61697-61703 Surgical Treatment Brain Aneurysm

INCLUDES   craniotomy

61697   **Surgery of complex intracranial aneurysm, intracranial approach; carotid circulation** 🅒 🞐 ▣ 🅟🅠
> *INCLUDES*   aneurysms bigger than 15 mm
> calcification of the aneurysm neck
> inclusion of normal vessels in aneurysm neck
> surgery needing temporary vessel occlusion, trapping, or cardiopulmonary bypass to treat aneurysm

💰 105.57   ⚕ 105.57   **Global Days 090**

🄰🄱/🄰🄱 Professional/Technical Component Only   🄰🄰/🄰🄰 Assist-at-Surgery Allowed/With Documentation   Unlisted   Not Covered
AMA: CPT Assistant References   🄰🄰-🅉🅉 ASC Payment Indicator   ♂ Male Only   ♀ Female Only   ⊘ Modifier 51 Exempt   🅟🅠 PQRI

236   CPT only © 2008 American Medical Association. All Rights Reserved. (Black Ink)   Medicare (Red Ink)   © 2008 Ingenix *(Blue Ink)*

61698   vertebrobasilar circulation   [C] [80] [□]
        [INCLUDES]   aneurysm bigger than 15 mm
                     calcification of aneurysm neck
                     inclusion of normal vessels into aneurysm
                         neck
                     surgery needing temporary vessel occlusion,
                         trapping, or cardiopulmonary bypass
                         to treat aneurysm

        ⚡ 113.18   ⚕ 113.18 Global Days 090

61700   Surgery of simple intracranial aneurysm, intracranial
        approach; carotid circulation   [C] [80] [□] [P0]
        ⚡ 89.01   ⚕ 89.01 Global Days 090
        AMA: 2008, Jan, 10-25; 2007, Jan, 13-27; 2007, Jan, 13-27; 2007,
        January, 13-27

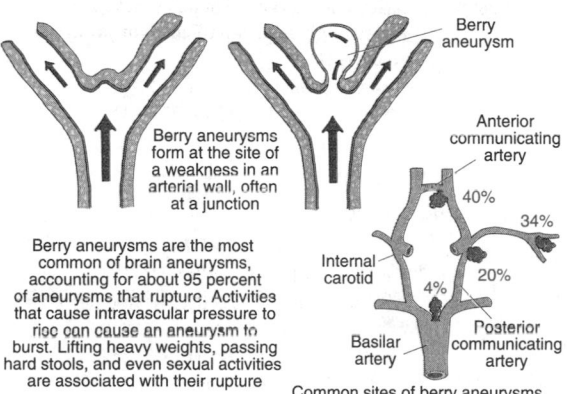

Berry aneurysms form at the site of a weakness in an arterial wall, often at a junction

Berry aneurysms are the most common of brain aneurysms, accounting for about 95 percent of aneurysms that rupture. Activities that cause intravascular pressure to rise can cause an aneurysm to burst. Lifting heavy weights, passing hard stools, and even sexual activities are associated with their rupture.

Berry aneurysm
Anterior communicating artery
40%
34%
Internal carotid
20%
4%
Basilar artery
Posterior communicating artery

Common sites of berry aneurysms in the circle of Willis arteries

61702   vertebrobasilar circulation   [C] [80] [□]
        ⚡ 98.46   ⚕ 98.46 Global Days 090

61703   Surgery of intracranial aneurysm, cervical approach by
        application of occluding clamp to cervical carotid artery
        (Selverstone-Crutchfield type)   [O] [80] [□]
        [EXCLUDES]   cervical approach for direct ligation of carotid
                     artery (37600-37606)
        ⚡ 33.87   ⚕ 33.87 Global Days 090

61705-61710 Other Procedures for Aneurysm, Arteriovenous Malformation, and Carotid-Cavernous Fistula

[INCLUDES]   craniotomy
[EXCLUDES]   ligation or gradual occlusion of internal common carotid artery
             (37605-37606)

61705   Surgery of aneurysm, vascular malformation or
        carotid-cavernous fistula; by intracranial and cervical
        occlusion of carotid artery   [C] [80] [□]
        ⚡ 65.30   ⚕ 65.30 Global Days 090

61708   by intracranial electrothrombosis   [C] [80] [□]
        [EXCLUDES]   ligation or gradual occlusion of internal or
                     common carotid artery (37605-37606)
        ⚡ 54.79   ⚕ 54.79 Global Days 090

61710   by intra-arterial embolization, injection procedure, or
        balloon catheter   [C] [80] [□]
        ⚡ 50.57   ⚕ 50.57 Global Days 090

61711 Extracranial-Intracranial Bypass

[INCLUDES]   craniotomy

61711   Anastomosis, arterial, extracranial-intracranial (eg,
        middle cerebral/cortical) arteries   [C] [80] [□]
        [EXCLUDES]   carotid or vertebral thromboendarterectomy
                     (35301)
                     operating microscope (69990)
        ⚡ 66.67   ⚕ 66.67 Global Days 090

61720-61791 Stereotactic Procedures of the Brain

CMS *100-3,160.4*   *Stereotactic Cingulotomy as a Means of Psychosurgery--Not
                         Covered*
CMS *100-3,160.5*   *Stereotaxic Depth Electrode Implantation*

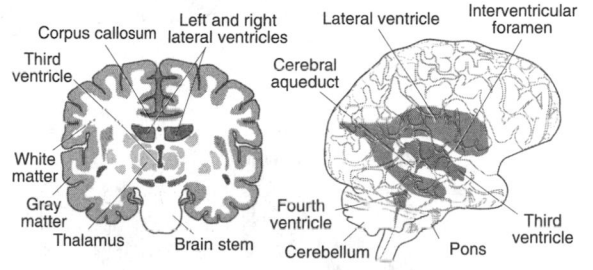

Corpus callosum
Left and right lateral ventricles
Lateral ventricle
Interventricular foramen
Third ventricle
Cerebral aqueduct
White matter
Gray matter
Thalamus
Brain stem
Fourth ventricle
Cerebellum
Pons
Third ventricle

Frontal section of the brain (left) and lateral view schematic showing the ventricular system in blue (right)

Cerebral spinal fluid (CSF) is secreted in the ventricles and flows generally from the laterals into the third ventricle via the interventricular foramina, and into the fourth ventricle via the cerebral aqueduct. Many brain disorders upset ventricular fluid pressures and shunts are employed to restore balance

61720   Creation of lesion by stereotactic method, including burr
        hole(s) and localizing and recording techniques, single
        or multiple stages; globus pallidus or thalamus   [T] [□]
        ⚡ 29.30   ⚕ 29.30 Global Days 090

61735   subcortical structure(s) other than globus pallidus or
        thalamus   [C] [□]
        ⚡ 35.75   ⚕ 35.75 Global Days 090

61750   Stereotactic biopsy, aspiration, or excision, including
        burr hole(s), for intracranial lesion;   [C] [□] [P0]
        ⚡ 35.57   ⚕ 35.57 Global Days 090

61751   with computed tomography and/or magnetic
        resonance guidance   [C] [□] [P0]
        ▨ 70450, 70460, 70470, 70551-70553
        ⚡ 34.66   ⚕ 34.66 Global Days 090
        AMA: 2008, Jan, 10-25; 2007, Jan, 13-27; 2007, Jan, 13-27, 2007,
        January, 13-27; 2004, Dec, 20; 2004, December, 20; 2004, Dec,
        20

61760   Stereotactic implantation of depth electrodes into the
        cerebrum for long-term seizure monitoring   [C] [□]
        ⚡ 39.21   ⚕ 39.21 Global Days 090

61770   Stereotactic localization, including burr hole(s), with
        insertion of catheter(s) or probe(s) for placement of
        radiation source   [T] [□]
        ⚡ 38.11   ⚕ 38.11 Global Days 090

61790   Creation of lesion by stereotactic method, percutaneous,
        by neurolytic agent (eg, alcohol, thermal, electrical,
        radiofrequency); gasserian ganglion   [A2] [T] [□]
        ⚡ 21.53   ⚕ 21.53 Global Days 090

61791   trigeminal medullary tract   [A2] [T] [80] [□]
        ⚡ 27.79   ⚕ 27.79 Global Days 090

● New Code   ▲ Revised Code   Ⓜ Maternity Edit   Ⓐ Age Edit   [A-Y] OPPS Status Indicator   ⚡ Facility RVU   ⚕ Non-Facility RVU
□ CCI Comprehensive Code   ⑳ Bilateral Procedure   + Add-on Indicator   ▣ Laboratory crosswalk   ▨ Radiology crosswalk

© 2008 Ingenix *(Blue Ink)*   CPT only © 2008 American Medical Association. All Rights Reserved. (Black Ink)   Medicare (Red Ink)   **237**

Nervous System

61793 — 61875

61793-61800 Stereotactic Radiosurgery (SRS): Brain

INCLUDES planning, dosimetry, targeting, positioning or blocking performed by the neurosurgen

EXCLUDES *intensity modulated beam delivery plan and treatment (77301, 77418)*
stereotactic body radiation therapy other than cranial or spinal (77435)
treatment planning, physics and dosimetry, and treatment delivery performed by the oncologist

Do not report radiation treatment management and radiosurgery by the same physician (77427-77435)
Do not report more than once per lesion for a course of treatment
Do not report with (20660)

~~61793 Stereotactic radiosurgery (particle beam, gamma ray or linear accelerator), one or more sessions~~
See 61796-61800, 63620-63621

+ 61795 Stereotactic computer-assisted volumetric (navigational) procedure, intracranial, extracranial, or spinal (List separately in addition to code for primary procedure) M N ▣
    Code first primary procedure
    Do not report with (61796-61799)
    🔗 6.47 ☒ 6.47 Global Days ZZZ
    AMA: 2008, Jan, 10-25; 2008, May, 9-11; 2008, Jul, 10&13; 2008, Oct, 10-11; 2007, Jan, 13-27; 2007, Jan, 13-27; 2007, Dec, 1-2; 2007, January, 13-27; 2006, Jan, 46-47; 2006, January, 46-47; 2006, Jan, 46-47

● 61796 Stereotactic radiosurgery (particle beam, gamma ray, or linear accelerator); 1 simple cranial lesion B 80
    INCLUDES lesions less than 3.5 cm
    EXCLUDES *brainstem lesions or lesions located <= 5 mm from the optic nerve, chasm, or tract (61798-61799)*
    Do not report more than once per treatment
    Do not report with (61795, 61798)
    🔗 20.28 ☒ 20.28 Global Days 090

+ ● 61797 each additional cranial lesion, simple (List separately in addition to code for primary procedure) B 80
    Do not report with (61795)
    INCLUDES lesions < 3.5 cm
    EXCLUDES *brainstem lesions or lesions located <= 5 mm from the optic nerve, chasm, or tract (61798-61799)*
    Code first (61796, or 61798)
    Do not report 61797 and 61799 more than four times in total per treatment course
    🔗 5.54 ☒ 5.54 Global Days ZZZ

● 61798 1 complex cranial lesion B 80
    INCLUDES all lesions involved in therapeutic lesion creation procedures
    arteriovenous malformations, cavernous sinus, parasellar, glomus, pineal region, pituary tumors, and Schwannomas
    brainstem lesions or lesions located <= 5 mm from the optic nerve, chasm, or tract
    lesions >= 3.5 cm
    Do not report more than once per lesion per treatment course
    Do not report with (61795-61796)
    🔗 20.28 ☒ 20.28 Global Days 090

+ ● 61799 each additional cranial lesion, complex (List separately in addition to code for primary procedure) B 80
    Do not report with (61795)
    INCLUDES all lesions created in therapeutic lesion creation procedures
    brainstem lesions or lesions located <= 5 mm from the optic nerve, chasm, or tract
    lesions >= 3.5 cm
    Code first (61798)
    Do not report more than once per lesion per treatment course
    Do not report 61797 and 61799 more than four times in total per treatment course
    🔗 7.66 ☒ 7.66 Global Days ZZZ

+ ● 61800 Application of stereotactic headframe for stereotactic radiosurgery (List separately in addition to code for primary procedure) B 80
    Code first (61796, 61798)
    🔗 3.93 ☒ 3.93 Global Days ZZZ

61850-61888 Intracranial Neurostimulation

CMS *100-3,160.7* *Electrical Nerve Stimulators*
CMS *100-3,160.2* *Treatment of Motor Function Disorders with Electric Nerve Stimulation*
CMS *100-4,32,50* *Deep Brain Stimulation for Essential Tremor and Parkinson's Disease*

INCLUDES microelectrode recording by same physician, if provided
EXCLUDES *electronic analysis and reprogramming of neurostimulator pulse generator (95970-95975)*
neurophysiological mapping by another physician (95961-95962)

61850 Twist drill or burr hole(s) for implantation of neurostimulator electrodes, cortical C 80 ▣
    🔗 24.74 ☒ 24.74 Global Days 090

61860 Craniectomy or craniotomy for implantation of neurostimulator electrodes, cerebral, cortical C 80 ▣
    🔗 39.35 ☒ 39.35 Global Days 090

61863 Twist drill, burr hole, craniotomy, or craniectomy with stereotactic implantation of neurostimulator electrode array in subcortical site (eg, thalamus, globus pallidus, subthalamic nucleus, periventricular, periaqueductal gray), without use of intraoperative microelectrode recording; first array C 80 50 ▣
    🔗 38.40 ☒ 38.40 Global Days 090

+ 61864 each additional array (List separately in addition to primary procedure) C 80 ▣
    Code first (61863)
    🔗 11.82 ☒ 11.82 Global Days ZZZ

61867 Twist drill, burr hole, craniotomy, or craniectomy with stereotactic implantation of neurostimulator electrode array in subcortical site (eg, thalamus, globus pallidus, subthalamic nucleus, periventricular, periaqueductal gray), with use of intraoperative microelectrode recording; first array C 80 50 ▣ P0
    🔗 55.74 ☒ 55.74 Global Days 090

+ 61868 each additional array (List separately in addition to primary procedure) C 80 ▣
    Code first (61867)
    🔗 16.68 ☒ 16.68 Global Days ZZZ

61870 Craniectomy for implantation of neurostimulator electrodes, cerebellar; cortical C 80 ▣
    🔗 29.96 ☒ 29.96 Global Days 090

61875 subcortical C 80 ▣
    🔗 28.91 ☒ 28.91 Global Days 090

61880 Revision or removal of intracranial neurostimulator electrodes   62 T 80 50 ☐
    🔧 13.77   ⚕ 13.77   Global Days 090

61885 Insertion or replacement of cranial neurostimulator pulse generator or receiver, direct or inductive coupling; with connection to a single electrode array   H9 S 80 50 ☐
     EXCLUDES   *open surgery to place cranial nerve neurostimulator electrode(s) (64573)*
        percutaneous procedure to place cranial nerve neurostimulator electrode(s) (64553)
        revision or removal of cranial nerve neurostimulator electrode(s) (64585)

     Code also (C1767, C1820)
     🔧 15.83   ⚕ 15.83   Global Days 090

61886 with connection to 2 or more electrode arrays   H9 S 80 ☐
     EXCLUDES   *open surgery to place cranial nerve neurostimulator electrode(s) (64573)*
        percutaneous procedure to place cranial nerve neurostimulator electrode(s) (64553)
        revision or removal of cranial nerve neurostimulator electrode(s) (64585)

     Code also (C1767)
     🔧 19.95   ⚕ 19.95   Global Days 090

61888 Revision or removal of cranial neurostimulator pulse generator or receiver   A2 T 50 ☐
     Do not report with (61885-61886)
     🔧 10.10   ⚕ 10.10   Global Days 010

62000-62148 Repair of Skull and/or Cerebrospinal Fluid Leaks

62000 Elevation of depressed skull fracture; simple, extradural   T ☐
     🔧 21.65   ⚕ 21.65   Global Days 090

62005 compound or comminuted, extradural   C 00 ☐
     🔧 31.31   ⚕ 31.31   Global Days 090

62010 with repair of dura and/or debridement of brain   C 80 ☐
     🔧 38.38   ⚕ 38.38   Global Days 090

62100 Craniotomy for repair of dural/cerebrospinal fluid leak, including surgery for rhinorrhea/otorrhea   C 80 ☐
     EXCLUDES   *repair of spinal fluid leak (63707, 63709)*
     🔧 40.65   ⚕ 40.65   Global Days 090

62115 Reduction of craniomegalic skull (eg, treated hydrocephalus); not requiring bone grafts or cranioplasty   C 80 ☐
     🔧 36.52   ⚕ 36.52   Global Days 090

62116 with simple cranioplasty   C 80 ☐
     🔧 45.04   ⚕ 45.04   Global Days 090

62117 requiring craniotomy and reconstruction with or without bone graft (includes obtaining grafts)   C 80 ☐
     🔧 47.93   ⚕ 47.93   Global Days 090

62120 Repair of encephalocele, skull vault, including cranioplasty   C 80 ☐
     🔧 45.20   ⚕ 45.20   Global Days 090

62121 Craniotomy for repair of encephalocele, skull base   C 80 ☐
     🔧 41.72   ⚕ 41.72   Global Days 090

62140 Cranioplasty for skull defect; up to 5 cm diameter   C 80 ☐
     🔧 26.54   ⚕ 26.54   Global Days 090

62141 larger than 5 cm diameter   C 80 ☐
     🔧 29.13   ⚕ 29.13   Global Days 090

62142 Removal of bone flap or prosthetic plate of skull   C 80 ☐
     🔧 22.16   ⚕ 22.16   Global Days 090

62143 Replacement of bone flap or prosthetic plate of skull   C 80 ☐
     🔧 26.01   ⚕ 26.01   Global Days 090

62145 Cranioplasty for skull defect with reparative brain surgery   C 80 ☐
     🔧 35.60   ⚕ 35.60   Global Days 090

62146 Cranioplasty with autograft (includes obtaining bone grafts); up to 5 cm diameter   C 80 ☐
     🔧 30.47   ⚕ 30.47   Global Days 090

62147 larger than 5 cm diameter   C 80 ☐
     🔧 36.19   ⚕ 36.19   Global Days 090

+ 62148 Incision and retrieval of subcutaneous cranial bone graft for cranioplasty (List separately in addition to code for primary procedure)   C ☐
     Code first (62140-62147)
     🔧 3.28   ⚕ 3.28   Global Days ZZZ

62160-62165 Neuroendoscopic Procedures of the Brain

INCLUDES   diagnostic endoscopy

+ 62160 Neuroendoscopy, intracranial, for placement or replacement of ventricular catheter and attachment to shunt system or external drainage (List separately in addition to code for primary procedure)   N ☐
     Code first (61107, 61210, 62220-62230, 62258)
     🔧 5.04   ⚕ 5.04   Global Days ZZZ
     AMA: 2008, Jan, 10-25; 2008, May, 9-11; 2007, Jun, 10-11; 2007, Jun, 10-11; 2007, June, 10-11

62161 Neuroendoscopy, intracranial; with dissection of adhesions, fenestration of septum pellucidum or intraventricular cysts (including placement, replacement, or removal of ventricular catheter)   C 80 ☐
     🔧 38.41   ⚕ 38.41   Global Days 090

62162 with fenestration or excision of colloid cyst, including placement of external ventricular catheter for drainage   U UU ☐
     🔧 47.58   ⚕ 47.58   Global Days 090

62163 with retrieval of foreign body   C 80 ☐
     🔧 30.88   ⚕ 30.88   Global Days 090

62164 with excision of brain tumor, including placement of external ventricular catheter for drainage   C 80 ☐
     🔧 50.42   ⚕ 50.42   Global Days 090

62165 with excision of pituitary tumor, transnasal or trans-sphenoidal approach   C 80 ☐
     🔧 38.74   ⚕ 38.74   Global Days 090

62180-62258 Cerebrospinal Fluid Diversion Procedures

62180 Ventriculocisternostomy (Torkildsen type operation)   C 80 ☐
     🔧 40.09   ⚕ 40.09   Global Days 090

62190 Creation of shunt; subarachnoid/subdural-atrial, -jugular, -auricular   C ☐
     🔧 22.81   ⚕ 22.81   Global Days 090

62192 subarachnoid/subdural-peritoneal, -pleural, other terminus   C 80 ☐
     🔧 24.32   ⚕ 24.32   Global Days 090

62194 Replacement or irrigation, subarachnoid/subdural catheter   A2 T 80 ☐
     🔧 9.82   ⚕ 9.82   Global Days 010

● New Code   ▲ Revised Code   M Maternity Edit   A Age Edit   A-V OPPS Status Indicator   🔧 Facility RVU   ⚕ Non-Facility RVU
☐ CCI Comprehensive Code   50 Bilateral Procedure   + Add-on Indicator   ▣ Laboratory crosswalk   ▦ Radiology crosswalk

Nervous System

62200 — 62269

62200 Ventriculocisternostomy, third ventricle; C 80 ▢
  INCLUDES Dandy ventriculocisternostomy

  🚑 34.79 ⚕ 34.79 Global Days 090

62201 stereotactic, neuroendoscopic method C ▢
  EXCLUDES intracranial neuroendoscopic surgery
    (62161-62165)

  🚑 29.77 ⚕ 29.77 Global Days 090
  AMA: 2008, Jan, 10-25; 2007, Aug, 15

62220 Creation of shunt; ventriculo-atrial, -jugular,
  -auricular C 80 ▢
  EXCLUDES intracranial neuroendoscopic ventricular
    catheter placement (62160)

  🚑 25.61 ⚕ 25.61 Global Days 090
  AMA: 2007, Jun, 10-11; 2007, Jun, 10-11; 2007, June, 10-11

62223 ventriculo-peritoneal, -pleural, other
  terminus C 80 ▢ PQ
  EXCLUDES intracranial neuroendoscopic ventricular
    catheter placement (62160)

  🚑 26.20 ⚕ 26.20 Global Days 090
  AMA: 2007, Jun, 10-11; 2007, Jun, 10-11; 2007, June, 10-11

62225 Replacement or irrigation, ventricular catheter A2 T ▢
  EXCLUDES intracranial neuroendoscopic ventricular
    catheter placement (62160)

  🚑 12.47 ⚕ 12.47 Global Days 090
  AMA: 2007, Jun, 10-11; 2007, Jun, 10-11; 2007, June, 10-11

62230 Replacement or revision of cerebrospinal fluid shunt,
  obstructed valve, or distal catheter in shunt
  system A2 T 80 ▢ PQ
    intracranial neuroendoscopic ventricular
    catheter placement (62160)

  🚑 21.15 ⚕ 21.15 Global Days 090
  AMA: 2007, Jun, 10-11; 2007, Jun, 10-11; 2007, June, 10-11

62252 Reprogramming of programmable cerebrospinal
  shunt P3 S 80 ▢
  EXCLUDES intracranial neuroendoscopic ventricular
    catheter insertion (62160)
    percutaneous irrigation or aspiraton of shunt
    reservoir (61070)

  🚑 2.60 ⚕ 2.60 Global Days XXX

62256 Removal of complete cerebrospinal fluid shunt system;
  without replacement C 80 ▢
  EXCLUDES intracranial neuroendoscopic ventricular
    catheter insertion (62160)
    percutaneous irrigation or aspiration of shunt
    reservoir (61070)
    reprogramming cerebrospinal fluid (SCF) shunt
    (62252)

  🚑 14.64 ⚕ 14.64 Global Days 090

62258 with replacement by similar or other shunt at same
  operation C 80 ▢
  EXCLUDES intracranial neuroendoscopic ventricular
    catheter placement (62160)
    percutaneous irrigation or aspiration of shunt
    reservoir (61070)
    reprogramming of a cerebrospinal fluid (CSF)
    shunt (62252)

  🚑 28.47 ⚕ 28.47 Global Days 090
  AMA: 2007, Jun, 10-11; 2007, Jun, 10-11; 2007, June, 10-11

62263-62264 Lysis of Epidural Lesions with Injection of Solution/Mechanical Methods
INCLUDES fluoroscopic guidance and epidurography (72275, 77003)

62263 Percutaneous lysis of epidural adhesions using solution
  injection (eg, hypertonic saline, enzyme) or mechanical
  means (eg, catheter) including radiologic localization
  (includes contrast when administered), multiple
  adhesiolysis sessions; 2 or more days A2 T ▢
  INCLUDES all adhesiolysis treatments, injections, and
    infusions during course of treatment
    contrast injection during fluoroscopic
    guidance/localization
    fluoroscopic guidance and epidurography
    (72275, 77003)
    percutaneous epidural catheter insertion
    and removal for neurolytic agent
    injections during serialized treatment
    sessions

  Do not report more than once for the complete series
    spanning two or more treatment days
  🚑 9.78 ⚕ 16.56 Global Days 010
  AMA: 2008, Jan, 10-25; 2008, Jun, 8-11; 2008, Jul, 9; 2007, Jan,
  13-27; 2007, Jan, 13-27; 2007, January, 13-27; 2005, Nov, 14-15;
  2005, November, 14-15; 2005, Nov, 14-15

62264 1 day A2 T ▢
  INCLUDES contrast injection during fluoroscopic
    guidance/localization
    multiple treatment sessions performed on
    the same day

  Do not report with (62263)
  🚑 5.98 ⚕ 10.14 Global Days 010
  AMA: 2008, Jan, 10-25; 2008, Jun, 8-11; 2008, Jul, 9; 2007, Jan,
  13-27; 2007, Jan, 13-27; 2007, January, 13-27; 2005, Nov, 14-15;
  2005, November, 14-15; 2005, Nov, 14-15

62267-62269 Percutaneous Procedures of Spinal Cord
EXCLUDES fluoroscopic guidance and localization unless a formal contrast study
    is performed (77003)

● **62267** Percutaneous aspiration within the nucleus pulposus,
  intervertebral disc, or paravertebral tissue for diagnostic
  purposes 62 T 80
  INCLUDES contrast injection during fluoroscopic
    guidance/localization

  Do not report with (10022, 20225, 62287, 62290-62291)
  🔀 77003, 77012
  🚑 4.38 ⚕ 6.61 Global Days 000

62268 Percutaneous aspiration, spinal cord cyst or
  syrinx A2 T ▢
  🔀 76942, 77002, 77012
  🚑 7.10 ⚕ 12.06 Global Days 000

62269 Biopsy of spinal cord, percutaneous needle A2 T 80 ▢
  EXCLUDES fine needle aspiration (10021-10022)
  🔀 76942, 77002, 77012
  🚑 7.20 ⚕ 13.05 Global Days 000

62270-62272 Spinal Puncture, Subarachnoid Space, Diagnostic/Therapeutic
INCLUDES contrast injection during fluoroscopic guidance/localization

EXCLUDES fluoroscopic guidance and localization unless a formal contrast study
    is performed (77003)

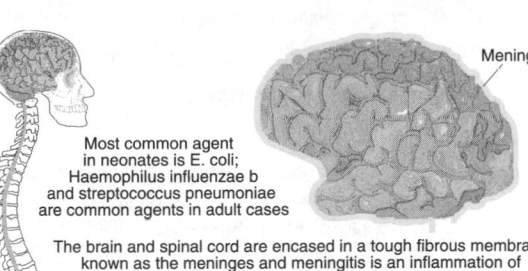

Most common agent
in neonates is E. coli;
Haemophilus influenzae b
and streptococcus pneumoniae
are common agents in adult cases

Meninges

The brain and spinal cord are encased in a tough fibrous membrane
known as the meninges; meningitis is an inflammation of
that tissue and commonly affects the underlying central nervous
system tissues and fluids; causes are numerous and classification
is based on type of infection; purulent refers to forms usually
caused by bacteria; chronic meningitis is usually caused by
mycobacteria and fungi; aseptic or abacterial meningitis is
commonly associated with a viral infection and is reported
with the underlying disease. Encephalitis is inflammation of
the brain and is also usually associated with a viral infection
and also is reported with the underlying disease

62270   **Spinal puncture, lumbar, diagnostic**   A2 T ▯
     INCLUDES   contrast injection during fluoroscopic
          guidance/localization

     ⚕ **2.04**   ⚕ **3.98**   **Global Days 000**
     AMA: 2007, Jul, 1-4; 2006, May, 1-9; 2006, May, 1-9; 2006, May, 1-9

62272   **Spinal puncture, therapeutic, for drainage of
       cerebrospinal fluid (by needle or catheter)**   A2 T ▯
     INCLUDES   contrast injection during fluoroscopic
          guidance/localization

     ⚕ **2.19**   ⚕ **4.72**   **Global Days 000**

62273 Epidural Blood Patch

EXCLUDES   *fluoroscopic guidance and localization unless a formal contrast study
     is performed (77003)
     injection of diagnostic or therapeutic material (62310-62311,
     62318-62319)*

62273   **Injection, epidural, of blood or clot patch**   A2 T ▯
     INCLUDES   contrast injection during fluoroscopic
          guidance/localization

     ⚕ **2.91**   ⚕ **4.24**   **Global Days 000**

62280-62282 Neurolysis

INCLUDES   contrast injection during fluoroscopic guidance/localization

EXCLUDES   *fluoroscopic guidance and localization unless a formal contrast study
     is performed (77003)
     injection of diagnostic or therapeutic material only (62310-62311,
     62318-62319)*

62280   **Injection/infusion of neurolytic substance (eg, alcohol,
       phenol, iced saline solutions), with or without other
       therapeutic substance; subarachnoid**   A2 T ▯
     ⚕ **4.03**   ⚕ **7.87**   **Global Days 010**
     AMA: 2008, Jul, 9

62281   **epidural, cervical or thoracic**   A2 T ▯
     ⚕ **3.85**   ⚕ **7.26**   **Global Days 010**
     AMA: 2008, Jul, 9

62282   **epidural, lumbar, sacral (caudal)**   A2 T ▯
     EXCLUDES   *fluoroscopic guidance and localization unless
          a formal contrast study is performed
          (77003)*

     ⚕ **3.55**   ⚕ **7.52**   **Global Days 010**
     AMA: 2008, Jan, 10-25; 2008, Jul, 9; 2007, Jan, 13-27; 2007, Jan,
     13-27; 2007, January, 13-27

62284-62294 Injection/Aspiration of Spine, Diagnostic/Therapeutic

62284   **Injection procedure for myelography and/or computed
       tomography, spinal (other than C1-C2 and posterior
       fossa)**   N1 N ▯
     EXCLUDES   *injection at C1-C2 (61055)*
     ⊞   *72126, 72129, 72132, 72240, 72255, 72265, 72270*
     ⚕ **2.41**   ⚕ **5.74**   **Global Days 000**
     AMA: 2008, Jan, 10-25; 2007, Jan, 13-27; 2007, Jan, 13-27; 2007,
     January, 13-27; 2004, Sep, 12; 2004, September, 12; 2004, Sep,
     12

▲ **62287**   **Decompression procedure, percutaneous, of nucleus
       pulposus of intervertebral disc, any method, single or
       multiple levels, lumbar (eg, manual or automated
       percutaneous discectomy, percutaneous laser
       discectomy)**   A2 T ▯
     EXCLUDES   *nonneurolytic injection (62310, 62311)*

     Do not report with (62267)
     ⊞   *77003*
     ⚕ **14.16**   ⚕ **14.16**   **Global Days 090**
     AMA: 2008, Jan, 10-25; 2008, Jun, 8-11; 2007, Jan, 13-27; 2007,
     Jan, 13-27; 2007, January, 13-27

62290   **Injection procedure for discography, each level;
       lumbar**   N1 N ▯
     ⊞   *72295*
     ⚕ **4.48**   ⚕ **8.38**   **Global Days 000**
     AMA: 2008, Jan, 10-25; 2007, Jan, 13-27; 2007, Jan, 13-27; 2007,
     January, 13-27

62291   **cervical or thoracic**   N1 N ▯
     ⊞   *72285*
     ⚕ **4.34**   ⚕ **7.86**   **Global Days 000**

62292   **Injection procedure for chemonucleolysis, including
       discography, intervertebral disc, single or multiple levels,
       lumbar**   R2 T 80 ▯
     ⚕ **12.83**   ⚕ **12.83**   **Global Days 090**
     AMA: 2008, Jan, 10-25; 2007, Jan, 13-27; 2007, Jan, 13-27; 2007,
     January, 13-27

62294   **Injection procedure, arterial, for occlusion of
       arteriovenous malformation, spinal**   A2 T ▯
     ⚕ **20.60**   ⚕ **20.60**   **Global Days 090**

62310-62319 Injection/Infusion Diagnostic/Therapeutic Material

EXCLUDES   *fluoroscopic guidance and localization unless a formal contrast study
     is performed (77003)
     daily management of continuous epidural or subarachnoid drug
     administration (01996)
     transforaminal epidural injection (64479-64484)*

62310   **Injection, single (not via indwelling catheter), not
       including neurolytic substances, with or without contrast
       (for either localization or epidurography), of diagnostic
       or therapeutic substance(s) (including anesthetic,
       antispasmodic, opioid, steroid, other solution), epidural
       or subarachnoid; cervical or thoracic**   A2 T ▯
     INCLUDES   contrast injection during fluoroscopic
          guidance/localization

     EXCLUDES   *fluoroscopic guidance and localization unless
          a formal contrast study is performed
          (77003)*

     ⚕ **2.64**   ⚕ **5.52**   **Global Days 000**
     AMA: 2008, Jan, 10-25; 2008, Jul, 9; 2007, Jan, 13-27; 2007, Jan,
     13-27; 2007, January, 13-27; 2004, Sep, 1; 2004, September, 1;
     2004, Sep, 1

Nervous System   **62270 — 62310**

● New Code   ▲ Revised Code   M Maternity Edit   ▯ Age Edit   A-V OPPS Status Indicator   ⚕ Facility RVU   ⚕ Non-Facility RVU

▯ CCI Comprehensive Code   50 Bilateral Procedure   + Add-on Indicator   ⊠ Laboratory crosswalk   ⊞ Radiology crosswalk

62311   lumbar, sacral (caudal)   [A2] [T] [▯]
> INCLUDES   contrast injection during fluoroscopic guidance/localization
>
> EXCLUDES   *fluoroscopic guidance and localization unless a formal contrast study is performed (77003)*

   ⚕ 2.19   ⚕ 4.87   Global Days 000
AMA: 2008, Jan, 10-25; 2008, Jul, 9; 2007, Jan, 13-27; 2007, Jan, 13-27; 2007, January, 13-27; 2004, Sep, 1; 2004, September, 1; 2004, Sep, 1

62318   Injection, including catheter placement, continuous infusion or intermittent bolus, not including neurolytic substances, with or without contrast (for either localization or epidurography), of diagnostic or therapeutic substance(s) (including anesthetic, antispasmodic, opioid, steroid, other solution), epidural or subarachnoid; cervical or thoracic   [A2] [T] [▯]
> INCLUDES   contrast injection during fluoroscopic guidance/localization
>
> EXCLUDES   *daily hospital management of epidural or subarachnoid infusion (01996)*
> *fluoroscopic guidance and localization unless a formal contrast study is performed (77003)*

   ⚕ 2.65   ⚕ 5.90   Global Days 000
AMA: 2008, Jan, 10-25; 2008, Jul, 9; 2007, Jan, 13-27; 2007, January, 13-27

62319   lumbar, sacral (caudal)   [A2] [T] [▯]
> INCLUDES   contrast injection during fluoroscopic guidance/localization
>
> EXCLUDES   *daily hospital management of epidural or subarachnoid infusion (01996)*
> *fluoroscopic guidance and localization unless a formal contrast study is performed (77003)*

   ⚕ 2.48   ⚕ 5.34   Global Days 000
AMA: 2008, Jan, 10-25; 2008, Jul, 9; 2007, Jan, 13-27; 2007, January, 13-27

62350-62368 Procedures Related to Epidural and Intrathecal Catheters

CMS *100-3,280.14*   *Infusion Pumps*
EXCLUDES   *infusion pump refilling and maintenance (95990-95991)*
percutaneous insertion of intrathecal or epidural catheter (62270-62273, 62280-62284, 62310-62319)

62350   Implantation, revision or repositioning of tunneled intrathecal or epidural catheter, for long-term medication administration via an external pump or implantable reservoir/infusion pump; without laminectomy   [A2] [T] [▯]
   ⚕ 10.11   ⚕ 10.11   Global Days 010

62351   with laminectomy   [T] [80] [▯]
   ⚕ 21.35   ⚕ 21.35   Global Days 090

62355   Removal of previously implanted intrathecal or epidural catheter   [A2] [T] [80] [▯]
   ⚕ 7.57   ⚕ 7.57   Global Days 010

62360   Implantation or replacement of device for intrathecal or epidural drug infusion; subcutaneous reservoir   [A2] [T] [80] [▯]
   ⚕ 7.17   ⚕ 7.17   Global Days 010

62361   nonprogrammable pump   [H8] [T] [80] [▯]
Code also (C1891, C2626)
   ⚕ 10.00   ⚕ 10.00   Global Days 010

62362   programmable pump, including preparation of pump, with or without programming   [H8] [T] [80] [▯]
Code also (C1772)
   ⚕ 10.66   ⚕ 10.66   Global Days 010
AMA: 2008, Jan, 10-25; 2007, Jan, 13-27; 2007, Jan, 13-27; 2007, January, 13-27

62365   Removal of subcutaneous reservoir or pump, previously implanted for intrathecal or epidural infusion   [A2] [T] [80] [▯]
   ⚕ 8.40   ⚕ 8.40   Global Days 010

62367   Electronic analysis of programmable, implanted pump for intrathecal or epidural drug infusion (includes evaluation of reservoir status, alarm status, drug prescription status); without reprogramming   [P3] [S] [80] [▯]
   ⚕ 0.63   ⚕ 0.99   Global Days XXX
AMA: 2006, Apr, 19-20; 2006, Apr, 19-20; 2006, April, 19-20

62368   with reprogramming   [P3] [S] [80] [▯]
   ⚕ 0.99   ⚕ 1.42   Global Days XXX
AMA: 2008, Jan, 10-25; 2007, Jan, 13-27; 2007, Jan, 13-27; 2007, January, 13-27; 2006, Apr, 19-20; 2006, April, 19-20; 2006, Apr, 19-20

63001-63048 Posterior Midline Approach: Laminectomy/Laminotomy/Decompression

EXCLUDES   *arthrodesis (22590-22614)*

63001   Laminectomy with exploration and/or decompression of spinal cord and/or cauda equina, without facetectomy, foraminotomy or discectomy (eg, spinal stenosis), 1 or 2 vertebral segments; cervical   [T] [80] [▯]
   ⚕ 31.20   ⚕ 31.20   Global Days 090
AMA: 2008, Jan, 10-25; 2007, Jan, 13-27; 2007, Jan, 13-27; 2007, Jun, 1-3; 2007, Jun, 1-3; 2007, January, 13-27; 2007, June, 1-3; 2005, Jun, 6-8; 2005, Jun, 6-8; 2005, June, 6-8

63003   thoracic   [T] [80] [▯]
   ⚕ 31.37   ⚕ 31.37   Global Days 090
AMA: 2008, Jan, 10-25; 2007, Jan, 13-27; 2007, Jan, 13-27; 2007, Jun, 1-3; 2007, Jun, 1-3; 2007, January, 13-27; 2007, June, 1-3; 2005, Jun, 6-8; 2005, Jun, 6-8; 2005, June, 6-8

63005   lumbar, except for spondylolisthesis   [T] [80] [▯]
   ⚕ 29.73   ⚕ 29.73   Global Days 090
AMA: 2008, Jan, 10-25; 2007, Jan, 13-27; 2007, Jan, 13-27; 2007, Jun, 1-3; 2007, Jun, 1-3; 2007, January, 13-27; 2007, June, 1-3; 2005, Jun, 6-8; 2005, Jun, 6-8; 2005, June, 6-8

63011   sacral   [T] [80] [▯]
   ⚕ 28.16   ⚕ 28.16   Global Days 090
AMA: 2008, Jan, 10-25; 2007, Jan, 13-27; 2007, Jan, 13-27; 2007, Jun, 1-3; 2007, Jun, 1-3; 2007, January, 13-27; 2007, June, 1-3; 2005, Jun, 6-8; 2005, Jun, 6-8; 2005, June, 6-8

63012   Laminectomy with removal of abnormal facets and/or pars inter-articularis with decompression of cauda equina and nerve roots for spondylolisthesis, lumbar (Gill type procedure)   [T] [80] [▯]
   ⚕ 30.27   ⚕ 30.27   Global Days 090
AMA: 2008, Jan, 10-25; 2007, Jan, 13-27; 2007, Jan, 13-27; 2007, Jun, 1-3; 2007, Jun, 1-3; 2007, January, 13-27; 2007, June, 1-3; 2005, Jun, 6-8; 2005, Jun, 6-8; 2005, June, 6-8

63015   Laminectomy with exploration and/or decompression of spinal cord and/or cauda equina, without facetectomy, foraminotomy or discectomy (eg, spinal stenosis), more than 2 vertebral segments; cervical   [T] [80] [▯] [P0]
   ⚕ 37.56   ⚕ 37.56   Global Days 090
AMA: 2008, Jan, 10-25; 2007, Jan, 13-27; 2007, Jan, 13-27; 2007, Jun, 1-3; 2007, Jun, 1-3; 2007, January, 13-27; 2007, June, 1-3; 2005, Jun, 6-8; 2005, Jun, 6-8; 2005, June, 6-8

---

[26]/[TC] Professional/Technical Component Only   [80]/[80] Assist-at-Surgery Allowed/With Documentation   Unlisted   Not Covered

AMA: CPT Assistant References   [A2]-[Z3] ASC Payment Indicator   ♂ Male Only   ♀ Female Only   ⊘ Modifier 51 Exempt   [P0] PQRI

242   CPT only © 2008 American Medical Association. All Rights Reserved. (Black Ink)   Medicare (Red Ink)   © 2008 Ingenix *(Blue Ink)*

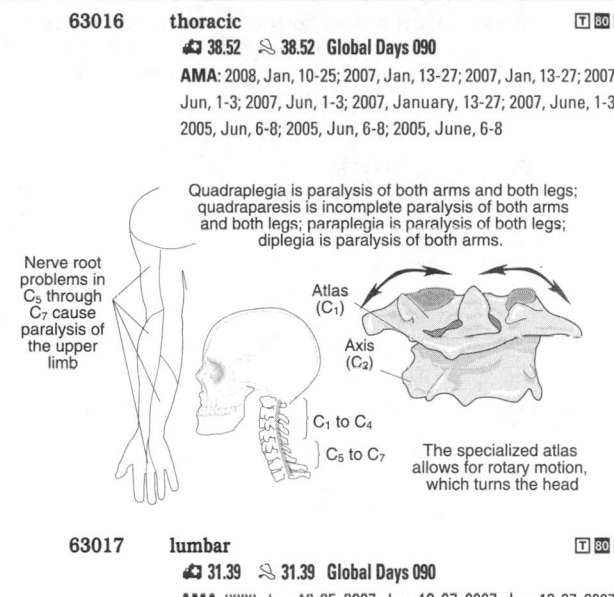

Quadraplegia is paralysis of both arms and both legs; quadraparesis is incomplete paralysis of both arms and both legs; paraplegia is paralysis of both legs; diplegia is paralysis of both arms.

Nerve root problems in C₅ through C₇ cause paralysis of the upper limb

Atlas (C₁)

Axis (C₂)

C₁ to C₄

C₅ to C₇

The specialized atlas allows for rotary motion, which turns the head

63016   thoracic   T 80 ▢
   🗘 38.52   ⌇ 38.52   Global Days 090
   AMA: 2008, Jan, 10-25; 2007, Jan, 13-27; 2007, Jan, 13-27; 2007, Jun, 1-3; 2007, Jun, 1-3; 2007, January, 13-27; 2007, June, 1-3; 2005, Jun, 6-8; 2005, Jun, 6-8; 2005, June, 6-8

63017   lumbar   T 80 ▢
   🗘 31.39   ⌇ 31.39   Global Days 090
   AMA: 2008, Jan, 10-25; 2007, Jan, 13-27; 2007, Jan, 13-27; 2007, Jun, 1-3; 2007, Jun, 1-3; 2007, January, 13-27; 2007, June, 1-3; 2005, Jun, 6-8; 2005, Jun, 6-8; 2005, June, 6-8

▲ 63020   Laminotomy (hemilaminectomy), with decompression of nerve root(s), including partial facetectomy, foraminotomy and/or excision of herniated intervertebral disc, including open and endoscopically-assisted approaches; 1 interspace, cervical   T 80 50 ▢ P0
   🗘 29.79   ⌇ 29.79   Global Days 090
   AMA: 2008, Jan, 10-25; 2007, Jan, 13-27; 2007, Jan, 13-27; 2007, Jun, 1-3; 2007, Jun, 1-3; 2007, January, 13-27; 2007, June, 1-3; 2005, Jun, 6-8; 2005, Jun, 6-8; 2005, June, 6-8

▲ 63030   1 interspace, lumbar   T 80 50 ▢ P0
   🗘 24.73   ⌇ 24.73   Global Days 090
   AMA: 2008, Jan, 10-25; 2008, Oct, 10-11; 2007, Jan, 13-27; 2007, Jan, 13-27; 2007, Jun, 1-3; 2007, June, 1-3; 2007, January, 13-27; 2007, Jun, 1-3; 2005, Jun, 6-8; 2005, June, 6-8; 2005, Jun, 6-8; 2004, Nov, 9; 2004, November, 9; 2004, Nov, 9

+ ▲ 63035   each additional interspace, cervical or lumbar (List separately in addition to code for primary procedure)   T 80 50 ▢
   Code first (63020-63030)
   🗘 5.30   ⌇ 5.30   Global Days ZZZ
   AMA: 2008, Jan, 10-25; 2007, Jan, 13-27; 2007, Jan, 13-27; 2007, Jun, 1-3; 2007, Jun, 1-3; 2007, January, 13-27; 2007, June, 1-3; 2005, Jun, 6-8; 2005, Jun, 6-8; 2005, June, 6-8

63040   Laminotomy (hemilaminectomy), with decompression of nerve root(s), including partial facetectomy, foraminotomy and/or excision of herniated intervertebral disc, reexploration, single interspace; cervical   T 80 50 ▢
   🗘 36.23   ⌇ 36.23   Global Days 090
   AMA: 2008, Jan, 10-25; 2007, Jan, 13-27; 2007, Jan, 13-27; 2007, Jun, 1-3; 2007, Jun, 1-3; 2007, January, 13-27; 2007, June, 1-3; 2005, Jun, 6-8; 2005, Jun, 6-8; 2005, June, 6-8

63042   lumbar   T 80 50 ▢ P0
   🗘 33.89   ⌇ 33.89   Global Days 090
   AMA: 2008, Jan, 10-25; 2008, Oct, 10-11; 2007, Jan, 13-27; 2007, Jan, 13-27; 2007, Jun, 1-3; 2007, Jun, 1-3; 2007, January, 13-27; 2007, June, 1-3; 2005, Jun, 6-8; 2005, Jun, 6-8; 2005, June, 6-8

+ 63043   each additional cervical interspace (List separately in addition to code for primary procedure)   C 80 50 ▢
   Code first (63040)
   🗘 0.00   ⌇ 0.00   Global Days ZZZ
   AMA: 2008, Jan, 10-25; 2007, Jan, 13-27; 2007, Jan, 13-27; 2007, Jun, 1-3; 2007, Jun, 1-3; 2007, January, 13-27; 2007, June, 1-3; 2005, Jun, 6-8; 2005, Jun, 6-8; 2005, June, 6-8

+ 63044   each additional lumbar interspace (List separately in addition to code for primary procedure)   C 80 50 ▢
   Code first (63042)
   🗘 0.00   ⌇ 0.00   Global Days ZZZ
   AMA: 2008, Jan, 10-25; 2007, Jan, 13-27; 2007, Jan, 13-27; 2007, Jun, 1-3; 2007, Jun, 1-3; 2007, January, 13-27; 2007, June, 1-3; 2005, Jun, 6-8; 2005, Jun, 6-8; 2005, June, 6-8

63045   Laminectomy, facetectomy and foraminotomy (unilateral or bilateral with decompression of spinal cord, cauda equina and/or nerve root[s], [eg, spinal or lateral recess stenosis]), single vertebral segment; cervical   T 80 ▢ P0
   🗘 32.34   ⌇ 32.34   Global Days 090
   AMA: 2008, Jan, 10-25; 2007, Jan, 13-27; 2007, Jan, 13-27; 2007, Jun, 1-3; 2007, Jun, 1-3; 2007, January, 13-27; 2007, June, 1-3; 2005, Jun, 6-8; 2005, Jun, 6-8; 2005, June, 6-8

63046   thoracic   T 80 ▢
   🗘 30.83   ⌇ 30.83   Global Days 090
   AMA: 2008, Jan, 10-25; 2007, Jan, 13-27; 2007, Jan, 13-27; 2007, Jun, 1-3; 2007, Jun, 1-3; 2007, January, 13-27; 2007, June, 1-3; 2005, Jun, 6-8; 2005, Jun, 6-8; 2005, June, 6-8

63047   lumbar   T 80 ▢ P0
   🗘 28.14   ⌇ 28.14   Global Days 090
   AMA: 2008, Apr, -11; 2008, Apr, -11; 2008, Jan, 10-25; 2008, Apr, -11; 2008, Oct, 10-11; 2008, Jul, 7-8&15; 2007, Jan, 13-27; 2007, Jan, 13-27; 2007, Jun, 1-3; 2007, June, 1-3; 2007, January, 13-27; 2007, Jun, 1-3; 2005, Jun, 6-8; 2005, June, 6-8; 2005, Jun, 6-8

+ 63048   each additional segment, cervical, thoracic, or lumbar (List separately in addition to code for primary procedure)   T 80 ▢
   Code first (63045-63047)
   🗘 5.66   ⌇ 5.66   Global Days ZZZ
   AMA: 2008, Jan, 10-25; 2007, Jan, 13-27; 2007, Jan, 13-27; 2007, Jun, 1-3; 2007, Jun, 1-3; 2007, January, 13-27; 2007, June, 1-3; 2005, Jun, 6-8; 2005, Jun, 6-8; 2005, June, 6-8

63050-63051 Cervical Laminoplasty: Posterior Midline Approach

Do not report with procedure performed on the same vertebral segment(s) (22600, 22614, 22840-22842, 63001, 63015, 63045, 63048, 63295)

63050   Laminoplasty, cervical, with decompression of the spinal cord, 2 or more vertebral segments;   C 80 ▢
   🗘 38.82   ⌇ 38.82   Global Days 090

63051   with reconstruction of the posterior bony elements (including the application of bridging bone graft and non-segmental fixation devices (eg, wire, suture, mini-plates), when performed)   C 80 ▢
   🗘 43.64   ⌇ 43.64   Global Days 090

63055-63066 Spinal Cord/Nerve Root Decompression: Costovertebral or Transpedicular Approach

63055   Transpedicular approach with decompression of spinal cord, equina and/or nerve root(s) (eg, herniated intervertebral disc), single segment; thoracic   T 80 ▢
   🗘 41.66   ⌇ 41.66   Global Days 090

Nervous System

63056 — 63180

63056 lumbar (including transfacet, or lateral extraforaminal approach) (eg, far lateral herniated intervertebral disc)　T 80 ▭ P0
🔲 38.43　🔲 38.43　Global Days 090

+ **63057** each additional segment, thoracic or lumbar (List separately in addition to code for primary procedure)　T 80 ▭
Code first (63055-63056)
🔲 8.71　🔲 8.71　Global Days ZZZ

63064 Costovertebral approach with decompression of spinal cord or nerve root(s) (eg, herniated intervertebral disc), thoracic; single segment　T 80 ▭
🔲 45.53　🔲 45.53　Global Days 090

+ **63066** each additional segment (List separately in addition to code for primary procedure)　T 80 ▭
EXCLUDES　laminectomy with intraspinal thoracic lesion removal (63266, 63271, 63276, 63281, 63286)

Code first (63064)
🔲 5.35　🔲 5.35　Global Days ZZZ

63075-63078 Discectomy: Anterior or Anterolateral Approach

INCLUDES　operating microscope (69990)

63075 Discectomy, anterior, with decompression of spinal cord and/or nerve root(s), including osteophytectomy; cervical, single interspace　T 80 ▭ P0
🔲 35.61　🔲 35.61　Global Days 090
AMA: 2008, Jan, 10-25; 2007, Jan, 13-27; 2007, Jan, 13-27; 2007, January, 13-27

+ **63076** cervical, each additional interspace (List separately in addition to code for primary procedure)　C 80 ▭
Code first (63075)
🔲 6.73　🔲 6.73　Global Days ZZZ
AMA: 2008, Jan, 10-25; 2007, Jan, 13-27; 2007, Jan, 13-27; 2007, January, 13-27

63077 thoracic, single interspace　C 80 ▭
🔲 38.68　🔲 38.68　Global Days 090
AMA: 2008, Jan, 10-25; 2007, Jan, 13-27; 2007, Jan, 13-27; 2007, January, 13-27

+ **63078** thoracic, each additional interspace (List separately in addition to code for primary procedure)　C 80 ▭
Code first (63077)
🔲 5.32　🔲 5.32　Global Days ZZZ
AMA: 2008, Jan, 10-25; 2007, Jan, 13-27; 2007, Jan, 13-27; 2007, January, 13-27

63081-63091 Vertebral Corpectomy, All Levels, Anterior Approach

INCLUDES　disc removal at the level below and/or above vertebral segment
EXCLUDES　arthrodesis (22548-22812)

Code also reconstruction (20930-20938, 22548-22812, 22840-22855)

63081 Vertebral corpectomy (vertebral body resection), partial or complete, anterior approach with decompression of spinal cord and/or nerve root(s); cervical, single segment　C 80 ▭ P0
EXCLUDES　transoral approach (61575-61576)
🔲 45.60　🔲 45.60　Global Days 090

+ **63082** cervical, each additional segment (List separately in addition to code for primary procedure)　C 80 ▭
EXCLUDES　transoral approach (61575-61576)
Code first (63081)
🔲 7.26　🔲 7.26　Global Days ZZZ

63085 Vertebral corpectomy (vertebral body resection), partial or complete, transthoracic approach with decompression of spinal cord and/or nerve root(s); thoracic, single segment　C 80 ▭
🔲 48.26　🔲 48.26　Global Days 090

+ **63086** thoracic, each additional segment (List separately in addition to code for primary procedure)　C 80 ▭
Code first (63085)
🔲 5.11　🔲 5.11　Global Days ZZZ

63087 Vertebral corpectomy (vertebral body resection), partial or complete, combined thoracolumbar approach with decompression of spinal cord, cauda equina or nerve root(s), lower thoracic or lumbar; single segment　C 80 ▭
🔲 61.78　🔲 61.78　Global Days 090

+ **63088** each additional segment (List separately in addition to code for primary procedure)　C 80 ▭
Code first (63087)
🔲 7.00　🔲 7.00　Global Days ZZZ

63090 Vertebral corpectomy (vertebral body resection), partial or complete, transperitoneal or retroperitoneal approach with decompression of spinal cord, cauda equina or nerve root(s), lower thoracic, lumbar, or sacral; single segment　C 80 ▭
🔲 50.28　🔲 50.28　Global Days 090

+ **63091** each additional segment (List separately in addition to code for primary procedure)　C 80 ▭
Code first (63090)
🔲 4.78　🔲 4.78　Global Days ZZZ

63101-63103 Corpectomy Lateral Extracavitary Approach

63101 Vertebral corpectomy (vertebral body resection), partial or complete, lateral extracavitary approach with decompression of spinal cord and/or nerve root(s) (eg, for tumor or retropulsed bone fragments); thoracic, single segment　C 80 ▭
🔲 57.88　🔲 57.88　Global Days 090

63102 lumbar, single segment　C 80 ▭
🔲 57.64　🔲 57.64　Global Days 090

+ **63103** thoracic or lumbar, each additional segment (List separately in addition to code for primary procedure)　C 80 ▭
Code first (63101-63102)
🔲 7.61　🔲 7.61　Global Days ZZZ

63170-63295 Laminectomies

63170 Laminectomy with myelotomy (eg, Bischof or DREZ type), cervical, thoracic, or thoracolumbar　C 80 ▭
🔲 39.12　🔲 39.12　Global Days 090

63172 Laminectomy with drainage of intramedullary cyst/syrinx; to subarachnoid space　C 80 ▭
🔲 35.26　🔲 35.26　Global Days 090

63173 to peritoneal or pleural space　C 80 ▭
🔲 43.52　🔲 43.52　Global Days 090

63180 Laminectomy and section of dentate ligaments, with or without dural graft, cervical; 1 or 2 segments　C 80 ▭
🔲 35.24　🔲 35.24　Global Days 090

63182   more than 2 segments   ☐C☐80☐
    🖐 38.08   ⚕ 38.08   Global Days 090

63185   **Laminectomy with rhizotomy; 1 or 2 segments**   ☐C☐80☐
    INCLUDES   Dana rhizotomy
               Stoffel rhizotomy
    🖐 28.55   ⚕ 28.55   Global Days 090

63190   more than 2 segments   ☐C☐80☐
    🖐 32.83   ⚕ 32.83   Global Days 090

63191   **Laminectomy with section of spinal accessory nerve**   ☐C☐80☐50☐
    EXCLUDES   *division of sternocleidomastoid muscle for torticollis (21720)*
    🖐 32.35   ⚕ 32.35   Global Days 090

63194   **Laminectomy with cordotomy, with section of 1 spinothalamic tract, 1 stage; cervical**   ☐C☐80☐
    🖐 37.17   ⚕ 37.17   Global Days 090

63195   thoracic   ☐C☐80☐
    🖐 38.14   ⚕ 38.14   Global Days 090

63196   **Laminectomy with cordotomy, with section of both spinothalamic tracts, 1 stage; cervical**   ☐C☐80☐
    🖐 44.89   ⚕ 44.89   Global Days 090

63197   thoracic   ☐C☐80☐
    🖐 42.75   ⚕ 42.75   Global Days 090

63198   **Laminectomy with cordotomy with section of both spinothalamic tracts, 2 stages within 14 days; cervical**   ☐C☐80☐
    INCLUDES   Keen laminectomy
    🖐 47.51   ⚕ 47.51   Global Days 090

63199   thoracic   ☐C☐80☐
    🖐 48.61   ⚕ 48.61   Global Days 090

63200   **Laminectomy, with release of tethered spinal cord, lumbar**   ☐C☐80☐
    🖐 38.29   ⚕ 38.29   Global Days 090

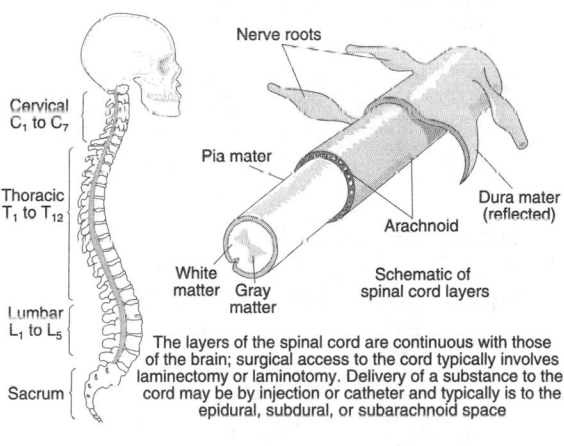

Nerve roots

Cervical
C₁ to C₇

Pia mater

Thoracic
T₁ to T₁₂

Dura mater
(reflected)

Arachnoid

White matter   Gray matter   Schematic of spinal cord layers

Lumbar
L₁ to L₅

The layers of the spinal cord are continuous with those of the brain; surgical access to the cord typically involves laminectomy or laminotomy. Delivery of a substance to the cord may be by injection or catheter and typically is to the epidural, subdural, or subarachnoid space

Sacrum

63250   **Laminectomy for excision or occlusion of arteriovenous malformation of spinal cord; cervical**   ☐C☐80☐
    🖐 74.04   ⚕ 74.04   Global Days 090

63251   thoracic   ☐C☐80☐
    🖐 77.20   ⚕ 77.20   Global Days 090

63252   thoracolumbar   ☐C☐80☐
    🖐 77.33   ⚕ 77.33   Global Days 090

63265   **Laminectomy for excision or evacuation of intraspinal lesion other than neoplasm, extradural; cervical**   ☐C☐80☐
    🖐 42.38   ⚕ 42.38   Global Days 090

63266   thoracic   ☐C☐80☐
    🖐 43.55   ⚕ 43.55   Global Days 090

63267   lumbar   ☐C☐80☐☐P0
    🖐 35.06   ⚕ 35.06   Global Days 090

63268   sacral   ☐C☐80☐
    🖐 34.96   ⚕ 34.96   Global Days 090

63270   **Laminectomy for excision of intraspinal lesion other than neoplasm, intradural; cervical**   ☐C☐80☐
    🖐 52.19   ⚕ 52.19   Global Days 090

63271   thoracic   ☐C☐80☐
    🖐 52.52   ⚕ 52.52   Global Days 090

63272   lumbar   ☐C☐80☐
    🖐 48.33   ⚕ 48.33   Global Days 090

63273   sacral   ☐C☐80☐
    🖐 45.60   ⚕ 45.60   Global Days 090

63275   **Laminectomy for biopsy/excision of intraspinal neoplasm; extradural, cervical**   ☐C☐80☐
    🖐 45.50   ⚕ 45.50   Global Days 090

63276   extradural, thoracic   ☐C☐80☐☐P0
    🖐 45.35   ⚕ 45.35   Global Days 090

63277   extradural, lumbar   ☐C☐80☐
    🖐 39.78   ⚕ 39.78   Global Days 090

63278   extradural, sacral   ☐C☐80☐
    🖐 38.82   ⚕ 38.82   Global Days 090

63280   intradural, extramedullary, cervical   ☐C☐80☐
    🖐 53.94   ⚕ 53.94   Global Days 090

63281   intradural, extramedullary, thoracic   ☐C☐80☐
    🖐 53.32   ⚕ 53.32   Global Days 090

63282   intradural, extramedullary, lumbar   ☐C☐80☐
    🖐 50.32   ⚕ 50.32   Global Days 090

63283   intradural, sacral   ☐C☐80☐
    🖐 47.63   ⚕ 47.63   Global Days 090

63285   intradural, intramedullary, cervical   ☐C☐80☐
    🖐 66.27   ⚕ 66.27   Global Days 090

63286   intradural, intramedullary, thoracic   ☐C☐80☐
    🖐 66.07   ⚕ 66.07   Global Days 090

63287   intradural, intramedullary, thoracolumbar   ☐C☐80☐
    🖐 69.59   ⚕ 69.59   Global Days 090

63290   **combined extradural-intradural lesion, any level**   ☐C☐80☐
    EXCLUDES   *drainage intermedullary cyst or syrinx (63172-63173)*
    🖐 70.25   ⚕ 70.25   Global Days 090

+   63295   **Osteoplastic reconstruction of dorsal spinal elements, following primary intraspinal procedure (List separately in addition to code for primary procedure)**   ☐C☐80
    Code first (63172-63173, 63185, 63190, 63200-63290)
    Do not report with procedure performed at the same vertebral segment(s) (22590-22614, 22840-22844, 63050-63051)
    🖐 8.34   ⚕ 8.34   Global Days ZZZ

63300-63308 Vertebral Corpectomy for Intraspinal Lesion: Anterior/Anterolateral Approach

EXCLUDES   *arthrodesis (22548-22585)*
    spinal reconstruction (20930-20938)

63300   **Vertebral corpectomy (vertebral body resection), partial or complete, for excision of intraspinal lesion, single segment: extradural, cervical**   ☐C☐80☐
    🖐 46.91   ⚕ 46.91   Global Days 090

63301   extradural, thoracic by transthoracic approach   ☐C☐80☐
    🖐 52.15   ⚕ 52.15   Global Days 090

● New Code   ▲ Revised Code   Ⓜ Maternity Edit   Ⓐ Age Edit   Ⓐ-Ⓥ OPPS Status Indicator   🖐 Facility RVU   ⚕ Non-Facility RVU
☐ CCI Comprehensive Code   50 Bilateral Procedure   + Add-on Indicator   Ⓛ Laboratory crosswalk   Ⓡ Radiology crosswalk

Nervous System

63302 — 63706

	63302	extradural, thoracic by thoracolumbar approach	C 80 ▢

51.89 ⚕ **51.89** Global Days 090

| | 63303 | extradural, lumbar or sacral by transperitoneal or retroperitoneal approach | C 80 ▢ |

53.86 ⚕ **53.86** Global Days 090

| | 63304 | intradural, cervical | C 80 ▢ |

57.69 ⚕ **57.69** Global Days 090

| | 63305 | intradural, thoracic by transthoracic approach | C 80 ▢ |

58.57 ⚕ **58.57** Global Days 090

| | 63306 | intradural, thoracic by thoracolumbar approach | C 80 ▢ |

62.30 ⚕ **62.30** Global Days 090

| | 63307 | intradural, lumbar or sacral by transperitoneal or retroperitoneal approach | C 80 ▢ |

56.63 ⚕ **56.63** Global Days 090

+ 63308 each additional segment (List separately in addition to codes for single segment)   C 80 ▢
Code first (63300-63307)

8.75 ⚕ **8.75** Global Days ZZZ

63600-63615 Stereotactic Procedures of the Spinal Cord

63600 Creation of lesion of spinal cord by stereotactic method, percutaneous, any modality (including stimulation and/or recording)   A2 T 80 ▢

21.31 ⚕ **21.31** Global Days 090

63610 Stereotactic stimulation of spinal cord, percutaneous, separate procedure not followed by other surgery   A2 T 80 ▢

11.41 ⚕ **34.26** Global Days 000

63615 Stereotactic biopsy, aspiration, or excision of lesion, spinal cord   A2 T ▢

28.98 ⚕ **28.98** Global Days 090

63620-63621 Stereotactic Radiosurgery (SRS): Spine

INCLUDES planning dosimetry, targeting, positioning, or blocking by neurosurgeon

EXCLUDES arteriovenous malformations (see Radiation Oncology Section)
intensity modulated beam delivery plan and treatment
stereotactic body radiation therapy for lesions other than cranial or spinal (77435)
treatment planning, physics, dosimetry, treatment delivery and management provided by the oncologist (77261-77790)

Do not report stereotactic radiosurgery services with radiation treat management by the same physician (77427-77432)

Do not report more than once per lesion per treatment course

● 63620 Stereotactic radiosurgery (particle beam, gamma ray, or linear accelerator); 1 spinal lesion   B 80

     INCLUDES computer-assisted planning

Do not report more than once per treatment course

Do not report with (61795)

20.28 ⚕ **20.28** Global Days 090

+ ● 63621 each additional spinal lesion (List separately in addition to code for primary procedure)   B 80
Code first (63620)

Do not report computer-assisted planning

Do not report more than once per lesion

Do not report more than twice per treatment course

Do not report with (61795)

6.37 ⚕ **6.37** Global Days ZZZ

63650-63688 Spinal Neurostimulation

CMS 100-3,160.7   *Electrical Nerve Stimulators*
CMS 100-3,160.2   *Treatment of Motor Function Disorders with Electric Nerve Stimulation*
EXCLUDES   *analysis and programming of neurostimulator pulse generator (95970-95975)*

63650 Percutaneous implantation of neurostimulator electrode array, epidural   H8 S ▢
     Code also (C1778, C1897)

10.51 ⚕ **10.51** Global Days 090

     AMA: 2008, Jan, 10-25; 2007, Jan, 13-27; 2007, Jan, 13-27; 2007, January, 13-27

63655 Laminectomy for implantation of neurostimulator electrodes, plate/paddle, epidural   J8 S 80 ▢
     Code also (C1778, C1897)

21.45 ⚕ **21.45** Global Days 090

63660 Revision or removal of spinal neurostimulator electrode percutaneous array(s) or plate/paddle(s)   A2 T ▢

11.17 ⚕ **11.17** Global Days 090

63685 Insertion or replacement of spinal neurostimulator pulse generator or receiver, direct or inductive coupling   H8 S 80 ▢
     Code also (C1767, C1820)

     Do not report with 63688 for the same pulse generator or receiver

10.27 ⚕ **10.27** Global Days 090

63688 Revision or removal of implanted spinal neurostimulator pulse generator or receiver   A2 T ▢

     Do not report with 63685 for the same pulse generator or receiver

9.19 ⚕ **9.19** Global Days 090

63700-63706 Repair Congenital Neural Tube Defects

EXCLUDES *complex skin repair (see appropriate integumentary closure code)*

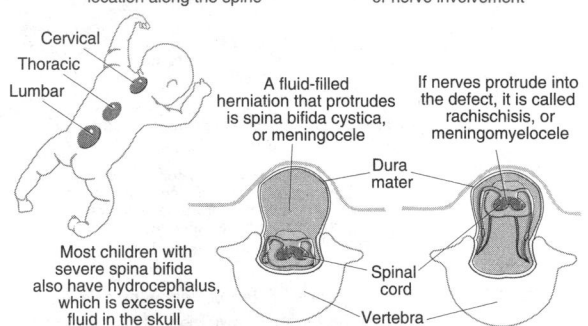

Spina bifida results from the defective closure of the spinal column during early fetal development; classification is according to location along the spine

Degree of disability is related to location and type; mild spina bifida may include only a bony abnormality with no meningeal or nerve involvement

Cervical
Thoracic
Lumbar

A fluid-filled herniation that protrudes is spina bifida cystica, or meningocele

If nerves protrude into the defect, it is called rachischisis, or meningomyelocele

Dura mater

Most children with severe spina bifida also have hydrocephalus, which is excessive fluid in the skull

Spinal cord

Vertebra

| | 63700 | Repair of meningocele; less than 5 cm diameter | C 80 ⊘ ▢ |

31.14 ⚕ **31.14** Global Days 090

| | 63702 | larger than 5 cm diameter | C 80 ⊘ ▢ |

35.08 ⚕ **35.08** Global Days 090

| | 63704 | Repair of myelomeningocele; less than 5 cm diameter | C 80 ⊘ ▢ |

39.06 ⚕ **39.06** Global Days 090

| | 63706 | larger than 5 cm diameter | C 80 ⊘ ▢ |

45.82 ⚕ **45.82** Global Days 090

63707-63710 Repair Dural Cerebrospinal Fluid Leak

63707 Repair of dural/cerebrospinal fluid leak, not requiring laminectomy　C 80 🖵
　🔂 22.98　🔨 22.98　Global Days 090

63709 Repair of dural/cerebrospinal fluid leak or pseudomeningocele, with laminectomy　C 80 🖵
　🔂 27.93　🔨 27.93　Global Days 090

63710 Dural graft, spinal　C 80 🖵
　　　EXCLUDES　*laminectomy and section of dentate ligament (63180, 63182)*
　🔂 28.01　🔨 28.01　Global Days 090

63740-63746 Cerebrospinal Fluid (CSF) Shunt: Lumbar

EXCLUDES　*placement of subarachnoid catheter with reservoir and/or pump:*
　not requiring laminectomy (62350, 62360-62362)
　with laminectomy (62351, 62360-62362)

63740 Creation of shunt, lumbar, subarachnoid-peritoneal, -pleural, or other; including laminectomy　C 80 🖵
　🔂 23.79　🔨 23.79　Global Days 090

63741 percutaneous, not requiring laminectomy　T 80 🖵
　🔂 15.36　🔨 15.36　Global Days 090

63744 Replacement, irrigation or revision of lumbosubarachnoid shunt　A2 T 80 🖵
　🔂 16.19　🔨 16.19　Global Days 090

63746 Removal of entire lumbosubarachnoid shunt system without replacement　A2 T 80 🖵
　🔂 14.10　🔨 14.10　Global Days 090

64400-64455 Nerve Blocks

EXCLUDES　*blood patch (62273)*
　diagnostic or therapeutic injection:
　cervical or thoracic (62310)
　lumbar (62311)
　nerve destruction (62280-62282, 64622-64627)

64400 Injection, anesthetic agent; trigeminal nerve, any division or branch　P3 T 50 🖵
　🔂 1.63　🔨 2.72　Global Days 000
　AMA: 2008, Jan, 10-25; 2008, Jun, 8-11; 2007, Jan, 13-27; 2007, Jan, 13-27, 2007, January, 13-27, 2005, Apr, 13-14, 2005, Apr, 13-14; 2005, April, 13-14; 2004, May, 15; 2004, May, 15; 2004, May, 15

64402 facial nerve　P3 T 50 🖵
　🔂 1.86　🔨 2.79　Global Days 000
　AMA: 2008, Jan, 10-26; 2008, Jun, 8-11; 2007, Jan, 13-27; 2007, Jan, 13-27; 2007, January, 13-27; 2005, Apr, 13-14; 2005, Apr, 13-14; 2005, April, 13-14; 2004, May, 15; 2004, May, 15; 2004, May, 15

64405 greater occipital nerve　P3 T 50 🖵
　🔂 1.90　🔨 2.63　Global Days 000
　AMA: 2008, Jan, 10-25; 2008, Jun, 8-11; 2007, Jan, 13-27; 2007, Jan, 13-27; 2007, January, 13-27; 2005, Apr, 13-14; 2005, Apr, 13-14; 2005, April, 13-14; 2004, May, 15; 2004, May, 15; 2004, May, 15

64408 vagus nerve　P3 T 80 50 🖵
　🔂 2.30　🔨 3.04　Global Days 000
　AMA: 2008, Jan, 10-25; 2008, Jun, 8-11; 2007, Jan, 13-27; 2007, Jan, 13-27; 2007, January, 13-27; 2005, Apr, 13-14; 2005, Apr, 13-14; 2005, April, 13-14; 2004, May, 15; 2004, May, 15; 2004, May, 15

64410 phrenic nerve　A2 T 80 50 🖵
　🔂 2.04　🔨 3.53　Global Days 000
　AMA: 2008, Jan, 10-25; 2008, Jun, 8-11; 2007, Jan, 13-27; 2007, Jan, 13-27; 2007, January, 13-27; 2005, Apr, 13-14; 2005, Apr, 13-14; 2005, April, 13-14; 2004, May, 15; 2004, May, 15; 2004, May, 15

64412 spinal accessory nerve　P3 T 50 🖵
　🔂 1.82　🔨 3.51　Global Days 000
　AMA: 2008, Jan, 10-25; 2008, Jun, 8-11; 2007, Jan, 13-27; 2007, Jan, 13-27; 2007, January, 13-27; 2007, Aug, 15; 2005, Apr, 13-14; 2005, Apr, 13-14; 2005, April, 13-14; 2004, May, 15; 2004, May, 15; 2004, May, 15

64413 cervical plexus　P3 T 50 🖵
　🔂 1.98　🔨 2.92　Global Days 000
　AMA: 2008, Jan, 10-25; 2008, Jun, 8-11; 2007, Jan, 13-27; 2007, Jan, 13-27; 2007, January, 13-27; 2007, Aug, 15; 2005, Apr, 13-14; 2005, Apr, 13-14; 2005, April, 13-14; 2004, May, 15; 2004, May, 15; 2004, May, 15

64415 brachial plexus, single　A2 T 50 🖵
　🔂 1.92　🔨 3.32　Global Days 000
　AMA: 2008, Jan, 10-25; 2008, Jun, 8-11; 2007, Jan, 13-27; 2007, Jan, 13-27, 2007, January, 13-27, 2006, Dec, 10-12, 2006, Dec, 10-12; 2006, Dec, 10-12; 2006, Dec, 10-12; 2006, Dec, 10-12; 2006, Dec, 10-12; 2006, Dec, 10-12; 2006, December, 10-12; 2006, December, 10-12; 2006, December, 10-12; 2006, Dec, 10-12; 2005, Apr, 13-14; 2005, April, 13-14; 2005, Apr, 13-14; 2004, May, 15; 2004, May, 15; 2004, February, 7; 2004, May, 15; 2004, Feb, 7; 2004, Feb, 7

▲ **64416** brachial plexus, continuous infusion by catheter (including catheter placement)　62 T 50 🖵
　Do not report with (01996)
　🔂 2.48　🔨 2.48　Global Days 000
　AMA: 2008, Jan, 10-25; 2008, Jun, 8-11; 2007, Jan, 13-27; 2007, Jan, 13-27; 2007, January, 13-27; 2005, Apr, 13-14; 2005, April, 13-14; 2005, Apr, 13-14; 2004, Feb, 7; 2004, February, 7; 2004, May, 15; 2004, Feb, 7; 2004, May, 15; 2004, May, 15

64417 axillary nerve　A2 T 50 🖵
　🔂 1.91　🔨 3.36　Global Days 000
　AMA: 2008, Jan, 10-25; 2008, Jun, 8-11; 2007, Jan, 13-27; 2007, Jan, 13-27; 2007, January, 13-27; 2005, Apr, 13-14; 2005, Apr, 13-14; 2005, April, 13-14; 2004, May, 15; 2004, May, 15; 2004, May, 15

64418 suprascapular nerve　P3 T 50 🖵
　🔂 1.89　🔨 3.41　Global Days 000
　AMA: 2008, Jan, 10-25; 2008, Jun, 8-11; 2007, Jan, 13-27; 2007, Jan, 13-27; 2007, January, 13-27; 2007, Aug, 15; 2005, Apr, 13-14; 2005, Apr, 13-14; 2005, April, 13-14; 2004, May, 15; 2004, May, 15; 2004, May, 15

64420 intercostal nerve, single　A2 T 🖵
　🔂 1.71　🔨 4.06　Global Days 000
　AMA: 2008, Jan, 10-25; 2008, Jun, 8-11; 2007, Jan, 13-27; 2007, Jan, 13-27; 2007, January, 13-27; 2005, Apr, 13-14; 2005, Apr, 13-14; 2005, April, 13-14; 2004, May, 15; 2004, May, 15; 2004, May, 15

64421 intercostal nerves, multiple, regional block　A2 T 50 🖵
　🔂 2.34　🔨 5.99　Global Days 000
　AMA: 2008, Jan, 10-25; 2008, Jun, 8-11; 2007, Jan, 13-27; 2007, Jan, 13-27; 2007, January, 13-27; 2005, Apr, 13-14; 2005, Apr, 13-14; 2005, April, 13-14; 2004, May, 15; 2004, May, 15; 2004, May, 15

Nervous System

64425 — 64479

64425   **ilioinguinal, iliohypogastric nerves**   P3 T 50 ▢
   ⌧ 2.43   ⚖ 3.28   Global Days 000
   AMA: 2008, Jan, 10-25; 2008, Jun, 8-11; 2007, Jan, 13-27; 2007, Jan, 13-27; 2007, January, 13-27; 2005, Apr, 13-14; 2005, Apr, 13-14; 2005, April, 13-14; 2004, May, 15; 2004, May, 15; 2004, May, 15

64430   **pudendal nerve**   A2 T ▢
   ⌧ 2.30   ⚖ 3.99   Global Days 000
   AMA: 2008, Jan, 10-25; 2008, Jun, 8-11; 2007, Jan, 13-27; 2007, Jan, 13-27; 2007, January, 13-27; 2005, Apr, 13-14; 2005, Apr, 13-14; 2005, April, 13-14; 2004, May, 15; 2004, May, 15; 2004, May, 15

64435   **paracervical (uterine) nerve**   ♀ P3 T 50 ▢
   ⌧ 2.22   ⚖ 3.72   Global Days 000
   AMA: 2008, Jan, 10-25; 2008, Jun, 8-11; 2007, Jan, 13-27; 2007, Jan, 13-27; 2007, January, 13-27; 2005, Apr, 13-14; 2005, Apr, 13-14; 2005, April, 13-14; 2004, May, 15; 2004, May, 15; 2004, May, 15

64445   **sciatic nerve, single**   P3 T 50 ▢
   ⌧ 2.09   ⚖ 3.45   Global Days 000
   AMA: 2008, Jun, 8-11; 2005, Apr, 13-14; 2005, Apr, 13-14; 2005, April, 13-14; 2004, May, 15; 2004, May, 15; 2004, May, 15; 2004, February, 7; 2004, Feb, 7; 2004, Feb, 7

▲ **64446**   **sciatic nerve, continuous infusion by catheter (including catheter placement)**   G2 T 50 ▢
   Do not report with (01996)
   ⌧ 2.44   ⚖ 2.44   Global Days 000
   AMA: 2008, Jun, 8-11; 2005, Apr, 13-14; 2005, Apr, 13-14; 2005, April, 13-14; 2004, May, 15; 2004, May, 15; 2004, May, 15; 2004, February, 7; 2004, Feb, 7; 2004, Feb, 7

64447   **femoral nerve, single**   A2 T 50 ▢
   Do not report with (01996)
   ⌧ 1.83   ⚖ 1.83   Global Days 000
   AMA: 2008, Jun, 8-11; 2005, Apr, 13-14; 2005, Apr, 13-14; 2005, April, 13-14; 2004, Feb, 7; 2004, Feb, 7; 2004, May, 15; 2004, February, 7; 2004, May, 15; 2004, May, 15

▲ **64448**   **femoral nerve, continuous infusion by catheter (including catheter placement)**   G2 T 50 ▢
   Do not report with (01996)
   ⌧ 2.16   ⚖ 2.16   Global Days 000
   AMA: 2008, Jun, 8-11; 2005, Apr, 13-14; 2005, Apr, 13-14; 2005, April, 13-14; 2004, Feb, 7; 2004, Feb, 7; 2004, February, 7; 2004, May, 15; 2004, May, 15; 2004, May, 15

▲ **64449**   **lumbar plexus, posterior approach, continuous infusion by catheter (including catheter placement)**   G2 T 50 ▢
   Do not report with (01996)
   ⌧ 2.40   ⚖ 2.40   Global Days 000
   AMA: 2008, Jun, 8-11; 2005, Apr, 13-14; 2005, Apr, 13-14; 2005, April, 13-14; 2004, May, 15; 2004, May, 15; 2004, May, 15

64450   **other peripheral nerve or branch**   P3 T 50 ▢
   EXCLUDES   *Morton's neuroma (64455, 64632)*
   ⌧ 1.89   ⚖ 2.65   Global Days 000
   AMA: 2008, Jan, 10-25; 2008, Jun, 8-11; 2007, Jan, 13-27; 2007, Jan, 13-27; 2007, January, 13-27; 2005, Apr, 13-14; 2005, Apr, 13-14; 2005, April, 13-14; 2004, May, 15; 2004, May, 15; 2004, May, 15

● **64455**   **Injection(s), anesthetic agent and/or steroid, plantar common digital nerve(s) (eg, Morton's neuroma)**   P3 T 80 50
   Do not report with (64632)
   ⌧ 1.08   ⚖ 1.36   Global Days 000

64470-64484 Paraspinal Nerve Injections

EXCLUDES   *epidural or caudal injection (62273, 62281-62282, 62310-62319)*
   nerve destruction (62280-62282, 64622-64627)
   subarachnoid or subdural injection (62280, 62310-62319)

Thoracic vertebra (superior view)
Spinous process
Transverse costal facet
Lamina
Pedicle
Superior articular facets
Superior costal facet
Vertebral body

Superior view of C7
Spinous process
Superior articular facets
Vertebral body

The articular facet joints of a single vertebral level are injected with an anesthetic agent or steroid. Report code 64470 for a single level cervical or thoracic injection. Report 64472 for each additional level in the cervical or thoracic regions

64470   **Injection, anesthetic agent and/or steroid, paravertebral facet joint or facet joint nerve; cervical or thoracic, single level**   A2 T 50 ▢
   ⌧ 77003
   ⌧ 2.69   ⚖ 6.64   Global Days 000
   AMA: 2008, Jun, 8-11; 2004, Sep, 1; 2004, Sep, 1; 2004, May, 15; 2004, May, 15; 2004, May, 15; 2004, September, 1

+ **64472**   **cervical or thoracic, each additional level (List separately in addition to code for primary procedure)**   A2 T 50 ▢
   ⌧ 77003
   Code first (64470)
   ⌧ 1.72   ⚖ 2.88   Global Days ZZZ
   AMA: 2008, Jun, 8-11; 2004, Sep, 1; 2004, Sep, 1; 2004, May, 15; 2004, May, 15; 2004, September, 1; 2004, May, 15

64475   **lumbar or sacral, single level**   A2 T 50 ▢
   ⌧ 77003
   ⌧ 2.12   ⚖ 5.95   Global Days 000
   AMA: 2008, Jan, 10-25; 2008, Jun, 8-11; 2007, Jan, 13-27; 2007, Jan, 13-27; 2007, January, 13-27; 2004, May, 15; 2004, May, 15; 2004, Sep, 1; 2004, September, 1; 2004, May, 15; 2004, May, 15; 2004, Sep, 1; 2004, May, 15; 2004, May, 15

+ **64476**   **lumbar or sacral, each additional level (List separately in addition to code for primary procedure)**   A2 T 50 ▢
   Code first (64475)
   ⌧ 77003
   ⌧ 1.29   ⚖ 2.42   Global Days ZZZ
   AMA: 2008, Jun, 8-11; 2004, Sep, 1; 2004, Sep, 1; 2004, May, 15; 2004, May, 15; 2004, May, 15; 2004, September, 1

64479   **Injection, anesthetic agent and/or steroid, transforaminal epidural; cervical or thoracic, single level**   A2 T 50 ▢
   ⌧ 77003
   ⌧ 3.18   ⚖ 7.03   Global Days 000
   AMA: 2008, Jun, 8-11; 2008, Jul, 9; 2004, May, 15; 2004, May, 15; 2004, Sep, 1; 2004, Sep, 1; 2004, September, 1; 2004, May, 15

+   **64480**   cervical or thoracic, each additional level (List separately in addition to code for primary procedure)   A2 T 50 ▢
Code first (64479)
➕ *77003*
🔷 2.08 ⚗ 3.54 **Global Days ZZZ**
AMA: 2008, Jan, 10-25; 2008, Jul, 9; 2007, Jan, 13-27; 2007, January, 13-27; 2005, Feb, 13-16; 2005, February, 13-16; 2005, Feb, 13-16; 2004, Sep, 1; 2004, May, 15; 2004, September, 1; 2004, Sep, 1; 2004, May, 15; 2004, May, 15

64483   lumbar or sacral, single level   A2 T 50 ▢
➕ *77003*
🔷 2.80 ⚗ 6.84 **Global Days 000**
AMA: 2008, Jun, 8-11; 2008, Jul, 9; 2004, Sep, 1; 2004, Sep, 1; 2004, May, 15; 2004, May, 15; 2004, September, 1; 2004, May, 15

+   **64484**   lumbar or sacral, each additional level (List separately in addition to code for primary procedure)   A2 T 50 ▢
Code first (64483)
➕ *77003*
🔷 1.77 ⚗ 3.47 **Global Days ZZZ**
AMA: 2008, Jan, 10-25; 2008, Jun, 8-11; 2008, Jul, 9; 2007, Jan, 13-27; 2007, Jan, 13-27; 2007, January, 13-27; 2005, Feb, 13-16; 2005, February, 13-16; 2005, Feb, 13-16; 2004, Sep, 1; 2004, September, 1; 2004, May, 15; 2004, Sep, 1; 2004, May, 15; 2004, May, 15

64505-64530 Sympathetic Nerve Blocks

64505   Injection, anesthetic agent; sphenopalatine ganglion   P3 T ▢
🔷 2.18 ⚗ 2.60 **Global Days 000**
AMA: 2008, Jan, 10-25; 2008, Jun, 8-11; 2007, Jan, 13-27; 2007, Jan, 13-27; 2007, January, 13-27; 2005, Apr, 13-14; 2005, Apr, 13-14; 2005, April, 13-14; 2004, May, 15; 2004, May, 15; 2004, May, 15

64508   carotid sinus (separate procedure)   P3 T 80 ▢
🔷 1.80 ⚗ 3.61 **Global Days 000**
AMA: 2008, Jun, 8-11; 2005, Apr, 13-14; 2005, Apr, 13-14; 2005, April, 13-14; 2004, May, 15; 2004, May, 15; 2004, May, 15

64510   stellate ganglion (cervical sympathetic)   A2 T ▢
🔷 1.75 ⚗ 3.59 **Global Days 000**
AMA: 2008, Jun, 8-11; 2005, Apr, 13-14; 2005, Apr, 13-14; 2005, April, 13-14; 2004, May, 15; 2004, May, 15; 2004, May, 15

64517   superior hypogastric plexus   A2 T ▢
🔷 3.07 ⚗ 4.32 **Global Days 000**
AMA: 2008, Jan, 10-25; 2008, Jun, 8-11; 2007, Jan, 13-27; 2007, Jan, 13-27; 2007, January, 13-27; 2005, Apr, 13-14; 2005, April, 13-14; 2005, Apr, 13-14; 2004, Nov, 11; 2004, November, 11; 2004, May, 15; 2004, Nov, 11; 2004, May, 15; 2004, May, 15

64520   lumbar or thoracic (paravertebral sympathetic)   A2 T ▢
🔷 1.98 ⚗ 4.70 **Global Days 000**
AMA: 2008, Jun, 8-11; 2005, Apr, 13-14; 2005, Apr, 13-14; 2005, April, 13-14; 2004, May, 15; 2004, May, 15; 2004, May, 15

64530   celiac plexus, with or without radiologic monitoring   A2 T ▢
🔷 2.34 ⚗ 4.86 **Global Days 000**
AMA: 2008, Jan, 10-25; 2008, Jun, 8-11; 2007, Jan, 13-27; 2007, Jan, 13-27; 2007, January, 13-27; 2005, Apr, 13-14; 2005, Apr, 13-14; 2005, April, 13-14; 2004, May, 15; 2004, May, 15; 2004, May, 15

64550 Transcutaneous Electrical Nerve Stimulation

CMS *100-3,280.13*   Transcutaneous Electrical Nerve Stimulators (TENS)
CMS *100-3,160.13*   Supplies Used for Transcutaneous Electrical Nerve Stimulation and Neuromuscular Electrical Stimulation (NMES)
CMS *100-3,160.7.1*   Assessing Patients Suitability for Electrical Nerve Stimulation Therapy
CMS *100-3,160.2*   Treatment of Motor Function Disorders with Electic Nerve Stimulation
CMS *100-4,4,20.5*   HCPCS Under OPPS
EXCLUDES   *analysis and programming neurostimulator pulse generator (95970-95975)*

64550   Application of surface (transcutaneous) neurostimulator   A ▢
🔷 0.24 ⚗ 0.40 **Global Days 000**
AMA: 2008, Jan, 10-25; 2007, Jan, 13-27; 2007, Jan, 13-27; 2007, January, 13-27

64553-64565 Electrical Nerve Stimulation: Insertion/Replacement/Removal/Revision

CMS *100-3,160.12*   Neuromuscular Electrical Stimulation (NMES)
CMS *100-3,160.13*   Supplies Used for Transcutaneous Electrical Nerve Stimulation and Neuromuscular Electrical Stimulation (NMES)
CMS *100-3,160.7.1*   Assessing Patients Suitability for Electrical Nerve Stimulation Therapy
CMS *100-3,160.7*   Electrical Nerve Stimulators
CMS *100-3,160.2*   Treatment of Motor Function Disorders with Electic Nerve Stimulation
CMS *100-4,32,40*   Sacral Nerve Stimulation
EXCLUDES   *analysis and programming of neurostimulator pulse generator (95970-95975)*

64553   Percutaneous implantation of neurostimulator electrodes; cranial nerve   H6 G 80 ▢
EXCLUDES   *open procedure (61885-61886)*
Code also (C1778, C1897)
🔷 4.07 ⚗ 5.17 **Global Days 010**

64555   peripheral nerve (excludes sacral nerve)   J8 S ▢
Code also (C1778, C1897)
🔷 4.01 ⚗ 6.49 **Global Days 010**

64560   autonomic nerve   J8 S 80 ▢
Code also (C1778, C1897)
🔷 4.14 ⚗ 5.45 **Global Days 010**

64561   sacral nerve (transforaminal placement)   H0 9 ▢
Code also (C1778, C1897)
🔷 11.22 ⚗ 29.62 **Global Days 010**

64565   neuromuscular   J8 S ▢
Code also (C1778, C1897)
🔷 3.06 ⚗ 4.33 **Global Days 010**
AMA: 2008, Jan, 10-25; 2007, Jan, 13-27; 2007, Jan, 13-27; 2007, January, 13-27

64573-64595 Implantation/Revision/Removal Neurostimulators: Incisional

64573   Incision for implantation of neurostimulator electrodes; cranial nerve   H6 S 80 ▢
EXCLUDES   *open procedure (61885-61886)*
removal or revision of cranial nerve neurostimulator pulse generator (61888)
Code also (C1778, C1897)
🔷 15.06 ⚗ 15.06 **Global Days 090**

64575   peripheral nerve (excludes sacral nerve)   H8 S ▢
Code also (C1778, C1897)
🔷 7.36 ⚗ 7.36 **Global Days 090**

64480 — 64575

● New Code   ▲ Revised Code   Ⓜ Maternity Edit   Ⓐ Age Edit   A-V OPPS Status Indicator   🔷 Facility RVU   ⚗ Non-Facility RVU
▢ CCI Comprehensive Code   50 Bilateral Procedure   + Add-on Indicator   ▣ Laboratory crosswalk   ➕ Radiology crosswalk

Nervous System

64577 — 64623

64577 autonomic nerve 〔H8〕〔S〕〔▣〕
Code also (C1778, C1897)
🔗 9.22 ✎ 9.22 **Global Days 090**

64580 neuromuscular 〔H8〕〔S〕〔80〕〔▣〕
Code also (C1778, C1897)
🔗 7.53 ✎ 7.53 **Global Days 090**

64581 sacral nerve (transforaminal placement) 〔H8〕〔S〕〔▣〕
Code also (C1778, C1897)
🔗 21.79 ✎ 21.79 **Global Days 090**

64585 Revision or removal of peripheral neurostimulator electrodes 〔A2〕〔T〕〔▣〕
🔗 4.16 ✎ 8.58 **Global Days 010**

64590 Insertion or replacement of peripheral or gastric neurostimulator pulse generator or receiver, direct or inductive coupling 〔H8〕〔S〕〔▣〕
Code also (C1767, C1820)
Do not report with (64595)
🔗 4.64 ✎ 8.05 **Global Days 010**
AMA: 2007, Mar, 4-5; 2007, Mar, 4-5; 2007, Apr, 7-10; 2007, Apr, 7-10; 2007, March, 4-5; 2007, April, 7-10; 2006, May, 12-15; 2006, May, 12-15; 2006, May, 12-15

64595 Revision or removal of peripheral or gastric neurostimulator pulse generator or receiver 〔A2〕〔T〕〔▣〕
Do not report with (64590)
🔗 3.68 ✎ 8.32 **Global Days 010**
AMA: 2008, Jan, 8-9; 2007, Mar, 4-5; 2007, Mar, 4-5; 2007, Apr, 7-10; 2007, Apr, 7-10; 2007, March, 4-5; 2007, April, 7-10; 2006, May, 12-15; 2006, May, 12-15; 2006, May, 12-15

64600-64610 Neurolysis Trigeminal Nerve

CMS 100-3,160.1 *Induced Lesions of Nerve Tracts*
〔EXCLUDES〕 *treatments that do not destroy the target nerve (64999)*
〔INCLUDES〕 injection of therapeutic medication

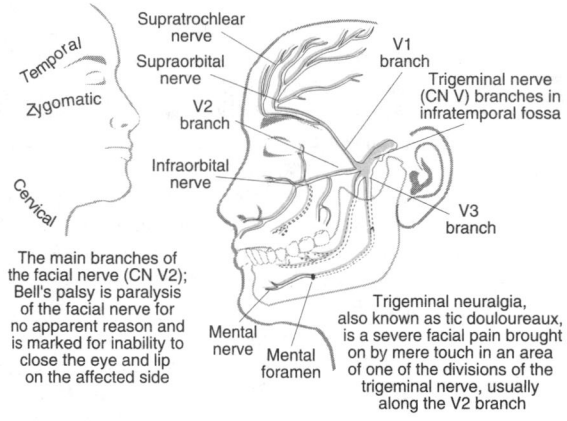

Supratrochlear nerve
Supraorbital nerve
V2 branch
V1 branch
Trigeminal nerve (CN V) branches in infratemporal fossa
Temporal
Zygomatic
Infraorbital nerve
V3 branch
Cervical
Mental nerve
Mental nerve
Mental foramen

The main branches of the facial nerve (CN VII); Bell's palsy is paralysis of the facial nerve for no apparent reason and is marked for inability to close the eye and lip on the affected side

Trigeminal neuralgia, also known as tic douloureaux, is a severe facial pain brought on by mere touch in an area of one of the divisions of the trigeminal nerve, usually along the V2 branch

64600 Destruction by neurolytic agent, trigeminal nerve; supraorbital, infraorbital, mental, or inferior alveolar branch 〔A2〕〔T〕〔▣〕
🔗 5.51 ✎ 10.24 **Global Days 010**
AMA: 2008, Jun, 8-11; 2005, Aug, 13-15; 2005, Aug, 13-15; 2005, August, 13-15

64605 second and third division branches at foramen ovale 〔A2〕〔T〕〔80〕〔▣〕
🔗 8.85 ✎ 14.51 **Global Days 010**
AMA: 2008, Jun, 8-11; 2005, Aug, 13-15; 2005, Aug, 13-15; 2005, August, 13-15

64610 second and third division branches at foramen ovale under radiologic monitoring 〔A2〕〔T〕〔▣〕
🔗 12.60 ✎ 17.85 **Global Days 010**
AMA: 2008, Jun, 8-11; 2005, Aug, 13-15; 2005, Aug, 13-15; 2005, August, 13-15

64612-64614 Chemical Denervation of Muscles

CMS 100-3,160.1 *Induced Lesions of Nerve Tracts*
〔INCLUDES〕 injection of therapeutic medication
〔EXCLUDES〕 *electromyography or muscle electric stimulation guidance (95873-95874)*
treatments that do not destroy the target nerve (64999)
nerve destruction of:
  anal sphincter (46505)
  extraocular muscles to treat strabismus (67345)

64612 Chemodenervation of muscle(s); muscle(s) innervated by facial nerve (eg, for blepharospasm, hemifacial spasm) 〔P3〕〔T〕〔50〕〔▣〕
🔗 3.45 ✎ 3.92 **Global Days 010**
AMA: 2008, Jan, 10-25; 2008, Jun, 8-11; 2007, Jan, 13-27; 2007, Jan, 13-27; 2007, January, 13-27; 2006, Sep, 5-8; 2006, Sep, 5-8; 2006, September, 5-8; 2005, Aug, 13-15; 2005, Aug, 13-15; 2005, August, 13-15

64613 neck muscle(s) (eg, for spasmodic torticollis, spasmodic dysphonia) 〔P3〕〔T〕〔50〕〔▣〕
🔗 3.26 ✎ 3.86 **Global Days 010**
AMA: 2008, Jan, 10-25; 2008, Jun, 8-11; 2007, Jan, 13-27; 2007, Jan, 13-27; 2007, January, 13-27; 2006, Sep, 5-8; 2006, Sep, 5-8; 2006, September, 5-8; 2005, Aug, 13-15; 2005, Aug, 13-15; 2005, August, 13-15

64614 extremity(s) and/or trunk muscle(s) (eg, for dystonia, cerebral palsy, multiple sclerosis) 〔P3〕〔T〕〔50〕〔▣〕
🔗 3.62 ✎ 4.32 **Global Days 010**
AMA: 2008, Jan, 10-25; 2008, Jun, 8-11; 2007, Jan, 13-27; 2007, Jan, 13-27; 2007, January, 13-27; 2006, Sep, 5-8; 2006, September, 5-8; 2006, Sep, 5-8; 2005, Aug, 13-15; 2005, August, 13-15; 2005, February, 13-16; 2005, Aug, 13-15; 2005, Feb, 13-16; 2005, Feb, 13-16

64620-64640 Neurolysis: Intercostal, Facet Joint, and Pudendal Nerve

CMS 100-3,160.1 *Induced Lesions of Nerve Tracts*
〔EXCLUDES〕 *treatments that do not destroy the target nerve (64999)*
〔INCLUDES〕 injection of therapeutic medication

64620 Destruction by neurolytic agent, intercostal nerve 〔A2〕〔T〕〔▣〕
🔗 4.28 ✎ 6.88 **Global Days 010**
AMA: 2008, Jun, 8-11; 2005, Aug, 13-15; 2005, Aug, 13-15; 2005, August, 13-15

64622 Destruction by neurolytic agent, paravertebral facet joint nerve; lumbar or sacral, single level 〔A2〕〔T〕〔50〕〔▣〕
🔗 77003
🔗 4.53 ✎ 8.22 **Global Days 010**
AMA: 2008, Jun, 8-11; 2005, Aug, 13-15; 2005, Aug, 13-15; 2005, August, 13-15; 2004, Sep, 1; 2004, September, 1; 2004, Sep, 1

+ **64623** lumbar or sacral, each additional level (List separately in addition to code for primary procedure) 〔A2〕〔T〕〔50〕〔▣〕
Code first (64622)
🔗 77003
🔗 1.28 ✎ 3.05 **Global Days ZZZ**
AMA: 2008, Jun, 8-11; 2005, Aug, 13-15; 2005, Aug, 13-15; 2005, August, 13-15; 2004, Sep, 1; 2004, September, 1; 2004, Sep, 1

64626   cervical or thoracic, single level   A2 T 50 ▭
   ▣ *77003*
   ⚐ 5.97   ⚕ 9.56   Global Days 010
   AMA: 2008, Jun, 8-11; 2005, Aug, 13-15; 2005, Aug, 13-15; 2005, August, 13-15; 2004, Sep, 1; 2004, September, 1; 2004, Sep, 1

+   64627   cervical or thoracic, each additional level (List separately in addition to code for primary procedure)   A2 T 50 ▭
   Code first (64626)
   ▣ *77003*
   ⚐ 1.50   ⚕ 4.16   Global Days ZZZ
   AMA: 2008, Jun, 8-11; 2005, Aug, 13-15; 2005, Aug, 13-15; 2005, August, 13-15; 2004, Sep, 1, 2004, September, 1, 2004, Sep, 1

64630   Destruction by neurolytic agent; pudendal nerve   A2 T 80 ▭
   ⚐ 4.98   ⚕ 5.97   Global Days 010
   AMA: 2008, Jun, 8-11; 2005, Aug, 13-15; 2005, Aug, 13-15; 2005, August, 13-15

● 64632   plantar common digital nerve   P3 T 80 50
   Do not report with (64455)
   ⚐ 1.88   ⚕ 2.20   Global Days 010

64640   other peripheral nerve or branch   M1 T 70 ▭
   ⚐ 4.59   ⚕ 5.90   Global Days 010
   AMA: 2008, Jun, 8-11; 2005, Aug, 13-15; 2005, Aug, 13-15; 2005, August, 13-15

64650-64653 Chemical Denervation Eccrine Glands

Code also medication provided
INCLUDES   injection of therapeutic medication

64650   Chemodenervation of eccrine glands; both axillae   P3 T 80
   ⚐ 1.03   ⚕ 1.71   Global Days 000
   AMA: 2008, Jun, 8-11; 2005, Aug, 13-15; 2005, Aug, 13-15; 2005, August, 13-15

64653   other area(s) (eg, scalp, face, neck), per day   P3 T 80
   EXCLUDES   *hands or feet (64999)*
   ⚐ 1.29   ⚕ 1.99   Global Days 000
   AMA: 2008, Jun, 8-11; 2005, Aug, 13-15; 2005, Aug, 13-15; 2005, August, 13-15

64680-64681 Neurolysis: Celiac Plexus, Superior Hypogastric Plexus

INCLUDES   injection of therapeutic medication
   only for lesions that abut the dura matter or that affect the spinal neural tissue
   planning, dosimetry, targeting, positioning, or blocking performed by the surgeon
   radiation treatment management by the same physician (77427-77432)

Do not report more than once per lesion per course of treatment
Do not report with (61795)

64680   Destruction by neurolytic agent, with or without radiologic monitoring; celiac plexus   A2 T ▭
   ⚐ 4.15   ⚕ 7.78   Global Days 010
   AMA: 2008, Jan, 10-25; 2008, Jun, 8-11; 2007, Jan, 13-27; 2007, Jan, 13-27; 2007, January, 13-27; 2005, Aug, 13-15; 2005, August, 13-15; 2005, Aug, 13-15

64681   superior hypogastric plexus   A2 T ▭
   ⚐ 5.59   ⚕ 10.06   Global Days 010
   AMA: 2007, Dec, 10-179; 2005, Aug, 13-15; 2005, Aug, 13-15; 2005, August, 13-15

64702-64727 Decompression and/or Transposition of Nerve

INCLUDES   neuroplasty with nerve wrapping
EXCLUDES   *facial nerve decompression (69720)*
   neuroplasty with operating microscope (64727)

64702   Neuroplasty; digital, 1 or both, same digit   A2 T ▭
   ⚐ 11.62   ⚕ 11.62   Global Days 090
   AMA: 2008, Jan, 10-25; 2007, Jan, 13-27; 2007, Jan, 13-27; 2007, January, 13-27

64704   nerve of hand or foot   A2 T 80 ▭
   ⚐ 8.60   ⚕ 8.60   Global Days 090
   AMA: 2008, Jan, 10-25; 2007, Jan, 13-27; 2007, Jan, 13-27; 2007, January, 13-27

64708   Neuroplasty, major peripheral nerve, arm or leg; other than specified   A2 T 80 ▭
   ⚐ 12.18   ⚕ 12.18   Global Days 090
   AMA: 2008, Jan, 10-25; 2007, Jan, 13-27; 2007, Jan, 13-27; 2007, January, 13-27

64712   sciatic nerve   A2 T 80 ▭
   ⚐ 13.94   ⚕ 13.94   Global Days 090
   AMA: 2008, Jan, 10-25; 2007, Jan, 13-27; 2007, Jan, 13-27; 2007, January, 13-27

64713   brachial plexus   A2 T 80 ▭
   ⚐ 19.66   ⚕ 19.66   Global Days 090
   AMA: 2008, Jan, 10-25; 2007, Jan, 13-27; 2007, Jan, 13-27; 2007, January, 13-27

64714   lumbar plexus   A2 T 80 ▭
   ⚐ 16.66   ⚕ 16.66   Global Days 090
   AMA: 2008, Jan, 10-25; 2007, Jan, 13-27; 2007, Jan, 13-27; 2007, January, 13-27

64716   Neuroplasty and/or transposition; cranial nerve (specify)   A2 T 80 ▭
   ⚐ 13.18   ⚕ 13.18   Global Days 090
   AMA: 2008, Jan, 10-25; 2007, Jan, 13-27; 2007, Jan, 13-27; 2007, January, 13-27

64718   ulnar nerve at elbow   A2 T 80 ▭
   ⚐ 14.34   ⚕ 14.34   Global Days 090
   AMA: 2008, Jan, 10-25; 2007, Jan, 13-27; 2007, Jan, 13-27; 2007, January, 13-27

64719   ulnar nerve at wrist   A2 T ▭
   ⚐ 9.96   ⚕ 9.96   Global Days 090
   AMA: 2008, Jan, 10-25; 2007, Jan, 13-27; 2007, Jan, 13-27; 2007, January, 13-27

64721   median nerve at carpal tunnel   A2 T 50 ▭
   EXCLUDES   *arthroscopic procedure (29848)*
   ⚐ 10.45   ⚕ 10.49   Global Days 090
   AMA: 2008, Jan, 10-25; 2007, Jan, 13-27; 2007, Jan, 13-27; 2007, January, 13-27; 2006, Dec, 10-12; 2006, Dec, 10-12; 2006, Dec, 10-12; 2006, Dec, 10-12; 2006, December, 10-12; 2006, December, 10-12; 2006, December, 10-12; 2006, December, 10-12; 2006, Dec, 10-12; 2006, Dec, 10-12; 2006, Dec, 10-12; 2006, Dec, 10-12

64722   Decompression; unspecified nerve(s) (specify)   A2 T 80 ▭
   ⚐ 8.46   ⚕ 8.46   Global Days 090
   AMA: 2008, Jan, 10-25; 2007, Jan, 13-27; 2007, Jan, 13-27; 2007, January, 13-27; 2004, Nov, 9; 2004, November, 9; 2004, Nov, 9

64726   plantar digital nerve   A2 T ▭
   ⚐ 7.49   ⚕ 7.49   Global Days 090
   AMA: 2008, Jan, 10-25; 2007, Jan, 13-27; 2007, Jan, 13-27; 2007, January, 13-27

● New Code   ▲ Revised Code   M Maternity Edit   A Age Edit   A-Y OPPS Status Indicator   ⚐ Facility RVU   ⚕ Non-Facility RVU
▭ CCI Comprehensive Code   50 Bilateral Procedure   + Add-on Indicator   ▣ Laboratory crosswalk   ▣ Radiology crosswalk

Nervous System

+ **64727** Internal neurolysis, requiring use of operating microscope (List separately in addition to code for neuroplasty) (Neuroplasty includes external neurolysis) ⒜2 ⓉⒽ▢

INCLUDES neuroplasty with nerve wrapping
operating microscope (69990)

🖐 4.92 ✂ 4.92 **Global Days ZZZ**
AMA: 2008, Jan, 10-25; 2007, Jan, 13-27; 2007, Jan, 13-27; 2007, January, 13-27

64732-64772 Surgical Avulsion/Transection of Nerve

CMS *100-3,160.1* *Induced Lesions of Nerve Tracts*
EXCLUDES *stereotactic lesion of gasserian ganglion (61790)*

64732 Transection or avulsion of; supraorbital nerve ⒜2 Ⓣ 80 ▢
🖐 9.82 ✂ 9.82 Global Days 090

64734 infraorbital nerve ⒜2 Ⓣ 80 ▢
🖐 10.55 ✂ 10.55 Global Days 090

64736 mental nerve ⒜2 Ⓣ 80 ▢
🖐 9.86 ✂ 9.86 Global Days 090

64738 inferior alveolar nerve by osteotomy ⒜2 Ⓣ 80 ▢
🖐 11.80 ✂ 11.80 Global Days 090

64740 lingual nerve ⒜2 Ⓣ 80 ▢
🖐 11.65 ✂ 11.65 Global Days 090

64742 facial nerve, differential or complete ⒜2 Ⓣ 80 ▢
🖐 11.92 ✂ 11.92 Global Days 090

64744 greater occipital nerve ⒜2 Ⓣ 80 50 ▢
🖐 10.64 ✂ 10.64 Global Days 090

64746 phrenic nerve ⒜2 Ⓣ 80 ▢ P0
EXCLUDES *section of recurrent unilateral laryngeal nerve (31595)*
🖐 11.33 ✂ 11.33 Global Days 090

64752 vagus nerve (vagotomy), transthoracic Ⓒ 80 ▢
🖐 12.82 ✂ 12.82 Global Days 090

64755 vagus nerves limited to proximal stomach (selective proximal vagotomy, proximal gastric vagotomy, parietal cell vagotomy, supra- or highly selective vagotomy) Ⓒ 80 ▢
EXCLUDES *laparoscopic procedure (43652)*
🖐 22.84 ✂ 22.84 Global Days 090

64760 vagus nerve (vagotomy), abdominal Ⓒ 80 ▢
EXCLUDES *laparoscopic procedure (43651)*
🖐 12.08 ✂ 12.08 Global Days 090

64761 pudendal nerve 62 Ⓣ 80 50 ▢
🖐 11.36 ✂ 11.36 Global Days 090

64763 Transection or avulsion of obturator nerve, extrapelvic, with or without adductor tenotomy 62 Ⓣ 80 50 ▢
🖐 13.87 ✂ 13.87 Global Days 090

64766 Transection or avulsion of obturator nerve, intrapelvic, with or without adductor tenotomy 62 Ⓣ 80 50 ▢
🖐 15.96 ✂ 15.96 Global Days 090

64771 Transection or avulsion of other cranial nerve, extradural ⒜2 Ⓣ 80 ▢
🖐 15.07 ✂ 15.07 Global Days 090

64772 Transection or avulsion of other spinal nerve, extradural ⒜2 Ⓣ 80 ▢
EXCLUDES *removal of tender scar and soft tissue including neuroma if necessary (11400-11446, 13100-13153)*
🖐 14.56 ✂ 14.56 Global Days 090

64774-64823 Excisional Nerve Procedures

EXCLUDES *Morton neuroma excision (28080)*

64774 Excision of neuroma; cutaneous nerve, surgically identifiable ⒜2 Ⓣ ▢
🖐 10.42 ✂ 10.42 Global Days 090

64776 digital nerve, 1 or both, same digit ⒜2 Ⓣ 80 ▢
🖐 10.03 ✂ 10.03 Global Days 090

+ **64778** digital nerve, each additional digit (List separately in addition to code for primary procedure) ⒜2 Ⓣ ▢
Code first (64776)
🖐 4.88 ✂ 4.88 Global Days ZZZ

64782 hand or foot, except digital nerve ⒜2 Ⓣ ▢
🖐 11.80 ✂ 11.80 Global Days 090

+ **64783** hand or foot, each additional nerve, except same digit (List separately in addition to code for primary procedure) ⒜2 Ⓣ ▢
Code first (64782)
🖐 5.82 ✂ 5.82 Global Days ZZZ

64784 major peripheral nerve, except sciatic ⒜2 Ⓣ 80 ▢
🖐 18.38 ✂ 18.38 Global Days 090

64786 sciatic nerve ⒜2 Ⓣ 80 ▢
🖐 27.76 ✂ 27.76 Global Days 090

+ **64787** Implantation of nerve end into bone or muscle (List separately in addition to neuroma excision) ⒜2 Ⓣ 80 ▢
Code first (64774-64786)
🖐 6.68 ✂ 6.68 Global Days ZZZ

64788 Excision of neurofibroma or neurolemmoma; cutaneous nerve ⒜2 Ⓣ ▢
🖐 9.80 ✂ 9.80 Global Days 090

64790 major peripheral nerve ⒜2 Ⓣ 80 ▢
🖐 21.20 ✂ 21.20 Global Days 090

64792 extensive (including malignant type) ⒜2 Ⓣ 80 ▢
🖐 27.41 ✂ 27.41 Global Days 090

64795 Biopsy of nerve ⒜2 Ⓣ ▢
🖐 5.03 ✂ 5.03 Global Days 000

64802 Sympathectomy, cervical ⒜2 Ⓣ 80 50 ▢
🖐 15.49 ✂ 15.49 Global Days 090

64804 Sympathectomy, cervicothoracic Ⓣ 80 50 ▢
🖐 23.66 ✂ 23.66 Global Days 090

64809 Sympathectomy, thoracolumbar Ⓒ 80 50 ▢
INCLUDES Leriche sympathectomy
🖐 22.05 ✂ 22.05 Global Days 090

64818 Sympathectomy, lumbar Ⓒ 80 50 ▢
🖐 17.17 ✂ 17.17 Global Days 090

64820 Sympathectomy; digital arteries, each digit 62 Ⓣ ▢
INCLUDES operating microscope (69990)
🖐 19.27 ✂ 19.27 Global Days 090
AMA: 2008, Jan, 10-25; 2007, Jan, 13-27; 2007, Jan, 13-27; 2007, January, 13-27; 2004, Jan, 27; 2004, January, 27; 2004, Jan, 27

64821 radial artery ⒜2 Ⓣ 50 ▢
INCLUDES operating microscope (69990)
🖐 17.36 ✂ 17.36 Global Days 090

64822 ulnar artery 62 Ⓣ 50 ▢
INCLUDES operating microscope (69990)
🖐 17.17 ✂ 17.17 Global Days 090

64823 superficial palmar arch 62 Ⓣ 50 ▢
INCLUDES operating microscope (69990)
🖐 19.53 ✂ 19.53 Global Days 090

64831-64907 Nerve Repair: Suture and Nerve Grafts

64831 Suture of digital nerve, hand or foot; 1 nerve   A2 T ⬛
    �3 17.27   ⚲ 17.27   Global Days 090

+ **64832** each additional digital nerve (List separately in addition to code for primary procedure)   A2 T 80 ⬛
    Code first (64831)
    �3 9.07   ⚲ 9.07   Global Days ZZZ

64834 Suture of one nerve; hand or foot, common sensory nerve   A2 T 80 ⬛
    �3 19.08   ⚲ 19.08   Global Days 090

64835 median motor thenar   A2 T 80 ⬛
    �3 20.71   ⚲ 20.71   Global Days 090

64836 ulnar motor   A2 T 80 ⬛
    �3 20.68   ⚲ 20.68   Global Days 090

+ **64837** Suture of each additional nerve, hand or foot (List separately in addition to code for primary procedure)   A2 T 80 ⬛
    Code first (64834-64836)
    �3 10.08   ⚲ 10.08   Global Days ZZZ

64840 Suture of posterior tibial nerve   A2 T 80 ⬛
    �3 23.34   ⚲ 23.34   Global Days 090

64856 Suture of major peripheral nerve, arm or leg, except sciatic; including transposition   A2 T ⬛
    �3 26.02   ⚲ 26.02   Global Days 090

64857 without transposition   A2 T 80 ⬛
    �3 27.20   ⚲ 27.20   Global Days 090

64858 Suture of sciatic nerve   A2 T 80 ⬛
    �3 31.63   ⚲ 31.63   Global Days 090

+ **64859** Suture of each additional major peripheral nerve (List separately in addition to code for primary procedure)   A2 T 80 ⬛
    Code first (64856-64857)
    �3 6.84   ⚲ 6.84   Global Days ZZZ

64861 Suture of; brachial plexus   A2 T 80 ⬛
    �3 35.77   ⚲ 35.77   Global Days 090

64862 lumbar plexus   A2 T 80 ⬛
    �3 35.13   ⚲ 35.13   Global Days 090

64864 Suture of facial nerve; extracranial   A2 T 80 ⬛
    �3 22.35   ⚲ 22.35   Global Days 090

64865 infratemporal, with or without grafting   A2 T 80 ⬛
    �3 29.54   ⚲ 29.54   Global Days 090

64866 Anastomosis; facial-spinal accessory   C 80 ⬛
    �3 30.87   ⚲ 30.87   Global Days 090

64868 facial-hypoglossal   C 80 ⬛
    INCLUDES   Korte-Ballance anastomosis
    �3 26.88   ⚲ 26.88   Global Days 090

64870 facial-phrenic   A2 T 80 ⬛
    �3 26.17   ⚲ 26.17   Global Days 090

+ **64872** Suture of nerve; requiring secondary or delayed suture (List separately in addition to code for primary neurorrhaphy)   A2 T 80 ⬛
    Code first (64831-64865)
    �3 3.20   ⚲ 3.20   Global Days ZZZ

+ **64874** requiring extensive mobilization, or transposition of nerve (List separately in addition to code for nerve suture)   A2 T 80 ⬛
    Code first (64831-64865)
    �3 4.70   ⚲ 4.70   Global Days ZZZ

+ **64876** requiring shortening of bone of extremity (List separately in addition to code for nerve suture)   A2 T 80 ⬛
    Code first (64831-64865)
    �3 5.13   ⚲ 5.13   Global Days ZZZ

64885 Nerve graft (includes obtaining graft), head or neck; up to 4 cm in length   A2 T 80 ⬛
    �3 29.10   ⚲ 29.10   Global Days 090
    AMA: 2008, Jan, 10-25; 2007, Jan, 13-27; 2007, Jan, 13-27; 2007, January, 13-27

64886 more than 4 cm length   A2 T 80 ⬛
    �3 34.58   ⚲ 34.58   Global Days 090
    AMA: 2008, Jan, 10-25; 2007, Jan, 13-27; 2007, Jan, 13-27; 2007, January, 13-27

64890 Nerve graft (includes obtaining graft), single strand, hand or foot; up to 4 cm length   A2 T 80 ⬛
    �3 28.03   ⚲ 28.03   Global Days 090

64891 more than 4 cm length   A2 T 80 ⬛
    �3 28.67   ⚲ 28.67   Global Days 090

64892 Nerve graft (includes obtaining graft), single strand, arm or leg; up to 4 cm length   A2 T 80 ⬛
    �3 27.35   ⚲ 27.35   Global Days 090

64893 more than 4 cm length   A2 T 80 ⬛
    �3 28.79   ⚲ 28.79   Global Days 090

64895 Nerve graft (includes obtaining graft), multiple strands (cable), hand or foot; up to 4 cm length   A2 T 80 ⬛
    �3 33.59   ⚲ 33.59   Global Days 090

64896 more than 4 cm length   A2 T 80 ⬛
    �3 37.18   ⚲ 37.18   Global Days 090

64897 Nerve graft (includes obtaining graft), multiple strands (cable), arm or leg; up to 4 cm length   A2 T 80 ⬛
    �3 32.54   ⚲ 32.54   Global Days 090

64898 more than 4 cm length   A2 T 80 ⬛
    �3 35.49   ⚲ 35.49   Global Days 090

+ **64901** Nerve graft, each additional nerve; single strand (List separately in addition to code for primary procedure)   A2 T 80 ⬛
    Code first (64885-64893)
    �3 15.97   ⚲ 15.97   Global Days ZZZ

+ **64902** multiple strands (cable) (List separately in addition to code for primary procedure)   A2 T 80 ⬛
    Code first (64885-64886, 64895-64898)
    �3 18.34   ⚲ 18.34   Global Days ZZZ

64905 Nerve pedicle transfer; first stage   A2 T 80 ⬛
    �3 26.03   ⚲ 26.03   Global Days 090

64907 second stage   A2 T 80 ⬛
    �3 34.38   ⚲ 34.38   Global Days 090

64910-64911 Nerve Repair: Synthetic and Vein Grafts

INCLUDES   operating microscope (69990)

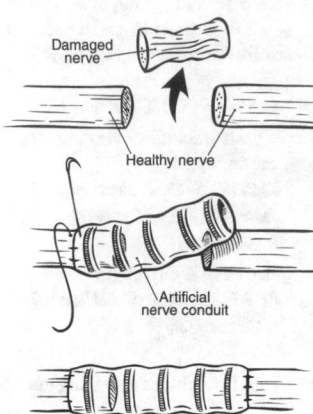

Damaged nerve

Healthy nerve

Artificial nerve conduit

A synthetic "bridge" is affixed to each end of a
severed nerve with sutures
This procedure is performed using an operating
microscope

64910   **Nerve repair; with synthetic conduit or vein allograft (eg, nerve tube), each nerve**   G2 T 80
        🚗 20.99   🔧 20.99   Global Days 090

64911   **with autogenous vein graft (includes harvest of vein graft), each nerve**   T 80
        Do not report with (64910-64911)
        🚗 25.25   🔧 25.25   Global Days 090

64999 Unlisted Procedure of the Nervous System

64999   **Unlisted procedure, nervous system**   T 80
        🚗 0.00   🔧 0.00   Global Days YYY
        AMA: 2008, Jan, 10-25; 2008, Jul, 9; 2008, Sep, 10☐-11; 2007, Jan, 13-27; 2007, Jan, 13-27; 2007, Dec, 7-8; 2007, January, 13-27; 2005, Apr, 13-14; 2005, Apr, 13-14; 2005, Aug, 13-15; 2005, Aug, 13-15; 2005, April, 13-14; 2005, September, 9-11; 2005, August, 13-15; 2005, Sep, 9-11; 2005, Sep, 9-11; 2004, Nov, 11; 2004, November, 11; 2004, Nov, 11

65091-65093 Surgical Removal of Eyeball Contents

CMS *100-2,15,120*   *Prosthetic Devices*
CMS *100-4,12,30*   *Correct Coding Policy*
INCLUDES   operating microscope (69990)

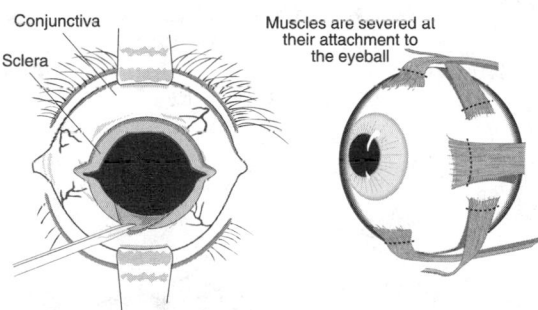

Conjunctiva

Sclera

Muscles are severed at their attachment to the eyeball

Evisceration involves removal of the contents of the eyeball: the vitreous; retina; choroid; lens; iris; and ciliary muscle. Only the scleral shell remains. A temporary or permanent implant is usually inserted

Enucleation involves severing the extraorbital muscles and optic nerve with removal of the eyeball. An implant is usually inserted and, if permanent, may involve attachment to the severed extraorbital muscles

65091   Evisceration of ocular contents; without implant   A2 T 80 50 ▭
    🗠 14.71   ⬧ 14.71   Global Days 090

65093   with implant   A2 I 50 ▭
    🗠 14.69   ⬧ 14.69   Global Days 090

65101-65105 Surgical Removal of Eyeball

CMS *100-2,15,120*   *Prosthetic Devices*
CMS *100-4,12,30*   *Correct Coding Policy*
INCLUDES   operating microscope (69990)
EXCLUDES   *conjunctivoplasty following enucleation (68320-68340)*

65101   Enucleation of eye; without implant   A2 T 50 ▭
    🗠 16.95   ⬧ 16.95   Global Days 090

65103   with implant, muscles not attached to implant   A2 T 50 ▭
    🗠 17.70   ⬧ 17.70   Global Days 090

65105   with implant, muscles attached to implant   A2 T 80 50 ▭
    🗠 19.53   ⬧ 19.53   Global Days 090

65110-65114 Surgical Removal of Orbital Contents

CMS *100-2,15,120*   *Prosthetic Devices*
CMS *100-4,12,30*   *Correct Coding Policy*
INCLUDES   operating microscope (69990)
EXCLUDES   *free full thickness graft (15260-15261)*
repair more extensive than skin (67930-67975)
skin graft (15120-15121)

65110   Exenteration of orbit (does not include skin graft), removal of orbital contents; only   A2 T 80 50 ▭
    🗠 28.52   ⬧ 28.52   Global Days 090

65112   with therapeutic removal of bone   A2 T 80 50 ▭
    🗠 33.70   ⬧ 33.70   Global Days 090

65114   with muscle or myocutaneous flap   A2 T 80 50 ▭
    🗠 34.92   ⬧ 34.92   Global Days 090

65125-65175 Implant Procedures: Insertion, Removal, and Revision

CMS *100-2,15,120*   *Prosthetic Devices*
CMS *100-4,12,30*   *Correct Coding Policy*
INCLUDES   operating microscope (69990)
EXCLUDES   *orbit implant insertion outside muscle cone (67550)*
orbital implant removal or revision outside muscle cone (67560)

65125   Modification of ocular implant with placement or replacement of pegs (eg, drilling receptacle for prosthesis appendage) (separate procedure)   G2 T 50 ▭
    🗠 6.69   ⬧ 10.57   Global Days 090

65130   Insertion of ocular implant secondary; after evisceration, in scleral shell   A2 T 50 ▭
    🗠 16.77   ⬧ 16.77   Global Days 090

65135   after enucleation, muscles not attached to implant   A2 T 50 ▭
    🗠 17.08   ⬧ 17.08   Global Days 090

65140   after enucleation, muscles attached to implant   A2 T 50 ▭
    🗠 18.61   ⬧ 18.61   Global Days 090

65150   Reinsertion of ocular implant; with or without conjunctival graft   A2 T 80 50 ▭
    🗠 13.50   ⬧ 13.50   Global Days 090

65155   with use of foreign material for reinforcement and/or attachment of muscles to implant   A2 T 50 ▭
    🗠 19.66   ⬧ 19.66   Global Days 090

65175   Removal of ocular implant   A2 T 50 ▭
    🗠 15.11   ⬧ 15.11   Global Days 090

65205-65265 Foreign Body Removal By Area of Eye

CMS *100-4,12,30*   *Correct Coding Policy*
INCLUDES   operating microscope (69990)
EXCLUDES   *removal:*
anterior segment implant (65920)
orbital implant outside muscle cone (67560)
posterior segment implant (67120)
removal of foreign body:
eyelid (67938)
frontal approach (67413)
lacrimal system (68530)
lateral approach (67430)
transcranial approach (61334)

65205   Removal of foreign body, external eye; conjunctival superficial   P3 S 50 ▭
    🞧 *70030, 76529*
    🗠 1.06   ⬧ 1.33   Global Days 000
    AMA: 2008, Jan, 10-25; 2007, Jan, 13-27; 2007, Jan, 13-27; 2007, January, 13-27; 2005, Mar, 16-17; 2005, March, 16-17; 2005, Mar, 16-17

65210   conjunctival embedded (includes concretions), subconjunctival, or scleral nonperforating   P3 S 50 ▭
    🞧 *70030, 76529*
    🗠 1.28   ⬧ 1.63   Global Days 000

65220   corneal, without slit lamp   G2 S 50 ▭
    EXCLUDES   *repair of corneal wound with foreign body (65275)*
    🞧 *70030, 76529*
    🗠 1.05   ⬧ 1.37   Global Days 000
    AMA: 2004, May, 9; 2004, May, 9; 2004, May, 9

65222 corneal, with slit lamp P3 S 50

EXCLUDES *repair of corneal wound with foreign body (65275)*

🔲 70030, 76529

⚙ **1.40** ⚕ **1.79 Global Days 000**

AMA: 2004, May, 9; 2004, May, 9; 2004, May, 9

65235 Removal of foreign body, intraocular; from anterior chamber of eye or lens A2 T 80 50 ▭

🔲 70030, 76529

⚙ **16.11** ⚕ **16.11 Global Days 090**

65260 from posterior segment, magnetic extraction, anterior or posterior route A2 T 80 50 ▭

🔲 70030, 76529

⚙ **22.11** ⚕ **22.11 Global Days 090**

65265 from posterior segment, nonmagnetic extraction A2 T 80 50 ▭

🔲 70030, 76529

⚙ **24.88** ⚕ **24.88 Global Days 090**

65270-65290 Laceration Repair External Eye

CMS *100-4,12,30*   *Correct Coding Policy*

INCLUDES conjunctival flap

operating microscope (69990)

restoration of anterior chamber with air or saline injection

EXCLUDES *repair:*

ciliary body or iris (66680)

eyelid laceration (12011-12018, 12051-12057, 13150-13160, 67930, 67935)

lacrimal system injury (68700)

surgical wound (66250)

treatment of orbit fracture (21385-21408)

65270 Repair of laceration; conjunctiva, with or without nonperforating laceration sclera, direct closure A2 T 80 50 ▭

⚙ **3.29** ⚕ **6.19 Global Days 010**

AMA: 2004, May, 9; 2004, May, 9; 2004, May, 9

65272 conjunctiva, by mobilization and rearrangement, without hospitalization A2 T 50 ▭

⚙ **7.99** ⚕ **11.42 Global Days 090**

AMA: 2004, May, 9; 2004, May, 9; 2004, May, 9

65273 conjunctiva, by mobilization and rearrangement, with hospitalization C 50 ▭

⚙ **8.78** ⚕ **8.78 Global Days 090**

AMA: 2004, May, 9; 2004, May, 9; 2004, May, 9

65275 cornea, nonperforating, with or without removal foreign body A2 T 80 50 ▭

⚙ **10.44** ⚕ **12.81 Global Days 090**

AMA: 2004, May, 9; 2004, May, 9; 2004, May, 9

65280 cornea and/or sclera, perforating, not involving uveal tissue A2 T 80 50 ▭

⚙ **15.40** ⚕ **15.40 Global Days 090**

AMA: 2004, May, 9; 2004, May, 9; 2004, May, 9

65285 cornea and/or sclera, perforating, with reposition or resection of uveal tissue A2 T 50 ▭

⚙ **24.03** ⚕ **24.03 Global Days 090**

AMA: 2004, May, 9; 2004, May, 9; 2004, May, 9

65286 application of tissue glue, wounds of cornea and/or sclera P2 T 50 ▭

⚙ **11.32** ⚕ **16.16 Global Days 090**

AMA: 2004, May, 9; 2004, May, 9; 2004, May, 9

65290 Repair of wound, extraocular muscle, tendon and/or Tenon's capsule A2 T 50 ▭

⚙ **11.32** ⚕ **11.32 Global Days 090**

AMA: 2004, May, 9; 2004, May, 9; 2004, May, 9

65400-65600 Removal Corneal Lesions

CMS *100-4,12,30*   *Correct Coding Policy*

INCLUDES operating microscope (69990)

65400 Excision of lesion, cornea (keratectomy, lamellar, partial), except pterygium A2 T 50 ▭

⚙ **13.65** ⚕ **15.38 Global Days 090**

AMA: 2004, May, 9; 2004, May, 9; 2004, May, 9

65410 Biopsy of cornea A2 T 80 50 ▭

⚙ **2.46** ⚕ **3.35 Global Days 000**

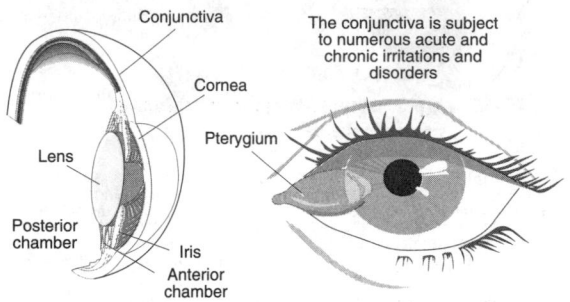

Conjunctiva

The conjunctiva is subject to numerous acute and chronic irritations and disorders

Cornea

Lens

Pterygium

Posterior chamber

Iris

Anterior chamber

Keratitis is an often painful inflammation of the cornea, the clear membrane covering the anterior segment of the eye

A pterygium is a wedge of excess tissue extending from the medial canthus toward the cornea

65420 Excision or transposition of pterygium; without graft A2 T 50 ▭

⚙ **8.62** ⚕ **11.87 Global Days 090**

AMA: 2007, Dec, 10-179

65426 with graft A2 T 50 ▭

⚙ **10.97** ⚕ **14.96 Global Days 090**

65430 Scraping of cornea, diagnostic, for smear and/or culture P2 S 50 ▭

⚙ **2.46** ⚕ **2.71 Global Days 000**

AMA: 2004, May, 9; 2004, May, 9; 2004, May, 9

65435 Removal of corneal epithelium; with or without chemocauterization (abrasion, curettage) P3 T 50 ▭

⚙ **1.64** ⚕ **1.87 Global Days 000**

AMA: 2004, May, 9; 2004, May, 9; 2004, May, 9

65436 with application of chelating agent (eg, EDTA) P3 T 50 ▭

⚙ **8.53** ⚕ **8.88 Global Days 090**

AMA: 2004, May, 9; 2004, May, 9; 2004, May, 9

65450 Destruction of lesion of cornea by cryotherapy, photocoagulation or thermocauterization G2 S 50 ▭

⚙ **7.26** ⚕ **7.35 Global Days 090**

AMA: 2004, May, 9; 2004, May, 9; 2004, May, 9

65600 Multiple punctures of anterior cornea (eg, for corneal erosion, tattoo) P3 T 50 ▭

⚙ **7.72** ⚕ **8.90 Global Days 090**

65710-65757 Corneal Transplants

CMS *100-3,80.7*   *Refractive Keratoplasty*
CMS *100-4,12,30*   *Correct Coding Policy*
INCLUDES   operating microscope (69990)
EXCLUDES   *processing, preserving and transporting corneal tissue (V2785)*

Do not report with (92025)

▲ **65710**   **Keratoplasty (corneal transplant); anterior lamellar**   A2 T 80 50 ▣
    INCLUDES   use and preparation of fresh or preserved graft
    EXCLUDES   *refractive keratoplasty surgery (65760, 65765, 65767)*
    📖 25.44   🔧 25.44   Global Days 090

▲ **65730**   **penetrating (except in aphakia or pseudophakia)**   A2 T 80 50 ▣
    INCLUDES   use and preparation of fresh or preserved graft
    EXCLUDES   *refractive keratoplasty surgery (65760, 65765, 65767)*
    📖 28.30   🔧 28.30   Global Days 090
    AMA: 2006, Feb, 1-6; 2006, Feb, 1-6; 2006, February, 1-6

65750   **penetrating (in aphakia)**   A2 T 80 50 ▣
    INCLUDES   use and preparation of fresh or preserved graft
    EXCLUDES   *refractive keratoplasty surgery (65760, 65765, 65767)*
    📖 28.70   🔧 28.70   Global Days 090

65755   **penetrating (in pseudophakia)**   A2 T 80 50 ▣
    INCLUDES   use and preparation of fresh or preserved graft
    EXCLUDES   *refractive keratoplasty surgery (65760, 65765, 65767)*
    📖 28.53   🔧 28.53   Global Days 090

● **65756**   **endothelial**   67 T 80 50
    Code also if appropriate (65757)
    📖 27.48   🔧 27.48   Global Days 090

+ ● **65757**   **Backbench preparation of corneal endothelial allograft prior to transplantation (List separately in addition to code for primary procedure)**   N 80
    Code first (65756)
    📖 0.00   🔧 0.00   Global Days ZZZ

65760-65775 Corneal Refractive Procedures

CMS *100-3,80.7*   *Refractive Keratoplasty*
INCLUDES   operating microscope (69990)

65760   **Keratomileusis**   E
    Do not report with (92025)
    📖 0.00   🔧 0.00   Global Days XXX

65765   **Keratophakia**   E
    Do not report with (92025)
    📖 0.00   🔧 0.00   Global Days XXX

65767   **Epikeratoplasty**   E
    Do not report with (92025)
    📖 0.00   🔧 0.00   Global Days XXX

65770   **Keratoprosthesis**   H8 T 80 50 ▣
    Code also (C1818, L8609)
    Do not report with (92025)
    📖 32.81   🔧 32.81   Global Days 090

65771   **Radial keratotomy**   E
    Do not report with (92025)
    📖 0.00   🔧 0.00   Global Days XXX

65772   **Corneal relaxing incision for correction of surgically induced astigmatism**   A2 T 50
    📖 9.25   🔧 10.29   Global Days 090

65775   **Corneal wedge resection for correction of surgically induced astigmatism**   A2 T 50
    EXCLUDES   *fitting of contact lens to treat disease (92070)*
    📖 12.64   🔧 12.64   Global Days 090

65780-65782 Corneal Surface Reconstruction

CMS *100-4,4,200.4*   *Billing for Amniotic Membrane*
CMS *100-4,12,30*   *Correct Coding Policy*
INCLUDES   operating microscope (69990)
EXCLUDES   *obtaining conjunctival allograft from a live donor (68371)*

65780   **Ocular surface reconstruction; amniotic membrane transplantation**   A2 T 50
    📖 20.36   🔧 20.36   Global Days 090
    AMA: 2008, Jan, 10-25; 2007, Jan, 13-27; 2007, Jan, 13-27; 2007, January, 13-27; 2004, May, 9; 2004, May, 9; 2004, May, 9

65781   **limbal stem cell allograft (eg, cadaveric or living donor)**   A2 T 80 50 ▣
    📖 30.82   🔧 30.82   Global Days 090
    AMA: 2004, May, 9; 2004, May, 9; 2004, May, 9

65782   **limbal conjunctival autograft (includes obtaining graft)**   A2 T 50 ▣
    📖 26.61   🔧 26.61   Global Days 090
    AMA: 2008, Jan, 10-25; 2007, Jan, 13-27; 2007, Jan, 13-27; 2007, January, 13-27; 2005, Feb, 13-16; 2005, February, 13-16; 2005, Feb, 13-16; 2004, May, 9; 2004, May, 9; 2004, February, 11; 2004, May, 9; 2004, Feb, 11; 2004, Feb, 11

65800-66030 Anterior Chamber Procedures

INCLUDES   operating microscope (69990)

65800   **Paracentesis of anterior chamber of eye (separate procedure); with diagnostic aspiration of aqueous**   A2 T 50 ▣
    📖 3.11   🔧 3.54   Global Days 000
    AMA: 2004, May, 9; 2004, May, 9; 2004, May, 9

65805   **with therapeutic release of aqueous**   A2 T 50 ▣
    📖 3.11   🔧 3.86   Global Days 000
    AMA: 2004, May, 9; 2004, May, 9; 2004, May, 9

65810   **with removal of vitreous and/or discission of anterior hyaloid membrane, with or without air injection**   A2 T 50 ▣
    📖 10.72   🔧 10.72   Global Days 090

65815   **with removal of blood, with or without irrigation and/or air injection**   A2 T 50 ▣
    EXCLUDES   *injection only (66020-66030)*
        removal of blood clot only (65930)
    📖 10.87   🔧 14.64   Global Days 090

65820   **Goniotomy**   A2 T 80 50 ⊙ ▣
    INCLUDES   Barkan's operation
    Code also ophthalmic endoscope if used (66990)
    📖 17.27   🔧 17.27   Global Days 090
    AMA: 2005, Sep, 5; 2005, Sep, 5; 2005, September, 5

65850   **Trabeculotomy ab externo**   A2 T 50 ▣
    📖 19.64   🔧 19.64   Global Days 090

● New Code   ▲ Revised Code   Maternity Edit   Age Edit   A-Y OPPS Status Indicator   📖 Facility RVU   🔧 Non-Facility RVU
▣ CCI Comprehensive Code   50 Bilateral Procedure   + Add-on Indicator   Laboratory crosswalk   Radiology crosswalk

65855 Trabeculoplasty by laser surgery, 1 or more sessions (defined treatment series) `P3` `T` `50` `▣`

    EXCLUDES   *re-treatment after several months for more extensive disease*
               trabeculectomy ab externo (66170)

    ✋ 6.93   ✂ 7.87 Global Days 010
    AMA: 2008, Jan, 10-25; 2007, Jan, 13-27; 2007, Jan, 13-27; 2007, January, 13-27

65860 Severing adhesions of anterior segment, laser technique (separate procedure) `P3` `T` `80` `50` `▣`
    ✋ 6.01   ✂ 7.27 Global Days 090

65865 Severing adhesions of anterior segment of eye, incisional technique (with or without injection of air or liquid) (separate procedure); goniosynechiae `A2` `50` `▣`

    EXCLUDES   *laser trabeculectomy (65855)*

    ✋ 10.99 ✂ 10.99 Global Days 090

65870 anterior synechiae, except goniosynechiae `A2` `50` `▣`
    ✋ 13.56 ✂ 13.56 Global Days 090

65875 posterior synechiae `A2` `50` `▣`
    Code also ophthalmic endoscope if used (66990)
    ✋ 14.40 ✂ 14.40 Global Days 090
    AMA: 2005, Sep, 5; 2005, Sep, 5; 2005, September, 5

65880 corneovitreal adhesions `A2` `50` `▣`
    ✋ 15.18 ✂ 15.18 Global Days 090

65900 Removal of epithelial downgrowth, anterior chamber of eye `A2` `T` `80` `50` `▣`
    ✋ 22.28 ✂ 22.28 Global Days 090

65920 Removal of implanted material, anterior segment of eye `A2` `T` `50` `▣`
    Code also ophthalmic endoscope if used (66990)
    ✋ 18.02 ✂ 18.02 Global Days 090
    AMA: 2005, Sep, 5; 2005, Sep, 5; 2005, September, 5

65930 Removal of blood clot, anterior segment of eye `A2` `T` `50` `▣`
    ✋ 14.84 ✂ 14.84 Global Days 090

66020 Injection, anterior chamber of eye (separate procedure); air or liquid `A2` `T` `50` `▣`
    ✋ 3.04   ✂ 4.31 Global Days 010

66030 medication `A2` `T` `50` `▣`
    ✋ 2.54   ✂ 3.81 Global Days 010

66130-66250 Scleral Procedures

CMS *100-4,12,30*   *Correct Coding Policy*
`INCLUDES` operating microscope (69990)

`EXCLUDES` *intraocular foreign body removal (65235)*
    scleral procedures with retinal procedures (67101-67228)
    surgery on posterior sclera (67250, 67255)

66130 Excision of lesion, sclera `A2` `T` `80` `50` `▣`
    ✋ 13.37 ✂ 16.33 Global Days 090

66150 Fistulization of sclera for glaucoma; trephination with iridectomy `A2` `T` `50` `▣`
    ✋ 19.83 ✂ 19.83 Global Days 090

66155 thermocauterization with iridectomy `A2` `T` `50` `▣`
    ✋ 19.75 ✂ 19.75 Global Days 090

66160 sclerectomy with punch or scissors, with iridectomy `A2` `T` `50` `▣`
    `INCLUDES` Knapp's operation
    ✋ 22.48 ✂ 22.48 Global Days 090

In 66165, the wick creates a permanent drainage route for the anterior chamber

66165 iridencleisis or iridotasis `A2` `T` `80` `50` `▣`
    ✋ 19.35 ✂ 19.35 Global Days 090

66170 trabeculectomy ab externo in absence of previous surgery `A2` `T` `80` `50` `▣`
    EXCLUDES   *dilation of Schlemm's canal (0176T-0177T)*
               repair of surgical wound (66250)
               trabeculectomy ab externo (65850)
    ✋ 27.22 ✂ 27.22 Global Days 090

66172 trabeculectomy ab externo with scarring from previous ocular surgery or trauma (includes injection of antifibrotic agents) `A2` `T` `80` `50` `▣`
    EXCLUDES   *fistulation of transciliary body sclera (0123T)*
    ✋ 34.20 ✂ 34.20 Global Days 090

66180 Aqueous shunt to extraocular reservoir (eg, Molteno, Schocket, Denver-Krupin) `A2` `T` `80` `50` `▣`
    `INCLUDES` Schocket implant
    ✋ 27.09 ✂ 27.09 Global Days 090

66185 Revision of aqueous shunt to extraocular reservoir `A2` `T` `80` `50` `▣`
    EXCLUDES   *implanted shunt removal (67120)*
    ✋ 17.10 ✂ 17.10 Global Days 090

66220 Repair of scleral staphyloma; without graft `A2` `T` `80` `50` `▣`
    ✋ 16.71 ✂ 16.71 Global Days 090

66225 with graft `A2` `T` `50` `▣`
    EXCLUDES   *scleral reinforcement (67250, 67255)*
    ✋ 21.50 ✂ 21.50 Global Days 090

66250 Revision or repair of operative wound of anterior segment, any type, early or late, major or minor procedure `A2` `T` `50` `▣`
    ✋ 12.69 ✂ 17.20 Global Days 090

66500-66505 Iridotomy With/Without Transfixion

CMS *100-4,12,30*   *Correct Coding Policy*
`INCLUDES` operating microscope (69990)

`EXCLUDES` *photocoagulation iridotomy (66761)*

66500 Iridotomy by stab incision (separate procedure); except transfixion `A2` `T` `50` `▣`
    ✋ 8.12   ✂ 8.12 Global Days 090

66505 with transfixion as for iris bombe `A2` `T` `50` `▣`
    ✋ 8.89   ✂ 8.89 Global Days 090

`26`/`TC` Professional/Technical Component Only   `80`/`80` Assist-at-Surgery Allowed/With Documentation   Unlisted   Not Covered

AMA: CPT Assistant References   `A2`-`Z3` ASC Payment Indicator ♂ Male Only ♀ Female Only ⊘ Modifier 51 Exempt `P0` PQRI

258   CPT only © 2008 American Medical Association. All Rights Reserved. (Black Ink)   Medicare (Red Ink)   © 2008 Ingenix *(Blue Ink)*

66600-66635 Iridectomy Procedures

CMS *100-4,12,30*   *Correct Coding Policy*
INCLUDES   operating microscope (69990)
EXCLUDES   *photocoagulation coreoplasty (66762)*

66600   Iridectomy, with corneoscleral or corneal section; for removal of lesion   A2 T 50 ☐
   📇 18.81   ⚕ 18.81   Global Days 090

66605   with cyclectomy   A2 T 50 ☐
   📇 24.50   ⚕ 24.50   Global Days 090

66625   peripheral for glaucoma (separate procedure)   A2 T 50 ☐
   📇 9.90   ⚕ 9.90   Global Days 090

66630   sector for glaucoma (separate procedure)   A2 T 50 ☐
   📇 13.01   ⚕ 13.01   Global Days 090

66635   optical (separate procedure)   A2 T 50 ☐
   📇 13.14   ⚕ 13.14   Global Days 090

66680-66770 Other Procedures of the Uveal Tract

CMS *100-4,12,30*   *Correct Coding Policy*
INCLUDES   operating microscope (69990)

66680   Repair of iris, ciliary body (as for iridodialysis)   A2 T 50 ☐
   📇 11.76   ⚕ 11.76   Global Days 090

66682   Suture of iris, ciliary body (separate procedure) with retrieval of suture through small incision (eg, McCannel suture)   A2 T 50 ☐
   📇 14.30   ⚕ 14.30   Global Days 090

66700   Ciliary body destruction; diathermy   A2 T 80 50 ☐
   INCLUDES   Heine's operation
   📇 9.10   ⚕ 10.32   Global Days 090

66710   cyclophotocoagulation, transscleral   A2 T 50 ☐
   📇 9.07   ⚕ 10.14   Global Days 090
   AMA: 2008, Jan, 10-25; 2007, Jan, 13-27; 2007, Jan, 13-27; 2007, January, 13-27; 2005, Mar, 16-17; 2005, Mar, 16-17; 2005, September, 5, 2005, March, 16-17; 2005, Sep; 2005, Sep, 5

66711   cyclophotocoagulation, endoscopic   A2 T 50 ☐
   INCLUDES   operating microscope (66990)
   📇 14.52   ⚕ 14.52   Global Days 090
   AMA: 2008, Jan, 10-25; 2007, Jan, 13-27; 2007, Jan, 13-27; 2007, January, 13-27; 2005, Mar, 16-17; 2005, Mar, 16-17; 2005, September, 5; 2005, March, 16-17; 2005, Sep, 5; 2005, Sep, 5

⊙ **66720**   cryotherapy   A2 T 50 ☐
   📇 9.61   ⚕ 10.65   Global Days 090
   AMA: 2006, Apr, 11-18; 2006, Apr, 11-18; 2006, April, 11-18

66740   cyclodialysis   A2 T 50 ☐
   📇 9.11   ⚕ 10.07   Global Days 090

66761   Iridotomy/iridectomy by laser surgery (eg, for glaucoma) (1 or more sessions)   P3 T 50 ☐
   📇 9.40   ⚕ 10.33   Global Days 090

66762   Iridoplasty by photocoagulation (1 or more sessions) (eg, for improvement of vision, for widening of anterior chamber angle)   P3 T 50 ☐
   📇 9.72   ⚕ 10.83   Global Days 090

66770   Destruction of cyst or lesion iris or ciliary body (nonexcisional procedure)   P2 T 50 ☐
   EXCLUDES   Excision:
      epithelial downgrowth (65900)
      iris, ciliary body lesion (66600-66605)
   📇 11.02   ⚕ 12.03   Global Days 090

66820-66825 Post-Cataract Surgery Procedures
INCLUDES   operating microscope (69990)

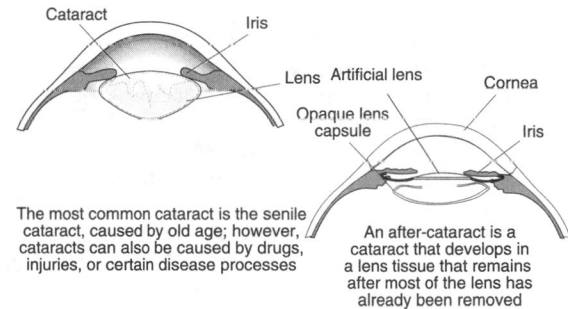

A cataract is a milky opacity on the normally clear lens of the eye; it obscures vision

Cataract — Iris — Lens — Artificial lens — Cornea — Opaque lens capsule — Iris

The most common cataract is the senile cataract, caused by old age; however, cataracts can also be caused by drugs, injuries, or certain disease processes

An after-cataract is a cataract that develops in a lens tissue that remains after most of the lens has already been removed

66820   Discission of secondary membranous cataract (opacified posterior lens capsule and/or anterior hyaloid); stab incision technique (Ziegler or Wheeler knife)   G2 T 50 ☐
   📇 9.12   ⚕ 9.12   Global Days 090

66821   laser surgery (eg, YAG laser) (1 or more stages)   A2 T 50 ☐
   📇 6.97   ⚕ 7.39   Global Days 090

66825   Repositioning of intraocular lens prosthesis, requiring an incision (separate procedure)   A2 T 80 50 ☐
   📇 17.51   ⚕ 17.51   Global Days 090

66830-66940 Cataract Extraction; Without Insertion Intraocular Lens

CMS *100-3,80.11*   *Vitrectomy*
CMS *100-3,80.10*   *Phacoemulsification Procedure--Cataract Extraction*
CMS *100-4,12,30*   *Correct Coding Policy*
INCLUDES   anterior and/or posterior capsulotomy
   enzymatic zonulysis
   iridectomy/iridotomy
   lateral canthotomy
   medications
   operating microscope (69990)
   subconjunctival injection
   subtenon injection
   use of viscoelastic material
EXCLUDES   *removal of intralenticular foreign body without lens excision (65235)*
   repair of surgical laceration (66250)

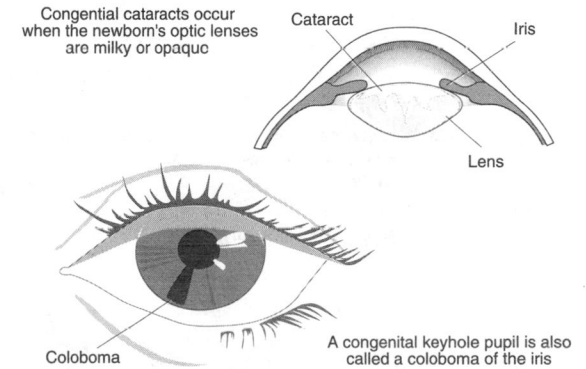

Congenital cataracts occur when the newborn's optic lenses are milky or opaque

Cataract — Iris — Lens

Coloboma — A congenital keyhole pupil is also called a coloboma of the iris

---

Eye and Ocular Adnexa

66830 — 67015

66830   Removal of secondary membranous cataract (opacified posterior lens capsule and/or anterior hyaloid) with corneo-scleral section, with or without iridectomy (iridocapsulotomy, iridocapsulectomy)   A2 T 50 ☐

     INCLUDES   Graefe's operation

     16.37   16.37   Global Days 090

66840   Removal of lens material; aspiration technique, 1 or more stages   A2 T 50 ☐ P0

     INCLUDES   Fukala's operation

     15.97   15.97   Global Days 090

66850   phacofragmentation technique (mechanical or ultrasonic) (eg, phacoemulsification), with aspiration   A2 T 50 ☐ P0

     18.23   18.23   Global Days 090

66852   pars plana approach, with or without vitrectomy   A2 T 80 50 ☐ P0

     19.51   19.51   Global Days 090

66920   intracapsular   A2 T 80 50 ☐ P0

     17.41   17.41   Global Days 090

66930   intracapsular, for dislocated lens   A2 T 80 50 ☐ P0

     19.78   19.78   Global Days 090

66940   extracapsular (other than 66840, 66850, 66852)   A2 T 80 50 ☐ P0

     17.96   17.96   Global Days 090

66982-66986 Cataract Extraction: With Insertion Intraocular Lens

CMS 100-3,80.12   *Intraocular Lenses (IOLs)*
CMS 100-3,80.10   *Phacoemulsification Procedure--Cataract Extraction*
CMS 100-4,12,30   *Correct Coding Policy*

INCLUDES   anterior or posterior capsulotomy
     enzymatic zonulysis
     iridectomy/iridotomy
     lateral canthotomy
     medications
     operating microscope (69990)
     subconjunctival injection
     subtenon injection
     use of viscoelastic material

EXCLUDES   *intraocular lens (99070, C1780, Q1003-Q1005, V2630-V2632, V2788)*

66982   Extracapsular cataract removal with insertion of intraocular lens prosthesis (one stage procedure), manual or mechanical technique (eg, irrigation and aspiration or phacoemulsification), complex, requiring devices or techniques not generally used in routine cataract surgery (eg, iris expansion device, suture support for intraocular lens, or primary posterior capsulorrhexis) or performed on patients in the amblyogenic developmental stage   A2 T 50 ☐ P0

     ☒ 76519

     24.72   24.72   Global Days 090

     AMA: 2008, Jan, 10-25; 2007, Jan, 13-27; 2007, Jan, 13-27; 2007, January, 13-27

66983   Intracapsular cataract extraction with insertion of intraocular lens prosthesis (1 stage procedure)   A2 T 50 ☐ P0

     ☒ 76519

     16.95   16.95   Global Days 090

66984   Extracapsular cataract removal with insertion of intraocular lens prosthesis (1 stage procedure), manual or mechanical technique (eg, irrigation and aspiration or phacoemulsification)   A2 T 50 ☐ P0

     EXCLUDES   *complex extracapsular cataract removal (66982)*

     ☒ 76519

     17.71   17.71   Global Days 090

     AMA: 2005, Mar, 11-15; 2005, Mar, 11-15; 2005, March, 11-15

66985   Insertion of intraocular lens prosthesis (secondary implant), not associated with concurrent cataract removal   A2 T 50 ☐

     EXCLUDES   *insertion of lens at the time of cataract procedure (66982-66984)*
                      secondary suture (66682)

     Code also ophthalmic endoscope if used (66990)

     ☒ 76519

     17.52   17.52   Global Days 090

     AMA: 2005, Sep, 5; 2005, Sep, 5; 2005, September, 5

66986   Exchange of intraocular lens   A2 T 50 ☐

     Code also ophthalmic endoscope if used (66990)

     ☒ 76519

     21.49   21.49   Global Days 090

     AMA: 2005, Sep, 5; 2005, Sep, 5; 2005, September, 5

66990 Ophthalmic Endoscopy

CMS 100-3,80.11   *Vitrectomy*
CMS 100-3,80.10   *Phacoemulsification Procedure--Cataract Extraction*
CMS 100-4,12,30   *Correct Coding Policy*

+   **66990**   Use of ophthalmic endoscope (List separately in addition to code for primary procedure)   N1 N ☐

     Code first (65820, 65875, 65920, 66985-66986, 67036-67043, 67112)

     2.20   2.20   Global Days ZZZ

     AMA: 2008, Jan, 10-25; 2008, Oct, 1-5; 2007, Jan, 13-27; 2007, Jan, 13-27; 2007, January, 13-27; 2005, Sep, 5; 2005, September, 5; 2005, Sep, 5

66999 Unlisted Anterior Segment Procedures

66999   Unlisted procedure, anterior segment of eye   T 80 50

     0.00   0.00   Global Days YYY

     AMA: 2004, May, 9; 2004, May, 9; 2004, May, 9

67005-67015 Vitrectomy: Partial and Subtotal

CMS 100-3,80.11   *Vitrectomy*
CMS 100-4,12,30   *Correct Coding Policy*

INCLUDES   operating microscope (69990)

67005   Removal of vitreous, anterior approach (open sky technique or limbal incision); partial removal   A2 T 50 ☐

     EXCLUDES   *anterior chamber vitrectomy by paracentesis (65810)*
                      severing of corneovitreal adhesions (65880)

     10.83   10.83   Global Days 090

67010   subtotal removal with mechanical vitrectomy   A2 T 50 ☐

     EXCLUDES   *anterior chamber vitrectomy by paracentesis (65810)*
                      severing of corneovitreal adhesions (65880)

     12.54   12.54   Global Days 090

67015   Aspiration or release of vitreous, subretinal or choroidal fluid, pars plana approach (posterior sclerotomy)   A2 T 50 ☐

     13.38   13.38   Global Days 090

67025-67028 Intravitreal Injection/Implantation

CMS *100-3,80.11*   *Vitrectomy*
CMS *100-4,12,30*   *Correct Coding Policy*
[INCLUDES]   operating microscope (69990)

67025   Injection of vitreous substitute, pars plana or limbal approach (fluid-gas exchange), with or without aspiration (separate procedure)   [A2] [T] [50] [□]
    🔧 14.42   ⚬ 16.62   **Global Days 090**

67027   Implantation of intravitreal drug delivery system (eg, ganciclovir implant), includes concomitant removal of vitreous   [A2] [T] [80] [50] [□]
    EXCLUDES   *removal of drug delivery system (67121)*
    🔧 19.77   ⚬ 19.77   **Global Days 090**
    AMA: 2007, Dec, 10-179

67028   Intravitreal injection of a pharmacologic agent (separate procedure)   [P3] [T] [50] [□]
    🔧 4.00   ⚬ 4.99   **Global Days 000**

67030-67031 Incision of Vitreous Strands/Membranes

CMS *100-4,12,30*   *Correct Coding Policy*
[INCLUDES]   operating microscope (69990)

67030   Discission of vitreous strands (without removal), pars plana approach   [A2] [T] [50] [□]
    🔧 11.94   ⚬ 11.94   **Global Days 090**

67031   Severing of vitreous strands, vitreous face adhesions, sheets, membranes or opacities, laser surgery (1 or more stages)   [A2] [T] [50] [□]
    🔧 8.10   ⚬ 8.83   **Global Days 090**

67036-67043 Pars Plana Mechanical Vitrectomy

CMS   *Vitrectomy*
CMS *100-4,12,30*   *Correct Coding Policy*
[INCLUDES]   operating microscope (69990)
EXCLUDES   *foreign body removal (65260, 65265)*
    lens removal (66850)
    vitrectomy in retinal detachment (67108, 67113)

Code also ophthalmic endoscope if used (66990)

67036   Vitrectomy, mechanical, pars plana approach;   [A2] [T] [80] [50] [□]
    Code also placement of intraocular radiation source applicator (0190T)
    🔧 22.32   ⚬ 22.32   **Global Days 090**
    AMA: 2008, Jan, 6 7; 2008, Oct, 1 5

67039   with focal endolaser photocoagulation   [A2] [T] [80] [50] [□]
    🔧 28.58   ⚬ 28.58   **Global Days 090**
    AMA: 2008, Jan, 10-25; 2008, Oct, 1-5; 2007, Jan, 13-27; 2007, Jan, 13-27; 2007, January, 13-27; 2005, Sep, 5; 2005, Sep, 5; 2005, September, 5; 2004, Jun, 10; 2004, Jun, 10; 2004, June, 10

67040   with endolaser panretinal photocoagulation   [A2] [T] [80] [50] [□]
    🔧 32.98   ⚬ 32.98   **Global Days 090**
    AMA: 2008, Jan, 10-25; 2008, Oct, 1-5; 2007, Jul, 12-13; 2005, Sep, 5; 2005, Sep, 5; 2005, September, 5

67041   with removal of preretinal cellular membrane (eg, macular pucker)   [62] [T] [80] [50]
    🔧 30.85   ⚬ 30.85   **Global Days 090**
    AMA: 2008, Oct, 1-5

67042   with removal of internal limiting membrane of retina (eg, for repair of macular hole, diabetic macular edema), includes, if performed, intraocular tamponade (ie, air, gas or silicone oil)   [62] [T] [80] [50]
    🔧 35.34   ⚬ 35.34   **Global Days 090**
    AMA: 2008, Oct, 1-5

67043   with removal of subretinal membrane (eg, choroidal neovascularization), includes, if performed, intraocular tamponade (ie, air, gas or silicone oil) and laser photocoagulation   [62] [T] [80] [50]
    🔧 37.08   ⚬ 37.08   **Global Days 090**
    AMA: 2008, Oct, 1-5

67101-67115 Detached Retina Repair

CMS *100-4,12,30*   *Correct Coding Policy*
[INCLUDES]   operating microscope (69990)

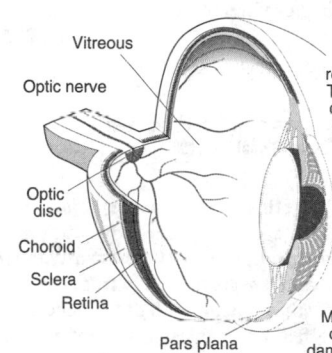

Vitreous   Optic nerve   Optic disc   Choroid   Sclera   Retina   Pars plana   Posterior chamber

The choroid is the vascular layer of the posterior chamber. It provides nourishment to the retina, to which it is firmly attached. The retina is a delicate membrane containing a light-sensitive neural layer fed by the optic nerve. This neural layer can delaminate (known as a detached retina). The optic nerve enters the chamber at the optic disc where the fibers spread throughout the retina. The vitreous is the transparent gel filling the interior of the posterior chamber.

Many surgeries to the posterior chamber center on repairing damage to the retina. Laser, zenon arc, cryoprobe, and diathermal probe are common techniques. Access to the retina is often via the pars plana

67101   Repair of retinal detachment, 1 or more sessions; cryotherapy or diathermy, with or without drainage of subretinal fluid   [P2] [T] [50] [□]
    🔧 15.43   ⚬ 17.80   **Global Days 090**

67105   photocoagulation, with or without drainage of subretinal fluid   [P2] [T] [50] [□]
    🔧 14.60   ⚬ 16.48   **Global Days 090**

67107   Repair of retinal detachment; scleral buckling (such as lamellar scleral dissection, imbrication or encircling procedure), with or without implant, with or without cryotherapy, photocoagulation, and drainage of subretinal fluid   [A2] [T] [80] [50] [□]
    [INCLUDES]   Gonin's operation
    🔧 26.07   ⚬ 26.07   **Global Days 090**

67108   with vitrectomy, any method, with or without air or gas tamponade, focal endolaser photocoagulation, cryotherapy, drainage of subretinal fluid, scleral buckling, and/or removal of lens by same technique   [A2] [T] [80] [50] [□]
    🔧 37.38   ⚬ 37.38   **Global Days 090**
    AMA: 2008, Jan, 10-25; 2008, Oct, 1-5; 2007, Jul, 12-13

67110   by injection of air or other gas (eg, pneumatic retinopexy)   [P3] [T] [50] [□]
    🔧 17.77   ⚬ 19.94   **Global Days 090**

● New Code   ▲ Revised Code   ▥ Maternity Edit   ◪ Age Edit   [A]-[Y] OPPS Status Indicator   🔧 Facility RVU   ⚬ Non-Facility RVU
▣ CCI Comprehensive Code   [50] Bilateral Procedure   + Add-on Indicator   ▨ Laboratory crosswalk   ▦ Radiology crosswalk

Eye and Ocular Adnexa

67112 — 67225

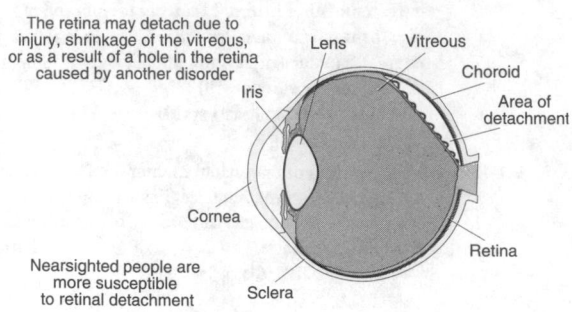

The retina may detach due to injury, shrinkage of the vitreous, or as a result of a hole in the retina caused by another disorder

Nearsighted people are more susceptible to retinal detachment

In retinal detachment, the photo-sensitive retinal layer of the eye separates from the blood-rich choroid layer; this can damage the retina and lead to blindness if not repaired

67112   **by scleral buckling or vitrectomy, on patient having previous ipsilateral retinal detachment repair(s) using scleral buckling or vitrectomy techniques**   A2 T 80 50 ▢

       EXCLUDES   *aspiration or drainage of subretinal or subchoroidal fluid (67015)*

       Code also ophthalmic endoscope if used (66990)

       30.84   30.84   Global Days 090

       AMA: 2008, Oct, 1-5

67113   **Repair of complex retinal detachment (eg, proliferative vitreoretinopathy, stage C-1 or greater, diabetic traction retinal detachment, retinopathy of prematurity, retinal tear of greater than 90 degrees), with vitrectomy and membrane peeling, may include air, gas, or silicone oil tamponade, cryotherapy, endolaser photocoagulation, drainage of subretinal fluid, scleral buckling, and/or removal of lens**   62 T 80 50

       EXCLUDES   *vitrectomy for other than retinal detachment, pars plana approach (67036-67043)*

       40.60   40.60   Global Days 090

       AMA: 2008, Oct, 1-5

67115   **Release of encircling material (posterior segment)**   A2 T 50 ▢

       11.29   11.29   Global Days 090

67120-67121 Removal of Previously Implanted Prosthetic Device

CMS *100-4,12,30*   *Correct Coding Policy*

INCLUDES   operating microscope (69990)

EXCLUDES   *foreign body removal (65260, 65265)*
removal of implanted material anterior segment (65920)

67120   **Removal of implanted material, posterior segment; extraocular**   A2 T 50 ▢

       12.72   15.01   Global Days 090

67121   **intraocular**   A2 T 80 50 ▢

       EXCLUDES   *removal from anterior segment (65920)*
removal of foreign body (65260, 65265)

       20.92   20.92   Global Days 090

67141-67145 Retinal Detachment: Preventative Procedures

CMS *100-4,12,30*   *Correct Coding Policy*

INCLUDES   operating microscope (69990)

       treatment at one or more sessions that may occur at different encounters

67141   **Prophylaxis of retinal detachment (eg, retinal break, lattice degeneration) without drainage, 1 or more sessions; cryotherapy, diathermy**   A2 T 50 ▢

       11.10   11.91   Global Days 090

       AMA: 2008, Oct, 1-5

67145   **photocoagulation (laser or xenon arc)**   P3 T 50 ▢

       11.35   12.01   Global Days 090

       AMA: 2008, Oct, 1-5

67208-67218 Destruction of Retinal Lesions

CMS *100-3,140.5*   *Laser Procedures*

CMS *100-4,12,30*   *Correct Coding Policy*

INCLUDES   operating microscope (69990)

       treatment at one or more sessions that may occur at different encounters

67208   **Destruction of localized lesion of retina (eg, macular edema, tumors), 1 or more sessions; cryotherapy, diathermy**   P3 T 50 ▢

       13.29   13.77   Global Days 090

       AMA: 2008, Oct, 1-5

67210   **photocoagulation**   P2 T 50 ▢

       15.57   16.10   Global Days 090

       AMA: 2008, Oct, 1-5

67218   **radiation by implantation of source (includes removal of source)**   A2 T 50 ▢

       32.66   32.66   Global Days 090

       AMA: 2008, Oct, 1-5

67220-67225 Destruction of Choroidal Lesions

CMS *100-3,80.3*   *Photosensitive Drugs*

CMS *100-3,80.2*   *Photodynamic Therapy*

CMS *100-3,140.5*   *Laser Procedures*

CMS *100-4,12,30*   *Correct Coding Policy*

INCLUDES   operating microscope (69990)

67220   **Destruction of localized lesion of choroid (eg, choroidal neovascularization); photocoagulation (eg, laser), 1 or more sessions**   P2 T 50 ▢

       EXCLUDES   *photocoagulation destruction of macular drusen (0017T)*
transpupillary thermotherapy choroid lesion destruction (0016T)

       23.57   24.71   Global Days 090

       AMA: 2008, Jan, 10-25; 2008, Oct, 1-5; 2007, Jan, 13-27; 2007, Jan, 13-27; 2007, January, 13-27

67221   **photodynamic therapy (includes intravenous infusion)**   P3 T ▢

       5.23   7.00   Global Days 000

       AMA: 2008, Jan, 10-25; 2007, Jan, 13-27; 2007, Jan, 13-27; 2007, January, 13-27

+   **67225**   **photodynamic therapy, second eye, at single session (List separately in addition to code for primary eye treatment)**   P3 T ▢

       Code first (67221)

       0.68   0.72   Global Days ZZZ

       AMA: 2008, Jan, 10-25; 2007, Jan, 13-27; 2007, Jan, 13-27; 2007, January, 13-27

67227-67229 Destruction Retinopathy

CMS 100-4,12,30   *Correct Coding Policy*

[INCLUDES]   operating microscope (69990)

treatment at one or more sessions that may occur at different encounters

67227   **Destruction of extensive or progressive retinopathy (eg, diabetic retinopathy), 1 or more sessions, cryotherapy, diathermy**   [A2] [T] [50] [□]

    🔷 13.13   ⚖ 14.02   Global Days 090

    AMA: 2008, Jan, 10-25; 2008, Oct, 1-5; 2007, Jan, 13-27; 2007, Jan, 13-27, 2007, January, 13-27; 2006, Apr, 11-18; 2006, Apr, 11 18; 2006, April, 11-18; 2004, Jun, 10; 2004, Jun, 10; 2004, June, 10

67228   **Treatment of extensive or progressive retinopathy, 1 or more sessions; (eg, diabetic retinopathy), photocoagulation**   [P2] [T] [50] [□]

    🔷 24.40   ⚖ 27.65   Global Days 090

    AMA: 2008, Oct, 1-5

67229   **preterm infant (less than 37 weeks gestation at birth), performed from birth up to 1 year of age (eg, retinopathy of prematurity), photocoagulation or cryotherapy**   [R2] [T] [50]

    🔷 26.71   ⚖ 26.71   Global Days 090

    AMA: 2008, Oct, 1-5

67250-67255 Reinforcement of Posterior Sclera

CMS 100-4,12,30   *Correct Coding Policy*

[INCLUDES]   operating microscope (69990)

[EXCLUDES]   *removal of lesion of sclera (66130)*
    repair scleral staphyloma (66220, 66225)

67250   **Scleral reinforcement (separate procedure); without graft**   [A2] [T] [50] [□]

    🔷 18.19   ⚖ 18.19   Global Days 090

67255   **with graft**   [A2] [T] [80] [50] [□]

    🔷 19.43   ⚖ 19.43   Global Days 090

67299 Unlisted Posterior Segment Procedure

67299   Unlisted procedure, posterior segment   [T] [80] [50]

    🔷 0.00   ⚖ 0.00   Global Days YYY

    AMA: 2007, Dec, 10-179

67311-67334 Strabismus Procedures on Extraocular Muscles

CMS 100-4,12,30   *Correct Coding Policy*

[INCLUDES]   operating microscope (69990)

Code also adjustable sutures (67335)

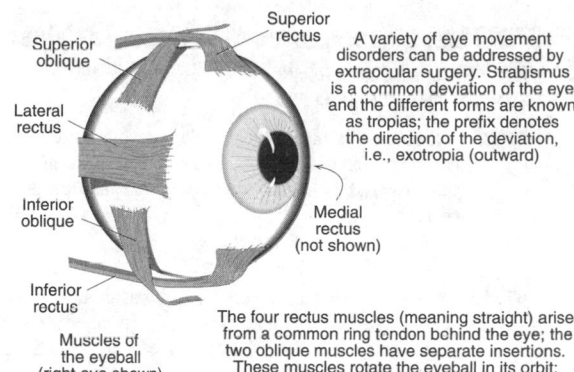

A variety of eye movement disorders can be addressed by extraocular surgery. Strabismus is a common deviation of the eye and the different forms are known as tropias; the prefix denotes the direction of the deviation, i.e., exotropia (outward)

Muscles of the eyeball (right eye shown)

The four rectus muscles (meaning straight) arise from a common ring tondon behind the eye; the two oblique muscles have separate insertions. These muscles rotate the eyeball in its orbit; paralysis of any one or more muscles results in diplopia, or double vision

67311   **Strabismus surgery, recession or resection procedure; 1 horizontal muscle**   [A2] [T] [50] [□]

    🔷 13.78   ⚖ 13.78   Global Days 090

    AMA: 2008, Jan, 10-25; 2007, Jan, 13-27; 2007, Jan, 13-27; 2007, January, 13-27

67312   **2 horizontal muscles**   [A2] [T] [50] [□]

    🔷 16.47   ⚖ 16.47   Global Days 090

    AMA: 2008, Jan, 10-25; 2007, Jan, 13-27; 2007, Jan, 13-27; 2007, January, 13-27

67314   **1 vertical muscle (excluding superior oblique)**   [A2] [T] [50] [□]

    🔷 15.44   ⚖ 15.44   Global Days 090

67316   **2 or more vertical muscles (excluding superior oblique)**   [A2] [T] [80] [50] [□]

    🔷 18.49   ⚖ 18.49   Global Days 090

67318   **Strabismus surgery, any procedure, superior oblique muscle**   [A2] [T] [50] [□]

    🔷 16.16   ⚖ 16.16   Global Days 090

+ 67320   **Transposition procedure (eg, for parctic extraocular muscle), any extraocular muscle (specify) (List separately in addition to code for primary procedure)**   [A2] [T]

    Code first (67311-67318)

    🔷 7.70   ⚖ 7.70   Global Days ZZZ

+ 67331   **Strabismus surgery on patient with previous eye surgery or injury that did not involve the extraocular muscles (List separately in addition to code for primary procedure)**   [A2] [T] [□]

    Code first (67311-67318)

    🔷 7.29   ⚖ 7.29   Global Days ZZZ

+ 67332   **Strabismus surgery on patient with scarring of extraocular muscles (eg, prior ocular injury, strabismus or retinal detachment surgery) or restrictive myopathy (eg, dysthyroid ophthalmopathy) (List separately in addition to code for primary procedure)**   [A2] [T] [□]

    Code first (67311-67318)

    🔷 7.93   ⚖ 7.93   Global Days ZZZ

+ 67334   **Strabismus surgery by posterior fixation suture technique, with or without muscle recession (List separately in addition to code for primary procedure)**   [A2] [T] [□]

    Code first (67311-67318)

    🔷 7.19   ⚖ 7.19   Global Days ZZZ

● New Code   ▲ Revised Code   □ Maternity Edit   ▲ Age Edit   [A]-[Y] OPPS Status Indicator   🔷 Facility RVU   ⚖ Non-Facility RVU

□ CCI Comprehensive Code   [50] Bilateral Procedure   + Add-on Indicator   ▣ Laboratory crosswalk   ▣ Radiology crosswalk

Eye and Ocular Adnexa

67335 — 67599

67335-67399 Other Procedures of Extraocular Muscles

CMS *100-4,12,30*   *Correct Coding Policy*
INCLUDES   operating microscope (69990)

+   67335   Placement of adjustable suture(s) during strabismus surgery, including postoperative adjustment(s) of suture(s) (List separately in addition to code for specific strabismus surgery)   A2 T ▭
     Code first (67311-67334)
     ⚕ 3.63   ⚕ 3.63 Global Days ZZZ

+   67340   Strabismus surgery involving exploration and/or repair of detached extraocular muscle(s) (List separately in addition to code for primary procedure)   A2 T 80 ▭
     INCLUDES   Hummelsheim operation
     Code first (67311-67334)
     ⚕ 8.57   ⚕ 8.57 Global Days ZZZ

     67343   Release of extensive scar tissue without detaching extraocular muscle (separate procedure)   A2 T 50 ▭
     Code also 67311-67340 if these procedures are performed on other than the affected muscle
     ⚕ 15.00   ⚕ 15.00 Global Days 090

     67345   Chemodenervation of extraocular muscle   P3 T 50 ▭
     EXCLUDES   nerve destruction for blepharospasm and other neurological disorders (64612-64613)
     ⚕ 4.99   ⚕ 5.48 Global Days 010

     67346   Biopsy of extraocular muscle   A2 T 80 50
     EXCLUDES   repair laceration extraocular muscle, tendon, or Tenon's capsule (65290)
     ⚕ 4.78   ⚕ 4.78 Global Days 000

     67399   Unlisted procedure, ocular muscle   T 80 50
     ⚕ 0.00   ⚕ 0.00 Global Days YYY

67400-67415 Frontal Orbitotomy

CMS *100-4,12,30*   *Correct Coding Policy*
INCLUDES   operating microscope (69990)

     67400   Orbitotomy without bone flap (frontal or transconjunctival approach); for exploration, with or without biopsy   A2 T 50 ▭
     ⚕ 21.64   ⚕ 21.64 Global Days 090

     67405   with drainage only   A2 T 50 ▭
     ⚕ 18.41   ⚕ 18.41 Global Days 090

     67412   with removal of lesion   A2 T 50 ▭
     ⚕ 20.02   ⚕ 20.02 Global Days 090

     67413   with removal of foreign body   A2 T 80 50 ▭
     ⚕ 20.04   ⚕ 20.04 Global Days 090

     67414   with removal of bone for decompression   62 T 80 50 ▭
     ⚕ 30.62   ⚕ 30.62 Global Days 090
     AMA: 2008, Jan, 10-25; 2007, Jan, 13-27; 2007, Jan, 13-27; 2007, January, 13-27

     67415   Fine needle aspiration of orbital contents   A2 T 80 50 ▭
     EXCLUDES   decompression optic nerve (67570)
                 exenteration, enucleation, and repair (65101-65114)
     ⚕ 2.54   ⚕ 2.54 Global Days 000

67420-67450 Lateral Orbitotomy

CMS *100-4,12,30*   *Correct Coding Policy*
INCLUDES   operating microscope (69990)
EXCLUDES   *eyeball removal or repair after removal (65091-65175)*
            orbital implant (67550, 67560)
            transcranial approach orbitotomy (61330-61334)

     67420   Orbitotomy with bone flap or window, lateral approach (eg, Kroenlein); with removal of lesion   A2 T 80 50 ▭
     ⚕ 38.29   ⚕ 38.29 Global Days 090

     67430   with removal of foreign body   A2 T 80 50 ▭
     ⚕ 29.12   ⚕ 29.12 Global Days 090

     67440   with drainage   A2 T 80 50 ▭
     ⚕ 28.03   ⚕ 28.03 Global Days 090

     67445   with removal of bone for decompression   A2 T 80 50 ▭
     EXCLUDES   *decompression optic nerve sheath (67570)*
     ⚕ 32.93   ⚕ 32.93 Global Days 090

     67450   for exploration, with or without biopsy   A2 T 80 50 ▭
     ⚕ 29.07   ⚕ 29.07 Global Days 090

67500-67515 Eye Injections

CMS *100-4,12,30*   *Correct Coding Policy*
INCLUDES   operating microscope (69990)

     67500   Retrobulbar injection; medication (separate procedure, does not include supply of medication)   62 S 50 ▭
     ⚕ 1.92   ⚕ 2.12 Global Days 000
     AMA: 2004, May, 9; 2004, May, 9; 2004, May, 9

     67505   alcohol   P3 T 50 ▭
     ⚕ 1.86   ⚕ 2.07 Global Days 000

     67515   Injection of medication or other substance into Tenon's capsule   P3 T 50 ▭
     EXCLUDES   *subconjunctival injection (68200)*
     ⚕ 2.02   ⚕ 2.19 Global Days 000
     AMA: 2004, May, 9; 2004, May, 9; 2004, May, 9

67550-67560 Orbital Implant

CMS *100-4,12,30*   *Correct Coding Policy*
INCLUDES   operating microscope (69990)
EXCLUDES   *fracture repair malar area, orbit (21355-21408)*
            ocular implant inside muscle cone (65093-65105, 65130-65175)

     67550   Orbital implant (implant outside muscle cone); insertion   A2 T 50 ▭
     ⚕ 22.60   ⚕ 22.60 Global Days 090

     67560   removal or revision   A2 T 80 50 ▭
     ⚕ 22.96   ⚕ 22.96 Global Days 090

67570-67599 Other and Unlisted Orbital Procedures

CMS *100-4,12,30*   *Correct Coding Policy*
INCLUDES   operating microscope (69990)

     67570   Optic nerve decompression (eg, incision or fenestration of optic nerve sheath)   A2 T 80 50 ▭
     ⚕ 26.97   ⚕ 26.97 Global Days 090

     67599   Unlisted procedure, orbit   T 80 50
     ⚕ 0.00   ⚕ 0.00 Global Days YYY

26/TC Professional/Technical Component Only   80/60 Assist-at-Surgery Allowed/With Documentation   Unlisted   Not Covered
AMA: CPT Assistant References   A2-Z3 ASC Payment Indicator   ♂ Male Only   ♀ Female Only   ⊘ Modifier 51 Exempt   P0 PQRI

67700-67715 Incisional Procedures of Eyelids

CMS *100-4,12,30*   *Correct Coding Policy*
INCLUDES   operating microscope (69990)

| 67700 | Blepharotomy, drainage of abscess, eyelid | P2 T 50 ▢ |
| | 🚑 2.66   ⚕ 6.18   Global Days 010 | |

| 67710 | Severing of tarsorrhaphy | P3 T 50 ▢ |
| | 🚑 2.22   ⚕ 5.21   Global Days 010 | |

| 67715 | Canthotomy (separate procedure) | A2 T 50 ▢ |

EXCLUDES   *canthoplasty (67950)*
      symblepharon division (68340)

🚑 2.51   ⚕ 5.49   Global Days 010

67800-67808 Excision of Chalazion (Meibomian Cyst)

CMS *100-4,12,30*   *Correct Coding Policy*
INCLUDES   lesion removal deeper than skin
      operating microscope (69990)
EXCLUDES   *blepharoplasty, graft, or reconstructive procedures (67930-67975)*
     lesion excision of skin (11310-11313, 11440-11446, 11640-11646, 17000-17004)

| 67800 | Excision of chalazion; single | P3 T ▢ |
| | 🚑 2.43   ⚕ 2.94   Global Days 010 | |

AMA: 2008, Jan, 10-25; 2007, Jan, 13-27; 2007, Jan, 13-27; 2007, January, 13-27

| 67801 | multiple, same lid | P3 T ▢ |
| | 🚑 3.15   ⚕ 3.77   Global Days 010 | |

| 67805 | multiple, different lids | P3 T ▢ |
| | 🚑 3.87   ⚕ 4.67   Global Days 010 | |

AMA: 2008, Jan, 10-25; 2007, Jan, 13-27; 2007, Jan, 13-27; 2007, January, 13-27

| 67808 | under general anesthesia and/or requiring hospitalization, single or multiple | A2 T ▢ |
| | 🚑 8.39   ⚕ 8.39   Global Days 090 | |

67810-67875 Other Eyelid Procedures

CMS *100-4,12,30*   *Correct Coding Policy*
INCLUDES   operating microscope (69990)

| 67810 | Biopsy of eyelid | P2 T 50 ▢ |
| | 🚑 2.26   ⚕ 5.31   Global Days 000 | |

AMA: 2008, Jan, 10-25; 2007, Jan, 13-27; 2007, Jan, 13-27; 2007, January, 13-27; 2004, Dec, 19; 2004, December, 19; 2004, Dec, 19

| 67820 | Correction of trichiasis; epilation, by forceps only | P3 S 50 ▢ |
| | 🚑 1.28   ⚕ 1.24   Global Days 000 | |

AMA: 2008, Jan, 10-25; 2007, Jan, 13-27; 2007, Jan, 13-27; 2007, January, 13-27

| 67825 | epilation by other than forceps (eg, by electrosurgery, cryotherapy, laser surgery) | P3 50 ▢ |
| | 🚑 2.80   ⚕ 2.98   Global Days 010 | |

AMA: 2008, Jan, 10-25; 2007, Jan, 13-27; 2007, Jan, 13-27; 2007, January, 13-27

| 67830 | incision of lid margin | A2 T 50 ▢ |
| | 🚑 3.20   ⚕ 6.19   Global Days 010 | |

| 67835 | incision of lid margin, with free mucous membrane graft | A2 T 00 50 ▢ |
| | 🚑 10.22   ⚕ 10.22   Global Days 090 | |

| 67840 | Excision of lesion of eyelid (except chalazion) without closure or with simple direct closure | P3 T 50 ▢ |

EXCLUDES   *eyelid removal and reconstruction (67961, 67966)*

🚑 3.71   ⚕ 6.48   Global Days 010

| 67850 | Destruction of lesion of lid margin (up to 1 cm) | P3 T 50 ▢ |

EXCLUDES   *Mohs micro procedures (17311-17315)*
      topical chemotherapy (99201-99215)

🚑 3.32   ⚕ 5.21   Global Days 010

| 67875 | Temporary closure of eyelids by suture (eg, Frost suture) | 62 T 50 ▢ |
| | 🚑 2.31   ⚕ 4.05   Global Days 000 | |

67880-67882 Suturing of the Eyelids

CMS *100-4,12,30*   *Correct Coding Policy*
INCLUDES   operating microscope (69990)
EXCLUDES   *canthoplasty (67950)*
      canthotomy (67715)
      severing of tarsorrhaphy (67710)

| 67880 | Construction of intermarginal adhesions, median tarsorrhaphy, or canthorrhaphy; | A2 T 50 ▢ |
| | 🚑 8.39   ⚕ 10.47   Global Days 090 | |

| 67882 | with transposition of tarsal plate | A2 T 50 ▢ |
| | 🚑 10.81   ⚕ 12.92   Global Days 090 | |

67900-67912 Repair of Ptosis/Retraction Eyelids, Eyebrows

CMS *100-2,16,120*   *Cosmetic Procedures*
CMS *100-4,12,30*   *Correct Coding Policy*
INCLUDES   operating microscope (69990)

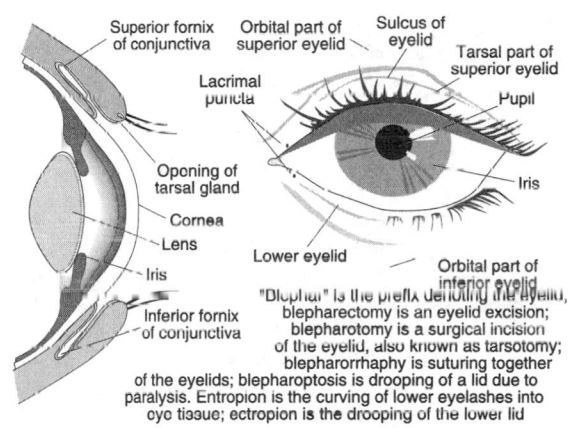

"Blephar" is the prefix denoting the eyelid; blepharectomy is an eyelid excision; blepharotomy is a surgical incision of the eyelid, also known as tarsotomy; of the eyelids; blepharorrhaphy is suturing together of the eyelids; blepharoptosis is drooping of a lid due to paralysis. Entropion is the curving of lower eyelashes into eye tissue; ectropion is the drooping of the lower lid

| 67900 | Repair of brow ptosis (supraciliary, mid-forehead or coronal approach) | A2 T 50 ▢ |

EXCLUDES   *forehead rhytidectomy (15824)*

🚑 11.98   ⚕ 14.97   Global Days 090

AMA: 2008, Jan, 10-25; 2007, Jan, 13-27; 2007, Jan, 13-27; 2007, January, 13-27; 2005, Jan, 46-47; 2005, January, 46-47; 2005, Jan, 46-47

| 67901 | Repair of blepharoptosis; frontalis muscle technique with suture or other material (eg, banked fascia) | A2 T 50 ▢ |
| | 🚑 13.48   ⚕ 16.21   Global Days 090 | |

| 67902 | frontalis muscle technique with autologous fascial sling (includes obtaining fascia) | A2 T 50 ▢ |
| | 🚑 16.66   ⚕ 16.66   Global Days 090 | |

| 67903 | (tarso) levator resection or advancement, internal approach | A2 T 50 ▢ |
| | 🚑 11.65   ⚕ 14.35   Global Days 090 | |

● New Code   ▲ Revised Code   M Maternity Edit   A Age Edit   Ⓣ-Ⓨ OPPS Status Indicator   🚑 Facility RVU   ⚕ Non-Facility RVU
▢ CCI Comprehensive Code   50 Bilateral Procedure   + Add-on Indicator   ◰ Laboratory crosswalk   ⊞ Radiology crosswalk

67904   (tarso) levator resection or advancement, external approach   A2 T 50 ▣
    INCLUDES   Everbusch's operation
    🔗 13.76   ✂ 16.92   Global Days 090

67906   superior rectus technique with fascial sling (includes obtaining fascia)   A2 T 50 ▣
    🔗 12.06   ✂ 12.06   Global Days 090

67908   conjunctivo-tarso-Muller's muscle-levator resection (eg, Fasanella-Servat type)   A2 T 50 ▣
    🔗 10.02   ✂ 11.40   Global Days 090

67909   Reduction of overcorrection of ptosis   A2 T 50 ▣
    🔗 10.26   ✂ 12.52   Global Days 090

67911   Correction of lid retraction   A2 T 50 ▣
    EXCLUDES   graft harvest (20920, 20922, 20926)
          mucous membrane graft repair of trichiasis (67835)
    🔗 12.84   ✂ 12.84   Global Days 090

67912   Correction of lagophthalmos, with implantation of upper eyelid lid load (eg, gold weight)   A2 T 50 ▣
    🔗 11.56   ✂ 21.11   Global Days 090
    AMA: 2008, Jan, 10-25; 2007, Jan, 13-27; 2007, Jan, 13-27; 2007, January, 13-27; 2004, May, 9; 2004, May, 9; 2004, May, 9; 2004, August, 10; 2004, Aug, 10; 2004, Aug, 10

67914-67924 Repair Ectropion/Entropion

CMS *100-4,12,30*   *Correct Coding Policy*
INCLUDES   operating microscope (69990)
EXCLUDES   *cicatricial ectropion or entropion with scar excision or graft (67961-67966)*

67914   Repair of ectropion; suture   A2 T 50 ▣
    🔗 6.75   ✂ 9.10   Global Days 090
    AMA: 2004, May, 9; 2004, May, 9; 2004, May, 9

67915   thermocauterization   P3 T 50 ▣
    🔗 5.96   ✂ 8.15   Global Days 090
    AMA: 2004, May, 9; 2004, May, 9; 2004, May, 9

67916   excision tarsal wedge   A2 T 50 ▣
    🔗 10.07   ✂ 12.53   Global Days 090
    AMA: 2008, Jan, 10-25; 2007, Jan, 13-27; 2007, Jan, 13-27; 2007, January, 13-27; 2005, Feb, 13-16; 2005, February, 13-16; 2005, Feb, 13-16; 2004, May, 9; 2004, May, 9; 2004, February, 11; 2004, May, 9; 2004, Feb, 11; 2004, Feb, 11

67917   extensive (eg, tarsal strip operations)   A2 T 50 ▣
    EXCLUDES   repair of everted punctum (68705)
    🔗 11.15   ✂ 13.71   Global Days 090
    AMA: 2008, Jan, 10-25; 2007, Jan, 13-27; 2007, Jan, 13-27; 2007, January, 13-27; 2005, Jan, 46-47; 2005, Jan, 46-47; 2005, January, 46-47; 2004, May, 9; 2004, May, 9; 2004, February, 11; 2004, May, 9; 2004, June, 10; 2004, Jun, 10; 2004, Jun, 10; 2004, Feb, 11; 2004, Feb, 11

67921   Repair of entropion; suture   A2 T 50 ▣
    🔗 6.31   ✂ 8.66   Global Days 090
    AMA: 2004, May, 9; 2004, May, 9; 2004, May, 9

67922   thermocauterization   P3 T 50 ▣
    🔗 5.74   ✂ 7.89   Global Days 090
    AMA: 2004, May, 9; 2004, May, 9; 2004, May, 9

67923   excision tarsal wedge   A2 T 50 ▣
    🔗 10.86   ✂ 13.21   Global Days 090
    AMA: 2004, May, 9; 2004, May, 9; 2004, May, 9

67924   extensive (eg, tarsal strip or capsulopalpebral fascia repairs operation)   A2 T 50 ▣
    🔗 10.50   ✂ 13.67   Global Days 090
    AMA: 2004, May, 9; 2004, May, 9; 2004, May, 9

67930-67935 Repair Eyelid Wound

CMS *100-4,12,30*   *Correct Coding Policy*
INCLUDES   operating microscope (69990)
EXCLUDES   *blepharoplasty for entropion or ectropion (67916-67917, 67923-67924)*
    correction of lid retraction and blepharoptosis (67901-67911)
    free graft (15120-15121, 15260-15261)
    graft preparation (15004)
    plastic repair of lacrimal canaliculi (68700)
    procedures more extensive than skin repair (12011-12018, 12051-12057, 13150-13153)
    removal of eyelid lesion (67800-67810, 67840-67850)
    repair involving skin and subcutaneous tissue (12011, 12051-12057, 13150-13153)
    repair of blepharochalasis (15820-15823)
    skin adjacent tissue transfer (14060-14061)
    tarsorrhaphy, canthorrhaphy (67880, 67882)

67930   Suture of recent wound, eyelid, involving lid margin, tarsus, and/or palpebral conjunctiva direct closure; partial thickness   P3 T 50 ▣
    🔗 5.79   ✂ 8.59   Global Days 010

67935   full thickness   A2 T 50 ▣
    🔗 10.60   ✂ 13.97   Global Days 090

67938-67999 Eyelid Reconstruction/Repair/Removal Deep Foreign Body

CMS *100-4,12,30*   *Correct Coding Policy*
INCLUDES   operating microscope (69990)
EXCLUDES   *blepharoplasty for entropion or ectropion (67916-67917, 67923-67924)*
    correction of lid retraction and blepharoptosis (67901-67911)
    free graft (15120-15121, 15260-15261)
    graft preparation (15004)
    plastic repair of lacrimal canaliculi (68700)
    procedures more extensive than skin repair (12011-12018, 12051-12053, 13150-13153)
    removal of eyelid lesion (67800-67810, 67840-67850)
    repair of blepharochalasis (15820-15823)
    skin adjacent tissue transfer (14060-14061)
    tarsorrhaphy, canthoplasty (67880, 67882)

67938   Removal of embedded foreign body, eyelid   P2 S 50 ▣
    🔗 2.67   ✂ 5.64   Global Days 010

67950   Canthoplasty (reconstruction of canthus)   A2 T 50 ▣
    🔗 10.95   ✂ 13.49   Global Days 090

67961   Excision and repair of eyelid, involving lid margin, tarsus, conjunctiva, canthus, or full thickness, may include preparation for skin graft or pedicle flap with adjacent tissue transfer or rearrangement; up to 1/4 of lid margin   A2 T 80 50 ▣
    🔗 10.69   ✂ 13.46   Global Days 090
    AMA: 2004, May, 9; 2004, May, 9; 2004, May, 9

67966   over 1/4 of lid margin   A2 T 50 ▣
    EXCLUDES   canthoplasty (67950)
          delay flap (15630)
          flap attachment (15650)
          free skin grafts (15120-15121, 15260-15261)
          tubed pedicle flap preparation (15576)
    🔗 15.10   ✂ 17.70   Global Days 090

67971   Reconstruction of eyelid, full thickness by transfer of tarsoconjunctival flap from opposing eyelid; up to 2/3 of eyelid, 1 stage or first stage   A2 T 50 🖵

    INCLUDES   Dupuy-Dutemp reconstruction
       Landboldt's operation

    🖀 17.09   ⚚ 17.09   Global Days 090

67973   total eyelid, lower, 1 stage or first stage   A2 T 80 50 🖵

    INCLUDES   Landboldt's operation

    🖀 22.16   ⚚ 22.16   Global Days 090

67974   total eyelid, upper, 1 stage or first stage   A2 T 80 50 🖵

    INCLUDES   Landboldt's operation

    🖀 22.07   ⚚ 22.07   Global Days 090

67975   second stage   A2 T 50 🖵

    INCLUDES   Landboldt's operation

    🖀 16.14   ⚚ 16.14   Global Days 090

67999   Unlisted procedure, eyelids   T 80 50

    🖀 0.00   ⚚ 0.00   Global Days YYY

    AMA: 2008, Jan, 10-25; 2007, Jan, 13-27; 2007, Jan, 13-27; 2007, January, 13-27; 2005, Jan, 46-47; 2005, January, 46-47; 2005, Jan, 46-47

68020-68200 Conjunctival Biopsy/Injection/Treatment of Lesions

CMS *100-4,12,30*   *Correct Coding Policy*

INCLUDES   operating microscope (69990)

68020   Incision of conjunctiva, drainage of cyst   P3 T 50 🖵

    🖀 2.57   ⚚ 2.76   Global Days 010

68040   Expression of conjunctival follicles (eg, for trachoma)   P3 S 50 🖵

    🖀 1.28   ⚚ 1.54   Global Days 000

68100   Biopsy of conjunctiva   P3 T 50 🖵

    🖀 2.33   ⚚ 4.02   Global Days 000

68110   Excision of lesion, conjunctiva; up to 1 cm   P3 T 50 🖵

    🖀 3.44   ⚚ 5.23   Global Days 010

68115   over 1 cm   A2 T 50 🖵

    🖀 4.29   ⚚ 7.26   Global Days 010

68130   with adjacent sclera   A2 T 50 🖵

    🖀 9.52   ⚚ 12.49   Global Days 090

68135   Destruction of lesion, conjunctiva   P3 T 50 🖵

    🖀 3.51   ⚚ 3.63   Global Days 010

68200   Subconjunctival injection   P3 S 50 🖵

    EXCLUDES   *retrobulbar or Tenon's capsule injection (67500-67515)*

    🖀 0.82   ⚚ 0.99   Global Days 000

    AMA: 2008, Jan, 10-25; 2007, Jan, 13-27; 2007, Jan, 13-27; 2007, January, 13-27; 2004, May, 9; 2004, May, 9; 2004, May, 9

68320-68340 Conjunctivoplasty Procedures

CMS *100-4,12,30*   *Correct Coding Policy*

EXCLUDES   *laceration repair (65270-65273)*

68320   Conjunctivoplasty; with conjunctival graft or extensive rearrangement   A2 T 50 🖵

    🖀 12.22   ⚚ 16.52   Global Days 090

    AMA: 2008, Jan, 10-25; 2007, Jan, 13-27; 2007, Jan, 13-27; 2007, Dec, 10-179; 2007, January, 13-27; 2004, Feb, 11; 2004, Feb, 11; 2004, May, 9; 2004, February, 11; 2004, May, 9; 2004, June, 10; 2004, May, 9; 2004, Jun, 10; 2004, Jun, 10

68325   with buccal mucous membrane graft (includes obtaining graft)   A2 T 50 🖵

    🖀 15.23   ⚚ 15.23   Global Days 090

    AMA: 2004, May, 9; 2004, May, 9; 2004, May, 9

68326   Conjunctivoplasty, reconstruction cul-de-sac; with conjunctival graft or extensive rearrangement   A2 T 50 🖵

    🖀 14.80   ⚚ 14.80   Global Days 090

    AMA: 2004, May, 9; 2004, May, 9; 2004, May, 9

68328   with buccal mucous membrane graft (includes obtaining graft)   A2 T 80 50 🖵

    🖀 16.58   ⚚ 16.58   Global Days 090

    AMA: 2004, May, 9; 2004, May, 9; 2004, May, 9

68330   Repair of symblepharon; conjunctivoplasty, without graft   A2 T 80 50 🖵

    🖀 10.51   ⚚ 13.88   Global Days 090

    AMA: 2004, May, 9; 2004, May, 9; 2004, May, 9

68335   with free graft conjunctiva or buccal mucous membrane (includes obtaining graft)   A2 T 50 🖵

    🖀 14.85   ⚚ 14.85   Global Days 090

    AMA: 2004, May, 9; 2004, May, 9; 2004, May, 9

68340   division of symblepharon, with or without insertion of conformer or contact lens   A2 T 80 50 🖵

    🖀 9.08   ⚚ 12.50   Global Days 090

    AMA: 2004, May, 9; 2004, May, 9; 2004, May, 9

68360-68399 Conjunctival Transplant and Unlisted Procedures

CMS *100-4,12,30*   *Correct Coding Policy*

INCLUDES   operating microscope (69990)

68360   Conjunctival flap; bridge or partial (separate procedure)   A2 T 50 🖵

    EXCLUDES   *conjunctival flap for injury (65280, 65285)*
       conjunctival foreign body removal (65205, 65210)
       surgical wound (66250)

    🖀 9.39   ⚚ 12.19   Global Days 090

    AMA: 2004, May, 9; 2004, May, 9; 2004, May, 9

68362   total (such as Gunderson thin flap or purse string flap)   A2 T 50 🖵

    EXCLUDES   *conjunctival flap for injury (65280, 65285)*
       conjunctival foreign body removal (65205, 65210)
       surgical wound (66250)

    🖀 15.05   ⚚ 15.05   Global Days 090

    AMA: 2004, May, 9; 2004, May, 9; 2004, May, 9

68371   Harvesting conjunctival allograft, living donor   A2 T 50 🖵

    🖀 9.75   ⚚ 9.75   Global Days 010

    AMA: 2004, May, 9; 2004, May, 9; 2004, May, 9

68399   Unlisted procedure, conjunctiva   T 80 50

    🖀 0.00   ⚚ 0.00   Global Days YYY

    AMA: 2004, May, 9; 2004, May, 9; 2004, May, 9

68400-68899 Nasolacrimal System Procedures

CMS *100-4,12,30*   *Correct Coding Policy*

INCLUDES   operating microscope (69990)

● New Code   ▲ Revised Code   M Maternity Edit   A Age Edit   A-Y OPPS Status Indicator   🖀 Facility RVU   ⚚ Non-Facility RVU

□ CCI Comprehensive Code   50 Bilateral Procedure   + Add-on Indicator   ⬛ Laboratory crosswalk   ⬛ Radiology crosswalk

Auditory System

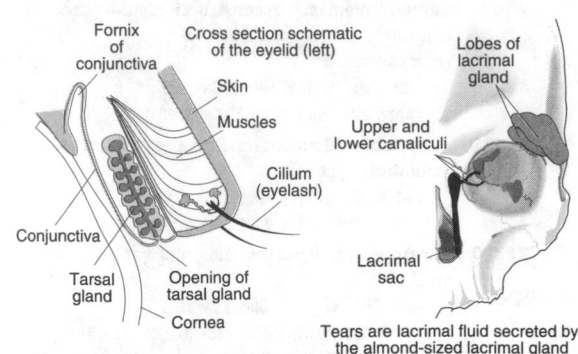

Fornix of conjunctiva

Cross section schematic of the eyelid (left)

Lobes of lacrimal gland

Skin

Muscles

Upper and lower canaliculi

Cilium (eyelash)

Conjunctiva

Tarsal gland

Opening of tarsal gland

Cornea

Lacrimal sac

The eyelid is a moveable fold covered by skin externally and highly vascularized conjunctiva internally. The tarsal glands secrete lubricant to the edges of the eyelid

Tears are lacrimal fluid secreted by the almond-sized lacrimal gland through ducts into the fornix of the conjunctiva; fluid is drained through the puncta and into the lacrimal sac and into the nose

68400   Incision, drainage of lacrimal gland   P2 T 50
          3.18   6.53   Global Days 010

68420   Incision, drainage of lacrimal sac (dacryocystotomy or dacryocystostomy)   P3 T 50
          4.08   7.45   Global Days 010

68440   Snip incision of lacrimal punctum   P3 T 50
          2.23   2.48   Global Days 010

68500   Excision of lacrimal gland (dacryoadenectomy), except for tumor; total   A2 T 50
          22.43   22.43   Global Days 090

68505   partial   A2 T 50
          22.57   22.57   Global Days 090

68510   Biopsy of lacrimal gland   A2 T 80 50
          6.99   10.65   Global Days 000

68520   Excision of lacrimal sac (dacryocystectomy)   A2 T 80 50
          15.88   15.88   Global Days 090

68525   Biopsy of lacrimal sac   A2 T 50
          6.43   6.43   Global Days 000

68530   Removal of foreign body or dacryolith, lacrimal passages   P2 T 50
          INCLUDES   Meller's excision
          6.16   10.15   Global Days 010

68540   Excision of lacrimal gland tumor; frontal approach   A2 T 50
          21.45   21.45   Global Days 090

68550   involving osteotomy   A2 T 50
          26.42   26.42   Global Days 090

68700   Plastic repair of canaliculi   A2 T 50
          13.84   13.84   Global Days 090

68705   Correction of everted punctum, cautery   P3 T 50
          3.86   5.53   Global Days 010
          AMA: 2004, May, 9; 2004, May, 9; 2004, May, 9

68720   Dacryocystorhinostomy (fistulization of lacrimal sac to nasal cavity)   A2 T 80 50
          17.58   17.58   Global Days 090
          AMA: 2008, Jan, 10-25; 2007, Jan, 13-27; 2007, January, 13-27

68745   Conjunctivorhinostomy (fistulization of conjunctiva to nasal cavity); without tube   A2 T 80 50
          17.68   17.68   Global Days 090

68750   with insertion of tube or stent   A2 T 80 50
          18.14   18.14   Global Days 090

68760   Closure of the lacrimal punctum; by thermocauterization, ligation, or laser surgery   P3 T 50
          3.38   4.69   Global Days 010

68761   by plug, each   P3 T 80 50
          2.74   3.41   Global Days 010
          AMA: 2008, Jan, 10-25; 2007, Jan, 28-31; 2007, Jan, 28-31; 2007, Jan, 13-27; 2007, Jan, 13-27; 2007, January, 28-31; 2007, January, 13-27

68770   Closure of lacrimal fistula (separate procedure)   A2 T 80 50
          13.69   13.69   Global Days 090

68801   Dilation of lacrimal punctum, with or without irrigation   P2 S 50
          2.45   2.83   Global Days 010

68810   Probing of nasolacrimal duct, with or without irrigation;   A2 S 50
          EXCLUDES   ophthalmological exam under anesthesia (92018)
          4.39   5.48   Global Days 010
          AMA: 2008, Oct, 1-5

68811   requiring general anesthesia   A2 T 50
          EXCLUDES   ophthalmological exam under anesthesia (92018)
          4.77   4.77   Global Days 010
          AMA: 2008, Jan, 10-25; 2008, Oct, 1-5; 2007, Jan, 13-27; 2007, Jan, 13-27; 2007, January, 13-27

68815   with insertion of tube or stent   A2 T 50
          EXCLUDES   ophthalmological exam under anesthesia (92018)
          6.01   10.32   Global Days 010
          AMA: 2008, Jan, 10-25; 2008, Oct, 1-5; 2007, Jan, 13-27; 2007, Jan, 13-27; 2007, January, 13-27

68816   with transluminal balloon catheter dilation   G2 T 50
          EXCLUDES   ophthalmological exam under anesthesia (92018)
          Do not report with (68810-68811, 68815)
          5.76   15.82   Global Days 010
          AMA: 2008, Oct, 1-5

68840   Probing of lacrimal canaliculi, with or without irrigation   P3 S 50
          2.59   2.88   Global Days 010

68850   Injection of contrast medium for dacryocystography   N1 N 50
          70170, 78660
          1.48   1.62   Global Days 000
          AMA: 2008, Jan, 10-25; 2007, Jan, 13-27; 2007, Jan, 13-27; 2007, January, 13-27

68899   Unlisted procedure, lacrimal system   T 80 50
          0.00   0.00   Global Days YYY

69000-69020 Treatment Abscess/Hematoma External

The external ear, or auricle, is a single elastic cartilage covered by skin and normal adnexal features (hair follicles, sweat glands, and sebaceous glands). The ridged nature of the auricle contributes to channeling sounds into the acoustic meatus. The semicircular depression leading into the middle ear is named the concha, Latin for shell.

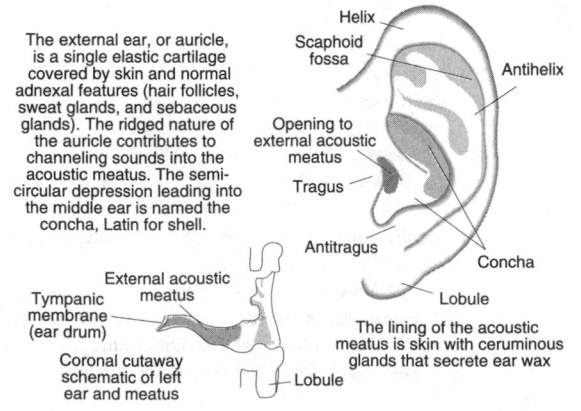

Helix

Scaphoid fossa

Antihelix

Opening to external acoustic meatus

Tragus

Antitragus

Concha

Lobule

External acoustic meatus

Tympanic membrane (ear drum)

Coronal cutaway schematic of left ear and meatus

Lobule

The lining of the acoustic meatus is skin with ceruminous glands that secrete ear wax

69000 Drainage external ear, abscess or hematoma; simple [P2] [T] [□]
  📇 2.94 ≷ 4.46 Global Days 010
  AMA: 2008, Jan, 10-25; 2007, Jan, 13-27; 2007, Jan, 13-27; 2007, January, 13-27

69005   complicated [P3] [T] [□]
  📇 4.00 ≷ 5.29 Global Days 010

69020 Drainage external auditory canal, abscess [P2] [T] [□]
  📇 3.58 ≷ 5.68 Global Days 010
  AMA: 2008, Jan, 10-25; 2007, Jan, 13-27; 2007, Jan, 13-27; 2007, January, 13-27

69090 Cosmetic Ear Piercing

CMS 100-2,16,120 *Cosmetic Procedures*
CMS 100-2,16,10 *Exclusions from Coverage*

69090 Ear piercing [E]
  📇 0.00 ≷ 0.00 Global Days XXX

69100-69222 Excisional Procedures External Ear/Auditory Canal

CMS 100-4,12,30 *Correct Coding Policy*
EXCLUDES *reconstruction of ear (see integumentary section codes)*

69100 Biopsy external ear [P3] [T] [□]
  📇 1.25 ≷ 2.64 Global Days 000

69105 Biopsy external auditory canal [P3] [□]
  📇 1.65 ≷ 3.47 Global Days 000

69110 Excision external ear; partial, simple repair [A2] [T] [□]
  EXCLUDES *reconstruction of ear (see integumentary section codes)*
  📇 8.26 ≷ 11.32 Global Days 090

69120   complete amputation [A2] [T] [□]
  📇 10.05 ≷ 10.05 Global Days 090

69140 Excision exostosis(es), external auditory canal [A2] [T] [80] [□]
  📇 21.91 ≷ 21.91 Global Days 090

69145 Excision soft tissue lesion, external auditory canal [A?] [T] [□]
  📇 6.22 ≷ 9.51 Global Days 090

69150 Radical excision external auditory canal lesion; without neck dissection [A2] [T] [□]
  EXCLUDES *skin graft (15004-15261) temporal bone resection (09535)*
  📇 26.86 ≷ 26.86 Global Days 090

69155   with neck dissection [C] [80] [□]
  📇 43.09 ≷ 43.09 Global Days 090

69200 Removal foreign body from external auditory canal; without general anesthesia [P2] [X] [□]
  📇 1.43 ≷ 3.02 Global Days 000

69205   with general anesthesia [A2] [T] [□]
  📇 2.57 ≷ 2.57 Global Days 010

69210 Removal impacted cerumen (separate procedure), 1 or both ears [P3] [X] [□]
  📇 0.85 ≷ 1.25 Global Days 000
  AMA: 2008, Jan, 10-25; 2007, Jan, 13-27; 2007, Jan, 13-27; 2007, January, 13-27; 2005, Jul, 13-16; 2005, July, 13-16; 2005, Jul, 13-16

69220 Debridement, mastoidectomy cavity, simple (eg, routine cleaning) [P2] [T] [50] [□]
  📇 1.60 ≷ 3.39 Global Days 000

69222 Debridement, mastoidectomy cavity, complex (eg, with anesthesia or more than routine cleaning) [P3] [T] [50] [□]
  📇 3.48 ≷ 5.44 Global Days 010

69300 Plastic Surgery for Prominent Ears

CMS 100-2,16,180 *Services Related to Noncovered Procedures*
CMS 100-2,16,120 *Cosmetic Procedures*

⊙ 69300 Otoplasty, protruding ear, with or without size reduction [A2] [T] [60] [50]
  📇 12.37 ≷ 16.34 Global Days YYY

69310-69399 Reconstruction Auditory Canal: Postaural Approach

CMS 100-4,12,30 *Correct Coding Policy*
EXCLUDES *suture of laceration of external ear (12011-14300)*

69310 Reconstruction of external auditory canal (meatoplasty) (eg, for stenosis due to injury, infection) (separate procedure) [A2] [T] [□]
  📇 27.36 ≷ 27.36 Global Days 090

69320 Reconstruction external auditory canal for congenital atresia, single stage [A2] [T] [80] [□]
  EXCLUDES *other reconstruction surgery with graft (13150-15760, 21230-21235) tympanoplasty (69631, 69641)*
  📇 39.04 ≷ 39.04 Global Days 090

69399 Unlisted procedure, external ear [T] [80]
  📇 0.00 ≷ 0.00 Global Days YYY

69400-69405 Treatment of Eustachian Tube Obstruction

CMS 100-4,12,30 *Correct Coding Policy*

69400 Eustachian tube inflation, transnasal; with catheterization [P3] [T] [□]
  📇 1.59 ≷ 3.52 Global Days 000

69401   without catheterization [P3] [T] [□]
  📇 1.27 ≷ 2.06 Global Days 000

69405 Eustachian tube catheterization, transtympanic [P3] [T] [80] [□]
  📇 4.95 ≷ 6.48 Global Days 010

69420-69450 Ear Drum Procedures

CMS 100-4,12,30 *Correct Coding Policy*

69420 Myringotomy including aspiration and/or eustachian tube inflation [P3] [T] [50] [□]
  📇 3.03 ≷ 4.71 Global Days 010

69421 Myringotomy including aspiration and/or eustachian tube inflation requiring general anesthesia [A2] [T] [50] [□]
  📇 3.84 ≷ 3.84 Global Days 010

69424 Ventilating tube removal requiring general anesthesia [P3] [T] [50] [□]
  Do not report with (69205, 69210, 69420-69421, 69433-69676, 69710-69745, 69801-69930)
  📇 1.60 ≷ 3.20 Global Days 000
  AMA: 2008, Jan, 10-25; 2007, Jan, 13-27; 2007, Jan, 13-27; 2007, January, 13-27; 2005, Mar, 16-17; 2005, March, 16-17; 2005, Mar, 16-17

69433 Tympanostomy (requiring insertion of ventilating tube), local or topical anesthesia [N] [T] [50] [□]
  📇 3.28 ≷ 4.91 Global Days 010

69436 Tympanostomy (requiring insertion of ventilating tube), general anesthesia [A2] [T] [50] [□]
  📇 4.18 ≷ 4.18 Global Days 010
  AMA: 2008, Sep, 10□-11

● New Code   ▲ Revised Code   [M] Maternity Edit   [A] Age Edit   [A]-[Y] OPPS Status Indicator   📇 Facility RVU   ≷ Non-Facility RVU
[□] CCI Comprehensive Code   [50] Bilateral Procedure   + Add-on Indicator   [L] Laboratory crosswalk   [R] Radiology crosswalk

69440   **Middle ear exploration through postauricular or ear canal incision**   ᴬ² T 50 ▣

     EXCLUDES   *atticotomy (69601-69605)*

     🔪 17.27   ✂ 17.27   Global Days 090

     AMA: 2008, Sep, 10☐-11

69450   **Tympanolysis, transcanal**   ᴬ² T 80 50 ▣

     🔪 13.55   ✂ 13.55   Global Days 090

     AMA: 2008, Sep, 10☐-11

69501-69535 Transmastoid Excision

CMS *100-4,12,30*   *Correct Coding Policy*

EXCLUDES   *mastoidectomy cavity debridement (69220, 69222)*
          skin graft (15004-15770)

69501   **Transmastoid antrotomy (simple mastoidectomy)**   ᴬ² T 50 ▣

     🔪 18.56   ✂ 18.56   Global Days 090

     AMA: 2004, Oct, 1; 2004, Oct, 1; 2004, October, 1

69502   **Mastoidectomy; complete**   ᴬ² T 80 50 ▣

     🔪 24.70   ✂ 24.70   Global Days 090

     AMA: 2004, Oct, 1; 2004, Oct, 1; 2004, October, 1

69505   **modified radical**   ᴬ² T 80 50 ▣

     🔪 30.49   ✂ 30.49   Global Days 090

     AMA: 2004, Oct, 1; 2004, Oct, 1; 2004, October, 1

69511   **radical**   ᴬ² T 80 50 ▣

     EXCLUDES   *debridement of mastoid cavity (69220, 69222)*
          skin graft (15004-15431)

     🔪 31.35   ✂ 31.35   Global Days 090

     AMA: 2004, Oct, 1; 2004, Oct, 1; 2004, October, 1

69530   **Petrous apicectomy including radical mastoidectomy**   ᴬ² T 80 50 ▣

     🔪 42.23   ✂ 42.23   Global Days 090

69535   **Resection temporal bone, external approach**   C 50 ▣

     EXCLUDES   *middle fossa approach (69950-69970)*

     🔪 68.75   ✂ 68.75   Global Days 090

69540-69554 Polyp and Glomus Tumor Removal

CMS *100-4,12,30*   *Correct Coding Policy*

69540   **Excision aural polyp**   P3 T 50 ▣

     🔪 3.20   ✂ 5.13   Global Days 010

69550   **Excision aural glomus tumor; transcanal**   ᴬ² T 80 50 ▣

     🔪 26.35   ✂ 26.35   Global Days 090

69552   **transmastoid**   ᴬ² T 80 50 ▣

     🔪 40.25   ✂ 40.25   Global Days 090

69554   **extended (extratemporal)**   C 80 50 ▣

     🔪 63.95   ✂ 63.95   Global Days 090

69601-69605 Revised Mastoidectomy

CMS *100-4,12,30*   *Correct Coding Policy*

EXCLUDES   *skin graft (15120-15121, 15260-15261)*

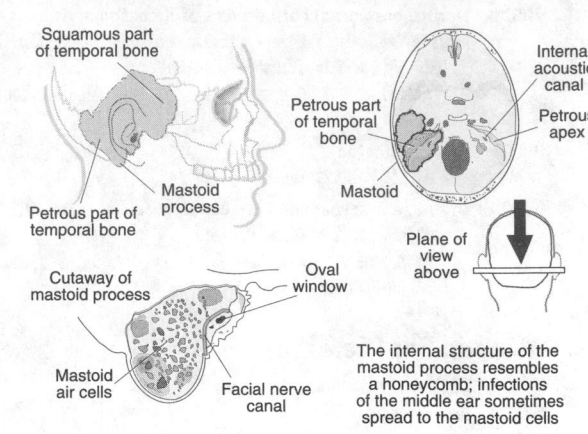

Squamous part of temporal bone · Internal acoustic canal · Petrous part of temporal bone · Petrous apex · Petrous part of temporal bone · Mastoid process · Mastoid · Cutaway of mastoid process · Oval window · Plane of view above · Mastoid air cells · Facial nerve canal

The internal structure of the mastoid process resembles a honeycomb; infections of the middle ear sometimes spread to the mastoid cells

69601   **Revision mastoidectomy; resulting in complete mastoidectomy**   ᴬ² T 80 50 ▣

     🔪 26.63   ✂ 26.63   Global Days 090

     AMA: 2004, Oct, 1; 2004, Oct, 1; 2004, October, 1

69602   **resulting in modified radical mastoidectomy**   ᴬ² T 80 50 ▣

     🔪 27.70   ✂ 27.70   Global Days 090

     AMA: 2004, Oct, 1; 2004, Oct, 1; 2004, October, 1

69603   **resulting in radical mastoidectomy**   ᴬ² T 80 50 ▣

     🔪 32.25   ✂ 32.25   Global Days 090

     AMA: 2004, Oct, 1; 2004, Oct, 1; 2004, October, 1

69604   **resulting in tympanoplasty**   ᴬ² T 50 ▣

     EXCLUDES   *secondary tympanoplasty following mastoidectomy (69631-69632)*

     🔪 28.58   ✂ 28.58   Global Days 090

     AMA: 2004, Oct, 1; 2004, Oct, 1; 2004, October, 1

69605   **with apicectomy**   ᴬ² T 80 50 ▣

     EXCLUDES   *skin graft (15120-15121, 15260-15261)*

     🔪 39.88   ✂ 39.88   Global Days 090

69610-69646 Eardrum Repair with/without Other Procedures

CMS *100-4,12,30*   *Correct Coding Policy*

69610   **Tympanic membrane repair, with or without site preparation of perforation for closure, with or without patch**   P3 T 50 ▣

     🔪 7.63   ✂ 9.90   Global Days 010

     AMA: 2008, Jan, 10-25; 2007, Jan, 13-27; 2007, Jan, 13-27; 2007, January, 13-27

69620   **Myringoplasty (surgery confined to drumhead and donor area)**   ᴬ² T 50 ▣

     🔪 12.41   ✂ 17.33   Global Days 090

     AMA: 2008, Jan, 10-25; 2007, Jan, 13-27; 2007, Jan, 13-27; 2007, January, 13-27

69631   **Tympanoplasty without mastoidectomy (including canalplasty, atticotomy and/or middle ear surgery), initial or revision; without ossicular chain reconstruction**   ᴬ² T 50 ▣

     🔪 22.22   ✂ 22.22   Global Days 090

     AMA: 2008, Jan, 10-25; 2007, Jan, 13-27; 2007, Jan, 13-27; 2007, Mar, 9-11; 2007, Mar, 9-11; 2007, January, 13-27; 2007, March, 9-11

69632   **with ossicular chain reconstruction (eg, postfenestration)**   ᴬ² T 50 ▣

     🔪 27.30   ✂ 27.30   Global Days 090

69633   with ossicular chain reconstruction and synthetic prosthesis (eg, partial ossicular replacement prosthesis [PORP], total ossicular replacement prosthesis [TORP])   A2 T 50 ▣
  💰 26.30   ✂ 26.30   Global Days 090

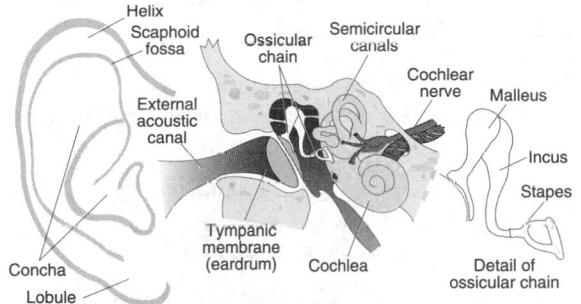

Helix
Scaphoid fossa
Ossicular chain
Semicircular canals
Cochlear nerve
Malleus
External acoustic canal
Incus
Stapes
Concha
Tympanic membrane (eardrum)
Cochlea
Detail of ossicular chain
Lobule

The tympanic membrane is a thin, sensitive tissue and is the gateway to the middle ear; the membrane vibrates in response to sound waves and the movement is transmitted via the ossicular chain to the internal ear. Many surgeries to the middle ear involve repair to the tympanic membrane and reconstruction to the various components of the ossicular chain

69635   Tympanoplasty with antrotomy or mastoidotomy (including canalplasty, atticotomy, middle ear surgery, and/or tympanic membrane repair); without ossicular chain reconstruction   A2 T 50 ▣
  💰 30.93   ✂ 30.93   Global Days 090
  AMA: 2004, Oct, 1; 2004, Oct, 1; 2004, October, 1

69636   with ossicular chain reconstruction   A2 T 80 50 ▣
  💰 35.05   ✂ 35.05   Global Days 090
  AMA: 2004, Oct, 1; 2004, Oct, 1; 2004, October, 1

69637   with ossicular chain reconstruction and synthetic prosthesis (eg, partial ossicular replacement prosthesis [PORP], total ossicular replacement prosthesis [TORP])   A2 T 80 50 ▣
  💰 34.89   ✂ 34.89   Global Days 090
  AMA: 2004, Oct, 1, 2004, Oct, 1, 2004, October, 1

69641   Tympanoplasty with mastoidectomy (including canalplasty, middle ear surgery, tympanic membrane repair); without ossicular chain reconstruction   A2 T 50 ▣
  💰 26.45   ✂ 26.45   Global Days 090
  AMA: 2004, Oct, 1; 2004, Oct, 1; 2004, October, 1

69642   with ossicular chain reconstruction   A2 T 50 ▣
  💰 34.12   ✂ 34.12   Global Days 090
  AMA: 2004, Oct, 1; 2004, Oct, 1; 2004, October, 1

69643   with intact or reconstructed wall, without ossicular chain reconstruction   A2 T 50 ▣
  💰 31.16   ✂ 31.16   Global Days 090
  AMA: 2004, Oct, 1; 2004, Oct, 1; 2004, October, 1

69644   with intact or reconstructed canal wall, with ossicular chain reconstruction   A2 T 50 ▣
  💰 37.73   ✂ 37.73   Global Days 090
  AMA: 2004, Oct, 1; 2004, Oct, 1; 2004, October, 1

69645   radical or complete, without ossicular chain reconstruction   A2 T 50 ▣
  💰 36.96   ✂ 36.96   Global Days 090
  AMA: 2004, Oct, 1; 2004, Oct, 1; 2004, October, 1

69646   radical or complete, with ossicular chain reconstruction   A2 T 80 50 ▣
  💰 39.30   ✂ 39.30   Global Days 090
  AMA: 2004, Oct, 1; 2004, Oct, 1; 2004, October, 1

69650-69662 Stapes Procedures

CMS 100-4,12,30   *Correct Coding Policy*

69650   **Stapes mobilization**   A2 T 50 ▣
  💰 20.14   ✂ 20.14   Global Days 090

69660   **Stapedectomy or stapedotomy with reestablishment of ossicular continuity, with or without use of foreign material;**   A2 T 50 ▣
  💰 23.70   ✂ 23.70   Global Days 090

69661   **with footplate drill out**   A2 T 80 50 ▣
  💰 31.00   ✂ 31.00   Global Days 090

69662   **Revision of stapedectomy or stapedotomy**   A2 T 50 ▣
  💰 29.72   ✂ 29.72   Global Days 090

69666-69700 Other Inner Ear Procedures

CMS 100-4,12,30   *Correct Coding Policy*

69666   **Repair oval window fistula**   A2 T 80 50 ▣
  💰 20.44   ✂ 20.44   Global Days 090

69667   **Repair round window fistula**   A2 T 80 50 ▣
  💰 20.51   ✂ 20.51   Global Days 090

69670   **Mastoid obliteration (separate procedure)**   A2 T 80 50 ▣
  💰 23.92   ✂ 23.92   Global Days 090

69676   **Tympanic neurectomy**   A2 T 50 ▣
  💰 21.09   ✂ 21.09   Global Days 090

69700   **Closure postauricular fistula, mastoid (separate procedure)**   A2 T 50 ▣
  💰 17.58   ✂ 17.58   Global Days 090

69710-69718 Procedures Related to Hearing Aids/Auditory Implants

CMS 100-2,16,100   *Hearing Devices*
CMS 100-2,16,180   *Services Related to Noncovered Procedures*

69710   **Implantation or replacement of electromagnetic bone conduction hearing device in temporal bone**   E
  INCLUDES   removal of existing device when performing replacement procedure
  💰 0.00   ✂ 0.00   Global Days XXX

69711   **Removal or repair of electromagnetic bone conduction hearing device in temporal bone**   A2 T 80 50 ▣
  💰 21.99   ✂ 21.99   Global Days 090

69714   **Implantation, osseointegrated implant, temporal bone, with percutaneous attachment to external speech processor/cochlear stimulator; without mastoidectomy**   H8 T 50 ▣
  💰 27.53   ✂ 27.53   Global Days 090

69715   **with mastoidectomy**   H8 T 50 ▣
  💰 34.27   ✂ 34.27   Global Days 090

69717   **Replacement (including removal of existing device), osseointegrated implant, temporal bone, with percutaneous attachment to external speech processor/cochlear stimulator; without mastoidectomy**   H8 T 50 ▣
  💰 29.00   ✂ 29.00   Global Days 090

69718   **with mastoidectomy**   H8 T 50 ▣
  💰 36.40   ✂ 36.40   Global Days 090

● New Code   ▲ Revised Code   ▣ Maternity Edit   ⬛ Age Edit   A-Y OPPS Status Indicator   💰 Facility RVU   ✂ Non-Facility RVU
▢ CCI Comprehensive Code   50 Bilateral Procedure   + Add-on Indicator   ◨ Laboratory crosswalk   ◧ Radiology crosswalk

Operating Microscope

69720 — 69990

69720-69799 Procedures of the Facial Nerve

CMS *100-4,12,30*   *Correct Coding Policy*
EXCLUDES   *extracranial suture of facial nerve (64864)*

69720 Decompression facial nerve, intratemporal; lateral to geniculate ganglion   A2 T 80 50 ▢ P0
   29.86   29.86   Global Days 090

69725 including medial to geniculate ganglion   T 80 50 ▢
   48.82   48.82   Global Days 090

69740 Suture facial nerve, intratemporal, with or without graft or decompression; lateral to geniculate ganglion   A2 T 80 50 ▢
   30.09   30.09   Global Days 090

69745 including medial to geniculate ganglion   A2 T 80 50 ▢
EXCLUDES   *extracranial suture of facial nerve (64864)*
   31.89   31.89   Global Days 090

69799 Unlisted procedure, middle ear   T 80 50
   0.00   0.00   Global Days YYY

69801-69915 Procedures of the Labyrinth

CMS *100-4,12,30*   *Correct Coding Policy*

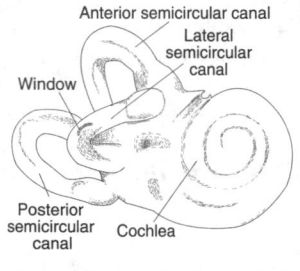

Anterior semicircular canal
Lateral semicircular canal
Window
Posterior semicircular canal
Cochlea

Side view schematic of semicircular canals (left). Sound (below) as registered in the cochlea
● Low tone
● Mid range
● High tones

The mastoid process is a bony protrusion of the petrous part of the temporal bone. It houses a honeycomb-like sinus that resonates sounds. The petrous apex lies deep in the inner ear and is drilled and drained during an apicectomy

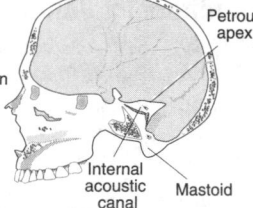

Petrous apex
Internal acoustic canal
Mastoid

69801 Labyrinthotomy, with or without cryosurgery including other nonexcisional destructive procedures or perfusion of vestibuloactive drugs (single or multiple perfusions); transcanal   A2 T 80 50 ▢
INCLUDES   initial and subsequent infusions
   18.92   18.92   Global Days 090
AMA: 2008, Jan, 10-25; 2007, Dec, 7-8

69802 with mastoidectomy   A2 T 80 50 ▢
   26.56   26.56   Global Days 090

69805 Endolymphatic sac operation; without shunt   A2 T 80 50 ▢
   26.94   26.94   Global Days 090

69806 with shunt   A2 T 50 ▢
   24.20   24.20   Global Days 090

69820 Fenestration semicircular canal   A2 T 80 50 ▢
INCLUDES   Lempert's fenestration
   21.96   21.96   Global Days 090

69840 Revision fenestration operation   A2 T 80 50 ▢
   23.03   23.03   Global Days 090

69905 Labyrinthectomy; transcanal   A2 T 50 ▢
   23.38   23.38   Global Days 090

69910 with mastoidectomy   A2 T 80 50 ▢
   26.16   26.16   Global Days 090

69915 Vestibular nerve section, translabyrinthine approach   A2 T 80 50 ▢
EXCLUDES   *transcranial approach (69950)*
   39.64   39.64   Global Days 090

69930-69949 Cochlear Implantation

CMS *100-3,50.3*   *Cochlear Implantation*
CMS *100-2,16,100*   *Hearing Devices*
CMS *100-4,32,100*   *Billing Requirements br Cochlear Implantation*

69930 Cochlear device implantation, with or without mastoidectomy   HB T 80 50 ▢ P0
Code also (L8614)
   31.86   31.86   Global Days 090

69949 Unlisted procedure, inner ear   T 80 50
   0.00   0.00   Global Days YYY

69950-69979 Inner Ear Procedures via Craniotomy

CMS *100-4,12,30*   *Correct Coding Policy*
EXCLUDES   *external approach (69535)*

69950 Vestibular nerve section, transcranial approach   C 80 50 ▢
   47.03   47.03   Global Days 090

69955 Total facial nerve decompression and/or repair (may include graft)   T 80 50 ▢ P0
   51.44   51.44   Global Days 090

69960 Decompression internal auditory canal   T 80 50 ▢ P0
   49.78   49.78   Global Days 090

69970 Removal of tumor, temporal bone   T 80 50 ▢ P0
   55.59   55.59   Global Days 090

69979 Unlisted procedure, temporal bone, middle fossa approach   T 80 50
   0.00   0.00   Global Days YYY

69990 Operating Microscope

CMS *100-4,12,30*   *Correct Coding Policy*
EXCLUDES   *magnifying loupes*

Code first primary procedure
+ **69990** Microsurgical techniques, requiring use of operating microscope (List separately in addition to code for primary procedure)   N1 N 80

Do not report with (0184T, 15756-15758, 15842, 19364, 19368, 20955-20962, 20969-20973, 22856-22861, 26551-26554, 26556, 31526, 31531, 31536, 31541, 31545-31546, 31561, 31571, 43116, 43496, 49906, 61548, 63075-63078, 64727, 64820-64823, 65091-68850)
   5.81   5.81   Global Days ZZZ
AMA: 2008, Jan, 10-25; 2008, Jan, 6-7; 2008, Sep, 10▢-11; 2007, Jan, 13-27; 2007, Jan, 13-27; 2007, January, 13-27; 2005, Aug, 1-3; 2005, Aug, 1-3; 2005, Jul, 13-16; 2005, July, 13-16; 2005, August, 1-3; 2005, March, 11-15; 2005, Jul, 13-16; 2005, Mar, 11-15; 2005, Mar, 11-15; 2004, May, 9; 2004, June, 10; 2004, June, 11; 2004, January, 27; 2004, May, 9; 2004, May, 9; 2004, Jan, 27; 2004, Jan, 27; 2004, Jun, 11; 2004, Jun, 11; 2004, Jun, 10; 2004, Jun, 10

70010-70015 Radiography: Neurodiagnostic

CMS 100-4,13,100	*Interpretation of Diagnostic Tests*
CMS 100-2,6,10	*Medical and Other Services Furnished to Inpatients*
CMS 100-4,3,10.4	*Payment of Nonphysician Services for Inpatients*
CMS 100-2,15,80	*Physician Supervision Requirements for Diagnostic Tests*

EXCLUDES *intrathecal injection procedures (61055, 62284)*

70010 **Myelography, posterior fossa, radiological supervision and interpretation** N1 02 80 ☐
    🛏 **4.74** ✎ **4.74 Global Days XXX**
       AMA: 2005, Mar, 11-15; 2005, Mar, 11-15; 2005, March, 11-15

70015 **Cisternography, positive contrast, radiological supervision and interpretation** N1 02 80 ☐
    🛏 **3.94** ✎ **3.94 Global Days XXX**

70030-70390 Radiography: Head, Neck, Orofacial Structures

CMS 100-4,13,100	*Interpretation of Diagnostic Tests*
CMS 100-2,6,10	*Medical and Other Services Furnished to Inpatients*
CMS 100-4,3,10.4	*Payment of Nonphysician Services for Inpatients*
CMS 100-2,15,80	*Physician Supervision Requirements for Diagnostic Tests*
CMS 100-4,13,10	*ICD-9-CM Coding for Diagnostic Tests*

INCLUDES minimum number of views or more views when needed to adequately complete the study
radiographs that have to be repeated during the encounter due to substandard quality; only one unit of service is reported

EXCLUDES *obtaining more films after review of initial films, based on the discretion of the radiologist, an order for the test, and a change in the patient's condition*

Do not report with a second interpretation by the requesting physician (included in E/M service)

70030 **Radiologic examination, eye, for detection of foreign body** Z3 X 80
    🛏 **0.77** ✎ **0.77 Global Days XXX**

70100 **Radiologic examination, mandible; partial, less than 4 views** Z1 X 80
    🛏 **0.83** ✎ **0.83 Global Days XXX**

70110 **complete, minimum of 4 views** Z3 X 80 ☐
    🛏 **1.08** ✎ **1.08 Global Days XXX**

70120 **Radiologic examination, mastoids; less than 3 views per side** Z0 X 80
    🛏 **0.91** ✎ **0.91 Global Days XXX**

70130 **complete, minimum of 3 views per side** Z2 X 80 ☐
    🛏 **1.50** ✎ **1.50 Global Days XXX**

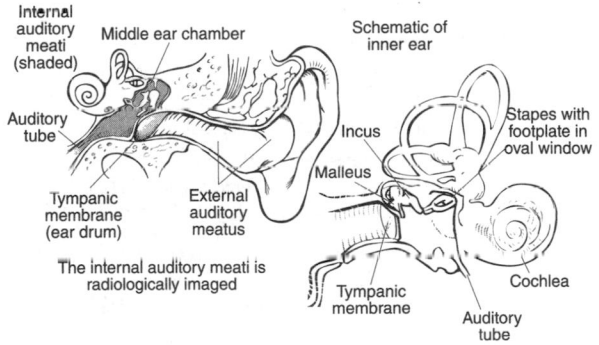

Internal auditory meati (shaded); Middle ear chamber; Schematic of inner ear; Auditory tube; Incus; Stapes with footplate in oval window; Malleus; Tympanic membrane (ear drum); External auditory meatus; Cochlea; The internal auditory meati is radiologically imaged; Tympanic membrane; Auditory tube

70134 **Radiologic examination, internal auditory meati, complete** Z3 X 80
    🛏 **1.29** ✎ **1.29 Global Days XXX**

Orbital rim; Frontal; Roof; Zygoma (malar); Ethmoid; Zygomatic arch; Lacrimal; Condylar process; Nasal; Maxilla; Palate; Coronoid process; Alveolar margins; Ramus; Mandible; Body; Angle; Symphysis

An x-ray of the facial bones is performed

70140 **Radiologic examination, facial bones; less than 3 views** Z3 X 80
    🛏 **0.82** ✎ **0.82 Global Days XXX**

70150 **complete, minimum of 3 views** Z2 X 80 ☐
    🛏 **1.17** ✎ **1.17 Global Days XXX**

70160 **Radiologic examination, nasal bones, complete, minimum of 3 views** Z3 X 80
    🛏 **0.87** ✎ **0.87 Global Days XXX**

70170 **Dacryocystography, nasolacrimal duct, radiological supervision and interpretation** N1 02 80 ☐
    EXCLUDES *procedure (68850)*
    🛏 **0.00** ✎ **0.00 Global Days XXX**

70190 **Radiologic examination; optic foramina** Z3 X 80
    🛏 **0.97** ✎ **0.97 Global Days XXX**

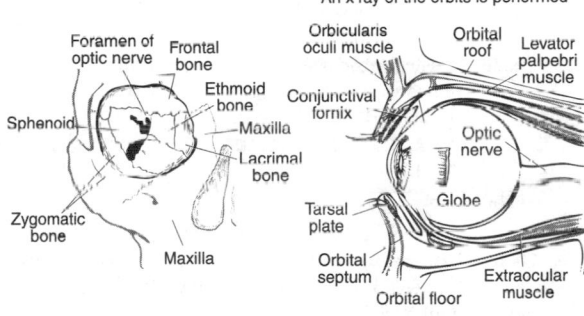

An x-ray of the orbits is performed

Foramen of optic nerve; Frontal bone; Orbicularis oculi muscle; Orbital roof; Levator palpebri muscle; Ethmoid bone; Conjunctival fornix; Sphenoid; Maxilla; Optic nerve; Lacrimal bone; Globe; Zygomatic bone; Tarsal plate; Maxilla; Orbital septum; Orbital floor; Extraocular muscle

70200 **orbits, complete, minimum of 4 views** Z2 X 80
    🛏 **1.21** ✎ **1.21 Global Days XXX**

70210 **Radiologic examination, sinuses, paranasal, less than 3 views** Z3 X 80
    🛏 **0.82** ✎ **0.82 Global Days XXX**

70220 **Radiologic examination, sinuses, paranasal, complete, minimum of 3 views** Z3 X 80 ☐
    🛏 **1.07** ✎ **1.07 Global Days XXX**

70240 **Radiologic examination, sella turcica** Z3 X 80
    🛏 **0.80** ✎ **0.80 Global Days XXX**

70250 **Radiologic examination, skull; less than 4 views** Z3 X 80
    🛏 **0.99** ✎ **0.99 Global Days XXX**

70260 **complete, minimum of 4 views** Z3 X 80 ☐
    🛏 **1.32** ✎ **1.32 Global Days XXX**

Radiology

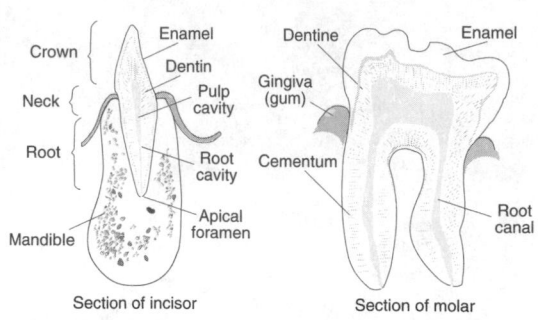

Crown — Enamel
Dentine — Enamel
Neck — Dentin
Gingiva (gum)
Root — Pulp cavity
Root cavity
Cementum
Apical foramen
Mandible
Root cavity
Root canal

Section of incisor   Section of molar

Normal adult dentition numbers 16 teeth in each jaw: four incisors, two canines, four premolars, and six molars. A common tooth eruption problem occurs with the third molars (wisdom teeth) which may be malposed and become impacted. Caries means "rotten" and is a decalcification of tooth enamel and sometimes penetration into the dentin and pulp. Disease processes may cause resorption of the dentin and cementum

70300 Radiologic examination, teeth; single view   Z3 X 80
🔲 0.39   ⚕ 0.39 Global Days XXX

70310   partial examination, less than full mouth   Z2 X 80 🔲
🔲 0.92   ⚕ 0.92 Global Days XXX

70320   complete, full mouth   Z2 X 80 🔲
🔲 1.30   ⚕ 1.30 Global Days XXX

70328 Radiologic examination, temporomandibular joint, open and closed mouth; unilateral   Z3 X 80
🔲 0.81   ⚕ 0.81 Global Days XXX

70330   bilateral   Z2 X 80 🔲
🔲 1.29   ⚕ 1.29 Global Days XXX

70332 Temporomandibular joint arthrography, radiological supervision and interpretation   N1 02 80 🔲

Do not report with fluoroscopic guidance (77002)
🔲 2.33   ⚕ 2.33 Global Days XXX
AMA: 2008, Jan, 10-25; 2008, Jun, 8-11; 2007, Feb, 10-11; 2007, Feb, 10-11; 2007, February, 10-11

70336 Magnetic resonance (eg, proton) imaging, temporomandibular joint(s)   Z2 03 80 🔲
🔲 14.14   ⚕ 14.14 Global Days XXX
AMA: 2008, Jan, 10-25; 2007, Jan, 13-27; 2007, Jan, 13-27; 2007, January, 13-27

70350 Cephalogram, orthodontic   Z3 X 80
🔲 0.56   ⚕ 0.56 Global Days XXX

70355 Orthopantogram   Z3 X 80 🔲
🔲 0.63   ⚕ 0.63 Global Days XXX

70360 Radiologic examination; neck, soft tissue   Z3 X 80
🔲 0.74   ⚕ 0.74 Global Days XXX

70370   pharynx or larynx, including fluoroscopy and/or magnification technique   Z2 X 80 🔲
🔲 2.03   ⚕ 2.03 Global Days XXX

70371 Complex dynamic pharyngeal and speech evaluation by cine or video recording   Z2 X 80 🔲
🔲 2.69   ⚕ 2.69 Global Days XXX
AMA: 2004, Dec, 14; 2004, Dec, 14; 2004, December, 14

70373 Laryngography, contrast, radiological supervision and interpretation   N1 02 80 🔲
🔲 2.21   ⚕ 2.21 Global Days XXX

70380 Radiologic examination, salivary gland for calculus   Z3 X 80
🔲 1.01   ⚕ 1.01 Global Days XXX

70390 Sialography, radiological supervision and interpretation   N1 02 80 🔲
🔲 2.73   ⚕ 2.73 Global Days XXX

70450-70492 Computerized Tomography: Head, Neck, Face

CMS 100-3,220.1   *Computerized Tomography*
CMS 100-4,13,100   *Interpretation of Diagnostic Tests*
CMS 100-2,6,10   *Medical and Other Services Furnished to Inpatients*
CMS 100-4,3,10.4   *Payment of Nonphysician Services for Inpatients*
CMS 100-2,15,80   *Physician Supervision Requirements for Diagnostic Tests*
CMS 100-4,13,10   *ICD-9-CM Coding for Diagnostic Tests*

INCLUDES   imaging using tomographic technique enhanced by computer imaging to create a cross-sectional plane of the body

EXCLUDES   *3D rendering (76376, 76377)*

70450 Computed tomography, head or brain; without contrast material   Z2 03 80 🔲 PQ
🔲 6.06   ⚕ 6.06 Global Days XXX
AMA: 2008, Jan, 10-25; 2007, Jan, 13-27; 2007, Jan, 13-27; 2007, January, 13-27; 2005, Mar, 11-15; 2005, March, 11-15; 2005, Mar, 11-15

70460   with contrast material(s)   Z2 03 80 🔲 PQ
🔲 7.83   ⚕ 7.83 Global Days XXX
AMA: 2008, Jan, 10-25; 2007, Jan, 13-27; 2007, Jan, 13-27; 2007, January, 13-27

70470   without contrast material, followed by contrast material(s) and further sections   Z2 03 80 🔲 PQ
🔲 9.48   ⚕ 9.48 Global Days XXX
AMA: 2008, Jan, 10-25; 2007, Jan, 13-27; 2007, Jan, 13-27; 2007, January, 13-27

70480 Computed tomography, orbit, sella, or posterior fossa or outer, middle, or inner ear; without contrast material   Z2 03 80 🔲
🔲 9.19   ⚕ 9.19 Global Days XXX

70481   with contrast material(s)   Z2 03 80 🔲
🔲 10.69   ⚕ 10.69 Global Days XXX
AMA: 2008, Apr, -11; 2008, Apr, -11; 2008, Apr, -11

70482   without contrast material, followed by contrast material(s) and further sections   Z2 03 80 🔲
🔲 12.25   ⚕ 12.25 Global Days XXX

70486 Computed tomography, maxillofacial area; without contrast material   Z2 03 80 🔲
🔲 7.78   ⚕ 7.78 Global Days XXX
AMA: 2008, Jan, 10-25; 2007, Jan, 13-27; 2007, Jan, 13-27; 2007, January, 13-27

70487   with contrast material(s)   Z2 03 80 🔲
🔲 9.41   ⚕ 9.41 Global Days XXX

70488   without contrast material, followed by contrast material(s) and further sections   Z2 03 80 🔲
🔲 11.45   ⚕ 11.45 Global Days XXX

70490 Computed tomography, soft tissue neck; without contrast material   Z2 03 80 🔲
EXCLUDES   *CT of the cervical spine (72125)*
🔲 7.71   ⚕ 7.71 Global Days XXX

70491   with contrast material(s)   Z2 03 80 🔲
EXCLUDES   *CT of the cervical spine (72126)*
🔲 9.25   ⚕ 9.25 Global Days XXX

70492   without contrast material followed by contrast material(s) and further sections   Z2 03 80 🔲
EXCLUDES   *CT of the cervical spine (72127)*
🔲 11.23   ⚕ 11.23 Global Days XXX

70300 — 70492

70496-70498 Computerized Tomographic Angiography: Head and Neck

CMS	100-3,220.1	Computerized Tomography
CMS	100-4,13,100	Interpretation of Diagnostic Tests
CMS	100-4,13,30	Computerized Axial Tomography (CT) Procedures
CMS	100-2,6,10	Medical and Other Services Furnished to Inpatients
CMS	100-4,3,10.4	Payment of Nonphysician Services for Inpatients
CMS	100-2,15,80	Physician Supervision Requirements for Diagnostic Tests
CMS	100-4,13,10	ICD-9-CM Coding for Diagnostic Tests

[INCLUDES] multiple rapid thin section CT scans to create cross-sectional images of bones, organs and tissues

70496 Computed tomographic angiography, head, with contrast material(s), including noncontrast images, if performed, and image postprocessing   Z2 03 80 ⊡
    ♨ 17.90   ⚘ 17.90   Global Days XXX
    AMA: 2007, Jan, 28-31; 2007, Jan, 28-31; 2007, January, 28-31; 2005, Dec, 7; 2005, December, 7; 2005, Dec, 7

70498 Computed tomographic angiography, neck, with contrast material(s), including noncontrast images, if performed, and image postprocessing   Z2 03 80 ⊡ P0
    ♨ 17.98   ⚘ 17.98   Global Days XXX
    AMA: 2007, Jan, 28-31; 2007, Jan, 28-31; 2007, January, 28-31; 2005, Dec, 7; 2005, December, 7; 2005, Dec, 7

70540-70543 Magnetic Resonance Imaging: Face, Neck, Orbits

CMS	100-4,13,100	Interpretation of Diagnostic Tests
CMS	100-4,13,40	Magnetic Resonance Imaging (MRI) Procedures
CMS	100-2,6,10	Medical and Other Services Furnished to Inpatients
CMS	100-4,3,10.4	Payment of Nonphysician Services for Inpatients
CMS	100-3,220.2	Magnetic Resonance Imaging
CMS	100-2,15,80	Physician Supervision Requirements for Diagnostic Tests

[INCLUDES] application of an external magnetic field that forces alignment of hydrogen atom nuclei in soft tissues which converts to sets of tomographic images that can be displayed as three-dimensional images

maximum frequency with which codes may be reported for each imaging session (once)

[EXCLUDES] *magnetic resonance angiography head/neck (70544-70549)*

70540 Magnetic resonance (eg, proton) imaging, orbit, face, and/or neck; without contrast material(s)   Z2 03 80 ⊡
    ♨ 15.24   ⚘ 15.24   Global Days XXX
    AMA: 2007, Mar, 7-8; 2007, Mar, 7-8; 2007, March, 7-8

70542 with contrast material(s)   Z2 03 80 ⊡
    ♨ 16.94   ⚘ 16.94   Global Days XXX

70543 without contrast material(s), followed by contrast material(s) and further sequences   Z2 03 80 ⊡
    ♨ 23.41   ⚘ 23.41   Global Days XXX

70544-70549 Magnetic Resonance Angiography: Head and Neck

CMS	100-4,13,40.1	Magnetic Resonance Angiography
CMS	100-4,13,100	Interpretation of Diagnostic Tests
CMS	100-4,13,40.1.1	Magnetic Resonance Angiography Coverage Summary
CMS	100-2,6,10	Medical and Other Services Furnished to Inpatients
CMS	100-4,3,10.4	Payment of Nonphysician Services for Inpatients
CMS	100-3,220.3	Magnetic Resonance Angiography
CMS	100-2,15,80	Physician Supervision Requirements for Diagnostic Tests
CMS	100-4,13,10	ICD-9-CM Coding for Diagnostic Tests

[INCLUDES] use of magnetic fields and radio waves to produce detailed cross-sectional images of internal body structures

70544 Magnetic resonance angiography, head; without contrast material(s)   Z2 03 80 ⊡
    ♨ 16.49   ⚘ 16.49   Global Days XXX
    AMA: 2007, Jan, 28-31; 2007, Jan, 28-31; 2007, January, 28-31; 2005, Dec, 7; 2005, December, 7; 2005, Dec, 7

70545 with contrast material(s)   Z2 03 80 ⊡
    ♨ 16.42   ⚘ 16.42   Global Days XXX
    AMA: 2007, Jan, 28-31; 2007, Jan, 28-31; 2007, January, 28-31; 2005, Dec, 7; 2005, December, 7; 2005, Dec, 7

70546 without contrast material(s), followed by contrast material(s) and further sequences   Z2 03 80 ⊡
    ♨ 26.04   ⚘ 26.04   Global Days XXX
    AMA: 2007, Jan, 28-31; 2007, Jan, 28-31; 2007, January, 28-31; 2005, Dec, 7; 2005, December, 7; 2005, Dec, 7

70547 Magnetic resonance angiography, neck; without contrast material(s)   Z2 03 80 ⊡ P0
    ♨ 16.45   ⚘ 16.45   Global Days XXX
    AMA: 2007, Jan, 28-31; 2007, Jan, 28-31; 2007, January, 28-31; 2005, Dec, 7; 2005, December, 7; 2005, Dec, 7

70548 with contrast material(s)   Z2 03 80 ⊡ P0
    ♨ 17.09   ⚘ 17.09   Global Days XXX
    AMA: 2007, Jan, 28-31; 2007, Jan, 28-31; 2007, January, 28-31; 2005, Dec, 7; 2005, December, 7; 2005, Dec, 7

70549 without contrast material(s), followed by contrast material(s) and further sequences   Z2 03 80 ⊡ P0
    ♨ 26.06   ⚘ 26.06   Global Days XXX
    AMA: 2007, Jan, 28-31; 2007, Jan, 28-31; 2007, January, 28-31; 2005, Dec, 7; 2005, December, 7; 2005, Dec, 7

70551-70553 Magnetic Resonance Imaging: Brain and Brain Stem

CMS		Magnetic Resonance Imaging
CMS	100-4,13,100	Interpretation of Diagnostic Tests
CMS	100-4,13,40	Magnetic Resonance Imaging (MRI) Procedures
CMS	100-4,13,20.1	Professional Component (PC)
CMS	100-2,6,10	Medical and Other Services Furnished to Inpatients
CMS	100-4,3,10.4	Payment of Nonphysician Services for Inpatients
CMS	100-2,15,80	Physician Supervision Requirements for Diagnostic Tests
CMS	100-4,13,10	ICD-9-CM Coding for Diagnostic Tests

[INCLUDES] application of an external magnetic field that forces alignment of hydrogen atom nuclei in soft tissues which converts to sets of tomographic images that can be displayed as three-dimensional images

[EXCLUDES] *magnetic spectroscopy (76390)*

70551 Magnetic resonance (eg, proton) imaging, brain (including brain stem); without contrast material   Z2 03 80 ⊡ P0
    ♨ 15.80   ⚘ 15.80   Global Days XXX
    AMA: 2008, Jan, 10-25; 2007, Jan, 13-27; 2007, Jan, 13-27; 2007, Feb, 6-7; 2007, Feb, 6-7; 2007, January, 13-27; 2007, February, 6-7; 2005, Mar, 16-17; 2005, Mar, 16-17; 2005, March, 16-17

● New Code   ▲ Revised Code   ⬜ Maternity Edit   ◩ Age Edit   A-Y OPPS Status Indicator   ♨ Facility RVU   ⚘ Non-Facility RVU
⊡ CCI Comprehensive Code   50 Bilateral Procedure   + Add-on Indicator   ◩ Laboratory crosswalk   ◩ Radiology crosswalk

70552 — 71060

| 70552 | with contrast material(s) | Z2 03 80 ▢ P0 |

🔲 17.67   ⅍ 17.67   Global Days XXX

AMA: 2008, Jan, 10-25; 2007, Jan, 13-27; 2007, Jan, 13-27; 2007, Feb, 6-7; 2007, Feb, 6-7; 2007, January, 13-27; 2007, February, 6-7; 2005, Mar, 16-17; 2005, Mar, 16-17; 2005, March, 16-17

| 70553 | without contrast material, followed by contrast material(s) and further sequences | Z2 03 80 ▢ P0 |

🔲 23.64   ⅍ 23.64   Global Days XXX

AMA: 2008, Jan, 10-25; 2007, Jan, 13-27; 2007, Jan, 13-27; 2007, Feb, 6-7; 2007, February, 6-7; 2007, January, 13-27; 2007, Feb, 6-7; 2005, Mar, 16-17; 2005, March, 11-15; 2005, March, 16-17; 2005, Mar, 16-17; 2005, Mar, 11-15; 2005, Mar, 11-15

70554-70555 Magnetic Resonance Imaging: Brain Mapping

INCLUDES   neuroimaging technique using MRI to identify and map signals related to brain activity

Do not report with the following codes unless a separate diagnostic MRI is performed (70551-70553)

| 70554 | Magnetic resonance imaging, brain, functional MRI; including test selection and administration of repetitive body part movement and/or visual stimulation, not requiring physician or psychologist administration | Z2 03 80 |

INCLUDES   testing performed by a technologist, nonphysician, or nonpsychologist

Do not report with functional brain mapping (96020)

🔲 17.17   ⅍ 17.17   Global Days XXX

AMA: 2007, Feb, 6-7; 2007, Feb, 6-7; 2007, Mar, 7-8; 2007, Mar, 7-8; 2007, February, 6-7; 2007, March, 7-8

| 70555 | requiring physician or psychologist administration of entire neurofunctional testing | Z2 S 80 |

INCLUDES   services provided by a physician or psychologist

Code also (96020)

🔲 0.00   ⅍ 0.00   Global Days XXX

AMA: 2007, Feb, 6-7; 2007, Feb, 6-7; 2007, Mar, 7-8; 2007, Mar, 7-8; 2007, February, 6-7; 2007, March, 7-8

70557-70559 Magnetic Resonance Imaging: Intraoperative

EXCLUDES   frequency greater than one for each code per operative session
intracranial lesion stereotaxic biopsy with magnetic resonance guidance (61751)

Code also only if a separate report is generated (70557-70559)
Do not report with (61751, 77021, 77022)

| 70557 | Magnetic resonance (eg, proton) imaging, brain (including brain stem and skull base), during open intracranial procedure (eg, to assess for residual tumor or residual vascular malformation); without contrast material | Z2 S 80 ▢ |

🔲 0.00   ⅍ 0.00   Global Days XXX

| 70558 | with contrast material(s) | Z2 S 80 ▢ |

🔲 0.00   ⅍ 0.00   Global Days XXX

| 70559 | without contrast material(s), followed by contrast material(s) and further sequences | Z2 S 80 ▢ |

🔲 0.00   ⅍ 0.00   Global Days XXX

71010-71130 Radiography: Thorax

CMS 100-4,13,100	Interpretation of Diagnostic Tests
CMS 100-2,6,10	Medical and Other Services Furnished to Inpatients
CMS 100-4,3,10.4	Payment of Nonphysician Services for Inpatients
CMS 100-2,15,80	Physician Supervision Requirements for Diagnostic Tests
CMS 100-4,13,10	ICD-9-CM Coding for Diagnostic Tests

EXCLUDES   needle placement guidance (76942, 77002)

| 71010 | Radiologic examination, chest; single view, frontal | Z6 X 80 ▢ |

EXCLUDES   Concurrent computer-aided detection (0174T)

Do not report with (99291-99292)

Do not report with remotely performed CAD (0175T)

🔲 0.66   ⅍ 0.66   Global Days XXX

AMA: 2008, Jan, 10-25; 2007, Feb, 10-11; 2007, Feb, 10-11; 2007, Jul, 6-10; 2007, February, 10-11; 2007, Jul, 1-4; 2005, Mar, 11-15; 2005, March, 11-15; 2005, Mar, 11-15

| 71015 | stereo, frontal | Z6 X 80 ▢ |

Do not report with (99291-99292)

🔲 0.81   ⅍ 0.81   Global Days XXX

AMA: 2007, Feb, 10-11; 2007, Feb, 10-11; 2007, February, 10-11; 2007, Jul, 1-4

| 71020 | Radiologic examination, chest, 2 views, frontal and lateral; | Z6 X 80 ▢ |

Do not report with (99291-99292)

🔲 0.88   ⅍ 0.88   Global Days XXX

AMA: 2007, Feb, 10-11; 2007, Feb, 10-11; 2007, Jul, 6-10; 2007, February, 10-11; 2007, Jul, 1-4; 2005, Mar, 11-15; 2005, March, 11-15; 2005, Mar, 11-15

| 71021 | with apical lordotic procedure | Z6 X 80 ▢ |

🔲 1.06   ⅍ 1.06   Global Days XXX

| 71022 | with oblique projections | Z2 X 80 ▢ |

🔲 1.27   ⅍ 1.27   Global Days XXX

AMA: 2007, Jul, 6-10

| 71023 | with fluoroscopy | Z6 X 80 ▢ |

🔲 1.83   ⅍ 1.83   Global Days XXX

AMA: 2008, Jan, 10-25; 2008, Jun, 8-11; 2007, Jan, 13-27; 2007, Jan, 13-27; 2007, January, 13-27

| 71030 | Radiologic examination, chest, complete, minimum of 4 views; | Z2 X 80 ▢ |

🔲 1.28   ⅍ 1.28   Global Days XXX

AMA: 2007, Jul, 6-10

| 71034 | with fluoroscopy | Z2 X 80 ▢ |

EXCLUDES   separate fluoroscopy of chest (76000)

🔲 2.52   ⅍ 2.52   Global Days XXX

AMA: 2008, Jan, 10-25; 2008, Jun, 8-11; 2007, Jan, 13-27; 2007, Jan, 13-27; 2007, January, 13-27

| 71035 | Radiologic examination, chest, special views (eg, lateral decubitus, Bucky studies) | Z3 X 80 |

🔲 0.94   ⅍ 0.94   Global Days XXX

| 71040 | Bronchography, unilateral, radiological supervision and interpretation | 01 02 80 ▢ |

EXCLUDES   procedure (31656, 31715)

🔲 2.63   ⅍ 2.63   Global Days XXX

| 71060 | Bronchography, bilateral, radiological supervision and interpretation | 01 02 80 ▢ |

EXCLUDES   procedure (31656, 31715)

🔲 3.83   ⅍ 3.83   Global Days XXX

71090 Insertion pacemaker, fluoroscopy and radiography, radiological supervision and interpretation `M` `N` `80` ⬜

EXCLUDES *pacemaker insertion procedure*

🔧 0.00 🔨 0.00 Global Days XXX
AMA: 2008, Jan, 10-25; 2008, May, 9-11; 2007, Jan, 13-27; 2007, Jan, 13-27; 2007, January, 13-27

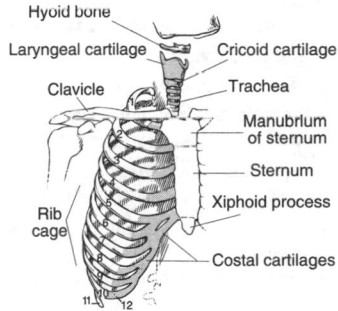

Hyoid bone
Laryngeal cartilage
Cricoid cartilage
Clavicle
Trachea
Manubrium of sternum
Sternum
Xiphoid process
Rib cage
Costal cartilages

An x-ray of the ribs is performed unilaterally (71100-71101) or bilaterally (71110-71111).

71100 Radiologic examination, ribs, unilateral; 2 views `73` `X` `80` ⬜

🔧 0.90 🔨 0.90 Global Days XXX

71101 including posteroanterior chest, minimum of 3 views `73` `X` `80` ⬜

🔧 1.08 🔨 1.08 Global Days XXX

71110 Radiologic examination, ribs, bilateral; 3 views `73` `X` `80` ⬜

🔧 1.12 🔨 1.12 Global Days XXX

71111 including posteroanterior chest, minimum of 4 views `73` `X` `80` ⬜

🔧 1.43 🔨 1.43 Global Days XXX

71120 Radiologic examination; sternum, minimum of 2 views `76` `X` `80`

🔧 0.90 🔨 0.90 Global Days XXX

71130 sternoclavicular joint or joints, minimum of 3 views `78` `Y` `80`

🔧 1.03 🔨 1.03 Global Days XXX

71250-71270 Computerized Tomography: Thorax

CMS 100-3,220.1 *Computerized Tomography*
CMS 100-4,13,100 *Interpretation of Diagnostic Tests*
CMS 100-4,13,30 *Computerized Axial Tomography (CT) Procedures*
CMS 100-2,6,10 *Medical and Other Services Furnished to Inpatients*
CMS 100-4,3,10.4 *Payment of Nonphysician Services for Inpatients*
CMS 100-2,15,80 *Physician Supervision Requirements for Diagnostic Tests*
CMS 100-4,13,10 *ICD-9-CM Coding for Diagnostic Tests*
INCLUDES imaging using tomographic technique enhanced by computer imaging to create a cross-sectional plane of the body

EXCLUDES *3D rendering (76376, 76377)*
cardiac computed tomography of the heart (0144T-0151T)

71250 Computed tomography, thorax; without contrast material `Z2` `03` `80` ⬜

🔧 7.90 🔨 7.90 Global Days XXX
AMA: 2008, Jan, 10-25; 2007, Jul, 12-13

71260 with contrast material(s) `Z2` `03` `80` ⬜

🔧 9.48 🔨 9.48 Global Days XXX
AMA: 2008, Jan, 10-25; 2007, Jul, 12-13; 2005, Mar, 11-15; 2005, Mar, 11-15; 2005, March, 11-15

71270 without contrast material, followed by contrast material(s) and further sections `Z2` `03` `80` ⬜

🔧 11.71 🔨 11.71 Global Days XXX
AMA: 2008, Jan, 10-25; 2007, Jan, 13-27; 2007, Jan, 13-27; 2007, January, 13-27; 2007, Jul, 12-13

71275 Computerized Tomographic Angiography: Thorax

CMS 100-3,220.1 *Computerized Tomography*
CMS 100-4,13,100 *Interpretation of Diagnostic Tests*
CMS 100-4,13,30 *Computerized Axial Tomography (CT) Procedures*
CMS 100-2,6,10 *Medical and Other Services Furnished to Inpatients*
CMS 100-4,3,10.4 *Payment of Nonphysician Services for Inpatients*
CMS 100-2,15,80 *Physician Supervision Requirements for Diagnostic Tests*
CMS 100-4,13,10 *ICD-9-CM Coding for Diagnostic Tests*
INCLUDES multiple rapid thin section CT scans to create cross-sectional images of bones, organs and tissues

EXCLUDES *computed tomographic angiography of coronary arteries (0146T-0149T)*

71275 Computed tomographic angiography, chest (noncoronary), with contrast material(s), including noncontrast images, if performed, and image postprocessing `Z2` `03` `80` ⬜

🔧 14.39 🔨 14.39 Global Days XXX
AMA: 2008, Jan, 10-25; 2007, Jan, 28-31; 2007, Jan, 28-31; 2007, Jan, 13-27; 2007, Mar, 7-8; 2007, January, 13-27; 2007, Jan, 13-27; 2007, Mar, 7-8; 2007, January, 28-31; 2007, March, 7-8; 2005, Dec, 7; 2005, Dec, 7; 2005, Jun, 9-11; 2005, December, 7; 2005, June, 9-11; 2005, Jun, 9-11

71550-71552 Magnetic Resonance Imaging: Thorax

CMS *Magnetic Resonance Imaging*
CMS 100-4,13,100 *Interpretation of Diagnostic Tests*
CMS 100-4,13,40 *Magnetic Resonance Imaging (MRI) Procedures*
CMS 100-2,6,10 *Medical and Other Services Furnished to Inpatients*
CMS 100-4,3,10.4 *Payment of Nonphysician Services for Inpatients*
CMS 100-2,15,80 *Physician Supervision Requirements for Diagnostic Tests*
CMS 100-4,13,10 *ICD-9-CM Coding for Diagnostic Tests*
INCLUDES application of an external magnetic field that forces alignment of hydrogen atom nuclei in soft tissues which converts to sets of tomographic images that can be displayed as three-dimensional images

EXCLUDES *MRI of the breast (77058, 77059)*

71550 Magnetic resonance (eg, proton) imaging, chest (eg, for evaluation of hilar and mediastinal lymphadenopathy); without contrast material(s) `Z2` `03` `80` ⬜

🔧 17.02 🔨 17.02 Global Days XXX

71551 with contrast material(s) `Z2` `03` `80` ⬜

🔧 19.10 🔨 19.10 Global Days XXX

71552 without contrast material(s), followed by contrast material(s) and further sequences `Z2` `03` `80` ⬜

🔧 26.19 🔨 26.19 Global Days XXX

71090 — 71552

71555 Magnetic Resonance Angiography: Thorax

CMS *100-4,13,40.1* *Magnetic Resonance Angiography*
CMS *Magnetic Resonance Angiography*
CMS *100-4,13,100* *Interpretation of Diagnostic Tests*
CMS *100-4,13,40.1.1* *Magnetic Resonance Angiography Coverage Summary*
CMS *100-2,6,10* *Medical and Other Services Furnished to Inpatients*
CMS *100-4,3,10.4* *Payment of Nonphysician Services for Inpatients*
CMS *100-2,15,80* *Physician Supervision Requirements for Diagnostic Tests*
CMS *100-4,13,10* *ICD-9-CM Coding for Diagnostic Tests*

71555 **Magnetic resonance angiography, chest (excluding myocardium), with or without contrast material(s)** B 80 🔲
🔳 16.78 ⚖ 16.78 Global Days XXX
AMA: 2008, Jul, 3&14; 2007, Jan, 28-31; 2007, Jan, 28-31; 2007, January, 28-31; 2005, Dec, 7; 2005, December, 7; 2005, Dec, 7

72010-72120 Radiography: Spine

CMS *100-4,13,100* *Interpretation of Diagnostic Tests*
CMS *100-2,6,10* *Medical and Other Services Furnished to Inpatients*
CMS *100-4,3,10.4* *Payment of Nonphysician Services for Inpatients*
CMS *100-2,15,80* *Physician Supervision Requirements for Diagnostic Tests*
CMS *100-4,13,10* *ICD-9-CM Coding for Diagnostic Tests*

INCLUDES minimum number of views or more views when needed to adequately complete the study
radiographs that have to be repeated during the encounter due to substandard quality; only one unit of service is reported

EXCLUDES *obtaining more films after review of initial films, based on the discretion of the radiologist, an order for the test, and a change in the patient's condition*

Do not report with a second interpretation by the requesting physician (included in E/M service)

72010 **Radiologic examination, spine, entire, survey study, anteroposterior and lateral** Z2 X 80 🔲
🔳 1.89 ⚖ 1.89 Global Days XXX
AMA: 2008, Jan, 10-25; 2007, Jan, 28-31; 2007, Jan, 28-31; 2007, Jan, 13-27; 2007, Jan, 13-27; 2007, January, 28-31; 2007, January, 13-27

72020 **Radiologic examination, spine, single view, specify level** Z3 X 80
🔳 0.65 ⚖ 0.65 Global Days XXX

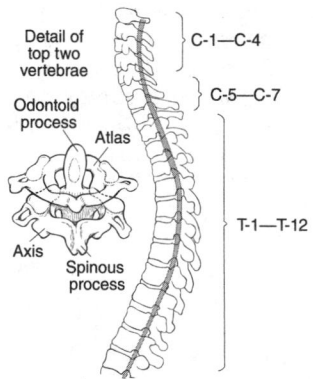

An x-ray of the cervical spine is performed

72040 **Radiologic examination, spine, cervical; 2 or 3 views** Z3 X 80
🔳 1.01 ⚖ 1.01 Global Days XXX

72050 **minimum of 4 views** Z3 X 80 🔲
🔳 1.43 ⚖ 1.43 Global Days XXX

72052 **complete, including oblique and flexion and/or extension studies** Z2 X 80 🔲
🔳 1.79 ⚖ 1.79 Global Days XXX

72069 **Radiologic examination, spine, thoracolumbar, standing (scoliosis)** Z3 X 80 🔲
🔳 0.95 ⚖ 0.95 Global Days XXX

72070 **Radiologic examination, spine; thoracic, 2 views** Z3 X 80 🔲
🔳 0.93 ⚖ 0.93 Global Days XXX

72072 **thoracic, 3 views** Z3 X 80 🔲
🔳 1.06 ⚖ 1.06 Global Days XXX

72074 **thoracic, minimum of 4 views** Z2 X 80 🔲
🔳 1.24 ⚖ 1.24 Global Days XXX

72080 **thoracolumbar, 2 views** Z3 X 80 🔲
🔳 0.97 ⚖ 0.97 Global Days XXX

72090 **scoliosis study, including supine and erect studies** Z3 X 80 🔲
🔳 1.27 ⚖ 1.27 Global Days XXX

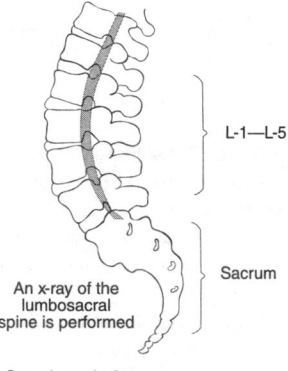

An x-ray of the lumbosacral spine is performed

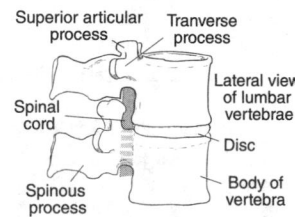

72100 **Radiologic examination, spine, lumbosacral; 2 or 3 views** Z3 X 80 🔲
🔳 1.06 ⚖ 1.06 Global Days XXX

72110 **minimum of 4 views** Z3 X 80 🔲
🔳 1.48 ⚖ 1.48 Global Days XXX

72114 **complete, including bending views** Z2 X 80 🔲
🔳 1.93 ⚖ 1.93 Global Days XXX

72120 **Radiologic examination, spine, lumbosacral, bending views only, minimum of 4 views** Z3 X 80 🔲
🔳 1.33 ⚖ 1.33 Global Days XXX

72125-72133 Computerized Tomography: Spine

CMS *100-3,220.1*   *Computerized Tomography*
CMS *100-4,13,100*   *Interpretation of Diagnostic Tests*
CMS *100-4,13,30*   *Computerized Axial Tomography (CT) Procedures*
CMS *100-2,6,10*   *Medical and Other Services Furnished to Inpatients*
CMS *100-2,15,80*   *Physician Supervision Requirements for Diagnostic Tests*
CMS *100-4,13,10*   *ICD-9-CM Coding for Diagnostic Tests*

[INCLUDES]   imaging using tomographic technique enhanced by computer imaging to create a cross-sectional plane of the body

[EXCLUDES]   *3D rendering (76376, 76377)*

Code also intrathecal injection procedure when performed (61055, 62284)

72125   **Computed tomography, cervical spine; without contrast material**   72 03 80 ▭
         ⊄ 7.92   ⅛ 7.92   Global Days XXX

72126   **with contrast material**   72 03 80 ▭
         ⊄ 9.46   ⅛ 9.46   Global Days XXX

72127   **without contrast material, followed by contrast material(s) and further sections**   72 03 80 ▭
         ⊄ 11.53   ⅛ 11.53   Global Days XXX

72128   **Computed tomography, thoracic spine; without contrast material**   72 03 80 ▭
         ⊄ 7.90   ⅛ 7.90   Global Days XXX

72129   **with contrast material**   72 03 80 ▭
         ⊄ 9.47   ⅛ 9.47   Global Days XXX

72130   **without contrast material, followed by contrast material(s) and further sections**   72 03 80 ▭
         ⊄ 11.56   ⅛ 11.56   Global Days XXX

72131   **Computed tomography, lumbar spine; without contrast material**   72 03 80 ▭
         ⊄ 7.89   ⅛ 7.89   Global Days XXX

72132   **with contrast material**   72 03 80 ▭
         ⊄ 9.46   ⅛ 9.46   Global Days XXX

72133   **without contrast material, followed by contrast material(s) and further sections**   72 03 80 ▭
         ⊄ 11.55   ⅛ 11.55   Global Days XXX

72141-72158 Magnetic Resonance Imaging: Spine

CMS   *Magnetic Resonance Imaging*
CMS *100-4,13,100*   *Interpretation of Diagnostic Tests*
CMS *100-4,13,40*   *Magnetic Resonance Imaging (MRI) Procedures*
CMS *100-2,6,10*   *Medical and Other Services Furnished to Inpatients*
CMS *100-4,3,10.4*   *Payment of Nonphysician Services for Inpatients*
CMS *100-2,15,80*   *Physician Supervision Requirements for Diagnostic Tests*
CMS *100-4,13,10*   *ICD-9-CM Coding for Diagnostic Tests*

[INCLUDES]   application of an external magnetic field that forces alignment of hydrogen atom nuclei in soft tissues which converts to sets of tomographic images that can be displayed as three-dimensional images

Code also intrathecal injection procedure when performed (61055, 62284)

72141   **Magnetic resonance (eg, proton) imaging, spinal canal and contents, cervical; without contrast material**   72 03 80 ▭
         ⊄ 14.46   ⅛ 14.46   Global Days XXX

72142   **with contrast material(s)**   72 03 80 ▭
         [EXCLUDES]   *MRI of cervical spinal canal performed without contrast followed by repeating the study with contrast (72156)*
         ⊄ 17.84   ⅛ 17.84   Global Days XXX

72146   **Magnetic resonance (eg, proton) imaging, spinal canal and contents, thoracic; without contrast material**   72 03 80 ▭
         ⊄ 14.84   ⅛ 14.84   Global Days XXX

72147   **with contrast material(s)**   72 03 80 ▭
         [EXCLUDES]   *MRI of thoracic spinal canal performed without contrast followed by repeating the study with contrast (72157)*
         ⊄ 16.33   ⅛ 16.33   Global Days XXX
         AMA: 2008, Jan, 10-25; 2007, Jan, 13-27; 2007, Jan, 13-27; 2007, January, 13-27

72148   **Magnetic resonance (eg, proton) imaging, spinal canal and contents, lumbar; without contrast material**   72 03 80 ▭
         ⊄ 14.66   ⅛ 14.66   Global Days XXX
         AMA: 2008, Jan, 10-25; 2007, Jan, 13-27; 2007, Jan, 13-27; 2007, January, 13-27; 2005, Mar, 11-15; 2005, Mar, 11-15; 2005, November, 14-15; 2005, March, 11-15; 2005, Nov, 14-15; 2005, Nov, 14-15

72149   **with contrast material(s)**   72 03 80 ▭
         [EXCLUDES]   *MRI of lumbar spinal canal performed without contrast followed by repeating the study with contrast (72158)*
         ⊄ 17.64   ⅛ 17.64   Global Days XXX

72156   **Magnetic resonance (eg, proton) imaging, spinal canal and contents, without contrast material, followed by contrast material(s) and further sequences; cervical**   72 03 80 ▭
         ⊄ 23.65   ⅛ 23.65   Global Days XXX

72157   **thoracic**   72 03 80 ▭
         ⊄ 22.49   ⅛ 22.49   Global Days XXX

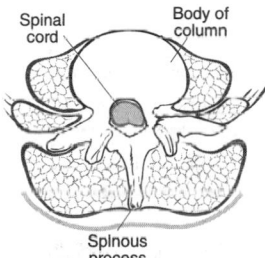

Superior view of thoracic spine and surrounding paraspinal muscles

An MRI of the lumbar spinal canal and its contents is performed without contrast material, and then with contrast. Report 72158 for the lumbar spine

72158   **lumbar**   72 03 80 ▭
         ⊄ 23.34   ⅛ 23.34   Global Days XXX

● New Code   ▲ Revised Code   ▥ Maternity Edit   ▧ Age Edit   Ⓐ-Ⓨ OPPS Status Indicator   ⊄ Facility RVU   ⅛ Non-Facility RVU

▱ CCI Comprehensive Code   ⑤ Bilateral Procedure   + Add-on Indicator   ▨ Laboratory crosswalk   ▨ Radiology crosswalk

Radiology

72159 Magnetic Resonance Angiography: Spine

CMS	Magnetic Resonance Angiography
CMS 100-4,13,100	Interpretation of Diagnostic Tests
CMS 100-4,13,40	Magnetic Resonance Imaging (MRI) Procedures
CMS 100-2,6,10	Medical and Other Services Furnished to Inpatients
CMS 100-4,3,10.4	Payment of Nonphysician Services for Inpatients
CMS 100-2,15,80	Physician Supervision Requirements for Diagnostic Tests
CMS 100-4,13,10	ICD-9-CM Coding for Diagnostic Tests

Code also intrathecal injection procedure when performed (61055, 62284)

72159 **Magnetic resonance angiography, spinal canal and contents, with or without contrast material(s)** [E]
 18.00 18.00 Global Days XXX
AMA: 2007, Jan, 28-31; 2007, Jan, 28-31; 2007, January, 28-31; 2005, Dec, 7; 2005, December, 7; 2005, Dec, 7

72170-72190 Radiography: Pelvis

CMS 100-4,13,100	Interpretation of Diagnostic Tests
CMS 100-2,6,10	Medical and Other Services Furnished to Inpatients
CMS 100-4,3,10.4	Payment of Nonphysician Services for Inpatients
CMS 100-2,15,80	Physician Supervision Requirements for Diagnostic Tests
CMS 100-4,13,10	ICD-9-CM Coding for Diagnostic Tests

INCLUDES   minimum number of views or more views when needed to adequately complete the study
radiographs that have to be repeated during the encounter due to substandard quality; only one unit of service is reported

EXCLUDES   obtaining more films after review of initial films, based on the discretion of the radiologist, an order for the test, and a change in the patient's condition
pelvimetry (74710)

Do not report with a second interpretation by the requesting physician (included in E/M service)

72170 **Radiologic examination, pelvis; 1 or 2 views** [26] [X] [80]
 0.71 0.71 Global Days XXX
AMA: 2008, Jan, 10-25; 2007, Jan, 13-27; 2007, Jan, 13-27; 2007, January, 13-27

72190 **complete, minimum of 3 views** [72] [X] [80] [□]
 1.08 1.08 Global Days XXX

72191 Computerized Tomographic Angiography: Pelvis

CMS 100-3,220.1	Computerized Tomography
CMS 100-4,13,100	Interpretation of Diagnostic Tests
CMS 100-4,13,30	Computerized Axial Tomography (CT) Procedures
CMS 100-2,6,10	Medical and Other Services Furnished to Inpatients
CMS 100-4,3,10.4	Payment of Nonphysician Services for Inpatients
CMS 100-2,15,80	Physician Supervision Requirements for Diagnostic Tests
CMS 100-4,13,10	ICD-9-CM Coding for Diagnostic Tests

INCLUDES   multiple rapid thin section CT scans to create cross-sectional images of bones, organs and tissues

EXCLUDES   CTA aorto-iliofemoral runoff (75635)

72191 **Computed tomographic angiography, pelvis, with contrast material(s), including noncontrast images, if performed, and image postprocessing** [72] [03] [80] [□]
 13.87 13.87 Global Days XXX
AMA: 2007, Jan, 28-31; 2007, Jan, 28-31; 2007, January, 28-31; 2005, Dec, 7; 2005, December, 7; 2005, Dec, 7

72192-72194 Computerized Tomography: Pelvis

CMS 100-3,220.1	Computerized Tomography
CMS 100-4,13,100	Interpretation of Diagnostic Tests
CMS 100-4,13,30	Computerized Axial Tomography (CT) Procedures
CMS 100-2,6,10	Medical and Other Services Furnished to Inpatients
CMS 100-4,3,10.4	Payment of Nonphysician Services for Inpatients
CMS 100-2,15,80	Physician Supervision Requirements for Diagnostic Tests
CMS 100-4,13,10	ICD-9-CM Coding for Diagnostic Tests

EXCLUDES   3D rendering (76376, 76377)
computed tomographic colonography (0066T, 0067T)

Do not report with (0066T, 0067T)

72192 **Computed tomography, pelvis; without contrast material** [72] [03] [80] [□]
 7.52 7.52 Global Days XXX
AMA: 2008, Jan, 10-25; 2007, Mar, 9-11; 2007, Mar, 9-11; 2007, March, 9-11; 2005, Mar, 1-6; 2005, Mar, 1-6; 2005, March, 1-6; 2004, Jul, 7; 2004, Jul, 7; 2004, July, 7

72193 **with contrast material(s)** [72] [03] [80] [□]
 9.00 9.00 Global Days XXX
AMA: 2007, Mar, 9-11; 2007, Mar, 9-11; 2007, March, 9-11; 2005, Mar, 11-15; 2005, Mar, 11-15; 2005, Mar, 1-6; 2005, March, 11-15; 2005, March, 1-6; 2005, Mar, 1-6; 2004, Jul, 7; 2004, July, 7; 2004, Jul, 7

72194 **without contrast material, followed by contrast material(s) and further sections** [72] [03] [80] [□]
EXCLUDES   3D rendering (76376, 76377)

Do not report with computed tomographic colonography (0066T, 0067T)

 11.47 11.47 Global Days XXX
AMA: 2008, Jan, 10-25; 2007, Mar, 9-11; 2007, Mar, 9-11; 2007, March, 9-11; 2005, Mar, 1-6; 2005, Mar, 1-6; 2005, March, 1-6; 2004, Jul, 7; 2004, Jul, 7; 2004, July, 7

72195-72197 Magnetic Resonance Imaging: Pelvis

CMS	Magnetic Resonance Imaging
CMS 100-4,13,100	Interpretation of Diagnostic Tests
CMS 100-4,13,40	Magnetic Resonance Imaging (MRI) Procedures
CMS 100-2,6,10	Medical and Other Services Furnished to Inpatients
CMS 100-4,3,10.4	Payment of Nonphysician Services for Inpatients
CMS 100-2,15,80	Physician Supervision Requirements for Diagnostic Tests
CMS 100-4,13,10	ICD-9-CM Coding for Diagnostic Tests

INCLUDES   application of an external magnetic field that forces alignment of hydrogen atom nuclei in soft tissues which converts to sets of tomographic images that can be displayed as three-dimensional images

72195 **Magnetic resonance (eg, proton) imaging, pelvis; without contrast material(s)** [72] [03] [80] [□]
 15.60 15.60 Global Days XXX
AMA: 2008, Jan, 10-25; 2007, Jan, 13-27; 2007, Jan, 13-27; 2007, January, 13-27; 2006, Jun, 16-17; 2006, June, 16-17; 2006, Jun, 16-17

72196 **with contrast material(s)** [72] [03] [80] [□]
 17.30 17.30 Global Days XXX
AMA: 2008, Jan, 10-25; 2007, Jan, 13-27; 2007, Jan, 13-27; 2007, January, 13-27; 2006, Jun, 16-17; 2006, June, 16-17; 2006, Jun, 16-17

72197 **without contrast material(s), followed by contrast material(s) and further sequences** [72] [03] [80] [□]
 23.77 23.77 Global Days XXX

72198 Magnetic Resonance Angiography: Pelvis

CMS *100-4,13,40.1* *Magnetic Resonance Angiography*
CMS *100-4,13,100* *Interpretation of Diagnostic Tests*
CMS *100-4,13,40.1.1* *Magnetic Resonance Angiography Coverage Summary*
CMS *100-2,6,10* *Medical and Other Services Furnished to Inpatients*
CMS *100-4,3,10.4* *Payment of Nonphysician Services for Inpatients*
CMS *100-3,220.3* *Magnetic Resonance Angiography*
CMS *100-2,15,80* *Physician Supervision Requirements for Diagnostic Tests*
CMS *100-4,13,10* *ICD-9-CM Coding for Diagnostic Tests*
[INCLUDES] use of magnetic fields and radio waves to produce detailed cross-sectional images of internal body structures

72198 Magnetic resonance angiography, pelvis, with or without contrast material(s) [R] [80] [⬜]
    🔹 16.68 ⚬ 16.68 Global Days XXX
    AMA: 2007, Jan, 28-31; 2007, Jan, 28-31; 2007, January, 28-31; 2005, Dec, 7; 2005, December, 7; 2005, Dec, 7

72200-72220 Radiography: Pelvisacral

CMS *100-4,13,100* *Interpretation of Diagnostic Tests*
CMS *100-2,6,10* *Medical and Other Services Furnished to Inpatients*
CMS *100-4,3,10.4* *Payment of Nonphysician Services for Inpatients*
CMS *100-2,15,80* *Physician Supervision Requirements for Diagnostic Tests*
CMS *100-4,13,10* *ICD-9-CM Coding for Diagnostic Tests*
[INCLUDES] minimum number of views or more views when needed to adequately complete the study
    radiographs that have to be repeated during the encounter due to substandard quality; only one unit of service is reported
[EXCLUDES] *obtaining more films after review of initial films, based on the discretion of the radiologist, an order for the test, and a change in the patient's condition*

Do not report with second interpretation by the requesting physician (included in E/M service)

72200 Radiologic examination, sacroiliac joints; less than 3 views [Z3] [X] [80]
    🔹 0.79 ⚬ 0.79 Global Days XXX

72202 3 or more views [Z3] [X] [80] [⬜]
    🔹 0.96 ⚬ 0.96 Global Days XXX

72220 Radiologic examination, sacrum and coccyx, minimum of 2 views [Z3] [X] [80]
    🔹 0.81 ⚬ 0.81 Global Days XXX

72240-72270 Radiography with Contrast: Spinal Cord

CMS *100-4,13,100* *Interpretation of Diagnostic Tests*
CMS *100-2,6,10* *Medical and Other Services Furnished to Inpatients*
CMS *100-4,3,10.4* *Payment of Nonphysician Services for Inpatients*
CMS *100-2,15,80* *Physician Supervision Requirements for Diagnostic Tests*
CMS *100-4,13,10* *ICD-9-CM Coding for Diagnostic Tests*
[INCLUDES] fluoroscopic guidance for subarachnoid puncture for diagnostic radiographic myelography

Code also injection procedure (61055, 62284)
Do not report with (77003)

72240 Myelography, cervical, radiological supervision and interpretation [N1] [02] [80] [⬜]
    🔹 4.39 ⚬ 4.39 Global Days XXX

72255 Myelography, thoracic, radiological supervision and interpretation [N1] [02] [80] [⬜]
    [INCLUDES] fluoroscopic guidance for subarachnoid puncture for diagnostic radiographic myelography (77003)
    🔹 4.01 ⚬ 4.01 Global Days XXX

72265 Myelography, lumbosacral, radiological supervision and interpretation [N1] [02] [80] [⬜]
    [INCLUDES] fluoroscopic guidance for subarachnoid puncture for diagnostic radiographic myelography (77003)
    🔹 4.08 ⚬ 4.08 Global Days XXX

72270 Myelography, 2 or more regions (eg, lumbar/thoracic, cervical/thoracic, lumbar/cervical, lumbar/thoracic/cervical), radiological supervision and interpretation [N1] [02] [80] [⬜]
    [INCLUDES] fluoroscopic guidance for subarachnoid puncture for diagnostic radiographic myelography (77003)
    🔹 6.36 ⚬ 6.36 Global Days XXX

72275 Radiography: Epidural Space

CMS *100-4,13,100* *Interpretation of Diagnostic Tests*
CMS *100-4,3,10.4* *Payment of Nonphysician Services for Inpatients*
CMS *100-2,15,80* *Physician Supervision Requirements for Diagnostic Tests*
CMS *100-4,13,10* *ICD-9-CM Coding for Diagnostic Tests*
[INCLUDES] epidurogram, documentation of images, formal written report
    fluoroscopic guidance (77003)

Code also injection procedure as appropriate (62280-62282, 62310-62319, 64479-64484)

72275 Epidurography, radiological supervision and interpretation [N1] [N] [⬜]
    [INCLUDES] fluoroscopic guidance (77003)
    🔹 2.90 ⚬ 2.90 Global Days XXX
    AMA: 2008, Jun, 8-11; 2008, Jul, 9

72285 Radiography: Intervertebral Disc (Cervical/Thoracic)

CMS *100-4,13,100* *Interpretation of Diagnostic Tests*
CMS *100-2,6,10* *Medical and Other Services Furnished to Inpatients*
CMS *100-4,3,10.4* *Payment of Nonphysician Services for Inpatients*
CMS *100-2,15,80* *Physician Supervision Requirements for Diagnostic Tests*
CMS *100-4,13,10* *ICD-9-CM Coding for Diagnostic Tests*
Code also discography injection procedure

72285 Discography, cervical or thoracic, radiological supervision and interpretation [N1] [02] [80] [⬜]
    🔹 4.96 ⚬ 4.96 Global Days XXX

72291-72292 Radiography: Percutaneous Vertebral Augmentation

Code also percutaneous vertebroplasty/vertebral augmentation procedure(s) as appropriate (22520-22522, 22523-22525)

72291 Radiological supervision and interpretation, percutaneous vertebroplasty or vertebral augmentation including cavity creation, per vertebral body; under fluoroscopic guidance [N1] [N] [80]
    🔹 0.00 ⚬ 0.00 Global Days XXX
    AMA: 2007, Mar, 7-8; 2007, Mar, 7-8; 2007, March, 7-8

72292 under CT guidance [N1] [N] [80]
    🔹 0.00 ⚬ 0.00 Global Days XXX
    AMA: 2007, Mar, 7-8; 2007, Mar, 7-8; 2007, March, 7-8

● New Code ▲ Revised Code Ⓜ Maternity Edit Ⓐ Age Edit A-V OPPS Status Indicator 🔹 Facility RVU ⚬ Non-Facility RVU
⬜ CCI Comprehensive Code 50 Bilateral Procedure + Add-on Indicator Ⓝ Laboratory crosswalk Ⓡ Radiology crosswalk

© 2008 Ingenix *(Blue Ink)* CPT only © 2008 American Medical Association. All Rights Reserved. (Black Ink) Medicare (Red Ink) **281**

72295 Radiography: Intervertebral Disc (Lumbar)

CMS *100-4,13,100*	Interpretation of Diagnostic Tests
CMS *100-2,6,10*	Medical and Other Services Furnished to Inpatients
CMS *100-4,3,10.4*	Payment of Nonphysician Services for Inpatients
CMS *100-2,15,80*	Physician Supervision Requirements for Diagnostic Tests
CMS *100-4,13,10*	ICD-9-CM Coding for Diagnostic Tests

Code also discography injection procedure (62291)

72295 **Discography, lumbar, radiological supervision and interpretation** N1 02 80 ▭
⊞ 4.42 ⚕ 4.42 **Global Days XXX**
AMA: 2008, Jan, 10-25; 2007, Jan, 13-27; 2007, Jan, 13-27; 2007, January, 13-27

73000-73085 Radiography: Shoulder and Upper Arm

CMS *100-4,13,100*	Interpretation of Diagnostic Tests
CMS *100-4,3,10.4*	Payment of Nonphysician Services for Inpatients
CMS *100-2,15,80*	Physician Supervision Requirements for Diagnostic Tests
CMS *100-4,13,10*	ICD-9-CM Coding for Diagnostic Tests

[INCLUDES] minimum number of views or more views when needed to adequately complete the study

radiographs that have to be repeated during the encounter due to substandard quality; only one unit of service is reported

[EXCLUDES] *obtaining more films after review of initial films, based on the discretion of the radiologist, an order for the test, and a change in the patient's condition*

stress views of upper body joint(s), when performed (77071)

Do not report with a second interpretation by the requesting physician (included in E/M service)

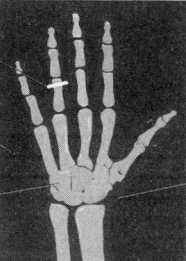
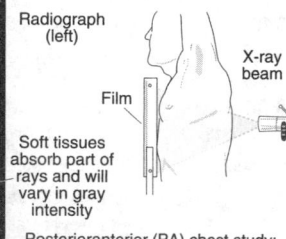

Gold wedding band absorbs all x-rays (white)

Air allows all rays to reach film (black)

Calcium in bone absorbs most of rays and is nearly white

Radiograph (left)

X-ray beam

Film

Soft tissues absorb part of rays and will vary in gray intensity

Posterioranterior (PA) chest study; lateral views also common

Traditional diagnostic radiography is defined by the x-ray. Radiographs, or x-rays, are "shadowgrams" of body structures and tissues and show radiopaque matter, such as bone, to be whiter and radiolucent substances, such as air, to be blacker. Each study is oriented by the direction path of the x-ray beam: e.g., PA, the most common, means the beam travels from posterior to anterior. Contrast agents are commonly used to highlight particular areas or structures

73000 **Radiologic examination; clavicle, complete** Z3 X 80
⊞ 0.75 ⚕ 0.75 **Global Days XXX**

73010 **scapula, complete** Z3 X 80
⊞ 0.77 ⚕ 0.77 **Global Days XXX**

73020 **Radiologic examination, shoulder; 1 view** Z3 X 80
⊞ 0.64 ⚕ 0.64 **Global Days XXX**

73030 **complete, minimum of 2 views** Z3 X 80 ▭
⊞ 0.82 ⚕ 0.82 **Global Days XXX**

73040 **Radiologic examination, shoulder, arthrography, radiological supervision and interpretation** N1 02 80 ▭
Code also arthrography injection procedure (23350)
Do not report with (77002)
⊞ 2.93 ⚕ 2.93 **Global Days XXX**
AMA: 2008, Jan, 10-25; 2008, Jun, 8-11; 2007, Feb, 10-11; 2007, Feb, 10-11; 2007, February, 10-11

73050 **acromioclavicular joints, bilateral, with or without weighted distraction** Z3 X 80
⊞ 0.98 ⚕ 0.98 **Global Days XXX**

73060 **humerus, minimum of 2 views** Z3 X 80
⊞ 0.80 ⚕ 0.80 **Global Days XXX**

73070 **Radiologic examination, elbow; 2 views** Z3 X 80
⊞ 0.73 ⚕ 0.73 **Global Days XXX**

73080 **complete, minimum of 3 views** Z3 X 80 ▭
⊞ 0.94 ⚕ 0.94 **Global Days XXX**

73085 **Radiologic examination, elbow, arthrography, radiological supervision and interpretation** N1 02 80 ▭
Do not report with (77002)
Code also arthrography injection procedure (24220)
⊞ 2.65 ⚕ 2.65 **Global Days XXX**
AMA: 2008, Jun, 8-11; 2007, Feb, 10-11; 2007, Feb, 10-11; 2007, February, 10-11

73090-73140 Radiography: Forearm and Hand

CMS *100-4,13,100*	Interpretation of Diagnostic Tests
CMS *100-4,3,10.4*	Payment of Nonphysician Services for Inpatients
CMS *100-2,15,80*	Physician Supervision Requirements for Diagnostic Tests
CMS *100-4,13,10*	ICD-9-CM Coding for Diagnostic Tests

[INCLUDES] minimum number of views or more views when needed to adequately complete the study

radiographs that have to be repeated during the encounter due to substandard quality; only one unit of service is reported

[EXCLUDES] *obtaining more films after review of initial films, based on the discretion of the radiologist, an order for the test, and a change in the patient's condition*

Code also stress views of upper body joint(s), when performed (77071)

Do not report with a second interpretation by the requesting physician (included in E/M service)

73090 **Radiologic examination; forearm, 2 views** Z3 X 80
⊞ 0.74 ⚕ 0.74 **Global Days XXX**

73092 **upper extremity, infant, minimum of 2 views** A Z3 X 80 ▭
⊞ 0.76 ⚕ 0.76 **Global Days XXX**

73100 **Radiologic examination, wrist; 2 views** Z3 X 80
⊞ 0.77 ⚕ 0.77 **Global Days XXX**

73110 **complete, minimum of 3 views** Z3 X 80 ▭
⊞ 0.92 ⚕ 0.92 **Global Days XXX**
AMA: 2008, Jan, 10-25; 2007, Jan, 13-27; 2007, Jan, 13-27; 2007, January, 13-27; 2006, Dec, 10-12; 2006, Dec, 10-12; 2006, Dec, 10-12; 2006, Dec, 10-12; 2006, December, 10-12; 2006, December, 10-12; 2006, December, 10-12; 2006, December, 10-12; 2006, Dec, 10-12; 2006, Dec, 10-12; 2006, Dec, 10-12; 2006, Dec, 10-12

73115 **Radiologic examination, wrist, arthrography, radiological supervision and interpretation** N1 02 80 ▭
Code also arthrography injection procedure (25246)
Do not report with (77002)
⊞ 2.80 ⚕ 2.80 **Global Days XXX**
AMA: 2008, Jun, 8-11; 2007, Feb, 10-11; 2007, Feb, 10-11; 2007, February, 10-11

73120 **Radiologic examination, hand; 2 views** Z3 X 80 ▭
⊞ 0.73 ⚕ 0.73 **Global Days XXX**

73130 **minimum of 3 views** Z3 X 80 ▭
⊞ 0.84 ⚕ 0.84 **Global Days XXX**

73140 **Radiologic examination, finger(s), minimum of 2 views** Z3 X 80
⊞ 0.78 ⚕ 0.78 **Global Days XXX**
AMA: 2007, Jan, 28-31; 2007, Jan, 28-31; 2007, January, 28-31

73200-73202 Computerized Tomography: Shoulder, Arm, Hand

CMS 100-3,220.1	Computerized Tomography
CMS 100-4,13,100	Interpretation of Diagnostic Tests
CMS 100-4,13,30	Computerized Axial Tomography (CT) Procedures
CMS 100-2,6,10	Medical and Other Services Furnished to Inpatients
CMS 100-4,3,10.4	Payment of Nonphysician Services for Inpatients
CMS 100-2,15,80	Physician Supervision Requirements for Diagnostic Tests
CMS 100-4,13,10	ICD-9-CM Coding for Diagnostic Tests

INCLUDES imaging using tomographic technique enhanced by computer imaging to create a cross-sectional plane of the body
intravascular injection of contrast material
intravascular, intrathecal, or intra-articular contrast materials when noted in code descriptor

EXCLUDES 3D rendering (76376-76377)

73200 Computed tomography, upper extremity; without contrast material ☲ 03 90 ▭
📑 7.48 ✂ 7.48 Global Days XXX

73201 with contrast material(s) ☲ 03 80 ▭
📑 8.98 ✂ 8.98 Global Days XXX

73202 without contrast material, followed by contrast material(s) and further sections ☲ 03 80 ▭
📑 11.49 ✂ 11.49 Global Days XXX

73206 Computerized Tomographic Angiography: Shoulder, Arm, and Hand

CMS 100-3,220.1	Computerized Tomography
CMS 100-4,13,100	Interpretation of Diagnostic Tests
CMS 100-4,13,30	Computerized Axial Tomography (CT) Procedures
CMS 100-2,6,10	Medical and Other Services Furnished to Inpatients
CMS 100-4,3,10.4	Payment of Nonphysician Services for Inpatients
CMS 100-2,15,80	Physician Supervision Requirements for Diagnostic Tests
CMS 100-4,13,10	ICD-9-CM Coding for Diagnostic Tests

INCLUDES intravascular injection of contrast material
intravascular, intrathecal, or intra-articular contrast materials when noted in code descriptor
multiple rapid thin section CT scans to create cross-sectional images of bones, organs and tissues

73206 Computed tomographic angiography, upper extremity, with contrast material(s), including noncontrast images, if performed, and image postprocessing ☲ 03 80 ▭
📑 13.29 ✂ 13.29 Global Days XXX
AMA: 2007, Jan, 28-31; 2007, Jan, 28-31; 2007, January, 28-31; 2005, Dec, 7; 2005, December, 7; 2005, Dec, 7

73218-73223 Magnetic Resonance Imaging: Shoulder, Arm, Hand

CMS	Magnetic Resonance Imaging
CMS 100-4,13,100	Interpretation of Diagnostic Tests
CMS 100-4,13,30	Computerized Axial Tomography (CT) Procedures
CMS 100-2,6,10	Medical and Other Services Furnished to Inpatients
CMS 100-4,3,10.4	Payment of Nonphysician Services for Inpatients
CMS 100-2,15,80	Physician Supervision Requirements for Diagnostic Tests
CMS 100-4,13,10	ICD-9-CM Coding for Diagnostic Tests

INCLUDES application of an external magnetic field that forces alignment of hydrogen atom nuclei in soft tissues which converts to sets of tomographic images that can be displayed as three-dimensional images
intravascular injection of contrast material
intravascular, intrathecal, or intra-articular contrast materials when noted in code descriptor

73218 Magnetic resonance (eg, proton) imaging, upper extremity, other than joint; without contrast material(s) ☲ 03 80 ▭
📑 15.59 ✂ 15.59 Global Days XXX

73219 with contrast material(s) ☲ 03 80 ▭
📑 17.13 ✂ 17.13 Global Days XXX

73220 without contrast material(s), followed by contrast material(s) and further sequences ☲ 03 80 ▭
📑 23.62 ✂ 23.62 Global Days XXX

73221 Magnetic resonance (eg, proton) imaging, any joint of upper extremity; without contrast material(s) ☲ 03 80 ▭
📑 14.76 ✂ 14.76 Global Days XXX

73222 with contrast material(s) ☲ 03 80 ▭
📑 16.29 ✂ 16.29 Global Days XXX

73223 without contrast material(s), followed by contrast material(s) and further sequences ☲ 03 80 ▭
📑 22.60 ✂ 22.60 Global Days XXX

73225 Magnetic Resonance Angiography: Shoulder, Arm, Hand

CMS 100-4,13,40.1	Magnetic Resonance Angiography
CMS 100-4,13,100	Interpretation of Diagnostic Tests
CMS 100-4,13,40.1.1	Magnetic Resonance Angiography Coverage Summary
CMS 100-2,6,10	Medical and Other Services Furnished to Inpatients
CMS 100-4,3,10.4	Payment of Nonphysician Services for Inpatients
CMS 100-3,220.3	Magnetic Resonance Angiography
CMS 100-2,15,80	Physician Supervision Requirements for Diagnostic Tests
CMS 100-4,13,10	ICD-9-CM Coding for Diagnostic Tests

INCLUDES intravascular injection of contrast material
intravascular, intrathecal, or intra-articular contrast materials when noted in code descriptor
use of magnetic fields and radio waves to produce detailed cross-sectional images of internal body structures

73225 Magnetic resonance angiography, upper extremity, with or without contrast material(s) 🅔
📑 17.54 ✂ 17.54 Global Days XXX
AMA: 2007, Jan, 28-31; 2007, Jan, 28-31; 2007, January, 28-31; 2005, Dec, 7; 2005, December, 7; 2005, Dec, 7

73500-73550 Radiography: Pelvic Region and Thigh

CMS 100-4,13,100	Interpretation of Diagnostic Tests
CMS 100-2,6,10	Medical and Other Services Furnished to Inpatients
CMS 100-4,3,10.4	Payment of Nonphysician Services for Inpatients
CMS 100-2,15,80	Physician Supervision Requirements for Diagnostic Tests
CMS 100-4,13,10	ICD-9-CM Coding for Diagnostic Tests

EXCLUDES stress views any joint (77071)

73500 Radiologic examination, hip, unilateral; 1 view ☲ X 80
📑 0.69 ✂ 0.69 Global Days XXX

● New Code ▲ Revised Code Ⓜ Maternity Edit Ⓐ Age Edit Ⓐ-Ⓥ OPPS Status Indicator 📑 Facility RVU ✂ Non-Facility RVU
▭ CCI Comprehensive Code 🔟 Bilateral Procedure + Add-on Indicator ▣ Laboratory crosswalk ☲ Radiology crosswalk

73510 complete, minimum of 2 views　[26] [X] [80] [▭]
　1.00　1.00　Global Days XXX
　　AMA: 2008, Jan, 10-25; 2007, Jan, 13-27; 2007, Jan, 13-27; 2007, January, 13-27

73520 Radiologic examination, hips, bilateral, minimum of 2 views of each hip, including anteroposterior view of pelvis　[26] [X] [80] [▭]
　1.08　1.08　Global Days XXX
　　AMA: 2008, Jan, 10-25; 2007, Jan, 13-27; 2007, Jan, 13-27; 2007, January, 13-27

73525 Radiologic examination, hip, arthrography, radiological supervision and interpretation　[N1] [02] [▭]
　Do not report with (77002)
　2.65　2.65　Global Days XXX
　　AMA: 2008, Jun, 8-11; 2007, Feb, 10-11; 2007, Feb, 10-11; 2007, February, 10-11

73530 Radiologic examination, hip, during operative procedure　[N1] [N] [80]
　0.00　0.00　Global Days XXX

73540 Radiologic examination, pelvis and hips, infant or child, minimum of 2 views　[A] [26] [X] [80] [▭]
　1.00　1.00　Global Days XXX

73542 Radiological examination, sacroiliac joint arthrography, radiological supervision and interpretation　[N1] [02] [▭]
　　EXCLUDES　*fluoroscopic guidance for sacroiliac joint injection (77003)*
　　　　　　　injection procedure (27096)
　Do not report with (77002)
　2.18　2.18　Global Days XXX
　　AMA: 2008, Jul, 9

73550 Radiologic examination, femur, 2 views　[26] [X] [80]
　0.78　0.78　Global Days XXX

73560-73660 Radiography: Lower Leg, Ankle, and Foot

CMS 100-4,13,100	*Interpretation of Diagnostic Tests*	
CMS 100-4,3,10.4	*Payment of Nonphysician Services for Inpatients*	
CMS 100-2,15,80	*Physician Supervision Requirements for Diagnostic Tests*	
CMS 100-4,13,10	*ICD-9-CM Coding for Diagnostic Tests*	
EXCLUDES	*stress views, any joint (77071)*	

73560 Radiologic examination, knee; 1 or 2 views　[26] [X] [80] [▭]
　0.77　0.77　Global Days XXX

73562 3 views　[26] [X] [80] [▭]
　0.93　0.93　Global Days XXX

73564 complete, 4 or more views　[26] [X] [80] [▭]
　1.08　1.08　Global Days XXX
　　AMA: 2008, Jan, 10-25; 2007, Jan, 13-27; 2007, Jan, 13-27; 2007, January, 13-27

73565 both knees, standing, anteroposterior　[26] [X] [80] [▭]
　0.82　0.82　Global Days XXX

73580 Radiologic examination, knee, arthrography, radiological supervision and interpretation　[N1] [02] [80] [▭]
　Do not report with (77002)
　3.30　3.30　Global Days XXX
　　AMA: 2008, Jun, 8-11; 2007, Feb, 10-11; 2007, Feb, 10-11; 2007, February, 10-11

73590 Radiologic examination; tibia and fibula, 2 views　[26] [X] [80] [▭]
　0.74　0.74　Global Days XXX

73592 lower extremity, infant, minimum of 2 views　[A] [26] [X] [80] [▭]
　0.76　0.76　Global Days XXX

73600 Radiologic examination, ankle; 2 views　[26] [X] [80] [▭]
　0.73　0.73　Global Days XXX

73610 complete, minimum of 3 views　[26] [X] [80] [▭]
　0.84　0.84　Global Days XXX

73615 Radiologic examination, ankle, arthrography, radiological supervision and interpretation　[N1] [02] [▭]
　Do not report with (77002)
　2.72　2.72　Global Days XXX
　　AMA: 2008, Jun, 8-11; 2007, Feb, 10-11; 2007, Feb, 10-11; 2007, February, 10-11

73620 Radiologic examination, foot; 2 views　[26] [X] [80] [▭]
　0.71　0.71　Global Days XXX

73630 complete, minimum of 3 views　[26] [X] [80] [▭]
　0.83　0.83　Global Days XXX

73650 calcaneus, minimum of 2 views　[26] [X] [80]
　0.72　0.72　Global Days XXX

73660 toe(s), minimum of 2 views　[26] [X] [80]
　0.74　0.74　Global Days XXX

73700-73702 Computerized Tomography: Leg, Ankle, and Foot

CMS 100-3,220.1	*Computerized Tomography*	
CMS 100-4,13,100	*Interpretation of Diagnostic Tests*	
CMS 100-2,6,10	*Medical and Other Services Furnished to Inpatients*	
CMS 100-4,3,10.4	*Payment of Nonphysician Services for Inpatients*	
CMS 100-2,15,80	*Physician Supervision Requirements for Diagnostic Tests*	
CMS 100-4,13,10	*ICD-9-CM Coding for Diagnostic Tests*	
EXCLUDES	*stress views, any joint (77071)*	

73700 Computed tomography, lower extremity; without contrast material　[Z2] [03] [80] [▭]
　7.49　7.49　Global Days XXX
　　AMA: 2007, Mar, 9-11; 2007, Mar, 9-11; 2007, March, 9-11

73701 with contrast material(s)　[Z2] [03] [80] [▭]
　9.04　9.04　Global Days XXX
　　AMA: 2007, Mar, 9-11; 2007, Mar, 9-11; 2007, March, 9-11

73702 without contrast material, followed by contrast material(s) and further sections　[Z2] [03] [▭]
　　EXCLUDES　*3D rendering (76376, 76377)*
　11.52　11.52　Global Days XXX
　　AMA: 2007, Mar, 9-11; 2007, Mar, 9-11; 2007, March, 9-11

73706 Computerized Tomographic Angiography: Leg, Ankle, and Foot

CMS 100-4,13,100	*Interpretation of Diagnostic Tests*	
CMS 100-2,6,10	*Medical and Other Services Furnished to Inpatients*	
CMS 100-4,3,10.4	*Payment of Nonphysician Services for Inpatients*	
CMS 100-2,15,80	*Physician Supervision Requirements for Diagnostic Tests*	
CMS 100-4,13,10	*ICD-9-CM Coding for Diagnostic Tests*	
EXCLUDES	*stress views, any joint (77071)*	

73706 Computed tomographic angiography, lower extremity, with contrast material(s), including noncontrast images, if performed, and image postprocessing　[Z2] [03] [80] [▭]
　　EXCLUDES　*computed tomographic angiography aorto-iliofemoral runoff (75635)*
　14.43　14.43　Global Days XXX
　　AMA: 2007, Jan, 28-31; 2007, Jan, 28-31; 2007, January, 28-31; 2005, Dec, 7; 2005, December, 7; 2005, Dec, 7

[26/TC] Professional/Technical Component Only　　[80/80] Assist-at-Surgery Allowed/With Documentation　　Unlisted　　Not Covered

AMA: CPT Assistant References　　[A2-Z3] ASC Payment Indicator　　♂ Male Only　　♀ Female Only　　Ⓢ Modifier 51 Exempt　　[PQ] PQRI

284　　CPT only © 2008 American Medical Association. All Rights Reserved. (Black Ink)　　Medicare (Red Ink)　　© 2008 Ingenix *(Blue Ink*

73718-73723 Magnetic Resonance Imaging: Leg, Ankle, and Foot

CMS 100-4,13,100　Interpretation of Diagnostic Tests
CMS 100-4,13,40　Magnetic Resonance Imaging (MRI) Procedures
CMS 100-2,6,10　Medical and Other Services Furnished to Inpatients
CMS 100-4,3,10.4　Payment of Nonphysician Services for Inpatients
CMS 100-3,220.2　Magnetic Resonance Imaging
CMS 100-2,15,80　Physician Supervision Requirements for Diagnostic Tests
CMS 100-4,13,10　ICD-9-CM Coding for Diagnostic Tests
EXCLUDES　stress views, any joint (77071)

73718 Magnetic resonance (eg, proton) imaging, lower extremity other than joint; without contrast material(s)
15.32　15.32　Global Days XXX

73719 with contrast material(s)
16.95　16.95　Global Days XXX

73720 without contrast material(s), followed by contrast material(s) and further sequences
23.61　23.61　Global Days XXX

73721 Magnetic resonance (eg, proton) imaging, any joint of lower extremity; without contrast material
15.01　15.01　Global Days XXX
AMA: 2008, Jan, 10-25; 2007, Jan, 13-27; 2007, Jan, 13-27; 2007, January, 13-27; 2006, Jun, 16-17; 2006, June, 16-17; 2006, Jun, 16-17

73722 with contrast material(s)
16.42　16.42　Global Days XXX
AMA: 2006, Jun, 16-17; 2006, Jun, 16-17; 2006, June, 16-17

73723 without contrast material(s), followed by contrast material(s) and further sequences
22.55　22.55　Global Days XXX

73725 Magnetic Resonace Angiography: Leg, Ankle, and Foot

CMS 100-4,13,40.1　Magnetic Resonance Angiography
CMS 100-4,13,100　Interpretation of Diagnostic Tests
CMS 100-4,13,40.1.1　Magnetic Resonance Angiography Coverage Summary
CMS 100-2,6,10　Medical and Other Services Furnished to Inpatients
CMS 100-4,3,10.4　Payment of Nonphysician Services for Inpatients
CMS 100-3,220.3　Magnetic Resonance Angiography
CMS 100-2,15,80　Physician Supervision Requirements for Diagnostic Tests
CMS 100-4,13,10　ICD-9-CM Coding for Diagnostic Tests

73725 Magnetic resonance angiography, lower extremity, with or without contrast material(s)
16.70　16.70　Global Days XXX
AMA: 2007, Jan, 28-31; 2007, Jan, 28-31; 2007, January, 28-31; 2005, Dec, 7; 2005, December, 7; 2005, Dec, 7

74000-74022 Radiography: Abdomen--General

CMS 100-4,13,100　Interpretation of Diagnostic Tests
CMS 100-4,3,10.4　Payment of Nonphysician Services for Inpatients
CMS 100-2,15,80　Physician Supervision Requirements for Diagnostic Tests
CMS 100-4,13,10　ICD-9-CM Coding for Diagnostic Tests

74000 Radiologic examination, abdomen; single anteroposterior view
0.70　0.70　Global Days XXX

74010 anteroposterior and additional oblique and cone views
1.03　1.03　Global Days XXX
AMA: 2007, Jan, 28-31; 2007, Jan, 28-31; 2007, January, 28-31

74020 complete, including decubitus and/or erect views
1.10　1.10　Global Days XXX

74022 complete acute abdomen series, including supine, erect, and/or decubitus views, single view chest
1.33　1.33　Global Days XXX

74150-74170 Computerized Tomography: Abdomen--General

CMS 100-3,220.1　Computerized Tomography
CMS 100-4,13,100　Interpretation of Diagnostic Tests
CMS 100-4,13,30　Computerized Axial Tomography (CT) Procedures
CMS 100-2,6,10　Medical and Other Services Furnished to Inpatients
CMS 100-4,3,10.4　Payment of Nonphysician Services for Inpatients
CMS 100-2,15,80　Physician Supervision Requirements for Diagnostic Tests
CMS 100-4,13,10　ICD-9-CM Coding for Diagnostic Tests
EXCLUDES　3D rendering (76376-76377)

Do not report with computed tomographic colonography (0066T-0067T)

74150 Computed tomography, abdomen; without contrast material
7.58　7.58　Global Days XXX
AMA: 2008, Jan, 10-25; 2007, Jan, 13-27; 2007, Jan, 13-27; 2007, January, 13-27; 2005, Mar, 1-6; 2005, Mar, 1-6; 2005, March, 1-6; 2004, Jul, 7; 2004, Jul, 7; 2004, July, 7

74160 with contrast material(s)
10.08　10.08　Global Days XXX
AMA: 2005, Mar, 1-6; 2005, Mar, 1-6; 2005, Mar, 11-15; 2005, Mar, 11-15; 2005, March, 1-6; 2005, March, 11-15; 2004, Jul, 7; 2004, Jul, 7; 2004, July, 7

74170 without contrast material, followed by contrast material(s) and further sections
13.19　13.19　Global Days XXX
AMA: 2005, Mar, 1-6; 2005, Mar, 1-6; 2005, March, 1-6; 2004, Jul, 7; 2004, July, 7; 2004, Jul, 7

74175 Computerized Tomographic Angiography: Abdomen--General

CMS 100-3,220.1　Computerized Tomography
CMS 100-4,13,100　Interpretation of Diagnostic Tests
CMS 100-4,13,30　Computerized Axial Tomography (CT) Procedures
CMS 100-2,6,10　Medical and Other Services Furnished to Inpatients
CMS 100-4,3,10.4　Payment of Nonphysician Services for Inpatients
CMS 100-2,15,80　Physician Supervision Requirements for Diagnostic Tests
CMS 100-4,13,10　ICD-9-CM Coding for Diagnostic Tests

74175 Computed tomographic angiography, abdomen, with contrast material(s), including noncontrast images, if performed, and image postprocessing
EXCLUDES　computed tomographic angiography aorto-iliofemoral runoff (75635)
14.67　14.67　Global Days XXX
AMA: 2007, Jan, 28-31; 2007, Jan, 28-31; 2007, January, 28-31; 2005, Dec, 7; 2005, December, 7; 2005, Dec, 7

74181-74183 Magnetic Resonance Imaging: Abdomen--General

CMS 100-4,13,100　Interpretation of Diagnostic Tests
CMS 100-4,13,40　Magnetic Resonance Imaging (MRI) Procedures
CMS 100-2,6,10　Medical and Other Services Furnished to Inpatients
CMS 100-4,3,10.4　Payment of Nonphysician Services for Inpatients
CMS 100-3,220.2　Magnetic Resonance Imaging
CMS 100-2,15,80　Physician Supervision Requirements for Diagnostic Tests
CMS 100-4,13,10　ICD-9-CM Coding for Diagnostic Tests

74181 Magnetic resonance (eg, proton) imaging, abdomen; without contrast material(s)
14.15　14.15　Global Days XXX
AMA: 2008, Jan, 10-25

74182 with contrast material(s)
18.76　18.76　Global Days XXX

● New Code　▲ Revised Code　Ⓜ Maternity Edit　🅰 Age Edit　A-Y OPPS Status Indicator　Facility RVU　Non-Facility RVU
🔲 CCI Comprehensive Code　50 Bilateral Procedure　+ Add-on Indicator　Laboratory crosswalk　Radiology crosswalk

74183 without contrast material(s), followed by with contrast material(s) and further sequences 🔲 🔲 🔲 🔲
🔳 23.79 ⚬ 23.79 Global Days XXX

74185 Magnetic Resonance Angiography: Abdomen--General

CMS *100-4,13,40.1*   *Magnetic Resonance Angiography*
CMS *100-4,13,100*   *Interpretation of Diagnostic Tests*
CMS *100-2,6,10*   *Medical and Other Services Furnished to Inpatients*
CMS *100-4,3,10.4*   *Payment of Nonphysician Services for Inpatients*
CMS *100-3,220.3*   *Magnetic Resonance Angiography*
CMS *100-2,15,80*   *Physician Supervision Requirements for Diagnostic Tests*
CMS *100-4,13,10*   *ICD-9-CM Coding for Diagnostic Tests*

74185 Magnetic resonance angiography, abdomen, with or without contrast material(s) 🔲 🔲 🔲
🔳 16.64 ⚬ 16.64 Global Days XXX
AMA: 2007, Jan, 28-31; 2007, Jan, 28-31; 2007, January, 28-31; 2005, Dec, 7; 2005, December, 7; 2005, Dec, 7

74190 Peritoneography

CMS *100-4,13,100*   *Interpretation of Diagnostic Tests*
CMS *100-4,3,10.4*   *Payment of Nonphysician Services for Inpatients*
CMS *100-2,15,80*   *Physician Supervision Requirements for Diagnostic Tests*
CMS *100-4,13,10*   *ICD-9-CM Coding for Diagnostic Tests*

74190 Peritoneogram (eg, after injection of air or contrast), radiological supervision and interpretation 🔲 🔲 🔲 🔲
EXCLUDES   *computed tomography, pelvis or abdomen (72192, 74150)*
injection procedure (49400)
🔳 0.00 ⚬ 0.00 Global Days XXX

74210-74235 Radiography: Throat and Esophagus

CMS *100-4,13,100*   *Interpretation of Diagnostic Tests*
CMS *100-4,3,10.4*   *Payment of Nonphysician Services for Inpatients*
CMS *100-2,15,80*   *Physician Supervision Requirements for Diagnostic Tests*
CMS *100-4,13,10*   *ICD-9-CM Coding for Diagnostic Tests*
EXCLUDES   *insertion of gastrostomy tube (43246)*
placement of gastrostomy tube, percutaneous (43246)

74210 Radiologic examination; pharynx and/or cervical esophagus 🔲 🔲 🔲
🔳 2.10 ⚬ 2.10 Global Days XXX
74220 esophagus 🔲 🔲 🔲 🔲
🔳 2.38 ⚬ 2.38 Global Days XXX
74230 Swallowing function, with cineradiography/videoradiography 🔲 🔲 🔲 🔲
🔳 2.45 ⚬ 2.45 Global Days XXX
AMA: 2004, Dec, 14; 2004, Dec, 14; 2004, December, 14
74235 Removal of foreign body(s), esophageal, with use of balloon catheter, radiological supervision and interpretation 🔲 🔲 🔲 🔲
EXCLUDES   *esophagoscopy/upper GI endoscopy (43215, 43247)*
🔳 0.00 ⚬ 0.00 Global Days XXX

74240-74283 Radiography: Intestines

CMS *100-4,13,100*   *Interpretation of Diagnostic Tests*
CMS *100-2,6,10*   *Medical and Other Services Furnished to Inpatients*
CMS *100-4,3,10.4*   *Payment of Nonphysician Services for Inpatients*
CMS *100-2,15,80*   *Physician Supervision Requirements for Diagnostic Tests*
CMS *100-4,13,10*   *ICD-9-CM Coding for Diagnostic Tests*
EXCLUDES   *insertion of gastrostomy tube (43246)*
placement of gastrostomy tube, percutaneous (43246)

74240 Radiologic examination, gastrointestinal tract, upper; with or without delayed films, without KUB 🔲 🔲 🔲 🔲
🔳 2.95 ⚬ 2.95 Global Days XXX
74241 with or without delayed films, with KUB 🔲 🔲 🔲 🔲
🔳 3.14 ⚬ 3.14 Global Days XXX
74245 with small intestine, includes multiple serial films 🔲 🔲 🔲 🔲
🔳 4.71 ⚬ 4.71 Global Days XXX
74246 Radiological examination, gastrointestinal tract, upper, air contrast, with specific high density barium, effervescent agent, with or without glucagon; with or without delayed films, without KUB 🔲 🔲 🔲 🔲
INCLUDES   Moynihan test
🔳 3.38 ⚬ 3.38 Global Days XXX
74247 with or without delayed films, with KUB 🔲 🔲 🔲 🔲
🔳 3.71 ⚬ 3.71 Global Days XXX
74249 with small intestine follow-through 🔲 🔲 🔲 🔲
🔳 5.05 ⚬ 5.05 Global Days XXX
74250 Radiologic examination, small intestine, includes multiple serial films; 🔲 🔲 🔲 🔲
🔳 2.77 ⚬ 2.77 Global Days XXX
74251 via enteroclysis tube 🔲 🔲 🔲 🔲
🔳 8.61 ⚬ 8.61 Global Days XXX
74260 Duodenography, hypotonic 🔲 🔲 🔲 🔲
🔳 7.18 ⚬ 7.18 Global Days XXX
▲ **74270** Radiologic examination, colon; contrast (eg, barium) enema, with or without KUB 🔲 🔲 🔲 🔲
🔳 3.98 ⚬ 3.98 Global Days XXX
AMA: 2008, Jan, 10-25; 2007, Jan, 13-27; 2007, Jan, 13-27; 2007, January, 13-27
74280 air contrast with specific high density barium, with or without glucagon 🔲 🔲 🔲 🔲
🔳 5.50 ⚬ 5.50 Global Days XXX
74283 Therapeutic enema, contrast or air, for reduction of intussusception or other intraluminal obstruction (eg, meconium ileus) 🔲 🔲 🔲
🔳 5.70 ⚬ 5.70 Global Days XXX

74290-74330 Radiography: Biliary Tract

CMS *100-4,13,100*   *Interpretation of Diagnostic Tests*
CMS *100-4,3,10.4*   *Payment of Nonphysician Services for Inpatients*
CMS *100-2,15,80*   *Physician Supervision Requirements for Diagnostic Tests*
CMS *100-4,13,10*   *ICD-9-CM Coding for Diagnostic Tests*
EXCLUDES   *insertion of gastrostomy tube (43246)*
placement of gastrostomy tube, percutaneous (43246)

74290 Cholecystography, oral contrast; 🔲 🔲 🔲
🔳 1.77 ⚬ 1.77 Global Days XXX
74291 additional or repeat examination or multiple day examination 🔲 🔲 🔲
🔳 1.52 ⚬ 1.52 Global Days XXX
74300 Cholangiography and/or pancreatography; intraoperative, radiological supervision and interpretation 🔲 🔲 🔲 🔲
🔳 0.00 ⚬ 0.00 Global Days XXX
AMA: 2008, Jan, 10-25; 2007, Jan, 13-27; 2007, Jan, 13-27; 2007, January, 13-27

+ **74301** additional set intraoperative, radiological supervision and interpretation (List separately in addition to code for primary procedure)   N1 N 60 🖵
Code first primary procedure (74300)
📧 0.00   ⚒ 0.00   Global Days ZZZ

74305 through existing catheter, radiological supervision and interpretation   N1 02 60 🖵
EXCLUDES   percutaneous biliary duct stone extraction (47630, 74327)
surgical procedure (47505, 47560, 47563, 48400-47561)
📧 0.00   ⚒ 0.00   Global Days XXX

74320 Cholangiography, percutaneous, transhepatic, radiological supervision and interpretation   N1 02 60 🖵
INCLUDES   needle placement with fluoroscopic guidance (77002)
📧 3.17   ⚒ 3.17   Global Days XXX
AMA: 2008, Jun, 8-11; 2007, Feb, 10-11; 2007, Feb, 10-11; 2007, February, 10-11

74327 Postoperative biliary duct calculus removal, percutaneous via T-tube tract, basket, or snare (eg, Burhenne technique), radiological supervision and interpretation   N1 N 60 🖵
EXCLUDES   percutaneous biliary duct stone extraction (47630)
📧 3.58   ⚒ 3.58   Global Days XXX

74328 Endoscopic catheterization of the biliary ductal system, radiological supervision and interpretation   N1 N 60 🖵
EXCLUDES   ERCP (43260-43272)
📧 0.00   ⚒ 0.00   Global Days XXX
AMA: 2008, May, 9-11

74329 Endoscopic catheterization of the pancreatic ductal system, radiological supervision and interpretation   N1 N 60 🖵
EXCLUDES   ERCP (43260-43272)
📧 0.00   ⚒ 0.00   Global Days XXX

74330 Combined endoscopic catheterization of the biliary and pancreatic ductal systems, radiological supervision and interpretation   N1 N 60 🖵
EXCLUDES   ERCP (43260-43272)
📧 0.00   ⚒ 0.00   Global Days XXX

74340-74363 Radiography: Bilidigestive Intubation

CMS 100-4,13,100   *Interpretation of Diagnostic Tests*
CMS 100-4,3,10.4   *Payment of Nonphysician Services for Inpatients*
CMS 100-2,15,80   *Physician Supervision Requirements for Diagnostic Tests*
CMS 100-4,13,10   *ICD-9-CM Coding for Diagnostic Tests*
EXCLUDES   *percutaneous insertion of gastrostomy tube (43246)*

74340 Introduction of long gastrointestinal tube (eg, Miller-Abbott), including multiple fluoroscopies and films, radiological supervision and interpretation   N1 N 60 🖵
EXCLUDES   placement of tube (44500)
📧 0.00   ⚒ 0.00   Global Days XXX

74355 Percutaneous placement of enteroclysis tube, radiological supervision and interpretation   N1 N 60 🖵
INCLUDES   needle placement with fluoroscopic guidance (77002)
📧 0.00   ⚒ 0.00   Global Days XXX
AMA: 2008, Jun, 8-11; 2007, Feb, 10-11; 2007, Feb, 10-11; 2007, February, 10-11

74360 Intraluminal dilation of strictures and/or obstructions (eg, esophagus), radiological supervision and interpretation   N1 N 60 🖵
📧 0.00   ⚒ 0.00   Global Days XXX
AMA: 2008, Oct, 6-7

74363 Percutaneous transhepatic dilation of biliary duct stricture with or without placement of stent, radiological supervision and interpretation   N1 N 60 🖵
EXCLUDES   surgical procedure (47510, 47511, 47555, 47556)
📧 0.00   ⚒ 0.00   Global Days XXX

74400-74775 Radiography: Urogenital

CMS 100-4,13,100   *Interpretation of Diagnostic Tests*
CMS 100-4,3,10.4   *Payment of Nonphysician Services for Inpatients*
CMS 100-2,15,80   *Physician Supervision Requirements for Diagnostic Tests*
CMS 100-4,13,10   *ICD-9-CM Coding for Diagnostic Tests*

74400 Urography (pyelography), intravenous, with or without KUB, with or without tomography   Z3 S 60 🖵
📧 3.01   ⚒ 3.01   Global Days XXX

74410 Urography, infusion, drip technique and/or bolus technique;   Z3 S 60 🖵
📧 3.17   ⚒ 3.17   Global Days XXX

74415 with nephrotomography   Z3 S 60 🖵
📧 3.63   ⚒ 3.63   Global Days XXX

74420 Urography, retrograde, with or without KUB   Z2 S 60 🖵
📧 0.00   ⚒ 0.00   Global Days XXX
AMA: 2008, Jan, 10-25; 2007, Jan, 13-27; 2007, Jan, 13-27; 2007, January, 13-27

74425 Urography, antegrade (pyelostogram, nephrostogram, loopogram), radiological supervision and interpretation   N1 02 60 🖵
📧 0.00   ⚒ 0.00   Global Days XXX
AMA: 2005, Oct, 18-22; 2005, Oct, 18-22; 2005, October, 18-22

74430 Cystography, minimum of 3 views, radiological supervision and interpretation   N1 02 60 🖵
📧 2.15   ⚒ 2.15   Global Days XXX

74440 Vasography, vesiculography, or epididymography, radiological supervision and interpretation   ♂ N1 02 60 🖵
📧 2.31   ⚒ 2.31   Global Days XXX

74445 Corpora cavernosography, radiological supervision and interpretation   ♂ N1 02 60 🖵
INCLUDES   needle placement with fluoroscopic guidance (77002)
📧 0.00   ⚒ 0.00   Global Days XXX
AMA: 2008, Jun, 8-11; 2007, Feb, 10-11; 2007, Feb, 10-11; 2007, February, 10-11

74450 Urethrocystography, retrograde, radiological supervision and interpretation   N1 02 60 🖵
📧 0.00   ⚒ 0.00   Global Days XXX

74455 Urethrocystography, voiding, radiological supervision and interpretation   N1 02 60 🖵
📧 2.50   ⚒ 2.50   Global Days XXX

74470 Radiologic examination, renal cyst study, translumbar, contrast visualization, radiological supervision and interpretation   N1 02 60 🖵
INCLUDES   needle placement with fluoroscopic guidance (77002)
📧 0.00   ⚒ 0.00   Global Days XXX
AMA: 2008, Jun, 8-11; 2007, Feb, 10-11; 2007, Feb, 10-11; 2007, February, 10-11; 2005, Oct, 18-22; 2005, October, 18-22; 2005, Oct, 18-22

● New Code   ▲ Revised Code   M Maternity Edit   A Age Edit   A-Y OPPS Status Indicator   📧 Facility RVU   ⚒ Non-Facility RVU
🖵 CCI Comprehensive Code   50 Bilateral Procedure   + Add-on Indicator   N Laboratory crosswalk   🔀 Radiology crosswalk

Radiology

74475 — 75564

74475   Introduction of intracatheter or catheter into renal pelvis for drainage and/or injection, percutaneous, radiological supervision and interpretation   M1 02 80 ▢
    INCLUDES   needle placement with fluoroscopic guidance (77002)
    📷 3.44   ✂ 3.44   Global Days XXX
    AMA: 2008, Jun, 8-11; 2007, Feb, 10-11; 2007, Feb, 10-11; 2007, February, 10-11; 2005, Oct, 18-22; 2005, October, 18-22; 2005, Oct, 18-22

74480   Introduction of ureteral catheter or stent into ureter through renal pelvis for drainage and/or injection, percutaneous, radiological supervision and interpretation   M1 02 80 ▢
    EXCLUDES   ureter/pelvis transurethral surgery (52320-52355)
    📷 3.45   ✂ 3.45   Global Days XXX
    AMA: 2005, Oct, 18-22; 2005, Oct, 18-22; 2005, October, 18-22

74485   Dilation of nephrostomy, ureters, or urethra, radiological supervision and interpretation   M1 02 80 ▢
    EXCLUDES   change of pyelostomy/nephrostomy tube (50398)
    ureter dilation without radiologic guidance (52341, 52344)
    📷 3.28   ✂ 3.28   Global Days XXX
    AMA: 2005, Oct, 18-22; 2005, Oct, 18-22; 2005, October, 18-22

74710   Pelvimetry, with or without placental localization   ♀ Z3 X 80
    EXCLUDES   imaging procedures on abdomen and pelvis (72170-72190, 74000-74170)
    📷 1.21   ✂ 1.21   Global Days XXX

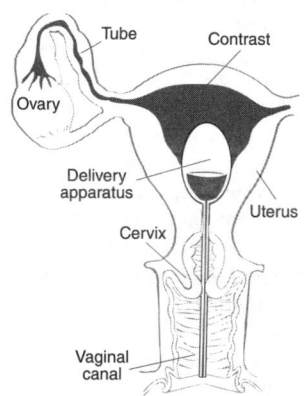

Tube
Contrast
Ovary
Delivery apparatus
Cervix
Uterus
Vaginal canal

Hysterosalpingography (imaging of the uterus and tubes) is performed. Report for radiological supervision and interpretation

74740   Hysterosalpingography, radiological supervision and interpretation   ♀ M1 02 80 ▢
    EXCLUDES   hysterosalpingography with introduction of saline/contrast (58340)
    imaging procedures on abdomen and pelvis (72170-72190, 74000-74170)
    📷 2.14   ✂ 2.14   Global Days XXX

74742   Transcervical catheterization of fallopian tube, radiological supervision and interpretation   ♀ M1 N 80 ▢
    EXCLUDES   surgical procedure (58345)
    imaging procedures on abdomen and pelvis (72170-72190, 74000-74170)
    📷 0.00   ✂ 0.00   Global Days XXX

74775   Perineogram (eg, vaginogram, for sex determination or extent of anomalies)   M ♀ Z2 S 80 ▢
    EXCLUDES   imaging procedures on abdomen and pelvis (72170-72190, 74000-74170)
    📷 0.00   ✂ 0.00   Global Days XXX

75557-75564 Magnetic Resonance Imaging: Heart Structure and Physiology

CMS 100-4,13,40   Magnetic Resonance Imaging (MRI) Procedures
CMS 100-4,3,10.4   Payment of Nonphysician Services for Inpatients
CMS 100-3,220.2   Magnetic Resonance Imaging
CMS 100-2,15,80   Physician Supervision Requirements for Diagnostic Tests
CMS 100-4,13,10   ICD-9-CM Coding for Diagnostic Tests
INCLUDES   physiologic evaluation of cardiac function
EXCLUDES   cardiac catheterization procedures (93501-93556)

Code also separate vascular injection (36000-36299)
Do not report with more than one code in this group per session
Do not report with (76376-76377)

75557   Cardiac magnetic resonance imaging for morphology and function without contrast material;   Z2 03 80
    📷 14.36   ✂ 14.36   Global Days XXX
    AMA: 2008, Jul, 3&14

75558   with flow/velocity quantification   E
    📷 17.47   ✂ 17.47   Global Days XXX
    AMA: 2008, Jul, 3&14

75559   with stress imaging   Z2 03 80
    INCLUDES   pharmacologic wall motion stress evaluation without contrast
    Code also stress test (93015-93018)
    📷 20.74   ✂ 20.74   Global Days XXX
    AMA: 2008, Jul, 3&14

75560   with flow/velocity quantification and stress   E
    INCLUDES   pharmacologic wall motion stress evaluation without contrast
    Code also stress test (93015-93018)
    📷 22.71   ✂ 22.71   Global Days XXX
    AMA: 2008, Jul, 3&14

75561   Cardiac magnetic resonance imaging for morphology and function without contrast material(s), followed by contrast material(s) and further sequences;   Z2 03 80
    📷 19.30   ✂ 19.30   Global Days XXX
    AMA: 2008, Jul, 3&14

75562   with flow/velocity quantification   E
    📷 22.51   ✂ 22.51   Global Days XXX
    AMA: 2008, Jul, 3&14

75563   with stress imaging   Z2 03 80
    INCLUDES   pharmacologic perfusion stress evaluation with contrast
    Code also stress test (93015-93018)
    📷 23.67   ✂ 23.67   Global Days XXX
    AMA: 2008, Jul, 3&14

75564   with flow/velocity quantification and stress   E
    INCLUDES   pharmacologic perfusion stress evaluation with contrast
    Code also stress test (93015-93018)
    📷 26.47   ✂ 26.47   Global Days XXX
    AMA: 2008, Jul, 3&14

75600-75790 Radiography: Arterial

CMS 100-4,13,100   *Interpretation of Diagnostic Tests*
CMS 100-4,3,10.4   *Payment of Nonphysician Services for Inpatients*
CMS 100-2,15,80   *Physician Supervision Requirements for Diagnostic Tests*
CMS 100-4,13,10   *ICD-9-CM Coding for Diagnostic Tests*

INCLUDES   diagnostic angiography specifically included in the interventional code description
the following diagnostic procedures with interventional supervision and interpretation:
     angiography
     contrast injection
     fluoroscopic guidance for intervention
     post-angioplasty/stent angiography
     roadmapping
     vessel measurement

EXCLUDES   *diagnostic angiogram during a separate encounter from the interventional procedure*
diagnostic angiography with interventional procedure if:
1. No previous catheter-based angiogram is accessible and a complete diagnostic procedure is performed and the decision to proceed with an interventional procedure is based on the diagnostic service, OR
2. The previous diagnostic angiogram is accessible but the documentation in the medical record specifies that:
     a. the patient's condition has changed
     b. there is insufficient imaging of the patient's anatomy and/or disease, OR
     c. there is a clinical change during the procedure that necessitates a new examination away from the site of the intervention
intra-arterial procedures (36100-36248)
intravenous procedures (36000-36013, 36400-36425)

75600   **Aortography, thoracic, without serialography, radiological supervision and interpretation**   N1 02 80 ▢
     EXCLUDES   *injection procedure (93544)*
     8.95   8.95   Global Days XXX

75605   **Aortography, thoracic, by serialography, radiological supervision and interpretation**   N1 02 80 ▢
     EXCLUDES   *injection procedure (93544)*
     7.68   7.68   Global Days XXX
     AMA: 2008, Jan, 10-25; 2007, Jan, 13-27; 2007, Jan, 13-27; 2007, January, 13-27

75625   **Aortography, abdominal, by serialography, radiological supervision and interpretation**   N1 02 80 ▢
     EXCLUDES   *injection procedure (93544)*
     7.58   7.58   Global Days XXX
     AMA: 2008, Apr, -11; 2008, Apr, -11; 2008, Jan, 10-25; 2008, Apr, -11; 2007, Jan, 13-27; 2007, Jan, 13-27; 2007, January, 13-27; 2007, Dec, 10-179

75630   **Aortography, abdominal plus bilateral iliofemoral lower extremity, catheter, by serialography, radiological supervision and interpretation**   N1 02 80 ▢
     8.79   8.79   Global Days XXX
     AMA: 2008, Apr, -11; 2008, Apr, -11; 2008, Jan, 10-25; 2008, Apr, -11; 2007, Jan, 13-27; 2007, Jan, 13-27; 2007, January, 13-27

75635   **Computed tomographic angiography, abdominal aorta and bilateral iliofemoral lower extremity runoff, with contrast material(s), including noncontrast images, if performed, and image postprocessing**   N1 02 80 ▢
     16.68   16.68   Global Days XXX
     AMA: 2007, Jan, 28-31; 2007, Jan, 28-31; 2007, January, 28-31; 2005, Dec, 7; 2005, December, 7; 2005, Dec, 7

75650   **Angiography, cervicocerebral, catheter, including vessel origin, radiological supervision and interpretation**   N1 02 80 ▢
     8.12   8.12   Global Days XXX

75658   **Angiography, brachial, retrograde, radiological supervision and interpretation**   N1 02 80 ▢
     8.03   8.03   Global Days XXX

75660   **Angiography, external carotid, unilateral, selective, radiological supervision and interpretation**   N1 02 80 ▢ P0
     8.17   8.17   Global Days XXX

75662   **Angiography, external carotid, bilateral, selective, radiological supervision and interpretation**   N1 02 80 ▢ P0
     9.35   9.35   Global Days XXX

75665   **Angiography, carotid, cerebral, unilateral, radiological supervision and interpretation**   N1 02 80 ▢ P0
     8.39   8.39   Global Days XXX

75671   **Angiography, carotid, cerebral, bilateral, radiological supervision and interpretation**   N1 02 80 ▢ P0
     9.47   9.47   Global Days XXX

75676   **Angiography, carotid, cervical, unilateral, radiological supervision and interpretation**   N1 02 80 ▢ P0
     8.18   8.18   Global Days XXX

75680   **Angiography, carotid, cervical, bilateral, radiological supervision and interpretation**   N1 02 80 ▢ P0
     9.10   9.10   Global Days XXX

75685   **Angiography, vertebral, cervical, and/or intracranial, radiological supervision and interpretation**   N1 02 80 ▢
     8.19   8.19   Global Days XXX

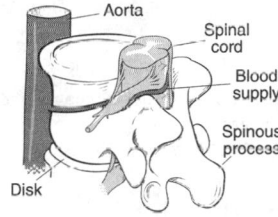

An angiography of a specific area of the spine is performed

75705   **Angiography, spinal, selective, radiological supervision and interpretation**   N1 02 80 ▢
     9.42   9.42   Global Days XXX

75710   **Angiography, extremity, unilateral, radiological supervision and interpretation**   N1 02 80 ▢
     8.01   8.01   Global Days XXX
     AMA: 2008, Jan, 10-25; 2007, Jan, 13-27; 2007, Jan, 13-27; 2007, January, 13-27

75716   **Angiography, extremity, bilateral, radiological supervision and interpretation**   N1 02 80 ▢
     8.91   8.91   Global Days XXX
     AMA: 2008, Apr, -11; 2008, Apr, -11; 2008, Jan, 10-25; 2008, Apr, -11; 2007, Jan, 13-27; 2007, Jan, 13-27; 2007, January, 13-27; 2007, Dec, 10-179

75722   **Angiography, renal, unilateral, selective (including flush aortogram), radiological supervision and interpretation**   N1 02 80 ▢
     7.91   7.91   Global Days XXX

75724   **Angiography, renal, bilateral, selective (including flush aortogram), radiological supervision and interpretation**   N1 02 80 ▢
     9.18   9.18   Global Days XXX

● New Code   ▲ Revised Code   Maternity Edit   Age Edit   A-Y OPPS Status Indicator   Facility RVU   Non-Facility RVU
CCI Comprehensive Code   50 Bilateral Procedure   + Add-on Indicator   Laboratory crosswalk   Radiology crosswalk

© 2008 Ingenix *(Blue Ink)*   CPT only © 2008 American Medical Association. All Rights Reserved. (Black Ink)   Medicare (Red Ink)   289

Radiology

75726 — 75820

+

75726 Angiography, visceral, selective or supraselective (with or without flush aortogram), radiological supervision and interpretation [N1] [02] [80] [▭]

    EXCLUDES *selective angiography, each additional visceral vessel studied after basic examination (75774)*

    🖩 7.92   ⚕ 7.92   Global Days XXX

75731 Angiography, adrenal, unilateral, selective, radiological supervision and interpretation [N1] [02] [80] [▭]

    🖩 8.19   ⚕ 8.19   Global Days XXX

75733 Angiography, adrenal, bilateral, selective, radiological supervision and interpretation [N1] [02] [80] [▭]

    🖩 9.25   ⚕ 9.25   Global Days XXX

75736 Angiography, pelvic, selective or supraselective, radiological supervision and interpretation [N1] [02] [80] [▭]

    🖩 7.99   ⚕ 7.99   Global Days XXX

75741 Angiography, pulmonary, unilateral, selective, radiological supervision and interpretation [N1] [02] [80] [▭]

    EXCLUDES *injection procedure (93541)*

    🖩 7.68   ⚕ 7.68   Global Days XXX

75743 Angiography, pulmonary, bilateral, selective, radiological supervision and interpretation [N1] [02] [80] [▭]

    EXCLUDES *injection procedure (93541)*

    🖩 8.39   ⚕ 8.39   Global Days XXX

75746 Angiography, pulmonary, by nonselective catheter or venous injection, radiological supervision and interpretation [N1] [02] [80] [▭]

    EXCLUDES *injection procedure (93541)*
    injection procedure, catheter introduction (93501-93533, 93539, 93540, 93545, 93556)

    🖩 7.75   ⚕ 7.75   Global Days XXX

75756 Angiography, internal mammary, radiological supervision and interpretation [N1] [02] [80] [▭]

    EXCLUDES *injection procedure, catheter introduction (93501-93533, 93545, 93556)*

    🖩 8.21   ⚕ 8.21   Global Days XXX

75774 Angiography, selective, each additional vessel studied after basic examination, radiological supervision and interpretation (List separately in addition to code for primary procedure) [N1] [N] [80] [▭]

    EXCLUDES *angiography (75600-75790)*
    catheterizations (36215-36248)
    injection procedure, catheter introduction (93501-93533, 93545, 93555, 93556)

    Code first initial vessel
    🖩 6.06   ⚕ 6.06   Global Days ZZZ
    AMA: 2007, Dec, 10-179

75790 Angiography, arteriovenous shunt (eg, dialysis patient), radiological supervision and interpretation [N1] [02] [▭]

    EXCLUDES *catheter introduction (36140, 36145, 36215-36217, 36245-36247)*

    🖩 4.84   ⚕ 4.84   Global Days XXX

75801-75893 Radiography: Lymphatic and Venous

CMS 100-4,13,100   *Interpretation of Diagnostic Tests*
CMS 100-4,3,10.4   *Payment of Nonphysician Services for Inpatients*
CMS 100-2,15,80   *Physician Supervision Requirements for Diagnostic Tests*
CMS 100-4,13,10   *ICD-9-CM Coding for Diagnostic Tests*

INCLUDES   diagnostic venography specifically included in the interventional code description
the following diagnostic procedures with interventional supervision and interpretation:
    contrast injection
    fluoroscopic guidance for intervention
    post-angioplasty/venography
    roadmapping
    venography
    vessel measurement

EXCLUDES   *diagnostic venogram during a separate encounter from the interventional procedure*
diagnostic venography with interventional procedure if:
   1. No previous catheter-based venogram is accessible and a complete diagnostic procedure is performed and the decision to proceed with an interventional procedure is based on the diagnostic service, OR
   2. The previous diagnostic venogram is accessible but the documentation in the medical record specifies that:
     a. the patient's condition has changed
     b. there is insufficient imaging of the patient's anatomy and/or disease, OR
     c. there is a clinical change during the procedure that necessitates a new examination away from the site of the intervention
intravenous procedures (36000-36015, 36400-36510)
lymphatic injection procedures (38790)

75801 Lymphangiography, extremity only, unilateral, radiological supervision and interpretation [N1] [02] [80] [▭]
    🖩 0.00   ⚕ 0.00   Global Days XXX

75803 Lymphangiography, extremity only, bilateral, radiological supervision and interpretation [N1] [02] [80] [▭]
    🖩 0.00   ⚕ 0.00   Global Days XXX

75805 Lymphangiography, pelvic/abdominal, unilateral, radiological supervision and interpretation [N1] [02] [80] [▭]
    🖩 0.00   ⚕ 0.00   Global Days XXX

75807 Lymphangiography, pelvic/abdominal, bilateral, radiological supervision and interpretation [N1] [02] [80] [▭]
    🖩 0.00   ⚕ 0.00   Global Days XXX

75809 Shuntogram for investigation of previously placed indwelling nonvascular shunt (eg, LeVeen shunt, ventriculoperitoneal shunt, indwelling infusion pump), radiological supervision and interpretation [N1] [02] [80] [▭]

    INCLUDES   needle placement with fluoroscopic guidance (77002)

    EXCLUDES   *surgical procedure (49427, 61070)*

    🖩 2.39   ⚕ 2.39   Global Days XXX
    AMA: 2008, Jun, 8-11; 2008, Jul, 10&13; 2008, Sep, 10☐-11; 2007, Feb, 10-11; 2007, Feb, 10-11; 2007, February, 10-11

75810 Splenoportography, radiological supervision and interpretation [N1] [02] [80] [▭]

    INCLUDES   needle placement with fluoroscopic guidance (77002)

    🖩 0.00   ⚕ 0.00   Global Days XXX
    AMA: 2008, Jun, 8-11; 2007, Feb, 10-11; 2007, Feb, 10-11; 2007, February, 10-11

75820 Venography, extremity, unilateral, radiological supervision and interpretation [N1] [02] [80] [▭]
    🖩 3.28   ⚕ 3.28   Global Days XXX
    AMA: 2008, Jan, 10-25; 2008, May, 9-11; 2007, Jan, 13-27; 2007, Jan, 13-27; 2007, January, 13-27

[26]/[TC] Professional/Technical Component Only   [80]/[80] Assist-at-Surgery Allowed/With Documentation   Unlisted   Not Covered

AMA: CPT Assistant References   [A2]-[Z3] ASC Payment Indicator   ♂ Male Only   ♀ Female Only   ⊘ Modifier 51 Exempt   [PQ] PQRI

290   CPT only © 2008 American Medical Association. All Rights Reserved. (Black Ink)   Medicare (Red Ink)   © 2008 Ingenix (Blue Ink)

75822 **Venography, extremity, bilateral, radiological supervision and interpretation** ⬛ 02 80 ▢
4.02 ⚲ 4.02 Global Days XXX

75825 **Venography, caval, inferior, with serialography, radiological supervision and interpretation** ⬛ 02 80 ▢
7.32 ⚲ 7.32 Global Days XXX
AMA: 2008, Oct, 10-11

75827 **Venography, caval, superior, with serialography, radiological supervision and interpretation** ⬛ 02 80 ▢
7.30 ⚲ 7.30 Global Days XXX

75831 **Venography, renal, unilateral, selective, radiological supervision and interpretation** ⬛ 02 80 ▢
7.40 ⚲ 7.40 Global Days XXX

75833 **Venography, renal, bilateral, selective, radiological supervision and interpretation** ⬛ 02 80 ▢
8.24 ⚲ 8.24 Global Days XXX

75840 **Venography, adrenal, unilateral, selective, radiological supervision and interpretation** ⬛ 02 80 ▢
7.34 ⚲ 7.34 Global Days XXX

75842 **Venography, adrenal, bilateral, selective, radiological supervision and interpretation** ⬛ 02 80 ▢
8.28 ⚲ 8.28 Global Days XXX

75860 **Venography, venous sinus (eg, petrosal and inferior sagittal) or jugular, catheter, radiological supervision and interpretation** ⬛ 02 80 ▢
7.54 ⚲ 7.54 Global Days XXX

75870 **Venography, superior sagittal sinus, radiological supervision and interpretation** ⬛ 02 80 ▢
7.48 ⚲ 7.48 Global Days XXX

75872 **Venography, epidural, radiological supervision and interpretation** ⬛ 02 80 ▢
8.17 ⚲ 8.17 Global Days XXX

75880 **Venography, orbital, radiological supervision and interpretation** ⬛ 02 00 ▢
3.31 ⚲ 3.31 Global Days XXX

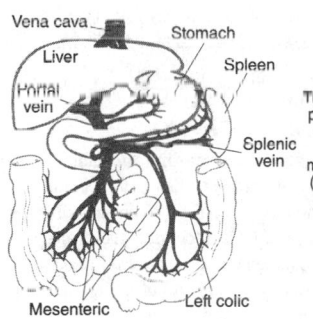

The portal vein is accessed by needle, percutaneously and through the liver, and contrast is delivered into the lumen. Measurement of blood movement through the vein are made (hemodynamic studies). Images are taken. Code 75885 reports the radiological supervision and interpretation of the studies

Schematic showing the portal vein

75885 **Percutaneous transhepatic portography with hemodynamic evaluation, radiological supervision and interpretation** ⬛ 02 80 ▢
INCLUDES needle placement with fluoroscopic guidance (77002)
7.86 ⚲ 7.86 Global Days XXX
AMA: 2008, Jan, 10-25; 2008, Jun, 8-11; 2007, Jan, 13-27; 2007, Jan, 13-27; 2007, Feb, 10-11; 2007, Feb, 10-11; 2007, January, 13-27; 2007, February, 10-11

75887 **Percutaneous transhepatic portography without hemodynamic evaluation, radiological supervision and interpretation** ⬛ 02 80 ▢
INCLUDES needle placement with fluoroscopic guidance (77002)
7.92 ⚲ 7.92 Global Days XXX
AMA: 2008, Jan, 10-25; 2008, Jun, 8-11; 2007, Jan, 13-27; 2007, Jan, 13-27; 2007, Feb, 10-11; 2007, Feb, 10-11; 2007, January, 13-27; 2007, February, 10-11; 2006, Apr, 11-18; 2006, Apr, 11-18; 2006, April, 11-18

75889 **Hepatic venography, wedged or free, with hemodynamic evaluation, radiological supervision and interpretation** ⬛ 02 80 ▢
7.42 ⚲ 7.42 Global Days XXX

75891 **Hepatic venography, wedged or free, without hemodynamic evaluation, radiological supervision and interpretation** ⬛ 02 80 ▢
7.42 ⚲ 7.42 Global Days XXX

75893 **Venous sampling through catheter, with or without angiography (eg, for parathyroid hormone, renin), radiological supervision and interpretation** ⬛ 02 80 ▢
EXCLUDES *surgical procedure (36500)*
6.54 ⚲ 6.54 Global Days XXX

75894-75946 Transcatheter Procedures

CMS 100-4,13,100   *Interpretation of Diagnostic Tests*
CM3 100-4,3,10.4   *Payment of Nonphysician Services for Inpatients*
CMS 100-3,20.28   *Therapeutic Embolization*
CMS 100-2,15,80   *Physician Supervision Requirements for Diagnostic Tests*
CMS 100-4,13,10   *ICD-9-CM Coding br Diagnostic Tests*
INCLUDES   the following diagnostic procedures with interventional supervision and interpretation:
angiography/venography
completion angiography/venography except for those services allowed by 75898
contrast injection
fluoroscopic guidance for intervention
roadmapping
vessel measurement
transurethral approach to the removal or replacement of an internally dwelling ureteral stent (50385-50386)
EXCLUDES   *diagnostic angiography/venography performed at the same session as transcatheter therapy unless it is specifically included in the code descriptor or is excluded in the venography/angiography notes (75600-75893)*
replacement of gastrostomy, duodenostomy, jejunostomy, gastrojejunostomy, or cecostomy tube, percutaneously, including guidance via fluoroscopy (49450-49452)

75894 **Transcatheter therapy, embolization, any method, radiological supervision and interpretation** ⬛ ⬛ 80 ▢
EXCLUDES   *obstetrical or postpartum hemorrhage embolization (37204)*
uterine fibroid embolization (37210)
0.00 ⚲ 0.00 Global Days XXX
AMA: 2008, Feb, 5-6; 2007, Jan, 7-10; 2007, Jan, 7-10; 2007, January, 7-10

75896 **Transcatheter therapy, infusion, any method (eg, thrombolysis other than coronary), radiological supervision and interpretation** ⬛ ⬛ 80 ▢
EXCLUDES   *coronary disease infusion (92975, 92977)*
0.00 ⚲ 0.00 Global Days XXX

● New Code   ▲ Revised Code   ⬛ Maternity Edit   ⬛ Age Edit   ⬛ OPPS Status Indicator   ⬛ Facility RVU   ⚲ Non-Facility RVU
▢ CCI Comprehensive Code   50 Bilateral Procedure   + Add-on Indicator   ⬛ Laboratory crosswalk   ⬛ Radiology crosswalk

© 2008 Ingenix *(Blue Ink)*   CPT only © 2008 American Medical Association. All Rights Reserved. (Black Ink)   Medicare (Red Ink)   **291**

75822 — 75896

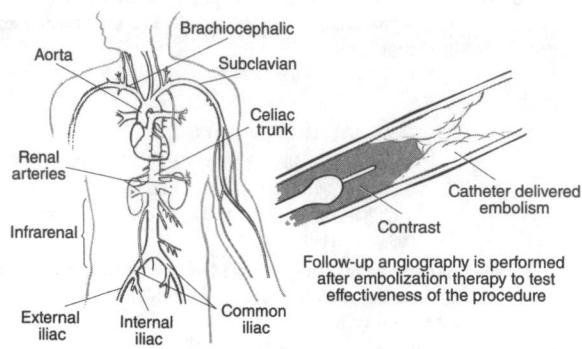

Brachiocephalic
Aorta
Subclavian
Celiac trunk
Renal arteries
Catheter delivered embolism
Infrarenal
Contrast
External iliac
Internal iliac
Common iliac
Follow-up angiography is performed after embolization therapy to test effectiveness of the procedure

75898 Angiography through existing catheter for follow-up study for transcatheter therapy, embolization or infusion

⌨ 0.00 ⚕ 0.00 **Global Days XXX**
AMA: 2007, Jan, 7-10; 2007, Jan, 7-10; 2007, January, 7-10; 2007, Dec, 10-179

75900 Exchange of a previously placed intravascular catheter during thrombolytic therapy with contrast monitoring, radiological supervision and interpretation
> ***EXCLUDES*** *surgical procedure (37209)*

⌨ 0.00 ⚕ 0.00 **Global Days XXX**

75901 Mechanical removal of pericatheter obstructive material (eg, fibrin sheath) from central venous device via separate venous access, radiologic supervision and interpretation
> ***EXCLUDES*** *surgical procedure (36595)*
> *venous catheterization (36010-36012)*

⌨ 4.82 ⚕ 4.82 **Global Days XXX**
AMA: 2004, Dec, 6; 2004, Dec, 6; 2004, December, 6

75902 Mechanical removal of intraluminal (intracatheter) obstructive material from central venous device through device lumen, radiologic supervision and interpretation
> ***EXCLUDES*** *surgical procedure (36596)*
> *venous catheterization (36010-36012)*

⌨ 2.82 ⚕ 2.82 **Global Days XXX**
AMA: 2004, Dec, 6; 2004, Dec, 6; 2004, December, 6

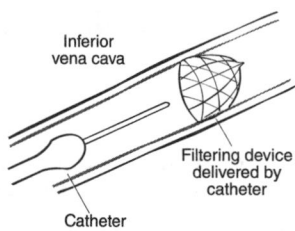

Inferior vena cava

Filtering device delivered by catheter

Catheter

A filtering device is placed by catheter into the inferior vena cava (IVC). Code 75940 reports radiological supervision and interpretation of procedure

75940 Percutaneous placement of IVC filter, radiological supervision and interpretation
⌨ 0.00 ⚕ 0.00 **Global Days XXX**
AMA: 2008, Jan, 10-25; 2008, Oct, 10-11; 2007, Jan, 13-27; 2007, Jan, 13-27; 2007, January, 13-27

75945 Intravascular ultrasound (non-coronary vessel), radiological supervision and interpretation; initial vessel
⌨ 0.00 ⚕ 0.00 **Global Days XXX**

+ **75946** each additional non-coronary vessel (List separately in addition to code for primary procedure)
Code first initial vessel (75945)
⌨ 0.00 ⚕ 0.00 **Global Days ZZZ**

75952-75959 Endovascular Aneurysm Repair
CMS *100-4,3,10.4* *Payment of Nonphysician Services for Inpatients*
INCLUDES the following diagnostic procedures with interventional supervision and interpretation:
angiography/venography
completion angiography/venography except for those services allowed by 75898
contrast injection
fluoroscopic guidance for intervention
roadmapping
vessel measurement
EXCLUDES *diagnostic angiography/venography performed at the same session as transcatheter therapy unless it is specifically included in the code descriptor or is excluded in the venography/angiography notes (75600-75893)*

75952 Endovascular repair of infrarenal abdominal aortic aneurysm or dissection, radiological supervision and interpretation
> ***EXCLUDES*** *endovascular repair of abdominal aortic aneurysm, radiologic supervision and interpretation (0078T-0081T)*
> *implantation endovascular grafts (34800-34808)*

⌨ 0.00 ⚕ 0.00 **Global Days XXX**

75953 Placement of proximal or distal extension prosthesis for endovascular repair of infrarenal aortic or iliac artery aneurysm, pseudoaneurysm, or dissection, radiological supervision and interpretation
> ***EXCLUDES*** *placement of endovascular extension prostheses (34825, 34826)*

⌨ 0.00 ⚕ 0.00 **Global Days XXX**

75954 Endovascular repair of iliac artery aneurysm, pseudoaneurysm, arteriovenous malformation, or trauma, radiological supervision and interpretation
> ***EXCLUDES*** *placement of endovascular graft (34900)*

⌨ 0.00 ⚕ 0.00 **Global Days XXX**

75956 Endovascular repair of descending thoracic aorta (eg, aneurysm, pseudoaneurysm, dissection, penetrating ulcer, intramural hematoma, or traumatic disruption); involving coverage of left subclavian artery origin, initial endoprosthesis plus descending thoracic aortic extension(s), if required, to level of celiac artery origin, radiological supervision and interpretation
> ***EXCLUDES*** *endovascular graft implantation (33880)*

⌨ 0.00 ⚕ 0.00 **Global Days XXX**
AMA: 2006, May, 10-11; 2006, May, 10-11; 2006, May, 10-11

75957 not involving coverage of left subclavian artery origin, initial endoprosthesis plus descending thoracic aortic extension(s), if required, to level of celiac artery origin, radiological supervision and interpretation
> ***EXCLUDES*** *endovascular graft implantation (33881)*

⌨ 0.00 ⚕ 0.00 **Global Days XXX**
AMA: 2006, May, 10-11; 2006, May, 10-11; 2006, May, 10-11

75958 Placement of proximal extension prosthesis for endovascular repair of descending thoracic aorta (eg, aneurysm, pseudoaneurysm, dissection, penetrating ulcer, intramural hematoma, or traumatic disruption), radiological supervision and interpretation C 80

INCLUDES corresponding services for placement of each proximal thoracic endovascular extension

EXCLUDES *placement of proximal endovascular extension (33883, 33884)*

🔧 0.00   🔧 0.00   Global Days XXX

AMA: 2006, May, 10-11; 2006, May, 10-11; 2006, May, 10-11

75959 Placement of distal extension prosthesis(s) (delayed) after endovascular repair of descending thoracic aorta, as needed, to level of celiac origin, radiological supervision and interpretation C 80

INCLUDES corresponding services for placement of distal thoracic endovascular extension(s) placed during procedure following the principal procedure

EXCLUDES *placement of distal endovascular extension (33886)*

Do not report with endovascular repair (75956, 75957)

🔧 0.00   🔧 0.00   Global Days XXX

AMA: 2006, May, 10-11; 2006, May, 10-11; 2006, May, 10-11

75960-75961 Transcatheter Insertion and Removal

CMS *100-4,13,100   Interpretation of Diagnostic Tests*
CMS *100-4,3,10.4   Payment of Nonphysician Services for Inpatients*
CMS *100-2,15,80   Physician Supervision Requirements for Diagnostic Tests*
CMS *100-4,13,10   ICD-9-CM Coding for Diagnostic Tests*

INCLUDES the following diagnostic procedures with interventional supervision and interpretation:
angiography/venography
completion angiography/venography except for those services allowed by 75898
contrast injection
fluoroscopic guidance for intervention
roadmapping
vessel measurement

EXCLUDES *diagnostic angiography/venography performed at the same session as transcatheter therapy unless it is specifically included in the code descriptor or is excluded in the venography/angiography notes (75600-75893)*

75960 Transcatheter introduction of intravascular stent(s) (except coronary, carotid, and vertebral vessel), percutaneous and/or open, radiological supervision and interpretation, each vessel M N 80 🔳

EXCLUDES *surgical procedure (37205-37208)*
transcatheter placement of extracranial vertebral/intrathoracic carotid artery stent(s) radiologic supervision and interpretation (0075T, 0076T)

🔧 7.43   🔧 7.43   Global Days XXX

75961 Transcatheter retrieval, percutaneous, of intravascular foreign body (eg, fractured venous or arterial catheter), radiological supervision and interpretation M N 80 🔳

EXCLUDES *surgical procedure (37203)*

🔧 11.54   🔧 11.54   Global Days XXX

AMA: 2008, Oct, 10-11

75962-75978 Percutaneous Transluminal Angioplasty

CMS *100-4,3,10.4   Payment of Nonphysician Services for Inpatients*
CMS *100-3,20.7   Percutaneous Transluminal Angioplasty (PTA)*

INCLUDES the following diagnostic procedures with interventional supervision and interpretation:
angiography/venography
completion angiography/venography except for those services allowed by 75898
contrast injection
fluoroscopic guidance for intervention
roadmapping
vessel measurement

EXCLUDES *diagnostic angiography/venography performed at the same session as transcatheter therapy unless it is specifically included in the code descriptor or is excluded in the venography/angiography notes (75600-75893)*

75962 Transluminal balloon angioplasty, peripheral artery, radiological supervision and interpretation M 02 80 🔳

Code also angioplasty catheter (C1725, C1885)

🔧 7.94   🔧 7.94   Global Days XXX

AMA: 2007, Dec, 10-179

+ **75964** Transluminal balloon angioplasty, each additional peripheral artery, radiological supervision and interpretation (List separately in addition to code for primary procedure) M N 80 🔳

Code first primary procedure (75962)

🔧 4.67   🔧 4.67   Global Days ZZZ

AMA: 2007, Dec, 10-179

75966 Transluminal balloon angioplasty, renal or other visceral artery, radiological supervision and interpretation N 02 80 🔳

Code also angioplasty catheter (C1725, C1885)

🔧 9.28   🔧 9.28   Global Days XXX

+ **75968** Transluminal balloon angioplasty, each additional visceral artery, radiological supervision and interpretation (List separately in addition to code for primary procedure) M N 80 🔳

EXCLUDES *percutaneous transluminal coronary angioplasty (92982-92984)*

Code first primary procedure (75966)

🔧 4.68   🔧 4.68   Global Days ZZZ

75970 Transcatheter biopsy, radiological supervision and interpretation M N 80 🔳

EXCLUDES *injection procedure only for transcatheter therapy or biopsy (36100-36299)*
percutaneous needle biopsy
  pancreas (48102)
  retroperitoneal lymph node/mass (49180)
  transcatheter renal/ureteral biopsy (52007)

🔧 0.00   🔧 0.00   Global Days XXX

75978 Transluminal balloon angioplasty, venous (eg, subclavian stenosis), radiological supervision and interpretation N 02 80 🔳

Code also angioplasty catheter (C1725, C1885)

🔧 7.81   🔧 7.81   Global Days XXX

● New Code   ▲ Revised Code   M Maternity Edit   A Age Edit   A Y OPPS Status Indicator   🔧 Facility RVU   🔧 Non-Facility RVU

🔳 CCI Comprehensive Code   50 Bilateral Procedure   + Add-on Indicator   🔳 Laboratory crosswalk   🔳 Radiology crosswalk

75980-75989 Percutaneous Drainage

CMS *100-3,220.1*   *Computerized Tomography*
CMS *100-4,3,10.4*   *Payment of Nonphysician Services for Inpatients*
CMS *100-3,220.5*   *Ultrasound Diagnostic Procedures*

INCLUDES the following diagnostic procedures with interventional supervision
and interpretation:
angiography/venography
completion angiography/venography except for those services
allowed by 75898
contrast injection
fluoroscopic guidance for intervention
roadmapping
vessel measurement

EXCLUDES *diagnostic angiography/venography performed at the same session*
as transcatheter therapy unless it is specifically included in the
code descriptor or is excluded in the venography/angiography
notes (75600-75893)

75980 **Percutaneous transhepatic biliary drainage with contrast
monitoring, radiological supervision and
interpretation** NI N 80 ▭

INCLUDES needle placement with fluoroscopic guidance
(77002)

🔲 0.00   ⚖ 0.00   **Global Days XXX**
AMA: 2008, Jun, 8-11; 2007, Feb, 10-11; 2007, Feb, 10-11; 2007,
February, 10-11

75982 **Percutaneous placement of drainage catheter for
combined internal and external biliary drainage or of a
drainage stent for internal biliary drainage in patients
with an inoperable mechanical biliary obstruction,
radiological supervision and interpretation** NI N 80 ▭

INCLUDES needle placement with fluoroscopic guidance
(77002)

🔲 0.00   ⚖ 0.00   **Global Days XXX**
AMA: 2008, Jun, 8-11; 2007, Feb, 10-11; 2007, Feb, 10-11; 2007,
February, 10-11

75984 **Change of percutaneous tube or drainage catheter with
contrast monitoring (eg, genitourinary system, abscess),
radiological supervision and interpretation** NI N 80 ▭

EXCLUDES *change only of nephrostomy/pyelostomy tube*
(50398)
change only of percutaneous biliary drainage
catheter (47525)
cholecystostomy, percutaneous (47490)
introduction procedure only for percutaneous
biliary drainage (47510, 47511)
nephrostolithotomy/pyelostolithotomy,
percutaneous (50080, 50081)
percutaneous replacement of gastrointestinal
tube using fluoroscopic guidance
(49450-49452)

🔲 3.16   ⚖ 3.16   **Global Days XXX**
AMA: 2005, Oct, 18-22; 2005, Oct, 18-22; 2005, October, 18-22

75989 **Radiological guidance (ie, fluoroscopy, ultrasound, or
computed tomography), for percutaneous drainage (eg,
abscess, specimen collection), with placement of catheter,
radiological supervision and interpretation** NI N 80 ▭

INCLUDES needle placement with fluoroscopic guidance
(77002)

🔲 4.00   ⚖ 4.00   **Global Days XXX**
AMA: 2008, Jun, 8-11; 2007, Feb, 10-11; 2007, Feb, 10-11; 2007,
February, 10-11

75992-75996 Noncoronary Transluminal Atherectomy

CMS *100-4,3,10.4*   *Payment of Nonphysician Services for Inpatients*

75992 **Transluminal atherectomy, peripheral artery, radiological
supervision and interpretation** NI N 80 ▭

EXCLUDES *surgical procedure (35481-35485,*
35491-35495)

🔲 0.00   ⚖ 0.00   **Global Days XXX**

+ 75993 **Transluminal atherectomy, each additional peripheral
artery, radiological supervision and interpretation (List
separately in addition to code for primary
procedure)** NI N 80 ▭

EXCLUDES *surgical procedure (35481-35485,*
35491-35495)

Code first primary procedure (75992)
🔲 0.00   ⚖ 0.00   **Global Days ZZZ**

75994 **Transluminal atherectomy, renal, radiological supervision
and interpretation** NI N 80 ▭

EXCLUDES *surgical procedure (35480, 35490)*

🔲 0.00   ⚖ 0.00   **Global Days XXX**

75995 **Transluminal atherectomy, visceral, radiological
supervision and interpretation** NI N 80 ▭

EXCLUDES *surgical procedure (35480, 35490)*

🔲 0.00   ⚖ 0.00   **Global Days XXX**

+ 75996 **Transluminal atherectomy, each additional visceral
artery, radiological supervision and interpretation (List
separately in addition to code for primary
procedure)** NI N 80 ▭

EXCLUDES *surgical procedure (35480, 35490)*

Code first primary procedure (75995)
🔲 0.00   ⚖ 0.00   **Global Days ZZZ**

76000-76150 Miscellaneous Techniques

CMS *100-4,3,10.4*   *Payment of Nonphysician Services for Inpatients*
EXCLUDES *arthrography:*
ankle (73615)
elbow (73085)
hip (73525)
knee (73580)
shoulder (73040)
wrist (73115)
CT cerebral perfusion test (0042T)

76000 **Fluoroscopy (separate procedure), up to 1 hour physician
time, other than 71023 or 71034 (eg, cardiac
fluoroscopy)** NI 01 80 ▭

🔲 2.64   ⚖ 2.64   **Global Days XXX**
AMA: 2008, Jan, 10-25; 2008, Jun, 8-11; 2008, Jul, 9; 2007, Jan,
13-27; 2007, Jan, 13-27; 2007, January, 13-27

76001 **Fluoroscopy, physician time more than 1 hour, assisting
a nonradiologic physician (eg, nephrostolithotomy, ERCP,
bronchoscopy, transbronchial biopsy)** NI N 80 ▭

🔲 0.00   ⚖ 0.00   **Global Days XXX**
AMA: 2008, Jun, 8-11; 2008, Jul, 9

76010 **Radiologic examination from nose to rectum for foreign
body, single view, child** A Z3 X 80 ▭

🔲 0.77   ⚖ 0.77   **Global Days XXX**

76080　Radiologic examination, abscess, fistula or sinus tract study, radiological supervision and interpretation 　N1 02 80 ⬚
　　　EXCLUDES　*contrast injections, radiology evaluation, and guidance via fluoroscopy of gastrostomy, duodenostomy, jejunostomy, gastro-jejunostomy, or cecostomy tube (49465)*
　　　🖫 1.76　🖎 1.76　Global Days XXX
　　　AMA: 2008, Jan, 10-25; 2007, Jan, 13-27; 2007, Jan, 13-27; 2007, January, 13-27; 2006, Dec, 10-12; 2006, Dec, 10-12; 2006, December, 10-12; 2006, December, 10-12; 2006, Dec, 10-12; 2006, Dec, 10-12

76098　Radiological examination, surgical specimen 　Z3 X 80
　　　🖫 0.55　🖎 0.55　Global Days XXX

76100　Radiologic examination, single plane body section (eg, tomography), other than with urography 　Z2 X 80 ⬚
　　　🖫 3.69　🖎 3.69　Global Days XXX

76101　Radiologic examination, complex motion (ie, hypercycloidal) body section (eg, mastoid polytomography), other than with urography; unilateral 　Z2 X 80
　　　🖫 5.10　🖎 5.10　Global Days XXX

76102　bilateral 　Z2 X 80 ⬚
　　　EXCLUDES　*nephrotomography (74415)*
　　　🖫 6.84　🖎 6.84　Global Days XXX

76120　Cineradiography/videoradiography, except where specifically included 　Z2 X 80 ⬚
　　　🖫 2.08　🖎 2.08　Global Days XXX
　　　AMA: 2004, Apr, 15; 2004, Apr, 15; 2004, April, 15

\+　76125　Cineradiography/videoradiography to complement routine examination (List separately in addition to code for primary procedure) 　N1 N 80 ⬚
　　　Code first primary procedure
　　　🖫 0.00　🖎 0.00　Global Days ZZZ

76140　Consultation on X-ray examination made elsewhere, written report 　E
　　　🖫 0.00　🖎 0.00　Global Days XXX
　　　AMA: 2008, Jan, 10-25; 2007, Jul, 12-13

76150　Xeroradiography 　Z3 X TC SU
　　　INCLUDES　non-mammographic studies only
　　　🖫 0.51　🖎 0.51　Global Days XXX

76350 Digital Subtraction Angiography

CMS *100-3,220.9*　　*Digital Subtraction Angiography*
EXCLUDES　*arthrography:*
　　ankle (73615)
　　elbow (73085)
　　hip (73525)
　　knee (73580)
　　shoulder (73040)
　　wrist (73115)
　CT cerebral perfusion test (0042T)

76350　Subtraction in conjunction with contrast studies 　N1 N TC 80
　　　EXCLUDES　*3D rendering (76376, 76377)*
　　　🖫 0.00　🖎 0.00　Global Days XXX

76376-76377 Three-dimensional Manipulation

CMS *100-4,3,10.4*　　*Payment of Nonphysician Services for Inpatients*
EXCLUDES　*arthrography:*
　　ankle (73615)
　　elbow (73085)
　　hip (73525)
　　knee (73580)
　　shoulder (73040)
　　wrist (73115)
　computer-aided detection of MRI data for lesion, breast MRI (0159T)
　CT cerebral perfusion test (0042T)

76376　3D rendering with interpretation and reporting of computed tomography, magnetic resonance imaging, ultrasound, or other tomographic modality; not requiring image postprocessing on an independent workstation 　N1 N 80
　　　INCLUDES　concurrent physician supervision of image postprocessing 3D manipulation of volumetric data set/image rendering
　　　Code also base imaging procedures
　　　Do not report with (0066T-0067T, 0144T-0151T, 0159T, 70496, 70498, 70544-70549, 71275, 71555, 72159, 72191, 72198, 73206, 73225, 73725, 74175, 74185, 75557-75564, 75635, 76377, 78000-78999)
　　　🖫 2.22　🖎 2.22　Global Days XXX
　　　AMA: 2008, Jan, 10-25; 2008, Jul, 3&14; 2007, Jan, 13-27; 2007, Jan, 13-27; 2007, Jan, 28-31; 2007, Jan, 28-31; 2007, January, 28-31; 2007, January, 13-27; 2005, Dec, 3-6; 2005, Dec, 3-6; 2005, December, 3-6; 2005, December, 7; 2005, December, 1-2; 2005, Dec, 1-2; 2005, Dec, 1-2; 2005, Dec, 7; 2005, Dec, 7

76377　requiring image postprocessing on an independent workstation 　N1 N 80
　　　Code also base imaging procedures
　　　🖫 3.16　🖎 3.16　Global Days XXX
　　　AMA: 2008, Jan, 10-25; 2008, Jul, 3&14; 2007, Jan, 28-31; 2007, Jan, 28-31; 2007, Jan, 13-27; 2007, Jan, 13-27; 2007, January, 13-27; 2007, January, 28-31; 2005, Dec, 3-6; 2005, Dec, 3-6; 2005, December, 3-6; 2005, December, 7; 2005, December, 1-2; 2005, Dec, 7; 2005, Dec, 7; 2005, Dec, 1-2; 2005, Dec, 1-2

76380 Computerized Tomography: Delimited

CMS *100-3,220.1*　　*Computerized Tomography*
EXCLUDES　*arthrography:*
　　ankle (73615)
　　elbow (73085)
　　hip (73525)
　　knee (73580)
　　shoulder (73040)
　　wrist (73115)
　CT cerebral perfusion test (0042T)

76380　Computed tomography, limited or localized follow-up study 　Z2 S 80
　　　🖫 5.68　🖎 5.68　Global Days XXX
　　　AMA: 2007, Jul, 12-13

Radiology

76390-76499 Magnetic Resonance Spectroscopy

CMS *100-3,220.2.1   Magnetic Resonance Spectroscopy*

EXCLUDES arthrography:
ankle (73615)
elbow (73085)
hip (73525)
knee (73580)
shoulder (73040)
wrist (73115)
CT cerebral perfusion test (0042T)

76390 Magnetic resonance spectroscopy   E
    EXCLUDES   MRI

    ⏚ 12.80   ⚕ 12.80 Global Days XXX

76496 Unlisted fluoroscopic procedure (eg, diagnostic, interventional)   Z2 X 80

    ⏚ 0.00   ⚕ 0.00 Global Days XXX

76497 Unlisted computed tomography procedure (eg, diagnostic, interventional)   Z2 S 80

    ⏚ 0.00   ⚕ 0.00 Global Days XXX
    AMA: 2008, Jan, 10-25; 2007, Jan, 13-27; 2007, Jan, 13-27; 2007, January, 13-27; 2005, Jun, 9-11; 2005, June, 9-11; 2005, Jun, 9-11

76498 Unlisted magnetic resonance procedure (eg, diagnostic, interventional)   Z2 S 80

    ⏚ 0.00   ⚕ 0.00 Global Days XXX
    AMA: 2008, Jul, 3&14

76499 Unlisted diagnostic radiographic procedure   Z2 X 80

    ⏚ 0.00   ⚕ 0.00 Global Days XXX
    AMA: 2008, Jan, 10-25; 2008, Mar, 14-15; 2007, Jan, 13-27; 2007, Jan, 13-27; 2007, January, 13-27; 2006, Dec, 10-12; 2006, Dec, 10-12; 2006, Dec, 10-12; 2006, Dec, 10-12; 2006, Dec, 10-12; 2006, December, 10-12; 2006, December, 10-12; 2006, December, 10-12; 2006, December, 10-12; 2006, Dec, 10-12; 2006, Dec, 10-12; 2006, Dec, 10-12; 2004, Apr, 15; 2004, Apr, 15; 2004, April, 15

76506 Ultrasound: Brain

CMS *100-3,220.5   Ultrasound Diagnostic Procedures*

INCLUDES required permanent documentation of ultrasound images except when diagnostic purpose is biometric measurement
written documentation

EXCLUDES doppler study of vessels, other than color flow (93875-93990)
focused ultrasound ablation of uterine leiomyomata (0071T-0072T)
noninvasive vascular studies, diagnostic (93875-93990)
ultrasound exam that does not include thorough assessment of organ or site, recorded image, and written report

76506 Echoencephalography, real time with image documentation (gray scale) (for determination of ventricular size, delineation of cerebral contents, and detection of fluid masses or other intracranial abnormalities), including A-mode encephalography as secondary component where indicated   Z2 S 80 🔲

    ⏚ 3.20   ⚕ 3.20 Global Days XXX
    AMA: 2007, Mar, 7-8; 2007, Mar, 7-8; 2007, March, 7-8; 2006, Dec, 10-12; 2006, Dec, 10-12; 2006, December, 10-12; 2006, December, 10-12; 2006, Dec, 10-12; 2006, Dec, 10-12

76510-76529 Ultrasound: Eyes

CMS *100-3,10.1   Visual Tests Prior to and General Anesthesia During Cataract Surgery*
CMS *100-3,220.5   Ultrasound Diagnostic Procedures*

INCLUDES required permanent documentation of ultrasound images except when diagnostic purpose is biometric measurement
written documentation

EXCLUDES doppler study of vessels, other than color flow (93875-93990)
focused ultrasound ablation of uterine leiomyomata (0071T-0072T)
ultrasound exam that does not include thorough assessment of organ or site, recorded image, and written report

76510 Ophthalmic ultrasound, diagnostic; B-scan and quantitative A-scan performed during the same patient encounter   Z3 T 80 🔲

    ⏚ 4.08   ⚕ 4.08 Global Days XXX
    AMA: 2005, Dec, 3-6; 2005, Dec, 3-6; 2005, December, 3-6

76511   quantitative A-scan only   Z3 S 80 🔲

    ⏚ 2.67   ⚕ 2.67 Global Days XXX
    AMA: 2005, Dec, 3-6; 2005, Dec, 3-6; 2005, December, 3-6; 2004, Jul, 12; 2004, July, 12; 2004, Jul, 12

76512   B-scan (with or without superimposed non-quantitative A-scan)   Z3 S 80 🔲

    ⏚ 2.51   ⚕ 2.51 Global Days XXX
    AMA: 2005, Dec, 3-6; 2005, Dec, 3-6; 2005, December, 3-6

76513   anterior segment ultrasound, immersion (water bath) B-scan or high resolution biomicroscopy   Z3 S 80 🔲
    EXCLUDES   computerized ophthalmic testing other than by ultrasound (0187T, 92135)

    ⏚ 2.32   ⚕ 2.32 Global Days XXX

76514   corneal pachymetry, unilateral or bilateral (determination of corneal thickness)   Z6 X 80

    ⏚ 0.35   ⚕ 0.35 Global Days XXX
    AMA: 2008, Jan, 10-25; 2007, Jan, 13-27; 2007, Jan, 13-27; 2007, January, 13-27; 2005, Feb, 13-16; 2005, Feb, 13-16; 2005, Jun, 9-11; 2005, Dec, 3-6; 2005, Jun, 9-11; 2005, Dec, 3-6; 2005, June, 9-11; 2005, December, 3-6; 2005, February, 13-16; 2004, Jun, 7; 2004, Jun, 7; 2004, June, 7; 2004, July, 12; 2004, Jul, 12; 2004, Jul, 12

76516 Ophthalmic biometry by ultrasound echography, A-scan;   Z3 S 80 🔲

    ⏚ 1.85   ⚕ 1.85 Global Days XXX
    AMA: 2008, Jan, 10-25; 2007, Jan, 13-27; 2007, Jan, 13-27; 2007, January, 13-27; 2005, Dec, 3-6; 2005, December, 3-6; 2005, Dec, 3-6

76519   with intraocular lens power calculation   Z3 S 80 🔲
    EXCLUDES   partial coherence interferometry (92136)

    ⏚ 1.98   ⚕ 1.98 Global Days XXX
    AMA: 2008, Jan, 10-25; 2007, Jan, 13-27; 2007, Jan, 13-27; 2007, January, 13-27; 2005, Dec, 3-6; 2005, December, 3-6; 2005, Dec, 3-6

76529 Ophthalmic ultrasonic foreign body localization   Z3 S 80 🔲

    ⏚ 1.88   ⚕ 1.88 Global Days XXX

76536-76800 Ultrasound: Neck, Thorax, Abdomen, and Spine

CMS *100-4,3,10.4*   *Payment of Nonphysician Services for Inpatients*
CMS *100-3,220.5*   *Ultrasound Diagnostic Procedures*
CMS *100-2,15,80*   *Physician Supervision Requirements for Diagnostic Tests*
[INCLUDES]   required permanent documentation of ultrasound images except
     when diagnostic purpose is biometric measurement
     written documentation

[EXCLUDES]   *focused ultrasound ablation of uterine leiomyomata (0071T-0072T)*
     ultrasound exam that does not include thorough assessment of organ
     or site, recorded image, and written report

76536   **Ultrasound, soft tissues of head and neck (eg, thyroid, parathyroid, parotid), real time with image documentation**   Z2 S 80 ▣
     🔷 **3.04**   🔷 **3.04**   **Global Days XXX**
     AMA: 2007, Mar, 7-8; 2007, Mar, 7-8; 2007, March, 7-8

76604   **Ultrasound, chest (includes mediastinum), real time with image documentation**   Z2 03 80 ▣
     🔷 **2.38**   🔷 **2.38**   **Global Days XXX**
     AMA: 2007, Mar, 7-8; 2007, Mar, 7-8; 2007, March, 7-8

76645   **Ultrasound, breast(s) (unilateral or bilateral), real time with image documentation**   Z2 S 80 ▣
     🔷 **2.51**   🔷 **2.51**   **Global Days XXX**
     AMA: 2007, Mar, 7-8; 2007, Mar, 7-8; 2007, March, 7-8

76700   **Ultrasound, abdominal, real time with image documentation; complete**   Z2 03 80 ▣
     [INCLUDES]   real time scans of:
         common bile duct
         gall bladder
         inferior vena cava
         kidneys
         liver
         pancreas
         spleen
         upper abdominal aorta
     🔷 **3.77**   🔷 **3.77**   **Global Days XXX**
     AMA: 2007, Mar, 7-8; 2007, Mar, 7-8; 2007, March, 7-8; 2005, Dec, 3-6; 2005, December, 3-6; 2005, Dec, 3-6

76705   **limited (eg, single organ, quadrant, follow-up)**   Z2 03 80 ▣
     🔷 **2.86**   🔷 **2.86**   **Global Days XXX**
     AMA: 2008, Jan, 10-25; 2007, Jan, 13-27; 2007, Jan, 13-27; 2007, January, 13-27; 2005, Dec, 3-6; 2005, December, 3-6; 2005, Dec, 3-6

76770   **Ultrasound, retroperitoneal (eg, renal, aorta, nodes), real time with image documentation; complete**   Z2 03 80 ▣
     [INCLUDES]   complete assessment of kidneys and bladder
         if history indicates urinary pathology
     real time scans of:
         abdominal aorta
         common iliac artery origins
         inferior vena cava
         kidneys
     🔷 **3.61**   🔷 **3.61**   **Global Days XXX**
     AMA: 2007, Mar, 7-8; 2007, Mar, 7-8; 2007, March, 7-8; 2005, Dec, 3-6; 2005, December, 3-6; 2005, Dec, 3-6

76775   **limited**   Z2 03 80 ▣
     🔷 **3.07**   🔷 **3.08**   **Global Days XXX**
     AMA: 2008, Jan, 10-25; 2007, Jan, 13-27; 2007, Jan, 13-27; 2007, January, 13-27; 2005, Dec, 3-6; 2005, December, 3-6; 2005, Dec, 3-6

76776   **Ultrasound, transplanted kidney, real time and duplex Doppler with image documentation**   Z2 03 80
     [EXCLUDES]   *transplanted kidney ultrasound without duplex doppler (76775)*
     Do not report with abdominal/pelvic/scrotal contents/retroperitoneal duplex scan (93975, 93976)
     🔷 **4.01**   🔷 **4.01**   **Global Days XXX**
     AMA: 2007, Mar, 7-8; 2007, Mar, 7-8; 2007, March, 7-8

76800   **Ultrasound, spinal canal and contents**   Z2 S 80 ▣
     🔷 **3.39**   🔷 **3.39**   **Global Days XXX**
     AMA: 2008, Jan, 10-25; 2007, Jan, 13-27; 2007, Jan, 13-27; 2007, January, 13-27

76801-76802 Ultrasound: Pregnancy Less Than 14 Weeks

CMS *100-4,3,10.4*   *Payment of Nonphysician Services for Inpatients*
CMS *100-3,220.5*   *Ultrasound Diagnostic Procedures*
CMS *100-2,15,80*   *Physician Supervision Requirements for Diagnostic Tests*
[INCLUDES]   determination of the number of gestational sacs and fetuses
     gestational sac/fetal measurement appropriate for gestational
       (younger than 14 weeks 0 days)
     inspection of the maternal uterus and adnexa
     quality analysis of amniotic fluid volume/gestational sac shape
     visualization of fetal and placental anatomic formation
     written documentation of each component of exam

[EXCLUDES]   *focused ultrasound ablation of uterine leiomyomata (0071T-0072T)*
     ultrasound exam that does not include thorough assessment of organ
     or site, recorded image, and written report

76801   **Ultrasound, pregnant uterus, real time with image documentation, fetal and maternal evaluation, first trimester (< 14 weeks 0 days), transabdominal approach; single or first gestation**   M ♀ Z2 S 80 ▣
     [EXCLUDES]   *fetal nuchal translucency measurement, first trimester (76813)*
     🔷 **3.62**   🔷 **3.62**   **Global Days XXX**
     AMA: 2008, Jan, 10-25; 2007, Jan, 13-27; 2007, Jan, 13-27; 2007, January, 13-27; 2005, Nov, 14-15; 2005, November, 14-15; 2005, Nov, 14-15

+ **76802**   **each additional gestation (List separately in addition to code for primary procedure)**   M ♀ AU U 80 ▣
     [EXCLUDES]   *fetal nuchal translucency measurement, first trimester (76814)*
     Code first single/first gestation (76801)
     🔷 **2.06**   🔷 **2.06**   **Global Days ZZZ**
     AMA: 2008, Jan, 10-25; 2007, Jan, 13-27; 2007, Jan, 13-27; 2007, January, 13-27; 2005, Nov, 14-15; 2005, November, 14-15; 2005, Nov, 14-15

● New Code   ▲ Revised Code   M Maternity Edit   A Age Edit   A-Y OPPS Status Indicator   🔷 Facility RVU   🔷 Non-Facility RVU
▣ CCI Comprehensive Code   50 Bilateral Procedure   + Add-on Indicator   N Laboratory crosswalk   Radiology crosswalk

76805-76810 Ultrasound: Pregnancy of 14 Weeks or More

CMS *100-4,3,10.4*   *Payment of Nonphysician Services for Inpatients*
CMS *100-3,220.5*   *Ultrasound Diagnostic Procedures*
CMS *100-2,15,80*   *Physician Supervision Requirements for Diagnostic Tests*

INCLUDES   determination of the number of gestational/chorionic sacs and fetuses
     evaluation of:
         amniotic fluid
         four chambered heart
         intracranial, spinal, abdominal anatomy
         placenta location
         umbilical cord insertion site
     examination of maternal adnexa if visible
     gestational sac/fetal measurement appropriate for gestational (older than or equal to 14 weeks 0 days)
     written documentation of each component of exam

EXCLUDES   *focused ultrasound ablation of uterine leiomyomata (0071T-0072T)*
     ultrasound exam that does not include thorough assessment of organ or site, recorded image, and written report

76805   **Ultrasound, pregnant uterus, real time with image documentation, fetal and maternal evaluation, after first trimester (> or = 14 weeks 0 days), transabdominal approach; single or first gestation**   M ♀ Z2 S 80 ▭
     4.03   4.03   Global Days XXX

\+   **76810**   **each additional gestation (List separately in addition to code for primary procedure)**   M ♀ Z3 S 80 ▭
     Code first single/first gestation (76805)
     2.82   2.82   Global Days ZZZ

76811-76812 Ultrasound: Pregnancy, with Additional Studies of Fetus

CMS *100-4,3,10.4*   *Payment of Nonphysician Services for Inpatients*
CMS *100-3,220.5*   *Ultrasound Diagnostic Procedures*

INCLUDES   determination of the number of gestational/chorionic sacs and fetuses
     evaluation of:
         abdominal organ specific anatomy
         amniotic fluid
         chest anatomy
         face
         fetal brain/ventricles
         four chambered heart
         heart/outflow tracts and chest anatomy
         intracranial, spinal, abdominal anatomy
         limbs including number, length, and architecture
         other fetal anatomy as indicated
         placenta
         umbilical cord insertion site
     examination of maternal adnexa if visible
     gestational sac/fetal measurement appropriate for gestational (older than or equal to 14 weeks 0 days)
     written documentation of each component of exam

EXCLUDES   *focused ultrasound ablation of uterine leiomyomata (0071T-0072T)*
     ultrasound exam that does not include thorough assessment organ or site, recorded image, and written report

76811   **Ultrasound, pregnant uterus, real time with image documentation, fetal and maternal evaluation plus detailed fetal anatomic examination, transabdominal approach; single or first gestation**   M ♀ Z2 S 80 ▭
     5.75   5.75   Global Days XXX

\+   **76812**   **each additional gestation (List separately in addition to code for primary procedure)**   M ♀ Z3 S 80 ▭
     Code first single/first gestation (76811)
     5.63   5.63   Global Days ZZZ

76813-76828 Ultrasound: Other Fetal Evaluations

CMS *100-4,3,10.4*   *Payment of Nonphysician Services for Inpatients*
CMS *100-3,220.5*   *Ultrasound Diagnostic Procedures*
CMS *100-2,15,80*   *Physician Supervision Requirements for Diagnostic Tests*

INCLUDES   required permanent documentation of ultrasound images except when diagnostic purpose is biometric measurement
     written documentation

EXCLUDES   *focused ultrasound ablation of uterine leiomyomata (0071T-0072T)*
     ultrasound exam that does not include thorough assessment of organ or site, recorded image, and written report

76813   **Ultrasound, pregnant uterus, real time with image documentation, first trimester fetal nuchal translucency measurement, transabdominal or transvaginal approach; single or first gestation**   Z2 S 80
     3.54   3.54   Global Days XXX
     AMA: 2007, Mar, 7-8; 2007, Mar, 7-8; 2007, March, 7-8

\+   **76814**   **each additional gestation (List separately in addition to code for primary procedure)**   Z3 S 80
     Code first single/first gestation (76813)
     2.32   2.32   Global Days XXX
     AMA: 2007, Mar, 7-8; 2007, Mar, 7-8; 2007, March, 7-8

76815   **Ultrasound, pregnant uterus, real time with image documentation, limited (eg, fetal heart beat, placental location, fetal position and/or qualitative amniotic fluid volume), 1 or more fetuses**   M ♀ Z2 S 80 ▭

     INCLUDES   focused "quick look" exam of one or more elements
         reporting only once per exam, instead of per element

     EXCLUDES   *fetal nuchal translucency measurement, first trimester (76813, 76814)*

     2.51   2.51   Global Days XXX
     AMA: 2008, Jan, 10-25; 2007, Jan, 13-27; 2007, Jan, 13-27; 2007, January, 13-27

76816   **Ultrasound, pregnant uterus, real time with image documentation, follow-up (eg, re-evaluation of fetal size by measuring standard growth parameters and amniotic fluid volume, re-evaluation of organ system(s) suspected or confirmed to be abnormal on a previous scan), transabdominal approach, per fetus**   M ♀ Z2 S 80 ▭
     Code also modifier 59 for examination of each additional fetus in a multiple pregnancy
     3.07   3.07   Global Days XXX

76817   **Ultrasound, pregnant uterus, real time with image documentation, transvaginal**   M ♀ Z2 S 80 ▭
     EXCLUDES   *transvaginal ultrasound, non-obstetrical (76830)*
     Code also transabdominal obstetrical ultrasound, if performed
     2.79   2.79   Global Days XXX

76818   **Fetal biophysical profile; with non-stress testing**   M ♀ Z2 S 80 ▭
     Code also modifier 59 for each additional fetus
     3.34   3.34   Global Days XXX
     AMA: 2008, Jan, 10-25; 2007, Jan, 13-27; 2007, Jan, 13-27; 2007, January, 13-27; 2004, Nov, 10; 2004, November, 10; 2004, Nov, 10

76819   **without non-stress testing**   M ♀ Z2 S 80 ▭
     EXCLUDES   *amniotic fluid index without non-stress test (76815)*
     Code also modifier 59 for each additional fetus
     2.59   2.59   Global Days XXX
     AMA: 2008, Jan, 10-25; 2007, Jan, 13-27; 2007, Jan, 13-27; 2007, January, 13-27

26/TC Professional/Technical Component Only   80/80 Assist-at-Surgery Allowed/With Documentation   Unlisted   Not Covered
AMA: CPT Assistant References   A2-Z3 ASC Payment Indicator   ♂ Male Only   ♀ Female Only   ⊘ Modifier-51 Exempt   P0 PQRI

298   **CPT only © 2008 American Medical Association. All Rights Reserved. (Black Ink)**   Medicare (Red Ink)   © 2008 Ingenix (Blue Ink)

76820   Doppler velocimetry, fetal; umbilical artery   ♀ Z3 S 80
    ↩ 1.52   ⚕ 1.52   Global Days XXX
    AMA: 2005, Dec, 3-6; 2005, Dec, 3-6; 2005, December, 3-6

76821   middle cerebral artery   ♀ Z2 S 80
    ↩ 2.70   ⚕ 2.70   Global Days XXX
    AMA: 2005, Dec, 3-6; 2005, Dec, 3-6; 2005, December, 3-6

76825   Echocardiography, fetal, cardiovascular system, real time with image documentation (2D), with or without M-mode recording;   M ♀ Z3 S 80
    ↩ 5.74   ⚕ 5.74   Global Days XXX

76826   follow-up or repeat study   M ♀ Z3 S 80
    ↩ 3.16   ⚕ 3.16   Global Days XXX

76827   Doppler echocardiography, fetal, pulsed wave and/or continuous wave with spectral display; complete   M ♀ Z2 S 80
    ↩ 2.00   ⚕ 2.00   Global Days XXX
    AMA: 2005, Dec, 3-6; 2005, Dec, 3-6; 2005, December, 3-6

76828   follow-up or repeat study   M ♀ Z3 S 80
    EXCLUDES   *color mapping (93325)*
    ↩ 1.48   ⚕ 1.48   Global Days XXX
    AMA: 2005, Dec, 3-6; 2005, Dec, 3-6; 2005, December, 3-6

76830-76886 Ultrasound: Male and Female Genitalia and Extremities

CMS *100-4,3,10.4*   *Payment of Nonphysician Services for Inpatients*
CMS *100-3,220.5*   *Ultrasound Diagnostic Procedures*
CMS *100-2,15,80*   *Physician Supervision Requirements for Diagnostic Tests*

INCLUDES   required permanent documentation of ultrasound images except when diagnostic purpose is biometric measurement
    written documentation

EXCLUDES   *focused ultrasound ablation of uterine leiomyomata (0071T-0072T)*
    ultrasound exam that does not include thorough assessment of organ or site, recorded image, and written report

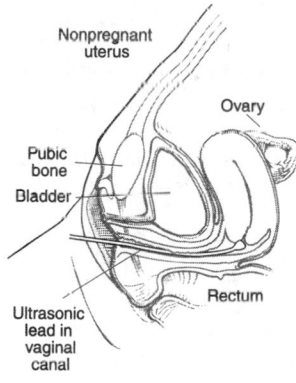

Nonpregnant uterus
Ovary
Pubic bone
Bladder
Rectum
Ultrasonic lead in vaginal canal

Ultrasound is performed in real time with image documentation by a transvaginal approach

76830   Ultrasound, transvaginal   ♀ Z2 S 80
    EXCLUDES   *transvaginal ultrasound, obstetric (76817)*
    Code also transabdominal non-obstetrical ultrasound, if performed
    ↩ 3.31   ⚕ 3.31   Global Days XXX
    AMA: 2008, Jan, 10-25; 2007, Jan, 13-27; 2007, Jan, 13-27; 2007, January, 13-27; 2005, Dec, 3-6; 2005, December, 3-6; 2005, Dec, 3-6

76831   Saline infusion sonohysterography (SIS), including color flow Doppler, when performed   ♀ Z3 03 80
    EXCLUDES   *saline introduction for saline infusion sonohysterography (58340)*
    ↩ 3.31   ⚕ 3.31   Global Days XXX
    AMA: 2005, Dec, 3-6; 2005, Dec, 3-6; 2005, December, 3-6

76856   Ultrasound, pelvic (nonobstetric), real time with image documentation; complete   Z2 03 80
    INCLUDES   total examination of the female pelvic anatomy which includes:
        bladder measurement
        description of any pelvic pathology
        description and measurement of the uterus and adnexa
        measurement of the endometrium
    total examination of the male pelvis which includes:
        bladder measurement
        description of any pelvic pathology
        evaluation of prostate and seminal vesicles
    ↩ 3.33   ⚕ 3.33   Global Days XXX
    AMA: 2008, Jan, 10-25; 2007, Jan, 13-27; 2007, Jan, 13-27; 2007, Mar, 7-8; 2007, March, 7-8; 2007, January, 13-27; 2007, Mar, 7-8; 2006, Mar, 15; 2006, March, 15; 2006, Mar, 15; 2005, Dec, 3-6; 2005, December, 3-6; 2005, Dec, 3-6

76857   limited or follow-up (eg, for follicles)   Z2 03 80
    INCLUDES   focused evaluation limited to:
        evaluation of one or more elements listed in 76856 and/or
        reevaluation of one or more pelvic abnormalities previously documented on ultrasound
        urinary bladder alone
    EXCLUDES   *bladder volume or post-voided residual measurement without imaging the bladder (51798)*
        urinary bladder and kidneys (76770)
    ↩ 2.77   ⚕ 2.77   Global Days XXX
    AMA: 2008, Jan, 10-25; 2007, Jan, 13-27; 2007, Jan, 13-27; 2007, January, 13-27; 2005, Dec, 3-6; 2005, December, 3-6; 2005, Dec, 3-6

76870   Ultrasound, scrotum and contents   ♂ Z2 03 80
    ↩ 3.30   ⚕ 3.30   Global Days XXX

76872   Ultrasound, transrectal;   Z2 S 80
    ↩ 3.93   ⚕ 3.93   Global Days XXX
    AMA: 2005, May, 3-6; 2005, May, 3-6; 2005, May, 3-6

76873   prostate volume study for brachytherapy treatment planning (separate procedure)   ♂ Z2 S
    ↩ 4.96   ⚕ 4.96   Global Days XXX

76880   Ultrasound, extremity, nonvascular, real time with image documentation   Z2 S 80
    ↩ 3.45   ⚕ 3.45   Global Days XXX
    AMA: 2007, Mar, 7-8; 2007, Mar, 7-8; 2007, March, 7-8

76885   Ultrasound, infant hips, real time with imaging documentation; dynamic (requiring physician manipulation)   A Z2 S 80
    ↩ 3.75   ⚕ 3.75   Global Days XXX

76886   limited, static (not requiring physician manipulation)   A Z2 G 80
    ↩ 2.77   ⚕ 2.77   Global Days XXX

● New Code   ▲ Revised Code   M Maternity Edit   A Age Edit   A-Y OPPS Status Indicator   ↩ Facility RVU   ⚕ Non-Facility RVU
▢ CCI Comprehensive Code   50 Bilateral Procedure   + Add-on Indicator   Laboratory crosswalk   Radiology crosswalk

© 2008 Ingenix *(Blue Ink)*   CPT only © 2008 American Medical Association. All Rights Reserved. **(Black Ink)**   Medicare (Red Ink)   **299**

76930-76970 Imaging Guidance: Ultrasound

CMS *100-4,3,10.4* *Payment of Nonphysician Services for Inpatients*
CMS *100-3,220.5* *Ultrasound Diagnostic Procedures*
INCLUDES required permanent documentation of ultrasound images except when diagnostic purpose is biometric measurement written documentation

EXCLUDES *focused ultrasound ablation of uterine leiomyomata (0071T-0072T)*
ultrasound exam that does not include thorough assessment of organ or site, recorded image, and written report

76930 **Ultrasonic guidance for pericardiocentesis, imaging supervision and interpretation** [N] [N] [80] [▭]
        🖪 2.72 ⚖ 2.72 Global Days XXX

76932 **Ultrasonic guidance for endomyocardial biopsy, imaging supervision and interpretation** [N1] [N] [80] [▭]
        🖪 0.00 ⚖ 0.00 Global Days XXX

76936 **Ultrasound guided compression repair of arterial pseudoaneurysm or arteriovenous fistulae (includes diagnostic ultrasound evaluation, compression of lesion and imaging)** [Z2] [S] [80] [▭]
        🖪 8.72 ⚖ 8.72 Global Days XXX

+ 76937 **Ultrasound guidance for vascular access requiring ultrasound evaluation of potential access sites, documentation of selected vessel patency, concurrent realtime ultrasound visualization of vascular needle entry, with permanent recording and reporting (List separately in addition to code for primary procedure)** [N1] [N] [80] [▭]

        EXCLUDES *extremity venous non-invasive vascular diagnostic study performed separately from venous access guidance (93965, 93970, 93971)*

        Code first primary procedure
        Do not report with ultrasonic guidance for needle placement (76942)
        🖪 1.02 ⚖ 1.02 Global Days ZZZ
        AMA: 2004, Dec, 6; 2004, Dec, 6; 2004, December, 6

76940 **Ultrasound guidance for, and monitoring of, parenchymal tissue ablation** [N1] [N] [80] [▭]
        EXCLUDES *ablation (32998, 47370-47382, 50592, 50593)*

        Do not report with intraoperative ultrasonic guidance (76998)
        🖪 0.00 ⚖ 0.00 Global Days XXX
        AMA: 2007, Mar, 7-8; 2007, Mar, 7-8; 2007, March, 7-8; 2006, Apr, 11-18; 2006, April, 11-18; 2006, Apr, 11-18

76941 **Ultrasonic guidance for intrauterine fetal transfusion or cordocentesis, imaging supervision and interpretation** [M] [♀] [N1] [N] [80] [▭]
        EXCLUDES *surgical procedure (36460, 59012)*
        🖪 0.00 ⚖ 0.00 Global Days XXX

76942 **Ultrasonic guidance for needle placement (eg, biopsy, aspiration, injection, localization device), imaging supervision and interpretation** [N1] [N] [80] [▭]
        Do not report with (43232, 43237, 43242, 45341, 45342, 76975)
        🖪 5.10 ⚖ 5.10 Global Days XXX
        AMA: 2008, Jan, 10-25; 2008, Jun, 8-11; 2007, Jan, 13-27; 2007, Jan, 13-27; 2007, May, 1-2; 2007, May, 1-2; 2007, Jun, 10-11; 2007, January, 13-27; 2007, June, 10-11; 2007, May, 1-2; 2007, Jun, 10-11; 2006, Apr, 11-18; 2006, April, 11-18; 2006, Apr, 11-18; 2005, Apr, 13-14; 2005, April, 13-14; 2005, Apr, 13-14; 2004, Dec, 6; 2004, Dec, 6; 2004, May, 6; 2004, May, 6; 2004, July, 7; 2004, December, 6; 2004, May, 6; 2004, Jul, 7; 2004, Jul, 7

76945 **Ultrasonic guidance for chorionic villus sampling, imaging supervision and interpretation** [M] [♀] [N1] [N] [80] [▭]
        EXCLUDES *surgical procedure (59015)*
        🖪 0.00 ⚖ 0.00 Global Days XXX

76946 **Ultrasonic guidance for amniocentesis, imaging supervision and interpretation** [M] [♀] [N1] [N] [80] [▭]
        🖪 1.25 ⚖ 1.25 Global Days XXX

76948 **Ultrasonic guidance for aspiration of ova, imaging supervision and interpretation** [♀] [N1] [N] [80] [▭]
        🖪 1.25 ⚖ 1.25 Global Days XXX

76950 **Ultrasonic guidance for placement of radiation therapy fields** [N1] [N] [80] [▭]
        🖪 1.96 ⚖ 1.96 Global Days XXX

76965 **Ultrasonic guidance for interstitial radioelement application** [N1] [N] [80] [▭]
        🖪 4.13 ⚖ 4.13 Global Days XXX

76970 **Ultrasound study follow-up (specify)** [Z2] [S] [80] [▭]
        🖪 2.29 ⚖ 2.29 Global Days XXX

76975 Endoscopic Ultrasound

CMS *100-4,12,30.1* *Upper Gastrointestinal Endoscopy Including Endoscopic Ultrasound (EUS)*
CMS *100-4,3,10.4* *Payment of Nonphysician Services for Inpatients*
CMS *100-3,220.5* *Ultrasound Diagnostic Procedures*
INCLUDES required permanent documentation of ultrasound images except when diagnostic purpose is biometric measurement written documentation

EXCLUDES *focused ultrasound ablation of uterine leiomyomata (0071T-0072T)*
ultrasound exam that does not include thorough assessment of organ or site, recorded image, and written report

76975 **Gastrointestinal endoscopic ultrasound, supervision and interpretation** [N1] [Z2] [80] [▭]
        Do not report with (43231, 43232, 43237, 43238, 43242, 43259, 45341, 45342, 76942)
        🖪 0.00 ⚖ 0.00 Global Days XXX
        AMA: 2004, May, 6; 2004, May, 6; 2004, May, 6

76977 Bone Density Measurements: Ultrasound

CMS *100-4,13,140* *Bone Mass Measurements (BMMs)*
CMS *100-3,220.5* *Ultrasound Diagnostic Procedures*
INCLUDES required permanent documentation of ultrasound images except when diagnostic purpose is biometric measurement written documentation

EXCLUDES *focused ultrasound ablation of uterine leiomyomata (0071T-0072T)*
ultrasound exam that does not include thorough assessment of organ or site, recorded image, and written report

76977 **Ultrasound bone density measurement and interpretation, peripheral site(s), any method** [Z3] [X] [80] [▭]
        🖪 0.40 ⚖ 0.40 Global Days XXX

76998-76999 Imaging Guidance During Surgery: Ultrasound

INCLUDES required permanent documentation of ultrasound images except when diagnostic purpose is biometric measurement written documentation

EXCLUDES *focused ultrasound ablation of uterine leiomyomata (0071T-0072T) ultrasound exam that does not include thorough assessment of organ or site, recorded image, and written report*

76998 Ultrasonic guidance, intraoperative   M N 80

   EXCLUDES *radiofrequency tissue ablation, open/laparoscopic, ultrasonic guidance (76940)*

   Do not report with (36475-36479, 47370-47382)

   🔷 0.00   ⚖ 0.00 Global Days XXX
   AMA: 2007, Mar, 7-8; 2007, Mar, 7-8; 2007, March, 7-8

76999 Unlisted ultrasound procedure (eg, diagnostic, interventional)   Z2 S 80

   🔷 0.00   ⚖ 0.00 Global Days XXX

77001-77022 Imaging Guidance Techniques

+ **77001** Fluoroscopic guidance for central venous access device placement, replacement (catheter only or complete), or removal (includes fluoroscopic guidance for vascular access and catheter manipulation, any necessary contrast injections through access site or catheter with related venography radiologic supervision and interpretation, and radiographic documentation of final catheter position) (List separately in addition to code for primary procedure)   M N 80

   EXCLUDES *formal extremity venography performed separately from venous access and interpreted separately (36005, 75820, 75822, 75825, 75827)*

   Do not report with (77002)

   🔷 2.88   ⚖ 2.88 Global Days ZZZ
   AMA: 2008, Jun, 8-11; 2008, Jul, 9; 2007, Mar, 7-8; 2007, March, 7-8

   77002 Fluoroscopic guidance for needle placement (eg, biopsy, aspiration, injection, localization device)   M N 80

   INCLUDES radiographic arthrography except for supervision and interpretation of CT and MRI arthrography

   EXCLUDES *surgical procedure*

   Do not report with (49440, 74320, 74355, 74445, 74470, 74475, 75809-75810, 75885, 75887, 75980, 75982, 75989)

   🔷 1.96   ⚖ 1.96 Global Days XXX
   AMA: 2008, Jan, 10-25; 2008, Jun, 8-11; 2008, Jul, 9; 2007, Feb, 10-11; 2007, Feb, 10-11; 2007, Mar, 7-8; 2007, Mar, 7-8; 2007, May, 1-2; 2007, May, 1-2; 2007, Jun, 10-11; 2007, Jun, 10-11; 2007, February, 10-11; 2007, March, 7-8; 2007, May, 1-2; 2007, June, 10-11

77003 Fluoroscopic guidance and localization of needle or catheter tip for spine or paraspinous diagnostic or therapeutic injection procedures (epidural, transforaminal epidural, subarachnoid, paravertebral facet joint, paravertebral facet joint nerve, or sacroiliac joint), including neurolytic agent destruction   M N

   EXCLUDES *injection and needle/catheter placement, epidural/subarachnoid (62270-62282, 62310-62319) injection, paravertebral facet joint (64470-64476) neurolytic agent destruction (64600-64680) sacroiliac joint arthrography (27096, 73542) transforaminal epidural needle placement/injection (64479-64484)*

   🔷 1.64   ⚖ 1.64 Global Days XXX
   AMA: 2008, Jun, 8-11; 2008, Jul, 9; 2007, Mar, 7-8; 2007, Mar, 7-8; 2007, March, 7-8

77011 Computed tomography guidance for stereotactic localization   M N 80

   🔷 18.71   ⚖ 18.71 Global Days XXX
   AMA: 2007, Mar, 7-8; 2007, Mar, 7-8; 2007, March, 7-8

77012 Computed tomography guidance for needle placement (eg, biopsy, aspiration, injection, localization device), radiological supervision and interpretation   M N 80

   🔷 5.56   ⚖ 5.56 Global Days XXX
   AMA: 2007, Mar, 7-8; 2007, Mar, 7-8; 2007, May, 1-2; 2007, May, 1-2, 2007, Jun, 10-11; 2007, Jun, 10-11; 2007, March, 7-8; 2007, May, 1-2; 2007, June, 10-11

77013 Computed tomography guidance for, and monitoring of, parenchymal tissue ablation   M N 80

   EXCLUDES *ablation, percutaneous radiofrequency (32998, 47382, 50592) percutaneous radiofrequency ablation (32998, 47382, 50592-50593)*

   Do not report with (20982)

   🔷 0.00   ⚖ 0.00 Global Days XXX
   AMA: 2007, Mar, 7-8; 2007, Mar, 7-8; 2007, March, 7-8

77014 Computed tomography guidance for placement of radiation therapy fields   M N 80

   EXCLUDES *placement of interstitial device(s) for radiation therapy guidance (55876)*

   🔷 5.13   ⚖ 5.13 Global Days XXX
   AMA: 2007, Mar, 7-8; 2007, Mar, 7-8; 2007, March, 7-8

77021 Magnetic resonance guidance for needle placement (eg, for biopsy, needle aspiration, injection, or placement of localization device) radiological supervision and interpretation   M N 80

   EXCLUDES *surgical procedure*

   🔷 12.42   ⚖ 12.42 Global Days XXX
   AMA: 2008, Jun, 8-11; 2007, Mar, 7-8; 2007, Mar, 7-8; 2007, May, 1-2; 2007, May, 1-2; 2007, Jun, 10-11; 2007, Jun, 10-11; 2007, March, 7-8; 2007, May, 1-2; 2007, June, 10-11

77022 Magnetic resonance guidance for, and monitoring of, parenchymal tissue ablation   M N 80

   EXCLUDES *ablation: percutaneous radiofrequency (32998, 47382, 50592-50593) uterine leiomyomata by focused ablation (0071T, 0072T)*

   🔷 0.00   ⚖ 0.00 Global Days XXX
   AMA: 2007, Mar, 7-8; 2007, Mar, 7-8; 2007, March, 7-8

77031 — 77081

77031-77059 Radiography: Breast

CMS 100-4,18,20 *Mammography Services*
CMS 100-4,18,20.4 *FI/A/B MAC Processing Mammography Services*
CMS 100-3,220.4 *Mammograms*
EXCLUDES *mammographic guidance for needle placement into lesion (77032)*

77031 Stereotactic localization guidance for breast biopsy or needle placement (eg, for wire localization or for injection), each lesion, radiological supervision and interpretation ⒨ Ⓝ 80

> **EXCLUDES** *sentinel node localization injection without lymphoscintigraphy (38792) surgical procedure (10022, 19000-19103, 19290, 19291)*

> 5.40 5.40 Global Days XXX
> **AMA:** 2007, Mar, 7-8; 2007, Mar, 7-8; 2007, March, 7-8

77032 Mammographic guidance for needle placement, breast (eg, for wire localization or for injection), each lesion, radiological supervision and interpretation ⒨ Ⓝ 80

> **EXCLUDES** *sentinel node localization injection without lymphoscintigraphy (38792) surgical procedure (10022, 19000, 19102, 19103, 19290, 19291)*

> 1.66 1.66 Global Days XXX
> **AMA:** 2007, Mar, 7-8; 2007, Mar, 7-8; 2007, March, 7-8

+ 77051 Computer-aided detection (computer algorithm analysis of digital image data for lesion detection) with further physician review for interpretation, with or without digitization of film radiographic images; diagnostic mammography (List separately in addition to code for primary procedure) Ⓐ 80

> Code first mammography (77055, 77056)
> 0.34 0.34 Global Days ZZZ
> **AMA:** 2007, Mar, 7-8; 2007, Mar, 7-8; 2007, Apr, 1-2; 2007, April, 1-2; 2007, March, 7-8; 2007, Apr, 1-2; 2006, Dec, 10-12; 2006, December, 10-12; 2006, December, 10-12; 2006, Dec, 10-12; 2006, Dec, 10-12; 2006, Dec, 10-12

+ 77052 screening mammography (List separately in addition to code for primary procedure) Ⓐ 80

> Code first screening mammography (77057)
> 0.34 0.34 Global Days ZZZ
> **AMA:** 2007, Mar, 7-8; 2007, Mar, 7-8; 2007, Apr, 1-2; 2007, April, 1-2; 2007, March, 7-8; 2007, Apr, 1-2; 2006, Dec, 10-12; 2006, December, 10-12; 2006, December, 10-12; 2006, Dec, 10-12; 2006, Dec, 10-12

77053 Mammary ductogram or galactogram, single duct, radiological supervision and interpretation ⒨ 02 80

> **EXCLUDES** *injection procedure (19030)*

> 2.13 2.13 Global Days XXX
> **AMA:** 2007, Mar, 7-8; 2007, Mar, 7-8; 2007, March, 7-8; 2006, Dec, 10-12; 2006, Dec, 10-12; 2006, December, 10-12; 2006, December, 10-12; 2006, Dec, 10-12; 2006, Dec, 10-12

77054 Mammary ductogram or galactogram, multiple ducts, radiological supervision and interpretation ⒨ 02 80

> 2.87 2.87 Global Days XXX
> **AMA:** 2007, Mar, 7-8; 2007, Mar, 7-8; 2007, March, 7-8

77055 Mammography; unilateral Ⓐ 80

> Code also computer-aided detection applied to diagnostic mammogram, if performed (77051)
> 2.35 2.35 Global Days XXX
> **AMA:** 2007, Mar, 7-8; 2007, Mar, 7-8; 2007, March, 7-8

77056 bilateral Ⓐ 80

> Code also computer-aided detection applied to diagnostic mammogram, if performed (77051)
> 2.98 2.98 Global Days XXX
> **AMA:** 2007, Mar, 7-8; 2007, Mar, 7-8; 2007, March, 7-8

77057 Screening mammography, bilateral (2-view film study of each breast) ♀ Ⓐ 80

> **EXCLUDES** *breast electrical impedance scan (76499)*

> Code also computer-aided detection applied to screening mammogram, if performed (77052)
> 2.26 2.26 Global Days XXX
> **AMA:** 2007, Mar, 7-8; 2007, Mar, 7-8; 2007, March, 7-8

77058 Magnetic resonance imaging, breast, without and/or with contrast material(s); unilateral Ⓑ 80

> 23.29 23.29 Global Days XXX
> **AMA:** 2007, Mar, 7-8; 2007, Mar, 7-8; 2007, March, 7-8; 2007, Jul, 6-10

77059 bilateral Ⓑ 80

> 25.09 25.09 Global Days XXX
> **AMA:** 2007, Mar, 7-8; 2007, Mar, 7-8; 2007, March, 7-8; 2007, Jul, 6-10

77071-77084 Additional Evaluations of Bones and Joints

77071 Manual application of stress performed by physician for joint radiography, including contralateral joint if indicated Z3 Ⓧ 26 80

> 1.09 1.09 Global Days XXX
> **AMA:** 2007, Mar, 7-8; 2007, Mar, 7-8; 2007, March, 7-8

77072 Bone age studies Z3 Ⓧ 80

> 0.65 0.65 Global Days XXX
> **AMA:** 2007, Mar, 7-8; 2007, Mar, 7-8; 2007, March, 7-8

77073 Bone length studies (orthoroentgenogram, scanogram) Z3 Ⓧ 80

> 1.04 1.04 Global Days XXX
> **AMA:** 2007, Mar, 7-8; 2007, Mar, 7-8; 2007, March, 7-8

77074 Radiologic examination, osseous survey; limited (eg, for metastases) Z3 Ⓧ 80

> 1.90 1.90 Global Days XXX
> **AMA:** 2007, Mar, 7-8; 2007, Mar, 7-8; 2007, March, 7-8

77075 complete (axial and appendicular skeleton) Z2 Ⓧ 80

> 2.75 2.75 Global Days XXX
> **AMA:** 2007, Mar, 7-8; 2007, Mar, 7-8; 2007, March, 7-8

77076 Radiologic examination, osseous survey, infant Z2 Ⓧ 80

> 2.56 2.56 Global Days XXX
> **AMA:** 2007, Mar, 7-8; 2007, Mar, 7-8; 2007, March, 7-8

77077 Joint survey, single view, 2 or more joints (specify) Z3 Ⓧ 80

> 1.18 1.18 Global Days XXX
> **AMA:** 2007, Mar, 7-8; 2007, Mar, 7-8; 2007, March, 7-8

77078 Computed tomography, bone mineral density study, 1 or more sites; axial skeleton (eg, hips, pelvis, spine) Z2 Ⓢ 80

> 4.72 4.72 Global Days XXX
> **AMA:** 2007, Mar, 7-8; 2007, Mar, 7-8; 2007, March, 7-8

77079 appendicular skeleton (peripheral) (eg, radius, wrist, heel) Z3 Ⓢ 80

> 1.59 1.59 Global Days XXX
> **AMA:** 2007, Mar, 7-8; 2007, Mar, 7-8; 2007, March, 7-8

77080 Dual-energy X-ray absorptiometry (DXA), bone density study, 1 or more sites; axial skeleton (eg, hips, pelvis, spine) Z2 Ⓢ 80

> 1.99 1.99 Global Days XXX
> **AMA:** 2007, Mar, 7-8; 2007, Mar, 7-8; 2007, March, 7-8

77081 appendicular skeleton (peripheral) (eg, radius, wrist, heel) Z3 Ⓢ 80

> 0.84 0.84 Global Days XXX
> **AMA:** 2007, Mar, 7-8; 2007, Mar, 7-8; 2007, March, 7-8

26/TC Professional/Technical Component Only   80/80 Assist-at-Surgery Allowed/With Documentation   Unlisted   Not Covered
AMA: CPT Assistant References   A2-Z3 ASC Payment Indicator   ♂ Male Only   ♀ Female Only   ⊘ Modifier 51 Exempt   PQRI

302   CPT only © 2008 American Medical Association. All Rights Reserved. (Black Ink)   Medicare (Red Ink)   © 2008 Ingenix *(Blue Ink)*

77082 vertebral fracture assessment ☒ Ⓧ 80

> **EXCLUDES** *dual-energy x-ray absorptiometry [DXA] body composition study (76499)*

> 📖 0.81 ⚖ 0.81 Global Days XXX
> **AMA:** 2007, Mar, 7-8; 2007, Mar, 7-8; 2007, March, 7-8

77083 Radiographic absorptiometry (eg, photodensitometry, radiogrammetry), 1 or more sites ☒ Ⓧ 80

> 📖 0.74 ⚖ 0.74 Global Days XXX
> **AMA:** 2007, Mar, 7-8; 2007, Mar, 7-8; 2007, March, 7-8

77084 Magnetic resonance (eg, proton) imaging, bone marrow blood supply ☒ Ⓢ 80

> 📖 16.05 ⚖ 16.05 Global Days XXX
> **AMA:** 2007, Mar, 7-8; 2007, Mar, 7-8; 2007, March, 7-8

77261-77263 Therapeutic Radiology: Treatment Planning

CMS *100-2,6,10*   *Medical and Other Services Furnished to Inpatients*
CMS *100-4,3,10.4*   *Payment of Nonphysician Services for Inpatients*

INCLUDES determination of:
> appropriate treatment devices
> number and size of treatment ports
> treatment method
> treatment time/dosage
> treatment volume
> interpretation of special testing
> tumor localization

77261 Therapeutic radiology treatment planning; simple Ⓑ 26 80 ▢

> **INCLUDES** planning for single treatment area included in a single port or simple parallel opposed ports with simple or no blocking

> 📖 1.97 ⚖ 1.97 Global Days XXX

77262 intermediate Ⓑ 26 80 ▢

> **INCLUDES** planning for three or more converging ports, two separate treatment sites, multiple blocks, or special time dose constraints

> 📖 2.96 ⚖ 2.96 Global Days XXX

77263 complex Ⓑ 26 80 ▢

> **INCLUDES** planning for very complex blocking, custom shielding blocks, tangential ports, special wedges or compensators, three or more separate treatment areas, rotational or special beam considerations, combination of treatment modalities

> 📖 4.39 ⚖ 4.39 Global Days XXX

77280-77299 Radiation Therapy Simulation

CMS *100-4,4,200.3.2*   *Additional Billing Instructions for IMRT Planning and Delivery*
CMS *100-2,6,10*   *Medical and Other Services Furnished to Inpatients*
CMS *100-4,3,10.4*   *Payment of Nonphysician Services for Inpatients*

INCLUDES simulation provided on a:
> dedicated simulator
> diagnostic x-ray machine
> radiation therapy treatment unit

77280 Therapeutic radiology simulation-aided field setting; simple ☒ Ⓧ 80 ▢

> **INCLUDES** simulation of a single treatment site with either a single port or parallel opposed ports with simple or no blocking

> 📖 5.11 ⚖ 5.11 Global Days XXX

77285 intermediate ☒ Ⓧ 80

> **INCLUDES** simulation of tangential portals, three or more treatment sites, rotation or arc therapy, complex blocking, custom shielding blocks, brachytherapy source verification, hyperthermia probe verification, any use of contrast materials

> 📖 8.80 ⚖ 8.80 Global Days XXX

77290 complex ☒ Ⓧ 80 ▢

> 📖 13.63 ⚖ 13.63 Global Days XXX

77295 3-dimensional ☒ Ⓧ 80 ▢

> **INCLUDES** computer-created 3D reconstruction of tumor and surrounding tissue from direct CT scans and/or MRI data

> 📖 19.17 ⚖ 19.17 Global Days XXX
> **AMA:** 2005, May, 7-12; 2005, May, 7-12; 2005, May, 7-12

77299 Unlisted procedure, therapeutic radiology clinical treatment planning ☒ Ⓧ 80

> 📖 0.00 ⚖ 0.00 Global Days XXX

77300-77370 Radiation Physics Services

CMS *100-4,4,200.3.1*   *Billing for IMRT Planning and Delivery*
CMS *100-4,4,200.3.2*   *Additional Billing Instructions for IMRT Planning and Delivery*
CMS *100-4,13,70.5*   *Radiation Physics Services*
CMS *100-4,4,220.2*   *Additional Billing Instructions for IMRT Planning*
CMS *100-4,3,10.4*   *Payment of Nonphysician Services for Inpatients*
CMS *100-4,3,10.4*   *Payment of Nonphysician Services for Inpatients*
CMS *100-4,4,61.2*   *Requirements for Specific Procedures to be Reported With Device Codes*

77300 Basic radiation dosimetry calculation, central axis depth dose calculation, TDF, NSD, gap calculation, off axis factor, tissue inhomogeneity factors, calculation of non-ionizing radiation surface and depth dose, as required during course of treatment, only when prescribed by the treating physician ☒ Ⓧ 80 ▢

> 📖 1.98 ⚖ 1.98 Global Days XXX

77301 Intensity modulated radiotherapy plan, including dose-volume histograms for target and critical structure partial tolerance specifications ☒ Ⓧ 80 ▢

> 📖 59.80 ⚖ 59.80 Global Days XXX
> **AMA:** 2005, Mar, 1-6; 2005, Mar, 1-6; 2005, May, 7-12; 2005, May, 7-12; 2005, March, 1-6; 2005, May, 7-12; 2004, Jul, 7; 2004, Jul, 7; 2004, July, 7

77305 Teletherapy, isodose plan (whether hand or computer calculated); simple (1 or 2 parallel opposed unmodified ports directed to a single area of interest) ☒ Ⓧ 80 ▢

> **INCLUDES** normal follow-up care during and three months after treatment

> 📖 2.05 ⚖ 2.05 Global Days XXX

77310 intermediate (3 or more treatment ports directed to a single area of interest) ☒ Ⓧ 80 ▢

> **INCLUDES** normal follow-up care during and three months after treatment

> 📖 2.84 ⚖ 2.84 Global Days XXX

77315 complex (mantle or inverted Y, tangential ports, the use of wedges, compensators, complex blocking, rotational beam, or special beam considerations) ☒ Ⓧ 80 ▢

> **INCLUDES** normal follow-up care during and three months after treatment

> 📖 4.13 ⚖ 4.13 Global Days XXX

77321 Special teletherapy port plan, particles, hemibody, total body ☒ Ⓧ 80 ▢

> 📖 3.42 ⚖ 3.42 Global Days XXX

● New Code   ▲ Revised Code   Ⓜ Maternity Edit   Ⓐ Age Edit   Ⓐ-Ⓥ OPPS Status Indicator   📖 Facility RVU   ⚖ Non-Facility RVU
▢ CCI Comprehensive Code   50 Bilateral Procedure   + Add-on Indicator   ☒ Laboratory crosswalk   ☒ Radiology crosswalk

77326 Brachytherapy isodose plan; simple (calculation made from single plane, 1 to 4 sources/ribbon application, remote afterloading brachytherapy, 1 to 8 sources) Z2 X 80 ▭
  🔀 3.96 ⚖ 3.96 Global Days XXX

77327 intermediate (multiplane dosage calculations, application involving 5 to 10 sources/ribbons, remote afterloading brachytherapy, 9 to 12 sources) Z3 X 80 ▭
  🔀 5.64 ⚖ 5.64 Global Days XXX

77328 complex (multiplane isodose plan, volume implant calculations, over 10 sources/ribbons used, special spatial reconstruction, remote afterloading brachytherapy, over 12 sources) Z2 X 80 ▭
  🔀 7.73 ⚖ 7.73 Global Days XXX

77331 Special dosimetry (eg, TLD, microdosimetry) (specify), only when prescribed by the treating physician Z3 X 80 ▭
  🔀 1.73 ⚖ 1.73 Global Days XXX

77332 Treatment devices, design and construction; simple (simple block, simple bolus) Z3 X 80 ▭
  🔀 2.16 ⚖ 2.16 Global Days XXX

77333 intermediate (multiple blocks, stents, bite blocks, special bolus) Z3 X 80 ▭
  🔀 1.93 ⚖ 1.93 Global Days XXX

77334 complex (irregular blocks, special shields, compensators, wedges, molds or casts) Z3 X 80 ▭
  🔀 4.40 ⚖ 4.40 Global Days XXX

77336 Continuing medical physics consultation, including assessment of treatment parameters, quality assurance of dose delivery, and review of patient treatment documentation in support of the radiation oncologist, reported per week of therapy Z3 X TC 80 ▭
  🔀 1.74 ⚖ 1.74 Global Days XXX

77370 Special medical radiation physics consultation Z2 X TC 80 ▭
  🔀 3.27 ⚖ 3.27 Global Days XXX

77371-77399 Stereotactic Radiosurgery (SRS) Planning and Delivery

CMS 100-4,4,200.3.3 Billing Multi-Source Photon Stereotactic Radiosurgey Planning and Delivery
CMS 100-4,13,70.5 Radiation Physics Services

77371 Radiation treatment delivery, stereotactic radiosurgery (SRS), complete course of treatment of cranial lesion(s) consisting of 1 session; multi-source Cobalt 60 based Z2 S TC 80
  🔀 0.00 ⚖ 0.00 Global Days XXX
  AMA: 2007, Mar, 7-8; 2007, Mar, 7-8; 2007, March, 7-8

77372 linear accelerator based B TC 80
  EXCLUDES   radiation treatment supervision (77432)
  🔀 22.43 ⚖ 22.43 Global Days XXX
  AMA: 2007, Mar, 7-8; 2007, Mar, 7-8; 2007, March, 7-8

77373 Stereotactic body radiation therapy, treatment delivery, per fraction to 1 or more lesions, including image guidance, entire course not to exceed 5 fractions B TC 80
  EXCLUDES   single fraction cranial lesion(s) (77371-77372)
  Do not report with (77401-77416, 77418)
  🔀 41.51 ⚖ 41.51 Global Days XXX
  AMA: 2007, Mar, 7-8; 2007, Mar, 7-8; 2007, March, 7-8

77399 Unlisted procedure, medical radiation physics, dosimetry and treatment devices, and special services Z2 X 80
  🔀 0.00 ⚖ 0.00 Global Days XXX

77401-77417 Radiation Treatment

CMS 100-4,13,70.3 Radiation Treatment Delivery
CMS 100-2,6,10 Medical and Other Services Furnished to Inpatients
CMS 100-4,3,10.4 Payment of Nonphysician Services for Inpatients
CMS 100-4,4,220.1 Billing for IMRT Planning and Delivery
INCLUDES   technical component and assorted energy levels

77401 Radiation treatment delivery, superficial and/or ortho voltage Z2 S 80 ▭
  🔀 0.90 ⚖ 0.90 Global Days XXX
  AMA: 2004, Jul, 7; 2004, Jul, 7; 2004, July, 7

77402 Radiation treatment delivery, single treatment area, single port or parallel opposed ports, simple blocks or no blocks; up to 5 MeV Z2 S TC 80 ▭
  🔀 3.76 ⚖ 3.76 Global Days XXX

77403 6-10 MeV Z2 S TC 80 ▭
  🔀 3.31 ⚖ 3.31 Global Days XXX

77404 11-19 MeV Z2 S TC 80 ▭
  🔀 3.64 ⚖ 3.64 Global Days XXX

77406 20 MeV or greater Z2 S TC 80 ▭
  🔀 3.67 ⚖ 3.67 Global Days XXX

77407 Radiation treatment delivery, 2 separate treatment areas, 3 or more ports on a single treatment area, use of multiple blocks; up to 5 MeV Z2 S TC 80 ▭
  🔀 5.88 ⚖ 5.88 Global Days XXX

77408 6-10 MeV Z2 S TC 80 ▭
  🔀 4.43 ⚖ 4.43 Global Days XXX

77409 11-19 MeV Z2 S TC 80 ▭
  🔀 4.88 ⚖ 4.88 Global Days XXX

77411 20 MeV or greater Z2 S TC 80 ▭
  🔀 4.85 ⚖ 4.85 Global Days XXX

77412 Radiation treatment delivery, 3 or more separate treatment areas, custom blocking, tangential ports, wedges, rotational beam, compensators, electron beam; up to 5 MeV Z2 S TC 80 ▭
  🔀 5.70 ⚖ 5.70 Global Days XXX

77413 6-10 MeV Z2 S TC 80 ▭
  🔀 5.74 ⚖ 5.74 Global Days XXX

77414 11-19 MeV Z2 S TC 80 ▭
  🔀 6.37 ⚖ 6.37 Global Days XXX

77416 20 MeV or greater Z2 S TC 80 ▭
  🔀 6.40 ⚖ 6.40 Global Days XXX
  AMA: 2004, Jul, 7; 2004, Jul, 7; 2004, July, 7

77417 Therapeutic radiology port film(s) N1 N TC 80 ▭
  🔀 0.45 ⚖ 0.45 Global Days XXX
  AMA: 2008, Jan, 10-25; 2007, Jan, 13-27; 2007, Jan, 13-27; 2007, January, 13-27; 2006, Feb, 16-18; 2006, February, 16-18; 2006, Feb, 16-18

77418 IMRT Delivery

CMS 100-2,6,10 Medical and Other Services Furnished to Inpatients
CMS 100-4,3,10.4 Payment of Nonphysician Services for Inpatients
CMS 100-4,4,220.1 Billing for IMRT Planning and Delivery
EXCLUDES   delivery of compensator-based beam modulation treatment (0073T) treatment planning (77301)

77418 Intensity modulated treatment delivery, single or multiple fields/arcs, via narrow spatially and temporally modulated beams, binary, dynamic MLC, per treatment session Z2 S TC 80 ▭
  🔀 14.33 ⚖ 14.33 Global Days XXX
  AMA: 2007, May, 1-2; 2007, May, 1-2; 2007, May, 1-2; 2005, Mar, 1-6; 2005, Mar, 1-6; 2005, Mar, 11-15; 2005, Mar, 11-15; 2005, March, 1-6; 2005, March, 11-15; 2005, May, 7-12; 2005, May, 7-12; 2005, May, 7-12; 2004, Jul, 7; 2004, July, 7; 2004, Jul, 7

26/TC Professional/Technical Component Only   80/80 Assist-at-Surgery Allowed/With Documentation   Unlisted   Not Covered
AMA: CPT Assistant References   A2-Z3 ASC Payment Indicator   ♂ Male Only   ♀ Female Only   ⊘ Modifier 51 Exempt   PQ PQRI

77421 Stereoscopic Imaging Guidance

CMS 100-2,6,10 *Medical and Other Services Furnished to Inpatients*
CMS 100-4,3,10.4 *Payment of Nonphysician Services for Inpatients*

77421 Stereoscopic X-ray guidance for localization of target volume for the delivery of radiation therapy Ⓜ Ⓝ 80

EXCLUDES *placement of interstitial devices(s) for radiation therapy guidance, prostate (55876)*

Do not report with (77432, 77435)

📌 3.14 ⚕ 3.14 Global Days XXX

77422-77423 Neutron Therapy

77422 High energy neutron radiation treatment delivery; single treatment area using a single port or parallel-opposed ports with no blocks or simple blocking Z2 S TC 80

📌 5.37 ⚕ 5.37 Global Days XXX

77423 1 or more isocenter(s) with coplanar or non-coplanar geometry with blocking and/or wedge, and/or compensator(s) Z2 S TC 80

📌 6.16 ⚕ 6.16 Global Days XXX

77427-77499 Radiation Therapy Management

CMS 100-4,13,70.1 *Weekly Radiation Therapy Management*

INCLUDES assessment of patient for medical evaluation and management
review of:
    dose delivery
    dosimetry
    patient treatment set-up
    port film
    treatment parameters
units of five fractions or treatment sessions regardless of time

77427 Radiation treatment management, 5 treatments B 26

INCLUDES fewer than two fractions at the end of a treatment period

📌 5.22 ⚕ 5.22 Global Days XXX
AMA: 2005, Mar, 11-15; 2005, Mar, 11-15; 2005, March, 11-15

77431 Radiation therapy management with complete course of therapy consisting of 1 or 2 fractions only B 26 80

📌 2.67 ⚕ 2.67 Global Days XXX

77432 Stereotactic radiation treatment management of cranial lesion(s) (complete course of treatment consisting of 1 session) B 26 80

EXCLUDES *stereotactic body radiation therapy treatment (77435)*

Do not report with stereotactic radiosurgery (61796-61800)

📌 11.11 ⚕ 11.11 Global Days XXX

77435 Stereotactic body radiation therapy, treatment management, per treatment course, to 1 or more lesions, including image guidance, entire course not to exceed 5 fractions Ⓜ Ⓝ 26 80

Do not report with stereotactic radiosurgery (63620, 63621)

Do not report with (77427-77432)

📌 18.43 ⚕ 18.43 Global Days XXX
AMA: 2007, Mar, 7-8; 2007, Mar, 7-8; 2007, March, 7-8

77470 Special treatment procedure (eg, total body irradiation, hemibody radiation, per oral, endocavitary or intraoperative cone irradiation) Z3 S 80

📌 7.20 ⚕ 7.20 Global Days XXX

77499 Unlisted procedure, therapeutic radiology treatment management B 80

📌 0.00 ⚕ 0.00 Global Days XXX

77520-77525 Proton Therapy

CMS 100-2,6,10 *Medical and Other Services Furnished to Inpatients*
CMS 100-4,3,10.4 *Payment of Nonphysician Services for Inpatients*

EXCLUDES *high dose rate electronic brachytherapy, per fraction (0182T)*

77520 Proton treatment delivery; simple, without compensation Z2 S TC 80

INCLUDES single treatment area using a single nontangential/oblique port

📌 0.00 ⚕ 0.00 Global Days XXX

77522 simple, with compensation Z2 S TC 80

INCLUDES single treatment area using a single nontangential/oblique port

📌 0.00 ⚕ 0.00 Global Days XXX

77523 intermediate Z2 S TC 80

INCLUDES proton therapy delivery to one or more treatment sites using two or more ports or one or more tangential/oblique ports, with custom blocks and compensators

📌 0.00 ⚕ 0.00 Global Days XXX

77525 complex Z2 S TC 80

INCLUDES proton therapy delivery to one or more treatment sites using two or more ports per treatment site with matching or patching fields and/or numerous isocenters, with custom blocks and compensators

📌 0.00 ⚕ 0.00 Global Days XXX

77600-77620 Hyperthermia Treatment

CMS 100-3,110.1 *Hyperthermia for Treatment of Cancer*

INCLUDES interstitial insertion of temperature sensors
management during the course of therapy
normal follow-up care for three months after completion
physics planning
use of heat generating devices

EXCLUDES *high dose rate electronic brachytherapy, per fraction (0182T)*
preliminary consultation (99241-99255)
radiation therapy treatment (77371-77373, 77401-77416, 77422-77423)

☉ **77600 Hyperthermia, externally generated; superficial (ie, heating to a depth of 4 cm or less)** Z2 S 80

📌 10.22 ⚕ 10.22 Global Days XXX

☉ **77605 deep (ie, heating to depths greater than 4 cm)** Z2 S 80

📌 18.27 ⚕ 18.27 Global Days XXX

☉ **77610 Hyperthermia generated by interstitial probe(s); 5 or fewer interstitial applicators** Z2 S 80

📌 17.04 ⚕ 17.04 Global Days XXX

☉ **77615 more than 5 interstitial applicators** Z2 S 80

📌 24.10 ⚕ 24.10 Global Days XXX

77620 Hyperthermia generated by intracavitary probe(s) Z2 S 80

📌 10.74 ⚕ 10.74 Global Days XXX

● New Code   ▲ Revised Code   Ⓜ Maternity Edit   Ⓐ Age Edit   Ⓐ-Ⓥ OPPS Status Indicator   📌 Facility RVU   ⚕ Non-Facility RVU
▢ CCI Comprehensive Code   50 Bilateral Procedure   + Add-on Indicator   Ⓛ Laboratory crosswalk   Ⓡ Radiology crosswalk

77750-77799 Brachytherapy

CMS *100-4,4,61.4.2*   *Definition of Brachytherapy Source for Separate Payment*
CMS *100-4,4,61.4.1*   *Brachytherapy Sources - General*
CMS *100-4,4,61.4.3*   *Brachytherapy Sources Ordered br a Specific Patient*
CMS *100-4,4,61.4.4*   *Billing br Brachytherapy Source Supervision, Handling, and Loading Costs*
CMS *100-4,13,70.4*   *Clinical Brachytherapy*

INCLUDES   hospital admission and daily visits

EXCLUDES   *high dose rate electronic brachytherapy, per fraction (0182T)*
placement of:
    Heyman capsules (58346)
    ovoids and tandems (57155)

Code also brachytherapy sources (C1716-C1719, C2616, C2634-C2643, C2698-C2699)

77750   **Infusion or instillation of radioelement solution (includes 3-month follow-up care)**   Z3 S 80 🖵

     EXCLUDES   *monoclonal antibody infusion (79403)*
       nonantibody radiopharmaceutical therapy
       infusion with follow-up care (79101)

    📇 9.40   ⚖ 9.40   Global Days 090
    AMA: 2005, Sep, 1-4; 2005, Sep, 1-4; 2005, September, 1-4

77761   **Intracavitary radiation source application; simple**   Z3 S 80 🖵
     INCLUDES   one to four sources/ribbons

    Do not report with (0182T)
    📇 9.74   ⚖ 9.74   Global Days 090
    AMA: 2008, Jan, 10-25; 2007, Jan, 13-27; 2007, Jan, 13-27; 2007, January, 13-27; 2005, Sep, 1-4; 2005, September, 1-4; 2005, Sep, 1-4

77762   **intermediate**   Z3 S 80 🖵
     INCLUDES   five to 10 sources/ribbons

    Do not report with (0182T)
    📇 13.29   ⚖ 13.29   Global Days 090
    AMA: 2005, Sep, 1-4; 2005, Sep, 1-4; 2005, September, 1-4

77763   **complex**   Z3 S 80 🖵
     INCLUDES   more than 10 sources/ribbons

    Do not report with (0182T)
    📇 18.80   ⚖ 18.80   Global Days 090
    AMA: 2005, Sep, 1-4; 2005, Sep, 1-4; 2005, September, 1-4

77776   **Interstitial radiation source application; simple**   Z3 S 80 🖵
     INCLUDES   one to four sources/ribbons

    📇 11.49   ⚖ 11.49   Global Days 090
    AMA: 2007, May, 1-2; 2007, May, 1-2; 2007, May, 1-2; 2005, Sep, 1-4; 2005, September, 1-4; 2005, Sep, 1-4

77777   **intermediate**   Z3 S 80 🖵
     INCLUDES   five to 10 sources/ribbons

    📇 15.92   ⚖ 15.92   Global Days 090
    AMA: 2007, May, 1-2; 2007, May, 1-2; 2007, May, 1-2; 2005, Sep, 1-4; 2005, September, 1-4; 2005, Sep, 1-4

77778   **complex**   Z3 Q3 80 🖵
     INCLUDES   more than 10 sources/ribbons

    📇 22.77   ⚖ 22.77   Global Days 090
    AMA: 2007, May, 1-2; 2007, May, 1-2; 2007, May, 1-2; 2005, Sep, 1-4; 2005, Sep, 1-4; 2005, September, 1-4; 2004, Apr, 6; 2004, Apr, 6; 2004, April, 6

~~**77781**~~   ~~**Remote afterloading high intensity brachytherapy; 1-4 source positions or catheters**~~
    See 77785-77786

~~**77782**~~   ~~**5-8 source positions or catheters**~~
    See 77785-77787

~~**77783**~~   ~~**9-12 source positions or catheters**~~
    See 77785-77787

~~**77784**~~   ~~**over 12 source positions or catheters**~~
    See 77785-77787

● **77785**   **Remote afterloading high dose rate radionuclide brachytherapy; 1 channel**   Z3 S 80
    📇 5.16   ⚖ 5.16   Global Days XXX

● **77786**   **2-12 channels**   Z3 S 80
    📇 15.47   ⚖ 15.47   Global Days XXX

● **77787**   **over 12 channels**   Z2 S 80
    📇 22.99   ⚖ 22.99   Global Days XXX

77789   **Surface application of radiation source**   Z3 S 80 🖵
    📇 2.89   ⚖ 2.89   Global Days 000
    AMA: 2005, Sep, 1-4; 2005, Sep, 1-4; 2005, September, 1-4

77790   **Supervision, handling, loading of radiation source**   N1 N 80 🖵
    📇 2.42   ⚖ 2.42   Global Days XXX
    AMA: 2005, Sep, 1-4; 2005, Sep, 1-4; 2005, September, 1-4

77799   **Unlisted procedure, clinical brachytherapy**   Z2 S 80
    📇 0.00   ⚖ 0.00   Global Days XXX
    AMA: 2005, Sep, 1-4; 2005, Sep, 1-4; 2005, September, 1-4

78000-78320 Nuclear Radiology Procedures

CMS *100-3,220.12*   *Single Photon Emission Tomography*
CMS *100-3,220.8*   *Nuclear Radiology Procedure*
EXCLUDES   *diagnostic services (see appropriate sections)*
    follow-up care (see appropriate section)
    radioimmunoassays (82000-84999)

Code also radiopharmaceuticals (A9500-A9605)

78000   **Thyroid uptake; single determination**   Z3 S 80 🖵
    📇 1.90   ⚖ 1.90   Global Days XXX
    AMA: 2008, Jan, 10-25; 2007, Jan, 28-31; 2007, Jan, 28-31; 2007, Jan, 13-27; 2007, Jan, 13-27; 2007, January, 28-31; 2007, January, 13-27; 2005, Dec, 7; 2005, Dec, 7; 2005, December, 7

78001   **multiple determinations**   Z2 S 80 🖵
    📇 2.41   ⚖ 2.41   Global Days XXX
    AMA: 2007, Jan, 28-31; 2007, Jan, 28-31; 2007, January, 28-31; 2005, Dec, 7; 2005, December, 7; 2005, Dec, 7

78003   **stimulation, suppression or discharge (not including initial uptake studies)**   Z3 S 80 🖵
    📇 2.10   ⚖ 2.10   Global Days XXX
    AMA: 2007, Jan, 28-31; 2007, Jan, 28-31; 2007, January, 28-31; 2005, Dec, 7; 2005, December, 7; 2005, Dec, 7

78006   **Thyroid imaging, with uptake; single determination**   Z2 S 80 🖵
    📇 5.92   ⚖ 5.92   Global Days XXX
    AMA: 2007, Jan, 28-31; 2007, Jan, 28-31; 2007, January, 28-31; 2005, Dec, 7; 2005, December, 7; 2005, Dec, 7

78007   **multiple determinations**   Z3 S 80 🖵
    📇 3.63   ⚖ 3.63   Global Days XXX
    AMA: 2007, Jan, 28-31; 2007, Jan, 28-31; 2007, January, 28-31; 2005, Dec, 7; 2005, December, 7; 2005, Dec, 7

26/TC Professional/Technical Component Only   80/80 Assist-at-Surgery Allowed/With Documentation   Unlisted   Not Covered
AMA: CPT Assistant References   A2-Z3 ASC Payment Indicator   ♂ Male Only   ♀ Female Only   ⊘ Modifier 51 Exempt   P0 PQRI

306   CPT only © 2008 American Medical Association. All Rights Reserved. (Black Ink)   Medicare (Red Ink)   © 2008 Ingenix *(Blue Ink)*

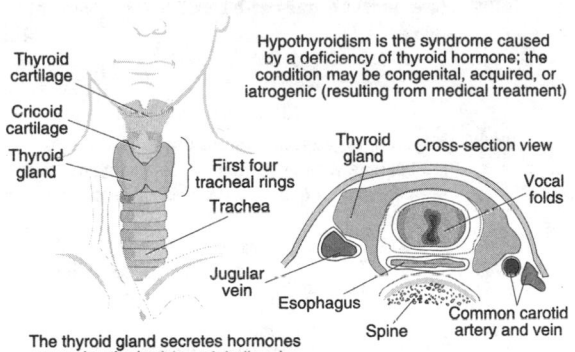

Hypothyroidism is the syndrome caused by a deficiency of thyroid hormone; the condition may be congenital, acquired, or iatrogenic (resulting from medical treatment)

The thyroid gland secretes hormones governing the body's metabolic rate; excess levels result in hyperthyroidism; abnormal enlargement of the gland is called goiter and there are numerous forms

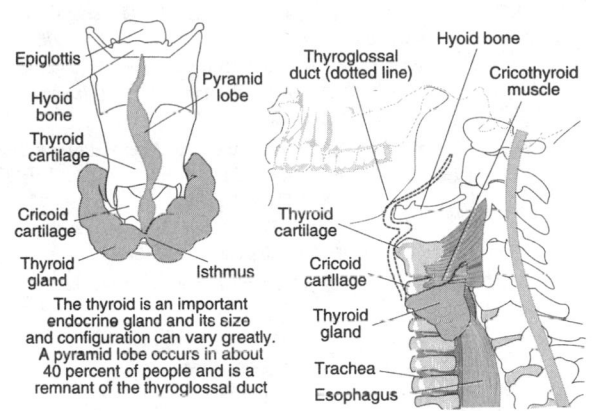

The thyroid is an important endocrine gland and its size and configuration can vary greatly. A pyramid lobe occurs in about 40 percent of people and is a remnant of the thyroglossal duct

78010 Thyroid imaging; only ⓩⓩ Ⓢ ⑧⓪ ▭

🔲 4.13 ⚖ 4.13 Global Days XXX

AMA: 2007, Jan, 28-31; 2007, Jan, 28-31; 2007, January, 28-31; 2005, Dec, 7; 2005, December, 7; 2005, Dec, 7

78011 with vascular flow ⓩⓩ Ⓢ ⑧⓪ ▭

🔲 4.70 ⚖ 4.70 Global Days XXX

AMA: 2007, Jan, 28-31; 2007, Jan, 28-31; 2007, January, 28-31; 2005, Dec, 7; 2005, December, 7; 2005, Dec, 7

78015 Thyroid carcinoma metastases imaging; limited area (eg, neck and chest only) ⓩⓩ Ⓢ ⑧⓪ ▭

🔲 5.58 ⚖ 5.58 Global Days XXX

AMA: 2007, Jan, 28-31; 2007, Jan, 28-31; 2007, January, 28-31; 2005, Dec, 7; 2005, December, 7; 2005, Dec, 7

78016 with additional studies (eg, urinary recovery) ⓩⓩ Ⓢ ⑧⓪ ▭

🔲 8.46 ⚖ 8.46 Global Days XXX

AMA: 2007, Jan, 28-31; 2007, Jan, 28-31; 2007, January, 28-31; 2005, Dec, 7; 2005, December, 7; 2005, Dec, 7

78018 whole body ⓩⓩ Ⓢ ⑧⓪ ▭

🔲 8.57 ⚖ 8.57 Global Days XXX

AMA: 2007, Jan, 28-31; 2007, Jan, 28-31; 2007, January, 28-31; 2005, Dec, 7; 2005, December, 7; 2005, Dec, 7

+ **78020 Thyroid carcinoma metastases uptake (List separately in addition to code for primary procedure)** ⓜ Ⓝ ⑧⓪ ▭

Code first (78018)

🔲 2.52 ⚖ 2.52 Global Days ZZZ

AMA: 2008, Jan, 10-25; 2007, Jan, 13-27; 2007, Jan, 13-27; 2007, Jan, 28-31; 2007, Jan, 28-31; 2007, January, 13-27; 2007, January, 28-31; 2005, Dec, 7; 2005, Dec, 7; 2005, December, 7

78070 Parathyroid imaging ⓩ③ Ⓢ ⑧⓪ ▭

🔲 4.73 ⚖ 4.73 Global Days XXX

AMA: 2007, Jan, 28-31; 2007, Jan, 28-31; 2007, January, 28-31; 2005, Dec, 7; 2005, December, 7; 2005, Dec, 7

78075 Adrenal imaging, cortex and/or medulla ⓩ③ Ⓢ ⑧⓪ ▭

🔲 11.11 ⚖ 11.11 Global Days XXX

AMA: 2007, Jan, 28-31; 2007, Jan, 28-31; 2007, January, 28-31; 2005, Dec, 7; 2005, December, 7; 2005, Dec, 7

78099 Unlisted endocrine procedure, diagnostic nuclear medicine ⓩⓩ Ⓢ ⑧⓪

🔲 0.00 ⚖ 0.00 Global Days XXX

AMA: 2007, Jan, 28-31; 2007, Jan, 28-31; 2007, January, 28-31; 2005, Dec, 7; 2005, December, 7; 2005, Dec, 7

78102 Bone marrow imaging; limited area ⓩ③ Ⓢ ⑧⓪ ▭

🔲 4.39 ⚖ 4.39 Global Days XXX

AMA: 2007, Jan, 28-31; 2007, Jan, 28-31; 2007, January, 28-31; 2005, Dec, 7; 2005, December, 7; 2005, Dec, 7

78103 multiple areas ⓩⓩ Ⓢ ⑧⓪ ▭

🔲 5.90 ⚖ 5.90 Global Days XXX

AMA: 2007, Jan, 28-31; 2007, Jan, 28-31; 2007, January, 28-31; 2005, Dec, 7; 2005, December, 7; 2005, Dec, 7

78104 whole body ⓩⓩ Ⓢ ⑧⓪ ▭

🔲 6.77 ⚖ 6.77 Global Days XXX

AMA: 2007, Jan, 28-31; 2007, Jan, 28-31; 2007, January, 28-31; 2005, Dec, 7; 2005, December, 7; 2005, Dec, 7

78110 Plasma volume, radiopharmaceutical volume-dilution technique (separate procedure); single sampling ⓩ③ Ⓢ ⑧⓪ ▭

🔲 2.10 ⚖ 2.10 Global Days XXX

AMA: 2007, Jan, 28-31; 2007, Jan, 28-31; 2007, January, 28-31; 2005, Dec, 7; 2005, December, 7; 2005, Dec, 7

78111 multiple samplings ⓩ③ Ⓢ ⑧⓪ ▭

🔲 2.70 ⚖ 2.70 Global Days XXX

AMA: 2007, Jan, 28-31; 2007, Jan, 28-31; 2007, January, 28-31; 2005, Dec, 7; 2005, December, 7; 2005, Dec, 7

78120 Red cell volume determination (separate procedure); single sampling ⓩ③ Ⓢ ⑧⓪ ▭

🔲 2.40 ⚖ 2.40 Global Days XXX

AMA: 2007, Jan, 28-31; 2007, Jan, 28-31; 2007, January, 28-31; 2005, Dec, 7; 2005, December, 7; 2005, Dec, 7

78121 multiple samplings ⓩ③ Ⓢ ⑧⓪ ▭

🔲 2.91 ⚖ 2.91 Global Days XXX

AMA: 2007, Jan, 28-31; 2007, Jan, 28-31; 2007, January, 28-31; 2005, Dec, 7; 2005, December, 7; 2005, Dec, 7

78122 Whole blood volume determination, including separate measurement of plasma volume and red cell volume (radiopharmaceutical volume-dilution technique) ⓩ③ Ⓢ ⑧⓪ ▭

🔲 3.63 ⚖ 3.63 Global Days XXX

AMA: 2007, Jan, 28-31; 2007, Jan, 28-31; 2007, January, 28-31; 2005, Dec, 7; 2005, December, 7; 2005, Dec, 7

78130 Red cell survival study; ⓩ③ Ⓢ ⑧⓪ ▭

🔲 4.20 ⚖ 4.20 Global Days XXX

AMA: 2007, Jan, 28-31; 2007, Jan, 28-31; 2007, January, 28-31; 2005, Dec, 7; 2005, December, 7; 2005, Dec, 7

● New Code ▲ Revised Code Ⓜ Maternity Edit Ⓐ Age Edit Ⓐ Ⓨ OPPS Status Indicator 🔲 Facility RVU ⚖ Non-Facility RVU

▭ CCI Comprehensive Code ⑧⓪ Bilateral Procedure + Add-on Indicator Ⓝ Laboratory crosswalk ⓩ Radiology crosswalk

Radiology

78135 — 78272

78135 differential organ/tissue kinetics (eg, splenic and/or hepatic sequestration) [72] [S] [80] [⊡]
    ⊞ 8.74   ⊠ 8.74   Global Days XXX
    AMA: 2007, Jan, 28-31; 2007, Jan, 28-31; 2007, January, 28-31; 2005, Dec, 7; 2005, December, 7; 2005, Dec, 7

78140 Labeled red cell sequestration, differential organ/tissue (eg, splenic and/or hepatic) [73] [S] [80] [⊡]
    ⊞ 4.09   ⊠ 4.09   Global Days XXX
    AMA: 2007, Jan, 28-31; 2007, Jan, 28-31; 2007, January, 28-31; 2005, Dec, 7; 2005, December, 7; 2005, Dec, 7

78185 Spleen imaging only, with or without vascular flow [73] [S] [80] [⊡]
    EXCLUDES   *liver imaging (78215-78216)*
    ⊞ 5.09   ⊠ 5.09   Global Days XXX
    AMA: 2007, Jan, 28-31; 2007, Jan, 28-31; 2007, January, 28-31; 2005, Dec, 7; 2005, December, 7; 2005, Dec, 7

78190 Kinetics, study of platelet survival, with or without differential organ/tissue localization [72] [S] [80] [⊡]
    ⊞ 10.02   ⊠ 10.02   Global Days XXX
    AMA: 2007, Jan, 28-31; 2007, Jan, 28-31; 2007, January, 28-31; 2005, Dec, 7; 2005, December, 7; 2005, Dec, 7

78191 Platelet survival study [72] [S] [80] [⊡]
    ⊞ 5.51   ⊠ 5.51   Global Days XXX
    AMA: 2007, Jan, 28-31; 2007, Jan, 28-31; 2007, January, 28-31; 2005, Dec, 7; 2005, December, 7; 2005, Dec, 7

78195 Lymphatics and lymph nodes imaging [72] [S] [80] [⊡]
    EXCLUDES   *sentinel node identification without scintigraphy (38792)*
                sentinel node removal (38500-38542)
    ⊞ 9.10   ⊠ 9.10   Global Days XXX
    AMA: 2008, Sep, 5-6; 2007, Jan, 28-31; 2007, Jan, 28-31; 2007, January, 28-31; 2005, Dec, 7; 2005, December, 7; 2005, Dec, 7

78199 Unlisted hematopoietic, reticuloendothelial and lymphatic procedure, diagnostic nuclear medicine [72] [S] [80]
    ⊞ 0.00   ⊠ 0.00   Global Days XXX
    AMA: 2007, Jan, 28-31; 2007, Jan, 28-31; 2007, January, 28-31; 2005, Dec, 7; 2005, December, 7; 2005, Dec, 7

78201 Liver imaging; static only [73] [S] [80] [⊡]
    EXCLUDES   *spleen imaging only (78185)*
    ⊞ 4.70   ⊠ 4.70   Global Days XXX
    AMA: 2007, Jan, 28-31; 2007, Jan, 28-31; 2007, January, 28-31; 2005, Dec, 7; 2005, December, 7; 2005, Dec, 7

78202 with vascular flow [72] [S] [80] [⊡]
    EXCLUDES   *spleen imaging only (78185)*
    ⊞ 5.42   ⊠ 5.42   Global Days XXX
    AMA: 2007, Jan, 28-31; 2007, Jan, 28-31; 2007, January, 28-31; 2005, Dec, 7; 2005, December, 7; 2005, Dec, 7

78205 Liver imaging (SPECT); [72] [S] [80] [⊡]
    ⊞ 6.53   ⊠ 6.53   Global Days XXX
    AMA: 2007, Jan, 28-31; 2007, Jan, 28-31; 2007, January, 28-31; 2005, Dec, 7; 2005, December, 7; 2005, Dec, 7

78206 with vascular flow [72] [S] [80] [⊡]
    ⊞ 9.08   ⊠ 9.08   Global Days XXX
    AMA: 2007, Jan, 28-31; 2007, Jan, 28-31; 2007, January, 28-31; 2005, Dec, 7; 2005, December, 7; 2005, Dec, 7

78215 Liver and spleen imaging; static only [73] [S] [80] [⊡]
    ⊞ 5.02   ⊠ 5.02   Global Days XXX
    AMA: 2007, Jan, 28-31; 2007, Jan, 28-31; 2007, January, 28-31; 2005, Dec, 7; 2005, December, 7; 2005, Dec, 7

78216 with vascular flow [73] [S] [80] [⊡]
    ⊞ 3.82   ⊠ 3.82   Global Days XXX
    AMA: 2007, Jan, 28-31; 2007, Jan, 28-31; 2007, January, 28-31; 2005, Dec, 7; 2005, December, 7; 2005, Dec, 7

78220 Liver function study with hepatobiliary agents, with serial images [73] [S] [80] [⊡]
    ⊞ 3.98   ⊠ 3.98   Global Days XXX
    AMA: 2007, Jan, 28-31; 2007, Jan, 28-31; 2007, January, 28-31; 2005, Dec, 7; 2005, December, 7; 2005, Dec, 7

78223 Hepatobiliary ductal system imaging, including gallbladder, with or without pharmacologic intervention, with or without quantitative measurement of gallbladder function [72] [S] [80] [⊡]
    ⊞ 8.39   ⊠ 8.39   Global Days XXX
    AMA: 2007, Jan, 28-31; 2007, Jan, 28-31; 2007, January, 28-31; 2005, Dec, 7; 2005, December, 7; 2005, Dec, 7

78230 Salivary gland imaging; [73] [S] [80] [⊡]
    ⊞ 4.28   ⊠ 4.28   Global Days XXX
    AMA: 2007, Jan, 28-31; 2007, Jan, 28-31; 2007, January, 28-31; 2005, Dec, 7; 2005, December, 7; 2005, Dec, 7

78231 with serial images [73] [S] [80] [⊡]
    ⊞ 3.67   ⊠ 3.67   Global Days XXX
    AMA: 2007, Jan, 28-31; 2007, Jan, 28-31; 2007, January, 28-31; 2005, Dec, 7; 2005, December, 7; 2005, Dec, 7

78232 Salivary gland function study [73] [S] [80] [⊡]
    ⊞ 3.74   ⊠ 3.74   Global Days XXX
    AMA: 2007, Jan, 28-31; 2007, Jan, 28-31; 2007, January, 28-31; 2005, Dec, 7; 2005, December, 7; 2005, Dec, 7

78258 Esophageal motility [72] [S] [80] [⊡]
    ⊞ 5.95   ⊠ 5.95   Global Days XXX
    AMA: 2007, Jan, 28-31; 2007, Jan, 28-31; 2007, January, 28-31; 2005, Dec, 7; 2005, December, 7; 2005, Dec, 7

78261 Gastric mucosa imaging [72] [S] [80] [⊡]
    ⊞ 6.59   ⊠ 6.59   Global Days XXX
    AMA: 2007, Jan, 28-31; 2007, Jan, 28-31; 2007, January, 28-31; 2005, Dec, 7; 2005, December, 7; 2005, Dec, 7

78262 Gastroesophageal reflux study [72] [S] [80] [⊡]
    ⊞ 6.50   ⊠ 6.50   Global Days XXX
    AMA: 2007, Jan, 28-31; 2007, Jan, 28-31; 2007, January, 28-31; 2005, Dec, 7; 2005, December, 7; 2005, Dec, 7

78264 Gastric emptying study [72] [S] [80] [⊡]
    ⊞ 7.47   ⊠ 7.47   Global Days XXX
    AMA: 2007, Jan, 28-31; 2007, Jan, 28-31; 2007, January, 28-31; 2005, Dec, 7; 2005, December, 7; 2005, Dec, 7

78267 Urea breath test, C-14 (isotopic); acquisition for analysis [A] [⊡]
    ⊞ 0.00   ⊠ 0.00   Global Days XXX
    AMA: 2007, Jan, 28-31; 2007, Jan, 28-31; 2007, January, 28-31; 2005, Dec, 7; 2005, December, 7; 2005, Dec, 7

78268 analysis [A] [⊡]
    ⊞ 0.00   ⊠ 0.00   Global Days XXX
    AMA: 2007, Jan, 28-31; 2007, Jan, 28-31; 2007, January, 28-31; 2005, Dec, 7; 2005, December, 7; 2005, Dec, 7

78270 Vitamin B-12 absorption study (eg, Schilling test); without intrinsic factor [73] [S] [80] [⊡]
    ⊞ 2.18   ⊠ 2.18   Global Days XXX
    AMA: 2007, Jan, 28-31; 2007, Jan, 28-31; 2007, January, 28-31; 2005, Dec, 7; 2005, December, 7; 2005, Dec, 7

78271 with intrinsic factor [73] [S] [80] [⊡]
    ⊞ 2.20   ⊠ 2.20   Global Days XXX
    AMA: 2007, Jan, 28-31; 2007, Jan, 28-31; 2007, January, 28-31; 2005, Dec, 7; 2005, December, 7; 2005, Dec, 7

78272 Vitamin B-12 absorption studies combined, with and without intrinsic factor [73] [S] [80] [⊡]
    ⊞ 2.50   ⊠ 2.50   Global Days XXX
    AMA: 2007, Jan, 28-31; 2007, Jan, 28-31; 2007, January, 28-31; 2005, Dec, 7; 2005, December, 7; 2005, Dec, 7

---

[26]/[16] Professional/Technical Component Only   [80]/[60] Assist-at-Surgery Allowed/With Documentation   Unlisted   Not Covered

AMA: CPT Assistant References   [A2]-[Z3] ASC Payment Indicator   ♂ Male Only   ♀ Female Only   ⊘ Modifier 51 Exempt   [P0] PQRI

308   CPT only © 2008 American Medical Association. All Rights Reserved. (Black Ink)   Medicare (Red Ink)   © 2008 Ingenix *(Blue Ink)*

78278 Acute gastrointestinal blood loss imaging Z2 S 80 ▱
⌨ 9.00 ⚲ 9.00 Global Days XXX
AMA: 2007, Jan, 28-31; 2007, Jan, 28-31; 2007, January, 28-31; 2005, Dec, 7; 2005, December, 7; 2005, Dec, 7

78282 Gastrointestinal protein loss Z2 S 80 ▱
⌨ 0.00 ⚲ 0.00 Global Days XXX
AMA: 2007, Jan, 28-31; 2007, Jan, 28-31; 2007, January, 28-31; 2005, Dec, 7; 2005, December, 7; 2005, Dec, 7

78290 Intestine imaging (eg, ectopic gastric mucosa, Meckel's localization, volvulus) Z2 S 80 ▱
⌨ 8.03 ⚲ 8.03 Global Days XXX
AMA: 2007, Jan, 28-31; 2007, Jan, 28-31; 2007, January, 28-31; 2005, Dec, 7; 2005, December, 7; 2005, Dec, 7

78291 Peritoneal-venous shunt patency test (eg, for LeVeen, Denver shunt) Z2 S 80 ▱
Code also (49427)
⌨ 6.55 ⚲ 6.55 Global Days XXX
AMA: 2007, Jan, 28-31; 2007, Jan, 28-31; 2007, January, 28-31; 2005, Dec, 7; 2005, December, 7; 2005, Dec, 7

78299 Unlisted gastrointestinal procedure, diagnostic nuclear medicine Z2 S 80
⌨ 0.00 ⚲ 0.00 Global Days XXX
AMA: 2007, Jan, 28-31; 2007, Jan, 28-31; 2007, January, 28-31; 2005, Dec, 7; 2005, December, 7; 2005, Dec, 7

78300 Bone and/or joint imaging; limited area Z3 S 80 ▱
⌨ 4.61 ⚲ 4.61 Global Days XXX
AMA: 2008, Jan, 10-25; 2007, Jan, 13-27; 2007, Jan, 13-27; 2007, Jan, 28-31; 2007, Jan, 28-31; 2007, January, 13-27; 2007, January, 28-31; 2005, Dec, 7; 2005, Dec, 7; 2005, December, 7

78305 multiple areas Z2 S 80 ▱
⌨ 6.13 ⚲ 6.13 Global Days XXX
AMA: 2007, Jan, 28-31; 2007, Jan, 28-31; 2007, January, 28-31; 2005, Dec, 7, 2005, December, 7, 2005, Dec, 7

78306 whole body Z7 S 80 ▱
⌨ 6.79 ⚲ 6.79 Global Days XXX
AMA: 2008, Jan, 10-25; 2007, Jan, 28-31; 2007, Jan, 28-31; 2007, Jan, 13-27; 2007, Jan, 13-27; 2007, January, 28-31; 2007, January, 13-27; 2005, Dec, 7; 2005, Dec, 7; 2005, December, 7

78315 3 phase study Z2 S 80 ▱
⌨ 8.01 ⚲ 8.01 Global Days XXX
AMA: 2008, Jan, 10-25; 2007, Jan, 13-27; 2007, Jan, 13-27; 2007, Jan, 28-31, 2007, Jan, 28-31, 2007, January, 28-31, 2007, January, 13-27; 2005, Dec, 7; 2005, Dec, 7; 2005, December, 7

78320 tomographic (SPECT) Z2 S 80 ▱
⌨ 6.99 ⚲ 6.99 Global Days XXX
AMA: 2008, Jan, 8-9; 2007, Jan, 28-31; 2007, Jan, 28-31; 2007, January, 28-31; 2005, Dec, 7; 2005, December, 7; 2005, Dec, 7

78350-78399 Nuclear Radiology: Bone Density Studies

CMS 100-3,220.8 Nuclear Radiology Procedure
CMS 100-3,150.3 Bone (Mineral) Density Studies
EXCLUDES radiographic bone density (photodensitometry) (77083)

78350 Bone density (bone mineral content) study, 1 or more sites; single photon absorptiometry E ▱
⌨ 0.93 ⚲ 0.93 Global Days XXX
AMA: 2007, Jan, 28-31; 2007, Jan, 28-31; 2007, January, 28-31; 2005, Dec, 7; 2005, December, 7; 2005, Dec, 7

78351 dual photon absorptiometry, 1 or more sites E
⌨ 0.42 ⚲ 0.42 Global Days XXX
AMA: 2007, Jan, 28-31; 2007, Jan, 28-31; 2007, January, 28-31; 2005, Dec, 7; 2005, December, 7; 2005, Dec, 7

78399 Unlisted musculoskeletal procedure, diagnostic nuclear medicine Z2 S 80
⌨ 0.00 ⚲ 0.00 Global Days XXX
AMA: 2007, Jan, 28-31; 2007, Jan, 28-31; 2007, January, 28-31; 2005, Dec, 7; 2005, December, 7; 2005, Dec, 7

78414-78499 Nuclear Radiology: Heart and Vascular

CMS 100-4,13,60.11 PET Scans for Perfusion of the Heart Using Ammonia N-13
CMS 100-4,13,60.9 Coverage of PET Scans for Myocardial Viability
CMS 100-4,13,60.4 PET Scans for Imaging of the Perfusion of the Heart Using Rubidium 82
CMS 100-4,13,60.2 Use of Gamma Cameras, Full and Partial Ring PET Scanners
CMS 100-4,13,60.3 PET Scan Qualifying Conditions
CMS 100-4,13,60.1 Billing for PET Scans
CMS 100-3,220.12 Single Photon Emission Tomography
CMS 100-3,220.8 Nuclear Radiology Procedure
CMS 100-3,220.6.8 PET (FDG) for Myocardial Viability
CMS 100-3,220.6.8 PET (FDG) for Myocardial Viability
CMS 100-3,220.6.1 PET for Perfusion of the Heart
CMS 100-3,220.6 Positron Emission Tomography (PET) Scans
CMS 100-4,13,60 Positron Emission Tomography (PET) Scans - General
EXCLUDES stress testing (93015-93018)

78414 Determination of central c-v hemodynamics (non-imaging) (eg, ejection fraction with probe technique) with or without pharmacologic intervention or exercise, single or multiple determinations Z2 S 80 ▱
⌨ 0.00 ⚲ 0.00 Global Days XXX
AMA: 2007, Jan, 28-31; 2007, Jan, 28-31; 2007, January, 28-31; 2005, Dec, 7; 2005, December, 7; 2005, Dec, 7

78428 Cardiac shunt detection Z3 S 80 ▱
⌨ 5.34 ⚲ 5.34 Global Days XXX
AMA: 2007, Jan, 28-31; 2007, Jan, 28-31; 2007, January, 28-31; 2005, Dec, 7; 2005, December, 7; 2005, Dec, 7

78445 Non-cardiac vascular flow imaging (ie, angiography, venography) Z2 S 80 ▱
⌨ 4.48 ⚲ 4.48 Global Days XXX
AMA: 2007, Jan, 28-31; 2007, Jan, 28-31; 2007, January, 28-31; 2005, Dec, 7; 2005, December, 7; 2005, Dec, 7

78456 Acute venous thrombosis imaging, peptide Z7 S ▱
⌨ 9.49 ⚲ 9.49 Global Days XXX
AMA: 2007, Jan, 28-31; 2007, Jan, 28-31; 2007, January, 28-31; 2005, Dec, 7; 2005, December, 7; 2005, Dec, 7

78457 Venous thrombosis imaging, venogram; unilateral Z2 S 80 ▱
⌨ 5.15 ⚲ 5.15 Global Days XXX
AMA: 2007, Jan, 28-31; 2007, Jan, 28-31; 2007, January, 28-31; 2005, Dec, 7, 2005, December, 7; 2005, Dec, 7

78458 bilateral Z2 S 80 ▱
⌨ 5.70 ⚲ 5.70 Global Days XXX
AMA: 2007, Jan, 28-31; 2007, Jan, 28-31; 2007, January, 28-31; 2005, Dec, 7; 2005, December, 7; 2005, Dec, 7

78459 Myocardial imaging, positron emission tomography (PET), metabolic evaluation Z2 S 80 ▱
⌨ 0.00 ⚲ 0.00 Global Days XXX
AMA: 2007, Jan, 28-31; 2007, Jan, 28-31; 2007, January, 28-31; 2005, Dec, 7; 2005, December, 7; 2005, Dec, 7

78460 Myocardial perfusion imaging; (planar) single study, at rest or stress (exercise and/or pharmacologic), with or without quantification Z3 S 80 ▱
⌨ 5.16 ⚲ 5.16 Global Days XXX
AMA: 2007, Jan, 28-31; 2007, Jan, 28-31; 2007, January, 28-31; 2005, Dec, 7; 2005, December, 7; 2005, Dec, 7

● New Code ▲ Revised Code ▯ Maternity Edit ▱ Age Edit A-Y OPPS Status Indicator ⌨ Facility RVU ⚲ Non-Facility RVU
▱ CCI Comprehensive Code 50 Bilateral Procedure + Add-on Indicator ▱ Laboratory crosswalk ▱ Radiology crosswalk

Radiology

78461 — 78580

78461   multiple studies (planar), at rest and/or stress (exercise and/or pharmacologic), and redistribution and/or rest injection, with or without quantification   Z3 S 80 ▢
  ⏱ 5.84   ⚕ 5.84 Global Days XXX
  AMA: 2007, Jan, 28-31; 2007, Jan, 28-31; 2007, January, 28-31; 2005, Dec, 7; 2005, December, 7; 2005, Dec, 7

78464   tomographic (SPECT), single study (including attenuation correction when performed), at rest or stress (exercise and/or pharmacologic), with or without quantification   Z3 S 80 ▢
  ⏱ 7.61   ⚕ 7.61 Global Days XXX
  AMA: 2007, Jan, 28-31; 2007, Jan, 28-31; 2007, January, 28-31; 2005, Dec, 7; 2005, December, 7; 2005, Dec, 7

78465   tomographic (SPECT), multiple studies (including attenuation correction when performed), at rest and/or stress (exercise and/or pharmacologic) and redistribution and/or rest injection, with or without quantification   Z3 S 80 ▢
  ⏱ 13.45   ⚕ 13.45 Global Days XXX
  AMA: 2008, Jan, 10-25; 2007, Jan, 13-27; 2007, Jan, 13-27; 2007, Jan, 28-31; 2007, Jan, 28-31; 2007, January, 28-31; 2007, January, 13-27; 2005, Mar, 11-15; 2005, Mar, 11-15; 2005, December, 7; 2005, March, 11-15; 2005, Dec, 7; 2005, Dec, 7; 2004, Oct, 15; 2004, October, 15; 2004, Oct, 15

78466   **Myocardial imaging, infarct avid, planar; qualitative or quantitative**   Z3 S 80 ▢
  ⏱ 4.92   ⚕ 4.92 Global Days XXX
  AMA: 2007, Jan, 28-31; 2007, Jan, 28-31; 2007, January, 28-31; 2005, Dec, 7; 2005, December, 7; 2005, Dec, 7

78468   with ejection fraction by first pass technique   Z3 S 80 ▢
  ⏱ 6.21   ⚕ 6.21 Global Days XXX
  AMA: 2007, Jan, 28-31; 2007, Jan, 28-31; 2007, January, 28-31; 2005, Dec, 7; 2005, December, 7; 2005, Dec, 7

78469   tomographic SPECT with or without quantification   Z2 S 80 ▢
  ⏱ 7.08   ⚕ 7.08 Global Days XXX
  AMA: 2007, Jan, 28-31; 2007, Jan, 28-31; 2007, January, 28-31; 2005, Dec, 7; 2005, December, 7; 2005, Dec, 7

78472   **Cardiac blood pool imaging, gated equilibrium; planar, single study at rest or stress (exercise and/or pharmacologic), wall motion study plus ejection fraction, with or without additional quantitative processing**   Z2 S 80 ▢
  ⏱ 7.21   ⚕ 7.21 Global Days XXX
  AMA: 2007, Jan, 28-31; 2007, Jan, 28-31; 2007, January, 28-31; 2005, Dec, 7; 2005, December, 7; 2005, Dec, 7

78473   multiple studies, wall motion study plus ejection fraction, at rest and stress (exercise and/or pharmacologic), with or without additional quantification   Z2 S 80 ▢
  ⏱ 9.86   ⚕ 9.86 Global Days XXX
  AMA: 2007, Jan, 28-31; 2007, Jan, 28-31; 2007, January, 28-31; 2005, Dec, 7; 2005, December, 7; 2005, Dec, 7

+ **78478**   **Myocardial perfusion study with wall motion, qualitative or quantitative study (List separately in addition to code for primary procedure)**   81 N 80 ▢
  Code first (78460-78461, 78464-78465)
  ⏱ 1.65   ⚕ 1.65 Global Days XXX
  AMA: 2008, Jan, 10-25; 2007, Jan, 28-31; 2007, Jan, 28-31; 2007, Jan, 13-27; 2007, Apr, 1-2; 2007, January, 13-27; 2007, April, 1-2; 2007, January, 28-31; 2007, Apr, 1-2; 2007, Jan, 13-27; 2005, Dec, 7; 2005, December, 7; 2005, March, 11-15; 2005, Dec, 7; 2005, Mar, 11-15; 2004, Oct, 15; 2004, Oct, 15; 2004, October, 15

+ **78480**   **Myocardial perfusion study with ejection fraction (List separately in addition to code for primary procedure)**   81 N 80 ▢
  Code first (78460-78461, 78464-78465)
  ⏱ 1.38   ⚕ 1.38 Global Days XXX
  AMA: 2008, Jan, 10-25; 2007, Jan, 28-31; 2007, Jan, 28-31; 2007, Jan, 13-27; 2007, Apr, 1-2; 2007, January, 28-31; 2007, April, 1-2; 2007, January, 13-27; 2007, Apr, 1-2; 2007, Jan, 13-27; 2005, Dec, 7; 2005, December, 7; 2005, March, 11-15; 2005, Dec, 7; 2005, Mar, 11-15; 2005, Mar, 11-15; 2004, Oct, 15; 2004, Oct, 15; 2004, October, 15

78481   **Cardiac blood pool imaging (planar), first pass technique; single study, at rest or with stress (exercise and/or pharmacologic), wall motion study plus ejection fraction, with or without quantification**   Z3 S 80 ▢
  ⏱ 6.33   ⚕ 6.33 Global Days XXX
  AMA: 2007, Jan, 28-31; 2007, Jan, 28-31; 2007, January, 28-31; 2005, Dec, 7; 2005, December, 7; 2005, Dec, 7

78483   multiple studies, at rest and with stress (exercise and/or pharmacologic), wall motion study plus ejection fraction, with or without quantification   Z2 S 80 ▢
  EXCLUDES   *blood flow studies of the brain (78610)*
  ⏱ 8.95   ⚕ 8.95 Global Days XXX
  AMA: 2007, Jan, 28-31; 2007, Jan, 28-31; 2007, January, 28-31; 2005, Dec, 7; 2005, December, 7; 2005, Dec, 7

78491   **Myocardial imaging, positron emission tomography (PET), perfusion; single study at rest or stress**   Z2 S 80 ▢
  ⏱ 0.00   ⚕ 0.00 Global Days XXX
  AMA: 2007, Jan, 28-31; 2007, Jan, 28-31; 2007, January, 28-31; 2005, Dec, 7; 2005, December, 7; 2005, Dec, 7

78492   multiple studies at rest and/or stress   Z2 S 80 ▢
  ⏱ 0.00   ⚕ 0.00 Global Days XXX
  AMA: 2007, Jan, 28-31; 2007, Jan, 28-31; 2007, January, 28-31; 2005, Dec, 7; 2005, December, 7; 2005, Dec, 7

78494   **Cardiac blood pool imaging, gated equilibrium, SPECT, at rest, wall motion study plus ejection fraction, with or without quantitative processing**   Z2 S 80 ▢
  ⏱ 7.86   ⚕ 7.86 Global Days XXX
  AMA: 2007, Jan, 28-31; 2007, Jan, 28-31; 2007, January, 28-31; 2005, Dec, 7; 2005, December, 7; 2005, Dec, 7

+ **78496**   **Cardiac blood pool imaging, gated equilibrium, single study, at rest, with right ventricular ejection fraction by first pass technique (List separately in addition to code for primary procedure)**   81 N 80 ▢
  Code first (78472)
  ⏱ 3.29   ⚕ 3.29 Global Days ZZZ
  AMA: 2008, Jan, 10-25; 2007, Jan, 28-31; 2007, Jan, 28-31; 2007, Jan, 13-27; 2007, Jan, 13-27; 2007, January, 28-31; 2007, January, 13-27; 2005, Dec, 7; 2005, Dec, 7; 2005, December, 7

78499   **Unlisted cardiovascular procedure, diagnostic nuclear medicine**   Z2 S
  ⏱ 0.00   ⚕ 0.00 Global Days XXX
  AMA: 2007, Jan, 28-31; 2007, Jan, 28-31; 2007, January, 28-31; 2005, Dec, 7; 2005, December, 7; 2005, Dec, 7

78580-78599 Nuclear Radiology: Lungs

CMS *100-3,220.8*   Nuclear Radiology Procedure
CMS *100-3,220.7*   Xenon Scan
CMS *100-4,3,10.4*   Payment of Nonphysician Services for Inpatients
CMS *100-2,15,80*   Physician Supervision Requirements for Diagnostic Tests

78580   **Pulmonary perfusion imaging, particulate**   Z2 S 80 ▢
  ⏱ 5.69   ⚕ 5.69 Global Days XXX
  AMA: 2007, Jan, 28-31; 2007, Jan, 28-31; 2007, January, 28-31; 2005, Dec, 7; 2005, December, 7; 2005, Dec, 7

---

26 /TC Professional/Technical Component Only   80 /80 Assist-at-Surgery Allowed/With Documentation   Unlisted   Not Covered

AMA: CPT Assistant References   A2 - Z3 ASC Payment Indicator   ♂ Male Only   ♀ Female Only   ⊘ Modifier 51 Exempt   PQ PQRI

CPT only © 2008 American Medical Association. All Rights Reserved. (Black Ink)   Medicare (Red Ink)   © 2008 Ingenix *(Blue Ink)*

78584 Pulmonary perfusion imaging, particulate, with ventilation; single breath ⚡Z3 S 80 🖵
    ⚡ 4.34   📐 4.34   Global Days XXX
    AMA: 2007, Jan, 28-31; 2007, Jan, 28-31; 2007, January, 28-31; 2005, Dec, 7; 2005, December, 7; 2005, Dec, 7

78585 rebreathing and washout, with or without single breath ⚡Z2 S 80 🖵
    ⚡ 9.39   📐 9.39   Global Days XXX
    AMA: 2007, Jan, 28-31; 2007, Jan, 28-31; 2007, January, 28-31; 2005, Dec, 7; 2005, December, 7; 2005, Dec, 7

78586 Pulmonary ventilation imaging, aerosol; single projection ⚡Z2 S 80 🖵
    ⚡ 4.34   📐 4.34   Global Days XXX
    AMA: 2007, Jan, 28-31; 2007, Jan, 28-31; 2007, January, 28-31; 2005, Dec, 7; 2005, December, 7; 2005, Dec, 7

78587 multiple projections (eg, anterior, posterior, lateral views) ⚡Z2 S 80 🖵
    ⚡ 5.45   📐 5.45   Global Days XXX
    AMA: 2007, Jan, 28-31; 2007, Jan, 28-31; 2007, January, 28-31; 2005, Dec, 7; 2005, December, 7; 2005, Dec, 7

78588 Pulmonary perfusion imaging, particulate, with ventilation imaging, aerosol, 1 or multiple projections ⚡Z2 S 80 🖵
    ⚡ 8.68   📐 8.68   Global Days XXX
    AMA: 2007, Jan, 28-31; 2007, Jan, 28-31; 2007, January, 28-31; 2005, Dec, 7; 2005, December, 7; 2005, Dec, 7

78591 Pulmonary ventilation imaging, gaseous, single breath, single projection ⚡Z2 S 80 🖵
    ⚡ 4.40   📐 4.40   Global Days XXX
    AMA: 2007, Jan, 28-31; 2007, Jan, 28-31; 2007, January, 28-31; 2005, Dec, 7; 2005, December, 7; 2005, Dec, 7

78593 Pulmonary ventilation imaging, gaseous, with rebreathing and washout with or without single breath; single projection ⚡Z2 S 80 🖵
    ⚡ 5.19   📐 5.19   Global Days XXX
    AMA: 2007, Jan, 28-31; 2007, Jan, 28-31; 2007, January, 28-31; 2005, Dec, 7; 2005, December, 7; 2005, Dec, 7

78594 multiple projections (eg, anterior, posterior, lateral views) ⚡Z2 G 80 🖵
    ⚡ 6.08   📐 6.08   Global Days XXX
    AMA: 2007, Jan, 28-31; 2007, Jan, 28-31; 2007, January, 28-31; 2005, Dec, 7; 2005, December, 7; 2005, Dec, 7

78596 Pulmonary quantitative differential function (ventilation/perfusion) study ⚡Z2 S 80 🖵
    ⚡ 10.10   📐 10.10   Global Days XXX
    AMA: 2007, Jan, 28-31; 2007, Jan, 28-31; 2007, January, 28-31; 2005, Dec, 7; 2005, December, 7; 2005, Dec, 7

78599 Unlisted respiratory procedure, diagnostic nuclear medicine ⚡Z2 S 80
    ⚡ 0.00   📐 0.00   Global Days XXX
    AMA: 2007, Jan, 28-31; 2007, Jan, 28-31; 2007, January, 28-31; 2005, Dec, 7; 2005, December, 7; 2005, Dec, 7

78600-78650 Diagnostic Imaging: Brain/Cerebrospinal Fluid

CMS 100-3,220.8   *Nuclear Radiology Procedure*
CMS 100-3,220.6.9   *FDG PET for Refractory Seizures*

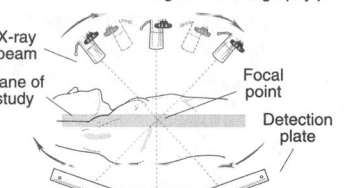
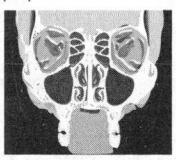

Diagram of tomography principal (left)

Schematic of frontal coronal CT section of skull

Tomogram is a general term for radiographic studies that focus on a single body plane, unimpeded by shadows cast by surrounding tissues and structures. The x-ray tube and the film are rotated around the patient during exposure of the focal point. Computed tomography (CT) offers a "slice" view of the study area and information is typically digitized and viewed on monitors. Magnetic resonance imaging (MRI) places a patient within the field of a powerful magnet while radio waves pass through the body; as with CT studies, views are usually of a "slice" of tissue. Ultrasound and nuclear imaging are other common radiological approaches

78600 Brain imaging, less than 4 static views; ⚡Z2 S 80 🖵
    ⚡ 4.72   📐 4.72   Global Days XXX
    AMA: 2007, Jan, 28-31; 2007, Jan, 28-31; 2007, January, 28-31; 2005, Dec, 7; 2005, December, 7; 2005, Dec, 7

78601 with vascular flow ⚡Z2 S 80 🖵
    ⚡ 5.62   📐 5.62   Global Days XXX
    AMA: 2007, Jan, 28-31; 2007, Jan, 28-31; 2007, January, 28-31; 2005, Dec, 7; 2005, December, 7; 2005, Dec, 7

78605 Brain imaging, minimum 4 static views; ⚡Z2 S 80 🖵
    ⚡ 5.26   📐 5.26   Global Days XXX
    AMA: 2007, Jan, 28-31; 2007, Jan, 28-31; 2007, January, 28-31; 2005, Dec, 7; 2005, December, 7; 2005, Dec, 7

78606 with vascular flow ⚡Z3 S 80 🖵
    ⚡ 8.22   📐 8.22   Global Days XXX
    AMA: 2007, Jan, 28-31; 2007, Jan, 28-31; 2007, January, 28-31; 2005, Dec, 7; 2005, December, 7; 2005, Dec, 7

78607 Brain imaging, tomographic (SPECT) ⚡Z3 S 80 🖵
    ⚡ 9.89   📐 9.89   Global Days XXX
    AMA: 2007, Jan, 28-31; 2007, Jan, 28-31; 2007, January, 28-31; 2005, Dec, 7; 2005, December, 7; 2005, Dec, 7

78608 Brain imaging, positron emission tomography (PET); metabolic evaluation ⚡Z2 S 80 🖵
    ⚡ 0.00   📐 0.00   Global Days XXX
    AMA: 2007, Jan, 28-31; 2007, Jan, 28-31; 2007, January, 28-31; 2005, Dec, 7; 2005, December, 7; 2005, Dec, 7

78609 perfusion evaluation E 🖵
    ⚡ 2.05   📐 2.05   Global Days XXX
    AMA: 2007, Jan, 28-31; 2007, Jan, 28-31; 2007, January, 28-31; 2005, Dec, 7; 2005, December, 7; 2005, Dec, 7

78610 Brain imaging, vascular flow only ⚡Z3 S 80 🖵
    ⚡ 4.75   📐 4.75   Global Days XXX
    AMA: 2007, Jan, 28-31; 2007, Jan, 28-31; 2007, January, 28-31; 2005, Dec, 7; 2005, December, 7; 2005, Dec, 7

78630 Cerebrospinal fluid flow, imaging (not including introduction of material); cisternography ⚡Z3 S 80 🖵
    Code also injection procedure (61000-61070, 62270-62319)
    ⚡ 8.74   📐 8.74   Global Days XXX
    AMA: 2007, Jan, 28-31; 2007, Jan, 28-31; 2007, January, 28-31; 2005, Dec, 7; 2005, December, 7; 2005, Dec, 7

78635 ventriculography ⚡Z3 S 80 🖵
    Code also injection procedure (61000-61070, 62270-62294)
    ⚡ 7.92   📐 7.92   Global Days XXX
    AMA: 2007, Jan, 28-31; 2007, Jan, 28-31; 2007, January, 28-31; 2005, Dec, 7; 2005, December, 7; 2005, Dec, 7

78645 shunt evaluation ⚡Z2 S 80 🖵
    Code also injection procedure (61000-61070, 62270-62294)
    ⚡ 8.03   📐 8.03   Global Days XXX
    AMA: 2007, Jan, 28-31; 2007, Jan, 28-31; 2007, January, 28-31; 2005, Dec, 7; 2005, December, 7; 2005, Dec, 7

● New Code   ▲ Revised Code   Ⓜ Maternity Edit   Ⓐ Age Edit   Ⓐ-Ⓨ OPPS Status Indicator   ⚡ Facility RVU   📐 Non-Facility RVU
🖵 CCI Comprehensive Code   50 Bilateral Procedure   + Add-on Indicator   Laboratory crosswalk   Radiology crosswalk

78647   tomographic (SPECT)   🔲 S 60 🔲
  🔳 9.23   ⚗ 9.23   Global Days XXX
  AMA: 2007, Jan, 28-31; 2007, Jan, 28-31; 2007, January, 28-31;
  2005, Dec, 7; 2005, December, 7; 2005, Dec, 7

78650   Cerebrospinal fluid leakage detection and
       localization   🔲 S 60 🔲
       Code also injection procedure (61000-61070, 62270-62294)
  🔳 8.52   ⚗ 8.52   Global Days XXX
  AMA: 2007, Jan, 28-31; 2007, Jan, 28-31; 2007, January, 28-31;
  2005, Dec, 7; 2005, December, 7; 2005, Dec, 7

78660-78699 Nuclear Radiology: Lacrimal Duct System

78660   Radiopharmaceutical dacryocystography   🔲 S 60 🔲
  🔳 4.44   ⚗ 4.44   Global Days XXX
  AMA: 2007, Jan, 28-31; 2007, Jan, 28-31; 2007, January, 28-31;
  2005, Dec, 7; 2005, December, 7; 2005, Dec, 7

78699   Unlisted nervous system procedure, diagnostic nuclear
       medicine   🔲 S 80
  🔳 0.00   ⚗ 0.00   Global Days XXX
  AMA: 2007, Jan, 28-31; 2007, Jan, 28-31; 2007, January, 28-31;
  2005, Dec, 7; 2005, December, 7; 2005, Dec, 7

78700-78725 Nuclear Radiology: Renal Anatomy and Function

CMS 100-3,220.12   *Single Photon Emission Tomography*
CMS 100-3,220.8   *Nuclear Radiology Procedure*
CMS 100-4,3,10.4   *Payment of Nonphysician Services for Inpatients*
CMS 100-2,15,80   *Physician Supervision Requirements for Diagnostic Tests*
*EXCLUDES   renal endoscopy with insertion of radioactive substances
       (77776-77778)*

78700   Kidney imaging morphology;   🔲 S 60 🔲
  🔳 4.69   ⚗ 4.69   Global Days XXX
  AMA: 2007, Jan, 28-31; 2007, Jan, 28-31; 2007, Mar, 7-8; 2007,
  Mar, 7-8; 2007, January, 28-31; 2007, March, 7-8; 2005, Dec, 7;
  2005, Dec, 7; 2005, December, 7

78701   with vascular flow   🔲 S 60 🔲
  🔳 5.61   ⚗ 5.61   Global Days XXX
  AMA: 2007, Jan, 28-31; 2007, Jan, 28-31; 2007, Mar, 7-8; 2007,
  Mar, 7-8; 2007, January, 28-31; 2007, March, 7-8; 2005, Dec, 7;
  2005, Dec, 7; 2005, December, 7

78707   with vascular flow and function, single study without
       pharmacological intervention   🔲 S 60 🔲
  🔳 6.54   ⚗ 6.54   Global Days XXX
  AMA: 2007, Jan, 28-31; 2007, Jan, 28-31; 2007, Mar, 7-8; 2007,
  Mar, 7-8; 2007, January, 28-31; 2007, March, 7-8; 2005, Dec, 7;
  2005, Dec, 7; 2005, December, 7

78708   with vascular flow and function, single study, with
       pharmacological intervention (eg, angiotensin
       converting enzyme inhibitor and/or
       diuretic)   🔲 S 60 🔲
  🔳 5.34   ⚗ 5.34   Global Days XXX
  AMA: 2007, Jan, 28-31; 2007, Jan, 28-31; 2007, Mar, 7-8; 2007,
  Mar, 7-8; 2007, January, 28-31; 2007, March, 7-8; 2005, Dec, 7;
  2005, Dec, 7; 2005, December, 7

78709   with vascular flow and function, multiple studies, with
       and without pharmacological intervention (eg,
       angiotensin converting enzyme inhibitor and/or
       diuretic)   🔲 S 60 🔲
  🔳 9.60   ⚗ 9.60   Global Days XXX
  AMA: 2007, Jan, 28-31; 2007, Jan, 28-31; 2007, Mar, 7-8; 2007,
  Mar, 7-8; 2007, January, 28-31; 2007, March, 7-8; 2005, Dec, 7;
  2005, Dec, 7; 2005, December, 7

78710   tomographic (SPECT)   🔲 S 60 🔲
  🔳 6.48   ⚗ 6.48   Global Days XXX
  AMA: 2007, Jan, 28-31; 2007, Jan, 28-31; 2007, Mar, 7-8; 2007,
  Mar, 7-8; 2007, January, 28-31; 2007, March, 7-8; 2005, Dec, 7;
  2005, Dec, 7; 2005, December, 7

78725   Kidney function study, non-imaging radioisotopic
       study   🔲 S 60 🔲
  🔳 2.73   ⚗ 2.73   Global Days XXX
  AMA: 2007, Jan, 28-31; 2007, Jan, 28-31; 2007, January, 28-31;
  2005, Dec, 7; 2005, December, 7; 2005, Dec, 7

78730-78799 Nuclear Radiology: Urogenital

CMS 100-3,220.8   *Nuclear Radiology Procedure*
CMS 100-4,3,10.4   *Payment of Nonphysician Services for Inpatients*
CMS 100-2,15,80   *Physician Supervision Requirements for Diagnostic Tests*

+ **78730**   Urinary bladder residual study (List separately in addition
       to code for primary procedure)   🔲 S 60 🔲
       *EXCLUDES   measurement of postvoid residual urine and
              /or bladder capacity using ultrasound
              (51798)
              ultrasound imaging of the bladder only with
              measurement of postvoid residual urine
              (76857)*
       Code first (78740)
  🔳 2.10   ⚗ 2.10   Global Days ZZZ
  AMA: 2007, Jan, 28-31; 2007, Jan, 28-31; 2007, Mar, 7-8; 2007,
  Mar, 7-8; 2007, January, 28-31; 2007, March, 7-8; 2005, Dec, 7;
  2005, Dec, 7; 2005, December, 7

78740   Ureteral reflux study (radiopharmaceutical voiding
       cystogram)   🔲 S 60 🔲
       EXCLUDES   catheterization (51701-51703)
       Code also urinary bladder residual study (78730)
  🔳 5.56   ⚗ 5.56   Global Days XXX
  AMA: 2007, Jan, 28-31; 2007, Jan, 28-31; 2007, January, 28-31;
  2005, Dec, 7; 2005, December, 7; 2005, Dec, 7

78761   Testicular imaging with vascular flow   ♂ 🔲 S 60 🔲
  🔳 5.59   ⚗ 5.59   Global Days XXX
  AMA: 2007, Jan, 28-31; 2007, Jan, 28-31; 2007, Mar, 7-8; 2007,
  Mar, 7-8; 2007, January, 28-31; 2007, March, 7-8; 2005, Dec, 7;
  2005, Dec, 7; 2005, December, 7

78799   Unlisted genitourinary procedure, diagnostic nuclear
       medicine   🔲 S 80
  🔳 0.00   ⚗ 0.00   Global Days XXX
  AMA: 2007, Jan, 28-31; 2007, Jan, 28-31; 2007, January, 28-31;
  2005, Dec, 7; 2005, December, 7; 2005, Dec, 7

78800-78804 Nuclear Radiology: Tumor Localization

CMS 100-3,220.12   *Single Photon Emission Tomography*
CMS 100-3,220.8   *Nuclear Radiology Procedure*
CMS 100-4,3,10.4   *Payment of Nonphysician Services for Inpatients*
CMS 100-2,15,80   *Physician Supervision Requirements for Diagnostic Tests*

78800   Radiopharmaceutical localization of tumor or distribution
       of radiopharmaceutical agent(s); limited area   🔲 S 60 🔲
       INCLUDES   ocular radiophosphorus tumor identification
       EXCLUDES   specific organ (see appropriate site)
  🔳 5.01   ⚗ 5.01   Global Days XXX
  AMA: 2007, Jan, 28-31; 2007, Jan, 28-31; 2007, January, 28-31;
  2005, Dec, 7; 2005, December, 7; 2005, Dec, 7

78801   multiple areas   🔲 S 60 🔲
  🔳 6.70   ⚗ 6.70   Global Days XXX
  AMA: 2007, Jan, 28-31; 2007, Jan, 28-31; 2007, January, 28-31;
  2005, Dec, 7; 2005, December, 7; 2005, Dec, 7

🔲 Professional/Technical Component Only   🔲 Assist-at-Surgery Allowed/With Documentation   Unlisted   Not Covered

AMA: CPT Assistant References   🔲-🔲 ASC Payment Indicator   ♂ Male Only   ♀ Female Only   ⊘ Modifier 51 Exempt   🔲 PQRI

CPT only © 2008 American Medical Association. All Rights Reserved. (Black Ink)   Medicare (Red Ink)   © 2008 Ingenix *(Blue Ink)*

78802 whole body, single day imaging 🔲 Ⓢ 🔳 ▢
🔲 8.77   ⚖ 8.77   Global Days XXX
AMA: 2007, Jan, 28-31; 2007, Jan, 28-31; 2007, January, 28-31; 2005, Dec, 7; 2005, December, 7; 2005, Dec, 7

78803 tomographic (SPECT) 🔲 Ⓢ 🔳 ▢
🔲 9.67   ⚖ 9.67   Global Days XXX
AMA: 2007, Jan, 28-31; 2007, Jan, 28-31; 2007, January, 28-31; 2005, Dec, 7; 2005, December, 7; 2005, Dec, 7

78804 whole body, requiring 2 or more days imaging 🔲 Ⓢ 🔳 ▢
🔲 15.38   ⚖ 15.38   Global Days XXX
AMA: 2007, Jan, 28-31; 2007, Jan, 28-31; 2007, January, 28-31; 2005, Dec, 7; 2005, December, 7; 2005, Dec, 7

78805-78807 Nuclear Radiology: Inflammation and Infection

CMS *100-3,220.12*   *Single Photon Emission Tomography*
CMS *100-3,220.8*   *Nuclear Radiology Procedure*
CMS *100-4,3,10.4*   *Payment of Nonphysician Services for Inpatients*
CMS *100-2,15,80*   *Physician Supervision Requirements for Diagnostic Tests*
EXCLUDES   *brain PET scan (78608-78609)*
imaging bone infectious or inflammatory disease with bone imaging radiopharmaceutical (78300, 78305-78306)
PET myocardial imaging (78459, 78491-78492)

78805 Radiopharmaceutical localization of inflammatory process; limited area 🔲 Ⓢ 🔳 ▢
🔲 5.02   ⚖ 5.02   Global Days XXX
AMA: 2007, Jan, 28-31; 2007, Jan, 28-31; 2007, January, 28-31; 2005, Dec, 7; 2005, December, 7; 2005, Dec, 7

78806 whole body 🔲 Ⓢ 🔳 ▢
🔲 9.19   ⚖ 9.19   Global Days XXX
AMA: 2007, Jan, 28-31; 2007, Jan, 28-31; 2007, January, 28-31; 2005, Dec, 7; 2005, December, 7; 2005, Dec, 7

78807 tomographic (SPECT) 🔲 Ⓢ 🔳 ▢
🔲 9.68   ⚖ 9.68   Global Days XXX
AMA: 2007, Jan, 28-31; 2007, Jan, 28-31; 2007, January, 28-31; 2005, Dec, 7; 2005, December, 7; 2005, Dec, 7

78808 Intravenous Injection for Radiopharmaceutical Localization

● **78808** Injection procedure for radiopharmaceutical localization by non-imaging probe study, intravenous (eg, parathyroid adenoma) 🔲 🔲 🔲
EXCLUDES   *identification of sentinel node (38792)*
🔲 1.23   ⚖ 1.23   Global Days XXX

78811-78999 Nuclear Radiology: Diagnosis, Staging, Restaging or Monitoring Cancer

CMS *100-4,13,60.3.1*   *Appropriate Codes for PET Scans*
CMS *100-4,13,60.3*   *PET Scan Qualifying Conditions*
CMS *100-4,3,10.4*   *Payment of Nonphysician Services for Inpatients*
EXCLUDES   *CT scan performed for other than attenuation correction and anatomical localization (report with the appropriate site-specific CT code)*
ocular radiophosphorus tumor identification (78800)

Do not report with procedure performed more than once per session

78811 Positron emission tomography (PET) imaging; limited area (eg, chest, head/neck) 🔲 Ⓢ 🔳 ▢
🔲 0.00   ⚖ 0.00   Global Days XXX
AMA: 2007, Jan, 28-31; 2007, Jan, 28-31; 2007, January, 28-31; 2005, Dec, 7; 2005, December, 7; 2005, Dec, 7

78812 skull base to mid-thigh 🔲 Ⓢ 🔳 ▢
🔲 0.00   ⚖ 0.00   Global Days XXX
AMA: 2007, Jan, 28-31; 2007, Jan, 28-31; 2007, January, 28-31; 2005, Dec, 7; 2005, December, 7; 2005, Dec, 7

78813 whole body 🔲 Ⓢ 🔳 ▢
🔲 0.00   ⚖ 0.00   Global Days XXX
AMA: 2007, Jan, 28-31; 2007, Jan, 28-31; 2007, January, 28-31; 2005, Dec, 7; 2005, December, 7; 2005, Dec, 7

78814 Positron emission tomography (PET) with concurrently acquired computed tomography (CT) for attenuation correction and anatomical localization imaging; limited area (eg, chest, head/neck) 🔲 Ⓢ 🔳 ▢
🔲 0.00   ⚖ 0.00   Global Days XXX
AMA: 2008, Jan, 10-25; 2007, Jan, 28-31; 2007, Jan, 28-31; 2007, Jan, 13-27; 2007, Jan, 13-27; 2007, January, 13-27; 2007, January, 28-31; 2005, Jun, 9-11; 2005, Jun, 9-11; 2005, June, 9-11; 2005, February, 13-16; 2005, December, 7; 2005, Dec, 7; 2005, Dec, 7; 2005, Feb, 13-16; 2005, Feb, 13-16

78815 skull base to mid-thigh 🔲 Ⓢ 🔳 ▢
🔲 0.00   ⚖ 0.00   Global Days XXX
AMA: 2008, Jan, 10-25; 2007, Jan, 28-31; 2007, Jan, 28-31; 2007, Jan, 13-27; 2007, Jan, 13-27; 2007, January, 13-27; 2007, January, 28-31; 2005, Jun, 9-11; 2005, Jun, 9-11; 2005, June, 9-11; 2005, February, 13-16; 2005, December, 7; 2005, Feb, 13-16; 2005, Feb, 13-16; 2005, Dec, 7; 2005, Dec, 7

78816 whole body 🔲 Ⓢ 🔳 ▢
🔲 0.00   ⚖ 0.00   Global Days XXX
AMA: 2008, Jan, 10-25; 2007, Jan, 28-31; 2007, Jan, 28-31; 2007, Jan, 13-27; 2007, Jan, 13-27; 2007, January, 13-27; 2007, January, 28-31; 2005, Jun, 9-11; 2005, Jun, 9-11; 2005, June, 9-11; 2005, February, 13-16; 2005, December, 7; 2005, Feb, 13-16; 2005, Feb, 13-16; 2005, Dec, 7; 2005, Dec, 7

~~**78890** Generation of automated data: interactive process involving nuclear physician and/or allied health professional personnel; simple manipulations and interpretation, not to exceed 30 minutes~~

~~**78891** complex manipulations and interpretation, exceeding 30 minutes~~

78999 Unlisted miscellaneous procedure, diagnostic nuclear medicine 🔲 Ⓢ 🔳
🔲 0.00   ⚖ 0.00   Global Days XXX
AMA: 2007, Jan, 28-31; 2007, Jan, 28-31; 2007, January, 28-31; 2005, Dec, 7; 2005, December, 7; 2005, Dec, 7

79005-79999 Systemic Radiopharmaceutical Therapy

CMS *100-3,220.8*   *Nuclear Radiology Procedure*
EXCLUDES   *imaging guidance*
intra-arterial, intra-cavitory, intra-articular injection (see appropriate injection codes)
radiological supervision and interpretation

79005 Radiopharmaceutical therapy, by oral administration 🔲 Ⓢ 🔳
EXCLUDES   *monoclonal antibody treatment (79403)*
🔲 4.26   ⚖ 4.26   Global Days XXX
AMA: 2005, Sep, 1-4; 2005, Sep, 1-4; 2005, September, 1-4

79101 Radiopharmaceutical therapy, by intravenous administration 🔲 Ⓢ 🔳 ▢
EXCLUDES   *administration of nonantibody radioelement solution including follow-up care (77750)*
radiolabeled monoclonal antibody IV infusion (79403)

Do not report with (36400, 36410, 79403, 96360, 96374-96375, 96409)
🔲 4.79   ⚖ 4.79   Global Days XXX

79200 Radiopharmaceutical therapy, by intracavitary administration 🔲 Ⓢ 🔳 ▢
🔲 4.86   ⚖ 4.86   Global Days XXX

● New Code   ▲ Revised Code   Ⓜ Maternity Edit   Ⓐ Age Edit   Ⓐ-Ⓨ OPPS Status Indicator   🔲 Facility RVU   ⚖ Non-Facility RVU
🔲 CCI Comprehensive Code   50 Bilateral Procedure   + Add-on Indicator   🔲 Laboratory crosswalk   🔲 Radiology crosswalk

79300 **Radiopharmaceutical therapy, by interstitial radioactive colloid administration** ZZ S 80 ▭
🚗 0.00   ⊘ 0.00   Global Days XXX

79403 **Radiopharmaceutical therapy, radiolabeled monoclonal antibody by intravenous infusion** Z3 S 80 ▭
EXCLUDES   pretreatment imaging (78802, 78804)

Do not report with (79101)
🚗 6.07   ⊘ 6.07   Global Days XXX
AMA: 2005, Sep, 1-4; 2005, Sep, 1-4; 2005, September, 1-4

79440 **Radiopharmaceutical therapy, by intra-articular administration** Z3 S 80 ▭
🚗 4.49   ⊘ 4.49   Global Days XXX

79445 **Radiopharmaceutical therapy, by intra-arterial particulate administration** ZZ S 80 ▭
EXCLUDES   procedural and radiological supervision and interpretation for angiographic and interventional procedures before intra-arterial radiopharmaceutical therapy

Do not report with (96373, 96420)
🚗 0.00   ⊘ 0.00   Global Days XXX
AMA: 2006, Dec, 10-12; 2006, Dec, 10-12; 2006, Dec, 10-12; 2006, Dec, 10-12; 2006, December, 10-12; 2006, December, 10-12

79999 **Radiopharmaceutical therapy, unlisted procedure** ZZ S 80
🚗 0.00   ⊘ 0.00   Global Days XXX
AMA: 2005, Mar, 11-15; 2005, Mar, 11-15; 2005, March, 11-15

26/TC Professional/Technical Component Only   80/80 Assist-at-Surgery Allowed/With Documentation   Unlisted   Not Covered
AMA: CPT Assistant References   A2-Z3 ASC Payment Indicator   ♂ Male Only   ♀ Female Only   ⊘ Modifier 51 Exempt   PQRI

314   CPT only © 2008 American Medical Association. All Rights Reserved. (Black Ink)   Medicare (Red Ink)   © 2008 Ingenix (Blue Ink)

79300 — 79999

80047-80076 Multi-test Laboratory Panels

CMS *100-2,6,10*   *Medical and Other Services Furnished to Inpatients*
CMS *100-4,3,10.4*   *Payment of Nonphysician Services for Inpatients*
CMS *100-2,15,80*   *Physician Supervision Requirements for Diagnostic Tests*
EXCLUDES   *test codes:*
        not specified by panel definition
        for testing performed at a frequency greater than the number
          specified by panel definition

80047   **Basic metabolic panel (Calcium, ionized)**   [A]
     INCLUDES   calcium, ionized (82330)
                carbon dioxide (82374)
                chloride (82435)
                creatinine (82565)
                glucose (82947)
                potassium (84132)
                sodium (84295)
                urea nitrogen (BUN) (84520)

     Do not report with (80053)

     📋 0.00   ✂ 0.00   Global Days XXX
     AMA: 2008, Apr, 5-7; 2008, Apr, 5-7; 2008, Apr, 5-7

▲ **80048**   **Basic metabolic panel (Calcium, total)**   [A][◻][✖]
     INCLUDES   calcium, total (82310)
                carbon dioxide (82374)
                chloride (82435)
                creatinine (82565)
                glucose (82947)
                potassium (84132)
                sodium (84295)
                urea nitrogen (BUN) (84520)

     Do not report with (80053)

     📋 0.00   ✂ 0.00   Global Days XXX
     AMA: 2008, Apr, 5-7; 2008, Apr, 5-7; 2008, Apr, 5-7; 2005, Aug,
     7-8; 2005, Aug, 7-8; 2005, July, 11-12; 2005, August, 7-8; 2005,
     August, 9-10; 2005, Aug, 9-10; 2005, Aug, 9-10; 2005, Jul, 11-12;
     2005, Jul, 11-12

80050   **General health panel**   [E]
     INCLUDES   complete blood count with differential (CBC)
                   (85004, or 85025, 85027)
                comprehensive metabolic profile OR (80053)
                complete blood count (CBC) automated and
                   appropriate manual differential WBC
                   count (85007, 85009, 85027)
                thyroid stimulating hormones (84443)

     📋 0.00   ✂ 0.00   Global Days XXX
     AMA: 2008, Jan, 10-25; 2007, Jan, 13-27; 2007, Jan, 13-27; 2007,
     January, 13-27; 2005, Aug, 9-10; 2005, Aug, 9-10; 2005, Aug,
     7-8; 2005, August, 9-10; 2005, August, 7-8; 2005, July, 11-12;
     2005, Aug, 7-8; 2005, Jul, 11-12; 2005, Jul, 11-12

80051   **Electrolyte panel**   [A][◻]
     INCLUDES   carbon dioxide (82374)
                chloride (82435)
                potassium (84132)
                sodium (84295)

     📋 0.00   ✂ 0.00   Global Days XXX
     AMA: 2008, Jan, 10-25; 2007, Jan, 13-27; 2007, Jan, 13-27; 2007,
     January, 13-27; 2005, Aug, 9-10; 2005, Aug, 9-10; 2005, Aug,
     7-8; 2005, August, 9-10; 2005, August, 7-8; 2005, July, 11-12;
     2005, Aug, 7-8; 2005, Jul, 11-12; 2005, Jul, 11-12

▲ **80053**   **Comprehensive metabolic panel**   [A][◻][✖]
     INCLUDES   albumin (82040)
                bilirubin, total (82247)
                calcium, total (82310)
                carbon dioxide (bicarbonate) (82374)
                chloride (82435)
                creatinine (82565)
                glucose (82947)
                phosphatase, alkaline (84075)
                potassium (84132)
                protein, total (84155)
                sodium (84295)
                transferase, alanine amino (ALT) (SGPT)
                   (84460)
                transferase, aspartate amino (AST) (SGOT)
                   (84450)
                urea nitrogen (BUN) (84520)

     Do not report with (80047-80048, 80076)

     📋 0.00   ✂ 0.00   Global Days XXX
     AMA: 2008, Apr, 5-7; 2008, Apr, 5-7; 2008, Apr, 5-7; 2008, Jan,
     10-25; 2007, Jan, 13-27; 2007, Jan, 13-27; 2007, January, 13-27;
     2005, Jul, 11-12; 2005, Jul, 11-12; 2005, July, 11-12; 2005, August,
     7-8; 2005, January, 46-47; 2005, August, 9-10; 2005, Aug, 9-10;
     2005, Aug, 9-10; 2005, Aug, 7-8; 2005, Aug, 7-8; 2005, Jan, 46-47;
     2005, Jan, 46-47

80055   **Obstetric panel**   [M][♀][E]
     INCLUDES   blood typing, ABO and Rh (86900-86901)
                CBC (85004, 85007, 85009, 85025, 85027)
                hepatitis B surface antigen (HBsAg) (87340)
                RBC antibody screen, each serum technique
                   (86850)
                rubella antibody (86762)
                syphilis test, qualitative (86592)

     📋 0.00   ✂ 0.00   Global Days XXX
     AMA: 2008, Jan, 10-25; 2007, Jan, 13-27; 2007, Jan, 13-27; 2007,
     January, 13-27; 2005, Jul, 11-12; 2005, Jul, 11-12; 2005, Aug,
     7-8; 2005, August, 9-10; 2005, August, 7-8; 2005, July, 11-12;
     2005, Aug, 7-8; 2005, Aug, 9-10; 2005, Aug, 9-10

80061   **Lipid panel**   [A][◻][✖]
     INCLUDES   cholesterol, serum, total (82465)
                lipoprotein, direct measurement, high
                   density cholesterol (HDL cholesterol)
                   (83718)
                triglycerides (84478)

     📋 0.00   ✂ 0.00   Global Days XXX
     AMA: 2008, Jan, 10-25; 2007, Jan, 13-27; 2007, Jan, 13-27; 2007,
     January, 13-27; 2005, Aug, 9-10; 2005, Aug, 9-10; 2005, Aug,
     7-8; 2005, Aug, 7-8; 2005, August, 7-8; 2005, August, 9-10; 2005,
     July, 11-12; 2005, February, 7-9; 2005, Feb, 7-9; 2005, Feb, 7-9;
     2005, Jul, 11-12; 2005, Jul, 11-12

▲ **80069**   **Renal function panel**   [A][◻]
     INCLUDES   albumin (82040)
                calcium, total (82310)
                carbon dioxide (82374)
                chloride (82435)
                creatinine (82565)
                glucose (82947)
                phosphorus inorganic (84100)
                potassium (84132)
                sodium (84295)
                urea nitrogen (BUN) (84520)

     📋 0.00   ✂ 0.00   Global Days XXX
     AMA: 2008, Jan, 10-25; 2007, Jan, 13-27; 2007, Jan, 13-27; 2007,
     January, 13-27; 2005, Jul, 11-12; 2005, Jul, 11-12; 2005, Aug,
     9-10; 2005, August, 9-10; 2005, August, 7-8; 2005, July, 11-12;
     2005, Aug, 9-10; 2005, Aug, 7-8; 2005, Aug, 7-8

⊛ Modifier 63 Exempt Code   ⊙ Moderate Sedation   + CPT Add-on Code   ⊘ Modifier 51 Exempt Code   ● New Code   ▲ Revised Code

[M] Maternity Edit   [A] Age Edit   [✖] CLIA Waived Test   [A]-[Y] APC Status Indicators   [◻] CCI Comprehensive Code   [50] Bilateral Procedure

© 2008 Ingenix *(Blue Ink)*   **CPT only © 2008 American Medical Association. All Rights Reserved. (Black Ink)**   Medicare (Red Ink)   315

80074 Acute hepatitis panel Ⓐ ▭

INCLUDES hepatitis A antibody (HAAb) IgM (86709)
hepatitis B core antibody (HBcAb), IgM (86705)
hepatitis B surface antigen (HBsAg) (87340)
hepatitis C antibody (86803)

🔲 0.00 🔲 0.00 **Global Days XXX**

AMA: 2008, Jan, 10-25; 2007, Jan, 13-27; 2007, Jan, 13-27; 2007, January, 13-27; 2005, Aug, 9-10; 2005, Aug, 9-10; 2005, Aug, 7-8; 2005, August, 9-10; 2005, August, 7-8; 2005, July, 11-12; 2005, Aug, 7-8; 2005, Jul, 11-12; 2005, Jul, 11-12

80076 Hepatic function panel Ⓐ ▭

INCLUDES albumin (82040)
bilirubin, direct (82248)
bilirubin, total (82247)
phosphatase, alkaline (84075)
protein, total (84155)
transferase, alanine amino (ALT) (SGPT) (84460)
transferase, aspartate amino (AST) (SGOT) (84450)

Do not report with (80053)

🔲 0.00 🔲 0.00 **Global Days XXX**

AMA: 2008, Jan, 10-25; 2007, Jan, 13-27; 2007, Jan, 13-27; 2007, January, 13-27; 2005, Aug, 7-8; 2005, Aug, 7-8; 2005, Jul, 11-12; 2005, July, 11-12; 2005, August, 7-8; 2005, August, 9-10; 2005, Jul, 11-12; 2005, Aug, 9-10; 2005, Aug, 9-10

80100-80103 Drug Screening Tests

CMS 100-2,6,10 *Medical and Other Services Furnished to Inpatients*
CMS 100-4,3,10.4 *Payment of Nonphysician Services for Inpatients*
CMS 100-2,15,80 *Physician Supervision Requirements for Diagnostic Tests*

INCLUDES qualitative test for drugs or drug classes such as:
alcohols
amphetamines
barbiturates
benzodiazepines
cocaine and metabolites
methadones
opiates
phencyclidines
phenothiazines
propoxyphenes
tetrahydrocannabinoids
tricyclic antidepressants
stationary and mobile chromatography

EXCLUDES *drug quantification (80150-80299, 82000-84999)*

80100 Drug screen, qualitative; multiple drug classes chromatographic method, each procedure Ⓐ ▭

🔲 0.00 🔲 0.00 **Global Days XXX**

AMA: 2005, Aug, 9-10; 2005, Aug, 9-10; 2005, Jul, 11-12; 2005, Jul, 11-12; 2005, Aug, 7-8; 2005, Aug, 7-8; 2005, August, 9-10; 2005, July, 11-12; 2005, August, 7-8

80101 single drug class method (eg, immunoassay, enzyme assay), each drug class Ⓐ ▭ ⊠

🔲 0.00 🔲 0.00 **Global Days XXX**

AMA: 2008, Jan, 10-25; 2007, Jan, 13-27; 2007, Jan, 13-27; 2007, January, 13-27; 2006, Dec, 10-12; 2006, Dec, 10-12; 2006, Dec, 10-12; 2006, Dec, 10-12; 2006, Dec, 10-12; 2006, Dec, 10-12; 2006, Dec, 10-12; 2006, December, 10-12; 2006, December, 10-12; 2006, December, 10-12; 2006, December, 10-12; 2006, Dec, 10-12; 2005, Aug, 9-10; 2005, Aug, 9-10; 2005, Jul, 11-12; 2005, July, 11-12; 2005, August, 7-8; 2005, August, 9-10; 2005, Jul, 11-12; 2005, Aug, 7-8; 2005, Aug, 7-8

80102 Drug confirmation, each procedure Ⓐ ▭

🔲 0.00 🔲 0.00 **Global Days XXX**

AMA: 2005, Aug, 7-8; 2005, Aug, 7-8; 2005, Jul, 11-12; 2005, Jul, 11-12; 2005, Aug, 9-10; 2005, Aug, 9-10; 2005, August, 9-10; 2005, July, 11-12; 2005, August, 7-8

80103 Tissue preparation for drug analysis Ⓝ

🔲 0.00 🔲 0.00 **Global Days XXX**

AMA: 2005, Aug, 9-10; 2005, Aug, 9-10; 2005, Aug, 7-8; 2005, Aug, 7-8; 2005, Jul, 11-12; 2005, Jul, 11-12; 2005, August, 9-10; 2005, July, 11-12; 2005, August, 7-8

80150-80299 Therapeutic Drug Levels

CMS 100-4,3,10.4 *Payment of Nonphysician Services for Inpatients*
CMS 100-2,15,80 *Physician Supervision Requirements for Diagnostic Tests*

INCLUDES *tests on specimens from any source*

EXCLUDES *nonquantitative testing (80100-80103)*

80150 Amikacin Ⓐ

🔲 0.00 🔲 0.00 **Global Days XXX**

AMA: 2005, Aug, 7-8; 2005, Aug, 7-8; 2005, Jul, 11-12; 2005, Jul, 11-12; 2005, Aug, 9-10; 2005, Aug, 9-10; 2005, August, 9-10; 2005, July, 11-12; 2005, August, 7-8

80152 Amitriptyline Ⓐ

🔲 0.00 🔲 0.00 **Global Days XXX**

AMA: 2005, Aug, 9-10; 2005, Aug, 9-10; 2005, Jul, 11-12; 2005, Jul, 11-12; 2005, Aug, 7-8; 2005, Aug, 7-8; 2005, August, 9-10; 2005, July, 11-12; 2005, August, 7-8

80154 Benzodiazepines Ⓐ

🔲 0.00 🔲 0.00 **Global Days XXX**

AMA: 2005, Aug, 9-10; 2005, Aug, 9-10; 2005, Jul, 11-12; 2005, Jul, 11-12; 2005, Aug, 7-8; 2005, Aug, 7-8; 2005, August, 9-10; 2005, July, 11-12; 2005, August, 7-8

80156 Carbamazepine; total Ⓐ

🔲 0.00 🔲 0.00 **Global Days XXX**

AMA: 2005, Aug, 7-8; 2005, Aug, 7-8; 2005, Jul, 11-12; 2005, Jul, 11-12; 2005, Aug, 9-10; 2005, Aug, 9-10; 2005, August, 9-10; 2005, July, 11-12; 2005, August, 7-8

80157 free Ⓐ

🔲 0.00 🔲 0.00 **Global Days XXX**

AMA: 2005, Aug, 7-8; 2005, Aug, 7-8; 2005, Aug, 9-10; 2005, Aug, 9-10; 2005, Jul, 11-12; 2005, Jul, 11-12; 2005, August, 9-10; 2005, July, 11-12; 2005, August, 7-8

80158 Cyclosporine Ⓐ

🔲 0.00 🔲 0.00 **Global Days XXX**

AMA: 2005, Aug, 7-8; 2005, Aug, 7-8; 2005, Jul, 11-12; 2005, Jul, 11-12; 2005, Aug, 9-10; 2005, Aug, 9-10; 2005, July, 11-12; 2005, August, 7-8; 2005, August, 9-10

80160 Desipramine Ⓐ

🔲 0.00 🔲 0.00 **Global Days XXX**

AMA: 2005, Aug, 9-10; 2005, Aug, 9-10; 2005, Aug, 7-8; 2005, Aug, 7-8; 2005, Jul, 11-12; 2005, Jul, 11-12; 2005, August, 9-10; 2005, August, 7-8; 2005, July, 11-12

80162 Digoxin Ⓐ

🔲 0.00 🔲 0.00 **Global Days XXX**

AMA: 2005, Aug, 9-10; 2005, Aug, 9-10; 2005, Jul, 11-12; 2005, Jul, 11-12; 2005, Aug, 7-8; 2005, Aug, 7-8; 2005, August, 9-10; 2005, August, 7-8

80164 Dipropylacetic acid (valproic acid) Ⓐ

🔲 0.00 🔲 0.00 **Global Days XXX**

AMA: 2005, Jul, 11-12; 2005, Jul, 11-12; 2005, Aug, 9-10; 2005, Aug, 9-10; 2005, Aug, 7-8; 2005, Aug, 7-8; 2005, July, 11-12; 2005, August, 9-10; 2005, August, 7-8

80166   **Doxepin**   Ⓐ
    🔾 0.00   🔾 0.00   Global Days XXX
    AMA: 2005, Jul, 11-12; 2005, Jul, 11-12; 2005, Aug, 7-8; 2005,
    Aug, 7-8; 2005, Aug, 9-10; 2005, Aug, 9-10; 2005, July, 11-12;
    2005, August, 9-10; 2005, August, 7-8

80168   **Ethosuximide**   Ⓐ
    🔾 0.00   🔾 0.00   Global Days XXX
    AMA: 2005, Aug, 7-8; 2005, Aug, 7-8; 2005, Jul, 11-12; 2005, Jul,
    11-12; 2005, Aug, 9-10; 2005, Aug, 9-10; 2005, July, 11-12; 2005,
    August, 9-10; 2005, August, 7-8

80170   **Gentamicin**   Ⓐ
    🔾 0.00   🔾 0.00   Global Days XXX
    AMA: 2005, Jul, 11-12; 2005, Jul, 11-12; 2005, Aug, 9-10; 2005,
    Aug, 9-10; 2005, Aug, 7-8; 2005, Aug, 7-8; 2005, July, 11-12; 2005,
    August, 9-10; 2005, August, 7 8

80172   **Gold**   Ⓐ
    🔾 0.00   🔾 0.00   Global Days XXX
    AMA: 2005, Aug, 9-10; 2005, Aug, 9-10; 2005, Aug, 7-8; 2005,
    Aug, 7-8; 2005, Jul, 11-12; 2005, Jul, 11-12; 2005, July, 11-12;
    2005, August, 9-10; 2005, August, 7-8

80173   **Haloperidol**   Ⓐ
    🔾 0.00   🔾 0.00   Global Days XXX
    AMA: 2005, Jul, 11-12; 2005, Jul, 11-12; 2005, Aug, 9-10; 2005,
    Aug, 9-10; 2005, Aug, 7-8; 2005, Aug, 7-8; 2005, July, 11-12; 2005,
    August, 9-10; 2005, August, 7-8

80174   **Imipramine**   Ⓐ
    🔾 0.00   🔾 0.00   Global Days XXX
    AMA: 2005, Aug, 9-10; 2005, Aug, 9-10; 2005, Aug, 7-8; 2005,
    Aug, 7-8; 2005, Jul, 11-12; 2005, Jul, 11-12; 2005, July, 11-12;
    2005, August, 9-10; 2005, August, 7-8

80176   **Lidocaine**   Ⓐ
    🔾 0.00   🔾 0.00   Global Days XXX
    AMA: 2005, Aug, 7-8; 2005, Aug, 7-8; 2005, Aug, 9-10; 2005, Aug,
    9-10; 2005, Jul, 11-12; 2005, Jul, 11-12; 2005, July, 11-12; 2005,
    August, 9-10; 2005, August, 7-8

80178   **Lithium**   Ⓐ ❌
    🔾 0.00   🔾 0.00   Global Days XXX
    AMA: 2005, Aug, 7-8; 2005, Aug, 7-8; 2005, Aug, 9-10; 2005, Aug,
    9-10; 2005, Jul, 11-12; 2005, Jul, 11-12; 2005, July, 11-12; 2005,
    August, 9-10; 2005, August, 7-8

80182   **Nortriptyline**   Ⓐ
    🔾 0.00   🔾 0.00   Global Days XXX
    AMA: 2005, Aug, 9-10; 2005, Aug, 9-10; 2005, Aug, 7-8; 2005,
    Aug, 7-8; 2005, Jul, 11-12; 2005, Jul, 11-12; 2005, July, 11-12;
    2005, August, 9-10; 2005, August, 7-8

80184   **Phenobarbital**   Ⓐ
    🔾 0.00   🔾 0.00   Global Days XXX
    AMA: 2005, Jul, 11-12; 2005, Jul, 11-12; 2005, Aug, 7-8; 2005,
    Aug, 7-8; 2005, Aug, 9-10; 2005, Aug, 9 10; 2005, July, 11-12;
    2005, August, 9-10; 2005, August, 7-8

80185   **Phenytoin; total**   Ⓐ
    🔾 0.00   🔾 0.00   Global Days XXX
    AMA: 2005, Aug, 9-10; 2005, Aug, 9-10; 2005, Jul, 11-12; 2005,
    Jul, 11-12; 2005, Aug, 7-8; 2005, Aug, 7-8; 2005, July, 11-12; 2005,
    August, 9-10; 2005, August, 7-8

80186   **free**   Ⓐ
    🔾 0.00   🔾 0.00   Global Days XXX
    AMA: 2005, Aug, 9-10; 2005, Aug, 9-10; 2005, Aug, 7-8; 2005,
    Aug, 7-8; 2005, Jul, 11-12; 2005, Jul, 11-12; 2005, July, 11-12;
    2005, August, 9-10; 2005, August, 7-8

80188   **Primidone**   Ⓐ
    🔾 0.00   🔾 0.00   Global Days XXX
    AMA: 2005, Jul, 11-12; 2005, Jul, 11-12; 2005, Aug, 7-8; 2005,
    Aug, 7-8; 2005, Aug, 9-10; 2005, Aug, 9-10; 2005, July, 11-12;
    2005, August, 9-10; 2005, August, 7-8

80190   **Procainamide;**   Ⓐ
    🔾 0.00   🔾 0.00   Global Days XXX
    AMA: 2005, Aug, 7-8; 2005, Aug, 7-8; 2005, Aug, 9-10; 2005, Aug,
    9-10; 2005, Jul, 11-12; 2005, Jul, 11-12; 2005, July, 11-12; 2005,
    August, 9-10; 2005, August, 7-8

80192   **with metabolites (eg, n-acetyl procainamide)**   Ⓐ ▫
    🔾 0.00   🔾 0.00   Global Days XXX
    AMA: 2005, Aug, 9-10; 2005, Aug, 9-10; 2005, Aug, 7 8; 2005,
    Aug, 7-8; 2005, Jul, 11-12; 2005, Jul, 11-12; 2005, July, 11-12;
    2005, August, 9-10; 2005, August, 7-8

80194   **Quinidine**   Ⓐ
    🔾 0.00   🔾 0.00   Global Days XXX
    AMA: 2005, Aug, 9-10; 2005, Aug, 9-10; 2005, Aug, 7-8; 2005,
    Aug, 7-8; 2005, Jul, 11-12; 2005, Jul, 11-12; 2005, July, 11-12;
    2005, August, 9-10; 2005, August, 7-8

80195   **Sirolimus**   Ⓐ
    🔾 0.00   🔾 0.00   Global Days XXX
    AMA: 2006, Mar, 6-9; 2006, Mar, 6-9; 2006, March, 6-9; 2005,
    Aug, 9-10; 2005, Aug, 9-10; 2005, August, 7-8; 2005, August,
    9-10; 2005, Aug, 7-8; 2005, Aug, 7-8

80196   **Salicylate**   Ⓐ
    🔾 0.00   🔾 0.00   Global Days XXX
    AMA: 2005, Jul, 11-12; 2005, Jul, 11-12; 2005, Aug, 9-10; 2005,
    Aug, 9-10; 2005, Aug, 7-8; 2005, Aug, 7-8; 2005, July, 11-12; 2005,
    August, 9-10; 2005, August, 7-8

80197   **Tacrolimus**   Ⓐ
    🔾 0.00   🔾 0.00   Global Days XXX
    AMA: 2005, Jul, 11-12; 2005, Jul, 11-12; 2005, Aug, 7-8; 2005,
    Aug, 7-8; 2005, Aug, 9-10; 2005, Aug, 9-10; 2005, August, 9-10;
    2005, August, 7-8; 2005, July, 11-12

80198   **Theophylline**   Ⓐ
    🔾 0.00   🔾 0.00   Global Days XXX
    AMA: 2005, Jul, 11-12; 2005, Jul, 11-12; 2005, Aug, 7-8; 2005,
    Aug, 7 8; 2005, Aug, 9-10; 2005, Aug, 9-10, 2005, July, 11-12;
    2005, August, 9-10; 2005, August, 7-8

80200   **Tobramycin**   Ⓐ
    🔾 0.00   🔾 0.00   Global Days XXX
    AMA: 2005, Aug, 9-10; 2005, Aug, 9-10; 2005, Aug, 7-8; 2005,
    Aug, 7-8; 2005, Jul, 11-12; 2005, Jul, 11-12; 2005, July, 11-12;
    2005, August, 9 10; 2005, August, 7-8

80201   **Topiramate**   Ⓐ
    🔾 0.00   🔾 0.00   Global Days XXX
    AMA: 2005, Aug, 7-8; 2005, Aug, 7-8; 2005, Aug, 9-10; 2005, Aug,
    9-10; 2005, Jul, 11-12; 2005, Jul, 11-12; 2005, July, 11-12; 2005,
    August, 9-10; 2005, August, 7-8

80202   **Vancomycin**   Ⓐ
    🔾 0.00   🔾 0.00   Global Days XXX
    AMA: 2005, Aug, 9-10; 2005, Aug, 9-10; 2005, Jul, 11-12; 2005,
    Jul, 11-12; 2005, Aug, 7-8; 2005, Aug, 7-8; 2005, July, 11-12; 2005,
    August, 9-10; 2005, August, 7-8

80299   **Quantitation of drug, not elsewhere specified**   Ⓐ
    🔾 0.00   🔾 0.00   Global Days XXX
    AMA: 2008, Jan, 10-25; 2007, Jan, 13-27; 2007, Jan, 13-27; 2007,
    January, 13-27; 2005, Aug, 9-10; 2005, Aug, 9-10; 2005, Aug,
    7-8; 2005, Aug, 7-8; 2005, July, 11-12; 2005, August, 7-8; 2005,
    August, 9-10; 2005, Jul, 11-12; 2005, Jul, 11-12; 2004, Oct, 14;
    2004, October, 14; 2004, Oct, 14

80400-80440 Stimulation and Suppression Test Panels

CMS *100-4,3,10.4*　*Payment of Nonphysician Services for Inpatients*
CMS *100-2,15,80*　*Physician Supervision Requirements for Diagnostic Tests*
EXCLUDES *administration of evocative or suppressive material (96365-96368, 96372-96376, C8957)*
evocative or suppression test substances (99070, J0120-J7599)
physician monitoring and attendance during the test (see Evaluation and Management codes)

80400　**ACTH stimulation panel; for adrenal insufficiency**　Ⓐ▯
　　INCLUDES　cortisol x 2 (82533)

　　🚑 0.00　🔧 0.00　**Global Days XXX**
　　AMA: 2005, Jul, 11-12; 2005, Jul, 11-12; 2005, Aug, 9-10; 2005, Aug, 9-10; 2005, Aug, 7-8; 2005, Aug, 7-8; 2005, July, 11-12; 2005, August, 9-10; 2005, August, 7-8

80402　**for 21 hydroxylase deficiency**　Ⓐ▯
　　INCLUDES　17 hydroxyprogesterone X 2 (83498)
　　　　　　cortisol x 2 (82533)

　　🚑 0.00　🔧 0.00　**Global Days XXX**
　　AMA: 2005, Aug, 7-8; 2005, Aug, 7-8; 2005, Jul, 11-12; 2005, Jul, 11-12; 2005, Aug, 9-10; 2005, Aug, 9-10; 2005, July, 11-12; 2005, August, 9-10; 2005, August, 7-8

80406　**for 3 beta-hydroxydehydrogenase deficiency**　Ⓐ▯
　　INCLUDES　17 hydroxypregnenolone x 2 (84143)
　　　　　　cortisol x 2 (82533)

　　🚑 0.00　🔧 0.00　**Global Days XXX**
　　AMA: 2005, Aug, 9-10; 2005, Aug, 9-10; 2005, Aug, 7-8; 2005, Aug, 7-8; 2005, Jul, 11-12; 2005, Jul, 11-12; 2005, July, 11-12; 2005, August, 9-10; 2005, August, 7-8

80408　**Aldosterone suppression evaluation panel (eg, saline infusion)**　Ⓐ▯
　　INCLUDES　aldosterone x 2 (82088)
　　　　　　renin x 2 (84244)

　　🚑 0.00　🔧 0.00　**Global Days XXX**
　　AMA: 2005, Aug, 9-10; 2005, Aug, 9-10; 2005, Aug, 7-8; 2005, Aug, 7-8; 2005, Jul, 11-12; 2005, Jul, 11-12; 2005, July, 11-12; 2005, August, 9-10; 2005, August, 7-8

80410　**Calcitonin stimulation panel (eg, calcium, pentagastrin)**　Ⓐ▯
　　INCLUDES　calcitonin x 3 (82308)

　　🚑 0.00　🔧 0.00　**Global Days XXX**
　　AMA: 2005, Aug, 9-10; 2005, Aug, 9-10; 2005, Aug, 7-8; 2005, Aug, 7-8; 2005, Jul, 11-12; 2005, Jul, 11-12; 2005, July, 11-12; 2005, August, 9-10; 2005, August, 7-8

80412　**Corticotropic releasing hormone (CRH) stimulation panel**　Ⓐ▯
　　INCLUDES　adrenocorticotropic hormone (ACTH) x 6 (82024)
　　　　　　cortisol x 6 (82533)

　　🚑 0.00　🔧 0.00　**Global Days XXX**
　　AMA: 2005, Aug, 9-10; 2005, Aug, 9-10; 2005, Jul, 11-12; 2005, Jul, 11-12; 2005, Aug, 7-8; 2005, Aug, 7-8; 2005, July, 11-12; 2005, August, 9-10; 2005, August, 7-8

80414　**Chorionic gonadotropin stimulation panel; testosterone response**　♀Ⓐ▯
　　INCLUDES　testosterone x 2 on three pooled blood samples (84403)

　　🚑 0.00　🔧 0.00　**Global Days XXX**
　　AMA: 2005, Jul, 11-12; 2005, Jul, 11-12; 2005, Aug, 7-8; 2005, Aug, 7-8; 2005, Aug, 9-10; 2005, Aug, 9-10; 2005, July, 11-12; 2005, August, 7-8; 2005, August, 9-10

80415　**estradiol response**　Ⓐ▯
　　INCLUDES　estradiol x 2 on three pooled blood samples (82670)

　　🚑 0.00　🔧 0.00　**Global Days XXX**
　　AMA: 2005, Aug, 9-10; 2005, Aug, 9-10; 2005, Aug, 7-8; 2005, Aug, 7-8; 2005, Jul, 11-12; 2005, Jul, 11-12; 2005, August, 9-10; 2005, August, 7-8

80416　**Renal vein renin stimulation panel (eg, captopril)**　Ⓐ▯
　　INCLUDES　renin x 6 (84244)

　　🚑 0.00　🔧 0.00　**Global Days XXX**
　　AMA: 2005, Aug, 7-8; 2005, Aug, 7-8; 2005, Jul, 11-12; 2005, Jul, 11-12; 2005, Aug, 9-10; 2005, Aug, 9-10; 2005, July, 11-12; 2005, August, 9-10; 2005, August, 7-8

80417　**Peripheral vein renin stimulation panel (eg, captopril)**　Ⓐ▯
　　INCLUDES　renin x 2 (84244)

　　🚑 0.00　🔧 0.00　**Global Days XXX**
　　AMA: 2005, Aug, 7-8; 2005, Aug, 7-8; 2005, Aug, 9-10; 2005, Aug, 9-10; 2005, Jul, 11-12; 2005, Jul, 11-12; 2005, July, 11-12; 2005, August, 9-10; 2005, August, 7-8

80418　**Combined rapid anterior pituitary evaluation panel**　Ⓐ▯
　　INCLUDES　adrenocorticotropic hormone (ACTH) x 4 (82024)
　　　　　　cortisol x 4 (82533)
　　　　　　follicle stimulating hormone (FSH) x 4 (83001)
　　　　　　human growth hormone x 4 (83003)
　　　　　　luteinizing hormone (LH) x 4 (83002)
　　　　　　prolactin x 4 (84146)
　　　　　　thyroid stimulating hormone (TSH) x 4 (84443)

　　🚑 0.00　🔧 0.00　**Global Days XXX**
　　AMA: 2005, Aug, 9-10; 2005, Aug, 9-10; 2005, Aug, 7-8; 2005, Aug, 7-8; 2005, Jul, 11-12; 2005, Jul, 11-12; 2005, July, 11-12; 2005, August, 9-10; 2005, August, 7-8

80420　**Dexamethasone suppression panel, 48 hour**　Ⓐ▯
　　INCLUDES　cortisol x 2 (82533)
　　　　　　free cortisol, urine x 2 (82530)
　　　　　　volume measurement for timed collection x 2 (81050)

　　EXCLUDES　*single dose dexamethasone (82533)*

　　🚑 0.00　🔧 0.00　**Global Days XXX**
　　AMA: 2005, Aug, 9-10; 2005, Aug, 9-10; 2005, Aug, 7-8; 2005, Aug, 7-8; 2005, Jul, 11-12; 2005, Jul, 11-12; 2005, July, 11-12; 2005, August, 9-10; 2005, August, 7-8

80422　**Glucagon tolerance panel; for insulinoma**　Ⓐ▯
　　INCLUDES　glucose x 3 (82947)
　　　　　　insulin x 3 (83525)

　　🚑 0.00　🔧 0.00　**Global Days XXX**
　　AMA: 2005, Aug, 9-10; 2005, Aug, 9-10; 2005, Aug, 7-8; 2005, Aug, 7-8; 2005, Jul, 11-12; 2005, Jul, 11-12; 2005, July, 11-12; 2005, August, 9-10; 2005, August, 7-8

80424　**for pheochromocytoma**　Ⓐ▯
　　INCLUDES　catecholamines, fractionated x 2 (82384)

　　🚑 0.00　🔧 0.00　**Global Days XXX**
　　AMA: 2005, Aug, 7-8; 2005, Aug, 7-8; 2005, Jul, 11-12; 2005, Jul, 11-12; 2005, Aug, 9-10; 2005, Aug, 9-10; 2005, July, 11-12; 2005, August, 9-10; 2005, August, 7-8

80426 Gonadotropin releasing hormone stimulation panel ⓐ▢
INCLUDES follicle stimulating hormone (FSH) x 4 (83001)
luteinizing hormone (LH) x 4 (83002)

💲 0.00 ✎ 0.00 Global Days XXX
AMA: 2005, Jul, 11-12; 2005, Jul, 11-12; 2005, Aug, 9-10; 2005, Aug, 9-10; 2005, Aug, 7-8; 2005, Aug, 7-8; 2005, July, 11-12; 2005, August, 9-10; 2005, August, 7-8

80428 Growth hormone stimulation panel (eg, arginine infusion, l-dopa administration) ⓐ▢
INCLUDES human growth hormone (HGH) x 4 (83003)

💲 0.00 ✎ 0.00 Global Days XXX
AMA: 2005, Aug, 9-10; 2005, Aug, 9-10; 2005, Aug, 7-8; 2005, Aug, 7-8; 2005, Jul, 11-12; 2005, Jul, 11-12; 2005, July, 11-12; 2005, August, 9-10; 2005, August, 7-8

80430 Growth hormone suppression panel (glucose administration) ⓐ▢
INCLUDES glucose x 3 (82947)
human growth hormone (HGH) x 4 (83003)

💲 0.00 ✎ 0.00 Global Days XXX
AMA: 2005, Jul, 11-12; 2005, Jul, 11-12; 2005, Aug, 7-8, 2005, Aug, 7-8; 2005, Aug, 9-10; 2005, Aug, 9-10; 2005, July, 11-12; 2005, August, 9-10; 2005, August, 7-8

80432 Insulin-induced C-peptide suppression panel ⓐ▢
INCLUDES C-peptide x 5 (84681)
glucose x 5 (82947)
insulin (83525)

💲 0.00 ✎ 0.00 Global Days XXX
AMA: 2005, Aug, 9-10; 2005, Aug, 9-10; 2005, Jul, 11-12; 2005, Jul, 11-12; 2005, Aug, 7-8; 2005, Aug, 7-8; 2005, July, 11-12; 2005, August, 9-10; 2005, August, 7-8

80434 Insulin tolerance panel; for ACTH insufficiency ⓐ▢
INCLUDES cortisol x 5 (82533)
glucose x 5 (82947)

💲 0.00 ✎ 0.00 Global Days XXX
AMA: 2005, Aug, 9-10; 2005, Aug, 9-10; 2005, Aug, 7-8; 2005, Aug, 7-8; 2005, Jul, 11-12; 2005, Jul, 11-12; 2005, July, 11-12; 2005, August, 9-10; 2005, August, 7-8

80435 for growth hormone deficiency ⓐ▢
INCLUDES glucose x 5 (82947)
human growth hormone (HGH) x 5 (83003)

💲 0.00 ✎ 0.00 Global Days XXX
AMA: 2005, Aug, 9-10; 2005, Aug, 9-10; 2005, Aug, 7-8; 2005, Aug, 7-8; 2005, Jul, 11-12; 2005, Jul, 11-12; 2005, July, 11-12; 2005, August, 7-8; 2005, August, 9-10

80436 Metyrapone panel ⓐ▢
INCLUDES 11 deoxycortisol x 2 (82634)
cortisol x 2 (82533)

💲 0.00 ✎ 0.00 Global Days XXX
AMA: 2005, Jul, 11-12; 2005, Jul, 11-12; 2005, Aug, 7-8; 2005, Aug, 7-8; 2005, Aug, 9-10; 2005, Aug, 9-10; 2005, August, 9-10; 2005, August, 7-8; 2005, July, 11-12

80438 Thyrotropin releasing hormone (TRH) stimulation panel; 1 hour ⓐ▢
INCLUDES thyroid stimulating hormone (TSH) x 3 (84443)

💲 0.00 ✎ 0.00 Global Days XXX
AMA: 2005, Jul, 11-12; 2005, Jul, 11-12; 2005, Aug, 9-10; 2005, Aug, 9-10; 2005, Aug, 7-8; 2005, Aug, 7-8; 2005, July, 11-12; 2005, August, 7-8

80439 2 hour ⓐ▢
INCLUDES thyroid stimulating hormone (TSH) x 4 (84443)

💲 0.00 ✎ 0.00 Global Days XXX
AMA: 2005, Jul, 11-12; 2005, Jul, 11-12; 2005, Aug, 9-10; 2005, Aug, 9-10; 2005, Aug, 7-8; 2005, Aug, 7-8; 2005, July, 11-12; 2005, August, 9-10; 2005, August, 7-8

80440 for hyperprolactinemia ⓐ▢
INCLUDES prolactin x 3 (84146)

💲 0.00 ✎ 0.00 Global Days XXX
AMA: 2005, Jul, 11-12; 2005, Jul, 11-12; 2005, Aug, 7-8; 2005, Aug, 7-8; 2005, Aug, 9-10; 2005, Aug, 9-10; 2005, July, 11-12; 2005, August, 9-10; 2005, August, 7-8

80500-80502 Consultation By Clinical Pathologist

CMS *100-4,12,60* *Payment for Pathology Services*
CMS *100-4,3,10.4* *Payment of Nonphysician Services for Inpatients*
CMS *100-2,15,80* *Physician Supervision Requirements for Diagnostic Tests*
INCLUDES pharmacokinetic consultations
written report by pathologist for tests requiring additional medical judgement

EXCLUDES *consultations that include examination of the patient (99241-99255)*

80500 Clinical pathology consultation; limited, without review of patient's history and medical records ⊠ ⑧₀ ▢
💲 0.50 ✎ 0.57 Global Days XXX
AMA: 2005, Jul, 11-12; 2005, Jul, 11-12; 2005, Aug, 9-10; 2005, Aug, 9-10; 2005, Aug, 7-8; 2005, Aug, 7-8; 2005, August, 9-10; 2005, August, 7-8; 2005, July, 11-12

80502 comprehensive, for a complex diagnostic problem, with review of patient's history and medical records ⊠ ⑧₀ ▢
💲 1.74 ✎ 1.78 Global Days XXX
AMA: 2005, Aug, 9-10; 2005, Aug, 9-10; 2005, Aug, 7-8; 2005, Aug, 7-8; 2005, Jul, 11-12; 2005, Jul, 11-12; 2005, July, 11-12; 2005, August, 9-10; 2005, August, 7-8

81000-81099 Urine Tests

CMS *100-4,3,10.4* *Payment of Nonphysician Services for Inpatients*
CMS *100-2,15,80* *Physician Supervision Requirements for Diagnostic Tests*

81000 Urinalysis, by dip stick or tablet reagent for bilirubin, glucose, hemoglobin, ketones, leukocytes, nitrite, pH, protein, specific gravity, urobilinogen, any number of these constituents; non-automated, with microscopy ⓐ▢
💲 0.00 ✎ 0.00 Global Days XXX
AMA: 2005, Aug, 7-8; 2005, Aug, 7-8; 2005, Aug, 9-10; 2005, Aug, 9-10; 2005, Jul, 11-12; 2005, Jul, 11-12; 2005, July, 11-12; 2005, August, 9-10; 2005, August, 7-8

81001 automated, with microscopy ⓐ▢
💲 0.00 ✎ 0.00 Global Days XXX
AMA: 2005, Aug, 9-10; 2005, Aug, 9-10; 2005, Jul, 11-12; 2005, Jul, 11-12; 2005, Aug, 7-8; 2005, Aug, 7-8; 2005, July, 11-12; 2005, August, 9-10; 2005, August, 7-8

81002 non-automated, without microscopy ⓐ▢⊠
INCLUDES Mosenthal test
💲 0.00 ✎ 0.00 Global Days XXX
AMA: 2007, Apr, 1-2; 2007, Apr, 1-2; 2007, April, 1-2; 2005, Aug, 7-8; 2005, Aug, 7-8; 2005, Jul, 11-12; 2005, August, 7-8; 2005, August, 9-10; 2005, July, 11-12; 2005, Jul, 11-12; 2005, Aug, 9-10; 2005, Aug, 9-10

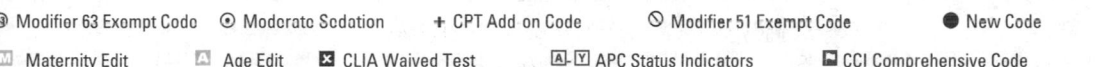

81003 automated, without microscopy [A] [▣] [✕]
 �ⁿ 0.00 ⚕ 0.00 Global Days XXX
 AMA: 2007, Apr, 1-2; 2007, Apr, 1-2; 2007, April, 1-2; 2005, Aug, 9-10; 2005, Aug, 9-10; 2005, Aug, 7-8; 2005, August, 7-8; 2005, July, 11-12; 2005, August, 9-10; 2005, Aug, 7-8; 2005, Jul, 11-12; 2005, Jul, 11-12

81005 Urinalysis; qualitative or semiquantitative, except immunoassays [A] [▣]
 INCLUDES Benedict test for dextrose
 EXCLUDES immunoassay, qualitative or semiquantitative (83518)
 microalbumin (82043-82044)
 nonimmunoassay reagent strip analysis (81000, 81002)

 �ⁿ 0.00 ⚕ 0.00 Global Days XXX
 AMA: 2005, Jul, 11-12; 2005, Jul, 11-12; 2005, Aug, 9-10; 2005, Aug, 9-10; 2005, Aug, 7-8; 2005, Aug, 7-8; 2005, July, 11-12; 2005, August, 9-10; 2005, August, 7-8

81007 bacteriuria screen, except by culture or dipstick [A] [▣] [✕]
 EXCLUDES culture (87086-87088)
 dipstick (81000-81002)

 �ⁿ 0.00 ⚕ 0.00 Global Days XXX
 AMA: 2005, Aug, 9-10; 2005, Aug, 9-10; 2005, Aug, 7-8; 2005, Aug, 7-8; 2005, Jul, 11-12; 2005, Jul, 11-12; 2005, July, 11-12; 2005, August, 9-10; 2005, August, 7-8

81015 microscopic only [A]
 EXCLUDES sperm evaluation for retrograde ejaculation (89331)

 �ⁿ 0.00 ⚕ 0.00 Global Days XXX
 AMA: 2008, Apr, 5-7; 2008, Apr, 5-7; 2008, Apr, 5-7; 2005, Aug, 9-10; 2005, Aug, 9-10; 2005, July, 11-12; 2005, August, 7-8; 2005, August, 9-10; 2005, Aug, 7-8; 2005, Aug, 7-8; 2005, Jul, 11-12; 2005, Jul, 11-12

81020 2 or 3 glass test [A] [▣]
 INCLUDES Valentine's test

 �ⁿ 0.00 ⚕ 0.00 Global Days XXX
 AMA: 2005, Aug, 7-8; 2005, Aug, 7-8; 2005, Jul, 11-12; 2005, Jul, 11-12; 2005, Aug, 9-10; 2005, Aug, 9-10; 2005, July, 11-12; 2005, August, 7-8; 2005, August, 9-10

81025 Urine pregnancy test, by visual color comparison methods [M] [♀] [A] [✕]
 🔿 0.00 ⚕ 0.00 Global Days XXX
 AMA: 2005, Aug, 7-8; 2005, Aug, 7-8; 2005, Jul, 11-12; 2005, Jul, 11-12; 2005, Aug, 9-10; 2005, Aug, 9-10; 2005, July, 11-12; 2005, August, 9-10; 2005, August, 7-8

81050 Volume measurement for timed collection, each [A]
 🔿 0.00 ⚕ 0.00 Global Days XXX
 AMA: 2005, Aug, 7-8; 2005, Aug, 7-8; 2005, Aug, 9-10; 2005, Aug, 9-10; 2005, Jul, 11-12; 2005, Jul, 11-12; 2005, July, 11-12; 2005, August, 9-10; 2005, August, 7-8

81099 Unlisted urinalysis procedure [A]
 🔿 0.00 ⚕ 0.00 Global Days XXX
 AMA: 2005, Aug, 9-10; 2005, Aug, 9-10; 2005, Jul, 11-12; 2005, Jul, 11-12; 2005, Aug, 7-8; 2005, Aug, 7-8; 2005, July, 11-12; 2005, August, 9-10; 2005, August, 7-8

82000-82030 Chemistry: Acetaldehyde--Adenosine

CMS 100-4,3,10.4   *Payment of Nonphysician Services for Inpatients*
CMS 100-2,15,80   *Physician Supervision Requirements for Diagnostic Tests*
INCLUDES mathematically calculated results
 quantitative analysis unless otherwise specified
 specimens from any source unless otherwise specified

EXCLUDES *organ or disease panels (80048-80076)*
 therapeutic drug assays (80150-80299)

82000 Acetaldehyde, blood [A]
 🔿 0.00 ⚕ 0.00 Global Days XXX
 AMA: 2005, Aug, 9-10; 2005, Aug, 9-10; 2005, Aug, 7-8; 2005, Aug, 7-8; 2005, Jul, 11-12; 2005, Jul, 11-12; 2005, July, 11-12; 2005, August, 9-10; 2005, August, 7-8

82003 Acetaminophen [A]
 🔿 0.00 ⚕ 0.00 Global Days XXX
 AMA: 2005, Aug, 9-10; 2005, Aug, 9-10; 2005, Aug, 7-8; 2005, Aug, 7-8; 2005, Jul, 11-12; 2005, Jul, 11-12; 2005, August, 9-10; 2005, August, 7-8; 2005, July, 11-12

82009 Acetone or other ketone bodies, serum; qualitative [A]
 🔿 0.00 ⚕ 0.00 Global Days XXX
 AMA: 2005, Jul, 11-12; 2005, Jul, 11-12; 2005, Aug, 9-10; 2005, Aug, 9-10; 2005, Aug, 7-8; 2005, Aug, 7-8; 2005, July, 11-12; 2005, August, 9-10; 2005, August, 7-8

82010 quantitative [A] [✕]
 🔿 0.00 ⚕ 0.00 Global Days XXX
 AMA: 2005, Jul, 11-12; 2005, Jul, 11-12; 2005, Aug, 7-8; 2005, Aug, 7-8; 2005, Aug, 9-10; 2005, Aug, 9-10; 2005, July, 11-12; 2005, August, 9-10; 2005, August, 7-8

82013 Acetylcholinesterase [A]
 🔿 0.00 ⚕ 0.00 Global Days XXX
 AMA: 2005, Aug, 9-10; 2005, Aug, 9-10; 2005, Aug, 7-8; 2005, Aug, 7-8; 2005, Jul, 11-12; 2005, Jul, 11-12; 2005, July, 11-12; 2005, August, 9-10; 2005, August, 7-8

82016 Acylcarnitines; qualitative, each specimen [A]
 🔿 0.00 ⚕ 0.00 Global Days XXX
 AMA: 2005, Aug, 9-10; 2005, Aug, 9-10; 2005, Aug, 7-8; 2005, Aug, 7-8; 2005, Jul, 11-12; 2005, Jul, 11-12; 2005, July, 11-12; 2005, August, 9-10; 2005, August, 7-8

82017 quantitative, each specimen [A] [▣]
 🔿 0.00 ⚕ 0.00 Global Days XXX
 AMA: 2005, Aug, 7-8; 2005, Aug, 7-8; 2005, Aug, 9-10; 2005, Aug, 9-10; 2005, Jul, 11-12; 2005, Jul, 11-12; 2005, July, 11-12; 2005, August, 9-10; 2005, August, 7-8

82024 Adrenocorticotropic hormone (ACTH) [A] [▣]
 🔿 0.00 ⚕ 0.00 Global Days XXX
 AMA: 2005, Jul, 11-12; 2005, Jul, 11-12; 2005, Aug, 9-10; 2005, Aug, 9-10; 2005, Aug, 7-8; 2005, Aug, 7-8; 2005, July, 11-12; 2005, August, 9-10; 2005, August, 7-8

82030 Adenosine, 5-monophosphate, cyclic (cyclic AMP) [A]
 🔿 0.00 ⚕ 0.00 Global Days XXX
 AMA: 2005, Aug, 9-10; 2005, Aug, 9-10; 2005, Aug, 7-8; 2005, Aug, 7-8; 2005, Jul, 11-12; 2005, Jul, 11-12; 2005, July, 11-12; 2005, August, 9-10; 2005, August, 7-8

Pathology and Laboratory

82040 — 82120

82040-82045 Chemistry: Albumin

CMS *100-3,190.10*   *Laboratory Tests--CRD Patients*
CMS *100-4,3,10.4*   *Payment of Nonphysician Services for Inpatients*
CMS *100-2,15,80*   *Physician Supervision Requirements for Diagnostic Tests*
INCLUDES   mathematically calculated results
   quantitative analysis unless otherwise specified
   specimens from any other sources unless otherwise specified

EXCLUDES   *organ or disease panels (80048-80076)*
   therapeutic drug assays (80150-80299)

▲ **82040**   **Albumin; serum, plasma or whole blood**   [A]
    0.00   0.00   **Global Days XXX**
    AMA: 2005, Jul, 11-12; 2005, Jul, 11-12; 2005, Aug, 9-10; 2005, Aug, 9-10; 2005, Aug, 7-8; 2005, Aug, 7-8; 2005, July, 11-12; 2005, August, 9-10; 2005, August, 7-8

82042   **urine or other source, quantitative, each specimen**   [A] [X]
    0.00   0.00   **Global Days XXX**
    AMA: 2005, Aug, 7-8; 2005, Aug, 7-8; 2005, Jul, 11-12; 2005, Jul, 11-12; 2005, Aug, 9-10; 2005, Aug, 9-10; 2005, July, 11-12; 2005, August, 7-8; 2005, August, 9-10

82043   **urine, microalbumin, quantitative**   [A] [▪]
    0.00   0.00   **Global Days XXX**
    AMA: 2005, Aug, 9-10; 2005, Aug, 9-10; 2005, Aug, 7-8; 2005, Aug, 7-8; 2005, Jul, 11-12; 2005, Jul, 11-12; 2005, July, 11-12; 2005, August, 9-10; 2005, August, 7-8

82044   **urine, microalbumin, semiquantitative (eg, reagent strip assay)**   [A] [X]
    EXCLUDES   *prealbumin (84134)*
    0.00   0.00   **Global Days XXX**
    AMA: 2008, Jan, 10-25; 2007, Jan, 13-27; 2007, Jan, 13-27; 2007, January, 13-27; 2005, Aug, 9-10; 2005, Aug, 9-10; 2005, Aug, 7-8; 2005, August, 9-10; 2005, August, 7-8; 2005, July, 11-12; 2005, Aug, 7-8; 2005, Jul, 11-12; 2005, Jul, 11-12

82045   **ischemia modified**   [A]
    0.00   0.00   **Global Days XXX**
    AMA: 2005, Aug, 9-10; 2005, Aug, 9-10; 2005, Jul, 11-12; 2005, Jul, 11-12; 2005, Aug, 7-8; 2005, Aug, 7-8; 2005, July, 11-12; 2005, August, 9-10; 2005, August, 7-8

82055-82107 Chemistry: Alcohol--Alpha-fetoprotein (AFP)

CMS *100-4,3,10.4*   *Payment of Nonphysician Services for Inpatients*
CMS *100-2,15,80*   *Physician Supervision Requirements for Diagnostic Tests*
INCLUDES   mathematically calculated results
   quantitative analysis unless otherwise specified
   specimens from any source unless otherwise specified

EXCLUDES   *organ or disease panels (80048-80076)*
   therapeutic drug assays (80150-80299)

82055   **Alcohol (ethanol); any specimen except breath**   [A] [X]
    EXCLUDES   *other types of alcohols, volatiles (84600)*
    0.00   0.00   **Global Days XXX**
    AMA: 2005, Jul, 11-12; 2005, Jul, 11-12; 2005, Aug, 9-10; 2005, Aug, 9-10; 2005, Aug, 7-8; 2005, Aug, 7-8; 2005, July, 11-12; 2005, August, 9-10; 2005, August, 7-8

82075   **breath**   [A]
    0.00   0.00   **Global Days XXX**
    AMA: 2005, Aug, 7-8; 2005, Aug, 7-8; 2005, Jul, 11-12; 2005, Jul, 11-12; 2005, Aug, 9-10; 2005, Aug, 9-10; 2005, July, 11-12; 2005, August, 9-10; 2005, August, 7-8

82085   **Aldolase**   [A]
    0.00   0.00   **Global Days XXX**
    AMA: 2005, Aug, 9-10; 2005, Aug, 9-10; 2005, Aug, 7-8; 2005, Aug, 7-8; 2005, Jul, 11-12; 2005, Jul, 11-12; 2005, July, 11-12; 2005, August, 9-10; 2005, August, 7-8

82088   **Aldosterone**   [A] [▪]
    0.00   0.00   **Global Days XXX**
    AMA: 2005, Aug, 9-10; 2005, Aug, 9-10; 2005, Jul, 11-12; 2005, Jul, 11-12; 2005, Aug, 7-8; 2005, Aug, 7-8; 2005, July, 11-12; 2005, August, 9-10; 2005, August, 7-8

82101   **Alkaloids, urine, quantitative**   [A]
    0.00   0.00   **Global Days XXX**
    AMA: 2005, Aug, 7-8; 2005, Aug, 7-8; 2005, Aug, 9-10; 2005, Aug, 9-10; 2005, Jul, 11-12; 2005, Jul, 11-12; 2005, July, 11-12; 2005, August, 9-10; 2005, August, 7-8

82103   **Alpha-1-antitrypsin; total**   [A]
    0.00   0.00   **Global Days XXX**
    AMA: 2005, Jul, 11-12; 2005, Jul, 11-12; 2005, Aug, 9-10; 2005, Aug, 9-10; 2005, Aug, 7-8; 2005, Aug, 7-8; 2005, July, 11-12; 2005, August, 9-10; 2005, August, 7-8

82104   **phenotype**   [A]
    0.00   0.00   **Global Days XXX**
    AMA: 2005, Aug, 9-10; 2005, Aug, 9-10; 2005, Jul, 11-12; 2005, Jul, 11-12; 2005, Aug, 7-8; 2005, July, 11-12; 2005, August, 9-10; 2005, August, 7-8

82105   **Alpha-fetoprotein (AFP); serum**   [A] [▪]
    0.00   0.00   **Global Days XXX**
    AMA: 2005, Aug, 7-8; 2005, Aug, 7-8; 2005, Jul, 11-12; 2005, Jul, 11-12; 2005, Aug, 9-10; 2005, Aug, 9-10; 2005, July, 11-12; 2005, August, 9-10; 2005, August, 7-8

82106   **amniotic fluid**   [M] [♀] [A] [▪]
    0.00   0.00   **Global Days XXX**
    AMA: 2005, Jul, 11-12; 2005, Jul, 11-12; 2005, Aug, 9-10; 2005, Aug, 9-10; 2005, Aug, 7-8; 2005, Aug, 7-8; 2005, July, 11-12; 2005, August, 9-10; 2005, August, 7-8

82107   **AFP-L3 fraction isoform and total AFP (including ratio)**   [A]
    0.00   0.00   **Global Days XXX**

82108 Chemistry: Aluminum

CMS *100-3,190.10*   *Laboratory Tests--CRD Patients*
CMS *100-4,3,10.4*   *Payment of Nonphysician Services for Inpatients*
CMS *100-2,15,80*   *Physician Supervision Requirements for Diagnostic Tests*
INCLUDES   mathematically calculated results
   quantitative analysis unless otherwise specified
   specimens from any source unless otherwise specified

EXCLUDES   *organ or disease panels (80048-80076)*
   therapeutic drug assays (80150-80299)

82108   **Aluminum**   [A]
    0.00   0.00   **Global Days XXX**
    AMA: 2005, Aug, 7-8; 2005, Aug, 7-8; 2005, Aug, 9-10; 2005, Aug, 9-10; 2005, Jul, 11-12; 2005, Jul, 11-12; 2005, July, 11-12; 2005, August, 7-8; 2005, August, 9-10

82120-82261 Chemistry: Amines--Biotinidase

CMS *100-4,3,10.4*   *Payment of Nonphysician Services for Inpatients*
CMS *100-2,15,80*   *Physician Supervision Requirements for Diagnostic Tests*
INCLUDES   mathematically calculated results
   quantitative analysis unless otherwise specified
   specimens from any source unless otherwise specified

EXCLUDES   *organ or disease panels (80048-80076)*
   therapeutic drug assays (80150-80299)

82120   **Amines, vaginal fluid, qualitative**   [♀] [A] [K]
    EXCLUDES   *combined pH and amines test for vaginitis (82120, 83986)*
    0.00   0.00   **Global Days XXX**
    AMA: 2005, Aug, 9-10; 2005, Aug, 9-10; 2005, Jul, 11-12; 2005, Jul, 11-12; 2005, Aug, 7-8; 2005, Aug, 7-8; 2005, July, 11-12; 2005, August, 9-10; 2005, August, 7-8

⊕ Modifier 63 Exempt Code   ⊙ Moderate Sedation   + CPT Add-on Code   ⊘ Modifier 51 Exempt Code   ● New Code   ▲ Revised Code

[M] Maternity Edit   [A] Age Edit   [X] CLIA Waived Test   [A]-[Y] APC Status Indicators   [▪] CCI Comprehensive Code   [50] Bilateral Procedure

© 2008 Ingenix *(Blue Ink)*   CPT only © 2008 American Medical Association. All Rights Reserved. (Black Ink)   Medicare *(Red Ink)*   **321**

82127 Amino acids; single, qualitative, each specimen [A]
0.00   0.00 Global Days XXX
AMA: 2005, Aug, 9-10; 2005, Aug, 9-10; 2005, Aug, 7-8; 2005, Aug, 7-8; 2005, Jul, 11-12; 2005, Jul, 11-12; 2005, July, 11-12; 2005, August, 9-10; 2005, August, 7-8

82128 multiple, qualitative, each specimen [A] [□]
0.00   0.00 Global Days XXX
AMA: 2005, Aug, 7-8; 2005, Aug, 7-8; 2005, Aug, 9-10; 2005, Aug, 9-10; 2005, Jul, 11-12; 2005, Jul, 11-12; 2005, August, 7-8; 2005, July, 11-12; 2005, August, 9-10

82131 single, quantitative, each specimen [A] [□]
INCLUDES   Van Slyke method

0.00   0.00 Global Days XXX
AMA: 2008, Jan, 10-25; 2007, Jan, 13-27; 2007, Jan, 13-27; 2007, January, 13-27; 2005, Aug, 9-10; 2005, Aug, 9-10; 2005, Aug, 7-8; 2005, July, 11-12; 2005, August, 9-10; 2005, August, 7-8; 2005, Aug, 7-8; 2005, Jul, 11-12; 2005, Jul, 11-12

82135 Aminolevulinic acid, delta (ALA) [A]
0.00   0.00 Global Days XXX
AMA: 2005, Aug, 7-8; 2005, Aug, 7-8; 2005, Aug, 9-10; 2005, Aug, 9-10; 2005, Jul, 11-12; 2005, Jul, 11-12; 2005, August, 7-8; 2005, July, 11-12; 2005, August, 9-10

82136 Amino acids, 2 to 5 amino acids, quantitative, each specimen [A] [□]
0.00   0.00 Global Days XXX
AMA: 2005, Aug, 7-8; 2005, Aug, 7-8; 2005, Aug, 9-10; 2005, Aug, 9-10; 2005, Jul, 11-12; 2005, Jul, 11-12; 2005, August, 7-8; 2005, July, 11-12; 2005, August, 9-10

82139 Amino acids, 6 or more amino acids, quantitative, each specimen [A] [□]
0.00   0.00 Global Days XXX
AMA: 2005, Aug, 9-10; 2005, Aug, 9-10; 2005, Jul, 11-12; 2005, Jul, 11-12; 2005, Aug, 7-8; 2005, Aug, 7-8; 2005, August, 7-8; 2005, July, 11-12; 2005, August, 9-10

82140 Ammonia [A]
0.00   0.00 Global Days XXX
AMA: 2005, Aug, 7-8; 2005, Aug, 7-8; 2005, Aug, 9-10; 2005, Aug, 9-10; 2005, Jul, 11-12; 2005, Jul, 11-12; 2005, August, 7-8; 2005, July, 11-12; 2005, August, 9-10

82143 Amniotic fluid scan (spectrophotometric) [M] [♀] [A]
EXCLUDES   L/S ratio (83661)

0.00   0.00 Global Days XXX
AMA: 2005, Jul, 11-12; 2005, Jul, 11-12; 2005, Aug, 7-8; 2005, Aug, 7-8; 2005, Aug, 9-10; 2005, Aug, 9-10; 2005, August, 7-8; 2005, July, 11-12; 2005, August, 9-10

82145 Amphetamine or methamphetamine [A]
EXCLUDES   qualitative testing (80100-80103)

0.00   0.00 Global Days XXX
AMA: 2005, Aug, 7-8; 2005, Aug, 7-8; 2005, Jul, 11-12; 2005, Jul, 11-12; 2005, Aug, 9-10; 2005, Aug, 9-10; 2005, August, 7-8; 2005, July, 11-12; 2005, August, 9-10

82150 Amylase [A] [✕]
0.00   0.00 Global Days XXX
AMA: 2005, Aug, 7-8; 2005, Aug, 7-8; 2005, Aug, 9-10; 2005, Aug, 9-10; 2005, Jul, 11-12; 2005, Jul, 11-12; 2005, August, 7-8; 2005, July, 11-12; 2005, August, 9-10

82154 Androstanediol glucuronide [A]
0.00   0.00 Global Days XXX
AMA: 2005, Aug, 9-10; 2005, Aug, 9-10; 2005, Jul, 11-12; 2005, Jul, 11-12; 2005, Aug, 7-8; 2005, Aug, 7-8; 2005, August, 9-10; 2005, July, 11-12; 2005, August, 7-8

82157 Androstenedione [A]
0.00   0.00 Global Days XXX
AMA: 2005, Aug, 7-8; 2005, Aug, 7-8; 2005, Aug, 9-10; 2005, Aug, 9-10; 2005, Jul, 11-12; 2005, Jul, 11-12; 2005, August, 7-8; 2005, July, 11-12; 2005, August, 9-10

82160 Androsterone [A]
0.00   0.00 Global Days XXX
AMA: 2005, Aug, 9-10; 2005, Aug, 9-10; 2005, Jul, 11-12; 2005, Jul, 11-12; 2005, Aug, 7-8; 2005, Aug, 7-8; 2005, August, 7-8; 2005, July, 11-12; 2005, August, 9-10

82163 Angiotensin II [A]
0.00   0.00 Global Days XXX
AMA: 2005, Aug, 7-8; 2005, Aug, 7-8; 2005, Aug, 9-10; 2005, Aug, 9-10; 2005, Jul, 11-12; 2005, Jul, 11-12; 2005, August, 9-10; 2005, July, 11-12

82164 Angiotensin I - converting enzyme (ACE) [A]
0.00   0.00 Global Days XXX
AMA: 2005, Aug, 9-10; 2005, Aug, 9-10; 2005, Jul, 11-12; 2005, Jul, 11-12; 2005, Aug, 7-8; 2005, Aug, 7-8; 2005, July, 11-12; 2005, August, 9-10

82172 Apolipoprotein, each [A]
0.00   0.00 Global Days XXX
AMA: 2005, Aug, 7-8; 2005, Aug, 7-8; 2005, Jul, 11-12; 2005, Jul, 11-12; 2005, Aug, 9-10; 2005, Aug, 9-10; 2005, August, 7-8; 2005, July, 11-12; 2005, August, 9-10

82175 Arsenic [A]
EXCLUDES   heavy metal screening (83015)

0.00   0.00 Global Days XXX
AMA: 2005, Aug, 9-10; 2005, Aug, 9-10; 2005, Aug, 7-8; 2005, Aug, 7-8; 2005, Jul, 11-12; 2005, Jul, 11-12; 2005, August, 7-8; 2005, July, 11-12; 2005, August, 9-10

82180 Ascorbic acid (Vitamin C), blood [A] [□]
0.00   0.00 Global Days XXX
AMA: 2005, Jul, 11-12; 2005, Jul, 11-12; 2005, Aug, 9-10; 2005, Aug, 9-10; 2005, Aug, 7-8; 2005, Aug, 7-8; 2005, August, 7-8; 2005, July, 11-12; 2005, August, 9-10

82190 Atomic absorption spectroscopy, each analyte [A]
0.00   0.00 Global Days XXX
AMA: 2005, Aug, 7-8; 2005, Aug, 7-8; 2005, Aug, 9-10; 2005, Aug, 9-10; 2005, Jul, 11-12; 2005, Jul, 11-12; 2005, August, 7-8; 2005, July, 11-12; 2005, August, 9-10

82205 Barbiturates, not elsewhere specified [A]
EXCLUDES   qualitative analysis (80100-80103)

0.00   0.00 Global Days XXX
AMA: 2005, Aug, 7-8; 2005, Aug, 7-8; 2005, Aug, 9-10; 2005, Aug, 9-10; 2005, Jul, 11-12; 2005, Jul, 11-12; 2005, August, 7-8; 2005, July, 11-12; 2005, August, 9-10

82232 Beta-2 microglobulin [A]
0.00   0.00 Global Days XXX
AMA: 2005, Jul, 11-12; 2005, Jul, 11-12; 2005, Aug, 9-10; 2005, Aug, 9-10; 2005, Aug, 7-8; 2005, Aug, 7-8; 2005, August, 7-8; 2005, July, 11-12; 2005, August, 9-10

82239 Bile acids; total [A]
0.00   0.00 Global Days XXX
AMA: 2005, Aug, 9-10; 2005, Aug, 9-10; 2005, Aug, 7-8; 2005, Aug, 7-8; 2005, Jul, 11-12; 2005, Jul, 11-12; 2005, August, 7-8; 2005, July, 11-12; 2005, August, 9-10

82240 cholylglycine [A]
EXCLUDES   bile pigments, urine (81000-81005)

0.00   0.00 Global Days XXX
AMA: 2005, Aug, 7-8; 2005, Aug, 7-8; 2005, Aug, 9-10; 2005, Aug, 9-10; 2005, Jul, 11-12; 2005, Jul, 11-12; 2005, July, 11-12; 2005, August, 9-10; 2005, August, 7-8

---

[26]/[TC] Professional/Technical Component Only   [80]/[80] Assist-at-Surgery Allowed/With Documentation   Unlisted   Not Covered   ⊠ Radiology crosswalk

MED: Pub 100/NCD References   **AMA:** CPT Assistant References   [A2]-[Z3] ASC Payment Indicator   ♂Male Only   ♀Female Only   ⊠ Laboratory crosswalk

322   CPT only © 2008 American Medical Association. All Rights Reserved. (Black Ink)   Medicare (Red Ink)   © 2008 Ingenix (Blue Ink)

82247 Bilirubin; total [A] [X]

INCLUDES Van Den Bergh test

📖 0.00 ✂ 0.00 Global Days XXX

AMA: 2005, Aug, 7-8; 2005, Aug, 7-8; 2005, Jul, 11-12; 2005, Jul, 11-12; 2005, Aug, 9-10; 2005, Aug, 9-10; 2005, August, 7-8; 2005, July, 11-12; 2005, August, 9-10

82248 direct [A]

📖 0.00 ✂ 0.00 Global Days XXX

AMA: 2005, Aug, 7-8; 2005, Aug, 7-8; 2005, Aug, 9-10; 2005, Aug, 9-10; 2005, Jul, 11-12; 2005, Jul, 11-12; 2005, August, 7-8; 2005, August, 9-10; 2005, July, 11-12

82252 feces, qualitative [A]

📖 0.00 ✂ 0.00 Global Days XXX

AMA: 2005, Jul, 11-12; 2005, Jul, 11-12; 2005, Aug, 9-10; 2005, Aug, 9-10; 2005, Aug, 7-8; 2005, Aug, 7-8; 2005, August, 7-8; 2005, July, 11-12; 2005, August, 9-10

82261 Biotinidase, each specimen [A]

📖 0.00 ✂ 0.00 Global Days XXX

AMA: 2005, Jul, 11-12; 2005, Jul, 11-12; 2005, Aug, 7-8; 2005, Aug, 7-8; 2005, Aug, 9-10; 2005, Aug, 9-10; 2005, August, 7-8; 2005, July, 11-12; 2005, August, 9-10

82270-82274 Chemistry: Occult Blood

CMS *100-3,190.34*   *Fecal Occult BloodTest (FOBT)*
CMS *100-4,18,60.6*   *Billing for Colorectal Screening Services*
CMS *100-4,18,60.2.1*   *Common Working File Edits: Colorectal Screening*
CMS *100-4,18,60.2*   *Frequency and Age Requirements for Colorectal Screening*
CMS *100-4,18,60.1*   *Payment for Colorectal Screening Services*
CMS *100-4,18,60*   *Colorectal Cancer Screening*
CMS *100-4,3,10.4*   *Payment of Nonphysician Services for Inpatients*
CMS *100-2,15,80*   *Physician Supervision Requirements for Diagnostic Tests*

INCLUDES mathematically calculated results
quantitative analysis unless otherwise specified
specimens from any source unless otherwise specified

EXCLUDES *organ or disease panels (80048-80076)*
therapeutic drug assays (80150-80299)

82270 Blood, occult, by peroxidase activity (eg, guaiac), qualitative; feces, consecutive collected specimens with single determination, for colorectal neoplasm screening (ie, patient was provided 3 cards or single triple card for consecutive collection) [A] [X]

INCLUDES Day test

📖 0.00 ✂ 0.00 Global Days XXX

AMA: 2008, Apr, 5-7; 2008, Apr, 5-7; 2008, Apr, 5-7; 2008, Jan, 10-25; 2007, Jan, 13-27; 2007, Jan, 13-27; 2007, January, 13-27; 2006, Feb, 7-9; 2006, Feb, 7-9; 2006, February, 7-9; 2005, Aug, 9-10; 2005, August, 9-10; 2005, July, 11-12; 2005, Aug, 9-10; 2005, Jul, 11-12; 2005, Jul, 11-12; 2005, August, 7-8; 2005, Aug, 7-8; 2005, Aug, 7-8

82271 other sources [A] [X]

📖 0.00 ✂ 0.00 Global Days XXX

AMA: 2006, Feb, 7-9; 2006, Feb, 7-9; 2006, February, 7-9; 2005, Aug, 7-8; 2005, Aug, 7-8; 2005, August, 9-10; 2005, August, 7-8; 2005, Aug, 9-10; 2005, Aug, 9-10

82272 Blood, occult, by peroxidase activity (eg, guaiac), qualitative, feces, 1-3 simultaneous determinations, performed for other than colorectal neoplasm screening [A] [X]

📖 0.00 ✂ 0.00 Global Days XXX

AMA: 2008, Apr, 5-7; 2008, Apr, 5-7; 2008, Apr, 5-7; 2006, Feb, 7-9; 2006, Feb, 7-9; 2006, February, 7-9; 2005, Aug, 7-8; 2005, August, 9-10; 2005, Aug, 7-8; 2005, Aug, 9-10; 2005, August, 7-8; 2005, Aug, 9-10

82274 Blood, occult, by fecal hemoglobin determination by immunoassay, qualitative, feces, 1-3 simultaneous determinations [A] [CCI] [X]

📖 0.00 ✂ 0.00 Global Days XXX

AMA: 2005, Aug, 9-10; 2005, Aug, 9-10; 2005, Jul, 11-12; 2005, Jul, 11-12; 2005, Aug, 7-8; 2005, Aug, 7-8; 2005, August, 7-8; 2005, July, 11-12; 2005, August, 9-10

82286-82308 Chemistry: Bradykinin--Calcitonin

CMS *100-4,3,10.4*   *Payment of Nonphysician Services for Inpatients*
CMS *100-2,15,80*   *Physician Supervision Requirements for Diagnostic Tests*

INCLUDES mathematically calculated results
quantitative analysis unless otherwise specified
specimens from any source unless otherwise specified

EXCLUDES *organ or disease panels (80048-80076)*
therapeutic drug assays (80150-80299)

82286 Bradykinin [A]

📖 0.00 ✂ 0.00 Global Days XXX

AMA: 2005, Jul, 11-12; 2005, Jul, 11-12; 2005, Aug, 9-10; 2005, Aug, 9-10; 2005, Aug, 7-8; 2005, Aug, 7-8; 2005, July, 11-12; 2005, August, 7-8; 2005, August, 9-10

82300 Cadmium [A]

📖 0.00 ✂ 0.00 Global Days XXX

AMA: 2005, Aug, 9-10; 2005, Aug, 9-10; 2005, Aug, 7-8; 2005, Aug, 7-8; 2005, Jul, 11-12; 2005, Jul, 11-12; 2005, July, 11-12; 2005, August, 7-8; 2005, August, 9-10

82306 Calcifediol (25-OH Vitamin D-3) [A] [CCI]

📖 0.00 ✂ 0.00 Global Days XXX

AMA: 2005, Jul, 11-12; 2005, Jul, 11-12; 2005, Aug, 9-10; 2005, Aug, 9-10; 2005, Aug, 7-8; 2005, Aug, 7-8; 2005, July, 11-12; 2005, August, 7-8; 2005, August, 9-10

82307 Calciferol (Vitamin D) [A] [CCI]

EXCLUDES *1, 25-Dihydroxyvitamin D (82652)*

📖 0.00 ✂ 0.00 Global Days XXX

AMA: 2005, Aug, 9-10; 2005, Aug, 9-10; 2005, Aug, 7-8; 2005, Aug, 7-8; 2005, Jul, 11-12; 2005, Jul, 11-12; 2005, August, 9-10; 2005, July, 11-12; 2005, August, 7-8

82308 Calcitonin [A] [CCI]

📖 0.00 ✂ 0.00 Global Days XXX

AMA: 2005, Aug, 7-8; 2005, Aug, 7-8; 2005, Aug, 9-10; 2005, Aug, 9-10; 2005, Jul, 11-12; 2005, Jul, 11-12; 2005, August, 9-10; 2005, July, 11-12; 2005, August, 7-8

82310 Chemistry: Total Calcium

CMS *100-3,190.10*   *Laboratory Tests--CRD Patients*
CMS *100-4,3,10.4*   *Payment of Nonphysician Services for Inpatients*
CMS *100-2,15,80*   *Physician Supervision Requirements for Diagnostic Tests*

INCLUDES mathematically calculated results
quantitative analysis unless otherwise specified
specimens from any source unless otherwise specified

EXCLUDES *organ or disease panels (80048-80076)*
therapeutic drug assays (80150-80299)

82310 Calcium; total [A] [CCI]

📖 0.00 ✂ 0.00 Global Days XXX

AMA: 2005, Jul, 11-12; 2005, Jul, 11-12; 2005, Aug, 9-10; 2005, Aug, 9-10; 2005, Aug, 7-8; 2005, Aug, 7-8; 2005, August, 9-10; 2005, August, 7-8; 2005, July, 11-12

⊛ Modifier 63 Exempt Code   ⊙ Moderate Sedation   + CPT Add-on Code   ⊘ Modifier 51 Exempt Code   ● New Code   ▲ Revised Code

Ⓜ Maternity Edit   A Age Edit   X CLIA Waived Test   [A] [Y] APC Status Indicators   CCI Comprehensive Code   50 Bilateral Procedure

82330-82373 Chemistry: Calcium, Ionized--Carbohydrate deficient transferrin

CMS *100-4,3,10.4*   *Payment of Nonphysician Services for Inpatients*
CMS *100-2,15,80*   *Physician Supervision Requirements for Diagnostic Tests*
[INCLUDES]   mathematically calculated results
    quantitative analysis unless otherwise specified
    specimens from any source unless otherwise specified
[EXCLUDES]   *organ or disease panels (80048-80076)*
    therapeutic drug assays (80150-80299)

82330   **Calcium; ionized**   A ✕
    [INCLUDES]   calcium, ionized (82330)

    💰 0.00   0.00   **Global Days XXX**
    AMA: 2005, Aug, 9-10; 2005, Aug, 9-10; 2005, Jul, 11-12; 2005, Jul, 11-12; 2005, Aug, 7-8; 2005, Aug, 7-8; 2005, August, 9-10; 2005, July, 11-12; 2005, August, 7-8

82331   **after calcium infusion test**   A ▭
    💰 0.00   0.00   **Global Days XXX**
    AMA: 2005, Aug, 9-10; 2005, Aug, 9-10; 2005, Jul, 11-12; 2005, Jul, 11-12; 2005, Aug, 7-8; 2005, Aug, 7-8; 2005, July, 11-12; 2005, August, 9-10; 2005, August, 7-8

82340   **urine quantitative, timed specimen**   A
    💰 0.00   0.00   **Global Days XXX**
    AMA: 2005, Jul, 11-12; 2005, Jul, 11-12; 2005, Aug, 7-8; 2005, Aug, 7-8; 2005, Aug, 9-10; 2005, Aug, 9-10; 2005, August, 9-10; 2005, August, 7-8; 2005, July, 11-12

82355   **Calculus; qualitative analysis**   A ▭
    💰 0.00   0.00   **Global Days XXX**
    AMA: 2005, Aug, 9-10; 2005, Aug, 9-10; 2005, Jul, 11-12; 2005, Jul, 11-12; 2005, Aug, 7-8; 2005, Aug, 7-8; 2005, July, 11-12; 2005, August, 9-10; 2005, August, 7-8

82360   **quantitative analysis, chemical**   A ▭
    💰 0.00   0.00   **Global Days XXX**
    AMA: 2005, Jul, 11-12; 2005, Jul, 11-12; 2005, Aug, 9-10; 2005, Aug, 9-10; 2005, Aug, 7-8; 2005, Aug, 7-8; 2005, July, 11-12; 2005, August, 7-8; 2005, August, 9-10

82365   **infrared spectroscopy**   A ▭
    💰 0.00   0.00   **Global Days XXX**
    AMA: 2005, Aug, 9-10; 2005, Aug, 9-10; 2005, Jul, 11-12; 2005, Jul, 11-12; 2005, Aug, 7-8; 2005, Aug, 7-8; 2005, July, 11-12; 2005, August, 9-10; 2005, August, 7-8

82370   **X-ray diffraction**   A ▭
    💰 0.00   0.00   **Global Days XXX**
    AMA: 2005, Aug, 7-8; 2005, Aug, 7-8; 2005, Jul, 11-12; 2005, Jul, 11-12; 2005, Aug, 9-10; 2005, Aug, 9-10; 2005, August, 9-10; 2005, August, 7-8; 2005, July, 11-12

82373   **Carbohydrate deficient transferrin**   A
    💰 0.00   0.00   **Global Days XXX**
    AMA: 2005, Jul, 11-12; 2005, Jul, 11-12; 2005, Aug, 7-8; 2005, Aug, 7-8; 2005, Aug, 9-10; 2005, Aug, 9-10; 2005, August, 9-10; 2005, August, 7-8; 2005, July, 11-12

82374 Chemistry: Carbon Dioxide

CMS *100-3,190.10*   *Laboratory Tests--CRD Patients*
CMS *100-4,3,10.4*   *Payment of Nonphysician Services for Inpatients*
CMS *100-2,15,80*   *Physician Supervision Requirements for Diagnostic Tests*
[INCLUDES]   mathematically calculated results
    quantitative analysis unless otherwise specified
    specimens from any source unless otherwise specified
[EXCLUDES]   *organ or disease panels (80048-80076)*
    therapeutic drug assays (80150-80299)

82374   **Carbon dioxide (bicarbonate)**   A ✕
    [EXCLUDES]   *blood gasses (82803)*

    💰 0.00   0.00   **Global Days XXX**
    AMA: 2005, Aug, 9-10; 2005, Aug, 9-10; 2005, Aug, 7-8; 2005, Aug, 7-8; 2005, Jul, 11-12; 2005, Jul, 11-12; 2005, August, 9-10; 2005, July, 11-12; 2005, August, 7-8

82375-82376 Chemistry: Carboxyhemoglobin (Carbon Monoxide)

CMS *100-4,3,10.4*   *Payment of Nonphysician Services for Inpatients*
CMS *100-2,15,80*   *Physician Supervision Requirements for Diagnostic Tests*
[INCLUDES]   mathematically calculated results
    specimens from any source unless otherwise specified
[EXCLUDES]   *organ or disease panels (80048-80076)*
    transcutaneous measurement of carboxyhemoglobin (88740)

▲ **82375**   **Carboxyhemoglobin; quantitative**   A
    💰 0.00   0.00   **Global Days XXX**
    AMA: 2005, Aug, 9-10; 2005, Aug, 9-10; 2005, Aug, 7-8; 2005, Aug, 7-8; 2005, Jul, 11-12; 2005, Jul, 11-12; 2005, August, 9-10; 2005, August, 7-8; 2005, July, 11-12

▲ **82376**   **qualitative**   A
    [EXCLUDES]   *transcutaneous measurement of carboxyhemoglobin (88740)*

    💰 0.00   0.00   **Global Days XXX**
    AMA: 2005, Jul, 11-12; 2005, Jul, 11-12; 2005, Aug, 7-8; 2005, Aug, 7-8; 2005, Aug, 9-10; 2005, Aug, 9-10; 2005, August, 9-10; 2005, August, 7-8; 2005, July, 11-12

82378 Chemistry: Carcinoembryonic Antigen (CEA)

CMS *100-3,190.26*   *Carcinoembryonic Antigen (CEA)*
CMS *100-4,3,10.4*   *Payment of Nonphysician Services for Inpatients*
CMS *100-2,15,80*   *Physician Supervision Requirements for Diagnostic Tests*

82378   **Carcinoembryonic antigen (CEA)**   A
    💰 0.00   0.00   **Global Days XXX**
    AMA: 2008, Jan, 10-25; 2007, Jan, 13-27; 2007, Jan, 13-27; 2007, January, 13-27; 2005, Jul, 11-12; 2005, Jul, 11-12; 2005, Aug, 9-10; 2005, August, 7-8; 2005, July, 11-12; 2005, August, 9-10; 2005, Aug, 9-10; 2005, Aug, 7-8; 2005, Aug, 7-8

26/TC Professional/Technical Component Only   80/80 Assist-at-Surgery Allowed/With Documentation   Unlisted   Not Covered   Radiology crosswalk
MED: Pub 100/NCD References   **AMA:** CPT Assistant References   A2-23 ASC Payment Indicator   ♂Male Only   ♀Female Only   Laboratory crosswalk

324   CPT only © 2008 American Medical Association. All Rights Reserved. (Black Ink)   Medicare (Red Ink)   © 2008 Ingenix *(Blue Ink)*

82379-82415 Chemistry: Carnitine--Chloramphenicol

CMS *100-4,3,10.4*   *Payment of Nonphysician Services for Inpatients*
CMS *100-2,15,80*   *Physician Supervision Requirements for Diagnostic Tests*
INCLUDES   mathematically calculated results
  quantitative analysis unless otherwise specified
  specimens from any source unless otherwise specified

EXCLUDES   *organ or disease panels (80048-80076)*
  therapeutic drug assays (80150-80299)

82379   **Carnitine (total and free), quantitative, each specimen**   A

    EXCLUDES   *acylcarnitine (82016-82017)*

    0.00   0.00   Global Days XXX
    AMA: 2005, Aug, 9-10; 2005, Aug, 9-10; 2005, Aug, 7-8; 2005, Aug, 7-8; 2005, Jul, 11-12; 2005, Jul, 11-12; 2005, August, 9-10; 2005, August, 7-8; 2005, July, 11-12

82380   **Carotene**   A

    0.00   0.00   Global Days XXX
    AMA: 2005, Aug, 9-10; 2005, Aug, 9-10; 2005, Aug, 7-8; 2005, Aug, 7-8; 2005, Jul, 11-12; 2005, Jul, 11-12; 2005, August, 9-10; 2005, July, 11-12; 2005, August, 7-8

82382   **Catecholamines; total urine**   A

    0.00   0.00   Global Days XXX
    AMA: 2005, Aug, 9-10; 2005, Aug, 9-10; 2005, Jul, 11-12; 2005, Jul, 11-12; 2005, Aug, 7-8; 2005, Aug, 7-8; 2005, August, 9-10; 2005, August, 7-8; 2005, July, 11-12

82383   **blood**   A

    0.00   0.00   Global Days XXX
    AMA: 2005, Aug, 7-8; 2005, Aug, 7-8; 2005, Jul, 11-12; 2005, Jul, 11-12; 2005, Aug, 9-10; 2005, Aug, 9-10; 2005, August, 9-10; August, 7-8; 2005, July, 11-12

82384   **fractionated**   A

    EXCLUDES   *urine metabolites (83835, 84585)*

    0.00   0.00   Global Days XXX
    AMA: 2005, Jul, 11-12; 2005, Jul, 11-12; 2005, Aug, 9-10; 2005, Aug, 7-8; 2005, Aug, 7-8; 2005, August, 9-10; 2005, August, 7-8; 2005, July, 11-12

82387   **Cathepsin-D**   A

    0.00   0.00   Global Days XXX
    AMA: 2005, Aug, 9-10; 2005, Aug, 9-10; 2005, Aug, 7-8; 2005, Aug, 7-8; 2005, Jul, 11-12; 2005, Jul, 11-12; 2005, August, 9-10; 2005, August, 7-8; 2005, July, 11-12

82390   **Ceruloplasmin**   A

    0.00   0.00   Global Days XXX
    AMA: 2005, Aug, 9-10; 2005, Aug, 9-10; 2005, Aug, 7-8; 2005, Aug, 7-8; 2005, Jul, 11-12; 2005, Jul, 11-12; 2005, August, 7-8; 2005, July, 11-12; 2005, August, 9-10

82397   **Chemiluminescent assay**   A

    0.00   0.00   Global Days XXX
    AMA: 2005, Aug, 9-10; 2005, Aug, 9-10; 2005, Aug, 7-8; 2005, Aug, 7-8; 2005, Jul, 11-12; 2005, Jul, 11-12; 2005, August, 9-10; 2005, August, 7-8; 2005, July, 11-12

82415   **Chloramphenicol**   A

    0.00   0.00   Global Days XXX
    AMA: 2005, Jul, 11-12; 2005, Jul, 11-12; 2005, Aug, 9-10; 2005, Aug, 9-10; 2005, Aug, 7-8; 2005, Aug, 7-8; 2005, August, 9-10; 2005, August, 7-8; 2005, July, 11-12

82435-82438 Chemistry: Chloride

CMS *100-3,190.10*   *Laboratory Tests--CRD Patients*
CMS *100-4,3,10.4*   *Payment of Nonphysician Services for Inpatients*
CMS *100-2,15,80*   *Physician Supervision Requirements for Diagnostic Tests*
INCLUDES   mathematically calculated results
  quantitative analysis unless otherwise specified
  specimens from any source unless otherwise specified

EXCLUDES   *organ or disease panels (80048-80076)*
  therapeutic drug assays (80150-80299)

82435   **Chloride; blood**   A X

    0.00   0.00   Global Days XXX
    AMA: 2005, Aug, 9-10; 2005, Aug, 9-10; 2005, Aug, 7-8; 2005, Aug, 7-8; 2005, Jul, 11-12; 2005, Jul, 11-12; 2005, August, 9-10; 2005, August, 7-8; 2005, July, 11-12

82436   **urine**   A

    0.00   0.00   Global Days XXX
    AMA: 2005, Jul, 11-12; 2005, Jul, 11-12; 2005, Aug, 9-10; 2005, Aug, 9-10; 2005, Aug, 7-8; 2005, Aug, 7-8; 2005, August, 9-10; 2005, August, 7-8; 2005, July, 11-12

82438   **other source**   A

    EXCLUDES   *sweat collections by iontophoresis (89230)*

    0.00   0.00   Global Days XXX
    AMA: 2005, Aug, 9-10; 2005, Aug, 9-10; 2005, Jul, 11-12; 2005, Jul, 11-12; 2005, Aug, 7-8; 2005, Aug, 7-8; 2005, August, 9-10; 2005, July, 11-12; 2005, August, 7-8

82441 Chemistry: Chlorinated Hydrocarbons

CMS *100-4,3,10.4*   *Payment of Nonphysician Services for Inpatients*
CMS *100-2,15,80*   *Physician Supervision Requirements for Diagnostic Tests*
INCLUDES   mathematically calculated results
  quantitative analysis unless otherwise specified
  specimens from any source unless otherwise specified

EXCLUDES   *organ or disease panels (80048-80076)*
  therapeutic drug assays (80150-80299)

82441   **Chlorinated hydrocarbons, screen**   A

    EXCLUDES   *chlorpromazine (84022)*
    cholecalciferol (vitamin D) (82307)

    0.00   0.00   Global Days XXX
    AMA: 2005, Jul, 11-12; 2005, Jul, 11-12; 2005, Aug, 9-10; 2005, Aug, 9-10; 2005, Aug, 7-8; 2005, Aug, 7-8; 2005, August, 9-10; 2005, July, 11-12; 2005, August, 7-8

82465 Chemistry: Cholesterol, Total

CMS *100-3,190.23*   *Lipid Testing*
CMS *100-4,3,10.4*   *Payment of Nonphysician Services for Inpatients*
CMS *100-2,15,80*   *Physician Supervision Requirements for Diagnostic Tests*
INCLUDES   mathematically calculated results
  quantitative analysis unless otherwise specified

EXCLUDES   *organ or disease panels (80048-80299)*

82465   **Cholesterol, serum or whole blood, total**   A X

    EXCLUDES   *high density lipoprotein (HDL) (83718)*

    0.00   0.00   Global Days XXX
    AMA: 2008, Jan, 10-25; 2007, Jan, 13-27; 2007, Jan, 13-27; 2007, January, 13-27; 2005, Aug, 9-10; 2005, Aug, 9-10; 2005, Feb, 7-9; 2005, Feb, 7-9; 2005, July, 11-12; 2005, August, 7-8; 2005, February, 7-9; 2005, August, 9-10; 2005, Aug, 7-8; 2005, Aug, 7-8; 2005, Jul, 11-12; 2005, Jul, 11-12

82480-82492 Chemistry: Cholinesterase--Chromatography

INCLUDES mathematically calculated results
quantitative analysis unless otherwise specified
specimens from any source unless otherwise specified

EXCLUDES *organ or disease panels (80048-80076)*
therapeutic drug assays (80048-80299)

82480 Cholinesterase; serum [A]
🔲 0.00 ⚕ 0.00 **Global Days XXX**
AMA: 2005, Aug, 9-10; 2005, Aug, 9-10; 2005, Aug, 7-8; 2005, Aug, 7-8; 2005, Jul, 11-12; 2005, Jul, 11-12; 2005, August, 9-10; 2005, July, 11-12; 2005, August, 7-8

82482 RBC [A]
🔲 0.00 ⚕ 0.00 **Global Days XXX**
AMA: 2005, Jul, 11-12; 2005, Jul, 11-12; 2005, Aug, 9-10; 2005, Aug, 9-10; 2005, Aug, 7-8; 2005, Aug, 7-8; 2005, August, 9-10; 2005, July, 11-12; 2005, August, 7-8

82485 Chondroitin B sulfate, quantitative [A]
🔲 0.00 ⚕ 0.00 **Global Days XXX**
AMA: 2005, Jul, 11-12; 2005, Jul, 11-12; 2005, Aug, 7-8; 2005, Aug, 7-8; 2005, Aug, 9-10; 2005, Aug, 9-10; 2005, August, 9-10; 2005, July, 11-12; 2005, August, 7-8

82486 Chromatography, qualitative; column (eg, gas liquid or HPLC), analyte not elsewhere specified [A]
🔲 0.00 ⚕ 0.00 **Global Days XXX**
AMA: 2005, Aug, 9-10; 2005, Aug, 9-10; 2005, Aug, 7-8; 2005, Aug, 7-8; 2005, Jul, 11-12; 2005, Jul, 11-12; 2005, August, 9-10; 2005, July, 11-12; 2005, August, 7-8

82487 paper, 1-dimensional, analyte not elsewhere specified [A]
🔲 0.00 ⚕ 0.00 **Global Days XXX**
AMA: 2005, Aug, 9-10; 2005, Aug, 9-10; 2005, Aug, 7-8; 2005, Aug, 7-8; 2005, Jul, 11-12; 2005, Jul, 11-12; 2005, August, 9-10; 2005, July, 11-12; 2005, August, 7-8

82488 paper, 2-dimensional, analyte not elsewhere specified [A]
🔲 0.00 ⚕ 0.00 **Global Days XXX**
AMA: 2005, Jul, 11-12; 2005, Jul, 11-12; 2005, Aug, 9-10; 2005, Aug, 9-10; 2005, Aug, 7-8; 2005, Aug, 7-8; 2005, July, 11-12; 2005, August, 7-8; 2005, August, 9-10

82489 thin layer, analyte not elsewhere specified [A]
🔲 0.00 ⚕ 0.00 **Global Days XXX**
AMA: 2005, Aug, 9-10; 2005, Aug, 9-10; 2005, Aug, 7-8; 2005, Aug, 7-8; 2005, Jul, 11-12; 2005, Jul, 11-12; 2005, August, 9-10; 2005, July, 11-12; 2005, August, 7-8

82491 Chromatography, quantitative, column (eg, gas liquid or HPLC); single analyte not elsewhere specified, single stationary and mobile phase [A]
🔲 0.00 ⚕ 0.00 **Global Days XXX**
AMA: 2005, Aug, 9-10; 2005, Aug, 9-10; 2005, Aug, 7-8; 2005, Aug, 7-8; 2005, Jul, 11-12; 2005, Jul, 11-12; 2005, August, 9-10; 2005, August, 7-8; 2005, July, 11-12

82492 multiple analytes, single stationary and mobile phase [A] 🔳
🔲 0.00 ⚕ 0.00 **Global Days XXX**
AMA: 2005, Jul, 11-12; 2005, Jul, 11-12; 2005, Aug, 9-10; 2005, Aug, 9-10; 2005, Aug, 7-8; 2005, Aug, 7-8; 2005, August, 9-10; 2005, August, 7-8; 2005, July, 11-12

82495-82520 Chemistry: Chromium--Cocaine

CMS 100-4,3,10.4 *Payment of Nonphysician Services for Inpatients*
CMS 100-2,15,80 *Physician Supervision Requirements for Diagnostic Tests*
INCLUDES mathematically calculated results
quantitative analysis unless otherwise specified
specimens from any source unless otherwise specified

EXCLUDES *organ or disease panels (80048-80076)*
therapeutic drug assays (80150-80299)

82495 Chromium [A]
🔲 0.00 ⚕ 0.00 **Global Days XXX**
AMA: 2005, Aug, 9-10; 2005, Aug, 9-10; 2005, Aug, 7-8; 2005, Aug, 7-8; 2005, Jul, 11-12; 2005, Jul, 11-12; 2005, August, 9-10; 2005, August, 7-8; 2005, July, 11-12

82507 Citrate [A]
🔲 0.00 ⚕ 0.00 **Global Days XXX**
AMA: 2005, Aug, 9-10; 2005, Aug, 9-10; 2005, Aug, 7-8; 2005, Aug, 7-8; 2005, Jul, 11-12; 2005, Jul, 11-12; 2005, August, 9-10; 2005, August, 7-8; 2005, July, 11-12

82520 Cocaine or metabolite [A]
EXCLUDES *cocaine, qualitative testing (80100-80103)*
🔲 0.00 ⚕ 0.00 **Global Days XXX**
AMA: 2005, Jul, 11-12; 2005, Jul, 11-12; 2005, Aug, 9-10; 2005, Aug, 9-10; 2005, Aug, 7-8; 2005, Aug, 7-8; 2005, August, 9-10; 2005, August, 7-8; 2005, July, 11-12

82523 Chemistry: Collagen Crosslinks, Any Method

CMS 100-3,190.19 *NCD for Collagen Crosslinks, Any Method*
CMS 100-4,3,10.4 *Payment of Nonphysician Services for Inpatients*
CMS 100-2,15,80 *Physician Supervision Requirements for Diagnostic Tests*
INCLUDES mathematically calculated results
quantitative analysis unless otherwise specified
specimens from any source unless otherwise specified

EXCLUDES *organ or disease panels (80048-80076)*
therapeutic drug assays (80150-80299)

82523 Collagen cross links, any method [A] [✗]
🔲 0.00 ⚕ 0.00 **Global Days XXX**
AMA: 2005, Aug, 9-10; 2005, Aug, 9-10; 2005, Aug, 7-8; 2005, Aug, 7-8; 2005, Jul, 11-12; 2005, Jul, 11-12; 2005, August, 9-10; 2005, August, 7-8; 2005, July, 11-12

82525-82946 Chemistry: Copper--Glucagon Tolerance Test

CMS 100-4,3,10.4 *Payment of Nonphysician Services for Inpatients*
CMS 100-2,15,80 *Physician Supervision Requirements for Diagnostic Tests*
INCLUDES mathematically calculated results
quantitative analysis unless otherwise specified
specimens from any source unless otherwise specified

EXCLUDES *organ or disease panels (80048-80076)*
therapeutic drug assays (80150-80299)

82525 Copper [A]
🔲 0.00 ⚕ 0.00 **Global Days XXX**
AMA: 2005, Aug, 7-8; 2005, Aug, 7-8; 2005, Jul, 11-12; 2005, Jul, 11-12; 2005, Aug, 9-10; 2005, Aug, 9-10; 2005, August, 9-10; 2005, July, 11-12; 2005, August, 7-8

82528 Corticosterone [A]
INCLUDES Porter-Silber test
🔲 0.00 ⚕ 0.00 **Global Days XXX**
AMA: 2005, Aug, 9-10; 2005, Aug, 9-10; 2005, Aug, 7-8; 2005, Aug, 7-8; 2005, Jul, 11-12; 2005, Jul, 11-12; 2005, August, 9-10; 2005, August, 7-8; 2005, July, 11-12

82633

Pathology and Laboratory

82530 — 82633

82530 Cortisol; free
🚗 0.00 ⚕ 0.00 Global Days XXX Ⓐ ▣
AMA: 2005, Aug, 7-8; 2005, Aug, 7-8; 2005, Aug, 9-10; 2005, Aug, 9-10; 2005, Jul, 11-12; 2005, Jul, 11-12; 2005, August, 9-10; 2005, August, 7-8; 2005, July, 11-12

82533 total
🚗 0.00 ⚕ 0.00 Global Days XXX Ⓐ ▣
AMA: 2005, Aug, 9-10; 2005, Aug, 9-10; 2005, Aug, 7-8; 2005, Aug, 7-8; 2005, Jul, 11-12; 2005, Jul, 11-12; 2005, August, 9-10; 2005, August, 7-8; 2005, July, 11-12

82540 Creatine
🚗 0.00 ⚕ 0.00 Global Days XXX Ⓐ
AMA: 2005, Aug, 9-10; 2005, Aug, 9-10; 2005, Aug, 7-8; 2005, Aug, 7-8; 2005, Jul, 11-12; 2005, Jul, 11-12; 2005, August, 9-10; 2005, August, 7-0; 2005, July, 11-12

82541 Column chromatography/mass spectrometry (eg, GC/MS, or HPLC/MS), analyte not elsewhere specified; qualitative, single stationary and mobile phase Ⓐ
🚗 0.00 ⚕ 0.00 Global Days XXX
AMA: 2005, Aug, 9-10; 2005, Aug, 9-10; 2005, Jul, 11-12; 2005, Jul, 11-12; 2005, Aug, 7-8; 2005, Aug, 7-8; 2005, August, 7-8; 2005, July, 11-12; 2005, August, 9-10

82542 quantitative, single stationary and mobile phase Ⓐ
🚗 0.00 ⚕ 0.00 Global Days XXX
AMA: 2005, Aug, 7-8; 2005, Aug, 7-8; 2005, Aug, 9-10; 2005, Aug, 9-10; 2005, Jul, 11-12; 2005, Jul, 11-12; 2005, August, 9-10, 2005, August, 7-8; 2005, July, 11-12

82543 stable isotope dilution, single analyte, quantitative, single stationary and mobile phase Ⓐ
🚗 0.00 ⚕ 0.00 Global Days XXX
AMA: 2005, Aug, 7-8; 2005, Aug, 7-8; 2005, Jul, 11-12; 2005, Jul, 11-12; 2005, Aug, 9-10; 2005, Aug, 9-10; 2005, August, 9-10; 2005, August, 7-8; 2005, July, 11-12

82544 stable isotope dilution, multiple analytes, quantitative, single stationary and mobile phase Ⓐ ▣
🚗 0.00 ⚕ 0.00 Global Days XXX
AMA: 2005, Aug, 9-10; 2005, Aug, 9-10; 2005, Jul, 11-12; 2005, Jul, 11-12; 2005, Aug, 7-8; 2005, Aug, 7-8; 2005, August, 9-10; 2005, August, 7-8; 2005, July, 11-12

82550 Creatine kinase (CK), (CPK); total Ⓐ ▣
🚗 0.00 ⚕ 0.00 Global Days XXX
AMA: 2005, Aug, 9-10; 2005, Aug, 9-10; 2005, Aug, 7-8; 2005, Aug, 7-8; 2005, Jul, 11-12; 2005, Jul, 11-12; 2005, August, 9-10; 2005, August, 7-8; 2005, July, 11-12

82552 isoenzymes Ⓐ ▣
🚗 0.00 ⚕ 0.00 Global Days XXX
AMA: 2005, Aug, 9-10; 2005, Aug, 9-10; 2005, Jul, 11-12; 2005, Jul, 11-12; 2005, Aug, 7-8; 2005, Aug, 7-8; 2005, August, 9-10; 2005, August, 7-8; 2005, July, 11-12

82553 MB fraction only Ⓐ ▣
🚗 0.00 ⚕ 0.00 Global Days XXX
AMA: 2005, Aug, 7-8; 2005, Aug, 7-8; 2005, Jul, 11-12; 2005, Jul, 11-12; 2005, Aug, 9-10; 2005, Aug, 9-10; 2005, August, 9-10; 2005, August, 7-8; 2005, July, 11-12

82554 isoforms Ⓐ ▣
🚗 0.00 ⚕ 0.00 Global Days XXX
AMA: 2005, Jul, 11-12; 2005, Jul, 11-12; 2005, Aug, 7-8; 2005, Aug, 7-8; 2005, Aug, 9-10; 2005, Aug, 9-10; 2005, August, 9-10; 2005, August, 7-8; 2005, July, 11-12

82565 Creatinine; blood Ⓐ
🚗 0.00 ⚕ 0.00 Global Days XXX
AMA: 2005, Aug, 9-10; 2005, Aug, 9-10; 2005, Aug, 7-8; 2005, Aug, 7-8; 2005, Jul, 11-12; 2005, Jul, 11-12; 2005, August, 9-10; 2005, July, 11-12; 2005, August, 7-8

82570 other source Ⓐ ▣
🚗 0.00 ⚕ 0.00 Global Days XXX
AMA: 2005, Aug, 9-10; 2005, Aug, 9-10; 2005, Aug, 7-8; 2005, Aug, 7-8; 2005, Jul, 11-12; 2005, Jul, 11-12; 2005, August, 9-10; 2005, July, 11-12; 2005, August, 7-8

82575 clearance Ⓐ ▣
INCLUDES   Holten test
🚗 0.00 ⚕ 0.00 Global Days XXX
AMA: 2005, Aug, 9-10; 2005, Aug, 9-10; 2005, Jul, 11-12; 2005, Jul, 11-12; 2005, Aug, 7-8; 2005, Aug, 7-8; 2005, August, 9-10; 2005, July, 11-12; 2005, August, 7-8

82585 Cryofibrinogen Ⓐ
🚗 0.00 ⚕ 0.00 Global Days XXX
AMA: 2005, Jul, 11-12; 2005, Jul, 11-12; 2005, Aug, 7-8; 2005, Aug, 7-8; 2005, Aug, 9-10; 2005, Aug, 9-10; 2005, August, 9-10; 2005, July, 11-12; 2005, August, 7-8

82595 Cryoglobulin, qualitative or semi-quantitative (eg, cryocrit) Ⓐ
EXCLUDES   quantitative, cryoglobulin (82784-82785)
🚗 0.00 ⚕ 0.00 Global Days XXX
AMA: 2005, Aug, 9-10; 2005, Aug, 9-10; 2005, Jul, 11-12; 2005, Jul, 11-12; 2005, Aug, 7-8; 2005, Aug, 7-8; 2005, August, 9-10; 2005, July, 11-12; 2005, August, 7-8

82600 Cyanide Ⓐ
🚗 0.00 ⚕ 0.00 Global Days XXX
AMA: 2005, Aug, 7-8; 2005, Aug, 7-8; 2005, Jul, 11-12; 2005, Jul, 11-12; 2005, Aug, 9-10; 2005, Aug, 9-10; 2005, August, 9-10; 2005, August, 7-8; 2005, July, 11-12

82607 Cyanocobalamin (Vitamin B-12); Ⓐ ▣
🚗 0.00 ⚕ 0.00 Global Days XXX
AMA: 2005, Aug, 9-10; 2005, Aug, 9-10; 2005, Aug, 7-8; 2005, Aug, 7-8; 2005, Jul, 11-12; 2005, Jul, 11-12; 2005, July, 11-12; 2005, August, 7-8; 2005, August, 9-10

82608 unsaturated binding capacity Ⓐ
🚗 0.00 ⚕ 0.00 Global Days XXX
AMA: 2005, Aug, 9-10; 2005, Aug, 9-10; 2005, Jul, 11-12; 2005, Jul, 11-12; 2005, Aug, 7-8; 2005, Aug, 7-8; 2005, August, 9-10; 2005, July, 11-12; 2005, August, 7-8

82610 Cystatin C Ⓐ
🚗 0.00 ⚕ 0.00 Global Days XXX
AMA: 2008, Apr, 5-7; 2008, Apr, 5-7; 2008, Apr, 5-7

82615 Cystine and homocystine, urine, qualitative Ⓐ
🚗 0.00 ⚕ 0.00 Global Days XXX
AMA: 2005, Jul, 11-12; 2005, Jul, 11-12; 2005, Aug, 7-8; 2005, Aug, 7-8; 2005, Aug, 9-10; 2005, Aug, 9-10; 2005, August, 9-10; 2005, July, 11-12; 2005, August, 7-8

82626 Dehydroepiandrosterone (DHEA) Ⓐ
🚗 0.00 ⚕ 0.00 Global Days XXX
AMA: 2005, Aug, 7-8; 2005, Aug, 7-8; 2005, Jul, 11-12; 2005, Jul, 11-12; 2005, Aug, 9-10; 2005, Aug, 9-10; 2005, August, 9-10; July, 11-12; 2005, August, 7-8

82627 Dehydroepiandrosterone-sulfate (DHEA-S) Ⓐ
🚗 0.00 ⚕ 0.00 Global Days XXX
AMA: 2005, Jul, 11-12; 2005, Jul, 11-12; 2005, Aug, 7-8; 2005, Aug, 7-8; 2005, Aug, 9-10; 2005, Aug, 9-10; 2005, August, 9-10; 2005, July, 11-12; 2005, August, 7-8

82633 Desoxycorticosterone, 11- Ⓐ
🚗 0.00 ⚕ 0.00 Global Days XXX
AMA: 2005, Aug, 7-8; 2005, Aug, 7-8; 2005, Jul, 11-12; 2005, Jul, 11-12; 2005, Aug, 9-10; 2005, Aug, 9-10; 2005, August, 9-10; 2005, August, 7-8; 2005, July, 11-12

⊕ Modifier 63 Exempt Code ☉ Moderate Sedation + CPT Add-on Code ⊘ Modifier 51 Exempt Code ● New Code ▲ Revised Code
Ⓜ Maternity Edit Ⓐ Age Edit ▣ CLIA Waived Test Ⓐ Ⓨ APC Status Indicators ▢ CCI Comprehensive Code 50 Bilateral Procedure

82634 **Deoxycortisol, 11-** [A] [▪]
0.00 0.00 **Global Days XXX**
AMA: 2005, Aug, 9-10; 2005, Aug, 9-10; 2005, Aug, 7-8; 2005, Aug, 7-8; 2005, Jul, 11-12; 2005, Jul, 11-12; 2005, August, 9-10; 2005, August, 7-8; 2005, July, 11-12

82638 **Dibucaine number** [A]
0.00 0.00 **Global Days XXX**
AMA: 2005, Aug, 9-10; 2005, Aug, 9-10; 2005, Jul, 11-12; 2005, Jul, 11-12; 2005, Aug, 7-8; 2005, Aug, 7-8; 2005, August, 9-10; 2005, July, 11-12; 2005, August, 7-8

82646 **Dihydrocodeinone** [A]
EXCLUDES *qualitative testing (80100-80103)*

0.00 0.00 **Global Days XXX**
AMA: 2005, Aug, 9-10; 2005, Aug, 9-10; 2005, Jul, 11-12; 2005, Jul, 11-12; 2005, Aug, 7-8; 2005, Aug, 7-8; 2005, August, 9-10; 2005, August, 7-8; 2005, July, 11-12

82649 **Dihydromorphinone** [A]
EXCLUDES *qualitative testing (80100-80103)*

0.00 0.00 **Global Days XXX**
AMA: 2005, Aug, 9-10; 2005, Aug, 9-10; 2005, Jul, 11-12; 2005, Jul, 11-12; 2005, Aug, 7-8; 2005, Aug, 7-8; 2005, August, 9-10; 2005, July, 11-12; 2005, August, 7-8

82651 **Dihydrotestosterone (DHT)** [A]
0.00 0.00 **Global Days XXX**
AMA: 2005, Aug, 7-8; 2005, Aug, 7-8; 2005, Jul, 11-12; 2005, Jul, 11-12; 2005, Aug, 9-10; 2005, Aug, 9-10; 2005, August, 9-10; 2005, July, 11-12; 2005, August, 7-8

82652 **Dihydroxyvitamin D, 1, 25-** [A] [▪]
0.00 0.00 **Global Days XXX**
AMA: 2005, Jul, 11-12; 2005, Jul, 11-12; 2005, Aug, 7-8; 2005, Aug, 7-8; 2005, Aug, 9-10; 2005, Aug, 9-10; 2005, August, 9-10; 2005, July, 11-12; 2005, August, 7-8

82654 **Dimethadione** [A]
EXCLUDES *qualitative testing (80100-80103)*

0.00 0.00 **Global Days XXX**
AMA: 2005, Aug, 9-10; 2005, Aug, 9-10; 2005, Jul, 11-12; 2005, Jul, 11-12; 2005, Aug, 7-8; 2005, Aug, 7-8; 2005, August, 9-10; 2005, July, 11-12; 2005, August, 7-8

82656 **Elastase, pancreatic (EL-1), fecal, qualitative or semi-quantitative** [A]
0.00 0.00 **Global Days XXX**
AMA: 2008, Jan, 10-25; 2007, Jan, 13-27; 2007, Jan, 13-27; 2007, January, 13-27; 2005, Jul, 11-12; 2005, Jul, 11-12; 2005, Aug, 7-8; 2005, Aug, 7-8; 2005, August, 7-8; 2005, August, 9-10; 2005, September, 9-11; 2005, July, 11-12; 2005, Sep, 9-11; 2005, Sep, 9-11; 2005, Aug, 9-10; 2005, Aug, 9-10

82657 **Enzyme activity in blood cells, cultured cells, or tissue, not elsewhere specified; nonradioactive substrate, each specimen** [A]
0.00 0.00 **Global Days XXX**
AMA: 2005, Aug, 9-10; 2005, Aug, 9-10; 2005, Jul, 11-12; 2005, Jul, 11-12; 2005, Aug, 7-8; 2005, Aug, 7-8; 2005, August, 9-10; 2005, August, 7-8; 2005, July, 11-12

82658 **radioactive substrate, each specimen** [A]
0.00 0.00 **Global Days XXX**
AMA: 2005, Aug, 9-10; 2005, Aug, 9-10; 2005, Jul, 11-12; 2005, Jul, 11-12; 2005, Aug, 7-8; 2005, Aug, 7-8; 2005, August, 9-10; 2005, July, 11-12; 2005, August, 7-8

82664 **Electrophoretic technique, not elsewhere specified** [A]
0.00 0.00 **Global Days XXX**
AMA: 2005, Jul, 11-12; 2005, Jul, 11-12; 2005, Aug, 7-8; 2005, Aug, 7-8; 2005, Aug, 9-10; 2005, Aug, 9-10; 2005, August, 9-10; 2005, July, 11-12; 2005, August, 7-8

82666 **Epiandrosterone** [A]
0.00 0.00 **Global Days XXX**
AMA: 2005, Aug, 7-8; 2005, Aug, 7-8; 2005, Aug, 9-10; 2005, Aug, 9-10; 2005, Jul, 11-12; 2005, Jul, 11-12; 2005, August, 9-10; 2005, August, 7-8; 2005, July, 11-12

82668 **Erythropoietin** [A]
0.00 0.00 **Global Days XXX**
AMA: 2005, Aug, 9-10; 2005, Aug, 9-10; 2005, Aug, 7-8; 2005, Aug, 7-8; 2005, Jul, 11-12; 2005, Jul, 11-12; 2005, August, 9-10; 2005, August, 7-8; 2005, July, 11-12

82670 **Estradiol** [A] [▪]
0.00 0.00 **Global Days XXX**
AMA: 2005, Aug, 9-10; 2005, Aug, 9-10; 2005, Jul, 11-12; 2005, Jul, 11-12; 2005, Aug, 7-8; 2005, Aug, 7-8; 2005, August, 9-10; 2005, July, 11-12; 2005, August, 7-8

82671 **Estrogens; fractionated** [A]
0.00 0.00 **Global Days XXX**
AMA: 2005, Aug, 9-10; 2005, Aug, 9-10; 2005, Aug, 7-8; 2005, Aug, 7-8; 2005, Jul, 11-12; 2005, Jul, 11-12; 2005, August, 9-10; 2005, July, 11-12; 2005, August, 7-8

82672 **total** [A]
0.00 0.00 **Global Days XXX**
AMA: 2005, Aug, 7-8; 2005, Aug, 7-8; 2005, Aug, 9-10; 2005, Aug, 9-10; 2005, Jul, 11-12; 2005, Jul, 11-12; 2005, August, 9-10; 2005, August, 7-8; 2005, July, 11-12

82677 **Estriol** [A]
0.00 0.00 **Global Days XXX**
AMA: 2005, Jul, 11-12; 2005, Jul, 11-12; 2005, Aug, 7-8; 2005, Aug, 7-8; 2005, Aug, 9-10; 2005, Aug, 9-10; 2005, August, 9-10; 2005, July, 11-12; 2005, August, 7-8

82679 **Estrone** [A] [✗]
0.00 0.00 **Global Days XXX**
AMA: 2005, Aug, 7-8; 2005, Aug, 7-8; 2005, Aug, 9-10; 2005, Aug, 9-10; 2005, Jul, 11-12; 2005, Jul, 11-12; 2005, August, 9-10; 2005, July, 11-12; 2005, August, 7-8

82690 **Ethchlorvynol** [A]
0.00 0.00 **Global Days XXX**
AMA: 2005, Jul, 11-12; 2005, Jul, 11-12; 2005, Aug, 7-8; 2005, Aug, 7-8; 2005, Aug, 9-10; 2005, Aug, 9-10; 2005, August, 9-10; 2005, July, 11-12; 2005, August, 7-8

82693 **Ethylene glycol** [A]
0.00 0.00 **Global Days XXX**
AMA: 2005, Jul, 11-12; 2005, Jul, 11-12; 2005, Aug, 9-10; 2005, Aug, 9-10; 2005, Aug, 7-8; 2005, Aug, 7-8; 2005, August, 9-10; 2005, July, 11-12; 2005, August, 7-8

82696 **Etiocholanolone** [A]
EXCLUDES *fractionation of ketosteroids (83593)*

0.00 0.00 **Global Days XXX**
AMA: 2005, Aug, 9-10; 2005, Aug, 9-10; 2005, Jul, 11-12; 2005, Jul, 11-12; 2005, Aug, 7-8; 2005, Aug, 7-8; 2005, July, 11-12; 2005, August, 7-8; 2005, August, 9-10

82705 **Fat or lipids, feces; qualitative** [A]
0.00 0.00 **Global Days XXX**
AMA: 2005, Aug, 9-10; 2005, Aug, 9-10; 2005, Jul, 11-12; 2005, Jul, 11-12; 2005, Aug, 7-8; 2005, Aug, 7-8; 2005, August, 9-10; 2005, July, 11-12; 2005, August, 7-8

82710 **quantitative** [A]
0.00 0.00 **Global Days XXX**
AMA: 2005, Aug, 7-8; 2005, Aug, 7-8; 2005, Aug, 9-10; 2005, Aug, 9-10; 2005, Jul, 11-12; 2005, Jul, 11-12; 2005, August, 9-10; 2005, July, 11-12; 2005, August, 7-8

82715 **Fat differential, feces, quantitative** [A]
0.00 0.00 **Global Days XXX**
AMA: 2005, Aug, 9-10; 2005, Aug, 9-10; 2005, Aug, 7-8; 2005, Aug, 7-8; 2005, Jul, 11-12; 2005, Jul, 11-12; 2005, August, 9-10; 2005, July, 11-12; 2005, August, 7-8

82725   Fatty acids, nonesterified   A
  📷 0.00   🔬 0.00   Global Days XXX
  AMA: 2005, Aug, 7-8; 2005, Aug, 7-8; 2005, Jul, 11-12; 2005, Jul, 11-12; 2005, Aug, 9-10; 2005, Aug, 9-10; 2005, August, 9-10; 2005, July, 11-12; 2005, August, 7-8

82726   Very long chain fatty acids   A
  EXCLUDES   *long-chain (C20-22) omega-3 fatty acids in red blood cell (RBC) membranes (0111T)*
  📷 0.00   🔬 0.00   Global Days XXX
  AMA: 2005, Aug, 9-10; 2005, Aug, 9-10; 2005, Jul, 11-12; 2005, Jul, 11-12; 2005, Aug, 7-8; 2005, Aug, 7-8; 2005, Jun, 6-8; 2005, Jun, 6-8; 2005, August, 9-10; 2005, June, 6-8; 2005, July, 11-12; 2005, August, 7-8

82728   Ferritin   A
  📷 0.00   🔬 0.00   Global Days XXX
  AMA: 2005, Aug, 7-8; 2005, Aug, 7-8; 2005, Aug, 9-10; 2005, Aug, 9-10; 2005, Jul, 11-12; 2005, Jul, 11-12; 2005, August, 9-10; 2005, July, 11-12; 2005, August, 7-8

82731   Fetal fibronectin, cervicovaginal secretions, semi-quantitative   M ♀ A
  📷 0.00   🔬 0.00   Global Days XXX
  AMA: 2005, Jul, 11-12; 2005, Jul, 11-12; 2005, Aug, 7-8; 2005, Aug, 7-8; 2005, Aug, 9-10; 2005, Aug, 9-10; 2005, July, 11-12; 2005, August, 9-10; 2005, August, 7-8

82735   Fluoride   A
  📷 0.00   🔬 0.00   Global Days XXX
  AMA: 2005, Aug, 9-10; 2005, Aug, 9-10; 2005, Aug, 7-8; 2005, Aug, 7-8; 2005, Jul, 11-12; 2005, Jul, 11-12; 2005, July, 11-12; 2005, August, 7-8; 2005, August, 9-10

82742   Flurazepam   A
  EXCLUDES   *qualitative testing (80100-80103)*
  📷 0.00   🔬 0.00   Global Days XXX
  AMA: 2005, Jul, 11-12; 2005, Jul, 11-12; 2005, Aug, 9-10; 2005, Aug, 9-10; 2005, Aug, 7-8; 2005, Aug, 7-8; 2005, August, 9-10; 2005, July, 11-12; 2005, August, 7-8

82746   Folic acid; serum   A
  📷 0.00   🔬 0.00   Global Days XXX
  AMA: 2005, Jul, 11-12; 2005, Jul, 11-12; 2005, Aug, 9-10; 2005, Aug, 9-10; 2005, Aug, 7-8; 2005, Aug, 7-8; 2005, August, 9-10; 2005, July, 11-12; 2005, August, 7-8

82747   RBC   A
  📷 0.00   🔬 0.00   Global Days XXX
  AMA: 2005, Aug, 7-8; 2005, Aug, 7-8; 2005, Aug, 9-10; 2005, Aug, 9-10; 2005, Jul, 11-12; 2005, Jul, 11-12; 2005, August, 9-10; 2005, July, 11-12; 2005, August, 7-8

82757   Fructose, semen   ♂ A
  EXCLUDES   *fructosamine (82985)*
            fructose, TLC screen (84375)
  📷 0.00   🔬 0.00   Global Days XXX
  AMA: 2005, Jul, 11-12; 2005, Jul, 11-12; 2005, Aug, 7-8; 2005, Aug, 7-8; 2005, Aug, 9-10; 2005, Aug, 9-10; 2005, August, 9-10; 2005, July, 11-12; 2005, August, 7-8

82759   Galactokinase, RBC   A
  📷 0.00   🔬 0.00   Global Days XXX
  AMA: 2005, Aug, 9-10; 2005, Aug, 9-10; 2005, Jul, 11-12; 2005, Jul, 11-12; 2005, Aug, 7-8; 2005, Aug, 7-8; 2005, August, 9-10; 2005, July, 11-12; 2005, August, 7-8

82760   Galactose   A
  📷 0.00   🔬 0.00   Global Days XXX
  AMA: 2005, Aug, 9-10; 2005, Aug, 9-10; 2005, Aug, 7-8; 2005, Aug, 7-8; 2005, Jul, 11-12; 2005, Jul, 11-12; 2005, August, 9-10; 2005, July, 11-12; 2005, August, 7-8

82775   Galactose-1-phosphate uridyl transferase; quantitative   A
  📷 0.00   🔬 0.00   Global Days XXX
  AMA: 2005, Aug, 9-10; 2005, Aug, 9-10; 2005, Aug, 7-8; 2005, Aug, 7-8; 2005, Jul, 11-12; 2005, Jul, 11-12; 2005, August, 9-10; 2005, August, 7-8; 2005, July, 11-12

82776   screen   A
  📷 0.00   🔬 0.00   Global Days XXX
  AMA: 2005, Jul, 11-12; 2005, Jul, 11-12; 2005, Aug, 9-10; 2005, Aug, 9-10; 2005, Aug, 7-8; 2005, Aug, 7-8; 2005, August, 9-10; 2005, August, 7-8; 2005, July, 11-12

82784   Gammaglobulin; IgA, IgD, IgG, IgM, each   A ▫
  INCLUDES   Farr test
  📷 0.00   🔬 0.00   Global Days XXX
  AMA: 2008, Jan, 10-25; 2007, Jan, 13-27; 2007, Jan, 13-27; 2007, January, 13-27; 2005, Jul, 11-12; 2005, Jul, 11-12; 2005, Aug, 7-8; 2005, August, 7-8; 2005, July, 11-12; 2005, August, 9-10; 2005, Aug, 7-8; 2005, Aug, 9-10; 2005, Aug, 9-10

82785   IgE   A ▫
  INCLUDES   Farr test
  EXCLUDES   *allergen specific, IgE (86003, 86005)*
  📷 0.00   🔬 0.00   Global Days XXX
  AMA: 2005, Aug, 9-10; 2005, Aug, 9-10; 2005, Aug, 7-8; 2005, Aug, 7-8; 2005, Jul, 11-12; 2005, Jul, 11-12; 2005, August, 9-10; 2005, August, 7-8; 2005, July, 11-12

82787   immunoglobulin subclasses (IgG1, 2, 3, or 4), each   A ▫
  EXCLUDES   *gamma-glutamyltransferase (GGT) (82977)*
  📷 0.00   🔬 0.00   Global Days XXX
  AMA: 2005, Aug, 9-10; 2005, Aug, 9-10; 2005, Aug, 7-8; 2005, Aug, 7-8; 2005, Jul, 11-12; 2005, Jul, 11-12; 2005, Aug, 9-10; 2005, August, 7-8; 2005, July, 11-12

82800   Gases, blood, pH only   A ▫
  📷 0.00   🔬 0.00   Global Days XXX
  AMA: 2005, Aug, 7-8; 2005, Aug, 7-8; 2005, Jul, 11-12; 2005, Jul, 11-12; 2005, Aug, 9-10; 2005, Aug, 9-10; 2005, August, 9-10; 2005, August, 7-8; 2005, July, 11-12

82803   Gases, blood, any combination of pH, pCO2, pO2, CO2, HCO3 (including calculated O2 saturation);   A ▫
  INCLUDES   two or more of the listed analytes
  📷 0.00   🔬 0.00   Global Days XXX
  AMA: 2005, Jul, 11-12; 2005, Jul, 11-12; 2005, Aug, 9-10; 2005, Aug, 9-10; 2005, Aug, 7-8; 2005, Aug, 7-8; 2005, August, 7-8; 2005, July, 11-12; 2005, August, 9-10

82805   with O2 saturation, by direct measurement, except pulse oximetry   A ▫
  📷 0.00   🔬 0.00   Global Days XXX
  AMA: 2005, Jul, 11-12; 2005, Jul, 11-12; 2005, Aug, 7-8; 2005, Aug, 7-8; 2005, Aug, 9-10; 2005, Aug, 9-10; 2005, Aug, 9-10; 2005, August, 7-8; 2005, July, 11-12

82810   Gases, blood, O2 saturation only, by direct measurement, except pulse oximetry   A ▫
  EXCLUDES   *pulse oximetry (94760)*
  📷 0.00   🔬 0.00   Global Days XXX
  AMA: 2005, Jul, 11-12; 2005, Jul, 11-12; 2005, Aug, 9-10; 2005, Aug, 9-10; 2005, Aug, 7-8; 2005, Aug, 7-8; 2005, August, 9-10; 2005, August, 7-8; 2005, July, 11-12

82820   Hemoglobin-oxygen affinity (pO2 for 50% hemoglobin saturation with oxygen)   A ▫
  📷 0.00   🔬 0.00   Global Days XXX
  AMA: 2005, Jul, 11-12; 2005, Jul, 11-12; 2005, Aug, 9-10; 2005, Aug, 9-10; 2005, Aug, 7-8; 2005, Aug, 7-8; 2005, August, 9-10; 2005, August, 7-8; 2005, July, 11-12

82926   **Gastric acid, free and total, each specimen**   A ▢
    0.00   0.00   **Global Days XXX**
    AMA: 2005, Aug, 7-8; 2005, Aug, 7-8; 2005, Jul, 11-12; 2005, Jul, 11-12; 2005, Aug, 9-10; 2005, Aug, 9-10; 2005, August, 9-10; 2005, August, 7-8; 2005, July, 11-12

82928   **Gastric acid, free or total, each specimen**   A
    0.00   0.00   **Global Days XXX**
    AMA: 2005, Aug, 9-10; 2005, Aug, 9-10; 2005, Jul, 11-12; 2005, Jul, 11-12; 2005, Aug, 7-8; 2005, Aug, 7-8; 2005, July, 11-12; 2005, August, 9-10; 2005, August, 7-8

82938   **Gastrin after secretin stimulation**   A
    0.00   0.00   **Global Days XXX**
    AMA: 2005, Aug, 9-10; 2005, Aug, 9-10; 2005, Aug, 7-8; 2005, Aug, 7-8; 2005, Jul, 11-12; 2005, Jul, 11-12; 2005, August, 9-10; 2005, July, 11-12; 2005, August, 7-8

82941   **Gastrin**   A
    0.00   0.00   **Global Days XXX**
    AMA: 2005, Aug, 7-8; 2005, Aug, 7-8; 2005, Jul, 11-12; 2005, Jul, 11-12; 2005, Aug, 9-10; 2005, Aug, 9-10; 2005, July, 11-12; 2005, August, 9-10; 2005, August, 7-8

82943   **Glucagon**   A
    0.00   0.00   **Global Days XXX**
    AMA: 2005, Jul, 11-12; 2005, Jul, 11-12; 2005, Aug, 7-8; 2005, Aug, 7-8; 2005, Aug, 9-10; 2005, Aug, 9-10; 2005, July, 11-12; 2005, August, 9-10; 2005, August, 7-8

82945   **Glucose, body fluid, other than blood**   A ▢
    0.00   0.00   **Global Days XXX**
    AMA: 2005, Aug, 9-10; 2005, Aug, 9-10; 2005, Aug, 7-8; 2005, Aug, 7-8; 2005, Jul, 11-12; 2005, Jul, 11-12; 2005, July, 11-12; 2005, August, 9-10; 2005, August, 7-8

82946   **Glucagon tolerance test**   A
    0.00   0.00   **Global Days XXX**
    AMA: 2005, Jul, 11-12; 2005, Jul, 11-12; 2005, Aug, 9-10; 2005, Aug, 9-10; 2005, Aug, 7-8; 2005, Aug, 7-8; 2005, July, 11-12; 2005, August, 9-10; 2005, August, 7-8

82947-82962 Chemistry: Glucose Testing

CMS *100-3,190.20*   *Blood Glucose Testing*
CMS *100-4,3,10.4*   *Payment of Nonphysician Services for Inpatients*
CMS *100-2,15,80*   *Physician Supervision Requirements for Diagnostic Tests*

INCLUDES   mathematically calculated results
    quantitative analysis unless otherwise specified
    specimens from any source unless otherwise specified

EXCLUDES   *organ or disease panels (80048-80076)*
    therapeutic drug assays (80150-80299)

Code also glucose administration injection (96374)

82947   **Glucose; quantitative, blood (except reagent strip)**   A ▢ ✕
    0.00   0.00   **Global Days XXX**
    AMA: 2005, Feb, 7-9; 2005, Feb, 7-9; 2005, Jul, 11-12; 2005, Jul, 11-12; 2005, Aug, 9-10; 2005, Aug, 9-10; 2005, Aug, 7-8; 2005, Aug, 7-8; 2005, February, 7-9; 2005, July, 11-12; 2005, August, 9-10; 2005, August, 7-8

82948   **blood, reagent strip**   A ▢
    0.00   0.00   **Global Days XXX**
    AMA: 2008, Jan, 10-25; 2007, Jan, 13-27; 2007, Jan, 13-27; 2007, January, 13-27; 2005, Jul, 11-12; 2005, Jul, 11-12; 2005, Aug, 9-10; 2005, August, 9-10; 2005, August, 7-8; 2005, July, 11-12; 2005, Aug, 9-10; 2005, Aug, 7-8; 2005, Aug, 7-8

82950   **post glucose dose (includes glucose)**   A ▢ ✕
    0.00   0.00   **Global Days XXX**
    AMA: 2008, Jan, 10-25; 2007, Jan, 13-27; 2007, Jan, 13-27; 2007, January, 13-27; 2005, Feb, 7-9; 2005, Feb, 7-9; 2005, Jul, 11-12; 2005, Jul, 11-12; 2005, August, 9-10; 2005, July, 11-12; 2005, August, 7-8; 2005, February, 7-9; 2005, Aug, 7-8; 2005, Aug, 7-8; 2005, Aug, 9-10; 2005, Aug, 9-10

82951   **tolerance test (GTT), 3 specimens (includes glucose)**   A ▢ ✕
    0.00   0.00   **Global Days XXX**
    AMA: 2008, Jan, 10-25; 2007, Jan, 13-27; 2007, Jan, 13-27; 2007, January, 13-27; 2005, Feb, 7-9; 2005, Feb, 7-9; 2005, Aug, 9-10; 2005, Aug, 9-10; 2005, July, 11-12; 2005, August, 9-10; 2005, August, 7-8; 2005, February, 7-9; 2005, Aug, 7-8; 2005, Aug, 7-8; 2005, Jul, 11-12; 2005, Jul, 11-12

82952   **tolerance test, each additional beyond 3 specimens**   A ▢ ✕
    0.00   0.00   **Global Days XXX**
    AMA: 2008, Jan, 10-25; 2007, Jan, 13-27; 2007, Jan, 13-27; 2007, January, 13-27; 2005, Jul, 11-12; 2005, Jul, 11-12; 2005, Aug, 7-8; 2005, August, 9-10; 2005, August, 7-8; 2005, July, 11-12; 2005, Aug, 7-8; 2005, Aug, 9-10; 2005, Aug, 9-10

82953   **tolbutamide tolerance test**   A ▢
    EXCLUDES   *semiquantitative urine glucose (81000, 81002, 81005, 81099)*
    0.00   0.00   **Global Days XXX**
    AMA: 2005, Jul, 11-12; 2005, Jul, 11-12; 2005, Aug, 9-10; 2005, Aug, 9-10; 2005, Aug, 7-8; 2005, Aug, 7-8; 2005, July, 11-12; 2005, August, 9-10; 2005, August, 7-8

82955   **Glucose-6-phosphate dehydrogenase (G6PD); quantitative**   A
    0.00   0.00   **Global Days XXX**
    AMA: 2005, Aug, 9-10; 2005, Aug, 9-10; 2005, Aug, 7-8; 2005, Aug, 7-8; 2005, Jul, 11-12; 2005, Jul, 11-12; 2005, August, 9-10; 2005, August, 7-8; 2005, July, 11-12

82960   **screen**   A
    Code also injection administration (96374)
    0.00   0.00   **Global Days XXX**
    AMA: 2005, Jul, 11-12; 2005, Jul, 11-12; 2005, Aug, 9-10; 2005, Aug, 9-10; 2005, Aug, 7-8; 2005, Aug, 7-8; 2005, July, 11-12; 2005, August, 9-10; 2005, August, 7-8

82962   **Glucose, blood by glucose monitoring device(s) cleared by the FDA specifically for home use**   A ▢ ✕
    0.00   0.00   **Global Days XXX**
    AMA: 2008, Jan, 10-25; 2007, Jan, 13-27; 2007, Jan, 13-27; 2007, January, 13-27; 2005, Jul, 11-12; 2005, Jul, 11-12; 2005, Aug, 7-8; 2005, August, 9-10; 2005, August, 7-8; 2005, July, 11-12; 2005, Aug, 7-8; 2005, Aug, 9-10; 2005, Aug, 9-10

82963-83690 Chemistry: Glucosidase--Lipase

CMS *100-4,3,10.4*   *Payment of Nonphysician Services for Inpatients*
CMS *100-2,15,80*   *Physician Supervision Requirements for Diagnostic Tests*

INCLUDES   mathematically calculated results
    quantitative analysis unless otherwise specified
    specimens from any source unless otherwise specified

EXCLUDES   *organ or disease panels (80048-80076)*
    therapeutic drug assays (80150-80299)

82963   **Glucosidase, beta**   A
    0.00   0.00   **Global Days XXX**
    AMA: 2005, Jul, 11-12; 2005, Jul, 11-12; 2005, Aug, 9-10; 2005, Aug, 9-10; 2005, Aug, 7-8; 2005, Aug, 7-8; 2005, July, 11-12; 2005, August, 9-10; 2005, August, 7-8

26/TC Professional/Technical Component Only   80/80 Assist-at-Surgery Allowed/With Documentation   Unlisted   Not Covered   ✕ Radiology crosswalk

MED: Pub 100/NCD References   **AMA:** CPT Assistant References   A2-Z3 ASC Payment Indicator   ♂Male Only   ♀Female Only   ◣ Laboratory crosswalk

330   CPT only © 2008 American Medical Association. All Rights Reserved. (Black Ink)   Medicare (Red Ink)   © 2008 Ingenix *(Blue Ink)*

82965 **Glutamate dehydrogenase** [A]
📋 0.00 ⚕ 0.00 Global Days XXX
AMA: 2005, Jul, 11-12; 2005, Jul, 11-12; 2005, Aug, 9-10; 2005, Aug, 9-10; 2005, Aug, 7-8; 2005, Aug, 7-8; 2005, July, 11-12; 2005, August, 9-10; 2005, August, 7-8

82975 **Glutamine (glutamic acid amide)** [A]
📋 0.00 ⚕ 0.00 Global Days XXX
AMA: 2005, Jul, 11-12; 2005, Jul, 11-12; 2005, Aug, 9-10; 2005, Aug, 9-10; 2005, Aug, 7-8; 2005, Aug, 7-8; 2005, August, 9-10; 2005, August, 7-8; 2005, July, 11-12

82977 **Glutamyltransferase, gamma (GGT)** [A] [X]
📋 0.00 ⚕ 0.00 Global Days XXX
AMA: 2005, Jul, 11-12; 2005, Jul, 11-12; 2005, Aug, 9-10; 2005, Aug, 9-10; 2005, Aug, 7-8; 2005, Aug, 7-8; 2005, July, 11-12; 2005, August, 9-10; 2005, August, 7-8

82978 **Glutathione** [A]
📋 0.00 ⚕ 0.00 Global Days XXX
AMA: 2005, Aug, 7-8; 2005, Aug, 7-8; 2005, Jul, 11-12; 2005, Jul, 11-12; 2005, Aug, 9-10; 2005, Aug, 9-10; 2005, July, 11-12; 2005, August, 9-10; 2005, August, 7-8

82979 **Glutathione reductase, RBC** [A]
📋 0.00 ⚕ 0.00 Global Days XXX
AMA: 2005, Jul, 11-12; 2005, Jul, 11-12; 2005, Aug, 9-10; 2005, Aug, 9-10; 2005, Aug, 7-8; 2005, Aug, 7-8; 2005, July, 11-12; 2005, August, 9-10; 2005, August, 7-8

82980 **Glutethimide** [A]
📋 0.00 ⚕ 0.00 Global Days XXX
AMA: 2005, Aug, 9-10; 2005, Aug, 9-10; 2005, Aug, 7-8; 2005, Aug, 7-8; 2005, Jul, 11-12; 2005, Jul, 11-12; 2005, July, 11-12; 2005, August, 9-10; 2005, August, 7-8

82985 **Glycated protein** [A] [C] [X]
EXCLUDES *gonadotropin, chorionic (hCG) (84702-84703)*
📋 0.00 ⚕ 0.00 Global Days XXX
AMA: 2005, Aug, 7-8; 2005, Aug, 7-8; 2005, Jul, 11-12; 2005, Jul, 11-12; 2005, Aug, 9-10; 2005, Aug, 9-10; 2005, July, 11-12; 2005, August, 7-8; 2005, August, 9-10

83001 **Gonadotropin; follicle stimulating hormone (FSH)** [A] [C] [X]
📋 0.00 ⚕ 0.00 Global Days XXX
AMA: 2005, Jul, 11-12; 2005, Jul, 11-12; 2005, Aug, 9-10; 2005, Aug, 9-10; 2005, Aug, 7-8; 2005, Aug, 7-8; 2005, July, 11-12; 2005, August, 9-10; 2005, August, 7-8

83002 **luteinizing hormone (LH)** [A] [C] [X]
EXCLUDES *luteinizing releasing factor (LRH) (83727)*
📋 0.00 ⚕ 0.00 Global Days XXX
AMA: 2005, Jul, 11-12; 2005, Jul, 11-12; 2005, Aug, 9-10; 2005, Aug, 9-10; 2005, Aug, 7-8; 2005, Aug, 7-8; 2005, July, 11-12; 2005, August, 9-10; 2005, August, 7-8

83003 **Growth hormone, human (HGH) (somatotropin)** [A] [C]
EXCLUDES *antibody to human growth hormone (86277)*
📋 0.00 ⚕ 0.00 Global Days XXX
AMA: 2005, Aug, 7-8; 2005, Aug, 7-8; 2005, Aug, 9-10; 2005, Aug, 9-10; 2005, Jul, 11-12; 2005, Jul, 11-12; 2005, July, 11-12; 2005, August, 9-10; 2005, August, 7-8

83008 **Guanosine monophosphate (GMP), cyclic** [A]
📋 0.00 ⚕ 0.00 Global Days XXX
AMA: 2005, Aug, 7-8; 2005, Aug, 7-8; 2005, Jul, 11-12; 2005, Jul, 11-12; 2005, Aug, 9-10; 2005, Aug, 9-10; 2005, July, 11-12; 2005, August, 7-8

83009 **Helicobacter pylori, blood test analysis for urease activity, non-radioactive isotope (eg, C-13)** [A]
EXCLUDES *H. pylori, breath test analysis for urease activity (83013-83014)*
📋 0.00 ⚕ 0.00 Global Days XXX
AMA: 2005, Jul, 11-12; 2005, Jul, 11-12; 2005, Aug, 9-10; 2005, Aug, 9-10; 2005, Aug, 7-8; 2005, Aug, 7-8; 2005, July, 11-12; 2005, August, 9-10; 2005, August, 7-8

83010 **Haptoglobin; quantitative** [A]
📋 0.00 ⚕ 0.00 Global Days XXX
AMA: 2005, Aug, 9-10; 2005, Aug, 9-10; 2005, Jul, 11-12; 2005, Jul, 11-12; 2005, Aug, 7-8; 2005, Aug, 7-8; 2005, July, 11-12; 2005, August, 9-10; 2005, August, 7-8

83012 **phenotypes** [A]
📋 0.00 ⚕ 0.00 Global Days XXX
AMA: 2005, Aug, 7-8; 2005, Aug, 7-8; 2005, Jul, 11-12; 2005, Jul, 11-12; 2005, Aug, 9-10; 2005, Aug, 9-10; 2005, July, 11-12; 2005, August, 9-10; 2005, August, 7-8

83013 **Helicobacter pylori; breath test analysis for urease activity, non-radioactive isotope (eg, C-13)** [A] [C]
📋 0.00 ⚕ 0.00 Global Days XXX
AMA: 2005, Jul, 11-12; 2005, Jul, 11-12; 2005, Aug, 9-10; 2005, Aug, 9-10; 2005, Aug, 7-8; 2005, Aug, 7-8; 2005, August, 9-10; 2005, August, 7-8; 2005, July, 11-12

83014 **drug administration** [A] [C]
EXCLUDES *H. pylori:*
blood test analysis for urease activity (83009)
enzyme immunoassay (87339)
liquid scintillation counter (78267-78268)
stool (87338)
📋 0.00 ⚕ 0.00 Global Days XXX
AMA: 2005, Jul, 11-12; 2005, Jul, 11-12; 2005, Aug, 7-8; 2005, Aug, 7-8; 2005, Aug, 9-10; 2005, Aug, 9-10; 2005, July, 11-12; 2005, August, 9-10; 2005, August, 7-8

83015 **Heavy metal (eg, arsenic, barium, beryllium, bismuth, antimony, mercury); screen** [A]
INCLUDES Reinsch test
📋 0.00 ⚕ 0.00 Global Days XXX
AMA: 2005, Aug, 9-10; 2005, Aug, 9-10; 2005, Aug, 7-8; 2005, Aug, 7-8; 2005, Jul, 11-12; 2005, Jul, 11-12; 2005, July, 11-12; 2005, August, 9-10; 2005, August, 7-8

83018 **quantitative, each** [A]
📋 0.00 ⚕ 0.00 Global Days XXX
AMA: 2005, Jul, 11-12; 2005, Jul, 11-12; 2005, Aug, 7-8; 2005, Aug, 7-8; 2005, Aug, 9-10; 2005, Aug, 9-10; 2005, July, 11-12; 2005, August, 9-10; 2005, August, 7-8

83020 **Hemoglobin fractionation and quantitation; electrophoresis (eg, A2, S, C, and/or F)** [A] [80] [C]
📋 0.00 ⚕ 0.00 Global Days XXX
AMA: 2005, Aug, 7-8; 2005, Aug, 7-8; 2005, Aug, 9-10; 2005, Aug, 9-10; 2005, Jul, 11-12; 2005, Jul, 11-12; 2005, July, 11-12; 2005, August, 9-10; 2005, August, 7-8

83021 **chromatography (eg, A2, S, C, and/or F)** [A] [C]
EXCLUDES *glycosylated (A1c) hemoglobin analysis by chromatography in the absence of an identified hemoglobin variant (83036)*
📋 0.00 ⚕ 0.00 Global Days XXX
AMA: 2005, Jul, 11-12; 2005, Jul, 11-12; 2005, Aug, 9-10; 2005, Aug, 9-10; 2005, Aug, 7-8; 2005, Aug, 7-8; 2005, July, 11-12; 2005, August, 7-8; 2005, August, 9-10

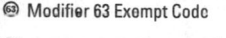

83026 Hemoglobin; by copper sulfate method, non-automated A X
  📷 0.00 ✂ 0.00 Global Days XXX
  AMA: 2005, Aug, 9-10; 2005, Aug, 9-10; 2005, Jul, 11-12; 2005, Jul, 11-12; 2005, Aug, 7-8; 2005, Aug, 7-8; 2005, July, 11-12; 2005, August, 9-10; 2005, August, 7-8

83030 F (fetal), chemical A ▭
  📷 0.00 ✂ 0.00 Global Days XXX
  AMA: 2005, Jul, 11-12; 2005, Jul, 11-12; 2005, Aug, 9-10; 2005, Aug, 9-10; 2005, Aug, 7-8; 2005, Aug, 7-8; 2005, July, 11-12; 2005, August, 9-10; 2005, August, 7-8

83033 F (fetal), qualitative A ▭
  📷 0.00 ✂ 0.00 Global Days XXX
  AMA: 2005, Aug, 9-10; 2005, Aug, 9-10; 2005, Aug, 7-8; 2005, Aug, 7-8; 2005, Jul, 11-12; 2005, Jul, 11-12; 2005, July, 11-12; 2005, August, 9-10; 2005, August, 7-8

83036 glycosylated (A1C) A X
  EXCLUDES glycosylated (A1c) hemoglobin analysis by chromatography in the setting of an identified hemoglobin variant (83021)
  📷 0.00 ✂ 0.00 Global Days XXX
  AMA: 2006, Feb, 7-9; 2006, Feb, 7-9; 2006, February, 7-9; 2005, Jul, 11-12; 2005, Jul, 11-12; 2005, Aug, 7-8; 2005, August, 9-10; 2005, August, 7-8; 2005, July, 11-12; 2005, Aug, 7-8; 2005, Aug, 9-10; 2005, Aug, 9-10

83037 glycosylated (A1C) by device cleared by FDA for home use A X
  📷 0.00 ✂ 0.00 Global Days XXX
  AMA: 2008, Jan, 10-25; 2007, Jan, 13-27; 2007, Jan, 13-27; 2007, January, 13-27; 2006, Feb, 7-9; 2006, February, 7-9; 2006, Feb, 7-9; 2005, Aug, 7-8; 2005, August, 7-8; 2005, August, 9-10; 2005, Aug, 7-8; 2005, Aug, 9-10; 2005, Aug, 9-10

83045 methemoglobin, qualitative A
  📷 0.00 ✂ 0.00 Global Days XXX
  AMA: 2005, Aug, 9-10; 2005, Aug, 9-10; 2005, Aug, 7-8; 2005, Aug, 7-8; 2005, Jul, 11-12; 2005, Jul, 11-12; 2005, July, 11-12; 2005, August, 9-10; 2005, August, 7-8

83050 methemoglobin, quantitative A
  EXCLUDES transcutaneous methemoglobin test (88741)
  📷 0.00 ✂ 0.00 Global Days XXX
  AMA: 2005, Jul, 11-12; 2005, Jul, 11-12; 2005, Aug, 9-10; 2005, Aug, 9-10; 2005, Aug, 7-8; 2005, Aug, 7-8; 2005, July, 11-12; 2005, August, 9-10; 2005, August, 7-8

83051 plasma A
  📷 0.00 ✂ 0.00 Global Days XXX
  AMA: 2005, Aug, 9-10; 2005, Aug, 9-10; 2005, Jul, 11-12; 2005, Jul, 11-12; 2005, Aug, 7-8; 2005, Aug, 7-8; 2005, July, 11-12; 2005, August, 9-10; 2005, August, 7-8

83055 sulfhemoglobin, qualitative A
  📷 0.00 ✂ 0.00 Global Days XXX
  AMA: 2005, Jul, 11-12; 2005, Jul, 11-12; 2005, Aug, 9-10; 2005, Aug, 9-10; 2005, Aug, 7-8; 2005, Aug, 7-8; 2005, July, 11-12; 2005, August, 9-10; 2005, August, 7-8

83060 sulfhemoglobin, quantitative A
  📷 0.00 ✂ 0.00 Global Days XXX
  AMA: 2005, Jul, 11-12; 2005, Jul, 11-12; 2005, Aug, 7-8; 2005, Aug, 7-8; 2005, Aug, 9-10; 2005, Aug, 9-10; 2005, August, 7-8; 2005, July, 11-12; 2005, August, 9-10

83065 thermolabile A
  📷 0.00 ✂ 0.00 Global Days XXX
  AMA: 2005, Aug, 7-8; 2005, Aug, 7-8; 2005, Aug, 9-10; 2005, Aug, 9-10; 2005, Jul, 11-12; 2005, Jul, 11-12; 2005, August, 7-8; 2005, July, 11-12; 2005, August, 9-10

83068 unstable, screen A ▭
  📷 0.00 ✂ 0.00 Global Days XXX
  AMA: 2005, Jul, 11-12; 2005, Jul, 11-12; 2005, Aug, 7-8; 2005, Aug, 7-8; 2005, Aug, 9-10; 2005, Aug, 9-10; 2005, August, 7-8; 2005, July, 11-12; 2005, August, 9-10

83069 urine A
  📷 0.00 ✂ 0.00 Global Days XXX
  AMA: 2005, Aug, 7-8; 2005, Aug, 7-8; 2005, Aug, 9-10; 2005, Aug, 9-10; 2005, Jul, 11-12; 2005, Jul, 11-12; 2005, August, 7-8; 2005, July, 11-12; 2005, August, 9-10

83070 Hemosiderin; qualitative A
  📷 0.00 ✂ 0.00 Global Days XXX
  AMA: 2005, Aug, 7-8; 2005, Aug, 7-8; 2005, Jul, 11-12; 2005, Jul, 11-12; 2005, Aug, 9-10; 2005, Aug, 9-10; 2005, August, 7-8; 2005, July, 11-12; 2005, August, 9-10

83071 quantitative A
  📷 0.00 ✂ 0.00 Global Days XXX
  AMA: 2005, Aug, 9-10; 2005, Aug, 9-10; 2005, Jul, 11-12; 2005, Jul, 11-12; 2005, Aug, 7-8; 2005, Aug, 7-8; 2005, August, 7-8; 2005, July, 11-12; 2005, August, 9-10

83080 b-Hexosaminidase, each assay A
  📷 0.00 ✂ 0.00 Global Days XXX
  AMA: 2005, Jul, 11-12; 2005, Jul, 11-12; 2005, Aug, 7-8; 2005, Aug, 7-8; 2005, Aug, 9-10; 2005, Aug, 9-10; 2005, August, 7-8; 2005, July, 11-12; 2005, August, 9-10

83088 Histamine A
  📷 0.00 ✂ 0.00 Global Days XXX
  AMA: 2005, Aug, 7-8; 2005, Aug, 7-8; 2005, Jul, 11-12; 2005, Jul, 11-12; 2005, Aug, 9-10; 2005, Aug, 9-10; 2005, August, 7-8; 2005, July, 11-12; 2005, August, 9-10

83090 Homocysteine A ▭
  📷 0.00 ✂ 0.00 Global Days XXX
  AMA: 2008, Jan, 10-25; 2007, Jan, 13-27; 2007, Jan, 13-27; 2007, January, 13-27; 2005, Aug, 7-8; 2005, Aug, 7-8; 2005, Jul, 11-12; 2005, August, 7-8; 2005, August, 9-10; 2005, July, 11-12; 2005, Jul, 11-12; 2005, Aug, 9-10; 2005, Aug, 9-10

83150 Homovanillic acid (HVA) A
  📷 0.00 ✂ 0.00 Global Days XXX
  AMA: 2005, Aug, 9-10; 2005, Aug, 9-10; 2005, Jul, 11-12; 2005, Jul, 11-12; 2005, Aug, 7-8; 2005, Aug, 7-8; 2005, July, 11-12; 2005, August, 7-8; 2005, August, 9-10

83491 Hydroxycorticosteroids, 17- (17-OHCS) A
  EXCLUDES cortisol (82530, 82533)
  deoxycortisol (82634)
  📷 0.00 ✂ 0.00 Global Days XXX
  AMA: 2005, Aug, 7-8; 2005, Aug, 7-8; 2005, Aug, 9-10; 2005, Aug, 9-10; 2005, Jul, 11-12; 2005, Jul, 11-12; 2005, August, 7-8; 2005, July, 11-12; 2005, August, 9-10

83497 Hydroxyindolacetic acid, 5-(HIAA) A
  EXCLUDES urine qualitative test (81005)
  📷 0.00 ✂ 0.00 Global Days XXX
  AMA: 2005, Jul, 11-12; 2005, Jul, 11-12; 2005, Aug, 7-8; 2005, Aug, 7-8; 2005, Aug, 9-10; 2005, Aug, 9-10; 2005, July, 11-12; 2005, August, 9-10; 2005, August, 7-8

83498 Hydroxyprogesterone, 17-d A ▭
  📷 0.00 ✂ 0.00 Global Days XXX
  AMA: 2005, Aug, 7-8; 2005, Aug, 7-8; 2005, Aug, 9-10; 2005, Aug, 9-10; 2005, Jul, 11-12; 2005, Jul, 11-12; 2005, August, 7-8; 2005, July, 11-12; 2005, August, 9-10

83499 Hydroxyprogesterone, 20- A
  📷 0.00 ✂ 0.00 Global Days XXX
  AMA: 2005, Aug, 7-8; 2005, Aug, 7-8; 2005, Jul, 11-12; 2005, Jul, 11-12; 2005, Aug, 9-10; 2005, Aug, 9-10; 2005, July, 11-12; 2005, August, 7-8; 2005, August, 9-10

26/TC Professional/Technical Component Only   80/60 Assist-at-Surgery Allowed/With Documentation   Unlisted   Not Covered   ✖ Radiology crosswalk
MED: Pub 100/NCD References   **AMA:** CPT Assistant References   A2-Z3 ASC Payment Indicator   ♂Male Only   ♀Female Only   ◣ Laboratory crosswalk

83500 Hydroxyproline; free [A]
 0.00 0.00 **Global Days XXX**
AMA: 2005, Jul, 11-12; 2005, Jul, 11-12; 2005, Aug, 7-8; 2005, Aug, 7-8; 2005, Aug, 9-10; 2005, Aug, 9-10; 2005, July, 11-12; 2005, August, 7-8; 2005, August, 9-10

83505 total [A]
 0.00 0.00 **Global Days XXX**
AMA: 2005, Jul, 11-12; 2005, Jul, 11-12; 2005, Aug, 9-10; 2005, Aug, 9-10; 2005, Aug, 7-8; 2005, Aug, 7-8; 2005, July, 11-12; 2005, August, 7-8; 2005, August, 9-10

83516 Immunoassay for analyte other than infectious agent antibody or infectious agent antigen, qualitative or semiquantitative; multiple step method [A] [□]
 0.00 0.00 **Global Days XXX**
AMA: 2005, Aug, 7-8; 2005, Aug, 7-8; 2005, Aug, 9-10; 2005, Aug, 9-10; 2005, Jul, 11-12; 2005, Jul, 11-12; 2005, July, 11-12; 2005, August, 7-8; 2005, August, 9-10

83518 single step method (eg, reagent strip) [A] [X]
 0.00 0.00 **Global Days XXX**
AMA: 2005, Jul, 11-12; 2005, Jul, 11-12; 2005, Aug, 9-10; 2005, Aug, 9-10; 2005, Aug, 7-8; 2005, Aug, 7-8; 2005, July, 11-12; 2005, August, 7-8; 2005, August, 9-10

83519 Immunoassay, analyte, quantitative; by radiopharmaceutical technique (eg, RIA) [A] [□]
 0.00 0.00 **Global Days XXX**
AMA: 2005, Aug, 7-8; 2005, Aug, 7-8; 2005, Aug, 9-10; 2005, Aug, 9-10; 2005, Jul, 11-12; 2005, Jul, 11-12; 2005, July, 11-12; 2005, August, 7-8; 2005, August, 9-10

83520 not otherwise specified [A] [□]
 0.00 0.00 **Global Days XXX**
AMA: 2005, Aug, 9-10; 2005, Aug, 9-10; 2005, Aug, 7-8; 2005, Aug, 7-8; 2005, Jul, 11-12; 2005, Jul, 11-12; 2005, July, 11-12; 2005, August, 7-8; 2005, August, 9-10

83525 Insulin; total [A] [□]
EXCLUDES   *proinsulin (84206)*
 0.00 0.00 **Global Days XXX**
AMA: 2005, Aug, 7-8; 2005, Aug, 7-8; 2005, Jul, 11-12; 2005, Jul, 11-12; 2005, Aug, 9-10; 2005, Aug, 9-10; 2005, July, 11-12; 2005, August, 7-8; 2005, August, 9-10

83527 free [A]
 0.00 0.00 **Global Days XXX**
AMA: 2005, Aug, 7-8; 2005, Aug, 7-8; 2005, Aug, 9-10; 2005, Aug, 9-10; 2005, Jul, 11-12; 2005, Jul, 11-12; 2005, July, 11-12; 2005, August, 7-8; 2005, August, 9-10

83528 Intrinsic factor [A]
EXCLUDES   *intrinsic factor antibodies (86340)*
 0.00 0.00 **Global Days XXX**
AMA: 2005, Jul, 11-12; 2005, Jul, 11-12; 2005, Aug, 9-10; 2005, Aug, 9-10; 2005, Aug, 7-8; 2005, Aug, 7-8; 2005, July, 11-12; 2005, August, 7-8; 2005, August, 9-10

83540 Iron [A]
 0.00 0.00 **Global Days XXX**
AMA: 2005, Aug, 7-8; 2005, Aug, 7-8; 2005, Jul, 11-12; 2005, Jul, 11-12; 2005, Aug, 9-10; 2005, Aug, 9-10; 2005, July, 11-12; 2005, August, 7-8; 2005, August, 9-10

83550 Iron binding capacity [A]
 0.00 0.00 **Global Days XXX**
AMA: 2005, Aug, 7-8; 2005, Aug, 7-8; 2005, Jul, 11-12; 2005, Jul, 11-12; 2005, Aug, 9-10; 2005, Aug, 9-10; 2005, August, 7-8; 2005, July, 11-12; 2005, August, 9-10

83570 Isocitric dehydrogenase (IDH) [A]
 0.00 0.00 **Global Days XXX**
AMA: 2005, Aug, 7-8; 2005, Aug, 7-8; 2005, Jul, 11-12; 2005, Jul, 11-12; 2005, Aug, 9-10; 2005, Aug, 9-10; 2005, August, 7-8; 2005, July, 11-12; 2005, August, 9-10

83582 Ketogenic steroids, fractionation [A]
 0.00 0.00 **Global Days XXX**
AMA: 2005, Jul, 11-12; 2005, Jul, 11-12; 2005, Aug, 7-8; 2005, Aug, 7-8; 2005, Aug, 9-10; 2005, Aug, 9-10; 2005, August, 7-8; 2005, July, 11-12; 2005, August, 9-10

83586 Ketosteroids, 17- (17-KS); total [A]
 0.00 0.00 **Global Days XXX**
AMA: 2005, Jul, 11-12; 2005, Jul, 11-12; 2005, Aug, 9 10; 2005, Aug, 9-10; 2005, Aug, 7-8; 2005, Aug, 7-8; 2005, August, 7-8; 2005, August, 9-10; 2005, July, 11-12

83593 fractionation [A]
 0.00 0.00 **Global Days XXX**
AMA: 2005, Aug, 7-8; 2005, Aug, 7-8; 2005, Jul, 11-12; 2005, Jul, 11-12; 2005, Aug, 9-10; 2005, Aug, 9-10; 2005, August, 7-8; 2005, August, 9-10; 2005, July, 11-12

83605 Lactate (lactic acid) [A] [X]
 0.00 0.00 **Global Days XXX**
AMA: 2005, Jul, 11-12; 2005, Jul, 11-12; 2005, Aug, 9-10; 2005, Aug, 9-10; 2005, Aug, 7-8; 2005, Aug, 7-8; 2005, August, 7-8; 2005, August, 9-10; 2005, July, 11-12

83615 Lactate dehydrogenase (LD), (LDH); [A]
 0.00 0.00 **Global Days XXX**
AMA: 2005, Aug, 7-8; 2005, Aug, 7-8; 2005, Aug, 9-10; 2005, Aug, 9-10; 2005, Jul, 11-12; 2005, Jul, 11-12; 2005, August, 7-8; 2005, August, 9-10; 2005, July, 11-12

83625 isoenzymes, separation and quantitation [A] [□]
 0.00 0.00 **Global Days XXX**
AMA: 2005, Aug, 7-8; 2005, Aug, 7-8; 2005, Aug, 9-10; 2005, Aug, 9-10; 2005, Jul, 11-12; 2005, Jul, 11-12; 2005, August, 7-8; 2005, August, 9-10; 2005, July, 11-12

83630 Lactoferrin, fecal; qualitative [A]
 0.00 0.00 **Global Days XXX**
AMA: 2006, Feb, 7-9; 2006, Feb, 7-9; 2006, February, 7-9; 2005, Aug, 9-10; 2005, Aug, 9 10; 2005, Aug, 7-8; 2005, August, 9-10; 2005, July, 11-12; 2005, August, 7-8; 2005, Aug, 7-8; 2005, Jul, 11-12; 2005, Jul, 11-12

83631 quantitative [A]
 0.00 0.00 **Global Days XXX**
AMA: 2008, Jan, 10-25; 2007, Jan, 28-31; 2007, Jan, 28-31; 2007, January, 28-31; 2006, Feb, 7-9; 2006, February, 7-9; 2006, Feb, 7-9; 2005, Aug, 7-8; 2005, August, 9-10; 2005, August, 7-8; 2005, Aug, 7-8, 2005, Aug, 9-10; 2005, Aug, 9-10

83632 Lactogen, human placental (HPL) human chorionic somatomammotropin [M] [♀] [A]
 0.00 0.00 **Global Days XXX**
AMA: 2005, Jul, 11-12; 2005, Jul, 11-12; 2005, Aug, 9-10; 2005, Aug, 9-10; 2005, Aug, 7 8; 2005, Aug, 7-8; 2005, August, 7-8; 2005, August, 9-10; 2005, July, 11-12

83633 Lactose, urine; qualitative [A]
 0.00 0.00 **Global Days XXX**
AMA: 2005, Aug, 7-8; 2005, Aug, 7-8; 2005, Aug, 9-10; 2005, Aug, 9-10; 2005, Jul, 11-12; 2005, Jul, 11-12; 2005, August, 7-8; 2005, August, 9-10; 2005, July, 11-12

83634 quantitative [A]
EXCLUDES   *breath hydrogen test for lactase deficiency (91065)*
            glucose tolerance test (GTT) (82951-82952)
 0.00 0.00 **Global Days XXX**
AMA: 2005, Aug, 9-10; 2005, Aug, 9-10; 2005, Aug, 7 8; 2005, Aug, 7-8; 2005, Jul, 11-12; 2005, Jul, 11-12; 2005, July, 11-12; 2005, August, 7-8; 2005, August, 9-10

83655 Lead [A] [X]
 0.00 0.00 **Global Days XXX**
AMA: 2005, Aug, 9-10; 2005, Aug, 9-10; 2005, Aug, 7-8; 2005, Aug, 7-8; 2005, Jul, 11-12; 2005, Jul, 11-12; 2005, August, 7-8; 2005, August, 9-10; 2005, July, 11-12

83661 Fetal lung maturity assessment; lecithin sphingomyelin (L/S) ratio ⊞ ♀ 🄰 ▣

📋 0.00 ✂ 0.00 **Global Days XXX**

AMA: 2005, Aug, 7-8; 2005, Aug, 7-8; 2005, Jul, 11-12; 2005, Jul, 11-12; 2005, Aug, 9-10; 2005, Aug, 9-10; 2005, August, 7-8; 2005, July, 11-12; 2005, August, 9-10

83662 foam stability test ⊞ ♀ 🄰 ▣

📋 0.00 ✂ 0.00 **Global Days XXX**

AMA: 2005, Aug, 7-8; 2005, Aug, 7-8; 2005, Jul, 11-12; 2005, Jul, 11-12; 2005, Aug, 9-10; 2005, Aug, 9-10; 2005, August, 7-8; 2005, July, 11-12; 2005, August, 9-10

83663 fluorescence polarization ⊞ ♀ 🄰 ▣

📋 0.00 ✂ 0.00 **Global Days XXX**

AMA: 2005, Aug, 9-10; 2005, Aug, 9-10; 2005, Jul, 11-12; 2005, Jul, 11-12; 2005, Aug, 7-8; 2005, Aug, 7-8; 2005, August, 7-8; 2005, July, 11-12; 2005, August, 9-10

83664 lamellar body density ⊞ ♀ 🄰 ▣

EXCLUDES *phosphatidylglycerol (84081)*

📋 0.00 ✂ 0.00 **Global Days XXX**

AMA: 2005, Jul, 11-12; 2005, Jul, 11-12; 2005, Aug, 9-10; 2005, Aug, 9-10; 2005, Aug, 7-8; 2005, Aug, 7-8; 2005, August, 7-8; 2005, July, 11-12; 2005, August, 9-10

83670 Leucine aminopeptidase (LAP) 🄰

📋 0.00 ✂ 0.00 **Global Days XXX**

AMA: 2005, Aug, 7-8; 2005, Aug, 7-8; 2005, Jul, 11-12; 2005, Jul, 11-12; 2005, Aug, 9-10; 2005, Aug, 9-10; 2005, August, 7-8; August, 9-10; 2005, July, 11-12

83690 Lipase 🄰

📋 0.00 ✂ 0.00 **Global Days XXX**

AMA: 2005, Aug, 7-8; 2005, Aug, 7-8; 2005, Jul, 11-12; 2005, Jul, 11-12; 2005, Aug, 9-10; 2005, Aug, 9-10; 2005, August, 7-8; 2005, July, 11-12; 2005, August, 9-10

83695-83727 Chemistry: Lipoprotein--Luteinizing Releasing Factor

CMS *100-3,190.23* Lipid Testing
CMS *100-4,3,10.4* Payment of Nonphysician Services for Inpatients
CMS *100-2,15,80* Physician Supervision Requirements for Diagnostic Tests
INCLUDES mathematically calculated results
quantitative analysis unless otherwise specified
specimens from any source unless otherwise specified
EXCLUDES *organ or disease panels (80048-80076)*
therapeutic drug assays

83695 Lipoprotein (a) 🄰

📋 0.00 ✂ 0.00 **Global Days XXX**

AMA: 2006, Feb, 7-9; 2006, Feb, 7-9; 2006, February, 7-9; 2005, Aug, 9-10; 2005, Aug, 9-10; 2005, August, 9-10; 2005, August, 7-8; 2005, Aug, 7-8; 2005, Aug, 7-8

83698 Lipoprotein-associated phospholipase A2 (Lp-PLA2) 🄰

📋 0.00 ✂ 0.00 **Global Days XXX**

83700 Lipoprotein, blood; electrophoretic separation and quantitation 🄰

📋 0.00 ✂ 0.00 **Global Days XXX**

AMA: 2006, Feb, 7-9; 2006, Feb, 7-9; 2006, February, 7-9; 2005, Aug, 9-10; 2005, Aug, 9-10; 2005, August, 9-10; 2005, August, 7-8; 2005, Aug, 7-8; 2005, Aug, 7-8

83701 high resolution fractionation and quantitation of lipoproteins including lipoprotein subclasses when performed (eg, electrophoresis, ultracentrifugation) 🄰

📋 0.00 ✂ 0.00 **Global Days XXX**

AMA: 2006, Feb, 7-9; 2006, Feb, 7-9; 2006, February, 7-9; 2005, Aug, 7-8; 2005, Aug, 7-8; 2005, August, 9-10; 2005, August, 7-8; 2005, Aug, 9-10; 2005, Aug, 9-10

83704 quantitation of lipoprotein particle numbers and lipoprotein particle subclasses (eg, by nuclear magnetic resonance spectroscopy) 🄰

📋 0.00 ✂ 0.00 **Global Days XXX**

AMA: 2006, Feb, 7-9; 2006, Feb, 7-9; 2006, February, 7-9; 2005, Aug, 9-10; 2005, Aug, 9-10; 2005, August, 9-10; 2005, August, 7-8; 2005, Aug, 7-8; 2005, Aug, 7-8

83718 Lipoprotein, direct measurement; high density cholesterol (HDL cholesterol) 🄰 ▣ ✗

📋 0.00 ✂ 0.00 **Global Days XXX**

AMA: 2008, Jan, 10-25; 2007, Jan, 13-27; 2007, Jan, 13-27; 2007, January, 13-27; 2005, Aug, 7-8; 2005, Aug, 7-8; 2005, Feb, 7-9; 2005, Feb, 7-9; 2005, February, 7-9; 2005, August, 9-10; 2005, July, 11-12; 2005, August, 7-8; 2005, Jul, 11-12; 2005, Jul, 11-12; 2005, Aug, 9-10; 2005, Aug, 9-10

83719 VLDL cholesterol 🄰 ▣

📋 0.00 ✂ 0.00 **Global Days XXX**

AMA: 2008, Jan, 10-25; 2007, Jan, 13-27; 2007, Jan, 13-27; 2007, January, 13-27; 2005, Aug, 7-8; 2005, Aug, 7-8; 2005, Jul, 11-12; 2005, July, 11-12; 2005, August, 9-10; 2005, August, 7-8; 2005, Jul, 11-12; 2005, Aug, 9-10; 2005, Aug, 9-10

83721 LDL cholesterol 🄰 ▣ ✗

EXCLUDES *fractionation by high resolution electrophoresis or ultracentrifugation (83701)*
lipoprotein particle numbers and subclasses analysis by nuclear magnetic resonance spectroscopy (83704)

📋 0.00 ✂ 0.00 **Global Days XXX**

AMA: 2008, Jan, 10-25; 2007, Jan, 13-27; 2007, Jan, 13-27; 2007, January, 13-27; 2005, Aug, 7-8; 2005, Aug, 7-8; 2005, Jul, 11-12; 2005, August, 9-10; 2005, August, 7-8; 2005, July, 11-12; 2005, Jul, 11-12; 2005, Aug, 9-10; 2005, Aug, 9-10

83727 Luteinizing releasing factor (LRH) 🄰

EXCLUDES *qualitative analysis (80100-80103)*

📋 0.00 ✂ 0.00 **Global Days XXX**

AMA: 2005, Aug, 7-8; 2005, Aug, 7-8; 2005, Jul, 11-12; 2005, Jul, 11-12; 2005, Aug, 9-10; 2005, Aug, 9-10; 2005, August, 7-8; July, 11-12; 2005, August, 9-10

83735-83887 Chemistry: Magnesium--Nicotine

CMS *100-4,3,10.4* Payment of Nonphysician Services for Inpatients
CMS *100-2,15,80* Physician Supervision Requirements for Diagnostic Tests
INCLUDES mathematically calculated results
quantitative analysis unless otherwise specified
specimens from any source unless otherwise specified
EXCLUDES *organ or disease panels (80048-80076)*
therapeutic drug assays (80150-80299)

83735 Magnesium 🄰

📋 0.00 ✂ 0.00 **Global Days XXX**

AMA: 2005, Aug, 9-10; 2005, Aug, 9-10; 2005, Jul, 11-12; 2005, Jul, 11-12; 2005, Aug, 7-8; 2005, Aug, 7-8; 2005, August, 7-8; 2005, July, 11-12; 2005, August, 9-10

83775 Malate dehydrogenase 🄰

📋 0.00 ✂ 0.00 **Global Days XXX**

AMA: 2005, Aug, 7-8; 2005, Aug, 7-8; 2005, Jul, 11-12; 2005, Jul, 11-12; 2005, Aug, 9-10; 2005, Aug, 9-10; 2005, August, 7-8; 2005, July, 11-12; 2005, August, 9-10

83785 Manganese 🄰

📋 0.00 ✂ 0.00 **Global Days XXX**

AMA: 2005, Aug, 7-8; 2005, Aug, 7-8; 2005, Aug, 9-10; 2005, Aug, 9-10; 2005, Jul, 11-12; 2005, Jul, 11-12; 2005, August, 7-8; 2005, July, 11-12; 2005, August, 9-10

㉖/🆃🄲 Professional/Technical Component Only   ⑧⓪/⑧⓪ Assist-at-Surgery Allowed/With Documentation   Unlisted   Not Covered   ❌ Radiology crosswalk

MED: Pub 100/NCD References   **AMA:** CPT Assistant References   🄰-🅉 ASC Payment Indicator   ♂Male Only   ♀Female Only   ◼ Laboratory crosswalk

334   CPT only © 2008 American Medical Association. All Rights Reserved. (Black Ink)   Medicare (Red Ink)   © 2008 Ingenix *(Blue Ink)*

83788 Mass spectrometry and tandem mass spectrometry (MS, MS/MS), analyte not elsewhere specified; qualitative, each specimen [A]

0.00   0.00 Global Days XXX

AMA: 2005, Jul, 11-12; 2005, Jul, 11-12; 2005, Aug, 7-8; 2005, Aug, 7-8; 2005, Aug, 9-10; 2005, Aug, 9-10; 2005, August, 7-8; 2005, July, 11-12; 2005, August, 9-10

83789 quantitative, each specimen [A] [CCI]

0.00   0.00 Global Days XXX

AMA: 2005, Jul, 11-12; 2005, Jul, 11-12; 2005, Aug, 9-10; 2005, Aug, 9-10; 2005, Aug, 7-8; 2005, Aug, 7-8; 2005, August, 7-8; 2005, July, 11-12; 2005, August, 9-10

83805 Meprobamate [A]

EXCLUDES   *qualitative analysis (80100-80103)*

0.00   0.00 Global Days XXX

AMA: 2005, Aug, 7-8; 2005, Aug, 7-8; 2005, Aug, 9-10; 2005, Aug, 9-10; 2005, Jul, 11-12; 2005, Jul, 11-12; 2005, August, 7-8; 2005, July, 11-12; 2005, August, 9-10

83825 Mercury, quantitative [A]

EXCLUDES   *mercury screen (83015)*

0.00   0.00 Global Days XXX

AMA: 2005, Aug, 7-8; 2005, Aug, 7-8; 2005, Aug, 9-10; 2005, Aug, 9-10; 2005, Jul, 11-12; 2005, Jul, 11-12; 2005, July, 11-12; 2005, August, 9-10; 2005, August, 7-8

83835 Metanephrines [A]

EXCLUDES   *catecholamines (82382-82384)*

0.00   0.00 Global Days XXX

AMA: 2005, Aug, 9-10; 2005, Aug, 9-10; 2005, Jul, 11-12; 2005, Jul, 11-12; 2005, Aug, 7-8; 2005, Aug, 7-8; 2005, August, 7-8; 2005, July, 11-12; 2005, August, 9-10

83840 Methadone [A]

EXCLUDES   *methadone qualitative analysis (80100-80103)*

0.00   0.00 Global Days XXX

AMA: 2005, Aug, 9-10; 2005, Aug, 9-10; 2005, Aug, 7-8; 2005, Aug, 7-8; 2005, Jul, 11-12; 2005, Jul, 11-12; 2005, August, 7-8; 2005, July, 11-12; 2005, August, 9-10

83857 Methemalbumin [A]

0.00   0.00 Global Days XXX

AMA: 2005, Aug, 7-8; 2005, Aug, 7-8; 2005, Jul, 11-12; 2005, Jul, 11-12; 2005, Aug, 9-10; 2005, Aug, 9-10; 2005, August, 7-8; 2005, July, 11-12; 2005, August, 9-10

83858 Methsuximide [A]

0.00   0.00 Global Days XXX

AMA: 2005, Aug, 9-10; 2005, Aug, 9-10; 2005, Aug, 7-8; 2005, Aug, 7-8; 2005, Jul, 11-12; 2005, Jul, 11-12; 2005, August, 7-8; 2005, July, 11-12; 2005, August, 9-10

83864 Mucopolysaccharides, acid; quantitative [A]

0.00   0.00 Global Days XXX

AMA: 2005, Aug, 7-8; 2005, Aug, 7-8; 2005, Jul, 11-12; 2005, Jul, 11-12; 2005, Aug, 9-10; 2005, Aug, 9-10; 2005, August, 7-8; 2005, July, 11-12; 2005, August, 9-10

83866 screen [A]

0.00   0.00 Global Days XXX

AMA: 2005, Aug, 7-8; 2005, Aug, 7-8; 2005, Aug, 9-10; 2005, Aug, 9-10; 2005, Jul, 11-12; 2005, Jul, 11-12; 2005, August, 7-8; 2005, July, 11-12; 2005, August, 9-10

83872 Mucin, synovial fluid (Ropes test) [A]

0.00   0.00 Global Days XXX

AMA: 2005, Aug, 9-10; 2005, Aug, 9-10; 2005, Aug, 7-8; 2005, Aug, 7-8; 2005, Jul, 11-12; 2005, Jul, 11-12; 2005, August, 7-8; 2005, July, 11-12; 2005, August, 9-10

83873 Myelin basic protein, cerebrospinal fluid [A]

EXCLUDES   *oligoclonal bands (83916)*

0.00   0.00 Global Days XXX

AMA: 2005, Aug, 7-8; 2005, Aug, 7-8; 2005, Aug, 9-10; 2005, Aug, 9-10; 2005, Jul, 11-12; 2005, Jul, 11-12; 2005, August, 7-8; 2005, August, 9-10; 2005, July, 11-12

83874 Myoglobin [A]

0.00   0.00 Global Days XXX

AMA: 2005, Jul, 11-12; 2005, Jul, 11-12; 2005, Aug, 9-10; 2005, Aug, 9-10; 2005, Aug, 7-8; 2005, Aug, 7-8; 2005, August, 7-8; 2005, August, 9-10; 2005, July, 11-12

● **83876** Myeloperoxidase (MPO) [A]

0.00   0.00 Global Days XXX

83880 Natriuretic peptide [A] [X]

0.00   0.00 Global Days XXX

AMA: 2005, Aug, 7-8; 2005, Aug, 7-8; 2005, Aug, 9-10; 2005, Aug, 9-10; 2005, Jul, 11-12; 2005, Jul, 11-12; 2005, August, 7-8; 2005, August, 9-10; 2005, July, 11-12

83883 Nephelometry, each analyte not elsewhere specified [A]

0.00   0.00 Global Days XXX

AMA: 2005, Jul, 11-12; 2005, Jul, 11-12; 2005, Aug, 7-8; 2005, Aug, 7-8; 2005, Aug, 9-10; 2005, Aug, 9-10; 2005, August, 7-8; 2005, August, 9-10; 2005, July, 11-12

83885 Nickel [A]

0.00   0.00 Global Days XXX

AMA: 2005, Aug, 7-8; 2005, Aug, 7-8; 2005, Jul, 11-12; 2005, Jul, 11-12; 2005, Aug, 9-10; 2005, Aug, 9-10; 2005, August, 7-8; 2005, August, 9-10; 2005, July, 11-12

83887 Nicotine [A]

0.00   0.00 Global Days XXX

AMA: 2005, Jul, 11-12; 2005, Jul, 11-12; 2005, Aug, 7-8; 2005, Aug, 7-8; 2005, Aug, 9-10; 2005, Aug, 9-10; 2005, July, 11-12; 2005, August, 9-10; 2005, August, 7-8

83890-83914 Chemistry: Nucleic Acid Diagnostics

CMS *100-4,3,10.4*   Payment of Nonphysician Services for Inpatients
CMS *100-2,15,80*   Physician Supervision Requirements for Diagnostic Tests
INCLUDES   molecular diagnostic techniques for analysis of nucleic acids tests reported by procedure instead of analyte

EXCLUDES   *array technology using more than 10 probes (88384-88386)*
digestate, undigested nucleic acid, or other individually modified nucleic acid sample
microbial identification (87470-87801)

▲ **83890** Molecular diagnostics; molecular isolation or extraction, each nucleic acid type (ie, DNA or RNA) [A] [CCI]

0.00   0.00 Global Days XXX

AMA: 2008, Apr, 5-7; 2008, Apr, 5-7; 2008, Apr, 5-7; 2006, Jan, 5-6,48; 2006, Jan, 5-6,48; 2006, February, 7-9; 2006, January, 5-6,48; 2006, Feb, 7-9; 2006, Feb, 7-9; 2005, Aug, 7-8; 2005, August, 7-8; 2005, August, 9-10; 2005, July, 1-8; 2005, July, 11-12; 2005, Aug, 7-8; 2005, Jul, 11-12; 2005, Jul, 11-12; 2005, Jul, 1-8; 2005, Jul, 1-8; 2005, Aug, 9-10; 2005, Aug, 9-10

▲ **83891** isolation or extraction of highly purified nucleic acid, each nucleic acid type (ie, DNA or RNA) [A] [CCI]

0.00   0.00 Global Days XXX

AMA: 2008, Apr, 5-7; 2008, Apr, 5-7; 2008, Apr, 5-7; 2006, Jan, 5-6,48; 2006, Jan, 5-6,48; 2006, January, 5-6,48; 2005, Aug, 9-10; 2005, Aug, 9-10; 2005, August, 7-8; 2005, July, 1-8; 2005, August, 9-10; 2005, July, 11-12; 2005, Aug, 7-8; 2005, Aug, 7-8; 2005, Jul, 1-8; 2005, Jul, 1-8; 2005, Jul, 11-12; 2005, Jul, 11-12

▲ 83892   enzymatic digestion, each enzyme treatment Ⓐ▫
    0.00   0.00 **Global Days XXX**
    AMA: 2008, Apr, 5-7; 2008, Apr, 5-7; 2008, Apr, 5-7; 2006, Jan, 5-6,48; 2006, Jan, 5-6,48; 2006, January, 5-6,48; 2005, Jul, 11-12; 2005, Jul, 11-12; 2005, August, 7-8; 2005, July, 1-8; 2005, August, 9-10; 2005, July, 11-12; 2005, Aug, 7-8; 2005, Aug, 7-8; 2005, Jul, 1-8; 2005, Jul, 1-8; 2005, Aug, 9-10; 2005, Aug, 9-10

▲ 83893   dot/slot blot production, each nucleic acid preparation Ⓐ▫
    0.00   0.00 **Global Days XXX**
    AMA: 2008, Apr, 5-7; 2008, Apr, 5-7; 2008, Apr, 5-7; 2006, Jan, 5-6,48; 2006, Jan, 5-6,48; 2006, January, 5-6,48; 2005, Aug, 7-8; 2005, Aug, 7-8; 2005, August, 7-8; 2005, July, 1-8; 2005, August, 9-10; 2005, July, 11-12; 2005, Jul, 11-12; 2005, Jul, 11-12; 2005, Aug, 9-10; 2005, Aug, 9-10; 2005, Jul, 1-8; 2005, Jul, 1-8

▲ 83894   separation by gel electrophoresis (eg, agarose, polyacrylamide), each nucleic acid preparation Ⓐ▫
    0.00   0.00 **Global Days XXX**
    AMA: 2008, Apr, 5-7; 2008, Apr, 5-7; 2008, Apr, 5-7; 2006, Jan, 5-6,48; 2006, Jan, 5-6,48; 2006, January, 5-6,48; 2005, Aug, 7-8; 2005, Aug, 7-8; 2005, August, 7-8; 2005, July, 1-8; 2005, August, 9-10; 2005, July, 1-8; 2005, Jul, 1-8; 2005, Aug, 9-10; 2005, Aug, 9-10; 2005, Jul, 11-12; 2005, Jul, 11-12

83896   nucleic acid probe, each Ⓐ▫
    0.00   0.00 **Global Days XXX**
    AMA: 2008, Apr, 5-7; 2008, Apr, 5-7; 2008, Apr, 5-7; 2008, Jan, 10-25; 2007, Jan, 13-27; 2007, Jan, 13-27; 2007, January, 13-27; 2006, Jan, 5-6,48; 2006, Jan, 5-6,48; 2006, January, 5-6,48; 2005, Aug, 7-8; 2005, August, 7-8; 2005, August, 9-10; 2005, July, 1-8; 2005, July, 11-12; 2005, Aug, 7-8; 2005, Jul, 11-12; 2005, Jul, 11-12; 2005, Aug, 9-10; 2005, Aug, 9-10; 2005, Jul, 1-8; 2005, Jul, 1-8

▲ 83897   nucleic acid transfer (eg, Southern, Northern), each nucleic acid preparation Ⓐ▫
    0.00   0.00 **Global Days XXX**
    AMA: 2008, Apr, 5-7; 2008, Apr, 5-7; 2008, Apr, 5-7; 2006, Jan, 5-6,48; 2006, Jan, 5-6,48; 2006, January, 5-6,48; 2005, Jul, 1-8; 2005, Jul, 1-8; 2005, August, 7-8; 2005, July, 11-12; 2005, August, 9-10; 2005, July, 1-8; 2005, Aug, 9-10; 2005, Aug, 9-10; 2005, Jul, 11-12; 2005, Jul, 11-12; 2005, Aug, 7-8; 2005, Aug, 7-8

83898   amplification, target, each nucleic acid sequence Ⓐ▫
    EXCLUDES   *multiple target amplification (83900-83901) signal amplification (83908)*
    0.00   0.00 **Global Days XXX**
    AMA: 2008, Apr, 5-7; 2008, Apr, 5-7; 2008, Apr, 5-7; 2006, Feb, 7-9; 2006, Feb, 7-9; 2006, February, 7-9; 2006, January, 5-6,48; 2006, Jan, 5-6,48; 2006, Jan, 5-6,48; 2005, Aug, 7-8; 2005, August, 7-8; 2005, August, 9-10; 2005, July, 11-12; 2005, July, 1-8; 2005, Aug, 7-8; 2005, Jul, 11-12; 2005, Jul, 11-12; 2005, Aug, 9-10; 2005, Aug, 9-10; 2005, Jul, 1-8; 2005, Jul, 1-8

83900   amplification, target, multiplex, first 2 nucleic acid sequences Ⓐ
    0.00   0.00 **Global Days XXX**
    AMA: 2008, Apr, 5-7; 2008, Apr, 5-7; 2008, Apr, 5-7; 2006, Feb, 7-9; 2006, Feb, 7-9; 2006, Jan, 5-6,48; 2006, Jan, 5-6,48; 2006, January, 5-6,48; 2006, February, 7-9; 2005, Aug, 7-8; 2005, Aug, 7-8; 2005, August, 7-8; 2005, August, 9-10; 2005, Aug, 9-10; 2005, Aug, 9-10

+ 83901   amplification, target, multiplex, each additional nucleic acid sequence beyond 2 (List separately in addition to code for primary procedure) Ⓐ▫
    Code first (83900)
    0.00   0.00 **Global Days XXX**
    AMA: 2008, Apr, 5-7; 2008, Apr, 5-7; 2008, Apr, 5-7; 2006, Feb, 7-9; 2006, Feb, 7-9; 2006, February, 7-9; 2006, January, 5-6,48; 2006, Jan, 5-6,48; 2006, Jan, 5-6,48; 2006, Jan, 5-6,48; 2005, Jul, 1-8; 2005, August, 7-8; 2005, July, 11-12; 2005, August, 9-10; 2005, July, 1-8; 2005, Jul, 1-8; 2005, Aug, 9-10; 2005, Aug, 9-10; 2005, Aug, 7-8; 2005, Jul, 11-12; 2005, Jul, 11-12

83902   reverse transcription Ⓐ▫
    0.00   0.00 **Global Days XXX**
    AMA: 2008, Apr, 5-7; 2008, Apr, 5-7; 2008, Apr, 5-7; 2006, Jan, 5-6,48; 2006, Jan, 5-6,48; 2006, January, 5-6,48; 2005, Aug, 7-8; 2005, Aug, 7-8; 2005, August, 7-8; 2005, July, 11-12; 2005, August, 9-10; 2005, July, 1-8; 2005, Jul, 1-8; 2005, Jul, 1-8; 2005, Aug, 9-10; 2005, Aug, 9-10; 2005, Jul, 11-12; 2005, Jul, 11-12

83903   mutation scanning, by physical properties (eg, single strand conformational polymorphisms [SSCP], heteroduplex, denaturing gradient gel electrophoresis [DGGE], RNA'ase A), single segment, each Ⓐ▫
    0.00   0.00 **Global Days XXX**
    AMA: 2008, Apr, 5-7; 2008, Apr, 5-7; 2008, Apr, 5-7; 2006, Jan, 5-6,48; 2006, Jan, 5-6,48; 2006, January, 5-6,48; 2005, Jul, 11-12; 2005, Jul, 11-12; 2005, August, 7-8; 2005, July, 1-8; 2005, August, 9-10; 2005, July, 11-12; 2005, Aug, 7-8; 2005, Aug, 7-8; 2005, Jul, 1-8; 2005, Jul, 1-8; 2005, Aug, 9-10; 2005, Aug, 9-10

83904   mutation identification by sequencing, single segment, each segment Ⓐ▫
    0.00   0.00 **Global Days XXX**
    AMA: 2008, Apr, 5-7; 2008, Apr, 5-7; 2008, Apr, 5-7; 2006, Jan, 5-6,48; 2006, Jan, 5-6,48; 2006, January, 5-6,48; 2005, Aug, 7-8; 2005, Aug, 7-8; 2005, August, 7-8; 2005, July, 1-8; 2005, August, 9-10; 2005, July, 11-12; 2005, Jul, 1-8; 2005, Jul, 1-8; 2005, Aug, 9-10; 2005, Aug, 9-10; 2005, Jul, 11-12; 2005, Jul, 11-12

83905   mutation identification by allele specific transcription, single segment, each segment Ⓐ▫
    0.00   0.00 **Global Days XXX**
    AMA: 2008, Apr, 5-7; 2008, Apr, 5-7; 2008, Apr, 5-7; 2006, Jan, 5-6,48; 2006, Jan, 5-6,48; 2006, January, 5-6,48; 2005, Jul, 1-8; 2005, Jul, 1-8; 2005, August, 7-8; 2005, July, 1-8; 2005, August, 9-10; 2005, July, 11-12; 2005, Aug, 7-8; 2005, Aug, 7-8; 2005, Aug, 9-10; 2005, Aug, 9-10; 2005, Jul, 11-12; 2005, Jul, 11-12

83906   mutation identification by allele specific translation, single segment, each segment Ⓐ▫
    0.00   0.00 **Global Days XXX**
    AMA: 2008, Apr, 5-7; 2008, Apr, 5-7; 2008, Apr, 5-7; 2006, Jan, 5-6,48; 2006, Jan, 5-6,48; 2006, January, 5-6,48; 2005, Aug, 7-8; 2005, Aug, 7-8; 2005, August, 7-8; 2005, July, 1-8; 2005, July, 11-12; 2005, August, 9-10; 2005, Jul, 11-12; 2005, Jul, 11-12; 2005, Jul, 1-8; 2005, Jul, 1-8; 2005, Aug, 9-10; 2005, Aug, 9-10

▲ 83907   lysis of cells prior to nucleic acid extraction (eg, stool specimens, paraffin embedded tissue), each specimen Ⓐ
    0.00   0.00 **Global Days XXX**
    AMA: 2008, Apr, 5-7; 2008, Apr, 5-7; 2008, Apr, 5-7; 2006, Feb, 7-9; 2006, Feb, 7-9; 2006, Jan, 5-6,48; 2006, Jan, 5-6,48; 2006, January, 5-6,48; 2006, February, 7-9; 2005, Aug, 7-8; 2005, August, 9-10; 2005, August, 7-8; 2005, Aug, 9-10; 2005, Aug, 9-10

26/TC Professional/Technical Component Only   80/80 Assist-at-Surgery Allowed/With Documentation   Unlisted   Not Covered   ✚ Radiology crosswalk

MED: Pub 100/NCD References   **AMA:** CPT Assistant References   A2-Z3 ASC Payment Indicator   ♂Male Only   ♀Female Only   ◣ Laboratory crosswalk

336   CPT only © 2008 American Medical Association. All Rights Reserved. (Black Ink)   Medicare (Red Ink)   © 2008 Ingenix *(Blue Ink)*

Pathology and Laboratory

83908 amplification, signal, each nucleic acid sequence Ⓐ
EXCLUDES *target amplification (83898-83901)*
🔲 0.00 🔲 0.00 Global Days XXX
AMA: 2008, Apr, 5-7; 2008, Apr, 5-7; 2008, Apr, 5-7; 2006, Jan, 5-6,48; 2006, Jan, 5-6,48; 2006, Feb, 7-9; 2006, Feb, 7-9; 2006, January, 5-6,48; 2006, February, 7-9; 2005, Aug, 9-10; 2005, Aug, 9-10; 2005, August, 7-8; 2005, August, 9-10; 2005, Aug, 7-8; 2005, Aug, 7-8

▲ 83909 separation and identification by high resolution technique (eg, capillary electrophoresis), each nucleic acid preparation Ⓐ
🔲 0.00 🔲 0.00 Global Days XXX
AMA: 2008, Apr, 5-7; 2008, Apr, 5-7; 2008, Apr, 5-7; 2006, Feb, 7-9; 2006, Feb, 7-9; 2006, Jan, 5-6,48; 2006, Jan, 5-6,48; 2006, January, 5-6,48; 2006, February, 7-9; 2005, Aug, 7-8; 2005, Aug, 7-8; 2005, August, 7-8; 2005, August, 9-10; 2005, Aug, 9-10; 2005, Aug, 9-10

83912 interpretation and report Ⓐ 80 🔲
🔲 0.00 🔲 0.00 Global Days XXX
AMA: 2008, Apr, 5-7; 2008, Apr, 5-7; 2008, Apr, 5-7; 2006, Jan, 5-6,48; 2006, Jan, 5-6,48; 2006, February, 7-9; 2006, January, 5-6,48; 2006, Feb, 7-9; 2006, Feb, 7-9; 2005, Aug, 7-8; 2005, August, 7-8; 2005, July, 1-8; 2005, July, 11-12; 2005, August, 9-10; 2005, Aug, 7-8; 2005, Jul, 11-12; 2005, Jul, 11-12; 2005, Aug, 9-10; 2005, Jul, 1-8; 2005, Jul, 1-8

83913 RNA stabilization Ⓐ
🔲 0.00 🔲 0.00 Global Days XXX
AMA: 2008, Apr, 5-7; 2008, Apr, 5-7; 2008, Apr, 5-7

83914 Mutation identification by enzymatic ligation or primer extension, single segment, each segment (eg, oligonucleotide ligation assay [OLA], single base chain extension [SBCE], or allele-specific primer extension [ASPE]) Ⓐ
🔲 0.00 🔲 0.00 Global Days XXX
AMA: 2008, Apr, 5-7; 2008, Apr, 5-7; 2008, Apr, 5-7; 2006, Jan, 5-6,48; 2006, Jan, 5-6,48; 2006, Feb, 7-9; 2006, Feb, 7-9; 2006, January, 5-6,48; 2006, February, 7-9; 2005, Aug, 7-8; 2005, Aug, 7-8; 2005, August, 7-8; 2005, August, 9-10; 2005, Aug, 9-10; 2005, Aug, 9-10

83915-84066 Chemistry: Nucleotidase 5'- Phosphatase (Acid)

CMS 100-4,3,10.4 *Payment of Nonphysician Services for Inpatients*
CMS 100-2,15,80 *Physician Supervision Requirements for Diagnostic Tests*
INCLUDES mathematically calculated results
quantitative analysis unless otherwise specified
specimens from any source unless otherwise specified
EXCLUDES *organ or disease panels (80048-80299)*
therapeutic drug assays (80150-80299)

83915 Nucleotidase 5'- Ⓐ
🔲 0.00 🔲 0.00 Global Days XXX
AMA: 2005, Jul, 11-12; 2005, Jul, 11-12; 2005, Aug, 9-10; 2005, Aug, 9-10; 2005, Aug, 7-8; 2005, Aug, 7-8; 2005, August, 7-8; 2005, August, 9-10; 2005, July, 11-12

83916 Oligoclonal immune (oligoclonal bands) Ⓐ 🔲
🔲 0.00 🔲 0.00 Global Days XXX
AMA: 2005, Aug, 7-8; 2005, Aug, 7-8; 2005, Aug, 9-10; 2005, Aug, 9-10; 2005, Jul, 11-12; 2005, Jul, 11-12; 2005, August, 7-8; 2005, August, 9-10; 2005, July, 11-12

83918 Organic acids; total, quantitative, each specimen Ⓐ 🔲
🔲 0.00 🔲 0.00 Global Days XXX
AMA: 2008, Jan, 10-25; 2007, Jan, 13-27; 2007, Jan, 13-27; 2007, January, 13-27; 2005, Jul, 11-12; 2005, Jul, 11-12; 2005, Aug, 9-10; 2005, August, 9-10; 2005, July, 11-12; 2005, August, 7-8; 2005, Aug, 9-10; 2005, Aug, 7-8; 2005, Aug, 7-8

83919 qualitative, each specimen Ⓐ
🔲 0.00 🔲 0.00 Global Days XXX
AMA: 2005, Jul, 11-12; 2005, Jul, 11-12; 2005, Aug, 9-10; 2005, Aug, 9-10; 2005, Aug, 7-8; 2005, Aug, 7-8; 2005, August, 7-8; 2005, August, 9-10; 2005, July, 11-12

83921 Organic acid, single, quantitative Ⓐ 🔲
🔲 0.00 🔲 0.00 Global Days XXX
AMA: 2005, Aug, 7-8; 2005, Aug, 7-8; 2005, Aug, 9-10; 2005, Aug, 9-10; 2005, Jul, 11-12; 2005, Jul, 11-12; 2005, August, 7-8; 2005, August, 9-10; 2005, July, 11-12

▲ 83925 Opiate(s), drug and metabolites, each procedure Ⓐ
🔲 0.00 🔲 0.00 Global Days XXX
AMA: 2005, Aug, 7-8; 2005, Aug, 7-8; 2005, Jul, 11-12; 2005, Jul, 11-12; 2005, Aug, 9-10; 2005, Aug, 9-10; 2005, August, 7-8; 2005, August, 9-10; 2005, July, 11-12

83930 Osmolality; blood Ⓐ
🔲 0.00 🔲 0.00 Global Days XXX
AMA: 2005, Aug, 7-8; 2005, Aug, 7-8; 2005, Jul, 11-12; 2005, Jul, 11-12; 2005, Aug, 9-10; 2005, Aug, 9-10; 2005, August, 7-8; 2005, August, 9-10; 2005, July, 11-12

83935 urine Ⓐ
🔲 0.00 🔲 0.00 Global Days XXX
AMA: 2005, Aug, 9-10; 2005, Aug, 9-10; 2005, Aug, 7-8; 2005, Aug, 7-8; 2005, Jul, 11-12; 2005, Jul, 11-12; 2005, August, 7-8; 2005, August, 9-10; 2005, July, 11-12

83937 Osteocalcin (bone g1a protein) Ⓐ
🔲 0.00 🔲 0.00 Global Days XXX
AMA: 2005, Jul, 11-12; 2005, Jul, 11-12; 2005, Aug, 9-10; 2005, Aug, 9-10; 2005, Aug, 7-8; 2005, Aug, 7-8; 2005, August, 9-10; 2005, July, 11-12; 2005, August, 7-8

83945 Oxalate Ⓐ
🔲 0.00 🔲 0.00 Global Days XXX
AMA: 2005, Aug, 7-8; 2005, Aug, 7-8; 2005, Jul, 11-12; 2005, Jul, 11-12; 2005, Aug, 9-10; 2005, Aug, 9-10; 2005, August, 7-8; 2005, August, 9-10; 2005, July, 11-12

▲ 83950 Oncoprotein; HER-2/neu Ⓐ 🔲
EXCLUDES *tissue (88342, 88365)*
🔲 0.00 🔲 0.00 Global Days XXX
AMA: 2005, Aug, 7-8; 2005, Aug, 7-8; 2005, Aug, 9-10; 2005, Aug, 9-10; 2005, Jul, 11-12; 2005, Jul, 11-12; 2005, August, 7-8; 2005, July, 11-12; 2005, August, 9-10

● 83951 Oncoprotein; des-gamma-carboxy-prothrombin (DCP) Ⓐ
🔲 0.00 🔲 0.00 Global Days XXX

83970 Parathormone (parathyroid hormone) Ⓐ
EXCLUDES *chlorinated hydrocarbons (82441)*
pesticide, quantitative (see code for specific method)
🔲 0.00 🔲 0.00 Global Days XXX
AMA: 2005, Aug, 7-8; 2005, Aug, 7-8; 2005, Jul, 11-12; 2005, Jul, 11-12; 2005, Aug, 9-10; 2005, Aug, 9-10; 2005, August, 7-8; 2005, August, 9-10; 2005, July, 11-12

83986 pH, body fluid, except blood Ⓐ ✕
EXCLUDES *blood pH (82800, 82803)*
🔲 0.00 🔲 0.00 Global Days XXX
AMA: 2005, Jul, 11-12; 2005, Jul, 11-12; 2005, Aug, 9-10; 2005, Aug, 9-10; 2005, Aug, 7-8; 2005, Aug, 7-8; 2005, August, 7-8; 2005, August, 9-10; 2005, July, 11-12

83992 Phencyclidine (PCP) Ⓐ
EXCLUDES *qualitative analysis (80100-80103)*
🔲 0.00 🔲 0.00 Global Days XXX
AMA: 2005, Aug, 7-8; 2005, Aug, 7-8; 2005, Aug, 9-10; 2005, Aug, 9-10; 2005, Jul, 11-12; 2005, Jul, 11-12; 2005, August, 7-8; 2005, August, 9-10; 2005, July, 11-12

83993 **Calprotectin, fecal** Ⓐ
📠 0.00 ⚕ 0.00 **Global Days XXX**
AMA: 2008, Apr, 5-7; 2008, Apr, 5-7; 2008, Apr, 5-7

84022 **Phenothiazine** Ⓐ
EXCLUDES *qualitative analysis (80100-80101)*

📠 0.00 ⚕ 0.00 **Global Days XXX**
AMA: 2005, Jul, 11-12; 2005, Jul, 11-12; 2005, Aug, 7-8; 2005, Aug, 7-8; 2005, Aug, 9-10; 2005, Aug, 9-10; 2005, August, 7-8; 2005, August, 9-10; 2005, July, 11-12

84030 **Phenylalanine (PKU), blood** Ⓐ
INCLUDES Guthrie test

EXCLUDES *phenylalanine-tyrosine ratio (84030, 84510)*

📠 0.00 ⚕ 0.00 **Global Days XXX**
AMA: 2005, Aug, 7-8; 2005, Aug, 7-8; 2005, Jul, 11-12; 2005, Jul, 11-12; 2005, Aug, 9-10; 2005, Aug, 9-10; 2005, August, 7-8; 2005, August, 9-10; 2005, July, 11-12

84035 **Phenylketones, qualitative** Ⓐ
📠 0.00 ⚕ 0.00 **Global Days XXX**
AMA: 2005, Aug, 7-8; 2005, Aug, 7-8; 2005, Aug, 9-10; 2005, Aug, 9-10; 2005, Jul, 11-12; 2005, Jul, 11-12; 2005, August, 7-8; 2005, August, 9-10; 2005, July, 11-12

84060 **Phosphatase, acid; total** Ⓐ
📠 0.00 ⚕ 0.00 **Global Days XXX**
AMA: 2005, Jul, 11-12; 2005, Jul, 11-12; 2005, Aug, 9-10; 2005, Aug, 9-10; 2005, Aug, 7-8; 2005, Aug, 7-8; 2005, August, 7-8; 2005, August, 9-10; 2005, July, 11-12

84061 **forensic examination** Ⓐ
📠 0.00 ⚕ 0.00 **Global Days XXX**
AMA: 2005, Aug, 7-8; 2005, Aug, 7-8; 2005, Aug, 9-10; 2005, Aug, 9-10; 2005, Jul, 11-12; 2005, Jul, 11-12; 2005, August, 7-8; 2005, July, 11-12; 2005, August, 9-10

84066 **prostatic** ♂ Ⓐ
📠 0.00 ⚕ 0.00 **Global Days XXX**
AMA: 2005, Jul, 11-12; 2005, Jul, 11-12; 2005, Aug, 9-10; 2005, Aug, 9-10; 2005, Aug, 7-8; 2005, Aug, 7-8; 2005, August, 7-8; 2005, July, 11-12; 2005, August, 9-10

84075-84080 Chemistry: Phosphatase (Alkaline)

CMS *100-3,190.10* *Laboratory Tests--CRD Patients*
CMS *100-4,3,10.4* *Payment of Nonphysician Services for Inpatients*
CMS *100-2,15,80* *Physician Supervision Requirements for Diagnostic Tests*
INCLUDES mathematically calculated results
quantitative analysis unless otherwise specified
specimens from any source unless otherwise specified

EXCLUDES *organ or disease panels (80048-80076)*

84075 **Phosphatase, alkaline;** Ⓐ ✖
📠 0.00 ⚕ 0.00 **Global Days XXX**
AMA: 2005, Aug, 7-8; 2005, Aug, 7-8; 2005, Aug, 9-10; 2005, Aug, 9-10; 2005, Jul, 11-12; 2005, Jul, 11-12; 2005, August, 7-8; 2005, July, 11-12; 2005, August, 9-10

84078 **heat stable (total not included)** Ⓐ
📠 0.00 ⚕ 0.00 **Global Days XXX**
AMA: 2005, Jul, 11-12; 2005, Jul, 11-12; 2005, Aug, 7-8; 2005, Aug, 7-8; 2005, Aug, 9-10; 2005, Aug, 9-10; 2005, July, 11-12; 2005, August, 9-10; 2005, August, 7-8

84080 **isoenzymes** Ⓐ ⬛
📠 0.00 ⚕ 0.00 **Global Days XXX**
AMA: 2005, Aug, 7-8; 2005, Aug, 7-8; 2005, Jul, 11-12; 2005, Jul, 11-12; 2005, Aug, 9-10; 2005, Aug, 9-10; 2005, August, 7-8; 2005, July, 11-12; 2005, August, 9-10

84081-84150 Chemistry: Phosphatidylglycerol--Prostaglandin

CMS *100-4,3,10.4* *Payment of Nonphysician Services for Inpatients*
CMS *100-2,15,80* *Physician Supervision Requirements for Diagnostic Tests*
INCLUDES mathematically calculated results
quantitative analysis unless otherwise specified
specimens from any source unless otherwise specified

EXCLUDES *organ or disease panels (80048-80076)*
therapeutic drug assays (80150-80299)

84081 **Phosphatidylglycerol** Ⓐ
📠 0.00 ⚕ 0.00 **Global Days XXX**
AMA: 2005, Aug, 7-8; 2005, Aug, 7-8; 2005, Jul, 11-12; 2005, Jul, 11-12; 2005, Aug, 9-10; 2005, Aug, 9-10; 2005, August, 7-8; 2005, July, 11-12; 2005, August, 9-10

84085 **Phosphogluconate, 6-, dehydrogenase, RBC** Ⓐ
📠 0.00 ⚕ 0.00 **Global Days XXX**
AMA: 2005, Jul, 11-12; 2005, Jul, 11-12; 2005, Aug, 7-8; 2005, Aug, 7-8; 2005, Aug, 9-10; 2005, Aug, 9-10; 2005, August, 7-8; 2005, July, 11-12; 2005, August, 9-10

84087 **Phosphohexose isomerase** Ⓐ
📠 0.00 ⚕ 0.00 **Global Days XXX**
AMA: 2005, Jul, 11-12; 2005, Jul, 11-12; 2005, Aug, 9-10; 2005, Aug, 9-10; 2005, Aug, 7-8; 2005, Aug, 7-8; 2005, August, 7-8; 2005, July, 11-12; 2005, August, 9-10

84100 **Phosphorus inorganic (phosphate);** Ⓐ
📠 0.00 ⚕ 0.00 **Global Days XXX**
AMA: 2005, Aug, 9-10; 2005, Aug, 9-10; 2005, Jul, 11-12; 2005, Jul, 11-12; 2005, Aug, 7-8; 2005, Aug, 7-8; 2005, August, 7-8; 2005, July, 11-12; 2005, August, 9-10

84105 **urine** Ⓐ
📠 0.00 ⚕ 0.00 **Global Days XXX**
AMA: 2005, Aug, 7-8; 2005, Aug, 7-8; 2005, Jul, 11-12; 2005, Jul, 11-12; 2005, Aug, 9-10; 2005, Aug, 9-10; 2005, August, 7-8; 2005, July, 11-12; 2005, August, 9-10

84106 **Porphobilinogen, urine; qualitative** Ⓐ
📠 0.00 ⚕ 0.00 **Global Days XXX**
AMA: 2005, Aug, 7-8; 2005, Aug, 7-8; 2005, Jul, 11-12; 2005, Jul, 11-12; 2005, Aug, 9-10; 2005, Aug, 9-10; 2005, August, 7-8; 2005, July, 11-12; 2005, August, 9-10

84110 **quantitative** Ⓐ
📠 0.00 ⚕ 0.00 **Global Days XXX**
AMA: 2005, Aug, 7-8; 2005, Aug, 7-8; 2005, Jul, 11-12; 2005, Jul, 11-12; 2005, Aug, 9-10; 2005, Aug, 9-10; 2005, August, 7-8; 2005, July, 11-12; 2005, August, 9-10

84119 **Porphyrins, urine; qualitative** Ⓐ
📠 0.00 ⚕ 0.00 **Global Days XXX**
AMA: 2005, Aug, 7-8; 2005, Aug, 7-8; 2005, Jul, 11-12; 2005, Jul, 11-12; 2005, Aug, 9-10; 2005, Aug, 9-10; 2005, August, 7-8; 2005, July, 11-12; 2005, August, 9-10

84120 **quantitation and fractionation** Ⓐ
📠 0.00 ⚕ 0.00 **Global Days XXX**
AMA: 2005, Jul, 11-12; 2005, Jul, 11-12; 2005, Aug, 9-10; 2005, Aug, 9-10; 2005, Aug, 7-8; 2005, Aug, 7-8; 2005, August, 7-8; 2005, July, 11-12; 2005, August, 9-10

84126 **Porphyrins, feces; quantitative** Ⓐ
📠 0.00 ⚕ 0.00 **Global Days XXX**
AMA: 2005, Jul, 11-12; 2005, Jul, 11-12; 2005, Aug, 9-10; 2005, Aug, 9-10; 2005, Aug, 7-8; 2005, Aug, 7-8; 2005, August, 7-8; 2005, July, 11-12; 2005, August, 9-10

84127 **qualitative** Ⓐ
EXCLUDES *porphyrin precursors (82135, 84106, 84110)*

📠 0.00 ⚕ 0.00 **Global Days XXX**
AMA: 2005, Aug, 7-8; 2005, Aug, 7-8; 2005, Jul, 11-12; 2005, Jul, 11-12; 2005, Aug, 9-10; 2005, Aug, 9-10; 2005, August, 7-8; 2005, July, 11-12; 2005, August, 9-10

▲ 84132 Potassium; serum, plasma or whole blood [A][X]
🚑 0.00 ✎ 0.00 Global Days XXX
AMA: 2005, Aug, 7-8; 2005, Aug, 7-8; 2005, Jul, 11-12; 2005, Jul, 11-12; 2005, Aug, 9-10; 2005, Aug, 9-10; 2005, August, 7-8; 2005, July, 11-12; 2005, August, 9-10

84133 urine [A]
🚑 0.00 ✎ 0.00 Global Days XXX
AMA: 2005, Jul, 11-12; 2005, Jul, 11-12; 2005, Aug, 9-10; 2005, Aug, 9-10; 2005, Aug, 7-8; 2005, Aug, 7-8; 2005, August, 7-8; 2005, July, 11-12; 2005, August, 9-10

84134 Prealbumin [A]
EXCLUDES microalbumin (82043-82044 (82043-82044)
🚑 0.00 ✎ 0.00 Global Days XXX
AMA: 2005, Aug, 7-8; 2005, Aug, 7-8; 2005, Jul, 11-12; 2005, Jul, 11-12; 2005, Aug, 9-10; 2005, Aug, 9-10; 2005, August, 7-8; 2005, August, 9-10; 2005, July, 11

84135 Pregnanediol [A]
🚑 0.00 ✎ 0.00 Global Days XXX
AMA: 2005, Jul, 11-12; 2005, Jul, 11-12; 2005, Aug, 9-10; 2005, Aug, 9-10; 2005, Aug, 7-8; 2005, Aug, 7-8; 2005, August, 7-8; 2005, August, 9-10; 2005, July, 11

84138 Pregnanetriol [A]
🚑 0.00 ✎ 0.00 Global Days XXX
AMA: 2005, Aug, 7-8; 2005, Aug, 7-8; 2005, Aug, 9-10; 2005, Aug, 9-10; 2005, Jul, 11-12; 2005, Jul, 11-12; 2005, July, 11-12; 2005, August, 7-8; 2005, August, 9-10

84140 Pregnenolone [A]
🚑 0.00 ✎ 0.00 Global Days XXX
AMA: 2005, Jul, 11-12; 2005, Jul, 11-12; 2005, Aug, 9-10; 2005, Aug, 9-10; 2005, Aug, 7-8; 2005, Aug, 7-8; 2005, August, 7-8; 2005, July, 11-12; 2005, August, 9-10

84143 17-hydroxypregnenolone [A]
🚑 0.00 ✎ 0.00 Global Days XXX
AMA: 2005, Aug, 7-8; 2005, Aug, 7-8; 2005, Aug, 9-10; 2005, Aug, 9-10; 2005, Jul, 11-12; 2005, Jul, 11-12; 2005, August, 7-8; 2005, July, 11-12; 2005, August, 9-10

84144 Progesterone [A]
EXCLUDES progesterone receptor assay (84234)
🚑 0.00 ✎ 0.00 Global Days XXX
AMA: 2005, Aug, 7-8; 2005, Aug, 7-8; 2005, Jul, 11-12; 2005, Jul, 11-12; 2005, Aug, 9-10; 2005, Aug, 9-10; 2005, August, 7-8; 2005, August, 9-10; 2005, July, 11-12

84146 Prolactin [A][▢]
🚑 0.00 ✎ 0.00 Global Days XXX
AMA: 2005, Jul, 11-12; 2005, Jul, 11-12; 2005, Aug, 9-10; 2005, Aug, 9-10; 2005, Aug, 7-8; 2005, Aug, 7-8; 2005, August, 7-8; 2005, July, 11-12, 2005, August, 9-10

84150 Prostaglandin, each [A]
🚑 0.00 ✎ 0.00 Global Days XXX
AMA: 2005, Jul, 11-12; 2005, Jul, 11-12; 2005, Aug, 9-10; 2005, Aug, 9-10; 2005, Aug, 7-8; 2005, Aug, 7-8; 2005, August, 7-8; 2005, July, 11-12; 2005, August, 9-10

84152-84154 Chemistry: Prostate Specific Antigen

CMS 100-3,190.31 Prostate Specific Antigen (PSA)
CMS 100-3,210.1 Prostate Cancer Screening Tests
CMS 100-4,3,10.4 Payment of Nonphysician Services for Inpatients
CMS 100-2,15,80 Physician Supervision Requirements for Diagnostic Tests
INCLUDES mathematically calculated results
quantitative analysis unless otherwise specified

84152 Prostate specific antigen (PSA); complexed (direct measurement) ♂ [A]
🚑 0.00 ✎ 0.00 Global Days XXX
AMA: 2005, Aug, 9-10; 2005, Aug, 9-10; 2005, Aug, 7-8; 2005, Aug, 7-8; 2005, Jul, 11-12; 2005, Jul, 11-12; 2005, August, 7-8; 2005, July, 11-12; 2005, August, 9-10

84153 total ♂ [A]
🚑 0.00 ✎ 0.00 Global Days XXX
AMA: 2008, Jan, 10-25; 2007, Jan, 13-27; 2007, Jan, 13-27; 2007, January, 13-27; 2005, Aug, 7-8; 2005, Aug, 7-8; 2005, Jul, 11-12; 2005, July, 11-12; 2005, August, 9-10; 2005, August, 7-8; Jul, 11-12; 2005, Aug, 9-10; 2005, Aug, 9-10

84154 free ♂ [A]
🚑 0.00 ✎ 0.00 Global Days XXX
AMA: 2008, Jan, 10-25; 2007, Jan, 13-27; 2007, Jan, 13-27; 2007, January, 13-27; 2005, Aug, 7-8; 2005, Aug, 7-8; 2005, Jul, 11-12; 2005, August, 9-10; 2005, July, 11-12; 2005, August, 7-8; 2005, Jul, 11-12; 2005, Aug, 9-10; 2005, Aug, 9-10

84155-84157 Chemistry: Protein, Total (Not by Refractometry)

CMS 100-3,190.10 Laboratory Tests--CRD Patients
CMS 100-4,3,10.4 Payment of Nonphysician Services for Inpatients
CMS 100-2,15,80 Physician Supervision Requirements for Diagnostic Tests
INCLUDES mathematically calculated results
EXCLUDES organ or disease panels (80048-80076)

▲ 84155 Protein, total, except by refractometry; serum, plasma or whole blood [A][▢]
🚑 0.00 ✎ 0.00 Global Days XXX
AMA: 2005, Aug, 7-8; 2005, Aug, 7-8; 2005, Jul, 11-12; 2005, Jul, 11-12; 2005, Aug, 9-10; 2005, Aug, 9-10; 2005, August, 7-8; 2005, July, 11-12; 2005, August, 9-10

84156 urine [A]
🚑 0.00 ✎ 0.00 Global Days XXX
AMA: 2005, Aug, 7-8; 2005, Aug, 7-8; 2005, Jul, 11-12; 2005, Jul, 11-12; 2005, Aug, 9-10; 2005, Aug, 9-10; 2005, August, 7-8; 2005, July, 11-12; 2005, August, 9-10

84157 other source (eg, synovial fluid, cerebrospinal fluid) [A][X]
🚑 0.00 ✎ 0.00 Global Days XXX
AMA: 2005, Jul, 11-12; 2005, Jul, 11-12; 2005, Aug, 9-10; 2005, Aug, 9-10; 2005, Aug, 7-8; 2005, Aug, 7-8; 2005, August, 7-8; 2005, August, 9-10; 2005, July, 11-12

84160-84432 Chemistry: Protein, Total (Refractometry)--Thyroglobulin

CMS *100-4,3,10.4* *Payment of Nonphysician Services for Inpatients*
CMS *100-2,15,80* *Physician Supervision Requirements for Diagnostic Tests*
INCLUDES mathematically calculated results
quantitative analysis unless otherwise specified
specimens from any source unless otherwise specified

EXCLUDES *organ or disease panels (80048-80076)*
therapeutic drug assays (80150-80299)

84160 **Protein, total, by refractometry, any source** [A] [⬛]
EXCLUDES *dipstick urine protein (81000-81003)*
🔲 0.00 ⚕ 0.00 **Global Days XXX**
AMA: 2005, Aug, 7-8; 2005, Aug, 7-8; 2005, Aug, 9-10; 2005, Aug, 9-10; 2005, Jul, 11-12; 2005, Jul, 11-12; 2005, August, 7-8; 2005, July, 11-12; 2005, August, 9-10

84163 **Pregnancy-associated plasma protein-A (PAPP-A)** ♀ [A]
🔲 0.00 ⚕ 0.00 **Global Days XXX**
AMA: 2005, Aug, 7-8; 2005, Aug, 7-8; 2005, Jul, 11-12; 2005, Jul, 11-12; 2005, Aug, 9-10; 2005, Aug, 9-10; 2005, July, 11-12; 2005, August, 9-10; 2005, August, 7-8

84165 **Protein; electrophoretic fractionation and quantitation, serum** [A] [80] [⬛]
🔲 0.00 ⚕ 0.00 **Global Days XXX**
AMA: 2005, Aug, 7-8; 2005, Aug, 7-8; 2005, Aug, 9-10; 2005, Aug, 9-10; 2005, Jul, 11-12; 2005, Jul, 11-12; 2005, August, 7-8; 2005, July, 11-12; 2005, August, 9-10

84166 **electrophoretic fractionation and quantitation, other fluids with concentration (eg, urine, CSF)** [A] [80] [⬛]
🔲 0.00 ⚕ 0.00 **Global Days XXX**
AMA: 2005, Jul, 11-12; 2005, Jul, 11-12; 2005, Aug, 7-8; 2005, Aug, 7-8; 2005, Aug, 9-10; 2005, Aug, 9-10; 2005, August, 7-8; 2005, July, 11-12; 2005, August, 9-10

84181 **Western Blot, with interpretation and report, blood or other body fluid** [A] [80] [⬛]
🔲 0.00 ⚕ 0.00 **Global Days XXX**
AMA: 2005, Jul, 11-12; 2005, Jul, 11-12; 2005, Aug, 9-10; 2005, Aug, 9-10; 2005, Aug, 7-8; 2005, Aug, 7-8; 2005, August, 7-8; 2005, July, 11-12; 2005, August, 9-10

84182 **Western Blot, with interpretation and report, blood or other body fluid, immunological probe for band identification, each** [A] [80] [⬛]
EXCLUDES *Western Blot tissue testing (88371)*
🔲 0.00 ⚕ 0.00 **Global Days XXX**
AMA: 2005, Aug, 7-8; 2005, Aug, 7-8; 2005, Jul, 11-12; 2005, Jul, 11-12; 2005, Aug, 9-10; 2005, Aug, 9-10; 2005, August, 7-8; 2005, July, 11-12; 2005, August, 9-10

84202 **Protoporphyrin, RBC; quantitative** [A]
🔲 0.00 ⚕ 0.00 **Global Days XXX**
AMA: 2005, Aug, 7-8; 2005, Aug, 7-8; 2005, Aug, 9-10; 2005, Aug, 9-10; 2005, Jul, 11-12; 2005, Jul, 11-12; 2005, August, 7-8; 2005, July, 11-12; 2005, August, 9-10

84203 **screen** [A]
🔲 0.00 ⚕ 0.00 **Global Days XXX**
AMA: 2005, Aug, 7-8; 2005, Aug, 7-8; 2005, Aug, 9-10; 2005, Aug, 9-10; 2005, Jul, 11-12; 2005, Jul, 11-12; 2005, August, 7-8; 2005, July, 11-12; 2005, August, 9-10

84206 **Proinsulin** [A]
🔲 0.00 ⚕ 0.00 **Global Days XXX**
AMA: 2005, Aug, 9-10; 2005, Aug, 9-10; 2005, Aug, 7-8; 2005, Aug, 7-8; 2005, Jul, 11-12; 2005, Jul, 11-12; 2005, August, 7-8; 2005, July, 11-12; 2005, August, 9-10

84207 **Pyridoxal phosphate (Vitamin B-6)** [A] [⬛]
🔲 0.00 ⚕ 0.00 **Global Days XXX**
AMA: 2005, Aug, 7-8; 2005, Aug, 7-8; 2005, Jul, 11-12; 2005, Jul, 11-12; 2005, Aug, 9-10; 2005, Aug, 9-10; 2005, August, 7-8; 2005, July, 11-12; 2005, August, 9-10

84210 **Pyruvate** [A]
🔲 0.00 ⚕ 0.00 **Global Days XXX**
AMA: 2005, Jul, 11-12; 2005, Jul, 11-12; 2005, Aug, 9-10; 2005, Aug, 9-10; 2005, Aug, 7-8; 2005, Aug, 7-8; 2005, August, 7-8; 2005, August, 9-10; 2005, July, 11-12

84220 **Pyruvate kinase** [A]
🔲 0.00 ⚕ 0.00 **Global Days XXX**
AMA: 2005, Aug, 7-8; 2005, Aug, 7-8; 2005, Jul, 11-12; 2005, Jul, 11-12; 2005, Aug, 9-10; 2005, Aug, 9-10; 2005, August, 7-8; 2005, July, 11-12; 2005, August, 9-10

84228 **Quinine** [A]
🔲 0.00 ⚕ 0.00 **Global Days XXX**
AMA: 2005, Aug, 9-10; 2005, Aug, 9-10; 2005, Aug, 7-8; 2005, Aug, 7-8; 2005, Jul, 11-12; 2005, Jul, 11-12; 2005, August, 7-8; 2005, August, 9-10; 2005, July, 11

84233 **Receptor assay; estrogen** [A] [⬛]
🔲 0.00 ⚕ 0.00 **Global Days XXX**
AMA: 2005, Aug, 7-8; 2005, Aug, 7-8; 2005, Jul, 11-12; 2005, Jul, 11-12; 2005, Aug, 9-10; 2005, Aug, 9-10; 2005, August, 7-8; 2005, August, 9-10

84234 **progesterone** [A] [⬛]
🔲 0.00 ⚕ 0.00 **Global Days XXX**
AMA: 2005, Aug, 7-8; 2005, Aug, 7-8; 2005, Jul, 11-12; 2005, Jul, 11-12; 2005, Aug, 9-10; 2005, Aug, 9-10; 2005, August, 7-8; 2005, August, 9-10

84235 **endocrine, other than estrogen or progesterone (specify hormone)** [A] [⬛]
🔲 0.00 ⚕ 0.00 **Global Days XXX**
AMA: 2005, Jul, 11-12; 2005, Jul, 11-12; 2005, Aug, 7-8; 2005, Aug, 7-8; 2005, Aug, 9-10; 2005, Aug, 9-10; 2005, July, 11-12; 2005, August, 7-8; 2005, August, 9-10

84238 **non-endocrine (specify receptor)** [A] [⬛]
🔲 0.00 ⚕ 0.00 **Global Days XXX**
AMA: 2008, Jan, 10-25; 2007, Jan, 13-27; 2007, Jan, 13-27; 2007, January, 13-27; 2006, Feb, 7-9; 2006, February, 7-9; 2006, Feb, 7-9; 2005, Aug, 7-8; 2005, Aug, 7-8; 2005, Jul, 11-12; 2005, July, 11-12; 2005, August, 9-10; 2005, November, 14-15; 2005, August, 7-8; 2005, Jul, 11-12; 2005, Aug, 9-10; 2005, Aug, 9-10; 2005, Nov, 14-15; 2005, Nov, 14-15

84244 **Renin** [A] [⬛]
🔲 0.00 ⚕ 0.00 **Global Days XXX**
AMA: 2005, Aug, 7-8; 2005, Aug, 7-8; 2005, Aug, 9-10; 2005, Aug, 9-10; 2005, Jul, 11-12; 2005, Jul, 11-12; 2005, August, 7-8; 2005, July, 11-12; 2005, August, 9-10

84252 **Riboflavin (Vitamin B-2)** [A] [⬛]
🔲 0.00 ⚕ 0.00 **Global Days XXX**
AMA: 2005, Aug, 9-10; 2005, Aug, 9-10; 2005, Aug, 7-8; 2005, Aug, 7-8; 2005, Jul, 11-12; 2005, Jul, 11-12; 2005, August, 7-8; 2005, July, 11-12; 2005, August, 9-10

84255 **Selenium** [A]
🔲 0.00 ⚕ 0.00 **Global Days XXX**
AMA: 2005, Aug, 7-8; 2005, Aug, 7-8; 2005, Jul, 11-12; 2005, Jul, 11-12; 2005, Aug, 9-10; 2005, Aug, 9-10; 2005, August, 7-8; 2005, July, 11-12; 2005, August, 9-10

84260 **Serotonin** [A]
EXCLUDES *urine metabolites (HIAA) (83497)*
🔲 0.00 ⚕ 0.00 **Global Days XXX**
AMA: 2005, Aug, 7-8; 2005, Aug, 7-8; 2005, Jul, 11-12; 2005, Jul, 11-12; 2005, Aug, 9-10; 2005, Aug, 9-10; 2005, August, 7-8; 2005, July, 11-12; 2005, August, 9-10

84270   **Sex hormone binding globulin (SHBG)**   A
        📠 0.00   ✄ 0.00 Global Days XXX
        AMA: 2005, Aug, 7-8; 2005, Aug, 7-8; 2005, Jul, 11-12; 2005, Jul,
        11-12; 2005, Aug, 9-10; 2005, Aug, 9-10; 2005, August, 7-8; 2005,
        July, 11-12; 2005, August, 9-10

84275   **Sialic acid**   A
        📠 0.00   ✄ 0.00 Global Days XXX
        AMA: 2005, Jul, 11-12; 2005, Jul, 11-12; 2005, Aug, 9-10; 2005,
        Aug, 9-10; 2005, Aug, 7-8; 2005, Aug, 7-8; 2005, August, 7-8;
        2005, July, 11-12; 2005, August, 9-10

84285   **Silica**   A
        📠 0.00   ✄ 0.00 Global Days XXX
        AMA: 2005, Aug, 7-8; 2005, Aug, 7-8; 2005, Jul, 11-12; 2005, Jul,
        11-12; 2005, Aug, 9-10; 2005, Aug, 9-10; 2005, August, 7-8; 2005,
        July, 11-12; 2005, August, 9-10

▲ 84295 **Sodium; serum, plasma or whole blood**   A ✖
        📠 0.00   ✄ 0.00 Global Days XXX
        AMA: 2005, Aug, 7-8; 2005, Aug, 7-8; 2005, Jul, 11-12; 2005, Jul,
        11-12; 2005, Aug, 9-10; 2005, Aug, 9-10; 2005, August, 7-8; 2005,
        July, 11-12; 2005, August, 9-10

84300   **urine**   A
        📠 0.00   ✄ 0.00 Global Days XXX
        AMA: 2005, Jul, 11-12; 2005, Jul, 11-12; 2005, Aug, 7-8; 2005,
        Aug, 7-8; 2005, Aug, 9-10; 2005, Aug, 9-10; 2005, August, 7-8;
        2005, July, 11-12; 2005, August, 9-10

84302   **other source**   A
        📠 0.00   ✄ 0.00 Global Days XXX
        AMA: 2005, Aug, 9-10; 2005, Aug, 9-10; 2005, Aug, 7-8; 2005,
        Aug, 7-8; 2005, Jul, 11-12; 2005, Jul, 11-12; 2005, August, 7-8;
        2005, July, 11-12; 2005, August, 9-10

84305   **Somatomedin**   A
        📠 0.00   ✄ 0.00 Global Days XXX
        AMA: 2005, Aug, 7-8; 2005, Aug, 7-8; 2005, Jul, 11-12; 2005, Jul,
        11-12; 2005, Aug, 9-10; 2005, Aug, 9-10; 2005, August, 7-8; 2005,
        July, 11-12; 2005, August, 9-10

84307   **Somatostatin**   A
        📠 0.00   ✄ 0.00 Global Days XXX
        AMA: 2005, Aug, 7-8; 2005, Aug, 7-8; 2005, Jul, 11-12; 2005, Jul,
        11-12; 2005, Aug, 9-10; 2005, Aug, 9-10; 2005, July, 11-12; 2005,
        August, 7-8; 2005, August, 9-10

84311   **Spectrophotometry, analyte not elsewhere specified**   A
        📠 0.00   ✄ 0.00 Global Days XXX
        AMA: 2005, Aug, 7-8; 2005, Aug, 7-8; 2005, Jul, 11-12; 2005, Jul,
        11-12; 2005, Aug, 9-10; 2005, Aug, 9-10; 2005, August, 7-8; 2005,
        July, 11-12; 2005, August, 9-10

84315   **Specific gravity (except urine)**   A
        EXCLUDES   *urine specific gravity (81000-81003)*
        📠 0.00   ✄ 0.00 Global Days XXX
        AMA: 2005, Jul, 11-12; 2005, Jul, 11-12; 2005, Aug, 9-10; 2005,
        Aug, 9-10; 2005, Aug, 7-8; 2005, Aug, 7-8; 2005, August, 7-8; 2005,
        August, 9-10; 2005, July, 11-12

84375   **Sugars, chromatographic, TLC or paper**
        chromatography   A
        📠 0.00   ✄ 0.00 Global Days XXX
        AMA: 2005, Jul, 11-12; 2005, Jul, 11-12; 2005, Aug, 7-8; 2005,
        Aug, 7-8; 2005, Aug, 9-10; 2005, Aug, 9-10; 2005, August, 7-8;
        2005, July, 11-12; 2005, August, 9-10

84376   **Sugars (mono-, di-, and oligosaccharides); single**
        qualitative, each specimen   A
        📠 0.00   ✄ 0.00 Global Days XXX
        AMA: 2005, Jul, 11-12; 2005, Jul, 11-12; 2005, Aug, 9-10; 2005,
        Aug, 9-10; 2005, Aug, 7-8; 2005, Aug, 7-8; 2005, August, 7-8;
        2005, July, 11-12; 2005, August, 9-10

84377   **multiple qualitative, each specimen**   A ▣
        📠 0.00   ✄ 0.00 Global Days XXX
        AMA: 2005, Aug, 7-8; 2005, Aug, 7-8; 2005, Aug, 9-10; 2005, Aug,
        9-10; 2005, Jul, 11-12; 2005, Jul, 11-12; 2005, August, 7-8;
        2005, July, 11-12; 2005, August, 9-10

84378   **single quantitative, each specimen**   A ▣
        📠 0.00   ✄ 0.00 Global Days XXX
        AMA: 2005, Aug, 9-10; 2005, Aug, 9-10; 2005, Aug, 7-8; 2005,
        Aug, 7-8; 2005, Jul, 11-12; 2005, Jul, 11-12; 2005, August, 7-8;
        2005, July, 11-12; 2005, August, 9-10

84379   **multiple quantitative, each specimen**   A ▣
        📠 0.00   ✄ 0.00 Global Days XXX
        AMA: 2005, Jul, 11-12; 2005, Jul, 11-12; 2005, Aug, 9-10; 2005,
        Aug, 9-10; 2005, Aug, 7-8; 2005, Aug, 7-8; 2005, August, 7-8;
        2005, July, 11-12; 2005, August, 9-10

84392   **Sulfate, urine**   A
        📠 0.00   ✄ 0.00 Global Days XXX
        AMA: 2005, Aug, 7-8; 2005, Aug, 7-8; 2005, Aug, 9-10; 2005, Aug,
        9-10; 2005, Jul, 11-12; 2005, Jul, 11-12; 2005, August, 7-8; 2005,
        July, 11-12; 2005, August, 9-10

84402   **Testosterone; free**   A
        📠 0.00   ✄ 0.00 Global Days XXX
        AMA: 2005, Aug, 7-8; 2005, Aug, 7-8; 2005, Jul, 11-12; 2005, Jul,
        11-12; 2005, Aug, 9-10; 2005, Aug, 9-10; 2005, August, 7-8; 2005,
        July, 11-12; 2005, August, 9-10

84403   **total**   A ▣
        📠 0.00   ✄ 0.00 Global Days XXX
        AMA: 2005, Aug, 7-8; 2005, Aug, 7-8; 2005, Aug, 9-10; 2005, Aug,
        9-10; 2005, Jul, 11-12; 2005, Jul, 11-12; 2005, August, 7-8; 2005,
        July, 11-12; 2005, August, 9-10

84425   **Thiamine (Vitamin B-1)**   A ▣
        📠 0.00   ✄ 0.00 Global Days XXX
        AMA: 2005, Aug, 9-10; 2005, Aug, 9-10; 2005, Aug, 7-8; 2005,
        Aug, 7-8; 2005, Jul, 11-12; 2005, Jul, 11-12; 2005, August, 7-8;
        2005, July, 11-12; 2005, August, 9-10

84430   **Thiocyanate**   A
        📠 0.00   ✄ 0.00 Global Days XXX
        AMA: 2005, Aug, 7-8; 2005, Aug, 7-8; 2005, Jul, 11-12; 2005, Jul,
        11-12; 2005, Aug, 9-10; 2005, Aug, 9-10; 2005, August, 7-8; 2005,
        July, 11-12; 2005, August, 9-10

84432   **Thyroglobulin**   A
        EXCLUDES   *thyroglobulin antibody (86800)*
        📠 0.00   ✄ 0.00 Global Days XXX
        AMA: 2005, Jul, 11-12; 2005, Jul, 11-12; 2005, Aug, 9-10; 2005,
        Aug, 9-10; 2005, Aug, 7-8; 2005, Aug, 7-8; 2005, August, 7-8;
        2005, July, 11-12; 2005, August, 9-10

84436-84445 Chemistry: Thyroid Tests

CMS *100-3,190.22*   *Thyroid Testing*
CMS *100 4,3,10.4*   *Payment of Nonphysician Services for Inpatients*
CMS *100-2,15,80*   *Physician Supervision Requirements for Diagnostic Tests*
INCLUDES   mathematically calculated results
           quantitative analysis unless otherwise specified
           specimens from any source unless otherwise specified
EXCLUDES   *organ or disease panels (00040-00070)*
           therapeutic drug assays (80150-80299)

84436   **Thyroxine; total**   A ▣
        📠 0.00   ✄ 0.00 Global Days XXX
        AMA: 2005, Aug, 7-8; 2005, Aug, 7-8; 2005, Aug, 9-10; 2005, Aug,
        9-10; 2005, Jul, 11-12; 2005, Jul, 11-12; 2005, July, 11-12; 2005,
        August, 9-10; 2005, August, 7-8

🅡 Modifier 63 Exempt Code   ⊙ Moderate Sedation   + CPT Add-on Code   ⊘ Modifier 51 Exempt Code   ● New Code   ▲ Revised Code

M Maternity Edit   A Age Edit   ✖ CLIA Waived Test   A Y APC Status Indicators   ▣ CCI Comprehensive Code   50 Bilateral Procedure

© 2008 Ingenix *(Blue Ink)*   CPT only © 2008 American Medical Association. All Rights Reserved. *(Black Ink)*   Medicare *(Red Ink)*   **341**

84437   requiring elution (eg, neonatal)   [A]
        📖 0.00 ⚕ 0.00 Global Days XXX
        AMA: 2005, Aug, 7-8; 2005, Aug, 7-8; 2005, Jul, 11-12; 2005, Jul,
        11-12; 2005, Aug, 9-10; 2005, Aug, 9-10; 2005, August, 7-8; 2005,
        July, 11-12; 2005, August, 9-10

84439   free   [A] [🔲]
        📖 0.00 ⚕ 0.00 Global Days XXX
        AMA: 2005, Jul, 11-12; 2005, Jul, 11-12; 2005, Aug, 9-10; 2005,
        Aug, 9-10; 2005, Aug, 7-8; 2005, Aug, 7-8; 2005, August, 7-8;
        2005, July, 11-12; 2005, August, 9-10

84442   Thyroxine binding globulin (TBG)   [A]
        📖 0.00 ⚕ 0.00 Global Days XXX
        AMA: 2005, Aug, 7-8; 2005, Aug, 7-8; 2005, Jul, 11-12; 2005, Jul,
        11-12; 2005, Aug, 9-10; 2005, Aug, 9-10; 2005, August, 7-8; 2005,
        July, 11-12; 2005, August, 9-10

84443   Thyroid stimulating hormone (TSH)   [A] [🔲] [🔲]
        📖 0.00 ⚕ 0.00 Global Days XXX
        AMA: 2005, Aug, 9-10; 2005, Aug, 9-10; 2005, Aug, 7-8; 2005,
        Aug, 7-8; 2005, Jul, 11-12; 2005, Jul, 11-12; 2005, August, 7-8;
        2005, July, 11-12; 2005, August, 9-10

84445   Thyroid stimulating immune globulins (TSI)   [A] [🔲]
        📖 0.00 ⚕ 0.00 Global Days XXX
        AMA: 2005, Aug, 7-8; 2005, Aug, 7-8; 2005, Jul, 11-12; 2005, Jul,
        11-12; 2005, Aug, 9-10; 2005, Aug, 9-10; 2005, August, 7-8; 2005,
        July, 11-12; 2005, August, 9-10

84446-84449 Chemistry: Tocopherol Alpha--Transcortin

CMS *100-4,3,10.4*   *Payment of Nonphysician Services for Inpatients*
CMS *100-2,15,80*   *Physician Supervision Requirements for Diagnostic Tests*
INCLUDES   mathematically calculated results
            quantitative analysis unless otherwise specified
            specimens from any source unless otherwise specified

EXCLUDES   *organ or disease panels (80048-80076)*
            therapeutic drug assays (80150-80299)

84446   Tocopherol alpha (Vitamin E)   [A] [🔲]
        📖 0.00 ⚕ 0.00 Global Days XXX
        AMA: 2005, Aug, 7-8; 2005, Aug, 7-8; 2005, Jul, 11-12; 2005, Jul,
        11-12; 2005, Aug, 9-10; 2005, Aug, 9-10; 2005, August, 7-8;
        July, 11-12; 2005, August, 9-10

84449   Transcortin (cortisol binding globulin)   [A]
        📖 0.00 ⚕ 0.00 Global Days XXX
        AMA: 2005, Aug, 7-8; 2005, Aug, 7-8; 2005, Jul, 11-12; 2005, Jul,
        11-12; 2005, Aug, 9-10; 2005, Aug, 9-10; 2005, August, 7-8; 2005,
        July, 11-12; 2005, August, 9-10

84450-84460 Chemistry: Transferase

CMS *100-3,190.10*   *Laboratory Tests--CRD Patients*
CMS *100-4,3,10.4*   *Payment of Nonphysician Services for Inpatients*
CMS *100-2,15,80*   *Physician Supervision Requirements for Diagnostic Tests*
INCLUDES   mathematically calculated results
            quantitative analysis unless otherwise specified

84450   Transferase; aspartate amino (AST) (SGOT)   [A] [🔲]
        📖 0.00 ⚕ 0.00 Global Days XXX
        AMA: 2005, Aug, 7-8; 2005, Aug, 7-8; 2005, Aug, 9-10; 2005, Aug,
        9-10; 2005, Jul, 11-12; 2005, Jul, 11-12; 2005, August, 7-8; 2005,
        July, 11-12; 2005, August, 9-10

84460   alanine amino (ALT) (SGPT)   [A] [🔲]
        📖 0.00 ⚕ 0.00 Global Days XXX
        AMA: 2005, Aug, 9-10; 2005, Aug, 9-10; 2005, Aug, 7-8; 2005,
        Aug, 7-8; 2005, Jul, 11-12; 2005, Jul, 11-12; 2005, August, 7-8;
        2005, August, 9-10; 2005, July, 11-12

84466 Chemistry: Transferrin

CMS *100-4,3,10.4*   *Payment of Nonphysician Services for Inpatients*
CMS *100-2,15,80*   *Physician Supervision Requirements for Diagnostic Tests*
INCLUDES   mathematically calculated results
            quantitative analysis unless otherwise specified

84466   Transferrin   [A] [🔲]
        EXCLUDES   *iron binding capacity (83550)*
        📖 0.00 ⚕ 0.00 Global Days XXX
        AMA: 2005, Aug, 9-10; 2005, Aug, 9-10; 2005, Jul, 11-12; 2005,
        Jul, 11-12; 2005, Aug, 7-8; 2005, Aug, 7-8; 2005, August, 7-8;
        2005, July, 11-12; 2005, August, 9-10

84478 Chemistry: Triglycerides

CMS *100-3,190.23*   *Lipid Testing*
CMS *100-4,3,10.4*   *Payment of Nonphysician Services for Inpatients*
CMS *100-2,15,80*   *Physician Supervision Requirements for Diagnostic Tests*
INCLUDES   mathematically calculated results
EXCLUDES   *organ or disease panels (80048-80076)*

84478   Triglycerides   [A] [🔲] [🔲]
        📖 0.00 ⚕ 0.00 Global Days XXX
        AMA: 2008, Jan, 10-25; 2007, Jan, 13-27; 2007, Jan, 13-27; 2007,
        January, 13-27; 2005, Feb, 7-9; 2005, Feb, 7-9; 2005, Aug, 9-10;
        2005, Aug, 9-10; 2005, February, 7-9; 2005, August, 9-10; 2005,
        July, 11-12; 2005, August, 7-8; 2005, Aug, 7-8; 2005, Aug, 7-8;
        2005, Jul, 11-12; 2005, Jul, 11-12

84479-84482 Chemistry: Thyroid Hormone--Triiodothyronine

CMS *100-3,190.22*   *Thyroid Testing*
CMS *100-4,3,10.4*   *Payment of Nonphysician Services for Inpatients*
CMS *100-2,15,80*   *Physician Supervision Requirements for Diagnostic Tests*
INCLUDES   mathematically calculated results
            quantitative analysis unless otherwise specified
            specimens from any source unless otherwise specified
EXCLUDES   *organ or disease panels (80048-80076)*

84479   Thyroid hormone (T3 or T4) uptake or thyroid hormone
         binding ratio (THBR)   [A] [🔲]
        📖 0.00 ⚕ 0.00 Global Days XXX
        AMA: 2005, Aug, 7-8; 2005, Aug, 7-8; 2005, Jul, 11-12; 2005, Jul,
        11-12; 2005, Aug, 9-10; 2005, Aug, 9-10; 2005, August, 7-8;
        July, 11-12; 2005, August, 9-10

84480   Triiodothyronine T3; total (TT-3)   [A] [🔲]
        📖 0.00 ⚕ 0.00 Global Days XXX
        AMA: 2005, Aug, 7-8; 2005, Aug, 7-8; 2005, Jul, 11-12; 2005, Jul,
        11-12; 2005, Aug, 9-10; 2005, Aug, 9-10; 2005, August, 7-8; 2005,
        July, 11-12; 2005, August, 9-10

84481   free   [A] [🔲]
        📖 0.00 ⚕ 0.00 Global Days XXX
        AMA: 2005, Aug, 7-8; 2005, Aug, 7-8; 2005, Jul, 11-12; 2005, Jul,
        11-12; 2005, Aug, 9-10; 2005, Aug, 9-10; 2005, July, 11-12; 2005,
        August, 9-10; 2005, August, 7-8

84482   reverse   [A] [🔲]
        📖 0.00 ⚕ 0.00 Global Days XXX
        AMA: 2005, Aug, 7-8; 2005, Aug, 7-8; 2005, Aug, 9-10; 2005, Aug,
        9-10; 2005, Jul, 11-12; 2005, Jul, 11-12; 2005, August, 7-8; 2005,
        July, 11-12; 2005, August, 9-10

84484-84512 Chemistry: Troponin (Quantitative)--Troponin (Qualitative)

CMS *100-4,3,10.4*   *Payment of Nonphysician Services for Inpatients*
CMS *100-2,15,80*   *Physician Supervision Requirements for Diagnostic Tests*
INCLUDES   mathematically calculated results
     specimens from any source unless otherwise specified

EXCLUDES   *organ or disease panels*

84484   **Troponin, quantitative**   [A]
     EXCLUDES   *qualitative troponin assay (84512)*
     0.00   0.00   Global Days XXX
     AMA: 2005, Jul, 11-12; 2005, Jul, 11-12, 2005, Aug, 9-10; 2005, Aug, 9-10, 2005, Aug, 7-8; 2005, Aug, 7-8; 2005, August, 7-8; 2005, July, 11-12; 2005, August, 9-10

84485   **Trypsin; duodenal fluid**   [A]
     0.00   0.00   Global Days XXX
     AMA: 2005, Aug, 7-8; 2005, Aug, 7-8; 2005, Jul, 11-12; 2005, Jul, 11-12; 2005, Aug, 9-10; 2005, Aug, 9-10; 2005, August, 7-8; 2005, July, 11-12; 2005, August, 9-10

84488   **feces, qualitative**   [A]
     0.00   0.00   Global Days XXX
     AMA: 2005, Aug, 7-8; 2005, Aug, 7-8; 2005, Aug, 9-10; 2005, Aug, 9-10; 2005, Jul, 11-12; 2005, Jul, 11-12; 2005, August, 7-8; 2005, July, 11-12; 2005, August, 9-10

84490   **feces, quantitative, 24-hour collection**   [A]
     0.00   0.00   Global Days XXX
     AMA: 2005, Aug, 7-8; 2005, Aug, 7-8; 2005, Aug, 9-10; 2005, Aug, 9-10; 2005, Jul, 11-12; 2005, Jul, 11-12; 2005, August, 7-8; 2005, July, 11-12; 2005, August, 9-10

84510   **Tyrosine**   [A]
     EXCLUDES   *urate crystal identification (89060)*
     0.00   0.00   Global Days XXX
     AMA: 2005, Aug, 7-8; 2005, Aug, 7-8; 2005, Jul, 11-12; 2005, Jul, 11-12; 2005, Aug, 9-10; 2005, Aug, 9-10; 2005, August, 7-8; 2005, July, 11-12; 2005, August, 9-10

84512   **Troponin, qualitative**   [A]
     EXCLUDES   *quantitative tropin assay (84484)*
     0.00   0.00   Global Days XXX
     AMA: 2005, Jul, 11-12; 2005, Jul, 11-12; 2005, Aug, 9-10; 2005, Aug, 9-10; 2005, Aug, 7-8; 2005, Aug, 7-8; 2005, August, 7-8; 2005, July, 11-12; 2005, August, 9-10

84520-84525 Chemistry: Urea Nitrogen (Blood)

CMS *100-3,190.10*   *Laboratory Tests--ESRD Patients*
CMS *100-4,3,10.4*   *Payment of Nonphysician Services for Inpatients*
CMS *100-2,15,80*   *Physician Supervision Requirements for Diagnostic Tests*
INCLUDES   mathematically calculated results
EXCLUDES   *organ or disease panels (80048-80076)*

84520   **Urea nitrogen; quantitative**   [A][X]
     0.00   0.00   Global Days XXX
     AMA: 2005, Aug, 9-10; 2005, Aug, 9-10; 2005, Aug, 7-8; 2005, Aug, 7-8; 2005, Jul, 11-12; 2005, Jul, 11-12; 2005, August, 7-8; 2005, July, 11-12; 2005, August, 9-10

84525   **semiquantitative (eg, reagent strip test)**   [A]
     INCLUDES   Patterson's test
     0.00   0.00   Global Days XXX
     AMA: 2005, Aug, 9-10; 2005, Aug, 9-10; 2005, Aug, 7-8; 2005, Aug, 7-8; 2005, Jul, 11-12; 2005, Jul, 11-12; 2005, August, 7-8; 2005, July, 11-12; 2005, August, 9-10

84540-84630 Chemistry: Urea Nitrogen (Urine)--Zinc

CMS *100-4,3,10.4*   *Payment of Nonphysician Services for Inpatients*
CMS *100-2,15,80*   *Physician Supervision Requirements for Diagnostic Tests*
INCLUDES   mathematically calculated results
     quantitative analysis unless otherwise specified
     specimens from any source unless otherwise specified

EXCLUDES   *organ or disease panels (80048-80076)*
     therapeutic drug assays (80150-80299)

84540   **Urea nitrogen, urine**   [A]
     0.00   0.00   Global Days XXX
     AMA: 2005, Aug, 7-8; 2005, Aug, 7-8; 2005, Jul, 11-12; 2005, Jul, 11-12; 2005, Aug, 9-10; 2005, Aug, 9-10; 2005, August, 7-8; 2005, July, 11-12; 2005, August, 9-10

84545   **Urea nitrogen, clearance**   [A]
     0.00   0.00   Global Days XXX
     AMA: 2005, Aug, 7-8; 2005, Aug, 7-8; 2005, Jul, 11-12; 2005, Jul, 11-12; 2005, Aug, 9-10; 2005, Aug, 9-10; 2005, August, 7-8; 2005, August, 9-10; 2005, July, 11-12

84550   **Uric acid; blood**   [A][X]
     0.00   0.00   Global Days XXX
     AMA: 2005, Jul, 11-12; 2005, Jul, 11-12; 2005, Aug, 9-10; 2005, Aug, 9-10; 2005, Aug, 7-8; 2005, Aug, 7-8; 2005, August, 7-8; 2005, July, 11-12; 2005, August, 9-10

84560   **other source**   [A]
     0.00   0.00   Global Days XXX
     AMA: 2005, Aug, 7-8; 2005, Aug, 7-8; 2005, Jul, 11-12; 2005, Jul, 11-12; 2005, Aug, 9-10; 2005, Aug, 9-10; 2005, August, 7-8; 2005, July, 11-12; 2005, August, 9-10

84577   **Urobilinogen, feces, quantitative**   [A]
     0.00   0.00   Global Days XXX
     AMA: 2005, Aug, 7-8; 2005, Aug, 7-8; 2005, Aug, 9-10; 2005, Aug, 9-10; 2005, Jul, 11-12; 2005, Jul, 11-12; 2005, August, 7-8; 2005, July, 11-12; 2005, August, 9-10

84578   **Urobilinogen, urine; qualitative**   [A]
     0.00   0.00   Global Days XXX
     AMA: 2005, Aug, 7-8; 2005, Aug, 7-8; 2005, Aug, 9-10; 2005, Aug, 9-10; 2005, Jul, 11-12; 2005, Jul, 11-12; 2005, August, 7-8; 2005, July, 11-12; 2005, August, 9-10

84580   **quantitative, timed specimen**   [A]
     0.00   0.00   Global Days XXX
     AMA: 2005, Aug, 9-10; 2005, Aug, 9-10; 2005, Jul, 11-12; 2005, Jul, 11-12; 2005, Aug, 7-8; 2005, Aug, 7-8; 2005, August, 7-8; 2005, July, 11-12; 2005, August, 9-10

84583   **semiquantitative**   [A]
     0.00   0.00   Global Days XXX
     AMA: 2005, Jul, 11-12; 2005, Jul, 11-12; 2005, Aug, 7-8; 2005, Aug, 7-8; 2005, Aug, 9-10; 2005, Aug, 9-10; 2005, August, 7-8; 2005, July, 11-12; 2005, August, 9-10

84585   **Vanillylmandelic acid (VMA), urine**   [A]
     0.00   0.00   Global Days XXX
     AMA: 2005, Aug, 7-8; 2005, Aug, 7-8; 2005, Jul, 11-12; 2005, Jul, 11-12; 2005, Aug, 9-10; 2005, Aug, 9-10; 2005, August, 7-8; 2005, July, 11-12; 2005, August, 9-10

84586   **Vasoactive intestinal peptide (VIP)**   [A]
     0.00   0.00   Global Days XXX
     AMA: 2005, Aug, 7-8; 2005, Aug, 7-8; 2005, Jul, 11-12; 2005, Jul, 11-12; 2005, Aug, 9-10; 2005, Aug, 9-10; 2005, August, 7-8; 2005, July, 11-12; 2005, August, 9-10

84588   **Vasopressin (antidiuretic hormone, ADH)**   [A]
     0.00   0.00   Global Days XXX
     AMA: 2005, Aug, 7-8; 2005, Aug, 7-8; 2005, Jul, 11-12; 2005, Jul, 11-12; 2005, Aug, 9-10; 2005, Aug, 9-10; 2005, August, 7-8; 2005, July, 11-12; 2005, August, 9-10

⊘ Modifier 63 Exempt Code   ⊙ Moderate Sedation   + CPT Add-on Code   ⊘ Modifier 51 Exempt Code   ● New Code   ▲ Revised Code

[M] Maternity Edit   [A] Age Edit   [X] CLIA Waived Test   [A][Y] APC Status Indicators   [□] CCI Comprehensive Code   [50] Bilateral Procedure

© 2008 Ingenix *(Blue Ink)*   CPT only © 2008 American Medical Association. All Rights Reserved. (Black Ink)   Medicare (Red Ink)   343

Pathology and Laboratory

84590 — 85009

84590   **Vitamin A**   Ⓐ ▫
         📋 0.00   ⚲ 0.00   **Global Days XXX**
         AMA: 2005, Aug, 9-10; 2005, Aug, 9-10; 2005, Jul, 11-12; 2005,
         Jul, 11-12; 2005, Aug, 7-8; 2005, Aug, 7-8; 2005, July, 11-12; 2005,
         August, 9-10; 2005, August, 7-8

84591   **Vitamin, not otherwise specified**   Ⓐ
         📋 0.00   ⚲ 0.00   **Global Days XXX**
         AMA: 2005, Jul, 11-12; 2005, Jul, 11-12; 2005, Aug, 9-10; 2005,
         Aug, 9-10; 2005, Aug, 7-8; 2005, Aug, 7-8; 2005, August, 7-8;
         2005, July, 11-12; 2005, August, 9-10

84597   **Vitamin K**   Ⓐ ▫
         📋 0.00   ⚲ 0.00   **Global Days XXX**
         AMA: 2005, Aug, 7-8; 2005, Aug, 7-8; 2005, Jul, 11-12; 2005, Jul,
         11-12; 2005, Aug, 9-10; 2005, Aug, 9-10; 2005, August, 7-8; 2005,
         July, 11-12; 2005, August, 9-10

84600   **Volatiles (eg, acetic anhydride, carbon tetrachloride,**
         dichloroethane, dichloromethane, diethylether, isopropyl
         alcohol, methanol)   Ⓐ
         EXCLUDES   *acetaldehyde (82000)*
         📋 0.00   ⚲ 0.00   **Global Days XXX**
         AMA: 2005, Aug, 7-8; 2005, Aug, 7-8; 2005, Jul, 11-12; 2005, Jul,
         11-12; 2005, Aug, 9-10; 2005, Aug, 9-10; 2005, August, 7-8; 2005,
         July, 11-12; 2005, August, 9-10

84620   **Xylose absorption test, blood and/or urine**   Ⓐ ▫
         EXCLUDES   *administration (99070)*
         📋 0.00   ⚲ 0.00   **Global Days XXX**
         AMA: 2005, Aug, 7-8; 2005, Aug, 7-8; 2005, Jul, 11-12; 2005, Jul,
         11-12; 2005, Aug, 9-10; 2005, Aug, 9-10; 2005, August, 7-8; 2005,
         July, 11-12; 2005, August, 9-10

84630   **Zinc**   Ⓐ
         📋 0.00   ⚲ 0.00   **Global Days XXX**
         AMA: 2005, Aug, 9-10; 2005, Aug, 9-10; 2005, Jul, 11-12; 2005,
         Jul, 11-12; 2005, Aug, 7-8; 2005, Aug, 7-8; 2005, August, 7-8;
         2005, July, 11-12; 2005, August, 9-10

84681-84999 Other and Unlisted Chemistry Tests

CMS *100-4,3,10.4*   *Payment of Nonphysician Services for Inpatients*
CMS *100-2,15,80*   *Physician Supervision Requirements for Diagnostic Tests*
INCLUDES   mathematically calculated results
              quantitative analysis unless otherwise specified
              specimens from any source unless otherwise specified

EXCLUDES   *organ or disease panels (80048-80076)*

84681   **C-peptide**   Ⓐ ▫
         📋 0.00   ⚲ 0.00   **Global Days XXX**
         AMA: 2005, Jul, 11-12; 2005, Jul, 11-12; 2005, Aug, 9-10; 2005,
         Aug, 9-10; 2005, Aug, 7-8; 2005, Aug, 7-8; 2005, August, 7-8;
         2005, July, 11-12; 2005, August, 9-10

84702   **Gonadotropin, chorionic (hCG); quantitative**   Ⓐ ▫
         📋 0.00   ⚲ 0.00   **Global Days XXX**
         AMA: 2005, Jul, 11-12; 2005, Jul, 11-12; 2005, Aug, 9-10; 2005,
         Aug, 9-10; 2005, Aug, 7-8; 2005, Aug, 7-8; 2005, August, 7-8;
         2005, July, 11-12; 2005, August, 9-10

84703   **qualitative**   Ⓐ ✖
             EXCLUDES   *urine pregnancy test by visual color*
                           comparison (81025)
             📋 0.00   ⚲ 0.00   **Global Days XXX**
             AMA: 2005, Aug, 7-8; 2005, Aug, 7-8; 2005, Jul, 11-12; 2005, Jul,
             11-12; 2005, Aug, 9-10; 2005, Aug, 9-10; 2005, August, 7-8; 2005,
             July, 11-12; 2005, August, 9-10

84704   **free beta chain**   Ⓐ
             📋 0.00   ⚲ 0.00   **Global Days XXX**
             AMA: 2008, Apr, 5-7; 2008, Apr, 5-7; 2008, Apr, 5-7

84830   **Ovulation tests, by visual color comparison methods for**
         human luteinizing hormone   ♀ Ⓐ ✖
         📋 0.00   ⚲ 0.00   **Global Days XXX**
         AMA: 2005, Aug, 7-8; 2005, Aug, 7-8; 2005, Jul, 11-12; 2005, Jul,
         11-12; 2005, Aug, 9-10; 2005, Aug, 9-10; 2005, August, 7-8; 2005,
         July, 11-12; 2005, August, 9-10

84999   **Unlisted chemistry procedure**   Ⓐ
         📋 0.00   ⚲ 0.00   **Global Days XXX**
         AMA: 2008, Jan, 10-25; 2007, Jan, 13-27; 2007, Jan, 13-27; 2007,
         January, 13-27; 2005, Jul, 11-12; 2005, Jul, 11-12; 2005, Aug,
         9-10; 2005, July, 11-12; 2005, August, 9-10; 2005, August, 7-8;
         2005, Aug, 9-10; 2005, Aug, 7-8; 2005, Aug, 7-8

85002 Bleeding Time Test

CMS *100-4,3,10.4*   *Payment of Nonphysician Services for Inpatients*
CMS *100-2,15,80*   *Physician Supervision Requirements for Diagnostic Tests*
EXCLUDES   *agglutinins (86000, 86156-86157)*
              antiplasmin (85410)
              antithrombin III (85300-85301)
              blood banking procedures (86850-86999)

85002   **Bleeding time**   Ⓐ
         📋 0.00   ⚲ 0.00   **Global Days XXX**
         AMA: 2005, Aug, 7-8; 2005, Aug, 7-8; 2005, Jul, 11-12; 2005, Jul,
         11-12; 2005, Aug, 9-10; 2005, Aug, 9-10; 2005, August, 7-8; 2005,
         July, 11-12; 2005, August, 9-10

85004-85049 Blood Counts

CMS *100-3,190.15*   *Blood Counts*
CMS *100-4,3,10.4*   *Payment of Nonphysician Services for Inpatients*
CMS *100-2,15,80*   *Physician Supervision Requirements for Diagnostic Tests*
EXCLUDES   *agglutinins (86000, 86156-86157)*
              antiplasmin (85410)
              antithrombin III (85300-85301)
              blood banking procedures (86850-86999)

85004   **Blood count; automated differential WBC count**   Ⓐ ▫
         📋 0.00   ⚲ 0.00   **Global Days XXX**
         AMA: 2008, Jan, 10-25; 2007, Jan, 13-27; 2007, Jan, 13-27; 2007,
         January, 13-27; 2005, Jul, 11-12; 2005, Jul, 11-12; 2005, Aug,
         9-10; 2005, Aug, 9-10; 2005, August, 7-8; 2005, August, 9-10;
         2005, July, 11-12; 2005, Aug, 7-8; 2005, Aug, 7-8; 2004, Jan, 26;
         2004, January, 26; 2004, Jan, 26

85007   **blood smear, microscopic examination with manual**
             differential WBC count   Ⓐ ▫
             📋 0.00   ⚲ 0.00   **Global Days XXX**
             AMA: 2008, Jan, 10-25; 2007, Jan, 13-27; 2007, Jan, 13-27; 2007,
             January, 13-27; 2005, Aug, 7-8; 2005, Aug, 7-8; 2005, Jul, 11-12;
             2005, Jul, 11-12; 2005, July, 11-12; 2005, August, 7-8; 2005,
             August, 9-10; 2005, Aug, 9-10; 2005, Aug, 9-10; 2004, Jan, 26;
             2004, January, 26; 2004, Jan, 26

85008   **blood smear, microscopic examination without manual**
             differential WBC count   Ⓐ ▫
             EXCLUDES   *cell count other fluids (eg, CSF) (89050-89051)*
             📋 0.00   ⚲ 0.00   **Global Days XXX**
             AMA: 2008, Jan, 10-25; 2007, Jan, 13-27; 2007, Jan, 13-27; 2007,
             January, 13-27; 2005, Jul, 11-12; 2005, Jul, 11-12; 2005, Aug,
             7-8; 2005, Aug, 7-8; 2005, August, 7-8; 2005, August, 9-10; 2005,
             July, 11-12; 2005, Aug, 9-10; 2005, Aug, 9-10; 2004, Jan, 26; 2004,
             January, 26; 2004, Jan, 26

85009   **manual differential WBC count, buffy coat**   Ⓐ ▫
             📋 0.00   ⚲ 0.00   **Global Days XXX**
             AMA: 2008, Jan, 10-25; 2007, Jan, 13-27; 2007, Jan, 13-27; 2007,
             January, 13-27; 2005, Aug, 7-8; 2005, Aug, 7-8; 2005, Jul, 11-12;
             2005, Jul, 11-12; 2005, August, 7-8; 2005, August, 9-10; 2005,
             July, 11-12; 2005, Aug, 9-10; 2005, Aug, 9-10; 2004, Jan, 26; 2004,
             January, 26; 2004, Jan, 26

85013　spun microhematocrit　Ⓐ ⊠
　　📷 0.00　🔲 0.00　Global Days XXX
　　AMA: 2005, Aug, 7-8; 2005, Aug, 7-8; 2005, Aug, 9-10; 2005, Aug, 9-10; 2005, Jul, 11-12; 2005, Jul, 11-12; 2005, August, 7-8; 2005, July, 11-12; 2005, August, 9-10

85014　hematocrit (Hct)　Ⓐ ▭ ⊠
　　📷 0.00　🔲 0.00　Global Days XXX
　　AMA: 2005, Jul, 11-12; 2005, Jul, 11-12; 2005, Aug, 9-10; 2005, Aug, 9-10; 2005, Aug, 7-8; 2005, Aug, 7-8; 2005, August, 7-8; 2005, July, 11-12; 2005, August, 9-10

85018　hemoglobin (Hgb)　Ⓐ ▭ ⊠
　　EXCLUDES　*immunoassay, hemoglobin, fecal (82274 (82274)*
　　　　　　other hemoglobin determination (83020-83069)

　　📷 0.00　🔲 0.00　Global Days XXX
　　AMA: 2005, Aug, 9-10; 2005, Aug, 9-10; 2005, Aug, 7-8; 2005, Aug, 7-8; 2005, Jul, 11-12; 2005, Jul, 11-12; 2005, August, 7-8; 2005, July, 11-12; 2005, August, 9-10

85025　complete (CBC), automated (Hgb, Hct, RBC, WBC and platelet count) and automated differential WBC count　Ⓐ ▭
　　📷 0.00　🔲 0.00　Global Days XXX
　　AMA: 2008, Jan, 10-25; 2007, Jan, 13-27; 2007, Jan, 13-27; 2007, January, 13-27; 2005, Aug, 7-8; 2005, Aug, 7-8; 2005, Jul, 11-12; 2005, Jul, 11-12; 2005, August, 7-8; 2005, August, 9-10; 2005, July, 11-12; 2005, Aug, 9-10; 2005, Aug, 9-10; 2004, Jan, 26; 2004, January, 26; 2004, Jan, 26

85027　complete (CBC), automated (Hgb, Hct, RBC, WBC and platelet count)　Ⓐ ▭
　　📷 0.00　🔲 0.00　Global Days XXX
　　AMA: 2005, Jul, 11-12; 2005, Jul, 11-12; 2005, Aug, 9-10; 2005, Aug, 9-10; 2005, Aug, 7-8; 2005, August, 7-8; 2005, August, 9-10; 2005, July, 11-12; 2005, Aug, 7-8; 2004, Jan, 26; 2004, January, 26; 2004, Jan, 26

85032　manual cell count (erythrocyte, leukocyte, or platelet) each　Ⓐ ▭
　　📷 0.00　🔲 0.00　Global Days XXX
　　AMA: 2008, Jan, 10-25; 2007, Jan, 13-27; 2007, Jan, 13-27; 2007, January, 13-27; 2005, Aug, 7-8; 2005, Aug, 7-8; 2005, Jul, 11-12; 2005, July, 11-12; 2005, August, 9-10; 2005, August, 7-8; 2005, Jul, 11-12; 2005, Aug, 9-10; 2005, Aug, 9-10

85041　red blood cell (RBC), automated　Ⓐ ▭
　　Do not report with (85025, 85027)
　　📷 0.00　🔲 0.00　Global Days XXX
　　AMA: 2005, Aug, 7-8; 2005, Aug, 7-8; 2005, Aug, 9-10; 2005, Aug, 9-10; 2005, Jul, 11-12; 2005, Jul, 11-12; 2005, August, 7-8; 2005, July, 11-12; 2005, August, 9-10

85044　reticulocyte, manual　Ⓐ
　　📷 0.00　🔲 0.00　Global Days XXX
　　AMA: 2005, Aug, 9-10; 2005, Aug, 9-10; 2005, Jul, 11-12, 2005, Jul, 11-12; 2005, Aug, 7-8; 2005, Aug, 7-8; 2005, August, 7-8; 2005, July, 11-12; 2005, August, 9-10

85045　reticulocyte, automated　Ⓐ ▭
　　📷 0.00　🔲 0.00　Global Days XXX
　　AMA: 2005, Jul, 11-12; 2005, Jul, 11-12; 2005, Aug, 9-10; 2005, Aug, 9-10; 2005, Aug, 7-8; 2005, Aug, 7-8; 2005, August, 7-8; 2005, July, 11-12; 2005, August, 9-10

85046　reticulocytes, automated, including one or more cellular parameters (eg, reticulocyte hemoglobin content [CHr], immature reticulocyte fraction [IRF], reticulocyte volume [MRV], RNA content), direct measurement　Ⓐ ▭
　　📷 0.00　🔲 0.00　Global Days XXX
　　AMA: 2005, Aug, 7-8; 2005, Aug, 7-8; 2005, Jul, 11-12; 2005, Jul, 11-12; 2005, Aug, 9-10; 2005, Aug, 9-10; 2005, July, 11-12; 2005, August, 9-10; 2005, August, 7-8

85048　leukocyte (WBC), automated　Ⓐ ▭
　　📷 0.00　🔲 0.00　Global Days XXX
　　AMA: 2005, Aug, 7-8; 2005, Aug, 7-8; 2005, Jul, 11-12; 2005, Jul, 11-12; 2005, Aug, 9-10; 2005, Aug, 9-10; 2005, August, 7-8; 2005, July, 11-12; 2005, August, 9-10

85049　platelet, automated　Ⓐ ▭
　　📷 0.00　🔲 0.00　Global Days XXX
　　AMA: 2005, Aug, 7-8; 2005, Aug, 7-8; 2005, Jul, 11-12; 2005, Jul, 11-12; 2005, Aug, 9-10; 2005, Aug, 9-10; 2005, August, 7-8; 2005, July, 11-12; 2005, August, 9-10

85055-85705 Coagulopathy Testing

CMS 100-4,3,20.7.3　*Payment for Blood Clotting Factor for Hemophilia Inpatients*
CMS 100-4,3,10.4　*Payment of Nonphysician Services for Inpatients*
CMS 100-2,15,80　*Physician Supervision Requirements for Diagnostic Tests*
EXCLUDES　*agglutinins (86000, 86156-86157)*
　　　　antiplasmin (85410)
　　　　antithrombin III (85300-85301)
　　　　blood banking procedures (86850-86999)

85055　Reticulated platelet assay　Ⓐ
　　📷 0.00　🔲 0.00　Global Days XXX
　　AMA: 2005, Aug, 9-10; 2005, Aug, 9-10; 2005, Aug, 7-8; 2005, Aug, 7-8; 2005, Jul, 11-12; 2005, Jul, 11-12; 2005, August, 7-8; 2005, July, 11-12; 2005, August, 9-10

85060　Blood smear, peripheral, interpretation by physician with written report　Ⓑ ⑧⓪
　　📷 0.62　🔲 0.62　Global Days XXX
　　AMA: 2005, Jul, 11-12; 2005, Jul, 11-12; 2005, Aug, 9-10; 2005, Aug, 9-10; 2005, Aug, 7-8; 2005, Aug, 7-8; 2005, August, 7-8; 2005, August, 9-10; 2005, July, 11-12

85097　Bone marrow, smear interpretation　Ⓐ ⑧⓪
　　EXCLUDES　*bone biopsy (20220, 20225, 20240, 20245, 20250-20251)*
　　　　　special stains (88312-88313)

　　📷 1.29　🔲 2.38　Global Days XXX
　　AMA: 2008, Jan, 10-25; 2007, Jan, 13-27; 2007, Jan, 13-27; 2007, January, 13-27; 2005, Aug, 7-8; 2005, Aug, 7-8; 2005, Jul, 11-12; 2005, July, 11-12; 2005, August, 9-10; 2005, August, 7-8; 2005, Jul, 11-12; 2005, Aug, 9-10; 2005, Aug, 9-10

85130　Chromogenic substrate assay　Ⓐ ▭
　　📷 0.00　🔲 0.00　Global Days XXX
　　AMA: 2005, Aug, 7-8; 2005, Aug, 7-8; 2005, Jul, 11-12; 2005, Jul, 11-12; 2005, Aug, 9-10; 2005, Aug, 9-10; 2005, August, 7-8; 2005, August, 9-10; 2005, July, 11-12

85170　Clot retraction　Ⓐ ▭
　　📷 0.00　🔲 0.00　Global Days XXX
　　AMA: 2005, Aug, 7-8; 2005, Aug, 7-8; 2005, Jul, 11-12; 2005, Jul, 11-12; 2005, Aug, 9-10; 2005, Aug, 9-10; 2005, August, 7-8; 2005, July, 11-12; 2005, August, 9-10

85175　Clot lysis time, whole blood dilution　Ⓐ ▭
　　📷 0.00　🔲 0.00　Global Days XXX
　　AMA: 2005, Aug, 9-10; 2005, Aug, 9-10; 2005, Jul, 11-12; 2005, Jul, 11-12; 2005, Aug, 7-8; 2005, Aug, 7-8; 2005, August, 7-8; 2005, July, 11-12; 2005, August, 9-10

⊛ Modifier 63 Exempt Code　⊙ Moderate Sedation　✛ CPT Add-on Code　　Ⓢ Modifier 51 Exempt Code　　● New Code　　▲ Revised Code

Ⓜ Maternity Edit　　Ⓐ Age Edit　　⊠ CLIA Waived Test　　Ⓐ-Ⓨ APC Status Indicators　　▭ CCI Comprehensive Code　　⑤⓪ Bilateral Procedure

© 2008 Ingenix *(Blue Ink)*　　CPT only © 2008 American Medical Association. All Rights Reserved. *(Black Ink)*　　Medicare *(Red Ink)*　　345

85210 Clotting; factor II, prothrombin, specific Ⓐ▢
EXCLUDES *prothrombin time (85610-85611)*
Russel viper venom time (85612-85613
(85612-85613)

📷 0.00 ⚕ 0.00 Global Days XXX
AMA: 2005, Aug, 7-8; 2005, Aug, 7-8; 2005, Jul, 11-12; 2005, Jul, 11-12; 2005, Aug, 9-10; 2005, Aug, 9-10; 2005, August, 7-8; 2005, July, 11-12; 2005, August, 9-10

85220 factor V (AcG or proaccelerin), labile factor Ⓐ▢
📷 0.00 ⚕ 0.00 Global Days XXX
AMA: 2005, Aug, 7-8; 2005, Aug, 7-8; 2005, Jul, 11-12; 2005, Jul, 11-12; 2005, Aug, 9-10; 2005, Aug, 9-10; 2005, August, 7-8; 2005, August, 9-10

85230 factor VII (proconvertin, stable factor) Ⓐ▢
📷 0.00 ⚕ 0.00 Global Days XXX
AMA: 2005, Aug, 7-8; 2005, Aug, 7-8; 2005, Jul, 11-12; 2005, Jul, 11-12; 2005, Aug, 9-10; 2005, Aug, 9-10; 2005, August, 7-8; 2005, August, 9-10; 2005, July, 11-12

85240 factor VIII (AHG), one stage Ⓐ▢
📷 0.00 ⚕ 0.00 Global Days XXX
AMA: 2005, Aug, 7-8; 2005, Aug, 7-8; 2005, Jul, 11-12; 2005, Jul, 11-12; 2005, Aug, 9-10; 2005, Aug, 9-10; 2005, August, 7-8; 2005, August, 9-10

85244 factor VIII related antigen Ⓐ▢
📷 0.00 ⚕ 0.00 Global Days XXX
AMA: 2005, Aug, 9-10; 2005, Aug, 9-10; 2005, Jul, 11-12; 2005, Jul, 11-12; 2005, Aug, 7-8; 2005, Aug, 7-8; 2005, August, 7-8; 2005, July, 11-12; 2005, August, 9-10

85245 factor VIII, VW factor, ristocetin cofactor Ⓐ▢
📷 0.00 ⚕ 0.00 Global Days XXX
AMA: 2005, Aug, 7-8; 2005, Aug, 7-8; 2005, Jul, 11-12; 2005, Jul, 11-12; 2005, Aug, 9-10; 2005, Aug, 9-10; 2005, July, 11-12; 2005, August, 9-10; 2005, August, 7-8

85246 factor VIII, VW factor antigen Ⓐ▢
📷 0.00 ⚕ 0.00 Global Days XXX
AMA: 2005, Aug, 7-8; 2005, Aug, 7-8; 2005, Aug, 9-10; 2005, Aug, 9-10; 2005, Jul, 11-12; 2005, Jul, 11-12; 2005, August, 7-8; 2005, July, 11-12; 2005, August, 9-10

85247 factor VIII, von Willebrand factor, multimetric analysis Ⓐ▢
📷 0.00 ⚕ 0.00 Global Days XXX
AMA: 2005, Jul, 11-12; 2005, Jul, 11-12; 2005, Aug, 9-10; 2005, Aug, 9-10; 2005, Aug, 7-8; 2005, Aug, 7-8; 2005, August, 7-8; 2005, July, 11-12; 2005, August, 9-10

85250 factor IX (PTC or Christmas) Ⓐ▢
📷 0.00 ⚕ 0.00 Global Days XXX
AMA: 2005, Aug, 7-8; 2005, Aug, 7-8; 2005, Jul, 11-12; 2005, Jul, 11-12; 2005, Aug, 9-10; 2005, Aug, 9-10; 2005, August, 7-8; 2005, July, 11-12; 2005, August, 9-10

85260 factor X (Stuart-Prower) Ⓐ▢
📷 0.00 ⚕ 0.00 Global Days XXX
AMA: 2005, Aug, 9-10; 2005, Aug, 9-10; 2005, Aug, 7-8; 2005, Aug, 7-8; 2005, Jul, 11-12; 2005, Jul, 11-12; 2005, August, 7-8; 2005, July, 11-12; 2005, August, 9-10

85270 factor XI (PTA) Ⓐ▢
📷 0.00 ⚕ 0.00 Global Days XXX
AMA: 2005, Aug, 7-8; 2005, Aug, 7-8; 2005, Aug, 9-10; 2005, Aug, 9-10; 2005, Jul, 11-12; 2005, Jul, 11-12; 2005, August, 7-8; 2005, July, 11-12; 2005, August, 9-10

85280 factor XII (Hageman) Ⓐ▢
📷 0.00 ⚕ 0.00 Global Days XXX
AMA: 2005, Aug, 7-8; 2005, Aug, 7-8; 2005, Jul, 11-12; 2005, Jul, 11-12; 2005, Aug, 9-10; 2005, Aug, 9-10; 2005, August, 7-8; 2005, July, 11-12; 2005, August, 9-10

85290 factor XIII (fibrin stabilizing) Ⓐ▢
📷 0.00 ⚕ 0.00 Global Days XXX
AMA: 2005, Aug, 7-8; 2005, Aug, 7-8; 2005, Jul, 11-12; 2005, Jul, 11-12; 2005, Aug, 9-10; 2005, Aug, 9-10; 2005, August, 7-8; 2005, July, 11-12; 2005, August, 9-10

85291 factor XIII (fibrin stabilizing), screen solubility Ⓐ▢
📷 0.00 ⚕ 0.00 Global Days XXX
AMA: 2005, Jul, 11-12; 2005, Jul, 11-12; 2005, Aug, 9-10; 2005, Aug, 9-10; 2005, Aug, 7-8; 2005, Aug, 7-8; 2005, August, 7-8; 2005, July, 11-12; 2005, August, 9-10

85292 prekallikrein assay (Fletcher factor assay) Ⓐ▢
📷 0.00 ⚕ 0.00 Global Days XXX
AMA: 2005, Aug, 7-8; 2005, Aug, 7-8; 2005, Jul, 11-12; 2005, Jul, 11-12; 2005, Aug, 9-10; 2005, Aug, 9-10; 2005, August, 7-8; 2005, August, 9-10; 2005, July, 11-12

85293 high molecular weight kininogen assay (Fitzgerald factor assay) Ⓐ▢
📷 0.00 ⚕ 0.00 Global Days XXX
AMA: 2005, Aug, 7-8; 2005, Aug, 7-8; 2005, Jul, 11-12; 2005, Jul, 11-12; 2005, Aug, 9-10; 2005, Aug, 9-10; 2005, August, 7-8; 2005, July, 11-12; 2005, August, 9-10

85300 Clotting inhibitors or anticoagulants; antithrombin III, activity Ⓐ▢
📷 0.00 ⚕ 0.00 Global Days XXX
AMA: 2005, Aug, 7-8; 2005, Aug, 7-8; 2005, Aug, 9-10; 2005, Aug, 9-10; 2005, Jul, 11-12; 2005, Jul, 11-12; 2005, August, 7-8; 2005, July, 11-12; 2005, August, 9-10

85301 antithrombin III, antigen assay Ⓐ▢
📷 0.00 ⚕ 0.00 Global Days XXX
AMA: 2005, Jul, 11-12; 2005, Jul, 11-12; 2005, Aug, 9-10; 2005, Aug, 9-10; 2005, Aug, 7-8; 2005, Aug, 7-8; 2005, August, 7-8; 2005, July, 11-12; 2005, August, 9-10

85302 protein C, antigen Ⓐ▢
📷 0.00 ⚕ 0.00 Global Days XXX
AMA: 2005, Jul, 11-12; 2005, Jul, 11-12; 2005, Aug, 7-8; 2005, Aug, 7-8; 2005, Aug, 9-10; 2005, Aug, 9-10; 2005, July, 11-12; 2005, August, 9-10; 2005, August, 7-8

85303 protein C, activity Ⓐ▢
📷 0.00 ⚕ 0.00 Global Days XXX
AMA: 2005, Jul, 11-12; 2005, Jul, 11-12; 2005, Aug, 9-10; 2005, Aug, 9-10; 2005, Aug, 7-8; 2005, Aug, 7-8; 2005, August, 7-8; 2005, July, 11-12; 2005, August, 9-10

85305 protein S, total Ⓐ▢
📷 0.00 ⚕ 0.00 Global Days XXX
AMA: 2005, Aug, 7-8; 2005, Aug, 7-8; 2005, Jul, 11-12; 2005, Jul, 11-12; 2005, Aug, 9-10; 2005, Aug, 9-10; 2005, August, 7-8; 2005, July, 11-12; 2005, August, 9-10

85306 protein S, free Ⓐ▢
📷 0.00 ⚕ 0.00 Global Days XXX
AMA: 2005, Aug, 7-8; 2005, Aug, 7-8; 2005, Jul, 11-12; 2005, Jul, 11-12; 2005, Aug, 9-10; 2005, Aug, 9-10; 2005, August, 7-8; 2005, July, 11-12; 2005, August, 9-10

85307 Activated Protein C (APC) resistance assay Ⓐ▢
📷 0.00 ⚕ 0.00 Global Days XXX
AMA: 2005, Jul, 11-12; 2005, Jul, 11-12; 2005, Aug, 7-8; 2005, Aug, 7-8; 2005, Aug, 9-10; 2005, Aug, 9-10; 2005, August, 7-8; 2005, August, 9-10; 2005, July, 11-12

85335 Factor inhibitor test Ⓐ▢
📷 0.00 ⚕ 0.00 Global Days XXX
AMA: 2005, Aug, 7-8; 2005, Aug, 7-8; 2005, Aug, 9-10; 2005, Aug, 9-10; 2005, Jul, 11-12; 2005, Jul, 11-12; 2005, August, 7-8; 2005, July, 11-12; 2005, August, 9-10

85337 Thrombomodulin [A] [▫]
EXCLUDES *mixing studies for inhibitors (85732)*
⟐ 0.00 ⚕ 0.00 Global Days XXX
AMA: 2005, Aug, 9-10; 2005, Aug, 9-10; 2005, Jul, 11-12; 2005, Jul, 11-12; 2005, Aug, 7-8; 2005, Aug, 7-8; 2005, August, 7-8; 2005, July, 11-12; 2005, August, 9-10

85345 Coagulation time; Lee and White [A] [▫]
⟐ 0.00 ⚕ 0.00 Global Days XXX
AMA: 2005, Aug, 7-8; 2005, Aug, 7-8; 2005, Aug, 9-10; 2005, Aug, 9-10; 2005, Jul, 11-12; 2005, Jul, 11-12; 2005, August, 7-8; 2005, July, 11-12; 2005, August, 9-10

85347 activated [A] [▫]
⟐ 0.00 ⚕ 0.00 Global Days XXX
AMA: 2005, Aug, 7-8; 2005, Aug, 7-8; 2005, Jul, 11-12; 2005, Jul, 11-12; 2005, Aug, 9-10; 2005, Aug, 9-10; 2005, August, 7-8; 2005, July, 11-12; 2005, August, 9-10

85348 other methods [A] [▫]
⟐ 0.00 ⚕ 0.00 Global Days XXX
AMA: 2005, Aug, 7-8; 2005, Aug, 7-8; 2005, Aug, 9-10; 2005, Aug, 9-10; 2005, Jul, 11-12; 2005, Jul, 11-12; 2005, August, 7-8; 2005, July, 11-12; 2005, August, 9-10

85360 Euglobulin lysis [A] [▫]
⟐ 0.00 ⚕ 0.00 Global Days XXX
AMA: 2005, Aug, 7-8; 2005, Aug, 7-8; 2005, Jul, 11-12; 2005, Jul, 11-12; 2005, Aug, 9-10; 2005, Aug, 9-10; 2005, August, 7-8; 2005, July, 11-12; 2005, August, 9-10

85362 Fibrin(ogen) degradation (split) products (FDP) (FSP); agglutination slide, semiquantitative [A] [▫]
⟐ 0.00 ⚕ 0.00 Global Days XXX
AMA: 2005, Jul, 11-12; 2005, Jul, 11-12; 2005, Aug, 9-10; 2005, Aug, 9-10; 2005, Aug, 7-8; 2005, Aug, 7-8; 2005, August, 7-8; 2005, July, 11-12; 2005, August, 9-10

85366 paracoagulation [A] [▫]
⟐ 0.00 ⚕ 0.00 Global Days XXX
AMA: 2005, Aug, 7-8; 2005, Aug, 7-8; 2005, Jul, 11-12; 2005, Jul, 11-12; 2005, Aug, 9-10; 2005, Aug, 9-10; 2005, August, 7-8; 2005, July, 11-12; 2005, August, 9-10

85370 quantitative [A] [▫]
⟐ 0.00 ⚕ 0.00 Global Days XXX
AMA: 2005, Aug, 7-8; 2005, Aug, 7-8; 2005, Aug, 9-10; 2005, Aug, 9-10; 2005, Jul, 11-12; 2005, Jul, 11-12; 2005, July, 11-12; 2005, August, 9-10; 2005, August, 7-8

85378 Fibrin degradation products, D-dimer; qualitative or semiquantitative [A] [▫]
⟐ 0.00 ⚕ 0.00 Global Days XXX
AMA: 2005, Aug, 7-8; 2005, Aug, 7-8; 2005, Aug, 9-10; 2005, Aug, 9-10; 2006, Jul, 11-12; 2005, Jul, 11-12; 2005, August, 7-8; 2005, July, 11-12; 2005, August, 9-10

85379 quantitative [A] [▫]
INCLUDES *ultrasensitive and standard sensitivity quantitative D-dimer*
⟐ 0.00 ⚕ 0.00 Global Days XXX
AMA: 2005, Aug, 7-8; 2005, Aug, 7-8; 2005, Jul, 11-12; 2005, Jul, 11-12; 2005, Aug, 9-10; 2005, Aug, 9-10; 2005, August, 7-8; 2005, July, 11-12; 2005, August, 9-10

85380 ultrasensitive (eg, for evaluation for venous thromboembolism), qualitative or semiquantitative [A] [▫]
⟐ 0.00 ⚕ 0.00 Global Days XXX
AMA: 2005, Aug, 7-8; 2005, Aug, 7-8; 2005, Jul, 11-12; 2005, Jul, 11-12; 2005, Aug, 9-10; 2005, Aug, 9-10; 2005, August, 7-8; 2005, August, 9-10; 2005, July, 11-12

85384 Fibrinogen; activity [A] [▫]
⟐ 0.00 ⚕ 0.00 Global Days XXX
AMA: 2005, Jul, 11-12; 2005, Jul, 11-12; 2005, Aug, 9-10; 2005, Aug, 9-10; 2005, Aug, 7-8; 2005, Aug, 7-8; 2005, August, 7-8; 2005, July, 11-12; 2005, August, 9-10

85385 antigen [A] [▫]
⟐ 0.00 ⚕ 0.00 Global Days XXX
AMA: 2005, Jul, 11-12; 2005, Jul, 11-12; 2005, Aug, 7-8; 2005, Aug, 7-8; 2005, Aug, 9-10; 2005, Aug, 9-10; 2005, August, 7-8; 2005, July, 11-12; 2005, August, 9-10

85390 Fibrinolysins or coagulopathy screen, interpretation and report [A] [60] [▫]
⟐ 0.00 ⚕ 0.00 Global Days XXX
AMA: 2005, Aug, 7-8; 2005, Aug, 7-8; 2005, Jul, 11-12; 2005, Jul, 11-12; 2005, Aug, 9-10; 2005, Aug, 9-10; 2005, August, 7-8; 2005, July, 11-12; 2005, August, 9-10

85396 Coagulation/fibrinolysis assay, whole blood (eg, viscoelastic clot assessment), including use of any pharmacologic additive(s), as indicated, including interpretation and written report, per day [N] [60]
⟐ 0.53 ⚕ 0.53 Global Days XXX
AMA: 2005, Aug, 7-8; 2005, Aug, 7-8; 2005, Jul, 11-12; 2005, Jul, 11-12; 2005, Aug, 9-10; 2005, Aug, 9-10; 2005, August, 7-8; 2005, July, 11-12; 2005, August, 9-10

● **85397** Coagulation and fibrinolysis, functional activity, not otherwise specified (eg, ADAMTS-13), each analyte [A]
⟐ 0.00 ⚕ 0.00 Global Days XXX

85400 Fibrinolytic factors and inhibitors; plasmin [A] [▫]
⟐ 0.00 ⚕ 0.00 Global Days XXX
AMA: 2005, Aug, 7-8; 2005, Aug, 7-8; 2005, Jul, 11-12; 2005, Jul, 11-12; 2005, Aug, 9-10; 2005, Aug, 9-10; 2005, August, 7-8; 2005, July, 11-12; 2005, August, 9-10

85410 alpha-2 antiplasmin [A] [▫]
⟐ 0.00 ⚕ 0.00 Global Days XXX
AMA: 2005, Jul, 11-12; 2005, Jul, 11-12; 2005, Aug, 9-10; 2005, Aug, 9-10; 2005, Aug, 7-8; 2005, Aug, 7-8; 2005, August, 7-8; 2005, July, 11-12; 2005, August, 9-10

85415 plasminogen activator [A] [▫]
⟐ 0.00 ⚕ 0.00 Global Days XXX
AMA: 2005, Jul, 11-12; 2005, Jul, 11-12; 2005, Aug, 9-10; 2005, Aug, 9-10; 2005, Aug, 7-8; 2005, Aug, 7-8; 2005, August, 7-8; 2005, July, 11-12; 2005, August, 9-10

85420 plasminogen, except antigenic assay [A] [▫]
⟐ 0.00 ⚕ 0.00 Global Days XXX
AMA: 2005, Jul, 11-12; 2005, Jul, 11-12; 2005, Aug, 9-10; 2005, Aug, 9-10; 2005, Aug, 7-8; 2005, Aug, 7-8; 2005, July, 11-12; 2005, August, 9-10

85421 plasminogen, antigenic assay [A] [▫]
⟐ 0.00 ⚕ 0.00 Global Days XXX
AMA: 2005, Aug, 7-8; 2005, Aug, 7-8; 2005, Jul, 11-12; 2005, Jul, 11-12; 2005, Aug, 9-10; 2005, Aug, 9-10; 2005, August, 7-8; 2005, July, 11-12; 2005, August, 9-10

85441 Heinz bodies; direct [A] [▫]
⟐ 0.00 ⚕ 0.00 Global Days XXX
AMA: 2005, Aug, 7-8; 2005, Aug, 7-8; 2005, Jul, 11-12; 2005, Jul, 11-12; 2005, Aug, 9-10; 2005, Aug, 9-10; 2005, August, 7-8; 2005, July, 11-12

85445 induced, acetyl phenylhydrazine [A] [▫]
⟐ 0.00 ⚕ 0.00 Global Days XXX
AMA: 2005, Aug, 9-10; 2005, Aug, 9-10; 2005, Jul, 11-12; 2005, Jul, 11-12; 2005, Aug, 7-8; 2005, Aug, 7-8; 2005, August, 7-8; 2005, July, 11-12; 2005, August, 9-10

⊕ Modifier 63 Exempt Code ⊙ Moderate Sedation + CPT Add-on Code ⊘ Modifier 51 Exempt Code ● New Code ▲ Revised Code

[M] Maternity Edit [A] Age Edit [X] CLIA Waived Test [A]-[Y] APC Status Indicators [▫] CCI Comprehensive Code [60] Bilateral Procedure

© 2008 Ingenix *(Blue Ink)*   CPT only © 2008 American Medical Association. All Rights Reserved. *(Black Ink)*   Medicare *(Red Ink)*   347

85460 Hemoglobin or RBCs, fetal, for fetomaternal hemorrhage; differential lysis (Kleihauer-Betke) Ⓜ♀Ⓐ🖻

EXCLUDES *hemoglobin F (83030, 83033)*
hemolysins (86940-86941)

💳 0.00 ⚖ 0.00 **Global Days XXX**
AMA: 2005, Aug, 7-8; 2005, Aug, 7-8; 2005, Jul, 11-12; 2005, Jul, 11-12; 2005, Aug, 9-10; 2005, Aug, 9-10; 2005, August, 7-8; 2005, July, 11-12; 2005, August, 9-10

85461 rosette Ⓜ♀Ⓐ🖻

💳 0.00 ⚖ 0.00 **Global Days XXX**
AMA: 2005, Aug, 9-10; 2005, Aug, 9-10; 2005, Aug, 7-8; 2005, Aug, 7-8; 2005, Jul, 11-12; 2005, Jul, 11-12; 2005, August, 7-8; 2005, July, 11-12; 2005, August, 9-10

85475 Hemolysin, acid Ⓐ🖻

INCLUDES Ham test

EXCLUDES *hemolysins and agglutinins (86940-86941)*

💳 0.00 ⚖ 0.00 **Global Days XXX**
AMA: 2005, Aug, 7-8; 2005, Aug, 7-8; 2005, Jul, 11-12; 2005, Jul, 11-12; 2005, Aug, 9-10; 2005, Aug, 9-10; 2005, August, 7-8; July, 11-12; 2005, August, 9-10

85520 Heparin assay Ⓐ🖻

💳 0.00 ⚖ 0.00 **Global Days XXX**
AMA: 2005, Aug, 7-8; 2005, Aug, 7-8; 2005, Aug, 9-10; 2005, Aug, 9-10; 2005, Jul, 11-12; 2005, Jul, 11-12; 2005, August, 7-8; July, 11-12; 2005, August, 9-10

85525 Heparin neutralization Ⓐ🖻

💳 0.00 ⚖ 0.00 **Global Days XXX**
AMA: 2005, Jul, 11-12; 2005, Jul, 11-12; 2005, Aug, 7-8; 2005, Aug, 7-8; 2005, Aug, 9-10; 2005, Aug, 9-10; 2005, August, 7-8; 2005, July, 11-12; 2005, August, 9-10

85530 Heparin-protamine tolerance test Ⓐ🖻

💳 0.00 ⚖ 0.00 **Global Days XXX**
AMA: 2005, Jul, 11-12; 2005, Jul, 11-12; 2005, Aug, 9-10; 2005, Aug, 9-10; 2005, Aug, 7-8; 2005, Aug, 7-8; 2005, August, 7-8; 2005, July, 11-12; 2005, August, 9-10

85536 Iron stain, peripheral blood Ⓐ🖻

EXCLUDES *iron stains on bone marrow or other tissues with physician evaluation (88313)*

💳 0.00 ⚖ 0.00 **Global Days XXX**
AMA: 2005, Aug, 7-8; 2005, Aug, 7-8; 2005, Jul, 11-12; 2005, Jul, 11-12; 2005, Aug, 9-10; 2005, Aug, 9-10; 2005, August, 7-8; 2005, August, 9-10; 2005, July, 11-12

85540 Leukocyte alkaline phosphatase with count Ⓐ🖻

💳 0.00 ⚖ 0.00 **Global Days XXX**
AMA: 2005, Aug, 9-10; 2005, Aug, 9-10; 2005, Jul, 11-12; 2005, Jul, 11-12; 2005, Aug, 7-8; 2005, Aug, 7-8; 2005, August, 7-8; 2005, July, 11-12; 2005, August, 9-10

85547 Mechanical fragility, RBC Ⓐ🖻

💳 0.00 ⚖ 0.00 **Global Days XXX**
AMA: 2005, Aug, 7-8; 2005, Aug, 7-8; 2005, Jul, 11-12; 2005, Jul, 11-12; 2005, Aug, 9-10; 2005, Aug, 9-10; 2005, August, 7-8; 2005, July, 11-12; 2005, August, 9-10

85549 Muramidase Ⓐ🖻

💳 0.00 ⚖ 0.00 **Global Days XXX**
AMA: 2005, Jul, 11-12; 2005, Jul, 11-12; 2005, Aug, 7-8; 2005, Aug, 7-8; 2005, Aug, 9-10; 2005, Aug, 9-10; 2005, August, 7-8; 2005, July, 11-12; 2005, August, 9-10

85555 Osmotic fragility, RBC; unincubated Ⓐ🖻

💳 0.00 ⚖ 0.00 **Global Days XXX**
AMA: 2005, Aug, 7-8; 2005, Aug, 7-8; 2005, Aug, 9-10; 2005, Aug, 9-10; 2005, Jul, 11-12; 2005, Jul, 11-12; 2005, August, 7-8; 2005, July, 11-12; 2005, August, 9-10

85557 incubated Ⓐ🖻

💳 0.00 ⚖ 0.00 **Global Days XXX**
AMA: 2005, Jul, 11-12; 2005, Jul, 11-12; 2005, Aug, 7-8; 2005, Aug, 7-8; 2005, Aug, 9-10; 2005, Aug, 9-10; 2005, July, 11-12; 2005, August, 9-10; 2005, August, 7-8

85576 Platelet, aggregation (in vitro), each agent Ⓐ🞱🖻✖

💳 0.00 ⚖ 0.00 **Global Days XXX**
AMA: 2008, Jan, 10-25; 2007, Jan, 13-27; 2007, Jan, 13-27; 2007, January, 13-27; 2005, Aug, 7-8; 2005, Aug, 7-8; 2005, Jul, 11-12; 2005, July, 11-12; 2005, August, 9-10; 2005, August, 7-8; 2005, Jul, 11-12; 2005, Aug, 9-10; 2005, Aug, 9-10

85597 Platelet neutralization Ⓐ🖻

💳 0.00 ⚖ 0.00 **Global Days XXX**
AMA: 2005, Jul, 11-12; 2005, Jul, 11-12; 2005, Aug, 9-10; 2005, Aug, 9-10; 2005, Aug, 7-8; 2005, Aug, 7-8; 2005, August, 7-8; 2005, July, 11-12; 2005, August, 9-10

85610 Prothrombin time; Ⓐ🖻✖

💳 0.00 ⚖ 0.00 **Global Days XXX**
AMA: 2005, Aug, 7-8; 2005, Aug, 7-8; 2005, Jul, 11-12; 2005, Jul, 11-12; 2005, Aug, 9-10; 2005, Aug, 9-10; 2005, August, 7-8; 2005, July, 11-12; 2005, August, 9-10

85611 substitution, plasma fractions, each Ⓐ🖻

💳 0.00 ⚖ 0.00 **Global Days XXX**
AMA: 2005, Aug, 7-8; 2005, Aug, 7-8; 2005, Jul, 11-12; 2005, Jul, 11-12; 2005, Aug, 9-10; 2005, Aug, 9-10; 2005, August, 7-8; 2005, July, 11-12; 2005, August, 9-10

85612 Russell viper venom time (includes venom); undiluted Ⓐ🖻

💳 0.00 ⚖ 0.00 **Global Days XXX**
AMA: 2005, Jul, 11-12; 2005, Jul, 11-12; 2005, Aug, 7-8; 2005, Aug, 7-8; 2005, Aug, 9-10; 2005, Aug, 9-10; 2005, August, 7-8; 2005, July, 11-12; 2005, August, 9-10

85613 diluted Ⓐ🖻

💳 0.00 ⚖ 0.00 **Global Days XXX**
AMA: 2005, Aug, 9-10; 2005, Aug, 9-10; 2005, Aug, 7-8; 2005, Aug, 7-8; 2005, Jul, 11-12; 2005, Jul, 11-12; 2005, August, 7-8; 2005, July, 11-12; 2005, August, 9-10

85635 Reptilase test Ⓐ🖻

💳 0.00 ⚖ 0.00 **Global Days XXX**
AMA: 2005, Aug, 7-8; 2005, Aug, 7-8; 2005, Aug, 9-10; 2005, Aug, 9-10; 2005, Jul, 11-12; 2005, Jul, 11-12; 2005, August, 7-8; 2005, July, 11-12; 2005, August, 9-10

85651 Sedimentation rate, erythrocyte; non-automated Ⓐ✖

💳 0.00 ⚖ 0.00 **Global Days XXX**
AMA: 2005, Aug, 7-8; 2005, Aug, 7-8; 2005, Jul, 11-12; 2005, Jul, 11-12; 2005, Aug, 9-10; 2005, Aug, 9-10; 2005, August, 7-8; 2005, July, 11-12; 2005, August, 9-10

85652 automated Ⓐ🖻

INCLUDES Westergren test

💳 0.00 ⚖ 0.00 **Global Days XXX**
AMA: 2005, Jul, 11-12; 2005, Jul, 11-12; 2005, Aug, 9-10; 2005, Aug, 9-10; 2005, Aug, 7-8; 2005, Aug, 7-8; 2005, August, 7-8; 2005, July, 11-12; 2005, August, 9-10

85660 Sickling of RBC, reduction Ⓐ🖻

EXCLUDES *hemoglobin electrophoresis (83020)*
smears (87207)

💳 0.00 ⚖ 0.00 **Global Days XXX**
AMA: 2005, Aug, 7-8; 2005, Aug, 7-8; 2005, Jul, 11-12; 2005, Jul, 11-12; 2005, Aug, 9-10; 2005, Aug, 9-10; 2005, August, 7-8; 2005, July, 11-12; 2005, August, 9-10

85670 Thrombin time; plasma Ⓐ🖻

💳 0.00 ⚖ 0.00 **Global Days XXX**
AMA: 2005, Jul, 11-12; 2005, Jul, 11-12; 2005, Aug, 7-8; 2005, Aug, 7-8; 2005, Aug, 9-10; 2005, Aug, 9-10; 2005, August, 7-8; 2005, July, 11-12; 2005, August, 9-10

85675　　titer　　Ⓐ ▣
🚗 0.00　🔖 0.00　Global Days XXX
AMA: 2005, Aug, 9-10; 2005, Aug, 9-10; 2005, Jul, 11-12; 2005,
Jul, 11-12; 2005, Aug, 7-8; 2005, Aug, 7-8; 2005, August, 7-8;
2005, August, 9-10; 2005, July, 11-12

85705　　Thromboplastin inhibition, tissue　　Ⓐ ▣
EXCLUDES　individual clotting factors (85245-85247)
🚗 0.00　🔖 0.00　Global Days XXX
AMA: 2005, Aug, 7-8; 2005, Aug, 7-8; 2005, Jul, 11-12; 2005, Jul,
11-12; 2005, Aug, 9-10; 2005, Aug, 9-10; 2005, July, 11-12; 2005,
August, 9-10; 2005, August, 7-8

85730-85732 Partial Thromboplastin Time (PTT)

CMS *100-3,190.16*　*Partial Thromboplastin Time (PTT)*
CMS *100-4,3,10.4*　*Payment of Nonphysician Services for Inpatients*
CMS *100-2,15,80*　*Physician Supervision Requirements for Diagnostic Tests*
EXCLUDES　agglutinins (86000, 86156-86157)
　　antiplasmin (85410)
　　antithrombin III (85300-85301)
　　blood banking procedures (86850-86999)

85730　　Thromboplastin time, partial (PTT); plasma or whole
　　blood　　Ⓐ ▣
　　INCLUDES　Hicks-Pitney test
🚗 0.00　🔖 0.00　Global Days XXX
AMA: 2005, Aug, 7-8; 2005, Aug, 7-8; 2005, Jul, 11-12; 2005, Jul,
11-12; 2005, Aug, 9-10; 2005, Aug, 9-10; 2005, August, 7-8; 2005,
July, 11-12; 2005, August, 9-10

85732　　substitution, plasma fractions, each　　Ⓐ ▣
🚗 0.00　🔖 0.00　Global Days XXX
AMA: 2005, Aug, 9-10; 2005, Aug, 9-10; 2005, Aug, 7-8; 2005,
Aug, 7-8; 2005, Jul, 11-12; 2005, Jul, 11-12; 2005, August, 7-8;
2005, July, 11-12; 2005, August, 9-10

85810-85999 Blood Viscosity and Unlisted Hematology Procedures

CMS *100-4,3,10.4*　*Payment of Nonphysician Services for Inpatients*
CMS *100-2,15,80*　*Physician Supervision Requirements for Diagnostic Tests*

85810　　Viscosity　　Ⓐ
🚗 0.00　🔖 0.00　Global Days XXX
AMA: 2005, Aug, 7-8; 2005, Aug, 7-8; 2005, Aug, 9-10; 2005, Aug,
9-10; 2005, Jul, 11-12; 2005, Jul, 11-12; 2005, August, 7-8; 2005,
July, 11-12; 2005, August, 9-10

85999　　Unlisted hematology and coagulation procedure　　Ⓐ
🚗 0.00　🔖 0.00　Global Days XXX
AMA: 2005, Aug, 7-8; 2005, Aug, 7-8; 2005, Jul, 11-12; 2005, Jul,
11-12; 2005, Aug, 9-10; 2005, Aug, 9-10; 2005, August, 7-8; 2005,
July, 11-12; 2005, August, 9-10

86000-86063 Antibody Testing

CMS *100-4,3,10.4*　*Payment of Nonphysician Services for Inpatients*
CMS *100-2,15,80*　*Physician Supervision Requirements for Diagnostic Tests*

86000　　Agglutinins, febrile (eg, Brucella, Francisella, Murine
　　typhus, Q fever, Rocky Mountain spotted fever, scrub
　　typhus), each antigen　　Ⓐ
🚗 0.00　🔖 0.00　Global Days XXX
AMA: 2005, Aug, 7-8; 2005, Aug, 7-8; 2005, Jul, 11-12; 2005, Jul,
11-12; 2005, Aug, 9-10; 2005, Aug, 9-10; 2005, August, 7-8; 2005,
July, 11-12; 2005, August, 9-10

86001　　Allergen specific IgG quantitative or semiquantitative,
　　each allergen　　Ⓐ ▣
🚗 0.00　🔖 0.00　Global Days XXX
AMA: 2005, Jul, 11-12; 2005, Jul, 11-12; 2005, Aug, 9-10; 2005,
Aug, 9-10; 2005, Aug, 7-8; 2005, Aug, 7-8; 2005, August, 7-8;
2005, July, 11-12; 2005, August, 9-10

86003　　Allergen specific IgE; quantitative or semiquantitative,
　　each allergen　　Ⓐ ▣
EXCLUDES　total quantitative IgE (82785)
🚗 0.00　🔖 0.00　Global Days XXX
AMA: 2005, Jul, 11-12; 2005, Jul, 11-12; 2005, Aug, 9-10; 2005,
Aug, 9-10; 2005, Aug, 7-8; 2005, Aug, 7-8; 2005, August, 7-8;
2005, July, 11-12; 2005, August, 9-10

86005　　qualitative, multiallergen screen (dipstick, paddle, or
　　disk)　　Ⓐ
EXCLUDES　total qualitative IgE (83518)
🚗 0.00　🔖 0.00　Global Days XXX
AMA: 2005, Aug, 7-8; 2005, Aug, 7-8; 2005, Jul, 11-12; 2005, Jul,
11-12; 2005, Aug, 9-10; 2005, Aug, 9-10; 2005, August, 7-8; 2005,
July, 11-12; 2005, August, 9-10

86021　　Antibody identification; leukocyte antibodies　　Ⓐ ▣
🚗 0.00　🔖 0.00　Global Days XXX
AMA: 2005, Aug, 7-8; 2005, Aug, 7-8; 2005, Jul, 11-12; 2005, Jul,
11-12; 2005, Aug, 9-10; 2005, Aug, 9-10; 2005, August, 7-8; 2005,
July, 11-12; 2005, August, 9-10

86022　　platelet antibodies　　Ⓐ ▣
🚗 0.00　🔖 0.00　Global Days XXX
AMA: 2005, Aug, 7-8; 2005, Aug, 7-8; 2005, Jul, 11-12; 2005, Jul,
11-12; 2005, Aug, 9-10; 2005, Aug, 9-10; 2005, August, 7-8; 2005,
August, 9-10; 2005, July, 11-12

86023　　platelet associated immunoglobulin assay　　Ⓐ ▣
🚗 0.00　🔖 0.00　Global Days XXX
AMA: 2005, Aug, 9-10; 2005, Aug, 9-10; 2005, Aug, 7-8; 2005,
Aug, 7-8; 2005, Jul, 11-12; 2005, Jul, 11-12; 2005, August, 7-8;
2005, July, 11-12; 2005, August, 9-10

86038　　Antinuclear antibodies (ANA);　　Ⓐ ▣
🚗 0.00　🔖 0.00　Global Days XXX
AMA: 2005, Jul, 11-12; 2005, Jul, 11-12; 2005, Aug, 9-10; 2005,
Aug, 9-10; 2005, Aug, 7-8; 2005, Aug, 7-8; 2005, July, 11-12; 2005,
August, 9-10; 2005, August, 7-8

86039　　titer　　Ⓐ ▣
🚗 0.00　🔖 0.00　Global Days XXX
AMA: 2005, Aug, 9-10; 2005, Aug, 9-10; 2005, Aug, 7-8; 2005,
Aug, 7-8; 2005, Jul, 11-12; 2005, Jul, 11-12; 2005, August, 7-8;
2005, July, 11-12; 2005, August, 9-10

86060　　Antistreptolysin O; titer　　Ⓐ ▣
🚗 0.00　🔖 0.00　Global Days XXX
AMA: 2005, Aug, 7-8; 2005, Aug, 7-8; 2005, Aug, 9-10; 2005, Aug,
9-10; 2005, Jul, 11-12; 2005, Jul, 11-12; 2005, August, 7-8; 2005,
July, 11-12; 2005, August, 9-10

86063　　screen　　Ⓐ
🚗 0.00　🔖 0.00　Global Days XXX
AMA: 2005, Aug, 7-8; 2005, Aug, 7-8; 2005, Aug, 9-10; 2005, Aug,
9-10; 2005, Jul, 11-12; 2005, Jul, 11-12; 2005, August, 7-8; 2005,
July, 11-12; 2005, August, 9-10

⊛ Modifier 63 Exempt Code　　⊙ Moderate Sedation　　+ CPT Add-on Code　　Ⓢ Modifier 51 Exempt Code　　● New Code　　▲ Revised Code

Ⓜ Maternity Edit　　Ⓐ Age Edit　　Ⓔ CLIA Waived Test　　Ⓐ-Ⓨ APC Status Indicators　　▣ CCI Comprehensive Code　　50 Bilateral Procedure

© 2008 Ingenix *(Blue Ink)*　　CPT only © 2008 American Medical Association. All Rights Reserved. (Black Ink)　　Medicare (Red Ink)　　349

Pathology and Laboratory

86077 — 86226

86077-86079 Blood Bank Services

CMS 100-4,12,60   *Payment for Pathology Services*
CMS 100-4,3,10.4   *Payment of Nonphysician Services for Inpatients*
CMS 100-2,15,80   *Physician Supervision Requirements for Diagnostic Tests*

86077   **Blood bank physician services; difficult cross match and/or evaluation of irregular antibody(s), interpretation and written report**   X 80
     1.29   1.35   **Global Days XXX**
     AMA: 2005, Aug, 7-8; 2005, Aug, 7-8; 2005, Aug, 9-10; 2005, Aug, 9-10; 2005, Jul, 11-12; 2005, Jul, 11-12; 2005, August, 7-8; 2005, August, 9-10; 2005, July, 11-12

86078   **investigation of transfusion reaction including suspicion of transmissible disease, interpretation and written report**   X 80
     1.29   1.37   **Global Days XXX**
     AMA: 2005, Aug, 7-8; 2005, Aug, 7-8; 2005, Jul, 11-12; 2005, Jul, 11-12; 2005, Aug, 9-10; 2005, Aug, 9-10; 2005, August, 7-8; 2005, July, 11-12; 2005, August, 9-10

86079   **authorization for deviation from standard blood banking procedures (eg, use of outdated blood, transfusion of Rh incompatible units), with written report**   X 80
     1.30   1.38   **Global Days XXX**
     AMA: 2005, Jul, 11-12; 2005, Jul, 11-12; 2005, Aug, 9-10; 2005, Aug, 9-10; 2005, Aug, 7-8; 2005, Aug, 7-8; 2005, August, 7-8; 2005, July, 11-12; 2005, August, 9-10

86140-86344 Diagnostic Immunology Testing

CMS 100-4,3,10.4   *Payment of Nonphysician Services for Inpatients*
CMS 100-2,15,80   *Physician Supervision Requirements for Diagnostic Tests*

86140   **C-reactive protein;**   A
     0.00   0.00   **Global Days XXX**
     AMA: 2005, Aug, 7-8; 2005, Aug, 7-8; 2005, Jul, 11-12; 2005, Jul, 11-12; 2005, Aug, 9-10; 2005, Aug, 9-10; 2005, August, 7-8; 2005, July, 11-12; 2005, August, 9-10

86141   **high sensitivity (hsCRP)**   A
     0.00   0.00   **Global Days XXX**
     AMA: 2005, Aug, 7-8; 2005, Aug, 7-8; 2005, Jul, 11-12; 2005, Jul, 11-12; 2005, Aug, 9-10; 2005, Aug, 9-10; 2005, August, 7-8; 2005, July, 11-12; 2005, August, 9-10

86146   **Beta 2 Glycoprotein I antibody, each**   A
     0.00   0.00   **Global Days XXX**
     AMA: 2005, Jul, 11-12; 2005, Jul, 11-12; 2005, Aug, 7-8; 2005, Aug, 7-8; 2005, Aug, 9-10; 2005, Aug, 9-10; 2005, August, 7-8; 2005, July, 11-12; 2005, August, 9-10

86147   **Cardiolipin (phospholipid) antibody, each Ig class**   A
     0.00   0.00   **Global Days XXX**
     AMA: 2005, Aug, 7-8; 2005, Aug, 7-8; 2005, Aug, 9-10; 2005, Aug, 9-10; 2005, Jul, 11-12; 2005, Jul, 11-12; 2005, August, 7-8; 2005, July, 11-12; 2005, August, 9-10

86148   **Anti-phosphatidylserine (phospholipid) antibody**   A
     EXCLUDES   *antiprothrombin (phospholipid cofactor) antibody (0030T)*
     0.00   0.00   **Global Days XXX**
     AMA: 2005, Jul, 11-12; 2005, Jul, 11-12; 2005, Aug, 9-10; 2005, Aug, 9-10; 2005, Aug, 7-8; 2005, Aug, 7-8; 2005, August, 7-8; 2005, July, 11-12; 2005, August, 9-10

86155   **Chemotaxis assay, specify method**   A
     0.00   0.00   **Global Days XXX**
     AMA: 2005, Aug, 7-8; 2005, Aug, 7-8; 2005, Jul, 11-12; 2005, Jul, 11-12; 2005, Aug, 9-10; 2005, Aug, 9-10; 2005, August, 7-8; 2005, July, 11-12; 2005, August, 9-10

86156   **Cold agglutinin; screen**   A
     0.00   0.00   **Global Days XXX**
     AMA: 2005, Aug, 9-10; 2005, Aug, 9-10; 2005, Aug, 7-8; 2005, Aug, 7-8; 2005, Jul, 11-12; 2005, Jul, 11-12; 2005, August, 7-8; 2005, July, 11-12; 2005, August, 9-10

86157   **titer**   A
     0.00   0.00   **Global Days XXX**
     AMA: 2005, Aug, 9-10; 2005, Aug, 9-10; 2005, Aug, 7-8; 2005, Aug, 7-8; 2005, Jul, 11-12; 2005, Jul, 11-12; 2005, August, 7-8; 2005, July, 11-12; 2005, August, 9-10

86160   **Complement; antigen, each component**   A
     0.00   0.00   **Global Days XXX**
     AMA: 2005, Aug, 7-8; 2005, Aug, 7-8; 2005, Jul, 11-12; 2005, Jul, 11-12; 2005, Aug, 9-10; 2005, Aug, 9-10; 2005, August, 7-8; 2005, July, 11-12; 2005, August, 9-10

86161   **functional activity, each component**   A
     0.00   0.00   **Global Days XXX**
     AMA: 2005, Aug, 7-8; 2005, Aug, 7-8; 2005, Aug, 9-10; 2005, Aug, 9-10; 2005, Jul, 11-12; 2005, Jul, 11-12; 2005, August, 7-8; 2005, July, 11-12; 2005, August, 9-10

86162   **total hemolytic (CH50)**   A
     0.00   0.00   **Global Days XXX**
     AMA: 2005, Aug, 9-10; 2005, Aug, 9-10; 2005, Aug, 7-8; 2005, Aug, 7-8; 2005, Jul, 11-12; 2005, Jul, 11-12; 2005, August, 7-8; 2005, July, 11-12; 2005, August, 9-10

86171   **Complement fixation tests, each antigen**   A
     0.00   0.00   **Global Days XXX**
     AMA: 2005, Jul, 11-12; 2005, Jul, 11-12; 2005, Aug, 9-10; 2005, Aug, 9-10; 2005, Aug, 7-8; 2005, Aug, 7-8; 2005, August, 7-8; 2005, July, 11-12; 2005, August, 9-10

86185   **Counterimmunoelectrophoresis, each antigen**   A
     0.00   0.00   **Global Days XXX**
     AMA: 2005, Jul, 11-12; 2005, Jul, 11-12; 2005, Aug, 9-10; 2005, Aug, 9-10; 2005, Aug, 7-8; 2005, Aug, 7-8; 2005, August, 7-8; 2005, July, 11-12; 2005, August, 9-10

86200   **Cyclic citrullinated peptide (CCP), antibody**   A
     0.00   0.00   **Global Days XXX**
     AMA: 2006, Mar, 6-9; 2006, Mar, 6-9; 2006, March, 6-9; 2005, Aug, 7-8; 2005, Aug, 7-8; 2005, August, 9-10; 2005, August, 7-8; 2005, Aug, 9-10; 2005, Aug, 9-10

86215   **Deoxyribonuclease, antibody**   A
     0.00   0.00   **Global Days XXX**
     AMA: 2005, Aug, 7-8; 2005, Aug, 7-8; 2005, Aug, 9-10; 2005, Aug, 9-10; 2005, Jul, 11-12; 2005, Jul, 11-12; 2005, August, 7-8; 2005, July, 11-12; 2005, August, 9-10

86225   **Deoxyribonucleic acid (DNA) antibody; native or double stranded**   A
     EXCLUDES   *echinococcus, antibodies (see code for specific method)*
     0.00   0.00   **Global Days XXX**
     AMA: 2005, Aug, 9-10; 2005, Aug, 9-10; 2005, Jul, 11-12; 2005, Jul, 11-12; 2005, Aug, 7-8; 2005, Aug, 7-8; 2005, July, 11-12; 2005, August, 9-10; 2005, August, 7-8

86226   **single stranded**   A
     EXCLUDES   *anti D.S, DNA, IFA, eg, using C. lucilae (86255-86256)*
     0.00   0.00   **Global Days XXX**
     AMA: 2005, Aug, 7-8; 2005, Aug, 7-8; 2005, Jul, 11-12; 2005, Jul, 11-12; 2005, Aug, 9-10; 2005, Aug, 9-10; 2005, July, 11-12; 2005, August, 9-10; 2005, August, 7-8

86235   Extractable nuclear antigen, antibody to, any method (eg, nRNP, SS-A, SS-B, Sm, RNP, Sc170, J01), each antibody   A ▣
    0.00   0.00 Global Days XXX
    AMA: 2005, Jul, 11-12; 2005, Jul, 11-12; 2005, Aug, 7-8; 2005, Aug, 7-8; 2005, Aug, 9-10; 2005, Aug, 9-10; 2005, July, 11-12; 2005, August, 9-10; 2005, August, 7-8

86243   Fc receptor   A
    EXCLUDES   *filaria antibodies to, (see code for specific method)*
    0.00   0.00 Global Days XXX
    AMA: 2005, Aug, 7-8; 2005, Aug, 7-8; 2005, Aug, 9-10; 2005, Aug, 9-10; 2005, Jul, 11-12; 2005, Jul, 11-12; 2005, July, 11-12; 2005, August, 9-10; 2005, August, 7-8

86255   Fluorescent noninfectious agent antibody; screen, each antibody   A 80 ▣
    0.00   0.00 Global Days XXX
    AMA: 2005, Jul, 11-12; 2005, Jul, 11-12; 2005, Aug, 9-10; 2005, Aug, 9-10; 2005, Aug, 7-8; 2005, Aug, 7-8; 2005, July, 11-12; 2005, August, 9-10; 2005, August, 7-8

86256   titer, each antibody   A 80 ▣
    EXCLUDES   *fluorescent technique for antigen identification in tissue (88346)*
        FTA (86781)
        gel (agar) diffusion tests (86331)
        indirect fluorescence (88347)
    0.00   0.00 Global Days XXX
    AMA: 2005, Aug, 7-8; 2005, Aug, 7-8; 2005, Jul, 11-12; 2005, Jul, 11-12; 2005, Aug, 9-10; 2005, Aug, 9-10; 2005, July, 11-12; 2005, August, 9-10; 2005, August, 7-8

86277   Growth hormone, human (HGH), antibody   A
    0.00   0.00 Global Days XXX
    AMA: 2005, Jul, 11-12; 2005, Jul, 11-12; 2005, Aug, 9-10; 2005, Aug, 9-10; 2005, Aug, 7-8; 2005, Aug, 7-8; 2005, July, 11-12; 2005, August, 9-10; 2005, August, 7-8

86280   Hemagglutination inhibition test (HAI)   A
    EXCLUDES   *antibodies to infectious agents (86602-86804)*
        rubella (86762)
    0.00   0.00 Global Days XXX
    AMA: 2005, Jul, 11-12; 2005, Jul, 11-12; 2005, Aug, 7-8; 2005, Aug, 7-8; 2005, Aug, 9-10; 2005, Aug, 9-10; 2005, July, 11-12; 2005, August, 9-10; 2005, August, 7-8

86294   Immunoassay for tumor antigen, qualitative or semiquantitative (eg, bladder tumor antigen)   A ▣
    0.00   0.00 Global Days XXX
    AMA: 2005, Jul, 11-12; 2005, Jul, 11-12; 2005, Aug, 9-10; 2005, Aug, 9-10; 2005, Aug, 7-8; 2005, Aug, 7-8; 2005, August, 9-10; 2005, August, 7-8; 2005, July, 11-12

86300   Immunoassay for tumor antigen, quantitative; CA 15-3 (27.29)   A ▣
    0.00   0.00 Global Days XXX
    AMA: 2005, Jul, 11-12; 2005, Jul, 11-12; 2005, Aug, 9-10; 2005, Aug, 9-10; 2005, Aug, 7-8; 2005, Aug, 7-8; 2005, July, 11-12; 2005, August, 9-10; 2005, August, 7-8

86301   CA 19-9   A ▣
    0.00   0.00 Global Days XXX
    AMA: 2005, Aug, 7-8; 2005, Aug, 7-8; 2005, Aug, 9-10; 2005, Aug, 9-10; 2005, Jul, 11-12; 2005, Jul, 11-12; 2005, July, 11-12; 2005, August, 9-10; 2005, August, 7-8

86304   CA 125   A ▣
    EXCLUDES   *measurement of serum HER-2/neu oncoprotein (83950)*
    0.00   0.00 Global Days XXX
    AMA: 2005, Aug, 7-8; 2005, Aug, 7-8; 2005, Aug, 9-10; 2005, Aug, 9-10; 2005, Jul, 11-12; 2005, Jul, 11-12; 2005, July, 11-12; 2005, August, 9-10; 2005, August, 7-8

86308   Heterophile antibodies; screening   A ▣
    EXCLUDES   *antibodies to infectious agents (86602-86804)*
    0.00   0.00 Global Days XXX
    AMA: 2005, Jul, 11-12; 2005, Jul, 11-12; 2005, Aug, 9-10; 2005, Aug, 9-10; 2005, Aug, 7-8; 2005, Aug, 7-8; 2005, July, 11-12; 2005, August, 9-10; 2005, August, 7-8

86309   titer   A
    EXCLUDES   *antibodies to infectious agents (86602-86804)*
    0.00   0.00 Global Days XXX
    AMA: 2005, Aug, 7-8; 2005, Aug, 7-8; 2005, Aug, 9-10; 2005, Aug, 9-10; 2005, Jul, 11-12; 2005, Jul, 11-12; 2005, July, 11-12; 2005, August, 9-10; 2005, August, 7-8

86310   titers after absorption with beef cells and guinea pig kidney   A
    EXCLUDES   *antibodies to infectious agents (86602-86804)*
    0.00   0.00 Global Days XXX
    AMA: 2005, Aug, 7-8; 2005, Aug, 7-8; 2005, Jul, 11-12; 2005, Jul, 11-12; 2005, Aug, 9-10; 2005, Aug, 9-10; 2005, August, 7-8; 2005, July, 11-12; 2005, August, 9-10

86316   Immunoassay for tumor antigen, other antigen, quantitative (eg, CA 50, 72-4, 549), each   A ▣
    0.00   0.00 Global Days XXX
    AMA: 2008, Jan, 10-25; 2007, Jan, 13-27; 2007, Jan, 13-27; 2007, January, 13-27; 2005, Aug, 7-8; 2005, Aug, 7-8; 2005, Jul, 11-12; 2005, July, 11-12; 2005, August, 9-10; 2005, August, 7-8; 2005, Jul, 11-12; 2005, Aug, 9-10; 2005, Aug, 9-10

86317   Immunoassay for infectious agent antibody, quantitative, not otherwise specified   A ▣
    0.00   0.00 Global Days XXX
    AMA: 2005, Jul, 11-12; 2005, Jul, 11-12; 2005, Aug, 7-8; 2005, Aug, 7-8; 2005, Aug, 9-10; 2005, Aug, 9-10; 2005, August, 7-8; 2005, July, 11-12; 2005, August, 9-10

86318   Immunoassay for infectious agent antibody, qualitative or semiquantitative, single step method (eg, reagent strip)   A ▣
    0.00   0.00 Global Days XXX
    AMA: 2008, Jan, 10-25; 2007, Mar, 9-11; 2007, Mar, 9-11; 2007, March, 9-11; 2005, Jul, 11-12; 2005, Jul, 11-12; 2005, Aug, 7-8; 2005, July, 11-12; 2005, August, 9-10; 2005, August, 7-8; 2005, Aug, 7-8; 2005, Aug, 9-10; 2005, Aug, 9-10

86320   Immunoelectrophoresis; serum   A 80 ▣
    0.00   0.00 Global Days XXX
    AMA: 2005, Jul, 11-12; 2005, Jul, 11-12; 2005, Aug, 9-10; 2005, Aug, 9-10; 2005, Aug, 7-8; 2005, Aug, 7-8; 2005, July, 11-12; 2005, August, 7-8; 2005, August, 9-10

86325   other fluids (eg, urine, cerebrospinal fluid) with concentration   A 80 ▣
    0.00   0.00 Global Days XXX
    AMA: 2005, Aug, 7-8; 2005, Aug, 7-8; 2005, Jul, 11-12; 2005, Jul, 11-12; 2005, Aug, 9-10; 2005, Aug, 9-10; 2005, July, 11-12; 2005, August, 7-8; 2005, August, 9-10

86327   crossed (2-dimensional assay)   A 80 ▣
    0.00   0.00 Global Days XXX
    AMA: 2005, Aug, 7-8; 2005, Aug, 7-8; 2005, Aug, 9-10; 2005, Aug, 9-10; 2005, Jul, 11-12; 2005, Jul, 11-12; 2005, August, 7-8; 2005, August, 9-10; 2005, July, 11-12

86329   Immunodiffusion; not elsewhere specified   A ▣
    0.00   0.00 Global Days XXX
    AMA: 2008, Jan, 10-25; 2007, Jan, 13-27; 2007, Jan, 13-27; 2007, January, 13-27; 2005, Aug, 9-10; 2005, Aug, 9-10; 2005, Jul, 11-12; 2005, August, 7-8; 2005, August, 9-10; 2005, July, 11-12; 2005, Jul, 11-12; 2005, Aug, 7-8; 2005, Aug, 7-8

Pathology and Laboratory

86331 — 86367

86331   gel diffusion, qualitative (Ouchterlony), each antigen or antibody   [A] [▣]

🔧 0.00   ✂ 0.00   **Global Days XXX**

AMA: 2005, Aug, 7-8; 2005, Aug, 7-8; 2005, Jul, 11-12; 2005, Jul, 11-12; 2005, Aug, 9-10; 2005, Aug, 9-10; 2005, August, 7-8; 2005, August, 9-10; 2005, July, 11-12

86332   Immune complex assay   [A]

🔧 0.00   ✂ 0.00   **Global Days XXX**

AMA: 2005, Jul, 11-12; 2005, Jul, 11-12; 2005, Aug, 9-10; 2005, Aug, 9-10; 2005, Aug, 7-8; 2005, Aug, 7-8; 2005, July, 11-12; 2005, August, 7-8; 2005, August, 9-10

86334   Immunofixation electrophoresis; serum   [A] [80] [▣]

🔧 0.00   ✂ 0.00   **Global Days XXX**

AMA: 2005, Aug, 7-8; 2005, Aug, 7-8; 2005, Jul, 11-12; 2005, Jul, 11-12; 2005, Aug, 9-10; 2005, Aug, 9-10; 2005, August, 7-8; 2005, August, 9-10; 2005, July, 11-12

86335   other fluids with concentration (eg, urine, CSF)   [A] [80] [▣]

🔧 0.00   ✂ 0.00   **Global Days XXX**

AMA: 2005, Aug, 7-8; 2005, Aug, 7-8; 2005, Jul, 11-12; 2005, Jul, 11-12; 2005, Aug, 9-10; 2005, Aug, 9-10; 2005, July, 11-12; 2005, August, 7-8; 2005, August, 9-10

86336   Inhibin A   [A]

🔧 0.00   ✂ 0.00   **Global Days XXX**

AMA: 2005, Aug, 9-10; 2005, Aug, 9-10; 2005, Jul, 11-12; 2005, Jul, 11-12; 2005, Aug, 7-8; 2005, Aug, 7-8; 2005, July, 11-12; 2005, Aug, 9-10; 2005, August, 7-8

86337   Insulin antibodies   [A]

🔧 0.00   ✂ 0.00   **Global Days XXX**

AMA: 2005, Aug, 7-8; 2005, Aug, 7-8; 2005, Aug, 9-10; 2005, Aug, 9-10; 2005, Jul, 11-12; 2005, Jul, 11-12; 2005, August, 7-8; 2005, August, 9-10; 2005, July, 11-12

86340   Intrinsic factor antibodies   [A]

🔧 0.00   ✂ 0.00   **Global Days XXX**

AMA: 2005, Aug, 7-8; 2005, Aug, 7-8; 2005, Jul, 11-12; 2005, Jul, 11-12; 2005, Aug, 9-10; 2005, Aug, 9-10; 2005, July, 11-12; 2005, August, 7-8; 2005, August, 9-10

86341   Islet cell antibody   [A]

🔧 0.00   ✂ 0.00   **Global Days XXX**

AMA: 2005, Jul, 11-12; 2005, Jul, 11-12; 2005, Aug, 9-10; 2005, Aug, 9-10; 2005, Aug, 7-8; 2005, Aug, 7-8; 2005, July, 11-12; 2005, August, 7-8; 2005, August, 9-10

86343   Leukocyte histamine release test (LHR)   [A]

🔧 0.00   ✂ 0.00   **Global Days XXX**

AMA: 2005, Aug, 7-8; 2005, Aug, 7-8; 2005, Jul, 11-12; 2005, Jul, 11-12; 2005, Aug, 9-10; 2005, Aug, 9-10; 2005, July, 11-12; 2005, August, 7-8; 2005, August, 9-10

86344   Leukocyte phagocytosis   [A] [▣]

🔧 0.00   ✂ 0.00   **Global Days XXX**

AMA: 2005, Aug, 7-8; 2005, Aug, 7-8; 2005, Jul, 11-12; 2005, Jul, 11-12; 2005, Aug, 9-10; 2005, Aug, 9-10; 2005, July, 11-12; 2005, August, 7-8; 2005, August, 9-10

86353 Lymphocyte Mitogen Response Assay

CMS 100-3,190.8   *Lymphocyte Mitogen Response Assays*
CMS 100-4,3,10.4   *Payment of Nonphysician Services for Inpatients*
CMS 100-2,15,80   *Physician Supervision Requirements for Diagnostic Tests*

86353   Lymphocyte transformation, mitogen (phytomitogen) or antigen induced blastogenesis   [A] [▣]

🔧 0.00   ✂ 0.00   **Global Days XXX**

AMA: 2005, Aug, 7-8; 2005, Aug, 7-8; 2005, Aug, 9-10; 2005, Aug, 9-10; 2005, Jul, 11-12; 2005, Jul, 11-12; 2005, July, 11-12; 2005, August, 7-8; 2005, August, 9-10

86355-86593 Additional Diagnostic Immunology Testing

CMS 100-4,3,10.4   *Payment of Nonphysician Services for Inpatients*
CMS 100-2,15,80   *Physician Supervision Requirements for Diagnostic Tests*

86355   B cells, total count   [A]

Do not report with flow cytometry interpretation (88187-88189)

🔧 0.00   ✂ 0.00   **Global Days XXX**

AMA: 2008, Apr, 5-7; 2008, Apr, 5-7; 2008, Apr, 5-7; 2006, Mar, 6-9; 2006, Mar, 6-9; 2006, March, 6-9; 2005, Aug, 9-10; 2005, August, 9-10; 2005, Aug, 9-10; 2005, Aug, 7-8; 2005, August, 7-8; 2005, Aug, 7-8

86356   Mononuclear cell antigen, quantitative (eg, flow cytometry), not otherwise specified, each antigen   [A]

Do not report with flow cytometry interpretation (88187-88189)

🔧 0.00   ✂ 0.00   **Global Days XXX**

AMA: 2008, Apr, 5-7; 2008, Apr, 5-7; 2008, Apr, 5-7

86357   Natural killer (NK) cells, total count   [A]

Do not report with flow cytometry interpretation (88187-88189)

🔧 0.00   ✂ 0.00   **Global Days XXX**

AMA: 2008, Apr, 5-7; 2008, Apr, 5-7; 2008, Apr, 5-7; 2006, Mar, 6-9; 2006, Mar, 6-9; 2006, March, 6-9; 2005, Aug, 9-10; 2005, August, 9-10; 2005, Aug, 9-10; 2005, Aug, 7-8; 2005, August, 7-8; 2005, Aug, 7-8

86359   T cells; total count   [A] [▣]

Do not report with flow cytometry interpretation (88187-88189)

🔧 0.00   ✂ 0.00   **Global Days XXX**

AMA: 2008, Apr, 5-7; 2008, Apr, 5-7; 2008, Apr, 5-7; 2005, Aug, 7-8; 2005, Aug, 7-8; 2005, July, 11-12; 2005, August, 7-8; 2005, August, 9-10; 2005, Aug, 9-10; 2005, Aug, 9-10; 2005, Jul, 11-12; 2005, Jul, 11-12

86360   absolute CD4 and CD8 count, including ratio   [A] [▣]

Do not report with flow cytometry interpretation (88187-88189)

🔧 0.00   ✂ 0.00   **Global Days XXX**

AMA: 2008, Apr, 5-7; 2008, Apr, 5-7; 2008, Apr, 5-7; 2007, Jan, 28-31; 2007, January, 28-31; 2007, Jan, 28-31; 2005, Aug, 7-8; 2005, July, 11-12; 2005, August, 9-10; 2005, August, 7-8; 2005, Aug, 7-8; 2005, Aug, 9-10; 2005, Aug, 9-10; 2005, Jul, 11-12; 2005, Jul, 11-12

86361   absolute CD4 count   [A] [▣]

Do not report with flow cytometry interpretation (88187-88189)

🔧 0.00   ✂ 0.00   **Global Days XXX**

AMA: 2008, Apr, 5-7; 2008, Apr, 5-7; 2008, Apr, 5-7; 2005, Aug, 7-8; 2005, Aug, 7-8; 2005, July, 11-12; 2005, August, 9-10; 2005, August, 7-8; 2005, Jul, 11-12; 2005, Jul, 11-12; 2005, Aug, 9-10; 2005, Aug, 9-10

86367   Stem cells (ie, CD34), total count   [A]

EXCLUDES   *flow cytometric immunophenotyping for the assessment of potential hematolymphoid neoplasia (88184-88189)*

Do not report with flow cytometry interpretation (88187-88189)

🔧 0.00   ✂ 0.00   **Global Days XXX**

AMA: 2008, Apr, 5-7; 2008, Apr, 5-7; 2008, Apr, 5-7; 2006, Mar, 6-9; 2006, Mar, 6-9; 2006, March, 6-9; 2005, Aug, 9-10; 2005, August, 9-10; 2005, Aug, 9-10; 2005, Aug, 7-8; 2005, August, 7-8; 2005, Aug, 7-8

[26]/[TC] Professional/Technical Component Only   [80]/[80] Assist-at-Surgery Allowed/With Documentation   Unlisted   Not Covered   ▣ Radiology crosswalk

MED: Pub 100/NCD References   **AMA:** CPT Assistant References   [A2]-[Z3] ASC Payment Indicator   ♂Male Only   ♀Female Only   ◣ Laboratory crosswalk

352   CPT only © 2008 American Medical Association. All Rights Reserved. (Black Ink)   Medicare (Red Ink)   © 2008 Ingenix (Blue Ink)

86376 Microsomal antibodies (eg, thyroid or liver-kidney), each   A ▫

    0.00   0.00 Global Days XXX

AMA: 2005, Jul, 11-12; 2005, Jul, 11-12; 2005, Aug, 9-10; 2005, Aug, 9-10; 2005, Aug, 7-8; 2005, Aug, 7-8; 2005, July, 11-12; 2005, August, 7-8; 2005, August, 9-10

86378 Migration inhibitory factor test (MIF)   A ▫

    0.00   0.00 Global Days XXX

AMA: 2005, Aug, 9-10; 2005, Aug, 9-10; 2005, Aug, 7-8; 2005, Aug, 7-8; 2005, Jul, 11-12; 2005, Jul, 11-12; 2005, July, 11-12; 2005, August, 7-8, 2005, August, 9-10

86382 Neutralization test, viral   A ▫

    0.00   0.00 Global Days XXX

AMA: 2005, Aug, 7-8; 2005, Aug, 7-8; 2005, Jul, 11-12; 2005, Jul, 11-12; 2005, Aug, 9-10; 2005, Aug, 9-10; 2005, August, 7-8; 2005, August, 9-10; 2005, July, 11-12

86384 Nitroblue tetrazolium dye test (NTD)   A ▫

    0.00   0.00 Global Days XXX

AMA: 2005, Aug, 7-8; 2005, Aug, 7-8; 2005, Aug, 9-10; 2005, Aug, 9-10; 2005, Jul, 11-12; 2005, Jul, 11-12; 2005, July, 11-12; 2005, August, 7-8; 2005, August, 9-10

86403 Particle agglutination; screen, each antibody   A

    0.00   0.00 Global Days XXX

AMA: 2005, Jul, 11-12; 2005, Jul, 11-12; 2005, Aug, 9-10; 2005, Aug, 9-10; 2005, Aug, 7-8; 2005, Aug, 7-8; 2005, July, 11-12; 2005, August, 7-8; 2005, August, 9-10

86406 titer, each antibody   A

    EXCLUDES   pregnancy test (84702-84703)
         rapid plasma reagin test (RPR) (86592-86593)

    0.00   0.00 Global Days XXX

AMA: 2005, Aug, 7-8; 2005, Aug, 7-8; 2005, Aug, 9-10; 2005, Aug, 9-10; 2005, Jul, 11-12; 2005, Jul, 11-12; 2005, July, 11-12; 2005, August, 7-8; 2005, August, 9-10

86430 Rheumatoid factor; qualitative   A

    0.00   0.00 Global Days XXX

AMA: 2005, Jul, 11-12; 2005, Jul, 11-12; 2005, Aug, 9-10; 2005, Aug, 9-10; 2005, Aug, 7-8; 2005, Aug, 7-8; 2005, July, 11-12; 2005, August, 7-8; 2005, August, 9-10

86431 quantitative   A

    0.00   0.00 Global Days XXX

AMA: 2005, Aug, 7-8; 2005, Aug, 7-8; 2005, Jul, 11-12; 2005, Jul, 11-12; 2005, Aug, 9-10, 2005, Aug, 9-10; 2005, July, 11-12; 2005, August, 7-8; 2005, August, 9-10

86480 Tuberculosis test, cell mediated immunity measurement of gamma interferon antigen response   A

    0.00   0.00 Global Days XXX

AMA: 2006, Mar, 6-9; 2006, Mar, 6-9; 2006, March, 6-9; 2005, Aug, 7-8; 2005, Aug, 7-8; 2005, August, 9-10; 2005, August, 7-8; 2005, Aug, 9-10; 2005, Aug, 9-10

86485 Skin test; candida   X TC 80

    0.00   0.00 Global Days XXX

AMA: 2005, Aug, 9-10; 2005, Aug, 9-10; 2005, Jul, 11-12; 2005, Jul, 11-12; 2005, Aug, 7-8; 2005, Aug, 7-8; 2005, July, 11-12; 2005, August, 9-10; 2005, August, 7-8

86486 unlisted antigen, each   X TC 80 ✖

    0.14   0.14 Global Days XXX

AMA: 2008, Apr, 5-7; 2008, Apr, 5-7; 2008, Apr, 5-7

86490 coccidioidomycosis   X TC 80

    0.19   0.19 Global Days XXX

AMA: 2005, Aug, 7-8; 2005, Aug, 7-8; 2005, Aug, 9-10; 2005, Aug, 9-10; 2005, Jul, 11-12; 2005, Jul, 11-12; 2005, August, 7-8; 2005, August, 9-10; 2005, July, 11-12

86510 histoplasmosis   X TC 80

    0.19   0.19 Global Days XXX

AMA: 2005, Jul, 11-12; 2005, Jul, 11-12; 2005, Aug, 9-10; 2005, Aug, 9-10; 2005, Aug, 7-8; 2005, Aug, 7-8; 2005, July, 11-12; 2005, August, 7-8; 2005, August, 9-10

86580 tuberculosis, intradermal   X TC 80 ▫

    INCLUDES   Heaf test
         intradermal Mantoux test

    EXCLUDES   skin test for allergy (95010-95199 (95010-95199)
         tuberculosis test, cell mediated immunity measurement of gamma interferon antigen response (86480 (86480)

    0.20   0.20 Global Days XXX

AMA: 2005, Jul, 11-12; 2005, Jul, 11-12; 2005, Aug, 9-10; 2005, Aug, 9-10; 2005, Aug, 7-8; 2005, Aug, 7-8; 2005, July, 11-12; 2005, August, 7-8; 2005, August, 9-10

86590 Streptokinase, antibody   A

    EXCLUDES   antibodies to infectious agents (86602-86804)
         streptolysin O antibody (86060, 86063)

    0.00   0.00 Global Days XXX

AMA: 2005, Aug, 9-10; 2005, Aug, 9-10; 2005, Aug, 7-8; 2005, Aug, 7-8; 2005, Jul, 11-12; 2005, Jul, 11-12; 2005, July, 11-12; 2005, August, 7-8; 2005, August, 9-10

86592 Syphilis test; qualitative (eg, VDRL, RPR, ART)   A

    INCLUDES   Wasserman test

    EXCLUDES   antibodies to infectious agents (86602-86804)

    0.00   0.00 Global Days XXX

AMA: 2005, Aug, 7-8; 2005, Aug, 7-8; 2005, Aug, 9-10; 2005, Aug, 9-10; 2005, Jul, 11-12; 2005, Jul, 11-12; 2005, July, 11-12; 2005, August, 7-8; 2005, August, 9-10

86593 quantitative   A

    EXCLUDES   antibodies to infectious agents (86602-86804)

    0.00   0.00 Global Days XXX

AMA: 2005, Jul, 11-12; 2005, Jul, 11-12; 2005, Aug, 7-8; 2005, Aug, 7-8; 2005, Aug, 9-10; 2005, Aug, 9-10; 2005, July, 11-12; 2005, August, 7-8; 2005, August, 9-10

86602-86698 Testing for Antibodies to Infectious Agents: Actinomyces--Histoplasma

CMS 100-4,3,10.4   Payment of Nonphysician Services for Inpatients
CMS 100-2,15,80   Physician Supervision Requirements for Diagnostic Tests

INCLUDES   qualitative or semiquantitative immunoassays performed by multiple-step methods for the detection of antibodies to infectious agents

EXCLUDES   detection of:
    antibodies other than those to infectious agents, see specific antibody or method (86021-86023, 86376, 86800, 86850-86870)
    infectious agent/antigen (87260-87899)
    immunoassays by single-step method (86318)

86602 Antibody; actinomyces   A

    0.00   0.00 Global Days XXX

AMA: 2005, Jul, 11-12; 2005, Jul, 11-12; 2005, Aug, 9-10; 2005, Aug, 9-10; 2005, Aug, 7-8; 2005, Aug, 7-8; 2005, July, 11-12; 2005, August, 7-8; 2005, August, 9-10

86603 adenovirus   A

    0.00   0.00 Global Days XXX

AMA: 2005, Aug, 7-8; 2005, Aug, 7-8; 2005, Aug, 9-10; 2005, Aug, 9-10; 2005, Jul, 11-12; 2005, Jul, 11-12; 2005, July, 11-12; 2005, August, 7-8; 2005, August, 9-10

Pathology and Laboratory

86606 — 86658

86606 **Aspergillus** [A]
🔲 0.00 ⚕ 0.00 **Global Days XXX**
AMA: 2005, Aug, 7-8; 2005, Aug, 7-8; 2005, Aug, 9-10; 2005, Aug, 9-10; 2005, Jul, 11-12; 2005, Jul, 11-12; 2005, July, 11-12; 2005, August, 7-8; 2005, August, 9-10

86609 **bacterium, not elsewhere specified** [A]
🔲 0.00 ⚕ 0.00 **Global Days XXX**
AMA: 2005, Jul, 11-12; 2005, Jul, 11-12; 2005, Aug, 7-8; 2005, Aug, 7-8; 2005, Aug, 9-10; 2005, Aug, 9-10; 2005, July, 11-12; 2005, August, 7-8; 2005, August, 9-10

86611 **Bartonella** [A]
🔲 0.00 ⚕ 0.00 **Global Days XXX**
AMA: 2005, Jul, 11-12; 2005, Jul, 11-12; 2005, Aug, 7-8; 2005, Aug, 7-8; 2005, Aug, 9-10; 2005, Aug, 9-10; 2005, August, 7-8; 2005, July, 11-12; 2005, August, 9-10

86612 **Blastomyces** [A]
🔲 0.00 ⚕ 0.00 **Global Days XXX**
AMA: 2005, Aug, 9-10; 2005, Aug, 9-10; 2005, Jul, 11-12; 2005, Jul, 11-12; 2005, Aug, 7-8; 2005, Aug, 7-8; 2005, July, 11-12; 2005, August, 9-10; 2005, August, 7-8

86615 **Bordetella** [A]
🔲 0.00 ⚕ 0.00 **Global Days XXX**
AMA: 2005, Jul, 11-12; 2005, Jul, 11-12; 2005, Aug, 7-8; 2005, Aug, 7-8; 2005, Aug, 9-10; 2005, Aug, 9-10; 2005, July, 11-12; 2005, August, 7-8; 2005, August, 9-10

86617 **Borrelia burgdorferi (Lyme disease) confirmatory test (eg, Western Blot or immunoblot)** [A]
🔲 0.00 ⚕ 0.00 **Global Days XXX**
AMA: 2005, Aug, 9-10; 2005, Aug, 9-10; 2005, Jul, 11-12; 2005, Jul, 11-12; 2005, Aug, 7-8; 2005, Aug, 7-8; 2005, July, 11-12; 2005, August, 7-8; 2005, August, 9-10

86618 **Borrelia burgdorferi (Lyme disease)** [A] [✕]
🔲 0.00 ⚕ 0.00 **Global Days XXX**
AMA: 2005, Jul, 11-12; 2005, Jul, 11-12; 2005, Aug, 7-8; 2005, Aug, 7-8; 2005, Aug, 9-10; 2005, Aug, 9-10; 2005, July, 11-12; 2005, August, 7-8; 2005, August, 9-10

86619 **Borrelia (relapsing fever)** [A]
🔲 0.00 ⚕ 0.00 **Global Days XXX**
AMA: 2005, Jul, 11-12; 2005, Jul, 11-12; 2005, Aug, 7-8; 2005, Aug, 7-8; 2005, Aug, 9-10; 2005, Aug, 9-10; 2005, July, 11-12; 2005, August, 7-8; 2005, August, 9-10

86622 **Brucella** [A]
🔲 0.00 ⚕ 0.00 **Global Days XXX**
AMA: 2005, Jul, 11-12; 2005, Jul, 11-12; 2005, Aug, 7-8; 2005, Aug, 7-8; 2005, Aug, 9-10; 2005, Aug, 9-10; 2005, July, 11-12; 2005, August, 7-8; 2005, August, 9-10

86625 **Campylobacter** [A]
🔲 0.00 ⚕ 0.00 **Global Days XXX**
AMA: 2005, Aug, 9-10; 2005, Aug, 9-10; 2005, Jul, 11-12; 2005, Jul, 11-12; 2005, Aug, 7-8; 2005, Aug, 7-8; 2005, August, 7-8; 2005, August, 9-10; 2005, July, 11-12

86628 **Candida** [A]
EXCLUDES *candida skin test (86485)*
🔲 0.00 ⚕ 0.00 **Global Days XXX**
AMA: 2005, Aug, 9-10; 2005, Aug, 9-10; 2005, Jul, 11-12; 2005, Jul, 11-12; 2005, Aug, 7-8; 2005, Aug, 7-8; 2005, July, 11-12; 2005, August, 7-8; 2005, August, 9-10

86631 **Chlamydia** [A]
🔲 0.00 ⚕ 0.00 **Global Days XXX**
AMA: 2005, Aug, 7-8; 2005, Aug, 7-8; 2005, Jul, 11-12; 2005, Jul, 11-12; 2005, Aug, 9-10; 2005, Aug, 9-10; 2005, August, 7-8; 2005, July, 11-12; 2005, August, 9-10

86632 **Chlamydia, IgM** [A]
EXCLUDES *chlamydia antigen (87270, 87320)*
fluorescent antibody technique (86255-86256)
🔲 0.00 ⚕ 0.00 **Global Days XXX**
AMA: 2005, Jul, 11-12; 2005, Jul, 11-12; 2005, Aug, 7-8; 2005, Aug, 7-8; 2005, Aug, 9-10; 2005, Aug, 9-10; 2005, July, 11-12; 2005, August, 7-8; 2005, August, 9-10

86635 **Coccidioides** [A]
🔲 0.00 ⚕ 0.00 **Global Days XXX**
AMA: 2005, Jul, 11-12; 2005, Jul, 11-12; 2005, Aug, 7-8; 2005, Aug, 7-8; 2005, Aug, 9-10; 2005, Aug, 9-10; 2005, July, 11-12; 2005, August, 7-8; 2005, August, 9-10

86638 **Coxiella burnetii (Q fever)** [A]
🔲 0.00 ⚕ 0.00 **Global Days XXX**
AMA: 2005, Jul, 11-12; 2005, Jul, 11-12; 2005, Aug, 7-8; 2005, Aug, 7-8; 2005, Aug, 9-10; 2005, Aug, 9-10; 2005, July, 11-12; 2005, August, 7-8; 2005, August, 9-10

86641 **Cryptococcus** [A]
🔲 0.00 ⚕ 0.00 **Global Days XXX**
AMA: 2005, Jul, 11-12; 2005, Jul, 11-12; 2005, Aug, 9-10; 2005, Aug, 9-10; 2005, Aug, 7-8; 2005, Aug, 7-8; 2005, July, 11-12; 2005, August, 7-8; 2005, August, 9-10

86644 **cytomegalovirus (CMV)** [A]
🔲 0.00 ⚕ 0.00 **Global Days XXX**
AMA: 2005, Aug, 9-10; 2005, Aug, 9-10; 2005, Aug, 7-8; 2005, Aug, 7-8; 2005, Jul, 11-12; 2005, Jul, 11-12; 2005, July, 11-12; 2005, August, 9-10; 2005, August, 7-8

86645 **cytomegalovirus (CMV), IgM** [A]
🔲 0.00 ⚕ 0.00 **Global Days XXX**
AMA: 2005, Aug, 7-8; 2005, Aug, 7-8; 2005, Jul, 11-12; 2005, Jul, 11-12; 2005, Aug, 9-10; 2005, Aug, 9-10; 2005, July, 11-12; 2005, August, 7-8; 2005, August, 9-10

86648 **Diphtheria** [A]
🔲 0.00 ⚕ 0.00 **Global Days XXX**
AMA: 2005, Jul, 11-12; 2005, Jul, 11-12; 2005, Aug, 9-10; 2005, Aug, 9-10; 2005, Aug, 7-8; 2005, Aug, 7-8; 2005, August, 7-8; 2005, August, 9-10; 2005, July, 11-12

86651 **encephalitis, California (La Crosse)** [A]
🔲 0.00 ⚕ 0.00 **Global Days XXX**
AMA: 2005, Jul, 11-12; 2005, Jul, 11-12; 2005, Aug, 7-8; 2005, Aug, 7-8; 2005, Aug, 9-10; 2005, Aug, 9-10; 2005, July, 11-12; 2005, August, 7-8; 2005, August, 9-10

86652 **encephalitis, Eastern equine** [A]
🔲 0.00 ⚕ 0.00 **Global Days XXX**
AMA: 2005, Jul, 11-12; 2005, Jul, 11-12; 2005, Aug, 7-8; 2005, Aug, 7-8; 2005, Aug, 9-10; 2005, Aug, 9-10; 2005, July, 11-12; 2005, August, 7-8; 2005, August, 9-10

86653 **encephalitis, St. Louis** [A]
🔲 0.00 ⚕ 0.00 **Global Days XXX**
AMA: 2005, Jul, 11-12; 2005, Jul, 11-12; 2005, Aug, 9-10; 2005, Aug, 9-10; 2005, Aug, 7-8; 2005, Aug, 7-8; 2005, August, 7-8; 2005, August, 9-10; 2005, July, 11-12

86654 **encephalitis, Western equine** [A]
🔲 0.00 ⚕ 0.00 **Global Days XXX**
AMA: 2005, Jul, 11-12; 2005, Jul, 11-12; 2005, Aug, 7-8; 2005, Aug, 7-8; 2005, Aug, 9-10; 2005, Aug, 9-10; 2005, July, 11-12; 2005, August, 7-8; 2005, August, 9-10

86658 **enterovirus (eg, coxsackie, echo, polio)** [A]
🔲 0.00 ⚕ 0.00 **Global Days XXX**
AMA: 2005, Jul, 11-12; 2005, Jul, 11-12; 2005, Aug, 9-10; 2005, Aug, 9-10; 2005, Aug, 7-8; 2005, Aug, 7-8; 2005, July, 11-12; 2005, August, 7-8; 2005, August, 9-10

86663 Epstein-Barr (EB) virus, early antigen (EA) [A]
📋 0.00 🔬 0.00 Global Days XXX
AMA: 2005, Jul, 11-12; 2005, Jul, 11-12; 2005, Aug, 7-8; 2005, Aug, 7-8; 2005, Aug, 9-10; 2005, Aug, 9-10; 2005, July, 11-12; 2005, August, 7-8; 2005, August, 9-10

86664 Epstein-Barr (EB) virus, nuclear antigen (EBNA) [A]
📋 0.00 🔬 0.00 Global Days XXX
AMA: 2005, Aug, 7-8; 2005, Aug, 7-8; 2005, Aug, 9-10; 2005, Aug, 9-10; 2005, Jul, 11-12; 2005, Jul, 11-12; 2005, July, 11-12; 2005, August, 7-8; 2005, August, 9-10

86665 Epstein-Barr (EB) virus, viral capsid (VCA) [A]
📋 0.00 🔬 0.00 Global Days XXX
AMA: 2005, Aug, 9-10; 2005, Aug, 9-10; 2005, Jul, 11-12; 2005, Jul, 11-12; 2005, Aug, 7-8; 2005, Aug, 7-8; 2005, July, 11-12; 2005, August, 7-8; 2005, August, 9-10

86666 Ehrlichia [A]
📋 0.00 🔬 0.00 Global Days XXX
AMA: 2005, Aug, 9-10; 2005, Aug, 9-10; 2005, Aug, 7-8; 2005, Aug, 7-8; 2005, Jul, 11-12; 2005, Jul, 11-12; 2005, July, 11-12; 2005, August, 7-8; 2005, August, 9-10

86668 Francisella tularensis [A]
📋 0.00 🔬 0.00 Global Days XXX
AMA: 2005, Jul, 11-12; 2005, Jul, 11-12; 2005, Aug, 7-8; 2005, Aug, 7-8; 2005, Aug, 9-10; 2005, Aug, 9-10; 2005, August, 7-8; 2005, August, 9-10; 2005, July, 11-12

86671 fungus, not elsewhere specified [A]
📋 0.00 🔬 0.00 Global Days XXX
AMA: 2005, Aug, 7-8; 2005, Aug, 7-8; 2005, Aug, 9-10; 2005, Aug, 9-10; 2005, Jul, 11-12; 2005, Jul, 11-12; 2005, July, 11-12; 2005, August, 9-10; 2005, August, 7-8

86674 Giardia lamblia [A]
📋 0.00 🔬 0.00 Global Days XXX
AMA: 2005, Aug, 7-8; 2005, Aug, 7-8; 2005, Aug, 9-10; 2005, Aug, 9-10; 2005, Jul, 11-12; 2005, Jul, 11-12; 2005, July, 11-12; 2005, August, 7-8; 2005, August, 9-10

86677 Helicobacter pylori [A]
📋 0.00 🔬 0.00 Global Days XXX
AMA: 2005, Jul, 11-12; 2005, Jul, 11-12; 2005, Aug, 7-8; 2005, Aug, 7-8; 2005, Aug, 9-10; 2005, Aug, 9-10; 2005, July, 11-12; 2005, August, 7-8; 2005, August, 9-10

86682 helminth, not elsewhere specified [A]
📋 0.00 🔬 0.00 Global Days XXX
AMA: 2005, Aug, 9-10; 2005, Aug, 9-10; 2005, Jul, 11-12; 2005, Jul, 11-12; 2005, Aug, 7-8; 2005, Aug, 7-8; 2005, July, 11-12; 2005, August, 7-8; 2005, August, 9-10

86684 Haemophilus influenza [A]
📋 0.00 🔬 0.00 Global Days XXX
AMA: 2005, Aug, 9-10; 2005, Aug, 9-10; 2005, Aug, 7-8; 2005, Aug, 7-8; 2005, Jul, 11-12; 2005, Jul, 11-12; 2005, July, 11-12; 2005, August, 7-8; 2005, August, 9-10

86687 HTLV-I [A]
📋 0.00 🔬 0.00 Global Days XXX
AMA: 2005, Aug, 7-8; 2005, Aug, 7-8; 2005, Aug, 9-10; 2005, Aug, 9-10; 2005, Jul, 11-12; 2005, Jul, 11-12; 2005, July, 11-12; 2005, August, 7-8; 2005, August, 9-10

86688 HTLV-II [A]
📋 0.00 🔬 0.00 Global Days XXX
AMA: 2005, Aug, 7-8; 2005, Aug, 7-8; 2005, Aug, 9-10; 2005, Aug, 9-10; 2005, Jul, 11-12; 2005, Jul, 11-12; 2005, July, 11-12; 2005, August, 7-8; 2005, August, 9-10

86689 HTLV or HIV antibody, confirmatory test (eg, Western Blot) [A]
📋 0.00 🔬 0.00 Global Days XXX
AMA: 2008, Mar, 3&7; 2005, Jul, 11-12; 2005, Jul, 11-12; 2005, Aug, 7-8; 2005, Aug, 7-8; 2005, Aug, 9-10; 2005, Aug, 9-10; 2005, July, 11-12; 2005, August, 7-8; 2005, August, 9-10

86692 hepatitis, delta agent [A]
EXCLUDES hepatitis delta agent, antigen (87380)
📋 0.00 🔬 0.00 Global Days XXX
AMA: 2005, Aug, 7-8; 2005, Aug, 7-8; 2005, Jul, 11-12; 2005, Jul, 11-12; 2005, Aug, 9-10; 2005, Aug, 9-10; 2005, July, 11-12; 2005, August, 7-8; 2005, August, 9-10

86694 herpes simplex, non-specific type test [A]
📋 0.00 🔬 0.00 Global Days XXX
AMA: 2005, Aug, 9-10; 2005, Aug, 9-10; 2005, Jul, 11-12; 2005, Jul, 11-12; 2005, Aug, 7-8; 2005, Aug, 7-8; 2005, July, 11-12; 2005, August, 7-8; 2005, August, 9-10

86695 herpes simplex, type 1 [A]
📋 0.00 🔬 0.00 Global Days XXX
AMA: 2005, Aug, 9-10; 2005, Aug, 9-10; 2005, Aug, 7-8; 2005, Aug, 7-8; 2005, Jul, 11-12; 2005, Jul, 11-12; 2005, July, 11-12; 2005, August, 7-8; 2005, August, 9-10

86696 herpes simplex, type 2 [A]
📋 0.00 🔬 0.00 Global Days XXX
AMA: 2005, Jul, 11-12; 2005, Jul, 11-12; 2005, Aug, 9-10; 2005, Aug, 9-10; 2005, Aug, 7-8; 2005, Aug, 7-8; 2005, July, 11-12; 2005, August, 7-8; 2005, August, 9-10

86698 histoplasma [A]
📋 0.00 🔬 0.00 Global Days XXX
AMA: 2005, Jul, 11-12; 2005, Jul, 11-12; 2005, Aug, 7-8; 2005, Aug, 7-8; 2005, Aug, 9-10; 2005, Aug, 9-10; 2005, August, 7-8; 2005, August, 9-10; 2005, July, 11-12

86701-86703 Testing for HIV Antibodies

CMS 100-3,190.14 Human Immunodeficiency Virus Testing (Diagnosis)
CMS 100-3,190.9 Serologic Testing for Acquired Immunodeficiency Syndrome (AIDS)
CMS 100-4,3,10.4 Payment of Nonphysician Services for Inpatients
CMS 100-2,15,80 Physician Supervision Requirements for Diagnostic Tests

INCLUDES qualitative or semiquantitative immunoassays performed by multiple-step methods for the detection of antibodies to infectious agents

EXCLUDES confirmatory test for HIV antibody (86689)
detection of:
antibodies other than those to infectious agents, see specific antibody or method (86021-86023, 86376, 86800, 86850-86870)
infectious agent/antigen (87260-87899)
HIV-1 antigen (87390)
HIV-2 antigen (87391)
immunoassays by single-step method (86318)

86701 Antibody; HIV-1 [A] [X]
📋 0.00 🔬 0.00 Global Days XXX
AMA: 2008, Apr, 5-7; 2008, Apr, 5-7; 2008, Mar, 3&7; 2008, Apr, 5-7; 2005, Jul, 11-12; 2005, Jul, 11-12; 2005, July, 11-12; 2005, August, 9-10; 2005, August, 7-8; 2005, Aug, 9-10; 2005, Aug, 9-10; 2005, Aug, 7-8; 2005, Aug, 7-8

86702 HIV-2 [A]
📋 0.00 🔬 0.00 Global Days XXX
AMA: 2008, Apr, 5-7; 2008, Apr, 5-7; 2008, Mar, 3&7; 2008, Apr, 5-7; 2005, Jul, 11-12; 2005, Jul, 11-12; 2005, July, 11-12; 2005, August, 7-8; 2005, August, 9-10; 2005, Aug, 7-8; 2005, Aug, 7-8; 2005, Aug, 9-10; 2005, Aug, 9-10

86703 HIV-1 and HIV-2, single assay [A] [X]
Code also modifier 92 when HIV antibody testing (86701-86703) is performed using a single use disposable kit or disposable analytic chamber in a transportable instrument.
📋 0.00 🔬 0.00 Global Days XXX
AMA: 2008, Apr, 5-7; 2008, Apr, 5-7; 2008, Mar, 3&7; 2008, Apr, 5-7; 2005, Aug, 7-8; 2005, Aug, 7-8; 2005, July, 11-12; 2005, August, 9-10; 2005, August, 7-8; 2005, Jul, 11-12; 2005, Jul, 11-12; 2005, Aug, 9-10; 2005, Aug, 9-10

86704-86804 Testing for Infectious Disease Antibodies: Hepatitis--Yersinia

CMS 100-4,3,10.4 *Payment of Nonphysician Services for Inpatients*
CMS 100-2,15,80 *Physician Supervision Requirements for Diagnostic Tests*

INCLUDES qualitative or semiquantitative immunoassays performed by multiple-step methods for the detection of antibodies to infectious agents

EXCLUDES detection of:
antibodies other than those to infectious agents, see specific antibody or method (86021-86023, 86376, 86800, 86850-86870)
infectious agent/antigen
immunoassays by single-step method (86318)

86704 Hepatitis B core antibody (HBcAb); total [A]
🔲 0.00 🔲 0.00 Global Days XXX
AMA: 2005, Jul, 11-12; 2005, Jul, 11-12; 2005, Aug, 9-10; 2005, Aug, 9-10; 2005, Aug, 7-8; 2005, Aug, 7-8; 2005, August, 7-8; 2005, August, 9-10; 2005, July, 11-12

86705 IgM antibody [A]
🔲 0.00 🔲 0.00 Global Days XXX
AMA: 2005, Aug, 7-8; 2005, Aug, 7-8; 2005, Aug, 9-10; 2005, Aug, 9-10; 2005, Jul, 11-12; 2005, Jul, 11-12; 2005, August, 7-8; 2005, July, 11-12; 2005, August, 9-10

86706 Hepatitis B surface antibody (HBsAb) [A]
🔲 0.00 🔲 0.00 Global Days XXX
AMA: 2005, Aug, 7-8; 2005, Aug, 7-8; 2005, Jul, 11-12; 2005, Jul, 11-12; 2005, Aug, 9-10; 2005, Aug, 9-10; 2005, August, 7-8; 2005, July, 11-12; 2005, August, 9-10

86707 Hepatitis Be antibody (HBeAb) [A]
🔲 0.00 🔲 0.00 Global Days XXX
AMA: 2005, Aug, 9-10; 2005, Aug, 9-10; 2005, Aug, 7-8; 2005, Aug, 7-8; 2005, Jul, 11-12; 2005, Jul, 11-12; 2005, August, 7-8; 2005, July, 11-12; 2005, August, 9-10

86708 Hepatitis A antibody (HAAb); total [A]
🔲 0.00 🔲 0.00 Global Days XXX
AMA: 2008, Jan, 10-25; 2007, Jan, 13-27; 2007, Jan, 13-27; 2007, January, 13-27; 2005, Jul, 11-12; 2005, Jul, 11-12; 2005, Aug, 7-8; 2005, August, 7-8; 2005, August, 9-10; 2005, July, 11-12; 2005, Aug, 7-8; 2005, Aug, 9-10; 2005, Aug, 9-10

86709 IgM antibody [A]
🔲 0.00 🔲 0.00 Global Days XXX
AMA: 2008, Jan, 10-25; 2007, Jan, 13-27; 2007, Jan, 13-27; 2007, January, 13-27; 2005, Jul, 11-12; 2005, Jul, 11-12; 2005, Aug, 9-10; 2005, August, 7-8; 2005, August, 9-10; 2005, July, 11-12; 2005, Aug, 9-10; 2005, Aug, 7-8; 2005, Aug, 7-8

86710 Antibody; influenza virus [A]
🔲 0.00 🔲 0.00 Global Days XXX
AMA: 2005, Aug, 7-8; 2005, Aug, 7-8; 2005, Jul, 11-12; 2005, Jul, 11-12; 2005, Aug, 9-10; 2005, Aug, 9-10; 2005, August, 7-8; 2005, July, 11-12; 2005, August, 9-10

86713 Legionella [A]
🔲 0.00 🔲 0.00 Global Days XXX
AMA: 2005, Aug, 9-10; 2005, Aug, 9-10; 2005, Jul, 11-12; 2005, Jul, 11-12; 2005, Aug, 7-8; 2005, Aug, 7-8; 2005, August, 7-8; 2005, July, 11-12; 2005, August, 9-10

86717 Leishmania [A]
🔲 0.00 🔲 0.00 Global Days XXX
AMA: 2005, Aug, 9-10; 2005, Aug, 9-10; 2005, Aug, 7-8; 2005, Aug, 7-8; 2005, Jul, 11-12; 2005, Jul, 11-12; 2005, August, 7-8; 2005, July, 11-12; 2005, August, 9-10

86720 Leptospira [A]
🔲 0.00 🔲 0.00 Global Days XXX
AMA: 2005, Jul, 11-12; 2005, Jul, 11-12; 2005, Aug, 7-8; 2005, Aug, 7-8; 2005, Aug, 9-10; 2005, Aug, 9-10; 2005, August, 7-8; 2005, July, 11-12; 2005, August, 9-10

86723 Listeria monocytogenes [A]
🔲 0.00 🔲 0.00 Global Days XXX
AMA: 2005, Jul, 11-12; 2005, Jul, 11-12; 2005, Aug, 7-8; 2005, Aug, 7-8; 2005, Aug, 9-10; 2005, Aug, 9-10; 2005, August, 7-8; 2005, July, 11-12; 2005, August, 9-10

86727 lymphocytic choriomeningitis [A]
🔲 0.00 🔲 0.00 Global Days XXX
AMA: 2005, Jul, 11-12; 2005, Jul, 11-12; 2005, Aug, 9-10; 2005, Aug, 9-10; 2005, Aug, 7-8; 2005, Aug, 7-8; 2005, July, 11-12; 2005, August, 9-10; 2005, August, 7-8

86729 lymphogranuloma venereum [A]
🔲 0.00 🔲 0.00 Global Days XXX
AMA: 2005, Jul, 11-12; 2005, Jul, 11-12; 2005, Aug, 9-10; 2005, Aug, 9-10; 2005, Aug, 7-8; 2005, Aug, 7-8; 2005, August, 7-8; 2005, July, 11-12; 2005, August, 9-10

86732 mucormycosis [A]
🔲 0.00 🔲 0.00 Global Days XXX
AMA: 2005, Jul, 11-12; 2005, Jul, 11-12; 2005, Aug, 7-8; 2005, Aug, 7-8; 2005, Aug, 9-10; 2005, Aug, 9-10; 2005, August, 7-8; 2005, July, 11-12; 2005, August, 9-10

86735 mumps [A]
🔲 0.00 🔲 0.00 Global Days XXX
AMA: 2008, Jan, 10-25; 2007, Jan, 13-27; 2007, Jan, 13-27; 2007, January, 13-27; 2006, Sep, 14-16; 2006, Sep, 14-16; 2006, September, 14-16; 2005, Aug, 7-8; 2005, Aug, 7-8; 2005, August, 9-10; 2005, July, 11-12; 2005, August, 7-8; 2005, Jul, 11-12; 2005, Aug, 9-10; 2005, Aug, 9-10

86738 mycoplasma [A]
🔲 0.00 🔲 0.00 Global Days XXX
AMA: 2005, Aug, 7-8; 2005, Aug, 7-8; 2005, Aug, 9-10; 2005, Aug, 9-10; 2005, Jul, 11-12; 2005, Jul, 11-12; 2005, August, 7-8; 2005, July, 11-12; 2005, August, 9-10

86741 Neisseria meningitidis [A]
🔲 0.00 🔲 0.00 Global Days XXX
AMA: 2005, Jul, 11-12; 2005, Jul, 11-12; 2005, Aug, 9-10; 2005, Aug, 9-10; 2005, Aug, 7-8; 2005, Aug, 7-8; 2005, August, 7-8; 2005, July, 11-12; 2005, August, 9-10

86744 Nocardia [A]
🔲 0.00 🔲 0.00 Global Days XXX
AMA: 2005, Aug, 7-8; 2005, Aug, 7-8; 2005, Aug, 9-10; 2005, Aug, 9-10; 2005, Jul, 11-12; 2005, Jul, 11-12; 2005, August, 7-8; 2005, July, 11-12; 2005, August, 9-10

86747 parvovirus [A]
🔲 0.00 🔲 0.00 Global Days XXX
AMA: 2005, Jul, 11-12; 2005, Jul, 11-12; 2005, Aug, 9-10; 2005, Aug, 9-10; 2005, Aug, 7-8; 2005, Aug, 7-8; 2005, August, 9-10; 2005, July, 11-12

86750 Plasmodium (malaria) [A]
🔲 0.00 🔲 0.00 Global Days XXX
AMA: 2005, Jul, 11-12; 2005, Jul, 11-12; 2005, Aug, 9-10; 2005, Aug, 9-10; 2005, Aug, 7-8; 2005, Aug, 7-8; 2005, August, 7-8; 2005, July, 11-12; 2005, August, 9-10

86753 protozoa, not elsewhere specified [A]
🔲 0.00 🔲 0.00 Global Days XXX
AMA: 2005, Jul, 11-12; 2005, Jul, 11-12; 2005, Aug, 7-8; 2005, Aug, 7-8; 2005, Aug, 9-10; 2005, Aug, 9-10; 2005, July, 11-12; 2005, August, 7-8; 2005, August, 9-10

86756 **respiratory syncytial virus** [A]
📇 0.00 ✂ 0.00 Global Days XXX
AMA: 2005, Jul, 11-12; 2005, Jul, 11-12; 2005, Aug, 7-8; 2005, Aug, 7-8; 2005, Aug, 9-10; 2005, Aug, 9-10; 2005, July, 11-12; 2005, August, 7-8; 2005, August, 9-10

86757 **Rickettsia** [A]
📇 0.00 ✂ 0.00 Global Days XXX
AMA: 2005, Jul, 11-12; 2005, Jul, 11-12; 2005, Aug, 9-10; 2005, Aug, 9-10; 2005, Aug, 7-8; 2005, Aug, 7-8; 2005, July, 11-12; 2005, August, 7-8; 2005, August, 9-10

86759 **rotavirus** [A]
📇 0.00 ✂ 0.00 Global Days XXX
AMA: 2005, Aug, 7-8; 2005, Aug, 7-8; 2005, Jul, 11-12; 2005, Jul, 11-12; 2005, Aug, 9-10; 2005, Aug, 9-10; 2005, July, 11-12; 2005, August, 7-8; 2005, August, 9-10

86762 **rubella** [A]
📇 0.00 ✂ 0.00 Global Days XXX
AMA: 2005, Aug, 9-10; 2005, Aug, 9-10; 2005, Aug, 7-8; 2005, Aug, 7-8; 2005, Jul, 11-12; 2005, Jul, 11-12; 2005, July, 11-12; 2005, August, 7-8; 2005, August, 9-10

86765 **rubeola** [A]
📇 0.00 ✂ 0.00 Global Days XXX
AMA: 2005, Jul, 11-12; 2005, Jul, 11-12; 2005, Aug, 7-8; 2005, Aug, 7-8; 2005, Aug, 9-10; 2005, Aug, 9-10; 2005, July, 11-12; 2005, August, 7-8; 2005, August, 9-10

86768 **Salmonella** [A]
📇 0.00 ✂ 0.00 Global Days XXX
AMA: 2005, Aug, 7-8; 2005, Aug, 7-8; 2005, Aug, 9-10; 2005, Aug, 9-10; 2005, Jul, 11-12; 2005, Jul, 11-12; 2005, July, 11-12; 2005, August, 7-8; 2005, August, 9-10

86771 **Shigella** [A]
📇 0.00 ✂ 0.00 Global Days XXX
AMA: 2005, Jul, 11-12; 2005, Jul, 11-12; 2005, Aug, 7-8; 2005, Aug, 7-8; 2005, Aug, 9-10; 2005, Aug, 9-10; 2005, July, 11-12; 2005, August, 7-8; 2005, August, 9-10

86774 **tetanus** [A]
📇 0.00 ✂ 0.00 Global Days XXX
AMA: 2005, Jul, 11-12; 2005, Jul, 11-12; 2005, Aug, 7-8; 2005, Aug, 7-8; 2005, Aug, 9-10; 2005, Aug, 9-10; 2005, July, 11-12; 2005, August, 7-8; 2005, August, 9-10

86777 **Toxoplasma** [A]
📇 0.00 ✂ 0.00 Global Days XXX
AMA: 2005, Jul, 11-12; 2005, Jul, 11-12; 2005, Aug, 7-8; 2005, Aug, 7-8; 2005, Aug, 9-10; 2005, Aug, 9-10; 2005, July, 11-12; 2005, August, 7-8; 2005, August, 9-10

86778 **Toxoplasma, IgM** [A]
📇 0.00 ✂ 0.00 Global Days XXX
AMA: 2005, Aug, 7-8; 2005, Aug, 7-8; 2005, Aug, 9-10; 2005, Aug, 9-10; 2005, Jul, 11-12; 2005, Jul, 11-12; 2005, July, 11-12; 2005, August, 7-8; 2005, August, 9-10

86781 **Treponema pallidum, confirmatory test (eg, FTA-abs)** [A]
📇 0.00 ✂ 0.00 Global Days XXX
AMA: 2005, Jul, 11-12; 2005, Jul, 11-12; 2005, Aug, 7-8; 2005, Aug, 7-8; 2005, Aug, 9-10; 2005, Aug, 9-10; 2005, July, 11-12; 2005, August, 7-8; 2005, August, 9-10

86784 **Trichinella** [A]
📇 0.00 ✂ 0.00 Global Days XXX
AMA: 2005, Jul, 11-12; 2005, Jul, 11-12; 2005, Aug, 7-8; 2005, Aug, 7-8; 2005, Aug, 9-10; 2005, Aug, 9-10; 2005, July, 11-12; 2005, August, 7-8; 2005, August, 9-10

86787 **varicella-zoster** [A]
📇 0.00 ✂ 0.00 Global Days XXX
AMA: 2005, Jul, 11-12; 2005, Jul, 11-12; 2005, Aug, 9-10; 2005, Aug, 9-10; 2005, Aug, 7-8; 2005, Aug, 7-8; 2005, July, 11-12; 2005, August, 9-10; 2005, August, 7-8

86788 **West Nile virus, IgM** [A]
📇 0.00 ✂ 0.00 Global Days XXX

86789 **West Nile virus** [A]
📇 0.00 ✂ 0.00 Global Days XXX

86790 **virus, not elsewhere specified** [A]
📇 0.00 ✂ 0.00 Global Days XXX
AMA: 2005, Jul, 11-12; 2005, Jul, 11-12; 2005, Aug, 9-10; 2005, Aug, 9-10; 2005, Aug, 7-8; 2005, Aug, 7-8; 2005, July, 11-12; 2005, August, 7-8; 2005, August, 9-10

86793 **Yersinia** [A]
📇 0.00 ✂ 0.00 Global Days XXX
AMA: 2005, Jul, 11-12; 2005, Jul, 11-12; 2005, Aug, 7-8; 2005, Aug, 7-8; 2005, Aug, 9-10; 2005, Aug, 9-10; 2005, July, 11-12; 2005, August, 7-8; 2005, August, 9-10

86800 **Thyroglobulin antibody** [A]
📇 0.00 ✂ 0.00 Global Days XXX
AMA: 2005, Jul, 11-12; 2005, Jul, 11-12; 2005, Aug, 7-8; 2005, Aug, 7-8; 2005, Aug, 9-10; 2005, Aug, 9-10; 2005, July, 11-12; 2005, August, 7-8; 2005, August, 9-10

86803 **Hepatitis C antibody;** [A]
📇 0.00 ✂ 0.00 Global Days XXX
AMA: 2005, Jul, 11-12; 2005, Jul, 11-12; 2005, Aug, 7-8; 2005, Aug, 7-8; 2005, Aug, 9-10; 2005, Aug, 9-10; 2005, July, 11-12; 2005, August, 7-8; 2005, August, 9-10

86804 **confirmatory test (eg, immunoblot)** [A]
📇 0.00 ✂ 0.00 Global Days XXX
AMA: 2005, Jul, 11-12; 2005, Jul, 11-12; 2005, Aug, 9-10; 2005, Aug, 9-10; 2005, Aug, 7-8; 2005, Aug, 7-8; 2005, July, 11-12; 2005, August, 7-8; 2005, August, 9-10

86805-86808 Pre-Transplant Antibody Cross Matching

CMS 100-4,3,10.4   *Payment of Nonphysician Services for Inpatients*
CMS 100-2,15,80   *Physician Supervision Requirements for Diagnostic Tests*

86805 **Lymphocytotoxicity assay, visual crossmatch; with titration** [A] 🔲
📇 0.00 ✂ 0.00 Global Days XXX
AMA: 2005, Jul, 11-12; 2005, Jul, 11-12; 2005, Aug, 9-10; 2005, Aug, 9-10; 2005, Aug, 7-8; 2005, Aug, 7-8; 2005, July, 11-12; 2005, August, 7-8; 2005, August, 9-10

86806 **without titration** [A]
📇 0.00 ✂ 0.00 Global Days XXX
AMA: 2005, Aug, 9-10; 2005, Aug, 9-10; 2005, Aug, 7-8; 2005, Aug, 7-8; 2005, Jul, 11-12; 2005, Jul, 11-12; 2005, August, 7-8; 2005, August, 9-10; 2005, July, 11-12

86807 **Serum screening for cytotoxic percent reactive antibody (PRA); standard method** [A]
📇 0.00 ✂ 0.00 Global Days XXX
AMA: 2008, Jan, 10-25; 2007, Jan, 13-27; 2007, Jan, 13-27; 2007, January, 13-27; 2005, Jul, 11-12; 2005, Jul, 11-12; 2005, Aug, 9-10; 2005, August, 7-8; 2005, August, 9-10; 2005, July, 11-12; 2005, Aug, 9-10; 2005, Aug, 7-8; 2005, Aug, 7-8

86808 **quick method** [A]
📇 0.00 ✂ 0.00 Global Days XXX
AMA: 2008, Jan, 10-25; 2007, Jan, 13-27; 2007, Jan, 13-27; 2007, January, 13-27; 2005, Jul, 11-12; 2005, Jul, 11-12; 2005, Aug, 7-8; 2005, August, 7-8; 2005, August, 9-10; 2005, July, 11-12; 2005, Aug, 7-8; 2005, Aug, 9-10; 2005, Aug, 9-10

86812-86849 Histocompatibility Testing

CMS *100-3,190.8*   *Lymphocyte Mitogen Response Assays*
CMS *100-4,3,10.4*   *Payment of Nonphysician Services for Inpatients*
CMS *100-3,190.1*   *Histocompatibility Testing*
CMS *100-2,15,80*   *Physician Supervision Requirements for Diagnostic Tests*

86812   **HLA typing; A, B, or C (eg, A10, B7, B27), single antigen**   Ⓐ
  💲 0.00   ⚕ 0.00   **Global Days XXX**
  AMA: 2008, Jan, 10-25; 2007, Jan, 13-27; 2007, Jan, 13-27; 2007, January, 13-27; 2006, Jun, 16-17; 2006, Jun, 16-17; 2006, June, 16-17; 2005, Jul, 11-12; 2005, Jul, 11-12; 2005, August, 7-8; 2005, August, 9-10; 2005, July, 11-12; 2005, Aug, 7-8; 2005, Aug, 7-8; 2005, Aug, 9-10; 2005, Aug, 9-10

86813   **A, B, or C, multiple antigens**   Ⓐ ▱
  💲 0.00   ⚕ 0.00   **Global Days XXX**
  AMA: 2008, Jan, 10-25; 2007, Jan, 13-27; 2007, Jan, 13-27; 2007, January, 13-27; 2006, Jun, 16-17; 2006, Jun, 16-17; 2006, June, 16-17; 2005, Jul, 11-12; 2005, Jul, 11-12; 2005, August, 7-8; 2005, August, 9-10; 2005, July, 11-12; 2005, Aug, 7-8; 2005, Aug, 7-8; 2005, Aug, 9-10; 2005, Aug, 9-10

86816   **DR/DQ, single antigen**   Ⓐ
  💲 0.00   ⚕ 0.00   **Global Days XXX**
  AMA: 2008, Jan, 10-25; 2007, Jan, 13-27; 2007, Jan, 13-27; 2007, January, 13-27; 2005, Aug, 7-8; 2005, Aug, 7-8; 2005, Jul, 11-12; 2005, August, 9-10; 2005, July, 11-12; 2005, August, 7-8; 2005, Jul, 11-12; 2005, Aug, 9-10; 2005, Aug, 9-10

86817   **DR/DQ, multiple antigens**   Ⓐ ▱
  💲 0.00   ⚕ 0.00   **Global Days XXX**
  AMA: 2008, Jan, 10-25; 2007, Jan, 13-27; 2007, Jan, 13-27; 2007, January, 13-27; 2005, Aug, 9-10; 2005, Aug, 9-10; 2005, Aug, 7-8; 2005, August, 9-10; 2005, August, 7-8; 2005, July, 11-12; 2005, Aug, 7-8; 2005, Jul, 11-12; 2005, Jul, 11-12

86821   **lymphocyte culture, mixed (MLC)**   Ⓐ
  💲 0.00   ⚕ 0.00   **Global Days XXX**
  AMA: 2008, Jan, 10-25; 2007, Jan, 13-27; 2007, Jan, 13-27; 2007, January, 13-27; 2005, Aug, 7-8; 2005, Aug, 7-8; 2005, Aug, 9-10; 2005, August, 7-8; 2005, August, 9-10; 2005, July, 11-12; 2005, Aug, 9-10; 2005, Jul, 11-12; 2005, Jul, 11-12

86822   **lymphocyte culture, primed (PLC)**   Ⓐ
  💲 0.00   ⚕ 0.00   **Global Days XXX**
  AMA: 2008, Jan, 10-25; 2007, Jan, 13-27; 2007, Jan, 13-27; 2007, January, 13-27; 2005, Aug, 9-10; 2005, Aug, 9-10; 2005, Aug, 7-8; 2005, August, 7-8; 2005, August, 9-10; 2005, July, 11-12; 2005, Aug, 7-8; 2005, Jul, 11-12; 2005, Jul, 11-12

86849   **Unlisted immunology procedure**   Ⓐ
  💲 0.00   ⚕ 0.00   **Global Days XXX**
  AMA: 2008, Jan, 10-25; 2007, Jan, 13-27; 2007, Jan, 13-27; 2007, January, 13-27; 2005, Jul, 11-12; 2005, Jul, 11-12; 2005, Aug, 9-10; 2005, July, 11-12; 2005, August, 9-10; 2005, August, 7-8; 2005, Aug, 9-10; 2005, Aug, 7-8; 2005, Aug, 7-8

EXCLUDES   *HLA typing by molecular pathology methods (83890-83914)*

86850-86999 Transfusion Services

CMS *100-4,3,10.4*   *Payment of Nonphysician Services for Inpatients*
CMS *100-3,110.8*   *Blood Platelet Transfusions*
CMS *100-3,110.7*   *Blood Transfusions*
CMS *100-3,110.5*   *Granulocyte Transfulsions*
CMS *100-2,15,80*   *Physician Supervision Requirements for Diagnostic Tests*
EXCLUDES   *apheresis (36511-36512)*
  therapeutic phlebotomy (99195)

86850   **Antibody screen, RBC, each serum technique**   Ⓧ
  💲 0.00   ⚕ 0.00   **Global Days XXX**
  AMA: 2008, Apr, 5-7; 2008, Apr, 5-7; 2008, Apr, 5-7; 2005, Aug, 7-8; 2005, Aug, 7-8; 2005, August, 7-8; 2005, August, 9-10; 2005, July, 11-12; 2005, Jul, 11-12; 2005, Jul, 11-12; 2005, Aug, 9-10; 2005, Aug, 9-10

86860   **Antibody elution (RBC), each elution**   Ⓧ
  💲 0.00   ⚕ 0.00   **Global Days XXX**
  AMA: 2005, Aug, 7-8; 2005, Aug, 7-8; 2005, Jul, 11-12; 2005, Jul, 11-12; 2005, Aug, 9-10; 2005, Aug, 9-10; 2005, July, 11-12; 2005, August, 7-8; 2005, August, 9-10

86870   **Antibody identification, RBC antibodies, each panel for each serum technique**   Ⓧ
  💲 0.00   ⚕ 0.00   **Global Days XXX**
  AMA: 2008, Apr, 5-7; 2008, Apr, 5-7; 2008, Jan, 10-25; 2008, Apr, 5-7; 2007, Jan, 13-27; 2007, January, 13-27; 2007, Jan, 13-27; 2005, Aug, 9-10; 2005, August, 7-8; 2005, July, 11-12; 2005, August, 9-10; 2005, Aug, 9-10; 2005, Jul, 11-12; 2005, Jul, 11-12; 2005, Aug, 7-8; 2005, Aug, 7-8

86880   **Antihuman globulin test (Coombs test); direct, each antiserum**   Ⓧ
  💲 0.00   ⚕ 0.00   **Global Days XXX**
  AMA: 2005, Jul, 11-12; 2005, Jul, 11-12; 2005, Aug, 9-10; 2005, Aug, 9-10; 2005, Aug, 7-8; 2005, Aug, 7-8; 2005, July, 11-12; 2005, August, 7-8; 2005, August, 9-10

86885   **indirect, qualitative, each reagent red cell**   Ⓧ
  💲 0.00   ⚕ 0.00   **Global Days XXX**
  AMA: 2008, Apr, 5-7; 2008, Apr, 5-7; 2008, Apr, 5-7; 2005, Aug, 7-8; 2005, Aug, 7-8; 2005, July, 11-12; 2005, August, 9-10; 2005, August, 7-8; 2005, Aug, 9-10; 2005, Aug, 9-10; 2005, Jul, 11-12; 2005, Jul, 11-12

86886   **indirect, each antibody titer**   Ⓧ
  EXCLUDES   *indirect antihuman globulin (Coombs) test for RBC antibody identification using reagent red cell panels (86870)*
  indirect antihuman globulin (Coombs) test for RBC antibody screening (86850)
  💲 0.00   ⚕ 0.00   **Global Days XXX**
  AMA: 2008, Apr, 5-7; 2008, Apr, 5-7; 2008, Apr, 5-7; 2005, Aug, 7-8; 2005, Aug, 7-8; 2005, August, 7-8; 2005, August, 9-10; 2005, July, 11-12; 2005, Aug, 9-10; 2005, Aug, 9-10; 2005, Jul, 11-12; 2005, Jul, 11-12

86890   **Autologous blood or component, collection processing and storage; predeposited**   Ⓧ ▱
  💲 0.00   ⚕ 0.00   **Global Days XXX**
  AMA: 2005, Jul, 11-12; 2005, Jul, 11-12; 2005, Aug, 9-10; 2005, Aug, 9-10; 2005, Aug, 7-8; 2005, Aug, 7-8; 2005, August, 7-8; 2005, July, 11-12; 2005, August, 9-10

86891   **intra- or postoperative salvage**   Ⓧ ▱
  EXCLUDES   *physician services to autologous donors (99201-99204)*
  💲 0.00   ⚕ 0.00   **Global Days XXX**
  AMA: 2005, Aug, 9-10; 2005, Aug, 9-10; 2005, Jul, 11-12; 2005, Jul, 11-12; 2005, Aug, 7-8; 2005, Aug, 7-8; 2005, August, 7-8; 2005, August, 9-10; 2005, July, 11-12

86900 Blood typing; ABO ☒
🔲 0.00 ⚕ 0.00 Global Days XXX
AMA: 2005, Aug, 7-8; 2005, Aug, 7-8; 2005, Jul, 11-12; 2005, Jul, 11-12; 2005, Aug, 9-10; 2005, Aug, 9-10; 2005, August, 7-8; 2005, July, 11-12; 2005, August, 9-10

86901 Rh (D) ☒
🔲 0.00 ⚕ 0.00 Global Days XXX
AMA: 2005, Aug, 7-8; 2005, Aug, 7-8; 2005, Aug, 9-10; 2005, Aug, 9-10; 2005, Jul, 11-12; 2005, Jul, 11-12; 2005, July, 11-12; 2005, August, 9-10; 2005, August, 7-8

86903 antigen screening for compatible blood unit using reagent serum, per unit screened ☒ 🔲
🔲 0.00 ⚕ 0.00 Global Days XXX
AMA: 2005, Aug, 7-8; 2005, Aug, 7-8; 2005, Jul, 11-12; 2005, Jul, 11-12; 2005, Aug, 9-10; 2005, Aug, 9-10; 2005, August, 7-8; 2005, July, 11-12; 2005, August, 9-10

86904 antigen screening for compatible unit using patient serum, per unit screened ☒
🔲 0.00 ⚕ 0.00 Global Days XXX
AMA: 2005, Aug, 9-10; 2005, Aug, 9-10; 2005, Aug, 7-8; 2005, Aug, 7-8; 2005, Jul, 11-12; 2005, Jul, 11-12; 2005, August, 7-8; 2005, July, 11-12; 2005, August, 9-10

86905 RBC antigens, other than ABO or Rh (D), each ☒
🔲 0.00 ⚕ 0.00 Global Days XXX
AMA: 2005, Aug, 9-10; 2005, Aug, 9-10; 2005, Jul, 11-12; 2005, Jul, 11-12; 2005, Aug, 7-8; 2005, Aug, 7-8; 2005, August, 7-8; 2005, July, 11-12; 2005, August, 9-10

86906 Rh phenotyping, complete ☒
🔲 0.00 ⚕ 0.00 Global Days XXX
AMA: 2005, Jul, 11-12; 2005, Jul, 11-12; 2005, Aug, 9-10; 2005, Aug, 9-10; 2005, Aug, 7-8; 2005, Aug, 7-8; 2005, August, 7-8; 2005, July, 11-12; 2005, August, 9-10

86910 Blood typing, for paternity testing, per individual; ABO, Rh and MN Ⓔ
🔲 0.00 ⚕ 0.00 Global Days XXX
AMA: 2005, Jul, 11-12; 2005, Jul, 11-12; 2005, Aug, 7-8; 2005, Aug, 7-8; 2005, Aug, 9-10; 2005, Aug, 9-10; 2005, August, 7-8; 2005, July, 11-12; 2005, August, 9-10

86911 each additional antigen system Ⓔ
🔲 0.00 ⚕ 0.00 Global Days XXX
AMA: 2005, Jul, 11-12; 2005, Jul, 11-12; 2005, Aug, 9-10; 2005, Aug, 9-10; 2005, Aug, 7-8; 2005, Aug, 7-8; 2005, August, 7-8; 2005, July, 11-12; 2005, August, 9-10

86920 Compatibility test each unit; immediate spin technique ☒
🔲 0.00 ⚕ 0.00 Global Days XXX
AMA: 2006, Mar, 6-9; 2006, Mar, 6-9; 2006, March, 6-9; 2005, Aug, 7-8; 2005, Aug, 7-8; 2005, Jul, 11-12; 2005, July, 11-12; 2005, August, 9-10; 2005, August, 7-8; 2005, Jul, 11-12; 2005, Aug, 9-10; 2005, Aug, 9-10

86921 incubation technique ☒
🔲 0.00 ⚕ 0.00 Global Days XXX
AMA: 2006, Mar, 6-9; 2006, Mar, 6-9; 2006, March, 6-9; 2005, Aug, 7-8; 2005, Aug, 7-8; 2005, Aug, 9-10; 2005, July, 11-12; 2005, August, 9-10; 2005, August, 7-8; 2005, Aug, 9-10; 2005, Jul, 11-12; 2005, Jul, 11-12

86922 antiglobulin technique ☒
🔲 0.00 ⚕ 0.00 Global Days XXX
AMA: 2006, Mar, 6-9; 2006, Mar, 6-9; 2006, March, 6-9; 2005, Aug, 7-8; 2005, Aug, 7-8; 2005, Jul, 11-12; 2005, July, 11-12; 2005, August, 9-10; 2005, August, 7-8; 2005, Jul, 11-12; 2005, Aug, 9-10; 2005, Aug, 9-10

86923 electronic ☒
Do not report with (86920-86922)
🔲 0.00 ⚕ 0.00 Global Days XXX
AMA: 2006, Mar, 6-9; 2006, Mar, 6-9; 2006, March, 6-9; 2005, Aug, 7-8; 2005, Aug, 7-8; 2005, August, 9-10; 2005, August, 7-8; 2005, Aug, 9-10; 2005, Aug, 9-10

86927 Fresh frozen plasma, thawing, each unit ☒
🔲 0.00 ⚕ 0.00 Global Days XXX
AMA: 2005, Aug, 9-10; 2005, Aug, 9-10; 2005, Jul, 11-12; 2005, Jul, 11-12; 2005, Aug, 7-8; 2005, Aug, 7-8; 2005, August, 7-8; 2005, July, 11-12; 2005, August, 9-10

86930 Frozen blood, each unit; freezing (includes preparation) ☒
🔲 0.00 ⚕ 0.00 Global Days XXX
AMA: 2005, Aug, 9-10; 2005, Aug, 9-10; 2005, Aug, 7-8; 2005, Aug, 7-8; 2005, Jul, 11-12; 2005, Jul, 11-12; 2005, July, 11-12; 2005, August, 7-8; 2005, August, 9-10

86931 thawing ☒ 🔲
🔲 0.00 ⚕ 0.00 Global Days XXX
AMA: 2005, Jul, 11-12; 2005, Jul, 11-12; 2005, Aug, 7-8; 2005, Aug, 7-8; 2005, Aug, 9-10; 2005, Aug, 9-10; 2005, July, 11-12; 2005, August, 7-8; 2005, August, 9-10

86932 freezing (includes preparation) and thawing ☒ 🔲
🔲 0.00 ⚕ 0.00 Global Days XXX
AMA: 2005, Jul, 11-12; 2005, Jul, 11-12; 2005, Aug, 7-8; 2005, Aug, 7-8; 2005, Aug, 9-10; 2005, Aug, 9-10; 2005, July, 11-12; 2005, August, 7-8; 2005, August, 9-10

86940 Hemolysins and agglutinins; auto, screen, each Ⓐ
🔲 0.00 ⚕ 0.00 Global Days XXX
AMA: 2005, Aug, 7-8; 2005, Aug, 7-8; 2005, Jul, 11-12; 2005, Jul, 11-12; 2005, Aug, 9-10; 2005, Aug, 9-10; 2005, July, 11-12; 2005, August, 7-8; 2005, August, 9-10

86941 incubated Ⓐ
🔲 0.00 ⚕ 0.00 Global Days XXX
AMA: 2005, Aug, 9-10; 2005, Aug, 9-10; 2005, Aug, 7-8; 2005, Aug, 7-8; 2005, Jul, 11-12; 2005, Jul, 11-12; 2005, July, 11-12; 2005, August, 7-8; 2005, August, 9-10

86945 Irradiation of blood product, each unit ☒
🔲 0.00 ⚕ 0.00 Global Days XXX
AMA: 2007, Dec, 10-179; 2005, Jul, 11-12; 2005, Jul, 11-12; 2005, Aug, 7-8; 2005, Aug, 7-8; 2005, Aug, 9-10; 2005, Aug, 9-10; 2005, July, 11-12; 2005, August, 7-8; 2005, August, 9-10

86950 Leukocyte transfusion ☒ 🔲
EXCLUDES leukapheresis (36511)
🔲 0.00 ⚕ 0.00 Global Days XXX
AMA: 2005, Aug, 7-8; 2005, Aug, 7-8; 2005, Aug, 9-10; 2005, Aug, 9-10; 2005, Jul, 11-12; 2005, Jul, 11-12; 2005, July, 11-12; 2005, August, 7-8; 2005, August, 9-10

86960 Volume reduction of blood or blood product (eg, red blood cells or platelets), each unit ☒
🔲 0.00 ⚕ 0.00 Global Days XXX
AMA: 2006, Mar, 6-9; 2006, Mar, 6-9; 2006, March, 6-9; 2005, Aug, 9-10; 2005, Aug, 9-10; 2005, August, 7-8; 2005, August, 9-10; 2005, Aug, 7-8; 2005, Aug, 7-8

86965 Pooling of platelets or other blood products ☒
🔲 0.00 ⚕ 0.00 Global Days XXX
AMA: 2005, Aug, 7-8; 2005, Aug, 7-8; 2005, Jul, 11-12; 2005, Jul, 11-12; 2005, Aug, 9-10; 2005, Aug, 9-10; 2005, August, 9-10; 2005, July, 11-12; 2005, August, 7-8

86970 Pretreatment of RBCs for use in RBC antibody detection, identification, and/or compatibility testing; incubation with chemical agents or drugs, each ☒
🔲 0.00 ⚕ 0.00 Global Days XXX
AMA: 2005, Aug, 9-10; 2005, Aug, 9-10; 2005, Aug, 7-8; 2005, Aug, 7-8; 2005, Jul, 11-12; 2005, Jul, 11-12; 2005, August, 9-10; 2005, July, 11-12; 2005, August, 7-8

86971 incubation with enzymes, each ☒
📷 0.00 🔪 0.00 **Global Days XXX**
AMA: 2005, Jul, 11-12; 2005, Jul, 11-12; 2005, Aug, 9-10; 2005, Aug, 9-10; 2005, Aug, 7-8; 2005, Aug, 7-8; 2005, July, 11-12; 2005, August, 7-8; 2005, August, 9-10

86972 by density gradient separation ☒
📷 0.00 🔪 0.00 **Global Days XXX**
AMA: 2005, Jul, 11-12; 2005, Jul, 11-12; 2005, Aug, 7-8; 2005, Aug, 7-8; 2005, Aug, 9-10; 2005, Aug, 9-10; 2005, August, 9-10; 2005, July, 11-12; 2005, August, 7-8

86975 Pretreatment of serum for use in RBC antibody identification; incubation with drugs, each ☒
📷 0.00 🔪 0.00 **Global Days XXX**
AMA: 2005, Aug, 9-10; 2005, Aug, 9-10; 2005, Aug, 7-8; 2005, Aug, 7-8; 2005, Jul, 11-12; 2005, Jul, 11-12; 2005, August, 9-10; 2005, July, 11-12; 2005, August, 7-8

86976 by dilution ☒
📷 0.00 🔪 0.00 **Global Days XXX**
AMA: 2005, Jul, 11-12; 2005, Jul, 11-12; 2005, Aug, 9-10; 2005, Aug, 9-10; 2005, Aug, 7-8; 2005, Aug, 7-8; 2005, August, 9-10; 2005, July, 11-12; 2005, August, 7-8

86977 incubation with inhibitors, each ☒
📷 0.00 🔪 0.00 **Global Days XXX**
AMA: 2005, Aug, 9-10; 2005, Aug, 9-10; 2005, Aug, 7-8; 2005, Aug, 7-8; 2005, Jul, 11-12; 2005, Jul, 11-12; 2005, August, 9-10; 2005, August, 7-8; 2005, July, 11-12

86978 by differential red cell absorption using patient RBCs or RBCs of known phenotype, each absorption ☒
📷 0.00 🔪 0.00 **Global Days XXX**
AMA: 2005, Aug, 9-10; 2005, Aug, 9-10; 2005, Aug, 7-8; 2005, Aug, 7-8; 2005, Jul, 11-12; 2005, Jul, 11-12; 2005, August, 9-10; 2005, July, 11-12; 2005, August, 7-8

86985 Splitting of blood or blood products, each unit ☒
📷 0.00 🔪 0.00 **Global Days XXX**
AMA: 2005, Jul, 11-12; 2005, Jul, 11-12; 2005, Aug, 7-8; 2005, Aug, 7-8; 2005, Aug, 9-10; 2005, Aug, 9-10; 2005, August, 9-10; 2005, July, 11-12; 2005, August, 7-8

86999 Unlisted transfusion medicine procedure ☒
📷 0.00 🔪 0.00 **Global Days XXX**
AMA: 2008, Jan, 10-25; 2007, Jan, 13-27; 2007, Jan, 13-27; 2007, January, 13-27; 2005, Jul, 11-12; 2005, Jul, 11-12; 2005, Nov, 14-15; 2005, Nov, 14-15; 2005, July, 11-12; 2005, November, 14-15; 2005, August, 7-8; 2005, August, 9-10; 2005, Aug, 9-10; 2005, Aug, 9-10; 2005, Aug, 7-8; 2005, Aug, 7-8

87001-87118 Identification of Microorganisms

CMS 100-3,190.12   *Urine Culture, Bacterial*
CMS 100-4,3,10.4   *Payment of Nonphysician Services for Inpatients*
CMS 100-2,15,80   *Physician Supervision Requirements for Diagnostic Tests*
[INCLUDES] bacteriology, mycology, parasitology, and virology

[EXCLUDES] *additional tests using molecular probes, chromatography, or immunologic techniques (87140-87158)*

87001 Animal inoculation, small animal; with observation Ⓐ
📷 0.00 🔪 0.00 **Global Days XXX**
AMA: 2005, Aug, 7-8; 2005, Aug, 7-8; 2005, Jul, 11-12; 2005, Jul, 11-12; 2005, Aug, 9-10; 2005, Aug, 9-10; 2005, August, 9-10; 2005, July, 11-12; 2005, August, 7-8

87003 with observation and dissection Ⓐ ▢
📷 0.00 🔪 0.00 **Global Days XXX**
AMA: 2005, Jul, 11-12; 2005, Jul, 11-12; 2005, Aug, 9-10; 2005, Aug, 9-10; 2005, Aug, 7-8; 2005, Aug, 7-8; 2005, August, 9-10; 2005, July, 11-12; 2005, August, 7-8

87015 Concentration (any type), for infectious agents Ⓐ
Do not report with (87177)
📷 0.00 🔪 0.00 **Global Days XXX**
AMA: 2005, Aug, 9-10; 2005, Aug, 9-10; 2005, Jul, 11-12; 2005, Jul, 11-12; 2005, Aug, 7-8; 2005, Aug, 7-8; 2005, August, 9-10; 2005, July, 11-12; 2005, August, 7-8

87040 Culture, bacterial; blood, aerobic, with isolation and presumptive identification of isolates (includes anaerobic culture, if appropriate) Ⓐ ▢
📷 0.00 🔪 0.00 **Global Days XXX**
AMA: 2008, Jan, 10-25; 2007, Jan, 13-27; 2007, Jan, 13-27; 2007, January, 13-27; 2005, Jul, 11-12; 2005, Jul, 11-12; 2005, Aug, 7-8; 2005, July, 11-12; 2005, August, 7-8; 2005, August, 9-10; 2005, Aug, 7-8; 2005, Aug, 9-10; 2005, Aug, 9-10

87045 stool, aerobic, with isolation and preliminary examination (eg, KIA, LIA), Salmonella and Shigella species Ⓐ ▢
📷 0.00 🔪 0.00 **Global Days XXX**
AMA: 2005, Aug, 9-10; 2005, Aug, 9-10; 2005, Jul, 11-12; 2005, Jul, 11-12; 2005, Aug, 7-8; 2005, Aug, 7-8; 2005, July, 11-12; 2005, August, 9-10; 2005, August, 7-8

87046 stool, aerobic, additional pathogens, isolation and presumptive identification of isolates, each plate Ⓐ ▢
📷 0.00 🔪 0.00 **Global Days XXX**
AMA: 2005, Jul, 11-12; 2005, Jul, 11-12; 2005, Aug, 7-8; 2005, Aug, 7-8; 2005, Aug, 9-10; 2005, Aug, 9-10; 2005, July, 11-12; 2005, August, 7-8; 2005, August, 9-10

87070 any other source except urine, blood or stool, aerobic, with isolation and presumptive identification of isolates Ⓐ
[EXCLUDES] *urine (87088)*
📷 0.00 🔪 0.00 **Global Days XXX**
AMA: 2008, Jan, 10-25; 2007, Jan, 13-27; 2007, Jan, 13-27; 2007, January, 13-27; 2005, Aug, 9-10; 2005, Aug, 9-10; 2005, Jul, 11-12; 2005, August, 9-10; 2005, August, 7-8; 2005, July, 11-12; 2005, Aug, 7-8; 2005, Aug, 7-8

87071 quantitative, aerobic with isolation and presumptive identification of isolates, any source except urine, blood or stool Ⓐ ▢
[EXCLUDES] *urine (87088)*
📷 0.00 🔪 0.00 **Global Days XXX**
AMA: 2005, Aug, 7-8; 2005, Aug, 7-8; 2005, Aug, 9-10; 2005, Aug, 9-10; 2005, Jul, 11-12; 2005, Jul, 11-12; 2005, July, 11-12; 2005, August, 9-10; 2005, August, 7-8

87073 quantitative, anaerobic with isolation and presumptive identification of isolates, any source except urine, blood or stool Ⓐ ▢
[EXCLUDES] *definitive identification of isolates (87076, or 87077)*
typing of isolates (87140-87158)
📷 0.00 🔪 0.00 **Global Days XXX**
AMA: 2005, Aug, 9-10; 2005, Aug, 9-10; 2005, Aug, 7-8; 2005, Aug, 7-8; 2005, Jul, 11-12; 2005, Jul, 11-12; 2005, July, 11-12; 2005, August, 9-10; 2005, August, 7-8

87075 any source, except blood, anaerobic with isolation and presumptive identification of isolates Ⓐ
📷 0.00 🔪 0.00 **Global Days XXX**
AMA: 2005, Aug, 7-8; 2005, Aug, 7-8; 2005, Aug, 9-10; 2005, Aug, 9-10; 2005, Jul, 11-12; 2005, Jul, 11-12; 2005, August, 7-8; 2005, July, 11-12; 2005, August, 9-10

㉖/🆃 Professional/Technical Component Only   �80/🅰🆂 Assist-at-Surgery Allowed/With Documentation   Unlisted   Not Covered   🅡 Radiology crosswalk

MED: Pub 100/NCD References   **AMA:** CPT Assistant References   🅰2/🆉3 ASC Payment Indicator   ♂Male Only   ♀Female Only   🅛 Laboratory crosswalk

360   CPT only © 2008 American Medical Association. All Rights Reserved. (Black Ink)   Medicare (Red Ink)   © 2008 Ingenix *(Blue Ink)*

87076   anaerobic isolate, additional methods required for definitive identification, each isolate   [A]

    EXCLUDES   *gas liquid chromatography (GLC) or high pressure liquid chromatography (HPLC) (87143)*

    📋 0.00   ⚕ 0.00   Global Days XXX

    AMA: 2005, Aug, 7-8; 2005, Aug, 7-8; 2005, Aug, 9-10; 2005, Aug, 9-10; 2005, Jul, 11-12; 2005, Jul, 11-12; 2005, August, 7-8; 2005, July, 11-12; 2005, August, 9-10

87077   aerobic isolate, additional methods required for definitive identification, each isolate   [A] [X]

    EXCLUDES   *gas liquid chromatography (GLC) or high pressure liquid chromatography (HPLC) (87143)*

    📋 0.00   ⚕ 0.00   Global Days XXX

    AMA: 2005, Aug, 7-8; 2005, Aug, 7-8; 2005, Jul, 11-12; 2005, Jul, 11-12; 2005, Aug, 9-10; 2005, Aug, 9-10; 2005, August, 7-8; 2005, July, 11-12; 2005, August, 9-10

87081   Culture, presumptive, pathogenic organisms, screening only;   [A] [CCI]

    📋 0.00   ⚕ 0.00   Global Days XXX

    AMA: 2005, Aug, 9-10; 2005, Aug, 9-10; 2005, Jul, 11-12; 2005, Jul, 11-12; 2005, Aug, 7-8; 2005, Aug, 7-8; 2005, August, 7-8; 2005, July, 11-12; 2005, August, 9-10

87084   with colony estimation from density chart   [A] [CCI]

    📋 0.00   ⚕ 0.00   Global Days XXX

    AMA: 2005, Aug, 7-8; 2005, Aug, 7-8; 2005, Jul, 11-12; 2005, Jul, 11-12; 2005, Aug, 9-10; 2005, Aug, 9-10; 2005, August, 7-8; 2005, July, 11-12; 2005, August, 9-10

87086   quantitative colony count, urine   [A] [CCI]

    📋 0.00   ⚕ 0.00   Global Days XXX

    AMA: 2005, Aug, 9-10; 2005, Aug, 9-10; 2005, Jul, 11-12; 2005, Jul, 11-12; 2005, Aug, 7-8; 2005, Aug, 7-8; 2005, August, 7-8; 2005, August, 9-10; 2005, July, 11-12

87088   with isolation and presumptive identification of each isolate, urine   [A] [CCI]

    📋 0.00   ⚕ 0.00   Global Days XXX

    AMA: 2005, Aug, 9-10; 2005, Aug, 9-10; 2005, Jul, 11-12; 2005, Jul, 11-12; 2005, Aug, 7-8; 2005, Aug, 7-8; 2005, August, 7-8; 2005, July, 11-12; 2005, August, 9-10

87101   Culture, fungi (mold or yeast) isolation, with presumptive identification of isolates; skin, hair, or nail   [A]

    📋 0.00   ⚕ 0.00   Global Days XXX

    AMA: 2008, Jan, 10-25; 2007, Jan, 13-27; 2007, Jan, 13-27; 2007, January, 13-27; 2005, Aug, 7-8; 2005, Aug, 7-8; 2005, Jul, 11-12; 2005, August, 9-10; 2005, July, 11-12; 2005, August, 7-8; Jul, 11-12; 2005, Aug, 9-10; 2005, Aug, 9-10

87102   other source (except blood)   [A]

    📋 0.00   ⚕ 0.00   Global Days XXX

    AMA: 2005, Aug, 7-8; 2005, Aug, 7-8; 2005, Jul, 11-12; 2005, Jul, 11-12; 2005, Aug, 9-10; 2005, Aug, 9-10; 2005, August, 9-10; 2005, July, 11-12; 2005, August, 7-8

87103   blood   [A]

    📋 0.00   ⚕ 0.00   Global Days XXX

    AMA: 2005, Aug, 9-10; 2005, Aug, 9-10; 2005, Jul, 11-12; 2005, Jul, 11-12; 2005, Aug, 7-8; 2005, Aug, 7-8; 2005, August, 7-8; 2005, August, 9-10; 2005, July, 11-12

87106   Culture, fungi, definitive identification, each organism; yeast   [A] [CCI]

    Code also (87101-87103)

    📋 0.00   ⚕ 0.00   Global Days XXX

    AMA: 2005, Aug, 7-8; 2005, Aug, 7-8; 2005, Aug, 9-10; 2005, Aug, 9-10; 2005, Jul, 11-12; 2005, Jul, 11-12; 2005, August, 7-8; July, 11-12; 2005, August, 9-10

87107   mold   [A]

    📋 0.00   ⚕ 0.00   Global Days XXX

    AMA: 2005, Aug, 9-10; 2005, Aug, 9-10; 2005, Jul, 11-12; 2005, Jul, 11-12; 2005, Aug, 7-8; 2005, Aug, 7-8; 2005, August, 7-8; 2005, August, 9-10; 2005, July, 11-12

87109   Culture, mycoplasma, any source   [A]

    📋 0.00   ⚕ 0.00   Global Days XXX

    AMA: 2005, Aug, 7-8; 2005, Aug, 7-8; 2005, Jul, 11-12; 2005, Jul, 11-12; 2005, Aug, 9-10; 2005, Aug, 9-10; 2005, August, 7-8; 2005, August, 9-10; 2005, July, 11-12

87110   Culture, chlamydia, any source   [A]

    EXCLUDES   *immunofluorescence staining of shell vials (87140)*

    📋 0.00   ⚕ 0.00   Global Days XXX

    AMA: 2005, Aug, 7-8; 2005, Aug, 7-8; 2005, Jul, 11-12; 2005, Jul, 11-12; 2005, Aug, 9-10; 2005, Aug, 9-10; 2005, August, 7-8; 2005, August, 9-10; 2005, July, 11-12

87116   Culture, tubercle or other acid-fast bacilli (eg, TB, AFB, mycobacteria) any source, with isolation and presumptive identification of isolates   [A]

    EXCLUDES   *concentration (87015)*

    📋 0.00   ⚕ 0.00   Global Days XXX

    AMA: 2005, Jul, 11-12; 2005, Jul, 11-12; 2005, Aug, 9-10; 2005, Aug, 9-10; 2005, Aug, 7-8; 2005, Aug, 7-8; 2005, August, 7-8; 2005, August, 9-10; 2005, July, 11-12

87118   Culture, mycobacterial, definitive identification, each isolate   [A]

    EXCLUDES   *GLC HPLC identification (87143)*   *nucleic acid probe identification (87149)*

    📋 0.00   ⚕ 0.00   Global Days XXX

    AMA: 2005, Jul, 11-12; 2005, Jul, 11-12; 2005, Aug, 9-10; 2005, Aug, 9-10; 2005, Aug, 7-8; 2005, Aug, 7-8; 2005, August, 7-8; 2005, August, 9-10; 2005, July, 11-12

87140-87158 Additional Culture Typing Techniques

CMS *100-4,3,10.4*   *Payment of Nonphysician Services for Inpatients*
CMS *100-2,15,80*   *Physician Supervision Requirements for Diagnostic Tests*
INCLUDES   bacteriology, mycology, parasitology, and virology

Code also definitive identification

87140   Culture, typing; immunofluorescent method, each antiserum   [A] [CCI]

    📋 0.00   ⚕ 0.00   Global Days XXX

    AMA: 2005, Aug, 7-8; 2005, Aug, 7-8; 2005, Jul, 11-12; 2005, Jul, 11-12; 2005, Aug, 9-10; 2005, Aug, 9-10; 2005, August, 7-8; 2005, August, 9-10; 2005, July, 11-12

87143   gas liquid chromatography (GLC) or high pressure liquid chromatography (HPLC) method   [A] [CCI]

    📋 0.00   ⚕ 0.00   Global Days XXX

    AMA: 2005, Aug, 9-10; 2005, Aug, 9-10; 2005, Jul, 11-12; 2005, Jul, 11-12; 2005, Aug, 7-8; 2005, Aug, 7-8; 2005, August, 9-10; 2005, July, 11-12

87147   immunologic method, other than immunofluoresence (eg, agglutination grouping), per antiserum   [A] [CCI]

    📋 0.00   ⚕ 0.00   Global Days XXX

    AMA: 2008, Jan, 10-25; 2007, Jan, 13-27; 2007, Jan, 13-27; 2007, January, 13-27; 2005, Aug, 7-8; 2005, Aug, 7-8; 2005, Jul, 11-12; 2005, August, 9-10; 2005, July, 11-12; 2005, August, 7-8; Jul, 11-12; 2005, Aug, 9-10; 2005, Aug, 9-10

87149   identification by nucleic acid probe   [A] [CCI]

    📋 0.00   ⚕ 0.00   Global Days XXX

    AMA: 2005, Aug, 7-8; 2005, Aug, 7-8; 2005, Jul, 11-12; 2005, Jul, 11-12; 2005, Aug, 9-10; 2005, Aug, 9-10; 2005, August, 7-8; 2005, August, 9-10; 2005, July, 11-12

⊛ Modifier 63 Exempt Code	☉ Moderate Sedation	✛ CPT Add-on Code
⃠ Modifier 51 Exempt Code	● New Code	▲ Revised Code
Ⓜ Maternity Edit	[A] Age Edit	☒ CLIA Waived Test
[A-Y] APC Status Indicators	[CCI] CCI Comprehensive Code	⑤⓪ Bilateral Procedure

87152   identification by pulse field gel typing   Ⓐ 🔲
 🔲 0.00   ⚕ 0.00   Global Days XXX
AMA: 2005, Aug, 9-10; 2005, Aug, 9-10; 2005, Jul, 11-12; 2005, Jul, 11-12; 2005, Aug, 7-8; 2005, Aug, 7-8; 2005, July, 11-12; 2005, August, 7-8; 2005, August, 9-10

87158   other methods   Ⓐ 🔲
 🔲 0.00   ⚕ 0.00   Global Days XXX
AMA: 2005, Jul, 11-12; 2005, Jul, 11-12; 2005, Aug, 7-8; 2005, Aug, 7-8; 2005, Aug, 9-10; 2005, Aug, 9-10; 2005, July, 11-12; 2005, August, 9-10; 2005, August, 7-8

87164-87255 Identification of Organism from Primary Source and Sensitivity Studies

CMS *100-4,3,10.4*   *Payment of Nonphysician Services for Inpatients*
CMS *100-2,15,80*   *Physician Supervision Requirements for Diagnostic Tests*
INCLUDES bacteriology, mycology, parasitology, and virology

EXCLUDES *additional tests using molecular probes, chromatography, or immunologic techniques (87140-87158)*

87164   **Dark field examination, any source (eg, penile, vaginal, oral, skin); includes specimen collection**   Ⓐ 80 🔲
 🔲 0.00   ⚕ 0.00   Global Days XXX
AMA: 2005, Aug, 7-8; 2005, Aug, 7-8; 2005, Aug, 9-10; 2005, Aug, 9-10; 2005, Jul, 11-12; 2005, Jul, 11-12; 2005, July, 11-12; 2005, August, 7-8; 2005, August, 9-10

87166   **without collection**   Ⓐ 🔲
 🔲 0.00   ⚕ 0.00   Global Days XXX
AMA: 2005, Aug, 7-8; 2005, Aug, 7-8; 2005, Aug, 9-10; 2005, Aug, 9-10; 2005, Jul, 11-12; 2005, Jul, 11-12; 2005, July, 11-12; 2005, August, 7-8; 2005, August, 9-10

87168   **Macroscopic examination; arthropod**   Ⓐ 🔲
 🔲 0.00   ⚕ 0.00   Global Days XXX
AMA: 2005, Jul, 11-12; 2005, Jul, 11-12; 2005, Aug, 7-8; 2005, Aug, 7-8; 2005, Aug, 9-10; 2005, Aug, 9-10; 2005, July, 11-12; 2005, August, 7-8; 2005, August, 9-10

87169   **parasite**   Ⓐ 🔲
 🔲 0.00   ⚕ 0.00   Global Days XXX
AMA: 2005, Aug, 7-8; 2005, Aug, 7-8; 2005, Jul, 11-12; 2005, Jul, 11-12; 2005, Aug, 9-10; 2005, Aug, 9-10; 2005, July, 11-12; 2005, August, 7-8; 2005, August, 9-10

87172   **Pinworm exam (eg, cellophane tape prep)**   Ⓐ 🔲
 🔲 0.00   ⚕ 0.00   Global Days XXX
AMA: 2005, Aug, 9-10; 2005, Aug, 9-10; 2005, Jul, 11-12; 2005, Jul, 11-12; 2005, Aug, 7-8; 2005, Aug, 7-8; 2005, July, 11-12; 2005, August, 7-8; 2005, August, 9-10

87176   **Homogenization, tissue, for culture**   Ⓐ
 🔲 0.00   ⚕ 0.00   Global Days XXX
AMA: 2005, Aug, 7-8; 2005, Aug, 7-8; 2005, Aug, 9-10; 2005, Aug, 9-10; 2005, Jul, 11-12; 2005, Jul, 11-12; 2005, August, 7-8; 2005, August, 9-10; 2005, July, 11-12

87177   **Ova and parasites, direct smears, concentration and identification**   Ⓐ 🔲
EXCLUDES *coccidia or microsporidia exam (87207)*
complex special stain (trichrome, iron hematoxylin) (87209)
direct smears from primary source (87207)
molecular diagnostics (83890-83898, 87470-87799)
nucleic acid probes in cytologic material (88365)

Do not report with (87015)
 🔲 0.00   ⚕ 0.00   Global Days XXX
AMA: 2008, Jan, 10-25; 2007, Jan, 13-27; 2007, Jan, 13-27; 2007, January, 13-27; 2006, Mar, 6-9; 2006, Mar, 6-9; 2006, March, 6-9; 2005, Aug, 9-10; 2005, Aug, 9-10; 2005, August, 9-10; 2005, July, 11-12; 2005, August, 7-8; 2005, Jul, 11-12; 2005, Jul, 11-12; 2005, Aug, 7-8; 2005, Aug, 7-8

87181   **Susceptibility studies, antimicrobial agent; agar dilution method, per agent (eg, antibiotic gradient strip)**   Ⓐ 🔲
 🔲 0.00   ⚕ 0.00   Global Days XXX
AMA: 2005, Aug, 7-8; 2005, Aug, 7-8; 2005, Aug, 9-10; 2005, Aug, 9-10; 2005, Jul, 11-12; 2005, Jul, 11-12; 2005, August, 7-8; 2005, August, 9-10; 2005, July, 11-12

87184   **disk method, per plate (12 or fewer agents)**   Ⓐ 🔲
 🔲 0.00   ⚕ 0.00   Global Days XXX
AMA: 2005, Jul, 11-12; 2005, Jul, 11-12; 2005, Aug, 9-10; 2005, Aug, 9-10; 2005, Aug, 7-8; 2005, Aug, 7-8; 2005, August, 7-8; 2005, August, 9-10; 2005, July, 11-12

87185   **enzyme detection (eg, beta lactamase), per enzyme**   Ⓐ 🔲
 🔲 0.00   ⚕ 0.00   Global Days XXX
AMA: 2005, Aug, 7-8; 2005, Aug, 7-8; 2005, Jul, 11-12; 2005, Jul, 11-12; 2005, Aug, 9-10; 2005, Aug, 9-10; 2005, August, 7-8; 2005, August, 9-10; 2005, July, 11-12

87186   **microdilution or agar dilution (minimum inhibitory concentration [MIC] or breakpoint), each multi-antimicrobial, per plate**   Ⓐ 🔲
 🔲 0.00   ⚕ 0.00   Global Days XXX
AMA: 2005, Aug, 9-10; 2005, Aug, 9-10; 2005, Jul, 11-12; 2005, Jul, 11-12; 2005, Aug, 7-8; 2005, Aug, 7-8; 2005, August, 7-8; 2005, August, 9-10; 2005, July, 11-12

+ 87187   **microdilution or agar dilution, minimum lethal concentration (MLC), each plate (List separately in addition to code for primary procedure)**   Ⓐ
Code first (87186, or 87188)
 🔲 0.00   ⚕ 0.00   Global Days XXX
AMA: 2005, Aug, 7-8; 2005, Aug, 7-8; 2005, Aug, 9-10; 2005, Aug, 9-10; 2005, Jul, 11-12; 2005, Jul, 11-12; 2005, August, 7-8; 2005, August, 9-10; 2005, July, 11-12

87188   **macrobroth dilution method, each agent**   Ⓐ 🔲
 🔲 0.00   ⚕ 0.00   Global Days XXX
AMA: 2005, Jul, 11-12; 2005, Jul, 11-12; 2005, Aug, 7-8; 2005, Aug, 7-8; 2005, Aug, 9-10; 2005, Aug, 9-10; 2005, August, 9-10; 2005, July, 11-12; 2005, August, 7-8

87190   **mycobacteria, proportion method, each agent**   Ⓐ
EXCLUDES *other mycobacterial susceptibility studies (87181, 87184, 87186, or 87188)*
 🔲 0.00   ⚕ 0.00   Global Days XXX
AMA: 2005, Aug, 7-8; 2005, Aug, 7-8; 2005, Aug, 9-10; 2005, Aug, 9-10; 2005, Jul, 11-12; 2005, Jul, 11-12; 2005, August, 7-8; 2005, August, 9-10; 2005, July, 11-12

87197   **Serum bactericidal titer (Schlicter test)**   Ⓐ
 🔲 0.00   ⚕ 0.00   Global Days XXX
AMA: 2005, Aug, 7-8; 2005, Aug, 7-8; 2005, Jul, 11-12; 2005, Jul, 11-12; 2005, Aug, 9-10; 2005, Aug, 9-10; 2005, August, 7-8; 2005, July, 11-12; 2005, August, 9-10

87205 Smear, primary source with interpretation; Gram or Giemsa stain for bacteria, fungi, or cell types   Ⓐ ▭

    📋 0.00 🔬 0.00 Global Days XXX

    AMA: 2005, Aug, 9-10; 2005, Aug, 9-10; 2005, Jul, 11-12; 2005, Jul, 11-12; 2005, Aug, 7-8; 2005, Aug, 7-8; 2005, August, 9-10; 2005, July, 11-12

87206 fluorescent and/or acid fast stain for bacteria, fungi, parasites, viruses or cell types   Ⓐ ▭

    📋 0.00 🔬 0.00 Global Days XXX

    AMA: 2005, Jul, 11-12; 2005, Jul, 11-12; 2005, Aug, 7-8; 2005, Aug, 7-8; 2005, Aug, 9-10; 2005, Aug, 9-10; 2005, August, 7-8; 2005, August, 9-10; 2005, July, 11-12

87207 special stain for inclusion bodies or parasites (eg, malaria, coccidia, microsporidia, trypanosomes, herpes viruses)   Ⓐ 🔟 ▭

    INCLUDES   Tzank smear

    EXCLUDES   *direct smears with concentration and identification (87177)*
        fat, meat, fibers, nasal eosinophils, and starch (see miscellaneous section)
        thick smear preparation (87015)

    📋 0.00 🔬 0.00 Global Days XXX

    AMA: 2006, Mar, 6-9; 2006, Mar, 6-9; 2006, March, 6-9; 2005, Aug, 7-8; 2005, Aug, 7-8; 2005, Aug, 9-10; 2005, August, 9-10; 2005, July, 11-12; 2005, August, 7-8; 2005, Aug, 9-10; 2005, Jul, 11-12; 2005, Jul, 11-12

87209 complex special stain (eg, trichrome, iron hemotoxylin) for ova and parasites   Ⓐ

    📋 0.00 🔬 0.00 Global Days XXX

    AMA: 2006, Mar, 6-9; 2006, Mar, 6-9; 2006, March, 6-9; 2005, Aug, 9-10; 2005, Aug, 9-10; 2005, August, 9-10, 2005, August, 7-8; 2005, Aug, 7-8; 2005, Aug, 7-8

87210 wet mount for infectious agents (eg, saline, India ink, KOH preps)   Ⓐ ▭ ⓧ

    EXCLUDES   *KOH evaluation of skin, hair, or nails (87220)*

    📋 0.00 🔬 0.00 Global Days XXX

    AMA: 2005, Aug, 7-8; 2005, Aug, 7-8; 2005, Aug, 9-10; 2005, Aug, 9-10; 2005, Jul, 11-12; 2005, Jul, 11-12; 2005, August, 7-8; 2005, August, 9-10; 2005, July, 11-12

87220 Tissue examination by KOH slide of samples from skin, hair, or nails for fungi or ectoparasite ova or mites (eg, scabies)   Ⓐ ▭

    📋 0.00 🔬 0.00 Global Days XXX

    AMA: 2005, Aug, 7-8; 2005, Aug, 7-8; 2005, Jul, 11-12; 2005, Jul, 11-12; 2005, Aug, 9-10; 2005, Aug, 9-10; 2005, August, 7-8; 2005, August, 9-10; 2005, July, 11-12

87230 Toxin or antitoxin assay, tissue culture (eg, Clostridium difficile toxin)   Ⓐ

    📋 0.00 🔬 0.00 Global Days XXX

    AMA: 2005, Jul, 11-12; 2005, Jul, 11-12; 2005, Aug, 7-8; 2005, Aug, 7-8; 2005, Aug, 9-10; 2005, August, 7-8; 2005, August, 9-10; 2005, July, 11-12

87250 Virus isolation; inoculation of embryonated eggs, or small animal, includes observation and dissection   Ⓐ

    📋 0.00 🔬 0.00 Global Days XXX

    AMA: 2005, Aug, 9-10; 2005, Aug, 9-10; 2005, Jul, 11-12; 2005, Jul, 11-12; 2005, Aug, 7-8; 2005, Aug, 7-8; 2005, August, 7-8; 2005, August, 9-10; 2005, July, 11-12

87252 tissue culture inoculation, observation, and presumptive identification by cytopathic effect   Ⓐ

    📋 0.00 🔬 0.00 Global Days XXX

    AMA: 2005, Aug, 7-8; 2005, Aug, 7-8; 2005, Aug, 9-10; 2005, Aug, 9-10; 2005, Jul, 11-12; 2005, Jul, 11-12; 2005, July, 11-12; 2005, August, 7-8; 2005, August, 9-10

87253 tissue culture, additional studies or definitive identification (eg, hemabsorption, neutralization, immunofluoresence stain), each isolate   Ⓐ ▭

    EXCLUDES   *electron microscopy (88348)*
        inclusion bodies in:
          fluids (88106)
          smears (87207-87210)
          tissue sections (88304-88309)

    📋 0.00 🔬 0.00 Global Days XXX

    AMA: 2005, Aug, 7-8; 2005, Aug, 7-8; 2005, Aug, 9-10; 2005, Aug, 9-10; 2005, Jul, 11-12; 2005, Jul, 11-12; 2005, July, 11-12; 2005, August, 7-8; 2005, August, 9-10

87254 centrifuge enhanced (shell vial) technique, includes identification with immunofluorescence stain, each virus   Ⓐ ▭

    Code also (87252)

    📋 0.00 🔬 0.00 Global Days XXX

    AMA: 2005, Jul, 11-12; 2005, Jul, 11-12; 2005, Aug, 7-8; 2005, Aug, 7-8; 2005, Aug, 9-10; 2005, Aug, 9-10; 2005, August, 9-10; 2005, July, 11-12; 2005, August, 7-8

87255 including identification by non-immunologic method, other than by cytopathic effect (eg, virus specific enzymatic activity)   Ⓐ ▭

    📋 0.00 🔬 0.00 Global Days XXX

    AMA: 2005, Aug, 7-8; 2005, Aug, 7-8; 2005, Jul, 11-12; 2005, Jul, 11-12; 2005, Aug, 9-10; 2005, Aug, 9-10; 2005, July, 11-12; 2005, August, 7-8; 2005, August, 9-10

87260-87300 Fluorescence Microscopy by Organism

  CMS *100-4,3,10.4*   *Payment of Nonphysician Services for Inpatients*
  CMS *100-2,15,80*   *Physician Supervision Requirements for Diagnostic Tests*

  INCLUDES   primary source code only

  EXCLUDES   *comparable tests on culture material (87140-87158)*
    identification of antibodies (86602-86804)
    nonspecific agent detection (87299, 87449, 87450, 87797-87799, 87899)
    separate assays performed for different species or strain(s) of organisms (report each separately with modifier 59)

87260 Infectious agent antigen detection by immunofluorescent technique; adenovirus   Ⓐ ▭

    📋 0.00 🔬 0.00 Global Days XXX

    AMA: 2005, Aug, 9-10; 2005, Aug, 9-10; 2005, Jul, 11-12; 2005, Jul, 11-12; 2005, Aug, 7-8; 2005, Aug, 7-8; 2005, July, 11-12; 2005, August, 7-8; 2005, August, 9-10

87265 Bordetella pertussis/parapertussis   Ⓐ ▭

    📋 0.00 🔬 0.00 Global Days XXX

    AMA: 2005, Aug, 7-8; 2005, Aug, 7-8; 2005, Aug, 9-10; 2005, Aug, 9-10; 2005, Jul, 11-12; 2005, Jul, 11-12; 2005, July, 11-12; 2005, August, 7-8; 2005, August, 9-10

87267 Enterovirus, direct fluorescent antibody (DFA)   Ⓐ ▭

    📋 0.00 🔬 0.00 Global Days XXX

    AMA: 2005, Jul, 11-12; 2005, Jul, 11-12; 2005, Aug, 7-8; 2005, Aug, 7-8; 2005, Aug, 9-10; 2005, Aug, 9-10; 2005, August, 7-8; 2005, August, 9-10; 2005, July, 11-12

87269 giardia   Ⓐ ▭

    📋 0.00 🔬 0.00 Global Days XXX

    AMA: 2005, Aug, 7-8; 2005, Aug, 7-8; 2005, Aug, 9-10; 2005, Aug, 9-10; 2005, Jul, 11-12; 2005, Jul, 11-12; 2005, July, 11-12; 2005, August, 7-8; 2005, August, 9-10

87270 Chlamydia trachomatis   Ⓐ ▭

    📋 0.00 🔬 0.00 Global Days XXX

    AMA: 2005, Jul, 11-12; 2005, Jul, 11-12; 2005, Aug, 7-8; 2005, Aug, 7-8; 2005, Aug, 9-10; 2005, Aug, 9-10; 2005, July, 11-12; 2005, August, 7-8; 2005, August, 9-10

| ⊛ Modifier 63 Exempt Code | ☉ Moderate Sedation | + CPT Add-on Code | ⊘ Modifier 51 Exempt Code | ● New Code | ▲ Revised Code |
| Ⓜ Maternity Edit | Ⓐ Age Edit | ⓧ CLIA Waived Test | Ⓐ-Ⓨ APC Status Indicators | ▭ CCI Comprehensive Code | 🔟 Bilateral Procedure |

© 2008 Ingenix *(Blue Ink)*   CPT only © 2008 American Medical Association. All Rights Reserved. (Black Ink)   Medicare (Red Ink)   **363**

87271   Cytomegalovirus, direct fluorescent antibody (DFA) 🅰 ▪
    0.00   0.00   Global Days XXX
    AMA: 2005, Aug, 7-8; 2005, Aug, 7-8; 2005, Jul, 11-12; 2005, Jul, 11-12; 2005, Aug, 9-10; 2005, Aug, 9-10; 2005, July, 11-12; 2005, August, 7-8; 2005, August, 9-10

87272   cryptosporidium 🅰 ▪
    0.00   0.00   Global Days XXX
    AMA: 2005, Aug, 9-10; 2005, Aug, 9-10; 2005, Jul, 11-12; 2005, Jul, 11-12; 2005, Aug, 7-8; 2005, Aug, 7-8; 2005, July, 11-12; 2005, August, 7-8; 2005, August, 9-10

87273   Herpes simplex virus type 2 🅰 ▪
    0.00   0.00   Global Days XXX
    AMA: 2005, Aug, 7-8; 2005, Aug, 7-8; 2005, Aug, 9-10; 2005, Aug, 9-10; 2005, Jul, 11-12; 2005, Jul, 11-12; 2005, July, 11-12; 2005, August, 7-8; 2005, August, 9-10

87274   Herpes simplex virus type 1 🅰 ▪
    0.00   0.00   Global Days XXX
    AMA: 2005, Aug, 9-10; 2005, Aug, 9-10; 2005, Jul, 11-12; 2005, Jul, 11-12; 2005, Aug, 7-8; 2005, Aug, 7-8; 2005, July, 11-12; 2005, August, 7-8; 2005, August, 9-10

87275   influenza B virus 🅰 ▪
    0.00   0.00   Global Days XXX
    AMA: 2005, Aug, 7-8; 2005, Aug, 7-8; 2005, Aug, 9-10; 2005, Aug, 9-10; 2005, Jul, 11-12; 2005, Jul, 11-12; 2005, July, 11-12; 2005, August, 7-8; 2005, August, 9-10

87276   influenza A virus 🅰 ▪
    0.00   0.00   Global Days XXX
    AMA: 2005, Jul, 11-12; 2005, Jul, 11-12; 2005, Aug, 9-10; 2005, Aug, 9-10; 2005, Aug, 7-8; 2005, Aug, 7-8; 2005, July, 11-12; 2005, August, 7-8; 2005, August, 9-10

87277   Legionella micdadei 🅰 ▪
    0.00   0.00   Global Days XXX
    AMA: 2005, Jul, 11-12; 2005, Jul, 11-12; 2005, Aug, 9-10; 2005, Aug, 9-10; 2005, Aug, 7-8; 2005, Aug, 7-8; 2005, July, 11-12; 2005, August, 9-10; 2005, August, 7-8

87278   Legionella pneumophila 🅰 ▪
    0.00   0.00   Global Days XXX
    AMA: 2005, Aug, 9-10; 2005, Aug, 9-10; 2005, Jul, 11-12; 2005, Jul, 11-12; 2005, Aug, 7-8; 2005, Aug, 7-8; 2005, July, 11-12; 2005, August, 7-8; 2005, August, 9-10

87279   Parainfluenza virus, each type 🅰 ▪
    0.00   0.00   Global Days XXX
    AMA: 2005, Aug, 7-8; 2005, Aug, 7-8; 2005, Aug, 9-10; 2005, Aug, 9-10; 2005, Jul, 11-12; 2005, Jul, 11-12; 2005, July, 11-12; 2005, August, 7-8; 2005, August, 9-10

87280   respiratory syncytial virus 🅰 ▪
    0.00   0.00   Global Days XXX
    AMA: 2005, Aug, 9-10; 2005, Aug, 9-10; 2005, Jul, 11-12; 2005, Jul, 11-12; 2005, Aug, 7-8; 2005, Aug, 7-8; 2005, July, 11-12; 2005, August, 7-8; 2005, August, 9-10

87281   Pneumocystis carinii 🅰 ▪
    0.00   0.00   Global Days XXX
    AMA: 2005, Aug, 7-8; 2005, Aug, 7-8; 2005, Jul, 11-12; 2005, Jul, 11-12; 2005, Aug, 9-10; 2005, Aug, 9-10; 2005, July, 11-12; 2005, August, 7-8; 2005, August, 9-10

87283   Rubeola 🅰 ▪
    0.00   0.00   Global Days XXX
    AMA: 2005, Aug, 7-8; 2005, Aug, 7-8; 2005, Jul, 11-12; 2005, Jul, 11-12; 2005, Aug, 9-10; 2005, Aug, 9-10; 2005, July, 11-12; 2005, August, 9-10

87285   Treponema pallidum 🅰 ▪
    0.00   0.00   Global Days XXX
    AMA: 2005, Jul, 11-12; 2005, Jul, 11-12; 2005, Aug, 9-10; 2005, Aug, 9-10; 2005, Aug, 7-8; 2005, Aug, 7-8; 2005, July, 11-12; 2005, August, 7-8; 2005, August, 9-10

87290   Varicella zoster virus 🅰 ▪
    0.00   0.00   Global Days XXX
    AMA: 2005, Aug, 9-10; 2005, Aug, 9-10; 2005, Jul, 11-12; 2005, Jul, 11-12; 2005, Aug, 7-8; 2005, Aug, 7-8; 2005, July, 11-12; 2005, August, 7-8; 2005, August, 9-10

87299   not otherwise specified, each organism 🅰 ▪
    0.00   0.00   Global Days XXX
    AMA: 2005, Aug, 9-10; 2005, Aug, 9-10; 2005, Jul, 11-12; 2005, Jul, 11-12; 2005, Aug, 7-8; 2005, Aug, 7-8; 2005, July, 11-12; 2005, August, 7-8; 2005, August, 9-10

87300   Infectious agent antigen detection by immunofluorescent technique, polyvalent for multiple organisms, each polyvalent antiserum 🅰 ▪
    EXCLUDES   *physician evaluation of infectious disease agents by immunofluorescence (88346)*
    0.00   0.00   Global Days XXX
    AMA: 2005, Aug, 7-8; 2005, Aug, 7-8; 2005, Jul, 11-12; 2005, Jul, 11-12; 2005, Aug, 9-10; 2005, Aug, 9-10; 2005, July, 11-12; 2005, August, 7-8; 2005, August, 9-10

87301-87451 Enzyme Immunoassay Technique by Organism

   EXCLUDES   *nonspecific agent detection (87449-87450, 87797-87799, 87899)*

87301   Infectious agent antigen detection by enzyme immunoassay technique, qualitative or semiquantitative, multiple-step method; adenovirus enteric types 40/41 🅰
    0.00   0.00   Global Days XXX
    AMA: 2005, Aug, 7-8; 2005, Aug, 7-8; 2005, Aug, 9-10; 2005, Aug, 9-10; 2005, Jul, 11-12; 2005, Jul, 11-12; 2005, July, 11-12; 2005, August, 7-8; 2005, August, 9-10

87305   Aspergillus 🅰
    0.00   0.00   Global Days XXX

87320   Chlamydia trachomatis 🅰 ▪
    0.00   0.00   Global Days XXX
    AMA: 2005, Aug, 7-8; 2005, Aug, 7-8; 2005, Aug, 9-10; 2005, Aug, 9-10; 2005, Jul, 11-12; 2005, Jul, 11-12; 2005, July, 11-12; 2005, August, 7-8; 2005, August, 9-10

87324   Clostridium difficile toxin(s) 🅰 ▪
    0.00   0.00   Global Days XXX
    AMA: 2005, Aug, 9-10; 2005, Aug, 9-10; 2005, Jul, 11-12; 2005, Jul, 11-12; 2005, Aug, 7-8; 2005, Aug, 7-8; 2005, July, 11-12; 2005, August, 7-8; 2005, August, 9-10

87327   Cryptococcus neoformans 🅰
    EXCLUDES   *Cryptococcus latex agglutination (86403)*
    0.00   0.00   Global Days XXX
    AMA: 2005, Jul, 11-12; 2005, Jul, 11-12; 2005, Aug, 9-10; 2005, Aug, 9-10; 2005, Aug, 7-8; 2005, Aug, 7-8; 2005, July, 11-12; 2005, August, 9-10; 2005, August, 7-8

87328   cryptosporidium 🅰 ▪
    0.00   0.00   Global Days XXX
    AMA: 2005, Aug, 7-8; 2005, Aug, 7-8; 2005, Aug, 9-10; 2005, Aug, 9-10; 2005, Jul, 11-12; 2005, Jul, 11-12; 2005, July, 11-12; 2005, August, 7-8; 2005, August, 9-10

87329   giardia 🅰 ▪
    0.00   0.00   Global Days XXX
    AMA: 2005, Aug, 7-8; 2005, Aug, 7-8; 2005, Aug, 9-10; 2005, Aug, 9-10; 2005, Jul, 11-12; 2005, Jul, 11-12; 2005, July, 11-12; 2005, August, 7-8; 2005, August, 9-10

87332   cytomegalovirus 🅰 ▪
    0.00   0.00   Global Days XXX
    AMA: 2005, Aug, 7-8; 2005, Aug, 7-8; 2005, Jul, 11-12; 2005, Jul, 11-12; 2005, Aug, 9-10; 2005, Aug, 9-10; 2005, July, 11-12; 2005, August, 7-8; 2005, August, 9-10

26/TC Professional/Technical Component Only   80/80 Assist-at-Surgery Allowed/With Documentation   Unlisted   Not Covered   Radiology crosswalk

MED: Pub 100/NCD References   **AMA:** CPT Assistant References   A2-Z3 ASC Payment Indicator   ♂Male Only   ♀Female Only   Laboratory crosswalk

364   CPT only © 2008 American Medical Association. All Rights Reserved. (Black Ink)   Medicare (Red Ink)   © 2008 Ingenix (Blue Ink)

87335   **Escherichia coli 0157**   A
    EXCLUDES   *giardia antigen (87329)*
    0.00   0.00   **Global Days XXX**
    AMA: 2005, Aug, 9-10; 2005, Aug, 9-10; 2005, Aug, 7-8; 2005, Aug, 7-8; 2005, Jul, 11-12; 2005, Jul, 11-12; 2005, August, 7-8; 2005, August, 9-10; 2005, July, 11-12

87336   **Entamoeba histolytica dispar group**   A
    0.00   0.00   **Global Days XXX**
    AMA: 2005, Jul, 11-12; 2005, Jul, 11-12; 2005, Aug, 9-10; 2005, Aug, 9-10; 2005, Aug, 7-8; 2005, Aug, 7-8; 2005, August, 7-8; 2005, August, 9-10; 2005, July, 11-12

87337   **Entamoeba histolytica group**   A
    0.00   0.00   **Global Days XXX**
    AMA: 2005, Aug, 9-10; 2005, Aug, 9-10; 2005, Jul, 11-12; 2005, Jul, 11-12; 2005, Aug, 7-8; 2005, Aug, 7-8; 2005, August, 7-8; 2005, August, 9-10; 2005, July, 11-12

87338   **Helicobacter pylori, stool**   A
    0.00   0.00   **Global Days XXX**
    AMA: 2005, Aug, 7-8; 2005, Aug, 7-8; 2005, Aug, 9-10; 2005, Aug, 9-10; 2005, Jul, 11-12; 2005, Jul, 11-12; 2005, August, 7-8; 2005, August, 9-10; 2005, July, 11-12

87339   **Helicobacter pylori**   A
    EXCLUDES   *H. pylori:*
       breath and blood by mass spectrometry (83013-83014)
       liquid scintillation counter (78267-78268)
       stool (87338)
    0.00   0.00   **Global Days XXX**
    AMA: 2005, Aug, 9-10; 2005, Aug, 9-10; 2005, Aug, 7-8; 2005, Aug, 7-8; 2005, Jul, 11-12; 2005, Jul, 11-12; 2005, August, 7-8; 2005, August, 9-10; 2005, July, 11-12

87340   **hepatitis B surface antigen (HBsAg)**   A
    0.00   0.00   **Global Days XXX**
    AMA: 2005, Aug, 7-8; 2005, Aug, 7-8; 2005, Aug, 9-10; 2005, Aug, 9-10; 2005, Jul, 11-12; 2005, Jul, 11-12; 2005, August, 7-8; 2005, August, 9-10, 2005, July, 11-12

87341   **hepatitis B surface antigen (HBsAg) neutralization**   A
    0.00   0.00   **Global Days XXX**
    AMA: 2005, Aug, 7-8; 2005, Aug, 7-8; 2005, Jul, 11-12; 2005, Jul, 11-12; 2005, Aug, 9-10; 2005, Aug, 9-10; 2005, August, 7-8; 2005, August, 9-10; 2005, July, 11-12

87350   **hepatitis Be antigen (HBeAg)**   A
    0.00   0.00   **Global Days XXX**
    AMA: 2005, Jul, 11-12; 2005, Jul, 11-12; 2005, Aug, 7-8; 2005, Aug, 7-8; 2005, Aug, 9-10; 2005, Aug, 9-10; 2005, August, 7-8; 2005, August, 9-10; 2005, July, 11-12

87380   **hepatitis, delta agent**   A
    0.00   0.00   **Global Days XXX**
    AMA: 2005, Aug, 7-8; 2005, Aug, 7-8; 2005, Jul, 11-12; 2005, Jul, 11-12; 2005, Aug, 9-10; 2005, Aug, 9-10; 2005, August, 7-8; 2005, July, 11-12; 2005, August, 9-10

87385   **Histoplasma capsulatum**   A
    0.00   0.00   **Global Days XXX**
    AMA: 2005, Jul, 11-12; 2005, Jul, 11-12; 2005, Aug, 9-10; 2005, Aug, 9-10; 2005, Aug, 7-8; 2005, Aug, 7-8; 2005, August, 9-10; 2005, July, 11-12; 2005, August, 7-8

87390   **HIV-1**   A
    0.00   0.00   **Global Days XXX**
    AMA: 2005, Aug, 7-8; 2005, Aug, 7-8; 2005, Jul, 11-12; 2005, Jul, 11-12; 2005, Aug, 9-10; 2005, Aug, 9-10; 2005, August, 7-8; 2005, August, 9-10; 2005, July, 11-12

87391   **HIV-2**   A
    0.00   0.00   **Global Days XXX**
    AMA: 2005, Aug, 7-8; 2005, Aug, 7-8; 2005, Aug, 9-10; 2005, Aug, 9-10; 2005, Jul, 11-12; 2005, Jul, 11-12; 2005, August, 7-8; 2005, August, 9-10; 2005, July, 11-12

87400   **Influenza, A or B, each**   A
    0.00   0.00   **Global Days XXX**
    AMA: 2008, Jan, 10-25; 2007, Jan, 13-27; 2007, Jan, 13-27; 2007, January, 13-27; 2005, Aug, 9-10; 2005, Aug, 9-10; 2005, Jul, 11-12; 2005, August, 9-10; 2005, July, 11-12; 2005, August, 7-8; 2005, Jul, 11-12; 2005, Aug, 7-8; 2005, Aug, 7-8

87420   **respiratory syncytial virus**   A
    0.00   0.00   **Global Days XXX**
    AMA: 2005, Jul, 11-12; 2005, Jul, 11-12; 2005, Aug, 9-10; 2005, Aug, 9-10; 2005, Aug, 7-8; 2005, Aug, 7-8; 2005, July, 11-12; 2005, August, 7-8; 2005, August, 9-10

87425   **rotavirus**   A
    0.00   0.00   **Global Days XXX**
    AMA: 2005, Aug, 7-8; 2005, Aug, 7-8; 2005, Aug, 9-10; 2005, Aug, 9-10; 2005, Jul, 11-12; 2005, Jul, 11-12; 2005, July, 11-12; 2005, August, 7-8; 2005, August, 9-10

87427   **Shiga-like toxin**   A
    0.00   0.00   **Global Days XXX**
    AMA: 2005, Aug, 9-10; 2005, Aug, 9-10; 2005, Aug, 7-8; 2005, Aug, 7-8; 2005, Jul, 11-12; 2005, Jul, 11-12; 2005, July, 11-12; 2005, August, 7-8; 2005, August, 9-10

87430   **Streptococcus, group A**   A
    0.00   0.00   **Global Days XXX**
    AMA: 2008, Jan, 10-25; 2007, Jan, 13-27; 2007, Jan, 13-27; 2007, January, 13-27; 2005, Jul, 11-12; 2005, Jul, 11-12; 2005, Aug, 7-8; 2005, July, 11-12; 2005, August, 9-10; 2005, August, 7-8; 2005, Aug, 7-8; 2005, Aug, 9-10; 2005, Aug, 9-10

87449   **Infectious agent antigen detection by enzyme immunoassay technique qualitative or semiquantitative; multiple step method, not otherwise specified, each organism**   A
    0.00   0.00   **Global Days XXX**
    AMA: 2008, Jan, 10-25; 2007, Jan, 13-27; 2007, Jan, 13-27; 2007, January, 13-27; 2005, Aug, 9-10; 2005, Aug, 9-10; 2005, Jul, 11-12; 2005, August, 9-10; 2005, July, 11-12; 2005, August, 7-8; 2005, Jul, 11-12; 2005, Aug, 7-8; 2005, Aug, 7-8

87450   **single step method, not otherwise specified, each organism**   A
    0.00   0.00   **Global Days XXX**
    AMA: 2005, Jul, 11-12; 2005, Jul, 11-12; 2005, Aug, 9-10; 2005, Aug, 9-10; 2005, Aug, 7-8; 2005, Aug, 7-8; 2005, August, 9-10; 2005, July, 11-12; 2005, August, 7-8

87451   **multiple step method, polyvalent for multiple organisms, each polyvalent antiserum**   A
    0.00   0.00   **Global Days XXX**
    AMA: 2005, Jul, 11-12; 2005, Jul, 11-12; 2005, Aug, 9-10; 2005, Aug, 9-10; 2005, Aug, 7-8; 2005, Aug, 7-8; 2005, August, 7-8; 2005, August, 9-10; 2005, July, 11-12

87470-87801 Detection Infectious Agent by Probe Techniques

87470   **Infectious agent detection by nucleic acid (DNA or RNA); Bartonella henselae and Bartonella quintana, direct probe technique**   A
    0.00   0.00   **Global Days XXX**
    AMA: 2005, Aug, 7-8; 2005, Aug, 7-8; 2005, Jul, 11-12; 2005, Jul, 11-12; 2005, Aug, 9-10; 2005, Aug, 9-10; 2005, August, 7-8; 2005, August, 9-10; 2005, July, 11-12

87471   Bartonella henselae and Bartonella quintana, amplified probe technique   Ⓐ ▣
   🔖 0.00   ⚕ 0.00   **Global Days XXX**
   AMA: 2005, Jul, 11-12; 2005, Jul, 11-12; 2005, Aug, 9-10; 2005, Aug, 9-10; 2005, Aug, 7-8; 2005, Aug, 7-8; 2005, August, 7-8; 2005, July, 11-12; 2005, August, 9-10

87472   Bartonella henselae and Bartonella quintana, quantification   Ⓐ ▣
   🔖 0.00   ⚕ 0.00   **Global Days XXX**
   AMA: 2005, Aug, 9-10; 2005, Aug, 9-10; 2005, Aug, 7-8; 2005, Aug, 7-8; 2005, Jul, 11-12; 2005, Jul, 11-12; 2005, August, 7-8; 2005, August, 9-10; 2005, July, 11-12

87475   Borrelia burgdorferi, direct probe technique   Ⓐ ▣
   🔖 0.00   ⚕ 0.00   **Global Days XXX**
   AMA: 2005, Aug, 9-10; 2005, Aug, 9-10; 2005, Aug, 7-8; 2005, Aug, 7-8; 2005, Jul, 11-12; 2005, Jul, 11-12; 2005, August, 7-8; 2005, August, 9-10; 2005, July, 11-12

87476   Borrelia burgdorferi, amplified probe technique   Ⓐ ▣
   🔖 0.00   ⚕ 0.00   **Global Days XXX**
   AMA: 2005, Jul, 11-12; 2005, Jul, 11-12; 2005, Aug, 9-10; 2005, Aug, 9-10; 2005, Aug, 7-8; 2005, Aug, 7-8; 2005, August, 7-8; 2005, August, 9-10; 2005, July, 11-12

87477   Borrelia burgdorferi, quantification   Ⓐ ▣
   🔖 0.00   ⚕ 0.00   **Global Days XXX**
   AMA: 2005, Aug, 7-8; 2005, Aug, 7-8; 2005, Jul, 11-12; 2005, Jul, 11-12; 2005, Aug, 9-10; 2005, Aug, 9-10; 2005, August, 7-8; 2005, August, 9-10; 2005, July, 11-12

87480   Candida species, direct probe technique   Ⓐ ▣
   🔖 0.00   ⚕ 0.00   **Global Days XXX**
   AMA: 2005, Aug, 9-10; 2005, Aug, 9-10; 2005, Jul, 11-12; 2005, Jul, 11-12; 2005, Aug, 7-8; 2005, Aug, 7-8; 2005, August, 7-8; 2005, August, 9-10; 2005, July, 11-12

87481   Candida species, amplified probe technique   Ⓐ ▣
   🔖 0.00   ⚕ 0.00   **Global Days XXX**
   AMA: 2005, Jul, 11-12; 2005, Jul, 11-12; 2005, Aug, 7-8; 2005, Aug, 7-8; 2005, Aug, 9-10; 2005, Aug, 9-10; 2005, August, 7-8; 2005, August, 9-10; 2005, July, 11-12

87482   Candida species, quantification   Ⓐ ▣
   🔖 0.00   ⚕ 0.00   **Global Days XXX**
   AMA: 2005, Jul, 11-12; 2005, Jul, 11-12; 2005, Aug, 7-8; 2005, Aug, 7-8; 2005, Aug, 9-10; 2005, Aug, 9-10; 2005, August, 7-8; 2005, August, 9-10; 2005, July, 11-12

87485   Chlamydia pneumoniae, direct probe technique   Ⓐ ▣
   🔖 0.00   ⚕ 0.00   **Global Days XXX**
   AMA: 2005, Jul, 11-12; 2005, Jul, 11-12; 2005, Aug, 9-10; 2005, Aug, 9-10; 2005, Aug, 7-8; 2005, Aug, 7-8; 2005, August, 7-8; 2005, August, 9-10; 2005, July, 11-12

87486   Chlamydia pneumoniae, amplified probe technique   Ⓐ ▣
   🔖 0.00   ⚕ 0.00   **Global Days XXX**
   AMA: 2005, Aug, 9-10; 2005, Aug, 9-10; 2005, Aug, 7-8; 2005, Aug, 7-8; 2005, Jul, 11-12; 2005, Jul, 11-12; 2005, August, 7-8; 2005, August, 9-10; 2005, July, 11-12

87487   Chlamydia pneumoniae, quantification   Ⓐ ▣
   🔖 0.00   ⚕ 0.00   **Global Days XXX**
   AMA: 2005, Jul, 11-12; 2005, Jul, 11-12; 2005, Aug, 9-10; 2005, Aug, 9-10; 2005, Aug, 7-8; 2005, Aug, 7-8; 2005, August, 9-10; 2005, July, 11-12; 2005, August, 7-8

87490   Chlamydia trachomatis, direct probe technique   Ⓐ ▣
   🔖 0.00   ⚕ 0.00   **Global Days XXX**
   AMA: 2005, Aug, 7-8; 2005, Aug, 7-8; 2005, Jul, 11-12; 2005, Jul, 11-12; 2005, Aug, 9-10; 2005, Aug, 9-10; 2005, August, 7-8; 2005, August, 9-10; 2005, July, 11-12

87491   Chlamydia trachomatis, amplified probe technique   Ⓐ ▣
   🔖 0.00   ⚕ 0.00   **Global Days XXX**
   AMA: 2005, Aug, 7-8; 2005, Aug, 7-8; 2005, Aug, 9-10; 2005, Aug, 9-10; 2005, Jul, 11-12; 2005, Jul, 11-12; 2005, August, 7-8; 2005, July, 11-12; 2005, August, 9-10

87492   Chlamydia trachomatis, quantification   Ⓐ ▣
   🔖 0.00   ⚕ 0.00   **Global Days XXX**
   AMA: 2005, Aug, 7-8; 2005, Aug, 7-8; 2005, Aug, 9-10; 2005, Aug, 9-10; 2005, Jul, 11-12; 2005, Jul, 11-12; 2005, August, 7-8; 2005, July, 11-12; 2005, August, 9-10

87495   cytomegalovirus, direct probe technique   Ⓐ ▣
   🔖 0.00   ⚕ 0.00   **Global Days XXX**
   AMA: 2005, Jul, 11-12; 2005, Jul, 11-12; 2005, Aug, 9-10; 2005, Aug, 9-10; 2005, Aug, 7-8; 2005, Aug, 7-8; 2005, August, 7-8; 2005, July, 11-12; 2005, August, 9-10

87496   cytomegalovirus, amplified probe technique   Ⓐ ▣
   🔖 0.00   ⚕ 0.00   **Global Days XXX**
   AMA: 2005, Jul, 11-12; 2005, Jul, 11-12; 2005, Aug, 9-10; 2005, Aug, 9-10; 2005, Aug, 7-8; 2005, Aug, 7-8; 2005, August, 7-8; 2005, July, 11-12; 2005, August, 9-10

87497   cytomegalovirus, quantification   Ⓐ ▣
   🔖 0.00   ⚕ 0.00   **Global Days XXX**
   AMA: 2005, Jul, 11-12; 2005, Jul, 11-12; 2005, Aug, 9-10; 2005, Aug, 9-10; 2005, Aug, 7-8; 2005, Aug, 7-8; 2005, August, 7-8; 2005, July, 11-12; 2005, August, 9-10

87498   enterovirus, amplified probe technique   Ⓐ
   🔖 0.00   ⚕ 0.00   **Global Days XXX**

87500   vancomycin resistance (eg, enterococcus species van A, van B), amplified probe technique   Ⓐ
   🔖 0.00   ⚕ 0.00   **Global Days XXX**
   AMA: 2008, Apr, 5-7; 2008, Apr, 5-7; 2008, Apr, 5-7

87510   Gardnerella vaginalis, direct probe technique   Ⓐ ▣
   🔖 0.00   ⚕ 0.00   **Global Days XXX**
   AMA: 2005, Aug, 7-8; 2005, Aug, 7-8; 2005, Jul, 11-12; 2005, Jul, 11-12; 2005, Aug, 9-10; 2005, Aug, 9-10; 2005, August, 7-8; 2005, July, 11-12; 2005, August, 9-10

87511   Gardnerella vaginalis, amplified probe technique   Ⓐ ▣
   🔖 0.00   ⚕ 0.00   **Global Days XXX**
   AMA: 2005, Aug, 7-8; 2005, Aug, 7-8; 2005, Jul, 11-12; 2005, Jul, 11-12; 2005, Aug, 9-10; 2005, Aug, 9-10; 2005, August, 7-8; 2005, July, 11-12; 2005, August, 9-10

87512   Gardnerella vaginalis, quantification   Ⓐ ▣
   🔖 0.00   ⚕ 0.00   **Global Days XXX**
   AMA: 2005, Jul, 11-12; 2005, Jul, 11-12; 2005, Aug, 9-10; 2005, Aug, 9-10; 2005, Aug, 7-8; 2005, Aug, 7-8; 2005, July, 11-12; 2005, August, 9-10

87515   hepatitis B virus, direct probe technique   Ⓐ ▣
   🔖 0.00   ⚕ 0.00   **Global Days XXX**
   AMA: 2005, Aug, 7-8; 2005, Aug, 7-8; 2005, Jul, 11-12; 2005, Jul, 11-12; 2005, Aug, 9-10; 2005, Aug, 9-10; 2005, July, 11-12; 2005, August, 9-10; 2005, August, 7-8

87516   hepatitis B virus, amplified probe technique   Ⓐ ▣
   🔖 0.00   ⚕ 0.00   **Global Days XXX**
   AMA: 2005, Aug, 9-10; 2005, Aug, 9-10; 2005, Jul, 11-12; 2005, Jul, 11-12; 2005, Aug, 7-8; 2005, Aug, 7-8; 2005, August, 9-10; 2005, July, 11-12

87517   hepatitis B virus, quantification   Ⓐ ▣
   🔖 0.00   ⚕ 0.00   **Global Days XXX**
   AMA: 2005, Aug, 7-8; 2005, Aug, 7-8; 2005, Aug, 9-10; 2005, Aug, 9-10; 2005, Jul, 11-12; 2005, Jul, 11-12; 2005, July, 11-12; 2005, August, 7-8; 2005, August, 9-10

㉖/ⓉⒸ Professional/Technical Component Only   ⑧⓪/⑧⓪ Assist-at-Surgery Allowed/With Documentation   Unlisted   Not Covered   ☒ Radiology crosswalk

MED: Pub 100/NCD References   **AMA:** CPT Assistant References   N2-Z3 ASC Payment Indicator   ♂ Male Only   ♀ Female Only   ◣ Laboratory crosswalk

366   CPT only © 2008 American Medical Association. All Rights Reserved. (Black Ink)   Medicare (Red Ink)   © 2008 Ingenix (Blue Ink)

87520   hepatitis C, direct probe technique   Ⓐ ▣
    📖 0.00   ✂ 0.00   Global Days XXX
    AMA: 2005, Jul, 11-12; 2005, Jul, 11-12; 2005, Aug, 7-8; 2005,
    Aug, 7-8; 2005, Aug, 9-10; 2005, Aug, 9-10; 2005, July, 11-12;
    2005, August, 7-8; 2005, August, 9-10

87521   hepatitis C, amplified probe technique   Ⓐ ▣
    📖 0.00   ✂ 0.00   Global Days XXX
    AMA: 2005, Aug, 7-8; 2005, Aug, 7-8; 2005, Aug, 9-10; 2005, Aug,
    9-10; 2005, Jul, 11-12; 2005, Jul, 11-12; 2005, July, 11-12; 2005,
    August, 7-8; 2005, August, 9-10

87522   hepatitis C, quantification   Ⓐ ▣
    📖 0.00   ✂ 0.00   Global Days XXX
    AMA: 2005, Aug, 7-8; 2005, Aug, 7-8; 2005, Jul, 11-12; 2005, Jul,
    11-12; 2005, Aug, 9-10; 2005, Aug, 9-10; 2005, July, 11-12; 2005,
    August, 7-8; 2005, August, 9-10

87525   hepatitis G, direct probe technique   Ⓐ ▣
    📖 0.00   ✂ 0.00   Global Days XXX
    AMA: 2005, Jul, 11-12; 2005, Jul, 11-12; 2005, Aug, 7-8; 2005,
    Aug, 7-8; 2005, Aug, 9-10; 2005, Aug, 9-10; 2005, July, 11-12;
    2005, August, 7-8; 2005, August, 9-10

87526   hepatitis G, amplified probe technique   Ⓐ ▣
    📖 0.00   ✂ 0.00   Global Days XXX
    AMA: 2005, Aug, 7-8; 2005, Aug, 7-8; 2005, Aug, 9-10; 2005, Aug,
    9-10; 2005, Jul, 11-12; 2005, Jul, 11-12; 2005, July, 11-12; 2005,
    August, 7-8; 2005, August, 9-10

87527   hepatitis G, quantification   Ⓐ ▣
    📖 0.00   ✂ 0.00   Global Days XXX
    AMA: 2005, Jul, 11-12; 2005, Jul, 11-12; 2005, Aug, 9-10; 2005,
    Aug, 9-10; 2005, Aug, 7-8; 2005, Aug, 7-8; 2005, July, 11-12; 2005,
    August, 7-8; 2005, August, 9-10

87528   Herpes simplex virus, direct probe technique   Ⓐ ▣
    📖 0.00   ✂ 0.00   Global Days XXX
    AMA: 2005, Aug, 7-8; 2005, Aug, 7-8; 2005, Aug, 9-10; 2005, Aug,
    9-10; 2005, Jul, 11-12; 2005, Jul, 11-12; 2005, July, 11-12; 2005,
    August, 7-8; 2005, August, 9-10

87529   Herpes simplex virus, amplified probe technique   Ⓐ ▣
    📖 0.00   ✂ 0.00   Global Days XXX
    AMA: 2005, Aug, 7-8; 2005, Aug, 7-8; 2005, Jul, 11-12; 2005, Jul,
    11-12, 2005, Aug, 8-10; 2005, Aug, 9-10; 2005, July, 11-12; 2005,
    August, 7-8; 2005, August, 9-10

87530   Herpes simplex virus, quantification   Ⓐ ▣
    📖 0.00   ✂ 0.00   Global Days XXX
    AMA: 2005, Aug, 7-8; 2005, Aug, 7-8; 2005, Jul, 11-12; 2005, Jul,
    11-12; 2005, Aug, 9-10; 2005, Aug, 9-10; 2005, July, 11-12; 2005,
    August, 7-8; 2005, August, 9-10

87531   Herpes virus-6, direct probe technique   Ⓐ ▣
    📖 0.00   ✂ 0.00   Global Days XXX
    AMA: 2005, Aug, 9-10; 2005, Aug, 9-10; 2005, Jul, 11-12; 2005,
    Jul, 11-12; 2005, Aug, 7-8; 2005, Aug, 7-8; 2005, July, 11-12; 2005,
    August, 7-8; 2005, August, 9-10

87532   Herpes virus-6, amplified probe technique   Ⓐ ▣
    📖 0.00   ✂ 0.00   Global Days XXX
    AMA: 2005, Jul, 11-12; 2005, Jul, 11-12; 2005, Aug, 7-8; 2005,
    Aug, 7-8; 2005, Aug, 9-10; 2005, Aug, 9-10; 2005, July, 11-12;
    2005, August, 9-10; 2005, August, 7-8

87533   Herpes virus-6, quantification   Ⓐ ▣
    📖 0.00   ✂ 0.00   Global Days XXX
    AMA: 2005, Aug, 7-8; 2005, Aug, 7-8; 2005, Jul, 11-12; 2005, Jul,
    11-12; 2005, Aug, 9-10; 2005, Aug, 9-10; 2005, July, 11-12; 2005,
    August, 7-8; 2005, August, 9-10

87534   HIV-1, direct probe technique   Ⓐ ▣
    📖 0.00   ✂ 0.00   Global Days XXX
    AMA: 2005, Aug, 7-8; 2005, Aug, 7-8; 2005, Aug, 9-10; 2005, Aug,
    9-10; 2005, Jul, 11-12; 2005, Jul, 11-12; 2005, July, 11-12; 2005,
    August, 7-8; 2005, August, 9-10

87535   HIV-1, amplified probe technique   Ⓐ ▣
    📖 0.00   ✂ 0.00   Global Days XXX
    AMA: 2008, Mar, 3&7; 2005, Aug, 7-8; 2005, Aug, 7-8; 2005, Jul,
    11-12; 2005, Jul, 11-12; 2005, Aug, 9-10; 2005, Aug, 9-10; 2005,
    August, 7-8; 2005, July, 11-12; 2005, August, 9-10

87536   HIV-1, quantification   Ⓐ ▣
    📖 0.00   ✂ 0.00   Global Days XXX
    AMA: 2005, Aug, 7-8; 2005, Aug, 7-8; 2005, Jul, 11-12; 2005, Jul,
    11-12; 2005, Aug, 9-10; 2005, Aug, 9-10; 2005, August, 7-8; 2005,
    July, 11-12; 2005, August, 9-10

87537   HIV-2, direct probe technique   Ⓐ ▣
    📖 0.00   ✂ 0.00   Global Days XXX
    AMA: 2005, Jul, 11-12; 2005, Jul, 11-12; 2005, Aug, 7-8; 2005,
    Aug, 7-8; 2005, Aug, 9-10; 2005, Aug, 9-10; 2005, August, 7-8;
    2005, July, 11-12; 2005, August, 9-10

87538   HIV-2, amplified probe technique   Ⓐ ▣
    📖 0.00   ✂ 0.00   Global Days XXX
    AMA: 2005, Aug, 7-8; 2005, Aug, 7-8; 2005, Aug, 9-10; 2005, Aug,
    9-10; 2005, Jul, 11-12; 2005, Jul, 11-12; 2005, August, 7-8; 2005,
    July, 11-12; 2005, August, 9-10

87539   HIV-2, quantification   Ⓐ ▣
    📖 0.00   ✂ 0.00   Global Days XXX
    AMA: 2005, Jul, 11-12; 2005, Jul, 11-12; 2005, Aug, 9-10; 2005,
    Aug, 9-10; 2005, Aug, 7-8; 2005, Aug, 7-8; 2005, August, 7-8;
    2005, July, 11-12; 2005, August, 9-10

87540   Legionella pneumophila, direct probe
    technique   Ⓐ ▣
    📖 0.00   ✂ 0.00   Global Days XXX
    AMA: 2005, Aug, 7-8; 2005, Aug, 7-8; 2005, Aug, 9-10; 2005, Aug,
    9-10; 2005, Jul, 11-12; 2005, Jul, 11-12; 2005, August, 7-8; 2005,
    July, 11-12; 2005, August, 9-10

87541   Legionella pneumophila, amplified probe
    technique   Ⓐ ▣
    📖 0.00   ✂ 0.00   Global Days XXX
    AMA: 2005, Aug, 7-8; 2005, Aug, 7-8; 2005, Jul, 11-12; 2005, Jul,
    11-12; 2005, Aug, 9-10; 2005, Aug, 9-10; 2005, August, 7-8; 2005,
    July, 11-12; 2005, August, 9-10

87542   Legionella pneumophila, quantification   Ⓐ ▣
    📖 0.00   ✂ 0.00   Global Days XXX
    AMA: 2005, Aug, 7-8; 2005, Aug, 7-8; 2005, Jul, 11-12; 2005, Jul,
    11-12; 2005, Aug, 9-10; 2005, Aug, 9-10; 2005, August, 7-8; 2005,
    July, 11-12; 2005, August, 9-10

87550   Mycobacteria species, direct probe technique   Ⓐ ▣
    📖 0.00   ✂ 0.00   Global Days XXX
    AMA: 2005, Aug, 7-8; 2005, Aug, 7-8; 2005, Aug, 9-10; 2005, Aug,
    9-10; 2005, Jul, 11-12; 2005, Jul, 11-12; 2005, Aug, 7-8; 2005,
    July, 11-12; 2005, August, 9-10

87551   Mycobacteria species, amplified probe
    technique   Ⓐ ▣
    📖 0.00   ✂ 0.00   Global Days XXX
    AMA: 2005, Aug, 7-8; 2005, Aug, 7-8; 2005, Aug, 9-10; 2005, Aug,
    9-10; 2005, Jul, 11-12; 2005, Jul, 11-12; 2005, August, 7-8; 2005,
    July, 11-12; 2005, August, 9-10

87552   Mycobacteria species, quantification   Ⓐ ▣
    📖 0.00   ✂ 0.00   Global Days XXX
    AMA: 2005, Aug, 7-8; 2005, Aug, 7-8; 2005, Jul, 11-12; 2005, Jul,
    11-12; 2005, Aug, 9-10; 2005, Aug, 9-10; 2005, July, 11-12; 2005,
    August, 9-10; 2005, August, 7-8

87555   Mycobacteria tuberculosis, direct probe
    technique   Ⓐ ▣
    📖 0.00   ✂ 0.00   Global Days XXX
    AMA: 2005, Jul, 11-12; 2005, Jul, 11-12; 2005, Aug, 9-10; 2005,
    Aug, 9-10; 2005, Aug, 7-8; 2005, Aug, 7-8; 2005, August, 7-8;
    2005, July, 11-12; 2005, August, 9-10

ⒻⒻ Modifier 63 Exempt Code   ⊙ Moderate Sedation   ＋ CPT Add-on Code   ⊘ Modifier 51 Exempt Code   ● New Code   ▲ Revised Code

Ⓜ Maternity Edit   Ⓐ Age Edit   ☒ CLIA Waived Test   Ⓐ-Ⓨ APC Status Indicators   ▣ CCI Comprehensive Code   🔟 Bilateral Procedure

87556 Mycobacteria tuberculosis, amplified probe technique 〔A〕〔▣〕
   📠 0.00   🔬 0.00   **Global Days XXX**
   AMA: 2005, Aug, 7-8; 2005, Aug, 7-8; 2005, Aug, 9-10; 2005, Aug, 9-10; 2005, Jul, 11-12; 2005, Jul, 11-12; 2005, August, 7-8; 2005, August, 9-10; 2005, July, 11-12

87557 Mycobacteria tuberculosis, quantification 〔A〕〔▣〕
   📠 0.00   🔬 0.00   **Global Days XXX**
   AMA: 2005, Aug, 7-8; 2005, Aug, 7-8; 2005, Aug, 9-10; 2005, Aug, 9-10; 2005, Jul, 11-12; 2005, Jul, 11-12; 2005, August, 7-8; 2005, July, 11-12; 2005, August, 9-10

87560 Mycobacteria avium-intracellulare, direct probe technique 〔A〕〔▣〕
   📠 0.00   🔬 0.00   **Global Days XXX**
   AMA: 2005, Aug, 7-8; 2005, Aug, 7-8; 2005, Jul, 11-12; 2005, Jul, 11-12; 2005, Aug, 9-10; 2005, Aug, 9-10; 2005, August, 7-8; 2005, July, 11-12; 2005, August, 9-10

87561 Mycobacteria avium-intracellulare, amplified probe technique 〔A〕〔▣〕
   📠 0.00   🔬 0.00   **Global Days XXX**
   AMA: 2005, Aug, 9-10; 2005, Aug, 9-10; 2005, Aug, 7-8; 2005, Aug, 7-8; 2005, Jul, 11-12; 2005, Jul, 11-12; 2005, August, 7-8; 2005, July, 11-12; 2005, August, 9-10

87562 Mycobacteria avium-intracellulare, quantification 〔A〕〔▣〕
   📠 0.00   🔬 0.00   **Global Days XXX**
   AMA: 2005, Jul, 11-12; 2005, Jul, 11-12; 2005, Aug, 9-10; 2005, Aug, 9-10; 2005, Aug, 7-8; 2005, Aug, 7-8; 2005, August, 7-8; 2005, July, 11-12; 2005, August, 9-10

87580 Mycoplasma pneumoniae, direct probe technique 〔A〕〔▣〕
   📠 0.00   🔬 0.00   **Global Days XXX**
   AMA: 2005, Aug, 7-8; 2005, Aug, 7-8; 2005, Jul, 11-12; 2005, Jul, 11-12; 2005, Aug, 9-10; 2005, Aug, 9-10; 2005, August, 7-8; 2005, July, 11-12; 2005, August, 9-10

87581 Mycoplasma pneumoniae, amplified probe technique 〔A〕〔▣〕
   📠 0.00   🔬 0.00   **Global Days XXX**
   AMA: 2005, Aug, 9-10; 2005, Aug, 9-10; 2005, Jul, 11-12; 2005, Jul, 11-12; 2005, Aug, 7-8; 2005, Aug, 7-8; 2005, August, 7-8; 2005, August, 9-10; 2005, July, 11-12

87582 Mycoplasma pneumoniae, quantification 〔A〕〔▣〕
   📠 0.00   🔬 0.00   **Global Days XXX**
   AMA: 2005, Aug, 7-8; 2005, Aug, 7-8; 2005, Jul, 11-12; 2005, Jul, 11-12; 2005, Aug, 9-10; 2005, Aug, 9-10; 2005, July, 11-12; 2005, August, 7-8; 2005, August, 9-10

87590 Neisseria gonorrhoeae, direct probe technique 〔A〕〔▣〕
   📠 0.00   🔬 0.00   **Global Days XXX**
   AMA: 2005, Aug, 9-10; 2005, Aug, 9-10; 2005, Aug, 7-8; 2005, Aug, 7-8; 2005, Jul, 11-12; 2005, Jul, 11-12; 2005, July, 11-12; 2005, August, 7-8; 2005, August, 9-10

87591 Neisseria gonorrhoeae, amplified probe technique 〔A〕〔▣〕
   📠 0.00   🔬 0.00   **Global Days XXX**
   AMA: 2005, Aug, 7-8; 2005, Aug, 7-8; 2005, Aug, 9-10; 2005, Aug, 9-10; 2005, Jul, 11-12; 2005, Jul, 11-12; 2005, July, 11-12; 2005, August, 7-8; 2005, August, 9-10

87592 Neisseria gonorrhoeae, quantification 〔A〕〔▣〕
   📠 0.00   🔬 0.00   **Global Days XXX**
   AMA: 2005, Jul, 11-12; 2005, Jul, 11-12; 2005, Aug, 7-8; 2005, Aug, 7-8; 2005, Aug, 9-10; 2005, Aug, 9-10; 2005, August, 7-8; 2005, August, 9-10; 2005, July, 11-12

87620 papillomavirus, human, direct probe technique 〔A〕〔▣〕
   📠 0.00   🔬 0.00   **Global Days XXX**
   AMA: 2008, Jan, 10-25; 2007, Jan, 13-27; 2007, Jan, 13-27; 2007, January, 13-27; 2005, Jul, 11-12; 2005, Jul, 11-12; 2005, Aug, 9-10; 2005, August, 7-8; 2005, August, 9-10; 2005, July, 11-12; 2005, Aug, 9-10; 2005, Aug, 7-8; 2005, Aug, 7-8

87621 papillomavirus, human, amplified probe technique 〔A〕〔▣〕
   📠 0.00   🔬 0.00   **Global Days XXX**
   AMA: 2005, Aug, 7-8; 2005, Aug, 7-8; 2005, Aug, 9-10; 2005, Aug, 9-10; 2005, Jul, 11-12; 2005, Jul, 11-12; 2005, July, 11-12; 2005, August, 9-10; 2005, August, 7-8

87622 papillomavirus, human, quantification 〔A〕〔▣〕
   📠 0.00   🔬 0.00   **Global Days XXX**
   AMA: 2005, Jul, 11-12; 2005, Jul, 11-12; 2005, Aug, 9-10; 2005, Aug, 9-10; 2005, Aug, 7-8; 2005, Aug, 7-8; 2005, August, 7-8; 2005, July, 11-12; 2005, August, 9-10

87640 Staphylococcus aureus, amplified probe technique 〔A〕
   📠 0.00   🔬 0.00   **Global Days XXX**
   AMA: 2007, Aug, 7-8

87641 Staphylococcus aureus, methicillin resistant, amplified probe technique 〔A〕
   EXCLUDES   *assays that detect methicillin resistance and identify Staphylococcus aureus using a single nucleic acid sequence (87641)*
   📠 0.00   🔬 0.00   **Global Days XXX**
   AMA: 2007, Aug, 7-8

87650 Streptococcus, group A, direct probe technique 〔A〕〔▣〕
   📠 0.00   🔬 0.00   **Global Days XXX**
   AMA: 2005, Jul, 11-12; 2005, Jul, 11-12; 2005, Aug, 9-10; 2005, Aug, 9-10; 2005, Aug, 7-8; 2005, Aug, 7-8; 2005, August, 7-8; 2005, July, 11-12; 2005, August, 9-10

87651 Streptococcus, group A, amplified probe technique 〔A〕〔▣〕
   📠 0.00   🔬 0.00   **Global Days XXX**
   AMA: 2007, Aug, 7-8; 2005, Aug, 7-8; 2005, Aug, 7-8; 2005, Jul, 11-12; 2005, Jul, 11-12; 2005, Aug, 9-10; 2005, Aug, 9-10; 2005, August, 7-8; 2005, August, 9-10; 2005, July, 11-12

87652 Streptococcus, group A, quantification 〔A〕〔▣〕
   📠 0.00   🔬 0.00   **Global Days XXX**
   AMA: 2005, Aug, 7-8; 2005, Aug, 7-8; 2005, Jul, 11-12; 2005, Jul, 11-12; 2005, Aug, 9-10; 2005, Aug, 9-10; 2005, July, 11-12; 2005, August, 7-8; 2005, August, 9-10

87653 Streptococcus, group B, amplified probe technique 〔A〕
   📠 0.00   🔬 0.00   **Global Days XXX**
   AMA: 2007, Aug, 7-8

87660 Trichomonas vaginalis, direct probe technique 〔A〕〔▣〕
   📠 0.00   🔬 0.00   **Global Days XXX**
   AMA: 2005, Aug, 7-8; 2005, Aug, 7-8; 2005, Jul, 11-12; 2005, Jul, 11-12; 2005, Aug, 9-10; 2005, Aug, 9-10; 2005, July, 11-12; 2005, August, 7-8; 2005, August, 9-10

87797 Infectious agent detection by nucleic acid (DNA or RNA), not otherwise specified; direct probe technique, each organism 〔A〕〔▣〕
   📠 0.00   🔬 0.00   **Global Days XXX**
   AMA: 2005, Aug, 9-10; 2005, Aug, 9-10; 2005, Jul, 11-12; 2005, Jul, 11-12; 2005, Aug, 7-8; 2005, Aug, 7-8; 2005, July, 11-12; 2005, August, 7-8; 2005, August, 9-10

87798 amplified probe technique, each organism 〔A〕〔▣〕
   📠 0.00   🔬 0.00   **Global Days XXX**
   AMA: 2007, Aug, 7-8; 2005, Aug, 9-10; 2005, Aug, 9-10; 2005, Aug, 7-8; 2005, Aug, 7-8; 2005, Jul, 11-12; 2005, Jul, 11-12; 2005, July, 11-12; 2005, August, 7-8; 2005, August, 9-10

㉖/⑩ Professional/Technical Component Only   ⑧⓪/⑧⓪ Assist-at-Surgery Allowed/With Documentation   Unlisted   Not Covered   ⊠ Radiology crosswalk

MED: Pub 100/NCD References   **AMA:** CPT Assistant References   🅰-🆉 ASC Payment Indicator   ♂Male Only   ♀Female Only   ⊠ Laboratory crosswalk

368   CPT only © 2008 American Medical Association. All Rights Reserved. (Black Ink)   Medicare (Red Ink)   © 2008 Ingenix *(Blue Ink)*

87799   quantification, each organism [A][□]
0.00   0.00 Global Days XXX
AMA: 2005, Aug, 9-10; 2005, Aug, 9-10; 2005, Aug, 7-8; 2005, Aug, 7-8; 2005, Jul, 11-12; 2005, Jul, 11-12; 2005, July, 11-12; 2005, August, 7-8; 2005, August, 9-10

87800   Infectious agent detection by nucleic acid (DNA or RNA), multiple organisms; direct probe(s) technique [A][□]
0.00   0.00 Global Days XXX
AMA: 2005, Aug, 7-8; 2005, Aug, 7-8; 2005, Aug, 9-10; 2005, Aug, 9-10; 2005, Jul, 11-12; 2005, Jul, 11-12; 2005, July, 11-12; 2005, August, 7-8; 2005, August, 9-10

87801   amplified probe(s) technique [A][□]
EXCLUDES detection of specific infectious agents not otherwise specified (87797-87799) each specific organism nucleic acid detection from a primary source (87470-87660)
0.00   0.00 Global Days XXX
AMA: 2005, Aug, 7-8; 2005, Aug, 7-8; 2005, Jul, 11-12; 2005, Jul, 11-12; 2005, Aug, 9-10; 2005, Aug, 9-10; 2005, July, 11-12; 2005, August, 7-8; 2005, August, 9-10

87802-87899 Detection Infectious Agent by Immunoassay with Direct Optical Observation

87802   Infectious agent antigen detection by immunoassay with direct optical observation; Streptococcus, group B [A][□]
0.00   0.00 Global Days XXX
AMA: 2005, Aug, 7-8; 2005, Aug, 7-8; 2005, Jul, 11-12; 2005, Jul, 11-12; 2005, Aug, 9-10; 2005, Aug, 9-10; 2005, July, 11-12; 2005, August, 7-8; 2005, August, 9-10

87803   Clostridium difficile toxin A [A][□]
0.00   0.00 Global Days XXX
AMA: 2005, Aug, 9-10; 2005, Aug, 9-10; 2005, Jul, 11-12; 2006, Jul, 11-12; 2005, Aug, 7-8; 2005, Aug, 7-8; 2005, July, 11-12; 2005, August, 7-8; 2005, August, 9-10

87804   Influenza [A][□][X]
0.00   0.00 Global Days XXX
AMA: 2007, Dec, 10-179; 2005, Aug, 9-10; 2005, Aug, 9-10; 2005, Aug, 7-8; 2005, Aug, 7-8; 2005, Jul, 11-12; 2005, Jul, 11-12; 2005, July, 11-12; 2005, August, 9-10; 2005, August, 7-8

87807   respiratory syncytial virus [A][□][X]
0.00   0.00 Global Days XXX
AMA: 2005, Aug, 7-8; 2005, Aug, 7-8; 2005, Aug, 9-10; 2005, Aug, 9-10; 2005, Jul, 11-12; 2005, Jul, 11-12; 2005, July, 11-12; 2005, August, 7-8; 2005, August, 9-10

87808   Trichomonas vaginalis [A][X]
0.00   0.00 Global Days XXX

87809   adenovirus [A]
0.00   0.00 Global Days XXX
AMA: 2008, Apr, 5-7; 2008, Apr, 5-7; 2008, Apr, 5-7

▲ 87810   Chlamydia trachomatis [A][□]
0.00   0.00 Global Days XXX
AMA: 2005, Aug, 7-8; 2005, Aug, 7-8; 2005, Aug, 9-10; 2005, Aug, 9-10; 2005, Jul, 11-12; 2005, Jul, 11-12; 2005, July, 11-12; 2005, August, 7-8; 2005, August, 9-10

▲ 87850   Neisseria gonorrhoeae [A][□]
0.00   0.00 Global Days XXX
AMA: 2005, Jul, 11-12; 2005, Jul, 11-12; 2005, Aug, 7-8; 2005, Aug, 7-8; 2005, Aug, 9-10; 2005, Aug, 9-10; 2005, July, 11-12; 2005, August, 7-8; 2005, August, 9-10

▲ 87880   Streptococcus, group A [A][□][X]
0.00   0.00 Global Days XXX
AMA: 2008, Jan, 10-25; 2007, Jan, 13-27; 2007, Jan, 13-27; 2007, January, 13-27; 2005, Aug, 7-8; 2005, Aug, 7-8; 2005, Aug, 9-10; 2005, August, 7-8; 2005, August, 9-10; 2005, July, 11-12; Aug, 9-10; 2005, Jul, 11-12; 2005, Jul, 11-12

▲ 87899   not otherwise specified [A][□][X]
0.00   0.00 Global Days XXX
AMA: 2008, Jan, 10-25; 2007, Jan, 13-27; 2007, Jan, 13-27; 2007, January, 13-27; 2005, Jul, 11-12; 2005, Jul, 11-12; 2005, Aug, 7-8; 2005, August, 7-8; 2005, August, 9-10; 2005, July, 11-12; 2005, Aug, 7-8; 2005, Aug, 9-10; 2005, Aug, 9-10

87900-87999 Drug Sensitivity Genotype/Phenotype

87900   Infectious agent drug susceptibility phenotype prediction using regularly updated genotypic bioinformatics [A]
0.00   0.00 Global Days XXX
AMA: 2006, Mar, 6-9; 2006, Mar, 6-9; 2006, March, 6-9; 2005, Aug, 9-10; 2005, Aug, 9-10; 2005, August, 9-10; 2005, August, 7-8; 2005, Aug, 7-8; 2005, Aug, 7-8

87901   Infectious agent genotype analysis by nucleic acid (DNA or RNA); HIV-1, reverse transcriptase and protease [A][□]
EXCLUDES infectious agent drug susceptibility phenotype prediction for HIV-1 (87900)
0.00   0.00 Global Days XXX
AMA: 2006, Mar, 6-9; 2006, Mar, 6-9; 2006, March, 6-9; 2005, Aug, 9-10; 2005, Aug, 9-10; 2005, Jul, 11-12; 2005, August, 9-10; 2005, July, 11-12; 2005, August, 7-8; 2005, Jul, 11-12; 2005, Aug, 7-8; 2005, Aug, 7-8

87902   Hepatitis C virus [A][□]
0.00   0.00 Global Days XXX
AMA: 2005, Aug, 7-8; 2005, Aug, 7-8; 2005, Aug, 9-10; 2005, Aug, 9-10; 2005, Jul, 11-12; 2005, Jul, 11-12; 2005, July, 11-12; 2005, August, 7-8; 2005, August, 9-10

87903   Infectious agent phenotype analysis by nucleic acid (DNA or RNA) with drug resistance tissue culture analysis, HIV 1; first through 10 drugs tested [A][□]
0.00   0.00 Global Days XXX
AMA: 2006, Mar, 6-9; 2006, Mar, 6-9; 2006, March, 6-9; 2005, Jul, 11-12; 2005, Jul, 11-12; 2005, Aug, 9-10; 2005, Aug, 9-10; 2005, July, 11-12; 2005, August, 9-10; 2005, August, 7-8; 2005, Aug, 7-8; 2005, Aug, 7-8; 2004, Apr, 15; 2004, April, 15; 2004, Apr, 15

+ 87904   each additional drug tested (List separately in addition to code for primary procedure) [A][□]
Code first (87903)
0.00   0.00 Global Days XXX
AMA: 2008, Jan, 10-25; 2007, Jan, 13-27; 2007, Jan, 13-27; 2007, January, 13-27; 2006, Mar, 6-9; 2006, March, 6-9; 2006, Mar, 6-9; 2005, Aug, 7-8; 2005, Aug, 7-8; 2005, Jul, 11-12; 2005, July, 11-12; 2005, August, 9-10; 2005, August, 7-8; 2005, Jul, 11-12; 2005, Aug, 9-10; 2005, Aug, 9-10, 2004, Apr, 15, 2004, Apr, 15; 2004, April, 15

● 87905   Infectious agent enzymatic activity other than virus (eg, sialidase activity in vaginal fluid) [A]
EXCLUDES isolation of a virus identified by a nonimmunologic method, and by noncytopathic effect (87255)
0.00   0.00 Global Days XXX

87999   Unlisted microbiology procedure [A][X]
0.00   0.00 Global Days XXX
AMA: 2005, Aug, 7-8; 2005, Aug, 7-8; 2005, Aug, 9-10; 2005, Aug, 9-10; 2005, Jul, 11-12; 2005, Jul, 11-12; 2005, July, 11-12; 2005, August, 7-8; 2005, August, 9-10

⊕ Modifier 63 Exempt Code   ⊙ Moderate Sedation   + CPT Add-on Code   ⊘ Modifier 51 Exempt Code   ● New Code   ▲ Revised Code
[M] Maternity Edit   [A] Age Edit   [X] CLIA Waived Test   [A]-[Y] APC Status Indicators   [□] CCI Comprehensive Code   [50] Bilateral Procedure

88000-88099 Autopsy Services

CMS 100-1,5,90.2   *Laboratory Defined*
CMS 100-2,15,80.1   *Payment for Clinical Laboratory Services*
CMS 100-2,15,80   *Physician Supervision Requirements for Diagnostic Tests*
CMS 100-4,16,110.4   *Carrier Contacts With Independent Clinical Laboratories*
CMS 100-4,16,10.1   *Laboratory Definitions*
CMS 100-4,16,10   *General Coverage: Diagnostic X-ray, Laboratory, and Other Tests*
[INCLUDES]   services for physicians only

88000   **Necropsy (autopsy), gross examination only; without CNS**   E

   0.00   0.00   Global Days XXX

   AMA: 2005, Aug, 9-10; 2005, Aug, 9-10; 2005, Aug, 7-8; 2005, Aug, 7-8; 2005, Jul, 11-12; 2005, Jul, 11-12; 2005, July, 11-12; 2005, August, 7-8; 2005, August, 9-10

88005   **with brain**   E

   0.00   0.00   Global Days XXX

   AMA: 2005, Aug, 9-10; 2005, Aug, 9-10; 2005, Jul, 11-12; 2005, Jul, 11-12; 2005, Aug, 7-8; 2005, Aug, 7-8; 2005, July, 11-12; 2005, August, 7-8; 2005, August, 9-10

88007   **with brain and spinal cord**   E

   0.00   0.00   Global Days XXX

   AMA: 2005, Jul, 11-12; 2005, Jul, 11-12; 2005, Aug, 7-8; 2005, Aug, 7-8; 2005, Aug, 9-10; 2005, Aug, 9-10; 2005, August, 7-8; 2005, August, 9-10; 2005, July, 11-12

88012   **infant with brain**   A E

   0.00   0.00   Global Days XXX

   AMA: 2005, Aug, 9-10; 2005, Aug, 9-10; 2005, Aug, 7-8; 2005, Aug, 7-8; 2005, Jul, 11-12; 2005, Jul, 11-12; 2005, July, 11-12; 2005, August, 7-8; 2005, August, 9-10

88014   **stillborn or newborn with brain**   A E

   0.00   0.00   Global Days XXX

   AMA: 2005, Aug, 7-8; 2005, Aug, 7-8; 2005, Aug, 9-10; 2005, Aug, 9-10; 2005, Jul, 11-12; 2005, Jul, 11-12; 2005, July, 11-12; 2005, August, 7-8; 2005, August, 9-10

88016   **macerated stillborn**   A E

   0.00   0.00   Global Days XXX

   AMA: 2005, Aug, 7-8; 2005, Aug, 7-8; 2005, Jul, 11-12; 2005, Jul, 11-12; 2005, Aug, 9-10; 2005, Aug, 9-10; 2005, July, 11-12; 2005, August, 9-10; 2005, August, 7-8

88020   **Necropsy (autopsy), gross and microscopic; without CNS**   E

   0.00   0.00   Global Days XXX

   AMA: 2005, Aug, 7-8; 2005, Aug, 7-8; 2005, Aug, 9-10; 2005, Aug, 9-10; 2005, Jul, 11-12; 2005, Jul, 11-12; 2005, July, 11-12; 2005, August, 7-8; 2005, August, 9-10

88025   **with brain**   E

   0.00   0.00   Global Days XXX

   AMA: 2005, Aug, 9-10; 2005, Aug, 9-10; 2005, Jul, 11-12; 2005, Jul, 11-12; 2005, Aug, 7-8; 2005, Aug, 7-8; 2005, July, 11-12; 2005, August, 7-8; 2005, August, 9-10

88027   **with brain and spinal cord**   E

   0.00   0.00   Global Days XXX

   AMA: 2005, Aug, 9-10; 2005, Aug, 9-10; 2005, Jul, 11-12; 2005, Jul, 11-12; 2005, Aug, 7-8; 2005, Aug, 7-8; 2005, July, 11-12; 2005, August, 9-10; 2005, August, 7-8

88028   **infant with brain**   A E

   0.00   0.00   Global Days XXX

   AMA: 2005, Aug, 9-10; 2005, Aug, 9-10; 2005, Aug, 7-8; 2005, Aug, 7-8; 2005, Jul, 11-12; 2005, Jul, 11-12; 2005, July, 11-12; 2005, August, 9-10; 2005, August, 7-8

88029   **stillborn or newborn with brain**   A E

   0.00   0.00   Global Days XXX

   AMA: 2005, Jul, 11-12; 2005, Jul, 11-12; 2005, Aug, 9-10; 2005, Aug, 9-10; 2005, Aug, 7-8; 2005, Aug, 7-8; 2005, July, 11-12; 2005, August, 9-10; 2005, August, 7-8

88036   **Necropsy (autopsy), limited, gross and/or microscopic; regional**   E

   0.00   0.00   Global Days XXX

   AMA: 2005, Aug, 7-8; 2005, Aug, 7-8; 2005, Aug, 9-10; 2005, Aug, 9-10; 2005, Jul, 11-12; 2005, Jul, 11-12; 2005, July, 11-12; 2005, August, 9-10; 2005, August, 7-8

88037   **single organ**   E

   0.00   0.00   Global Days XXX

   AMA: 2005, Aug, 9-10; 2005, Aug, 9-10; 2005, Jul, 11-12; 2005, Jul, 11-12; 2005, Aug, 7-8; 2005, Aug, 7-8; 2005, July, 11-12; 2005, August, 9-10; 2005, August, 7-8

88040   **Necropsy (autopsy); forensic examination**   E

   0.00   0.00   Global Days XXX

   AMA: 2005, Aug, 7-8; 2005, Aug, 7-8; 2005, Aug, 9-10; 2005, Aug, 9-10; 2005, Jul, 11-12; 2005, July, 11-12; 2005, August, 9-10; 2005, August, 7-8

88045   **coroner's call**   E

   0.00   0.00   Global Days XXX

   AMA: 2005, Aug, 9-10; 2005, Aug, 9-10; 2005, Aug, 7-8; 2005, Aug, 7-8; 2005, Jul, 11-12; 2005, Jul, 11-12; 2005, July, 11-12; 2005, August, 9-10; 2005, August, 7-8

88099   **Unlisted necropsy (autopsy) procedure**   E

   0.00   0.00   Global Days XXX

   AMA: 2005, Aug, 9-10; 2005, Aug, 9-10; 2005, Aug, 7-8; 2005, Aug, 7-8; 2005, Jul, 11-12; 2005, Jul, 11-12; 2005, August, 7-8; 2005, August, 9-10

88104-88140 Cytopathology: Other Than Cervical/Vaginal

CMS 100-4,12,60   *Payment for Pathology Services*
CMS 100-4,3,10.4   *Payment of Nonphysician Services for Inpatients*
CMS 100-2,15,80   *Physician Supervision Requirements for Diagnostic Tests*

88104   **Cytopathology, fluids, washings or brushings, except cervical or vaginal; smears with interpretation**   X 80 ☐

   1.68   1.68   Global Days XXX

   AMA: 2008, Jun, 14-15; 2005, Jul, 11-12; 2005, Jul, 11-12; 2005, Aug, 7-8; 2005, Aug, 9-10; 2005, Aug, 9-10; 2005, July, 11-12; 2005, August, 9-10; 2005, August, 7-8

88106   **simple filter method with interpretation**   X 80

   2.09   2.09   Global Days XXX

   AMA: 2005, Jul, 11-12; 2005, Jul, 11-12; 2005, Aug, 9-10; 2005, Aug, 9-10; 2005, Aug, 7-8; 2005, Aug, 7-8; 2005, July, 11-12; 2005, August, 9-10; 2005, August, 7-8

88107   **smears and simple filter preparation with interpretation**   X 80 ☐

   [EXCLUDES]   *nongynecological selective cellular enhancement including filter transfer techniques (88112)*

   2.63   2.63   Global Days XXX

   AMA: 2005, Aug, 9-10; 2005, Aug, 9-10; 2005, Jul, 11-12; 2005, Jul, 11-12; 2005, Aug, 7-8; 2005, Aug, 7-8; 2005, August, 9-10; 2005, August, 7-8; 2005, July, 11-12

88108   **Cytopathology, concentration technique, smears and interpretation (eg, Saccomanno technique)**   X 80 ☐

   [EXCLUDES]   *cervical or vaginal smears (88150-88155) gastric intubation with lavage (89130-89141, 91055)*

   74340

   1.98   1.98   Global Days XXX

   AMA: 2005, Aug, 9-10; 2005, Aug, 9-10; 2005, Aug, 7-8; 2005, Aug, 7-8; 2005, Jul, 11-12; 2005, Jul, 11-12; 2005, July, 11-12; 2005, August, 9-10; 2005, August, 7-8

26/TC Professional/Technical Component Only   80/80 Assist-at-Surgery Allowed/With Documentation   Unlisted   Not Covered   Radiology crosswalk

MED: Pub 100/NCD References   **AMA:** CPT Assistant References   A2 Z3 ASC Payment Indicator   ♂Male Only   ♀Female Only   Laboratory crosswalk

370   CPT only © 2008 American Medical Association. All Rights Reserved. (Black Ink)   Medicare (Red Ink)   © 2008 Ingenix (Blue Ink)

88112 Cytopathology, selective cellular enhancement technique with interpretation (eg, liquid based slide preparation method), except cervical or vaginal　　　X 80 ▭

Do not report with (88108)

🗪 2.79　⚲ 2.79　Global Days XXX

AMA: 2005, Aug, 9-10; 2005, Aug, 9-10; 2005, Aug, 7-8; 2005, Aug, 7-8; 2005, Jul, 11-12; 2005, Jul, 11-12; 2005, July, 11-12; 2005, August, 9-10; 2005, August, 7-8

88125 Cytopathology, forensic (eg, sperm)　　　X 80

🗪 0.59　⚲ 0.59　Global Days XXX

AMA: 2005, Jul, 11-12; 2005, Jul, 11-12; 2005, Aug, 7-8; 2005, Aug, 7-8; 2005, Aug, 9-10; 2005, Aug, 9-10; 2005, August, 9-10; 2005, August, 7-8; 2005, July, 11-12

88130 Sex chromatin identification; Barr bodies　　　A

🗪 0.00　⚲ 0.00　Global Days XXX

AMA: 2005, Aug, 9-10; 2005, Aug, 9-10; 2005, Aug, 7-8; 2005, Aug, 7-8; 2005, Jul, 11-12; 2005, Jul, 11-12; 2005, July, 11-12; 2005, August, 9-10; 2005, August, 7-8

88140 peripheral blood smear, polymorphonuclear drumsticks　　　A
> EXCLUDES　Guard stain (88313)

🗪 0.00　⚲ 0.00　Global Days XXX

AMA: 2006, Mar, 6-9; 2006, Mar, 6-9; 2006, March, 6-9; 2005, Aug, 9-10; 2005, Aug, 9-10; 2005, Jul, 11-12; 2005, August, 9-10; 2005, August, 7-8; 2005, July, 11-12; 2005, Jul, 11-12; 2005, Aug, 7-8; 2005, Aug, 7-8

88141-88155 Pap Smears

CMS 100-3,210.2　Screening Pap Smears/Pelvic Examinations for Early Detection Cervical/Vaginal Cancer
CMS 100-3,190.2　Diagnostic Pap Smears
CMS 100-4,3,10.4　Payment of Nonphysician Services for Inpatients
CMS 100-2,15,80　Physician Supervision Requirements for Diagnostic Tests

88141 Cytopathology, cervical or vaginal (any reporting system), requiring interpretation by physician　　　♀ N 26 80 ▭

Code also (88142-88154, 88164-88167, 88174-88175)

🗪 0.75　⚲ 0.75　Global Days XXX

AMA: 2008, Jan, 10-25; 2007, Jan, 13-27; 2007, Jan, 13-27; 2007, January, 13-27; 2005, Mar, 16-17; 2005, Mar, 16-17; 2005, Aug, 7-8; 2005, Aug, 7-8; 2005, Aug, 9-10; 2005, July, 11-12; 2005, August, 9-10; 2005, August, 7-8; 2005, March, 16-17; 2005, Jul, 11-12; 2005, Jul, 11-12; 2005, Aug, 9-10; 2004, Mar, 4; 2004, Mar, 4; 2004, March, 4

88142 Cytopathology, cervical or vaginal (any reporting system), collected in preservative fluid, automated thin layer preparation; manual screening under physician supervision　　　♀ A ▭
> INCLUDES　Bethesda or non-Bethesda method

🗪 0.00　⚲ 0.00　Global Days XXX

AMA: 2005, Jul, 11-12; 2005, Jul, 11-12; 2005, Aug, 7-8; 2005, Aug, 7-8; 2005, Aug, 9-10; 2005, July, 11-12; 2005, August, 7-8; 2005, August, 9-10; 2005, Aug, 9-10; 2004, Mar, 4; 2004, March, 4; 2004, Mar, 4

88143 with manual screening and rescreening under physician supervision　　　♀ A ▭
> INCLUDES　Bethesda or non-Bethesda method
> EXCLUDES　automated screening of automated thin layer preparation (88174-88175)

🗪 0.00　⚲ 0.00　Global Days XXX

AMA: 2008, Jan, 10-25; 2007, Jan, 13-27; 2007, Jan, 13-27; 2007, January, 13-27; 2005, Mar, 16-17; 2005, Mar, 16-17; 2005, Jul, 11-12; 2005, Jul, 11-12; 2005, Aug, 9-10; 2005, March, 16-17; 2005, August, 9-10; 2005, August, 7-8; 2005, July, 11-12; 2005, Aug, 7-8; 2005, Aug, 7-8; 2005, Aug, 9-10; 2004, Mar, 4; 2004, Mar, 4; 2004, March, 4

88147 Cytopathology smears, cervical or vaginal; screening by automated system under physician supervision　　　♀ A ▭

🗪 0.00　⚲ 0.00　Global Days XXX

AMA: 2008, Jan, 10-25; 2007, Jan, 13-27; 2007, Jan, 13-27; 2007, January, 13-27; 2005, Jul, 11-12; 2005, Jul, 11-12; 2005, Aug, 9-10; 2005, Aug, 9-10; 2005, July, 11-12; 2005, August, 7-8; 2005, August, 9-10; 2005, Aug, 7-8; 2005, Aug, 7-8; 2004, Mar, 4; 2004, March, 4; 2004, Mar, 4

88148 screening by automated system with manual rescreening under physician supervision　　　♀ A ▭

🗪 0.00　⚲ 0.00　Global Days XXX

AMA: 2005, Aug, 9-10; 2005, Aug, 9-10; 2005, Jul, 11-12; 2005, Jul, 11-12; 2005, Aug, 7-8; 2005, July, 11-12; 2005, August, 9-10; 2005, August, 7-8; 2005, Aug, 7-8; 2004, Mar, 4; 2004, March, 4; 2004, Mar, 4

88150 Cytopathology, slides, cervical or vaginal; manual screening under physician supervision　　　♀ A ▭
> EXCLUDES　Bethesda method Pap smears (88164-88167)

🗪 0.00　⚲ 0.00　Global Days XXX

AMA: 2005, Jul, 11-12; 2005, Jul, 11-12; 2005, Aug, 9-10; 2005, Aug, 9-10; 2005, Aug, 7-8; 2005, August, 9-10; 2005, August, 7-8; 2005, July, 11-12; 2005, Aug, 7-8; 2004, Mar, 4; 2004, March, 4; 2004, Mar, 4

88152 with manual screening and computer-assisted rescreening under physician supervision　　　♀ A ▭
> EXCLUDES　Bethesda method Pap smears (88164-88167)

🗪 0.00　⚲ 0.00　Global Days XXX

AMA: 2005, Aug, 7-8; 2005, Aug, 7-8; 2005, Aug, 9-10; 2005, Aug, 9-10; 2005, Jul, 11-12; 2005, August, 9-10; 2005, August, 7-8; 2005, July, 11-12; 2005, Jul, 11-12; 2004, Mar, 4; 2004, March, 4; 2004, Mar, 4

88153 with manual screening and rescreening under physician supervision　　　♀ A ▭
> EXCLUDES　Bethesda method Pap smears (88164-88167)

🗪 0.00　⚲ 0.00　Global Days XXX

AMA: 2008, Jan, 10-25; 2007, Jan, 13-27; 2007, Jan, 13-27; 2007, January, 13-27; 2005, Mar, 16-17; 2005, Mar, 16-17; 2005, Aug, 7-8; 2005, Aug, 7-8; 2005, Aug, 9-10; 2005, March, 16-17; 2005, August, 9-10; 2005, August, 7-8; 2005, July, 11-12; 2005, Jul, 11-12; 2005, Jul, 11-12; 2005, Aug, 9-10; 2004, Mar, 4; 2004, Mar, 4; 2004, March, 4

88154 with manual screening and computer-assisted rescreening using cell selection and review under physician supervision　　　♀ A ▭
> EXCLUDES　Bethesda method Pap smears (88164-88167)

🗪 0.00　⚲ 0.00　Global Days XXX

AMA: 2005, Aug, 9-10; 2005, Aug, 9-10; 2005, Jul, 11-12; 2005, Jul, 11-12; 2005, Aug, 7-8; 2005, July, 11-12; 2005, August, 7-8; 2005, August, 9-10; 2005, Aug, 7-8; 2004, Mar, 4; 2004, March, 4; 2004, Mar, 4

+ 88155 Cytopathology, slides, cervical or vaginal, definitive hormonal evaluation (eg, maturation index, karyopyknotic index, estrogenic index) (List separately in addition to code[s] for other technical and interpretation services)　　　♀ A ▭

Code first (88142-88154, 88164-88167, 88174-88175)

🗪 0.00　⚲ 0.00　Global Days XXX

AMA: 2005, Jul, 11-12; 2005, Jul, 11-12; 2005, Aug, 7-8; 2005, Aug, 7-8; 2005, Aug, 9-10; 2005, July, 11-12; 2005, August, 7-8; 2005, August, 9-10; 2005, Aug, 9-10; 2004, Mar, 4; 2004, March, 4

® Modifier 63 Exempt Code　⊙ Moderate Sedation　+ CPT Add-on Code　Ⓢ Modifier 51 Exempt Code　● New Code　▲ Revised Code

M Maternity Edit　A Age Edit　X CLIA Waived Test　A Y APC Status Indicators　▭ CCI Comprehensive Code　50 Bilateral Procedure

© 2008 Ingenix (Blue Ink)　　CPT only © 2008 American Medical Association. All Rights Reserved. (Black Ink)　　Medicare (Red Ink)　　371

88160-88162 Cytopathology Smears (Other Than Pap)

CMS *100-4,12,60*   *Payment for Pathology Services*
CMS *100-2,15,80*   *Physician Supervision Requirements for Diagnostic Tests*

88160   **Cytopathology, smears, any other source; screening and interpretation**   ⊠ 80 ▭

     ⏱ **1.42**   ⚕ **1.42**   **Global Days XXX**

     AMA: 2006, Dec, 10-12; 2006, Dec, 10-12; 2006, Dec, 10-12; 2006, Dec, 10-12; 2006, December, 10-12; 2005, Aug, 9-10; 2005, Aug, 9-10; 2005, August, 7-8; 2005, July, 11-12; 2005, Aug, 7-8; 2005, Aug, 7-8; 2005, Jul, 11-12; 2005, Jul, 11-12

88161   **preparation, screening and interpretation**   ⊠ 80 ▭

     ⏱ **1.48**   ⚕ **1.48**   **Global Days XXX**

     AMA: 2006, Dec, 10-12; 2006, Dec, 10-12; 2006, Dec, 10-12; 2006, Dec, 10-12; 2006, December, 10-12; 2006, December, 10-12; 2005, Aug, 7-8; 2005, Aug, 7-8; 2005, August, 9-10; 2005, August, 7-8; 2005, July, 11-12; 2005, Aug, 9-10; 2005, Aug, 9-10; 2005, Jul, 11-12; 2005, Jul, 11-12

88162   **extended study involving over 5 slides and/or multiple stains**   ⊠ 80 ▭

     EXCLUDES   *aerosol collection of sputum (89220)*
                 special stains (88312-88314)

     ⏱ **2.14**   ⚕ **2.14**   **Global Days XXX**

     AMA: 2005, Jul, 11-12; 2005, Jul, 11-12; 2005, Aug, 7-8; 2005, Aug, 7-8; 2005, Aug, 9-10; 2005, Aug, 9-10; 2005, July, 11-12; 2005, August, 9-10; 2005, August, 7-8

88164-88167 Pap Smears: Bethesda System

CMS *100-3,210.2*   *Screening Pap Smears/Pelvic Examinations for Early Detection Cervical/Vaginal Cancer*
CMS *100-3,190.2*   *Diagnostic Pap Smears*
CMS *100-4,3,10.4*   *Payment of Nonphysician Services for Inpatients*
CMS *100-2,15,80*   *Physician Supervision Requirements for Diagnostic Tests*

EXCLUDES   *non-Bethesda method (88150-88154)*

88164   **Cytopathology, slides, cervical or vaginal (the Bethesda System); manual screening under physician supervision**   ♀ A ▭

     ⏱ **0.00**   ⚕ **0.00**   **Global Days XXX**

     AMA: 2005, Aug, 9-10; 2005, Aug, 9-10; 2005, Jul, 11-12; 2005, Jul, 11-12; 2005, Aug, 7-8; 2005, July, 11-12; 2005, August, 7-8; 2005, August, 9-10; 2005, Aug, 7-8; 2004, Mar, 4; 2004, March, 4; 2004, Mar, 4

88165   **with manual screening and rescreening under physician supervision**   ♀ A ▭

     ⏱ **0.00**   ⚕ **0.00**   **Global Days XXX**

     AMA: 2008, Jan, 10-25; 2007, Jan, 13-27; 2007, Jan, 13-27; 2007, January, 13-27; 2005, Mar, 16-17; 2005, Mar, 16-17; 2005, Jul, 11-12; 2005, Jul, 11-12; 2005, Aug, 9-10; 2005, July, 11-12; 2005, August, 7-8; 2005, March, 16-17; 2005, August, 9-10; 2005, Aug, 7-8; 2005, Aug, 9-10; 2004, Mar, 4; 2004, Mar, 4; 2004, March, 4

88166   **with manual screening and computer-assisted rescreening under physician supervision**   ♀ A ▭

     ⏱ **0.00**   ⚕ **0.00**   **Global Days XXX**

     AMA: 2005, Jul, 11-12; 2005, Jul, 11-12; 2005, Aug, 7-8; 2005, Aug, 7-8; 2005, Aug, 9-10; 2005, July, 11-12; 2005, August, 7-8; 2005, August, 9-10; 2005, Aug, 9-10; 2004, Mar, 4; 2004, March, 4; 2004, Mar, 4

88167   **with manual screening and computer-assisted rescreening using cell selection and review under physician supervision**   ♀ A ▭

     EXCLUDES   *collection of specimen via fine needle aspiration (10021-10022)*

     ⏱ **0.00**   ⚕ **0.00**   **Global Days XXX**

     AMA: 2005, Jul, 11-12; 2005, Jul, 11-12; 2005, Aug, 9-10; 2005, Aug, 9-10; 2005, Aug, 7-8; 2005, July, 11-12; 2005, August, 7-8; 2005, August, 9-10; 2005, Aug, 7-8; 2004, Mar, 4; 2004, March, 4; 2004, Mar, 4

88172-88173 Cytopathology of Needle Biopsy

CMS *100-4,12,60*   *Payment for Pathology Services*
CMS *100-4,3,10.4*   *Payment of Nonphysician Services for Inpatients*
CMS *100-2,15,80*   *Physician Supervision Requirements for Diagnostic Tests*

88172   **Cytopathology, evaluation of fine needle aspirate; immediate cytohistologic study to determine adequacy of specimen(s)**   ⊠ 80 ▭

     Do not report with same specimen (88333-88334)

     ⏱ **1.44**   ⚕ **1.44**   **Global Days XXX**

     AMA: 2008, Jan, 10-25; 2007, Jan, 13-27; 2007, Jan, 13-27; 2007, Aug, 15; 2007, January, 13-27; 2005, Jul, 11-12; 2005, Jul, 11-12; 2005, Aug, 9-10; 2005, August, 7-8; 2005, August, 9-10; 2005, July, 11-12; 2005, Aug, 9-10; 2005, Aug, 7-8; 2005, Aug, 7-8

88173   **interpretation and report**   ⊠ 80 ▭

     EXCLUDES   *fine needle aspiration (10021-10022)*

     Do not report with same specimen (88333-88334)

     ⏱ **3.65**   ⚕ **3.65**   **Global Days XXX**

     AMA: 2008, Jan, 10-25; 2007, Jan, 13-27; 2007, Jan, 13-27; 2007, January, 13-27; 2005, Jul, 11-12; 2005, Jul, 11-12; 2005, Aug, 9-10; 2005, August, 9-10; 2005, August, 7-8; 2005, July, 11-12; 2005, Aug, 9-10; 2005, Aug, 7-8; 2005, Aug, 7-8

88174-88175 Pap Smears: Automated Screening

CMS *100-3,210.2*   *Screening Pap Smears/Pelvic Examinations for Early Detection Cervical/Vaginal Cancer*
CMS *100-3,190.2*   *Diagnostic Pap Smears*
CMS *100-4,3,10.4*   *Payment of Nonphysician Services for Inpatients*
CMS *100-2,15,80*   *Physician Supervision Requirements for Diagnostic Tests*

88174   **Cytopathology, cervical or vaginal (any reporting system), collected in preservative fluid, automated thin layer preparation; screening by automated system, under physician supervision**   ♀ A ▭

     INCLUDES   Bethesda or non-Bethesda method

     ⏱ **0.00**   ⚕ **0.00**   **Global Days XXX**

     AMA: 2005, Jul, 11-12; 2005, Jul, 11-12; 2005, Aug, 9-10; 2005, Aug, 9-10; 2005, Aug, 7-8; 2005, July, 11-12; 2005, August, 7-8; 2005, August, 9-10; 2005, Aug, 7-8; 2004, Mar, 4; 2004, March, 4; 2004, Mar, 4

88175   **with screening by automated system and manual rescreening or review, under physician supervision**   ♀ A ▭

     INCLUDES   Bethesda or non-Bethesda method

     EXCLUDES   *manual screening (88142-88143)*

     ⏱ **0.00**   ⚕ **0.00**   **Global Days XXX**

     AMA: 2006, Mar, 6-9; 2006, Mar, 6-9; 2006, March, 6-9; 2005, Aug, 7-8; 2005, Aug, 7-8; 2005, Jul, 11-12; 2005, Jul, 11-12; 2005, July, 11-12; 2005, August, 7-8; 2005, August, 9-10; 2005, Aug, 9-10; 2005, Aug, 9-10; 2004, Mar, 4; 2004, March, 4; 2004, Mar, 4

26 /TC Professional/Technical Component Only	80 /80 Assist-at-Surgery Allowed/With Documentation	Unlisted Not Covered	⊠ Radiology crosswalk
MED: Pub 100/NCD References **AMA:** CPT Assistant References	A2 -Z3 ASC Payment Indicator	♂Male Only ♀Female Only	◨ Laboratory crosswalk

372   CPT only © 2008 American Medical Association. All Rights Reserved. (Black Ink)   Medicare (Red Ink)   © 2008 Ingenix *(Blue Ink)*

88182-88199 Cytopathology Using the Fluorescence-Activated Cell Sorter

CMS *100-4,12,60*	*Payment for Pathology Services*
CMS *100-4,3,10.4*	*Payment of Nonphysician Services for Inpatients*
CMS *100-2,15,80*	*Physician Supervision Requirements for Diagnostic Tests*

88182 Flow cytometry, cell cycle or DNA analysis Ⓧ ⑩ ▭

  EXCLUDES *DNA ploidy analysis by morphometric technique (88358)*

  📖 2.80 ⚒ 2.80 **Global Days XXX**

  AMA: 2005, Jul, 11-12; 2005, Jul, 11-12; 2005, Aug, 9-10; 2005, Aug, 9-10; 2005, Aug, 7-8; 2005, Aug, 7-8; 2005, August, 9-10; 2005, August, 7-8; 2005, July, 11-12

88184 Flow cytometry, cell surface, cytoplasmic, or nuclear marker, technical component only; first marker Ⓧ ᴛᴄ ⑧ ▭

  📖 2.17 ⚒ 2.17 **Global Days XXX**

  AMA: 2007, Dec, 10-179; 2005, Aug, 7-8; 2005, Aug, 7-8; 2005, Jul, 11-12; 2005, Jul, 11-12; 2005, Aug, 9-10; 2005, Aug, 9-10; 2005, July, 11-12; 2005, August, 9-10; 2005, August, 7-8

+ **88185** each additional marker (List separately in addition to code for first marker) Ⓧ ᴛᴄ ⑧

  Code first (88184)

  📖 1.29 ⚒ 1.29 **Global Days ZZZ**

  AMA: 2007, Dec, 10-179; 2005, Aug, 9-10; 2005, Aug, 9-10; 2005, Jul, 11-12; 2005, Jul, 11-12; 2005, Aug, 7-8; 2005, Aug, 7-8; 2005, July, 11-12; 2005, August, 9-10; 2005, August, 7-8

88187 Flow cytometry, interpretation; 2 to 8 markers Ⓧ ②⑥ ⑧ ▭

  EXCLUDES *interpretation (86355-86357, 86359-86361, 86367)*

  📖 1.78 ⚒ 1.78 **Global Days XXX**

  AMA: 2008, Apr, 5-7; 2008, Apr, 5-7; 2008, Apr, 5-7; 2008, Jan, 10-25; 2007, Jan, 13-27; 2007, Jan, 13-27; 2007, January, 13-27; 2005, Apr, 13-14; 2005, Apr, 13-14; 2005, April, 13-14; 2005, August, 7-8; 2005, July, 11-12; 2005, August, 9-10; 2005, Aug, 9-10; 2005, Aug, 9-10; 2005, Jul, 11-12; 2005, Jul, 11-12; 2005, Aug, 7-8; 2005, Aug, 7-8

88188 9 to 15 markers Ⓧ ②⑥ ⑧ ▭

  EXCLUDES *interpretation (86355-86357, 86359-86361, 86367)*

  📖 2.19 ⚒ 2.19 **Global Days XXX**

  AMA: 2008, Apr, 5-7; 2008, Apr, 5-7; 2008, Apr, 5-7; 2008, Jan, 10-25; 2007, Jan, 13-27; 2007, Jan, 13-27; 2007, January, 13-27; 2005, Apr, 13-14; 2005, Apr, 13-14; 2005, July, 11-12; 2005, August, 7-8; 2005, August, 9-10; 2005, April, 13-14; 2005, Aug, 9-10; 2005, Aug, 9-10; 2005, Aug, 7-8; 2005, Aug, 7-8; 2005, Jul, 11-12; 2005, Jul, 11-12

88189 16 or more markers Ⓧ ②⑥ ⑧ ▭

  EXCLUDES *interpretation (86355-86357, 86359-86361, 86367)*

  📖 2.79 ⚒ 2.79 **Global Days XXX**

  AMA: 2008, Apr, 5-7; 2008, Apr, 5-7; 2008, Apr, 5-7; 2008, Jan, 10-25; 2007, Jan, 13-27; 2007, Jan, 13-27; 2007, January, 13-27; 2005, Jul, 11-12; 2005, Jul, 11-12; 2005, July, 11-12; 2005, August, 7-8; 2005, April, 13-14; 2005, August, 9-10; 2005, Apr, 13-14; 2005, Apr, 13-14; 2005, Aug, 7-8; 2005, Aug, 7-8; 2005, Aug, 9-10; 2005, Aug, 9-10

88199 Unlisted cytopathology procedure Ⓧ ⑧

  📖 0.00 ⚒ 0.00 **Global Days XXX**

  AMA: 2005, Jul, 11-12; 2005, Jul, 11-12; 2005, Aug, 9-10; 2005, Aug, 9-10; 2005, Aug, 7-8; 2005, Aug, 7-8; 2005, July, 11-12; 2005, August, 9-10; 2005, August, 7-8

88230-88299 Cytogenic Studies

CMS *100-3,190.3*	*Cytogenic Studies*
CMS *100-4,3,10.4*	*Payment of Nonphysician Services for Inpatients*
CMS *100-1,5,90.2*	*Laboratory Defined*
CMS *100-2,15,80.1*	*Payment for Clinical Laboratory Services*
CMS *100-2,15,80*	*Physician Supervision Requirements for Diagnostic Tests*
CMS *100-4,16,110.4*	*Carrier Contacts With Independent Clinical Laboratories*
CMS *100-4,16,10.1*	*Laboratory Definitions*
CMS *100-4,16,10*	*General Coverage: Diagnostic X-ray, Laboratory, and Other Tests*

Code also genetic testing modifiers for oncologic or inherited disorder

88230 Tissue culture for non-neoplastic disorders; lymphocyte Ⓐ

  📖 0.00 ⚒ 0.00 **Global Days XXX**

  AMA: 2008, May, 5-8; 2005, Jul, 11-12; 2005, Jul, 11-12; 2005, Aug, 9-10; 2005, Aug, 9-10; 2005, Aug, 7-8; 2005, Aug, 7-8; 2005, July, 11-12; 2005, August, 9-10; 2005, August, 7-8

88233 skin or other solid tissue biopsy Ⓐ

  📖 0.00 ⚒ 0.00 **Global Days XXX**

  AMA: 2008, May, 5-8; 2005, Jul, 11-12; 2005, Jul, 11-12; 2005, Aug, 9-10; 2005, Aug, 9-10; 2005, Aug, 7-8; 2005, Aug, 7-8; 2005, August, 9-10; 2005, August, 7-8; 2005, July, 11-12

88235 amniotic fluid or chorionic villus cells Ⓜ ♀ Ⓐ

  📖 0.00 ⚒ 0.00 **Global Days XXX**

  AMA: 2008, May, 5-8; 2005, Aug, 9-10; 2005, Aug, 9-10; 2005, Jul, 11-12; 2005, Jul, 11-12; 2005, Aug, 7-8; 2005, Aug, 7-8; 2005, July, 11-12; 2005, August, 9-10; 2005, August, 7-8

88237 Tissue culture for neoplastic disorders; bone marrow, blood cells Ⓐ

  📖 0.00 ⚒ 0.00 **Global Days XXX**

  AMA: 2008, May, 5-8; 2005, Jul, 11-12; 2005, Jul, 11-12; 2005, Aug, 9-10; 2005, Aug, 9-10; 2005, Aug, 7-8; 2005, Aug, 7-8; 2005, July, 11-12; 2005, August, 9-10; 2005, August, 7-8

88239 solid tumor Ⓐ

  📖 0.00 ⚒ 0.00 **Global Days XXX**

  AMA: 2008, May, 5-8; 2005, Jul, 11-12; 2005, Jul, 11-12; 2005, Aug, 9-10; 2005, Aug, 9-10; 2005, Aug, 7-8; 2005, Aug, 7-8; 2005, July, 11-12; 2005, August, 7-8; 2005, August, 9-10

88240 Cryopreservation, freezing and storage of cells, each cell line Ⓐ ▭

  EXCLUDES *therapeutic cryopreservation and storage (38207)*

  📖 0.00 ⚒ 0.00 **Global Days XXX**

  AMA: 2005, Jul, 11-12; 2005, Jul, 11-12; 2005, Aug, 7-8; 2005, Aug, 7-8; 2005, Aug, 9-10; 2005, Aug, 9-10; 2005, July, 11-12; 2005, August, 9-10; 2005, August, 7-8

88241 Thawing and expansion of frozen cells, each aliquot Ⓐ ▭

  EXCLUDES *therapeutic thawing of previous harvest (38208)*

  📖 0.00 ⚒ 0.00 **Global Days XXX**

  AMA: 2005, Aug, 9-10; 2005, Aug, 9-10; 2005, Jul, 11-12; 2005, Jul, 11-12; 2005, Aug, 7-8; 2005, Aug, 7-8; 2005, July, 11-12; 2005, August, 9-10; 2005, August, 7-8

88245 Chromosome analysis for breakage syndromes; baseline Sister Chromatid Exchange (SCE), 20-25 cells Ⓐ ▭

  📖 0.00 ⚒ 0.00 **Global Days XXX**

  AMA: 2008, May, 5-8; 2005, Jul, 11-12; 2005, Jul, 11-12; 2005, Jul, 1-8; 2005, Jul, 1-8; 2005, Aug, 7-8; 2005, Aug, 7-8; 2005, Aug, 9-10; 2005, Aug, 9-10; 2005, July, 11-12; 2005, July, 1-8; 2005, August, 9-10; 2005, August, 7-8

® Modifier 63 Exempt Code ⊙ Moderate Sedation + CPT Add-on Code ⊘ Modifier 51 Exempt Code ● New Code ▲ Revised Code

Ⓜ Maternity Edit Ⓐ Age Edit ⊠ CLIA Waived Test Ⓐ-Ⓨ APC Status Indicators ▭ CCI Comprehensive Code ⑤⓪ Bilateral Procedure

© 2008 Ingenix *(Blue Ink)* CPT only © 2008 American Medical Association. All Rights Reserved. (Black Ink) Medicare (Red Ink) 373

88248 baseline breakage, score 50-100 cells, count 20 cells, 2 karyotypes (eg, for ataxia telangiectasia, Fanconi anemia, fragile X) Ⓐ ▣
 0.00   0.00 Global Days XXX
AMA: 2008, May, 5-8; 2005, Aug, 9-10; 2005, Jul, 11-12; 2005, Jul, 11-12; 2005, Jul, 1-8; 2005, Jul, 1-8; 2005, Aug, 7-8; 2005, Aug, 7-8; 2005, July, 1-8; 2005, August, 9-10; 2005, August, 7-8

88249 score 100 cells, clastogen stress (eg, diepoxybutane, mitomycin C, ionizing radiation, UV radiation) Ⓐ ▣
 0.00   0.00 Global Days XXX
AMA: 2008, May, 5-8; 2005, Jul, 11-12; 2005, Jul, 1-8; 2005, Jul, 1-8; 2005, Aug, 7-8; 2005, Aug, 7-8; 2005, Aug, 9-10; 2005, Aug, 9-10; 2005, July, 11-12; 2005, July, 1-8; 2005, August, 9-10; 2005, August, 7-8

88261 Chromosome analysis; count 5 cells, 1 karyotype, with banding Ⓐ ▣
 0.00   0.00 Global Days XXX
AMA: 2008, May, 5-8; 2007, Dec, 10-179; 2005, Aug, 9-10; 2005, Aug, 9-10; 2005, Jul, 1-8; 2005, Jul, 1-8; 2005, Aug, 7-8; 2005, Aug, 7-8; 2005, Jul, 11-12; 2005, Jul, 11-12; 2005, July, 11-12; 2005, July, 1-8; 2005, August, 9-10; 2005, August, 7-8

88262 count 15-20 cells, 2 karyotypes, with banding Ⓐ ▣
 0.00   0.00 Global Days XXX
AMA: 2008, May, 5-8; 2007, Dec, 10-179; 2005, Jul, 1-8; 2005, Jul, 1-8; 2005, Aug, 7-8; 2005, Aug, 7-8; 2005, Aug, 9-10; 2005, Aug, 9-10; 2005, Jul, 11-12; 2005, Jul, 11-12; 2005, July, 11-12; 2005, July, 1-8; 2005, August, 9-10; 2005, August, 7-8

88263 count 45 cells for mosaicism, 2 karyotypes, with banding Ⓐ ▣
 0.00   0.00 Global Days XXX
AMA: 2008, May, 5-8; 2005, Aug, 9-10; 2005, Aug, 9-10; 2005, Jul, 1-8; 2005, Jul, 1-8; 2005, Jul, 11-12; 2005, Jul, 11-12; 2005, Aug, 7-8; 2005, Aug, 7-8; 2005, July, 11-12; 2005, July, 1-8; 2005, August, 9-10; 2005, August, 7-8

88264 analyze 20-25 cells Ⓐ ▣
 0.00   0.00 Global Days XXX
AMA: 2008, May, 5-8; 2005, Jul, 1-8; 2005, Jul, 1-8; 2005, Aug, 9-10; 2005, Aug, 9-10; 2005, Aug, 7-8; 2005, Aug, 7-8; 2005, Jul, 11-12; 2005, Jul, 11-12; 2005, July, 11-12; 2005, July, 1-8; 2005, August, 9-10; 2005, August, 7-8

88267 Chromosome analysis, amniotic fluid or chorionic villus, count 15 cells, 1 karyotype, with banding Ⓜ ♀ Ⓐ ▣
 0.00   0.00 Global Days XXX
AMA: 2008, May, 5-8; 2005, Jul, 11-12; 2005, Jul, 11-12; 2005, Aug, 7-8; 2005, Aug, 7-8; 2005, Aug, 9-10; 2005, Aug, 9-10; 2005, Jul, 1-8; 2005, Jul, 1-8; 2005, July, 11-12; 2005, July, 1-8; 2005, August, 9-10; 2005, August, 7-8

88269 Chromosome analysis, in situ for amniotic fluid cells, count cells from 6-12 colonies, 1 karyotype, with banding Ⓜ ♀ Ⓐ ▣
 0.00   0.00 Global Days XXX
AMA: 2008, May, 5-8; 2005, Jul, 11-12; 2005, Jul, 11-12; 2005, Jul, 1-8; 2005, Jul, 1-8; 2005, Aug, 7-8; 2005, Aug, 7-8; 2005, Aug, 9-10; 2005, Aug, 9-10; 2005, July, 11-12; 2005, July, 1-8; 2005, August, 9-10; 2005, August, 7-8

88271 Molecular cytogenetics; DNA probe, each (eg, FISH) Ⓐ ▣
 0.00   0.00 Global Days XXX
AMA: 2008, Jan, 10-25; 2008, May, 5-8; 2007, Jan, 13-27; 2007, Jan, 13-27; 2007, January, 13-27; 2005, Aug, 9-10; 2005, Aug, 9-10; 2005, Jul, 1-8; 2005, Jul, 1-8; 2005, July, 11-12; 2005, August, 7-8; 2005, August, 9-10; 2005, July, 1-8; 2005, Aug, 7-8; 2005, Aug, 7-8; 2005, Jul, 11-12; 2005, Jul, 11-12

88272 chromosomal in situ hybridization, analyze 3-5 cells (eg, for derivatives and markers) Ⓐ ▣
 0.00   0.00 Global Days XXX
AMA: 2008, Jan, 10-25; 2008, May, 5-8; 2007, Jan, 13-27; 2007, Jan, 13-27; 2007, January, 13-27; 2005, Aug, 9-10; 2005, Aug, 9-10; 2005, Jul, 1-8; 2005, Jul, 1-8; 2005, July, 1-8; 2005, August, 7-8; 2005, August, 9-10; 2005, July, 11-12; 2005, Jul, 11-12; 2005, Jul, 11-12; 2005, Aug, 7-8; 2005, Aug, 7-8

88273 chromosomal in situ hybridization, analyze 10-30 cells (eg, for microdeletions) Ⓐ ▣
 0.00   0.00 Global Days XXX
AMA: 2008, Jan, 10-25; 2008, May, 5-8; 2007, Jan, 13-27; 2007, Jan, 13-27; 2007, January, 13-27; 2005, Aug, 7-8; 2005, Aug, 7-8; 2005, Aug, 9-10; 2005, Aug, 9-10; 2005, July, 1-8; 2005, August, 7-8; 2005, August, 9-10; 2005, July, 11-12; 2005, Jul, 11-12; 2005, Jul, 11-12; 2005, Jul, 1-8; 2005, Jul, 1-8

88274 interphase in situ hybridization, analyze 25-99 cells Ⓐ ▣
 0.00   0.00 Global Days XXX
AMA: 2008, Jan, 10-25; 2008, May, 5-8; 2007, Jan, 13-27; 2007, Jan, 13-27; 2007, January, 13-27; 2005, Aug, 9-10; 2005, Aug, 9-10; 2005, Jul, 1-8; 2005, Jul, 1-8; 2005, July, 1-8; 2005, August, 9-10; 2005, August, 7-8; 2005, July, 11-12; 2005, Aug, 7-8; 2005, Aug, 7-8; 2005, Jul, 11-12; 2005, Jul, 11-12

88275 interphase in situ hybridization, analyze 100-300 cells Ⓐ ▣
 0.00   0.00 Global Days XXX
AMA: 2008, Jan, 10-25; 2008, May, 5-8; 2007, Jan, 13-27; 2007, Jan, 13-27; 2007, January, 13-27; 2005, Jul, 1-8; 2005, Jul, 1-8; 2005, Aug, 7-8; 2005, Aug, 7-8; 2005, July, 11-12; 2005, August, 7-8; 2005, August, 9-10; 2005, July, 1-8; 2005, Jul, 11-12; 2005, Jul, 11-12; 2005, Aug, 9-10; 2005, Aug, 9-10

88280 additional karyotypes, each study Ⓐ ▣
 0.00   0.00 Global Days XXX
AMA: 2008, May, 5-8; 2005, Aug, 9-10; 2005, Aug, 9-10; 2005, Jul, 11-12; 2005, Jul, 11-12; 2005, Aug, 7-8; 2005, Aug, 7-8; 2005, Jul, 1-8; 2005, Jul, 1-8; 2005, July, 1-8; 2005, July, 1-8; 2005, August, 9-10; 2005, August, 7-8

88283 additional specialized banding technique (eg, NOR, C-banding) Ⓐ ▣
 0.00   0.00 Global Days XXX
AMA: 2008, May, 5-8; 2005, Jul, 11-12; 2005, Jul, 11-12; 2005, Aug, 7-8; 2005, Aug, 7-8; 2005, Aug, 9-10; 2005, Aug, 9-10; 2005, Jul, 1-8; 2005, Jul, 1-8; 2005, July, 11-12; 2005, July, 1-8; 2005, August, 9-10; 2005, August, 7-8

88285 additional cells counted, each study Ⓐ ▣
 0.00   0.00 Global Days XXX
AMA: 2008, May, 5-8; 2007, Dec, 10-179; 2005, Aug, 9-10; 2005, Aug, 9-10; 2005, Jul, 11-12; 2005, Jul, 11-12; 2005, Jul, 1-8; 2005, Jul, 1-8; 2005, Aug, 7-8; 2005, Aug, 7-8; 2005, July, 11-12; 2005, July, 1-8; 2005, August, 9-10; 2005, August, 7-8

88289 additional high resolution study Ⓐ ▣
 0.00   0.00 Global Days XXX
AMA: 2008, May, 5-8; 2005, Jul, 1-8; 2005, Jul, 1-8; 2005, Aug, 7-8; 2005, Aug, 7-8; 2005, Aug, 9-10; 2005, Aug, 9-10; 2005, Jul, 11-12; 2005, Jul, 11-12; 2005, July, 11-12; 2005, July, 1-8; 2005, August, 9-10; 2005, August, 7-8

88291 Cytogenetics and molecular cytogenetics, interpretation and report Ⓜ ㉖ ⑳
 0.79   0.79 Global Days XXX
AMA: 2008, May, 5-8; 2005, Jul, 11-12; 2005, Jul, 11-12; 2005, Aug, 9-10; 2005, Aug, 9-10; 2005, Jul, 1-8; 2005, Jul, 1-8; 2005, Aug, 7-8; 2005, Aug, 7-8; 2005, July, 11-12; 2005, July, 1-8; 2005, August, 9-10; 2005, August, 7-8

㉖/ⓉⒸ Professional/Technical Component Only   ⑧⓪/⑧⓪ Assist-at-Surgery Allowed/With Documentation   Unlisted   Not Covered   ☒ Radiology crosswalk

MED: Pub 100/NCD References   **AMA:** CPT Assistant References   Ⓐ₂–Ⓩ₉ ASC Payment Indicator   ♂Male Only   ♀Female Only   ☒ Laboratory crosswalk

374   CPT only © 2008 American Medical Association. All Rights Reserved. (Black Ink)   Medicare (Red Ink)   © 2008 Ingenix (Blue Ink)

88299   **Unlisted cytogenetic study**   ☒ 80
         ⏱ 0.00   ⚖ 0.00 Global Days XXX
         AMA: 2005, Jul, 11-12; 2005, Jul, 11-12; 2005, Aug, 7-8; 2005,
         Aug, 7-8; 2005, Aug, 9-10; 2005, Aug, 9-10; 2005, July, 11-12;
         2005, August, 9-10; 2005, August, 7-8

88300 Evaluation of Surgical Specimen: Gross Anatomy

CMS *100-4,12,60*   *Payment for Pathology Services*
CMS *100-1,5,90.2*   *Laboratory Defined*
INCLUDES   attainment, examination, and reporting
            unit of service is the specimen

EXCLUDES   *additional procedures (88311-88365, 88399)*

88300   **Level I - Surgical pathology, gross examination
         only**   ☒ 80
              EXCLUDES *microscopic exam (88302-88309)*

              ⏱ 0.64   ⚖ 0.64 Global Days XXX
              AMA: 2008, Jan, 10-25; 2007, Jan, 13-27; 2007, Jan, 13-27; 2007,
              January, 13-27; 2005, Jul, 11-12; 2005, Jul, 11-12; 2005, Aug,
              9-10; 2005, August, 9-10; 2005, August, 7-8; 2005, July, 11-12;
              2005, Aug, 9-10; 2005, Aug, 7-8; 2005, Aug, 7-8

88302-88309 Evaluation of Surgical Specimens: Gross and Microscopic Anatomy

CMS *100-4,12,60*   *Payment for Pathology Services*
CMS *100-1,5,90.2*   *Laboratory Defined*
INCLUDES   attainment, examination, and reporting
            unit of service is the specimen

EXCLUDES   *additional procedures (88311-88365, 88399)*

Do not report with Mohs surgery (17311-17315)

88302   **Level II - Surgical pathology, gross and microscopic
         examination**   ☒ 80
              INCLUDES appendix, incidental
                        confirming identification and absence of
                             disease
                        fallopian tube, sterilization
                        fingers or toes traumatic amputation
                        foreskin, newborn
                        hernia sac, any site
                        hydrocele sac
                        nerve
                        skin, plastic repair
                        sympathetic ganglion
                        testis, castration
                        vaginal mucosa, incidental
                        vas deferense, sterilization

              ⏱ 1.34   ⚖ 1.34 Global Days XXX
              AMA: 2008, Jan, 10-25; 2007, Jan, 13-27; 2007, Jan, 13-27; 2007,
              Jan, 28-31; 2007, January, 13-27; 2007, January, 28-31; 2007,
              Jan, 28-31; 2006, Dec, 1-3; 2006, Dec, 1-3; 2006, Dec, 1-3; 2006,
              Dec, 1-3; 2006, Dec, 1-3; 2006, Dec, 1-3; 2006, Dec, 1-3; 2006,
              December, 1-3; 2006, December, 1-3; 2006, December, 1-3;
              2006, December, 1-3; 2006, Dec, 1-3; 2005, Aug, 9-10; 2005, Aug,
              9-10; 2005, Aug, 7-8; 2005, August, 9-10; 2005, August, 7-8; 2005,
              July, 11-12; 2005, Aug, 7-8; 2005, Jul, 11-12; 2005, Jul, 11-12

88304   **Level III - Surgical pathology, gross and microscopic
         examination**   ☒ 80 ▢
              INCLUDES abortion, induced
                        abscess
                        anal tag
                        aneurysm-atrial/ventricular
                        appendix, other than incidental
                        artery, atheromatous plaque
                        Bartholin's gland cyst
                        bone fragment(s), other than pathologic
                             fracture
                        bursa/ synovial cyst
                        carpal tunnel tissue
                        cartilage, shavings
                        cholesteatoma
                        colon, colostomy stoma
                        conjunctiva-biopsy/pterygium
                        cornea
                        diverticulum-esophagus/small intestine
                        Dupuytren's contracture tissue
                        femoral head, other than fracture
                        fissure/fistula
                        foreskin, other than newborn
                        gallbladder
                        ganglion cyst
                        hematoma
                        hemorrhoids
                        hydatid of Morgagni
                        intervertebral disc
                        joint, loose body
                        meniscus
                        mucocele, salivary
                        neuroma-Morton's/traumatic
                        pilonidal cyst/sinus
                        polyps, inflammatory nasal/sinusoidal
                        skin-cyst/tag/debridement
                        soft tissue, debridement
                        soft tissue, lipoma
                        spermatocele
                        tendon/tendon sheath
                        testicular appendage
                        thrombus or embolus
                        tonsil and/or adenoids
                        varicocele
                        vas deferens, other than sterilization
                        vein, varicosity

              ⏱ 1.70   ⚖ 1.70 Global Days XXX
              AMA: 2008, Jan, 10-25; 2007, Jan, 13-27; 2007, Jan, 13-27; 2007,
              Jan, 28-31; 2007, January, 13-27; 2007, January, 28-31; 2007,
              Jan, 28-31; 2006, Dec, 1-3; 2006, Dec, 1-3; 2006, Dec, 1-3; 2006,
              Dec, 1-3; 2006, Dec, 1-3; 2006, Dec, 1-3; 2006, Dec, 1-3; 2006,
              December, 1-3; 2006, December, 1-3; 2006, December, 1-3;
              2006, December, 1-3; 2006, Dec, 1-3; 2005, Aug, 9-10; 2005, Aug,
              9-10; 2005, Aug, 7-8; 2005, August, 9-10; 2005, August, 7-8; 2005,
              July, 11-12; 2005, Aug, 7-8; 2005, Jul, 11-12; 2005, Jul, 11-12

Pathology and Laboratory

88305 — 88307

88305 **Level IV - Surgical pathology, gross and microscopic examination** ☒ 80 ▭

INCLUDES

abortion, spontaneous/missed
artery, biopsy
bone exostosis
bone marrow, biopsy
brain/meninges, other than for tumor resection
breast biopsy without microscopic assessment of surgical margin
breast reduction mammoplasty
bronchus, biopsy
cell block, any source
cervix, biopsy
colon, biopsy
duodenum, biopsy
endocervix, curettings/biopsy
endometrium, curettings/biopsy
esophagus, biopsy
extremity, amputation, traumatic
fallopian tube, biopsy
fallopian tube, ectopic pregnancy
femoral head, fracture
finger/toes, amputation, nontraumatic
gingiva/oral mucosa, biopsy
heart valve
joint resection
kidney biopsy
larynx biopsy
leiomyoma(s), uterine myomectomy-without uterus
lip, biopsy/wedge resection
lung, transbronchial biopsy
lymph node, biopsy
muscle, biopsy
nasal mucosa, biopsy
nasopharynx/oropharynx, biopsy
nerve biopsy
odontogenic/dental cyst
omentum, biopsy
ovary, biopsy/wedge resection
ovary with or without tube, nonneoplastic
parathyroid gland
peritoneum, biopsy
pituitary tumor
placenta, other than third trimester
pleura/pericardium-biopsy/tissue
polyp:
   cervical/endometrial
   colorectal
   stomach/small intestine
prostate:
   needle biopsy
   TUR
salivary gland, biopsy
sinus, paranasal biopsy
skin, other than cyst/tag/debridement/plastic repair
small intestine, biopsy
soft tissue, other than tumor/mas/lipoma/debridement
spleen
stomach biopsy
synovium
testis, other than tumor/biopsy, castration
thyroglossal duct/brachial cleft cyst
tongue, biopsy
tonsil, biopsy
trachea biopsy
ureter, biopsy
urethra, biopsy
urinary bladder, biopsy
uterus, with or without tubes and ovaries, for prolapse
vagina biopsy
vulva/labial biopsy

🚗 2.88 🔍 2.88 **Global Days XXX**

AMA: 2008, Jan, 10-25; 2007, Jan, 28-31; 2007, Jan, 28-31; 2007, Jan, 13-27; 2007, January, 28-31; 2007, Jan, 13-27; 2007, January, 13-27; 2006, Dec, 1-3; 2006, Dec, 1-3; 2006, Dec, 1-3; 2006, Dec, 1-3; 2006, December, 1-3; 2006, December, 1-3; 2006, December, 1-3; 2006, December, 1-3; 2006, Dec, 1-3; 2006, Dec, 1-3; 2006, Dec, 1-3; 2005, Mar, 11-15; 2005, Mar, 11-15; 2005, Jul, 13-16; 2005, August, 7-8; 2005, August, 9-10; 2005, July, 13-16; 2005, March, 11-15; 2005, July, 11-12; 2005, Jul, 13-16; 2005, Aug, 9-10; 2005, Aug, 9-10; 2005, Aug, 7-8; 2005, Aug, 7-8; 2005, Jul, 11-12; 2005, Jul, 11-12

88307 **Level V - Surgical pathology, gross and microscopic examination** ☒ 80 ▭

INCLUDES

adrenal resection
bone, biopsy/curettings
bone fragment(s), pathologic fractures
brain, biopsy
brain meninges, tumor resection
breast, excision of lesion, requiring microscopic evaluation of surgical margins
breast, mastectomy-partial/simple
cervix, conization
colon, segmental resection, other than for tumor
extremity, amputation, nontraumatic
eye, enucleation
kidney, partial/total nephrectomy
larynx, partial/total resection
liver, biopsy-needle, wedge
lung, wedge biopsy
lymph nodes, regional resection
mediastinum, mass
myocardium, biopsy
odontogenic tumor
ovary with or without tube, neoplastic
pancreas, biopsy
placenta, third trimester
prostate, except radical resection
salivary gland
sentinel lymph node
small intestine, resection, other than for tumor
soft tissue mass (except lipoma)-biopsy/simple excision
stomach-subtotal/total resection, other than for tumor
testis, biopsy
thymus, tumor
thyroid, total/lobe
ureter, resection
urinary bladder, TUR
uterus, with or without tubes and ovaries, other than neoplastic/prolapse

🚗 5.76 🔍 5.76 **Global Days XXX**

AMA: 2008, Jan, 10-25; 2007, Jan, 13-27; 2007, Jan, 13-27; 2007, Jan, 28-31; 2007, January, 13-27; 2007, January, 28-31; 2007, Jan, 28-31; 2006, Dec, 1-3; 2006, Dec, 1-3; 2006, Dec, 1-3; 2006, Dec, 1-3; 2006, Dec, 1-3; 2006, Dec, 1-3; 2006, Dec, 1-3; 2006, December, 1-3; 2006, December, 1-3; 2006, December, 1-3; 2006, December, 1-3; 2006, Dec, 1-3; 2005, Aug, 9-10; 2005, Aug, 9-10; 2005, Jul, 11-12; 2005, August, 9-10; 2005, August, 7-8; 2005, July, 11-12; 2005, Jul, 11-12; 2005, Aug, 7-8; 2005, Aug, 7-8

26/TC Professional/Technical Component Only   80/80 Assist-at-Surgery Allowed/With Documentation   Unlisted   Not Covered   🔀 Radiology crosswalk

MED: Pub 100/NCD References   **AMA:** CPT Assistant References   A2-Z3 ASC Payment Indicator   ♂Male Only   ♀Female Only   🔀 Laboratory crosswalk

376   CPT only © 2008 American Medical Association. All Rights Reserved. (Black Ink)   Medicare (Red Ink)   © 2008 Ingenix (Blue Ink)

88309   Level VI - Surgical pathology, gross and microscopic
         examination   X 60 ▢
         INCLUDES   bone resection
                    breast, mastectomy-with regional lymph
                       nodes
                    colon:
                       total resection
                       segmental resection for tumor
                    esophagus, partial/total resection
                    extremity, disarticulation
                    fetus, with dissection
                    larynx, partial/total resection-with regional
                       lymph nodes
                    lung-total/lobe/segment resection
                    pancreas, total/subtotal resection
                    prostate, radical resection
                    small intestine, resection for tumor
                    soft tissue tumor, extensive resection
                    stomach, subtotal/total resection for tumor
                    testis, tumor
                    tongue/tonsil, resection for tumor
                    urinary bladder, partial/total resection
                    uterus, with or without tubes and ovaries,
                       neoplastic
                    vulva, total/subtotal resection

         EXCLUDES   *evaluation of fine needle aspirate
                       (88172-88173)*
                    fine needle aspiration (10021-10022)

         ⏢ 8.66   ⚖ 8.66 Global Days XXX
         AMA: 2008, Jan, 10-25; 2007, Jan, 13-27; 2007, Jan, 13-27; 2007,
         Jan, 28-31; 2007, January, 13-27; 2007, January, 28-31; 2007,
         Jan, 28-31; 2006, Dec, 1-3; 2006, Dec, 1-3; 2006, Dec, 1-3; 2006,
         Dec, 1-3; 2006, Dec, 1-3; 2006, Dec, 1-3; 2006, Dec, 1-3; 2006,
         December, 1-3; 2006, December, 1-3; 2006, December, 1-3;
         2006, December, 1-3; 2006, Dec, 1-3; 2005, Aug, 7-8; 2005, Aug,
         7-8; 2005, Aug, 9-10; 2005, August, 7-8; 2005, August, 9-10; 2005,
         July, 11-12; 2005, Aug, 9-10; 2005, Jul, 11-12; 2005, Jul, 11-12

88311-88399 Additional Surgical Pathology Services

CMS *100-4,12,60*   *Payment for Pathology Services*

+   88311   Decalcification procedure (List separately in addition to
              code for surgical pathology examination)   X 80
              Code first Code also surgical pathology exam
                 (88302-88309)
              ⏢ 0.50   ⚖ 0.50 Global Days XXX
              AMA: 2008, Jan, 10-25; 2007, Jan, 13-27; 2007, Jan, 13-27; 2007,
              January, 13-27; 2006, Dec, 1-3; 2006, Dec, 1-3; 2006, Dec, 1-3;
              2006, Dec, 1-3; 2006, December, 1-3; 2006, December, 1-3; 2006,
              December, 1-3; 2006, December, 1-3; 2006, Dec, 1-3; 2006, Dec,
              1-3; 2006, Dec, 1-3; 2006, Dec, 1-3; 2005, Aug, 9-10; 2005, August,
              7-8; 2005, August, 9-10; 2005, July, 11-12; 2005, Aug, 9-10; 2005,
              Jul, 11-12; 2005, Jul, 11-12; 2005, Aug, 7-8; 2005, Aug, 7-8; 2004,
              Jul, 1; 2004, July, 1; 2004, Jul, 1

+   88312   Special stains (List separately in addition to code for
              primary service); Group I for microorganisms (eg, Gridley,
              acid fast, methenamine silver), each   X 80
              Code first primary pathology procedure
              ⏢ 2.71   ⚖ 2.71 Global Days XXX
              AMA: 2008, Jan, 10-25; 2007, Jan, 13-27; 2007, Jan, 13-27; 2007,
              January, 13-27; 2006, Mar, 6-9; 2006, Mar, 6-9; 2006, Dec, 1-3;
              2006, Dec, 1-3; 2006, Dec, 1-3; 2006, Dec, 1-3; 2006, Dec, 1-3;
              2006, Dec, 1-3; 2006, Dec, 1-3; 2006, December, 1-3; 2006,
              December, 1-3; 2006, December, 1-3; 2006, December, 1-3;
              2006, March, 6-9; 2006, Dec, 1-3; 2005, Aug, 9-10; 2005, Aug,
              9-10; 2005, Jul, 11-12; 2005, August, 9-10; 2005, August, 7-8;
              2005, July, 11-12; 2005, Jul, 11-12; 2005, Aug, 7-8; 2005, Aug,
              1-8

+   88313   Group II, all other (eg, iron, trichrome), except
              immunocytochemistry and immunoperoxidase stains,
              each   X 60 ▢
              Code first primary pathology procedure
              EXCLUDES   *immunocytochemistry and immunoperoxidase
                         tissue studies (88342)*
              ⏢ 1.98   ⚖ 1.98 Global Days XXX
              AMA: 2008, Jan, 10-25; 2007, Jan, 13-27; 2007, Jan, 13-27; 2007,
              January, 13-27; 2006, Mar, 6-9; 2006, Mar, 6-9; 2006, Jun, 16-17;
              2006, Dec, 1-3; 2006, Dec, 1-3; 2006, Dec, 1-3; 2006, Jun, 16-17;
              2006, Dec, 1-3; 2006, Dec, 1-3; 2006, December, 1-3; 2006,
              December, 1-3; 2006, December, 1-3; 2006, December, 1-3;
              2006, June, 16-17; 2006, March, 6-9; 2006, Dec, 1-3; 2006, Dec,
              1-3; 2006, Dec, 1-3; 2005, Aug, 7-8; 2005, Aug, 7-8; 2005, August,
              9-10; 2005, August, 7-8; 2005, July, 11-12; 2005, Aug, 9-10; 2005,
              Aug, 9-10; 2005, Jul, 11-12; 2005, Jul, 11-12

+   88314   histochemical staining with frozen section(s)   X 80
              Code first primary pathology procedure
              Do not report with routine frozen section stain during
                 Mohs surgery (17311-17315)
              ⏢ 2.42   ⚖ 2.42 Global Days XXX
              AMA: 2006, Dec, 1-3; 2006, Dec, 1-3; 2006, Dec, 1-3; 2006, Dec,
              1-3; 2006, Dec, 1-3; 2006, December, 1-3; 2006, December, 1-3;
              2006, December, 1-3; 2006, December, 1-3; 2006, Dec, 1-3; 2006,
              Dec, 1-3; 2006, Dec, 1-3; 2005, Aug, 7-8; 2005, August, 7-8; 2005,
              August, 9-10; 2005, July, 11-12; 2005, Aug, 7-8; 2005, Aug, 9-10;
              2005, Aug, 9-10; 2005, Jul, 11-12; 2005, Jul, 11-12; 2004, Jul, 1;
              2004, July, 1; 2004, Jul, 1

88318   Determinative histochemistry to identify chemical
         components (eg, copper, zinc)   X 80
         ⏢ 2.72   ⚖ 2.72 Global Days XXX
         AMA: 2005, Aug, 9-10; 2005, Aug, 9-10; 2005, Jul, 11-12; 2005,
         Jul, 11-12; 2005, Aug, 7-8; 2005, Aug, 7-8; 2005, August, 9-10;
         2005, August, 7-8; 2005, July, 11-12

88319   Determinative histochemistry or cytochemistry to
         identify enzyme constituents, each   X 80
         ⏢ 3.78   ⚖ 3.78 Global Days XXX
         AMA: 2005, Jul, 11-12; 2005, Jul, 11-12; 2005, Aug, 7-8; 2005,
         Aug, 7-8; 2005, Aug, 9-10; 2005, Aug, 9-10; 2005, July, 11-12;
         2005, August, 9-10; 2005, August, 7-8

88321   Consultation and report on referred slides prepared
         elsewhere   X 60 ▢
         ⏢ 2.18   ⚖ 2.42 Global Days XXX
         AMA: 2008, Jan, 10-25; 2007, Jan, 13-27; 2007, Jan, 13-27; 2007,
         January, 13-27; 2005, Aug, 9-10; 2005, Aug, 9-10; 2005, Jul,
         11-12; 2005, August, 9-10; 2005, August, 7-8; 2005, July, 11-12;
         2005, Jul, 11-12; 2005, Aug, 7-8; 2005, Aug, 7-8

88323   Consultation and report on referred material requiring
         preparation of slides   X 60 ▢
         ⏢ 3.92   ⚖ 3.92 Global Days XXX
         AMA: 2008, Jan, 10-25; 2007, Jan, 13-27; 2007, Jan, 13-27; 2007,
         January, 13-27; 2005, Aug, 7-8; 2005, Aug, 7-8; 2005, Aug, 9-10;
         2005, July, 11-12; 2005, August, 7-8; 2005, August, 9-10; 2005,
         Aug, 9-10; 2005, Jul, 11-12; 2005, Jul, 11-12

88325   Consultation, comprehensive, with review of records and
         specimens, with report on referred material   X 60 ▢
         ⏢ 3.39   ⚖ 5.21 Global Days XXX
         AMA: 2008, Jan, 10-25; 2007, Jan, 13-27; 2007, Jan, 13-27; 2007,
         January, 13-27; 2005, Aug, 9-10; 2005, Aug, 9-10; 2005, Aug,
         7-8; 2005, July, 11-12; 2005, August, 7-8; 2005, August, 9-10;
         2005, Aug, 7-8; 2005, Jul, 11-12; 2005, Jul, 11-12

Ⓖ Modifier 63 Exempt Code   ⊙ Moderate Sedation   + CPT Add-on Code   Ⓢ Modifier 51 Exempt Code   ● New Code   ▲ Revised Code

M Maternity Edit   A Age Edit   X CLIA Waived Test   A Y APC Status Indicators   ▢ CCI Comprehensive Code   50 Bilateral Procedure

© 2008 Ingenix *(Blue Ink)*   CPT only © 2008 American Medical Association. All Rights Reserved. (Black Ink)   Medicare (Red Ink)   377

88329 Pathology consultation during surgery; ☒ 80 ▢

📖 0.92 ⚕ 1.35 **Global Days XXX**

AMA: 2008, Jan, 10-25; 2007, Jan, 13-27; 2007, Jan, 13-27; 2007, Jan, 28-31; 2007, Jan, 28-31; 2007, January, 13-27; 2007, January, 28-31; 2005, Jul, 11-12; 2005, Jul, 11-12; 2005, July, 11-12; 2005, August, 7-8; 2005, August, 9-10; 2005, Aug, 9-10; 2005, Aug, 9-10; 2005, Aug, 7-8; 2005, Aug, 7-8

88331 first tissue block, with frozen section(s), single specimen ☒ 80 ▢

📖 2.46 ⚕ 2.46 **Global Days XXX**

AMA: 2007, Jan, 28-31; 2007, Jan, 28-31; 2007, January, 28-31; 2006, Mar, 6-9; 2006, Mar, 6-9; 2006, Dec, 1-3; 2006, Dec, 1-3; 2006, Dec, 1-3; 2006, December, 1-3; 2006, December, 1-3; 2006, December, 1-3; 2006, December, 1-3; 2006, March, 6-9; 2006, Dec, 1-3; 2006, Dec, 1-3; 2006, Dec, 1-3; 2006, Dec, 1-3; 2005, Jul, 11-12; 2005, August, 7-8; 2005, July, 11-12; 2005, August, 9-10; 2005, Jul, 11-12; 2005, Aug, 7-8; 2005, Aug, 7-8; 2005, Aug, 9-10; 2005, Aug, 9-10; 2004, Jul, 1; 2004, July, 1; 2004, Jul, 1

88332 each additional tissue block with frozen section(s) ☒ 80 ▢

📖 1.10 ⚕ 1.10 **Global Days XXX**

AMA: 2007, Jan, 28-31; 2007, Jan, 28-31; 2007, January, 28-31; 2006, Mar, 6-9; 2006, Mar, 6-9; 2006, Dec, 1-3; 2006, Dec, 1-3; 2006, Dec, 1-3; 2006, December, 1-3; 2006, December, 1-3; 2006, December, 1-3; 2006, December, 1-3; 2006, March, 6-9; 2006, Dec, 1-3; 2006, Dec, 1-3; 2006, Dec, 1-3; 2006, Dec, 1-3; 2005, Jul, 11-12; 2005, August, 7-8; 2005, July, 11-12; 2005, August, 9-10; 2005, Jul, 11-12; 2005, Aug, 9-10; 2005, Aug, 9-10; 2005, Aug, 7-8; 2005, Aug, 7-8; 2004, Jul, 1; 2004, July, 1; 2004, Jul, 1

88333 cytologic examination (eg, touch prep, squash prep), initial site ☒ 80

EXCLUDES *intraprocedural cytologic evaluation of fine needle aspirate (88172)*
nonintraoperative cytologic examination (88160-88162)

📖 2.52 ⚕ 2.52 **Global Days XXX**

AMA: 2008, Jun, 14-15; 2007, Jan, 28-31; 2007, Jan, 28-31; 2007, January, 28-31; 2006, Mar, 6-9; 2006, March, 6-9; 2006, Mar, 6-9; 2005, Aug, 9-10; 2005, August, 7-8; 2005, August, 9-10; 2005, Aug, 9-10; 2005, Aug, 7-8; 2005, Aug, 7-8

88334 cytologic examination (eg, touch prep, squash prep), each additional site ☒ 80

EXCLUDES *intraoperative consultation on a specimen requiring both frozen section and cytologic evaluation (88331, 88334)*
intraprocedural cytologic evaluation of fine needle aspirate (88172)
nonintraoperative cytologic examination (88160-88162)
percutaneous needle biopsy requiring intraprocedural cytologic examination (88333)

📖 1.52 ⚕ 1.52 **Global Days XXX**

AMA: 2007, Jan, 28-31; 2007, Jan, 28-31; 2007, January, 28-31; 2006, Mar, 6-9; 2006, March, 6-9; 2006, Mar, 6-9; 2005, Aug, 9-10; 2005, August, 9-10; 2005, August, 7-8; 2005, Aug, 9-10; 2005, Aug, 7-8; 2005, Aug, 7-8

88342 Immunohistochemistry (including tissue immunoperoxidase), each antibody ☒ 80 ▢

EXCLUDES *quantitative or semiquantitative immunohistochemistry (88360-88361)*

Do not report with testing on the same antibody (88360-88361)

📖 2.72 ⚕ 2.72 **Global Days XXX**

AMA: 2008, Jan, 10-25; 2007, Jan, 13-27; 2007, Jan, 13-27; 2007, January, 13-27; 2006, Dec, 1-3; 2006, Dec, 1-3; 2006, Dec, 1-3; 2006, Dec, 1-3; 2006, December, 1-3; 2006, December, 1-3; 2006, December, 1-3; 2006, December, 1-3; 2006, Dec, 1-3; 2006, Dec, 1-3; 2006, Dec, 1-3; 2005, Aug, 9-10; 2005, August, 7-8; 2005, July, 11-12; 2005, August, 9-10; 2005, Aug, 9-10; 2005, Jul, 11-12; 2005, Jul, 11-12; 2005, Aug, 7-8; 2005, Aug, 7-8; 2004, Jul, 1; 2004, July, 1; 2004, Jul, 1

88346 Immunofluorescent study, each antibody; direct method ☒ 80

📖 2.73 ⚕ 2.73 **Global Days XXX**

AMA: 2005, Aug, 7-8; 2005, Aug, 7-8; 2005, Aug, 9-10; 2005, Aug, 9-10; 2005, Jul, 11-12; 2005, Jul, 11-12; 2005, July, 11-12; 2005, August, 9-10; 2005, August, 7-8

88347 indirect method ☒ 80

📖 2.16 ⚕ 2.16 **Global Days XXX**

AMA: 2005, Jul, 11-12; 2005, Jul, 11-12; 2005, Aug, 7-8; 2005, Aug, 7-8; 2005, Aug, 9-10; 2005, Aug, 9-10; 2005, July, 11-12; 2005, August, 9-10; 2005, August, 7-8

88348 Electron microscopy; diagnostic ☒ 80 ▢

📖 17.12 ⚕ 17.12 **Global Days XXX**

AMA: 2005, Aug, 7-8; 2005, Aug, 7-8; 2005, Aug, 9-10; 2005, Aug, 9-10; 2005, Jul, 11-12; 2005, Jul, 11-12; 2005, July, 11-12; 2005, August, 9-10; 2005, August, 7-8

88349 scanning ☒ 80

📖 8.15 ⚕ 8.15 **Global Days XXX**

AMA: 2005, Aug, 9-10; 2005, Aug, 9-10; 2005, Aug, 7-8; 2005, Aug, 7-8; 2005, Jul, 11-12; 2005, Jul, 11-12; 2005, July, 11-12; 2005, August, 9-10; 2005, August, 7-8

88355 Morphometric analysis; skeletal muscle ☒ 80 ▢

📖 6.55 ⚕ 6.55 **Global Days XXX**

AMA: 2005, Jul, 11-12; 2005, Jul, 11-12; 2005, Aug, 9-10; 2005, Aug, 9-10; 2005, Aug, 7-8; 2005, Aug, 7-8; 2005, July, 11-12; 2005, August, 9-10; 2005, August, 7-8

88356 nerve ☒ 80 ▢

📖 7.94 ⚕ 7.94 **Global Days XXX**

AMA: 2005, Jul, 11-12; 2005, Jul, 11-12; 2005, Aug, 7-8; 2005, Aug, 7-8; 2005, Aug, 9-10; 2005, Aug, 9-10; 2005, July, 11-12; 2005, August, 9-10; 2005, August, 7-8

88358 tumor (eg, DNA ploidy) ☒ 80 ▢

Do not report with 88313 unless each procedure is for a different special stain (88313)

📖 2.15 ⚕ 2.15 **Global Days XXX**

AMA: 2008, Jan, 10-25; 2007, Jan, 13-27; 2007, Jan, 13-27; 2007, January, 13-27; 2006, Jun, 16-17; 2006, Jun, 16-17; 2006, June, 16-17; 2005, Jul, 11-12; 2005, Jul, 11-12; 2005, August, 9-10; 2005, August, 7-8; 2005, July, 11-12; 2005, Aug, 9-10; 2005, Aug, 9-10; 2005, Aug, 7-8; 2005, Aug, 7-8

88360 Morphometric analysis, tumor immunohistochemistry (eg, Her-2/neu, estrogen receptor/progesterone receptor), quantitative or semiquantitative, each antibody; manual ☒ 80 ▢

Do not report with 88342 unless each test is for different antibody (88342)

📖 3.29 ⚕ 3.29 **Global Days XXX**

AMA: 2005, Jul, 11-12; 2005, Jul, 11-12; 2005, Aug, 7-8; 2005, Aug, 7-8; 2005, Aug, 9-10; 2005, Aug, 9-10; 2005, August, 9-10; 2005, July, 11-12; 2005, August, 7-8

26/TC Professional/Technical Component Only   80/80 Assist-at-Surgery Allowed/With Documentation   Unlisted   Not Covered   ☒ Radiology crosswalk

MED: Pub 100/NCD References   AMA: CPT Assistant References   A2-Z3 ASC Payment Indicator   ♂Male Only   ♀Female Only   ◼ Laboratory crosswalk

378   CPT only © 2008 American Medical Association. All Rights Reserved. (Black Ink)   Medicare (Red Ink)   © 2008 Ingenix *(Blue Ink)*

88361   **using computer-assisted technology**   ⓧ 80 ▭

> EXCLUDES   *morphometric analysis using in situ hybridization techniques (88367-88368)*

Do not report with 88342 unless each test is for different antibody (88342)

🚗 4.17   ⚖ 4.17   Global Days XXX
AMA: 2005, Jul, 11-12; 2005, Jul, 11-12; 2005, Aug, 9-10; 2005, Aug, 9-10; 2005, Aug, 7-8; 2005, Aug, 7-8; 2005, August, 9-10; 2005, July, 11-12; 2005, August, 7-8

88362   **Nerve teasing preparations**   ⓧ 80 ▭

🚗 7.19   ⚖ 7.19   Global Days XXX
AMA: 2005, Aug, 7-8; 2005, Aug, 7-8; 2005, Aug, 9-10; 2005, Aug, 9-10; 2005, Jul, 11-12; 2005, Jul, 11-12; 2005, August, 9-10; 2005, July, 11-12; 2005, August, 7-8

88365   **In situ hybridization (eg, FISH), each probe**   ⓧ 80 ▭

Do not report with 88367-88368 for the same probe (88367-88368)

🚗 4.28   ⚖ 4.28   Global Days XXX
AMA: 2008, Jan, 10-25; 2007, Jan, 13-27; 2007, Jan, 13-27; 2007, January, 13-27; 2005, Jul, 11-12; 2005, Jul, 11-12; 2005, Aug, 9-10; 2005, Aug, 9-10; 2005, March, 16-17; 2005, August, 7-8; 2005, July, 11-12; 2005, August, 9-10; 2005, Mar, 16-17; 2005, Mar, 16-17; 2005, Aug, 7-8; 2005, Aug, 7-8

88367   **Morphometric analysis, in situ hybridization (quantitative or semi-quantitative) each probe; using computer-assisted technology**   ⓧ 80 ▭

🚗 6.58   ⚖ 6.58   Global Days XXX
AMA: 2008, Jan, 10-25; 2007, Jan, 13-27; 2007, Jan, 13-27; 2007, January, 13-27; 2005, Jul, 11-12; 2005, Jul, 11-12; 2005, Mar, 16-17; 2005, Mar, 16-17; 2005, March, 16-17; 2005, August, 7-8; 2005, August, 9-10; 2005, July, 11-12; 2005, Aug, 9-10; 2005, Aug, 9-10; 2005, Aug, 7-8; 2005, Aug, 7-8

88368   **manual**   ⓧ 80 ▭

🚗 5.79   ⚖ 5.79   Global Days XXX
AMA: 2008, Jan, 10-25; 2007, Jan, 13-27; 2007, Jan, 13-27; 2007, January, 13-27; 2005, Aug, 9-10; 2005, Aug, 9-10; 2005, Aug, 7-8, 2005, Aug, 7-8; 2005, March, 16-17; 2005, August, 9-10; 2005, August, 7-8; 2005, July, 11-12; 2005, Mar, 16-17; 2005, Mar, 16-17; 2005, Jul, 11-12; 2005, Jul, 11-12

88371   **Protein analysis of tissue by Western Blot, with interpretation and report;**   Ⓐ 80 ▭

🚗 0.00   ⚖ 0.00   Global Days XXX
AMA: 2005, Jul, 11-12; 2005, Jul, 11-12; 2005, Aug, 9-10; 2005, Aug, 9-10; 2005, Aug, 7-8; 2005, Aug, 7-8; 2005, July, 11-12; 2005, August, 9-10; 2005, August, 7-8

88372   **immunological probe for band identification, each**   Ⓐ 80 ▭

🚗 0.00   ⚖ 0.00   Global Days XXX
AMA: 2005, Jul, 11-12; 2005, Jul, 11-12; 2005, Aug, 7-8; 2005, Aug, 7-8; 2005, Aug, 9-10; 2005, July, 11-12; 2005, August, 9-10; 2005, August, 7-8

88380   **Microdissection (ie, sample preparation of microscopically identified target); laser capture**   Ⓝ 80

🚗 5.39   ⚖ 5.39   Global Days XXX
AMA: 2008, Apr, 5-7; 2008, Apr, 5-7; 2008, Apr, 5-7; 2005, Jul, 11-12; 2006, Jul, 11-12; 2005, July, 11-12; 2005, August, 7-8; 2005, August, 9-10; 2005, Aug, 9-10; 2005, Aug, 9-10; 2005, Aug, 7-8; 2005, Aug, 7-8

88381   **manual**   Ⓝ 80

Do not report with 88381

🚗 5.87   ⚖ 5.87   Global Days XXX
AMA: 2008, Apr, 5-7; 2008, Apr, 5-7; 2008, Apr, 5-7

88384   **Array-based evaluation of multiple molecular probes; 11 through 50 probes**   ⓧ 80

🚗 0.00   ⚖ 0.00   Global Days XXX
AMA: 2006, Jan, 5-6,48; 2006, Jan, 5-6,48; 2006, Mar, 6-9; 2006, March, 6-9; 2006, January, 5-6,48; 2006, Mar, 6-9; 2005, Aug, 9-10; 2005, August, 7-8; 2005, August, 9-10; 2005, Aug, 9-10; 2005, Aug, 7-8; 2005, Aug, 7-8

88385   **51 through 250 probes**   ⓧ 80

🚗 14.36   ⚖ 14.36   Global Days XXX
AMA: 2008, May, 5-8; 2006, Mar, 6-9; 2006, Mar, 6-9; 2006, Jan, 5-6,48; 2006, March, 6-9; 2006, January, 5-6,48; 2006, Jan, 5-6,48; 2005, Aug, 9-10; 2005, August, 7-8; 2005, August, 9-10; 2005, Aug, 9-10; 2005, Aug, 7-8; 2005, Aug, 7-8

88386   **251 through 500 probes**   ⓧ 80

> EXCLUDES   *preparation and analysis of fewer than 11 probes (83890-83914)*
> *preparation of array-based evaluation (83890-83892, 83898-83901)*

🚗 18.39   ⚖ 18.39   Global Days XXX
AMA: 2008, May, 5-8; 2008, May, 9-11; 2006, Jan, 5-6,48; 2006, Jan, 5-6,48; 2006, Mar, 6-9; 2006, March, 6-9; 2006, January, 5-6,48; 2006, Mar, 6-9; 2005, Aug, 9-10; 2005, August, 7-8; 2005, August, 9-10; 2005, Aug, 9-10; 2005, Aug, 7-8; 2005, Aug, 7-8

88399   **Unlisted surgical pathology procedure**   ⓧ 80

🚗 0.00   ⚖ 0.00   Global Days XXX
AMA: 2008, May, 9-11; 2005, Jul, 11-12; 2005, Jul, 11-12; 2005, Aug, 9-10; 2005, Aug, 9-10; 2005, Aug, 7-8; 2005, July, 11-12; 2005, August, 9-10; 2005, August, 7-8

88720-88741 Transcutaneous Procedures

● **88720**   **Bilirubin, total, transcutaneous**   Ⓐ

> EXCLUDES   *transdermal oxygen saturation testing (94760-94762)*

🚗 0.00   ⚖ 0.00   Global Days XXX

● **88740**   **Hemoglobin, quantitative, transcutaneous, per day; carboxyhemoglobin**   Ⓐ

> EXCLUDES   *in vitro carboxyhemoglobin measurement (82375)*

🚗 0.00   ⚖ 0.00   Global Days XXX

● **88741**   **methemoglobin**   Ⓐ

> EXCLUDES   *in vitro quantitative methemoglobin measurement (83050)*

🚗 0.00   ⚖ 0.00   Global Days XXX

89049-89240 Other Pathology Services

CMS *100-4,3,10.4*   *Payment of Nonphysician Services for Inpatients*

89049   **Caffeine halothane contracture test (CHCT) for malignant hyperthermia susceptibility, including interpretation and report**   ⓧ 80

🚗 1.88   ⚖ 6.53   Global Days XXX
AMA: 2008, Jan, 10-25; 2007, Jan, 13-27; 2007, Jan, 13-27; 2007, January, 13-27; 2006, Mar, 6-9; 2006, Mar, 6-9; 2006, March, 6-9; 2006, May, 16-20; 2006, May, 16-20; 2006, May, 16-20; 2005, Aug, 7-8; 2005, Aug, 7-8; 2005, Aug, 9-10; 2005, August, 7-8; 2005, August, 9-10; 2005, Aug, 9-10

89050   **Cell count, miscellaneous body fluids (eg, cerebrospinal fluid, joint fluid), except blood;**   Ⓐ ▭

🚗 0.00   ⚖ 0.00   Global Days XXX
AMA: 2005, Aug, 9-10; 2005, Aug, 9-10; 2005, Aug, 7-8; 2005, Aug, 7-8; 2005, Jul, 11-12; 2005, Jul, 11-12; 2005, July, 11-12; 2005, August, 9-10; 2005, August, 7-8

---

63 Modifier 63 Exempt Code   ⊙ Moderate Sedation   + CPT Add on Code   ⦰ Modifier 51 Exempt Code   ● New Code   ▲ Revised Code

Ⓜ Maternity Edit   Ⓐ Age Edit   ⓧ CLIA Waived Test   Ⓐ-Ⓨ APC Status Indicators   ▭ CCI Comprehensive Code   80 Bilateral Procedure

89051   with differential count   Ⓐ ▭
    🚗 0.00   ⚕ 0.00   **Global Days XXX**

AMA: 2005, Jul, 11-12; 2005, Jul, 11-12; 2005, Aug, 9-10; 2005, Aug, 9-10; 2005, Aug, 7-8; 2005, Aug, 7-8; 2005, July, 11-12; 2005, August, 9-10; 2005, August, 7-8

89055   Leukocyte assessment, fecal, qualitative or semiquantitative   Ⓐ
    🚗 0.00   ⚕ 0.00   **Global Days XXX**

AMA: 2005, Jul, 11-12; 2005, Jul, 11-12; 2005, Aug, 9-10; Aug, 9-10; 2005, Aug, 7-8; 2005, Aug, 7-8; 2005, July, 11-12; 2005, August, 9-10; 2005, August, 7-8

89060   Crystal identification by light microscopy with or without polarizing lens analysis, tissue or any body fluid (except urine)   80 ▭
      EXCLUDES   *crystal identification on paraffin embedded tissue (89060)*
    🚗 0.00   ⚕ 0.00   **Global Days XXX**

AMA: 2005, Aug, 7-8; 2005, Aug, 7-8; 2005, Jul, 11-12; 2005, Jul, 11-12; 2005, Aug, 9-10; 2005, Aug, 9-10; 2005, July, 11-12; 2005, August, 7-8; 2005, August, 9-10

89100   Duodenal intubation and aspiration; single specimen (eg, simple bile study or afferent loop culture) plus appropriate test procedure   Ⓧ 80 ▭
    🚗 1.07   ⚕ 6.62   **Global Days XXX**

AMA: 2005, Aug, 9-10; 2005, Aug, 9-10; 2005, Jul, 11-12; 2005, Jul, 11-12; 2005, Aug, 7-8; 2005, Aug, 7-8; 2005, July, 11-12; 2005, August, 9-10; 2005, August, 7-8

89105   collection of multiple fractional specimens with pancreatic or gallbladder stimulation, single or double lumen tube   Ⓧ 80 ▭
      EXCLUDES   *chemical analyses (see chemistry codes)*
        electrocardiogram (93000-93268)
        esophagus acid perfusion test (Berstein) (91030)

    ⬚ *74340*
    🚗 0.91   ⚕ 6.80   **Global Days XXX**

AMA: 2005, Jul, 11-12; 2005, Jul, 11-12; 2005, Aug, 7-8; 2005, Aug, 7-8; 2005, Aug, 9-10; 2005, Aug, 9-10; 2005, July, 11-12; 2005, August, 9-10; 2005, August, 7-8

89125   Fat stain, feces, urine, or respiratory secretions   Ⓐ ▭
    🚗 0.00   ⚕ 0.00   **Global Days XXX**

AMA: 2005, Aug, 9-10; 2005, Aug, 9-10; 2005, Jul, 11-12; 2005, Jul, 11-12; 2005, Aug, 7-8; 2005, Aug, 7-8; 2005, July, 11-12; 2005, August, 9-10; 2005, August, 7-8

89130   Gastric intubation and aspiration, diagnostic, each specimen, for chemical analyses or cytopathology;   Ⓧ 80 ▭
    🚗 0.79   ⚕ 5.76   **Global Days XXX**

AMA: 2005, Aug, 9-10; 2005, Aug, 9-10; 2005, Aug, 7-8; 2005, Aug, 7-8; 2005, Jul, 11-12; 2005, Jul, 11-12; 2005, July, 11-12; 2005, August, 9-10; 2005, August, 7-8

89132   after stimulation   Ⓧ 80 ▭
    🚗 0.50   ⚕ 6.56   **Global Days XXX**

AMA: 2005, Aug, 7-8; 2005, Aug, 7-8; 2005, Aug, 9-10; 2005, Aug, 9-10; 2005, Jul, 11-12; 2005, Jul, 11-12; 2005, July, 11-12; 2005, August, 9-10; 2005, August, 7-8

89135   Gastric intubation, aspiration, and fractional collections (eg, gastric secretory study); 1 hour   Ⓧ 80 ▭
    🚗 1.41   ⚕ 7.84   **Global Days XXX**

AMA: 2005, Aug, 7-8; 2005, Aug, 7-8; 2005, Aug, 9-10; 2005, Aug, 9-10; 2005, Jul, 11-12; 2005, Jul, 11-12; 2005, July, 11-12; 2005, August, 9-10; 2005, August, 7-8

89136   2 hours   Ⓧ 80 ▭
    🚗 0.47   ⚕ 5.56   **Global Days XXX**

AMA: 2005, Aug, 9-10; 2005, Aug, 9-10; 2005, Jul, 11-12; 2005, Jul, 11-12; 2005, Aug, 7-8; 2005, Aug, 7-8; 2005, August, 9-10; 2005, August, 7-8; 2005, July, 11-12

89140   2 hours including gastric stimulation (eg, histalog, pentagastrin)   Ⓧ 80 ▭
    🚗 1.43   ⚕ 6.51   **Global Days XXX**

AMA: 2005, Aug, 9-10; 2005, Aug, 9-10; 2005, Aug, 7-8; 2005, Aug, 7-8; 2005, Jul, 11-12; 2005, Jul, 11-12; 2005, July, 11-12; 2005, August, 9-10; 2005, August, 7-8

89141   3 hours, including gastric stimulation   Ⓧ 80 ▭
      EXCLUDES   *chemical analyses (82926, 82928)*
        joint fluid chemistry (see chemistry codes)
        therapeutic gastric lavage (91105)

    ⬚ *74340*
    🚗 1.35   ⚕ 6.73   **Global Days XXX**

AMA: 2005, Jul, 11-12; 2005, Jul, 11-12; 2005, Aug, 7-8; 2005, Aug, 7-8; 2005, Aug, 9-10; 2005, Aug, 9-10; 2005, July, 11-12; 2005, August, 9-10; 2005, August, 7-8

89160   Meat fibers, feces   Ⓐ ▭
    🚗 0.00   ⚕ 0.00   **Global Days XXX**

AMA: 2005, Aug, 7-8; 2005, Aug, 7-8; 2005, Aug, 9-10; 2005, Aug, 9-10; 2005, Jul, 11-12; 2005, Jul, 11-12; 2005, July, 11-12; 2005, August, 9-10; 2005, August, 7-8

89190   Nasal smear for eosinophils   Ⓐ ▭
      EXCLUDES   *occult blood, feces (82270)*
        paternity tests (86910)
    🚗 0.00   ⚕ 0.00   **Global Days XXX**

AMA: 2005, Aug, 9-10; 2005, Aug, 9-10; 2005, Aug, 7-8; 2005, Aug, 7-8; 2005, Jul, 11-12; 2005, Jul, 11-12; 2005, July, 11-12; 2005, August, 9-10; 2005, August, 7-8

89220   Sputum, obtaining specimen, aerosol induced technique (separate procedure)   Ⓧ TC 80
    🚗 0.41   ⚕ 0.41   **Global Days XXX**

AMA: 2005, Aug, 9-10; 2005, Aug, 9-10; 2005, Jul, 11-12; 2005, Jul, 11-12; 2005, Aug, 7-8; 2005, Aug, 7-8; 2005, July, 11-12; 2005, August, 9-10; 2005, August, 7-8

89225   Starch granules, feces   Ⓐ ▭
    🚗 0.00   ⚕ 0.00   **Global Days XXX**

AMA: 2005, Jul, 11-12; 2005, Jul, 11-12; 2005, Aug, 7-8; 2005, Aug, 7-8; 2005, Aug, 9-10; 2005, Aug, 9-10; 2005, July, 11-12; 2005, August, 7-8; 2005, August, 9-10

89230   Sweat collection by iontophoresis   Ⓧ TC 80 ▭
    🚗 0.11   ⚕ 0.11   **Global Days XXX**

AMA: 2005, Jul, 11-12; 2005, Jul, 11-12; 2005, Aug, 9-10; 2005, Aug, 9-10; 2005, Aug, 7-8; 2005, Aug, 7-8; 2005, August, 9-10; 2005, July, 11-12; 2005, August, 7-8

89235   Water load test   Ⓐ ▭
    🚗 0.00   ⚕ 0.00   **Global Days XXX**

AMA: 2005, Aug, 7-8; 2005, Aug, 7-8; 2005, Jul, 11-12; 2005, Jul, 11-12; 2005, Aug, 9-10; 2005, Aug, 9-10; 2005, August, 9-10; 2005, July, 11-12; 2005, August, 7-8

89240   Unlisted miscellaneous pathology test   Ⓧ 80
    🚗 0.00   ⚕ 0.00   **Global Days XXX**

AMA: 2008, Jan, 10-25; 2007, Jan, 13-27; 2007, Jan, 13-27; 2007, January, 13-27; 2005, Jul, 11-12; 2005, Jul, 11-12; 2005, Aug, 7-8; 2005, Aug, 7-8; 2005, July, 11-12; 2005, November, 14-15; 2005, August, 7-8; 2005, August, 9-10; 2005, Nov, 14-15; 2005, Nov, 14-15; 2005, Aug, 9-10; 2005, Aug, 9-10

26/TC Professional/Technical Component Only   80/80 Assist-at-Surgery Allowed/With Documentation   Unlisted   Not Covered   ☢ Radiology crosswalk

MED: Pub 100/NCD References   **AMA:** CPT Assistant References   A2-Z3 ASC Payment Indicator   ♂Male Only   ♀Female Only   ◣ Laboratory crosswalk

380   CPT only © 2008 American Medical Association. All Rights Reserved. (Black Ink)   Medicare **(Red Ink)**   © 2008 Ingenix *(Blue Ink)*

89250-89356 Infertility Treatment Services

CMS 100-2,1,100   *Treatment for Infertility*
CMS 100-4,3,10.4   *Payment of Nonphysician Services for Inpatients*

89250   Culture of oocyte(s)/embryo(s), less than 4 days;   ♀ ☒
   📠 0.00   ✂ 0.00   Global Days XXX
   AMA: 2008, Jan, 10-25; 2007, Jan, 13-27; 2007, Jan, 13-27; 2007, January, 13-27; 2005, Jul, 11-12; 2005, Jul, 11-12; 2005, Aug, 7-8; 2005, August, 9-10; 2005, August, 7-8; 2005, July, 11-12; 2005, Aug, 9-10; 2005, Aug, 9-10; 2005, Aug, 7-8; 2004, May, 16; 2004, June, 7; 2004, May, 16; 2004, Apr, 1; 2004, Apr, 1; 2004, April, 1; 2004, May, 16; 2004, Jun, 7; 2004, Jun, 7

89251   with co-culture of oocyte(s)/embryos   ♀ ☒ ▢
   EXCLUDES   *extended culture of oocyte(s)/embryo(s) (89272)*
   📠 0.00   ✂ 0.00   Global Days XXX
   AMA: 2008, Jan, 10-25; 2007, Jan, 13-27; 2007, Jan, 13-27; 2007, January, 13-27; 2005, Aug, 9-10; 2005, Aug, 9-10; 2005, Jul, 11-12; 2005, Aug, 7-8; 2005, Jul, 11-12; 2005, Aug, 7-8; 2005, August, 9-10; 2005, August, 7-8; 2005, July, 11-12; 2004, May, 16; 2004, May, 16; 2004, May, 16; 2004, April, 1; 2004, Apr, 1; 2004, Apr, 1

89253   Assisted embryo hatching, microtechniques (any method)   ☒
   📠 0.00   ✂ 0.00   Global Days XXX
   AMA: 2008, Jan, 10-25; 2007, Jan, 13-27; 2007, Jan, 13-27; 2007, January, 13-27; 2005, Jul, 11-12; 2005, Jul, 11-12; 2005, Aug, 7-8; 2005, Aug, 9-10; 2005, Aug, 7-8; 2005, Aug, 9-10; 2005, August, 9-10; 2005, August, 7-8; 2005, July, 11-12; 2004, Apr, 1; 2004, Apr, 1; 2004, May, 16; 2004, April, 1; 2004, May, 16; 2004, May, 16

89254   Oocyte identification from follicular fluid   ♀ ☒
   📠 0.00   ✂ 0.00   Global Days XXX
   AMA: 2008, Jan, 10-25; 2007, Jan, 13-27; 2007, Jan, 13-27; 2007, January, 13-27; 2005, Aug, 7-8; 2005, Aug, 7-8; 2005, Aug, 9-10; 2005, Jul, 11-12; 2005, Aug, 9-10; 2005, Jul, 11-12; 2005, August, 9-10; 2005, August, 7-8; 2005, July, 11-12; 2004, May, 16; 2004, May, 16; 2004, May, 16; 2004, April, 1; 2004, Apr, 1; 2004, Apr, 1

89255   Preparation of embryo for transfer (any method)   ☒
   📠 0.00   ✂ 0.00   Global Days XXX
   AMA: 2008, Jan, 10-25; 2007, Jan, 13-27; 2007, Jan, 13-27; 2007, January, 13-27; 2005, Aug, 7-8; 2005, Aug, 7-8; 2005, Aug, 9-10; 2005, Jul, 11-12; 2005, Aug, 9-10; 2005, Jul, 11-12; 2005, August, 9-10; 2005, August, 7-8; 2005, July, 11-12; 2004, May, 16; 2004, May, 16; 2004, April, 1; 2004, May, 16; 2004, Apr, 1; 2004, Apr, 1

89257   Sperm identification from aspiration (other than seminal fluid)   ☒ ▢
   EXCLUDES   *semen analysis (89300-89320)*
         sperm identification from testis tissue (89264)
   📠 0.00   ✂ 0.00   Global Days XXX
   AMA: 2008, Jan, 10-25; 2007, Jan, 13-27; 2007, Jan, 13-27; 2007, January, 13-27; 2005, Aug, 9-10; 2005, Aug, 9-10; 2005, Aug, 7-8; 2005, Jul, 11-12; 2005, Aug, 7-8; 2005, Jul, 11-12; 2005, August, 7-8; 2005, July, 11-12; 2005, August, 9-10; 2004, Apr, 1; 2004, Apr, 1; 2004, May, 16; 2004, April, 1; 2004, May, 16; 2004, May, 16

89258   Cryopreservation; embryo(s)   ☒
   📠 0.00   ✂ 0.00   Global Days XXX
   AMA: 2008, Jan, 10-25; 2007, Jan, 13-27; 2007, Jan, 13-27; 2007, January, 13-27; 2005, Aug, 7-8; 2005, Aug, 7-8; 2005, Aug, 9-10; 2005, Jul, 11-12; 2005, Aug, 9-10; 2005, Jul, 11-12; 2005, August, 9-10; 2005, August, 7-8; 2005, July, 11-12; 2004, May, 16; 2004, May, 16; 2004, May, 16; 2004, April, 1; 2004, Apr, 1; 2004, Apr, 1

89259   sperm   ☒
   EXCLUDES   *cryopreservation of testicular reproductive tissue (89335)*
   📠 0.00   ✂ 0.00   Global Days XXX
   AMA: 2008, Jan, 10-25; 2007, Jan, 13-27; 2007, Jan, 13-27; 2007, January, 13-27; 2005, Aug, 9-10; 2005, Aug, 9-10; 2005, Jul, 11-12; 2005, Aug, 7-8; 2005, Jul, 11-12; 2005, Aug, 7-8; 2005, August, 9-10; 2005, August, 7-8; 2005, July, 11-12; 2004, Apr, 1; 2004, Apr, 1; 2004, April, 1; 2004, May, 16; 2004, May, 16; 2004, May, 16

89260   Sperm isolation; simple prep (eg, sperm wash and swim-up) for insemination or diagnosis with semen analysis   ☒ ▢
   📠 0.00   ✂ 0.00   Global Days XXX
   AMA: 2008, Jan, 10-25; 2007, Jan, 13-27; 2007, Jan, 13-27; 2007, January, 13-27; 2005, Jul, 11-12; 2005, Jul, 11-12; 2005, Aug, 7-8; 2005, Aug, 9-10; 2005, Aug, 7-8; 2005, Aug, 9-10; 2005, August, 9-10; 2005, August, 7-8; 2005, July, 11-12; 2004, May, 16; 2004, May, 16; 2004, May, 16; 2004, April, 1; 2004, Apr, 1; 2004, Apr, 1

89261   complex prep (eg, Percoll gradient, albumin gradient) for insemination or diagnosis with semen analysis   ☒ ▢
   EXCLUDES   *semen analysis without sperm wash or swim-up (89320)*
   📠 0.00   ✂ 0.00   Global Days XXX
   AMA: 2008, Jan, 10-25; 2007, Jan, 13-27; 2007, Jan, 13-27; 2007, January, 13-27; 2005, Jul, 11-12; 2005, Jul, 11-12; 2005, Aug, 7-8; 2005, Aug, 9-10; 2005, Aug, 7-8; 2005, Aug, 9-10; 2005, August, 9-10; 2005, August, 7-8; 2005, July, 11-12; 2004, May, 16; 2004, May, 16; 2004, May, 16; 2004, April, 1; 2004, Apr, 1; 2004, Apr, 1

89264   Sperm identification from testis tissue, fresh or cryopreserved   ☒ ▢
   EXCLUDES   *biopsy of testis (54500, 54505)*
         semen analysis (89300-89320)
         sperm identification from aspiration (89257)
   📠 0.00   ✂ 0.00   Global Days XXX
   AMA: 2008, Jan, 10-25; 2007, Jan, 13-27; 2007, Jan, 13-27; 2007, January, 13-27; 2005, Jul, 11-12; 2005, Jul, 11-12; 2005, Aug, 7-8; 2005, Aug, 9-10; 2005, Aug, 7-8; 2005, Aug, 9-10; 2005, August, 7-8; 2005, July, 11-12; 2005, August, 9-10; 2004, May, 16; 2004, May, 16; 2004, May, 16; 2004, April, 1; 2004, Apr, 1; 2004, Apr, 1

89268   Insemination of oocytes   ♀ ☒
   📠 0.00   ✂ 0.00   Global Days XXX
   AMA: 2008, Jan, 10-25; 2007, Jan, 13-27; 2007, Jan, 13-27; 2007, January, 13-27; 2005, Jul, 11-12; 2005, Jul, 11-12; 2005, Aug, 9-10; 2005, Aug, 7-8; 2005, Aug, 9-10; 2005, Aug, 7-8; 2005, August, 9-10; 2005, August, 7-8; 2005, July, 11-12; 2004, Apr, 1; 2004, Apr, 1; 2004, May, 16; 2004, April, 1; 2004, May, 16; 2004, May, 16

89272   Extended culture of oocyte(s)/embryo(s), 4-7 days   ♀ ☒
   📠 0.00   ✂ 0.00   Global Days XXX
   AMA: 2008, Jan, 10-25; 2007, Jan, 13-27; 2007, Jan, 13-27; 2007, January, 13-27; 2005, Aug, 9-10; 2005, Aug, 9-10; 2005, Jul, 11-12; 2005, Aug, 7-8; 2005, Jul, 11-12; 2005, Aug, 7-8; 2005, August, 9-10; 2005, August, 7-8; 2005, July, 11-12; 2004, Apr, 1; 2004, Apr, 1; 2004, April, 1; 2004, May, 16; 2004, May, 16; 2004, May, 16

89280 Assisted oocyte fertilization, microtechnique; less than or equal to 10 oocytes ♀ ⓧ

🖩 0.00 🔍 0.00 **Global Days XXX**
AMA: 2008, Jan, 10-25; 2007, Jan, 13-27; 2007, Jan, 13-27; 2007, January, 13-27; 2005, Aug, 7-8; 2005, Aug, 7-8; 2005, Aug, 9-10; 2005, Jul, 11-12; 2005, Aug, 9-10; 2005, Jul, 11-12; 2005, August, 9-10; 2005, August, 7-8; 2005, July, 11-12; 2004, Apr, 1; 2004, Apr, 1; 2004, May, 16; 2004, April, 1; 2004, May, 16; 2004, May, 16

89281 greater than 10 oocytes ♀ ⓧ

🖩 0.00 🔍 0.00 **Global Days XXX**
AMA: 2008, Jan, 10-25; 2007, Jan, 13-27; 2007, Jan, 13-27; 2007, January, 13-27; 2005, Aug, 7-8; 2005, Aug, 7-8; 2005, Aug, 9-10; 2005, Jul, 11-12; 2005, Aug, 9-10; 2005, Jul, 11-12; 2005, August, 9-10; 2005, August, 7-8; 2005, July, 11-12; 2004, Apr, 1; 2004, Apr, 1; 2004, April, 1; 2004, May, 16; 2004, May, 16; 2004, May, 16

89290 Biopsy, oocyte polar body or embryo blastomere, microtechnique (for pre-implantation genetic diagnosis); less than or equal to 5 embryos ♀ ⓧ

🖩 0.00 🔍 0.00 **Global Days XXX**
AMA: 2008, Jan, 10-25; 2007, Jan, 13-27; 2007, Jan, 13-27; 2007, January, 13-27; 2005, Aug, 7-8; 2005, Aug, 7-8; 2005, Aug, 9-10; 2005, Jul, 11-12; 2005, Aug, 9-10; 2005, Jul, 11-12; 2005, August, 9-10; 2005, August, 7-8; 2005, July, 11-12; 2004, May, 16; 2004, May, 16; 2004, May, 16; 2004, April, 1; 2004, Apr, 1; 2004, Apr, 1

89291 greater than 5 embryos ♀ ⓧ

🖩 0.00 🔍 0.00 **Global Days XXX**
AMA: 2008, Jan, 10-25; 2007, Jan, 13-27; 2007, Jan, 13-27; 2007, January, 13-27; 2005, Jul, 11-12; 2005, Jul, 11-12; 2005, Aug, 7-8; 2005, Aug, 9-10; 2005, Aug, 7-8; 2005, Aug, 9-10; 2005, August, 9-10; 2005, August, 7-8; 2005, July, 11-12; 2004, May, 16; 2004, May, 16; 2004, May, 16; 2004, April, 1; 2004, Apr, 1; 2004, Apr, 1

89300 Semen analysis; presence and/or motility of sperm including Huhner test (post coital) ♂ Ⓐ ▪ ⓧ

🖩 0.00 🔍 0.00 **Global Days XXX**
AMA: 2008, Apr, 5-7; 2008, Apr, 5-7; 2008, Apr, 5-7; 2008, Jan, 10-25; 2007, Jan, 13-27; 2007, Jan, 13-27; 2007, January, 13-27; 2005, Jul, 11-12; 2005, Jul, 11-12; 2005, Aug, 9-10; 2005, Aug, 7-8; 2005, August, 7-8; 2005, August, 9-10; 2005, July, 11-12; 2005, Aug, 9-10; 2005, Aug, 7-8; 2004, May, 16; 2004, May, 16; 2004, April, 1; 2004, May, 16; 2004, Apr, 1; 2004, Apr, 1

89310 motility and count (not including Huhner test) Ⓐ ▪

🖩 0.00 🔍 0.00 **Global Days XXX**
AMA: 2008, Apr, 5-7; 2008, Apr, 5-7; 2008, Apr, 5-7; 2008, Jan, 10-25; 2007, Jan, 13-27; 2007, Jan, 13-27; 2007, January, 13-27; 2005, Jul, 11-12; 2005, Jul, 11-12; 2005, Aug, 7-8; 2005, Aug, 9-10; 2005, August, 9-10; 2005, July, 11-12; 2005, Aug, 7-8; 2005, Aug, 9-10; 2004, Apr, 1; 2004, May, 16; 2004, April, 1; 2004, Apr, 1; 2004, May, 16; 2004, May, 16

89320 volume, count, motility, and differential Ⓐ ▪

🖩 0.00 🔍 0.00 **Global Days XXX**
AMA: 2008, Apr, 5-7; 2008, Apr, 5-7; 2008, Apr, 5-7; 2008, Jan, 10-25; 2007, Jan, 13-27; 2007, Jan, 13-27; 2007, January, 13-27; 2005, Aug, 9-10; 2005, Aug, 9-10; 2005, Aug, 7-8; 2005, Jul, 11-12; 2005, August, 7-8; 2005, August, 9-10; 2005, July, 11-12; 2005, Aug, 7-8; 2005, Jul, 11-12; 2004, Apr, 1; 2004, May, 16; 2004, April, 1; 2004, Apr, 1; 2004, May, 16; 2004, May, 16

89321 sperm presence and motility of sperm, if performed ♂ Ⓐ ▪

EXCLUDES *Hyaluronan binding assay (HBA) (0087T)*

🖩 0.00 🔍 0.00 **Global Days XXX**
AMA: 2008, Apr, 5-7; 2008, Apr, 5-7; 2008, Apr, 5-7; 2008, Jan, 10-25; 2007, Jan, 13-27; 2007, Jan, 13-27; 2007, January, 13-27; 2005, Aug, 7-8; 2005, Aug, 7-8; 2005, Aug, 9-10; 2005, Jul, 11-12; 2005, July, 11-12; 2005, August, 7-8; 2005, August, 9-10; 2005, Aug, 9-10; 2005, Jul, 11-12; 2004, May, 16; 2004, May, 16; 2004, April, 1; 2004, May, 16; 2004, Apr, 1; 2004, Apr, 1

89322 volume, count, motility, and differential using strict morphologic criteria (eg, Kruger) ♂ Ⓐ

🖩 0.00 🔍 0.00 **Global Days XXX**
AMA: 2008, Apr, 5-7; 2008, Apr, 5-7; 2008, Apr, 5-7; 2008, Jan, 10-25

89325 Sperm antibodies Ⓐ ▪

EXCLUDES *medicolegal identification of sperm (88125)*

🖩 0.00 🔍 0.00 **Global Days XXX**
AMA: 2008, Jan, 10-25; 2007, Jan, 13-27; 2007, Jan, 13-27; 2007, January, 13-27; 2005, Jul, 11-12; 2005, Jul, 11-12; 2005, Aug, 9-10; 2005, Aug, 7-8; 2005, Aug, 9-10; 2005, Aug, 7-8; 2005, August, 9-10; 2005, August, 7-8; 2005, July, 11-12; 2004, May, 16; 2004, May, 16; 2004, May, 16; 2004, April, 1; 2004, Apr, 1; 2004, Apr, 1

89329 Sperm evaluation; hamster penetration test Ⓐ ▪

🖩 0.00 🔍 0.00 **Global Days XXX**
AMA: 2008, Jan, 10-25; 2007, Jan, 13-27; 2007, Jan, 13-27; 2007, January, 13-27; 2005, Jul, 11-12; 2005, Jul, 11-12; 2005, Aug, 7-8; 2005, Aug, 9-10; 2005, Aug, 7-8; 2005, Aug, 9-10; 2005, August, 9-10; 2005, August, 7-8; 2005, July, 11-12; 2004, Apr, 1; 2004, Apr, 1; 2004, May, 16; 2004, April, 1; 2004, May, 16; 2004, May, 16

89330 cervical mucus penetration test, with or without spinnbarkeit test ♂ Ⓐ ▪

🖩 0.00 🔍 0.00 **Global Days XXX**
AMA: 2008, Jan, 10-25; 2007, Jan, 13-27; 2007, Jan, 13-27; 2007, January, 13-27; 2005, Aug, 7-8; 2005, Aug, 7-8; 2005, Aug, 9-10; 2005, Nov, 14-15; 2005, Aug, 9-10; 2005, Nov, 14-15; 2005, Jul, 11-12; 2005, August, 7-8; 2005, August, 9-10; 2005, November, 14-15; 2005, July, 11-12; 2005, Jul, 11-12; 2004, Apr, 1; 2004, Apr, 1; 2004, April, 1; 2004, May, 16; 2004, May, 16; 2004, May, 16

89331 Sperm evaluation, for retrograde ejaculation, urine (sperm concentration, motility, and morphology, as indicated) ♂ Ⓐ

EXCLUDES *detection of sperm in urine (81015)*

Code also semen analysis on concurrent sperm specimen (89300-89322)

🖩 0.00 🔍 0.00 **Global Days XXX**
AMA: 2008, Apr, 5-7; 2008, Apr, 5-7; 2008, Apr, 5-7; 2008, Jan, 10-25

89335 Cryopreservation, reproductive tissue, testicular ⓧ

EXCLUDES *cryopreservation of:*
embryo(s) (89258)
sperm (89259)

🖩 0.00 🔍 0.00 **Global Days XXX**
AMA: 2008, Jan, 10-25; 2007, Jan, 13-27; 2007, Jan, 13-27; 2007, January, 13-27; 2005, Aug, 7-8; 2005, Aug, 7-8; 2005, Aug, 9-10; 2005, Jul, 11-12; 2005, Aug, 9-10; 2005, Jul, 11-12; 2005, August, 9-10; 2005, August, 7-8; 2005, July, 11-12; 2004, Apr, 1; 2004, Apr, 1; 2004, May, 16; 2004, April, 1; 2004, May, 16; 2004, May, 16

89342 **Storage (per year); embryo(s)** ☒
0.00 0.00 Global Days XXX
AMA: 2008, Jan, 10-25; 2007, Jan, 13-27; 2007, Jan, 13-27; 2007, January, 13-27; 2005, Jul, 11-12; 2005, Jul, 11-12; 2005, Aug, 9-10; 2005, Aug, 7-8; 2005, Aug, 9-10; 2005, Aug, 7-8; 2005, August, 9-10; 2005, August, 7-8; 2005, July, 11-12; 2004, May, 16; 2004, May, 16; 2004, May, 16; 2004, April, 1; 2004, Apr, 1; 2004, Apr, 1

89343 **sperm/semen** ☒
0.00 0.00 Global Days XXX
AMA: 2008, Jan, 10-25; 2007, Jan, 13-27; 2007, Jan, 13-27; 2007, January, 13-27; 2005, Jul, 11-12; 2005, Jul, 11-12; 2005, Aug, 7-8; 2005, Aug, 9-10; 2005, Aug, 7-8; 2005, Aug, 9-10; 2005, August, 7-8; 2005, August, 9-10; 2005, July, 11-12; 2004, May, 16; 2004, May, 16; 2004, May, 16; 2004, April, 1; 2004, Apr, 1; 2004, Apr, 1

89344 **reproductive tissue, testicular/ovarian** ☒
0.00 0.00 Global Days XXX
AMA: 2008, Jan, 10-25; 2007, Jan, 13-27; 2007, Jan, 13-27; 2007, January, 13-27; 2005, Aug, 7-8; 2005, Aug, 7-8; 2005, Aug, 9-10; 2005, Jul, 11-12; 2005, Aug, 9-10; 2005, Jul, 11-12; 2005, August, 9-10; 2005, August, 7-8; 2005, July, 11-12; 2004, Apr, 1; 2004, Apr, 1; 2004, May, 16; 2004, April, 1; 2004, May, 16; 2004, May, 16

89346 **oocyte(s)** ♀ ☒
0.00 0.00 Global Days XXX
AMA: 2008, Jan, 10-25; 2007, Jan, 13-27; 2007, Jan, 13-27; 2007, January, 13-27; 2005, Aug, 9-10; 2005, Aug, 9-10; 2005, Aug, 7-8; 2005, Jul, 11-12; 2005, Aug, 7-8; 2005, Jul, 11-12; 2005, August, 9-10; 2005, August, 7-8; 2005, July, 11-12; 2004, Apr, 1; 2004, Apr, 1; 2004, May, 16; 2004, April, 1; 2004, May, 16; 2004, May, 16

89352 **Thawing of cryopreserved; embryo(s)** ☒
0.00 0.00 Global Days XXX
AMA: 2008, Jan, 10-25; 2007, Jan, 13-27; 2007, Jan, 13-27; 2007, January, 13-27; 2005, Aug, 9-10; 2005, Aug, 9-10; 2005, Jul, 11-12; 2005, Aug, 7-8; 2005, Jul, 11-12; 2005, Aug, 7-8; 2005, August, 9-10; 2005, August, 7-8; 2005, July, 11-12; 2004, Apr, 1; 2004, Apr, 1; 2004, April, 1; 2004, May, 16; 2004, May, 16; 2004, May, 16

89353 **sperm/semen, each aliquot** ☒
0.00 0.00 Global Days XXX
AMA: 2008, Jan, 10-25; 2007, Jan, 13-27; 2007, Jan, 13-27; 2007, January, 13-27; 2005, Jul, 11-12; 2005, Jul, 11-12; 2005, Aug, 7-8, 2005, Aug, 9-10, 2005, Aug, 7-8; 2005, Aug, 9-10; 2005, August, 9-10; 2005, August, 7-8; 2005, July, 11-12; 2004, May, 16; 2004, May, 16; 2004, May, 16; 2004, April, 1; 2004, Apr, 1; 2004, Apr, 1

89354 **reproductive tissue, testicular/ovarian** ☒
0.00 0.00 Global Days XXX
AMA: 2008, Jan, 10-25; 2007, Jan, 13-27; 2007, Jan, 13-27; 2007, January, 13-27; 2005, Aug, 7-8; 2005, Aug, 7-8; 2005, Aug, 9-10; 2005, Jul, 11-12; 2005, Aug, 9-10; 2005, Jul, 11-12; 2005, August, 9-10; 2005, August, 7-8; 2005, July, 11-12; 2004, Apr, 1; 2004, Apr, 1; 2004, May, 16; 2004, April, 1; 2004, May, 16; 2004, May, 16

89356 **oocytes, each aliquot** ☒
0.00 0.00 Global Days XXX
AMA: 2008, Jan, 10-25; 2007, Jan, 13-27; 2007, Jan, 13-27; 2007, January, 13-27; 2005, Jul, 11-12; 2005, Jul, 11-12; 2005, Aug, 7-8; 2005, August, 9-10; 2005, August, 7-8; 2005, July, 11-12; 2005, Aug, 9-10; 2005, Aug, 9-10; 2005, Aug, 7-8; 2004, May, 16; 2004, June, 7; 2004, May, 16; 2004, Jun, 7; 2004, Jun, 7; 2004, April, 1; 2004, May, 16; 2004, Apr, 1; 2004, Apr, 1

90281-90399 Immunoglobulin Products

CMS *100-2,15,50* — *Drugs and Biologicals*
CMS *100-4,4,20.5* — *HCPCS Under OPPS*
[INCLUDES] immune globulin product only
immune globulins/antioxins/various isoantibodies:
anti-infective
broad-spectrum

Code also (96365-96368, 96372, 96374-96375)

⊘ **90281** Immune globulin (Ig), human, for intramuscular use ᴱ
💊 0.00 🔖 0.00 Global Days XXX
AMA: 2008, Jan, 10-25; 2007, Jan, 13-27; 2007, Jan, 13-27; 2007, January, 13 27

⊘ **90283** Immune globulin (IgIV), human, for intravenous use ᴱ
💊 0.00 🔖 0.00 Global Days XXX
AMA: 2008, Jan, 10-25

⊘ **90284** Immune globulin (SCIg), human, for use in subcutaneous infusions, 100 mg, each ᴱ
💊 0.00 🔖 0.00 Global Days XXX
AMA: 2008, Jan, 10-25

⊘ **90287** Botulinum antitoxin, equine, any route ᴱ
💊 0.00 🔖 0.00 Global Days XXX
AMA: 2008, Jan, 10-25

⊘ **90288** Botulism immune globulin, human, for intravenous use ᴱ
💊 0.00 🔖 0.00 Global Days XXX
AMA: 2008, Jan, 10-25

⊘ **90291** Cytomegalovirus immune globulin (CMV-IgIV), human, for intravenous use ᴱ
💊 0.00 🔖 0.00 Global Days XXX
AMA: 2008, Jan, 10-25

⊘ **90296** Diphtheria antitoxin, equine, any route K2 K
💊 0.00 🔖 0.00 Global Days XXX
AMA: 2008, Jan, 10-25

⊘ **90371** Hepatitis B immune globulin (HBIg), human, for intramuscular use K2 K
💊 0.00 🔖 0.00 Global Days XXX
AMA: 2008, Jan, 10-25

⊘ **90375** Rabies immune globulin (RIg), human, for intramuscular and/or subcutaneous use K2 K 🔲
💊 0.00 🔖 0.00 Global Days XXX
AMA: 2008, Jan, 10-25

⊘ **90376** Rabies immune globulin, heat-treated (RIg-HT), human, for intramuscular and/or subcutaneous use K2 K
💊 0.00 🔖 0.00 Global Days XXX
AMA: 2008, Jan, 10-25

⊘ **90378** Respiratory syncytial virus immune globulin (RSV-IgIM), for intramuscular use, 50 mg, each K2 K 🔲
💊 0.00 🔖 0.00 Global Days XXX
AMA: 2008, Jan, 10-25

⊘ **90379** Respiratory syncytial virus immune globulin (RSV-IgIV), human, for intravenous use ᴱ
💊 0.00 🔖 0.00 Global Days XXX
AMA: 2008, Jan, 10-25

⊘ **90384** Rho(D) immune globulin (RhIg), human, full-dose, for intramuscular use ᴱ
💊 0.00 🔖 0.00 Global Days XXX
AMA: 2008, Jan, 10-25

⊘ **90385** Rho(D) immune globulin (RhIg), human, mini-dose, for intramuscular use N1 N
💊 0.00 🔖 0.00 Global Days XXX
AMA: 2008, Jan, 10-25

⊘ **90386** Rho(D) immune globulin (RhIgIV), human, for intravenous use ᴱ
💊 0.00 🔖 0.00 Global Days XXX
AMA: 2008, Jan, 10-25

⊘ **90389** Tetanus immune globulin (TIg), human, for intramuscular use ᴱ
💊 0.00 🔖 0.00 Global Days XXX
AMA: 2008, Jan, 10-25

⊘ **90393** Vaccinia immune globulin, human, for intramuscular use N1 N
💊 0.00 🔖 0.00 Global Days XXX
AMA: 2008, Jan, 10-25

⊘ **90396** Varicella-zoster immune globulin, human, for intramuscular use K2 K
💊 0.00 🔖 0.00 Global Days XXX
AMA: 2008, Jan, 10-25

⊘ **90399** Unlisted immune globulin ᴱ
💊 0.00 🔖 0.00 Global Days XXX
AMA: 2008, Jan, 10-25

90465-90468 Injections Provided with Physician Counseling

CMS *100-2,16,90* — *Routine Services and Appliances*
[INCLUDES] patient/family face-to-face counseling
[EXCLUDES] *allergy testing (95004-95075)*
bacterial/viral/fungal skin tests (86485-86580)
diagnostic and therapeutic injections (96372-96379)

Code also significant, separately identifiable preventive medicine services (99381-99429)

Code also significant separately identifiable evaluation and management service if performed (99201-99215)

Code also therapeutic or diagnostic injections (96372-96379)

Code also toxoid/vaccine (90476-90749)

90465 Immunization administration younger than 8 years of age (includes percutaneous, intradermal, subcutaneous, or intramuscular injections) when the physician counsels the patient/family; first injection (single or combination vaccine/toxoid), per day A B 80 🔲
Do not report with intranasal/oral administration (90467)
💊 0.58 🔖 0.58 Global Days XXX
AMA: 2005, Nov, 1-9; 2005, Nov, 1-9; 2005, Apr, 1-5; 2005, Apr, 1-5; 2005, Aug, 13-15; 2005, Aug, 13-15; 2005, Apr, 1; 2005, Apr, 1; 2005, Nov, 1; 2005, Nov, 1; 2005, Aug, 13, 2005, Aug, 13; 2005, April, 1-5; 2005, August, 13-15; 2005, November, 1-9

+ **90466** each additional injection (single or combination vaccine/toxoid), per day (List separately in addition to code for primary procedure) A B 80
Code first initial administration/injection (90465, 90467)
💊 0.22 🔖 0.29 Global Days ZZZ
AMA: 2005, Aug, 13-15; 2005, Aug, 13-15; 2005, Apr, 1-5; 2005, Apr, 1-5; 2005, Nov, 1-9; 2005, Nov, 1-9; 2005, Apr, 1; 2005, Apr, 1; 2005, Nov, 1; 2005, Nov, 1; 2005, Aug, 13, 2005, Aug, 13; 2005, April, 1-5; 2005, August, 13-15; 2005, November, 1-9

90467 Immunization administration younger than age 8 years (includes intranasal or oral routes of administration) when the physician counsels the patient/family; first administration (single or combination vaccine/toxoid), per day A B 80 🔲
Do not report with percutaneous/intradermal/subcutaneous/intramuscular injection (90465)
💊 0.26 🔖 0.38 Global Days XXX
AMA: 2005, Apr, 1-5; 2005, Apr, 1-5; 2005, Aug, 13-15; 2005, Aug, 13-15; 2005, Apr, 1; 2005, Apr, 1; 2005, Aug, 13; 2005, Aug, 13; 2005, August, 13-15; 2005, April, 1-5

⊛ Modifier 63 Exempt Code ⊙ Moderate Sedation + CPT Add-on Code ⊘ Modifier 51 Exempt Code ● New Code ▲ Revised Code

Ⓜ Maternity Edit Ⓐ Age Edit Ⓐ-Ⓨ APC Status Indicators 🔲 CCI Comprehensive Code ⁄ Drug Not Approved by FDA 80 Bilateral Procedure

© 2008 Ingenix *(Blue Ink)* CPT only © 2008 American Medical Association. All Rights Reserved. (Black Ink) Medicare (Red Ink) **385**

+ 90468 each additional administration (single or combination vaccine/toxoid), per day (List separately in addition to code for primary procedure) [A] [B] [80]
Code first initial administration/injection (90465, 90467)
🔾 0.21 ⚖ 0.28 Global Days ZZZ

> **AMA:** 2005, Apr, 1-5; 2005, Apr, 1-5; 2005, Aug, 13-15; 2005, Aug, 13-15; 2005, Apr, 1; 2005, Apr, 1; 2005, Aug, 13; 2005, Aug, 13; 2005, April, 1-5; 2005, August, 13-15

90471-90474 Injections and Other Routes of Administration Without Physician Counseling

CMS *100-4,18,10.2.1* *Vaccines and Administation*
CMS *100-2,16,90* *Routine Services and Appliances*
CMS *100-2,15,50* *Drugs and Biologicals*
EXCLUDES *allergy testing (95004-95075)*
bacterial/viral/fungal skin tests (86485-86580)
injections, diagnostic/therapeutic (96372-96379)
patient/family face-to-face counseling

Code also significant, separately identifiable preventive medicine services (99381-99429)

Code also significant separately identifiable evaluation and management service if performed (99201-99215)

Code also toxoid/vaccine (90476-90749)

90471 Immunization administration (includes percutaneous, intradermal, subcutaneous, or intramuscular injections); 1 vaccine (single or combination vaccine/toxoid) [S] [80] [▭]

> Do not report with intranasal/oral administration (90473)
🔾 0.58 ⚖ 0.58 Global Days XXX

> **AMA:** 2008, Jan, 10-25; 2007, Jul, 12-13; 2005, Apr, 1-5; 2005, Apr, 1-5; 2005, Nov, 1-9; 2005, Nov, 1; 2005, Nov, 1-9; 2005, Nov, 1; 2005, Apr, 1; 2005, April, 1-5; 2005, November, 1-9; 2005, Apr, 1; 2004, Mar, 11; 2004, Mar, 11; 2004, March, 11; 2004, Mar, 11; 2004, Mar, 11

+ 90472 each additional vaccine (single or combination vaccine/toxoid) (List separately in addition to code for primary procedure) [S] [80]
EXCLUDES *BCG vaccine, intravesical administration (51720, 90586)*
immune globulin administration (96365-96368, 96372-96375)
immune globulin product (90281-90399)

> Code first initial vaccine (90471, 90473)
🔾 0.22 ⚖ 0.29 Global Days ZZZ

> **AMA:** 2008, Jan, 10-25; 2007, Jul, 12-13; 2005, Apr, 1-5; 2005, Apr, 1-5; 2005, Nov, 1-9; 2005, Nov, 1-9; 2005, Apr, 1; 2005, November, 1-9; 2005, April, 1-5; 2005, Apr, 1; 2005, Nov, 1; 2005, Nov, 1; 2004, Mar, 11; 2004, March, 11; 2004, April, 14; 2004, Mar, 11; 2004, Apr, 14; 2004, Apr, 14; 2004, Mar, 11; 2004, Mar, 11; 2004, Apr, 14; 2004, Apr, 14

90473 Immunization administration by intranasal or oral route; 1 vaccine (single or combination vaccine/toxoid) [S] [80] [▭]

> Do not report with percutaneous/intradermal/subcutaneous/intramuscular injections (90471)
🔾 0.23 ⚖ 0.38 Global Days XXX

> **AMA:** 2005, Apr, 1-5; 2005, Apr, 1-5; 2005, Apr, 1; 2005, April, 1-5; 2005, Apr, 1; 2004, Apr, 14; 2004, April, 14; 2004, Apr, 14; 2004, Apr, 14; 2004, Apr, 14

+ 90474 each additional vaccine (single or combination vaccine/toxoid) (List separately in addition to code for primary procedure) [S] [80]
Code first initial vaccine (90471, 90473)
🔾 0.21 ⚖ 0.25 Global Days ZZZ

> **AMA:** 2005, Apr, 1-5; 2005, Apr, 1-5; 2005, Apr, 1; 2005, April, 1-5; 2005, Apr, 1; 2004, Apr, 14; 2004, April, 14; 2004, Apr, 14; 2004, Apr, 14; 2004, Apr, 14

90476-90749 Vaccination Products

CMS *100-2,16,90* *Routine Services and Appliances*
CMS *100-2,15,50* *Drugs and Biologicals*
CMS *100-4,4,20.5* *HCPCS Under OPPS*
INCLUDES *vaccine product only*
EXCLUDES *immune globulins and adminstration (90281-90399, 96365, 96372-96375)*

Code also administration of vaccine (90465-90474)

Code also office/other outpatient (99201-99215)

Code also preventive medicine (99381-99429)

Code also significant separately identifiable evaluation and management service if performed

90476 Adenovirus vaccine, type 4, live, for oral use [M] [N]
🔾 0.00 ⚖ 0.00 Global Days XXX

> **AMA:** 2008, Jan, 10-25; 2007, Jan, 13-27; 2007, Jan, 13-27; 2007, Feb, 10-11; 2007, Feb, 10-11; 2007, January, 13-27; 2007, February, 10-11

90477 Adenovirus vaccine, type 7, live, for oral use [M] [N]
🔾 0.00 ⚖ 0.00 Global Days XXX

> **AMA:** 2008, Jan, 10-25

90581 Anthrax vaccine, for subcutaneous use [M] [N] [▭]
INCLUDES BioThrax
🔾 0.00 ⚖ 0.00 Global Days XXX

> **AMA:** 2008, Jan, 10-25

90585 Bacillus Calmette-Guerin vaccine (BCG) for tuberculosis, live, for percutaneous use [K2] [K] [▭]
INCLUDES Mycobax
🔾 0.00 ⚖ 0.00 Global Days XXX

> **AMA:** 2008, Jan, 10-25

90586 Bacillus Calmette-Guerin vaccine (BCG) for bladder cancer, live, for intravesical use [B]
INCLUDES TheraCys
TICE BCG
🔾 0.00 ⚖ 0.00 Global Days XXX

> **AMA:** 2008, Jan, 10-25

90632 Hepatitis A vaccine, adult dosage, for intramuscular use [M] [N] [▭]
INCLUDES HAVRIX 1440EL.U/1mL
VAQTA 50U/1mL
🔾 0.00 ⚖ 0.00 Global Days XXX

> **AMA:** 2008, Jan, 10-25

90633 Hepatitis A vaccine, pediatric/adolescent dosage-2 dose schedule, for intramuscular use [M] [N] [▭]
INCLUDES HAVRIX 720EL.U/0.5mL
VAQTA 25U/0.5mL
🔾 0.00 ⚖ 0.00 Global Days XXX

> **AMA:** 2008, Jan, 10-25

90634 Hepatitis A vaccine, pediatric/adolescent dosage-3 dose schedule, for intramuscular use [M] [N] [▭]
🔾 0.00 ⚖ 0.00 Global Days XXX

> **AMA:** 2008, Jan, 10-25

---

[26] [TC] Professional/Technical Component Only [89] [80] Assist-at-Surgery Allowed/With Documentation Unlisted Not Covered ⬡ Radiology crosswalk

MED: Pub 100/NCD References **AMA:** CPT Assistant References [A2] [Z3] ASC Payment Indicator ♂Male Only ♀Female Only ⬡ Laboratory crosswalk

386 CPT only © 2008 American Medical Association. All Rights Reserved. (Black Ink) Medicare (Red Ink) © 2008 Ingenix (Blue Ink)

Medicine

90636 Hepatitis A and hepatitis B vaccine (HepA-HepB), adult dosage, for intramuscular use ⓂⓃ▱
INCLUDES TWINRIX

🔲 0.00 🔲 0.00 Global Days XXX

AMA: 2008, Jan, 10-25

90645 Hemophilus influenza b vaccine (Hib), HbOC conjugate (4 dose schedule), for intramuscular use ⓂⓃ▱
🔲 0.00 🔲 0.00 Global Days XXX

AMA: 2008, Jan, 10-25

90646 Hemophilus influenza b vaccine (Hib), PRP-D conjugate, for booster use only, intramuscular use ⓂⓃ▱
🔲 0.00 🔲 0.00 Global Days XXX

AMA: 2008, Jan, 10-25

90647 Hemophilus influenza b vaccine (Hib), PRP-OMP conjugate (3 dose schedule), for intramuscular use ⓂⓃ▱
INCLUDES PedvaxHIB

🔲 0.00 🔲 0.00 Global Days XXX

AMA: 2008, Jan, 10-25

90648 Hemophilus influenza b vaccine (Hib), PRP-T conjugate (4 dose schedule), for intramuscular use ⓂⓃ▱
INCLUDES ActHIB

🔲 0.00 🔲 0.00 Global Days XXX

AMA: 2008, Jan, 10-25

90649 Human Papilloma virus (HPV) vaccine, types 6, 11, 16, 18 (quadrivalent), 3 dose schedule, for intramuscular use Ⓑ
INCLUDES GARDASIL

🔲 0.00 🔲 0.00 Global Days XXX

AMA: 2008, Jan, 10-25; 2007, Jul, 12-13; 2006, Jun, 8-10; 2006, Jun, 8-10; 2006, Jun, 8; 2006, June, 8-10; 2006, Jun, 8; 2005, Dec, 9-11; 2005, December, 9-11; 2005, Dec, 9; 2005, Dec, 9; 2005, Dec, 9-11

✐ **90650** Human Papillomavirus (HPV) vaccine, types 16 and 18, bivalent, 3 dose schedule, for intramuscular use Ⓐ Ⓔ
🔲 0.00 🔲 0.00 Global Days XXX

AMA: 2008, Jan, 10-25

90655 Influenza virus vaccine, split virus, preservative free, when administered to children 6-35 months of age, for intramuscular use Ⓐ ⓊⓁ▱
INCLUDES Fluzone, no preservative, pediatric dose

🔲 0.00 🔲 0.00 Global Days XXX

AMA: 2008, Apr, 8-9; 2008, Apr, 8-9; 2008, Jan, 10-25; 2008, Apr, 8-9; 2007, Apr, 11-12; 2007, April, 11-12; 2007, Apr, 11-12; 2004, Feb, 3; 2004, February, 1; 2004, February, 3; 2004, Feb, 3; 2004, Feb, 1; 2004, Feb, 1; 2004, Feb, 1; 2004, Feb, 1

90656 Influenza virus vaccine, split virus, preservative free, when administered to individuals 3 years and older, for intramuscular use Ⓐ ⓊⓁ▱
INCLUDES AFLURIA (prefilled syringe)
FLUARIX
Fluvirin (prefilled syringe)
Fluzone, no preservative
Fluzone®, Influenza Virus Vaccine, No Preservative

🔲 0.00 🔲 0.00 Global Days XXX

AMA: 2008, Apr, 8-9; 2008, Apr, 8-9; 2008, Apr, 8-9; 2008, Jan, 10-25; 2004, Feb, 3; 2004, Feb, 3; 2004, February, 1; 2004, February, 3; 2004, Feb, 1; 2004, Feb, 1; 2004, Feb, 1; 2004, Feb, 1

90657 Influenza virus vaccine, split virus, when administered to children 6-35 months of age, for intramuscular use Ⓐ ⓊⓁ▱
INCLUDES Fluzone, 0.25 mL

🔲 0.00 🔲 0.00 Global Days XXX

AMA: 2008, Apr, 8-9; 2008, Apr, 8-9; 2008, Apr, 8-9; 2008, Jan, 10-25; 2007, Feb, 10; 2007, February, 10-11; 2007, Feb, 10; 2007, Feb, 10-11; 2007, Feb, 10-11; 2005, Apr, 1-5; 2005, April, 1-5; 2005, Apr, 1-5; 2004, Feb, 1; 2004, Feb, 1; 2004, February, 1; 2004, Feb, 1; 2004, Feb, 1

90658 Influenza virus vaccine, split virus, when administered to individuals 3 years of age and older, for intramuscular use Ⓐ ⓊⓁ▱
INCLUDES AFLURIA, 0.5mL
FLULAVAL
Fluvirin, 0.5mL
Fluzone, 0.5 mL
Fluzone®, Influenza Virus Vaccine (5mL vial [0.5mL dose])

🔲 0.00 🔲 0.00 Global Days XXX

AMA: 2008, Apr, 8-9; 2008, Apr, 8-9; 2008, Apr, 8-9; 2008, Jan, 10-25; 2007, Feb, 10; 2007, Feb, 10; 2007, Feb, 10-11; 2007, Apr, 11-12; 2007, Feb, 10-11; 2007, April, 11-12; 2007, February, 10-11; 2007, Apr, 11-12; 2004, Feb, 1; 2004, Feb, 1; 2004, February, 1; 2004, Feb, 1; 2004, Feb, 1

90660 Influenza virus vaccine, live, for intranasal use ⓊⓁ▱
INCLUDES FluMist

🔲 0.00 🔲 0.00 Global Days XXX

2008, Apr, 8-9; 2008, Apr, 8-9; 2008, Apr, 8-9; 2008, Jan, 10-25;

✐ **90661** Influenza virus vaccine, derived from cell cultures, subunit, preservative and antibiotic free, for intramuscular use Ⓔ
🔲 0.00 🔲 0.00 Global Days XXX

AMA: 2008, Apr, 8-9; 2008, Apr, 8-9; 2008, Apr, 8-9; 2008, Jan, 10-25

✐ **90662** Influenza virus vaccine, split virus, preservative free, enhanced immunogenicity via increased antigen content, for intramuscular use Ⓔ
🔲 0.00 🔲 0.00 Global Days XXX

AMA: 2008, Apr, 8-9; 2008, Apr, 8-9; 2008, Apr, 8-9; 2008, Jan, 10-25

✐ **90663** Influenza virus vaccine, pandemic formulation Ⓔ
🔲 0.00 🔲 0.00 Global Days XXX

AMA: 2008, Apr, 8-9; 2008, Apr, 8-9; 2008, Apr, 8-9; 2008, Jan, 10-25

90665 Lyme disease vaccine, adult dosage, for intramuscular use Ⓚ²Ⓚ▱
🔲 0.00 🔲 0.00 Global Days XXX

AMA: 2008, Jan, 10-25; 2007, Feb, 10; 2007, Feb, 10; 2007, Feb, 10-11; 2007, Feb, 10-11; 2007, February, 10-11

90669 Pneumococcal conjugate vaccine, polyvalent, when administered to children younger than 5 years, for intramuscular use ⓊⓁ
INCLUDES Prevnar

🔲 0.00 🔲 0.00 Global Days XXX

AMA: 2008, Jan, 10-25; 2007, Feb, 10; 2007, Feb, 10; 2007, Feb, 10-11; 2007, Feb, 10-11; 2007, February, 10-11

90675 Rabies vaccine, for intramuscular use Ⓚ²Ⓚ▱
INCLUDES IMOVAX
RabAvert

🔲 0.00 🔲 0.00 Global Days XXX

AMA: 2008, Jan, 10-25; 2007, Feb, 10; 2007, Feb, 10; 2007, Feb, 10-11; 2007, Feb, 10-11; 2007, February, 10-11

90676   Rabies vaccine, for intradermal use   K2 K ▢
         📷 0.00 ✂ 0.00 **Global Days XXX**
         AMA: 2008, Jan, 10-25; 2007, Feb, 10; 2007, Feb, 10; 2007, Feb,
         10-11; 2007, Feb, 10-11; 2007, February, 10-11

90680   Rotavirus vaccine, pentavalent, 3 dose schedule, live,
         for oral use   N1 N
         INCLUDES   RotaTeq

         📷 0.00 ✂ 0.00 **Global Days XXX**
         AMA: 2008, Jan, 10-25; 2007, Feb, 10; 2007, Feb, 10; 2007, Feb,
         10-11; 2007, February, 10-11; 2007, Feb, 10-11; 2006, Jun, 8-10;
         2006, June, 8-10; 2006, Jun, 8-10; 2006, Jun, 8; 2006, Jun, 8;
         2005, Jun, 6-8; 2005, December, 9-11; 2005, June, 6-8; 2005,
         Jun, 6-8; 2005, Jun, 6; 2005, Dec, 9; 2005, Dec, 9; 2005, Jun, 6;
         2005, Dec, 9-11; 2005, Dec, 9-11

90681   Rotavirus vaccine, human, attenuated, 2 dose schedule,
         live, for oral use   K2 K
         INCLUDES   Rotarix

         📷 0.00 ✂ 0.00 **Global Days XXX**
         AMA: 2008, Jan, 10-25

90690   Typhoid vaccine, live, oral   N1 N
         INCLUDES   Vivotif

         📷 0.00 ✂ 0.00 **Global Days XXX**
         AMA: 2008, Jan, 10-25; 2007, Feb, 10; 2007, Feb, 10; 2007, Feb,
         10-11; 2007, Feb, 10-11; 2007, February, 10-11

90691   Typhoid vaccine, Vi capsular polysaccharide (ViCPs), for
         intramuscular use   N1 N ▢
         INCLUDES   Typhim Vi

         📷 0.00 ✂ 0.00 **Global Days XXX**
         AMA: 2008, Jan, 10-25; 2007, Feb, 10; 2007, Feb, 10; 2007, Feb,
         10-11; 2007, Feb, 10-11; 2007, February, 10-11

90692   Typhoid vaccine, heat- and phenol-inactivated (H-P), for
         subcutaneous or intradermal use   N1 N ▢
         📷 0.00 ✂ 0.00 **Global Days XXX**
         AMA: 2008, Jan, 10-25; 2007, Feb, 10; 2007, Feb, 10; 2007, Feb,
         10-11; 2007, Feb, 10-11; 2007, February, 10-11

90693   Typhoid vaccine, acetone-killed, dried (AKD), for
         subcutaneous use (U.S. military)   B ▢
         📷 0.00 ✂ 0.00 **Global Days XXX**
         AMA: 2008, Jan, 10-25; 2007, Jan, 13-27; 2007, Jan, 13-27; 2007,
         Feb, 10-11; 2007, Feb, 10-11; 2007, January, 13-27; 2007,
         February, 10-11

✎ 90696   Diphtheria, tetanus toxoids, acellular pertussis vaccine
         and poliovirus vaccine, inactivated (DTaP-IPV), when
         administered to children 4 years through 6 years of age,
         for intramuscular use   A K2 K
         INCLUDES   KINRIX

         📷 0.00 ✂ 0.00 **Global Days XXX**
         AMA: 2008, Jan, 10-25

90698   Diphtheria, tetanus toxoids, acellular pertussis vaccine,
         haemophilus influenza Type B, and poliovirus vaccine,
         inactivated (DTaP - Hib - IPV), for intramuscular
         use   N1 N
         INCLUDES   Pentacel

         📷 0.00 ✂ 0.00 **Global Days XXX**
         AMA: 2008, Jan, 10-25; 2007, Feb, 10; 2007, Feb, 10; 2007, Feb,
         10; 2007, Feb, 10; 2007, Feb, 10-11; 2007, February, 10-11; 2007,
         Feb, 10-11; 2006, Jun, 8-10; 2006, June, 8-10; 2006, Jun, 8-10

90700   Diphtheria, tetanus toxoids, and acellular pertussis
         vaccine (DTaP), when administered to individuals younger
         than 7 years, for intramuscular use   A N1 N ▢
         INCLUDES   DAPTACEL
                     INFANRIX
                     Tripedia

         📷 0.00 ✂ 0.00 **Global Days XXX**
         AMA: 2008, Jan, 10-25; 2007, Feb, 10; 2007, Feb, 10; 2007, Feb,
         10-11; 2007, Feb, 10-11; 2007, February, 10-11

90701   Diphtheria, tetanus toxoids, and whole cell pertussis
         vaccine (DTP), for intramuscular use   N1 N ▢
         📷 0.00 ✂ 0.00 **Global Days XXX**
         AMA: 2008, Jan, 10-25; 2007, Feb, 10; 2007, Feb, 10; 2007, Feb,
         10-11; 2007, Feb, 10-11; 2007, February, 10-11

90702   Diphtheria and tetanus toxoids (DT) adsorbed when
         administered to individuals younger than 7 years, for
         intramuscular use   A N1 N ▢
         INCLUDES   Diphtheria and Tetanus Toxoids Adsorbed
                     USP (For Pediatric Use)

         📷 0.00 ✂ 0.00 **Global Days XXX**
         AMA: 2008, Jan, 10-25; 2007, Feb, 10; 2007, Feb, 10; 2007, Feb,
         10-11; 2007, Feb, 10-11; 2007, February, 10-11

90703   Tetanus toxoid adsorbed, for intramuscular use   N1 N ▢
         INCLUDES   Tetanus Toxoid Adsorbed

         📷 0.00 ✂ 0.00 **Global Days XXX**
         AMA: 2008, Jan, 10-25; 2007, Feb, 10; 2007, Feb, 10; 2007, Feb,
         10-11; 2007, Feb, 10-11; 2007, February, 10-11

90704   Mumps virus vaccine, live, for subcutaneous
         use   N1 N ▢
         INCLUDES   MUMPSVAX

         📷 0.00 ✂ 0.00 **Global Days XXX**
         AMA: 2008, Jan, 10-25; 2007, Feb, 10; 2007, Feb, 10; 2007, Feb,
         10-11; 2007, Feb, 10-11; 2007, February, 10-11

90705   Measles virus vaccine, live, for subcutaneous
         use   N1 N ▢
         INCLUDES   ATTENUVAX

         📷 0.00 ✂ 0.00 **Global Days XXX**
         AMA: 2008, Jan, 10-25; 2007, Feb, 10; 2007, Feb, 10; 2007, Feb,
         10-11; 2007, Feb, 10-11; 2007, February, 10-11

90706   Rubella virus vaccine, live, for subcutaneous
         use   N1 N ▢
         INCLUDES   MERUVAX II

         📷 0.00 ✂ 0.00 **Global Days XXX**
         AMA: 2008, Jan, 10-25; 2007, Feb, 10; 2007, Feb, 10; 2007, Feb,
         10-11; 2007, Feb, 10-11; 2007, February, 10-11

90707   Measles, mumps and rubella virus vaccine (MMR), live,
         for subcutaneous use   N1 N ▢
         INCLUDES   M-M-R II

         📷 0.00 ✂ 0.00 **Global Days XXX**
         AMA: 2008, Jan, 10-25; 2007, Feb, 10; 2007, Feb, 10; 2007, Feb,
         10-11; 2007, February, 10-11; 2007, Feb, 10-11; 2005, Apr, 1-5;
         2005, April, 1-5; 2005, Apr, 1-5; 2005, Apr, 1; 2005, Apr, 1

90708   Measles and rubella virus vaccine, live, for subcutaneous
         use   N1 N ▢
         📷 0.00 ✂ 0.00 **Global Days XXX**
         AMA: 2008, Jan, 10-25; 2007, Feb, 10; 2007, Feb, 10; 2007, Feb,
         10-11; 2007, Feb, 10-11; 2007, February, 10-11; 2005, Apr, 1; 2005,
         Apr, 1

26 /TC Professional/Technical Component Only   80 /80 Assist-at-Surgery Allowed/With Documentation   Unlisted   Not Covered   ☒ Radiology crosswalk

MED: Pub 100/NCD References   **AMA:** CPT Assistant References   A2 Z3 ASC Payment Indicator   ♂Male Only   ♀Female Only   ☒ Laboratory crosswalk

388   CPT only © 2008 American Medical Association. All Rights Reserved. (Black Ink)   Medicare (Red Ink)   © 2008 Ingenix *(Blue Ink)*

90710 Measles, mumps, rubella, and varicella vaccine (MMRV), live, for subcutaneous use M N ▭
INCLUDES ProQuad

📖 0.00 ✂ 0.00 Global Days XXX
AMA: 2008, Jan, 10-25; 2007, Feb, 10; 2007, Feb, 10; 2007, Feb, 10-11; 2007, February, 10-11; 2007, Feb, 10-11; 2006, Jun, 8-10; 2006, Jun, 8-10; 2006, Jun, 8; 2006, Jun, 8; 2006, June, 8-10; 2005, Dec, 9-11; 2005, Apr, 1; 2005, Dec, 9; 2005, Dec, 9; 2005, December, 9-11; 2005, Apr, 1; 2005, Dec, 9-11

90712 Poliovirus vaccine, (any type[s]) (OPV), live, for oral use M N ▭

📖 0.00 ✂ 0.00 Global Days XXX
AMA: 2008, Jan, 10-25; 2007, Feb, 10; 2007, Feb, 10; 2007, Feb, 10-11; 2007, Feb, 10-11; 2007, February, 10-11

90713 Poliovirus vaccine, inactivated (IPV), for subcutaneous or intramuscular use M N ▭
INCLUDES IPOL

📖 0.00 ✂ 0.00 Global Days XXX
AMA: 2008, Jan, 10-25; 2007, Feb, 10; 2007, Feb, 10; 2007, Feb, 10-11; 2007, February, 10-11; 2007, Feb, 10-11; 2005, Jun, 6-8; 2005, June, 6-8; 2005, Jun, 6-8; 2005, Jun, 6; 2005, Jun, 6

90714 Tetanus and diphtheria toxoids (Td) adsorbed, preservative free, when administered to individuals 7 years or older, for intramuscular use M N
INCLUDES DECAVAC

📖 0.00 ✂ 0.00 Global Days XXX
AMA: 2008, Jan, 10-25; 2007, Feb, 10; 2007, Feb, 10; 2007, Feb, 10-11; 2007, February, 10-11; 2007, Feb, 10-11; 2005, Jun, 6-8; 2005, June, 6-8; 2005, Jun, 6-8; 2005, Jun, 6; 2005, Jun, 6

90715 Tetanus, diphtheria toxoids and acellular pertussis vaccine (Tdap), when administered to individuals 7 years or older, for intramuscular use M N
INCLUDES Adacel
BOOSTRIX

📖 0.00 ✂ 0.00 Global Days XXX
AMA: 2008, Jan, 10-25; 2007, Feb, 10; 2007, Feb, 10; 2007, Feb, 10-11; 2007, February, 10-11; 2007, Feb, 10-11; 2006, Jun, 8-10; 2006, June, 8-10; 2006, Jun, 8-10; 2006, Jun, 8; 2006, Jun, 8; 2005, Jun, 6-8; 2005, June, 6-8; 2005, December, 9-11; 2005, Jun, 6-8; 2005, Dec, 9; 2005, Jun, 6; 2005, Jun, 6; 2005, Dec, 9; 2005, Dec, 9-11; 2005, Dec, 9-11

90716 Varicella virus vaccine, live, for subcutaneous use B ▭
INCLUDES VARIVAX

📖 0.00 ✂ 0.00 Global Days XXX
AMA: 2008, Jan, 10-25; 2007, Feb, 10; 2007, Feb, 10; 2007, Feb, 10-11; 2007, Feb, 10-11; 2007, February, 10-11

90717 Yellow fever vaccine, live, for subcutaneous use M N ▭
INCLUDES YF-VAX

📖 0.00 ✂ 0.00 Global Days XXX
AMA: 2008, Jan, 10-25; 2007, Feb, 10; 2007, Feb, 10; 2007, Jan, 13; 2007, Jan, 13; 2007, Jan, 13-27; 2007, Jan, 13-27; 2007, Feb, 10-11; 2007, Feb, 10-11; 2007, January, 13-27; 2007, February, 10-11

90718 Tetanus and diphtheria toxoids (Td) adsorbed when administered to individuals 7 years or older, for intramuscular use A M N ▭
INCLUDES Tetanus and Diphtheria Toxoids Adsorbed for Adult Use

📖 0.00 ✂ 0.00 Global Days XXX
AMA: 2008, Jan, 10-25; 2007, Jan, 13-27; 2007, Jan, 13-27; 2007, Feb, 10-11; 2007, Feb, 10-11; 2007, January, 13-27; 2007, February, 10-11

90719 Diphtheria toxoid, for intramuscular use M N ▭

📖 0.00 ✂ 0.00 Global Days XXX
AMA: 2008, Jan, 10-25; 2007, Jan, 13-27; 2007, Jan, 13-27; 2007, Feb, 10-11; 2007, Feb, 10-11; 2007, January, 13-27; 2007, February, 10-11

90720 Diphtheria, tetanus toxoids, and whole cell pertussis vaccine and Hemophilus influenza B vaccine (DTP-Hib), for intramuscular use M N ▭

📖 0.00 ✂ 0.00 Global Days XXX
AMA: 2008, Jan, 10-25; 2007, Jan, 13-27; 2007, Jan, 13-27; 2007, Feb, 10-11; 2007, Feb, 10-11; 2007, January, 13-27; 2007, February, 10-11

90721 Diphtheria, tetanus toxoids, and acellular pertussis vaccine and Hemophilus influenza B vaccine (DtaP-Hib), for intramuscular use M N ▭
INCLUDES TriHIBit

📖 0.00 ✂ 0.00 Global Days XXX
AMA: 2008, Jan, 10-25; 2007, Jan, 13-27; 2007, Jan, 13-27; 2007, Feb, 10-11; 2007, Feb, 10-11; 2007, January, 13-27; 2007, February, 10-11

90723 Diphtheria, tetanus toxoids, acellular pertussis vaccine, Hepatitis B, and poliovirus vaccine, inactivated (DtaP-HepB-IPV), for intramuscular use E
INCLUDES PEDIARIX

📖 0.00 ✂ 0.00 Global Days XXX
AMA: 2008, Jan, 10-25; 2007, Jan, 13-27; 2007, Jan, 13-27; 2007, Feb, 10-11; 2007, Feb, 10-11; 2007, January, 13-27; 2007, February, 10-11

90725 Cholera vaccine for injectable use M N ▭

📖 0.00 ✂ 0.00 Global Days XXX
AMA: 2008, Jan, 10-25; 2007, Jan, 13-27; 2007, Jan, 13-27; 2007, Feb, 10-11; 2007, Feb, 10-11; 2007, January, 13-27; 2007, February, 10-11

90727 Plague vaccine, for intramuscular use M N ▭

📖 0.00 ✂ 0.00 Global Days XXX
AMA: 2008, Jan, 10-25; 2007, Jan, 13-27; 2007, Jan, 13-27; 2007, Feb, 10-11; 2007, Feb, 10-11; 2007, January, 13-27; 2007, February, 10-11

90732 Pneumococcal polysaccharide vaccine, 23-valent, adult or immunosuppressed patient dosage, when administered to individuals 2 years or older, for subcutaneous or intramuscular use A L ▭
INCLUDES PNEUMOVAX 23

📖 0.00 ✂ 0.00 Global Days XXX
AMA: 2008, Jan, 10-25; 2007, Jan, 13-27; 2007, Jan, 13-27; 2007, Feb, 10-11; 2007, Feb, 10-11; 2007, January, 13-27; 2007, February, 10-11

90733 Meningococcal polysaccharide vaccine (any group(s)), for subcutaneous use K2 K ▭
INCLUDES Menomune-A/C/Y/W-135

📖 0.00 ✂ 0.00 Global Days XXX
AMA: 2008, Jan, 10-25; 2007, Jan, 13-27; 2007, Jan, 13-27; 2007, Feb, 10-11; 2007, Feb, 10-11; 2007, January, 13-27; 2007, February, 10-11

90734 Meningococcal conjugate vaccine, serogroups A, C, Y and W-135 (tetravalent), for intramuscular use K2 K ▭
INCLUDES Menactra

📖 0.00 ✂ 0.00 Global Days XXX
AMA: 2008, Jan, 10-25; 2007, Jan, 13-27; 2007, Jan, 13-27; 2007, Feb, 10-11; 2007, Feb, 10-11; 2007, January, 13-27; 2007, February, 10-11

90735 Japanese encephalitis virus vaccine, for subcutaneous use ☐☐

INCLUDES JE-VAX

🔲 0.00 ⚖ 0.00 Global Days XXX
AMA: 2008, Jan, 10-25; 2007, Jan, 13-27; 2007, Jan, 13-27; 2007, Feb, 10-11; 2007, Feb, 10-11; 2007, January, 13-27; 2007, February, 10-11

90736 Zoster (shingles) vaccine, live, for subcutaneous injection ☐

INCLUDES ZOSTAVAX

🔲 0.00 ⚖ 0.00 Global Days XXX
AMA: 2008, Jan, 10-25; 2007, Jan, 13-27; 2007, Jan, 13-27; 2007, Feb, 10-11; 2007, February, 10-11; 2007, Jul, 12-13; 2007, January, 13-27; 2007, Feb, 10-11; 2006, Jun, 8-10; 2006, June, 8-10; 2006, Jun, 8-10; 2005, Dec, 9-11; 2005, December, 9-11; 2005, Dec, 9-11

90738 Japanese encephalitis virus vaccine, inactivated, for intramuscular use ☐

🔲 0.00 ⚖ 0.00 Global Days XXX

90740 Hepatitis B vaccine, dialysis or immunosuppressed patient dosage (3 dose schedule), for intramuscular use ☐☐

INCLUDES RECOMBIVAX HB 40mcg/1mL (dialysis formulation)

🔲 0.00 ⚖ 0.00 Global Days XXX
AMA: 2008, Jan, 10-25; 2007, Jan, 13-27; 2007, Jan, 13-27; 2007, Feb, 10-11; 2007, Feb, 10-11; 2007, January, 13-27; 2007, February, 10-11

90743 Hepatitis B vaccine, adolescent (2 dose schedule), for intramuscular use ☐☐

INCLUDES RECOMBIVAX HB 10mcg/1mL

🔲 0.00 ⚖ 0.00 Global Days XXX
AMA: 2008, Jan, 10-25; 2007, Jan, 13-27; 2007, Jan, 13-27; 2007, Feb, 10-11; 2007, Feb, 10-11; 2007, January, 13-27; 2007, February, 10-11

90744 Hepatitis B vaccine, pediatric/adolescent dosage (3 dose schedule), for intramuscular use ☐☐

INCLUDES ENGERIX-B 10mcg/0.5mL
RECOMBIVAX HB 5mcg/0.5mL

🔲 0.00 ⚖ 0.00 Global Days XXX
AMA: 2008, Jan, 10-25; 2007, Jan, 13-27; 2007, Jan, 13-27; 2007, Feb, 10-11; 2007, Feb, 10-11; 2007, January, 13-27; 2007, February, 10-11; 2005, Apr, 1-5; 2005, Apr, 1-5; 2005, April, 1-5

90746 Hepatitis B vaccine, adult dosage, for intramuscular use ☐☐

INCLUDES ENGERIX-B 20mcg/1mL
RECOMBIVAX HB 10mcg/1mL

🔲 0.00 ⚖ 0.00 Global Days XXX
AMA: 2008, Jan, 10-25; 2007, Jan, 13-27; 2007, Jan, 13-27; 2007, Feb, 10-11; 2007, Feb, 10-11; 2007, January, 13-27; 2007, February, 10-11

90747 Hepatitis B vaccine, dialysis or immunosuppressed patient dosage (4 dose schedule), for intramuscular use ☐☐

INCLUDES ENGERIX-B 20mcg/1mL x 2 - 40mcg/2mL each dose

🔲 0.00 ⚖ 0.00 Global Days XXX
AMA: 2008, Jan, 10-25; 2007, Jan, 13-27; 2007, Jan, 13-27; 2007, Feb, 10-11; 2007, Feb, 10-11; 2007, January, 13-27; 2007, February, 10-11

90748 Hepatitis B and Hemophilus influenza b vaccine (HepB-Hib), for intramuscular use ☐

INCLUDES COMVAX

🔲 0.00 ⚖ 0.00 Global Days XXX
AMA: 2008, Jan, 10-25; 2007, Jan, 13-27; 2007, Jan, 13-27; 2007, Feb, 10-11; 2007, Feb, 10-11; 2007, January, 13-27; 2007, February, 10-11

90749 Unlisted vaccine/toxoid ☐☐

🔲 0.00 ⚖ 0.00 Global Days XXX
AMA: 2008, Jan, 10-25; 2007, Feb, 10-11; 2007, Feb, 10-11; 2007, February, 10-11

90760-90761 Intravenous Fluid Infusion for Hydration (Nonchemotherapy)

~~90760~~ ~~Intravenous infusion, hydration; initial, 31 minutes to 1 hour~~
See 96360

~~90761~~ ~~each additional hour (List separately in addition to code for primary procedure)~~
See 96361

90765-90771 Infusions: Diagnostic/Preventive/Therapeutic

~~90765~~ ~~Intravenous infusion, for therapy, prophylaxis, or diagnosis (specify substance or drug); initial, up to 1 hour~~
See 96365

~~90766~~ ~~each additional hour (List separately in addition to code for primary procedure)~~
See 96366

~~90767~~ ~~additional sequential infusion, up to 1 hour (List separately in addition to code for primary procedure)~~
See 96367

~~90768~~ ~~concurrent infusion (List separately in addition to code for primary procedure)~~
See 96368

~~90769~~ ~~Subcutaneous infusion for therapy or prophylaxis (specify substance or drug); initial, up to one hour, including pump set-up and establishment of subcutaneous infusion site(s)~~
See 96369

~~90770~~ ~~each additional hour (List separately in addition to code for primary procedure)~~
See 96370

~~90771~~ ~~additional pump set-up with establishment of new subcutaneous infusion site(s) (List separately in addition to code for primary procedure)~~
See 96371

90772-90779 Injections: Diagnostic/Preventive/Therapeutic

~~90772~~ ~~Therapeutic, prophylactic or diagnostic injection (specify substance or drug); subcutaneous or intramuscular~~
See 96372

~~90773~~ ~~intra-arterial~~
See 96373

~~90774~~ ~~intravenous push, single or initial substance/drug~~
See 96374

90775 ~~each additional sequential intravenous push of a new substance/drug (List separately in addition to code for primary procedure)~~
See 96375

90776 ~~each additional sequential intravenous push of the same substance/drug provided in a facility (List separately in addition to code for primary procedure)~~
See 96376

90779 ~~Unlisted therapeutic, prophylactic or diagnostic intravenous or intra-arterial injection or infusion~~
See 96379

90801-90802 Interactive Psychiatric Evaluation

CMS 100-4,12,150 Clinical Social Worker (CSW) Services
CMS 100-4,12,170.1 Payment for Clinical Psychologist Services
CMS 100-4,12,170 Clinical Psychologist Services
CMS 100-4,12,160.1 Payment for Independent Psychologists' Services
CMS 100-4,12,210 Outpatient Mental Health Limitation
CMS 100-4,12,160 Independent Psychologist Services
CMS 100-4,12,110.2 Outpatient Mental Health Limitation

90801 **Psychiatric diagnostic interview examination**
INCLUDES communication with family/other sources
disposition
history
mental status
ordering/interpretation of lab studies
ordering/interpretation of other medical diagnostic studies

3.55 4.24 Global Days XXX
AMA: 2007, Jul, 6-10; 2006, Dec, 8-9; 2006, Dec, 8-9; 2006, Dec, 8-9; 2006, Dec, 8-9; 2006, Dec, 8-9; 2006, Dec, 8-9; 2006, Dec, 8-9; 2006, Dec, 8-9; 2006, December, 8-9; 2006, December, 8-9; 2006, December, 8-9; 2006, December, 8 9; 2005, Mar, 11-15; 2005, Mar, 11-15; 2005, May, 1-2; 2005, March, 11-15; 2005, May, 1-2; 2005, May, 1-2

90802 **Interactive psychiatric diagnostic interview examination using play equipment, physical devices, language interpreter, or other mechanisms of communication**
INCLUDES non-verbal communication
physical aids
services furnished to:
children
other individuals lacking
expressive/receptive communication skills

3.82 4.52 Global Days XXX
AMA: 2005, May, 1-2; 2005, May, 1-2; 2005, May, 1-2

90804-90809 Individual Outpatient Psychotherapy

CMS 100-3,130.7 Withdrawal Treatments for Narcotic Addictions
CMS 100-3,130.5 Treatment of Alcoholism/Drug Abuse in a Freestanding Clinic
CMS 100-3,130.6 Treatment of Drug Abuse (Chemical Dependency)
CMS 100-3,130.2 Outpatient Hospital Services for Alcoholism
CMS 100-3,130.1 Inpatient Stays for Alcoholism Treatment
CMS 100-4,12,150 Clinical Social Worker (CSW) Services
CMS 100-4,12,170.1 Payment for Clinical Psychologist Services
CMS 100-4,12,170 Clinical Psychologist Services
CMS 100-4,12,160.1 Payment for Independent Psychologists' Services
CMS 100-4,12,210 Outpatient Mental Health Limitation
CMS 100-4,12,160 Independent Psychologist Services
CMS 100-4,12,110.2 Outpatient Mental Health Limitation
INCLUDES drug management
face-to-face time
insight oriented/behavior modifying/supportive psychotherapy:
cognitive discussion of reality
development of insight/affective understanding
supportive interactions
use of behavior modification
interpretation of lab/other diagnostic studies/observations
medical diagnostic evaluation:
comorbid medical conditions
drug interactions
physical examination
physician orders
psychotherapy only
psychotherapy with medical evaluation and management services
services provided in office or other outpatient facility
treatment for:
behavior disturbances
mental illness

90804 **Individual psychotherapy, insight oriented, behavior modifying and/or supportive, in an office or outpatient facility, approximately 20 to 30 minutes face-to-face with the patient;**
1.50 1.77 Global Days XXX
AMA: 2008, Jan, 10-25; 2007, Jan, 13-27; 2007, Jan, 13-27; 2007, January, 13-27; 2005, May, 1-2; 2005, May, 1-2; 2005, May, 1-2

90805 **with medical evaluation and management services**
1.69 1.97 Global Days XXX
AMA: 2005, May, 1-2; 2005, May, 1-2; 2005, May, 1-2

90806 **Individual psychotherapy, insight oriented, behavior modifying and/or supportive, in an office or outpatient facility, approximately 45 to 50 minutes face-to-face with the patient;**
2.30 2.47 Global Days XXX
AMA: 2008, Jan, 10-25; 2007, Jan, 13-27; 2007, Jan, 13-27; 2007, January, 13-27; 2005, Mar, 11-15; 2005, Mar, 11-15; 2005, May, 1-2; 2005, Mar, 16-17; 2005, May, 1-2; 2005, Mar, 16-17; 2005, March, 16-17; 2005, May, 1-2; 2005, March, 11-15; 2004, Sep, 13; 2004, Sep, 13; 2004, September, 13; 2004, September, 13; 2004, Sep, 13; 2004, Sep, 13

90807 **with medical evaluation and management services**
2.50 2.77 Global Days XXX
AMA: 2005, May, 1-2; 2005, May, 1-2; 2005, May, 1-2

90808 **Individual psychotherapy, insight oriented, behavior modifying and/or supportive, in an office or outpatient facility, approximately 75 to 80 minutes face-to-face with the patient;**
3.46 3.63 Global Days XXX
AMA: 2005, May, 1-2; 2005, May, 1-2; 2005, May, 1-2

Medicine

90809 — 90822

90809   with medical evaluation and management services   🄌 🔳 ▭ 🄿🄾
     📖 3.66   ⚕ 3.92   Global Days XXX
      AMA: 2005, May, 1-2; 2005, May, 1-2; 2005, May, 1-2

90810-90815 Individual Outpatient Interactive Psychotherapy

CMS *100-3,130.7*   *Withdrawal Treatments for Narcotic Addictions*
CMS *100-3,130.5*   *Treatment of Alcoholism/Drug Abuse in a Freestanding Clinic*
CMS *100-3,130.6*   *Treatment of Drug Abuse (Chemical Dependency)*
CMS *100-3,130.2*   *Outpatient Hospital Services for Alcoholism*
CMS *100-4,12,150*   *Clinical Social Worker (CSW) Services*
CMS *100-4,12,170*   *Clinical Psychologist Services*
CMS *100-4,12,160*   *Independent Psychologist Services*
CMS *100-4,12,110.2*   *Outpatient Mental Health Limitation*

INCLUDES   drug management
      face-to-face time
      interactive psychotherapy:
         physical aids/non-verbal communication for individuals lacking expressive/receptive communication skills
         usually provided to children
      interpretation of lab/other diagnostic studies/observations
      medical diagnostic evaluation:
         comorbid medical conditions
         drug interactions
         physical examination
      physician orders
      psychotherapy only
      psychotherapy with medical evaluation and management services
      services provided in office or other outpatient facility
      treatment for:
         behavior disturbances
         mental illness

90810   **Individual psychotherapy, interactive, using play equipment, physical devices, language interpreter, or other mechanisms of non-verbal communication, in an office or outpatient facility, approximately 20 to 30 minutes face-to-face with the patient;**   🄌 🔳 ▭
     📖 1.64   ⚕ 1.88   Global Days XXX
      AMA: 2005, May, 1-2; 2005, May, 1-2; 2005, May, 1-2

90811   with medical evaluation and management services   🄌 🔳 ▭
     📖 1.84   ⚕ 2.19   Global Days XXX
      AMA: 2005, May, 1-2; 2005, May, 1-2; 2005, May, 1-2

90812   **Individual psychotherapy, interactive, using play equipment, physical devices, language interpreter, or other mechanisms of non-verbal communication, in an office or outpatient facility, approximately 45 to 50 minutes face-to-face with the patient;**   🄌 🔳 ▭
     📖 2.44   ⚕ 2.69   Global Days XXX
      AMA: 2005, May, 1-2; 2005, May, 1-2; 2005, May, 1-2

90813   with medical evaluation and management services   🄌 🔳 ▭
     📖 2.64   ⚕ 2.99   Global Days XXX
      AMA: 2005, May, 1-2; 2005, May, 1-2; 2005, May, 1-2

90814   **Individual psychotherapy, interactive, using play equipment, physical devices, language interpreter, or other mechanisms of non-verbal communication, in an office or outpatient facility, approximately 75 to 80 minutes face-to-face with the patient;**   🄌 🔳 ▭
     📖 3.66   ⚕ 3.90   Global Days XXX
      AMA: 2005, May, 1-2; 2005, May, 1-2; 2005, May, 1-2

90815   with medical evaluation and management services   🄌 🔳 ▭
     📖 3.79   ⚕ 4.14   Global Days XXX
      AMA: 2005, May, 1-2; 2005, May, 1-2; 2005, May, 1-2

90816-90822 Individual Inpatient Psychotherapy

CMS *100-3,130.7*   *Withdrawal Treatments for Narcotic Addictions*
CMS *100-3,130.6*   *Treatment of Drug Abuse (Chemical Dependency)*
CMS *100-3,130.1*   *Inpatient Stays for Alcoholism Treatment*
CMS *100-4,12,150*   *Clinical Social Worker (CSW) Services*
CMS *100-4,12,170.1*   *Payment for Clinical Psychologist Services*
CMS *100-4,12,170*   *Clinical Psychologist Services*
CMS *100-4,12,160.1*   *Payment for Independent Psychologists' Services*
CMS *100-4,12,210*   *Outpatient Mental Health Limitation*
CMS *100-4,12,160*   *Independent Psychologist Services*
CMS *100-4,12,110.2*   *Outpatient Mental Health Limitation*

INCLUDES   drug management
      face-to-face time
      insight oriented/behavior modifying/supportive psychotherapy:
         cognitive discussion of reality
         development of insight/affective understanding
         supportive interactions
         use of behavior modification
      interpretation of lab/other diagnostic studies/observations
      medical diagnostic evaluation:
         comorbid medical conditions
         drug interactions
         physical examination
      physician orders
      psychotherapy only
      psychotherapy with medical evaluation and management services
      services provided in inpatient hospital/partial hospital/residential care facility
      treatment for:
         behavior disturbances
         mental illiness

90816   **Individual psychotherapy, insight oriented, behavior modifying and/or supportive, in an inpatient hospital, partial hospital or residential care setting, approximately 20 to 30 minutes face-to-face with the patient;**   🄿 🔳 ▭
     📖 1.64   ⚕ 1.64   Global Days XXX
      AMA: 2005, May, 1-2; 2005, May, 1-2; 2005, May, 1-2

90817   with medical evaluation and management services   🄿 🔳 ▭
     📖 1.82   ⚕ 1.82   Global Days XXX
      AMA: 2005, May, 1-2; 2005, May, 1-2; 2005, May, 1-2

90818   **Individual psychotherapy, insight oriented, behavior modifying and/or supportive, in an inpatient hospital, partial hospital or residential care setting, approximately 45 to 50 minutes face-to-face with the patient;**   🄿 🔳 ▭
     📖 2.44   ⚕ 2.44   Global Days XXX
      AMA: 2005, May, 1-2; 2005, May, 1-2; 2005, May, 1-2

90819   with medical evaluation and management services   🄿 🔳 ▭
     📖 2.62   ⚕ 2.62   Global Days XXX
      AMA: 2005, May, 1-2; 2005, May, 1-2; 2005, May, 1-2

90821   **Individual psychotherapy, insight oriented, behavior modifying and/or supportive, in an inpatient hospital, partial hospital or residential care setting, approximately 75 to 80 minutes face-to-face with the patient;**   🄿 🔳 ▭
     📖 3.60   ⚕ 3.60   Global Days XXX
      AMA: 2005, May, 1-2; 2005, May, 1-2; 2005, May, 1-2

90822   with medical evaluation and management services   🄿 🔳 ▭
     📖 3.79   ⚕ 3.79   Global Days XXX
      AMA: 2005, May, 1-2; 2005, May, 1-2; 2005, May, 1-2

🄼🄲/🄣🄲 Professional/Technical Component Only   🄰🄾/🄶🄾 Assist-at-Surgery Allowed/With Documentation   Unlisted   Not Covered   ⊠ Radiology crosswalk

MED: Pub 100/NCD References   **AMA:** CPT Assistant References   🄰🄸-🅉🅉 ASC Payment Indicator   ♂Male Only   ♀Female Only   ⊠ Laboratory crosswalk

392   CPT only © 2008 American Medical Association. All Rights Reserved. (Black Ink)   Medicare (Red Ink)   © 2008 Ingenix *(Blue Ink)*

90823-90829 Inpatient Individual Psychotherapy: Interactive

CMS *100-3,130.7*   *Withdrawal Treatments for Narcotic Addictions*
CMS *100-3,130.6*   *Treatment of Drug Abuse (Chemical Dependency)*
CMS *100-3,130.1*   *Inpatient Stays for Alcoholism Treatment*
CMS *100-4,12,150*   *Clinical Social Worker (CSW) Services*
CMS *100-4,12,170*   *Clinical Psychologist Services*
CMS *100-4,12,160.1*   *Payment for Independent Psychologists' Services*
CMS *100-4,12,160*   *Independent Psychologist Services*
CMS *100-4,12,110.2*   *Outpatient Mental Health Limitation*

INCLUDES   drug management
face-to-face time
interactive psychotherapy:
physical aids/non-verbal communication for individuals lacking
expressive/receptive communication skills
usually provided to children
interpretation of lab/other diagnostic studies/observations
medical diagnostic evaluation:
comorbid medical conditions
drug interactions
physical examination
physician orders
psychotherapy only
psychotherapy with medical evaluation and management services
services provided in inpatient hospital/partial hospital/residential
care facility
treatment for:
behavior disturbances
mental illness

90823   Individual psychotherapy, interactive, using play
equipment, physical devices, language interpreter, or
other mechanisms of non-verbal communication, in an
inpatient hospital, partial hospital or residential care
setting, approximately 20 to 30 minutes face-to-face with
the patient;   P 80 ▭
  1.77   1.77   Global Days XXX
AMA: 2005, May, 1-2; 2005, May, 1-2; 2005, May, 1-2

90824   with medical evaluation and management
services   P 80 ▭
  1.97   1.97   Global Days XXX
AMA: 2005, May, 1-2; 2005, May, 1-2; 2005, May, 1-2

90826   Individual psychotherapy, interactive, using play
equipment, physical devices, language interpreter, or
other mechanisms of non-verbal communication, in an
inpatient hospital, partial hospital or residential care
setting, approximately 45 to 50 minutes face-to-face with
the patient;   P 80 ▭
  2.59   2.59   Global Days XXX
AMA: 2005, May, 1-2; 2005, May, 1-2; 2005, May, 1-2

90827   with medical evaluation and management
services   P 80 ▭
  2.75   2.75   Global Days XXX
AMA: 2005, May, 1-2; 2005, May, 1-2; 2005, May, 1-2

90828   Individual psychotherapy, interactive, using play
equipment, physical devices, language interpreter, or
other mechanisms of non-verbal communication, in an
inpatient hospital, partial hospital or residential care
setting, approximately 75 to 80 minutes face-to-face with
the patient;   P 80 ▭
  3.74   3.74   Global Days XXX
AMA: 2005, May, 1-2; 2005, May, 1-2; 2005, May, 1-2

90829   with medical evaluation and management
services   P 80 ▭
  3.91   3.91   Global Days XXX
AMA: 2005, May, 1-2; 2005, May, 1-2; 2005, May, 1-2

90845-90862 Additional Psychotherapy Services

CMS *100-2,15,160*   *Clinical Psychologist Services*
CMS *100-3,130.7*   *Withdrawal Treatments for Narcotic Addictions*
CMS *100-3,130.5*   *Treatment of Alcoholism/Drug Abuse in a Freestanding Clinic*
CMS *100-3,130.6*   *Treatment of Drug Abuse (Chemical Dependency)*
CMS *100-3,130.2*   *Outpatient Hospital Services for Alcoholism*
CMS *100-3,130.1*   *Inpatient Stays for Alcoholism Treatment*
CMS *100-4,12,150*   *Clinical Social Worker (CSW) Services*
CMS *100-4,12,170.1*   *Payment for Clinical Psychologist Services*
CMS *100-4,12,170*   *Clinical Psychologist Services*
CMS *100-4,12,160.1*   *Payment for Independent Psychologists' Services*
CMS *100-4,12,160*   *Independent Psychologist Services*
CMS *100-4,12,110.2*   *Outpatient Mental Health Limitation*

90845   Psychoanalysis   03 80 ▭
  2.22   2.27   Global Days XXX
AMA: 2008, Jan, 10-25; 2007, Jan, 13-27; 2007, Jan, 13-27; 2007,
January, 13-27; 2006, Feb, 16-18; 2006, Feb, 16-18; 2006,
February, 16-18; 2005, May, 1-2; 2005, May, 1-2; 2005, May, 1-2

90846   Family psychotherapy (without the patient
present)   03 80 ▭
  2.36   2.42   Global Days XXX
AMA: 2005, May, 1-2; 2005, May, 1-2; 2005, May, 1-2

90847   Family psychotherapy (conjoint psychotherapy) (with
patient present)   00 00 ▭
  2.83   3.01   Global Days XXX
AMA: 2005, May, 1-2; 2005, May, 1-2; 2005, May, 1-2

90849   Multiple-family group psychotherapy   03 80 ▭
  0.83   0.91   Global Days XXX
AMA: 2005, May, 1-2; 2005, May, 1-2; 2005, May, 1-2

90853   Group psychotherapy (other than of a multiple-family
group)   03 00 ▭
  0.81   0.86   Global Days XXX
AMA: 2005, May, 1-2; 2005, May, 1-2; 2005, May, 1-2

90857   Interactive group psychotherapy   03 80 ▭
  0.86   0.97   Global Days XXX
AMA: 2005, May, 1-2; 2005, May, 1-2; 2005, May, 1-2

90862   Pharmacologic management, including prescription, use,
and review of medication with no more than minimal
medical psychotherapy   03 80 ▭ P0
  EXCLUDES   *analysis/programming of neurostimulators
for vagus nerve stimulation therapy
(95970, 95974, 95975)
repetitive transcranial magnetic stimulation
for treatment of clinical depression
(0160T, 0161T)*
  1.25   1.53   Global Days XXX
AMA: 2006, Dec, 10-12; 2006, Dec, 10-12; 2006, Dec, 10-12; 2006,
December, 10-12; 2006, December, 10-12; 2006, Dec, 10-12;
2005, May, 1-2; 2005, March, 11-15; 2005, May, 1-2; 2005, May,
1-2; 2005, Mar, 11-15; 2005, Mar, 11-15

90865-90870 Psychiatric Treatment with Drugs or Electroshock

CMS 100-4,12,150   Clinical Social Worker (CSW) Services
CMS 100-4,12,170.1 Payment for Clinical Psychologist Services
CMS 100-4,12,170   Clinical Psychologist Services
CMS 100-4,12,160.1 Payment for Independent Psychologists' Services
CMS 100-4,12,210   Outpatient Mental Health Limitation
CMS 100-4,12,160   Independent Psychologist Services
CMS 100-4,12,110.2 Outpatient Mental Health Limitation

EXCLUDES analysis/programming of neurostimulators for vagus nerve stimulation therapy (95970, 95974, 95975)

repetitive transcranial magnetic stimulation for treatment of clinical depression (0160T-0161T)

90865 Narcosynthesis for psychiatric diagnostic and therapeutic purposes (eg, sodium amobarbital (Amytal) interview) 03 80 ▣

   3.69   4.29 Global Days XXX
   AMA: 2005, May, 1-2; 2005, May, 1-2; 2005, May, 1-2

90870 Electroconvulsive therapy (includes necessary monitoring) S 80 ▣

   2.36   3.79 Global Days 000
   AMA: 2005, May, 1-2; 2005, May, 1-2; 2005, May, 1-2

90875-90880 Psychiatric Therapy with Biofeedback or Hypnosis

CMS 100-3,30.1   Biofeedback Therapy
CMS 100-4,12,150   Clinical Social Worker (CSW) Services
CMS 100-4,12,170.1 Payment for Clinical Psychologist Services
CMS 100-4,12,170   Clinical Psychologist Services
CMS 100-4,12,160.1 Payment for Independent Psychologists' Services
CMS 100-4,12,210   Outpatient Mental Health Limitation
CMS 100-4,12,160   Independent Psychologist Services
CMS 100-4,12,110.2 Outpatient Mental Health Limitation

EXCLUDES analysis/programming of neurostimulators for vagus nerve stimulation therapy (95970, 95974, 95975)

repetitive transcranial magnetic stimulation for treatment of clinical depression (0160T, 0161T)

90875 Individual psychophysiological therapy incorporating biofeedback training by any modality (face-to-face with the patient), with psychotherapy (eg, insight oriented, behavior modifying or supportive psychotherapy); approximately 20-30 minutes E

   1.66   1.97 Global Days XXX
   AMA: 2008, Jan, 10-25; 2007, Jan, 13-27; 2007, Jan, 13-27; 2007, January, 13-27; 2005, Mar, 16-17; 2005, Mar, 16-17; 2005, March, 16-17; 2005, May, 1-2; 2005, May, 1-2; 2005, May, 1-2

90876 approximately 45-50 minutes E

   2.61   2.91 Global Days XXX
   AMA: 2005, Mar, 16-17; 2005, Mar, 16-17; 2005, May, 1-2; 2005, May, 1-2; 2005, May, 1-2; 2005, March, 16-17

90880 Hypnotherapy 03 80 ▣

   2.72   2.94 Global Days XXX
   AMA: 2005, May, 1-2; 2005, May, 1-2; 2005, Mar, 16-17; 2005, Mar, 16-17; 2005, May, 1-2; 2005, March, 16-17

90882-90899 Psychiatric Services without Patient Face-to-Face Contact

CMS 100-1,3,30.3   Mental Health Diagnostic Services
CMS 100-4,12,150   Clinical Social Worker (CSW) Services
CMS 100-4,12,170.1 Payment for Clinical Psychologist Services
CMS 100-4,12,170   Clinical Psychologist Services
CMS 100-4,12,160.1 Payment for Independent Psychologists' Services
CMS 100-4,12,210   Outpatient Mental Health Limitation
CMS 100-4,12,160   Independent Psychologist Services
CMS 100-4,12,110.2 Outpatient Mental Health Limitation

EXCLUDES analysis/programming of neurostimulators for vagus nerve stimulation therapy (95970, 95974, 95975)

repetitive transcranial magnetic stimulation for treatment of clinical depression (0160T, 0161T)

90882 Environmental intervention for medical management purposes on a psychiatric patient's behalf with agencies, employers, or institutions E

   0.00   0.00 Global Days XXX
   AMA: 2005, Mar, 16-17; 2005, Mar, 16-17; 2005, May, 1-2; 2005, May, 1-2; 2005, May, 1-2; 2005, March, 16-17

90885 Psychiatric evaluation of hospital records, other psychiatric reports, psychometric and/or projective tests, and other accumulated data for medical diagnostic purposes N

   1.33   1.33 Global Days XXX
   AMA: 2008, Jan, 10-25; 2007, Jan, 13-27; 2007, Jan, 13-27; 2007, January, 13-27; 2005, May, 1-2; 2005, May, 1-2; 2005, Mar, 16-17; 2005, March, 16-17; 2005, May, 1-2; 2005, Mar, 16-17; 2004, Nov, 10; 2004, November, 10; 2004, Nov, 10

90887 Interpretation or explanation of results of psychiatric, other medical examinations and procedures, or other accumulated data to family or other responsible persons, or advising them how to assist patient N

   2.03   2.32 Global Days XXX
   AMA: 2008, Jan, 10-25; 2007, Jan, 13-27; 2007, Jan, 13-27; 2007, January, 13-27; 2005, Mar, 16-17; 2005, Mar, 16-17; 2005, May, 1-2; 2005, March, 16-17; 2005, May, 1-2; 2005, May, 1-2

90889 Preparation of report of patient's psychiatric status, history, treatment, or progress (other than for legal or consultative purposes) for other physicians, agencies, or insurance carriers N

   0.00   0.00 Global Days XXX
   AMA: 2005, May, 1-2; 2005, May, 1-2; 2005, Mar, 16-17; 2005, Mar, 16-17; 2005, May, 1-2; 2005, March, 16-17

90899 Unlisted psychiatric service or procedure 03 80

   0.00   0.00 Global Days XXX
   AMA: 2005, May, 1-2; 2005, May, 1-2; 2005, Mar, 16-17; 2005, May, 1-2; 2005, March, 16-17

90901-90911 Biofeedback Therapy

CMS 100-3,30.1.1   Biofeedback for Urinary Incontinence
CMS 100-3,30.1   Biofeedback Therapy

EXCLUDES psychophysiological therapy utilizing biofeedback training (90875, 90876)

90901 Biofeedback training by any modality A 80 ▣

   0.55   0.93 Global Days 000
   AMA: 2008, Jan, 10-25; 2007, Jan, 13-27; 2007, Jan, 13-27; 2007, January, 13-27; 2005, Mar, 16-17; 2005, March, 16-17; 2005, Mar, 16-17; 2004, Sep, 13; 2004, September, 13; 2004, September, 13; 2004, Sep, 13; 2004, Sep, 13; 2004, Sep, 13

90911 Biofeedback training, perineal muscles, anorectal or urethral sphincter, including EMG and/or manometry 〔T〕〔80〕▭

EXCLUDES *rectal sensation/tone/compliance testing (91120)*

treatment for incontinence, pulsed magnetic neuromodulation (53899)

🚗 1.27 ⚕ 2.38 Global Days 000
AMA: 2008, Jan, 10-25; 2007, Jan, 13-27; 2007, Jan, 13-27; 2007, January, 13-27; 2005, Mar, 16-17; 2005, March, 16-17; 2005, Mar, 16-17

90918-90921 End-stage Renal Disease (ESRD) Services: Full Month

90918 ~~End-stage renal disease (ESRD) related services per full month; for patients younger than two years of age to include monitoring for the adequacy of nutrition, assessment of growth and development, and counseling of parents~~
See 90951-90953, 90963, 90967

90919 ~~for patients between two and eleven years of age to include monitoring for the adequacy of nutrition, assessment of growth and development, and counseling of parents~~
See 90954-90956, 90964, 90968

90920 ~~for patients between twelve and nineteen years of age to include monitoring for the adequacy of nutrition, assessment of growth and development, and counseling of parents~~
See 90957-90959, 90965, 90969

90921 ~~for patients twenty years of age and older~~
See 90960-90962, 90966, 90970

90922-90925 End-stage Renal Disease (ESRD) Services: Partial Month

90922 ~~End-stage renal disease (ESRD) related services (less than full month), per day; for patients younger than two years of age~~
See 90951-90953, 90963, 90967

90923 ~~for patients between two and eleven years of age~~
See 90954-90956, 90964, 90968

90924 ~~for patients between twelve and nineteen years of age~~
See 90957-90959, 90965, 90969

90925 ~~for patients twenty years of age and older~~
See 90960-90962, 90966, 90970

90935-90940 Hemodialysis Services: Inpatient ESRD and Outpatient Non-ESRD

CMS *100-3,130.8* Hemodialysis for Schizophrenia
CMS *100-3,230.14* Ultrafiltration Monitor
CMS *100-3,190.10* Laboratory Tests--CRD Patients
CMS *100-2,1,10* Inpatient Hospital Services Covered Under Part A
CMS *100-2,11,20* Coverage of Outpatient Maintenance Dialysis
CMS *100-4,3,100.6* Inpatient Renal Services

EXCLUDES *blood specimen collection from partial/complete implantable venous access device (36591)*
declotting of cannula (36831, 36833, 36860, 36861)
hemodialysis home visit by non-physician health care professional (99512)
physician attendance for a prolonged period of time (99354-99360)
thrombolytic agent declotting of implanted vascular access device/catheter (36593)

Code also significant separately identifiable evaluation and management service not related to dialysis procedure or renal failure, with modifier 25

90935 Hemodialysis procedure with single physician evaluation 〔S〕〔80〕▭〔PQ〕

INCLUDES all evaluation and management services related to the patient's renal disease rendered on a day dialysis is performed:
inpatient ESRD and non-ESRD procedures
only one evaluation of the patient related to hemodialysis procedure
outpatient non-ESRD dialysis

🚗 1.84 ⚕ 1.84 Global Days 000
AMA: 2005, Mar, 16-17; 2005, Mar, 16-17; 2005, March, 16-17

90937 Hemodialysis procedure requiring repeated evaluation(s) with or without substantial revision of dialysis prescription 〔B〕〔80〕▭〔PQ〕

INCLUDES all evaluation and management services related to the patient's renal disease rendered on a day dialysis is performed:
Inpatient ESRD and non-ESRD procedures
outpatient non-ESRD dialysis
re-evaluation of the patient during hemodialysis procedure

🚗 3.02 ⚕ 3.02 Global Days 000
AMA: 2005, Mar, 16-17; 2005, Mar, 16-17; 2005, March, 16-17

90940 Hemodialysis access flow study to determine blood flow in grafts and arteriovenous fistulae by an indicator method 〔N〕▭

EXCLUDES *hemodialysis access duplex scan (93990)*

🚗 0.00 ⚕ 0.00 Global Days XXX
AMA: 2008, Jan, 10-25; 2007, Jan, 13-27; 2007, Jan, 13-27; 2007, January, 13-27; 2006, May, 16-20; 2006, May, 16-20; 2006, May, 16-20; 2005, Mar, 16-17; 2005, Mar, 16-17; 2005, March, 16-17

Medicine

90945 — 90962

90945-90947 Dialysis Techniques Other Than Hemodialysis

CMS *100-3,110.15*   *Ultrafiltration, Hemoperfusion, and Hemofiltration*
CMS *100-3,190.10*   *Laboratory Tests--CRD Patients*
CMS *100-2,1,10*   *Inpatient Hospital Services Covered Under Part A*
CMS *100-3,240.6*   *Transvenous (Catheter) Pulmonary Embolectomy*
CMS *100-4,3,100.6* *Inpatient Renal Services*
CMS *100-4,4,20.5*   *HCPCS Under OPPS*

EXCLUDES   *intraperitoneal cannula/catheter insertion (49420, 49421)*
physician attendance for a prolonged period of time (99354-99360)

90945   **Dialysis procedure other than hemodialysis (eg, peritoneal dialysis, hemofiltration, or other continuous renal replacement therapies), with single physician evaluation**   V 80 ▣

   INCLUDES   all evaluation and management services related to the patient's renal disease rendered on a day dialysis is performed:
   continuous renal replacement therapies
   hemofiltration
   only one evaluation of the patient related to the procedure
   peritoneal dialysis

   EXCLUDES   *hemodialysis*
   peritoneal dialysis home infusion (99601, 99602)

   Code also significant separately identifiable evaluation and management service not related to dialysis procedure or renal failure, with modifier 25
   ⚷ 1.91   ⚷ 1.91   Global Days 000
   AMA: 2008, Jan, 10-25; 2007, Jan, 13-27; 2007, Jan, 13-27; 2007, January, 13-27; 2005, Mar, 16-17; 2005, March, 16-17; 2005, Mar, 16-17

90947   **Dialysis procedure other than hemodialysis (eg, peritoneal dialysis, hemofiltration, or other continuous renal replacement therapies) requiring repeated physician evaluations, with or without substantial revision of dialysis prescription**   B 80 ▣

   INCLUDES   all evaluation and management services related to the patient's renal disease rendered on a day dialysis is performed:
   continuous renal replacement therapies
   hemofiltration
   peritoneal dialysis
   re-evaluation during a procedure

   EXCLUDES   *hemodialysis*

   Code also significant separately identifiable evaluation and management service not related to dialysis procedure or renal failure, with modifier 25
   ⚷ 3.09   ⚷ 3.09   Global Days 000
   AMA: 2008, Jan, 10-25; 2007, Jan, 13-27; 2007, Jan, 13-27; 2007, January, 13-27; 2005, Mar, 16-17; 2005, March, 16-17; 2005, Mar, 16-17

90951-90962 End-stage Renal Disease Monthly Outpatient Services

CMS *100-3,230.14*   *Ultrafiltration Monitor*
CMS *100-3,190.10*   *Laboratory Tests--CRD Patients*

INCLUDES   establishing dialyzing cycle
management of dialysis visits
outpatient evaluation
patient management
telephone calls

EXCLUDES   *ESRD/non-ESRD dialysis services performed in an inpatient setting (90935-90937, 90945-90947)*
non-ESRD dialysis services performed in an outpatient setting (90935-90937, 90945-90947)
non-ESRD related evaluation and management services that cannot be performed during the dialysis session
dialysis services provided during an inpatient hospitalization (90935-90937, 90945-90947)

● **90951**   **End-stage renal disease (ESRD) related services monthly, for patients younger than 2 years of age to include monitoring for the adequacy of nutrition, assessment of growth and development, and counseling of parents; with 4 or more face-to-face physician visits per month**   A M 80
   ⚷ 26.67   ⚷ 26.67   Global Days XXX

● **90952**   **with 2-3 face-to-face physician visits per month**   A M 80
   ⚷ 0.00   ⚷ 0.00   Global Days XXX

● **90953**   **with 1 face-to-face physician visit per month**   A M 80
   ⚷ 0.00   ⚷ 0.00   Global Days XXX

● **90954**   **End-stage renal disease (ESRD) related services monthly, for patients 2-11 years of age to include monitoring for the adequacy of nutrition, assessment of growth and development, and counseling of parents; with 4 or more face-to-face physician visits per month**   A M 80
   ⚷ 21.85   ⚷ 21.85   Global Days XXX

● **90955**   **with 2-3 face-to-face physician visits per month**   A M 80
   ⚷ 12.39   ⚷ 12.39   Global Days XXX

● **90956**   **with 1 face-to-face physician visit per month**   A M 80
   ⚷ 8.39   ⚷ 8.39   Global Days XXX

● **90957**   **End-stage renal disease (ESRD) related services monthly, for patients 12-19 years of age to include monitoring for the adequacy of nutrition, assessment of growth and development, and counseling of parents; with 4 or more face-to-face physician visits per month**   A M 80
   ⚷ 17.55   ⚷ 17.55   Global Days XXX

● **90958**   **with 2-3 face-to-face physician visits per month**   A M 80
   ⚷ 11.85   ⚷ 11.85   Global Days XXX

● **90959**   **with 1 face-to-face physician visit per month**   A M 80
   ⚷ 7.77   ⚷ 7.77   Global Days XXX

● **90960**   **End-stage renal disease (ESRD) related services monthly, for patients 20 years of age and older; with 4 or more face-to-face physician visits per month**   A M 80
   ⚷ 7.81   ⚷ 7.81   Global Days XXX

● **90961**   **with 2-3 face-to-face physician visits per month**   A M 80
   ⚷ 6.30   ⚷ 6.30   Global Days XXX

● **90962**   **with 1 face-to-face physician visit per month**   A M 80
   ⚷ 4.55   ⚷ 4.55   Global Days XXX

90963-90966 End-stage Renal Disease Monthly Home Dialysis Services

INCLUDES ESRD services for home dialysis patients
services provided for a full month services

● **90963** End-stage renal disease (ESRD) related services for home dialysis per full month, for patients younger than 2 years of age to include monitoring for the adequacy of nutrition, assessment of growth and development, and counseling of parents M 80
  15.06   15.06   Global Days XXX

● **90964** End-stage renal disease (ESRD) related services for home dialysis per full month, for patients 2-11 years of age to include monitoring for the adequacy of nutrition, assessment of growth and development, and counseling of parents A M 80
  12.55   12.55   Global Days XXX

● **90965** End-stage renal disease (ESRD) related services for home dialysis per full month, for patients 12-19 years of age to include monitoring for the adequacy of nutrition, assessment of growth and development, and counseling of parents A M 80
  11.93   11.93   Global Days XXX

● **90966** End-stage renal disease (ESRD) related services for home dialysis per full month, for patients 20 years of age and older A M 80
  6.23   6.23   Global Days XXX

90967-90970 End-stage Renal Disease (ESRD) Services: Partial Month

CMS 100-3,230.14 *Ultrafiltration Monitor*
CMS 100-3,190.10 *Laboratory Tests--CRD Patients*
INCLUDES ESRD services for less than a full month, such as:
a patient who is transient, dies, recovers, or undergoes kidney transplant
outpatient ESRD-related services initiated prior to completion of assessment
patient spending part of the month as a hospital inpatient
services reported on a daily basis, less the days of hospitalization

● **90967** End-stage renal disease (ESRD) related services for dialysis less than a full month of service, per day; for patients younger than 2 years of age A M 80
  0.54   0.54   Global Days XXX

● **90968** for patients 2-11 years of age A M 80
  0.42   0.42   Global Days XXX

● **90969** for patients 12-19 years of age A M 80
  0.41   0.41   Global Days XXX

● **90970** for patients 20 years of age and older A M 80
  0.22   0.22   Global Days XXX

90989-90993 Dialysis Training Services

90989 Dialysis training, patient, including helper where applicable, any mode, completed course B
  0.00   0.00   Global Days XXX
AMA: 2008, Jan, 10-25; 2007, Jan, 13-27; 2007, Jan, 13-27; 2007, January, 13-27

90993 Dialysis training, patient, including helper where applicable, any mode, course not completed, per training session B
  0.00   0.00   Global Days XXX
AMA: 2008, Jan, 10-25; 2007, Jan, 13-27; 2007, Jan, 13-27; 2007, January, 13-27

90997-90999 Hemoperfusion and Unlisted Dialysis Procedures

90997 Hemoperfusion (eg, with activated charcoal or resin) B 80
  2.46   2.46   Global Days 000

90999 Unlisted dialysis procedure, inpatient or outpatient B 80
  0.00   0.00   Global Days XXX

91000 Esophageal Intubation for Cytology Washings

EXCLUDES anoscopy (46600-46615)
colonoscopy (45355-45385)
duodenal intubation/aspiration (89100-89105)
esophagoscopy (43200-43228)
insertion of:
esophageal tamponade tube (43460)
Miller-Abbott tube (44500)
proctosigmoidoscopy (45300-45321)
radiologic services, gastrointestinal (74210-74363)
sigmoidoscopy (45330-45339)
small intestine/stomal endoscopy (44360-44393)
upper gastrointestinal endoscopy (43234-43259)

91000 Esophageal intubation and collection of washings for cytology, including preparation of specimens (separate procedure) X 80
  2.42   2.42   Global Days 000

91010-91022 Manometry

CMS 100-3,100.4 *Esophageal Manometry*
EXCLUDES anoscopy (46600-46615)
colonoscopy (45355-45385)
duodenal intubation/aspiration (89100-89105)
esophagoscopy (43200-43228)
insertion of:
esophageal tamponade tube (43460)
Miller-Abbott tube (44500)
proctosigmoidoscopy (45300-45321)
radiologic services, gastrointestinal (74210-74363)
sigmoidoscopy (45330-45339)
small intestine/stomal endoscopy (44360-44393)
upper gastrointestinal endoscopy (43234-43259)

91010 Esophageal motility (manometric study of the esophagus and/or gastroesophageal junction) study; X 80
  5.13   5.13   Global Days 000
AMA: 2005, May, 3-6; 2005, May, 3-6; 2005, May, 3-6

91011 with mecholyl or similar stimulant X 80
  6.86   6.86   Global Days 000

91012 with acid perfusion studies X 80
  6.97   6.97   Global Days 000

Medicine

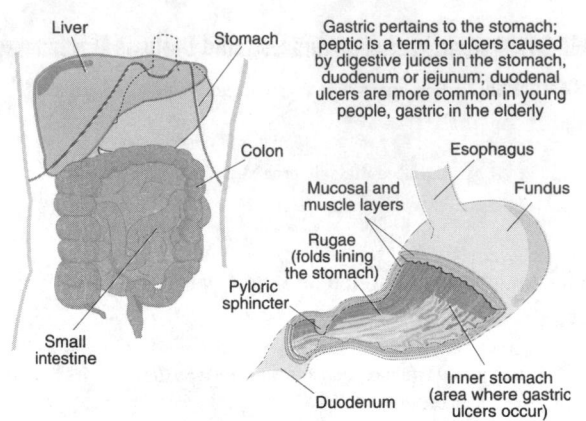

Liver

Stomach

Gastric pertains to the stomach; peptic is a term for ulcers caused by digestive juices in the stomach, duodenum or jejunum; duodenal ulcers are more common in young people, gastric in the elderly

Colon

Esophagus

Mucosal and muscle layers

Fundus

Rugae (folds lining the stomach)

Pyloric sphincter

Small intestine

Duodenum

Inner stomach (area where gastric ulcers occur)

91020   **Gastric motility (manometric) studies**   X 80 ▭
         6.23   6.23   Global Days 000

91022   **Duodenal motility (manometric) study**   X 80
         EXCLUDES   *fluoroscopy (76000)*
                       gastric motility study (91020)
         5.13   5.13   Global Days 000

91030-91040 Esophageal Reflux Tests

EXCLUDES   *anoscopy (46600-46615)*
              colonoscopy (45355-45385)
              duodenal intubation/aspiration (89100-89105)
              esophagoscopy (43200-43228)
              insertion of:
                  esophageal tamponade tube (43460)
                  Miller-Abbott tube (44500)
              proctosigmoidoscopy (45300-45321)
              radiologic services, gastrointestinal (74210-74363)
              sigmoidoscopy (45330-45339)
              small intestine/stomal endoscopy (44360-44393)
              upper gastrointestinal endoscopy (43234-43259)

91030   **Esophagus, acid perfusion (Bernstein) test for**
         esophagitis   X 80 ▭
         3.73   3.73   Global Days 000

91034   **Esophagus, gastroesophageal reflux test; with nasal**
         catheter pH electrode(s) placement, recording, analysis
         and interpretation   X 80 ▭
         5.38   5.38   Global Days 000
         AMA: 2005, May, 3-6; 2005, May, 3-6; 2005, May, 3-6

91035   **with mucosal attached telemetry pH electrode**
         placement, recording, analysis and
         interpretation   X 80 ▭
         12.63   12.63 Global Days 000
         AMA: 2005, May, 3-6; 2005, May, 3-6; 2005, May, 3-6

91037   **Esophageal function test, gastroesophageal reflux test**
         with nasal catheter intraluminal impedance electrode(s)
         placement, recording, analysis and
         interpretation;   X 80 ▭
         4.32   4.32   Global Days 000
         AMA: 2005, May, 3-6; 2005, May, 3-6; 2005, May, 3-6

91038   **prolonged (greater than 1 hour, up to 24**
         hours)   X 80 ▭
         3.81   3.81   Global Days 000
         AMA: 2005, May, 3-6; 2005, May, 3-6; 2005, May, 3-6

91040   **Esophageal balloon distension provocation**
         study   X 80 ▭
         EXCLUDES   *endoscopic balloon dilation (43220, 43249,*
                       43456, 43458)
         10.23   10.23 Global Days 000
         AMA: 2005, May, 3-6; 2005, May, 3-6; 2005, May, 3-6

91052 Gastric Analysis for pH of Stomach Secretions

CMS *100-3,30.6*   *Intravenous Histamine Therapy*
EXCLUDES   *anoscopy (46600-46615)*
              colonoscopy (45355-45385)
              duodenal intubation/aspiration (89100-89105)
              esophagoscopy (43200-43228)
              insertion of:
                  esophageal tamponade tube (43460)
                  Miller-Abbott tube (44500)
              proctosigmoidoscopy (45300-45321)
              radiologic services, gastrointestinal (74210-74363)
              sigmoidoscopy (45330-45339)
              small intestine/stomal endoscopy (44360-44393)
              upper gastrointestinal endoscopy (43234-43259)

91052   **Gastric analysis test with injection of stimulant of gastric**
         secretion (eg, histamine, insulin, pentagastrin, calcium
         and secretin)   X 80 ▭
         EXCLUDES   *stomach biopsy by capsule/peroral/via tube,*
                       one or more specimens (43600)

         ◢   *89130-89141*
         3.32   3.32   Global Days 000

91055 Gastric Intubation for Cytology Washings

EXCLUDES   *anoscopy (46600-46615)*
              colonoscopy (45355-45385)
              duodenal intubation/aspiration (89100-89105)
              esophagoscopy (43200-43228)
              insertion of:
                  esophageal tamponade tube (43460)
                  Miller-Abbott tube (44500)
              proctosigmoidoscopy (45300-45321)
              radiologic services, gastrointestinal (74210-74363)
              sigmoidoscopy (45330-45339)
              small intestine/stomal endoscopy (44360-44393)
              upper gastrointestinal endoscopy (43234-43259)

91055   **Gastric intubation, washings, and preparing slides for**
         cytology (separate procedure)   X 80 ▭
         INCLUDES   Hollander test
                       Rehfuss' test
         EXCLUDES   *intestinal biopsy by capsule/mouth/tube, one*
                       or more specimens (44100)
                       therapeutic gastric lavage (91105)
         3.59   3.59   Global Days 000

91020 — 91055

91065 Breath Analysis

CMS *100-3,100.5*   *Diagnostic Breath Analysis*

EXCLUDES   *anoscopy (46600-46615)*
    colonoscopy (45355-45385)
    duodenal intubation/aspiration (89100-89105)
    esophagoscopy (43200-43228)
    H. pylori breath test analysis, radioactive (C-14) or nonradioactive (C-13) (78268, or 83013)
    insertion of:
      esophageal tamponade tube (43460)
      Miller-Abbott tube (44500)
    proctosigmoidoscopy (45300-45321)
    radiologic services, gastrointestinal (74210-74363)
    sigmoidoscopy (45330-45339)
    small intestine/stomal endoscopy (44360-44393)
    upper gastrointestinal endoscopy (43234-43259)

91065   **Breath hydrogen test (eg, for detection of lactase deficiency, fructose intolerance, bacterial overgrowth, or oro-cecal gastrointestinal transit)**   X 80 □

    EXCLUDES   *H. pylori breath test analysis nonreactive isotope (C-13) (83013) radioactive isotope (C-14) (78268)*

    1.77   1.77   **Global Days 000**
    AMA: 2005, May, 3-6; 2005, May, 3-6; 2005, May, 3-6

91100 Intestinal Intubation

~~**91100**   **Intestinal bleeding tube, passage, positioning and monitoring**~~
    See 43460, 44500

91105 Gastric Lavage and Aspiration

CMS *100-4,12,30.6.12 Critical Care Visits*

EXCLUDES   *anoscopy (46600-46615)*
    colonoscopy (45355-45385)
    duodenal intubation/aspiration (89100-89105)
    esophagoscopy (43200-43228)
    proctosigmoidoscopy (45300-45321)
    radiologic services, gastrointestinal (74210-74363)
    sigmoidoscopy (45330-45339)
    small intestine/stomal endoscopy (44360-44393)
    upper gastrointestinal endoscopy (43234-43259)

91105   **Gastric intubation, and aspiration or lavage for treatment (eg, for ingested poisons)**   X 80 □

    EXCLUDES   *cholangiography (47500, 74320) paracentesis, abdominal (49080, 49081)*
      with medication instillation (96440, 96445)
    peritoneoscopy (49320)
      with biopsy (49321)
    peritoneoscopy with guided transhepatic cholangiography (47560)
      with biopsy (47561)
    splenoportography (38200, 75810)

    0.47   2.14   **Global Days 000**
    AMA: 2008, Jan, 10-25; 2007, Jan, 13-27; 2007, Jan, 13-27; 2007, Feb, 10-11; 2007, Feb, 10-11; 2007, January, 13-27; 2007, February, 10-11; 2007, Jul, 1-4

91110-91299 Additional Gastrointestinal Diagnostic/Therapeutic Procedures

EXCLUDES   *anoscopy (46600-46615)*
    colonoscopy (45355-45385)
    duodenal intubation/aspiration (89100-89105)
    esophagoscopy (43200-43228)
    proctosigmoidoscopy (45300-45321)
    radiologic services, gastrointestinal (74210-74363)
    sigmoidoscopy (45330-45339)
    small intestine/stomal endoscopy (44360-44393)
    upper gastrointestinal endoscopy (43234-43259)

91110   **Gastrointestinal tract imaging, intraluminal (eg, capsule endoscopy), esophagus through ileum, with physician interpretation and report**   T 80

    Code also modifier 52 if ileum is not visualized
    Do not report with visualization of the colon separately

    24.30   24.30   **Global Days XXX**
    AMA: 2008, Jan, 10-25; 2007, Jan, 13-27; 2007, Jan, 13-27; 2007, January, 13-27; 2005, Aug, 13-15; 2005, Aug, 13-15; 2005, August, 13-15; 2004, Oct, 15; 2004, Oct, 15; 2004, October, 15

91111   **Gastrointestinal tract imaging, intraluminal (eg, capsule endoscopy), esophagus with physician interpretation and report**   T 80

    Do not report with imaging, esophagus through ileum (91110)

    18.97   18.97   **Global Days XXX**

91120   **Rectal sensation, tone, and compliance test (ie, response to graded balloon distention)**   T 80

    EXCLUDES   *anorectal manometry (91122) biofeedback training (90911)*

    10.48   10.48   **Global Days XXX**
    AMA: 2005, May, 3-6; 2005, May, 3-6; 2005, May, 3-6

91122   **Anorectal manometry**   T 80 □
    6.29   6.29   **Global Days 000**

91123   **Pulsed irrigation of fecal impaction**   N
    0.00   0.00   **Global Days XXX**

91132   **Electrogastrography, diagnostic, transcutaneous;**   X 80 □
    0.00   0.00   **Global Days XXX**

91133   **with provocative testing**   X 80 □
    0.00   0.00   **Global Days XXX**

91299   **Unlisted diagnostic gastroenterology procedure**   X 80
    0.00   0.00   **Global Days XXX**
    AMA: 2005, Aug, 13-15; 2005, Aug, 13-15; 2005, August, 13-15

Medicine

92002 — 92012

92002-92014 Ophthalmic Medical Services

CMS 100-4,4,160   *Clinic and EmergencyVisits Under OPPS*
CMS 100-4,4,20.5   *HCPCS Under OPPS*
[INCLUDES]   routine ophthalmoscopy
[EXCLUDES]   *surgical procedures on the eye/ocular adnexa (65091-68899)*

92002   **Ophthalmological services: medical examination and evaluation with initiation of diagnostic and treatment program; intermediate, new patient**   [V] [80] [□] [PQ]
  [INCLUDES]   evaluation of new/existing condition complicated by new diagnostic or management problem
      integrated services where medical decision making cannot be separated from examination methods
      problems not related to primary diagnosis
      services provided to patients who have received no professional services from this physician or other same-specialty physicians within the same group practice within the past three years
      the following for intermediate services:
        biomicroscopy
        external ocular/adnexal examination
        general medical observation
        history
        mydriasis
        ophthalmoscopy
        other diagnostic procedures
        tonometry

  🔲 1.20 ⚖ 1.86 **Global Days XXX**
  AMA: 2008, Jan, 1-3; 2008, Jan, 10-25; 2008, Sep, 7-8; 2007, Jan, 28-31; 2007, Jan, 28-31; 2007, January, 28-31; 2005, Jun, 9-11; 2005, Jun, 9-11; 2005, Dec, 9-11; 2005, June, 9-11; 2005, December, 9-11; 2005, Dec, 9-11; 2004, Mar, 7; 2004, March, 7; 2004, Mar, 7

92004   **comprehensive, new patient, 1 or more visits**   [V] [80] [□] [PQ]
  [INCLUDES]   general evaluation of complete visual system
      integrated services where medical decision making cannot be separated from examination methods
      services provided to patients who have received no professional services from this physician or other same-specialty physicians within the same group practice within the past three years
      single service that need not be performed at one session
      the following for comprehensive services:
        basic sensorimotor examination
        biomicroscopy
        consultations
        dilation (cycloplegia)
        external examinations
        general medical observation
        gross visual fields
        history
        initiation of diagnostic/treatment programs
        laboratory services
        mydriasis
        ophthalmoscopic examinations
        other diagnostic procedures
        prescription of medication
        radiological services
        special diagnostic/treatment services
        tonometry

  🔲 2.49 ⚖ 3.50 **Global Days XXX**
  AMA: 2008, Jan, 1-3; 2008, Sep, 7-8; 2007, Jan, 28-31; 2007, Jan, 28-31; 2007, January, 28-31; 2005, Mar, 11-15; 2005, Mar, 11-15; 2005, Jun, 9-11; 2005, Jun, 9-11; 2005, March, 11-15; 2005, December, 9-11; 2005, June, 9-11; 2005, Dec, 9-11; 2005, Dec, 9-11; 2004, Mar, 7; 2004, March, 7; 2004, Mar, 7

92012   **Ophthalmological services: medical examination and evaluation, with initiation or continuation of diagnostic and treatment program; intermediate, established patient**   [V] [80] [□] [PQ]
  [INCLUDES]   evaluation of new/existing condition complicated by new diagnostic or management problem
      integrated services where medical decision making cannot be separated from examination methods
      problems not related to primary diagnosis
      services provided to patients who have received professional services from this physician or other same-specialty physicians within the same group practice within the past three years
      the following for intermediate services:
        external ocular/adnexal examination
        general medical observation
        history
        other diagnostic procedures
        biomicroscopy
        mydriasis
        ophthalmoscopy
        tonometry

  🔲 1.27 ⚖ 1.96 **Global Days XXX**
  AMA: 2008, Jan, 1-3; 2008, Sep, 7-8; 2007, Jan, 28-31; 2007, Jan, 28-31; 2007, January, 28-31; 2005, Mar, 11-15; 2005, Mar, 11-15; 2005, Dec, 9-11; 2005, Dec, 9-11; 2005, March, 11-15; 2005, June, 9-11; 2005, December, 9-11; 2005, Jun, 9-11; 2005, Jun, 9-11; 2004, Mar, 7; 2004, March, 7; 2004, Mar, 7

92014 comprehensive, established patient, 1 or more visits ▣ 80 ▣ 80
  INCLUDES general evaluation of complete visual system
    integrated services where medical decision making cannot be separated from examination methods
    services provided to patients who have received professional services from this physician or other same-specialty physicians within the same group practice within the past three years
    single service that need not be performed at one session
    the following for comprehensive services:
      basic sensorimotor examination
      biomicroscopy
      consultations
      dilation (cycloplegia)
      external examinations
      general medical observation
      gross visual fields
      history
      initiation of diagnostic/treatment programs
      laboratory services
      mydriasis
      ophthalmoscopic examinations
      other diagnostic procedures
      prescription of medication
      radiological services
      special diagnostic/treatment services
      tonometry

  🔲 1.95 🔲 2.86 Global Days XXX
  AMA: 2008, Jan, 1-3; 2008, Jan, 10-25; 2008, Sep, 7-8; 2007, Jan, 28-31; 2007, Jan, 28-31; 2007, Jan, 13-27; 2007, January, 20-31; 2007, Jan, 13-27, 2007, January, 13-27; 2005, Dec, 9-11; 2005, Dec, 9-11; 2005, Mar, 11-15; 2005, March, 11-15; 2005, December, 9-11; 2005, June, 9-11; 2005, Mar, 11-15; 2005, Jun, 9-11; 2005, Jun, 9-11; 2004, Mar, 7; 2004, Mar, 7; 2004, March, 7

92015-92287 Ophthalmic Diagnostic and Other Special Services

CMS 100-3,80.9 *Computer Enhanced Perimetry*
CMS 100-3,80.8 *Endothelial Cell Photography*
CMS 100-3,80.6 *Intraocular Photography*
CMS 100-3,80.4 *Hydrophilic Contact Lens*
CMS 100 3,80.1 *Hydrophilic Contact lens or Corneal Bandage*
CMS 100-2,16,90 *Routine Services and Appliances*
CMS 100-3,80.2 *Photodynamic Therapy*
INCLUDES routine ophthalmoscopy

EXCLUDES *surgical procedures on the eye/ocular adnexa (65091-68899)*

Code also evaluation and management services (99201-99499)
general ophthalmological services (92002-92014)

92015 Determination of refractive state E
  INCLUDES lens prescription
    absorptive factor
    axis
    impact resistance
    lens power
    prism
    specification of lens type
    monofocal
    bifocal

  🔲 0.52 🔲 0.87 Global Days XXX
  AMA: 2008, Jan, 10-25; 2007, Jan, 13-27; 2007, Jan, 13-27; 2007, January, 13-27; 2006, Aug, 12-14; 2006, August, 12-14; 2006, Aug, 12-14

92018 Ophthalmological examination and evaluation, under general anesthesia, with or without manipulation of globe for passive range of motion or other manipulation to facilitate diagnostic examination; complete ▣ 80 ▣
  🔲 3.54 🔲 3.54 Global Days XXX

92019 limited ▣ 80 ▣
  🔲 1.76 🔲 1.76 Global Days XXX

92020 Gonioscopy (separate procedure) ⓢ 80 ▣
  EXCLUDES *gonioscopy under general anesthesia (92018)*
  🔲 0.52 🔲 0.66 Global Days XXX

92025 Computerized corneal topography, unilateral or bilateral, with interpretation and report ⓢ 80
  EXCLUDES *manual keratoscopy*

  Do not report with (65710-65771)
  🔲 0.86 🔲 0.86 Global Days XXX

92060 Sensorimotor examination with multiple measurements of ocular deviation (eg, restrictive or paretic muscle with diplopia) with interpretation and report (separate procedure) ⓢ 80 ▣
  🔲 1.49 🔲 1.49 Global Days XXX

92065 Orthoptic and/or pleoptic training, with continuing medical direction and evaluation ⓢ 80 ▣
  🔲 1.17 🔲 1.17 Global Days XXX
  AMA: 2008, Jan, 10-25; 2007, Jan, 13-27; 2007, Jan, 13-27; 2007, January, 13-27

92070 Fitting of contact lens for treatment of disease, including supply of lens ▣ 80 ▣
  🔲 0.98 🔲 1.67 Global Days XXX

92081 Visual field examination, unilateral or bilateral, with interpretation and report; limited examination (eg, tangent screen, Autoplot, arc perimeter, or single stimulus level automated test, such as Octopus 3 or 7 equivalent) ⓢ 80 ▣
  🔲 1.33 🔲 1.33 Global Days XXX

92082 intermediate examination (eg, at least 2 isopters on Goldmann perimeter, or semiquantitative, automated suprathreshold screening program, Humphrey suprathreshold automatic diagnostic test, Octopus program 33) ⓒ 80 ▣
  🔲 1.76 🔲 1.76 Global Days XXX

92083 extended examination (eg, Goldmann visual fields with at least 3 isopters plotted and static determination within the central 30°, or quantitative, automated threshold perimetry, Octopus program G 1, 32 or 42, Humphrey visual field analyzer full threshold programs 30-2, 24-2, or 30/60-2) ⓢ 80 ▣
  EXCLUDES *gross visual field testing/confrontation testing*
  🔲 2.01 🔲 2.01 Global Days XXX
  AMA: 2005, Mar, 11-15; 2005, Mar, 11-15; 2005, March, 11-15

92100 Serial tonometry (separate procedure) with multiple measurements of intraocular pressure over an extended time period with interpretation and report, same day (eg, diurnal curve or medical treatment of acute elevation of intraocular pressure) ▣ 80 ▣
  🔲 1.26 🔲 2.23 Global Days XXX
  AMA: 2008, Jan, 10-25; 2007, Jan, 13-27; 2007, Jan, 13-27; 2007, January, 13-27

92120 Tonography with interpretation and report, recording indentation tonometer method or perilimbal suction method ⓢ 80 ▣
  🔲 1.12 🔲 1.84 Global Days XXX

92130 Tonography with water provocation ⓢ 80 ▣
  🔲 1.14 🔲 2.03 Global Days XXX

Medicine

92135 — 92312

92135 **Scanning computerized ophthalmic diagnostic imaging, posterior segment, (eg, scanning laser) with interpretation and report, unilateral** Ⓢ🖥
📷 1.17 ✂ 1.17 Global Days XXX
AMA: 2008, Jan, 10-25; 2008, Jan, 1-3; 2007, Jan, 13-27; 2007, Jan, 13-27; 2007, January, 13-27; 2005, Mar, 11-15; 2005, March, 11-15; 2005, Mar, 11-15

92136 **Ophthalmic biometry by partial coherence interferometry with intraocular lens power calculation** Ⓢ80🖥
📷 2.10 ✂ 2.10 Global Days XXX
AMA: 2008, Jan, 10-25; 2007, Jan, 13-27; 2007, Jan, 13-27; 2007, January, 13-27

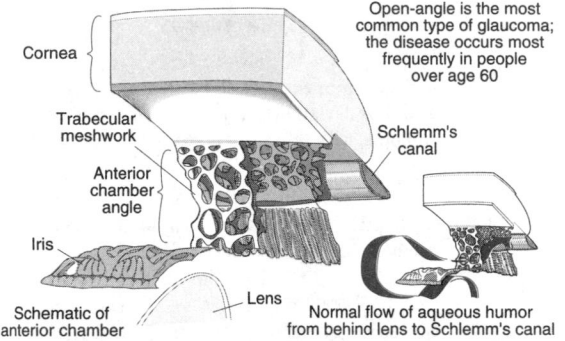

Cornea

Open-angle is the most common type of glaucoma; the disease occurs most frequently in people over age 60

Trabecular meshwork

Schlemm's canal

Anterior chamber angle

Iris

Lens

Schematic of anterior chamber

Normal flow of aqueous humor from behind lens to Schlemm's canal

Glaucoma is caused by excessive intraocular pressure and abnormal accumulation of aqueous humor in the anterior chamber of the eye; pressure reduces blood supply to the optic nerve and causes nerve damage

92140 **Provocative tests for glaucoma, with interpretation and report, without tonography** Ⓢ80🖥
📷 0.68 ✂ 1.44 Global Days XXX

92225 **Ophthalmoscopy, extended, with retinal drawing (eg, for retinal detachment, melanoma), with interpretation and report; initial** Ⓢ80🖥
EXCLUDES *ophthalmoscopy under general anesthesia (92018)*
📷 0.53 ✂ 0.63 Global Days XXX
AMA: 2008, Jan, 10-25; 2007, Jan, 13-27; 2007, Jan, 13-27; 2007, January, 13-27

92226 **subsequent** Ⓢ80🖥
📷 0.47 ✂ 0.57 Global Days XXX

92230 **Fluorescein angioscopy with interpretation and report** Ⓢ80🖥
📷 0.83 ✂ 1.52 Global Days XXX

92235 **Fluorescein angiography (includes multiframe imaging) with interpretation and report** Ⓢ80🖥
📷 3.24 ✂ 3.24 Global Days XXX
AMA: 2008, Jan, 1-3; 2005, Mar, 11-15; 2005, Mar, 11-15; 2005, March, 11-15

92240 **Indocyanine-green angiography (includes multiframe imaging) with interpretation and report** Ⓢ80🖥
📷 6.00 ✂ 6.00 Global Days XXX
AMA: 2008, Jan, 1-3

92250 **Fundus photography with interpretation and report** Ⓢ80🖥
📷 1.81 ✂ 1.81 Global Days XXX
AMA: 2008, Jan, 1-3

92260 **Ophthalmodynamometry** Ⓢ80🖥
EXCLUDES *ophthalmoscopy under general anesthesia (92018)*
📷 0.29 ✂ 0.45 Global Days XXX

92265 **Needle oculoelectromyography, 1 or more extraocular muscles, 1 or both eyes, with interpretation and report** Ⓢ80🖥
📷 1.97 ✂ 1.97 Global Days XXX

92270 **Electro-oculography with interpretation and report** Ⓢ80🖥
📷 2.26 ✂ 2.26 Global Days XXX

92275 **Electroretinography with interpretation and report** Ⓢ80🖥
EXCLUDES *vestibular function tests/electronystagmography (92541-92548)*
⊞ 76511-76529
📷 3.37 ✂ 3.37 Global Days XXX

92283 **Color vision examination, extended, eg, anomaloscope or equivalent** Ⓢ80🖥
INCLUDES Farnsworth-Munsell color test Ishihara test
📷 1.15 ✂ 1.15 Global Days XXX

92284 **Dark adaptation examination with interpretation and report** Ⓢ80🖥
📷 1.54 ✂ 1.54 Global Days XXX

92285 **External ocular photography with interpretation and report for documentation of medical progress (eg, close-up photography, slit lamp photography, goniophotography, stereo-photography)** Ⓢ80🖥
📷 1.06 ✂ 1.06 Global Days XXX
AMA: 2008, Jan, 1-3; 2008, Jan, 10-25; 2007, Jan, 13-27; 2007, Jan, 13-27; 2007, January, 13-27

92286 **Special anterior segment photography with interpretation and report; with specular endothelial microscopy and cell count** Ⓢ80🖥
📷 3.02 ✂ 3.02 Global Days XXX
AMA: 2008, Jan, 1-3

92287 **with fluorescein angiography** Ⓢ80🖥
📷 1.14 ✂ 2.86 Global Days XXX

92310-92326 Services Related to Contact Lenses

CMS *100-3,80.4* *Hydrophilic Contact Lens*
CMS *100-3,80.1* *Hydrophilic Contact lens br Corneal Bandage*
CMS *100-2,15,120* *Prosthetic Devices*
CMS *100-2,15,30.4* *Optometrist's Services*
CMS *100-4,4,20.5* *HCPCS Under OPPS*

INCLUDES incidental revision of lens during training period
patient training/instruction
specification of optical/physical characteristics:
curvature
flexibility
gas-permeabililty
power
size

EXCLUDES *extended wear lenses follow up (92012-92014)*
general ophthalmological services
therapeutic/surgical use of contact lens (68340, 92070)

92310 **Prescription of optical and physical characteristics of and fitting of contact lens, with medical supervision of adaptation; corneal lens, both eyes, except for aphakia** Ⓔ
Code also modifier 52 for one eye
📷 1.62 ✂ 2.44 Global Days XXX

92311 **corneal lens for aphakia, 1 eye** Ⓢ80🖥
📷 1.45 ✂ 2.36 Global Days XXX

92312 **corneal lens for aphakia, both eyes** Ⓢ80🖥
📷 1.70 ✂ 2.68 Global Days XXX

92313 corneoscleral lens ⑤ 80 🖵
  📖 1.26 ⚖ 2.27 Global Days XXX

92314 Prescription of optical and physical characteristics of contact lens, with medical supervision of adaptation and direction of fitting by independent technician; corneal lens, both eyes except for aphakia Ⓔ
  Code also modifier 52 for one eye
  📖 0.94 ⚖ 1.91 Global Days XXX

92315 corneal lens for aphakia, 1 eye ⑤ 80 🖵
  📖 0.60 ⚖ 1.64 Global Days XXX

92316 corneal lens for aphakia, both eyes ⑤ 80 🖵
  📖 0.95 ⚖ 2.14 Global Days XXX

92317 corneoscleral lens ⑤ 80 🖵
  📖 0.59 ⚖ 1.69 Global Days XXX

92325 Modification of contact lens (separate procedure), with medical supervision of adaptation ⑤ 80 🖵
  📖 0.73 ⚖ 0.73 Global Days XXX

92326 Replacement of contact lens ⑤ 80 🖵
  EXCLUDES *prescription/fitting/medical supervision of ocular prosthetic adaptation by the physician (92002-92014, 99201-99499)*
  📖 1.01 ⚖ 1.01 Global Days XXX

92340-92499 Services Related to Eyeglasses

CMS *100-4,1,30.3.5* *Effect of Assignment on Cataract Glasses from Participating Physician/Supplier*
CMS *100-2,15,120* *Prosthetic Devices*
CMS *100-2,15,120* *Prosthetic Devices*
CMS *100-2,15,30.4* *Optometrist's Services*
CMS *100-4,4,20.5* *HCPCS Under OPPS*
CMS *100-4,4,20.5* *HCPCS Under OPPS*
INCLUDES anatomical facial characteristics measurement
  final adjustment of spectacles to visual axes/anatomical topography
  written laboratory specifications

EXCLUDES *supply of materials*

92340 Fitting of spectacles, except for aphakia; monofocal Ⓕ
  📖 0.51 ⚖ 0.94 Global Days XXX

92341 bifocal Ⓔ
  📖 0.04 ⚖ 1.08 Global Days XXX

92342 multifocal, other than bifocal Ⓔ
  📖 0.73 ⚖ 1.16 Global Days XXX

92352 Fitting of spectacle prosthesis for aphakia; monofocal ⑤
  📖 0.51 ⚖ 1.04 Global Days XXX

92353 multifocal ⑤
  📖 0.69 ⚖ 1.22 Global Days XXX

92354 Fitting of spectacle mounted low vision aid; single element system ⑤
  📖 2.56 ⚖ 2.56 Global Days XXX

92355 telescopic or other compound lens system ⑤
  📖 1.47 ⚖ 1.47 Global Days XXX

92358 Prosthesis service for aphakia, temporary (disposable or loan, including materials) ⑤
  📖 0.49 ⚖ 0.49 Global Days XXX

92370 Repair and refitting spectacles; except for aphakia Ⓔ
  📖 0.45 ⚖ 0.82 Global Days XXX

92371 spectacle prosthesis for aphakia ⑤
  📖 0.38 ⚖ 0.38 Global Days XXX

92499 Unlisted ophthalmological service or procedure ⑤ 80
  📖 0.00 ⚖ 0.00 Global Days XXX

92502-92548 Special Procedures of the Ears/Nose/Throat

CMS *100-2,15,230.3* *Practice of Speech-Language Pathology*
CMS *100-2,15,80.3* *Audiological Diagnostic Testing*
CMS *100-4,4,20.5* *HCPCS Under OPPS*
INCLUDES diagnostic/treatment services not generally included in a comprehensive otorhinolaryngologic evaluation or office visit (92502-92700)

EXCLUDES *laryngoscopy with stroboscopy (31579)*

Do not report anterior rhinoscopy, tuning fork testing, otoscopy, or removal of cerumen (non-impacted) separately

92502 Otolaryngologic examination under general anesthesia Ⓣ 80 🖵
  📖 2.53 ⚖ 2.53 Global Days 000

92504 Binocular microscopy (separate diagnostic procedure) Ⓝ 80 🖵
  📖 0.26 ⚖ 0.76 Global Days XXX
  AMA: 2008, Jan, 10-25; 2007, Jan, 13-27; 2007, Jan, 13-27; 2007, January, 13-27; 2005, Jul, 13-16; 2005, Jul, 13-16; 2005, January, 46-47; 2005, July, 13-16; 2005, Jan, 46-47; 2005, Jan, 46-47

92506 Evaluation of speech, language, voice, communication, and/or auditory processing Ⓐ 80 🖵
  INCLUDES evaluation of:
    expressive language abilities
    receptive language
    speech production
  examination of:
    appropriate formulation/utterance of expressive thought
    articulatory movements of oral musculature
    capability of understanding the meaning/intent of written/verbal expressions
    speech sound production
  📖 1.21 ⚖ 4.08 Global Days XXX
  AMA: 2008, Jan, 10-25; 2007, Jan, 13-27; 2007, Jan, 13-27; 2007, January, 13-27; 2006, Jan, 7-10,47; 2006, Jan, 7-10,47; 2006, January, 7-10,47; 2005, Mar, 7-10; 2005, Mar, 7-10; 2005, March, 7-10; 2004, Dec, 14; 2004, Dec, 14; 2004, Sep, 13; 2004, December, 14; 2004, September, 13; 2004, Sep, 13

92507 Treatment of speech, language, voice, communication, and/or auditory processing disorder; individual Ⓐ 80 🖵
  EXCLUDES *auditory rehabilitation:*
    postlingual hearing loss (92633)
    prelingual hearing loss (92630)
    programming of cochlear implant (92601-92604)
  📖 0.72 ⚖ 1.70 Global Days XXX
  AMA: 2006, Jan, 7-10,47; 2006, Jan, 7-10,47; 2006, January, 7-10,47; 2004, Dec, 14; 2004, December, 14; 2004, Dec, 14

92508 group, 2 or more individuals Ⓐ 80 🖵
  EXCLUDES *auditory rehabilitation:*
    postlingual hearing loss (92633)
    prelingual hearing loss (92630)
    programming of cochlear implant (92601-92604)
  📖 0.37 ⚖ 0.81 Global Days XXX
  AMA: 2004, Dec, 14; 2004, Dec, 14; 2004, December, 14

92511 Nasopharyngoscopy with endoscope (separate procedure) Ⓣ 80 🖵
  📖 1.57 ⚖ 4.01 Global Days 000

92512 Nasal function studies (eg, rhinomanometry) Ⓧ 80
  📖 0.76 ⚖ 1.59 Global Days XXX

Medicine

92516 — 92567

92516 Facial nerve function studies (eg, electroneuronography) ⊠ 80
🔹 0.61 ⚬ 1.64 **Global Days XXX**

92520 Laryngeal function studies (ie, aerodynamic testing and acoustic testing) ⊠ 80 ▭
EXCLUDES *other laryngeal function testing (92700) swallowing/laryngeal sensory testing with flexible fiberoptic endoscope (92611-92617)*

Code also modifier 52 for single test
🔹 1.07 ⚬ 1.62 **Global Days XXX**
AMA: 2006, Jan, 7-10,47; 2006, Jan, 7-10,47; 2006, January, 7-10,47; 2004, Dec, 14; 2004, December, 14; 2004, Dec, 14

92526 Treatment of swallowing dysfunction and/or oral function for feeding A 80 ▭
🔹 0.75 ⚬ 2.17 **Global Days XXX**

92531 Spontaneous nystagmus, including gaze N
Do not report with evaluation and management services
🔹 0.00 ⚬ 0.00 **Global Days XXX**

92532 Positional nystagmus test N
Do not report with evaluation and management services
🔹 0.00 ⚬ 0.00 **Global Days XXX**

92533 Caloric vestibular test, each irrigation (binaural, bithermal stimulation constitutes 4 tests) N
INCLUDES Barany caloric test
🔹 0.00 ⚬ 0.00 **Global Days XXX**

92534 Optokinetic nystagmus test N
🔹 0.00 ⚬ 0.00 **Global Days XXX**

92541 Spontaneous nystagmus test, including gaze and fixation nystagmus, with recording ⊠ 80 ▭
🔹 1.58 ⚬ 1.58 **Global Days XXX**
AMA: 2005, Feb, 13-16; 2005, Feb, 13-16; 2005, February, 13-16; 2004, May, 14; 2004, May, 14; 2004, May, 14

92542 Positional nystagmus test, minimum of 4 positions, with recording ⊠ 80
🔹 1.64 ⚬ 1.64 **Global Days XXX**
AMA: 2005, Feb, 13-16; 2005, Feb, 13-16; 2005, February, 13-16; 2004, May, 14; 2004, May, 14; 2004, May, 14

92543 Caloric vestibular test, each irrigation (binaural, bithermal stimulation constitutes 4 tests), with recording ⊠ 80 ▭
🔹 0.76 ⚬ 0.76 **Global Days XXX**
AMA: 2008, Jan, 10-25; 2007, Jan, 13-27; 2007, Jan, 13-27; 2007, January, 13-27; 2006, Sep, 14-16; 2006, Sep, 14-16; 2006, September, 14-16; 2005, Feb, 13-16; 2005, Feb, 13-16; 2005, February, 13-16; 2004, May, 14; 2004, May, 14; 2004, Nov, 10; 2004, May, 14; 2004, November, 10; 2004, Nov, 10

92544 Optokinetic nystagmus test, bidirectional, foveal or peripheral stimulation, with recording ⊠ 80
🔹 1.32 ⚬ 1.32 **Global Days XXX**
AMA: 2005, Feb, 13-16; 2005, Feb, 13-16; 2005, February, 13-16; 2004, May, 14; 2004, May, 14; 2004, May, 14

92545 Oscillating tracking test, with recording ⊠ 80
🔹 1.24 ⚬ 1.24 **Global Days XXX**
AMA: 2005, Feb, 13-16; 2005, Feb, 13-16; 2005, February, 13-16; 2004, May, 14; 2004, May, 14; 2004, May, 14

92546 Sinusoidal vertical axis rotational testing ⊠ 80
🔹 2.22 ⚬ 2.22 **Global Days XXX**
AMA: 2008, Jan, 10-25; 2007, Jan, 13-27; 2007, Jan, 13-27; 2007, January, 13-27; 2005, Feb, 13-16; 2005, Feb, 13-16; 2005, February, 13-16; 2004, May, 14; 2004, May, 14; 2004, September, 13; 2004, September, 13; 2004, May, 14; 2004, Sep, 13; 2004, Sep, 13; 2004, Sep, 13

+ 92547 Use of vertical electrodes (List separately in addition to code for primary procedure) N TC 80
Code first vestibular function tests with recording/medical diagnostic evaluation (92541-92546)
🔹 0.16 ⚬ 0.16 **Global Days ZZZ**
AMA: 2008, Jan, 10-25; 2007, Jan, 13-27; 2007, Jan, 13-27; 2007, January, 13-27; 2005, Feb, 13-16; 2005, Feb, 13-16; 2005, February, 13-16; 2004, May, 14; 2004, May, 14; 2004, May, 14

92548 Computerized dynamic posturography ⊠ 80
🔹 2.55 ⚬ 2.55 **Global Days XXX**

92551-92596 Hearing and Speech Tests

CMS 100-4,5,10.2   *Financial Limitation for Outpatient Rehabilitation Services*
CMS 100-4,12,30.3   *Audiological DiagnosticTests, Speech-Language Evaluations and Treatments*
CMS 100-2,15,230.3 *Practice of Speech-Language Pathology*
CMS 100-2,15,80.3   *Audiological DiagnosticTesting*
CMS 100-4,4,20.5   *HCPCS Under OPPS*
CMS 100-4,4,20.5   *HCPCS Under OPPS*

INCLUDES diagnostic/treatment services not generally included in a comprehensive otorhinolaryngologic evaluation or office visit
use of calibrated electronic equipment, recording of results, and a report with interpretation
testing of both ears. When one ear is tested, append modifier 52.

EXCLUDES *evaluation of speech/language/hearing problems using observation/assessment of performance*

Do not report tuning fork or whispered voice hearing tests separately

92551 Screening test, pure tone, air only E
🔹 0.29 ⚬ 0.29 **Global Days XXX**

92552 Pure tone audiometry (threshold); air only ⊠ TC 80 ▭
🔹 0.59 ⚬ 0.59 **Global Days XXX**

92553 air and bone ⊠ TC 80 ▭
🔹 0.79 ⚬ 0.79 **Global Days XXX**

92555 Speech audiometry threshold; ⊠ TC 80 ▭
🔹 0.44 ⚬ 0.44 **Global Days XXX**

92556 with speech recognition ⊠ TC 80 ▭
🔹 0.68 ⚬ 0.68 **Global Days XXX**

92557 Comprehensive audiometry threshold evaluation and speech recognition (92553 and 92556 combined) ⊠ 80 ▭
EXCLUDES *evaluation/selection of hearing aid (92590-92595)*
🔹 1.18 ⚬ 1.25 **Global Days XXX**

92559 Audiometric testing of groups E
🔹 0.00 ⚬ 0.00 **Global Days XXX**

92560 Bekesy audiometry; screening E
🔹 0.00 ⚬ 0.00 **Global Days XXX**

92561 diagnostic ⊠ TC 80 ▭
🔹 0.77 ⚬ 0.77 **Global Days XXX**

92562 Loudness balance test, alternate binaural or monaural ⊠ TC 80 ▭
INCLUDES ABLB test
🔹 0.62 ⚬ 0.62 **Global Days XXX**
AMA: 2005, Mar, 7-10; 2005, Mar, 7-10; 2005, March, 7-10

92563 Tone decay test ⊠ TC 80 ▭
🔹 0.56 ⚬ 0.56 **Global Days XXX**

92564 Short increment sensitivity index (SISI) ⊠ TC 80 ▭
🔹 0.54 ⚬ 0.54 **Global Days XXX**

92565 Stenger test, pure tone ⊠ TC 80 ▭
🔹 0.35 ⚬ 0.35 **Global Days XXX**

92567 Tympanometry (impedance testing) ⊠ 80 ▭
🔹 0.44 ⚬ 0.49 **Global Days XXX**

92568 **Acoustic reflex testing; threshold** ☒ 80 🖵
📖 0.50 ≤ 0.50 Global Days XXX
AMA: 2008, Jan, 10-25; 2007, Jan, 13-27; 2007, Jan, 13-27; 2007, January, 13-27; 2006, Jan, 7-10,47; 2006, Jan, 7-10,47; 2006, January, 7-10,47; 2004, Jun, 10; 2004, Jun, 10; 2004, June, 10

92569 **decay** ☒ 80 🖵
📖 0.40 ≤ 0.40 Global Days XXX
AMA: 2006, Jan, 7-10,47; 2006, Jan, 7-10,47; 2006, January, 7-10,47

92571 **Filtered speech test** ☒ TC 80 🖵
📖 0.45 ≤ 0.45 Global Days XXX
AMA: 2005, Mar, 7-10; 2005, Mar, 7-10; 2005, March, 7-10

92572 **Staggered spondaic word test** ☒ TC 80 🖵
📖 0.47 ≤ 0.47 Global Days XXX
AMA: 2005, Mar, 7-10; 2005, Mar, 7-10; 2005, March, 7-10

92575 **Sensorineural acuity level test** ☒ TC 80 🖵
📖 0.95 ≤ 0.95 Global Days XXX

92576 **Synthetic sentence identification test** ☒ TC 80 🖵
📖 0.58 ≤ 0.58 Global Days XXX
AMA: 2005, Mar, 7-10; 2005, Mar, 7-10; 2005, March, 7-10

92577 **Stenger test, speech** ☒ TC 80 🖵
📖 0.48 ≤ 0.48 Global Days XXX

92579 **Visual reinforcement audiometry (VRA)** ☒ 80 🖵
📖 1.13 ≤ 1.21 Global Days XXX

92582 **Conditioning play audiometry** ☒ TC 80 🖵
📖 1.12 ≤ 1.12 Global Days XXX

92583 **Select picture audiometry** ☒ TC 80 🖵
📖 0.91 ≤ 0.91 Global Days XXX

92584 **Electrocochleography** ☒ TC 80 🖵
📖 1.86 ≤ 1.86 Global Days XXX

92585 **Auditory evoked potentials for evoked response audiometry and/or testing of the central nervous system; comprehensive** ☒ 80 🖵
📖 2.76 ≤ 2.76 Global Days XXX

92586 **limited** ☒ TC 80 🖵
📖 1.71 ≤ 1.71 Global Days XXX

92587 **Evoked otoacoustic emissions; limited (single stimulus level, either transient or distortion products)** ☒ 80 🖵
📖 1.07 ≤ 1.07 Global Days XXX

92588 **comprehensive or diagnostic evaluation (comparison of transient and/or distortion product otoacoustic emissions at multiple levels and frequencies)** ☒ 80 🖵
EXCLUDES *evaluation of central auditory function (92620, 92621)*
📖 1.74 ≤ 1.74 Global Days XXX

92590 **Hearing aid examination and selection; monaural** E
📖 0.00 ≤ 0.00 Global Days XXX

92591 **binaural** E
📖 0.00 ≤ 0.00 Global Days XXX

92592 **Hearing aid check; monaural** E
📖 0.00 ≤ 0.00 Global Days XXX

92593 **binaural** E
📖 0.00 ≤ 0.00 Global Days XXX

92594 **Electroacoustic evaluation for hearing aid; monaural** E
📖 0.00 ≤ 0.00 Global Days XXX

92595 **binaural** E
📖 0.00 ≤ 0.00 Global Days XXX

92596 **Ear protector attenuation measurements** ☒ TC 80 🖵
📖 0.95 ≤ 0.95 Global Days XXX

92597 Services Related to Voice Prosthesis

INCLUDES diagnostic/treatment services not generally included in a comprehensive otorhinolaryngologic evaluation or office visit use of calibrated electronic equipment

92597 **Evaluation for use and/or fitting of voice prosthetic device to supplement oral speech** A 80 🖵
EXCLUDES *communication device services, augmentative/alternative (92605, 92607, 92608)*

📖 1.23 ≤ 2.78 Global Days XXX
AMA: 2004, Dec, 14; 2004, Dec, 14; 2004, December, 14

92601-92609 Services Related to Hearing and Speech Devices

CMS *100-3,50.2*   *Electronic Speech Aids*
CMS *100-3,50.1*   *Speech Generating Devices*
CMS *100-3,50.3*   *Cochlear Implantation*
CMS *100-4,32,100*   *Billing Requirements for Cochlear Implantation*
CMS *100-2,15,80.3*   *Audiological Diagnostic Testing*
INCLUDES diagnostic/treatment services not generally included in a comprehensive otorhinolaryngologic evaluation or office visit

92601 **Diagnostic analysis of cochlear implant, patient younger than 7 years of age; with programming** A ☒ 80 🖵
INCLUDES connection to cochlear implant
postoperative analysis/fitting of previously placed external devices
stimulator programming
EXCLUDES *cochlear implant placement (69930)*

📖 3.85 ≤ 4.21 Global Days XXX
AMA: 2006, Jan, 7-10,47; 2006, Jan, 7-10,47; 2006, January, 7-10,47

92602 **subsequent reprogramming** A ☒ 80 🖵
INCLUDES internal stimulator re-programming
subsequent sessions for external transmitter measurements/adjustment
EXCLUDES *aural rehabilitation services after a cochlear implant (92626-92627, 92630-92633)*
cochlear implant placement (69930)

Do not report with 92601
📖 2.31 ≤ 2.64 Global Days XXX
AMA: 2008, Jan, 10-25; 2007, Jan, 13-27; 2007, Jan, 13-27; 2007, January, 13-27; 2006, Jan, 7-10,47; 2006, January, 7-10,47; 2006, Jan, 7-10,47

92603 **Diagnostic analysis of cochlear implant, age 7 years or older; with programming** ☒ 80 🖵
INCLUDES connection to cochlear implant
post-operative analysis/fitting of previously placed external devices
stimulator programming
EXCLUDES *cochlear implant placement (69930)*

📖 3.46 ≤ 3.79 Global Days XXX
AMA: 2006, Jan, 7-10,47; 2006, Jan, 7-10,47; 2006, January, 7-10,47

92604 **subsequent reprogramming** ☒ 80 🖵
INCLUDES internal stimulator re-programming
subsequent sessions for external transmitter measurements/adjustment
EXCLUDES *cochlear implant placement (69930)*

Do not report with 92603
📖 1.99 ≤ 2.26 Global Days XXX
AMA: 2008, Jan, 10-25; 2007, Jan, 13-27; 2007, Jan, 13-27; 2007, January, 13-27; 2006, Jan, 7-10,47; 2006, January, 7-10,47; 2006, Jan, 7-10,47

Medicine

92605 — 92625

92605 Evaluation for prescription of non-speech-generating augmentative and alternative communication device [A]
📞 0.00 ⚕ 0.00 Global Days XXX

92606 Therapeutic service(s) for the use of non-speech-generating device, including programming and modification [A]
📞 0.00 ⚕ 0.00 Global Days XXX

92607 Evaluation for prescription for speech-generating augmentative and alternative communication device, face-to-face with the patient; first hour [A] [80] [⌐]
EXCLUDES *evaluation for prescription of non-speech generating device (92605)*
📞 4.17 ⚕ 4.17 Global Days XXX
AMA: 2004, Dec, 14; 2004, Dec, 14; 2004, December, 14

+ **92608** each additional 30 minutes (List separately in addition to code for primary procedure) [A] [80] [⌐]
Code first initial hour (92607)
📞 0.81 ⚕ 0.81 Global Days XXX
AMA: 2004, Dec, 14; 2004, Dec, 14; 2004, December, 14

92609 Therapeutic services for the use of speech-generating device, including programming and modification [A] [80] [⌐]
EXCLUDES *therapeutic services for use of non-speech generating device (92606)*
📞 2.22 ⚕ 2.22 Global Days XXX
AMA: 2004, Dec, 14; 2004, Dec, 14; 2004, December, 14

92610-92617 Swallowing Evaluations

CMS *100-3,170.3* *Speech-language Pathology Services for the Treatment of Dysphagia*
CMS *100-2,15,230.3* *Practice of Speech-Language Pathology*

92610 Evaluation of oral and pharyngeal swallowing function [A] [80] [⌐]
EXCLUDES *evaluation with flexible endoscope (92612-92617)*
motion fluoroscopic evaluation of swallowing function (92611)
📞 2.16 ⚕ 2.16 Global Days XXX
AMA: 2004, Dec, 14; 2004, Dec, 14; 2004, December, 14

92611 Motion fluoroscopic evaluation of swallowing function by cine or video recording [A] [80] [⌐]
EXCLUDES *diagnostic flexible fiberoptic laryngoscopy (31575)*
evaluation of oral/pharyngeal swallowing function (92610)
📷 *74230*
📞 2.35 ⚕ 2.35 Global Days XXX
AMA: 2006, Jan, 7-10,47; 2006, Jan, 7-10,47; 2006, January, 7-10,47; 2004, Dec, 14; 2004, December, 14; 2004, Dec, 14

92612 Flexible fiberoptic endoscopic evaluation of swallowing by cine or video recording; [A] [80] [⌐]
EXCLUDES *flexible fiberoptic endoscopic examination/testing without cine or video recording (92700)*
Do not report with diagnostic flexible fiberoptic laryngoscopy (31575)
📞 1.81 ⚕ 4.20 Global Days XXX
AMA: 2008, Jan, 10-25; 2007, Jan, 13-27; 2007, Jan, 13-27; 2007, January, 13-27; 2006, Jan, 7-10,47; 2006, Jan, 7-10,47; 2006, January, 7-10,47; 2004, Nov, 10; 2004, Nov, 10; 2004, November, 10

92613 physician interpretation and report only [B] [80] [⌐]
EXCLUDES *oral/pharyngeal swallowing function examination (92610)*
swallowing function motion fluoroscopic examination (92611)
Do not report with diagnostic flexible fiberoptic laryngoscopy (31575)
📞 1.05 ⚕ 1.05 Global Days XXX
AMA: 2006, Jan, 7-10,47; 2006, Jan, 7-10,47; 2006, January, 7-10,47

92614 Flexible fiberoptic endoscopic evaluation, laryngeal sensory testing by cine or video recording; [A] [80] [⌐]
EXCLUDES *flexible fiberoptic endoscopic examination/testing without cine or video recording (92700)*
Do not report with diagnostic flexible fiberoptic laryngoscopy (31575)
📞 1.81 ⚕ 3.74 Global Days XXX
AMA: 2006, Jan, 7-10,47; 2006, Jan, 7-10,47; 2006, January, 7-10,47

92615 physician interpretation and report only [E] [80] [⌐]
Do not report with diagnostic flexible fiberoptic laryngoscopy (31575)
📞 0.94 ⚕ 0.94 Global Days XXX
AMA: 2006, Jan, 7-10,47; 2006, Jan, 7-10,47; 2006, January, 7-10,47

92616 Flexible fiberoptic endoscopic evaluation of swallowing and laryngeal sensory testing by cine or video recording; [A] [80] [⌐]
EXCLUDES *flexible fiberoptic endoscopic examination/testing without cine or video recording (92700)*
Do not report with diagnostic flexible fiberoptic laryngoscopy (31575)
📞 2.67 ⚕ 5.14 Global Days XXX
AMA: 2006, Jan, 7-10,47; 2006, Jan, 7-10,47; 2006, January, 7-10,47

92617 physician interpretation and report only [E] [80] [⌐]
Do not report with diagnostic flexible fiberoptic laryngoscopy (31575)
📞 1.15 ⚕ 1.15 Global Days XXX
AMA: 2006, Jan, 7-10,47; 2006, Jan, 7-10,47; 2006, January, 7-10,47

92620-92700 Diagnostic Hearing Evaluations and Rehabilitation

INCLUDES *diagnostic/treatment services not generally included in a comprehensive otorhinolaryngologic evaluation or office visit*

92620 Evaluation of central auditory function, with report; initial 60 minutes [X] [80] [⌐]
Do not report with (92506)
📞 1.98 ⚕ 1.98 Global Days XXX
AMA: 2005, Mar, 7-10; 2005, Mar, 7-10; 2005, March, 7-10

92621 each additional 15 minutes [N] [80] [⌐]
Code first initial hour (92620)
Do not report with (92506)
📞 0.46 ⚕ 0.46 Global Days ZZZ
AMA: 2005, Mar, 7-10; 2005, Mar, 7-10; 2005, March, 7-10

92625 Assessment of tinnitus (includes pitch, loudness matching, and masking) [X] [80] [⌐]
Code also modifier 52 for unilateral procedure
Do not report with (92562)
📞 1.57 ⚕ 1.57 Global Days XXX
AMA: 2005, Mar, 7-10; 2005, Mar, 7-10; 2005, March, 7-10

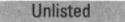
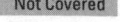

92626 **Evaluation of auditory rehabilitation status; first hour** ⓧ 80
INCLUDES   face-to-face time spent with the patient or family
the ability of the patient to use residual hearing in order to identify acoustic characteristics of sounds associated with speech communication

🖩 2.17   ✎ 2.17 Global Days XXX
AMA: 2006, Jan, 7-10,47; 2006, Jan, 7-10,47; 2006, January, 7-10,47

+ 92627 **each additional 15 minutes (List separately in addition to code for primary procedure)** Ⓝ 80
INCLUDES   face-to-face time spent with the patient or family
the ability of the patient to use residual hearing in order to identify acoustic characteristics of sounds associated with speech communication

Code first initial hour (92626)
🖩 0.53   ✎ 0.53 Global Days ZZZ
AMA: 2006, Jan, 7-10,47; 2006, Jan, 7-10,47; 2006, January, 7-10,47

92630 **Auditory rehabilitation; prelingual hearing loss** Ⓔ
🖩 0.00   ✎ 0.00 Global Days XXX
AMA: 2006, Jan, 7-10,47; 2006, Jan, 7-10,47; 2006, January, 7-10,47

92633 **postlingual hearing loss** Ⓔ
🖩 0.00   ✎ 0.00 Global Days XXX
AMA: 2006, Jan, 7-10,47; 2006, Jan, 7-10,47; 2006, January, 7-10,47

92640 **Diagnostic analysis with programming of auditory brainstem implant, per hour** ⓧ 80
EXCLUDES   nonprogramming services (cardiac monitoring)

🖩 2.07   ✎ 2.07 Global Days XXX

92700 **Unlisted otorhinolaryngological service or procedure** ⓧ 80
INCLUDES   Lombard test
🖩 0.00   ✎ 0.00 Global Days XXX
AMA: 2008, Jan, 10-25; 2007, Jan, 13-27; 2007, Jan, 13-27; 2007, January, 13-27; 2006, Jan, 7-10,47; 2006, Jan, 7-10,47; 2006, January, 7-10,47; 2006, September, 14-16; 2006, Sep, 14-16; 2006, Sep, 14-16; 2004, Nov, 10; 2004, September, 13; 2004, November, 10; 2004, November, 10; 2004, Nov, 10; 2004, Sep, 13; 2004, Sep, 13; 2004, Nov, 10; 2004, Nov, 10

92950-92953 Emergency Cardiac Procedures

CMS *100-4,12,30.4*   *Cardiovascular System*

92950 **Cardiopulmonary resuscitation (eg, in cardiac arrest)** Ⓢ 80
EXCLUDES   critical care (99291, 99292)

🖩 4.91   ✎ 7.49 Global Days 000
AMA: 2008, Jan, 10-25; 2007, Jan, 13-27; 2007, Jan, 13-27; 2007, January, 13-27; 2004, Oct, 14; 2004, October, 14; 2004, Oct, 14

⊙ 92953 **Temporary transcutaneous pacing** Ⓢ ⓜ
EXCLUDES   physician direction of ambulance/rescue personnel outside of the hospital (99288)

🖩 0.33   ✎ 0.33 Global Days 000
AMA: 2007, Feb, 10-11; 2007, Feb, 10-11; 2007, February, 10-11; 2007, Jul, 1-4

92960-92961 Cardioversion

CMS *100-4,12,30.4*   *Cardiovascular System*

⊙ 92960 **Cardioversion, elective, electrical conversion of arrhythmia; external** Ⓢ 80
🖩 3.70   ✎ 7.07 Global Days 000
AMA: 2008, Jan, 10-25; 2007, Jan, 13-27; 2007, Jan, 13-27; 2007, January, 13-27

⊙ 92961 **internal (separate procedure)** Ⓢ
Do not report with (93282-93283, 93289, 93292, 93295, 93618-93624, 93631, 93640-93642, 93650, 93651, 93652, 93662)
🖩 7.27   ✎ 7.27 Global Days 000

92970-92971 Circulatory Assist: External/Internal

EXCLUDES   atrial septostomy, balloon (92992)
catheter placement for use in circulatory assist devices (intra-aortic balloon pump) (33970)

92970 **Cardioassist-method of circulatory assist; internal** Ⓒ 80
🖩 5.04   ✎ 5.04 Global Days 000

92971 **external** Ⓒ 80
🖩 2.87   ✎ 2.87 Global Days 000

92973-92979 Intravascular Coronary Procedures: Insert Brachytherapy Device; Treatment of Thrombosis; Ultrasound

CMS *100-4,12,30.4*   *Cardiovascular System*

+ ⊙ 92973 **Percutaneous transluminal coronary thrombectomy (List separately in addition to code for primary procedure)** Ⓣ 80
Code first primary procedure (92980, 92982)
🖩 5.16   ✎ 5.16 Global Days ZZZ
AMA: 2008, Jan, 10-25; 2007, Jan, 13-27; 2007, Jan, 13-27; 2007, January, 13-27; 2004, Mar, 10; 2004, March, 10; 2004, Mar, 10

+ ⊙ 92974 **Transcatheter placement of radiation delivery device for subsequent coronary intravascular brachytherapy (List separately in addition to code for primary procedure)** Ⓣ 80
EXCLUDES   application of intravascular radioelement (77785-77787)

Code first primary procedure (92980, 92982, 92995, 93508)
🖩 4.73   ✎ 4.73 Global Days ZZZ

⊙ 92975 **Thrombolysis, coronary; by intracoronary infusion, including selective coronary angiography** Ⓒ 80
EXCLUDES   thrombolysis, cerebral (37195)
thrombolysis other than coronary (37201, 75896)

🖩 11.33   ✎ 11.33 Global Days 000

92977 **by intravenous infusion** Ⓣ 80
EXCLUDES   thrombolysis, cerebral (37195)
thrombolysis other than coronary (37201, 75896)

🖩 3.72   ✎ 3.72 Global Days XXX

+ ⊙ 92978 **Intravascular ultrasound (coronary vessel or graft) during diagnostic evaluation and/or therapeutic intervention including imaging supervision, interpretation and report; initial vessel (List separately in addition to code for primary procedure)** Ⓝ 80
Code also (C1753)
Code first primary procedure
🖩 0.00   ✎ 0.00 Global Days ZZZ
AMA: 2008, Jan, 10-25

㊿ Modifier 63 Exempt Code   ⊙ Moderate Sedation   + CPT Add on Code   Ⓢ Modifier 51 Exempt Code   ● New Code   ▲ Revised Code

Ⓜ Maternity Edit   Ⓐ Age Edit   Ⓐ Ⓨ APC Status Indicators   ▢ CCI Comprehensive Code   ⊬ Drug Not Approved by FDA   50 Bilateral Procedure

Medicine

92979 — 92995

+ ⊙   92979   **each additional vessel (List separately in addition to code for primary procedure)**   N 80
       INCLUDES   transducer manipulations/repositioning in the vessel examined, before and after therapeutic intervention

     Code first initial vessel (92978)
     🔲 0.00   ✂ 0.00   Global Days ZZZ

92980-92984 Percutaneous Transluminal Angioplasty and Stent Placement

CMS 100-4,12,30.4   *Cardiovascular System*
CMS 100-3,20.7   *Percutaneous Transluminal Angioplasty (PTA)*

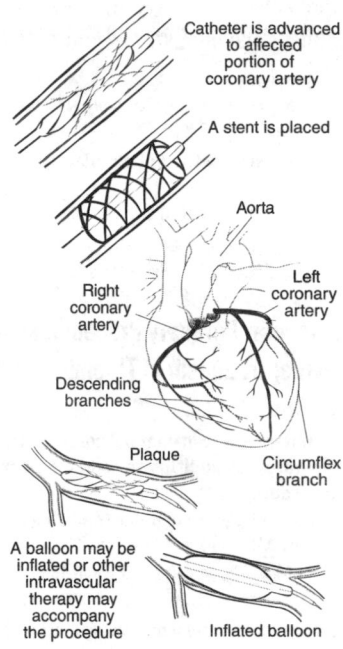

Catheter is advanced to affected portion of coronary artery

A stent is placed

Aorta

Right coronary artery

Left coronary artery

Descending branches

Plaque

Circumflex branch

A balloon may be inflated or other intravascular therapy may accompany the procedure

Inflated balloon

⊙   92980   **Transcatheter placement of an intracoronary stent(s), percutaneous, with or without other therapeutic intervention, any method; single vessel**   T 80 🔲
       INCLUDES   coronary angioplasty/atherectomy in the same artery
                  coronary artery stenting
       EXCLUDES   *coronary brachytherapy (92974)*
                  intravascular ultrasound (92978, 92979)
                  percutaneous transluminal coronary thrombectomy (92973)

     Code also (C1874, C1875, C1876, C1877)
     🔲 23.51   ✂ 23.51   Global Days 000
     AMA: 2008, Jan, 10-25; 2007, Jan, 13-27; 2007, Jan, 13-27; 2007, January, 13-27; 2005, Mar, 11-15; 2005, Mar, 11-15; 2005, April, 13-14; 2005, March, 11-15; 2005, Apr, 13-14; 2005, Apr, 13-14

+ ⊙   92981   **each additional vessel (List separately in addition to code for primary procedure)**   T 80 🔲
       INCLUDES   coronary angioplasty/atherectomy in the same artery
                  coronary artery stenting
       EXCLUDES   *additional vessels treated by only angioplasty or atherectomy during the same session (92984, 92996)*
                  transcatheter placement of radiation delivery device for coronary intravascular brachytherapy (92974)

     Code also (C1874, C1875, C1876, C1877)
     Code first single vessel (92980)
     🔲 6.54   ✂ 6.54   Global Days ZZZ
     AMA: 2008, Jan, 10-25; 2007, Jan, 13-27; 2007, Jan, 13-27; 2007, January, 13-27

⊙   92982   **Percutaneous transluminal coronary balloon angioplasty; single vessel**   T 80 🔲
     Code also (C1725, C1874, C1876, C1885)
     🔲 17.43   ✂ 17.43   Global Days 000
     AMA: 2008, Jan, 10-25; 2007, Jan, 13-27; 2007, Jan, 13-27; 2007, January, 13-27; 2005, Apr, 13-14; 2005, April, 13-14; 2005, Apr, 13-14

+ ⊙   92984   **each additional vessel (List separately in addition to code for primary procedure)**   T 80 🔲
       EXCLUDES   *application of intravascular radioelement (77785-77787)*
                  placement of stent after angioplasty/atherectomy completion (92980, 92981)
                  transcatheter placement of radiation delivery device for coronary intravascular brachytherapy (92974)

     Code also (C1725, C1874, C1876, C1885)
     Code first single vessel (92980, 92982, 92995)
     🔲 4.67   ✂ 4.67   Global Days ZZZ
     AMA: 2008, Jan, 10-25; 2007, Jan, 13-27; 2007, Jan, 13-27; 2007, January, 13-27; 2005, Apr, 13-14; 2005, April, 13-14; 2005, Apr, 13-14

92986-92993 Percutaneous Procedures of Heart Valves and Septum

CMS 100-4,12,30.4   *Cardiovascular System*

⊙   92986   **Percutaneous balloon valvuloplasty; aortic valve**   T 80 🔲
     🔲 38.57   ✂ 38.57   Global Days 090

⊙   92987   **mitral valve**   T 80 🔲
     🔲 39.93   ✂ 39.93   Global Days 090

       92990   **pulmonary valve**   T 80 🔲
     🔲 30.72   ✂ 30.72   Global Days 090

       92992   **Atrial septectomy or septostomy; transvenous method, balloon (eg, Rashkind type) (includes cardiac catheterization)**   C 80 🔲
     🔲 0.00   ✂ 0.00   Global Days 090
     AMA: 2008, Jan, 10-25

       92993   **blade method (Park septostomy) (includes cardiac catheterization)**   C 80 🔲
     🔲 0.00   ✂ 0.00   Global Days 090

92995-92996 Percutaneous Coronary Atherectomy

CMS 100-4,12,30.4   *Cardiovascular System*
Code also (C1714, C1724, C1885)

⊙   92995   **Percutaneous transluminal coronary atherectomy, by mechanical or other method, with or without balloon angioplasty; single vessel**   T 80 🔲
     🔲 19.21   ✂ 19.21   Global Days 000

+ ⊙ 92996 each additional vessel (List separately in addition to code for primary procedure) [T] [80] ▢
EXCLUDES *additional vessels treated by only angioplasty during the same session (92984)*
placement of stent after angioplasty/atherectomy completion (92980, 92981)

Code first single vessel (92980, 92982, 92995)
🔧 5.00   ⚒ 5.00   Global Days ZZZ

92997-92998 Percutaneous Angioplasty: Pulmonary Artery

CMS *100-4,12,30.4   Cardiovascular System*
Code also (C1725, C1874, C1885, C2625)

92997 Percutaneous transluminal pulmonary artery balloon angioplasty; single vessel [T] [80] ▢
🔧 17.63   ⚒ 17.63   Global Days 000

+ 92998 each additional vessel (List separately in addition to code for primary procedure) [T] [80] ▢
Code first single vessel (92997)
🔧 9.06   ⚒ 9.06   Global Days ZZZ

93000-93014 Electrocardiographic Services

CMS *100-4,12,30.4   Cardiovascular System*
CMS *100-3,20.15   Electrocardiographic Services*
INCLUDES specific order for the service, a separate written and signed report, and documentation of medical necessity
EXCLUDES *acoustic heart sound recording (00681-00701)*
echocardiography (93303-93350)
EKG with 64 or more leads, graphic presentation, and analysis (0178T-0180T)
use of these codes for the review of telemetry monitoring strips

93000 Electrocardiogram, routine ECG with at least 12 leads; with interpretation and report [M] [80] ▢
EXCLUDES *ECG monitoring (99354-99360)*
🔧 0.58   ⚒ 0.58   Global Days XXX
AMA: 2008, Jul, 3&14; 2005, Feb, 7-9; 2005, Feb, 7-9; 2005, Mar, 11-15; 2005, Mar, 1-6; 2005, February, 7-9; 2005, Mar, 11-15; 2005, Mar, 1-6; 2005, March, 1-6; 2005, March, 11-15, 2004, Jul, 7, 2004, Jul, 7, 2004, Apr, 8; 2004, April, 8; 2004, July, 7; 2004, Apr, 8

93005 tracing only, without interpretation and report [S] [TC] [80] ▢
EXCLUDES *ECG monitoring (99354-99360)*
🔧 0.33   ⚒ 0.33   Global Days XXX
AMA: 2005, Mar, 1-6; 2005, Mar, 1-6; 2005, March, 1-6; 2004, Jul, 7; 2004, Jul, 7; 2004, April, 8; 2004, July, 7; 2004, Apr, 0; 2004, Apr, 8

93010 interpretation and report only [B] [26] [80] ▢
EXCLUDES *ECG monitoring (99354-99360)*
🔧 0.25   ⚒ 0.25   Global Days XXX
AMA: 2007, Apr, 1-2; 2007, Apr, 1-2; 2007, April, 1-2; 2005, Mar, 1-6; 2005, Mar, 1-6; 2005, March, 1-6; 2005, Mar, 11-15; 2005, Mar, 11-15; 2005, March, 11-15; 2004, Jul, 7; 2004, Jul, 7; 2004, Apr, 8; 2004, April, 8; 2004, July, 7; 2004, Apr, 8

93012 Telephonic transmission of post-symptom electrocardiogram rhythm strip(s), 24-hour attended monitoring, per 30 day period of time; tracing only [N] [TC] [80] ▢
🔧 5.05   ⚒ 5.05   Global Days XXX
AMA: 2005, Oct, 14-17; 2005, Oct, 14-17; 2005, October, 14-17; 2004, Apr, 8; 2004, April, 8; 2004, Apr, 8

93014 physician review with interpretation and report only [B] [26] ▢
Do not report with (93228-93229)
🔧 0.77   ⚒ 0.77   Global Days XXX
AMA: 2005, Oct, 14-17; 2005, Oct, 14-17; 2005, October, 14-17; 2004, Apr, 8; 2004, April, 8; 2004, Apr, 8

93015-93018 Stress Test

CMS *100-4,12,30.4   Cardiovascular System*
CMS *100-3,20.15   Electrocardiographic Services*
CMS *100-3,20.10   Cardiac Rehabilitation Programs*
EXCLUDES *inert gas rebreathing measurement (0104T, 0105T)*

93015 Cardiovascular stress test using maximal or submaximal treadmill or bicycle exercise, continuous electrocardiographic monitoring, and/or pharmacological stress; with physician supervision, with interpretation and report [B] [80] ▢
🔧 2.78   ⚒ 2.78   Global Days XXX
AMA: 2008, Jan, 10-25; 2008, Jul, 3&14; 2007, Jan, 13-27; 2007, Jan, 13-27; 2007, January, 13-27; 2005, Mar, 11-15; 2005, Mar, 11-15; 2005, March, 11-15; 2004, Apr, 8; 2004, Apr, 8; 2004, April, 8

93016 physician supervision only, without interpretation and report [B] [26] [80] ▢
🔧 0.68   ⚒ 0.68   Global Days XXX
AMA: 2008, Jan, 10-25; 2008, Jul, 3&14; 2007, Jan, 13-27; 2007, Jan, 10 27, 2007, January, 13-27, 2004, Apr, 8, 2004, April, 8, 2004, Apr, 8

93017 tracing only, without interpretation and report [X] [TC] [80] ▢
🔧 1.65   ⚒ 1.65   Global Days XXX
AMA: 2008, Jan, 10-25; 2008, Jul, 3&14; 2007, Jan, 13-27; 2007, Jan, 13-27; 2007, January, 13-27; 2004, Apr, 8; 2004, April, 8; 2004, Apr, 8

93018 interpretation and report only [B] [26] [80] ▢
🔧 0.45   ⚒ 0.45   Global Days XXX
AMA: 2008, Jan, 10-25; 2008, Jul, 3&14; 2007, Jan, 13-27; 2007, Jan, 13-27; 2007, January, 13-27; 2004, Apr, 8; 2004, April, 8; 2004, Apr, 8

93024 Provocation Test for Coronary Vasospasm

CMS *100-4,12,30.4   Cardiovascular System*
CMS *100-3,20.15   Electrocardiographic Services*

93024 Ergonovine provocation test [X] [80] ▢
🔧 3.38   ⚒ 3.38   Global Days XXX

93025 Microvolt T-Wave Alternans

CMS *100-3,20.30   Microvolt T-Wave Alternans (MTWA)*
CMS *100-4,12,30.4   Cardiovascular System*
INCLUDES specific order for the service, a separate written and signed report, and documentation of medical necessity
EXCLUDES *echocardiography (93303-93350)*
EKG with 64 or more leads, graphic presentation, and analysis (0178T-0180T)
use of these codes for the review of telemetry monitoring strips

93025 Microvolt T-wave alternans for assessment of ventricular arrhythmias [X] [80] ▢
🔧 5.91   ⚒ 5.91   Global Days XXX

⊛ Modifier 63 Exempt Code   ⊙ Moderate Sedation   + CPT Add-on Code   ⊘ Modifier 51 Exempt Code   ● New Code   ▲ Revised Code
[M] Maternity Edit   [A] Age Edit   [A]-[Y] APC Status Indicators   ▢ CCI Comprehensive Code   ⁄ Drug Not Approved by FDA   [50] Bilateral Procedure

Medicine

93040 — 93236

93040-93042 Rhythm Strips

CMS 100-4,12,30.4 *Cardiovascular System*
CMS 100-3,20.15 *Electrocardiographic Services*
EXCLUDES *echocardiography (93303-93350)*
EKG with 64 or more leads, graphic presentation, and analysis (0178T-0180T)
specific order for the service, a separate written and signed report, and documentation of medical necessity
use of these codes for the review of telemetry monitoring strips

93040 **Rhythm ECG, 1-3 leads; with interpretation and report** B 80 ▢
    🔾 0.37 🔾 0.37 Global Days XXX
    AMA: 2004, Apr, 8; 2004, Apr, 8; 2004, April, 8

93041 **tracing only without interpretation and report** X TC 80
    🔾 0.15 🔾 0.15 Global Days XXX
    AMA: 2004, Apr, 8; 2004, Apr, 8; 2004, April, 8

93042 **interpretation and report only** B 26 80 ▢
    🔾 0.22 🔾 0.22 Global Days XXX
    AMA: 2004, Apr, 8; 2004, Apr, 8; 2004, April, 8

93224-93272 Ambulatory ECG Monitoring

CMS 100-4,12,30.4 *Cardiovascular System*
CMS 100-3,20.15 *Electrocardiographic Services*
INCLUDES wearable mobile cardiovascular monitoring that transmits to a surveillance center for up to 30 days
wearable mobile cardiovascular monitoring that does transmit to an attended surveillance center
EXCLUDES *echocardiography (93303-93350)*
EKG with 64 or more leads, graphic presentation, and analysis (0178T-0180T)
implantable patient activated cardiac event recorders (33282, 93285, 93291, 93298)

▲ 93224 **Wearable electrocardiographic rhythm derived monitoring for 24 hours by continuous original waveform recording and storage, with visual superimposition scanning; includes recording, scanning analysis with report, physician review and interpretation** M 80 ▢
    🔾 3.31 🔾 3.31 Global Days XXX
    AMA: 2008, Mar, 4-5; 2007, Apr, 3-6; 2007, Apr, 3-6; 2007, April, 3-6; 2005, Oct, 14-17; 2005, October, 14-17; 2005, Oct, 14-17

▲ 93225 **recording (includes connection, recording, and disconnection)** X TC 80 ▢
    🔾 0.99 🔾 0.99 Global Days XXX
    AMA: 2008, Mar, 4-5; 2007, Apr, 3-6; 2007, Apr, 3-6; 2007, April, 3-6; 2005, Oct, 14-17; 2005, October, 14-17; 2005, Oct, 14-17

▲ 93226 **scanning analysis with report** X TC 80 ▢
    🔾 1.53 🔾 1.53 Global Days XXX
    AMA: 2008, Mar, 4-5; 2007, Apr, 3-6; 2007, Apr, 3-6; 2007, April, 3-6; 2005, Oct, 14-17; 2005, October, 14-17; 2005, Oct, 14-17

▲ 93227 **physician review and interpretation** M 26 80 ▢
    🔾 0.79 🔾 0.79 Global Days XXX
    AMA: 2008, Mar, 4-5; 2007, Apr, 3-6; 2007, Apr, 3-6; 2007, April, 3-6; 2005, Oct, 14-17; 2005, October, 14-17; 2005, Oct, 14-17

● 93228 **Wearable mobile cardiovascular telemetry with electrocardiographic recording, concurrent computerized real time data analysis and greater than 24 hours of accessible ECG data storage (retrievable with query) with ECG triggered and patient selected events transmitted to a remote attended surveillance center for up to 30 days; physician review and interpretation with report** M 26 80
    Do not report when monitoring period is less than 10 days
    INCLUDES reporting only once in a 30-day period
    Do not report with (93014)
    🔾 0.71 🔾 0.71 Global Days XXX

● 93229 **technical support for connection and patient instructions for use, attended surveillance, analysis and physician prescribed transmission of daily and emergent data reports** S TC 80
    INCLUDES reporting only once in a 30-day period
    Do not report with (93014)
    🔾 0.00 🔾 0.00 Global Days XXX

▲ 93230 **Wearable electrocardiographic rhythm derived monitoring for 24 hours by continuous original waveform recording and storage without superimposition scanning utilizing a device capable of producing a full miniaturized printout; includes recording, microprocessor-based analysis with report, physician review and interpretation** M 80 ▢
    🔾 3.39 🔾 3.39 Global Days XXX
    AMA: 2008, Mar, 4-5; 2007, Apr, 3-6; 2007, Apr, 3-6; 2007, April, 3-6; 2005, Oct, 14-17; 2005, Oct, 14-17; 2005, October, 14-17; 2004, Apr, 8; 2004, Apr, 8; 2004, April, 8

▲ 93231 **recording (includes connection, recording, and disconnection)** X TC 80 ▢
    🔾 1.00 🔾 1.00 Global Days XXX
    AMA: 2008, Mar, 4-5; 2007, Apr, 3-6; 2007, Apr, 3-6; 2007, April, 3-6; 2005, Oct, 14-17; 2005, Oct, 14-17; 2005, October, 14-17; 2004, Apr, 8; 2004, Apr, 8; 2004, April, 8

▲ 93232 **microprocessor-based analysis with report** X TC 80 ▢
    🔾 1.63 🔾 1.63 Global Days XXX
    AMA: 2008, Mar, 4-5; 2007, Apr, 3-6; 2007, Apr, 3-6; 2007, April, 3-6; 2005, Oct, 14-17; 2005, Oct, 14-17; 2005, October, 14-17; 2004, Apr, 8; 2004, Apr, 8; 2004, April, 8

▲ 93233 **physician review and interpretation** M 26 80 ▢
    🔾 0.76 🔾 0.76 Global Days XXX
    AMA: 2008, Mar, 4-5; 2007, Apr, 3-6; 2007, Apr, 3-6; 2007, April, 3-6; 2005, Oct, 14-17; 2005, Oct, 14-17; 2005, October, 14-17; 2004, Apr, 8; 2004, Apr, 8; 2004, April, 8

▲ 93235 **Wearable electrocardiographic rhythm derived monitoring for 24 hours by continuous computerized monitoring and non-continuous recording, and real-time data analysis utilizing a device capable of producing intermittent full-sized waveform tracings, possibly patient activated; includes monitoring and real-time data analysis with report, physician review and interpretation** M 80 ▢
    INCLUDES Holter monitor procedure
    🔾 0.00 🔾 0.00 Global Days XXX
    AMA: 2008, Mar, 4-5; 2007, Apr, 3-6; 2007, Apr, 3-6; 2007, April, 3-6; 2005, Oct, 14-17; 2005, Oct, 14-17; 2005, October, 14-17; 2004, Apr, 8; 2004, Apr, 8; 2004, April, 8

▲ 93236 **monitoring and real-time data analysis with report** X TC 80 ▢
    🔾 0.00 🔾 0.00 Global Days XXX
    AMA: 2008, Mar, 4-5; 2007, Apr, 3-6; 2007, Apr, 3-6; 2007, April, 3-6; 2005, Oct, 14-17; 2005, Oct, 14-17; 2005, October, 14-17; 2004, Apr, 8; 2004, Apr, 8; 2004, April, 8

---

26 TC Professional/Technical Component Only   80 /80 Assist-at-Surgery Allowed/With Documentation   Unlisted   Not Covered   ☒ Radiology crosswalk
MED: Pub 100/NCD References   **AMA:** CPT Assistant References   A2 - Z3 ASC Payment Indicator   ♂Male Only   ♀Female Only   ☒ Laboratory crosswalk

▲ 93237   **physician review and interpretation**   M 26 80
       0.68   0.68 **Global Days XXX**
       AMA: 2008, Mar, 4-5; 2007, Apr, 3-6; 2007, Apr, 3-6; 2007, April, 3-6; 2005, Oct, 14-17; 2005, Oct, 14-17; 2005, October, 14-17; 2004, Apr, 8; 2004, Apr, 8; 2004, April, 8

▲ 93268   **Wearable patient activated electrocardiographic rhythm derived event recording with presymptom memory loop, 24-hour attended monitoring, per 30 day period of time; includes transmission, physician review and interpretation**   M 80
       EXCLUDES   *implanted patient activated cardiac event recording (33282, 93285, 93291, 93298)*
                postsymptom recording (93012, 93014)

       7.36   7.36 **Global Days XXX**
       AMA: 2008, Mar, 4-5; 2007, Apr, 3-6; 2007, Apr, 3-6; 2007, April, 3-6; 2005, Oct, 14-17; 2005, Oct, 14-17; 2005, October, 14-17; 2004, Apr, 8; 2004, Apr, 8; 2004, April, 8

▲ 93270   **recording (includes connection, recording, and disconnection)**   X TC 80
       0.60   0.60 **Global Days XXX**
       AMA: 2008, Mar, 4-5; 2007, Apr, 3-6; 2007, Apr, 3-6; 2007, April, 3-6; 2005, Oct, 14-17; 2005, Oct, 14-17; 2005, October, 14-17; 2004, Apr, 8; 2004, Apr, 8; 2004, April, 8

▲ 93271   **monitoring, receipt of transmissions, and analysis**   S TC 80
       6.00   6.00 **Global Days XXX**
       AMA: 2008, Mar, 4-5; 2007, Apr, 3-6; 2007, Apr, 3-6; 2007, April, 3-6; 2005, Oct, 14-17; 2005, Oct, 14-17; 2005, October, 14-17; 2004, Apr, 8; 2004, Apr, 8; 2004, April, 8

▲ 93272   **physician review and interpretation**   M 26 80
       0.76   0.76 **Global Days XXX**
       AMA: 2008, Jan, 10-25; 2008, Mar, 4-5; 2007, Jan, 13-27; 2007, Jan, 13-27; 2007, Apr, 3-6; 2007, April, 3-6; 2007, January, 13-27; 2007, Apr, 3-6; 2005, Oct, 14-17; 2005, October, 14-17; 2005, Oct, 14-17; 2004, Apr, 8; 2004, April, 8; 2004, Apr, 8

93278 Signal-averaged Electrocardiography

CMS *100-4,12,30.4*   *Cardiovascular System*
CMS *100-3,20.15*   *Electrocardiographic Services*
EXCLUDES   *echocardiography (93303-93350)*
       EKG with 64 or more leads, graphic presentation, and analysis (0178T-0180T)

      93278   **Signal-averaged electrocardiography (SAECG), with or without ECG**   X 80
            1.13   1.13 **Global Days XXX**
            AMA: 2008, Mar, 4-5

93279-93299 Monitoring of Cardiovascular Devices

INCLUDES   interrogation evaluation of device
       cardioverter-defibrillator (ICD) interrogation:
          battery
          capture and sensing functions
          leads
          presence or absence of therapy for ventricular tachyarrhythmias
          programmed parameters
          underlying heart rhythm
       implantable cardiovascular monitor (ICM) interrogation:
          analysis of at least one recorded physiologic cardiovascular data element from either internal or external sensors
          programmed parameters
       implantable loop recorder (ILR) interrogation:
          heart rate and rhythm during recorded episodes from both patient-initiated and device detected events
          programmed parameters
       pacemaker interrogation:
          battery
          capture and sensing functions
          heart rhythm
          leads
          programmed parameters
       time period established by the initiation of remote monitoring or the 91st day of ICD or pacemaker monitoring or the 31st day of ILR monitoring and extends for the succeeding 30 or 90 day period

EXCLUDES   *wearable device monitoring (93224-93272)*

Do not report in-person and remote interrogation of the same device during the same period
Do not report programming and in-person interrogation on the same day by the same physician

●   93279   **Programming device evaluation with iterative adjustment of the implantable device to test the function of the device and select optimal permanent programmed values with physician analysis, review and report; single lead pacemaker system**   S 80
            Do not report with (93286, 93288)
            1.55   1.55 **Global Days XXX**

●   93280   **dual lead pacemaker system**   S 80
            Do not report with (93286, 93288)
            1.83   1.83 **Global Days XXX**

●   93281   **multiple lead pacemaker system**   S 80
            Do not report with (93286, 93288)
            2.14   2.14 **Global Days XXX**

●   93282   **single lead implantable cardioverter-defibrillator system**   S 80
            Do not report with (93287, 93289, 93745)
            1.98   1.98 **Global Days XXX**

●   93283   **dual lead implantable cardioverter-defibrillator system**   S 80
            Do not report with (93287, 93289)
            2.41   2.41 **Global Days XXX**

●   93284   **multiple lead implantable cardioverter-defibrillator system**   S 80
            Do not report with (93287, 93289)
            2.82   2.82 **Global Days XXX**

●   93285   **implantable loop recorder system**   S 80
            Do not report with (33282, 93279-93284, 93291)
            1.34   1.34 **Global Days XXX**

⊚ Modifier 63 Exempt Code   ⊙ Moderate Sedation   + CPT Add-on Code   ⊘ Modifier 51 Exempt Code   ● New Code   ▲ Revised Code

M Maternity Edit   A Age Edit   A-Y APC Status Indicators   ☐ CCI Comprehensive Code   ✒ Drug Not Approved by FDA   50 Bilateral Procedure

- 93286 Peri-procedural device evaluation and programming of device system parameters before or after a surgery, procedure, or test with physician analysis, review and report; single, dual, or multiple lead pacemaker system [N] [80]
  INCLUDES one evaluation and programming (if performed once before and once after, report as two units)

  Do not report with (93279-93281, 93288)
  🔧 0.76 ⚒ 0.76 Global Days XXX

- 93287 single, dual, or multiple lead implantable cardioverter-defibrillator system [N] [80]
  INCLUDES one evaluation and programming (if performed once before and once after, report as two units)

  Do not report with (93282-93284, 93289)
  🔧 1.00 ⚒ 1.00 Global Days XXX

- 93288 Interrogation device evaluation (in person) with physician analysis, review and report, includes connection, recording and disconnection per patient encounter; single, dual, or multiple lead pacemaker system [S] [80]
  INCLUDES correct operation of:
  heart rhythm
  capture and sensing
  battery
  lead(s)
  programmed settings

  Do not report with (93012, 93014, 93040-93042, 93279-93281, 93286, 93294, 93296)
  🔧 1.20 ⚒ 1.20 Global Days XXX

- 93289 single, dual, or multiple lead implantable cardioverter-defibrillator system, including analysis of heart rhythm derived data elements [S] [80]
  EXCLUDES monitoring physiologic cardiovascular data elements derived from an ICD (93290)

  Do not report with (93282-93284, 93287, 93295-93296)
  🔧 1.84 ⚒ 1.84 Global Days XXX

- 93290 implantable cardiovascular monitor system, including analysis of 1 or more recorded physiologic cardiovascular data elements from all internal and external sensors [S] [80]
  EXCLUDES heart rhythm derived data (93289)

  Do not report with (93297, 93299)
  🔧 0.89 ⚒ 0.89 Global Days XXX

- 93291 implantable loop recorder system, including heart rhythm derived data analysis [S] [80]
  Do not report with (33282, 93288-93290, 93298-93299)
  🔧 1.15 ⚒ 1.15 Global Days XXX

- 93292 wearable defibrillator system [S] [80]
  Do not report with (93745)
  🔧 1.04 ⚒ 1.04 Global Days XXX

- 93293 Transtelephonic rhythm strip pacemaker evaluation(s) single, dual, or multiple lead pacemaker system, includes recording with and without magnet application with physician analysis, review and report(s), up to 90 days [S] [80]
  EXCLUDES in-person evaluation (93040-93042)

  Do not report more than once in a 90 day period
  Do not report when monitoring period is less than 30 days
  Do not report with (93294)
  🔧 1.66 ⚒ 1.66 Global Days XXX

- 93294 Interrogation device evaluation(s) (remote), up to 90 days; single, dual, or multiple lead pacemaker system with interim physician analysis, review(s) and report(s) [M] [26] [80]
  Do not report more than once in a 90 day period
  Do not report when monitoring period is less than 30 days
  Do not report with (93288, 93293)
  🔧 1.02 ⚒ 1.02 Global Days XXX

- 93295 single, dual, or multiple lead implantable cardioverter-defibrillator system with interim physician analysis, review(s) and report(s) [M] [26] [80]
  EXCLUDES remote monitoring of physiological cardiovascular ICD data (93297)

  Do not report more than once in a 90 day period
  Do not report when monitoring period is less than 30 days
  Do not report with (93289)
  🔧 1.84 ⚒ 1.84 Global Days XXX

- 93296 single, dual, or multiple lead pacemaker system or implantable cardioverter-defibrillator system, remote data acquisition(s), receipt of transmissions and technician review, technical support and distribution of results [S] [TC] [80]
  Do not report more than once in a 90 day period
  Do not report with (93288-93289, 93299)
  🔧 1.01 ⚒ 1.01 Global Days XXX

- 93297 Interrogation device evaluation(s), (remote) up to 30 days; implantable cardiovascular monitor system, including analysis of 1 or more recorded physiologic cardiovascular data elements from all internal and external sensors, physician analysis, review(s) and report(s) [M] [26] [80]
  EXCLUDES heart rhythm derived data (93295)

  Do not report more than once in a 30 day period
  Do not report when monitoring period is less than 10 days
  Do not report with (93290, 93298)
  🔧 0.71 ⚒ 0.71 Global Days XXX

- 93298 implantable loop recorder system, including analysis of recorded heart rhythm data, physician analysis, review(s) and report(s) [M] [26] [80]
  Do not report more than once in a 30 day period
  Do not report when monitoring period is less than 10 days
  Do not report with (33282, 93291, 93297)
  🔧 0.82 ⚒ 0.82 Global Days XXX

- 93299 implantable cardiovascular monitor system or implantable loop recorder system, remote data acquisition(s), receipt of transmissions and technician review, technical support and distribution of results [S] [TC] [80]
  Do not report more than once in a 30 day period
  Do not report when monitoring period is less than 10 days
  Do not report with (93290-93291, 93296)
  🔧 0.00 ⚒ 0.00 Global Days XXX

[26]/[TC] Professional/Technical Component Only   [80]/[80] Assist-at-Surgery Allowed/With Documentation    Unlisted   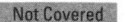 Not Covered   ☒ Radiology crosswalk

MED: Pub 100/NCD References   **AMA:** CPT Assistant References   [A2]-[Z3] ASC Payment Indicator   ♂Male Only   ♀Female Only   ☒ Laboratory crosswalk

412   CPT only © 2008 American Medical Association. All Rights Reserved. (Black Ink)   Medicare (Red Ink)   © 2008 Ingenix *(Blue Ink)*

93303-93352 Echocardiography

CMS *100-4,4,200.7.1 Cardiac Echocardiogaphy Without Contrast*
CMS *100-4,12,30.4 Cardiovascular System*

INCLUDES   interpretation and report
obtaining ultrasonic signals from heart/great arteries
report of study which includes:
    description of recognized abnormalities
    documentation of all clinically relevent findings which includes
      obtained quantitative measurements
    interpretation of all information obtained
two-dimensional image/doppler ultrasonic signal documentation
ultrasound exam of:
    adjacent great vessels
    cardiac chambers/valves
    pericardium

EXCLUDES   *echocardiography, fetal (76825-76828)*
contrast agents and/or drugs used for pharmacogical stress
ultrasound without thorough examination of the organ(s) or anatomic region/documentation of the image/final written report

93303   **Transthoracic echocardiography for congenital cardiac anomalies; complete**   S 80 ▯
   🖩 6.05   📐 6.05   Global Days XXX
   AMA: 2008, Jan, 10-25; 2008, Mar, 4-5; 2007, Jan, 13-27; 2007, Jan, 13-27; 2007, January, 13-27; 2004, Apr, 8; 2004, April, 8; 2004, Apr, 8

93304   **follow-up or limited study**   S 80 ▯
   🖩 3.74   📐 3.74   Global Days XXX
   AMA: 2008, Mar, 4-5; 2004, Apr, 8; 2004, Apr, 8; 2004, April, 8

● **93306**   **Echocardiography, transthoracic, real-time with image documentation (2D), includes M-mode recording, when performed, complete, with spectral Doppler echocardiography, and with color flow Doppler echocardiography**   S 80
     EXCLUDES   *transthoracic without spectral and color doppler (93307)*
   🖩 7.42   📐 7.42   Global Days XXX

▲ **93307**   **Echocardiography, transthoracic, real-time with image documentation (2D), includes M-mode recording, when performed, complete, without spectral or color Doppler echocardiography**   S 80 ▯
     INCLUDES   2-dimensional/selected M-mode exam of:
      adjacent portions of the aorta
      aortic/mitral/tricuspid valves
      left/right atria
      left/right ventricles
      pericardium
      obtaining/recording appropriate
        measurements
      using multiple views as required to obtain a
        complete functional/anatomic
        evaluation

     Do not report with (93320-93321, 93325)
   🖩 4.91   📐 4.91   Global Days XXX
   AMA: 2008, Jan, 10-25; 2008, Mar, 4-5; 2007, Jan, 13-27; 2007, Jan, 13-27, 2007, January, 13-27; 2005, Mar, 11-15; 2005, Mar, 11-15; 2005, Sep, 9-11; 2005, March, 11-15; 2005, September, 9-11; 2005, Sep, 9-11; 2004, Apr, 8; 2004, April, 8; 2004, Apr, 8

▲ **93308**   **Echocardiography, transthoracic, real-time with image documentation (2D), includes M-mode recording, when performed, follow-up or limited study**   S 80 ▯
     INCLUDES   an exam that does not evaluate/document the attempt to evaluate all the structures that comprise the complete echocardiographic exam

   🖩 3.10   📐 3.10   Global Days XXX
   AMA: 2008, Jan, 10-25; 2008, Mar, 4-5; 2007, Jan, 13-27; 2007, Jan, 13-27; 2007, January, 13-27; 2005, Sep, 9-11; 2005, Sep, 9-11; 2005, September, 9-11; 2004, Apr, 8; 2004, Apr, 8; 2004, April, 8

⊙ **93312**   **Echocardiography, transesophageal, real-time with image documentation (2D) (with or without M-mode recording); including probe placement, image acquisition, interpretation and report**   S 80 ▯
   🖩 9.03   📐 9.03   Global Days XXX
   AMA: 2008, Jan, 10-25; 2008, Mar, 4-5; 2007, Jan, 13-27; 2007, Jan, 13-27; 2007, January, 13-27

⊙ **93313**   **placement of transesophageal probe only**   S 80 ▯
   🖩 1.15   📐 1.15   Global Days XXX
   AMA: 2008, Mar, 4-5

⊙ **93314**   **image acquisition, interpretation and report only**   N 80 ▯
   🖩 7.77   📐 7.77   Global Days XXX
   AMA: 2008, Mar, 4-5

⊙ **93315**   **Transesophageal echocardiography for congenital cardiac anomalies; including probe placement, image acquisition, interpretation and report**   S 80 ▯
   🖩 0.00   📐 0.00   Global Days XXX
   AMA: 2008, Mar, 4-5

⊙ **93316**   **placement of transesophageal probe only**   S 80 ▯
   🖩 1.26   📐 1.26   Global Days XXX
   AMA: 2008, Mar, 4-5

⊙ **93317**   **image acquisition, interpretation and report only**   N 80 ▯
   🖩 0.00   📐 0.00   Global Days XXX
   AMA: 2008, Mar, 4-5

⊙ **93318**   **Echocardiography, transesophageal (TEE) for monitoring purposes, including probe placement, real time 2-dimensional image acquisition and interpretation leading to ongoing (continuous) assessment of (dynamically changing) cardiac pumping function and to therapeutic measures on an immediate time basis**   S 80 ▯
   🖩 0.00   📐 0.00   Global Days XXX
   AMA: 2008, Mar, 4-5

+ **93320**   **Doppler echocardiography, pulsed wave and/or continuous wave with spectral display (List separately in addition to codes for echocardiographic imaging); complete**   N 80 ▯
   Code first (93303-93304, 93312, 93314-93315, 93317, 93350-93351)
   🖩 2.17   📐 2.17   Global Days ZZZ
   AMA: 2008, Mar, 4-5; 2005, Mar, 11-15; 2005, Mar, 11-15; 2005, March, 11-15; 2004, Apr, 8; 2004, April, 8; 2004, Apr, 8

+ **93321**   **follow-up or limited study (List separately in addition to codes for echocardiographic imaging)**   N 80 ▯
   Code first (93303-93304, 93308, 93312, 93314-93315, 93317, 93350-93351)
   🖩 0.97   📐 0.97   Global Days ZZZ
   AMA: 2008, Mar, 4-5; 2004, Apr, 8; 2004, Apr, 8; 2004, April, 8

⊜ Modifier 63 Exempt Code   ⊙ Moderate Sedation   + CPT Add-on Code   ⊘ Modifier 51 Exempt Code   ● New Code   ▲ Revised Code

M Maternity Edit   A Age Edit   A-Y APC Status Indicators   ▯ CCI Comprehensive Code   ✗ Drug Not Approved by FDA   50 Bilateral Procedure

© 2008 Ingenix *(Blue Ink)*   CPT only © 2008 American Medical Association. All Rights Reserved. (Black Ink)   Medicare (Red Ink)   413

\+ 93325 **Doppler echocardiography color flow velocity mapping (List separately in addition to codes for echocardiography)** N 80 □
Code first (76825-76828, 93303-93304, 93308, 93312, 93314-93315, 93317, 93350-93351)
⚕ 1.50 ⚖ 1.50 **Global Days ZZZ**
AMA: 2008, Mar, 4-5; 2005, Mar, 11-15; 2005, Mar, 11-15; 2005, March, 11-15; 2004, Apr, 8; 2004, April, 8; 2004, Apr, 8

▲ 93350 **Echocardiography, transthoracic, real-time with image documentation (2D), includes M-mode recording, when performed, during rest and cardiovascular stress test using treadmill, bicycle exercise and/or pharmacologically induced stress, with interpretation and report;** S 80 □
Code also exercise stress testing (93015-93018)
⚕ 5.87 ⚖ 5.87 **Global Days XXX**
AMA: 2008, Jan, 10-25; 2008, Mar, 4-5; 2007, Jan, 13-27; 2007, Jan, 13-27; 2007, January, 13-27; 2004, Apr, 8; 2004, April, 8; 2004, Apr, 8

● 93351 **including performance of continuous electrocardiographic monitoring, with physician supervision** S 80
Do not report with (93015-93018, 93350)
⚕ 7.68 ⚖ 7.68 **Global Days XXX**

\+ ● 93352 **Use of echocardiographic contrast agent during stress echocardiography (List separately in addition to code for primary procedure)** M 80
Code also (93350, 93351)
Do not report more than once for each stress echocardiogram
⚕ 1.07 ⚖ 1.07 **Global Days XXX**

93501-93562 Heart Catheterization and Injection Procedures

CMS 100-4,12,30.4   *Cardiovascular System*
INCLUDES   catheter(s):
  introduction
  positioning
  repositioning
  final evalution
  intracardiac pressure recording
  intravascular pressure recording
  obtaining blood samples
  report
EXCLUDES   *selective injection procedures without cardiac catheterization (36011-36015, 36215-36218)*

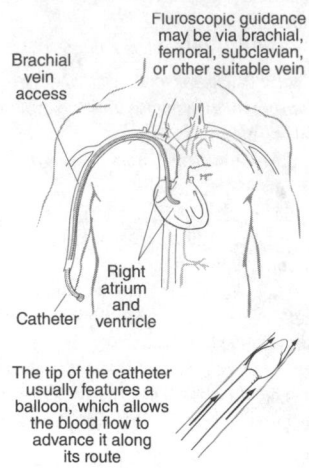

Brachial vein access

Fluroscopic guidance may be via brachial, femoral, subclavian, or other suitable vein

Right atrium and ventricle

Catheter

The tip of the catheter usually features a balloon, which allows the blood flow to advance it along its route

Right side catheterization usually takes pressure measurements at several sites.

⊙ 93501 **Right heart catheterization** T 80 □
EXCLUDES   *bundle of His recording (93600)*
⚕ 22.29 ⚖ 22.29 **Global Days 000**
AMA: 2008, Jan, 10-25; 2008, Mar, 4-5; 2007, Jan, 13-27; 2007, Jan, 13-27; 2007, January, 13-27

⊘ 93503 **Insertion and placement of flow directed catheter (eg, Swan-Ganz) for monitoring purposes** T 80 □
EXCLUDES   *subsequent monitoring (99356-99357)*
⚕ 3.11 ⚖ 3.11 **Global Days 000**
AMA: 2008, Mar, 4-5

⊙ 93505 **Endomyocardial biopsy** T 80 □
⚕ 20.70 ⚖ 20.70 **Global Days 000**
AMA: 2008, Jan, 10-25; 2008, Mar, 4-5; 2007, Jan, 13-27; 2007, Jan, 13-27; 2007, January, 13-27

⊙ 93508 **Catheter placement in coronary artery(s), arterial coronary conduit(s), and/or venous coronary bypass graft(s) for coronary angiography without concomitant left heart catheterization** T 80 □
INCLUDES   reporting only once per procedure
EXCLUDES   *application of intravascular radioelement (77785-77787)*
  left heart catheterization (93510, 93511, 93524, 93526)
  transcatheter placement of radiation delivery device for coronary intravascular brachytherapy (92974)
Code also imaging supervision, interpretation and report (93556)
Code also injection procedures (93539, 93540, 93544, 93545)
⚕ 29.41 ⚖ 29.41 **Global Days 000**
AMA: 2008, Jan, 10-25; 2008, Mar, 4-5; 2007, Jan, 13-27; 2007, Jan, 13-27; 2007, January, 13-27; 2007, Dec, 10-179

⊙ 93510 **Left heart catheterization, retrograde, from the brachial artery, axillary artery or femoral artery; percutaneous** T 80 □
⚕ 36.98 ⚖ 36.98 **Global Days 000**
AMA: 2008, Mar, 4-5; 2005, Mar, 11-15; 2005, Mar, 11-15; 2005, March, 11-15

⊙ 93511 **by cutdown** T 80 □
⚕ 0.00 ⚖ 0.00 **Global Days 000**
AMA: 2008, Mar, 4-5

⊙ 93514 Left heart catheterization by left ventricular puncture T 80 🖵
   🔧 0.00 ✂ 0.00 Global Days 000
   AMA: 2008, Mar, 4-5

⊙ 93524 Combined transseptal and retrograde left heart catheterization T 80 🖵
   🔧 0.00 ✂ 0.00 Global Days 000
   AMA: 2008, Mar, 4-5

⊙ 93526 Combined right heart catheterization and retrograde left heart catheterization T 80 🖵
   🔧 47.46 ✂ 47.46 Global Days 000
   AMA: 2008, Mar, 4-5

⊙ 93527 Combined right heart catheterization and transseptal left heart catheterization through intact septum (with or without retrograde left heart catheterization) T 80 🖵
   🔧 0.00 ✂ 0.00 Global Days 000
   AMA: 2008, Mar, 4-5

⊙ 93528 Combined right heart catheterization with left ventricular puncture (with or without retrograde left heart catheterization) T 80 🖵
   🔧 0.00 ✂ 0.00 Global Days 000
   AMA: 2008, Mar, 4-5

⊙ 93529 Combined right heart catheterization and left heart catheterization through existing septal opening (with or without retrograde left heart catheterization) T 80 🖵
   🔧 0.00 ✂ 0.00 Global Days 000
   AMA: 2008, Mar, 4-5

⊙ 93530 Right heart catheterization, for congenital cardiac anomalies T 80 🖵
   🔧 0.00 ✂ 0.00 Global Days 000
   AMA: 2008, Jan, 10-25; 2008, Mar, 4-5; 2007, Jan, 13-27; 2007, Jan, 13-27; 2007, January, 13-27

93531 Combined right heart catheterization and retrograde left heart catheterization, for congenital cardiac anomalies T 80 🖵
   🔧 0.00 ✂ 0.00 Global Days 000
   AMA: 2008, Mar, 4-5

93532 Combined right heart catheterization and transseptal left heart catheterization through intact septum with or without retrograde left heart catheterization, for congenital cardiac anomalies T 80 🖵
   🔧 0.00 ✂ 0.00 Global Days 000
   AMA: 2008, Jan, 10-25; 2008, Mar, 4-5; 2007, Jan, 13-27; 2007, January, 13-27

93533 Combined right heart catheterization and transseptal left heart catheterization through existing septal opening, with or without retrograde left heart catheterization, for congenital cardiac anomalies T 80 🖵
   🔧 0.00 ✂ 0.00 Global Days 000
   AMA: 2008, Mar, 4-5

⊘ ⊙ 93539 Injection procedure during cardiac catheterization; for selective opacification of arterial conduits (eg, internal mammary), whether native or used for bypass N 80 🖵
   ⊠ 93556
   🔧 0.61 ✂ 2.22 Global Days 000
   AMA: 2008, Jan, 10-25; 2008, Mar, 4-5; 2007, Jan, 13-27; 2007, Jan, 13-27; 2007, January, 13-27; 2007, Dec, 10-179

⊘ ⊙ 93540 for selective opacification of aortocoronary venous bypass grafts, 1 or more coronary arteries N 80 🖵
   ⊠ 93556
   🔧 0.66 ✂ 6.62 Global Days 000
   AMA: 2008, Mar, 4-5; 2007, Dec, 10-179

⊙ 93541 for pulmonary angiography N 80 🖵
   ⊠ 93556
   🔧 0.44 ✂ 0.44 Global Days 000
   AMA: 2008, Mar, 4-5; 2007, Dec, 10-179

⊙ 93542 for selective right ventricular or right atrial angiography N 80 🖵
   ⊠ 93555
   🔧 0.44 ✂ 4.02 Global Days 000
   AMA: 2008, Mar, 4-5; 2007, Dec, 10-179

⊙ 93543 for selective left ventricular or left atrial angiography N 80 🖵
   ⊠ 93555
   🔧 0.44 ✂ 2.20 Global Days 000
   AMA: 2008, Mar, 4-5; 2007, Dec, 10-179

⊘ ⊙ 93544 for aortography N 80 🖵
   ⊠ 93556
   🔧 0.39 ✂ 1.60 Global Days 000
   AMA: 2008, Mar, 4-5; 2007, Dec, 10-179

⊘ ⊙ 93545 for selective coronary angiography (injection of radiopaque material may be by hand) N 80 🖵
   ⊠ 93556
   🔧 0.61 ✂ 4.63 Global Days 000
   AMA: 2008, Jan, 10-25; 2008, Mar, 4-5; 2007, Jan, 13-27; 2007, Jan, 13-27; 2007, January, 13-27; 2007, Dec, 10-179

⊘ ⊙ 93555 Imaging supervision, interpretation and report for injection procedure(s) during cardiac catheterization; ventricular and/or atrial angiography N 80 🖵
   Code also (93542, 93543)
   🔧 3.27 ✂ 3.27 Global Days XXX
   AMA: 2008, Jan, 10-25; 2008, Mar, 4-5; 2007, Jan, 13-27; 2007, Jan, 13-27; 2007, January, 13-27

⊘ ⊙ 93556 pulmonary angiography, aortography, and/or selective coronary angiography including venous bypass grafts and arterial conduits (whether native or used in bypass) N 80 🖵
   Code also (93539-93541, 93544-93545)
   🔧 4.57 ✂ 4.57 Global Days XXX
   AMA: 2008, Jan, 10-25; 2008, Mar, 4-5; 2007, Jan, 13-27; 2007, Jan, 13-27; 2007, January, 13-27; 2007, Dec, 10-179

⊙ 93561 Indicator dilution studies such as dye or thermal dilution, including arterial and/or venous catheterization; with cardiac output measurement (separate procedure) N 80 🖵
   EXCLUDES *cardiac output, radioisotope method (78472, 78473, 78481)*

   Do not report with cardiac catheterization codes
   🔧 0.00 ✂ 0.00 Global Days 000
   AMA: 2008, Jan, 10-25; 2008, Mar, 4-5; 2007, Feb, 10-11; 2007, Feb, 10-11; 2007, February, 10-11; 2007, Jul, 1-4

⊙ 93562 subsequent measurement of cardiac output N 80 🖵
   EXCLUDES *cardiac output, radioisotope method (78472, 78473, 78481)*

   Do not report with cardiac catheterization codes
   🔧 0.00 ✂ 0.00 Global Days 000
   AMA: 2008, Mar, 4-5; 2007, Feb, 10-11; 2007, Feb, 10-11; 2007, February, 10-11; 2007, Jul, 1-4

93571-93572 Coronary Artery Doppler Studies

CMS *100-4,12,30.4* *Cardiovascular System*

INCLUDES doppler transducer manipulations/repositioning within the vessel examined, during coronary angiography/therapeutic intervention (angioplasty)

+ ⊙ **93571** **Intravascular Doppler velocity and/or pressure derived coronary flow reserve measurement (coronary vessel or graft) during coronary angiography including pharmacologically induced stress; initial vessel (List separately in addition to code for primary procedure)** N 80 ▭

Code first primary procedure
💰 0.00 ⚕ 0.00 Global Days ZZZ
AMA: 2008, Mar, 4-5

+ ⊙ **93572** **each additional vessel (List separately in addition to code for primary procedure)** N 80

Code first initial vessel (93571)
💰 0.00 ⚕ 0.00 Global Days ZZZ
AMA: 2008, Mar, 4-5

93580-93581 Percutaneous Repair of Septal Defect

CMS *100-4,12,30.4* *Cardiovascular System*

INCLUDES injection of contrast for atrial/ventricular angiograms
right heart catheterization

EXCLUDES *closure of ventricular septal defect with transmyocardial implant delivery (0166T, 0167T)*
echocardiography (93303-93317, 93662)

Do not report with (93501, 93529-93533, 93539, 93543, 93555)

93580 **Percutaneous transcatheter closure of congenital interatrial communication (ie, Fontan fenestration, atrial septal defect) with implant** T 80 ▭

💰 28.25 ⚕ 28.25 Global Days 000
AMA: 2008, Jan, 10-25; 2008, Mar, 4-5; 2007, Jan, 13-27; 2007, Jan, 13-27; 2007, January, 13-27

93581 **Percutaneous transcatheter closure of a congenital ventricular septal defect with implant** T 80 ▭

💰 37.00 ⚕ 37.00 Global Days 000
AMA: 2008, Jan, 10-25; 2008, Mar, 4-5; 2007, Jan, 13-27; 2007, Jan, 13-27; 2007, January, 13-27

93600-93603 Recording of Intracardiac Electrograms

CMS *100-4,12,30.4* *Cardiovascular System*
CMS *100-3,20.13* *HIS Bundle Study*

INCLUDES unusual situations where there may be recording/pacing/attempt at arrhythmia induction from only one side of the heart

⊘ **93600** **Bundle of His recording** S 80 ▭

Code also (C1730, C1731, C1732, C1733, C1766, C1892, C1893, C1894, C2629, C2630)
💰 0.00 ⚕ 0.00 Global Days 000
AMA: 2008, Jan, 10-25; 2008, Mar, 4-5; 2007, Jan, 13-27; 2007, Jan, 13-27; 2007, Dec, 10-179; 2007, January, 13-27; 2005, Aug, 13-15; 2005, August, 13-15; 2005, Aug, 13-15; 2004, Jul, 13; 2004, April, 8; 2004, July, 13; 2004, Jul, 13; 2004, Apr, 8; 2004, Apr, 8

⊘ **93602** **Intra-atrial recording** S 80 ▭

Code also (C1730, C1731, C1732, C1733, C1766, C1892, C1893, C1894, C2629, C2630)
💰 0.00 ⚕ 0.00 Global Days 000
AMA: 2008, Jan, 10-25; 2008, Mar, 4-5; 2007, Jan, 13-27; 2007, Jan, 13-27; 2007, January, 13-27; 2005, Aug, 13-15; 2005, August, 13-15; 2005, Aug, 13-15; 2004, Apr, 8; 2004, April, 8; 2004, July, 13; 2004, Apr, 8; 2004, Jul, 13; 2004, Jul, 13

⊘ **93603** **Right ventricular recording** S 80 ▭

Code also (C1730, C1731, C1732, C1733, C1766, C1892, C1893, C1894, C2629, C2630)
💰 0.00 ⚕ 0.00 Global Days 000
AMA: 2008, Mar, 4-5; 2005, Aug, 13-15; 2005, Aug, 13-15; 2005, August, 13-15; 2004, Apr, 8; 2004, Apr, 8; 2004, April, 8; 2004, July, 13; 2004, Jul, 13; 2004, Jul, 13

93609-93613 Intracardiac Mapping and Pacing

CMS *100-4,12,30.4* *Cardiovascular System*
CMS *100-3,20.12* *Diagnostic Endocardial Electrical Stimulation (Pacing)*

+ ⊙ **93609** **Intraventricular and/or intra-atrial mapping of tachycardia site(s) with catheter manipulation to record from multiple sites to identify origin of tachycardia (List separately in addition to code for primary procedure)** N 80 ▭

Code also (C1730, C1731, C1733, C2629, C2630)
Code first comprehensive electrophysiologic evaluation or intracardiac catheter ablation (93620, 93651, 93652)

Do not report with (93613)
💰 0.00 ⚕ 0.00 Global Days ZZZ
AMA: 2008, Mar, 4-5; 2005, Aug, 13-15; 2005, Aug, 13-15; 2005, August, 13-15; 2004, Apr, 8; 2004, April, 8; 2004, Apr, 8

⊘ **93610** **Intra-atrial pacing** S 80 ▭

INCLUDES unusual situations where there may be recording/pacing/attempt at arrhythmia induction from only one side of the heart

Code also (C1730, C1731, C1732, C1733, C1766, C1892, C1893, C1894, C2629, C2630)
💰 0.00 ⚕ 0.00 Global Days 000
AMA: 2008, Mar, 4-5; 2005, Aug, 13-15; 2005, Aug, 13-15; 2005, August, 13-15; 2004, Jul, 13; 2004, Jul, 13; 2004, April, 8; 2004, July, 13; 2004, Apr, 8; 2004, Apr, 8

⊘ **93612** **Intraventricular pacing** S 80 ▭

INCLUDES unusual situations where there may be recording/pacing/attempt at arrhythmia induction from only one side of the heart

Code also (C1730, C1731, C1732, C1733, C1766, C1892, C1893, C1894, C2629, C2630)
Do not report with (93620-93622)
💰 0.00 ⚕ 0.00 Global Days 000
AMA: 2008, Mar, 4-5; 2005, Aug, 13-15; 2005, Aug, 13-15; 2005, August, 13-15; 2004, Jul, 13; 2004, Jul, 13; 2004, April, 8; 2004, July, 13; 2004, Apr, 8; 2004, Apr, 8

+ ⊙ **93613** **Intracardiac electrophysiologic 3-dimensional mapping (List separately in addition to code for primary procedure)** N 80 ▭

Code also (C1730, C1731, C1732, C1733, C2630)
Code first comprehensive electrophysiologic evaluation or intracardiac catheter ablation (93620, 93651, 93652)

Do not report with (93609)
💰 10.96 ⚕ 10.96 Global Days ZZZ
AMA: 2008, Mar, 4-5; 2005, Aug, 13-15; 2005, Aug, 13-15; 2005, August, 13-15; 2004, Apr, 8; 2004, April, 8; 2004, Apr, 8

93615-93616 Recording and Pacing via Esophagus

CMS *100-4,12,30.4* *Cardiovascular System*

Code also (C1730-C1733, C1766, C1892-C1894, C2629, C2630)

⊘ ⊙   **93615**   **Esophageal recording of atrial electrogram with or without ventricular electrogram(s);**   Ⓢ 80 ▱

🚑 0.00   ⚕ 0.00   **Global Days 000**

AMA: 2008, Mar, 4-5; 2005, Aug, 13-15; 2005, Aug, 13-15; 2005, August, 13-15; 2004, Apr, 8; 2004, April, 8; 2004, Apr, 8

⊘ ⊙   **93616**   **with pacing**   Ⓢ 80 ▱

Code also (C1756)

🚑 0.00   ⚕ 0.00   **Global Days 000**

AMA: 2008, Mar, 4-5; 2005, Aug, 13-15; 2005, Aug, 13-15; 2005, August, 13-15; 2004, Apr, 8; 2004, April, 8; 2004, Apr, 8

93618 Pacing to Produce an Arrhythmia

CMS *100-4,12,30.4* *Cardiovascular System*

INCLUDES   unusual situations where there may be recording/pacing/attempt at arrhythmia induction from only one side of the heart

EXCLUDES   *intracardiac phonocardiogram (93799)*

Code also (C1730-C1733, C1766, C1892-C1894, C2629, C2630)

⊘ ⊙   **93618**   **Induction of arrhythmia by electrical pacing**   Ⓢ 80 ▱

INCLUDES   unusual situations where there may be recording/pacing/attempt at arrhythmia induction from only one side of the heart

EXCLUDES   *intracardiac phonocardiogram (93799)*

Code also (C1730, C1731, C1732, C1733, C1766, C1892, C1893, C1894, C2629, C2630)

🚑 0.00   ⚕ 0.00   **Global Days 000**

AMA: 2008, Jan, 10-25, 2008, Mar, 4-5, 2007, Jan, 13-27, 2007, Jan, 13-27; 2007, Dec, 10-179; 2007, January, 13-27; 2005, Aug, 13-15; 2005, August, 13-15; 2005, Aug, 13-15; 2004, Apr, 8; 2004, July, 13; 2004, April, 8; 2004, Apr, 8; 2004, Jul, 13; 2004, Jul, 13

93619-93623 Comprehensive Electrophysiological Studies

CMS *100-4,12,30.4* *Cardiovascular System*
CMS *100-3,20.12* *Diagnostic Endocardial Electical Stimulation (Pacing)*

⊙   **93619**   **Comprehensive electrophysiologic evaluation with right atrial pacing and recording, right ventricular pacing and recording, His bundle recording, including insertion and repositioning of multiple electrode catheters, without induction or attempted induction of arrhythmia**   03 80 ▱

INCLUDES   evaluation of sinus node/atrioventricular node/His-Purkinje conduction system without arrhythmia induction

Code also (C1730, C1731, C1732, C1733, C1766, C1892, C1893, C1894, C2629, C2630)

Do not report with (93600, 93602, 93610, 93612, 93618, 93620-93622)

🚑 0.00   ⚕ 0.00   **Global Days 000**

AMA: 2008, Jan, 10-25; 2008, Mar, 4-5; 2007, Jan, 13-27; 2007, Jan, 13-27; 2007, Dec, 10-179; 2007, January, 13-27; 2005, Aug, 13-15; 2005, August, 13-15; 2005, Aug, 13-15; 2004, Apr, 8; 2004, April, 8; 2004, July, 13; 2004, Apr, 8; 2004, Jul, 13; 2004, Jul, 13

⊙   **93620**   **Comprehensive electrophysiologic evaluation including insertion and repositioning of multiple electrode catheters with induction or attempted induction of arrhythmia; with right atrial pacing and recording, right ventricular pacing and recording, His bundle recording**   03 80 ▱

INCLUDES   recording/pacing/attempted arrhythmia induction from one or more site(s) in the heart

Code also (C1730, C1731, C1732, C1733, C1766, C1892, C1893, C1894, C2629, C2630)

Do not report with (93600, 93602, 93610, 93612, 93618, 93619)

🚑 0.00   ⚕ 0.00   **Global Days 000**

AMA: 2008, Jan, 10-25; 2008, Mar, 4-5; 2008, Oct, 10-11; 2007, Jan, 13-27; 2007, Jan, 13-27; 2007, Dec, 10-179; 2007, January, 13-27; 2005, Aug, 13-15; 2005, August, 13-15; 2005, Aug, 13-15; 2004, Apr, 8; 2004, April, 8; 2004, July, 13; 2004, Apr, 8; 2004, Jul, 13; 2004, Jul, 13

+ ⊙   **93621**   **with left atrial pacing and recording from coronary sinus or left atrium (List separately in addition to code for primary procedure)**   Ⓝ 80 ▱

INCLUDES   recording/pacing/attempted arrhythmia induction from one or more site(s) in the heart

Code also (C1730, C1731, C1732, C1733, C1766, C1892, C1893, C1894, C2629, C2630)

Code first right atrial/ventricular pacing/recording (93620)

🚑 0.00   ⚕ 0.00   **Global Days ZZZ**

AMA: 2008, Jan, 10-25; 2008, Mar, 4-5; 2008, Oct, 10-11; 2007, Jan, 13-27; 2007, Jan, 13-27; 2007, Dec, 10-179; 2007, January, 13-27; 2005, Aug, 13-15; 2005, August, 13-15; 2005, Aug, 13-15; 2004, Apr, 8; 2004, July, 13; 2004, April, 8; 2004, Apr, 8; 2004, Jul, 13; 2004, Jul, 13

+ ⊙   **93622**   **with left ventricular pacing and recording (List separately in addition to code for primary procedure)**   Ⓝ 80 ▱

Code also (C1730, C1731, C1732, C1733, C1766, C1892, C1893, C1894, C2629, C2630)

Code first right atrial/ventricular pacing/recording (93620)

🚑 0.00   ⚕ 0.00   **Global Days ZZZ**

AMA: 2008, Jan, 10-25; 2008, Mar, 4-5; 2007, Jan, 13-27; 2007, Jan, 13-27; 2007, Dec, 10-179; 2007, January, 13-27; 2005, Aug, 13-15; 2005, August, 13-15; 2005, Aug, 13-15; 2004, Apr, 8; 2004, July, 13; 2004, April, 8; 2004, Apr, 8; 2004, Jul, 13; 2004, Jul, 13

+   **93623**   **Programmed stimulation and pacing after intravenous drug infusion (List separately in addition to code for primary procedure)**   Ⓝ 80 ▱

INCLUDES   recording/pacing/attempted arrhythmia induction from one or more site(s) in the heart

Code also (C1730, C1731, C1732, C1733, C1766, C1892, C1893, C1894, C2629, C2630)

Code first comprehensive eletrophysiologic evaluation (93619, 93620)

🚑 0.00   ⚕ 0.00   **Global Days ZZZ**

AMA: 2008, Mar, 4-5; 2008, Oct, 10-11; 2007, Dec, 10-179; 2005, Aug, 13-15; 2005, Aug, 13-15; 2005, August, 13-15; 2004, Apr, 8; 2004, April, 8; 2004, Apr, 8

⊚ Modifier 63 Exempt Code   ⊙ Moderate Sedation   + CPT Add-on Code   ⊘ Modifier 51 Exempt Code   ● New Code   ▲ Revised Code

Ⓜ Maternity Edit   Ⓐ Age Edit   Ⓐ-Ⓨ APC Status Indicators   ▱ CCI Comprehensive Code   ⚕ Drug Not Approved by FDA   50 Bilateral Procedure

93624-93631 Followup and Intraoperative Electrophysiologic Studies

CMS *100-3,20.11*   *Intraoperative Ventricular Mapping*
CMS *100-4,12,30.4*   *Cardiovascular System*
CMS *100-3,20.12*   *Diagnostic Endocardial Electrical Stimulation (Pacing)*

⊙   **93624**   **Electrophysiologic follow-up study with pacing and recording to test effectiveness of therapy, including induction or attempted induction of arrhythmia**   T 80 ▭

    INCLUDES   recording/pacing/attempted arrhythmia induction from one or more site(s) in the heart

    Code also (C1730, C1731, C1732, C1733, C1766, C1892, C1893, C1894)

    🔄 0.00   📎 0.00   **Global Days 000**
    AMA: 2008, Mar, 4-5; 2007, Dec, 10-179; 2005, Aug, 13-15; 2005, Aug, 13-15; 2005, August, 13-15; 2004, Apr, 8; 2004, April, 8; 2004, Apr, 8

⊘   **93631**   **Intra-operative epicardial and endocardial pacing and mapping to localize the site of tachycardia or zone of slow conduction for surgical correction**   N 80 ▭

    EXCLUDES   *operative ablation of an arrhythmogenic focus or pathway by a separate provider (33250-33261)*

    Code also (C1730, C1731, C1732, C1733, C1766, C1892, C1893, C1894, C2629, C2630)

    🔄 0.00   📎 0.00   **Global Days 000**
    AMA: 2008, Mar, 4-5; 2007, Dec, 10-179; 2005, Aug, 13-15; 2005, Aug, 13-15; 2005, August, 13-15; 2004, Apr, 8; 2004, April, 8; 2004, Apr, 8

93640-93642 Electrophysiologic Studies of Pacing Cardioverter-Defibrillators

CMS *100-4,12,30.4*   *Cardiovascular System*
CMS *100-3,20.12*   *Diagnostic Endocardial Electrical Stimulation (Pacing)*
CMS *100-3,20.8.2*   *Self-contained Pacemaker Monitors*
INCLUDES   recording/pacing/attempted arrhythmia induction from one or more site(s) in the heart

⊙   **93640**   **Electrophysiologic evaluation of single or dual chamber pacing cardioverter-defibrillator leads including defibrillation threshold evaluation (induction of arrhythmia, evaluation of sensing and pacing for arrhythmia termination) at time of initial implantation or replacement;**   N 80 ▭

    🔄 0.00   📎 0.00   **Global Days 000**
    AMA: 2008, Mar, 4-5; 2005, Aug, 13-15; 2005, Aug, 13-15; 2005, August, 13-15; 2004, Apr, 8; 2004, April, 8; 2004, Apr, 8

⊙   **93641**   **with testing of single or dual chamber pacing cardioverter-defibrillator pulse generator**   N 80 ▭

    EXCLUDES   *single/dual chamber pacing cardioverter-defibrillators reprogramming/electronic analysis, subsequent/periodic (93282-93283, 93289, 93292, 93295, 93642)*

    🔄 0.00   📎 0.00   **Global Days 000**
    AMA: 2008, Mar, 4-5; 2005, Aug, 13-15; 2005, Aug, 13-15; 2005, August, 13-15; 2004, Apr, 8; 2004, April, 8; 2004, Apr, 8

⊙   **93642**   **Electrophysiologic evaluation of single or dual chamber pacing cardioverter-defibrillator (includes defibrillation threshold evaluation, induction of arrhythmia, evaluation of sensing and pacing for arrhythmia termination, and programming or reprogramming of sensing or therapeutic parameters)**   S 80 ▭

    🔄 13.11   📎 13.11   **Global Days 000**
    AMA: 2008, Mar, 4-5; 2005, Aug, 13-15; 2005, Aug, 13-15; 2005, August, 13-15; 2004, Apr, 8; 2004, April, 8; 2004, Apr, 8

93650-93652 Intracardiac Ablation

CMS *100-4,12,30.4*   *Cardiovascular System*
Code also (C1732, C1733, C1766, C1892-C1894, C2629, C2630)

⊙   **93650**   **Intracardiac catheter ablation of atrioventricular node function, atrioventricular conduction for creation of complete heart block, with or without temporary pacemaker placement**   03 80 ▭

    🔄 16.69   📎 16.69   **Global Days 000**
    AMA: 2008, Mar, 4-5; 2005, Aug, 13-15; 2005, Aug, 13-15; 2005, August, 13-15; 2004, Apr, 8; 2004, April, 8; 2004, Apr, 8

⊙   **93651**   **Intracardiac catheter ablation of arrhythmogenic focus; for treatment of supraventricular tachycardia by ablation of fast or slow atrioventricular pathways, accessory atrioventricular connections or other atrial foci, singly or in combination**   03 80 ▭

    INCLUDES   delivery of radiofrequency energy to the area to selectively destroy cardiac tissue services that may be performed independently on a date subsequent to or at the same time as a diagnostic electrophysiologic study/tachycardia(s) induction/mapping

    Code also electrophysiology catheter (C2630)
    🔄 25.39   📎 25.39   **Global Days 000**
    AMA: 2008, Mar, 4-5; 2007, Dec, 10-179; 2005, Aug, 13-15; 2005, Aug, 13-15; 2005, August, 13-15; 2004, Apr, 8; 2004, April, 8; 2004, Apr, 8

⊙   **93652**   **for treatment of ventricular tachycardia**   03 80 ▭

    INCLUDES   delivery of radiofrequency energy to the area to selectively destroy cardiac tissue services that may be performed independently on a date subsequent to or at the same time as a diagnostic electrophysiologic study/tachycardia(s) induction/mapping

    🔄 27.63   📎 27.63   **Global Days 000**
    AMA: 2008, Jan, 10-25; 2008, Mar, 4-5; 2007, Jan, 13-27; 2007, Jan, 13-27; 2007, January, 13-27; 2005, Aug, 13-15; 2005, Aug, 13-15; 2005, August, 13-15; 2004, Apr, 8; 2004, Apr, 8; 2004, April, 8

93660-93662 Other Tests for Cardiac Function

CMS *100-4,12,30.4*   *Cardiovascular System*

    93660   **Evaluation of cardiovascular function with tilt table evaluation, with continuous ECG monitoring and intermittent blood pressure monitoring, with or without pharmacological intervention**   S 80 ▭

    EXCLUDES   *autonomic nervous system function testing (95921-95923)*

    🔄 4.75   📎 4.75   **Global Days 000**
    AMA: 2008, Mar, 4-5

| 26/1C Professional/Technical Component Only | 80/80 Assist-at-Surgery Allowed/With Documentation | Unlisted | Not Covered | 🔆 Radiology crosswalk |
| MED: Pub 100/NCD References | AMA: CPT Assistant References | A2-Z3 ASC Payment Indicator | ♂Male Only   ♀Female Only | 🔬 Laboratory crosswalk |

418   CPT only © 2008 American Medical Association. All Rights Reserved. (Black Ink)   Medicare (Red Ink)   © 2008 Ingenix (Blue Ink)

+ 93662 Intracardiac echocardiography during therapeutic/diagnostic intervention, including imaging supervision and interpretation (List separately in addition to code for primary procedure) [N] [80] [▢]

Code also (C1759)

Code first 92987, 93527, 93532, 93580, 93581, 93621, 93622, 93651, 93652

Do not report with internal cardioversion (92961)

🔲 0.00 ◇ 0.00 Global Days ZZZ

AMA: 2008, Jan, 10-25; 2008, Mar, 4-5; 2007, Jan, 13-27; 2007, Jan, 13-27; 2007, January, 13-27

93668 Rehabilitation Services: Peripheral Arterial Disease

[INCLUDES] 45-60 minutes per session
monitoring:
other cardiovascular limitations for adjustment of workload
patient's claudication threshold
motorized treadmill or track
supervision by exercise physiologist/nurse

Code also evaluation and managment service, if appropriate

93668 Peripheral arterial disease (PAD) rehabilitation, per session [E]

🔲 0.47 ◇ 0.47 Global Days XXX

AMA: 2008, Mar, 4-5

93701 Thoracic Electrical Bioimpedance

CMS 100-3,20.16 Cardiac Output Monitoring by Thoracic Electrical Bioimpedance (TEB)
CMS 100-4,12,30.4 Cardiovascular System

93701 Bioimpedance, thoracic, electrical [S] [80]

🔲 0.94 ◇ 0.94 Global Days XXX

AMA: 2008, Mar, 4-5

93720-93722 Total Body Plethysmography

CMS 100-3,20.14 Plethysmography
[EXCLUDES] penile plethysmography (54240)
regional plethysmography (93875-93931)

93720 Plethysmography, total body; with interpretation and report [B] [80] [▢]

🔲 1.28 ◇ 1.28 Global Days XXX

AMA: 2008, Jan, 10-25; 2008, Mar, 4-5; 2007, Jan, 13-27; 2007, Jan, 13-27; 2007, January, 13-27

93721 tracing only, without interpretation and report [X] [TC] [80]

🔲 1.05 ◇ 1.05 Global Days XXX

AMA: 2008, Mar, 4-5

93722 interpretation and report only [B] [26] [80]

🔲 0.23 ◇ 0.23 Global Days XXX

AMA: 2008, Mar, 4-5

93724-93736 Electronic Analysis of Pacemaker Function

CMS 100-4,12,30.4 Cardiovascular System
CMS 100-3,20.8.1 Cardiac Pacemaker Evaluation Services
CMS 100-3,20.8 Cardiac Pacemakers
CMS 100-3,20.14 Plethysmography
[EXCLUDES] arterial cannulization/recording of direct arterial pressure (36620)
chemotherapy (96409-96549)
hemodialysis vascular cannulization (36800-36821)
radiographic injection services (36000-36299)

93724 Electronic analysis of antitachycardia pacemaker system (includes electrocardiographic recording, programming of device, induction and termination of tachycardia via implanted pacemaker, and interpretation of recordings) [S] [80] [▢]

🔲 9.28 ◇ 9.28 Global Days 000

AMA: 2008, Mar, 4-5

~~93727~~ ~~Electronic analysis of implantable loop recorder (ILR) system (includes retrieval of recorded and stored ECG data, physician review and interpretation of retrieved ECG data and reprogramming)~~
See 93285, 93291, 93298

~~93731~~ ~~Electronic analysis of dual-chamber pacemaker system (includes evaluation of programmable parameters at rest and during activity where applicable, using electrocardiographic recording and interpretation of recordings at rest and during exercise, analysis of event markers and device response); without reprogramming~~
See 93280, 93288, 93294

~~93732~~ ~~with reprogramming~~
See 93280, 93288, 93294

~~93733~~ ~~Electronic analysis of dual chamber internal pacemaker system (may include rate, pulse amplitude and duration, configuration of wave form, and/or testing of sensory function of pacemaker); telephonic analysis~~
See 93293

~~93734~~ ~~Electronic analysis of single-chamber pacemaker system (includes evaluation of programmable parameters at rest and during activity where applicable, using electrocardiographic recording and interpretation of recordings at rest and during exercise, analysis of event markers and device response); without reprogramming~~
See 93279, 93288, 93294

~~93735~~ ~~with reprogramming~~
See 93279, 93288, 93294

~~93736~~ ~~Electronic analysis of single chamber internal pacemaker system (may include rate, pulse amplitude and duration, configuration of wave form, and/or testing of sensory function of pacemaker); telephonic analysis~~
See 93293

93740 Temperature Gradient Assessment

CMS 100-4,12,30.4 Cardiovascular System

93740 Temperature gradient studies [X]

🔲 0.27 ◇ 0.27 Global Days XXX

⊚ Modifier 63 Exempt Code	⊙ Moderate Sedation	✛ CPT Add-on Code	⊘ Modifier 51 Exempt Code	● New Code	▲ Revised Code
[M] Maternity Edit	[A] Age Edit	[A-Y] APC Status Indicators	[▢] CCI Comprehensive Code	✗ Drug Not Approved by FDA	[50] Bilateral Procedure

93741-93744 Analysis of Pacing Cardioverter-Defibrillator Function

CMS *100-4,12,30.4*   *Cardiovascular System*
CMS *100-3,20.8.1*   *Cardiac Pacemaker Evaluation Services*
CMS *100-3,20.8*   *Cardiac Pacemakers*

~~93741~~ ~~Electronic analysis of pacing cardioverter-defibrillator (includes interrogation, evaluation of pulse generator status, evaluation of programmable parameters at rest and during activity where applicable, using electrocardiographic recording and interpretation of recordings at rest and during exercise, analysis of event markers and device response); single chamber or wearable cardioverter-defibrillator system, without reprogramming~~
See 93282, 93289, 93292, 93295

~~93742~~ ~~single chamber or wearable cardioverter-defibrillator system, with reprogramming~~
See 93282, 93289, 93292, 93295

~~93743~~ ~~dual chamber, without reprogramming~~
See 93283, 93289, 93295

~~93744~~ ~~dual chamber, with reprogramming~~
See 93283, 93289, 93295

93745 Wearable Cardioverter-Defibrillator System Services

CMS *100-4,12,30.4*   *Cardiovascular System*
EXCLUDES *arterial cannulization/recording of direct arterial pressure (36620)*
chemotherapy (96409-96549)
hemodialysis vascular cannulization (36800-36821)
radiographic injection services (36000-36299)

93745 **Initial set-up and programming by a physician of wearable cardioverter-defibrillator includes initial programming of system, establishing baseline electronic ECG, transmission of data to data repository, patient instruction in wearing system and patient reporting of problems or events** S 80 ▯

Do not report with (93282, 93292)
🔁 0.00   ⚖ 0.00   Global Days XXX

~~93760~~ ~~Thermogram; cephalic~~

~~93762~~ ~~peripheral~~

93770 Peripheral Venous Blood Pressure Assessment

CMS *100-4,12,30.4*   *Cardiovascular System*

93770 **Determination of venous pressure** N
    EXCLUDES *cannulization, central venous (36500, 36555-36556)*

🔁 0.24   ⚖ 0.24   Global Days XXX

93784-93790 Ambulatory Blood Pressure Monitoring

CMS *100-4,32,10.1*   *Ambulatory Blood Pressure Monitoring Billing Requirements*
CMS *100-3,20.19*   *Ambulatory Blood Pressure Monitoring*
CMS *100-4,12,30.4*   *Cardiovascular System*
EXCLUDES *arterial cannulization/recording of direct arterial pressure (36620)*
chemotherapy (96409-96549)
hemodialysis vascular cannulization (36800-36821)
radiographic injection services (36000-36299)

93784 **Ambulatory blood pressure monitoring, utilizing a system such as magnetic tape and/or computer disk, for 24 hours or longer; including recording, scanning analysis, interpretation and report** E 80 ▯
🔁 1.81   ⚖ 1.81   Global Days XXX

93786 **recording only** X TC 80
🔁 0.82   ⚖ 0.82   Global Days XXX

93788 **scanning analysis with report** X TC 80
🔁 0.46   ⚖ 0.46   Global Days XXX

93790 **physician review with interpretation and report** M 26 80
🔁 0.53   ⚖ 0.53   Global Days XXX

93797-93799 Cardiac Rehabilitation

CMS *100-4,4,200.5*   *Cardiac Rehabilitation Services*
CMS *100-4,12,30.4*   *Cardiovascular System*
CMS *100-3,20.10*   *Cardiac Rehabilitation Programs*
EXCLUDES *arterial cannulization/recording of direct arterial pressure (36620)*
chemotherapy (96409)
hemodialysis vascular cannulization (36800-36821)
radiographic injection services (36000-36299)

93797 **Physician services for outpatient cardiac rehabilitation; without continuous ECG monitoring (per session)** S 80 ▯
🔁 0.27   ⚖ 0.50   Global Days 000

93798 **with continuous ECG monitoring (per session)** S 80 ▯
🔁 0.42   ⚖ 0.72   Global Days 000
AMA: 2005, Nov, 1-9; 2005, Nov, 1-9; 2005, November, 1-9

93799 **Unlisted cardiovascular service or procedure** X 80
🔁 0.00   ⚖ 0.00   Global Days XXX
AMA: 2008, Jan, 10-25; 2007, Jan, 13-27; 2007, Jan, 13-27; 2007, January, 13-27; 2005, Nov, 14-15; 2005, November, 14-15; 2005, Nov, 14-15

93875-93893 Noninvasive Tests Extracranial/Intracranial Arteries

CMS *100-3,20.17*   *Noninvasive Tests of Carotid Function*

93875 **Noninvasive physiologic studies of extracranial arteries, complete bilateral study (eg, periorbital flow direction with arterial compression, ocular pneumoplethysmography, Doppler ultrasound spectral analysis)** S 80 ▯
   INCLUDES   *evaluation of*
     doppler analysis of bi-directional blood flow
     non-imaging physiologic recordings of pressures
     oxygen tension measurements
     plethysmography

🔁 2.81   ⚖ 2.81   Global Days XXX
AMA: 2008, Jan, 10-25; 2007, Jan, 13-27; 2007, Jan, 13-27; 2007, January, 13-27; 2005, Dec, 3-6; 2005, December, 3-6; 2005, Dec, 3-6

93880 **Duplex scan of extracranial arteries; complete bilateral study** S 80 ▯ P0
🔁 6.89   ⚖ 6.89   Global Days XXX
AMA: 2005, Mar, 11-15; 2005, Mar, 11-15; 2005, Dec, 3-6; 2005, Dec, 3-6; 2005, March, 11-15; 2005, December, 3-6

93882 **unilateral or limited study** S 80 ▯ P0
   EXCLUDES *common carotid intima-media thickness study for coronary heart disease risk factor assessment or evaluation of atherosclerotic burden (0126T)*

🔁 4.54   ⚖ 4.54   Global Days XXX
AMA: 2005, Dec, 3-6; 2005, Dec, 3-6; 2005, December, 3-6

93886 **Transcranial Doppler study of the intracranial arteries; complete study** [S] [80] [▭]

> INCLUDES complete transcranial doppler (TCD) study
> ultrasound evaluation of right/left anterior circulation territories and posterior circulation territory

📷 8.26 ≥ 8.26 Global Days XXX
AMA: 2005, Dec, 3-6; 2005, Dec, 3-6; 2005, December, 3-6

93888 **limited study** [S] [80] [▭]

> INCLUDES limited TCD study
> ultrasound examination of two or fewer of these territories (right/left anterior circulation, posterior circulation)

📷 5.63 ≥ 5.63 Global Days XXX
AMA: 2005, Dec, 3-6; 2005, Dec, 3-6; 2005, December, 3-6

93890 **vasoreactivity study** [S] [80] [▭]

Do not report with limited TCD study (93888)

📷 7.26 ≥ 7.26 Global Days XXX
AMA: 2005, Dec, 3-6; 2005, Dec, 3-6; 2005, December, 3-6

93892 **emboli detection without intravenous microbubble injection** [S] [80] [▭]

Do not report with limited TCD study (93888)

📷 7.95 ≥ 7.95 Global Days XXX
AMA: 2005, Dec, 3-6; 2005, Dec, 3-6; 2005, December, 3-6

93893 **emboli detection with intravenous microbubble injection** [S] [80] [▭]

Do not report with limited TCD study (93888)

📷 7.93 ≥ 7.93 Global Days XXX
AMA: 2005, Dec, 3-6; 2005, Dec, 3-6; 2005, December, 3-6

93922-93990 Noninvasive Vascular Studies: Abdomen/Extremities/Thorax

CMS 100-3,20.14   *Plethysmography*

INCLUDES patient care required to perform/supervise studies and interpret results
use of simple hand-held devices

93922 **Noninvasive physiologic studies of upper or lower extremity arteries, single level, bilateral (eg, ankle/brachial indices, Doppler waveform analysis, volume plethysmography, transcutaneous oxygen tension measurement)** [S] [80] [▭]

> INCLUDES evaluation of:
> doppler analysis of bi-directional blood flow
> nonimaging physiologic recordings of pressures
> oxygen tension measurements
> plethysmography

📷 3.34 ≥ 3.34 Global Days XXX
AMA: 2005, Dec, 3-6; 2005, Dec, 3-6; 2005, December, 3-6

93923 **Noninvasive physiologic studies of upper or lower extremity arteries, multiple levels or with provocative functional maneuvers, complete bilateral study (eg, segmental blood pressure measurements, segmental Doppler waveform analysis, segmental volume plethysmography, segmental transcutaneous oxygen tension measurements, measurements with postural provocative tests, measurements with reactive hyperemia)** [S] [80] [▭]

> INCLUDES evaluation of
> doppler analysis of bi-directional blood flow
> non-imaging physiologic recordings of pressures
> oxygen tension measurements
> plethysmography

📷 5.16 ≥ 5.16 Global Days XXX
AMA: 2008, Jan, 10-25; 2007, Jan, 13-27; 2007, Jan, 13-27; 2007, January, 13-27; 2005, Dec, 3-6; 2005, December, 3-6; 2005, Dec, 3-6

93924 **Noninvasive physiologic studies of lower extremity arteries, at rest and following treadmill stress testing, complete bilateral study** [6] [80] [▭]

> INCLUDES evaluation of
> doppler analysis of bi-directional blood flow
> non-imaging physiologic recordings of pressures
> oxygen tension measurements
> plethysmography

📷 6.35 ≥ 6.35 Global Days XXX
AMA: 2005, Dec, 3-6; 2005, Dec, 3-6; 2005, December, 3-6

93925 **Duplex scan of lower extremity arteries or arterial bypass grafts; complete bilateral study** [S] [80] [▭]
📷 8.55 ≥ 8.55 Global Days XXX
AMA: 2005, Dec, 3-6; 2005, Dec, 3-6; 2005, December, 3-6

93926 **unilateral or limited study** [6] [80] [▭]
📷 5.46 ≥ 5.46 Global Days XXX
AMA: 2005, Dec, 3-6; 2005, Dec, 3-6; 2005, December, 3-6

93930 **Duplex scan of upper extremity arteries or arterial bypass grafts; complete bilateral study** [S] [80] [▭]
📷 6.77 ≥ 6.77 Global Days XXX
AMA: 2005, Dec, 3-6; 2005, Dec, 3-6; 2005, December, 3-6

93931 **unilateral or limited study** [S] [80] [▭]
📷 4.53 ≥ 4.53 Global Days XXX
AMA: 2005, Dec, 3-6; 2005, Dec, 3-6; 2005, December, 3-6

93965 **Noninvasive physiologic studies of extremity veins, complete bilateral study (eg, Doppler waveform analysis with responses to compression and other maneuvers, phleborheography, impedance plethysmography)** [S] [80] [▭]

> INCLUDES evaluation of:
> doppler analysis of bi-directional blood flow
> nonimaging physiologic recordings of pressures
> oxygen tension measurements
> plethysmography

📷 3.41 ≥ 3.41 Global Days XXX
AMA: 2005, Dec, 3-6; 2005, Dec, 3-6; 2005, December, 3-6

93970 **Duplex scan of extremity veins including responses to compression and other maneuvers; complete bilateral study** [S] [80] [▭]
📷 7.04 ≥ 7.04 Global Days XXX
AMA: 2005, Dec, 3-6; 2005, Dec, 3-6; 2005, December, 3-6

93971 unilateral or limited study ⑤ 80 ▭
🔧 4.66 ⚖ 4.66 **Global Days XXX**
AMA: 2008, Jan, 10-25; 2007, Jan, 13-27; 2007, Jan, 13-27; 2007, January, 13-27; 2005, Dec, 3-6; 2005, December, 3-6; 2005, Dec, 3-6

93975 Duplex scan of arterial inflow and venous outflow of abdominal, pelvic, scrotal contents and/or retroperitoneal organs; complete study ⑤ 80 ▭
🔧 10.49 ⚖ 10.49 **Global Days XXX**
AMA: 2008, Jan, 10-25; 2007, Jan, 13-27; 2007, Jan, 13-27; 2007, January, 13-27; 2005, Dec, 3-6; 2005, December, 3-6; 2005, Dec, 3-6

93976 limited study ⑤ 80 ▭
🔧 6.05 ⚖ 6.05 **Global Days XXX**
AMA: 2008, Jan, 10-25; 2007, Jan, 13-27; 2007, Jan, 13-27; 2007, January, 13-27; 2005, Dec, 3-6; 2005, December, 3-6; 2005, Dec, 3-6

93978 Duplex scan of aorta, inferior vena cava, iliac vasculature, or bypass grafts; complete study ⑤ 80 ▭
🔧 6.62 ⚖ 6.62 **Global Days XXX**
AMA: 2005, Dec, 3-6; 2005, Dec, 3-6; 2005, December, 3-6

93979 unilateral or limited study ⑤ 80 ▭
🔧 4.57 ⚖ 4.57 **Global Days XXX**
AMA: 2005, Dec, 3-6; 2005, Dec, 3-6; 2005, December, 3-6

93980 Duplex scan of arterial inflow and venous outflow of penile vessels; complete study ♂ ⑤ 80 ▭
🔧 5.13 ⚖ 5.13 **Global Days XXX**
AMA: 2005, Dec, 3-6; 2005, Dec, 3-6; 2005, December, 3-6

93981 follow-up or limited study ♂ ⑤ 80 ▭
🔧 3.61 ⚖ 3.61 **Global Days XXX**
AMA: 2005, Dec, 3-6; 2005, Dec, 3-6; 2005, December, 3-6

93982 Noninvasive physiologic study of implanted wireless pressure sensor in aneurysmal sac following endovascular repair, complete study including recording, analysis of pressure and waveform tracings, interpretation and report Ⓧ 80
Do not report with (34806)
🔧 1.10 ⚖ 1.10 **Global Days XXX**

93990 Duplex scan of hemodialysis access (including arterial inflow, body of access and venous outflow) ⑤ 80 ▭
EXCLUDES hemodialysis access flow measurement by indicator method (90940)
🔧 5.35 ⚖ 5.35 **Global Days XXX**
AMA: 2005, Dec, 3-6; 2005, Dec, 3-6; 2005, December, 3-6

94002-94005 Ventilator Management Services

94002 Ventilation assist and management, initiation of pressure or volume preset ventilators for assisted or controlled breathing; hospital inpatient/observation, initial day ⑤ 80
Do not report with (99201-99499)
🔧 2.43 ⚖ 2.43 **Global Days XXX**
AMA: 2008, Jan, 10-25; 2007, Feb, 10-11; 2007, Feb, 10-11; 2007, Mar, 9-11; 2007, Mar, 9-11; 2007, Apr, 3-6; 2007, Apr, 3-6; 2007, February, 10-11; 2007, March, 9-11; 2007, April, 3-6; 2007, Jul, 1-4

94003 hospital inpatient/observation, each subsequent day ⑤ 80
Do not report with (99201-99499)
🔧 1.76 ⚖ 1.76 **Global Days XXX**
AMA: 2007, Feb, 10-11; 2007, Feb, 10-11; 2007, Apr, 3-6; 2007, Apr, 3-6; 2007, February, 10-11; 2007, April, 3-6; 2007, Jul, 1-4

94004 nursing facility, per day Ⓑ 80
Do not report with (99201-99499)
🔧 1.28 ⚖ 1.28 **Global Days XXX**
AMA: 2007, Feb, 10-11; 2007, Feb, 10-11; 2007, Apr, 3-6; 2007, Apr, 3-6; 2007, February, 10-11; 2007, April, 3-6; 2007, Jul, 1-4

94005 Home ventilator management care plan oversight of a patient (patient not present) in home, domiciliary or rest home (eg, assisted living) requiring review of status, review of laboratories and other studies and revision of orders and respiratory care plan (as appropriate), within a calendar month, 30 minutes or more Ⓜ
Do not report with (99339-99340, 99374-99378)
🔧 2.45 ⚖ 2.45 **Global Days XXX**
AMA: 2008, Jan, 10-25; 2007, Mar, 9-11; 2007, Mar, 9-11; 2007, Apr, 3-6; 2007, Apr, 3-6; 2007, March, 9-11; 2007, April, 3-6; 2007, Jul, 1-4

94010-94799 Respiratory Services: Diagnostic and Therapeutic

INCLUDES laboratory procedure(s)
test results interpretation

EXCLUDES *separate identifiable evaluation and management service (99201-99499)*

94010 Spirometry, including graphic record, total and timed vital capacity, expiratory flow rate measurement(s), with or without maximal voluntary ventilation Ⓧ 80 ▭
🔧 0.91 ⚖ 0.91 **Global Days XXX**
AMA: 2008, Jan, 10-25; 2007, Jan, 13-27; 2007, Jan, 13-27; 2007, January, 13-27; 2005, Jul, 11-12; 2005, July, 11-12; 2005, Jul, 11-12

94014 Patient-initiated spirometric recording per 30-day period of time; includes reinforced education, transmission of spirometric tracing, data capture, analysis of transmitted data, periodic recalibration and physician review and interpretation Ⓧ 80 ▭
🔧 1.34 ⚖ 1.34 **Global Days XXX**
AMA: 2005, Jul, 11-12; 2005, Jul, 11-12; 2005, July, 11-12

94015 recording (includes hook-up, reinforced education, data transmission, data capture, trend analysis, and periodic recalibration) Ⓧ TC 80 ▭
🔧 0.65 ⚖ 0.65 **Global Days XXX**
AMA: 2005, Jul, 11-12; 2005, Jul, 11-12; 2005, July, 11-12

94016 physician review and interpretation only Ⓐ 26 80 ▭
🔧 0.69 ⚖ 0.69 **Global Days XXX**
AMA: 2005, Jul, 11-12; 2005, Jul, 11-12; 2005, July, 11-12

94060 Bronchodilation responsiveness, spirometry as in 94010, pre- and post-bronchodilator administration ⑤ 80 ▭
EXCLUDES *bronchospasm prolonged exercise test with pre- and post-spirometry (94620)*
Code also bronchodilator supply with appropriate supply code or 99070
🔧 1.60 ⚖ 1.60 **Global Days XXX**
AMA: 2008, Jan, 10-25; 2007, Jan, 13-27; 2007, Jan, 13-27; 2007, January, 13-27; 2005, Jul, 11-12; 2005, July, 11-12; 2005, Jul, 11-12

94070 Bronchospasm provocation evaluation, multiple spirometric determinations as in 94010, with administered agents (eg, antigen[s], cold air, methacholine) Ⓧ 80 ▭
Code also antigen(s) administration with appropriate supply code or 99070
🔧 1.67 ⚖ 1.67 **Global Days XXX**
AMA: 2005, Jul, 11-12; 2005, Jul, 11-12; 2005, July, 11-12

94150 Vital capacity, total (separate procedure) Ⓧ
🔧 0.62 ⚖ 0.62 **Global Days XXX**
AMA: 2005, Jul, 11-12; 2005, Jul, 11-12; 2005, July, 11-12

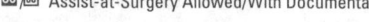

94200   Maximum breathing capacity, maximal voluntary ventilation   [X][80]
   0.62   0.62   Global Days XXX
AMA: 2008, Jan, 10-25; 2007, Jan, 13-27; 2007, Jan, 13-27; 2007, January, 13-27; 2005, Jul, 11-12; 2005, July, 11-12; 2005, Jul, 11-12

94240   Functional residual capacity or residual volume: helium method, nitrogen open circuit method, or other method   [X][80][▭]
   1.08   1.08   Global Days XXX
AMA: 2005, Jul, 11-12; 2005, Jul, 11-12, 2005, July, 11-12

94250   Expired gas collection, quantitative, single procedure (separate procedure)   [X][80]
   0.67   0.67   Global Days XXX
AMA: 2005, Jul, 11-12; 2005, Jul, 11-12; 2005, July, 11-12

94260   Thoracic gas volume   [X][80][▭]
EXCLUDES   plethysmography (93720-93722)
   0.87   0.87   Global Days XXX
AMA: 2005, Jul, 11-12; 2005, Jul, 11-12; 2005, July, 11-12

94350   Determination of maldistribution of inspired gas: multiple breath nitrogen washout curve including alveolar nitrogen or helium equilibration time   [X][80][▭]
   0.96   0.96   Global Days XXX
AMA: 2005, Jul, 11-12; 2005, Jul, 11-12; 2005, July, 11-12

94360   Determination of resistance to airflow, oscillatory or plethysmographic methods   [X][80][▭]
   1.20   1.20   Global Days XXX
AMA: 2005, Jul, 11-12; 2005, Jul, 11-12; 2005, July, 11-12

94370   Determination of airway closing volume, single breath tests   [X][80][▭]
   0.92   0.92   Global Days XXX
AMA: 2005, Jul, 11-12; 2005, Jul, 11-12; 2005, July, 11-12

94375   Respiratory flow volume loop   [X][80][▭]
   1.02   1.02   Global Days XXX
AMA: 2007, Jul, 1-4; 2006, May, 1-9; 2006, May, 1-9; 2006, May, 1-9; 2005, Jul, 11-12; 2005, July, 11-12; 2005, Jul, 11-12

94400   Breathing response to CO2 (CO2 response curve)   [X][80][▭]
   1.46   1.46   Global Days XXX
AMA: 2005, Jul, 11-12; 2005, Jul, 11-12; 2005, July, 11-12

94450   Breathing response to hypoxia (hypoxia response curve)   [X][80][▭]
EXCLUDES   HAST - high altitude simulation test (94452, 94453)
   1.39   1.39   Global Days XXX
AMA: 2005, Jul, 11-12; 2005, Jul, 11-12; 2005, July, 11-12

94452   High altitude simulation test (HAST), with physician interpretation and report;   [X][80][▭] +
EXCLUDES   obtaining arterial blood gases (36600)
Do not report with (94453, 94760-94761)
   1.53   1.53   Global Days XXX
AMA: 2005, Jul, 11-12; 2005, Jul, 11-12; 2005, July, 11-12

94453   with supplemental oxygen titration   [X][80][▭]
EXCLUDES   obtaining arterial blood gases (36600)
Do not report with (94452, 94760-94761)
   2.04   2.04   Global Days XXX
AMA: 2005, Jul, 11-12; 2005, Jul, 11-12; 2005, July, 11-12

94610   Intrapulmonary surfactant administration by a physician through endotracheal tube   [S][80]
INCLUDES   reporting once per dosing episode
EXCLUDES   intubation, endotracheal (31500)
Do not report with (99468-99469)
   1.79   1.79   Global Days XXX
AMA: 2008, Jul, 7-8&15; 2007, Apr, 3-6; 2007, Apr, 3-6; 2007, April, 3-6; 2007, Jul, 1-4

94620   Pulmonary stress testing; simple (eg, 6-minute walk test, prolonged exercise test for bronchospasm with pre- and post-spirometry and oximetry)   [X][80][▭]
   1.99   1.99   Global Days XXX
AMA: 2008, Jan, 10-25; 2007, Jan, 13-27; 2007, Apr, 3-6; 2007, Jun, 10-11; 2007, January, 13-27; 2007, Juno, 10-11; 2007, April, 3-6; 2007, Jun, 10-11; 2007, Apr, 3-6; 2005, Jul, 13-16; 2005, July, 13-16; 2005, July, 11-12; 2005, Jul, 13-16; 2005, Jul, 11-12; 2005, Jul, 11-12; 2004, Mar, 10; 2004, Mar, 10; 2004, March, 10

94621   complex (including measurements of CO2 production, O2 uptake, and electrocardiographic recordings)   [X][80][▭]
   4.46   4.46   Global Days XXX
AMA: 2008, Jan, 10-25; 2007, Jan, 13-27; 2007, Jan, 13-27; 2007, January, 13-27; 2005, Jul, 11-12; 2005, July, 11-12; 2005, Jul, 11-12

94640   Pressurized or nonpressurized inhalation treatment for acute airway obstruction or for sputum induction for diagnostic purposes (eg, with an aerosol generator, nebulizer, metered dose inhaler or intermittent positive pressure breathing [IPPB] device)   [S][80][▭]
EXCLUDES   1 hour or more of continuous inhalation treatment (94644, 94645)
Code also modifier 76 when more than 1 inhalation treatment is performed on the same date
   0.37   0.37   Global Days XXX
AMA: 2008, Jan, 10-25; 2007, Jan, 13-27; 2007, Jan, 13-27; 2007, Apr, 3-6; 2007, Apr, 3-6; 2007, January, 13-27; 2007, April, 3-6; 2005, Jul, 11-12; 2005, Jul, 11-12; 2005, July, 11-12

94642   Aerosol inhalation of pentamidine for pneumocystis carinii pneumonia treatment or prophylaxis   [S][80][▭]
   0.00   0.00   Global Days XXX
AMA: 2005, Jul, 11-12; 2005, Jul, 11-12; 2005, July, 11-12

94644   Continuous inhalation treatment with aerosol medication for acute airway obstruction; first hour   [X][80]
EXCLUDES   services that are less than 1 hour (94640)
   0.94   0.94   Global Days XXX
AMA: 2007, Apr, 3-6; 2007, Apr, 3-6; 2007, April, 3-6

94645   each additional hour (List separately in addition to code for primary procedure)   [X][80]
Code first initial hour (94644)
   0.37   0.37   Global Days XXX
AMA: 2007, Apr, 3-6; 2007, Apr, 3-6; 2007, April, 3-6

94660   Continuous positive airway pressure ventilation (CPAP), initiation and management   [S][80]
   1.00   1.55   Global Days XXX
AMA: 2008, Jan, 10-25; 2007, Jan, 13-27; 2007, Jan, 13-27; 2007, Feb, 10-11; 2007, February, 10-11; 2007, Jul, 1-4; 2007, January, 13-27; 2007, Feb, 10-11; 2006, May, 1-9; 2006, May, 1-9; 2006, May, 1-9; 2005, Jul, 11-12; 2005, July, 11-12, 2005, Jul, 11-12

94662   Continuous negative pressure ventilation (CNP), initiation and management   [S][80][▭]
   0.99   0.99   Global Days XXX
AMA: 2008, Jan, 10-25; 2007, Jan, 13-27; 2007, Jan, 13-27; 2007, Feb, 10-11; 2007, Feb, 10-11; 2007, January, 13-27; 2007, Jul, 1-4; 2007, February, 10-11; 2005, Jul, 11-12; 2005, Jul, 11-12; 2005, July, 11-12

⊕ Modifier 63 Exempt Code   ⊙ Moderate Sedation   + CPT Add-on Code   ⊘ Modifier 51 Exempt Code   ● New Code   ▲ Revised Code
[M] Maternity Edit   [A] Age Edit   [A-Y] APC Status Indicators   [▭] CCI Comprehensive Code   ✗ Drug Not Approved by FDA   [50] Bilateral Procedure

Medicine

94664 — 94776

94664 Demonstration and/or evaluation of patient utilization of an aerosol generator, nebulizer, metered dose inhaler or IPPB device [S] [80] [▢]

INCLUDES reporting only one time per day of service

🔧 0.41 ✎ 0.41 Global Days XXX

AMA: 2008, Jan, 10-25; 2007, Jan, 13-27; 2007, Jan, 13-27; 2007, January, 13-27; 2005, Jul, 11-12; 2005, July, 11-12; 2005, Jul, 11-12

94667 Manipulation chest wall, such as cupping, percussing, and vibration to facilitate lung function; initial demonstration and/or evaluation [S] [80] [▢]

🔧 0.57 ✎ 0.57 Global Days XXX

AMA: 2005, Jul, 11-12; 2005, Jul, 11-12; 2005, July, 11-12

94668 subsequent [S] [80] [▢]

🔧 0.53 ✎ 0.53 Global Days XXX

AMA: 2005, Jul, 11-12; 2005, Jul, 11-12; 2005, July, 11-12

94680 Oxygen uptake, expired gas analysis; rest and exercise, direct, simple [X] [80] [▢]

🔧 1.59 ✎ 1.59 Global Days XXX

AMA: 2005, Jul, 11-12; 2005, Jul, 11-12; 2005, July, 11-12

94681 including CO_2 output, percentage oxygen extracted [X] [80] [▢]

🔧 1.74 ✎ 1.74 Global Days XXX

AMA: 2005, Jul, 11-12; 2005, Jul, 11-12; 2005, July, 11-12

94690 rest, indirect (separate procedure) [X] [80] [▢]

EXCLUDES arterial puncture (36600)

🔧 1.39 ✎ 1.39 Global Days XXX

AMA: 2005, Jul, 11-12; 2005, Jul, 11-12; 2005, July, 11-12

94720 Carbon monoxide diffusing capacity (eg, single breath, steady state) [X] [80] [▢]

🔧 1.42 ✎ 1.42 Global Days XXX

AMA: 2005, Jul, 11-12; 2005, Jul, 11-12; 2005, July, 11-12

94725 Membrane diffusion capacity [X] [80] [▢]

🔧 1.85 ✎ 1.85 Global Days XXX

AMA: 2005, Jul, 11-12; 2005, Jul, 11-12; 2005, July, 11-12

94750 Pulmonary compliance study (eg, plethysmography, volume and pressure measurements) [X] [80] [▢]

🔧 1.95 ✎ 1.95 Global Days XXX

AMA: 2005, Jul, 11-12; 2005, Jul, 11-12; 2005, July, 11-12

94760 Noninvasive ear or pulse oximetry for oxygen saturation; single determination [N] [TC] [80] [▢]

EXCLUDES blood gases (82803-82810)

🔧 0.08 ✎ 0.08 Global Days XXX

AMA: 2008, Jan, 10-25; 2007, Jan, 13-27; 2007, Jan, 13-27; 2007, Feb, 10-11; 2007, Apr, 1-2; 2007, January, 13-27; 2007, April, 1-2; 2007, Jul, 1-4; 2007, February, 10-11; 2007, Apr, 1-2; 2007, Feb, 10-11; 2006, Feb, 10-15; 2006, February, 10-15; 2006, May, 1-9; 2006, Feb, 10-15; 2006, May, 1-9; 2006, May, 1-9; 2005, Jul, 11-12; 2005, Jul, 11-12; 2005, July, 11-12

94761 multiple determinations (eg, during exercise) [N] [TC] [80] [▢]

🔧 0.16 ✎ 0.16 Global Days XXX

AMA: 2008, Jan, 10-25; 2007, Jan, 13-27; 2007, Jan, 13-27; 2007, Feb, 10-11; 2007, Apr, 1-2; 2007, Jun, 10-11; 2007, February, 10-11; 2007, June, 10-11; 2007, Jul, 1-4; 2007, April, 1-2; 2007, January, 13-27; 2007, Apr, 1-2; 2007, Feb, 10-11; 2007, Jun, 10-11; 2006, Feb, 10-15; 2006, May, 1-9; 2006, Feb, 10-15; 2006, May, 1-9; 2006, May, 1-9; 2006, February, 10-15; 2005, Jul, 11-12; 2005, Jul, 11-12; 2005, July, 11-12

94762 by continuous overnight monitoring (separate procedure) [Q1] [TC] [80] [▢]

🔧 0.82 ✎ 0.82 Global Days XXX

AMA: 2007, Feb, 10-11; 2007, Feb, 10-11; 2007, Apr, 1-2; 2007, Apr, 1-2; 2007, Jul, 1-4; 2007, April, 1-2; 2007, February, 10-11; 2006, May, 1-9; 2006, May, 1-9; 2006, February, 10-15; 2006, May, 1-9; 2006, Feb, 10-15; 2006, Feb, 10-15; 2005, Jul, 11-12; 2005, July, 11-12; 2005, Jul, 11-12

94770 Carbon dioxide, expired gas determination by infrared analyzer [X] [80] [▢]

EXCLUDES arterial catheterization/cannulation (36620)
arterial puncture (36600)
bronchoscopy (31622-31656)
flow directed catheter placement (93503)
needle biopsy of the lung (32405)
orotracheal/nasotracheal intubation (31500)
placement of central venous catheter (36555-36556)
therapeutic phlebotomy (99195)
thoracentesis (32421)
venipuncture (36410)

🔧 1.01 ✎ 1.01 Global Days XXX

AMA: 2005, Jul, 11-12; 2005, Jul, 11-12; 2005, July, 11-12

94772 Circadian respiratory pattern recording (pediatric pneumogram), 12-24 hour continuous recording, infant [A] [X] [80] [▢]

EXCLUDES separate procedure codes for electromyograms/EEG/ECG/respiration recordings

🔧 0.00 ✎ 0.00 Global Days XXX

AMA: 2005, Jul, 11-12; 2005, Jul, 11-12; 2005, July, 11-12

94774 Pediatric home apnea monitoring event recording including respiratory rate, pattern and heart rate per 30-day period of time; includes monitor attachment, download of data, physician review, interpretation, and preparation of a report [B] [80]

INCLUDES oxygen saturation monitoring

EXCLUDES sleep testing (95805-95811)

Do not report with (93224-93272, 94775-94777)

🔧 0.00 ✎ 0.00 Global Days YYY

AMA: 2008, Mar, 4-5; 2007, Apr, 3-6; 2007, Apr, 3-6; 2007, April, 3-6

94775 monitor attachment only (includes hook-up, initiation of recording and disconnection) [X] [TC] [80]

INCLUDES oxygen saturation monitoring

EXCLUDES sleep testing (95805-95811)

Do not report with 93224-93272

🔧 0.00 ✎ 0.00 Global Days YYY

AMA: 2008, Mar, 4-5; 2007, Apr, 3-6; 2007, Apr, 3-6; 2007, April, 3-6

94776 monitoring, download of information, receipt of transmission(s) and analyses by computer only [X] [TC] [80]

INCLUDES oxygen saturation monitoring

EXCLUDES sleep testing (95805-95811)

Do not report with 93224-93272

🔧 0.00 ✎ 0.00 Global Days YYY

AMA: 2008, Mar, 4-5; 2007, Apr, 3-6; 2007, Apr, 3-6; 2007, April, 3-6

[26] [TC] Professional/Technical Component Only   [80] [80] Assist-at-Surgery Allowed/With Documentation   Unlisted   Not Covered   ⊠ Radiology crosswalk

MED: Pub 100/NCD References   **AMA:** CPT Assistant References   [I2] [Z3] ASC Payment Indicator   ♂Male Only   ♀Female Only   ⊠ Laboratory crosswalk

424   CPT only © 2008 American Medical Association. All Rights Reserved. (Black Ink)   Medicare (Red Ink)   © 2008 Ingenix (Blue Ink)

94777 physician review, interpretation and preparation of report only B 26 80

INCLUDES oxygen saturation monitoring

EXCLUDES *sleep testing (95805-95811)*

Do not report with (93224-93272)

🔀 0.00 🔀 0.00 Global Days YYY

AMA: 2008, Mar, 4-5; 2007, Apr, 3-6; 2007, Apr, 3-6; 2007, April, 3-6

94799 Unlisted pulmonary service or procedure X 80

🔀 0.00 🔀 0.00 Global Days XXX

AMA: 2008, Jan, 10-25; 2007, Jan, 13-27; 2007, Jan, 13-27; 2007, January, 13-27; 2005, Jul, 11-12; 2005, July, 11-12; 2005, Jul, 11-12

95004-95075 Allergy Tests

CMS *100-3,110.13* Cytotoxic Food Tests
CMS *100-3,110.12* Challenge Ingestion Food Testing
CMS *100-3,110.11* Food Allergy Testing and Treatment
CMS *100-4,12,200* Allergy Testing and Immunotherapy
CMS *100-2,15,20.2* Physician Expense for Allergy Treatment

EXCLUDES *intractable/severe allergic disease therapy (96365-96368, 96372, 96374-96375)*

Do not report with codes for evaluation and management services when reporting test interpretation/report
Code also significant, separately identifiable E/M services using modifier 25

95004 Percutaneous tests (scratch, puncture, prick) with allergenic extracts, immediate type reaction, including test interpretation and report by a physician, specify number of tests X 80 🔲

🔳 *86000-86999*

🔀 0.16 🔀 0.16 Global Days XXX

AMA: 2007, Dec, 9

▲ 95010 Percutaneous tests (scratch, puncture, prick) sequential and incremental, with drugs, biologicals or venoms, immediate type reaction, including test interpretation and report by a physician, specify number of tests X 80 🔲

🔳 *86000-86999*

🔀 0.47 🔀 0.47 Global Days XXX

95012 Nitric oxide expired gas determination X 80

EXCLUDES *determination nitric oxide with spectroscopy (0064T)*

🔳 *86000-86999*

🔀 0.54 🔀 0.54 Global Days XXX

AMA: 2008, Jan, 10-25; 2007, Mar, 9-11; 2007, Mar, 9-11; 2007, Apr, 3-6; 2007, Apr, 3-6; 2007, March, 9-11; 2007, April, 3-6

▲ 95015 Intracutaneous (intradermal) tests, sequential and incremental, with drugs, biologicals, or venoms, immediate type reaction, including test interpretation and report by a physician, specify number of tests X 80 🔲

🔳 *86000-86999*

🔀 0.35 🔀 0.35 Global Days XXX

95024 Intracutaneous (intradermal) tests with allergenic extracts, immediate type reaction, including test interpretation and report by a physician, specify number of tests X 80 🔲

🔳 *86000-86999*

🔀 0.19 🔀 0.19 Global Days XXX

AMA: 2007, Dec, 9

95027 Intracutaneous (intradermal) tests, sequential and incremental, with allergenic extracts for airborne allergens, immediate type reaction, including test interpretation and report by a physician, specify number of tests X 80 🔲

🔳 *86000-86999*

🔀 0.13 🔀 0.13 Global Days XXX

AMA: 2008, Jan, 10-25; 2007, Jan, 13-27; 2007, Jan, 13-27; 2007, January, 13-27; 2007, Dec, 9

95028 Intracutaneous (intradermal) tests with allergenic extracts, delayed type reaction, including reading, specify number of tests X TC 80 🔲

🔳 *86000-86999*

🔀 0.30 🔀 0.30 Global Days XXX

95044 Patch or application test(s) (specify number of tests) X 80 🔲

🔳 *86000-86999*

🔀 0.17 🔀 0.17 Global Days XXX

95052 Photo patch test(s) (specify number of tests) X 80 🔲

🔳 *86000-86999*

🔀 0.19 🔀 0.19 Global Days XXX

95056 Photo tests X 80 🔲

🔳 *86000-86999*

🔀 0.95 🔀 0.95 Global Days XXX

95060 Ophthalmic mucous membrane tests X TC 80 🔲

🔳 *86000-86999*

🔀 0.64 🔀 0.64 Global Days XXX

95065 Direct nasal mucous membrane test X TC 80 🔲

🔳 *86000-86999*

🔀 0.58 🔀 0.58 Global Days XXX

95070 Inhalation bronchial challenge testing (not including necessary pulmonary function tests); with histamine, methacholine, or similar compounds X TC 80 🔲

EXCLUDES *pulmonary function tests (94060, 94070)*

🔳 *86000-86999*

🔀 1.18 🔀 1.18 Global Days XXX

95071 with antigens or gases, specify X TC 80 🔲

EXCLUDES *pulmonary function tests (94060, 94070)*

🔳 *86000-86999*

🔀 1.46 🔀 1.46 Global Days XXX

95075 Ingestion challenge test (sequential and incremental ingestion of test items, eg, food, drug or other substance such as metabisulfite) X 80

🔳 *86000-86999*

🔀 1.30 🔀 1.72 Global Days XXX

AMA: 2008, Jan, 10-25; 2007, Jan, 13-27; 2007, Jan, 13-27; 2007, January, 13-27

® Modifier 63 Exempt Code ⊙ Moderate Sedation + CPT Add-on Code ⊘ Modifier 51 Exempt Code ● New Code ▲ Revised Code

M Maternity Edit A Age Edit A-Y APC Status Indicators 🔲 CCI Comprehensive Code ✗ Drug Not Approved by FDA 50 Bilateral Procedure

© 2008 Ingenix *(Blue Ink)*   CPT only © 2008 American Medical Association. All Rights Reserved. (Black Ink)   Medicare (Red Ink)   425

Medicine

95115 — 95199

95115-95199 Allergy Immunotherapy

CMS *100-3,110.9*   *Antigens Prepared for Sublingual Administration*
CMS *100-4,12,200*   *Allergy Testing and Immunotherapy*
CMS *100-2,15,20.2*   *Physician Expense for Allergy Treatment*

[INCLUDES]   allergen immunotherapy professional services

[EXCLUDES]   *bacterial/viral/fungal extracts skin testing (86485-86486, 95028)*
special reports for allergy patients (99080)
the following procedures for testing (see Pathology/Immunology section or 95199)
>*leukocyte histamine release (LHR)*
>*lymphocytic transformation test (LTT)*
>*mast cell degranulation test (MCDT)*
>*migration inhibitory factor test (MIF)*
>*nitroblue tetrazolium dye test (NTD)*
>*radioallergosorbent testing (RAST)*
>*rat mast cell technique (RMCT)*
>*transfer factor test (TFT)*

Code also significantly separate identifiable evaluation and management services, if provided

95115   **Professional services for allergen immunotherapy not including provision of allergenic extracts; single injection**   S 80 ▭
   0.29   0.29   Global Days XXX
   AMA: 2007, Dec, 9; 2006, Dec, 10-12; 2006, Dec, 10-12; 2006, Dec, 10-12; 2006, Dec, 10-12; 2006, Dec, 10-12; 2006, Dec, 10-12; 2006, Dec, 10-12; 2006, Dec, 10-12; 2006, December, 10-12; 2006, December, 10-12; 2006, December, 10-12; 2005, Nov, 1-9; 2005, Nov, 1-9; 2005, February, 10-12; 2005, November, 1-9; 2005, Feb, 10-12

95117   **2 or more injections**   S 80 ▭
   0.35   0.35   Global Days XXX
   AMA: 2008, Jan, 10-25; 2007, Jan, 13-27; 2007, Jan, 13-27; 2007, January, 13-27; 2007, Dec, 9; 2006, Dec, 10-12; 2006, Dec, 10-12; 2006, Dec, 10-12; 2006, Dec, 10-12; 2006, Dec, 10-12; 2006, Dec, 10-12; 2006, Dec, 10-12; 2006, December, 10-12; 2006, December, 10-12; 2006, December, 10-12; 2006, December, 10-12; 2006, Dec, 10-12; 2005, Nov, 1-9; 2005, Nov, 1-9; 2005, November, 1-9; 2005, February, 10-12; 2005, Feb, 10-12; 2005, Feb, 10-12

95120   **Professional services for allergen immunotherapy in prescribing physicians office or institution, including provision of allergenic extract; single injection**   E
   0.00   0.00   Global Days XXX
   AMA: 2005, Feb, 10-12; 2005, Feb, 10-12; 2005, February, 10-12

95125   **2 or more injections**   E
   0.00   0.00   Global Days XXX
   AMA: 2008, Jan, 10-25; 2007, Jan, 13-27; 2007, Jan, 13-27; 2007, January, 13-27; 2005, Feb, 10-12; 2005, February, 10-12; 2005, Feb, 10-12

95130   **single stinging insect venom**   E
   0.00   0.00   Global Days XXX
   AMA: 2008, Jan, 10-25; 2007, Jan, 13-27; 2007, Jan, 13-27; 2007, January, 13-27; 2005, Feb, 10-12; 2005, February, 10-12; 2005, Feb, 10-12

95131   **2 stinging insect venoms**   E
   0.00   0.00   Global Days XXX
   AMA: 2008, Jan, 10-25; 2007, Jan, 13-27; 2007, Jan, 13-27; 2007, January, 13-27; 2005, Feb, 10-12; 2005, February, 10-12; 2005, Feb, 10-12

95132   **3 stinging insect venoms**   E
   0.00   0.00   Global Days XXX
   AMA: 2008, Jan, 10-25; 2007, Jan, 13-27; 2007, Jan, 13-27; 2007, January, 13-27; 2005, Feb, 10-12; 2005, February, 10-12; 2005, Feb, 10-12

95133   **4 stinging insect venoms**   E
   0.00   0.00   Global Days XXX
   AMA: 2008, Jan, 10-25; 2007, Jan, 13-27; 2007, Jan, 13-27; 2007, January, 13-27; 2005, Feb, 10-12; 2005, February, 10-12; 2005, Feb, 10-12

95134   **5 stinging insect venoms**   E
   0.00   0.00   Global Days XXX
   AMA: 2008, Jan, 10-25; 2007, Jan, 13-27; 2007, Jan, 13-27; 2007, January, 13-27; 2005, Feb, 10-12; 2005, February, 10-12; 2005, Feb, 10-12

95144   **Professional services for the supervision of preparation and provision of antigens for allergen immunotherapy, single dose vial(s) (specify number of vials)**   S 80 ▭
   [INCLUDES]   single dose vial/single dose of antigen administered in one injection
   0.09   0.32   Global Days XXX
   AMA: 2008, Jan, 10-25; 2007, Jan, 13-27; 2007, Jan, 13-27; 2007, January, 13-27; 2005, Feb, 10-12; 2005, February, 10-12; 2005, Feb, 10-12

95145   **Professional services for the supervision of preparation and provision of antigens for allergen immunotherapy (specify number of doses); single stinging insect venom**   S 80 ▭
   0.09   0.42   Global Days XXX
   AMA: 2008, Jan, 10-25; 2007, Jan, 13-27; 2007, Jan, 13-27; 2007, January, 13-27; 2005, Feb, 10-12; 2005, February, 10-12; 2005, Feb, 10-12

95146   **2 single stinging insect venoms**   S 80 ▭
   0.09   0.69   Global Days XXX
   AMA: 2005, Feb, 10-12; 2005, Feb, 10-12; 2005, February, 10-12

95147   **3 single stinging insect venoms**   S 80 ▭
   0.09   0.67   Global Days XXX
   AMA: 2005, Feb, 10-12; 2005, Feb, 10-12; 2005, February, 10-12

95148   **4 single stinging insect venoms**   S 80 ▭
   0.09   0.94   Global Days XXX
   AMA: 2005, Feb, 10-12; 2005, Feb, 10-12; 2005, February, 10-12

95149   **5 single stinging insect venoms**   S 80 ▭
   0.09   1.23   Global Days XXX
   AMA: 2005, Feb, 10-12; 2005, Feb, 10-12; 2005, February, 10-12

95165   **Professional services for the supervision of preparation and provision of antigens for allergen immunotherapy; single or multiple antigens (specify number of doses)**   S 80 ▭
   0.09   0.32   Global Days XXX
   AMA: 2008, Jan, 10-25; 2007, Jan, 13-27; 2007, Jan, 13-27; 2007, January, 13-27; 2005, Feb, 10-12; 2005, Feb, 10-12; 2005, February, 10-12; 2005, June, 9-11; 2005, Jun, 9-11; 2005, Jun, 9-11

95170   **whole body extract of biting insect or other arthropod (specify number of doses)**   S 80 ▭
   [INCLUDES]   a dose which is the amount of antigen(s) administered in a single injection from a multiple dose vial
   0.09   0.25   Global Days XXX
   AMA: 2008, Jan, 10-25; 2007, Jan, 13-27; 2007, Jan, 13-27; 2007, January, 13-27; 2005, Jun, 9-11; 2005, Jun, 9-11; 2005, February, 10-12; 2005, June, 9-11; 2005, Feb, 10-12; 2005, Feb, 10-12

95180   **Rapid desensitization procedure, each hour (eg, insulin, penicillin, equine serum)**   X 80 ▭
   2.91   3.85   Global Days XXX

95199   **Unlisted allergy/clinical immunologic service or procedure**   X 80
   0.00   0.00   Global Days XXX

95250-95251 Glucose Monitoring By Subcutaneous Device

Do not report with physiologic data collection/interpretation (99091)

▲ **95250** **Ambulatory continuous glucose monitoring of interstitial tissue fluid via a subcutaneous sensor for a minimum of 72 hours; sensor placement, hook-up, calibration of monitor, patient training, removal of sensor, and printout of recording** ⓥ ⓘ 80 ▭

Do not report more than once per month

Do not report with (99091)

⏴ 3.56 ⚕ 3.56 Global Days XXX

▲ **95251** **interpretation and report** Ⓑ 26 80

Do not report more than once per month

Do not report with (99091)

⏴ 1.10 ⚕ 1.10 Global Days XXX

95803-95811 Sleep Studies

CMS 100-2,6,50 *Sleep Disorder Clinics*

INCLUDES diagnosis of sleep disorders

evaluation of patient's response to therapies

physician:
    interpretation
    recording
    report
    review

simultaneous/continuous monitoring/recording of physiological/pathophysiological sleep parameters of 6 hours or more

EXCLUDES *clinical depression treatment by repetitive transcranial magnetic stimulation (0160T-0161T)*

consultation services (99241-99255)

evaluation and management services (99201-99499)

Code also modifier 26 for interpretation only

Code also modifier 52 for less than 6 hours of recording or other reduced services

● **95803** **Actigraphy testing, recording, analysis, interpretation, and report (minimum of 72 hours to 14 consecutive days of recording)** Ⓢ 60

EXCLUDES *unattended sleep studies (95806)*

Do not report more than once in any 14 day period

Do not report with (95806-95811)

⏴ 0.00 ⚕ 0.00 Global Days XXX

95805 **Multiple sleep latency or maintenance of wakefulness testing, recording, analysis and interpretation of physiological measurements of sleep during multiple trials to assess sleepiness** Ⓢ 80 ▭

EXCLUDES *polysomnography (95808-95811)*

sleep study, not attended (95806)

⏴ 11.69 ⚕ 11.69 Global Days XXX

AMA: 2008, Mar, 4-5

95806 **Sleep study, simultaneous recording of ventilation, respiratory effort, ECG or heart rate, and oxygen saturation, unattended by a technologist** Ⓢ 80 ▭

EXCLUDES *polysomnography (95808-95811)*

⏴ 5.80 ⚕ 5.80 Global Days XXX

AMA: 2008, Jan, 10-25; 2008, Mar, 4-5; 2007, Jan, 13-27; 2007, Jan, 13-27; 2007, January, 13-27

95807 **Sleep study, simultaneous recording of ventilation, respiratory effort, ECG or heart rate, and oxygen saturation, attended by a technologist** Ⓢ 80 ▭

EXCLUDES *polysomnography (95808-95811)*

sleep study, not attended (95806)

⏴ 13.68 ⚕ 13.68 Global Days XXX

AMA: 2008, Mar, 4-5

95808 **Polysomnography; sleep staging with 1-3 additional parameters of sleep, attended by a technologist** Ⓢ 80 ▭

EXCLUDES *sleep study, not attended (95806)*

⏴ 17.89 ⚕ 17.89 Global Days XXX

AMA: 2008, Jan, 10-25; 2008, Mar, 4-5; 2007, Jan, 13-27; 2007, Jan, 13-27; 2007, January, 13-27

95810 **sleep staging with 4 or more additional parameters of sleep, attended by a technologist** Ⓢ 80 ▭

EXCLUDES *sleep study, not attended (95806)*

⏴ 21.28 ⚕ 21.28 Global Days XXX

AMA: 2008, Mar, 4-5

95811 **sleep staging with 4 or more additional parameters of sleep, with initiation of continuous positive airway pressure therapy or bilevel ventilation, attended by a technologist** Ⓢ 80 ▭

EXCLUDES *sleep study, not attended (95806)*

⏴ 23.44 ⚕ 23.44 Global Days XXX

AMA: 2008, Mar, 4-5

95812-95830 Evaluation of Brain Activity by Electroencephalogram

EXCLUDES *clinical depression treatment by repetitive transcranial magnetic stimulation (0160T-0161T)*

consultation services (99241-99255)

evaluation and management services (99201-99499)

95812 **Electroencephalogram (EEG) extended monitoring; 41-60 minutes** Ⓢ 80 ▭

INCLUDES hyperventilation
photic stimulation
physician interpretation
recording of 41-60 minutes
report

EXCLUDES *EEG digital analysis (95957)*
EEG during nonintracranial surgery (95955)
EEG monitoring, 24-hour (95950-95953, 95956)
Wada test (95958)

Code also modifier 26 for physician interpretation only

⏴ 6.52 ⚕ 6.52 Global Days XXX

95813 **greater than 1 hour** Ⓢ 80 ▭

INCLUDES hyperventilation
photic stimulation
physician interpretation
recording of 61 minutes or more
report

EXCLUDES *EEG digital analysis (95957)*
EEG during nonintracranial surgery (95955)
EEG monitoring, 24-hour (95950-95953, 95956)
Wada test (95958)

Code also modifier 26 for physician interpretation only

⏴ 7.99 ⚕ 7.99 Global Days XXX

95816   Electroencephalogram (EEG); including recording awake and drowsy   S 80 ▭

INCLUDES   photic stimulation
physician interpretation
recording of 20-40 minutes
report

EXCLUDES   *EEG digital analysis (95957)*
EEG during nonintracranial surgery (95955)
EEG monitoring, 24-hour (95950-95953, 95956)
Wada test (95958)

Code also modifier 26 for physician interpretation only
🚑 5.98   ⚕ 5.98   **Global Days XXX**
AMA: 2008, Jan, 10-25; 2007, Jan, 13-27; 2007, Jan, 13-27; 2007, January, 13-27

95819   including recording awake and asleep   S 80 ▭

INCLUDES   hyperventilation
photic stimulation
physician interpretation
recording of 20-40 minutes
report

EXCLUDES   *EEG digital analysis (95957)*
EEG during nonintracranial surgery (95955)
EEG monitoring, 24-hour (95950-95953, 95956)
Wada test (95958)

Code also modifier 26 for interpretation only
🚑 6.42   ⚕ 6.42   **Global Days XXX**

95822   recording in coma or sleep only   S 80

INCLUDES   hyperventilation
photic stimulation
physician interpretation
recording of 20-40 minutes
report

EXCLUDES   *EEG digital analysis (95957)*
EEG during nonintracranial surgery (95955)
EEG monitoring, 24-hour (95950-95953, 95956)
Wada test (95958)

Code also modifier 26 for interpretation only
🚑 6.40   ⚕ 6.40   **Global Days XXX**

95824   cerebral death evaluation only   S 80 ▭

INCLUDES   physician interpretation
recording
report

EXCLUDES   *EEG digital analysis (95957)*
EEG during nonintracranial surgery (95955)
EEG monitoring, 24-hour (95950-95953, 95956)
Wada test (95958)

Code also modifier 26 for physician interpretation only
🚑 0.00   ⚕ 0.00   **Global Days XXX**

95827   all night recording   S 80 ▭

INCLUDES   physician interpretation
recording
report

EXCLUDES   *EEG digital analysis (95957)*
EEG during nonintracranial surgery (95955)
EEG monitoring, 24-hour (95950-95953, 95956)
Wada test (95958)

Code also modifier 26 for interpretation only
🚑 10.33   ⚕ 10.33   **Global Days XXX**

95829   Electrocorticogram at surgery (separate procedure)   N 80 ▭

INCLUDES   physician interpretation
recording
report

Code also modifier 26 for interpretation only
🚑 33.20   ⚕ 33.20   **Global Days XXX**

95830   Insertion by physician of sphenoidal electrodes for electroencephalographic (EEG) recording   B 80 ▭
🚑 2.35   ⚕ 4.83   **Global Days XXX**

95831-95857 Evaluation of Muscles and Range of Motion

EXCLUDES   *clinical depression treatment by repetitive transcranial magnetic stimulation (0160T-0161T)*
consultation services (99241-99255)
evaluation and management services (99201-99499)

95831   Muscle testing, manual (separate procedure) with report; extremity (excluding hand) or trunk   A 80 ▭
🚑 0.39   ⚕ 0.70   **Global Days XXX**
AMA: 2008, Jan, 10-25; 2008, May, 9-11; 2007, Jan, 13-27; 2007, Jan, 13-27; 2007, January, 13-27; 2004, Feb, 5; 2004, February, 5; 2004, Feb, 5

95832   hand, with or without comparison with normal side   A 80 ▭
🚑 0.41   ⚕ 0.66   **Global Days XXX**
AMA: 2008, Jan, 10-25; 2008, May, 9-11; 2007, Jan, 13-27; 2007, Jan, 13-27; 2007, January, 13-27; 2004, Feb, 5; 2004, February, 5; 2004, Feb, 5

95833   total evaluation of body, excluding hands   A 80 ▭
🚑 0.65   ⚕ 0.97   **Global Days XXX**
AMA: 2008, May, 9-11; 2004, Feb, 5; 2004, Feb, 5; 2004, February, 5

95834   total evaluation of body, including hands   A 80 ▭
🚑 0.82   ⚕ 1.15   **Global Days XXX**
AMA: 2008, May, 9-11; 2004, Feb, 5; 2004, Feb, 5; 2004, February, 5

95851   Range of motion measurements and report (separate procedure); each extremity (excluding hand) or each trunk section (spine)   A 80
🚑 0.22   ⚕ 0.45   **Global Days XXX**
AMA: 2008, Jan, 10-25; 2008, May, 9-11; 2007, Jan, 13-27; 2007, Jan, 13-27; 2007, Dec, 10-179; 2007, January, 13-27; 2004, Feb, 5; 2004, February, 5; 2004, Feb, 5

95852   hand, with or without comparison with normal side   A 80
🚑 0.16   ⚕ 0.35   **Global Days XXX**
AMA: 2008, May, 9-11; 2004, Feb, 5; 2004, Feb, 5; 2004, February, 5

95857   Tensilon test for myasthenia gravis   S 80 ▭
🚑 0.74   ⚕ 1.13   **Global Days XXX**

95860-95920 Evaluation of Nerve and Muscle Function: Electromyography/Nerve Conduction Studies

CMS *100-3,160.10*   *Evoked Response Tests*
CMS *100-2,15,80*   *Physician Supervision Requirements for Diagnostic Tests*

INCLUDES   physician interpretation
            recording
            report

EXCLUDES   *clinical depression treatment by repetitive transcranial magnetic*
            stimulation (0160T-0161T)
            consultation services (99241-99255)
            evaluation and management services (99201-99499)

95860   **Needle electromyography; 1 extremity with or without related paraspinal areas**   S 80 ▭
            EXCLUDES   *dynamic electromyography during motion analysis studies (96002-96003)*

            Do not report with (95873, 95874, 96000-96004)
            📷 2.23   ⚖ 2.23   Global Days XXX
            AMA: 2008, Jan, 10-25; 2007, Jan, 13-27; 2007, Jan, 13-27; 2007, January, 13-27; 2006, Jun, 8-10; 2006, Jun, 8-10; 2006, September, 5-8; 2006, June, 8-10; 2006, Sep, 5-8; 2006, Sep, 5-8; 2004, Jul, 6; 2004, February, 4; 2004, October, 15; 2004, July, 6; 2004, Jul, 6; 2004, Feb, 4; 2004, Feb, 4; 2004, Oct, 15; 2004, Oct, 15

95861   **2 extremities with or without related paraspinal areas**   S 80 ▭
            EXCLUDES   *dynamic electromyography during motion analysis studies (96002-96003)*

            Do not report with (95873, 95874, 96000-96004)
            📷 3.24   ⚖ 3.24   Global Days XXX
            AMA: 2008, Jan, 10-25; 2007, Jan, 13-27; 2007, Jan, 13-27; 2007, January, 13-27; 2006, Sep, 5-8; 2006, Sep, 5-8; 2006, Jun, 8-10; 2006, September, 5-8; 2006, June, 8-10; 2006, Jun, 8-10; 2005, Jun, 9-11; 2005, June, 9-11; 2005, Jun, 9-11; 2004, Jul, 6; 2004, October, 15; 2004, Jul, 6; 2004, Oct, 15; 2004, Oct, 15; 2004, February, 4; 2004, July, 6; 2004, Feb, 4; 2004, Feb, 4

95863   **3 extremities with or without related paraspinal areas**   S 80 ▭
            Do not report with (95873-95874, 96000-96004)
            📷 3.86   ⚖ 3.86   Global Days XXX
            AMA: 2008, Jan, 10-25; 2007, Jan, 13-27; 2007, Jan, 13-27; 2007, January, 13-27; 2006, Sep, 5-8; 2006, Sep, 5-8; 2006, September, 5-8; 2006, June, 8-10; 2006, Jun, 8-10; 2006, Jun, 8-10; 2004, Oct, 15; 2004, October, 15; 2004, July, 6; 2004, February, 4; 2004, Oct, 15; 2004, Jul, 6; 2004, Jul, 6; 2004, Feb, 4; 2004, Feb, 4

95864   **4 extremities with or without related paraspinal areas**   S 80 ▭
            Do not report with (95873-95874, 96000-96004)
            📷 4.44   ⚖ 4.44   Global Days XXX
            AMA: 2008, Jan, 10-25; 2007, Jan, 13-27; 2007, Jan, 13-27; 2007, January, 13-27; 2006, Sep, 5-8; 2006, Sep, 5-8; 2006, September, 5-8; 2006, June, 8-10; 2006, Jun, 8-10; 2006, Jun, 8-10; 2004, Feb, 4; 2004, July, 6; 2004, February, 4; 2004, October, 15; 2004, Feb, 4; 2004, Jul, 6; 2004, Jul, 6; 2004, Oct, 15; 2004, Oct, 15

95865   **larynx**   S 80
            Do not report with (95873-95874, 96000-96004)
            📷 3.10   ⚖ 3.10   Global Days XXX
            AMA: 2008, Jan, 10-25; 2007, Jan, 13-27; 2007, Jan, 13-27; 2007, Dec, 10-179; 2007, January, 13-27; 2006, Sep, 5-8; 2006, September, 5-8; 2006, Sep, 5-8

95866   **hemidiaphragm**   S 80 50
            Do not report with (95873-95874, 96000-96004)
            📷 2.54   ⚖ 2.54   Global Days XXX
            AMA: 2008, Jan, 10-25; 2007, Jan, 13-27; 2007, Jan, 13-27; 2007, January, 13-27; 2006, Sep, 5-8; 2006, September, 5-8; 2006, Sep, 5-8

95867   **cranial nerve supplied muscle(s), unilateral**   S 80 ▭
            Do not report with (95873-95874, 96000-96004)
            📷 1.94   ⚖ 1.94   Global Days XXX
            AMA: 2008, Jan, 10-25; 2007, Jan, 13-27; 2007, Jan, 13-27; 2007, Dec, 10-179; 2007, January, 13-27; 2006, Jun, 8-10; 2006, Jun, 8-10; 2006, September, 5-8; 2006, Sep, 5-8; 2006, Sep, 5-8; 2006, June, 8-10; 2004, Feb, 4; 2004, Feb, 4; 2004, Jul, 6; 2004, July, 6; 2004, February, 4; 2004, Jul, 6

95868   **cranial nerve supplied muscles, bilateral**   S 80 ▭
            Do not report with (95873-95874, 96000-96004)
            📷 2.66   ⚖ 2.66   Global Days XXX
            AMA: 2008, Jan, 10-25; 2007, Jan, 13-27; 2007, Jan, 13-27; 2007, Dec, 10-179; 2007, January, 13-27; 2006, Sep, 5-8; 2006, Sep, 5-8; 2006, September, 5-8; 2006, Jun, 8-10; 2006, Jun, 8-10; 2006, June, 8-10; 2004, Feb, 4; 2004, Feb, 4; 2004, Jul, 6; 2004, July, 6; 2004, February, 4; 2004, Jul, 6

95869   **thoracic paraspinal muscles (excluding T1 or T12)**   S 80 ▭
            Do not report with (95873-95874, 96000-96004)
            📷 1.24   ⚖ 1.24   Global Days XXX
            AMA: 2008, Jan, 10-25; 2007, Jan, 13-27; 2007, Jan, 13-27; 2007, January, 13-27; 2006, Sep, 5-8; 2006, Sep, 5-8; 2006, September, 5-8; 2006, June, 8-10; 2006, Jun, 8-10; 2006, Jun, 8-10; 2004, Feb, 4; 2004, July, 6; 2004, October, 15; 2004, February, 4; 2004, Feb, 4; 2004, Jul, 6; 2004, Jul, 6; 2004, Oct, 15; 2004, Oct, 15

95870   **limited study of muscles in 1 extremity or non-limb (axial) muscles (unilateral or bilateral), other than thoracic paraspinal, cranial nerve supplied muscles, or sphincters**   S 80
            INCLUDES   Adson test
            EXCLUDES   *anal/urethral*
                        sphincter/detrusor/urethra/perineum
                        musculature (51785-51792)
                        complete study of extremities (95860-95864)
                        eye muscles (92265)

            Do not report with (95873-95874, 96000-96004)
            📷 1.21   ⚖ 1.21   Global Days XXX
            AMA: 2008, Jan, 10-25; 2007, Jan, 13-27; 2007, Jan, 13-27; 2007, January, 13-27; 2006, Jun, 8-10; 2006, Jun, 8-10; 2006, September, 5-8; 2006, June, 8-10; 2006, Sep, 5-8; 2006, Sep, 5-8; 2005, Jun, 9-11; 2005, Jun, 9-11; 2005, June, 9-11; 2004, Feb, 4; 2004, Feb, 4; 2004, February, 4; 2004, July, 6; 2004, Jul, 6; 2004, Jul, 6

95872   **Needle electromyography using single fiber electrode, with quantitative measurement of jitter, blocking and/or fiber density, any/all sites of each muscle studied**   S 80
            Do not report with motion analysis (96000-96004)
            📷 4.55   ⚖ 4.55   Global Days XXX
            AMA: 2008, Jan, 10-25; 2007, Jan, 13-27; 2007, Jan, 13-27; 2007, January, 13-27; 2006, Sep, 5-8; 2006, September, 5-8; 2006, Sep, 5-8

Medicine

95873 — 95922

+ 95873   **Electrical stimulation for guidance in conjunction with chemodenervation (List separately in addition to code for primary procedure)** [N] [80]

Do not report with (95860-95870, 95874, 96000-96004)

Code first chemodenervation (64612-64614)

🔧 1.26   ⚕ 1.26   **Global Days ZZZ**

AMA: 2008, Jan, 10-25; 2007, Jan, 13-27; 2007, Jan, 13-27; 2007, January, 13-27; 2006, Sep, 5-8; 2006, September, 5-8; 2006, Sep, 5-8

+ 95874   **Needle electromyography for guidance in conjunction with chemodenervation (List separately in addition to code for primary procedure)** [N] [80]

Do not report with (95860-95870, 95873, 96000-96004)

Code first chemodenervation (64612-64614)

🔧 1.19   ⚕ 1.19   **Global Days ZZZ**

AMA: 2008, Jan, 10-25; 2007, Jan, 13-27; 2007, Jan, 13-27; 2007, January, 13-27; 2006, Sep, 5-8; 2006, September, 5-8; 2006, Sep, 5-8

95875   **Ischemic limb exercise test with serial specimen(s) acquisition for muscle(s) metabolite(s)** [S] [80] 🖵

Do not report with (96000-96004)

🔧 2.55   ⚕ 2.55   **Global Days XXX**

AMA: 2008, Jan, 10-25; 2007, Jan, 13-27; 2007, Jan, 13-27; 2007, January, 13-27

⊘ 95900   **Nerve conduction, amplitude and latency/velocity study, each nerve; motor, without F-wave study** [S] [80]

[INCLUDES]   reporting this service only once when multiple sites on the same nerve are stimulated/recorded

🔧 1.45   ⚕ 1.45   **Global Days XXX**

AMA: 2008, Jan, 10-25; 2008, Feb, 2; 2008, Feb, 1; 2007, Jan, 13-27; 2007, Jan, 13-27; 2007, January, 13-27; 2006, Sep, 5-8; 2006, Sep, 5-8; 2006, September, 5-8; 2006, June, 8-10; 2006, Jun, 8-10; 2006, Jun, 8-10; 2005, Mar, 16-17; 2005, March, 16-17; 2005, December, 9-11; 2005, Mar, 16-17; 2005, Dec, 9-11; 2005, Dec, 9-11; 2004, Jul, 13; 2004, Jul, 13; 2004, July, 13

⊘ 95903   **motor, with F-wave study** [S] [80] 🖵

[INCLUDES]   reporting this service only once when multiple sites on the same nerve are stimulated/recorded

🔧 1.70   ⚕ 1.70   **Global Days XXX**

AMA: 2008, Jan, 10-25; 2008, Feb, 2; 2008, Feb, 1; 2007, Jan, 13-27; 2007, Jan, 13-27; 2007, January, 13-27; 2006, Sep, 5-8; 2006, Sep, 5-8; 2006, September, 5-8; 2006, Jun, 8-10; 2006, Jun, 8-10; 2006, June, 8-10; 2005, Mar, 16-17; 2005, Mar, 16-17; 2005, Dec, 9-11; 2005, December, 9-11; 2005, March, 16-17; 2005, Dec, 9-11

⊘ 95904   **sensory** [S] [80]

[INCLUDES]   reporting this service only once when multiple sites on the same nerve are stimulated/recorded

🔧 1.28   ⚕ 1.28   **Global Days XXX**

AMA: 2008, Jan, 10-25; 2008, Feb, 2; 2008, Feb, 1; 2007, Jan, 13-27; 2007, Jan, 13-27; 2007, Jul, 12-13; 2007, January, 13-27; 2006, Sep, 5-8; 2006, Sep, 5-8; 2006, September, 5-8; 2006, Jun, 8-10; 2006, Jun, 8-10; 2006, June, 8-10; 2005, Mar, 16-17; 2005, Mar, 16-17; 2005, Dec, 9-11; 2005, March, 16-17; 2005, December, 9-11; 2005, Dec, 9-11

+ 95920   **Intraoperative neurophysiology testing, per hour (List separately in addition to code for primary procedure)** [N] [80] 🖵

[INCLUDES]   electrophysiologic testing/monitoring that is ongoing while surgical procedures are performed

ongoing electrophysiologic monitoring time that is distinct from:

performance of specific type(s) of baseline electrophysiologic study(s) (95860, 95861, 95867, 95868, 95870, 95900, 95904, 95928, 95929, 95933-95937)

interpretation of specific type(s) of baseline electrophysiologic study(s) (92585, 95822, 95870, 95925-95928, 95929, 95930)

use of baseline electrophysiologic study(s) only once per operative session

use of code only once per hour, even if multiple electrophysiologic studies are performed

EXCLUDES   *electrocorticography (95829)*
intraoperative:
   EEG during nonintracranial surgery (95955)
   functional cortical/subcortical mapping (95961-95962)
   neurostimulator programming/analysis (95970-95975)
   time spent performing/interpreting baseline electrophysiologic study(s)

Code first primary procedure (92585, 95822, 95860, 95861, 95867, 95868, 95870, 95900, 95904, 95925-95937)

🔧 4.16   ⚕ 4.16   **Global Days ZZZ**

AMA: 2008, Jan, 10-25; 2007, Jan, 13-27; 2007, Jan, 13-27; 2007, January, 13-27; 2005, Jun, 9-11; 2005, June, 9-11; 2005, Jun, 9-11

95921-95923 Evaluation of Autonomic Nervous System

[INCLUDES]   physician interpretation
recording
report

EXCLUDES   *clinical depression treatment by repetitive transcranial magnetic stimulation (0160T-0161T)*

95921   **Testing of autonomic nervous system function; cardiovagal innervation (parasympathetic function), including 2 or more of the following: heart rate response to deep breathing with recorded R-R interval, Valsalva ratio, and 30:15 ratio** [S] [80] 🖵

🔧 2.01   ⚕ 2.01   **Global Days XXX**

AMA: 2008, Jan, 10-25; 2007, Jan, 13-27; 2007, Jan, 13-27; 2007, January, 13-27; 2006, Feb, 16-18; 2006, February, 16-18; 2006, Feb, 16-18

95922   **vasomotor adrenergic innervation (sympathetic adrenergic function), including beat-to-beat blood pressure and R-R interval changes during Valsalva maneuver and at least 5 minutes of passive tilt** [S] [80] 🖵

🔧 2.41   ⚕ 2.41   **Global Days XXX**

AMA: 2008, Jan, 10-25; 2007, Jan, 13-27; 2007, Jan, 13-27; 2007, January, 13-27; 2006, Feb, 16-18; 2006, Feb, 16-18; 2006, Dec, 10-12; 2006, Dec, 10-12; 2006, Dec, 10-12; 2006, December, 10-12; 2006, December, 10-12; 2006, December, 10-12; 2006, December, 10-12; 2006, February, 16-18; 2006, Dec, 10-12; 2006, Dec, 10-12; 2006, Dec, 10-12; 2006, Dec, 10-12

26/ 🆃 Professional/Technical Component Only   80/ 80 Assist-at-Surgery Allowed/With Documentation    Unlisted   Not Covered   ❎ Radiology crosswalk

MED: Pub 100/NCD References   **AMA:** CPT Assistant References   A2- Z3 ASC Payment Indicator   ♂Male Only   ♀Female Only   ◪ Laboratory crosswalk

430   CPT only © 2008 American Medical Association. All Rights Reserved. (Black Ink)   Medicare (Red Ink)   © 2008 Ingenix *(Blue Ink)*

95923   sudomotor, including 1 or more of the following: quantitative sudomotor axon reflex test (QSART), silastic sweat imprint, thermoregulatory sweat test, and changes in sympathetic skin potential   S 80 ▢

    3.16   3.16   Global Days XXX

    AMA: 2008, Jan, 10-25; 2007, Jan, 13-27; 2007, Jan, 13-27; 2007, January, 13-27; 2006, Feb, 16-18; 2006, February, 16-18; 2006, Feb, 16-18

95925-95937 Neurotransmission Studies

95925   Short-latency somatosensory evoked potential study, stimulation of any/all peripheral nerves or skin sites, recording from the central nervous system; in upper limbs   S 80

    EXCLUDES   *auditory evoked potentials (92585)*

    3.22   3.22   Global Days XXX

95926   in lower limbs   S 80

    EXCLUDES   *auditory evoked potentials (92585)*

    3.16   3.16   Global Days XXX

    AMA: 2008, Jan, 10-25; 2007, Jan, 13-27; 2007, Jan, 13-27; 2007, January, 13-27

95927   in the trunk or head   S 80

    EXCLUDES   *auditory evoked potentials (92585)*

    3.24   3.24   Global Days XXX

95928   Central motor evoked potential study (transcranial motor stimulation); upper limbs   S 80

    5.13   5.13   Global Days XXX

95929   lower limbs   S 80

    5.41   5.41   Global Days XXX

95930   Visual evoked potential (VEP) testing central nervous system, checkerboard or flash   S 80

    2.84   2.84   Global Days XXX

95933   Orbicularis oculi (blink) reflex, by electrodiagnostic testing   S 80

    1.76   1.76   Global Days XXX

95934   H-reflex, amplitude and latency study; record gastrocnemius/soleus muscle   S 80 50

    1.31   1.31   Global Days XXX

    AMA: 2008, Jan, 10-25; 2007, Jan, 13-27; 2007, Jan, 13-27; 2007, January, 13-27; 2006, Jun, 8-10; 2006, June, 8-10; 2006, Jun, 8-10

95936   record muscle other than gastrocnemius/soleus muscle   S 80 50

    1.16   1.16   Global Days XXX

    AMA: 2006, Jun, 8-10; 2006, Jun, 8-10; 2006, June, 8-10

95937   Neuromuscular junction testing (repetitive stimulation, paired stimuli), each nerve, any 1 method   S 80 ▢

    1.57   1.57   Global Days XXX

    AMA: 2006, Jun, 8-10; 2006, Jun, 8-10; 2006, June, 8-10

95950-95962 Electroencephalography For Seizure Monitoring/Intraoperative Use

EXCLUDES   *clinical depression treatment by repetitive transcranial magnetic stimulation (0160T-0161T)*
consultation services (99241-99255)
evaluation and management services (99201-99499)

95950   Monitoring for identification and lateralization of cerebral seizure focus, electroencephalographic (eg, 8 channel EEG) recording and interpretation, each 24 hours   S 80 ▢

    6.58   6.58   Global Days XXX

95951   Monitoring for localization of cerebral seizure focus by cable or radio, 16 or more channel telemetry, combined electroencephalographic (EEG) and video recording and interpretation (eg, for presurgical localization), each 24 hours   S 80 ▢

    0.00   0.00   Global Days XXX

    AMA: 2008, Jan, 10-25; 2007, Jan, 13-27; 2007, Jan, 13-27; 2007, January, 13-27; 2004, Dec, 18; 2004, December, 18; 2004, Dec, 18

95953   Monitoring for localization of cerebral seizure focus by computerized portable 16 or more channel EEG, electroencephalographic (EEG) recording and interpretation, each 24 hours   S 80 ▢

    11.06   11.06   Global Days XXX

95954   Pharmacological or physical activation requiring physician attendance during EEG recording of activation phase (eg, thiopental activation test)   S 80 ▢

    6.75   6.75   Global Days XXX

95955   Electroencephalogram (EEG) during nonintracranial surgery (eg, carotid surgery)   N 80 ▢

    3.79   3.79   Global Days XXX

95956   Monitoring for localization of cerebral seizure focus by cable or radio, 16 or more channel telemetry, electroencephalographic (EEG) recording and interpretation, each 24 hours   S 80 ▢

    19.42   19.42   Global Days XXX

95957   Digital analysis of electroencephalogram (EEG) (eg, for epileptic spike analysis)   N 80 ▢

    7.11   7.11   Global Days XXX

95958   Wada activation test for hemispheric function, including electroencephalographic (EEG) monitoring   C 80 ▢

    10.47   10.47   Global Days XXX

95961   Functional cortical and subcortical mapping by stimulation and/or recording of electrodes on brain surface, or of depth electrodes, to provoke seizures or identify vital brain structures; initial hour of physician attendance   S 80 ▢

    6.42   6.42   Global Days XXX

+ 95962   each additional hour of physician attendance (List separately in addition to code for primary procedure)   S 80 ▢

    Code first initial hour (95961)

    5.89   5.89   Global Days ZZZ

◎ Modifier 63 Exempt Code   ⊙ Moderate Sedation   + CPT Add-on Code   ⊘ Modifier 51 Exempt Code   ● New Code   ▲ Revised Code

M Maternity Edit   A Age Edit   A-Y APC Status Indicators   ▢ CCI Comprehensive Code   ✗ Drug Not Approved by FDA   50 Bilateral Procedure

© 2008 Ingenix *(Blue Ink)*   CPT only © 2008 American Medical Association. All Rights Reserved. (Black Ink)   Medicare (Red Ink)   431

Medicine

95965 — 95972

95965-95967 Magnetoencephalography

INCLUDES   physician interpretation
recording
report

EXCLUDES   *clinical depression treatment by repetitive transcranial magnetic stimulation (0160T-0161T)*
consultation services (99241-99255)
CT provided along with magnetoencephalography (70450-70470, 70496)
electroencephalography provided along with magnetoencephalography (95812-95827)
evaluation and management services (99201-99499)
MRI provided along with magnetoencephalography (70551-70553)
somatosensory evoked potentials/auditory evoked potentials/visual evoked potentials provided along with magnetic evoked field responses (92585, 95925, 95926, 95930)

95965   Magnetoencephalography (MEG), recording and analysis; for spontaneous brain magnetic activity (eg, epileptic cerebral cortex localization) [S] [80] [▣]
⏍ 0.00   ⚚ 0.00   Global Days XXX

95966   for evoked magnetic fields, single modality (eg, sensory, motor, language, or visual cortex localization) [S] [80] [▣]
⏍ 0.00   ⚚ 0.00   Global Days XXX

+ **95967   for evoked magnetic fields, each additional modality (eg, sensory, motor, language, or visual cortex localization) (List separately in addition to code for primary procedure)** [S] [80]
Code first single modality (95966)
⏍ 0.00   ⚚ 0.00   Global Days ZZZ

95970-95982 Evaluation of Implanted Neurostimulator

CMS *100-3,160.12   Neuromuscular Electrical Stimulation (NMES)*
CMS *100-3,160.13   Supplies Used for Transcutaneous Electrical Nerve Stimulation and Neuromuscular Electrical Stimulation (NMES)*
CMS *100-4,32,50   Deep Brain Stimulation for Essential Tremor and Parkinson's Disease*

INCLUDES   simple neurostimulator (three or less of the following); or complex neurostimulator (three or more of the following):
8 or more electrode contacts
alternating electrode polarities
cycling
dose time
more than 1 clinical feature
number of channels
number of programs
pulse amplitude
pulse duration
pulse frequency
stimulation train duration
train spacing

EXCLUDES   *clinical depression treatment by repetitive transcranial magnetic stimulation (0160T-0161T)*
consultation services (99241-99255)
evaluation and management services (99201-99499)
neurostimulator electrodes:
implantation (0155T-0157T, 43647, 43881, 61850-61875, 63650-63655, 64553-64580)
revision/removal (0156T, 0158T, 43648, 43882, 61880, 63660, 64585)
neurostimulator pulse generator/receiver
insertion (61885, 63685, 64590)
revision/removal (61888, 63688, 64595)

95970   Electronic analysis of implanted neurostimulator pulse generator system (eg, rate, pulse amplitude and duration, configuration of wave form, battery status, electrode selectability, output modulation, cycling, impedance and patient compliance measurements); simple or complex brain, spinal cord, or peripheral (ie, cranial nerve, peripheral nerve, autonomic nerve, neuromuscular) neurostimulator pulse generator/transmitter, without reprogramming [S] [80] [▣]
⏍ 0.61   ⚚ 1.36   Global Days XXX
AMA: 2008, Jan, 10-25; 2007, Jan, 13-27; 2007, Jan, 13-27; 2007, January, 13-27; 2006, Dec, 10-12; 2006, Dec, 10-12; 2006, December, 10-12; 2006, Dec, 10-12; 2006, Dec, 10-12; 2006, December, 10-12; 2005, Sep, 9-11; 2005, Sep, 9-11; 2005, Aug, 7-8; 2005, August, 7-8; 2005, September, 9-11; 2005, Aug, 7-8

95971   simple spinal cord, or peripheral (ie, peripheral nerve, autonomic nerve, neuromuscular) neurostimulator pulse generator/transmitter, with intraoperative or subsequent programming [S] [80] [▣]
⏍ 1.11   ⚚ 1.57   Global Days XXX
AMA: 2005, Aug, 7-8; 2005, Aug, 7-8; 2005, August, 7-8

95972   complex spinal cord, or peripheral (except cranial nerve) neurostimulator pulse generator/transmitter, with intraoperative or subsequent programming, first hour [S] [80] [▣]
⏍ 2.11   ⚚ 2.80   Global Days XXX
AMA: 2006, May, 12-15; 2006, May, 12-15; 2006, May, 12-15; 2005, Aug, 7-8; 2005, August, 7-8; 2005, Aug, 7-8

+ 95973 complex spinal cord, or peripheral (except cranial nerve) neurostimulator pulse generator/transmitter, with intraoperative or subsequent programming, each additional 30 minutes after first hour (List separately in addition to code for primary procedure) [S] [80]

Code first initial hour (95972)

📷 1.25 � 1.53 Global Days ZZZ

AMA: 2006, May, 12-15; 2006, May, 12-15; 2006, May, 12-15; 2005, Aug, 7-8; 2005, August, 7-8; 2005, Aug, 7-8

95974 complex cranial nerve neurostimulator pulse generator/transmitter, with intraoperative or subsequent programming, with or without nerve interface testing, first hour [S] [80]

📷 4.10 � 4.68 Global Days XXX

AMA: 2008, Jan, 10-25; 2007, Jan, 13-27; 2007, Jan, 13-27; 2007, January, 13-27; 2006, Dec, 10-12; 2006, Dec, 10-12; 2006, Dec, 10-12; 2006, December, 10-12; 2006, December, 10-12; 2006, Dec, 10-12; 2005, Sep, 9-11; 2005, September, 9-11; 2005, Sep, 9-11

+ 95975 complex cranial nerve neurostimulator pulse generator/transmitter, with intraoperative or subsequent programming, each additional 30 minutes after first hour (List separately in addition to code for primary procedure) [S] [80]

Code first initial hour (95974)

📷 2.37 � 2.60 Global Days ZZZ

AMA: 2008, Jan, 10-25; 2007, Jan, 13-27; 2007, Jan, 13-27; 2007, January, 13-27; 2006, Dec, 10-12; 2006, Dec, 10-12; 2006, Dec, 10-12; 2006, December, 10-12; 2006, December, 10-12; 2006, Dec, 10-12; 2005, Sep, 9-11; 2005, September, 9-11; 2005, Sep, 9-11

95978 Electronic analysis of implanted neurostimulator pulse generator system (eg, rate, pulse amplitude and duration, battery status, electrode selectability and polarity, impedance and patient compliance measurements), complex deep brain neurostimulator pulse generator/transmitter, with initial or subsequent programming; first hour [S] [80] [▣]

📷 4.81 � 5.56 Global Days XXX

AMA: 2005, Aug, 7-8; 2005, Aug, 7-8; 2005, August, 7-8

+ 95979 each additional 30 minutes after first hour (List separately in addition to code for primary procedure) [S] [80]

Code first initial hour (95978)

📷 2.26 � 2.49 Global Days ZZZ

AMA: 2005, Aug, 7-8; 2005, Aug, 7-8; 2005, August, 7-8

95980 Electronic analysis of implanted neurostimulator pulse generator system (eg, rate, pulse amplitude and duration, configuration of wave form, battery status, electrode selectability, output modulation, cycling, impedance and patient measurements) gastric neurostimulator pulse generator/transmitter; intraoperative, with programming [N] [80]

INCLUDES gastric neurostimulator of lesser curvature (95980-95982)

📷 1.12 � 1.12 Global Days XXX

AMA: 2008, Jan, 8-9

95981 subsequent, without reprogramming [S] [80]

📷 0.44 � 0.76 Global Days XXX

AMA: 2008, Jan, 8-9

95982 subsequent, with reprogramming [S] [80]

📷 0.90 � 1.19 Global Days XXX

AMA: 2008, Jan, 8-9

95990-95991 Refill/Upkeep of Implanted Drug Delivery Pump to Central Nervous System

CMS 100-3,280.14 *Infusion Pumps*

EXCLUDES *clinical depression treatment by repetitive transcranial magnetic stimulation (0160T-0161T)*
consultation services (99241-99255)
evaluation and management services (99201-99499)

95990 Refilling and maintenance of implantable pump or reservoir for drug delivery, spinal (intrathecal, epidural) or brain (intraventricular); [S] [80] [▣]

EXCLUDES *analysis/reprogramming of implanted pump for infusion (62367-62368)*
refilling/maintenance implantable drug delivery pump (96522)

📷 1.62 � 1.62 Global Days XXX

AMA: 2008, Jan, 10-25; 2007, Jan, 13-27; 2007, Jan, 13-27; 2007, January, 13-27; 2006, Apr, 19-20; 2006, April, 19-20; 2006, Apr, 19-20; 2005, Jan, 46-47; 2005, November, 1-9; 2005, January, 46-47; 2005, Jan, 46-47; 2005, Nov, 1-9; 2005, Nov, 1-9

95991 administered by physician [S] [▣▣] [▣]

📷 1.01 � 2.40 Global Days XXX

AMA: 2006, Apr, 19-20; 2006, Apr, 19-20; 2006, April, 19-20; 2005, Nov, 1-9; 2005, November, 1-9; 2005, Nov, 1-9

95992-95999 Other and Unlisted Neurological Procedures

⊘ ● 95992 Canalith repositioning procedure(s) (eg, Epley maneuver, Semont maneuver), per day [A]

Do not report with (92531-92532)

📷 1.02 � 1.13 Global Days XXX

06000 Unlisted neurological or neuromuscular diagnostic procedure [S] [80]

📷 0.00 � 0.00 Global Days XXX

AMA: 2008, Jan, 10-25; 2007, Jan, 13-27; 2007, Jan, 13-27; 2007, Mar, 4-5; 2007, Mar, 4-5; 2007, Apr, 7-10; 2007, Apr, 7-10; 2007, January, 13-27; 2007, March, 4-5; 2007, April, 7-10

96000-96004 Motion Analysis Studies

CMS 100-2,15,230.4 *Services By a Physical/OccupationalTherapist in Private Practice*
CMS 100-2,15,80 *Physician Supervision Requirements for Diagnostic Tests*

INCLUDES services provided as part of major therapeutic/diagnostic decision making
services provided in a dedicated motion analysis department capable of
3-D kinetics/dynamic electromyography
computerized 3-D kinematics
videotaping from the front/back/both sides

EXCLUDES *clinical depression treatment by repetitive transcranial magnetic stimulation (0160T-0161T)*
consultation services (99241-99255)
evaluation and management services (99201-99499)
gait training (97116)
needle electromyography (95860-95875)

96000 Comprehensive computer-based motion analysis by video-taping and 3D kinematics; [S] [80] [▣]

📷 2.40 � 2.40 Global Days XXX

AMA: 2007, May, 3-4; 2007, May, 3-4; 2007, May, 3-4

96001 with dynamic plantar pressure measurements during walking [S] [80] [▣]

📷 2.83 � 2.83 Global Days XXX

⑥ Modifier 63 Exempt Code   ⊙ Moderate Sedation   + CPT Add-on Code   ⊘ Modifier 51 Exempt Code   ● New Code   ▲ Revised Code

[M] Maternity Edit   [A] Age Edit   [A-Y] APC Status Indicators   [▣] CCI Comprehensive Code   ⁄ Drug Not Approved by FDA   [50] Bilateral Procedure

© 2008 Ingenix *(Blue Ink)*   CPT only © 2008 American Medical Association. All Rights Reserved. (Black Ink)   Medicare (Red Ink)   433

96002 Dynamic surface electromyography, during walking or other functional activities, 1-12 muscles ⓢ 80 ▭

Do not report with (95860-95864, 95869-95872)

🚗 0.56 ⚖ 0.56 Global Days XXX

96003 Dynamic fine wire electromyography, during walking or other functional activities, 1 muscle ⓢ 80 ▭

Do not report with (95860-95864, 95869-95872)

🚗 0.49 ⚖ 0.49 Global Days XXX

96004 Physician review and interpretation of comprehensive computer-based motion analysis, dynamic plantar pressure measurements, dynamic surface electromyography during walking or other functional activities, and dynamic fine wire electromyography, with written report Ⓑ 26 80 ▭

🚗 3.04 ⚖ 3.04 Global Days XXX

96020 Neurofunctional Brain Testing

96020 Neurofunctional testing selection and administration during noninvasive imaging functional brain mapping, with test administered entirely by a physician or psychologist, with review of test results and report Ⓝ 80

INCLUDES selection/administration of testing of:
cognition
determination of validity of
neurofunctional testing relative to
separately interpreted functional
magnetic resonance images
functional neuroimaging
language
memory
monitoring performance of testing
movement
other neurological functions
sensation

EXCLUDES *clinical depression treatment by repetitive transcranial magnetic stimulation (0160T-0161T)*
consultation services (99241-99255)
evaluation and management services (99201-99499)

Do not report with (70554, 96101-96103, 96116-96120, 99201-99499)

📧 *70555*

🚗 0.00 ⚖ 0.00 Global Days XXX

AMA: 2007, Feb, 6-7; 2007, Feb, 6-7; 2007, February, 6-7

96040 Genetic Counseling Services

INCLUDES analysis for genetic risk assessment
counseling of patient/family
counseling services
face-to-face interviews
obtaining structured family genetic history
pedigree construction
review of medical data/family information
services provided by trained genetic counselor
services provided during one or more sessions

EXCLUDES *education/genetic counseling by a physician to a group (99078)*
education/genetic counseling by a physician to an individual (99201-99499)
education regarding genetic risks by a nonphysician to a group (98961, 98962)
genetic counseling and/or risk factor reduction intervention from a physician, provided to patients without symptoms/diagnosis (99401-99412)

96040 Medical genetics and genetic counseling services, each 30 minutes face-to-face with patient/family Ⓑ

INCLUDES analysis for genetic risk assessment
counseling of patient/family
counseling services
face-to-face interviews
obtaining structured family genetic history
pedigree construction
review of medical data/family information
services provided by trained genetic counselor
services provided during one or more sessions

🚗 1.11 ⚖ 1.11 Global Days XXX

AMA: 2007, Aug, 9-12

26/ⓉⒸ Professional/Technical Component Only   80/80 Assist-at-Surgery Allowed/With Documentation   Unlisted   Not Covered   🏥 Radiology crosswalk

MED: Pub 100/NCD References   **AMA:** CPT Assistant References   A2 Z3 ASC Payment Indicator   ♂Male Only   ♀Female Only   🔬 Laboratory crosswalk

434   CPT only © 2008 American Medical Association. All Rights Reserved. (Black Ink)   Medicare (Red Ink)   © 2008 Ingenix *(Blue Ink)*

CPC EXPERT MEDICINE · 96120

Medicine

96101 — 96120

96101-96125 Cognitive Capability Assessments

CMS *100-2,15,80.2*   *Psychological and Neuropsychological Tests*
CMS *100-1,3,30.2*   *Disorders Subject to Mental Health Limitation*
CMS *100-1,3,30.1*   *Application of Mental Health Limitation - Status of Patient*
CMS *100-1,3,30*   *Outpatient Mental Health Treatment Limitation*
CMS *100-2,15,160*   *Clinical Psychologist Services*
CMS *100-4,12,150*   *Clinical Social Worker (CSW) Services*
CMS *100-4,12,170.1*   *Payment for Clinical Psychologist Services*
CMS *100-4,12,170*   *Clinical Psychologist Services*
CMS *100-4,12,210*   *Outpatient Mental Health Limitation*
CMS *100-4,12,160*   *Independent Psychologist Services*

[INCLUDES] cognitive function testing of the central nervous system

[EXCLUDES] *cognitive skills development (97532, 97533)*
physician conducted mini-mental status examination (99201-99499)

96101   **Psychological testing (includes psychodiagnostic assessment of emotionality, intellectual abilities, personality and psychopathology, eg, MMPI, Rorschach, WAIS), per hour of the psychologist's or physician's time, both face-to-face time administering tests to the patient and time interpreting these test results and preparing the report** [03] [80]

> [INCLUDES] situations when more time is needed to assimilate other clinical data sources including tests administered by a technician or computer and previously reported

> [EXCLUDES] *interpretation and report of (96102-96103)*

📹 2.33   ⚖ 2.34   Global Days XXX

AMA: 2006, Dec, 8-9; 2006, Dec, 8-9; 2006, Dec, 8-9, 2006, Dec, 8-9; 2006, Dec, 8-9; 2006, Dec, 8-9; 2006, Dec, 8-9; 2006, Dec, 8-9; 2006, December, 8-9; 2006, December, 8-9; 2006, December, 8-9; 2006, December, 8-9

96102   **Psychological testing (includes psychodiagnostic assessment of emotionality, intellectual abilities, personality and psychopathology, eg, MMPI and WAIS), with qualified health care professional interpretation and report, administered by technician, per hour of technician time, face-to-face** [03] [80]

📹 0.63   ⚖ 1.42   Global Days XXX

AMA: 2006, Dec, 8-9; 2006, Dec, 8-9; 2006, Dec, 8-9; 2006, Dec, 8-9; 2006, Dec, 8-9; 2006, Dec, 8-9; 2006, Dec, 8-9; 2006, Dec, 8-9; 2006, December, 8-9; 2006, December, 8-9; 2006, December, 8-9; 2006, December, 8-9

96103   **Psychological testing (includes psychodiagnostic assessment of emotionality, intellectual abilities, personality and psychopathology, eg, MMPI), administered by a computer, with qualified health care professional interpretation and report** [03] [80]

📹 0.66   ⚖ 1.28   Global Days XXX

AMA: 2006, Dec, 8-9; 2006, Dec, 8-9; 2006, Dec, 8-9; 2006, Dec, 8-9; 2006, Dec, 8-9; 2006, Dec, 8-9; 2006, December, 8-9; 2006, December, 8-9; 2006, December, 8-9; 2006, December, 8-9

96105   **Assessment of aphasia (includes assessment of expressive and receptive speech and language function, language comprehension, speech production ability, reading, spelling, writing, eg, by Boston Diagnostic Aphasia Examination) with interpretation and report, per hour** [A] [80] [▫]

📹 2.04   ⚖ 2.04   Global Days XXX

AMA: 2005, May, 1-2; 2005, May, 1-2; 2005, May, 1-2

96110   **Developmental testing; limited (eg, Developmental Screening Test II, Early Language Milestone Screen), with interpretation and report** [03] [80] [▫]

📹 0.36   ⚖ 0.36   Global Days XXX

AMA: 2005, May, 1-2; 2005, May, 1-2; 2005, May, 1-2

96111   **extended (includes assessment of motor, language, social, adaptive and/or cognitive functioning by standardized developmental instruments) with interpretation and report** [03] [80] [▫]

📹 3.53   ⚖ 3.61   Global Days XXX

AMA: 2005, May, 1-2; 2005, May, 1-2; 2005, May, 1-2

96116   **Neurobehavioral status exam (clinical assessment of thinking, reasoning and judgment, eg, acquired knowledge, attention, language, memory, planning and problem solving, and visual spatial abilities), per hour of the psychologist's or physician's time, both face-to-face time with the patient and time interpreting test results and preparing the report** [03] [80]

📹 2.51   ⚖ 2.65   Global Days XXX

AMA: 2008, Jan, 10-25; 2007, Jan, 13-27; 2007, Jan, 13-27; 2007, January, 13-27; 2006, Sep, 14-16; 2006, Sep, 14-16; 2006, Dec, 8-9; 2006, Dec, 8-9; 2006, Dec, 8-9; 2006, December, 8-9; 2006, December, 8-9; 2006, December, 8-9; 2006, December, 8-9; 2006, September, 14-16; 2006, Dec, 8-9; 2006, Dec, 8-9; 2006, Dec, 8-9; 2006, Dec, 8-9; 2006, Dec, 8-9

96118   **Neuropsychological testing (eg, Halstead-Reitan Neuropsychological Battery, Wechsler Memory Scales and Wisconsin Card Sorting Test), per hour of the psychologist's or physician's time, both face-to-face time administering tests to the patient and time interpreting these test results and preparing the report** [03] [80]

> [EXCLUDES] *interpretation and report of (96119-96120)*

> [INCLUDES] situations when more time is needed to assimilate other clinical data sources including tests administered by a technician or computer and previously reported

📹 2.45   ⚖ 3.00   Global Days XXX

AMA: 2008, Sep, 14-16; 2006, Sep, 14-16; 2006, Dec, 8-9; 2006, Dec, 8-9; 2006, Dec, 8-9; 2006, Dec, 8-9; 2006, Dec, 8-9; 2006, Dec, 8-9; 2006, Dec, 8-9; 2006, September, 14-16; 2006, December, 8-9; 2006, December, 8-9; 2006, December, 8-9; 2006, December, 8-9

96119   **Neuropsychological testing (eg, Halstead-Reitan Neuropsychological Battery, Wechsler Memory Scales and Wisconsin Card Sorting Test), with qualified health care professional interpretation and report, administered by technician, per hour of technician time, face-to-face** [03] [80]

📹 0.86   ⚖ 2.06   Global Days XXX

AMA: 2006, Sep, 14-16; 2006, Sep, 14-16; 2006, Dec, 8-9; 2006, Dec, 8-9; 2006, Dec, 8-9; 2006, Dec, 8-9; 2006, Dec, 8-9; 2006, Dec, 8-9; 2006, Dec, 8-9; 2006, September, 14-16; 2006, December, 8-9; 2006, December, 8-9; 2006, December, 8-9; 2006, December, 8-9

96120   **Neuropsychological testing (eg, Wisconsin Card Sorting Test), administered by a computer, with qualified health care professional interpretation and report** [03] [80]

📹 0.66   ⚖ 1.90   Global Days XXX

AMA: 2008, Jan, 10-25; 2007, Jan, 13-27; 2007, Jan, 13-27; 2007, January, 13-27; 2006, Sep, 14-16; 2006, Sep, 14-16; 2006, Dec, 8-9; 2006, Dec, 8-9; 2006, Dec, 8-9; 2006, December, 8-9; 2006, December, 8-9; 2006, December, 8-9; 2006, December, 8-9; 2006, September, 14-16; 2006, Dec, 8-9; 2006, Dec, 8-9; 2006, Dec, 8-9; 2006, Dec, 8-9; 2006, Dec, 8-9

ⓔ Modifier 63 Exempt Code   ⊙ Moderate Sedation   + CPT Add-on Code   ⦸ Modifier 51 Exempt Code   ● New Code   ▲ Revised Code

[M] Maternity Edit   [A] Age Edit   [A][Y] APC Status Indicators   [□] CCI Comprehensive Code   ⁄ Drug Not Approved by FDA   [50] Bilateral Procedure

© 2008 Ingenix *(Blue Ink)*   CPT only © 2008 American Medical Association. All Rights Reserved. (Black Ink)   Medicare (Red Ink)   **435**

Medicine

96125   Standardized cognitive performance testing (eg, Ross Information Processing Assessment) per hour of a qualified health care professional's time, both face-to-face time administering tests to the patient and time interpreting these test results and preparing the report   Ⓐ 80

> *EXCLUDES*   *neuropsychological testing by a physician or psychologist (96118-96120)*
> *psychological testing by a physician or psychologist (96101-96103)*

   📖 2.24   ⚕ 2.63   Global Days XXX

96150-96155 Biopsychosocial Assessment/Intervention

INCLUDES   services for patients that have primary physical illnesses/diagnoses/symptoms who may benefit from assessments/interventions that focus on the biopsychosocial factors related to the patient's health status
services used to identify the following factors which are important to the prevention/treatment/management of physical health problems:
behavioral
cognitive
emotional
psychological
social

EXCLUDES   *health and behavior assessment/intervention done by a physician (99201-99499)*
preventive medicine counseling/risk factor reduction/behavioral change (99401-99412)

Do not report evaluation and management service codes, including 99401-99412, on the same day
Do not report with (90801-90899, 99401-99404, 99411-99412)

96150   Health and behavior assessment (eg, health-focused clinical interview, behavioral observations, psychophysiological monitoring, health-oriented questionnaires), each 15 minutes face-to-face with the patient; initial assessment   03 80 🔲

   📖 0.62   ⚕ 0.63   Global Days XXX
   AMA: 2008, Jan, 10-25; 2007, Jan, 13-27; 2007, Jan, 13-27; 2007, January, 13-27; 2005, Jun, 9-11; 2005, Jun, 9-11; 2005, June, 9-11; 2005, May, 1-2; 2005, May, 1-2; 2005, May, 1-2; 2004, Mar, 10; 2004, Mar, 10; 2004, Feb, 11; 2004, February, 11; 2004, March, 10; 2004, Feb, 11

96151   re-assessment   03 80 🔲

   📖 0.60   ⚕ 0.61   Global Days XXX
   AMA: 2008, Jan, 10-25; 2007, Jan, 13-27; 2007, Jan, 13-27; 2007, January, 13-27; 2005, May, 1-2; 2005, May, 1-2; 2005, May, 1-2; 2005, Jun, 9-11; 2005, Jun, 9-11; 2005, June, 9-11; 2004, Feb, 11; 2004, Feb, 11; 2004, Mar, 10; 2004, February, 11; 2004, March, 10; 2004, Mar, 10

96152   Health and behavior intervention, each 15 minutes, face-to-face; individual   03 80 🔲

   📖 0.57   ⚕ 0.58   Global Days XXX
   AMA: 2008, Jan, 10-25; 2007, Jan, 13-27; 2007, Jan, 13-27; 2007, January, 13-27; 2005, May, 1-2; 2005, May, 1-2; 2005, June, 9-11; 2005, Jun, 9-11; 2005, Jun, 9-11; 2005, May, 1-2; 2004, Feb, 11; 2004, Feb, 11; 2004, Mar, 10; 2004, February, 11; 2004, March, 10; 2004, Mar, 10

96153   group (2 or more patients)   03 80 🔲

   📖 0.13   ⚕ 0.14   Global Days XXX
   AMA: 2008, Jan, 10-25; 2007, Jan, 13-27; 2007, Jan, 13-27; 2007, January, 13-27; 2005, Jun, 9-11; 2005, Jun, 9-11; 2005, May, 1-2; 2005, May, 1-2; 2005, May, 1-2; 2005, June, 9-11; 2004, Mar, 10; 2004, Mar, 10; 2004, Feb, 11; 2004, February, 11; 2004, March, 10; 2004, Feb, 11

96154   family (with the patient present)   03 80 🔲

   📖 0.56   ⚕ 0.57   Global Days XXX
   AMA: 2008, Jan, 10-25; 2007, Jan, 13-27; 2007, Jan, 13-27; 2007, January, 13-27; 2005, Jun, 9-11; 2005, Jun, 9-11; 2005, May, 1-2; 2005, May, 1-2; 2005, May, 1-2; 2005, June, 9-11; 2004, Feb, 11; 2004, Feb, 11; 2004, Mar, 10; 2004, March, 10; 2004, February, 11; 2004, Mar, 10

96155   family (without the patient present)   Ⓔ

   📖 0.61   ⚕ 0.62   Global Days XXX
   AMA: 2008, Jan, 10-25; 2007, Jan, 13-27; 2007, Jan, 13-27; 2007, January, 13-27; 2005, May, 1-2; 2005, May, 1-2; 2005, May, 1-2; 2005, Jun, 9-11; 2005, Jun, 9-11; 2005, June, 9-11; 2004, Feb, 11; 2004, Feb, 11; 2004, Mar, 10; 2004, February, 11; 2004, March, 10; 2004, Mar, 10

96360-96361 Intravenous Fluid Infusion for Hydration (Nonchemotherapy)

CMS *100-4,12,30.5*   *Payment for Injections and Infusions: Chemotherapy and Nonchemotherapy*

INCLUDES   coding hierarchy rules for facility reporting only:
diagnostic, prophylactic, and therapeutic services are primary to hydration services
chemotherapy services are primary to diagnostic, prophylactic, and therapeutic services
infusions are primary to pushes
pushes are primary to injections
direct physician supervision:
direction of personnel
minimal supervision for:
consent
safety oversight
supervision of personnel
pre-packaged fluid/electrolytes
the following if done to facilitate the injection/infusion:
flush at the end of infusion
indwelling IV, subcutaneous catheter/port access
local anesthesia
start of IV
supplies/tubing/syringes
treatment plan verification

EXCLUDES   *catheter/port declotting (36593)*
drugs/other substances
reporting by the physician in the facility setting
significant separately identifiable evaluation and management service if performed

Do not report with infusion for hydration that is 30 minutes or less

● **96360**   Intravenous infusion, hydration; initial, 31 minutes to 1 hour   Ⓢ 80

   Do not report hydration infusions of 30 minutes or less

   Do not report if performed as a concurrent infusion

   📖 1.57   ⚕ 1.57   Global Days XXX

● **96361**   each additional hour (List separately in addition to code for primary procedure)   Ⓢ 80

> *INCLUDES*   hydration infusion of more than 30 minutes beyond 1 hour
> hydration provided as a secondary or subsequent service after a different initial service via the same IV access site

   Code first (96360)
   📖 0.46   ⚕ 0.46   Global Days ZZZ

96125 — 96361

96365-96371 Infusions: Diagnostic/Preventive/Therapeutic

CMS *100-4,20,160.1*   *Billing for Total Parenteral Nutrition Furnished to Part B Inpatients*
CMS *100-4,12,30.5*   *Payment for Injections and Infusions: Chemotherapy and Nonchemotherapy*

[INCLUDES]   administration of fluid
administration of substances/drugs
an infusion of 15 minutes or less
coding heirarchy rules for facility reporting:
     chemotherapy services are primary to diagnostic, prophylactic, and therapeutic services
     diagnostic, prophylactic, and therapeutic services are primary to hydration services
     infusions are primary to pushes
     pushes are primary to injections
constant presence of health care professional administering the substance/drug
direct physician supervision:
     consent
     direction of personnel
     patient assessment
     safety oversight
     supervision of personnel
the following if done to facilitate the injection/infusion:
     flush at the end of infusion
     indwelling IV, subcutaneous catheter/port access
     local anesthesia
     supplics/tubing/syringes
     start of IV
training to assess patient and monitor vital signs
training to prepare/dose/dispose
treatment plan verification

EXCLUDES   *catheter/port declotting (36593)*
significant separately identifiable evaluation and management service if performed

Code also drugs/materials

Do not report with codes for which IV push or infusion is an integral part of the procedure

● **96365** **Intravenous infusion, for therapy, prophylaxis, or diagnosis (specify substance or drug); initial, up to 1 hour** [S] [80]
     1.91   1.91   Global Days XXX

+ ● **96366** **each additional hour (List separately in addition to code for primary procedure)** [S] [80]
     [INCLUDES]   additional hours of sequential infusion infusion intervals of more than 30 minutes beyond one hour

     Code first (96365, 96367)
     0.61   0.61   Global Days ZZZ

+ ● **96367** **additional sequential infusion, up to 1 hour (List separately in addition to code for primary procedure)** [S] [80]
     [INCLUDES]   a secondary or subsequent service after a different initial service via the same IV access

     Code also (90305, 90374, 90409, 96413)
     Do not report more than once per sequential infusion of the same mix
     0.96   0.96   Global Days ZZZ

+ ● **96368** **concurrent infusion (List separately in addition to code for primary procedure)** [N] [80]
     Code also (96365, 96366, 96413, 96415, 96416)
     Do not report more than once per encounter
     0.57   0.57   Global Days ZZZ

● **96369** **Subcutaneous infusion for therapy or prophylaxis (specify substance or drug); initial, up to 1 hour, including pump set-up and establishment of subcutaneous infusion site(s)** [S] [80]
     EXCLUDES   *infusions of 15 minutes or less (96372)*

     4.15   4.15   Global Days XXX

+ ● **96370** **each additional hour (List separately in addition to code for primary procedure)** [S] [80]
     [INCLUDES]   infusions of more than 30 minutes beyond one hour

     Code first (96369)
     Do not report more than once per encounter
     0.44   0.44   Global Days ZZZ

+ ● **96371** **additional pump set-up with establishment of new subcutaneous infusion site(s) (List separately in addition to code for primary procedure)** [S] [80]
     Code also (96369)
     Do not report more than once per encounter
     2.01   2.01   Global Days ZZZ

⊛ Modifier 63 Exempt Code   ⊙ Moderate Sedation   + CPT Add on Code   ⊘ Modifier 51 Exempt Code   ● New Code   ▲ Revised Code

[M] Maternity Edit   [A] Age Edit   [A]-[Y] APC Status Indicators   [▣] CCI Comprehensive Code   ✗ Drug Not Approved by FDA   [50] Bilateral Procedure

© 2008 Ingenix *(Blue Ink)*   CPT only © 2008 American Medical Association. All Rights Reserved. (Black Ink)   Medicare (Red Ink)   437

96372-96379 Injections: Diagnostic/Preventive/Therapeutic

CMS *100-4,12,30.5*   *Payment for Injections and Infusions: Chemotherapy and Nonchemotherapy*
CMS *100-4,4,20.5*   *HCPCS Under OPPS*

INCLUDES   administration of fluid
administration of substances/drugs
coding heirarchy rules for facility reporting:
     chemotherapy services are primary to diagnostic, prophylactic, and therapeutic services
     infusions are primary to pushes
     pushes are primary to injections
constant presence of health care professional administering the substance/drug
direct physician supervision:
     consent
     direction of personnel
     patient assessment
     safety oversight
     supervision of personnel
infusion of 15 minutes or less
the following if done to facilitate the injection/infusion:
     flush at the end of infusion
     indwelling IV, subcutaneous catheter/port access
     local anesthesia
     start of IV
     supplies/tubing/syringes
training to assess patient and monitor vital signs
training to prepare/dose/dispose
treatment plan verification

EXCLUDES   *catheter/port declotting (36593)*
significant separately identifiable evaluation and management service if performed

Code also drugs/materials

Do not report with codes for which IV push or infusion is an integral part of the procedure

● **96372**   **Therapeutic, prophylactic, or diagnostic injection (specify substance or drug); subcutaneous or intramuscular**   S 80

     INCLUDES   direct physician supervision when reported by the physician. When reported by a hospital, physician need not be present.

     EXCLUDES   *administration of vaccines/toxiods (90465, 90466, 90471, 90472)*
allergen immunotherapy injections (95115-95117)
antineoplastic hormonal injections (96402)
antineoplastic nonhormonal injections (96401)
hormonal therapy injections (non-antineoplastic) (96372)

     0.58   0.58   **Global Days XXX**

● **96373**   **intra-arterial**   S 80
     0.50   0.50   **Global Days XXX**

● **96374**   **intravenous push, single or initial substance/drug**   S 80
     1.51   1.51   **Global Days XXX**

+ ● **96375**   **each additional sequential intravenous push of a new substance/drug (List separately in addition to code for primary procedure)**   S 80

     INCLUDES   IV push of a new substance/drug provided as a secondary or subsequent service after a different initial service via same IV access site

Code also (96365, 96374, 96409, 96413)
     0.66   0.66   **Global Days ZZZ**

+ ● **96376**   **each additional sequential intravenous push of the same substance/drug provided in a facility (List separately in addition to code for primary procedure)**   N

     INCLUDES   facilities only

     EXCLUDES   *services performed by any provider that is not a facility*

Do not report a push performed within 30 minutes of a reported push of the same substance or drug
     0.00   0.00   **Global Days ZZZ**

● **96379**   **Unlisted therapeutic, prophylactic, or diagnostic intravenous or intra-arterial injection or infusion**   S 80
     0.00   0.00   **Global Days XXX**

96401-96411 Chemotherapy and Other Complex Drugs, Biologicals: Injection

CMS *100-3,110.6*   *Scalp Hypothermia During Chemotherapy, to Prevent Hair Loss*
CMS *100-3,110.2*   *Certain Drugs Distributed by the National Cancer Institute*
CMS *100-4,4,230.2.2*   *Chemotherapy Drug Administration*
CMS *100-4,12,30.5*   *Payment for Injections and Infusions: Chemotherapy and Nonchemotherapy*

INCLUDES   highly complex services that require direct supervision for:
     consent
     patient assessment
     safety oversight
     supervision
intravenous/intra-arterial push
an infusion of 15 minutes or less
constant presence of the health care professional administering the drug or substance
parenteral administration of:
     anti-neoplastic agents for noncancer diagnoses
     monoclonal antibody agents
     nonradionuclide antineoplastic drugs
     other biologic response modifiers
more intense physician work and monitoring of clinical staff due to greater risk of severe patient reactions.

Do not report with physician services provided in the facility setting with these codes.

96401   **Chemotherapy administration, subcutaneous or intramuscular; non-hormonal anti-neoplastic**   S 80 P0
     1.87   1.87   **Global Days XXX**
     AMA: 2008, Jan, 10-25; 2007, Jan, 28-31; 2007, Jan, 28-31; 2007, Jan, 13-27; 2007, Jan, 13-27; 2007, May, 3-4; 2007, Jun, 4-6; 2007, January, 28-31; 2007, May, 3-4; 2007, June, 4-6; 2007, January, 13-27; 2007, Jun, 4-6; 2007, May, 3-4; 2005, Nov, 1-9; 2005, November, 1-9; 2005, Nov, 1-9

96402   **hormonal anti-neoplastic**   S 80 P0
     1.02   1.02   **Global Days XXX**
     AMA: 2008, Jan, 10-25; 2007, Jan, 13-27; 2007, Jan, 13-27; 2007, Jan, 28-31; 2007, Jan, 28-31; 2007, May, 3-4; 2007, Jun, 4-6; 2007, January, 13-27; 2007, May, 3-4; 2007, June, 4-6; 2007, January, 28-31; 2007, Jun, 4-6; 2007, May, 3-4; 2005, Nov, 1-9; 2005, November, 1-9; 2005, Nov, 1-9

96405 Chemotherapy administration; intralesional, up to and
including 7 lesions   S ▣ P0

🛇 0.80 ⚖ 2.34 **Global Days 000**

AMA: 2008, Jan, 10-25; 2007, Jan, 28-31; 2007, Jan, 28-31; 2007,
Jan, 13-27; 2007, May, 3-4; 2007, Jan, 13-27; 2007, May, 3-4;
2007, Jun, 4-6; 2007, Jun, 4-6; 2007, January, 13-27; 2007, June,
4-6; 2007, May, 3-4; 2007, January, 28-31; 2005, Nov, 1-9; 2005,
November, 1-9; 2005, Nov, 1-9; 2004, Mar, 7; 2004, Mar, 7; 2004,
March, 7

96406 intralesional, more than 7 lesions   S ▣ P0

🛇 1.16 ⚖ 3.23 **Global Days 000**

AMA: 2008, Jan, 10-25; 2007, Jan, 28-31; 2007, Jan, 28-31; 2007,
Jan, 13-27; 2007, May, 3-4; 2007, Jan, 13-27; 2007, May, 3-4;
2007, Jun, 4-6; 2007, Jun, 4-6; 2007, January, 28-31; 2007, June,
4-6; 2007, May, 3-4; 2007, January, 13-27; 2005, Nov, 1-9; 2005,
November, 1-9; 2005, Nov, 1-9; 2004, Mar, 7; 2004, Mar, 7; 2004,
March, 7

96409 intravenous, push technique, single or initial
substance/drug   S 80 P0

Do not report with 36823

🛇 3.10 ⚖ 3.10 **Global Days XXX**

AMA: 2008, Jan, 10-25; 2007, Jan, 28-31; 2007, Jan, 28-31; 2007,
Jan, 13-27; 2007, Jan, 13-27; 2007, May, 3-4; 2007, Jun, 4-6;
2007, January, 13-27; 2007, May, 3-4; 2007, June, 4-6; 2007,
January, 28-31; 2007, Jun, 4-6; 2007, May, 3-4; 2005, Nov, 1-9;
2005, November, 1-9; 2005, Nov, 1-9

+ 96411 intravenous, push technique, each additional
substance/drug (List separately in addition to code
for primary procedure)   S 80 P0

Code first initial substance/drug (96409, 96413)

Do not report with 36823

🛇 1.77 ⚖ 1.77 **Global Days ZZZ**

AMA: 2008, Jan, 10-25; 2007, Jan, 28-31; 2007, Jan, 28-31; 2007,
Jan, 13-27; 2007, Jan, 13-27; 2007, May, 3-4; 2007, Jun, 4-6;
2007, January, 13-27; 2007, May, 3-4; 2007, June, 4-6; 2007,
January, 28-31; 2007, Jun, 4-6; 2007, May, 3-4; 2005, Nov, 1-9;
2005, November, 1-9; 2005, Nov, 1-9

96413-96417 Chemotherapy and Complex Drugs, Biologicals: Intravenous Infusion

CMS *100-4,4,230.2*   *Coding and Payment for Drug Administration*
CMS *100-3,110.6*   *Scalp Hypothermia During Chemotherapy, to Prevent Hair Loss*
CMS *100-3,110.2*   *Certain Drugs Distributed by the National Cancer Institute*
CMS *100-4,4,230.2.2*   *Chemotherapy Drug Administration*
CMS *100-4,12,30.5*   *Payment for Injections and Infusions: Chemotherapy and Nonchemotherapy*

INCLUDES   an infusion of 15 minutes or less

constant presence of the health care professional administering the
drug or substance

highly complex services that require direct supervision for:
consent
patient assessment
safety oversight
supervision

intravenous/intra-arterial push

more intense physician work and monitoring of clinical staff due to
greater risk of severe patient reactions

parenteral administration of:
anti-neoplastic agents for noncancer diagnoses
monoclonal antibody agents
nonradionuclide antineoplastic drugs
other biologic response modifiers

the following in the administration:
access to IV/catheter/port
drug preparation
flushing at the completion of the infusion
hydration fluid
routine tubing/syringe/supplies
starting the IV
use of local anesthesia

EXCLUDES   *administration of nonchemotherapy agents such as
antibiotics/steriods/analgesics*
declotting of catheter/port (36593)
home infusion (99601-99602)

Code also drug or substance

Code also significant separately identifiable evaluation and management service,
if performed

Do not report with 36823

Do not report with physician services provided in the facility setting with these
codes.

96413 Chemotherapy administration, intravenous infusion
technique; up to 1 hour, single or initial
substance/drug   S 80 P0

EXCLUDES   *hydration administered as secondary or
subsequent service via same IV access
site (96361)*
*therapeutic/prophylactic/diagnostic drug
infusion/injection through the same
intravenous access (96366, 96367,
96375)*

🛇 4.09 ⚖ 4.09 **Global Days XXX**

AMA: 2008, Jan, 10-25; 2007, Jan, 13-27; 2007, Jan, 13-27; 2007,
Jan, 28-31; 2007, Jan, 28-31; 2007, May, 3-4; 2007, Jun, 4-6;
2007, January, 13-27; 2007, May, 3-4; 2007, Dec, 10-179; 2007,
June, 4-6; 2007, January, 28-31; 2007, Jun, 4-6; 2007, May, 3-4;
2005, Nov, 1-9; 2005, November, 1-9; 2005, Nov, 1-9

🄫 Modifier 63 Exempt Code   ⊙ Moderate Sedation   + CPT Add on Code   🚫 Modifier 51 Exempt Code   ● New Code   ▲ Revised Code

Ⓜ Maternity Edit   Ⓐ Age Edit   Ⓐ Ⓨ APC Status Indicators   ▢ CCI Comprehensive Code   ✗ Drug Not Approved by FDA   50 Bilateral Procedure

© 2008 Ingenix *(Blue Ink)*   CPT only © 2008 American Medical Association. All Rights Reserved. (Black Ink)   Medicare (Red Ink)   **439**

Medicine

96415 — 96422

+ 96415   each additional hour (List separately in addition to code for primary procedure) [S] [80] [P0]
    INCLUDES infusion intervals of more than 30 minutes past 1-hour increments

    Code first initial hour (96413)
    ⚕ 0.93   ⚖ 0.93   Global Days ZZZ
    AMA: 2008, Jan, 10-25; 2007, Jan, 13-27; 2007, Jan, 13-27; 2007, Jan, 28-31; 2007, Jan, 28-31; 2007, May, 3-4; 2007, Jun, 4-6; 2007, January, 13-27; 2007, May, 3-4; 2007, Dec, 10-179; 2007, June, 4-6; 2007, January, 28-31; 2007, Jun, 4-6; 2007, May, 3-4; 2005, Nov, 1-9; 2005, November, 1-9; 2005, Nov, 1-9

96416   initiation of prolonged chemotherapy infusion (more than 8 hours), requiring use of a portable or implantable pump [S] [80] [P0]
    EXCLUDES portable or implantable infusion pump/reservoir refilling/maintenance for drug delivery (96521-96523)

    ⚕ 4.46   ⚖ 4.46   Global Days XXX
    AMA: 2008, Jan, 10-25; 2007, Jan, 28-31; 2007, Jan, 28-31; 2007, Jan, 13-27; 2007, Jan, 13-27; 2007, May, 3-4; 2007, Jun, 4-6; 2007, January, 13-27; 2007, May, 3-4; 2007, Dec, 10-179; 2007, June, 4-6; 2007, January, 28-31; 2007, Jun, 4-6; 2007, May, 3-4; 2005, Nov, 1-9; 2005, November, 1-9; 2005, Nov, 1-9

+ 96417   each additional sequential infusion (different substance/drug), up to 1 hour (List separately in addition to code for primary procedure) [S] [80] [P0]
    INCLUDES reporting only once per sequential infusion
    EXCLUDES additional hour(s) of sequential infusion (96415)

    Code first initial substance/drug (96413)
    ⚕ 2.04   ⚖ 2.04   Global Days ZZZ
    AMA: 2008, Jan, 10-25; 2007, Jan, 28-31; 2007, Jan, 28-31; 2007, Jan, 13-27; 2007, Jan, 13-27; 2007, May, 3-4; 2007, Jun, 4-6; 2007, January, 28-31; 2007, May, 3-4; 2007, June, 4-6; 2007, January, 13-27; 2007, Jun, 4-6; 2007, May, 3-4; 2005, Nov, 1-9; 2005, November, 1-9; 2005, Nov, 1-9

96420-96425 Chemotherapy and Complex Drugs, Biologicals: Intra-arterial

CMS 100-4,4,230.2   *Coding and Payment for Drug Administration*
CMS 100-3,110.6   *Scalp Hypothermia During Chemotherapy, to Prevent Hair Loss*
CMS 100-3,110.2   *Certain Drugs Distributed by the National Cancer Institute*
CMS 100-4,4,230.2.2 *Chemotherapy Drug Administration*
CMS 100-4,12,30.5   *Payment for Injections and Infusions: Chemotherapy and Nonchemotherapy*

INCLUDES highly complex services that require direct supervision for:
    consent
    patient assessment
    safety oversight
    supervision
  more intense physician work and monitoring of clinical staff due to greater risk of severe patient reactions
  parenteral administration of:
    anti-neoplastic agents for noncancer diagnoses
    monoclonal antibody agents
    non-radionuclide antineoplastic drugs
    other biologic response modifiers
  the following in the administration:
    access to IV/catheter/port
    drug preparation
    flushing at the completion of the infusion
    hydration fluid
    routine tubing/syringe/supplies
    starting the IV
    use of local anesthesia

EXCLUDES administration of non-chemotherapy agents such as antibiotics/steriods/analgesics
    declotting of catheter/port (36593)
    home infusion (99601-99602)

Code also drug or substance
    significant separately identifiable evaluation and management service, if performed
Do not report with physician services provided in the facility setting with these codes.

96420   Chemotherapy administration, intra-arterial; push technique [S] [80] [📷] [P0]
    INCLUDES regional chemotherapy perfusion
    EXCLUDES placement of intra-arterial catheter

    Do not report with 36823
    ⚕ 2.99   ⚖ 2.99   Global Days XXX
    AMA: 2008, Jan, 10-25; 2007, Jan, 28-31; 2007, Jan, 28-31; 2007, Jan, 13-27; 2007, Jan, 13-27; 2007, Jun, 4-6; 2007, January, 28-31; 2007, June, 4-6; 2007, May, 3-4; 2007, January, 13-27; 2007, Jun, 4-6; 2007, May, 3-4; 2007, May, 3-4; 2006, Dec, 10-12; 2006, December, 10-12; 2006, December, 10-12; 2006, Dec, 10-12; 2006, Dec, 10-12; 2006, Dec, 10-12; 2005, Nov, 1-9; 2005, November, 1-9; 2005, Nov, 1-9; 2004, Mar, 7; 2004, March, 7; 2004, Mar, 7

96422   infusion technique, up to one hour [S] [80] [📷] [P0]
    INCLUDES regional chemotherapy perfusion
    EXCLUDES placement of intra-arterial catheter

    Do not report with 36823
    ⚕ 4.82   ⚖ 4.82   Global Days XXX
    AMA: 2008, Jan, 10-25; 2007, Jan, 28-31; 2007, Jan, 28-31; 2007, Jan, 13-27; 2007, May, 3-4; 2007, Jan, 13-27; 2007, May, 3-4; 2007, Jun, 4-6; 2007, Jun, 4-6; 2007, January, 28-31; 2007, Dec, 10-179; 2007, June, 4-6; 2007, May, 3-4; 2007, January, 13-27; 2005, Nov, 1-9; 2005, November, 1-9; 2005, Nov, 1-9; 2004, Mar, 7; 2004, Mar, 7; 2004, March, 7

---

[26] [TC] Professional/Technical Component Only   [80] [80] Assist-at-Surgery Allowed/With Documentation   Unlisted   Not Covered   ⬛ Radiology crosswalk

MED: Pub 100/NCD References   **AMA:** CPT Assistant References   [N2] [Z3] ASC Payment Indicator   ♂Male Only   ♀Female Only   ⬛ Laboratory crosswalk

440   CPT only © 2008 American Medical Association. All Rights Reserved. (Black Ink)   Medicare (Red Ink)   © 2008 Ingenix *(Blue Ink)*

+ **96423** infusion technique, each additional hour (List separately in addition to code for primary procedure) [S] [80] [□] [P0]

> INCLUDES   infusion intervals of more than 30 minutes past 1-hour increments
> regional chemotherapy perfusion

> EXCLUDES   *arterial/venous cannula insertion with regional chemotherapy perfusion to an extremity (36823)*
> *placement of intra-arterial catheter*

Code first initial hour (96422)

Do not report with 36823

🔢 2.15   🔢 2.15   Global Days ZZZ

AMA: 2008, Jan, 10-25; 2007, Jan, 13-27; 2007, Jan, 13-27; 2007, Jan, 28-31; 2007, May, 3-4; 2007, Jan, 28-31; 2007, May, 3 4; 2007, Jun, 4-6; 2007, Jun, 4-6; 2007, January, 28-31; 2007, Dec, 10-179; 2007, June, 4-6; 2007, May, 3-4; 2007, January, 13-27; 2005, Nov, 1-9; 2005, November, 1-9; 2005, Nov, 1-9; 2004, Mar, 7; 2004, Mar, 7; 2004, March, 7

96425 infusion technique, initiation of prolonged infusion (more than 8 hours), requiring the use of a portable or implantable pump [S] [80] [□] [P0]

> INCLUDES   regional chemotherapy perfusion

> EXCLUDES   *placement of intra-arterial catheter*
> *portable or implantable infusion pump/reservoir refilling/maintenance for drug delivery (96521-96523)*

Do not report with 36823

🔢 4.75   🔢 4.75   Global Days XXX

AMA: 2008, Jan, 10-25; 2007, Jan, 28-31; 2007, Jan, 28-31; 2007, Jan, 13-27; 2007, May, 3-4; 2007, Jan, 13-27; 2007, May, 3-4; 2007, Jun, 4-6; 2007, Jun, 4-6; 2007, January, 28-31; 2007, June, 4-6; 2007, May, 3-4; 2007, January, 13-27; 2005, Nov, 1-9; 2005, November, 1-9; 2005, Nov, 1-9; 2004, Mar, 7; 2004, Mar, 7; 2004, March, 7

96440-96450 Chemotherapy Administration: Intrathecal/Peritoneal Cavity/Pleural Cavity

96440 Chemotherapy administration into pleural cavity, requiring and including thoracentesis [S] [80] [□] [P0]

> EXCLUDES   *blood specimen collection from completely implantable venous access device (36591)*

🔢 3.67   🔢 16.58   Global Days 000

AMA: 2008, Jan, 10-25; 2007, Jan, 28-31; 2007, Jan, 28-31; 2007, Jan, 13 27; 2007, May, 3 4; 2007, Jan, 13-27; 2007, May, 3-4; 2007, Jun, 4-6; 2007, Jun, 4-6; 2007, January, 28-31; 2007, June, 4 6; 2007, May, 3-4; 2007, January, 13-27; 2005, Nov, 1-9; 2005, November, 1-9; 2005, Nov, 1-9; 2004, Mar, 7; 2004, Mar, 7; 2004, March, 7

96445 Chemotherapy administration into peritoneal cavity, requiring and including peritoneocentesis [S] [80] [□] [P0]

> EXCLUDES   *blood specimen collection from completely implantable venous access device (36591)*

🔢 3.24   🔢 7.91   Global Days 000

AMA: 2008, Jan, 10-25; 2007, Jan, 13-27; 2007, Jan, 13-27; 2007, Jan, 28-31; 2007, May, 3-4; 2007, Jan, 28-31; 2007, May, 3-4; 2007, May, 9-11; 2007, Jun, 4-6; 2007, Jun, 4-6; 2007, June, 4-6; 2007, May, 9-11; 2007, May, 3-4; 2007, January, 28-31; 2007, January, 13-27; 2007, May, 9-11; 2005, Nov, 1-9; 2005, Nov, 1-9; 2005, November, 1-9; 2004, Mar, 7; 2004, Mar, 7; 2004, March, 7

96450 Chemotherapy administration, into CNS (eg, intrathecal), requiring and including spinal puncture [S] [80] [□] [P0]

> EXCLUDES   *blood specimen collection from completely implantable venous access device (36591)*
> *chemotherapy administration, intravesical/bladder (51720)*
> *insertion of catheter/reservoir*
>   *intraventricular (61210, 61215)*
>   *subarachnoid (62350, 62351, 62360-62362)*

🔢 2.44   🔢 5.77   Global Days 000

AMA: 2008, Jan, 10-25; 2007, Jan, 28-31; 2007, Jan, 28-31; 2007, Jan, 13-27; 2007, May, 3-4; 2007, Jan, 13-27; 2007, May, 3-4; 2007, Jun, 4-6; 2007, Jun, 4-6; 2007, January, 28-31; 2007, June, 4-6; 2007, May, 3-4; 2007, January, 13-27; 2005, Nov, 1-9; 2005, November, 1-9; 2005, Nov, 1-9; 2004, Mar, 7; 2004, Mar, 7; 2004, March, 7

96521-96523 Refill/Upkeep of Drug Delivery Device

CMS *100-4,4,230.2   Coding and Payment for Drug Administration*

> INCLUDES   highly complex services that require direct supervision for:
>   consent
>   patient assessment
>   safety oversight
>   supervision
> parenteral administration of:
>   anti-neoplastic agents for noncancer diagnoses
>   monoclonal antibody agents
>   non-radionuclide antineoplastic drugs
>   other biologic response modifiers
> the following in the administration:
>   access to IV/catheter/port
>   drug preparation
>   flushing at the completion of the infusion
>   hydration fluid
>   routine tubing/syringe/supplies
>   starting the IV
>   use of local anesthesia
> therapeutic drugs other than chemotherapy

> EXCLUDES   *administratoin of non-chemotherapy agents such as antibiotics/steriods/analgesics*
> *blood specimen collection from completely implantable venous access device (36591)*
> *declotting of catheter/port (36593)*
> *home infusion (99601-99602)*

Code also drug or substance

> significant separately identifiable evaluation and management service, if performed

96521 Refilling and maintenance of portable pump [S] [80] [P0]

🔢 3.52   🔢 3.52   Global Days XXX

AMA: 2007, Jan, 28-31; 2007, Jan, 28-31; 2007, May, 3-4; 2007, May, 3-4; 2007, Jun, 4 6; 2007, January, 28-31; 2007, June, 4-6; 2007, May, 3-4; 2007, Jun, 4-6; 2005, Nov, 1-9; 2005, November, 1-9; 2005, Nov, 1-9

⊕ Modifier 63 Exempt Code   ⊙ Moderate Sedation   + CPT Add-on Code   Ⓢ Modifier 51 Exempt Code   ● New Code   ▲ Revised Code

Ⓜ Maternity Edit   Ⓐ Age Edit   Ⓐ-Ⓨ APC Status Indicators   □ CCI Comprehensive Code   ✗ Drug Not Approved by FDA   50 Bilateral Procedure

© 2008 Ingenix *(Blue Ink)*   CPT only © 2008 American Medical Association. All Rights Reserved. (Black Ink)   Medicare (Red Ink)   **441**

96522 **Refilling and maintenance of implantable pump or reservoir for drug delivery, systemic (eg, intravenous, intra-arterial)** ⬚S ⬚80 ⬚P0

EXCLUDES *implantable infusion pump refilling/maintenance for spinal/brain drug delivery (95990-95991)*

⚙ 2.99 ⚖ 2.99 Global Days XXX
AMA: 2007, Jan, 28-31; 2007, Jan, 28-31; 2007, May, 3-4; 2007, Jun, 4-6; 2007, January, 28-31; 2007, May, 3-4; 2007, Jun, 4-6; 2007, May, 3-4; 2007, June, 4-6; 2006, Apr, 19-20; 2006, Apr, 19-20; 2006, April, 19-20; 2005, Nov, 1-9; 2005, November, 1-9; 2005, Nov, 1-9

96523 **Irrigation of implanted venous access device for drug delivery systems** ⬚Q1 ⬚80 ⬚P0

EXCLUDES *direct physician supervision*

Do not report with any other services on the same date of service.

⚙ 0.70 ⚖ 0.70 Global Days XXX
AMA: 2007, Jan, 28-31; 2007, Jan, 28-31; 2007, May, 3-4; 2007, May, 3-4; 2007, Jun, 4-6; 2007, January, 28-31; 2007, June, 4-6; 2007, May, 3-4; 2007, Jun, 4-6; 2005, Nov, 1-9; 2005, November, 1-9; 2005, Nov, 1-9

96542-96549 Chemotherapy Injection Into Brain

CMS *100-3,110.2* *Certain Drugs Distributed by the National Cancer Institute*
CMS *100-4,4,230.2.2* *Chemotherapy Drug Administration*
CMS *100-4,12,30.5* *Payment for Injections and Infusions: Chemotherapy and Nonchemotherapy*

INCLUDES highly complex services that require direct supervision for:
consent
patient assessment
safety oversight
supervision
parenteral administration of:
anti-neoplastic agents for noncancer diagnoses
monoclonal antibody agents
non-radionuclide antineoplastic drugs
other biologic response modifiers
the following in the administration:
access to IV/catheter/port
drug preparation
flushing at the completion of the infusion
hydration fluid
routine tubing/syringe/supplies
starting the IV
use of local anesthesia

EXCLUDES *administration of non-chemotherapy agents such as antibiotics/steriods/analgesics*
blood specimen collection from completely implantable venous access device (36591)
declotting of catheter/port (36593)
home infusion (99601-99602)

Code also drug or substance
Code also significant separately identifiable evaluation and management service, if performed

96542 **Chemotherapy injection, subarachnoid or intraventricular via subcutaneous reservoir, single or multiple agents** ⬚S ⬚80 ⬚☐ ⬚P0

🔬 *79005*

⚙ 1.26 ⚖ 3.72 Global Days XXX
AMA: 2007, Jan, 28-31; 2007, Jan, 28-31; 2007, May, 3-4; 2007, May, 3-4; 2007, Jun, 4-6; 2007, January, 28-31; 2007, June, 4-6; 2007, May, 3-4; 2007, Jun, 4-6; 2005, Nov, 1-9; 2005, November, 1-9; 2005, Nov, 1-9

96549 **Unlisted chemotherapy procedure** ⬚S ⬚80 ⬚P0

⚙ 0.00 ⚖ 0.00 Global Days XXX
AMA: 2008, Jan, 10-25; 2007, Jan, 28-31; 2007, Jan, 28-31; 2007, May, 3-4; 2007, May, 3-4; 2007, Jun, 4-6; 2007, January, 28-31; 2007, June, 4-6; 2007, May, 3-4; 2007, Jun, 4-6; 2005, Nov, 1-9; 2005, November, 1-9; 2005, Nov, 1-9

96567-96571 Destruction of Lesions: Photodynamic Therapy

EXCLUDES *ocular photodynamic therapy (67221)*

96567 **Photodynamic therapy by external application of light to destroy premalignant and/or malignant lesions of the skin and adjacent mucosa (eg, lip) by activation of photosensitive drug(s), each phototherapy exposure session** ⬚T ⬚80 ⬚☐

⚙ 3.24 ⚖ 3.24 Global Days XXX

+ 96570 **Photodynamic therapy by endoscopic application of light to ablate abnormal tissue via activation of photosensitive drug(s); first 30 minutes (List separately in addition to code for endoscopy or bronchoscopy procedures of lung and esophagus)** ⬚T ⬚☐

Code first (31641, 43228)
⚙ 1.61 ⚖ 1.61 Global Days ZZZ
AMA: 2008, Oct, 6-7

+ 96571 **each additional 15 minutes (List separately in addition to code for endoscopy or bronchoscopy procedures of lung and esophagus)** ⬚T

Code first (31641, 43228)
⚙ 0.77 ⚖ 0.77 Global Days ZZZ
AMA: 2008, Oct, 6-7

96900-96999 Diagnostic/Therapeutic Skin Procedures

CMS *100-3,190.6* *Hair Analysis*
CMS *100-3,250.4* *Treatment of Actinic Keratosis*
CMS *100-3,250.1* *Treatment of Psoriasis*
EXCLUDES *consultation services (99241-99255)*
evaluation and management services (99201-99499)
injection, intralesional (11900-11901)

96900 **Actinotherapy (ultraviolet light)** ⬚S ⬚80 ⬚☐

🔬 *88160-88161*

⚙ 0.54 ⚖ 0.54 Global Days XXX
AMA: 2008, Jan, 10-25; 2007, Jan, 13-27; 2007, Jan, 13-27; 2007, January, 13-27; 2006, Aug, 12-14; 2006, Aug, 12-14; 2006, Dec, 10-12; 2006, December, 10-12; 2006, December, 10-12; 2006, August, 12-14; 2006, Dec, 10-12; 2006, Dec, 10-12; 2006, Dec, 10-12

96902 **Microscopic examination of hairs plucked or clipped by the examiner (excluding hair collected by the patient) to determine telogen and anagen counts, or structural hair shaft abnormality** ⬚N

🔬 *88160-88161*

⚙ 0.56 ⚖ 0.58 Global Days XXX

96904 **Whole body integumentary photography, for monitoring of high risk patients with dysplastic nevus syndrome or a history of dysplastic nevi, or patients with a personal or familial history of melanoma** ⬚N ⬚80

🔬 *88160-88161*

⚙ 1.78 ⚖ 1.78 Global Days XXX
AMA: 2006, Dec, 10-12; 2006, Dec, 10-12; 2006, Dec, 10-12; 2006, Dec, 10-12; 2006, December, 10-12; 2006, December, 10-12

96910 **Photochemotherapy; tar and ultraviolet B (Goeckerman treatment) or petrolatum and ultraviolet B** ⬚S ⬚80 ⬚☐

🔬 *88160-88161*

⚙ 1.74 ⚖ 1.74 Global Days XXX

96912	**psoralens and ultraviolet A (PUVA)**	S 80 ▭

📺 *88160-88161*

💾 2.23   🔧 2.23   Global Days XXX

96913	**Photochemotherapy (Goeckerman and/or PUVA) for severe photoresponsive dermatoses requiring at least 4 to 8 hours of care under direct supervision of the physician (includes application of medication and dressings)**	S 80 ▭

📺 *88160-88161*

💾 3.10   🔧 3.10   Global Days XXX

96920	**Laser treatment for inflammatory skin disease (psoriasis); total area less than 250 sq cm**	T ▭

📺 *88160-88161*

💾 1.76   🔧 4.44   Global Days 000

96921	**250 sq cm to 500 sq cm**	T ▭

📺 *88160-88161*

💾 1.75   🔧 4.35   Global Days 000

96922	**over 500 sq cm**	T ▭

📺 *88160-88161*

💾 3.12   🔧 6.44   Global Days 000

96999	**Unlisted special dermatological service or procedure**	T A0

💾 0.00   🔧 0.00   Global Days XXX

97001-97006 Physical Medicine Assessments

CMS *100-4,5,10.2*   Financial Limitation for Outpatient Rehabilitation Services
CMS *100-4,5,20*   HCPCS Coding Requirement
CMS *100-4,5,10*   Part B Outpatient Rehabilitation/Comprehensive Outpatient Rehabilitation Facility Services
CMS *100-2,15,230.4*   Services By a Physical/OccupationalTherapist in Private Practice
CMS *100-3,20.10*   Cardiac Rehabilitation Programs
EXCLUDES   EMG biofeedback training (90901)
muscle/range of motion testing and electromyography (95831-95904)
TNS - transcutaneous nerve stimulation (64550)

⊘	97001	**Physical therapy evaluation**	A 80 ▭ P0

💾 1.94   🔧 1.94   Global Days XXX

AMA: 2008, Jan, 10-25; 2008, May, 9-11; 2007, Jan, 13-27; 2007, Jan, 13-27; 2007, January, 13-27; 2006, Aug, 12-14; 2006, Aug, 12-14; 2006, August, 12-14; 2004, Feb, 5; 2004, Feb, 5; 2004, February, 5

⊘	97002	**Physical therapy re-evaluation**	A 80 ▭ P0

💾 1.04   🔧 1.04   Global Days XXX

AMA: 2008, Jan, 10-25; 2008, May, 9-11; 2007, Jan, 13-27; 2007, Jan, 13-27; 2007, January, 13-27; 2004, Feb, 5; 2004, February, 5; 2004, Feb, 5

⊘	97003	**Occupational therapy evaluation**	A 80 ▭ P0

💾 2.06   🔧 2.06   Global Days XXX

AMA: 2008, Jan, 10-25; 2008, May, 9-11; 2007, Jan, 13-27; 2007, Jan, 13-27; 2007, January, 13-27; 2006, Aug, 12-14; 2006, Aug, 12-14; 2006, August, 12-14; 2004, Feb, 5; 2004, Feb, 5; 2004, February, 5

⊘	97004	**Occupational therapy re-evaluation**	A 80 ▭ P0

💾 1.19   🔧 1.19   Global Days XXX

AMA: 2008, Jan, 10-25; 2008, May, 9-11; 2007, Jan, 13-27; 2007, Jan, 13-27; 2007, January, 13-27; 2004, Feb, 5; 2004, February, 5; 2004, Feb, 5

⊘	97005	**Athletic training evaluation**	E

💾 0.00   🔧 0.00   Global Days XXX

AMA: 2004, Feb, 5; 2004, Feb, 5; 2004, February, 5

⊘	97006	**Athletic training re-evaluation**	E

💾 0.00   🔧 0.00   Global Days XXX

AMA: 2004, Feb, 5; 2004, Feb, 5; 2004, February, 5

97010-97028 Physical Therapy Treatment Modalities: Supervised

CMS *100-4,5,10.2*   Financial Limitation for Outpatient Rehabilitation Services
CMS *100-4,5,20*   HCPCS Coding Requirement
CMS *100-4,5,10*   Part B Outpatient Rehabilitation/Comprehensive Outpatient Rehabilitation Facility Services
CMS *100-2,15,230.1*   Practice of Physical Therapy
CMS *100-2,15,230*   Practice of Physical Therapy, OccupationalTherapy, and Speech-Language Pathology
CMS *100-2,15,230.4*   Services By a Physical/OccupationalTherapist in Private Practice
CMS *100-3,20.10*   Cardiac Rehabilitation Programs
EXCLUDES   direct patient contact by the provider
EMG biofeedback training (90901)
muscle/range of motion testing and electromyography (95831-95904)
TNS - transcutaneous nerve stimulation (64550)

⊘	97010	**Application of a modality to 1 or more areas; hot or cold packs**	A

💾 0.13   🔧 0.13   Global Days XXX

AMA: 2008, Jan, 10-25; 2007, Jan, 13-27; 2007, Jan, 13-27; 2007, January, 13-27; 2006, Aug, 12-14; 2006, August, 12-14; 2006, Aug, 12-14

⊘	97012	**traction, mechanical**	A 80 ▭

💾 0.40   🔧 0.40   Global Days XXX

AMA: 2008, Jan, 10-25; 2007, Jan, 13-27; 2007, Jan, 13-27; 2007, January, 13-27; 2004, Nov, 9; 2004, November, 9; 2004, Nov, 9

⊘	97014	**electrical stimulation (unattended)**	E

EXCLUDES   acupuncture with electrical stimulation (97813, 97814)

💾 0.37   🔧 0.37   Global Days XXX

AMA: 2008, Jan, 10-25; 2007, Jan, 13-27; 2007, Jan, 13-27; 2007, January, 13-27

⊘	97016	**vasopneumatic devices**	A 80 ▭

💾 0.42   🔧 0.42   Global Days XXX

AMA: 2005, May, 13-14; 2005, May, 13-14; 2005, May, 13-14

⊘	97018	**paraffin bath**	A 80 ▭

💾 0.22   🔧 0.22   Global Days XXX

⊘	97022	**whirlpool**	A 80 ▭

💾 0.48   🔧 0.48   Global Days XXX

⊘	97024	**diathermy (eg, microwave)**	A 80 ▭

💾 0.15   🔧 0.15   Global Days XXX

⊘	97026	**infrared**	A 80 ▭

💾 0.14   🔧 0.14   Global Days XXX

⊘	97028	**ultraviolet**	A 80 ▭

💾 0.17   🔧 0.17   Global Days XXX

⊛ Modifier 63 Exempt Code   ⊙ Moderate Sedation   + CPT Add-on Code   ⊘ Modifier 51 Exempt Code   ● New Code   ▲ Revised Code

M Maternity Edit   A Age Edit   A-Y APC Status Indicators   ▭ CCI Comprehensive Code   ∦ Drug Not Approved by FDA   50 Bilateral Procedure

© 2008 Ingenix *(Blue Ink)*   CPT only © 2008 American Medical Association. All Rights Reserved. (Black Ink)   Medicare (Red Ink)   **443**

Medicine

97032 — 97124

97032-97039 Physical Therapy Treatment Modalities: Constant Attendance

CMS *100-4,5,10.2*   *Financial Limitation for Outpatient Rehabilitation Services*
CMS *100-4,5,20*   *HCPCS Coding Requirement*
CMS *100-4,5,10*   *Part B Outpatient Rehabilitation/Comprehensive Outpatient Rehabilitation Facility Services*
CMS *100-2,15,230.2*   *Practice of Occupational Therapy*
CMS *100-2,15,230.1*   *Practice of Physical Therapy*
CMS *100-2,15,230*   *Practice of Physical Therapy, Occupational Therapy, and Speech-Language Pathology*
CMS *100-2,15,230.4*   *Services By a Physical/Occupational Therapist in Private Practice*
CMS *100-3,20.10*   *Cardiac Rehabilitation Programs*

INCLUDES   direct patient contact by the provider

EXCLUDES   *EMG biofeedback training (90901)*
muscle/range of motion testing and electromyography (95831-95904)
TNS - transcutaneous nerve stimulation (64550)

⊘   **97032**   **Application of a modality to 1 or more areas; electrical stimulation (manual), each 15 minutes**   A 80 ▣
     🖩 0.45   ⚖ 0.45   **Global Days XXX**
     AMA: 2008, Jan, 10-25; 2007, Jan, 13-27; 2007, Jan, 13-27; 2007, January, 13-27; 2004, Jul, 13; 2004, July, 13; 2004, Jul, 13

⊘   **97033**   **iontophoresis, each 15 minutes**   A 80 ▣
     🖩 0.67   ⚖ 0.67   **Global Days XXX**

⊘   **97034**   **contrast baths, each 15 minutes**   A 80 ▣
     🖩 0.41   ⚖ 0.41   **Global Days XXX**

⊘   **97035**   **ultrasound, each 15 minutes**   A 80 ▣
     🖩 0.32   ⚖ 0.32   **Global Days XXX**
     AMA: 2008, Jan, 10-25; 2007, Jan, 13-27; 2007, Jan, 13-27; 2007, January, 13-27

⊘   **97036**   **Hubbard tank, each 15 minutes**   A 80 ▣
     🖩 0.70   ⚖ 0.70   **Global Days XXX**

  97039   **Unlisted modality (specify type and time if constant attendance)**   A 88 ▣
     🖩 0.00   ⚖ 0.00   **Global Days XXX**
     AMA: 2008, Jan, 10-25; 2007, Jan, 13-27; 2007, Jan, 13-27; 2007, January, 13-27; 2005, May, 13-14; 2005, May, 13-14; 2005, May, 13-14

97110-97546 Additional Therapeutic Techniques With Direct Patient Contact

CMS *100-4,5,10.2*   *Financial Limitation for Outpatient Rehabilitation Services*
CMS *100-4,5,20*   *HCPCS Coding Requirement*
CMS *100-4,5,10*   *Part B Outpatient Rehabilitation/Comprehensive Outpatient Rehabilitation Facility Services*
CMS *100-2,15,230.2*   *Practice of Occupational Therapy*
CMS *100-2,15,230.1*   *Practice of Physical Therapy*
CMS *100-2,15,230*   *Practice of Physical Therapy, Occupational Therapy, and Speech-Language Pathology*
CMS *100-2,15,230.4*   *Services By a Physical/Occupational Therapist in Private Practice*
CMS *100-3,20.10*   *Cardiac Rehabilitation Programs*

INCLUDES   application of clinical skills/services to improve function
        direct patient contact by the provider

EXCLUDES   *EMG biofeedback training (90901)*
muscle/range of motion testing and electromyography (95831-95904)
TNS - transcutaneous nerve stimulation (64550)

⊘   **97110**   **Therapeutic procedure, 1 or more areas, each 15 minutes; therapeutic exercises to develop strength and endurance, range of motion and flexibility**   A 80 ▣
     🖩 0.78   ⚖ 0.78   **Global Days XXX**
     AMA: 2008, Jan, 10-25; 2008, May, 9-11; 2007, Jan, 13-27; 2007, Jan, 13-27; 2007, January, 13-27; 2006, Aug, 12-14; 2006, Aug, 12-14; 2006, Mar, 15; 2006, August, 12-14; 2006, March, 15; 2006, Mar, 15; 2005, Mar, 11-15; 2005, Mar, 11-15; 2005, March, 11-15; 2005, August, 11-12; 2005, December, 8; 2005, April, 13-14; 2005, Dec, 8; 2005, Dec, 8; 2005, Apr, 13-14; 2005, Apr, 13-14; 2005, Aug, 11-12; 2005, Aug, 11-12

⊘   **97112**   **neuromuscular reeducation of movement, balance, coordination, kinesthetic sense, posture, and/or proprioception for sitting and/or standing activities**   A 80 ▣
     🖩 0.80   ⚖ 0.80   **Global Days XXX**
     AMA: 2008, Jan, 10-25; 2008, May, 9-11; 2007, Jan, 13-27; 2007, Jan, 13-27; 2007, January, 13-27; 2006, Mar, 15; 2006, Mar, 15; 2006, March, 15; 2006, Aug, 12-14; 2006, Aug, 12-14; 2006, August, 12-14; 2005, Aug, 11-12; 2005, Aug, 11-12; 2005, Apr, 13-14; 2005, August, 11-12; 2005, April, 13-14; 2005, Apr, 13-14

⊘   **97113**   **aquatic therapy with therapeutic exercises**   A 80 ▣
     🖩 0.95   ⚖ 0.95   **Global Days XXX**
     AMA: 2008, Jan, 10-25; 2008, May, 9-11; 2007, Jan, 13-27; 2007, Jan, 13-27; 2007, January, 13-27; 2006, Aug, 12-14; 2006, Aug, 12-14; 2006, Mar, 15; 2006, March, 15; 2006, August, 12-14; 2006, Mar, 15; 2005, Apr, 13-14; 2005, April, 13-14; 2005, Apr, 13-14

⊘   **97116**   **gait training (includes stair climbing)**   A 80 ▣
     EXCLUDES   *comprehensive gait/motion analysis (96000-96003)*
     🖩 0.68   ⚖ 0.68   **Global Days XXX**
     AMA: 2008, Jan, 10-25; 2008, May, 9-11; 2007, Jan, 13-27; 2007, Jan, 13-27; 2007, Feb, 8-9; 2007, Feb, 8-9; 2007, February, 8-9; 2007, January, 13-27; 2006, Aug, 12-14; 2006, Aug, 12-14; 2006, March, 15; 2006, August, 12-14; 2006, Mar, 15; 2006, Mar, 15; 2005, Apr, 13-14; 2005, April, 13-14; 2005, Apr, 13-14

⊘   **97124**   **massage, including effleurage, petrissage and/or tapotement (stroking, compression, percussion)**   A 80 ▣
     EXCLUDES   *myofascial release (97140)*
     🖩 0.62   ⚖ 0.62   **Global Days XXX**
     AMA: 2008, Jan, 10-25; 2008, May, 9-11; 2007, Jan, 13-27; 2007, Jan, 13-27; 2007, January, 13-27; 2006, Aug, 12-14; 2006, Aug, 12-14; 2006, March, 15; 2006, Mar, 15; 2006, Mar, 15; 2006, August, 12-14; 2005, Apr, 13-14; 2005, Apr, 13-14; 2005, May, 13-14; 2005, May, 13-14; 2005, April, 13-14; 2005, May, 13-14

97139 Unlisted therapeutic procedure (specify) A 80 🖵
📠 0.00 🔍 0.00 **Global Days XXX**
AMA: 2008, Jan, 10-25; 2008, May, 9-11; 2007, Jan, 13-27; 2007, Jan, 13-27; 2007, January, 13-27; 2006, Aug, 12-14; 2006, Aug, 12-14; 2006, August, 12-14; 2005, Apr, 13-14; 2005, Apr, 13-14; 2005, April, 13-14

⊘ **97140** Manual therapy techniques (eg, mobilization/ manipulation, manual lymphatic drainage, manual traction), 1 or more regions, each 15 minutes A 80 🖵
📠 0.72 🔍 0.72 **Global Days XXX**
AMA: 2008, Jan, 10-25; 2008, May, 9-11; 2007, Jan, 13-27; 2007, Jan, 13-27; 2007, January, 13-27; 2005, Jan, 46-47; 2005, Jan, 46-47; 2005, March, 11-15; 2005, January, 46-47; 2005, Mar, 11-15; 2005, Mar, 11-15

⊘ **97150** Therapeutic procedure(s), group (2 or more individuals) A 80 🖵
INCLUDES   constant attendance by the physician/therapist reporting this procedure for each member of group
EXCLUDES   osteopathic manipulative treatment (98925-98929)
📠 0.49 🔍 0.49 **Global Days XXX**
AMA: 2008, Jan, 10-25; 2008, May, 9-11; 2007, Jan, 13-27; 2007, Jan, 13-27; 2007, January, 13-27; 2006, Aug, 12-14; 2006, Aug, 12-14; 2006, August, 12-14; 2005, Apr, 13-14; 2005, Apr, 13-14; 2005, April, 13-14

⊘ **97530** Therapeutic activities, direct (one-on-one) patient contact by the provider (use of dynamic activities to improve functional performance), each 15 minutes A 80 🖵
📠 0.82 🔍 0.82 **Global Days XXX**
AMA: 2008, Jan, 10-25; 2008, May, 9-11; 2007, Jan, 13-27; 2007, Jan, 13-27; 2007, January, 13-27; 2005, Aug, 11-12; 2005, August, 11-12; 2005, Aug, 11-12

⊘ **97532** Development of cognitive skills to improve attention, memory, problem solving (includes compensatory training), direct (one-on-one) patient contact by the provider, each 15 minutes A 80 🖵
📠 0.67 🔍 0.67 **Global Days XXX**
AMA: 2008, May, 9-11

⊘ **97533** Sensory integrative techniques to enhance sensory processing and promote adaptive responses to environmental demands, direct (one-on-one) patient contact by the provider, each 15 minutes A 80 🖵
📠 0.72 🔍 0.72 **Global Days XXX**
AMA: 2008, May, 9-11

⊘ **97535** Self-care/home management training (eg, activities of daily living (ADL) and compensatory training, meal preparation, safety procedures, and instructions in use of assistive technology devices/adaptive equipment) direct one-on-one contact by provider, each 15 minutes A 80 🖵
📠 0.82 🔍 0.82 **Global Days XXX**
AMA: 2008, Jan, 10-25; 2008, May, 9-11; 2007, Jan, 13-27; 2007, Jan, 13-27; 2007, January, 13-27

⊘ **97537** Community/work reintegration training (eg, shopping, transportation, money management, avocational activities and/or work environment/modification analysis, work task analysis, use of assistive technology device/adaptive equipment), direct one-on-one contact by provider, each 15 minutes A 80 🖵
EXCLUDES   wheelchair management/propulsion training (97542)
📠 0.74 🔍 0.74 **Global Days XXX**
AMA: 2008, May, 9-11

⊘ **97542** Wheelchair management (eg, assessment, fitting, training), each 15 minutes A 80 🖵
📠 0.75 🔍 0.75 **Global Days XXX**
AMA: 2008, May, 9-11

⊘ **97545** Work hardening/conditioning; initial 2 hours A 80 🖵
📠 0.00 🔍 0.00 **Global Days XXX**
AMA: 2008, Jan, 10-25; 2008, May, 9-11; 2007, Jan, 13-27; 2007, Jan, 13-27; 2007, January, 13-27

+ **97546** each additional hour (List separately in addition to code for primary procedure) A 80
Code first initial 2 hours (97545)
📠 0.00 🔍 0.00 **Global Days ZZZ**
AMA: 2008, May, 9-11

97597-97606 Treatment of Wounds

CMS 100-3,270.3   *Blood-derived Products for Chronic Nonhealing Wounds*
CMS 100-3,270.2   *Noncontact Normothermic Wound Therapy*
CMS 100-3,270.1   *Electrical Stimulation and Electromagnetic Therapy for the Treatment of Wounds*
CMS 100-4,5,20   *HCPCS Coding Requirement*
CMS 100-4,5,10   *Part B Outpatient Rehabilitation/Comprehensive Outpatient Rehabilitation Facility Services*
CMS 100-2,15,230.4   *Services By a Physical/Occupational Therapist in Private Practice*
CMS 100-3,270.4   *Treatment of Decubitus*

⊘ **97597** Removal of devitalized tissue from wound(s), selective debridement, without anesthesia (eg, high pressure waterjet with/without suction, sharp selective debridement with scissors, scalpel and forceps), with or without topical application(s), wound assessment, and instruction(s) for ongoing care, may include use of a whirlpool, per session; total wound(s) surface area less than or equal to 20 square centimeters T 80 🖵
INCLUDES   direct patient contact removing devitalized/necrotic tissue and promoting healing
Do not report with debridement (11040-11044)
📠 0.89 🔍 1.62 **Global Days XXX**
AMA: 2008, Jan, 10-25; 2007, Jan, 13-27; 2007, Jan, 13-27; 2007, January, 13-27; 2005, Jun, 9-11; 2005, Jun, 9-11; 2005, June, 9-11; 2005, June, 1-4; 2005, Jun, 1-4; 2005, Jun, 1-4

⊘ **97598** total wound(s) surface area greater than 20 square centimeters T 80 🖵
INCLUDES   direct patient contact removing devitalized/necrotic tissue and promoting healing
Do not report with debridement (11040-11044)
📠 1.18 🔍 2.00 **Global Days XXX**
AMA: 2005, Jun, 9-11; 2005, Jun, 9-11; 2005, Jun, 1-4; 2005, Jun, 1-4; 2005, June, 1-4; 2005, June, 9-11

⊘ **97602** Removal of devitalized tissue from wound(s), non-selective debridement, without anesthesia (eg, wet-to-moist dressings, enzymatic, abrasion), including topical application(s), wound assessment, and instruction(s) for ongoing care, per session T
INCLUDES   direct patient contact removing devitalized/necrotic tissue and promoting healing
Do not report with debridement (11040-11044)
📠 0.00 🔍 0.00 **Global Days XXX**
AMA: 2008, Sep, 10-11; 2005, Jun, 1-4; 2005, Jun, 1-4; 2005, Jun, 9-11; 2005, Jun, 9-11; 2005, June, 1-4; 2005, June, 9-11

◎ Modifier 63 Exempt Code   ⊙ Moderate Sedation   + CPT Add-on Code   ⊘ Modifier 51 Exempt Code   ● New Code   ▲ Revised Code
Ⓜ Maternity Edit   Ⓐ Age Edit   A Y APC Status Indicators   🖵 CCI Comprehensive Code   ✗ Drug Not Approved by FDA   50 Bilateral Procedure

© 2008 Ingenix (Blue Ink)   CPT only © 2008 American Medical Association. All Rights Reserved. (Black Ink)   Medicare (Red Ink)   445

Medicine

97605 — 97810

⊘ **97605** **Negative pressure wound therapy (eg, vacuum assisted drainage collection), including topical application(s), wound assessment, and instruction(s) for ongoing care, per session; total wound(s) surface area less than or equal to 50 square centimeters** ⊤ 80

INCLUDES   direct patient contact
removing devitalized/necrotic tissue and
promoting healing

⊞ 0.72   ⚕ 0.96   Global Days XXX

AMA: 2008, Jan, 10-25; 2007, Jan, 13-27; 2007, Jan, 13-27; 2007, January, 13-27; 2005, Jun, 1-4; 2005, Jun, 1-4; 2005, Apr, 13-14; 2005, April, 13-14; 2005, June, 9-11; 2005, June, 1-4; 2005, Apr, 13-14; 2005, Jun, 9-11; 2005, Jun, 9-11

⊘ **97606** **total wound(s) surface area greater than 50 square centimeters** ⊤ 80

INCLUDES   direct patient contact
removing devitalized/necrotic tissue and
promoting healing

⊞ 0.79   ⚕ 1.03   Global Days XXX

AMA: 2008, Jan, 10-25; 2007, Jan, 13-27; 2007, Jan, 13-27; 2007, January, 13-27; 2005, Jun, 1-4; 2005, Jun, 1-4; 2005, Apr, 13-14; 2005, April, 13-14; 2005, June, 9-11; 2005, June, 1-4; 2005, Apr, 13-14; 2005, Jun, 9-11; 2005, Jun, 9-11

97750-97799 Assessments and Training

CMS 100-4,5,20   *HCPCS Coding Requirement*
CMS 100-4,5,10   *Part B Outpatient Rehabilitation/Comprehensive Outpatient Rehabilitation Facility Services*
CMS 100-2,15,230.2   *Practice of OccupationalTherapy*
CMS 100-2,15,230.1   *Practice of Physical Therapy*
CMS 100-2,15,230   *Practice of Physical Therapy, OccupationalTherapy, and Speech-Language Pathology*
CMS 100-2,15,230.4   *Services By a Physical/OccupationalTherapist in Private Practice*
CMS 100-3,20.10   *Cardiac Rehabilitation Programs*

⊘ **97750** **Physical performance test or measurement (eg, musculoskeletal, functional capacity), with written report, each 15 minutes** A 80 ▢

INCLUDES   direct patient contact

EXCLUDES   *muscle/range of motion testing and electromyography/nerve velocity determination (95831-95904)*

⊞ 0.80   ⚕ 0.80   Global Days XXX

AMA: 2008, Jan, 10-25; 2008, May, 9-11; 2007, Jan, 13-27; 2007, Jan, 13-27; 2007, Feb, 10-11; 2007, Feb, 10-11; 2007, January, 13-27; 2007, February, 10-11; 2004, Feb, 5; 2004, Feb, 5; 2004, February, 5

⊘ **97755** **Assistive technology assessment (eg, to restore, augment or compensate for existing function, optimize functional tasks and/or maximize environmental accessibility), direct one-on-one contact by provider, with written report, each 15 minutes** A 80 ▢

INCLUDES   direct patient contact

EXCLUDES   *augmentative/alternative communication device (92605, 92607)*
muscle/range of motion testing and electromyography/nerve velocity determination (95831-95904)

⊞ 0.92   ⚕ 0.92   Global Days XXX

97760 **Orthotic(s) management and training (including assessment and fitting when not otherwise reported), upper extremity(s), lower extremity(s) and/or trunk, each 15 minutes** A 80

Do not report with gait training, if performed on the same extremity (97116)

⊞ 0.89   ⚕ 0.89   Global Days XXX

AMA: 2007, Feb, 8-9; 2007, Feb, 8-9; 2007, February, 8-9; 2005, Dec, 8; 2005, December, 8; 2005, Dec, 8

97761 **Prosthetic training, upper and/or lower extremity(s), each 15 minutes** A 80

⊞ 0.79   ⚕ 0.79   Global Days XXX

AMA: 2008, Jan, 10-25; 2007, Jan, 13-27; 2007, Jan, 13-27; 2007, Feb, 8-9; 2007, Feb, 8-9; 2007, January, 13-27; 2007, February, 8-9; 2005, Dec, 8; 2005, Dec, 8; 2005, December, 8

97762 **Checkout for orthotic/prosthetic use, established patient, each 15 minutes** A 80

⊞ 0.92   ⚕ 0.92   Global Days XXX

AMA: 2007, Feb, 8-9; 2007, Feb, 8-9; 2007, February, 8-9; 2005, Dec, 8; 2005, December, 8; 2005, Dec, 8

97799 **Unlisted physical medicine/rehabilitation service or procedure** A 80

⊞ 0.00   ⚕ 0.00   Global Days XXX

97802-97804 Medical Nutrition Therapy Services

CMS 100-4,4,300   *Medical Nutrition Therapy Services*
CMS 100-3,180.1   *Medical Nutrition Therapy*
CMS 100-3,40.1   *Diabetes Outpatient Self-managementTraining*
CMS 100-3,40.5   *Treatment of Obesity*

EXCLUDES   *physician provided medical nutrition therapy assessment/intervention (99201-99499)*

97802 **Medical nutrition therapy; initial assessment and intervention, individual, face-to-face with the patient, each 15 minutes** A 80 ▢ P0

⊞ 0.76   ⚕ 0.81   Global Days XXX

97803 **re-assessment and intervention, individual, face-to-face with the patient, each 15 minutes** A 80 ▢ P0

⊞ 0.66   ⚕ 0.71   Global Days XXX

97804 **group (2 or more individual(s)), each 30 minutes** A 80 P0

⊞ 0.36   ⚕ 0.36   Global Days XXX

97810-97814 Acupuncture

CMS 100-3,30.3.2   *Acupuncture for Osteoarthritis*
CMS 100-3,30.3.1   *Acupuncture for Fibromyalgia*
CMS 100-3,30.3   *Acupuncture*

INCLUDES   15 minute increments of face-to-face contact with the patient reporting only one code for each 15 minute increment

Code also evaluation and mangement time, if performed

Code also significant separately identifiable evaluation and management code (99201-99499)

97810 **Acupuncture, 1 or more needles; without electrical stimulation, initial 15 minutes of personal one-on-one contact with the patient** E

EXCLUDES   *electrical stimulation (97813-97814)*

Do not report with (97813)

⊞ 0.84   ⚕ 0.97   Global Days XXX

AMA: 2008, Jan, 10-25; 2007, Jan, 13-27; 2007, Jan, 13-27; 2007, January, 13-27; 2006, Jun, 16-17; 2006, Jun, 16-17; 2006, August, 3-5; 2006, Aug, 3-5; 2006, Aug, 3-5; 2006, June, 16-17; 2005, Jan, 16-18; 2005, Jan, 16-18; 2005, Jun, 5; 2005, January, 16-18; 2005, June, 5; 2005, Jun, 5

26/TC Professional/Technical Component Only   80/80 Assist-at-Surgery Allowed/With Documentation   Unlisted   Not Covered   Radiology crosswalk

MED: Pub 100/NCD References   AMA: CPT Assistant References   A2-Z3 ASC Payment Indicator   ♂Male Only   ♀Female Only   Laboratory crosswalk

446   CPT only © 2008 American Medical Association. All Rights Reserved. (Black Ink)   Medicare (Red Ink)   © 2008 Ingenix (Blue Ink)

+ 97811 **without electrical stimulation, each additional 15 minutes of personal one-on-one contact with the patient, with re-insertion of needle(s) (List separately in addition to code for primary procedure)** E

EXCLUDES *electrical stimulation (97813-97814)*

Code first initial 15 minutes (97810, 97813)

🚑 0.70 ◈ 0.75 Global Days ZZZ

AMA: 2006, Aug, 3-5; 2006, Aug, 3-5; 2006, August, 3-5; 2005, Jan, 16-18; 2005, Jan, 16-18; 2005, January, 16-18; 2005, June, 5; 2005, Jun, 5; 2005, Jun, 5

97813 **with electrical stimulation, initial 15 minutes of personal one-on-one contact with the patient** E

INCLUDES *electrical stimulation*

Do not report with (97810)

🚑 0.91 ◈ 1.04 Global Days XXX

AMA: 2006, Aug, 3-5; 2006, Aug, 3-5; 2006, Jun, 16-17; 2006, June, 16-17; 2006, August, 3-5; 2006, Jun, 16-17; 2005, Jun, 5; 2005, January, 16-18; 2005, June, 5; 2005, Jun, 5; 2005, Jan, 16-18; 2005, Jan, 16-18

+ 97814 **with electrical stimulation, each additional 15 minutes of personal one-on-one contact with the patient, with re-insertion of needle(s) (List separately in addition to code for primary procedure)** E

INCLUDES *electrical stimulation*

Code first initial 15 minutes (97810, 97813)

🚑 0.77 ◈ 0.84 Global Days ZZZ

AMA: 2006, Aug, 3-5; 2006, Aug, 3-5; 2006, August, 3-5; 2005, Jun, 5; 2005, Jun, 5; 2005, January, 16-18; 2005, June, 5; 2005, Jan, 16-18; 2005, Jan, 16-18

98925-98929 Osteopathic Manipulation

CMS *100-3,150.1   Manipulation*

INCLUDES physician applied manual treatment done to eliminate/alleviate somatic dysfunction and related disorders using a variety of techniques

the following body regions:
abdomen/viscera region
cervical region
head region
lower extremities
lumbar region
pelvic region
rib cage region
sacral region
thoracic region
upper extremities

Code also significant separately identifiable evaluation and management service (99201-99499)

98925 **Osteopathic manipulative treatment (OMT); 1-2 body regions involved** S 80 ▢

🚑 0.60 ◈ 0.77 Global Days 000

AMA: 2008, Jan, 10-25; 2007, Jan, 13-27; 2007, Jan, 13-27; 2007, January, 13-27

98926 **3-4 body regions involved** S 80 ▢

🚑 0.88 ◈ 1.06 Global Days 000

AMA: 2008, Jan, 10-25; 2007, Jan, 13-27; 2007, Jan, 13-27; 2007, January, 13-27

98927 **5-6 body regions involved** S 80 ▢

🚑 1.15 ◈ 1.37 Global Days 000

AMA: 2008, Jan, 10-25; 2007, Jan, 13-27; 2007, Jan, 13-27; 2007, January, 13-27

98928 **7-8 body regions involved** S 80 ▢

🚑 1.36 ◈ 1.61 Global Days 000

AMA: 2008, Jan, 10-25; 2007, Jan, 13-27; 2007, Jan, 13-27; 2007, January, 13-27

98929 **9-10 body regions involved** S 80 ▢

🚑 1.58 ◈ 1.85 Global Days 000

AMA: 2008, Jan, 10-25; 2007, Jan, 13-27; 2007, Jan, 13-27; 2007, January, 13-27

98940-98943 Chiropractic Manipulation

CMS *100-1,5,70.6   Chiropractors*
CMS *100-2,15,240   Chiropractic Services - General*
CMS *100-3,150.1   Manipulation*

INCLUDES form of manual treatment performed to influence joint/neurophysical function

the following five extraspinal regions:
abdomen
head, including temporomandibular joint, excluding atlanto-occipital region
lower extremities
rib cage, not including costotransverse/costovertebral joints
upper extremities

the following five spinal regions:
cervical region (atlanto-occipital joint)
lumbar region
pelvic region (sacro-iliac joint)
sacral region
thoracic region (costovertebral/costotransverse joints)

Code also signficant separately identifiable evaluation and management service (99201-99499)

98940 **Chiropractic manipulative treatment (CMT); spinal, 1-2 regions** S 80 ▢

🚑 0.58 ◈ 0.68 Global Days 000

AMA: 2008, Jan, 10-25; 2007, Jan, 13-27; 2007, Jan, 13-27; 2007, Dec, 10-179; 2007, January, 13-27; 2006, Mar, 15; 2006, March, 15; 2006, Mar, 15; 2005, Mar, 11-15; 2005, March, 11-15; 2005, January, 46-47; 2005, Mar, 11-15; 2005, Jan, 46-47; 2005, Jan, 46-47

98941 **spinal, 3-4 regions** S 80 ▢

🚑 0.84 ◈ 0.94 Global Days 000

AMA: 2008, Jan, 10-25; 2007, Jan, 13-27; 2007, Jan, 13-27; 2007, Dec, 10-179; 2007, January, 13-27; 2006, Mar, 15; 2006, March, 15; 2006, Mar, 15; 2005, Mar, 11-15; 2005, January, 46-47; 2005, March, 11-15; 2005, Mar, 11-15; 2005, Jan, 46-47; 2005, Jan, 46-47

98942 **spinal, 5 regions** S 80 ▢

🚑 1.13 ◈ 1.23 Global Days 000

AMA: 2008, Jan, 10-25; 2007, Jan, 13-27; 2007, Jan, 13-27; 2007, January, 13-27; 2007, Dec, 10-179; 2006, Mar, 15; 2006, Mar, 15; 2006, March, 15; 2005, Jan, 46-47; 2005, Jan, 46-47; 2005, January, 46-47

98943 **extraspinal, 1 or more regions** E

🚑 0.55 ◈ 0.64 Global Days XXX

AMA: 2008, Jan, 10-25; 2007, Jan, 13-27; 2007, Jan, 13-27; 2007, January, 13-27; 2007, Dec, 10-179; 2006, Mar, 15; 2006, Mar, 15; 2006, March, 15; 2005, Jan, 46-47; 2005, Jan, 46-47; 2005, January, 46-47

🅢 Modifier 63 Exempt Code   ⊙ Moderate Sedation   + CPT Add-on Code   ⊘ Modifier 51 Exempt Code   ● New Code   ▲ Revised Code

Ⓜ Maternity Edit   🅐 Age Edit   Ⓐ-Ⓨ APC Status Indicators   ▢ CCI Comprehensive Code   ⚕ Drug Not Approved by FDA   50 Bilateral Procedure

© 2008 Ingenix *(Blue Ink)*   CPT only © 2008 American Medical Association. All Rights Reserved. *(Black Ink)*   Medicare *(Red Ink)*   447

Medicine

98960 — 99024

98960-98962 Self-Management Training

INCLUDES
education/training services:
prescribed by a physician
provided by a qualified nonphysician health care provider
standardized curriculum that may be modified as necessary for:
clinical needs
cultural norms
health literacy
teaching the patient how to manage the illness/delay the comorbidity(s)

EXCLUDES
genetic counseling education services (96040)
health/behavior assessment (96150-96155)
medical nutrition therapy (97802-97804)
the following services provided by physicians:
counseling/education to a group (99078)
counseling/education to individuals (99201-99499)
counseling/risk factor reduction without symptoms/established disease (99401-99412)

98960 **Education and training for patient self-management by a qualified, nonphysician health care professional using a standardized curriculum, face-to-face with the patient (could include caregiver/family) each 30 minutes; individual patient** ⊑
♻ 0.66 ⚖ 0.66 Global Days XXX

98961 **2-4 patients** ⊑
INCLUDES group education regarding genetic risks
♻ 0.32 ⚖ 0.32 Global Days XXX
AMA: 2007, Aug, 9-12

98962 **5-8 patients** ⊑
INCLUDES group education regarding genetic risks
♻ 0.24 ⚖ 0.24 Global Days XXX
AMA: 2007, Aug, 9-12

98966-98968 Nonphysician Telephone Services

CMS *100-1,5,70* *Definition of Physician*
INCLUDES
assessment and management services provided by telephone by a qualified health care professional
episode of care initiated by an established patient or his/her guardian

EXCLUDES
call initiated by the qualified health care professional
calls during the postoperative period of a procedure
decision to see the patient at the next available urgent care appointment
decision to see the patient within 24 hours of the call
telephone services provided by a physician (99441-99443)
telephone services that are considered a part of a previous or subsequent service

Do not report with 98966-98968, 98969 if performed in the seven preceding days

98966 **Telephone assessment and management service provided by a qualified nonphysician health care professional to an established patient, parent, or guardian not originating from a related assessment and management service provided within the previous 7 days nor leading to an assessment and management service or procedure within the next 24 hours or soonest available appointment; 5-10 minutes of medical discussion** ⊑
♻ 0.34 ⚖ 0.38 Global Days XXX
AMA: 2008, Mar, 6-7

98967 **11-20 minutes of medical discussion** ⊑
♻ 0.69 ⚖ 0.72 Global Days XXX
AMA: 2008, Mar, 6-7

98968 **21-30 minutes of medical discussion** ⊑
♻ 1.03 ⚖ 1.06 Global Days XXX
AMA: 2008, Mar, 6-7

98969 Nonphysician Online Service

INCLUDES
on-line assessment and management service provided by a qualified health care professional
timely reply to the patient as well as:
ordering laboratory services
permanent record of the service; either hard copy or electronic
providing a prescription
related telephone calls

EXCLUDES
on-line evaluation service:
provided during the postoperative period of a procedure
provided more than once in a seven day period
related to a service provided in the previous seven days

Do not report with (99339-99340, 99363-99364, 99374-99380)
Do not report with (99363-99364)

98969 **Online assessment and management service provided by a qualified nonphysician health care professional to an established patient, guardian, or health care provider not originating from a related assessment and management service provided within the previous 7 days, using the Internet or similar electronic communications network** ⊑
♻ 0.00 ⚖ 0.00 Global Days XXX

99000-99091 Supplemental Services and Supplies

INCLUDES
supplemental reporting for services adjunct to the basic service provided

99000 **Handling and/or conveyance of specimen for transfer from the physician's office to a laboratory** ⊑
♻ 0.00 ⚖ 0.00 Global Days XXX
AMA: 2008, Jan, 10-25; 2007, Jan, 13-27; 2007, Jan, 13-27; 2007, Jan, 28-31; 2007, January, 13-27; 2007, January, 28-31; 2007, Jan, 28-31; 2006, Sep, 14-16; 2006, September, 14-16; 2006, August, 6-8; 2006, Sep, 14-16; 2006, Aug, 6-8; 2006, Aug, 6-8

99001 **Handling and/or conveyance of specimen for transfer from the patient in other than a physician's office to a laboratory (distance may be indicated)** ⊑
♻ 0.00 ⚖ 0.00 Global Days XXX
AMA: 2008, Jan, 10-25; 2007, Jan, 28-31; 2007, Jan, 28-31; 2007, Jan, 13-27; 2007, January, 13-27; 2007, January, 28-31; 2007, Jan, 13-27; 2006, Aug, 6-8; 2006, September, 14-16; 2006, August, 6-8; 2006, Aug, 6-8; 2006, Sep, 14-16; 2006, Sep, 14-16

99002 **Handling, conveyance, and/or any other service in connection with the implementation of an order involving devices (eg, designing, fitting, packaging, handling, delivery or mailing) when devices such as orthotics, protectives, prosthetics are fabricated by an outside laboratory or shop but which items have been designed, and are to be fitted and adjusted by the attending physician** Ⓑ
EXCLUDES *venous blood routine collection (36415)*
♻ 0.00 ⚖ 0.00 Global Days XXX
AMA: 2008, Jan, 10-25; 2007, Jan, 28-31; 2007, Jan, 28-31; 2007, Jan, 13-27; 2007, January, 28-31; 2007, January, 13-27; 2007, Jan, 13-27; 2006, Sep, 14-16; 2006, September, 14-16; 2006, August, 6-8; 2006, Sep, 14-16; 2006, Aug, 6-8; 2006, Aug, 6-8

99024 **Postoperative follow-up visit, normally included in the surgical package, to indicate that an evaluation and management service was performed during a postoperative period for a reason(s) related to the original procedure** Ⓑ
♻ 0.00 ⚖ 0.00 Global Days XXX
AMA: 2008, Jan, 10-25; 2007, Jan, 13-27; 2007, Jan, 13-27; 2007, Jan, 28-31; 2007, January, 13-27; 2007, January, 28-31; 2007, Jan, 28-31; 2006, Sep, 14-16; 2006, September, 14-16; 2006, August, 6-8; 2006, Sep, 14-16; 2006, Aug, 6-8; 2006, Aug, 6-8

99026 Hospital mandated on call service; in-hospital, each hour ⒠

  EXCLUDES *physician stand-by services with prolonged physician attendance (99360)*

  🖐 0.00 ✂ 0.00 **Global Days XXX**
  AMA: 2008, Jan, 10-25; 2007, Jan, 28-31; 2007, Jan, 28-31; 2007, Jan, 13-27; 2007, January, 13-27; 2007, January, 28-31; 2007, Jan, 13-27; 2006, Aug, 6-8; 2006, September, 14-16; 2006, August, 6-8; 2006, Aug, 6-8; 2006, Sep, 14-16; 2006, Sep, 14-16

99027 out-of-hospital, each hour ⒠

  EXCLUDES *physician stand-by services with prolonged physician attendance (99360)*

  🖐 0.00 ✂ 0.00 **Global Days XXX**
  AMA: 2008, Jan, 10-25; 2007, Jan, 13-27; 2007, Jan, 13-27; 2007, Jan, 28-31; 2007, January, 13-27; 2007, January, 28-31; 2007, Jan, 28-31; 2006, Aug, 6-8; 2006, September, 14-16; 2006, August, 6-8; 2006, Aug, 6-8; 2006, Sep, 14-16; 2006, Sep, 14-16

99050 Services provided in the office at times other than regularly scheduled office hours, or days when the office is normally closed (eg, holidays, Saturday or Sunday), in addition to basic service ⒝

  🖐 0.00 ✂ 0.00 **Global Days XXX**
  AMA: 2008, Jan, 10-25; 2007, Jan, 13-27; 2007, Jan, 13-27; 2007, Jan, 28-31; 2007, Jan, 28-31; 2007, January, 13-27; 2007, January, 28-31; 2006, Sep, 14-16; 2006, Sep, 14-16; 2006, May, 16-20, 2006, September, 14-16; 2006, August, 6-8; 2006, Aug, 6-8; 2006, Aug, 6-8; 2006, May, 16-20; 2006, May, 16-20

99051 Service(s) provided in the office during regularly scheduled evening, weekend, or holiday office hours, in addition to basic service ⒝

  🖐 0.00 ✂ 0.00 **Global Days XXX**
  AMA: 2008, Jan, 10-25; 2007, Jan, 28-31; 2007, Jan, 28-31; 2007, Jan, 13-27; 2007, Jan, 13-27; 2007, January, 13-27; 2007, January, 28-31; 2006, Sep, 14-16; 2006, Sep, 14-16; 2006, May, 16-20; 2006, September, 14-16; 2006, August, 6-8; 2006, May, 16-20; 2006, May, 16-20, 2006, Aug, 6-8; 2006, Aug, 6-8

99053 Service(s) provided between 10:00 PM and 8:00 AM at 24-hour facility, in addition to basic service ⒝

  🖐 0.00 ✂ 0.00 **Global Days XXX**
  AMA: 2008, Jan, 10-25; 2007, Jan, 13-27; 2007, Jan, 13-27; 2007, Jan, 28-31; 2007, Jan, 28-31; 2007, January, 13-27; 2007, January, 28-31; 2006, May, 16-20; 2006, May, 16-20; 2006, May, 16-20; 2006, September, 14-16; 2006, August, 6-8; 2006, Aug, 6-8; 2006, Aug, 6-8; 2006, Sep, 14-16; 2006, Sep, 14-16

99056 Service(s) typically provided in the office, provided out of the office at request of patient, in addition to basic service ⒝

  🖐 0.00 ✂ 0.00 **Global Days XXX**
  AMA: 2008, Jan, 10-25; 2007, Jan, 13-27; 2007, Jan, 13-27; 2007, Jan, 28-31; 2007, Jan, 28-31; 2007, January, 13-27; 2007, January, 28-31; 2006, Sep, 14-16; 2006, Sep, 14-16; 2006, August, 6-8; 2006, May, 16-20; 2006, September, 14-16; 2006, Aug, 6-8; 2006, Aug, 6-8; 2006, May, 16-20; 2006, May, 16-20

99058 Service(s) provided on an emergency basis in the office, which disrupts other scheduled office services, in addition to basic service ⒝

  🖐 0.00 ✂ 0.00 **Global Days XXX**
  AMA: 2008, Jan, 10-25; 2007, Jan, 13-27; 2007, Jan, 13-27; 2007, Jan, 28-31; 2007, January, 28-31; 2007, January, 13-27; 2006, May, 16-20; 2006, May, 16-20; 2006, August, 6-8; 2006, May, 16-20; 2006, September, 14-16; 2006, Aug, 6-8; 2006, Aug, 6-8; 2006, Sep, 14-16

99060 Service(s) provided on an emergency basis, out of the office, which disrupts other scheduled office services, in addition to basic service ⒝

  🖐 0.00 ✂ 0.00 **Global Days XXX**
  AMA: 2008, Jan, 10-25; 2007, Jan, 28-31; 2007, Jan, 28-31; 2007, Jan, 13-27; 2007, Jan, 13-27; 2007, January, 13-27; 2007, January, 28-31; 2006, May, 16-20; 2006, May, 16-20; 2006, May, 16-20; 2006, September, 14-16; 2006, August, 6-8; 2006, Aug, 6-8; 2006, Sep, 14-16; 2006, Sep, 14-16

99070 Supplies and materials (except spectacles), provided by the physician over and above those usually included with the office visit or other services rendered (list drugs, trays, supplies, or materials provided) ⒝

  EXCLUDES *spectacles supply*

  🖐 0.00 ✂ 0.00 **Global Days XXX**
  AMA: 2008, Jan, 10-25; 2008, Sep, 10☐-11; 2007, Jan, 13-27; 2007, Jan, 13-27; 2007, Jan, 28-31; 2007, Jan, 28-31; 2007, Feb, 8-9; 2007, January, 28-31; 2007, February, 8-9; 2007, January, 13-27; 2007, Feb, 8-9; 2006, Sep, 14-16; 2006, Sep, 14-16; 2006, Aug, 6-8; 2006, September, 14-16; 2006, April, 19-20; 2006, August, 6-8; 2006, Apr, 19-20; 2006, Aug, 6-8; 2006, Apr, 19-20; 2005, Jun, 1-4; 2005, July, 11-12; 2005, June, 1-4; 2005, Jun, 1-4; 2005, Jul, 11-12; 2005, Jul, 11-12

99071 Educational supplies, such as books, tapes, and pamphlets, provided by the physician for the patient's education at cost to physician ⒝

  🖐 0.00 ✂ 0.00 **Global Days XXX**
  AMA: 2008, Jan, 10-25; 2007, Jan, 13-27; 2007, Jan, 13-27; 2007, Jan, 28-31; 2007, January, 13-27; 2007, January, 28-31; 2007, Jan, 28-31; 2006, Sep, 14-16; 2006, September, 14-16; 2006, August, 6-8; 2006, Sep, 14-16; 2006, Aug, 6-8; 2006, Aug, 6-8

99075 Medical testimony ⒠

  🖐 0.00 ✂ 0.00 **Global Days XXX**
  AMA: 2008, Jan, 10-25; 2007, Jan, 13-27; 2007, Jan, 13-27; 2007, Jan, 28-31; 2007, January, 13-27; 2007, January, 28-31; 2007, Jan, 28-31; 2006, Sep, 14-16; 2006, September, 14-16; 2006, August, 6-8; 2006, Sep, 14-16; 2006, Aug, 6-8; 2006, Aug, 6-8

99078 Physician educational services rendered to patients in a group setting (eg, prenatal, obesity, or diabetic instructions) ⒩

  🖐 0.00 ✂ 0.00 **Global Days XXX**
  AMA: 2008, Jan, 10-25; 2007, Jan, 13-27; 2007, Jan, 13-27; 2007, Jan, 28-31; 2007, Jan, 28-31; 2007, Aug, 9-12; 2007, January, 13-27; 2007, January, 28-31; 2006, Sep, 14-16; 2006, Sep, 14-16; 2006, August, 6-8; 2006, September, 14-16; 2006, Aug, 6-8; 2006, Aug, 6-8; 2004, Aug, 1; 2004, August, 1; 2004, Aug, 1

99080 Special reports such as insurance forms, more than the information conveyed in the usual medical communications or standard reporting form ⒝

  Do not report with 99455, 99456 for completion of workmen's compensation forms

  🖐 0.00 ✂ 0.00 **Global Days XXX**
  AMA: 2008, Jan, 10-25; 2007, Jan, 13-27; 2007, Jan, 28-31; 2007, January, 13-27; 2007, January, 28-31; 2007, Jan, 28-31; 2006, Aug, 6-8; 2006, September, 14-16; 2006, August, 6-8; 2006, Aug, 6-8; 2006, Sep, 14-16; 2006, Sep, 14-16

99082 Unusual travel (eg, transportation and escort of patient) ⒝ ⑸⓪

  🖐 0.00 ✂ 0.00 **Global Days XXX**
  AMA: 2008, Jan, 10-25; 2007, Jan, 28-31; 2007, Jan, 28-31; 2007, Jan, 13-27; 2007, January, 13-27; 2007, January, 28-31; 2007, Jan, 13-27; 2006, Aug, 6-8; 2006, September, 14-16; 2006, August, 6-8; 2006, Aug, 6-8; 2006, Sep, 14-16; 2006, Sep, 14-16

99090 Analysis of clinical data stored in computers (eg, ECGs, blood pressures, hematologic data) B

EXCLUDES *collection/interpretation by health care professional/physician of physiologic data stored/transmitted by patient or caregiver (99091)*

this service if there exists a more specific CPT code for cardiographic services, glucose monitoring or musculoskeletal function testing (93014, 93227, 93233, 93272, 95250, 97750)

0.00   0.00 Global Days XXX

AMA: 2008, Jan, 10-25; 2008, Jan, 6-7; 2007, Jan, 13-27; 2007, Jan, 13-27; 2007, Jan, 28-31; 2007, Feb, 10-11; 2007, January, 28-31; 2007, Jan, 28-31; 2007, Feb, 10-11; 2007, January, 13-27; 2007, Jul, 1-4; 2007, February, 10-11; 2006, Sep, 14-16; 2006, Sep, 14-16; 2006, Aug, 6-8; 2006, September, 14-16; 2006, August, 6-8; 2006, Aug, 6-8

99091 Collection and interpretation of physiologic data (eg, ECG, blood pressure, glucose monitoring) digitally stored and/or transmitted by the patient and/or caregiver to the physician or other qualified health care professional, requiring a minimum of 30 minutes of time N

INCLUDES *reporting only once in a 30-day period*

EXCLUDES *this service if there exists a more specific CPT code for cardiographic services or glucose monitoring (93014, 93227, 93233, 93272, 95250)*

transfer/interpretation of data from hospital/clinical laboratory computers

Do not report with care plan oversight services if within 30 days (99374-99380)

1.51   1.51 Global Days XXX

AMA: 2008, Jan, 10-25; 2007, Jan, 13-27; 2007, Jan, 13-27; 2007, Jan, 28-31; 2007, January, 13-27; 2007, January, 28-31; 2007, Jan, 28-31; 2006, Aug, 6-8; 2006, September, 14-16; 2006, August, 6-8; 2006, Aug, 6-8; 2006, Sep, 14-16; 2006, Sep, 14-16

99100-99140 Modifying Factors for Anesthesia Services

CMS *100-4,12,140.3.2 Calculation of Anesthesia Time*
CMS *100-4,12,140.2 Payment for CRNA Services*
CMS *100-4,12,140 Certified Registered Nurse Anesthetist Services*
CMS *100-4,12,50 Anesthesia Services*

+ **99100** Anesthesia for patient of extreme age, younger than 1 year and older than 70 (List separately in addition to code for primary anesthesia procedure) B

EXCLUDES *services performed on infants that are less that 1 year old at the time of surgery (00326, 00561, 00834, 00836)*

Code first primary anesthesia procedure
0.00   0.00 Global Days ZZZ
AMA: 2008, Apr, 3-4; 2008, Apr, 3-4; 2008, Apr, 3-4

+ **99116** Anesthesia complicated by utilization of total body hypothermia (List separately in addition to code for primary anesthesia procedure) B

Code first primary anesthesia procedure
0.00   0.00 Global Days ZZZ
AMA: 2008, Apr, 3-4; 2008, Apr, 3-4; 2008, Apr, 3-4

+ **99135** Anesthesia complicated by utilization of controlled hypotension (List separately in addition to code for primary anesthesia procedure) B

Code first primary anesthesia procedure
0.00   0.00 Global Days ZZZ
AMA: 2008, Apr, 3-4; 2008, Apr, 3-4; 2008, Apr, 3-4

+ **99140** Anesthesia complicated by emergency conditions (specify) (List separately in addition to code for primary anesthesia procedure) B

INCLUDES *circumstances where a delay in treatment would lead to a significant increase in the threat to life or body part*

Code first primary anesthesia procedure
0.00   0.00 Global Days ZZZ
AMA: 2008, Apr, 3-4; 2008, Apr, 3-4; 2008, Jan, 10-25; 2008, Apr, 3-4; 2007, Jan, 13-27; 2007, Jan, 13-27; 2007, January, 13-27

99143-99150 Moderate Sedation Services

INCLUDES administration of medication
IV access
maintenance of sedation
monitoring of oxygen saturation/heart rate/blood pressure
patient assessment
recovery (not included in intraservice time)

EXCLUDES *minimal sedation/anxiolysis/deep sedation/monitored anesthesia care (00100-01999)*

Do not report with pulse oximetry (94760-94762)

⊘ **99143** Moderate sedation services (other than those services described by codes 00100-01999) provided by the same physician performing the diagnostic or therapeutic service that the sedation supports, requiring the presence of an independent trained observer to assist in the monitoring of the patient's level of consciousness and physiological status; younger than 5 years of age, first 30 minutes intra-service time N 80

0.00   0.00 Global Days XXX
AMA: 2008, Jan, 10-25; 2008, Feb, 5-6; 2007, Jan, 13-27; 2007, Jan, 13-27; 2007, January, 13-27; 2006, May, 16-20; 2006, May, 16-20; 2006, Feb, 10-15; 2006, September, 1-4; 2006, May, 16-20; 2006, February, 10-15; 2006, Feb, 10-15; 2006, Sep, 1-4; 2006, Sep, 1-4

⊘ **99144** age 5 years or older, first 30 minutes intra-service time A N 80

0.00   0.00 Global Days XXX
AMA: 2008, Feb, 5-6; 2006, Feb, 10-15; 2006, Feb, 10-15; 2006, Sep, 1-4; 2006, Sep, 1-4; 2006, May, 16-20; 2006, May, 16-20; 2006, February, 10-15; 2006, May, 16-20; 2006, September, 1-4

+ **99145** each additional 15 minutes intra-service time (List separately in addition to code for primary service) N 80

Code first initial 30 minutes (99143, 99144)
0.00   0.00 Global Days ZZZ
AMA: 2008, Feb, 5-6; 2006, May, 16-20; 2006, May, 16-20; 2006, Sep, 1-4; 2006, Sep, 1-4; 2006, Feb, 10-15; 2006, Feb, 10-15; 2006, February, 10-15; 2006, May, 16-20; 2006, September, 1-4

99148 Moderate sedation services (other than those services described by codes 00100-01999), provided by a physician other than the health care professional performing the diagnostic or therapeutic service that the sedation supports; younger than 5 years of age, first 30 minutes intra-service time N 80

0.00   0.00 Global Days XXX
AMA: 2008, Jan, 10-25; 2007, Jan, 13-27; 2007, Jan, 13-27; 2007, January, 13-27; 2006, May, 16-20; 2006, May, 16-20; 2006, May, 16-20; 2006, February, 10-15; 2006, Feb, 10-15; 2006, Feb, 10-15

99149 age 5 years or older, first 30 minutes intra-service time A N 80

0.00   0.00 Global Days XXX
AMA: 2006, May, 16-20; 2006, May, 16-20; 2006, Feb, 10-15; 2006, Feb, 10-15; 2006, May, 16-20; 2006, February, 10-15

+   99150   each additional 15 minutes intra-service time (List separately in addition to code for primary service) N 80
Code first initial 30 minutes (99148, 99149)
🔧 0.00 ⚕ 0.00 Global Days ZZZ
AMA: 2006, Feb, 10-15; 2006, Feb, 10-15; 2006, May, 16-20; 2006, May, 16-20; 2006, February, 10-15; 2006, May, 16-20

99170 Specialized Examination of Child

99170   Anogenital examination with colposcopic magnification in childhood for suspected trauma A T 🔲
EXCLUDES   *conscious sedation (99143-99150)*
🔧 2.61 ⚕ 3.94 Global Days 000
AMA: 2006, Apr, 1-7; 2006, Apr, 1-7; 2006, April, 1-7

99172-99173 Visual Acuity Screening Tests

CMS 100-2,16,90   *Routine Services and Appliances*
99172   Visual function screening, automated or semi-automated bilateral quantitative determination of visual acuity, ocular alignment, color vision by pseudoisochromatic plates, and field of vision (may include all or some screening of the determination[s] for contrast sensitivity, vision under glare) E
INCLUDES   graduated visual acuity stimuli that allow a quantitative determination of visual acuity
ocular photoscreening

Do not report with (99173)

Do not report with evaluation and management service or general ophthalmological service (92002-92014, 99201-99499)
🔧 0.00 ⚕ 0.00 Global Days XXX
AMA: 2008, Jan, 10-25; 2007, Jan, 13-27; 2007, Jan, 13-27; 2007, January, 13-27; 2005, Mar, 1-6; 2005, Mar, 1-6; 2005, March, 1-6; 2004, Jul, 7; 2004, Jul, 7; 2004, July, 7

99173   Screening test of visual acuity, quantitative, bilateral E
INCLUDES   graduated visual acuity stimuli that allow a quantitative estimate of visual acuity
ocular photoscreening

Do not report with (99172)
🔧 0.07 ⚕ 0.07 Global Days XXX
AMA: 2005, Mar, 1-6; 2005, Mar, 1-6; 2005, March, 1-6; 2004, Jul, 7; 2004, July, 7; 2004, Jul, 7

99174 Screening For Amblyogenic Factors

Do not report with (92002-92014, 99172-99173)
99174   Ocular photoscreening with interpretation and report, bilateral E
🔧 0.70 ⚕ 0.70 Global Days XXX

99175 Drug Administration to Induce Vomiting

99175   Ipecac or similar administration for individual emesis and continued observation until stomach adequately emptied of poison N 80
EXCLUDES   *diagnostic gastric lavage (91055)*
diagnostic intubation (82926-82928, 89130-89141)
🔧 0.72 ⚕ 0.72 Global Days XXX

99183 Hyperbaric Oxygen Therapy

CMS 100-3,20.29   *Hyperbaric Oxygen Therapy*
99183   Physician attendance and supervision of hyperbaric oxygen therapy, per session B 80
EXCLUDES   *evaluation and management services if performed*
other procedures such as wound debridement, if performed
🔧 3.14 ⚕ 5.25 Global Days XXX
AMA: 2008, Jan, 10-25; 2007, Jan, 13-27; 2007, Jan, 13-27; 2007, January, 13-27

99185-99186 Hypothermia Treatment

CMS 100-3,110.6   *Scalp Hypothermia During Chemotherapy, to Prevent Hair Loss*
99185   Hypothermia; regional N 80
🔧 1.56 ⚕ 1.56 Global Days XXX
99186   total body N 80 🔲
🔧 2.12 ⚕ 2.12 Global Days XXX

99190-99192 Assemble and Manage Pump with Oxygenator/Heat Exchange

99190   Assembly and operation of pump with oxygenator or heat exchanger (with or without ECG and/or pressure monitoring); each hour C 🔲
🔧 0.00 ⚕ 0.00 Global Days XXX
99191   45 minutes C 🔲
🔧 0.00 ⚕ 0.00 Global Days XXX
99192   30 minutes C 🔲
🔧 0.00 ⚕ 0.00 Global Days XXX

99195-99199 Therapeutic Phlebotomy and Unlisted Procedures

99195   Phlebotomy, therapeutic (separate procedure) X 80 🔲
🔧 1.95 ⚕ 1.95 Global Days XXX
AMA: 2008, Jan, 10-25; 2007, Jan, 13-27; 2007, Jan, 13-27; 2007, January, 13-27
99199   Unlisted special service, procedure or report B 80
🔧 0.00 ⚕ 0.00 Global Days XXX

99500-99602 Home Visit By Non-Physician Professionals

INCLUDES   services performed by non-physician providers
services provided in patient's:
assisted living apartment
custodial care facility
group home
non-traditional private home
residence
school

EXCLUDES   *home visits performed by physicians (99341-99350)*
other services/procedures provided by physicians to patients at home

Code also home visit evaluation and management codes if health care provider is authorized to use (99341-99350)

Code also significant separately identifiable evaluation and management service

99500   Home visit for prenatal monitoring and assessment to include fetal heart rate, non-stress test, uterine monitoring, and gestational diabetes monitoring M ♀ E
🔧 0.00 ⚕ 0.00 Global Days XXX
AMA: 2008, Jan, 10-25; 2007, Jan, 28-31; 2007, Jan, 28-31; 2007, January, 28-31

99501 Home visit for postnatal assessment and follow-up care ♀ E
📋 0.00 ✂ 0.00 Global Days XXX
AMA: 2007, Jan, 28-31; 2007, Jan, 28-31; 2007, January, 28-31

99502 Home visit for newborn care and assessment A E
📋 0.00 ✂ 0.00 Global Days XXX
AMA: 2007, Jan, 28-31; 2007, Jan, 28-31; 2007, January, 28-31

99503 Home visit for respiratory therapy care (eg, bronchodilator, oxygen therapy, respiratory assessment, apnea evaluation) E
📋 0.00 ✂ 0.00 Global Days XXX
AMA: 2007, Jan, 28-31; 2007, Jan, 28-31; 2007, January, 28-31

99504 Home visit for mechanical ventilation care E
📋 0.00 ✂ 0.00 Global Days XXX
AMA: 2007, Jan, 28-31; 2007, Jan, 28-31; 2007, January, 28-31

99505 Home visit for stoma care and maintenance including colostomy and cystostomy E
📋 0.00 ✂ 0.00 Global Days XXX
AMA: 2007, Jan, 28-31; 2007, Jan, 28-31; 2007, January, 28-31

99506 Home visit for intramuscular injections E
📋 0.00 ✂ 0.00 Global Days XXX
AMA: 2007, Jan, 28-31; 2007, Jan, 28-31; 2007, January, 28-31

99507 Home visit for care and maintenance of catheter(s) (eg, urinary, drainage, and enteral) E
📋 0.00 ✂ 0.00 Global Days XXX
AMA: 2007, Jan, 28-31; 2007, Jan, 28-31; 2007, January, 28-31

99509 Home visit for assistance with activities of daily living and personal care E
EXCLUDES *medical nutrition therapy/assessment home services (97802-97804)*
self-care/home management training (97535)
speech therapy home services (92507-92508)
📋 0.00 ✂ 0.00 Global Days XXX
AMA: 2007, Jan, 28-31; 2007, Jan, 28-31; 2007, January, 28-31

99510 Home visit for individual, family, or marriage counseling E
📋 0.00 ✂ 0.00 Global Days XXX
AMA: 2007, Jan, 28-31; 2007, Jan, 28-31; 2007, January, 28-31

99511 Home visit for fecal impaction management and enema administration E
📋 0.00 ✂ 0.00 Global Days XXX
AMA: 2007, Jan, 28-31; 2007, Jan, 28-31; 2007, January, 28-31

99512 Home visit for hemodialysis E
EXCLUDES *peritoneal dialysis home infusion (99601, 99602)*
📋 0.00 ✂ 0.00 Global Days XXX
AMA: 2007, Jan, 28-31; 2007, Jan, 28-31; 2007, January, 28-31

99600 Unlisted home visit service or procedure E
📋 0.00 ✂ 0.00 Global Days XXX
AMA: 2008, Jan, 10-25; 2007, Jan, 28-31; 2007, Jan, 28-31; 2007, January, 28-31

99601 Home infusion/specialty drug administration, per visit (up to 2 hours); E
📋 0.00 ✂ 0.00 Global Days XXX
AMA: 2005, Nov, 1-9; 2005, Nov, 1-9; 2005, November, 1-9

+ **99602** each additional hour (List separately in addition to code for primary procedure) E
Code first initial 2 hours (99601)
📋 0.00 ✂ 0.00 Global Days XXX
AMA: 2005, Nov, 1-9; 2005, Nov, 1-9; 2005, November, 1-9

99605-99607 Medication Management By Pharmacist

INCLUDES direct (face-to-face) assessment and intervention by a pharmacist for the purpose of:
managing medication complications and/or interactions
maximizing the patient's response to drug therapy
documenting the following required elements:
advice given regarding improvement of treatment compliance and outcomes
profile of medications (prescription and nonprescription)
review of applicable patient history

EXCLUDES *routine tasks associated with dispensing and related activities (e.g., providing product information)*

99605 Medication therapy management service(s) provided by a pharmacist, individual, face-to-face with patient, with assessment and intervention if provided; initial 15 minutes, new patient E
📋 0.00 ✂ 0.00 Global Days XXX

99606 initial 15 minutes, established patient E
📋 0.00 ✂ 0.00 Global Days XXX

+ **99607** each additional 15 minutes (List separately in addition to code for primary service) E
Code first (99605, 99606)
📋 0.00 ✂ 0.00 Global Days XXX

Evaluation and Management (E/M) Services Guidelines

In addition to the information presented in the Introduction, several other items unique to this section are defined or identified here.

CLASSIFICATION OF EVALUATION AND MANAGEMENT (E/M) SERVICES

The E/M section is divided into broad categories such as office visits, hospital visits, and consultations. Most of the categories are further divided into two or more subcategories of E/M services. For example, there are two subcategories of office visits (new patient and established patient) and there are two subcategories of hospital visits (initial and subsequent). The subcategories of E/M services are further classified into levels of E/M services that are identified by specific codes. This classification is important because the nature of physician work varies by type of service, place of service, and the patient's status.

The basic format of the levels of E/M services is the same for most categories. First, a unique code number is listed. Second, the place and/or type of service is specified, eg, office consultation. Third, the content of the service is defined, eg, comprehensive history and comprehensive examination. Fourth, the nature of the presenting problem(s) usually associated with a given level is described. Fifth, the time typically required to provide the service is specified.

DEFINITIONS OF COMMONLY USED TERMS

Certain key words and phrases are used throughout the E/M section. The following definitions are intended to reduce the potential for differing interpretations and to increase the consistency of reporting by physicians in differing specialties. E/M services may also be reported by other qualified health care professionals who are authorized to perform such services within the scope of their practice.

New and Established Patient

Solely for the purposes of distinguishing between new and established patients, professional services are those face-to-face services rendered by a physician and reported by a specific CPT code(s). A new patient is one who has not received any professional services from the physician or another physician of the same specialty who belongs to the same group practice, within the past three years.

An established patient is one who has received professional services from the physician or another physician of the same specialty who belongs to the same group practice, within the past three years.

In the instance where a physician is on call for or covering for another physician, the patient's encounter will be classified as it would have been by the physician who is not available.

No distinction is made between new and established patients in the emergency department. E/M services in the emergency department category may be reported for any new or established patient who presents for treatment in the emergency department.

The decision tree is provided to aid in determining whether to report the E/M service provided as a new or an established patient encounter.

Chief Complaint

A chief complaint is a concise statement describing the symptom, problem, condition, diagnosis, or other factor that is the reason for the encounter, usually stated in the patient's words.

Concurrent Care

Concurrent care is the provision of similar services, eg, hospital visits, to the same patient by more than one physician on the same day. When concurrent care is provided, no special reporting is required.

Counseling

Counseling is a discussion with a patient and/or family concerning one or more of the following areas:

- Diagnostic results, impressions, and/or recommended diagnostic studies

- Prognosis

- Risks and benefits of management (treatment) options

- Instructions for management (treatment) and/or follow-up

- Importance of compliance with chosen management (treatment) options

- Risk factor reduction

- Patient and family education

(For psychotherapy, see 90804-90857)

Family History

A review of medical events in the patient's family that includes significant information about:

- The health status or cause of death of parents, siblings, and children

- Specific diseases related to problems identified in the Chief Complaint or History of the Present Illness, and/or System Review

- Diseases of family members that may be hereditary or place the patient at risk

History of Present Illness

A chronological description of the development of the patient's present illness from the first sign and/or symptom to the present. This includes a description of location, quality, severity, timing, context, modifying factors, and associated signs and symptoms significantly related to the presenting problem(s).

Levels of E/M Services

Within each category or subcategory of E/M service, there are three to five levels of E/M services available for reporting purposes. Levels of E/M services are not interchangeable among the different categories or subcategories of service. For example, the first level of E/M services in the subcategory of office visit, new patient, does not have the same definition as the first level of E/M services in the subcategory of office visit, established patient.

The levels of E/M services include examinations, evaluations, treatments, conferences with or concerning patients, preventive pediatric and adult health supervision, and similar medical services, such as the determination of the need and/or location for appropriate care. Medical screening includes the history, examination, and medical decision-making required to determine the need and/or location for appropriate care and treatment of the patient (eg, office and other outpatient setting, emergency department, nursing facility). The levels of E/M services encompass the wide variations in skill, effort, time, responsibility, and medical knowledge required for the prevention or diagnosis and treatment of illness or injury and the promotion of optimal health. Each level of E/M services may be used by all physicians.

The descriptors for the levels of E/M services recognize seven components, six of which are used in defining the levels of E/M services. These components are:

- History

- Examination

- Medical decision making

- Counseling

- Coordination of care

- Nature of presenting problem

- Time

The first three of these components (history, examination, and medical decision making) are considered the key components in selecting a level of E/M services.

The next three components (counseling, coordination of care, and the nature of the presenting problem) are considered contributory factors in the majority of encounters. Although the first two of these contributory factors are important E/M services, it is not required that these services be provided at every patient encounter.

Coordination of care with other providers or agencies without a patient encounter on that day is reported using the case management codes.

Decision Tree for New vs. Established patients

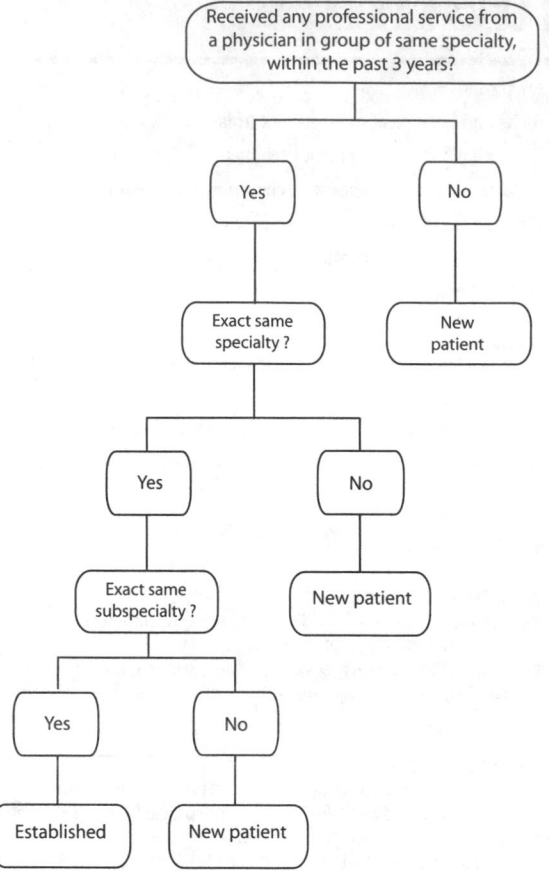

The final component, time, is discussed in detail.

Any specifically identifiable procedure (ie, identified with a specific CPT code) performed on or subsequent to the date of initial or subsequent E/M services should be reported separately.

The actual performance and/or interpretation of diagnostic tests/studies ordered during a patient encounter are not included in the levels of E/M services. Physician performance of diagnostic tests/studies for which specific CPT codes are available may be reported separately, in addition to the appropriate E/M code. The physician's interpretation of the results of diagnostic tests/studies (ie, professional component) with preparation of a separate distinctly identifiable signed written report may also be reported separately, using the appropriate CPT code with modifier 26 appended.

The physician may need to indicate that on the day a procedure or service identified by a CPT code was performed, the patient's condition required a significant separately identifiable E/M service above and beyond other services provided or beyond the usual preservice and postservice care associated with the procedure that was performed. The E/M service may be caused or prompted by the symptoms or condition for which the procedure and/or service was provided. This circumstance may be reported by adding modifier 25 to the appropriate level of E/M service. As such, different diagnoses are not required for reporting of the procedure and the E/M services on the same date.

Nature of Presenting Problem
A presenting problem is a disease, condition, illness, injury, symptom, sign, finding, complaint, or other reason for encounter, with or without a diagnosis being established at the time of the encounter. The E/M codes recognize five types of presenting problems that are defined as follows:

Minimal: A problem that may not require the presence of the physician, but service is provided under the physician's supervision.

Self-limited or minor: A problem that runs a definite and prescribed course, is transient in nature, and is not likely to permanently alter health status OR has a good prognosis with management/compliance.

Low severity: A problem where the risk of morbidity without treatment is low; there is little to no risk of mortality without treatment; full recovery without functional impairment is expected.

Moderate severity: A problem where the risk of morbidity without treatment is moderate; there is moderate risk of mortality without treatment; uncertain prognosis OR increased probability of prolonged functional impairment.

High severity: A problem where the risk of morbidity without treatment is high to extreme; there is a moderate to high risk of mortality without treatment OR high probability of severe, prolonged functional impairment.

Past History
A review of the patient's past experiences with illnesses, injuries, and treatments that includes significant information about:

- Prior major illnesses and injuries
- Prior operations
- Prior hospitalizations
- Current medications
- Allergies (eg, drug, food)
- Age appropriate immunization status
- Age appropriate feeding/dietary status

Social History
An age appropriate review of past and current activities that includes significant information about:

- Marital status and/or living arrangements
- Current employment
- Occupational history
- Use of drugs, alcohol, and tobacco
- Level of education
- Sexual history
- Other relevant social factors

System Review (Review of Systems)
An inventory of body systems obtained through a series of questions seeking to identify signs and/or symptoms that the patient may be experiencing or has experienced. For the purposes of the CPT codebook the following elements of a system review have been identified:

- Constitutional symptoms (fever, weight loss, etc)
- Eyes
- Ears, nose, mouth, throat
- Cardiovascular
- Respiratory
- Gastrointestinal
- Genitourinary
- Musculoskeletal
- Integumentary (skin and/or breast)
- Neurological
- Psychiatric
- Endocrine
- Hematologic/lymphatic
- Allergic/immunologic

The review of systems helps define the problem, clarify the differential diagnosis, identify needed testing, or serves as baseline data on other systems that might be affected by any possible management options.

Time
The inclusion of time in the definitions of levels of E/M services has been implicit in prior editions of the CPT codebook. The inclusion of time as an

explicit factor beginning in CPT 1992 is done to assist physicians in selecting the most appropriate level of E/M services. It should be recognized that the specific times expressed in the visit code descriptors are averages and, therefore, represent a range of times that may be higher or lower depending on actual clinical circumstances.

Time is not a descriptive component for the emergency department levels of E/M services because emergency department services are typically provided on a variable intensity basis, often involving multiple encounters with several patients over an extended period of time. Therefore, it is often difficult for physicians to provide accurate estimates of the time spent face-to-face with the patient.

Studies to establish levels of E/M services employed surveys of practicing physicians to obtain data on the amount of time and work associated with typical E/M services. Since "work" is not easily quantifiable, the codes must rely on other objective, verifiable measures that correlate with physicians' estimates of their "work." It has been demonstrated that physicians' estimations of intraservice time (as explained on the next page), both within and across specialties, is a variable that is predictive of the "work" of E/M services. This same research has shown there is a strong relationship between intraservice time and total time for E/M services. Intraservice time, rather than total time, was chosen for inclusion with the codes because of its relative ease of measurement and because of its direct correlation with measurements of the total amount of time and work associated with typical E/M services.

Intraservice times are defined as face-to-face time for office and other outpatient visits and as unit/floor time for hospital and other inpatient visits. This distinction is necessary because most of the work of typical office visits takes place during the face-to-face time with the patient, while most of the work of typical hospital visits takes place during the time spent on the patient's floor or unit.

Face-to-face time (office and other outpatient visits and office consultations): For coding purposes, face-to-face time for these services is defined as only that time that the physician spends face-to-face with the patient and/or family. This includes the time in which the physician performs such tasks as obtaining a history, performing an examination, and counseling the patient.

Physicians also spend time doing work before or after the face-to-face time with the patient, performing such tasks as reviewing records and tests, arranging for further services, and communicating further with other professionals and the patient through written reports and telephone contact.

This non-face-to-face time for office services—also called pre- and postencounter time—is not included in the time component described in the E/M codes. However, the pre- and post-face-to-face work associated with an encounter was included in calculating the total work of typical services in physician surveys.

Thus, the face-to-face time associated with the services described by any E/M code is a valid proxy for the total work done before, during, and after the visit.

Unit/floor time (hospital observation services, inpatient hospital care, initial and follow-up hospital consultations, nursing facility): For reporting purposes, intraservice time for these services is defined as unit/floor time, which includes the time that the physician is present on the patient's hospital unit and at the bedside rendering services for that patient. This includes the time in which the physician establishes and/or reviews the patient's chart, examines the patient, writes notes, and communicates with other professionals and the patient's family.

In the hospital, pre- and post-time includes time spent off the patient's floor performing such tasks as reviewing pathology and radiology findings in another part of the hospital.

This pre- and postvisit time is not included in the time component described in these codes. However, the pre- and postwork performed during the time spent off the floor or unit was included in calculating the total work of typical services in physician surveys.

Thus, the unit/floor time associated with the services described by any code is a valid proxy for the total work done before, during, and after the visit.

UNLISTED SERVICE

An E/M service may be provided that is not listed in this section of the CPT codebook. When reporting such a service, the appropriate "Unlisted" code may be used to indicate the service, identifying it by "Special Report," as

discussed in the following paragraph. The "Unlisted Services" and accompanying codes for the E/M section are as follows:

    99429   Unlisted preventive medicine service

    99499   Unlisted evaluation and management service

SPECIAL REPORT

An unlisted service or one that is unusual, variable, or new may require a special report demonstrating the medical appropriateness of the service. Pertinent information should include an adequate definition or description of the nature, extent, and need for the procedure and the time, effort, and equipment necessary to provide the service. Additional items that may be included are complexity of symptoms, final diagnosis, pertinent physical findings, diagnostic and therapeutic procedures, concurrent problems, and follow-up care.

INSTRUCTIONS FOR SELECTING A LEVEL OF E/M SERVICE

Identify the Category and Subcategory of Service
The categories and subcategories of codes available for reporting E/M services are shown in Table 1.

Review the Reporting Instructions for the Selected Category or Subcategory
Most of the categories and many of the subcategories of service have special guidelines or instructions unique to that category or subcategory. Where these are indicated, eg, "Inpatient Hospital Care," special instructions will be presented preceding the levels of E/M services.

Review the Level of E/M Service Descriptors and Examples in the Selected Category or Subcategory
The descriptors for the levels of E/M services recognize seven components, six of which are used in defining the levels of E/M services. These components are:

- History
- Examination
- Medical decision making
- Counseling
- Coordination of care
- Nature of presenting problem
- Time

The first three of these components (ie, history, examination, and medical decision making) should be considered the key components in selecting the level of E/M services. An exception to this rule is in the case of visits that consist predominantly of counseling or coordination of care.

The nature of the presenting problem and time are provided in some levels to assist the physician in determining the appropriate level of E/M service.

Determine the Extent of History Obtained
The extent of the history is dependent upon clinical judgment and on the nature of the presenting problems(s). The levels of E/M services recognize four types of history that are defined as follows:

Problem focused: Chief complaint; brief history of present illness or problem.

Expanded problem focused: Chief complaint; brief history of present illness; problem pertinent system review.

Detailed: Chief complaint; extended history of present illness; problem pertinent system review extended to include a review of a limited number of additional systems; pertinent past, family, and/or social history directly related to the patient's problems.

Comprehensive: Chief complaint; extended history of present illness; review of systems that is directly related to the problem(s) identified in the history of the present illness plus a review of all additional body systems; complete past, family, and social history.

The comprehensive history obtained as part of the preventive medicine E/M service is not problem-oriented and does not involve a chief complaint or present illness. It does, however, include a comprehensive system review and comprehensive or interval past, family, and social history as well as a comprehensive assessment/history of pertinent risk factors.

Determine the Extent of Examination Performed

The extent of the examination performed is dependent on clinical judgment and on the nature of the presenting problem(s). The levels of E/M services recognize four types of examination that are defined as follows:

Problem focused: A limited examination of the affected body area or organ system.

Expanded problem focused: A limited examination of the affected body area or organ system and other symptomatic or related organ system(s).

Detailed: An extended examination of the affected body area(s) and other symptomatic or related organ system(s).

Comprehensive: A general multisystem examination or a complete examination of a single organ system. Note: The comprehensive examination performed as part of the preventive medicine E/M service is multisystem, but its extent is based on age and risk factors identified.

For the purposes of these CPT definitions, the following body areas are recognized:

- Head, including the face
- Neck
- Chest, including breasts and axilla
- Abdomen
- Genitalia, groin, buttocks
- Back
- Each extremity

For the purposes of these CPT definitions, the following organ systems are recognized:

- Eyes
- Ears, nose, mouth, and throat
- Cardiovascular
- Respiratory
- Gastrointestinal
- Genitourinary
- Musculoskeletal
- Skin
- Neurologic
- Psychiatric

- Hematologic/lymphatic/immunologic

Determine the Complexity of Medical Decision Making

Medical decision making refers to the complexity of establishing a diagnosis and/or selecting a management option as measured by:

- The number of possible diagnoses and/or the number of management options that must be considered

- The amount and/or complexity of medical records, diagnostic tests, and/or other information that must be obtained, reviewed, and analyzed

- The risk of significant complications, morbidity, and/or mortality, as well as comorbidities, associated with the patient's presenting problems(s), the diagnostic procedure(s), and/or the possible management options

Four types of medical decision making are recognized: straightforward, low complexity, moderate complexity, and high complexity. To qualify for a given type of decision making, two of the three elements in Table 2 must be met or exceeded.

Comorbidities/underlying diseases, in and of themselves, are not considered in selecting a level of E/M services unless their presence significantly increases the complexity of the medical decision making.

Select the Appropriate Level of E/M Services Based on the Following

1. For the following categories/subcategories, all of the key components, ie, history, examination, and medical decision making, must meet or exceed the stated requirements to qualify for a particular level of E/M service: office, new patient; hospital observation services; initial hospital care; office consultations; initial inpatient consultations; emergency department services; initial nursing facility care; domiciliary care, new patient; and home, new patient.

2. For the following categories/subcategories, two of the three key components (ie, history, examination, and medical decision making) must meet or exceed the stated requirements to qualify for a particular level of E/M services: office, established patient; subsequent hospital care; subsequent nursing facility care; domiciliary care, established patient; and home, established patient.

3. When counseling and/or coordination of care dominates (more than 50%) the physician/patient and/or family encounter (face-to-face time in the office or other outpatient setting or floor/unit time in the hospital or nursing facility), then time may be considered the key or controlling factor to qualify for a particular level of E/M services. This includes time spent with parties who have assumed responsibility for the care of the patient or decision making whether or not they are family members (eg, foster parents, person acting in loco parentis, legal guardian). The extent of counseling and/or coordination of care must be documented in the medical record.

TABLE 1

Categories and Subcategories of Service

Category/Subcategory	Code Numbers
Office or Other Outpatient Services	
New Patient	99201-99205
Established Patient	99211-99215
Hospital Observation Services	
Hospital Observation Discharge Services	99217
Initial Hospital Observation Services	99218-99220
Hospital Observation or Inpatient Care Services (Including Admission and Discharge Services)	99234-99236
Hospital Inpatient Services	
Initial Hospital Care	99221-99223
Subsequent Hospital Care	99231-99233
Hospital Discharge Services	99238-99239
Consultations	
Office Consultations	99241-99245
Inpatient Consultations	99251-99255
Emergency Department Services	99281-99288
Critical Care Services	
Adult (over 24 months of age)	99291-99292
Nursing Facility Services	
Initial Nursing Facility Care	99304-99306
Subsequent Nursing Facility Care	99307-99310
Nursing Facility Discharge Services	99315-99316
Other Nursing Facility Services	99318
Domiciliary, Rest Home or Custodial Care Services	
New Patient	99324-99328
Established Patient	99334-99337
Domiciliary, Rest Home (eg, Assisted Living Facility), or Home Care Plan	

Category/Subcategory	Code Numbers
Oversight Services	99339-99340
Home Services	
New Patient	99341-99345
Established Patient	99347-99350
Prolonged Services	
With Direct Patient Contact	99354-99357
Without Direct Patient Contact	99358-99359
Standby Services	99360
Case Management Services	
Anticoagulant Management	99363-99364
Medical Team Conferences	99366-99368
Care Plan Oversight Services	99374-99380
Medical Team Conferences	99366-99368
Preventive Medicine Services	
New Patient	99381-99387
Established Patient	99391-99397
Individual Counseling	99401-99404
Group Counseling	99411-99412
Other	99420-99429
Non-Face-to-Face Physician Services	
Telephone Services	99441-99443
Online Medical Evaluation	99444
Special E/M Services	99450-99456
▲ Newborn Care	99460-99463
Delivery/Birthing Room Attendance	99464-99465
Neonatal and Pediatric Critical Care Services	
Pediatric Patient Transport	99466-99467
Inpatient Neonatal Critical Care Services	99468-99469
Inpatient Pediatric Critical Care Services	99471-99476
Initial and Continuing Intensive Care Services	99477-99480
Other E/M Services	99499

TABLE 2

Complexity of Medical Decision Making

Number of Diagnoses or Management Options	Amount and/or Complexity of Data to be Reviewed	Risk of Complications and/or Morbidity or Mortality	Type of Decision Making
minimal	minimal or none	minimal	straightforward
limited	limited	low	low complexity
multiple	moderate	moderate	moderate complexity
extensive	extensive	high	high complexity

Evaluation and Management

99201 — 99204

99201-99215 Outpatient and Other Visits

CMS *100-3,70.3*   *Physician's Offices Within an Institution--"Incident-to" Provision*
CMS *100-4,12,30.6.7*   *Payment for Office or Other Outpatient Evaluation and Management (E/M) Visits*

INCLUDES   established patients: received prior care from the physician or another physician in the practice of the same specialty in the previous three years (99211-99215)

new patients: have not received care from the physician or any other physician in the same practice within the same specialty in the previous three years (99201-99205)

office visits

outpatient services prior to formal admission to a facility

EXCLUDES   *office/outpatient services that require more than the customary E/M service (99354-99355, 99358-99359)*

99201   **Office or other outpatient visit for the evaluation and management of a new patient, which requires these 3 key components: A problem focused history; A problem focused examination; Straightforward medical decision making. Counseling and/or coordination of care with other providers or agencies are provided consistent with the nature of the problem(s) and the patient's and/or family's needs. Usually, the presenting problem(s) are self limited or minor. Physicians typically spend 10 minutes face-to-face with the patient and/or family.** V 80 ▢ PQ

   0.65   1.02   **Global Days XXX**

AMA: 2008, Jan, 10-25; 2007, Jan, 13-27; 2007, Jan, 13-27; 2007, Mar, 9-11; 2007, Apr, 11-12; 2007, January, 13-27; 2007, Mar, 9-11; 2007, Apr, 11-12; 2007, March, 9-11; 2007, Jul, 1-4; 2007, April, 11-12; 2006, May, 1-9; 2006, May, 1-9; 2006, Jun, 1-7; 2006, June, 1-7; 2006, May, 1-9; 2006, Jun, 1-7; 2005, May, 1-2; 2005, May, 1-2; 2005, Mar, 11-15; 2005, Dec, 9-11; 2005, Jun, 9-11; 2005, Dec, 9-11; 2005, Mar, 11-15; 2005, Jun, 9-11; 2005, Feb, 1-6; 2005, December, 9-11; 2005, June, 9-11; 2005, April, 1-5; 2005, February, 1-6; 2005, March, 11-15; 2005, May, 1-2; 2005, Apr, 1-5; 2005, Apr, 1-5; 2005, Feb, 1-6; 2004, Nov, 11; 2004, Nov, 11; 2004, November, 11; 2004, August, 1; 2004, March, 7; 2004, Mar, 7; 2004, Mar, 7; 2004, Aug, 1; 2004, Aug, 1

99202   **Office or other outpatient visit for the evaluation and management of a new patient, which requires these 3 key components: An expanded problem focused history; An expanded problem focused examination; Straightforward medical decision making. Counseling and/or coordination of care with other providers or agencies are provided consistent with the nature of the problem(s) and the patient's and/or family's needs. Usually, the presenting problem(s) are of low to moderate severity. Physicians typically spend 20 minutes face-to-face with the patient and/or family.** V 80 ▢ PQ

   1.25   1.76   **Global Days XXX**

AMA: 2008, Jan, 10-25; 2007, Jan, 13-27; 2007, Jan, 13-27; 2007, Mar, 9-11; 2007, Apr, 11-12; 2007, January, 13-27; 2007, Mar, 9-11; 2007, Apr, 11-12; 2007, March, 9-11; 2007, Jul, 1-4; 2007, April, 11-12; 2006, May, 1-9; 2006, May, 1-9; 2006, Jun, 1-7; 2006, June, 1-7; 2006, May, 1-9; 2006, Jun, 1-7; 2005, Mar, 11-15; 2005, Mar, 11-15; 2005, Feb, 1-6; 2005, Jun, 9-11; 2005, May, 1-2; 2005, Jun, 9-11; 2005, Feb, 1-6; 2005, May, 1-2; 2005, Apr, 1-5; 2005, February, 1-6; 2005, December, 9-11; 2005, May, 1-2; 2005, June, 9-11; 2005, April, 1-5; 2005, March, 11-15; 2005, Dec, 9-11; 2005, Dec, 9-11; 2005, Apr, 1-5; 2004, Mar, 7; 2004, Mar, 7; 2004, November, 11; 2004, August, 1; 2004, March, 7; 2004, Aug, 1; 2004, Aug, 1; 2004, Nov, 11; 2004, Nov, 11

99203   **Office or other outpatient visit for the evaluation and management of a new patient, which requires these 3 key components: A detailed history; A detailed examination; Medical decision making of low complexity. Counseling and/or coordination of care with other providers or agencies are provided consistent with the nature of the problem(s) and the patient's and/or family's needs. Usually, the presenting problem(s) are of moderate severity. Physicians typically spend 30 minutes face-to-face with the patient and/or family.** V 80 ▢ PQ

   1.89   2.55   **Global Days XXX**

AMA: 2008, Jan, 10-25; 2007, Jan, 13-27; 2007, Jan, 13-27; 2007, Mar, 9-11; 2007, Mar, 9-11; 2007, Apr, 11-12; 2007, March, 9-11; 2007, Jul, 1-4; 2007, April, 11-12; 2007, January, 13-27; 2007, Apr, 11-12; 2006, May, 1-9; 2006, May, 1-9; 2006, Jun, 1-7; 2006, June, 1-7; 2006, May, 1-9; 2006, Jun, 1-7; 2005, Apr, 1-5; 2005, Apr, 1-5; 2005, Jun, 9-11; 2005, Jun, 9-11; 2005, Feb, 1-6; 2005, Dec, 9-11; 2005, Feb, 7-9; 2005, December, 9-11; 2005, February, 7-9; 2005, February, 1-6; 2005, March, 11-15; 2005, May, 1-2; 2005, June, 9-11; 2005, April, 1-5; 2005, Mar, 11-15; 2005, Mar, 11-15; 2005, Feb, 7-9; 2005, Dec, 9-11; 2005, Feb, 1-6; 2005, May, 1-2; 2005, May, 1-2; 2004, Mar, 7; 2004, November, 11; 2004, August, 1; 2004, November, 5; 2004, March, 7; 2004, Mar, 7; 2004, Nov, 5; 2004, Nov, 5; 2004, Aug, 1; 2004, Aug, 1; 2004, Nov, 11; 2004, Nov, 11

99204   **Office or other outpatient visit for the evaluation and management of a new patient, which requires these 3 key components: A comprehensive history; A comprehensive examination; Medical decision making of moderate complexity. Counseling and/or coordination of care with other providers or agencies are provided consistent with the nature of the problem(s) and the patient's and/or family's needs. Usually, the presenting problem(s) are of moderate to high severity. Physicians typically spend 45 minutes face-to-face with the patient and/or family.** V 80 ▢ PQ

   3.16   3.93   **Global Days XXX**

AMA: 2008, Jan, 10-25; 2007, Jan, 13-27; 2007, Jan, 13-27; 2007, Mar, 9-11; 2007, Apr, 11-12; 2007, January, 13-27; 2007, Mar, 9-11; 2007, Apr, 11-12; 2007, March, 9-11; 2007, Jul, 1-4; 2007, April, 11-12; 2006, May, 1-9; 2006, May, 1-9; 2006, Jun, 1-7; 2006, June, 1-7; 2006, May, 1-9; 2006, Jun, 1-7; 2005, May, 1-2; 2005, May, 1-2; 2005, Jun, 9-11; 2005, Dec, 9-11; 2005, Feb, 1-6; 2005, Dec, 9-11; 2005, Jun, 9-11; 2005, Feb, 1-6; 2005, Apr, 1-5; 2005, February, 1-6; 2005, December, 9-11; 2005, June, 9-11; 2005, March, 11-15; 2005, May, 1-2; 2005, April, 1-5; 2005, Mar, 11-15; 2005, Mar, 11-15; 2005, Apr, 1-5; 2004, Mar, 7; 2004, Mar, 7; 2004, August, 1; 2004, November, 11; 2004, March, 7; 2004, Nov, 11; 2004, Nov, 11; 2004, Aug, 1; 2004, Aug, 1

99205 Office or other outpatient visit for the evaluation and management of a new patient, which requires these 3 key components: A comprehensive history; A comprehensive examination; Medical decision making of high complexity. Counseling and/or coordination of care with other providers or agencies are provided consistent with the nature of the problem(s) and the patient's and/or family's needs. Usually, the presenting problem(s) are of moderate to high severity. Physicians typically spend 60 minutes face-to-face with the patient and/or family. [03] [80] [□] [P0]

　🔖 4.11   ✄ 4.96   **Global Days XXX**
AMA: 2008, Jan, 10-25; 2007, Jan, 13-27; 2007, Jan, 13-27; 2007, Mar, 9-11; 2007, Apr, 11-12; 2007, January, 13-27; 2007, Mar, 9-11; 2007, Apr, 11-12; 2007, March, 9-11; 2007, Jul, 1-4; 2007, April, 11-12; 2006, Jun, 1-7; 2006, Jun, 1-7; 2006, May, 1-9; 2006, June, 1-7; 2006, May, 1-9; 2006, May, 1-9; 2005, Mar, 11-15; 2005, Mar, 11-15; 2005, Jun, 9-11; 2005, Dec, 9-11; 2005, Feb, 1-6; 2005, Dec, 9-11; 2005, Jun, 9-11; 2005, Feb, 1-6; 2005, May, 1-2; 2005, December, 9-11; 2005, February, 1-6; 2005, April, 1-5; 2005, June, 9-11; 2005, March, 11-15; 2005, May, 1-2; 2005, Apr, 1-5; 2005, Apr, 1-5; 2005, May, 1-2; 2004, Nov, 11; 2004, Nov, 11; 2004, August, 1; 2004, March, 7; 2004, November, 11; 2004, Mar, 7; 2004, Mar, 7; 2004, Aug, 1; 2004, Aug, 1

99211 Office or other outpatient visit for the evaluation and management of an established patient, that may not require the presence of a physician. Usually, the presenting problem(s) are minimal. Typically, 5 minutes are spent performing or supervising these services. [V] [80] [□] [P0]

　🔖 0.24   ✄ 0.52   **Global Days XXX**
AMA: 2008, Jan, 10-25; 2008, Mar, 3&7; 2007, Jan, 13-27; 2007, Jan, 13-27; 2007, Mar, 9-11; 2007, Apr, 11-12; 2007, January, 13-27; 2007, April, 11-12; 2007, Dec, 9; 2007, Jul, 1-4; 2007, March, 9-11; 2007, Apr, 11-12; 2007, Mar, 9-11; 2006, May, 16-20; 2006, May, 16-20; 2006, June, 1-7; 2006, May, 1-9; 2006, May, 16-20; 2006, May, 1-9; 2006, May, 1-9; 2006, Jun, 1-7; 2006, Jun, 1-7; 2005, May, 1-2; 2005, May, 1-2; 2005, Jun, 9-11; 2005, Jun, 9-11; 2005, Apr, 1-5; 2005, Nov, 1-9; 2005, Dec, 9-11; 2005, Feb, 13-16; 2005, Mar, 11-15; 2005, November, 1-9; 2005, April, 1-5; 2005, December, 9-11; 2005, February, 13-16; 2005, February, 1-6; 2005, June, 9-11; 2005, March, 11-15; 2005, May, 1-2; 2005, Mar, 11-15; 2005, Feb, 13-16; 2005, Dec, 9-11; 2005, Nov, 1-9; 2005, Apr, 1-5; 2005, Feb, 1-6; 2005, Feb, 1-6; 2004, Mar, 7; 2004, August, 1; 2004, November, 11; 2004, March, 7; 2004, April, 14; 2004, Mar, 7; 2004, Nov, 11; 2004, Nov, 11; 2004, Apr, 14; 2004, Aug, 1; 2004, Aug, 1

99212 Office or other outpatient visit for the evaluation and management of an established patient, which requires at least 2 of these 3 key components: A problem focused history; A problem focused examination; Straightforward medical decision making. Counseling and/or coordination of care with other providers or agencies are provided consistent with the nature of the problem(s) and the patient's and/or family's needs. Usually, the presenting problem(s) are self limited or minor. Physicians typically spend 10 minutes face-to-face with the patient and/or family. [V] [80] [□] [P0]

　🔖 0.64   ✄ 1.03   **Global Days XXX**
AMA: 2008, Jan, 10-25; 2008, Mar, 3&7; 2007, Jan, 13-27; 2007, Jan, 13-27; 2007, Mar, 9-11; 2007, Apr, 11-12; 2007, Mar, 9-11; 2007, Apr, 11-12; 2007, March, 9-11; 2007, Jul, 1-4; 2007, April, 11-12; 2007, January, 13-27; 2006, Jun, 11-15; 2006, Jun, 11-15; 2006, May, 1-9; 2006, Jun, 1-7; 2006, May, 1-9; 2006, May, 1-9; 2006, June, 1-7; 2006, June, 11-15; 2006, September, 9-13; 2006, Jun, 1-7; 2006, Sep, 9-13; 2006, Sep, 9-13; 2005, Apr, 1-5; 2005, Apr, 1-5; 2005, Mar, 11-15; 2005, Mar, 11-15; 2005, Dec, 9-11; 2005, December, 9-11; 2005, April, 1-5; 2005, February, 1-6; 2005, June, 9-11; 2005, March, 11-15; 2005, May, 1-2; 2005, May, 1-2; 2005, Feb, 1-6; 2005, Feb, 1-6; 2005, May, 1-2; 2005, Dec, 9-11; 2005, Jun, 9-11; 2005, Jun, 9-11; 2004, Apr, 14; 2004, November, 11; 2004, August, 1; 2004, March, 7; 2004, April, 14; 2004, Apr, 14; 2004, Mar, 7; 2004, Mar, 7; 2004, Nov, 11; 2004, Aug, 1; 2004, Aug, 1

99213 Office or other outpatient visit for the evaluation and management of an established patient, which requires at least 2 of these 3 key components: An expanded problem focused history; An expanded problem focused examination; Medical decision making of low complexity. Counseling and coordination of care with other providers or agencies are provided consistent with the nature of the problem(s) and the patient's and/or family's needs. Usually, the presenting problem(s) are of low to moderate severity. Physicians typically spend 15 minutes face-to-face with the patient and/or family. [V] [80] [□] [P0]

　🔖 1.24   ✄ 1.70   **Global Days XXX**
AMA: 2008, Jan, 10-25; 2008, Mar, 3&7; 2007, Jan, 13-27; 2007, Jan, 13-27; 2007, Mar, 9-11; 2007, Apr, 11-12; 2007, January, 13-27; 2007, Apr, 11-12; 2007, Mar, 9-11; 2007, March, 9-11; 2007, Jul, 1-4; 2007, April, 11-12; 2006, Sep, 9-13; 2006, Sep, 9-13; 2006, May, 1-9; 2006, Jun, 11-15; 2006, Jun, 1-7; 2006, Jun, 11-15; 2006, May, 1-9; 2006, June, 1-7; 2006, June, 11-15; 2006, May, 1-9; 2006, September, 9-13; 2006, Jun, 1-7; 2005, Mar, 11-15; 2005, Mar, 11-15; 2005, Feb, 1-6; 2005, Feb, 1-6; 2005, Apr, 1-5; 2005, Jun, 9-11; 2005, May, 1-2; 2005, December, 9-11; 2005, May, 1-2; 2005, April, 1-5; 2005, February, 1-6; 2005, June, 9-11; 2005, March, 11-15; 2005, Dec, 9-11; 2005, Dec, 9-11; 2005, May, 1-2; 2005, Jun, 9-11; 2005, Apr, 1-5; 2004, Nov, 5; 2004, Nov, 5; 2004, Nov, 11; 2004, April, 14; 2004, August, 1; 2004, November, 5; 2004, November, 11; 2004, March, 7; 2004, Nov, 11; 2004, Aug, 1; 2004, Aug, 1; 2004, Mar, 7; 2004, Mar, 7; 2004, Apr, 14; 2004, Apr, 14

99214 Office or other outpatient visit for the evaluation and management of an established patient, which requires at least 2 of these 3 key components: A detailed history; A detailed examination; Medical decision making of moderate complexity. Counseling and/or coordination of care with other providers or agencies are provided consistent with the nature of the problem(s) and the patient's and/or family's needs. Usually, the presenting problem(s) are of moderate to high severity. Physicians typically spend 25 minutes face-to-face with the patient and/or family. V 80 PQ

1.92 2.56 Global Days XXX

AMA: 2008, Jan, 10-25; 2008, Mar, 3&7; 2008, Jun, 12&15; 2007, Jan, 13-27; 2007, Jan, 13-27; 2007, Mar, 9-11; 2007, Mar, 9-11; 2007, March, 9-11; 2007, Jul, 1-4; 2007, April, 11-12; 2007, January, 13-27; 2007, Apr, 11-12; 2007, Apr, 11-12; 2006, Jun, 11-15; 2006, Jun, 11-15; 2006, Sep, 9-13; 2006, May, 1-9; 2006, Sep, 14-16; 2006, May, 1-9; 2006, Sep, 9-13; 2006, Sep, 14-16; 2006, Jun, 1-7; 2006, June, 1-7; 2006, June, 11-15; 2006, May, 1-9; 2006, September, 14-16; 2006, September, 9-13; 2006, Jun, 1-7; 2005, May, 1-2; 2005, May, 1-2; 2005, Jun, 9-11; 2005, Jun, 9-11; 2005, Feb, 1-6; 2005, Dec, 9-11; 2005, Mar, 11-15; 2005, April, 1-5; 2005, December, 9-11; 2005, February, 1-6; 2005, June, 9-11; 2005, March, 11-15; 2005, May, 1-2; 2005, Apr, 1-5; 2005, Apr, 1-5; 2005, Mar, 11-15; 2005, Dec, 9-11; 2005, Feb, 1-6; 2004, Mar, 7; 2004, Mar, 7; 2004, Aug, 1; 2004, August, 1; 2004, November, 5; 2004, November, 11; 2004, March, 7; 2004, April, 14; 2004, Aug, 1; 2004, Apr, 14; 2004, Apr, 14; 2004, Nov, 11; 2004, Nov, 11; 2004, Nov, 5; 2004, Nov, 5

99215 Office or other outpatient visit for the evaluation and management of an established patient, which requires at least 2 of these 3 key components: A comprehensive history; A comprehensive examination; Medical decision making of high complexity. Counseling and/or coordination of care with other providers or agencies are provided consistent with the nature of the problem(s) and the patient's and/or family's needs. Usually, the presenting problem(s) are of moderate to high severity. Physicians typically spend 40 minutes face-to-face with the patient and/or family. 03 80 PQ

2.73 3.46 Global Days XXX

AMA: 2008, Jan, 10-25; 2008, Mar, 3&7; 2007, Jan, 13-27; 2007, Jan, 13-27; 2007, Mar, 9-11; 2007, Apr, 11-12; 2007, January, 13-27; 2007, Apr, 11-12; 2007, Mar, 9-11; 2007, March, 9-11; 2007, Jul, 1-4; 2007, April, 11-12; 2006, Sep, 9-13; 2006, Sep, 9-13; 2006, Jun, 11-15; 2006, Jun, 1-7; 2006, May, 1-9; 2006, Jun, 1-7; 2006, Jun, 11-15; 2006, June, 1-7; 2006, June, 11-15; 2006, May, 1-9; 2006, September, 9-13; 2006, May, 1-9; 2005, Mar, 11-15; 2005, Mar, 11-15; 2005, Jun, 9-11; 2005, Jun, 9-11; 2005, Dec, 9-11; 2005, Nov, 10-13; 2005, May, 1-2; 2005, February, 1-6; 2005, December, 9-11; 2005, November, 10-13; 2005, April, 1-5; 2005, June, 9-11; 2005, March, 11-15; 2005, May, 1-2; 2005, Apr, 1-5; 2005, Apr, 1-5; 2005, May, 1-2; 2005, Nov, 10-13; 2005, Dec, 9-11; 2005, Feb, 1-6; 2005, Feb, 1-6; 2004, Mar, 7; 2004, August, 1; 2004, April, 14; 2004, November, 11; 2004, March, 7; 2004, Mar, 7; 2004, Nov, 11; 2004, Nov, 11; 2004, Aug, 1; 2004, Aug, 1; 2004, Apr, 14; 2004, Apr, 14

99217-99220 Facility Observation Visits: Initial and Discharge

CMS *100-3,70.1* *Consultations with a Beneficiary's Family and Associates*
CMS *100-2,15,30* *Physician Services*
CMS *100-1,5,70* *Definition of Physician*
CMS *100-4,12,30.6.8* *Payment for Hospital Observation Services*

INCLUDES services provided on the same date in other settings (e.g, emergency department, physician's office) associated with the observation status admission
services provided to new and established patients admitted to a hospital specifically for observation (not required to be a designated area of the hospital)

EXCLUDES *post-surgical care services*
services provided by physicians other than the admitting physician (99241-99245)
services provided to patients who are admitted and discharged from observation status on the same date (99234-99236)

99217 Observation care discharge day management (This code is to be utilized by the physician to report all services provided to a patient on discharge from "observation status" if the discharge is on other than the initial date of "observation status." To report services to a patient designated as "observation status" or "inpatient status" and discharged on the same date, use the codes for Observation or Inpatient Care Services [including Admission and Discharge Services, 99234-99236 as appropriate.]) B 80 PQ

INCLUDES discussing the observation admission with the patient
final patient evaluation
discharge instructions
sign off on discharge medical records

Do not report with hospital discharge day management services (99238-99239)

Do not report with observation/inpatient admission/discharge on the same date (99234-99236)

1.85 1.85 Global Days XXX

AMA: 2007, Mar, 9-11; 2007, Mar, 9-11; 2007, March, 9-11; 2007, Jul, 1-4; 2006, Sep, 9-13; 2006, Sep, 9-13; 2006, May, 1-9; 2006, Dec, 14-15; 2006, Dec, 14-15; 2006, Dec, 14-15; 2006, May, 1-9; 2006, December, 14-15; 2006, December, 14-15; 2006, September, 9-13; 2006, May, 1-9; 2006, Dec, 14-15; 2005, May, 1-2; 2005, May, 1-2; 2005, Nov, 10-13; 2005, February, 1-6; 2005, November, 10-13; 2005, May, 1-2; 2005, Nov, 10-13; 2005, Feb, 1-6; 2005, Feb, 1-6

99218 Initial observation care, per day, for the evaluation and management of a patient which requires these 3 key components: A detailed or comprehensive history; A detailed or comprehensive examination; and Medical decision making that is straightforward or of low complexity. Counseling and/or coordination of care with other providers or agencies are provided consistent with the nature of the problem(s) and the patient's and/or family's needs. Usually, the problem(s) requiring admission to "observation status" are of low severity.   B 80 ▢ P0

     ◪ 1.74   ⚬ 1.74   Global Days XXX

     AMA: 2008, Jan, 10-25; 2007, Jan, 13-27; 2007, Jan, 13-27; 2007, Mar, 9-11; 2007, January, 13-27; 2007, Mar, 9-11; 2007, March, 9-11; 2007, Jul, 1-4; 2006, Sep, 9-13; 2006, Sep, 9-13; 2006, May, 1-9; 2006, May, 1-9; 2006, December, 14-15; 2006, December, 14-15; 2006, September, 9-13; 2006, May, 1-9; 2006, Dec, 14-15; 2006, Dec, 14-15; 2006, Dec, 14-15; 2006, Dec, 14-15; 2005, Feb, 1-6; 2005, November, 10-13; 2005, February, 1-6; 2005, May, 1-2; 2005, Feb, 1-6; 2005, May, 1-2; 2005, May, 1-2; 2005, Nov, 10-13; 2005, Nov, 10-13; 2004, Aug, 11; 2004, August, 11; 2004, Aug, 11

99219 Initial observation care, per day, for the evaluation and management of a patient, which requires these 3 key components: A comprehensive history; A comprehensive examination; and Medical decision making of moderate complexity. Counseling and/or coordination of care with other providers or agencies are provided consistent with the nature of the problem(s) and the patient's and/or family's needs. Usually, the problem(s) requiring admission to "observation status" are of moderate severity.   B 80 ▢ P0

     ◪ 2.88   ⚬ 2.88   Global Days XXX

     AMA: 2008, Jan, 10-25; 2007, Jan, 13-27; 2007, Jan, 13-27; 2007, Mar, 9-11; 2007, January, 13-27; 2007, Mar, 9-11; 2007, March, 9-11; 2007, Jul, 1-4; 2006, May, 1-9; 2006, May, 1-9; 2006, Sep, 9-13; 2006, May, 1-9; 2006, December, 14-15; 2006, December, 14-15; 2006, September, 9-13; 2006, Sep, 9-13; 2006, Dec, 14-15; 2006, Dec, 14-15; 2006, Dec, 14-15; 2006, Dec, 14-15; 2005, May, 1-2; 2005, November, 10-13; 2005, February, 1-6; 2005, May, 1-2; 2005, May, 1-2; 2005, Nov, 10-13; 2005, Nov, 10-13; 2005, Feb, 1-6; 2005, Feb, 1-6; 2004, Aug, 11; 2004, August, 11; 2004, Aug, 11

99220 Initial observation care, per day, for the evaluation and management of a patient, which requires these 3 key components: A comprehensive history; A comprehensive examination; and Medical decision making of high complexity. Counseling and/or coordination of care with other providers or agencies are provided consistent with the nature of the problem(s) and the patient's and/or family's needs. Usually, the problem(s) requiring admission to "observation status" are of high severity.   B 80 ▢ P0

     ◪ 4.04   ⚬ 4.04   Global Days XXX

     AMA: 2008, Jan, 10-25; 2007, Jan, 13-27; 2007, Jan, 13-27; 2007, Mar, 9-11; 2007, January, 13-27; 2007, Mar, 9-11; 2007, March, 9-11; 2007, Jul, 1-4; 2006, Sep, 9-13; 2006, Sep, 9-13; 2006, May, 1-9; 2006, May, 1-9; 2006, December, 14-15; 2006, December, 14-15; 2006, September, 9-13; 2006, May, 1-9; 2006, Dec, 14-15; 2006, Dec, 14-15; 2006, Dec, 14-15; 2006, Dec, 14-15; 2005, May, 1-2; 2005, November, 10-13; 2005, May, 1-2; 2005, February, 1-6; 2005, May, 1-2; 2005, Nov, 10-13; 2005, Nov, 10-13; 2005, Feb, 1-6; 2005, Feb, 1-6; 2004, Aug, 11; 2004, August, 11; 2004, Aug, 11

99221-99233 Inpatient Hospital Visits: Initial and Subsequent

CMS 100-3,70.1   *Consultations with a Beneficiary's Family and Associates*
CMS 100-2,15,30   *Physician Services*
CMS 100-1,5,70   *Definition of Physician*
CMS 100-4,12,30.6.9.1 *Initial Hospital Care and Observation or Inpatient Care Services*
CMS 100-4,12,30.6.9 *Hospital Visit and Critical Care on Same Day*
CMS 100-4,12,30.6.8 *Payment for Hospital Observation Services*

INCLUDES   all services provided on the date of admission in other sites of service (e.g., emergency department, physician's office, nursing facility)

     initial physician services provided to the patient in the hospital or "partial" hospital settings (99221-99223)

     services provided to a new or established patient

EXCLUDES   *consultation services provided by other than the admitting physician (99251)*

     inpatient E/M services provided by other than the admitting physician (99231-99233)

     observation/inpatient care when the patient is admitted/discharged on the same date (99234-99236)

     physician services provided to the patient in the hospital or "partial" hospital settings after the initial care (99231-99233)

99221 Initial hospital care, per day, for the evaluation and management of a patient, which requires these 3 key components: A detailed or comprehensive history; A detailed or comprehensive examination; and Medical decision making that is straightforward or of low complexity. Counseling and/or coordination of care with other providers or agencies are provided consistent with the nature of the problem(s) and the patient's and/or family's needs. Usually, the problem(s) requiring admission are of low severity. Physicians typically spend 30 minutes at the bedside and on the patient's hospital floor or unit.   B 80 ▢ P0

     ◪ 2.49   ⚬ 2.49   Global Days XXX

     AMA: 2008, Jan, 10-25; 2007, Jan, 13-27; 2007, Jan, 13-27; 2007, Mar, 9-11; 2007, March, 9-11; 2007, January, 13-27; 2007, Mar, 9-11; 2007, Jul, 1-4; 2007, Jul, 12-13; 2006, Sep, 9-13; 2006, September, 9-13; 2006, Sep, 9-13; 2005, May, 1-2; 2005, May, 1-2; 2005, Feb, 1-6; 2005, February, 1-6; 2005, May, 1-2; 2005, Feb, 1-6; 2004, Aug, 11; 2004, Aug, 11; 2004, Aug, 1; 2004, August, 11; 2004, August, 1; 2004, April, 14; 2004, Aug, 1; 2004, Apr, 14; 2004, Apr, 14

99222 Initial hospital care, per day, for the evaluation and management of a patient, which requires these 3 key components: A comprehensive history; A comprehensive examination; and Medical decision making of moderate complexity. Counseling and/or coordination of care with other providers or agencies are provided consistent with the nature of the problem(s) and the patient's and/or family's needs. Usually, the problem(s) requiring admission are of moderate severity. Physicians typically spend 50 minutes at the bedside and on the patient's hospital floor or unit.   B 80 ▢ P0

     ◪ 3.40   ⚬ 3.40   Global Days XXX

     AMA: 2008, Jan, 10-25; 2007, Jan, 13-27; 2007, Jan, 13-27; 2007, Mar, 9-11; 2007, January, 13-27; 2007, Jul, 12-13; 2007, Jul, 1-4; 2007, March, 9-11; 2007, Mar, 9-11; 2006, Sep, 9-13; 2006, Sep, 9-13; 2006, September, 9-13; 2005, Feb, 1-6; 2005, Feb, 1-6; 2005, Mar, 11-15; 2005, May, 1-2; 2005, May, 1-2; 2005, March, 11-15; 2005, February, 1-6; 2005, May, 1-2; 2005, Mar, 11-15; 2004, Apr, 14; 2004, Apr, 14; 2004, Aug, 11; 2004, August, 11; 2004, August, 1; 2004, April, 14; 2004, Aug, 11; 2004, Aug, 1; 2004, Aug, 1

● New Code   ▲ Revised Code   M Maternity Edit   A Age Edit   A-Y OPPS Status Indicator   ◪ Facility RVU   ⚬ Non-Facility RVU
▢ CCI Comprehensive Code   50 Bilateral Procedure   + Add-on Indicator   ▣ Laboratory crosswalk   ▣ Radiology crosswalk

© 2008 Ingenix *(Blue Ink)*   CPT only © 2008 American Medical Association. All Rights Reserved. (Black Ink)   Medicare (Red Ink)   461

Evaluation and Management

99223 — 99234

99223   Initial hospital care, per day, for the evaluation and management of a patient, which requires these 3 key components: A comprehensive history; A comprehensive examination; and Medical decision making of high complexity. Counseling and/or coordination of care with other providers or agencies are provided consistent with the nature of the problem(s) and the patient's and/or family's needs. Usually, the problem(s) requiring admission are of high severity. Physicians typically spend 70 minutes at the bedside and on the patient's hospital floor or unit.   B 80 ▭ PQ

   ✂ 5.00   ⚕ 5.00   **Global Days XXX**

   AMA: 2008, Jan, 10-25; 2007, Jan, 13-27; 2007, Jan, 13-27; 2007, Mar, 9-11; 2007, January, 13-27; 2007, Jul, 12-13; 2007, Jul, 1-4; 2007, March, 9-11; 2007, Mar, 9-11; 2006, Sep, 9-13; 2006, Sep, 9-13; 2006, September, 9-13; 2005, Mar, 11-15; 2005, Mar, 11-15; 2005, Feb, 1-6; 2005, May, 1-2; 2005, May, 1-2; 2005, February, 1-6; 2005, March, 11-15; 2005, May, 1-2; 2005, Feb, 1-6; 2004, Apr, 14; 2004, Apr, 14; 2004, Aug, 1; 2004, August, 1; 2004, April, 14; 2004, August, 11; 2004, Aug, 1; 2004, Aug, 11; 2004, Aug, 11

99231   Subsequent hospital care, per day, for the evaluation and management of a patient, which requires at least 2 of these 3 key components: A problem focused interval history; A problem focused examination; Medical decision making that is straightforward or of low complexity. Counseling and/or coordination of care with other providers or agencies are provided consistent with the nature of the problem(s) and the patient's and/or family's needs. Usually, the patient is stable, recovering or improving. Physicians typically spend 15 minutes at the bedside and on the patient's hospital floor or unit.   B 80 ▭ PQ

   ✂ 1.03   ⚕ 1.03   **Global Days XXX**

   AMA: 2008, Jan, 10-25; 2007, Jan, 13-27; 2007, Jan, 13-27; 2007, Mar, 9-11; 2007, January, 13-27; 2007, Mar, 9-11; 2007, March, 9-11; 2007, Jul, 1-4; 2006, Jun, 1-7; 2006, Jun, 1-7; 2006, May, 16-20; 2006, May, 1-9; 2006, June, 1-7; 2006, May, 16-20; 2006, May, 1-9; 2006, May, 16-20; 2006, May, 1-9; 2005, Feb, 1-6; 2005, Feb, 1-6; 2005, May, 1-2; 2005, Mar, 11-15; 2005, Mar, 11-15; 2005, February, 1-6; 2005, March, 11-15; 2005, May, 1-2; 2005, May, 1-2; 2004, Apr, 14; 2004, Apr, 14; 2004, Aug, 1; 2004, August, 11; 2004, August, 1; 2004, April, 14; 2004, Aug, 1; 2004, Aug, 11; 2004, Aug, 11

99232   Subsequent hospital care, per day, for the evaluation and management of a patient, which requires at least 2 of these 3 key components: An expanded problem focused interval history; An expanded problem focused examination; Medical decision making of moderate complexity. Counseling and/or coordination of care with other providers or agencies are provided consistent with the nature of the problem(s) and the patient's and/or family's needs. Usually, the patient is responding inadequately to therapy or has developed a minor complication. Physicians typically spend 25 minutes at the bedside and on the patient's hospital floor or unit.   B 80 ▭ PQ

   ✂ 1.85   ⚕ 1.85   **Global Days XXX**

   AMA: 2008, Jan, 10-25; 2008, Jun, 12&15; 2007, Jan, 13-27; 2007, Jan, 13-27; 2007, Mar, 9-11; 2007, January, 13-27; 2007, Mar, 9-11; 2007, March, 9-11; 2007, Jul, 1-4; 2006, May, 1-9; 2006, May, 1-9; 2006, Jun, 1-7; 2006, May, 16-20; 2006, June, 1-7; 2006, May, 16-20; 2006, May, 1-9; 2006, Jun, 1-7; 2006, May, 16-20; 2005, May, 1-2; 2005, May, 1-2; 2005, Feb, 1-6; 2005, Mar, 11-15; 2005, Mar, 11-15; 2005, February, 1-6; 2005, March, 11-15; 2005, May, 1-2; 2005, Feb, 1-6; 2004, Aug, 11; 2004, Aug, 11; 2004, Apr, 14; 2004, August, 11; 2004, August, 1; 2004, April, 14; 2004, Apr, 14; 2004, Aug, 1; 2004, Aug, 1

99233   Subsequent hospital care, per day, for the evaluation and management of a patient, which requires at least 2 of these 3 key components: A detailed interval history; A detailed examination; Medical decision making of high complexity. Counseling and/or coordination of care with other providers or agencies are provided consistent with the nature of the problem(s) and the patient's and/or family's needs. Usually, the patient is unstable or has developed a significant complication or a significant new problem. Physicians typically spend 35 minutes at the bedside and on the patient's hospital floor or unit.   B 80 ▭ PQ

   ✂ 2.65   ⚕ 2.65   **Global Days XXX**

   AMA: 2008, Jan, 10-25; 2007, Mar, 9-11; 2007, Mar, 9-11; 2007, March, 9-11; 2007, Jul, 1-4; 2006, May, 1-9; 2006, May, 1-9; 2006, Jun, 1-7; 2006, May, 16-20; 2006, Jun, 1-7; 2006, June, 1-7; 2006, May, 16-20; 2006, May, 1-9; 2006, May, 16-20; 2005, Mar, 11-15; 2005, Mar, 11-15; 2005, Feb, 1-6; 2005, May, 1-2; 2005, May, 1-2; 2005, February, 1-6; 2005, March, 11-15; 2005, May, 1-2; 2005, Feb, 1-6; 2004, Apr, 14; 2004, Apr, 14; 2004, Aug, 1; 2004, August, 11; 2004, August, 1; 2004, April, 14; 2004, Aug, 1; 2004, Aug, 11; 2004, Aug, 11

99234-99236 Observation/Inpatient Visits: Admitted/Discharged on Same Date

CMS *100-3,70.1*   *Consultations with a Beneficiary's Family and Associates*
CMS *100-2,15,30*   *Physician Services*
CMS *100-1,5,70*   *Definition of Physician*
CMS *100-4,12,30.6.9.1 Initial Hospital Care and Observation or Inpatient Care Services*
CMS *100-4,12,30.6.9 Hospital Visit and Critical Care on Same Day*
CMS *100-4,12,30.6.8 Payment for Hospital Observation Services*
CMS *100-4,12,40.2   Global Surgery Billing Requirements*

INCLUDES   admission to observation and discharge services on the same date
   all services provided by admitting physician on same date of service, even when initiated in another setting (e.g., emergency department, nursing facility, physician's office)

EXCLUDES   *inpatient discharge services (99238-99239)*
   inpatient subsequent care services (99231-99233)
   services provided to patients admitted to observation and discharged on a different date (99217-99220)

99234   Observation or inpatient hospital care, for the evaluation and management of a patient including admission and discharge on the same date, which requires these 3 key components: A detailed or comprehensive history; A detailed or comprehensive examination; and Medical decision making that is straightforward or of low complexity. Counseling and/or coordination of care with other providers or agencies are provided consistent with the nature of the problem(s) and the patient's and/or family's needs. Usually the presenting problem(s) requiring admission are of low severity.   B 80 ▭ PQ

   ✂ 3.53   ⚕ 3.53   **Global Days XXX**

   AMA: 2008, Jan, 10-25; 2007, Jan, 13-27; 2007, Jan, 13-27; 2007, Mar, 9-11; 2007, March, 9-11; 2007, Jul, 1-4; 2007, January, 13-27; 2007, Mar, 9-11; 2006, May, 1-9; 2006, May, 1-9; 2006, Sep, 9-13; 2006, Dec, 14-15; 2006, Dec, 14-15; 2006, Dec, 14-15; 2006, Sep, 9-13; 2006, December, 14-15; 2006, December, 14-15; 2006, May, 1-9; 2006, September, 9-13; 2006, Dec, 14-15; 2005, Feb, 1-6; 2005, Feb, 1-6; 2005, May, 1-2; 2005, February, 1-6; 2005, November, 10-13; 2005, May, 1-2; 2005, May, 1-2; 2005, Nov, 10-13; 2005, Nov, 10-13

26/TC Professional/Technical Component Only   80/80 Assist-at-Surgery Allowed/With Documentation   Unlisted   Not Covered
AMA: CPT Assistant References   A2-Z3 ASC Payment Indicator   ♂ Male Only   ♀ Female Only   ⊘ Modifier 51 Exempt   PQ PQRI

462   CPT only © 2008 American Medical Association. All Rights Reserved. (Black Ink)   Medicare (Red Ink)   © 2008 Ingenix (Blue Ink)

99235   Observation or inpatient hospital care, for the evaluation and management of a patient including admission and discharge on the same date, which requires these 3 key components: A comprehensive history; A comprehensive examination; and Medical decision making of moderate complexity. Counseling and/or coordination of care with other providers or agencies are provided consistent with the nature of the problem(s) and the patient's and/or family's needs. Usually the presenting problem(s) requiring admission are of moderate severity. ☒ ☒ ☒ ☒

     4.63   4.63   Global Days XXX

     AMA: 2008, Jan, 10-25; 2007, Jan, 13-27; 2007, Jan, 13-27; 2007, Mar, 9-11; 2007, March, 9-11; 2007, Jul, 1-4; 2007, January, 13-27; 2007, Mar, 9-11; 2006, May, 1-9; 2006, May, 1-9; 2006, Sep, 9-13; 2006, Dec, 14-15; 2006, Dec, 14-15; 2006, Dec, 14-15; 2006, Sep, 9-13; 2006, December, 14-15; 2006, December, 14-15; 2006, May, 1-9; 2006, September, 9-13; 2006, Dec, 14-15; 2005, Feb, 1-6; 2005, Feb, 1-6; 2005, Nov, 10-13; 2005, February, 1-6; 2005, November, 10-13; 2005, May, 1-2; 2005, Nov, 10-13; 2005, May, 1-2; 2005, May, 1-2

99236   Observation or inpatient hospital care, for the evaluation and management of a patient including admission and discharge on the same date, which requires these 3 key components: A comprehensive history; A comprehensive examination; and Medical decision making of high complexity. Counseling and/or coordination of care with other providers or agencies are provided consistent with the nature of the problem(s) and the patient's and/or family's needs. Usually the presenting problem(s) requiring admission are of high severity. ☒ ☒ ☒ ☒

     5.75   5.75   Global Days XXX

     AMA: 2008, Jan, 10-25; 2007, Jan, 13-27; 2007, Jan, 13-27; 2007, Mar, 9-11; 2007, March, 9-11; 2007, Jul, 1-4; 2007, January, 13-27; 2007, Mar, 9-11; 2006, May, 1-9; 2006, May, 1-9; 2006, Sep, 9-13; 2006, Dec, 14-15; 2006, Dec, 14-15; 2006, Dec, 14-15; 2006, Sep, 9-13; 2006, December, 14-15; 2006, December, 14-15; 2006, May, 1-9; 2006, September, 9-13; 2006, Dec, 14-15; 2005, May, 1-2; 2005, May, 1-2; 2005, Nov, 10-13; 2005, February, 1-6; 2005, November, 10-13; 2005, May, 1-2; 2005, Nov, 10-13; 2005, Feb, 1-6; 2005, Feb, 1-6

99238-99239 Inpatient Hospital Discharge Services

CMS *100-4,12,30.6.9.2 Hospital Discharge Management*

INCLUDES   discharge instructions
     final preparation of the pateint's medical records
     provision of prescriptions/referrals, as needed
     review of the inpatient admission

EXCLUDES   *discharge from observation (99217)*
     admission/discharge on same date (99234-99236)
     discharge from nursing facility (99315, 99316)
     discharge services for newborns admitted and discharged the same day (99463)
     final patient evaluation
     healthy newborn evaluated and discharged on same date (99463)
     services provided by other than attending physician on date of discharge (99231-99233)

99238   Hospital discharge day management; 30 minutes or less ☒ ☒ ☒ ☒

     1.84   1.84   Global Days XXX

     AMA: 2008, Jan, 10-25; 2007, Jan, 13-27; 2007, Jan, 13-27; 2007, Mar, 9-11; 2007, March, 9-11; 2007, January, 13-27; 2007, Mar, 9-11; 2007, Jul, 1-4; 2006, Sep, 9-13; 2006, September, 9-13; 2006, Sep, 9-13; 2005, Mar, 11-15; 2005, Mar, 11-15; 2005, May, 1-2; 2005, February, 1-6; 2005, March, 11-15; 2005, May, 1-2; 2005, May, 1-2; 2005, Feb, 1-6; 2005, Feb, 1-6; 2004, Aug, 11; 2004, Aug, 11; 2004, August, 11

99239   more than 30 minutes ☒ ☒ ☒ ☒

     2.67   2.67   Global Days XXX

     AMA: 2008, Jan, 10-25; 2007, Jan, 13-27; 2007, Jan, 13-27; 2007, Mar, 9-11; 2007, March, 9-11; 2007, January, 13-27; 2007, Mar, 9-11; 2007, Jul, 1-4; 2006, Sep, 9-13; 2006, September, 9-13; 2006, Sep, 9-13; 2005, May, 1-2; 2005, May, 1-2; 2005, May, 1-2; 2005, February, 1-6; 2005, March, 11-15; 2005, Feb, 1-6; 2005, Feb, 1-6; 2005, Mar, 11-15; 2005, Mar, 11-15; 2004, Aug, 11; 2004, Aug, 11; 2004, August, 11

99241-99255 Consultations

CMS *100-3,70.1*   *Consultations with a Beneficiary's Family and Associates*
CMS *100-2,15,30*   *Physician Services*
CMS *100-1,5,70*   *Definition of Physician*
CMS *100-4,12,30.6.10*   *Consultation Services*

INCLUDES   a third-party mandated consultation
     one consultation per consultant
     provision by a physician or qualified nonphysician practitioner whose advice, opinion, recommendation, suggestion, direction, or counsel, etc. is requested for evaluating/treating a patient since that individual's expertise in a specific medical area is beyond the scope of knowledge of the requesting physician
     documentation of a request for a consultation from an appropriate source
     documentation of the need for consultation in the patient's medical record
     provision of a written report of findings/recommendations from the consultant to the referring physician

EXCLUDES   *another appropriately requested and documented consultation pertaining to the same/new problem: repeat use of consultation codes*
     any distinctly recognizable procedure/service provided on or following the consultation
     assumption of care (all or partial): report subsequent codes as appropriate for the place of service (99211-99215, 99231-99233, 99307-99310)
     consultation prompted by the patient/family: report codes for office, domiciliary/rest home, or home visits instead (99201-99215, 99324-99337, 99341-99350)

99241   Office consultation for a new or established patient, which requires these 3 key components: A problem focused history; A problem focused examination; and Straightforward medical decision making. Counseling and/or coordination of care with other providers or agencies are provided consistent with the nature of the problem(s) and the patient's and/or family's needs. Usually, the presenting problem(s) are self limited or minor. Physicians typically spend 15 minutes face-to-face with the patient and/or family. ☒ ☒ ☒ ☒

     0.92   1.35   Global Days XXX

     AMA: 2008, Jan, 10-25; 2007, Jan, 13-27; 2007, Jan, 13-27; 2007, Mar, 9-11; 2007, Mar, 9-11; 2007, Apr, 11-12; 2007, March, 9-11; 2007, Jul, 1-4; 2007, April, 11-12; 2007, January, 13-27; 2007, Apr, 11-12; 2006, May, 1-9; 2006, May, 1-9; 2006, Jun, 1-7; 2006, May, 16-20; 2006, June, 1-7; 2006, May, 1-9; 2006, September, 9-13; 2006, Jun, 1-7; 2006, May, 16-20; 2006, Sep, 9-13; 2006, Sep, 9-13; 2006, May, 16-20; 2005, May, 1-2; 2005, May, 1-2; 2005, Feb, 1-6; 2005, December, 9-11; 2005, February, 1-6; 2005, May, 1-2; 2005, Dec, 9-11; 2005, Feb, 1-6; 2005, Dec, 9-11; 2004, Mar, 7; 2004, August, 1; 2004, March, 7; 2004, Mar, 7; 2004, Aug, 1; 2004, Aug, 1

99242 Office consultation for a new or established patient, which requires these 3 key components: An expanded problem focused history; An expanded problem focused examination; and Straightforward medical decision making. Counseling and/or coordination of care with other providers or agencies are provided consistent with the nature of the problem(s) and the patient's and/or family's needs. Usually, the presenting problem(s) are of low severity. Physicians typically spend 30 minutes face-to-face with the patient and/or family. ▣ ▣ ▣ ▣

◪ 1.94 ◪ 2.52 Global Days XXX

AMA: 2008, Jan, 10-25; 2007, Jan, 13-27; 2007, Jan, 13-27; 2007, Mar, 9-11; 2007, Apr, 11-12; 2007, Mar, 9-11; 2007, Apr, 11-12; 2007, March, 9-11; 2007, Jul, 1-4; 2007, April, 11-12; 2007, January, 13-27; 2006, Sep, 9-13; 2006, Sep, 9-13; 2006, May, 16-20; 2006, May, 1-9; 2006, May, 16-20; 2006, May, 1-9; 2006, September, 9-13; 2006, May, 16-20; 2006, June, 1-7; 2006, May, 1-9; 2006, Jun, 1-7; 2006, Jun, 1-7; 2005, May, 1-2; 2005, May, 1-2; 2005, Feb, 1-6; 2005, Dec, 9-11; 2005, Feb, 1-6; 2005, March, 11-15; 2005, December, 9-11; 2005, February, 1-6; 2005, May, 1-2; 2005, Dec, 9-11; 2005, Mar, 11-15; 2005, Mar, 11-15; 2004, Aug, 1; 2004, August, 1; 2004, March, 7; 2004, Aug, 1; 2004, Mar, 7; 2004, Mar, 7

99243 Office consultation for a new or established patient, which requires these 3 key components: A detailed history; A detailed examination; and Medical decision making of low complexity. Counseling and/or coordination of care with other providers or agencies are provided consistent with the nature of the problem(s) and the patient's and/or family's needs. Usually, the presenting problem(s) are of moderate severity. Physicians typically spend 40 minutes face-to-face with the patient and/or family. ▣ ▣ ▣ ▣

◪ 2.70 ◪ 3.46 Global Days XXX

AMA: 2008, Jan, 10-25; 2007, Jan, 13-27; 2007, Jan, 13-27; 2007, Mar, 9-11; 2007, Apr, 11-12; 2007, Mar, 9-11; 2007, Apr, 11-12; 2007, March, 9-11; 2007, Jul, 1-4; 2007, April, 11-12; 2007, January, 13-27; 2006, Sep, 9-13; 2006, Sep, 9-13; 2006, May, 16-20; 2006, May, 1-9; 2006, May, 16-20; 2006, May, 16-20; 2006, June, 1-7; 2006, May, 1-9; 2006, September, 9-13; 2006, May, 1-9; 2006, Jun, 1-7; 2006, Jun, 1-7; 2005, May, 1-2; 2005, May, 1-2; 2005, Feb, 1-6; 2005, Dec, 9-11; 2005, Feb, 1-6; 2005, December, 9-11; 2005, February, 1-6; 2005, March, 11-15; 2005, May, 1-2; 2005, Dec, 9-11; 2005, Mar, 11-15; 2005, Mar, 11-15; 2004, Mar, 7; 2004, March, 7; 2004, August, 1; 2004, Mar, 7; 2004, Aug, 1; 2004, Aug, 1

99244 Office consultation for a new or established patient, which requires these 3 key components: A comprehensive history; A comprehensive examination; and Medical decision making of moderate complexity. Counseling and/or coordination of care with other providers or agencies are provided consistent with the nature of the problem(s) and the patient's and/or family's needs. Usually, the presenting problem(s) are of moderate to high severity. Physicians typically spend 60 minutes face-to-face with the patient and/or family. ▣ ▣ ▣ ▣

◪ 4.27 ◪ 5.11 Global Days XXX

AMA: 2008, Jan, 10-25; 2007, Jan, 13-27; 2007, Jan, 13-27; 2007, Mar, 9-11; 2007, Apr, 11-12; 2007, Mar, 9-11; 2007, Apr, 11-12; 2007, March, 9-11; 2007, Jul, 1-4; 2007, April, 11-12; 2007, January, 13-27; 2006, May, 1-9; 2006, May, 1-9; 2006, Jun, 1-7; 2006, Sep, 9-13; 2006, Jun, 1-7; 2006, May, 16-20; 2006, June, 1-7; 2006, May, 1-9; 2006, September, 9-13; 2006, Sep, 9-13; 2006, May, 16-20; 2006, Mar, 11-15; 2005, Mar, 11-15; 2005, Feb, 1-6; 2005, Dec, 9-11; 2005, Feb, 1-6; 2005, March, 11-15; 2005, December, 9-11; 2005, February, 1-6; 2005, May, 1-2; 2005, Dec, 9-11; 2005, May, 1-2; 2005, May, 1-2; 2004, Mar, 7; 2004, August, 1; 2004, March, 7; 2004, Mar, 7; 2004, Aug, 1; 2004, Aug, 1

99245 Office consultation for a new or established patient, which requires these 3 key components: A comprehensive history; A comprehensive examination; and Medical decision making of high complexity. Counseling and/or coordination of care with other providers or agencies are provided consistent with the nature of the problem(s) and the patient's and/or family's needs. Usually, the presenting problem(s) are of moderate to high severity. Physicians typically spend 80 minutes face-to-face with the patient and/or family. ▣ ▣ ▣ ▣

◪ 5.33 ◪ 6.28 Global Days XXX

AMA: 2008, Jan, 10-25; 2007, Jan, 13-27; 2007, Jan, 13-27; 2007, Mar, 9-11; 2007, Apr, 11-12; 2007, Mar, 9-11; 2007, Apr, 11-12; 2007, March, 9-11; 2007, Jul, 1-4; 2007, April, 11-12; 2007, January, 13-27; 2006, Sep, 9-13; 2006, Sep, 9-13; 2006, Jun, 1-7; 2006, May, 16-20; 2006, Jun, 1-7; 2006, May, 16-20; 2006, June, 1-7; 2006, May, 1-9; 2006, September, 9-13; 2006, May, 16-20; 2006, May, 1-9; 2006, May, 1-9; 2005, Mar, 11-15; 2005, Mar, 11-15; 2005, Feb, 1-6; 2005, Dec, 9-11; 2005, Feb, 1-6; 2005, December, 9-11; 2005, February, 1-6; 2005, March, 11-15; 2005, May, 1-2; 2005, Dec, 9-11; 2005, May, 1-2; 2005, May, 1-2; 2004, Aug, 1; 2004, August, 1; 2004, March, 7; 2004, Aug, 1; 2004, Mar, 7; 2004, Mar, 7

99251 Inpatient consultation for a new or established patient, which requires these 3 key components: A problem focused history; A problem focused examination; and Straightforward medical decision making. Counseling and/or coordination of care with other providers or agencies are provided consistent with the nature of the problem(s) and the patient's and/or family's needs. Usually, the presenting problem(s) are self limited or minor. Physicians typically spend 20 minutes at the bedside and on the patient's hospital floor or unit. ▣ ▣ ▣ ▣

◪ 1.35 ◪ 1.35 Global Days XXX

AMA: 2008, Jan, 10-25; 2007, Jan, 13-27; 2007, Jan, 13-27; 2007, Mar, 9-11; 2007, Mar, 9-11; 2007, Jul, 1-4; 2007, March, 9-11; 2007, January, 13-27; 2006, May, 1-9; 2006, May, 1-9; 2006, May, 1-9; 2006, June, 1-7; 2006, May, 16-20; 2006, Jun, 1-7; 2006, Jun, 1-7; 2006, May, 16-20; 2006, May, 16-20; 2005, May, 1-2; 2005, December, 9-11; 2005, February, 1-6; 2005, May, 1-2; 2005, May, 1-2; 2005, Feb, 1-6; 2005, Feb, 1-6; 2005, Dec, 9-11; 2005, Dec, 9-11; 2004, Aug, 1; 2004, August, 1; 2004, Aug, 1

99252 Inpatient consultation for a new or established patient, which requires these 3 key components: An expanded problem focused history; An expanded problem focused examination; and Straightforward medical decision making. Counseling and/or coordination of care with other providers or agencies are provided consistent with the nature of the problem(s) and the patient's and/or family's needs. Usually, the presenting problem(s) are of low severity. Physicians typically spend 40 minutes at the bedside and on the patient's hospital floor or unit. ▣ ▣ ▣ ▣

◪ 2.10 ◪ 2.10 Global Days XXX

AMA: 2008, Jan, 10-25; 2007, Jan, 13-27; 2007, Jan, 13-27; 2007, Mar, 9-11; 2007, Mar, 9-11; 2007, January, 13-27; 2007, Jul, 1-4; 2007, March, 9-11; 2006, May, 1-9; 2006, May, 1-9; 2006, Jun, 1-7; 2006, May, 1-9; 2006, June, 1-7; 2006, May, 16-20; 2006, Jun, 1-7; 2006, May, 16-20; 2006, May, 16-20; 2005, Mar, 11-15; 2005, Mar, 11-15; 2005, Feb, 1-6; 2005, December, 9-11; 2005, February, 1-6; 2005, March, 11-15; 2005, May, 1-2; 2005, Feb, 1-6; 2005, Dec, 9-11; 2005, May, 1-2; 2005, May, 1-2; 2005, Dec, 9-11; 2004, Aug, 1; 2004, August, 1; 2004, Aug, 1

99253   Inpatient consultation for a new or established patient, which requires these 3 key components: A detailed history; A detailed examination; and Medical decision making of low complexity. Counseling and/or coordination of care with other providers or agencies are provided consistent with the nature of the problem(s) and the patient's and/or family's needs. Usually, the presenting problem(s) are of moderate severity. Physicians typically spend 55 minutes at the bedside and on the patient's hospital floor or unit.   C 80 ▢ P0

    3.18   3.18   Global Days XXX

    AMA: 2008, Jan, 10-25; 2007, Jan, 13-27; 2007, Jan, 13-27; 2007, Mar, 9-11; 2007, Mar, 9-11; 2007, January, 13-27; 2007, Jul, 1-4; 2007, March, 9-11; 2006, May, 16-20; 2006, May, 16-20; 2006, May, 1-9; 2006, May, 1-9; 2006, June, 1-7; 2006, May, 16-20; 2006, May, 1-9; 2006, Jun, 1-7; 2006, Jun, 1-7; 2005, May, 1-2; 2005, May, 1-2; 2005, Feb, 1-6; 2005, December, 9-11; 2005, February, 1-6; 2005, March, 11-15; 2005, May, 1-2; 2005, Feb, 1-6; 2005, Mar, 11-15; 2005, Dec, 9-11; 2005, Dec, 9-11; 2005, Mar, 11-15; 2004, Aug, 1; 2004, August, 1; 2004, Aug, 1

99254   Inpatient consultation for a new or established patient, which requires these 3 key components: A comprehensive history; A comprehensive examination; and Medical decision making of moderate complexity. Counseling and/or coordination of care with other providers or agencies are provided consistent with the nature of the problem(s) and the patient's and/or family's needs. Usually, the presenting problem(s) are of moderate to high severity. Physicians typically spend 80 minutes at the bedside and on the patient's hospital floor or unit.   C 80 ▢ P0

    4.59   4.59   Global Days XXX

    AMA: 2008, Jan, 10-25; 2007, Jan, 13-27; 2007, Jan, 13-27; 2007, Mar, 9-11; 2007, Mar, 9-11; 2007, January, 13-27; 2007, Jul, 1-4; 2007, March, 9-11; 2006, May, 1-9; 2006, May, 1-9; 2006, Jun, 1-7; 2006, June, 1-7; 2006, May, 16-20; 2006, May, 1-9; 2006, Jun, 1-7; 2006, May, 16-20; 2006, May, 16-20; 2005, May, 1-2; 2005, May, 1-2; 2005, Feb, 1-6; 2005, December, 9-11; 2005, February, 1-6; 2005, March, 11-15; 2005, May, 1-2; 2005, Feb, 1-6; 2005, Dec, 9-11; 2005, Mar, 11-15; 2005, Mar, 11-15; 2005, Dec, 9-11; 2004, Aug, 1; 2004, August, 1; 2004, Aug, 1

99255   Inpatient consultation for a new or established patient, which requires these 3 key components: A comprehensive history; A comprehensive examination; and Medical decision making of high complexity. Counseling and/or coordination of care with other providers or agencies are provided consistent with the nature of the problem(s) and the patient's and/or family's needs. Usually, the presenting problem(s) are of moderate to high severity. Physicians typically spend 110 minutes at the bedside and on the patient's hospital floor or unit.   C 80 ▢ P0

    5.60   5.60   Global Days XXX

    AMA: 2008, Jan, 10-25; 2007, Jan, 13-27; 2007, Jan, 13-27; 2007, Mar, 9-11; 2007, Mar, 9-11; 2007, January, 13-27; 2007, Jul, 1-4; 2007, March, 9-11; 2006, May, 16-20; 2006, May, 16-20; 2006, Jun, 1-7; 2006, May, 1-9; 2006, June, 1-7; 2006, May, 16-20; 2006, Jun, 1-7; 2006, May, 1-9; 2006, May, 1-9; 2005, May, 1-2; 2005, May, 1-2; 2005, Feb, 1-6; 2005, December, 9-11; 2005, February, 1-6; 2005, March, 11-15; 2005, May, 1-2; 2005, Feb, 1-6; 2005, Dec, 9-11; 2005, Mar, 11-15; 2005, Mar, 11-15; 2005, Dec, 9-11; 2004, Aug, 1; 2004, August, 1; 2004, Aug, 1

99281-99288 Emergency Department Visits

CMS 100-3,70.1   *Consultations with a Beneficiary's Family and Associates*
CMS 100-2,15,30   *Physician Services*
CMS 100-1,5,70   *Definition of Physician*
CMS 100-4,12,30.6.11 *Emergency Department Visits*

INCLUDES   any amount of time spent with the patient, which usually involves a series of encounters while the patient is in the emergency department
    care provided to new and established patients

EXCLUDES   *critical care services (99291-99292)*
    observation services (99217-99220, 99234-99236)

99281   Emergency department visit for the evaluation and management of a patient, which requires these 3 key components: A problem focused history; A problem focused examination; and Straightforward medical decision making. Counseling and/or coordination of care with other providers or agencies are provided consistent with the nature of the problem(s) and the patient's and/or family's needs. Usually, the presenting problem(s) are self limited or minor.   V 80 ▢ P0

    0.56   0.56   Global Days XXX

    AMA: 2008, Jan, 10-25; 2007, Jan, 13-27; 2007, Jan, 13-27; 2007, Mar, 9-11; 2007, Mar, 9-11; 2007, January, 13-27; 2007, Jul, 1-4; 2007, Dec, 10-179; 2007, March, 9-11; 2006, Feb, 16-18; 2006, Feb, 16-18; 2006, Dec, 14-15; 2006, December, 14-15; 2006, December, 14-15; 2006, February, 16-18; 2006, Dec, 14-15; 2006, Dec, 14-15; 2006, Dec, 14-15; 2005, Nov, 10-13; 2005, Nov, 10-13; 2005, Feb, 1-6; 2005, November, 10-13; 2005, February, 1-6; 2005, May, 1-2; 2005, May, 1-2; 2005, Feb, 1-6; 2005, May, 1-2; 2004, Mar, 7; 2004, March, 7; 2004, August, 1; 2004, Mar, 7; 2004, Aug, 1; 2004, Aug, 1

99282   Emergency department visit for the evaluation and management of a patient, which requires these 3 key components: An expanded problem focused history; An expanded problem focused examination; and Medical decision making of low complexity. Counseling and/or coordination of care with other providers or agencies are provided consistent with the nature of the problem(s) and the patient's and/or family's needs. Usually, the presenting problem(s) are of low to moderate severity.   V 80 ▢ P0

    1.09   1.09   Global Days XXX

    AMA: 2008, Jan, 10-25; 2007, Jan, 13-27; 2007, Jan, 13-27; 2007, Mar, 9-11; 2007, Mar, 9-11; 2007, January, 13-27; 2007, Jul, 1-4; 2007, Dec, 10-179; 2007, March, 9-11; 2006, Feb, 16-18; 2006, Feb, 16-18; 2006, Dec, 14-15; 2006, December, 14-15; 2006, December, 14-15; 2006, February, 16-18; 2006, Dec, 14-15; 2006, Dec, 14-15; 2006, Dec, 14-15; 2005, Feb, 1-6; 2005, Feb, 1-6; 2005, May, 1-2; 2005, November, 10-13; 2005, May, 1-2; 2005, February, 1-6; 2005, Nov, 10-13; 2005, May, 1-2; 2005, Nov, 10-13; 2004, Mar, 7; 2004, August, 1; 2004, March, 7; 2004, Mar, 7; 2004, Aug, 1; 2004, Aug, 1

● New Code   ▲ Revised Code   M Maternity Edit   Age Edit   A-V OPPS Status Indicator   Facility RVU   Non-Facility RVU
▢ CCI Comprehensive Code   50 Bilateral Procedure   + Add-on Indicator   Laboratory crosswalk   Radiology crosswalk

© 2008 Ingenix *(Blue Ink)*   CPT only © 2008 American Medical Association. All Rights Reserved. (Black Ink)   Medicare (Red Ink)   465

99283 Emergency department visit for the evaluation and management of a patient, which requires these 3 key components: An expanded problem focused history; An expanded problem focused examination; and Medical decision making of moderate complexity. Counseling and/or coordination of care with other providers or agencies are provided consistent with the nature of the problem(s) and the patient's and/or family's needs. Usually, the presenting problem(s) are of moderate severity.　　　　　　　　　　　V 80 ⌨ PQ

🔪 1.70 　 ⚖ 1.70 　Global Days XXX

AMA: 2008, Jan, 10-25; 2007, Jan, 13-27; 2007, Jan, 13-27; 2007, Mar, 9-11; 2007, January, 13-27; 2007, Mar, 9-11; 2007, March, 9-11; 2007, Dec, 10-179; 2007, Jul, 1-4; 2006, Feb, 16-18; 2006, Feb, 16-18; 2006, Dec, 14-15; 2006, Dec, 14-15; 2006, December, 14-15; 2006, December, 14-15; 2006, February, 16-18; 2006, Dec, 14-15; 2006, Dec, 14-15; 2005, Feb, 1-6; 2005, Feb, 1-6; 2005, Nov, 10-13; 2005, Mar, 11-15; 2005, Nov, 10-13; 2005, November, 10-13; 2005, February, 1-6; 2005, March, 11-15; 2005, May, 1-2; 2005, Mar, 11-15; 2005, May, 1-2; 2005, May, 1-2; 2004, Mar, 7; 2004, August, 1; 2004, March, 7; 2004, Mar, 7; 2004, Aug, 1; 2004, Aug, 1

99284 Emergency department visit for the evaluation and management of a patient, which requires these 3 key components: A detailed history; A detailed examination; and Medical decision making of moderate complexity. Counseling and/or coordination of care with other providers or agencies are provided consistent with the nature of the problem(s) and the patient's and/or family's needs. Usually, the presenting problem(s) are of high severity, and require urgent evaluation by the physician but do not pose an immediate significant threat to life or physiologic function.　　　　　03 80 ⌨ PQ

🔪 3.17 　 ⚖ 3.17 　Global Days XXX

AMA: 2008, Jan, 10-25; 2007, Jan, 13-27; 2007, Jan, 13-27; 2007, Mar, 9-11; 2007, January, 13-27; 2007, Mar, 9-11; 2007, March, 9-11; 2007, Dec, 10-179; 2007, Jul, 1-4; 2006, Feb, 16-18; 2006, Feb, 16-18; 2006, Dec, 14-15; 2006, Dec, 14-15; 2006, December, 14-15; 2006, December, 14-15; 2006, February, 16-18; 2006, Dec, 14-15; 2006, Dec, 14-15; 2005, May, 1-2; 2005, May, 1-2; 2005, Nov, 10-13; 2005, Mar, 11-15; 2005, Nov, 10-13; 2005, November, 10-13; 2005, February, 1-6; 2005, March, 11-15; 2005, May, 1-2; 2005, Mar, 11-15; 2005, Feb, 1-6; 2005, Feb, 1-6; 2004, Mar, 7; 2004, August, 1; 2004, March, 7; 2004, Mar, 7; 2004, Aug, 1; 2004, Aug, 1

99285 Emergency department visit for the evaluation and management of a patient, which requires these 3 key components within the constraints imposed by the urgency of the patient's clinical condition and/or mental status: A comprehensive history; A comprehensive examination; and Medical decision making of high complexity. Counseling and/or coordination of care with other providers or agencies are provided consistent with the nature of the problem(s) and the patient's and/or family's needs. Usually, the presenting problem(s) are of high severity and pose an immediate significant threat to life or physiologic function.　　　　　03 80 ⌨ PQ

🔪 4.72 　 ⚖ 4.72 　Global Days XXX

AMA: 2008, Jan, 10-25; 2007, Jan, 13-27; 2007, Jan, 13-27; 2007, Mar, 9-11; 2007, January, 13-27; 2007, Mar, 9-11; 2007, March, 9-11; 2007, Dec, 10-179; 2007, Jul, 1-4; 2006, Feb, 16-18; 2006, Feb, 16-18; 2006, Dec, 14-15; 2006, Dec, 14-15; 2006, December, 14-15; 2006, December, 14-15; 2006, February, 16-18; 2006, Dec, 14-15; 2006, Dec, 14-15; 2005, May, 1-2; 2005, May, 1-2; 2005, Nov, 10-13; 2005, Mar, 11-15; 2005, Nov, 10-13; 2005, November, 10-13; 2005, February, 1-6; 2005, March, 11-15; 2005, May, 1-2; 2005, Mar, 11-15; 2005, Feb, 1-6; 2005, Feb, 1-6; 2004, Aug, 1; 2004, August, 1; 2004, March, 7; 2004, Aug, 1; 2004, Mar, 7; 2004, Mar, 7

99288 Physician direction of emergency medical systems (EMS) emergency care, advanced life support　　　B

[INCLUDES]　management provided by an emergency/intensive care based physician via voice contact to ambulance/rescue staff for services such as heart monitoring and drug administration

🔪 0.00 　 ⚖ 0.00 　Global Days XXX

AMA: 2007, Mar, 9-11; 2007, Mar, 9-11; 2007, March, 9-11; 2007, Jul, 1-4; 2005, Feb, 1-6; 2005, Feb, 1-6; 2005, February, 1-6; 2005, May, 1-2; 2005, May, 1-2; 2005, May, 1-2

99289-99290 Critical Care Transport Age 24 Months or Younger

~~99289~~ ~~Critical care services delivered by a physician, face-to-face, during an interfacility transport of critically ill or critically injured pediatric patient; 24 months of age or less; first 30-74 minutes of hands on care during transport~~

99466 99466

~~99290~~ ~~each additional 30 minutes (List separately in addition to code for primary service)~~

See 99467

99291-99292 Critical Care Visits: Patients 25 Months of Age and Older

CMS *100-3,70.1* *Consultations with a Beneficiary's Family and Associates*
CMS *100-2,15,30* *Physician Services*
CMS *100-1,5,70* *Definition of Physician*
CMS *100-4,12,30.6.12* *Critical Care Visits*
CMS *100-4,12,30.6.9* *Hospital Visit and Critical Care on Same Day*

[INCLUDES] 30 minutes or more of direct care provided by the physician to a critically ill or injured patient, regardless of the location
all time spent exclusively with patient/family/caregivers on the nursing unit or elsewhere
blood gases (82800-82810)
chest films (71010-71020)
customary monitoring, blood gases
gastric intubation (43752, 91105)
includes physician presence during interfacility transfer for critically ill/injured patients over 24 months of age
measurement of cardiac output (93561-93562)
other computer stored information (99090)
outpatient critical care provided to neonates and pediatric patients up through 71 months of age
pulse oximetry (94760-94762)
transcutaneous pacing, temporary (92953)
venous access, arterial puncture (36000, 36410, 36415, 36591, 36600)
ventilation assistance and management, includes CPAP, CNP (94002-94004, 94660, 94662)

[EXCLUDES] *all services that are less than 30 minutes; report appropriate E/M code*
critical care services provided via remote real-time interactive videoconferencing (0188T, 0189T)
inpatient critical care services provided to neonates that are age 28 days or less (99468-99469)
other procedures not listed as included performed by the physician rendering critical care
physician presence during interfacility transfer for critically ill/injured patients under 24 months of age (99466, 99467)

Do not report activities performed outside of the unit or off the floor

99291 Critical care, evaluation and management of the critically ill or critically injured patient; first 30-74 minutes [93] [80] [□] [P0]
     🚑 5.88 ⚖ 7.04 **Global Days XXX**
     AMA: 2008, Jan, 10-25; 2008, Jul, 7-8&15; 2007, Jan, 13-27; 2007, Jan, 13-27; 2007, Mar, 9-11; 2007, Mar, 9-11; 2007, January, 13-27; 2007, Jul, 1-4; 2007, March, 9-11; 2006, May, 1-9; 2006, May, 1-9; 2006, Dec, 13; 2006, December, 13; 2006, May, 1-9; 2006, Dec, 13; 2006, Dec, 13; 2005, Feb, 1-6; 2005, Feb, 1-6; 2005, Nov, 10-13; 2005, November, 10-13; 2005, July, 13-16; 2005, February, 1-6; 2005, March, 11-15; 2005, May, 1-2; 2005, Nov, 10-13; 2005, Jul, 13-16; 2005, Mar, 11-15; 2005, Mar, 11-15; 2005, Jul, 13-16; 2005, May, 1-2; 2005, May, 1-2; 2004, Mar, 7; 2004, October, 14; 2004, August, 7; 2004, August, 10; 2004, March, 7; 2004, Mar, 7; 2004, Aug, 7; 2004, Aug, 7; 2004, Oct, 14; 2004, Oct, 14; 2004, Aug, 10; 2004, Aug, 10

+ **99292** each additional 30 minutes (List separately in addition to code for primary service) [N] [80] [□] [P0]
     Code first (99291)
     🚑 2.94 ⚖ 3.18 **Global Days ZZZ**
     AMA: 2008, Jan, 10-25; 2008, Jul, 7-8&15; 2007, Jan, 13-27; 2007, Jan, 13-27; 2007, Mar, 9-11; 2007, Mar, 9-11; 2007, January, 13-27; 2007, March, 9-11; 2007, Jul, 1-4; 2006, May, 1-9; 2006, May, 1-9; 2006, Dec, 13; 2006, Dec, 13; 2006, Dec, 13; 2006, December, 13; 2006, December, 13; 2006, May, 1-9; 2006, Dec, 13; 2005, Feb, 1-6; 2005, Feb, 1-6; 2005, Jul, 13-16; 2005, May, 1-2; 2005, Nov, 10-13; 2005, May, 1-2; 2005, Jul, 13-16; 2005, July, 13-16; 2005, November, 10-13; 2005, May, 1-2; 2005, February, 1-6; 2005, Nov, 10-13; 2004, Aug, 10; 2004, Aug, 10; 2004, Aug, 7; 2004, August, 10; 2004, August, 7; 2004, October, 14; 2004, Aug, 7; 2004, Oct, 14; 2004, Oct, 14

99293-99296 Critical Care for Neonate or Child

99293 ~~Initial inpatient pediatric critical care, per day, for the evaluation and management of a critically ill infant or young child, 29 days through 24 months of age~~
See 99471

99294 ~~Subsequent inpatient pediatric critical care, per day, for the evaluation and management of a critically ill infant or young child, 29 days through 24 months of age~~
See 99472

99295 ~~Initial inpatient neonatal critical care, per day, for the evaluation and management of a critically ill neonate, 28 days of age or less~~
See 99468

99296 ~~Subsequent inpatient neonatal critical care, per day, for the evaluation and management of a critically ill neonate, 28 days of age or less~~
See 99469

99298-99300 Intensive Care Low Birth Weight Infant

99298 ~~Subsequent intensive care, per day, for the evaluation and management of the recovering very low birth weight infant (present body weight less than 1500 g)~~
See 99478

99299 ~~Subsequent intensive care, per day, for the evaluation and management of the recovering low birth weight infant (present body weight of 1500-2500 g)~~
See 99479

99300 ~~Subsequent intensive care, per day, for the evaluation and management of the recovering infant (present body weight of 2501-5000 g)~~
See 99480

● New Code   ▲ Revised Code   Ⓜ Maternity Edit   🅐 Age Edit   🅐 🆅 OPPS Status Indicator   🚑 Facility RVU   ⚖ Non-Facility RVU
◻ CCI Comprehensive Code   🗿 Bilateral Procedure   + Add-on Indicator   ◼ Laboratory crosswalk   ◼ Radiology crosswalk

99304-99318 Nursing Facility Visits

CMS 100-4,12,30.6.9 *Swing BedVisits*
CMS 100-3,70.3 *Physician's OfficesWithin an Institution--"Incident-to" Provision*
CMS 100-3,70.2 *Consultation by a Podiatrist in a Skilled Nursing Facility*
CMS 100-3,70.1 *Consultations with a Beneficiary's Family and Associates*
CMS 100-2,15,30 *Physician Services*
CMS 100-1,5,70 *Definition of Physician*
CMS 100-4,12,30.6.13 *Nursing Facility Visits*

INCLUDES all E/M services provided by the admitting physican on the date of nursing facility admission in other locations (e.g, office, emergency department)

discharge services include all time spent by the physician for:

initial care, subsequent care, discharge, and yearly assessments

initial services include patient assessment and physician participation in developing a plan of care (99304-99306)

services provided to new and established patients in a nursing facility (skilled, intermediate, and long-term care facilities)

subsequent services include physician review of medical records, reassessment, review of test results (99307-99310)

EXCLUDES *care plan oversight services (99379-99380)*

99304 Initial nursing facility care, per day, for the evaluation and management of a patient, which requires these 3 key components: A detailed or comprehensive history; A detailed or comprehensive examination; and Medical decision making that is straightforward or of low complexity. Counseling and/or coordination of care with other providers or agencies are provided consistent with the nature of the problem(s) and the patient's and/or family's needs. Usually, the problem(s) requiring admission are of low severity. Physicians typically spend 25 minutes with the patient and/or family or caregiver. B 80 PQ

📖 2.22 ⚖ 2.22 Global Days XXX

AMA: 2007, Mar, 9-11; 2007, Mar, 9-11; 2007, Jul, 1-4; 2007, March, 9-11; 2006, Jun, 1-7; 2006, June, 1-7; 2006, Jun, 1-7

99305 Initial nursing facility care, per day, for the evaluation and management of a patient, which requires these 3 key components: A comprehensive history; A comprehensive examination; and Medical decision making of moderate complexity. Counseling and/or coordination of care with other providers or agencies are provided consistent with the nature of the problem(s) and the patient's and/or family's needs. Usually, the problem(s) requiring admission are of moderate severity. Physicians typically spend 35 minutes with the patient and/or family or caregiver. B 80 PQ

📖 3.10 ⚖ 3.10 Global Days XXX

AMA: 2007, Mar, 9-11; 2007, Mar, 9-11; 2007, Jul, 1-4; 2007, March, 9-11; 2006, Jun, 1-7; 2006, June, 1-7; 2006, Jun, 1-7

99306 Initial nursing facility care, per day, for the evaluation and management of a patient, which requires these 3 key components: A comprehensive history; A comprehensive examination; and Medical decision making of high complexity. Counseling and/or coordination of care with other providers or agencies are provided consistent with the nature of the problem(s) and the patient's and/or family's needs. Usually, the problem(s) requiring admission are of high severity. Physicians typically spend 45 minutes with the patient and/or family or caregiver. B 80 PQ

📖 3.98 ⚖ 3.98 Global Days XXX

AMA: 2007, Mar, 9-11; 2007, Mar, 9-11; 2007, Jul, 1-4; 2007, March, 9-11; 2006, Jun, 1-7; 2006, June, 1-7; 2006, Jun, 1-7

99307 Subsequent nursing facility care, per day, for the evaluation and management of a patient, which requires at least 2 of these 3 key components: A problem focused interval history; A problem focused examination; Straightforward medical decision making. Counseling and/or coordination of care with other providers or agencies are provided consistent with the nature of the problem(s) and the patient's and/or family's needs. Usually, the patient is stable, recovering, or improving. Physicians typically spend 10 minutes with the patient and/or family or caregiver. B 80 PQ

📖 1.10 ⚖ 1.10 Global Days XXX

AMA: 2008, Jan, 10-25; 2007, Mar, 9-11; 2007, Mar, 9-11; 2007, Jul, 1-4; 2007, March, 9-11; 2006, May, 1-9; 2006, May, 1-9; 2006, Jun, 1-7; 2006, June, 1-7; 2006, May, 16-20; 2006, May, 1-9; 2006, Jun, 1-7; 2006, May, 16-20; 2006, May, 16-20

99308 Subsequent nursing facility care, per day, for the evaluation and management of a patient, which requires at least 2 of these 3 key components: An expanded problem focused interval history; An expanded problem focused examination; Medical decision making of low complexity. Counseling and/or coordination of care with other providers or agencies are provided consistent with the nature of the problem(s) and the patient's and/or family's needs. Usually, the patient is responding inadequately to therapy or has developed a minor complication. Physicians typically spend 15 minutes with the patient and/or family or caregiver. B 80 PQ

📖 1.68 ⚖ 1.68 Global Days XXX

AMA: 2007, Mar, 9-11; 2007, Mar, 9-11; 2007, Jul, 1-4; 2007, March, 9-11; 2006, May, 16-20; 2006, May, 16-20; 2006, Jun, 1-7; 2006, June, 1-7; 2006, May, 16-20; 2006, May, 1-9; 2006, Jun, 1-7; 2006, May, 1-9; 2006, May, 1-9

99309 Subsequent nursing facility care, per day, for the evaluation and management of a patient, which requires at least 2 of these 3 key components: A detailed interval history; A detailed examination; Medical decision making of moderate complexity. Counseling and/or coordination of care with other providers or agencies are provided consistent with the nature of the problem(s) and the patient's and/or family's needs. Usually, the patient has developed a significant complication or a significant new problem. Physicians typically spend 25 minutes with the patient and/or family or caregiver. B 80 PQ

📖 2.23 ⚖ 2.23 Global Days XXX

AMA: 2007, Mar, 9-11; 2007, Mar, 9-11; 2007, Jul, 1-4; 2007, March, 9-11; 2006, May, 16-20; 2006, May, 16-20; 2006, May, 1-9; 2006, May, 1-9; 2006, June, 1-7; 2006, May, 16-20; 2006, May, 1-9; 2006, Jun, 1-7; 2006, Jun, 1-7

99310 Subsequent nursing facility care, per day, for the evaluation and management of a patient, which requires at least 2 of these 3 key components: A comprehensive interval history; A comprehensive examination; Medical decision making of high complexity. Counseling and/or coordination of care with other providers or agencies are provided consistent with the nature of the problem(s) and the patient's and/or family's needs. The patient may be unstable or may have developed a significant new problem requiring immediate physician attention. Physicians typically spend 35 minutes with the patient and/or family or caregiver. B 80 PQ

📖 3.29 ⚖ 3.29 Global Days XXX

AMA: 2008, Jan, 10-25; 2007, Mar, 9-11; 2007, Mar, 9-11; 2007, Jul, 1-4; 2007, March, 9-11; 2006, May, 1-9; 2006, May, 1-9; 2006, Jun, 1-7; 2006, May, 1-9; 2006, June, 1-7; 2006, May, 16-20; 2006, Jun, 1-7; 2006, May, 16-20; 2006, May, 16-20

99315   Nursing facility discharge day management; 30 minutes
          or less   B 80 ▢
              🖩 1.61   ⚖ 1.61 Global Days XXX
              AMA: 2008, Jan, 10-25; 2007, Jan, 13-27; 2007, Jan, 13-27; 2007,
              Mar, 9-11; 2007, March, 9-11; 2007, Jul, 1-4; 2007, January,
              13-27; 2007, Mar, 9-11; 2005, Feb, 1-6; 2005, February, 1-6; 2005,
              May, 1-2; 2005, Feb, 1-6; 2005, May, 1-2; 2005, May, 1-2

99316   more than 30 minutes   B 80 ▢
              🖩 2.10   ⚖ 2.10 Global Days XXX
              AMA: 2008, Jan, 10-25; 2007, Jan, 13-27; 2007, Jan, 13-27; 2007,
              Mar, 9-11; 2007, March, 9-11; 2007, Jul, 1-4; 2007, January,
              13-27; 2007, Mar, 9-11; 2005, May, 1-2; 2005, May, 1-2; 2005,
              February, 1-6; 2005, May, 1-2; 2005, Feb, 1-6; 2005, Feb, 1-6

99318   Evaluation and management of a patient involving an
          annual nursing facility assessment, which requires these
          3 key components: A detailed interval history; A
          comprehensive examination; and Medical decision making
          that is of low to moderate complexity. Counseling and/or
          coordination of care with other providers or agencies are
          provided consistent with the nature of the problem(s)
          and the patient's and/or family's needs. Usually, the
          patient is stable, recovering, or improving. Physicians
          typically spend 30 minutes with the patient and/or family
          or caregiver.   B 80
                  Do not report with the same date of service as
                              (99304-99316)
              🖩 2.32   ⚖ 2.32 Global Days XXX
              AMA: 2007, Mar, 9-11; 2007, Mar, 9-11; 2007, Jul, 1-4; 2007,
              March, 9-11; 2006, Jun, 1-7; 2006, June, 1-7; 2006, Jun, 1-7

99324-99337 Domiciliary Care, Rest Home, Assisted Living Visits

CMS *100-3,70.1   Consultations with a Beneficiary's Family and Associates*
CMS *100-4,12,30.6.14 Domiciliary Care, Rest Home, Assisted Living Visits*
[INCLUDES]   E/M services for patients residing in assisted living, domiciliary care,
              and rest homes where medical care is not included
              services provided to new patients or established patients
              (99324-99328, or 99334-99337)
[EXCLUDES]   *rest home/home care plan oversight services (99339-99340)*

99324   Domiciliary or rest home visit for the evaluation and
          management of a new patient, which requires these 3
          key components: A problem focused history; A problem
          focused examination; and Straightforward medical
          decision making. Counseling and/or coordination of care
          with other providers or agencies are provided consistent
          with the nature of the problem(s) and the patient's and/or
          family's needs. Usually, the presenting problem(s) are of
          low severity. Physicians typically spend 20 minutes with
          the patient and/or family or caregiver.   B 80 P0
              🖩 1.50   ⚖ 1.50 Global Days XXX
              AMA: 2007, Mar, 9-11; 2007, Mar, 9-11; 2007, Jul, 1-4; 2007,
              March, 9-11; 2006, Jun, 1-7; 2006, June, 1-7; 2006, Jun, 1-7

99325   Domiciliary or rest home visit for the evaluation and
          management of a new patient, which requires these 3
          key components: An expanded problem focused history;
          An expanded problem focused examination; and Medical
          decision making of low complexity. Counseling and/or
          coordination of care with other providers or agencies are
          provided consistent with the nature of the problem(s)
          and the patient's and/or family's needs. Usually, the
          presenting problem(s) are of moderate severity.
          Physicians typically spend 30 minutes with the patient
          and/or family or caregiver.   B 80 P0
              🖩 2.18   ⚖ 2.18 Global Days XXX
              AMA: 2007, Mar, 9-11; 2007, Mar, 9-11; 2007, Jul, 1-4; 2007,
              March, 9-11; 2006, Jun, 1-7; 2006, June, 1-7; 2006, Jun, 1-7

99326   Domiciliary or rest home visit for the evaluation and
          management of a new patient, which requires these 3
          key components: A detailed history; A detailed
          examination; and Medical decision making of moderate
          complexity. Counseling and/or coordination of care with
          other providers or agencies are provided consistent with
          the nature of the problem(s) and the patient's and/or
          family's needs. Usually, the presenting problem(s) are of
          moderate to high severity. Physicians typically spend 45
          minutes with the patient and/or family or
          caregiver.   B 80 P0
              🖩 3.59   ⚖ 3.59 Global Days XXX
              AMA: 2007, Mar, 9-11; 2007, Mar, 9-11; 2007, Jul, 1-4; 2007,
              March, 9-11; 2006, Jun, 1-7; 2006, June, 1-7; 2006, Jun, 1-7

99327   Domiciliary or rest home visit for the evaluation and
          management of a new patient, which requires these 3
          key components: A comprehensive history; A
          comprehensive examination; and Medical decision making
          of moderate complexity. Counseling and/or coordination
          of care with other providers or agencies are provided
          consistent with the nature of the problem(s) and the
          patient's and/or family's needs. Usually, the presenting
          problem(s) are of high severity. Physicians typically spend
          60 minutes with the patient and/or family or
          caregiver.   B 80 P0
              🖩 4.68   ⚖ 4.68 Global Days XXX
              AMA: 2007, Mar, 9-11; 2007, Mar, 9-11; 2007, Jul, 1-4; 2007,
              March, 9-11; 2006, Jun, 1-7; 2006, June, 1-7; 2006, Jun, 1-7

99328   and Medical decision making of high complexity.
          Counseling and/or coordination of care with other
          providers or agencies are provided consistent with
          the nature of the problem(s) and the patient's and/or
          family's needs. Usually, the patient is unstable or has
          developed a significant new problem requiring
          immediate physician attention. Physicians typically
          spend 75 minutes with the patient and/or family or
          caregiver.   B 80 P0
              🖩 5.51   ⚖ 5.51 Global Days XXX
              AMA: 2007, Mar, 9-11; 2007, Mar, 9-11; 2007, Jul, 1-4; 2007,
              March, 9-11; 2006, Jun, 1-7; 2006, June, 1-7; 2006, Jun, 1-7

99334   Domiciliary or rest home visit for the evaluation and
          management of an established patient, which requires
          at least 3 of these 3 key components: A problem focused
          interval history; A problem focused examination;
          Straightforward medical decision making. Counseling
          and/or coordination of care with other providers or
          agencies are provided consistent with the nature of the
          problem(s) and the patient's and/or family's needs.
          Usually, the presenting problem(s) are self-limited or
          minor. Physicians typically spend 15 minutes with the
          patient and/or family or caregiver.   B 80 P0
              🖩 1.54   ⚖ 1.54 Global Days XXX
              AMA: 2007, Mar, 9-11; 2007, Mar, 9-11; 2007, Jul, 1-4; 2007,
              March, 9-11; 2006, Jun, 1-7; 2006, June, 1-7; 2006, Jun, 1-7

99335   Domiciliary or rest home visit for the evaluation and
          management of an established patient, which requires
          at least 2 of these 3 key components: An expanded
          problem focused interval history; An expanded problem
          focused examination; Medical decision making of low
          complexity. Counseling and/or coordination of care with
          other providers or agencies are provided consistent with
          the nature of the problem(s) and the patient's and/or
          family's needs. Usually, the presenting problem(s) are of
          low to moderate severity. Physicians typically spend 25
          minutes with the patient and/or family or
          caregiver.   B 80 P0
              🖩 2.38   ⚖ 2.38 Global Days XXX
              AMA: 2007, Mar, 9-11; 2007, Mar, 9-11; 2007, Jul, 1-4; 2007,
              March, 9-11; 2006, Jun, 1-7; 2006, June, 1-7; 2006, Jun, 1-7

● New Code   ▲ Revised Code   Ⓜ Maternity Edit   Ⓐ Age Edit   Ⓐ Ⓣ OPPS Status Indicator   🖩 Facility RVU   ⚖ Non-Facility RVU
▢ CCI Comprehensive Code   50 Bilateral Procedure   + Add-on Indicator   ▣ Laboratory crosswalk   ▣ Radiology crosswalk

99336   Domiciliary or rest home visit for the evaluation and management of an established patient, which requires at least 2 of these 3 key components: A detailed interval history; A detailed examination; Medical decision making of moderate complexity. Counseling and/or coordination of care with other providers or agencies are provided consistent with the nature of the problem(s) and the patient's and/or family's needs. Usually, the presenting problem(s) are of moderate to high severity. Physicians typically spend 40 minutes with the patient and/or family or caregiver.   ⬛ 🔲 🔲

    💳 3.35   ✂ 3.35   **Global Days XXX**

     AMA: 2007, Mar, 9-11; 2007, Mar, 9-11; 2007, Jul, 1-4; 2007, March, 9-11; 2006, Jun, 1-7; 2006, June, 1-7; 2006, Jun, 1-7

99337   Domiciliary or rest home visit for the evaluation and management of an established patient, which requires at least 2 of these 3 key components: A comprehensive interval history; A comprehensive examination; Medical decision making of moderate to high complexity. Counseling and/or coordination of care with other providers or agencies are provided consistent with the nature of the problem(s) and the patient's and/or family's needs. Usually, the presenting problem(s) are of moderate to high severity. The patient may be unstable or may have developed a significant new problem requiring immediate physician attention. Physicians typically spend 60 minutes with the patient and/or family or caregiver.   ⬛ 🔲 🔲

    💳 4.81   ✂ 4.81   **Global Days XXX**

     AMA: 2007, Mar, 9-11; 2007, Mar, 9-11; 2007, Jul, 1-4; 2007, March, 9-11; 2006, Jun, 1-7; 2006, June, 1-7; 2006, Jun, 1-7

99339-99340 Care Plan Oversight: Rest Home, Domiciliary Care, Assisted Living, and Home

CMS *100-4,12,30.6.14 Domiciliary Care, Rest Home, Assisted Living Visits*

INCLUDES   care plan oversight for patients residing in assisted living, domiciliary care, private residences, and rest homes

EXCLUDES   *care plan oversight services furnished under a home health agency, nursing facility, or hospice (99374-99380)*

Do not report with (98966-98969, 99441-99444)

99339   Individual physician supervision of a patient (patient not present) in home, domiciliary or rest home (eg, assisted living facility) requiring complex and multidisciplinary care modalities involving regular physician development and/or revision of care plans, review of subsequent reports of patient status, review of related laboratory and other studies, communication (including telephone calls) for purposes of assessment or care decisions with health care professional(s), family member(s), surrogate decision maker(s) (eg, legal guardian) and/or key caregiver(s) involved in patient's care, integration of new information into the medical treatment plan and/or adjustment of medical therapy, within a calendar month; 15-29 minutes   ⬛

    Do not report with time peroid reported for (98966-98969, 99441-99444)

    💳 2.05   ✂ 2.05   **Global Days XXX**

     AMA: 2008, Mar, 6-7; 2008, Sep, 3-4; 2007, Mar, 9-11; 2007, Mar, 9-11; 2007, Apr, 3-6; 2007, April, 3-6; 2007, Jul, 1-4; 2007, March, 9-11; 2007, Apr, 3-6; 2006, Dec, 4-7; 2006, December, 4-7; 2006, December, 4-7; 2006, Dec, 4-7; 2006, Dec, 4-7; 2006, Dec, 4-7

99340   30 minutes or more   ⬛

    Do not report with time peroid reported for (98966-98969, 99441-99444)

    💳 2.86   ✂ 2.86   **Global Days XXX**

     AMA: 2008, Mar, 6-7; 2008, Sep, 3-4; 2007, Mar, 9-11; 2007, Mar, 9-11; 2007, Apr, 3-6; 2007, April, 3-6; 2007, Jul, 1-4; 2007, March, 9-11; 2007, Apr, 3-6; 2006, Dec, 4-7; 2006, December, 4-7; 2006, December, 4-7; 2006, Dec, 4-7; 2006, Dec, 4-7; 2006, Dec, 4-7

99341-99350 Home Visits

CMS *100-4,12,30.6.14.1 Home Visits*

INCLUDES   services for a new patient or an established patient (99341-99345, or 99347-99350)

           services provided to a patient in a private home

EXCLUDES   *services provided to patients under home health agency or hospice care (99374-99378)*

99341   Home visit for the evaluation and management of a new patient, which requires these 3 key components: A problem focused history; A problem focused examination; and Straightforward medical decision making. Counseling and/or coordination of care with other providers or agencies are provided consistent with the nature of the problem(s) and the patient's and/or family's needs. Usually, the presenting problem(s) are of low severity. Physicians typically spend 20 minutes face-to-face with the patient and/or family.   ⬛ 🔲 🔲 🔲

    💳 1.50   ✂ 1.50   **Global Days XXX**

     AMA: 2007, Jan, 28-31; 2007, Jan, 28-31; 2007, Mar, 9-11; 2007, January, 28-31; 2007, Mar, 9-11; 2007, March, 9-11; 2007, Jul, 1-4; 2006, Jan, 2-4,48; 2006, Jan, 2-4,48; 2006, January, 2-4,48; 2005, Feb, 1-6; 2005, May, 1-2; 2005, February, 1-6; 2005, Feb, 1-6; 2005, May, 1-2; 2005, May, 1-2; 2004, Aug, 1; 2004, Aug, 1; 2004, August, 1

99342   Home visit for the evaluation and management of a new patient, which requires these 3 key components: An expanded problem focused history; An expanded problem focused examination; and Medical decision making of low complexity. Counseling and/or coordination of care with other providers or agencies are provided consistent with the nature of the problem(s) and the patient's and/or family's needs. Usually, the presenting problem(s) are of moderate severity. Physicians typically spend 30 minutes face-to-face with the patient and/or family.   ⬛ 🔲 🔲 🔲

    💳 2.18   ✂ 2.18   **Global Days XXX**

     AMA: 2007, Jan, 28-31; 2007, Jan, 28-31; 2007, Mar, 9-11; 2007, January, 28-31; 2007, Mar, 9-11; 2007, March, 9-11; 2007, Jul, 1-4; 2006, Jan, 2-4,48; 2006, Jan, 2-4,48; 2006, January, 2-4,48; 2005, May, 1-2; 2005, February, 1-6; 2005, May, 1-2; 2005, May, 1-2; 2005, Feb, 1-6; 2005, Feb, 1-6; 2004, Aug, 1; 2004, Aug, 1; 2004, August, 1

99343   Home visit for the evaluation and management of a new patient, which requires these 3 key components: A detailed history; A detailed examination; and Medical decision making of moderate complexity. Counseling and/or coordination of care with other providers or agencies are provided consistent with the nature of the problem(s) and the patient's and/or family's needs. Usually, the presenting problem(s) are of moderate to high severity. Physicians typically spend 45 minutes face-to-face with the patient and/or family.   ⬛ 🔲 🔲 🔲

    💳 3.50   ✂ 3.50   **Global Days XXX**

     AMA: 2007, Jan, 28-31; 2007, Jan, 28-31; 2007, Mar, 9-11; 2007, January, 28-31; 2007, Mar, 9-11; 2007, March, 9-11; 2007, Jul, 1-4; 2006, Jan, 2-4,48; 2006, Jan, 2-4,48; 2006, January, 2-4,48; 2005, Feb, 1-6; 2005, May, 1-2; 2005, February, 1-6; 2005, Feb, 1-6; 2005, May, 1-2; 2005, May, 1-2; 2004, Aug, 1; 2004, Aug, 1; 2004, August, 1

99344   Home visit for the evaluation and management of a new patient, which requires these 3 key components: A comprehensive history; A comprehensive examination; and Medical decision making of moderate complexity. Counseling and/or coordination of care with other providers or agencies are provided consistent with the nature of the problem(s) and the patient's and/or family's needs. Usually, the presenting problem(s) are of high severity. Physicians typically spend 60 minutes face-to-face with the patient and/or family.   B 80 ☐ P0

     🔌 4.59   ᨏ 4.59   Global Days XXX

     AMA: 2007, Jan, 28-31; 2007, Jan, 28-31; 2007, Mar, 9-11; 2007, January, 28-31; 2007, Mar, 9-11; 2007, March, 9-11; 2007, Jul, 1-4; 2006, Jan, 2-4,48; 2006, Jan, 2-4,48; 2006, January, 2-4,48; 2005, May, 1-2; 2005, May, 1-2; 2005, February, 1-6; 2005, May, 1-2; 2005, Feb, 1-6; 2005, Feb, 1-6; 2004, Aug, 1; 2004, Aug, 1; 2004, August, 1

99345   and Medical decision making of high complexity. Counseling and/or coordination of care with other providers or agencies are provided consistent with the nature of the problem(s) and the patient's and/or family's needs. Usually, the patient is unstable or has developed a significant new problem requiring immediate physician attention. Physicians typically spend 75 minutes face-to-face with the patient and/or family.   B 80 ☐ P0

     🔌 5.52   ᨏ 5.52   Global Days XXX

     AMA: 2007, Jan, 28-31; 2007, Jan, 28-31; 2007, Mar, 9-11; 2007, January, 28-31; 2007, Mar, 9-11; 2007, March, 9-11; 2007, Jul, 1-4; 2006, Jan, 2-4,48; 2006, Jan, 2-4,48; 2006, January, 2-4,48; 2005, Feb, 1-6; 2005, May, 1-2; 2005, February, 1-6; 2005, Feb, 1-6; 2005, May, 1-2; 2005, May, 1-2; 2004, Aug, 1; 2004, Aug, 1; 2004, August, 1

99347   Home visit for the evaluation and management of an established patient, which requires at least 2 of these 3 key components: A problem focused interval history; A problem focused examination; Straightforward medical decision making. Counseling and/or coordination of care with other providers or agencies are provided consistent with the nature of the problem(s) and the patient's and/or family's needs. Usually, the presenting problem(s) are self limited or minor. Physicians typically spend 15 minutes face-to-face with the patient and/or family.   B 80 ☐ P0

     🔌 1.46   ᨏ 1.46   Global Days XXX

     AMA: 2007, Jan, 28-31; 2007, Jan, 28-31; 2007, Mar, 9-11; 2007, January, 28-31; 2007, Mar, 9-11; 2007, March, 9-11; 2007, Jul, 1-4; 2006, Jan, 2-4,48; 2006, Jan, 2-4,48; 2006, January, 2-4,48; 2005, Feb, 1-6; 2005, May, 1-2; 2005, February, 1-6; 2005, Feb, 1-6; 2005, May, 1-2; 2005, May, 1-2; 2004, Aug, 1; 2004, Aug, 1; 2004, August, 1

99348   Home visit for the evaluation and management of an established patient, which requires at least 2 of these 3 key components: An expanded problem focused interval history; An expanded problem focused examination; Medical decision making of low complexity. Counseling and/or coordination of care with other providers or agencies are provided consistent with the nature of the problem(s) and the patient's and/or family's needs. Usually, the presenting problem(s) are of low to moderate severity. Physicians typically spend 25 minutes face-to-face with the patient and/or family.   B 80 ☐ P0

     🔌 2.20   ᨏ 2.20   Global Days XXX

     AMA: 2007, Jan, 28-31; 2007, Jan, 28-31; 2007, Mar, 9-11; 2007, January, 28-31; 2007, Mar, 9-11; 2007, March, 9-11; 2007, Jul, 1-4; 2006, Jan, 2-4,48; 2006, Jan, 2-4,48; 2006, January, 2-4,48; 2005, May, 1-2; 2005, May, 1-2; 2005, February, 1-6; 2005, May, 1-2; 2005, Feb, 1-6; 2005, Feb, 1-6; 2004, Aug, 1; 2004, Aug, 1; 2004, August, 1

99349   Home visit for the evaluation and management of an established patient, which requires at least 2 of these 3 key components: A detailed interval history; A detailed examination; Medical decision making of moderate complexity. Counseling and/or coordination of care with other providers or agencies are provided consistent with the nature of the problem(s) and the patient's and/or family's needs. Usually, the presenting problem(s) are moderate to high severity. Physicians typically spend 40 minutes face-to-face with the patient and/or family.   B 80 ☐ P0

     🔌 3.20   ᨏ 3.20   Global Days XXX

     AMA: 2007, Jan, 28-31; 2007, Jan, 28-31; 2007, Mar, 9-11; 2007, January, 28-31; 2007, Mar, 9-11; 2007, March, 9-11; 2007, Jul, 1-4; 2006, Jan, 2-4,48; 2006, Jan, 2-4,48; 2006, January, 2-4,48; 2005, May, 1-2; 2005, May, 1-2; 2005, February, 1-6; 2005, May, 1-2; 2005, Feb, 1-6; 2005, Feb, 1-6; 2004, Aug, 1; 2004, Aug, 1; 2004, August, 1

99350   Home visit for the evaluation and management of an established patient, which requires at least 2 of these 3 key components: A comprehensive interval history; A comprehensive examination; Medical decision making of moderate to high complexity. Counseling and/or coordination of care with other providers or agencies are provided consistent with the nature of the problem(s) and the patient's and/or family's needs. Usually, the presenting problem(s) are of moderate to high severity. The patient may be unstable or may have developed a significant new problem requiring immediate physician attention. Physicians typically spend 60 minutes face-to-face with the patient and/or family.   B 80 ☐ P0

     🔌 4.46   ᨏ 4.46   Global Days XXX

     AMA: 2007, Jan, 28-31; 2007, Jan, 28-31; 2007, Mar, 9-11; 2007, January, 28-31; 2007, Mar, 9-11; 2007, March, 9-11; 2007, Jul, 1-4; 2006, Jan, 2-4,48; 2006, Jan, 2-4,48; 2006, January, 2-4,48; 2005, May, 1-2; 2005, May, 1-2; 2005, February, 1-6; 2005, May, 1-2; 2005, Feb, 1-6; 2005, Feb, 1-6; 2004, Aug, 1; 2004, Aug, 1; 2004, August, 1

99354-99359 Prolonged Services Outside Customary Services

CMS *100-2,15,30*   *Physician Services*
CMS *100-1,5,70*   *Definition of Physician*
CMS *100-4,12,30.6.15.2 Prolonged Services Without Face to Face Service*
CMS *100-4,12,30.6.15.1 Prolonged Services With Direct Face-to-Face Patient Contact*
CMS *100-4,12,30.6.15 Extended Services Outside Customary Services*
[INCLUDES]   personal contact with the patient (99354-99357)

     services provided prior to and after personal contact with the patient (99358, 99359)

     services that extend beyond the customary service provided in the inpatient or outpatient setting

     time spent providing prolonged services on a date of service, even when the time is not continuous

Do not report any service less than 30 minutes
Do not report any service that fails to extend into the next time period by 15 minutes or more

+   ▲   **99354**   Prolonged physician service in the office or other outpatient setting requiring direct (face-to-face) patient contact beyond the usual service; first hour (List separately in addition to code for office or other outpatient Evaluation and Management service)   N 80 ☐

     Code first (90809, 90815, 99201-99215, 99241-99245, 99324-99337, 99341-99350)

     🔌 2.41   ᨏ 2.55   Global Days ZZZ

     AMA: 2008, Jun, 12&15; 2008, Sep, 3-4; 2007, Mar, 9-11; 2007, Mar, 9-11; 2007, Jul, 1-4; 2007, March, 9-11; 2005, May, 1-2; 2005, May, 1-2; 2005, Nov, 10-13; 2005, February, 1-6; 2005, November, 10-13; 2005, May, 1-2; 2005, Nov, 10-13; 2005, Feb, 1-6; 2005, Feb, 1-6

● New Code   ▲ Revised Code   Ⓜ Maternity Edit   Ⓐ Age Edit   Ⓐ Ⓨ OPPS Status Indicator   🔌 Facility RVU   ᨏ Non-Facility RVU

☐ CCI Comprehensive Code   50 Bilateral Procedure   + Add-on Indicator   Ⓢ Laboratory crosswalk   ⊞ Radiology crosswalk

Evaluation and Management

99355 — 99364

+ ▲ **99355** each additional 30 minutes (List separately in addition to code for prolonged physician service) Ⓝ 🔢
  Code first (99354)
  📖 2.38   ✂ 2.52   **Global Days ZZZ**
  AMA: 2008, Jun, 12&15; 2008, Sep, 3-4; 2007, Mar, 9-11; 2007, Mar, 9-11; 2007, Jul, 1-4; 2007, March, 9-11; 2005, Feb, 1-6; 2005, Feb, 1-6; 2005, Nov, 10-13; 2005, February, 1-6; 2005, November, 10-13; 2005, May, 1-2; 2005, Nov, 10-13; 2005, May, 1-2; 2005, May, 1-2

+ ▲ **99356** Prolonged physician service in the inpatient setting, requiring unit/floor time beyond the usual service; first hour (List separately in addition to code for inpatient Evaluation and Management service) Ⓒ 🔢 🖥
  Code first (90822, 90829, 99221-99233, 99251-99255, 99304-99310)
  📖 2.32   ✂ 2.32   **Global Days ZZZ**
  AMA: 2008, Jun, 12&15; 2008, Sep, 3-4; 2007, Mar, 9-11; 2007, Mar, 9-11; 2007, Jul, 1-4; 2007, March, 9-11; 2005, Feb, 1-6; 2005, Feb, 1-6; 2005, Nov, 10-13; 2005, February, 1-6; 2005, November, 10-13; 2005, May, 1-2; 2005, Nov, 10-13; 2005, May, 1-2; 2005, May, 1-2

+ ▲ **99357** each additional 30 minutes (List separately in addition to code for prolonged physician service) Ⓒ 🔢 🖥
  Code first (99356)
  📖 2.34   ✂ 2.34   **Global Days ZZZ**
  AMA: 2008, Jun, 12&15; 2008, Sep, 3-4; 2007, Mar, 9-11; 2007, Mar, 9-11; 2007, Jul, 1-4; 2007, March, 9-11; 2005, May, 1-2; 2005, May, 1-2; 2005, Nov, 10-13; 2005, February, 1-6; 2005, November, 10-13; 2005, May, 1-2; 2005, Nov, 10-13; 2005, Feb, 1-6; 2005, Feb, 1-6

+ **99358** Prolonged evaluation and management service before and/or after direct (face-to-face) patient care (eg, review of extensive records and tests, communication with other professionals and/or the patient/family); first hour (List separately in addition to code(s) for other physician service(s) and/or inpatient or outpatient Evaluation and Management service) Ⓝ
  EXCLUDES   *telephone evaluation and management services (99441-99443)*
  📖 2.93   ✂ 2.93   **Global Days ZZZ**
  AMA: 2008, Jun, 12&15; 2008, Sep, 3-4; 2007, Mar, 9-11; 2007, Mar, 9-11; 2007, Jul, 1-4; 2007, March, 9-11; 2005, May, 1-2; 2005, May, 1-2; 2005, Feb, 1-6; 2005, February, 1-6; 2005, November, 10-13; 2005, May, 1-2; 2005, Feb, 1-6; 2005, Nov, 10-13; 2005, Nov, 10-13

+ **99359** each additional 30 minutes (List separately in addition to code for prolonged physician service) Ⓝ
  EXCLUDES   *telephone evaluation and management services (99441-99443)*
  Code first (99358)
  📖 1.41   ✂ 1.41   **Global Days ZZZ**
  AMA: 2008, Jun, 12&15; 2008, Sep, 3-4; 2007, Mar, 9-11; 2007, Mar, 9-11; 2007, Jul, 1-4; 2007, March, 9-11; 2005, May, 1-2; 2005, May, 1-2; 2005, Feb, 1-6; 2005, February, 1-6; 2005, November, 10-13; 2005, May, 1-2; 2005, Feb, 1-6; 2005, Nov, 10-13; 2005, Nov, 10-13

99360 Standby Services

CMS *100-4,12,30.6.15.3 Standby Services*

INCLUDES   services requested by another physician that involve no direct pateint contact

EXCLUDES   *history/examination of normal newborn (99460-99461, 99463)*
less than 30 minutes of standby time
oncall services ordered by the hospital (99026, 99027)
resuscitation of newborn (99465)

Do not report with (99464)

99360 Physician standby service, requiring prolonged physician attendance, each 30 minutes (eg, operative standby, standby for frozen section, for cesarean/high risk delivery, for monitoring EEG) Ⓑ 🖥
  EXCLUDES   *hospital mandated on call services (99026-99027)*
  Code also as appropriate (99460, 99465)
  Do not report with (99464)
  📖 1.65   ✂ 1.65   **Global Days XXX**
  AMA: 2008, Jan, 10-25; 2008, Mar, 14-15; 2007, Jan, 13-27; 2007, Jan, 13-27; 2007, Mar, 9-11; 2007, January, 13-27; 2007, Mar, 9-11; 2007, March, 9-11; 2007, Jul, 1-4; 2006, Dec, 10-12; 2006, Dec, 10-12; 2006, Dec, 10-12; 2006, December, 10-12; 2006, December, 10-12; 2006, December, 10-12; 2006, December, 10-12; 2006, Dec, 10-12; 2006, Dec, 10-12; 2006, Dec, 10-12; 2006, Dec, 10-12; 2006, Dec, 10-12; 2005, May, 1-2; 2005, November, 10-13; 2005, February, 1-6; 2005, May, 1-2; 2005, May, 1-2; 2005, Nov, 10-13; 2005, Nov, 10-13; 2005, Feb, 1-6; 2005, Feb, 1-6; 2004, Aug, 7; 2004, August, 7; 2004, Aug, 7

99363-99364 Supervision of Warfarin Therapy

INCLUDES   services provided on an outpatient basis only
supervision of therapy with warfarin: ordering, dosage adjustments, analysis of International Normalized Ration (INR) tests, patient discussion

EXCLUDES   *initial services provided/continued in the hospital or in observation: new period of subsequent therapy starts with discharge (99364)*
services provided for less than 60 uninterrupted days
services that fail to meet the required criteria (e.g., at least 8 INR tests/initial 90 days; 3 INR tests/each following 90 days
warfarin therapy supervision accomplished online or via telephone contact (98969, 99444)

Do not report with (99217-99239, 99291-99292, 99304-99318, 99471-99480)

99363 Anticoagulant management for an outpatient taking warfarin, physician review and interpretation of International Normalized Ratio (INR) testing, patient instructions, dosage adjustment (as needed), and ordering of additional tests; initial 90 days of therapy (must include a minimum of 8 INR measurements) Ⓑ
  📖 2.27   ✂ 3.28   **Global Days XXX**
  AMA: 2008, Mar, 6-7; 2007, Mar, 9-11; 2007, Mar, 9-11; 2007, March, 9-11; 2007, Jul, 1-4

99364 each subsequent 90 days of therapy (must include a minimum of 3 INR measurements) Ⓑ
  📖 0.88   ✂ 1.14   **Global Days XXX**
  AMA: 2008, Mar, 6-7; 2007, Mar, 9-11; 2007, Mar, 9-11; 2007, March, 9-11; 2007, Jul, 1-4

99366-99368 Interdisciplinary Conferences

CMS 100-4,11,40.1.3   *Attending Physician Services Under Hospice*
CMS 100-2,15,30   *Physician Services*
CMS 100-1,5,70   *Definition of Physician*

INCLUDES   documentation of participation, contribution, and recommendations of the conference
face-to-face participation by minimum of three qualified people from different specialties or disciplines
only participants who have performed face-to-face evaluations or direct treatment to the patient within the previous 60 days
start of the review of an individual patient and ends at conclusion of review

EXCLUDES   *conferences of less than 30 minutes (not reportable)*
more than one individual from the same specialty at the same encounter
time spent record keeping or writing a report.

99366   **Medical team conference with interdisciplinary team of health care professionals, face-to-face with patient and/or family, 30 minutes or more, participation by nonphysician qualified health care professional**   N
   INCLUDES   team conferences of 30 minutes or more
   EXCLUDES   *team conferences by a physician with patient or family present (99201-99499)*
   1.15   1.17   Global Days XXX
   AMA: 2008, Jun, 14-15; 2008, Sep, 3-4

99367   **Medical team conference with interdisciplinary team of health care professionals, patient and/or family not present, 30 minutes or more; participation by physician**   N
   INCLUDES   team conferences of 30 minutes or more
   1.52   1.52   Global Days XXX
   AMA: 2008, Sep, 3-4

99368   **participation by nonphysician qualified health care professional**   N
   INCLUDES   team conferences of 30 minutes or more
   0.99   0.99   Global Days XXX
   AMA: 2008, Jun, 14-15; 2008, Sep, 3-4

99374-99380 Care Plan Oversight: Patient Under Care of HHA, Hospice, or Nursing Facility

CMS 100-4,11,40.1.3.1 *CPO Services with Hospice Care*
CMS 100-4,12,180.1   *Billing for Care Plan Oversight (CPO)*
CMS 100-4,12,180   *Payment of Care Plan Oversight (CPO)*

INCLUDES   analysis of reports, diagnostic tests, treatment plans
discussions with other health care providers, outside of the practice, involved in the patient's care
establishment of and revisions to care plans within a 30-day period
payment to one physician per month for covered care plan oversight services (must be the same one who signed the plan of care)

EXCLUDES   *care plan oversight services provided in assisted living, domiciliary care, or private residence, not under care of a home health agency or hospice (99339, 99340)*
routine postoperative care provided during a global surgery period
time discussing treatment with patient and/or caregivers

Code also office/outpatient visits, hospital, home, nursing facility, domiciliary, or non-face-to-face services
Do not report with (98966-98969, 99441-99444)

99374   **Physician supervision of a patient under care of home health agency (patient not present) in home, domiciliary or equivalent environment (eg, Alzheimer's facility) requiring complex and multidisciplinary care modalities involving regular physician development and/or revision of care plans, review of subsequent reports of patient status, review of related laboratory and other studies, communication (including telephone calls) for purposes of assessment or care decisions with health care professional(s), family member(s), surrogate decision maker(s) (eg, legal guardian) and/or key caregiver(s) involved in patient's care, integration of new information into the medical treatment plan and/or adjustment of medical therapy, within a calendar month; 15-29 minutes**   B
   1.53   1.84   Global Days XXX
   AMA: 2008, Mar, 6-7; 2008, Sep, 3-4; 2007, Mar, 9-11; 2007, Mar, 9-11; 2007, Apr, 3-6; 2007, March, 9-11; 2007, Apr, 3-6; 2007, April, 3-6; 2007, Jul, 1-4; 2006, Dec, 4-7; 2006, Dec, 4-7; 2006, Dec, 4-7; 2006, Dec, 4-7; 2006, December, 4-7; 2006, December, 4-7; 2005, Feb, 1-6; 2005, Feb, 1-6; 2005, May, 1-2; 2005, February, 1-6; 2005, May, 1-2; 2005, May, 1-2

99375   **30 minutes or more**   E
   2.62   2.91   Global Days XXX
   AMA: 2008, Mar, 6-7; 2008, Sep, 3-4; 2007, Mar, 9-11; 2007, Mar, 9-11; 2007, Apr, 3-6; 2007, March, 9-11; 2007, Apr, 3-6; 2007, April, 3-6; 2007, Jul, 1-4; 2006, Dec, 4-7; 2006, Dec, 4-7; 2006, Dec, 4-7; 2006, Dec, 4-7; 2006, December, 4-7; 2006, December, 4-7; 2005, Feb, 1-6; 2005, Feb, 1-6; 2005, May, 1-2; 2005, February, 1-6; 2005, May, 1-2; 2005, May, 1-2

Evaluation and Management

99377 — 99387

99377 Physician supervision of a hospice patient (patient not present) requiring complex and multidisciplinary care modalities involving regular physician development and/or revision of care plans, review of subsequent reports of patient status, review of related laboratory and other studies, communication (including telephone calls) for purposes of assessment or care decisions with health care professional(s), family member(s), surrogate decision maker(s) (eg, legal guardian) and/or key caregiver(s) involved in patient's care, integration of new information into the medical treatment plan and/or adjustment of medical therapy, within a calendar month; 15-29 minutes   B

    📖 1.53 🔪 1.84 **Global Days XXX**
    AMA: 2008, Mar, 6-7; 2008, Sep, 3-4; 2007, Mar, 9-11; 2007, Mar, 9-11; 2007, Apr, 3-6; 2007, March, 9-11; 2007, Apr, 3-6; 2007, April, 3-6; 2007, Jul, 1-4; 2006, Dec, 4-7; 2006, Dec, 4-7; 2006, Dec, 4-7; 2006, Dec, 4-7; 2006, December, 4-7; 2006, December, 4-7; 2005, May, 1-2; 2005, May, 1-2; 2005, February, 1-6; 2005, May, 1-2; 2005, Feb, 1-6; 2005, Feb, 1-6

99378 30 minutes or more   E

    📖 2.72 🔪 3.01 **Global Days XXX**
    AMA: 2008, Mar, 6-7; 2008, Sep, 3-4; 2007, Mar, 9-11; 2007, Mar, 9-11; 2007, Apr, 3-6; 2007, March, 9-11; 2007, Apr, 3-6; 2007, April, 3-6; 2007, Jul, 1-4; 2006, Dec, 4-7; 2006, Dec, 4-7; 2006, Dec, 4-7; 2006, Dec, 4-7; 2006, December, 4-7; 2006, December, 4-7; 2005, Feb, 1-6; 2005, Feb, 1-6; 2005, May, 1-2; 2005, February, 1-6; 2005, May, 1-2; 2005, May, 1-2

99379 Physician supervision of a nursing facility patient (patient not present) requiring complex and multidisciplinary care modalities involving regular physician development and/or revision of care plans, review of subsequent reports of patient status, review of related laboratory and other studies, communication (including telephone calls) for purposes of assessment or care decisions with health care professional(s), family member(s), surrogate decision maker(s) (eg, legal guardian) and/or key caregiver(s) involved in patient's care, integration of new information into the medical treatment plan and/or adjustment of medical therapy, within a calendar month; 15-29 minutes   B

    📖 1.52 🔪 1.83 **Global Days XXX**
    AMA: 2008, Mar, 6-7; 2008, Sep, 3-4; 2007, Mar, 9-11; 2007, Mar, 9-11; 2007, Jul, 1-4; 2007, March, 9-11; 2006, Dec, 4-7; 2006, Dec, 4-7; 2006, December, 4-7; 2006, Dec, 4-7; 2006, Dec, 4-7; 2006, December, 4-7; 2005, May, 1-2; 2005, May, 1-2; 2005, Feb, 1-6; 2005, May, 1-2; 2005, February, 1-6; 2005, Feb, 1-6

99380 30 minutes or more   B

    📖 2.39 🔪 2.76 **Global Days XXX**
    AMA: 2008, Mar, 6-7; 2008, Sep, 3-4; 2007, Mar, 9-11; 2007, Mar, 9-11; 2007, Jul, 1-4; 2007, March, 9-11; 2006, Dec, 4-7; 2006, Dec, 4-7; 2006, December, 4-7; 2006, Dec, 4-7; 2006, Dec, 4-7; 2006, December, 4-7; 2005, May, 1-2; 2005, May, 1-2; 2005, Feb, 1-6; 2005, February, 1-6; 2005, May, 1-2; 2005, Feb, 1-6

99381-99397 Preventive Medicine Visits

CMS 100-4,12,30.6.2 *Medically Necessary and Preventive Medicine Service on Same Date*
CMS 100-2,15,30 *Physician Services*
CMS 100-1,5,70 *Definition of Physician*
INCLUDES   care of a small problem or preexisting condition that requires no extra work
    new patients or established patients (99381-99387, or 99391-99397)
    regular preventive care (e.g., well-child exams) for all age groups
EXCLUDES *counseling/risk factor reduction interventions not provided with a preventive medical examination (99401-99412)*
    diagnostic tests and other procedures
    immunizations (90465-90474, 90476-90749)
    substantial problems that require additional work

▲ **99381** Initial comprehensive preventive medicine evaluation and management of an individual including an age and gender appropriate history, examination, counseling/anticipatory guidance/risk factor reduction interventions, and the ordering of laboratory/diagnostic procedures, new patient; infant (age younger than 1 year)   A E

    📖 1.65 🔪 2.51 **Global Days XXX**
    AMA: 2008, Jan, 10-25; 2007, Jan, 13-27; 2007, Jan, 13-27; 2007, Mar, 9-11; 2007, Mar, 9-11; 2007, Jul, 1-4; 2007, March, 9-11; 2007, January, 13-27; 2005, May, 1-2; 2005, May, 1-2; 2005, May, 1-2; 2005, August, 13-15; 2005, February, 1-6; 2005, Feb, 1-6; 2005, Feb, 1-6; 2005, Aug, 13-15; 2005, Aug, 13-15

▲ **99382** early childhood (age 1 through 4 years)   A E PQ

    📖 1.88 🔪 2.73 **Global Days XXX**
    AMA: 2007, Mar, 9-11; 2007, Mar, 9-11; 2007, Jul, 1-4; 2007, March, 9-11; 2005, May, 1-2; 2005, May, 1-2; 2005, Feb, 1-6; 2005, February, 1-6; 2005, August, 13-15; 2005, May, 1-2; 2005, Feb, 1-6; 2005, Aug, 13-15; 2005, Aug, 13-15

▲ **99383** late childhood (age 5 through 11 years)   A E PQ

    📖 1.88 🔪 2.71 **Global Days XXX**
    AMA: 2007, Mar, 9-11; 2007, Mar, 9-11; 2007, Jul, 1-4; 2007, March, 9-11; 2005, Feb, 1-6; 2005, Feb, 1-6; 2005, May, 1-2; 2005, May, 1-2; 2005, August, 13-15; 2005, February, 1-6; 2005, May, 1-2; 2005, Aug, 13-15; 2005, Aug, 13-15

▲ **99384** adolescent (age 12 through 17 years)   A E PQ

    📖 2.12 🔪 2.95 **Global Days XXX**
    AMA: 2007, Mar, 9-11; 2007, Mar, 9-11; 2007, Jul, 1-4; 2007, March, 9-11; 2005, Aug, 13-15; 2005, Aug, 13-15; 2005, May, 1-2; 2005, February, 1-6; 2005, August, 13-15; 2005, May, 1-2; 2005, May, 1-2; 2005, Feb, 1-6; 2005, Feb, 1-6

▲ **99385** 18-39 years   A E PQ

    📖 2.12 🔪 2.95 **Global Days XXX**
    AMA: 2007, Mar, 9-11; 2007, Mar, 9-11; 2007, Jul, 1-4; 2007, March, 9-11; 2005, May, 1-2; 2005, May, 1-2; 2005, Feb, 1-6; 2005, May, 1-2; 2005, August, 13-15; 2005, February, 1-6; 2005, Feb, 1-6; 2005, Aug, 13-15; 2005, Aug, 13-15

▲ **99386** 40-64 years   A E PQ

    📖 2.60 🔪 3.45 **Global Days XXX**
    AMA: 2007, Mar, 9-11; 2007, Mar, 9-11; 2007, Jul, 1-4; 2007, March, 9-11; 2005, Aug, 13-15; 2005, Aug, 13-15; 2005, May, 1-2; 2005, February, 1-6; 2005, August, 13-15; 2005, May, 1-2; 2005, May, 1-2; 2005, Feb, 1-6; 2005, Feb, 1-6

▲ **99387** 65 years and older   A E PQ

    📖 2.85 🔪 3.78 **Global Days XXX**
    AMA: 2007, Mar, 9-11; 2007, Mar, 9-11; 2007, Jul, 1-4; 2007, March, 9-11; 2005, Feb, 1-6; 2005, Feb, 1-6; 2005, Aug, 13-15; 2005, May, 1-2; 2005, August, 13-15; 2005, February, 1-6; 2005, Aug, 13-15; 2005, May, 1-2; 2005, May, 1-2

▲ 99391   Periodic comprehensive preventive medicine reevaluation and management of an individual including an age and gender appropriate history, examination, counseling/anticipatory guidance/risk factor reduction interventions, and the ordering of laboratory/diagnostic procedures, established patient; infant (age younger than 1 year)   A E

    1.41   2.09   Global Days XXX

    AMA: 2007, Mar, 9-11; 2007, Mar, 9-11; 2007, Jul, 1-4; 2007, March, 9-11; 2005, May, 1-2; 2005, May, 1-2; 2005, Feb, 1-6; 2005, February, 1-6; 2005, August, 13-15; 2005, May, 1-2; 2005, Feb, 1-6; 2005, Aug, 13-15; 2005, Aug, 13-15

▲ 99392   early childhood (age 1 through 4 years)   A E P0

    1.65   2.33   Global Days XXX

    AMA: 2007, Mar, 9-11; 2007, Mar, 9-11; 2007, Jul, 1-4; 2007, March, 9-11; 2005, Feb, 1-6; 2005, Feb, 1-6; 2005, May, 1-2; 2005, May, 1-2; 2005, August, 13-15; 2005, February, 1-6; 2005, May, 1-2; 2005, Aug, 13-15; 2005, Aug, 13-15

▲ 99393   late childhood (age 5 through 11 years)   A E P0

    1.65   2.32   Global Days XXX

    AMA: 2007, Mar, 9-11; 2007, Mar, 9-11; 2007, Jul, 1-4; 2007, March, 9-11; 2005, Feb, 1-6; 2005, Feb, 1-6; 2005, Aug, 13-15; 2005, February, 1-6; 2005, August, 13-15; 2005, May, 1-2; 2005, Aug, 13-15; 2005, May, 1-2; 2005, May, 1-2

▲ 99394   adolescent (age 12 through 17 years)   A E P0

    1.88   2.55   Global Days XXX

    AMA: 2007, Mar, 9-11; 2007, Mar, 9-11; 2007, Jul, 1-4; 2007, March, 9-11; 2005, Feb, 1-6; 2005, Feb, 1-6; 2005, May, 1-2; 2005, May, 1-2; 2005, August, 13-15; 2005, February, 1-6; 2005, May, 1-2; 2005, Aug, 13-15; 2005, Aug, 13-15

▲ 99395   18-39 years   A E P0

    1.88   2.56   Global Days XXX

    AMA: 2008, Mar, 3&7; 2007, Mar, 9-11; 2007, Mar, 9-11; 2007, Jul, 1-4; 2007, March, 9-11; 2005, May, 1-2; 2005, May, 1-2; 2005, Aug, 13-15; 2005, February, 1-6; 2005, August, 13-15; 2005, May, 1-2; 2005, Aug, 13-15; 2005, Feb, 1-6; 2005, Feb, 1-6

▲ 99396   40-64 years   A E P0

    2.12   2.80   Global Days XXX

    AMA: 2007, Mar, 9-11; 2007, Mar, 9-11; 2007, Jul, 1-4; 2007, March, 9-11; 2005, May, 1-2; 2005, May, 1-2; 2005, Aug, 13-15; 2005, May, 1-2; 2005, August, 13-15; 2005, February, 1-6; 2005, Aug, 13-15; 2005, Feb, 1-6; 2005, Feb, 1-6

▲ 99397   65 years and older   A E P0

    2.37   3.14   Global Days XXX

    AMA: 2000, Jan, 10-25, 2007, Jan, 13-27; 2007, Jan, 13-27; 2007, Mar, 9-11; 2007, Mar, 9-11; 2007, Jul, 1-4; 2007, March, 9-11; 2007, January, 13-27; 2005, Feb, 1-6; 2005, Feb, 1-6; 2005, August, 13-15; 2005, February, 1-6; 2005, May, 1-2; 2005, Aug, 13-15; 2005, Aug, 13-15; 2005, May, 1-2; 2005, May, 1-2

99401-99429 Counseling Services: Risk Factor and Behavioral Change Modification

CMS 100-4,32,12.3	*FI Billing: Smoking and Tobacco Use Cessation Counseling*	
CMS 100-4,32,12.2	*Carrier Billing: Smoking and Tobacco Use Cessation Counseling*	
CMS 100-4,32,12.1	*Smoking And Tobacco- Use Cessation Counseling*	
CMS 100-4,4,200.6	*Alcohol and/or Substance Abuse Assessment and Intervention Services*	
CMS 100-3,210.4	*Smoking and Tobacco-Use Cessation Counseling*	
CMS 100-4,32,12	*Smoking and Tobacco-Use Cessation Counseling Services*	
CMS 100-4,12,10	*General Processing Instructions*	
CMS 100-2,16,90	*Routine Services and Appliances*	
CMS 100-2,15,30	*Physician Services*	
CMS 100-1,5,70	*Definition of Physician*	

INCLUDES   administration and analysis of a health risk assessment (99420)

    face-to-face services for new and established patients based on time increments of 15 to 60 minutes

    issues such as a healthy diet, exercise, alcohol and drug abuse

    services provided by a physician or other qualified healthcare professional for the purpose of promoting health and reducing illness and injury

EXCLUDES   *counseling and risk factor reduction interventions included in preventive medicine services (99381-99397)*

    counseling services provided to patient groups with existing symptoms or illness (99078)

Code also distinct evaluation and management services when performed in addition

Do not report with heath and behavioral services (96150-96155)

99401   Preventive medicine counseling and/or risk factor reduction intervention(s) provided to an individual (separate procedure); approximately 15 minutes   A E P0

    0.66   0.97   Global Days XXX

    AMA: 2007, Mar, 9-11; 2007, Mar, 9-11; 2007, Jul, 1-4; 2007, March, 9-11; 2007, Aug, 9-12; 2005, Feb, 1-6; 2005, Feb, 1-6; 2005, May, 1-2; 2005, February, 1-6; 2005, May, 1-2; 2005, May, 1-2; 2004, Aug, 1; 2004, August, 1; 2004, Aug, 1

99402   approximately 30 minutes   E P0

    1.34   1.67   Global Days XXX

    AMA: 2007, Mar, 9-11; 2007, Mar, 9-11; 2007, March, 9-11; 2007, Aug, 9-12; 2007, Jul, 1-4; 2005, May, 1-2; 2005, May, 1-2, 2005, February, 1-6; 2005, May, 1-2; 2005, Feb, 1-6; 2005, Feb, 1-6

99403   approximately 45 minutes   E P0

    2.01   2.35   Global Days XXX

    AMA: 2007, Mar, 9-11; 2007, Mar, 9-11; 2007, March, 9-11; 2007, Aug, 9-12; 2007, Jul, 1-4; 2005, May, 1-2; 2005, May, 1-2; 2005, February, 1-6; 2005, May, 1-2; 2005, Feb, 1-6; 2005, Feb, 1-6

99404   approximately 60 minutes   E P0

    2.68   3.03   Global Days XXX

    AMA: 2007, Mar, 9-11; 2007, Mar, 9-11; 2007, March, 9-11; 2007, Aug, 9-12; 2007, Jul, 1-4; 2005, May, 1-2; 2005, May, 1-2; 2005, February, 1-6; 2005, May, 1-2; 2005, Feb, 1-6; 2005, Feb, 1-6

99406   Smoking and tobacco use cessation counseling visit; intermediate, greater than 3 minutes up to 10 minutes   X 80

    0.32   0.36   Global Days XXX

    AMA: 2008, Jan, 1-3

99407   intensive, greater than 10 minutes   X 80

    Do not report with (99406)

    0.66   0.69   Global Days XXX

    AMA: 2008, Jan, 1-3

● New Code   ▲ Revised Code   M Maternity Edit   A Age Edit   A-Y OPPS Status Indicator   Facility RVU   Non-Facility RVU

CCI Comprehensive Code   50 Bilateral Procedure   + Add-on Indicator   Laboratory crosswalk   Radiology crosswalk

Evaluation and Management

99408 — 99443

99408 Alcohol and/or substance (other than tobacco) abuse structured screening (eg, AUDIT, DAST), and brief intervention (SBI) services; 15 to 30 minutes 〔E〕
  INCLUDES only initial screening and brief intervention services of 15 minutes or more.

  Do not report with (99420)
  〔〕 0.88　〔〕 0.92　Global Days XXX
  AMA: 2008, May, 3-4; 2008, Jul, 11-13

99409 greater than 30 minutes 〔E〕
  INCLUDES only initial screening and brief intervention

  Do not report with (99408, 99420)
  〔〕 1.77　〔〕 1.81　Global Days XXX
  AMA: 2008, May, 3-4; 2008, Jul, 11-13

99411 Preventive medicine counseling and/or risk factor reduction intervention(s) provided to individuals in a group setting (separate procedure); approximately 30 minutes 〔E〕〔PQ〕
  〔〕 0.21　〔〕 0.40　Global Days XXX
  AMA: 2007, Mar, 9-11; 2007, Mar, 9-11; 2007, March, 9-11; 2007, Aug, 9-12; 2007, Jul, 1-4; 2005, May, 1-2; 2005, May, 1-2; 2005, February, 1-6; 2005, May, 1-2; 2005, Feb, 1-6; 2005, Feb, 1-6

99412 approximately 60 minutes 〔E〕〔PQ〕
  〔〕 0.35　〔〕 0.54　Global Days XXX
  AMA: 2007, Mar, 9-11; 2007, Mar, 9-11; 2007, Jul, 1-4; 2007, March, 9-11; 2007, Aug, 9-12; 2005, Feb, 1-6; 2005, Feb, 1-6; 2005, May, 1-2; 2005, May, 1-2; 2005, February, 1-6; 2005, May, 1-2; 2004, Aug, 1; 2004, August, 1; 2004, Aug, 1

99420 Administration and interpretation of health risk assessment instrument (eg, health hazard appraisal) 〔E〕〔PQ〕
  〔〕 0.26　〔〕 0.26　Global Days XXX
  AMA: 2007, Mar, 9-11; 2007, Mar, 9-11; 2007, March, 9-11; 2007, Jul, 1-4; 2005, Feb, 1-6; 2005, Feb, 1-6; 2005, February, 1-6; 2005, May, 1-2; 2005, May, 1-2; 2005, May, 1-2

99429 Unlisted preventive medicine service 〔E〕〔PQ〕
  〔〕 0.00　〔〕 0.00　Global Days XXX
  AMA: 2007, Mar, 9-11; 2007, Mar, 9-11; 2007, March, 9-11; 2007, Jul, 1-4; 2005, May, 1-2; 2005, May, 1-2; 2005, February, 1-6; 2005, May, 1-2; 2005, Feb, 1-6; 2005, Feb, 1-6

99431-99440 Newborn Care

99431 ~~History and examination of the normal newborn infant; initiation of diagnostic and treatment programs and preparation of hospital records. (This code should also be used for birthing room deliveries.)~~
  See 99460

99432 ~~Normal newborn care in other than hospital or birthing room setting, including physical examination of baby and conference(s) with parent(s)~~
  See 99461

99433 ~~Subsequent hospital care, for the evaluation and management of a normal newborn, per day~~
  See 99462

99435 ~~History and examination of the normal newborn infant; including the preparation of medical records. (This code should only be used for newborns assessed and discharged from the hospital or birthing room on the same date.)~~
  See 99463

99436 ~~Attendance at delivery (when requested by delivering physician) and initial stabilization of newborn~~
  See 99464

99440 ~~Newborn resuscitation: provision of positive pressure ventilation and/or chest compressions in the presence of acute inadequate ventilation and/or cardiac output~~
  See 99465

99441-99443 Telephone Calls for Patient Management

CMS 100-4,12,10　General Processing Instructions
CMS 100-4,11,40.1.3　Attending Physician Services Under Hospice
CMS 100-2,15,30　Physician Services
CMS 100-1,5,70　Definition of Physician
INCLUDES episodes of care initiated by an established patient or the patient or guardian of an established patient
  non-face-to-face evaluation and management services provided by a physician

EXCLUDES *services provided by a qualified nonphysician healthcare professional (98966-98968)*

Do not report with a related evaluation and management visit within the next 24 hours or as the next available urgent visit
Do not report with a related evaluation and management service performed and reported within the previous seven days or within the postoperative period of a completed procedure
Do not report with a related evaluation and management service perfomed in the previous seven days (99441-99444)
Do not report with the same call reported with codes: (99339-99340, 99374-99380)
Do not report with anticoagulation management reported with codes: (99363-99364)

99441 Telephone evaluation and management service provided by a physician to an established patient, parent, or guardian not originating from a related E/M service provided within the previous 7 days nor leading to an E/M service or procedure within the next 24 hours or soonest available appointment; 5-10 minutes of medical discussion 〔E〕
  〔〕 0.35　〔〕 0.39　Global Days XXX
  AMA: 2008, Mar, 6-7

99442 11-20 minutes of medical discussion 〔E〕
  〔〕 0.69　〔〕 0.72　Global Days XXX
  AMA: 2008, Mar, 6-7

99443 21-30 minutes of medical discussion 〔E〕
  〔〕 1.03　〔〕 1.06　Global Days XXX
  AMA: 2008, Mar, 6-7

99444 Online Patient Management Services

INCLUDES   all related communications such as related phone calls, prescription and lab orders

permanent electronic or hardcopy storage

physician evaluation and management services provided via the internet in response to a patient's on-line inquiry

the physician's personal timely response

Do not report with more than once per seven day period for the same episode of care

Do not report with when related to an evaluation service performed and reported within the previous seven days

Do not report with when within the postoperative period of a previously completed procedure

99444   **Online evaluation and management service provided by a physician to an established patient, guardian, or health care provider not originating from a related E/M service provided within the previous 7 days, using the Internet or similar electronic communications network**   E

EXCLUDES   *on-line medical evaluation by a qualified nonphysician healthcare professional (98969)*

Do not report with (99339-99340, 99363-99364, 99374-99380)

🔹 0.00   🔹 0.00 Global Days XXX

99450-99456 Life/Disability Insurance Eligibility Visits

CMS *100-2,15,30*   *Physician Services*
CMS *100-1,5,70*   *Definition of Physician*
INCLUDES   assessment services for insurance eligibility and work-related disability without medical management of the patient's illness/injury

services provided to new/established patients at any site of service

EXCLUDES   *any additional E/M services or procedures performed on the same date of service: report with appropriate code*

99450   **Basic life and/or disability examination that includes: Measurement of height, weight, and blood pressure; Completion of a medical history following a life insurance pro forma; Collection of blood sample and/or urinalysis complying with "chain of custody" protocols; and Completion of necessary documentation/certificates.**   E

🔹 0.00   🔹 0.00 Global Days XXX

AMA: 2007, Mar, 9-11; 2007, Mar, 9-11; 2007, March, 9-11, 2007, Jul, 1-4; 2005, Feb, 1-6; 2005, Feb, 1-6; 2005, May, 1-2; 2005, February, 1-6; 2005, May, 1-2; 2005, May, 1-2

99455   **Work related or medical disability examination by the treating physician that includes: Completion of a medical history commensurate with the patient's condition; Performance of an examination commensurate with the patient's condition; Formulation of a diagnosis, assessment of capabilities and stability, and calculation of impairment; Development of future medical treatment plan; and Completion of necessary documentation/certificates and report.**   B 80 ▭

Do not report with (99080)

🔹 0.00   🔹 0.00 Global Days XXX

AMA: 2007, Mar, 9-11; 2007, Mar, 9-11; 2007, March, 9-11; 2007, Jul, 1-4; 2005, Feb, 1-6; 2005, Feb, 1-6; 2005, February, 1-6; 2005, May, 1-2; 2005, May, 1-2; 2005, May, 1-2

99456   **Work related or medical disability examination by other than the treating physician that includes: Completion of a medical history commensurate with the patient's condition; Performance of an examination commensurate with the patient's condition; Formulation of a diagnosis, assessment of capabilities and stability, and calculation of impairment; Development of future medical treatment plan; and Completion of necessary documentation/certificates and report.**   B 80 ▭

Do not report with (99080)

🔹 0.00   🔹 0.00 Global Days XXX

AMA: 2007, Mar, 9-11; 2007, Mar, 9-11; 2007, March, 9-11; 2007, Jul, 1-4; 2005, May, 1-2; 2005, May, 1-2; 2005, February, 1-6; 2005, May, 1-2; 2005, Feb, 1-6; 2005, Feb, 1-6

99460-99463 Evaluation and Management Services for Age 28 Days or Less

INCLUDES   family consultation

healthy newborn history and physical

medical record documentation

ordering of diagnostic test and treatments

services provied to healthy newborns age 28 days or less

EXCLUDES   *attendance at delivery (99464)*

circumcision (54150)

emergency resuscitation services (99465)

neonatal intensive and critical care services (99466-99469, 99477-99480)

● 99460   **Initial hospital or birthing center care, per day, for evaluation and management of normal newborn infant**   A V 80

🔹 1.56   🔹 1.56 Global Days XXX

● 99461   **Initial care, per day, for evaluation and management of normal newborn infant seen in other than hospital or birthing center**   A M 80

🔹 1.75   🔹 2.34 Global Days XXX

● 99462   **Subsequent hospital care, per day, for evaluation and management of normal newborn**   A C 80

🔹 0.83   🔹 0.83 Global Days XXX

● 99463   **Initial hospital or birthing center care, per day, for evaluation and management of normal newborn infant admitted and discharged on the same date**   A V 80

EXCLUDES   *services to newborns admitted and discharged on a date other than the admission date (99238-99239)*

🔹 2.09   🔹 2.09 Global Days XXX

99464-99465 Newborn Delivery Attendance/Resuscitation

● 99464   **Attendance at delivery (when requested by the delivering physician) and initial stabilization of newborn**   N 80

Code also (99460, 99468, 99477)

Do not report with (99465)

🔹 1.96   🔹 1.96 Global Days XXX

● 99465   **Delivery/birthing room resuscitation, provision of positive pressure ventilation and/or chest compressions in the presence of acute inadequate ventilation and/or cardiac output**   S 80

Code also any necessary procedures performed as part of the resuscitation

Code also as appropriate (99460, 99468, 99477)

Do not report with (99464)

🔹 4.02   🔹 4.02 Global Days XXX

● New Code   ▲ Revised Code   M Maternity Edit   A Age Edit   A V OPPS Status Indicator   🔹 Facility RVU   🔹 Non-Facility RVU

▭ CCI Comprehensive Code   50 Bilateral Procedure   + Add-on Indicator   N Laboratory crosswalk   R Radiology crosswalk

Evaluation and Management

99466 — 99499

99466-99467 Critical Care Transport Age 24 Months or Younger

INCLUDES   all services included for neonatal and pediatric critical care
physician presence during interfacility transfer of critically ill/injured patient 24 months of age or less

EXCLUDES   *patient critical care transport services with personal contact with patient of less than 30 minutes*
physician directed emergency care via two-way voice communication with transporting staff (99288)

Do not report for services less than 30 minutes duration (see evaluation and management codes)

● **99466**   **Critical care services delivered by a physician, face-to-face, during an interfacility transport of critically ill or critically injured pediatric patient, 24 months of age or less; first 30-74 minutes of hands-on care during transport**   A N 80
🚑 6.43   ⚕ 6.43   Global Days XXX

+ ● **99467**   **each additional 30 minutes (List separately in addition to code for primary service)**   A N 80
Code first (99466)
🚑 3.21   ⚕ 3.21   Global Days ZZZ

99468-99476 Critical Care Age 5 Years or Younger

INCLUDES   all services included in codes 99291-99292 as well as:
administration of blood/blood components (36430, 36440)
administration of intravenous fluids (96360-96361)
administration of surfactant (94610)
bladder aspiration, suprapubic (51100)
bladder catheterization (51701, 51702)
catheterization umbillical artery (36660)
catheterization umbillical vein (36510)
central venous catheter, centrally inserted (36555)
endotracheal intubation (31500)
lumbar puncture (62270)
oral or nasogastric tube placement (43752)
pulmonary function testing, performed at the bedside (94375)
pulse or ear oximetry (94760-94762)
vascular access, arteries (36140, 36620)
vascular access, venous (36400-36406, 36420)
ventilatory management (94002-94004, 94660)
initial and subsequent care provided to a critically ill infant or child

EXCLUDES   *critical care services for patients 6 years of age or older (99291-99292)*
critical care services provided by a second physician or physician of a different specialty (99291-99292)
critical care services to an outpatient (99291-99292)

Do not report with remote critical care (0188T-0189T)

● **99468**   **Initial inpatient neonatal critical care, per day, for the evaluation and management of a critically ill neonate, 28 days of age or less**   A C 80
🚑 24.14   ⚕ 24.14   Global Days XXX

● **99469**   **Subsequent inpatient neonatal critical care, per day, for the evaluation and management of a critically ill neonate, 28 days of age or less**   A C 80
🚑 10.52   ⚕ 10.52   Global Days XXX

● **99471**   **Initial inpatient pediatric critical care, per day, for the evaluation and management of a critically ill infant or young child, 29 days through 24 months of age**   A C 80
🚑 21.57   ⚕ 21.57   Global Days XXX

● **99472**   **Subsequent inpatient pediatric critical care, per day, for the evaluation and management of a critically ill infant or young child, 29 days through 24 months of age**   A C 80
🚑 10.65   ⚕ 10.65   Global Days XXX

● **99475**   **Initial inpatient pediatric critical care, per day, for the evaluation and management of a critically ill infant or young child, 2 through 5 years of age**   A C 80
🚑 14.87   ⚕ 14.87   Global Days XXX

● **99476**   **Subsequent inpatient pediatric critical care, per day, for the evaluation and management of a critically ill infant or young child, 2 through 5 years of age**   A C 80
🚑 8.83   ⚕ 8.83   Global Days XXX

99477-99499 Initial Inpatient Neonatal Intensive Care and Other Services

INCLUDES   initial and subsequent services for non-critically ill infants and neonates that continue to require any of the following:
adjustments to enteral and/or parenteral nutrition
constant and/or frequent montoring of vitals signs
continuous observation by the healthcare team
heat maintenance
intensive cardiac or respiratory monitoring
monitoring of laboratory and oxygen values

EXCLUDES   *subsequent care of a sick neonate, under 28 days of age, more than 5000 grams, not requiring critical or intensive care services (99231-99233)*

99477   **Initial hospital care, per day, for the evaluation and management of the neonate, 28 days of age or less, who requires intensive observation, frequent interventions, and other intensive care services**   A C 80
EXCLUDES   *initiation of care of a critically ill neonate (99468)*
initiation of inpatient care of a normal newborn (99460)
initiation of inpatient hospital care of a neonate not requiring:
frequent interventions
intensive observation
other intensive services
🚑 9.37   ⚕ 9.37   Global Days XXX
AMA: 2008, Jan, 1-3; 2008, Jan, 8-9; 2008, Jul, 10&13

● **99478**   **Subsequent intensive care, per day, for the evaluation and management of the recovering very low birth weight infant (present body weight less than 1500 grams)**   A C 80
🚑 3.83   ⚕ 3.83   Global Days XXX

● **99479**   **Subsequent intensive care, per day, for the evaluation and management of the recovering low birth weight infant (present body weight of 1500-2500 grams)**   A C 80
🚑 3.37   ⚕ 3.37   Global Days XXX

● **99480**   **Subsequent intensive care, per day, for the evaluation and management of the recovering infant (present body weight of 2501-5000 grams)**   A C 80
🚑 3.24   ⚕ 3.24   Global Days XXX

99499   **Unlisted evaluation and management service**   B 80 PQ
🚑 0.00   ⚕ 0.00   Global Days XXX
AMA: 2008, Jan, 10-25; 2007, Jan, 13-27; 2007, Jan, 13-27; 2007, Mar, 9-11; 2007, March, 9-11; 2007, Jul, 1-4; 2007, January, 13-27; 2007, Mar, 9-11; 2006, Sep, 9-13; 2006, September, 9-13; 2006, January, 46-47; 2006, Sep, 9-13; 2006, Jan, 46-47; 2006, Jan, 46-47; 2005, May, 1-2; 2005, February, 1-6; 2005, May, 1-2; 2005, Feb, 1-6; 2005, Feb, 1-6; 2005, March, 11-15; 2005, May, 1-2; 2005, Mar, 11-15; 2005, Mar, 11-15

0001F-0015F Quality Measures with Multiple Components

INCLUDES   several measures grouped within a single code descriptor to make possible reporting for clinical conditions when all of the components have been met

0001F   Heart failure assessed (includes assessment of all the following components)(CAD, HF)[1]: Blood pressure measured (2000F)[1] Level of activity assessed (1003F)[1] Clinical symptoms of volume overload (excess) assessed (1004F)[1] Weight, recorded (2001F)[1] Clinical signs of volume overload (excess) assessed (2002F)[1]

INCLUDES   blood pressure measured[1] (2000F)
clinical signs of volume overload (excess) assessed[1] (2002F)
clinical symptoms of volume overload (excess) assessed[1] (1004F)
level of activity assessed[1] (1003F)
weight recorded[1] (2001F)

🖪 0.00   ⚖ 0.00   Global Days XXX
AMA: 2006, Dec, 10-12; 2006, Dec, 10-12; 2006, December, 10-12; 2006, December, 10-12; 2006, December, 10-12; 2005, Oct, 1-5; 2005, October, 1-5; 2005, October, 1-5; 2005, October, 1-5; 2005, Oct, 1-5

0005F   Osteoarthritis assessed (OA)[1] Includes assessment of all the following components: Osteoarthritis symptoms and functional status assessed (1006F)[1] Use of anti-inflammatory or over-the-counter (OTC) analgesic medications assessed (1007F)[1] Initial examination of the involved joint(s) (includes visual inspection, palpation, range of motion) (2004F)[1]   Ⓜ

INCLUDES   initial examination of the involved joint(s) (includes visual inspection/palpation/range of motion)[1] (2004F)
osteoarthritis symptoms and functional status assessed (1006F)
use of anti-inflammatory or over-the-counter (OTC) analgesic medications assessed[1] (1007F)

EXCLUDES   *tobacco use cessation intervention (1001F)*

🖪 0.00   ⚖ 0.00   Global Days XXX
AMA: 2005, Oct, 1-5; 2005, Oct, 1-5; 2005, October, 1-5; 2005, October, 1-5; 2005, October, 1-5; 2005, October, 1-5

0012F   Community-acquired bacterial pneumonia assessment (includes all of the following components) (CAP)[1]: Co-morbid conditions assessed (1026F)[1] Vital signs recorded (2010F)[1] Mental status assessed (2014F)[1] Hydration status assessed (2018F)[1]   Ⓜ

INCLUDES   co-morbid conditions assessed[1] (1026F)
hydration status assessed[1] (2018F)
mental status assessed[1] (2014F)
vital signs recorded[1] (2010F)

🖪 0.00   ⚖ 0.00   Global Days XXX

0014F   Comprehensive preoperative assessment performed for cataract surgery with intraocular lens (IOL) placement (includes assessment of all of the following components) (EC)[5]: Dilated fundus evaluation performed within 12 months prior to cataract surgery (2020F)[5] Pre-surgical (cataract) axial length, corneal power measurement and method of intraocular lens power calculation documented (must be performed within 12 months prior to surgery) (3073F)[5] Preoperative assessment of functional or medical indication(s) for surgery prior to the cataract surgery with intraocular lens placement (must be performed within 12 months prior to cataract surgery) (3325F)[5]   Ⓜ

INCLUDES   evaluation of dilated fundus done within 12 months prior to surgery (2020F)
preoperative assessment of functional or medical indications done within 12 months prior to sugery (3325F)
presurgical measurement of axial length and corneal power and IOL power calculation performed within 12 months prior to sugery (3325F)

🖪 0.00   ⚖ 0.00   Global Days XXX
AMA: 2008, Mar, 8-12

0015F   Melanoma follow-up completed (includes assessment of all of the following components) (ML)[5]: History obtained regarding new or changing moles (1050F)[5] Complete physical skin exam performed (2029F)[5] Patient counseled to perform a monthly self skin examination (5005F)[5]   Ⓜ

INCLUDES   complete physical skin exam (2029F)
counseling to perform monthly skin self-examination (5005F)
history obtained of new or changing moles (1050F)

🖪 0.00   ⚖ 0.00   Global Days XXX
AMA: 2008, Mar, 8-12

0500F-0575F Care Provided According to Prevailing Guidelines

INCLUDES   measures of utilization or patient care provided for certain clinical purposes

0500F   Initial prenatal care visit (report at first prenatal encounter with health care professional providing obstetrical care. Report also date of visit and, in a separate field, the date of the last menstrual period - LMP) (Prenatal)[2]   Ⓜ ♀ Ⓜ

🖪 0.00   ⚖ 0.00   Global Days XXX
AMA: 2005, Oct, 1-5; 2005, Oct, 1-5; 2005, October, 1-5; 2004, Nov, 1; 2004, November, 1, 2004, Nov, 1

0501F   Prenatal flow sheet documented in medical record by first prenatal visit (documentation includes at minimum blood pressure, weight, urine protein, uterine size, fetal heart tones, and estimated date of delivery). Report also: date of visit and, in a separate field, the date of the last menstrual period - LMP (Note: If reporting 0501F Prenatal flow sheet, it is not necessary to report 0500F Initial prenatal care visit) (Prenatal)[1]   Ⓜ ♀ Ⓜ

🖪 0.00   ⚖ 0.00   Global Days XXX
AMA: 2004, Nov, 1; 2004, Nov, 1; 2004, November, 1

FOOTNOTES:
[1]   Physician Consortium for Performance Improvement, www. physicianconsortium.org
[2]   National Committee on Quality Assurance (NCOA), Health Employer Data Information Set (HEDIS®), www.ncqa.org
[5]   Joint measure from The Physician Consortium for Performance Improvement, www.physicianconsortium.org and National Committee

---

● New Code   ▲ Revised Code   Ⓜ Maternity Edit   🄰 Age Edit   Ⓐ-Ⓨ OPPS Status Indicator   🖪 Facility RVU   ⚖ Non-Facility RVU
🄲 CCI Comprehensive Code   🔟 Bilateral Procedure   + Add-on Indicator   🅛 Laboratory crosswalk   🅡 Radiology crosswalk

Category II Codes

0502F — 1022F

0502F Subsequent prenatal care visit (Prenatal)[2] Ⓜ♀ Ⓜ
  EXCLUDES patients seen for an unrelated pregnancy/prenatal care condition (e.g., upper respiratory infection; patients seen for consultation only, not for continuing care)
  🕮 0.00 ⚘ 0.00 Global Days XXX
  AMA: 2004, Nov, 1; 2004, Nov, 1; 2004, November, 1

0503F Postpartum care visit (Prenatal)[2] Ⓜ♀ Ⓜ
  🕮 0.00 ⚘ 0.00 Global Days XXX
  AMA: 2004, Nov, 1; 2004, Nov, 1; 2004, November, 1

0505F Hemodialysis plan of care documented (ESRD)[1] Ⓜ
  🕮 0.00 ⚘ 0.00 Global Days XXX
  AMA: 2008, Mar, 8-12

0507F Peritoneal dialysis plan of care documented (ESRD)[1] Ⓜ
  🕮 0.00 ⚘ 0.00 Global Days XXX
  AMA: 2008, Mar, 8-12

0509F Urinary incontinence plan of care documented (GER)[5] Ⓜ PQ
  🕮 0.00 ⚘ 0.00 Global Days XXX

0513F Elevated blood pressure plan of care documented (CKD)[1] Ⓜ
  🕮 0.00 ⚘ 0.00 Global Days XXX
  AMA: 2008, Mar, 8-12

0514F Plan of care for elevated hemoglobin level documented for patient receiving Erythropoiesis-Stimulating Agent (ESA) therapy (CKD)[1] Ⓜ
  🕮 0.00 ⚘ 0.00 Global Days XXX
  AMA: 2008, Mar, 8-12

0516F Anemia plan of care documented (ESRD)[1] Ⓜ
  🕮 0.00 ⚘ 0.00 Global Days XXX
  AMA: 2008, Mar, 8-12

0517F Glaucoma plan of care documented (EC)[5] Ⓜ
  🕮 0.00 ⚘ 0.00 Global Days XXX
  AMA: 2008, Mar, 8-12

0518F Falls plan of care documented (GER)[5] Ⓜ
  🕮 0.00 ⚘ 0.00 Global Days XXX
  AMA: 2008, Mar, 8-12

0519F Planned chemotherapy regimen, including at a minimum: drug(s) prescribed, dose, and duration, documented prior to initiation of a new treatment regimen (ONC)[1] Ⓜ
  🕮 0.00 ⚘ 0.00 Global Days XXX
  AMA: 2008, Mar, 8-12

▲ 0520F Radiation dose limits to normal tissues established prior to the initiation of a course of 3D conformal radiation for a minimum of 2 tissues/organs (ONC)[1] Ⓜ
  🕮 0.00 ⚘ 0.00 Global Days XXX
  AMA: 2008, Mar, 8-12

0521F Plan of care to address pain documented (ONC)[1] Ⓜ
  🕮 0.00 ⚘ 0.00 Global Days XXX
  AMA: 2008, Mar, 8-12

0525F Initial visit for episode (BkP)[2] Ⓜ
  🕮 0.00 ⚘ 0.00 Global Days XXX
  AMA: 2008, Mar, 8-12

0526F Subsequent visit for episode (BkP)[2] Ⓜ
  🕮 0.00 ⚘ 0.00 Global Days XXX
  AMA: 2008, Mar, 8-12

● 0575F HIV RNA control plan of care, documented (HIV)[5] Ⓜ
  🕮 0.00 ⚘ 0.00 Global Days XXX

1000F-1220F Elements of History/Review of Systems

INCLUDES measures for specific aspects of patient history or review of systems

1000F Tobacco use assessed (CAD, CAP, COPD, PV)[1] (DM)[4] Ⓜ
  🕮 0.00 ⚘ 0.00 Global Days XXX
  AMA: 2005, Oct, 1-5; 2005, Oct, 1-5; 2005, Oct, 1-5; 2005, October, 1-5; 2005, Oct, 1-5; 2004, Nov, 1; 2004, November, 1; 2004, Nov, 1; 2004, Nov, 1; 2004, Nov, 1

1002F Anginal symptoms and level of activity assessed (CAD)[1] Ⓜ
  🕮 0.00 ⚘ 0.00 Global Days XXX
  AMA: 2004, Nov, 1; 2004, Nov, 1; 2004, November, 1

1003F Level of activity assessed (HF)[1] Ⓜ
  🕮 0.00 ⚘ 0.00 Global Days XXX
  AMA: 2006, Dec, 10-12; 2006, Dec, 10-12; 2006, Dec, 10-12; 2006, Dec, 10-12; 2006, December, 10-12; 2006, December, 10-12

1004F Clinical symptoms of volume overload (excess) assessed (HF)[1] Ⓜ
  🕮 0.00 ⚘ 0.00 Global Days XXX
  AMA: 2006, Dec, 10-12; 2006, Dec, 10-12; 2006, Dec, 10-12; 2006, Dec, 10-12; 2006, December, 10-12; 2006, December, 10-12

1005F Asthma symptoms evaluated (includes physician documentation of numeric frequency of symptoms or patient completion of an asthma assessment tool/survey/questionnaire) (Asthma)[1] Ⓜ PQ
  🕮 0.00 ⚘ 0.00 Global Days XXX

1006F Osteoarthritis symptoms and functional status assessed (may include the use of a standardized scale or the completion of an assessment questionnaire, such as the SF-36, AAOS Hip & Knee Questionnaire) (OA)[1] [Instructions: Report when osteoarthritis is addressed during the patient encounter] Ⓜ
  INCLUDES osteoarthritis when it is addressed during the patient encounter
  🕮 0.00 ⚘ 0.00 Global Days XXX

1007F Use of anti-inflammatory or analgesic over-the-counter (OTC) medications for symptom relief assessed (OA)[1] Ⓜ
  🕮 0.00 ⚘ 0.00 Global Days XXX

1008F Gastrointestinal and renal risk factors assessed for patients on prescribed or OTC non-steroidal anti-inflammatory drug (NSAID) (OA)[1] Ⓜ
  🕮 0.00 ⚘ 0.00 Global Days XXX

1015F Chronic obstructive pulmonary disease (COPD) symptoms assessed (Includes assessment of at least 1 of the following: dyspnea, cough/sputum, wheezing), or respiratory symptom assessment tool completed (COPD)[1] Ⓜ
  🕮 0.00 ⚘ 0.00 Global Days XXX

1018F Dyspnea assessed, not present (COPD)[1] Ⓜ
  🕮 0.00 ⚘ 0.00 Global Days XXX

1019F Dyspnea assessed, present (COPD)[1] Ⓜ
  🕮 0.00 ⚘ 0.00 Global Days XXX

1022F Pneumococcus immunization status assessed (CAP, COPD)[1] Ⓜ
  🕮 0.00 ⚘ 0.00 Global Days XXX
  AMA: 2008, Mar, 8-12

FOOTNOTES:

[1] Physician Consortium for Performance Improvement, www. physicianconsortium.org

[2] National Committee on Quality Assurance (NCOA), Health Employer Data Information Set (HEDIS®), www.ncqa.org

[4] National Diabetes Quality Improvement Alliance (NDQIA), www.nationaldiabetesalliance.org

[5] Joint measure from The Physician Consortium for Performance Improvement, www.physicianconsortium.org and National Committee

26/Ⓣ Professional/Technical Component Only   80/80 Assist-at-Surgery Allowed/With Documentation   Unlisted   Not Covered
AMA: CPT Assistant References   A2/Z3 ASC Payment Indicator   ♂ Male Only   ♀ Female Only   ⊘Modifier 51 Exempt   PQ PQRI

1026F Co-morbid conditions assessed (eg, includes assessment for presence or absence of: malignancy, liver disease, congestive heart failure, cerebrovascular disease, renal disease, chronic obstructive pulmonary disease, asthma, diabetes, other co-morbid conditions) (CAP)[1] M
🔧 0.00 ✂ 0.00 Global Days XXX

1030F Influenza immunization status assessed (CAP)[1] M
🔧 0.00 ✂ 0.00 Global Days XXX
AMA: 2008, Mar, 8-12

1034F Current tobacco smoker (CAD, CAP, COPD, PV)[1] (DM)[4] M
🔧 0.00 ✂ 0.00 Global Days XXX
AMA: 2008, Mar, 8-12

1035F Current smokeless tobacco user (eg, chew, snuff) (PV)[1] M
🔧 0.00 ✂ 0.00 Global Days XXX
AMA: 2008, Mar, 8-12

1036F Current tobacco non-user (CAD, CAP, COPD, PV)[1] (DM)[4] M
🔧 0.00 ✂ 0.00 Global Days XXX
AMA: 2008, Mar, 8-12

1038F Persistent asthma (mild, moderate or severe) (Asthma)[1] M PO
🔧 0.00 ✂ 0.00 Global Days XXX

1039F Intermittent asthma (Asthma)[1] M PO
🔧 0.00 ✂ 0.00 Global Days XXX

1040F DSM-IV™ criteria for major depressive disorder documented at the initial evaluation (MDD)[1] M
🔧 0.00 ✂ 0.00 Global Days XXX
AMA: 2008, Mar, 8-12

1050F History obtained regarding new or changing moles (ML)[5] M PO
🔧 0.00 ✂ 0.00 Global Days XXX
AMA: 2008, Mar, 8-12

1055F Visual functional status assessed (EC)[5] M PO
🔧 0.00 ✂ 0.00 Global Days XXX

1060F Documentation of permanent OR persistent OR paroxysmal atrial fibrillation (STR)[5] M
🔧 0.00 ✂ 0.00 Global Days XXX

1061F Documentation of absence of permanent AND persistent AND paroxysmal atrial fibrillation (STR)[5] M
🔧 0.00 ✂ 0.00 Global Days XXX

1065F Ischemic stroke symptom onset of less than 3 hours prior to arrival (STR)[5] M PO
🔧 0.00 ✂ 0.00 Global Days XXX

1066F Ischemic stroke symptom onset greater than or equal to 3 hours prior to arrival (STR)[5] M PO
🔧 0.00 ✂ 0.00 Global Days XXX

1070F Alarm symptoms (involuntary weight loss, dysphagia, or gastrointestinal bleeding) assessed; none present (GERD)[5] M PO
🔧 0.00 ✂ 0.00 Global Days XXX

1071F Alarm symptoms (involuntary weight loss, dysphagia, or gastrointestinal bleeding) assessed; 1 or more present (GERD)[5] M PO
🔧 0.00 ✂ 0.00 Global Days XXX

~~**1080F** Surrogate decision maker or advance care plan documented in the medical record (GER)[5]~~
See 1123F-1124F

1090F Presence or absence of urinary incontinence assessed (GER)[5] M PO
🔧 0.00 ✂ 0.00 Global Days XXX

1091F Urinary incontinence characterized (eg frequency, volume, timing, type of symptoms, how bothersome) (GER)[5] M PO
🔧 0.00 ✂ 0.00 Global Days XXX

1100F Patient screened for future fall risk; documentation of 2 or more falls in the past year or any fall with injury in the past year (GER)[5] M PO
🔧 0.00 ✂ 0.00 Global Days XXX
AMA: 2008, Mar, 8-12

1101F Patient screened for future fall risk; documentation of no falls in the past year or only 1 fall without injury in the past year (GER)[5] M PU
🔧 0.00 ✂ 0.00 Global Days XXX
AMA: 2008, Mar, 8-12

1110F Patient discharged from an inpatient facility (eg hospital, skilled nursing facility, or rehabilitation facility) within the last 60 days (GER)[5] M PO
🔧 0.00 ✂ 0.00 Global Days XXX

1111F Discharge medications reconciled with the current medication list in outpatient medical record (GER)[5] M PO
🔧 0.00 ✂ 0.00 Global Days XXX

1116F Auricular or periauricular pain assessed (AOE)[1] M
🔧 0.00 ✂ 0.00 Global Days XXX
AMA: 2008, Mar, 8-12

1118F GERD symptoms assessed after 12 months of therapy (GERD)[5] M
🔧 0.00 ✂ 0.00 Global Days XXX
AMA: 2008, Mar, 8-12

1119F Initial evaluation for condition (HEP C)[1] M
🔧 0.00 ✂ 0.00 Global Days XXX
AMA: 2008, Mar, 8-12

1121F Subsequent evaluation for condition (HEP C)[1] M
🔧 0.00 ✂ 0.00 Global Days XXX
AMA: 2008, Mar, 8-12

1123F Advance care planning discussed and documented; advance care plan or surrogate decision maker documented in the medical record (GER)[5] M
🔧 0.00 ✂ 0.00 Global Days XXX
AMA: 2008, Mar, 8-12

1124F Advance care planning discussed and documented in the medical record; patient did not wish or was not able to name a surrogate decision maker or provide an advance care plan (GER)[5] M
🔧 0.00 ✂ 0.00 Global Days XXX
AMA: 2008, Mar, 8-12

1125F Pain severity quantified; pain present (ONC)[1] M
🔧 0.00 ✂ 0.00 Global Days XXX
AMA: 2008, Mar, 8-12

1126F Pain severity quantified; no pain present (ONC)[1] M
🔧 0.00 ✂ 0.00 Global Days XXX
AMA: 2008, Mar, 8-12

1127F New episode for condition (ML)[5] M
🔧 0.00 ✂ 0.00 Global Days XXX
AMA: 2008, Mar, 8-12

FOOTNOTES:
[1] Physician Consortium for Performance Improvement, www. physicianconsortium.org
[4] National Diabetes Quality Improvement Alliance (NDQIA), www.nationaldiabetesalliance.org
[5] Joint measure from The Physician Consortium for Performance Improvement, www.physicianconsortium.org and National Committee

---

● New Code   ▲ Revised Code   M Maternity Edit   A Age Edit   A-Y OPPS Status Indicator   🔧 Facility RVU   ✂ Non-Facility RVU
▣ CCI Comprehensive Code   50 Bilateral Procedure   + Add-on Indicator   ▮ Laboratory crosswalk   ▮ Radiology crosswalk

Category II Codes

1128F — 2035F

1128F Subsequent episode for condition (ML)[5]   M
    0.00   0.00   Global Days XXX
    AMA: 2008, Mar, 8-12

1130F Back pain and function assessed, including all of the following: Pain assessment AND functional status AND patient history, including notation of presence or absence of "red flags" (warning signs) AND assessment of prior treatment and response, AND employment status (BkP)[2]   M
    0.00   0.00   Global Days XXX
    AMA: 2008, Mar, 8-12

1134F Episode of back pain lasting 6 weeks or less (BkP)[2]   M
    0.00   0.00   Global Days XXX
    AMA: 2008, Mar, 8-12

1135F Episode of back pain lasting longer than 6 weeks (BkP)[2]   M
    0.00   0.00   Global Days XXX
    AMA: 2008, Mar, 8-12

1136F Episode of back pain lasting 12 weeks or less (BkP)2   M
    0.00   0.00   Global Days XXX
    AMA: 2008, Mar, 8-12

1137F Episode of back pain lasting longer than 12 weeks (BkP)[2]   M
    0.00   0.00   Global Days XXX
    AMA: 2008, Mar, 8-12

● **1180F** All specified thromboembolic risk factors assessed (AFIB)[1]   E
    0.00   0.00   Global Days XXX

● **1220F** Patient screened for depression (SUD)[5]   M
    0.00   0.00   Global Days XXX

2000F-2044F Elements of Examination

INCLUDES   components of clinical assessment or physical exam

2000F Blood pressure measured (CAD, CKD, HF, HTN)[1](DM)[2,4]   M PQ
    0.00   0.00   Global Days XXX
    AMA: 2008, Mar, 8-12; 2006, Dec, 10-12; 2006, Dec, 10-12; 2006, Dec, 10-12; 2006, December, 10-12; 2006, December, 10-12; 2006, Dec, 10-12; 2005, Oct, 1-5; 2005, October, 1-5; 2005, Oct, 1-5; 2004, Nov, 1; 2004, November, 1; 2004, Nov, 1

2001F Weight recorded (HF, PAG)[1]   M
    0.00   0.00   Global Days XXX
    AMA: 2006, Dec, 10-12; 2006, Dec, 10-12; 2006, Dec, 10-12; 2006, Dec, 10-12; 2006, December, 10-12; 2006, December, 10-12

2002F Clinical signs of volume overload (excess) assessed (HF)[1]   M
    0.00   0.00   Global Days XXX
    AMA: 2006, Dec, 10-12; 2006, Dec, 10-12; 2006, Dec, 10-12; 2006, Dec, 10-12; 2006, December, 10-12; 2006, December, 10-12

2004F Initial examination of the involved joint(s) (includes visual inspection, palpation, range of motion) (OA)[1] [Instructions: Report only for initial osteoarthritis visit or for visits for new joint involvement]   M
    INCLUDES   visits for initial osteoarthritis examination or new joint involvement
    0.00   0.00   Global Days XXX
    AMA: 2004, Feb, 3; 2004, Feb, 3; 2004, February, 3

2010F Vital signs (temperature, pulse, respiratory rate, and blood pressure) documented and reviewed (CAP)[2] (EM)[5]   M PQ
    0.00   0.00   Global Days XXX

2014F Mental status assessed (CAP)[1] (EM) [5]   M PQ
    0.00   0.00   Global Days XXX

2018F Hydration status assessed (normal/mildly dehydrated/severely dehydrated) (CAP)[1]   M
    0.00   0.00   Global Days XXX

2019F Dilated macular exam performed, including documentation of the presence or absence of macular thickening or hemorrhage AND the level of macular degeneration severity (EC)[5]   M PQ
    0.00   0.00   Global Days XXX

2020F Dilated fundus evaluation performed within 12 months prior to cataract surgery (EC)[5]   M PQ
    0.00   0.00   Global Days XXX
    AMA: 2008, Mar, 8-12

2021F Dilated macular or fundus exam performed, including documentation of the presence or absence of macular edema AND level of severity of retinopathy (EC)[5]   M PQ
    0.00   0.00   Global Days XXX

2022F Dilated retinal eye exam with interpretation by an ophthalmologist or optometrist documented and reviewed (DM)[2,4]   M
    0.00   0.00   Global Days XXX
    AMA: 2008, Mar, 8-12

2024F 7 standard field stereoscopic photos with interpretation by an ophthalmologist or optometrist documented and reviewed (DM)[2,4]   M
    0.00   0.00   Global Days XXX
    AMA: 2008, Mar, 8-12

2026F Eye imaging validated to match diagnosis from 7 standard field stereoscopic photos results documented and reviewed (DM)[2,4]   M
    0.00   0.00   Global Days XXX
    AMA: 2008, Mar, 8-12

2027F Optic nerve head evaluation performed (EC)[5]   M PQ
    0.00   0.00   Global Days XXX

2028F Foot examination performed (includes examination through visual inspection, sensory exam with monofilament, and pulse exam – report when any of the 3 components are completed) (DM)[4]   M
    0.00   0.00   Global Days XXX

2029F Complete physical skin exam performed (ML)[5]   M PQ
    0.00   0.00   Global Days XXX
    AMA: 2008, Mar, 8-12

2030F Hydration status documented, normally hydrated (PAG)[1]   M
    0.00   0.00   Global Days XXX

2031F Hydration status documented, dehydrated (PAG)[1]   M
    0.00   0.00   Global Days XXX

2035F Tympanic membrane mobility assessed with pneumatic otoscopy or tympanometry (OME)[1]   M
    0.00   0.00   Global Days XXX
    AMA: 2008, Mar, 8-12

FOOTNOTES:

[1] Physician Consortium for Performance Improvement, www. physicianconsortium.org

[2] National Committee on Quality Assurance (NCOA), Health Employer Data Information Set (HEDIS®), www.ncqa.org

[4] National Diabetes Quality Improvement Alliance (NDQIA), www.nationaldiabetesalliance.org

[5] Joint measure from The Physician Consortium for Performance Improvement, www.physicianconsortium.org and National Committee

2040F Physical examination on the date of the initial visit for low back pain performed, in accordance with specifications (BkP)[2]   M

   💷 0.00   ⚖ 0.00 Global Days XXX
   AMA: 2008, Mar, 8-12

2044F Documentation of mental health assessment prior to intervention (back surgery or epidural steroid injection) or for back pain episode lasting longer than 6 weeks (BkP)[2]   M

   💷 0.00   ⚖ 0.00 Global Days XXX
   AMA: 2008, Mar, 8-12

3006F-3573F Findings from Diagnostic Tests

INCLUDES ordered test results and medical decision making:of:
   clinical laboratory tests
   other procedural examinations
   radiological examinations

3006F Chest X-ray results documented and reviewed (CAP)[1]   M

   💷 0.00   ⚖ 0.00 Global Days XXX

3011F Lipid panel results documented and reviewed (must include total cholesterol, HDL-C, triglycerides and calculated LDL-C) (CAD)[1]   M

   💷 0.00   ⚖ 0.00 Global Days XXX

3014F Screening mammography results documented and reviewed (PV)[1,2]   M

   💷 0.00   ⚖ 0.00 Global Days XXX
   AMA: 2008, Mar, 8-12

3017F Colorectal cancer screening results documented and reviewed (PV)[1,2]   M

   💷 0.00   ⚖ 0.00 Global Days XXX
   AMA: 2008, Mar, 8-12

3020F Left ventricular function (LVF) assessment (eg, echocardiography, nuclear test, or ventriculography) documented in the medical record (includes: quantitative or qualitative assessment results) (HF)[1]   M

   💷 0.00   ⚖ 0.00 Global Days XXX
   AMA: 2006, Dec, 10-12; 2006, Dec, 10-12; 2006, Dec, 10-12; 2006, Dec, 10-12; 2006, December, 10-12; 2006, December, 10-12

● 3021F Left ventricular ejection fraction (LVEF) less than 40% or documentation of moderately or severely depressed left ventricular systolic function (CAD, HF)[1]   M PO

   💷 0.00   ⚖ 0.00 Global Days XXX

3022F Left ventricular ejection fraction (LVEF) greater than or equal to 40% or documentation as normal or mildly depressed left ventricular systolic function (CAD, HF)[1]   M PO

   💷 0.00   ⚖ 0.00 Global Days XXX

3023F Spirometry results documented and reviewed (COPD)[1]   M PO

   💷 0.00   ⚖ 0.00 Global Days XXX

● 3025F Spirometry test results demonstrate FEV_1/FVC less than 70% with COPD symptoms (eg, dyspnea, cough/sputum, wheezing) (CAP, COPD)[1]   M PO

   💷 0.00   ⚖ 0.00 Global Days XXX

3027F Spirometry test results demonstrate FEV_1/FVC greater than or equal to 70% or patient does not have COPD symptoms (COPD)[1]   M PO

   💷 0.00   ⚖ 0.00 Global Days XXX

3028F Oxygen saturation results documented and reviewed (includes assessment through pulse oximetry or arterial blood gas measurement) (CAP, COPD)[1] (EM)[5]   M PO

   💷 0.00   ⚖ 0.00 Global Days XXX

3035F Oxygen saturation less than or equal to 88 % or a PaO_2 less than or equal to 55 mm Hg (COPD)[1]   M

   💷 0.00   ⚖ 0.00 Global Days XXX

3037F Oxygen saturation greater than 88% or PaO_2 greater than 55 mmHg (COPD)[1]   M

   💷 0.00   ⚖ 0.00 Global Days XXX

3040F Functional expiratory volume (FEV_1) less than 40% of predicted value (COPD)[1]   M

   💷 0.00   ⚖ 0.00 Global Days XXX

3042F Functional expiratory volume (FEV_1) greater than or equal to 40% of predicted value (COPD)[1]   M

   💷 0.00   ⚖ 0.00 Global Days XXX

3044F Most recent hemoglobin A1c (HbA1c) level less than 7.0% (DM)[2,4]   M PO

   💷 0.00   ⚖ 0.00 Global Days XXX

3045F Most recent hemoglobin A1c (HbA1c) level 7.0 – 9.0 % (DM)[2,4]   M PO

   💷 0.00   ⚖ 0.00 Global Days XXX

3046F Most recent hemoglobin A1c level greater than 9.0% (DM)[4]   M PO

   💷 0.00   ⚖ 0.00 Global Days XXX

3048F Most recent LDL-C less than 100 mg/dL (DM)[4]   M PO
   💷 0.00   ⚖ 0.00 Global Days XXX

3049F Most recent LDL-C 100-129 mg/dL (DM)[4]   M PO
   💷 0.00   ⚖ 0.00 Global Days XXX

3050F Most recent LDL-C greater than or equal to 130 mg/dL (DM)[4]   M PO

   💷 0.00   ⚖ 0.00 Global Days XXX

3060F Positive microalbuminuria test result documented and reviewed (DM)[2,4]   M

   💷 0.00   ⚖ 0.00 Global Days XXX

3061F Negative microalbuminuria test result documented and reviewed (DM)[2,4]   M

   💷 0.00   ⚖ 0.00 Global Days XXX

3062F Positive macroalbuminuria test result documented and reviewed (DM)[2,4]   M

   💷 0.00   ⚖ 0.00 Global Days XXX

3066F Documentation of treatment for nephropathy (eg, patient receiving dialysis, patient being treated for ESRD, CRF, ARF, or renal insufficiency, any visit to a nephrologist) (DM)[2,4]   M

   💷 0.00   ⚖ 0.00 Global Days XXX

3072F Low risk for retinopathy (no evidence of retinopathy in the prior year) (DM)[2,4]   M

   💷 0.00   ⚖ 0.00 Global Days XXX
   AMA: 2008, Mar, 8-12

▲ 3073F Pre-surgical (cataract) axial length, corneal power measurement and method of intraocular lens power calculation documented (must be performed within 12 months prior to surgery) (EC)[5]   M PO

   💷 0.00   ⚖ 0.00 Global Days XXX
   AMA: 2008, Mar, 8-12

FOOTNOTES:

[1] Physician Consortium for Performance Improvement, www. physicianconsortium.org

[2] National Committee on Quality Assurance (NCOA), Health Employer Data Information Set (HEDIS®), www.ncqa.org

[4] National Diabetes Quality Improvement Alliance (NDQIA), www.nationaldiabetesalliance.org

[5] Joint measure from The Physician Consortium for Performance Improvement, www.physicianconsortium.org and National Committee

● New Code   ▲ Revised Code   M Maternity Edit   A Age Edit   A/Y OPPS Status Indicator   💷 Facility RVU   ⚖ Non-Facility RVU
CCI Comprehensive Code   50 Bilateral Procedure   + Add-on Indicator   N Laboratory crosswalk   R Radiology crosswalk

3074F Most recent systolic blood pressure less than 130 mm Hg (DM)[2,4], (HTN, CKD)[1]   M P0
   0.00   0.00 Global Days XXX
   AMA: 2008, Mar, 8-12

3075F Most recent systolic blood pressure 130 to 139 mm Hg (DM)[2,4] (HTN, CKD)[1]   M P0
   0.00   0.00 Global Days XXX
   AMA: 2008, Mar, 8-12

3077F Most recent systolic blood pressure >= 140 mm Hg (DM)[2,4] (HTN, CKD)[1]   M P0
   0.00   0.00 Global Days XXX
   AMA: 2008, Mar, 8-12

3078F Most recent diastolic blood pressure < 80 mm Hg (DM)[2,4] (HTN, CKD)[1]   M P0
   0.00   0.00 Global Days XXX
   AMA: 2008, Mar, 8-12

3079F Most recent diastolic blood pressure 80 - 89 mm Hg (DM)[2,4] (HTN, CKD)[1]   M P0
   0.00   0.00 Global Days XXX
   AMA: 2008, Mar, 8-12

3080F Most recent diastolic blood pressure >= 90 mm Hg (DM)[2,4] (HTN, CKD)[1]   M P0
   0.00   0.00 Global Days XXX
   AMA: 2008, Mar, 8-12

3082F Kt/V less than 1.2 (Clearance of urea [Kt]/volume [V]) (ESRD)[1]   M
   0.00   0.00 Global Days XXX
   AMA: 2008, Mar, 8-12

3083F Kt/V equal to or greater than 1.2 and less than 1.7 (Clearance of urea [Kt]/volume [V]) (ESRD)[1]   M
   0.00   0.00 Global Days XXX
   AMA: 2008, Mar, 8-12

3084F Kt/V greater than or equal to 1.7 (Clearance of urea [Kt]/volume [V]) (ESRD)[1]   M
   0.00   0.00 Global Days XXX
   AMA: 2008, Mar, 8-12

3085F Suicide risk assessed (MDD)[1]   M
   0.00   0.00 Global Days XXX

3088F Major depressive disorder, mild (MDD)[1]   M
   0.00   0.00 Global Days XXX

3089F Major depressive disorder, moderate (MDD)[1]   M
   0.00   0.00 Global Days XXX

3090F Major depressive disorder, severe without psychotic features (MDD)[1]   M
   0.00   0.00 Global Days XXX

3091F Major depressive disorder, severe with psychotic features (MDD)[1]   M
   0.00   0.00 Global Days XXX

3092F Major depressive disorder, in remission (MDD)[1]   M
   0.00   0.00 Global Days XXX

3093F Documentation of new diagnosis of initial or recurrent episode of major depressive disorder (MDD)[1]   M
   0.00   0.00 Global Days XXX
   AMA: 2008, Mar, 8-12

3095F Central dual-energy X-Ray Absorptiometry (DXA) results documented (OP)[5]   M P0
   0.00   0.00 Global Days XXX

3096F Central dual-energy X-Ray Absorptiometry (DXA) ordered (OP)[5]   M P0
   0.00   0.00 Global Days XXX

3100F Carotid imaging study report includes direct or indirect reference to measurements of distal internal carotid diameter as the denominator for stenosis measurement (STR, RAD)[5]   M P0
   0.00   0.00 Global Days XXX
   AMA: 2008, Mar, 8-12

3110F Presence or absence of hemorrhage and mass lesion and acute infarction documented in final CT or MRI report (STR)[5]   M P0
   0.00   0.00 Global Days XXX

3111F CT or MRI of the brain performed within 24 hours of arrival to the hospital (STR)[5]   M P0
   0.00   0.00 Global Days XXX

3112F CT or MRI of the brain performed greater than 24 hours after arrival to the hospital (STR)[5]   M P0
   0.00   0.00 Global Days XXX

3120F 12-Lead ECG Performed (EM)[5]   M P0
   0.00   0.00 Global Days XXX

3130F Upper gastrointestinal endoscopy performed (GERD)[5]   M P0
   0.00   0.00 Global Days XXX

3132F Documentation of referral for upper gastrointestinal endoscopy (GERD)[5]   M P0
   0.00   0.00 Global Days XXX

3140F Upper gastrointestinal endoscopy report indicates suspicion of Barrett's esophagus (GERD)[5]   M P0
   0.00   0.00 Global Days XXX

3141F Upper gastrointestinal endoscopy report indicates no suspicion of Barrett's esophagus (GERD)[5]   M P0
   0.00   0.00 Global Days XXX

3142F Barium swallow test ordered (GERD)[5]   M P0
   0.00   0.00 Global Days XXX

3150F Forceps esophageal biopsy performed (GERD)[5]   M P0
   0.00   0.00 Global Days XXX

3155F Cytogenetic testing performed on bone marrow at time of diagnosis or prior to initiating treatment (HEM)[1]   M P0
   0.00   0.00 Global Days XXX

3160F Documentation of iron stores prior to initiating erythropoietin therapy (HEM)[1]   M P0
   0.00   0.00 Global Days XXX
   AMA: 2008, Mar, 8-12

3170F Flow cytometry studies performed at time of diagnosis or prior to initiating treatment (HEM)[1]   M P0
   0.00   0.00 Global Days XXX
   AMA: 2008, Mar, 8-12

3200F Barium swallow test not ordered (GERD)[5]   M P0
   0.00   0.00 Global Days XXX

3210F Group A Strep Test Performed (PHAR)[2]   M P0
   0.00   0.00 Global Days XXX
   AMA: 2008, Mar, 8-12

3215F Patient has documented immunity to Hepatitis A (HEP-C)[1]   M
   0.00   0.00 Global Days XXX
   AMA: 2008, Mar, 8-12

FOOTNOTES:

[1] Physician Consortium for Performance Improvement, www. physicianconsortium.org
[2] National Committee on Quality Assurance (NCOA), Health Employer Data Information Set (HEDIS®), www.ncqa.org
[4] National Diabetes Quality Improvement Alliance (NDQIA), www.nationaldiabetesalliance.org
[5] Joint measure from The Physician Consortium for Performance Improvement, www.physicianconsortium.org and National Committee

3216F Patient has documented immunity to Hepatitis B (HEP-C)[1]   [M]

    📠 0.00   🔬 0.00 Global Days XXX

    AMA: 2008, Mar, 8-12

3218F RNA testing for Hepatitis C documented as performed within 6 months prior to initiation of antiviral treatment for Hepatitis C (HEP-C)[1]   [M]

    📠 0.00   🔬 0.00 Global Days XXX

    AMA: 2008, Mar, 8-12

3220F Hepatitis C quantitative RNA testing documented as performed at 12 weeks from initiation of antiviral treatment (HEP-C)[1]   [M]

    📠 0.00   🔬 0.00 Global Days XXX

    AMA: 2008, Mar, 8-12

3230F Documentation that hearing test was performed within 6 months prior to tympanostomy tube insertion (OME)[1]   [M]

    📠 0.00   🔬 0.00 Global Days XXX

    AMA: 2008, Mar, 8-12

● **3250F** Specimen biopsy site other than anatomic location of primary tumor (eg, liver biopsy, lymph node biopsy) (PATH)[1]   [M]

    📠 0.00   🔬 0.00 Global Days XXX

3260F pT category (primary tumor), pN category (regional lymph nodes), and histologic grade documented in pathology report (PATH)[1]   [M]

    📠 0.00   🔬 0.00 Global Days XXX

    AMA: 2008, Mar, 8-12

3265F Ribonucleic acid (RNA) testing for Hepatitis C viremia ordered or results documented (HEP C)[1]   [M]

    📠 0.00   🔬 0.00 Global Days XXX

    AMA: 2008, Mar, 8-12

3266F Hepatitis C genotype testing documented as performed prior to initiation of antiviral treatment for Hepatitis C (HEP C)[1]   [M]

    📠 0.00   🔬 0.00 Global Days XXX

    AMA: 2008, Mar, 8-12

3268F Prostate-specific antigen (PSA), AND primary tumor (T) stage, AND Gleason score documented prior to initiation of treatment (PRCA)[1]   [M]

    📠 0.00   🔬 0.00 Global Days XXX

3269F Bone scan performed prior to initiation of treatment or at any time since diagnosis of prostate cancer (PRCA)[1]   [M]

    📠 0.00   🔬 0.00 Global Days XXX

    AMA: 2008, Mar, 8-12

3270F Bone scan not performed prior to initiation of treatment nor at any time since diagnosis of prostate cancer (PRCA)[1]   [M]

    📠 0.00   🔬 0.00 Global Days XXX

    AMA: 2008, Mar, 8-12

3271F Low risk of recurrence, prostate cancer (PRCA)[1]   [M]

    📠 0.00   🔬 0.00 Global Days XXX

    AMA: 2008, Mar, 8-12

3272F Intermediate risk of recurrence, prostate cancer (PRCA)[1]   [M]

    📠 0.00   🔬 0.00 Global Days XXX

    AMA: 2008, Mar, 8-12

3273F High risk of recurrence, prostate cancer (PRCA)[1]   [M]

    📠 0.00   🔬 0.00 Global Days XXX

    AMA: 2008, Mar, 8-12

3274F Prostate cancer risk of recurrence not determined or neither low, intermediate nor high (PRCA)[1]   ♂ [M]

    📠 0.00   🔬 0.00 Global Days XXX

    AMA: 2008, Mar, 8-12

3278F Serum levels of calcium, phosphorus, intact Parathyroid Hormone (PTH) and lipid profile ordered (CKD)[1]   [M]

    📠 0.00   🔬 0.00 Global Days XXX

    AMA: 2008, Mar, 8-12

3279F Hemoglobin level greater than or equal to 13 g/dL (CKD, ESRD)[1]   [M]

    📠 0.00   🔬 0.00 Global Days XXX

    AMA: 2008, Mar, 8-12

3280F Hemoglobin level 11 g/dL to 12.9 g/dL (CKD, ESRD)[1]   [M]

    📠 0.00   🔬 0.00 Global Days XXX

    AMA: 2008, Mar, 8-12

3281F Hemoglobin level less than 11 g/dL (CKD, ESRD)[1]   [M]

    📠 0.00   🔬 0.00 Global Days XXX

    AMA: 2008, Mar, 8-12

3284F Intraocular pressure (IOP) reduced by a value of greater than or equal to 15% from the pre-intervention level (EC)[5]   [M]

    📠 0.00   🔬 0.00 Global Days XXX

    AMA: 2008, Mar, 8-12

3285F Intraocular pressure (IOP) reduced by a value less than 15% from the pre-intervention level (EC)[5]   [M]

    📠 0.00   🔬 0.00 Global Days XXX

    AMA: 2008, Mar, 8-12

3288F Falls risk assessment documented (GER)[5]   [M]

    📠 0.00   🔬 0.00 Global Days XXX

    AMA: 2008, Mar, 8-12

3290F Patient is D (Rh) negative and unsensitized (PRENATAL)[1]   [M]

    📠 0.00   🔬 0.00 Global Days XXX

    AMA: 2008, Mar, 8-12

3291F Patient is D (Rh) positive or sensitized (PRENATAL)[1]   [M]

    📠 0.00   🔬 0.00 Global Days XXX

    AMA: 2008, Mar, 8-12

3292F HIV testing ordered or documented and reviewed during the first or second prenatal visit (PRENATAL)[1]   [M]

    📠 0.00   🔬 0.00 Global Days XXX

▲ **3300F** American Joint Committee on Cancer (AJCC) stage documented and reviewed (ONC)[1]   [M]

    📠 0.00   🔬 0.00 Global Days XXX

    AMA: 2008, Mar, 8-12

▲ **3301F** Cancer stage documented in medical record as metastatic and reviewed (ONC)[1]   [M]

    📠 0.00   🔬 0.00 Global Days XXX

    AMA: 2008, Mar, 8-12

~~**3302F** AJCC Cancer Stage 0, documented (ONC)[1], (ML)[5]~~

    See 3321F-3390F

~~**3303F** AJCC Cancer Stage IA, documented (ONC)[1], (ML)[5]~~

    See 3321F-3390F

~~**3304F** AJCC Cancer Stage IB, documented (ONC)[1], (ML)[5]~~

    See 3321F-3390F

FOOTNOTES:

[1] Physician Consortium for Performance Improvement, www.physicianconsortium.org

[5] Joint measure from The Physician Consortium for Performance Improvement, www.physicianconsortium.org and National Committee

---

● New Code   ▲ Revised Code   [M] Maternity Edit   [A] Age Edit   [A] [Y] OPPS Status Indicator   📠 Facility RVU   🔬 Non-Facility RVU

[CCI] CCI Comprehensive Code   [50] Bilateral Procedure   + Add-on Indicator   [N] Laboratory crosswalk   [R] Radiology crosswalk

~~3305F~~ ~~AJCC Cancer Stage IC, documented (ONC)¹, (ML)⁵~~
See 3321F-3390F

~~3306F~~ ~~AJCC Cancer Stage IIA, documented (ONC)¹, (ML)⁵~~
See 3321F-3390F

~~3307F~~ ~~AJCC Cancer Stage IIB, documented (ONC)¹, (ML)⁵~~
See 3321F-3390F

~~3308F~~ ~~AJCC Cancer Stage IIC, documented (ONC)¹, (ML)⁵~~
See 3321F-3390F

~~3309F~~ ~~AJCC Cancer Stage IIIA, documented (ONC)¹, (ML)⁵~~
See 3321F-3390F

~~3310F~~ ~~AJCC Cancer Stage IIIB, documented (ONC)¹, (ML)⁵~~
See 3321F-3390F

~~3311F~~ ~~AJCC Cancer Stage IIIC, documented (ONC)¹, (ML)⁵~~
See 3321F-3390F

~~3312F~~ ~~AJCC Cancer Stage IV, documented (ONC)¹, (ML)⁵~~
See 3321F-3390F

~~3313F~~ ~~AJCC Cancer Stage IVB, documented (ONC)¹, (ML)⁵~~
See 3321F-3390F

~~3314F~~ ~~AJCC Cancer Stage IVC, documented (ONC)¹, (ML)⁵~~
See 3321F-3390F

3315F Estrogen receptor (ER) or progesterone receptor (PR) positive breast cancer (ONC)[1] [M]
0.00 0.00 Global Days XXX
AMA: 2008, Mar, 8-12

3316F Estrogen receptor (ER) and progesterone receptor (PR) negative breast cancer (ONC)[1] [M]
0.00 0.00 Global Days XXX
AMA: 2008, Mar, 8-12

3317F Pathology report confirming malignancy documented in the medical record and reviewed prior to the initiation of chemotherapy (ONC)[1] [M]
0.00 0.00 Global Days XXX
AMA: 2008, Mar, 8-12

3318F Pathology report confirming malignancy documented in the medical record and reviewed prior to the initiation of radiation therapy (ONC)[1] [M]
0.00 0.00 Global Days XXX
AMA: 2008, Mar, 8-12

3319F One of the following diagnostic imaging studies ordered: (chest X-ray, CT, Ultrasound, MRI, PET, or nuclear medicine scans) (ML)[5] [M]
0.00 0.00 Global Days XXX
AMA: 2008, Mar, 8-12

3320F None of the following diagnostic imaging studies ordered: (chest X-ray, CT, Ultrasound, MRI, PET, or nuclear medicine scans) (ML)[5] [M]
0.00 0.00 Global Days XXX
AMA: 2008, Mar, 8-12

● **3321F** AJCC Cancer Stage 0 or 1A Melanoma, documented (ML)[5] [E]
0.00 0.00 Global Days XXX

● **3322F** Melanoma greater than AJCC Stage 0 or IA (ML)[5] [E]
0.00 0.00 Global Days XXX

3325F Preoperative assessment of functional or medical indication(s) for surgery prior to the cataract surgery with intraocular lens placement (must be performed within 12 months prior to cataract surgery) (EC)[5] [M]
0.00 0.00 Global Days XXX
AMA: 2008, Mar, 8-12

3330F Imaging study ordered (BkP)[2] [M]
0.00 0.00 Global Days XXX
AMA: 2008, Mar, 8-12

3331F Imaging study not ordered (BkP)[2] [M]
0.00 0.00 Global Days XXX
AMA: 2008, Mar, 8-12

▲ **3340F** Mammogram assessment category of "incomplete: need additional imaging evaluation", documented (RAD)[5] ♀[M]
0.00 0.00 Global Days XXX
AMA: 2008, Mar, 8-12

▲ **3341F** Mammogram assessment category of "negative", documented(RAD) ♀[M]
0.00 0.00 Global Days XXX
AMA: 2008, Mar, 8-12

▲ **3342F** Mammogram assessment category of "benign", documented (RAD)[5] ♀[M]
0.00 0.00 Global Days XXX
AMA: 2008, Mar, 8-12

▲ **3343F** Mammogram assessment category of "probably benign", documented (RAD)[5] ♀[M]
0.00 0.00 Global Days XXX
AMA: 2008, Mar, 8-12

▲ **3344F** Mammogram assessment category of "suspicious", documented (RAD)[5] ♀[M]
0.00 0.00 Global Days XXX
AMA: 2008, Mar, 8-12

▲ **3345F** Mammogram assessment category of "highly suggestive of malignancy", documented (RAD)[5] ♀[M]
0.00 0.00 Global Days XXX
AMA: 2008, Mar, 8-12

● **3350F** Mammogram assessment category of "known biopsy proven malignancy", documented (RAD)[5] ♀[M]
0.00 0.00 Global Days XXX
AMA: 2008, Mar, 8-12

● **3351F** Negative screen for depressive symptoms as categorized by using a standardized depression screening/assessment tool (MDD)[2] [E]
0.00 0.00 Global Days XXX

● **3352F** No significant depressive symptoms as categorized by using a standardized depression assessment tool (MDD)[2] [E]
0.00 0.00 Global Days XXX

● **3353F** Mild to moderate depressive symptoms as categorized by using a standardized depression screening/assessment tool (MDD)[2] [E]
0.00 0.00 Global Days XXX

● **3354F** Clinically significant depressive symptoms as categorized by using a standardized depression screening/assessment tool (MDD)[2] [E]
0.00 0.00 Global Days XXX

FOOTNOTES:

[1] Physician Consortium for Performance Improvement, www. physicianconsortium.org

[2] National Committee on Quality Assurance (NCOA), Health Employer Data Information Set (HEDIS®), www.ncqa.org

[5] Joint measure from The Physician Consortium for Performance Improvement, www.physicianconsortium.org and National Committee

● 3370F AJCC Breast Cancer Stage 0, documented (ONC)[1] M
    📋 0.00 🔧 0.00 Global Days XXX

● 3372F AJCC Breast Cancer Stage I: T1mic, T1a or T1b (tumor size <= 1 cm), documented (ONC)[1] M
    📋 0.00 🔧 0.00 Global Days XXX

● 3374F AJCC Breast Cancer Stage I: T1c (tumor size > 1 cm to 2 cm), documented (ONC)[1] M
    📋 0.00 🔧 0.00 Global Days XXX

● 3376F AJCC Breast Cancer Stage II, documented (ONC)[1] M
    📋 0.00 🔧 0.00 Global Days XXX

● 3378F AJCC Breast Cancer Stage III, documented (ONC)[1] M
    📋 0.00 🔧 0.00 Global Days XXX

● 3380F AJCC Breast Cancer Stage IV, documented (ONC)[1] M
    📋 0.00 🔧 0.00 Global Days XXX

● 3382F AJCC colon cancer, Stage 0, documented (ONC)[1] M
    📋 0.00 🔧 0.00 Global Days XXX

● 3384F AJCC colon cancer, Stage I, documented (ONC)[1] M
    📋 0.00 🔧 0.00 Global Days XXX

● 3386F AJCC colon cancer, Stage II, documented (ONC)[1] M
    📋 0.00 🔧 0.00 Global Days XXX

● 3388F AJCC colon cancer, Stage III, documented (ONC)[1] M
    📋 0.00 🔧 0.00 Global Days XXX

● 3390F AJCC colon cancer, Stage IV, documented (ONC)[1] M
    📋 0.00 🔧 0.00 Global Days XXX

● 3500F CD4+ cell count or CD4+ cell percentage documented as performed (HIV)[5] M
    📋 0.00 🔧 0.00 Global Days XXX

● 3502F HIV RNA viral load below limits of quantification (HIV)[5] M
    📋 0.00 🔧 0.00 Global Days XXX

● 3503F HIV RNA viral load not below limits of quantification (HIV)[5] M
    📋 0.00 🔧 0.00 Global Days XXX

● 3510F Documentation that tuberculosis (TB) screening test performed and results interpreted (HIV)[5] E
    📋 0.00 🔧 0.00 Global Days XXX

● 3511F Chlamydia and gonorrhea screenings documented as performed (HIV)[5] E
    📋 0.00 🔧 0.00 Global Days XXX

● 3512F Syphilis screening documented as performed (HIV)[5] E
    📋 0.00 🔧 0.00 Global Days XXX

● 3513F Hepatitis B screening documented as performed (HIV)[5] E
    📋 0.00 🔧 0.00 Global Days XXX

● 3514F Hepatitis C screening documented as performed (HIV)[5] E
    📋 0.00 🔧 0.00 Global Days XXX

● 3515F Patient has documented immunity to Hepatitis C (HIV)[5] E
    📋 0.00 🔧 0.00 Global Days XXX

● 3550F Low risk for thromboembolism (AFIB)[1] E
    📋 0.00 🔧 0.00 Global Days XXX

● 3551F Intermediate risk for thromboembolism (AFIB)[1] E
    📋 0.00 🔧 0.00 Global Days XXX

● 3552F High risk for thromboembolism (AFIB)[1] E
    📋 0.00 🔧 0.00 Global Days XXX

● 3555F Patient had International Normalized Ratio (INR) measurement performed (AFIB)[1] E
    📋 0.00 🔧 0.00 Global Days XXX

● 3570F Final report for bone scintigraphy study includes correlation with existing relevant imaging studies (eg, x-ray, MRI, CT) corresponding to the same anatomical region in question (NUC_MED)[1] E
    📋 0.00 🔧 0.00 Global Days XXX

● 3572F Patient considered to be potentially at risk for fracture in a weight-bearing site (NUC_MED)[1] E
    📋 0.00 🔧 0.00 Global Days XXX

● 3573F Patient not considered to be potentially at risk for fracture in a weight-bearing site (NUC_MED)[1] F
    📋 0.00 🔧 0.00 Global Days XXX

4000F-4320F Therapies Provided (Includes Preventive Services)

INCLUDES behavioral/pharmacologic/procedural therapies preventive services including patient education/counseling

▲ 4000F Tobacco use cessation intervention, counseling (COPD, CAP, CAD)[1] (DM)[4] (PV)[2] M
    📋 0.00 🔧 0.00 Global Days XXX
    AMA: 2008, Mar, 8-12; 2005, Oct, 1-5; 2005, Oct, 1-5; 2005, October, 1-5; 2004, Nov, 1; 2004, November, 1; 2004, Nov, 1

▲ 4001F Tobacco use cessation intervention, pharmacologic therapy (COPD, CAP, CAD)[1] (DM)[4] (PV)[2] M
    📋 0.00 🔧 0.00 Global Days XXX
    AMA: 2008, Mar, 8-12; 2004, Nov, 1; 2004, Nov, 1; 2004, November, 1

4002F Statin therapy, prescribed (CAD)[1] M
    📋 0.00 🔧 0.00 Global Days XXX
    AMA: 2004, Nov, 1; 2004, Nov, 1; 2004, November, 1

4003F Patient education, written/oral, appropriate for patients with heart failure, performed (HF)[1] M
    📋 0.00 🔧 0.00 Global Days XXX
    AMA: 2004, Nov, 1; 2004, Nov, 1; 2004, November, 1

4005F Pharmacologic therapy (other than minerals/vitamins) for osteoporosis prescribed (OP)[5] M PO
    📋 0.00 🔧 0.00 Global Days XXX

4006F Beta-blocker therapy, prescribed (CAD, HF)[1] M PO
    📋 0.00 🔧 0.00 Global Days XXX

4009F Angiotensin converting enzyme (ACE) inhibitor or Angiotensin Receptor Blocker (ARB) therapy, prescribed (HF, CAD, CKD)[1], (DM)[2] M PO
    📋 0.00 🔧 0.00 Global Days XXX
    AMA: 2008, Mar, 8-12; 2004, Nov, 1; 2004, Nov, 1; 2004, November, 1

4011F Oral antiplatelet therapy prescribed (eg, aspirin, clopidogrel/Plavix, or combination of aspirin and dipyridamole/Aggrenox) (CAD)[1] M PO
    📋 0.00 🔧 0.00 Global Days XXX
    AMA: 2004, Nov, 1; 2004, Nov, 1; 2004, November, 1

▲ 4012F Warfarin therapy prescribed (HF)[1] M
    📋 0.00 🔧 0.00 Global Days XXX

FOOTNOTES:

[1] Physician Consortium for Performance Improvement, www. physicianconsortium.org

[2] National Committee on Quality Assurance (NCOA), Health Employer Data Information Set (HEDIS®), www.ncqa.org

[5] Joint measure from The Physician Consortium for Performance Improvement, www.physicianconsortium.org and National Committee

---

● New Code ▲ Revised Code M Maternity Edit Age Edit OPPS Status Indicator Facility RVU Non-Facility RVU
CCI Comprehensive Code 50 Bilateral Procedure + Add-on Indicator Laboratory crosswalk Radiology crosswalk

4014F Written discharge instructions provided to heart failure patients discharged home. (Instructions include all of the following components: activity level, diet, discharge medications, follow-up appointment, weight monitoring, what to do if symptoms worsen(HF)[3] (Excludes patients less than 18 years of age) Ⓐ Ⓜ

> **EXCLUDES** *patients younger than 18 years of age*

💬 0.00 👁 0.00 Global Days XXX

▲ **4015F** Persistent asthma, preferred long term control medication or an acceptable alternative treatment, prescribed (Asthma)[1] (Note: There are no medical exclusion criteria) Ⓜ Ⓟ

> Code also modifier 2P for patient reasons for not prescribing
>
> Do not report with with modifier 1P

💬 0.00 👁 0.00 Global Days XXX

▲ **4016F** Anti-inflammatory/analgesic agent prescribed (OA)[1] (Use for prescribed or continued medication[s], including over-the-counter medication[s]) Ⓜ

> **INCLUDES** over-the-counter medication(s) prescribed/continued medication(s)

💬 0.00 👁 0.00 Global Days XXX

4017F Gastrointestinal prophylaxis for NSAID use prescribed (OA)[1] Ⓜ

💬 0.00 👁 0.00 Global Days XXX

4018F Therapeutic exercise for the involved joint(s) instructed or physical or occupational therapy prescribed (OA)[1] Ⓜ

💬 0.00 👁 0.00 Global Days XXX

4019F Documentation of receipt of counseling on exercise AND either both calcium and vitamin D use or counseling regarding both calcium and vitamin D use (OP)[5] Ⓜ Ⓟ

💬 0.00 👁 0.00 Global Days XXX

4025F Inhaled bronchodilator prescribed (COPD)[1] Ⓜ Ⓟ

💬 0.00 👁 0.00 Global Days XXX

4030F Long-term oxygen therapy prescribed (more than 15 hours per day) (COPD)[1] Ⓜ

💬 0.00 👁 0.00 Global Days XXX

4033F Pulmonary rehabilitation exercise training recommended (COPD)[1] Ⓜ

> Code also dyspnea assessed, present (1019F)

💬 0.00 👁 0.00 Global Days XXX

4035F Influenza immunization recommended (COPD)[1] Ⓜ

💬 0.00 👁 0.00 Global Days XXX

AMA: 2008, Mar, 8-12

4037F Influenza immunization ordered or administered (COPD, PV, CKD, ESRD)[1] Ⓜ

💬 0.00 👁 0.00 Global Days XXX

AMA: 2008, Mar, 8-12

4040F Pneumococcal vaccine administered or previously received (COPD)[1], (PV)[2] Ⓜ

💬 0.00 👁 0.00 Global Days XXX

AMA: 2008, Mar, 8-12

4041F Documentation of order for cefazolin OR cefuroxime for antimicrobial prophylaxis (PERI 2)[5] Ⓜ Ⓟ

💬 0.00 👁 0.00 Global Days XXX

4042F Documentation that prophylactic antibiotics were neither given within 4 hours prior to surgical incision nor given intraoperatively (PERI 2)[5] Ⓜ Ⓟ

💬 0.00 👁 0.00 Global Days XXX

4043F Documentation that an order was given to discontinue prophylactic antibiotics within 48 hours of surgical end time, cardiac procedures (PERI 2)[5] Ⓜ Ⓟ

💬 0.00 👁 0.00 Global Days XXX

4044F Documentation that an order was given for venous thromboembolism (VTE) prophylaxis to be given within 24 hrs prior to incision time or 24 hours after surgery end time (PERI 2)[5] Ⓜ Ⓟ

💬 0.00 👁 0.00 Global Days XXX

4045F Appropriate empiric antibiotic prescribed (CAP)[1], (EM)[5] Ⓜ Ⓟ

💬 0.00 👁 0.00 Global Days XXX

4046F Documentation that prophylactic antibiotics were given within 4 hours prior to surgical incision or given intraoperatively (PERI 2)[5] Ⓜ Ⓟ

💬 0.00 👁 0.00 Global Days XXX

4047F Documentation of order for prophylactic antibiotics to be given within 1 hour (if fluoroquinolone or vancomycin, 2 hours) prior to surgical incision (or start of procedure when no incision is required) (PERI 2)[5] Ⓜ Ⓟ

💬 0.00 👁 0.00 Global Days XXX

4048F Documentation that prophylactic antibiotic was given within 1 hour (if fluoroquinolone or vancomycin, 2 hours) prior to surgical incision (or start of procedure when no incision is required) (PERI 2)[5] Ⓜ Ⓟ

💬 0.00 👁 0.00 Global Days XXX

4049F Documentation that order was given to discontinue prophylactic antibiotics within 24 hours of surgical end time, non-cardiac procedure (PERI 2)[5] Ⓜ Ⓟ

💬 0.00 👁 0.00 Global Days XXX

4050F Hypertension plan of care documented as appropriate (HTN)[1] Ⓜ

💬 0.00 👁 0.00 Global Days XXX

4051F Referred for an arteriovenous (AV) fistula (ESRD, CKD)[1] Ⓜ

💬 0.00 👁 0.00 Global Days XXX

AMA: 2008, Mar, 8-12

4052F Hemodialysis via functioning arteriovenous (AV) fistula (ESRD)[1] Ⓜ

💬 0.00 👁 0.00 Global Days XXX

AMA: 2008, Mar, 8-12

4053F Hemodialysis via functioning arteriovenous (AV) graft (ESRD)[1] Ⓜ

💬 0.00 👁 0.00 Global Days XXX

AMA: 2008, Mar, 8-12

4054F Hemodialysis via catheter (ESRD)[1] Ⓜ

💬 0.00 👁 0.00 Global Days XXX

AMA: 2008, Mar, 8-12

4055F Patient receiving peritoneal dialysis (ESRD)[1] Ⓜ

💬 0.00 👁 0.00 Global Days XXX

AMA: 2008, Mar, 8-12

4056F Appropriate oral rehydration solution recommended (PAG)[1] Ⓜ

💬 0.00 👁 0.00 Global Days XXX

FOOTNOTES:

[1] Physician Consortium for Performance Improvement, www. physicianconsortium.org

[2] National Committee on Quality Assurance (NCOA), Health Employer Data Information Set (HEDIS®), www.ncqa.org

[3] Joint Commission on Accreditation of Healthcare Organizations (JCAHO), ORYX Initiative Performance Measures, www.JointCommission.org

[5] Joint measure from The Physician Consortium for Performance Improvement, www.physicianconsortium.org and National Committee

---

4058F　Pediatric gastroenteritis education provided to caregiver (PAG)[1]　　M
　　　　📠 0.00　　≋ 0.00　Global Days XXX

4060F　Psychotherapy services provided (MDD)[1]　　M
　　　　📠 0.00　　≋ 0.00　Global Days XXX

4062F　Patient referral for psychotherapy documented (MDD)[1]　　M
　　　　📠 0.00　　≋ 0.00　Global Days XXX

4064F　Antidepressant pharmacotherapy prescribed (MDD)[1]　　M
　　　　📠 0.00　　≋ 0.00　Global Days XXX

4065F　Antipsychotic pharmacotherapy prescribed (MDD)[1]　　M
　　　　📠 0.00　　≋ 0.00　Global Days XXX

4066F　Electroconvulsive therapy (ECT) provided (MDD)[1]　　M
　　　　📠 0.00　　≋ 0.00　Global Days XXX

4067F　Patient referral for electroconvulsive therapy (ECT) documented (MDD)[1]　　M
　　　　📠 0.00　　≋ 0.00　Global Days XXX

4070F　Deep vein thrombosis (DVT) prophylaxis received by end of hospital day 2 (STR)[5]　　M P0
　　　　📠 0.00　　≋ 0.00　Global Days XXX

4073F　Oral antiplatelet therapy prescribed at discharge (STR)[5]　　M P0
　　　　📠 0.00　　≋ 0.00　Global Days XXX

4075F　Anticoagulant therapy prescribed at discharge (STR)[5]　　M P0
　　　　📠 0.00　　≋ 0.00　Global Days XXX

4077F　Documentation that tissue plasminogen activator (t-PA) administration was considered (STR)[5]　　M P0
　　　　📠 0.00　　≋ 0.00　Global Days XXX

4079F　Documentation that rehabilitation services were considered (STR)[5]　　M P0
　　　　📠 0.00　　≋ 0.00　Global Days XXX

4084F　Aspirin received within 24 hours before emergency department arrival or during emergency department stay (EM)[5]　　M P0
　　　　📠 0.00　　≋ 0.00　Global Days XXX

4090F　Patient receiving erythropoietin therapy (HEM)[1]　　M P0
　　　　📠 0.00　　≋ 0.00　Global Days XXX
　　　　AMA: 2008, Mar, 8-12

4095F　Patient not receiving erythropoietin therapy (HEM)[1]　　M P0
　　　　📠 0.00　　≋ 0.00　Global Days XXX
　　　　AMA: 2008, Mar, 8-12

4100F　Bisphosphonate therapy, intravenous, ordered or received (HEM)[1]　　M P0
　　　　📠 0.00　　≋ 0.00　Global Days XXX
　　　　AMA: 2008, Mar, 8-12

4110F　Internal mammary artery graft performed for primary, isolated coronary artery bypass graft procedure (CABG)[6]　　M P0
　　　　📠 0.00　　≋ 0.00　Global Days XXX

4115F　Beta blocker administered within 24 hours prior to surgical incision (CABG)[6]　　M P0
　　　　📠 0.00　　≋ 0.00　Global Days XXX

4120F　Antibiotic prescribed or dispensed (URI, PHAR, A-BRONCH)[2]　　M P0
　　　　📠 0.00　　≋ 0.00　Global Days XXX
　　　　AMA: 2008, Mar, 8-12

4124F　Antibiotic neither prescribed nor dispensed (URI, PHAR, A-BRONCH)[2]　　M P0
　　　　📠 0.00　　≋ 0.00　Global Days XXX
　　　　AMA: 2008, Mar, 8-12

4130F　Topical preparations (including OTC) prescribed for acute otitis externa (AOE)[1]　　M
　　　　📠 0.00　　≋ 0.00　Global Days XXX
　　　　AMA: 2008, Mar, 8-12

4131F　Systemic antimicrobial therapy prescribed (AOE)[1]　　M
　　　　📠 0.00　　≋ 0.00　Global Days XXX
　　　　AMA: 2008, Mar, 8-12

4132F　Systemic antimicrobial therapy not prescribed (AOE)[1]　　M
　　　　📠 0.00　　≋ 0.00　Global Days XXX
　　　　AMA: 2008, Mar, 8-12

4133F　Antihistamines or decongestants prescribed or recommended (OME)[1]　　M
　　　　📠 0.00　　≋ 0.00　Global Days XXX
　　　　AMA: 2008, Mar, 8-12

4134F　Antihistamines or decongestants neither prescribed nor recommended (OME)[1]　　M
　　　　📠 0.00　　≋ 0.00　Global Days XXX
　　　　AMA: 2008, Mar, 8-12

4135F　Systemic corticosteroids prescribed (OME)[1]　　M
　　　　📠 0.00　　≋ 0.00　Global Days XXX
　　　　AMA: 2008, Mar, 8-12

4136F　Systemic corticosteroids not prescribed (OME)[1]　　M
　　　　📠 0.00　　≋ 0.00　Global Days XXX
　　　　AMA: 2008, Mar, 8-12

● 4148F　Hepatitis A vaccine injection administered or previously received (HEP-C)[1]　　E
　　　　📠 0.00　　≋ 0.00　Global Days XXX

● 4149F　Hepatitis B vaccine injection administered or previously received (HEP-C)[1]　　E
　　　　📠 0.00　　≋ 0.00　Global Days XXX

4150F　Patient receiving antiviral treatment for Hepatitis C (HEP-C)[1]　　M
　　　　📠 0.00　　≋ 0.00　Global Days XXX
　　　　AMA: 2008, Mar, 8-12

4151F　Patient not receiving antiviral treatment for Hepatitis C (HEP-C)[1]　　M
　　　　📠 0.00　　≋ 0.00　Global Days XXX
　　　　AMA: 2008, Mar, 8-12

~~4152F　Documentation that combination peginterferon and ribavirin therapy considered (HEP-C)[1]~~

4153F　Combination peginterferon and ribavirin therapy prescribed (HEP-C)[1]　　M
　　　　📠 0.00　　≋ 0.00　Global Days XXX
　　　　AMA: 2008, Mar, 8-12

~~4154F　Hepatitis A vaccine series recommended (HEP-C)[1]~~

4155F　Hepatitis A vaccine series previously received (HEP-C)[1]　　M
　　　　📠 0.00　　≋ 0.00　Global Days XXX
　　　　AMA: 2008, Mar, 8-12

~~4156F　Hepatitis B vaccine series recommended (HEP-C)[1]~~

FOOTNOTES:

[1]　Physician Consortium for Performance Improvement, www. physicianconsortium.org

[2]　National Committee on Quality Assurance (NCOA), Health Employer Data Information Set (HEDIS®), www.ncqa.org

[5]　Joint measure from The Physician Consortium for Performance Improvement, www.physicianconsortium.org and National Committee

[6]　The Society of Thoracic Surgeons, http://www.sts.org, National Quality Forum, http://www.qualityforum.org

---

● New Code　　▲ Revised Code　　M Maternity Edit　　A Age Edit　　A-Y OPPS Status Indicator　　📠 Facility RVU　　≋ Non-Facility RVU
C CCI Comprehensive Code　　50 Bilateral Procedure　　+ Add-on Indicator　　N Laboratory crosswalk　　R Radiology crosswalk

4157F Hepatitis B vaccine series previously received (HEP-C)[1] Ⓜ
    📞 0.00 ⚕ 0.00 Global Days XXX
    AMA: 2008, Mar, 8-12

4158F Patient counseled about risks of alcohol use (HEP-C)[1] Ⓜ
    📞 0.00 ⚕ 0.00 Global Days XXX
    AMA: 2008, Mar, 8-12

4159F Counseling regarding contraception received prior to initiation of antiviral treatment (HEP-C)[1] Ⓜ
    📞 0.00 ⚕ 0.00 Global Days XXX
    AMA: 2008, Mar, 8-12

4163F Patient counseling at a minimum on all of the following treatment options for clinically localized prostate cancer: active surveillance, AND interstitial prostate brachytherapy, AND external beam radiotherapy, AND radical prostatectomy, provided prior to initiation of treatment (PRCA)[1] Ⓜ
    📞 0.00 ⚕ 0.00 Global Days XXX
    AMA: 2008, Mar, 8-12

4164F Adjuvant (ie, in combination with external beam radiotherapy to the prostate for prostate cancer) hormonal therapy (gonadotropin-releasing hormone [GnRH] agonist or antagonist) prescribed/administered (PRCA)[1] Ⓜ
    📞 0.00 ⚕ 0.00 Global Days XXX
    AMA: 2008, Mar, 8-12

4165F Three-dimensional conformal radiotherapy (3D-CRT) or intensity modulated radiation therapy (IMRT) received (PRCA)[1] Ⓜ
    📞 0.00 ⚕ 0.00 Global Days XXX
    AMA: 2008, Mar, 8-12

4167F Head of bed elevation (30-45 degrees) on first ventilator day ordered (CRIT)[1] Ⓜ
    📞 0.00 ⚕ 0.00 Global Days XXX
    AMA: 2008, Mar, 8-12

4168F Patient receiving care in the intensive care unit (ICU) and receiving mechanical ventilation, 24 hours or less (CRIT)[1] Ⓜ
    📞 0.00 ⚕ 0.00 Global Days XXX
    AMA: 2008, Mar, 8-12

4169F Patient either not receiving care in the intensive care unit (ICU) OR not receiving mechanical ventilation OR receiving mechanical ventilation greater than 24 hours (CRIT)[1] Ⓜ
    📞 0.00 ⚕ 0.00 Global Days XXX
    AMA: 2008, Mar, 8-12

4171F Patient receiving Erythropoiesis-Stimulating Agents (ESA) therapy (CKD)[1] Ⓜ
    📞 0.00 ⚕ 0.00 Global Days XXX
    AMA: 2008, Mar, 8-12

4172F Patient not receiving Erythropoiesis-Stimulating Agents (ESA) therapy (CKD)[1] Ⓜ
    📞 0.00 ⚕ 0.00 Global Days XXX
    AMA: 2008, Mar, 8-12

4174F Counseling about the potential impact of glaucoma on visual functioning and quality of life, and importance of treatment adherence provided to patient and/or caregiver(s) (EC)[5] Ⓜ
    📞 0.00 ⚕ 0.00 Global Days XXX
    AMA: 2008, Mar, 8-12

4175F Best-corrected visual acuity of 20/40 or better (distance or near) achieved within the 90 days following cataract surgery (EC)[5] Ⓜ
    📞 0.00 ⚕ 0.00 Global Days XXX
    AMA: 2008, Mar, 8-12

4176F Counseling about value of protection from UV light and lack of proven efficacy of nutritional supplements in prevention or progression of cataract development provided to patient and/or caregiver(s) (EC) Ⓜ
    📞 0.00 ⚕ 0.00 Global Days XXX

4177F Counseling about the benefits and/or risks of the Age-Related Eye Disease Study (AREDS) formulation for preventing progression of age-related macular degeneration (AMD) provided to patient and/or caregiver(s) (EC)[5] Ⓜ
    📞 0.00 ⚕ 0.00 Global Days XXX
    AMA: 2008, Mar, 8-12

4178F Anti-D immune globulin received between 26 and 30 weeks gestation (PRENATAL)[1] Ⓜ ♀ Ⓜ
    📞 0.00 ⚕ 0.00 Global Days XXX
    AMA: 2008, Mar, 8-12

4179F Tamoxifen or aromatase inhibitor (AI) prescribed (ONC)[1] Ⓜ
    📞 0.00 ⚕ 0.00 Global Days XXX
    AMA: 2008, Mar, 8-12

4180F Adjuvant chemotherapy referred, prescribed, or previously received for Stage III colon cancer (ONC)[1] Ⓜ
    📞 0.00 ⚕ 0.00 Global Days XXX
    AMA: 2008, Mar, 8-12

4181F Conformal radiation therapy received (NMA-No Measure Assoc.)[1] Ⓜ
    📞 0.00 ⚕ 0.00 Global Days XXX

4182F Conformal radiation therapy not received (NMA-No Measure Assoc.)[1] Ⓜ
    📞 0.00 ⚕ 0.00 Global Days XXX

4185F Continuous (12-months) therapy with proton pump inhibitor (PPI) or histamine H2 receptor antagonist (H2RA) received (GERD)[5] Ⓜ
    📞 0.00 ⚕ 0.00 Global Days XXX

4186F No continuous (12-months) therapy with either proton pump inhibitor (PPI) or histamine H2 receptor antagonist (H2RA) received (GERD)[5] Ⓜ
    📞 0.00 ⚕ 0.00 Global Days XXX
    AMA: 2008, Mar, 8-12

4187F Disease modifying anti-rheumatic drug therapy prescribed or dispensed (RA)[2] Ⓜ
    📞 0.00 ⚕ 0.00 Global Days XXX

4188F Appropriate angiotensin converting enzyme (ACE)/angiotensin receptor blockers (ARB) therapeutic monitoring test ordered or performed (AM)[2] Ⓜ
    📞 0.00 ⚕ 0.00 Global Days XXX
    AMA: 2008, Mar, 8-12

FOOTNOTES:

[1] Physician Consortium for Performance Improvement, www. physicianconsortium.org

[2] National Committee on Quality Assurance (NCOA), Health Employer Data Information Set (HEDIS®), www.ncqa.org

[5] Joint measure from The Physician Consortium for Performance Improvement, www.physicianconsortium.org and National Committee

---

4189F   Appropriate digoxin therapeutic monitoring test ordered or performed (AM)[2]   M

    0.00   0.00   Global Days XXX
    AMA: 2008, Mar, 8-12

4190F   Appropriate diuretic therapeutic monitoring test ordered or performed (AM)[2]   M

    0.00   0.00   Global Days XXX
    AMA: 2008, Mar, 8-12

4191F   Appropriate anticonvulsant therapeutic monitoring test ordered or performed (AM)[2]   M

    0.00   0.00   Global Days XXX
    AMA: 2008, Mar, 8-12

▲ 4200F   External beam radiotherapy as primary therapy to the prostate with or without nodal irradiation (PRCA)[1]   M

    0.00   0.00   Global Days XXX
    AMA: 2008, Mar, 8-12

▲ 4201F   External beam radiotherapy with or without nodal irradiation as adjuvant or salvage therapy for prostate cancer patient (PRCA)[1]   M

    0.00   0.00   Global Days XXX
    AMA: 2008, Mar, 8-12

4210F   Angiotensin converting enzyme (ACE) or angiotensin receptor blockers (ARB) medication therapy for 6 months or more (MM)[2]   M

    0.00   0.00   Global Days XXX
    AMA: 2008, Mar, 8-12

4220F   Digoxin medication therapy for 6 months or more (MM)[2]   M

    0.00   0.00   Global Days XXX
    AMA: 2008, Mar, 8-12

4221F   Diuretic medication therapy for 6 months or more (MM)[2]   M

    0.00   0.00   Global Days XXX
    AMA: 2008, Mar, 8-12

4230F   Anticonvulsant medication therapy for 6 months or more (MM)[2]   M

    0.00   0.00   Global Days XXX
    AMA: 2008, Mar, 8-12

4240F   Instruction in therapeutic exercise with follow-up by the physician provided to patients during episode of back pain lasting longer than 12 weeks (BkP)[2]   M

    0.00   0.00   Global Days XXX
    AMA: 2008, Mar, 8-12

4242F   Counseling for supervised exercise program provided to patients during episode of back pain lasting longer than 12 weeks (BkP)[2]   M

    0.00   0.00   Global Days XXX
    AMA: 2000, Mar, 8-12

4245F   Patient counseled during the initial visit to maintain or resume normal activities (BkP)[2]   M

    0.00   0.00   Global Days XXX
    AMA: 2008, Mar, 8-12

4248F   Patient counseled during the initial visit for an episode of back pain against bed rest lasting 4 days or longer (BkP)[2]   M

    0.00   0.00   Global Days XXX
    AMA: 2008, Mar, 8-12

▲ 4250F   Active warming used intraoperatively for the purpose of maintaining normothermia, OR at least 1 body temperature equal to or greater than 36 degrees Centigrade (or 96.8 degrees Fahrenheit) recorded within the 30 minutes immediately before or the 15 minutes immediately after anesthesia end time (CRIT)[1]   M

    0.00   0.00   Global Days XXX
    AMA: 2008, Mar, 8-12

● 4270F   Patient receiving potent antiretroviral therapy for 6 months or longer (HIV)[5]   M

    0.00   0.00   Global Days XXX

● 4271F   Patient receiving potent antiretroviral therapy for less than 6 months or not receiving potent antiretroviral therapy (HIV)[5]   M

    0.00   0.00   Global Days XXX

● 4274F   Influenza immunization administered or previously received (HIV)[5]   M

    0.00   0.00   Global Days XXX

● 4275F   Hepatitis B vaccine injection administered or previously received (HIV)[5]   E

    0.00   0.00   Global Days XXX

● 4290F   Patient screened for injection drug use (HIV)[5]   E

    0.00   0.00   Global Days XXX

● 4293F   Patient screened for high-risk sexual behavior (HIV)[5]   E

    0.00   0.00   Global Days XXX

● 4300F   Patient receiving warfarin therapy for nonvalvular atrial fibrillation or atrial flutter (AFIB)[1]   E

    0.00   0.00   Global Days XXX

● 4301F   Patient not receiving warfarin therapy for nonvalvular atrial fibrillation or atrial flutter (AFIB)[1]   E

    0.00   0.00   Global Days XXX

● 4320F   Patient counseled regarding psychosocial AND pharmacologic treatment options for alcohol dependence (SUD)[5]   E

    0.00   0.00   Global Days XXX

5005F-5062F Results Conveyed and Documented

INCLUDES   patient's:
    functional status
    morbidity/mortality
    satisfaction/experience with care
  review/communication of test results to patients

5005F   Patient counseled on self-examination for new or changing moles (ML)[5]   M PO

    0.00   0.00   Global Days XXX
    AMA: 2008, Mar, 8-12

5010F   Findings of dilated macular or fundus exam communicated to the physician managing the diabetes care (EC)[5]   M PO

    0.00   0.00   Global Days XXX

5015F   Documentation of communication that a fracture occurred and that the patient was or should be tested or treated for osteoporosis (OP)[5]   M PO

    0.00   0.00   Global Days XXX

▲ 5020F   Treatment summary report communicated to physician(s) managing continuing care and to the patient within 1 month of completing treatment (ONC)[1]   E

    0.00   0.00   Global Days XXX
    AMA: 2008, Mar, 8-12

FOOTNOTES:

[1] Physician Consortium for Performance Improvement, www. physicianconsortium.org

[2] National Committee on Quality Assurance (NCOA), Health Employer Data Information Set (HEDIS®), www.ncqa.org

[5] Joint measure from The Physician Consortium for Performance Improvement, www.physicianconsortium.org and National Committee

---

● New Code   ▲ Revised Code   M Maternity Edit   A Age Edit   A-Y OPPS Status Indicator   Facility RVU   Non-Facility RVU
CCI Comprehensive Code   50 Bilateral Procedure   + Add-on Indicator   Laboratory crosswalk   Radiology crosswalk

5050F   Treatment plan communicated to provider(s) managing continuing care within 1 month of diagnosis (ML)[5]   M

     0.00   0.00   Global Days XXX
     AMA: 2008, Mar, 8-12

5060F   Findings from diagnostic mammogram communicated to practice managing patient's ongoing care within 3 business days of exam interpretation (RAD)[5]   ♀ M

     0.00   0.00   Global Days XXX
     AMA: 2008, Mar, 8-12

▲ **5062F**   Findings from diagnostic mammogram communicated to the patient within 5 days of exam interpretation (RAD)[5]   ♀ M

     0.00   0.00   Global Days XXX
     AMA: 2008, Mar, 8-12

6005F-6045F Elements Related to Patient Safety Processes

INCLUDES   patient safety practices

6005F   Rationale (eg, severity of illness and safety) for level of care (eg, home, hospital) documented (CAP)[1]   M

     0.00   0.00   Global Days XXX

6010F   Dysphagia screening conducted prior to order for or receipt of any foods, fluids or medication by mouth (STR)[5]   M PQ

     0.00   0.00   Global Days XXX

6015F   Patient receiving or eligible to receive foods, fluids or medication by mouth (STR)[5]   M PQ

     0.00   0.00   Global Days XXX

6020F   NPO (nothing by mouth) ordered (STR)[5]   M PQ

     0.00   0.00   Global Days XXX

6030F   All elements of maximal sterile barrier technique including: cap AND mask AND sterile gown AND sterile gloves AND a large sterile sheet AND hand hygiene AND 2% chlorhexidine for cutaneous antisepsis, followed (CRIT)[1]   M

     0.00   0.00   Global Days XXX
     AMA: 2008, Mar, 8-12

6040F   Use of appropriate radiation dose reduction devices OR manual techniques for appropriate moderation of exposure, documented (RAD)[5]   M

     0.00   0.00   Global Days XXX

6045F   Radiation exposure or exposure time in final report for procedure using fluoroscopy, documented (RAD)[5]   M

     0.00   0.00   Global Days XXX
     AMA: 2008, Mar, 8-12

7010F-7025F Recall/Reminder System in Place

INCLUDES   capabilities of the provider
            measures that address the setting or system of care provided

7010F   Patient information entered into a recall system with the target date for the next exam specified (ML)[5]   M

     0.00   0.00   Global Days XXX
     AMA: 2008, Mar, 8-12

▲ **7020F**   Mammogram assessment category [eg, Mammography Quality Standards Act (MQSA), Breast Imaging Reporting and Data System (BI-RADS®), or FDA approved equivalent categories] entered into an internal database to allow for analysis of abnormal interpretation (recall) rate (RAD)[5]   ♀

     0.00   0.00   Global Days XXX
     AMA: 2008, Mar, 8-12

7025F   Patient information entered into a reminder system with a target due date for the next mammogram (RAD)[5]   ♀ M

     0.00   0.00   Global Days XXX
     AMA: 2008, Mar, 8-12

FOOTNOTES:

[1]   Physician Consortium for Performance Improvement, www. physicianconsortium.org

[5]   Joint measure from The Physician Consortium for Performance Improvement, www.physicianconsortium.org and National Committee

---

0016T

    0016T Destruction of localized lesion of choroid (eg, choroidal neovascularization), transpupillary thermotherapy   R2 T 80 50 ▭
      🗁 0.00   ☖ 0.00   Global Days XXX

0017T

CMS 100-3,140.5   *Laser Procedures*
    0017T Destruction of macular drusen, photocoagulation   R2 T 80 50 ▭
      🗁 0.00   ☖ 0.00   Global Days XXX

0019T-0047T

    0019T Extracorporeal shock wave involving musculoskeletal system, not otherwise specified, low energy   A 80
      EXCLUDES   high energy:
             extracorporeal shock wave (0101T)
             lateral humeral epicondyle extracorporeal shock wave (0102T)

      🗁 0.00   ☖ 0.00   Global Days XXX
      AMA: 2006, Mar, 1-5; 2006, Mar, 1-5; 2006, March, 1-5; 2005, Jun, 6-8; 2005, June, 6-8; 2005, Jun, 6-8

    ~~**0026T** Lipoprotein, direct measurement, intermediate density lipoproteins (IDL) (remnant lipoproteins)~~
    See 84999

    ~~**0027T** Endoscopic lysis of epidural adhesions with direct visualization using mechanical means (eg, spinal endoscopic catheter system) or solution injection (eg, normal saline) including radiologic localization and epidurography~~
    See 64999

    ~~**0028T** Dual energy x-ray absorptiometry (DEXA) body composition study, one or more sites~~
    See 76499

    ~~**0029T** Treatment(s) for incontinence, pulsed magnetic neuromodulation, per day~~
    See 53899

    0030T Antiprothrombin (phospholipid cofactor) antibody, each Ig class   A 80
      🗁 0.00   ☖ 0.00   Global Days XXX

    ~~**0031T** Speculoscopy;~~
    ~~**0032T** with directed sampling~~
    See 58999

    ~~**0041T** Urinalysis infectious agent detection, semi-quantitative analysis of volatile compounds~~
    See 81099

    0042T Cerebral perfusion analysis using computed tomography with contrast administration, including post-processing of parametric maps with determination of cerebral blood flow, cerebral blood volume, and mean transit time   N1 N 80 ▭ P0
      🗁 0.00   ☖ 0.00   Global Days XXX

    ~~**0043T** Carbon monoxide, expired gas analysis (eg, ETCOc/hemolysis breath test)~~
    See 84999

    ~~**0046T** Catheter lavage of a mammary duct(s) for collection of cytology specimen(s), in high risk individuals (GAIL risk scoring or prior personal history of breast cancer), each breast; single duct~~
    See 19499

    ~~**0047T** each additional duct~~
    See 19499

0048T-0053T

CMS 100-4,3,90.2.1   *Artificial Hearts and Related Devices*
    0048T Implantation of a ventricular assist device, extracorporeal, percutaneous transseptal access, single or dual cannulation   C 80 ▭
      🗁 0.00   ☖ 0.00   Global Days XXX
      AMA: 2004, Jul, 7; 2004, Jul, 7; 2004, July, 7

    ~~**0049T** Prolonged extracorporeal percutaneous transseptal ventricular assist device, greater than 24 hours, each subsequent 24 hour period (List separately in addition to code for primary procedure)~~
    See 33999

    0050T Removal of a ventricular assist device, extracorporeal, percutaneous transseptal access, single or dual cannulation   C 80 ▭
      🗁 0.00   ☖ 0.00   Global Days XXX
      AMA: 2004, Jul, 7; 2004, Jul, 7; 2004, July, 7

    0051T Implantation of a total replacement heart system (artificial heart) with recipient cardiectomy   C 80 ▭
      EXCLUDES   *ventricular assist device implant (33975-33976)*
      🗁 0.00   ☖ 0.00   Global Days XXX
      AMA: 2004, Jun, 7; 2004, Jun, 7; 2004, June, 7

    0052T Replacement or repair of thoracic unit of a total replacement heart system (artificial heart)   C 80 ▭
      EXCLUDES   *exchange or repair of other artificial heart components (0053T)*
      🗁 0.00   ☖ 0.00   Global Days XXX
      AMA: 2004, Jun, 7; 2004, Jun, 7; 2004, June, 7

    0053T Replacement or repair of implantable component or components of total replacement heart system (artificial heart), excluding thoracic unit   C 80 ▭
      EXCLUDES   *exchange or repair of thoracic unit of artificial heart (0052T)*
      🗁 0.00   ☖ 0.00   Global Days XXX
      AMA: 2004, Jun, 7; 2004, Jun, 7; 2004, June, 7

0054T-0061T

+   ● **0054T** Computer-assisted musculoskeletal surgical navigational orthopedic procedure, with image-guidance based on fluoroscopic images (List separately in addition to code for primary procedure)   N 80 ▭
      Code first primary procedure
      🗁 0.00   ☖ 0.00   Global Days XXX
      AMA: 2007, Jan, 13-27; 2007, Jan, 13-27; 2007, January, 13-27; 2004, Jun, 7; 2004, Jun, 7; 2004, May, 14; 2004, June, 7; 2004, May, 14; 2004, May, 14

Category III Codes

0055T — 0072T

+ ● **0055T** Computer-assisted musculoskeletal surgical navigational orthopedic procedure, with image-guidance based on CT/MRI images (List separately in addition to code for primary procedure)   N 80 ▢

     INCLUDES   performance of both CT and MRI in same session (1 unit)

     Code first Code also primary procedure

     0.00   0.00   Global Days XXX

     AMA: 2007, Jan, 13-27; 2007, Jan, 13-27; 2007, January, 13-27; 2004, Jun, 7; 2004, Jun, 7; 2004, May, 14; 2004, June, 7; 2004, May, 14; 2004, May, 14

     ~~0058T~~   ~~Cryopreservation; reproductive tissue, ovarian~~
     See 89240

     ~~0059T~~   ~~oocyte(s)~~
     See 89240

     ~~0060T~~   ~~Electrical impedance scan of the breast, bilateral (risk assessment device for breast cancer)~~
     See 76499

     ~~0061T~~   ~~Destruction/reduction of malignant breast tumor including breast carcinoma cells in the margins, microwave phased array thermotherapy, disposable catheter with combined temperature monitoring probe and microwave sensor, externally applied microwave energy, including interstitial placement of sensor~~
     See 19499

0062T-0063T

     EXCLUDES   *intradiscal electrothermal annuloplasty (22526-22527)*

     0062T Percutaneous intradiscal annuloplasty, any method except electrothermal, unilateral or bilateral including fluoroscopic guidance; single level   E 80 ▢

          77012, 77021

          0.00   0.00   Global Days XXX

          AMA: 2008, Jan, 10-25; 2007, Jan, 13-27; 2007, Jan, 13-27; 2007, Mar, 7-8; 2007, Mar, 7-8; 2007, March, 7-8; 2007, January, 13-27; 2005, Mar, 1-6; 2005, Mar, 1-6; 2005, March, 1-6; 2005, April, 13-14; 2005, Apr, 13-14; 2005, Apr, 13-14; 2004, Jul, 7; 2004, July, 7; 2004, Jul, 7

+ **0063T** 1 or more additional levels (List separately in addition to 0062T for primary procedure)   E 80

          77012, 77021

          Code first (0062T)

          0.00   0.00   Global Days XXX

          AMA: 2007, Mar, 7-8; 2007, Mar, 7-8; 2007, March, 7-8; 2005, Mar, 1-6; 2005, Mar, 1-6; 2005, March, 1-6; 2004, Jul, 7; 2004, July, 7

0064T

     0064T Spectroscopy, expired gas analysis (eg, nitric oxide/carbon dioxide test)   X 80

          0.00   0.00   Global Days XXX

          AMA: 2007, Mar, 9-11; 2007, Mar, 9-11; 2007, Apr, 3-6; 2007, April, 3-6; 2007, March, 9-11; 2007, Apr, 3-6; 2005, Mar, 1-6; 2005, March, 1-6; 2005, Mar, 1-6; 2004, Jul, 7; 2004, July, 7; 2004, Jul, 7

0066T-0067T

Do not report with (72192-72194, 74150-74170)

     0066T Computed tomographic (CT) colonography (ie, virtual colonoscopy); screening   E

          0.00   0.00   Global Days XXX

          AMA: 2007, Jan, 28-31; 2007, Jan, 28-31; 2007, January, 28-31; 2005, Dec, 7; 2005, Dec, 7; 2005, Mar, 1-6; 2005, March, 1-6; 2005, December, 7; 2005, Mar, 1-6; 2004, Jul, 7; 2004, July, 7; 2004, Jul, 7

     0067T diagnostic   Z2 03 80

          0.00   0.00   Global Days XXX

          AMA: 2007, Jan, 28-31; 2007, Jan, 28-31; 2007, January, 28-31; 2005, Dec, 7; 2005, Dec, 7; 2005, Mar, 1-6; 2005, March, 1-6; 2005, December, 7; 2005, Mar, 1-6; 2004, Jul, 7; 2004, July, 7; 2004, Jul, 7

0068T-0070T

     0068T Acoustic heart sound recording and computer analysis; with interpretation and report   B 80

          0.00   0.00   Global Days XXX

          AMA: 2006, Dec, 8-9; 2006, Dec, 8-9; 2006, Dec, 8-9; 2006, December, 8-9; 2006, December, 8-9; 2006, Dec, 8-9; 2005, Mar, 1-6; 2005, March, 1-6; 2005, Mar, 1-6; 2004, Jul, 7; 2004, July, 7; 2004, Jul, 7

     0069T acoustic heart sound recording and computer analysis only   N 80

          0.00   0.00   Global Days XXX

          AMA: 2006, Dec, 8-9; 2006, Dec, 8-9; 2006, December, 8-9; 2006, December, 8-9; 2006, Dec, 8-9; 2005, Mar, 1-6; 2005, March, 1-6; 2005, Mar, 1-6; 2004, Jul, 7; 2004, July, 7; 2004, Jul, 7

     0070T interpretation and report only   B 80

          0.00   0.00   Global Days XXX

          AMA: 2006, Dec, 8-9; 2006, Dec, 8-9; 2006, Dec, 8-9; 2006, December, 8-9; 2006, December, 8-9; 2006, Dec, 8-9; 2005, Mar, 1-6; 2005, March, 1-6; 2005, Mar, 1-6; 2004, Jul, 7; 2004, July, 7; 2004, Jul, 7

0071T-0072T

Do not report with (51702, 77022)

     0071T Focused ultrasound ablation of uterine leiomyomata, including MR guidance; total leiomyomata volume less than 200 cc of tissue   ♀ S 80 ▢

          0.00   0.00   Global Days XXX

          AMA: 2005, Dec, 3-6; 2005, Dec, 3-6; 2005, Mar, 1-6; 2005, Mar, 1-6; 2005, December, 3-6; 2005, March, 1-6; 2004, Jul, 7; 2004, July, 7

     0072T total leiomyomata volume greater or equal to 200 cc of tissue   ♀ S 80 ▢

          0.00   0.00   Global Days XXX

          AMA: 2005, Mar, 1-6; 2005, Mar, 1-6; 2005, Dec, 3-6; 2005, Dec, 3-6; 2005, March, 1-6; 2005, December, 3-6; 2004, Jul, 7; 2004, July, 7

0073T

CMS 100-4,4,220.1   *Billing for IMRT Planning and Delivery*

0073T   **Compensator-based beam modulation treatment delivery of inverse planned treatment using 3 or more high resolution (milled or cast) compensator convergent beam modulated fields, per treatment session** ⓩ Ⓢ Ⓣ 80 ▭

     EXCLUDES   *radiotherapy treatment planning (77301)*

    Do not report with other treatment delivery (77401-77416, 77418)

    🗲 14.33   ⚕ 14.33   Global Days XXX

    AMA: 2005, May, 7-12; 2005, May, 7-12; 2005, Mar, 1-6; 2005, Mar, 1-6; 2005, March, 1-6; 2005, May, 7-12; 2004, Jul, 7; 2004, Jul, 7; 2004, July, 7

0075T-0077T

0075T   **Transcatheter placement of extracranial vertebral or intrathoracic carotid artery stent(s), including radiologic supervision and interpretation, percutaneous; initial vessel** Ⓒ 80 ▭

     INCLUDES   all diagnostic services for stenting ipsilateral extracranial vertebral or intrathoraic selective carotid when confirming the need for stenting

     EXCLUDES   *selective catheterization and imaging when stenting is not required (report only slective catheteriation codes)*

    🗲 0.00   ⚕ 0.00   Global Days XXX

    AMA: 2005, May, 7-12; 2005, May, 7-12; 2005, May, 7-12

+   0076T   **each additional vessel (List separately in addition to code for primary procedure)** Ⓒ 80

    Code first 0075T

    🗲 0.00   ⚕ 0.00   Global Days XXX

    AMA: 2005, May, 7-12; 2005, May, 7-12; 2005, May, 7-12

0077T   **Implanting and securing cerebral thermal perfusion probe, including twist drill or burr hole, to measure absolute cerebral tissue perfusion** Ⓒ 80 ▭

     INCLUDES   endovascular abdominal aneurysm repair guidelines (34800-34826)

    🗲 0.00   ⚕ 0.00   Global Days XXX

    AMA: 2005, May, 7-12; 2005, May, 7-12; 2005, May, 7-12

0078T-0081T

Code also when performed outside the endoprosthesis target zone (35454, 37205-37208)

Do not report with (34800-34805, 35081, 35102, 35452, 35454, 35472, 37205-37208)

0078T   **Endovascular repair using prosthesis of abdominal aortic aneurysm, pseudoaneurysm or dissection, abdominal aorta involving visceral branches (superior mesenteric, celiac and/or renal artery[s])** Ⓒ 80 ▭

    Code also when performed outside the target area of the endoprosthesis (35454, 37205)

    🗲 0.00   ⚕ 0.00   Global Days XXX

    AMA: 2005, May, 7-12; 2005, May, 7-12; 2005, Jun, 6-8; 2005, Jun, 6-8; 2005, June, 6-8; 2005, May, 7-12

+   0079T   **Placement of visceral extension prosthesis for endovascular repair of abdominal aortic aneurysm involving visceral vessels, each visceral branch (List separately in addition to code for primary procedure)** Ⓒ 80 ▭

    Code first (0078T)

    🗲 0.00   ⚕ 0.00   Global Days XXX

    AMA: 2005, May, 7-12; 2005, May, 7-12; 2005, Jun, 6-8; 2005, Jun, 6-8; 2005, June, 6-8; 2005, May, 7-12

0080T   **Endovascular repair of abdominal aortic aneurysm, pseudoaneurysm or dissection, abdominal aorta involving visceral vessels (superior mesenteric, celiac or renal), using fenestrated modular bifurcated prosthesis (2 docking limbs), radiological supervision and interpretation** Ⓒ 80 ▭

    🗲 0.00   ⚕ 0.00   Global Days XXX

    AMA: 2005, May, 7-12; 2005, May, 7-12; 2005, Jun, 6-8; 2005, Jun, 6-8; 2005, June, 6-8; 2005, May, 7-12

+   0081T   **Placement of visceral extension prosthesis for endovascular repair of abdominal aortic aneurysm involving visceral vessels, each visceral branch, radiological supervision and interpretation (List separately in addition to code for primary procedure)** Ⓒ 80 ▭

    Code first 0080T

    🗲 0.00   ⚕ 0.00   Global Days XXX

    AMA: 2005, Jun, 6-8; 2005, Jun, 6-8; 2005, May, 7-12; 2005, May, 7-12; 2005, June, 6-8; 2005, May, 7-12

0084T-0090T

0084T   **Insertion of a temporary prostatic urethral stent** ♂ Ⓡ Ⓣ 80 ▭

    🗲 0.00   ⚕ 0.00   Global Days XXX

    AMA: 2005, May, 7-12; 2005, May, 7-12; 2005, May, 7-12

0085T   **Breath test for heart transplant rejection** Ⓧ 80

    🗲 0.00   ⚕ 0.00   Global Days XXX

    AMA: 2005, May, 7-12; 2005, May, 7-12; 2005, May, 7-12

0086T   **Left ventricular filling pressure indirect measurement by computerized calibration of the arterial waveform response to Valsalva maneuver** Ⓝ

    🗲 0.00   ⚕ 0.00   Global Days XXX

    AMA: 2005, May, 7-12; 2005, May, 7-12; 2005, May, 7-12

0087T   **Sperm evaluation, Hyaluronan sperm binding test** ♂ Ⓧ 80

    🗲 0.00   ⚕ 0.00   Global Days XXX

    AMA: 2006, Dec, 8-9; 2006, Dec, 8-9; 2006, Dec, 8-9; 2006, Dec, 8-9; 2006, December, 8-9; 2006, December, 8-9; 2005, May, 7-12; 2005, May, 7-12; 2005, May, 7-12

0088T   ~~Submucosal radiofrequency tissue volume reduction of tongue base, one or more sites; per session (ie, for treatment of obstructive sleep apnea syndrome)~~
See 41530

0089T   ~~Actigraphy testing, recording, analysis and interpretation (minimum of three-day recording)~~
See 95803

0090T   ~~Total disc arthroplasty (artificial disc), anterior approach, including discectomy to prepare interspace (other than for decompression) cervical; single interspace~~
See 22856

● New Code   ▲ Revised Code   Ⓜ Maternity Edit   Ⓐ Age Edit   Ⓐ-Ⓨ OPPS Status Indicator   🗲 Facility RVU   ⚕ Non-Facility RVU
▭ CCI Comprehensive Code   50 Bilateral Procedure   + Add-on Indicator   ◼ Laboratory crosswalk   Ⓡ Radiology crosswalk

0092T-0098T

INCLUDES   fluoroscopy

Do not report with these procedures when performed at the same level (22851, 49010)

+ ▲ **0092T**   **Total disc arthroplasty (artificial disc), anterior approach, including discectomy with end plate preparation (includes osteophytectomy for nerve root or spinal cord decompression and microdissection), each additional interspace, cervical (List separately in addition to code for primary procedure)**   C 80

       EXCLUDES   *lumbar arthroplasty (0163T)*

       Code first 0090T (22856)

       Do not report with total disc arthroplasty (22851)

       🔲 0.00   ⚚ 0.00   **Global Days XXX**

       AMA: 2006, Feb, 1-6; 2006, Feb, 1-6; 2006, February, 1-6; 2005, Jun, 6-8; 2005, June, 6-8; 2005, Jun, 6-8

~~**0093T** Removal of total disc arthroplasty, anterior approach cervical; single interspace~~
       See 22864

+ ▲ **0095T**   **Removal of total disc arthroplasty (artificial disc), anterior approach, each additional interspace, cervical (List separately in addition to code for primary procedure)**   C 80

       EXCLUDES   *lumbar disc (0164T)*
                   total disc arthroplasty removal (22865)

       Code first (22864)

       🔲 0.00   ⚚ 0.00   **Global Days XXX**

       AMA: 2006, Feb, 1-6; 2006, Feb, 1-6; 2006, February, 1-6; 2005, Jun, 6-8; 2005, June, 6-8; 2005, Jun, 6-8

~~**0096T** Revision of total disc arthroplasty, anterior approach cervical; single interspace~~
       See 22861

+ ▲ **0098T**   **Revision including replacement of total disc arthroplasty (artificial disc), anterior approach, each additional interspace, cervical (List separately in addition to code for primary procedure)**   C 80

       EXCLUDES   *spinal cord decompression (63001-63048)*

       Code first (22861)

       Do not report with instrumentation at the same level (22851)

       Do not report with (0095T, 22861)

       🔲 0.00   ⚚ 0.00   **Global Days XXX**

       AMA: 2006, Feb, 1-6; 2006, Feb, 1-6; 2006, February, 1-6; 2005, Jun, 6-8; 2005, June, 6-8; 2005, Jun, 6-8

0099T-0140T

0099T   **Implantation of intrastromal corneal ring segments**   62 T 80

       🔲 0.00   ⚚ 0.00   **Global Days XXX**

       AMA: 2006, Feb, 1-6; 2006, Feb, 1-6; 2006, February, 1-6; 2005, Jun, 6-8; 2005, June, 6-8; 2005, Jun, 6-8

0100T   **Placement of a subconjunctival retinal prosthesis receiver and pulse generator, and implantation of intra-ocular retinal electrode array, with vitrectomy**   62 T 80

       🔲 0.00   ⚚ 0.00   **Global Days XXX**

       AMA: 2006, Feb, 1-6; 2006, Feb, 1-6; 2006, February, 1-6; 2005, Jun, 6-8; 2005, June, 6-8; 2005, Jun, 6-8

0101T   **Extracorporeal shock wave involving musculoskeletal system, not otherwise specified, high energy**   62 T 80

       EXCLUDES   *low energy extracorporeal shock wave (0019T)*

       🔲 0.00   ⚚ 0.00   **Global Days XXX**

       AMA: 2006, Mar, 1-5; 2006, Mar, 1-5; 2006, March, 1-5; 2005, Jun, 6-8; 2005, June, 6-8; 2005, Jun, 6-8

0102T   **Extracorporeal shock wave, high energy, performed by a physician, requiring anesthesia other than local, involving lateral humeral epicondyle**   62 T 80

       EXCLUDES   *low energy extracorporeal shock wave (0019T)*

       🔲 0.00   ⚚ 0.00   **Global Days XXX**

       AMA: 2006, Mar, 1-5; 2006, Mar, 1-5; 2006, March, 1-5; 2005, Jun, 6-8; 2005, June, 6-8; 2005, Jun, 6-8

0103T   **Holotranscobalamin, quantitative**   A 80

       🔲 0.00   ⚚ 0.00   **Global Days XXX**

       AMA: 2006, Mar, 1-5; 2006, Mar, 1-5; 2006, March, 1-5; 2005, Jun, 6-8; 2005, June, 6-8; 2005, Jun, 6-8

0104T   **Inert gas rebreathing for cardiac output measurement; during rest**   A 80

       🔲 0.00   ⚚ 0.00   **Global Days XXX**

       AMA: 2006, Mar, 1-5; 2006, Mar, 1-5; 2006, March, 1-5; 2005, Jun, 6-8; 2005, June, 6-8; 2005, Jun, 6-8

0105T   **during exercise**   A 80

       🔲 0.00   ⚚ 0.00   **Global Days XXX**

       AMA: 2006, Mar, 1-5; 2006, Mar, 1-5; 2006, March, 1-5; 2005, Jun, 6-8; 2005, June, 6-8; 2005, Jun, 6-8

0106T   **Quantitative sensory testing (QST), testing and interpretation per extremity; using touch pressure stimuli to assess large diameter sensation**   X 80

       🔲 0.00   ⚚ 0.00   **Global Days XXX**

       AMA: 2006, Mar, 1-5; 2006, Mar, 1-5; 2006, March, 1-5; 2005, Jun, 6-8; 2005, June, 6-8; 2005, Jun, 6-8

0107T   **using vibration stimuli to assess large diameter fiber sensation**   X 80

       🔲 0.00   ⚚ 0.00   **Global Days XXX**

       AMA: 2006, Mar, 1-5; 2006, Mar, 1-5; 2006, March, 1-5; 2005, Jun, 6-8; 2005, June, 6-8; 2005, Jun, 6-8

0108T   **using cooling stimuli to assess small nerve fiber sensation and hyperalgesia**   X 80

       🔲 0.00   ⚚ 0.00   **Global Days XXX**

       AMA: 2006, Mar, 1-5; 2006, Mar, 1-5; 2006, March, 1-5; 2005, Jun, 6-8; 2005, June, 6-8; 2005, Jun, 6-8

0109T   **using heat-pain stimuli to assess small nerve fiber sensation and hyperalgesia**   X 80

       🔲 0.00   ⚚ 0.00   **Global Days XXX**

       AMA: 2006, Mar, 1-5; 2006, Mar, 1-5; 2006, March, 1-5; 2005, Jun, 6-8; 2005, June, 6-8; 2005, Jun, 6-8

0110T   **using other stimuli to assess sensation**   X 80

       🔲 0.00   ⚚ 0.00   **Global Days XXX**

       AMA: 2006, Mar, 1-5; 2006, Mar, 1-5; 2006, March, 1-5; 2005, Jun, 6-8; 2005, June, 6-8; 2005, Jun, 6-8

0111T   **Long-chain (C20-22) omega-3 fatty acids in red blood cell (RBC) membranes**   A 80

       EXCLUDES   *very long chain fatty acids (82726)*

       🔲 0.00   ⚚ 0.00   **Global Days XXX**

       AMA: 2006, Mar, 1-5; 2006, Mar, 1-5; 2006, March, 1-5; 2005, Jun, 6-8; 2005, June, 6-8; 2005, Jun, 6-8

0123T   **Fistulization of sclera for glaucoma, through ciliary body**   62 T 80

       🔲 0.00   ⚚ 0.00   **Global Days XXX**

       AMA: 2006, Apr, 11-18; 2006, Apr, 11-18; 2006, April, 11-18

0124T Conjunctival incision with posterior extrascleral placement of pharmacological agent (does not include supply of medication) Ⓡ₂ Ⓣ ⑧₀
  EXCLUDES *Suprachoroidal delivery of medication (0186T)*

  Code also medication
  💰 0.00   ⚗ 0.00 Global Days XXX
  AMA: 2008, Jan, 6-7; 2006, Apr, 11-18; 2006, Apr, 11-18; 2006, April, 11-18

0126T Common carotid intima-media thickness (IMT) study for evaluation of atherosclerotic burden or coronary heart disease risk factor assessment Ⓜ Ⓠ₁ ⑧₀
  💰 0.00   ⚗ 0.00 Global Days XXX
  AMA: 2006, Apr, 11-18; 2006, Apr, 11-18; 2006, April, 11-18

0130T Validated, statistically reliable, randomized, controlled, single-patient clinical investigation of FDA approved chronic care drugs, provided by a pharmacist, interpretation and report to the prescribing health care professional Ⓑ ⑧₀
  💰 0.00   ⚗ 0.00 Global Days XXX
  AMA: 2006, Apr, 11-18; 2006, Apr, 11-18; 2006, April, 11-18

~~0137T~~ ~~Biopsy, prostate, needle, saturation sampling for prostate mapping~~
  See 55706

0140T Exhaled breath condensate pH Ⓐ ⑧₀
  💰 0.00   ⚗ 0.00 Global Days XXX
  AMA: 2006, Apr, 11-18; 2006, Apr, 11-18; 2006, April, 11-18

0141T-0143T

INCLUDES administration and management of:
  antibiotics
  immunotherapy
  islet cells
  pain medication
  sedation
  recovery services
  all other therapeutic, infusions, and injections during islet cell infusion
  blood glucose and insulin therapy
  portal and hemodynamics

0141T Pancreatic islet cell transplantation through portal vein, percutaneous Ⓔ
  EXCLUDES *catheterization of portal vein (36481)*
     laparoscopic procedure (0143T)
     open procedure (0142T)

  ☒ 75887
  💰 0.00   ⚗ 0.00 Global Days XXX
  AMA: 2007, Jun, 7-9; 2007, Jun, 7-9; 2007, June, 7-9; 2006, Apr, 11-18; 2006, April, 11-18; 2006, Apr, 11-18

0142T Pancreatic islet cell transplantation through portal vein, open Ⓔ
  EXCLUDES *laparoscopic procedure (0143T)*
     percutaneous procedure (0141T)

  Do not report with (49000, 49002)
  💰 0.00   ⚗ 0.00 Global Days XXX
  AMA: 2007, Jun, 7-9; 2007, Jun, 7-9; 2007, June, 7-9; 2006, Apr, 11-18; 2006, April, 11-18; 2006, Apr, 11-18

0143T Laparoscopy, surgical, pancreatic islet cell transplantation through portal vein Ⓔ
  EXCLUDES *open procedure (0142T)*
     percutaneous procedure (0141T)

  Do not report with diagnostic laparoscopy (49320)
  💰 0.00   ⚗ 0.00 Global Days XXX
  AMA: 2007, Jun, 7-9; 2007, Jun, 7-9; 2007, June, 7-9; 2006, Apr, 11-18; 2006, April, 11-18; 2006, Apr, 11-18

0144T-0151T

0144T Computed tomography, heart, without contrast material, including image postprocessing and quantitative evaluation of coronary calcium Ⓩ₂ Ⓢ ⑧₀
  Do not report with (0145T-0151T)
  💰 0.00   ⚗ 0.00 Global Days XXX
  AMA: 2007, Jan, 28-31; 2007, Jan, 28-31; 2007, Jun, 7-9; 2007, Jun, 7-9; 2007, January, 28-31; 2007, June, 7-9; 2006, Apr, 11-18; 2006, Apr, 11-18; 2006, April, 11-18

0145T Computed tomography, heart, with contrast material(s), including noncontrast images, if performed, cardiac gating and 3D image postprocessing; cardiac structure and morphology Ⓩ₂ Ⓢ ⑧₀
  EXCLUDES *test for congenital heart disease (0150T)*
  💰 0.00   ⚗ 0.00 Global Days XXX
  AMA: 2007, Jan, 28-31; 2007, Jan, 28-31; 2007, Jun, 7-9; 2007, Jun, 7-9; 2007, January, 28-31; 2007, June, 7-9; 2006, Apr, 11-18; 2006, Apr, 11-18; 2006, April, 11-18

0146T computed tomographic angiography of coronary arteries (including native and anomalous coronary arteries, coronary bypass grafts), without quantitative evaluation of coronary calcium Ⓩ₂ Ⓢ ⑧₀
  💰 0.00   ⚗ 0.00 Global Days XXX
  AMA: 2007, Jan, 28-31; 2007, Jan, 28-31; 2007, Jun, 7-9; 2007, Jun, 7-9; 2007, January, 28-31; 2007, June, 7-9; 2006, Apr, 11-18; 2006, Apr, 11-18; 2006, April, 11-18

0147T computed tomographic angiography of coronary arteries (including native and anomalous coronary arteries, coronary bypass grafts), with quantitative evaluation of coronary calcium Ⓩ₂ Ⓢ ⑧₀
  Do not report with (0144T)
  💰 0.00   ⚗ 0.00 Global Days XXX
  AMA: 2007, Jan, 28-31; 2007, Jan, 28-31; 2007, Jun, 7-9; 2007, Jun, 7-9; 2007, January, 28-31; 2007, June, 7-9; 2006, Apr, 11-18; 2006, Apr, 11-18; 2006, April, 11-18

0148T cardiac structure and morphology and computed tomographic angiography of coronary arteries (including native and anomalous coronary arteries, coronary bypass grafts), without quantitative evaluation of coronary calcium Ⓩ₂ Ⓢ ⑧₀
  💰 0.00   ⚗ 0.00 Global Days XXX
  AMA: 2007, Jan, 28-31; 2007, Jan, 28-31; 2007, Jun, 7-9; 2007, Jun, 7-9; 2007, January, 28-31; 2007, June, 7-9; 2006, Apr, 11-18; 2006, April, 11-18

0149T cardiac structure and morphology and computed tomographic angiography of coronary arteries (including native and anomalous coronary arteries, coronary bypass grafts), with quantitative evaluation of coronary calcium Ⓩ₂ Ⓢ ⑧₀
  Do not report with (0144T)
  💰 0.00   ⚗ 0.00 Global Days XXX
  AMA: 2007, Jan, 28-31; 2007, Jan, 28-31; 2007, Jun, 7-9; 2007, Jun, 7-9; 2007, January, 28-31; 2007, June, 7-9; 2006, Apr, 11-18; 2006, April, 11-18

0150T cardiac structure and morphology in congenital heart disease Ⓩ₂ Ⓢ ⑧₀
  💰 0.00   ⚗ 0.00 Global Days XXX
  AMA: 2007, Jan, 28-31; 2007, Jan, 28-31; 2007, Jun, 7-9; 2007, Jun, 7-9; 2007, January, 28-31; 2007, June, 7-9; 2006, Apr, 11-18; 2006, April, 11-18

● New Code   ▲ Revised Code   Ⓜ Maternity Edit   Ⓐ Age Edit   Ⓐ-Ⓨ OPPS Status Indicator   💰 Facility RVU   ⚗ Non-Facility RVU
▣ CCI Comprehensive Code   ⑤₀ Bilateral Procedure   + Add-on Indicator   Ⓝ Laboratory crosswalk   ☒ Radiology crosswalk

Category III Codes

0151T — 0164T

+   **0151T**   Computed tomography, heart, with contrast material(s), including noncontrast images, if performed, cardiac gating and 3D image postprocessing, function evaluation (left and right ventricular function, ejection-fraction and segmental wall motion) (List separately in addition to code for primary procedure)   72 S 80
     Code first 0145T-0150T
     0.00   0.00   Global Days XXX

       AMA: 2007, Jan, 28-31; 2007, Jan, 28-31; 2007, Jun, 7-9; 2007, Jun, 7-9; 2007, January, 28-31; 2007, June, 7-9; 2006, Apr, 11-18; 2006, Apr, 11-18; 2006, April, 11-18

0155T-0156T

EXCLUDES   *electronic study and programming of gastric neurostimulator pulse generator (95999)*
     open procedure (0157T-0158T)

     0155T   Laparoscopy, surgical; implantation or replacement of gastric stimulation electrodes, lesser curvature (ie, morbid obesity)   T 80
       0.00   0.00   Global Days XXX

       AMA: 2007, Mar, 4-5; 2007, Mar, 4-5; 2007, Apr, 7-10; 2007, Apr, 7-10; 2007, March, 4-5; 2007, April, 7-10; 2006, May, 12-15; 2006, May, 12-15; 2006, May, 12-15

     0156T   revision or removal of gastric stimulation electrodes, lesser curvature (ie, morbid obesity)   T 80
       EXCLUDES   *electronic analysis and programming of:*
         antral gastric neurostimulator pulse generator (95980-95982)
         insertion, revision or removal of gastric neurostimulator pulse generator (64590, 64595)
         laproscopic or open insertion, revision, or removal of antral gastric neurostimulator (43647-43648, 43881-43882)
         open approach (0157T-0158T)

       0.00   0.00   Global Days XXX

       AMA: 2007, Mar, 4-5; 2007, Mar, 4-5; 2007, Apr, 7-10; 2007, Apr, 7-10; 2007, March, 4-5; 2007, April, 7-10; 2006, May, 12-15; 2006, May, 12-15; 2006, May, 12-15

0157T-0158T

EXCLUDES   *electronic analysis and programming of antral gastric neurostimulator pulse generator (95980-95982)*
     laparoscopic procedure (0155T-0156T)
     placement of gastric neurostimulator pulse generator (64590)
     revision or removal of gastric neurostimulator pulse generator (64595)

     0157T   Laparotomy, implantation or replacement of gastric stimulation electrodes, lesser curvature (ie, morbid obesity)   C 80
       0.00   0.00   Global Days XXX

       AMA: 2007, Apr, 7-10; 2007, Apr, 7-10; 2007, April, 7-10; 2006, May, 12-15; 2006, May, 12-15; 2006, May, 12-15

     0158T   Laparotomy, revision or removal of gastric stimulation electrodes, lesser curvature (ie, morbid obesity)   C 80
       0.00   0.00   Global Days XXX

       AMA: 2007, Apr, 7-10; 2007, Apr, 7-10; 2007, April, 7-10; 2006, May, 12-15; 2006, May, 12-15; 2006, May, 12-15

0159T

+   **0159T**   Computer-aided detection, including computer algorithm analysis of MRI image data for lesion detection/characterization, pharmacokinetic analysis, with further physician review for interpretation, breast MRI (List separately in addition to code for primary procedure)   M1 N 80
     Do not report with (76376-76377)
     ⟳ *76376-76377, 77058-77059*
     0.00   0.00   Global Days ZZZ

       AMA: 2007, Mar, 7-8; 2007, Mar, 7-8; 2007, March, 7-8; 2007, Jul, 6-10; 2006, May, 12-15; 2006, May, 12-15; 2006, April, 11-18; 2006, Apr, 11-18; 2006, Apr, 11-18

0160T-0162T

     0160T   Therapeutic repetitive transcranial magnetic stimulation treatment planning   S 80
       INCLUDES   pretreatment:
         determination of magnetic field strength
         stimulation limits
         treatment site

       0.00   0.00   Global Days XXX

       AMA: 2007, Jul, 6-10; 2006, May, 12-15; 2006, May, 12-15; 2006, Dec, 10-12; 2006, Dec, 10-12; 2006, Dec, 10-12; 2006, Dec, 10-12; 2006, May, 12-15; 2006, December, 10-12; 2006, December, 10-12

     0161T   Therapeutic repetitive transcranial magnetic stimulation treatment delivery and management, per session   S 80
       INCLUDES   monitoring
         treatment limit review

       0.00   0.00   Global Days XXX

       AMA: 2007, Jul, 6-10; 2006, May, 12-15; 2006, May, 12-15; 2006, Dec, 10-12; 2006, Dec, 10-12; 2006, Dec, 10-12; 2006, Dec, 10-12; 2006, May, 12-15; 2006, December, 10-12; 2006, December, 10-12

     ~~0162T~~   ~~Electronic analysis and programming, reprogramming of gastric neurostimulator (ie, morbid obesity)~~
     See 95980-95982

0163T-0165T

INCLUDES   *fluoroscopy*

EXCLUDES   *cervical disc procedures (0090T-0098T)*
     decompression (63001-63048)

Do not report with these procedures when performed at the same level (22851, 49010)

+   ▲   **0163T**   Total disc arthroplasty (artificial disc), anterior approach, including discectomy to prepare interspace (other than for decompression), each additional interspace, lumbar (List separately in addition to code for primary procedure)   C 80
     Code first 22857
     0.00   0.00   Global Days YYY

       AMA: 2007, Jun, 1-3; 2007, Jun, 1-3; 2007, June, 1-3

+   ▲   **0164T**   Removal of total disc arthroplasty, (artificial disc), anterior approach, each additional interspace, lumbar (List separately in addition to code for primary procedure) .   C 80
     Code first 22865
     0.00   0.00   Global Days YYY

       AMA: 2007, Jun, 1-3; 2007, Jun, 1-3; 2007, June, 1-3

26/TC Professional/Technical Component Only   80/80 Assist-at-Surgery Allowed/With Documentation   Unlisted   Not Covered

AMA: CPT Assistant References   A2 Z3 ASC Payment Indicator   ♂ Male Only   ♀ Female Only   ⊘ Modifier 51 Exempt   PQRI

\+ ▲ **0165T** Revision including replacement of total disc arthroplasty (artificial disc), anterior approach, each additional interspace, lumbar (List separately in addition to code for primary procedure)   C 80

Code first 22862

💷 0.00   ✂ 0.00   Global Days YYY

AMA: 2007, Jun, 1-3; 2007, Jun, 1-3; 2007, June, 1-3

0166T-0167T

EXCLUDES   *percutaneous ventricular septal defect repair (93581)*

Do not report with (32551, 33210-33211)

0166T Transmyocardial transcatheter closure of ventricular septal defect, with implant; without cardiopulmonary bypass   C 80

EXCLUDES   *ventricular septal defect closure via percutaneous transcatheter implant delivery (93581)*

💷 0.00   ✂ 0.00   Global Days XXX

AMA: 2007, Jul, 6-10; 2006, Dec, 8-9; 2006, Dec, 8-9; 2006, Dec, 8-9; 2006, Dec, 8-9; 2006, December, 8-9; 2006, December, 8-9

0167T with cardiopulmonary bypass   C 80

EXCLUDES   *ventricular septal defect closure via percutaneous transcatheter implant delivery (93581)*

💷 0.00   ✂ 0.00   Global Days XXX

AMA: 2007, Jul, 6-10; 2006, Dec, 8-9; 2006, Dec, 8-9; 2006, Dec, 8-9; 2006, Dec, 8-9; 2006, December, 8-9; 2006, December, 8-9

0168T-0177T

0168T Rhinophototherapy, intranasal application of ultraviolet and visible light, bilateral   T 80

💷 0.00   ✂ 0.00   Global Days XXX

AMA: 2007, Jul, 6-10; 2006, Dec, 8-9; 2006, Dec, 8-9; 2006, Dec, 8-9; 2006, Dec, 8-9; 2006, December, 8-9; 2006, December, 8-9

0169T Stereotactic placement of infusion catheter(s) in the brain for delivery of therapeutic agent(s), including computerized stereotactic planning and burr hole(s)   C 80

Do not report with (20660, 61107, 61795)

💷 0.00   ✂ 0.00   Global Days XXX

AMA: 2008, May, 9-11, 2008, Jul, 4; 2007, Jul, 6-10; 2006, Dec, 8-9; 2006, Dec, 8-9; 2006, Dec, 8-9; 2006, December, 8-9; 2006, December, 8-9

0170T Repair of anorectal fistula with plug (eg, porcine small intestine submucosa [SIS])   G2 T 80

EXCLUDES   *repair with fibrin glue (46706)*

Do not report with acellular xenograft implant (15430-15431)

💷 0.00   ✂ 0.00   Global Days XXX

AMA: 2007, Jul, 6-10; 2006, Dec, 8-9; 2006, Dec, 8-9; 2006, Dec, 8-9; 2006, Dec, 8-9; 2006, December, 8-9; 2006, December, 8-9

0171T Insertion of posterior spinous process distraction device (including necessary removal of bone or ligament for insertion and imaging guidance), lumbar; single level   T 80

💷 0.00   ✂ 0.00   Global Days XXX

AMA: 2007, Jul, 6-10; 2006, Dec, 8-9; 2006, Dec, 8-9; 2006, Dec, 8-9; 2006, Dec, 8-9; 2006, December, 8-9; 2006, December, 8-9

\+ **0172T** each additional level (List separately in addition to code for primary procedure)   T 80

Code first 0171T

💷 0.00   ✂ 0.00   Global Days XXX

AMA: 2007, Jul, 6-10; 2006, Dec, 8-9; 2006, Dec, 8-9; 2006, Dec, 8-9; 2006, Dec, 8-9; 2006, December, 8-9; 2006, December, 8-9

\+ **0173T** Monitoring of intraocular pressure during vitrectomy surgery (List separately in addition to code for primary procedure)   N 80

Code first (67036, 67039-67043, 67108, 67112)

💷 0.00   ✂ 0.00   Global Days XXX

AMA: 2008, Oct, 1-5; 2007, Jul, 6-10; 2006, Dec, 8-9; 2006, Dec, 8-9; 2006, Dec, 8-9; 2006, Dec, 8-9; 2006, December, 8-9; 2006, December, 8-9

\+ **0174T** Computer-aided detection (CAD) (computer algorithm analysis of digital image data for lesion detection) with further physician review for interpretation and report, with or without digitization of film radiographic images, chest radiograph(s), performed concurrent with primary interpretation (List separately in addition to code for primary procedure)   M N 80

Code first primary procedure

📷 71010, 71020-71022, 71030

💷 0.00   ✂ 0.00   Global Days XXX

AMA: 2007, Mar, 7-8; 2007, Mar, 7-8; 2007, March, 7-8; 2007, Jul, 6-10; 2006, Dec, 8-9; 2006, Dec, 8-9; 2006, December, 8-9; 2006, December, 8-9; 2006, Dec, 8-9; 2006, Dec, 8-9

0175T Computer-aided detection (CAD) (computer algorithm analysis of digital image data for lesion detection) with further physician review for interpretation and report, with or without digitization of film radiographic images, chest radiograph(s), performed remote from primary interpretation   M N 80

Do not report with (71010, 71020-71022, 71030)

💷 0.00   ✂ 0.00   Global Days XXX

AMA: 2007, Mar, 7-8; 2007, Mar, 7-8; 2007, March, 7-8; 2007, Jul, 6-10; 2006, Dec, 8-9; 2006, Dec, 8-9; 2006, December, 8-9; 2006, December, 8-9; 2006, Dec, 8-9; 2006, Dec, 8-9

0176T Transluminal dilation of aqueous outflow canal; without retention of device or stent   A2 T 80

💷 0.00   ✂ 0.00   Global Days XXX

AMA: 2007, Jul, 6-10; 2006, Dec, 8-9; 2006, Dec, 8-9; 2006, Dec, 8-9; 2006, December, 8-9; 2006, December, 8-9

0177T with retention of device or stent   A2 T 80

💷 0.00   ✂ 0.00   Global Days XXX

AMA: 2007, Jul, 6-10; 2006, Dec, 8-9; 2006, Dec, 8-9; 2006, Dec, 8-9; 2006, December, 8-9; 2006, December, 8-9

0178T-0180T

EXCLUDES   *separately performed 12-lead electrocardiogram (93000-93010)*

0178T Electrocardiogram, 64 leads or greater, with graphic presentation and analysis; with interpretation and report   R 80

💷 0.00   ✂ 0.00   Global Days XXX

0179T tracing and graphics only, without interpretation and report   X TC 80

💷 0.00   ✂ 0.00   Global Days XXX

0180T interpretation and report only   B 26 80

💷 0.00   ✂ 0.00   Global Days XXX

0181T-0187T

0181T Corneal hysteresis determination, by air impulse stimulation, bilateral, with interpretation and report   S 80

💷 0.00   ✂ 0.00   Global Days XXX

● New Code   ▲ Revised Code   M Maternity Edit   A Age Edit   A T OPPS Status Indicator   💷 Facility RVU   ✂ Non-Facility RVU

☐ CCI Comprehensive Code   50 Bilateral Procedure   \+ Add-on Indicator   ☒ Laboratory crosswalk   📷 Radiology crosswalk

Category III Codes

0182T — 0192T

0182T High dose rate electronic brachytherapy, per fraction ⬚ S ⬚
EXCLUDES *placement or removal of an applicator into breast for radiation therapy (C9726)*

Do not report with (77761-77763, 77776-77778, 77785-77787, 77789)
💲 0.00   ⚖ 0.00   Global Days XXX

0183T Low frequency, non-contact, non-thermal ultrasound, including topical application(s), when performed, wound assessment, and instruction(s) for ongoing care, per day   T ⬚
💲 0.00   ⚖ 0.00   Global Days XXX

● **0184T** Excision of rectal tumor, transanal endoscopic microsurgical approach (ie, TEMS)   C ⬚
EXCLUDES *nonendoscopic excision of rectal tumor (45160, 45170)*
INCLUDES operating microscope (66990)

Do not report with (45300-45327)
💲 0.00   ⚖ 0.00   Global Days XXX
AMA: 2008, Jan, 6-7

● **0185T** Multivariate analysis of patient specific findings with quantifiable computer probability assessment, including report   N N ⬚
Do not report with (99090)
💲 0.00   ⚖ 0.00   Global Days XXX
AMA: 2008, Jan, 6-7

● **0186T** Suprachoroidal delivery of pharmacologic agent (does not include supply of medication)   G2 T ⬚
💲 0.00   ⚖ 0.00   Global Days XXX
AMA: 2008, Jan, 6-7

● **0187T** Scanning computerized ophthalmic diagnostic imaging, anterior segment, with interpretation and report, unilateral   S ⬚
💲 0.00   ⚖ 0.00   Global Days XXX
AMA: 2008, Jan, 6-7

0188T-0189T

INCLUDES 30 minutes or more of direct medical care by a physician(s) to a critically ill or critically injured patient from an off-site location.
additional on-site critical care services when a critically ill or injured patient requires critical care resources not available on-site
real time ability to:
  document the remote care services in the medical record
  enter orders electronically
  evaluate patients with high fidelity audio/video capabilities
  talk to patients and family members
  videoconference with the health care team on-site in the patient's room
real-time access to the patient's:
  clinical laboratory test results
  diagnostic test results
  medical records
  radiographic images
review and/or interpretation of all diagnostic information
time spent with the patient, family, or surrogate decision makers to obtain a medical history, review the patient's condition/prognosis, or discuss treatment options from the remote site

Do not report for time spent away from the remotes site without real-time capabilities
Do not report time spent for services that do not directly contribute to patient treatment

● **0188T** Remote real-time interactive videoconferenced critical care, evaluation and management of the critically ill or critically injured patient; first 30- 74 minutes   M
INCLUDES first 30 to 74 minutes of remote critical care each day

Do not report remote critical care less than 30 minutes total duration
💲 0.00   ⚖ 0.00   Global Days XXX
AMA: 2008, Jan, 6-7

+ ● **0189T** each additional 30 minutes (List separately in addition to code for primary service)   M
INCLUDES up to 30 minutes each beyond the first 74 minutes

Code first (0188T)
💲 0.00   ⚖ 0.00   Global Days XXX
AMA: 2008, Jan, 6-7

0190T-0194T

+ ● **0190T** Placement of intraocular radiation source applicator (List separately in addition to primary procedure)   G2 T ⬚
EXCLUDES *insertion of brachytherapy source by radiation oncologist (see Clinical Brachytherapy Section)*

Code first (67036)
Code also brachytherapy source
💲 0.00   ⚖ 0.00   Global Days XXX
AMA: 2008, Jan, 6-7

● **0191T** Insertion of anterior segment aqueous drainage device, without extraocular reservoir; internal approach   G2 T ⬚
💲 0.00   ⚖ 0.00   Global Days XXX
AMA: 2008, Jan, 6-7

● **0192T** external approach   G2 T ⬚
💲 0.00   ⚖ 0.00   Global Days XXX
AMA: 2008, Jan, 6-7

● 0193T **Transurethral, radiofrequency micro-remodeling of the female bladder neck and proximal urethra for stress urinary incontinence**   ♀ T 80

  Do not report with (51701)

  🔧 0.00   ⬦ 0.00 Global Days XXX

● 0194T **Procalcitonin (PCT)**   A 80

  🔧 0.00   ⬦ 0.00 Global Days XXX

0195T-0196T

Do not report with (22558, 22845, 22851, 76000, 76380, 76496, 76497)

● 0195T **Arthrodesis, pre-sacral interbody technique, including instrumentation, imaging (when performed), and discectomy to prepare interspace, lumbar; single interspace**   C 80

  🔧 0.00   ⬦ 0.00 Global Days XXX

+ ● 0196T **each additional interspace (List separately in addition to code for primary procedure)**   C 80

  Code first (0195T)

  🔧 0.00   ⬦ 0.00 Global Days XXX

0197T-0198T

● 0197T **Intra-fraction localization and tracking of target or patient motion during delivery of radiation therapy (eg, 3D positional tracking, gating, 3D surface tracking), each fraction of treatment**   N 80

  🔧 0.00   ⬦ 0.00 Global Days XXX

● 0198T **Measurement of ocular blood flow by repetitive intraocular pressure sampling, with interpretation and report**   S 80

  🔧 0.00   ⬦ 0.00 Global Days XXX

● New Code   ▲ Revised Code   ▣ Maternity Edit   ▣ Age Edit   A V OPPS Status Indicator   🔧 Facility RVU   ⬦ Non-Facility RVU

▣ CCI Comprehensive Code   50 Bilateral Procedure   + Add-on Indicator   ▣ Laboratory crosswalk   ▣ Radiology crosswalk

501

APPENDIX A — MODIFIERS

CPT Modifiers

A modifier is a two-position alpha or numeric code that is appended to a CPT code to clarify the services being billed. Modifiers provide a means by which a service can be altered without changing the procedure code. They add more information, such as the anatomical site, to the code. In addition, they help to eliminate the appearance of duplicate billing and unbundling. Modifiers are used to increase accuracy in reimbursement, coding consistency, editing, and to capture payment data.

22 Increased Procedural Services: When the work required to provide a service is substantially greater than typically required, it may be identified by adding modifier 22 to the usual procedure code. Documentation must support the substantial additional work and the reason for the additional work (ie, increased intensity, time, technical difficulty of procedure, severity of patient's condition, physical and mental effort required).

> **Note:** This modifier should not be appended to an E/M service.

23 Unusual Anesthesia: Occasionally, a procedure, which usually requires either no anesthesia or local anesthesia, because of unusual circumstances must be done under general anesthesia. This circumstance may be reported by adding modifier 23 to the procedure code of the basic service.

24 Unrelated Evaluation and Management Service by the Same Physician During a Postoperative Period: The physician may need to indicate that an evaluation and management service was performed during a postoperative period for a reason(s) unrelated to the original procedure. This circumstance may be reported by adding modifier 24 to the appropriate level of E/M service.

25 Significant, Separately Identifiable Evaluation and Management Service by the Same Physician on the Same Day of the Procedure or Other Service: It may be necessary to indicate that on the day a procedure or service identified by a CPT code was performed, the patient's condition required a significant, separately identifiable E/M service above and beyond the other service provided or beyond the usual preoperative and postoperative care associated with the procedure that was performed. A significant, separately identifiable E/M service is defined or substantiated by documentation that satisfies the relevant criteria for the respective E/M service to be reported (see Evaluation and Management Services Guidelines for instructions on determining level of E/M service). The E/M service may be prompted by the symptom or condition for which the procedure and/or service was provided. As such, different diagnoses are not required for reporting of the E/M services on the same date. This circumstance may be reported by adding modifier 25 to the appropriate level of E/M service. Note: This modifier is not used to report an E/M service that resulted in a decision to perform surgery. See modifier 57. For significant, separately identifiable non-E/M services, see modifier 59.

26 Professional Component: Certain procedures are a combination of a physician component and a technical component. When the physician component is reported separately, the service may be identified by adding modifier 26 to the usual procedure number.

32 Mandated Services: Services related to mandated consultation and/or related services (eg, third-party payer, governmental, legislative or regulatory requirement) may be identified by adding modifier 32 to the basic procedure.

47 Anesthesia by Surgeon: Regional or general anesthesia provided by the surgeon may be reported by adding modifier 47 to the basic service. (This does not include local anesthesia.) Note: Modifier 47 would not be used as a modifier for the anesthesia procedures 00100-01999.

50 Bilateral Procedure: Unless otherwise identified in the listings, bilateral procedures that are performed at the same operative session should be identified by adding modifier 50 to the appropriate five digit code.

51 Multiple Procedures: When multiple procedures, other than Evaluation and Management Services, are performed at the same session by the same provider, the primary procedure or service may be reported as listed. The additional procedure(s) or service(s) may be identified by appending modifier 51 to the additional procedure or

service code(s). Note: This modifier should not be appended to designated "add-on" codes.

52 Reduced Services: Under certain circumstances a service or procedure is partially reduced or eliminated at the physician's discretion. Under these circumstances the service provided can be identified by its usual procedure number and the addition of modifier 52, signifying that the service is reduced. This provides a means of reporting reduced services without disturbing the identification of the basic service. Note: For hospital outpatient reporting of a previously scheduled procedure/service that is partially reduced or cancelled as a result of extenuating circumstances or those that threaten the well-being of the patient prior to or after administration of anesthesia, see modifiers 73 and 74 (see modifiers approved for ASC hospital outpatient use).

53 Discontinued Procedure: Under certain circumstances, the physician may elect to terminate a surgical or diagnostic procedure. Due to extenuating circumstances or those that threaten the well being of the patient, it may be necessary to indicate that a surgical or diagnostic procedure was started but discontinued. This circumstance may be reported by adding modifier 53 to the code reported by the physician for the discontinued procedure. Note: This modifier is not used to report the elective cancellation of a procedure prior to the patient's anesthesia induction and/or surgical preparation in the operating suite. For outpatient hospital/ambulatory surgery center (ASC) reporting of a previously scheduled procedure/service that is partially reduced or cancelled as a result of extenuating circumstances or those that threaten the well being of the patient prior to or after administration of anesthesia, see modifiers 73 and 74 (see modifiers approved for ASC hospital outpatient use).

54 Surgical Care Only: When one physician performs a surgical procedure and another provides preoperative and/or postoperative management, surgical services may be identified by adding modifier 54 to the usual procedure number.

55 Postoperative Management Only: When one physician performs the postoperative management and another physician has performed the surgical procedure, the postoperative component may be identified by adding modifier 55 to the usual procedure number.

56 Preoperative Management Only: When one physician performs the preoperative care and evaluation and another physician performs the surgical procedure, the preoperative component may be identified by adding modifier 56 to the usual procedure number.

57 Decision for Surgery: An evaluation and management service that resulted in the initial decision to perform the surgery may be identified by adding modifier 57 to the appropriate level of E/M service.

58 Staged or Related Procedure or Service by the Same Physician During the Postoperative Period: It may be necessary to indicate that the performance of a procedure or service during the postoperative period was (a) planned or anticipated (staged); (b) more extensive than the original procedure; or (c) for therapy following a surgical procedure. This circumstance may be reported by adding modifier 58 to the staged or related procedure. Note: For treatment of a problem that requires a return to the operating or procedure room (eg, unanticipated clinical condition), see modifier 78.

59 Distinct Procedural Service: Under certain circumstances, it may be necessary to indicate that a procedure or service was distinct or independent from other non-E/M services performed on the same day. Modifier 59 is used to identify procedures or services, other than E/M services, that are not normally reported together but are appropriate under the circumstances. Documentation must support a different session, different procedure or surgery, different site or organ system, separate incision or excision, separate lesion, or separate injury (or area of injury in extensive injuries) not ordinarily encountered or performed on the same day by the same individual. However, when another already established modifier is appropriate it should be used rather than modifier 59. Only if no more descriptive modifier is available and the use of modifier 59 best explains the circumstances should modifier 59 be used.

> **Note:** Modifier 59 should not be appended to an E/M service. To report a separate and distinct E/M service with a non-E/M service performed on the same date, see modifier 25.

62 Two Surgeons: When two surgeons work together as primary surgeons performing distinct part(s) of a procedure, each surgeon should report his/her distinct operative work by adding modifier 62 to the procedure code and any associated add-on code(s) for that procedure as long as both surgeons continue to work together as primary surgeons. Each surgeon should report the co-surgery once using the same procedure code. If an additional procedure(s) (including an add-on procedure(s)) is performed during the same surgical session, a separate code(s) may be reported with the modifier 62 added.

Note: If a co-surgeon acts as an assistant in the performance of an additional procedure(s) during the same surgical session, the service(s) may be reported using a separate procedure code(s) with modifier 80 or modifier 82 added, as appropriate.

63 Procedure Performed on Infants less than 4 kg: Procedures performed on neonates and infants up to a present body weight of 4 kg may involve significantly increased complexity and physician work commonly associated with these patients. This circumstance may be reported by adding the modifier 63 to the procedure number.

Note: Unless otherwise designated, this modifier may only be appended to procedures/services listed in the 20000-69999 code series. Modifier 63 should not be appended to any CPT codes in the **Evaluation and Management Services, Anesthesia, Radiology, Pathology/Laboratory or Medicine** sections.

66 Surgical Team: Under some circumstances, highly complex procedures (requiring the concomitant services of several physicians, often of different specialties, plus other highly skilled, specially trained personnel, various types of complex equipment) are carried out under the "surgical team" concept. Such circumstances may be identified by each participating physician with the addition of modifier 66 to the basic procedure number used for reporting services.

76 Repeat Procedure or Service by Same Physician It may be necessary to indicate that a procedure or service was repeated subsequent to the original procedure or service. This circumstance may be reported by adding modifier 76 to the repeated procedure or service.

77 Repeat Procedure by Another Physician: The physician may need to indicate that a basic procedure or service performed by another physician had to be repeated. This situation may be reported by adding modifier 77 to the repeated procedure/service.

78 Unplanned Return to the Operating/Procedure Room by the Same Physician Following Initial Procedure for a Related Procedure During the Postoperative Period: It may be necessary to indicate that another procedure was performed during the postoperative period of the initial procedure (unplanned procedure following initial procedure). When this procedure is related to the first and requires the use of an operating or procedure room, it may be reported by adding modifier 78 to the related procedure. (For repeat procedures, see modifier 76.)

79 Unrelated Procedure or Service by the Same Physician During the Postoperative Period: The physician may need to indicate that the performance of a procedure or service during the postoperative period was unrelated to the original procedure. This circumstance may be reported by using modifier 79. (For repeat procedures on the same day, see modifier 76.)

80 Assistant Surgeon: Surgical assistant services may be identified by adding modifier 80 to the usual procedure number(s).

81 Minimum Assistant Surgeon: Minimum surgical assistant services are identified by adding modifier 81 to the usual procedure number.

82 Assistant Surgeon (when qualified resident surgeon not available): The unavailability of a qualified resident surgeon is a prerequisite for use of modifier 82 appended to the usual procedure code number(s).

90 Reference (Outside) Laboratory: When laboratory procedures are performed by a party other than the treating or reporting physician, the procedure may be identified by adding modifier 90 to the usual procedure number.

91 Repeat Clinical Diagnostic Laboratory Test: In the course of treatment of the patient, it may be necessary to repeat the same laboratory test on the same day to obtain subsequent (multiple) test results. Under these circumstances, the laboratory test performed can be identified by its usual procedure number and the addition of modifier 91.

Note: This modifier may not be used when tests are rerun to confirm initial results; due to testing problems with specimens or equipment; or for any other reason when a normal, one-time, reportable result is all that is required. This modifier may not be used when another code(s) describes a series of test results (eg, glucose tolerance tests, evocative/suppression testing). This modifier may only be used for a laboratory test(s) performed more than once on the same day on the same patient.

92 Alternative Laboratory Platform Testing When laboratory testing is being performed using a kit or transportable instrument that wholly or in part consists of a single use, disposable analytical chamber, the service may be identified by adding modifier 92 to the usual laboratory procedure code (HIV testing 86701-86703). The test does not require permanent dedicated space; hence by its design it may be hand carried or transported to the vicinity of the patient for immediate testing at that site, although location of the testing is not in itself determinative of the use of this modifier.

99 Multiple Modifiers: Under certain circumstances two or more modifiers may be necessary to completely delineate a service. In such situations, modifier 99 should be added to the basic procedure and other applicable modifiers may be listed as part of the description of the service.

Anesthesia Physical Status Modifiers

All anesthesia services are reported by use of the five-digit anesthesia procedure code with the appropriate physical status modifier appended.

Under certain circumstances, when other modifier(s) are appropriate, they should be reported in addition to the physical status modifier.

P1 A normal healthy patient

P2 A patient with mild systemic disease

P3 A patient with severe systemic disease

P4 A patient with severe systemic disease that is a constant threat to life

P5 A moribund patient who is not expected to survive without the operation

P6 A declared brain-dead patient whose organs are being removed for donor purposes

MODIFIERS APPROVED FOR AMBULATORY SURGERY CENTER (ASC) HOSPITAL OUTPATIENT USE

CPT Level I Modifiers

25 Significant, Separately Identifiable Evaluation and Management Service by the Same Physician on the Same Day of the Procedure or Other Service: It may be necessary to indicate that on the day a procedure or service identified by a CPT code was performed, the patient's condition required a significant, separately identifiable E/M service above and beyond the other service provided or beyond the usual preoperative and postoperative care associated with the procedure that was performed. A significant, separately identifiable E/M service is defined or substantiated by documentation that satisfies the relevant criteria for the respective E/M service to be reported (see **Evaluation and Management Services Guidelines** for instructions on determining level of E/M service). The E/M service may be prompted by the symptom or condition for which the procedure and/or service was provided. As such, different diagnoses are not required for reporting of the E/M services on the same date. This circumstance may be reported by adding modifier 25 to the appropriate level of E/M service.

Note: This modifier is not used to report an E/M service that resulted in a decision to perform surgery. See modifier 57. For significant, separately identifiable non-E/M services, see modifier 59.

27 Multiple Outpatient Hospital E/M Encounters on the Same Date: For hospital outpatient reporting purposes, utilization of hospital resources related to separate and distinct E/M encounters performed in multiple outpatient hospital settings on the same date may be reported by adding modifier 27 to each appropriate level outpatient and/or emergency department E/M code(s). This modifier provides a means of reporting circumstances involving evaluation and management services provided by a physician(s) in more than one (multiple) outpatient hospital setting(s) (eg, hospital emergency department, clinic). Note: This modifier is not to be used for physician reporting of multiple E/M services performed by the same physician on the same date. For physician reporting of all outpatient evaluation and management services provided by the same physician on the same date and performed in multiple outpatient settings (eg, hospital emergency department, clinic), see **Evaluation and Management, Emergency Department, or Preventive Medicine Services** codes.

50   **Bilateral Procedure:** Unless otherwise identified in the listings, bilateral procedures that are performed at the same operative session should be identified by adding modifier 50 to the appropriate five digit code.

52   **Reduced Services:** Under certain circumstances a service or procedure is partially reduced or eliminated at the physician's discretion. Under these circumstances the service provided can be identified by its usual procedure number and the addition of modifier 52, signifying that the service is reduced. This provides a means of reporting reduced services without disturbing the identification of the basic service. Note: For hospital outpatient reporting of a previously scheduled procedure/service that is partially reduced or cancelled as a result of extenuating circumstances or those that threaten the well-being of the patient prior to or after administration of anesthesia, see modifiers 73 and 74 (see modifiers approved for ASC hospital outpatient use).

58   **Staged or Related Procedure or Service by the Same Physician During the Postoperative Period:** It may be necessary to indicate that the performance of a procedure or service during the postoperative period was (a) planned or anticipated (staged); (b) more extensive than the original procedure; or (c) for therapy following a surgical procedure. This circumstance may be reported by adding modifier 58 to the staged or related procedure

Note: For treatment of a problem that requires a return to the operating or procedure room (eg, unanticipated clinical condition), see modifier 78.

59   **Distinct Procedural Service:** Under certain circumstances, it may be necessary to indicate that a procedure or service was distinct or independent from other non-E/M services performed on the same day. Modifier 59 is used to identify procedures or services, other than E/M services, that are not normally reported together but are appropriate under the circumstances. Documentation must support a different session, different procedure or surgery, different site or organ system, separate incision or excision, separate lesion, or separate injury (or area of injury in extensive injuries) not ordinarily encountered or performed on the same day by the same individual. However, when another already established modifier is appropriate it should be used rather than modifier 59. Only if no more descriptive modifier is available and the use of modifier 59 best explains the circumstances should modifier 59 be used. Note: Modifier 59 should not be appended to an E/M service. To report a separate and distinct E/M service with a non-E/M service performed on the same date, see modifier 25.

73   **Discontinued Out-Patient Hospital/Ambulatory Surgery Center (ASC) Procedure Prior to the Administration of Anesthesia:** Due to extenuating circumstances or those that threaten the well being of the patient, the physician may cancel a surgical or diagnostic procedure subsequent to the patient's surgical preparation (including sedation when provided, and being taken to the room where the procedure is to be performed), but prior to the administration of anesthesia (local, regional block(s), or general). Under these circumstances, the intended service that is prepared for but cancelled can be reported by its usual procedure number and the addition of modifier 73. Note: The elective cancellation of a service prior to the administration of anesthesia and/or surgical preparation of the patient should not be reported. For physician reporting of a discontinued procedure, see modifier 53.

74   **Discontinued Out-Patient Hospital/Ambulatory Surgery Center (ASC) Procedure After Administration of Anesthesia:** Due to extenuating circumstances or those that threaten the well being of the patient, the physician may terminate a surgical or

diagnostic procedure after the administration of anesthesia (local, regional block(s), general) or after the procedure was started (incision made, intubation started, scope inserted, etc.). Under these circumstances, the procedure started but terminated can be reported by its usual procedure number and the addition of modifier 74. Note: The elective cancellation of a service prior to the administration of anesthesia and/or surgical preparation of the patient should not be reported. For physician reporting of a discontinued procedure, see modifier 53.

76   **Repeat Procedure or Service by Same Physician:** It may be necessary to indicate that a procedure or service was repeated subsequent to the original procedure or service. This circumstance may be reported by adding modifier 76 to the repeated procedure or service.

77   **Repeat Procedure by Another Physician:** The physician may need to indicate that a basic procedure or service performed by another physician had to be repeated. This situation may be reported by adding modifier 77 to the repeated procedure/service.

78   **Unplanned Return to the Operating/Procedure Room by the Same Physician Following Initial Procedure for a Related Procedure During the Postoperative Period:** It may be necessary to indicate that another procedure was performed during the postoperative period of the initial procedure (unplanned procedure following initial procedure). When this procedure is related to the first and requires the use of an operating or procedure room, it may be reported by adding modifier 78 to the related procedure. (For repeat procedures, see modifier 76.)

79   **Unrelated Procedure or Service by the Same Physician During the Postoperative Period:** The physician may need to indicate that the performance of a procedure or service during the postoperative period was unrelated to the original procedure. This circumstance may be reported by using modifier 79. (For repeat procedures on the same day, see modifier 76.)

91   **Repeat Clinical Diagnostic Laboratory Test:** In the course of treatment of the patient, it may be necessary to repeat the same laboratory test on the same day to obtain subsequent (multiple) test results. Under these circumstances, the laboratory test performed can be identified by its usual procedure number and the addition of modifier 91. Note: This modifier may not be used when tests are rerun to confirm initial results; due to testing problems with specimens or equipment; or for any other reason when a normal, one-time, reportable result is all that is required. This modifier may not be used when another code(s) describe a series of test results (eg, glucose tolerance tests, evocative/suppression testing). This modifier may only be used for a laboratory test(s) performed more than once on the same day on the same patient.

Level II (HCPCS/National) Modifiers

Anatomical Modifiers

E1	Upper left, eyelid
E2	Lower left, eyelid
E3	Upper right, eyelid
E4	Lower right, eyelid
F1	Left hand, second digit
F2	Left hand, third digit
F3	Left hand, fourth digit
F4	Left hand, fifth digit
F5	Right hand, thumb
F6	Right hand, second digit
F7	Right hand, third digit
F8	Right hand, fourth digit
F9	Right hand, fifth digit
FA	Left hand, thumb
LT	Left side (used to identify procedures performed on the left side of the body)
RT	Right side (used to identify procedures performed on the right side of the body)
T1	Left foot, second digit
T2	Left foot, third digit

T3 Left foot, fourth digit

T4 Left foot, fifth digit

T5 Right foot, great toe

T6 Right foot, second digit

T7 Right foot, third digit

T8 Right foot, fourth digit

T9 Right foot, fifth digit

TA Left foot, great toe

Anesthesia Modifiers

AA Anesthesia services performed personally by anesthesiologist

AD Medical supervision by a physician: more than four concurrent anesthesia procedures

G8 Monitored anesthesia care (MAC) for deep complex, complicated, or markedly invasive surgical procedure

G9 Monitored anesthesia care for patient who has history of severe cardio-pulmonary condition

QK Medical direction of two, three, or four concurrent anesthesia procedures involving qualified individuals

QS Monitored anesthesia care service

QX CRNA service: with medical direction by a physician

QY Medical direction of one certified registered nurse anesthetist (CRNA) by an anesthesiologist

QZ CRNA service: without medical direction by a physician

P1 A normal healthy patient

P2 A patient with mild systemic disease

P3 A patient with severe systemic disease

P4 A patient with severe systemic disease that is a constant threat to life

P5 A moribund patient who is not expected to survive without the operation

P6 A declared brain-dead patient whose organs are being removed for donor purposes

Coronary Artery Modifiers

LC Left circumflex coronary artery (Hospitals use with codes 92980-92984, 92995, 92996)

LD Left anterior descending coronary artery (Hospitals use with codes 92980-92984, 92995, 92996)

RC Right coronary artery (Hospitals use with codes 92980-92984, 92995, 92996)

Ophthalmology Modifiers

AP Determination of refractive state was not performed in the course of diagnostic ophthalmological examination

LS FDA-monitored intraocular lens implant

PL Progressive addition lenses

VP Aphakic patient

Other Modifiers

AE Registered dietician

AF Specialty physician

AG Primary physician

AH Clinical psychologist

AJ Clinical social worker

AK Nonparticipating physician

AM Physician, team member service

AQ Physician providing a service in an unlisted health professional shortage area (HPSA)

AR Physician provider services in a physician scarcity area

AS Physician assistant, nurse practitioner, or clinical nurse specialist services for assistant at surgery

AT Acute treatment (this modifier should be used when reporting service 98940, 98941, 98942)

CA Procedure payable only in the inpatient setting when performed emergently on an outpatient who expires prior to admission

CB Service ordered by a renal dialysis facility (RDF) physician as part of the ESRD beneficiary's dialysis benefit, is not part of the composite rate, and is separately reimbursable

CC Procedure code change (use 'CC' when the procedure code submitted was changed either for administrative reasons or because an incorrect code was filed)

CG Policy criteria applied

CR Catastrophe/disaster related

EP Service provided as part of Medicaid early periodic screening diagnosis and treatment (EPSDT) program

ET Emergency services

EY No physician or other licensed health care provider order for this item or service

FB Item provided without cost to provider, supplier or practitioner, or full credit received for replaced device (examples, but not limited to covered under warranty, replaced due to defect, free samples)

FC Partial credit received for replacement device

FP Service provided as part of family planning program

G7 Pregnancy resulted from rape or incest or pregnancy certified by physician as life threatening

GA Waiver of liability statement on file

GB Claim being resubmitted for payment because it is no longer covered under a global payment demonstration

GC This service has been performed in part by a resident under the direction of a teaching physician

GD Units of service exceeds medically unlikely edit value and represents reasonable and necessary services

GE This service has been performed by a resident without the presence of a teaching physician under the primary care exception

GF Non-physician (e.g. nurse practitioner (NP), certified registered nurse anesthetist (CRNA), certified registered nurse (CRN), clinical nurse specialist (CNS), physician assistant (PA)) services in a critical access hospital

GG Performance and payment of a screening mammogram and diagnostic mammogram on the same patient, same day

GH Diagnostic mammogram converted from screening mammogram on same day

GJ Opt out physician or practitioner emergency or urgent service

GK Reasonable and necessary item/service associated with GA or GZ modifier

GN Service delivered under an outpatient speech-language pathology plan of care

GO Service delivered an outpatient occupational therapy plan of care

GP Service delivered under an outpatient physical therapy plan of care

GQ Via asynchronous telecommunications system

GR This service was performed in whole or in part by a resident in a department of veterans affairs medical center or clinic, supervised in accordance with VA policy

GT Via interactive audio and video telecommunication systems

GV Attending physician not employed or paid under arrangement by the patient's hospice provider

GW Service not related to the hospice patient's terminal condition

GY Item or service statutorily excluded, does not meet the definition of any Medicare benefit or for non-Medicare insurers, is not a contract benefit

GZ Item or service expected to be denied as not reasonable and necessary

H9 Court-ordered

HA Child/adolescent program

HB Adult program, nongeriatric

HC Adult program, geriatric

HD Pregnant/parenting women's program

HE Mental health program

HF Substance abuse program

HG   Opioid addiction treatment program

HH   Integrated mental health/substance abuse program

HI   Integrated mental health and mental retardation/developmental disabilities program

HJ   Employee assistance program

HK   Specialized mental health programs for high-risk populations

HL   Intern

HM   Less than bachelor degree level

HN   Bachelors degree level

HO   Masters degree level

HP   Doctoral level

HQ   Group setting

HR   Family/couple with client present

HS   Family/couple without client present

HT   Multi-disciplinary team

HU   Funded by child welfare agency

HV   Funded state addictions agency

HW   Funded by state mental health agency

HX   Funded by county/local agency

HY   Funded by juvenile justice agency

HZ   Funded by criminal justice agency

KB   Beneficiary requested upgrade for ABN, more than four modifiers identified on claim

KX   Requirements specified in the medical policy have been met

KZ   New coverage not implemented by managed care

LR   Laboratory round trip

M2   Medicare secondary payer (MSP)

Q0   Investigational clinical service provided in a clinical research study that is in an approved clinical research study

Q1   Routine clinical service provided in a clinical research study that is in an approved clinical research study

Q2   HCFA/ORD demonstration project procedure/service

Q3   Live kidney donor surgery and related services

Q4   Service for ordering/referring physician qualifies as a service exemption

Q5   Service furnished by a substitute physician under a reciprocal billing arrangement

Q6   Service furnished by a locum tenens physician

Q7   One Class A finding

Q8   Two Class B findings

Q9   One Class B and two Class C findings

QC   Single channel monitoring

QD   Recording and storage in solid state memory by a digital recorder

QJ   Services/items provided to a prisoner or patient in state or local custody, however the state or local government, as applicable, meets the requirements in 42 CRF 411.4 (B)

QP   Documentation is on file showing that the laboratory test(s) was ordered individually or ordered as a CPT-recognized panel other than automated profile codes 80002-80019, G0058, G0059, and G0060

QT   Recording and storage on tape by an analog tape recorder

QW   CLIA waived test

RE   Furnished in full compliance with FDA-mandated risk evaluation and mitigation strategy (REMS)

SA   Nurse practitioner rendering service in collaboration with a physician

SB   Nurse Midwife

SC   Medically necessary service or supply

SD   Services provided by registered nurse with specialized, highly technical home infusion training

SE   State and/or federally funded programs/services

SF   Second opinion ordered by a professional review organization (PRO) per section 9401, P.L.99-272 (100% reimbursement - no Medicare deductible or coinsurance)

SG   Ambulatory surgical center (ASC) facility service

SH   Second concurrently administered infusion therapy

SJ   Third or more concurrently administered infusion therapy

SK   Member of high risk population (use only with codes for immunization)

SL   State supplied vaccine

SM   Second surgical opinion

SN   Third surgical opinion

SQ   Item ordered by home health

SS   Home infusion services provided in the infusion suite of the IV therapy provider

ST   Related to trauma or injury

SU   Procedure performed in physician's office (to denote use of facility and equipment)

SW   Services provided by a certified diabetic educator

SY   Persons who are in close contact with member of high risk population (use only with codes for immunization)

TC   Technical component. Under certain circumstances, a charge may be made for the technical component alone. Under those circumstances the technical component charge is identified by adding modifier 'TC' to the usual procedure number. Technical component charges are institutional charges and not billed separately by physicians. However, portable x-ray suppliers only bill for technical component and should utilize modifier TC. The charge data from portable x-ray suppliers will then be used to build customary and prevailing profiles.

TD   RN

TE   LPN/LVN

TF   Intermediate level of care

TG   Complex/high level of care

TH   Obstetrical treatment/services, prenatal or postpartum

TJ   Program group, child and/or adolescent

TK   Extra patient or passenger, nonambulance

TL   Early intervention/individualized family service plan (IFSP)

TM   Individualized education program (IEP)

TN   Rural/outside providers' customary service area

TR   School-based individualized education program (IEP) services provided outside the public school district responsible for the student

TS   Follow-up service

TT   Individualized service provided to more than one patient in same setting

TU   Special payment rate, overtime

TV   Special payment rates, holidays/weekends

U1   Medicaid level of care 1, as defined by each state

U2   Medicaid level of care 2, as defined by each state

U3   Medicaid level of care 3, as defined by each state

U4   Medicaid level of care 4, as defined by each state

U5   Medicaid level of care 5, as defined by each state

U6   Medicaid level of care 6, as defined by each state

U7   Medicaid level of care 7, as defined by each state

U8   Medicaid level of care 8, as defined by each state

U9   Medicaid level of care 9, as defined by each state

UA   Medicaid level of care 10, as defined by each state

UB   Medicaid level of care 11, as defined by each state

UC   Medicaid level of care 12, as defined by each state

UD   Medicaid level of care 13, as defined by each state

UF   Services provided in the morning

UG   Services provided in the afternoon

UH Services provided in the evening

UJ Services provided at night

UK Services provided on behalf of the client to someone other than the client (collateral relationship)

UN Two patients served

UP Three patients served

UQ Four patients served

UR Five patients served

US Six or more patients served

Category II Modifiers

1P Performance measure exclusion modifier due to medical reasons

Includes:

- Not indicated (absence of organ/limb, already received/performed, other)
- Contraindicated (patient allergic history, potential adverse drug interaction, other)
- Other medical reasons

2P Performance measure exclusion modifier due to patient reasons

Includes:

- Patient declined
- Economic, social, or religious reasons
- Other patient reasons

3P Performance measure exclusion modifier due to system reasons

Includes:

- Resources to perform the services not available (eg, equipment, supplies)
- Insurance coverage or payer-related limitations
- Other reasons attributable to health care delivery system

8P Performance measure reporting modifier - action not performed, reason not otherwise specified

Includes:

- Reporting of circumstances that describe a service in the measure's numerator is not performed and the reason is not otherwise specified

Dental Modifiers

ET Emergency services (dental procedures performed in emergency situations should show the modifier ET)

ESRD Modifiers

CD AMCC test has been ordered by an ESRD facility or MCP physician that is a part of the composite rate and is not separately billable

CE AMCC test has been ordered by an ESRD facility or MCP physician that is a composite rate test but is beyond the normal frequency covered under the rate and is separately reimbursable based on medically necessary

CF AMCC test has been ordered by an ESRD facility or MCP physician that is not part of the composite rate and is separately billable

G6 ESRD patient for whom less than six dialysis sessions have been provided in a month

GS Dosage of EPO or darbepoietin alfa has been reduced and maintained in response to hematocrit or hemoglobin level

Q3 Live kidney donor: services associated with postoperative medical complications directly related to the donation

Genetic Testing Modifiers

Neoplasia (Solid Tumor, Excluding Sarcoma and Lymphoma)

0A BRCA1 (Hereditary breast/ovarian cancer)

0B BRCA2 (Hereditary breast cancer)

0C Neurofibromin (Neurofibromatosis, type 1)

0D Merlin (Neurofibromatosis, type 2)

0E c-RET (Multiple endocrine neoplasia, types 2A/B, familial medullary thyroid carcinoma)

0F VHL (Von Hippel Lindau disease, renal carcinoma)

0G SDHD (Hereditary paraganglioma)

0H SDHB (Hereditary paraganglioma)

0I ERRB2, commonly called Her-2/neu

0J MLH1 (HNPCC mismatch repair genes)

0K MSH2, MSH6, or PMS2 (HNPCC, mismatch repair genes)

0L APC (Hereditary polyposis coli)

0M Rb (Retinoblastoma)

0N TP53, commonly called p53

0O PTEN (Cowden's syndrome)

0P KIT, also called CD 117 (gastrointestinal stromal tumor)

0Z Solid tumor gene, not otherwise specified

Neoplasia (Sarcoma)

1A WT1 or WT2 (Wilm's tumor)

1B PAX3, PAX7, or FOX01A (Alveolar rhabdomyosarcoma)

1C FLI1, ERG, ETV1, or EWSR1 (Ewing's sarcoma, desmoplastic round cell)

1D DDIT3 or FUS (Myxoid liposarcoma)

1E NR4A3, RBF56, or TCF12 (Myxoid chondrosarcoma)

1F SSX1, SSX2, or SYT (Synovial sarcoma)

1G MYCN (Neuroblastoma)

1H COL1A1 or PDGFB (Dermatofibrosarcoma protuberans)

1I TFE3 or ASPSCR1 (Alveolar soft parts sarcoma)

1J JAZF1 or JJAZ1 (Endometrial stromal sarcoma)

1Z Sarcoma gene, not otherwise specified

Neoplasia (Lymphoid/Hemtopoietic)

2A RUNX1 or CBFA2T1, commonly called AML1 or ETO, (genes associated with t(8;21) AML1–also ETO (Acute myeloid leukemia)

2B BCR or ABL, genes associated with t(9;22) (Chronic myelogenous or acute leukemia) BCR—also ABL (Chronic myeloid, acute lymphoid leukemia)

2C PBX1 or TCF3, genes associated with t(1;19) (Acute lymphoblastic leukemia) CGF1

2D CBFB or MYH11, genes associated with inv 16 (Acute myelogenous leukemia) CBF betas (leukemia)

2E MML (Acute leukemia)

2F PML or RARA, genes associated with t (15;17) (Acute promyelocytic leukemia)PML/RAR alpha (Promyelocytic leukemia)

2G ETV6, commonly called TEL, gene associated with t (12;210 (acute leukemia) EL (Leukemia)

2H BCL2 (B cell lymphoma, follicle center cell origin) BCL-2 (Lymphoma)

2I CCND1, commonly called BCL1, cyclin D1 (Mantle cell lymphoma, myeloma) BCL-1 (Lymphoma)

2J Myc (Burkitt lymphoma) c-Myc (Lymphoma)

2K IgH (Lymphoma/leukemia)

2L IGK (Lymphoma/leukemia)

2M TRB, T cell receptor beta (Lymphoma/leukemia)

2N TRG, T cell receptor gamma (Lymphoma/leukemia)

2O SIL or TAL1 (T cell leukemia)

2T BCL6 (B cell lymphoma)

2Q API1 or MALT1 (MALT lymphoma)

2R NPM or ALK, genes associated with t (2;5) (anaplastic large cell lymphoma)

2S FLT3 (Acute myelogenous leukemia)

2Z Lymphoid/hematopoetic neoplasia, not otherwise specified

Non-Neoplastic Hematology/Coagulation

3A F5, commonly called Factor V (Leiden, others) (Hypercoagulable state)

3B FACC (Fanconi anemia)

3C FACD (Fanconi anemia)

3D HBB, Beta globin (Thalassemia, sickle cell anemia, other hemoglobinopathies)

© 2008 Ingenix

3E   HBA, commonly called alpha globin (thalassemia)

3F   MTHFR (Elevated homocysteine)

3G   F2, commonly called prothrombin (20210, others) (Hypercoagulable state) prothrombin (Factor II, 20210A) (Hypercoagulable state)

3H   F8, commonly called Factor VII (Hemophilia A/VWF)

3I   F9, commonly called Factor IX (Hemophilia B)

3K   F13, commonly called Factor XII (bleeding or hypercoagulable state) beta globin

3Z   Non-neoplastic hematology/coagulation, not otherwise specified

Histocompatibility/Blood Typing/Identity/Microsatellite
4A   HLA-A

4B   HLA-B

4C   HLA-C

4D   HLA-D

4E   HLA-DR

4F   HLA-DQ

4G   HLA-DP

4H   Kell

4I   Fingerprint for engraftment (post-allogenic progenitor cell transplant)

4J   Fingerprint for donor allelotype (allogeneic transplant)

4K   Fingerprint for recipient allelotype (allogeneic transplant)

4L   Fingerprint for leukocyte chimerism (allogeneic solid organ transplant)

4M   Fingerprint for maternal versus fetal origin

4N   Microsatellite instability

4O   Microsatelite loss (loss of heterozygosity)

4Z   Histocompatibility/blood typing, not otherwise specified

Neurologic, Non-Neoplastic
5A   ASPA, commonly called Aspartoacylase A (Canavan disease)

5B   FMR-1 (Fragile X, FRAXA, syndrome)

5C   FRDA, commonly called Frataxin (Freidreich's ataxia)

5D   HD, commonly called Huntington (Huntington's disease)

5E   GABRA, NIPA1, UBE3A, or ANCR GABRA (Prader Willi-Angelman syndrome)

5F   GJB2, commonly called Connexin 26 (Hereditary hearing loss) Connexin-26 (GJB2) (Hereditary deafness)

5G   GJB1, commonly called Connexin-32 (X-linked Charcot-Marie-Tooth disease)

5H   SNRPN (Prader Willi-Angelman syndrome)

5I   SCA1, commonly called Ataxin-1 (Spinocerebellar ataxia, type 1)

5J   SCA2, commonly called Ataxin-2 (Spinocerebellar ataxia, type 2)

5K   MJD, commonly called Ataxin-3 (Spinocerebellar ataxia, type 3, Machado-Joseph disease)

5L   CACNA1A (Spinocerebellar ataxia, type 6)

5M   ATXN7 Ataxin-7 (Spinocerebellar ataxia, type 7)

5N   PMP-22 (Charcot-Marie-Tooth disease, type 1A)

5O   MECP1 (Rett syndrome)

5Z   Neurologic, non-neoplastic, not otherwise specified

Muscular, Non-Neoplastic
6A   DMD, commonly called Dystrophin (Duchenne/Becker muscular dystrophy)

6B   DMPK (Myotonic dystrophy, type 1)

6C   ZNF-9 (Myotonic dystrophy, type 2)

6D   SMN1/SMN2 (Autosomal recessive spinal muscular atrophy)

6E   MTTK, commonly called tRNAlys (mytonic epilepsy, MERRF)

6F   MTTL1, commonly called tRNAleu (mitochondrialencephalomyopathy, MELAS)

6Z   Muscular, not otherwise specified

Metabolic, Other
7A   APOE, commonly called Apolipoprotein E (Cardiovascular disease, Alzheimer's disease)

7B   NPC1 or NPC2, commonly called sphingomyelin phosphodiesterase (Nieman-Pick disease)

7C   GBA, commonly called Acid Beta Glucosidase (Gaucher disease)

7D   HFE (Hemochromatosis)

7E   HEXA, commonly called Hexosaminidase A (Tay-Sachs disease)

7F   ACADM (medium chain acyl CoA dehydrogenase deficiency)

7Z   Metabolic, other, not otherwise specified

Metabolic, Transport
8A   CFTR (Cystic fibrosis)

8B   PRSS1 (Hereditary pancreatitis)

8C   Long QT syndrome, KCN (Jervell and Lange-Nielsen syndromes, types 1, 2, 5, and 6) and SCN (Brugada syndrome, SIDS and type 3)

8Z   Metabolic, transport, not otherwise specified)

Metabolic-Pharmacogenetics
9A   TPMT, commonly called (thiopurine methyltransferase) (patients on antimetabolite therapy)

9B   CYP2 genes, commonly called cytochrome p450 (drug metabolism)

9C   ABCB1, commonly called MDR1 or p-glycoprotein (drug transport)

9D   NAT2 (drug metabolism)

9L   Metabolic-pharmacogenetics, not otherwise specified

Dysmorphology
9M   FGFR-1 (Pfeiffer and Kallmann syndromes)

9N   FGFR2 (Crouzon, Jackson-Weiss, Apert, Saethre-Chotzen syndromes)

9O   FGFR3 (Achondroplasia, Hypochondroplasia, Thanatophoric dysplasia, types I and II, Crouzon syndrome with acanthosis nigricans, Muencke syndromes)

9P   TWIST (Saethre-Chotzen syndrome)

9Q   DCGR, commonly called CATCH-22 (DiGeorge and 22q11 deletion syndromes)

9Z   Dysmorphology, not otherwise specified

APPENDIX B — NEW, CHANGED, DELETED, AND MODIFIED CODES

The following lists include codes ear-marked as new, changed, and deleted. Codes specified as add-on, exempt from Modifier 51 and 63, and include conscious sedation are listed. The lists are designed to be read left to right rather than vertically

New Codes

00211 Anesthesia for intracranial procedures; craniotomy or craniectomy for evacuation of hematoma

00567 Anesthesia for direct coronary artery bypass grafting; with pump oxygenator

20696 Application of multiplane (pins or wires in more than 1 plane), unilateral, external fixation with stereotactic computer-assisted adjustment (eg, spatial frame), including imaging; initial and subsequent alignment(s), assessment(s), and computation(s) of adjustment schedule(s)

20697 Application of multiplane (pins or wires in more than 1 plane), unilateral, external fixation with stereotactic computer-assisted adjustment (eg, spatial frame), including imaging; exchange (ie, removal and replacement) of strut, each

22856 Total disc arthroplasty (artificial disc), anterior approach, including discectomy with end plate preparation (includes osteophytectomy for nerve root or spinal cord decompression and microdissection), single interspace, cervical

22861 Revision including replacement of total disc arthroplasty (artificial disc), anterior approach, single interspace; cervical

22864 Removal of total disc arthroplasty (artificial disc), anterior approach, single interspace; cervical

27027 Decompression fasciotomy(ies), pelvic (buttock) compartment(s) (eg, gluteus medius-minimus, gluteus maximus, iliopsoas, and/or tensor fascia lata muscle), unilateral

27057 Decompression fasciotomy(ies), pelvic (buttock) compartment(s) (eg, gluteus medius-minimus, gluteus maximus, iliopsoas, and/or tensor fascia lata muscle) with debridement of nonviable muscle, unilateral

35535 Bypass graft, with vein; hepatorenal

35570 Bypass graft, with vein; tibial-tibial, peroneal-tibial, or tibial/peroneal trunk-tibial

35632 Bypass graft, with other than vein; ilio-celiac

35633 Bypass graft, with other than vein; ilio-mesenteric

35634 Bypass graft, with other than vein; iliorenal

41512 Tongue base suspension, permanent suture technique

41530 Submucosal ablation of the tongue base, radiofrequency, 1 or more sites, per session

43273 Endoscopic cannulation of papilla with direct visualization of common bile duct(s) and/or pancreatic duct(s) (List separately in addition to code(s) for primary procedure)

43279 Laparoscopy, surgical, esophagomyotomy (Heller type), with fundoplasty, when performed

46930 Destruction of internal hemorrhoid(s) by thermal energy (eg, infrared coagulation, cautery, radiofrequency)

49652 Laparoscopy, surgical, repair, ventral, umbilical, spigelian or epigastric hernia (includes mesh insertion, when performed); reducible

49653 Laparoscopy, surgical, repair, ventral, umbilical, spigelian or epigastric hernia (includes mesh insertion, when performed); incarcerated or strangulated

49654 Laparoscopy, surgical, repair, incisional hernia (includes mesh insertion, when performed); reducible

49655 Laparoscopy, surgical, repair, incisional hernia (includes mesh insertion, when performed); incarcerated or strangulated

49656 Laparoscopy, surgical, repair, recurrent incisional hernia (includes mesh insertion, when performed); reducible

49657 Laparoscopy, surgical, repair, recurrent incisional hernia (includes mesh insertion, when performed); incarcerated or strangulated

55706 Biopsies, prostate, needle, transperineal, stereotactic template guided saturation sampling, including imaging guidance

61796 Stereotactic radiosurgery (particle beam, gamma ray, or linear accelerator); 1 simple cranial lesion

61797 Stereotactic radiosurgery (particle beam, gamma ray, or linear accelerator); each additional cranial lesion, simple (List separately in addition to code for primary procedure)

61798 Stereotactic radiosurgery (particle beam, gamma ray, or linear accelerator); 1 complex cranial lesion

61799 Stereotactic radiosurgery (particle beam, gamma ray, or linear accelerator); each additional cranial lesion, complex (List separately in addition to code for primary procedure)

61800 Application of stereotactic headframe for stereotactic radiosurgery (List separately in addition to code for primary procedure)

62267 Percutaneous aspiration within the nucleus pulposus, intervertebral disc, or paravertebral tissue for diagnostic purposes

63620 Stereotactic radiosurgery (particle beam, gamma ray, or linear accelerator); 1 spinal lesion

63621 Stereotactic radiosurgery (particle beam, gamma ray, or linear accelerator); each additional spinal lesion (List separately in addition to code for primary procedure)

64455 Injection(s), anesthetic agent and/or steroid, plantar common digital nerve(s) (eg, Morton's neuroma)

64632 Destruction by neurolytic agent; plantar common digital nerve

65756 Keratoplasty (corneal transplant); endothelial

65757 Backbench preparation of corneal endothelial allograft prior to transplantation (List separately in addition to code for primary procedure)

77785 Remote afterloading high dose rate radionuclide brachytherapy; 1 channel

77786 Remote afterloading high dose rate radionuclide brachytherapy; 2-12 channels

77787 Remote afterloading high dose rate radionuclide brachytherapy; over 12 channels

78808 Injection procedure for radiopharmaceutical localization by non-imaging probe study, intravenous (eg, parathyroid adenoma)

83876 Myeloperoxidase (MPO)

83951 Oncoprotein; des-gamma-carboxy-prothrombin (DCP)

85397 Coagulation and fibrinolysis, functional activity, not otherwise specified (eg, ADAMTS-13), each analyte

87905 Infectious agent enzymatic activity other than virus (eg, sialidase activity in vaginal fluid)

88720 Bilirubin, total, transcutaneous

88740 Hemoglobin, quantitative, transcutaneous, per day; carboxyhemoglobin

88741 Hemoglobin, quantitative, transcutaneous, per day; methemoglobin

90738 Japanese encephalitis virus vaccine, inactivated, for intramuscular use

90951 End-stage renal disease (ESRD) related services monthly, for patients younger than 2 years of age to include monitoring for the adequacy of nutrition, assessment of growth and development, and counseling of parents; with 4 or more face-to-face physician visits per month

90952 End-stage renal disease (ESRD) related services monthly, for patients younger than 2 years of age to include monitoring for the adequacy of nutrition, assessment of growth and development, and counseling of parents; with 2-3 face-to-face physician visits per month

90953 End-stage renal disease (ESRD) related services monthly, for patients younger than 2 years of age to include monitoring for the adequacy of nutrition, assessment of growth and development, and counseling of parents; with 1 face-to-face physician visit per month

90954 End-stage renal disease (ESRD) related services monthly, for patients 2-11 years of age to include monitoring for the adequacy of nutrition, assessment of growth and development, and counseling of parents; with 4 or more face-to-face physician visits per month

90955 End-stage renal disease (ESRD) related services monthly, for patients 2-11 years of age to include monitoring for the adequacy of nutrition, assessment of growth and development, and counseling of parents; with 2-3 face-to-face physician visits per month

 © 2008 Ingenix

New Codes (continued)

90956 End-stage renal disease (ESRD) related services monthly, for patients 2-11 years of age to include monitoring for the adequacy of nutrition, assessment of growth and development, and counseling of parents; with 1 face-to-face physician visit per month

90957 End-stage renal disease (ESRD) related services monthly, for patients 12-19 years of age to include monitoring for the adequacy of nutrition, assessment of growth and development, and counseling of parents; with 4 or more face-to-face physician visits per month

90958 End-stage renal disease (ESRD) related services monthly, for patients 12-19 years of age to include monitoring for the adequacy of nutrition, assessment of growth and development, and counseling of parents; with 2-3 face-to-face physician visits per month

90959 End-stage renal disease (ESRD) related services monthly, for patients 12-19 years of age to include monitoring for the adequacy of nutrition, assessment of growth and development, and counseling of parents; with 1 face-to-face physician visit per month

90960 End-stage renal disease (ESRD) related services monthly, for patients 20 years of age and older; with 4 or more face-to-face physician visits per month

90961 End-stage renal disease (ESRD) related services monthly, for patients 20 years of age and older; with 2-3 face-to-face physician visits per month

90962 End-stage renal disease (ESRD) related services monthly, for patients 20 years of age and older; with 1 face-to-face physician visit per month

90963 End-stage renal disease (ESRD) related services for home dialysis per full month, for patients younger than 2 years of age to include monitoring for the adequacy of nutrition, assessment of growth and development, and counseling of parents

90964 End-stage renal disease (ESRD) related services for home dialysis per full month, for patients 2-11 years of age to include monitoring for the adequacy of nutrition, assessment of growth and development, and counseling of parents

90965 End-stage renal disease (ESRD) related services for home dialysis per full month, for patients 12-19 years of age to include monitoring for the adequacy of nutrition, assessment of growth and development, and counseling of parents

90966 End-stage renal disease (ESRD) related services for home dialysis per full month, for patients 20 years of age and older

90967 End-stage renal disease (ESRD) related services for dialysis less than a full month of service, per day; for patients younger than 2 years of age

90968 End-stage renal disease (ESRD) related services for dialysis less than a full month of service, per day; for patients 2-11 years of age

90969 End-stage renal disease (ESRD) related services for dialysis less than a full month of service, per day; for patients 12-19 years of age

90970 End-stage renal disease (ESRD) related services for dialysis less than a full month of service, per day; for patients 20 years of age and older

93228 Wearable mobile cardiovascular telemetry with electrocardiographic recording, concurrent computerized real time data analysis and greater than 24 hours of accessible ECG data storage (retrievable with query) with ECG triggered and patient selected events transmitted to a remote attended surveillance center for up to 30 days; physician review and interpretation with report

93229 Wearable mobile cardiovascular telemetry with electrocardiographic recording, concurrent computerized real time data analysis and greater than 24 hours of accessible ECG data storage (retrievable with query) with ECG triggered and patient selected events transmitted to a remote attended surveillance center for up to 30 days; technical support for connection and patient instructions for use, attended surveillance, analysis and physician prescribed transmission of daily and emergent data reports

93279 Programming device evaluation with iterative adjustment of the implantable device to test the function of the device and select optimal permanent programmed values with physician analysis, review and report; single lead pacemaker system

93280 Programming device evaluation with iterative adjustment of the implantable device to test the function of the device and select optimal permanent programmed values with physician analysis, review and report; dual lead pacemaker system

93281 Programming device evaluation with iterative adjustment of the implantable device to test the function of the device and select optimal permanent programmed values with physician analysis, review and report; multiple lead pacemaker system

93282 Programming device evaluation with iterative adjustment of the implantable device to test the function of the device and select optimal permanent programmed values with physician analysis, review and report; single lead implantable cardioverter-defibrillator system

93283 Programming device evaluation with iterative adjustment of the implantable device to test the function of the device and select optimal permanent programmed values with physician analysis, review and report; dual lead implantable cardioverter-defibrillator system

93284 Programming device evaluation with iterative adjustment of the implantable device to test the function of the device and select optimal permanent programmed values with physician analysis, review and report; multiple lead implantable cardioverter-defibrillator system

93285 Programming device evaluation with iterative adjustment of the implantable device to test the function of the device and select optimal permanent programmed values with physician analysis, review and report; implantable loop recorder system

93286 Peri-procedural device evaluation and programming of device system parameters before or after a surgery, procedure, or test with physician analysis, review and report; single, dual, or multiple lead pacemaker system

93287 Peri-procedural device evaluation and programming of device system parameters before or after a surgery, procedure, or test with physician analysis, review and report; single, dual, or multiple lead implantable cardioverter-defibrillator system

93288 Interrogation device evaluation (in person) with physician analysis, review and report, includes connection, recording and disconnection per patient encounter; single, dual, or multiple lead pacemaker system

93289 Interrogation device evaluation (in person) with physician analysis, review and report, includes connection, recording and disconnection per patient encounter; single, dual, or multiple lead implantable cardioverter-defibrillator system, including analysis of heart rhythm derived data elements

93290 Interrogation device evaluation (in person) with physician analysis, review and report, includes connection, recording and disconnection per patient encounter; implantable cardiovascular monitor system, including analysis of 1 or more recorded physiologic cardiovascular data elements from all internal and external sensors

93291 Interrogation device evaluation (in person) with physician analysis, review and report, includes connection, recording and disconnection per patient encounter; implantable loop recorder system, including heart rhythm derived data analysis

93292 Interrogation device evaluation (in person) with physician analysis, review and report, includes connection, recording and disconnection per patient encounter; wearable defibrillator system

93293 Transtelephonic rhythm strip pacemaker evaluation(s) single, dual, or multiple lead pacemaker system, includes recording with and without magnet application with physician analysis, review and report(s), up to 90 days

93294 Interrogation device evaluation(s) (remote), up to 90 days; single, dual, or multiple lead pacemaker system with interim physician analysis, review(s) and report(s)

93295 Interrogation device evaluation(s) (remote), up to 90 days; single, dual, or multiple lead implantable cardioverter-defibrillator system with interim physician analysis, review(s) and report(s)

93296 Interrogation device evaluation(s) (remote), up to 90 days; single, dual, or multiple lead pacemaker system or implantable cardioverter-defibrillator system, remote data acquisition(s), receipt of transmissions and technician review, technical support and distribution of results

93297 Interrogation device evaluation(s), (remote) up to 30 days; implantable cardiovascular monitor system, including analysis of 1 or more recorded physiologic cardiovascular data elements from all internal and external sensors, physician analysis, review(s) and report(s)

New Codes (continued)

93298 Interrogation device evaluation(s), (remote) up to 30 days; implantable loop recorder system, including analysis of recorded heart rhythm data, physician analysis, review(s) and report(s)

93299 Interrogation device evaluation(s), (remote) up to 30 days; implantable cardiovascular monitor system or implantable loop recorder system, remote data acquisition(s), receipt of transmissions and technician review, technical support and distribution of results

93306 Echocardiography, transthoracic, real-time with image documentation (2D), includes M-mode recording, when performed, complete, with spectral Doppler echocardiography, and with color flow Doppler echocardiography

93351 Echocardiography, transthoracic, real-time with image documentation (2D), includes M-mode recording, when performed, during rest and cardiovascular stress test using treadmill, bicycle exercise and/or pharmacologically induced stress, with interpretation and report; including performance of continuous electrocardiographic monitoring, with physician supervision

93352 Use of echocardiographic contrast agent during stress echocardiography (List separately in addition to code for primary procedure)

95803 Actigraphy testing, recording, analysis, interpretation, and report (minimum of 72 hours to 14 consecutive days of recording)

95992 Canalith repositioning procedure(s) (eg, Epley maneuver, Semont maneuver), per day

96360 Intravenous infusion, hydration; initial, 31 minutes to 1 hour

96361 Intravenous infusion, hydration; each additional hour (List separately in addition to code for primary procedure)

96365 Intravenous infusion, for therapy, prophylaxis, or diagnosis (specify substance or drug); initial, up to 1 hour

96366 Intravenous infusion, for therapy, prophylaxis, or diagnosis (specify substance or drug); each additional hour (List separately in addition to code for primary procedure)

96367 Intravenous infusion, for therapy, prophylaxis, or diagnosis (specify substance or drug); additional sequential infusion, up to 1 hour (List separately in addition to code for primary procedure)

96368 Intravenous infusion, for therapy, prophylaxis, or diagnosis (specify substance or drug); concurrent infusion (List separately in addition to code for primary procedure)

96369 Subcutaneous infusion for therapy or prophylaxis (specify substance or drug); initial, up to 1 hour, including pump set-up and establishment of subcutaneous infusion site(s)

96370 Subcutaneous infusion for therapy or prophylaxis (specify substance or drug); each additional hour (List separately in addition to code for primary procedure)

96371 Subcutaneous infusion for therapy or prophylaxis (specify substance or drug); additional pump set-up with establishment of new subcutaneous infusion site(s) (List separately in addition to code for primary procedure)

96372 Therapeutic, prophylactic, or diagnostic injection (specify substance or drug); subcutaneous or intramuscular

96373 Therapeutic, prophylactic, or diagnostic injection (specify substance or drug); intra-arterial

96374 Therapeutic, prophylactic, or diagnostic injection (specify substance or drug); intravenous push, single or initial substance/drug

96375 Therapeutic, prophylactic, or diagnostic injection (specify substance or drug); each additional sequential intravenous push of a new substance/drug (List separately in addition to code for primary procedure)

96376 Therapeutic, prophylactic, or diagnostic injection (specify substance or drug); each additional sequential intravenous push of the same substance/drug provided in a facility (List separately in addition to code for primary procedure)

96379 Unlisted therapeutic, prophylactic, or diagnostic intravenous or intra-arterial injection or infusion

99460 Initial hospital or birthing center care, per day, for evaluation and management of normal newborn infant

99461 Initial care, per day, for evaluation and management of normal newborn infant seen in other than hospital or birthing center

99462 Subsequent hospital care, per day, for evaluation and management of normal newborn

99463 Initial hospital or birthing center care, per day, for evaluation and management of normal newborn infant admitted and discharged on the same date

99464 Attendance at delivery (when requested by the delivering physician) and initial stabilization of newborn

99465 Delivery/birthing room resuscitation, provision of positive pressure ventilation and/or chest compressions in the presence of acute inadequate ventilation and/or cardiac output

99466 Critical care services delivered by a physician, face-to-face, during an interfacility transport of critically ill or critically injured pediatric patient, 24 months of age or less; first 30-74 minutes of hands-on care during transport

99467 Critical care services delivered by a physician, face-to-face, during an interfacility transport of critically ill or critically injured pediatric patient, 24 months of age or less; each additional 30 minutes (List separately in addition to code for primary service)

99468 Initial inpatient neonatal critical care, per day, for the evaluation and management of a critically ill neonate, 28 days of age or less

99469 Subsequent inpatient neonatal critical care, per day, for the evaluation and management of a critically ill neonate, 28 days of age or less

99471 Initial inpatient pediatric critical care, per day, for the evaluation and management of a critically ill infant or young child, 29 days through 24 months of age

99472 Subsequent inpatient pediatric critical care, per day, for the evaluation and management of a critically ill infant or young child, 29 days through 24 months of age

99475 Initial inpatient pediatric critical care, per day, for the evaluation and management of a critically ill infant or young child, 2 through 5 years of age

99476 Subsequent inpatient pediatric critical care, per day, for the evaluation and management of a critically ill infant or young child, 2 through 5 years of age

99478 Subsequent intensive care, per day, for the evaluation and management of the recovering very low birth weight infant (present body weight less than 1500 grams)

99479 Subsequent intensive care, per day, for the evaluation and management of the recovering low birth weight infant (present body weight of 1500-2500 grams)

99480 Subsequent intensive care, per day, for the evaluation and management of the recovering infant (present body weight of 2501-5000 grams)

0184T Excision of rectal tumor, transanal endoscopic microsurgical approach (ie, TEMS)

0185T Multivariate analysis of patient specific findings with quantifiable computer probability assessment, including report

0186T Suprachoroidal delivery of pharmacologic agent (does not include supply of medication)

0187T Scanning computerized ophthalmic diagnostic imaging, anterior segment, with interpretation and report, unilateral

0188T Remote real-time interactive videoconferenced critical care, evaluation and management of the critically ill or critically injured patient; first 30-74 minutes

0189T Remote real-time interactive videoconferenced critical care, evaluation and management of the critically ill or critically injured patient; each additional 30 minutes (List separately in addition to code for primary service)

0190T Placement of intraocular radiation source applicator (List separately in addition to primary procedure)

0191T Insertion of anterior segment aqueous drainage device, without extraocular reservoir; internal approach

0192T Insertion of anterior segment aqueous drainage device, without extraocular reservoir; external approach

0193T Transurethral, radiofrequency micro-remodeling of the female bladder neck and proximal urethra for stress urinary incontinence

0194T Procalcitonin (PCT)

© 2008 Ingenix

New Codes (continued)

0195T　Arthrodesis, pre-sacral interbody technique, including instrumentation, imaging (when performed), and discectomy to prepare interspace, lumbar; single interspace

0196T　Arthrodesis, pre-sacral interbody technique, including instrumentation, imaging (when performed), and discectomy to prepare interspace, lumbar; each additional interspace (List separately in addition to code for primary procedure)

0197T　Intra-fraction localization and tracking of target or patient motion during delivery of radiation therapy (eg, 3D positional tracking, gating, 3D surface tracking), each fraction of treatment

0198T　Measurement of ocular blood flow by repetitive intraocular pressure sampling, with interpretation and report

0575F　HIV RNA control plan of care, documented (HIV)5

1180F　All specified thromboembolic risk factors assessed (AFIB)1

1220F　Patient screened for depression (SUD)5

3250F　Specimen biopsy site other than anatomic location of primary tumor (eg, liver biopsy, lymph node biopsy) (PATH)1

3321F　AJCC Cancer Stage 0 or 1A Melanoma, documented (ML)5

3322F　Melanoma greater than AJCC Stage 0 or IA (ML)5

3350F　Mammogram assessment category of "known biopsy proven malignancy", documented (RAD)5

3351F　Negative screen for depressive symptoms as categorized by using a standardized depression screening/assessment tool (MDD)2

3352F　No significant depressive symptoms as categorized by using a standardized depression assessment tool (MDD)2

3353F　Mild to moderate depressive symptoms as categorized by using a standardized depression screening/assessment tool (MDD)2

3354F　Clinically significant depressive symptoms as categorized by using a standardized depression screening/assessment tool (MDD)2

3370F　AJCC Breast Cancer Stage 0, documented (ONC)1

3372F　AJCC Breast Cancer Stage I: T1mic, T1a or T1b (tumor size <= 1 cm), documented (ONC)1

3374F　AJCC Breast Cancer Stage I: T1c (tumor size > 1 cm to 2 cm), documented (ONC)1~

3376F　AJCC Breast Cancer Stage II, documented (ONC)1

3378F　AJCC Breast Cancer Stage III, documented (ONC)1

3380F　AJCC Breast Cancer Stage IV, documented (ONC)1

3382F　AJCC colon cancer, Stage 0, documented (ONC)1

3384F　AJCC colon cancer, Stage I, documented (ONC)1

3386F　AJCC colon cancer, Stage II, documented (ONC)1

3388F　AJCC colon cancer, Stage III, documented (ONC)1

3390F　AJCC colon cancer, Stage IV, documented (ONC)1

3500F　CD4+ cell count or CD4+ cell percentage documented as performed (HIV)5

3502F　HIV RNA viral load below limits of quantification (HIV)5

3503F　HIV RNA viral load not below limits of quantification (HIV)5

3510F　Documentation that tuberculosis (TB) screening test performed and results interpreted (HIV)5

3511F　Chlamydia and gonorrhea screenings documented as performed (HIV)5

3512F　Syphilis screening documented as performed (HIV)5

3513F　Hepatitis B screening documented as performed (HIV)5

3514F　Hepatitis C screening documented as performed (HIV)5

3515F　Patient has documented immunity to Hepatitis C (HIV)5

3550F　Low risk for thromboembolism (AFIB)1

3551F　Intermediate risk for thromboembolism (AFIB)1

3552F　High risk for thromboembolism (AFIB)1

3555F　Patient had International Normalized Ratio (INR) measurement performed (AFIB)1

3570F　Final report for bone scintigraphy study includes correlation with existing relevant imaging studies (eg, x-ray, MRI, CT) corresponding to the same anatomical region in question (NUC_MED)1

3572F　Patient considered to be potentially at risk for fracture in a weight-bearing site (NUC_MED)1

3573F　Patient not considered to be potentially at risk for fracture in a weight-bearing site (NUC_MED)1

4148F　Hepatitis A vaccine injection administered or previously received (HEP-C)1

4149F　Hepatitis B vaccine injection administered or previously received (HEP-C)1

4270F　Patient receiving potent antiretroviral therapy for 6 months or longer (HIV)5

4271F　Patient receiving potent antiretroviral therapy for less than 6 months or not receiving potent antiretroviral therapy (HIV)5

4274F　Influenza immunization administered or previously received (HIV)5

4275F　Hepatitis B vaccine injection administered or previously received (HIV)5

4290F　Patient screened for injection drug use (HIV)5

4293F　Patient screened for high-risk sexual behavior (HIV)5

4300F　Patient receiving warfarin therapy for nonvalvular atrial fibrillation or atrial flutter (AFIB)1

4301F　Patient not receiving warfarin therapy for nonvalvular atrial fibrillation or atrial flutter (AFIB)1

4320F　Patient counseled regarding psychosocial AND pharmacologic treatment options for alcohol dependence (SUD)5

Changed Codes

00562　Anesthesia for procedures on heart, pericardial sac, and great vessels of chest; with pump oxygenator, age 1 year or older, for all non-coronary bypass procedures (eg, valve procedures) or for re-operation for coronary bypass more than 1 month after original operation

00566　Anesthesia for direct coronary artery bypass grafting; without pump oxygenator

11001　Debridement of extensive eczematous or infected skin; each additional 10% of the body surface, or part thereof (List separately in addition to code for primary procedure)

11201　Removal of skin tags, multiple fibrocutaneous tags, any area; each additional 10 lesions, or part thereof (List separately in addition to code for primary procedure)

11922　Tattooing, intradermal introduction of insoluble opaque pigments to correct color defects of skin, including micropigmentation; each additional 20.0 sq cm, or part thereof (List separately in addition to code for primary procedure)

12031　Repair, intermediate, wounds of scalp, axillae, trunk and/or extremities (excluding hands and feet); 2.5 cm or less

12032　Repair, intermediate, wounds of scalp, axillae, trunk and/or extremities (excluding hands and feet); 2.6 cm to 7.5 cm

12034　Repair, intermediate, wounds of scalp, axillae, trunk and/or extremities (excluding hands and feet); 7.6 cm to 12.5 cm

12035　Repair, intermediate, wounds of scalp, axillae, trunk and/or extremities (excluding hands and feet); 12.6 cm to 20.0 cm

12036　Repair, intermediate, wounds of scalp, axillae, trunk and/or extremities (excluding hands and feet); 20.1 cm to 30.0 cm

12037　Repair, intermediate, wounds of scalp, axillae, trunk and/or extremities (excluding hands and feet); over 30.0 cm

12041　Repair, intermediate, wounds of neck, hands, feet and/or external genitalia; 2.5 cm or less

12042　Repair, intermediate, wounds of neck, hands, feet and/or external genitalia; 2.6 cm to 7.5 cm

12044　Repair, intermediate, wounds of neck, hands, feet and/or external genitalia; 7.6 cm to 12.5 cm

12045　Repair, intermediate, wounds of neck, hands, feet and/or external genitalia; 12.6 cm to 20.0 cm

12046　Repair, intermediate, wounds of neck, hands, feet and/or external genitalia; 20.1 cm to 30.0 cm

12047　Repair, intermediate, wounds of neck, hands, feet and/or external genitalia; over 30.0 cm

Changed Codes (continued)

12051 Repair, intermediate, wounds of face, ears, eyelids, nose, lips and/or mucous membranes; 2.5 cm or less

12052 Repair, intermediate, wounds of face, ears, eyelids, nose, lips and/or mucous membranes; 2.6 cm to 5.0 cm

12053 Repair, intermediate, wounds of face, ears, eyelids, nose, lips and/or mucous membranes; 5.1 cm to 7.5 cm

12054 Repair, intermediate, wounds of face, ears, eyelids, nose, lips and/or mucous membranes; 7.6 cm to 12.5 cm

12055 Repair, intermediate, wounds of face, ears, eyelids, nose, lips and/or mucous membranes; 12.6 cm to 20.0 cm

12056 Repair, intermediate, wounds of face, ears, eyelids, nose, lips and/or mucous membranes; 20.1 cm to 30.0 cm

12057 Repair, intermediate, wounds of face, ears, eyelids, nose, lips and/or mucous membranes; over 30.0 cm

15003 Surgical preparation or creation of recipient site by excision of open wounds, burn eschar, or scar (including subcutaneous tissues), or incisional release of scar contracture, trunk, arms, legs; each additional 100 sq cm, or part thereof, or each additional 1% of body area of infants and children (List separately in addition to code for primary procedure)

15005 Surgical preparation or creation of recipient site by excision of open wounds, burn eschar, or scar (including subcutaneous tissues), or incisional release of scar contracture, face, scalp, eyelids, mouth, neck, ears, orbits, genitalia, hands, feet and/or multiple digits; each additional 100 sq cm, or part thereof, or each additional 1% of body area of infants and children (List separately in addition to code for primary procedure)

15201 Full thickness graft, free, including direct closure of donor site, trunk; each additional 20 sq cm, or part thereof (List separately in addition to code for primary procedure)

15221 Full thickness graft, free, including direct closure of donor site, scalp, arms, and/or legs; each additional 20 sq cm, or part thereof (List separately in addition to code for primary procedure)

15241 Full thickness graft, free, including direct closure of donor site, forehead, cheeks, chin, mouth, neck, axillae, genitalia, hands, and/or feet; each additional 20 sq cm, or part thereof (List separately in addition to code for primary procedure)

15261 Full thickness graft, free, including direct closure of donor site, nose, ears, eyelids, and/or lips; each additional 20 sq cm, or part thereof (List separately in addition to code for primary procedure)

15341 Tissue cultured allogeneic skin substitute; each additional 25 sq cm, or part thereof (List separately in addition to code for primary procedure)

19296 Placement of radiotherapy afterloading expandable catheter (single or multichannel) into the breast for interstitial radioelement application following partial mastectomy, includes imaging guidance; on date separate from partial mastectomy

19297 Placement of radiotherapy afterloading expandable catheter (single or multichannel) into the breast for interstitial radioelement application following partial mastectomy, includes imaging guidance; concurrent with partial mastectomy (List separately in addition to code for primary procedure)

20985 Computer-assisted surgical navigational procedure for musculoskeletal procedures, image-less (List separately in addition to code for primary procedure)

22857 Total disc arthroplasty (artificial disc), anterior approach, including discectomy to prepare interspace (other than for decompression), single interspace, lumbar

22862 Revision including replacement of total disc arthroplasty (artificial disc), anterior approach, single interspace; lumbar

22865 Removal of total disc arthroplasty (artificial disc), anterior approach, single interspace; lumbar

23585 Open treatment of scapular fracture (body, glenoid or acromion) includes internal fixation, when performed

27215 Open treatment of iliac spine(s), tuberosity avulsion, or iliac wing fracture(s), unilateral, for pelvic bone fracture patterns that do not disrupt the pelvic ring, includes internal fixation, when performed

27216 Percutaneous skeletal fixation of posterior pelvic bone fracture and/or dislocation, for fracture patterns that disrupt the pelvic ring, unilateral (includes ipsilateral ilium, sacroiliac joint and/or sacrum)

27217 Open treatment of anterior pelvic bone fracture and/or dislocation for fracture patterns that disrupt the pelvic ring, unilateral, includes internal fixation, when performed (includes pubic symphysis and/or ipsilateral superior/inferior rami)

27218 Open treatment of posterior pelvic bone fracture and/or dislocation, for fracture patterns that disrupt the pelvic ring, unilateral, includes internal fixation, when performed (includes ipsilateral ilium, sacroiliac joint and/or sacrum)

27396 Transplant or transfer (with muscle redirection or rerouting), thigh (eg, extensor to flexor); single tendon

27397 Transplant or transfer (with muscle redirection or rerouting), thigh (eg, extensor to flexor); multiple tendons

27457 Osteotomy, proximal tibia, including fibular excision or osteotomy (includes correction of genu varus [bowleg] or genu valgus [knock-knee]); after epiphyseal closure

34806 Transcatheter placement of wireless physiologic sensor in aneurysmal sac during endovascular repair, including radiological supervision and interpretation, instrument calibration, and collection of pressure data (List separately in addition to code for primary procedure)

47144 Backbench standard preparation of cadaver donor whole liver graft prior to allotransplantation, including cholecystectomy, if necessary, and dissection and removal of surrounding soft tissues to prepare the vena cava, portal vein, hepatic artery, and common bile duct for implantation; with trisegment split of whole liver graft into 2 partial liver grafts (ie, left lateral segment [segments II and III] and right trisegment [segments I and IV through VIII])

47145 Backbench standard preparation of cadaver donor whole liver graft prior to allotransplantation, including cholecystectomy, if necessary, and dissection and removal of surrounding soft tissues to prepare the vena cava, portal vein, hepatic artery, and common bile duct for implantation; with lobe split of whole liver graft into 2 partial liver grafts (ie, left lobe [segments II, III, and IV] and right lobe [segments I and V through VIII])

49568 Implantation of mesh or other prosthesis for open incisional or ventral hernia repair or mesh for closure of debridement for necrotizing soft tissue infection (List separately in addition to code for the incisional or ventral hernia repair)

52630 Transurethral resection; residual or regrowth of obstructive prostate tissue including control of postoperative bleeding, complete (vasectomy, meatotomy, cystourethroscopy, urethral calibration and/or dilation, and internal urethrotomy are included)

57400 Dilation of vagina under anesthesia (other than local)

57410 Pelvic examination under anesthesia (other than local)

57415 Removal of impacted vaginal foreign body (separate procedure) under anesthesia (other than local)

62287 Decompression procedure, percutaneous, of nucleus pulposus of intervertebral disc, any method, single or multiple levels, lumbar (eg, manual or automated percutaneous discectomy, percutaneous laser discectomy)

63020 Laminotomy (hemilaminectomy), with decompression of nerve root(s), including partial facetectomy, foraminotomy and/or excision of herniated intervertebral disc, including open and endoscopically-assisted approaches; 1 interspace, cervical

63030 Laminotomy (hemilaminectomy), with decompression of nerve root(s), including partial facetectomy, foraminotomy and/or excision of herniated intervertebral disc, including open and endoscopically-assisted approaches; 1 interspace, lumbar

63035 Laminotomy (hemilaminectomy), with decompression of nerve root(s), including partial facetectomy, foraminotomy and/or excision of herniated intervertebral disc, including open and endoscopically-assisted approaches; each additional interspace, cervical or lumbar (List separately in addition to code for primary procedure)

64416 Injection, anesthetic agent; brachial plexus, continuous infusion by catheter (including catheter placement)

64446 Injection, anesthetic agent; sciatic nerve, continuous infusion by catheter (including catheter placement)

Changed Codes (continued)

64448   Injection, anesthetic agent; femoral nerve, continuous infusion by catheter (including catheter placement)

64449   Injection, anesthetic agent; lumbar plexus, posterior approach, continuous infusion by catheter (including catheter placement)

65710   Keratoplasty (corneal transplant); anterior lamellar

65730   Keratoplasty (corneal transplant); penetrating (except in aphakia or pseudophakia)

67145   Prophylaxis of retinal detachment (eg, retinal break, lattice degeneration) without drainage, 1 or more sessions; photocoagulation (laser or xenon arc)

67210   Destruction of localized lesion of retina (eg, macular edema, tumors), 1 or more sessions; photocoagulation

67218   Destruction of localized lesion of retina (eg, macular edema, tumors), 1 or more sessions; radiation by implantation of source (includes removal of source)

74270   Radiologic examination, colon; contrast (eg, barium) enema, with or without KUB

80048   Basic metabolic panel (Calcium, total) This panel must include the following: Calcium, total (82310) Carbon dioxide (82374) Chloride (82435) Creatinine (82565) Glucose (82947) Potassium (84132) Sodium (84295) Urea nitrogen (BUN) (84520)

80053   Comprehensive metabolic panel This panel must include the following: Albumin (82040) Bilirubin, total (82247) Calcium, total (82310) Carbon dioxide (bicarbonate) (82374) Chloride (82435) Creatinine (82565) Glucose (82947) Phosphatase, alkaline (84075) Potassium (84132) Protein, total (84155) Sodium (84295) Transferase, alanine amino (ALT) (SGPT) (84460) Transferase, aspartate amino (AST) (SGOT) (84450) Urea nitrogen (BUN) (84520)

80069   Renal function panel This panel must include the following: Albumin (82040) Calcium, total (82310) Carbon dioxide (bicarbonate) (82374) Chloride (82435) Creatinine (82565) Glucose (82947) Phosphorus inorganic (phosphate) (84100) Potassium (84132) Sodium (84295) Urea nitrogen (BUN) (84520)

82040   Albumin; serum, plasma or whole blood

82375   Carboxyhemoglobin; quantitative

82376   Carboxyhemoglobin; qualitative

83890   Molecular diagnostics; molecular isolation or extraction, each nucleic acid type (ie, DNA or RNA)

83891   Molecular diagnostics; isolation or extraction of highly purified nucleic acid, each nucleic acid type (ie, DNA or RNA)

83892   Molecular diagnostics; enzymatic digestion, each enzyme treatment

83893   Molecular diagnostics; dot/slot blot production, each nucleic acid preparation

83894   Molecular diagnostics; separation by gel electrophoresis (eg, agarose, polyacrylamide), each nucleic acid preparation

83897   Molecular diagnostics; nucleic acid transfer (eg, Southern, Northern), each nucleic acid preparation

83907   Molecular diagnostics; lysis of cells prior to nucleic acid extraction (eg, stool specimens, paraffin embedded tissue), each specimen

83909   Molecular diagnostics; separation and identification by high resolution technique (eg, capillary electrophoresis), each nucleic acid preparation

83925   Opiate(s), drug and metabolites, each procedure

83950   Oncoprotein; HER-2/neu

84132   Potassium; serum, plasma or whole blood

84155   Protein, total, except by refractometry; serum, plasma or whole blood

84295   Sodium; serum, plasma or whole blood

87810   Infectious agent antigen detection by immunoassay with direct optical observation; Chlamydia trachomatis

87850   Infectious agent antigen detection by immunoassay with direct optical observation; Neisseria gonorrhoeae

87880   Infectious agent antigen detection by immunoassay with direct optical observation; Streptococcus, group A

93224   Wearable electrocardiographic rhythm derived monitoring for 24 hours by continuous original waveform recording and storage, with visual superimposition scanning; includes recording, scanning analysis with report, physician review and interpretation

93225   Wearable electrocardiographic rhythm derived monitoring for 24 hours by continuous original waveform recording and storage, with visual superimposition scanning; recording (includes connection, recording, and disconnection)

93226   Wearable electrocardiographic rhythm derived monitoring for 24 hours by continuous original waveform recording and storage, with visual superimposition scanning; scanning analysis with report

93227   Wearable electrocardiographic rhythm derived monitoring for 24 hours by continuous original waveform recording and storage, with visual superimposition scanning; physician review and interpretation

93230   Wearable electrocardiographic rhythm derived monitoring for 24 hours by continuous original waveform recording and storage without superimposition scanning utilizing a device capable of producing a full miniaturized printout; includes recording, microprocessor-based analysis with report, physician review and interpretation

93231   Wearable electrocardiographic rhythm derived monitoring for 24 hours by continuous original waveform recording and storage without superimposition scanning utilizing a device capable of producing a full miniaturized printout; recording (includes connection, recording, and disconnection)

93232   Wearable electrocardiographic rhythm derived monitoring for 24 hours by continuous original waveform recording and storage without superimposition scanning utilizing a device capable of producing a full miniaturized printout; microprocessor-based analysis with report

93233   Wearable electrocardiographic rhythm derived monitoring for 24 hours by continuous original waveform recording and storage without superimposition scanning utilizing a device capable of producing a full miniaturized printout; physician review and interpretation

93235   Wearable electrocardiographic rhythm derived monitoring for 24 hours by continuous computerized monitoring and non-continuous recording, and real-time data analysis utilizing a device capable of producing intermittent full-sized waveform tracings, possibly patient activated; includes monitoring and real-time data analysis with report, physician review and interpretation

93236   Wearable electrocardiographic rhythm derived monitoring for 24 hours by continuous computerized monitoring and non-continuous recording, and real-time data analysis utilizing a device capable of producing intermittent full-sized waveform tracings, possibly patient activated; monitoring and real-time data analysis with report

93237   Wearable electrocardiographic rhythm derived monitoring for 24 hours by continuous computerized monitoring and non-continuous recording, and real-time data analysis utilizing a device capable of producing intermittent full-sized waveform tracings, possibly patient activated; physician review and interpretation

93268   Wearable patient activated electrocardiographic rhythm derived event recording with presymptom memory loop, 24-hour attended monitoring, per 30 day period of time; includes transmission, physician review and interpretation

93270   Wearable patient activated electrocardiographic rhythm derived event recording with presymptom memory loop, 24-hour attended monitoring, per 30 day period of time; recording (includes connection, recording, and disconnection)

93271   Wearable patient activated electrocardiographic rhythm derived event recording with presymptom memory loop, 24-hour attended monitoring, per 30 day period of time; monitoring, receipt of transmissions, and analysis

93272   Wearable patient activated electrocardiographic rhythm derived event recording with presymptom memory loop, 24-hour attended monitoring, per 30 day period of time; physician review and interpretation

93307   Echocardiography, transthoracic, real-time with image documentation (2D), includes M-mode recording, when performed, complete, without spectral or color Doppler echocardiography

93308   Echocardiography, transthoracic, real-time with image documentation (2D), includes M-mode recording, when performed, follow-up or limited study

Changed Codes (continued)

93313 Echocardiography, transesophageal, real-time with image documentation (2D) (with or without M-mode recording); placement of transesophageal probe only

93350 Echocardiography, transthoracic, real-time with image documentation (2D), includes M-mode recording, when performed, during rest and cardiovascular stress test using treadmill, bicycle exercise and/or pharmacologically induced stress, with interpretation and report;

95010 Percutaneous tests (scratch, puncture, prick) sequential and incremental, with drugs, biologicals or venoms, immediate type reaction, including test interpretation and report by a physician, specify number of tests

95015 Intracutaneous (intradermal) tests, sequential and incremental, with drugs, biologicals, or venoms, immediate type reaction, including test interpretation and report by a physician, specify number of tests

95250 Ambulatory continuous glucose monitoring of interstitial tissue fluid via a subcutaneous sensor for a minimum of 72 hours; sensor placement, hook-up, calibration of monitor, patient training, removal of sensor, and printout of recording

95251 Ambulatory continuous glucose monitoring of interstitial tissue fluid via a subcutaneous sensor for a minimum of 72 hours; interpretation and report

99354 Prolonged physician service in the office or other outpatient setting requiring direct (face-to-face) patient contact beyond the usual service; first hour (List separately in addition to code for office or other outpatient Evaluation and Management service)

99355 Prolonged physician service in the office or other outpatient setting requiring direct (face-to-face) patient contact beyond the usual service; each additional 30 minutes (List separately in addition to code for prolonged physician service)

99356 Prolonged physician service in the inpatient setting, requiring unit/floor time beyond the usual service; first hour (List separately in addition to code for inpatient Evaluation and Management service)

99357 Prolonged physician service in the inpatient setting, requiring unit/floor time beyond the usual service; each additional 30 minutes (List separately in addition to code for prolonged physician service)

99381 Initial comprehensive preventive medicine evaluation and management of an individual including an age and gender appropriate history, examination, counseling/anticipatory guidance/risk factor reduction interventions, and the ordering of laboratory/diagnostic procedures, new patient; infant (age younger than 1 year)

99382 Initial comprehensive preventive medicine evaluation and management of an individual including an age and gender appropriate history, examination, counseling/anticipatory guidance/risk factor reduction interventions, and the ordering of laboratory/diagnostic procedures, new patient; early childhood (age 1 through 4 years)

99383 Initial comprehensive preventive medicine evaluation and management of an individual including an age and gender appropriate history, examination, counseling/anticipatory guidance/risk factor reduction interventions, and the ordering of laboratory/diagnostic procedures, new patient; late childhood (age 5 through 11 years)

99384 Initial comprehensive preventive medicine evaluation and management of an individual including an age and gender appropriate history, examination, counseling/anticipatory guidance/risk factor reduction interventions, and the ordering of laboratory/diagnostic procedures, new patient; adolescent (age 12 through 17 years)

99385 Initial comprehensive preventive medicine evaluation and management of an individual including an age and gender appropriate history, examination, counseling/anticipatory guidance/risk factor reduction interventions, and the ordering of laboratory/diagnostic procedures, new patient; 18-39 years

99386 Initial comprehensive preventive medicine evaluation and management of an individual including an age and gender appropriate history, examination, counseling/anticipatory guidance/risk factor reduction interventions, and the ordering of laboratory/diagnostic procedures, new patient; 40-64 years

99387 Initial comprehensive preventive medicine evaluation and management of an individual including an age and gender appropriate history, examination, counseling/anticipatory guidance/risk factor reduction interventions, and the ordering of laboratory/diagnostic procedures, new patient; 65 years and older

99391 Periodic comprehensive preventive medicine reevaluation and management of an individual including an age and gender appropriate history, examination, counseling/anticipatory guidance/risk factor reduction interventions, and the ordering of laboratory/diagnostic procedures, established patient; infant (age younger than 1 year)

99392 Periodic comprehensive preventive medicine reevaluation and management of an individual including an age and gender appropriate history, examination, counseling/anticipatory guidance/risk factor reduction interventions, and the ordering of laboratory/diagnostic procedures, established patient; early childhood (age 1 through 4 years)

99393 Periodic comprehensive preventive medicine reevaluation and management of an individual including an age and gender appropriate history, examination, counseling/anticipatory guidance/risk factor reduction interventions, and the ordering of laboratory/diagnostic procedures, established patient; late childhood (age 5 through 11 years)

99394 Periodic comprehensive preventive medicine reevaluation and management of an individual including an age and gender appropriate history, examination, counseling/anticipatory guidance/risk factor reduction interventions, and the ordering of laboratory/diagnostic procedures, established patient; adolescent (age 12 through 17 years)

99395 Periodic comprehensive preventive medicine reevaluation and management of an individual including an age and gender appropriate history, examination, counseling/anticipatory guidance/risk factor reduction interventions, and the ordering of laboratory/diagnostic procedures, established patient; 18-39 years

99396 Periodic comprehensive preventive medicine reevaluation and management of an individual including an age and gender appropriate history, examination, counseling/anticipatory guidance/risk factor reduction interventions, and the ordering of laboratory/diagnostic procedures, established patient; 40-64 years

99397 Periodic comprehensive preventive medicine reevaluation and management of an individual including an age and gender appropriate history, examination, counseling/anticipatory guidance/risk factor reduction interventions, and the ordering of laboratory/diagnostic procedures, established patient; 65 years and older

0092T Total disc arthroplasty (artificial disc), anterior approach, including discectomy with end plate preparation (includes osteophytectomy for nerve root or spinal cord decompression and microdissection), each additional interspace, cervical (List separately in addition to code for primary procedure)

0095T Removal of total disc arthroplasty (artificial disc), anterior approach, each additional interspace, cervical (List separately in addition to code for primary procedure)

0098T Revision including replacement of total disc arthroplasty (artificial disc), anterior approach, each additional interspace, cervical (List separately in addition to code for primary procedure)

0163T Total disc arthroplasty (artificial disc), anterior approach, including discectomy to prepare interspace (other than for decompression), each additional interspace, lumbar (List separately in addition to code for primary procedure)

0164T Removal of total disc arthroplasty, (artificial disc), anterior approach, each additional interspace, lumbar (List separately in addition to code for primary procedure)

0165T Revision including replacement of total disc arthroplasty (artificial disc), anterior approach, each additional interspace, lumbar (List separately in addition to code for primary procedure)

0520F Radiation dose limits to normal tissues established prior to the initiation of a course of 3D conformal radiation for a minimum of two tissues/organs (ONC)1

3073F Pre-surgical (cataract) axial length, corneal power measurement and method of intraocular lens power calculation documented (must be performed within twelve months prior to surgery) (EC)5

Changed Codes (continued)

3300F American Joint Committee on Cancer (AJCC) stage documented and reviewed (ONC)1

3301F Cancer stage documented in medical record as metastatic and reviewed (ONC)1

3340F Mammogram assessment category of "incomplete: need additional imaging evaluation", documented (RAD)5

3341F Mammogram assessment category of "negative", documented (RAD)5

3342F Mammogram assessment category of "benign", documented (RAD)5"

3343F Mammogram assessment category of "probably benign", documented (RAD)5

3344F Mammogram assessment category of "suspicious", documented (RAD)5

3345F Mammogram assessment category of "highly suggestive of malignancy", documented (RAD)5

4001F Tobacco use cessation intervention, pharmacologic therapy (COPD, CAP, CAD) (DM) (PV)

4012F Warfarin therapy prescribed (HF)

4015F Persistent asthma, preferred long term control medication or an acceptable alternative treatment, prescribed (Asthma) (Note: There are no medical exclusion criteria)

4016F Anti-inflammatory/analgesic agent prescribed (OA) (Use for prescribed or continued medication[s], including over-the-counter medication[s])

4158F Patient counseled about risks of alcohol use (HEP-C)1

4180F Adjuvant chemotherapy referred, prescribed, or previously received for Stage III colon cancer (ONC)1

4182F Conformal radiation therapy not received (NMA-No Measure Assoc.)

4200F External beam radiotherapy as primary therapy to the prostate with or without nodal irradiation (PRCA)1

4201F External beam radiotherapy with or without nodal irradiation as adjuvant or salvage therapy for prostate cancer patient(PRCA)1

4250F Active warming used intraoperatively for the purpose of maintaining normothermia, OR at least one body temperature equal to or greater than 36 degrees Centigrade (or 96.8 degrees Fahrenheit) recorded within the 30 minutes immediately before or the 15 minutes immediately after anesthesia end time (CRIT)1

5020F Treatment summary report communicated to physician(s) managing continuing care and to the patient within one month of completing treatment (ONC)1

5062F Findings from diagnostic mammogram communicated to the patient within 5 days of exam interpretation (RAD)5

7020F Mammogram assessment category [eg, Mammography Quality Standards Act (MQSA), Breast Imaging Reporting and Data System (BI-RADS(R)), or FDA approved equivalent categories] entered into an internal database to allow for analysis of abnormal interpretation (recall) rate (RAD)5

Deleted Codes

20986	20987	46934	46935	46936	52606	52612
52614	52620	53853	61793	77781	77782	77783
77784	78890	78891	88400	90760	90761	90765
90766	90767	90768	90769	90770	90771	90772
90773	90774	90775	90776	90779	90918	90919
90920	90921	90922	90923	90924	90925	91100
93727	93731	93732	93733	93734	93735	93736
93741	93742	93743	93744	93760	93762	99289
99290	99293	99294	99295	99296	99298	99299
99300	99431	99432	99433	99435	99436	99440
0026T	0027T	0028T	0029T	0031T	0032T	0041T
0043T	0046T	0047T	0049T	0058T	0059T	0060T
0061T	0088T	0089T	0090T	0093T	0096T	0137T
0162T	1080F	3302F	3303F	3304F	3305F	3306F
3307F	3308F	3309F	3310F	3311F	3312F	3313F
3314F	4152F	4154F	4156F			

Add-On Codes

0049T	0054T	0055T	0063T	0076T	0079T	0081T
0092T	0095T	0098T	0151T	0159T	0163T	0164T
0165T	0172T	0173T	0174T	0189T	0190T	01953
01968	01969	0196T	11001	11008	11101	11201
11732	11922	13102	13122	13133	13153	15003
15005	15101	15111	15116	15121	15131	15136
15151	15152	15156	15157	15171	15176	15201
15221	15241	15261	15301	15321	15331	15336
15341	15361	15366	15401	15421	15431	15787
15847	16036	17003	17312	17314	17315	19001
19126	19291	19295	19297	20930	20931	20936
20937	20938	20985	20986	20987	22103	22116
22208	22216	22226	22328	22522	22525	22527
22534	22585	22614	22632	22840	22841	22842
22843	22844	22845	22846	22847	22848	22851
26125	26861	26863	27358	27692	31620	31632
31633	31637	32501	33141	33225	33257	33258
33259	33508	33517	33518	33519	33521	33522
33523	33530	33572	33768	33884	33924	33961
34806	34808	34813	34826	35306	35390	35400
35500	35572	35600	35681	35682	35683	35685
35686	35697	35700	36218	36248	36476	36479
37185	37186	37206	37208	37250	37251	38102
38746	38747	43273	43635	44015	44121	44128
44139	44203	44213	44701	44955	47001	47550
48400	49326	49435	49568	49905	51797	56606
57267	58110	58611	59525	60512	61316	61517
61609	61610	61611	61612	61641	61642	61795
61799	61800	61864	61868	62148	62160	63035
63043	63044	63048	63057	63066	63076	63078
63082	63086	63088	63091	63103	63295	63308
63621	64472	64476	64480	64484	64623	64627
64727	64778	64783	64787	64832	64837	64859
64872	64874	64876	64901	64902	65757	66990
67225	67320	67331	67332	67334	67335	67340
69990	74301	75774	75946	75964	75968	75993
75996	76125	76802	76810	76812	76814	76937
77001	77051	77052	78020	78478	78480	78496
78730	83901	87187	87904	88155	88185	88311
88312	88313	88314	90466	90468	90472	90474
90761	90766	90767	90768	90770	90771	90775
90776	92547	92608	92627	92973	92974	92978
92979	92981	92984	92996	92998	93320	93321
93325	93352	93571	93572	93609	93613	93621
93622	93623	93662	94645	95873	95874	95920
95962	95967	95973	95975	95979	96366	96367
96368	96370	96371	96375	96376	96411	96415
96417	96423	96570	96571	97546	97811	97814
99100	99116	99135	99140	99145	99150	99290
99292	99354	99355	99356	99357	99358	99359
99467	99602	99607				

Modifier 51 Exempt Codes

17004	20697	20974	20975	31500	36620	44500
61107	90281	90283	90284	90287	90288	90291
90296	90371	90375	90376	90378	90379	90384
90385	90386	90389	90393	90396	90399	93503
93539	93540	93544	93545	93555	93556	93600
93602	93603	93610	93612	93615	93616	93618
93631	94610	95900	95903	95904	95992	97001
97002	97003	97004	97005	97006	97010	97012
97014	97016	97018	97022	97024	97026	97028
97032	97033	97034	97035	97036	97110	97112
97113	97116	97124	97140	97150	97530	97532
97533	97535	97537	97542	97545	97546	97597
97598	97602	97605	97606	97750	97755	99143
99144						

Modifier 63 Exempt Codes

30540	30545	31520	33401	33403	33470	33472
33502	33503	33505	33506	33610	33611	33619
33647	33670	33690	33694	33730	33732	33735
33736	33750	33755	33762	33778	33786	33922
33960	33961	36415	36420	36450	36460	36510
36660	39503	43313	43314	43520	43831	44055

44126	44127	44128	46070	46705	46715	46716
46730	46735	46740	46742	46744	47700	47701
49215	49491	49492	49495	49496	49600	49605
49606	49610	49611	53025	54000	54150	54160
63700	63702	63704	63706	65820		

Moderate Sedation Codes

19298	20982	22526	22527	31615	31620	31622
31623	31624	31625	31628	31629	31635	31645
31646	31656	31725	32201	32550	32551	33010
33011	33206	33207	33208	33210	33211	33212
33213	33214	33216	33217	33218	33220	33222
33223	33233	33234	33235	33240	33241	33244
33249	35470	35471	35472	35473	35474	35475
35476	36555	36557	36558	36560	36561	36563
36565	36566	36568	36570	36571	36576	36578
36581	36582	36583	36585	36590	36870	37184
37185	37186	37187	37188	37203	37210	37215
37216	43200	43201	43202	43204	43205	43215
43216	43217	43219	43220	43226	43227	43228
43231	43232	43234	43235	43236	43237	43238
43239	43240					

APPENDIX C — CROSSWALK OF DELETED CODES

Deleted CPT 2008 Codes	CPT 2009 Code	Deleted CPT 2008 Codes	CPT 2009 Code	Deleted CPT 2008 Codes	CPT 2009 Code
0026T	84999	46934	46930, 46999	90923	90954-90956, 90964, 90968
0027T	64999	52606	52214	90924	90957-90959, 90965, 90969
0028T	76499	52612	52601		
0029T	53899	52614	52601	90925	90960-90962, 90966, 90970
0032T	58999	52620	52630		
0041T	81099	53853	55899	91100	43460, 44500
0043T	84999	61793	61796-61800, 63620-63621	93727	93285, 93291, 93298
0046T	19499			93731	93280, 93288, 93294
0047T	19499	77781	77785-77786	93732	93280, 93288, 93294
0049T	33999	77782	77785-77787	93733	93293
0058T	89240	77783	77785-77787	93734	93279, 93288, 93294
0059T	89240	77784	77785-77787	93735	93279, 93288, 93294
0060T	76499	88400	88720	93736	93293
0061T	19499	90760	96360	93741	93282, 93289, 93292, 93295
0088T	41530	90761	96361		
0089T	95803	90765	96365	93742	93282, 93289, 93292, 93295
0090T	22856	90766	96366		
0093T	22864	90767	96367	93743	93283, 93289, 93295
0096T	22861	90768	96368	93744	93283, 93289, 93295
0137T	55706	90769	96369	99289	99466-99466
0162T	95980-95982	90770	96370	99290	99467
20086	0054T-0055T	90771	96371	99293	99471
20987	0054T-0055T	90772	96372	99294	99472
3302F	3321F-3390F	90773	96373	99295	99468
3303F	3321F-3390F	90774	96374	99296	99469
3304F	3321F-3390F	90775	96375	99298	99478
3305F	3321F-3390F	90776	96376	99299	99479
3306F	3321F-3390F	90779	96379	99300	99480
3307F	3321F-3390F	90918	90951-90953, 90963, 90967	99431	99460
3308F	3321F-3390F			99432	99461
3309F	3321F-3390F	90919	90954-90956, 90964, 90968	99433	99462
3310F	3321F-3390F			99435	99463
3311F	3321F-3390F	90920	90957-90959, 90965, 90969	99436	99464
3312F	3321F-3390F			99440	99465
3313F	3321F-3390F	90921	90960-90962, 90966, 90970	3076F	3074F-3075F
3314F	3321F-3390F				
		90922	90951-90953, 90963, 90967		

APPENDIX D — PLACE OF SERVICE AND TYPE OF SERVICE

Place-of-Service Codes for Professional Claims

Listed below are place of service codes and descriptions. These codes should be used on professional claims to specify the entity where service(s) were rendered. Check with individual payers (e.g., Medicare, Medicaid, other private insurance) for reimbursement policies regarding these codes. To comment on a code(s) or description(s), please send your request to posinfo@cms.hhs.gov.

01 Pharmacy A facility or location where drugs and other medically related items and services are sold, dispensed, or otherwise provided directly to patients.

02 Unassigned N/A

03 School A facility whose primary purpose is education.

04 Homeless shelter A facility or location whose primary purpose is to provide temporary housing to homeless individuals (e.g., emergency shelters, individual or family shelters).

05 Indian Health Service freestanding facility A facility or location, owned and operated by the Indian Health Service, which provides diagnostic, therapeutic (surgical and non-surgical), and rehabilitation services to American Indians and Alaska natives who do not require hospitalization.

06 Indian Health Service provider-based facility A facility or location, owned and operated by the Indian Health Service, which provides diagnostic, therapeutic (surgical and nonsurgical), and rehabilitation services rendered by, or under the supervision of, physicians to American Indians and Alaska natives admitted as inpatients or outpatients.

07 Tribal 638 freestanding facility A facility or location owned and operated by a federally recognized American Indian or Alaska native tribe or tribal organization under a 638 agreement, which provides diagnostic, therapeutic (surgical and nonsurgical), and rehabilitation services to tribal members who do not require hospitalization.

08 Tribal 638 Provider-based Facility A facility or location owned and operated by a federally recognized American Indian or Alaska native tribe or tribal organization under a 638 agreement, which provides diagnostic, therapeutic (surgical and nonsurgical), and rehabilitation services to tribal members admitted as inpatients or outpatients.

09 Prison/correctional facility A prison, jail, reformatory, work farm, detention center, or any other similar facility maintained by either federal, state or local authorities for the purpose of confinement or rehabilitation of adult or juvenile criminal offenders.

10 Unassigned N/A

11 Office Location, other than a hospital, skilled nursing facility (SNF), military treatment facility, community health center, State or local public health clinic, or intermediate care facility (ICF), where the health professional routinely provides health examinations, diagnosis, and treatment of illness or injury on an ambulatory basis.

12 Home Location, other than a hospital or other facility, where the patient receives care in a private residence.

13 Assisted living facility Congregate residential facility with self-contained living units providing assessment of each resident's needs and on-site support 24 hours a day, 7 days a week, with the capacity to deliver or arrange for services including some health care and other services.

14 Group home A residence, with shared living areas, where clients receive supervision and other services such as social and/or behavioral services, custodial service, and minimal services (e.g., medication administration).

15 Mobile unit A facility/unit that moves from place-to-place equipped to provide preventive, screening, diagnostic, and/or treatment services.

16 Temporary lodging A short-term accommodation such as a hotel, campground, hostel, cruise ship or resort where the patient receives care, and which is not identified by any other POS code.

17-19 Unassigned N/A

20 Urgent care facility Location, distinct from a hospital emergency room, an office, or a clinic, whose purpose is to diagnose and treat illness or injury for unscheduled, ambulatory patients seeking immediate medical attention.

21 Inpatient hospital A facility, other than psychiatric, which primarily provides diagnostic, therapeutic (both surgical and nonsurgical), and rehabilitation services by, or under, the supervision of physicians to patients admitted for a variety of medical conditions.

22 Outpatient hospital A portion of a hospital which provides diagnostic, therapeutic (both surgical and nonsurgical), and rehabilitation services to sick or injured persons who do not require hospitalization or institutionalization.

23 Emergency room—hospital A portion of a hospital where emergency diagnosis and treatment of illness or injury is provided.

24 Ambulatory surgical center A freestanding facility, other than a physician's office, where surgical and diagnostic services are provided on an ambulatory basis.

25 Birthing center A facility, other than a hospital's maternity facilities or a physician's office, which provides a setting for labor, delivery, and immediate post-partum care as well as immediate care of new born infants.

26 Military treatment facility A medical facility operated by one or more of the uniformed services. Military treatment facility (MTF) also refers to certain former U.S. Public Health Service (USPHS) facilities now designated as uniformed service treatment facilities (USTF).

27-30 Unassigned N/A

31 Skilled nursing facility A facility which primarily provides inpatient skilled nursing care and related services to patients who require medical, nursing, or rehabilitative services but does not provide the level of care or treatment available in a hospital.

32	Nursing facility	A facility which primarily provides to residents skilled nursing care and related services for the rehabilitation of injured, disabled, or sick persons, or, on a regular basis, health-related care services above the level of custodial care to other than mentally retarded individuals.
33	Custodial care facility	A facility which provides room, board, and other personal assistance services, generally on a long-term basis, and which does not include a medical component.
34	Hospice	A facility, other than a patient's home, in which palliative and supportive care for terminally ill patients and their families are provided.
35-40	Unassigned	N/A
41	Ambulance—land	A land vehicle specifically designed, equipped and staffed for lifesaving and transporting the sick or injured.
42	Ambulance—air or water	An air or water vehicle specifically designed, equipped and staffed for lifesaving and transporting the sick or injured.
43-48	Unassigned	N/A
49	Independent clinic	A location, not part of a hospital and not described by any other place-of-service code, that is organized and operated to provide preventive, diagnostic, therapeutic, rehabilitative, or palliative services to outpatients only.
50	Federally qualified health center	A facility located in a medically underserved area that provides Medicare beneficiaries preventive primary medical care under the general direction of a physician.
51	Inpatient psychiatric facility	A facility that provides inpatient psychiatric services for the diagnosis and treatment of mental illness on a 24-hour basis, by or under the supervision of a physician.
52	Psychiatric facility-partial hospitalization	A facility for the diagnosis and treatment of mental illness that provides a planned therapeutic program for patients who do not require full time hospitalization, but who need broader programs than are possible from outpatient visits to a hospital-based or hospital-affiliated facility.
53	Community mental health center	A facility that provides the following services: outpatient services, including specialized outpatient services for children, the elderly, individuals who are chronically ill, and residents of the CMHC's mental health services area who have been discharged from inpatient treatment at a mental health facility; 24 hour a day emergency care services; day treatment, other partial hospitalization services, or psychosocial rehabilitation services; screening for patients being considered for admission to state mental health facilities to determine the appropriateness of such admission; and consultation and education services.
54	Intermediate care facility/mentally retarded	A facility which primarily provides health-related care and services above the level of custodial care to mentally retarded individuals but does not provide the level of care or treatment available in a hospital or SNF.
55	Residential substance abuse treatment facility	A facility which provides treatment for substance (alcohol and drug) abuse to live-in residents who do not require acute medical care. Services include individual and group therapy and counseling, family counseling, laboratory tests, drugs and supplies, psychological testing, and room and board.
56	Psychiatric residential treatment center	A facility or distinct part of a facility for psychiatric care which provides a total 24-hour therapeutically planned and professionally staffed group living and learning environment.
57	Non-residential substance abuse treatment facility	A location which provides treatment for substance (alcohol and drug) abuse on an ambulatory basis. Services include individual and group therapy and counseling, family counseling, laboratory tests, drugs and supplies, and psychological testing.
58-59	Unassigned	N/A
60	Mass immunization center	A location where providers administer pneumococcal pneumonia and influenza virus vaccinations and submit these services as electronic media claims, paper claims, or using the roster billing method. This generally takes place in a mass immunization setting, such as, a public health center, pharmacy, or mall but may include a physician office setting.
61	Comprehensive inpatient rehabilitation facility	A facility that provides comprehensive rehabilitation services under the supervision of a physician to inpatients with physical disabilities. Services include physical therapy, occupational therapy, speech pathology, social or psychological services, and orthotics and prosthetics services.
62	Comprehensive outpatient rehabilitation facility	A facility that provides comprehensive rehabilitation services under the supervision of a physician to outpatients with physical disabilities. Services include physical therapy, occupational therapy, and speech pathology services.
63-64	Unassigned	N/A
65	End-stage renal disease treatment facility	A facility other than a hospital, which provides dialysis treatment, maintenance, and/or training to patients or caregivers on an ambulatory or home-care basis.
66-70	Unassigned	N/A
71	Public health clinic	A facility maintained by either state or local health departments that provides ambulatory primary medical care under the general direction of a physician.
72	Rural health clinic	A certified facility which is located in a rural medically underserved area that provides ambulatory primary medical care under the general direction of a physician
73-80	Unassigned	N/A
81	Independent laboratory	A laboratory certified to perform diagnostic and/or clinical tests independent of an institution or a physician's office.
82-98	Unassigned	N/A
99	Other place of service	Other place of service not identified above.

Type of Service
Common Working File Type of Service (TOS) Indicators

For submitting a claim to the Common Working File (CWF), use the following table to assign the proper TOS. Some procedures may have more than one applicable TOS. CWF will reject alerts on codes with incorrect TOS designations. CWF is rejecting codes with incorrect TOS designations.

The only exceptions to this table are:

- Surgical services billed for dates of service through December 31, 2007, containing the ASC facility service modifier SG must be reported as TOS F. Effective for services on or after January 1, 2008, the SG modifier is no longer applicable for Medicare services. ASC providers should discontinue applying the SG modifier on ASC facility claims. The indicator F does not appear in the TOS table because its use depends upon claims submitted with POS 24 (ASC facility) from an ASC (specialty 49). This became effective for dates of service January 1, 2008, or after.

- Surgical services billed with an assistant-at-surgery modifier (80-82, AS,) must be reported with TOS 8. The 8 indicator does not appear on the TOS table because its use is dependent upon the use of the appropriate modifier. (See Pub. 100-4 *Medicare Claims Processing Manual*, chapter 12, "Physician/Practitioner Billing," for instructions on when assistant-at-surgery is allowable.)

- Psychiatric treatment services that are subject to the outpatient mental health treatment limitation should be reported with TOS T.

- TOS H appears in the list of descriptors. However, it does not appear in the table. In CWF, "H" is used only as an indicator for hospice. The carrier should not submit TOS H to CWF at this time.

- For outpatient services, when a transfusion medicine code appears on a claim that also contains a blood product, the service is paid under reasonable charge at 80 percent; coinsurance and deductible apply. When transfusion medicine codes are paid under the clinical laboratory fee schedule they are paid at 100 percent; coinsurance and deductible do not apply.

Note: For injection codes with more than one possible TOS designation, use the following guidelines when assigning the TOS:

When the choice is L or 1:

- Use TOS L when the drug is used related to ESRD; or
- Use TOS 1 when the drug is not related to ESRD and is administered in the office.

When the choice is G or 1:

- Use TOS G when the drug is an immunosuppressive drug; or
- Use TOS 1 when the drug is used for other than immunosuppression.

When the choice is P or 1:

- Use TOS P if the drug is administered through durable medical equipment (DME); or
- Use TOS 1 if the drug is administered in the office.

The place of service or diagnosis may be considered when determining the appropriate TOS. The descriptors for each of the TOS codes listed in the following table are:

0   Whole blood

1   Medical care

2   Surgery

3   Consultation

4   Diagnostic radiology

5   Diagnostic laboratory

6   Therapeutic radiology

7   Anesthesia

8   Assistant at surgery

9   Other medical items or services

A   Used DME

B   High risk screening mammography

C   Low risk screening mammography

D   Ambulance

E   Enteral/parenteral nutrients/supplies

F   Ambulatory surgical center (facility usage for surgical services)

G   Immunosuppressive drugs

H   Hospice

J   Diabetic shoes

K   Hearing items and services

L   ESRD supplies

M   Monthly capitation payment for dialysis

N   Kidney donor

P   Lump sum purchase of DME, prosthetics, orthotics

Q   Vision items or services

R   Rental of DME

S   Surgical dressings or other medical supplies

T   Outpatient mental health treatment limitation

U   Occupational therapy

V   Pneumococcal/flu vaccine

W   Physical therapy

Berenson-Eggers Type of Service (BETOS) Codes

The BETOS coding system was developed primarily for analyzing the growth in Medicare expenditures. The coding system covers all HCPCS codes; assigns a HCPCS code to only one BETOS code; consists of readily understood clinical categories (as opposed to statistical or financial categories); consists of categories that permit objective assignment; is stable over time; and is relatively immune to minor changes in technology or practice patterns.

BETOS Codes and Descriptions:

1.   Evaluation and Management

1.	M1A	Office visits—new
2.	M1B	Office visits—established
3.	M2A	Hospital visit—initial
4.	M2B	Hospital visit—subsequent
5.	M2C	Hospital visit—critical care
6.	M3	Emergency room visit
7.	M4A	Home visit
8.	M4B	Nursing home visit
9.	M5A	Specialist—pathology
10.	M5B	Specialist—psychiatry
11.	M5C	Specialist—ophthalmology
12.	M5D	Specialist—other
13.	M6	Consultations

2.   Procedures

1.	P0	Anesthesia
2.	P1A	Major procedure—breast
3.	P1B	Major procedure—colectomy
4.	P1C	Major procedure—cholecystectomy
5.	P1D	Major procedure—TURP
6.	P1E	Major procedure—hysterectomy
7.	P1F	Major procedure—explor/decompr/excis disc
8.	P1G	Major procedure—other
9.	P2A	Major procedure, cardiovascular—CABG
10.	P2B	Major procedure, cardiovascular—aneurysm repair
11.	P2C	Major procedure, cardiovascular—thromboendarterectomy
12.	P2D	Major procedure, cardiovascular—coronary angioplasty (PTCA)
13.	P2E	Major procedure, cardiovascular—pacemaker insertion
14.	P2F	Major procedure, cardiovascular—other

© 2008 Ingenix

15.	P3A	Major procedure, orthopedic—hip fracture repair
16.	P3B	Major procedure, orthopedic—hip replacement
17.	P3C	Major procedure, orthopedic—knee replacement
18.	P3D	Major procedure, orthopedic—other
19.	P4A	Eye procedure—corneal transplant
20.	P4B	Eye procedure—cataract removal/lens insertion
21.	P4C	Eye procedure—retinal detachment
22.	P4D	Eye procedure—treatment of retinal lesions
23.	P4E	Eye procedure—other
24.	P5A	Ambulatory procedures—skin
25.	P5B	Ambulatory procedures—musculoskeletal
26.	P5C	Ambulatory procedures—groin hernia repair
27.	P5D	Ambulatory procedures—lithotripsy
28.	P5E	Ambulatory procedures—other
29.	P6A	Minor procedures—skin
30.	P6B	Minor procedures—musculoskeletal
31.	P6C	Minor procedures—other (Medicare fee schedule)
32.	P6D	Minor procedures—other (non-Medicare fee schedule)
33.	P7A	Oncology—radiation therapy
34.	P7B	Oncology—other
35.	P8A	Endoscopy—arthroscopy
36.	P8B	Endoscopy—upper gastrointestinal
37.	P8C	Endoscopy—sigmoidoscopy
38.	P8D	Endoscopy—colonoscopy
39.	P8E	Endoscopy—cystoscopy
40.	P8F	Endoscopy—bronchoscopy
41.	P8G	Endoscopy—laparoscopic cholecystectomy
42.	P8H	Endoscopy—laryngoscopy
43.	P8I	Endoscopy—other
44.	P9A	Dialysis services (Medicare fee schedule)
45.	P9B	Dialysis services (non-Medicare fee schedule)

3. Imaging

1.	I1A	Standard imaging—chest
2.	I1B	Standard imaging—musculoskeletal
3.	I1C	Standard imaging—breast
4.	I1D	Standard imaging—contrast gastrointestinal
5.	I1E	Standard imaging—nuclear medicine
6.	I1F	Standard imaging—other
7.	I2A	Advanced imaging—CAT/CT/CTA; brain/head/neck
8.	I2B	Advanced imaging—CAT/CT/CTA; other
9.	I2C	Advanced imaging—MRI/MRA; brain/head/neck
10.	I2D	Advanced imaging—MRI/MRA; other
11.	I3A	Echography—eye

12.	I3B	Echography—abdomen/pelvis
13.	I3C	Echography—heart
14.	I3D	Echography—carotid arteries
15.	I3E	Echography—prostate, transrectal
16.	I3F	Echography—other
17.	I4A	Imaging/procedure—heart, including cardiac catheterization
18.	I4B	Imaging/procedure—other

4. Tests

1.	T1A	Lab tests—routine venipuncture (non-Medicare fee schedule)
2.	T1B	Lab tests—automated general profiles
3.	T1C	Lab tests—urinalysis
4.	T1D	Lab tests—blood counts
5.	T1E	Lab tests—glucose
6.	T1F	Lab tests—bacterial cultures
7.	T1G	Lab tests—other (Medicare fee schedule)
8.	T1H	Lab tests—other (non-Medicare fee schedule)
9.	T2A	Other tests—electrocardiograms
10.	T2B	Other tests—cardiovascular stress tests
11.	T2C	Other tests—EKG monitoring
12.	T2D	Other tests—other

5. Durable Medical Equipment

1.	D1A	Medical/surgical supplies
2.	D1B	Hospital beds
3.	D1C	Oxygen and supplies
4.	D1D	Wheelchairs
5.	D1E	Other DME
6.	D1F	Prosthetic/orthotic devices
7.	D1G	Drugs administered through DME

6. Other

1.	O1A	Ambulance
2.	O1B	Chiropractic
3.	O1C	Enteral and parenteral
4.	O1D	Chemotherapy
5.	O1E	Other drugs
6.	O1F	Hearing and speech services
7.	O1G	Immunizations/vaccinations

7. Exceptions/Unclassified

1.	Y1	Other—Medicare fee schedule
2.	Y2	Other—Non-Medicare fee schedule
3.	Z1	Local codes
4.	Z2	Undefined codes

APPENDIX E — PUB 100 REFERENCES

The Centers for Medicare and Medicaid Services restructured its paper-based manual system as a web-based system on October 1, 2003. Called the online CMS manual system, it combines all of the various program instructions into internet-only manuals (IOMs), which are used by all CMS programs and contractors. Complete versions of all of the manuals can be found at http://www.cms.hhs.gov/manuals.

Effective with implementation of the IOMs, the former method of publishing program memoranda (PMs) to communicate program instructions was replaced by the following four templates:

- One-time notification
- Manual revisions
- Business requirements
- Confidential requirements

The web-based system has been organized by functional area (e.g., eligibility, entitlement, claims processing, benefit policy, program integrity) in an effort to eliminate redundancy within the manuals, simplify updating, and make CMS program instructions available more quickly. The web-based system contains the functional areas included below:

Pub. 100	Introduction
Pub. 100-1	Medicare General Information, Eligibility, and Entitlement Manual
Pub. 100-2	Medicare Benefit Policy Manual
Pub. 100-3	Medicare National Coverage Determinations Manual
Pub. 100-4	Medicare Claims Processing Manual
Pub. 100-5	Medicare Secondary Payer Manual
Pub. 100-6	Medicare Financial Management Manual
Pub. 100-7	State Operations Manual
Pub. 100-8	Medicare Program Integrity Manual
Pub. 100-9	Medicare Contractor Beneficiary and Provider Communications Manual
Pub. 100-10	Quality Improvement Organization Manual
Pub. 100-11	Reserved
Pub. 100-12	State Medicaid Manual (under development)
Pub. 100-13	Medicaid State Children's Health Insurance Program (under development)
Pub. 100-14	Medicare ESRD Network Organizations Manual
Pub. 100-15	State Buy-In Manual
Pub. 100-16	Medicare Managed Care Manual
Pub. 100-17	CMS/Business Partners Systems Security Manual
Pub. 100-18	Reserved
Pub. 100-19	Demonstrations
Pub. 100-20	One-Time Notification
Pub. 100-21	Recurring Update Notification

A brief description of the Medicare manuals primarily used for *CPC Expert* follows:

The **National Coverage Determinations Manual** (NCD), is organized according to categories such as diagnostic services, supplies, and medical procedures. The table of contents lists each category and subject within that category. Revision transmittals identify any new or background material, recap the changes, and provide an effective date for the change.

When complete, the manual will contain two chapters. Chapter 1 currently includes a description of CMS's national coverage determinations. When available, chapter 2 will contain a list of HCPCS codes related to each coverage determination. The manual is organized in accordance with CPT category sequences.

The **Medicare Benefit Policy Manual** contains Medicare general coverage instructions that are not national coverage determinations. As a general rule, in the past these instructions have been found in chapter II of the **Medicare**

Carriers Manual, the **Medicare Intermediary Manual**, other provider manuals, and program memoranda.

The **Medicare Claims Processing Manual** contains instructions for processing claims for contractors and providers.

The **Medicare Program Integrity Manual** communicates the priorities and standards for the Medicare integrity programs.

MEDICARE IOM REFERENCES

100-1, 3, 20.5
Blood Deductibles (Part A and Part B)

Program payment may not be made for the first 3 pints of whole blood or equivalent units of packed red cells received under Part A and Part B combined in a calendar year. However, blood processing (e.g., administration, storage) is not subject to the deductible.

The blood deductibles are in addition to any other applicable deductible and coinsurance amounts for which the patient is responsible.

The deductible applies only to the first 3 pints of blood furnished in a calendar year, even if more than one provider furnished blood.

100-1, 3, 20.5.2
Part B Blood Deductible

Blood is furnished on an outpatient basis or is subject to the Part B blood deductible and is counted toward the combined limit. It should be noted that payment for blood may be made to the hospital under Part B only for blood furnished in an outpatient setting. Blood is not covered for inpatient Part B services.

100-1, 3, 20.5.3
Items Subject to Blood Deductibles

The blood deductibles apply only to whole blood and packed red cells. The term whole blood means human blood from which none of the liquid or cellular components have been removed. Where packed red cells are furnished, a unit of packed red cells is considered equivalent to a pint of whole blood. Other components of blood such as platelets, fibrinogen, plasma, gamma globulin, and serum albumin are not subject to the blood deductible. However, these components of blood are covered as biologicals.

Refer to Pub. 100-04, Medicare Claims Processing Manual, chapter 4, Sec.231 regarding billing for blood and blood products under the Hospital Outpatient Prospective Payment System (OPPS).

100-1, 3, 30
Outpatient Mental Health Treatment Limitation

Regardless of the actual expenses a beneficiary incurs for treatment of mental, psychoneurotic, and personality disorders while the beneficiary is not an inpatient of a hospital at the time such expenses are incurred, the amount of those expenses that may be recognized for Part B deductible and payment purposes is limited to 62.5 percent of the Medicare allowed amount for these services. The limitation is called the outpatient mental health treatment limitation. Since Part B deductible also applies the program pays for about half of the allowed amount recognized for mental health therapy services.

Expenses for diagnostic services (e.g., psychiatric testing and evaluation to diagnose the patient's illness) are not subject to this limitation. This limitation applies only to therapeutic services and to services performed to evaluate the progress of a course of treatment for a diagnosed condition.

100-1, 3, 30.1
Application of Mental Health Limitation - Status of Patient

The limitation is applicable to expenses incurred in connection with the treatment of an individual who is not an inpatient of a hospital. Thus, the limitation applies to mental health services furnished to a person in a physician's office, in the patient's home, in a skilled nursing facility, as an outpatient, and so forth. The term "hospital" in this context means an institution which is primarily engaged in providing to inpatients, by or under the supervision of a physician(s):

- Diagnostic and therapeutic services for medical diagnosis, and treatment, and care of injured, disabled, or sick persons;
- Rehabilitation services for injured, disabled, or sick persons; or
- Psychiatric services for the diagnosis and treatment of mentally ill patients.

100-1, 3, 30.2
Disorders Subject to Mental Health Limitation

The term "mental, psychoneurotic, and personality disorders" is defined as the specific psychiatric conditions described in the American Psychiatric Association's Diagnostic and Statistical Manual of Mental Disorders, Third Edition - Revised (DSM-III-R).

If the treatment services rendered are for both a psychiatric condition and one or more nonpsychiatric conditions, the charges are separated to apply the limitation only to the mental health charge. Normally HCPCS code and diagnoses are used. Where HCPCS code is not available on the claim, revenue code is used.

If the service is primarily on the basis of a diagnosis of Alzheimer's Disease (coded 331.0 in the International Classification of Diseases, 9th Revision) or Alzheimer's or other disorders (coded 290.XX in DSM-III-R), treatment typically represents medical management of the patient's condition (rather than psychiatric treatment) and is not subject to the limitation.

© 2008 Ingenix

100-1, 3, 30.3
Diagnostic Services

The mental health limitation does not apply to tests and evaluations performed to establish or confirm the patient's diagnosis. Diagnostic services include psychiatric or psychological tests and interpretations, diagnostic consultations, and initial evaluations. However, testing services performed to evaluate a patient's progress during treatment are considered part of treatment and are subject to the limitation.

100-1, 5, 70
Physician Defined

Physician means doctor of medicine, doctor of osteopathy (including osteopathic practitioner), doctor of dental surgery or dental medicine (within the limitations in subsection Sec.70.2), doctor of podiatric medicine (within the limitations in subsection Sec.70.3), or doctor of optometry (within the limitations of subsection Sec.70.5), and, with respect to certain specified treatment, a doctor of chiropractic legally authorized to practice by a State in which he/she performs this function. The services performed by a physician within these definitions are subject to any limitations imposed by the State on the scope of practice. The issuance by a State of a license to practice medicine constitutes legal authorization. Temporary State licenses also constitute legal authorization to practice medicine. If State law authorizes local political subdivisions to establish higher standards for medical practitioners than those set by the State licensing board, the local standards determine whether a particular physician has legal authorization. If State licensing law limits the scope of practice of a particular type of medical practitioner, only the services within the limitations are covered. The issuance by a State of a license to practice medicine constitutes legal authorization. Temporary State licenses also constitute legal authorization to practice medicine. If State law authorizes local political subdivisions to establish higher standards for medical practitioners than those set by the State licensing board, the local standards determine whether a particular physician has legal authorization. If State licensing law limits the scope of practice of a particular type of medical practitioner, only the services within the limitations are covered. NOTE:The term physician does not include such practitioners as a Christian Science practitioner or naturopath.

100-1, 5 , 70.6
Chiropractors

A. General

A licensed chiropractor who meets uniform minimum standards (see subsection C) is a physician for specified services. Coverage extends only to treatment by means of manual manipulation of the spine to correct a subluxation demonstrated by X-ray, provided such treatment is legal in the State where performed. All other services furnished or ordered by chiropractors are not covered. An X-ray obtained by a chiropractor for his or her own diagnostic purposes before commencing treatment may suffice for claims documentation purposes. This means that if a chiropractor orders, takes, or interprets an X-ray to demonstrate a subluxation of the spine, the X-ray can be used for claims processing purposes. However, there is no coverage or payment for these services or for any other diagnostic or therapeutic service ordered or furnished by the chiropractor. In addition, in performing manual manipulation of the spine, some chiropractors use manual devices that are hand-held with the thrust of the force of the device being controlled manually. While such manual manipulation may be covered, there is no separate payment permitted for use of this device.

B. Licensure and Authorization to Practice

A chiropractor must be licensed or legally authorized to furnish chiropractic services by the State or jurisdiction in which the services are furnished.

C. Uniform Minimum Standards

I. Prior to July 1, 1974, Chiropractors licensed or authorized to practice prior to July 1, 1974, and those individuals who commenced their studies in a chiropractic college before that date must meet all of the following minimum standards to render payable services under the program:

   a. Preliminary education equal to the requirements for graduation from an accredited high school or other secondary school;

   b. Graduation from a college of chiropractic approved by the State's chiropractic examiners that included the completion of a course of study covering a period of not less than 3 school years of 6 months each year in actual continuous attendance covering adequate course of study in the subjects of anatomy, physiology, symptomatology and diagnosis, hygiene and sanitation, chemistry, histology, pathology, and principles and practice of chiropractic, including clinical instruction in vertebral palpation, nerve tracing and adjusting; and

   c. Passage of an examination prescribed by the State's chiropractic examiners covering the subjects listed in subsection b.

2. After June 30, 1974 - Individuals commencing their studies in a chiropractic college after June 30, 1974, must meet all of the following additional requirements:

   a. Satisfactory completion of 2 years of pre-chiropractic study at the college level;

   b. Satisfactory completion of a 4-year course of 8 months each year (instead of a 3-year course of 6 months each year) at a college or school of chiropractic that includes not less than 4,000 hours in the scientific and chiropractic courses specified in subsection 1.b, plus courses in the use and effect of X-ray and chiropractic analysis; and

   c. The practitioner must be over 21 years of age.

100-1, 5, 90.2
Laboratory Defined

Laboratory means a facility for the biological, microbiological, serological, chemical, immuno-hematological, hematological, biophysical, cytological, pathological, or other examination of materials derived from the human body for the purpose of providing information for the diagnosis, prevention, or treatment of any disease or impairment of, or the assessment of the health of, human beings. These examinations also include procedures to determine, measure, or otherwise describe the presence or absence of various substances or organisms in the body. Facilities only collecting or preparing specimens (or both) or only serving as a mailing service and not performing testing are not considered laboratories.

100-2, 1, 10
Covered Inpatient Hospital Services Covered Under Part A

A3-3101, HO-210

Patients covered under hospital insurance are entitled to have payment made on their behalf for inpatient hospital services. (Inpatient hospital services do not include extended care services provided by hospitals pursuant to swing bed approvals. See Pub. 100-1, Chapter 8, Sec.10.1, "Hospital Providers of Extended Care Services.") However, both inpatient hospital and inpatient SNF benefits are provided under Part A - Hospital Insurance Benefits for the Aged and Disabled, of Title XVIII).

Additional information concerning the following topics can be found in the following manual chapters:

- Benefit periods is found in Chapter 3, "Duration of Covered Inpatient Services";
- Copayment days is found in Chapter 2, "Duration of Covered Inpatient Services";
- Lifetime reserve days is found in Chapter 5, "Lifetime Reserve Days";
- Related payment information is housed in the Provider Reimbursement Manual.

Blood must be furnished on a day which counts as a day of inpatient hospital services to be covered as a Part A service and to count toward the blood deductible. Thus, blood is not covered under Part A and does not count toward the Part A blood deductible when furnished to an Inpatient after the inpatient has exhausted all benefit days in a benefit period, or where the individual has elected not to use lifetime reserve days. However, where the patient is discharged on their first day of entitlement or on the hospital's first day of participation, the hospital is permitted to submit a billing form with no accommodation charge, but with ancillary charges including blood.

The records for all Medicare hospital inpatient discharges are maintained in CMS for statistical analysis and use in determining future PPS DRG classifications and rates.

Non-PPS hospitals do not pay for noncovered services generally excluded from coverage in the Medicare Program. This may result in denial of a part of the billed charges or in denial of the entire admission, depending upon circumstance. In PPS hospitals, the following are also possible.

1. In appropriately admitted cases where a noncovered procedure was performed, denied services may result in payment of a different DRG (i.e., one which excludes payment for the noncovered procedure); or

2. In appropriately admitted cases that become cost outlier cases, denied services may lead to denial of some or all of an outlier payment.

The following examples illustrate this principle. If care is noncovered because a patient does not need to be hospitalized, the intermediary denies the admission and makes no Part A (i.e., PPS) payment unless paid under limitation on liability. Under limitation on liability, Medicare payment may be made when the provider and the beneficiary were not aware the services were not necessary and could not reasonably be expected to know that the services were not necessary. For detailed instructions, see the Medicare Claims Processing Manual, Chapter 30,"Limitation on Liability." If a patient is appropriately hospitalized but receives (beyond routine services) only noncovered care, the admission is denied.

NOTE: The intermediary does not deny an admission that includes covered care, even if noncovered care was also rendered. Under PPS, Medicare assumes that it is paying for only the covered care rendered whenever covered services needed to treat and/or diagnose the illness were in fact provided.

If a noncovered procedure is provided along with covered nonroutine care, a DRG change rather than an admission denial might occur. If noncovered procedures are elevating costs into the cost outlier category, outlier payment is denied in whole or in part.

When the hospital is included in PPS, most of the subsequent discussion regarding coverage of inpatient hospital services is relevant only in the context of determining the appropriateness of admissions, which DRG, if any, to pay, and the appropriateness of payment for any outlier cases.

If a patient receives items or services in excess of, or more expensive than, those for which payment can be made, payment is made only for the covered items or services or for only the appropriate prospective payment amount. This provision applies not only to inpatient services, but also to all hospital services under Parts A and B of the program. If the items or services were requested by the patient, the hospital may charge him the difference between the amount customarily charged for the services requested and the amount customarily charged for covered services.

An inpatient is a person who has been admitted to a hospital for bed occupancy for purposes of receiving inpatient hospital services. Generally, a patient is considered an inpatient if formally admitted as inpatient with the expectation that he or she will remain at least overnight and occupy a bed even though it later develops that the patient can be discharged or transferred to another hospital and not actually use a hospital bed overnight.

The physician or other practitioner responsible for a patient's care at the hospital is also responsible for deciding whether the patient should be admitted as an inpatient. Physicians should use a 24-hour period as a benchmark, i.e., they should order admission for patients who are expected to need hospital care for 24 hours or more, and treat other patients on an outpatient basis. However, the decision to admit a patient is a complex medical judgment which can be made only after the physician has considered a number of factors, including the patient's medical history and current medical needs, the types of facilities available to inpatients and to outpatients, the hospital's by-laws and admissions policies, and the relative appropriateness of treatment in each setting. Factors to be considered when making the decision to admit include such things as:

- The severity of the signs and symptoms exhibited by the patient;
- The medical predictability of something adverse happening to the patient;
- The need for diagnostic studies that appropriately are outpatient services (i.e., their performance does not ordinarily require the patient to remain at the hospital for 24 hours or more) to assist in assessing whether the patient should be admitted; and
- The availability of diagnostic procedures at the time when and at the location where the patient presents.

Admissions of particular patients are not covered or noncovered solely on the basis of the length of time the patient actually spends in the hospital. In certain specific situations coverage of services on an inpatient or outpatient basis is determined by the following rules:

Minor Surgery or Other Treatment - When patients with known diagnoses enter a hospital for a specific minor surgical procedure or other treatment that is expected to keep them in the hospital for only a few hours (less than 24), they are considered outpatients for coverage purposes regardless of: the hour they came to the hospital, whether they used a bed, and whether they remained in the hospital past midnight.

Renal Dialysis - Renal dialysis treatments are usually covered only as outpatient services but may under certain circumstances be covered as inpatient services depending on the patient's condition. Patients staying at home, who are ambulatory, whose conditions are stable and who come to the hospital for routine chronic dialysis treatments, and not for a diagnostic workup or a change in therapy, are considered outpatients. On the other hand, patients undergoing short-term dialysis until their kidneys recover from an acute illness (acute dialysis), or persons with borderline renal failure who develop acute renal failure every time they have an illness and require dialysis (episodic dialysis) are usually inpatients. A patient may begin dialysis as an inpatient and then progress to an outpatient status.

Under original Medicare, the Quality Improvement Organization (QIO), for each hospital is responsible for deciding, during review of inpatient admissions on a case-by-case basis, whether the admission was medically necessary. Medicare law authorizes the QIO to make these judgments, and the judgments are binding for purposes of Medicare coverage. In making these judgments, however, QIOs consider only the medical evidence which was available to the physician at the time an admission decision had to be made. They do not take into account other information (e.g., test results) which became available only after admission, except in cases where considering the post-admission information would support a finding that an admission was medically necessary.

Refer to Parts 4 and 7 of the QIO Manual with regard to initial determinations for these services. The QIO will review the swing bed services in these PPS hospitals as well.

NOTE: When patients requiring extended care services are admitted to beds in a hospital, they are considered inpatients of the hospital. In such cases, the services furnished in the hospital will not be considered extended care services, and payment may not be made under the program for such services unless the services are extended care services furnished pursuant to a swing bed agreement granted to the hospital by the Secretary of Health and Human Services.

100-2, 1, 90

Termination of Pregnancy
B3-4276.1,.2

Effective for services furnished on or after October 1, 1998, Medicare will cover abortions procedures in the following situations:

1. If the pregnancy is the result of an act or rape or incest; or
2. In the case where a woman suffers from a physical disorder, physical injury, or physical illness, including a life-endangering physical condition caused by the pregnancy itself that would, as certified by a physician, place the woman in danger of death unless an abortion is performed.

NOTE: The "G7" modifier must be used with the following CPT codes in order for these services to be covered when the pregnancy resulted from rape or incest, or the pregnancy is certified by a physician as life threatening to the mother:

59840, 59841, 59850, 59851, 59852, 59855, 59856, 59857, 59866

100-2, 1, 100

Treatment for Infertility
A3-3101.13

Effective for services rendered on or after January 15, 1980, reasonable and necessary services associated with treatment for infertility are covered under Medicare. Like pregnancy (see Sec. 80 above), infertility is a condition sufficiently at variance with the usual state of health to make it appropriate for a person who normally would be expected to be fertile to seek medical consultation and treatment. Contractors should coordinate with QIOs to see that utilization guidelines are established for this treatment if inappropriate utilization or abuse is suspected.

100-2 , 6, 10

Medical and Other Health Services Furnished to Inpatients of Participating Hospitals

Payment may be made under Part B for physician services and for the nonphysician medical and other health services listed below when furnished by a participating hospital (either directly or under arrangements) to an inpatient of the hospital, but only if payment for these services cannot be made under Part A.

In PPS hospitals, this means that Part B payment could be made for these services if:

- No Part A prospective payment is made at all for the hospital stay because of patient exhaustion of benefit days before admission;
- The admission was disapproved as not reasonable and necessary (and waiver of liability payment was not made);
- The day or days of the otherwise covered stay during which the services were provided were not reasonable and necessary (and no payment was made under waiver of liability);
- The patient was not otherwise eligible for or entitled to coverage under Part A (See the Medicare Benefit Policy Manual, Chapter 1, Sec.150, for services received as a result of noncovered services); or
- No Part A day outlier payment is made (for discharges before October 1997) for one or more outlier days due to patient exhaustion of benefit days after admission but before the case's arrival at outlier status, or because outlier days are otherwise not covered and waiver of liability payment is not made.

However, if only day outlier payment is denied under Part A (discharges before October 1997), Part B payment may be made for only the services covered under Part B and furnished on the denied outlier days.

In non-PPS hospitals, Part B payment may be made for services on any day for which Part A payment is denied (i.e., benefit days are exhausted; services are not at the hospital level of care; or patient is not otherwise eligible or entitled to payment under Part A).

Services payable are:

- Diagnostic x-ray tests, diagnostic laboratory tests, and other diagnostic tests;
- X-ray, radium, and radioactive isotope therapy, including materials and services of technicians;
- Surgical dressings, and splints, casts, and other devices used for reduction of fractures and dislocations;
- Prosthetic devices (other than dental) which replace all or part of an internal body organ (including contiguous tissue), or all or part of the function of a permanently inoperative or malfunctioning internal body organ, including replacement or repairs of such devices;
- Leg, arm, back, and neck braces, trusses, and artificial legs, arms, and eyes including adjustments, repairs, and replacements required because of breakage, wear, loss, or a change in the patient's physical condition;
- Outpatient physical therapy, outpatient speech-language pathology services, and outpatient occupational therapy (see the Medicare Benefit Policy Manual, Chapter 15, "Covered Medical and Other Health Services," Sec.Sec.220 and 230);
- Screening mammography services;
- Screening pap smears;
- Influenza, pneumococcal pneumonia, and hepatitis B vaccines;
- Colorectal screening;
- Bone mass measurements;
- Diabetes self-management;
- Prostate screening;
- Ambulance services;
- Hemophilia clotting factors for hemophilia patients competent to use these factors without supervision);
- Immunosuppressive drugs;
- Oral anti-cancer drugs;
- Oral drug prescribed for use as an acute anti-emetic used as part of an anti-cancer chemotherapeutic regimen; and Epoetin Alfa (EPO).

Coverage rules for these services are described in the Medicare Benefit Policy Manual, Chapters: 11, "End Stage Renal Disease (ESRD);" 14, "Medical Devices;" or 15, "Medical and Other Health Services."

For services to be covered under Part A or Part B, a hospital must furnish nonphysician services to its inpatients directly or under arrangements. A nonphysician service is one which does not meet the criteria defining physicians' services specifically provided for in regulation at 42 CFR 415.102. Services "incident to" physicians' services (except for the services of nurse anesthetists employed by anesthesiologists) are nonphysician services for purposes of this provision. This provision is applicable to all hospitals participating in Medicare, including those paid under alternative arrangements such as State cost control systems, and to emergency hospital services furnished by nonparticipating hospitals.

In all hospitals, every service provided to a hospital inpatient other than those listed in the next paragraph must be treated as an inpatient hospital service to be paid for under Part A, if Part A coverage is available and the beneficiary is entitled to Part A. This is because every hospital must provide directly or arrange for any nonphysician service rendered to its inpatients, and a hospital can be paid under Part B for a service provided in this manner only if Part A coverage does not exist.

These services, when provided to a hospital inpatient, may be covered under Part B, even though the patient has Part A coverage for the hospital stay. This is because these services are covered under Part B and not covered under Part A. They are.

- Physicians' services (including the services of residents and interns in unapproved teaching programs);
- Influenza vaccine;
- Pneumoccocal vaccine and its administration;
- Hepatitis B vaccine and its administration;
- Screening mammography services;
- Screening pap smears and pelvic exams;
- Colorectal screening;
- Bone mass measurements;
- Diabetes self management training services; and
- Prostate screening.

However, note that in order to have any Medicare coverage at all (Part A or Part B), any nonphysician service rendered to a hospital inpatient must be provided directly or arranged for by the hospital.

100-2, 6, 50
Sleep Disorder Clinics
A3-3112.5

Sleep disorder clinics are facilities in which certain conditions are diagnosed through the study of sleep. Such clinics are for diagnosis, therapy, and research. Sleep disorder clinics may provide some diagnostic or therapeutic services that are covered under Medicare. These clinics may be affiliated either with a hospital or a freestanding facility. Whether a clinic is hospital-affiliated or freestanding, coverage for diagnostic services under some circumstances is covered under provisions of the law different from those for coverage of therapeutic services.

100-2, 11, 20
Coverage of Outpatient Maintenance Dialysis
A3-3167, B3-2230.2, RDF-202, SOM-2272, RDF-317.1, PM AB-03 001

Medicare covers maintenance dialysis treatments when they are provided to ESRD patients by an approved hospital-based dialysis facility, an independent dialysis facility, or a special purpose dialysis facility. Outpatient dialysis treatments are covered in various settings: hospital outpatient facility, independent dialysis facility, or the patient's home. Dialysis treatments at dialysis facilities differ according to the types of patients being treated, the types of equipment and supplies used, the preferences of the treating physician, and the capability and makeup of the staff. Although not all facilities provide an identical range of services, the most common elements of a dialysis treatment are:

a. Personnel services;

b. Equipment and supplies - dialysis machine and its maintenance;

c. Administrative services;

d. Overhead costs;

e. Monitoring access and related declotting the access or referring the patient;

f. ESRD related laboratory tests; and

g. Biologicals.

Direct nursing services include registered nurses, licensed practical nurses, technicians, social workers, and dietitians. Facilities with self-dialysis units must meet specific health and safety requirements. Certain standards applicable to staff assisted dialysis have been adjusted for self-dialysis units in consideration of the differences in the two modalities. Before participating in self-dialysis, patients must have completed an appropriate training program in emergency procedures and have a safe storage area for their supplies. Access to the self-dialysis unit is limited to patients for whom the facility maintains patient care plans in order to exclude transient patients who might not be familiar with the facility's equipment or emergency procedures. The self-dialysis unit need not be physically separate from the rest of the facility nor operate on a separate shift.

100-2, 13, 30
Rural Health Clinic and Federally Qualified Health Center Service Defined
Payments for covered RHC/FQHC services furnished to Medicare beneficiaries are made on the basis of an all-inclusive rate per covered visit (except for pneumococcal and influenza vaccines and their administration, which is paid at 100 percent of reasonable cost). The term "visit" is defined as a face-to-face encounter between the patient and a physician, physician assistant, nurse practitioner, certified nurse midwife, visiting nurse, clinical psychologist, or clinical social worker during which an RHC/FQHC service is rendered. As a result of section 5114 of the Deficit Reduction Act of 2005 (DRA), the FQHC definition of a face-to-face encounter is expanded to include encounters with qualified practitioners of Outpatient Diabetes Self-Management Training Services (DSMT) and medical nutrition therapy (MNT) services when the FQHC meets all relevant program requirements for the provision of such services.

Encounters with (1) more than one health professional; and (2) multiple encounters with the same health professional which take place on the same day and at a single location, constitute a single visit. An exception occurs in cases in which the patient, subsequent to the first encounter, suffers an illness or injury requiring additional diagnosis or treatment.

100-2, 15, 20.1
Physician Expense for Surgery, Childbirth, and Treatment for Infertility
B3-2005.I

A. Surgery and Childbirth
Skilled medical management is covered throughout the events of pregnancy, beginning with diagnosis, continuing through delivery and ending after the necessary postnatal care. Similarly, in the event of termination of pregnancy, regardless of whether terminated spontaneously or for therapeutic reasons (i.e., where the life of the mother would be endangered if the fetus were brought to term), the need for skilled medical management and/or medical services is equally important as in those cases carried to full term. After the infant is delivered and is a separate individual, items and services furnished to the infant are not covered on the basis of the mother's eligibility.

Most surgeons and obstetricians bill patients an all-inclusive package charge intended to cover all services associated with the surgical procedure or delivery of the child. All expenses for surgical and obstetrical care, including preoperative/prenatal examinations and tests and post-operative/postnatal services, are considered incurred on the date of surgery or delivery, as appropriate. This policy applies whether the physician bills on a package charge basis, or itemizes the bill separately for these items.

Occasionally, a physician's bill may include charges for additional services not directly related to the surgical procedure or the delivery. Such charges are considered incurred on the date the additional services are furnished.

The above policy applies only where the charges are imposed by one physician or by a clinic on behalf of a group of physicians. Where more than one physician imposes charges for surgical or obstetrical services, all preoperative/prenatal and post-operative/postnatal services performed by the physician who performed the surgery or delivery are considered incurred on the date of the surgery or delivery. Expenses for services rendered by other physicians are considered incurred on the date they were performed.

B. Treatment for Infertility
Reasonable and necessary services associated with treatment for infertility are covered under Medicare. Infertility is a condition sufficiently at variance with the usual state of health to make it appropriate for a person who normally is expected to be fertile to seek medical consultation and treatment.

100-2, 15, 20.2
Physician Expense for Allergy Treatment
B3-2005.2, B3-4145 Allergists commonly bill separately for the initial diagnostic workup and for the treatment (See Sec.60.2). Where it is necessary to provide treatment over an extended period, the allergist may submit a single bill for all of the treatments, or may bill periodically. In either case the Form CMS-1500 claim shows the Healthcare Common Procedure Coding System (HCPCS) codes and from and through dates of service, or the Form CMS-1450 outpatient claim shows the HCPCS code and date of service (except for critical access hospital (CAH) claims).

100 2, 15, 20.3
Artificial Limbs, Braces, and Other Custom Made Items Ordered But Not Furnished
B3-2005.3

A. Date of Incurred Expense
If a custom-made item was ordered but not furnished to a beneficiary because the individual died or because the order was canceled by the beneficiary or because the beneficiary's condition changed and the item was no longer reasonable and necessary or appropriate, payment can be made based on the supplier's expenses. (See subsection B for determination of the allowed amount.) In such cases, the expense is considered incurred on the date the beneficiary died or the date the supplier learned of the cancellation or that the item was no longer reasonable and necessary or appropriate for the beneficiary's condition. If the beneficiary died or the beneficiary's condition changed and the item was no longer reasonable and necessary or appropriate, payment can be made on either an assigned or unassigned claim. If the beneficiary, for any other reason, canceled the order, payment can be made to the supplier only.

B. Determination of Allowed Amount
The allowed amount is based on the services furnished and materials used, up to the date the supplier learned of the beneficiary's death or of the cancellation of the order or that the item was no longer reasonable and necessary or appropriate. The Durable Medical Equipment Regional Carrier (DMERC), carrier or intermediary, as appropriate, determines the services performed and the allowable amount appropriate in the particular situation. It takes into account any salvage value of the device to the supplier. Where a supplier breaches an agreement to make a prosthesis, brace, or other custom-made device for a Medicare beneficiary, e.g., an unexcused failure to provide the article within the time specified in the contract, payment may not be made for any work or material expended on the item. Whether a particular supplier has lived up to its agreement, of course, depends on the facts in the individual case.

100-2, 15, 30
Physician Services
B3-2020, B3-4142

A. General
Physician services are the professional services performed by a physician or physicians for a patient including diagnosis, therapy, surgery, consultation, and care plan oversight. The physician must render the service for the service to be covered. (See Publication 100-1, the Medicare General Information, Eligibility, and Entitlement Manual, Chapter 5, Sec.70, for definition of physician.) A service may be considered to be a physician's service where the physician either examines the patient in person or is able to visualize some aspect of the patient's condition without the interposition of a third person's judgment. Direct visualization would be possible by means of x-rays, electrocardiogram and electroencephalogram tapes, tissue samples, etc. For example, the interpretation by a physician of an actual

electrocardiogram or electroencephalogram reading that has been transmitted via telephone (i.e., electronically rather than by means of a verbal description) is a covered service. Professional services of the physician are covered if provided within the United States, and may be performed in a home, office, institution, or at the scene of an accident. A patient's home, for this purpose, is anywhere the patient makes his or her residence, e.g., home for the aged, a nursing home, a relative's home.

B. Telephone Services

Services by means of a telephone call between a physician and a beneficiary, or between a physician and a member of a beneficiary's family, are covered under Medicare, but carriers may not make separate payment for these services under the program. The physician work resulting from telephone calls is considered to be an integral part of the prework and postwork of other physician services, and the fee schedule amount for the latter services already includes payment for the telephone calls. See the Medicare Benefit Policy Manual, Chapter 15, "Covered Medical and Other Health Services," Sec.270, for coverage of telehealth services.

C. Consultations

A consultation may be paid when the consulting physician initiates treatment on the same day as the consultation. It is only after a transfer of care has occurred that evaluation and management (E&M) services may not be billed as consultations; they must be billed as subsequent office/outpatient visits. Therefore, if covered, a consultation is reimbursable when it is a professional service furnished a patient by a second physician at the request of the attending physician. Such a consultation includes the history and examination of the patient as well as the written report, which is furnished to the attending physician for inclusion in the patient's permanent medical record. These reports must be prepared and submitted to the provider for retention when they involve patients of institutions responsible for maintaining such records, and submitted to the attending physician's office for other patients. To reimburse laboratory consultations, the services must: Be requested by the patient's attending physician; Relate to a test result that lies outside of the clinically significant normal or expected/established range relative to the condition of the patient; Result in a written narrative report included in the patient's medical record; andRequire medical judgment by the consultant physician. A consultation must involve a medical judgment that ordinarily requires a physician. Where a nonphysician laboratory specialist could furnish the information, the service of the physician is not a consultation payable under Part B. The following indicators can ordinarily distinguish attending physician's claims:Therapeutic services are included on the bill in addition to an examination;The patient's history is before the examiner while the claim is reviewed and the billing physician has previously rendered other services to the patient; orInformation in the file indicates that the patient was not referred. The attending physician may remove himself from the care of the patient and turn the patient over to the person who performed a consultation service. In this situation, the initial examination would be a consultation if the above requirements were met at that time.

D. Patient-Initiated Second Opinions

Patient-initiated second opinions that relate to the medical need for surgery or for major nonsurgical diagnostic and therapeutic procedures (e.g., invasive diagnostic techniques such as cardiac catheterization and gastroscopy) are covered under Medicare. In the event that the recommendation of the first and second physician differs regarding the need for surgery (or other major procedure), a third opinion is also covered. Second and third opinions are covered even though the surgery or other procedure, if performed, is determined not covered. Payment may be made for the history and examination of the patient, and for other covered diagnostic services required to properly evaluate the patient's need for a procedure and to render a professional opinion. In some cases, the results of tests done by the first physician may be available to the second physician.

E. Concurrent Care

Concurrent care exists where more than one physician renders services more extensive than consultative services during a period of time. The reasonable and necessary services of each physician rendering concurrent care could be covered where each is required to play an active role in the patient's treatment, for example, because of the existence of more than one medical condition requiring diverse specialized medical services. In order to determine whether concurrent physicians' services are reasonable and necessary, the carrier must decide the following:

1. Whether the patient's condition warrants the services of more than one physician on an attending (rather than consultative) basis, and

2. Whether the individual services provided by each physician are reasonable and necessary.

In resolving the first question, the carrier should consider the specialties of the physicians as well as the patient's diagnosis, as concurrent care is usually (although not always) initiated because of the existence of more than one medical condition requiring diverse specialized medical or surgical services. The specialties of the physicians are an indication of the necessity for concurrent services, but the patient's condition and the inherent reasonableness and necessity of the services, as determined by the carrier's medical staff in accordance with locality norms, must also be considered. For example, although cardiology is a sub-specialty of internal medicine, the treatment of both diabetes and of a serious heart condition might require the concurrent services of two physicians, each practicing in internal medicine but specializing in different sub-specialties.

While it would not be highly unusual for concurrent care performed by physicians in different specialties (e.g., a surgeon and an internist) or by physicians in different sub-specialties of the same specialty (e.g., an allergist and a cardiologist) to be found medically necessary, the need for such care by physicians in the same specialty or sub-specialty (e.g., two internists or two cardiologists) would occur infrequently since in most cases both physicians would possess the skills and knowledge necessary to treat the patient. However, circumstances could arise which would necessitate such care. For example, a patient may require the services of two physicians in the same specialty or sub-specialty when one physician has further limited his or her practice to some unusual aspect of that specialty, e.g., tropical medicine. Similarly, concurrent services

provided by a family physician and an internist may or may not be found to be reasonable and necessary, depending on the circumstances of the specific case. If it is determined that the services of one of the physicians are not warranted by the patient's condition, payment may be made only for the other physician's (or physicians') services.

Once it is determined that the patient requires the active services of more than one physician, the individual services must be examined for medical necessity, just as where a single physician provides the care. For example, even if it is determined that the patient requires the concurrent services of both a cardiologist and a surgeon, payment may not be made for any services rendered by either physician which, for that condition, exceed normal frequency or duration unless there are special circumstances requiring the additional care.

The carrier must also assure that the services of one physician do not duplicate those provided by another, e.g., where the family physician visits during the post-operative period primarily as a courtesy to the patient.

Hospital admission services performed by two physicians for the same beneficiary on the same day could represent reasonable and necessary services, provided, as stated above, that the patient's condition necessitates treatment by both physicians. The level of difficulty of the service provided may vary between the physicians, depending on the severity of the complaint each one is treating and that physician's prior contact with the patient. For example, the admission services performed by a physician who has been treating a patient over a period of time for a chronic condition would not be as involved as the services performed by a physician who has had no prior contact with the patient and who has been called in to diagnose and treat a major acute condition.

Carriers should have sufficient means for identifying concurrent care situations. A correct coverage determination can be made on a concurrent care case only where the claim is sufficiently documented for the carrier to determine the role each physician played in the patient's care (i.e., the condition or conditions for which the physician treated the patient). If, in any case, the role of each physician involved is not clear, the carrier should request clarification.

F. Completion of Claims Forms

Separate charges for the services of a physician in completing a Form CMS-1500, a statement in lieu of a Form CMS-1500, or an itemized bill are not covered. Payment for completion of the Form CMS-1500 claim form is considered included in the fee schedule amount.

G. Care Plan Oversight Services

Care plan oversight is supervision of patients under care of home health agencies or hospices that require complex and multidisciplinary care modalities involving regular physician development and/or revision of care plans, review of subsequent reports of patient status, review of laboratory and other studies, communication with other health professionals not employed in the same practice who are involved in the patient's care, integration of new information into the care plan, and/or adjustment of medical therapy.

Such services are covered for home health and hospice patients, but are not covered for patients of skilled nursing facilities (SNFs), nursing home facilities, or hospitals. These services are covered only if all the following requirements are met:

1. The beneficiary must require complex or multi-disciplinary care modalities requiring ongoing physician involvement in the patient's plan of care;

2. The care plan oversight (CPO) services should be furnished during the period in which the beneficiary was receiving Medicare covered HHA or hospice services;

3. The physician who bills CPO must be the same physician who signed the home health or hospice plan of care;

4. The physician furnished at least 30 minutes of care plan oversight within the calendar month for which payment is claimed. Time spent by a physician's nurse or the time spent consulting with one's nurse is not countable toward the 30-minute threshold. Low-intensity services included as part of other evaluation and management services are not included as part of the 30 minutes required for coverage;

5. The work included in hospital discharge day management (codes 99238-99239) and discharge from observation (code 99217) is not countable toward the 30 minutes per month required for work on the same day as discharge but only for those services separately documented as occurring after the patient is actually physically discharged from the hospital;

6. The physician provided a covered physician service that required a face-to-face encounter with the beneficiary within the six months immediately preceding the first care plan oversight service. Only evaluation and management services are acceptable prerequisite face-to-face encounters for CPO. EKG, lab, and surgical services are not sufficient face-to-face services for CPO;

7. The care plan oversight billed by the physician was not routine post-operative care provided in the global surgical period of a surgical procedure billed by the physician;

8. If the beneficiary is receiving home health agency services, the physician did not have a significant financial or contractual interest in the home health agency. A physician who is an employee of a hospice, including a volunteer medical director, should not bill CPO services. Payment for the services of a physician employed by the hospice is included in the payment to the hospice;

9. The physician who bills the care plan oversight services is the physician who furnished them;

10. Services provided incident to a physician's service do not qualify as CPO and do not count toward the 30-minute requirement;

11. The physician is not billing for the Medicare end stage renal disease (ESRD) capitation payment for the same beneficiary during the same month; and

12. The physician billing for CPO must document in the patient's record the services furnished and the date and length of time associated with those services.

100-2, 15, 30.4
Optometrist's Services
B3-2020.25

Effective April 1, 1987, a doctor of optometry is considered a physician with respect to all services the optometrist is authorized to perform under State law or regulation. To be covered under Medicare, the services must be medically reasonable and necessary for the diagnosis or treatment of illness or injury, and must meet all applicable coverage requirements. See the Medicare Benefit Policy Manual, Chapter 16, "General Exclusions from Coverage," for exclusions from coverage that apply to vision care services, and the Medicare Claims Processing Manual, Chapter 12, "Physician/Practitioner Billing," for information dealing with payment for items and services furnished by optometrists.

A. FDA Monitored Studies of Intraocular Lenses
Special coverage rules apply to situations in which an ophthalmologist is involved in a Food and Drug Administration (FDA) monitored study of the safety and efficacy of an investigational Intraocular Lens (IOL). The investigation process for IOLs is unique in that there is a core period and an adjunct period. The core study is a traditional, well-controlled clinical investigation with full record keeping and reporting requirements. The adjunct study is essentially an extended distribution phase for lenses in which only limited safety data are compiled. Depending on the lens being evaluated, the adjunct study may be an extension of the core study or may be the only type of investigation to which the lens may be subject.

All eye care services related to the investigation of the IOL must be provided by the investigator (i.e., the implanting ophthalmologist) or another practitioner (including a doctor of optometry) who provides services at the direction or under the supervision of the investigator and who has an agreement with the investigator that information on the patient is given to the investigator so that he or she may report on the patient to the IOL manufacturer. Eye care services furnished by anyone other than the investigator (or a practitioner who assists the investigator, as described in the preceding paragraph) are not covered during the period the IOL is being investigated, unless the services are not related to the investigation.

B. Concurrent Care
Where more than one practitioner furnishes concurrent care, services furnished to a beneficiary by both an ophthalmologist and another physician (including an optometrist) may be recognized for payment if it is determined that each practitioner's services were reasonable and necessary. (See Sec.30.E

100-2, 15, 30.5
Chiropractor's Services
B3-2020.26

A chiropractor must be licensed or legally authorized to furnish chiropractic services by the State or jurisdiction in which the services are furnished. In addition, a licensed chiropractor must meet the following uniform minimum standards to be considered a physician for Medicare coverage. Coverage extends only to treatment by means of manual manipulation of the spine to correct a subluxation provided such treatment is legal in the State where performed. All other services furnished or ordered by chiropractors are not covered. If a chiropractor orders, takes, or interprets an x-ray or other diagnostic procedure to demonstrate a subluxation of the spine, the x-ray can be used for documentation. However, there is no coverage or payment for these services or for any other diagnostic or therapeutic service ordered or furnished by the chiropractor. For detailed information on using x-rays to determine subluxation, see Sec.240.1.2. In addition, in performing manual manipulation of the spine, some chiropractors use manual devices that are hand-held with the thrust of the force of the device being controlled manually. While such manual manipulation may be covered, there is no separate payment permitted for use of this device.

A. Uniform Minimum Standards
Prior to July 1, 1974 Chiropractors licensed or authorized to practice prior to July 1, 1974, and those individuals who commenced their studies in a chiropractic college before that date must meet all of the following three minimum standards to render payable services under the program:

Preliminary education equal to the requirements for graduation from an accredited high school or other secondary school;Graduation from a college of chiropractic approved by the State's chiropractic examiners that included the completion of a course of study covering a period of not less than 3 school years of 6 months each year in actual continuous attendance covering adequate course of study in the subjects of anatomy, physiology, symptomatology and diagnosis, hygiene and sanitation, chemistry, histology, pathology, and principles and practice of chiropractic, including clinical instruction in vertebral palpation, nerve tracing, and adjusting; andPassage of an examination prescribed by the State's chiropractic examiners covering the subjects listed above.

After June 30, 1974Individuals commencing their studies in a chiropractic college after June 30, 1974, must meet all of the above three standards and all of the following additional requirements:Satisfactory completion of 2 years of pre-chiropractic study at the college level;Satisfactory completion of a 4-year course of 8 months each year (instead of a 3-year course of 6 months each year) at a college or school of chiropractic that includes not less than 4,000 hours in the scientific and chiropractic courses specified in the second bullet under "Prior to July 1, 1974" above, plus courses in the use and effect of x-ray and chiropractic analysis; andThe practitioner must be over 21 years of age.

B. Maintenance Therapy
Under the Medicare program, Chiropractic maintenance therapy is not considered to be medically reasonable or necessary, and is therefore not payable. Maintenance therapy is defined as a treatment plan that seeks to prevent disease, promote health, and prolong and enhance the quality of life; or therapy that is performed to maintain or prevent deterioration of a chronic condition. When further clinical improvement cannot reasonably be expected from continuous ongoing care, and the chiropractic treatment becomes supportive rather than corrective in nature, the treatment is then considered maintenance therapy. For information on how to indicate on a claim a treatment is or is not maintenance, see Sec.240.1.

100-2, 15, 50
Drugs and Biologicals
B3-2049, A3-3112.4.B, HO-230.4.B

The Medicare program provides limited benefits for outpatient drugs. The program covers drugs that are furnished "incident to" a physician's service provided that the drugs are not usually self-administered by the patients who take them. Generally, drugs and biologicals are covered only if all of the following requirements are met:

- They meet the definition of drugs or biologicals (see Sec.50.1);

- They are of the type that are not usually self-administered. (see Sec.50.2);

- They meet all the general requirements for coverage of items as incident to a physician's services (see Sec.Sec.50.1 and 50.3);

- They are reasonable and necessary for the diagnosis or treatment of the illness or injury for which they are administered according to accepted standards of medical practice (see Sec.50.4);

- They are not excluded as noncovered immunizations (see Sec.50.4.4.2); and

- They have not been determined by the FDA to be less than effective. (See Sec.Sec.50.4.4).

Medicare Part B does generally not cover drugs that can be self-administered, such as those in pill form, or are used for self-injection. However, the statute provides for the coverage of some self-administered drugs. Examples of self-administered drugs that are covered include blood-clotting factors, drugs used in immunosuppressive therapy, erythropoietin for dialysis patients, osteoporosis drugs for certain homebound patients, and certain oral cancer drugs. (See Sec.110.3 for coverage of drugs, which are necessary to the effective use of Durable Medical Equipment (DME) or prosthetic devices.)

100-2, 15, 50.4.4.2
Immunizations
A3-3157.A, B3-2049.4, HO-230.4.C

Vaccinations or inoculations are excluded as immunizations unless they are directly related to the treatment of an injury or direct exposure to a disease or condition, such as anti-rabies treatment, tetanus antitoxin or booster vaccine, botulin antitoxin, antivenin sera, or immune globulin. In the absence of injury or direct exposure, preventive immunization (vaccination or inoculation) against such diseases as smallpox, polio, diphtheria, etc., is not covered. However, pneumococcal, hepatitis B, and influenza virus vaccines are exceptions to this rule. (See items A, B, and C below.) In cases where a vaccination or inoculation is excluded from coverage, related charges are also not covered.

A. Pneumococcal Pneumonia Vaccinations
Effective for services furnished on or after May 1, 1981, the Medicare Part B program covers pneumococcal pneumonia vaccine and its administration when furnished in compliance with any applicable State law by any provider of services or any entity or individual with a supplier number. This includes revaccination of patients at highest risk of pneumococcal infection. Typically, these vaccines are administered once in a lifetime except for persons at highest risk. Effective July 1, 2000, Medicare does not require for coverage purposes that a doctor of medicine or osteopathy order the vaccine. Therefore, the beneficiary may receive the vaccine upon request without a physician's order and without physician supervision.

An initial vaccine may be administered only to persons at high risk (see below) of pneumococcal disease. Revaccination may be administered only to persons at highest risk of serious pneumococcal infection and those likely to have a rapid decline in pneumococcal antibody levels, provided that at least five years have [passed since the previous doe of pneumococcal vaccine. Persons at high risk for whom an initial vaccine may be administered include all people age 65 and older; immunocompetent adults who are at increased risk of pneumococcal disease or its complications because of chronic illness (e.g., cardiovascular disease, pulmonary disease, diabetes mellitus, alcoholism, cirrhosis, or cerebrospinal fluid leaks); and individuals with compromised immune systems (e.g., splenic dysfunction or anatomic asplenia, Hodgkin's disease, lymphoma, multiple myeloma, chronic renal failure, HIV infection, nephrotic syndrome, sickle cell disease, or organ transplantation). Persons at highest risk and those most likely to have rapid declines in antibody levels are those for whom revaccination may be appropriate. This group includes persons with functional or anatomic asplenia (e.g., sickle cell disease, splenectomy), HIV infection, leukemia, lymphoma, Hodgkin's disease, multiple myeloma, generalized malignancy, chronic renal failure, nephrotic syndrome, or other conditions associated with immunosuppression such as organ or bone marrow transplantation, and those receiving immunosuppressive chemotherapy. It is not appropriate for routine revaccination of people age 65 or older that are not at highest risk. Those administering the vaccine should not require the patient to present an immunization record prior to administering the pneumococcal vaccine, nor should they feel compelled to review the patient's complete medical record if it is not available. Instead, provided that the patient is competent, it is acceptable to rely on the patient's verbal history to determine prior vaccination status. If the patient is uncertain about his or her vaccination history in the past five years, the vaccine should be given. However, if the patient is certain he/she was were vaccinated in the last five years, the vaccine should not be given. If the patient is certain that the vaccine was given more than five years ago, revaccination is covered only if the patient is at high risk.

B. Hepatitis B Vaccine
Effective for services furnished on or after September 1, 1984, P.L. 98-369 provides coverage under Part B for hepatitis B vaccine and its administration, furnished to a Medicare beneficiary who is at high or intermediate risk of contracting hepatitis B. This coverage is effective for services furnished on or after September 1, 1984. High-risk groups currently identified include (see exception below):ESRD patients;Hemophiliacs who receive Factor VIII or IX concentrates;Clients of institutions for the mentally retarded;Persons who live in the same household as an Hepatitis B Virus (HBV) carrier;Homosexual men; andIllicit injectable drug abusers.

Intermediate risk groups currently identified include:Staff in institutions for the mentally retarded; andWorkers in health care professions who have frequent contact with blood or blood-derived body fluids during routine work. EXCEPTION: Persons in both of the above-listed groups in paragraph B, would not be considered at high or intermediate risk of contracting.hepatitis B, however, if there were laboratory evidence positive for antibodies to hepatitis B. (ESRD patients are routinely tested for hepatitis B antibodies as part of their continuing monitoring and therapy.) For Medicare program purposes, the vaccine may be administered upon the order of a doctor of medicine or osteopathy, by a doctor of medicine or osteopathy, or by home health agencies, skilled nursing facilities, ESRD facilities, hospital outpatient departments, and persons recognized under the incident to physicians' services provision of law. A charge separate from the ESRD composite rate will be recognized and paid for administration of the vaccine to ESRD patients.

C. Influenza Virus Vaccine

Effective for services furnished on or after May 1, 1993, the Medicare Part B program covers influenza virus vaccine and its administration when furnished in compliance with any applicable State law by any provider of services or any entity or individual with a supplier number. Typically, these vaccines are administered once a year in the fall or winter. Medicare does not require, for coverage purposes, that a doctor of medicine or osteopathy order the vaccine. Therefore, the beneficiary may receive the vaccine upon request without a physician's order and without physician supervision.

100-2, 15, 50.5

Self-Administered Drugs and Biologicals

B3-2049.5 Medicare Part B does not cover drugs that are usually self-administered by the patient unless the statute provides for such coverage. The statute explicitly provides coverage, for blood clotting factors, drugs used in immunosuppressive therapy, erythropoietin for dialysis patients, certain oral anti-cancer drugs and anti-emetics used in certain situations.

100-2, 15, 60.3

Incident to Physician's Service in Clinic

B3-2050.3

Services and supplies incident to a physician's service in a physician directed clinic or group association are generally the same as those described above.

A physician directed clinic is one where:

1. A physician (or a number of physicians) is present to perform medical (rather than administrative) services at all times the clinic is open;

2. Each patient is under the care of a clinic physician; and

3. The nonphysician services are under medical supervision.

In highly organized clinics, particularly those that are departmentalized, direct physician supervision may be the responsibility of several physicians as opposed to an individual attending physician. In this situation, medical management of all services provided in the clinic is assured. The physician ordering a particular service need not be the physician who is supervising the service. Therefore, services performed by auxiliary personnel and other aides are covered even though they are performed in another department of the clinic. Supplies provided by the clinic during the course of treatment are also covered. When the auxiliary personnel perform services outside the clinic premises, the services are covered only if performed under the direct supervision of a clinic physician. If the clinic refers a patient for auxiliary services performed by personnel who are not supervised by clinic physicians, such services are not incident to a physician's servic

100-2, 15, 80

Requirements for Diagnostic X-Ray, Diagnostic Laboratory, and Other Diagnostic Tests

This section describes the levels of physician supervision required for furnishing the technical component of diagnostic tests for a Medicare beneficiary who is not a hospital inpatient or outpatient. Section 410.32(b) of the Code of Federal Regulations (CFR) requires that diagnostic tests covered under Sec.1861(s)(3) of the Act and payable under the physician fee schedule, with certain exceptions listed in the regulation, have to be performed under the supervision of an individual meeting the definition of a physician (Sec.1861(r) of the Act) to be considered reasonable and necessary and, therefore, covered under Medicare. The regulation defines these levels of physician supervision for diagnostic tests as follows:

General Supervision - means the procedure is furnished under the physician's overall direction and control, but the physician's presence is not required during the performance of the procedure. Under general supervision, the training of the nonphysician personnel who actually performs the diagnostic procedure and the maintenance of the necessary equipment and supplies are the continuing responsibility of the physician.

Direct Supervision - in the office setting means the physician must be present in the office suite and immediately available to furnish assistance and direction throughout the performance of the procedure. It does not mean that the physician must be present in the room when the procedure is performed.

Personal Supervision - means a physician must be in attendance in the room during the performance of the procedure.

One of the following numerical levels is assigned to each CPT or HCPCS code in the Medicare Physician Fee Schedule Database:

0   Procedure is not a diagnostic test or procedure is a diagnostic test which is not subject to the physician supervision policy.

1   Procedure must be performed under the general supervision of a physician.

2   Procedure must be performed under the direct supervision of a physician.

3   Procedure must be performed under the personal supervision of a physician.

4   Physician supervision policy does not apply when procedure is furnished by a qualified, independent psychologist or a clinical psychologist or furnished under the general supervision of a clinical psychologist; otherwise must be performed under the general supervision of a physician.

5   Physician supervision policy does not apply when procedure is furnished by a qualified audiologist; otherwise must be performed under the general supervision of a physician.

6   Procedure must be performed by a physician or by a physical therapist (PT) who is certified by the American Board of Physical Therapy Specialties (ABPTS) as a qualified electrophysiologic clinical specialist and is permitted to provide the procedure under State law.

6a   Supervision standards for level 66 apply; in addition, the PT with ABPTS certification may supervise another PT but only the PT with ABPTS certification may bill.

7a   Supervision standards for level 77 apply; in addition, the PT with ABPTS certification may supervise another PT but only the PT with ABPTS certification may bill.

9   Concept does not apply.

21   Procedure must be performed by a technician with certification under general supervision of a physician; otherwise must be performed under direct supervision of a physician.

22   Procedure may be performed by a technician with on-line real-time contact with physician.

66   Procedure must be performed by a physician or by a PT with ABPTS certification and certification in this specific procedure.

77   Procedure must be performed by a PT with ABPTS certification or by a PT without certification under direct supervision of a physician, or by a technician with certification under general supervision of a physician.

Nurse practitioners, clinical nurse specialists, and physician assistants are not defined as physicians under Sec.1861(r) of the Act. Therefore, they may not function as supervisory physicians under the diagnostic tests benefit (Sec.1861(s)(3) of the Act). However, when these practitioners personally perform diagnostic tests as provided under Sec.1861(s)(2)(K) of the Act, Sec.1861(s)(3) does not apply and they may perform diagnostic tests pursuant to State scope of practice laws and under the applicable State requirements for physician supervision or collaboration. Because the diagnostic tests benefit set forth in Sec.1861(s)(3) of the Act is separate and distinct from the incident to benefit set forth in Sec.1861(s)(2) of the Act, diagnostic tests need not meet the incident to requirements. Diagnostic tests may be furnished under situations that meet the incident to requirements but this is not required. However, carriers must not scrutinize claims for diagnostic tests utilizing the incident to requirements.

100-2, 15, 80.1

Clinical Laboratory Services

Section 1833 and 1861 of the Act provides for payment of clinical laboratory services under Medicare Part B. Clinical laboratory services involve the biological, microbiological, serological, chemical, immunohematological, hematological, biophysical, cytological, pathological, or other examination of materials derived from the human body for the diagnosis, prevention, or treatment of a disease or assessment of a medical condition. Laboratory services must meet all applicable requirements of the Clinical Laboratory Improvement Amendments of 1988 (CLIA), as set forth at 42 CFR part 493. Section 1862(a)(1)(A) of the Act provides that Medicare payment may not be made for services that are not reasonable and necessary. Clinical laboratory services must be ordered and used promptly by the physician who is treating the beneficiary as described in 42 CFR 410.32(a), or by a qualified nonphysician practitioner, as described in 42 CFR 410.32(a)(3).

See section 80.6 of this manual for related physician ordering instructions.

See the Medicare Claims Processing Manual Chapter 16 for related claims processing instructions.

100-2, 15, 80.2

Psychological Tests and Neuropsychological Tests

Medicare Part B coverage of psychological tests and neuropsychological tests is authorized under section 1861(s)(3) of the Social Security Act. Payment for psychological and neuropsychological tests is authorized under section 1842(b)(2)(A) of the Social Security Act. The payment amounts for the new psychological and neuropsychological tests (CPT codes 96102, 96103, 96119 and 96120) that are effective January 1, 2006, and are billed for tests administered by a technician or a computer reflect a site of service payment differential for the facility and non-facility settings.

Additionally, there is no authorization for payment for diagnostic tests when performed on an "incident to" basis.

Under the diagnostic tests provision, all diagnostic tests are assigned a certain level of supervision. Generally, regulations governing the diagnostic tests provision require that only physicians can provide the assigned level of supervision for diagnostic tests.

However, there is a regulatory exception to the supervision requirement for diagnostic psychological and neuropsychological tests in terms of who can provide the supervision.

That is, regulations allow a clinical psychologist (CP) or a physician to perform the general supervision assigned to diagnostic psychological and neuropsychological tests.

In addition, nonphysician practitioners such as nurse practitioners (NPs), clinical nurse specialists (CNSs) and physician assistants (PAs) who personally perform diagnostic psychological and neuropsychological tests are excluded from having to perform these tests under the general supervision of a physician or a CP. Rather, NPs and CNSs must perform such tests under the requirements of their respective benefit instead of the requirements for diagnostic psychological and neuropsychological tests. Accordingly, NPs and CNSs must perform tests in collaboration (as defined under Medicare law at section 1861(aa)(6) of the Act) with a physician. PAs perform tests under the general supervision of a physician as required for services furnished under the PA benefit.

Furthermore, physical therapists (PTs), occupational therapists (OTs) and speech language pathologists (SLPs) are authorized to bill three test codes as "sometimes therapy" codes. Specifically, CPT codes 96105, 96110 and 96111 may be performed by these therapists. However, when PTs, OTs and SLPs perform these three tests, they must be performed under the general supervision of a physician or a CP.

Who May Bill for Diagnostic Psychological and Neuropsychological Tests

- CPs - see qualifications under chapter 15, section 160 of the Benefits Policy Manual, Pub. 100-02.

- NPs -to the extent authorized under State scope of practice. See qualifications under chapter 15, section 200 of the Benefits Policy Manual, Pub. 100-02.

- CNSs -to the extent authorized under State scope of practice. See qualifications under chapter 15, section 210 of the Benefits Policy Manual, Pub. 100-02.

- PAs - to the extent authorized under State scope of practice. See qualifications under chapter 15, section 190 of the Benefits Policy Manual, Pub. 100-02.

- Independently Practicing Psychologists (IPPs)

- PTs, OTs and SLPs - see qualifications under chapter 15, sections 220-230.6 of the Benefits Policy Manual, Pub. 100-02.

Psychological and neuropsychological tests performed by a psychologist (who is not a CP) practicing independently of an institution, agency, or physician's office are covered when a physician orders such tests. An IPP is any psychologist who is licensed or certified to practice psychology in the State or jurisdiction where furnishing services or, if the jurisdiction does not issue licenses, if provided by any practicing psychologist. (It is CMS' understanding that all States, the District of Columbia, and Puerto Rico license psychologists, but that some trust territories do not. Examples of psychologists, other than CPs, whose psychological and neuropsychological tests are covered under the diagnostic tests provision include, but are not limited to, educational psychologists and counseling psychologists.)

The carrier must secure from the appropriate State agency a current listing of psychologists holding the required credentials to determine whether the tests of a particular IPP are covered under Part B in States that have statutory licensure or certification. In States or territories that lack statutory licensing or certification, the carrier checks individual qualifications before provider numbers are issued. Possible reference sources are the national directory of membership of the American Psychological Association, which provides data about the educational background of individuals and indicates which members are board-certified, the records and directories of the State or territorial psychological association, and the National Register of Health Service Providers. If qualification is dependent on a doctoral degree from a currently accredited program, the carrier verifies the date of accreditation of the school involved, since such accreditation is not retroactive. If the listed reference sources do not provide enough information (e.g., the psychologist is not a member of one of these sources), the carrier contacts the psychologist personally for the required information. Generally, carriers maintain a continuing list of psychologists whose qualifications have been verified.

NOTE: When diagnostic psychological tests are performed by a psychologist who is not practicing independently, but is on the staff of an institution, agency, or clinic, that entity bills for the psychological tests.

The carrier considers psychologists as practicing independently when:

- They render services on their own responsibility, free of the administrative and professional control of an employer such as a physician, institution or agency;

- The persons they treat are their own patients; and

- They have the right to bill directly, collect and retain the fee for their services.

A psychologist practicing in an office located in an institution may be considered an independently practicing psychologist when both of the following conditions exist:

- The office is confined to a separately-identified part of the facility which is used solely as the psychologist's office and cannot be construed as extending throughout the entire institution; and

- The psychologist conducts a private practice, i.e., services are rendered to patients from outside the institution as well as to institutional patients.

Payment for Diagnostic Psychological and Neuropsychological Tests Expenses for diagnostic psychological and neuropsychological tests are not subject to the outpatient mental health treatment limitation, that is, the payment limitation on treatment services for mental, psychoneurotic and personality disorders as authorized under Section 1833(c) of the Act. The payment amount for the new psychological and neuropsychological tests (CPT codes 96102, 96103, 96119 and 96120) that are billed for tests performed by a technician or a computer reflect a site of service payment differential for the facility and non-facility settings. CPs, NPs, CNSs and PAs are required by law to accept assigned payment for psychological and neuropsychological tests. However, while IPPs are not required by law to accept assigned payment for these tests, they must report the name and address of the physician who ordered the test on the claim form when billing for tests.

CPT Codes for Diagnostic Psychological and Neuropsychological Tests The range of CPT codes used to report psychological and neuropsychological tests is 96101-96120. CPT codes 96101, 96102, 96103, 96105, 96110, and 96111 are appropriate for use when billing for psychological tests. CPT codes 96116, 96118, 96119 and 96120 are appropriate for use when billing for neuropsychological tests.

All of the tests under this CPT code range 96101-96120 are indicated as active codes under the physician fee schedule database and are covered if medically necessary.

Payment and Billing Guidelines for Psychological and Neuropsychological Tests The technician and computer CPT codes for psychological and neuropsychological tests include practice expense, malpractice expense and professional work relative value units.

Accordingly, CPT psychological test code 96101 should not be paid when billed for the same tests or services performed under psychological test codes 96102 or 96103. CPT neuropsychological test code 96118 should not be paid when billed for the same tests or services performed under neuropsychological test codes 96119 or 96120. However, CPT codes 96101 and 96118 can be paid separately on the rare occasion when billed on the same date of service for different and separate tests from 96102, 96103, 96119 and 96120.

Under the physician fee schedule, there is no payment for services performed by students or trainees. Accordingly, Medicare does not pay for services represented by CPT codes 96102 and 96119 when performed by a student or a trainee. However, the presence of a student or a trainee while the test is being administered does not prevent a physician, CP, IPP, NP, CNS or PA from performing and being paid for the psychological test under 96102 or the neuropsychological test under 96119.

100-2, 15, 80.3
Audiological Diagnostic Testing

References.

1861(ll)(3)(B) of the Social Security Act for qualifications of audiologists.

Pub. 100-04, chapter 12, section 30.3 for coding and billing information related to audiological services and aural rehabilitation.

Pub. 100-02, chapter 15, sections 220 and 230 for the physical therapy and speech-language pathology policies relative to aural rehabilitation and balance, section 60 for services incident to a physician, and section 80.5 for policies relevant to ordering for diagnostic tests.

Pub. 100-02, chapter 16, section 100 for hearing aid policies.

Benefit.
Audiological diagnostic testing refers to tests of the audiological and vestibular systems, e.g., hearing, balance, auditory processing, tinnitus and diagnostic programming of certain prosthetic devices, performed by qualified audiologists. Audiological testing is covered as "other diagnostic tests" under Sec.1861(s)(3) of the Act when a physician orders such testing for the purpose of obtaining information necessary for the physician's diagnostic medical evaluation or to determine the appropriate medical or surgical treatment of a hearing deficit or related medical problem. For the purposes of ordering audiological diagnostic tests, a nonphysician practitioner may perform the same service as a physician when the nonphysician practitioner orders diagnostic tests within their scope of practice, State and local laws and any policies applicable to the setting. See subsections of section 80 of this chapter for policies relative to ordering diagnostic tests.

Audiological diagnostic tests are not covered under the benefit for incident to a physician (described in Pub. 100-02, chapter 15, section 60), because they have their own benefit as "other diagnostic tests". See Pub. 100-04, chapter 13 for diagnostic test policies.

Orders
If a beneficiary undergoes diagnostic testing performed by an audiologist without a physician order, the tests are not covered even if the audiologist discovers a pathologic condition. See the policies on ordering diagnostic tests in section 80.6 of this chapter.

When a qualified physician or qualified nonphysician practitioner orders a specific audiological test using the CPT descriptor for the test, only that test may be provided on that order. Further orders are necessary if the ordered test indicates that other tests are necessary to evaluate, for example, the type or cause of the condition. Orders for specific tests are required for technicians. When the qualified physician or qualified nonphysician practitioner orders diagnostic audiological tests by an audiologist without naming specific tests, the audiologist may select the appropriate battery of tests.

Coverage and Payment for Audiological Services.
Diagnostic services performed by a qualified audiologist and meeting the requirements at Sec.1861(ll)(3)(B) are payable as "other diagnostic tests." Audiological diagnostic tests are not covered as services incident to physician's services or as services incident to audiologist's services.

The payment for audiological diagnostic tests is determined by the reason the tests were performed, rather than by the diagnosis or the patient's condition.

Payment for audiological diagnostic tests is not allowed by virtue of Sec.1862(a)(7) when:

- The type and severity of the current hearing, tinnitus or balance status needed to determine the appropriate medical or surgical treatment is known to the physician before the test; or

- The test was ordered for the specific purpose of fitting or modifying a hearing aid.

Payment of audiological diagnostic tests is allowed for other reasons (see Documentation subsection below) and is not limited, for example, by:

- Any information resulting from the test including, for example:

  - Confirmation of a prior diagnosis;

  - Post-evaluation diagnoses; or

  - Treatment provided after diagnosis, including hearing aids, or

- The type of evaluation or treatment the physician anticipates before the diagnostic test; or

- Timing of re-evaluation. Re-evaluation is appropriate at a schedule dictated by the ordering physician when the information provided by the diagnostic test is required, for example, to determine changes in hearing, to evaluate the appropriate medical or surgical treatment or evaluate the results of treatment. For example, re-evaluation may be appropriate, even when the evaluation was recent, in cases where the hearing loss, balance or tinnitus may be progressive or fluctuating, the patient or caregiver complains of new symptoms, or treatment (such as medication or surgery) may have changed the patient's audiological condition with or without awareness by the patient.

Payment for these services is based on the physician fee schedule amount except for audiology services furnished in a hospital outpatient department, which are paid under the Outpatient Prospective Payment System.

Computer-administered hearing tests are screening tests, do not require the skilled services of an audiologist and are not covered or payable using codes for diagnostic audiological testing. Examples include, but are not limited to "otograms" and pure tone or immitance screening devices that do not require the skills of an audiologist.

Diagnostic analysis of cochlear or brainstem implant and programming are audiology diagnostic services covered under the "other diagnostic test" benefit. Audiological diagnostic tests before and periodically after implantation of auditory prosthetic devices are covered services.

For descriptions of hearing aids and auditory prosthetic devices including osseointegrated devices, see Pub. 100-02, chapter16, section 100.

If a physician refers a beneficiary to an audiologist for testing related to signs or symptoms associated with hearing loss, balance disorder, tinnitus, ear disease, or ear injury, the audiologist's diagnostic testing services should be covered even if the only outcome is the prescription of a hearing aid.

Individuals Who Provide Audiological Tests.
Some diagnostic audiological tests require, for both the technical and professional components, the skills of an audiologist to perform the test and interpret not only the data output, but also the manner of the patient's response to the test. These tests must be personally furnished by an audiologist or a physician. The skills of an audiologist required when furnishing the ordered diagnostic tests involve skilled judgment or assessment including but not limited to:

- Interpretation, comparison or consideration of the anatomical or physiological implications of test results or patient responsiveness to stimuli during the test;

- Modification of the stimulus based on responses obtained during the test;

- Choices for subsequent presentations of stimuli, or tests in a battery of tests;

- Tests related to implantation of auditory prosthetic devices, central auditory processing, contralateral masking; and/or

- Tests designed to identify central auditory processing disorders, tinnitus, or nonorganic hearing loss.

The technical components of certain audiological diagnostic tests i.e., tympanometry (92567) and vestibular function tests (e.g., 92541) that do not require the skills of an audiologist may be performed by a qualified technician or by an audiologist, physician or nonphysician practitioner acting within their scope of practice. If performed by a technician, the service must be provided under the direct supervision [42 CFR Sec.410.32(3)] of a physician or qualified nonphysician practitioner who is responsible for all clinical judgment and for the appropriate provision of the service. The physician or qualified nonphysician practitioner bills the directly supervised service as a diagnostic test.

Documenting for Audiological Tests.
The "other diagnostic tests" benefit requires an order from a physician, or, where allowed by State and local law, by a non-physician practitioner. See section 80.6 of this chapter for policies concerning orders for diagnostic tests.

The reason for the test should be documented either on the order, on the audiological evaluation report, or in the patient's medical record. (See subsection of this section titled "Benefit".) Examples of appropriate reasons include but are not limited to:

- Evaluation of suspected change in hearing, tinnitus, or balance;

- Evaluation of the cause of disorders of hearing, tinnitus, or balance.

- Determination of the effect of medication, surgery or other treatment;

Reevaluation to follow-up changes in hearing, tinnitus or balance that may be caused for example, but not limited to otosclerosis, atelectatic tympanic membrane, tymposclerosis, cholesteatoma, resolving middle ear infection, Meniere's disease, sudden idiopathic sensorineural hearing loss, autoimmune inner ear disease, acoustic neuroma, demyelinating diseases, ototoxicity secondary to medications, genetic, vascular and viral conditions. Screening tests are not payable, but failure of a screening test may be an appropriate reason for diagnostic audiological tests.

The medical record shall identify the name and professional identity of the person who ordered and the person who actually performed the service. When the medical record is subject to medical review, it is necessary that the contractor determine that the service qualifies as an audiological diagnostic test that requires the skills of an audiologist. A technician must meet qualifications determined by the Medicare contractor to whom the claim is billed. At a minimum, the qualifications must include the requirements of any applicable State or local laws, and successful completion of a curriculum including both classroom training and supervised clinical experience in administration of the audiological service.

If a technician performs the technical component of a service that does not require the skills of an audiologist, the physician supervisor shall provide and document the physician's professional component of the service including, e.g., clinical decision making, and other active participation in the delivery of the service. This participation may not also be billed as evaluation and management or as part of other billed services.

Audiological Treatment.
There is no provision in the law for Medicare to pay audiologists for therapeutic services. For example, vestibular treatment, auditory rehabilitation and auditory processing treatment, while they are within the scope of practice of audiologists, are not diagnostic tests, and therefore, shall not be billed by audiologists to Medicare. Services related to hearing aid evaluation and fitting are not covered regardless of how they are billed. Services identified as "always" therapy in Pub. 100-04 chapter 5, section 20 may not be billed when provided by audiologists. (See also Pub 100-04, chapter 12, section 30.3.)

Services that are not diagnostic tests and are also not "always" therapy (according to the list and the policy in Pub.100-04, chapter 5, section 20) and are provided by qualified personnel (who may be audiologists), may be billed "incident to" when all other appropriate requirements are met. (See policies in Pub. 100-02, chapter 15, sections 60, 200, and 230.)

Treatment related to hearing may be covered under the speech-language pathology benefit when the services are provided by speech-language pathologists. Treatment related to balance (e.g., using "always therapy" codes 97001-97004, 97110, 97112, 97116, and 97750) may be covered under the physical therapy or occupational therapy benefit when the services are provided by physical or occupational therapists or their assistants, where appropriate. Covered therapy services incident to a physician's service must conform to policies in chapter 15, sections 60, 220 and 230. Audiological treatment provided under the benefit for physical therapy and speech-language pathology services may be personally provided and billed by physicians and nonphysician practitioners when the services are within their scope of practice and consistent with State and local laws.

For example, aural rehabilitation and signed communication training may be payable according to the benefit for speech-language pathology services or as speech-language pathology services incident to a physician's or nonphysician practitioner's service. Treatment for balance disorders may be payable according to the benefit for physical therapy services or as a physical therapy service incident to the services of a physician or nonphysician practitioner. See the policies in Pub 100-02, chapter 15, section 220 and 230 for details.

Assignment.
Nonhospital entities billing for the audiologist's services may accept assignment under the usual procedure or, if not accepting assignment, may charge the patient and submit a nonassigned claim on their beha

100-2, 15, 80.5.4
Conditions for Coverage
Medicare covers BMM under the following conditions:

1. Is ordered by the physician or qualified nonphysician practitioner who is treating the beneficiary following an evaluation of the need for a BMM and determination of the appropriate BMM to be used. A physician or qualified nonphysician practitioner treating the beneficiary for purposes of this provision is one who furnishes a consultation or treats a beneficiary for a specific medical problem, and who uses the results in the management of the patient. For the purposes of the BMM benefit, qualified nonphysician practitioners include physician assistants, nurse practitioners, clinical nurse specialists, and certified nurse midwives.

2. Is performed under the appropriate level of physician supervision as defined in 42 CFR 410.32(b).

3. Is reasonable and necessary for diagnosing and treating the condition of a beneficiary who meets the conditions described in Sec.80.5.6.

4. In the case of an individual being monitored to assess the response to or efficacy of an FDA-approved osteoporosis drug therapy, is performed with a dual-energy x-ray absorptiometry system (axial skeleton).

5. In the case of any individual who meets the conditions of 80.5.6 and who has a confirmatory BMM, is performed by a dual-energy x-ray absorptiometry system (axial skeleton) if the initial BMM was not performed by a dual-energy x-ray absorptiometry system (axial skeleton). A confirmatory baseline BMM is not covered if the initial BMM was performed by a dual-energy x-ray absorptiometry system (axial skeleton).

100-2, 15, 80.5.5
Frequency Standards
Medicare pays for a screening BMM once every 2 years (at least 23 months have passed since the month the last covered BMM was performed).

When medically necessary, Medicare may pay for more frequent BMMs. Examples include, but are not limited to, the following medical circumstances: Monitoring beneficiaries on long-term glucocorticoid (steroid) therapy of more than 3 months.

Confirming baseline BMMs to permit monitoring of beneficiaries in the future.

100-2, 15, 80.5.6
Beneficiaries Who May be Covered
To be covered, a beneficiary must meet at least one of the five conditions listed below:

1. A woman who has been determined by the physician or qualified nonphysician practitioner treating her to be estrogen-deficient and at clinical risk for osteoporosis, based on her medical history and other findings.

   NOTE: Since not every woman who has been prescribed estrogen replacement therapy (ERT) may be receiving an "adequate" dose of the therapy, the fact that a woman is receiving ERT should not preclude her treating physician or other qualified treating nonphysician practitioner from ordering a bone mass measurement for her. If a BMM is ordered for a woman following a careful evaluation of her medical need, however, it is expected that the ordering treating physician (or other qualified treating nonphysician practitioner) will document in her medical record why he or she believes that the woman is estrogen-deficient and at clinical risk for osteoporosis.

2. An individual with vertebral abnormalities as demonstrated by an x-ray to be indicative of osteoporosis, osteopenia, or vertebral fracture.

3. An individual receiving (or expecting to receive) glucocorticoid (steroid) therapy equivalent to an average of 5.0 mg of prednisone, or greater, per day, for more than 3 months.

4. An individual with primary hyperparathyroidism.

5. An individual being monitored to assess the response to or efficacy of an FDAapproved osteoporosis drug therapy.

100-2, 15, 100

Surgical Dressings, Splints, Casts, and Other Devices Used for Reductions of Fractures and Dislocations

B3-2079, A3-3110.3, HO-228.3

Surgical dressings are limited to primary and secondary dressings required for the treatment of a wound caused by, or treated by, a surgical procedure that has been performed by a physician or other health care professional to the extent permissible under State law. In addition, surgical dressings required after debridement of a wound are also covered, irrespective of the type of debridement, as long as the debridement was reasonable and necessary and was performed by a health care professional acting within the scope of his/her legal authority when performing this function. Surgical dressings are covered for as long as they are medically necessary.

Primary dressings are therapeutic or protective coverings applied directly to wounds or lesions either on the skin or caused by an opening to the skin. Secondary dressing materials that serve a therapeutic or protective function and that are needed to secure a primary dressing are also covered. Items such as adhesive tape, roll gauze, bandages, and disposable compression material are examples of secondary dressings. Elastic stockings, support hose, foot coverings, leotards, knee supports, surgical leggings, gauntlets, and pressure garments for the arms and hands are examples of items that are not ordinarily covered as surgical dressings. Some items, such as transparent film, may be used as a primary or secondary dressing.

If a physician, certified nurse midwife, physician assistant, nurse practitioner, or clinical nurse specialist applies surgical dressings as part of a professional service that is billed to Medicare, the surgical dressings are considered incident to the professional services of the health care practitioner. (See Sec. 60.1, 180, 190, 200, and 210.) When surgical dressings are not covered incident to the services of a health care practitioner and are obtained by the patient from a supplier (e.g., a drugstore, physician, or other health care practitioner that qualifies as a supplier) on an order from a physician or other health care professional authorized under State law or regulation to make such an order, the surgical dressings are covered separately under Part B.

Splints and casts, and other devices used for reductions of fractures and dislocations are covered under Part B of Medicare. This includes dental splints.

100-2, 15, 120

Prosthetic Devices

B3-2130, A3-3110.4, HO-228.4, A3-3111, HO-229

A. General
Prosthetic devices (other than dental) which replace all or part of an internal body organ (including contiguous tissue), or replace all or part of the function of a permanently inoperative or malfunctioning internal body organ are covered when furnished on a physician's order. This does not require a determination that there is no possibility that the patient's condition may improve sometime in the future. If the medical record, including the judgment of the attending physician, indicates the condition is of long and indefinite duration, the test of permanence is considered met. (Such a device may also be covered under Sec.60.l as a supply when furnished incident to a physician's service.)

Examples of prosthetic devices include artificial limbs, parenteral and enteral (PEN) nutrition, cardiac pacemakers, prosthetic lenses (see subsection B), breast prostheses (including a surgical brassiere) for postmastectomy patients, maxillofacial devices, and devices which replace all or part of the ear or nose. A urinary collection and retention system with or without a tube is a prosthetic device replacing bladder function in case of permanent urinary incontinence. The foley catheter is also considered a prosthetic device when ordered for a patient with permanent urinary incontinence. However, chucks, diapers, rubber sheets, etc., are supplies that are not covered under this provision. Although hemodialysis equipment is a prosthetic device, payment for the rental or purchase of such equipment in the home is made only for use under the provisions for payment applicable to durable medical equipment.

An exception is that if payment cannot be made on an inpatient's behalf under Part A, hemodialysis equipment, supplies, and services required by such patient could be covered under Part B as a prosthetic device, which replaces the function of a kidney. See the Medicare Benefit Policy Manual, Chapter 11, "End Stage Renal Disease," for payment for hemodialysis equipment used in the home. See the Medicare Benefit Policy Manual, Chapter 1, "Inpatient Hospital Services," Sec.10, for additional instructions on hospitalization for renal dialysis.

NOTE: Medicare does not cover a prosthetic device dispensed to a patient prior to the time at which the patient undergoes the procedure that makes necessary the use of the device. For example, the carrier does not make a separate Part B payment for an intraocular lens (IOL) or pacemaker that a physician, during an office visit prior to the actual surgery, dispenses to the patient for his or her use. Dispensing a prosthetic device in this manner raises health and safety issues. Moreover, the need for the device cannot be clearly established until the procedure that makes its use possible is successfully performed. Therefore, dispensing a prosthetic device in this manner is not considered reasonable and necessary for the treatment of the patient's condition.

Colostomy (and other ostomy) bags and necessary accouterments required for attachment are covered as prosthetic devices. This coverage also includes irrigation and flushing equipment and other items and supplies directly related to ostomy care, whether the attachment of a bag is required. Accessories and/or supplies which are used directly with an enteral or parenteral device to achieve the therapeutic benefit of the prosthesis or to assure the proper functioning of the device may also be covered under the prosthetic device benefit subject to the additional guidelines in the Medicare National Coverage Determinations Manual.

Covered items include catheters, filters, extension tubing, infusion bottles, pumps (either food or infusion), intravenous (I.V.) pole, needles, syringes, dressings, tape, Heparin Sodium (parenteral only), volumetric monitors (parenteral only), and parenteral and enteral nutrient solutions. Baby food and other regular grocery products that can be blenderized and used with the enteral system are not covered. Note that some of these items, e.g., a food pump and an I.V. pole, qualify as DME. Although coverage of the enteral and parenteral nutritional therapy systems is provided on the basis of the prosthetic device benefit, the payment rules relating to lump sum or monthly payment for DME apply to such items.

The coverage of prosthetic devices includes replacement of and repairs to such devices as explained in subsection D.

Finally, the Benefits Improvement and Protection Act of 2000 amended Sec.1834(h)(1) of the Act by adding a provision (1834 (h)(1)(G)(i)) that requires Medicare payment to be made for the replacement of prosthetic devices which are artificial limbs, or for the replacement of any part of such devices, without regard to continuous use or useful lifetime restrictions if an ordering physician determines that the replacement device, or replacement part of such a device, is necessary.

Payment may be made for the replacement of a prosthetic device that is an artificial limb, or replacement part of a device if the ordering physician determines that the replacement device or part is necessary because of any of the following:

1. A change in the physiological condition of the patient;
2. An irreparable change in the condition of the device, or in a part of the device; or
3. The condition of the device, or the part of the device, requires repairs and the cost of such repairs would be more than 60 percent of the cost of a replacement device, or, as the case may be, of the part being replaced.

This provision is effective for items replaced on or after April 1, 2001. It supersedes any rule that that provided a 5-year or other replacement rule with regard to prosthetic devices.

B. Prosthetic Lenses
The term "internal body organ" includes the lens of an eye. Prostheses replacing the lens of an eye include post-surgical lenses customarily used during convalescence from eye surgery in which the lens of the eye was removed. In addition, permanent lenses are also covered when required by an individual lacking the organic lens of the eye because of surgical removal or congenital absence. Prosthetic lenses obtained on or after the beneficiary's date of entitlement to supplementary medical insurance benefits may be covered even though the surgical removal of the crystalline lens occurred before entitlement.

1. Prosthetic Cataract Lenses
   One of the following prosthetic lenses or combinations of prosthetic lenses furnished by a physician (see Sec.30.4 for coverage of prosthetic lenses prescribed by a doctor of optometry) may be covered when determined to be reasonable and necessary to restore essentially the vision provided by the crystalline lens of the eye:
   - Prosthetic bifocal lenses in frames;
   - Prosthetic lenses in frames for far vision, and prosthetic lenses in frames for near vision; or
   - When a prosthetic contact lens(es) for far vision is prescribed (including cases of binocular and monocular aphakia), make payment for the contact lens(es) and prosthetic lenses in frames for near vision to be worn at the same time as the contact lens(es), and prosthetic lenses in frames to be worn when the contacts have been removed.

   Lenses which have ultraviolet absorbing or reflecting properties may be covered, in lieu of payment for regular (untinted) lenses, if it has been determined that such lenses are medically reasonable and necessary for the individual patient.

   Medicare does not cover cataract sunglasses obtained in addition to the regular (untinted) prosthetic lenses since the sunglasses duplicate the restoration of vision function performed by the regular prosthetic lenses.
2. Payment for Intraocular Lenses (IOLs) Furnished in Ambulatory Surgical Centers (ASCs)
   Effective for services furnished on or after March 12, 1990, payment for intraocular lenses (IOLs) inserted during or subsequent to cataract surgery in a Medicare certified ASC is included with the payment for facility services that are furnished in connection with the covered surgery.

   Refer to the Medicare Claims Processing Manual, Chapter 14, "Ambulatory Surgical Centers," for more information.
3. Limitation on Coverage of Conventional Lenses One pair of conventional eyeglasses or conventional contact lenses furnished after each cataract surgery with insertion of an IOL is covered.

C. Dentures
Dentures are excluded from coverage. However, when a denture or a portion of the denture is an integral part (built-in) of a covered prosthesis (e.g., an obturator to fill an opening in the palate), it is covered as part of that prosthesis.

D. Supplies, Repairs, Adjustments, and Replacement
Supplies are covered that are necessary for the effective use of a prosthetic device (e.g., the batteries needed to operate an artificial larynx). Adjustment of prosthetic devices required by wear or by a change in the patient's condition is covered when ordered by a physician. General provisions relating to the repair and replacement of durable medical equipment in Sec.110.2 for the repair and replacement of prosthetic devices are applicable. (See the Medicare Benefit Policy Manual, Chapter 16, "General Exclusions from Coverage," Sec.40.4, for payment for devices replaced under a warranty.) Replacement of conventional eyeglasses or contact lenses furnished in accordance with Sec.120.B.3 is not covered. Necessary supplies, adjustments, repairs, and replacements are covered even when the device had been in use before the user enrolled in Part B of the program, so long as the device continues to be medically required.

100-2, 15, 150

Dental Services

B3-2136

As indicated under the general exclusions from coverage, items and services in connection with the care, treatment, filling, removal, or replacement of teeth or structures directly supporting the teeth are not covered. "Structures directly supporting the teeth" means the periodontium, which includes the gingivae, dentogingival junction, periodontal membrane, cementum of the teeth, and alveolar process.

In addition to the following, see Pub 100-01, the Medicare General Information, Eligibility, and Entitlement Manual, Chapter 5, Definitions and Pub 3, the Medicare National Coverage Determinations Manual for specific services which may be covered when furnished by a dentist. If an otherwise noncovered procedure or service is performed by a dentist as incident to and as an integral part of a covered procedure or service performed by the dentist, the total service performed by the dentist on such an occasion is covered.

EXAMPLE 1: The reconstruction of a ridge performed primarily to prepare the mouth for dentures is a noncovered procedure. However, when the reconstruction of a ridge is performed as a result of and at the same time as the surgical removal of a tumor (for other than dental purposes), the totality of surgical procedures is a covered service.

EXAMPLE 2: Medicare makes payment for the wiring of teeth when this is done in connection with the reduction of a jaw fracture.

The extraction of teeth to prepare the jaw for radiation treatment of neoplastic disease is also covered. This is an exception to the requirement that to be covered, a noncovered procedure or service performed by a dentist must be an incident to and an integral part of a covered procedure or service performed by the dentist. Ordinarily, the dentist extracts the patient's teeth, but another physician, e.g., a radiologist, administers the radiation treatments.

When an excluded service is the primary procedure involved, it is not covered, regardless of its complexity or difficulty. For example, the extraction of an impacted tooth is not covered. Similarly, an alveoplasty (the surgical improvement of the shape and condition of the alveolar process) and a frenectomy are excluded from coverage when either of these procedures is performed in connection with an excluded service, e.g., the preparation of the mouth for dentures. In a like manner, the removal of a torus palatinus (a bony protuberance of the hard palate) may be a covered service. However, with rare exception, this surgery is performed in connection with an excluded service, i.e., the preparation of the mouth for dentures. Under such circumstances, Medicare does not pay for this procedure.

Dental splints used to treat a dental condition are excluded from coverage under 1862(a)(12) of the Act. On the other hand, if the treatment is determined to be a covered medical condition (i.e., dislocated upper/lower jaw joints), then the splint can be covered.

Whether such services as the administration of anesthesia, diagnostic x-rays, and other related procedures are covered depends upon whether the primary procedure being performed by the dentist is itself covered. Thus, an x-ray taken in connection with the reduction of a fracture of the jaw or facial bone is covered. However, a single x-ray or x-ray survey taken in connection with the care or treatment of teeth or the periodontium is not covered.

Medicare makes payment for a covered dental procedure no matter where the service is performed. The hospitalization or nonhospitalization of a patient has no direct bearing on the coverage or exclusion of a given dental procedure.

Payment may also be made for services and supplies furnished incident to covered dental services. For example, the services of a dental technician or nurse who is under the direct supervision of the dentist or physician are covered if the services are included in the dentist's or physician's bill.

100-2, 15, 160

Clinical Psychologist Services

A. Clinical Psychologist (CP) Defined

To qualify as a clinical psychologist (CP), a practitioner must meet the following requirements:

- Hold a doctoral degree in psychology;

- Be licensed or certified, on the basis of the doctoral degree in psychology, by the State in which he or she practices, at the independent practice level of psychology to furnish diagnostic, assessment, preventive, and therapeutic services directly to individuals.

B. Qualified Clinical Psychologist Services Defined

Effective July 1, 1990, the diagnostic and therapeutic services of CPs and services and supplies furnished incident to such services are covered as the services furnished by a physician or as incident to physician's services are covered. However, the CP must be legally authorized to perform the services under applicable licensure laws of the State in which they are furnished.

C. Types of Clinical Psychologist Services That May Be Covered

Diagnostic and therapeutic services that the CP is legally authorized to perform in accordance with State law and/or regulation. Carriers pay all qualified CPs based on the physician fee schedule for the diagnostic and therapeutic services. (Psychological tests by practitioners who do not meet the requirements for a CP may be covered under the provisions for diagnostic tests as described in Sec.80.2.

Services and supplies furnished incident to a CP's services are covered if the requirements that apply to services incident to a physician's services, as described in Sec.60 are met. These services must be:

- Mental health services that are commonly furnished in CPs' offices;

- An integral, although incidental, part of professional services performed by the CP;

- Performed under the direct personal supervision of the CP; i.e., the CP must be physically present and immediately available;

- Furnished without charge or included in the CP's bill; and

- Performed by an employee of the CP (or an employee of the legal entity that employs the supervising CP) under the common law control test of the Act, as set forth in 20 CFR 404.1007 and Sec.RS 2101.020 of the Retirement and Survivors Insurance part of the Social Security Program Operations Manual System.

- Diagnostic psychological testing services when furnished under the general supervision of a CP.

Carriers are required to familiarize themselves with appropriate State laws and/or regulations governing a CP's scope of practice.

D. Noncovered Services

The services of CPs are not covered if the service is otherwise excluded from Medicare coverage even though a clinical psychologist is authorized by State law to perform them.

For example, Sec.1862(a)(1)(A) of the Act excludes from coverage services that are not "reasonable and necessary for the diagnosis or treatment of an illness or injury or to improve the functioning of a malformed body member." Therefore, even though the services are authorized by State law, the services of a CP that are determined to be not reasonable and necessary are not covered. Additionally, any therapeutic services that are billed by CPs under CPT psychotherapy codes that include medical evaluation and management services are not covered.

E. Requirement for Consultation

When applying for a Medicare provider number, a CP must submit to the carrier a signed Medicare provider/supplier enrollment form that indicates an agreement to the effect that, contingent upon the patient's consent, the CP will attempt to consult with the patient's attending or primary care physician in accordance with accepted professional ethical norms, taking into consideration patient confidentiality.

If the patient assents to the consultation, the CP must attempt to consult with the patient's physician within a reasonable time after receiving the consent. If the CP's attempts to consult directly with the physician are not successful, the CP must notify the physician within a reasonable time that he or she is furnishing services to the patient. Additionally, the CP must document, in the patient's medical record, the date the patient consented or declined consent to consultations, the date of consultation, or, if attempts to consult did not succeed, that date and manner of notification to the physician.

The only exception to the consultation requirement for CPs is in cases where the patient's primary care or attending physician refers the patient to the CP. Also, neither a CP nor a primary care nor attending physician may bill Medicare or the patient for this required consultation.

F. Outpatient Mental Health Services Limitation

All covered therapeutic services furnished by qualified CPs are subject to the outpatient mental health services limitation in Pub 100-01, Medicare General Information, Eligibility, and Entitlement Manual, Chapter 3, "Deductibles, Coinsurance Amounts, and Payment Limitations," Sec.30, (i.e., only 62 1/2 percent of expenses for these services are considered incurred expenses for Medicare purposes). The limitation does not apply to diagnostic services.

G. Assignment Requirement

Assignment Sec. required.

100-2, 15, 170

Clinical Social Worker (CSW) Services

B3-2152

See the Medicare Claims Processing Manual Chapter 12, Physician/Nonphysician Practitioners, Sec.150, "Clinical Social Worker Services," for payment requirements.

A. Clinical Social Worker Defined

Section 1861(hh) of the Act defines a "clinical social worker" as an individual who:

- Possesses a master's or doctor's degree in social work;

- Has performed at least two years of supervised clinical social work; and

- Is licensed or certified as a clinical social worker by the State in which the services are performed; or

- In the case of an individual in a State that does not provide for licensure or certification, has completed at least 2 years or 3,000 hours of post master's degree supervised clinical social work practice under the supervision of a master's level social worker in an appropriate setting such as a hospital, SNF, or clinic.

B. Clinical Social Worker Services Defined

Section 1861(hh)(2) of the Act defines "clinical social worker services" as those services that the CSW is legally authorized to perform under State law (or the State regulatory mechanism provided by State law) of the State in which such services are performed for the diagnosis and treatment of mental illnesses. Services furnished to an inpatient of a hospital or an inpatient of a SNF that the SNF is required to provide as a requirement for participation are not included. The services that are covered are those that are otherwise covered if furnished by a physician or as incident to a physician's professional service.

C. Covered Services

Coverage is limited to the services a CSW is legally authorized to perform in accordance with State law (or State regulatory mechanism established by State law). The services of a CSW may be covered under Part B if they are: The type of services that are otherwise covered if furnished by a physician, or as incident to a physician's service. (See Sec.30 for a description of physicians' services and Sec.70 of Pub 100-1, the Medicare General Information, Eligibility, and Entitlement Manual, Chapter 5, for the definition of a physician.); Performed by a person who meets the definition of a CSW (See subsection A.); and Not otherwise excluded from coverage. Carriers should become familiar with the State law or regulatory mechanism governing a CSW's scope of practice in their service area.

D. Noncovered Services

Services of a CSW are not covered when furnished to inpatients of a hospital or to inpatients of a SNF if the services furnished in the SNF are those that the SNF is required to furnish as a condition of participation in Medicare. In addition, CSW services are not covered if they are otherwise excluded from Medicare coverage even though a CSW is authorized by State law to perform them. For example, the Medicare law excludes from coverage services that are not "reasonable and necessary for the diagnosis or treatment of an illness or injury or to improve the functioning of a malformed body member."

E. Outpatient Mental Health Services

Limitation All covered therapeutic services furnished by qualified CSWs are subject to the outpatient psychiatric services limitation in Pub 100-01, Medicare General Information, Eligibility, and Entitlement Manual, Chapter 3, "Deductibles, Coinsurance Amounts, and Payment Limitations," Sec.30, (i.e., only 62 1/2 percent of expenses for these services are considered incurred expenses for Medicare purposes) The limitation does not apply to diagnostic services.

F. Assignment Requirement

Assignment is required.

100-2, 15, 180

Nurse-Midwife (CNM) Services

B3-2154

A. General

Effective on or after July 1, 1988, the services provided by a certified nurse-midwife or incident to the certified nurse-midwife's services are covered. Payment is made under assignment only. See the Medicare Claims Processing Manual, Chapter 12, "Physician and Nonphysician Practitioners," Sec.130, for payment methodology for nurse midwife services.

B. Certified Nurse-Midwife Defined

A certified nurse-midwife is a registered nurse who has successfully completed a program of study and clinical experience in nurse-midwifery, meeting guidelines prescribed by the Secretary, or who has been certified by an organization recognized by the Secretary. The Secretary has recognized certification by the American College of Nurse Midwives and State qualifying requirements in those States that specify a program of education and clinical experience for nurse-midwives for these purposes. A nurse-midwife must:

- Be currently licensed to practice in the State as a registered professional nurse; and

- Meet one of the following requirements:

  1. Be legally authorized under State law or regulations to practice as a nurse-midwife and have completed a program of study and clinical experience for nurse-midwives, as specified by the State; or

  2. If the State does not specify a program of study and clinical experience that nurse-midwives must complete to practice in that State, the nurse-midwife must:

     a. Be currently certified as a nurse-midwife by the American College of Nurse-Midwives;

     b. Have satisfactorily completed a formal education program (of at least one academic year) that, upon completion, qualifies the nurse to take the certification examination offered by the American College of Nurse-Midwives; or

     c. Have successfully completed a formal education program for preparing registered nurses to furnish gynecological and obstetrical care to women during pregnancy, delivery, and the postpartum period, and care to normal newborns, and have practiced as a nurse-midwife for a total of 12 months during any 18-month period from August 8, 1976, to July 16, 1982.

C. Covered Services

1. General - Effective January 1, 1988, through December 31, 1993, the coverage of nurse-midwife services was restricted to the maternity cycle. The maternity cycle is a period that includes pregnancy, labor, and the immediate postpartum period

   Beginning with services furnished on or after January 1, 1994, coverage is no longer limited to the maternity cycle. Coverage is available for services furnished by a nurse-midwife that he or she is legally authorized to perform in the State in which the services are furnished and that would otherwise be covered if furnished by a physician, including obstetrical and gynecological services.

2. Incident To- Services and supplies furnished incident to a nurse midwife's service are covered if they would have been covered when furnished incident to the services of a doctor of medicine or osteopathy, as described in Sec.60.

D. Noncovered Services

The services of nurse-midwives are not covered if they are otherwise excluded from Medicare coverage even though a nurse-midwife is authorized by State law to perform them. For example, the Medicare program excludes from coverage routine physical checkups and services that are not reasonable and necessary for the diagnosis or treatment of an illness or injury or to improve the functioning of a malformed body member. Coverage of service to the newborn continues only to the point that the newborn is or would normally be treated medically as a separate individual. Items and services furnished the newborn from that point are not covered on the basis of the mother's eligibility.

E. Relationship With Physician

Most States have licensure and other requirements applicable to nurse-midwives. For example, some require that the nurse-midwife have an arrangement with a physician for the referral of the patient in the event a problem develops that requires medical attention. Others may require that the nurse-midwife function under the general supervision of a physician. Although these and similar State requirements must be met in order for the nurse-midwife to provide Medicare

covered care, they have no effect on the nurse-midwife's right to personally bill for and receive direct Medicare payment. That is, billing does not have to flow through a physician or facility. See Sec.60.2 for coverage of services performed by nurse-midwives incident to the service of physicians.

F. Place of Service

There is no restriction on place of service. Therefore, nurse-midwife services are covered if provided in the nurse-midwife's office, in the patient's home, or in a hospital or other facility, such as a clinic or birthing center owned or operated by a nurse-midwife.

G. Assignment Requirement

Assignment is required.

100-2, 15, 230

Practice of Physical Therapy, Occupational Therapy, and Speech-Language Pathology

A. Group Therapy Services.

Contractors pay for outpatient physical therapy services (which includes outpatient speech-language pathology services) and outpatient occupational therapy services provided simultaneously to two or more individuals by a practitioner as group therapy services (97150). The individuals can be, but need not be performing the same activity. The physician or therapist involved in group therapy services must be in constant attendance, but one-on-one patient contact is not required.

B. Therapy Students

1. General

   Only the services of the therapist can be billed and paid under Medicare Part B. The services performed by a student are not reimbursed even if provided under "line of sight" supervision of the therapist; however, the presence of the student "in the room" does not make the service unbillable. Pay for the direct (one-to-one) patient contact services of the physician or therapist provided to Medicare Part B patients. Group therapy services performed by a therapist or physician may be billed when a student is also present "in the room".

   EXAMPLES:

   Therapists may bill and be paid for the provision of services in the following scenarios:

   - The qualified practitioner is present and in the room for the entire session. The student participates in the delivery of services when the qualified practitioner is directing the service, making the skilled judgment, and is responsible for the assessment and treatment.

   - The qualified practitioner is present in the room guiding the student in service delivery when the therapy student and the therapy assistant student are participating in the provision of services, and the practitioner is not engaged in treating another patient or doing other tasks at the same time

   - The qualified practitioner is responsible for the services and as such, signs all documentation. (A student may, of course, also sign but it is not necessary since the Part B payment is for the clinician's service, not for the student's services).

2. Therapy Assistants as Clinical Instructors

   Physical therapist assistants and occupational therapy assistants are not precluded from serving as clinical instructors for therapy students, while providing services within their scope of work and performed under the direction and supervision of a licensed physical or occupational therapist to a Medicare beneficiary.

3. Services Provided Under Part A and Part B

   The payment methodologies for Part A and B therapy services rendered by a student are different. Under the MPFS (Medicare Part B), Medicare pays for services provided by physicians and practitioners that are specifically authorized by statute. Students do not meet the definition of practitioners under Medicare Part B. Under SNF PPS, payments are based upon the case mix or Resource Utilization Group (RUG) category that describes the patient. In the rehabilitation groups, the number of therapy minutes delivered to the patient determines the RUG category. Payment levels for each category are based upon the costs of caring for patients in each group rather than providing pecific payment for each therapy service as is done in Medicare Part B.

100-2, 15, 230.1

Practice of Physical Therapy

A. General

Physical therapy services are those services provided within the scope of practice of physical therapists and necessary for the diagnosis and treatment of impairments, functional limitations, disabilities or changes in physical function and health status. (See Pub. 100-03, the Medicare National Coverage Determinations Manual, for specific conditions or services.) For descriptions of aquatic therapy in a community center pool see section 220C of this chapter.

B. Qualified Physical Therapist Defined

Reference: 42CFR484.4

The new personnel qualifications for physical therapists were discussed in the 2008 Physician Fee Schedule. See the Federal Register of November 27, 2007, for the full text. See also the correction notice for this rule, published in the Federal Register on January 15, 2008.

The regulation provides that a qualified physical therapist (PT) is a person who is licensed, if applicable, as a PT by the state in which he or she is practicing unless licensure does not apply, has graduated from an accredited PT education program and passed a national examination approved by the state in which PT services are provided. The phrase, "by the state in which practicing" includes any authorization to practice provided by the same state in which the service is provided, including temporary licensure, regardless of the location of the entity billing the services. The curriculum accreditation is provided by the Commission on Accreditation in

Physical Therapy Education (CAPTE) or, for those who graduated before CAPTE, curriculum approval was provided by the American Physical Therapy Association (APTA). For internationally educated PTs, curricula are approved by a credentials evaluation organization either approved by the APTA or identified in 8 CFR 212.15(e) as it relates to PTs. For example, in 2007, 8 CFR 212.15(e) approved the credentials evaluation provided by the Federation of State Boards of Physical Therapy (FSBPT) and the Foreign Credentialing Commission on Physical Therapy (FCCPT). The requirements above apply to all PTs effective January 1, 2010, if they have not met any of the following requirements prior to January 1, 2010.

Physical therapists whose current license was obtained on or prior to December 31, 2009, qualify to provide PT services to Medicare beneficiaries if they:

- graduated from a CAPTE approved program in PT on or before December 31, 2009 (examination is not required); or,

- graduated on or before December 31, 2009, from a PT program outside the U.S. that is determined to be substantially equivalent to a U.S. program by a credentials evaluating organization approved by either the APTA or identified in 8 CFR 212.15(e) and also passed an examination for PTs approved by the state in which practicing.

Or, PTs whose current license was obtained before January 1, 2008, may meet the requirements in place on that date (i.e., graduation from a curriculum approved by either the APTA, the Committee on Allied Health Education and Accreditation of the American Medical Association, or both).

Or, PTs meet the requirements who are currently licensed and were licensed or qualified as a PT on or before December 31, 1977, and had 2 years appropriate experience as a PT, and passed a proficiency examination conducted, approved, or sponsored by the U.S. Public Health Service.

Or, PTs meet the requirements if they are currently licensed and before January 1, 1966, they were:

- admitted to membership by the APTA; or

- admitted to registration by the American Registry of Physical Therapists; or

- graduated from a 4-year PT curriculum approved by a State Department of Education; or

- licensed or registered and prior to January 1, 1970, they had 15 years of fulltime experience in PT under the order and direction of attending and referring doctors of medicine or osteopathy.

Or, PTs meet requirements if they are currently licensed and they were trained outside the U.S. before January 1, 2008, and after 1928 graduated from a PT curriculum approved in the country in which the curriculum was located, if that country had an organization that was a member of the World Confederation for Physical Therapy, and that PT qualified as a member of the organization.

For outpatient PT services that are provided incident to the services of physicians/NPPs, the requirement for PT licensure does not apply; all other personnel qualifications do apply. The qualified personnel providing PT services incident to the services of a physician/NPP must be trained in an accredited PT curriculum. For example, a person who, on or before December 31, 2009, graduated from a PT curriculum accredited by CAPTE, but who has not passed the national examination or obtained a license, could provide Medicare outpatient PT therapy services incident to the services of a physician/NPP if the physician assumes responsibility for the services according to the incident to policies. On or after January 1, 2010, although licensure does not apply, both education and examination requirements that are effective January 1, 2010, apply to qualified personnel who provide PT services incident to the services of a physician/NPP.

C. Services of Physical Therapy Support Personnel

Reference: 42CFR 484.4

Personnel Qualifications. The new personnel qualifications for physical therapist assistants (PTA) were discussed in the 2008 Physician Fee Schedule. See the Federal Register of November 27, 2007, for the full text. See also the correction notice for this rule, published in the Federal Register on January 15, 2008.

The regulation provides that a qualified PTA is a person who is licensed as a PTA unless licensure does not apply, is registered or certified, if applicable, as a PTA by the state in which practicing, and graduated from an approved curriculum for PTAs, and passed a national examination for PTAs. The phrase, "by the state in which practicing" includes any authorization to practice provided by the same state in which the service is provided, including temporary licensure, regardless of the location or the entity billing for the services. Approval for the curriculum is provided by CAPTE or, if internationally or military trained PTAs apply, approval will be through a credentialing body for the curriculum for PTAs identified by either the American Physical Therapy Association or identified in 8 CFR 212.15(e). A national examination for PTAs is, for example the one furnished by the Federation of State Boards of Physical Therapy. These requirements above apply to all PTAs effective January 1, 2010, if they have not met any of the following requirements prior to January 1, 2010.

Those PTAs also qualify who, on or before December 31, 2009, are licensed, registered or certified as a PTA and met one of the two following requirements:

1. Is licensed or otherwise regulated in the state in which practicing; or

2. In states that have no licensure or other regulations, or where licensure does not apply, PTAs have:

- graduated on or before December 31, 2009, from a 2-year college-level program approved by the APTA or CAPTE; and

- effective January 1, 2010, those PTAs must have both graduated from a CAPTE approved curriculum and passed a national examination for PTAs; or

PTAs may also qualify if they are licensed, registered or certified as a PTA, if applicable and meet requirements in effect before January 1, 2008, that is,

- they have graduated before January 1, 2008, from a 2 year college level program approved by the APTA; or

- on or before December 31, 1977, they were licensed or qualified as a PTA and passed a proficiency examination conducted, approved, or sponsored by the U.S. Public Health Service.

Services. The services of PTAs used when providing covered therapy benefits are included as part of the covered service. These services are billed by the supervising physical therapist. PTAs may not provide evaluation services, make clinical judgments or decisions or take responsibility for the service. They act at the direction and under the supervision of the treating physical therapist and in accordance with state laws.

A physical therapist must supervise PTAs. The level and frequency of supervision differs by setting (and by state or local law). General supervision is required for PTAs in all settings except private practice (which requires direct supervision) unless state practice requirements are more stringent, in which case state or local requirements must be followed. See specific settings for details. For example, in clinics, rehabilitation services, either on or off the organization's premises, those services are supervised by a qualified physical therapist who makes an onsite supervisory visit at least once every 30 days or more frequently if required by state or local laws or regulation.

The services of a PTA shall not be billed as services incident to a physician/NPP's service, because they do not meet the qualifications of a therapist.

The cost of supplies (e.g., theraband, hand putty, electrodes) used in furnishing covered therapy care is included in the payment for the HCPCS codes billed by the physical therapist, and are, therefore, not separately billable. Separate coverage and billing provisions apply to items that meet the definition of brace in Sec.130.

Services provided by aides, even if under the supervision of a therapist, are not therapy services and are not covered by Medicare. Although an aide may help the therapist by providing unskilled services, those services that are unskilled are not covered by Medicare and shall be denied as not reasonable and necessary if they are billed as therapy services.

D. Application of Medicare Guidelines to PT Services

This subsection will be used in the future to illustrate the application of the above guidelines to some of the physical therapy modalities and procedures utilized in the treatment of patient

100-2, 15, 230.2

Practice of Occupational Therapy

(Rev. 88, Issued: 05-07-08, Effective: 01-01-08, Implementation: 06-09-08)

A. General

Occupational therapy services are those services provided within the scope of practice of occupational therapists and necessary for the diagnosis and treatment of impairments, functional disabilities or changes in physical function and health status. (See Pub. 100- 03, the Medicare National Coverage Determinations Manual, for specific conditions or services.)

Occupational therapy is medically prescribed treatment concerned with improving or restoring functions which have been impaired by illness or injury or, where function has been permanently lost or reduced by illness or injury, to improve the individual's ability to perform those tasks required for independent functioning. Such therapy may involve:

The evaluation, and reevaluation as required, of a patient's level of function by administering diagnostic and prognostic tests;

The selection and teaching of task-oriented therapeutic activities designed to restore physical function; e.g., use of woodworking activities on an inclined table to restore shoulder, elbow, and wrist range of motion lost as a result of burns;

The planning, implementing, and supervising of individualized therapeutic activity programs as part of an overall "active treatment" program for a patient with a diagnosed psychiatric illness; e.g., the use of sewing activities which require following a pattern to reduce confusion and restore reality orientation in a schizophrenic patient;

The planning and implementing of therapeutic tasks and activities to restore sensoryintegrative function; e.g., providing motor and tactile activities to increase sensory input and improve response for a stroke patient with functional loss resulting in a distorted body image;

The teaching of compensatory technique to improve the level of independence in the activities of daily living, for example:

- Teaching a patient who has lost the use of an arm how to pare potatoes and chop vegetables with one hand;

- Teaching an upper extremity amputee how to functionally utilize a prosthesis;

- Teaching a stroke patient new techniques to enable the patient to perform feeding, dressing, and other activities as independently as possible; or

- Teaching a patient with a hip fracture/hip replacement techniques of standing tolerance and balance to enable the patient to perform such functional activities as dressing and homemaking tasks.

The designing, fabricating, and fitting of orthotics and self-help devices; e.g., making a hand splint for a patient with rheumatoid arthritis to maintain the hand in a functional position or constructing a device which would enable an individual to hold a utensil and feed independently; or Vocational and prevocational assessment and training, subject to the limitations specified in item B below.

Only a qualified occupational therapist has the knowledge, training, and experience required to evaluate and, as necessary, reevaluate a patient's level of function, determine whether an occupational therapy program could reasonably be expected to improve, restore, or compensate for lost function and, where appropriate, recommend to the physician/NPP a plan of treatment.

B. Qualified Occupational Therapist Defined
Reference: 42CFR484.4 The new personnel qualifications for occupational therapists (OT) were discussed in the 2008 Physician Fee Schedule. See the Federal Register of November 27, 2007, for the full text. See also the correction notice for this rule, published in the Federal Register on January 15, 2008.

The regulation provides that a qualified OT is an individual who is licensed, if licensure applies, or otherwise regulated, if applicable, as an OT by the state in which practicing, and graduated from an accredited education program for OTs, and is eligible to take or has passed the examination for OTs administered by the National Board for Certification in Occupational Therapy, Inc. (NBCOT). The phrase, "by the state in which practicing" includes any authorization to practice provided by the same state in which the service is provided, including temporary licensure, regardless of the location of the entity billing the services. The education program for U.S. trained OTs is accredited by the Accreditation Council for Occupational Therapy Education (ACOTE). The requirements above apply to all OTs effective January 1, 2010, if they have not met any of the following requirements prior to January 1, 2010.

The OTs may also qualify if on or before December 31, 2009:

- they are licensed or otherwise regulated as an OT in the state in which practicing (regardless of the qualifications they met to obtain that licensure or regulation); or

- when licensure or other regulation does not apply, OTs have graduated from an OT education program accredited by ACOTE and are eligible to take, or have successfully completed the NBCOT examination for OTs.

Also, those OTs who met the Medicare requirements for OTs that were in 42CFR484.4 prior to January 1, 2008, qualify to provide OT services for Medicare beneficiaries if:

- on or before January 1, 2008, they graduated an OT program approved jointly by the American Medical Association and the AOTA, or

- they are eligible for the National Registration Examination of AOTA or the National Board for Certification in OT.

Also, they qualify who on or before December 31, 1977, had 2 years of appropriate experience as an occupational therapist, and had achieved a satisfactory grade on a proficiency examination conducted, approved, or sponsored by the U.S. Public Health Service.

Those educated outside the U.S. may meet the same qualifications for domestic trained OTs. For example, they qualify if they were licensed or otherwise regulated by the state in which practicing on or before December 31, 2009. Or they are qualified if they:

- graduated from an OT education program accredited as substantially equivalent to a U.S. OT education program by ACOTE, the World Federation of Occupational Therapists, or a credentialing body approved by AOTA; and

- passed the NBCOT examination for OT; and

- Effective January 1, 2010, are licensed or otherwise regulated, if applicable as an OT by the state in which practicing.

For outpatient OT services that are provided incident to the services of physicians/NPPs, the requirement for OT licensure does not apply; all other personnel qualifications do apply. The qualified personnel providing OT services incident to the services of a physician/NPP must be trained in an accredited OT curriculum. For example, a person who, on or before December 31, 2009, graduated from an OT curriculum accredited by ACOTE and is eligible to take or has successfully completed the entry level certification examination for OTs developed and administered by NBCOT, could provide Medicare outpatient OT services incident to the services of a physician/NPP if the physician assumes responsibility for the services according to the incident to policies. On or after January 1, 2010, although licensure does not apply, both education and examination requirements that are effective January 1, 2010, apply to qualified personnel who provide OT services incident to the services of a physician/NPP.

C. Services of Occupational Therapy Support Personnel
Reference: 42CFR 484.4

The new personnel qualifications for occupational therapy assistants were discussed in the 2008 Physician Fee Schedule. See the Federal Register of November 27, 2007, for the full text. See also the correction notice for this rule, published in the Federal Register on January 15, 2008.

The regulation provides that an occupational therapy assistant is a person who is licensed, unless licensure does not apply, or otherwise regulated, if applicable, as an OTA by the state in which practicing, and graduated from an OTA education program accredited by ACOTE and is eligible to take or has successfully completed the NBCOT examination for OTAs. The phrase, "by the state in which practicing" includes any authorization to practice provided by the same state in which the service is provided, including temporary licensure, regardless of the location of the entity billing the services.

If the requirements above are not met, an OTA may qualify if, on or before December 31, 2009, the OTA is licensed or otherwise regulated as an OTA, if applicable, by the state in which practicing, or meets any qualifications defined by the state in which practicing.

Or, where licensure or other state regulation does not apply, OTAs may qualify if they have, on or before December 31, 2009:

- completed certification requirements to practice as an OTA established by a credentialing organization approved by AOTA; and

- after January 1, 2010, they have also completed an education program accredited by ACOTE and passed the NBCOT examination for OTAs.

OTAs who qualified under the policies in effect prior to January 1, 2008, continue to qualify to provide OT directed and supervised OTA services to Medicare beneficiaries.

Therefore, OTAs qualify who after December 31, 1977, and on or before December 31, 2007:

- completed certification requirements to practice as an OTA established by a credentialing organization approved by AOTA; or

- completed the requirements to practice as an OTA applicable in the state in which practicing.

Those OTAs who were educated outside the U.S. may meet the same requirements as domestically trained OTAs. Or, if educated outside the U.S. on or after January 1, 2008, they must have graduated from an OTA program accredited as substantially equivalent to OTA entry level education in the U.S. by ACOTE, its successor organization, or the World Federation of Occupational Therapists or a credentialing body approved by AOTA. In addition, they must have passed an exam for OTAs administered by NBCOT.

Services. The services of OTAs used when providing covered therapy benefits are included as part of the covered service. These services are billed by the supervising occupational therapist. OTAs may not provide evaluation services, make clinical judgments or decisions or take responsibility for the service. They act at the direction and under the supervision of the treating occupational therapist and in accordance with state laws.

An occupational therapist must supervise OTAs. The level and frequency of supervision differs by setting (and by state or local law). General supervision is required for OTAs in all settings except private practice (which requires direct supervision) unless state practice requirements are more stringent, in which case state or local requirements must be followed. See specific settings for details. For example, in clinics, rehabilitation agencies, and public health agencies, 42CFR485.713 indicates that when an OTA provides services, either on or off the organization's premises, those services are supervised by a qualified occupational therapist who makes an onsite supervisory visit at least once every 30 days or more frequently if required by state or local laws or regulation.

The services of an OTA shall not be billed as services incident to a physician/NPP's service, because they do not meet the qualifications of a therapist.

The cost of supplies (e.g., looms, ceramic tiles, or leather) used in furnishing covered therapy care is included in the payment for the HCPCS codes billed by the occupational therapist and are, therefore, not separately billable. Separate coverage and billing provisions apply to items that meet the definition of brace in Sec.130 of this manual.

Services provided by aides, even if under the supervision of a therapist, are not therapy services in the outpatient setting and are not covered by Medicare. Although an aide may help the therapist by providing unskilled services, those services that are unskilled are not covered by Medicare and shall be denied as not reasonable and necessary if they are billed as therapy services.

D. Application of Medicare Guidelines to Occupational Therapy Services
Occupational therapy may be required for a patient with a specific diagnosed psychiatric illness. If such services are required, they are covered assuming the coverage criteria are met. However, where an individual's motivational needs are not related to a specific diagnosed psychiatric illness, the meeting of such needs does not usually require an individualized therapeutic program. Such needs can be met through general activity programs or the efforts of other professional personnel involved in the care of the patient. Patient motivation is an appropriate and inherent function of all health disciplines, which is interwoven with other functions performed by such personnel for the patient. Accordingly, since the special skills of an occupational therapist are not required, an occupational therapy program for individuals who do not have a specific diagnosed psychiatric illness is not to be considered reasonable and necessary for the treatment of an illness or injury. Services furnished under such a program are not covered.

Occupational therapy may include vocational and prevocational assessment and training. When services provided by an occupational therapist are related solely to specific employment opportunities, work skills, or work settings, they are not reasonable or necessary for the diagnosis or treatment of an illness or injury and are not covered. However, carriers and intermediaries exercise care in applying this exclusion, because the assessment of level of function and the teaching of compensatory techniques to improve the level of function, especially in activities of daily living, are services which occupational therapists provide for both vocational and nonvocational purposes. For example, an assessment of sitting and standing tolerance might be nonvocational for a mother of young children or a retired individual living alone, but could also be a vocational test for a sales clerk. Training an amputee in the use of prosthesis for telephoning is necessary for everyday activities as well as for employment purposes. Major changes in life style may be mandatory for an individual with a substantial disability. The techniques of adjustment cannot be considered exclusively vocational or nonvocational.

100-2, 15, 230.3
Practice of Speech-Language Pathology
A. General
Speech-language pathology services are those services provided within the scope of practice of speech-language pathologists and necessary for the diagnosis and treatment of speech and language disorders, which result in communication disabilities and for the diagnosis and treatment of swallowing disorders (dysphagia), regardless of the presence of a communication disability. (See Pub. 100-03, chapter 1, Sec.170.3)

B. Qualified Speech-Language Pathologist Defined
A qualified speech-language pathologist for program coverage purposes meets one of the following requirements:

- The education and experience requirements for a Certificate of Clinical Competence in (speech-language pathology) granted by the American Speech- Language Hearing Association; or

- Meets the educational requirements for certification and is in the process of accumulating the supervised experience required for certification.

For outpatient speech-language pathology services that are provided incident to the services of physicians/NPPs, the requirement for speech-language pathology licensure does not apply; all other personnel qualifications do apply. Therefore, qualified personnel providing speech-language pathology services incident to the services of a physician/NPP must meet the above qualifications.

C. Services of Speech-Language Pathology Support Personnel
Services of speech-language pathology assistants are not recognized for Medicare coverage. Services provided by speech-language pathology assistants, even if they are licensed to provide services in their states, will be considered unskilled services and denied as not reasonable and necessary if they are billed as therapy services.

Services provided by aides, even if under the supervision of a therapist, are not therapy services and are not covered by Medicare. Although an aide may help the therapist by providing unskilled services, those services are not covered by Medicare and shall be denied as not reasonable and necessary if they are billed as therapy services.

D. Application of Medicare Guidelines to Speech-Language Pathology Services

1. Evaluation Services
   Speech-language pathology evaluation services are covered if they are reasonable and necessary and not excluded as routine screening by Sec.1862(a)(7) of the Act. The speechlanguage pathologist employs a variety of formal and informal speech, language, and dysphagia assessment tests to ascertain the type, causal factor(s), and severity of the speech and language or swallowing disorders. Reevaluation of patients for whom speech, language and swallowing were previously contraindicated is covered only if the patient exhibits a change in medical condition. However, monthly reevaluations; e.g., a Western Aphasia Battery, for a patient undergoing a rehabilitative speech-language pathology program, are considered a part of the treatment session and shall not be covered as a separate evaluation for billing purposes. Although hearing screening by the speechlanguage pathologist may be part of an evaluation, it is not billable as a separate service.
2. Therapeutic Services
   The following are examples of common medical disorders and resulting communication deficits, which may necessitate active rehabilitative therapy. This list is not all-inclusive:
   - Cerebrovascular disease such as cerebral vascular accidents presenting with dysphagia, aphasia/dysphasia, apraxia, and dysarthria;
   - Neurological disease such as Parkinsonism or
   - Multiple Sclerosis with dysarthria, dysphagia, inadequate respiratory volume/control, or voice disorder; or
   - Laryngeal carcinoma requiring laryngectomy resulting in aphonia.
3. Impairments of the Auditory System
   The terms, aural rehabilitation, auditory rehabilitation, auditory processing, lipreading and speech reading are among the terms used to describe covered services related to perception and comprehension of sound through the auditory system. See Pub. 100-04, chapter 12, section 30.3 for billing instructions. For example:
   - Auditory processing evaluation and treatment may be covered and medically necessary. Examples include but are not limited to services for certain neurological impairments or the absence of natural auditory stimulation that results in impaired ability to process sound. Certain auditory processing disorders require diagnostic audiological tests in addition to speech-language pathology evaluation and treatment.
   - Evaluation and treatment for disorders of the auditory system may be covered and medically necessary, for example, when it has been determined by a speechlanguage pathologist in collaboration with an audiologist that the hearing impaired beneficiary's current amplification options (hearing aid, other amplification device or cochlear implant) will not sufficiently meet the patient's functional communication needs. Audiologists and speech-language pathologists both evaluate beneficiaries for disorders of the auditory system using different skills and techniques, but only speech-language pathologists may provide treatment.

Assessment for the need for rehabilitation of the auditory system (but not the vestibular system) may be done by a speech language pathologist. Examples include but are not limited to: evaluation of comprehension and production of language in oral, signed or written modalities, speech and voice production, listening skills, speech reading, communications strategies, and the impact of the hearing loss on the patient/client and family.

Examples of rehabilitation include but are not limited to treatment that focuses on comprehension, and production of language in oral, signed or written modalities; speech and voice production, auditory training, speech reading, multimodal (e.g., visual, auditory-visual, and tactile) training, communication strategies, education and counseling. In determining the necessity for treatment, the beneficiary's performance in both clinical and natural environment should be considered.

4. Dysphagia
Dysphagia, or difficulty in swallowing, can cause food to enter the airway, resulting in coughing, choking, pulmonary problems, aspiration or inadequate nutrition and hydration with resultant weight loss, failure to thrive, pneumonia and death. It is most often due to complex neurological and/or structural impairments including head and neck trauma, cerebrovascular accident, neuromuscular degenerative diseases, head and neck cancer, dementias, and encephalopathies. For these reasons, it is important that only qualified professionals with specific training and experience in this disorder provide evaluation and treatment.

The speech-language pathologist performs clinical and instrumental assessments and analyzes and integrates the diagnostic information to determine candidacy for intervention as well as appropriate compensations and rehabilitative therapy techniques.

The equipment that is used in the examination may be fixed, mobile or portable.

Professional guidelines recommend that the service be provided in a team setting with a physician/NPP who provides supervision of the radiological examination and interpretation of medical conditions revealed in it.

Swallowing assessment and rehabilitation are highly specialized services. The professional rendering care must have education, experience and demonstrated competencies. Competencies include but are not limited to: identifying abnormal upper aerodigestive tract structure and function; conducting an oral, pharyngeal, laryngeal and respiratory function examination as it relates to the functional assessment of swallowing; recommending methods of oral intake and risk precautions; and developing a treatment plan employing appropriate compensations and therapy techniques.

100-2, 15, 230.4

Services Furnished by a Physical or Occupational Therapist in Private Practice

A. General
In order to qualify to bill Medicare directly as a therapist, each individual must be enrolled as a private practitioner and employed in one of the following practice types: an unincorporated solo practice, unincorporated partnership, unincorporated group practice, physician/NPP group or groups that are not professional corporations, if allowed by state and local law. Physician/NPP group practices may employ physical therapists in private practice (PTPP) and/or occupational therapists in private practice (OTPP) if state and local law permits this employee relationship.

For purposes of this provision, a physician/NPP group practice is defined as one or more physicians/NPPs enrolled with Medicare who may bill as one entity. For further details on issues concerning enrollment, see the provider enrollment Web site at www.cms.hhs.gov/providers/enrollment.

Private practice also includes therapists who are practicing therapy as employees of another supplier, of a professional corporation or other incorporated therapy practice. Private practice does not include individuals when they are working as employees of an institutional provider.

Services should be furnished in the therapist's or group's office or in the patient's home. The office is defined as the location(s) where the practice is operated, in the state(s) where the therapist (and practice, if applicable) is legally authorized to furnish services, during the hours that the therapist engages in the practice at that location. If services are furnished in a private practice office space, that space shall be owned, leased, or rented by the practice and used for the exclusive purpose of operating the practice. For descriptions of aquatic therapy in a community center pool see section 220C of this chapter.

Therapists in private practice must be approved as meeting certain requirements, but do not execute a formal provider agreement with the Secretary.

If therapists who have their own Medicare Personal Identification number (PIN) or National Provider Identifier (NPI) are employed by therapist groups, physician/NPP groups, or groups that are not professional organizations, the requirement that therapy space be owned, leased, or rented may be satisfied by the group that employs the therapist. Each physical or occupational therapist employed by a group should enroll as a PT or OT in private practice.

When therapists with a Medicare PIN/NPI provide services in the physician's/NPP's office in which they are employed, and bill using their PIN/NPI for each therapy service, then the direct supervision requirement for PTAs and OTAs apply.

When the PT or OT who has a Medicare PIN/ NPI is employed in a physician's/NPP's office the services are ordinarily billed as services of the PT or OT, with the PT or OT identified on the claim as the supplier of services. However, services of the PT or OT who has a Medicare PIN/NPI may also be billed by the physician/NPP as services incident to the physician's/NPP's service. (See Sec.230.5 for rules related to PTA and OTA services incident to a physician.) In that case, the physician/NPP is the supplier of service, the Unique Provider Identification Number (UPIN) or NPI of the physician/NPP (ordering or supervising, as indicated) is reported on the claim with the service and all the rules for incident to services (Sec.230.5) must be followed.

B. Private Practice Defined
Reference: Federal Register November, 1998, pages 58863-58869; 42CFR 410.38(b)

The carrier considers a therapist to be in private practice if the therapist maintains office space at his or her own expense and furnishes services only in that space or the patient's home. Or, a therapist is employed by another supplier and furnishes services in facilities provided at the expense of that supplier.

The therapist need not be in full-time private practice but must be engaged in private practice on a regular basis; i.e., the therapist is recognized as a private practitioner and for that purpose has access to the necessary equipment to provide an adequate program of therapy.

The physical or occupational therapy services must be provided either by or under the direct supervision of the therapist in private practice. Each physical or occupational therapist in a practice should be enrolled as a Medicare provider. If a physical or occupational therapist is not enrolled, the services of that therapist must be directly supervised by an enrolled physical or occupational therapist. Direct supervision requires that the supervising private practice therapist be present in the office suite at the time the service is performed. These direct supervision requirements apply only in the private practice setting and only for physical therapists and occupational therapists and their assistants. In other outpatient settings, supervision rules differ. The services of support personnel must be included in the therapist's bill. The supporting personnel, including other therapists, must be W-2 or 1099 employees of the therapist in private practice or other qualified employer.

Coverage of outpatient physical therapy and occupational therapy under Part B includes the services of a qualified therapist in private practice when furnished in the therapist's office or the beneficiary's home. For this purpose, "home" includes an institution that is used as a home, but not a hospital, CAH or SNF, (Federal Register Nov. 2, 1998, pg 58869). Place of Service (POS) includes:

- 03/School, only if residential,
- 04/Homeless Shelter,

- 12/Home, other than a facility that is a private residence,
- 14/Group Home, 33/Custodial Care Facility.

C. Assignment
Reference: Nov. 2, 1998 Federal Register, pg. 58863

See also Pub. 100-04 chapter 1, Sec.30.2.

When physicians, NPPs, PTPPs or OTPPs obtain provider numbers, they have the option of accepting assignment (participating) or not accepting assignment (nonparticipating). In contrast, providers, such as outpatient hospitals, SNFs, rehabilitation agencies, and CORFs, do not have the option. For these providers, assignment is mandatory.

If physicians/NPPs, PTPPs or OTPPs accept assignment (are participating), they must accept the Medicare Physician Fee Schedule amount as payment. Medicare pays 80% and the patient is responsible for 20%. In contrast, if they do not accept assignment, Medicare will only pay 95% of the fee schedule amount. However, when these services are not furnished on an assignment-related basis, the limiting charge applies. (See Sec.1848(g)(2)(c) of the Act.)

NOTE: Services furnished by a therapist in the therapist's office under arrangements with hospitals in rural communities and public health agencies (or services provided in the beneficiary's home under arrangements with a provider of outpatient physical or occupational therapy services) are not covered under this provision. See section 230.6.

100-2, 15, 240
Chiropractic Services - General
B3-2250, B3-4118

The term "physician" under Part B includes a chiropractor who meets the specified qualifying requirements set forth in Sec.30.5 but only for treatment by means of manual manipulation of the spine to correct a subluxation.

Effective for claims with dates of services on or after January 1, 2000, an x-ray is not required to demonstrate the subluxation.

Implementation of the chiropractic benefit requires an appreciation of the differences between chiropractic theory and experience and traditional medicine due to fundamental differences regarding etiology and theories of the pathogenesis of disease. Judgments about the reasonableness of chiropractic treatment must be based on the application of chiropractic principles. So that Medicare beneficiaries receive equitable adjudication of claims based on such principles and are not deprived of the benefits intended by the law, carriers may use chiropractic consultation in carrier review of Medicare chiropractic claims.

Payment is based on the physician fee schedule and made to the beneficiary or, on assignment, to the chiropractor.

A. Verification of Chiropractor's Qualifications
Carriers must establish a reference file of chiropractors eligible for payment as physicians under the criteria in Sec.30.1. They pay only chiropractors on file. Information needed to establish such files is furnished by the CMS RO.

The RO is notified by the appropriate State agency which chiropractors are licensed and whether each meets the national uniform standards.

100-2, 15, 260
Ambulatory Surgical Center Services
Facility services furnished by ambulatory surgical centers (ASCs) in connection with certain surgical procedures are covered under Part B. To receive coverage of and payment for its services under this provision, a facility must be certified as meeting the requirements for an ASC and enter into a written agreement with CMS. Medicare periodically updates the list of covered procedures and related payment amounts through release of regulations and Program Memoranda. The ASC must accept Medicare's payment for such procedures as payment in full with respect to those services defined as ASC facility services.

Where services are performed in an ASC, the physician and others who perform covered services may also be paid for his/her professional services; however, the "professional" rate is then adjusted since the ASC incurs the facility costs.

100-2, 15, 290
Foot Care
A. Treatment of Subluxation of Foot
Subluxations of the foot are defined as partial dislocations or displacements of joint surfaces, tendons ligaments, or muscles of the foot. Surgical or nonsurgical treatments undertaken for the sole purpose of correcting a subluxated structure in the foot as an isolated entity are not covered.

However, medical or surgical treatment of subluxation of the ankle joint (talo-crural joint) is covered. In addition, reasonable and necessary medical or surgical services, diagnosis, or treatment for medical conditions that have resulted from or are associated with partial displacement of structures is covered. For example, if a patient has osteoarthritis that has resulted in a partial displacement of joints in the foot, and the primary treatment is for the osteoarthritis, coverage is provided.

B. Exclusions from Coverage
The following foot care services are generally excluded from coverage under both Part A and Part B. (See Sec.290.F and Sec.290.G for instructions on applying foot care exclusions.)

1. Treatment of Flat Foot

    The term "flat foot" is defined as a condition in which one or more arches of the foot have flattened out. Services or devices directed toward the care or correction of such conditions, including the prescription of supportive devices, are not covered.

2. Routine Foot Care

Except as provided above, routine foot care is excluded from coverage. Services that normally are considered routine and not covered by Medicare include the following:

- The cutting or removal of corns and calluses;
- The trimming, cutting, clipping, or debriding of nails; and
- Other hygienic and preventive maintenance care, such as cleaning and soaking the feet, the use of skin creams to maintain skin tone of either ambulatory or bedfast patients, and any other service performed in the absence of localized illness, injury, or symptoms involving the foot.

3. Supportive Devices for Feet

    Orthopedic shoes and other supportive devices for the feet generally are not covered. However, this exclusion does not apply to such a shoe if it is an integral part of a leg brace, and its expense is included as part of the cost of the brace. Also, this exclusion does not apply to therapeutic shoes furnished to diabetics.

C. Exceptions to Routine Foot Care Exclusion

1. Necessary and Integral Part of Otherwise Covered Services

    In certain circumstances, services ordinarily considered to be routine may be covered if they are performed as a necessary and integral part of otherwise covered services, such as diagnosis and treatment of ulcers, wounds, or infections.

2. Treatment of Warts on Foot

    The treatment of warts (including plantar warts) on the foot is covered to the same extent as services provided for the treatment of warts located elsewhere on the body.

3. Presence of Systemic Condition

    The presence of a systemic condition such as metabolic, neurologic, or peripheral vascular disease may require scrupulous foot care by a professional that in the absence of such condition(s) would be considered routine (and, therefore, excluded from coverage). Accordingly, foot care that would otherwise be considered routine may be covered when systemic condition(s) result in severe circulatory embarrassment or areas of diminished sensation in the individual's legs or feet. (See subsection A.)

    In these instances, certain foot care procedures that otherwise are considered routine (e.g., cutting or removing corns and calluses, or trimming, cutting, clipping, or debriding nails) may pose a hazard when performed by a nonprofessional person on patients with such systemic conditions. (See Sec.290.G for procedural instructions.)

4. Mycotic Nails

    In the absence of a systemic condition, treatment of mycotic nails may be covered.

    The treatment of mycotic nails for an ambulatory patient is covered only when the physician attending the patient's mycotic condition documents that (1) there is clinical evidence of mycosis of the toenail, and (2) the patient has marked limitation of ambulation, pain, or secondary infection resulting from the thickening and dystrophy of the infected toenail plate.

    The treatment of mycotic nails for a nonambulatory patient is covered only when the physician attending the patient's mycotic condition documents that (1) there is clinical evidence of mycosis of the toenail, and (2) the patient suffers from pain or secondary infection resulting from the thickening and dystrophy of the infected toenail plate.

    For the purpose of these requirements, documentation means any written information that is required by the carrier in order for services to be covered. Thus, the information submitted with claims must be substantiated by information found in the patient's medical record. Any information, including that contained in a form letter, used for documentation purposes is subject to carrier verification in order to ensure that the information adequately justifies coverage of the treatment of mycotic nails.

D. Systemic Conditions That Might Justify Coverage
Although not intended as a comprehensive list, the following metabolic, neurologic, and peripheral vascular diseases (with synonyms in parentheses) most commonly represent the underlying conditions that might justify coverage for routine foot care.

- Diabetes mellitus *
- Arteriosclerosis obliterans (A.S.O., arteriosclerosis of the extremities, occlusive peripheral arteriosclerosis)
- Buerger's disease (thromboangiitis obliterans)
- Chronic thrombophlebitis *
- Peripheral neuropathies involving the feet -

    Associated with malnutrition and vitamin deficiency *

    - Malnutrition (general, pellagra)
    - Alcoholism
    - Malabsorption (celiac disease, tropical sprue)
    - Pernicious anemia

        Associated with carcinoma *

        Associated with diabetes mellitus *

        Associated with drugs and toxins *

        Associated with multiple sclerosis *

        Associated with uremia (chronic renal disease) *

        Associated with traumatic injury

        Associated with leprosy or neurosyphilis

        Associated with hereditary disorders

- Hereditary sensory radicular neuropathy
- Angiokeratoma corporis diffusum (Fabry's)
- Amyloid neuropathy

When the patient's condition is one of those designated by an asterisk (*), routine procedures are covered only if the patient is under the active care of a doctor of medicine or osteopathy who documents the condition.

E. Supportive Devices for Feet

Orthopedic shoes and other supportive devices for the feet generally are not covered. However, this exclusion does not apply to such a shoe if it is an integral part of a leg brace, and its expense is included as part of the cost of the brace. Also, this exclusion does not apply to therapeutic shoes furnished to diabetics.

F. Presumption of Coverage

In evaluating whether the routine services can be reimbursed, a presumption of coverage may be made where the evidence available discloses certain physical and/or clinical findings consistent with the diagnosis and indicative of severe peripheral involvement. For purposes of applying this presumption the following findings are pertinent:

Class A Findings

- Nontraumatic amputation of foot or integral skeletal portion thereof.

Class B Findings

- Absent posterior tibial pulse;
- Advanced trophic changes as: hair growth (decrease or absence) nail changes (thickening) pigmentary changes (discoloration) skin texture (thin, shiny) skin color (rubor or redness) (Three required); and
- Absent dorsalis pedis pulse.

Class C Findings

- Claudication;
- Temperature changes (e.g., cold feet);
- Edema;
- Paresthesias (abnormal spontaneous sensations in the feet); and
- Burning.

The presumption of coverage may be applied when the physician rendering the routine foot care has identified:

1. A Class A finding;
2. Two of the Class B findings; or
3. One Class B and two Class C findings.

Cases evidencing findings falling short of these alternatives may involve podiatric treatment that may constitute covered care and should be reviewed by the intermediary's medical staff and developed as necessary.

For purposes of applying the coverage presumption where the routine services have been rendered by a podiatrist, the contractor may deem the active care requirement met if the claim or other evidence available discloses that the patient has seen an M.D. or D.O. for treatment and/or evaluation of the complicating disease process during the 6-month period prior to the rendition of the routine-type services. The intermediary may also accept the podiatrist's statement that the diagnosing and treating M.D. or D.O. also concurs with the podiatrist's findings as to the severity of the peripheral involvement indicated.

Services ordinarily considered routine might also be covered if they are performed as a necessary and integral part of otherwise covered services, such as diagnosis and treatment of diabetic ulcers, wounds, and infections.

G. Application of Foot Care Exclusions to Physician's Services

The exclusion of foot care is determined by the nature of the service. Thus, payment for an excluded service should be denied whether performed by a podiatrist, osteopath, or a doctor of medicine, and without regard to the difficulty or complexity of the procedure.

When an itemized bill shows both covered services and noncovered services not integrally related to the covered service, the portion of charges attributable to the noncovered services should be denied. (For example, if an itemized bill shows surgery for an ingrown toenail and also removal of calluses not necessary for the performance of toe surgery, any additional charge attributable to removal of the calluses should be denied.)

In reviewing claims involving foot care, the carrier should be alert to the following exceptional situations:

1. Payment may be made for incidental noncovered services performed as a necessary and integral part of, and secondary to, a covered procedure. For example, if trimming of toenails is required for application of a cast to a fractured foot, the carrier need not allocate and deny a portion of the charge for the trimming of the nails. However, a separately itemized charge for such excluded service should be disallowed. When the primary procedure is covered the administration of anesthesia necessary for the performance of such procedure is also covered.

2. Payment may be made for initial diagnostic services performed in connection with a specific symptom or complaint if it seems likely that its treatment would be covered even though the resulting diagnosis may be one requiring only noncovered care.

The name of the M.D. or D.O. who diagnosed the complicating condition must be submitted with the claim. In those cases, where active care is required, the approximate date the beneficiary was last seen by such physician must also be indicated.

NOTE: Section 939 of P.L. 96-499 removed "warts" from the routine foot care exclusion effective July 1, 1981.

Relatively few claims for routine-type care are anticipated considering the severity of conditions contemplated as the basis for this exception. Claims for this type of foot care should not be paid in the absence of convincing evidence that nonprofessional performance of the service would have been hazardous for the beneficiary because of an underlying systemic disease. The mere statement of a diagnosis such as those mentioned in Sec.D above does not of itself indicate the severity of the condition. Where development is indicated to verify diagnosis and/or severity the carrier should follow existing claims processing practices which may include review of carrier's history and medical consultation as well as physician contacts.

The rules in Sec.290.F concerning presumption of coverage also apply.

Codes and policies for routine foot care and supportive devices for the feet are not exclusively for the use of podiatrists. These codes must be used to report foot care services regardless of the specialty of the physician who furnishes the services. Carriers must instruct physicians to use the most appropriate code available when billing for routine foot care.

100-2, 16, 10

General Exclusions From Coverage

A3-3150, HO-260, HHA-232, B3-2300

No payment can be made under either the hospital insurance or supplementary medical insurance program for certain items and services, when the following conditions exist:

- Not reasonable and necessary (Sec.20);
- No legal obligation to pay for or provide (Sec.40);
- Paid for by a governmental entity (Sec.50);
- Not provided within United States (Sec.60);
- Resulting from war (Sec.70);
- Personal comfort (Sec.80);
- Routine services and appliances (Sec.90);
- Custodial care (Sec.110);
- Cosmetic surgery (Sec.120);
- Charges by immediate relatives or members of household (Sec.130);
- Dental services (Sec.140);
- Paid or expected to be paid under workers' compensation (Sec.150);
- Nonphysician services provided to a hospital inpatient that were not provided directly or arranged for by the hospital (Sec.170);
- Services Related to and Required as a Result of Services Which are not Covered Under Medicare (Sec.180);
- Excluded foot care services and supportive devices for feet (Sec.30); or
- Excluded investigational devices (See Chapter 14, Sec.30).

100-2, 16, 20

Services Not Reasonable and Necessary

A3-3151, HO-260.1, B3-2303, AB-00-52 - 6/00

Items and services which are not reasonable and necessary for the diagnosis or treatment of illness or injury or to improve the functioning of a malformed body member are not covered, e.g., payment cannot be made for the rental of a special hospital bed to be used by the patient in their home unless it was a reasonable and necessary part of the patient's treatment. See also Sec.80.

A health care item or service for the purpose of causing, or assisting to cause, the death of any individual (assisted suicide) is not covered. This prohibition does not apply to the provision of an item or service for the purpose of alleviating pain or discomfort, even if such use may increase the risk of death, so long as the item or service is not furnished for the specific purpose of causing death.

100-2, 16, 90

Routine Services and Appliances

A3-3157, HO-260.7, B3-2320, R-1797A3 - 5/00

Routine physical checkups; eyeglasses, contact lenses, and eye examinations for the purpose of prescribing, fitting, or changing eyeglasses; eye refractions by whatever practitioner and for whatever purpose performed; hearing aids and examinations for hearing aids; and immunizations are not covered.

The routine physical checkup exclusion applies to (a) examinations performed without relationship to treatment or diagnosis for a specific illness, symptom, complaint, or injury; and (b) examinations required by third parties such as insurance companies business establishments, or Government agencies.

If the claim is for a diagnostic test or examination performed solely for the purpose of establishing a claim under title IV of Public Law 91-173, "Black Lung Benefits," the service is not covered under Medicare and the claimant should be advised to contact their Social Security office regarding the filing of a claim for reimbursement under the "Black Lung" program.

The exclusions apply to eyeglasses or contact lenses, and eye examinations for the purpose of prescribing, fitting, or changing eyeglasses or contact lenses for refractive errors. The exclusions do not apply to physicians' services (and services incident to a physicians' service) performed in conjunction with an eye disease, as for example, glaucoma or cataracts, or to post-surgical prosthetic lenses which are customarily cured during convalescence from eye surgery in which the lens of the eye was removed, or to permanent prosthetic lenses required by an individual lacking the organic lens of the eye whether by surgical removal or congenital disease. Such prosthetic lens is a replacement for an internal body organ - the lens of the eye. (See the Medicare Benefit Policy Manual, Chapter 15, "Covered Medical and Other Health Services," Sec.120). Expenses for all refractive procedures, whether performed by an ophthalmologist (or any other physician) or an optometrist and without regard to the reason for performance of the refraction, are excluded from coverage.

A. Immunizations

Vaccinations or inoculations are excluded as immunizations unless they are either

- Directly related to the treatment of an injury or direct exposure to a disease or condition, such as antirabies treatment, tetanus antitoxin or booster vaccine, botulin antitoxin, antivenin sera, or immune globulin. (In the absence of injury or direct exposure, preventive immunization (vaccination or inoculation) against such diseases as smallpox, polio, diphtheria, etc., is not covered.); or

- Specifically covered by statute, as described in the Medicare Benefit Policy Manual, Chapter 15, "Covered Medical and Other Health Services," Sec.50.

B. Antigens

Prior to the Omnibus Reconciliation Act of 1980, a physician who prepared an antigen for a patient could not be reimbursed for that service unless the physician also administered the antigen to the patient. Effective January 1, 1981, payment may be made for a reasonable supply of antigens that have been prepared for a particular patient even though they have not been administered to the patient by the same physician who prepared them if:

- The antigens are prepared by a physician who is a doctor of medicine or osteopathy, and

- The physician who prepared the antigens has examined the patient and has determined a plan of treatment and a dosage regimen.

A reasonable supply of antigens is considered to be not more than a 12-week supply of antigens that has been prepared for a particular patient at any one time. The purpose of the reasonable supply limitation is to assure that the antigens retain their potency and effectiveness over the period in which they are to be administered to the patient. (See the Medicare Benefit Policy Manual, Chapter 15, "Covered Medical and Other Health Services," Sec.50.4.4.2)

100-2, 16, 100

Hearing Aids and Auditory Implants

Section 1862(a)(7) of the Social Security Act states that no payment may be made under part A or part B for any expenses incurred for items or services "where such expenses are for . . . hearing aids or examinations therefore. . . ." This policy is further reiterated at 42 CFR 411.15(d) which specifically states that "hearing aids or examination for the purpose of prescribing, fitting, or changing hearing aids" are excluded from coverage.

Hearing aids are amplifying devices that compensate for impaired hearing. Hearing aids include air conduction devices that provide acoustic energy to the cochlea via stimulation of the tympanic membrane with amplified sound. They also include bone conduction devices that provide mechanical energy to the cochlea via stimulation of the scalp with amplified mechanical vibration or by direct contact with the tympanic membrane or middle ear ossicles.

Certain devices that produce perception of sound by replacing the function of the middle ear, cochlea or auditory nerve are payable by Medicare as prosthetic devices. These devices are indicated only when hearing aids are medically inappropriate or cannot be utilized due to congenital malformations, chronic disease, severe sensorineural hearing loss or surgery. The following are prosthetic devices:

- Cochlear implants and auditory brainstem implants, i.e., devices that replace the function of cochlear structures or auditory nerve and provide electrical energy to auditory nerve fibers and other neural tissue via implanted electrode arrays.

- Osseointegrated implants, i.e., devices implanted in the skull that replace the function of the middle ear and provide mechanical energy to the cochlea via a mechanical transducer.

Medicare contractors deny payment for an item or service that is associated with any hearing aid as defined above. See Sec.180 for policy for the medically necessary treatment of complications of implantable hearing aids, such as medically necessary removals of implantable hearing aids due to infection.

100-2, 16, 120

Cosmetic Surgery

A3-3160, HO-260.11, B3-2329

Cosmetic surgery or expenses incurred in connection with such surgery is not covered. Cosmetic surgery includes any surgical procedure directed at improving appearance, except when required for the prompt (i.e., as soon as medically feasible) repair of accidental injury or for the improvement of the functioning of a malformed body member. For example, this exclusion does not apply to surgery in connection with treatment of severe burns or repair of the face following a serious automobile accident, or to surgery for therapeutic purposes which coincidentally also serves some cosmetic purpose.

100-2, 16, 180

Services Related to and Required as a Result of Services Which Are Not Covered Under Medicare

B3-2300.1, A3-3101.14, HO-210.12

Medical and hospital services are sometimes required to treat a condition that arises as a result of services that are not covered because they are determined to be not reasonable and necessary or because they are excluded from coverage for other reasons. Services "related to" noncovered services (e.g., cosmetic surgery, noncovered organ transplants, noncovered artificial organ implants, etc.), including services related to follow-up care and complications of noncovered services which require treatment during a hospital stay in which the noncovered service was performed, are not covered services under Medicare. Services "not related to" noncovered services are covered under Medicare.

Following are examples of services "related to" and "not related to" noncovered services while the beneficiary is an inpatient:

- A beneficiary was hospitalized for a noncovered service and broke a leg while in the hospital. Services related to care of the broken leg during this stay is a clear example of "not related to" services and are covered under Medicare.

- A beneficiary was admitted to the hospital for covered services, but during the course of hospitalization became a candidate for a noncovered transplant or implant and actually received the transplant or implant during that hospital stay. When the original admission was entirely unrelated to the diagnosis that led to a recommendation for a noncovered transplant or implant, the services related to the admitting condition would be covered.

- A beneficiary was admitted to the hospital for covered services related to a condition which ultimately led to identification of a need for transplant and receipt of a transplant during the same hospital stay. If, on the basis of the nature of the services and a comparison of the date they are received with the date on which the beneficiary is identified as a transplant candidate, the services could reasonably be attributed to preparation for the noncovered transplant, the services would be "related to" noncovered services and would also be noncovered.

Following is an example of services received subsequent to a noncovered inpatient stay:

- After a beneficiary has been discharged from the hospital stay in which the beneficiary received noncovered services, medical and hospital services required to treat a condition or complication that arises as a result of the prior noncovered services may be covered when they are reasonable and necessary in all respects. Thus, coverage could be provided for subsequent inpatient stays or outpatient treatment ordinarily covered by Medicare, even if the need for treatment arose because of a previous noncovered procedure. Some examples of services that may be found to be covered under this policy are the reversal of intestinal bypass surgery for obesity, repair of complications from transsexual surgery or from cosmetic surgery, removal of a noncovered bladder stimulator, or treatment of any infection at the surgical site of a noncovered transplant that occurred following discharge from the hospital.

However, any subsequent services that could be expected to have been incorporated into a global fee are considered to have been paid in the global fee, and may not be paid again. Thus, where a patient undergoes cosmetic surgery and the treatment regimen calls for a series of postoperative visits to the surgeon for evaluating the patient's progress, these visits are not paid.

100-3, 10.1

NCD for Use of Visual Tests Prior to and General Anesthesia During Cataract Surgery (10.1)

A - Pre-Surgery Evaluations

Cataract surgery with an intraocular lens (IOL) implant is a high volume Medicare procedure. Along with the surgery, a substantial number of preoperative tests are available to the surgeon. In most cases, a comprehensive eye examination (ocular history and ocular examination) and a single scan to determine the appropriate pseudophakic power of the IOL are sufficient. In most cases involving a simple cataract, a diagnostic ultrasound A-scan is used. For patients with a dense cataract, an ultrasound B-scan may be used.

Accordingly, where the only diagnosis is cataract(s), Medicare does not routinely cover testing other than one comprehensive eye examination (or a combination of a brief/intermediate examination not to exceed the charge of a comprehensive examination) and an A-scan or, if medically justified, a B-scan. Claims for additional tests are denied as not reasonable and necessary unless there is an additional diagnosis and the medical need for the additional tests is fully documented.

Because cataract surgery is an elective procedure, the patient may decide not to have the surgery until later, or to have the surgery performed by a physician other than the diagnosing physician. In these situations, it may be medically appropriate for the operating physician to conduct another examination. To the extent the additional tests are considered reasonable and necessary by the carrier's medical staff, they are covered.

B - General Anesthesia

The use of general anesthesia in cataract surgery may be considered reasonable and necessary if, for particular medical indications, it is the accepted procedure among ophthalmologists in the local community to use general anesthesia.

100-3, 10.2

NCD for Transcutaneous Electrical Nerve Stimulation (TENS) for Acute Post-Operative Pain (10.2)

The use of TENS for the relief of acute post-operative pain is covered under Medicare. TENS may be covered whether used as an adjunct to the use of drugs, or as an alternative to drugs, in the treatment of acute pain resulting from surgery.

TENS devices, whether durable or disposable, may be used in furnishing this service. When used for the purpose of treating acute post-operative pain, TENS devices are considered supplies. As such they may be hospital supplies furnished inpatients covered under Part A, or supplies incident to a physician's service when furnished in connection with surgery done on an outpatient basis, and covered under Part B.

It is expected that TENS, when used for acute post-operative pain, will be necessary for relatively short periods of time, usually 30 days or less. In cases when TENS is used for longer periods, contractors should attempt to ascertain whether TENS is no longer being used for acute pain but rather for chronic pain, in which case the TENS device may be covered as durable medical equipment as described in 280.13.

100-3, 10.3

NCD for Inpatient Hospital Pain Rehabilitation Programs (10.3)

Since pain rehabilitation programs of a lesser scope than that described above would raise a question as to whether the program could be provided in a less intensive setting than on an inpatient hospital basis, carefully evaluate such programs to determine whether the program does, in fact, necessitate a hospital level of care. Some pain rehabilitation programs may utilize services and devices which are excluded from coverage, e.g., acupuncture (see 35-8), biofeedback (see 35-27), dorsal column stimulator (see 65-8), and family counseling services (see 35-14). In determining whether the scope of a pain program does necessitate inpatient hospital care, evaluate only those services and devices which are covered. Although diagnostic tests may be an appropriate part of pain rehabilitation programs, such tests would be covered in an individual case only where they can be reasonably related to a patient's illness, complaint, symptom, or injury and where they do not represent an unnecessary duplication of tests previously performed.

An inpatient program of 4 weeks' duration is generally required to modify pain behavior. After this period it would be expected that any additional rehabilitation services which might be required could be effectively provided on an outpatient basis under an outpatient pain rehabilitation program (see 10.4 of the NCD Manual) or other outpatient program. The first 7-10 days of such an inpatient program constitute, in effect, an evaluation period. If a patient is unable to adjust to the program within this period, it is generally concluded that it is unlikely that the program will be effective and the patient is discharged from the program. On occasions a program longer than 4 weeks may be required in a particular case. In such a case there should be documentation to substantiate that inpatient care beyond a 4-week period was reasonable and necessary. Similarly, where it appears that a patient participating in a program is being granted frequent outside passes, a question would exist as to whether an inpatient program is reasonable and necessary for the treatment of the patient's condition.

An inpatient hospital stay for the purpose of participating in a pain rehabilitation program would be covered as reasonable and necessary to the treatment of a patient's condition where the pain is attributable to a physical cause, the usual methods of treatment have not been successful in alleviating it, and a significant loss of ability to function independently has resulted from the pain. Chronic pain patients often have psychological problems which accompany or stem from the physical pain and it is appropriate to include psychological treatment in the multidisciplinary approach. However, patients whose pain symptoms result from a mental condition, rather than from any physical cause, generally cannot be succesfully treated in a pain rehabilitation program.

100-3, 10.4

NCD for Outpatient Hospital Pain Rehabilitation Programs (10.4)

Coverage of services furnished under outpatient hospital pain rehabilitation programs, including services furnished in group settings under individualized plans of treatment, is available if the patient's pain is attributable to a physical cause, the usual methods of treatment have not been successful in alleviating it, and a significant loss of ability by the patient to function independently has resulted from the pain. If a patient meets these conditions and the program provides services of the types discussed in 10.3 of the NCD Manual, the services provided under the program may be covered. Noncovered services (e.g., vocational counseling, meals for outpatients, or acupuncture) continue to be excluded from coverage, and intermediaries would not be precluded from finding, in the case of particular patients, that the pain rehabilitation program is not reasonable and necessary under 1862(a)(1) of the Act for the treatment of their conditions.

100-3, 10.5

NCD for Autogenous Epidural Blood Graft (10.5)

Autogenous epidural blood grafts are considered a safe and effective remedy for severe headaches that may occur after performance of spinal anesthesia, spinal taps or myelograms, and are covered.

100-3, 10.6

The use of general or monitored anesthesia during transvenous cardiac pacemaker surgery may be reasonable and necessary and therefore covered under Medicare only if adequate documentation of medical necessity is provided on a case-by-case basis. The contractor obtains advice from its medical consultants or from appropriate specialty physicians or groups in its locality regarding the adequacy of documentation before deciding whether a particular claim should be covered.

A second type of pacemaker surgery that is sometimes performed involves the use of the thoracic method of implantation which requires open surgery. Where the thoracic method is employed, general anesthesia is always used and should not require special medical documentation.

100-3, 20.1

NCD for Vertebral Artery Surgery (20.1)

- These procedures can be medically reasonable and necessary, but only if each of the following conditions is met:
- Symptoms of vertebral artery obstruction exist;
- Other causes have been considered and ruled out;
- There is radiographic evidence of a valid vertebral artery obstruction; and
- Contraindications to the procedure do not exist, such as coexistent obstructions of multiple cerebral vessels.

Angiograms documenting a valid obstruction should show not only the aortic arch with the vessels off the arch, but also show the vessels in the neck and head (providing biplane views of the carotid and vertebral vascular system). In addition, serial views are needed to diagnose "subclavian steal," the condition in which subclavian artery obstruction causes the symptoms of vertebral artery obstruction. Because the symptoms are not specific for vertebral artery

obstruction, other causes must be considered. In addition to vertebral artery obstruction, the differential diagnosis should include various degenerative disorders of the brain, orthostatic hypotension, acoustic neuroma, labyrinthitis, diabetes mellitus and hypoglycemia related disorders.

Obstructions which can cause symptoms of blocked vertebral artery blood flow and which can be documented by an angiogram include:

- Intravascular obstructions - arteriosclerotic lesions within the vertebral artery or in other arteries.
- Extravascular obstructions.
- Bony tissue or osteophytes, located laterally in the C6(C7)-C2 cervical vertebral area course of the vertebral artery, most commonly at C5 -C6.
- Anatomical variations - Anomalous location of the origin of the vertebral artery, a congenital aberration, and tortuosity and kinks of the vertebral artery.
- Fibrous tissue - Tissue changed as a result of manipulation of the neck for neck pain or injury associated with hematoma; external bands, tendinous slings, and fibrous bands.

The most controversial obstructions include vertebral artery tortuosity and kinks and connective tissue along the course of the vertebral artery, and variously called external bands, tendinous slings and fibrous bands. In the absence of symptoms of vertebral artery obstruction, vascular surgeons feel such abnormalities are insignificant. Vascular surgery experts, however, agree that these abnormalities in very rare cases do cause symptoms of vertebral artery obstruction and do necessitate surgical correction.

Vertebral artery construction and vertebral artery surgery are phrases which most physicians interpret to include only surgical cleaning (endarterectomy) and bypass (resection) procedures. However, some physicians who use these terms mean all operative manipulations which remove vertebral artery blood flow obstructions. Also, some physicians use general terms of vascular surgery, such as endarterectomy when vertebral artery related surgery is performed. Use of the above terminology specifies neither the surgical procedure performed nor its relationship to the vertebral artery. Therefore, in developing claims for this type of procedure, require specific identification of the obstruction in question and the surgical procedure performed. Also, in view of the specific coverage criteria given, develop all claims for vertebral artery surgery on a case-by-case basis.

Make payment for a surgical procedure listed above if: (1) it is reasonable and necessary for the individual patient to have the surgery performed to remove or relieve an obstruction to vertebral artery flow, and (2) the four conditions noted are met.

In all other cases, these procedures cannot be considered reasonable and necessary within the meaning of Sec.1862(a)(1) of the Act and are not reimbursable under the program.

100-3, 20.3

NCD for Thoracic Duct Drainage (TDD) in Renal Transplants (20.3)

TDD is performed on an inpatient basis, and the inpatient stay is covered for patients admitted for treatment in advance of a kidney transplant as well as for those receiving it post-transplant. TDD is a covered technique when furnished to a kidney transplant recipient or an individual approved to receive kidney transplantation in a hospital approved to perform kidney transplantation.

100-3, 20.4

NCD for Implantable Automatic Defibrillators (20.4)

A. General

The implantable automatic defibrillator is an electronic device designed to detect and treat life-threatening tachyarrhythmias. The device consists of a pulse generator and electrodes for sensing and defibrillating.

B. Covered Indications

1. Documented episode of cardiac arrest due to ventricular fibrillation (VF), not due to a transient or reversible cause (effective July 1, 1991).

2. Documented sustained ventricular tachyarrhythmia (VT), either spontaneous or induced by an electrophysiology (EP) study, not associated with an acute myocardial infarction (MI) and not due to a transient or reversible cause (effective July 1, 1999).

3. Documented familial or inherited conditions with a high risk of life-threatening VT, such as long QT syndrome or hypertrophic cardiomyopathy (effective July 1, 1999).

   Additional indications effective for services performed on or after October 1, 2003:

4. Coronary artery disease with a documented prior MI, a measured left ventricular ejection fraction (LVEF) <0.35, and inducible, sustained VT or VF at EP study. (The MI must have occurred more than 40 days prior to defibrillator insertion. The EP test must be performed more than 4 weeks after the qualifying MI.)

5. Documented prior MI and a measured LVEF <0.30 and a QRS duration of >120 milliseconds (the QRS restriction does not apply to services performed on or after January 27, 2005) . Patients must not have:

   a. New York Heart Association (NYHC) classification IV;

   b. Cardiogenic shock or symptomatic hypotension while in a stable baseline rhythm;

   c. Had a coronary artery bypass graft (CABG) or percutaneous transluminal coronary angioplasty (PTCA) within past 3 months;

   d. Had an enzyme positive MI within past month (Effective for services on or after January 27, 2005, patients must not have an acute MI in the past 40 days);

   e. Clinical symptoms or findings that would make them a candidate for coronary revascularization; or

f. Any disease, other than cardiac disease (e.g., cancer, uremia, liver failure), associated with a likelihood of survival less than 1 year.

Additional indications effective for services performed on or after January 27, 2005:

6. Patients with ischemic dilated cardiomyopathy (IDCM), documented prior MI, NYHA Class II and III heart failure, and measured LVEF <35%;

7. Patients with non-ischemic dilated cardiomyopathy (NIDCM) >9 months, NYHA Class II and III heart failure, and measured LVEF <35%;

8. Patients who meet all current Centers for Medicare & Medicaid Services (CMS) coverage requirements for a cardiac resynchronization therapy (CRT) device and have NYHA Class IV heart failure;

All indications must meet the following criteria:

a. Patients must not have irreversible brain damage from preexisting cerebral disease;

b. MIs must be documented and defined according to the consensus document of the Joint European Society of Cardiology/American College of Cardiology Committee for the Redefinition of Myocardial Infarction[1];

Either one of the following criteria satisfies the diagnosis for an acute, evolving or recent MI:

1. Typical rise and gradual fall (troponin) or more rapid rise and fall (CK-MB) of biochemical markers of myocardial necrosis with at least one of the following:

    a. ischemic symptoms;

    b. development of pathologic Q waves on the ECG;

    c. ECG changes indicative of ischemia (ST segment elevation or depression); or

    d. coronary artery intervention (e.g., coronary angioplasty).

2. Pathologic findings of an acute MI.

    Criteria for established MI.

    Any one of the following criteria satisfies the diagnosis for established MI:

    Indications 3-8 (primary prevention of sudden cardiac death) must also meet the following critera:

    a. Patients must be able to give informed consent;

    b. Patients must have:

    • Cardiogenic shock or symptomatic hypotension while in a stable baseline rhythm;

    • Had a CABG or PTCA within the past 3 months;

    • Had an acute MI within the past 40 days;

    • Clinical symptoms or findings that would make them a candidate for coronary revascularization;

    • Any disease, other than cardiac disease (e.g., cancer, uremia, liver failure), associated with a likelihood of survival less than 1 year;

    c. Ejection fractions must be measured by angiography, radionuclide scanning, or echocardiography;

    d. The beneficiary receiving the defibrillator implantation for primary prevention is enrolled in either a Food and Drug Administration (FDA)-approved category B investigational device exemption (IDE) clinical trial (42 CFR Sec.405.201), a trial under the CMS Clinical Trial Policy (National Coverage Determination (NCD) Manual Sec.310.1) or a qualifying data collection system including approved clinical trials and registries. Initially, an implantable cardiac defibrillator (ICD) database will be maintained using a data submission mechanism that is already in use by Medicare participating hospitals to submit data to the Iowa Foundation for Medical Care (IFMC)--a Quality Improvement Organization (QIO) contractor--for determination of reasonable and necessary and quality improvement. Initial hypothesis and data elements are specified in this decision (Appendix VI) and are the minimum necessary to ensure that the device is reasonable and necessary. Data collection will be completed using the ICDA (ICD Abstraction Tool) and transmitted via QNet (Quality Network Exchange) to the IFMC who will collect and maintain the database. Additional stakeholder-developed data collection systems to augment or replace the initial QNet system, addressing at a minimum the hypotheses specified in this decision, must meet the following basic criteria:

    • Written protocol on file;

        1) Development of new pathologic Q waves on serial ECGs. The patient may or may not remember previous symptoms. Biochemical markers of myocardial necrosis may have normalized, depending on the length of time that has passed since the infarct developed.

        2) Pathologic findings of a healed or healing MI.

            • Institutional review board review and approval;

            • Scientific review and approval by two or more qualified individuals who are not part of the research team;

            • Certification that investigators have not been disqualified.

e. For purposes of this coverage decision, CMS will determine whether specific registries or clinical trials meet these criteria.

f. Providers must be able to justify the medical necessity of devices other than single lead devices. This justification should be available in the patient's medical record.

9. Patients with NIDCM >3 months, NYHA Class II or III heart failure, and measured LVEF = 35%, only if the following additional criteria are also met:

    a. Patients must be able to give informed consent;

    b. Patients must not have:

    • Cardiogenic shock or symptomatic hypotension while in a stable baseline rhythm;

    • Had a CABG or PTCA within the past 3 months;

    • Had an acute MI within the past 40 days;

    • Clinical symptoms or findings that would make them a candidate for coronary revascularization;

    • Irreversible brain damage from preexisting cerebral disease;

    • Any disease, other than cardiac disease (e.g. cancer, uremia, liver failure), associated with a likelihood of survival less than 1 year;

    c. Ejection fractions must be measured by angiography, radionuclide scanning, or echocardiography;

    d. MIs must be documented and defined according to the consensus document of the Joint European Society of Cardiology/American College of Cardiology Committee for the Redefinition of Myocardial Infarction[2]

    e. The beneficiary receiving the defibrillator implantation for this indication is enrolled in either an FDA-approved category B IDE clinical trial (42 CFR §405.201), a trial under the CMS Clinical Trial Policy (NCD Manual §310.1), or a prospective data collection system meeting the following basic criteria:

    • Written protocol on file;

    • Institutional Review Board review and approval;

    • Scientific review and approval by two or more qualified individuals who are not part of the research team;

    • Certification that investigators have not been disqualified.

For purposes of this coverage decision, CMS will determine whether specific registries or clinical trials meet these criteria.

d. Providers must be able to justify the medical necessity of devices other than single lead devices. This justification should be available in the patient's medical record.

C. Other Indications
All other indications for implantable automatic defibrillators not currently covered in accordance with this decision will continue to be covered under Category B IDE trials (42 CFR §405.201) and the CMS routine clinical trials policy (NCD §310.1).

(This NCD last reviewed February 2005.)

100-3, 20.5
NCD for Extracorporeal Immunoadsorption (ECI) Using Protein A Columns (20.5)
For claims with dates of service on or after January 1, 2001, Medicare covers the use of Protein A columns for the treatment of ITP. In addition, Medicare will cover Protein A columns for the treatment of rheumatoid arthritis (RA) under the following conditions:

• Patient has severe RA. Patient disease is active, having >5 swollen joints, >20 tender joints, and morning stiffness >60 minutes.

• Patient has failed an adequate course of a minimum of 3 Disease Modifying Anti-Rheumatic Drugs (DMARDs). Failure does not include intolerance.

Other uses of these columns are currently considered to be investigational and, therefore, not reasonable and necessary under the Medicare law. (See Sec.1862(a)(1)(A) of the Act.)

100-3, 20.6
NCD for Transmyocardial Revascularization (TMR) (20.6)
CMS therefore covers TMR as a late or last resort for patients with severe (Canadian Cardiovascular Society classification Classes III or IV) angina (stable or unstable), which has been found refractory to standard medical therapy, including drug therapy at the maximum tolerated or maximum safe dosages. In addition, the angina symptoms must be caused by areas of the heart not amenable to surgical therapies such as percutaneous transluminal coronary angioplasty, stenting, coronary atherectomy or coronary bypass. Coverage is further limited to those uses of the laser used in performing the procedure which have been approved by the Food and Drug Administration for the purpose for which they are being used.

Patients would have to meet the following additional selection guidelines:

• An ejection fraction of 25% or greater;

• Have areas of viable ischemic myocardium (as demonstrated by diagnostic study) which are not capable of being revascularized by direct coronary intervention; and

• Have been stabilized, or have had maximal efforts to stabilize acute conditions such as severe ventricular arrhythmias, decompensated congestive heart failure or acute myocardial infarction.

---

1. Alpert and Thygesen et al., 2000. Criteria for acute, evolving or recent MI.

2. Ibid.

Coverage is limited to physicians who have been properly trained in the procedure. Providers of this service is performed must also document that all ancillary personnel, including physicians, nurses, operating room personnel and technicians, are trained in the procedure and the proper use of the equipment involved. Coverage is further limited to providers which have dedicated cardiac care units, including the diagnostic and support services necessary for care of patients undergoing this therapy. In addition, these providers must conform to the standards for laser safety set by the American National Standards Institute, ANSIZ1363.

100-3, 20.7

NCD for Percutaneous Transluminal Angioplasty (PTA) (20.7)

A. General

This procedure involves inserting a balloon catheter into a narrow or occluded blood vessel to recanalize and dilate the vessel by inflating the balloon. The objective of PTA is to improve the blood flow through the diseased segment of a vessel so that vessel patency is increased and embolization is decreased. With the development and use of balloon angioplasty for treatment of atherosclerotic and other vascular stenoses, PTA (with and without the placement of a stent) is a widely used technique for dilating lesions of peripheral, renal, and coronary arteries.

Indications and Limitations of Coverage

B. Nationally Covered Indications

The PTA is covered when used under the following conditions:

1. Treatment of Atherosclerotic Obstructive Lesions

    In the lower extremities, i.e., the iliac, femoral, and popliteal arteries, or in the upper extremities, i.e., the innominate, subclavian, axillary, and brachial arteries. The upper extremities do not include head or neck vessels.

    Of a single coronary artery for patients for whom the likely alternative treatment is coronary bypass surgery and who exhibit the following characteristics:

    *   Angina refractory to optimal medical management;

    *   Objective evidence of myocardial ischemia; and

    *   Lesions amenable to angioplasty.

    Of the renal arteries for patients in whom there is an inadequate response to a thorough medical management of symptoms and for whom surgery is the likely alternative. The PTA for this group of patients is an alternative to surgery, not simply an addition to medical management.

    Of arteriovenous dialysis fistulas and grafts when performed through either a venous or arterial approach.

2. Concurrent with Carotid Stent Placement Food and Drug Administration(FDA)-Approved Category B Investigational Device Exemption(IDE) Clinical Trials

    Effective July 1, 2001, Medicare covers PTA of the carotid artery concurrent with carotid stent placement when furnished in accordance with the Food and Drug Administration (FDA)-approved protocols governing Category B Investigational Device Exemption (IDE) clinical trials. The PTA of the carotid artery, when provided solely for the purpose of carotid artery dilation concurrent with carotid stent placement, is considered to be a reasonable and necessary service only when provided in the context of such a clinical trial.

3. Concurrent With Carotid Stent Placement in FDA-Approved Post Approval Studies

    Effective October 12, 2004, Medicare covers PTA of the carotid artery concurrent with the placement of an FDA-approved carotid stent for an FDA-approved indication when furnished in accordance with FDA-approved protocols governing post-approval studies. CMS determines that coverage of PTA of the carotid artery is reasonable and necessary under these circumstances.

4. Concurrent With Carotid Stent Placement in Patients at High Risk for Carotid Endarterectomy (CEA)

    Effective March 17, 2005, Medicare covers PTA of the carotid artery concurrent with the placement of an FDA-approved carotid stent with embolic protection for the following:

    *   Patients who are at high risk for CEA and who also have symptomatic carotid artery stenosis >70 percent. Coverage is limited to procedures performed using FDA-approved carotid artery stenting systems and embolic protection devices;

    *   Patients who are at high risk for CEA and have symptomatic carotid artery stenosis between 50 percent and 70 percent, in accordance with the Category B IDE clinical trials regulation (42 CFR 405.201), as a routine cost under the clinical trials policy (Medicare NCD Manual 310.1), or in accordance with the NCD on carotid artery stenting (CAS) post-approval studies (Medicare NCD Manual 20.7);

    *   Patients who are at high risk for CEA and have asymptomatic carotid artery stenosis >80 percent, in accordance with the Category B IDE clinical trials regulation (42 CFR 405.201), as a routine cost under the clinical trials policy (Medicare NCD Manual 310.1), or in accordance with the NCD on CAS post-approval studies (Medicare NCD Manual 20.7).

    Coverage is limited to procedures performed using FDA approved carotid artery stents and embolic protection devices.

    The use of a distal embolic protection device is required. If deployment of the distal embolic protection device is not technically possible, then the procedure should be aborted given the risks of CAS without distal embolic protection.

    Patients at high risk for CEA are defined as having significant comorbidities and/or anatomic risk factors (i.e., recurrent stenosis and/or previous radical neck dissection), and would be poor candidates for CEA. Significant comorbid conditions include but are not limited to:

    *   Congestive heart failure (CHF) class III/IV;

    *   Left ventricular ejection fraction (LVEF) < 30 percent;

    *   Unstable angina;

    *   Contralateral carotid occlusion;

    *   Recent myocardial infarction (MI);

    *   Previous CEA with recurrent stenosis;

    *   Prior radiation treatment to the neck; and

    *   Other conditions that were used to determine patients at high risk for CEA in the prior carotid artery stenting trials and studies, such as ARCHER, CABERNET, SAPPHIRE, BEACH, and MAVERIC II.

    Symptoms of carotid artery stenosis include carotid transient ischemic attack (distinct focal neurological dysfunction persisting less than 24 hours), focal cerebral ischemia producing a non-disabling stroke (modified Rankin scale >3) shall be excluded from coverage.

    The determination that a patient is at high risk for CEA and the patient's symptoms of carotid artery stenosis shall be available in the patient medical records prior to performing any procedure.

    The degree of carotid artery stenosis shall be measured by duplex Doppler ultrasound or carotid artery angiography and recorded in the patient's medical records. If the stenosis is measured by ultrasound prior to the procedure, then the degree of stenosis must be

    confirmed by angiography at the start of the procedure. If the stenosis is determined to be less than 70 percent by angiography, then CAS should not proceed.

    In addition, CMS has determined that CAS with embolic protection is reasonable and necessary only if performed in facilities that have been determined to be competent in performing the evaluation, procedure and follow-up necessary to ensure optimal patient outcomes. Standards to determine competency include specific physician training standards, facility support requirements and data collection to evaluate outcomes during a required reevaluation.

    The CMS has created a list of minimum standards modeled in part on professional society statements on competency. All facilities must at least meet CMS's standards in order to receive coverage for carotid artery stenting for high-risk patients.

    *   Facilities must have necessary imaging equipment, device inventory, staffing, and infrastructure to support a dedicated carotid stent program. Specifically, high-quality x-ray imaging equipment is a critical component of any carotid interventional suite, such as high-resolution digital imaging systems with the capability of subtraction, magnification, road mapping, and orthogonal angulation.

    *   Advanced physiologic monitoring must be available in the interventional suite. This includes real time and archived physiologic, hemodynamic, and cardiac rhythm monitoring equipment, as well as support staff who are capable of interpreting the findings and responding appropriately.

    *   Emergency management equipment and systems must be readily available in the interventional suite such as resuscitation equipment, a defibrillator, vasoactive and antiarrhythmic drugs, endotracheal intubation capability, and anesthesia support.

    *   Each institution shall have a clearly delineated program for granting carotid stent privileges and for monitoring the quality of the individual interventionalists and the program as a whole. The oversight committee for this program shall be empowered to identify the minimum case volume for an operator to maintain privileges, as well as the (risk-adjusted) threshold for complications that the institution will allow before suspending privileges or instituting measures for remediation. Committees are encouraged to apply published standards from national specialty societies recognized by the American Board of Medical Specialties to determine appropriate physician qualifications. Examples of standards and clinical competence guidelines include those published in the December 2004 edition of the American Journal of Neuroradiology, and those published in the August 18, 2004, Journal of the American College of Cardiology.

    *   To continue to receive Medicare payment for CAS under this decision, the facility or a contractor to the facility must collect data on all carotid artery stenting procedures done at that particular facility. This data must be analyzed routinely to ensure patient safety. This data must be made available to CMS upon request. The interval for data analysis will be determined by the facility but shall not be less frequent than every 6 months.

    Since there currently is no recognized entity that evaluates CAS facilities, CMS has established a mechanism for evaluating facilities. Facilities must provide written documentation to CMS that the facility meets one of the following:

    1. The facility was an FDA approved site that enrolled patients in prior CAS IDE trials, such as SAPPHIRE, and ARCHER;

    2. The facility is an FDA approved site that is participating and enrolling patients in ongoing CAS IDE trials, such as CREST;

    3. The facility is an FDA approved site for one or more FDA post approval studies; or

    4. The facility has provided a written affidavit to CMS attesting that the facility has met the minimum facility standards. This should be sent to:

        Director, Coverage and Analysis Group
        7500 Security Boulevard, Mailstop C1-09-06
        Baltimore, MD 21244

    The letter must include the following information:

    *   Facility's name and complete address;

    *   Facility's national provider identifier (formerly referred to as the Medicare provider number);

    *   Point-of-contact for questions with telephone number;

    *   Discussion of how each standard has been met by the hospital;

- Mechanism of data collection of CAS procedures; and

- Signature of a senior facility administrative official.

A list of certified facilities will be made available and viewable at: http://www.cms.hhs.gov/coverage/carotid-stent-facilities.asp. In addition, CMS will publish a list of approved facilities in the Federal Register.

Facilities must recertify every two (2) years in order to maintain Medicare coverage of CAS procedures. Recertification will occur when the facility documents that and describes how it continues to meet the CMS standards.

The process for recertification is as follows:

1. At 23 months after initial certification:

    - Submission of a letter to CMS stating how the facility continues to meet the minimum facility standards as listed above.

2   At 27 months after initial certification:

    - Submission of required data elements for all CAS procedures performed on patients during the previous two (2) years of certification.

    - Data elements:

    a. Patients' Medicare identification number if a Medicare beneficiary;

    b. Patients' date of birth;

    c. Date of procedure;

    d. Does the patient meet high surgical risk criteria (defined below)?

        - Age >80;

        - Recent (< 30 days) Myocardial Infarction (MI);

        - Left Ventricle Ejection Fraction (LVEF) < 30 percent;

        - Contralateral carotid occlusion;

        - New York Heart Association (NYHA) Class III or IV congestive heart failure;

        - Unstable angina: Canadian Cardiovascular Society (CCS) Class III/IV;

        - Renal failure: end stage renal disease on dialysis;

        - Common Carotid Artery (CCA) lesion(s) below clavicle;

        - Severe chronic lung disease;

        - Previous neck radiation;

        - High cervical Internal Carotid Artery (ICA) lesion(s);

        - Restenosis of prior carotid endarterectomy (CEA);

        - Tracheostomy;

        - Contralateral laryngeal nerve palsy.

    e. Is the patient symptomatic (defined below)?

        - Carotid Transient Ischemic Attack (TIA) persisting less than 24 hours;

        - Non-disabling stroke: Modified Rankin Scale

        - Transient monocular blindness:amaurosis fugax.

    f. Modified Rankin Scale score if the patient experienced a stroke.

    g. Percent stenosis of stented lesion(s) by angiography.

    h. Was embolic protection used?

    i. Were there any complications during hospitalization (defined below)?

        - All stroke: an ischemic neurologic deficit that persisted more than 24 hours;

        - MI;

        - All death.

Recertification is effective for two (2) additional years during which facilities will be required to submit the requested data every April 1 and October 1.

The CMS will consider the approval of national carotid artery stenting registries that provide CMS with a comprehensive overview of the registry and its capabilities, and the manner in which the registry meets CMS data collection and evaluation requirements. Specific standards for CMS approval are listed below. Facilities enrolled in a CMS approved national carotid artery stenting registry will automatically meet the data collection standards required for initial and continued facility certification. Hospitals' contracts with an approved registry may include authority for the registry to submit required data to CMS for the hospital. A list of approved registries will be available on the CMS Coverage Web Site.

National Registries

As noted above, CMS will approve national registries developed by professional societies and other organizations and allow these entities to collect and submit data to CMS on behalf of participating facilities to meet facility certification and recertification requirements. To be eligible to perform these functions and become a CMS approved registry, the national registry, at a minimum, must be able to:

1. Enroll facilities in every U.S. state and territory;

2. Assure data confidentiality and compliance with HIPPA;

3. Collect the required CMS data elements as listed in the above section;

4. Assure data quality and data completeness;

5. Address deficiencies in the facility data collection, quality, and submission;

6. Validate the data submitted by facilities as needed;

7. Track long term outcomes such as stroke and death;

8. Conduct data analyses and produce facility specific data reports and summaries;

9. Submit data to CMS on behalf of the individual facilities; and

10. Provide quarterly reports to CMS on facilities that do not meet or no longer meet the CMS facility certification and recertification requirements pertaining to data collection and analysis.

Registries wishing to receive this designation from CMS must submit evidence that they meet or exceed our standards. Though the registry requirements pertain to CAS, CMS strongly encourages all national registries to establish a similar mechanism to collect

comparable data on CEA. Having both CAS and CEA data will help answer questions about carotid revascularization, in general, in the Medicare population.

The CAS for patients who are not at high risk for CEA remains covered only in FDA-approved Category B IDE clinical trials under 42 CFR 405.201.

The CMS has determined that PTA of the carotid artery concurrent with the placement of an FDA-approved carotid stent is not reasonable and necessary for all other patients.

Concurrent with Intracranial Stent Placement in FDA-Approved Category B IDE Clinical Trials

Effective November 6, 2006, Medicare covers PTA and stenting of intracranial arteries for the treatment of cerebral artery stenosis >50 percent in patients with intracranial atherosclerotic disease when furnished in accordance with the FDA-approved protocols governing Category B IDE clinical trials. CMS determines that coverage of intracranial PTA and stenting is reasonable and necessary under these circumstances.

C. Nationally Non-covered Indications

All other indications for PTA with or without stenting to treat obstructive lesions of the vertebral and cerebral arteries remain non-covered. The safety and efficacy of these procedures are not established.

All other indications for PTA without stenting for which CMS has not specifically indicated coverage remain non-covered.

D. Other

Coverage of PTA with stenting not specifically addressed or discussed in this NCD is at local Medicare contractor discretion.

(This NCD last reviewed May 2008.)

100-3, 20.8

NCD for Cardiac Pacemakers (20.8)

Cardiac pacemakers are self-contained, battery-operated units that send electrical stimulation to the heart. They are generally implanted to alleviate symptoms of decreased cardiac output related to abnormal heart rate and/or rhythm. Pacemakers are generally used for persistent symptomatic second- or third-degree atrioventricular (AV) block and symptomatic sinus bradycardia.

Cardiac pacemakers are covered as prosthetic devices under the Medicare program, subject to the following conditions and limitations. While cardiac pacemakers have been covered under Medicare for many years, there were no specific guidelines for their use other than the general Medicare requirement that covered services be reasonable and necessary for the treatment of the condition. Services rendered for cardiac pacing on or after the effective dates of this instruction are subject to these guidelines, which are based on certain assumptions regarding the clinical goals of cardiac pacing. While some uses of pacemakers are relatively certain or unambiguous, many other uses require considerable expertise and judgment.

Consequently, the medical necessity for permanent cardiac pacing must be viewed in the context of overall patient management. The appropriateness of such pacing may be conditional on other diagnostic or therapeutic modalities having been undertaken. Although significant complications and adverse side effects of pacemaker use are relatively rare, they cannot be ignored when considering the use of pacemakers for dubious medical conditions, or marginal clinical benefit.

These guidelines represent current concepts regarding medical circumstances in which permanent cardiac pacing may be appropriate or necessary. As with other areas of medicine, advances in knowledge and techniques in cardiology are expected. Consequently, judgments about the medical necessity and acceptability of new uses for cardiac pacing in new classes of patients may change as more more conclusive evidence becomes available. This instruction applies only to permanent cardiac pacemakers, and does not address the use of temporary, non-implanted pacemakers.

The two groups of conditions outlined below deal with the necessity for cardiac pacing for patients in general. These are intended as guidelines in assessing the medical necessity for pacing therapies, taking into account the particular circumstances in each case. However, as a general rule, the two groups of current medical concepts may be viewed as representing:

Group I: Single-Chamber Cardiac Pacemakers – a) conditions under which single chamber pacemaker claims may be considered covered without further claims development; and b) conditions under which single-chamber pacemaker claims would be denied unless further claims development shows that they fall into the covered category, or special medical circumstances exist of the sufficiency to convince the contractor that the claim should be paid.

Group II: Dual-Chamber Cardiac Pacemakers - a) conditions under which dual-chamber pacemaker claims may be considered covered without further claims development, and b) conditions under which dual-chamber pacemaker claims would be denied unless further claims development shows that they fall into the covered categories for single- and dual-chamber pacemakers, or special medical circumstances exist sufficient to convince the contractor that the claim should be paid.

The CMS opened the NCD on Cardiac Pacemakers to afford the public an opportunity to comment on the proposal to revise the language contained in the instruction. The revisions transfer the focus of the NCD from the actual pacemaker implantation procedure itself to the reasonable and necessary medical indications that justify cardiac

pacing. This is consistent with our findings that pacemaker implantation is no longer considered routinely harmful or an experimental procedure.

Group I: Single-Chamber Cardiac Pacemakers (Effective March 16, 1983)

A. Nationally Covered Indications

Conditions under which cardiac pacing is generally considered acceptable or necessary, provided that the conditions are chronic or recurrent and not due to transient causes such as acute myocardial infarction, drug toxicity, or electrolyte imbalance. (In cases where there is a rhythm disturbance, if the rhythm disturbance is chronic or recurrent, a single episode of a symptom such as syncope or seizure is adequate to establish medical necessity.)

1. Acquired complete (also referred to as third-degree) AV heart block.

2. Congenital complete heart block with severe bradycardia (in relation to age), or significant physiological deficits or significant symptoms due to the bradycardia.

3. Second-degree AV heart block of Type II (i.e., no progressive prolongation of P-R interval prior to each blocked beat. P-R interval indicates the time taken for an impulse to travel from the atria to the ventricles on an electrocardiogram).

4. Second-degree AV heart block of Type I (i.e., progressive prolongation of P-R interval prior to each blocked beat) with significant symptoms due to hemodynamic instability associated with the heart block.

5. Sinus bradycardia associated with major symptoms (e.g., syncope, seizures, congestive heart failure); or substantial sinus bradycardia (heart rate less than 50) associated with dizziness or confusion. The correlation between symptoms and bradycardia must be documented, or the symptoms must be clearly attributable to the bradycardia rather than to some other cause.

6. In selected and few patients, sinus bradycardia of lesser severity (heart rate 50-59) with dizziness or confusion. The correlation between symptoms and bradycardia must be documented, or the symptoms must be clearly attributable to the bradycardia rather than to some other cause.

7. Sinus bradycardia is the consequence of long-term necessary drug treatment for which there is no acceptable alternative when accompanied by significant symptoms (e.g., syncope, seizures, congestive heart failure, dizziness or confusion). The correlation between symptoms and bradycardia must be documented, or the symptoms must be clearly attributable to the bradycardia rather than to some other cause.

8. Sinus node dysfunction with or without tachyarrhythmias or AV conduction block (i.e., the bradycardia-tachycardia syndrome, sino-atrial block, sinus arrest) when accompanied by significant symptoms (e.g., syncope, seizures, congestive heart failure, dizziness or confusion).

9. Sinus node dysfunction with or without symptoms when there are potentially life-threatening ventricular arrhythmias or tachycardia secondary to the bradycardia (e.g., numerous premature ventricular contractions, couplets, runs of premature ventricular contractions, or ventricular tachycardia).

10. Bradycardia associated with supraventricular tachycardia (e.g., atrial fibrillation, atrial flutter, or paroxysmal atrial tachycardia) with high-degree AV block which is unresponsive to appropriate pharmacological management and when the bradycardia is associated with significant symptoms (e.g., syncope, seizures, congestive heart failure, dizziness or confusion).

11. The occasional patient with hypersensitive carotid sinus syndrome with syncope due to bradycardia and unresponsive to prophylactic medical measures.

12. Bifascicular or trifascicular block accompanied by syncope which is attributed to transient complete heart block after other plausible causes of syncope have been reasonably excluded.

13. Prophylactic pacemaker use following recovery from acute myocardial infarction during which there was temporary complete (third-degree) and/or Mobitz Type II second-degree AV block in association with bundle branch block.

14. In patients with recurrent and refractory ventricular tachycardia, "overdrive pacing" (pacing above the basal rate) to prevent ventricular tachycardia.

    (Effective May 9, 1985)

15. Second-degree AV heart block of Type I with the QRS complexes prolonged.

B. Nationally Noncovered Indications

Conditions which, although used by some physicians as a basis for permanent cardiac pacing, are considered unsupported by adequate evidence of benefit and therefore should not generally be considered appropriate uses for single-chamber pacemakers in the absence of the above indications. Contractors should review claims for pacemakers with these indications to determine the need for further claims development prior to denying the claim, since additional claims development may be required. The object of such further development is to establish whether the particular claim actually meets the conditions in a) above. In claims where this is not the case or where such an event appears unlikely, the contractor may deny the claim

1   Syncope of undetermined cause.

2. Sinus bradycardia without significant symptoms.

3. Sino-atrial block or sinus arrest without significant symptoms.

4. Prolonged P-R intervals with atrial fibrillation (without third-degree AV block) or with other causes of transient ventricular pause.

5. Bradycardia during sleep.

6. Right bundle branch block with left axis deviation (and other forms of fascicular or bundle branch block) without syncope or other symptoms of intermittent AV block).

7. Asymptomatic second-degree AV block of Type I unless the QRS complexes are prolonged or electrophysiological studies have demonstrated that the block is at or beyond the level of the His bundle (a component of the electrical conduction system of the heart).

    Effective October 1, 2001

8. Asymptomatic bradycardia in post-mycardial infarction patients about to initiate long-term beta-blocker drug therapy.

C. Other

All other indications for single-chamber cardiac pacing for which CMS has not specifically indicated coverage remain nationally noncovered, except for Category B Investigational Device Exemption (IDE) clinical trials, or as routine costs of single-chamber cardiac pacing associated with clinical trials, in accordance with section 310.1 of the NCD Manual.

Group II: Dual-Chamber Cardiac Pacemakers – (Effective May 9, 1985)

A. Nationally Covered Indications

Conditions under dual-chamber cardiac pacing are considered acceptable or necessary in the general medical community unless conditions 1 and 2 under Group II. B., are present:

1. Patients in who single-chamber (ventricular pacing) at the time of pacemaker insertion elicits a definite drop in blood pressure, retrograde conduction, or discomfort.

2. Patients in whom the pacemaker syndrome (atrial ventricular asynchrony), with significant symptoms, has already been experienced with a pacemaker that is being replaced.

3. Patients in whom even a relatively small increase in cardiac efficiency will importantly improve the quality of life, e.g., patients with congestive heart failure despite adequate other medical measures.

4. Patients in whom the pacemaker syndrome can be anticipated, e.g., in young and active people, etc.

Dual-chamber pacemakers may also be covered for the conditions, as listed in Group I. A., if the medical necessity is sufficiently justified through adequate claims development. Expert physicians differ in their judgments about what constitutes appropriate criteria for dual-chamber pacemaker use. The judgment that such a pacemaker is warranted in the patient meeting accepted criteria must be based upon the individual needs and characteristics of that patient, weighing the magnitude and likelihood of anticipated benefits against the magnitude and likelihood of disadvantages to the patient.

B. Nationally Noncovered Indications

Whenever the following conditions (which represent overriding contraindications) are present, dual-chamber pacemakers are not covered:

1. Ineffective atrial contractions (e.g., chronic atrial fibrillation or flutter, or giant left atrium).

2. Frequent or persistent supraventricular tachycardias, except where the pacemaker is specifically for the control of the tachycardia.

3. A clinical condition in which pacing takes place only intermittently and briefly, and which is not associated with a reasonable likelihood that pacing needs will become prolonged, e.g., the occasional patient with hypersensitive carotid sinus syndrome with syncope due to bradycardia and unresponsive to prophylactic medical measures.

4. Prophylactic pacemaker use following recovery from acute myocardial infarction during which there was temporary complete (third-degree) and/or Type II second-degree AV block in association with bundle branch block.

C. Other

All other indications for dual-chamber cardiac pacing for which CMS has not specifically indicated coverage remain nationally noncovered, except for Category B IDE clinical trials, or as routine costs of dual-chamber cardiac pacing associated with clinical trials, in accordance with section 310.1 of the NCD Manual.

(This NCD last reviewed June 2004.)

100-3, 20.8.1

NCD for Cardiac Pacemaker Evaluation Services (20.8.1)

Medicare covers a variety of services for the post-implant follow-up and evaluation of implanted cardiac pacemakers. The following guidelines are designed to assist contractors in identifying and processing claims for such services.

NOTE: These new guidelines are limited to lithium battery-powered pacemakers, because mercury-zinc battery-powered pacemakers are no longer being manufactured and virtually all have been replaced by lithium units. Contractors still receiving claims for monitoring such units should continue to apply the guidelines published in 1980 to those units until they are replaced.

One fact of which contractors should be aware is that many dual-chamber units may be programmed to pace only the ventricles; this may be done either at the time the pacemaker is implanted or at some time afterward. In such cases, a dual-chamber unit, when programmed or reprogrammed for ventricular pacing, should be treated as a single-chamber pacemaker in applying screening guidelines.

The decision as to how often any patient's pacemaker should be monitored is the responsibility of the patient's physician who is best able to take into account the condition and circumstances of the individual patient. These may vary over time, requiring modifications of the frequency with which the patient should be monitored. In cases where monitoring is done by some entity other than the patient's physician, such as a commercial monitoring service or hospital outpatient department, the physician's prescription for monitoring is required and should be periodically renewed (at least annually) to assure that the frequency of monitoring is proper for the patient. When a patient is monitered both during clinica visits and transtelephonically, the contractor should be sure to include frequency data on both ypes of monitoring in evaluating the reasonableness of the frequency of monitoring services received by the patient.

Since there are over 200 pacemaker models in service at any given point, and a variety of patient conditions that give rise to the need for pacemakers, the question of the appropriate frequency of monitorings is a complex one. Nevertheless, it is possible to develop guidelines within which the vast majority of pacemaker monitorings will fall and contractors should do this, using their own data and experience, as well as the frequency guidelines which follow, in order to limit extensive claims development to those cases requiring special attention.

100-3, 20.8.2
NCD for Self-Contained Pacemaker Monitors (20.8.2)
Self-contained pacemaker monitors are accepted devices for monitoring cardiac pacemakers. Accordingly, program payment may be made for the rental or purchase of either of the following pacemaker monitors when it is prescribed by a physician for a patient with a cardiac pacemaker:

A. Digital Electronic Pacemaker Monitor.
This device provides the patient with an instantaneous digital readout of his pacemaker pulse rate. Use of this device does not involve professional services until there has been a change of five pulses (or more) per minute above or below the initial rate of the pacemaker; when such change occurs, the patient contacts his physician.

B. Audible/Visible Signal Pacemaker Monitor.
This device produces an audible and visible signal which indicates the pacemaker rate. Use of this device does not involve professional services until a change occurs in these signals; at such time, the patient contacts his physician.

NOTE: The design of the self-contained pacemaker monitor makes it possible for the patient to monitor his pacemaker periodically and minimizes the need for regular visits to the outpatient department of the provider.

Therefore, documentation of the medical necessity for pacemaker evaluation in the outpatient department of the provider should be obtained where such evaluation is employed in addition to the self-contained pacemaker monitor used by the patient in his home.

100-3, 20.10
NCD for Cardiac Rehabilitation Programs (20.10)
A. General
Phase II cardiac rehabilitation, as described by the U.S. Public Health Service, is a comprehensive, long-term program including medical evaluation, prescribed exercise, cardiac risk factor modification, education, and counseling. Phase II refers to outpatient, medically supervised programs that are typically initiated 1-3 weeks after hospital discharge and provide appropriate electrocardiographic monitoring.

B. Nationally Covered Indications
Effective for services performed on or after March 22, 2006, Medicare coverage of cardiac rehabilitation programs is considered reasonable and necessary only for patients who: (1) have a documented diagnosis of acute myocardial infarction within the preceding 12 months; or (2) have had coronary bypass surgery; or (3) have stable angina pectoris; or (4) have had heart valve repair/replacement; or (5) have had percutaneous transluminal coronary angioplasty (PTCA) or coronary stenting; or (6) have had a heart or heart-lung transplant.

1. Program Requirements
   a. Duration

      Services provided in connection with a cardiac rehabilitation exercise program may be considered reasonable and necessary for up to 36 sessions. Patients generally receive 2 to 3 sessions per week for 12 to 18 weeks. Coverage of additional sessions is discussed in section D below.

   b. Components

      Cardiac rehabilitation programs must be comprehensive and to be comprehensive they must include a medical evaluation, a program to modify cardiac risk factors (e.g., nutritional counseling), prescribed exercise, education, and counseling.

   c. Facility

      The facility must have available for immediate use the necessary cardio-pulmonary, emergency, diagnostic, and therapeutic life-saving equipment accepted by the medical community as medically necessary, e.g., oxygen, cardiopulmonary resuscitation equipment, or defibrillator.

   d. Staff

      The program must be staffed by personnel necessary to conduct the program safely and effectively, who are trained in both basic and advanced life support techniques and in exercise therapy for coronary disease. The program must be under the direct supervision of a physician, as defined in 42 CFR Sec.410.26(a)(2) (defined through cross reference to 42 CFR Sec.410.32(b)(3)(ii), or 42 CFR Sec.410.27(f)).

C. Nationally Non-Covered Indications
Except as provided in section D., all other indications are not covered.

D. Other
The contractor has the discretion to cover cardiac rehabilitation services beyond 18 weeks. Coverage must not exceed a total of 72 sessions for 36 weeks.

(This NCD last reviewed March 2006.)

100-3, 20.11
NCD for Intraoperative Ventricular Mapping (20.11)
Intraoperative ventricular mapping is the technique of recording cardiac electrical activity directly from the heart. The recording sites are usually identified from an anatomical grid and may consist of epicardial, intramural, and endocardial sites. A probe with electrodes is used to explore these surfaces and generate a map that displays the sequence of electrical activation. This information is used by the surgeon to locate precisely the site of an operative intervention.

The intraoperative ventricular mapping procedure is covered under Medicare only for the uses and medical conditions described below:

- Localize accessory pathways associated with the Wolff-Parkinson-White (WPW) and other preexcitation syndromes;

- Map the sequence of atrial and ventricular activation for drug-resistant supraventricular tachycardias;

- Delineate the anatomical course of His bundle and/or bundle branches during corrective cardiac surgery for congenital heart diseases; and

- Direct the surgical treatment of patients with refractory ventricular tachyarrhythmias.

100-3, 20.12
NCD for Diagnostic Endocardial Electrical Stimulation (Pacing) (20.12)
Diagnostic endocardial electrical stimulation (EES), also called programmed electrical stimulation of the heart, is covered under Medicare when used for patients with severe cardiac arrhythmias.

100-3, 20.13
NCD for HIS Bundle Study (20.13)
Medicare coverage of the procedure would be limited to selected patients: those with complex ongoing acute arrhythmias, those with intermittent or permanent heart block in whom pacemaker implantation is being considered, and those patients who have recently developed heart block secondary to a myocardial infarction. When heart catheterization and the HIS Bundle Study are performed at the same time, the program will cover only one catheterization and a small additional charge for the study.

When a HIS bundle cardiogram is obtained as part of a diagnostic endocardial electrical stimulation, no separate charge will be recognized for the His bundle study.

100-3, 20.14
NCD for Plethysmography (20.14)
Medicare coverage is extended to those procedures listed in Category I below when used for the accepted medical indications mentioned above. The procedures in Category II are still considered experimental and are not covered at this time. Denial of claims because a noncovered procedure was used or because there was no medical indication for plethysmographic evaluation of any type should be based on Sec.1862(a)(1) of the Act.

Category I - Covered
Segmental Plethysmography - Included under this procedure are services performed with a regional plethysmograph, differential plethysmograph, recording oscillometer, and a pulse volume recorder.

Electrical Impedance Plethysmography

Ultrasonic Measurement of Blood Flow (Doppler) - While not strictly a plethysmographic method, this is also a useful tool in the evaluation of suspected peripheral vascular disease or preoperative screening of podiatric patients with suspected peripheral vascular compromise. (See Sec.50-7 for the applicable coverage policy on this procedure.)

Oculoplethysmography - See NCD on Noninvasive Tests of Carotid Function, Sec.20.17.

Strain Gauge Plethysmography - This test is based on recording the non-pulsatile aspects of inflowing blood at various points on an extremity by a mercury-in-silastic strain gauge sensor. The instrument consists of a chart recorder, an automatic cuff inflation and deflation system, and a recording manometer.

Category II - Experimental
The following methods have not yet reached a level of development such as to allow their routine use in the evaluation of suspected peripheral vascular disease.

Inductance Plethysmography - This method is considered experimental and does not provide reproducible results.

Capacitance Plethysmography - This method is considered experimental and does not provide reproducible results.

Mechanical Oscillometry - This is a non-standardized method which offers poor sensitivity and is not considered superior to the simple measurement of peripheral blood pressure.

Photoelectric Plethysmography - This method is considered useful only in determining whether or not a pulse is present and does not provide reproducible measurements of blood flow.

Differential plethysmography, on the other hand, is a system which uses an impedance technique to compare pulse pressures at various points along a limb, with a reference pressure at the mid-brachial or wrist level. It is not clear whether this technique, as usually performed in the physician's office, meets the definition of plethysmography because quantitative measurements of blood flow are usually not made. It has been concluded, in any event, that the differential plethysmography system is a blood pulse recorder of undetermined value, which has the potential for significant overutilization. Therefore, reimbursement for studies done by techniques other than venous occlusive pneumoplethysmography should be denied, at least until additional data on these devices, including controlled clinical studies, become available.

100-3, 20.15

NCD for Electrocardiographic (EKG) Services (20.15)

Nationally Covered Indications

The following indications are covered nationally unless otherwise indicated:

1. Computer analysis of EKGs when furnished in a setting and under the circumstances required for coverage of other EKG services.

2. EKG services rendered by an independent diagnostic testing facility (IDTF), including physician review and interpretation. Separate physician services are not covered unless he/she is the patient's attending or consulting physician.

3. Emergency EKGs (i.e., when the patient is or may be experiencing a lifethreatening event) performed as a laboratory or diagnostic service by a portable x-ray supplier only when a physician is in attendance at the time the service is performed or immediately thereafter.

4. Home EKG services with documentation of medical necessity.

5. Trans-telephonic EKG transmissions (effective March 1, 1980) as a diagnostic service for the indications described below, when performed with equipment meeting the standards described below, subject to the limitations and conditions specified below. Coverage is further limited to the amounts payable with respect to the physician's service in interpreting the results of such transmissions, including charges for rental of the equipment. The device used by the beneficiary is part of a total diagnostic system and is not considered DME separately. Covered uses are to:

   a. Detect, characterize, and document symptomatic transient arrhythmias;

   b. Initiate, revise, or discontinue arrhythmic drug therapy; or,

   c. Carry out early post-hospital monitoring of patients discharged after myocardial infarction (MI); (only if 24-hour coverage is provided, see C.5. below).

   Certain uses other than those specified above may be covered if, in the judgment of the local contractor, such use is medically necessary.

   Additionally, the transmitting devices must meet at least the following criteria:

   a. They must be capable of transmitting EKG Leads, I, II, or III; and,

   b. The tracing must be sufficiently comparable to a conventional EKG.

24-hour attended coverage used as early post-hospital monitoring of patients discharged after MI is only covered if provision is made for such 24-hour attended coverage in the manner described below:

24-hour attended coverage means there must be, at a monitoring site or central data center, an EKG technician or other non-physician, receiving calls and/or EKG data; tape recording devices do not meet this requirement. Further, such technicians should have immediate, 24-hour access to a physician to review transmitted data and make clinical decisions regarding the patient. The technician should also be instructed as to when and how to contact available facilities to assist the patient in case of emergencies.

C. Nationally Non-covered Indications

The following indications are non-covered nationally unless otherwise specified below:

1. The time-sampling mode of operation of ambulatory EKG cardiac event monitoring/recording.

2. Separate physician services other than those rendered by an IDTF unless rendered by the patient's attending or consulting physician.

3. Home EKG services without documentation of medical necessity.

4. Emergency EKG services by a portable x-ray supplier without a physician in attendance at the time of service or immediately thereafter.

5. 24-hour attended coverage used as early post-hospital monitoring of patients discharged after MI unless provision is made for such 24-hour attended coverage in the manner described in section B.5. above.

6. Any marketed Food and Drug Administration (FDA)-approved ambulatory cardiac monitoring device or service that cannot be categorized according to the framework below.

D. Other

Ambulatory cardiac monitoring performed with a marketed, FDA-approved device, is eligible for coverage if it can be categorized according to the framework below. Unless there is a specific NCD for that device or service, determination as to whether a device or service that fits into the framework is reasonable and necessary is according to local contractor discretion.

Electrocardiographic Services Framework

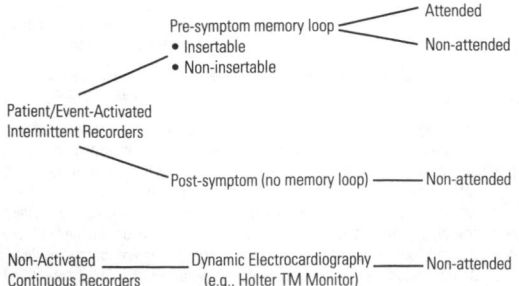

(This NCD last reviewed December 2004.)

100-3, 20.17

NCD for Noninvasive Tests of Carotid Function (20.17)

It is important to note that the names of these tests are not standardized. Following are some of the acceptable tests, recognizing that this list is not inclusive and that local medical consultants should make determinations:

Direct Tests

- Carotid Phonoangiography
- Direct Bruit Analysis
- Spectral Bruit Analysis
- Doppler Flow Velocity
- Ultrasound Imaging including Real Time
- B-Scan and Doppler Devices

Indirect Tests

- Periorbital Directional Doppler Ultrasonography
- Oculoplethysmography
- Ophthalmodynamometry

100-3, 20.18

NCD for Carotid Body Resection/Carotid Body Denervation (20.18)

Carotid body resection is occasionally used to relieve pulmonary symptoms, including asthma, but has been shown to lack general acceptance of the professional medical community. In addition, controlled clinical studies establishing the safety and effectiveness of this procedure are needed. Therefore, all carotid body resections to relieve pulmonary symptoms must be considered investigational and cannot be considered reasonable and necessary within the meaning of section 1862(a)(I) of the law. No program reimbursement may be made in such cases.

There is, however, one instance where carotid body resection has been accepted by the medical community as effective. That instance is when evidence of a mass in the carotid body,with or without symptoms, indicates the need for surgery to remove the carotid body tumor.

Denervation of a carotid sinus to treat hypersensitive carotid sinus reflex is another procedure performed in the area of the carotid body. In the case of hypersensitive carotid sinus, light pressure on the upper part of the neck (such as might be experienced when turning or raising one's head) results in symptoms such as dizziness or syncope due to hypotension and slowed heart rate. Failure of medical therapy and continued deterioration in the condition of the patient in such cases may indicate need for surgery. Denervation of the carotid sinus is rarely performed, but when elected as the therapy of choice with the above indications, this procedure may be considered reasonable and necessary.

100-3, 20.19

NCD for Ambulatory Blood Pressure Monitoring (20.19)

ABPM must be performed for at least 24 hours to meet coverage criteria.

ABPM is only covered for those patients with suspected white coat hypertension. Suspected white coat hypertension is defined as

1) office blood pressure >140/90 mm Hg on at least three separate clinic/office visits with two separate measurements made at each visit;

2) at least two documented blood pressure measurements taken outside the office which are <140/90 mm Hg; and

3) no evidence of end-organ damage.

The information obtained by ABPM is necessary in order to determine the appropriate management of the patient. ABPM is not covered for any other uses. In the rare circumstance that ABPM needs to be performed more than once in a patient, the qualifying criteria described above must be met for each subsequent ABPM test.

For those patients that undergo ABPM and have an ambulatory blood pressure of <135/85 with no evidence of end-organ damage, it is likely that their cardiovascular risk is similar to that of normotensives. They should be followed over time. Patients for which ABPM demonstrates a blood pressure of >135/85 may be at increased cardiovascular risk, and a physician may wish to consider antihypertensive therapy.

100-3, 20.23

NCD for Fabric Wrapping of Abdominal Aneurysms (20.23)

Fabric wrapping of abdominal aneurysms is not a covered Medicare procedure. This is a treatment for abdominal aneurysms which involves wrapping aneurysms with cellophane or fascia lata. This procedure has not been shown to prevent eventual rupture. In extremely rare instances, external wall reinforcement may be indicated when the current accepted treatment (excision of the aneurysm and reconstruction with synthetic materials) is not a viable alternative, but external wall reinforcement is not fabric wrapping. Accordingly, fabric wrapping of abdominal aneurysms is not considered reasonable and necessary within the meaning of Sec.1862(a)(1) of the Act.

100-3, 20.25

NCD for Cardiac Catheterization Performed in Other than a Hospital Setting (20.25)

(Effective January 12, 2006 - Repealed)

100-3, 20.28

NCD for Therapeutic Embolization (20.28)

Therapeutic embolization is covered when done for hemorrhage, and for other conditions amenable to treatment by the procedure, when reasonable and necessary for the individual patient. Renal embolization for the treatment of renal adenocarcinoma continues to be covered, effective December 15, 1978, as one type of therapeutic embolization, to:

- Reduce tumor vascularity preoperatively;
- Reduce tumor bulk in inoperable cases; or
- Palliate specific symptoms.

100-3, 20.29

NCD for Hyperbaric Oxygen Therapy (20.29)
A. Covered Conditions

Program reimbursement for HBO therapy will be limited to that which is administered in a chamber (including the one man unit) and is limited to the following conditions:

1. Acute carbon monoxide intoxication,
2. Decompression illness,
3. Gas embolism,
4. Gas gangrene,
5. Acute traumatic peripheral ischemia. HBO therapy is a valuable adjunctive treatment to be used in combination with accepted standard therapeutic measures when loss of function, limb, or life is threatened.
6. Crush injuries and suturing of severed limbs. As in the previous conditions, HBO therapy would be an adjunctive treatment when loss of function, limb, or life is threatened.
7. Progressive necrotizing infections (necrotizing fasciitis),
8. Acute peripheral arterial insufficiency,
9. Preparation and preservation of compromised skin grafts (not for primary management of wounds),
10. Chronic refractory osteomyelitis, unresponsive to conventional medical and surgical management,
11. Osteoradionecrosis as an adjunct to conventional treatment,
12. Soft tissue radionecrosis as an adjunct to conventional treatment,
13. Cyanide poisoning,
14. Actinomycosis, only as an adjunct to conventional therapy when the disease process is refractory to antibiotics and surgical treatment,
15. Diabetic wounds of the lower extremities in patients who meet the following three criteria:
    a. Patient has type I or type II diabetes and has a lower extremity wound that is due to diabetes;
    b. Patient has a wound classified as Wagner grade III or higher; and
    c. Patient has failed an adequate course of standard wound therapy.

The use of HBO therapy is covered as adjunctive therapy only after there are no measurable signs of healing for at least 30 -days of treatment with standard wound therapy and must be used in addition to standard wound care. Standard wound care in patients with diabetic wounds includes: assessment of a patient's vascular status and correction of any vascular problems in the affected limb if possible, optimization of nutritional status, optimization of glucose control, debridement by any means to remove devitalized tissue, maintenance of a clean, moist bed of granulation tissue with appropriate moist dressings, appropriate off-loading, and necessary treatment to resolve any infection that might be present. Failure to respond to standard wound care occurs when there are no measurable signs of healing for at least 30 consecutive days. Wounds must be evaluated at least every 30 days during administration of HBO therapy. Continued treatment with HBO therapy is not covered if measurable signs of healing have not been demonstrated within any 30-day period of treatment.

B. Noncovered Conditions
All other indications not specified under Sec.270.4(A) are not covered under the Medicare program. No program payment may be made for any conditions other than those listed in Sec.270.4(A).

No program payment may be made for HBO in the treatment of the following conditions:

1. Cutaneous, decubitus, and stasis ulcers.
2. Chronic peripheral vascular insufficiency.
3. Anaerobic septicemia and infection other than clostridial.
4. Skin burns (thermal).
5. Senility.
6. Myocardial infarction.
7. Cardiogenic shock.
8. Sickle cell anemia.
9. Acute thermal and chemical pulmonary damage, i.e., smoke inhalation with pulmonary insufficiency.
10. Acute or chronic cerebral vascular insufficiency.
11. Hepatic necrosis.

12. Aerobic septicemia.
13. Nonvascular causes of chronic brain syndrome (Pick's disease, Alzheimer's disease, Korsakoff's disease).
14. Tetanus.
15. Systemic aerobic infection.
16. Organ transplantation.
17. Organ storage.
18. Pulmonary emphysema.
19. Exceptional blood loss anemia.
20. Multiple Sclerosis.
21. Arthritic Diseases.
22. Acute cerebral edema.

C. Topical Application of Oxygen
This method of administering oxygen does not meet the definition of HBO therapy as stated above. Also, its clinical efficacy has not been established. Therefore, no Medicare reimbursement may be made for the topical application of oxygen.

100-3, 30.1

NCD for Biofeedback Therapy (30.1)

Biofeedback therapy is covered under Medicare only when it is reasonable and necessary for the individual patient for muscle re-education of specific muscle groups or for treating pathological muscle abnormalities of spasticity, incapacitating muscle spasm, or weakness, and more conventional treatments (heat, cold, massage, exercise, support) have not been successful. This therapy is not covered for treatment of ordinary muscle tension states or for psychosomatic conditions. (See the Medicare Benefit Policy Manual, Chapter 15, for general coverage requirements about physical therapy requirements.)

100-3, 30.1.1

NCD for Biofeedback Therapy for the Treatment of Urinary Incontinence (30.1.1)

This policy applies to biofeedback therapy rendered by a practitioner in an office or other facility setting.

Biofeedback is covered for the treatment of stress and/or urge incontinence in cognitively intact patients who have failed a documented trial of pelvic muscle exercise (PME)training. Biofeedback is not a treatment, per se, but a tool to help patients learn how to perform PME. Biofeedback-assisted PME incorporates the use of an electronic or mechanical device to relay visual and/or auditory evidence of pelvic floor muscle tone, in order to improve awareness of pelvic floor musculature and to assist patients in the performance of PME.

A failed trial of PME training is defined as no clinically significant improvement in urinary incontinence after completing 4 weeks of an ordered plan of pelvic muscle exercises to increase periurethral muscle strength.

Contractors may decide whether or not to cover biofeedback as an initial treatment modality.

Home use of biofeedback therapy is not covered.

100-3, 30.5

NCD for Transcendental Meditation (TM) (30.5)

After review of this issue, CMS has concluded that the evidence concerning the medical efficacy of TM is incomplete at best and does not demonstrate effectiveness and that a professional level of skill is not required for the training of patients to engage in TM.

Although many articles have been written about application of TM for patients with certain forms of hypertension and anxiety, there are no rigorous scientific studies that demonstrate the effectiveness of TM for use as an adjunct medical therapy for such conditions. Accordingly, neither TM nor the training of patients for its use are covered under the Medicare program.

100-3, 30.6

NCD for Intravenous Histamine Therapy (30.6)

However, there is no scientifically valid clinical evidence that histamine therapy is effective for any condition regardless of the method of administration, nor is it accepted or widely used by the medical profession. Therefore, histamine therapy cannot be considered reasonable and necessary, and program payment for such therapy is not made.

100-3, 40.1

NCD for Diabetes Outpatient Self-Management Training (40.1)

Please refer to 42 CFR 410.140 - 410.146 for conditions that must be met for Medicare coverage.

100-3, 40.5

NCD for Treatment of Obesity (40.5)
B. Nationally Covered Indications

Certain designated surgical services for the treatment of obesity are covered for Medicare beneficiaries who have a BMI >=35, have at least one co-morbidity related to obesity and have been previously unsuccessful with the medical treatment of obesity. See Sec.100.1.

C. Nationally Noncovered Indications

1. Treatments for obesity alone remain non-covered.
2. Supplemented fasting is not covered under the Medicare program as a general treatment for obesity (see section D. below for discretionary local coverage).

D. Other

Where weight loss is necessary before surgery in order to ameliorate the complications posed by obesity when it coexists with pathological conditions such as cardiac and respiratory diseases, diabetes, or hypertension (and other more conservative techniques to achieve this end are not regarded as appropriate), supplemented fasting with adequate monitoring of the patient is eligible for coverage on a case-by-case basis or pursuant to a local coverage determination. The risks associated with the achievement of rapid weight loss must be carefully balanced against the risk posed by the condition requiring surgical treatment.

(This NCD last reviewed February 2006.)

100-3, 50.1

NCD for Speech Generating Devices (50.1)

Effective January 1, 2001, augmentative and alternative communication devices or communicators, which are hereafter referred to as "speech generating devices" are now considered to fall within the DME benefit category established by Sec.1861(n) of the Act. They may be covered if the contractor's medical staff determines that the patient suffers from a severe speech impairment and that the medical condition warrants the use of a device based on the definitions above.

100-3, 50.2

NCD for Electronic Speech Aids (50.2)

Electronic speech aids are covered under Part B as prosthetic devices when the patient has had a laryngectomy or his larynx is permanently inoperative.

100-3, 50.3

NCD for Cochlear Implantation (50.3)

B. Nationally Covered Indications

1. Effective for services performed on or after April 4, 2005, cochlear implantation may be covered for treatment of bilateral pre- or post-linguistic, sensorineural, moderate-to-profound hearing loss in individuals who demonstrate limited benefit from amplification. Limited benefit from amplification is defined by test scores of less than or equal to 40% correct in the best-aided listening condition on tape-recorded tests of open-set sentence cognition. Medicare coverage is provided only for those patients who meet all of the following selection guidelines.

   - Diagnosis of bilateral moderate-to-profound sensorineural hearing impairment with limited benefit from appropriate hearing (or vibrotactile) aids;

   - Cognitive ability to use auditory clues and a willingness to undergo an extended program of rehabilitation;

   - Freedom from middle ear infection, an accessible cochlear lumen that is structurally suited to implantation, and freedom from lesions in the auditory nerve and acoustic areas of the central nervous system;

   - No contraindications to surgery; and

   - The device must be used in accordance with Food and Drug Administration (FDA)-approved labeling.

2. Effective for services performed on or after April 4, 2005, cochlear implantation may be covered for individuals meeting the selection guidelines above and with hearing test scores of greater than 40% and less than or equal to 60% only when the provider is participating in, and patients are enrolled in, either an FDA-approved category B investigational device exemption clinical trial as defined at 42 CFR 405.201, a trial under the Centers for Medicare & Medicaid (CMS) Clinical Trial Policy as defined at section 310.1 of the National Coverage Determinations Manual, or a prospective, controlled comparative trial approved by CMS as consistent with the evidentiary requirements for National Coverage Analyses and meeting specific quality standards.

C. Nationally Noncovered Indications

Medicare beneficiaries not meeting all of the coverage criteria for cochlear implantation listed are deemed not eligible for Medicare coverage under section 1862(a)(1)(A) of the Social Security Act.

D. Other

All other indications for cochlear implantation not otherwise indicated as nationally covered or non-covered above remain at local contractor discretion.

(This NCD last reviewed May 2005.)

100-3, 70.1

NCD for Consultations with a Beneficiary's Family and Associates (70.1)

In certain types of medical conditions, including when a patient is withdrawn and uncommunicative due to a mental disorder or comatose, the physician may contact relatives and close associates to secure background information to assist in diagnosis and treatment planning. When a physician contacts his patient's relatives or associates for this purpose, expenses of such interviews are properly chargeable as physician's services to the patient on whose behalf the information was secured. If the beneficiary is not an inpatient of a hospital, Part B reimbursement for such an interview is subject to the special limitation on payments for physicians' services in connection with mental, psychoneurotic, and personality disorders.

A physician may also have contacts with a patient's family and associates for purposes other than securing background information. In some cases, the physician will provide counseling to members of the household. Family counseling services are covered only where the primary purpose of such counseling is the treatment of the patient's condition. For example, two situations where family counseling services would be appropriate are as follows: (1) where there is a need to observe the patient's interaction with family members; and/or (2) where there is a need to assess the capability of and assist the family members in aiding in the management of the patient. Counseling principally concerned with the effects of the patient's condition on the individual being interviewed would not be reimbursable as part of the physician's personal services to the patient. While to a limited degree, the counseling described in the second situation may be used to modify the behavior of the family members, such services nevertheless are covered because they relate primarily to the management of the patient's problems and not to the treatment of the family member's problems.

100-3, 70.2

NCD for Consultation Services Rendered by a Podiatrist in a Skilled Nursing Facility (70.2)

Consultation services rendered by a podiatrist in a skilled nursing facility are covered if the services are reasonable and necessary and do not come within any of the specific statutory exclusions. Section 1862(a)(13) of the Act excludes payment for the treatment of flat foot conditions, the treatment of subluxations of the foot, and routine foot care. To determine whether the consultation comes within the foot care exclusions, apply the same rule as for initial diagnostic examinations, i.e., where services are performed in connection with specific symptoms or complaints which suggest the need for covered services, the services are covered regardless of the resulting diagnosis. The exclusion of routine physician examinations is also pertinent and would generally exclude podiatric consultation performed on all patients in a skilled nursing facility on a routine basis for screening purposes, except in those cases where a specific foot ailment is involved. Section 1862(a)(7) of the Act excludes payment for routine physical checkups.

100-3, 70.2.1

NCD for Services Provided for the Diagnosis and Treatment of Diabetic Sensory Neuropathy with Loss of Protective Sensation (AKA Diabetic Peripheral Neuropathy) (70.2.1)

Diabetic sensory neuropathy with LOPS is a localized illness of the feet and falls within the regulation's exception to the general exclusionary rule (see 42 CFR Sec.411.15(l)(1)(i)). Foot exams for people with diabetic sensory neuropathy with LOPS are reasonable and necessary to allow for early intervention in serious complications that typically afflict diabetics with the disease.

Effective for services furnished on or after July 1, 2002, Medicare covers, as a physician service, an evaluation (examination and treatment) of the feet no more often than every six months for individuals with a documented diagnosis of diabetic sensory neuropathy and LOPS, as long as the beneficiary has not seen a foot care specialist for some other reason in the interim. LOPS shall be diagnosed through sensory testing with the 5.07 monofilament using established guidelines, such as those developed by the National Institute of Diabetes and Digestive and Kidney Diseases guidelines. Five sites should be tested on the plantar surface of each foot, according to the National Institute of Diabetes and Digestive and Kidney Diseases guidelines. The areas must be tested randomly since the loss of protective sensation may be patchy in distribution, and the patient may get clues if the test is done rhythmically. Heavily callused areas should be avoided. As suggested by the American Podiatric Medicine Association, an absence of sensation at two or more sites out of 5 tested on either foot when tested with the 5.07 Semmes-Weinstein monofilament must be present and documented to diagnose peripheral neuropathy with loss of protective sensation.

The examination includes:

1. A patient history.
2. A physical examination that must consist of at least the following elements:
   - Visual inspection of forefoot and hindfoot (including toe web spaces).
   - Evaluation of protective sensation.
   - Evaluation of foot structure and biomechanics.
   - Evaluation of vascular status and skin integrity.
   - Evaluation of the need for special footwear.
3. Patient education.

A. Treatment includes, but is not limited to:

- Local care of superficial wounds.
- Debridement of corns and calluses.
- Trimming and debridement of nails.

The diagnosis of diabetic sensory neuropathy with LOPS should be established and documented prior to coverage of foot care. Other causes of peripheral neuropathy should be considered and investigated by the primary care physician prior to initiating or referring for foot care for persons with LOPS.

100-3, 80.1

NCD for Hydrophilic Contact Lens For Corneal Bandage (80.1)

Payment may be made under Sec.1861(s)(2) of the Act for a hydrophilic contact les approved by the Food and Drug Administration (FDA) and used as a supply incident to a pphysician's service. Payment for the lens is included in the payment for the physician's service to which the lens is incident. Contractors are authorized to accept an FDA letter of approval or other FDA published material as evidence of FDA approval. (See Sec.80.4 of the NCD Manual for coverage of a hydrophilic contact lens as prosthetic device.)

100-3, 80.2
Photodynamic Therapy
(Rev. 1, 10-03-03)

CIM 35-100

Photodynamic therapy is a medical procedure which involves the infusion of a photosensitive (light-activated) drug with a very specific absorption peak. This drug is chemically designed to have a unique affinity for the diseased tissue intended for treatment. Once introduced to the body, the drug accumulates and is retained in diseased tissue to a greater degree than in normal tissue. Infusion is followed by the targeted irradiation of this tissue with a non-thermal laser, calibrated to emit light at a wavelength that corresponds to the drug's absorption peak. The drug then becomes active and locally treats the diseased tissue.

Ocular photodynamic therapy (OPT)
The OPT is used in the treatment of ophthalmologic diseases. OPT is only covered when used in conjunction with verteporfin (see §80.3, "Photosensitive Drugs").

- Classic Subfoveal Choroidal Neovascular (CNV) Lesions - OPT is covered with a diagnosis of neovascular age-related macular degeneration (AMD) with predominately classic subfoveal choroidal neovascular (CNV) lesions (where the area of classic CNV occupies . 50 percent of the area of the entire lesion) at the initial visit as determined by a fluorescein angiogram. Subsequent follow-up visits will require a fluorescein angiogram prior to treatment. There are no requirements regarding visual acuity, lesion size, and number of re-treatments.

- Occult Subfoveal Choroidal Neovascular (CNV) Lesions - OPT is noncovered for patients with a diagnosis of age-related macular degeneration (AMD) with occult and no classic CNV lesions.

- Other Conditions - Use of OPT with verteporfin for other types of AMD (e.g., patients with minimally classic CNV lesions, atrophic, or dry AMD) is noncovered. OPT with verteporfin for other ocular indications such as pathologic myopia or presumed ocular histoplasmosis syndrome, is eligible for coverage through individual contractor discretion.

100-3, 80.4
NCD for Hydrophilic Contact Lenses (80.4)
Hydrophilic contact lenses are eyeglasses within the meaning of the exclusion in Sec.1862(a)(7) of the Act and are not covered when used in the treatment of nondiseased eyes with spherical ametrophia, refractive astigmatism, and/or corneal astigmatism. Payment may be made under the prosthetic device benefit, however, for hydrophilic contact lenses when prescribed for an aphakic patient.

Contractors are authorized to accept an FDA letter of approval or other FDA published material as evidence of FDA approval. (See Sec.80.1 of the NCD Manual for coverage of a hydrophilic lens as a corneal bandage.)

100-3, 80.6
NCD for Intraocular Photography (80.6)
Intraocular photography is covered when used for the diagnosis of such conditions as macular degeneration, retinal neoplasms, choroid disturbances and diabetic retinopathy, or to identify glaucoma, multiple sclerosis and other central nervous system abnormalities. Make Medicare payment for the use of this procedure by an opthalmologist in these situations when it is reasonable and necessary for the individual patient to receive these services.

100-3, 80.7
NCD for Refractive Keratoplasty (80.7)
The correction of common refractive errors by eyeglasses, contact lenses or other prosthetic devices is specifically excluded from coverage. The use of radial keratotomy and/or keratoplasty for the purpose of refractive error compensation is considered a substitute or alternative to eye glasses or contact lenses, which are specifically excluded by Sec.1862(a)(7) of the Act (except in certain cases in connection with cataract surgery). In addition, many in the medical community consider such procedures cosmetic surgery, which is excluded by section Sec.1862(a)(10) of the Act. Therefore, radial keratotomy and keratoplasty to treat refractive defects are not covered.

Keratoplasty that treats specific lesions of the cornea, such as phototherapeutic keratectomy that removes scar tissue from the visual field, deals with an abnormality of the eye and is not cosmetic surgery. Such cases may be covered under Sec.1862(a)(1)(A) of the Act.

The use of lasers to treat ophthalmic disease constitutes opthalmalogic surgery. Coverage is restricted to practitioners who have completed an approved training program in ophthalmologic surgery.

100-3, 80.8
NCD for Endothelial Cell Photography (80.8)
Endothelial cell photography is a covered procedure under Medicare when reasonable and necessary for patients who meet one or more of the following criteria:

- Have slit lamp evidence of endothelial dystrophy (cornea guttata),
- Have slit lamp evidence of corneal edema (unilateral or bilateral),
- Are about to undergo a secondary intraocular lens implantation,
- Have had previous intraocular surgery and require cataract surgery,
- Are about to undergo a surgical procedure associated with a higher risk to corneal endothelium; i.e., phacoemulsification, or refractive surgery (see Sec.80.7 for excluded refractive procedures),
- With evidence of posterior polymorphous dystrophy of the cornea or irido-corneal-endothelium syndrome, or
- Are about to be fitted with extended wear contact lenses after intraocular surgery.

When a pre-surgical examination for cataract surgery is performed and the conditions of this section are met, if the only visual problem is cataracts, endothelial cell photography is covered as part of the presurgical comprehensive eye examination or combination brief/intermediate examination provided prior to cataract surgery, and not in addition to it. (See Sec.10.1.)

100-3, 80.9
NCD for Computer Enhanced Perimetry (80.9)
It is a covered service when used in assessing visual fields in patients with glaucoma or other neuropathologic defects.

100-3, 80.10
NCD for Phaco-Emulsification procedure - cataract extraction (80.10)
In view of recommendations of authoritative sources in the field of ophthalmology, the subject technique is viewed as an accepted procedure for removal of cataracts. Accordingly, program reimbursement may be made for necessary services furnished in connection with cataract extraction utilizing the phaco-emulsification procedure.

100-3, 80.11
NCD for Vitrectomy (80.11)
Vitrectomy may be considered reasonable and necessary for the following conditions: vitreous loss incident to cataract surgery, vitreous opacities due to vitreous hemorrhage or other causes, retinal detachments secondary to vitreous strands, proliferative retinopathy, and vitreous retraction. See Chapter 23 of the Medicare Claims Manual for how to determine payment for physician vitrectomy services and Chapter 14 Sec.40 for how to determine payment for ASC facility vitrectomy services. Also, see Chapter 23 Sec.20.9 to identify when, for Medicare payment purposes, certain vitrectomy codes are included in other codes or when codes for other services include vitrectomy codes.

100-3, 80.12
NCD for Intraocular Lenses (IOLs) (80.12)
Intraocular lens implantation services, as well as the lens itself, may be covered if reasonable and necessary for the individual. Implantation services may include hospital, surgical, and other medical services, including pre-implantation ultrasound (A-scan) eye measurement of one or both eyes.

100-3, 100.1
NCD for Bariatric Surgery for Treatment of Morbid Obesity (100.1)
Indications and Limitations of Coverage

B. Nationally Covered Indications
Open and laparoscopic Roux-en-Y gastric bypass (RYGBP), open and laparoscopic Biliopancreatic Diversion with Duodenal Switch (BPD/DS), and laparoscopic adjustable gastric banding (LAGB) are covered for Medicare beneficiaries who have a body-mass index >35, have at least one co-morbidity related to obesity, and have been previously unsuccessful with medical treatment for obesity. These procedures are only covered when performed at facilities that are: (1) certified by the American College of Surgeons as a Level 1 Bariatric Surgery Center (program standards and requirements in effect on February 15, 2006); or (2) certified by the American Society for Bariatric Surgery as a Bariatric Surgery Center of Excellence (program standards and requirements in effect on February 15, 2006).

A list of approved facilities and their approval dates are listed and maintained on the CMS Coverage Web site at http://www.cms.hhs.gov/center/coverage.asp , and published in the Federal Register.

C. Nationally Non-covered Indications
The following bariatric surgery procedures are non-covered for all Medicare beneficiaries:
- Open adjustable gastric banding
- Open and laparoscopic sleeve gastrectomy; and
- Open and laparoscopic vertical banded gastroplasty.

The two previously non-coverage determinations remain unchanged - Gastric Balloon (Section 100.11) and Intestinal Bypass (Section 100.8).

D. Other
(This NCD last reviewed February 2006.)

100-3, 100.2
NCD for Endoscopy (100.2)
Endoscopic procedures are covered when reasonable and necessary for the individual patient.

100-3, 100.4
NCD for Esophageal Manometry (100.4)
Esophageal manometry is covered under Medicare where it is determined to be reasonable and necessary for the individual patient.

100-3, 100.5
NCD for Diagnostic Breath Analyses (100.5)
The Following Breath Test is Covered:
- Lactose breath hydrogen to detect lactose malabsorption .

The Following Breath Tests are Excluded from Coverage:
- Lactulose breath hydrogen for diagnosing small bowel bacterial overgrowth and measuring small bowel transit time.
- CO_2 for diagnosing bile acid malabsorption.
- CO_2 for diagnosing fat malabsorption.

100-3, 100.8

NCD for Intestinal By-Pass Surgery (100.8)

The safety of intestinal bypass surgery for treatment of obesity has not been demonstrated. Severe adverse reactions such as steatorrhea, electrolyte depletion, liver failure, arthralgia, hypoplasia of bone marrow, and avitaminosis have sometimes occurred as a result of this procedure. It does not meet the reasonable and necessary provisions of Sec.1862(a)(1) of the Act and is not a covered Medicare procedure.

100-3, 100.9

NCD for Implantation of Anti-Gastroesophageal Reflux Device (100.9)

The implantation of this device may be considered reasonable and necessary in specific clinical situations where a conventional valvuloplasty procedure is contraindicated. The implantation of an anti-gastroesophageal reflux device is covered only for patients with documented severe or life threatening gastroesophageal reflux disease whose conditions have been resistant to medical treatment and who also:

- have esophageal involvement with progressive systemic sclerosis; or
- have foreshortening of the esophagus such that insufficient tissue exists to permit a valve reconstruction; or
- are poor surgical risks for a valvuloplasty procedure; or
- have failed previous attempts at surgical treatment with valvuloplasty procedures.

100-3, 100.10

NCD for Injection Sclerotherapy for Esophageal Variceal Bleeding (100.10)

This procedure is covered under Medicare.

100-3, 100.12

NCD for Gastrophotography (100.12)

Gastrophotography is an accepted procedure for diagnosis and treatment of gastrointestinal disorders. The photographic record provided by this procedure is often necessary for consultation and/or followup purposes and when required for such purposes, is more valuable than a conventional gastroscopic examination. Such a record facilitates the documentation and evaluation (healing or worsening) of lesions such as the gastric ulcer, facilitates consultation between physicians concerning difficult-to-interpret lesions, provides preoperative characterization for the surgeon, and permits better diagnosis of postoperative gastric bleeding to help determine whether there is a need for reoperation. Therefore, program reimbursement may be made for this procedure.

100-3, 100.13

NCD for Laparoscopic Cholecystectomy (100.13)

Laparoscopic cholecystectomy is a covered surgical procedure in which a diseased gall bladder is removed through the use of instruments introduced via cannulae, with vision of the operative field maintained by use of a high-resolution television camera-monitor system (video laparoscope). For inpatient claims, use ICD-9-CM code 51.23, Laparoscopic cholecystectomy. For all other claims, use CPT codes 49310 for laparoscopy, surgical; cholecystectomy (any method), and 49311 for laparoscopy, surgical: cholecystectomy with cholangiography.

100-3, 110.1

NCD for Hyperthermia for Treatment of Cancer (110.1)

Local hyperthermia is covered under Medicare when used in connection with radiation therapy for the treatment of primary or metastatic cutaneous or subcutaneous superficial malignancies. It is not covered when used alone or in connection with chemotherapy.

100-3, 110.2

NCD for Certain Drugs Distributed by the National Cancer Institute (110.2)

A physician is eligible to receive Group C drugs from the Divison of Cancer Treatment only if the following requirements are met:

- A physician must be registered with the NCI as an investigator by having completed an FD-Form 1573;
- A written request for the drug, indicating the disease to be treated, must be submitted to the NCI;
- The use of the drug must be limited to indications outlined in the NCI's guidelines; and
- All adverse reactions must be reported to the Investigational Drug Branch of the Division of Cancer Treatment.

In view of these NCI controls on distribution and use of Group C drugs, intermediaries may assume, in the absence of evidence to the contrary, that a Group C drug and the related hospital stay are covered if all other applicable coverage requirements are satisfied.

If there is reason to question coverage in a particular case, the matter should be resolved with the assistance of the Quality improvemetn organization (QIO), or if there is none, the assistance of your medical consultants.

Information regarding those drugs which are classified as Group C drugs may be obtained from:

Office of the Chief, Investigational Drug Branch
Division of Cancer Treatment, CTEP, Landow Building
Room 4C09, National Cancer Institute
Bethesda, Maryland 20205

100-3, 110.3

NCD for Anti-Inhibitor Coagulant Complex (AICC) (110.3)

Anti-inhibitor coagulant complex, AICC, is a drug used to treat hemophilia in patients with factor VIII inhibitor antibodies. AICC has been shown to be safe and effective and has Medicare coverage when furnished to patients with hemophilia A and inhibitor antibodies to factor VIII who have major bleeding episodes and who fail to respond to other, less expensive therapies.

100-3, 110.4

NCD for Extracorporeal Photopheresis (110.4)

B. Nationally Covered Indications

The CMS has determined that extracorporeal photopheresis is reasonable and necessary under Sec.1862(a)(1)(A) of the Social Security Act under the following circumstances:

1. Effective April 8, 1988, Medicare provides coverage for:

   Palliative treatment of skin manifestations of CTCL that has not responded to other therapy.

2. Effective December 19, 2006, Medicare also provides coverage for:

   Patients with acute cardiac allograft rejection whose disease is refractory to standard immunosuppressive drug treatment; and

   Patients with chronic graft versus host disease whose disease is refractory to standard immunosuppressive drug treatment.

C. Nationally Noncovered Indications

All other indications for extracorporeal photopheresis remain noncovered.

D. Other

Claims processing instructions can be found in chapter 32, section 190 of the Medicare Claims Processing Manual.

(This NCD last reviewed December 2006.)

100-3, 110.5

NCD for Granulocyte Transfusions (110.5)

Granulocyte transfusions to patients suffering from severe infection and granulocytopenia are a covered service under Medicare. Granulocytopenia is usually identified as fewer than 500 granulocytes/mm 3 whole blood. Accepted indications for granulocyte transfusions include:

Granulocytopenia with evidence of gram negative sepsis; and

Granulocytopenia in febrile patients with local progressive infections unresponsive to appropriate antibiotic therapy, thought to be due to gram negative organisms.

100-3, 110.6

NCD for Scalp Hypothermia During Chemotherapy, to Prevent Hair Loss (110.6)

While ice-filled bags or bandages or other devices used for scalp hypothermia during chemotherapy may be covered as supplies of the kind commonly furnished without a separate charge, no separate charge for them would be recognized.

100-3, 110.7

NCD for Blood Transfusions (110.7)

B. Policy Governing Transfusions

For Medicare coverage purposes, it is important to distinguish between a transfusion itself and preoperative blood services; e.g., collection, processing, storage. Medically necessary transfusion of blood, regardless of the type, may generally be a covered service under both Part A and Part B of Medicare. Coverage does not make a distinction between the transfusion of homologous, autologous, or donor-directed blood. With respect to the coverage of the services associated with the preoperative collection, processing, and storage of autologous and donor-directed blood, the following policies apply.

1. Hospital Part A and B Coverage and Payment

   Under Sec.1862(a)(14) of the Act, non-physician services furnished to hospital patients are covered and paid for as hospital services. As provided in Sec.1886 of the Act, under the prospective [payment system (PPS), the diganosis related group (DRG) payment to the hospital includes all covered blood and blood processing expenses, whether or not the blood is eventually used.

   Under its provider agreement, a hospital is required to furnish or arrange for all covered services furnished to hospital patients. medicare payment is made to the hospital, under PPS or cost reimbursement for covered inpatient services, and it is intended to reflect payment for all costs of furnishing those services.

2. Nonhospital Part B Coverage

   Under Part B, to be eligible for separate coverage, a service must fit the definition of one of the services authorized by Sec.1832 of the Act. These services are defined in 42 CFR 410.10 and do not include a separate category for a supplier's services associated with blood donation services, either autologous or donor-directed. That is, the collection, processing, and storage of blood for later transfusion into the beneficiary is not recognized as a separate service under Part B. Therefore, there is no avenue through which a blood supplier can receive direct payment under Part B for blood donation services.

C. Perioperative Blood Salvage

When the perioperative blood salvage process is used in surgery on a hospital patient, payment made to the hospital (under PPS or through cost reimbursement) for the procedure in which that process is used is intended to encompass payment for all costs relating to that process.

           © 2008 Ingenix

100-3, 110.8
NCD for Blood Platelet Transfusions (110.8)
Blood platelet transplants are safe and effective for the correction of thrombocytopenia and other blood defects. It is covered under Medicare when treatment is reasonable and necessary for the individual patient.

100-3, 110.8.1
NCD for Stem Cell Transplantation (110.8.1)
1. Allogeneic Stem Cell Transplantation

   Allogeneic stem cell transplantation is a procedure in which a portion of a healthy donor's stem cell or bone marrow is obtained and prepared for intravenous infusion.

   a. Covered Indications

   The following uses of allogeneic bone marrow transplantation are covered under Medicare:

   - Effective for services performed on or after August 1, 1978, for the treatment of leukemia, leukemia in remission, or aplastic anemia when it is reasonable and necessary; and

   - Effective for services performed on or after June 3, 1985, for the treatment of severe combined immunodeficiency disease (SCID), and for the treatment of Wiskott-Aldrich syndrome.

   b. Noncovered Indications

   Effective for services performed on or after May 24, 1996, allogeneic stem cell transplantation is not covered as treatment for multiple myeloma.

2. Autologous Stem Cell Transplantation (AuSCT)

   Autologous stem cell transplantation (AuSCT) is a technique for restoring stem cells using the patient's own previously stored cells.

   a. Covered Indications

   Effective for services performed on or after April 28, 1989, AuSCT is considered reasonable and necessary under Sec.1862(a)(1)(A) of the Social Security Act (the Act) for the following conditions and is covered under Medicare for patients with:

   - Acute leukemia in remission who have a high probability of relapse and who have no human leucocyte antigens (HLA)-matched;

   - Resistant non-Hodgkin's lymphomas or those presenting with poor prognostic features following an initial response;

   - Recurrent or refractory neuroblastoma; or

   - Advanced Hodgkin's disease who have failed conventional therapy and have no HLA-matched donor.

   Effective October 1, 2000, single AuSCT is only covered for Durie-Salmon Stage II or III patients that fit the following requirements:

   - Newly diagnosed or responsive multiple myeloma. This includes those patients with previously untreated disease, those with at least a partial response to prior chemotherapy (defined as a 50% decrease either in measurable paraprotein [serum and/or urine] or in bone marrow infiltration, sustained for at least 1 month), and those in responsive relapse; and

   - Adequate cardiac, renal, pulmonary, and hepatic function.

   Effective for services performed on or after March 15, 2005, when recognized clinical risk factors are employed to select patients for transplantation, high dose melphalan (HDM) together with AuSCT is reasonable and necessary for Medicare beneficiaries of any age group with primary amyloid light chain (AL) amyloidosis who meet the following criteria:

   - Amyloid deposition in 2 or fewer organs; and,

   - Cardiac left ventricular ejection fraction (EF) greater than 45%

   b. Noncovered Indications

   Insufficient data exist to establish definite conclusions regarding the efficacy of AuSCT for the following conditions:

   - Acute leukemia not in remission;

   - Chronic granulocytic leukemia;

   - Solid tumors (other than neuroblastoma);

   - Up to October 1, 2000, multiple myeloma;

   - Tandem transplantation (multiple rounds of AuSCT) for patients with multiple myeloma;

   - Effective October 1, 2000, non primary AL amyloidosis; and,

   - Effective October 1, 2000, thru March 14, 2005, primary AL amyloidosis for Medicare beneficiaries age 64 or older.

   In these cases, AuSCT is not considered reasonable and necessary within the meaning of Sec.1862(a)(1)(A) of the Act and is not covered under Medicare.

B. Other
All other indications for stem cell transplantation not otherwise noted above as covered or noncovered nationally remain at local contractor discretion.

(This NCD last reviewed November 2005.)

100-3, 110.9
NCD for Antigens Prepared for Sublingual Administration (110.9)
For antigens provided to patients on or after November 17, 1996, Medicare does not cover such antigens if they are to be administered sublingually, i.e., by placing drops under the patient's tongue. This kind of allergy therapy has not been proven to be safe and effective. Antigens are covered only if they are administered by injection.

100-3, 110.10
NCD for Intravenous Iron Therapy (110.10)
Effective December 1, 2000, Medicare covers sodium ferric gluconate complex in sucrose injection as a first line treatment of iron deficiency anemia when furnished intravenously to patients undergoing chronic hemodialysis who are receiving supplemental erythropoietin therapy.

Effective October 1, 2001, Medicare also covers iron sucrose injection as a first line treatment of iron deficiency anemia when furnished intravenously to patients undergoing chronic hemodialysis who are receiving supplemental erythropoeitin therapy.

100-3, 110.12
NCD for Challenge Ingestion Food Testing (110.12)
This procedure is covered when it is used on an outpatient basis if it is reasonable and necessary for the individual patient.

Challenge ingestion food testing has not been proven to be effective in the diagnosis of rheumatoid arthritis, depression, or respiratory disorders. Accordingly, its use in the diagnosis of these conditions is not reasonable and necessary within the meaning of section 1862(a)(1) of the Medicare law, and no program payment is made for this procedure when it is so used.

100-3, 110.14
NCD for Apheresis (Therapeutic Pheresis) (110.14)
B. Indications
Apheresis is covered for the following indications:

- Plasma exchange for acquired myasthenia gravis;

- Leukapheresis in the treatment of leukemia

- Plasmapheresis in the treatment of primary macroglobulinemia (Waldenstrom);

- Treatment of hyperglobulinemias, including (but not limited to) multiple myelomas, cryoglobulinemia and hyperviscosity syndromes;

- Plasmapheresis or plasma exchange as a last resort treatment of thrombotic thrombocytopenic purpura (TTP);

- Plasmapheresis or plasma exchange in the last resort treatment of life threatening rheumatoid vasculitis;

- Plasma perfusion of charcoal filters for treatment of pruritis of cholestatic liver disease;

- Plasma exchange in the treatment of Goodpasture's Syndrome;

- Plasma exchange in the treatment of glomerulonephritis associated with antiglomerular basement membrane antibodies and advancing renal failure or pulmonary hemorrhage;

- Treatment of chronic relapsing polyneuropathy for patients with severe or life threatening symptoms who have failed to respond to conventional therapy;

- Treatment of life threatening scleroderma and polymyositis when the patient is unresponsive to conventional therapy;

- Treatment of Guillain-Barre Syndrome; and

- Treatment of last resort for life threatening systemic lupus erythematosus (SLE) when conventional therapy has failed to prevent clinical deterioration.

C. Settings
Apheresis is covered only when performed in a hospital setting (either inpatient or outpatient), or in a nonhospital setting, e.g. physician directed clinic when the following conditions are met:

- A physician (or a number of physicians) is present to perform medical services and to respond to medical emergencies at all times during patient care hours;

- Each patient is under the care of a physician; and

- All nonphysician services are furnished under the direct, personal supervision of a physician.

100-3, 110.15
NCD for Ultrafiltration, Hemoperfusion and Hemofiltration (110.15)
A. Ultrafiltration.
This is a process for removing excess fluid from the blood through the dialysis membrane by means of pressure. It is not a substitute for dialysis. Ultrafiltration is utilized in cases where excess fluid cannot be removed easily during the regular course of hemodialysis. When it is performed, it is commonly done during the first hour or two of each hemodialysis on patients who, e.g., have refractory edema. Ultrafiltration is a covered procedure under the Medicare program (effective for services performed on and after 9/1/79).

Predialysis Ultrafiltration.--While this procedure requires additional staff care, the facility dialysis rate is intended to cover the full range of complicated and uncomplicated nonacute dialysis treatments. Therefore, no additional facility charge is recognized for predialysis ultrafiltration. The physician's role in ultrafiltration varies with the stability of the patient's condition. In unstable patients, the physician may need to be present at the initiation of dialysis, and available either in- house or in close proximity to monitor the patient carefully. In patients who are relatively stable, but who seem to accumulate excessive weight gain, the procedure requires only a modest increase in physician involvement over routine outpatient hemodialysis.

Occasionally, medical complications may occur which require that ultrafiltration be performed separate from the dialysis treatment, and in these cases an additional charge can be recognized. However, the claim must be documented as to why the ultrafiltration could not have been performed at the same time as the dialysis.

B. Hemoperfusion.
This is a process which removes substances from the blood using a charcoal or resin artificial kidney. When used in the treatment of life threatening drug overdose, hemoperfusion is a covered service for patients with or without renal failure (effective for services performed on and after 9/1/79). Hemoperfusion generally requires a physician to be present to initiate treatment and to be present in the hospital or an adjacent medical office during the entire procedure, as changes may be sudden. Special staff training and equipment are required.

Develop charges for hemoperfusion in the same manner as for any new or unusual service. One or two treatments are usually all that is necessary to remove the toxic compound; document additional treatments. Hemoperfusion may be performed concurrently with dialysis, and in those cases payment for the hemoperfusion reflects only the additional care rendered over and above the care given with dialysis.

The effects of using hemoperfusion to improve the results of chronic hemodialysis are not known. Therefore, hemoperfusion is not a covered service when used to improve the results of hemodialysis. In addition, it has not been demonstrated that the use of hemoperfusion in conjunction with deferoxamine (DFO), in treating symptomatic patients with iron overload, is efficacious. There is also a paucity of data regarding its efficacy in treating asymptomatic patients with iron overload. Therefore, hemoperfusion used in conjunction with DFO in treating patients with iron overload is not a covered service; i.e., it is not considered reasonable and necessary within the meaning of Sec.1862(a)(1) of the Act.

However, the use of hemoperfusion in conjunction with DFO for the treatment of patients with aluminum toxicity has been demonstrated to be clinically efficacious and is therefore regarded as a covered service.

C. Hemofiltration.
This is a process which removes fluid, electrolytes and other low molecular weight toxic substances from the blood by filtration through hollow artificial membranes and may be routinely performed in 3 weekly sessions. Hemofiltration (which is also known as diafiltration) is a covered procedure under Medicare and is a safe and effective technique for the treatment of ESRD patients and an alternative to peritoneal dialysis and hemodialysis (effective for services performed on and after August 20, 1987). In contrast to both hemodialysis and peritoneal dialysis treatments, which eliminate dissolved substances via diffusion across semipermeable membranes, hemofiltration mimics the filtration process of the normal kidney. The technique requires an arteriovenous access. Hemofiltration may be performed either in facility or at home.

The procedure is most advantageous when applied to high-risk unstable patients, such as older patients with cardiovascular diseases or diabetes, because there are fewer side effects such as hypotension, hypertension or volume overload.

100-3, 110.16

NCD for Nonselective (Random) Transfusions and Living Related Donor Specific Transfusions (DST) in Kidney Transplantation (110.16)

These pretransplant transfusions are covered under Medicare without a specific limitation on the number of transfusions, subject to the normal Medicare blood deductible provisions. Where blood is given directly to the transplant patient; e.g., in the case of donor specific transfusions, the blood is considered replaced for purposes of the blood deductible provisions.

100-3, 130.1

NCD for Inpatient Hospital Stays for the Treatment of Alcoholism (130.1)

A. Inpatient Hospital Stay for Alcohol Detoxification
Many hospitals provide detoxification services during the more acute stages of alcoholism or alcohol withdrawal. When the high probability or occurrence of medical complications (e.g., delirium, confusion, trauma, or unconsciousness) during detoxification for acute alcoholism or alcohol withdrawal necessitates the constant availability of physicians and/or complex medical equipment found only in the hospital setting, inpatient hospital care during this period is considered reasonable and necessary and is therefore covered under the program. Generally, detoxification can be accomplished within 2-3 days with an occasional need for up to 5 days where the patient's condition dictates. This limit (5 days) may be extended in an individual case where there is a need for a longer period for detoxification for a particular patient. In such cases, however, there should be documentation by a physician which substantiates that a longer period of detoxification was reasonable and necessary. When the detoxification needs of an individual no longer require an inpatient hospital setting, coverage should be denied on the basis that inpatient hospital care is not reasonable and necessary as required by section l862(a)(l) of the Act. Following detoxification a patient may be transferred to an inpatient rehabilitation unit or discharged to a residential treatment program or outpatient treatment setting.

B. Inpatient Hospital Stay for Alcohol Rehabilitation
Hospitals may also provide structured inpatient alcohol rehabilitation programs to the chronic alcoholic. These programs are composed primarily of coordinated educational and psychotherapeutic services provided on a group basis. Depending on the subject matter, a series of lectures, discussions, films, and group therapy sessions are led by either physicians, psychologists, or alcoholism counselors from the hospital or various outside organizations. In addition, individual psychotherapy and family counseling (see Sec.70.1 of the NCD Manual) may be provided in selected cases. These programs are conducted under the supervision and direction of a physician. Patients may directly enter an inpatient hospital rehabilitation program after having undergone detoxification in the same hospital or in another hospital or may enter an inpatient hospital rehabilitation program without prior hospitalization for detoxification.

Alcohol rehabilitation can be provided in a variety of settings other than the hospital setting. In order for an inpatient hospital stay for alcohol rehabilitation to be covered under Medicare it must be medically necessary for the care to be provided in the inpatient hospital setting rather than in a less costly facility or on an outpatient basis. Inpatient hospital care for receipt of an alcohol rehabilitation program would generally be medically necessary where either (l) there is documentation by the physician that recent alcohol rehabilitation services in a less intensive setting or on an outpatient basis have proven unsuccessful and, as a consequence, the patient requires the supervision and intensity of services which can only be found in the controlled environment of the hospital, or (2) only the hospital environment can assure the medical management or control of the patient's concomitant conditions during the course of alcohol rehabilitation. (However, a patient's concomitant condition may make the use of certain alcohol treatment modalities medically inappropriate.) In addition, the "active treatment" criteria (see the Medicare Benefit Policy Manual, Chapter 2, "Inpatient Psychiatric Hospital Services," Sec.20) should be applied to psychiatric care in the general hospital as well as to psychiatric care in a psychiatric hospital. Since alcoholism is classifiable as a psychiatric condition the "active treatment" criteria must also be met in order for alcohol rehabilitation services to be covered under Medicare. (Thus, it is the combined need for "active treatment" and for covered care which can only be provided in the inpatient hospital setting, rather than the fact that rehabilitation immediately follows a period of detoxification, which provides the basis for coverage of inpatient hospital alcohol rehabilitation programs.)

Generally 16-19 days of rehabilitation services are sufficient to bring a patient to a point where care could be continued in other than an inpatient hospital setting. An inpatient hospital stay for alcohol rehabilitation may be extended beyond this limit in an individual case where a longer period of alcohol rehabilitation is medically necessary. In such cases, however, there should be documentation by a physician which substantiates the need for such care. Where the rehabilitation needs of an individual no longer require an inpatient hospital setting, coverage should be denied on the basis that inpatient hospital care is not reasonable and necessary as required by section l862(a)(l) of the Act..

Subsequent admissions to the inpatient hospital setting for alcohol rehabilitation followup, reinforcement, or "recap" treatments are considered to be readmissions (rather than an extension of the original stay) and must meet the requirements of this section for coverage under Medicare. Prior admissions to the inpatient hospital setting--either in the same hospital or in a different hospital--may be an indication that the "active treatment" requirements are not met (i.e., there is no reasonable expectation of improvement) and the stay should not be covered. Accordingly, there should be documentation to establish that "readmission" to the hospital setting for alcohol rehabilitation services can reasonably be expected to result in improvement of the patient's condition. For example, the documentation should indicate what changes in the patient's medical condition, social or emotional status, or treatment plan make improvement likely, or why the patient's initial hospital treatment was not sufficient.

C. Combined Alcohol Detoxification/Rehabilitation Programs.
Fiscal intermediaries should apply the guidelines in A. and B. above to both phases of a combined inpatient hospital alcohol detoxification/rehabilitation program. Not all patients who require the inpatient hospital setting for detoxification also need the inpatient hospital setting for rehabilitation. (See Sec.130.1 of the NCD Manual for coverage of outpatient hospital alcohol rehabilitation services.) Where the inpatient hospital setting is medically necessary for both alcohol detoxification and rehabilitation, generally a 3-week period is reasonable and necessary to bring the patient to the point where care can be continued in other than an inpatient hospital setting.

Decisions regarding reasonableness and necessity of treatment, the need for an inpatient hospital level of care, and length of treatment should be made by intermediaries based on accepted medical practice with the advice of their medical consultant. (In hospitals under PSRO review, PSRO determinations of medical necessity of services and appropriateness of the level of care at which services are provided are binding on the title XVIII fiscal intermediaries for purposes of adjudicating claims for payment.)

100-3, 130.2

NCD for Outpatient Hospital Services for Treatment of Alcoholism (130.2)

Coverage is available for both diagnostic and therapeutic services furnished for the treatment of alcoholism by the hospital to outpatients subject to the same rules applicable to outpatient hospital services in general. While there is no coverage for day hospitalization programs, per se, individual services which meet the requirements in the Medicare Benefit Policy Manual, Chapter 6, Sec.20 may be covered. (Meals, transportation and recreational and social activities do not fall within the scope of covered outpatient hospital services under Medicare.)

All services must be reasonable and necessary for diagnosis or treatment of the patient's condition (see the Medicare Benefit Policy Manual, chapter 16 Sec.20). Thus, educational services and family counseling would only be covered where they are directly related to treatment of the patient's condition. The frequency of treatment and period of time over which it occurs must also be reasonable and necessary.

100-3, 130.3

NCD for Chemical Aversion Therapy for Treatment of Alcoholism (130.3)

Available evidence indicates that chemical aversion therapy may be an effective component of certain alcoholism treatment programs, particularly as part of multimodality treatment programs which include other behavioral techniques and therapies, such as psychotherapy. Based on this evidence, CMS's medical consultants have recommended that chemical aversion therapy be covered under Medicare. However, since chemical aversion therapy is a demanding therapy which may not be appropriate for all Medicare beneficiaries needing treatment for alcoholism, a physician should certify to the appropriateness of chemical aversion therapy in the individual case. Therefore, if chemical aversion therapy for treatment of alcoholism is determined to be reasonable and necessary for an individual patient, it is covered under Medicare.

When it is medically necessary for a patient to receive chemical aversion therapy as a hospital inpatient, coverage for care in that setting is available. (See Sec.130.1 regarding coverage of multimodality treatment programs.) Followup treatments for chemical aversion therapy can generally be provided on an outpatient basis. Thus, where a patient is admitted as an inpatient for receipt of chemical aversion therapy, there must be documentation by the physician of the need in the individual case for the inpatient hospital admission.

Decisions regarding reasonableness and necessity of treatment and the need for an inpatient hospital level of care should be made by intermediaries based on accepted medical practice with the advice of their medical consultant. (In hospitals under QIO review, QIO determinations of medical necessity of services and appropriateness of the level of care at which services are provided are binding on the title XVIII fiscal intermediaries for purposes of adjudicating claims for payment.)

100-3, 130.4
NCD for Electrical Aversion Therapy for Treatment of Alcoholism (130.4)
Electrical aversion therapy has not been shown to be safe and effective and therefore is excluded from coverage.

100-3, 130.5
NCD for Treatment of Alcoholism and Drug Abuse in a Freestanding Clinic (130.5)
Coverage is available for alcoholism or drug abuse treatment services (such as drug therapy, psychotherapy, and patient education) that are provided incident to a physician's professional service in a freestanding clinic to patients who, for example, have been discharged from an inpatient hospital stay for the treatment of alcoholism or drug abuse or to individuals who are not in the acute stages of alcoholism or drug abuse but require treatment. The coverage available for these services is subject to the same rules generally applicable to the coverage of clinic services. Of course, the services also must be reasonable and necessary for the diagnosis or treatment of the individual's alcoholism or drug abuse. The Part B psychiatric limitation would apply to alcoholism or drug abuse treatment services furnished by physicians to individuals who are not hospital inpatients.

100-3, 130.6
NCD for Treatment of Drug Abuse (Chemical Dependency) (130.6)
Accordingly, when it is medically necessary for a patient to receive detoxification and/or rehabilitation for drug substance abuse as a hospital inpatient, coverage for care in that setting is available. Coverage is also available for treatment services that are provided in the outpatient department of a hospital to patients who, for example, have been discharged from an inpatient stay for the treatment of drug substance abuse or who require treatment but do not require the availability and intensity of services found only in the inpatient hospital setting. The coverage available for these services is subject to the same rules generally applicable to the coverage of outpatient hospital services. The services must also be reasonable and necessary for treatment of the individual's condition. Decisions regarding reasonableness and necessity of treatment, the need for an inpatient hospital level of care, and length of treatment should be made by intermediaries based on accepted medical practice with the advice of their medical consultant. (In hospitals under QIO review, QIO determinations of medical necessity of services and appropriateness of the level of care at which services are provided are binding on the title XVIII fiscal intermediaries for purposes of adjudicating claims for payment.)

100-3, 130.7
NCD for Withdrawal Treatments for Narcotic Addictions (130.7)
Withdrawal is an accepted treatment for narcotic addiction, and Part B payment can be made for these services if they are provided by the physician directly or under his personal supervision and if they are reasonable and necessary. In reviewing claims, reasonableness and necessity are determined with the aid of the contractor's medical staff.

Drugs that the physician provides in connection with this treatment are also covered if they cannot be self-administered and meet all other statutory requirements.

100-3, 130.8
NCD for Hemodialysis for Treatment of Schizophrenia (130.8)
Scientific evidence supporting use of hemodialysis as a safe and effective means of treatment for schizophrenia is inconclusive at this time. Accordingly, Medicare does not cover hemodialysis for treatment of schizophrenia.

100-3, 140.1
NCD for Abortion (140.1)
Abortions are not covered Medicare procedures except:

1. If the pregnancy is the result of an act of rape or incest; or

2. In the case where a woman suffers from a physical disorder, physical injury, or physical illness, including a life-endangering physical condition caused by or arising from the pregnancy itself, that would, as certified by a physician, place the woman in danger of death unless an abortion is performed.

100-3, 140.2
NCD for Breast Reconstruction Following Mastectomy (140.2)
Reconstruction of the affected and the contralateral unaffected breast following a medically necessary mastectomy is considered a relatively safe and effective noncosmetic procedure. Accordingly, program payment may be made for breast reconstruction surgery following removal of a breast for any medical reason.

Program payment may not be made for breast reconstruction for cosmetic reasons. (Cosmetic surgery is excluded from coverage under Sec.1862(a)(I0) of the Social Security Act.)

100-3, 140.3
NCD for Transsexual Surgery (140.3)
Transsexual surgery for sex reassignment of transsexuals is controversial. Because of the lack of well controlled, long term studies of the safety and effectiveness of the surgical procedures and attendant therapies for transsexualism, the treatment is considered experimental. Moreover, there is a high rate of serious complications for these surgical procedures. For these reasons, transsexual surgery is not covered.

100-3, 140.4
NCD for Plastic Surgery to Correct "Moon Face" (140.4)
The cosmetic surgery exclusion precludes payment for any surgical procedure directed at improving appearance. The condition giving rise to the patient's preoperative appearance is generally not a consideration. The only exception to the exclusion is surgery for the prompt repair of an accidental injury or for the improvement of a malformed body member which coincidentally serves some cosmetic purpose. Since surgery to correct a condition of "moon face" which developed as a side effect of cortisone therapy does not meet the exception to the exclusion, it is not covered under Medicare (Sec.1862(a)(10) of the Act).

100-3, 140.5
NCD for Laser Procedures (140.5)
Medicare recognizes the use of lasers for many medical indications. Procedures performed with lasers are sometimes used in place of more conventional techniques. In the absence of a specific noncoverage instruction, and where a laser has been approved for marketing by the Food and Drug Administration, contractor discretion may be used to determine whether a procedure performed with a laser is reasonable and necessary and, therefore, covered.

The determination of coverage for a procedure performed using a laser is made on the basis that the use of lasers to alter, revise, or destroy tissue is a surgical procedure. Therefore, coverage of laser procedures is restricted to practitioners with training in the surgical management of the disease or condition being treated.

100-3, 150.1
NCD for Manipulation (150.1)
A. Manipulation of the Rib Cage.
Manual manipulation of the rib cage contributes to the treatment of respiratory conditions such as bronchitis, emphysema, and asthma as part of a regimen which includes other elements of therapy, and is covered only under such circumstances.

B. Manipulation of the Head.
Manipulation of the occipitocervical or temporomandibular regions of the head when indicated for conditions affecting those portions of the head and neck is a covered service.

100-3, 150.2
NCD for Osteogenic Stimulators (150.2)
Electrical Osteogenic Stimulators
B. Nationally Covered Indications

1. Noninvasive Stimulator.

   The noninvasive stimulator device is covered only for the following indications:
   - Nonunion of long bone fractures;
   - Failed fusion, where a minimum of nine months has elapsed since the last surgery;
   - Congenital pseudarthroses; and
   - Effective July 1, 1996, as an adjunct to spinal fusion surgery for patients at high risk of pseudarthrosis due to previously failed spinal fusion at the same site or for those undergoing multiple level fusion. A multiple level fusion involves 3 or more vertebrae (e.g., L3-L5, L4-S1, etc).
   - Effective September 15, 1980, nonunion of long bone fractures is considered to exist only after 6 or more months have elapsed without healing of the fracture.
   - Effective April 1, 2000, nonunion of long bone fractures is considered to exist only when serial radiographs have confirmed that fracture healing has ceased for 3 or more months prior to starting treatment with the electrical osteogenic stimulator. Serial radiographs must include a minimum of 2 sets of radiographs, each including multiple views of the fracture site, separated by a minimum of 90 days.

2. Invasive (Implantable) Stimulator.

   The invasive stimulator device is covered only for the following indications:
   - Nonunion of long bone fractures
   - Effective July 1, 1996, as an adjunct to spinal fusion surgery for patients at high risk of pseudarthrosis due to previously failed spinal fusion at the same site or for those undergoing multiple level fusion. A multiple level fusion involves 3 or more vertebrae (e.g., L3-5, L4-S1, etc.)
   - Effective September 15, 1980, nonunion of long bone fractures is considered to exist only after 6 or more months have elapsed without healing of the fracture.
   - Effective April 1, 2000, non union of long bone fractures is considered to exist only when serial radiographs have confirmed that fracture healing has ceased for 3 or more months prior to starting treatment with the electrical osteogenic stimulator. Serial radiographs must include a minimum of 2 sets of radiographs, each including multiple views of the fracture site, separated by a minimum of 90 days.
   - Effective for services performed on or after January 1, 2001, ultrasonic osteogenic stimulators are covered as medically reasonable and necessary for the treatment of non-union fractures. In demonstrating nonunion of fractures, we would expect:
   - A minimum of two sets of radiographs obtained prior to starting treatment with the osteogenic stimulator, separated by a minimum of 90 days. Each radiograph must include multiple views of the fracture site accompanied with a written interpretation by a physician stating that there has been no clinically significant evidence of fracture healing between the two sets of radiographs.
   - Indications that the patient failed at least one surgical intervention for the treatment of the fracture.

- Effective April 27, 2005, upon the recommendation of the ultrasound stimulation for nonunion fracture healing, CMS determins that the evidence is adequate to condlude that noninvasive ultrasound stimulation for the treatment of nonunion bone fractures prior to surfical intervention is reasonable and necessary. In demonstrating non-union fracturs, CMS expects:

- A minimum of 2 sets of radiographs, obtained prior to starting treating with the osteogenic stimulator, separated by a minimum of 90 days. Each radiograph set must include multiple views of the fracture site accompanied with a written interpretation by a physician stating that there has been no clinically significant evidence of fracture healing between the 2 sets of radiographs.

C. Nationally Non-Covered Indications

Nonunion fractures of the skull, vertebrae and those that are tumor-related are excluded from coverage.

Ultrasonic osteogenic stimulators may not be used concurrently with other non-invasive osteogenic devices.

Ultrasonic osteogenic stimulators for fresh fracturs and delayed unions remain non-covered.

(This NCD last reviewed June 2005)

100-3, 150.3
NCD for Bone (Mineral) Density Studies (150.3)

Conditions for coverage of bone mass measurements are now contained in chapter 15, section 80.5 of Pub. 100-02, Medicare Benefit Policy Manual . Claims processing instructions can be found in chapter 13, section 140 of Pub. 100-04, Medicare Claims Processing Manual .

100-3, 150.5
NCD for Diathermy Treatment (150.5)

High energy pulsed wave diathermy machines have been found to produce some degree of therapeutic benefit for essentially the same conditions and to the same extent as standard diathermy. Accordingly, where the contractor's medical staff has determined that the pulsed wave diathermy apparatus used is one which is considered therapeutically effective, the treatments are considered a covered service, but only for those conditions for which standard diathermy is medically indicated and only when rendered by a physician or incident to a physician's professional services.

100-3, 150.6
NCD for Vitamin B12 Injections to Strengthen Tendons, Ligaments, etc., of the Foot (150.6)

Vitamin B12 injections to strengthen tendons, ligaments, etc., of the foot are not covered under Medicare because (1) there is no evidence that vitamin B12 injections are effective for the purpose of strengthening weakened tendons and ligaments, and (2) this is nonsurgical treatment under the subluxation exclusion. Accordingly, vitamin B12 injections are not considered reasonable and necessary within the meaning of Sec.1862(a)(1) of the Act.

100-3, 150.7
NCD for Prolotherapy, Joint Sclerotherapy, and Ligamentous Injections with Sclerosing Agents (150.7)

The medical effectiveness of the above therapies has not been verified by scientifically controlled studies. Accordingly, reimbursement for these modalities should be denied on the ground that they are not reasonable and necessary as required by Sec.1862(a)(1) of the Act.

100-3, 160.1
NCD for Induced Lesions of Nerve Tracts (160.1)

Accordingly, program payment may be made for these denervation procedures when used in selected cases (concurred in by contractor's medical staff) to treat chronic pain.

100-3, 160.2
NCD for Treatment of Motor Function Disorders with Electric Nerve Stimulation (160.2)

Where electric nerve stimulation is employed to treat motor function disorders, no reimbursement may be made for the stimulator or for the services related to its implantation since this treatment cannot be considered reasonable and necessary.

Note: For Medicare coverage of deep brain stimulation for essential tremor and Parkinson's disease, see Sec.160.24 of the NCD Manual.

100-3, 160.4
NCD for Stereotactic Cingulotomy as a Means of Psychosurgery (160.4)

Stereotactic cingulotomy is not covered under Medicare because the procedure is considered to be investigational.

100-3, 160.5
NCD for Stereotaxic Depth Electrode Implantation (160.5)

Stereotaxic depth electrode implantation prior to surgical treatment of focal epilepsy for patients who are unresponsive to anticonvulsant medications has been found both safe and effective for diagnosing resectable seizure foci that may go undetected by conventional scalp electroencephalographs (EEGs).

100-3, 160.6
NCD for Carotid Sinus Nerve Stimulator (160.6)

Implantation of the carotid sinus nerve stimulator is indicated for relief of angina pectoris in carefully selected patients who are refractory to medical therapy and who after undergoing coronary angiography study either are poor candidates for or refuse to have coronary bypass surgery. In such cases, Medicare reimbursement may be made for this device and for the related services required for its implantation.

However, the use of the carotid sinus nerve stimulator in the treatment of paroxysmal supraventricular tachycardia is considered investigational and is not in common use by the medical community. The device and related services in such cases cannot be considered as reasonable and necessary for the treatment of an illness or injury or to improve the functioning of a malformed body member as required by Sec.1862(a)(1) of the Act.

100-3, 160.7
NCD for Electrical Nerve Stimulators (160.7)

Two general classifications of electrical nerve stimulators are employed to treat chronic intractable pain: peripheral nerve stimulators and central nervous system stimulators.

A. Implanted Peripheral Nerve Stimulators

Payment may be made under the prosthetic device benefit for implanted peripheral nerve stimulators. Use of this stimulator involves implantation of electrodes around a selected peripheral nerve. The stimulating electrode is connected by an insulated lead to a receiver unit which is implanted under the skin at a depth not greater than 1/2 inch. Stimulation is induced by a generator connected to an antenna unit which is attached to the skin surface over the receiver unit. Implantation of electrodes requires surgery and usually necessitates an operating room.

Note: Peripheral nerve stimulators may also be employed to assess a patient's suitability for continued treatment with an electric nerve stimulator. As explained in Sec.160.7.1, such use of the stimulator is covered as part of the total diagnostic service furnished to the beneficiary rather than as a prosthesis.

B. Central Nervous System Stimulators (Dorsal Column and Depth Brain Stimulators)

The implantation of central nervous system stimulators may be covered as therapies for the relief of chronic intractable pain, subject to the following conditions:

1. Types of Implantations

    There are two types of implantations covered by this instruction:

    Dorsal Column (Spinal Cord) Neurostimulation - The surgical implantation of neurostimulator electrodes within the dura mater (endodural) or the percutaneous insertion of electrodes in the epidural space is covered.

    Depth Brain Neurostimulation - The stereotactic implantation of electrodes in the deep brain (e.g., thalamus and periaqueductal gray matter) is covered.

2. Conditions for Coverage

    No payment may be made for the implantation of dorsal column or depth brain stimulators or services and supplies related to such implantation, unless all of the conditions listed below have been met:

    The implantation of the stimulator is used only as a late resort (if not a last resort) for patients with chronic intractable pain;

    With respect to item a, other treatment modalities (pharmacological, surgical, physical, or psychological therapies) have been tried and did not prove satisfactory, or are judged to be unsuitable or contraindicated for the given patient;

    Patients have undergone careful screening, evaluation and diagnosis by a multidisciplinary team prior to implantation. (Such screening must include psychological, as well as physical evaluation);

    All the facilities, equipment, and professional and support personnel required for the proper diagnosis, treatment training, and followup of the patient (including that required to satisfy item c) must be available; and

    Demonstration of pain relief with a temporarily implanted electrode precedes permanent implantation.

    Contractors may find it helpful to work with QIOs to obtain the information needed to apply these conditions to claims.

100-3, 160.7.1
NCD for Assessing Patient's Suitability for Electrical Nerve Stimulation Therapy (160.7.1)
Indications and Limitations of Coverage

CIM 35-46

Electrical nerve stimulation is an accepted modality for assessing a patient's suitability for ongoing treatment with a transcutaneous or an implanted nerve stimulator.

Accordingly, program payment may be made for the following techniques when used to determine the potential therapeutic usefulness of an electrical nerve stimulator:

A. Transcutaneous Electrical Nerve Stimulation(TENS)

This technique involves attachment of a transcutaneous nerve stimulator to the surface of the skin over the peripheral nerve to be stimulated. It is used by the patient on a trial basis and its effectiveness in modulating pain is monitored by the physician, or physical therapist. Generally, the physician or physical therapist is able to determine whether the patient is likely to derive a significant therapeutic benefit from continuous use of a transcutaneous stimulator within a trial period of 1 month; in a few cases this determination may take longer to make. Document the medical necessity for such services which are furnished beyond the first month. (See Sec.160.13 for an explanation of coverage of medically necessary supplies for the effective use of TENS.)

If TENS significantly alleviates pain, it may be considered as primary treatment; if it produces no relief or greater discomfort than the original pain electrical nerve stimulation therapy is ruled out. However, where TENS produces incomplete relief, further evaluation with percutaneous electrical nerve stimulation may be considered to determine whether an implanted peripheral nerve stimulator would provide significant relief from pain.

Usually, the physician or physical therapist providing the services will furnish the equipment necessary for assessment. Where the physician or physical therapist advises the patient to rent the TENS from a supplier during the trial period rather than supplying it himself/herself, program payment may be made for rental of the TENS as well as for the services of the physician or physical therapist who is evaluating its use. However, the combined program payment which is made for the physician's or physical therapist's services and the rental of the stimulator from a supplier should not exceed the amount which would be payable for the total service, including the stimulator, furnished by the physician or physical therapist alone.

B. Percutaneous Electrical Nerve Stimulation (PENS)
This diagnostic procedure which involves stimulation of peripheral nerves by a needle electrode inserted through the skin is performed only in a physician's office, clinic, or hospital outpatient department. Therefore, it is covered only when performed by a physician or incident to physician's service. If pain is effectively controlled by percutaneous stimulation, implantation of electrodes is warranted.

As in the case of TENS (described in subsection A), generally the physician should be able to determine whether the patient is likely to derive a significant therapeutic benefit from continuing use of an implanted nerve stimulator within a trial period of 1 month. In a few cases, this determination may take longer to make. The medical necessity for such diagnostic services which are furnished beyond the first month must be documented.

NOTE. Electrical nerve stimulators do not prevent pain but only alleviate pain as it occurs. A patient can be taught how to employ the stimulator, and once this is done, can use it safely and effectively without direct physician supervision. Consequently, it is inappropriate for a patient to visit his/her physician, physical therapist, or an outpatient clinic on a continuing basis for treatment of pain with electrical nerve stimulation. Once it is determined that electrical nerve stimulation should be continued as therapy and the patient has been trained to use the stimulator, it is expected that a stimulator will be implanted or the patient will employ the TENS on a continual basis in his/her home. Electrical nerve stimulation treatments furnished by a physician in his/her office, by a physical therapist or outpatient clinic are excluded from coverage by Sec.1862(a)(1) of the Act. (See Sec.160.7 for an explanation of coverage of the therapeutic use of implanted peripheral nerve stimulators under the prosthetic devices benefit. See Sec.280.13 for an explanation of coverage of the therapeutic use of TENS under the durable medical equipment benefit.)

100-3, 160.8

NCD for Electroencephalographic (EEG) Monitoring During Surgical Procedures Involving the Cerebral Vasculature (160.8)
CIM 35-57

Electroencephalographic (EEG) monitoring is a safe and reliable technique for the assessment of gross cerebral blood flow during general anesthesia and is covered under Medicare. Very characteristic changes in the EEG occur when cerebral perfusion is inadequate for cerebral function. EEG monitoring as an indirect measure of cerebral perfusion requires the expertise of an electroencephalographer, a neurologist trained in EEG, or an advanced EEG technician for its proper interpretation.

The EEG monitoring may be covered routinely in carotid endarterectomies and in other neurological procedures where cerebral perfusion could be reduced. Such other procedures might include aneurysm surgery where hypotensive anesthesia is used or other cerebral vascular procedures where cerebral blood flow may be interrupted.

100-3, 160.9

NCD for Electroencephalographic (EEG) Monitoring during Open-Heart Surgery (160.9)
The value of EEG monitoring during open heart surgery and in the immediate post-operative period is debatable because there are little published data based on well designed studies regarding its clinical effectiveness. The procedure is not frequently used and does not enjoy widespread acceptance of benefit.

Accordingly, Medicare does not cover EEG monitoring during open heart surgery and during the immediate post operative period.

100-3, 160.10

NCD for Evoked Response Tests (160.10)
Evoked response tests, including brain stem evoked response and visual evoked response tests, are generally accepted as safe and effective diagnostic tools. Program payment may be made for these procedures.

100-3, 160.12

NCD for Neuromuscular Electrical Stimulaton (NMES) (160.12)
Indications and Limitations of Coverage

Treatment of Muscle Atrophy
Coverage of NMES to treat muscle atrophy is limited to the treatment of disuse atrophy where nerve supply to the muscle is intact, including brain, spinal cord and peripheral nerves, and other non-neurological reasons for disuse atrophy. Some examples would be casting or splinting of a limb, contracture due to scarring of soft tissue as in burn lesions, and hip replacement surgery (until orthotic training begins). (See Sec.160.13 of the NCD Manual for an explanation of coverage of medically necessary supplies for the effective use of NMES.)

Use for Walking in Patients with Spinal Cord Injury (SCI)
The type of NMES that is use to enhance the ability to walk of SCI patients is commonly referred to as functional electrical stimulation (FES). These devices are surface units that use electrical impulses to activate paralyzed or weak muscles in precise sequence. Coverage for the use of NMES/FES is limited to SCI patients for walking, who have completed a training program which consists of at least 32 physical therapy sessions with the device over a period of three months. The trial period of physical therapy will enable the physician treating the patient for his or her spinal cord injury to properly evaluate the person's ability to use these devices frequently and for the long term. Physical therapy necessary to perform this training must be directly performed by the physical therapist as part of a one-on-one training program.

The goal of physical therapy must be to train SCI patients on the use of NMES/FES devices to achieve walking, not to reverse or retard muscle atrophy.

Coverage for NMES/FES for walking will be covered in SCI patients with all of the following characteristics:

- Persons with intact lower motor unite (L1 and below) (both muscle and peripheral nerve);
- Persons with muscle and joint stability for weight bearing at upper and lower extremities that can demonstrate balance and control to maintain an upright support posture independently;
- Persons that demonstrate brisk muscle contraction to NMES and have sensory perception electrical stimulation sufficient for muscle contraction;
- Persons that possess high motivation, commitment and cognitive ability to use such devices for walking;
- Persons that can transfer independently and can demonstrate independent standing tolerance for at least 3 minutes;
- Persons that can demonstrate hand and finger function to manipulate controls;
- Persons with at least 6-month post recovery spinal cord injury and restorative surgery;
- Persons with hip and knee degenerative disease and no history of long bone fracture secondary to osteoporosis; and
- Persons who have demonstrated a willingness to use the device long-term.

NMES/FES for walking will not be covered in SCI patient with any of the following:

- Persons with cardiac pacemakers;
- Severe scoliosis or severe osteoporosis;
- Skin disease or cancer at area of stimulation;
- Irreversible contracture; or
- Autonomic dysflexia.

The only settings where therapists with the sufficient skills to provide these services are employed, are inpatient hospitals; outpatient hospitals; comprehensive outpatient rehabilitation facilities; and outpatient rehabilitation facilities. The physical therapy necessary to perform this training must be part of a one-on-one training program.

Additional therapy after the purchase of the DME would be limited by our general policies in converge of skilled physical therapy.

100-3, 160.13

NCD for Supplies Used in the Delivery of Transcutaneous Electrical Nerve Stimulation (TENS) and Neuromuscular Electrical Stimulation (NMES) (160.13)
A form-fitting conductive garment (and medically necessary related supplies) may be covered under the program only when:

1. It has received permission or approval for marketing by the Food and Drug Administration;
2. It has been prescribed by a physician for use in delivering covered TENS or NMES treatment; and
3. One of the medical indications outlined below is met:
   - The patient cannot manage without the conductive garment because there is such a large area or so many sites to be stimulated and the stimulation would have to be delivered so frequently that it is not feasible to use conventional electrodes, adhesive tapes and lead wires;
   - The patient cannot manage without the conductive garment for the treatment of chronic intractable pain because the areas or sites to be stimulated are inaccessible with the use of conventional electrodes, adhesive tapes and lead wires;
   - The patient has a documented medical condition such as skin problems that preclude the application of conventional electrodes, adhesive tapes and lead wires;
   - The patient requires electrical stimulation beneath a cast either to treat disuse atrophy, where the nerve supply to the muscle is intact, or to treat chronic intractable pain; or
   - The patient has a medical need for rehabilitation strengthening (pursuant to a written plan of rehabilitation) following an injury where the nerve supply to the muscle is intact.

A conductive garment is not covered for use with a TENS device during the trial period specified in Sec.160.3 unless:

- The patient has a documented skin problem prior to the start of the trial period; and
- The carrier's medical consultants are satisfied that use of such an item is medically necessary for the patient.

100-3, 160.15

NCD for Electrotherapy for Treatment of Facial Nerve Paralysis (Bell's Palsy) (160.15)

Electrotherapy for the treatment of facial nerve paralysis, commonly known as Bell's Palsy, is not covered under Medicare because its clinical effectiveness has not been established.

100-3, 160.17

NCD for L-DOPA (160.17)

A - Part A Payment for L-Dopa and Associated Inpatient Hospital Services

A hospital stay and related ancillary services for the administration of L-Dopa are covered if medically required for this purpose. Whether a drug represents an allowable inpatient hospital cost during such stay depends on whether it meets the definition of a drug in Sec.1861(t) of the Act; i.e., on its inclusion in the compendia named in the Act or approval by the hospital's pharmacy and drug therapeutics (P&DT) or equivalent committee. (Levodopa (L-Dopa) has been favorably evaluated for the treatment of Parkinsonism by A.M.A. Drug Evaluations, First Edition 1971, the replacement compendia for "New Drugs.")

Inpatient hospital services are frequently not required in many cases when L-Dopa therapy is initiated. Therefore, determine the medical need for inpatient hospital services on the basis of medical facts in the individual case. It is not necessary to hospitalize the typical, well-functioning, ambulatory Parkinsonian patient who has no concurrent disease at the start of L-Dopa treatment. It is reasonable to provide inpatient hospital services for Parkinsonian patients with concurrent diseases, particularly of the cardiovascular, gastrointestinal, and neuropsychiatric systems. Although many patients require hospitalization for a period of under 2 weeks, a 4-week period of inpatient care is not unreasonable.

Laboratory tests in connection with the administration of L-Dopa - The tests medically warranted in connection with the achievement of optimal dosage and the control of the side effects of L-Dopa include a complete blood count, liver function tests such as SGOT, SGPT, and/or alkaline phosphatase, BUN or creatinine and urinalysis, blood sugar, and electrocardiogram.

Whether or not the patient is hospitalized, laboratory tests in certain cases are reasonable at weekly intervals although some physicians prefer to perform the tests much less frequently.

Physical therapy furnished in connection with administration of L-Dopa - Where, following administration of the drug, the patient experiences a reduction of rigidity which permits the reestablishment of a restorative goal for him/her, physical therapy services required to enable him/her to achieve this goal are payable provided they require the skills of a qualified physical therapist and are furnished by or under the supervision of such a therapist. However, once the individual's restoration potential has been achieved, the services required to maintain him/her at this level do not generally require the skills of a qualified physical therapist. In such situations, the role of the therapist is to evaluate the patient's needs in consultation with his/her physician and design a program of exercise appropriate to the capacity and tolerance of the patient and treatment objectives of the physician, leaving to others the actual carrying out of the program. While the evaluative services rendered by a qualified physical therapist are payable as physical therapy, services furnished by others in connection with the carrying out of the maintenance program established by the therapist are not.

B - Part A Reimbursement for L-Dopa Therapy in SNFs

Initiation of L-Dopa therapy can be appropriately carried out in the SNF setting, applying the same guidelines used for initiation of L-Dopa therapy in the hospital, including the types of patients who should be covered for inpatient services, the role of physical therapy, and the use of laboratory tests. (See subsection A.)

Where inpatient care is required and L-Dopa therapy is initiated in the SNF, limit the stay to a maximum of 4 weeks; but in many cases the need may be no longer than 1 or 2 weeks, depending upon the patient's condition. However, where L-Dopa therapy is begun in the hospital and the patient is transferred to an SNF for continuation of the therapy, a combined length of stay in hospital and SNF of no longer than 4 weeks is reasonable (i.e., 1 week hospital stay followed by 3 weeks SNF stay; or 2 weeks hospital stay followed by 2 weeks SNF stay; etc.). Medical need must be demonstrated in cases where the combined length of stay in hospital and SNF is longer than 4 weeks. The choice of hospital or SNF, and the decision regarding the relative length of time spent in each, should be left to the medical judgment of the treating physician.

C - L-Dopa Coverage Under Part B

Part B reimbursement may not be made for the drug L-Dopa since it is a self-administrable drug. However, physician services rendered in connection with its administration and control of its side effects are covered if determined to be reasonable and necessary. Initiation of L-Dopa therapy on an outpatient basis is possible in most cases. Visit frequency ranging from every week to every 2 or 3 months is acceptable. However, after half a year of therapy, visits more frequent than every month would usually not be reasonable.

100-3, 160.18

NCD for Vagus Nerve Stimulation for Treatment of Seizures (160.18)

B. Nationally Covered Indications

Effective for services performed on or after July 1, 1999, VNS is reasonable and necessary for patients with medically refractory partial onset seizures for whom surgery is not recommended or for whom surgery has failed.

C. Nationally Non-Covered Indications

Effective for services performed on or after July 1, 1999, VNS is not reasonable and necessary for all other types of seizure disorders which are medically refractory and for whom surgery is not recommended or for whom surgery has failed.

Effective for services performed on or after May 4, 2007, VNS is not reasonable and necessary for resistant depression. (Information on the national coverage analysis leading to this determination can be found at: http://www.cms.hhs.gov/mcd/viewnca.asp?where=index&nca_id= 195.)

D. Other

Also see Sec.160, "Electrical Nerve Stimulators."

(This NCD last reviewed May 2007.)

100-3, 160.20

NCD for Transfer Factor for Treatment of Multiple Sclerosis (160.20)

Transfer factor is the dialysate of an extract from sensitized leukocytes which increases cellular immune activity in the recipient. It is not covered as a treatment for multiple sclerosis because its use for the purpose is still experimental.

100-3, 160.21

NCD for Telephone Transmission of Electroencephalograms (EEGs) (160.21)

Telephone transmission of electroencephalograms (EEGs) is covered as a physician's service or as incident to a physician's service when reasonable and necessary for the individual patient, under appropriate circumstances. The service is safe, and may save time and cost in sending EEGs from remote areas without special competence in neurology, neurosurgery, and electroencephalography, by avoiding the need to transport patients to large medical centers for standard EEG testing.

100-3, 160.22

NCD for Ambulatory EEG Monitoring (160.22)

Ambulatory EEG monitoring is a diagnostic procedure for patients in whom a seizure diathesis is suspected but not defined by history, physical or resting EEG. Ambulatory EEG can be utilized in the differential diagnosis of syncope and transient ischemic attacks if not elucidated by conventional studies. Ambulatory EEG should always be preceded by a resting EEG.

Ambulatory EEG monitoring is considered an established technique and covered under Medicare for the above purposes.

100-3, 170.3

NCD for Speech Pathology Services for the Treatment of Dysphagia (170.3)

Speech -language pathology services are covered under Medicare for the treatment of dysphagia, regardless of the presence of a communication disability.

100-3, 180.1

NCD for Medical Nutrition Therapy (180.1)

Effective October 1, 2002, basic coverage of MNT for the first year a beneficiary receives MNT with either a diagnosis of renal disease or diabetes as defined at 42 CFR Sec.410.130 is 3 hours. Also effective October 1, 2002, basic coverage in subsequent years for renal disease or diabetes is 2 hours. The dietitian/nutritionist may choose how many units are performed per day as long as all of the other requirements in this NCD and 42 CFR Secs.410.130-410.134 are met. Pursuant to the exception at 42 CFR Sec.410.132(b)(5), additional hours are considered to be medically necessary and covered if the treating physician determines that there is a change in medical condition, diagnosis, or treatment regimen that requires a change in MNT and orders additional hours during that episode of care.

Effective October 1, 2002, if the treating physician determines that receipt of both MNT and DSMT is medically necessary in the same episode of care, Medicare will cover both DSMT and MNT initial and subsequent years without decreasing either benefit as long as DSMT and MNT are not provided on the same date of service. The dietitian/nutritionist may choose how many units are performed per day as long as all of the other requirements in the NCD and 42 CFR Secs.410.130-410.134 are met. Pursuant to the exception at 42 CFR 410.132(b)(5), additional hours are considered to be medically necessary and covered if the treating physician determines that there is a change in medical condition, diagnosis, or treatment regimen that requires a change in MNT and orders additional hours during that episode of care.

100-3, 190.1

NCD for Histocompatibility Testing (190.1)

This testing is safe and effective when it is performed on patients:

- In preparation for a kidney transplant;
- In preparation for bone marrow transplantation;
- In preparation for blood platelet transfusions (particularly where multiple infusions are involved); or
- Who are suspected of having ankylosing spondylitis.

This testing is covered under Medicare when used for any of the indications listed in A, B, and C and if it is reasonable and necessary for the patient.

It is covered for ankylosing spondylitis in cases where other methods of diagnosis would not be appropriate or have yielded inconclusive results. Request documentation supporting the medical necessity of the test from the physician in all cases where ankylosing spondylitis is indicated as the reason for the test.

100-3, 190.2

NCD for Diagnostic Pap Smears (190.2)

CIM 50-20, CIM 50-20.1

A diagnostic pap smear and related medically necessary services are covered under Medicare Part B when ordered by a physician under one of the following conditions:

- Previous cancer of the cervix, uterus, or vagina that has been or is presently being treated;
- Previous abnormal pap smear;
- Any abnormal findings of the vagina, cervix, uterus, ovaries, or adnexa;
- Any significant complaint by the patient referable to the female reproductive system; or

- Any signs or symptoms that might in the physician's judgment reasonably be related to a gynecologic disorder.

Screening Pap Smears and Pelvic Examinations for Early Detection of Cervical or Vaginal Cancer. (See section 210.2.)

100-3, 190.3

NCD for Cytogenetic Studies (190.3)

Medicare covers these tests when they are reasonable and necessary for the diagnosis or treatment of the following conditions:

Genetic disorders (e.g., mongolism) in a fetus (See Medicare Benefit Policy Manual, Chapter 15, "Covered medical and Other health Services," Sec.20.1)

Failure of sexual development;

Chronic myelogenous leukemia;

Acute leukemias lymphoid (FAB L1-L3), myeloid (FAB M0-M7), and unclassified; or

Mylodysplasia

100-3, 190.4

NCD for Electron Microscope (190.4)

The electron microscope has been used in the examination of biopsies for years; its efficacy, and therefore its Medicare coverage, is not being questioned. However, there are less expensive methods for examining biopsies which are normally adequate. The additional expense for the electron microscope is normally warranted only when distinguishing different types of nephritis from renal needle biopsies or when there is an uncertain diagnosis from the pathologist. When an uncertain diagnosis from the pathologists results from a less expensive method of examination and an electron microscope examination is therefore necessary, both biopsy examinations are covered. Where the additional expense for an electron microscope examination is not warranted, payment is based upon the less costly methods of examining biopsies.

100-3, 190.5

NCD for Sweat Test (190.5)
Indications and Limitations of Coverage

The sweat test is an important diagnostic tool in cystic fibrosis and may be covered when used for that purpose. Usage of the sweat test as a predictor of efficacy of sympathectomy in peripheral vascular disease is unproven and, therefore, is not covered.

100-3, 190.6

NCD for Hair Analysis (190.6)
Indications and Limitations of Coverage

Hair analysis to detect mineral traces as an aid in diagnosing human disease is not a covered service under Medicare.

The correlation of hair analysis to the chemical state of the whole body is not possible at this time, and therefore this diagnostic procedure cannot be considered to be reasonable and necessary under Sec.1862(a)(1) of the Act.

100-3, 190.8

NCD for Lymphocyte Mitogen Response Assays (190.8)

It is a covered test under Medicare when it is medically necessary to assess lymphocytic function in diagnosed immunodeficiency diseases and to monitor immunotherapy.

It is not covered when it is used to monitor the treatment of cancer, because its use for that purpose is experimental.

100-3, 190.9

NCD for Serologic Testing for Acquired Immunodeficiency Syndrome (AIDS) (190.9)

These tests may be covered when performed to help determine a diagnosis for symptomaticpatients. They are not covered when furnished as part of a screening program for asymptomatic persons.

Note: Two enzyme-linked immunosorbent assay (ELISA) tests that were conducted on the same specimen must both be positive before Medicare will cover the Western blot test.

100-3, 190.10

NCD for Laboratory Tests - CRD Patients (190.10)

Laboratory tests are essential to monitor the progress of CRD patients. The following list and frequencies of tests constitute the level and types of routine laboratory tests that are covered. Bills for other types of tests are considered nonroutine. Routine tests at greater frequencies must include medical justification. Nonroutine tests generally are justified by the diagnosis.

The routinely covered regimen includes the following tests:

Per Dialysis

- All hematocrit or hemoglobin and clotting time tests furnished incident to dialysis treatments.

Per Week

- Prothrombin time for patients on anticoagulant therapy
- Serum Creatinine

Per Week or Thirteen Per Quarter

- BUN

Monthly

- CBC
- Serum Calcium
- Serum Potassium
- Serum Chloride
- Serum Bicarbonate
- Serum Phosphorous
- Total Protein
- Serum Albumin
- Alkaline Phospatase
- AST, SGOT
- LDH

Guidelines for tests other than those routinely performed include:

- Serum Aluminum - one every 3 months
- Serum Ferritin - one every 3 months

The following tests for hepatitis B are covered when patients first enter a dialysis facility:

- Hepatitis B surface antigen (HBsAg)
- Anti-HBs

Coverage of future testing in these patients depends on their serologic status and on whether they have been successfully immunized against hepatitis B virus. The following table summarizes the frequency of serologic surveillance for hepatitis B. Tests furnished according to this table do not require additional documentation and are paid separately because payment for maintenance dialysis treatments does not take them into account.

Frequency of Screening

	Vaccination and Serologic Status	HbsAg Patients	Anti-HBs Patients
Unvaccinated	Susceptible	Monthly	Semiannually
Unvaccinated	HBsAg Carrier	Annually	None
Unvaccinated	Anti-HBs-Positive (1)	None	Annually
Vaccinated	Anti-HBs-Positive (1)	None	Annually
Vaccinated	Low Level or No Anti HBs	Monthly	Semiannually

(1) At least 10 sample ration units by radioimmunoassay or positive by enzyme immunoassay.

Patients who are in the process of receiving hepatitis B vaccines, but have not received the complete series, should continue to be routinely screened as susceptible. Between one and six months after the third dose, all vaccines should be tested for anti-HBs to confirm their response to the vaccine. Patients who have a level of anti-HBs of at least 10 sample ratio units (SRUs) by radioimmunoassay (RIA) or who are positive by enzyme immunoassay (EIA) are considered adequate responders to vaccine and need only be tested for anti-HBs annually to verify their immune status. If anti-HBs drops below 10 SRUs by RIA or is negative by EIA, a booster dose of hepatitis B vaccine should be given.

Laboratory tests are subject to the normal coverage requirements. If the laboratory services are performed by a free-standing facility, be sure it meets the conditions of coverage for independent laboratories.

100-3, 190.11

NCD for Home Prothrombin Time International Normalized Ratio (INR) Monitoring for Anticoagulation Management (190.11)

For services furnished on or after July 1, 2002, Medicare will cover for the use of home prothrombin time INR monitoring for anticoagulation management for patients with mechanical heart valves on Warfarin. Home prothrombin monitoring with the use of INR devices is covered only for patients with mechanical heart valves. The monitor and the home testing must be prescribed by a treating physician as provided at 42 CFR 410.32(a) and the following requirements must be met: The patient must have been anticoagulated for at least three months prior to use of the home INR device;

The patient must undergo an educational program on anticoagulation management and the use of the device prior to its use in the home; and

Self-testing with the device should not occur more frequently than once a week.

100-3, 190.12

NCD for Urine Culture, Bacterial (190.12)
Indications

1. A patient's urinalysis is abnormal suggesting urinary tract infection, for example, abnormal microscopic (hematuria, pyuria, bacteriuria); abnormal biochemical urinalysis (positive leukocyte esterase, nitrite, protein, blood); a Gram's stain positive for microorganisms; positive bacteriuria screen by a non?culture technique; or other significant abnormality of a urinalysis. While it is not essential to evaluate a urine specimen by one of these methods before a urine culture is performed, certain clinical presentations with highly suggestive signs and symptoms may lend themselves to an antecedent urinalysis procedure where follow-up culture depends upon an initial positive or abnormal test result.

2. A patient has clinical signs and symptoms indicative of a possible urinary tract infection (UTI). Acute lower UTI may present with urgency, frequency, nocturia, dysuria, discharge or

incontinence. These findings may also be noted in upper UTI with additional systemic symptoms (for example, fever, chills, lethargy); or pain in the costovertebral, abdominal, or pelvic areas. Signs and symptoms may overlap considerably with other inflammatory conditions of the genitourinary tract (for example, prostatitis, urethritis, vaginitis, or cervicitis). Elderly or immunocompromised patients, or patients with neurologic disorders may present atypically (for example, general debility, acute mental status changes, declining functional status).

3. The patient is being evaluated for suspected urosepsis, fever of unknown origin, or other systemic manifestations of infection but without a known source. Signs and symptoms used to define sepsis have been well established.

4. A test-of cure is generally not indicated in an uncomplicated infection. However, it may be indicated if the patient is being evaluated for response to therapy and there is a complicating co-existing urinary abnormality including structural or functional abnormalities, calculi, foreign bodies, or ureteral/renal stents or there is clinical or laboratory evidence of failure to respond as described in Indications 1 and 2.

5. In surgical procedures involving major manipulations of the genitourinary tract, preoperative examination to detect occult infection may be indicated in selected cases (for example, prior to renal transplantation, manipulation or removal of kidney stones, or transurethral surgery of the bladder or prostate).

6. Urine culture may be indicated to detect occult infection in renal transplant recipients on immunosuppressive therapy.

Limitations

1. CPT 87086 may be used one time per encounter.

2. Colony count restrictions on coverage of CPT 87088 do not apply as they may be highly variable according to syndrome or other clinical circumstances (for example, antecedent therapy, collection time, degree of hydration).

3. CPT 87088, 87184, and 87186 may be used multiple times in association with or independent of 87086, as urinary tract infections may be polymicrobial.

4. Testing for asymptomatic bacteriuria as part of a prenatal evaluation may be medically appropriate but is considered screening and, therefore, not covered by Medicare. The US Preventive Services Task Force has concluded that screening for asymptomatic bacteriuria outside of the narrow indication for pregnant women is generally not indicated. There are insufficient data to recommend screening in ambulatory elderly patients including those with diabetes. Testing may be clinically indicated on other grounds including likelihood of recurrence or potential adverse effects of antibiotics, but is considered screening in the absence of clinical or laboratory evidence of infection.

100-3, 190.13
NCD for Human Immunodeficiency Virus (HIV) Testing (Prognosis Including Monitoring) (190.13)
Indications

1. A plasma HIV RNA baseline level may be medically necessary in any patient with confirmed HIV infection.

2. Regular periodic measurement of plasma HIV RNA levels may be medically necessary to determine risk for disease progression in an HIV-infected individual and to determine when to initiate or modify antiretroviral treatment regimens.

3. In clinical situations where the risk of HIV infection is significant and initiation of therapy is anticipated, a baseline HIV quantification may be performed. These situations include:

   a. Persistence of borderline or equivocal serologic reactivity in an at-risk individual.

   b. Signs and symptoms of acute retroviral syndrome characterized by fever, malaise, lymphadenopathy and rash in an at-risk individual.

Limitations

1. Viral quantification may be appropriate for prognostic use including baseline determination, periodic monitoring, and monitoring of response to therapy. Use as a diagnostic test method is not indicated.

2. Measurement of plasma HIV RNA levels should be performed at the time of establishment of an HIV infection diagnosis. For an accurate baseline, 2 specimens in a 2-week period are appropriate.

3. For prognosis including anti-retroviral therapy monitoring, regular, periodic measurements are appropriate. The frequency of viral load testing should be consistent with the most current Centers for Disease Control and Prevention guidelines for use of anti-retroviral agents in adults and adolescents or pediatrics.

4. Because differences in absolute HIV copy number are known to occur using different assays, plasma HIV RNA levels should be measured by the same analytical method. A change in assay method may necessitate re-establishment of a baseline.

5. Nucleic acid quantification techniques are representative of rapidly emerging and evolving new technologies. As such, users are advised to remain current on FDA-approval status.

100-3, 190.14
NCD for Human Immunodeficiency Virus (HIV) Testing (Diagnosis) (190.14)
Indications and Limitations of Coverage

Indications

Diagnostic testing to establish HIV infection may be indicated when there is a strong clinical suspicion supported by one or more of the following clinical findings:

1. The patient has a documented, otherwise unexplained, AIDS-defining or AIDS-associated opportunistic infection.

2. The patient has another documented sexually transmitted disease which identifies significant risk of exposure to HIV and the potential for an early or subclinical infection.

4. The patient has documented acute or chronic hepatitis B or C infection that identifies a significant risk of exposure to HIV and the potential for an early or subclinical infection.

5. The patient has a documented AIDS-defining or AIDS-associated neoplasm.

6. The patient has a documented AIDS-associated neurologic disorder or otherwise unexplained dementia.

7. The patient has another documented AIDS-defining clinical condition, or a history of other severe, recurrent, or persistent conditions which suggest an underlying immune deficiency (for example, cutaneous or mucosal disorders).

8. The patient has otherwise unexplained generalized signs and symptoms suggestive of a chronic process with an underlying immune deficiency (for example, fever, weight loss, malaise, fatigue, chronic diarrhea, failure to thrive, chronic cough, hemoptysis, shortness of breath, or lymphadenopathy).

9. The patient has otherwise unexplained laboratory evidence of a chronic disease process with an underlying immune deficiency (for example, anemia, leukopenia, pancytopenia, lymphopenia, or low CD4+ lymphocyte count).

10. The patient has signs and symptoms of acute retroviral syndrome with fever, malaise, lymphadenopathy, and skin rash.

11. The patient has documented exposure to blood or body fluids known to be capable of transmitting HIV (for example, needlesticks and other significant blood exposures) and antiviral therapy is initiated or anticipated to be initiated.

12. The patient is undergoing treatment for rape. (HIV testing is a part of the rape treatment protocol.)

Limitations

1. HIV antibody testing in the United States is usually performed using HIV-1 or HIV-¾ combination tests. HIV-2 testing is indicated if clinical circumstances suggest HIV-2 is likely (that is, compatible clinical findings and HIV-1 test negative). HIV-2 testing may also be indicated in areas of the country where there is greater prevalence of HIV-2 infections.

2. The Western Blot test should be performed only after documentation that the initial EIA tests are repeatedly positive or equivocal on a single sample.

3. The HIV antigen tests currently have no defined diagnostic usage.

4. Direct viral RNA detection may be performed in those situations where serologic testing does not establish a diagnosis but strong clinical suspicion persists (for example, acute retroviral syndrome, nonspecific serologic evidence of HIV, or perinatal HIV infection).

5. If initial serologic tests confirm an HIV infection, repeat testing is not indicated.

6. If initial serologic tests are HIV EIA negative and there is no indication for confirmation of infection by viral RNA detection, the interval prior to retesting is 3-6 months.

7. Testing for evidence of HIV infection using serologic methods may be medically appropriate in situations where there is a risk of exposure to HIV. However, in the absence of a documented AIDS defining or HIV- associated disease, an HIV associated sign or symptom, or documented exposure to a known HIV-infected source, the testing is considered by Medicare to be screening and thus is not covered by Medicare (for example, history of multiple blood component transfusions, exposure to blood or body fluids not resulting in consideration of therapy, history of transplant, history of illicit drug use, multiple sexual partners, same-sex encounters, prostitution, or contact with prostitutes).

8. The CPT Editorial Panel has issued a number of codes for infectious agent detection by direct antigen or nucleic acid probe techniques that have not yet been developed or are only being used on an investigational basis. Laboratory providers are advised to remain current on FDA-approval status for these tests

100-3, 190.15
NCD for Blood Counts (190.15)
Indications

Indications for a CBC or hemogram include red cell, platelet, and white cell disorders. Examples of these indications are enumerated individually below.

1. Indications for a CBC generally include the evaluation of bone marrow dysfunction as a result of neoplasms, therapeutic agents, exposure to toxic substances, or pregnancy. The CBC is also useful in assessing peripheral destruction of blood cells, suspected bone marrow failure or bone marrow infiltrate, suspected myeloproliferative, myelodysplastic, or lymphoproliferative processes, and immune disorders.

2. Indications for hemogram or CBC related to red cell (RBC) parameters of the hemogram include signs, symptoms, test results, illness, or disease that can be associated with anemia or other red blood cell disorder (e.g., pallor, weakness, fatigue, weight loss, bleeding, acute injury associated with blood loss or suspected blood loss, abnormal menstrual bleeding, hematuria, hematemesis, hematochezia, positive fecal occult blood test, malnutrition, vitamin deficiency, malabsorption, neuropathy, known malignancy, presence of acute or chronic disease that may have associated anemia, coagulation or hemostatic disorders, postural dizziness, syncope, abdominal pain, change in bowel habits, chronic marrow hypoplasia or decreased RBC production, tachycardia, systolic heart murmur, congestive heart failure, dyspnea, angina, nailbed deformities, growth retardation, jaundice, hepatomegaly, splenomegaly, lymphadenopathy, ulcers on the lower extremities).

3. Indications for hemogram or CBC related to red cell (RBC) parameters of the hemogram include signs, symptoms, test results, illness, or disease that can be associated with polycythemia (for example, fever, chills, ruddy skin, conjunctival redness, cough, wheezing, cyanosis, clubbing of the fingers, orthopnea, heart murmur, headache, vague cognitive changes including memory changes, sleep apnea, weakness, pruritus, dizziness, excessive sweating, visual symptoms, weight loss, massive obesity, gastrointestinal bleeding,

paresthesias, dyspnea, joint symptoms, epigastric distress, pain and erythema of the fingers or toes, venous or arterial thrombosis, thromboembolism, myocardial infarction, stroke, transient ischemic attacks, congenital heart disease, chronic obstructive pulmonary disease, increased erythropoietin production associated with neoplastic, renal or hepatic disorders, androgen or diuretic use, splenomegaly, hepatomegaly, diastolic hypertension.)

4. Specific indications for CBC with differential count related to the WBC include signs, symptoms, test results, illness, or disease associated with leukemia, infections or inflammatory processes, suspected bone marrow failure or bone marrow infiltrate, suspected myeloproliferative, myelodysplastic or lymphoproliferative disorder, use of drugs that may cause leukopenia, and immune disorders (e.g., fever, chills, sweats, shock, fatigue, malaise, tachycardia, tachypnea, heart murmur, seizures, alterations of consciousness, meningismus, pain such as headache, abdominal pain, arthralgia, odynophagia, or dysuria, redness or swelling of skin, soft tissue bone, or joint, ulcers of the skin or mucous membranes, gangrene, mucous membrane discharge, bleeding, thrombosis, respiratory failure, pulmonary infiltrate, jaundice, diarrhea, vomiting, hepatomegaly, splenomegaly, lymphadenopathy, opportunistic infection such as oral candidiasis.)

5. Specific indications for CBC related to the platelet count include signs, symptoms, test results, illness or disease associated with increased or decreased platelet production and destruction, or platelet dysfunction (e.g., gastrointestinal bleeding, genitourinary tract bleeding, bilateral epistaxis, thrombosis, ecchymosis, purpura, jaundice, petechiae, fever, heparin therapy, suspected DIC, shock, pre-eclampsia, neonate with maternal ITP, massive transfusion, recent platelet transfusion, cardiopulmonary bypass, hemolytic uremic syndrome, renal diseases, lymphadenopathy, hepatomegaly, splenomegaly, hypersplenism, neurologic abnormalities, viral or other infection, myeloproliferative, myelodysplastic, or lymphoproliferative disorder, thrombosis, exposure to toxic agents, excessive alcohol ingestion, autoimmune disorders (SLE, RA and other).

6. Indications for hemogram or CBC related to red cell (RBC) parameters of the hemogram include, in addition to those already listed, thalassemia, suspected hemoglobinopathy, lead poisoning, arsenic poisoning, and spherocytosis.

7. Specific indications for CBC with differential count related to the WBC include, in addition to those already listed, storage diseases; mucopolysaccharidoses, and use of drugs that cause leukocytosis such as G-CSF or GM-CSF.

8. Specific indications for CBC related to platelet count include, in addition to those already listed, May-Hegglin syndrome and Wiskott-Aldrich syndrome.

Limitations

1. Testing of patients who are asymptomatic, or who do not have a condition that could be expected to result in a hematological abnormality, is screening and is not a covered service.

2. In some circumstances it may be appropriate to perform only a hemoglobin or hematocrit to assess the oxygen carrying capacity of the blood. When the ordering provider requests only a hemoglobin or hematocrit, the remaining components of the CBC are not covered.

3. When a blood count is performed for an end-stage renal disease (ESRD) patient, and is billed outside the ESRD rate, documentation of the medical necessity for the blood count must be submitted with the claim.

4. In some patients presenting with certain signs, symptoms or diseases, a single CBC may be appropriate. Repeat testing may not be indicated unless abnormal results are found, or unless there is a change in clinical condition. If repeat testing is performed, a more descriptive diagnosis code (e.g., anemia) should be reported to support medical necessity. However, repeat testing may be indicated where results are normal in patients with conditions where there is a continued risk for the development of hematologic abnormality.

100-3, 190.16

NCD for Partial Thromboplastin Time (PTT) (190.16)
Indications and Limitations of Coverage

Indications

1. The PTT is most commonly used to quantitate the effect of therapeutic unfractionated heparin and to regulate its dosing. Except during transitions between heparin and warfarin therapy, in general both the PTT and PT are not necessary together to assess the effect of anticoagulation therapy. PT and PTT must be justified separately.

2. A PTT may be used to assess patients with signs or symptoms of hemorrhage or thrombosis. For example: abnormal bleeding, hemorrhage or hematoma petechiae or other signs of thrombocytopenia that could be due to disseminated intravascular coagulation; swollen extremity with or without prior trauma.

3. A PTT may be useful in evaluating patients who have a history of a condition known to be associated with the risk of hemorrhage or thrombosis that is related to the intrinsic coagulation pathway. Such abnormalities may be genetic or acquired. For example: dysfibrinogenemia; afibrinogenemia (complete); acute or chronic liver dysfunction or failure, including Wilson's disease; hemophilia; liver disease and failure; infectious processes; bleeding disorders; disseminated intravascular coagulation; lupus erythematosus or other conditions associated with circulating inhibitors, e.g., Factor VIII Inhibitor, lupus-like anticoagulant, etc.; sepsis; von Willebrand's disease; arterial and venous thrombosis, including the evaluation of hypercoagulable states; clinical conditions associated with nephrosis or renal failure; other acquired and congenital coagulopathies as well as thrombotic states.

4. A PTT may be used to assess the risk of thrombosis or hemorrhage in patients who are going to have a medical intervention known to be associated with increased risk of bleeding or thrombosis. An example is as follows: evaluation prior to invasive procedures or operations of patients with personal or family history of bleeding or who are on heparin therapy.

Limitations

1. The PTT is not useful in monitoring the effects of warfarin on a patient's coagulation routinely. However, a PTT may be ordered on a patient being treated with warfarin as heparin therapy is being discontinued. A PTT may also be indicated when the PT is markedly prolonged due to warfarin toxicity.

2. The need to repeat this test is determined by changes in the underlying medical condition and/or the dosing of heparin.

3. Testing prior to any medical intervention associated with a risk of bleeding and thrombosis (other than thrombolytic therapy) will generally be considered medically necessary only where there are signs or symptoms of a bleeding or thrombotic abnormality or a personal history of bleeding, thrombosis or a condition associated with a coagulopathy. Hospital/clinic-specific policies, protocols, etc., in and of themselves, cannot alone justify coverage.

100-3, 190.17

NCD for Prothrombin Time (PT) (190.17)
Indications

1. A PT may be used to assess patients taking warfarin. The prothrombin time is generally not useful in monitoring patients receiving heparin who are not taking warfarin.

2. A PT may be used to assess patients with signs or symptoms of abnormal bleeding or thrombosis. For example: swollen extremity with or without prior trauma; unexplained bruising; abnormal bleeding, hemorrhage or hematoma; petechiae or other signs of thrombocytopenia that could be due to disseminated intravascular coagulation.

3. A PT may be useful in evaluating patients who have a history of a condition known to be associated with the risk of bleeding or thrombosis that is related to the extrinsic coagulation pathway. Such abnormalities may be genetic or acquired. For example: dysfibrinogenemia; afibrinogenemia (complete); acute or chronic liver dysfunction or failure, including Wilson's disease and Hemochromatosis; disseminated intravascular coagulation (DIC); congenital and acquired deficiencies of factors II, V, VII, X; vitamin K deficiency; lupus erythematosus; hypercoagulable state; paraproteinemia; lymphoma; amyloidosis; acute and chronic leukemias; plasma cell dyscrasia; HIV infection; malignant neoplasms; hemorrhagic fever; salicylate poisoning; obstructive jaundice; intestinal fistula; malabsorption syndrome; colitis; chronic diarrhea; presence of peripheral venous or arterial thrombosis or pulmonary emboli or myocardial infarction; patients with bleeding or clotting tendencies; organ transplantation; presence of circulating coagulation inhibitors.

4. A PT may be used to assess the risk of hemorrhage or thrombosis in patients who are going to have a medical intervention known to be associated with increased risk of bleeding or thrombosis. For example: evaluation prior to invasive procedures or operations of patients with personal history of bleeding or a condition associated with coagulopathy prior to the use of thrombolytic medication.

Limitations

1. When an ESRD patient is tested for PT, testing more frequently than weekly requires documentation of medical necessity, e.g., other than chronic renal failure or renal failure, unspecified.

2. The need to repeat this test is determined by changes in the underlying medical condition and/or the dosing of warfarin. In a patient on stable warfarin therapy, it is ordinarily not necessary to repeat testing more than every two to three weeks. When testing is performed to evaluate a patient with signs or symptoms of abnormal bleeding or thrombosis and the initial test result is normal, it is ordinarily not necessary to repeat testing unless there is a change in the patient's medical status.

3. Since the INR is a calculation, it will not be paid in addition to the PT when expressed in seconds, and is considered part of the conventional prothrombin time.

4. Testing prior to any medical intervention associated with a risk of bleeding and thrombosis (other than thrombolytic therapy) will generally be considered medically necessary only where there are signs or symptoms of a bleeding or thrombotic abnormality or a personal history of bleeding, thrombosis or a condition associated with a coagulopathy. Hospital/clinic-specific policies, protocols, etc., in and of themselves, cannot alone justify coverage.

100-3, 190.18

100-3, 190.18
Indications

1. Ferritin (82728), iron (83540) and either iron binding capacity (83550) or transferrin (84466) are useful in the differential diagnosis of iron deficiency, anemia, and for iron overload conditions.

   a. The following presentations are examples that may support the use of these studies for evaluating iron deficiency:

   • Certain abnormal blood count values (i.e., decreased mean corpuscular volume (MCV), decreased hemoglobin/hematocrit when the MCV is low or normal, or increased red cell distribution width (RDW) and low or normal MCV);

   • Abnormal appetite (pica);

   • Acute or chronic gastrointestinal blood loss;

   • Hematuria;

   • Menorrhagia;

   • Malabsorption;

   • Status post-gastrectomy;

   • Status post-gastrojejunostomy;

- Malnutrition;
- Preoperative autologous blood collection(s);
- Malignant, chronic inflammatory and infectious conditions associated with anemia which may present in a similar manner to iron deficiency anemia;
- Following a significant surgical procedure where blood loss had occurred and had not been repaired with adequate iron replacement.

b. The following presentations are examples that may support the use of these studies for evaluating iron overload:

- Chronic Hepatitis;
- Diabetes;
- Hyperpigmentation of skin;
- Arthropathy;
- Cirrhosis;
- Hypogonadism;
- Hypopituitarism;
- Impaired porphyrin metabolism;
- Heart failure;
- Multiple transfusions;
- Sideroblastic anemia;
- Thalassemia major;
- Cardiomyopathy, cardiac dysrhythmias and conduction disturbances.

2. Follow-up testing may be appropriate to monitor response to therapy, e.g., oral or parenteral iron, ascorbic acid, and erythropoietin.

3. Iron studies may be appropriate in patients after treatment for other nutritional deficiency anemias, such as folate and vitamin B12, because iron deficiency may not be revealed until such a nutritional deficiency is treated.

4. Serum ferritin may be appropriate for monitoring iron status in patients with chronic renal disease with or without dialysis.

5. Serum iron may also be indicated for evaluation of toxic effects of iron and other metals (e.g., nickel, cadmium, aluminum, lead) whether due to accidental, intentional exposure or metabolic causes.

Limitations

1. Iron studies should be used to diagnose and manage iron deficiency or iron overload states. These tests are not to be used solely to assess acute phase reactants where disease management will be unchanged. For example, infections and malignancies are associated with elevations in acute phase reactants such as ferritin, and decreases in serum iron concentration, but iron studies would only be medically necessary if results of iron studies might alter the management of the primary diagnosis or might warrant direct treatment of an iron disorder or condition.

2. If a normal serum ferritin level is documented, repeat testing would not ordinarily be medically necessary unless there is a change in the patient's condition, and ferritin assessment is needed for the ongoing management of the patient. For example, a patient presents with new onset insulin-dependent diabetes mellitus and has a serum ferritin level performed for the suspicion of hemochromatosis. If the ferritin level is normal, the repeat ferritin for diabetes mellitus would not be medically necessary.

3. When an End Stage Renal Disease (ESRD) patient is tested for ferritin, testing more frequently than every three months (the frequency authorized by 3167.3, Fiscal Intermediary manual) requires documentation of medical necessity [e.g., other than "Chronic Renal Failure" (ICD-9-CM 585) or "Renal Failure, Unspecified" (ICD-9-CM 586)].

4. It is ordinarily not necessary to measure both transferrin and TIBC at the same time because TIBC is an indirect measure of transferrin. When transferrin is ordered as part of the nutritional assessment for evaluating malnutrition, it is not necessary to order other iron studies unless iron deficiency or iron overload is suspected as well.

5. It is not ordinarily necessary to measure both iron/TIBC (or transferrin) and ferritin in initial patient testing. If clinically indicated after evaluation of the initial iron studies, it may be appropriate to perform additional iron studies either on the initial specimen or on a subsequently obtained specimen. After a diagnosis of iron deficiency or iron overload is established, either iron/TIBC (or transferrin) or ferritin may be medically necessary for monitoring, but not both.

6. It would not ordinarily be considered medically necessary to do a ferritin as a preoperative test except in the presence of anemia or recent autologous blood collections prior to the surgery.

100-3, 190.19

Collagen Crosslinks, Any Method

Indications

Generally speaking, collagen crosslink testing is useful mostly in "fast losers" of bone. The age when these bone markers can help direct therapy is often pre-Medicare. By the time a fast loser of bone reaches age 65, she will most likely have been stabilized by appropriate therapy or have lost so much bone mass that further testing is useless. Coverage for bone marker assays may be

established, however, for younger Medicare beneficiaries and for those men and women who might become fast losers because of some other therapy such as glucocorticoids. Safeguards should be incorporated to prevent excessive use of tests in patients for whom they have no clinical relevance.

Collagen crosslinks testing is used to:

1. Identify individuals with elevated bone resorption, who have osteoporosis in whom response to treatment is being monitored;

2. Predict response (as assessed by bone mass measurements) to FDA approved antiresorptive therapy in postmenopausal women; and

3. Assess response to treatment of patients with osteoporosis, Paget's disease of the bone, or risk for osteoporosis where treatment may include FDA approved antiresorptive agents, anti-estrogens or selective estrogen receptor moderators.

Limitations

Because of significant specimen to specimen collagen crosslink physiologic variability (15-20%), current recommendations for appropriate utilization include: one or two base-line assays from specified urine collections on separate days; followed by a repeat assay about three months after starting anti-resorptive therapy; followed by a repeat assay in 12 months after the three-month assay; and thereafter not more than annually, unless there is a change in therapy in which circumstance an additional test may be indicated three months after the initiation of new therapy.

Some collagen crosslink assays may not be appropriate for use in some disorders, according to FDA labeling restrictions.

100-3, 190.20

NCD for Blood Glucose Testing (190.20)

Indications

Blood glucose values are often necessary for the management of patients with diabetes mellitus, where hyperglycemia and hypoglycemia are often present. They are also critical in the determination of control of blood glucose levels in the patient with impaired fasting glucose (FPG 110-125 mg/dL), the patient with insulin resistance syndrome and/or carbohydrate intolerance (excessive rise in glucose following ingestion of glucose or glucose sources of food), in the patient with a hypoglycemic disorder such as nesidioblastosis or insulinoma, and in patients with a catabolic or malnutrition state. In addition to those conditions already listed, glucose testing may be medically necessary in patients with tuberculosis, unexplained chronic or recurrent infections, alcoholism, coronary artery disease (especially in women), or unexplained skin conditions (including pruritis, local skin infections, ulceration and gangrene without an established cause).

Many medical conditions may be a consequence of a sustained elevated or depressed glucose level. These include comas, seizures or epilepsy, confusion, abnormal hunger, abnormal weight loss or gain, and loss of sensation. Evaluation of glucose may also be indicated in patients on medications known to affect carbohydrate metabolism.

Effective January 1, 2005, the Medicare law expanded coverage to diabetic screening services. Some forms of blood glucode testing covered under this national coverage determination may be covered for screening purposes subject to specified frequencies. See 42 CFR 410.18 and section 90, chapter 18 of the Claims Processing Manual, for a full description of this screening benefit.

Limitations

Frequent home blood glucose testing by diabetic patients should be encouraged. In stable, non-hospitalized patients who are unable or unwilling to do home monitoring, it may be reasonable and necessary to measure quantitative blood glucose up to four times annually.

Depending upon the age of the patient, type of diabetes, degree of control, complications of diabetes, and other co-morbid conditions, more frequent testing than four times annually may be reasonable and necessary.

In some patients presenting with nonspecific signs, symptoms, or diseases not normally associated with disturbances in glucose metabolism, a single blood glucose test may be medically necessary. Repeat testing may not be indicated unless abnormal results are found or unless there is a change in clinical condition. If repeat testing is performed, a specific diagnosis code (e.g., diabetes) should be reported to support medical necessity. However, repeat testing may be indicated where results are normal in patients with conditions where there is a confirmed continuing risk of glucose metabolism abnormality (e.g., monitoring glucocorticoid therapy).

100-3, 190.21

NCD for Glycated Hemoglobin/Glycated Protein (190.21)

Indications

Glycated hemoglobin/protein testing is widely accepted as medically necessary for the management and control of diabetes. It is also valuable to assess hyperglycemia, a history of hyperglycemia or dangerous hypoglycemia. Glycated protein testing may be used in place of glycated hemoglobin in the management of diabetic patients, and is particularly useful in patients who have abnormalities of erythrocytes such as hemolytic anemia or hemoglobinopathies.

Limitations

It is not considered reasonable and necessary to perform glycated hemoglobin tests more often than every three months on a controlled diabetic patient to determine whether the patient's metabolic control has been on average within the target range. It is not considered reasonable and necessary for these tests to be performed more frequently than once a month for diabetic pregnant women. Testing for uncontrolled type one or two diabetes mellitus may require testing more than four times a year. The above Description Section provides the clinical basis for those situations in which testing more frequently than four times per annum is indicated, and medical necessity documentation must support such testing in excess of the above guidelines.

Many methods for the analysis of glycated hemoglobin show significant interference from elevated levels of fetal hemoglobin or by variant hemoglobin molecules. When the glycated hemoglobin assay is initially performed in these patients, the laboratory may inform the ordering physician of a possible analytical interference. Alternative testing, including glycated protein, for example, fructosamine, may be indicated for the monitoring of the degree of glycemic control in this situation. It is therefore conceivable that a patient will have both a glycated hemoglobin and glycated protein ordered on the same day. This should be limited to the initial assay of glycated hemoglobin, with subsequent exclusive use of glycated protein. These tests are not considered to be medically necessary for the diagnosis of diabetes.

100-3, 190.22
NCD for Thyroid Testing (190.22)
Indications
Thyroid function tests are used to define hyper function, euthyroidism, or hypofunction of thyroid disease. Thyroid testing may be reasonable and necessary to:

- Distinguish between primary and secondary hypothyroidism;
- Confirm or rule out primary hypothyroidism;
- Monitor thyroid hormone levels (for example, patients with goiter, thyroid nodules, or thyroid cancer);
- Monitor drug therapy in patients with primary hypothyroidism;
- Confirm or rule out primary hyperthyroidism; and
- Monitor therapy in patients with hyperthyroidism.

Thyroid function testing may be medically necessary in patients with disease or neoplasm of the thyroid and other endocrine glands. Thyroid function testing may also be medically necessary in patients with metabolic disorders; malnutrition; hyperlipidemia; certain types of anemia; psychosis and non-psychotic personality disorders; unexplained depression; ophthalmologic disorders; various cardiac arrhythmias; disorders of menstruation; skin conditions; myalgias; and a wide array of signs and symptoms, including alterations in consciousness; malaise; hypothermia; symptoms of the nervous and musculoskeletal system; skin and integumentary system; nutrition and metabolism; cardiovascular; and gastrointestinal system.

It may be medically necessary to do follow-up thyroid testing in patients with a personal history of malignant neoplasm of the endocrine system and in patients on long-term thyroid drug therapy.

Limitations
Testing may be covered up to two times a year in clinically stable patients; more frequent testing may be reasonable and necessary for patients whose thyroid therapy has been altered or in whom symptoms or signs of hyperthyroidism or hypothyroidism are noted.

100-3, 190.23
NCD for Lipid Testing (190.23)
Indications and Limitations of Coverage

Indications
The medical community recognizes lipid testing as appropriate for evaluating atherosclerotic cardiovascular disease. Conditions in which lipid testing may be indicated include:

- Assessment of patients with atherosclerotic cardiovascular disease.
- Evaluation of primary dyslipidemia.
- Any form of atherosclerotic disease, or any disease leading to the formation of atherosclerotic disease.
- Diagnostic evaluation of diseases associated with altered lipid metabolism, such as: nephrotic syndrome, pancreatitis, hepatic disease, and hypo and hyperthyroidism.
- Secondary dyslipidemia, including diabetes mellitus, disorders of gastrointestinal absorption, chronic renal failure.
- Signs or symptoms of dyslipidemias, such as skin lesions.
- As follow-up to the initial screen for coronary heart disease (total cholesterol + HDL cholesterol) when total cholesterol is determined to be high (>240 mg/dL), or borderline-high (200-240 mg/dL) plus two or more coronary heart disease risk factors, or an HDL cholesterol, <35 mg/dl.

To monitor the progress of patients on anti-lipid dietary management and pharmacologic therapy for the treatment of elevated blood lipid disorders, total cholesterol, HDL cholesterol and LDL cholesterol may be used. Triglycerides may be obtained if this lipid fraction is also elevated or if the patient is put on drugs (for example, thiazide diuretics, beta blockers, estrogens, glucocorticoids, and tamoxifen) which may raise the triglyceride level.

When monitoring long term anti-lipid dietary or pharmacologic therapy and when following patients with borderline high total or LDL cholesterol levels, it may be reasonable to perform the lipid panel annually. A lipid panel at a yearly interval will usually be adequate while measurement of the serum total cholesterol or a measured LDL should suffice for interim visits if the patient does not have hypertriglyceridemia.

Any one component of the panel or a measured LDL may be reasonable and necessary up to six times the first year for monitoring dietary or pharmacologic therapy. More frequent total cholesterol HDL cholesterol, LDL cholesterol and triglyceride testing may be indicated for marked elevations or for changes to anti-lipid therapy due to inadequate initial patient response to dietary or pharmacologic therapy. The LDL cholesterol or total cholesterol may be measured three times yearly after treatment goals have been achieved.

Electrophoretic or other quantitation of lipoproteins may be indicated if the patient has a primary disorder of lipoid metabolism.

Effective January 1, 2005, the Medicare law expanded coverage to cardiovascular screening services. Several of the procedures included in this NCD may be covered for screening purposes subject to specified frequencies. See 42 CFR 410.17 and section 100, chapter 18, of the Claims Processing Manual, for a full description of this benefit.Limitations

Limitations
Lipid panel and hepatic panel testing may be used for patients with severe psoriasis which has not responded to conventional therapy and for which the retinoid etretinate has been prescribed and who have developed hyperlipidemia or hepatic toxicity. Specific examples include erythrodermia and generalized pustular type and psoriasis associated with arthritis.

Routine screening and prophylactic testing for lipid disorder are not covered by Medicare. While lipid screening may be medically appropriate, Medicare by statute does not pay for it. Lipid testing in asymptomatic individuals is considered to be screening regardless of the presence of other risk factors such as family history, tobacco use, etc.

Once a diagnosis is established, one or several specific tests are usually adequate for monitoring the course of the disease. Less specific diagnoses (for example, other chest pain) alone do not support medical necessity of these tests

When monitoring long term anti-lipid dietary or pharmacologic therapy and when following patients with borderline high total or LDL cholesterol levels, it is reasonable to perform the lipid panel annually. A lipid panel at a yearly interval will usually be adequate while measurement of the serum total cholesterol or a measured LDL should suffice for interim visits if the patient does not have hypertriglyceridemia.

Any one component of the panel or a measured LDL may be medically necessary up to six times the first year for monitoring dietary or pharmacologic therapy. More frequent total cholesterol HDL cholesterol, LDL cholesterol and triglyceride testing may be indicated for marked elevations or for changes to anti-lipid therapy due to inadequate initial patient response to dietary or pharmacologic therapy. The LDL cholesterol or total cholesterol may be measured three times yearly after treatment goals have been achieved.

If no dietary or pharmacological therapy is advised, monitoring is not necessary.

When evaluating non-specific chronic abnormalities of the liver (for example, elevations of transaminase, alkaline phosphatase, abnormal imaging studies, etc.), a lipid panel would generally not be indicated more than twice per year

100-3, 190.24
NCD for Digoxin Therapeutic Drug Assay (190.24)
Indications and Limitations of Coverage

Indications
Digoxin levels may be performed to monitor drug levels of individuals receiving digoxin therapy because the margin of safety between side effects and toxicity is narrow or because the blood level may not be high enough to achieve the desired clinical effect.

Clinical indications may include individuals on digoxin:

- With symptoms, signs or electrocardiogram (ECG) suggestive of digoxin toxicity.
- Taking medications that influence absorption, bioavailability, distribution, and/or elimination of digoxin.
- With impaired renal, hepatic, gastrointestinal, or thyroid function.
- With pH and/or electrolyte abnormalities.
- With unstable cardiovascular status, including myocarditis.
- Requiring monitoring of patient compliance.

Clinical indications may include individuals:

- Suspected of accidental or intended overdose.
- Who have an acceptable cardiac diagnosis (as listed) and for whom an accurate history of use of digoxin is unobtainable.

The value of obtaining regular serum digoxin levels is uncertain, but it may be reasonable to check levels once yearly after a steady state is achieved. In addition, it may be reasonable to check the level if:

- Heart failure status worsens.
- Renal function deteriorates.
- Additional medications are added that could affect the digoxin level.
- Signs or symptoms of toxicity develop.

Steady state will be reached in approximately 1 week in patients with normal renal function, although 2?3 weeks may be needed in patients with renal impairment. After changes in dosages or the addition of a medication that could affect the digoxin level, it is reasonable to check the digoxin level one week after the change or addition. Based on the clinical situation, in cases of digoxin toxicity, testing may need to be done more than once a week.

Digoxin is indicated for the treatment of patients with heart failure due to systolic dysfunction and for reduction of the ventricular response in patients with atrial fibrillation or flutter. Digoxin may also be indicated for the treatment of other supraventricular arrhythmias, particularly in the presence of heart failure.

Limitations
This test is not appropriate for patients on digitoxin or treated with digoxin FAB (fragment antigen binding) antibody.

100-3, 190.25
NCD for Alpha-fetoprotein (AFP) (190.25)
Indications and Limitations of Coverage

AFP is useful for the diagnosis of hepatocellular carcinoma in high-risk patients (such as alcoholic cirrhosis, cirrhosis of viral etiology, hemochromatosis, and alpha 1-antitrypsin deficiency) and in separating patients with benign hepatocellular neoplasms or metastases from those with hepatocellular carcinoma and, as a non-specific tumor associated antigen, serves in marking germ cell neoplasms of the testis, ovary, retro peritoneum, and mediastinum.

100-3, 190.26
NCD for Carcinoembryonic Antigen (CEA) (190.26)
Indications

CEA may be medically necessary for follow-up of patients with colorectal carcinoma. It would however only be medically necessary at treatment decision?making points. In some clinical situations (e.g. adenocarcinoma of the lung, small cell carcinoma of the lung, and some gastrointestinal carcinomas) when a more specific marker is not expressed by the tumor, CEA may be a medically necessary alternative marker for monitoring. Preoperative CEA may also be helpful in determining the post?operative adequacy of surgical resection and subsequent medical management. In general, a single tumor marker will suffice in following patients with colorectal carcinoma or other malignancies that express such tumor markers.

In following patients who have had treatment for colorectal carcinoma, ASCO guideline suggests that if resection of liver metastasis would be indicated, it is recommended that post-operative CEA testing be performed every two to three months in patients with initial stage II or stage III disease for at least two years after diagnosis.

For patients with metastatic solid tumors which express CEA, CEA may be measured at the start of the treatment and with subsequent treatment cycles to assess the tumor's response to therapy.

Limitations

Serum CEA determinations are generally not indicated more frequently than once per chemotherapy treatment cycle for patients with metastatic solid tumors which express CEA or every two months post-surgical treatment for patients who have had colorectal carcinoma. However, it may be proper to order the test more frequently in certain situations, for example, when there has been a significant change from prior CEA level or a significant change in patient status which could reflect disease progression or recurrence.

Testing with a diagnosis of an in situ carcinoma is not reasonably done more frequently than once, unless the result is abnormal, in which case the test may be repeated once.

100-3, 190.27
NCD for Human Chorionic Gonadotropin (hCG) (190.27)
Indications and Limitations of Coverage

Indications

hCG is useful for monitoring and diagnosis of germ cell neoplasms of the ovary, testis, mediastinum, retroperitoneum, and central nervous system. In addition, hCG is useful for monitoring pregnant patients with vaginal bleeding, hypertension and/or suspected fetal loss.

Limitations

It is not reasonable and necessary to perform hCG testing more than once per month for diagnostic purposes. It may be performed as needed for monitoring of patient progress and treatment. Qualitative hCG assays are not appropriate for medically managing patients with known or suspected germ cell neoplasms.

100-3, 190.28
NCD for Tumor Antigen by Immunoassay - CA125 (190.28)
Indications

CA 125 is a high molecular weight serum tumor marker elevated in 80% of patients who present with epithelial ovarian carcinoma. It is also elevated in carcinomas of the fallopian tube, endometrium, and endocervix. An elevated level may also be associated with the presence of a malignant mesothelioma or primary peritoneal carcinoma.

A CA125 level may be obtained as part of the initial pre-operative work-up for women presenting with a suspicious pelvic mass to be used as a baseline for purposes of post-operative monitoring. Initial declines in CA 125 after initial surgery and/or chemotherapy for ovarian carcinoma are also measured by obtaining three serum levels during the first month post treatment to determine the patient's CA 125 half-life, which has significant prognostic implications.

The CA 125 levels are again obtained at the completion of chemotherapy as an index of residual disease. Surveillance CA125 measurements are generally obtained every 3 months for 2 years, every 6 months for the next 3 years, and yearly thereafter. CA 125 levels are also an important indicator of a patient's response to therapy in the presence of advanced or recurrent disease. In this setting, CA 125 levels may be obtained prior to each treatment cycle.

Limitations

These services are not covered for the evaluation of patients with signs or symptoms suggestive of malignancy. The service may be ordered at times necessary to assess either the presence of recurrent disease or the patient's response to treatment with subsequent treatment cycles.

The CA 125 is specifically not covered for aiding in the differential diagnosis of patients with a pelvic mass as the sensitivity and specificity of the test is not sufficient. In general, a single "tumor marker" will suffice in following a patient with one of these malignancies.

100-3, 190.29
NCD for Tumor Antigen by Immunoassay CA 15-3/CA 27.29 (190.29)
Indications

Multiple tumor markers are available for monitoring the response of certain malignancies to therapy and assessing whether residual tumor exists post-surgical therapy.

CA 15-3 is often medically necessary to aid in the management of patients with breast cancer. Serial testing must be used in conjunction with other clinical methods for monitoring breast cancer. For monitoring, if medically necessary, use consistently either CA 15-3 or CA 27.29, not both.

CA 27.29 is equivalent to CA 15-3 in its usage in management of patients with breast cancer.

Limitations

These services are not covered for the evaluation of patients with signs or symptoms suggestive of malignancy. The service may be ordered at times necessary to assess either the presence of recurrent disease or the patient's response to treatment with subsequent treatment cycles.

100-3, 190.30
NCD for Tumor Antigen by Immunoassay CA 19-9 (190.30)
Indications

Multiple tumor markers are available for monitoring the response of certain malignancies to therapy and assessing whether residual tumor exists post-surgical therapy.

Levels are useful in following the course of patients with established diagnosis of pancreatic and biliary ductal carcinoma. The test is not indicated for diagnosing these two diseases.

Limitations

These services are not covered for the evaluation of patients with signs or symptoms suggestive of malignancy. The service may be ordered at times necessary to assess either the presence of recurrent disease or the patient's response to treatment with subsequent treatment cycles.

100-3, 190.31
NCD for Prostate Specific Antigen (PSA) (190.31)
Indications

PSA is of proven value in differentiating benign from malignant disease in men with lower urinary tract signs and symptoms (e.g., hematuria, slow urine stream, hesitancy, urgency, frequency, nocturia and incontinence) as well as with patients with palpably abnormal prostate glands on physician exam, and in patients with other laboratory or imaging studies that suggest the possibility of a malignant prostate disorder. PSA is also a marker used to follow the progress of prostate cancer once a diagnosis has been established, such as in detecting metastatic or persistent disease in patients who may require additional treatment. PSA testing may also be useful in the differential diagnosis of men presenting with as yet undiagnosed disseminated metastatic disease.

Limitations

Generally, for patients with lower urinary tract signs or symptoms, the test is performed only once per year unless there is a change in the patient's medical condition.

Testing with a diagnosis of in situ carcinoma is not reasonably done more frequently than once, unless the result is abnormal, in which case the test may be repeated once.

100-3, 190.32
NCD for Gamma Glutamyl Transferase (GGT) (190.32)
Indications

1. To provide information about known or suspected hepatobiliary disease, for example:
   a. Following chronic alcohol or drug ingestion.
   b. Following exposure to hepatotoxins.
   c. When using medication known to have a potential for causing liver toxicity (e.g., following the drug manufacturer's recommendations).
   d. Following infection (e.g., viral hepatitis and other specific infections such as amoebiasis, tuberculosis, psittacosis, and similar infections).
2. To assess liver injury/function following diagnosis of primary or secondary malignant neoplasms.
3. To assess liver injury/function in a wide variety of disorders and diseases known to cause liver involvement (e.g., diabetes mellitus, malnutrition, disorders of iron and mineral metabolism, sarcoidosis, amyloidosis, lupus, and hypertension).
4. To assess liver function related to gastrointestinal disease.
5. To assess liver function related to pancreatic disease.
6. To assess liver function in patients subsequent to liver transplantation.
7. To differentiate between the different sources of elevated alkaline phosphatase activity.

Limitations

When used to assess liver dysfunction secondary to existing non-hepatobiliary disease with no change in signs, symptoms, or treatment, it is generally not necessary to repeat a GGT determination after a normal result has been obtained unless new indications are present.

If the GGT is the only "liver" enzyme abnormally high, it is generally not necessary to pursue further evaluation for liver disease for this specific indication.

When used to determine if other abnormal enzyme tests reflect liver abnormality rather than other tissue, it generally is not necessary to repeat a GGT more than one time per week.

Because of the extreme sensitivity of GGT as a marker for cytochrome oxidase induction or cell membrane permeability, it is generally not useful in monitoring patients with known liver disease.

100-3, 190.33
NCD for Hepatitis Panel/Acute Hepatitis Panel (190.33)
Indications

1. To detect viral hepatitis infection when there are abnormal liver function test results, with or without signs or symptoms of hepatitis.

2. Prior to and subsequent to liver transplantation.

Limitations

After a hepatitis diagnosis has been established, only individual tests, rather than the entire panel, are needed.

100-3, 190.34
NCD for Fecal Occult Blood Test (FOBT) (190.34)
NCD for Fecal Occult Blood Test (FOBT) (190.34)

Indications

1. To evaluate known or suspected alimentary tract conditions that might cause bleeding into the intestinal tract.

2. To evaluate unexpected anemia.

3. To evaluate abnormal signs, symptoms, or complaints that might be associated with loss of blood.

4. To evaluate patient complaints of black or red-tinged stools.

Limitations

1. The FOBT is reported once for the testing of up to three separate specimens (comprising either one or two tests per specimen).

2. In patients who are taking non-steroidal anti-inflammatory drugs and have a history of gastrointestinal bleeding but no other signs, symptoms, or complaints associated with gastrointestinal blood loss, testing for occult blood may generally be appropriate no more than once every three months.

When testing is done for the purpose of screening for colorectal cancer in the absence of signs, symptoms, conditions, or complaints associated with gastrointestinal blood loss, report the HCPCS code for colorectal cancer screening; fecal-occult blood test, 1-3 simultaneous determinations should be used.

100-3, 210.1
NCD for Prostate Cancer Screening Tests (210.1)
Indications and Limitations of Coverage

CIM 50-55

Covered

A. General

Section 4103 of the Balanced Budget Act of 1997 provides for coverage of certain prostate cancer screening tests subject to certain coverage, frequency, and payment limitations. Medicare will cover prostate cancer screening tests/procedures for the early detection of prostate cancer. Coverage of prostate cancer screening tests includes the following procedures furnished to an individual for the early detection of prostate cancer:

- Screening digital rectal examination; and
- Screening prostate specific antigen blood test

B. Screening Digital Rectal Examinations

Screening digital rectal examinations are covered at a frequency of once every 12 months for men who have attained age 50 (at least 11 months have passed following the month in which the last Medicare-covered screening digital rectal examination was performed). Screening digital rectal examination means a clinical examination of an individual's prostate for nodules or other abnormalities of the prostate. This screening must be performed by a doctor of medicine or osteopathy (as defined in §1861(r)(1) of the Act), or by a physician assistant, nurse practitioner, clinical nurse specialist, or certified nurse midwife (as defined in §1861(aa) and §1861(gg) of the Act) who is authorized under State law to perform the examination, fully knowledgeable about the beneficiary's medical condition, and would be responsible for using the results of any examination performed in the overall management of the beneficiary's specific medical problem.

C. Screening Prostate Specific Antigen Tests

Screening prostate specific antigen tests are covered at a frequency of once every 12 months for men who have attained age 50 (at least 11 months have passed following the month in which the last Medicare-covered screening prostate specific antigen test was performed). Screening prostate specific antigen tests (PSA) means a test to detect the marker for adenocarcinoma of prostate. PSA is a reliable immunocytochemical marker for primary and metastatic adenocarcinoma of prostate. This screening must be ordered by the beneficiary's physician or by the beneficiary's physician assistant, nurse practitioner, clinical nurse specialist, or certified nurse midwife (the term "attending physician" is defined in §1861(r)(1) of the Act to mean a doctor of medicine or osteopathy and the terms "physician assistant, nurse practitioner, clinical nurse specialist, or certified nurse midwife" are defined in §1861(aa) and §1861(gg) of the Act) who is fully knowledgeable about the beneficiary's medical condition, and who would be responsible for using the results of any examination (test) performed in the overall management of the beneficiary's specific medica

100-3, 210.2
NCD for Screening Pap Smears and Pelvic Examinations for Early Detection of Cervical or Vaginal Cancer (210.2)
Indications and Limitations of Coverage

CIM 50-20.1

Screening Pap Smear

A screening pap smear and related medically necessary services provided to a woman for the early detection of cervical cancer (including collection of the sample of cells and a physician's interpretation of the test results) and pelvic examination (including clinical breast examination) are covered under Medicare Part B when ordered by a physician (or authorized practitioner) under one of the following conditions:

- She has not had such a test during the preceding two years or is a woman of childbearing age (§1861(nn) of the Act).

- There is evidence (on the basis of her medical history or other findings) that she is at high risk of developing cervical cancer and her physician (or authorized practitioner) recommends that she have the test performed more frequently than every two years.

High risk factors for cervical and vaginal cancer are:

- Early onset of sexual activity (under 16 years of age).
- Multiple sexual partners (five or more in a lifetime).
- History of sexually transmitted disease (including HIV infection).
- Fewer than three negative or any pap smears within the previous 7 years.; and
- DES (diethylstilbestrol) - exposed daughters of women who took DES during pregnancy.

NOTE: Claims for pap smears must indicate the beneficiary's low or high risk status by including the appropriate ICD-9-CM on the line item (Item 24E of the Form CMS-1500).

Definitions

- A woman as described in §1861(nn) of the Act is a woman who is of childbearing age and has had a pap smear test during any of the preceding three years that indicated the presence of cervical or vaginal cancer or other abnormality, or is at high risk of developing cervical or vaginal cancer.

- A woman of childbearing age is one who is premenopausal and has been determined by a physician or other qualified practitioner to be of childbearing age, based upon the medical history or other findings.

- Other qualified practitioner, as defined in 42 CFR 410.56(a) includes a certified nurse midwife (as defined in §1861(gg) of the Act), or a physician assistant, nurse practitioner, or clinical nurse specialist (as defined in §1861(aa) of the Act) who is authorized under State law to perform the examination.

Screening Pelvic Examination

Section 4102 of the Balanced Budget Act of 1997 provides for coverage of screening pelvic examinations (including a clinical breast examination) for all female beneficiaries, subject to certain frequency and other limitations. A screening pelvic examination (including a clinical breast examination) should include at least seven of the following eleven elements:

- Inspection and palpation of breasts for masses or lumps, tenderness, symmetry, or nipple discharge.

- Digital rectal examination including sphincter tone, presence of hemorrhoids, and rectal masses. Pelvic examination (with or without specimen collection for smears and cultures) including:

- External genitalia (for example, general appearance, hair distribution, or lesions).
- Urethral maetus (for example, size, location, lesions, or prolapse).
- Urethra (for example, masses, tenderness, or scarring).
- Bladder (for example, fullness, masses, or tenderness).
- Vagina (for example, general appearance, estrogen effect, discharge lesions, pelvic support, cystocele, or rectocele).
- Cervix (for example, general appearance, lesions, or discharge).
- Uterus (for example, size, contour, position, mobility, tenderness, consistency, descent, or support).
- Adnexa/parametria (for example, masses, tenderness, organomegaly, or nodularity).
- Anus and perineum.

This description is from Documentation Guidelines for Evaluation and Management Services, published in May 1997 and was developed by the Centers for Medicare and Medicaid

100-3, 220.1
NCD for Computerized Tomography (220.1)
A. General

Diagnostic examinations of the head (head scans) and of other parts of the body (body scans) performed by computerized tomography (CT) scanners are covered if you find that the medical and scientific literature and opinion support the effective use of a scan for the condition, and the scan is: (1) reasonable and necessary for the individual patient; and (2) performed on a model of CT equipment that meets the criteria in C below.

CT scans have become the primary diagnostic tool for many conditions and symptoms. CT scanning used as the primary diagnostic tool can be cost effective because it can eliminate the need for a series of other tests, is non-invasive and thus virtually eliminates complications, and does not require hospitalization.

B. Determining Whether a CT Scan Is Reasonable and Necessary

Sufficient information must be provided with claims to differentiate CT scans from other radiology services and to make coverage determinations. Carefully review claims to insure that a scan is reasonable and necessary for the individual patient; i.e., the use must be found to be medically appropriate considering the patient's symptoms and preliminary diagnosis.

There is no general rule that requires other diagnostic tests to be tried before CT scanning is used. However, in an individual case the contractor's medical staff may determine that use of a CT scan as the initial diagnostic test was not reasonable and necessary because it was not supported by the patient's symptoms or complaints stated on the claim form; e.g., "periodic headaches."

Claims for CT scans are reviewed for evidence of abuse which might include the absence of reasonable indications for the scans, an excessive number of scans or unnecessarily expensive types of scans considering the facts in the particular cases.

C-Approved Models of CT Equipment

1. Criteria for Approval

    In the absence of evidence to the contrary, you may assume that a CT scan for which payment is requested has been performed on equipment that meets the following criteria:

    a. The model must be known to the Food and Drug Administration, and

    b. Must be in the full market release phase of development.

    Should it be necessary to confirm that those criteria are met, ask the manufacturer to submit the information in subsection C.2. If manufacturers inquire about obtaining Medicare approval for their equipment, inform them of the foregoing criteria.

2. Evidence of Approval

    a. The letter sent by the Bureau of Radiological Health, Food and Drug Administration (FDA), to the manufacturer acknowledging the FDA's receipt of information on the specific CT scanner system model submitted as required under Public Law 90-602, "The Radiation Control for Health and Safety Act of 1968."

    b. A letter signed by the chief executive officer or other officer acting in a similar capacity for the manufacturer which:

       1) Furnishes the CT scanner system model number, all names that hospitals and physicians' offices may use to refer to the CT scanner system on claims, and the accession number assigned by FDA to the specific model; \

       2) Specifies whether the scanner performs head scans only, body scans only (i.e., scans of parts of the body other than the head), or head and body scans;

       3) States that the company or corporation is satisfied with the results of the developmental stages that preceded the full market release phase of the equipment, that the equipment is in the full market release phase, and the date on which it was decided to put the product into the full market release phase.

D-Mobile Ct Equipment

CT scans performed on mobile units are subject to the same Medicare coverage requirements applicable to scans performed on stationary units, as well as certain health and safety requirements recommended by PHS. As with scans performed on stationary units, the scans must be determined medically necessary for the individual patient. The scans must be performed on types of CT scanning equipment that have been approved for use as stationary units (see C above), and must be in compliance with applicable State laws and regulations for control of radiation.

1. Hospital Setting

    The hospital must assume responsibility for the quality of the scan furnished to inpatients and outpatients and must assure that a radiologist or other qualified physician is in charge of the procedure. The radiologist or other physician (i.e., one who is with the mobile unit) who is responsible for the procedure must be approved by the hospital for similar privileges.

2. Ambulatory Setting

    If mobile CT scan services are furnished at an ambulatory health care facility other than a hospital-based facility, e.g., a freestanding physician-directed clinic, the diagnostic procedure must be performed by or under the direct personal supervision of a radiologist or other qualified physician. In addition, the facility must maintain a record of the attending physician's order for a scan performed on a mobile unit.

3. Billing for Mobile CT Scans

    Hospitals, hospital-associated radiologists, ambulatory health care facilities, and physician owner/operators of mobile units may bill for mobile scans as they would for scans performed on stationary equipment.

4. Claims Review

    Evidence of compliance with applicable State laws and regulations for control of radiation should be requested from owners of mobile CT scan units upon receipt of the first claims. All mobile scan claims should be reviewed very carefully in accordance with instructions applicable to scans performed on fixed units, with particular emphasis on the medical necessity for scans performed in an ambulatory setting.

E-Multi-Planar Diagnostic Imaging (MPDI)

In usual computerized tomography (CT) scanning procedures, a series of transverse or axial images are reproduced. These transverse images are routinely translated into coronal and/or sagittal views. Multiplanar diagnostic imaging (MPDI) is a process which further translates the data produced by CT scanning by providing reconstructed oblique images which can contribute to diagnostic information. MPDI, also known as planar image reconstruction or reformatted imaging, is covered under Medicare when provided as a service to an entity performing a covered CT scan.

100-3, 220.2

NCD for Magnetic Resonance Imaging (MRI) (220.2)

B - Nationally Covered Indications (Effective November 22, 1985)

Although several uses of MRI are still considered investigational and some uses are clearly contraindicated (see subsection D), MRI is considered medically efficacious for a number of uses. Use the following descriptions as general guidelines or examples of what may be considered covered rather than as a restrictive list of specific covered indications. Coverage is limited to MRI units that have received FDA premarket approval, and such units must be operated within the parameters specified by the approval. In addition, the services must be reasonable and necessary for the diagnosis or treatment of the specific patient involved.

The MRI is useful in examining the head, central nervous system, and spine. Multiple sclerosis can be diagnosed with MRI and the contents of the posterior fossa are visible. The inherent tissue contrast resolution of MRI makes it an appropriate standard diagnostic modality for general neuroradiology.

The MRI can assist in the differential diagnosis of mediastinal and retroperitoneal masses, including abnormalities of the large vessels such as aneurysms and dissection. When a clinical need exists to visualize the parenchyma of solid organs to detect anatomic disruption or neoplasia, this can be accomplished in the liver, urogenital system, adrenals, and pelvic organs without the use of radiological contrast materials. When MRI is considered reasonable and necessary, the use of paramagnetic contrast materials may be covered as part of the study. MRI may also be used to detect and stage pelvic and retroperitoneal neoplasms and to evaluate disorders of cancellous bone and soft tissues. It may also be used in the detection of pericardial thickening. Primary and secondary bone neoplasm and aseptic necrosis can be detected at an early stage and monitored with MRI. Patients with metallic prostheses, especially of the hip, can be imaged in order to detect the early stages of infection of the bone to which the prothesis is attached.

Disc Disease Diagnosis (Effective March 22, 1994)

The MRI may also be covered to diagnose disc disease without regard to whether radiological imaging has been tried first to diagnose the problem.

Gating Devices and Surface Coils (Effective March 4, 1991)

Gating devices that eliminate distorted images caused by cardiac and respiratory movement cycles are now considered state of the art techniques and may be covered. Surface and other specialty coils may also be covered, as they are used routinely for high resolution imaging where small limited regions of the body are studied. They produce high signal-to-noise ratios resulting in images of enhanced anatomic detail.

C - Contraindications and Nationally Noncovered Indications

1. Contraindications

    The MRI is not covered when the following patient-specific contraindications are present. It is not covered for patients with cardiac pacemakers or with metallic clips on vascular aneurysms. MRI during a viable pregnancy is also contraindicated at this time. The danger inherent in bringing ferromagnetic materials within range of MRI units generally constrains the use of MRI on acutely ill patients requiring life support systems and monitoring devices that employ ferromagnetic materials. In addition, the long imaging time and the enclosed position of the patient may result in claustrophobia, making patients who have a history of claustrophobia unsuitable candidates for MRI procedures.

2. Nationally Noncovered Indications

    The CMS has determined that blood flow measurement, imaging of cortical bone and calcifications, and procedures involving spatial resolution of bone and calcifications, are not considered reasonable and necessary indications within the meaning of section 1862(a)(1)(A) of the Social Security Act, and are therefore noncovered.

D. Other

All other uses of MRI for which CMS has not specifically indicated coverage or noncoverage continue to be eligible for coverage through individual local contractor discretion.

(This NCD last reviewed September 2004.)

100-3, 220.3

NCD for Magnetic Resonance Angiography (MRA) (220.3)

B. Nationally Covered Indications

1. Head and Neck

    Studies have proven that MRA is effective for evaluating flow in internal carotid vessels of the head and neck. However, not all potential applications of MRA have been shown to be reasonable and necessary. All of the following criteria must apply in order for Medicare to provide coverage for MRA of the head and neck:

    a. MRA is used to evaluate the carotid arteries, the circle of Willis, the anterior, middle or posterior cerebral arteries, the vertebral or basilar arteries or the venous sinuses;

    b. MRA is performed on patients with conditions of the head and neck for which surgery is anticipated and may be found to be appropriate based on the MRA. These conditions include, but are not limited to, tumor, aneurysms, vascular malformations, vascular occlusion or thrombosis. Within this broad category of disorders, medical necessity is the underlying determinant of the need for an MRA in specific diseases. The medical records should clearly justify and demonstrate the existence of medical necessity; and

    c. MRA and contrast angiography (CA) are not expected to be performed on the same patient for diagnostic purposes prior to the application of anticipated therapy. Only one of these tests will be covered routinely unless the physician can demonstrate the medical need to perform both tests.

2. Peripheral Arteries of Lower Extremities

    Studies have proven that MRA of peripheral arteries is useful in determining the presence and extent of peripheral vascular disease in lower extremities. This procedure is noninvasive and has been shown to find occult vessels in some patients for which those vessels were not apparent when CA was performed. Medicare will cover either MRA or CA to evaluate peripheral arteries of the lower extremities. However, both MRA and CA may be useful is some cases, such as:

a. A patient has had CA and this test was unable to identify a viable run-off vessel for bypass. When exploratory surgery is not believed to be a reasonable medical course of action for this patient, MRA may be performed to identify the viable runoff vessel; or

b. A patient has had MRA, but the results are inconclusive.

3. Abdomen and Pelvis

a. Pre-operative Evaluation of Patients Undergoing Elective Abdominal Aortic Aneurysm (AAA) Repair (Effective July 1, 1999)

The MRA is covered for pre-operative evaluation of patients undergoing elective AAA repair if the scientific evidence reveals MRA is considered comparable to CA in determining the extent of AAA, as well as in evaluating aortoiliac occlusion disease and renal artery pathology that may be necessary in the surgical planning of AAA repair. These studies also reveal that MRA could provide a net benefit to the patient. If preoperative CA is avoided, then patients are not exposed to the risks associated with invasive procedures, contrast media, end-organ damage, or arterial injury.

b. Imaging the Renal Arteries and the Aortoiliac Arteries in the Absence of AAA or Aortic Dissection (Effective July 1, 2003)

The MRA coverage is expanded to include imaging the renal arteries and the aortoiliac arteries in the absence of AAA or aortic dissection. MRA should be obtained in those circumstances in which using MRA is expected to avoid obtaining CA, when physician history, physical examination, and standard assessment tools provide insufficient information for patient management, and obtaining an MRA has a high probability of positively affecting patient management. However, CA may be ordered after obtaining the results of an MRA in those rare instances where medical necessity is demonstrated.

4. Chest

a. Diagnosis of Pulmonary Embolism

Current scientific data has shown that diagnostic pulmonary MRAs are improving due to recent developments such as faster imaging capabilities and gadolinium-enhancement. However, these advances in MRA are not significant enough to warrant replacement of pulmonary angiography in the diagnosis of pulmonary embolism for patients who have no contraindication to receiving intravenous iodinated contrast material. Patients who are allergic to iodinated contrast material face a high risk of developing complications if they undergo pulmonary angiography or computed tomography angiography. Therefore, Medicare will cover MRA of the chest for diagnosing a suspected pulmonary embolism when it is contraindicated for the patient to receive intravascular iodinated contrast material.

b. Evaluation of Thoracic Aortic Dissection and Aneurysm

Studies have shown that MRA of the chest has a high level of diagnostic accuracy for pre-operative and post-operative evaluation of aortic dissection of aneurysm. Depending on the clinical presentation, MRA may be used as an alternative to other non-invasive imaging technologies, such as transesophageal echocardiography and CT. Generally, Medicare will provide coverage only for MRA or for CA when used as a diagnostic test. However, if both MRA and CA of the chest are used, the physician must demonstrate the medical need for performing these tests.

While the intent of this policy is to provide reimbursement for either MRA or CA, CMS is also allowing flexibility for physicians to make appropriate decisions concerning the use of these tests based on the needs of individual patients. CMS anticipates, however, low utilization of the combined use of MRA and CA. As a result, CMS encourages contractors to monitor the use of these tests and, where indicated, requires evidence of the need to perform both MRA and CA.

C. Nationally Noncovered Indications

All other uses of MRA for which CMS has not specifically indicated coverage continue to be noncovered.

D. Other

Not applicable.

(This NCD last reviewe

100-3, 220.5

NCD for Ultrasound Diagnostic Procedures (220.5)

A. General

Ultrasound diagnostic procedures utilizing low energy sound waves are being widely employed to determine the composition and contours of nearly all body tissues except bone and air-filled spaces. This technique permits noninvasive visualization of even the deepest structures in the body. The use of the ultrasound technique is sufficiently developed that it can be considered essential to good patient care in diagnosing a wide variety of conditions.

Ultrasound diagnostic procedures are listed below and are divided into two categories. Medicare coverage is extended to the procedures listed in Category I. Periodic claims review by the intermediary's medical consultants should be conducted to ensure that the techniques are medically appropriate and the general indications specified in these categories are met. Techniques in Category II are considered experimental and should not be covered at this time.

Indications and Limitations of Coverage

B. Nationally Covered Indications

Category I - (Clinically effective, usually part of initial patient evaluation, may be an adjunct to radiologic and nuclear medicine diagnostic technique)

- Echoencephalography, (Diencephalic Midline) (A-Mode).
- Echoencephalography, Complete (Diencephalic Midline and Ventricular Size).
- Ocular and Orbital Echography (A-Mode).
- Covered procedures include efforts to determine the suitability of aphakic patients for implantation of an artificial lens (pseudophakoi) following cataract surgery.
- Ocular and Orbital Sonography (B-Mode).
- Echocardiography, Pericardial Effusion (M-Mode).
- Pericardiocentesis, by Ultrasonic Guidance.
- Echocardiography, Cardiac Valve(s) (M-Mode).
- Echocardiography, Complete (M-Mode).
- Echocardiography, limited (e.g., follow-up or limited study) (M-Mode).
- Pleural Effusion Echography.
- Thoracentesis, by Ultrasonic Guidance.
- Abdominal Sonography, complete survey study (B-Scan).
- Abdominal Sonography, limited (e.g., follow-up or limited study) (B-Scan).
- Abdominal Sonography is not synonymous with ultrasound examination of individual organs.
- Renal Cyst Aspiration, by Ultrasonic Guidance.
- Renal Biopsy, by Ultrasonic Guidance.
- Pancreas Sonography (B-Scan).
- Pancreatic Sonography has proven effective in diagnosing pseudocysts.
- Spleen Sonography (B-Scan).
- Abdominal Aorta Echography (A-Mode).
- Abdominal Aorta Sonography (B-Scan).
- Retroperitoneal Sonography (B-Scan).
- Retroperitoneal Sonography does not include planning of fields for radiation therapy.
- Urinary Bladder Sonography (B-Scan).
- Urinary bladder Sonography does not include staging of bladder tumors.
- Pregnancy Diagnosis Sonography (B-Scan).
- Fetal Age Determination (Biparietal Diameter) Sonography (B-Scan).
- Fetal Growth Rate Sonography (B-Scan).
- Placenta Localization Sonography (B-Scan).
- Pregnancy Sonography, Complete (B-Scan).
- Molar Pregnancy Diagnosis Sonography (B-Scan).
- Ectopic Pregnancy Diagnosis Sonography (B-Scan).
- Passive Testing (Antepartum Monitoring of Fetal Heart Rate In the Resting Fetus)
- Intrauterine Contraceptive Device Sonography (B-Scan).
- Pelvic Mass Diagnosis Sonography (B-Scan).
- Amniocentesis, by Ultrasonic Guidance.
- Arterial Flow Study, Peripheral (Doppler).
- Venous Flow Study, Peripheral (Doppler).
- Arterial Aneurysm, Peripheral (B-Scan).
- Radiation Therapy Planning Sonography (B-Scan).
- Thyroid Echography (A-Mode).
- Thyroid Sonography (B-Scan).
- Breast Echography (A-Mode).
- Breast Sonography (B-Scan).
- Hepatic Sonography (B-Scan).
- Gallbladder Sonography.
- Renal Sonography.
- Two-Dimensional Echocardiography (B-Mode).
- Monitoring of cardiac output(Esophageal Doppler) for ventilated patients in the ICU and operative patients with a need for intra-operative fluid optimization

C. Nationally Non-Covered Indications

Category II - (Clinical reliability and efficacy not proven):

- B-Scan for atherosclerotic narrowing of peripheral arteries.

D. Other

Uses for ultrasound diagnostic procedures not listed in Category I or II above are left to local contractor discretion. In view of the rapid changes in the field of ultrasound diagnosis, uses for ultrasound diagnostic procedures other than those listed under Categories I and II should be carefully reviewed before payment. Medical justification may be required.

(This NCD last reviewed June 2007.)

100-3, 220.6

NCD for PET Scans (220.6)

The following indications may be covered for PET under certain circumstances. Details of Medicare PET coverage are discussed later in this section. Unless otherwise indicated, the clinical conditions below are covered when PET utilizes FDG as a tracer.

NOTE: This manual section 220.6 lists all Medicare-covered uses of PET scans. Except as set forth below in cancer indications listed as "Coverage with Evidence Development", a particular use of PET scans is not covered unless this manual specifically provides that such use is covered. Although this section 220.6 lists some non-covered uses of PET scans, it does not constitute an exhaustive list of all non-covered uses.

Clinical Condition	Effective Date	Coverage
Solitary Pulmonary Nodules (SPNs)	January 1, 1998	Characterization
Lung Cancer (Non Small Cell)	January 1, 1998	Initial staging
Lung Cancer (Non Small Cell)	July 1, 2001	Diagnosis, staging, restaging
Esophageal Cancer	July 1, 2001	Diagnosis, staging, restaging
Colorectal Cancer	July 1, 1999	Determining location of tumors if rising CEA level suggests recurrence
Colorectal Cancer	July 1, 2001	Diagnosis, staging, restaging
Lymphoma	July 1, 1999	Staging and restaging only when used as alternative to Gallium scan
Lymphoma	July 1, 2001	Diagnosis, staging and restaging
Melanoma	July 1, 1999	Evaluating recurrence prior to surgery as alternative to Gallium scan
Melanoma	July 1, 2001	Diagnosis, staging, restaging; Noncovered for evaluating regional nodes
Breast Cancer	October 1, 2002	As an adjunct to standard imaging modalities for staging patients with distant metastasis or restaging patients with loco-regional recurrence or metastasis; as an adjunct to standard imaging modalities for monitoring tumor response to treatment for women with locally advanced and metastatic breast cancer when a change in therapy is anticipated
Head and Neck Cancers (excluding CNS and thyroid)	July 1, 2001	Diagnosis, staging, restaging
Thyroid Cancer	October 1, 2003	Restaging of recurrent or residual thyroid cancers of follicular cell origin previously treated by thyroidectomy and radioiodine ablation and have a serum thyroglobulin >10ng/ml and negative I-131 whole body scan performed
Myocardial Viability	July 1, 2001 to September 30,	
2002	Only following inconclusive SPECT	
Myocardial Viability	October 1, 2002	Primary or initial diagnosis, or following an inconclusive SPECT prior to revascularization. SPECT may not be used following an inconclusive PET scan
Refractory Seizures	July 1, 2001	Pre-surgical evaluation only
Perfusion of the heart using Rubidium 82* tracer	March 14, 1995	Noninvasive imaging of the perfusion of the heart
Perfusion of the heart using ammonia N-13* tracer	October 1, 2003	Noninvasive imaging of the perfusion of the heart

*Not FDG-PET.

EFFECTIVE JANUARY 28, 2005: This manual section lists Medicare-covered uses of PET scans effective for services performed on or after January 28, 2005. Except as set forth below in cancer indications listed as "coverage with evidence development", a particular use of PET scans is not covered unless this manual specifically provides that such use is covered. Although this section 220.6 lists some non-covered uses of PET scans, it does not constitute an exhaustive list of all non-covered uses.

For cancer indications listed as "coverage with evidence development" CMS determines that the evidence is sufficient to conclude that an FDG PET scan is reasonable and necessary only when the provider is participating in, and patients are enrolled in, one of the following types of prospective clinical studies that is designed to collect additional information at the time of the scan to assist in patient management:

- A clinical trial of FDG PET that meets the requirements of Food and Drug Administration (FDA) category B investigational device exemption (42 CFR 405.201);

- An FDG PET clinical study that is designed to collect additional information at the time of the scan to assist in patient management. Qualifying clinical studies must ensure that specific hypotheses are addressed; appropriate data elements are collected; hospitals and providers are qualified to provide the PET scan and interpret the results; participating hospitals and providers accurately report data on all enrolled patients not included in other qualifying trials through adequate auditing mechanisms; and, all patient confidentiality, privacy, and other Federal laws must be followed.

Effective January 28, 2005: For PET services identified as "Coverage with Evidence Development." Medicare shall notify providers and beneficiaries where these services can be accessed, as they become available, via the following:

- Federal Register Notice
- CMS coverage Web site at: www.cms.gov/coverage

Indication	Covered[1]	Nationally Non-covered[2]	Coverage with Evidence Development[3]
Brain			X
Breast			
• Diagnosis		X	
• Initial staging of axillary nodes		X	
• Staging of distant metastasis	X		
• Restaging, monitoring *	X		
Cervoca;			
• Staging as adjunct to conventional imaging	X		
• Other staging			X
• Diagnosis, restaging, monitoring *			X
Colorectal			
• Diagnosis, staging, restaging	X		
• Monitoring *			X
Esophagus			
• Diagnosis, staging, restaging	X		
• Monitoring *			X
Head and Neck (non-CNS/thyroid)			
• Diagnosis, staging, restaging	X		
• Monitoring *			X
Lymphoma			
• Diagnosis, staging, restaging	X		
• Monitoring *	X		X
Melanoma			
• Diagnosis, staging, restaging	X		
• Monitoring *			X
Non-Small Cell Lung			
• Diagnosis, staging, restaging	X		
• Monitoring *			X
Ovarian			X
Pancreatic			X
Small Cell Lung			X
Soft Tissue Sarcoma			X
Solitary Pulmonary Nodule (characterization)	X		

1   Covered nationally based on evidence of benefit. Refer to National Coverage Determination Manual Section 220.6 in its entirety for specific coverage language and limitations for each indication.

2   Non-covered nationally based on evidence of harm or no benefit.

3   Covered only in specific settings discussed above if certain patient safeguards are provided. Otherwise, non-covered nationally based on lack of evidence sufficient to establish either benefit or harm or no prior decision addressing this cancer. Medicare shall notify providers and beneficiaries where these services can be accessed, as they become available, via the following:
    Federal Register Notice
    CMS coverage Web site at: www.cms.gov/coverage

*   Monitoring = monitoring response to treatment when a change in therapy is anticipated.

© 2008 Ingenix

Indication	Covered[1]	Nationally Non-covered[2]	Coverage with Evidence Development[3]
Thyroid			
• Staging of follicular cell tumors	X		
• Restaging of medullary cell tumors			X
• Diagnosis, other staging & restaging			X
• Monitoring *			
Testicular			X
All other cancers not listed herein (all indications)			X

1. Covered nationally based on evidence of benefit. Refer to National Coverage Determination Manual Section 220.6 in its entirety for specific coverage language and limitations for each indication.
2. Non-covered nationally based on evidence of harm or no benefit.
3. Covered only in specific settings discussed above if certain patient safeguards are provided. Otherwise, non-covered nationally based on lack of evidence sufficient to establish either benefit or harm or no prior decision addressing this cancer. Medicare shall notify providers and beneficiaries where these services can be accessed, as they become available, via the following:
   Federal Register Notice
   CMS coverage Web site at: www.cms.gov/coverage
* Monitoring = monitoring response to treatment when a change in therapy is anticipated.

II. General Conditions of Coverage for FDG PET

Allowable FDG PET Systems

A. Definitions: For purposes of this section:

- "Any FDA-approved" means all systems approved or cleared for marketing by the Food and Drug Administration (FDA) to image radionuclides in the body.
- "FDA-approved" means that the system indicated has been approved or cleared for marketing by the FDA to image radionuclides in the body.
- "Certain coincidence systems" refers to the systems that have all the following features:
  - Crystal at least 5/8-inch thick;
  - Techniques to minimize or correct for scatter and/or randoms; and
  - Digital detectors and iterative reconstruction.

Scans performed with gamma camera PET systems with crystals thinner than 5/8" will not be covered by Medicare. In addition, scans performed with systems with crystals greater than or equal to 5/8" in thickness, but that do not meet the other listed design characteristics are not covered by Medicare. B. Allowable PET systems by covered clinical indication:

Covered Clinical Condition	Prior to July 1, 2001	July 1, 2001 through December 31, 2001	On or after January 1, 2002
Characterization of single pulmonary nodules	Effective 1/1/1998, any FDA-approved	Any FDA-approved	FDA-approved: Full/Partial ring, certain coincidence systems
Initial staging of lung cancer (non small cell)	Effective 1/1/1998, any FDA-approved	Any FDA-approved	FDA-approved: Full/Partial ring, certain coincidence systems
Determining location of colorectal tumors if rising CEA level suggests recurrence	Effective 7/1/1999, any FDA-approved	Any FDA-approved	FDA approved: Full/Partial ring, certain coincidence systems
Staging or restaging of lymphoma only when used as alternative to gallium scan	Effective 7/1/1999, any FDA-approved	Any FDA-approved	FDA-approved: Full/Partial ring, certain coincidence systems
Evaluating recurrence of melanoma prior to surgery as alternative to gallium scan	Effective 7/1/1999, any FDA-approved.	Any FDA-approved	FDA-approved: Full/Partial ring, certain coincidence systems
Diagnosis, staging, restaging of colorectal cancer	Not covered by Medicare	Full ring	FDA-approved: Full/Partial ring
Diagnosis, staging, restaging of esophageal cancer	Not covered by Medicare	Full ring	FDA-approved: Full/Partial ring
Diagnosis, staging, restaging of head and neck cancers (excluding CNS and thyroid)	Not covered by Medicare	Full ring	FDA-approved: Full/Partial ring

Covered Clinical Condition	Prior to July 1, 2001	July 1, 2001 through December 31, 2001	On or after January 1, 2002
Diagnosis, staging, restaging of lung cancer (non small cell)	Not covered by Medicare	Full ring	FDA-approved: Full/Partial ring
Diagnosis, staging, restaging of lymphoma	Not covered by Medicare	Full ring	FDA-approved: Full/Partial ring
Diagnosis, staging, restaging of melanoma (non-covered for evaluating regional nodes)	Not covered by Medicare	Full ring	FDA-approved: Full/Partial ring
Determination of myocardial viability only following inconclusive SPECT	Not covered by Medicare	Full ring	FDA-approved: Full/Partial ring
Pre-surgical evaluation of refractory seizures	Not covered by Medicare	Full ring	FDA-approved: Full/Partial ring
Breast Cancer	Not covered	Not covered	Effective October 1, 2002, Full/Partial ring
Thyroid Cancer	Not covered	Not covered	Effective October 1, 2003, Full/Partial ring
Myocardial Viability Primary or initial diagnosis prior to revascularization	Not covered	Not covered	Effective October 1, 2002, Full/Partial ring
All other oncology indications not previously specified	Not covered	Not covered	Effective January 28, 2005, Full/Partial ring

C. Regardless of any other terms or conditions, all uses of FDG PET scans, in order to be covered by the Medicare program, must meet the following general conditions prior to June 30, 2001:

- Submission of claims for payment must include any information Medicare requires to ensure the PET scans performed were: (a) medically necessary, (b) did not unnecessarily duplicate other covered diagnostic tests, and (c) did not involve investigational drugs or procedures using investigational drugs, as determined by the FDA.
- The PET scan entity submitting claims for payment must keep such patient records as Medicare requires on file for each patient for whom a PET scan claim is made.
- Regardless of any other terms or conditions, all uses of FDG PET scans, in order to be covered by the Medicare program, must meet the following general conditions as of July 1, 2001:
  - The provider of the PET scan should maintain on file the doctor's referral and documentation that the procedure involved only FDA-approved drugs and devices, as is normal business practice.
  - The ordering physician is responsible for documenting the medical necessity of the study and ensuring that it meets the conditions specified in the instructions. The physician should have documentation in the beneficiary's medical record to support the referral to the PET scan provider.

III. Covered Indications for PET Scans and Limitations/Requirements for Usage

For all uses of PET relating to malignancies the following conditions apply:

A. Diagnosis: PET is covered only in clinical situations in which: (1) the PET results may assist in avoiding an invasive diagnostic procedure, or in which (2) the PET results may assist in determining the optimal anatomical location to perform an invasive diagnostic procedure. In general, for most solid tumors, a tissue diagnosis is made prior to the performance of PET scanning. PET scans following a tissue diagnosis are generally performed for staging rather than diagnosis.

PET is not covered as a screening test (i.e., testing patients without specific signs and symptoms of disease).

B. Staging: PET is covered for staging in clinical situations in which: (1)(a) the stage of the cancer remains in doubt after completion of a standard diagnostic workup, including conventional imaging (computed tomography (CT), magnetic resonance imaging (MRI), or ultrasound), or (1)(b) it could potentially replace one or more conventional imaging studies when it is expected that conventional study information is insufficient for the clinical management of the patient, and 2) clinical management of the patient would differ depending on the stage of the cancer identified.

C. Restaging: PET is covered for restaging: (1) after completion of treatment for the purpose of detecting residual disease, (2) for detecting suspected recurrence or metastasis, (3) to determine the extent of a known recurrence, or (4) if it could potentially replace one or more conventional imaging studies when it is expected that conventional study information is insufficient for the clinical management of the patient. Restaging applies to testing after a course of treatment is completed, and is covered subject to the conditions above.

D. Monitoring: This refers to use of PET to monitor tumor response to treatment during the planned course of therapy (i.e., when a change in therapy is anticipated).

NOTE: In the absence of national frequency limitations, contractors, should, if necessary, develop frequency requirements on any or all of the indications covered on and after July 1, 2001.

(This N

100-3, 220.6.6

NCD for PET (FDG) for Melanoma (220.6.6)

1. Evaluation of Recurrent Melanoma Prior to Surgery As Alternative to Gallium Scan (Effective July 1, 1999)

Effective for services performed on or after July 1, 1999, FDG PET (when used as an alternative to a Gallium scan) is covered for patients with recurrent melanoma prior to surgery for tumor evaluation. FDG PET is not covered for the evaluation of regional nodes.

Frequency Limitations: Whole body PET scans cannot be ordered more frequently than once every 12 months, unless medical necessity documentation, maintained in the beneficiary's medical record, supports the specific need for anatomic localization of possible recurrent tumor within this period.

Limitations: The FDG PET scan is covered only as an alternative to a Gallium scan. PET scans can not be covered in cases where they are performed within 50 days of a Gallium scan performed by the same PET facility where the patient has remained under the care of the same facility during the 50-day period. Gallium scans performed by another facility less than 50 days prior to the PET scan will not be counted against this screen. The purpose of this screen is to ensure that PET scans are covered only as an alternative to a Gallium scan within the same facility. The CMS is aware that, in order to ensure proper patient care, the treating physician may conclude that previously performed Gallium scans are either inconclusive or not sufficiently reliable to make the determination covered by this provision. Therefore, CMS will apply this 50-day rule only to PET scans performed by the same facility that performed the Gallium scan.

Effective for services performed on or after July 1, 2001, documentation should be maintained in the beneficiary's medical file at the referring physician's office to support the medical necessity of the procedure, as is normal business practice.

2. Diagnosis, Staging, and Restaging (Effective July 1, 2001)

Effective for services performed on or after July 1, 2001, FDG PET is covered for the diagnosis, staging, and restaging of melanoma. FDG PET is not covered for the evaluation of regional nodes.

3. Monitoring Response to Treatment (Effective January 28, 2005)

Effective for services performed on or after January 28, 2005, Medicare only covers FDG PET for monitoring response to treatment for melanoma as "coverage with evidence development".

Medicare shall notify providers and beneficiaries where these services can be accessed, as they become available, via the following:

Federal Register Notice

CMS coverage Web site at: www.cms.gov/coverage

Requirements: PET is covered in any/all of the following circumstances:

A. Diagnosis: PET is covered only in clinical situations in which: (1) the PET results may assist in avoiding an invasive diagnostic procedure, or (2) the PET results may assist in determining the optimal anatomical location to perform an invasive diagnostic procedure. In general, for most solid tumors, a tissue diagnosis is made prior to the performance of PET scanning. PET scans following a tissue diagnosis are generally performed for staging rather than diagnosis.

B. Staging and/or Restaging: PET is covered for staging in clinical situations in which: (1) (a) the stage of the cancer remains in doubt after completion of a standard diagnostic workup, including conventional imaging (computed tomography, magnetic resonance imaging, or ultrasound), or (1)(b) the use of PET could potentially replace one or more conventional imaging studies when it is expected that conventional study information is insufficient for the clinical management of the patient, and (2) clinical management of the patient would differ depending on the stage of the cancer identified.

PET is covered for restaging after the completion of treatment for the purpose of: (1) detecting residual disease, (2) detecting suspected recurrence, (3) determining the extent of a known recurrence, or (4) potentially replacing one or more conventional imaging studies when it is expected that conventional study information is insufficient for the clinical management of the patient.

C. Monitoring Response to Treatment: PET is covered for monitoring response to treatment when a change in therapy is anticipated.

Documentation that these conditions are met should be maintained by the referring physician in the beneficiary's medical file, as is normal business practice.

(This NCD last reviewed March 2005.)

100-3, 220.6.7

NCD for PET (FDG) for Head and Neck Cancers (220.6.7)

Effective for services performed on or after July 1, 2001, Medicare covers FDG PET for diagnosis, staging and restaging of cancer of the head and neck, excluding the central nervous system (CNS) and thyroid. The head and neck cancers encompass a diverse set of malignancies of which the majority is squamous cell carcinomas. Patients may present with metastases to cervical lymph nodes but conventional forms of diagnostic imaging fail to identify the primary tumor. Patients that present with cancer of the head and neck are left with two options - either to have a neck dissection or to have radiation of both sides of the neck with random biopsies. PET scanning attempts to reveal the site of primary tumor to prevent the adverse effects of random biopsies or unnecessary radiation.

Limitations: PET scans for head and neck cancers are not covered for CNS or thyroid cancers prior to October 1, 2003. Refer to section 220.6.11 for coverage for thyroid cancer effective October 1, 2003.

Effective for services performed on or after January 28, 2005, Medicare only covers FDG PET for monitoring response to treatment for head and neck cancers as "coverage with evidence development".

Medicare shall notify providers and beneficiaries where these services can be accessed, as they become available, via the following: Federal Register Notice

CMS coverage Web site at: www.cms.gov/coverage

Requirements: PET is covered in any/all of the following circumstances:

A. Diagnosis:
PET is covered only in clinical situations in which: (1) the PET results may assist in avoiding an invasive diagnostic procedure, or (2) the PET results may assist in determining the optimal anatomical location to perform an invasive diagnostic procedure. In general, for most solid tumors a tissue diagnosis is made prior to the performance of PET scanning. PET scans following a tissue diagnosis are generally performed for staging rather than diagnosis.

B. Staging and/or Restaging:
PET is covered for staging in clinical situations in which: (1)(a) the stage of the cancer remains in doubt after completion of a standard diagnostic workup, including conventional imaging (computed tomography, magnetic resonance imaging, or ultrasound), or (1)(b) the use of PET could potentially replace one or more conventional imaging studies when it is expected that conventional study information is insufficient for the clinical management of the patient, and (2) clinical management of the patient would differ depending on the stage of the cancer identified.

PET is covered for restaging after completion of treatment for the purpose of: (1) detecting residual disease, (2) detecting suspected recurrence, (3) determining the extent of a known recurrence, or (4) potentially replacing one or more conventional imaging studies when it is expected that conventional study information is insufficient for the clinical management of the patient.

C. Monitoring Response to Treatment: PET is covered for monitoring response to treatment when a change in therapy is anticipated.
Documentation that these conditions are met should be maintained by the referring physician in the beneficiary's medical record, as is normal business practice.

(This NCD last reviewed March 2005.)

100-3, 220.6.8

NCD for PET (FDG) for Myocardial Viability (220.6.8)

1. FDG PET is covered for the determination of myocardial viability following an inconclusive single photon emission computed tomography (SPECT) test from July 1, 2001, through September 30, 2002. Only full ring PET scanners are covered from July 1, 2001, through December 31, 2001. However, as of January 1, 2002, full and partial ring scanners are covered.

2. Beginning October 1, 2002, Medicare covers FDG PET for the determination of myocardial viability as a primary or initial diagnostic study prior to revascularization, or following an inconclusive SPECT. Studies performed by full and partial ring scanners are covered.

Limitations
In the event a patient receives a SPECT test with inconclusive results, a PET scan may be covered. However, if a patient receives a FDG PET study with inconclusive results, a follow up SPECT test is not covered.

Documentation that these conditions are met should be maintained by the referring physician in the beneficiary's medical record, as is normal business practice.

(This NCD last reviewed September 2002.)

100-3, 220.6.10

NCD for PET (FDG) for Breast Cancer (220.6.10)

Effective for services performed on or after October 1, 2002, Medicare covers FDG PET only as an adjunct to other imaging modalities for: (1) staging breast cancer patients with distant metastasis, (2) restaging patients with loco-regional recurrence or metastasis, or (3) monitoring tumor response to treatment for women with locally advanced and metastatic breast cancer when a change in therapy is contemplated.

Limitations
Medicare continues to nationally non-cover initial diagnosis of breast cancer and staging of axillary lymph nodes.

Documentation that these conditions are met should be maintained by the referring physician in the beneficiary's medical record, as is normal business practice.

(This NCD last reviewed September 2002.)

100-3, 220.6.11

FDG PET for Thyroid Cancer (Various Effective Dates Below)

(Rev. 31, Issued: 04-04-05; Effective: 01-28-05; Implementation: 04-18-05)

1. Effective for services performed on or after October 1, 2003, Medicare covers the use of FDG PET for thyroid cancer only for restaging of recurrent or residual thyroid cancers of follicular cell origin that have been previously treated by thyroidectomy and radioiodine ablation and have a serum thyroglobulin >10ng/ml and negative I-131 whole body scan performed.

2. Effective for services performed on or after January 28, 2005, Medicare only covers FDG PET for diagnosis, other staging and restaging, restaging of medullary cell tumors, and monitoring response to treatment as "coverage with evidence development"

Medicare shall notify providers and beneficiaries where these services can be accessed, as they become available, via the following:

• Federal Register Notice

• The CMS coverage Web site at: www.cms.gov/coverage

Requirements: PET is covered in any/all of the following circumstances:

A. Diagnosis: PET is covered only in clinical situations in which: (1) the PET results may assist in avoiding an invasive diagnostic procedure, or (2) the PET results may assist in determining the optimal anatomical location to perform an invasive diagnostic procedure. In general, for most solid tumors a tissue diagnosis is made prior to the performance of PET scanning. PET scans following a tissue diagnosis are generally performed for staging rather than diagnosis.

B. Staging and/or Restaging: PET is covered for staging in clinical situations in which: (1)(a) the stage of the cancer remains in doubt after completion of a standard diagnostic workup, including conventional imaging (computed tomography, magnetic resonance imaging, or ultrasound), or (1)(b) the use of PET could potentially replace one or more conventional imaging studies when it is expected that conventional study information is insufficient for the clinical management of the patient, and (2) clinical management of the patient would differ depending on the stage of the cancer identified.

The PET is covered for restaging after completion of treatment for the purpose of: (1) detecting residual disease, (2) detecting suspected recurrence, (3) determining the extent of a known recurrence, or (4) potentially replacing one or more conventional imaging studies when it is expected that conventional study information is insufficient for the clinical management of the patient.

C. Monitoring Response to Treatment: PET is covered for monitoring response to treatment when a change in therapy is anticipated.

Documentation that these conditions are met should be maintained by the referring physician in the beneficiary's medical record, as is normal business practice.

(This NCD last reviewed March 2005.)

100-3, 220.7
NCD for Xenon Scan (220.7)
Program payment may be made for this diagnostic procedure which involves perfusion lung imaging with 133 xenon. However, review for evidence of abuse which might include absence of reasonable indications, inappropriate sequence, or excessive number or kinds of procedures used in the care of individual patients.

100-3, 220.8
NCD for Nuclear Radiology Procedure (220.8)
Nuclear radiology procedures, including nuclear examinations performed with mobile radiological equipment, are covered if reasonable and necessary for the individual patient. Although these procedures may not be widely used, they are generally accepted. Review claims for these procedures for evidence of abuse which might absence of reasonable indications, inappropriate sequence, or excessive number or kinds of procedures used in the care of individual patients.

100-3, 220.12
NCD for Single Photon Emission Computed Tomography (SPECT) (220.12)
Frequency limitations: Contractor discretion.

In the case of myocardial viability, FDG PET may be used following a SPECT that was found to be inconclusive. However, SPECT may not be used following an inconclusive FDG PET performed to evaluate myocardial viability.

100-3, 220.13
NCD for Percutaneous Image-Guided Breast Biopsy (220.13)
The Breast Imaging Reporting and Data System (or BIRADS system) employed by the American College of Radiology provides a standardized lexicon with which radiologists may report their interpretation of a mammogram. The BIRADS grading of mammograms is as follows: Grade I-Negative, Grade II-Benign finding, Grade III-Probably benign, Grade IV-Suspicious abnormality, and Grade V-Highly suggestive of malignant neoplasm.

A. Nonpalpable Breast Lesions.
Effective January 1, 2003, Medicare covers percutaneous image-guided breast biopsy using stereotactic or ultrasound imaging for a radiographic abnormality that is nonpalpable and is graded as a BIRADS III, IV, or V.

B. Palpable Breast Lesions.
Effective January 1, 2003, Medicare covers percutaneous image guided breast biopsy using stereotactic or ultrasound imaging for palpable lesions that are difficult to biopsy using palpation alone. Contractors have the discretion to decide what types of palpable lesions are difficult to biopsy using palpation.

100-3, 230.1
NCD for Treatment of Kidney Stones (230.1)
In addition to the traditional surgical/endoscopic techniques for the treatment of kidney stones, the following lithotripsy techniques are also covered for services rendered on or after March 15, 1985.

A. Extracorporeal Shock Wave Lithotripsy.
Extracorporeal Shock Wave Lithotripsy (ESWL) is a non-invasive method of treating kidney stones using a device called a lithotriptor. The lithotriptor uses shock waves generated outside of the body to break up upper urinary tract stones. It focuses the shock waves specifically on stones under X-ray visualization, pulverizing them by repeated shocks. ESWL is covered under Medicare for use in the treatment of upper urinary tract kidney stones.

B. Percutaneous Lithotripsy.
Percutaneous lithotripsy (or nephrolithotomy) is an invasive method of treating kidney stones by using ultrasound, electrohydraulic or mechanical lithotripsy. A probe is inserted through an incision in the skin directly over the kidney and applied to the stone. A form of lithotripsy is then used to fragment the stone. Mechanical or electrohydraulic lithotripsy may be used as an alternative or adjunct to ultrasonic lithotripsy. Percutaneous lithotripsy of kidney stones by ultrasound or by the related techniques of electrohydraulic or mechanical lithotripsy is covered under Medicare.

The following is covered for services rendered on or after January 16, 1988.

C. Transurethral Ureteroscopic Lithotripsy.
Transurethral ureteroscopic lithotripsy is a method of fragmenting and removing ureteral and renal stones through a cystoscope. The cystoscope is inserted through the urethra into the bladder. Catheters are passed through the scope into the opening where the ureters enter the bladder. Instruments passed through this opening into the ureters are used to manipulate and ultimately disintegrate stones, using either mechanical crushing, transcystoscopic electrohydraulic shock waves, ultrasound or laser. Transurethral ureteroscopic lithotripsy for the treatment of urinary tract stones of the kidney or ureter is covered under Medicare.

100-3, 230.2
NCD for Uroflowmetric Evaluations (230.2)
Uroflowmetric evaluations (also referred to as urodynamic voiding or urodynamic flow studies) are covered under Medicare for diagnosing various urological dysfunctions, including bladder outlet obstructions.

100-3, 230.3
NCD for Sterilization (230.3)
- Payment may be made only where sterilization is a necessary part of the treatment of an illness or injury, e.g., removal of a uterus because of a tumor, removal of diseased ovaries (bilateral oophorectomy), or bilateral orchidectomy in a case of cancer of the prostate. Deny claims when the pathological evidence of the necessity to perform any such procedures to treat an illness or injury is absent; and

- Sterilization of a mentally retarded beneficiary is covered if it is a necessary part of the treatment of an illness or injury.

- Monitor such surgeries closely and obtain the information needed to determine whether in fact the surgery was performed as a means of treating an illness or injury or only to achieve sterilization.

- **B - Noncovered Conditions**
  Elective hysterectomy, tubal ligation, and vasectomy, if the stated reason for these procedures is sterilization;

- A sterilization that is performed because a physician believes another pregnancy would endanger the overall general health of the woman is not considered to be reasonable and necessary for the diagnosis or treatment of illness or injury within the meaning of Sec.1862(a)(1) of the Act. The same conclusion would apply where the sterilization is performed only as a measure to prevent the possible development of, or effect on, a mental condition should the individual become pregnant; and Sterilization of a mentally retarded person where the purpose is to prevent conception, rather than the treatment of an illness or injury.

100-3, 230.4
NCD for Diagnosis and Treatment of Impotence (230.4)
Program payment may be made for diagnosis and treatment of sexual impotence.¬

100-3, 230.6
NCD for Vabra Aspirator (230.6)
Program payment cannot be made for the aspirator or the related diagnostic services when furnished in connection with the examination of an asymptomatic patient. Payment for routine physical checkups is precluded under the statute (Sec.1862(a)(7) of the Act).

100-3, 230.9
NCD for Cryosurgery of Prostate (230.9)
Cryosurgery of the prostate as a salvage therapy is not covered for any services performed prior to June 30, 2001.

Salvage Cryosurgery of Prostate After Radiation Failure. Salvage cryosurgery of the prostate for recurrent cancer is medically necessary and appropriate only for those patients with localized disease who:

1. Have failed a trial of radiation therapy as their primary treatment; and

2. Meet one of the following conditions: Stage T2B or below, Gleason score <9, PSA <8 ng/mL.

Cryosurgery as salvage therapy is therefore not covered under Medicare after failure of other therapies as the primary treatment. Cryosurgery as salvage is only covered after the failure of a trial of radiation therapy, under the conditions noted above.

100-3, 230.10
NCD for Incontinence Control Devices (230.10)
A - Mechanical/Hydraulic Incontinence Control Devices
Mechanical/hydraulic incontinence control devices are accepted as safe and effective in the management of urinary incontinence in patients with permanent anatomic and neurologic dysfunctions of the bladder. This class of devices achieves control of urination by compression of the urethra. The materials used and the success rate may vary somewhat from device to device. Such a device is covered when its use is reasonable and necessary for the individual patient.

B - Collagen Implant

A collagen implant, which is injected into the submucosal tissues of the urethra and/or the bladder neck and into tissues adjacent to the urethra, is a prosthetic device used in the treatment of stress urinary incontinence resulting from intrinsic sphincter deficiency (ISD). ISD is a cause of stress urinary incontinence in which the urethral sphincter is unable to contract and generate sufficient resistance in the bladder, especially during stress maneuvers.

Prior to collagen implant therapy, a skin test for collagen sensitivity must be administered and evaluated over a 4 week period.

In male patients, the evaluation must include a complete history and physical examination and a simple cystometrogram to determine that the bladder fills and stores properly. The patient then is asked to stand upright with a full bladder and to cough or otherwise exert abdominal pressure on his bladder. If the patient leaks, the diagnosis of ISD is established.

In female patients, the evaluation must include a complete history and physical examination (including a pelvic exam) and a simple cystometrogram to rule out abnormalities of bladder compliance and abnormalities of urethral support. Following that determination, an abdominal leak point pressure (ALLP) test is performed. Leak point pressure, stated in cm H2O, is defined as the intra-abdominal pressure at which leakage occurs from the bladder (around a catheter) when the bladder has been filled with a minimum of 150 cc fluid. If the patient has an ALLP of less than 100 cm H2O, the diagnosis of ISD is established.

To use a collagen implant, physicians must have urology training in the use of a cystoscope and must complete a collagen implant training program.

Coverage of a collagen implant, and the procedure to inject it, is limited to the following types of patients with stress urinary incontinence due to ISD:

- Male or female patients with congenital sphincter weakness secondary to conditions such as myelomeningocele or epispadias;
- Male or female patients with acquired sphincter weakness secondary to spinal cord lesions;
- Male patients following trauma, including prostatectomy and/or radiation; and
- Female patients without urethral hypermobility and with abdominal leak point pressures of 100 cm H2O or less.

Patients whose incontinence does not improve with 5 injection procedures (5 separate treatment sessions) are considered treatment failures, and no further treatment of urinary incontinence by collagen implant is covered. Patients who have a reoccurrence of incontinence following successful treatment with collagen implants in the past (e.g., 6-12 months previously) may benefit from additional treatment sessions. Coverage of additional sessions may be allowed but must be supported by medical justification.

100-3, 230.12

NCD for Dimethyl Sulfoxide (DMSO) (230.12)

The Food and Drug Administration has determined that the only purpose for which DMSO is safe and effective for humans is in the treatment of the bladder condition, interstitial cystitis. Therefore, the use of DMSO for all other indications is not considered to be reasonable and necessary. Payment may be made for its use only when reasonable and necessary for a patient in the treatment of interstitial cystitis.

100-3, 230.14

NCD for Ultrafiltration Monitor (230.14)

Covered:

Ultrafiltration and ultrafiltration monitoring as a component of hemodialysis has an established and critical role in maintaining the well-being of ESRD patients and is a covered service. The Ultrafiltration Monitor is covered under the Medicare program when it is used to calculate fluid rates for those recipients who present difficult fluid management problems. Determine the medical necessity of this device on a case-by-case basis.

Not Covered:

Ultrafiltration, independent of conventional dialysis, is considered experimental, and technology exclusively designed for this purpose is not covered under Medicare.

100-3, 240.3

NCD for Heat Treatment, including the Use of Diathermy and Ultrasound for Pulmonary Conditions (240.3)

There is no physiological rationale or valid scientific documentation of effectiveness of diathermy or ultrasound heat treatments for asthma, bronchitis, or any other pulmonary condition and for such purpose this treatment cannot be considered reasonable and necessary within the meaning of section 1862(a)(1) of the Act.

100-3, 240.6

NCD for Transvenous (Catheter) Pulmonary Embolectomy (240.6)

It is not covered under Medicare because it is still experimental.

100-3, 240.7

NCD for Postural Drainage Procedures and Pulmonary Exercises (240.7)

In most cases, postural drainage procedures and pulmonary exercises can be carried out safely and effectively by nursing personnel. However, in some cases patients may have acute or severe pulmonary conditions involving complex situations in which these procedures or exercises require the knowledge and skills of a physical therapist or a respiratory therapist. Therefore, if the attending physician determines as part of his/her plan of treatment that for the safe and effective administration of such services the procedures or exercises in question need to be performed by a physical therapist, the services of such a therapist constitute covered physical therapy when provided as an inpatient hospital service, extended care service, home health service, or outpatient physical therapy service.

NOTE: Physical therapy furnished in the outpatient department of a hospital is covered under the outpatient physical therapy benefit.

If the attending physician determines that the services should be performed by a respiratory therapist, the services of such a therapist constitute covered respiratory therapy when provided as an inpatient hospital service, outpatient hospital service, or extended care service, assuming that such services are furnished to the skilled nursing facility by a hospital with which the facility has a transfer agreement. Since the services of a respiratory therapist are not covered under the home health benefit, payment may not be made under the home health benefit for visits by a respiratory therapist to a patient's home to provide such services. Postural drainage procedures and pulmonary exercises are also covered when furnished by a physical therapist or a respiratory therapist as incident to a physician's professional service.

100-3, 250.1

NCD for Treatment of Psoriasis (250.1)

Psoriasis is a chronic skin disease, for which several conventional methods of treatment have been recognized as covered. These include topical application of steroids or other drugs; ultraviolet light (actinotherapy); and coal tar alone or in combination with ultraviolet B light (Goeckerman treatment).

A newer treatment for psoriasis uses a psoralen derivative drug in combination with ultraviolet A light, known as PUVA. PUVA therapy is covered for treatment of intractable, disabling psoriasis, but only after the psoriasis has not responded to more conventional treatment. The contractor should document this before paying for PUVA therapy.

In addition, reimbursement for PUVA therapy should be limited to amounts paid for other types of photochemotherapy; ordinarily, payment should not be allowed for more than 30 days of treatment, unless improvement is documented.

100-3, 250.3

NCD for Intravenous Immune Globulin for the Treatment of Autoimmune Mucocutaneous Blistering Diseases (250.3)

Effective October 1, 2002, IVIg is covered for the treatment of biopsy-proven (1) Pemphigus Vulgaris, (2) Pemphigus Foliaceus, (3) Bullous Pemphigoid, (4) Mucous Membrane Pemphigoid (a.k.a. Cicatricial Pemphigoid), and (5) Epidermolysis Bullosa Acquisita for the following patient subpopulations:

- Patients who have failed conventional therapy. Contractors have the discretion to define what constitutes failure of conventional therapy;
- Patients in whom conventional therapy is otherwise contraindicated. Contractors have the discretion to define what constitutes contraindications to conventional therapy; or
- Patients with rapidly progressive disease in whom a clinical response could not be affected quickly enough using conventional agents. In such situations IVIg therapy would be given along with conventional treatment(s) and the IVIg would be used only until the conventional therapy could take effect.

In addition, IVIg for the treatment of autoimmune mucocutaneous blistering diseases must be used only for short-term therapy and not as a maintenance therapy. Contractors have the discretion to decide what constitutes short-term therapy.

100-3, 250.4

NCD for Treatment of Actinic Keratosis (AKs) (250.4)

Actinic keratoses (AKs), also known as solar keratoses, are common, sun-induced skin lesions that are confined to the epidermis and have the potential to become a skin cancer.

Various options exist for treating AKs. Clinicians should select an appropriate treatment based on the patient's medical history, the lesion's characteristics, and on the patient's preference for a specific treatment. Commonly performed treatments for AKs include cryosurgery with liquid nitrogen, topical drug therapy, and curettage. Less commonly performed treatments for AK include dermabrasion, excision, chemical peels, laser therapy, and photodynamic therapy (PDT). An alternative approach to treating AKs is to observe the lesions over time and remove them only if they exhibit specific clinical features suggesting possible transformation to invasive squamous cell carcinoma (SCC).

Effective for services performed on and after November 26, 2001, Medicare covers the destruction of actinic keratoses without restrictions based on lesion or patient characteristics.

100-3, 260.1

NCD for Adult Liver Transplantation (260.1)
A - General

Effective July 15, 1996, adult liver transplantation when performed on beneficiaries with end stage liver disease other than hepatitis B or malignancies is covered under Medicare when performed in a facility which is approved by CMS as meeting institutional coverage criteria.

Effective December 10, 1999, adult liver transplantation when performed on beneficiaries with end stage liver disease other than malignancies is covered under Medicare when performed in a facility which is approved by CMS as meeting institutional coverage criteria.

Effective September 1, 2001, Medicare covers adult liver transplantation for hepatocellular carcinoma when the following conditions are met:

- The patient is not a candidate for subtotal liver resection;
- The patient's tumor(s) is less than or equal to 5 cm in diameter;
- There is no macrovascular involvement;
- There is no identifiable extrahepatic spread of tumor to surrounding lymph nodes, lungs, abdominal organs or bone; and
- The transplant is furnished in a facility which is approved by CMS as meeting institutional coverage criteria for liver transplants (See 65 FR 15006).

Adult liver transplantation for other malignancies remains excluded from coverage.

Coverage of adult liver transplantation is effective as of the date of the facility's approval, but for applications received before July 13, 1991, can be effective as early as March 8, 1990. (See "Federal Register" 56 FR 15006 dated April 12, 1991.)

B - Follow-up Care

Follow-up care or retransplantation (ICD-9-M 996.82, Complications of Transplanted Organ, Liver required as a result of a covered liver transplant is covered, provided such services are otherwise reasonable and necessary. Follow-up care is also covered for patients who have been discharged from a hospital after receiving noncovered liver transplant. Coverage for follow-up care is for items and services that are reasonable and necessary as determined by Medicare guidelines.

C - Immunosuppressive Drugs

See the Medicare Benefit Policy Manual, Chapter 15, "Covered Medical and Other Health Services," Sec.50.5.1 and the Medicare Claims Processing Manual, Chapter 17, "Drugs and Biologicals," Sec.80.3.

100-3, 260.2

NCD for Pediatric Liver Transplantation (260.2)

Liver transplantation is covered for children (under age 18) with extrahepatic biliary atresia or any other form of end stage liver disease, except that coverage is not provided for children with a malignancy extending beyond the margins of the liver or those with persistent viremia.

Liver transplantation is covered for Medicare beneficiaries when performed in a pediatric hospital that performs pediatric liver transplants if the hospital submits an application which CMS approves documenting that:

The hospital's pediatric liver transplant program is operated jointly by the hospital and another facility that has been found by CMS to meet the institutional coverage criteria in the "Federal Register" notice of April 12, 1991;

- The unified program shares the same transplant surgeons and quality assurance program (including oversight committee, patient protocol, and patient selection criteria); and
- The hospital is able to provide the specialized facilities, services, and personnel that are required by pediatric liver transplant patients.

100-3, 260.3

NCD for Pancreas Transplants (260.3)

B. Nationally Covered Indications

Effective for services performed on or after July 1, 1999, whole organ pancreas transplantation is nationally covered by Medicare when performed simultaneous with or after a kidney transplant. If the pancreas transplant occurs after the kidney transplant, immunosuppressive therapy begins with the date of discharge from the inpatient stay for the pancreas transplant.

Effective for services performed on or after April 26, 2006, pancreas transplants alone (PA) are reasonable and necessary for Medicare beneficiaries in the following limited circumstances:

1. PA will be limited to those facilities that are Medicare-approved for kidney transplantation. (Approved centers can be found at http://www.cms.hhs.gov/ESRDGeneralInformation/02_Data.asp#TopOfPage
2. Patients must have a diagnosis of type I diabetes: ul.mylist2 li{list-style-type : circle}
   - Patient with diabetes must be beta cell autoantibody positive; or
   - Patient must demonstrate insulinopenia defined as a fasting C-peptide level that is less than or equal to 110% of the lower limit of normal of the laboratory's measurement method. Fasting C-peptide levels will only be considered valid with a concurrently obtained fasting glucose <225 mg/dL;
3. Patients must have a history of medically-uncontrollable labile (brittle) insulin-dependent diabetes mellitus with documented recurrent, severe, acutely life-threatening metabolic complications that require hospitalization. Aforementioned complications include frequent hypoglycemia unawareness or recurring severe ketoacidosis, or recurring severe hypoglycemic attacks;
4. Patients must have been optimally and intensively managed by an endocrinologist for at least 12 months with the most medically-recognized advanced insulin formulations and delivery systems;
5. Patients must have the emotional and mental capacity to understand the significant risks associated with surgery and to effectively manage the lifelong need for immunosuppression; and,
6. Patients must otherwise be a suitable candidate for transplantation.

C. Nationally Non-Covered Indications

The following procedure is not considered reasonable and necessary within the meaning of section 1862(a)(1)(A) of the Social Security Act:

1. Transplantation of partial pancreatic tissue or islet cells (except in the context of a clinical trial (see section 260.3.1 of the National Coverage Determinations Manual).

D. Other

Not applicable.

(This NCD last reviewed April 2006.)

100-3, 260.7

NCD for Lymphocyte Immune Globulin, Anti-Thymocyte Globulin (Equine) (260.7)

The FDA has approved one lymphocyte immune globulin preparation for marketing, lymphocyte immune globulin, anti-thymocyte globulin (equine). This drug is indicated for the management of allograft rejection episodes in renal transplantation. It is covered under Medicare when used for this purpose. Other forms of lymphocyte globulin preparation which the FDA approves for this indication in the future may be covered under Medicare.

100-3, 260.9

NCD for Heart Transplants (260.9)

A - General

Cardiac transplantation is covered under Medicare when performed in a facility which is approved by Medicare as meeting institutional coverage criteria. (See CMS Ruling 87-1.)

B - Exceptions

In certain limited cases, exceptions to the criteria may be warranted if there is justification and if the facility ensures our objectives of safety and efficacy. Under no circumstances will exceptions be made for facilities whose transplant programs have been in existence for less than two years, and applications from consortia will not be approved.

Although consortium arrangements will not be approved for payment of Medicare heart transplants, consideration will be given to applications from heart transplant facilities that consist of more than one hospital where all of the following conditions exist:

The hospitals are under the common control or have a formal affiliation arrangement with each other under the auspices of an organization such as a university or a legally-constituted medical research institute; and

The hospitals share resources by routinely using the same personnel or services in their transplant programs. The sharing of resources must be supported by the submission of operative notes or other information that documents the routine use of the same personnel and services in all of the individual hospitals. At a minimum, shared resources means:

- The individual members of the transplant team, consisting of the cardiac transplant surgeons, cardiologists and pathologists, must practice in all the hospitals and it can be documented that they otherwise function as members of the transplant team;
- The same organ procurement organization, immunology, and tissue-typing services must be used by all the hospitals;
- The hospitals submit, in the manner required (Kaplan-Meier method) their individual and pooled experience and survival data; and
- The hospitals otherwise meet the remaining Medicare criteria for heart transplant facilities; that is, the criteria regarding patient selection, patient management, program commitment, etc.

C - Pediatric Hospitals

Cardiac transplantation is covered for Medicare beneficiaries when performed in a pediatric hospital that performs pediatric heart transplants if the hospital submits an application which CMS approves as documenting that:

- The hospital's pediatric heart transplant program is operated jointly by the hospital and another facility that has been found by CMS to meet the institutional coverage criteria in CMS Ruling 87-1;
- The unified program shares the same transplant surgeons and quality assurance program (including oversight committee, patient protocol, and patient selection criteria); and
- The hospital is able to provide the specialized facilities, services, and personnel that are required by pediatric heart transplant patients.

D - Follow-Up Care

Follow up care required as a result of a covered heart transplant is covered, provided such services are otherwise reasonable and necessary. Follow-up care is also covered for patients who have been discharged from a hospital after receiving a noncovered heart transplant. Coverage for follow-up care would be for items and services that are reasonable and necessary, as determined by Medicare guidelines. (See the Medicare Benefit Policy Manual, Chapter 16, "General Exclusions from Coverage," Sec.180.)

E - Immunosuppressive Drugs

See the Medicare Claims Processing Manual, Chapter 17, "Drugs and Biologicals," Sec.80.3.1, and Chapter 8, "Outpatient ESRD Hospital, Independent Facility, and Physician/Supplier Claims," Sec.120.1.

F - Artificial Hearts

Medicare does not cover the use of artificial hearts as a permanent replacement for a human heart or as a temporary life-support system until a human heart becomes available for transplant (often referred to as a "bridge to transplant"). Medicare does cover a ventricular assist device (VAD) when used in conjunction with specific criteria listed in Sec.20.9 of the NCD Manual.

100-3, 270.1

NCD for Electrical Stimulation (ES) and Electromagnetic Therapy for the Treatment of Wounds (270.1)

A. Nationally Covered Indications

The use of ES and electromagnetic therapy for the treatment of wounds are considered adjunctive therapies, and will only be covered for chronic Stage III or Stage IV pressure ulcers, arterial ulcers, diabetic ulcers, and venous stasis ulcers. Chronic ulcers are defined as ulcers that have not healed within 30 days of occurrence. ES or electromagnetic therapy will be covered only after appropriate standard wound therapy has been tried for at least 30 days and there are no measurable signs of improved healing. This 30-day period may begin while the wound is acute.

Standard wound care includes: optimization of nutritional status, debridement by any means to remove devitalized tissue, maintenance of a clean, moist bed of granulation tissue with appropriate moist dressings, and necessary treatment to resolve any infection that may be present. Standard wound care based on the specific type of wound includes: frequent repositioning of a patient with pressure ulcers (usually every 2 hours), offloading of pressure and good glucose control for diabetic ulcers, establishment of adequate circulation for arterial ulcers, and the use of a compression system for patients with venous ulcers.

Measurable signs of improved healing include: a decrease in wound size (either surface area or volume), decrease in amount of exudates, and decrease in amount of necrotic tissue. ES or electromagnetic therapy must be discontinued when the wound demonstrates 100% epithelialized wound bed.

ES and electromagnetic therapy services can only be covered when performed by a physician, physical therapist, or incident to a physician service. Evaluation of the wound is an integral part of wound therapy. When a physician, physical therapist, or a clinician incident to a physician, performs ES or electromagnetic therapy, the practitioner must evaluate the wound and contact the treating physician if the wound worsens. If ES or electromagnetic therapy is being used, wounds must be evaluated at least monthly by the treating physician.

B. Nationally Noncovered Indications

1. ES and electromagnetic therapy will not be covered as an initial treatment modality.

2. Continued treatment with ES or electromagnetic therapy is not covered if measurable signs of healing have not been demonstrated within any 30-day period of treatment.

3. Unsupervised use of ES or electromagnetic therapy for wound therapy will not be covered, as this use has not been found to be medically reasonable and necessary.

C. Other

All other uses of ES and electromagnetic therapy not otherwise specified for the treatment of wounds remain at local contractor discretion.

(This NCD last reviewed March 2004.)

100-3, 270.2

NCD for Noncontact Normothermic Wound Therapy (NNWT) (270.2)

There is insufficient scientific or clinical evidence to consider this device as reasonable and necessary for the treatment of wounds within the meaning of Sec.1862(a)(1)(A) of the Social Security Act and will not be covered by Medicare.

100-3, 270.4

NCD for Treatment of Decubitus Ulcers (270.4)

An accepted procedure for healing decubitus ulcers is to remove dead tissue from the lesions and to keep them clean to promote the growth of new tissue. This may be accomplished by hydrotherapy (whirlpool) treatments. Hydrotherapy (whirlpool) treatment for decubitus ulcers is a covered service under Medicare for patients when treatment is reasonable and necessary. Some other methods of treating decubitus ulcers, the safety and effectiveness of which have not been established, are not covered under the Medicare program. Some examples of these types of treatments are: ultraviolet light, low intensity direct current, topical application of oxygen, and topical dressings with Balsam of Peru in castor oil.

100-3, 270.5

NCD for Porcine Skin and Gradient Pressure Dressings (270.5)

Porcine (pig) skin dressings are covered, if reasonable and necessary for the individual patient as an occlusive dressing for burns, donor sites of a homograft, and decubiti and other ulcers.

100-3, 280.13

NCD for Transcutaneous Electrical Nerve Stimulators (TENS) (280.13)

(Rev. 1, 10-03-03)

CIM 60-20

The TENS is a type of electrical nerve stimulator that is employed to treat chronic intractable pain. This stimulator is attached to the surface of the patient's skin over the peripheral nerve to be stimulated. It may be applied in a variety of settings (in the patient's home, a physician's office, or in an outpatient clinic). Payment for TENS may be made under the durable medical equipment benefit. (See §160.13 for an explanation of coverage of medically necessary supplies for the effective use of TENS and §10.2 for an explanation of coverage of TENS for acute post-operative pain.)

100-3, 280.14

NCD for Infusion Pumps (280.14)

B. Nationally Covered Indications

The following indications for treatment using infusion pumps are covered under Medicare:

1. External Infusion Pumps

   a. Iron Poisoning (Effective for Services Performed On or After September 26, 1984)

      When used in the administration of deferoxamine for the treatment of acute iron poisoning and iron overload, only external infusion pumps are covered.

   b. Thromboembolic Disease (Effective for Services Performed On or After September 26, 1984)

      When used in the administration of heparin for the treatment of thromboembolic disease and/or pulmonary embolism, only external infusion pumps used in an institutional setting are covered.

   c. Chemotherapy for Liver Cancer (Effective for Services Performed On or After January 29, 1985)

      The external chemotherapy infusion pump is covered when used in the treatment of primary hepatocellular carcinoma or colorectal cancer where this disease is unresectable; OR, where the patient refuses surgical excision of the tumor.

   d. Morphine for Intractable Cancer Pain (Effective for Services Performed On or After April 22, 1985)

Morphine infusion via an external infusion pump is covered when used in the treatment of intractable pain caused by cancer (in either an inpatient or outpatient setting, including a hospice).

   e. Continuous Subcutaneous Insulin Infusion (CSII) Pumps (Effective for Services Performed On or after December 17, 2004)

      Continuous subcutaneous insulin infusion (CSII) and related drugs/supplies are covered as medically reasonable and necessary in the home setting for the treatment of diabetic patients who: (1) either meet the updated fasting C-Peptide testing requirement, or, are beta cell autoantibody positive; and, (2) satisfy the remaining criteria for insulin pump therapy as described below. Patients must meet either Criterion A or B as follows:

      Criterion A: The patient has completed a comprehensive diabetes education program, and has been on a program of multiple daily injections of insulin (i.e., at least 3 injections per day), with frequent self-adjustments of insulin doses for at least 6 months prior to initiation of the insulin pump, and has documented frequency of glucose self-testing an average of at least 4 times per day during the 2 months prior to initiation of the insulin pump, and meets one or more of the following criteria while on the multiple daily injection regimen:

      - Glycosylated hemoglobin level (HbAlc) > 7.0 percent;
      - History of recurring hypoglycemia;
      - Wide fluctuations in blood glucose before mealtime;
      - Dawn phenomenon with fasting blood sugars frequently exceeding 200 mg/dl; or,
      - History of severe glycemic excursions.

      Criterion B: The patient with diabetes has been on a pump prior to enrollment in Medicare and has documented frequency of glucose self-testing an average of at least 4 times per day during the month prior to Medicare enrollment.

      General CSII Criteria

      In addition to meeting Criterion A or B above, the following general requirements must be met:

      The patient with diabetes must be insulinopenic per the updated fasting C-peptide testing requirement, or, as an alternative, must be beta cell autoantibody positive.

      Updated fasting C-peptide testing requirement:

      - Insulinopenia is defined as a fasting C-peptide level that is less than or equal to 110% of the lower limit of normal of the laboratory's measurement method.
      - For patients with renal insufficiency and creatinine clearance (actual or calculated from age, gender, weight, and serum creatinine) <50 ml/minute, insulinopenia is defined as a fasting C-peptide level that is less than or equal to 200% of the lower limit of normal of the laboratory's measurement method.
      - Fasting C-peptide levels will only be considered valid with a concurrently obtained fasting glucose <225 mg/dL.
      - Levels only need to be documented once in the medical records.

      Continued coverage of the insulin pump would require that the patient be seen and evaluated by the treating physician at least every 3 months.

      The pump must be ordered by and follow-up care of the patient must be managed by a physician who manages multiple patients with CSII and who works closely with a team including nurses, diabetes educators, and dietitians who are knowledgeable in the use of CSII.

      Other Uses of CSII

      The CMS will continue to allow coverage of all other uses of CSII in accordance with the Category B investigational device exemption (IDE) clinical trials regulation (42 CFR 405.201) or as a routine cost under the clinical trials policy (Medicare National Coverage Determinations (NCD) Manual 310.1).

   f. Other Uses

      Other uses of external infusion pumps are covered if the contractor's medical staff verifies the appropriateness of the therapy and the prescribed pump for the individual patient.

      NOTE: Payment may also be made for drugs necessary for the effective use of a covered external infusion pump as long as the drug being used with the pump is itself reasonable and necessary for the patient's treatment.

2. Implantable Infusion Pumps

   a. Chemotherapy for Liver Cancer (Effective for Services Performed On or After September 26, 1984)

      The implantable infusion pump is covered for intra-arterial infusion of 5-FUdR for the treatment of liver cancer for patients with primary hepatocellular carcinoma or Duke's Class D colorectal cancer, in whom the metastases are limited to the liver, and where: (1) the disease is unresectable, or (2) the patient refuses surgical excision of the tumor.

   b. Anti-Spasmodic Drugs for Severe Spasticity

      An implantable infusion pump is covered when used to administer anti-spasmodic drugs intrathecally (e.g., baclofen) to treat chronic intractable spasticity in patients who have proven unresponsive to less invasive medical therapy as determined by the following criteria:

      As indicated by at least a 6-week trial, the patient cannot be maintained on noninvasive methods of spasm control, such as oral anti-spasmodic drugs, either because these methods fail to control adequately the spasticity or produce intolerable side effects, and prior to pump implantation, the patient must have responded favorably to a trial intrathecal dose of the anti-spasmodic drug.

c. Opioid Drugs for Treatment of Chronic Intractable Pain

An implantable infusion pump is covered when used to administer opioid drugs (e.g., morphine) intrathecally or epidurally for treatment of severe chronic intractable pain of malignant or nonmalignant origin in patients who have a life expectancy of at least 3 months, and who have proven unresponsive to less invasive medical therapy as determined by the following criteria:

The patient's history must indicate that he/she would not respond adequately to noninvasive methods of pain control, such as systemic opioids (including attempts to eliminate physical and behavioral abnormalities which may cause an exaggerated reaction to pain); and a preliminary trial of intraspinal opioid drug administration must be undertaken with a temporary intrathecal/epidural catheter to substantiate adequately acceptable pain relief and degree of side effects (including effects on the activities of daily living) and patient acceptance.

d. Coverage of Other Uses of Implanted Infusion Pumps

Determinations may be made on coverage of other uses of implanted infusion pumps if the contractor's medical staff verifies that:

- The drug is reasonable and necessary for the treatment of the individual patient;
- It is medically necessary that the drug be administered by an implanted infusion pump; and,
- The Food and Drug Administration (FDA)-approved labeling for the pump must specify that the drug being administered and the purpose for which it is administered is an indicated use for the pump.

e. Implantation of Infusion Pump Is Contraindicated

The implantation of an infusion pump is contraindicated in the following patients:

- With a known allergy or hypersensitivity to the drug being used (e.g., oral baclofen, morphine, etc.);
- Who have an infection;
- Whose body size is insufficient to support the weight and bulk of the device; and,
- With other implanted programmable devices since crosstalk between devices may inadvertently change the prescription.

NOTE: Payment may also be made for drugs necessary for the effective use of an implantable infusion pump as long as the drug being used with the pump is itself reasonable and necessary for the patient's treatment.

C. Nationally Noncovered Indications
The following indications for treatment using infusion pumps are not covered under Medicare:

1. External Infusion Pumps

a. Vancomycin (Effective for Services Beginning On or After September 1, 1996)

Medicare coverage of vancomycin as a durable medical equipment infusion pump benefit is not covered. There is insufficient evidence to support the necessity of using an external infusion pump, instead of a disposable elastomeric pump or the gravity drip method, to administer vancomycin in a safe and appropriate manner

2. Implantable Infusion Pump

a. Thromboembolic Disease (Effective for Services Performed On or After September 26, 1984)

According to the Public Health Service, there is insufficient published clinical data to support the safety and effectiveness of the heparin implantable pump. Therefore, the use of an implantable infusion pump for infusion of heparin in the treatment of recurrent thromboembolic disease is not covered.

b. Diabetes

An implanted infusion pump for the infusion of insulin to treat diabetes is not covered. The data does not demonstrate that the pump provides effective administration of insulin.

D. Other
Not applicable.

(This NCD last reviewed January 2005.)

100-3, 300.1
NCD for Obsolete or Unreliable Diagnostic Tests (300.1)
CIM 50-34

A. Diagnostic Tests
Do not routinely pay for the following diagnostic tests because they are obsolete and have been replaced by more advanced procedures. The listed tests may be paid for only if the medical need for the procedure is satisfactorily justified by the physician who performs it. When the services are subject to the Quality Improvement Organization (QIO) Review, the QIO is responsible for determining that satisfactory medical justification exists. When the services are not subject to QIO review, the intermediary or carrier is responsible for determining that satisfactory medical justification exists. This includes:

- Amylase, blood isoenzymes, electrophoretic,
- Chromium, blood,

- Guanase, blood,
- Zinc sulphate turbidity, blood,
- Skin test, cat scratch fever,
- Skin test, lymphopathia venereum,
- Circulation time, one test,
- Cephalin flocculation,
- Congo red, blood,
- Hormones, adrenocorticotropin quantitative animal tests,
- Hormones, adrenocorticotropin quantitative bioassay,
- Thymol turbidity, blood,
- Skin test, actinomycosis,
- Skin test, brucellosis,
- Skin test, psittacosis,
- Skin test, trichinosis,
- Calcium, feces, 24-hour quantitative,
- Starch, feces, screening,
- Chymotrypsin, duodenal contents,
- Gastric analysis, pepsin,
- Gastric analysis, tubeless,
- Calcium saturation clotting time,
- Capillary fragility test (Rumpel-Leede),
- Colloidal gold,
- Bendien's test for cancer and tuberculosis,
- Bolen's test for cancer.
- Rehfuss test for gastric acidity, and
- Serum seromucoid assay for cancer and other diseases.

B. Cardiovascular Tests
Do not pay for the following phonocardiography and vectorcardiography diagnostic tests because they have been determined to be outmoded and of little clinical value. They include:

- Phonocardiogram with or without ECG lead; with supervision during recording with interpretation and report (when equipment is supplied by the physician),
- Phonocardiogram; tracing only, without interpretation and report (e.g., when equipment is supplied by the hospital, clinic),
- Phonocardiogram; interpretation and report,
- Phonocardiogram with ECG lead, with indirect carotid artery and/or jugular vein tracing, and/or apex cardiogram, with interpretation and report,
- Phonocardiogram; without interpretation and report,
- Phonocardiogram; interpretation and report only,
- Intracardiac,
- Vectorcardiogram (VCG), with or without ECG; with interpretation and report,
- Vectorcardiogram; tracing only, without interpretation and report, and
- Vectorcardiogram; interpretation and report only.

100-4, 1, 30.3.5
Effect of Assignment Upon Purchase of Cataract Glasses From Participating Physician or Supplier on Claims Submitted to Carriers
B3-3045.4

A pair of cataract glasses is comprised of two distinct products: a professional product (the prescribed lenses) and a retail commercial product (the frames). The frames serve not only as a holder of lenses but also as an article of personal apparel. As such, they are usually selected on the basis of personal taste and style. Although Medicare will pay only for standard frames, most patients want deluxe frames. Participating physicians and suppliers cannot profitably furnish such deluxe frames unless they can make an extra (noncovered) charge for the frames even though they accept assignment.

Therefore, a participating physician or supplier (whether an ophthalmologist, optometrist, or optician) who accepts assignment on cataract glasses with deluxe frames may charge the Medicare patient the difference between his/her usual charge to private pay patients for glasses with standard frames and his/her usual charge to such patients for glasses with deluxe frames, in addition to the applicable deductible and coinsurance on glasses with standard frames, if all of the following requirements are met:

A. The participating physician or supplier has standard frames available, offers them for sale to the patient, and issues and ABN to the patient that explains the price and other differences between standard and deluxe frames. Refer to Chapter 30.

B. The participating physician or supplier obtains from the patient (or his/her representative) and keeps on file the following signed and dated statement:

_____

Name of Patient   Medicare Claim Number

Having been informed that an extra charge is being made by the physician or supplier for deluxe frames, that this extra charge is not covered by Medicare, and that standard frames are available for purchase from the physician or supplier at no extra charge, I have chosen to purchase deluxe frames.

_____   _____
Signature   Date

C. The participating physician or supplier itemizes on his/her claim his/her actual charge for the lenses, his/her actual charge for the standard frames, and his/her actual extra charge for the deluxe frames (charge differential). Once the assigned claim for deluxe frames has been processed, the carrier will follow the ABN instructions as described in Sec.60.

100-4, 3, 10.4
Payment of Nonphysician Services for Inpatients
All items and nonphysician services furnished to inpatients must be furnished directly by the hospital or billed through the hospital under arrangements. This provision applies to all hospitals, regardless of whether they are subject to PPS.

Other Medical Items, Supplies, and Services the following medical items, supplies, and services furnished to inpatients are covered under Part A. Consequently, they are covered by the prospective payment rate or reimbursed as reasonable costs under Part A to hospitals excluded from PPS.

- Laboratory services (excluding anatomic pathology services and certain clinical pathology services);

- Pacemakers and other prosthetic devices including lenses, and artificial limbs, knees, and hips;

- Radiology services including computed tomography (CT) scans furnished to inpatients by a physician's office, other hospital, or radiology clinic;

- Total parenteral nutrition (TPN) services; and

- Transportation, including transportation by ambulance, to and from another hospital or freestanding facility to receive specialized diagnostic or therapeutic services not available at the facility where the patient is an inpatient.

The hospital must include the cost of these services in the appropriate ancillary service cost center, i.e., in the cost of the diagnostic or therapeutic service. It must not show them separately under revenue code 0540.

EXCEPTIONS

- Pneumococcal Vaccine -is payable under Part B only and is billed by the hospital on the Form CMS-1450.

- Ambulance Service For purposes of this section "hospital inpatient" means beneficiary who has been formally admitted it does not include a beneficiary who is in the process of being transferred from one hospital to another. Where the patient is transferred from one hospital to another, and is admitted as an inpatient to the second, the ambulance service is payable under only Part B. If transportation is by a hospital owned and operated ambulance, the hospital bills separately on Form CMS-1450 as appropriate. Similarly, if the hospital arranges for the ambulance transportation with an ambulance operator, including paying the ambulance operator, it bills separately. However, if the hospital does not assume any financial responsibility, the billing is to the carrier by the ambulance operator or beneficiary, as appropriate, if an ambulance is used for the transportation of a hospital inpatient to another facility for diagnostic tests or special treatment the ambulance trip is considered part of the DRG, and not separately billable, if the resident hospital is under PPS.

- Part B Inpatient Services Where Part A benefits are not payable, payment maybe made to the hospital under Part B for certain medical and other health services. See Chapter 4 for a description of Part B inpatient services.

- Anesthetist Services "Incident to" Physician Services-If a physician's practice was to employ anesthetists and to bill on a reasonable charge basis for these services and that practice was in effect as of the last day of the hospital's most recent 12-month cost reporting period ending before September 30, 1983, the physician may continue that practice through cost reporting periods beginning October 1, 1984. However, if the physician chooses to continue this practice, the hospital may not add costs of the anesthetist's service to its base period costs for purposes of its transition payment rates. If it is the existing or new practice of the physician to employ certified registered nurse anesthetists (CRNAs) and other qualified anesthetists and include charges for their services in the physician bills for anesthesiology services for the hospital's cost report periods beginning on or after October 1, 1984, and before October 1, 1987, the physician may continue to do so.

B. Exceptions/Waivers
These provisions were waived before cost reporting periods beginning on or after October1, 1986, under certain circumstances. The basic criteria for waiver was that services furnished by outside suppliers are so extensive that a sudden change in billing practices would threaten the stability of patient care. Specific criteria for waiver and processing procedures are in Sec.2804 of the Provider Reimbursement Manual (CMS Pub. 15-1).

100-4, 3, 20.1.2.8
Special Outlier Payments for Burn Cases
For discharges occurring on or after April 1, 1988, the additional payment amount for the DRGs related to burn cases, which are identified in the most recent annual notice of prospective payment rates is computed using the same methodology (as stated above in section 20.1.2.3) except that the payment is made using a marginal cost factor of 90 percent instead of 80 percent.

100-4, 3, 20.2.1
Medicare Code Editor (MCE)
A. General
The MCE edits claims to detect incorrect billing data. In determining the appropriate DRG for a Medicare patient, the age, sex, discharge status, principal diagnosis, secondary diagnosis, and procedures performed must be reported accurately to the Grouper program. The logic of the Grouper software assumes that this information is accurate and the Grouper does not make any attempt to edit the data for accuracy. Only where extreme inconsistencies occur in the patient information will a patient not be assigned to a DRG. Therefore, the MCE is used to improve the quality of information given to Grouper.

The MCE addresses three basic types of edits which will support the DRG assignment:

- Code Edits - Examines a record for the correct use of ICD-9-CM codes that describe a patient's diagnoses and procedures. They include basic consistency checks on the interrelationship among a patient's age, sex, and diagnoses and procedures.

- Coverage Edits - Examines the type of patient and procedures performed to determine if the services where covered.

- Clinical Edits - Examines the clinical consistency of the diagnostic and procedural information on the medical claim to determine if they are clinically reasonable and, therefore, should be paid.

B. Implementation Requirements
The FI processes all inpatient Part A discharge/transfer bills for both PPS and non-PPS facilities (including waiver States, long-term care hospitals, and excluded units) through the MCE. It processes claims that have been reviewed by the QIO prior to billing through the MCE only for edit types 1, 2, 3, 4, 7, and 12. It does not process the following kinds of bills through the MCE:

- Where no Medicare payment is due (amounts reported by value codes 12, 13, 14, 15, or 16 equal or exceed charges).

- Where no Medicare payment is being made. Where partial payment is made, editing is required.

- Where QIO reviewed prior to billing (code C1 or C3 in FL 24-30). It may process these exceptions through the program and ignore development codes or bypass the program.

The MCE software contains multiple versions. The version of the MCE accessed by the program depends upon the patient discharge date entered on the claim.

C. Bill System/MCE Interface
The FI installs the MCE online, if possible, so that prepayment edit requirements identified in subsection C can be directed to hospitals without clerical handling.

The MCE needs the following data elements to analyze the bill:

- Age;

- Sex;

- Discharge status;

- Diagnosis (9 maximum - principal diagnosis and up to 8 additional diagnoses);

- Procedures (6 maximum); and

- Discharge date.

The MCE provides the FI an analysis of "errors" on the bill as described in subsection D. The FI develops its own interface program to provide data to MCE and receive data from it.

The MCE Installation Manual describes the installation and operation of the program, including data base formats and locations.

D. Processing Requirements
The hospital must follow the procedure described below for each error code. For bills returned to the provider, the FI considers the bill improperly completed for control and processing time purposes. (See chapter 1.)

1. Invalid Diagnosis or Procedure Code
   The MCE checks each diagnosis code, including the admitting diagnosis, and each procedure code against a table of valid ICD-9-CM codes. An admitting diagnosis, a principle diagnosis, and up to eight additional diagnoses may be reported. Up to six total procedure codes may be reported on an inpatient claim. If the recorded code is not in this table, the code is invalid, and the FI returns the bill to the provider.

   For a list of all valid ICD-9-CM codes see "International Classification of Diseases, 9th Revision, Clinical Modification (ICD-9-CM), January 1979, Volume I (Diseases)" and "Volume 3 (Procedures)," and the "Addendum/Errata" and new codes furnished by the FI. The hospital must review the medical record and/or face sheet and enter the correct diagnosis/procedure codes before returning the bill.

2. Invalid Fourth or Fifth Digit
   The MCE identifies any diagnosis code, including the admitting diagnosis or any procedure that requires a fourth or fifth digit, which is either missing or not valid for the code in question.

   For a list of all valid fourth and fifth digit ICD-9-CM codes see "International Classification of Diseases, 9th Revision, Clinical Modification (ICD-9-CM), January 1979, Volume 1 (Diseases)" and "Volume 3 (Procedures)," and the "Addendum/Errata" and new codes furnished by the FI. The FI returns claims edited for this reason to the hospital. The hospital must review the medical record and/or face sheet and enter the correct diagnosis/procedure before returning the bill.

3. E-Code as Principal Diagnosis
   E-codes describe the circumstances that caused an injury, not the nature of the injury, and therefore are not recognized by the Grouper program as acceptable principal diagnoses. E-codes are all ICD-9-CM diagnosis codes that begin with the letter E. For a list of all E-codes,

see "International Classification of Diseases, 9th Revision, Clinical Modification (ICD-9-CM), January 1979, Volume I (Diseases)." The hospital must review the medical record and/or face sheet and enter the correct diagnosis before returning the bill.

4. Duplicate of PDX

Any secondary diagnosis that is the same code as the principal diagnosis is identified as a duplicate of the principal diagnoses. This is unacceptable because the secondary diagnosis may cause an erroneous assignment to a higher severity MS-DRG. Hospitals may not repeat a diagnosis code. The FI will delete the duplicate secondary diagnosis and process the bill.

5. Age Conflict

The MCE detects inconsistencies between a patient's age and any diagnosis on the patient's record. Examples are:

- A 5-year-old patient with benign prostatic hypertrophy.

- A 78-year-old delivery.

In the above cases, the diagnosis is clinically impossible in a patient of the stated age. Therefore, either the diagnosis or age is presumed to be incorrect. Four age code categories are described below.

- A subset of diagnoses is intended only for newborns and neonates. These are "Newborn" diagnoses. For "Newborn" diagnoses, the patient's age must be 0 years.

- Certain diagnoses are considered reasonable only for children between the ages of 0 and 17. These are "Pediatric" diagnoses.

- Diagnoses identified as "Maternity" are coded only for patients between the ages of 12 and 55 years.

- A subset of diagnoses is considered valid only for patients over the age of 14. These are "Adult" diagnoses. For "Adult" diagnoses the age range is 15 through 124.

The diagnoses described in the Medicare Code Editor, posted on the CMS Webpage at: http://www.cms.hhs.gov/AcuteInpatientPPS/FFD/itemdetail.asp?filterType=none&filterByDID=-99&sortByDID=2&sortOrder=ascending&itemID=CMS1206058&intNumPerPage=10 are acceptable only for the age categories shown. If the FI edits online, it will return such bills for a proper diagnosis or correction of age as applicable. If the FI edits in batch operations after receipt of the admission query response, it uses the age based on CMS records and returns bills that fail this edit. The hospital must review the medical record and/or face sheet and enter the proper diagnosis or patient's age before returning the bill.

6. Sex Conflict

The MCE detects inconsistencies between a patient's sex and a diagnosis or procedure on the patient's record. Examples are:

- Male patient with cervical cancer (diagnosis).

- Male patient with a hysterectomy (procedure).

In both instances, the indicated diagnosis or the procedure conflicts with the stated sex of the patient. Therefore, either the patient's diagnosis, procedure or sex is incorrect.

The Medicare Code Editor contains listings of male and female related ICD-9-CM diagnosis and procedure codes and the corresponding English descriptions. The hospital should review the medical record and/or face sheet and enter the proper sex, diagnosis, and procedure before returning the bill.

7. Manifestation Code As Principal Diagnosis

A manifestation code describes the manifestation of an underlying disease, not the disease itself, and therefore, cannot be a principal diagnosis. The Medicare Code Editor contains listings of ICD-9-CM diagnoses identified as manifestation codes. The hospital should review the medical record and/or face sheet and enter the proper diagnosis before returning the bill.

8. Nonspecific Principal Diagnosis

Effective October 1, 2007 (FY 2008), the non-specific principal diagnosis edit was discontinued and will appear for claims processed using MCE version 2.0-23.0 only.

9. Questionable Admission

There are some diagnoses which are not usually sufficient justification for admission to an acute care hospital. For example, if a patient is given a principal diagnosis of:

> 4011 - Benign Hypertension

then this patient would have a questionable admission, since benign hypertension is not normally sufficient justification for admission.

The Medicare Code Editor contains a listing of ICD-9-CM diagnosis codes identified as "Questionable Admission" when used as principal diagnosis.

The A/B MACs or the FIs may review on a post-payment basis all questionable admission cases. Where the A/B MACs or the FIs determines the denial rate is sufficiently high to warrant, it may review the claim before payment.

10. Unacceptable Principal Diagnosis

There are selected codes that describe a circumstance which influences an individual's health status but is not a current illness or injury; therefore, they are unacceptable as a principal diagnosis. For example, VI73 (Family History of Ischemic Heart Disease) is an unacceptable principal diagnosis.

In a few cases, there are codes that are acceptable if a secondary diagnosis is coded. If no secondary diagnosis is present for them, MCE returns the message "requires secondary dx." The A/B MAC or the FI may review claims with diagnosis V571, V5721, V5722, V573, V5789, and V579 and a secondary diagnosis. A/B MACs or FIs may choose to review as a principal diagnosis if data analysis deems it a priority.

If these codes are identified without a secondary diagnosis, the FI returns the bill to the hospital and requests a secondary diagnosis that describes the origin of the impairment. Also, bills containing other "unacceptable principal diagnosis" codes are returned.

The hospital reviews the medical record and/or face sheet and enters the principal diagnosis that describes the illness or injury before returning the bill.

11. Nonspecific O.R. Procedures

Effective October 1, 2007 (FY 2008), the non-specific O.R. procedure edit was discontinued and will appear for claims processed using MCE version 2.0-23.0 only.

12. Noncovered O.R. Procedures

There are some O.R. procedures for which Medicare does not provide payment. The FI will return the bill requesting either:

- A no pay bill, or

- A correction in the procedure code.

- A bill indicating the covered and noncovered procedures.

If the hospital indicates that there are covered and noncovered procedures, the FI refers the bill to the QIO for prepayment review. Upon receipt of the QIOs response, it either deletes the noncovered procedures and charges or requires the hospital to delete them. It does not process the noncovered procedures through Grouper or the noncovered charges through Pricer.

13. Open Biopsy Check

Biopsies can be performed as open (i.e., a body cavity is entered surgically), percutaneously, or endoscopically. The DRG Grouper logic assign a patient to different DRGs depending upon whether or not the biopsy was open. In general, for most organ systems, open biopsies are performed infrequently.

Effective October 1, 1987, there are revised biopsy codes that distinguish between open and closed biopsies. To make sure that hospitals are using ICD-9-CM codes correctly, the FI requests O.R. reports on a sample of 10 percent of claims with open biopsy procedures for review on a post payment basis.

If the O.R. report reveals that the biopsy was closed (performed percutaneously, endoscopically, etc.) the FI changes the procedure code on the bill to the closed biopsy code and processes an adjustment bill. Some biopsy codes (3328 and 5634) have two related closed biopsy codes, one for closed endoscopic and for closed percutaneous biopsies. The FI assigns the appropriate closed biopsy code after reviewing the medical information.

14. Medicare as Secondary Payer - MSP Alert

The MCE identifies situations that may involve automobile medical, no-fault or liability insurance. The hospital must develop other insurance coverage as provided in the Medicare Secondary Payer Manuals, before billing Medicare.

15. Bilateral Procedure

There are codes that do not accurately reflect performed procedures in one admission on two or more different bilateral joints of the lower extremities. A combination of these codes show a bilateral procedure when, in fact, they could be single joint procedures (i.e., duplicate procedures).

If two or more of these procedures are coded, and the principal diagnosis is in MDC 8, the claim is flagged for post-pay development. The FI processes the bill as coded but requests an O.R. report. If the report substantiates bilateral surgery, no further action is necessary. If the O.R. report does not substantiate bilateral surgery, an adjustment bill is processed.

If the error rate for any provider is sufficiently high, the FI may develop claims prior to payment on a provider-specific basis.

16. Invalid Age

If the report reports an age over 124, the FI requests the hospital to determine if it made a bill preparation error. If the beneficiary's age is established at over 124, the hospital enters 123.

17. Invalid Sex

A patient's sex is sometimes necessary for appropriate DRG determination. Usually the FI can resolve the issue without hospital assistance. The sex code reported must be either 1 (male) or 2 (female).

18. Invalid Discharge Status

A patient's discharge status is sometimes necessary for appropriate DRG determination. Discharge status must be coded according to the Form CMS-1450 conventions. See Chapter 25.

19. Invalid Discharge Date

An invalid discharge date is a discharge date that does not fall into the acceptable range of numbers to represent, either the month, day or year (e.g., 13/03/01, 12/32/01). If no discharge date is entered, it is also invalid. MCE reports when an invalid discharge date is entered.

20. Limited Coverage

Effective October 1, 2003, for certain procedures whose medical complexity and serious nature incur extraordinary associated costs, Medicare limits coverage. The edit message indicates the type of limited coverage (e.g., LVRS, heart transplant, etc). The procedures receiving limited coverage edits previously were listed as non-covered procedures, but were covered under Medicare in certain circumstances. The FIs will handle these procedures as they had previously.

100-4, 3, 20.7.3

Payment for Blood Clotting Factor Administered to Hemophilia Patients

Section 6011 of Public Law (P.L.) 101-239 amended Sec.1886(a)(4) of the Social Security Act (the Act) to provide that prospective payment system (PPS) hospitals receive anadditional payment for the costs of administering blood clotting factor to Medicare hemophiliacs who are hospital inpatients. Section 6011(b) of P.L. 101.239 specified that the payment be based on a predetermined price per unit of clotting factor multiplied by the number of units provided. This add-on payment originally was effective for blood clotting factors furnished on or after June 19, 1990, and before December 19, 1991. Section 13505 of P.L. 103-66 amended Sec.6011 (d) of P.L.

101-239 to extend the period covered by the add-on payment for blood clotting factors administered to Medicare inpatients with hemophilia through September 30, 1994. Section 4452 of P.L. 105-33 amended Sec.6011(d) of P.L. 101-239 to reinstate the add-on payment for the costs of administering blood clotting factor to Medicare beneficiaries who have hemophilia and who are hospital inpatients for discharges occurring on or after October 1, 1998.

Local carriers shall process non-institutional blood clotting factor claims.

The FIs shall process institutional blood clotting factor claims payable under either Part A or Part B.

A. Inpatient Bills

Under the Inpatient Prospective Payment System (PPS), hospitals receive a special add-on payment for the costs of furnishing blood clotting factors to Medicare inpatients with hemophilia, admitted as inpatients of PPS hospitals. The clotting factor add-on payment is calculated using the number of units (as defined in the HCPCS code long descriptor) billed by the provider under special instructions for units of service.

The PPS Pricer software does not calculate the payment amount. The Fiscal Intermediary Standard System (FISS) calculates the payment amount and subtracts the charges from those submitted to Pricer so that the clotting factor charges are not included in cost outlier computations.

Blood clotting factors not paid on a cost or PPS basis are priced as a drug/biological under the Medicare Part B Drug Pricing File effective for the specific date of service. As of January 1, 2005, the average sales price (ASP) plus 6 percent shall be used.

If a beneficiary is in a covered Part A stay in a PPS hospital, the clotting factors are paid in addition to the DRG/HIPPS payment (For FY 2004, this payment is based on 95 percent of average wholesale price.) For a SNF subject to SNF/PPS, the payment is bundled into the SNF/PPS rate.

For SNF inpatient Part A, there is no add-on payment for blood clotting factors.

The codes for blood-clotting factors are found on the Medicare Part B Drug Pricing File. This file is distributed on a quarterly basis.

For discharges occurring on or after October 1, 2000, and before December 31, 2005, report HCPCS Q0187 based on 1 billing unit per 1.2 mg. Effective January 1, 2006, HCPCS code J7189 replaces Q0187 and is defined as 1 billing unit per 1 microgram (mcg).

The examples below include the HCPCS code and indicate the dosage amount specified in the descriptor of that code. Facilities use the units field as a multiplier to arrive at the dosage amount.

EXAMPLE 1

HCPCS	Drug	Dosage
J7189	Factor VIIa	1 mcg

Actual dosage: 13,365 mcg

On the bill, the facility shows J7189 and 13,365 in the units field (13,365 mcg divided by 1 mcg = 13,365 units).

NOTE: The process for dealing with one international unit (IU) is the same as the process of dealing with one microgram.

EXAMPLE 2

HCPCS	Drug	Dosage
J9355	Trastuzumab	10 mg

Actual dosage: 140 mg

On the bill, the facility shows J9355 and 14 in the units field (140 mg divided by 10mg = 14 units).

When the dosage amount is greater than the amount indicated for the HCPCS code, the facility rounds up to determine units. When the dosage amount is less than the amount indicated for the HCPCS code, use 1 as the unit of measure.

EXAMPLE 3

HCPCS	Drug	Dosage
J3100	Tenecteplase	50 mg

Actual Dosage: 40 mg

The provider would bill for 1 unit, even though less than 1 full unit was furnished.

At times, the facility provides less than the amount provided in a single use vial and there is waste, i.e.; some drugs may be available only in packaged amounts that exceed the needs of an individual patient. Once the drug is reconstituted in the hospital's pharmacy, it may have a limited shelf life. Since an individual patient may receive less than the fully reconstituted amount, we encourage hospitals to schedule patients in such a way that the hospital can use the drug most efficiently. However, if the hospital must discard the remainder of a vial after administering part of it to a Medicare patient, the provider may bill for the amount of drug discarded plus the amount administered.

Example 1:

Drug X is available only in a 100-unit size. A hospital schedules three Medicare patients to receive drug X on the same day within the designated shelf life of the product. An appropriate hospital staff member administers 30 units to each patient. The remaining 10 units are billed to Medicare on the account of the last patient. Therefore, 30 units are billed on behalf of the first patient seen and 30 units are billed on behalf of the second patient seen. Forty units are billed on behalf of the last patient seen because the hospital had to discard 10 units at that point.

Example 2:

An appropriate hospital staff member must administer 30 units of drug X to a Medicare patient, and it is not practical to schedule another patient who requires the same drug. For example, the hospital has only one patient who requires drug X, or the hospital sees the patient for the first time and did not know the patient's condition. The hospital bills for 100 units on behalf of the patient, and Medicare pays for 100 units.

When the number of units of blood clotting factor administered to hemophiliac inpatients exceeds 99,999, the hospital reports the excess as a second line for revenue code 0636 and repeats the HCPCS code. One hundred thousand fifty (100,050) units are reported on one line as 99,999, and another line shows 1,051.

Revenue Code 0636 is used. It requires HCPCS. Some other inpatient drugs continue to be billed without HCPCS codes under pharmacy.

No changes in beneficiary notices are required. Coverage is applicable to hospital Part A claims only. Coverage is also applicable to inpatient Part B services in SNFs and all types of hospitals, including CAHs. Separate payment is not made to SNFs for beneficiaries in an inpatient Part A stay.

B. FI Action

The FI is responsible for the following:

- It accepts HCPCS codes for inpatient services;

- It edits to require HCPCS codes with Revenue Code 0636. Multiple iterations of the revenue code are possible with the same or different HCPCS codes. It does not edit units except to ensure a numeric value;

- It reduces charges forwarded to Pricer by the charges for hemophilia clotting factors in revenue code 0636. It retains the charges and revenue and HCPCS codes for CWF; and

- It modifies data entry screens to accept HCPCS codes for hospital (including CAH) swing bed, and SNF inpatient claims (bill types 11X, 12X, 18x, 21x and, 22x).

The September 1, 1993, IPPS final rule (58 FR 46304) states that payment will be made for the blood clotting factor only if an ICD-9-CM diagnosis code for hemophilia is included on the bill.

Since inpatient blood-clotting factors are covered only for beneficiaries with hemophilia, the FI must ensure that one of the following hemophilia diagnosis codes is listed on the bill before payment is made:

286.0 Congenital factor VIII disorder

286.1 Congenital factor IX disorder

286.2 Congenital factor IX disorder

286.3 Congenital deficiency of other clotting factor

286.4 von Willebrands' disease

Effective for discharges on or after August 1, 2001, payment may also be made if one of the following diagnosis codes is reported:

286.5 Hemorrhagic disorder due to circulating anticoagulants

286.7 Acquired coagulation factor deficiency

C. Part A Remittance Advice

1. X12.835 Ver. 003030M
   For remittance reporting PIP and/or non-PIP payments, the Hemophilia Add on will be reported in a claims level 2-090-CAS segment (CAS is the element identifier) exhibiting an "OA" Group Code and adjustment reason code "97" (payment is included in the allowance for the basic service/ procedure) followed by the associated dollar amount (POSITIVE) and units of service. For this version of the 835, "OA" group coded line level CAS segments are informational and are not included in the balancing routine. The Hemophilia Add On amount will always be included in the 2-010-CLP04 Claim Payment Amount.

   For remittance reporting PIP payments, the Hemophilia Add On will also be reported in the provider level adjustment (element identifier PLB) segment with the provider level adjustment reason code "CA" (Manual claims adjustment) followed by the associated dollar amount (NEGATIVE).

   NOTE: A data maintenance request will be submitted to ANSI ASC X12 for a new PLB adjustment reason code specifically for PIP payment Hemophilia Add On situations for future use. However, continue to use adjustment reason code "CA" until further notice.

   . The FIs enter MA103 (Hemophilia Add On) in an open MIA (element identifier) remark code data element. This will alert the provider that the reason code 97 and PLB code "CA" adjustments are related to the Hemophilia Add On.

2. X12.835 Ver. 003051
   For remittances reporting PIP and/or non-PIP payments, Hemophilia Add On information will be reported in the claim level 2-062-AMT and 2-064-QTY segments. The 2-062-AMT01 element will carry a "ZK" (Federal Medicare claim MANDATE - Category 1) qualifier code followed by the total claim level Hemophilia Add On amount (POSITIVE). The 2-064QTY01 element will carry a "FL" (Units) qualifier code followed by the number of units approved for

the Hemophilia Add On for the claim. The Hemophilia Add On amount will always be included in the 2-010-CLP04 Claim Payment Amount.

NOTE: A data maintenance request will be submitted to ANSI ASC X12 for a new AMT qualifier code specifically for the Hemophilia Add On for future use. However, continue to use adjustment reason code "ZK" until further notice.

For remittances reporting PIP payments, the Hemophilia Add On will be reported in the provider level adjustment PLB segment with the provider level adjustment reason "ZZ" followed by the associated dollar amount (NEGATIVE).

NOTE: A data maintenance request will be submitted to ANSI ASC X12 for a new PLB, adjustment reason code specifically for the Hemophilia Add On for future use. However, continue to use PLB adjustment reason code "ZZ" until further notice. The FIs enter MA103 (Hemophilia Add On) in an open MIA remark code data element. This will alert the provider that the ZK, FL and ZZ entries are related to the Hemophilia Add On. (Effective with version 4010 of the 835, report ZK in lieu of FL in the QTY segment.)

3. Standard Hard Copy Remittance Advice
For paper remittances reporting non-PIP payments involving Hemophilia Add On, add a "Hemophilia Add On" category to the end of the "Pass Thru Amounts" listings in the "Summary" section of the paper remittance. Enter the total of the Hemophilia Add On amounts due for the claims covered by this remittance next to the Hemophilia Add On heading.

The FIs add the Remark Code "MA103" (Hemophilia Add On) to the remittance advice under the REM column for those claims that qualify for Hemophilia Add On payments.

This will be the full extent of Hemophilia Add On reporting on paper remittance notices; providers wishing more detailed information must subscribe to the Medicare Part A specifications for the ANSI ASC X12N 835, where additional information is available.

See chapter 22, for detailed instructions and definitions.

100-4, 3, 40.2.2
Charges to Beneficiaries for Part A Services
The hospital submits a bill even where the patient is responsible for a deductible which covers the entire amount of the charges for non-PPS hospitals, or in PPS hospitals, where the DRG payment amount will be less than the deductible.

A hospital receiving payment for a covered hospital stay (or PPS hospital that includes at least one covered day, or one treated as covered under guarantee of payment or limitation on liability) may charge the beneficiary, or other person, for items and services furnished during the stay only as described in subsections A through H. If limitation of liability applies, a beneficiary's liability for payment is governed by the limitation on liability notification rules in Chapter 30 of this manual. For related notices for inpatient hospitals, see CMS Transmittal 594, Change Request3903, dated June 24, 2005.

A. Deductible and Coinsurance
The hospital may charge the beneficiary or other person for applicable deductible and coinsurance amounts. The deductible is satisfied only by charges for covered services. The FI deducts the deductible and coinsurance first from the PPS payment. Where the deductible exceeds the PPS amount, the excess will be applied to a subsequent payment to the hospital. (See Chapter 3 of the Medicare General Information, Eligibility, and Entitlement Manual for specific policies.)

B. Blood Deductible
The Part A blood deductible provision applies to whole blood and red blood cells, and reporting of the number of pints is applicable to both PPS and non-PPS hospitals. (See Chapter 3 of the Medicare General Information, Eligibility, and Entitlement Manual for specific policies.) Hospitals shall report charges for red blood cells using revenue code 381, and charges for whole blood using revenue code 382.

C. Inpatient Care No Longer Required
The hospital may charge for services that are not reasonable and necessary or that constitute custodial care. Notification may be required under limitation of liability. See CMS Transmittal 594, Change Request3903, dated June 24, 2005, section V. of the attachment, for specific notification requirements. Note this transmittal will be placed in Chapter 30 of this manual at a future point. Chapter 1, section 150 of this manual also contains related billing information in addition to that provided below.

In general, after proper notification has occurred, and assuming an expedited decision is received from a Quality Improvement Organization (QIO), the following entries are required on the bill the hospital prepares:

- Occurrence code 3I (and date) to indicate the date the hospital notified the patient in accordance with the first bullet above;
- Occurrence span code 76 (and dates) to indicate the period of noncovered care for which it is charging the beneficiary;
- Occurrence span code 77 (and dates) to indicate the period of noncovered care for which the provider is liable, when it is aware of this prior to billing; and
- Value code 3I (and amount) to indicate the amount of charges it may bill the beneficiary for days for which inpatient care was no longer required. They are included as noncovered charges on the bill.

D. Change in the Beneficiary's Condition
If the beneficiary remains in the hospital after receiving notice as described in subsection C, and the hospital, the physician who concurred in the hospital's determination, or the QIO, subsequently determines that the beneficiary again requires inpatient hospital care, the hospital may not charge the beneficiary or other person for services furnished after the beneficiary again required inpatient hospital care until proper notification occurs (see subsection C).

If a patient who needs only a SNF level of care remains in the hospital after the SNF bed becomes available, and the bed ceases to be available, the hospital may continue to charge the beneficiary. It need not provide the beneficiary with another notice when the patient chose not to be discharged to the SNF bed.

E. Admission Denied
If the entire hospital admission is determined to be not reasonable or necessary, limitation of liability may apply. See 2005 CMS transmittal 594, section V. of the attachment, for specific notification requirements.

NOTE: This transmittal will be placed in Chapter 30 of this manual at a future point.

In such cases the following entries are required on the bill:

- Occurrence code 3I (and date) to indicate the date the hospital notified the beneficiary.
- Occurrence span code 76 (and dates) to indicate the period of noncovered care for which the hospital is charging the beneficiary.
- Occurrence span code 77 (and dates) to indicate any period of noncovered care for which the provider is liable (e.g., the period between issuing the notice and the time it may charge the beneficiary) when the provider is aware of this prior to billing.
- Value code 3I (and amount) to indicate the amount of charges the hospital may bill the beneficiary for hospitalization that was not necessary or reasonable. They are included as noncovered charges on the bill.

F. Procedures, Studies and Courses of Treatment That Are Not Reasonable or Necessary
If diagnostic procedures, studies, therapeutic studies and courses of treatment are excluded from coverage as not reasonable and necessary (even though the beneficiary requires inpatient hospital care) the hospital may charge the beneficiary or other person for the services or care according to the procedures given in CMS Transmittal 594, Change Request3903, dated June 24, 2005.

The following bill entries apply to these circumstances:

- Occurrence code 32 (and date) to indicate the date the hospital provided the notice to the beneficiary.
- Value code 3I (and amount) to indicate the amount of such charges to be billed to the beneficiary. They are included as noncovered charges on the bill.

G. Nonentitlement Days and Days after Benefits Exhausted
If a hospital stay exceeds the day outlier threshold, the hospital may charge for some, or all, of the days on which the patient is not entitled to Medicare Part A, or after the Part A benefits are exhausted (i.e., the hospital may charge its customary charges for services furnished on those days). It may charge the beneficiary for the lesser of:

- The number of days on which the patient was not entitled to benefits or after the benefits were exhausted; or
- The number of outlier days. (Day outliers were discontinued at the end of FY 1997.)

If the number of outlier days exceeds the number of days on which the patient was not entitled to benefits, or after benefits were exhausted, the hospital may charge for all days on which the patient was not entitled to benefits or after benefits were exhausted. If the number of days on which the beneficiary was not entitled to benefits, or after benefits were exhausted, exceeds the number of outlier days, the hospital determines the days for which it may charge by starting with the last day of the stay (i.e., the day before the day of discharge) and identifying and counting off in reverse order, days on which the patient was not entitled to benefits or after the benefits were exhausted, until the number of days counted off equals the number of outlier days. The days counted off are the days for which the hospital may charge.

H. Contractual Exclusions
In addition to receiving the basic prospective payment, the hospital may charge the beneficiary for any services that are excluded from coverage for reasons other than, or in addition to, absence of medical necessity, provision of custodial care, non-entitlement to Part A, or exhaustion of benefits. For example, it may charge for most cosmetic and dental surgery.

I. Private Room Care
Payment for medically necessary private room care is included in the prospective payment. Where the beneficiary requests private room accommodations, the hospital must inform the beneficiary of the additional charge. (See the Medicare Benefit Policy Manual, Chapter 1.) When the beneficiary accepts the liability, the hospital will supply the service, and bill the beneficiary directly. If the beneficiary believes the private room was medically necessary, the beneficiary has a right to a determination and may initiate a Part A appeal.

J. Deluxe Item or Service
Where a beneficiary requests a deluxe item or service, i.e., an item or service which is more expensive than is medically required for the beneficiary's condition, the hospital may collect the additional charge if it informs the beneficiary of the additional charge. That charge is the difference between the customary charge for the item or service most commonly furnished by the hospital to private pay patients with the beneficiary's condition, and the charge for the more expensive item or service requested. If the beneficiary believes that the more expensive item or service was medically necessary, the beneficiary has a right to a determination and may initiate a Part A appeal.

K. Inpatient Acute Care Hospital Admission Followed By a Death or Discharge Prior To Room Assignment
A patient of an acute care hospital is considered an inpatient upon issuance of written doctor's orders to that effect. If a patient either dies or is discharged prior to being assigned and/or occupying a room, a hospital may enter an appropriate room and board charge on the claim. If a patient leaves of their own volition prior to being assigned and/or occupying a room, a hospital may enter an appropriate room and board charge on the claim as well as a patient status code 07 which indicates they left against medical advice. A hospital is not required to enter a room and board charge, but failure to do so may have a minimal impact on future DRG weight calculations.

100-4, 3, 40.3
Outpatient Services Treated as Inpatient Services
A3-3610.3, HO-415.6, HO-400D, A-03-008, A-03-013, A-03-054

A Outpatient Services Followed by Admission Before Midnight of the Following Day
(Effective For Services Furnished Before October 1, 1991)

When a beneficiary receives outpatient hospital services during the day immediately preceding the hospital admission, the outpatient hospital services are treated as inpatient services if the beneficiary has Part A coverage. Hospitals and FIs apply this provision only when the beneficiary is admitted to the hospital before midnight of the day following receipt of outpatient services. The day on which the patient is formally admitted as an inpatient is counted as the first inpatient day.

When this provision applies, services are included in the applicable PPS payment and not billed separately. When this provision applies to hospitals and units excluded from the hospital PPS, services are shown on the bill and included in the Part A payment. See Chapter 1 for FI requirements for detecting duplicate claims in such cases.

B Preadmission Diagnostic Services
(Effective for Services Furnished On or After January 1, 1991)

Diagnostic services (including clinical diagnostic laboratory tests) provided to a beneficiary by the admitting hospital, or by an entity wholly owned or wholly operated by the admitting hospital (or by another entity under arrangements with the admitting hospital), within 3 days prior to and including the date of the beneficiary's admission, are deemed to be inpatient services and included in the inpatient payment, unless there is no Part A coverage. For example, if a patient is admitted on a Wednesday, outpatient services provided by the hospital on Sunday, Monday, Tuesday, or Wednesday are included in the inpatient Part A payment.

This provision does not apply to ambulance services and maintenance renal dialysis services (see the Medicare Benefit Policy Manual, Chapters 10 and 11, respectively). Additionally, Part A services furnished by skilled nursing facilities, home health agencies, and hospices are excluded from the payment window provisions.

For services provided before October 31, 1994, this provision applies to both hospitals subject to the hospital inpatient prospective payment system (IPPS) as well as those hospitals and units excluded from IPPS.

For services provided on or after October 31, 1994, for hospitals and units excluded from IPPS, this provision applies only to services furnished within one day prior to and including the date of the beneficiary's admission. The hospitals and units that are excluded from IPPS are: psychiatric hospitals and units; inpatient rehabilitation facilities (IRF) and units; long-term care hospitals (LTCH); children's hospitals; and cancer hospitals.

Critical access hospitals (CAHs) are not subject to the 3-day (nor 1-day) DRG payment window.

An entity is considered to be "wholly owned or operated" by the hospital if the hospital is the sole owner or operator. A hospital need not exercise administrative control over a facility in order to operate it. A hospital is considered the sole operator of the facility if the hospital has exclusive responsibility for implementing facility policies (i.e., conducting or overseeing the facility's routine operations), regardless of whether it also has the authority to make the policies.

For this provision, diagnostic services are defined by the presence on the bill of the following revenue and/or CPT codes:

0254 -	Drugs incident to other diagnostic services
0255 -	Drugs incident to radiology
030X -	Laboratory
031X -	Laboratory pathological
032X -	Radiology diagnostic
0341, 0343 -	Nuclear medicine, diagnostic/Diagnostic Radiopharmaceuticals
035X -	CT scan
0371 -	Anesthesia incident to Radiology
0372 -	Anesthesia incident to other diagnostic services
040X -	Other imaging services
046X -	Pulmonary function
0471 -	Audiology diagnostic
0481, 0489-	Cardiology, Cardiac Catheter Lab/Other Cardiology with CPT codes 93501, 93503, 93505, 93508, 93510, 93526, 93541, 93542, 93543, 93544, 93556, 93561, or 93562 diagnostic
0482-	Cardiology, Stress Test
0483-	Cardiology, Echocardiology
053X -	Osteopathic services
061X -	MRT
062X -	Medical/surgical supplies, incident to radiology or other diagnostic services
073X -	EKG/ECG
074X -	EEG
0918-	Testing- Behavioral Health
092X -	Other diagnostic services

The CWF rejects services furnished January 1, 1991, or later when outpatient bills for diagnostic services with through dates or last date of service (occurrence span code 72) fall on the day of admission or any of the 3 days immediately prior to admission to an IPPS or IPPS-excluded hospital. This reject applies to the bill in process, regardless of whether the outpatient or inpatient bill is processed first. Hospitals must analyze the two bills and report appropriate corrections. For services on or after October 31, 1994, for hospitals and units excluded from IPPS, CWF will reject outpatient diagnostic bills that occur on the day of or one day before admission. For IPPS hospitals, CWF will continue to reject outpatient diagnostic bills for services that occur on the day of or any of the 3 days prior to admission. Effective for dates of service on or after July 1, 2008, CWF will reject diagnostic services when the line item date of service (LIDOS) falls on the day of admission or any of the 3 days immediately prior to an admission to an IPPS hospital or on the day of admission or one day prior to admission for hospitals excluded from IPPS.

Hospitals in Maryland that are under the jurisdiction of the Health Services Cost Review Commission are subject to the 3-day payment window.

C Other Preadmission Services
(Effective for Services Furnished On or After October 1, 1991)

Nondiagnostic outpatient services that are related to a patient's hospital admission and that are provided by the hospital, or by an entity wholly owned or wholly operated by the admitting hospital (or by another entity under arrangements with the admitting hospital), to the patient during the 3 days immediately preceding and including the date of the patient's admission are deemed to be inpatient services and are included in the inpatient payment. Effective March 13, 1998, we defined nondiagnostic preadmission services as being related to the admission only when there is an exact match (for all digits) between the ICD-9-CM principal diagnosis code assigned for both the preadmission services and the inpatient stay. Thus, whenever Part A covers an admission, the hospital may bill nondiagnostic preadmission services to Part B as outpatient services only if they are not related to the admission. The FI shall assume, in the absence of evidence to the contrary, that such bills are not admission related and, therefore, are not deemed to be inpatient (Part A) services. If there are both diagnostic and nondiagnostic preadmission services and the nondiagnostic services are unrelated to the admission, the hospital may separately bill the nondiagnostic preadmission services to Part B. This provision applies only when the patient has Part A coverage. This provision does not apply to ambulance services and maintenance renal dialysis. Additionally, Part A services furnished by skilled nursing facilities, home health agencies, and hospices are excluded from the payment window provisions.

For services provided before October 31, 1994, this provision applies to both hospitals subject to IPPS as well as those hospitals and units excluded from IPPS (see section B above).

For services provided on or after October 31, 1994, for hospitals and units excluded from IPPS, this provision applies only to services furnished within one day prior to and including the date of the beneficiary's admission.

Critical access hospitals (CAHs) are not subject to the 3-day (nor 1-day) DRG payment window.

Hospitals in Maryland that are under the jurisdiction of the Health Services Cost Review Commission are subject to the 3-day payment window.

Effective for dates of service on or after July 1, 2008, CWF will reject therapeutic services when the line item date of service (LIDOS) falls on the day of admission or any of the 3 days immediately prior to an admission to an IPPS hospital or on the day of admission or one day prior to admission for hospitals excluded from IPPS.

100-4, 3, 90.1
Kidney Transplant - General
A3-3612, HO-E414

A major treatment for patients with ESRD is kidney transplantation. This involves removing a kidney, usually from a living relative of the patient or from an unrelated person who has died, and surgically placing the kidney into the patient. After the beneficiary receives a kidney transplant, Medicare pays the transplant hospital for the transplant and appropriate standard acquisition charges. Special provisions apply to payment. For the list of approved Medicare certified transplant facilities, refer to the following Web site: http://www.cms.hhs.gov/CertificationandComplianc/20_Transplant.asp#TopOfPage

A transplant hospital may acquire cadaver kidneys by:

• Excising kidneys from cadavers in its own hospital; and

• Arrangements with a freestanding organ procurement organization (OPO) that provides cadaver kidneys to any transplant hospital or by a hospital based OPO.

A transplant hospital that is also a certified organ procurement organization may acquire cadaver kidneys by:

• Having its organ procurement team excise kidneys from cadavers in other hospitals;

• Arrangements with participating community hospitals, whether they excise kidneys on a regular or irregular basis; and

• Arrangements with an organ procurement organization that services the transplant hospital as a member of a network.

When the transplant hospital also excises the cadaver kidney, the cost of the procedure is included in its kidney acquisition costs and is considered in arriving at its standard cadaver kidney acquisition charge. When the transplant hospital excises a kidney to provide another hospital, it may use its standard cadaver kidney acquisition charge or its standard detailed departmental charges to bill that hospital.

When the excising hospital is not a transplant hospital, it bills its customary charges for services used in excising the cadaver kidney to the transplant hospital or organ procurement agency.

If the transplanting hospital's organ procurement team excises the cadaver kidney at another hospital, the cost of operating such a team is included in the transplanting hospital's kidney acquisition costs, along with the reasonable charges billed by the other hospital of its services.

100-4, 3, 90.1.1

The Standard Kidney Acquisition Charge

A3-3612.1, A3-3612.3, HO-E417, HO-406, HO-E408, HO-E410, HO-E412, HO-E416,HO-E418, HO-E420

There are two basic standard charges that must be developed by transplant hospitals fromcosts expected to be incurred in the acquisition of kidneys:

- The standard charge for acquiring a live donor kidney; and
- The standard charge for acquiring a cadaver kidney.

The standard charge is not a charge representing the acquisition cost of a specific kidney;rather, it is a charge that reflects the average cost associated with each type of kidney acquisition.When the transplant hospital bills the program for the transplant, it shows its standard kidney acquisition charge on a separate line on the billing form.Acquisition services are billed from the excising hospital to the transplant hospital. A billing form is not submitted from the excising hospital to the FI. The transplant hospital keeps an itemized statement that identifies the services furnished, the charges, the person receiving the service (donor/recipient), and whether this is a potential transplant donor orrecipient. These charges are reflected in the transplant hospital's kidney acquisition costcenter and are used in determining the hospital's standard charge for acquiring a live donor's kidney or a cadaver's kidney. The standard charge is not a charge representing theacquisition cost of a specific kidney. Rather, it is a charge that reflects the average costassociated with each type of kidney acquisition. Also, it is an all-inclusive charge for allservices required in acquisition of a kidney, i.e., tissue typing, post-operative evaluation.

A. Billing For Blood And Tissue Typing of the Transplant Recipient Whether or NotMedicare Entitlement Is Established

Tissue typing and pre-transplant evaluation can be reflected only through the kidney acquisition charge of the hospital where the transplant will take place. The transplant hospital includes in its kidney acquisition cost center the reasonable charges it pays to the independent laboratory or other hospital which typed the potential transplant recipient,either before or after his entitlement. It also includes reasonable charges paid for physician tissue typing services, applicable to live donors and recipients (during the preentitlement period and after entitlement, but prior to hospital admission for transplantation).

B. Billing for Blood and Tissue Typing and Other Pre-Transplant Evaluation of LiveDonors

The entitlement date of the beneficiary who will receive the transplant is not aconsideration in reimbursing for the services to donors, since no bill is submitted directly to Medicare. All charges for services to donors prior to admission into the hospital for excision are "billed" indirectly to Medicare through the live donor acquisition charge oftransplanting hospitals.

C. Billing Donor And Recipient Pre-Transplant Services (Performed by Transplant Hospitals or Other Providers) to the Kidney Acquisition Cost Center

The transplant hospital prepares an itemized statement of the services rendered for submittal to its cost accounting department. Regular Medicare billing forms are not necessary for this purpose, since no bills are submitted to the FI at this point.The itemized statement should contain information that identifies the person receiving theservice (donor/recipient), the health care insurance number, the service rendered and the charge for the service, as well as a statement as to whether this is a potential transplantdonor or recipient. If it is a potential donor, the provider must identify the prospective recipient.

EXAMPLE:

Mary Jones
Health care insurance number
200 Adams St.
Anywhere, MS

Transplant donor evaluation services for recipient:
John Jones
Health care insurance number
200 Adams St.
Anywhere, MS

Services performed in a hospital other than the potential transplant hospital or by an independent laboratory are billed by that facility to the potential transplant hospital. This holds true regardless of where in the United States the service is performed. For example, if the donor services are performed in a Florida hospital and the transplant is to take place in a California hospital, the Florida hospital bills the California hospital (as described inabove). The Florida hospital is paid by the California hospital, which recoups the monies through the kidney acquisition cost center.

D. Billing for Cadaveric Donor Services

Normally, various tests are performed to determine the type and suitability of a cadaver kidney. Such tests may be performed by the excising hospital (which may also be a transplant hospital) or an independent laboratory. When the excising-only hospital performs the tests, it includes the related charges on its bill to the transplant hospital or tothe organ procurement agency.When the tests are performed by the transplant hospital, it uses the related costs in establishing the standard charge for acquiring the cadaver kidney. The transplant hospitalincludes the costs and charges in the appropriate departments for final cost settlementpurposes.When the tests are performed by an independent laboratory for the excising-only hospital or the transplant hospital, the laboratory bills the hospital that engages its services or the organ procurement agency. The excising-only hospital includes such charges in itscharges to the transplant hospital, which then

includes the charges in developing its standard charge for acquiring the cadaver kidney. It is the transplant hospitals'responsibility to assure that the independent laboratory does not bill both hospitals.The cost of these services cannot be billed directly to the program, since such tests andother procedures performed on a cadaver are not identifiable to a specific patient.

E. Billing For Physicians' Services Prior to Transplantation

Physicians' services applicable to kidney excisions involving live donors and recipients (during the pre-entitlement period and after entitlement, but prior to entrance into the hospital for transplantation) as well as all physicians' services applicable to cadavers are considered Part A hospital services (kidney acquisition costs).

F. Billing for Physicians' Services After Transplantation

All physicians' services rendered to the living donor and all physicians' services renderedto the transplant recipient are billed to the Medicare program in the same manner as all Medicare Part B services are billed. All donor physicians' services must be billed to the account of the recipient (i.e., the recipient's Medicare number).

G. Billing For Physicians' Renal Transplantation Services

To ensure proper payment when submitting a Part B bill for the renal surgeon's services to the recipient, the appropriate HCPCS codes must be submitted, including HCPCS codes for concurrent surgery, as applicable.The bill must include all living donor physicians' services, e.g., Revenue Center code 081X.

100-4, 3, 90.1.2

Billing for Kidney Transplant and Acquisition Services

Applicable standard kidney acquisition charges are identified separately in FL 42 by revenue code 0811 (Living Donor Kidney Acquisition) or 0812 (Cadaver Donor Kidney Acquisition). Where interim bills are submitted, the standard acquisition charge appears on the billing form for the period during which the transplant took place. This charge is in addition to the hospital's charges for services rendered directly to the Medicare recipient.

The contractor deducts kidney acquisition charges for PPS hospitals for processing through Pricer. These costs, incurred by approved kidney transplant hospitals, are not included in the prospective payment DRG 302 (kidney transplant). They are paid on a reasonable cost basis. Interim payment is paid as a "pass through" item. (See the Provider Reimbursement Manual, Part 1, Sec.2802 B.8.) The contractor includes kidney acquisition charges under the appropriate revenue code in CWF.

Bill Review Procedures

The Medicare Code Editor (MCE) creates a Limited Coverage edit for procedure code 55.69 (kidney transplant). Where this procedure code is identified by MCE, the contractor checks the provider number to determine if the provider is an approved transplant center, and checks the effective approval date. The contractor shall also determine if the facility is certified for adults and/or pediatric transplants dependent upon the patient's age. If payment is appropriate (i.e., the center is approved and the service is on or after the approval date) it overrides the limited coverage edit.

100-4, 3, 90.2

Heart Transplants

A3 3613, HO 416

Cardiac transplantation is covered under Medicare when performed in a facility which is approved by Medicare as meeting institutional coverage criteria. On April 6, 1987, CMS Ruling 87-1, "Criteria for Medicare Coverage of Heart Transplants" was published in the "Federal Register." For Medicare coverage purposes, heart transplants are medically reasonable and necessary when performed in facilities that meet these criteria. If a hospital wishes to bill Medicare for heart transplants, it must submit an application and documentation, showing its ongoing compliance with each criterion.

If a contractor has any questions concerning the effective or approval dates of its hospitals, it should contact its RO.

For a complete list of approved transplant centers, visit:
http://www.cms.hhs.gov/CertificationandComplianc/20_Transplant.asp#TopOfPage

A. Effective Dates

The effective date of coverage for heart transplants performed at facilities applying after July 6, 1987, is the date the facility receives approval as a heart transplant facility. Coverage is effective for discharges October 1/, 1986 for facilities that would have qualified and that applied by July 6, 1987. All transplant hospitals will be recertified under the final rule, Federal Register / Vol. 72, No. 61 / Friday, March 30, 2007, / Rules and Regulations.

The CMS informs each hospital of its effective date in an approval letter.

B. Drugs

Medicare Part B covers immunosuppressive drugs following a covered transplant in an approved facility.

C. Noncovered Transplants

Medicare will not cover transplants or re-transplants in facilities that have not been approved as meeting the facility criteria. If a beneficiary is admitted for and receives a heart transplant from a hospital that is not approved, physicians' services, and inpatient services associated with the transplantation procedure are not covered.

If a beneficiary received a heart transplant from a hospital while it was not an approved facility and later requires services as a result of the noncovered transplant, the services are covered when they are reasonable and necessary in all other respects.

D. Charges for Heart Acquisition Services

The excising hospital bills the OPO, who in turn bills the transplant (implant) hospital for applicable services. It should not submit a bill to its contractor. The transplant hospital must keep an itemized statement that identifies the services rendered, the charges, the person receiving the service (donor/recipient), and whether this person is a potential transplant donor or recipient.

These charges are reflected in the transplant hospital's heart acquisition cost center and are used in determining its standard charge for acquiring a donor's heart. The standard charge is not a charge representing the acquisition cost of a specific heart; rather, it reflects the average cost associated with each type of heart acquisition. Also, it is an all inclusive charge for all services required in acquisition of a heart, i.e., tissue typing, post-operative evaluation, etc.

E. Bill Review Procedures
The contractor takes the following actions to process heart transplant bills. It may accomplish them manually or modify its MCE and Grouper interface programs to handle the processing.

1. Change in MCE Interface
   The MCE creates a Limited Coverage edit for procedure code 37.51 (heart transplant). Where this procedure code is identified by MCE, the contractor checks the provider number to determine if the provider is an approved transplant center, and checks the effective approval date. The contractor shall also determine if the facility is certified for adults and/or pediatric transplants dependent upon the patient's age. If payment is appropriate (i.e., the center is approved and the service is on or after the approval date) it overrides the limited coverage edit.

2. Handling Heart Transplant Billings From Nonapproved Hospitals
   Where a heart transplant and covered services are provided by a nonapproved hospital, the bill data processed through Grouper and Pricer must exclude transplant procedure codes and related charges.

100-4, 3, 90.2.1
Artificial Hearts and Related Devices

Effective for discharges before May 1, 2008, Medicare does not cover the use of artificial hearts, either as a permanent replacement for a human heart or as a temporary life-support system until a human heart becomes available for transplant (often referred to a "bridge to transplant").

Medicare does cover a Ventricular Assist Device (VAD). A VAD is used to assist a damaged or weakened heart in pumping blood. VADs are used as a bridge to a heart transplant, for support of blood circulation postcardiotomy or destination therapy. Refer to the NCD Manual, section 20.9 for coverage criteria.

The MCE creates a Limited Coverage edit for procedure code 37.66. This procedure code has limited coverage due to the stringent conditions that must be met by hospitals. Where this procedure code is identified by MCE, the FI shall determine if coverage criteria is met and override the MCE if appropriate.

Effective for discharges on or after May 1, 2008, the use of artificial hearts will be covered by Medicare under Coverage with Evidence Development when beneficiaries are enrolled in a clinical study that meets all of the criteria listed in Pub. 100-03, Medicare NCD Manual, section 20.9.

100-4, 3, 90.3
Stem Cell Transplantation

Stem cell transplantation is a process in which stem cells are harvested from either a patient's or donor's bone marrow or peripheral blood for intravenous infusion. Autologous stem cell transplants (AuSCT) must be used to effect hematopoietic reconstitution following severely myelotoxic doses of chemotherapy (HDCT) and/or radiotherapy used to treat various malignancies. Allogeneic stem cell transplant may also be used to restore function in recipients having an inherited or acquired deficiency or defect.

Bone marrow and peripheral blood stem cell transplantation is a process which includes mobilization, harvesting, and transplant of bone marrow or peripheral blood stem cells and the administration of high dose chemotherapy or radiotherapy prior to the actual transplant. When bone marrow or peripheral blood stem cell transplantation is covered, all necessary steps are included in coverage. When bone marrow or peripheral blood stem cell transplantation is non-covered, none of the steps are covered.

Allogeneic and autologous stem cell transplants are covered under Medicare for specific diagnoses. Effective October 1, 1990, these cases were assigned to MS-DRG 009, Bone Marrow Transplant.

The FI's Medicare Code Editor (MCE) will edit stem cell transplant procedure codes 4101, 4102, 4103, 4104, 4105, 4107, 4108, and 4109 against diagnosis codes to determine which cases meet specified coverage criteria. Cases with a diagnosis code for a covered condition will pass (as covered) the MCE noncovered procedure edit. When a stem cell transplant case is selected for review based on the random selection of beneficiaries, the QIO will review the case on a post-payment basis to assure proper coverage decisions.

Procedure code 41.00 (bone marrow transplant, not otherwise specified) will be classified as noncovered and the claim will be returned to the hospital for a more specific procedure code.

The A/B MACs or the FI may choose to review if data analysis deems it a priority.

100-4, 3, 90.3.1
Allogeneic Stem Cell Transplantation
A3-3614.1, HO-416.2, A3-3614.2, HO-416.3

A. General
Allogeneic stem cell transplantation (ICD-9-CM Procedure Codes 41.02, 41.03, 41.05, and 41.08, CPT-4 Code 38240) is a procedure in which a portion of a healthy donor's stem cells are obtained and prepared for intravenous infusion to restore normal hematopoietic function in recipients having an inherited or acquired hematopoietic deficiency or defect.

See the National Coverage Determinations Manual for more information.

Expenses incurred by a donor are a covered benefit to the recipient/beneficiary but, except for physician services, are not paid separately. Services to the donor include physician services, hospital care in connection with screening the stem cell, and ordinary follow-up care.

B. Covered Conditions

1. Effective for services performed on or after August 1, 1978:
   - For the treatment of leukemia, leukemia in remission (ICD-9-CM codes 204.00 through 208.91), or aplastic anemia (ICD-9-CM codes 284.0 through 284.9) when it is reasonable and necessary; and

2. Effective for services performed on or after June 3, 1985:
   - For the treatment of severe combined immunodeficiency disease (SCID) (ICD-9-CM code 279.2), and for the treatment of Wiskott - Aldrich syndrome (ICD-9-CM 279.12).

C. Noncovered Conditions

3. Effective for services performed on or after May 24, 1996:
   - Allogeneic stem cell transplantation is not covered as treatment for multiple myeloma (ICD-9-CM codes 203.00 and 203.01).

NOTE: Coverage for conditions other than these specifically designated as covered or noncovered in this section or National Coverage Determination Manual are left to individual FI's discretion.

100-4, 3, 90.3.2
Autologous Stem Cell Transplantation (AuSCT)
A. General
Autologous stem cell transplantation (AuSCT) (ICD-9-CM procedure code 41.01, 41.04, 41.07, and 41.09 and CPT-4 code 38241) is a technique for restoring stem cells using the patient's own previously stored cells. AuSCT must be used to effect hematopoietic reconstitution following severely myelotoxic doses of chemotherapy (high dose chemotherapy (HDCT)) and/or radiotherapy used to treat various malignancies.

B. Covered Conditions

1. Effective for services performed on or after April 28, 1989:
   - Acute leukemia in remission (ICD-9-CM codes 204.01, lymphoid; 205.01, myeloid; 206.01, monocytic; 207.01, acute erythremia and erythroleukemia; and 208.01 unspecified cell type) patients who have a high probability of relapse and who have no human leucocyte antigens (HLA)-matched;
   - Resistant non-Hodgkin's lymphomas (ICD-9-CM codes 200.00-200.08, 200.10-200.18, 200.20-200.28, 200.80-200.88, 202.00-202.08, 202.80-202.88, and 202.90-202.98) or those presenting with poor prognostic features following an initial response;
   - Recurrent or refractory neuroblastoma (see ICD-9-CM Neoplasm by site, malignant); or
   - Advanced Hodgkin's disease (ICD-9-CM codes 201.00-201.98) patients who have failed conventional therapy and have no HLA-matched donor.

2. Effective for services performed on or after October 1, 2000:
   - Durie-Salmon Stage II or III that fit the following requirement: Newly diagnosed or responsive multiple myeloma (ICD-9-CM codes 203.00 and 238.6). This includes those patients with previously untreated disease, those with at least a partial response to prior chemotherapy (defined as a 50% decrease either in measurable paraprotein [serum and/or urine] or in bone marrow infiltration, sustained for at least 1 month), and those in responsive relapse, and adequate cardiac, renal, pulmonary, and hepatic function.

3. Effective for services performed on or after March 15, 2005, when recognized clinical risk factors are employed to select patients for transplantation, high-dose melphalan (HDM), together with AuSCT, in treating Medicare beneficiaries of any age group with primary amyloid light-chain (AL) amyloidosis who meet the following criteria:
   1. Amyloid deposition in 2 or fewer organs; and,
   2. Cardiac left ventricular ejection fraction (EF) of 45% or greater.

C. Noncovered Conditions
Insufficient data exist to establish definite conclusions regarding the efficacy of autologous stem cell transplantation for the following conditions:

- Acute leukemia not in remission (ICD-9-CM codes 204.00, 205.00, 206.00, 207.00 and 208.00);
- Chronic granulocytic leukemia (ICD-9-CM codes 205.10 and 205.11);
- Solid tumors (other than neuroblastoma) (ICD-9-CM codes 140.0-199.1);
- Multiple myeloma (ICD-9-CM code 203.00 and 238.6), through September 30, 2000.
- Tandem transplantation (multiple rounds of autologous stem cell transplantation) for patients with multiple myeloma (ICD-9-CM code 203.00 and 238.6)
- Non-primary (AL) amyloidosis (ICD-9-CM code 277.3), effective October 1, 2000; or
- Primary (AL) amyloidosis (ICD-9-CM code 277.3) for Medicare beneficiaries age 64 or older, effective October 1, 2000, through March 14, 2005.

NOTE: Coverage for conditions other than these specifically designated as covered or non-covered is left to the FI's discretion.

100-4, 3, 90.3.3
Billing for Stem Cell Transplantation
A. Billing for Acquisition Services
The hospital identifies stem cell acquisition charges separately in FL 42 of Form CMS-1450 by using revenue code 0819 (Other Organ Acquisition). The FI does not make separate payment for these acquisition charges, since they are included in the DRG payment.

For allogeneic stem cell transplants (procedure codes 41.02 or 41.03) where the hospital submits interim bills, the acquisition charge will appear on the billing form for the period during which the transplant took place. Since claims for stem cell transplants are paid using PPS, the hospital submits an adjustment bill whenever an interim bill has been processed. Charges will appear on the transplant bill if there are no interim bills involved.

The transplant hospital keeps an itemized statement that identifies the services furnished, the charges, the person receiving the service (donor/recipient), and whether this is a potential transplant donor or recipient. These charges will be reflected in the transplant hospital's stem cell/bone marrow acquisition cost center. Revenue code 0819 is to include all services required in acquisition of stem cell, e.g., tissue typing or post-operative evaluation.

For allogeneic stem cell transplants (procedure codes 41.02 and 41.03, 41.05, or 41.08), the hospital includes charges for acquisition and any applicable storage charges on the recipient's transplant bill.

Acquisition charges do not apply to autologous stem cell acquisitions. On the transplant bill, the hospital reports the charges, cost report days, and utilization days for the stay in which the stem cell was obtained.

B. Billing for Allogeneic Stem Cell Transplants
The donor is covered for medically necessary inpatient hospital days of care in connection with the bone marrow transplant operation. Expenses incurred for complications are covered only if they are directly and immediately attributable to the stem cell donation procedure

If the donor receives hospital services in connection with a stem cell transplant, they are covered under Part A. The hospital reports the charges on the billing form for the recipient. It does not charge the donor's days of care against the recipient's utilization record. For cost reporting purposes, it includes the covered donor days and charges as Medicare days and charges.

The hospital shows charges for the transplant itself in revenue center code 0362. Selection of the cost center is up to the hospital.

C. Billing for Autologous Stem Cell Transplants
Since there are no covered acquisition charges for autologous stem cell transplant, the hospital shows all charges in the usual manner. It shows charges for the transplant, procedure code 41.01, in revenue center code 0362 or other appropriate cost center.

100-4, 3, 90.4
Liver Transplants
A. Background
For Medicare coverage purposes, liver transplants are considered medically reasonable and necessary for specified conditions when performed in facilities that meet specific criteria.

To review the current list of approved Liver Transplant Centers, see
http://www.cms.hhs.gov/CertificationandCompliance/20_Transplant.asp#TopOfPage

100-4, 3, 90.4.1
Standard Liver Acquisition Charge
A3-3615.1, A3-3615.3

Each transplant facility must develop a standard charge for acquiring a cadaver liver from costs it expects to incur in the acquisition of livers.

This standard charge is not a charge that represents the acquisition cost of a specific liver. Rather, it is a charge that reflects the average cost associated with a liver acquisition.

Services associated with liver acquisition are billed from the organ procurement organization or, in some cases, the excising hospital to the transplant hospital. The excising hospital does not submit a billing form to the FI. The transplant hospital keeps an itemized statement that identifies the services furnished, the charges, the person receiving the service (donor/recipient), and the potential transplant donor. These charges are reflected in the transplant hospital's liver acquisition cost center and are used in determining the hospital's standard charge for acquiring a cadaver's liver. The standard charge is not a charge representing the acquisition cost of a specific liver. Rather, it is a charge that reflects the average cost associated with liver acquisition. Also, it is an all inclusive charge for all services required in acquisition of a liver, e.g., tissue typing, transportation of organ, and surgeons' retrieval fees.

100-4, 3, 90.4.2
Billing for Liver Transplant and Acquisition Services
Form CMS-1450 or its electronic equivalent is completed in accordance with instructions in chapter 25 for the beneficiary who receives a covered liver transplant. Applicable standard liver acquisition charges are identified separately in FL 42 by revenue code 0817 (Donor-Liver). Where interim bills are submitted, the standard acquisition charge appears on the billing form for the period during which the transplant took place. This charge is in addition to the hospital's charge for services furnished directly to the Medicare recipient.

The contractor deducts liver acquisition charges for IPPS hospitals prior to processing through Pricer. Costs of liver acquisition incurred by approved liver transplant facilities are not included in prospective payment DRG 480 (Liver Transplant). They are paid on a reasonable cost basis. This item is a "pass-through" cost for which interim payments are made. (See the Provider Reimbursement Manual, Part 1, Sec.2802 B.8.) The contractor includes liver acquisition charges under revenue code 0817 in the HUIP record that it sends to CWF and the QIO.

A. Bill Review Procedures
The contractor takes the following actions to process liver transplant bills.

1. Operative Report
   The contractor requires the operative report with all claims for liver transplants, or sends a development request to the hospital for each liver transplant with a diagnosis code for a covered condition.

2. MCE Interface
   Code 50.51 (Auxiliary liver transplant) is always a non-covered procedure. However, the MCE contains a limited coverage edit for procedure code 50.59 (liver transplant). Where procedure code 50.59 is identified by the MCE, the contractor shall check the provider number and effective date to determine if the provider is an approved liver transplant facility at the time of the transplant, and the contractor shall also determine if the facility is certified for adults and/or pediatric transplants dependent upon the patient's age. If yes, the claim is suspended for review of the operative report to determine whether the beneficiary has at least one of the covered conditions when the diagnosis code is for a covered condition. If payment is appropriate (i.e., the facility is approved, the service is furnished on or after the approval date, and the beneficiary has a covered condition), the contractor sends the claim to Grouper and Pricer.

   If none of the diagnoses codes are for a covered condition, or if the provider is not an approved liver transplant facility, the contractor denies the claim.

   NOTE: Some non-covered conditions are included in the covered diagnostic codes. (The diagnostic codes are broader than the covered conditions. For example, primary biliary cirrhosis is a covered condition, secondary biliary cirrhosis is not a covered condition. Both primary and secondary biliary cirrhosis have the same diagnosis code ICD 9 571.6) Do not pay for noncovered conditions.

3. Grouper
   If the bill shows a discharge date before March 8, 1990, the liver transplant procedure is not covered. If the discharge date is March 8, 1990 or later, the contractor processes the bill through Grouper and Pricer. If the discharge date is after March 7, 1990, and before October 1, 1990, Grouper assigned CMS DRG 191 or 192. The contractor sent the bill to Pricer with review code 08. Pricer would then overlay CMS DRG 191 or 192 with CMS DRG 480 and the weights and thresholds for CMS DRG 480 to price the bill. If the discharge date is after September 30, 1990, Grouper assigns CMS DRG 480 and Pricer is able to price without using review code 08. If the discharge date is after September 30, 2007, Grouper assigns MS-DRG 005 or 006 (Liver transplant with MCC or Intestinal Transplant or Liver transplant without MCC, respectively) and Pricer is able to price without using review code 08.

4. Liver Transplant Billing From Non-approved Hospitals
   Where a liver transplant and covered services are provided by a non-approved hospital, the bill data processed through Grouper and Pricer must exclude transplant procedure codes and related charges.

   When CMS approves a hospital to furnish liver transplant services, it informs the hospital of the effective date in the approval letter. The contractor will receive a copy of the letter.

100-4, 3, 90.5
Pancreas Transplants Kidney Transplants
A. Background
Effective July 1, 1999, Medicare covered pancreas transplantation when performed simultaneously with or following a kidney transplant (ICD-9-CM procedure code 55.69). Pancreas transplantation is performed to induce an insulin independent, euglycemic state in diabetic patients. The procedure is generally limited to those patients with severe secondary complications of diabetes including kidney failure. However, pancreas transplantation is sometimes performed on patients with labile diabetes and hypoglycemic unawareness.

Medicare has had a policy of not covering pancreas transplantation. The Office of Health Technology Assessment performed an assessment on pancreas-kidney transplantation in 1994. They found reasonable graft survival outcomes for patients receiving either simultaneous pancreas-kidney (SPK) transplantation or pancreas after kidney (PAK) transplantation. For a list of facilities approved to perform SPK or PAK, refer to the following Web site:
http://www.cms.hhs.gov/CertificationandCompliance/20_Transplant.asp#TopOfPage

B. Billing for Pancreas Transplants
There are no special provisions related to managed care participants. Managed care plans are required to provide all Medicare covered services. Medicare does not restrict which hospitals or physicians may perform pancreas transplantation.

The transplant procedure and revenue code 0360 for the operating room are paid under these codes. Procedures must be reported using the current ICD-9-CM procedure codes for pancreas and kidney transplants. Providers must place at least one of the following transplant procedure codes on the claim:

   52.80 Transplant of pancreas

   52.82 Homotransplant of pancreas

The Medicare Code Editor (MCE) has been updated to include 52.80 and 52.82 as limited coverage procedures. The contractor must determine if the facility is approved for the transplant and certified for either pediatric or adult transplants dependent upon the age of the patient.

Effective October 1, 2000, ICD 9 CM code 52.83 was moved in the MCE to non-covered. The contractor must override any deny edit on claims that came in with 52.82 prior to October 1, 2000 and adjust, as 52.82 is the correct code.

If the discharge date is July 1, 1999, or later: the contractor processes the bill through Grouper and Pricer.

Pancreas transplantation is reasonable and necessary for the following diagnosis codes. However, since this is not an all-inclusive list, the contractor is permitted to determine if any additional diagnosis codes will be covered for this procedure.

Diabetes Diagnosis Codes

   250.00 Diabetes mellitus without mention of complication, type II (non-insulin dependent) (NIDDM) (adult onset) or unspecified type, not stated as uncontrolled.

   250.01 Diabetes mellitus without mention of complication, type I (insulin dependent) (IDDM) (juvenile), not stated as uncontrolled.

250.02 Diabetes mellitus without mention of complication, type II (non-insulin dependent) (NIDDM) (adult onset) or unspecified type, uncontrolled.

250.03 Diabetes mellitus without mention of complication, type I (insulin dependent) (IDDM) (juvenile), uncontrolled.

250.1X Diabetes with ketoacidosis

250.2X Diabetes with hyperosmolarity

250.3X Diabetes with coma

250.4X Diabetes with renal manifestations

250.5X Diabetes with ophthalmic manifestations

250.6X Diabetes with neurological manifestations

250.7X Diabetes with peripheral circulatory disorders

250.8X Diabetes with other specified manifestations

250.9X Diabetes with unspecified complication

NOTE: X=0-3

Hypertensive Renal Diagnosis Codes:

403.01 Malignant hypertensive renal disease, with renal failure

403.11 Benign hypertensive renal disease, with renal failure

403.91 Unspecified hypertensive renal disease, with renal failure

404.02 Malignant hypertensive heart and renal disease, with renal failure

404.03 Malignant hypertensive heart and renal disease, with congestive heart failure or renal failure

404.12 Benign hypertensive heart and renal disease, with renal failure

404.13 Benign hypertensive heart and renal disease, with congestive heart failure or renal failure

404.92 Unspecified hypertensive heart and renal disease, with renal failure

404.93 Unspecified hypertensive heart and renal disease, with congestive heart failure or renal failure

585.1-585.6, 585.9 Chronic Renal Failure Code

NOTE: If a patient had a kidney transplant that was successful, the patient no longer has chronic kidney failure, therefore it would be inappropriate for the provider to bill 585.1 - 585.6, 585.9 on such a patient. In these cases one of the following V-codes should be present on the claim or in the beneficiary's history.

The provider uses the following V-codes only when a kidney transplant was performed before the pancreas transplant:

V42.0 Organ or tissue replaced by transplant kidney

V43.89 Organ tissue replaced by other means, kidney or pancreas

NOTE: If a kidney and pancreas transplants are performed simultaneously, the claim should contain a diabetes diagnosis code and a renal failure code or one of the hypertensive renal failure diagnosis codes. The claim should also contain two transplant procedure codes. If the claim is for a pancreas transplant only, the claim should contain a diabetes diagnosis code and a V-code to indicate a previous kidney transplant. If the V-code is not on the claim for the pancreas transplant, the contractor will search the beneficiary's claim history for a V-code.

C. Drugs
If the pancreas transplant occurs after the kidney transplant, immunosuppressive therapy will begin with the date of discharge from the inpatient stay for the pancreas transplant.

D. Charges for Pancreas Acquisition Services
A separate organ acquisition cost center has been established for pancreas transplantation. The Medicare cost report will include a separate line to account for pancreas transplantation costs. The 42 CFR 412.2(e)(4) was changed to include pancreas in the list of organ acquisition costs that are paid on a reasonable cost basis.

Acquisition costs for pancreas transplantation as well as kidney transplants will occur in Revenue Center 081X. The contractor overrides any claims that suspend due to repetition of revenue code 081X on the same claim if the patient had a simultaneous kidney/pancreas transplant. It pays for acquisition costs for both kidney and pancreas organs if transplants are performed simultaneously. It will not pay for more than two organ acquisitions on the same claim.

E. Medicare Summary Notices (MSN) and Remittance Advice Messages
If the provider submits a claim for simultaneous pancreas kidney transplantation or pancreas transplantation following a kidney transplant, and omits one of the appropriate diagnosis/procedure codes, the contractor rejects the claim, using the following MSN:

- MSN 16.32, "Medicare does not pay separately for this service."

- Use the following Remittance Advice Message:

- Claim adjustment reason code B15, "Claim/service denied/reduced because this procedure or service is not paid separately."

- If a claim is denied because no evidence of a prior kidney transplant is presented, use the following MSN message:

- MSN 15.4, "The information provided does not support the need for this service or item."

The contractor uses the following Remittance Advice Message:

- Claim adjustment reason code 50, "These are non-covered services because this is not deemed a 'medical necessity' by the payer."

To further clarify the situation, the contractor should also use new claim level remark code MA 126, "Pancreas transplant not covered unless kidney transplant performed."

100-4, 3, 90.6
Intestinal and Multi-Visceral Transplants
A. Background
Effective for services on or after April 1, 2001, Medicare covers intestinal and multi-visceral transplantation for the purpose of restoring intestinal function in patients with irreversible intestinal failure. Intestinal failure is defined as the loss of absorptive capacity of the small bowel secondary to severe primary gastrointestinal disease or surgically induced short bowel syndrome. Intestinal failure prevents oral nutrition and may be associated with both mortality and profound morbidity. Multi-Visceral transplantation includes organs in the digestive system (stomach, duodenum, liver, and intestine). See Sec.260.5 of the National Coverage Determinations Manual for further information.

B. Approved Transplant Facilities
Medicare will cover intestinal transplantation if performed in an approved facility. The approved facilities are located at:
http://www.cms.hhs.gov/CertificationandComplianc/20_Transplant.asp#TopOfPage

C. Billing
ICD-9-CM procedure code 46.97 is effective for discharges on or after April 1, 2001. The Medicare Code Editor (MCE) lists this code as a limited coverage procedure. The contractor shall override the MCE when this procedure code is listed and the coverage criteria are met in an approved transplant facility, and also determine if the facility is certified for adults and/or pediatric transplants dependent upon the patient's age.

For this procedure where the provider is approved as transplant facility and certified for the adult and/or pediatric population, and the service is performed on or after the transplant approval date, the contractor must suspend the claim for clerical review of the operative report to determine whether the beneficiary has at least one of the covered conditions listed when the diagnosis code is for a covered condition.

This review is not part of the contractor's medical review workload. Instead, the contractor should complete this review as part of its claims processing workload.

Charges for ICD-9-CM procedure code 46.97 should be billed under revenue code 0360, Operating Room Services.

For discharge dates on or after October 1, 2001, acquisition charges are billed under revenue code 081X, Organ Acquisition. For discharge dates between April 1, 2001, and September 30, 2001, hospitals were to report the acquisition charges on the claim, but there was no interim pass-through payment made for these costs.

Bill the procedure used to obtain the donor's organ on the same claim, using appropriate ICD-9-CM procedure codes.

The 11X bill type should be used when billing for intestinal transplants.

Immunosuppressive therapy for intestinal transplantation is covered and should be billed consistent with other organ transplants under the current rules.

There is no specific ICD-9-CM diagnosis code for intestinal failure. Diagnosis codes exist to capture the causes of intestinal failure. Some examples of intestinal failure include, but are not limited to:

- Volvulus 560.2,

- Volvulus gastroschisis 756.79, other [congenital] anomalies of abdominal wall,

- Volvulus gastroschisis 569.89, other specified disorders of intestine,

- Necrotizing enterocolitis 777.5, necrotizing enterocolitis in fetus or newborn,

- Necrotizing enterocolitis 014.8, other tuberculosis of intestines, peritoneum, and mesenteric,

- Necrotizing enterocolitis and splanchnic vascular thrombosis 557.0, acute vascular insufficiency of intestine,

- Inflammatory bowel disease 569.9, unspecified disorder of intestine,

- Radiation enteritis 777.5, necrotizing enterocolitis in fetus or newborn, and

- Radiation enteritis 558.1.

D. Acquisition Costs
A separate organ acquisition cost center was established for acquisition costs incurred on or after October 1, 2001. The Medicare Cost Report will include a separate line to account for these transplantation costs. For intestinal and multi-visceral transplants performed between April 1, 2001, and October 1, 2001, the DRG payment was payment in full for all hospital services related to this procedure.

E. Medicare Summary Notices (MSN), Remittance Advice Messages, and Notice of Utilization Notices (NOU)
If an intestinal transplant is billed by an unapproved facility after April 1, 2001, the contractor shall deny the claim and use MSN message 21.6, "This item or service is not covered when performed, referred, or ordered by this provider;" 21.18, "This item or service is not covered when performed or ordered by this provider;" or, 16.2, "This service cannot be paid when provided in this location/facility;" and Remittance Advice Message, Claim Adjustment Reason Code 52, "The referring/prescribing/rendering provider is not eligible to refer/prescribe/order/perform the service billed."

100-4, 3, 100.1
Billing for Abortion Services
A3-3652

Effective October 1, 1998, abortions are not covered under the Medicare program except for instances where the pregnancy is a result of an act of rape or incest; or the woman suffers from a physical disorder, physical injury, or physical illness, including a life endangering physical condition caused by the pregnancy itself that would, as certified by a physician, place the woman in danger of death unless an abortion is performed.

A. "G" Modifier

The "G7" modifier is defined as "the pregnancy resulted from rape or incest, or pregnancy certified by physician as life threatening."

Beginning July 1, 1999, providers should bill for abortion services using the new Modifier G7. This modifier can be used on claims with dates of services October 1, 1998, and after. CWF will be able to recognize the modifier beginning July 1, 1999.

B. FI Billing Instructions

1. Hospital Inpatient Billing
   Hospitals will bill the FI on Form CMS-1450 using bill type 11X. Medicare will pay only when condition code A7 or A8 is used in FLs 24-30 of UB92 along with an appropriate ICD-9-CM principal diagnosis code that will group to DRG 380 or with an appropriate ICD-9-CM principal diagnosis code and one of the four appropriate ICD-9-CM operating room procedure codes listed below that will group to DRG 381.

   69.01 69.02 69.51 74.91

   Providers must use ICD-9-CM codes 69.01 and 69.02 to describe exactly the procedure or service performed.

   The FI must manually review claims with the above ICD-9-CM procedure codes to verify that all of the above conditions are met.

2. Outpatient Billing
   Hospitals will bill the FI on Form CMS-1450 using bill type 13X, 83X and 85X.

   Medicare will pay only if one of the following CPT codes is used with the "G7" modifier.

   59840 59851 59856

   59841 59852 59857

   59850 59855 59866

C. Common Working File (CWF) Edits

For hospital outpatient claims, CWF will bypass its edits for a managed care beneficiary who is having an abortion outside their plan and the claim is submitted with the "G7" modifier and one of the above CPT codes.

For hospital inpatient claims, CWF will bypass its edits for a managed care beneficiary who is having an abortion outside their plan and the claim is submitted with one of the above ICD-9-CM procedure codes.

D. Medicare Summary Notices (MSN)/Explanation of Your Medicare Benefits
Remittance Advice Message

If a claim is submitted with one of the above CPT procedure codes but no "G7" modifier, the claim is denied. The FI states on the MSN the following message:

This service was denied because Medicare covers this service only under certain circumstances." (MSN Message 21.21).

For the remittance advice the FI uses existing American National Standard Institute (ANSI) X12-835 claim adjustment reason code B5, "Claim/service denied/reduced because coverage guidelines were not met or were exceeded."

100-4, 3, 100.2

Payment for CRNA or AA Services
A3-3660.9

Anesthesia services furnished on or after January 1, 1990, at a qualified rural hospital by a hospital employed or contracted CRNA or AA can be paid on a reasonable cost basis. The FI determines the hospital's qualification using the following criteria.

The hospital must be located in a rural area (as defined for PPS purposes) to be considered. A rural hospital that qualified and was paid on a reasonable cost basis for CRNA or AA services during calendar year 1989 could continue to be paid on a reasonable cost basis for these services furnished during calendar year 1990 if it could establish before January 1, 1990, that it did not provide more than 500 surgical procedures, both inpatient and outpatient, requiring anesthesia services during 1989.

A rural hospital that was not paid on a reasonable cost basis for CRNA or AA services during calendar year 1989 could be paid on a reasonable cost basis for these services furnished during calendar year 1990 if it established before January 1, 1990, that:

- As of January 1, 1988, it employed or contracted with a CRNA or AA (but not more than one full-time equivalent CRNA or AA); and

- In both 1987 and 1989, it had a volume of 500 or fewer surgical procedures, including inpatient and outpatient procedures, requiring anesthesia services.

Each CRNA or AA employed by, or under contract with the hospital, must agree in writing not to bill on a fee schedule basis for services furnished at the hospital. A rural hospital can qualify and continue to be paid on a reasonable cost basis for qualified CRNA or AA services for a calendar year beyond 1990 if it could establish before January 1 of that year that it did not provide more than 500 surgical procedures, both inpatient and outpatient, requiring anesthesia services during the preceding year. For a calendar year beyond 1990, it must make its election after September 30, but before January 1. The FI determines the number of anesthetics by annualizing the number of surgical procedures for the 9-month period ending September 30.

A rural hospital that first elects reasonable cost payment for CRNA services for a calendar year after 1990 must demonstrate that:

- It had a volume of 500 or fewer surgical procedures, including inpatient and outpatient, requiring anesthesia services in the preceding year; and

- It meets the criteria that would have been met by a rural hospital first electing reasonable cost in calendar year 1990.

To prevent duplicate payments, the FI informs carriers of the names of CRNAs or AAs, the hospitals with which they have agreements, and the effective dates of the agreements. If the CRNA or AA bills Part B for anesthesia services furnished prior to the hospital's election of reasonable cost payments, the carrier must recover the overpayment from the CRNA or AA.

100-4, 3, 100.6

Inpatient Renal Services
HO-E400

Section 405.103I of Subpart J of Regulation 5 stipulates that only approved hospitals may bill for ESRD services. Hence, to allow hospitals to bill and be reimbursed for inpatient dialysis services furnished under arrangements, both facilities participating in the arrangement must meet the conditions of 405.2120 and 405.2160 of Subpart U of Regulation 5. In order for renal dialysis facilities to have a written arrangement with each other to provide inpatient dialysis care both facilities must meet the minimum utilization rate requirement, i.e., two dialysis stations with a performance capacity of at least four dialysis treatments per week.

Dialysis may be billed by an SNF as a service if: (a) it is provided by a hospital with which the facility has a transfer agreement in effect, and that hospital is approved to provide staff-assisted dialysis for the Medicare program; or (b) it is furnished directly by an SNF meeting all nonhospital maintenance dialysis facility requirements, including minimum utilization requirements. (See 1861(h)(6), 1861(h)(7), title XVIII.)

100-4, 3, 100.7

Lung Volume Reduction Surgery (LVRS) (also known as reduction pneumoplasty, lung shaving, or lung contouring) is an invasive surgical procedure to reduce the volume of a hyperinflated lung in order to allow the underlying compressed lung to expand, and thus, establish improved respiratory function.
Effective for discharges on or after January 1, 2004, Medicare will cover LVRS under certain conditions as described in 240 of Pub. 100-03, "National Coverage Determinations".

The Medicare Code Editor (MCE) creates a Limited Coverage edit for procedure code 32.22. This procedure code has limited coverage due to the stringent conditions that must be met by hospitals. Where this procedure code is identified by MCE, the FI shall determine if coverage criteria is met and override the MCE if appropriate.

The LVRS can only be performed in the facilities listed on the following Web site: www.cms.hhs.gov/coverage/lvrsfacility.pdf

Medicare previously only covered LVRS as part of the National Emphysema Treatment Trial (NETT). The study was limited to 18 hospitals, and patients were randomized into two arms, either medical management and LVRS or medical management. The study was conducted by The National Heart, Lung, and Blood Institute of the National Institutes of Health and coordinated by Johns Hopkins University (JHU). Hospital claims for patients in the NETT were identified by the presence of Condition Code EY. The JHU instructed hospitals of the correct billing procedures for billing claims under the NETT.

100-4, 4, 10.4

Packaging
Under the OPPS, packaged services are items and services that are considered to be an integral part of another service that is paid under the OPPS. No separate payment is made for packaged services, because the cost of these items and services is included in the APC payment for the service of which they are an integral part. For example, routine supplies, anesthesia, recovery room use, and most drugs are considered to be an integral part of a surgical procedure so payment for these items is packaged into the APC payment for the surgical procedure.

A. Packaging for Claims Resulting In APC Payments
If a claim contains services that result in an APC payment but also contains packaged services, separate payment for the packaged services is not made since payment is included in the APC. However, charges related to the packaged services are used for outlier and Transitional Corridor Payments (TOPs) as well as for future rate setting.

Therefore, it is extremely important that hospitals report all HCPCS codes and all charges for all services they furnish, whether payment for the services is made separately paid or is packaged.

B. Packaging for Claims Resulting in No APC Payments
If the claim contains only services payable under cost reimbursement, such as corneal tissue, and services that would be packaged services if an APC were payable, then the packaged services are not separately payable. In addition, these charges for the packaged services are not used to calculate TOPs.

If the claim contains only services payable under a fee schedule, such as clinical diagnostic laboratory tests, and also contains services that would be packaged services if an APC were payable, the packaged services are not separately payable. In addition, the charges are not used to calculate TOPs.

If a claim contains services payable under cost reimbursement, services payable under a fee schedule, and services that would be packaged services if an APC were payable, the packaged services are not separately payable. In addition, the charges are not used to calculate TOPs payments.

C. Packaging Types Under the OPPS
1. Unconditionally packaged services are services for which separate payment is never made because the payment for the service is always packaged into the payment for other services. Unconditionally packaged services are identified in the OPPS Addendum B with status

indictor of N. See the OPPS Web site at http://www.cms.hhs.gov/HospitalOutpatientPPS/ for the most recent Addendum B (HCPCS codes with status indicators). In general, the charges for unconditionally packaged services are used to calculate outlier and TOPS payments when they appear on a claim with a service that is separately paid under the OPPS because the packaged service is considered to be part of the package of services for which payment is being made through the APC payment for the separately paid service.

2. STVX-packaged services are services for which separate payment is made only if there is no service with status indicator S, T, V or X reported with the same date of service on the same claim. If a claim includes a service that is assigned status indicator S, T, V, or X reported on the same date of service as the STVXpackaged service, the payment for the STVX-packaged service is packaged into the payment for the service(s) with status indicator S, T, V or X and no separate payment is made for the STVX-packaged service. STVX-packaged services are assigned status indicator Q. See the OPPS Webpage at http://www.cms.hhs.gov/HospitalOutpatientPPS/ for identification of STVXpackaged codes.

3. T-packaged services are services for which separate payment is made only if there is no service with status indicator T reported with the same date of service on the same claim. When there is a claim that includes a service that is assigned status indicator T reported on the same date of service as the T-packaged service, the payment for the T-packaged service is packaged into the payment for the service(s) with status indicator T and no separate payment is made for the T-packaged service. T-packaged services are assigned status indicator Q. See the OPPS Web site at http://www.cms.hhs.gov/HospitalOutpatientPPS/ for identification of T-packaged codes.

4. A service that is assigned to a composite APC is a major component of a single episode of care. The hospital receives one payment through a composite APC for multiple major separately identifiable services. Services mapped to composite APCs are assigned status indicator Q. See the discussion of composite APCs in section 10.2.1.

100-4, 4, 10.5
Discounting

- Fifty percent of the full OPPS amount is paid if a procedure for which anesthesia is planned is discontinued after the patient is prepared and taken to the room where the procedure is to be performed but before anesthesia is provided.

- Fifty percent of the full OPPS amount is paid if a procedure for which anesthesia is not planned is discontinued after the patient is prepared and taken to the room where the procedure is to be performed.

- Multiple surgical procedures furnished during the same operative session are discounted.

  - The full amount is paid for the surgical procedure with the highest weight;

  - Fifty percent is paid for any other surgical procedure(s) performed at the same time;

  - Similar discounting occurs now under the physician fee schedule and the payment system for ASCs;

- When multiple surgical procedures are performed during the same operative session, beneficiary coinsurance is discounted in proportion to the APC payment.

100-4, 4, 10.10
Biweekly Interim Payments for Certain Hospital OutpatientItems and Services That Are Paid on a Cost Basis, and Direct Medical Education Payments, Not Included in the Hospital Outpatient Prospective Payment System
A-01-32

For hospitals subject to the OPPS, payment for certain items that are not paid under the OPPS, but which are reimbursable in addition to OPPS, are made through biweekly interim payments subject to retrospective adjustment based on a settled cost report.

These payments include:

- Direct medical education payments;

- Costs of nursing and allied health programs;

- Costs associated with interns and residents not in an approved teaching program as described in 42 CFR 415.202;

- Teaching physicians costs attributable to Part B services for hospitals that elect cost-based reimbursement for teaching physicians under 42 CFR 415.160;

- CRNA services;

- For hospitals that meet the requirements under 42 CFR 412.113(c), the reasonable costs of anesthesia services furnished to hospital outpatients by qualified nonphysician anesthetists (i.e., certified registered nurse anesthetists and anesthesiologists' assistants) employed by the hospital or obtained under arrangements;

- Bad debts for uncollectible deductibles and coinsurance;

- Organ acquisition costs paid under Part B.

For hospitals that are paid under the OPPS, interim payments for these items attributable to both hospital outpatients, as well as inpatients whose services are paid under Part B of the Medicare program are made on a biweekly basis. The FI determines the amount of the biweekly payment by estimating a hospital's reimbursement amount for these items for the cost reporting period by using:

- Medicare principles of cost reimbursement for cost-based items; and

- Medicare rules for determining payment for graduate medical education for direct medical education, and dividing the total annual estimated amount for these items into 26 equal biweekly payments.

The estimated annual amount is based on the most current data available. Biweekly interim payments are reviewed and, if necessary, adjusted at least twice during the reporting period, with final settlement based on a submitted cost report. Because hospitals subject to the OPPS have not received payment for these items attributable to services furnished on or after August 1, 2000, the date the OPPS was implemented, the first payment to each hospital included all the payments due to the hospital retroactive to August 1, 2000. Thereafter, FIs continue to make payment on a biweekly basis. Each payment is made two weeks after the end of a biweekly period of services. The FI was required to make retroactive payments and begin making biweekly interim payments to all hospitals that are due these payments no later than 60 days after March 8, 2001.

These biweekly payments may be combined with the inpatient biweekly payments that the FI makes under 2405.2 of the Medicare Provider Reimbursement Manual (CMS Pub.15-I). However, if a single payment is made, for purposes of final cost report settlement, they must maintain records to separately identify the amount of the hospital's combined payment that is paid out of the Part A or Part B trust fund.

100-4, 4, 61.4.1
Billing for Brachytherapy Sources - General

Brachytherapy sources (e.g., brachytherapy devices or seeds, solutions) are paid separately from the services to administer and deliver brachytherapy in the OPPS, per section 1833(t)(2)(H) of the Act, reflecting the number, isotope, and radioactive intensity of devices furnished, as well as stranded versus non-stranded configurations of sources. Therefore, providers must bill for brachytherapy sources in addition to the brachytherapy services with which the sources are applied, in order to receive payment for the sources. The list of separately payable sources is found in Addendum B of the most recent OPPS annual update published in the Federal Register, as well as in the recurring update notifications of the current year for billing purposes. New sources meeting the OPPS definition of a brachytherapy source may be added for payment beginning any quarter, and the new source codes and descriptors are announced in the recurring update notifications. Each unit of a billable source is identified by the unit measurement in the respective source's long descriptor. Seed-like sources are generally billed and paid "per source" based on the number of units of the source HCPCS code reported, including the billing of the number of sources within a stranded configuration of sources. Providers therefore must bill the number of units of a source used with the brachytherapy service rendered.

100-4, 4, 61.4.2
Definition of Brachytherapy Source for Separate Payment

Brachytherapy sources eligible for separate billing and payment must be radioactive sources, meaning that the source contains a radioactive isotope. Separate brachytherapy source payments reflect the number, isotope, and radioactive intensity of sources furnished to patients, as well as stranded and non-stranded configurations.

100-4, 4, 61.4.3
Billing of Brachytherapy Sources Ordered for a Specific Patient

A hospital may report and charge Medicare and the Medicare beneficiary for all brachytherapy sources that are ordered by the physician for a specific patient, acquired by the hospital, and used in the care of the patient. Specifically, brachytherapy sources prescribed by the physician in accordance with high quality clinical care, acquired by the hospital, and actually implanted in the patient may be reported and charged. In the case where most, but not all, prescribed sources are implanted in the patient, CMS will consider the relatively few brachytherapy sources that were ordered but not implanted due to specific clinical considerations to be used in the care of the patient and billable to Medicare under the following circumstances. The hospital may charge for all sources if they were specifically acquired by the hospital for the particular patient according to a physician's prescription for the sources that was consistent with standard clinical practice and high quality brachytherapy treatment, in order to ensure that the clinically appropriate number of sources was available for the implantation procedure, and they were not implanted in any other patient. Those sources that were not implanted must have been disposed of in accordance with all appropriate requirements for their handling.

In general, the number of sources used in the care of the patient but not implanted would not be expected to constitute more than a small fraction of the sources actually implanted in the patient. Under these circumstances, the beneficiary is liable for the copayment for all the sources billed to Medicare.

100-4, 4, 61.4.4
Billing for Brachytherapy Source Supervision, Handling and Loading Costs
Providers should report charges related to supervision, handling, and loading of radiation sources, including brachytherapy sources, in one of two ways:

1. Report the charge separately using CPT code 77790 (Supervision, handling, loading of radiation source), in addition to reporting the associated HCPCS procedure code(s) for application of the radiation source;

2. Include the supervision, handling, and/or loading charges as part of the charge reported with the HCPCS procedure code(s) for application of the radiation source.

Do not bill a separate charge for brachytherapy source storage costs. These costs are treated as part of the department's overhead costs.

100-4, 4, 160
Clinic and Emergency Visits
CMS has acknowledged from the beginning of the OPPS that CMS believes that CPT Evaluation and Management (E/M) codes were designed to reflect the activities of physicians and do not describe well the range and mix of services provided by hospitals during visits of clinic and emergency department patients. While awaiting the development of a national set of facility-specific codes and guidelines, providers should continue to apply their current internal guidelines to the existing CPT codes. Each hospital's internal guidelines should follow the intent of the CPT

code descriptors, in that the guidelines should be designed to reasonably relate the intensity of hospital resources to the different levels of effort represented by the codes. Hospitals should ensure that their guidelines accurately reflect resource distinctions between the five levels of codes.

Effective January 1, 2007, CMS is distinguishing between two types of emergency departments: Type A emergency departments and Type B emergency departments.

A Type A emergency department is defined as an emergency department that is available 24 hours a day, 7 days a week and is either licensed by the State in which it is located or applicable State law as an emergency room or emergency department or it is held out to the public (by name, posted signs, advertising, or other means) as a place that provides care for emergency medical conditions on an urgent basis without requiring a previously scheduled appointment.

A Type B emergency department is defined as an emergency department that meets the definition of a "dedicated emergency department" as defined in 42 CFR 489.24 under the EMTALA regulations. It must meet at least one of the following requirements.

(1) It is licensed by the State in which it is located under applicable State law as an emergency room or emergency department;

(2) It is held out to the public (by name, posted signs, advertising, or other means) as a place that provides care for emergency medical conditions on an urgent basis without requiring a previously scheduled appointment; or

(3) During the calendar year immediately preceding the calendar year in which a determination under 42 CFR 489.24 is being made, based on a representative sample of patient visits that occurred during that calendar year, it provides at least one-third of all of its outpatient visits for the treatment of emergency medical conditions on an urgent basis without requiring a previously scheduled appointment.

Hospitals must bill for visits provided in Type A emergency departments using CPT emergency department E/M codes. Hospitals must bill for visits provided in Type B emergency departments using the G-codes that describe visits provided in Type B emergency departments.

Hospitals that will be billing the new Type B ED visit codes may need to update their internal guidelines to report these codes.

Emergency department and clinic visits are paid in some cases separately and in other cases as part of a composite APC payment. See section 10.2.1 of this chapter for further details.

100-4, 4, 160.1
Critical Care Services

Beginning January 1, 2007, critical care services will be paid at two levels, depending on the presence or absence of trauma activation. Providers will receive one payment rate for critical care without trauma activation and will receive additional payment when critical care is associated with trauma activation.

To determine whether trauma activation occurs, follow the National Uniform Billing Committee (NUBC) guidelines in the Claims Processing Manual, Pub 100-04, Chapter 25, Sec 75.4 related to the reporting of the trauma revenue codes in the 68x series. The revenue code series 68x can be used only by trauma centers/hospitals as licensed or designated by the state or local government authority authorized to do so, or as verified by the American College of Surgeons. Different subcategory revenue codes are reported by designated Level 1-4 hospital trauma centers. Only patients for whom there has been prehospital notification based on triage information from prehospital caregivers, who meet either local, state or American College of Surgeons field triage criteria, or are delivered by inter-hospital transfers, and are given the appropriate team response can be billed a trauma activation charge.

When critical care services are provided without trauma activation, the hospital may bill CPT code 99291, Critical care, evaluation and management of the critically ill or critically injured patient; first 30-74 minutes (and 99292, if appropriate). If trauma activation occurs under the circumstances described by the NUBC guidelines that would permit reporting a charge under 68x, the hospital may also bill one unit of code G0390, which describes trauma activation associated with hospital critical care services. Revenue code 68x must be reported on the same date of service. The OCE will edit to ensure that G0390 appears with revenue code 68x on the same date of service and that only one unit of G0390 is billed. CMS believes that trauma activation is a one-time occurrence in association with critical care services, and therefore, CMS will only pay for one unit of G0390 per day.

The CPT code 99291 is defined by CPT as the first 30-74 minutes of critical care. This 30 minute minimum has always applied under the OPPS. The CPT code 99292, Critical care, evaluation and management of the critically ill or critically injured patient; each additional 30 minutes, remains a packaged service under the OPPS, so that hospitals do not have the ongoing administrative burden of reporting precisely the time for each critical service provided. As the CPT guidelines indicate, hospitals that provide less than 30 minutes of critical care should bill for a visit, typically an emergency department visit, at a level consistent with their own internal guidelines.

Under the OPPS, the time that can be reported as critical care is the time spent by a physician and/or hospital staff engaged in active face-to-face care of a critically ill or critically injured patient. If the physician and hospital staff or multiple hospital staff members are simultaneously engaged in this active face-to-face care, the time involved can only be counted once.

- In CY 2007 hospitals may continue to report a charge with RC 68x without any HCPCS code when trauma team activation occurs. In order to receive additional payment when critical care services are associated with trauma activation, the hospital must report G0390 on the same date of service as RC 68x, in addition to CPT code 99291 (or 99292, if appropriate.)

In CY 2007 hospitals should continue to report 99291 (and 99292 as appropriate) for critical care services furnished without trauma team activation. CPT 99291 maps to APC 0617 (Critical Care). (CPT 99292 is packaged and not paid separately, but should be reported if provided.)

Critical care services are paid in some cases separately and in other cases as part of a composite APC payment. See Section 10.2.1 of this chapter for further details.

100-4, 4, 180.3
Unlisted Service or Procedure

This section does not apply to OPPS hospitals.

There may be services or procedures performed that are not found in HCPCS. These are typically services that are rarely provided, unusual, variable, or new. A number of specific code numbers have been designated for reporting unlisted procedures. When an unlisted procedure code is used, a report describing the service is submitted with the claim. Pertinent information includes a definition or description of the nature, extent, and need for the procedure and the time, effort, and equipment necessary to provide the service.

When an FI receives a claim with an unlisted procedure code, it reviews it to verify that there is no existing code that adequately describes the procedure. If it determines that an adequately descriptive code is contained in HCPCS, it advises the hospital of the proper code and processes the claim. If it determines that no existing code is sufficiently descriptive, it pays the claim using the unlisted procedure code. If the frequency of the procedure warrants assignment of a local code, the FI forwards a copy and the operative report to the RO HCPCS coordinator for a code determination. When it receives a determination, the FI informs the hospital of the correct code for future reporting. Local codes are not accepted under OPPS and line items for local codes are no longer paid on cost.

NOTE:If the claim is submitted via EMC or identified after the bill has been processed, an operative report, the provider number, revenue codes, and charges are sufficient.

The "Unlisted Procedures" and codes for surgery are:

HCPCS code	Unlisted Procedure
15999	Unlisted procedure, excision pressure ulcer
17999	Unlisted procedure, skin, mucous membrane and subcutaneous tissue
19499	Unlisted procedure, breast
20999	Unlisted procedure, musculoskeletal system, general
21299	Unlisted craniofacial and maxillofacial procedures
21499	Unlisted orthopedic procedure, head
21899	Unlisted procedure, neck or thorax
22899	Unlisted procedure, spine
22999	Unlisted procedure, abdomen, musculoskeletal system
23929	Unlisted procedure, shoulder
24999	Unlisted procedure, humerus or elbow
25999	Unlisted procedure, forearm or wrist
26989	Unlisted procedure, hands or fingers
27299	Unlisted procedure, pelvis or hip joint
27599	Unlisted procedure, femur or knee
27899	Unlisted procedure, leg or ankle
28899	Unlisted procedure, foot or toes
29799	Unlisted procedure, casting or strapping
29909	Unlisted procedure, arthroscopy
30999	Unlisted procedure, nose
31299	Unlisted procedure, accessory sinuses
31599	Unlisted procedure, larynx
31899	Unlisted procedure, trachea, bronchi
32999	Unlisted procedure, lungs, and pleura
33999	Unlisted procedure, cardiac surgery
36299	Unlisted procedure, vascular injection
37799	Unlisted procedure, vascular surgery
38999	Unlisted procedure, hemic or lymphatic system
39499	Unlisted procedure, mediastinum
39599	Unlisted procedure, diaphragm
40799	Unlisted procedure, lips
40899	Unlisted procedure, vestibule of mouth
41599	Unlisted procedure, tongue, floor of mouth
41899	Unlisted procedure, dentoalveolar structures
42299	Unlisted procedure, palate, uvula
42699	Unlisted procedure, salivary glands or ducts
42999	Unlisted procedure, pharynx, adenoids, or tonsils
43499	Unlisted procedure, esophag
43999	Unlisted procedure, stomach
44799	Unlisted procedure, intestine
44899	Unlisted procedure, Meckel's diverticulum and the mesentery
45999	Unlisted procedure, rectum

HCPCS code	Unlisted Procedure
46999	Unlisted procedure, anus
47399	Unlisted procedure, liver
47999	Unlisted procedure, biliary tract
48999	Unlisted procedure, pancreas
49999	Unlisted procedure, abdomen, peritoneum, and omentum
53899	Unlisted procedure, urinary system
55899	Unlisted procedure, male genital system
56399	Unlisted procedure, laparoscopy, hysteroscopy
58999	Unlisted procedure, female genital system non-obstetrical
59899	Unlisted procedure, maternity care and delivery
60699	Unlisted procedure, endocrine system
64999	Unlisted procedure, nervous system
66999	Unlisted procedure, anterior segment of eye
67299	Unlisted procedure, posterior segment
67399	Unlisted procedure, ocular muscle
67599	Unlisted procedure, orbit
67999	Unlisted procedure, eyelids
68399	Unlisted procedure, conjunctiva
68899	Unlisted procedure, lacrimal system
69399	Unlisted procedure, external ear
69799	Unlisted procedure, middle ear
69949	Unlisted procedure, inner ear
69979	Unlisted procedure, temporal bone, middle fossa approach

100-4, 4, 200, 3.1

Billing for IMRT Planning and Delivery

Effective for services furnished on or after April 1, 2002, HCPCS codes G0174 (IMRT delivery) and G0178 (IMRT planning) are no longer valid codes. HCPCS code G0174 has been replaced with CPT codes 77418 and 0073T for IMRT delivery and HCPCS code G0178 with CPT code 77301. Therefore, hospitals must use CPT codes 77418 or 0073T for IMRT delivery and CPT code 77301 for IMRT planning. Any of the CPT codes 77401 through 77416 or 77418 may be reported on the same day as long as the services are furnished at separate treatment sessions. In these cases, modifier -59 must be appended to the appropriate codes. Additionally, in the context of billing 77301, regardless of the same or different dates of service, CPT codes 77014, 77280-77295, 77305-77321, 77331, 77336, and 77370 may only be billed in addition to 77301 if they are not provided as part of developing the IMRT treatment plan.

- 7730   Intensity modulated radiotherapy plan, including dose-volume histograms for target and critical structure partial tolerance specifications

- 77418   Intensity modulated treatment delivery, single or multiple fields/arcs, via narrow spatially and temporally modulated beams, binary, dynamic MLC, per treatment session

- 0073T   Compensator-based beam modulation treatment delivery of inverse planned treatment using three or more high resolution (milled or cast) compensator convergent beam modulated fields, per treatment session

100-4, 4, 200.3.2

Additional Billing Instructions for IMRT Planning

Payment for the services identified by CPT codes 77014, 77280-77295, 77305-77321, 77331, 77336, and 77370 is included in the APC payment for IMRT planning when these services are performed as part of developing an IMRT plan that is reported using CPT code 77301. Under those circumstances, these codes should not be billed in addition to CPT code 77301 for IMRT planning.

100-4, 4, 200.3.3

Billing for Multi-Source Photon (Cobalt 60-Based) Stereotactic

Radiosurgery (SRS) Planning and Delivery

Effective for services furnished on or after January 1, 2006, hospitals must bill for multisource photon (cobalt 60-based) SRS planning using existing CPT codes that most accurately describe the service furnished, and HCPCS code G0243 for the delivery. For CY 2007, HCPCS code G0243 is no longer be reportable under the hospital OPPS because the code has been deleted and replaced with CPT code 77371, effective January 1, 2007.

- 77371   Radiation treatment delivery, stereotactic radiosurgery (SRS) (complete course of treatment of cerebral lesion[s] consisting of 1 session); multisource Cobalt 60 based.

Payment for CPT code 20660 is included in CPT code 77371; therefore, hospitals should not report 20660 separately.

100-4, 4, 200.4

Billing for Amniotic Membrane

Hospitals should report HCPCS code V2790 (Amniotic membrane for surgical reconstruction, per procedure) to report amniotic membrane tissue when the tissue is used. A specific procedure code associated with use of amniotic membrane tissue is CPT code 65780 (Ocular surface reconstruction; amniotic membrane transplantation).

Payment for the amniotic membrane tissue is packaged into payment for CPT code 65780 or other procedures with which the amniotic membrane is used.

100-4, 4, 200.5

Billing and Payment for Cardiac Rehabilitation Services

The National Coverage Determination for cardiac rehabilitation programs requires that programs must be comprehensive and to be comprehensive they must include a medical evaluation, a program to modify cardiac risk factors (e.g., nutritional counseling), prescribed exercise, education, and counseling. See the National Coverage Determination (NCD) Manual, Pub. 100-03, section 20.10, for more information. A cardiac rehabilitation session may include more than one aspect of the comprehensive program. For CY 2008, hospitals will continue to use CPT code 93797 (Physician services for outpatient cardiac rehabilitation, without continuous ECG monitoring (per session)) and CPT code 93798 (Physician services for outpatient cardiac rehabilitation, with continuous ECG monitoring (per session)) to report cardiac rehabilitation services.

However, effective for dates of service on or after January 1, 2008, hospitals may report more than one unit of HCPCS code 93797 or 97398 for a date of service if more than one cardiac rehabilitation session lasting at least 1 hour each is provided on the same day.

In order to report more than one session for a given date of service, each session must last a minimum of 60 minutes. For example, if the cardiac rehabilitation services provided on a given day total 1 hour and 50 minutes, then only one session should be billed to report the cardiac rehabilitation services provided on that day.

100-4, 4, 200.6

Billing and Payment for Alcohol and/or Substance Abuse Assessment and Intervention Services

For CY 2008, the CPT Editorial Panel has created two new Category I CPT codes for reporting alcohol and/or substance abuse screening and intervention services. They are CPT code 99408 (Alcohol and/or substance (other than tobacco) abuse structured screening (e.g., AUDIT, DAST), and brief intervention (SBI) services; 15 to 30 minutes); and CPT code 99409 (Alcohol and/or substance (other than tobacco) abuse structured screening (e.g., AUDIT, DAST), and brief intervention (SBI) services; greater than 30 minutes). However, screening services are not covered by Medicare without specific statutory authority, such as has been provided for mammography, diabetes, and colorectal cancer screening. Therefore, beginning January 1, 2008, the OPPS recognizes two parallel G-codes (HCPCS codes G0396 and G0397) to allow for appropriate reporting and payment of alcohol and substance abuse structured assessment and intervention services that are not provided as screening services, but that are performed in the context of the diagnosis or treatment of illness or injury.

Contractors shall make payment under the OPPS for HCPCS code G0396 (Alcohol and/or substance (other than tobacco) abuse structured assessment (e.g., AUDIT, DAST) and brief intervention, 15 to 30 minutes) and HCPCS code G0397, (Alcohol and/or substance(other than tobacco) abuse structured assessment (e.g., AUDIT, DAST) and intervention greater than 30 minutes), only when reasonable and necessary (i.e., when the service is provided to evaluate patients with signs/symptoms of illness or injury) as per section 1862(a)(1)(A) of the Act.

HCPCS codes G0396 and G0397 are to be used for structured alcohol and/or substance (other than tobacco) abuse assessment and intervention services that are distinct from other clinic and emergency department visit services performed during the same encounter. Hospital resources expended performing services described by HCPCS codes G0396 and G0397 may not be counted as resources for determining the level of a visit service and vice versa (i.e., hospitals may not double count the same facility resources in order to reach a higher level clinic or emergency department visit). However, alcohol and/or substance structured assessment or intervention services lasting less than 15 minutes should not be reported using these HCPCS codes, but the hospital resources expended should be included in determining the level of the visit service reported.

100-4, 4, 200.7.1

Cardiac Echocardiography Without Contrast

Hospitals are instructed to bill for echocardiograms without contrast in accordance with the CPT code descriptors and guidelines associated with the applicable Level I CPT code(s) (93303-93350).

100-4, 4, 230.2

Coding and Payment for Drug Administration

A. Overview

Drug administration services furnished under the Hospital Outpatient Prospective Payment System (OPPS) during CY 2005 were reported using CPT codes 90780, 90781, and 96400-96459.

Effective January 1, 2006, some of these CPT codes were replaced with more detailed CPT codes incorporating specific procedural concepts, as defined and described by the CPT manual, such as initial, concurrent, and sequential.

Hospitals are instructed to use the full set of CPT codes, including those codes referencing concepts of initial, concurrent, and sequential, to bill for drug administration services furnished in the hospital outpatient department beginning January 1, 2007. In addition, hospitals are instructed to continue billing the HCPCS codes that most accurately describe the service(s) provided.

Hospitals are reminded to bill a separate Evaluation and Management code (with modifier 25) only if a significant, separately identifiable E/M service is performed in the same encounter with OPPS drug administration services.

B. Billing for Infusions and Injections

In CY 2007, hospitals are instructed to use the full set of drug administration CPT codes (90760-90779; 96401-96549) when billing for drug administration services provided in the hospital outpatient department. In addition, hospitals are to continue to bill HCPCS code C8957 (Intravenous infusion for therapy/diagnosis; initiation of prolonged infusion (more than 8 hours), requiring use of portable or implantable pump) when appropriate.

Hospitals are expected to report all drug administration CPT codes in a manner consistent with their descriptors, CPT instructions, and correct coding principles. Hospitals should note the conceptual changes between CY 2006 drug administration codes effective under the OPPS and the CY 2007 CPT codes in order to ensure accurate billing under the OPPS.

Medicare's general policy regarding physician supervision within hospital outpatient departments meets the physician supervision requirements for use of CPT codes 90760- 90779, 96401-96549. (Reference: Medicare Benefit Policy Manual, Pub.100-02, Chapter 6, Sec.20.4.1.)

C. Payments For Drug Administration Services

For CY 2007, OPPS drug administration APCs have been restructured resulting in a sixlevel hierarchy where active HCPCS codes have been assigned according to their clinical coherence and resource use. Contrary to the CY 2006 payment structure that bundled payment for several instances of a type of service (non-chemotherapy, chemotherapy by infusion, non-infusion chemotherapy) into a per-encounter APC payment, the CY 2007 structure provides a separate APC payment for each reported unit of a separately payable HCPCS code.

Hospitals should note that the transition to the full set of CPT drug administration codes provides for conceptual differences when reporting, such as those noted below.

- In CY 2006, hospitals were instructed to bill for the first hour (and any additional hours) by each type of infusion service (non-chemotherapy, chemotherapy by infusion, non-infusion chemotherapy). In CY 2007, the first hour concept no longer exists. CY 2007 CPT codes allow for only one initial service per encounter, for each vascular access site, no matter how many types of infusion services are provided; however, hospitals will receive an APC payment for the initial service and separate APC payment(s) for additional hours of infusion or other drug administration services provided that are separately payable .

- In CY 2006, hospitals providing infusion services of different types (nonchemotherapy, chemotherapy by infusion, non-infusion chemotherapy) received payment for the associated per-encounter infusion APC even if these infusions occurred during the same time period. In CY 2007, CPT instructions allow reporting of only one initial drug administration service, including infusion services, per encounter for each distinct vascular access site, with other services through the same vascular access site being reported via the sequential, concurrent or additional hour codes.

(NOTE: This list provides a brief overview of a limited number of the conceptual changes between CY 2006 OPPS drug administration codes and CY 2007 OPPS drug administration codes - this list is not comprehensive and does not include all items hospitals will need to consider during this transition) For CY 2007 APC payment rates, refer to Addendum B on the CMS Web site at http://www.cms.hhs.gov/HospitalOutpatientPPS/.

D. Infusions Started Outside the Hospital

Hospitals may receive Medicare beneficiaries for outpatient services who are in the process of receiving an infusion at their time of arrival at the hospital (e.g. a patient who arrives via ambulance with an ongoing intravenous infusion initiated by paramedics during transport). Hospitals are reminded to bill for all services provided using the HCPCS code(s) that most accurately describe the service(s) they provided. This includes hospitals reporting an initial hour of infusion, even if the hospital did not initiate the infusion, and additional HCPCS codes for additional or sequential infusion services if needed.

100-4, 4, 231.4

Billing for Split Unit of Blood

HCPCS code P9011 was created to identify situations where one unit of blood or a blood product is split and some portion of the unit is transfused to one patient and the other portions are transfused to other patients or to the same patient at other times. When a patient receives a transfusion of a split unit of blood or blood product, OPPS providers should bill P9011 for the blood product transfused, as well as CPT 86985 (Splitting, blood products) for each splitting procedure performed to prepare the blood product for a specific patient.

Providers should bill split units of packed red cells and whole blood using Revenue Code 389 (Other blood), and should not use Revenue Codes 381 (Packed red cells) or 382 (Whole blood). Providers should bill split units of other blood products using the applicable revenue codes for the blood product type, such as 383 (Plasma) or 384 (Platelets), rather than 389. Reporting revenue codes according to these specifications will ensure the Medicare beneficiary's blood deductible is applied correctly.

EXAMPLE: OPPS provider splits off a 100cc aliquot from a 250 cc unit of leukocytereduced red blood cells for a transfusion to Patient X. The hospital then splits off an 80cc aliquot of the remaining unit for a transfusion to Patient Y. At a later time, the remaining 70cc from the unit is transfused to Patient Z.

In billing for the services for Patient X and Patient Y, the OPPS provider should report the charges by billing P9011 and 86985 in addition to the CPT code for the transfusion service, because a specific splitting service was required to prepare a split unit for transfusion to each of those patients. However, the OPPS provider should report only P9011 and the CPT code for the transfusion service for Patient Z because no additional splitting was necessary to prepare the split unit for transfusion to Patient Z. The OPPS provider should bill Revenue Code 0389 for each split unit of the leukocyte-reduced red blood cells that was transfused.

100-4, 4, 231.9

Billing for Pheresis and Apheresis Services

Apheresis/pheresis services are billed on a per visit basis and not on a per unit basis. OPPS providers should report the charge for an Evaluation and Management (E&M) visit only if there is a separately identifiable E&M service performed which extends beyond the evaluation and management portion of a typical apheresis/pheresis service. If the OPPS provider is billing an E&M visit code in addition to the apheresis/pheresis service, it may be appropriate to use the HCPCS modifier -25.

100-4, 4, 240

Inpatient Part B Hospital Services

Inpatient Part B services which are paid under OPPS include:

- Diagnostic x-ray tests, and other diagnostic tests (excluding clinical diagnostic laboratory tests);

- X-ray, radium, and radioactive isotope therapy, including materials and services of technicians;

- Surgical dressings applied during an encounter at the hospital and splints, casts, and other devices used for reduction of fractures and dislocations (splints and casts, etc., include dental splints);

- Implantable prosthetic devices;

- Hepatitis B vaccine and its administration, and certain preventive screening services (pelvic exams, screening sigmoidoscopies, screening colonoscopies, bone mass measurements, and prostate screening.)

- Bone Mass measurements;

- Prostate screening;

- Immunosuppressive drugs;

- Oral anti-cancer drugs;

- Oral drug prescribed for use as an acute anti-emetic used as part of an anti-cancer chemotherapeutic regimen; and

- Epoetin Alfa (EPO)

NOTE: Payment for some of these services is packaged into the payment rate of other separately payable services.

Inpatient Part B services paid under other payment methods include:

- Clinical diagnostic laboratory tests, prosthetic devices other than implantable ones and other than dental which replace all or part of an internal body organ (including contiguous tissue), or all or part of the function of a permanently inoperative or malfunctioning internal body organ, including replacement or repairs of such devices;

- Leg, arm, back and neck braces; trusses and artificial legs; arms and eyes including adjustments, repairs, and replacements required because of breakage, wear, loss, or a change in the patient's physical condition; take home surgical dressings; outpatient physical therapy; outpatient occupational therapy; and outpatient speech-language pathology services;

- Ambulance services;

- Screening pap smears, screening colorectal tests, and screening mammography;

- Influenza virus vaccine and its administration, pneumococcal vaccine and its administration;

- Diabetes self-management;

- Hemophilia clotting factors for hemophilia patients competent to use these factors without supervision).

See Chapter 6 of the Medicare Benefit Policy Manual for a discussion of the circumstances under which the above services may be covered as Part B Inpatient services.

100-4, 4, 250.3.2

Physician Rendering Anesthesia in a Hospital Outpatient Setting

When a medically necessary anesthesia service is furnished within a HPSA area by a physician, a HPSA bonus is payable. In addition to using the PC/TC indicator on the CORF extract of the MPFS Summary File to identify HPSA services, pay physicians the HPSA bonus when CPT codes 00100 through 01999 are billed with the following modifiers: QY, QK, AA, or GC and "QB" or "QU" in revenue code 963. Modifier QB or QU must be submitted to receive payment of the HPSA bonus for claims with dates of service prior to January 01, 2006. Effective for claims with dates of service on or after January 01, 2006, the modifier AQ, physician providing a service in a health professional shortage area, may be required to receive the HPSA bonus. Refer to 250.2.2 of this chapter for more information on when modifier AQ is required.

The modifiers signify that a physician performed an anesthesia service. Using the Anesthesia File (See Section above) the physician service will be 115 percent times the payment amount to be paid to a CAH on Method II payment plus 10 percent HPSA bonus payment.

Anesthesiology modifiers:

AA	anesthesia services performed personally by anesthesiologist.
GC	service performed, in part, by a resident under the direction of a teaching physician.
QK	medical direction of two, three, or four concurrent anesthesia procedures involving qualified individuals.
QY	medical direction of one CRNA by an anesthesiologist.

Modifiers AA and GC result in physician payment at 80% of the allowed amount. Modifiers QK and QY result in physician payment at 50% of the allowed amount.

Data elements needed to calculate payment:

- HCPCS plus Modifier,
- Base Units,
- Time units, based on standard 15 minute intervals,
- locality specific anesthesia Conversion factor, and
- Allowed amount minus applicable deductions and coinsurance amount.

Formula 1: Calculate payment for a physician performing anesthesia alone

HCPCS = xxxxx

Modifier = AA

Base Units = 4

Anesthesia Time is 60 minutes. Anesthesia time units = 4 (60/15)

Sum of Base Units plus Time Units = 4 + 4 = 8

Locality specific Anesthesia conversion factor = $17.00 (varies by localities)

Coinsurance = 20%

Example 1: Physician personally performs the anesthesia case

Base Units plus time units - 4+4=8

Total units multiplied by the anesthesia conversion factor times .80

8 x $17= ($136.00 - (deductible*) x .80 = $108.80

Payment amount times 115 percent for the CAH method II payment.

$108.80 x 1.15 = $125.12 (Payment amount)

$125.12 x .10 = $12.51 (HPSA bonus payment)

*Assume the Part B deductible has already been met for the calendar year

Formula 2: Calculate the payment for the physician's medical direction service when the physician directs two concurrent cases involving CRNAs. The medical direction allowance is 50% of the allowance for the anesthesia service personally performed by the physician.

HCPCS = xxxxx

Modifier = QK

Base Units = 4

Time Units 60/15=4

Sum of base units plus time units = 8

Locality specific anesthesia conversion factor = $17(varies by localities)

Coinsurance = 20 %

(Allowed amount adjusted for applicable deductions and coinsurance and to reflect payment percentage for medical direction).

Example 2: Physician medically directs two concurrent cases involving CRNAs

Base units plus time - 4+4=8

Total units multiplied by the anesthesia conversion factor times. 50 equal allowed amount minus any remaining deductible

8 x $17 = $136 x .50 = $68.00 -(deductible*) = $68.00

Allowed amount Times 80 percent times 1.15

$68.00 x .80 = $54.40 x 1.15 = 62.56 (Payment amount)

$62.56 x .10 = $6.26 (HPSA bonus payment)

*Assume the deductible has already been met for the calendar year.

100-4, 4, 290.5.1

Billing and Payment for Observation Services Beginning January 1, 2008

Observation services are reported using HCPCS code G0378 (Hospital observation service, per hour). Beginning January 1, 2008, HCPCS code G0378 for hourly observation services is assigned status indicator N, signifying that its payment is always packaged. No separate payment is made for observation services reported with HCPCS code G0378, and APC 0339 is deleted as of January 1, 2008. In most circumstances, observation services are supportive and ancillary to the other services provided to a patient. In certain circumstances when observation care is billed in conjunction with a high level clinic visit (Level 5), high level emergency department visit (Level 4 or 5), critical care services, or direct admission as an integral part of a patient's extended encounter of care, payment may be made for the entire extended care encounter through one of two composite APCs when certain criteria are met. For information about payment for extended assessment and management composite APCs, see Sec.10.2.1 (Composite APCs) of this chapter.

APC 8002 (Level I Extended Assessment and Management Composite) describes an encounter for care provided to a patient that includes a high level (Level 5) clinic visit or direct admission to observation in conjunction with observation services of substantial duration (8 or more hours). APC 8003 (Level II Extended Assessment and Management Composite) describes an encounter for care provided to a patient that includes a high level (Level 4 or 5) emergency department visit or critical care services in conjunction with observation services of substantial duration. There is no limitation on diagnosis for payment of these composite APCs; however, composite APC payment will not be made when observation services are reported in association with a surgical procedure (T status procedure) or the hours of observation care reported are less than 8. The

I/OCE evaluates every claim received to determine if payment through a composite APC is appropriate. If payment through a composite APC is inappropriate, the I/OCE, in conjunction with the Pricer, determines the appropriate status indicator, APC, and payment for every code on a claim.

All of the following requirements must be met in order for a hospital to receive an APC payment for an extended assessment and management composite APC:

1. Observation Time
   a. Observation time must be documented in the medical record.
   b. A beneficiary's time in observation (and hospital billing) begins with the beneficiary's admission to an observation bed.
   c. A beneficiary's time in observation (and hospital billing) ends when all clinical or medical interventions have been completed, including follow-up care furnished by hospital staff and physicians that may take place after a physician has ordered the patient be released or admitted as an inpatient.
   d. The number of units reported with HCPCS code G0378 must equal or exceed 8 hours.
2. Additional Hospital Services
   a. The claim for observation services must include one of the following services in addition to the reported observation services. The additional services listed below must have a line item date of service on the same day or the day before the date reported for observation:
      - An emergency department visit (CPT code 99284 or 99285) or
      - A clinic visit (CPT code 99205 or 99215); or
      - Critical care (CPT code 99291); or
      - Direct admission to observation reported with HCPCS code G0379 (APC 0604) must be reported on the same date of service as the date reported for observation services.
   b. No procedure with a T status indicator can be reported on the same day or day before observation care is provided.
3. Physician Evaluation
   a. The beneficiary must be in the care of a physician during the period of observation, as documented in the medical record by admission, discharge, and other appropriate progress notes that are timed, written, and signed by the physician.
   b. The medical record must include documentation that the physician explicitly assessed patient risk to determine that the beneficiary would benefit from observation care.

Criteria 1 and 3 related to observation care beginning and ending time and physician evaluation apply regardless of whether the hospital believes that observation services will be packaged or will meet the criteria for extended assessment and management composite payment.

Only observation services that are billed on a 13X bill type may be considered for a composite APC payment.

Non-repetitive services provided on the same day as either direct admission to observation care or observation services must be reported on the same claim because the OCE claim-by-claim logic cannot function properly unless all services related to the episode of observation care, including hospital clinic visits, emergency department visits, critical care services, and T status procedures, are reported on the same claim.

Additional guidance can be found in Change Request 4047, Transmittal 763, issued on November 25, 2005.

If a claim for services providing during an extended assessment and management encounter including observation care does not meet all of the requirements listed above, then the usual APC logic will apply to separately payable items and services on the claim; the special logic for direct admission will apply, and payment for the observation care will be packaged into payments for other separately payable services provided to the beneficiary in the same encounter.

100-4, 4, 300

Medical Nutrition Therapy (MNT) Services

Section 105 of the Medicare, Medicaid, and SCHIP Benefits Improvement and Protection Act of 2000 (BIPA) permits Medicare coverage of Medical Nutrition Therapy (MNT) services when furnished by a registered dietitian or nutrition professional meeting certain requirements. The benefit is available for beneficiaries with diabetes or renal disease, when referral is made by a physician as defined in Sec.1861(r)(I) of the Act. It also allows registered dietitians and nutrition professionals to receive direct Medicare reimbursement for the first time. The effective date of this provision is January 1, 2002.

The benefit consists of an initial visit for an assessment; follow-up visits for interventions; and reassessments as necessary during the 12-month period beginning with the initial assessment ("episode of care") to assure compliance with the dietary plan. Effective October 1, 2002, basic coverage of MNT for the first year a beneficiary receives MNT with either a diagnosis of renal disease or diabetes as defined at 42 CFR, 410.130 is 3 hours. Also effective October 1, 2002, basic coverage in subsequent years for renal disease is 2 hours.

For the purposes of this benefit, renal disease means chronic renal insufficiency or the medical condition of a beneficiary who has been discharged from the hospital after a successful renal transplant within the last 6 months. Chronic renal insufficiency means a reduction in renal function not severe enough to require dialysis or transplantation (glomerular filtration rate (GFR) 13-50 ml/min/1.73m~ð). Effective January 1, 2004, CMS updated the definition of diabetes to be as follows: Diabetes is defined as diabetes mellitus, a condition of abnormal glucose metabolism diagnosed using the following criteria: a fasting blood sugar greater than or equal to 126 mg/dL on two different occasions; a 2 hour post-glucose challenge greater than or equal to 200 mg/dL on 2 different occasions; or a random glucose test over 200 mg/dL for a person with symptoms of uncontrolled diabetes.

The MNT benefit is a completely separate benefit from the diabetes self-management training (DSMT) benefit. CMS had originally planned to limit how much of both benefits a beneficiary might receive in the same time period. However, the national coverage decision, published May 1, 2002, allows a beneficiary to receive the full amount of both benefits in the same period. Therefore, a beneficiary can receive the full 10 hours of initial DSMT and the full 3 hours of MNT. However, providers are not allowed to bill for both DSMT and MNT on the same date of service for the same beneficiary

100-4, 5, 10

Part B Outpatient Rehabilitation and Comprehensive Outpatient Rehabilitation Facility (CORF) Services - General

Section 4541(a)(2) of the Balanced Budget Act (BBA) (P.L. 105-33), which added 1834(k)(5) to the Social Security Act (the Act), required that all claims for outpatient rehabilitation, certain audiology services and comprehensive outpatient rehabilitation facility (CORF) services, be reported using a uniform coding system. The CMS chose HCPCS (Healthcare Common Procedure Coding System) as the coding system to be used for the reporting of these services. This coding requirement is effective for all claims for outpatient rehabilitation services including certain audiology services and CORF services submitted on or after April 1, 1998.

The BBA also required payment under a prospective payment system for outpatient rehabilitation services including audiology and CORF services. Effective for claims with dates of service on or after January 1, 1999, the Medicare Physician Fee Schedule (MPFS) became the method of payment for outpatient physical therapy (which includes outpatient speech-language pathology) services furnished by:

- Comprehensive Outpatient Rehabilitation Facilities (CORFs);
- Outpatient Physical Therapy Providers (OPTs);
- Other Rehabilitation Facilities (ORFs);
- Hospitals (to outpatients and inpatients who are not in a covered Part A stay);
- Skilled Nursing Facilities (SNFs) (to residents not in a covered Part A stay and to nonresidents who receive outpatient rehabilitation services from the SNF); and
- Home Health Agencies (HHAs) (to individuals who are not homebound or otherwise are not receiving services under a home health plan of care (POC)).

The MPFS is used as a method of payment for outpatient rehabilitation services furnished under arrangement with any of these providers.

In addition, the MPFS is used as the payment system for audiology and CORF services identified by the HCPCS codes in 20 Assignment is mandatory.

The Medicare allowed charge for the services is the lower of the actual charge or the MPFS amount. The Medicare payment for the services is 80 percent of the allowed charge after the Part B deductible is met. Coinsurance is made at 20 percent of the lower of the actual charge or the MPFS amount. The general coinsurance rule (20 percent of the actual charges) does not apply when making payment under the MPFS. This is a final payment.

The MPFS does not apply to outpatient rehabilitation services furnished by critical access hospitals (CAHs). CAHs are to be paid on a reasonable cost basis.

Fiscal Intermediaries (FIs) process outpatient rehabilitation claims from hospitals, including CAHs, SNFs, CORFs, outpatient rehabilitation agencies, and outpatient physical therapy providers for which they have received a tie in notice from the RO.

Carriers process claims from physicians, certain nonphysician practitioners (NPPs), and physical and occupational therapists in private practice (PTPPs and OTPPs). A physician-directed clinic that bills for services furnished incident to a physician's service (see Chapter 15 in Pub. 100-02, Medicare Benefit Policy Manual for a definition of "incident to") bills the carrier.

There are different fee rates for nonfacility and facility services. Chapter 23 describes the differences in these two rates. (See fields 28 and 29 of the record therein described).

Facility rates apply to professional services performed in a facility other than the professional's office. Nonfacility rates apply when the service is performed in the professional's office. The nonfacility rate (that is paid when the provider performs the services in its own facility) accommodates overhead and indirect expenses the provider incurs by operating its own facility. Thus it is somewhat higher than the facility rate.

FIs pay the nonfacility rate for services performed in the provider's facility. Carriers may pay the facility or nonfacility rate depending upon where the service is performed (place of service on the claim), and the provider specialty.

Carriers pay the codes in 20 under the MPFS regardless of whether they may be considered rehabilitation services. However, FIs must use this list to determine whether to pay under outpatient rehabilitation rules or whether payment rules for other types of service may apply, e.g., OPPS for hospitals, reasonable costs for CAHs.

Note that because a service is considered an outpatient rehabilitation service does not automatically imply payment for that service. Additional criteria, including coverage, plan of care and physician certification must also be met. These criteria are described in Pub. 100-02, Medicare Benefit Policy Manual, Chapters 1 and 15.

Payment for rehabilitation services provided to Part A inpatients of hospitals or SNFs is included in the respective PPS rate. Also, for SNFs (but not hospitals), if the beneficiary has Part B, but not Part A coverage (e.g., Part A benefits are exhausted), the SNF must bill the FI for any rehabilitation service (except audiologic function services).

Independent audiologists may bill the carrier directly for services rendered to Part B Medicare entitled beneficiaries residing in a SNF, but not in a SNF Part A covered stay.

Payment is made based on the MPFS, whether by the carrier or the FI. For beneficiaries not in a covered Part A SNF stay, who are sometimes referred to as beneficiaries in a Part B SNF stay, audiologic function tests are payable under Part B when billed by the SNF as type of bill 22X, or when billed directly to the carrier by the provider or supplier of the service. For tests that include both a professional component and technical component, the SNF may elect to bill the technical component to the FI, but is not required to bill the service. (The professional component of a service is the direct patient care provided by the physician or audiologist, e.g., the interpretation of a test.) Payment for rehabilitation services provided by home health agencies under a home health plan of care is included in the home health PPS rate. HHAs may submit bill type 34X and be paid under the MPFS if there are no home health services billed under a home health plan of care at the same time, and there is a valid rehabilitation POC (e.g., the patient is not homebound).

An institutional employer (other than a SNF) of the PTPPs, OTPPs, or physician performing outpatient services, (e.g., hospital, CORF, etc.), or a clinic billing on behalf of the physician or therapist may bill the carrier on Form CMS-1500.

The MPFS is the basis of payment for outpatient rehabilitation services furnished by PTPPs and OTPPs, physicians, and certain nonphysician practitioners or for diagnostic tests provided incident to the services of such physicians or nonphysician practitioners.

(See Pub. 100-02, Medicare Benefit Policy Manual, Chapter 15, for a definition of "incident to.") Such services are billed to the Part B carrier. Assignment is mandatory.

The following table identifies the provider types or physician/nonphysician and to which contractor they may submit bills.

"Provider/Service" Type	Bill to	Bill Type	Comment
Inpatient hospital Part A	FI	11X	Included in PPS
Inpatient SNF Part A	FI	21X	Included in PPS
Inpatient hospital Part B	FI	12X	Hospital may obtain services under arrangements and bill, or rendering provider may bill.
Inpatient SNF Part B except for audiology function tests.	FI	22X	SNF must provide and bill, or obtain under arrangements and bill.
Inpatient SNF Part B audiology function tests only.	FI	22X	SNF may bill the FI or provider of service may bill the carrier.
Outpatient hospital	FI	13X	Hospital may provide and bill or obtain under arrangements and bill, or rendering provider may bill
Outpatient SNF	FI	23X	SNF must provide and bill or obtain under arrangements and "Provider/Service" Type Bill to Bill Type Comment bill
HHA billing for services rendered under a Part A or Part B home health plan of care.	FI	32X	Service is included in PPS rate. OMO determines whether payment is from Part A or Part B trust fund.
HHA billing for services not rendered under a Part A or Part B home health plan of care, but rendered under a therapy plan of care.	FI	34X	Service not under home health plan of care.
Other Rehabilitation Facility (ORF)	FI	74X	Paid MPFS for outpatient rehabilitation services effective January 1, 1999, and all other services except drugs effective July 1, 2000. Starting April 1, 2002, drugs are paid 95% of the AWP. For claims with dates of service on or after July 1, 2003, drugs and biologicals do not apply in an OPT setting. Therefore, FIs are to advise their OPTs not to bill for them.
Comprehensive Outpatient Rehabilitation Facility (CORF)	FI	75X	Paid MPFS for outpatient rehabilitation services effective January 1, 1999, and all other services except drugs effective July 1, 2000. Starting April 1, 2002, drugs are paid 95% of the AWP.
Physician, NPPs, PTPPs, OTPPs, and, for diagnostic tests only, audiologists (service in hospital or SNF)	Carrier	See Chapter 26 for place of service, and type of service coding.	Payment may not be made for therapy services to Part A inpatients of hospitals or SNFs, or for Part B SNF residents. Otherwise, carrier billing. Note that physician/ NPP/PTPP/OTPP employee of facility may assign benefits to the facility, enabling the facility to bill for physician/therapist to "Provider/Service" Type Bill to Bill Type Comment carrier

"Provider/Service" Type	Bill to	Bill Type	Comment
Physician/NPP/PTPP/OTPP office, independent clinic or patient's home	Carrier	See Chapter 26 for place of service, and type of service coding.	Paid via Physician fee schedule.
Practicing audiologist for services defined as diagnostic tests only	Carrier	See Chapter 26 for place of service, and type of service coding.	Some audiologists tests provided in hospitals are considered other diagnostic tests and are subject to HOPPS instead of MPFS for outpatient therapy fee schedule.
Critical Access Hospital - inpatient Part A	FI	85X	Rehabilitation services are paid cost.
Critical Access Hospital - inpatient Part B	FI	85X	Rehabilitation services are paid cost.
Critical Access Hospital - outpatient Part B	FI	85X	Rehabilitation services are paid cost.

Complete Claim form completion requirements are contained in Chapters 25 and 26.

For a list of the outpatient rehabilitation HCPCS codes see 20.

If an FI receives a claim for one of the these HCPCS codes with dates of service on or after July 1, 2003, that does not appear on the supplemental file it currently uses to pay the therapy claims, it contacts its local carrier to obtain the price in order to pay the claim.

When requesting the pricing data, it advises the carrier to provide it with the nonfacility fee.

NOTE:The list of codes in 20 contains commonly utilized codes for outpatient rehabilitation services. FIs may consider other codes for payment under the MPFS as outpatient rehabilitation services to the extent that such codes are determined to be medically reasonable and necessary and those that could be performed within the scope of practice of the therapist providing the service.

100-4, 5, 10.2

A. Financial Limitation Prior to the Balanced Budget Refinement Act (BBRA)

Section 4541(a)(2) of the Balanced Budget Act (BBA) (P.L. 105-33) of 1997, which added §1834(k)(5) to the Act, required payment under a prospective payment system for outpatient rehabilitation services (except those furnished by or under arrangements with a hospital). Outpatient rehabilitation services include the following services:

- Physical therapy (which includes outpatient speech-language pathology); and

- Occupational therapy.

Section 4541(c) of the BBA required application of a financial limitation to all outpatient rehabilitation services (except those furnished by or under arrangements with a hospital). In 1999, an annual per beneficiary limit of $1,500 applied to all outpatient physical therapy services (including speech-language pathology services). A separate limit applied to all occupational therapy services. The limit is based on incurred expenses and includes applicable deductible and coinsurance. The BBA provided that the limits be indexed by the Medicare Economic Index (MEI) each year beginning in 2002.

The limitation is based on therapy services the Medicare beneficiary receives, not the type of practitioner who provides the service. Physical therapists, speech-language pathologists, occupational therapists as well as physicians and certain nonphysician practitioners could render a therapy service.

As a transitional measure, effective in 1999, providers/suppliers were instructed to keep track of the allowed incurred expenses. This process was put in place to assure providers/suppliers did not bill Medicare for patients who exceeded the annual limitations for physical therapy, and for occupational therapy services rendered by individual providers/suppliers. In 2003 and later, the limitation was applied through CMS systems.

B. Moratoria and Exceptions for Therapy Claims

Section 221 of the BBRA of 1999 placed a 2-year moratorium on the application of the financial limitation for claims for therapy services with dates of service January 1, 2000, through December 31, 2001.

Section 421 of the Medicare, Medicaid, and SCHIP Benefits Improvement and Protection Act (BIPA) of 2000, extended the moratorium on application of the financial limitation to claims for outpatient rehabilitation services with dates of service January 1, 2002, through December 31, 2002. Therefore, the moratorium was for a 3-year period and applied to outpatient rehabilitation claims with dates of service January 1, 2000, through December 31, 2002.

=In 2003, there was not a moratorium on therapy caps. Implementation was delayed until September 1, 2003. Therapy caps were in effect for services rendered on September 1, 2003 through December 7, 2003.

Congress re-enacted a moratorium on financial limitations on outpatient therapy services on December 8, 2003 that extended through December 31, 2005. Caps were implemented again on January 1, 2006 and policies were modified to allow exceptions as directed by the Deficit Reduction Act of 2005 only for calendar year 2006. The Tax Relief and Health Care Act of 2006 extended the cap exceptions process through calendar year 2007. The Medicare, Medicaid, and SCHIP Extension Act of 2007 extended the cap exceptions process for services furnished through June 30, 2008.

Future exceptions. The cap exception for therapy services billed by outpatient hospitals was part of the original legislation and applies as long as caps are in effect. Exceptions to caps based on the medical necessity of the service are in effect only when Congress legislates the exceptions, as they did for 2007. References to the exceptions process in subsection C of this section apply only when the exceptions are in effect.

C. Application of Financial Limitations

Financial limitations on outpatient therapy services, as described above, began for therapy services rendered on or after on January 1, 2006. See C 1 to C 7 of this section when exceptions to therapy caps apply. The limits were $1740 in 2006 and $1780 in 2007. For 2008, the annual limit on the allowed amount for outpatient physical therapy and speech-language pathology combined is $1810; the limit for occupational therapy is $1810. Limits apply to outpatient Part B therapy services from all settings except outpatient hospital (place of service code 22 on carrier claims) and hospital emergency room (place of service code 23 on carrier claims). These excluded hospital services are reported on types of bill 12x or 13x on intermediary claims.

Contractors apply the financial limitations to the Medicare Physician Fee Schedule (MPFS) amount (or the amount charged if it is smaller) for therapy services for each beneficiary.

As with any Medicare payment, beneficiaries pay the coinsurance (20 percent) and any deductible that may apply. Medicare will pay the remaining 80 percent of the limit after the deductible is met. These amounts will change each calendar year. Medicare Contractors shall publish the financial limitation amount in educational articles. It is also available at 1-800-Medicare.

Medicare shall apply these financial limitations in order, according to the dates when the claims were received. When limitations apply, the Common Working File (CWF) tracks the limits. Shared System Maintainers are not responsible for tracking the dollar amounts of incurred expenses of rehabilitation services for each therapy limit.

In processing claims where Medicare is the secondary payer, the shared system takes the lowest secondary payment amount from MSPPAY and sends this amount on to CWF as the amount applied to therapy limits.

1. Exceptions to Therapy Caps - General
   The Tax Relief and Health Care Act of 2006 directed CMS to extend a process to allow for exceptions to the caps for services received in CY2007 in cases where continued therapy services are medically necessary. The following policies concerning exceptions to caps due to medical necessity apply only when the exceptions process is in effect. With the exception of the use of the KX modifier, the guidance in this section concerning medical necessity applies as well to services provided before caps are reached.

   Instructions for contractors to manage automatic process for exceptions will be found in the Program Integrity Manual, chapter 3, section 3.4.1.2. Provider and supplier information concerning exceptions is in this manual and in IOM Pub. 100-02, chapter 15, section 220.3. Exceptions shall be identified by a modifier on the claim and supported by documentation.

   Since the providers and suppliers will take an active role in obtaining an exception for a beneficiary, this manual section is written to address them as well as Medicare contractors.

   The beneficiary may qualify for use of the cap exceptions at any time during the episode when documented medically necessary services exceed caps. All covered and medically necessary services qualify for exceptions to caps.

   In 2006, the Exception Processes fell into two categories, Automatic Process Exceptions, and Manual Process Exceptions. Beginning January 1, 2007, there is no manual process for exceptions. All services that require exceptions to caps shall be processed using the automatic process. All requests for exception are in the form of a KX modifier added to claim lines. (See subsection C6 for use of the KX modifier.)

   Use of the automatic process for exceptions increases the responsibility of the provider/supplier for determining and documenting that services are appropriate.

   Also, use of the automatic process for exception does not exempt services from manual or other medical review processes as described in 100-08, Chapter 3, Section 3.4.1.1.1. Rather, atypical use of the automatic exception process may invite contractor scrutiny. Particular care should be taken to document improvement and avoid billing for services that do not meet the requirements for skilled services, or for services which are maintenance rather than rehabilitative treatment (See Pub. 100-02, chapter 15, sections 220.2, 220.3, and 230).

   The KX modifier, described in subsection C6, is added to claim lines to indicate that the clinician attests that services are medically necessary and justification is documented in the medical record.

2. Automatic Process Exceptions
   The term "automatic process exceptions" indicates that the claims processing for the exception is automatic, and not that the exception is automatic. An exception may be made when the patient's condition is justified by documentation indicating that the beneficiary requires continued skilled therapy, i.e., therapy beyond the amount payable under the therapy cap, to achieve their prior functional status or maximum expected functional status within a reasonable amount of time.

   No special documentation is submitted to the contractor for automatic process exceptions. The clinician is responsible for consulting guidance in the Medicare manuals and in the professional literature to determine if the beneficiary may qualify for the automatic process exception when documentation justifies medically necessary services above the caps. The clinician's opinion is not binding on the Medicare contractor who makes the final determination concerning whether the claim is payable.

   Documentation justifying the services shall be submitted in response to any Additional Documentation Request (ADR) for claims that are selected for medical review. Follow the documentation requirements in Pub. 100-02, chapter 15, section 220.3. If medical records are requested for review, clinicians may include, at their discretion, a summary that specifically addresses the justification for therapy cap exception.

In making a decision about whether to utilize the automatic process exception, clinicians shall consider, for example, whether services are appropriate to--

- The patient's condition including the diagnosis, complexities and severity (A list of the excepted evaluation codes are in C.2.a. A list of the ICD-9 codes for conditions and complexities that might qualify a beneficiary for exception to caps is in 10.2 C3. The list is a guideline and neither assures that services on the list will be excepted nor limits provision of covered and medically necessary services for conditions not on the list);

- The services provided including their type, frequency and duration;

- The interaction of current active conditions and complexities that directly and significantly influence the treatment such that it causes services to exceed caps.

In addition, the following should be considered before using the automatic exception process:

a. Exceptions for Services

Evaluation. The CMS will except therapy evaluations from caps after the therapy caps are reached when evaluation is necessary, e.g., to determine if the current status of the beneficiary requires therapy services. For example, the following evaluation procedures may be appropriate:

92506, 92597, 92607, 92608, 92610, 92611, 92612, 92614, 92616, 96105, 97001, 97002, 97003, 97004.

These codes will continue to be reported as outpatient therapy procedures as described in the Claims Processing Manual, Chapter 5, Section 20(B) "Applicable Outpatient Rehabilitation HCPCS Codes." They are not diagnostic tests. Definition of evaluations and documentation is found in Pub 100-02, sections 220 and 230.

Other Services. There are a number of sources that suggest the amount of certain services that may be typical, either per service, per episode, per condition, or per discipline. For example, see the CSC- Utilization and Edit Report, 2006, Appendices at www.cms.hhs.gov/TherapyServices (Studies and Reports). Professional literature and guidelines from professional associations also provide a basis on which to estimate whether the type, frequency and intensity of services are appropriate to an individual. Clinicians and contractors should utilize available evidence related to the patient's condition to justify provision of medically necessary services to individual beneficiaries, especially when they exceed caps. Contractors shall not limit medically necessary services that are justified by scientific research applicable to the beneficiary. Neither contractors nor clinicians shall utilize professional literature and scientific reports to justify payment for continued services after an individual's goals have been met earlier than is typical. Conversely, professional literature and scientific reports shall not be used as justification to deny payment to patients whose needs are greater than is typical or when the patient's condition is not represented by the literature.

b. Exceptions for Conditions or Complexities Identified by ICD-9 codes.

Clinicians may utilize the automatic process for exception for any diagnosis for which they can justify services exceeding the cap. Based upon analysis of claims data, research and evidence based practice guidelines, CMS has identified conditions and complexities represented by ICD-9 codes that may be more likely than others to require therapy services that exceed therapy caps. This list appears in 10.2 C3. Clinicians may use the automatic process of exception for beneficiaries who do not have a condition or complexity on this list when they justify the provision of therapy services that exceed caps for that patient's condition.

NOT ALL patients who have a condition or complexity on the list are "automatically" excepted from therapy caps. See Pub. 100-02, chapter 15, section 230.3 for documenting the patient's condition and complexities. Contractors may scrutinize claims from providers whose services exceed caps more frequently than is typical.

Regardless of the condition, the patient must also meet other requirements for coverage. For example, the patient must require skilled treatment for a covered, medically necessary service; the services must be appropriate in type, frequency and duration for the patient's condition and service must be documented appropriately. Guidelines for utilization of therapy services may be found in Medicare manuals, Local Coverage Determinations of Medicare contractors, and professional guidelines issued by associations and states.

Bill the most relevant diagnosis. As always, when billing for therapy services, the ICD-9 code that best relates to the reason for the treatment shall be on the claim, unless there is a compelling reason. For example, when a patient with diabetes is being treated for gait training due to amputation, the preferred diagnosis is abnormality of gait (which characterizes the treatment). Where it is possible in accordance with State and local laws and the contractors Local Coverage Determinations, avoid using vague or general diagnoses. When a claim includes several types of services, or where the physician/NPP must supply the diagnosis, it may not be possible to use the most relevant therapy code in the primary position. In that case, the relevant code should, if possible, be on the claim in another position.

Codes representing the medical condition that caused the treatment are used when there is no code representing the treatment. Complicating conditions are preferably used in non-primary positions on the claim and are billed in the primary position only in the rare circumstance that there is no more relevant code.

The condition or complexity that caused treatment to exceed caps must be related to the therapy goals and must either be the condition that is being treated or a complexity that directly and significantly impacts the rate of recovery of the condition being treated such that it is appropriate to exceed the caps. Codes marked as complexities represented by ICD-9 codes on the list below are unlikely to require therapy services that would exceed the caps unless they occur in a patient who also has another condition (either listed or not listed). Therefore, documentation for an exception should indicate how the complexity (or combination of complexities) directly and significantly affects treatment

for a therapy condition. For example, if the condition underlying the reason for therapy is V43.64, hip replacement, the treatment may have a goal to ambulate 60' with stand-by assistance and a KX modifier may be appropriate for gait training (assuming the severity of the patient is such that the services exceed the cap). Alternatively, it would not be appropriate to use the KX modifier for a patient who recovered from hip replacement last year and is being treated this year for a sprain of a severity which does not justify extensive therapy exceeding caps.

3. ICD-9 Codes That are Likely to Qualify for the Automatic Process Therapy Cap Exception Based Upon Clinical Condition or Complexity

When using this table, refer to the ICD-9 code book for coding instructions. Some contractors' Local Coverage Determinations do not allow the use of some of the codes on this list in the primary diagnosis position on a claim. If the contractor has determined that these codes do not characterize patients who require medically necessary services, providers/suppliers may not use these codes, but must utilize a billable diagnosis code allowed by their contractor to describe the patient's condition. Contractors shall not apply therapy caps to services based on the patient's condition, but only on the medical necessity of the service for the condition. If a service is payable before the cap is reached and is still medically necessary after the cap is reached, that service is excepted. Providers/suppliers may use the automatic process for exception for medically necessary services when the patient has a billable condition that is not on the list below. The diagnosis on the list below may be put in a secondary position on the claim and/or in the medical records, as the contractor directs.

When two codes are listed in the left cell in a row, all the codes between them are also eligible for exception. If one code is in the cell, only that one code is likely to qualify for exception. The descriptions in the table are not always identical to those in the ICD-9 code book, but may be summaries. Contact your contractor for interpretation if you are not sure that a condition or complexity is applicable for automatic process exception.

It is very important to recognize that most of the conditions on this list would not ordinarily result in services exceeding the cap. Use the KX modifier only in cases where the condition of the individual patient is such that services are APPROPRIATELY provided in an episode that exceeds the cap. In most cases, the severity of the condition, comorbidities, or complexities will contribute to the necessity of services exceeding the cap, and these should be documented. Routine use of the KX modifier for all patients with these conditions will likely show up on data analysis as aberrant and invite inquiry. Be sure that documentation is sufficiently detailed to support the use of the modifier.

The following ICD-9 codes describe the conditions (etiology or underlying medical conditions) that may result in excepted conditions (marked X) and complexities (marked *) that MIGHT cause medically necessary therapy services to qualify for the automatic process exception for each discipline separately. When the field corresponding to the therapy discipline treating and the diagnosis code is marked with a dash (Äì) services by that discipline are not appropriate for that diagnosis and, therefore, services do not qualify for exception to caps.

These codes are grouped only to facilitate reference to them. The codes may be used only when the code is applicable to the condition being actively treated. For example, an exception should not be claimed for a diagnosis of hip replacement when the service provided is for an unrelated dysphagia.

ICD-9 Cluster	ICD-9 (Cluster) Description	PT	OT	SLP
V43.61-V43.69	Joint Replacement	X	X	--
V45.4	Arthrodesis Status	*	*	--
V45.81-V45.82 and V45.89	Other Postprocedural Status	*	*	--
V49-61-V49.67	Upper Limb Amputation Status	X	X	--
V49.71-V49.77	Lower Limb Amputation Status	X	X	--
V54.10-V54.29	Aftercare for Healing Traumatic or Pathologic Fracture	X	X	--
V58.71-V58.78	Aftercare Following Surgery to Specified Body Systems, Not Elsewhere Classified	*	*	*
244.0-244.9	Acquired Hypothyroidism	*	*	*
250.00-251.9	Diabetes Mellitus and Other Disorders of Pancreatic Internal Secretion	*	*	*
276.0-276.9	Disorders of Fluid, Electrolyte, and Acid-Base Balance	*	*	*
278.00-278.01	Obesity and Morbid Obesity	*	*	*
280.0-289.9	Diseases of the blood and blood-forming organs	*	*	*
290.0-290.43	Dementias	*	*	*
294.0-294.9	Persistent Mental Disorders due to Conditions Classified Elsewhere	*	*	*
295.00-299.91	Other Psychoses	*	*	*
300.00-300.9	Anxiety, Disassociative and Somatoform Disorders	*	*	*
310.0-310.9	Specific Nonpsychotic Mental Disorders due to Brain Damage	*	*	*

Key
Automatic (only ICD-9 needed on claim) = X
Complexity (requires another ICD-9 on claim) = *
Does not serve as qualifying ICD-9 on claim = --

ICD-9 Cluster	ICD-9 (Cluster) Description	PT	OT	SLP
311	Depressive Disorder, Not Elsewhere Classified	*	*	*
315.00-315.9	Specific delays in Development	*	*	*
317	Mild Mental Retardation	*	*	*
320.0-326	Inflammatory Diseases of the Central Nervous System	*	*	*
330.0-337.9	Hereditary and Degenerative Diseases of the Central Nervous System	X	X	X
340-345.91 and 348.0-349.9	Other Disorders of the Central Nervous System	X	X	X
353.0-359.9	Disorders of the Peripheral Nervous system	X	X	--
365.00-365.9	Glaucoma	*	*	*
369.00-369.9	Blindness and Low Vision	*	*	*
386.00-386.9	Vertiginous Syndromes and Other Disorders of Vestibular System	*	*	*
389.00-389.9	Hearing Loss	*	*	*
401.0-405.99	Hypertensive Disease	*	*	*
410.00-414.9	Ischemic Heart Disease	*	*	*
415.0-417.9	Diseases of Pulmonary Circulation	*	*	*
420.0-429.9	Other Forms of Heart Disease	*	*	*
430-438.9	Cerebrovascular Disease	X	X	X
440.0-448.9	Diseases of Arteries, Arterioles, and Capillaries	*	*	*
451.0-453.9 and 456.0-459.9	Diseases of Veins and Lymphatics, and Other Diseases of Circulatory System	*	*	*
465.00-466.19	Acute Respiratory Infections	*	*	*
478.30-478.5	Paralysis, Polyps, or Other Diseases of Vocal Cords	*	*	*
480.0-486	Pneumonia	*	*	*
490-496	Chronic Obstructive Pulmonary Disease and Allied Conditions	*	*	*
507.0-507.8	Pneumonitis due to solids and liquids	*	*	*
510.0-519.9	Other Diseases of Respiratory System	*	*	*
560.0-560.9	Intestinal Obstruction Without Mention of Hernia	*	*	*
578.0-578.9	Gastrointestinal Hemorrhage	*	*	*
584.5-586	Renal Failure and Chronic Kidney Disease	*	*	*
590.00-599.9	Other Diseases of Urinary System	*	*	*
682.0-682.8	Other Cellulitis and Abscess	*	*	--
707.00-707.9	Chronic Ulcer of Skin	*	*	--
710.0-710.9	Diffuse Diseases of Connective Tissue	*	*	*
711.00-711.99	Arthropathy Associated with Infections	*	*	--
712.10-713.8	Crystal Arthropathies and Arthropathy Associated with Other Disorders Classified Elsewhere	*	*	--
714.0-714.9	Rheumatoid Arthritis and Other Inflammatory Polyarthropathies	*	*	--
715.00-715.98	Osteoarthrosis and Allied Disorders (Complexity except as listed below)	*	*	--
715.09	Osteoarthritis and allied disorders, multiple sites	X	X	--
715.11	Osteoarthritis, localized, primary, shoulder region	X	X	--
715.15	Osteoarthritis, localized, primary, pelvic region and thigh	X	X	--
715.16	Osteoarthritis, localized, primary, lower leg	X	X	--
715.91	Osteoarthritis, unspecified id gen. or local, shoulder	X	X	--
715.96	Osteoarthritis, unspecified if gen. or local, lower leg	X	X	--
716.00-716.99	Other and Unspecified Arthropathies	*	*	--
717.0-717.9	Internal Derangement of Knee	*	*	--

ICD-9 Cluster	ICD-9 (Cluster) Description	PT	OT	SLP
718.00-718.99	Other Derangement of Joint (Complexity except as listed below)	*	*	--
718.49	Contracture of Joint, Multiple Sites	X	X	--
719.00-719.99	Other and Unspecified Disorders of Joint (Complexity except as listed below)	*	*	--
719.7	Difficulty Walking	X	X	--
720.0-724.9	Dorsopathies	*	*	--
725-729.9	Rheumatism, Excluding Back (Complexity except as listed below)	*	*	--
726.10-726.19	Rotator Cuff Disorder and Allied Syndromes	X	X	--
727.61-727.62	Rupture of Tendon, Nontraumatic	X	X	--
730.00-739.9	Osteopathies, Chondropathies, and Acquired Musculoskeletal Deformities (Complexity except as listed below)	*	*	--
733.00	Osteoporosis	X	X	--
741.00-742.9 and 745.0-748.9 and 754.0-756.9	Congenital Anomalies	*	*	*
780.31-780.39	Convulsions	*	*	*
780.71-780.79	Malaise and Fatigue	*	*	*
780.93	Memory Loss	*	*	*
781.0-781.99	Symptoms Involving Nervous and Musculoskeletal System (Complexity except as listed below)	*	*	*
781.2	Abnormality of Gait	X	X	--
781.3	Lack of Coordination	X	X	-
783.0-783.9	Symptoms Concerning Nutrition, Metabolism, and Development	*	*	*
784.3-784.69	Aphasia, Voice and Other Speech Disturbance, Other Symbolic Dysfunction	*	*	X
785.4	Gangrene	*	*	--
786.00-786.9	Symptoms involving Respiratory System and Other Chest Symptoms	*	*	*
787.2	Dysphagia	*	*	X
800.00-828.1	Fractures (Complexity except as listed below)	*	*	--
806.00-806.9	Fracture of Vertebral Column With Spinal Cord Injury	X	X	--
810.11-810.13	Fracture of Clavicle	X	X	--
811.00-811.19	Fracture of Scapula	X	X	--
812.00-812.59	Fracture of Humerus	X	X	--
813.00-813.93	Fracture of Radius and Ulna	X	X	--
820.00-820.9	Fracture of Neck of Femur	X	X	--
821.00-821.39	Fracture of Other and Unspecified Parts of Femur	X	X	--
828.0-828.1	Multiple Fractures Involving Both Lower Limbs, Lower with Upper Limb, and Lower Limb(s) with Rib(s) and Sternum	X	X	--
830.0-839.9	Dislocations	X	X	--
840.0-848.8	Sprains and Strains of Joints and Adjacent Muscles	*	*	--
851.00-854.19	Intracranial Injury, excluding those With Skull Fracture	X	X	X
880.00-884.2	Open Wound of Upper Limb	*	*	--
885.0-887.7	Traumatic Amputation, Thumb(s), Finger(s), Arm and Hand (complete)(partial)	X	X	--
890.0-894.2	Open Wound Lower Limb	*	*	--
895.0-897.7	Traumatic Amputation, Toe(s), Foot/Feet, Leg(s) (complete)(partial)	X	X	--
905.0-905.9	Late Effects of Musculoskeletal and Connective Tissue Injuries	*	*	*
907.0-907.9	Late Effects of Injuries to the Nervous System	*	*	*

Key
Automatic (only ICD-9 needed on claim) = X
Complexity (requires another ICD-9 on claim) = *
Does not serve as qualifying ICD-9 on claim = --

Key
Automatic (only ICD-9 needed on claim) = X
Complexity (requires another ICD-9 on claim) = *
Does not serve as qualifying ICD-9 on claim = --

ICD-9 Cluster	ICD-9 (Cluster) Description	PT	OT	SLP
941.00-949.5	Burns	*	*	*
952.00-952.9	Spinal Cord Injury Without Evidence of Spinal Bone Injury	X	X	X
953.0-953.8	Injury to Nerve Roots and Spinal Plexus	X	X	*
959.01	Head Injury, Unspecified	X	X	X

Key

Automatic (only ICD-9 needed on claim) = X
Complexity (requires another ICD-9 on claim) = *
Does not serve as qualifying ICD-9 on claim = --

4. Additional Considerations for Exceptions

In justifying exceptions for therapy caps, clinicians and contractors should not only consider the medical diagnoses and medical complications that might directly and significantly influence the amount of treatment required. Other variables (such as the availability of a caregiver at home) that affect appropriate treatment shall also be considered. Factors that influence the need for treatment should be supportable by published research, clinical guidelines from professional sources, and/or clinical/common sense. See Pub. 100-02, chapter 15, section 230.3 subsections related to documentation of the evaluation, and section 220.2 medical necessity for some factors that complicate treatment.

Note that the patient's lack of access to outpatient hospital therapy services alone does not justify excepted services. Residents of skilled nursing facilities prevented by consolidated billing from accessing hospital services, debilitated patients for whom transportation to the hospital is a physical hardship or lack of therapy services at hospitals in the beneficiary's county may or may not qualify for continued services above the caps. The patient's condition and complexities might justify extended services, but their location does not.

5. Appeals Related to Disapproval of Cap Exceptions

Disapproval of Exception from Caps. The DRA allows that certain services that would not be covered due to caps, but are medically necessary, may be covered if they meet certain criteria. Therefore, when a service beyond the cap is determined to be medically necessary, it is covered and payable. But, when a service provided beyond the cap (outside the benefit) is determined to be NOT medically necessary, it is denied as a benefit category denial. Contractors may review claims with KX modifiers to determine whether the services are medically necessary, or for other reasons. Services that exceed therapy caps but do not meet Medicare criteria for medically necessary services are not payable even when clinicians recommend and furnish and these services.

Services without a Medicare benefit may be billed to Medicare with a GY modifier for the purpose of obtaining a denial that can be used with other insurers. See CMS IOM Pub. 100-04 Chapter 1, Section 60 for appropriate use of modifiers.

APPEALS –If a beneficiary whose excepted services do not meet the Medicare criteria for medical necessity elects to receive such services and a claim is submitted for such services, the resulting determination would be subject to the administrative appeals process. Further details concerning appeals are found in CMS IOM Pub. 100-04, chapter 29.

6. Use of the KX Modifier for Therapy Cap Exceptions

When exceptions are in effect and when the beneficiary qualifies for a therapy cap exception, the provider shall add a KX modifier to the therapy HCPCS subject to the cap limits The KX modifier shall not be added to any line of service that is not a medically necessary service; this applies to services that, according to a Local Coverage Determination by the contractor, are not medically necessary services.

The codes subject to the therapy cap tracking requirements are listed in a table in the Claims Processing Manual, Pub. 100-04, chapter 5, section 20(D), "Applicable Outpatient Rehabilitation HCPCS Codes."

The GN, GO, or GP therapy modifiers are currently required. In addition to the KX modifier, the GN, GP and GO modifiers shall continue to be used. Providers may report the modifiers on claims in any order. If there is insufficient room on a claim line for multiple modifiers, additional modifiers may be reported in the remarks field. Follow the routine procedure for placing HCPCS modifiers on a claim as described below.

- For professional claims, sent to the carrier, refer to:

  - Pub.100-04 Medicare Claims Processing Manual, Chapter 26, for more detail regarding completing the CMS- Form 1500 claim form, including the placement of HCPCS modifiers. Note that the CMS-Form1500 claim form currently has space for providing two modifiers in block 24D, but, if you have more than two to report, you can do so by placing the -99 modifier (which indicates multiple modifiers) in block 24D and placing the additional modifiers in block 19.

You may access the Medicare Claims Processing Manual at this web address http://www.cms.hhs.gov/Manuals/

From this site, click the links to Internet-Only Manuals (IOMs), then Pub. 100-04 to reach the Medicare Claims Processing Manual.

- The ASC X12N 837 Health Care Claim: Professional Implementation Guide, Version 4010A1, for more detail regarding how to electronically submit a health care claim transaction, including the placement of HCPCS modifiers. The ASC X12N 837 implementation guides are the standards adopted under the Health Insurance Portability and Accountability Act of 1996 (HIPAA) for submitting health care claims electronically. The 837 professional transaction currently permits the placement of up to four modifiers, in the 2400 loop, SV1 segment, data elements SV101-3, SV101-4, SV101-5, and SV101-6. You may obtain copies of the ASC X12N 837 implementation guides from the Washington Publishing Company.

- For claims paid to carriers, it is only appropriate to use a KX for a service that reasonably may exceed the cap. Use of the KX modifier when there is no indication that the cap is likely to be exceeded is abusive. For example, use of the KX modifier for low cost services early in an episode when there is no evidence of a previous episode that might have exceeded the cap is inappropriate.

  - For institutional claims, sent to the FI:

    - When the cap is exceeded by at least one line on the claim, use the KX modifier on all of the lines on that institutional claim that refer to the same therapy cap (PT/SLP or, OT,) regardless of whether the other services exceed the cap. For example, if one PT service line exceeds the cap, use the KX on all the PT and SLP service lines (also identified with the GP or GN modifier) for that claim. (When the PT/SLP cap is exceeded by PT services, the SLP lines on the claim may meet the requirements for an exception due to the complexity of two episodes of service. Use the KX on either all or none of the SLP lines on the claim, as appropriate.) In contrast, if all the OT lines on the claim are below the cap, do not use the KX modifier on any of the OT lines, even when the KX is appropriately used on all of the PT lines.

    - Refer to Pub.100-04 Medicare Claims Processing Manual, Chapter 25, for more detail regarding completing the CMS- Form 1450 claim form, including the placement of HCPCS modifiers.

You may access the Medicare Claims Processing Manual at this web address http://www.cms.hhs.gov/Manuals/. From this site, click the links to Internet-Only Manuals (IOMs), then Pub. 100-04 to reach the Medicare Claims Processing Manual.

- By attaching the KX modifier, the provider is attesting that the services billed:

  - Are reasonable and necessary services that require the skills of a therapist; (See CMS Pub. 100-02, chapter 15, section 220.2 B); and

  - Are justified by appropriate documentation in the medical record, (See CMS Pub. 100-02, chapter 15, section 220.3); and

  - Qualify for an exception using the automatic process exception.

If this attestation is determined to be inaccurate, the provider/supplier is subject to sanctions resulting from providing inaccurate information on a claim.

- When the KX modifier is attached to a therapy HCPCS, the contractor will override the CWF system reject for services that exceed the caps and pay the claim if it is otherwise payable.

- Providers and suppliers shall continue to attach correct coding initiative (CCI) HCPCS modifiers under current instructions.

- If a claim is submitted without KX modifiers and the cap is exceeded, those services will be denied. In cases where the KX would have been appropriate, contractors may reopen and/or adjust the claim, if it is brought to their attention.

- Services billed after the cap has been exceeded which are not eligible for exceptions may be billed for the purpose of obtaining a denial using condition code 21.

D. MSN Messages

Existing MSN message 38.18 shall continue to appear on all Medicare MSN forms. It has been updated to the following:

- ALERT. Coverage by Medicare is limited to $1,780 in 2007 and $1,810 in 2008 for outpatient physical therapy and speech-language pathology combined. Occupational therapy services have the same limits. Medicare pays up to 80 percent of the limits after the deductible has been met. Exceptions to these limits apply to therapy billed by hospital outpatient departments and may also apply to medically necessary services.

Existing MSN messages 17.13, 17.18 and 17.19 shall be issued on all claims containing outpatient rehabilitation services as noted in this manual. Add applied amount for individual beneficiaries and the generic limit amount (e.g., $1740 in 2006, $1780 in 2007, and $1810 in 2008) to all MSN that require them.

- 17.13 - Medicare approves a limited dollar amount each year for physical therapy and speech-language pathology services and a separate limit each year for occupational therapy services when billed by providers, physical and occupational therapists, physicians, and other non-physician practitioners. Medically necessary therapy over these limits is covered when received at a hospital outpatient department or when approved by Medicare.

- 17.18 - ($) has been applied during this calendar year (CCYY) towards the ($) limit on outpatient physical therapy and speech-language pathology benefits.

- 17.19 ($) has been applied during this calendar year (CCYY) towards the ($) limit on outpatient occupational therapy benefits.

Carriers and intermediaries shall use the existing Medicare Summary Notice message 17.6 to inform the beneficiaries that they have reached the financial limitation. Apply this message at the line level:

- 17.6 - Full payment was not made for this service because the yearly limit has been met.

E. FI Requirements

1. General Requirements

Regardless of financial limits on therapy services, CMS requires modifiers (See Sec. 20.1 of this chapter) on specific codes for the purpose of data analysis. Edit to ensure that the therapy modifiers are present on a claim based on the presence of revenue codes 042X, 043X, or 044X. Claims containing revenue codes 042X, 043X, or 044X without a therapy modifier GN, GP, or GO should be returned to the provider.

Beneficiaries may not be simultaneously covered by Medicare as an outpatient of a hospital and as a patient in another facility. They must be discharged from the other setting and registered as a hospital outpatient in order to receive payment for outpatient rehabilitation services in a hospital outpatient setting after the limitation has been reached.

A hospital may bill for services of a facility as hospital outpatient services if that facility meets the requirements of a department of the provider (hospital) under 42 CFR 413.65. Facilities that do not meet those requirements are not considered to be part of the hospital and may not bill under the hospital's provider number, even if they are owned by the hospital. For example, services of a Comprehensive Outpatient Rehabilitation Facility (CORF) must be billed as CORF services and not a hospital outpatient services, even if the CORF is owned by the hospital. Only services billed by the hospital as bill type 12X or 13X are exempt from limitations on therapy services.

2. When Financial Limits Are in Effect
    The CWF applies the financial limitation to the following bill types 22X, 23X, 34X, 74X and 75X using the MPFS allowed amount (before adjustment for beneficiary liability).

    For SNFs, the financial limitation does apply to rehabilitation services furnished to those SNF residents in noncovered stays (bill type 22X) who are in a Medicare-certified section of the facility—i.e., one that is either certified by Medicare alone, or is dually certified (by Medicare as a SNF and by Medicaid as a nursing facility (NF). For SNF residents, consolidated billing requires all outpatient rehabilitation services be billed to Part B by the SNF. If a resident has reached the financial limitation, and remains in the Medicarecertified section of the SNF, no further payment will be made to the SNF or any other entity. Therefore, SNF residents who are subject to consolidated billing may not obtain services from an outpatient hospital after the cap has been exceeded.

    Once the financial limitation has been reached, SNF residents who are in a **non- Medicare certified** section of the facility—i.e., one that is certified only by Medicaid as a NF or that is not certified at all by either program—FIs use bill type 23X. For SNF residents in non-Medicare certified portions of the facility and SNF nonresidents who go to the SNF for outpatient treatment (bill type 23X), medically necessary outpatient therapy may be covered at an outpatient hospital facility after the financial limitation has been exceeded.

    Limitations do not apply for SNF residents in a covered Part A stay, including swing beds. Rehabilitation services are included within the global Part A per diem payment that the SNF receives under the PPS for the covered stay. Also, limitations do not apply to any therapy services billed under PPS Home Health, or inpatient hospitals including critical access hospitals.

F. Carrier Requirements when Financial Limits are in Effect
Claims containing any of the "Applicable Outpatient Rehabilitation HCPCS Codes" in section 20 below marked "always therapy" (underlined) codes should contain one of the therapy modifiers (GN, GO, GP). All claims submitted for codes underlined but without a therapy modifier shall be returned as unprocessable.

When any code on the list of "Applicable Outpatient Rehabilitation HCPCS Codes" codes are submitted with specialty codes "65" (physical therapist in private practice), and "67" (occupational therapist in private practice), they always represent therapy services, because they are provided by therapists. Carriers shall return claims for these services when they do not contain therapy modifiers for the applicable HCPCS codes.

The "Applicable Outpatient Rehabilitation HCPCS Codes in section 20 of this chapter that are marked (+) are sometimes therapy codes. Claims from physicians (all specialty codes) and nonphysician practitioners, including specialty codes "50," "89," and "97" may be processed without therapy modifiers. On review of these claims, services that are not accompanied by a therapy modifier must be documented, reasonable and necessary, and payable as physician or nonphysician practitioner services, and not services that the contractor interprets as therapy services.

The CWF will capture the amount and apply it to the limitation whenever a service is billed using the GN, GO, or GP modifier, except when the place of service code is 22 (outpatient hospital) or 23 (emergency room-hospital). The CWF has disabled the edit involving specialty codes "65" and "67" and Type of Service W or U.

G. FI Action Based on CWF Trailer During the Time Therapy Limits are in Effect
Upon receipt of the CWF error code/trailer, FIs are responsible for assuring that payment does not exceed the financial limitations, when the limits are in effect, except as noted below.

In cases where a claim line partially exceeds the limit, the FI must adjust the line based on information contained in the CWF trailer. For example, where the MPFS allowed amount is greater than the financial limitation available, always report the MPFS allowed amount in the "Financial Limitation" field of the CWF record and include the CWF override code. See example below for situations where the claim contains multiple lines that exceed the limit.

EXAMPLE: Based on the 2007 limit of $1780 for a beneficiary who has paid the deductible and the coinsurance:

Services received to date $1765 ($15 under the limit)

Incoming claim: Line 1 MPFS allowed amount is $50.

Line 2 MPFS allowed amount is $25.

Line 3, MPFS allowed amount is $30.

Based on this example, lines 1 and 3 are denied and line 2 is paid. The FI reports in the "Financial Limitation" field of the CWF record "$25.00 along with the CWF override code. The FI always applies the amount that would least exceed the limit. Since the FI systems cannot split the payment on a line, CWF will allow payment on the line that least exceeds the limit and deny other lines.

H. Additional Information for Carriers and FIs During the Time Financial Limits Are in Effect With or Without Exceptions
Once the limit is reached, if a claim is submitted, CWF returns an error code stating the financial limitation has been met. Over applied lines will be identified at the line level. The outpatient rehabilitation therapy services that exceed the limit should be denied. The FIs and carriers use group code PR and claim adjustment reason code 119 - Benefit maximum for this time period or occurrence has been reached- in the provider remittance advice to establish the reason for denial.

In situations where a beneficiary is close to reaching the financial limitation and a particular claim might exceed the limitation, the provider/supplier should bill the usual and customary charges for the services furnished even though such charges might exceed the limit. The CWF will return an error code/trailer that will identify the line that exceeds the limitation.

Because CWF applies the financial limitation according to the date when the claim was received (when the date of service is within the effective date range for the limitation), it is possible that the financial limitation will have been met before the date of service of a given claim. Such claims will prompt the CWF error code and subsequent contractor denial.

When the provider/supplier knows that the limit has been reached, further billing should not occur. The provider/supplier should inform the beneficiary of the limit and their option of receiving further covered services from an outpatient hospital (unless consolidated billing rules prevent the use of the outpatient hospital setting). If the beneficiary chooses to continue treatment at a setting other than the outpatient hospital where medically necessary services may be covered, the services may be billed at the rate the provider/supplier determines. Services provided in a capped setting after the limitation has been reached are not Medicare benefits and are not governed by Medicare policies.

If a beneficiary elects to receive services that exceed the cap limitation and a claim is submitted for such services, the resulting determination is subject to the administrative appeals process as described in subsection C.6 of this section and Pub. 100-04, chapter 29.

I. Provider Notification for Beneficiaries Exceeding Therapy Limits
Contractors will advise providers/suppliers to notify beneficiaries of the therapy financial limitations at their first therapy encounter with the beneficiary. Providers/suppliers should inform beneficiaries that beneficiaries are responsible for 100 percent of the costs of therapy services above each respective therapy limit, unless this outpatient care is furnished directly or under arrangements by a hospital. Patients who are residents in a Medicare certified part of a SNF may not utilize outpatient hospital services for therapy services over the financial limits, because consolidated billing rules require all services to be billed by the SNF. However, when therapy cap exceptions apply, SNF residents may qualify for exceptions that allow billing within the consolidated billing rules. NEMB It is the provider's responsibility to present each beneficiary with accurate information about the therapy limits, and that, where necessary, appropriate care above the limits can be obtained at a hospital outpatient therapy department. Although use of the NEMB form is not a Medicare requirement, Medicare contractors shall advise providers/suppliers to use the Notice of Exclusion from Medicare Benefits (NEMB Form No. CMS 20007 & Formulario No. CMS 20007) form, or a similar form of their own design to inform beneficiaries of the therapy financial limitation and the cap exclusion process.

The NEMB form can be found at: http://www.cms.hhs.gov/medicare/bni/

When using the NEMB form, the practitioner checks box number 1 and writes the reason for denial in the space provided at the top of the form. The following reason is suggested: "Services do not qualify for exception to therapy caps. Medicare will not pay for physical therapy and speech-language pathology services over (add the dollar amount of the cap and the year or the dates of service to which it applies, e.g., $1810 in 2008) unless the beneficiary qualifies for a cap exception." Providers are to supply this same information for occupational therapy services over the limit for the same time period, as appropriate.

ABN

An Advance Beneficiary Notice (ABN) is required to be given to a beneficiary whenever the treating clinician determines that the services being provided are no longer expected to be covered because they do not satisfy Medicare's medical necessity requirements. The ABN informs the beneficiary of their potential financial obligation to the provider and provides guidance regarding appeal rights. ABN applies to services that are provided BEFORE the cap is exceeded.

After the cap is exceeded, only the NEMB is appropriate, regardless of whether the services were excepted from the cap. For example, if services are provided over the cap for an excepted condition, when the therapist determines that the services no longer meet the criteria for reasonable and necessary services, an NEMB and not an ABN is provided to the patient.

At the time the clinician determines that skilled services are not necessary, the clinical goals have been met, or that there is no longer potential for the rehabilitation of health and/or function in a reasonable time, the beneficiary should be informed. If the beneficiary requests further services, inform the beneficiary that Medicare will not likely provide additional coverage. Use the ABN form for this purpose if the services are within the cap, and use the NEMB for services after the cap is exceeded.

Access to Accrued Amount

All providers and contractors may access the accrued amount of therapy services from the ELGA screen inquiries into CWF. Provider/suppliers may access remaining therapy services limitation dollar amount through the 270/271 eligibility inquiry and response transaction. Providers who bill to FIs will also find the amount a beneficiary has accrued toward the financial limitations on the HIQA. Some suppliers and providers billing to carriers may, in addition, have access the accrued amount of therapy services from the ELGB screen inquiries into CWF. Suppliers who do not have access to these inquiries may call the contractor to obtain the amount accrued.

100-4 , 5, 20
HCPCS Coding Requirement
A. Uniform Coding

Section 1834(k)(5) of the Act requires that all claims for outpatient rehabilitation therapy services and all comprehensive outpatient rehabilitation facility (CORF) services be reported using a uniform coding system. The Healthcare Common Procedure Coding System/Current Procedural Terminology is the coding system used for the reporting of these services. The uniform coding requirement in the Act is specific to payment for all CORF services and outpatient rehabilitation therapy services - including physical therapy, occupational therapy, and speech-language pathology - that is provided and billed to carriers and fiscal intermediaries (FIs). The Medicare physician fee schedule (MPFS) is used to make payment for these therapy services at the nonfacility rate.

Effective for claims submitted on or after April 1, 1998, providers that had not previously reported HCPCS/CPT for outpatient rehabilitation and CORF services began using HCPCS to report these services. This requirement does not apply to outpatient rehabilitation services provided by:

- Critical access hospitals, which are paid on a cost basis, not MPFS;
- RHCs, and FQHCs for which therapy is included in the all-inclusive rate; or
- Providers that do not furnish therapy services.

The following "providers of services" must bill the FI for outpatient rehabilitation services using HCPCS codes:

- Hospitals (to outpatients and inpatients who are not in a covered Part A1stay);
- Skilled nursing facilities (SNFs) (to residents not in a covered Part A1stay and to nonresidents who receive outpatient rehabilitation services from the SNF);
- Home health agencies (HHAs) (to individuals who are not homebound or otherwise are not receiving services under a home health plan of care2(POC);
- Comprehensive outpatient rehabilitation facilities (CORFs); and
- Providers of outpatient physical therapy and speech-language pathology services (OPTs), also known as rehabilitation agencies (previously termed outpatient physical therapy facilities in this instruction).

Note 1. The requirements for hospitals and SNFs apply to inpatient Part B and outpatient services only. Inpatient Part A services are bundled into the respective prospective payment system payment; no separate payment is made.

Note 2. For HHAs, HCPCS/CPT coding for outpatient rehabilitation services is required only when the HHA provides such service to individuals that are not homebound and, therefore, not under a Home Health plan of care.

The following practitioners must bill the carriers for outpatient rehabilitation therapy services using HCPCS/CPT codes:

- Physical therapists in private practice (PTPPs),
- Occupational therapists in private practice (OTPPs),
- Physicians, including MDs, DOs, podiatrists and optometrists, and
- Certain nonphysician practitioners (NPPs), acting within their State scope of practice, e.g., nurse practitioners and clinical nurse specialists.

Providers billing to intermediaries shall report:

- The date the therapy plan of care was either established or last reviewed (see 220.1.3B) in Occurrence Code 17, 29, or 30.
- The first day of treatment in Occurrence Code 35, 44, or 45.

B. Applicable Outpatient Rehabilitation HCPCS Codes

The CMS identifies the following codes as therapy services, regardless of the presence of a financial limitation. Therapy services include only physical therapy, occupational therapy and speech-language pathology services. Therapist means only a physical therapist, occupational therapist or speech-language pathologist. Therapy modifiers are GP for physical therapy, GO for occupational therapy, and GN for speech-language pathology. Check the notes below the chart for details about each code.

When in effect, any financial limitation will also apply to services represented by the following codes, except as noted below.

NOTE:Listing of the following codes does not imply that services are covered or applicable to all provider settings.ider settings.

64550+	90901+	92506▲	92507▲	92508	92526
92597	92605****	92606****	92607	92608	92609
92610+	92611+	92612+	92614+	92616+	95831+
95832+	95833+	95834+	95851+	95852+	96105+
96110+✓	96111+✓	97001	97002	97003	97004
97010****	97012	97016	97018	97022	97024
97026	97028	97032	97033	97034	97035
97036	97039*◆	97110	97112	97113	97116
97124	97139*◆	97140	97150	97530	97532+
97533	97535	97537	97542	97597+✗	97598+✗
97602+****✗	97605+✗	97606+✗	97750	97755	97760**▲
97761	97762	97799*	G0281	G0283	G0329
0019T+***	0029T+***				

*   The physician fee schedule abstract file does not contain a price for CPT codes 97039, 97139, or 97799, since the carrier prices them. Therefore, the FI must contact the carrier to obtain the appropriate fee schedule amount in order to make proper payment for these codes.

◆   Effective January 1, 2006, these codes will no longer be valued under the MPFS. They will be priced by the carriers.

▲   Effective January 1, 2006, the code descriptors for these services have been changed.

**   CPT code 97760 should not be reported with CPT code 97116 for the same extremity.

***   The physician fee schedule abstract file does not contain a price for CPT codes 0019T or 0029T since they are priced by the carrier. In addition, the carrier determines coverage for these codes. Therefore, the FI contacts the carrier to obtain the appropriate fee schedule amount.

****   These HCPCS codes are bundled under the MPFS. They are bundled with any therapy codes. Regardless of whether they are billed alone or in conjunction with another therapy code, never make payment separately for these codes. If billed alone, HCPCS/CPT codes marked as "****" shall be denied using the existing MSN language. For remittance advice notices, use group code CO and claim adjustment reason code 97 that says: "Payment is included in the allowance for another service/procedure." Use reason code 97 to deny a procedure code that should have been bundled. Alternatively, reason code B15, which has the same intent, may also be used.

✓   If billed by an outpatient hospital department, these HCPCS codes are paid using the Outpatient Prospective Payment System (OPPS).
Underlined codes are "always therapy" services, regardless of who performs them. These codes always require therapy modifiers (GP, GO, GN).

✗   If billed by a hospital subject to OPPS on an outpatient service, these HCPCS codes – also indicated as "sometimes therapy" services - will be paid under the OPPS when the service is not performed by a qualified therapist and it is inappropriate to bill the service under a therapy plan of care. The requirements for other "sometimes therapy" codes, described below, apply.

+   These HCPCS/CPT codes sometimes represent therapy services. However, these codes always represent therapy services and require the use of a therapy modifier when performed by therapists.

There are some circumstances when these codes will not be considered representative of therapy services and therapy limits (when they are in effect) will not apply. Codes marked + are not therapy services when:

- It is not appropriate to bill the service under a therapy plan of care, and
- They are billed by practitioners/providers of services who are not therapists, i.e., physicians, clinical nurse specialists, nurse practitioners and psychologists; or they are billed to fiscal intermediaries by hospitals for outpatient services which are performed by non-therapists as noted in Note ✗ above.

While the "+" designates that a particular HCPCS/CPT code will not of itself always indicate that a therapy service was rendered, these codes always represent therapy services when rendered by therapists or by practitioners who are not therapists in situations where the service provided is integral to an outpatient rehabilitation therapy plan of care. For those situations, these codes must always have a therapy modifier. For example, when the service is rendered by either a doctor of medicine or a nurse practitioner (acting within the scope of his or her license when performing such service), with the goal of rehabilitation, a modifier is required. When there is doubt about whether a service should be part of a therapy plan of care, the contractor shall make that determination.

"Outpatient rehabilitation therapy" refers to skilled therapy services, requiring the skills of qualified therapists, performed for restorative purposes and generally involving ongoing treatments as part of a therapy plan of care. In contrast, a non-therapy service is a service performed by non-therapist practitioners. without an appropriate rehabilitative plan or goals, e.g., application of a surface (transcutaneous) neurostimulator - CPT code 64550, and biofeedback training by any modality - CPT code 90901. When performed by therapists, these are "always" therapy services. Contractors have discretion to determine whether circumstances describe a therapy service or require a rehabilitation plan of care.

The underlined HCPCS codes on the above list do not have a + sign because they are considered "always therapy" codes and always require a therapy modifier. Therapy services, whether represented by "always therapy" codes, or + codes in the above list performed as outpatient rehabilitation therapy services, must follow all the policies for therapy services (e.g., Pub. 100-04, chapter 5; Pub. 100-02, chapters 12 and 15).

C. Additional HCPCS Codes

Some HCPCS/CPT codes that are not on the list of therapy services should not be billed with a modifier. For example, outpatient non-rehabilitation HCPCS codes G0237, G0238, and G0239 should be billed without therapy modifiers. These HCPCS codes describe services for the improvement of respiratory function and may represent either "incident to" services or respiratory therapy services that may be appropriately billed in the CORF setting. When the services described by these G-codes are provided by physical therapists (PTs) or occupational therapists (OTs) treating respiratory conditions, they are considered therapy services and must meet the other conditions for physical and occupational therapy. The PT or OT would use the appropriate HCPCS/CPT code(s) in the 97000 - 97799 series and the corresponding therapy modifier, GP or GO, must be used.

Another example of codes that are not on the list of therapy services and should not be billed with a therapy modifier includes the following HCPCS codes: 95860, 95861, 95863, 95864, 95867, 95869, 95870, 95900, 95903, 95904, and 95934. These services represent diagnostic services - not therapy services; they must be appropriately billed and shall not include therapy modifiers.

Other codes not on the above list, and not paid under another fee schedule, are appropriately billed with therapy modifiers when the services are furnished by therapists or provided under a therapy plan of care and where the services are covered and appropriately delivered (e.g., the therapist is qualified to provide the service). One example of non-listed codes where a therapy modifier is indicated, regards the provision of services described in the CPT code series, 29000 through 29590, for the application of casts and strapping. Some of these codes previously appeared on the above list, but were deleted because we determined that they represented services that are most often performed outside a therapy plan of care. However, when these services are provided by therapists or as an integral part of a therapy plan of care, the CPT code must be accompanied with the appropriate therapy modifier.

NOTE:The above lists of HCPCS/CPT codes are intended to facilitate the contractor's ability to pay claims under the MPFS. It is not intended to be an exhaustive list of covered services, imply applicability to provider settings, and does not assure coverage of these services.

100-4, 5, 100.10
Group Therapy Services (Code 97150)
Policies for group therapy services for CORF are the same as group therapy services for other Part B outpatient services. See Pub 100-02, chapter 15, section 230.

100-4, 8, 140
Monthly Capitation Payment Method for Physicians' Services Furnished to Patients on Maintenance Dialysis
Physicians and practitioners managing patients on dialysis (center based) are paid a monthly capitation payment (MCP) for most outpatient dialysis-related physician services furnished to a Medicare end stage renal disease (ESRD) beneficiary. The payment amount varies based on the number of visits provided within each month and the age of the ESRD beneficiary. Physicians and practitioners managing ESRD patients who dialyze at home are paid a single monthly rate based on the age of the ESRD beneficiary, regardless of the number of face-to-face physician or practitioner visits. The MCP is reported once per month for services performed in an outpatient setting that are related to the patients' ESRD.

Physicians and practitioners may receive payment for managing patients on dialysis for less than a full month of care in specific circumstances as discussed in section 140.2. Payment for ESRD related services, less than a full month, is made on a per diem bases.

Payment for ESRD-related services is made at 80 percent of the Medicare approved amount (lesser of the actual charge or applicable Medicare fee schedule amount) after the beneficiary's Part B deductible is met. The beneficiary is responsible for the Part B deductible and the 20 percent coinsurance for physician and practitioner ESRD-related services.

A. Services Included in Monthly Capitation Payment
The following physician services are included in the MCP:

- Assessment of the need for a specified diet and the need for nutritional supplementation for the control of chronic renal failure. Specification of the quantity of total protein, high biologic protein, sodium, potassium, and amount of fluids to be allowed during a given time period. For diabetic patients with chronic renal failure, the prescription usually specifies the number of calories in the diet.

- Assessment of which mode(s) of chronic dialysis (types of hemodialysis or peritoneal dialysis) are suitable for a given patient and recommendation of the type(s) of therapy for a given patient.

- Assessment and determination of which type of dialysis access is best suited for a given patient and arrangement for creation of dialysis access.

- Assessment of whether the patient meets preliminary criteria as a renal transplant candidate and presentation of this assessment to the patient and family.

- Prescription of the parameters of intradialytic management. For chronic hemodialysis therapies, this includes the type of dialysis access, the type and amount of anticoagulant to be employed, blood flow rates, dialysate flow rate, ultrafiltration rate, dialysate temperature, type of dialysate (acetate versus bicarbonate) and composition of the electrolytes in the dialysate, size of hemodialyzer (surface area) and composition of the dialyzer membrane (conventional versus high flux), duration and frequency of treatments, the type and frequency of measuring indices of clearance, and intradialytic medications to be administered. For chronic peritoneal dialysis therapies, this includes the type of peritoneal dialysis, the volume of dialysate, concentration of dextrose in the dialysate, electrolyte composition of the dialysate, duration of each exchange, and addition of medication to the dialysate, such as heparin, and the type and frequency of measuring indices of clearance. For diabetics, the quantity of insulin to be added to each exchange is prescribed.

- Assessment of whether the patient has significant renal failure-related anemia, determination of the etiology(ies) for the anemia based on diagnostic tests, and prescription of therapy for correction of the anemia, such as vitamins, oral or parenteral iron, and hormonal therapy such as erythropoietin.

- Assessment of whether the patient has hyperparathyroidism and/or renal osteodystrophy secondary to chronic renal failure and prescription of appropriate therapy, such as calcium and phosphate binders for control of hyperphosphatemia. Based upon assessment of parahormone levels, serum calcium levels, and evaluation for the presence of metabolic bone disease, the physician determines whether oral or parenteral therapy with vitamin D or its analogs is indicated and prescribes the appropriate therapy. Based upon assessment and diagnosis of bone disease, the physician may prescribe specific chelation therapy with deferoxamine and the use of hemoperfusion for removal of aluminum and the chelation.

- Assessment of whether the patient has dialysis-related arthropathy or neuropathy and adjustment of the patient's prescription accordingly. Referral of the patient for any additional needed specialist evaluation and management of these endorgan problems.

- Assessment of whether the patient has fluid overload resulting from renal failure and establishment of an estimated "ideal (dry) weight." The physician determines the need for fluid removal independent of the dialysis prescription and implements these measures when indicated.

- Determination of the need for and prescription of antihypertensive medications and their timing relative to dialysis when the patient is hypertensive in spite of correction of fluid overload.

- Periodic review of the dialysis records to ascertain whether the patient is receiving the prescribed amount of dialysis and ordering of indices of clearance, such as urea kinetics, in order to ascertain whether the dialysis prescription is producing adequate dialysis. If the indices of clearance suggest that the prescription requires alteration, the physician orders changes in the hemodialysis prescription, such as blood flow rate, dialyzer surface area, dialysis frequency, and/or dialysis duration (length of treatment). For peritoneal dialysis patients, the physician may order changes in the volume of dialysate, dextrose concentration of the dialysate, and duration of the exchanges.

- Periodic visits (at least one per month) to the patient during dialysis to ascertain whether the dialysis is working well and whether the patient is tolerating the procedure well (physiologically and psychologically). During these visits, the physician determines whether alteration in any aspect of a given patient's prescription is indicated, such as changes in the estimate of the patient's dry weight. Review of the treatment with the nurse or technician performing the therapy is also included. The frequency of these visits will vary depending upon the patient's medical status, complicating conditions, and other determinants.

- Performance of periodic physical assessments, based upon the patient's clinical stability, in order to determine the necessity for alterations in various aspects of the patient's prescription. Similarly, the physician reviews the results of periodic laboratory testing in order to determine the need for alterations in the patient's prescription, such as changes in the amount and timing of phosphate binders or dose of erythropoietin.

- Periodic assessment of the adequacy and function of the patient's dialysis access appropriate tests and antibiotic therapy.

- Interpretations of the following tests:
  - Bone mineral density studies (CPT codes 76070, 76075, 78350, and 78351);
  - Noninvasive vascular diagnostic studies of hemodialysis access (CPT codes 93925, 93926, 93930, 93931, and 93990);
  - Nerve conduction studies (CPT codes 95900, 95903, 95904, 95925, 95926, 95927, 95934, 95935, and 95936);
  - Electromyography studies (CPT codes 95860, 95861, 95863, 95864, 95867, 95869, and 95872).

- Periodic review and update of the patient's short-term and long-term care plans with staff.

- Coordination and direction of the care of patients by other professional staff, such as dieticians and social workers.

- Certification of the need for items and services such as durable medical equipment and home health care services. Care plan oversight services described by CPT code 99375 are included in the MCP and may not be separately reported.

B. Services Excluded from Monthly Capitation Payment
The following physician services furnished to the physician's ESRD patients are excluded from the MCP and should be paid in accordance with the physician fee schedule:

1. Administration of hepatitis B vaccine.

2. Surgical services such as:
   - Temporary or permanent hemodialysis catheter placement;
   - Temporary or permanent peritoneal dialysis catheter placement;
   - Repair of existing dialysis accesses;
   - Placement of catheter(s) for thrombolytic therapy;
   - Thrombolytic therapy (systemic, regional, or access catheter only; hemodialysis or peritoneal dialysis);
   - Thrombectomy of clotted cannula;
   - Arthrocentesis;
   - Bone marrow aspiration; and
   - Bone marrow biopsy.

3. Interpretation of tests that have a professional component such as:
   - Electrocardiograms (12 lead, Holter monitor, stress tests, etc.);
   - Echocardiograms;
   - 24-hour blood pressure monitor;
   - Biopsies; and
   - Spirometry and complete pulmonary function tests.

4. Complete evaluation for renal transplantation. While the physician assessment of whether the patient meets preliminary criteria as a renal transplant candidate is included under the MCP, the complete evaluation for renal transplantation is excluded from the MCP.

5. Evaluation of potential living transplant donors.

6. The training of patients to perform home hemodialysis, self hemodialysis, and the various forms of self peritoneal dialysis.

7. Non-renal related physician's services. These services may be furnished by the physician providing renal care or by another physician. They may not be incidental to services furnished during a dialysis session or office visit necessitated by the renal condition. The physician must provide documentation that the illness is not related to the renal condition and that the added visits are required. The contractor's medical staff determines whether additional reimbursement is warranted for treatment of the unrelated illness. For example, the medical management of diabetes mellitus that is not related to the dialysis or furnished during a dialysis session is excluded.

                    © 2008 Ingenix

8. Covered physician services furnished to hospital inpatients.

9. All physician services that antedate the initiation of outpatient dialysis.

10. Covered physician services furnished by another physician when the patient is not available to receive the outpatient services as usual; for example, when the patient is traveling out of tow

100-4, 11, 10

Overview

Medicare beneficiaries entitled to hospital insurance (Part A) who have terminal illnesses and a life expectancy of six months or less have the option of electing hospice benefits in lieu of standard Medicare coverage for treatment and management of their terminal condition. Only care provided by a Medicare certified hospice is covered under the hospice benefit provisions.

Hospice care is available for two 90-day periods and an unlimited number of 60-day periods during the remainder of the hospice patient's lifetime. However, a beneficiary may voluntarily terminate his hospice election period. Election/termination dates are retained on CWF.

When hospice coverage is elected, the beneficiary waives all rights to Medicare Part B payments for services that are related to the treatment and management of his/her terminal illness during any period his/her hospice benefit election is in force, except for professional services of an attending physician, which may include a nurse practitioner. If the attending physician, who may be a nurse practitioner, is an employee of the designated hospice, he or she may not receive compensation from the hospice for those services under Part B. These physician professional services are billed to Medicare Part A by the hospice.

To be covered, hospice services must be reasonable and necessary for the palliation or management of the terminal illness and related conditions. The individual must elect hospice care and a certification that the individual is terminally ill must be completed by the patient's attending physician (if there is one), and the Medical Director (or the physician member of the Interdisciplinary Group (IDG)). Nurse practitioners serving as the attending physician may not certify or re-certify the terminal illness. A plan of care must be established before services are provided. To be covered, services must be consistent with the plan of care. Certification of terminal illness is based on the physician's or medical director's clinical judgment regarding the normal course of an individual's illness. It should be noted that predicting life expectancy is not always exact.

See the Medicare Benefit Policy Manual, Chapter 9, for additional general information about the Hospice benefit.

See Chapter 29 of this manual for information on the appeals process that should be followed when an entity is dissatisfied with the determination made on a claim.

See Chapter 9 of the Medicare Benefit Policy Manual for hospice eligibility requirements and election of hospice care.

100-4, 11, 40.1.3

Attending Physician Services

When hospice coverage is elected, the beneficiary waives all rights to Medicare Part B payments for professional services that are related to the treatment and management of his/her terminal illness during any period his/her hospice benefit election is in force, except for professional services of an "attending physician," who is not an employee of the designated hospice nor receives compensation from the hospice for those services. For purposes of administering the hospice benefit provisions, an "attending physician" means an individual who:

• Is a doctor of medicine or osteopathy or

• A nurse practitioner (for professional services related to the terminal illness that are furnished on or after December 8, 2003); and

• Is identified by the individual, at the time he/she elects hospice coverage, as having the most significant role in the determination and delivery of their medical care.

Even though a beneficiary elects hospice coverage, he/she may designate and use an attending physician, who is not employed by nor receives compensation from the hospice for professional services furnished, in addition to the services of hospice-employed physicians. The professional services of an attending physician, who may be a nurse practitioner as defined in Chapter 9, that are reasonable and necessary for the treatment and management of a hospice patient's terminal illness are not considered hospice services.

Where the service is considered a hospice service (i.e., a service related to the hospice patient's terminal illness that was furnished by someone other than the designated "attending physician" [or a physician substituting for the attending physician]) the physician or other provider must look to the hospice for payment.

Professional services related to the hospice patient's terminal condition that were furnished by the "attending physician", who may be a nurse practitioner, are billed to carriers. When the attending physician furnishes a terminal illness related service that includes both a professional and technical component (e.g., x-rays), he/she bills the professional component of such services to the carrier and looks to the hospice for payment for the technical component. Likewise, the attending physician, who may be a nurse practitioner, would look to the hospice for payment for terminal illness related services furnished that have no professional component (e.g., clinical lab tests). The remainder of this section explains this in greater detail.

When a Medicare beneficiary elects hospice coverage he/she may designate an attending physician, who may be a nurse practitioner, not employed by the hospice, in addition to receiving care from hospice-employed physicians. The professional services of a non-hospice affiliated attending physician for the treatment and management of a hospice patient's terminal illness are not considered "hospice services." These attending physician services are billed to the carrier, provided they were not furnished under a payment arrangement with the hospice. The attending physician codes services with the GV modifier "Attending physician not employed or paid under

agreement by the patient's hospice provider" when billing his/her professional services furnished for the treatment and management of a hospice patient's terminal condition. Carriers make payment to the attending physician or beneficiary, as appropriate, based on the payment and deductible rules applicable to each covered service.

Payments for the services of attending physician are not counted in determining whether the hospice cap amount has been exceeded because services provided by an independent attending physician are not part of the hospice's care.

Services provided by an independent attending physician who may be a nurse practitioner must be coordinated with any direct care services provided by hospice physicians.

Only the direct professional services of an independent attending physician, who may be a nurse practitioner, to a patient may be billed; the costs for services such as lab or x-rays are not to be included in the bill.

If another physician covers for a hospice patient's designated attending physician, the services of the substituting physician are billed by the designated attending physician under the reciprocal or locum tenens billing instructions. In such instances, the attending physician bills using the GV modifier in conjunction with either the Q5 or Q6 modifier.

When services related to a hospice patient's terminal condition are furnished under a payment arrangement with the hospice by the designated attending physician who may be a nurse practitioner, the physician must look to the hospice for payment. In this situation the physicians' services are hospice services and are billed by the hospice to its FI.

Carriers must process and pay for covered, medically necessary Part B services that physicians furnish to patients after their hospice benefits are revoked even if the patient remains under the care of the hospice. Such services are billed without the GV or GW modifiers. Make payment based on applicable Medicare payment and deductible rules for each covered service even if the beneficiary continues to be treated by the hospice after hospice benefits are revoked.

The CWF response contains the period of hospice entitlement. This information is a permanent part of the notice and is furnished on all CWF replies and automatic notices. Carriers use the CWF reply for validating dates of hospice coverage and to research, examine and adjudicate services coded with the GV or GW modifiers.

100-4, 11, 40.1.3.1

Care Plan Oversight

Care plan oversight (CPO) exists where there is physician supervision of patients under care of hospices that require complex and multidisciplinary care modalities involving regular physician development and/or revision of care plans. Implicit in the concept of CPO is the expectation that the physician has coordinated an aspect of the patient's care with the hospice during the month for which CPO services were billed.

For a physician or NP employed by or under arrangement with a hospice agency, CPO functions are incorporated and are part of the hospice per diem payment and as such may not be separately billed.

For information on separately billable CPO services by the attending physician or nurse practitioner see Chapter 12, 180 of this manual.

100-4, 12, 30

Correct Coding Policy
B3-15068

The Correct Coding Initiative was developed to promote national correct coding methodologies and to control improper coding leading to inappropriate payment in Part B claims. Refer to Chapter 23 for additional information on the initiative.

The principles for the correct coding policy are:

• The service represents the standard of care in accomplishing the overall procedure;

• The service is necessary to successfully accomplish the comprehensive procedure.

• Failure to perform the service may compromise the success of the procedure; and

• The service does not represent a separately identifiable procedure unrelated to the comprehensive procedure planned.

For a detailed description of the correct coding policy, refer to http://www.cms.hhs.gov/medlearn/ncci.asp.

The CMS as well as many third party payers have adopted the HCPCS/CPT coding system for use by physicians and others to describe services rendered. The system contains three levels of codes. Level I contains the American Medical Association's Current Procedural Terminology (CPT) numeric codes. Level II contains alpha-numeric codes primarily for items and services not included in CPT. Level III contains carrier specific codes that are not included in either Level I or Level II. For a list of CPT and HCPCS codes refer to the CMS Web site.

The following general coding policies encompass coding principles that are to be applied in the review of Medicare claims. They are the basis for the correct coding edits that are installed in the claims processing systems effective January 1, 1996.

A. Coding Based on Standards of Medical/Surgical Practice

All services integral to accomplishing a procedure are considered bundled into that procedure and, therefore, are considered a component part of the comprehensive code. Many of these generic activities are common to virtually all procedures and, on other occasions, some are integral to only a certain group of procedures, but are still essential to accomplish these particular procedures. Accordingly, it is inappropriate to separately report these services based on standard medical and surgical principles.

Because many services are unique to individual CPT coding sections, the rationale for rebundling is described in that particular section of the detailed coding narratives that are transmitted to carriers periodically.

B. CPT Procedure Code Definition

The format of the CPT manual includes descriptions of procedures, which are, in order to conserve space, not listed in their entirety for all procedures. The partial description is indented under the main entry. The main entry then encompasses the portion of the description preceding the semicolon. The main entry applies to and is a part of all indented entries, which follow with their codes.

In the course of other procedure descriptions, the code definition specifies other procedures that are included in this comprehensive code. In addition, a code description may define a rebundling relationship where one code is a part of another based on the language used in the descriptor.

C. CPT Coding Manual Instruction/Guideline

Each of the six major subsections include guidelines that are unique to that section.

These directions are not all inclusive of nor limited to, definitions of terms, modifiers, unlisted procedures or services, special or written reports, details about reporting separate, and multiple or starred procedures and qualifying circumstances.

D. Coding Services Supplemental to Principal Procedure (Add-On Codes) Code

Generally, these are identified with the statement "list separately in addition to code for primary procedure" in parentheses, and other times the supplemental code is used only with certain primary codes, which are parenthetically identified. The reason for these CPT codes is to enable physicians and others to separately identify a service that is performed in certain situations as an additional service. Incidental services that are necessary to accomplish the primary procedure (e.g., lysis of adhesions in the course of an open cholecystectomy) are not separately billed.

E. Separate Procedures

The narrative for many CPT codes includes a parenthetical statement that the procedure represents a "separate procedure."

The inclusion of this statement indicates that the procedure, while possible to perform separately, is generally included in a more comprehensive procedure, and the service is not to be billed when a related, more comprehensive, service is performed. The "separate procedure" designation is used with codes in the surgery (CPT codes 10000-69999), radiology (CPT codes 70000-79999), and medicine (CPT codes 90000-99199) sections.

When a related procedure from the same section, subsection, category, or subcategory is performed, a code with the designation of "separate procedure" is not to be billed with the primary procedure.

F. Designation of Sex

Many procedure codes have a sex designation within their narrative. These codes are not billed with codes having an opposite sex designation because this would reflect a conflict in sex classification either by the definition of the code descriptions themselves, or by the fact that the performance of these procedures on the same beneficiary would be anatomically impossible.

G. Family of Codes

In a family of codes, there are two or more component codes that are not billed separately because they are included in a more comprehensive code as members of the code family.

Comprehensive codes include certain services that are separately identifiable by other component codes. The component codes as members of the comprehensive code family represent parts of the procedure that should not be listed separately when the complete procedure is done. However, the component codes are considered individually if performed independently of the complete procedure and if not all the services listed in the comprehensive codes were rendered to make up the total service.

H. Most Extensive Procedures

When procedures are performed together that are basically the same or performed on the same site but are qualified by an increased level of complexity, the less extensive procedure is bundled into the more extensive procedure.

I. Sequential Procedures

An initial approach to a procedure may be followed at the same encounter by a second, usually more invasive approach. There may be separate CPT codes describing each service. The second procedure is usually performed because the initial approach was unsuccessful in accomplishing the medically necessary service. These procedures are considered "sequential procedures." Only the CPT code for one of the services, generally the more invasive service, should be billed.

J. With/Without Procedures

In the CPT manual, there are various procedures that have been separated into two codes with the definitional difference being "with" versus "without" (e.g., with and without contrast). Both procedure codes cannot be billed. When done together, the "without" procedure is bundled into the "with" procedure.

K. Laboratory Panels

When components of a specific organ or disease oriented laboratory panel (e.g., codes 80061 and 80059) or automated multi-channel tests (e.g., codes 80002 - 80019) are billed separately, they must be bundled into the comprehensive panel or automated multichannel test code as appropriate that includes the multiple component tests. The individual tests that make up a panel or can be performed on an automated multi-channel test analyzer are not to be separately billed.

L Mutually Exclusive Procedures

There are numerous procedure codes that are not billed together because they are mutually exclusive of each other. Mutually exclusive codes are those codes that cannot reasonably be done in the same session.

An example of a mutually exclusive situation is when the repair of the organ can be performed by two different methods. One repair method must be chosen to repair the organ and must be billed. Another example is the billing of an "initial" service and a subsequent" service. It is contradictory for a service to be classified as an initial and a subsequent service at the same time.

CPT codes which are mutually exclusive of one another based either on the CPT definition or the medical impossibility/improbability that the procedures could be performed at the same session can be identified as code pairs. These codes are not necessarily linked to one another with one code narrative describing a more comprehensive procedure compared to the component code, but can be identified as code pairs which should not be billed together.

M. Use of Modifiers

When certain component codes or mutually exclusive codes are appropriately furnished, such as later on the same day or on a different digit or limb, it is appropriate that these services be reported using a HCPCS code modifier. Such modifiers are modifiers E1 -E4, FA, F1 - F9, TA, T1 - T9, LT, RT, LC, LD, RC, -58, -78, -79, and -94.

Modifier -59 is not appropriate to use with weekly radiation therapy management codes (77427) or with evaluation and management services codes (99201 - 99499).

Application of these modifiers prevent erroneous denials of claims for several procedures performed on different anatomical sites, on different sides of the body, or at different sessions on the same date of service. The medical record must reflect that the modifier is being used appropriately to describe separate services.

100-4, 12, 30.1

Digestive System (Codes 40000 - 49999)

B3-15100

A. Upper Gastrointestinal Endoscopy Including Endoscopic Ultrasound (EUS) (Code 43259)

If the person performing the original diagnostic endoscopy has access to the EUS and the clinical situation requires an EUS, the EUS may be done at the same time. The procedure, diagnostic and EUS, is reported under the same code, CPT 43259. This code conforms to CPT guidelines for the indented codes. The service represented by the indented code, in this case code 43259 for EUS, includes the service represented by the unintended code preceding the list of indented codes. Therefore, when a diagnostic examination of the upper gastrointestinal tract "including esophagus, stomach, and either the duodenum or jejunum as appropriate," includes the use of endoscopic ultrasonography, the service is reported by a single code, namely 43259.

Interpretation, whether by a radiologist or endoscopist, is reported under CPT code 76975-26. These codes may both be reported on the same day.

B. Incomplete Colonoscopies (Codes 45330 and 45378)

An incomplete colonoscopy, e.g., the inability to extend beyond the splenic flexure, is billed and paid using colonoscopy code 45378 with modifier "-53." The Medicare physician fee schedule database has specific values for code 45378-53. These values are the same as for code 45330, sigmoidoscopy, as failure to extend beyond the splenic flexure means that a sigmoidoscopy rather than a colonoscopy has been performed.

However, code 45378-53 should be used when an incomplete colonoscopy has been done because other MPFSDB indicators are different for codes 45378 and 45330.

100-4, 12, 30.2

Urinary and Male Genital Systems (Codes 50010 - 55899)

B3-15200

A. Cystourethroscopy With Ureteral Catheterization (Code 52005)

Code 52005 has a zero in the bilateral field (payment adjustment for bilateral procedure does not apply) because the basic procedure is an examination of the bladder and urethra (cystourethroscopy), which are not paired organs. The work RVUs assigned take into account that it may be necessary to examine and catheterize one or both ureters. No additional payment is made when the procedure is billed with bilateral modifier "-50." Neither is any additional payment made when both ureters are examined and code 52005 is billed with multiple surgery modifier "-51." It is inappropriate to bill code 52005 twice, once by itself and once with modifier "-51," when both ureters are examined.

B. Cystourethroscopy With Fulgration and/or Resection of Tumors (Codes 52234, 52235, and 52240)

The descriptors for codes 52234 through 52240 include the language "tumor(s)." This means that regardless of the number of tumors removed, only one unit of a single code can be billed on a given date of service. It is inconsistent to allow payment for removal of a small (code 52234) and a large (code 52240) tumor using two codes when only one code is allowed for the removal of more than one large tumor. For these three codes only one unit may be billed for any of these codes, only one of the codes may be billed, and the billed code reflects the size of the largest tumor removed.

100-4, 12, 30.3

Audiological Diagnostic Tests, Speech-Language Evaluations and Treatments

A. Correct Coding

Contact the Medicare contractor for guidance if the CPT codebook changes the description of codes mentioned in this section.

Speech-Language Pathology Services. Speech-language pathology (SLP) services are included in the list of therapy services in Pub. 100-04, Chapter 5, Sec.20. Policies for outpatient therapy services are in Pub. 100-02, Chapter 15, Secs.220 and 230. Most of the CPT codes that apply to SLP services are untimed codes that may only be billed once for each encounter. A common error is the billing of untimed codes for multiple units of time. For example, the evaluation code 92506 is billed once a day regardless of the number of types of evaluation included or the length of time that is involved. Bill the code that most appropriately describes the service that is being provided.

Audiology Services. Policies concerning audiology services are found in Pub. 100-02, Chapter 15, Sec.80.3.

Audiologists shall bill for the global service if they perform both technical and professional components of the diagnostic tests that have both components.

Audiologists are to be encouraged to enroll as soon as possible after they obtain their National Provider Identifier (NPI). For audiologists who are enrolled and bill independently for services they render, the audiologist's NPI is required on all claims.

Audiologists must be enrolled and use their NPI on all claims for services they render on or after October 1, 2008, (for additional information about enrollment, please refer to Chapter 10 of the Program Integrity Manual, Pub.100-08). Before October 1, 2008, audiologists who are not yet enrolled may continue to have their services billed by a physician or group who employs the audiologist. Audiologists shall use the billing instructions in the Medicare manuals; for example, see this manual, Chapter 1, Sec.30.

See the most recent Physician Fee Schedule for pricing and supervision levels for audiology services: http://www.cms.hhs.gov/PFSlookup/01_Overview.asp#TopOfPage.

B. Implant Processing
Payment for diagnostic testing of implants, such as cochlear, osseointegrated or brainstem implants, including programming or reprogramming following implantation surgery is not included in the global fee for the surgery.

The diagnostic analysis of a cochlear implant shall be billed using CPT codes 92601 through 92604.

Osseointegrated prosthetic devices should be billed and paid for under provisions of the applicable payment system. For example, payment may differ depending upon whether the device is furnished on an inpatient or outpatient basis, and by a hospital subject to the OPPS, or by a Critical Access Hospital, physician's clinic, or a Federally Qualified Health Center.

C. Aural Rehabilitation Services
General Policy for Evaluation and Treatment of Conditions Related to the Auditory System.

For evaluation of auditory processing disorders and speech-reading or lip-reading, by a speech-language pathologists use the untimed code 92506 with "1" as the unit of service, regardless of the duration of the service on a given day. This "always therapy" evaluation code must be provided by speech-language pathologists according to the policies in Pub. 100-02, Chapter 15, Secs.220 and 230. The codes 92620 and 92621 are diagnostic audiological tests and may not be used for SLP services.

For treatment of auditory processing disorders or auditory rehabilitation/auditory training (including speech-reading or lip-reading), 92507, and 92508 are used to report a single encounter with "1" as the unit of service, regardless of the duration of the service on a given day. These codes always represent SLP services. See Pub. 100-02, Chapter 15, Sec.220 and 230 for SLP policies. These SLP evaluation and treatment services are not covered when performed or billed by audiologists, even if they are supervised by physicians or nonphysician practitioners.

For evaluation of auditory rehabilitation to instruct the use of residual hearing provided by an implant or hearing aid related to hearing loss, the timed codes 92626 and 92627 are used. These are not "always therapy" codes. Evaluation of auditory rehabilitation shall be appropriately provided by an audiologist or speech-language pathologist. Evaluation services may be billed by an audiologist. Also, these services may be provided incident to a physician or nonphysician practitioner's service by a speech-language pathologist, or personally by a physician or nonphysician practitioner within their scope of practice. Evaluation of auditory rehabilitation is a covered diagnostic test when performed and billed by an audiologist and is a SLP evaluation service covered under the SLP benefit when performed by a speech-language pathologist.

General Policies for Post implant Services.
The services of a speech-language pathologist may be covered for SLP services provided after implantation of auditory devices. For example, a speech-language pathologist may provide evaluation and treatment of speech, language, cognition, voice, and auditory processing using code 92506 and 92507. Use 92626 and 92627 for auditory (aural) rehabilitation evaluation following cochlear implantation or for other hearing impairments.

For diagnostic testing of cochlear implants, audiologists use codes 92601, 92602, 92603 and 92604. These services may not be provided by speech-language pathologists or others, with the exception of physicians and non-physician practitioners who may personally provide the services that are within their scope of practice.

D. Computer Administered Hearing Testing
Services using devices that do not require the skills of an audiologist are not covered audiological diagnostic tests. See Pub. 100-02, Chapter 15 concerning descriptions of services that require the skills of an audiologist.

There are some computerized testing devices (e.g., certain audiometers, Bekesy audiometry - 92561) that may be used to produce diagnostic tests when personally performed by an audiologist or physician. Codes for audiological diagnostic tests may be used when an audiologist or physician utilizes an audiometer to furnish a diagnostic test, even if the audiometer has some computerized functions, if the skills of an audiologist are applied to complete the test. (See Pub 100-02, Chapter 15, Sec.80.3.)

Otograms. This is one example of the use of computer-administered hearing tests. Otograms may be coded as unlisted otorhinolaryngological services or procedures (92700). However, these computer-administered hearing tests do not require the skills of an audiologist and are not payable.

Comprehensive audiometry threshold evaluation and speech recognition. Comprehensive audiometry threshold evaluation and speech recognition (92557) are not payable when a computer administers the test e.g., tracks or evaluates responses, automatically adjusts the stimulus or suggests a diagnosis.

100-4, 12, 30.4
Cardiovascular System (Codes 92950-93799)
A. Echocardiography Contrast Agents
Effective October 1, 2000, physicians may separately bill for contrast agents used in echocardiography. Physicians should use HCPCS Code A9700 (Supply of Injectable Contrast Material for Use in Echocardiography, per study). The type of service code is 9. This code will be carrier-priced.

B. Electronic Analyses of Implantable Cardioverter-defibrillators and Pacemakers
The CPT codes 93731, 93734, 93741 and 93743 are used to report electronic analyses of single or dual chamber pacemakers and single or dual chamber implantable cardioverterdefibrillators. In the office, a physician uses a device called a programmer to obtain information about the status and performance of the device and to evaluate the patient's cardiac rhythm and response to the implanted device. Advances in information technology now enable physicians to evaluate patients with implanted cardiac devices without requiring the patient to be present in the physician's office. Using a manufacturer's specific monitor/transmitter, a patient can send complete device data and specific cardiac data to a distant receiving station or secure Internet server. The electronic analysis of cardiac device data that is remotely obtained provides immediate and long-term data on the device and clinical data on the patient's cardiac functioning equivalent to that obtained during an in-office evaluation. Physicians should report the electronic analysis of an implanted cardiac device using remotely obtained data as described above with CPT code 93731, 93734, 93741 or 93743, depending on the type of cardiac device implanted in the patient.

100-4, 12, 30.5
Payment for Codes for Chemotherapy Administration and Nonchemotherapy Injections and Infusions
A. General
Codes for Chemotherapy administration and nonchemotherapy injections and infusions include the following three categories of codes in the American Medical Association's Current Procedural Terminology (CPT):

1. Hydration;

2. Therapeutic, prophylactic, and diagnostic injections and infusions (excluding chemotherapy); and

3. Chemotherapy administration.

Physician work related to hydration, injection, and infusion services involves the affirmation of the treatment plan and the supervision (pursuant to incident to requirements) of nonphysician clinical staff.

B. Hydration
The hydration codes are used to report a hydration IV infusion which consists of a prepackaged fluid and /or electrolytes (e.g. normal saline, D5-1/2 normal saline +30 mg EqKC1/liter) but are not used to report infusion of drugs or other substances.

C. Therapeutic, prophylactic, and diagnostic injections and infusions (excluding chemotherapy)
A therapeutic, prophylactic, or diagnostic IV infusion or injection, other than hydration, is for the administration of substances/drugs. The fluid used to administer the drug (s) is incidental hydration and is not separately payable.

If performed to facilitate the infusion or injection or hydration, the following services and items are included and are not separately billable.

1. Use of local anesthesia;

2. IV start;

3. Access to indwelling IV, subcutaneous catheter or port;

4. Flush at conclusion of infusion; and

5. Standard tubing, syringes and supplies.

Payment for the above is included in the payment for the chemotherapy administration or nonchemotherapy injection and infusion service.

If a significant separately identifiable evaluation and management service is performed, the appropriate E & M code should be reported utilizing modifier 25 in addition to the chemotherapy administration or nonchemotherapy injection and infusion service. For an evaluation and management service provided on the same day, a different diagnosis is not required.

The CPT 2006 includes a parenthetical remark immediately following CPT code 90772 (Therapeutic, prophylactic or diagnostic injection; (specify substance or drug); subcutaneous or intramuscular.) It states, "Do not report 90772 for injections given without direct supervision. To report, use 99211." This coding guideline does not apply to Medicare patients. If the RN, LPN or other auxiliary personnel furnishes the injection in the office and the physician is not present in the office to meet the supervision requirement, which is one of the requirements for coverage of an incident to service, then the injection is not covered. The physician would also not report 99211 as this would not be covered as an incident to service.

D. Chemotherapy Administration
Chemotherapy administration codes apply to parenteral administration of nonradionuclide anti-neoplastic drugs; and also to anti-neoplastic agents provided for treatment of noncancer diagnoses (e.g., cyclophosphamide for auto-immune conditions) or to substances such as monoclonal antibody agents, and other biologic response modifiers. The following drugs are commonly considered to fall under the category of monoclonal antibodies: infliximab, rituximab, alemtuzumb, gemtuzumab, and trastuzumab. Drugs commonly considered to fall under the category of hormonal antineoplastics include leuprolide acetate and goserelin acetate. The drugs cited are not intended to be a complete list of drugs that may be administered using the chemotherapy administration codes. Local carriers may provide additional guidance as to which drugs may be considered to be chemotherapy drugs under Medicare.

The administration of anti-anemia drugs and anti-emetic drugs by injection or infusion for cancer patients is not considered chemotherapy administration.

If performed to facilitate the chemotherapy infusion or injection, the following services and items are included and are not separately billable:

1. Use of local anesthesia;

2. IV access;

3. Access to indwelling IV, subcutaneous catheter or port;

4. Flush at conclusion of infusion;

5. Standard tubing, syringes and supplies; and

6. Preparation of chemotherapy agent(s).

Payment for the above is included in the payment for the chemotherapy administration service.

If a significant separately identifiable evaluation and management service is performed, the appropriate E & M code should be reported utilizing modifier 25 in addition to the chemotherapy code. For an evaluation and management service provided on the same day, a different diagnosis is not required.

E. Coding Rules for Chemotherapy Administration and Nonchemotherapy Injections and Infusion Services

Instruct physicians to follow the CPT coding instructions to report chemotherapy administration and nonchemotherapy injections and infusion services with the exception listed in subsection C for CPT code 90772. The physician should be aware of the following specific rules.

When administering multiple infusions, injections or combinations, the physician should report only one "initial" service code unless protocol requires that two separate IV sites must be used. The initial code is the code that best describes the key or primary reason for the encounter and should always be reported irrespective of the order in which the infusions or injections occur. If an injection or infusion is of a subsequent or concurrent nature, even if it is the first such service within that group of services, then a subsequent or concurrent code should be reported. For example, the first IV push given subsequent to an initial one-hour infusion is reported using a subsequent IV push code.

If more than one "initial" service code is billed per day, the carrier shall deny the second initial service code unless the patient has to come back for a separately identifiable service on the same day or has two IV lines per protocol. For these separately identifiable services, instruct the physician to report with modifier 59.

The CPT includes a code for a concurrent infusion in addition to an intravenous infusion for therapy, prophylaxis or diagnosis. Allow only one concurrent infusion per patient per encounter. Do not allow payment for the concurrent infusion billed with modifier 59 unless it is provided during a second encounter on the same day with the patient and is documented in the medical record.

For chemotherapy administration and therapeutic, prophylactic and diagnostic injections and infusions, an intravenous or intra-arterial push is defined as: 1.) an injection in which the healthcare professional is continuously present to administer the substance/drug and observe the patient; or 2.) an infusion of 15 minutes or less.

The physician may report the infusion code for "each additional hour" only if the infusion interval is greater than 30 minutes beyond the 1 hour increment. For example if the patient receives an infusion of a single drug that lasts 1 hour and 45 minutes, the physician would report the "initial" code up to 1 hour and the add-on code for the additional 45 minutes.

Several chemotherapy administration and nonchemotherapy injection and infusion service codes have the following parenthetical descriptor included as a part of the CPT code, "List separately in addition to code for primary procedure." Each of these codes has a physician fee schedule indicator of "ZZZ" meaning this service is allowed if billed with another chemotherapy administration or nonchemotherapy injection and infusion service code.

Do not interpret this parenthetical descriptor to mean that the add-on code can be billed only if it is listed with another drug administration primary code. For example, code 90761 will be ordinarily billed with code 90760. However, there may be instances when only the add-on code, 90761, is billed because an "initial" code from another section in the drug administration codes, instead of 90760, is billed as the primary code.

Pay for code 96523, "Irrigation of implanted venous access device for drug delivery systems," if it is the only service provided that day. If there is a visit or other chemotherapy administration or nonchemotherapy injection or infusion service provided on the same day, payment for 96523 is included in the payment for the other service.

F. Chemotherapy Administration (or Nonchemotherapy Injection and Infusion) and Evaluation and Management Services Furnished on the Same Day

For services furnished on or after January 1, 2004, do not allow payment for CPT code 99211, with or without modifier 25, if it is billed with a nonchemotherapy drug infusion code or a chemotherapy administration code. Apply this policy to code 99211 when it is billed with a diagnostic or therapeutic injection code on or after January 1, 2005.

Physicians providing a chemotherapy administration service or a nonchemotherapy drug infusion service and evaluation and management services, other than CPT code 99211, on the same day must bill in accordance with 30.6.6 using modifier 25. The carriers pay for evaluation and management services provided on the same day as the chemotherapy administration services or a nonchemotherapy injection or infusion service if the evaluation and management service meets the requirements of section 30.6.6 even though the underlying codes do not have global periods. If a chemotherapy service and a significant separately identifiable evaluation and management service are provided on the same day, a different diagnosis is not required.

In 2005, the Medicare physician fee schedule status database indicators for therapeutic and diagnostic injections were changed from T to A. Thus, beginning in 2005, the policy on evaluation and management services, other than 99211, that is applicable to a chemotherapy or a nonchemotherapy injection or infusion service applies equally to these codes.

100-4, 12, 30.6.1

Selection of Level of Evaluation and Management Service

A. Use of CPT Codes

Advise physicians to use CPT codes (level 1 of HCPCS) to code physician services, including evaluation and management services. Medicare will pay for E/M services for specific non-physician practitioners (i.e., nurse practitioner (NP), clinical nurse specialist (CNS) and certified nurse midwife (CNM)) whose Medicare benefit permits them to bill these services. A physician assistant (PA) may also provide a physician service, however, the physician collaboration and general supervision rules as well as all billing rules apply to all the above non-physician practitioners. The service provided must be medically necessary and the service must be within the scope of practice for a nonphysician practitioner in the State in which he/she practices. Do not pay for CPT evaluation and management codes billed by physical therapists in independent practice or by occupational therapists in independent practice.

Medical necessity of a service is the overarching criterion for payment in addition to the individual requirements of a CPT code. It would not be medically necessary or appropriate to bill a higher level of evaluation and management service when a lower level of service is warranted. The volume of documentation should not be the primary influence upon which a specific level of service is billed. Documentation should support the level of service reported. The service should be documented during, or as soon as practicable after it is provided in order to maintain an accurate medical record.

B. Selection of Level Of Evaluation and Management Service

Instruct physicians to select the code for the service based upon the content of the service. The duration of the visit is an ancillary factor and does not control the level of the service to be billed unless more than 50 percent of the face-to-face time (for non-inpatient services) or more than 50 percent of the floor time (for inpatient services) is spent providing counseling or coordination of care as described in subsection C.

Any physician or non-physician practitioner (NPP) authorized to bill Medicare services will be paid by the carrier at the appropriate physician fee schedule amount based on the rendering UPIN/PIN.

"Incident to" Medicare Part B payment policy is applicable for office visits when the requirements for "incident to" are met (refer to sections 60.1, 60.2, and 60.3, chapter 15 in IOM 100-02).

SPLIT/SHARED E/M SERVICE

Office/Clinic Setting

In the office/clinic setting when the physician performs the E/M service the service must be reported using the physician's UPIN/PIN. When an E/M service is a shared/split encounter between a physician and a non-physician practitioner (NP, PA, CNS or CNM), the service is considered to have been performed "incident to" if the requirements for "incident to" are met and the patient is an established patient. If "incident to" requirements are not met for the shared/split E/M service, the service must be billed under the NPP's UPIN/PIN, and payment will be made at the appropriate physician fee schedule payment.

Hospital Inpatient/Outpatient/Emergency Department Setting When a hospital inpatient/hospital outpatient or emergency department E/M is shared between a physician and an NPP from the same group practice and the physician provides any face-to-face portion of the E/M encounter with the patient, the service may be billed under either the physician's or the NPP's UPIN/PIN number. However, if there was no face-to-face encounter between the patient and the physician (e.g., even if the physician participated in the service by only reviewing the patient's medical record) then the service may only be billed under the NPP's UPIN/PIN. Payment will be made at the appropriate physician fee schedule rate based on the UPIN/PIN entered on the claim.

EXAMPLES OF SHARED VISITS

1. If the NPP sees a hospital inpatient in the morning and the physician follows with a later face-to-face visit with the patient on the same day, the physician or the NPP may report the service.

2. In an office setting the NPP performs a portion of an E/M encounter and the physician completes the E/M service. If the "incident to" requirements are met, the physician reports the service. If the "incident to" requirements are not met, the service must be reported using the NPP's UPIN/PIN.

In the rare circumstance when a physician (or NPP) provides a service that does not reflect a CPT code description, the service must be reported as an unlisted service with CPT code 99499. A description of the service provided must accompany the claim. The carrier has the discretion to value the service when the service does not meet the full terms of a CPT code description (e.g., only a history is performed). The carrier also determines the payment based on the applicable percentage of the physician fee schedule depending on whether the claim is paid at the physician rate or the non-physician practitioner rate. CPT modifier -52 (reduced services) must not be used with an evaluation and management service. Medicare does not recognize modifier -52 for this purpose.

C. Selection Of Level Of Evaluation and Management Service Based On Duration Of Coordination Of Care and/or Counseling

Advise physicians that when counseling and/or coordination of care dominates (more than 50 percent) the face-to-face physician/patient encounter or the floor time (in the case of inpatient services), time is the key or controlling factor in selecting the level of service.

In general, to bill an E/M code, the physician must complete at least 2 out of 3 criteria applicable to the type/level of service provided. However, the physician may document time spent with the patient in conjunction with the medical decision-making involved and a description of the coordination of care or counseling provided. Documentation must be in sufficient detail to support the claim.

EXAMPLE:A cancer patient has had all preliminary studies completed and a medical decision to implement chemotherapy. At an office visit the physician discusses the treatment options and subsequent lifestyle effects of treatment the patient may encounter or is experiencing. The physician need not complete a history and physical examination in order to select the level of service. The time spent in counseling/coordination of care and medical decision-making will determine the level of service billed.

The code selection is based on the total time of the face-to-face encounter or floor time, not just the counseling time. The medical record must be documented in sufficient detail to justify the selection of the specific code if time is the basis for selection of the code.

In the office and other outpatient setting, counseling and/or coordination of care must be provided in the presence of the patient if the time spent providing those services is used to determine the level of service reported. Face to face time refers to the time with the physician only. Counseling by other staff is not considered to be part of the face-to-face physician/patient encounter time. Therefore, the time spent by the other staff is not considered in selecting the appropriate level of service. The code used depends upon the physician service provided.

In an inpatient setting, the counseling and/or coordination of care must be provided at the bedside or on the patient's hospital floor or unit that is associated with an individual patient. Time spent counseling the patient or coordinating the patient's care after the patient has left the office or the physician has left the patient's floor or begun to care for another patient on the floor is not considered when selecting the level of service to be reported.

The duration of counseling or coordination of care that is provided face-to-face or on the floor may be estimated but that estimate, along with the total duration of the visit, must be recorded when time is used for the selection of the level of a service that involves predominantly coordination of care or counseling.

D. Use of Highest Levels of Evaluation and Management Codes
Carriers must advise physicians that to bill the highest levels of visit and consultation codes, the services furnished must meet the definition of the code (e.g., to bill a Level 5 new patient visit, the history must meet CPT's definition of a comprehensive history).

The comprehensive history must include a review of all the systems and a complete past (medical and surgical) family and social history obtained at that visit. In the case of an established patient, it is acceptable for a physician to review the existing record and update it to reflect only changes in the patient's medical, family, and social history from the last encounter, but the physician must review the entire history for it to be considered a comprehensive history.

The comprehensive examination may be a complete single system exam such as cardiac, respiratory, psychiatric, or a complete multi-system examination.

100-4, 12, 30.6.2

Billing for Medically Necessary Visit on Same Occasion as Preventive Medicine Service

See Chapter 18 for payment for covered preventive services.

When a physician furnishes a Medicare beneficiary a covered visit at the same place and on the same occasion as a noncovered preventive medicine service (CPT codes 99381- 99397), consider the covered visit to be provided in lieu of a part of the preventive medicine service of equal value to the visit. A preventive medicine service (CPT codes 99381-99397) is a noncovered service. The physician may charge the beneficiary, as a charge for the noncovered remainder of the service, the amount by which the physician's current established charge for the preventive medicine service exceeds his/her current established charge for the covered visit. Pay for the covered visit based on the lesser of the fee schedule amount or the physician's actual charge for the visit. The physician is not required to give the beneficiary written advance notice of noncoverage of the part of the visit that constitutes a routine preventive visit. However, the physician is responsible for notifying the patient in advance of his/her liability for the charges for services that are not medically necessary to treat the illness or injury.

There could be covered and noncovered procedures performed during this encounter (e.g., screening x-ray, EKG, lab tests.). These are considered individually. Those procedures which are for screening for asymptomatic conditions are considered noncovered and, therefore, no payment is made. Those procedures ordered to diagnose or monitor a symptom, medical condition, or treatment are evaluated for medical necessity and, if covered, are paid.

100-4, 12, 30.6.4

Evaluation and Management (E/M) Services Furnished Incident to Physician's Service by Nonphysician Practitioners

When evaluation and management services are furnished incident to a physician's service by a nonphysician practitioner, the physician may bill the CPT code that describes the evaluation and management service furnished.

When evaluation and management services are furnished incident to a physician's service by a nonphysician employee of the physician, not as part of a physician service, the physician bills code 99211 for the service.

A physician is not precluded from billing under the "incident to" provision for services provided by employees whose services cannot be paid for directly under the Medicare program. Employees of the physician may provide services incident to the physician's service, but the physician alone is permitted to bill Medicare.

Services provided by employees as "incident to" are covered when they meet all the requirements for incident to and are medically necessary for the individual needs of the patien

100-4, 12, 30.6.7

Payment for Office or Other Outpatient Evaluation and Management (E/M) Visits (Codes 99201 - 99215)

A Definition of New Patient for Selection of E/M Visit Code
Interpret the phrase "new patient" to mean a patient who has not received any professional services, i.e., E/M service or other face-to-face service (e.g., surgical procedure) from the physician or physician group practice (same physician specialty) within the previous 3 years. For example, if a professional component of a previous procedure is billed in a 3 year time period, e.g., a lab interpretation is billed and no E/M service or other face-to-face service with the patient is performed, then this patient remains a new patient for the initial visit. An interpretation of a diagnostic test, reading an x-ray or EKG etc., in the absence of an E/M service or other face-to-face service with the patient does not affect the designation of a new patient.

B. Office/Outpatient E/M Visits Provided on Same Day for Unrelated Problems
As for all other E/M services except where specifically noted, carriers may not pay two E/M office visits billed by a physician (or physician of the same specialty from the same group practice) for the same beneficiary on the same day unless the physician documents that the visits were for unrelated problems in the office or outpatient setting which could not be provided during the same encounter (e.g., office visit for blood pressure medication evaluation, followed five hours later by a visit for evaluation of leg pain following an accident).

C. Office/Outpatient or Emergency Department E/M Visit on Day of Admission to Nursing Facility
Carriers may not pay a physician for an emergency department visit or an office visit and a comprehensive nursing facility assessment on the same day. Bundle E/M visits on the same date provided in sites other than the nursing facility into the initial nursing facility care code when performed on the same date as the nursing facility admission by the same physician.

D. Drug Administration Services and E/M Visits Billed on Same Day of Service
Carriers must advise physicians that CPT code 99211 cannot be paid if it is billed with a drug administration service such as a chemotherapy or nonchemotherapy drug infusion code (effective January 1, 2004). This drug administration policy was expanded in the Physician Fee Schedule Final Rule, November 15, 2004, to also include a therapeutic or diagnostic injection code (effective January 1, 2005). Therefore, when a medically necessary, significant and separately identifiable E/M service (which meets a higher complexity level than CPT code 99211) is performed, in addition to one of these drug administration services, the appropriate E/M CPT code should be reported with modifier -25. Documentation should support the level of E/M service billed. For an E/M service provided on the same day, a different diagnosis is not required.

100-4, 12, 30.6.8

Payment for Hospital Observation Services (Codes 99217‚Äì 99220) and Observation or Inpatient Care Services (Including Admission and Discharge Services–(Codes 99234–99236))

A. Who May Bill Initial Observation Care
Contractors pay for initial observation care billed by only the physician who admitted the patient to hospital observation and was responsible for the patient during his/her stay in observation. A physician who does not have inpatient admitting privileges but who is authorized to admit a patient to observation status may bill these codes.

For a physician to bill the initial observation care codes, there must be a medical observation record for the patient which contains dated and timed physician's admitting orders regarding the care the patient is to receive while in observation, nursing notes, and progress notes prepared by the physician while the patient was in observation status.

This record must be in addition to any record prepared as a result of an emergency department or outpatient clinic encounter.

Payment for an initial observation care code is for all the care rendered by the admitting physician on the date the patient was admitted to observation. All other physicians who see the patient while he or she is in observation must bill the office and other outpatient service codes or outpatient consultation codes as appropriate when they provide services to the patient.

For example, if an internist admits a patient to observation and asks an allergist for a consultation on the patient's condition, only the internist may bill the initial observation care code. The allergist must bill using the outpatient consultation code that best represents the services he or she provided. The allergist cannot bill an inpatient consultation since the patient was not a hospital inpatient.

B. Physician Billing for Observation Care Following Admission to Observation
When a patient is admitted for observation care for less than 8 hours on the same calendar date, the Initial Observation Care, from CPT code range 99218 - 99220, shall be reported by the physician. The Observation Care Discharge Service, CPT code 99217, shall not be reported for this scenario.

When a patient is admitted for observation care and then discharged on a different calendar date, the physician shall report Initial Observation Care, from CPT code range 99218 - 99220 and CPT observation care discharge CPT code 99217.

When a patient has been admitted for observation care for a minimum of 8 hours, but less than 24 hours and discharged on the same calendar date, Observation or Inpatient Care Services (Including Admission and Discharge Services) from CPT code range 99234 - 99236, shall be reported. The observation discharge, CPT code 99217, cannot also be reported for this scenario.

C. Documentation Requirements for Billing Observation or Inpatient Care Services (Including Admission and Discharge Services (Codes 99234 - 99236))
The physician shall satisfy the E/M documentation guidelines for admission to and discharge from observation care or inpatient hospital care. In addition to meeting the documentation requirements for history, examination, and medical decision making documentation in the medical record shall include:

- Documentation stating the stay for observation care or inpatient hospital care involves 8 hours, but less than 24 hours;

- Documentation identifying the billing physician was present and personally performed the services; and

- Documentation identifying the admission and discharge notes were written by the billing physician.

In the rare circumstance when a patient is held in observation status for more than 2 calendar dates, the physician shall bill a visit furnished before the discharge date using the outpatient/office visit codes. The physician may not use the subsequent hospital care codes since the patient is not an inpatient of the hospital.

D. Admission to Inpatient Status from Observation

If the same physician who admitted a patient to observation status also admits the patient to inpatient status from observation before the end of the date on which the patient was admitted to observation, pay only an initial hospital visit for the evaluation and management services provided on that date. Medicare payment for the initial hospital visit includes all services provided to the patient on the date of admission by that physician, regardless of the site of service. The physician may not bill an initial observation care code for services on the date that he or she admits the patient to inpatient status. If the patient is admitted to inpatient status from observation subsequent to the date of admission to observation, the physician must bill an initial hospital visit for the services provided on that date. The physician may not bill the hospital observation discharge management code (code 99217) or an outpatient/office visit for the care provided in observation on the date of admission to inpatient status.

E. Hospital Observation During Global Surgical Period

The global surgical fee includes payment for hospital observation (codes 99217, 99218, 99219, and 99220, 99234, 99235, 99236) services unless the criteria for use of CPT modifiers "-24," "-25," or "-57" are met. Contractors must pay for these services in addition to the global surgical fee only if both of the following requirements are met:

- The hospital observation service meets the criteria needed to justify billing it with CPT modifiers "-24," "-25," or "-57" (decision for major surgery); and

- The hospital observation service furnished by the surgeon meets all of the criteria for the hospital observation code billed.

Examples of the decision for surgery during a hospital observation period are:

- A patient is admitted by an emergency department physician to an observation unit for observation of a head injury. A neurosurgeon is called in to do a consultation on the need for surgery while the patient is in the observation unit and decides that the patient requires surgery. The surgeon would bill an outpatient consultation with the "-57" modifier to indicate that the decision for surgery was made during the consultation. The surgeon must bill an outpatient consultation because the patient in an observation unit is not an inpatient of the hospital. Only the physician who admitted the patient to hospital observation may bill for initial observation care.

- A patient is admitted by a neurosurgeon to a hospital observation unit for observation of a head injury. During the observation period, the surgeon makes the decision for surgery. The surgeon would bill the appropriate level of hospital observation code with the "-57" modifier to indicate that the decision for surgery was made while the surgeon was providing hospital observation care.

Examples of hospital observation services during the postoperative period of a surgery are:

- A patient at the 80th day following a TURP is admitted to observation with abdominal pain from a kidney stone by the surgeon who performed the procedure.The surgeon decides that the patient does not require surgery. The surgeon would bill the observation code with CPT modifier "-24" and documentation to support that the observation services are unrelated to the surgery.

- A patient at the 80th day following a TURP is admitted to observation with abdominal pain by the surgeon who performed the procedure. While the patient is in hospital observation, the surgeon decides that the patient requires kidney surgery. The surgeon would bill the observation code with HCPCS modifier "-57" to indicate that the decision for surgery was made while the patient was in hospital observation. The subsequent surgical procedure would be reported with modifier "-79."

- A patient at the 20th day following a resection of the colon is admitted to observation for abdominal pain by the surgeon who performed the surgery. The surgeon determines that the patient requires no further colon surgery and discharges the patient. The surgeon may not bill for the observation services furnished during the global period because they were related to the previous surgery.

An example of a billable hospital observation service on the same day as a procedure is a patient is admitted to the hospital observation unit for observation of a head injury by a physician who repaired a laceration of the scalp in the emergency department. The physician would bill the observation code with a CPT modifier 25 and the procedure

100-4, 12, 30.6.9

Payment for Inpatient Hospital Visits - General (Codes 99221 - 99239)

A. Hospital Visit and Critical Care on Same Day

When a hospital inpatient or office/outpatient evaluation and management service (E/M) are furnished on a calendar date at which time the patient does not require critical care and the patient subsequently requires critical care both the critical Care Services (CPT codes 99291 and 99292) and the previous E/M service may be paid on the same date of service. Hospital emergency department services are not paid for the same date as critical care services when provided by the same physician to the same patient.

During critical care management of a patient those services that do not meet the level of critical care shall be reported using an inpatient hospital care service with CPT Subsequent Hospital Care using a code from CPT code range 99231 - 99233.

Both Initial Hospital Care (CPT codes 99221 - 99223) and Subsequent Hospital Care codes are "per diem" services and may be reported only once per day by the same physician or physicians of the same specialty from the same group practice.

Physicians and qualified nonphysician practitioners (NPPs) are advised to retain documentation for discretionary contractor review should claims be questioned for both hospital care and critical care claims. The retained documentation shall support claims for critical care when the same physician or physicians of the same specialty in a group practice report critical care services for the same patient on the same calendar date as other E/M services.

B. Two Hospital Visits Same Day

Contractors pay a physician for only one hospital visit per day for the same patient, whether the problems seen during the encounters are related or not. The inpatient hospital visit descriptors contain the phrase "per day" which means that the code and the payment established for the code represent all services provided on that date. The physician should select a code that reflects all services provided during the date of the service.

C. Hospital Visits Same Day But by Different Physicians

In a hospital inpatient situation involving one physician covering for another, if physician A sees the patient in the morning and physician B, who is covering for A, sees the same patient in the evening, carriers do not pay physician B for the second visit. The hospital visit descriptors include the phrase "per day" meaning care for the day.

If the physicians are each responsible for a different aspect of the patient's care, pay both visits if the physicians are in different specialties and the visits are billed with different diagnoses. There are circumstances where concurrent care may be billed by physicians of the same specialty.

D. Visits to Patients in Swing Beds

If the inpatient care is being billed by the hospital as inpatient hospital care, the hospital care codes apply. If the inpatient care is being billed by the hospital as nursing facility care, then the nursing facility codes apply.

100-4, 12, 30.6.9.1

Payment for Initial Hospital Care Services (Codes 99221–99223 and Observation or Inpatient Care Services (Including Admission and Discharge Services) (Codes 99234–99236)

A. Initial Hospital Care From Emergency Room

Contractors pay for an initial hospital care service or an initial inpatient consultation if a physician sees his/her patient in the emergency room and decides to admit the person to the hospital. They do not pay for both E/M services. Also, they do not pay for an emergency department visit by the same physician on the same date of service. When the patient is admitted to the hospital via another site of service (e.g., hospital emergency department, physician's office, nursing facility), all services provided by the physician in conjunction with that admission are considered part of the initial hospital care when performed on the same date as the admission.

B. Initial Hospital Care on Day Following Visit

Contractors pay both visits if a patient is seen in the office on one date and admitted to the hospital on the next date, even if fewer than 24 hours has elapsed between the visit and the admission.

C. Initial Hospital Care and Discharge on Same Day

When the patient is admitted to inpatient hospital care for less than 8 hours on the same date, then Initial Hospital Care, from CPT code range 99221 - 99223, shall be reported by the physician. The Hospital Discharge Day Management service, CPT codes 99238 or 99239, shall not be reported for this scenario.

When a patient is admitted to inpatient initial hospital care and then discharged on a different calendar date, the physician shall report an Initial Hospital Care from CPT code range 99221 - 99223 and a Hospital Discharge Day Management service, CPT code 99238 or 99239.

When a patient has been admitted to inpatient hospital care for a minimum of 8 hours but less than 24 hours and discharged on the same calendar date, Observation or Inpatient Hospital Care Services (Including Admission and Discharge Services), from CPT code range 99234 - 99236, shall be reported.

D. Documentation Requirements for Billing Observation or Inpatient Care Services (Including Admission and Discharge Services), CPT codes 99234 - 99236

The physician shall satisfy the E/M documentation guidelines for admission to and discharge from inpatient observation or hospital care. In addition to meeting the documentation requirements for history, examination and medical decision making documentation in the medical record shall include:

- Documentation stating the stay for hospital treatment or observation care status involves 8 hours but less than 24 hours;

- Documentation identifying the billing physician was present and personally performed the services; and

- Documentation identifying the admission and discharge notes were written by the billing physician.

E. Physician Services Involving Transfer From One Hospital to Another; Transfer Within Facility to Prospective Payment System (PPS) Exempt Unit of Hospital; Transfer From One Facility to Another Separate Entity Under Same Ownership and/or Part of Same Complex; or Transfer From One Department to Another Within Single Facility

Physicians may bill both the hospital discharge management code and an initial hospital care code when the discharge and admission do not occur on the same day if the transfer is between:

- Different hospitals;

- Different facilities under common ownership which do not have merged records; or

- Between the acute care hospital and a PPS exempt unit within the same hospital when there are no merged records.

In all other transfer circumstances, the physician should bill only the appropriate level of subsequent hospital care for the date of transfer.

F. Initial Hospital Care Service History and Physical That Is Less Than Comprehensive
When a physician performs a visit or consultation that meets the definition of a Level 5 office visit or consultation several days prior to an admission and on the day of admission performs less than a comprehensive history and physical, he or she should report the office visit or consultation that reflects the services furnished and also report the lowest level initial hospital care code (i.e., code 99221) for the initial hospital admission. Contractors pay the office visit as billed and the Level 1 initial hospital care code.

G. Initial Hospital Care Visits by Two Different M.D.s or D.O.s When They Are Involved in Same Admission
Physicians use the initial hospital care codes (codes 99221-99223) to report the first hospital inpatient encounter with the patient when he or she is the admitting physician.

Contractors consider only one M.D. or D.O. to be the admitting physician and permit only the admitting physician to use the initial hospital care codes. Physicians that participate in the care of a patient but are not the admitting physician of record should bill the inpatient evaluation and management services codes that describe their participation in the patient's care (i.e., subsequent hospital visit or inpatient consultation).

H. Initial Hospital Care and Nursing Facility Visit on Same Day
Pay only the initial hospital care code if the patient is admitted to a hospital following a nursing facility visit on the same date by the same physician. Instruct physicians that they may not report a nursing facility service and an initial hospital care service on the same day. Payment for the initial hospital care service includes all work performed by in all sites of service on that dat

100-4, 12, 30.6.9.2
Subsequent Hospital Visit and Hospital Discharge Day Management (Codes 99231 - 99239)

A. Subsequent Hospital Visits During the Global Surgery Period
(Refer to Secs.40-40.4 on global surgery)

The Medicare physician fee schedule payment amount for surgical procedures includes all services (e.g., evaluation and management visits) that are part of the global surgery payment; therefore, contractors shall not pay more than that amount when a bill is fragmented for staged procedures.

B. Hospital Discharge Day Management Service
Hospital Discharge Day Management Services, CPT code 99238 or 99239 is a face-to-face evaluation and management (E/M) service between the attending physician and the patient. The E/M discharge day management visit shall be reported for the date of the actual visit by the physician or qualified nonphysician practitioner even if the patient is discharged from the facility on a different calendar date. Only one hospital discharge day management service is payable per patient per hospital stay.

Only the attending physician of record reports the discharge day management service. Physicians or qualified nonphysician practitioners, other than the attending physician, who have been managing concurrent health care problems not primarily managed by the attending physician, and who are not acting on behalf of the attending physician, shall use Subsequent Hospital Care (CPT code range 99231 - 99233) for a final visit.

Medicare pays for the paperwork of patient discharge day management through the pre- and post- service work of an E/M service.

C. Subsequent Hospital Visit and Discharge Management on Same Day
Pay only the hospital discharge management code on the day of discharge (unless it is also the day of admission, in which case, refer to Sec.30.6.9.1 C for the policy on Observation or Inpatient Care Services (Including Admission and Discharge Services CPT Codes 99234 - 99236). Contractors do not pay both a subsequent hospital visit in addition to hospital discharge day management service on the same day by the same physician. Instruct physicians that they may not bill for both a hospital visit and hospital discharge management for the same date of service.

D. Hospital Discharge Management (CPT Codes 99238 and 99239) and Nursing Facility Admission Code When Patient Is Discharged From Hospital and Admitted to Nursing Facility on Same Day
Contractors pay the hospital discharge code (codes 99238 or 99239) in addition to a nursing facility admission code when they are billed by the same physician with the same date of service.

If a surgeon is admitting the patient to the nursing facility due to a condition that is not as a result of the surgery during the postoperative period of a service with the global surgical period, he/she bills for the nursing facility admission and care with a modifier "-24" and provides documentation that the service is unrelated to the surgery (e.g., return of an elderly patient to the nursing facility in which he/she has resided for five years following discharge from the hospital for cholecystectomy).

Contractors do not pay for a nursing facility admission by a surgeon in the postoperative period of a procedure with a global surgical period if the patient's admission to the nursing facility is to receive post operative care related to the surgery (e.g., admission to a nursing facility to receive physical therapy following a hip replacement). Payment for the nursing facility admission and subsequent nursing facility services are included in the global fee and cannot be paid separately.

E. Hospital Discharge Management and Death Pronouncement
Only the physician who personally performs the pronouncement of death shall bill for the face-to-face Hospital Discharge Day Management Service, CPT code 99238 or 99239. The date of the pronouncement shall reflect the calendar date of service on the day it was performed even if the paperwork is delayed to a subsequent date.

100-4, 12, 30.6.10
Consultation Services (Codes 99241 - 99255)
A. Consultation Services versus Other Evaluation and Management (E/M) Visits
Carriers pay for a reasonable and medically necessary consultation service when all of the following criteria for the use of a consultation code are met:

- Specifically, a consultation service is distinguished from other evaluation and management (E/M) visits because it is provided by a physician or qualified nonphysician practitioner (NPP) whose opinion or advice regarding evaluation and/or management of a specific problem is requested by another physician or other appropriate source. The qualified NPP may perform consultation services within the scope of practice and licensure requirements for NPPs in the State in which he/she practices. Applicable collaboration and general supervision rules apply as well as billing rules;

- A request for a consultation from an appropriate source and the need for consultation (i.e., the reason for a consultation service) shall be documented by the consultant in the patient's medical record and included in the requesting physician or qualified NPP's plan of care in the patient's medical record; and

- After the consultation is provided, the consultant shall prepare a written report of his/her findings and recommendations, which shall be provided to the referring physician.

The intent of a consultation service is that a physician or qualified NPP or other appropriate source is asking another physician or qualified NPP for advice, opinion, a recommendation, suggestion, direction, or counsel, etc. in evaluating or treating a patient because that individual has expertise in a specific medical area beyond the requesting professional's knowledge. Consultations may be billed based on time if the counseling/coordination of care constitutes more than 50 percent of the face-to-face encounter between the physician or qualified NPP and the patient. The preceding requirements (request, evaluation (or counseling/coordination) and written report) shall also be met when the consultation is based on time for counseling/coordination.

A consultation shall not be performed as a split/shared E/M visit.

B. Consultation Followed by Treatment
A physician or qualified NPP consultant may initiate diagnostic services and treatment at the initial consultation service or subsequent visit. Ongoing management, following the initial consultation service by the consultant physician, shall not be reported with consultation service codes. These services shall be reported as subsequent visits for the appropriate place of service and level of service. Payment for a consultation service shall be made regardless of treatment initiation unless a transfer of care occurs.

Transfer of Care A transfer of care occurs when a physician or qualified NPP requests that another physician or qualified NPP take over the responsibility for managing the patients' complete care for the condition and does not expect to continue treating or caring for the patient for that condition.

When this transfer is arranged, the requesting physician or qualified NPP is not asking for an opinion or advice to personally treat this patient and is not expecting to continue treating the patient for the condition. The receiving physician or qualified NPP shall document this transfer of the patient's care, to his/her service, in the patient's medical record or plan of care.

In a transfer of care the receiving physician or qualified NPP would report the appropriate new or established patient visit code according to the place of service and level of service performed and shall not report a consultation service.

C. Initial and Follow-Up Consultation Services
Initial Consultation Service
In the hospital setting, the consulting physician or qualified NPP shall use the appropriate Initial Inpatient Consultation codes (99251 - 99255) for the initial consultation service.

In the nursing facility setting, the consulting physician or qualified NPP shall use the appropriate Initial Inpatient Consultation codes (99251 - 99255) for the initial consultation service.

The Initial Inpatient Consultation may be reported only once per consultant per patient per facility admission.

In the office or other outpatient setting, the consulting physician or qualified NPP shall use the appropriate Office or Other Outpatient Consultation (new or established patient) codes (99241 - 99245) for the initial consultation service.

If an additional request for an opinion or advice, regarding the same or a new problem with the same patient, is received from the same or another physician or qualified NPP and documented in the medical record, the Office or Other Outpatient Consultation (new or established patient) codes (99241 - 99245) may be used again. However, if the consultant continues to care for the patient for the original condition following his/her initial consultation, repeat consultation services shall not be reported by this physician or qualified NPP during his/her ongoing management of this condition.

Follow-Up Consultation Service
Effective January 1, 2006, the follow-up inpatient consultation codes (99261 - 99263) are deleted.

In the hospital setting, following the initial consultation service, the Subsequent Hospital Care codes (99231 - 99233) shall be reported for additional follow-up visits.

In the nursing facility setting, following the initial consultation service, the Subsequent Nursing Facility (NF) Care codes (new CPT codes 99307 - 99310) shall be reported for additional follow-up visits. Effective January 1, 2006, CPT codes 99311 - 99313 are deleted and not valid for Subsequent NF visits.

In the office or other outpatient setting, following the initial consultation service, the Office or Other Outpatient Established Patient codes (99212 - 99215) shall be reported for additional follow-up visits. The CPT code 99211 shall not be reported as a consultation service. The CPT code 99211 is not included by Medicare for a consultation service since this service typically does not require the presence of a physician or qualified NPP and would not meet the consultation service criteria.

D. Second Opinion E/M Service Requests
Effective January 1, 2006, the Confirmatory Consultation codes (99271 - 99275) are deleted.

A second opinion E/M service is a request by the patient and/or family or mandated (e.g., by a third-party payer) and is not requested by a physician or qualified NPP. A consultation service requested by a physician, qualified NPP or other appropriate source that meets the requirements stated in Section A shall be reported using the initial consultation service codes as discussed in Section C. A written report is not required by Medicare to be sent to a physician when an evaluation for a second opinion has been requested by the patient and/or family.

A second opinion, for Medicare purposes, is generally performed as a request for a second or third opinion of a previously recommended medical treatment or surgical procedure. A second opinion E/M service initiated by a patient and/or family is not reported using the consultation codes.

In both the inpatient hospital setting and the NF setting, a request for a second opinion would be made through the attending physician or physician of record. If an initial consultation is requested of another physician or qualified NPP by the attending physician and meets the requirements for a consultation service (as identified in Section A) then the appropriate Initial Inpatient Consultation code shall be reported by the consultant. If the service does not meet the consultation requirements, then the E/M service shall be reported using the Subsequent Hospital Care codes (99231 - 99233) in the inpatient hospital setting and the Subsequent NF Care codes (99307 - 99310) in the NF setting.

A second opinion E/M service performed in the office or other outpatient setting shall be reported using the Office or Other Outpatient new patient codes (99201 - 99205) for a new patient and established patient codes (99212 - 99215) for an established patient, as appropriate. The 3 year rule regarding "new patient" status applies. Any medically necessary follow-up visits shall be reported using the appropriate subsequent visit/established patient E/M visit codes.

The CPT modifier -32 (Mandated Services) is not recognized as a payment modifier in Medicare. A second opinion evaluation service to satisfy a requirement for a third party payer is not a covered service in Medicare.

E. Consultations Requested by Members of Same Group
Carriers pay for a consultation if one physician or qualified NPP in a group practice requests a consultation from another physician in the same group practice when the consulting physician or qualified NPP has expertise in a specific medical area beyond the requesting professional's knowledge. A consultation service shall not be reported on every patient as a routine practice between physicians and qualified NPPs within a group practice setting.

F. Documentation for Consultation Services
Consultation Request
A written request for a consultation from an appropriate source and the need for a consultation must be documented in the patient's medical record. The initial request may be a verbal interaction between the requesting physician and the consulting physician; however, the verbal conversation shall be documented in the patient's medical record, indicating a request for a consultation service was made by the requesting physician or qualified NPP.

The reason for the consultation service shall be documented by the consultant (physician or qualified NPP) in the patient's medical record and included in the requesting physician or qualified NPP's plan of care. The consultation service request may be written on a physician order form by the requestor in a shared medical record.

Consultation Report
A written report shall be furnished to the requesting physician or qualified NPP.

In an emergency department or an inpatient or outpatient setting in which the medical record is shared between the referring physician or qualified NPP and the consultant, the request may be documented as part of a plan written in the requesting physician or qualified NPP's progress note, an order in the medical record, or a specific written request for the consultation. In these settings, the report may consist of an appropriate entry in the common medical record.

In an office setting, the documentation requirement may be met by a specific written request for the consultation from the requesting physician or qualified NPP or if the consultant's records show a specific reference to the request. In this setting, the consultation report is a separate document communicated to the requesting physician or qualified NPP.

In a large group practice, e.g., an academic department or a large multi-specialty group, in which there is often a shared medical record, it is acceptable to include the consultant's report in the medical record documentation and not require a separate letter from the consulting physician or qualified NPP to the requesting physician or qualified NPP. The written request and the consultation evaluation, findings and recommendations shall be available in the consultation report.

G. Consultation for Preoperative Clearance
Preoperative consultations are payable for new or established patients performed by any physician or qualified NPP at the request of a surgeon, as long as all of the requirements for performing and reporting the consultation codes are met and the service is medically necessary and not routine screening.

H. Postoperative Care by Physician Who Did Preoperative Clearance Consultation
If subsequent to the completion of a preoperative consultation in the office or hospital, the consultant assumes responsibility for the management of a portion or all of the patient's condition(s) during the postoperative period, the consultation codes should not be used postoperatively. In the hospital setting, the physician or qualified NPP who has performed a preoperative consultation and assumes responsibility for the management of a portion or all of the patient's condition(s) during the postoperative period should use the appropriate subsequent hospital care codes to bill for the concurrent care he or she is providing. In the office setting, the appropriate established patient visit codes should be used during the postoperative period.

A physician (primary care or specialist) or qualified NPP who performs a postoperative evaluation of a new or established patient at the request of the surgeon may bill the appropriate consultation code for evaluation and management services furnished during the postoperative period following surgery when all of the criteria for the use of the consultation codes are met and that same physician has not already performed a preoperative consultation.

I. Surgeon's Request That Another Physician Participate In Postoperative Care
If the surgeon asks a physician or qualified NPP who had been treating the patient preoperatively or who had not seen the patient for a preoperative consultation to take responsibility for the management of an aspect of the patient's condition during the postoperative period, the physician or qualified NPP may not bill a consultation because the surgeon is not asking the physician or qualified NPP's opinion or advice for the surgeon's use in treating the patient. The physician or qualified NPP's services would constitute concurrent care and should be billed using the appropriate subsequent hospital care codes in the hospital inpatient setting, subsequent NF care codes in the SNF/NF setting or the appropriate office or other outpatient visit codes in the office or outpatient settings.

J. Examples That Meet the Criteria for Consultation Services
For brevity, the consultation request and the consultation written report is not repeated in each of these examples. Criteria for consultation services shall always include a request and a written report in the medical record as described above.

EXAMPLE 1: An internist sees a patient that he has followed for 20 years for mild hypertension and diabetes mellitus. He identifies a questionable skin lesion and asks a dermatologist to evaluate the lesion. The dermatologist examines the patient and decides the lesion is probably malignant and needs to be removed. He removes the lesion which is determined to be an early melanoma. The dermatologist dictates and forwards a report to the internist regarding his evaluation and treatment of the patient. Modifier -25 shall be used with the consultation service code in addition to the procedure code. Modifier -25 is required to identify the consultation service as a significant, separately identifiable E/M service in addition to the procedure code reported for the incision/removal of lesion. The internist resumes care of the patient and continues surveillance of the skin on the advice of the dermatologist.

EXAMPLE 2: A rural family practice physician examines a patient who has been under his care for 20 years and diagnoses a new onset of atrial fibrillation. The family practitioner sends the patient to a cardiologist at an urban cardiology center for advice on his care and management. The cardiologist examines the patient, suggests a cardiac catheterization and other diagnostic tests which he schedules and then sends a written report to the requesting physician. The cardiologist subsequently periodically sees the patient once a year as follow-up. Subsequent visits provided by the cardiologist should be billed as an established patient visit in the office or other outpatient setting, as appropriate.

Following the advice and intervention by the cardiologist the family practice physician resumes the general medical care of the patient.

EXAMPLE 3: A family practice physician examines a female patient who has been under his care for some time and diagnoses a breast mass. The family practitioner sends the patient to a general surgeon for advice and management of the mass and related patient care. The general surgeon examines the patient and recommends a breast biopsy, which he schedules, and then sends a written report to the requesting physician. The general surgeon subsequently performs a biopsy and then periodically sees the patient once a year as follow-up. Subsequent visits provided by the surgeon should be billed as an established patient visit in the office or other outpatient setting, as appropriate.

Following the advice and intervention by the surgeon the family practice physician resumes the general medical care of the patient.

I. Examples That Do Not Meet the Criteria for Consultation Services
EXAMPLE 1: Standing orders in the medical record for consultations.

EXAMPLE 2: No order for a consultation.

EXAMPLE 3: No written report of a consultation.

EXAMPLE 4: The emergency room physician treats the patient for a sprained ankle.

The patient is discharged and instructed to visit the orthopedic clinic for follow-up. The physician in the orthopedic clinic shall not report a consultation service because advice or opinion is not required by the emergency room physician. The orthopedic physician shall report the appropriate office or other outpatient visit code.

100-4, 12, 30.6.11
Emergency Department Visits (Codes 99281 - 99288)
B3-15507

A. Use of Emergency Department Codes by Physicians Not Assigned to Emergency Department
Any physician seeing a patient registered in the emergency department may use emergency department visit codes (for services matching the code description). It is not required that the physician be assigned to the emergency department.

B. Use of Emergency Department Codes In Office
Emergency department coding is not appropriate if the site of service is an office or outpatient setting or any sight of service other than an emergency department. The emergency department codes should only be used if the patient is seen in the emergency department and the services described by the HCPCS code definition are provided. The emergency department is defined as an organized hospital-based facility for the provision of unscheduled or episodic services to patients who present for immediate medical attention.

C. Use of Emergency Department Codes to Bill Nonemergency Services
Services in the emergency department may not be emergencies. However the codes (99281 - 99288) are payable if the described services are provided.

However, if the physician asks the patient to meet him or her in the emergency department as an alternative to the physician's office and the patient is not registered as a patient in the emergency department, the physician should bill the appropriate office/outpatient visit codes. Normally a lower level emergency department code would be reported for a nonemergency condition.

D. Emergency Department or Office/Outpatient Visits on Same Day As Nursing Facility Admission
Emergency department visit provided on the same day as a comprehensive nursing facility assessment are not paid. Payment for evaluation and management services on the same date provided in sites other than the nursing facility are included in the payment for initial nursing facility care when performed on the same date as the nursing facility admission.

E. Physician Billing for Emergency Department Services Provided to Patient by Both Patient's Personal Physician and Emergency Department Physician
If a physician advises his/her own patient to go to an emergency department (ED) of a hospital for care and the physician subsequently is asked by the ED physician to come to the hospital to evaluate the patient and to advise the ED physician as to whether the patient should be admitted to the hospital or be sent home, the physicians should bill as follows:

- If the patient is admitted to the hospital by the patient's personal physician, then the patient's regular physician should bill only the appropriate level of the initial hospital care (codes 99221 - 99223) because all evaluation and management services provided by that physician in conjunction with that admission are considered part of the initial hospital care when performed on the same date as the admission. The ED physician who saw the patient in the emergency department should bill the appropriate level of the ED codes.

- If the ED physician, based on the advice of the patient's personal physician who came to the emergency department to see the patient, sends the patient home, then the ED physician should bill the appropriate level of emergency department service. The patient's personal physician should also bill the level of emergency department code that describes the service he or she provided in the emergency department. The patient's personal physician would not bill a consultation because he or she is not providing information to the emergency department physician for his or her use in treating the patient. If the patient's personal physician does not come to the hospital to see the patient, but only advises the emergency department physician by telephone, then the patient's personal physician may not bill.

F. Emergency Department Physician Requests Another Physician to See the Patient in Emergency Department or Office/Outpatient Setting
If the emergency department physician requests that another physician evaluate a given patient, the other physician should bill a consultation if the criteria for consultation are met. If the criteria for a consultation are not met and the patient is discharged from the Emergency Department or admitted to the hospital by another physician, the physician contacted by the Emergency Department physician should bill an emergency department visit. If the consulted physician admits the patient to the hospital and the criteria for a consultation are not met, he/she should bill an initial hospital care code.

100-4, 12, 30.6.12
Critical Care Visits and Neonatal Intensive Care (Codes 99291 - 99292)
CRITICAL CARE SERVICES (CODES 99291-99292)

A. Use of Critical Care Codes
Pay for services reported with CPT codes 99291 and 99292 when all the criteria for critical care and critical care services are met. Critical care is defined as the direct delivery by a physician(s) medical care for a critically ill or critically injured patient. A critical illness or injury acutely impairs one or more vital organ systems such that there is a high probability of imminent or life threatening deterioration in the patient's condition.

Critical care involves high complexity decision making to assess, manipulate, and support vital system function(s) to treat single or multiple vital organ system failure and/or to prevent further life threatening deterioration of the patient's condition.

Examples of vital organ system failure include, but are not limited to: central nervous system failure, circulatory failure, shock, renal, hepatic, metabolic, and/or respiratory failure. Although critical care typically requires interpretation of multiple physiologic parameters and/or application of advanced technology(s), critical care may be provided in life threatening situations when these elements are not present.

Providing medical care to a critically ill, injured, or post-operative patient qualifies as a critical care service only if both the illness or injury and the treatment being provided meet the above requirements.

Critical care is usually, but not always, given in a critical care area such as a coronary care unit, intensive care unit, respiratory care unit, or the emergency department. However, payment may be made for critical care services provided in any location as long as the care provided meets the definition of critical care.

Consult the American Medical Association (AMA) CPT Manual for the applicable codes and guidance for critical care services provided to neonates, infants and children.

B. Critical Care Services and Medical Necessity
Critical care services must be medically necessary and reasonable. Services provided that do not meet critical care services or services provided for a patient who is not critically ill or injured in accordance with the above definitions and criteria but who happens to be in a critical care, intensive care, or other specialized care unit should be reported using another appropriate E/M code (e.g., subsequent hospital care, CPT codes 99231 - 99233).

As described in Section A, critical care services encompass both treatment of "vital organ failure" and "prevention of further life threatening deterioration of the patient's condition." Therefore, although critical care may be delivered in a moment of crisis or upon being called to the patient's bedside emergently, this is not a requirement for providing critical care service. The treatment and management of the patient's condition, while not necessarily emergent, shall be required, based on the threat of imminent deterioration (i.e., the patient shall be critically ill or injured at the time of the physician's visit).

Chronic Illness and Critical Care:

Examples of patients whose medical condition may not warrant critical care services:

1. Daily management of a patient on chronic ventilator therapy does not meet the criteria for critical care unless the critical care is separately identifiable from the chronic long term management of the ventilator dependence.

2. Management of dialysis or care related to dialysis for a patient receiving ESRD hemodialysis does not meet the criteria for critical care unless the critical care is separately identifiable from the chronic long term management of the dialysis dependence (refer to Chapter 8, Sec.160.4). When a separately identifiable condition (e.g., management of seizures or pericardial tamponade related to renal failure) is being managed, it may be billed as critical care if critical care requirements are met. Modifier -25 should be appended to the critical care code when applicable in this situation.

Examples of patients whose medical condition may warrant critical care services:

1. An 81 year old male patient is admitted to the intensive care unit following abdominal aortic aneurysm resection. Two days after surgery he requires fluids and pressors to maintain adequate perfusion and arterial pressures. He remains ventilator dependent.

2. A 67 year old female patient is 3 days status post mitral valve repair. She develops petechiae, hypotension and hypoxia requiring respiratory and circulatory support.

3. A 70 year old admitted for right lower lobe pneumococcal pneumonia with a history of COPD becomes hypoxic and hypotensive 2 days after admission.

4. A 68 year old admitted for an acute anterior wall myocardial infarction continues to have symptomatic ventricular tachycardia that is marginally responsive to antiarrhythmic therapy.

Examples of patients who may not satisfy Medicare medical necessity criteria, or do not meet critical care criteria or who do not have a critical care illness or injury and therefore not eligible for critical care payment:

1. Patients admitted to a critical care unit because no other hospital beds were available;

2. Patients admitted to a critical care unit for close nursing observation and/or frequent monitoring of vital signs (e.g., drug toxicity or overdose); and

3. Patients admitted to a critical care unit because hospital rules require certain treatments (e.g., insulin infusions) to be administered in the critical care unit.

Providing medical care to a critically ill patient should not be automatically deemed to be a critical care service for the sole reason that the patient is critically ill or injured. While more than one physician may provide critical care services to a patient during the critical care episode of an illness or injury each physician must be managing one or more critical illness(es) or injury(ies) in whole or in part.

> EXAMPLE: A dermatologist evaluates and treats a rash on an ICU patient who is maintained on a ventilator and nitroglycerine infusion that are being managed by an intensivist. The dermatologist should not report a service for critical care.

C. Critical Care Services and Full Attention of the Physician
The duration of critical care services to be reported is the time the physician spent evaluating, providing care and managing the critically ill or injured patient's care. That time must be spent at the immediate bedside or elsewhere on the floor or unit so long as the physician is immediately available to the patient.

For example, time spent reviewing laboratory test results or discussing the critically ill patient's care with other medical staff in the unit or at the nursing station on the floor may be reported as critical care, even when it does not occur at the bedside, if this time represents the physician's full attention to the management of the critically ill/injured patient.

For any given period of time spent providing critical care services, the physician must devote his or her full attention to the patient and, therefore, cannot provide services to any other patient during the same period of time.   D. Critical Care Services and Qualified Non-Physician Practitioners (NPP) Critical care services may be provided by qualified NPPs and reported for payment under the NPP's National Provider Identifier (NPI) when the services meet the definition and requirements of critical care services in Sections A and B. The provision of critical care services must be within the scope of practice and licensure requirements for the State in which the qualified NPP practices and provides the service(s). Collaboration, physician supervision and billing requirements must also be met. A physician assistant shall meet the general physician supervision requirements.

E. Critical Care Services and Physician Time
Critical care is a time-based service, and for each date and encounter entry, the physician's progress note(s) shall document the total time that critical care services were provided. More than one physician can provide critical care at another time and be paid if the service meets critical care, is medically necessary and is not duplicative care. Concurrent care by more than one physician (generally representing different physician specialties) is payable if these requirements are met (refer to the Medicare Benefit Policy Manual, Pub. 100-02, Chapter 15, Sec.30 for concurrent care policy discussion).

The CPT critical care codes 99291 and 99292 are used to report the total duration of time spent by a physician providing critical care services to a critically ill or critically injured patient, even if the time spent by the physician on that date is not continuous. Non-continuous time for medically necessary critical care services may be aggregated. Reporting CPT code 99291 is a prerequisite to reporting CPT code 99292. Physicians of the same specialty within the same group practice bill and are paid as though they were a single physician (Sec.30.6.5).

1. Off the Unit/Floor
Time spent in activities (excluding those identified previously in Section C) that occur outside of the unit or off the floor (i.e., telephone calls, whether taken at home, in the office, or elsewhere in the hospital) may not be reported as critical care because the physician is not immediately available to the patient. This time is regarded as pre- and post service work bundled in evaluation and management services.

2. Split/Shared Service
A split/shared E/M service performed by a physician and a qualified NPP of the same group practice (or employed by the same employer) cannot be reported as a critical care service. Critical care services are reflective of the care and management of a critically ill or critically injured patient by an individual physician or qualified non-physician practitioner for the specified reportable period of time.

Unlike other E/M services where a split/shared service is allowed the critical care service reported shall reflect the evaluation, treatment and management of a patient by an individual physician or qualified non-physician practitioner and shall not be representative of a combined service between a physician and a qualified NPP.

When CPT code time requirements for both 99291 and 99292 and critical care criteria are met for a medically necessary visit by a qualified NPP the service shall be billed using the appropriate individual NPI number. Medically necessary visit(s) that do not meet these requirements shall be reported as subsequent hospital care services.

3. Unbundled Procedures
Time involved performing procedures that are not bundled into critical care (i.e., billed and paid separately) may not be included and counted toward critical care time. The physician's progress note(s) in the medical record should document that time involved in the performance of separately billable procedures was not counted toward critical care time.

4. Family Counseling/Discussions
Critical care CPT codes 99291 and 99292 include pre and post service work. Routine daily updates or reports to family members and or surrogates are considered part of this service. However, time involved with family members or other surrogate decision makers, whether to obtain a history or to discuss treatment options (as described in CPT), may be counted toward critical care time when these specific criteria are met:

a) The patient is unable or incompetent to participate in giving a history and/or making treatment decisions, and

b) The discussion is necessary for determining treatment decisions.

For family discussions, the physician should document:

a. The patient is unable or incompetent to participate in giving history and/or making treatment decisions

b. The necessity to have the discussion (e.g., "no other source was available to obtain a history" or "because the patient was deteriorating so rapidly I needed to immediately discuss treatment options with the family",

c. Medically necessary treatment decisions for which the discussion was needed, and

d. A summary in the medical record that supports the medical necessity of the discussion All other family discussions, no matter how lengthy, may not be additionally counted towards critical care. Telephone calls to family members and or surrogate decision-makers may be counted towards critical care time, but only if they meet the same criteria as described in the aforementioned paragraph.

5. Inappropriate Use of Time for Payment of Critical Care Services.
Time involved in activities that do not directly contribute to the treatment of the critically ill or injured patient may not be counted towards the critical care time, even when they are performed in the critical care unit at a patient's bedside (e.g., review of literature, and teaching sessions with physician residents whether conducted on hospital rounds or in other venues).

F. Hours and Days of Critical Care that May Be Billed
Critical care service is a time-based service provided on an hourly or fraction of an hour basis. Payment should not be restricted to a fixed number of hours, a fixed number of physicians, or a fixed number of days, on a per patient basis, for medically necessary critical care services. Time counted towards critical care services may be continuous or intermittent and aggregated in time increments (e.g., 50 minutes of continuous clock time or (5) 10 minute blocks of time spread over a given calendar date). Only one physician may bill for critical care services during any one single period of time even if more than one physician is providing care to a critically ill patient.

For Medicare Part B physician services paid under the physician fee schedule, critical care is not a service that is paid on a "shift" basis or a "per day" basis. Documentation may be requested for any claim to determine medical necessity. Examples of critical care billing that may require further review could include: claims from several physicians submitting multiple units of critical care for a single patient, and submitting claims for more than 12 hours of critical care time by a physician for one or more patients on the same given calendar date. Physicians assigned to a critical care unit (e.g., hospitalist, intensivist, etc.) may not report critical care for patients based on a "per shift" basis.

The CPT code 99291 is used to report the first 30 - 74 minutes of critical care on a given calendar date of service. It should only be used once per calendar date per patient by the same physician or physician group of the same specialty. CPT code 99292 is used to report additional block(s) of time, of up to 30 minutes each beyond the first 74 minutes of critical care (See table below). Critical care of less than 30 minutes total duration on a given calendar date is not reported separately using the critical care codes. This service should be reported using another appropriate E/M code such as subsequent hospital care.

Clinical Example of Correct Billing of Time:
A patient arrives in the emergency department in cardiac arrest. The emergency department physician provides 40 minutes of critical care services. A cardiologist is called to the ED and assumes responsibility for the patient, providing 35 minutes of critical care services. The patient stabilizes and is transferred to the CCU. In this instance, the ED physician provided 40 minutes of critical care services and reports only the critical care code (CPT code 99291) and not also emergency department services. The cardiologist may report the 35 minutes of critical care services (also CPT code 99291) provided in the ED. Additional critical care services by the cardiologist in the CCU may be reported on the same calendar date using 99292 or another appropriate E/M code depending on the clock time involved.

G. Counting of Units of Critical Care Services
The CPT code 99291 (critical care, first hour) is used to report the services of a physician providing full attention to a critically ill or critically injured patient from 30-74 minutes on a given date. Only one unit of CPT code 99291 may be billed by a physician for a patient on a given date. Physicians of the same specialty within the same group practice bill and are paid as though they were a single physician and would not each report CPT 99291on the same date of service.

The following illustrates the correct reporting of critical care services:

Total Duration of Critical Care	Code(s)
Less than 30 minutes	99232 or 99233 or other appropriate E/M code
30-74 minutes	99291 x 1
75-104 minutes	99291 x 1 and 99292 x 1
105-134 minutes	99291 x 1 and 99292 x 2
135-164 minutes	99291 x 1 and 99292 x 3
165-194 minutes	99291 x 1 and 99292 x 4
194 minutes or longer	99291 - 99292 as appropriate (per the above illustrations)

H. Critical Care Services and Other Evaluation and Management Services Provided on Same Day
When critical care services are required upon the patient's presentation to the hospital emergency department, only critical care codes 99291 - 99292 may be reported. An emergency department visit code may not also be reported.

When critical care services are provided on a date where an inpatient hospital or office/outpatient evaluation and management service was furnished earlier on the same date at which time the patient did not require critical care, both the critical care and the previous evaluation and management service may be paid. Hospital emergency department services are not payable for the same calendar date as critical care services when provided by the same physician to the same patient.

Physicians are advised to submit documentation to support a claim when critical care is additionally reported on the same calendar date as when other evaluation and management services are provided to a patient by the same physician or physicians of the same specialty in a group practice.

I. Critical Care Services Provided by Physicians in Group Practice(s)
Medically necessary critical care services provided on the same calendar date to the same patient by physicians representing different medical specialties that are not duplicative services are payable. The medical specialists may be from the same group practice or from different group practices.

Critically ill or critically injured patients may require the care of more than one physician medical specialty. Concurrent critical care services provided by each physician must be medically necessary and not provided during the same instance of time. Medical record documentation must support the medical necessity of critical care services provided by each physician (or qualified NPP). Each physician must accurately report the service(s) he/she provided to the patient in accordance with any applicable global surgery rules or concurrent care rules. (Refer to Medicare Claims Processing Manual, Pub. 100-04, Chapter 12, Sec.40, and the Medicare Benefit Policy Manual, Pub. 100-02, Chapter 15, Sec.30.)

CPT Code 99291
The initial critical care time, billed as CPT code 99291, must be met by a single physician or qualified NPP. This may be performed in a single period of time or be cumulative by the same physician on the same calendar date. A history or physical exam performed by one group partner for another group partner in order for the second group partner to make a medical decision would not represent critical care services.

CPT Code 99292
Subsequent critical care visits performed on the same calendar date are reported using CPT code 99292. The service may represent aggregate time met by a single physician or physicians in the same group practice with the same medical specialty in order to meet the duration of minutes required for CPT code 99292. The aggregated critical care visits must be medically necessary and each aggregated visit must meet the definition of critical care in order to combine the times.

Physicians in the same group practice who have the same specialty may not each report CPT initial critical care code 99291 for critical care services to the same patient on the same calendar date. Medicare payment policy states that physicians in the same group practice who are in the same specialty must bill and be paid as though each were the single physician. (Refer to the Medicare Claims Processing Manual, Pub. 100-04, Chapter 12, Sec.30.6.) Physician specialty means the self-designated primary specialty by which the physician bills Medicare and is known to the contractor that adjudicates the claims. Physicians in the same group practice who have different medical specialties may bill and be paid without regard to their membership in the same group. For example, if a cardiologist and an endocrinologist are group partners and the critical care services of each are medically necessary and not duplicative, the critical care services may be reported by each regardless of their group practice relationship.

Two or more physicians in the same group practice who have different specialties and who provide critical care to a critically ill or critically injured patient may not in all cases each report the initial critical care code (CPT 99291) on the same date. When the group physicians are providing care that is unique to his/her individual medical specialty and managing at least one of the patient's critical illness(es) or critical injury(ies) then the initial critical care service may be payable to each.

However, if a physician or qualified NPP within a group provides "staff coverage" or "follow-up" for each other after the first hour of critical care services was provided on the same calendar date by the previous group clinician (physician or qualified NPP), the subsequent visits by the "covering" physician or qualified NPP in the group shall be billed using CPT critical care add-on code 99292. The appropriate individual NPI number shall be reported on the claim. The services will be paid at the specific physician fee schedule rate for the individual clinician (physician or qualified NPP) billing the service.

Clinical Examples of Critical Care Services

1. Drs. Smith and Jones, pulmonary specialists, share a group practice. On Tuesday Dr. Smith provides critical care services to Mrs. Benson who is comatose and has been in the intensive care unit for 4 days following a motor vehicle accident. She has multiple organ dysfunction including cerebral hematoma, flail chest and pulmonary contusion. Later on the same calendar date Dr. Jones covers for Dr. Smith and provides critical care services. Medically necessary critical care services provided at the different time periods may be reported by both Drs. Smith and Jones. Dr. Smith would report CPT code 99291 for the initial visit and Dr. Jones, as part of the same group practice would report CPT code 99292 on the same calendar date if the appropriate time requirements are met.

2. Mr. Marks, a 79 year old comes to the emergency room with vague joint pains and lethargy. The ED physician evaluates Mr. Marks and phones his primary care physician to discuss his medical evaluation. His primary care physician visits the ER and admits Mr. Marks to the observation unit for monitoring, and diagnostic and laboratory tests. In observation Mr. Marks has a cardiac arrest. His primary care physician provides 50 minutes of critical care services. Mr. Marks' is admitted to the intensive care unit. On the same calendar day Mr. Marks' condition deteriorates and he requires intermittent critical care services. In this scenario the ED physician should report an emergency department visit and the primary care physician should report both an initial hospital visit and critical care services.

J. Critical Care Services and Other Procedures Provided on the Same Day by the Same Physician as Critical Care Codes 99291 - 99292

The following services when performed on the day a physician bills for critical care are included in the critical care service and should not be reported separately:

- The interpretation of cardiac output measurements (CPT 93561, 93562);
- Chest x-rays, professional component (CPT 71010, 71015, 71020);
- Blood draw for specimen (CPT 36415);
- Blood gases, and information data stored in computers (e.g., ECGs, blood pressures, hematologic data-CPT 99090);
- Gastric intubation (CPT 43752, 91105);
- Pulse oximetry (CPT 94760, 94761, 94762);
- Temporary transcutaneous pacing (CPT 92953);
- Ventilator management (CPT 94002 - 94004, 94660, 94662); and
- Vascular access procedures (CPT 36000, 36410, 36415, 36591, 36600).

No other procedure codes are bundled into the critical care services. Therefore, other medically necessary procedure codes may be billed separately.

K. Global Surgery

Critical care services shall not be paid on the same calendar date the physician also reports a procedure code with a global surgical period unless the critical care is billed with CPT modifier -25 to indicate that the critical care is a significant, separately identifiable evaluation and management service that is above and beyond the usual pre and post operative care associated with the procedure that is performed.

Services such as endotracheal intubation (CPT code 31500) and the insertion and placement of a flow directed catheter e.g., Swan-Ganz (CPT code 93503) are not bundled into the critical care codes. Therefore, separate payment may be made for critical care in addition to these services if the critical care was a significant, separately identifiable service and it was reported with modifier -25. The time spent performing the pre, intra, and post procedure work of these unbundled services, e.g., endotracheal intubation, shall be excluded from the determination of the time spent providing critical care.

This policy applies to any procedure with a 0, 10 or 90 day global period including cardiopulmonary resuscitation (CPT code 92950). CPR has a global period of 0 days and is not bundled into critical care codes. Therefore, critical care may be billed in addition to CPR if critical care was a significant, separately identifiable service and it was reported with modifier -25. The time spent performing CPR shall be excluded from the determination of the time spent providing critical care. In this instance it must be the physician who performs the resuscitation who bills for this service. Members of a code team must not each bill Medicare Part B for this service.

When postoperative critical care services (for procedures with a global surgical period) are provided by a physician other than the surgeon, no modifier is required unless all surgical postoperative care has been officially transferred from the surgeon to the physician performing the critical care services. In this situation, CPT modifiers "-54" (surgical care only) and "-55"(postoperative management only) must be used by the surgeon and intensivist who are submitting claims. Medical record documentation by the surgeon and the physician who assumes a transfer (e.g., intensivist) is required to support claims for services when CPT modifiers -54 and -55 are used indicating the transfer of care from the surgeon to the intensivist. Critical care services must meet all the conditions previously described in this manual section.

L. Critical Care Services Provided During Preoperative Portion and Postoperative Portion of Global Period of Procedure with 90 Day Global Period in Trauma and Burn Cases

Preoperative

Preoperative critical care may be paid in addition to a global fee if the patient is critically ill and requires the full attention of the physician, and the critical care is unrelated to the specific anatomic injury or general surgical procedure performed. Such patients may meet the definition of being critically ill and criteria for conditions where there is a high probability of imminent or life threatening deterioration in the patient's condition.

Preoperatively, in order for these services to be paid, two reporting requirements must be met. Codes 99291 - 99292 and modifier -25 (significant, separately identifiable evaluation and management services by the same physician on the day of the procedure) must be used, and documentation identifying that the critical care was unrelated to the specific anatomic injury or general surgical procedure performed shall be submitted. An ICD-9-CM code in the range 800.0 through 959.9 (except 930.0 - 939.9), which clearly indicates that the critical care was unrelated to the surgery, is acceptable documentation.

Postoperative

Postoperatively, in order for critical care services to be paid, two reporting requirements must be met. Codes 99291 - 99292 and modifier -24 (unrelated evaluation and management service by the same physician during a postoperative period) must be used, and documentation that the critical care was unrelated to the specific anatomic injury or general surgical procedure performed must be submitted. An ICD-9-CM code in the range 800.0 through 959.9 (except 930.0 - 939.9), which clearly indicates that the critical care was unrelated to the surgery, is acceptable documentation.

Medicare policy allows separate payment to the surgeon for postoperative critical care services during the surgical global period when the patient has suffered trauma or burns. When the surgeon provides critical care services during the global period, for reasons unrelated to the surgery, these are separately payable as well.

M. Teaching Physician Criteria

In order for the teaching physician to bill for critical care services the teaching physician must meet the requirements for critical care described in the preceding sections. For CPT codes determined on the basis of time, such as critical care, the teaching physician must be present for the entire period of time for which the claim is submitted. For example, payment will be made for 35 minutes of critical care services only if the teaching physician is present for the full 35 minutes. (See IOM, Pub 100-04, Chapter12, Sec. 100.1.4)

1. Teaching
   Time spent teaching may not be counted towards critical care time. Time spent by the resident, in the absence of the teaching physician, cannot be billed by the teaching physician as critical care or other time-based services. Only time spent by the resident and teaching physician together with the patient or the teaching physician alone with the patient can be counted toward critical care time.

2. Documentation
   A combination of the teaching physician's documentation and the resident's documentation may support critical care services. Provided that all requirements for critical care services are met, the teaching physician documentation may tie into the resident's documentation. The teaching physician may refer to the resident's documentation for specific patient history, physical findings and medical assessment. However, the teaching physician medical record documentation must provide substantive information including: (1) the time the teaching physician spent providing critical care, (2) that the patient was critically ill during the time the teaching physician saw the patient, (3) what made the patient critically ill, and (4) the nature of the treatment and management provided by the teaching physician. The medical review criteria are the same for the teaching physician as for all physicians. (See the Medicare Claims Processing, Pub. 100-04, Chapter 12, Sec.100.1.1 for teaching physician documentation guidance.)

Unacceptable Example of Documentation:

"I came and saw (the patient) and agree with (the resident)".

Acceptable Example of Documentation:

"Patient developed hypotension and hypoxia; I spent 45 minutes while the patient was in this condition, providing fluids, pressor drugs, and oxygen. I reviewed the resident's documentation and I agree with the resident's assessment and plan of care."

N. Ventilator Management

Medicare recognizes the ventilator codes (CPT codes 94002 - 94004, 94660 and 94662) as physician services payable under the physician fee schedule. Medicare Part B under the physician fee schedule does not pay for ventilator management services in addition to an evaluation and management service (e.g., critical care services, CPT codes 99291 - 99292) on the same day for the patient even when the evaluation and management service is billed with CPT modifier -2

100-4, 12, 30.6.13

Nursing Facility Services (Codes 99304 - 99318)

A. Visits to Perform the Initial Comprehensive Assessment and Annual Assessments

The distinction made between the delegation of physician visits and tasks in a skilled nursing facility (SNF) and in a nursing facility (NF) is based on the Medicare Statute. Section 1819 (b) (6) (A) of the Social Security Act (the Act) governs SNFs while section 1919 (b) (6) (A) of the Act governs NFs. For further information refer to Medlearn Matters article number SE0418 at www.cms.hhs.gov/medlearn/matters The initial visit in a SNF and NF must be performed by the physician except as otherwise permitted (42 CFR 483.40 (c) (4)). The initial visit is defined in S&C-04-08 (see www.cms.hhs.gov/medlearn/matters) as the initial comprehensive assessment visit during which the physician completes a thorough assessment, develops a plan of care and writes or verifies admitting orders for the nursing facility resident. For Survey and Certification requirements, a visit must occur no later than 30 days after admission.

Further, per the Long Term Care regulations at 42 CFR 483.40 (c)(4) and (e) (2), the physician may not delegate a task that the physician must personally perform. Therefore, as stated in S&C-04-08 the physician may not delegate the initial visit in a SNF. This also applies to the NF with one exception.

The only exception, as to who performs the initial visit, relates to the NF setting. In the NF setting, a qualified NPP (i.e., a nurse practitioner (NP), physician assistant (PA), or a clinical nurse specialist (CNS), who is not employed by the facility, may perform the initial visit when the State law permits this. The evaluation and management (E/M) visit shall be within the State scope of practice and licensure requirements where the E/M visit is performed and the requirements for physician collaboration and physician supervision shall be met.

Under Medicare Part B payment policy, other medically necessary E/M visits may be performed and reported prior to and after the initial visit, if the medical needs of the patient require an E/M visit. A qualified NPP may perform medically necessary E/M visits prior to and after the initial visit if all the requirements for collaboration, general physician supervision, licensure and billing are met.

The CPT Nursing Facility Services codes shall be used with place of service (POS) 31 (SNF) if the patient is in a Part A SNF stay. They shall be used with POS 32 (nursing facility) if the patient does not have Part A SNF benefits or if the patient is in a NF or in a non-covered SNF stay (e.g., there was no preceding 3-day hospital stay). The CPT Nursing Facility code definition also includes POS 54 (Intermediate Care Facility/Mentally Retarded) and POS 56 (Psychiatric Residential Treatment Center). For further guidance on POS codes and associated CPT codes refer to Sec.30.6.14.

Effective January 1, 2006, the Initial Nursing Facility Care codes 99301- 99303 are deleted.

Beginning January 1, 2006, the new CPT codes, Initial Nursing Facility Care, per day, (99304 - 99306) shall be used to report the initial visit. Only a physician may report

these codes for an initial visit performed in a SNF or NF (with the exception of the qualified NPP in the NF setting who is not employed by the facility and when State law permits, as explained above).

A readmission to a SNF or NF shall have the same payment policy requirements as an initial admission in both the SNF and NF settings.

A physician who is employed by the SNF/NF may perform the E/M visits and bill independently to Medicare Part B for payment. An NPP who is employed by the SNF or NF may perform and bill Medicare Part B directly for those services where it is permitted as discussed above. The employer of the PA shall always report the visits performed by the PA. A physician, NP or CNS has the option to bill Medicare directly or to reassign payment for his/her professional service to the facility.

As with all E/M visits for Medicare Part B payment policy, the E/M documentation guidelines apply.

B. Visits to Comply With Federal Regulations (42 CFR 483.40 (c) (1)) in the SNF and NF
Payment is made under the physician fee schedule by Medicare Part B for federally mandated visits. Following the initial visit by the physician, payment shall be made for federally mandated visits that monitor and evaluate residents at least once every 30 days for the first 90 days after admission and at least once every 60 days thereafter.

Effective January 1, 2006, the Subsequent Nursing Facility Care, per day, codes 99311- 99313 are deleted.

Beginning January 1, 2006, the new CPT codes, Subsequent Nursing Facility Care, per day, (99307 - 99310) shall be used to report federally mandated physician E/M visits and medically necessary E/M visits.

Carriers shall not pay for more than one E/M visit performed by the physician or qualified NPP for the same patient on the same date of service. The Nursing Facility Services codes represent a "per day" service.

The federally mandated E/M visit may serve also as a medically necessary E/M visit if the situation arises (i.e., the patient has health problems that need attention on the day the scheduled mandated physician E/M visit occurs). The physician/qualified NPP shall bill only one E/M visit.

Beginning January 1, 2006, the new CPT code, Other Nursing Facility Service (99318), may be used to report an annual nursing facility assessment visit on the required schedule of visits on an annual basis. For Medicare Part B payment policy, an annual nursing facility assessment visit code may substitute as meeting one of the federally mandated physician visits if the code requirements for CPT code 99318 are fully met and in lieu of reporting a Subsequent Nursing Facility Care, per day, service (codes 99307 - 99310). It shall not be performed in addition to the required number of federally mandated physician visits. The new CPT annual assessment code does not represent a new benefit service for Medicare Part B physician services.

Qualified NPPs, whether employed or not by the SNF, may perform alternating federally mandated physician visits, at the option of the physician, after the initial visit by the physician in a SNF.

Qualified NPPs in the NF setting, who are not employed by the NF, may perform federally mandated physician visits, at the option of the State, after the initial visit by the physician.

Medicare Part B payment policy does not pay for additional E/M visits that may be required by State law for a facility admission or for other additional visits to satisfy facility or other administrative purposes. E/M visits, prior to and after the initial physician visit, that are reasonable and medically necessary to meet the medical needs of the individual patient (unrelated to any State requirement or administrative purpose) are payable under Medicare Part B.

C. Visits by Qualified Nonphysician Practitioners
All E/M visits shall be within the State scope of practice and licensure requirements where the visit is performed and all the requirements for physician collaboration and physician supervision shall be met when performed and reported by qualified NPPs. General physician supervision and employer billing requirements shall be met for PA services in addition to the PA meeting the State scope of practice and licensure requirements where the E/M visit is performed.

Medically Necessary Visits Qualified NPPs may perform medically necessary E/M visits prior to and after the physician's initial visit in both the SNF and NF. Medically necessary E/M visits for the diagnosis or treatment of an illness or injury or to improve the functioning of a malformed body member are payable under the physician fee schedule under Medicare Part B. CPT codes, Subsequent Nursing Facility Care, per day (99307 - 99310), shall be reported for these E/M visits even if the visits are provided prior to the initial visit by the physician.

SNF Setting--Place of Service Code 31

Following the initial visit by the physician, the physician may delegate alternate federally mandated physician visits to a qualified NPP who meets collaboration and physician supervision requirements and is licensed as such by the State and performing within the scope of practice in that State.

NF Setting--Place of Service Code 32

Per the regulations at 42 CFR 483.40 (f), a qualified NPP, who meets the collaboration and physician supervision requirements, the State scope of practice and licensure requirements, and who is not employed by the NF, may at the option of the State, perform the initial visit in a NF, and may perform any other federally mandated physician visit in a NF in addition to performing other medically necessary E/M visits.

Questions pertaining to writing orders or certification and recertification issues in the SNF and NF settings shall be addressed to the appropriate State Survey and Certification Agency departments for clarification.

D. Medically Complex Care
Payment is made for E/M visits to patients in a SNF who are receiving services for medically complex care upon discharge from an acute care facility when the visits are reasonable and medically necessary and documented in the medical record. Physicians and qualified NPPs shall report E/M visits using the Subsequent Nursing Facility Care, per day (codes 99307 - 99310) for these E/M visits even if the visits are provided prior to the initial visit by the physician.

E. Incident to Services
Where a physician establishes an office in a SNF/NF, the "incident to" services and requirements are confined to this discrete part of the facility designated as his/her office. "Incident to" E/M visits, provided in a facility setting, are not payable under the Physician Fee Schedule for Medicare Part B. Thus, visits performed outside the designated "office" area in the SNF/NF would be subject to the coverage and payment rules applicable to SNF/NF setting and shall not be reported using the CPT codes for office or other outpatient visits or use place of service code 11.

F. Use of the Prolonged Services Codes and Other Time-Related Services
Beginning January 1, 2008, typical/average time units for E/M visits in the SNF/NF settings are reestablished. Medically necessary prolonged services for E/M visits (codes 99356 and 99357) in a SNF or NF may be billed with the Nursing Facility Services in the code ranges (99304 - 99306, 99307 - 99310 and 99318).

Counseling and Coordination of Care Visits With the reestablishment of typical/average time units, medically necessary E/M visits for counseling and coordination of care, for Nursing Facility Services in the code ranges (99304 - 99306, 99307 - 99310 and 99318) that are time-based services, may be billed with the appropriate prolonged services codes (99356 and 99357).

G. Gang Visits
The complexity level of an E/M visit and the CPT code billed must be a covered and medically necessary visit for each patient (refer to Secs.1862 (a)(1)(A) of the Act). Claims for an unreasonable number of daily E/M visits by the same physician to multiple patients at a facility within a 24-hour period may result in medical review to determine medical necessity for the visits. The E/M visit (Nursing Facility Services) represents a "per day" service per patient as defined by the CPT code. The medical record must be personally documented by the physician or qualified NPP who performed the E/M visit and the documentation shall support the specific level of E/M visit to each individual patient.

H. Split/Shared E/M Visit
A split/shared E/M visit cannot be reported in the SNF/NF setting. A split/shared E/M visit is defined by Medicare Part B payment policy as a medically necessary encounter with a patient where the physician and a qualified NPP each personally perform a substantive portion of an E/M visit face-to-face with the same patient on the same date of service. A substantive portion of an E/M visit involves all or some portion of the history, exam or medical decision making key components of an E/M service. The physician and the qualified NPP must be in the same group practice or be employed by the same employer. The split/shared E/M visit applies only to selected E/M visits and settings (i.e., hospital inpatient, hospital outpatient, hospital observation, emergency department, hospital discharge, office and non facility clinic visits, and prolonged visits associated with these E/M visit codes). The split/shared E/M policy does not apply to consultation services, critical care services or procedures.

I. SNF/NF Discharge Day Management Service
Medicare Part B payment policy requires a face-to-face visit with the patient provided by the physician or the qualified NPP to meet the SNF/NF discharge day management service as defined by the CPT code. The E/M discharge day management visit shall be reported for the date of the actual visit by the physician or qualified NPP even if the patient is discharged from the facility on a different calendar date. The CPT codes 99315 - 99316 shall be reported for this visit. The Discharge Day Management Service may be reported using CPT code 99315 or 99316, depending on the code requirement, for a patient who has expired, but only if the physician or qualified NPP personally performed the death pronouncement.

100-4, 12, 30.6.14

Home Care and Domiciliary Care Visits (Codes 99324- 99350)

Physician Visits to Patients Residing in Various Places of Service

The American Medical Association's Current Procedural Terminology (CPT) 2006 new patient codes 99324 - 99328 and established patient codes 99334 - 99337(new codes beginning January 2006), for Domiciliary, Rest Home (e.g., Boarding Home), or Custodial Care Services, are used to report evaluation and management (E/M) services to residents residing in a facility which provides room, board, and other personal assistance services, generally on a long-term basis. These CPT codes are used to report E/M services in facilities assigned places of service (POS) codes 13 (Assisted Living Facility), 14 (Group Home), 33 (Custodial Care Facility) and 55 (Residential Substance Abuse Facility). Assisted living facilities may also be known as adult living facilities.

Physicians and qualified nonphysician practitioners (NPPs) furnishing E/M services to residents in a living arrangement described by one of the POS listed above must use the correct level of service code in the CPT code range 99324 - 99337 to report the service they provide. The CPT codes 99321 - 99333 for Domiciliary, Rest Home (e.g., Boarding Home), or Custodial Care Services are deleted beginning January, 2006.

Beginning in 2006, reasonable and medically necessary, face-to-face, prolonged services, represented by CPT codes 99354 - 99355, may be reported with the appropriate companion E/M codes when a physician or qualified NPP, provides a prolonged service involving direct (face-to-face) patient contact that is beyond the usual E/M visit service for a Domiciliary, Rest Home (e.g., Boarding Home) or Custodial Care Service. All the requirements for prolonged services at Sec.30.6.15.1 must be met.

The CPT codes 99341 through 99350, Home Services codes, are used to report E/M services furnished to a patient residing in his or her own private residence (e.g., private home, apartment, town home) and not residing in any type of congregate/shared facility living arrangement including assisted living facilities and group homes. The Home Services codes apply only to the specific 2-digit POS 12 (Home). Home Services codes may not be used for billing E/M services provided in settings other than in the private residence of an individual as described above.

Beginning in 2006, E/M services provided to patients residing in a Skilled Nursing Facility (SNF) or a Nursing Facility (NF) must be reported using the appropriate CPT level of service code within the range identified for Initial Nursing Facility Care (new CPT codes 99304 - 99306) and Subsequent Nursing Facility Care (new CPT codes 99307 - 99310). Use the CPT code, Other Nursing Facility Services (new CPT code 99318), for an annual nursing facility assessment. Use CPT codes 99315 - 99316 for SNF/NF discharge services. The CPT codes 99301 - 99303 and 99311 - 99313 are deleted beginning January, 2006. The Home Services codes should not be used for these places of service.

The CPT SNF/NF code definition includes intermediate care facilities (ICFs) and long term care facilities (LTCFs). These codes are limited to the specific 2-digit POS 31 (SNF), 32 (Nursing Facility), 54 (Intermediate Care Facility/Mentally Retarded) and 56 (Psychiatric Residential Treatment Center).

The CPT nursing facility codes should be used with POS 31 (SNF) if the patient is in a Part A SNF stay and POS 32 (nursing facility) if the patient does not have Part A SNF benefits. There is no longer a different payment amount for a Part A or Part B benefit period in these POS settings.

100-4, 12, 30.6.14.1

Home Services (Codes 99341 - 99350)

B3-15515, B3-15066

A. Requirement for Physician Presence

Home services codes 99341-99350 are paid when they are billed to report evaluation and management services provided in a private residence. A home visit cannot be billed by a physician unless the physician was actually present in the beneficiary's home.

B. Homebound Status

Under the home health benefit the beneficiary must be confined to the home for services to be covered. For home services provided by a physician using these codes, the beneficiary does not need to be confined to the home. The medical record must document the medical necessity of the home visit made in lieu of an office or outpatient visit.

C. Fee Schedule Payment for Services to Homebound Patients under General Supervision

Payment may be made in some medically underserved areas where there is a lack of medical personnel and home health services for injections, EKGs, and venipunctures that are performed for homebound patients under general physician supervision by nurses and paramedical employees of physicians or physician-directed clinics. Section 10 provides additional information on the provision of services to homebound Medicare patients.

100-4, 12, 30.6.15.1

Prolonged Services With Direct Face-to-Face Patient Contact Service (Codes 99354 - 99357) (ZZZ codes)

A. Definition

Prolonged physician services (CPT code 99354) in the office or other outpatient setting with direct face-to-face patient contact which require one hour beyond the usual service are payable when billed on the same day by the same physician or qualified nonphysician practitioner (NPP) as the companion evaluation and management codes. The time for usual service refers to the typical/average time units associated with the companion evaluation and management service as noted in the CPT code. Each additional 30 minutes of direct face-to-face patient contact following the first hour of prolonged services may be reported by CPT code 99355.

Prolonged physician services (code 99356) in the inpatient setting, with direct face-to-face patient contact which require one hour beyond the usual service are payable when they are billed on the same day by the same physician or qualified NPP as the companion evaluation and management codes. Each additional 30 minutes of direct face-to-face patient contact following the first hour of prolonged services may be reported by CPT code 99357.

Prolonged service of less than 30 minutes total duration on a given date is not separately reported because the work involved is included in the total work of the evaluation and management codes.

Code 99355 or 99357 may be used to report each additional 30 minutes beyond the first hour of prolonged services, based on the place of service. These codes may be used to report the final 15 - 30 minutes of prolonged service on a given date, if not otherwise billed. Prolonged service of less than 15 minutes beyond the first hour or less than 15 minutes beyond the final 30 minutes is not reported separately.

B. Required Companion Codes

- The companion evaluation and management codes for 99354 are the Office or Other Outpatient visit codes (99201 - 99205, 99212 - 99215), the Office or Other Outpatient Consultation codes (99241 - 99245), the Domiciliary, Rest Home, or Custodial Care Services codes (99324 - 99328, 99334 - 99337), the Home Services codes (99341 - 99345, 99347 - 99350);

- The companion codes for 99355 are 99354 and one of the evaluation and management codes required for 99354 to be used;

- The companion evaluation and management codes for 99356 are the Initial Hospital Care codes and Subsequent Hospital Care codes (99221 - 99223, 99231 - 99233), the Inpatient Consultation codes (99251 - 99255); Nursing Facility Services codes (99304 -99318) or

- The companion codes for 99357 are 99356 and one of the evaluation and management codes required for 99356 to be used.

Prolonged services codes 99354 - 99357 are not paid unless they are accompanied by the companion codes as indicated.

C. Requirement for Physician Presence

Physicians may count only the duration of direct face-to-face contact between the physician and the patient (whether the service was continuous or not) beyond the typical/average time of the visit code billed to determine whether prolonged services can be billed and to determine the prolonged services codes that are allowable. In the case of prolonged office services, time spent by office staff with the patient, or time the patient remains unaccompanied in the office cannot be billed. In the case of prolonged hospital services, time spent reviewing charts or discussion of a patient with house medical staff and not with direct face-to-face contact with the patient, or waiting for test results, for changes in the patient's condition, for end of a therapy, or for use of facilities cannot be billed as prolonged services.

D. Documentation

Documentation is not required to accompany the bill for prolonged services unless the physician has been selected for medical review. Documentation is required in the medical record about the duration and content of the medically necessary evaluation and management service and prolonged services billed. The medical record must be appropriately and sufficiently documented by the physician or qualified NPP to show that the physician or qualified NPP personally furnished the direct face-to-face time with the patient specified in the CPT code definitions. The start and end times of the visit shall be documented in the medical record along with the date of service.

E. Use of the Codes

Prolonged services codes can be billed only if the total duration of all physician or qualified NPP direct face-to-face service (including the visit) equals or exceeds the threshold time for the evaluation and management service the physician or qualified NPP provided (typical/average time associated with the CPT E/M code plus 30 minutes). If the total duration of direct face-to-face time does not equal or exceed the threshold time for the level of evaluation and management service the physician or qualified NPP provided, the physician or qualified NPP may not bill for prolonged services.

F. Threshold Times for Codes 99354 and 99355 (Office or Other Outpatient Setting)

If the total direct face-to-face time equals or exceeds the threshold time for code 99354, but is less than the threshold time for code 99355, the physician should bill the evaluation and management visit code and code 99354. No more than one unit of 99354 is acceptable. If the total direct face-to-face time equals or exceeds the threshold time for code 99355 by no more than 29 minutes, the physician should bill the visit code 99354 and one unit of code 99355. One additional unit of code 99355 is billed for each additional increment of 30 minutes extended duration. Contractors use the following threshold times to determine if the prolonged services codes 99354 and/or 99355 can be billed with the office or other outpatient settings including outpatient consultation services and domiciliary, rest home, or custodial care services and home services codes.

Threshold Time for Prolonged Visit Codes 99354 and/or 99355 Billed with Office/Outpatient and Consultation Codes

Code	Typical Time for Code	Threshold Time to Bill Code 99354	Threshold Time to Bill Codes 99354 and 99355
99201	10	40	85
99202	20	50	95
99203	30	60	105
99204	45	75	120
99205	60	90	135
99212	10	40	85

Code	Typical Time for Code	Threshold Time to Bill Code 99354	Threshold Time to Bill Codes 99354 and 99355
99213	15	45	90
99214	25	55	100
99215	40	70	115
99241	15	45	90
99242	30	60	105
99243	40	70	115
99244	60	90	135
99245	80	110	155
99324	20	50	95
99325	30	60	105
99326	45	75	120
99327	60	90	135
99328	75	105	150
99334	15	45	90
99335	25	55	100
99336	40	70	115
99337	60	90	135
99341	20	50	95
99342	30	60	105
99343	45	75	120
99344	60	90	135
99345	75	105	150
99347	15	45	90
99348	25	55	100
99349	40	70	115
99350	60	90	135

Add 30 minutes to the threshold time for billing codes 99354 and 99355 to get the threshold time for billing code 99354 and two units of code 99355. For example, to bill code 99354 and two units of code 99355 when billing a code 99205, the threshold time is 150 minutes.

G. Threshold Times for Codes 99356 and 99357 (Inpatient Setting)

If the total direct face-to-face time equals or exceeds the threshold time for code 99356, but is less than the threshold time for code 99357, the physician should bill the visit and code 99356. Contractors do not accept more than one unit of code 99356. If the total direct face-to-face time equals or exceeds the threshold time for code 99356 by no more than 29 minutes, the physician bills the visit code 99356 and one unit of code 99357. One additional unit of code 99357 is billed for each additional increment of 30 minutes extended duration. Contractors use the following threshold times to determine if the prolonged services codes 99356 and/or 99357 can be billed with the inpatient setting codes.

Threshold Time for Prolonged Visit Codes 99356 and/or 99357 Billed with Inpatient Setting Codes

Code	Typical Time for Code	Threshold Time to Bill Code 99356	Threshold Time to Bill Codes 99356 and 99357
99221	30	60	105
99222	50	80	125
99223	70	100	145
99231	15	45	90
99232	25	55	100
99233	35	65	110
99251	20	50	95
99252	40	70	115
99253	55	85	130
99254	80	110	155
99255	110	140	185
99304	25	55	100
99305	35	65	110
99306	45	75	120
99307	10	40	85
99308	15	45	90
99309	25	55	100
99310	35	65	110
99318	30	60	105

Add 30 minutes to the threshold time for billing codes 99356 and 99357 to get the threshold time for billing code 99356 and two units of 99357.

H. Prolonged Services Associated With Evaluation and Management Services Based on Counseling and/or Coordination of Care (Time-Based)

When an evaluation and management service is dominated by counseling and/or coordination of care (the counseling and/or coordination of care represents more than 50% of the total time with the patient) in a face-to-face encounter between the physician or qualified NPP and the patient in the office/clinic or the floor time (in the scenario of an inpatient service), then the evaluation and management code is selected based on the typical/average time associated with the code levels. The time approximation must meet or exceed the specific CPT code billed (determined by the typical/average time associated with the evaluation and management code) and should not be "rounded" to the next higher level.

In those evaluation and management services in which the code level is selected based on time, prolonged services may only be reported with the highest code level in that family of codes as the companion code.

I. Examples of Billable Prolonged Services

EXAMPLE 1. A physician performed a visit that met the definition of an office visit code 99213 and the total duration of the direct face-to-face services (including the visit) was 65 minutes. The physician bills code 99213 and one unit of code 99354.

EXAMPLE 2. A physician performed a visit that met the definition of a domiciliary, rest home care visit code 99327 and the total duration of the direct face-to-face contact (including the visit) was 140 minutes. The physician bills codes 99327, 99354, and one unit of code 99355.

EXAMPLE 3. A physician performed an office visit to an established patient that was predominantly counseling, spending 75 minutes (direct face-to-face) with the patient. The physician should report CPT code 99215 and one unit of code 99354.

J. Examples of Nonbillable Prolonged Services

EXAMPLE 1. A physician performed a visit that met the definition of visit code 99212 and the total duration of the direct face-to-face contact (including the visit) was 35 minutes. The physician cannot bill prolonged services because the total duration of direct face-to-face service did not meet the threshold time for billing prolonged services.

EXAMPLE 2. A physician performed a visit that met the definition of code 99213 and, while the patient was in the office receiving treatment for 4 hours, the total duration of the direct face-to-face service of the physician was 40 minutes. The physician cannot bill prolonged services because the total duration of direct face-to-face service did not meet the threshold time for billing prolonged services.

EXAMPLE 3. A physician provided a subsequent office visit that was predominantly counseling, spending 60 minutes (face-to-face) with the patient. The physician cannot code 99214, which has a typical time of 25 minutes, and one unit of code 99354. The physician must bill the highest level code in the code family (99215 which has 40 minutes typical/average time units associated with it). The additional time spent beyond this code is 20 minutes and does not meet the threshold time for billing prolonged services.

100-4, 12, 30.6.15.2
Prolonged Services Without Direct Face-to-Face Patient Contact Service (Codes 99358–99359)

Contractors may not pay prolonged services codes 99358 and 99359, which do not require any direct patient face-to-face contact (e.g., telephone calls). Payment for these services is included in the payment for direct face-to-face services that physicians bill. The physician cannot bill the patient for these services since they are Medicare covered services and payment is included in the payment for other billable services.

100-4, 12, 30.6.15.3
Physician Standby Service (Code 99360)

Standby services are not payable to physicians. Physicians may not bill Medicare or beneficiaries for standby services. Payment for standby services is included in the Part A payment to the facility. Such services are a part of hospital costs to provide quality care.

If hospitals pay physicians for standby services, such services are part of hospital costs to provide quality care.

100-4, 12, 30.6.16
Case Management Services (Codes 99362 and 99371 - 99373)
A. Team Conferences

Team conferences (codes 99361-99362) may not be paid separately. Payment for these services is included in the payment for the services to which they relate.

B. Telephone Calls

Telephone calls (codes 99371-99373) may not be paid separately. Payment for telephone calls is included in payment for billable services (e.g., visit, surgery, diagnostic procedure results).

100-4, 12, 40.2
Billing Requirements for Global Surgeries

To ensure the proper identification of services that are, or are not, included in the global package, the following procedures apply.

A. Procedure Codes and Modifiers

Use of the modifiers in this section apply to both major procedures with a 90-day postoperative period and minor procedures with a 10-day postoperative period (and/or a zero day postoperative period in the case of modifiers "-22" and "-25").

1. Physicians Who Furnish the Entire Global Surgical Package
   Physicians who perform the surgery and furnish all of the usual pre-and postoperative work

bill for the global package by entering the appropriate CPT code for the surgical procedure only. Billing is not allowed for visits or other services that are included in the global package.

2. Physicians in Group Practice

When different physicians in a group practice participate in the care of the patient, the group bills for the entire global package if the physicians reassign benefits to the group. The physician who performs the surgery is shown as the performing physician. (For dates of service prior to January 1, 1994, however, where a new physician furnishes the entire postoperative care, the group billed for the surgical care and the postoperative care as separate line items with the appropriate modifiers.)

3. Physicians Who Furnish Part of a Global Surgical Package

Where physicians agree on the transfer of care during the global period, the following modifiers are used:

- "-54" for surgical care only; or

- "-55" for postoperative management only.

Both the bill for the surgical care only and the bill for the postoperative care only, will contain the same date of service and the same surgical procedure code, with the services distinguished by the use of the appropriate modifier.

Providers need not specify on the claim that care has been transferred. However, the date on which care was relinquished or assumed, as applicable, must be shown on the claim. This should be indicated in the remarks field/free text segment on the claim form/format. Both the surgeon and the physician providing the postoperative care must keep a copy of the written transfer agreement in the beneficiary's medical record.

Where a transfer of postoperative care occurs, the receiving physician cannot bill for any part of the global services until he/she has provided at least one service. Once the physician has seen the patient, that physician may bill for the period beginning with the date on which he/she assumes care of the patient.

EXCEPTIONS:

- Where a transfer of care does not occur, occasional post-discharge services of a physician other than the surgeon are reported by the appropriate evaluation and management code. No modifiers are necessary on the claim.

- If the transfer of care occurs immediately after surgery, the physician other than the surgeon who provides the in-hospital postoperative care bills using subsequent hospital care codes for the inpatient hospital care and the surgical code with the "-55" modifier for the post-discharge care. The surgeon bills the surgery code with the "-54" modifier.

- Physicians who provide follow-up services for minor procedures performed in emergency departments bill the appropriate level of office visit code. The physician who performs the emergency room service bills for the surgical procedure without a modifier.

- If the services of a physician other than the surgeon are required during a postoperative period for an underlying condition or medical complication, the other physician reports the appropriate evaluation and management code. No modifiers are necessary on the claim. An example is a cardiologist who manages underlying cardiovascular conditions of a patient.

4. Evaluation and Management Service Resulting in the Initial Decision to Perform Surgery

Evaluation and management services on the day before major surgery or on the day of major surgery that result in the initial decision to perform the surgery are not included in the global surgery payment for the major surgery and, therefore, may be billed and paid separately.

In addition to the CPT evaluation and management code, modifier "-57" (decision for surgery) is used to identify a visit which results in the initial decision to perform surgery. (Modifier "-QI" was used for dates of service prior to January 1, 1994.)

If evaluation and management services occur on the day of surgery, the physician bills using modifier "-57," not "-25." The "-57" modifier is not used with minor surgeries because the global period for minor surgeries does not include the day prior to the surgery. Moreover, where the decision to perform the minor procedure is typically done immediately before the service, it is considered a routine preoperative service and a visit or consultation is not billed in addition to the procedure.

5. Return Trips to the Operating Room During the Postoperative Period

When treatment for complications requires a return trip to the operating room, physicians must bill the CPT code that describes the procedure(s) performed during the return trip. If no such code exists, use the unspecified procedure code in the correct series, i.e., 47999 or 64999. The procedure code for the original surgery is not used except when the identical procedure is repeated.

In addition to the CPT code, physicians use CPT modifier "-78" for these return trips (return to the operating room for a related procedure during a postoperative period.)

The physician may also need to indicate that another procedure was performed during the postoperative period of the initial procedure. When this subsequent procedure is related to the first procedure and requires the use of the operating room, this circumstance may be reported by adding the modifier "-78" to the related procedure.

NOTE: The CPT definition for this modifier does not limit its use to treatment for complications.

6. Staged or Related Procedures

Modifier "-58" was established to facilitate billing of staged or related surgical procedures done during the postoperative period of the first procedure. This modifier is not used to report the treatment of a problem that requires a return to the operating room.

The physician may need to indicate that the performance of a procedure or service during the postoperative period was:

a. Planned prospectively or at the time of the original procedure;

b. More extensive than the original procedure; or

c. For therapy following a diagnostic surgical procedure.

These circumstances may be reported by adding modifier "-58" to the staged procedure. A new postoperative period begins when the next procedure in the series is billed.

7. Unrelated Procedures or Visits During the Postoperative Period

Two CPT modifiers were established to simplify billing for visits and other procedures which are furnished during the postoperative period of a surgical procedure, but which are not included in the payment for the surgical procedure.

Modifier "-79": Reports an unrelated procedure by the same physician during a postoperative period. The physician may need to indicate that the performance of a procedure or service during a postoperative period was unrelated to the original procedure.

A new postoperative period begins when the unrelated procedure is billed.

Modifier "-24": Reports an unrelated evaluation and management service by same physician during a postoperative period. The physician may need to indicate that an evaluation and management service was performed during the postoperative period of an unrelated procedure. This circumstance is reported by adding the modifier "-24" to the appropriate level of evaluation and management service.

Services submitted with the "-24" modifier must be sufficiently documented to establish that the visit was unrelated to the surgery. An ICD-9-CM code that clearly indicates that the reason for the encounter was unrelated to the surgery is acceptable documentation.

A physician who is responsible for postoperative care and has reported and been paid using modifier "-55" also uses modifier "-24" to report any unrelated visits.

8. Significant Evaluation and Management on the Day of a Procedure

Modifier "-25" is used to facilitate billing of evaluation and management services on the day of a procedure for which separate payment may be made.

It is used to report a significant, separately identifiable evaluation and management service by same physician on the day of a procedure. The physician may need to indicate that on the day of a procedure or service that is identified with a CPT code was performed, the patient's condition required a significant, separately identifiable evaluation and management service above and beyond the usual preoperative and postoperative care associated with the procedure or service that was performed. This circumstance may be reported by adding the modifier "-25" to the appropriate level of evaluation and management service.

Claims containing evaluation and management codes with modifier "-25" are not subject to prepayment review except in the following situations:

- Effective January 1, 1995, all evaluation and management services provided on the same day as inpatient dialysis are denied without review with the exception of CPT Codes 99221-9223, 99251-99255, and 99238. These codes may be billed with modifier "-25" and reviewed for possible allowance if the evaluation and management service is unrelated to the treatment of ESRD and was not, and could not, have been provided during the dialysis treatment;

- When preoperative critical care codes are being billed for within a global surgical period; and

- When carriers have conducted a specific medical review process and determined, after reviewing the data, that an individual or group have high statistics in terms of the use of modifier "-25," have done a case-by-case review of the records to verify that the use of modifier "-25" was inappropriate, and have educated the individual or group as to the proper use of this modifier.

9. Critical Care

Critical care services provided during a global surgical period for a seriously injured or burned patient are not considered related to a surgical procedure and may be paid separately under the following circumstances.

Preoperative and postoperative critical care may be paid in addition to a global fee if:

- The patient is critically ill and requires the constant attendance of the physician; and

- The critical care is above and beyond, and, in most instances, unrelated to the specific anatomic injury or general surgical procedure performed.

Such patients are potentially unstable or have conditions that could pose a significant threat to life or risk of prolonged impairment.

In order for these services to be paid, two reporting requirements must be met:

- Codes 99291/99292 and modifier "-25" (for preoperative care) or "-24" (for postoperative care) must be used; and

- Documentation that the critical care was unrelated to the specific anatomic injury or general surgical procedure performed must be submitted. An ICD-9-CM code in the range 800.0 through 959.9 (except 930-939), which clearly indicates that the critical care was unrelated to the surgery, is acceptable documentation.

10. Unusual Circumstances

Surgeries for which services performed are significantly greater than usually required may be billed with the "-22" modifier added to the CPT code for the procedure. Surgeries for which services performed are significantly less than usually required may be billed with the "-52" modifier. The biller must provide:

- A concise statement about how the service differs from the usual; and

- An operative report with the claim.

Modifier "-22" should only be reported with procedure codes that have a global period of 0, 10, or 90 days. There is no such restriction on the use of modifier "-52."

B. Date(s) of Service

Physicians, who bill for the entire global surgical package or for only a portion of the care, must enter the date on which the surgical procedure was performed in the "From/To" date of service field. This will enable carriers to relate all appropriate billings to the correct surgery. Physicians who share postoperative management with another physician must submit additional information showing when they assumed and relinquished responsibility for the postoperative care. If the physician who performed the surgery relinquishes care at the time of discharge, he or she need only show the date of surgery when billing with modifier "-54."

However, if the surgeon also cares for the patient for some period following discharge, the surgeon must show the date of surgery and the date on which postoperative care was relinquished to another physician. The physician providing the remaining postoperative care must show the date care was assumed. This information should be shown in Item 19 on the paper Form CMS-1500, in the narrative portion of the HAO record on the National Standard Format, and in the NTE segment for ANSI X12N electronic claims.

C. Care Provided in Different Payment Localities

If portions of the global period are provided in different payment localities, the services should be billed to the carriers servicing each applicable payment locality. For example, if the surgery is performed in one state and the postoperative care is provided in another state, the surgery is billed with modifier "-54" to the carrier servicing the payment locality where the surgery was performed and the postoperative care is billed with modifier "-55" to the carrier servicing the payment locality where the postoperative care was performed. This is true whether the services were performed by the same physician/group or different physicians/groups.

D. Health Professional Shortage Area (HPSA) Payments for Services Which are Subject to the Global Surgery Rules

HPSA bonus payments may be made for global surgeries when the services are provided in HPSAs. The following are guidelines for the appropriate billing procedures:

- If the entire global package is provided in a HPSA, physicians should bill for the appropriate global surgical code with the applicable HPSA modifier.

- If only a portion of the global package is provided in a HPSA, the physician should bill using a HPSA modifier for the portion which is provided in the HPSA.

EXAMPLE

The surgical portion of the global service is provided in a non-HPSA and the postoperative portion is provided in a HPSA. The surgical portion should be billed with the "-54" modifier and no HPSA modifier. The postoperative portion should be billed with the "-55" modifier and the appropriate HPSA modifier. The 10 percent bonus will be paid on the appropriate postoperative portion only. If a claim is submitted with a global surgical code and a HPSA modifier, the carrier assumes that the entire global service was provided in a HPSA in the absence of evidence otherwise.

NOTE: The sum of the payments made for the surgical and postoperative services provided in different localities will not equal the global amount in either of the localities because of geographic adjustments made through the Geographic Practice Cost Indices.

100-4, 12, 40.6

Claims for Multiple Surgeries

B3-4826, B3-15038, B3-15056

A. General

Multiple surgeries are separate procedures performed by a single physician or physicians in the same group practice on the same patient at the same operative session or on the same day for which separate payment may be allowed. Co-surgeons, surgical teams, or assistants-at-surgery may participate in performing multiple surgeries on the same patient on the same day.

Multiple surgeries are distinguished from procedures that are components of or incidental to a primary procedure. These intra-operative services, incidental surgeries, or components of more major surgeries are not separately billable. See Chapter 23 for a description of mandatory edits to prevent separate payment for those procedures. Major surgical procedures are determined based on the MFSDB approved amount and not on the submitted amount from the providers. The major surgery, as based on the MFSDB, may or may not be the one with the larger submitted amount.

Also, see subsection D below for a description of the standard payment policy on multiple surgeries. However, these standard payment rules are not appropriate for certain procedures. Field 21 of the MFSDB indicates whether the standard payment policy rules apply to a multiple surgery, or whether special payment rules apply. Site of service payment adjustments (codes with an indicator of "1" in Field 27 of the MFSDB) should be applied before multiple surgery payment adjustments.

B. Billing Instructions

The following procedures apply when billing for multiple surgeries by the same physician on the same day.

- Report the more major surgical procedure without the multiple procedures modifier "-51."
- Report additional surgical procedures performed by the surgeon on the same day with modifier "-51."

There may be instances in which two or more physicians each perform distinctly different, unrelated surgeries on the same patient on the same day (e.g., in some multiple trauma cases). When this occurs, the payment adjustment rules for multiple surgeries may not be appropriate. In such cases, the physician does not use modifier "-51" unless one of the surgeons individually performs multiple surgeries.

C. Carrier Claims Processing System Requirements

Carriers must be able to:

1. Identify multiple surgeries by both of the following methods:

- The presence on the claim form or electronic submission of the "-51" modifier; and

- The billing of more than one separately payable surgical procedure by the same physician performed on the same patient on the same day, whether on different lines or with a number greater than 1 in the units column on the claim form or inappropriately billed with modifier "-78" (i.e., after the global period has expired);

2. Access Field 34 of the MFSDB to determine the Medicare fee schedule payment amount for each surgery;

3. Access Field 21 for each procedure of the MFSDB to determine if the payment rules for multiple surgeries apply to any of the multiple surgeries billed on the same day;

4. If Field 21 for any of the multiple procedures contains an indicator of "0," the multiple surgery rules do not apply to that procedure. Base payment on the lower of the billed amount or the fee schedule amount (Field 34 or 35) for each code unless other payment adjustment rules apply;

5. For dates of service prior to January 1, 1995, if Field 21 contains an indicator of "1," the standard rules for pricing multiple surgeries apply (see items 6-8 below);

6. Rank the surgeries subject to the standard multiple surgery rules (indicator "1") in descending order by the Medicare fee schedule amount;

7. Base payment for each ranked procedure on the lower of the billed amount, or:

- 100 percent of the fee schedule amount (Field 34 or 35) for the highest valued procedure;

- 50 percent of the fee schedule amount for the second highest valued procedure; and

- 25 percent of the fee schedule amount for the third through the fifth highest valued procedures;

8. If more than five procedures are billed, pay for the first five according to the rules listed in 5, 6, and 7 above and suspend the sixth and subsequent procedures for manual review and payment, if appropriate, "by report." Payment determined on a "by report" basis for these codes should never be lower than 25 percent of the full payment amount;

9. For dates of service on or after January 1, 1995, new standard rules for pricing multiple surgeries apply. If Field 21 contains an indicator of "2," these new standard rules apply (see items 10-12 below);

10. Rank the surgeries subject to the multiple surgery rules (indicator "2") in descending order by the Medicare fee schedule amount;

11. Base payment for each ranked procedure (indicator "2") on the lower of the billed amount:

- 100 percent of the fee schedule amount (Field 34 or 35) for the highest valued procedure; and

- 50 percent of the fee schedule amount for the second through the fifth highest valued procedures; or

12. If more than five procedures with an indicator of "2" are billed, pay for the first five according to the rules listed in 9, 10, and 11 above and suspend the sixth and subsequent procedures for manual review and payment, if appropriate, "by report." Payment determined on a "by report" basis for these codes should never be lower than 50 percent of the full payment amount. Pay by the unit for services that are already reduced (e.g., 17003). Pay for 17340 only once per session, regardless of how many lesions were destroyed;

NOTE: For dates of service prior to January 1, 1995, the multiple surgery indicator of "2" indicated that special dermatology rules applied. The payment rules for these codes have not changed. The rules were expanded, however, to all codes that previously had a multiple surgery indicator of "1." For dates of service prior to January 1, 1995, if a dermatological procedure with an indicator of "2" was billed with the "-51" modifier with other procedures that are not dermatological procedures (procedures with an indicator of "1" in Field 21), the standard multiple surgery rules applied. Pay no less than 50 percent for the dermatological procedures with an indicator of "2." See 40.6.C.6-8 for required actions.

13. If Field 21 contains an indicator of "3," and multiple endoscopies are billed, the special rules for multiple endoscopic procedures apply. Pay the full value of the highest valued endoscopy, plus the difference between the next highest and the base endoscopy. Access Field 31A of the MFSDB to determine the base endoscopy.

EXAMPLE

In the course of performing a fiber optic colonoscopy (CPT code 45378), a physician performs a biopsy on a lesion (code 45380) and removes a polyp (code 45385) from a different part of the colon. The physician bills for codes 45380 and 45385. The value of codes 45380 and 45385 have the value of the diagnostic colonoscopy (45378) built in.

Rather than paying 100 percent for the highest valued procedure (45385) and 50 percent for the next (45380), pay the full value of the higher valued endoscopy (45385), plus the difference between the next highest endoscopy (45380) and the base endoscopy (45378).

Carriers assume the following fee schedule amounts for these codes:

45378 - $255.40

45380 - $285.98

45385 - $374.56

Pay the full value of 45385 ($374.56), plus the difference between 45380 and 45378 ($30.58), for a total of $405.14.

NOTE: If an endoscopic procedure with an indicator of "3" is billed with the "-51" modifier with other procedures that are not endoscopies (procedures with an indicator of "1" in Field 21), the standard multiple surgery rules apply. See 40.6.C.6-8 for required actions.

14. Apply the following rules where endoscopies are performed on the same day as unrelated endoscopies or other surgical procedures:

- Two unrelated endoscopies (e.g., 46606 and 43217): Apply the usual multiple surgery rules;

- Two sets of unrelated endoscopies (e.g., 43202 and 43217; 46606 and 46608): Apply the special endoscopy rules to each series and then apply the multiple surgery rules. Consider the total payment for each set of endoscopies as one service;

- Two related endoscopies and a third, unrelated procedure: Apply the special endoscopic rules to the related endoscopies, and, then apply the multiple surgery rules. Consider the total payment for the related endoscopies as one service and the unrelated endoscopy as another service.

15. If two or more multiple surgeries are of equal value, rank them in descending dollar order billed and base payment on the percentages listed above (i.e., 100 percent for the first billed procedure, 50 percent for the second, etc.);

16. If any of the multiple surgeries are bilateral surgeries, consider the bilateral procedure at 150 percent as one payment amount, rank this with the remaining procedures, and apply the appropriate multiple surgery reductions. See 40.7 for bilateral surgery payment instructions);

17. Round all adjusted payment amounts to the nearest cent;

18. If some of the surgeries are subject to special rules while others are subject to the standard rules, automate pricing to the extent possible. If necessary, price manually;

19. In cases of multiple interventional radiological procedures, both the radiology code and the primary surgical code are paid at 100 percent of the fee schedule amount. The subsequent surgical procedures are paid at the standard multiple surgical percentages (50 percent, 50 percent, 50 percent and 50 percent);

20. Apply the requirements in 40 on global surgeries to multiple surgeries;

21. Retain the "-51" modifier in history for any multiple surgeries paid at less than the full global amount; and

22. Follow the instructions on adjudicating surgery claims submitted with the "-22" modifier. Review documentation to determine if full payment should be made for those distinctly different, unrelated surgeries performed by different physicians on the same day.

D. Ranking of Same Day Multiple Surgeries When One Surgery Has a "-22" Modifier and Additional Payment is Allowed

B3-4826

If the patient returns to the operating room after the initial operative session on the same day as a result of complications from the original surgery, the complications rules apply to each procedure required to treat the complications from the original surgery. The multiple surgery rules would not apply.

However, if the patient is returned to the operating room during the postoperative period of the original surgery, not on the same day of the original surgery, for multiple procedures that are required as a result of complications from the original surgery, the complications rules would apply. The multiple surgery rules would also not apply.

Multiple surgeries are defined as separate procedures performed by a single physician or physicians in the same group practice on the same patient at the same operative session or on the same day for which separate payment may be allowed. Co-surgeons, surgical teams, or assistants-at-surgery may participate in performing multiple surgeries on the same patient on the same day.

Multiple surgeries are distinguished from procedures that are components of or incidental to a primary procedure. These intra-operative services, incidental surgeries, or components of more major surgeries are not separately billable. See Chapter 23 for a description of mandatory edits to prevent separate payment for those procedures.

100-4, 12, 40.7
Claims for Bilateral Surgeries
B3-4827, B3-15040

A. General
Bilateral surgeries are procedures performed on both sides of the body during the same operative session or on the same day.

The terminology for some procedure codes includes the terms "bilateral" (e.g., code 27395; Lengthening of the hamstring tendon; multiple, bilateral.) or "unilateral or bilateral" (e.g., code 52290; cystourethroscopy; with ureteral meatotomy, unilateral or bilateral). The payment adjustment rules for bilateral surgeries do not apply to procedures identified by CPT as "bilateral" or "unilateral or bilateral" since the fee schedule reflects any additional work required for bilateral surgeries.

Field 22 of the MFSDB indicates whether the payment adjustment rules apply to a surgical procedure.

B. Billing Instructions for Bilateral Surgeries
If a procedure is not identified by its terminology as a bilateral procedure (or unilateral or bilateral), physicians must report the procedure with modifier "-50." They report such procedures as a single line item. (NOTE: This differs from the CPT coding guidelines which indicate that bilateral procedures should be billed as two line items.)

If a procedure is identified by the terminology as bilateral (or unilateral or bilateral), as in codes 27395 and 52290, physicians do not report the procedure with modifier "-50."

C. Claims Processing System Requirements
Carriers must be able to:

1. Identify bilateral surgeries by the presence on the claim form or electronic submission of the "-50" modifier or of the same code on separate lines reported once with modifier "-LT" and once with modifier "-RT";

2. Access Field 34 or 35 of the MFSDB to determine the Medicare payment amount;

3. Access Field 22 of the MFSDB:

   - If Field 22 contains an indicator of "0," "2," or "3," the payment adjustment rules for bilateral surgeries do not apply. Base payment on the lower of the billed amount or 100 percent of the fee schedule amount (Field 34 or 35) unless other payment adjustment rules apply.

     NOTE: Some codes which have a bilateral indicator of "0" in the MFSDB may be performed more than once on a given day. These are services that would never be considered bilateral and thus should not be billed with modifier "-50." Where such a code is billed on multiple line items or with more than 1 in the units field and carriers have determined that the code may be reported more than once, bypass the "0" bilateral indicator and refer to the multiple surgery field for pricing;

   - If Field 22 contains an indicator of "1," the standard adjustment rules apply. Base payment on the lower of the billed amount or 150 percent of the fee schedule amount (Field 34 or 35). (Multiply the payment amount in Field 34 or 35 for the surgery by 150 percent and round to the nearest cent.)

4. Apply the requirements 40 - 40.4 on global surgeries to bilateral surgeries; and

5. Retain the "-50" modifier in history for any bilateral surgeries paid at the adjusted amount. (NOTE: The "-50" modifier is not retained for surgeries which are bilateral by definition such as code 27395.)

100-4, 12, 40.8
Claims for Co-Surgeons and Team Surgeons
B3 4828, B3 15046

A. General
Under some circumstances, the individual skills of two or more surgeons are required to perform surgery on the same patient during the same operative session. This may be required because of the complex nature of the procedure(s) and/or the patient's condition.

In these cases, the additional physicians are not acting as assistants-at-surgery.

B. Billing Instructions
The following billing procedures apply when billing for a surgical procedure or procedures that required the use of two surgeons or a team of surgeons:

- If two surgeons (each in a different specialty) are required to perform a specific procedure, each surgeon bills for the procedure with a modifier "-62." Co-surgery also refers to surgical procedures involving two surgeons performing the parts of the procedure simultaneously, i.e., heart transplant or bilateral knee replacements. Documentation of the medical necessity for two surgeons is required for certain services identified in the MFSDB. (See 40.8.C.5.);

- If a team of surgeons (more than 2 surgeons of different specialties) is required to perform a specific procedure, each surgeon bills for the procedure with a modifier "-66." Field 25 of the MFSDB identifies certain services submitted with a "-66" modifier which must be sufficiently documented to establish that a team was medically necessary. All claims for team surgeons must contain sufficient information to allow pricing "by report."

- If surgeons of different specialties are each performing a different procedure (with specific CPT codes), neither co-surgery nor multiple surgery rules apply (even if the procedures are performed through the same incision). If one of the surgeons performs multiple procedures, the multiple procedure rules apply to that surgeon's services. (See 40.6 for multiple surgery payment rules.)

For co-surgeons (modifier 62), the fee schedule amount applicable to the payment for each co-surgeon is 62.5 percent of the global surgery fee schedule amount. Team surgery (modifier 66) is paid for on a "By Report" basis.

C. Claims Processing System Requirements
Carriers must be able to:

1. Identify a surgical procedure performed by two surgeons or a team of surgeons by the presence on the claim form or electronic submission of the "-62" or "-66" modifier;

2. Access Field 34 or 35 of the MFSDB to determine the fee schedule payment amount for the surgery;

3. Access Field 24 or 25, as appropriate, of the MFSDB. These fields provide guidance on whether two or team surgeons are generally required for the surgical procedure;

4. If the surgery is billed with a "-62" or "-66" modifier and Field 24 or 25 contains an indicator of "0," payment adjustment rules for two or team surgeons do not apply:

   - Carriers pay the first bill submitted, and base payment on the lower of the billed amount or 100 percent of the fee schedule amount (Field 34 or 35) unless other payment adjustment rules apply;

   - Carriers deny bills received subsequently from other physicians and use the appropriate MSN message in 40.8.D. As these are medical necessity denials, the instructions in the Program Integrity Manual regarding denial of unassigned claims for medical necessity are applied;

5. If the surgery is billed with a "-62" modifier and Field 24 contains an indicator of "1," suspend the claim for manual review of any documentation submitted with the claim. If the documentation supports the need for co-surgeons, base payment for each physician on the lower of the billed amount or 62.5 percent of the fee schedule amount (Field 34 or 35);

6. If the surgery is billed with a "-62" modifier and Field 24 contains an indicator of "2," payment rules for two surgeons apply. Carriers base payment for each physician on the lower of the billed amount or 62.5 percent of the fee schedule amount (Field 34 or 35);

7. If the surgery is billed with a "-66" modifier and Field 25 contains an indicator of "1," carriers suspend the claim for manual review. If carriers determine that team surgeons were medically necessary, each physician is paid on a "by report" basis;

8. If the surgery is billed with a "-66" modifier and Field 25 contains an indicator of "2," carriers pay "by report";

NOTE: A Medicare fee may have been established for some surgical procedures that are billed with the "-66" modifier. In these cases, all physicians on the team must agree on the percentage of the Medicare payment amount each is to receive.If carriers receive a bill with a "-66" modifier after carriers have paid one surgeon the full Medicare payment amount (on a bill without the modifier), deny the subsequent claim.

9. Apply the rules global surgical packages to each of the physicians participating in a co- or team surgery; and

10. Retain the "-62" and "-66" modifiers in history for any co- or team surgeries.

D. Beneficiary Liability on Denied Claims for Assistant, Co- surgeon and Team Surgeons

MSN message 23.10 which states "Medicare does not pay for a surgical assistant for this kind of surgery," was established for denial of claims for assistant surgeons. Where such payment is denied because the procedure is subject to the statutory restriction against payment for assistants-at-surgery. Carriers include the following statement in the MSN:

"You cannot be charged for this service." (Unnumbered add-on message.)

Carriers use Group Code CO on the remittance advice to the physician to signify that the beneficiary may not be billed for the denied service and that the physician could be subject to penalties if a bill is issued to the beneficiary.

If Field 23 of the MFSDB contains an indicator of "0" or "1" (assistant-at-surgery may not be paid) for procedures CMS has determined that an assistant surgeon is not generally medically necessary.

For those procedures with an indicator of "0," the limitation on liability provisions described in Chapter 30 apply to assigned claims. Therefore, carriers include the appropriate limitation of liability language from Chapter 21. For unassigned claims, apply the rules in the Program Integrity Manual concerning denial for medical necessity.

Where payment may not be made for a co- or team surgeon, use the following MSN message (MSN message number 15.13):

Medicare does not pay for team surgeons for this procedure.

Where payment may not be made for a two surgeons, use the following MSN message (MSN message number 15.12):

Medicare does not pay for two surgeons for this procedure.

Also see limitation of liability remittance notice REF remark codes M25, M26, and M27.

Use the following message on the remittance notice:

Multiple physicians/assistants are not covered in this case. (Reason code 54.)

100-4, 12, 50

Payment for Anesthesiology Services

A. General Payment Rule

The fee schedule amount for physician anesthesia services furnished on or after January 1, 1992 is, with the exceptions noted, based on allowable base and time units multiplied by an anesthesia conversion factor specific to that locality. The base unit for each anesthesia procedure is communicated to the carriers by means of the HCPCS file released annually. The public can access the base units on the CMS homepage through the anesthesiologists center. The way in which time units are calculated is described in 50.G. CMS releases the conversion factor annually.

B. Payment at Personally Performed Rate

Carriers must determine the fee schedule payment, recognizing the base unit for the anesthesia code and one time unit per 15 minutes of anesthesia time if:

- The physician personally performed the entire anesthesia service alone;

- The physician is involved with one anesthesia case with a resident, the physician is a teaching physician as defined in 100, and the service is furnished on or after January 1, 1996;

- The physician is continuously involved in a single case involving a student nurse anesthetist;

- The physician is continuously involved in one anesthesia case involving a CRNA (or AA) and the service was furnished prior to January 1, 1998. If the physician is involved with a single case with a CRNA (or AA) and the service was furnished on or after January 1, 1998, carriers may pay the physician service and the CRNA (or AA) service in accordance with the medical direction payment policy; or

- The physician and the CRNA (or AA) are involved in one anesthesia case and the services of each are found to be medically necessary. Documentation must be submitted by both the CRNA and the physician to support payment of the full fee for each of the two providers. The physician reports the "AA" modifier and the CRNA reports the "QZ" modifier for a nonmedically directed case.

C. Payment at the Medically Directed Rate

Carriers determine payment for the physician's medical direction service furnished on or after January 1, 1998, on the basis of 50 percent of the allowance for the service performed by the physician alone. Medical direction occurs if the physician medically directs qualified individuals in two, three, or four concurrent cases and the physician performs the following activities.

- Performs a pre-anesthetic examination and evaluation;

- Prescribes the anesthesia plan;

- Personally participates in the most demanding procedures in the anesthesia plan, including induction and emergence;

- Ensures that any procedures in the anesthesia plan that he or she does not perform are performed by a qualified anesthetist;

- Monitors the course of anesthesia administration at frequent intervals;

- Remains physically present and available for immediate diagnosis and treatment of emergencies; and

- Provides indicated-post-anesthesia care.

Prior to January 1, 1999, the physician was required to participate in the most demanding procedures of the anesthesia plan, including induction and emergence.

For medical direction services furnished on or after January 1, 1999, the physician must participate only in the most demanding procedures of the anesthesia plan, including, if applicable, induction and emergence. Also for medical direction services furnished on or after January 1, 1999, the physician must document in the medical record that he or she performed the pre-anesthetic examination and evaluation. Physicians must also document that they provided indicated post-anesthesia care, were present during some portion of the anesthesia monitoring, and were present during the most demanding procedures, including induction and emergence, where indicated.

For services furnished on or after January 1, 1994, the physician can medically direct two, three, or four concurrent procedures involving qualified individuals, all of whom could be CRNAs, AAs, interns, residents or combinations of these individuals. The medical direction rules apply to cases involving student nurse anesthetists if the physician directs two concurrent cases, each of which involves a student nurse anesthetist, or the physician directs one case involving a student nurse anesthetist and another involving a CRNA, AA, intern or resident.

If anesthesiologists are in a group practice, one physician member may provide the pre-anesthesia examination and evaluation while another fulfills the other criteria. Similarly, one physician member of the group may provide post-anesthesia care while another member of the group furnishes the other component parts of the anesthesia service. However, the medical record must indicate that the services were furnished by physicians and identify the physicians who furnished them.

A physician who is concurrently directing the administration of anesthesia to not more than four surgical patients cannot ordinarily be involved in furnishing additional services to other patients. However, addressing an emergency of short duration in the immediate area, administering an epidural or caudal anesthetic to ease labor pain, or periodic, rather than continuous, monitoring of an obstetrical patient does not substantially diminish the scope of control exercised by the physician in directing the administration of anesthesia to surgical patients. It does not constitute a separate service for the purpose of determining whether the medical direction criteria are met. Further, while directing concurrent anesthesia procedures, a physician may receive patients entering the operating suite for the next surgery, check or discharge patients in the recovery room, or handle scheduling matters without affecting fee schedule payment.

However, if the physician leaves the immediate area of the operating suite for other than short durations or devotes extensive time to an emergency case or is otherwise not available to respond to the immediate needs of the surgical patients, the physician's services to the surgical patients are supervisory in nature. Carriers may not make payment under the fee schedule.

See 50.J for a definition of concurrent anesthesia procedures.

D. Payment at Medically Supervised Rate

Carriers may allow only three base units per procedure when the anesthesiologist is involved in furnishing more than four procedures concurrently or is performing other services while directing the concurrent procedures. An additional time unit may be recognized if the physician can document he or she was present at induction.

E. Billing and Payment for Multiple Anesthesia Procedures

Physicians bill for the anesthesia services associated with multiple bilateral surgeries by reporting the anesthesia procedure with the highest base unit value with the multiple procedure modifier "-51." They report the total time for all procedures in the line item with the highest base unit value.

If the same anesthesia CPT code applies to two or more of the surgical procedures, billers enter the anesthesia code with the "-51" modifier and the number of surgeries to which the modified CPT code applies.

Payment can be made under the fee schedule for anesthesia services associated with multiple surgical procedures or multiple bilateral procedures. Payment is determined based on the base unit of the anesthesia procedure with the highest base unit value and time units based on the actual anesthesia time of the multiple procedures. See 40.6-40.7 for a definition and appropriate billing and claims processing instructions for multiple and bilateral surgeries.

F. Payment for Medical and Surgical Services Furnished in Addition to Anesthesia Procedure

Payment may be made under the fee schedule for specific medical and surgical services furnished by the anesthesiologist as long as these services are reasonable and medically necessary or provided that other rebunding provisions (see 30 and Chapter 23) do not preclude separate payment. These services may be furnished in conjunction with the anesthesia procedure to the patient or may be furnished as single services, e.g., during the day of or the day before the anesthesia service. These services include the insertion of a Swan Ganz catheter, the insertion of central venous pressure lines, emergency intubation, and critical care visits.

G. Anesthesia Time and Calculation of Anesthesia Time Units

Anesthesia time is defined as the period during which an anesthesia practitioner is present with the patient. It starts when the anesthesia practitioner begins to prepare the patient for anesthesia services in the operating room or an equivalent area and ends when the anesthesia practitioner is no longer furnishing anesthesia services to the patient, that is, when the patient may be placed safely under postoperative care. Anesthesia time is a continuous time period from the start of anesthesia to the end of an anesthesia service. In counting anesthesia time for services furnished on or after January 1, 2000, the anesthesia practitioner can add blocks of time around an interruption in anesthesia time as long as the anesthesia practitioner is furnishing continuous anesthesia care within the time periods around the interruption.

Actual anesthesia time in minutes is reported on the claim. For anesthesia services furnished on or after January 1, 1994, carriers compute time units by dividing reported anesthesia time by 15 minutes. Round the time unit to one decimal place. Carriers do not recognize time units for CPT codes 01995 or 01996.

For purposes of this section, anesthesia practitioner means a physician who performs the anesthesia service alone, a CRNA who is not medically directed, or a CRNA or AA, who is medically directed. The physician who medically directs the CRNA or AA would ordinarily report the same time as the CRNA or AA reports for the CRNA service.

H. Base Unit Reduction for Concurrent Medically Directed Procedures
If the physician medically directs concurrent medically directed procedures prior to January 1, 1994, reduce the number of base units for each concurrent procedure as follows.

- For two concurrent procedures, the base unit on each procedure is reduced 10 percent.
- For three concurrent procedures, the base unit on each procedure is reduced 25 percent.
- For four concurrent procedures, the base on each concurrent procedure is reduced 40 percent.
- If the physician medically directs concurrent procedures prior to January 1, 1994, and any of the concurrent procedures are cataract or iridectomy anesthesia, reduce the base units for each cataract or iridectomy procedure by 10 percent.

I. Monitored Anesthesia Care
Carriers pay for reasonable and medically necessary monitored anesthesia care services on the same basis as other anesthesia services. Anesthesiologists use modifier QS to report monitored anesthesia care cases. Monitored anesthesia care involves the intra-operative monitoring by a physician or qualified individual under the medical direction of a physician or of the patient's vital physiological signs in anticipation of the need for administration of general anesthesia or of the development of adverse physiological patient reaction to the surgical procedure. It also includes the performance of a pre-anesthetic examination and evaluation, prescription of the anesthesia care required, administration of any necessary oral or parenteral medications (e.g., atropine, demerol, valium) and provision of indicated postoperative anesthesia care.

Payment is made under the fee schedule using the payment rules in subsection B if the physician personally performs the monitored anesthesia care case or under the rules in subsection C if the physician medically directs four or fewer concurrent cases and monitored anesthesia care represents one or more of these concurrent cases.

J. Definition of Concurrent Medically Directed Anesthesia Procedures
Concurrency is defined with regard to the maximum number of procedures that the physician is medically directing within the context of a single procedure and whether these other procedures overlap each other. Concurrency is not dependent on each of the cases involving a Medicare patient. For example, if an anesthesiologist directs three concurrent procedures, two of which involve non-Medicare patients and the remaining a Medicare patient, this represents three concurrent cases. The following example illustrates this concept and guides physicians in determining how many procedures they are directing.

EXAMPLE.

Procedures A through E are medically directed procedures involving CRNAs and furnished between January 1, 1992 and December 31, 1997 (1998 concurrent instructions can be found in subsection C.) The starting and ending times for each procedure represent the periods during which anesthesia time is counted. Assume that none of the procedures were cataract or iridectomy anesthesia.

Procedure A begins at 8:00 a.m. and lasts until 8:20 a.m.

Procedure B begins at 8:10 a.m. and lasts until 8:45 a.m.

Procedure C begins at 8:30 a.m. and lasts until 9:15 a.m.

Procedure D begins at 9:00 a.m. and lasts until 12:00 noon.

Procedure E begins at 9:10 a.m. and lasts until 9:55 a.m.

Procedure	Number of Concurrent Medically Directed Procedures	Base Unit Reduction Percentage
A	2	10%
B	2	10%
C	3	25%
D	3	25%
E	3	25%

From 8:00 a.m. to 8:20 a.m., the length of procedure A, the anesthesiologist medically directed two concurrent procedures, A and B. From 8:10 a.m. to 8:45 a.m., the length of procedure B, the anesthesiologist medically directed two concurrent procedures.

From 8:10 to 8:20 a.m., the anesthesiologist medically directed procedures A and B. From 8:20 to 8:30 a.m., the anesthesiologist medically directed only procedure B. From 8:30 to 8:45 a.m., the anesthesiologist medically directed procedures B and C. Thus, during procedure B, the anesthesiologist medically directed, at most, two concurrent procedures.

From 8:30 a.m. to 9:15 a.m., the length of procedure C, the anesthesiologist medically directed three concurrent procedures.

From 8:30 to 8:45 a.m., the anesthesiologist medically directed procedures B and C. From 8:45 to 9:00 a.m., the anesthesiologist medically directed procedure C. From 9:00 to 9:10 a.m., the anesthesiologist medically directed procedures C and D. From 9:10 to 9:15 a.m., the anesthesiologist medically directed procedures C, D and E. Thus, during procedure C, the anesthesiologist medically directed, at most, three concurrent procedures.

The same analysis shows that during procedure D or E, the anesthesiologist medically directed, at most, three concurrent procedures.

K. Anesthesia Claims Modifiers
Physicians report the appropriate anesthesia modifier to denote whether the service was personally performed, medically directed, or medically supervised.

Specific anesthesia modifiers include:

- AA Anesthesia Services performed personally by the anesthesiologist
- AD Medical Supervision by a physician, more than 4 concurrent anesthesia procedures;
- G8 Monitored anesthesia care (MAC) for deep complex complicated, or markedly invasive surgical procedures;
- G9 Monitored anesthesia care for patient who has a history of severe cardio-pulmonary condition
- QK Medical direction of two, three or four concurrent anesthesia procedures involving qualified individuals
- QS Monitored anesthesia care service
- QX CRNA service; with medical direction by a physician
- QY Medical direction of one certified registered nurse anesthetist by an anesthesiologist
- QZ CRNA service: Without medical direction by a physician.

The QS modifier is for informational purposes. Providers must report actual anesthesia time on the claim.

Carriers must determine payment for anesthesia in accordance with these instructions. They must be able to determine the uniform base unit that is assigned to the anesthesia code and apply the appropriate reduction where the anesthesia procedure is medically directed. They must also be able to determine the number of anesthesia time units from actual anesthesia time reported on the claim. Carriers must multiply allowable units by the anesthesia-specific conversion factor used to determine fee schedule payment for the payment area.

L. Anesthesia and Medical/Surgical Service Provided by the Same Physician
Anesthesia services range in complexity. The continuum of anesthesia services, from least intense to most intense in complexity is as follows: local or topical anesthesia, moderate (conscious) sedation, regional anesthesia and general anesthesia. Prior to 2006, Medicare did not recognize separate payment if the same physician provided the medical or surgical procedure and the anesthesia needed for the procedure.

Moderate sedation is a drug induced depression of consciousness during which the patient responds purposefully to verbal commands, either alone or accompanied by light

tactile stimulation. Moderate sedation does not include minimal sedation, deep sedation or monitored anesthesia care. In 2006, the CPT added new codes 99143 to 99150 for moderate or conscious sedation. The moderate (conscious) sedation codes are carrier priced under the Medicare physician fee schedule.

CPT codes 99143 to 99145 describe moderate sedation provided by the same physician performing the diagnostic or therapeutic service that the sedation supports, requiring the presence of an independent trained observer to assist in the monitoring of the patient's level of consciousness and physiological status. The physician can bill the conscious sedation codes 99143 to 99145 as long as the procedure with it is billed is not listed in Appendix G of CPT. CPT codes 99148 to 99150 describe moderate sedation provided by a physician other than the health care professional performing the diagnostic or therapeutic service that the sedation supports.

The CPT includes Appendix G, Summary of CPT Codes That Include Moderate (Conscious) Sedation. This appendix lists those procedures for which moderate (conscious) sedation is an inherent part of the procedure itself. CPT coding guidelines instruct practices not to report CPT codes 99143 to 99145 in conjunction with codes listed in Appendix G. The National Correct Coding Initiative has established edits that bundle CPT codes 99143 and 99144 into the procedures listed in Appendix G.

In the unusual event when a second physician other than the health care professional performing the diagnostic or therapeutic services provides moderate sedation in the facility setting for the procedures listed in Appendix G, the second physician can bill 99148 to 99150. The term, facility, includes those places of service listed in Chapter 23 Addendum -- field 29. However, when these services are performed by the second physician in the nonfacility setting, CPT codes 99148 to 99150 are not to be reported.

If the anesthesiologist or CRNA provides anesthesia for diagnostic or therapeutic nerve blocks or injections and a different provider performs the block or injection, then the anesthesiologist or CRNA may report the anesthesia service using CPT code 01991. The service must meet the criteria for monitored anesthesia care. If the anesthesiologist or CRNA provides both the anesthesia service and the block or injection, then the anesthesiologist or CRNA may report the anesthesia service using the conscious sedation code and the injection or block. However, the anesthesia service must meet the requirements for conscious sedation and if a lower level complexity anesthesia service is provided, then the conscious sedation code should not be reported.

If the physician performing the medical or surgical procedure also provides a level of anesthesia lower in intensity than moderate or conscious sedation, such as a local or topical anesthesia, then the conscious sedation code should not be reported and no payment should be allowed by the carrier. There is no CPT code for the performance of local anesthesia and as payment for this service is considered in the payment for the underlying medical or surgical service.

100-4, 12, 60

Payment for Pathology Services

B3-15020, AB-01-47 (CR1499)

A. General Payment Rule

Payment may be made under the fee schedule for the professional component of physician laboratory or physician pathology services furnished to hospital inpatients or outpatients by hospital physicians or by independent laboratories, if they qualify as the reassignee for the physician service.. Payment may be made under the fee schedule, as noted below, for the technical component (TC) of pathology services furnished by an independent laboratory to hospital inpatients or outpatients. Payment may be made under the fee schedule for the technical component of physician pathology services furnished by an independent laboratory, or a hospital if it is acting as an independent laboratory, to non-hospital patients. The Medicare physician fee schedule identifies those physician laboratory or physician pathology services that have a technical component service.

CMS published a final regulation in 1999 that would no longer allow independent laboratories to bill under the physician fee schedule for the TC of physician pathology services. The implementation of this regulation was delayed by Section 542 of the Benefits and Improvement and Protection Act of 2000 (BIPA). Section 542 allows the Medicare carrier to continue to pay for the TC of physician pathology services when an independent laboratory furnishes this service to an inpatient or outpatient of a covered hospital. This provision is applicable to TC services furnished in 2001, 2002, 2003, 2004, 2005 or 2006.

For this provision, a covered hospital is a hospital that had an arrangement with an independent laboratory that was in effect as of July 22, 1999, under which a laboratory furnished the TC of physician pathology services to fee-for-service Medicare beneficiaries who were hospital inpatients or outpatients, and submitted claims for payment for the TC to a carrier. The TC could have been submitted separately or combined with the professional component and reported as a combined service.

The term, fee-for-service Medicare beneficiary, means an individual who:

Is entitled to benefits under Part A or enrolled under Part B of title XVIII or both; and

Is not enrolled in any of the following: A Medicare + Choice plan under Part C of such title; a plan offered by an eligible organization under 1876 of the Social Security Act; a program of all-inclusive care for the elderly under 1894; or a social health maintenance organization demonstration project established under Section 4108 of the Omnibus Budget Reconciliation Act of 1987.

In implementing Section 542, the carriers should consider as independent laboratories those entities that it has previously recognized as independent laboratories. An independent laboratory that has acquired another independent laboratory that had an arrangement of July 22, 1999, with a covered hospital, can bill the TC of physician pathology services for that hospital's inpatients and outpatients under the physician fee schedule.

An independent laboratory that furnishes the TC of physician pathology services to inpatients or outpatients of a hospital that is not a covered hospital may not bill the carrier for the TC of physician pathology services during the time 542 is in effect.

If the arrangement between the independent laboratory and the covered hospital limited the provision of TC physician pathology services to certain situations or at particular times, then the independent laboratory can bill the carrier only for these limited services.

The carrier shall require independent laboratories that had an arrangement, on or prior to July 22, 1999 with a covered hospital, to bill for the technical component of physician pathology services to provide a copy of this agreement, or other documentation substantiating that an arrangement was in effect between the hospital and the independent laboratory as of this date. The independent laboratory must submit this documentation for each covered hospital that the independent laboratory services.

See Chapter 16 for additional instruction on laboratory services including clinical diagnostic laboratory services.

Physician laboratory and pathology services are limited to:

- Surgical pathology services;
- Specific cytopathology, hematology and blood banking services that have been identified to require performance by a physician and are listed below;
- Clinical consultation services that meet the requirements in subsection D below;
- and
- Clinical laboratory interpretation services that meet the requirements and which are specifically listed in subsection E below.

B. Surgical Pathology Services

Surgical pathology services include the gross and microscopic examination of organ tissue performed by a physician, except for autopsies, which are not covered by Medicare. Surgical pathology services paid under the physician fee schedule are reported under the following CPT codes:

88300, 88302, 88304, 88305, 88307, 88309, 88311, 88312, 88313, 88314, 88318, 88319, 88321, 88323, 88325, 88329, 88331, 88332, 88342, 88346, 88347, 88348, 88349, 88355, 88356, 88358, 88361, 88362, 88365, 88380.

Depending upon circumstances and the billing entity, the carriers may pay professional component, technical component or both.

C. Specific Hematology, Cytopathology and Blood Banking Services

Cytopathology services include the examination of cells from fluids, washings, brushings or smears, but generally excluding hematology. Examining cervical and vaginal smears are the most common service in cytopathology. Cervical and vaginal smears do not require interpretation by a physician unless the results are or appear to be abnormal. In such cases, a physician personally conducts a separate microscopic evaluation to determine the nature of an abnormality. This microscopic evaluation ordinarily does require performance by a physician. When medically necessary and when furnished by a physician, it is paid under the fee schedule.

These codes include 88104, 88106, 88107, 88108, 88112, 88125, 88141, 88160, 88161, 88162, 88172, 88173, 88180, 88182.

For services furnished prior to January 1, 1999, carriers pay separately under the physician fee schedule for the interpretation of an abnormal pap smear furnished to a hospital inpatient by a physician. They must pay under the clinical laboratory fee schedule for pap smears furnished in all other situations. This policy also applies to screening pap smears requiring a physician interpretation. For services furnished on or after January 1, 1999, carriers allow separate payment for a physician's interpretation of a pap smear to any patient (i.e., hospital or non-hospital) as long as: (1) the laboratory's screening personnel suspect an abnormality; and (2) the physician reviews and interprets the pap smear.

This policy also applies to screening pap smears requiring a physician interpretation and described in the National Coverage Determination Manual and Chapter 18. These services are reported under codes P3000 or P3001.

Physician hematology services include microscopic evaluation of bone marrow aspirations and biopsies. It also includes those limited number of peripheral blood smears which need to be referred to a physician to evaluate the nature of an apparent abnormality identified by the technologist. These codes include 85060, 38220, 85097, and 38221.

Carriers pay the professional component for the interpretation of an abnormal blood smear (code 85060) furnished to a hospital inpatient by a hospital physician or an independent laboratory.

For the other listed hematology codes, payment may be made for the professional component if the service is furnished to a patient by a hospital physician or independent laboratory. In addition, payment may be made for these services furnished to patients by an independent laboratory.

Codes 38220 and 85097 represent professional-only component services and have no technical component values.

Blood banking services of hematologists and pathologists are paid under the physician fee schedule when analyses are performed on donor and/or patient blood to determine compatible donor units for transfusion where cross matching is difficult or where contamination with transmissible disease of donor is suspected.

The blood banking codes are 86077, 86078, and 86079 and represent professional component only services. These codes do not have a technical component.

D. Clinical Consultation Services

Clinical consultations are paid under the physician fee schedule only if they:

- Are requested by the patient's attending physician;
- Relate to a test result that lies outside the clinically significant normal or expected range in view of the condition of the patient;
- Result in a written narrative report included in the patient's medical record; and
- Require the exercise of medical judgment by the consultant physician.

Clinical consultations are professional component services only. There is no technical component. The clinical consultation codes are 80500 and 80502.

Routine conversations held between a laboratory director and an attending physician about test orders or results do not qualify as consultations unless all four requirements are met. Laboratory personnel, including the director, may from time to time contact attending physicians to report test results or to suggest additional testing or be contacted by attending physicians on similar matters. These contacts do not constitute clinical consultations. However, if in the course of such a contact, the attending physician requests a consultation from the pathologist, and if that consultation meets the other criteria and is properly documented, it is paid under the fee schedule.

EXAMPLE: A pathologist telephones a surgeon about a patient's suitability for surgery based on the results of clinical laboratory test results. During the course of their conversation, the surgeon ask the pathologist whether, based on test results, patient history and medical records, the patient is a candidate for surgery. The surgeon's request requires the pathologist to render a medical judgment and provide a consultation. The athologist follows up his/her oral advice with a written report and the surgeon notes in the patient's medical record that he/she requested a consultation. This consultation is paid under the fee schedule.

In any case, if the information could ordinarily be furnished by a nonphysician laboratory specialist, the service of the physician is not a consultation payable under the fee schedule.

See the Program Integrity Manual for guidelines for related data analysis to identify inappropriate patterns of billing for consultations.

E. Clinical Laboratory Interpretation Services

Only clinical laboratory interpretation services listed below and which meet the criteria in subsections D.1, D.3, and D.4 for clinical consultations and, as a result, are billable under the fee schedule. These services are reported under the clinical laboratory code with modifier 26. These services can be paid under the physician fee schedule if they are furnished to a patient by a hospital pathologist or an independent laboratory. Note that a hospital's standing order policy can be used as a substitute for the individual request by the patient's attending physician. Carriers are not allowed to revise CMS's list to accommodate local medical practice. The CMS periodically reviews this list and adds or deletes clinical laboratory codes as warranted.

Clinical Laboratory Interpretation Services

Code	Definition
83020	Hemoglobin; electrophoresis
83912	Nucleic acid probe, with electrophoresis, with examination and report
84165	Protein, total, serum; electrophoretic fractionation and quantitation
84181	Protein; Western Blot with interpretation and report, blood or other body fluid
84182	Protein; Western Blot, with interpretation and report, blood or other body fluid, immunological probe for band identification; each
85390	Fibrinolysin; screening
85576	Platelet; aggregation (in vitro), any agent
86255	Fluorescent antibody; screen
86256	Fluorescent antibody; titer
86320	Immunoelectrophoresis; serum, each specimen
86325	Immunoelectrophoresis; other fluids (e.g.urine) with concentration, each specimen
86327	Immunoelectrophoresis; crossed (2 dimensional assay)
86334	Immunofixation electrophoresis
87164	Dark field examination, any source (e.g. penile, vaginal, oral, skin); includes specimen collection
87207	Smear, primary source, with interpretation; special stain for inclusion bodies or intracellular parasites (e.g. malaria, kala azar, herpes)
88371	Protein analysis of tissue by Western Blot, with interpretation and report.
88372	Protein analysis of tissue by Western Blot, immunological probe for band identification; each
89060	Crystal identification by light microscopy with or without polarizing lens analysis, any body fluid (except urine)

100-4, 12, 80.3
Unusual Travel (CPT Code 99082)

B3 15026 In general, travel has been incorporated in the MPFSDB individual fees and is thus not separately payable. Carriers must pay separately for unusual travel (CPT code 99082) only when the physician submits documentation to demonstrate that the travel was very unusual.

100-4, 12, 90.3
Physicians' Services Performed in Ambulatory Surgical Centers (ASC)

B3-2265, B3-2265.4

See Chapter 14, for a description of services that may be billed by an ASC and services separately billed by physicians.

The ASC payment does not include the professional services of the physician. These are billed separately by the physician. Physicians' services include the services of anesthesiologists administering or supervising the administration of anesthesia to ASC patients and the patients' recovery from the anesthesia. The term physicians' services also includes any routine pre- or postoperative services, such as office visits, consultations, diagnostic tests, removal of stitches, changing of dressings, and other services which the individual physician usually performs.

The physician must enter the place of service code (POS) 24 on the claim to show that the procedure was performed in an ASC.

The carrier pays the "facility" fee from the MPFSDB to the physician. The facility fee is for services done in a facility other than the physician's office and is less then the nonfacility fee for services performed in the physician's office.

100-4, 12, 100
Teaching Physician Services
Definitions
For purposes of this section, the following definitions apply.

Resident -An individual who participates in an approved graduate medical education (GME) program or a physician who is not in an approved GME program but who is authorized to practice only in a hospital setting. The term includes interns and fellows in GME programs recognized as approved for purposes of direct GME payments made by the FI. Receiving a staff or faculty appointment or participating in a fellowship does not by itself alter the status of "resident". Additionally, this status remains unaffected regardless of whether a hospital includes the physician in its full time equivalency count of residents.

Student- An individual who participates in an accredited educational program (e.g., a medical school) that is not an approved GME program. A student is never considered to be an intern or a resident. Medicare does not pay for any service furnished by a student. See 100.1.1B for a discussion concerning E/M service documentation performed by students.

Teaching Physician -A physician (other than another resident) who involves residents in the care of his or her patients.

Direct Medical and Surgical Services -Services to individual beneficiaries that are either personally furnished by a physician or furnished by a resident under the supervision of a physician in a teaching hospital making the reasonable cost election for physician services furnished in teaching hospitals. All payments for such services are made by the FI for the hospital.

Teaching Hospital -A hospital engaged in an approved GME residency program in medicine, osteopathy, dentistry, or podiatry.

Teaching Setting -Any provider, hospital-based provider, or nonprovider setting in which Medicare payment for the services of residents is made by the FI under the direct graduate medical education payment methodology or freestanding SNF or HHA in which such payments are made on a reasonable cost basis.

Critical or Key Portion- That part (or parts) of a service that the teaching physician determines is (are) a critical or key portion(s). For purposes of this section, these terms are interchangeable.

Documentation- Notes recorded in the patient's medical records by a resident, and/or teaching physician or others as outlined in the specific situations below regarding the service furnished. Documentation may be dictated and typed or hand-written, or computer-generated and typed or handwritten. Documentation must be dated and include a legible signature or identity. Pursuant to 42 CFR 415.172 (b), documentation must identify, at a minimum, the service furnished, the participation of the teaching physician in providing the service, and whether the teaching physician was physically present. In the context of an electronic medical record, the term 'macro' means a command in a computer or dictation application that automatically generates predetermined text that is not edited by the user.

When using an electronic medical record, it is acceptable for the teaching physician to use a macro as the required personal documentation if the teaching physician adds it personally in a secured (password protected) system. In addition to the teaching physician's macro, either the resident or the teaching physician must provide customized information that is sufficient to support a medical necessity determination. The note in the electronic medical record must sufficiently describe the specific services furnished to the specific patient on the specific date. It is insufficient documentation if both the resident and the teaching physician use macros only.

Physically Present- The teaching physician is located in the same room (or partitioned or curtained area, if the room is subdivided to accommodate multiple patients) as the patient and/or performs a face-to-face service.

100-4, 12, 110.2
Outpatient Mental Health Limitation

B3-4112, B3-2472.4 The carrier must apply the outpatient mental health limitation to all covered mental health therapeutic services furnished by PAs. The reduction is 62.5 percent applied after the 85 percent.

Refer to 210 below for a complete discussion of the outpatient mental health limitation.

100-4, 12, 140
Certified Registered Nurse Anesthetist (CRNA) Services

B3-10003, B3-10003 A, B3-3040.4, B3-4172 Section 9320 of OBRA 1986 provides for payment under a fee schedule to certified registered nurse anesthetists (CRNAs) and anesthesia assistants (AAs). CRNAs and AAs may bill Medicare directly for their services or have payment made to an employer or an entity under which they have a contract. This could be a hospital, physician or ASC. This provision is effective for services rendered on or after January 1, 1989. Anesthesia services are subject to the usual Part B coinsurance and deductible and when furnished on or after January 1, 1992 by a qualified nurse anesthetist and are paid at the lesser of the actual charge, the physician fee schedule, or the CRNA fee schedule. Payment for CRNA services is made only on an assignment basis.

100-4, 12, 140.2
Entity or Individual to Whom CRNA Fee Schedule is Payable

B3-16003.C, B3-4830.A

Payment for the services of a CRNA may be made to the CRNA who furnished the anesthesia services or to a hospital, physician, group practice, or ASC with which the CRNA has an employment or contractual relationship.

100-4, 12, 140.3.2
Anesthesia Time and Calculation of Anesthesia Time Units

B3-15018.G Anesthesia time means the time during which a CRNA is present with the patient. It starts when the CRNA begins to prepare the patient for anesthesia services in the operating room or an equivalent area and ends when the CRNA is no longer furnishing anesthesia services to the patient, that is, when the patient may be placed safely under postoperative care. Anesthesia time is a continuous time period from the start of anesthesia to the end of an anesthesia service. In counting anesthesia time for services furnished on or after January 1, 2000, the CRNA can add blocks of time around an interruption in anesthesia time as long as the CRNA is furnishing continuous anesthesia care within the time periods around the interruption.

100-4, 12, 150
Clinical Social Worker (CSW) Services

B3-2152, B3-17000 See Medicare Benefit Policy Manual, Chapter 15, for coverage requirements.

Assignment of benefits is required.

Payment is at 75 percent of the physician fee schedule.

CSWs are identified on the provider file by specialty code 80 and provider type 56.

Medicare applies the outpatient mental health limitation to all covered therapeutic services furnished by qualified CSWs. Refer to 210, below, for a discussion of the outpatient mental health limitation. The modifier "AJ" must be applied on CSW services.

100-4, 12, 160
Independent Psychologist Services

B3-2150, B3-2070.2 See the Medicare Benefit Policy Manual, Chapter 15, for coverage requirements.

There are a number of types of psychologists. Educational psychologists engage in identifying and treating education-related issues. In contrast, counseling psychologists provide services that include a broader realm including phobias, familial issues, etc.

Psychometrists are psychologists who have been trained to administer and interpret tests.

However, clinical psychologists are defined as a provider of diagnostic and therapeutic services. Because of the differences in services provided, services provided by psychologists who do not provide clinical services are subject to different billing guidelines. One service often provided by nonclinical psychologist is diagnostic testing.

NOTE:Diagnostic psychological testing services performed by persons who meet these requirements are covered as other diagnostic tests. When, however, the psychologist is not practicing independently, but is on the staff of an institution, agency, or clinic, that entity bills for the diagnostic services.

Expenses for such testing are not subject to the payment limitation on treatment for mental, psychoneurotic, and personality disorders. Independent psychologists are not required by law to accept assignment when performing psychological tests. However, regardless of whether the psychologist accepts assignment, he or she must report on the claim form the name and address of the physician who ordered the test.

100-4, 12, 160.1
Payment

Diagnostic testing services are not subject to the outpatient mental health limitation. Refer to §210, below, for a discussion of the outpatient mental health limitation.

The diagnostic testing services performed by a psychologist (who is not a clinical psychologist) practicing independently of an institution, agency, or physician's office are covered as other diagnostic tests if a physician orders such testing. Medicare covers this type of testing as an outpatient service if furnished by any psychologist who is licensed or certified to practice psychology in the State or jurisdiction where he or she is furnishing services or, if the jurisdiction does not issue licenses, if provided by any practicing psychologist. (It is CMS' understanding that all States, the District of Columbia, and Puerto Ricolicense psychologists, but that some trust territories do not. Examples of psychologists, other than clinical psychologists, whose services are covered under this provision include, but are not limited to, educational psychologists and counseling psychologists.)

To determine whether the diagnostic psychological testing services of a particular independent psychologist are covered under Part B in States which have statutory licensure or certification, carriers must secure from the appropriate State agency a current listing of psychologists holding the required credentials. In States or territories which lack statutory licensing and certification, carriers must check individual qualifications as claims are submitted. Possible reference sources are the national directory of membership of the American Psychological Association, which provides data about the educational background of individuals and indicates which members are board-certified, and records and directories of the State or territorial psychological association. If qualification is dependent on a doctoral degree from a currently accredited program, carriers must verify the date of accreditation of the school involved, since such accreditation is not retroactive. If the reference sources listed above do not provide enough information (e.g., the psychologist is not a member of the association), carriers must contact the psychologist personally for the required information. Carriers may wish to maintain a continuing list of psychologists whose qualifications have been verified.

Medicare excludes expenses for diagnostic testing from the payment limitation on treatment for mental/psychoneurotic/personality disorders.

Carriers must identify the independent psychologist's choice whether or not to accept assignment when performing psychological tests.

Carriers must accept an independent psychologist claim only if the psychologist reports the name/UPIN of the physician who ordered a test.

Carriers pay nonparticipating independent psychologists at 95 percent of the physician fee schedule allowed amount. Carriers pay participating independent psychologists at 100 percent of the physician fee schedule allowed amount.

Independent psychologists are identified on the provider file by specialty code 62 and provider type 35.

100-4, 12, 170
Clinical Psychologist Services

B3-2150 See Medicare Benefit Policy Manual, Chapter 15, for general coverage requirements.

Direct payment may be made under Part B for professional services. However, services furnished incident to the professional services of CPs to hospital patients remain bundled.

Therefore, payment must continue to be made to the hospital (by the FI) for such "incident to" services.

100-4, 12, 170.1
Payment

B3-2150, B3-17001.1 All covered therapeutic services furnished by qualified CPs are subject to the outpatient mental health services limitation (i.e., only 62 1/2 percent of expenses for these services are considered incurred expenses for Medicare purposes). The limitation does not apply to diagnostic services. Refer to 210 below for a discussion of the outpatient mental health limitation.

Payment for the services of CPs is made on the basis of a fee schedule or the actual charge, whichever is less, and only on the basis of assignment.

CPs are identified by specialty code 68 and provider type 27. Modifier "AH" is required on CP services.

100-4, 12, 180
Care Plan Oversight Services

The Medicare Benefit Policy Manual, Chapter 15, contains requirements for coverage for medical and other health services including those of physicians and non-physician practitioners.

Care plan oversight (CPO) is the physician supervision of a patient receiving complex and/or multidisciplinary care as part of Medicare-covered services provided by a participating home health agency or Medicare approved hospice.

CPO services require complex or multidisciplinary care modalities involving:

- Regular physician development and/or revision of care plans;
- Review of subsequent reports of patient status;
- Review of related laboratory and other studies;
- Communication with other health professionals not employed in the same practice who are involved in the patient's care;
- Integration of new information into the medical treatment plan; and/or
- Adjustment of medical therapy.

The CPO services require recurrent physician supervision of a patient involving 30 or more minutes of the physician's time per month. Services not countable toward the 30 minutes threshold that must be provided in order to bill for CPO include, but are not limited to:

- Time associated with discussions with the patient, his or her family or friends to adjust medication or treatment;
- Time spent by staff getting or filing charts;
- Travel time; and/or
- Physician's time spent telephoning prescriptions into the pharmacist unless the telephone conversation involves discussions of pharmaceutical therapies.

Implicit in the concept of CPO is the expectation that the physician has coordinated an aspect of the patient's care with the home health agency or hospice during the month for which CPO services were billed. The physician who bills for CPO must be the same physician who signs the plan of care.

Nurse practitioners, physician assistants, and clinical nurse specialists, practicing within the scope of State law, may bill for care plan oversight. These non-physician practitioners must have been providing ongoing care for the beneficiary through evaluation and management services. These non-physician practitioners may not bill for CPO if they have been involved only with the delivery of the Medicare-covered home health or hospice service.

A. Home Health CPO

Non-physician practitioners can perform CPO only if the physician signing the plan of care provides regular ongoing care under the same plan of care as does the NPP billing for CPO and either:

- The physician and NPP are part of the same group practice; or
- If the NPP is a nurse practitioner or clinical nurse specialist, the physician signing the plan of care also has a collaborative agreement with the NPP; or
- If the NPP is a physician assistant, the physician signing the plan of care is also the physician who provides general supervision of physician assistant services for the practice.

Billing may be made for care plan oversight services furnished by an NPP when:

- The NPP providing the care plan oversight has seen and examined the patient;
- The NPP providing care plan oversight is not functioning as a consultant whose participation is limited to a single medical condition rather than multidisciplinary coordination of care; and
- The NPP providing care plan oversight integrates his or her care with that of the physician who signed the plan of care.

NPPs may not certify the beneficiary for home health care.

B. Hospice CPO

The attending physician or nurse practitioner (who has been designated as the attending physician) may bill for hospice CPO when they are acting as an "attending physician".

An "attending physician" is one who has been identified by the individual, at the time he/she elects hospice coverage, as having the most significant role in the determination and delivery of their medical care. They are not employed nor paid by the hospice. The care plan oversight services are billed using Form CMS-1500 or electronic equivalent.

For additional information on hospice CPO, see Chapter 11, 40.1.3.1 of this manual.

100-4, 12, 180.1
Care Plan Oversight Billing Requirements
A. Codes for Which Separate Payment May Be Made

Effective January 1, 1995, separate payment may be made for CPO oversight services for 30 minutes or more if the requirements specified in the Medicare Benefits Policy Manual, Chapter 15 are met.

Providers billing for CPO must submit the claim with no other services billed on that claim and may bill only after the end of the month in which the CPO services were rendered. CPO services may not be billed across calendar months and should be submitted (and paid) only for one unit of service.

Physicians may bill and be paid separately for CPO services only if all the criteria in the Medicare Benefit Policy Manual, Chapter 15 are met.

B. Physician Certification and Recertification of Home Health Plans of Care

Effective 2001, two new HCPCS codes for the certification and recertification and development of plans of care for Medicare-covered home health services were created.

See the Medicare General Information, Eligibility, and Entitlement Manual, Pub. 100-01, Chapter 4, "Physician Certification and Recertification of Services," 10-60, and the Medicare Benefit Policy Manual, Pub. 100-02, Chapter 7, "Home Health Services", 30.

The home health agency certification code can be billed only when the patient has not received Medicare-covered home health services for at least 60 days. The home health agency recertification code is used after a patient has received services for at least 60 days (or one certification period) when the physician signs the certification after the initial certification period. The home health agency recertification code will be reported only once every 60 days, except in the rare situation when the patient starts a new episode before 60 days elapses and requires a new plan of care to start a new episode.

C. Provider Number of Home Health Agency (HHA) or Hospice

For claims for CPO submitted on or after January 1, 1997, physicians must enter on the Medicare claim form the 6-character Medicare provider number of the HHA or hospice providing Medicare-covered services to the beneficiary for the period during which CPO services was furnished and for which the physician signed the plan of care. Physicians are responsible for obtaining the HHA or hospice Medicare provider numbers.

Additionally, physicians should provide their UPIN to the HHA or hospice furnishing services to their patient.

NOTE: There is currently no place on the HIPAA standard ASC X12N 837 professional format to specifically include the HHA or hospice provider number required for a care plan oversight claim. For this reason, the requirement to include the HHA or hospice provider number on a care plan oversight claim is temporarily waived until a new version of this electronic standard format is adopted under HIPAA and includes a place to provide the HHA and hospice provider numbers for care plan oversight claims.

100-4, 12, 190.3

List of Medicare Telehealth Services

The use of a telecommunications system may substitute for a face-to-face, "hands on" encounter for consultation, office visits, individual psychotherapy, pharmacologic management, psychiatric diagnostic interview examination, end stage renal disease related services, and individual medical nutrition therapy. These services and corresponding current procedure terminology (CPT) or Healthcare Common Procedure Coding System (HCPCS) codes are listed below.

- Consultations (CPT codes 99241 - 99275) - Effective October 1, 2001 - December 31, 2005;
- Consultations (CPT codes 99241 - 99255) - Effective January 1, 2006;
- Office or other outpatient visits (CPT codes 99201 - 99215);
- Individual psychotherapy (CPT codes 90804 - 90809);
- Pharmacologic management (CPT code 90862); and
- Psychiatric diagnostic interview examination (CPT code 90801) - Effective March 1, 2003.
- End Stage Renal Disease (ESRD) related services (HCPCS codes G0308, G0309, G0311, G0312, G0314, G0315, G0317, and G0318) - Effective January 1, 2005.
- Individual Medical Nutrition Therapy (HCPCS codes G0270, 97802, and 97803) (Effective January 1, 2006).
- Neurobehavioral status exam (CPT code 96116) (Effective January 1, 2008).

100-4, 12, 190.7

Contractor Editing of Telehealth Claims

Medicare telehealth services (as listed in section 190.3) are billed with either the "GT" or "GQ" modifier. The contractor shall approve covered telehealth services if the physician or practitioner is licensed under State law to provide the service. Contractors must familiarize themselves with licensure provisions of States for which they process claims and disallow telehealth services furnished by physicians or practitioners who are not authorized to furnish the applicable telehealth service under State law. For example, if a nurse practitioner is not licensed to provide individual psychotherapy under State law, he or she would not be permitted to receive payment for individual psychotherapy under Medicare. The contractor shall install edits to ensure that only properly licensed physicians and practitioners are paid for covered telehealth services.

If a contractor receives claims for professional telehealth services coded with the "GQ" modifier (representing "via asynchronous telecommunications system"), it shall approve/pay for these services only if the physician or practitioner is affiliated with a Federal telemedicine demonstration conducted in Alaska or Hawaii. The contractor may require the physician or practitioner at the distant site to document his or her participation in a Federal telemedicine demonstration program conducted in Alaska or Hawaii prior to paying for telehealth services provided via asynchronous, store and forward technologies.

If a contractor denies telehealth services because the physician or practitioner may not bill for them, the contractor uses MSN message 21.18: "This item or service is not covered when performed or ordered by this practitioner." The contractor uses remittance advice message 52 when denying the claim based upon MSN message 21.18.

If a service is billed with one of the telehealth modifiers and the procedure code is not designated as a covered telehealth service, the contractor denies the service using MSN message 9.4: "This item or service was denied because information required to make payment was incorrect." The remittance advice message depends on what is incorrect, e.g., B18 if procedure code or modifier is incorrect, 125 for submission billing errors, 4-12 for difference inconsistencies. The contractor uses B18 as the explanation for the denial of the claim.

The only claims from institutional facilities that FIs shall pay for telehealth services at the distant site, except for MNT services, are for physician or practitioner services when the distant site is located in a CAH that has elected Method II, and the physician or practitioner has reassigned his/her benefits to the CAH. The CAH bills its regular FI for the professional services provided at the distant site via a telecommunications system, in any of the revenue codes 096x, 097x or 098x. All requirements for billing distant site telehealth services apply.

Claims from hospitals or CAHs for MNT services are submitted to the hospital's or CAH's regular FI. Payment is based on the non-facility amount on the Medicare Physician Fee Schedule for the particular HCPCS codes.

100-4, 12, 200

Allergy Testing and Immunotherapy

B3-15050

A. Allergy Testing

The MPFSDB fee amounts for allergy testing services billed under codes 95004-95078 are established for single tests. Therefore, the number of tests must be shown on the claim.

EXAMPLE: If a physician performs 25 percutaneous tests (scratch, puncture, or prick) with allergenic extract, the physician must bill code 95004 and specify 25 in the units field of Form CMS-1500 (paper claims or electronic format). To compute payment, the Medicare carrier multiplies the payment for one test (i.e., the payment listed in the fee schedule) by the quantity listed in the units field.

B. Allergy Immunotherapy

For services rendered on or after January 1, 1995, all antigen/allergy immunotherapy services are paid for under the Medicare physician fee schedule. Prior to that date, only the antigen injection services, i.e., only codes 95115 and 95117, were paid for under the fee schedule. Codes representing antigens and their preparation and single codes representing both the antigens and their injection were paid for under the Medicare reasonable charge system. A legislative change brought all of these services under the fee schedule at the beginning of 1995 and the following policies are effective as of January 1, 1995:

1. CPT codes 95120 through 95134 are not valid for Medicare. Codes 95120 through 95134 represent complete services, i.e., services that include both the injection service as well as the antigen and its preparation.

2. Separate coding for injection only codes (i.e., codes 95115 and 95117) and/or the codes representing antigens and their preparation (i.e., codes 95144 through 95170) must be used.

   If both services are provided both codes are billed.

   This includes allergists who provide both services through the use of treatment boards.

3. If a physician bills both an injection code plus either codes 95165 or 95144, carriers pay the appropriate injection code (i.e., code 95115 or code 95117) plus the code 95165 rate. When a provider bills for codes 95115 or 95117 plus code 95144, carriers change 95144 to 95165 and pay accordingly. Code 95144 (single dose vials of antigen) should be billed only if the physician providing the antigen is providing it to be injected by some other entity. Single dose vials, which should be used only as a means of insuring proper dosage amounts for injections, are more costly than multiple dose vials (i.e., code 95165) and therefore their payment rate is higher. Allergists who prepare antigens are assumed to be able to administer proper doses from the less costly multiple dose vials. Thus, regardless of whether they use or bill for single or multiple dose vials at the same time that they are billing for an injection service, they are paid at the multiple dose vial rate.

4. The fee schedule amounts for the antigen codes (95144 through 95170) are for a single dose. When billing those codes, physicians are to specify the number of doses provided. When making payment, carriers multiply the fee schedule amount by the number of doses specified in the units field.

5. If a patient's doses are adjusted, e.g., because of patient reaction, and the antigen provided is actually more or fewer doses than originally anticipated, the physician is to make no change in the number of doses for which he or she bills. The number of doses anticipated at the time of the antigen preparation is the number of doses to be billed. This is consistent with the notes on page 30 of the Spring 1994 issue of the American Medical Association's CPT Assistant. Those notes indicate that the antigen codes mean that the physician is to identify the number of doses "prospectively planned to be provided." The physician is to "identify the number of doses scheduled when the vial is provided." This means that in cases where the patient actually gets more doses than originally anticipated (because dose amounts were decreased during treatment) and in cases where the patient gets fewer doses (because dose amounts were increased), no change is to be made in the billing. In the first case, carriers are not to pay more because the number of doses provided in the original vial(s) increased. In the second case, carriers are not to seek recoupment (if carriers have already made payment) because the number of doses is less than originally planned. This is the case for both venom and nonvenom antigen codes.

6. Venom Doses and Catch-Up Billing - Venom doses are prepared in separate vials and not mixed together - except in the case of the three vespid mix (white and yellow hornets and yellow jackets). A dose of code 95146 (the two-venom code) means getting some of two venoms. Similarly, a dose of code 95147 means getting some of three venoms; a dose of code 95148 means getting some of four venoms; and a dose of 95149 means getting some of five venoms. Some amount of each of the venoms must be provided. Questions arise when the administration of these venoms does not remain synchronized because of dosage adjustments due to patient reaction. For example, a physician prepares ten doses of code 95148 (the four venom code) in two vials - one containing 10 doses of three vespid mix and another containing 10 doses of wasp venom. Because of dose adjustment, the three vespid mix doses last longer, i.e., they last for 15 doses. Consequently, questions arise regarding the amount of "replacement" wasp venom antigen that should be prepared and how it should be billed. Medicare pricing amounts have savings built into the use of the higher venom codes. Therefore, if a patient is in two venom, three venom, four venom or five venom therapy, the carrier objective is to pay at the highest venom level possible. This means that,

to the greatest extent possible, code 95146 is to be billed for a patient in two venom therapy, code 95147 is to be billed for a patient in three venom therapy, code 95148 is to be billed for a patient in four venom therapy, and code 95149 is to be billed for a patient in five venom therapy. Thus, physicians are to be instructed that the venom antigen preparation, after dose adjustment, must be done in a manner that, as soon as possible, synchronizes the preparation back to the highest venom code possible. In the above example, the physician should prepare and bill for only 5 doses of "replacement" wasp venom - billing five doses of code 95145 (the one venom code). This will permit the physician to get back to preparing the four venoms at one time and therefore billing the doses of the "cheaper" four venom code. Use of a code below the venom treatment number for the particular patient should occur only for the purpose of "catching up."

7. Code 95165 Doses. - Code 95165 represents preparation of vials of non-venom antigens. As in the case of venoms, some non-venom antigens cannot be mixed together, i.e., they must be prepared in separate vials. An example of this is mold and pollen. Therefore, some patients will be injected at one time from one vial - containing in one mixture all of the appropriate antigens - while other patients will be injected at one time from more than one vial. In establishing the practice expense component for mixing a multidose vial of antigens, we observed that the most common practice was to prepare a 10 cc vial; we also observed that the most common use was to remove aliquots with a volume of 1 cc. Our PE computations were based on those facts. Therefore, a physician's removing 10 1cc aliquot doses captures the entire PE component for the service.

This does not mean that the physician must remove 1 cc aliquot doses from a multidose vial. It means that the practice expenses payable for the preparation of a 10cc vial remain the same irrespective of the size or number of aliquots removed from the vial. Therefore, a physician may not bill this vial preparation code for more than 10 doses per vial; paying more than 10 doses per multidose vial would significantly overpay the practice expense component attributable to this service. (Note that this code does not include the injection of antigen(s); injection of antigen(s) is separately billable.) When a multidose vial contains less than 10cc, physicians should bill Medicare for the number of 1 cc aliquots that may be removed from the vial. That is, a physician may bill Medicare up to a maximum of 10 doses per multidose vial, but should bill Medicare for fewer than 10 doses per vial when there is less than 10cc in the vial.

If it is medically necessary, physicians may bill Medicare for preparation of more than one multidose vial.

EXAMPLES:

(1) If a 10cc multidose vial is filled to 6cc with antigen, the physician may bill Medicare for 6 doses since six 1cc aliquots may be removed from the vial.

(2) If a 5cc multidose vial is filled completely, the physician may bill Medicare for 5 doses for this vial.

(3) If a physician removes ¬¾ cc aliquots from a 10cc multidose vial for a total of 20 doses from one vial, he/she may only bill Medicare for 10 doses. Billing for more than 10 doses would mean that Medicare is overpaying for the practice expense of making the vial.

(4) If a physician prepares two 10cc multidose vials, he/she may bill Medicare for 20 doses. However, he/she may remove aliquots of any amount from those vials. For example, the physician may remove ¬¾ aliquots from one vial, and 1cc aliquots from the other vial, but may bill no more than a total of 20 doses.

(5) If a physician prepares a 20cc multidose vial, he/she may bill Medicare for 20 doses, since the practice expense is calculated based on the physician's removing 1cc aliquots from a vial. If a physician removes 2cc aliquots from this vial, thus getting only 10 doses, he/she may nonetheless bill Medicare for 20 doses because the PE for 20 doses reflects the actual practice expense of preparing the vial.

(6) If a physician prepares a 5cc multidose vial, he may bill Medicare for 5 doses, based on the way that the practice expense component is calculated. However, if the physician removes ten ¬¾ cc aliquots from the vial, he/she may still bill only 5 doses because the practice expense of preparing the vial is the same, without regard to the number of additional doses that are removed from the vial.

C. Allergy Shots and Visit Services on the Same Day
At the outset of the physician fee schedule, the question was posed as to whether visits should be billed on the same day as an allergy injection (CPT codes 95115-95117), since these codes have status indicators of A rather than T. Visits should not be billed with allergy injection services 95115 or 95117 unless the visit represents another separately identifiable service. This language parallels CPT editorial language that accompanies the allergen immunotherapy codes, which include codes 9515 and 95117. Prior to January 1, 1995, you appeared to be enforcing this policy through three (3) different means:

- Advising physician to use modifier 25 with the visit service;
- Denying payment for the visit unless documentation has been provided; and
- Paying for both the visit and the allergy shot if both are billed for.

For services rendered on or after January 1, 1995, you are to enforce the requirement that visits not be billed and paid for on the same day as an allergy injection through the following means. Effective for services rendered on or after that date, the global surgery policies will apply to all codes in the allergen immunotherapy series, including the allergy shot codes 95115 and 95117. To accomplish this, CMS changed the global surgery indicator for allergen immunotherapy codes from XXX, which meant that the global surgery concept did not apply to those codes, to 000, which means that the global surgery concept applies, but that there are no days in the postoperative global period.

Now that the global surgery policies apply to these services, you are to rely on the use of modifier 25 as the only means through which you can make payment for visit services provided on the same day as allergen immunotherapy services. In order for a physician to receive payment for a visit service provided on the same day that the physician also provides a service in the allergen immunotherapy series (i.e., any service in the series from 95115 through 95199), the physician is to bill a modifier 25 with the visit code, indicating that the patient's condition required a significant, separately identifiable visit service above and beyond the allergen immunotherapy service provided.

D. Reasonable Supply of Antigens
See CMS Manual System, Internet Only Manual, Medicare Benefits Policy Manual, CMS Pub. 100-02 Chapter 15, section 50.4.4, regarding the coverage of antigens, including what constitutes a reasonable supply of antige

100-4, 12, 210
Outpatient Mental Health Limitation
B3-2470

Regardless of the actual expenses a beneficiary incurs for treatment of mental, psychoneurotic, and personality disorders while the beneficiary is not an inpatient of a hospital at the time such expenses are incurred, the amount of those expenses that may be recognized for Part B deductible and payment purposes is limited to 62.5 percent of the Medicare allowed amount for those services. This limitation is called the outpatient mental health treatment limitation. Expenses for diagnostic services (e.g., psychiatric testing and evaluation to diagnose the patient's illness) are not subject to this limitation.

This limitation applies only to therapeutic services and to services performed to evaluate the progress of a course of treatment for a diagnosed condition.

100-4, 13, 10
ICD-9-CM Coding for Diagnostic Tests
The ICD-9-CM Coding Guidelines for Outpatient Services (hospital-based and physician office) have instructed physicians to report diagnoses based on test results. Instructions and examples for coding specialists, contractors, physicians, hospitals, and other health care providers to use in determining the use of ICD-9-CM codes for coding diagnostic test results is found in Chapter 23.

100-4, 13, 30
Computerized Axial Tomography (CT) Procedures
Carriers do not reduce or deny payment for medically necessary multiple CT scans of different areas of the body that are performed on the same day.

The TC RVUs for CT procedures that specify "with contrast" include payment for high osmolar contrast media. When separate payment is made for low osmolar contrast media under the conditions set forth in 30.1.1, reduce payment for the contrast media as set forth in 30.1.2.

100-4, 13, 40
Magnetic Resonance Imaging (MRI) Procedures
Prior to January 1, 2007

Carriers do not make additional payments for three or more MRI sequences. The RVUs reflect payment levels for two sequences.

The TC RVUs for MRI procedures that specify "with contrast" include payment for paramagnetic contrast media. Carriers do not make separate payment under code A4647.

A diagnostic technique has been developed under which an MRI of the brain or spine is first performed without contrast material, then another MRI is performed with a standard (0.1mmol/kg) dose of contrast material and, based on the need to achieve a better image, a third MRI is performed with an additional double dosage (0.2mmol/kg) of contrast material. When the high-dose contrast technique is utilized, carriers:

- Do not pay separately for the contrast material used in the second MRI procedure;
- Pay for the contrast material given for the third MRI procedure through supply code Q9952, the replacement code for A4643, when billed with CPT codes 70553, 72156, 72157, and 72158;
- Do not pay for the third MRI procedure. For example, in the case of an MRI of the brain, if CPT code 70553 (without contrast material, followed by with contrast material(s) and further sequences) is billed, make no payment for CPT code 70551 (without contrast material(s)), the additional procedure given for the purpose of administering the double dosage, furnished during the same session. Medicare does not pay for the third procedure (as distinguished from the contrast material) because the CPT definition of code 70553 includes all further sequences; and
- Do not apply the payment criteria for low osmolar contrast media in 30.1.2 to billings for code Q9952, the replacement code for A4643.

Effective January 1, 2007

With the implementation for calendar year 2007 of a bottom-up methodology, which utilizes the direct inputs to determine the practice expense (PE) relative value units (RVUs), the cost of the contrast media is not included in the PE RVUs. Therefore, a separate payment for the contrast media used in various imaging procedures is paid. In addition to the CPT code representing the imaging procedure, separately bill the appropriate HCPCS "Q" code (Q9945 - Q9954; Q9958-Q9964) for the contrast medium utilized in performing the service.

100-4, 13, 40.1.1

Magnetic Resonance Angiography Coverage Summary

Section 1861(s)(2)(C) of the Act provides for coverage of diagnostic testing. Coverage of magnetic resonance angiography (MRA) of the head and neck, and MRA of the peripheral vessels of the lower extremities is limited as described in the Medicare National Coverage Determinations Manual. This instruction has been revised as of July 1, 2003, based on a determination that coverage is reasonable and necessary in additional circumstances. Under that instruction, MRA is generally covered only to the extent that it is used as a substitute for contrast angiography, except to the extent that there are documented circumstances consistent with that instruction that demonstrate the medical necessity of both tests. There is no coverage of MRA outside of the indications and circumstances described in that instruction.

Because the status codes for HCPCS codes 71555, 71555-TC, 71555-26, 74185, 74185- TC, and 74185-26 were changed in the MPFSDB from N to R on April 1, 1998, any MRA claims with those HCPCS codes with dates of service between April 1, 1998, and June 30, 1999, are to be processed according to the contractor's discretionary authority to determine payment in the absence of national policy.

100-4, 13, 60

Positron Emission Tomography (PET) Scans - General Information

Positron emission tomography (PET) is a noninvasive imaging procedure that assesses perfusion and the level of metabolic activity in various organ systems of the human body.

A positron camera (tomograph) is used to produce cross-sectional tomographic images which are obtained by detecting radioactivity from a radioactive tracer substance (radiopharmaceutical) that emits a radioactive tracer substance (radiopharmaceutical FDG) such as 2 -[F-18] flouro-D-glucose FDG, that is administered intravenously to the patient.

The Medicare National Coverage Determinations (NCD) Manual, Chapter 1, 220.6, contains additional coverage instructions to indicate the conditions under which a PET scan is performed.

A. Definitions

For all uses of PET, excluding Rubidium 82 for perfusion of the heart, myocardial viability and refractory seizures, the following definitions apply:

- Diagnosis: PET is covered only in clinical situations in which the PET results may assist in avoiding an invasive diagnostic procedure, or in which the PET results may assist in determining the optimal anatomical location to perform an invasive diagnostic procedure. In general, for most solid tumors, a tissue diagnosis is made prior to the performance of PET scanning. PET scans following a tissue diagnosis are generally performed for the purpose of staging, rather than diagnosis. Therefore, the use of PET in the diagnosis of lymphoma, esophageal and colorectal cancers, as well as in melanoma, should be rare. PET is not covered for other diagnostic uses, and is not covered for screening (testing of patients without specific signs and symptoms of disease).

- Staging: PET is covered in clinical situations in which (1) (a) the stage of the cancer remains in doubt after completion of a standard diagnostic workup, including conventional imaging (computed tomography, magnetic resonance imaging, or ultrasound) or, (b) the use of PET would also be considered reasonable and necessary if it could potentially replace one or more conventional imaging studies when it is expected that conventional study information is insufficient for the clinical management of the patient and, (2) clinical management of the patient would differ depending on the stage of the cancer identified.

- Restaging: PET will be covered for restaging: (1) after the completion of treatment for the purpose of detecting residual disease, (2) for detecting suspected recurrence, or metastasis, (3) to determine the extent of a known recurrence, or (4) if it could potentially replace one or more conventional imaging studies when it is expected that conventional study information is to determine the extent of a known recurrence, or if study information is insufficient for the clinical management of the patient. Restaging applies to testing after a course of treatment is completed and is covered subject to the conditions above.

- Monitoring: Use of PET to monitor tumor response to treatment during the planned course of therapy (i.e., when a change in therapy is anticipated).

B. Limitations

For staging and restaging: PET is covered in either/or both of the following circumstances:

- The stage of the cancer remains in doubt after completion of a standard diagnostic workup, including conventional imaging (computed tomography, magnetic resonance imaging, or ultrasound); and/or

- The clinical management of the patient would differ depending on the stage of the cancer identified. PET will be covered for restaging after the completion of treatment for the purpose of detecting residual disease, for detecting suspected recurrence, or to determine the extent of a known recurrence. Use of PET would also be considered reasonable and necessary if it could potentially replace one or more conventional imaging studies when it is expected that conventional study information is insufficient for the clinical management of the patient.

The PET is not covered for other diagnostic uses, and is not covered for screening (testing of patients without specific symptoms). Use of PET to monitor tumor response during the planned course of therapy (i.e. when no change in therapy is being contemplated) is not covered.

100-4, 13, 60.1

Billing Instructions

A. Billing and Payment Instructions or Responsibilities for Carriers

Claims for PET scan services must be billed on Form-CMS 1500 or the electronic equivalent with the appropriate HCPCS or CPT code and diagnosis codes to the local carrier. Effective for claims received on or after July 1, 2001, PET modifiers were discontinued and are no longer a claims processing requirement for PET scan claims.

Therefore, July 1, 2001, and after the MSN messages regarding the use of PET modifiers can be discontinued. The type of service (TOS) for the new PET scan procedure codes is TOS 4, Diagnostic Radiology. Payment is based on the Medicare Physician Fee Schedule.

B. Billing and Payment Instructions or Responsibilities for FIs

Claims for PET scan procedures must be billed to the FI on Form CMS-1450 (UB-92) or the electronic equivalent with the appropriate diagnosis and HCPCS "G" code or CPT code to indicate the conditions under which a PET scan was done. These codes represent the technical component costs associated with these procedures when furnished to hospital and SNF outpatients. They are paid as follows:

- under OPPS for hospitals subject to OPPS
- under current payment methodologies for hospitals not subject to OPPS
- on a reasonable cost basis for critical access hospitals.
- on a reasonable cost basis for skilled nursing facilities.

Institutional providers bill these codes under Revenue Code 0404 (PET Scan).

Medicare contractors shall pay claims submitted for services provided by a critical access hospital (CAH) as follows: Method I technical services are paid at 101% of reasonable cost; Method II technical services are paid at 101% of reasonable cost, and professional services are paid at 115% of the Medicare Physician Fee Schedule Data Base.

C. Frequency

In the absence of national frequency limitations, for all indications covered on and after July 1, 2001, contractors can, if necessary, develop frequency limitations on any or all covered PET scan services.

D. Post-Payment Review for PET Scans

As with any claim, but particularly in view of the limitations on this coverage, Medicare may decide to conduct post-payment reviews to determine that the use of PET scans is consistent with coverage instructions. Pet scanning facilities must keep patient record information on file for each Medicare patient for whom a PET scan claim is made. These medical records can be used in any post-payment reviews and must include the information necessary to substantiate the need for the PET scan. These records must include standard information (e.g., age, sex, and height) along with sufficient patient histories to allow determination that the steps required in the coverage instructions were followed. Such information must include, but is not limited to, the date, place and results of previous diagnostic tests (e.g., cytopathology and surgical pathology reports, CT), as well as the results and reports of the PET scan(s) performed at the center. If available, such records should include the prognosis derived from the PET scan, together with information regarding the physician or institution to which the patient proceeded following the scan for treatment or evaluation. The ordering physician is responsible for forwarding appropriate clinical data to the PET scan facility.

Effective for claims received on or after July 1, 2001, CMS no longer requires paper documentation to be submitted up front with PET scan claims. Contractors shall be aware and advise providers of the specific documentation requirements for PET scans for dementia and neurodegenerative diseases. This information is outlined in section 60.12.

Documentation requirements such as physician referral and medical necessity determination are to be maintained by the provider as part of the beneficiary's medical record. This information must be made available to the carrier or FI upon request of additional documentation to determine appropriate payment of an individual claim.

100-4, 13, 60.2

Use of Gamma Cameras and Full Ring and Partial Ring PET Scanners for PET Scans

See the Medicare NCD Manual, Section 220.6, concerning 2-[F-18] Fluoro-D-Glucose (FDG) PET scanners and details about coverage.

On July 1, 2001, HCPCS codes G0210 - G0230 were added to allow billing for all currently covered indications for FDG PET. Although the codes do not indicate the type of PET scanner, these codes were used until January 1, 2002, by providers to bill for services in a manner consistent with the coverage policy.

Effective January 1, 2002, HCPCS codes G0210 - G0230 were updated with new descriptors to properly reflect the type of PET scanner used. In addition, four new HCPCS codes became effective for dates of service on and after January 1, 2002, (G0231, G0232, G0233, G0234) for covered conditions that may be billed if a gamma camera is used for the PET scan. For services performed from January 1, 2002, through January 27, 2005, providers should bill using the revised HCPCS codes G0210 - G0234.

Beginning January 28, 2005 providers should bill using the appropriate CPT code.

100-4, 13, 60.3

PET Scan Qualifying Conditions and HCPCS Code Chart

Below is a summary of all covered PET scan conditions, with effective dates.

NOTE: The G codes below except those a # can be used to bill for PET Scan services through January 27, 2005. Effective for dates of service on or after January 28, 2005, providers must bill for PET scan services using the appropriate CPT codes. See section 60.3.1. The G codes with a # can continue to be used for billing after January 28, 2005 and these remain non-covered by Medicare. (NOTE: PET Scanners must be FDA-approved.)

Conditions	Coverage Effective Date	****HCPCS/ CPT
*Myocardial perfusion imaging (following previous PET G0030-G0047) single study, rest or stress (exercise and/or pharmacologic)	3/14/95	G0030
*Myocardial perfusion imaging (following previous PET G0030-G0047) multiple studies, rest or stress (exercise and/or pharmacologic)	3/14/95	G0031
*Myocardial perfusion imaging (following rest SPECT, 78464); single study, rest or stress (exercise and/or pharmacologic)	'3/14/95	G0032
*Myocardial perfusion imaging (following rest SPECT 78464); multiple studies, rest or stress (exercise and/or pharmacologic)	3/14/95	G0033
*Myocardial perfusion (following stress SPECT 78465); single study, rest or stress (exercise and/or pharmacologic)	3/14/95	G0034
*Myocardial Perfusion Imaging (following stress SPECT 78465); multiple studies, rest or stress (exercise and/or pharmacologic)	3/14/95	G0035
*Myocardial Perfusion Imaging (following coronary angiography 93510-93529); single study, rest or stress (exercise and/or pharmacologic)	3/14/95	G0036
*Myocardial Perfusion Imaging, (following coronary angiography), 93510-93529); multiple studies, rest or stress (exercise and/or pharmacologic)	3/14/95	G0037
*Myocardial Perfusion Imaging (following stress planar myocardial perfusion, 78460); single study, rest or stress (exercise and/or pharmacologic)	3/14/95	G0038
*Myocardial Perfusion Imaging (following stress planar myocardial perfusion, 78460); multiple studies, rest or stress (exercise and/or pharmacologic)	3/14/95	G0039
*Myocardial Perfusion Imaging (following stress echocardiogram 93350); single study, rest or stress (exercise and/or pharmacologic)	3/14/95	G0040
*Myocardial Perfusion Imaging (following stress echocardiogram, 93350); multiple studies, rest or stress (exercise and/or pharmacologic)	3/14/95	G0041
*Myocardial Perfusion Imaging (following stress nuclear ventriculogram 78481 or 78483); single study, rest or stress (exercise and/or pharmacologic)	3/14/95	G0042
*Myocardial Perfusion Imaging (following stress nuclear ventriculogram 78481 or 78483); multiple studies, rest or stress (exercise and/or pharmacologic)	3/14/95	G0043
*Myocardial Perfusion Imaging (following stress ECG, 93000); single study, rest or stress (exercise and/or pharmacologic)	3/14/95	G0044
*Myocardial perfusion (following stress ECG, 93000), multiple studies; rest or stress (exercise and/or pharmacologic)	3/14/95	G0045
*Myocardial perfusion (following stress ECG, 93015), single study; rest or stress (exercise and/or pharmacologic)	3/14/95	G0046
*Myocardial perfusion (following stress ECG, 93015); multiple studies, rest or stress (exercise and/or pharmacologic)	3/14/95	G0047
PET imaging regional or whole body; single pulmonary nodule	1/1/98	G0125
Lung cancer, non-small cell (PET imaging whole body) Diagnosis, Initial Staging, Restaging	7/1/01	G0210 G0211 G0212
Colorectal cancer (PET imaging whole body) Diagnosis, Initial Staging, Restaging	7/1/01	G0213 G0214 G0215
Melanoma (PET imaging whole body) Diagnosis, Initial Staging, Restaging	7/1/01	G0216 G0217 G0218
Melanoma for non-covered indications	7/1/01	G0219
Lymphoma (PET imaging whole body) Diagnosis, Initial Staging, Restaging	7/1/01	G0220 G0221 G0222
Head and neck cancer; excluding thyroid and CNS cancers (PET imaging whole body or regional) Diagnosis, Initial Staging, Restaging	7/1/01	G0223 G0224 G0225

* Carriers must report A4641 for the tracer Rubidium 82 when used with PET scan codes G0030 through G0047 for services performed on or before January 27, 2005

** Not FDG PET

*** For dates of service October 1, 2003, through December 31, 2003, use temporary code Q4078 for billing this radiopharmaceutical.

Conditions	Coverage Effective Date	****HCPCS/ CPT
Esophageal cancer (PET imaging whole body) Diagnosis, Initial Staging, Restaging	7/1/01	G0226 G0227 G0228
Metabolic brain imaging for pre-surgical evaluation of refractory seizures	7/1/01	G0229
Metabolic assessment for myocardial viability following inconclusive SPECT study	7/1/01	G0230
Recurrence of colorectal or colorectal metastatic cancer (PET whole body, gamma cameras only)	1/1/02	G0231
Staging and characterization of lymphoma (PET whole body, gamma cameras only)	1/1/02	G0232
Recurrence of melanoma or melanoma metastatic cancer (PET whole body, gamma cameras only)	1/1/02	G0233
Regional or whole body, for solitary pulmonary nodule following CT, or for initial staging of nonsmall cell lung cancer (gamma cameras only)	1/1/02	G0234
Non-Covered Service PET imaging, any site not otherwise specified	1/28/05	G0235
Non-Covered Service Initial diagnosis of breast cancer and/or surgical planning for breast cancer (e.g., initial staging of axillary lymph nodes), not covered (full- and partialring PET scanners only)	10/1/02	G0252
Breast cancer, staging/restaging of local regional recurrence or distant metastases, i.e., staging/restaging after or prior to course of treatment (full- and partial-ring PET scanners only)	10/1/02	G0253
Breast cancer, evaluation of responses to treatment, performed during course of treatment (full- and partial-ring PET scanners only)	10/1/02	G0254
Myocardial imaging, positron emission tomography (PET), metabolic evaluation)	10/1/02	78459
Restaging or previously treated thyroid cancer of follicular cell origin following negative I-131 whole body scan (full- and partial-ring PET scanner only)	10/1/03	G0296
Tracer Rubidium**82 (Supply of Radiopharmaceutical Diagnostic Imaging Agent) (This is only billed through Outpatient Perspective Payment System, OPPS.) (Carriers must use HCPCS Code A4641).	10/1/03	Q3000
Supply of Radiopharmaceutical Diagnostic Imaging Agent, Ammonia N-13	01/1/04	A9526
PET imaging, brain imaging for the differential diagnosis of Alzheimer's disease with aberrant features vs. fronto-temporal dementia	09/15/04	Appropriate CPT Code from section 60.3.1
PET Cervical Cancer Staging as adjunct to conventional imaging, other staging, diagnosis, restaging, monitoring	1/28/05	Appropriate CPT Code from section 60.3.1

* Carriers must report A4641 for the tracer Rubidium 82 when used with PET scan codes G0030 through G0047 for services performed on or before January 27, 2005

** Not FDG PET

*** For dates of service October 1, 2003, through December 31, 2003, use temporary code Q4078 for billing this radiopharmaceutical.

100-4, 13, 60.3.1

Appropriate CPT Codes Effective for PET Scans for Services Performed on or After January 28, 2005

NOTE: All PET scan services require the use of a radiopharmaceutical diagnostic imaging agent (tracer). The applicable tracer code should be billed when billing for a PET scan service. See section 60.3.2 below for applicable tracer codes.

CPT Code	Description
78459	Myocardial imaging, positron emission tomography (PET), metabolic evaluation
78491	Myocardial imaging, positron emission tomography (PET), perfusion, single study at rest or stress
78492	Myocardial imaging, positron emission tomography (PET), perfusion, multiple studies at rest and/or stress
78608	Brain imaging, positron emission tomography (PET); metabolic evaluation
78811	Tumor imaging, positron emission tomography (PET); limited area (eg, chest, head/neck)
78812	Tumor imaging, positron emission tomography (PET); skull base to mid-thigh
78813	Tumor imaging, positron emission tomography (PET); whole body

© 2008 Ingenix

CPT Code	Description
78814	Tumor imaging, positron emission tomography (PET) with concurrently acquired computed tomography (CT) for attenuation correction and anatomical localization; limited area (eg, chest, head/neck)
78815	Tumor imaging, positron emission tomography (PET) with concurrently acquired computed tomography (CT) for attenuation correction and anatomical localization; skull base to mid-thigh
78816	Tumor imaging, positron emission tomography (PET) with concurrently acquired computed tomography (CT) for attenuation correction and anatomical localization; whole body

100-4, 13, 60.3.2

Tracer Codes Required for PET Scans

The following tracer codes are applicable only to CPT 78491 and 78492. They can not be reported with any other code.

Institutional providers billing the fiscal intermediary.

HCPCS	Description
*A9555	Rubidium Rb-82, Diagnostic, Per study dose, Up To 60 Millicuries
* Q3000 (Deleted effective 12/31/05)	Supply of Radiopharmaceutical Diagnostic Imaging Agent, Rubidium Rb-82, per dose
A9526	Nitrogen N-13 Ammonia, Diagnostic, Per study dose, Up To 40 Millicuries

NOTE: For claims with dates of service prior to 1/01/06, providers report Q3000 for supply of radiopharmaceutical diagnostic imaging agent, Rubidium Rb-82. For claims with dates of service 1/01/06 and later, providers report A9555 for radiopharmaceutical diagnostic imaging agent, Rubidium Rb-82 in place of Q3000.

Physicians / practitioners billing the carrier:

*A4641	Supply of Radiopharmaceutical Diagnostic Imaging Agent, Not Otherwise Classified
A9526	Nitrogen N-13 Ammonia, Diagnostic, Per study dose, Up To 40 Millicuries
A9555	Rubidium Rb-82, Diagnostic, Per study dose, Up To 60 Millicuries

*   NOTE: Effective January 1, 2008, tracer code A4641 is not applicable for PET Scans. The following tracer codes are applicable only to CPT 78459, 78608, 78811-78816. They can not be reported with any other code:

Institutional providers billing the fiscal intermediary:

* A9552	Fluorodeoxyglucose F18, FDG, Diagnostic, Per study dose, Up To 45 Millicuries
" C1775 (Deleted effective 12/31/05)	Supply of Radiopharmaceutical Diagnostic Imaging Agent Fluorodeoxyglucose F18, (2-Deoxy-2-18F Fluoro-D-Glucose), Per dose (4-40 Mci/Ml)
**A4641	Supply of Radiopharmaceutical Diagnostic Imaging Agent, Not Otherwise Classified

*   NOTE: For claims with dates of service prior to 1/01/06, OPPS hospitals report C1775 for supply of radiopharmaceutical diagnostic imaging agent, Fluorodeoxyglucose F18. For claims with dates of service 1/01/06 and later, providers report A9552 for radiopharmaceutical diagnostic imaging agent, Fluorodeoxyglucose F18 in place of C1775.

** NOTE: Effective January 1, 2008, tracer code A4641 is not applicable for PET Scans.

Physicians / practitioners billing the carrier:

| A9552 | Fluorodeoxyglucose F18, FDG, Diagnostic, Per study dose, Up To 45 Millicuries |
| *A4641 | Supply of Radiopharmaceutical Diagnostic Imaging Agent, Not Otherwise Classified |

*   NOTE: Effective January 1, 2008, tracer code A4641 is not applicable for PET Scans.

100-4, 13, 60.4

PET Scans for Imaging of the Perfusion of the Heart Using Rubidium 82 (Rb 82)(Rev. 223, Issued: 07-02-04) (Effective/Implementation: Not Applicable)

For dates of service on or after March 14, 1995, Medicare covers one PET scan for imaging of the perfusion of the heart using Rubidium 82 (Rb 82), provided that the following conditions are met:

- The PET is done at a PET imaging center with a PET scanner that has been approved by the FDA;
- The PET scan is a rest alone or rest with pharmacologic stress PET scan, used for noninvasive imaging of the perfusion of the heart for the diagnosis and management of patients with known or suspected coronary artery disease, using Rb 82; and
- Either the PET scan is used in place of, but not in addition to, a single photon emission computed tomography (SPECT) or the PET scan is used following a SPECT that was found inconclusive.

100-4, 13, 60.9

Coverage of PET Scans for Myocardial Viability

FDG PET is covered for the determination of myocardial viability following an inconclusive single photon computed tomography test (SPECT) from July 1, 2001, through September 30, 2002. Only full ring scanners are covered as the scanning medium for this service from July 1, 2001, through December 31, 2001. However, as of January 1, 2002, full and partial ring scanners are covered for myocardial viability following an inconclusive SPECT.

Beginning October 1, 2002, Medicare will cover FDG PET for the determination of myocardial viability as a primary or initial diagnostic study prior to revascularization, and will continue to cover FDG PET when used as a follow-up to an inconclusive SPECT.

However, if a patient received a FDG PET study with inconclusive results, a follow-up SPECT is not covered. FDA full and partial ring PET scanners are covered. In the event that a patient receives a SPECT with inconclusive results, a PET scan may be performed and covered by Medicare. However, a SPECT is not covered following a FDG PET with inconclusive results. See the Medicare National Coverage Determinations Manual, Section 220.6 for specific frequency limitations for Myocardial Viability following an inconclusive SPECT.

Documentation that these conditions are met should be maintained by the referring provider as part of the beneficiary's medical record.

HCPCS Code for PET Scan for Myocardial Viability

78459   Myocardial imaging, positron emission tomography (PET), metabolic evaluation

100-4, 13, 60.11

Coverage of PET Scans for Perfusion of the Heart Using Ammonia N-13

Effective for service performed on or after October 1, 2003, PET scans performed at rest or with pharmacological stress used for noninvasive imaging of the perfusion of the heart for the diagnosis and management of patients with known or suspected coronary artery disease using the FDA-approved radiopharmaceutical ammonia N-13 are covered, provided the following requirements are met.

100-4, 13, 60.12

Coverage for PET Scans for Dementia and Neurodegenerative Diseases

Effective for dates of service on or after September 15, 2004, Medicare will cover FDG PET scans for a differential diagnosis of fronto-temporal dementia (FTD) and Alzheimer's disease OR; its use in a CMS-approved practical clinical trial focused on the utility of FDG-PET in the diagnosis or treatment of dementing neurodegenerative diseases. Refer to Pub. 100-03, NCD Manual, section 220.6.13, for complete coverage conditions and clinical trial requirements and section 60.15 of this manual for claims processing information.

A. Carrier and FI Billing Requirements for PET Scan Claims for FDG-PET for the Differential Diagnosis of Fronto-temporal Dementia and Alzheimer's Disease:

- CPT Code for PET Scans for Dementia and Neurodegenerative Diseases

  Contractors shall advise providers to use the appropriate CPT code from section 60.3.1 for dementia and neurodegenerative diseases for services performed on or after January 28, 2005.

- Diagnosis Codes for PET Scans for Dementia and Neurodegenerative Diseases

  The contractor shall ensure one of the following appropriate diagnosis codes is present on claims for PET Scans for AD:

  - 290.0, 290.10 - 290.13, 290.20   290, 21, 290.3, 331.0, 331.11, 331.19, 331.2, 331.9, 780.93

  Medicare contractors shall use an appropriate Medicare Summary Notice (MSN) message such as 16.48, "Medicare does not pay for this item or service for this condition" to deny claims when submitted with an appropriate CPT code from section 60.3.1 and with a diagnosis code other than the range of codes listed above. Also, contractors shall use an appropriate Remittance Advice (RA) such as 11, "The diagnosis is inconsistent with the procedure."

  Medicare contractors shall instruct providers to issue an Advanced Beneficiary Notice to beneficiaries advising them of potential financial liability prior to delivering the service if one of the appropriate diagnosis codes will not be present on the claim.

- Provider Documentation Required with the PET Scan Claim

  Medicare contractors shall inform providers to ensure the conditions mentioned in the NCD Manual, section 220.6.13, have been met. The information must also be maintained in the beneficiary's medical record:

  - Date of onset of symptoms;
  - Diagnosis of clinical syndrome (normal aging, mild cognitive impairment or MCI: mild, moderate, or severe dementia);
  - Mini mental status exam (MMSE) or similar test score;
  - Presumptive cause (possible, probably, uncertain AD);
  - Any neuropsychological testing performed;
  - Results of any structural imaging (MRI, CT) performed;
  - Relevant laboratory tests (B12, thyroid hormone); and,
  - Number and name of prescribed medications.

100-4, 13, 70.1

Weekly Radiation Therapy Management (CPT 77419 - 77430)

Carriers must pay for a physician's weekly treatment management services under code 77427. Billing entities must indicate on each claim the number of fractions for which payment is sought.

A weekly unit of treatment management is equal to five fractions or treatment sessions.

A week for the purpose of making payments under these codes is comprised of five fractions regardless of the actual time period in which the services are furnished. It is not necessary that the radiation therapist personally examine the patient during each fraction for the weekly treatment management code to be payable. Multiple fractions representing two or more treatment sessions furnished on the same day may be counted as long as there has been a distinct break in therapy sessions, and the fractions are of the character usually furnished on different days. If, at the final billing of the treatment course, there are three or four fractions beyond a multiple of five, those three or four fractions are paid for as a week. If there are one or two fractions beyond a multiple of five, payment for these services is considered as having been made through prior payments.

EXAMPLE:

18 fractions = 4 weekly services

62 fractions = 12 weekly services

8 fractions = 2 weekly services

6 fractions = 1 weekly service

If billings have occurred which indicate that the treatment course has ended (and, therefore, the number of residual fractions has been determined), but treatments resume, adjust carrier payments for the additional services consistent with the above policy.

EXAMPLE:

8 fractions = payment for 2 weeks

2 additional fractions are furnished by the same physician. No additional Medicare payment is made for the 2 additional fractions.

A. SNF Treatment Management Delivery Services
A SNF may not bill weekly treatment management services for its outpatients (codes 77419, 77420, 77425, 77430, and 77431). Instead, the SNF should bill for radiation treatment delivery (codes 77401 - 77404, 77406 - 77409, 77411 - 77414, and 77416).

Also, SNFs bill for therapeutic radiology port film (code 77417), which was previously a part of the weekly services. They enter the number of services in the units field.

100-4, 13, 70.3
Radiation Treatment Delivery (CPT 77401 - 77417)
Carriers pay for these TC services on a daily basis under CPT codes 77401-77416 for radiation treatment delivery. They do not use local codes and RVUs in paying for the TC of radiation oncology services. Multiple treatment sessions on the same day are payable as long as there has been a distinct break in therapy services, and the individual sessions are of the character usually furnished on different days. Carriers pay for CPT code 77417 (Therapeutic radiology port film(s)) on a weekly (five fractions) basis.

100-4, 13, 70.4
Clinical Brachytherapy (CPT Codes 77750 - 77799)
Carriers must apply the bundled services policy to procedures in this family of codes other than CPT code 77776. For procedures furnished in settings in which TC payments are made, carriers must pay separately for the expendable source associated with these procedures under CPT code 79900 except in the case of remote after-loading high intensity brachytherapy procedures (CPT codes 77781-77784). In the four codes cited, the expendable source is included in the RVUs for the TC of the procedures.

100-4, 13, 70.5
Radiation Physics Services (CPT Codes 77300 - 77399)
Carriers pay for the PC and TC of CPT codes 77300-77334 and 77399 on the same basis as they pay for radiologic services generally. For professional component billings in all settings, carriers presume that the radiologist participated in the provision of the service, e.g., reviewed/validated the physicist's calculation. CPT codes 77336 and 77370 are technical services only codes that are payable by carriers in settings in which only technical component is are payable.

100-4, 13, 80.1
Physician Presence
Radiologic supervision and interpretation (S&I) codes are used to describe the personal supervision of the performance of the radiologic portion of a procedure by one or more physicians and the interpretation of the findings. In order to bill for the supervision aspect of the procedure, the physician must be present during its performance. This kind of personal supervision of the performance of the procedure is a service to an individual beneficiary and differs from the type of general supervision of the radiologic procedures performed in a hospital for which FIs pay the costs as physician services to the hospital. The interpretation of the procedure may be performed later by another physician. In situations in which a cardiologist, for example, bills for the supervision (the "S") of the S&I code, and a radiologist bills for the interpretation (the "I") of the code, both physicians should use a "-52" modifier indicating a reduced service, e.g., only one of supervision and/or interpretation. Payment for the fragmented S&I code is no more than if a single physician furnished both aspects of the procedure.

100-4, 13, 80.2
Multiple Procedure Reduction
Carriers make no multiple procedure reductions in the S&I or primary non-radiologic codes in these types of procedures, or in any procedure codes for which the descriptor and RVUs reflect a multiple service reduction. For additional procedure codes that do not reflect such a reduction, carriers apply the multiple procedure reductions.

100-4, 13, 100
Interpretation of Diagnostic Tests
B3-15023

100-4, 13, 140
Bone Mass Measurements (BMMs)
Sections H1861(s)(15)H and H(rr)(1)H of the Social Security Act (the Act) (as added by 4106 of the Balanced Budget Act (BBA) of 1997) standardize Medicare coverage of medically necessary bone mass measurements by providing for uniform coverage under Medicare Part B. This coverage is effective for claims with dates of service furnished on or after July 1, 1998.

Effective for dates of service on and after January 1, 2007, the CY 2007 Physician Fee Schedule final rule expanded the number of beneficiaries qualifying for BMM by reducing the dosage requirement for glucocorticoid (steroid) therapy from 7.5 mg of prednisone per day to 5.0 mg. It also changed the definition of BMM by removing coverage for a single-photon absorptiometry as it is not considered reasonable and necessary under section 1862 (a)(1)(A) of the Act. Finally, it required that in the case of monitoring and confirmatory baseline BMMs, they be performed with a dual-energy xray absorptiometry (axial) test.

Conditions of Coverage for BMMs are located in Pub.100-02, Medicare Benefit Policy Manual, chapter 15.

100-4, 13, 140.1
Payment Methodology and HCPCS Coding
Carriers pay for BMM procedures based on the Medicare physician fee schedule. Claims from physicians, other practitioners, or suppliers where assignment was not taken are subject to the Medicare limiting charge.

The FIs pay for BMM procedures under the current payment methodologies for radiology services according to the type of provider.

Do not pay BMM procedure claims for dual photon absorptiometry, CPT procedure code 78351.

Deductible and coinsurance apply.

Any of the following CPT procedure codes may be used when billing for BMMs through December 31, 2006. All of these codes are bone densitometry measurements except code 76977, which is bone sonometry measurements. CPT procedure codes are applicable to billing FIs and carriers.

76070 76071 76075 76076 76078 76977 78350 G0130

Effective for dates of services on and after January 1, 2007, the following changes apply to BMM:

- New 2007 CPT bone mass procedure codes have been assigned for BMM. The following codes will replace current codes, however the CPT descriptors for the services remain the same:

  77078 replaces 76070

  77079 replaces 76071

  77080 replaces 76075

  77081 replaces 76076

  77083 replaces 76078

- Certain BMM tests are covered when used to screen patients for osteoporosis subject to the frequency standards described in chapter 15, section 80.5.5 of the Medicare Benefit Policy Manual.
  - Contractors will pay claims for screening tests when coded as follows:
    - Contains CPT procedure code 77078, 77079, 77080, 77081, 77083, 76977 or G0130, and
    - Contains a valid ICD-9-CM diagnosis code indicating the reason for the test is postmenopausal female, vertebral fracture, hyperparathyroidism, or steroid therapy. Contractors are to maintain local lists of valid codes for the benefit's screening categories.
  - Contractors will deny claims for screening tests when coded as follows:
    - Contains CPT procedure code 77078, 77079, 77081, 77083, 76977 or G0130, but
    - Does not contain a valid ICD-9-CM diagnosis code from the local lists of valid ICD-9-CM diagnosis codes maintained by the contractor for the benefit's screening categories indicating the reason for the test is postmenopausal female, vertebral fracture, hyperparathyroidism, or steroid therapy.
- Dual-energy x-ray absorptiometry (axial) tests are covered when used to monitor FDA-approved osteoporosis drug therapy subject to the 2-year frequency standards described in chapter 15, section 80.5.5 of the Medicare Benefit Policy Manual.
  - Contractors will pay claims for monitoring tests when coded as follows:
    - Contains CPT procedure code 77080, and
    - Contains 733.00, 733.01, 733.02, 733.03, 733.09, 733.90, or 255.0 as the ICD-9-CM diagnosis code.
  - Contractors will deny claims for monitoring tests when coded as follows:
    - Contains CPT procedure code 77078, 77079, 77081, 77083, 76977 or G0130, and
    - Contains 733.00, 733.01, 733.02, 733.03, 733.09, 733.90, or 255.0 as the ICD-9-CM diagnosis code, but

- Does not contain a valid ICD-9-CM diagnosis code from the local lists of valid ICD-9-CM diagnosis codes maintained by the contractor for the benefit's screening categories indicating the reason for the test is postmenopausal female, vertebral fracture, hyperparathyroidism, or steroid therapy.

- Single photon absorptiometry tests are not covered. Contractors will deny CPT procedure code 78350.

The FIs are billed using the ANSI X12N 837 I or hardcopy Form CMS-1450. The appropriate bill types are: 12X, 13X, 22X, 23X, 34X, 71X (Provider-based and independent), 72X, 73X (Provider-based and freestanding), 83X, and 85X. Effective April 1, 2006, type of bill 14X is for non-patient laboratory specimens and is no longer applicable for bone mass measurements. Information regarding the claim form locators that correspond to the HCPCS/CPT code or Type of Bill and a table to crosswalk its CMS-1450 form locators to the 837 transaction are found in Chapter 25.

Providers must report HCPCS codes for bone mass measurements under revenue code 320 with number of units and line item dates of service per revenue code line for each bone mass measurement reported.

Carriers are billed for bone mass measurement procedures using the ANSI X12N 837 P or hardcopy Form CMS-1500.

100-4, 14, 10
General
Payment is made under Part B for certain surgical procedures that are furnished in ASCs and are approved for being furnished in an ASC. These procedures are those that generally do not exceed 90 minutes in length and do not require more than four hours recovery or convalescent time.

To be paid under this provision, a facility must be certified as meeting the requirements for an ASC and must enter into a written agreement with the Centers for Medicare & Medicaid Services (CMS). The certification process is described in the State Operations Manual.

Medicare will not pay an ASC for those procedures that require more than an ASC level of care, or for minor procedures that are normally performed in a physician's office.

The CMS publishes updates to the list of procedures for which an ASC may be paid each year. The complete list of procedures is available through the Public Use files (PUF) at http://www.cms.hhs.gov/researchers/. This includes applicable codes, payment groups, and payment amounts for each ASC group before adjustments for regional wage variations. Applicable wage indices are also published via program memorandum.

ASCs must accept Medicare's payment for such procedures as payment in full for the facility service with respect to those services defined as ASC facility services. The physician and anesthesiologist may bill and be paid for the professional component of the service also.

Certain other services may be performed in an ASC facility, billed by the appropriate certified provider/supplier, or in certain cases by the ASC facility itself, and paid outside of the facility rate.

100-4, 16, 10
Background
B3-2070, B3-2070.1, B3-4110.3, B3-5114

Diagnostic X-ray, laboratory, and other diagnostic tests, including materials and the services of technicians, are covered under the Medicare program. Some clinical laboratory procedures or tests require Food and Drug Administration (FDA) approval before coverage is provided.

A diagnostic laboratory test is considered a laboratory service for billing purposes, regardless of whether it is performed in:

A physician's office, by an independent laboratory;

By a hospital laboratory for its outpatients or nonpatients;

In a rural health clinic; or

In an HMO or Health Care Prepayment Plan (HCPP) for a patient who is not a member.

When a hospital laboratory performs laboratory tests for nonhospital patients, the laboratory is functioning as an independent laboratory, and still bills the fiscal intermediary (FI). Also, when physicians and laboratories perform the same test, whether manually or with automated equipment, the services are deemed similar. Laboratory services furnished by an independent laboratory are covered under SMI if the laboratory is an approved Independent Clinical Laboratory. However, as is the case of all diagnostic services, in order to be covered these services must be related to a patient's illness or injury (or symptom or complaint) and ordered by a physician. A small number of laboratory tests can be covered as a preventive screening service.

See the Medicare Benefit Policy Manual, Chapter 15, for detailed coverage requirements.

See the Medicare Program Integrity Manual, Chapter 10, for laboratory/supplier enrollment guidelines.

See the Medicare State Operations Manual for laboratory/supplier certification requirements.

100-4, 17, 20.5.7
Injection Services
Where the sole purpose of an office visit was for the patient to receive an injection, payment may be made only for the injection service (if it is covered). Conversely, injection services (codes 90782, 90783, 90784, 90788, and 90799) included in the Medicare Physician Fee Schedule (MPFS) are not paid for separately, if the physician is paid for any other physician fee schedule service furnished at the same time. Pay separately for those injection services only if no other

physician fee schedule service is being paid. However, pay separately for cancer chemotherapy injections (CPT codes 96400-96549) in addition to the visit furnished on the same day. In either case, the drug is separately payable. All injection claims must include the specific name of the drug and dosage. Identification of the drug enables you to pay for the services.

100-4, 18, 10.2.1
Healthcare Common Procedure Coding System (HCPCS) Codes
Vaccines and their administration are reported using separate codes. The following codes are for reporting the vaccines only.

HCPCS	Definition
90655	Influenza virus vaccine, split virus, preservative free, for children 6-35 months of age, for intramuscular use;
90656	Influenza virus vaccine, split virus, preservative free, for use in individuals 3 years and above, for intramuscular use;
90657	Influenza virus vaccine, split virus, for children 6-35 months of age, for intramuscular use;
90658	Influenza virus vaccine, split virus, for use in individuals 3 years of age and above, for intramuscular use;
90659	Influenza virus vaccine, whole virus, for intramuscular or jet injection use (Discontinued December 31, 2003);
90660	Influenza virus vaccine, live, for intranasal use;
90669	Pneumococcal conjugate vaccine, polyvalent, for children under 5 years, for intramuscular use
90732	Pneumococcal polysaccharide vaccine, 23-valent, adult or immunosuppressed patient dosage, for use in individuals 2 years or older, for subcutaneous or intramuscular use;
90740	Hepatitis B vaccine, dialysis or immunosuppressed patient dosage (3 dose schedule), for intramuscular use;
90743	Hepatitis B vaccine, adolescent (2 dose schedule), for intramuscular use;
90744	Hepatitis B vaccine, pediatric/adolescent dosage (3 dose schedule), for intramuscular use;
90746	Hepatitis B vaccine, adult dosage, for intramuscular use; and
90747	Hepatitis B vaccine, dialysis or immunosuppressed patient dosage (4 dose schedule), for intramuscular use.

The following codes are for reporting administration of the vaccines only. The administration of the vaccines is billed using:

HCPCS	Definition
G0008	Administration of influenza virus vaccine;
G0009	Administration of pneumococcal vaccine; and
*G0010	Administration of hepatitis B vaccine.
*90471	Immunization administration. (For OPPS hospitals billing for the hepatitis B vaccine administration)
*90472	Each additional vaccine. (For OPPS hospitals billing for the hepatitis B vaccine administration)

* NOTE: For claims with dates of service prior to January 1, 2006, OPPS and non-OPPS hospitals report G0010 for Hepatitis B vaccine administration. For claims with dates of service January 1, 2006 and later, OPPS hospitals report 90471 or 90472 for hepatitis B vaccine administration as appropriate in place of G0010.

One of the following diagnosis codes must be reported as appropriate. If the sole purpose for the visit is to receive a vaccine or if a vaccine is the only service billed on a claim the applicable following diagnosis code may be used.

Diagnosis Code	Description
V03.82	Pneumococcus
V04.81**	Influenza
V06.6***	Pneumococcus and Influenza
V05.3	Hepatitis B

** Effective for influenza virus claims with dates of service October 1, 2003 and later.

*** Effective October 1, 2006, providers may report diagnosis code V06.6 on claims for pneumococcus and/or influenza virus vaccines when the purpose of the visit was to receive both vaccines.

If a diagnosis code for pneumococcus, hepatitis B, or influenza virus vaccination is not reported on a claim, contractors may not enter the diagnosis on the claim. Contractors must follow current resolution processes for claims with missing diagnosis codes.

If the diagnosis code and the narrative description are correct, but the HCPCS code is incorrect, the carrier or intermediary may correct the HCPCS code and pay the claim. For example, if the reported diagnosis code is V04.81 and the narrative description (if annotated on the claim) says "flu shot" but the HCPCS code is incorrect, contractors may change the HCPCS code and pay for the flu vaccine. Effective October 1, 2006, carriers/AB MACs should follow the instructions in Pub. 100-04, Chapter 1, Section 80.3.2.1.1 (Carrier Data Element Requirements) for claims submitted without a HCPCS code.

Claims for Hepatitis B vaccinations must report the I.D. Number of referring physician. In addition, if a doctor of medicine or osteopathy does not order the influenza virus vaccine, the intermediary claims require:

- UPIN code SLF000 to be reported on claims submitted prior to the date when Medicare will no longer accept identifiers other than NPIs, or

- The provider's own NPI to be reported in the NPI field for the attending physician on claims submitted when NPI requirements are implemented.

100-4, 18, 10.2.2.1

FI /AB MAC Payment for Pneumococcal Pneumonia Virus, and Hepatitis B Virus Vaccines and Their Administration

Payment for Vaccines

Payment for all of these vaccines is on a reasonable cost basis for hospitals, home health agencies (HHAs), skilled nursing facilities (SNFs), critical access hospitals (CAHs), and hospital-based renal dialysis facilities (RDFs). Payment for comprehensive outpatient rehabilitation facilities (CORFs), Indian Health Service hospitals (IHS), IHS CAHs and independent RDFs is based on 95 percent of the average wholesale price (AWP). Section 10.2.4 of this chapter contains information on payment of these vaccines when provided by RDFs or hospices. See Sec.10.2.2.2 for payment to independent and provider- based Rural Health Centers and Federally Qualified Health Clinics.

Payment for these vaccines is as follows:

Facility	Type of Bill	Payment
Hospitals, other than Indian Health Service (IHS) Hospitals and Critical Access Hospitals (CAHs)	12x, 13x	Reasonable cost
IHS Hospitals	12x, 13x, 83x	95% of AWP
IHS CAHs	85x	95% of AWP
CAHs Method I and Method II	85x	Reasonable cost
Skilled Nursing Facilities	22x, 23x	Reasonable cost
Home Health Agencies	34x	Reasonable cost
Comprehensive Outpatient Rehabilitation Facilities	75x	95% of the AWP
Independent Renal Dialysis Facilities	72x	95% of the AWP
Hospital-based Renal Dialysis Facilities	72x	Reasonable cost

Payment for Vaccine Administration

Payment for the administration of Influenza Virus and PPV vaccines is as follows:

Facility	Type of Bill	Payment
Hospitals, other than IHS Hospitals and CAHs	12x, 13x	Outpatient Prospective Payment System (OPPS) for hospitals subject to OPPS. Reasonable cost for hospitals not subject to OPPS
IHS Hospitals	12x, 13x, 83x	MPFS as indicated in guidelines below.
IHS CAHs	85x	MPFS as indicated in guidelines below.
CAHs Method I and II	85x	Reasonable cost
Skilled Nursing Facilities	22x, 23x	MPFS as indicated in the guidelines below
Home Health Agencies	34x	OPPS
Comprehensive Outpatient Rehabilitation Facilities	75x	MPFS as indicated in the guidelines below
Independent RDFs	72x	MPFS as indicated in the guidelines below
Hospital-based RDFs	72x	Reasonable cost

Guidelines for pricing PPV and Influenza vaccine administration under the MPFS.

Make reimbursement based on the rate in the MPFS associated with the CPT code 90782 or 90471 as follows:

HCPCS code	Effective prior to March 1, 2003	Effective on and after March 1, 2003
G0008	90782	90471
G0009	90782	90471

See Sec.10.2.2.2 for payment to independent and provider based Rural Health Centers and Federally Qualified Health Clinics.

Payment for the administration of Hepatitis B vaccine is as follows:

Facility	Type of Bill	Payment
Hospitals other than IHS hospitals and CAHs	12x, 13x	Outpatient Prospective Payment System (OPPS) for hospitals subject to OPPS. Reasonable cost for hospitals not subject to OPPS
IHS Hospitals	12x, 13x, 83x	MPFS as indicated in the guidelines below
CAHs Method I and II	85x	Reasonable cost
IHS CAHs	85x	MPFS as indicated in guidelines below.
Skilled Nursing Facilities	22x, 23x	MPFS as indicated in the chart below
Home Health Agencies	34x	OPPS
Comprehensive Outpatient Rehabilitation Facilities	75x	MPFS as indicated in the guidelines below
Independent RDFs	72x	MPFS as indicated in the chart below
Hospital-based RDFs	72x	Reasonable cost

Guidelines for pricing Hepatitis B vaccine administration under the MPFS.

Make reimbursement based on the rate in the MPFS associated with the CPT code 90782 or 90471 as follows:

HCPCS code	Effective prior to March 1, 2003	Effective on and after March 1, 2003
G0010	90782	90471

See Sec.10.2.2.2 for payment to independent and provider based Rural Health Centers and Federally Qualified Health Clinics.

100-4, 18, 10.4

CWF Edits

In order to prevent duplicate payments for influenza virus and pneumococcal vaccination claims by the local contractor/AB MAC and the centralized billing contractor, effective for claims received on or after July 1, 2002, CWF has implemented a number of edits.

NOTE: 90659 was discontinued December 31, 2003.

CWF returns information in Trailer 13 information from the history claim. The following fields are returned to the contractor:

- Trailer Code;
- Contractor Number;
- Document Control Number;
- First Service Date;
- Last Service Date;
- Provider, Physician, Supplier Number;
- Claim Type; Procedure code;
- Alert Code (where applicable); and,
- More history (where applicable.)

100-4, 18, 10.4.1

CWF Edits on FI/AB MAC Claims

(Rev. 1586, Issued: 09-05-08, Effective: 10-06-08, Implementation: 10-06-08)

In order to prevent duplicate payment by the same FI/AB MAC, CWF edits by line item on the FI/AB MAC number, the beneficiary Health Insurance Claim (HIC) number, and the date of service, the influenza virus procedure codes 90657, 90658, or 90659, the pneumonia procedure code 90732, and the administration codes G0008 or G0009.

If CWF receives a claim with either HCPCS codes 90657, 90658 or 90659, and it already has on record a claim with the same HIC number, same FI/AB MAC number, same date of service, and any one of those HCPCS codes, the second claim submitted to CWF rejects.

If CWF receives a claim with HCPCS code 90732 and it already has on record a claim with the same HIC number, same FI/AB MAC number, same date of service, and the same HCPCS code, the second claim submitted to CWF rejects when all four items match.

If CWF receives a claim with HCPCS administration codes G0008 or G0009 and it already has on record a claim with the same HIC number, same FI/AB MAC number, same date of service, and same procedure code, CWF rejects the second claim submitted when all four items match.

CWF returns to the FI/AB MAC a reject code "7262" for this edit. FIs/AB MACs must deny the second claim and use the same messages they currently use for the denial of duplicate claims.

100-4, 18, 20

Mammography Services (Screening and Diagnostic)

A. Screening Mammography

Beginning January 1, 1991, Medicare provides Part B coverage of screening mammographies for women. Screening mammographies are radiologic procedures for early detection of breast cancer and include a physician's interpretation of the results. A doctor's prescription or referral is not necessary for the procedure to be covered.

© 2008 Ingenix

Whether payment can be made is determined by a woman's age and statutory frequency parameter. See Pub. 100-02, Medicare Benefit Policy Manual, chapter 15, section 280.3 for additional coverage information for a screening mammography.

Section 4101 of the Balanced Budget Act (BBA) of 1997 provides for annual screening mammographies for women over age 39 and waives the Part B deductible. Coverage applies as follows:

Age Groups	Screening Period
Under age 35	No payment allowed for screening mammography.
35-39	Baseline (pay for only one screening mammography performed on a woman between her 35th and 40th birthday)
Over age 39	Annual (11 full months have elapsed following the month of last screening

NOTE: Count months between screening mammographies beginning the month after the date of the examination. For example, if Mrs. Smith received a screening mammography examination in January 2005, begin counting the next month (February 2005) until 11 months have elapsed. Payment can be made for another screening mammography in January 2006.

B. Diagnostic Mammography

A diagnostic mammography is a radiological mammogram and is a covered diagnostic test under the following conditions:

- A patient has distinct signs and symptoms for which a mammogram is indicated,
- A patient has a history of breast cancer; or
- A patient is asymptomatic, but based on the patient's history and other factors the physician considers significant, the physician's judgment is that a mammogram is appropriate.

Beginning January 1, 2005, Medicare Prescription Drug, Improvement, and Modernization Act (MMA) of 2003, Sec. 644, Public Law 108-173 has changed the way Medicare pays for diagnostic mammography. Medicare will pay based on the MPFS in lieu of OPPS or the lower of the actual change.

100-4, 18, 20.4

Billing Requirements - FI/A/B MAC Claims

Contractors use the weekly-updated MQSA file to verify that the billing facility is certified by the FDA to perform mammography services, and has the appropriate certification to perform the type of mammogram billed (film and/or digital). (See Sec.20.1.) FIs/A/B MACs use the provider number submitted on the claim to identify the facility and use the MQSA data file to verify the facility's certification(s). FIs/A/B MACs complete the following activities in processing mammography claims:

- If the provider number on the claim does not correspond with a certified mammography facility on the MQSA file, then intermediaries/A/B MACs deny the claim.
- When a film mammography HCPCS code is on a claim, the claim is checked for a "1" film indicator.
- If a film mammography HCPCS code comes in on a claim and the facility is certified for film mammography, the claim is paid if all other relevant Medicare criteria are met.
- If a film mammography HCPCS code is on a claim and the facility is certified for digital mammography only, the claim is denied.
- When a digital mammography HCPCS code is on a claim, the claim is checked for "2" digital indicator.
- If a digital mammography HCPCS code is on a claim and the facility is certified for digital mammography, the claim is paid if all other relevant Medicare criteria are met.
- If a digital mammography HCPCS code is on a claim and the facility is certified for film mammography only, the claim is denied.

NOTE: The Common Working File (CWF) no longer receives the mammography file for editing purposes.

Except as provided in the following sections for RHCs and FQHCs, the following procedures apply to billing for screening mammographies: The technical component portion of the screening mammography is billed on Form CMS-1450 under bill type 12X, 13X, 14X**, 22X, 23X or 85X using revenue code 0403 and HCPCS code 77057* (76092*).

The technical component portion of the diagnostic mammography is billed on Form CMS-1450 under bill type 12X, 13X, 14X**, 22X, 23X or 85X using revenue code 0401 and HCPCS code 77055* (76090*), 77056* (76091*), G0204 and G0206.

Separate bills are required for claims for screening mammographies with dates of service prior to January 1, 2002. Providers include on the bill only charges for the screening mammography. Separate bills are not required for claims for screening mammographies with dates of service on or after January 1, 2002.

See separate instructions below for rural health clinics (RHCs) and federally qualified health centers (FQHCs).

* For claims with dates of service prior to January 1, 2007, providers report CPT codes 76090, 76091, and 76092. For claims with dates of service January 1, 2007 and later, providers report CPT codes 77055, 77056, and 77057 respectively.

** For claims with dates of service April 1, 2005 and later, hospitals bill for all mammography services under the 13X type of bill or for dates of service April 1, 2007 and later, 12X or 13X as appropriate. The 14X type of bill is no longer applicable. Appropriate bill types for providers other than hospitals are 22X, 23X, and 85X.

In cases where screening mammography services are self-referred and as a result an attending physician NPI is not available, the provider shall duplicate their facility NPI in the attending physician identifier field on the claim.

100-4, 18, 20.5

Carrier Processing Requirements

Contractors use the weekly-updated file to verify that the billing facility is certified by the FDA to perform mammography services, and has the appropriate certification to perform the type of mammogram billed (film and/or digital). Carriers/B MACs match the FDA assigned, 6 digit mammography certification number on the claim to the FDA mammography certification number appearing on the file for the billing facility. Carriers/B MACs complete the following activities in processing mammography claims: If the claim does not contain the facility's 6-digit certification number, or if a 6-digit certification number is not reported in item 32 of the Form CMS-1500 for paper claims, or in the 2400 loop (REF 02 segment, where 01=EW segment) of the ASC X12N 837 professional claim format, version 4010A1, for electronic claims, then carriers/B MACs return the claim as unprocessable.

- If the claim contains a 6-digit certification number that is reported in the proper field or segment (as specified in the previous bullet) but such number does not correspond to the number specified in the MQSA file for the facility, then Carriers/B MACs deny the claim.
- When a film mammography HCPCS code is on a claim, the claim is checked for a "1" film indicator.
- If a film mammography HCPCS code comes in on a claim and the facility is certified for film mammography, the claim is paid if all other relevant Medicare criteria are met.
- If a film mammography HCPCS code is on a claim and the facility is certified for digital mammography only, the claim is denied.
- When a digital mammography HCPCS code is on a claim, the claim is checked for "2" digital indicator.
- If a digital mammography HCPCS code is on a claim and the facility is certified for digital mammography, the claim is paid if all other relevant Medicare criteria are met.
- If a digital mammography HCPCS code is on a claim and the facility is certified for film mammography only, the claim is denied.
- Process the claim to the point of payment based on the information provided on the claim and in carrier claims history.
- Identify the claim as a screening mammography claim by the CPT-4 code listed in field 24D and the diagnosis code(s) listed in field 21 of Form CMS-1500.
- Assign physician specialty code 45 to facilities that are certified to perform only screening mammography.
- Ensure that entities that bill globally for screening mammography contain a blank in modifier position #1.
- Ensure that entities that bill for the technical component use only HCPCS modifier "-TC." Ensure that physicians who bill the professional component separately use HCPCS modifier "-26." Send the mammography modifier to CWF in the first modifier position on the claim. If more than one modifier is necessary, e.g., if the service was performed in a rural Health Manpower Shortage Area (HMSA) facility, instruct providers to bill the mammography modifier in modifier position 1 and the rural (or other) modifier in modifier position 2.
- Ensure all those who are qualified include the 6-digit FDA-assigned certification number of the screening center in field 32 of Form CMS-1500 and in the REF02
- segment (where 01 = EW segment) of the 2400 loop for the ASC X12N 837 professional claim format, version 4010A1. Carriers/B MACs retain this number in their provider files.
- Waive Part B deductible and apply coinsurance for a screening mammography.
- Add diagnosis code V76.12 if a claim comes in for screening mammography without a diagnosis and the carrier file data shows this is appropriate. If there are other diagnoses on the claim, but not code V76.12, add it. (Do not change or overlay code V76.12 but ADD it). At a minimum, edit for age, frequency, and place of service (POS).
- After May 23, 2008, accept the screening mammography facility's NPI number in place of the attending/referring physician NPI number for self-referred mammography claims.

NOTE: Beginning October 1, 2003, carriers/B MACs are no longer permitted to add the ICD-9 code for a screening mammography when the screening mammography claim has no diagnosis code. Screening mammography claims with no diagnosis code must be returned as unprocessable for assigned claims. For unassigned claims, deny the claim.

Carrier Provider Education

- Educate providers that when a screening mammography turns to a diagnostic mammography on the same day for the same beneficiary, add the "GG" modifier to the diagnostic code and bill both codes on the same claim. Both services are reimbursable by Medicare.
- Educate providers that they cannot bill an add-on code without also billing for the appropriate mammography code. If just the add-on code is billed, the service will be denied. Both the add-on code and the appropriate mammography code should be on the same claim.
- Educate providers to submit their own NPI in place of an attending/referring physician NPI in cases where screening mammography services are self-referred.

100-4, 18, 60.1

Payment

Payment (contractor) is under the MPFS except as follows:

- Fecal occult blood tests (82270* (G0107*) and G0328) are paid under the clinical diagnostic lab fee schedule except reasonable cost is paid to all non-OPPS hospitals, including CAHs, but not IHS hospitals billing on TOB 83x. IHS hospitals billing on TOB 83x are paid the ASC payment amount. Other IHS hospitals (billing on TOB 13x) are paid the OMB approved AIR, or the facility specific per visit amount as applicable. Deductible and coinsurance do not apply for these tests. See section A below for payment to Maryland waiver on TOB 13X. Payment from all hospitals for non-patient laboratory specimens on TOB 14X will be based on the clinical diagnostic fee schedule, including CAHs and Maryland waiver hospitals

- Flexible sigmoidoscopy (code G0104) is paid under OPPS for hospital outpatient departments and on a reasonable cost basis for CAHs; or current payment methodologies for hospitals not subject to OPPS.

- Colonoscopies (G0105 and G0121) and barium enemas (G0106 and G0120) are paid under OPPS for hospital outpatient departments and on a reasonable costs basis for CAHs or current payment methodologies for hospitals not subject to OPPS. Also colonoscopies may be done in an Ambulatory Surgical Center (ASC) and when done in an ASC the ASC rate applies. The ASC rate is the same for diagnostic and screening colonoscopies. The ASC rate is paid to IHS hospitals when the service is billed on TOB 83x.

Prior to January 1, 2007, deductible and coinsurance apply to HCPCS codes G0104, G0105, G0106, G0120, and G0121. Beginning with services provided on or after January 1, 2007, Section 5113 of the Deficit Reduction Act of 2005 waives the requirement of the annual Part B deductible for these screening services. Coinsurance still applies. Coinsurance and deductible applies to the diagnostic colorectal service codes listed below.

The following screening codes must be paid at rates consistent with the diagnostic codes indicated.

Screening Code	Diagnostic Code
G0104	45330
G0105 and G0121	45378
G0106 and G0120	74280

A. Special Payment Instructions for TOB 13X Maryland Waiver Hospitals
For hospitals in Maryland under the jurisdiction of the Health Services Cost Review Commission, screening colorectal services HCPCS codes G0104, G0105, G0106, 82270* (G0107*), G0120, G0121 and G0328 are paid according to the terms of the waiver, that is 94% of submitted charges minus any unmet existing deductible, co-insurance and non-covered charges. Maryland Hospitals bill TOB 13X for outpatient colorectal cancer screenings.

B. Special Payment Instructions for Non-Patient Laboratory Specimen (TOB 14X) for all hospitals
Payment for colorectal cancer screenings (82270* (G0107*) and G0328) to a hospital for a non-patient laboratory specimen (TOB 14X), is the lesser of the actual charge, the fee schedule amount, or the National Limitation Amount (NLA), (including CAHs and Maryland Waiver hospitals). Part B deductible and coinsurance do not apply.

*NOTE: For claims with dates of service prior to January 1, 2007, physicians, suppliers, and providers report HCPCS code G0107. Effective January 1, 2007, code G0107 is discontinued and replaced with CPT code 82270.

100-4, 18, 60.2
HCPCS Codes, Frequency Requirements, and Age Requirements (If Applicable)
Effective for services furnished on or after January 1, 1998, the following codes are used for colorectal cancer screening services:

- 82270* (G0107*) - Colorectal cancer screening; fecal-occult blood tests, 1-3 simultaneous determinations;

- G0104 - Colorectal cancer screening; flexible sigmoidoscopy;

- G0105 - Colorectal cancer screening; colonoscopy on individual at high risk;

- G0106 - Colorectal cancer screening; barium enema; as an alternative to G0104, screening sigmoidoscopy;

- G0120 - Colorectal cancer screening; barium enema; as an alternative to G0105, screening colonoscopy.

Effective for services furnished on or after July 1, 2001, the following codes are used for colorectal cancer screening services:

- G0121 - Colorectal cancer screening; colonoscopy on individual not meeting criteria for high risk. Note that the description for this code has been revised to remove the term "noncovered."

- G0122 - Colorectal cancer screening; barium enema (noncovered).

Effective for services furnished on or after January 1, 2004, the following code is used for colorectal cancer screening services as an alternative to 82270* (G0107*):

- G0328 - Colorectal cancer screening; immunoassay, fecal-occult blood test, 1-3 simultaneous determinations

*NOTE: For claims with dates of service prior to January 1, 2007, physicians, suppliers, and providers report HCPCS code G0107. Effective January 1, 2007, code G0107 is discontinued and replaced with CPT code 82270.

G0104 - Colorectal Cancer Screening; Flexible Sigmoidoscopy
Screening flexible sigmoidoscopies (code G0104) may be paid for beneficiaries who have attained age 50, when performed by a doctor of medicine or osteopathy at the frequencies noted below.

For claims with dates of service on or after January 1, 2002, contractors pay for screening flexible sigmoidoscopies (code G0104) for beneficiaries who have attained age 50 when these services were performed by a doctor of medicine or osteopathy, or by a physician assistant, nurse practitioner, or clinical nurse specialist (as defined in Sec.1861(aa)(5) of the Act and in the

Code of Federal Regulations at42 CFR 410.74, 410.75, and410.76) at the frequencies noted above. For claims with dates of service prior to January 1, 2002, contractors pay for these services under the conditions noted only when a doctor of medicine or osteopathy performs them.

For services furnished from January 1, 1998, through June 30, 2001, inclusive:

- Once every 48 months (i.e., at least 47 months have passed following the month in which the last covered screening flexible sigmoidoscopy was done).

For services furnished on or after July 1, 2001:

- Once every 48 months as calculated above unless the beneficiary does not meet the criteria for high risk of developing colorectal cancer (refer to Sec.60.3 of this chapter) and he/she has had a screening colonoscopy (code G0121) within the preceding 10 years. If such a beneficiary has had a screening colonoscopy within the preceding 10 years, then he or she can have covered a screening flexible sigmoidoscopy only after at least 119 months have passed following the month that he/she received the screening colonoscopy (code G0121).

NOTE:If during the course of a screening flexible sigmoidoscopy a lesion or growth is detected which results in a biopsy or removal of the growth; the appropriate diagnostic procedure classified as a flexible sigmoidoscopy with biopsy or removal should be billed and paid rather than code G0104.

G0105 - Colorectal Cancer Screening; Colonoscopy on Individual at High Risk
Screening colonoscopies (code G0105) may be paid when performed by a doctor of medicine or osteopathy at a frequency of once every 24 months for beneficiaries at high risk for developing colorectal cancer (i.e., at least 23 months have passed following the month in which the last covered G0105 screening colonoscopy was performed). Refer to Sec.60.3of this chapter for the criteria to use in determining whether or not an individual is at high risk for developing colorectal cancer.

NOTE: If during the course of the screening colonoscopy, a lesion or growth is detected which results in a biopsy or removal of the growth, the appropriate diagnostic procedure classified as a colonoscopy with biopsy or removal should be billed and paid rather than code G0105.

A. Colonoscopy Cannot be Completed Because of Extenuating Circumstances
1. FIs
   When a covered colonoscopy is attempted but cannot be completed because of extenuating circumstances, Medicare will pay for the interrupted colonoscopy as long as the coverage conditions are met for the incomplete procedure. However, the frequency standards associated with screening colonoscopies will not be applied by CWF. When a covered colonoscopy is next attempted and completed, Medicare will pay for that colonoscopy according to its payment methodology for this procedure as long as coverage conditions are met, and the frequency standards will be applied by CWF. This policy is applied to both screening and diagnostic colonoscopies.

   When submitting a facility claim for the interrupted colonoscopy, providers are to suffix the colonoscopy HCPCS codes with a modifier of "-73" or "-74" as appropriate to indicate that the procedure was interrupted. Payment for covered incomplete screening colonoscopies shall be consistent with payment methodologies currently in place for complete screening colonoscopies, including those contained in42 CFR 419.44(b). In situations where a critical access hospital (CAH) has elected payment Method II for CAH patients, payment shall be consistent with payment methodologies currently in place as outlined in Chapter 3. As such, instruct CAHs that elect Method II to use modifier "-53" to identify an incomplete screening colonoscopy (physician professional service(s) billed in revenue code 096X, 097X, and/or 098X). Such CAHs will also bill the technical or facility component of the interrupted colonoscopy in revenue code 075X (or other appropriate revenue code) using the "-73" or "-74" modifier as appropriate.

   Note that Medicare would expect the provider to maintain adequate information in the patient's medical record in case it is needed by the contractor to document the incomplete procedure.

2. Carriers
   When a covered colonoscopy is attempted but cannot be completed because of extenuating circumstances (see Chapter 12), Medicare will pay for the interrupted colonoscopy at a rate consistent with that of a flexible sigmoidoscopy as long as coverage conditions are met for the incomplete procedure. When a covered colonoscopy is next attempted and completed, Medicare will pay for that colonoscopy according to its payment methodology for this procedure as long as coverage conditions are met. This policy is applied to both screening and diagnostic colonoscopies.

   When submitting a claim for the interrupted colonoscopy, professional providers are to suffix the colonoscopy code with a modifier of "-53" to indicate that the procedure was interrupted. When submitting a claim for the facility fee associated with this procedure, Ambulatory Surgical Centers (ASCs) are to suffix the colonoscopy code with "-73" or "-74" as appropriate. Payment for covered screening colonoscopies, including that for the associated ASC facility fee when applicable, shall be consistent with payment for diagnostic colonoscopies, whether the procedure is complete or incomplete.

   Note that Medicare would expect the provider to maintain adequate information in the patient's medical record in case it is needed by the contractor to document the incomplete procedure.

G0106 - Colorectal Cancer Screening; Barium Enema; as an Alternative to G0104, Screening Sigmoidoscopy
Screening barium enema examinations may be paid as an alternative to a screening sigmoidoscopy (code G0104). The same frequency parameters for screening sigmoidoscopies (see those codes above) apply. In the case of an individual aged 50 or over, payment may be made for a screening barium enema examination (code G0106) performed after at least 47 months have passed following the month in which the last screening barium enema or screening flexible sigmoidoscopy was performed. For example, the beneficiary received a screening barium enema examination as an alternative to a screening flexible sigmoidoscopy in January 1999.

Start counts beginning February 1999. The beneficiary is eligible for another screening barium enema in January 2003. The screening barium enema must be ordered in writing after a determination that the test is the appropriate screening test. Generally, it is expected that this will be a screening double contrast enema unless the individual is unable to withstand such an exam. This means that in the case of a particular individual, the attending physician must determine that the estimated screening potential for the barium enema is equal to or greater than the screening potential that has been estimated for a screening flexible sigmoidoscopy for the same individual. The screening single contrast barium enema also requires a written order from the beneficiary's attending physician in the same manner as described above for the screening double contrast barium enema examination.

82270* (G0107*) - Colorectal Cancer Screening; Fecal-Occult Blood Test, 1-3 Simultaneous Determinations
Effective for services furnished on or after January 1, 1998, screening FOBT (code 82270* (G0107*) may be paid for beneficiaries who have attained age 50, and at a frequency of once every 12 months (i.e., at least 11 months have passed following the month in which the last covered screening FOBT was performed). This screening FOBT means a guaiac-based test for peroxidase activity, in which the beneficiary completes it by taking samples from two different sites of three consecutive stools. This screening requires a written order from the beneficiary's attending physician. (The term "attending physician" is defined to mean a doctor of medicine or osteopathy (as defined in Sec.1861(r)(1)of the Act) who is fully knowledgeable about the beneficiary's medical condition, and who would be responsible for using the results of any examination performed in the overall management of the beneficiary's specific medical problem.)

Effective for services furnished on or after January 1, 2004, payment may be made for a immunoassay-based FOBT (G0328, described below) as an alternative to the guaiacbased FOBT, 82270* (G0107*). Medicare will pay for only one covered FOBT per year, either 82270* (G0107*) or G0328, but not both.

*NOTE: For claims with dates of service prior to January 1, 2007, physicians, suppliers, and providers report HCPCS code G0107. Effective January 1, 2007, code G0107 is discontinued and replaced with CPT code 82270.

G0328 - Colorectal Cancer Screening; Immunoassay, Fecal-Occult Blood Test, 1-3 Simultaneous Determinations
Effective for services furnished on or after January 1, 2004, screening FOBT, (code G0328) may be paid as an alternative to 82270* (G0107*) for beneficiaries who have attained age 50. Medicare will pay for a covered FOBT (either 82270* (G0107*) or G0328, but not both) at a frequency of once every 12 months (i.e., at least 11 months have passed following the month in which the last covered screening FOBT was performed). Screening FOBT, immunoassay, includes the use of a spatula to collect the appropriate number of samples or the use of a special brush for the collection of samples, as determined by the individual manufacturer's instructions. This screening requires a written order from the beneficiary's attending physician. (The term "attending physician" is defined to mean a doctor of medicine or osteopathy (as defined in Sec.1861(r)(1) of the Act) who is fully knowledgeable about the beneficiary's medical condition, and who would be responsible for using the results of any examination performed in the overall management of the beneficiary's specific medical problem.)

G0120 - Colorectal Cancer Screening; Barium Enema; as an Alternative to or G0105, Screening Colonoscopy
Screening barium enema examinations may be paid as an alternative to a screening colonoscopy (code G0105) examination. The same frequency parameters for screening colonoscopies (see those codes above) apply. In the case of an individual who is at high risk for colorectal cancer, payment may be made for a screening barium enema examination (code G0120) performed after at least 23 months have passed following the month in which the last screening barium enema or the last screening colonoscopy was performed. For example, a beneficiary at high risk for developing colorectal cancer received a screening barium enema examination (code G0120) as an alternative to a screening colonoscopy (code G0105) in January 2000. Start counts beginning February 2000. The beneficiary is eligible for another screening barium enema examination (code G0120) in January 2002. The screening barium enema must be ordered in writing after a determination that the test is the appropriate screening test. Generally, it is expected that this will be a screening double contrast enema unless the individual is unable to withstand such an exam. This means that in the case of a particular individual, the attending physician must determine that the estimated screening potential for the barium enema is equal to or greater than the screening potential that has been estimated for a screening colonoscopy, for the same individual. The screening single contrast barium enema also requires a written order from the beneficiary's attending physician in the same manner as described above for the screening double contrast barium enema examination.

G0121 - Colorectal Screening; Colonoscopy on Individual Not Meeting Criteria for High Risk - Applicable On and After July 1, 2001
Effective for services furnished on or after July 1, 2001, screening colonoscopies (code G0121) performed on individuals not meeting the criteria for being at high risk for developing colorectal cancer (refer to Sec.60.3 of this chapter) may be paid under the following conditions:

- At a frequency of once every 10 years (i.e., at least 119 months have passed following the month in which the last covered G0121 screening colonoscopy was performed.)
- If the individual would otherwise qualify to have covered a G0121 screening colonoscopy based on the above but has had a covered screening flexible sigmoidoscopy (code G0104), then he or she may have covered a G0121 screening colonoscopy only after at least 47 months have passed following the month in which the last covered G0104 flexible sigmoidoscopy was performed.

NOTE: If during the course of the screening colonoscopy, a lesion or growth is detected which results in a biopsy or removal of the growth, the appropriate diagnostic procedure classified as a colonoscopy with biopsy or removal should be billed and paid rather than code G0121.

G0122 - Colorectal Cancer Screening; Barium Enema
The code is not covered by Medicare.

100-4, 18, 60.6
Billing Requirements for Claims Submitted to FIs
Follow the general bill review instructions in Chapter 25. Hospitals use the ANSI X12N 837I to bill the FI or on the hardcopy Form CMS-1450. Hospitals bill revenue codes and HCPCS codes as follows:

Screening Test/Procedure	Revenue Code	HCPCS Code	TOB
Fecal Occult blood test	030X	82270*** (G0107***), G0328	13X, 14X**, 22X, 23X, 83X, 85X
Barium enema	032X	G0106, G0120, G0122	13X, 22X, 23X, 85X****
Flexible Sigmoidoscopy	*	G0104	13X, 22X, 23X, 83X, 85X****
Colonoscopy high risk	*	G0105, G0121	13X, 22X, 23X, 83X, 85X**** *

*　　The appropriate revenue code when reporting any other surgical procedure.

**　 14X is only applicable for non-patient laboratory specimens.

***　For claims with dates of service prior to January 1, 2007, physicians, suppliers, and providers report HCPCS code G0107. Effective January 1, 2007, code G0107, is discontinued and replaced with CPT code 82270.

**** CAHs that elect Method II bill revenue code 096X, 097X, and/or 098X for professional services and 075X (or other appropriate revenue code) for the technical or facility component.

A Special Billing Instructions for Hospital Inpatients
When these tests/procedures are provided to inpatients of a hospital, they are covered under this benefit. However, the provider bills on bill type 13X using the discharge date of the hospital stay to avoid editing in the Common Working File (CWF) as a result of the hospital bundling rules.

100-4, 20, 100.2.2
Evidence of Medical Necessity for Parenteral and Enteral Nutrition (PEN) Therapy
The PEN coverage is determined by information provided by the treating physician and the PEN supplier. A completed certification of medical necessity (CMN) must accompany and support initial claims for PEN to establish whether coverage criteria are met and to ensure that the PEN therapy provided is consistent with the attending or ordering physician's prescription.

Contractors ensure that the CMN contains pertinent information from the treating physician. Uniform specific medical data facilitate the review and promote consistency in coverage determinations and timelier claims processing.The medical and prescription information on a PEN CMN can be most appropriatelycompleted by the treating physician or from information in the patient's records by an employee of the physician for the physician's review and signature.

Although PEN suppliers sometimes may assist in providing the PEN services, they cannot complete the CMN since they do not have the same access to patient information needed to properly enter medical or prescription information. Contractors use appropriate professional relations issuances, training sessions, and meetings to ensure that all persons and PEN suppliers are aware of this limitation of their role. When properly completed, the PEN CMN includes the elements of a prescription as well as other data needed to determine whether Medicare coverage is possible. This practice will facilitate prompt delivery of PEN services and timely submittal of the related claim.

100-4, 32, 10.1
Ambulatory Blood Pressure Monitoring (ABPM) Billing Requirements
A. Coding Applicable to Local Carriers & Fiscal Intermediaries (FIs)
Effective April 1, 2002, a National Coverage Decision was made to allow for Medicare coverage of ABPM for those beneficiaries with suspected "white coat hypertension" (WCH). ABPM involves the use of a non-invasive device, which is used to measure blood pressure in 24-hour cycles. These 24-hour measurements are stored in the device and are later interpreted by a physician. Suspected "WCH" is defined as: (1) Clinic/office blood pressure >140/90 mm Hg on at least three separate clinic/office visits with two separate measurements made at each visit; (2) At least two documented separate blood pressure measurements taken outside the clinic/office which are < 140/90 mm Hg; and (3) No evidence of end-organ damage. ABPM is not covered for any other uses. Coverage policy can be found in Medicare National Coverage Determinations Manual, Chapter 1, Section 20.19. (www.cms.hhs.gov/masnuals/103 cov determ/ncd103index.asp).

The ABPM must be performed for at least 24 hours to meet coverage criteria. Payment is not allowed for institutionalized beneficiaries, such as those receiving Medicare covered skilled nursing in a facility. In the rare circumstance that ABPM needs to be performed more than once for a beneficiary, the qualifying criteria described above must be met for each subsequent ABPM test.

Effective dates for applicable Common Procedure Coding System (HCPCS) codes for ABPM for suspected WCH and their covered effective dates are as follows:

HCPCS	Definition	Effective Date
93784	ABPM, utilizing a system such as magnetic tape and/or computer disk, for 24 hours or longer; including recording, scanning analysis, interpretation and report.	04/01/2002
93786	ABPM, utilizing a system such as magnetic tape and/or computer disk, for 24 hours or longer; recording only.	04/01/2002
93788	ABPM, utilizing a system such as magnetic tape and/or computer disk, for 24 hours or longer; scanning analysis with report.	01/01/2004

HCPCS Definition Effective Date

93790	ABPM, utilizing a system such as magnetic tape and/or computer disk, for 24 hours or longer; physician review with interpretation and report.	04/01/2002

In addition, the following diagnosis code must be present:

Diagnosis Code	Description
796.2	Elevated blood pressure reading without diagnosis of hypertension.

B. FI Billing Instructions

The applicable types of bills acceptable when billing for ABPM services are 13X, 23X, 71X, 73X, 75X, and 85X. Chapter 25 of this manual provides general billing instructions that must be followed for bills submitted to FIs. The FIs pay for hospital outpatient ABPM services billed on a 13X type of bill with HCPCS 93786 and/or 93788 as follows: (1) Outpatient Prospective Payment System (OPPS) hospitals pay based on the Ambulatory Payment Classification (APC); (2) non-OPPS hospitals (Indian Health Services Hospitals, Hospitals that provide Part B services only, and hospitals located in American Samoa, Guam, Saipan and the Virgin Islands) pay based on reasonable cost, except for Maryland Hospitals which are paid based on a percentage of cost. Effective 4/1/06, type of bill 14X is for non-patient laboratory specimens and is no longer applicable for ABPM.

The FIs pay for comprehensive outpatient rehabilitation facility (CORF) ABPM services billed on a 75x type of bill with HCPCS code 93786 and/or 93788 based on the Medicare Physician Fee Schedule (MPFS) amount for that HCPCS code.

The FIs pay for ABPM services for critical access hospitals (CAHs) billed on a 85x type of bill as follows: (1) for CAHs that elected the Standard Method and billed HCPCS code 93786 and/or 93788, pay based on reasonable cost for that HCPCS code; and (2) for CAHs that elected the Optional Method and billed any combination of HCPCS codes 93786, 93788 and 93790 pay based on reasonable cost for HCPCS 93786 and 93788 and pay 115% of the MPFS amount for HCPCS 93790.

The FIs pay for ABPM services for skilled nursing facility (SNF) outpatients billed on a 23x type of bill with HCPCS code 93786 and/or 93788, based on the MPFS.

The FIs accept independent and provider-based rural health clinic (RHC) bills for visits under the all-inclusive rate when the RHC bills on a 71x type of bill with revenue code 052x for providing the professional component of ABPM services. The FIs should not make a separate payment to a RHC for the professional component of ABPM services in

addition to the all-inclusive rate. RHCs are not required to use ABPM HCPCS codes for professional services covered under the all-inclusive rate.

The FIs accept free-standing and provider-based federally qualified health center (FQHC) bills for visits under the all-inclusive rate when the FQHC bills on a 73x type of bill with revenue code 052x for providing the professional component of ABPM services.

The FIs should not make a separate payment to a FQHC for the professional component of ABPM services in addition to the all-inclusive rate. FQHCs are not required to use ABPM HCPCS codes for professional services covered under the all-inclusive rate.

The FIs pay provider-based RHCs/FQHCs for the technical component of ABPM services when billed under the base provider's number using the above requirements for that particular base provider type, i.e., a OPPS hospital based RHC would be paid for the ABPM technical component services under the OPPS using the APC for code 93786 and/or 93788 when billed on a 13x type of bill.

Independent and free-standing RHC/FQHC practitioners are only paid for providing the technical component of ABPM services when billed to the carrier following the carrier instructions.

C. Carrier Claims

Local carriers pay for ABPM services billed with diagnosis code 796.2 and HCPCS codes 93784 or for any combination of 93786, 93788 and 93790, based on the MPFS for the specific HCPCS code billed.

D. Coinsurance and Deductible

The FIs and local carriers shall apply coinsurance and deductible to payments for ABPM services except for services billed to the FI by FQHCs. For FQHCs only co-insurance applies.

100-4, 32, 12

Smoking and Tobacco-Use Cessation Counseling Services

Background: Effective for services furnished on or after March 22, 2005, a National Coverage Determination (NCD) provides for coverage of smoking and tobacco-use cessation counseling services. Conditions of Medicare Part A and Medicare Part B coverage for smoking and tobacco-use cessation counseling services are located in the Medicare National Coverage Determinations Manual, Publication 100-3, section 210.4.

100-4, 32, 12.1

HCPCS and Diagnosis Coding

The following HCPCS codes should be reported when billing for smoking and tobacco-use cessation counseling services:

99406   Smoking and tobacco-use cessation counseling visit; intermediate, greater than 3 minutes up to 10 minutes

99407   Smoking and tobacco-use cessation counseling visit; intensive, greater than 10 minutes

Note the above codes are payable for dates of service on or after January 1, 2008. Codes G0375 and G0376, below, are not valid or payable for dates of service on or after January 1, 2008.

G0375   Smoking and tobacco-use cessation counseling visit; intermediate, greater than 3 minutes up to 10 minutes

Short Descriptor: Smoke/Tobacco counseling 3-10

G0376   Smoking and tobacco-use cessation counseling visit; intensive, greater than 10 minutes

Short Descriptor: Smoke/Tobacco counseling greater than 10

NOTE: The above G codes will NOT be active in contractors' systems until July 5, 2005. Therefore, contractors shall advise providers to use unlisted code 99199 to bill for smoking and tobacco-use cessation counseling services during the interim period of March 22, 2005, through July 4, 2005, and received prior to July 5, 2005.

On July 5, 2005, contractors' systems will accept the new G codes for services performed on and after March 22, 2005.

Contractors shall allow payment for a medically necessary E/M service on the same day as the smoking and tobacco-use cessation counseling service when it is clinically appropriate. Physicians and qualified non-physician practitioners shall use an appropriate HCPCS code, such as HCPCS 99201- 99215, to report an E/M service with modifier 25 to indicate that the E/M service is a separately identifiable service from G0375 or G0376.

Contractors shall only pay for 8 Smoking and Tobacco-Use Cessation Counseling sessions in a 12-month period. The beneficiary may receive another 8 sessions during a second or subsequent year after 11 full months have passed since the first Medicare covered cessation session was performed. To start the count for the second or subsequent 12-month period, begin with the month after the month in which the first Medicare covered cessation session was performed and count until 11 full months have elapsed.

Claims for smoking and tobacco use cessation counseling services shall be submitted with an appropriate diagnosis code. Diagnosis codes should reflect: the condition the patient has that is adversely affected by tobacco use or the condition the patient is being treated for with a therapeutic agent whose metabolism or dosing is affected by tobacco use.

NOTE: This decision does not modify existing coverage for minimal cessation counseling (defined as 3 minutes or less in duration) which is already considered to be covered as part of each Evaluation and Management (E/M) visit and is not separately billable.

100-4, 32, 12.2

Carrier Billing:

Carriers shall pay for counseling services billed with codes 99406 and 99407 for dates of service on or after January 1, 2008. Carriers shall pay for counseling services billed with codes G0375 and G0376 for dates of service performed on and after March 22, 2005 through Dec. 31, 2007. The type of service (TOS) for each of the new codes is 1.

Carriers pay for counseling services billed based on the Medicare Physician Fee Schedule (MPFS). Deductible and coinsurance apply. Claims from physicians or other providers where assignment was not taken are subject to the Medicare limiting charge, which means that charges to the beneficiary may be no more than 115 percent of the allowed amount.

Physicians or qualified non-physician practitioners shall bill the carrier for smoking and tobacco-use cessation counseling services on the Form CMS-1500 or an approved electronic format.

100-4, 32, 12.3

FI Billing Requirements

FIs shall pay for Smoking and Tobacco-Use Cessation Counseling services with codes 99406 and 99407 for dates of service on or after January 1, 2008. FIs shall pay for counseling services billed with codes G0375 and G0376 for dates of service performed on or after March 22, 2005 through December 31, 2007.

A. Claims for Smoking and Tobacco-Use Cessation Counseling Services should be submitted on Form CMS-1450 or its electronic equivalent.

The applicable bill types are 12X, 13X, 22X, 23X, 34X, 71X, 73X, 74X, 75X, 83X, and 85X. Effective 4/1/06, type of bill 14X is for non-patient laboratory specimens and is no longer applicable for Smoking and Tobacco-Use Cessation Counseling services.

Applicable revenue codes are as follows:

Provider Type	Revenue Code
Rural Health Centers (RHCs)/Federally Qualified Health Centers (FQHCs)	052X
Indian Health Services (IHS)	0510
Critical Access Hospitals (CAHs) Method II	096X, 097X, 098X
All Other Providers	0942

NOTE: When these services are provided by a Clinical Nurse Specialist in the RHC/FQHC setting, they are considered "incident to" and do not constitute a billable visit.

Payment for outpatient services is as follows:

Type of Facility	Method of Payment
Rural Health Centers (RHCs)/Federally Qualified Health Centers (FQHCs)	All-inclusive rate (AIR) for the encounter
Indian Health Service (IHS)/Tribally owned or operated hospitals and hospital- based facilities	All-inclusive rate (AIR)

Type of Facility	Method of Payment
IHS/Tribally owned or operated non-hospital-based facilities	Medicare Physician Fee Schedule (MPFS)
IHS/Tribally owned or operated Critical Access Hospitals (CAHs)	Facility Specific Visit Rate
Hospitals subject to the Outpatient Prospective Payment System (OPPS)	Ambulatory Payment Classification (APC)
Hospitals not subject to OPPS	Payment is made under current methodologies
Skilled Nursing Facilities (SNFs) NOTE: Included in Part A PPS for skilled patients.	Medicare Physician Fee Schedule (MPFS)
Comprehensive Outpatient Rehabilitation Facilities (CORFs)	Medicare Physician Fee Schedule (MPFS)
Home Health Agencies (HHAs)	Medicare Physician Fee Schedule (MPFS)
Critical Access Hospitals (CAHs)	Method I: Technical services are paid at 101% of reasonable cost. Method II: technical services are paid at 101% of reasonable cost, and Professional services are paid at 115% of the MMPFS Data Base
Maryland Hospitals	Payment is based according to the Health Services Cost Review Commission (HSCRC). That is 94% of submitted charges subject to any unmet deductible, coinsurance, and non-covered charges policies.

NOTE: Inpatient claims submitted with Smoking and Tobacco-Use Cessation Counseling Services are processed under the current payment methodologies.

100-4, 32, 40
Sacral Nerve Stimulation
A sacral nerve stimulator is a pulse generator that transmits electrical impulses to the sacral nerves through an implanted wire. These impulses cause the bladder muscles to contract, which gives the patient ability to void more properly.

100-4, 32, 50
Deep Brain Stimulation for Essential Tremor and Parkinson's Disease
Deep brain stimulation (DBS) refers to high-frequency electrical stimulation of anatomic regions deep within the brain utilizing neurosurgically implanted electrodes. These DBS electrodes are stereotactically placed within targeted nuclei on one (unilateral) or both (bilateral) sides of the brain. There are currently three targets for DBS -- the thalamic ventralis intermedius nucleus (VIM), subthalamic nucleus (STN) and globus pallidus interna (GPi).

Essential tremor (ET) is a progressive, disabling tremor most often affecting the hands. ET may also affect the head, voice and legs. The precise pathogenesis of ET is unknown. While it may start at any age, ET usually peaks within the second and sixth decades. Beta-adrenergic blockers and anticonvulsant medications are usually the first line treatments for reducing the severity of tremor. Many patients, however, do not adequately respond or cannot tolerate these medications. In these medically refractory ET patients, thalamic VIM DBS may be helpful for symptomatic relief of tremor.

Parkinson's disease (PD) is an age-related progressive neurodegenerative disorder involving the loss of dopaminergic cells in the substantia nigra of the midbrain. The disease is characterized by tremor, rigidity, bradykinesia and progressive postural instability. Dopaminergic medication is typically used as a first line treatment for reducing the primary symptoms of PD. However, after prolonged use, medication can become less effective and can produce significant adverse events such as dyskinesias and other motor function complications. For patients who become unresponsive to medical treatments and/or have intolerable side effects from medications, DBS for symptom relief may be considere

100-4, 32, 90
Stem Cell Transplantation
Stem cell transplantation is a process in which stem cells are harvested from either a patient's or donor's bone marrow or peripheral blood for intravenous infusion. Autologous stem cell transplantation (AuSCT) must be used to effect hematopoietic reconstitution following severely myelotoxic doses of chemotherapy (HDCT) and/or radiotherapy used to treat various malignancies. Allogeneic stem cell transplant may also be used to restore function in recipients having an inherited or acquired deficiency or defect.

Bone marrow and peripheral blood stem cell transplantation is a process which includes mobilization, harvesting, and transplant of bone marrow or peripheral blood stem cells and the administration of high dose chemotherapy or radiotherapy prior to the actual transplant. When bone marrow or peripheral blood stem cell transplantation is covered, all necessary steps are included in coverage. When bone marrow or peripheral blood stem cell transplantation is non-covered, none of the steps are covered.

Allogeneic and autologous stem cell transplants are covered under Medicare for specific diagnoses. See Pub. 100-03, National Coverage Determinations Manual, section 110.8.1, for a complete description of covered and noncovered conditions. The following sections contain claims processing instructions for carrier claims. For institutional claims processing instructions, please refer to Pub. 100-04, chapter 3, section 90.3.

100-4, 32, 100
Billing Requirements for Expanded Coverage of Cochlear Implantation
Effective for dates of services on and after April 4, 2005, the Centers for Medicare & Medicaid Services (CMS) has expanded the coverage for cochlear implantation to cover moderate-to-profound hearing loss in individuals with hearing test scores equal to or less than 40% correct in the best aided listening condition on tape-recorded tests of open-set sentence recognition and who demonstrate limited benefit from amplification. (See Publication 100-03, chapter 1, section 50.3, for specific coverage criteria).

In addition CMS is covering cochlear implantation for individuals with open-set sentence recognition test scores of greater than 40% to less than or equal to 60% correct but only when the provider is participating in, and patients are enrolled in, either:

A Food and Drug Administration (FDA)-approved category B investigational device exemption (IDE) clinical trial; or

A trial under the CMS clinical trial policy (see Pub. 100-03, section 310.1); or

A prospective, controlled comparative trial approved by CMS as consistent with the evidentiary requirements for national coverage analyses and meeting specific quality standards.

APPENDIX F — GLOSSARY

abdominal lymphadenectomy. Surgical removal of the abdominal lymph nodes grouping, with or without para-aortic and vena cava nodes.

ablation. Removal or destruction of a body part or tissue or its function. Ablation may be performed by surgical means, hormones, drugs, radiofrequency, heat, chemical application, or other methods.

absorbable sutures. Strands prepared from collagen or a synthetic polymer and capable of being absorbed by tissue over time. Examples include surgical gut and collagen sutures; or synthetics like polydioxanone (PDS), polyglactin 910 (Vicryl), poliglecaprone 25 (Monocryl), polyglyconate (Maxon), and polyglycolic acid (Dexon). For wound repair, see CPT codes 12001-13160. Correct code assignment is dependent upon the type of closure performed (i.e., simple, intermediate, or complex), the anatomical site, and the wound size.

acetabuloplasty. Surgical repair or reconstruction of the large cup-shaped socket in the hipbone (acetabulum) with which the head of the femur articulates.

actigraphy. Science of monitoring activity levels, particularly during sleep. In most cases, the patient wears a wristband that records motion while sleeping. The data are recorded, analyzed, and interpreted to study sleep/wake patterns and circadian rhythms.

air conduction. Transportation of sound from the air, through the external auditory canal, to the tympanic membrane and ossicular chain. Air conduction hearing is tested by presenting an acoustic stimulus through earphones or a loudspeaker to the ear.

air puff device. Instrument that measures intraocular pressure by evaluating the force of a reflected amount of air blown against the cornea.

allograft. Graft from one individual to another of the same species.

amniocentesis. Surgical puncture through the abdominal wall, with a specialized needle and under ultrasonic guidance, into the interior of the pregnant uterus and directly into the amniotic sac to collect fluid for diagnostic analysis or therapeutic reduction of fluid levels.

anastomosis. Surgically created connection between ducts, blood vessels, or bowel segments to allow flow from one to the other.

angioplasty. Reconstruction or repair of a diseased or damaged blood vessel.

annuloplasty. Surgical plication of weakened tissue of the heart, to improve its muscular function. Annuli are thick, fibrous rings and one is found surrounding each of the cardiac chambers. The atrial and ventricular muscle fibers attach to the annuli. In annuloplasty, weakened annuli may be surgically plicated, or tucked, to improve muscular functions.

anorectal anometry. Measurement of pressure generated by anal sphincter to diagnose incontinence.

anterior chamber lenses. Lenses inserted into the anterior chamber following intracapsular cataract extraction.

applanation tonometer. Instrument that measures intraocular pressure by recording the force required to flatten an area of the cornea.

aspirate. To withdraw fluid or air from a body cavity by suction.

atrial septal defect. Cardiac anomaly consisting of a patent opening in the atrial septum due to a fusion failure, classified as ostium secundum type, ostium primum defect, or endocardial cushion defect.

attended surveillance. The ability of a technician at a remote surveillance center or location to respond immediately to patient transmissions regarding rhythm or device alerts as they are produced and received at the remote location. These transmissions may originate from either wearable or implanted therapy or monitoring devices.

auricle. External ear, which is a single elastic cartilage covered in skin and normal adnexal features (hair follicles, sweat glands, and sebaceous glands), shaped to channel sound waves into the acoustic meatus.

autogenous transplant. Tissue, such as bone, that is harvested from the patient and used for transplantation back into the same patient.

autograft. Any tissue harvested from one anatomical site of a person and grafted to another anatomical site of the same person. Most commonly, blood vessels, skin, tendons, fascia, and bone are used as autografts.

backbench preparation. Procedures performed on a donor organ following procurement to prepare the organ for transplant into the recipient. Excess fat and other tissue may be removed, the organ may be perfused, and vital arteries may be sized, repaired, or modified to fit the patient. These procedures are done on a back table in the operating room before transplantation can begin.

Bartholin's gland. Mucous-producing gland found in the vestibular bulbs on either side of the vaginal orifice and connected to the mucosal membrane at the opening by a duct.

Bartholin's gland abscess. Pocket of pus and surrounding cellulitis caused by infection of the Bartholin's gland and causing localized swelling and pain in the posterior labia majora that may extend into the lower vagina.

Berman locator. Small, sensitive tool used to detect the location of a metallic foreign body in the eye.

bifurcated. Having two branches or divisions, such as the left pulmonary veins that split off from the left atrium to carry oxygenated blood away from the heart.

biopsy. Tissue or fluid removed for diagnostic purposes through analysis of the cells in the biopsy material.

Blalock-Hanlon procedure. Excision of a segment of the right atrium, creating an atrial septal defect.

Blalock-Taussig procedure. Anastomosis of the left subclavian artery to the left pulmonary artery or the right subclavian artery to the right pulmonary artery in order to shunt some of the blood flow from the systemic to the pulmonary circulation.

blepharorrhaphy. Suture of a portion or all of the opposing eyelids to shorten the palpebral fissure or close it entirely.

blue baby. Infant born with bluish discoloration due to cyanosis.

bone conduction. Transportation of sound through the bones of the skull to the inner ear.

bone mass measurement. Radiologic or radioisotopic procedure or other procedure approved by the FDA for identifying bone mass, detecting bone loss, or determining bone quality. The procedure includes a physician's interpretation of the results. Qualifying individuals must be an estrogen-deficient woman at clinical risk for osteoporosis with vertebral abnormalities.

Bristow procedure. Anterior capsulorrhaphy prevents chronic separation of the shoulder. In this procedure, the bone block is affixed to the anterior glenoid rim with a screw.

buccal mucosa. Tissue from the mucous membrane on the inside of the cheek.

Caldwell-Luc operation. Intraoral antrostomy approach into the maxillary sinus for the removal of tooth roots or tissue, or for packing the sinus to reduce zygomatic fractures by creating a window above the teeth in the canine fossa area.

cardiopulmonary bypass. Venous blood is diverted to a heart-lung machine, which mechanically pumps and oxygenates the blood temporarily so the heart can be bypassed while an open procedure on the heart or coronary arteries is performed. During bypass, the lungs are deflated and immobile.

cardioverter-defibrillator. Device that uses both low energy cardioversion or defibrillating shocks and antitachycardia pacing to treat ventricular tachycardia or ventricular fibrillation.

care plan oversight services. Physician's ongoing review and revision of a patient's care plan involving complex or multidisciplinary care modalities.

case management services. Physician case management is a process of involving direct patient care as well as coordinating and controlling access to the patient or initiating and/or supervising other necessary health care services.

cataract extraction. Most common surgical procedure performed on adults. Most ophthalmologists perform cataract surgery in an ambulatory surgical setting. Anterior chamber lenses are inserted in conjunction with intracapsular cataract extraction and posterior chamber lenses are inserted in conjunction with extracapsular cataract extraction. *NCD Reference: 10.1, 80.10.*

certified nurse midwife. Registered nurse who has successfully completed a program of study and clinical experience or has been certified by a recognized organization for the care of pregnant or delivering patients.

cervical cap. Contraceptive device similar in form and function to the diaphragm but that can be left in place for 48 hours.

choanal atresia. Congenital, membranous, or bony closure of one or both posterior nostrils due to failure of the embryonic bucconasal membrane to rupture and open up the nasal passageway.

cholecystectomy. Surgical removal of the gallbladder and its contents. Cholecystectomy may be performed by an open incision into the abdominal cavity or laparoscopically via instruments inserted through small incisions into the peritoneum for video-controlled imaging. *NCD Reference: 100.13.*

chorionic villus sampling. Aspiration of a placental sample through a catheter, under ultrasonic guidance. The specialized needle is placed transvaginally through the cervix or transabdominally into the uterine cavity.

chronic pain management services. Distinct services frequently performed by anesthesiologists who have additional training in pain management procedures. Pain management services include initial and subsequent evaluation and management (E/M) services, trigger point injections, spine and spinal cord injections, and nerve blocks.

cineplastic amputation. Amputation in which muscles and tendons of the remaining portion of the extremity are arranged so that they may be utilized for motor functions. Following this type of amputation, a specially constructed prosthetic device allows the individual to execute more complex movements because the muscles and tendons are able to communicate independent movements to the device.

circadian. Relating to a cyclic, 24-hour period.

clinical social worker. Individual who possesses a master's or doctor's degree in social work and, after obtaining the degree, has performed at least two years of supervised clinical social work. A clinical social worker must be licensed by the state or, in the case of states without licensure, must completed at least two years or 3,000 hours of post-master's degree supervised clinical social work practice under the supervision of a master's level social worker.

CO2 laser. Carbon dioxide laser that emits an invisible beam and vaporizes water-rich tissue. The vapor is suctioned from the site.

colostomy. Artificial surgical opening anywhere along the length of the colon to the skin surface for the diversion of feces.

commissurotomy. Surgical division or disruption of any two parts that are joined to form a commissure in order to increase the opening. The procedure most often refers to opening the adherent leaflet bands of fibrous tissue in a stenosed mitral valve.

community mental health center. Facility providing outpatient mental health day treatment, assessments, and education as appropriate to community members.

computerized corneal topography. Digital imaging and analysis by computer of the shape of the corneal.

conjunctivodacryocystostomy. Surgical connection of the lacrimal sac directly to the conjunctival sac.

conjunctivorhinostomy. Correction of an obstruction of the lacrimal canal achieved by suturing the posterior flaps and removing any lacrimal obstruction, preserving the conjunctiva.

consultation. Advice or an opinion regarding diagnosis and treatment of a patient rendered by a medical professional at the request of the primary care provider.

core needle biopsy. Large-bore biopsy needle inserted into a mass and a core of tissue is removed for diagnostic study.

corpectomy. Removal of the body of a bone, such as a vertebra.

costochondral. Pertaining to the ribs and the scapula.

covered osteoporosis drug. Injectable drug approved for treating post-menopausal osteoporosis provided to an individual that has suffered a bone fracture related to post-menopausal osteoporosis.

craniosynostosis. Congenital condition in which one or more of the cranial sutures fuse prematurely, creating a deformed or aberrant head shape.

craterization. Excision of a portion of bone creating a crater-like depression to facilitate drainage from infected areas of bone.

cricoid. Circular cartilage around the trachea.

cryolathe. Tool used for reshaping a button of corneal tissue.

cryosurgery. Application of intense cold, usually produced using liquid nitrogen, to locally freeze diseased or unwanted tissue and induce tissue necrosis without causing harm to adjacent tissue.

cutdown. Small, incised opening in the skin to expose a blood vessel, especially over a vein (venous cutdown) to allow venipuncture and permit a needle or cannula to be inserted for the withdrawal of blood or administration of fluids.

cytogenetic studies. Procedures in CPT that are related to the branch of genetics that studies cellular (cyto) structure and function as it relates to heredity (genetics). White blood cells, specifically T-lymphocytes, are the most commonly used specimen for chromosome analysis. *NCD Reference: 190.3.*

dacryocystotome. Instrument used for incising the lacrimal duct strictures.

debride. To remove all foreign objects and devitalized or infected tissue from a burn or wound to prevent infection and promote healing.

dermis graft. Skin graft that has been separated from the epidermal tissue and the underlying subcutaneous fat, used primarily as a substitute for fascia grafts in plastic surgery.

desensitization. 1) Administration of extracts of allergens periodically to build immunity in the patient. 2) Application of medication to decrease the symptoms, usually pain, associated with a dental condition or disease.

destruction. Ablation or eradication of a structure or tissue.

diabetes outpatient self-management training services. Educational and training services furnished by a certified provider in an outpatient setting. The physician managing the individual's diabetic condition must certify that the services are needed under a comprehensive plan of care and provide the patient with the skills and knowledge necessary for therapeutic program compliance (including skills related to the self-administration of injectable drugs). The provider must meet applicable standards established by the National Diabetes Advisory or be recognized by an organization that represents individuals with diabetes as meeting standards for furnishing the services. *NCD Reference: 40.1.*

diagnostic procedures. Procedure performed on a patient to obtain information to assess the medical condition of the patient or to identify a disease and to determine the nature and severity of an illness or injury.

diaphragm. 1) Muscular wall separating the thorax and its structures from the abdomen. 2) Flexible disk inserted into the vagina and against the cervix as a method of birth control.

diaphysectomy. Surgical removal of a portion of the shaft of a long bone, often done to facilitate drainage from infected bone.

diathermy. Applying heat to body tissues by various methods for therapeutic treatment or surgical purposes to coagulate and seal tissue. *NCD References: 150.5, 240.3.*

dilation. Artificial increase in the diameter of an opening or lumen made by medication or by instrumentation.

dissect. Cut apart or separate tissue for surgical purposes or for visual or microscopic study.

dorsal. Pertaining to the back or posterior aspect.

drugs and biologicals. Drugs and biologicals included - or approved for inclusion - in the United States Pharmacopocia, the National Formulary, the United States Homeopathic Pharmacopoeia, in New Drugs or Accepted Dental Remedies, or approved by the pharmacy and drug therapeutics committee of the medical staff of the hospital. Also included are medically accepted and FDA approved drugs used in an anticancer chemotherapeutic regimen. The carrier determines medical acceptance based on supportive clinical evidence.

Dual-lead device. Implantable cardiac device (pacemaker or implantable cardioverter-defibrillator [ICD]) in which pacing and sensing components are placed in only two chambers of the heart.

DuToit staple capsulorrhaphy. Reattachment of the capsule of the shoulder and glenoid labrum to the glenoid lip using staples to anchor the avulsed capsule and glenoid labrum.

DXA. Dual energy x-ray absorptiometry. Radiological technique for bone density measurement using a two-dimensional projection system in which two x-ray beams with different levels of energy are pulsed alternately and the results are given in two scores, reported as standard deviations from peak bone mass density.

ECMO. Extracorporeal membrane oxygenation.

ectropion. Drooping of the lower eyelid away from the eye or outward turning or eversion of the edge of the eyelid, exposing the palpebral conjunctiva and causing irritation.

Eden-Hybinette procedure. Anterior shoulder repair using an anterior bone block to augment the bony anterior glenoid lip.

EDTA. Drug used to inhibit damage to the cornea by collagenase. EDTA is especially effective in alkali burns as it neutralizes soluable alkali, including lye.

effusion. Escape of fluid from within a body cavity.

Electrocardiographic rhythm derived. Analysis of data obtained from readings of the heart's electrical activation, to include heart rate and rhythm, variability of heart rate, ST analysis, and T-wave alternans. Other data may also be assessed when warranted.

electrocautery. Division or cutting of tissue using high-frequency electrical current to produce heat, which destroys cells.

emergency. Serious medical condition or symptom (including severe pain) resulting from injury, sickness, or mental illness that arises suddenly and requires immediate care and treatment, generally received within 24 hours of onset, to avoid jeopardy to the life, limb, or health of a covered person.

empyema. Accumulation of pus within the respiratory, or pleural, cavity.

endarterectomy. Removal of the thickened, endothelial lining of a diseased or damaged artery.

entropion. Inversion of the eyelid, turning the edge in toward the eyeball and causing irritation from contact of the lashes with the surface of the eye.

enucleation. Removal of a growth or organ cleanly so as to extract it in one piece.

epiphysiodesis. Surgical fusion of an epiphysis performed to prematurely stop further bone growth.

escharotomy. Surgical incision into the scab or crust resulting from a severe burn in order to relieve constriction and allow blood flow to the distal unburned tissue.

established patient. Patient who has received professional services in a face-to-face setting within the last three years from the same physician or another physician of the same specialty who belongs to the same group practice.

evacuation. Removal or purging of waste material.

evaluation and management codes. Assessment and management of a patient's health care using CPT codes 99201-99499.

evaluation and management service components. Key components of history, examination, and medical decision making that are key to selecting the correct E/M codes. Other non-key components include counseling, coordination of care, nature of presenting problem, and time.

exenteration. Surgical removal of the entire contents of a body cavity, such as the pelvis or orbit.

extended care services. Items and services provided to an inpatient of a skilled nursing facility, including nursing care, physical or occupational therapy, speech pathology, drugs and supplies, and medical social services.

external electrical capacitor device. External electrical stimulation device designed to promote bone healing. This device may also promote neural regeneration, revascularization, epiphyseal growth, and ligament maturation.

external pulsating electromagnetic field. External stimulation device designed to promote bone healing. This device may also promote neural regeneration, revascularization, epiphyseal growth, and ligament maturation.

extracorporeal. Located or taking place outside the body.

Eyre-Brook capsulorrhaphy. Reattachment of the capsule of the shoulder and glenoid labrum to the glenoid lip.

fascia. Fibrous sheet or band of tissue that envelops organs, muscles, and groupings of muscles.

fasciectomy. Excision of fascia or strips of fascial tissue.

fasciotomy. Incision or transection of fascial tissue.

fat graft. Graft composed of fatty tissue completely freed from surrounding tissue that is used primarily to fill in depressions.

fistulization. Creation of a communication between two structures that were not previously connected.

fluoroscopy. Radiology technique that allows visual examination of part of the body or a function of an organ using a device that projects an x-ray image on a fluorescent screen.

focal length. Distance between the object in focus and the lens.

free flap. Tissue that is completely detached from the donor site and transplanted to the recipient site, receiving its blood supply from capillary ingrowth at the recipient site.

free microvascular flap. Tissue that is completely detached from the donor site following careful dissection and preservation of the blood vessels, then attached to the recipient site with the transferred blood vessels anastomosed to the vessels in the recipient bed.

fulguration. Destruction of living tissue by using sparks from a high-frequency electric current.

gas tamponade. Absorbable gas may be injected to force the retina against the choroid. Common gases include room air, short-acting sulfahexafluoride, intermediate-acting perfluoroethane, or long-acting perfluorooctane.

hemilaminectomy. Excision of a portion of the vertebral lamina.

hemodialysis. Cleansing of wastes and contaminating elements from the blood by virtue of different diffusion rates through a semipermeable membrane, which separates blood from a filtration solution that diffuses other elements out of the blood.

hemoperitoneum. Effusion of blood into the peritoneal cavity, the space between the continuous membrane lining the abdominopelvic walls and encasing the visceral organs.

heterologous transplant. Tissue from another species, such as porcine from a pig, that is grafted into a human recipient.

heterotopic transplant. Tissue transplanted from a different anatomical site for usage as is natural for that tissue, for example, buccal mucosa to a conjunctival site.

home health services. Services furnished to patients in their homes under the care of physicians. These services include part-time or intermittent skilled nursing care, physical therapy, medical social services, medical supplies and some rehabilitation equipment. Home health supplies and services must be prescribed by a physician, and the beneficiary must be confined at home in order for Medicare to pay the benefits in full.

homograft. Graft from one individual to another of the same species.

hospice care. Items and services provided to a terminally ill individual by a hospice program under a written plan established and periodically reviewed by the individual's attending physician and by the medical director: Nursing care provided by or under the supervision of a registered professional nurse; Physical or occupational therapy or speech-language pathology services; Medical social services under the direction of a physician; Services of a home health aide who has successfully completed a training program; Medical supplies (including drugs and biologicals) and the use of medical appliances; Physicians' services; Short-term inpatient care (including both respite care and procedures necessary for pain control and acute and chronic symptom management) in an inpatient facility on an intermittent basis and not consecutively over longer than five days; Counseling (including dietary counseling) with respect to care of the terminally ill individual and adjustment to his death; Any item or service which is specified in the plan and for which payment may be made.

hospital. Institution that provides, under the supervision of physicians, diagnostic, therapeutic, and rehabilitation services for medical diagnosis, treatment, and care of patients. Hospitals receiving federal funds must maintain clinical records on all patients, provide 24-hour nursing services, and have a discharge planning process in place. The term "hospital" also includes religious nonmedical health care institutions and facilities of 50 beds or less located in rural areas.

ICD. Implantable cardioverter defibrillator.

ICM. Implantable cardiovascular monitor.

ileostomy. Artificial surgical opening that brings the end of the ileum out through the abdominal wall to the skin surface for the diversion of feces through a stoma.

ILR. Implantable loop recorder.

implantable cardiovascular monitor (ICM). Implantable electronic device that stores cardiovascular physiologic data such as intracardiac pressure waveforms collected from internal sensors or data such as weight and blood pressure collected from external sensors. The information stored in these devices is used as an aid in managing patients with heart failure and other cardiac conditions that are nonrhythm related. The data may be transmitted via local telemetry or remotely to a surveillance technician or an internet-based file server.

implantable cardioverter-defibrillator (ICD). Implantable electronic cardiac device used to control rhythm abnormalities such as tachycardia, fibrillation, or bradycardia by producing high- or low-energy stimulation and pacemaker functions. It may also have the capability to provide the functions of an implantable loop recorder or implantable cardiovascular monitor.

implantable loop recorder (ILR). Implantable electronic cardiac device that constantly monitors and records electrocardiographic rhythm. It may be triggered by the patient when a symptomatic episode occurs or activated automatically by rapid or slow heart rates. This may be the sole purpose of the device or it may be a component of another cardiac device such as a pacemaker or implantable cardioverter-defibrillator. The data can be transmitted via local telemetry or remotely to a surveillance technician or an internet-based file server.

infundibulectomy. Excision of the anterosuperior portion of the right ventricle of the heart.

internal direct current stimulator. Electrostimulation device placed directly into the surgical site designed to promote bone regeneration by encouraging cellular healing response in bone and ligaments.

interrogation device evaluation (in person). Face-to-face assessment of an implantable cardiac device (pacemaker, cardioverter-defibrillator, cardiovascular monitor, or loop recorder) in which collected data about the patient's heart rate and rhythm, battery and pulse generator function, and any leads or sensors present, is retrieved and evaluated. Determinations regarding device programming and appropriate treatment settings are made based on the findings. CPT provides specific required components for evaluation of the various types of devices.

intramedullary implants. Nail, rod, or pin placed into the intramedullary canal at the fracture site. Intramedullary implants not only provide a method of aligning the fracture, they also act as a splint and may reduce fracture pain. Implants may be rigid or flexible. Rigid implants are preferred for prophylactic treatment of diseased bone, while flexible implants are preferred for traumatic injuries.

intravenous. Within a vein or veins.

irrigation. To wash out or cleanse a body cavity, wound, or tissue with water or other fluid.

krypton laser. Laser light energy that uses ionized krypton by electric current as the active source, has a radiation beam between the visible yellow-red spectrum, and is effective in photocoagulation of retinal bleeding, macular lesions, and vessel aberrations of the choroid.

lacrimal punctum. Opening of the lacrimal papilla of the eyelid through which tears flow to the canaliculi to the lacrimal sac.

lacrimotome. Knife for cutting the lacrimal sac or duct.

lacrimotomy. Incision of the lacrimal sac or duct.

larynx. Musculocartilaginous structure between the trachea and the pharynx that functions as the valve preventing food and other particles from entering the respiratory tract, as well as the voice mechanism. Also called the voicebox, the larynx is composed of three single cartilages: cricoid, epiglottis, and thyroid; and three paired cartilages: arytenoid, corniculate, and cuneiform.

laser surgery. Use of concentrated, sharply defined light beams to cut, cauterize, coagulate, seal, or vaporize tissue. The color and wavelength of the laser light is produced by its active medium, such as argon, CO2, potassium titanyl phosphate (KTP), Krypton, and Nd:YAG, which determines which type of tissues it can best treat. *NCD Reference: 140.5.*

LEEP. Loop electrode excision procedure. Biopsy specimen or cone shaped wedge of cervical tissue is removed using a hot cautery wire loop with an electrical current running through it.

levonorgestrel. Drug inhibiting ovulation and preventing sperm from penetrating cervical mucus. It is delivered subcutaneously in polysiloxone capsules. The capsules can be effective for up to five years, and provide a cumulative pregnancy rate of less than 2 percent. The capsules are not biodegradable, and therefore must be removed. Removal is more difficult than insertion of levonorgestrel capsules because fibrosis develops around the capsules. Normal hormonal activity and a return to fertility begins immediately upon removal.

ligation. Tying off a blood vessel or duct with a suture or a soft, thin wire.

lysis. Destruction, breakdown, dissolution, or decomposition of cells or substances by a specific catalyzing agent.

Magnuson-Stack procedure. Treatment for recurrent anterior dislocation of the shoulder that involves tightening and realigning the subscapularis tendon.

marsupialization. Creation of a pouch in surgical treatment of a cyst in which one wall is resected and the remaining cut edges are sutured to adjacent tissue creating an open pouch of the previously enclosed cyst.

mastectomy. Surgical removal of one or both breasts.

McDonald procedure. Polyester tape is placed around the cervix with a running stitch to assist in the prevention of pre-term delivery. Tape is removed at term for vaginal delivery.

mitral valve. Valve with two cusps that is between the left atrium and left ventricle of the heart.

Mohs micrographic surgery. Special technique used to treat complex or ill-defined skin cancer and requires a single physician to provide two distinct services. The first service is surgical and involves the destruction of the lesion by a combination of chemosurgery and excision. The second service is that of a pathologist and includes mapping, color coding of specimens, microscopic examination of specimens, and complete histopathologic preparation.

multiple-lead device. Implantable cardiac device (pacemaker or implantable cardioverter-defibrillator [ICD]) in which pacing and sensing components are placed in at least three chambers of the heart.

Mustard procedure. Corrective measure for transposition of great vessels involves an intra-atrial baffle made of pericardial tissue or synthetic material. The baffle is secured between pulmonary veins and mitral valve and between mitral and tricuspid valves. The baffle directs systemic venous flow into the left ventricle and lungs and pulmonary venous flow into the right ventricle and aorta.

myasthenia gravis. Autoimmune neuromuscular disorder caused by antibodies to the acetylcholine receptors at the neuromuscular junction, interfering with proper binding of the neurotransmitter from the neuron to the target muscle, causing muscle weakness, fatigue, and exhaustion, without pain or atrophy.

myotomy. Surgical cutting of a muscle to gain access to underlying tissues or for therapeutic reasons.

nasal polyp. Fleshy outgrowth projecting from the mucous membrane of the nose or nasal sinus cavity that may obstruct ventilation or affect the sense of smell.

nasal sinus. Air-filled cavities in the cranial bones lined with mucous membrane and continuous with the nasal cavity, draining fluids through the nose.

nasopharynx. Membranous passage above the level of the soft palate.

Nd:YAG laser. Laser light energy that uses an yttrium, aluminum, and garnet crystal doped with neodymium ions as the active source, has a radiation beam nearing the infrared spectrum, and is effective in photocoagulation, photoablation, cataract extraction, and lysis of vitreous strands.

neurectomy. Excision of all or a portion of a nerve.

new patient. Patient who, for the first time in three years, is receiving face-to-face care from the provider or another physician of the same specialty who belongs to the same group practice.

Nissen fundoplasty. Surgical repair technique that involves the fundus of the stomach being wrapped around the lower end of the esophagus to treat reflux esophagitis.

nonabsorbable sutures. Strands of natural or synthetic material that resist absorption into living tissue and are removed once healing is under way. Nonabsorbable sutures are commonly used to close skin wounds and repair tendons or collagenous tissue.

oophorectomy. Surgical removal of all or part of one or both ovaries, either as open procedure or laparoscopically. Menstruation and childbearing ability continues when one ovary is removed.

pacemaker. Implantable cardiac device that controls the heart's rhythm and maintains regular beats by artificial electric discharges. This device consists of the pulse generator with a battery and the electrodes, or leads, which are placed in single or dual chambers of the heart, usually transvenously.

paratenon graft. Graft composed of the fatty tissue found between a tendon and its sheath.

pedicle flap. Full-thickness skin and subcutaneous tissue for grafting that remains partially attached to the donor site by a pedicle or stem in which the blood vessels supplying the flap remain intact.

percutaneous intradiscal electrothermal annuloplasty. Procedure corrects tears in the vertebral annulus by applying heat to the collagen disc walls percutaneously through a catheter. The heat contracts and thickens the wall, which may contract and close any annular tears.

percutaneous skeletal fixation. Treatment that is neither open nor closed. In this procedure, the injury site is not directly visualized. Instead, fixation devices (pins, screws) are placed to stabilize the dislocation using x-ray guidance.

pericardium. Thin and slippery case in which the heart lies that is lined with fluid so that the heart is free to pulse and move as it beats.

photocoagulation. Application of an intense laser beam of light to disrupt tissue and condense protein material to a residual mass, used especially for treating ocular conditions.

physical status modifiers. Alphanumeric modifier used to identify the patient's health status as it affects the work related to providing the anesthesia service.

physical therapy modality. Therapeutic agent or regimen applied or used to provide appropriate treatment of the musculoskeletal system.

pleurodesis. Injection of a sclerosing agent into the pleural space for creating adhesions between the parietal and the visceral pleura to treat a collapsed lung caused by air trapped in the pleural cavity, or severe cases of pleural effusion.

plication. Surgical technique involving folding, tucking, or pleating to reduce the size of a hollow structure or organ.

Potts-Smith-Gibson procedure. A side-to-side anastomosis of the aorta and left pulmonary artery creating a shunt that enlarges as the child grows.

profunda. Denotes a part of a structure that is deeper from the surface of the body than the rest of the structure.

prolonged physician services. Extended pre- or post-service care provided to a patient whose condition requires services beyond the usual.

provider of services. Institution, individual, or organization that provides health care.

psychiatric hospital. Specialized institution that provides, under the supervision of physicians, services for the diagnosis and treatment of mentally ill persons.

pulmonary artery banding. Surgical constriction of the pulmonary artery to prevent irreversible pulmonary vascular obstructive changes and overflow into the left ventricle.

Putti-Platt procedure. Realignment of the subscapularis tendon to treat recurrent anterior dislocation, thereby partially eliminating external rotation. The anterior capsule is also tightened and reinforced.

pyloroplasty. Enlargement and reconstruction of the lower portion of the stomach opening into the duodenum performed after vagotomy to speed gastric emptying and treat duodenal ulcers.

radioactive substances. Materials used in the diagnosis and treatment of disease that emit high-speed particles and energy-containing rays.

radiology services. Services that include diagnostic and therapeutic radiology, nuclear medicine, CT scan procedures, magnetic resonance imaging services, ultrasound, and other imaging procedures.

Rashkind procedure. Transvenous balloon atrial septectomy or septostomy performed by cardiac catheterization. A balloon catheter is inserted into the heart either to create or enlarge an opening in the interatrial septal wall.

repair. Surgical closure of a wound. The wound may be a result of injury/trauma or it may be a surgically created defect. Repairs are divided into three categories: simple, intermediate, and complex. Simple repair is performed when the wound is superficial and only requires simple, one layer, primary suturing. Intermediate repair is performed for wounds and lacerations in which one or more of the deeper layers of subcutaneous tissue and non-muscle fascia are repaired in addition to the skin and subcutaneous tissue. Complex repair includes repair of wounds requiring more than layered closure.

ribbons. In oncology, small plastic tubes containing radioactive sources for interstitial placement that may be cut into specific lengths tailored to the size of the area receiving ionizing radiation treatment.

rural health clinic. Clinic in an area where there is a shortage of health services staffed by a nurse practitioner, physician assistant, or certified nurse midwife under physician direction that provides routine diagnostic services, including clinical laboratory services, drugs, and biologicals and that has prompt access to additional diagnostic services from facilities meeting federal requirements.

saucerization. Creation of a shallow, saucer-like depression in the bone to facilitate drainage of infected areas.

Schiotz tonometer. Instrument that measures intraocular pressure by recording the depth of an indentation on the cornea by a plunger of known weight.

screening mammography. Radiologic images taken of the female breast for the purpose of early detection of breast cancer.

screening pap smear. Diagnostic laboratory test consisting of a routine exfoliative cytology test (Papanicolaou test) provided to a woman for the purpose of early detection of cervical or vaginal cancer. The exam includes a clinical breast examination and a physician's interpretation of the results.

seeds. Small (1 mm or less) sources of radioactive material that are permanently placed directly into tumors.

senning procedure. Flaps of intra-atrial septum and right atrial wall are used to create two interatrial channels to divert the systemic and pulmonary venous circulation.

sensitivity tests. Number of methods of applying selective suspected allergens to the skin or mucous.

sensorineural conduction. Transportation of sound from the cochlea to the acoustic nerve and central auditory pathway to the brain.

separate procedures. Services commonly carried out as a fundamental part of a total service, and as such usually do not warrant a separate identification. They are noted in the CPT book with the parenthetical phrase (separate procedure) at the end of the description, and are payable only when they are performed alone.

Shirodkar procedure. Treatment of an incompetent cervical os by placing nonabsorbent suture material in purse-string sutures as a cerclage to support the cervix.

single-lead device. Implantable cardiac device (pacemaker or implantable cardioverter-defibrillator [ICD]) in which pacing and sensing components are placed in only one chamber of the heart.

sinus of Valsalva. Any of three sinuses corresponding to the individual cusps of the aortic valve, located in the most proximal part of the aorta just above the cusps. These structures are contained within the pericardium and appear as distinct but subtle outpouchings or dilations of the aortic wall between each of the semilunar cusps of the valve.

speculoscopy. Viewing the cervix utilizing a magnifier and a special wavelength of light, allowing detection of abnormalities that may not be discovered on a routine Pap smear.

sphincteroplasty. Surgical repair done to correct, augment, or improve the muscular function of a sphincter, such as the anus or intestines.

spirometry. Measurement of the lungs' breathing capacity.

stent. Tube to provide support in a body cavity or lumen.

stereotactic radiosurgery. Delivery of externally-generated ionizing radiation to specific targets for destruction or inactivation. Most often utilized in the treatment of brain or spinal tumors, high-resolution stereotactic imaging is used to identify the target and then deliver the treatment. Computer-assisted planning may also be employed. Simple and complex cranial lesions and spinal lesions are typically treated in a single planning and treatment session, although a maximum of five sessions may be required. No incision is made for stereotactic radiosurgery procedures.

strabismus. Misalignment of the eyes due to an imbalance in extraocular muscles.

surgical package. Normal, uncomplicated performance of specific surgical services, with the assumption that, on average, all surgical procedures of a given type are similar with respect to skill level, duration, and length of normal follow-up care.

sympathectomy. Surgical interruption or transection of a sympathetic nervous system pathway.

tarsocheiloplasty. Plastic operation upon the edge of the eyelid for the treatment of trichiasis.

tarsorrhaphy. Suture of a portion or all of the opposing eyelids together for the purpose of shortening the palpebral fissure or closing it entirely.

tendon allograft. Allografts are tissues obtained from another individual of the same species. Tendon allografts are usually obtained from cadavers and frozen or freeze dried for later use in soft tissue repairs where the physician elects not to obtain an autogenous graft (a graft obtained from the individual on whom the surgery is being performed).

tendon suture material. Tendons are composed of fibrous tissue consisting primarily of collagen and containing few cells or blood vessels. This tissue heals more slowly than tissues with more vascularization. Because of this, tendons are usually repaired with nonabsorbable suture material. Examples include surgical silk, surgical cotton, linen, stainless steel, surgical nylon, polyester fiber, polybutester (Novafil), polyethylene (Dermalene), and polypropylene (Prolene, Surilene).

tenon's capsule. Connective tissue that forms the capsule enclosing the posterior eyeball, extending from the conjunctival fornix and continuous with the muscular fascia of the eye.

tensilon. Edrophonium chloride. Agent used for evaluation and treatment of myasthenia gravis.

terminally ill. Individual whose medical prognosis for life expectancy is six months or less.

tetralogy of Fallot. Specific combination of congenital cardiac defects: obstruction of the right ventricular outflow tract with pulmonary stenosis, interventricular septal defect, malposition of the aorta, overriding the interventricular septum and receiving blood from both the venous and arterial systems, and enlargement of the right ventricle.

therapeutic services. Services performed for treatment of a specific diagnosis. These services include performance of the procedure, various incidental elements, and normal, related follow-up care.

thoracentesis. Surgical puncture of the chest cavity with a specialized needle or hollow tubing to aspirate fluid from within the pleural space for diagnostic or therapeutic reasons.

thoracic lymphadenectomy. Procedure to cut out the lymph nodes near the lungs, around the heart, and behind the trachea.

thoracostomy. Creation of an opening in the chest wall for drainage.

thyroglossal duct. Embryonic duct at the front of the neck, which becomes the pyramidal lobe of the thyroid gland with obliteration of the remaining duct, but may form a cyst or sinus in adulthood if it persists.

total disc arthroplasty with artificial disc. Removal of an intravertebral disc and its replacement with an implant. The implant is an artificial disc consisting of two metal plates with a weight-bearing surface of polyethylene between the plates. The plates are anchored to the vertebral immediately above and below the affected disc.

total shoulder replacement. Prosthetic replacement of the entire shoulder joint, including the humeral head and the glenoid fossa.

trabeculae carneae cordis. Bands of muscular tissue that line the walls of the ventricles in the heart.

tracheostomy. Formation of a tracheal opening on the neck surface with tube insertion to allow for respiration in cases of obstruction or decreased patency. A tracheostomy may be planned or performed on an emergency basis for temporary or long-term use.

tracheotomy. Formation of a tracheal opening on the neck surface with tube insertion to allow for respiration in cases of obstruction or decreased patency. A tracheotomy may be planned or performed on an emergency basis for temporary or long-term use.

transcranial magnetic stimulation. Application of electromagnetic energy to the brain through a coil placed on the scalp. The procedure stimulates cortical neurons and is intended to activate and normalize their processes.

trephine. 1) Specialized round saw for cutting circular holes in bone, especially the skull. 2) Instrument that removes small disc-shaped buttons of corneal tissue for transplanting.

tricuspid atresia. Congenital absence of the valve that may occur with other defects, such as atrial septal defect, pulmonary atresia, and transposition of great vessels.

turbinates. Scroll or shell-shaped elevations from the wall of the nasal cavity, the inferior turbinate being a separate bone, while the superior and middle turbinates are of the ethmoid bone.

tympanic membrane. Thin, sensitive membrane across the entrance to the middle ear that vibrates in response to sound waves, allowing the waves to be transmitted via the ossicular chain to the internal ear.

vagotomy. Division of the vagus nerves, interrupting impulses resulting in lower gastric acid production and hastening gastric emptying.

vasectomy. Surgical procedure involving the removal of all or part of the vas deferens, usually performed for sterilization or in conjunction with a prostatectomy.

ventricular septal defect. Congenital cardiac anomaly resulting in a continual opening in the septum between the ventricles that, in severe cases, causes oxygenated blood to flow back into the lungs, resulting in pulmonary hypertension.

vertebral interspace. Non-bony space between two adjacent vertebral bodies that contains the cushioning intervertebral disk.

volar. Palm of the hand (palmar) or sole of the foot (plantar).

Waterston procedure. Type of aortopulmonary shunting done to increase pulmonary blood flow where the ascending aorta is anastomosed to the right pulmonary artery.

Wharton's ducts. Salivary ducts below the mandible.

wick catheter. Device used to monitor interstitial fluid pressure, and sometimes used intraoperatively during fasciotomy procedures to evaluate the effectiveness of the decompression.

xenograft. Tissue that is nonhuman and harvested from one species and grafted to another. Pigskin is the most common xenograft for human skin and is applied to a wound as a temporary closure until a permanent option is performed.

z-plasty. Plastic surgery technique used primarily to release tension or elongate contracted scar tissue in which a Z-shaped incision is made with the middle line of the Z crossing the area of greatest tension. The triangular flaps are then rotated so that they cross the incision line in the opposite direction, creating a reversed Z.

APPENDIX G — LISTING OF SENSORY, MOTOR, AND MIXED NERVES

This summary assigns each sensory, motor, and mixed nerve with its appropriate nerve conduction study code in order to enhance accurate reporting of codes 95900, 95903, and 95904. Each nerve constitutes one unit of service.

Motor Nerves Assigned to Codes 95900 and 95903.

I. Upper extremity, cervical plexus, and brachial plexus motor nerves
    A. Axillary motor nerve to the deltoid
    B. Long thoracic motor nerve to the serratus anterior
    C. Median nerve
        1. Median motor nerve to the abductor pollicis brevis
        2. Median motor nerve, anterior interosseous branch, to the flexor pollicis longus
        3. Median motor nerve, anterior interosseous branch, to the pronator quadratus
        4. Median motor nerve to the first lumbrical
        5. Median motor nerve to the second lumbrical
    D. Musculocutaneous motor nerve to the biceps brachii
    E. Radial nerve
        1. Radial motor nerve to the extensor carpi ulnaris
        2. Radial motor nerve to the extensor digitorum communis
        3. Radial motor nerve to the extensor indicis proprius
        4. Radial motor nerve to the brachioradialis
    F. Suprascapular nerve
        1. Suprascapular motor nerve to the supraspinatus
        2. Suprascapular motor nerve to the infraspinatus
    G. Thoracodorsal motor nerve to the latissimus dorsi
    H. Ulnar nerve
        1. Ulnar motor nerve to the abductor digiti minimi
        2. Ulnar motor nerve to the palmar interosseous
        3. Ulnar motor nerve to the first dorsal interosseous
        4. Ulnar motor nerve to the flexor carpi ulnaris
    I. Other
II. Lower extremity motor nerves
    A. Femoral motor nerve to the quadriceps
        1. Femoral motor nerve to the vastus medialis
        2. Femoral motor nerve to vastus lateralis
        3. Femoral motor nerve to vastus intermedialis
        4. Femoral motor nerve to rectus femoris
    B. Ilioinguinal motor nerve
    C. Peroneal (fibular) nerve
        1. Peroneal motor nerve to the extensor digitorum brevis
        2. Peroneal motor nerve to the peroneus brevis
        3. Peroneal motor nerve to the peroneus longus
        4. Peroneal motor nerve to the tibialis anterior
    D. Plantar motor nerve
    E. Sciatic nerve
    F. Tibial nerve
        1. Tibial motor nerve, inferior calcaneal branch, to the abductor digiti minimi
        2. Tibial motor nerve, medial plantar branch, to the abductor hallucis
        3. Tibial motor nerve, lateral plantar branch, to the flexor digiti minimi brevis

    G. Other
III. Cranial nerves and trunk
    A. Cranial nerve VII (facial motor nerve)
        1. Facial nerve to the frontalis
        2. Facial nerve to the nasalis
        3. Facial nerve to the orbicularis oculi
        4. Facial nerve to the orbicularis oris
    B. Cranial nerve XI (spinal accessory motor nerve)
    C. Cranial nerve XII (hypoglossal motor nerve)
    D. Intercostal motor nerve
    E. Phrenic motor nerve to the diaphragm
    F. Recurrent laryngeal nerve
    G. Other
IV. Nerve Roots
    A. Cervical nerve root stimulation
        1. Cervical level 5 (CT)
        2. Cervical level 6 (C6)
        3. Cervical level 7 (C7)
        4. Cervical level 8 (C8)
    B. Thoracic nerve root stimulation
        1. Thoracic level 1 (T1)
        2. Thoracic level 2 (T2)
        3. Thoracic level 3 (T3)
        4. Thoracic level 4 (T4)
        5. Thoracic level 5 (T5)
        6. Thoracic level 6 (T6)
        7. Thoracic level 7 (T7)
        8. Thoracic level 8 (T8)
        9. Thoracic level 9 (T9)
        10. Thoracic level 10 (T10)
        11. Thoracic level 11 (T11)
        12. Thoracic level 12 (T12)
    C. Lumbar nerve root stimulation
        1. Lumbar level 1 (L1)
        2. Lumbar level 2 (L2)
        3. Lumbar level 3 (L3)
        4. Lumbar level 4 (L4)
        5. Lumbar level 5 (L5)
    D. Sacral nerve root stimulation
        1. Sacral level 1 (S1)
        2. Sacral level 2 (S2)
        3. Sacral level 3 (S3)
        4. Sacral level 4 (S4)

SENSORY AND MIXED NERVES ASSIGNED TO CODE 95904

I. Upper extremity sensory and mixed nerves
    A. Lateral antebrachial cutaneous sensory nerve
    B. Medial antebrachial cutaneous sensory nerve
    C. Medial brachial cutaneous sensory nerve
    D. Median nerve
        1. Median sensory nerve to the first digit
        2. Median sensory nerve to the second digit
        3. Median sensory nerve to the third digit

4. Median sensory nerve to the fourth digit

5. Median palmar cutaneous sensory nerve

6. Median palmar mixed nerve

E. Posterior antebrachial cutaneous sensory nerve

F. Radial sensory nerve

   1. Radial sensory nerve to the base of the thumb

   2. Radial sensory nerve to digit 1

G. Ulnar nerve

   1. Ulnar dorsal cutaneous sensory nerve

   2. Ulnar sensory nerve to the fourth digit

   3. Ulnar sensory nerve to the fifth digit

   4. Ulnar palmar mixed nerve

H. Intercostal sensory nerve

I. Other

II. Lower extremity sensory and mixed nerves

A. Lateral femoral cutaneous sensory nerve

B. Medical calcaneal sensory nerve

C. Medial femoral cutaneous sensory nerve

D. Peroneal nerve

   1. Deep peroneal sensory nerve

   2. Superficial peroneal sensory nerve, medial dorsal cutaneous branch

   3. Superficial peroneal sensory nerve, intermediate dorsal cutaneous branch

E. Posterior femoral cutaneous sensory nerve

F. Saphenous nerve

   1. Saphenous sensory nerve (distal technique)

   2. Saphenous sensory nerve (proximal technique)

G. Sural nerve

   1. Sural sensory nerve, lateral dorsal cutaneous branch

   2. Sural sensory nerve

H. Tibial sensory nerve (digital nerve to toe 1)

I. Tibial sensory nerve (medial plantar nerve)

J. Tibial sensory nerve (lateral plantar nerve)

K. Other

III. Head and trunk sensory nerves

A. Dorsal nerve of the penis

B. Greater auricular nerve

C. Ophthalmic branch of the trigeminal nerve

D. Pudendal sensory nerve

E. Suprascapular sensory nerves

F. Other

The following table provides a reasonable maximum number of studies performed per diagnostic category necessary for a physician to arrive at a diagnosis in 90% of patients with that final diagnosis. The numbers in each column represent the number of studies recommended. The appropriate number of studies to be performed is based upon the physician's discretion.

		Type of Study/Maximum Number of Studies			
		Nerve Conduction Studies (95900, 95903, 95904)		Other EMG Studies (95934, 95936, 95937)	
Indication	Needle EMG (95860-95864, 95867-95870)	Motor NCS With and/or Without F wave	Sensory NCS	H-Reflex	Neuromuscular Junction Testing (Repetitive Stimulation)
Carpal Tunnel (Unilateral)	1	3	4	—	—
Carpal Tunnel (Bilateral)	2	4	6	—	—
Radiculopathy	2	3	2	2	—
Mononeuropathy	1	3	3	2	—
Polyneuropathy/Mononeuropathy Multiplex	3	4	4	2	—
Myopathy	2	2	2	—	2
Motor Neuronopathy (e.g., ALS)	4	4	2	—	2
Plexopathy	2	4	6	2	-
Neuromuscular Junction	2	2	2	—	3
Tarsal Tunnel Syndrome (Unilateral)	1	4	4	—	—
Tarsal Tunnel Syndrome (Bilateral)	2	5	6	—	—
Weakness, Fatigue, Cramps, or Twitching (Focal)	2	3	4	—	2
Weakness, Fatigue, Cramps, or Twitching (General)	4	4	4	—	2
Pain, Numbness, or Tingling (Unilateral)	1	3	4	2	—
Pain, Numbness, or Tingling (Bilateral)	2	4	6	2	—

APPENDIX H — VASCULAR FAMILIES

This table assumes that the starting point is catheterization of the aorta. This categorization would not be accurate, for instance, if a femoral or carotid artery were catheterized with the blood's flow.

First Order	Second Order Branch	Third Order Branch	Beyond Third Order Branches
Innominate	**Right Common Carotid**	**Right Internal Carotid**	Right Ophthalmic Right Posterior Communicating Right Middle Cerebral Right Anterior Cerebral
		Right External Carotid	Right Superior Thyroid Right Ascending Pharyngeal Right Facial Right Lingual Right Occipital Right Posterior Auricular Right Superficial Temporal Right Internal Maxillary Right Middle Meningeal
	Right Subclavian and	**Right Vertebral**	Basilar
		Right Internal Thoracic (Internal Mammary)	
		Right Thyrocervical Trunk	Right Inferior Thyroid Right Surascapular Right Transverse Cervical
		Right Costocervical Trunk	Right Highest Intercostal Right Deep Cervical
		Right Lateral Thoracic Right Thoracromial Right Humeral Circumflex (A/P)	
		Right Subcapular	Right Circumflex Scapular
		Right Brachial	
		Right Deep Brachial	Right Ulnar Right Radial Right Interosseous Right Deep Palmar Arch Right Superficial Palmar Arch Right Metacarpals and Digitals
Left Common Carotid	**Left Internal Carotid**	Left Ophthalmic Left Posterior Communicating Left Middle Cerebral Left Anterior Cerebral	
	Left External Carotid	Left Superior Thyroid Left Ascending Pharyngeal Left Facial Left Lingual Left Occipital Left Posterior Auricular Left Superficial Temporal	
		Left Internal Maxillary	Left Middle Meningeal

First Order	Second Order Branch	Third Order Branch	Beyond Third Order Branches

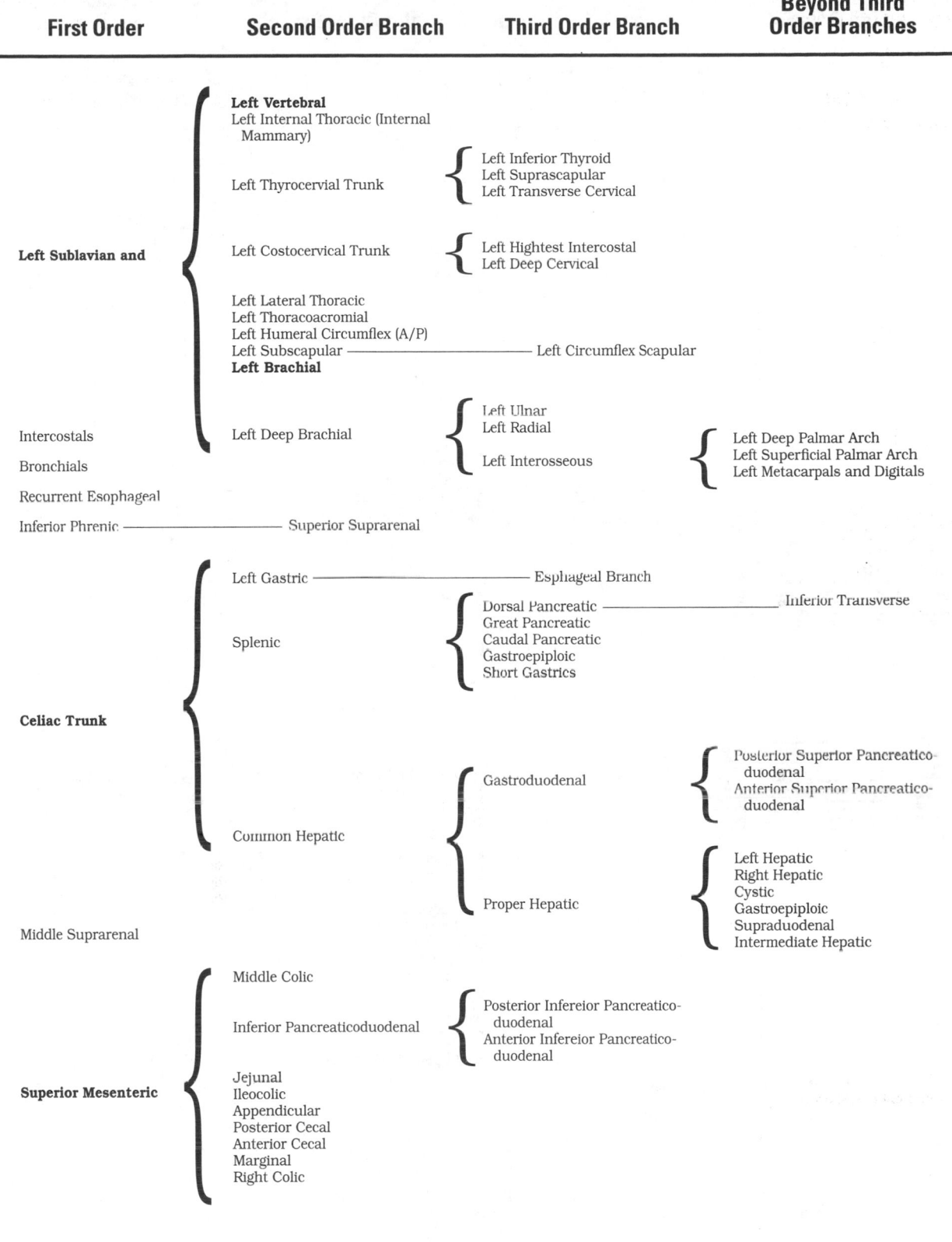

Left Vertebral
Left Internal Thoracic (Internal Mammary)

Left Thyrocervial Trunk
{ Left Inferior Thyroid
Left Suprascapular
Left Transverse Cervical

Left Sublavian and

Left Costocervical Trunk
{ Left Hightest Intercostal
Left Deep Cervical

Left Lateral Thoracic
Left Thoracoacromial
Left Humeral Circumflex (A/P)
Left Subscapular —————————— Left Circumflex Scapular
Left Brachial

Left Deep Brachial
{ Left Ulnar
Left Radial
Left Interosseous
{ Left Deep Palmar Arch
Left Superficial Palmar Arch
Left Metacarpals and Digitals

Intercostals

Bronchials

Recurrent Esophageal

Inferior Phrenic ———————— Superior Suprarenal

Left Gastric ———————————— Esphageal Branch

Splenic
{ Dorsal Pancreatic ———————— Inferior Transverse
Great Pancreatic
Caudal Pancreatic
Gastroepiploic
Short Gastrics

Celiac Trunk

Common Hepatic
Gastroduodenal
{ Posterior Superior Pancreatico-duodenal
Anterior Superior Pancreatico-duodenal

Proper Hepatic
{ Left Hepatic
Right Hepatic
Cystic
Gastroepiploic
Supraduodenal
Intermediate Hepatic

Middle Suprarenal

Middle Colic

Inferior Pancreaticoduodenal
{ Posterior Infereior Pancreatico-duodenal
Anterior Infereior Pancreatico-duodenal

Superior Mesenteric

Jejunal
Ileocolic
Appendicular
Posterior Cecal
Anterior Cecal
Marginal
Right Colic

Appendix H — Vascular Families

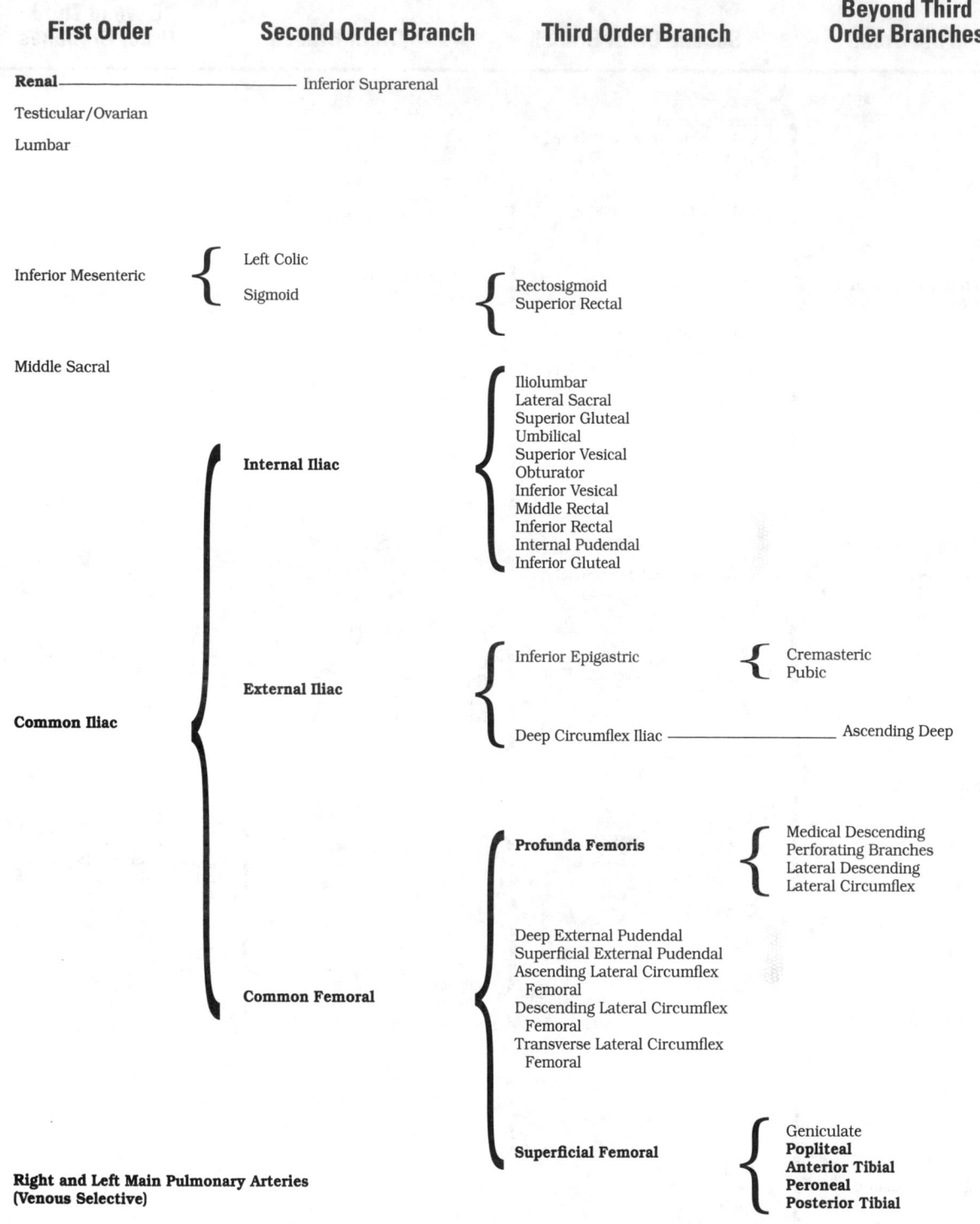

First Order	Second Order Branch	Third Order Branch	Beyond Third Order Branches
Renal ————————————	Inferior Suprarenal		
Testicular/Ovarian			
Lumbar			
Inferior Mesenteric	{ Left Colic Sigmoid	{ Rectosigmoid Superior Rectal	
Middle Sacral			
	Internal Iliac	{ Iliolumbar Lateral Sacral Superior Gluteal Umbilical Superior Vesical Obturator Inferior Vesical Middle Rectal Inferior Rectal Internal Pudendal Inferior Gluteal	
	External Iliac	{ Inferior Epigastric Deep Circumflex Iliac —————	{ Cremasteric Pubic Ascending Deep
Common Iliac			
	Common Femoral	**Profunda Femoris**	{ Medical Descending Perforating Branches Lateral Descending Lateral Circumflex

		Deep External Pudendal
		 Superficial External Pudendal
		 Ascending Lateral Circumflex
		  Femoral
		 Descending Lateral Circumflex
		  Femoral
		 Transverse Lateral Circumflex
		  Femoral	

		Superficial Femoral	{ Geniculate **Popliteal** **Anterior Tibial** **Peroneal** **Posterior Tibial**
Right and Left Main Pulmonary Arteries **(Venous Selective)**			

Reference: Kadir S. *Atlas of Normal and Variant Angiographic Anatomy.* Philadelphia, Pa: WB Saunders Co; 1991

APPENDIX I — PHYSICIAN QUALITY REPORTING INITIATIVE (PQRI)

Numerator	Associated Diagnostic Denominator	Associated Procedure Denominator	Associated Modifiers
0505F	585.6	90935, 90937, G0314, G0315, G0316, G0317, G0318, G0319	8P
0507F	585.6	90945, 90947, G0322, G0323, G0326, G0327	8P
0509F	307.6, 625.6, 788.30-788.39	99201-99205, 99212-99215, 99241 99245	8P
0513F	585.4, 585.5	G8476-G8478, 99201-99205, 99212-99215, 99241-99245	8P
0514F, 3279F, 3280F, 4171F, 4172F	585.4, 585.5	G8476-G8478, 99201-99205, 99212-99215, 99241-99245	8P
0516F	585.6	90935, 90937, 90947, G0314-G0319, G0322-G0323, G0326-G0327	
0519F	153.0-153.9, 154.0-154.3, 154.8, 174.0-174.3, 174.5-174.6, 174.8-174.9	96401-96402, 96405-96406, 96409-96411, 96413-96417, 96420, 96422, 96425, 96440, 96445, 96450, 96521-96523, 96542, 96549, 99201-99205, 99212-99215	8p
1000F	N/A	99201-99205, 99212-99215	8P
1005F	493.00-493.02, 493.10-493.12, 493.20-493.22, 493.81, 493.82, 493.90, 493.92	99201-99205, 99212-99215, 99241-99245, 99354, 99355, 99383-99386, 99393-99396, 99401-99404	8P
1006F	715.00, 715.04, 715.09, 712.10-715.18, 715.20-715.28, 715.30-715.38, 715.80, 715.89, 715.90-715.98	99201-99205, 99212-99215, 99241-99245	8P
1034F	N/A	99201-99205, 99212-99215	
1035F	N/A	99201-99205, 99212-99215	
1036F	N/A	99201-99205, 99212-99215	
1038F, 1039F	493.00-493.02, 493.10-493.12, 493.20-493.22, 493.81, 493.82, 493.90, 493.92	99201-99205, 99212-99215, 99241-99245, 99354, 99355, 99383-99386, 99393-99396, 99401-99404	
1040F	292.20-296.24, 296.30-296.34	90801-90802, 90804-90815, 90845, 90862, 99201-99205, 99212-99215, 99241-99245	8P
1065F	433.01, 433.11, 433.21, 433.81, 433.91, 434.01, 434.11, 434.91	99221-99223 99251-99255	8P
1066F	433.01, 433.11, 433.21, 433.81, 433.91, 434.01, 434.11, 434.91	99221-99223 99251-99255	
1090F	N/A	99201-99205, 99212-99215	1P, 8P
1091F	307.6, 625.6, 788.30-788.31, 788.33-788.39	99201-99205, 99212-99215, 99241-99245	8P
1100F, 1101F	N/A	97001-97004, 97002, 99201-99205, 99212-99215, 99304-99310, 99324-99328, 99334-99337, 99341-99345, 99347-99350	1P, 8P
1110F, 1111F	N/A	99201-99205, 99212-99215	8P
1116F	380.10-380.13, 380.22	99201-99205, 99212-99215, 99241-99245	1P, 8P
1118F	530.10-530.12, 530.79, 830.81	99201-99205, 99212-99215, 99241-99245	1P, 8P
1119F	070.51, 070.54, 070.70	530.10-530.12, 530.19, 530.81	
1121F	070.51, 070.54, 070.70	530.10-530.12, 530.19, 530.81	
1123F	N/A	99201-99205, 99212-99215, 99218-99219, 99220-99223, 99231-99236, 99291, 99304-99310, 99324-99328, 99334-99337-99341, 99345, 99347-99350	
1124F	N/A	99201-99205, 99212-99215, 99218-99219, 99220-99223, 99231-99236, 99291, 99304-99310, 99324-99328, 99334-99337, 99341-99345, 99347-99350	
2000F	250.00-250.93, 648.00-648.04	97802-97804, 99201-99205, 99211-99215, 99304-99310, 99324-99328, 99334- 99337, 99341-99345, 99347-99350	8P
2010F	481, 482.0-482.2, 482.30-482.32, 482.39, 482.40, 482.41, 482.49, 482.81-482.84, 482.89, 482.9, 483.0, 483.1, 483.8, 485, 486, 487.0	99201-99205, 99212-99215, 99241-99245, 99281-99285, 99291	8P
2014F	481, 482.0-482.2, 482.30-482.32, 482.39, 482.40, 482.41, 482.49, 482.81-482.84, 482.89, 482.9, 483.0, 483.1, 483.8, 485, 486, 487.0	99201-99205, 99212-99215, 99241-99245, 99281-99285, 99291	8P
2019F	362.50-362.52	92002, 92004, 92012, 92014, 99201-99205, 99212-99215, 99241-99245, 99304-99310, 99324-99328, 99334-99337	1P, 2P, 3P, 8P
2021F	362.01-362.06	92002, 92004, 92012, 92014, 99201-99205, 99212-99215, 99241-99245, 99304-99310, 99324-99328, 99334-99337	1P, 2P, 3P, 8P
2022F, 2024F, 2026F	250.00-250.93, 357.2, 362.01-362.07, 366.41, 648.00-648.04	92002, 92004, 92012, 92014, 99201-99205, 99212-99215, 99241-99245, 99455-99456	8P

Numerator	Associated Diagnostic Denominator	Associated Procedure Denominator	Associated Modifiers
2027F	365.01, 365.10, 365.11, 365.12, 365.15	99201-99205, 99212-99215, 99241-99245, 92002, 92004, 92012, 92014	1P, 3P, 8P
2035F	380.10-380.13, 380.22	99201-99205, 99212-99215, 99241-99245	
2111F	431, 433.01, 433.11, 433.21, 433.31, 433.81, 433.91, 434.01, 434.11, 434.91, 435.0-435.3, 435.8, 435.9, 997.02	70450, 70460, 70470, 70551-70553, 0042T	8P
3014F		99201-99205, 99212-99215, 99241-99245	1P, 8P
3017F		99201-99205, 99212-99215, 99241-99245, 99304-99310, 99324-99328, 99334-99337	1P, 8P
3021F, 3022F	402.01, 402.11, 402.91, 404.01, 404.03, 404.11, 404.13, 404.91, 404.93 428.0, 428.1, 428.20-428.23, 428.30-428.33, 428.40-428.43, 428.9	99201-99205, 99212-99215. 99238, 99239, 99241-99345, 99304-99310 , 99324-99328, 99334-99337, 99341-99350	1P, 2P, 3P, 8P
3023F	491.0, 491.1, 491.20-491.22, 491.8, 491.9, 492.0, 492.8, 496	99201-99205, 99212-99215, 99241-99245,	1P, 2P, 3P, 8P
3025F, 3027F	491.0, 491.1, 491.20-491.22, 491.8, 491.9, 492.0, 492.8, 496	99201-99205, 99212-99215, 99241-99245,	1P
3028F	481, 482.0-482.2, 482.30-482.32, 482.39, 482.40, 482.41, 482.49, 482.81-482.84, 482.89, 482.9, 483.0, 483.1, 483.8, 485, 486, 487.0	99201-99205, 99212-99215, 99241-99245, 99281-99285, 99291	1P, 2P, 3P, 8P
3044F, 3045F, 3046F, 3048F, 3049F, 3050F, 3074F, 3075F, 3077F, 3078F, 3079F, 3080F,	250.00-250.93, 648.00-648.04	99201-99205, 99211-99215, 99341-99345, 99347-99350, 99304-99310, 99324-99328, 99334-99337	8P
3060F, 3061F, 3062F, 3066F, 4009F	250.00-250.93, 357.2, 362.01-362.07, 648.00-648.04	92002, 92004, 99201-99205, 99211-99215, 99217-99220, 99241-99245, 99455-99456	8P
3072F	250.00-250.93, 357.2, 362.01-362.07, 366.41, 648.00-648.04	92002, 92004, 92012, 92014, 99201-99205, 99212-99215, 99241-99245, 99455-99456	
3082F	585.6	90945, 90947, G0322, G0323, G0326, G0327	
3083F	585.6	90945, 90947, G0322, G0323, G0326, G0327	
3084F	585.6	90945, 90947, G0322, G0323, G0326, G0327	8P
3085F, 3092F, 3093F	296.20-296.24, 296.30-296.34	90801-90802, 90804-90815, 90845, 90862, 99201-99205, 99212-99215, 99241-99245	
3095F, 3096F, 4005F	733.12-73314, 805.00-805-08, 805.10-805.18, 805.2, 805.4, 805.6, 805.8, 813.40-813.45, 813.50-813.54, 820.00-820.03, 820.09, 820.10-820.11, 820.13, 820.20-820.22, 820.9, 820.9	22305, 22310, 22315, 22318-22319, 22325-22327, 22520-22521, 22523-22524, 25600, 25605-25609, 27230, 27232, 27235-27236, 27238, 27240, 27244-27246, 27248, 99201-99205, 99212-99215, 22941-99245	1P, 2P, 3P, 8P
3100F	433.01, 433.11, 433.21, 433.31, 433.81, 433.91, 434.01, 434.11, 434.91, 435.0-435.3, 435.8, 435.9, 997.02	70547-70549, 70498, 75660, 75662, 75665, 75671, 75676, 75680, 93880, 93882	1P, 8P
3110F, 3111F, 3112F	4368.12, 368.2, 386.2, 431, 433.01, 433.11, 433.21, 433.31, 433.81, 433.91, 434.01, 434.11, 434.91, 435.0-435.3, 435.8, 435.9, 437.7, 780.02, 781.3-781.4, 781.94, 782.0, 784.3, 784.5	70450, 70460, 70470, 70551-70553,	8P
3120F	780.2, 786.50-786.52, 786.59, 413.0, 413.1, 413.9	99281-99285, 99291	1P, 2P, 8P
3130F	413.0, 413.1, 413.9, 786.50-786.52, 786.59	99281-99285, 99291	1P, 2P, 8P
3155F	204.00, 205.00, 206.00, 207.00, 207.20, 208.00, 238.72-238.75	99201-99205, 99212-99215, 99241-99245	1P, 2P, 3P, 8P
3160F	238.72-238.75	99201-99205, 99212-99215, 99241-99245, 99354, 99355	3P, 8P
3170F	204.10	99201-99205, 99212-99215, 99241-99245	1P, 2P, 3P, 8P
3210F	034.0, 462, 463	99201-99205, 99211-99215, 99241-99245	1P, 8P
3215F, 3216F, 4154F, 4155F, 4156F, 4157F	070.51, 070.54, 070.70	99201-99205, 99211-99215, 99241-99245	1P, 8P
3218F, 4150F	070.54	99201-99205, 99211-99215, 99241-99245	1P, 8P
3220F	070.54	99201-99205, 99211-99215, 99241-99245	1P, 8P
3230F	381.10, 381.19, 381.20, 381.29, 381.3, 381.4	69433, 69436	1P, 3P

Numerator	Associated Diagnostic Denominator	Associated Procedure Denominator	Associated Modifiers
3260F	153.5-153.9, 154.0-154.1, 154.8, 174.0, 174.2-174.6, 174.8-174.9, 175.0, 175.9	88307, 88309	1P, 8P
3265F	070.51, 070.54, 070.70	99201-99205, 99211-99215, 99241-99245	1P, 2P, 8P
3266F	070.54	99201-99205, 99211-99215, 99241-99245	8P
3268F, 3269F, 3270F, 3271F, 3272F, 3273F, 3274F	185	55810, 55812, 55815, 55840, 55842, 55845, 55866, 55873, 77411-77414, 77416, 77418, 77427, 77776-77778, 77784	1P, 8P
3278F	585.4-585.5	99201-99205, 99211-99215, 99241-99245	1P, 2P, 8P
3305F, 3306 , 3307F, 3309F, 3310F, 3311F, 3315F, 3316F, 4179F	174.0-174.6, 174.8-174.9	99201-99205, 99212-99215	
4005F	733.12-73314, 805.00-805-08, 805.10-805.18, 805.2, 805.4, 805.6, 805.8, 813.40-813.45, 813.50-813.54, 820.00-820.03, 820.09, 820.10-820.11, 820.13, 820.20-820.22, 820.9, 820.9	22305, 22310, 22315, 22318-22319, 22325-22327, 22520-22521, 22523-22524, 25600, 25605-25609, 27230, 27232, 27235-27236, 27238, 27240, 27244-27246, 27248, 99201-99205, 99212-99215, 22941-99245	1P, 2P, 3P, 8P
4006F	410.00-410.02, 410.10-410.22, 410.30-410.32, 410.40-410.42, 410.50-410.52, 410.60-410.62, 410.70-410.72, 410.80-410.82, 410.90-410.92411.0-411.1, 411.81, 411.89, 412, 413.0-413.1, 413.9, 414.00-414.0-414.07, 414.8, 414.9, V54.81, V54.82	99201-99205, 99212-99215, 99238-99239, 99241-99245, 99304-99310, 99324-99328, 99334-99337, 99341-99350	1P, 2P, 3P, 8P
4009F	402.01, 402.11, 402.91 , 404.01, 404.03, 404.11, 404.13, 404.91, 404.93 , 428.0, 428.1, 428.20-428.23, 428.30-428.33, 428.40-428.43, 428.9	99201-99205, 99212-99215 99221-99223 99238, 9923999241-99245, 99251-99255 99304-99310, 99324-99328, 99334-99337, 99341-99345, 99347-99350	1P, 2P, 3P, 8P
4011F	414.00-414.07, 414.8, 414.9, 410.00 410.92 412 , 411.0-411.89, 413.0-413.9, V45.81, V45.82,	99201-99205, 99212-99215, 99221-99223 99238, 99239, 99241-99245 99251-99255, 99304-99310 99324-99328, 99334-99337, 99341-99345, 99347-99350	1P, 2P, 3P, 8P
4015F	493.00-493.02, 493.10-493.12, 493.20-493.22, 493.81, 493.82, 493.90, 493.92	99201-99205, 99212-99215, 99241-99245, 99354, 99355, 99383-99386, 99393-99396, 99401-99404	2P, 8P
4025F	491.0, 491.1, 491.20-491.22, 491.8, 491.9, 492.0, 492.8, 496	99201-99205, 99212-99215, 99241-99245,	1P, 2p, 3p, 8p
4037F	585.6	09035, 90997, 90046, 90047, G0314-G0319, G0322-G0323, G0326-G3027	1P, 2P, 3P, 8P
4040F	N/A	99201-99205, 99211-99215, 99218-99220, 99241-99245, 99324-99328, 99334-99337, 99341-99345, 99347-99350, 99356, 99357	

Numerator	Associated Diagnostic Denominator	Associated Procedure Denominator	Associated Modifiers
4041F	N/A	15734, 15738, 19120, 19125, 19260, 19271, 19272, 19272, 19301-19307, 19361, 19364, 19366-19369, 21627, 21632, 21740, 21750, 21805, 21825, 22325, 22524, 22554, 22558, 22600, 22612, 22612, 22630, 22630, 22800, 22802, 22804, 27125, 27130, 27132, 27134, 27137, 27138, 27235, 27236, 27244, 27245, 27440-27443, 27445-27447, 27758, 27759, 27766, 27792, 27814, 31760, 31766, 31770, 31775, 31786, 31805, 32035, 32036, 32095, 32100, 32110, 32120, 32124, 32140, 32141, 32150, 32200, 32215, 32220, 32225, 32310, 32320, 32402, 32440, 32442, 32445, 32480, 32482, 32484, 32486, 32488, 32491, 32500, 32501, 32540, 32601-32606, 32650-32665, 32800, 32810, 32815, 32900, 32905, 32906, 32940, 33020, 33025, 33030, 33031, 33050, 33120, 33130, 33140, 33141, 33202, 33203, 33250, 33251, 33254, 33255, 33256, 33261, 33300, 33305, 33310, 33315, 33320-33322, 33332, 33335, 33400, 33401, 33403-33406, 33410, 33411, 33413, 33416, 33422, 33425-33427, 33430, 33460, 33463-33465, 33475, 33496, 33510-33519, 33521-33523, 33530, 33533-33536, 33542, 33545, 33548, 33572, 33877, 33880, 33881, 33883, 33886, 33891, 34051, 34800, 34802-34805, 34825, 34830-34832, 34900, 35021, 35021, 35081, 35091, 35102, 35131, 35141, 35151, 35211, 35216, 35216, 35241, 35246, 35246, 35271, 35276, 35276, 35301, 35311, 35311, 35481, 35526, 35601, 35606, 35612, 35616, 35621, 35623, 35626, 35631, 35636-35638, 35642, 35645-35647, 35650, 35651, 35654, 35656, 35661, 35663, 35665, 35666, 35671, 35820, 36830, 37616, 38100, 38101, 38115, 38120, 38381, 38746, 38747, 39000, 39010, 39200, 39220, 39545, 39561, 43045, 43100, 43101, 43107, 43108, 43112, 43113, 43116-43118, 43121-43124, 43130, 43135, 43280, 43300, 43305, 43310, 43312, 43313, 43320, 43324-43326, 43330, 43331, 43340, 43341, 43350, 43651-43653, 43360, 43361, 43400, 43401, 43405, 43410, 43415, 43420, 43425, 43496, 43500-43502, 43510, 43520, 43600, 43605, 43610, 43611, 43620-43622, 43631-43634, 43640, 43641, 43800, 43810, 43820, 43825, 43830-43832, 43845-43848, 43840, 43842, 43843, 43850, 43855, 43860, 43865, 43870, 43880, 44005, 44010, 44020, 44021, 44025, 44050, 44055, 44100, 44110, 44111, 47719-47721, 44120, 44125-44127, 44130, 44132, 44133, 44135, 44136, 47133, 47135, 47136, 47140-47142, 47420, 47425, 47460, 47480, 47490, 47510, 47511, 47525, 47530, 47560, 47561, 47570, 47600, 47605, 47610, 47612, 47620, 47630, 47700, 47701, 47711, 47712, 47715, 47740, 47741, 47760, 47765, 47780, 47785, 47800-47802, 47900, 48001, 48020, 48100, 48102, 48120, 48152-48155, 48152-48155, 48140, 48145, 48146, 48148, 48150, 48160, 48500, 48510, 48511, 48520, 48540, 48545, 48547, 48548, 48550, 48554, 48556, 49000, 49002, 49010, 49180, 49200, 49201, 49215, 50300, 50320, 50340, 50360, 50365, 50370, 50380, 58150, 58152, 58180, 58200, 58210, 58260, 58262, 58263, 58267, 58270, 58275, 58280, 58285, 58290-58294, 60521, 60522, 61154, 61312, 61313, 61315, 61510, 61512, 61518, 61548, 61697, 61700, 61750, 61751, 61867, 62223, 62230, 63015, 63020, 63030, 63030, 63042, 63042, 63045, 63047, 63056, 63075, 63081, 63267, 63276, 64746	1P, 8P

Numerator	Associated Diagnostic Denominator	Associated Procedure Denominator	Associated Modifiers
4042F, 4043F, 4046F	N/A	15734, 15738, 19120, 19125, 19260, 19271, 19272, 19272, 19301-19307, 19361, 19364, 19366-19369, 21346-21348, 21422, 21423, 21432, 21433, 21435, 21436, 21454, 21461, 21462, 21465, 21470, 21627, 21632, 21740, 21750, 21805, 21825, 22325, 22524, 22554, 22558, 22600, 22612, 22612, 22630, 22630, 22800, 22802, 22804, 27125, 27130, 27132, 27134, 27137, 27138, 27235, 27236, 27244, 27245, 27440-27443, 27445-27447, 27758, 27759, 27766, 27792, 27814, 31360, 31365, 31367, 31368, 31370, 31375, 31380, 31382, 31390, 31395, 31760, 31766, 31770, 31775, 31786, 31805, 32035, 32036, 32095, 32100, 32110, 32120, 32124, 32140, 32141, 32150, 32200, 32215, 32220, 32225, 32310, 32320, 32402, 32440, 32442, 32445, 32480, 32482, 32484, 32486, 32488, 32491, 32500, 32501, 32540, 32601-32606, 32650-32665, 32800, 32810, 32815, 32900, 32905, 32906, 32940, 33020, 33025, 33030, 33031, 33050, 33203, 33206-33208, 33210-33218, 33220, 33222-33226, 33233-33238, 33240, 33241, 33243, 33244, 33249, 33254, 33255, 33300, 33310, 33320, 33877, 33880, 33881, 33883, 33886, 33891, 34051, 34800, 34802-34805, 34825, 34830-34832, 34900, 35021, 35081, 35091, 35102, 35131, 35141, 35151, 35216, 35246, 35276, 35301, 35311, 35481, 35526, 35601, 35606, 35612, 35616, 35621, 35623, 35626, 35631, 35636-35638, 35642, 35645-35647, 35650, 35651, 35654, 35656, 35661, 35663, 35665, 35666, 35671, 36830, 37616, 38100, 38101, 38115, 38120, 38381, 38746, 38747, 39000, 39010, 39200, 39220, 39545, 39561, 41130, 41135, 41140, 41145, 41150, 41153, 41155, 43045, 43100, 43101, 43107, 43108, 43112, 43113, 43116-43118, 43121-43124, 43130, 43135, 43280, 43300, 43305, 43310, 43312, 43313, 43320, 43324-43326, 43330, 43331, 43340, 43341, 43350, 43351, 43352, 43360, 43361, 43400, 43401, 43405, 43410, 43415, 43420, 43425, 43496, 43500-43502, 43510, 43520, 43600, 43605, 43610, 43611, 43620-43622, 43631-43634, 43640, 43641, 43651-43653, 43800, 43810, 43820, 43830-43832, 43825, 43840, 43842, 43843, 43845-43848, 43850, 43855, 43860, 43865, 43870, 43880, 44005, 44010, 44020, 44021, 44025, 44050, 44055, 44100, 44110, 44111, 44120, 44125-44127, 44130, 44132, 44133, 44135, 44136, 44140, 44141, 44143-44147, 44150, 44151, 44155-44158, 44160, 44202, 44204-44208, 44210-44212, 44300, 44310, 44312, 44314, 44316, 44320, 44322, 44340, 44345, 43460, 44602-44605, 44615, 44620, 44625, 44626, 44640, 44650, 44660, 44661, 44680, 44700, 44800, 44820, 44850, 44950, 44960, 44970, 45108, 45110-45114, 45116, 45119-45121, 45123, 45126, 45130, 45135, 45136, 45150, 45160, 45170, 45190, 45500, 45505, 45520, 45540, 45541, 45550, 45560, 45562, 45563, 45800, 45805, 45820, 45825, 47133, 47135, 47136, 47140-47142, 47420, 47425, 47460, 47480, 47490, 47510, 47511, 47525, 47530, 47560, 47561, 47570, 47600, 47605, 47610, 47612, 47620, 47630, 47700, 47701, 47711, 47712, 47715, 47719-47721, 47740, 47741, 47760, 47765, 47780, 47785, 47719-47721, 47900, 48001, 48020, 48100, 48102, 48120, 48140, 48145, 48146, 48148, 48150, 48152-48155, 48160, 48500, 48510, 48511, 48520, 48540, 48545, 48547, 48548, 48550, 48554, 48556, 49000, 49002, 49010, 49180, 49200, 49201, 49215, 50300, 50320, 50340, 50360, 50365, 50370, 50380, 58150, 58152, 58180, 58200, 58210, 58260, 58262, 58263, 58267, 58270, 58275, 58280, 58285, 58290-58294, 60521, 60522, 61154, 61312, 61313, 61315, 61510, 61512, 61518, 61520, 61526, 61530, 61548, 61591, 61595, 61596, 61598, 61606, 61616, 61618, 61619, 61697, 61700, 61750, 61751, 61867, 62223, 62230, 63015, 63020, 63030, 63030, 63042, 63042, 63045, 63047, 63056, 63075, 63081, 63267, 63276, 64746, 69720, 69930, 69955, 69960, 69970	1P, 8P

Numerator	Associated Diagnostic Denominator	Associated Procedure Denominator	Associated Modifiers
4045F, 4049F	N/A	15734, 15738, 19120, 19125, 19260, 19271, 19272, 19272, 19301-19307, 19361, 19364, 19366-19369, 21346-21348, 21422, 21423, 21432, 21433, 21435, 21436, 21454, 21461, 21462, 21465, 21470, 21627, 21632, 21740, 21750, 21805, 21825, 22325, 22524, 22554, 22558, 22600, 22612, 22612, 22630, 22630, 22800, 22802, 22804, 27125, 27130, 27132, 27134, 27137, 27138, 27235, 27236, 27244, 27245, 27440-27443, 27445-27447, 27758, 27759, 27766, 27792, 27814, 31360, 31365, 31367, 31368, 31370, 31375, 31380, 31382, 31390, 31395, 31760, 31766, 31770, 31775, 31786, 31805, 32035, 32036, 32095, 32100, 32110, 32120, 32124, 32140, 32141, 32150, 32200, 32215, 32220, 32225, 32310, 32320, 32402, 32440, 32442, 32445, 32480, 32482, 32484, 32486, 32488, 32491, 32500, 32501, 32540, 32601-32606, 32650-32665, 32800, 32810, 32815, 32900, 32905, 32906, 32940, 33020, 33025, 33030, 33031, 33050, 33203, 33206-33208, 33210-33218, 33220, 33222-33226, 33233-33238, 33240, 33241, 33243, 33244, 33249, 33254, 33255, 33300, 33310, 33320, 33877, 33880, 33881, 33883, 33886, 33891, 34051, 34800, 34802-34805, 34825, 34830-34832, 34900, 35021, 35081, 35091, 35102, 35131, 35141, 35151, 35216, 35246, 35276, 35301, 35311, 35481, 35526, 35601, 35606, 35612, 35616, 35621, 35623, 35626, 35631, 35636-35638, 35642, 35645-35647, 35650, 35651, 35654, 35656, 35661, 35663, 35665, 35666, 35671, 36830, 37616, 38100, 38101, 38115, 38120, 38381, 38746, 38747, 39000, 39010, 39200, 39220, 39545, 39561, 41130, 41135, 41140, 41145, 41150, 41153, 41155, 43045, 43100, 43101, 43107, 43108, 43112, 43113, 43116-43118, 43121-43124, 43130, 43135, 43280, 43300, 43305, 43310, 43312, 43313, 43320, 43324-43326, 43330, 43331, 43340, 43341, 43350, 43351, 43352, 43360, 43361, 43400, 43401, 43405, 43410, 43415, 43420, 43425, 43496, 43500-43502, 43510, 43520, 43600, 43605, 43610, 43611, 43620-43622, 43631-43634, 43640, 43641, 43651-43653, 43800, 43810, 43820, 43830-43832, 43825, 43840, 43842, 43843, 43845-43848, 43850, 43855, 43860, 43865, 43870, 43880, 44005, 44010, 44020, 44021, 44025, 44050, 44055, 44100, 44110, 44111, 44120, 44125-44127, 44130, 44132, 44133, 44135, 44136, 44140, 44141, 44143-44147, 44150, 44151, 44155-44158, 44160, 44202, 44204-44208, 44210-44212, 44300, 44310, 44312, 44314, 44316, 44320, 44322, 44340, 44345, 43460, 44602-44605, 44615, 44620, 44625, 44626, 44640, 44650, 44660, 44661, 44680, 44700, 44800, 44820, 44850, 44950, 44960, 44970, 45108, 45110-45114, 45116,45119-45121, 45123, 45126, 45130, 45135, 45136, 45150, 45160, 45170, 45190, 45500, 45505, 45520, 45540, 45541, 45550, 45560, 45562, 45563, 45800, 45805, 45820, 45825, 47133, 47135, 47136, 47140-47142, 47420, 47425, 47460, 47480, 47490, 47510, 47511, 47525, 47530, 47560, 47561, 47570, 47600, 47605, 47610, 47612, 47620, 47630, 47700, 47701, 47711, 47712, 47715, 47719-47721, 47740, 47741, 47760, 47765, 47780, 47785, 47719-47721, 47900, 48001, 48020, 48100, 48102, 48120, 48140, 48145, 48146, 48148, 48150, 48152-48155, 48160, 48500, 48510, 48511, 48520, 48540, 48545, 48547, 48548, 48554, 48556, 49000, 49002, 49010, 49180, 49200, 49201, 49215, 50300, 50320, 50340, 50360, 50365, 50370, 50380, 58150, 58152, 58180, 58200, 58210, 58260, 58262, 58263, 58267, 58270, 58275, 58280, 58285, 58290-58294, 60521, 60522, 61154, 61312, 61313, 61315, 61510, 61512, 61518, 61520, 61526, 61530, 61548, 61591, 61595, 61596, 61598, 61606, 61616, 61618, 61619, 61697, 61700, 61750, 61751, 61867, 62223, 62230, 63015, 63020, 63030, 63030, 63042, 63042, 63045, 63047, 63056, 63075, 63081, 63267, 63276, 64746, 69720, 69930, 69955, 69960, 69970	1P, 8P

Numerator	Associated Diagnostic Denominator	Associated Procedure Denominator	Associated Modifiers
4044F	N/A	19260, 19301-19307, 19271, 19272, 19316, 19318, 19324, 19325, 19328, 19330, 19342, 19350, 19355, 19357, 19361, 19364, 19366-19371, 19380, 22558, 22600, 22612, 22630, 27125, 27130, 27132, 27134, 27137, 27138, 27235, 27236, 27440-27443, 27244, 27245, 27445-27447, 38100, 38101, 38115, 38120, 38571, 38572, 38700, 38720, 38724, 38740, 38745, 38747, 38760, 38765, 38770, 38780, 39501-39503, 39520, 39530, 39531, 39540, 39541, 39545, 39560, 39561, 43020, 43030, 43045, 43100, 43101, 43107, 43108, 43112, 43113, 43116-43118, 43121-43124, 43130, 43135, 43280, 43300, 43305, 43310, 43312-43314, 43320, 43324-43326, 43330, 43331, 43340, 43341, 43350-43352, 43360, 43361, 43400, 43401, 43405, 43410, 43415, 43420, 43425, 43496, 43500-43502, 43510, 43520, 43605, 43610, 43611, 43620-43622, 43631-43634, 43640, 43641, 43644, 43645, 43651-43653, 43770-43774, 43800, 43810, 43820, 43825, 43830, 43832, 43840, 43842, 43843, 43845-43848, 43850, 43855, 43860, 43865, 43870, 43880, 43886-43888, 44005, 44010, 44020, 44021, 44025, 44050, 44055, 44110, 44111, 44120, 44125-44127, 44130, 44140, 44141, 44143-44147, 44150, 44151, 44155-44158, 44160, 44180, 44186-44188, 44202, 44204-44208, 44210-44212, 44227, 44300, 44310, 44312, 44314, 44316, 44320, 44322, 44340, 44345, 44346, 44602-44605, 44615, 44620, 44625, 44626, 44640, 44650, 44660, 44661, 44680, 44700, 44800, 48152-48155, 44820, 44850, 44900, 44950, 44960, 44970, 45000, 45020, 45100, 45108, 45110-45114, 45116, 45119-45121, 45123, 45126, 45130, 45135, 45136, 45150, 45160, 45170, 45190, 45395, 45397, 45400, 45402, 45500, 45505, 45550, 45560, 45562, 45563, 45800, 45805, 45820, 45825, 46715, 46716, 46730, 46735, 46740, 46742, 46744, 46746, 46748, 46750, 46751, 46753, 46754, 46760, 46761, 46762, 47010, 47100, 47120, 47122, 47125, 47130, 47135, 47136, 47140-47142, 47300, 47350, 47360-47362, 47370, 47371, 47380-47382, 47400, 47420, 47425, 47460, 47480, 47500, 47505, 47560-47564, 47570, 47600, 47605, 47610, 47612, 47620, 47630, 47700, 47701, 47711, 47712, 47715, 47720, 47721, 47740, 47741, 47760, 47765, 47780, 47785, 47800-47802, 47900, 48000, 48001, 48020, 48100, 48105, 48120, 48140, 48145, 48146, 48148, 48150, 48500, 48510, 48520, 48540, 48545, 48547, 48548, 48554, 48556, 49000, 49002, 49010, 49020, 49040, 49060, 49200, 49201, 49215, 49220, 49250, 49255, 49320-49323, 49560, 49561, 49565, 49566, 49570, 50020, 50220, 50225, 50230, 50234, 50236, 50240, 50320, 50320, 50340, 50360, 50360, 50365, 50365, 50370, 50370, 50380, 50380, 50543, 50545, 50546, 50547, 50548, 50715, 50722, 50725, 50727, 50728, 50760, 50770, 50780, 50782, 50783, 50785, 50800, 50810, 50815, 50820, 50947, 50948, 51550, 51555, 51565, 51570, 51575, 51580, 51585, 51590, 51595-51597, 51800, 51820, 51900, 51920, 51952, 51960, 55810, 55812, 55815, 55821, 55831, 55840, 55842, 55845, 55866, 56630-56634, 56637, 56640, 58200, 58210, 58240, 58285, 58951, 58953, 58954, 58956, 60200, 60210, 60212, 60220, 60225, 60240, 60252, 60254, 60260, 60270, 60271, 60280, 60281, 60500, 60502, 60505, 60520-60522, 60540, 60545, 60600, 60605, 60650, 61313, 61510, 61512, 61518, 61548, 61697, 61700, 62230, 63015, 63020, 63047, 63056, 63081, 63267, 63276	1P, 8P
4045F	481, 482.0-482.2, 482.30-482.32, 482.39, 482.40, 482.41, 482.49, 482.81-482.84, 482.89, 482.9, 483.0, 483.1, 483.8, 485, 486, 487.0	99201-99205, 99212 99215, 99241-99245, 99281-99285, 99291	1P, 2P, 3P, 8P
4046F	N/A	33120, 33130, 33140, 33141, 33202, 33250, 33251, 33256, 33261, 33300, 33305, 33310, 33315, 33320-33322, 33332, 33335, 33400, 33401, 33403-33406, 33410, 33411, 33413, 33416, 33422, 33425-33427, 33430, 33460, 33463-33465, 33475, 33496, 33510 33519, 33521-33523, 33530, 33533-33536, 33542, 33545, 33548, 33572, 35021, 35211, 35216, 35241, 35246, 35271, 35276, 35311, 35820	1P, 8P

Numerator	Associated Diagnostic Denominator	Associated Procedure Denominator	Associated Modifiers
4047F, 4048F	N/A	15734, 15738, 19120, 19125, 19260, 19271, 19272, 19272, 19301-19307, 19361, 19364, 19301-19307, 21346-21348, 21422, 21423, 21432, 21433, 21435, 21436, 21454, 21461, 21462, 21465, 21470, 21627, 21632, 21740, 21750, 21805, 21825, 22325, 22524, 22554, 22558, 22600, 22612, 22612, 22630, 22630, 22800, 22802, 22804, 27125, 27130, 27132, 27134, 27137, 27138, 27235, 27236, 27244, 27245, 27440-27443, 27445-27447, 27758, 27759, 27766, 27792, 27814, 31360, 31365, 31367, 31368, 31370, 31375, 31380, 31382, 31390, 31395, 31760, 31766, 31770, 31775, 31786, 31805, 32035, 32036, 32095, 32100, 32110, 32120, 32124, 32140, 32141, 32150, 32200, 32215, 32220, 32225, 32310, 32320, 32402, 32440, 32442, 32445, 32480, 32482, 32484, 32486, 32488, 32491, 32500, 32501, 32540, 32601-32606, 32650-32665, 32800, 32810, 32815, 32900, 32905, 32906, 32940, 33020, 33025, 33030, 33031, 33050, 33120, 33130, 33140, 33141, 33202, 33203, 33206-33208, 33210-33218, 33220, 33222-33226, 33233-33238, 33240, 33241, 33243, 33244, 33249, 33250, 33251, 33254, 33255, 33256, 33261, 33300, 33300, 33305, 33310, 33310, 33315, 33320-33322, 33332, 33335, 33400, 33401, 33403-33406, 33410, 33411, 33413, 33416, 33422, 33425-33427, 33430, 33460, 33463-33465, 33475, 33496, 33510-33519, 33521-33523, 33530, 33533-33536, 33542, 33545, 33548, 33572, 33877, 33880, 33881, 33883, 33886, 33891, 34051, 34800, 34802-34805, 34825, 34830-34832, 34900, 35021, 35021, 35081, 35091, 35102, 35131, 35141, 35151, 35211, 35216, 35216, 35241, 35246, 35246, 35271, 35276, 35276, 35301, 35311, 35481, 35526, 35601, 35606, 35612, 35616, 35621, 35623, 35626, 35631, 35636-35638, 35642, 35645-35647, 35650, 35651, 35654, 35656, 35661, 35663, 35665, 35666, 35671, 35820, 36830, 37616, 38100, 38101, 38115, 38120, 38381, 38746, 38747, 39000, 39010, 39200, 39220, 39545, 39561, 41130, 41135, 41140, 41145, 41150, 41153, 41155, 43045, 43100, 43101, 43107, 43108, 43112, 43113, 43116-43118, 43121-43124, 43130, 43135, 43280, 43300, 43305, 43310, 43312, 43313, 43320, 43324-43326, 43330, 43331, 43340, 43341, 43350, 43351, 43352, 43360, 43361, 43400, 43401, 43405, 43410, 43415, 43425, 43496, 43500-43502, 43510, 43520, 43600, 43605, 43610, 43611, 43620-43622, 43631-43634, 43640, 43641, 43651-43653, 43800, 43810, 43820, 43825, 43830-43832, 43840, 43842, 43843, 43845-43848, 43850, 43855, 43860, 43865, 43870, 43880, 44005, 44010, 44020, 44021, 44025, 44050, 44055, 44100, 44110, 44111, 44120, 44125-44127, 44130, 44132, 44133, 44135, 44136, 44140, 44141, 44143-44147, 44150, 44151, 44155-44158, 44160, 44210-44212, 44202, 44204-44208, 44300, 44310, 44314, 44316, 44320, 44322, 44340, 44345, 44346, 45119-45121, 44602-44605, 44615, 44620, 44625, 44626, 44640, 44650, 44660, 44661, 44680, 44700, 44800, 44820, 44850, 44950, 44960, 44970, 45108, 45110-45114, 45116, 45123, 45126, 45130, 45135, 45136, 45150, 45160, 45170, 45190, 45500, 45505, 45520, 45540, 45541, 45550, 45560, 45562, 45563, 45800, 45805, 45820, 45825, 47133, 47135, 47136, 47140-47142, 47420, 47425, 47460, 47480, 47490, 47510, 47511, 47525, 47530, 47560, 47561, 47570, 47600, 47605, 47610, 47612, 47620, 47630, 47700, 47701, 47711, 47712, 47715, 47719-47721, 47740, 47741, 47760, 47765, 47780, 47785, 47800-47802, 47900, 48001, 48020, 48100, 48102, 48120, 48140, 48145, 48146, 48148, 48150, 48152-48155, 48160, 48500, 48510, 48511, 48520, 48540, 48545, 48547, 48548, 48550, 48554, 48556, 49000, 49002, 49010, 49180, 49200, 49201, 49215, 50080, 50081, 50300, 50320, 50340, 50360, 50365, 50370, 50380, 50551, 50553, 50555, 50557, 50561, 50562, 50570, 50572, 50574-50576, 50580, 50951, 50953, 50955, 50957, 50961, 50970, 50972, 50974, 50976, 50980, 51550, 51555, 51565, 51570, 51575, 51580, 51585, 51590, 51595, 51596, 51597, 51840, 51841, 51845, 51920, 51925, 51990, 51992, 52450, 52601, 52612, 52614, 52620, 52630, 52647, 52648, 53230, 53240, 54401, 54405, 54406, 54408, 54410, 54411, 54415, 54416, 54417, 55801, 55810, 55812, 55815, 55821, 55831, 55840, 55842, 55845, 55866, 55873, 55875, 58150, 58152, 58180, 58200, 58210, 58260, 58262, 58263, 58267, 58270, 58275, 58280, 58285, 58290-58294, 60521, 60522, 61154, 61312, 61313, 61315, 61510, 61512, 61518, 61520, 61526, 61530, 61548, 61591, 61595, 61596, 61598, 61606, 61616, 61618, 61619, 61697, 61700, 61750, 61751, 61867, 62223, 62230, 63015, 63020, 63030, 63030, 63042, 63042, 63045, 63047, 63056, 63075, 63081, 63267, 63276, 64746, 69720, 69930, 69955, 69960, 69970	1P, 8P,
4051F, 4052F, 4053F, 4054F	585.6	99035, 99037, G0314-G0319	1P, 2P, 8P
4067F	431, 433.01, 433.11, 433.21, 433.31, 433.81, 433.91, 434.01, 434.11, 434.91	99221-99223, 99251-99255, 99291	1P, 2P, 8P
4070F	431, 433.01, 433.11, 433.21, 433.31, 433.81, 433.91, 434.01, 434.11, 434.91, 435.9, 436, 438.2, 438.89, 438.9, 997.02	99221-99223, 99231-99233, 99238-99239, 99251-99255 99291	1P, 2P, 8P

Numerator	Associated Diagnostic Denominator	Associated Procedure Denominator	Associated Modifiers
4073F	433.01, 433.11, 433.21, 433.31, 433.81, 433.91, 434.01, 434.11, 434.91, 435.0-435.3, 435.8, 435.9, 436, 438.2, 438.89, 438.9, 997.02	99218-99220, 99221-99223 99231-99233, 99238, 99239, 99251-99255, 99281-99285, 99291	1P, 2P, 8P
4075F	433.01, 433.11, 433.21, 433.31, 433.81, 433.91, 434.01, 434.11, 434.91, 435.0-435.3, 435.8, 435.9, 436, 438.2, 438.89, 438.9, 997.02, 427.31	99218-99220, 99221-99223 99231-99233, 99238, 99239, 99251-99255, 99281-99285, 99291	1P, 2P, 8P
4077F	433.01, 433.11, 433.21, 433.31, 433.81, 433.91, 434.01, 434.11, 434.91, 997.02	99221-99223 99251-99255	N/A
4079F	431, 433.01, 433.11, 433.21, 433.81, 433.91, 434.01, 434.11, 434.91,	99220, 99221-99223 99231-99233, 99234-99236, 99238, 99239, 99251-99255	8P
4084F	410.01, 410.11, 410.21, 410.31, 410.41, 410.51, 410.61, 410.71, 410.81, 410.91	99281-99285, 99291	1P, 2P, 8P
4090F, 4095F	238.72-238.75	99201-99205, 99212-99215, 99241-99245, 99354, 99355	3P, 8P
4100F	203.00	99201-99205, 99212-99215, 99241-99245, 99354, 99355	1P, 2P, 8P
4110F	N/A	33517-33519, 33521-33523, 33533-33536	1P, 8P
4115F	N/A	33510-33514, 33516, 33533-33536	1P, 8P
4120F, 4124F	034.0, 462, 463	99201-99205, 99211-99215, 99241 99245	1P, 2P, 8P
4130F	380.10-380.13, 380.22	99201-99205, 99212-99215, 99241-99245	1P, 23P, 8P
4131F	380.10-380.13, 380.22	99201-99205, 99212-99215, 99241-99245	1P
4132F	380.10-380.13, 380.22	99201-99205, 99212-99215, 99241-99245	
4133F, 4135F, 4136F	381.10, 381.19, 381.20, 381.29, 381.3, 381.4	99201-99205, 99212-99215, 99241-99245	1P
4134F	381.10, 381.19, 381.20, 381.29, 381.3, 381.4	99201-99205, 99212-99215, 99241-99245	
4152F	070.54	99201-99205, 99212-99215, 99241-99245	8P
4153F, 4159f	070.54	99201-99205, 99212-99215, 99241-99245	
4158F	070.51, 070.54, 070.70	99201-99205, 99212-99215, 99241-99245	8P
4163F	185, 197.0-197.8, 198.0-198.82, 198.89	55810, 55812, 55815, 55840, 55842, 55845, 55866, 55873, 77261-77263	1P, 8P
4164F	185	77407, 77408-77409, 77411-77416, 77418, 77427	1P, 2P, 8P
4165F	185, 197.0-197.8, 198.0-198.82, 198.89	77401-77404, 77406-77409, 77411-77414, 77416, 77418, 77427	8p
4167F	N/A	99291	1P, 8P
4168F	N/A	99291	
4180F	153.0-153.9	99201-99205, 99212 99215	1P, 2P, 3P, 8P
4182F	530.10-530.12, 530.19, 530.81		
4185F	530.10-530.12, 530.19, 530.81	99201-99205, 99212-99215, 99241-99245	
4186F	N/A	99201-99205, 99212-99215, 99241-99245	
4187F	714.0-714.2, 714.81	99201-99205, 99212-99215, 99217-99220, 99241-99245, 99255-99256	1P, 8P
4200F, 4201F	185, 197.0-197.8, 198.0-198.82, 198.89	77401-77404, 77406-77409, 77411-77414, 77416, 77418, 77427	
4220F, 4201F	185, 197.0-197.8, 198.0-198.82, 198.89	77401-77404, 77406 77409, 77411-77414, 77416, 77418, 77427	
5010F	362.01-362.06	99201-99205, 99212-99215, 99241-99245, 92002, 92004, 92012, 92014	1P, 2P, 8P
5015F	733.12-733.14, 805.00-805.08, 805.10-805.18, 805.2, 805.4, 805.6, 805.8, 813.40-813.42, 813.44, 813.45, 813.50-813.52, 813.54, 820.00-820.03, 820.09-820.11, 820.13, 820.20-820.22, 820.8, 820.9	99024, 99201-99205, 99212-99215, 99241-99245, 99354, 99355 22305-22327, 22520, 22521, 22523, 22524, 25600-25609, 27230-27248	1P, 2P, 8P
6010F, 6015F, 6020F	431, 433.01, 433.11, 433.21, 433.31, 433.81, 433.91, 434.01, 434.11, 434.91, 435.9, 436, 438.2, 438.89, 438.9, 997.02	99218-99220, 99281-99285, 99221-99223, 99231-99233, 99251-99255	1P, 8P
6030F	N/A	36555-36558, 36560-36561, 36563, 36566, 36568-36571, 36578, 36580-36585	1P, 8P

APPENDIX J — MEDICALLY UNLIKELY EDITS (MUES)

The Centers for Medicare & Medicaid Services (CMS) began to publish many of the edits used in the medically unlikely edits (MUE) program for the first time effective October 2008. What follows below is a list of the published CPT codes that have MUEs assigned to them and the number of units allowed with each code. CMS will subsequently publish the updates on a quarterly basis. Not all MUEs will be published, however. MUEs intended to detect and discourage any questionable payments will not be published as the agency feels the efficacy of these edits would be compromised.

The quarterly updates will be published on the CMS website at http://www.cms.hhs.gov/NationalCorrectCodInitEd/08_MUE.asp#TopOfPage.

PROFESSIONAL

CPT	MUE	CPT	MUE	CPT	MUE	CPT	MUE	CPT	MUE	CPT	MUE	CPT	MUE	CPT	MUE
0016T	2	0126T	1	11976	1	15150	1	15876	1	19340	2	21049	2	21246	2
0017T	2	0130T	1	11980	1	15151	1	15877	1	19342	2	21076	1	21247	2
0026T	1	0137T	1	11981	1	15155	1	15878	2	19350	2	21077	2	21255	2
0027T	1	0140T	1	11982	1	15156	1	15879	2	19355	1	21079	1	21256	2
0028T	1	0144T	1	11983	1	15170	1	15920	1	19357	2	21080	1	21260	1
0031T	1	0145T	1	12001	1	15175	1	15922	1	19361	2	21081	1	21261	1
0032T	1	0146T	1	12002	1	15200	1	15931	1	19364	2	21082	1	21263	1
0041T	1	0147T	1	12004	1	15220	1	15933	1	19366	2	21083	1	21267	1
0042T	1	0148T	1	12005	1	15240	1	15934	1	19367	2	21084	1	21268	2
0043T	1	0149T	1	12006	1	15260	1	15935	1	19368	2	21085	1	21270	2
0046T	2	0150T	1	12007	1	15300	1	15936	1	19369	2	21086	2	21275	1
0047T	2	0151T	1	12011	1	15320	1	15937	1	19370	2	21087	1	21280	1
0048T	1	0159T	2	12013	1	15330	1	15940	2	19371	2	21088	1	21282	1
0049T	1	0174T	1	12014	1	15335	1	15941	2	19380	2	21100	1	21295	2
0050T	1	0177T	2	12015	1	15340	1	15944	2	19396	2	21110	2	21296	2
0051T	1	10040	1	12016	1	15360	1	15945	2	20150	2	21116	2	21310	1
0052T	1	10060	1	12017	1	15365	1	15946	2	20526	2	21120	1	21315	1
0053T	1	10061	1	12018	1	15400	1	15950	2	20552	1	21121	1	21320	1
0058T	1	10080	1	12020	3	15420	1	15951	2	20553	1	21122	1	21325	1
0059T	1	10081	1	12021	3	15430	1	15952	2	20660	1	21123	1	21330	1
0060T	1	10180	3	12031	1	15570	3	15953	2	20661	1	21125	2	21335	1
0061T	2	11000	1	12032	1	15572	2	15956	2	20662	1	21127	2	21336	1
0062T	1	11004	1	12034	1	15574	2	15958	2	20663	1	21137	1	21337	1
0063T	1	11005	1	12035	1	15576	2	16000	1	20664	1	21138	1	21338	1
0064T	1	11006	1	12036	1	15600	2	16020	1	20665	1	21139	1	21339	1
0067T	1	11008	1	12037	1	15610	2	16025	1	20802	2	21141	1	21340	1
0068T	1	11010	1	12041	1	15620	2	16030	1	20805	2	21142	1	21343	1
0069T	1	11011	1	12042	1	15630	2	16035	1	20808	2	21143	1	21344	1
0070T	1	11012	1	12044	1	15650	1	17000	1	20824	2	21145	1	21345	1
0071T	1	11055	1	12045	1	15740	3	17004	1	20827	2	21146	1	21346	1
0072T	1	11056	1	12046	1	15750	2	17106	1	20838	2	21147	1	21347	1
0073T	2	11057	1	12047	1	15757	3	17107	1	20900	2	21150	1	21348	1
0075T	1	11100	1	12051	1	15758	3	17108	1	20912	1	21151	1	21355	2
0076T	2	11200	1	12052	1	15760	2	17110	1	20920	2	21154	1	21356	2
0077T	2	11201	1	12053	1	15770	2	17111	1	20922	2	21155	1	21360	2
0078T	1	11446	3	12054	1	15775	1	17276	3	20926	2	21159	1	21365	2
0080T	1	11450	2	12055	1	15776	1	17286	3	20937	3	21160	1	21366	2
0084T	1	11451	2	12056	1	15780	1	17340	1	20938	3	21172	1	21385	2
0085T	1	11462	2	12057	1	15786	1	17360	1	20969	2	21175	1	21386	2
0086T	1	11463	2	13100	1	15787	3	19000	2	20970	2	21179	1	21387	2
0087T	1	11646	3	13101	1	15788	1	19020	2	20972	2	21180	1	21390	2
0088T	1	11719	1	13120	1	15789	1	19030	2	20973	2	21181	1	21395	2
0089T	1	11720	1	13121	1	15819	1	19290	3	20974	1	21182	2	21400	2
0090T	1	11721	1	13131	1	15824	1	19296	2	20975	1	21183	2	21401	2
0092T	1	11730	1	13132	1	15825	1	19297	2	20979	1	21184	2	21406	2
0093T	1	11770	1	13150	1	15826	1	19298	2	20982	1	21188	1	21407	2
0095T	1	11771	1	13151	1	15828	1	19300	2	21015	1	21193	1	21408	2
0096T	1	11772	1	13152	1	15830	1	19301	2	21025	2	21194	1	21421	1
0098T	1	11900	1	13160	3	15832	2	19302	2	21026	2	21195	1	21422	1
0099T	2	11901	1	14300	3	15833	2	19303	2	21029	1	21196	1	21423	1
0100T	2	11920	1	15002	1	15834	2	19304	2	21030	2	21198	1	21431	1
0101T	1	11921	1	15004	1	15835	1	19305	2	21031	2	21199	1	21432	1
0102T	2	11922	1	15040	1	15836	2	19306	2	21032	1	21206	1	21433	1
0103T	1	11950	1	15050	1	15838	1	19307	2	21034	1	21215	2	21435	1
0104T	1	11951	1	15100	1	15841	2	19316	2	21040	2	21235	2	21436	1
0105T	1	11952	1	15110	1	15842	2	19318	2	21044	1	21240	2	21440	2
0111T	1	11954	1	15115	1	15845	2	19324	2	21045	1	21242	2	21445	2
0123T	2	11960	3	15120	1	15851	1	19325	2	21046	2	21243	2	21450	1
0124T	2	11970	2	15130	1	15852	2	19328	2	21047	2	21244	1	21451	1
		11971	1	15135	1	15860	1	19330	2	21048	2	21245	2	21452	1

CPT	MUE	CPT	MUE	CPT	MUE	CPT	MUE	CPT	MUE	CPT	MUE	CPT	MUE	CPT	MUE
21453	1	22556	1	23332	2	24102	2	24666	2	25430	2	26025	2	27006	2
21454	1	22558	1	23350	2	24105	2	24670	2	25440	2	26030	2	27030	2
21461	1	22590	1	23395	1	24115	2	24675	2	25441	2	26034	2	27033	2
21462	1	22595	1	23397	1	24120	2	24685	2	25442	2	26035	3	27035	2
21465	2	22600	1	23400	1	24130	2	24800	2	25443	2	26037	2	27036	2
21470	1	22610	1	23405	2	24138	2	24802	2	25444	2	26040	2	27040	2
21480	2	22612	1	23406	2	24140	2	24900	2	25445	2	26045	2	27041	3
21485	2	22630	1	23410	2	24145	2	24920	2	25446	2	26070	3	27048	2
21490	2	22800	1	23412	2	24147	2	24925	2	25449	2	26100	2	27049	2
21495	1	22802	1	23415	2	24149	2	24930	2	25450	2	26105	2	27050	2
21497	1	22804	1	23420	2	24150	1	24931	2	25455	2	26110	3	27052	2
21501	3	22808	1	23430	2	24152	1	24935	2	25490	2	26117	2	27054	2
21557	1	22810	1	23440	2	24153	1	24940	2	25491	2	26121	2	27060	2
21615	2	22812	1	23450	2	24155	1	25000	2	25492	2	26123	2	27062	2
21616	2	22818	1	23455	2	24160	2	25001	2	25500	2	26185	1	27065	2
21620	1	22819	1	23460	2	24164	2	25020	2	25505	2	26205	2	27066	2
21627	1	22830	1	23462	2	24200	3	25023	2	25515	2	26215	2	27067	2
21630	1	22840	1	23465	2	24201	3	25024	2	25520	2	26230	3	27070	2
21632	1	22842	1	23466	2	24220	2	25025	2	25525	2	26236	3	27071	2
21685	1	22843	1	23470	2	24300	2	25035	2	25526	2	26250	2	27075	1
21700	2	22844	1	23472	2	24301	2	25040	2	25530	2	26255	2	27076	2
21705	2	22845	1	23480	2	24320	2	25077	2	25535	2	26260	2	27077	2
21720	1	22846	1	23485	2	24330	2	25085	2	25545	2	26261	2	27078	2
21725	1	22847	1	23490	2	24331	2	25100	2	25560	2	26262	2	27079	2
21740	1	22848	1	23491	2	24332	2	25101	2	25565	2	26357	3	27080	1
21742	1	22849	1	23500	2	24340	2	25105	2	25574	2	26358	3	27086	2
21743	1	22850	1	23505	2	24342	2	25107	2	25575	2	26390	3	27087	2
21750	1	22852	1	23515	2	24343	2	25111	2	25600	2	26392	3	27090	2
21805	3	22855	1	23520	2	24344	2	25112	2	25605	2	26416	2	27091	2
21810	1	22857	1	23525	2	24345	2	25115	2	25606	2	26428	2	27093	2
21820	1	22862	1	23530	2	24346	2	25116	2	25607	2	26432	2	27095	2
21825	1	22865	1	23532	2	24360	2	25119	2	25608	2	26433	2	27097	2
21920	3	22900	3	23540	2	24361	2	25120	2	25609	2	26434	3	27098	2
21925	3	23000	2	23545	2	24362	2	25130	2	25622	2	26494	2	27100	2
21935	1	23020	2	23550	2	24363	2	25135	2	25624	2	26496	2	27105	2
22010	2	23030	2	23552	2	24365	2	25136	2	25628	2	26497	2	27110	2
22015	2	23031	2	23570	2	24366	2	25210	2	25630	2	26498	2	27111	2
22100	1	23035	2	23575	2	24400	2	25215	2	25635	2	26508	2	27120	2
22101	1	23040	2	23585	2	24410	2	25230	2	25650	2	26516	2	27122	2
22102	1	23044	2	23600	2	24420	2	25240	2	25651	2	26517	2	27125	2
22103	3	23065	2	23605	2	24430	2	25246	2	25652	2	26518	2	27130	2
22110	1	23066	2	23615	2	24435	2	25250	2	25660	2	26548	3	27132	2
22112	1	23076	2	23616	2	24470	2	25251	2	25670	2	26550	2	27134	2
22114	1	23100	2	23620	2	24495	2	25259	2	25671	2	26551	2	27137	2
22116	3	23101	2	23625	2	24498	2	25300	2	25675	2	26553	2	27138	2
22210	1	23105	2	23630	2	24500	2	25301	2	25676	2	26554	2	27140	2
22212	1	23106	2	23650	2	24505	2	25315	2	25680	2	26555	2	27146	2
22214	1	23107	2	23655	2	24515	2	25316	2	25685	2	26556	2	27147	2
22220	1	23120	2	23660	2	24516	2	25320	2	25690	2	26560	2	27151	2
22222	1	23125	2	23665	2	24530	2	25332	2	25695	2	26561	2	27156	2
22224	1	23130	2	23670	2	24535	2	25335	2	25800	2	26562	2	27158	1
22305	1	23150	1	23675	2	24538	2	25337	2	25805	2	26580	2	27161	2
22310	1	23155	1	23680	2	24545	2	25350	2	25810	2	26641	2	27165	2
22315	1	23156	1	23700	2	24546	2	25355	2	25820	2	26645	2	27170	2
22318	1	23170	1	23800	2	24560	2	25360	2	25825	2	26650	2	27175	2
22319	1	23172	1	23802	2	24565	2	25365	2	25830	2	26665	2	27176	2
22325	1	23174	1	23900	1	24576	2	25370	2	25900	2	26740	3	27177	2
22326	1	23180	1	23920	2	24577	2	25375	2	25905	2	26742	3	27178	2
22327	1	23182	1	23921	2	24586	2	25390	2	25907	2	26746	3	27179	2
22505	1	23184	1	23930	2	24587	2	25391	2	25909	2	26820	2	27181	2
22520	1	23190	1	23931	2	24600	2	25392	2	25915	2	26841	2	27185	2
22521	1	23195	1	23935	2	24605	2	25393	2	25920	2	26842	2	27187	2
22523	1	23200	1	24000	2	24615	2	25394	2	25922	2	26860	1	27193	1
22524	1	23210	1	24006	2	24620	2	25400	2	25924	2	26862	1	27194	1
22532	1	23220	1	24065	2	24635	2	25405	2	25927	2	26990	2	27200	1
22533	1	23221	1	24066	2	24640	2	25415	2	25929	2	26991	2	27202	1
22534	3	23222	1	24077	2	24650	2	25420	2	25931	2	26992	2	27216	1
22548	1	23330	2	24100	2	24655	2	25425	2	26010	3	27000	2	27217	1
22554	1	23331	2	24101	2	24665	2	25426	2	26011	3	27005	2	27218	1

CPT	MUE	CPT	MUE	CPT	MUE	CPT	MUE	CPT	MUE	CPT	MUE	CPT	MUE	CPT	MUE
27220	2	27405	2	27558	2	27730	2	28106	2	28505	2	29700	2	29898	2
27222	2	27407	2	27560	2	27732	2	28107	2	28530	2	29705	2	29899	2
27226	2	27409	2	27562	2	27734	2	28108	2	28531	2	29710	2	29900	2
27227	2	27412	2	27566	2	27740	2	28110	2	28540	2	29715	1	29901	2
27228	2	27415	2	27570	2	27742	2	28111	2	28545	2	29720	1	29902	2
27230	2	27418	2	27580	2	27745	2	28113	2	28546	2	29730	2	30000	1
27232	2	27420	2	27590	2	27750	2	28114	2	28555	2	29740	1	30020	1
27235	2	27422	2	27591	2	27752	2	28116	2	28570	2	29800	2	30100	3
27236	2	27424	2	27592	2	27756	2	28118	2	28575	2	29804	2	30117	2
27238	2	27425	2	27594	2	27758	2	28119	2	28576	2	29805	2	30118	2
27240	2	27427	2	27596	2	27759	2	28120	2	28585	2	29806	2	30120	1
27244	2	27428	2	27598	2	27760	2	28130	2	28600	3	29807	2	30124	2
27245	2	27429	2	27600	2	27762	2	28171	2	28605	3	29819	2	30125	1
27246	2	27430	2	27601	2	27766	2	28173	2	28630	3	29820	2	30130	2
27248	2	27435	2	27602	2	27780	2	28175	2	28705	2	29821	2	30140	2
27250	2	27437	2	27604	2	27781	2	28192	2	28715	2	29822	2	30150	1
27252	2	27438	2	27605	2	27784	2	28193	2	28725	2	29823	2	30160	1
27253	2	27440	2	27606	2	27786	2	28202	2	28730	2	29824	2	30200	1
27254	2	27441	2	27607	2	27788	2	28210	2	28735	2	29825	2	30210	1
27256	2	27442	2	27610	2	27792	2	28220	2	28737	2	29826	2	30220	1
27257	2	27443	2	27612	2	27808	2	28222	2	28750	2	29827	2	30300	1
27258	2	27445	2	27615	2	27810	2	28225	2	28755	2	29830	2	30310	1
27259	2	27446	2	27620	2	27814	2	28226	2	28760	2	29834	2	30320	1
27265	2	27447	2	27625	2	27816	2	28230	2	28800	2	29835	2	30400	1
27266	2	27454	2	27626	2	27818	2	28238	2	28805	2	29836	2	30410	1
27275	2	27465	2	27630	2	27822	2	28240	2	28890	2	29837	2	30420	1
27282	1	27466	2	27635	2	27823	2	28250	2	29000	1	29838	2	30430	1
27284	2	27468	2	27637	2	27824	2	28260	2	29010	1	29840	2	30435	1
27286	2	27470	2	27638	2	27825	2	28261	2	29015	1	29843	2	30450	1
27290	1	27472	2	27640	2	27826	2	28262	2	29020	1	29844	2	30460	1
27295	2	27475	2	27641	2	27827	2	28264	2	29025	1	29845	2	30462	1
27303	2	27477	2	27645	1	27828	2	28280	2	29035	1	29846	2	30520	1
27305	2	27479	2	27646	1	27829	2	28286	2	29040	1	29847	2	30540	1
27306	2	27485	2	27647	2	27830	2	28289	2	29044	1	29848	2	30545	1
27307	2	27486	2	27648	2	27831	2	28290	2	29046	1	29850	2	30560	1
27310	2	27487	2	27650	2	27832	2	28292	2	29049	1	29851	2	30580	2
27325	1	27488	2	27652	2	27840	2	28293	2	29055	1	29855	2	30600	1
27326	1	27495	2	27654	2	27842	2	28294	2	29065	2	29856	2	30620	1
27329	2	27496	2	27656	2	27846	2	28296	2	29075	2	29860	2	30630	1
27330	2	27497	2	27658	2	27848	2	28297	2	29085	2	29861	2	30801	1
27331	2	27498	2	27659	2	27860	2	28298	2	29086	2	29862	2	30802	1
27332	2	27499	2	27664	2	27870	2	28299	2	29105	2	29863	2	30905	1
27333	2	27500	2	27665	2	27871	2	28300	2	29125	2	29866	2	30906	1
27334	2	27501	2	27675	2	27880	2	28302	2	29126	2	29867	2	30915	1
27335	2	27502	2	27676	2	27881	2	28304	2	29200	1	29868	2	30920	1
27340	2	27503	2	27680	3	27882	2	28305	2	29220	1	29870	2	31002	2
27345	2	27506	2	27681	2	27884	2	28306	2	29240	2	29871	2	31040	2
27347	2	27507	2	27685	2	27886	2	28307	2	29260	2	29873	2	31050	2
27350	2	27508	2	27686	2	27888	2	28309	2	29280	2	29874	2	31051	2
27355	2	27509	2	27687	2	27889	2	28310	2	29305	1	29875	2	31070	2
27356	2	27510	2	27690	2	27892	2	28315	2	29325	1	29876	2	31075	2
27357	2	27511	2	27691	2	27893	2	28320	2	29345	2	29877	2	31080	2
27358	2	27513	2	27695	2	27894	2	28322	2	29355	2	29879	2	31081	2
27365	2	27514	2	27696	2	28001	2	28340	2	29358	2	29880	2	31084	2
27370	2	27516	2	27698	2	28002	3	28341	2	29365	2	29881	2	31085	2
27380	2	27517	2	27700	2	28003	2	28344	2	29405	2	29882	2	31086	2
27381	2	27519	2	27702	2	28005	3	28360	2	29425	2	29883	2	31087	2
27385	2	27520	2	27703	2	28035	2	28400	2	29435	2	29884	2	31090	2
27386	2	27524	2	27704	2	28052	2	28405	2	29440	2	29885	2	31200	2
27390	2	27530	2	27705	2	28054	2	28406	2	29445	2	29886	2	31201	2
27391	1	27532	2	27707	2	28060	2	28415	2	29450	2	29887	2	31205	2
27392	1	27535	2	27709	2	28062	2	28420	2	29505	2	29888	2	31225	2
27393	2	27536	2	27712	2	28086	2	28430	2	29515	2	29889	2	31230	2
27394	1	27538	2	27715	2	28088	2	28435	2	29520	2	29891	2	31231	1
27395	1	27540	2	27720	2	28090	2	28436	2	29530	2	29892	2	31233	2
27396	2	27550	2	27722	2	28092	2	28445	2	29540	2	29893	2	31235	2
27397	2	27552	2	27724	2	28100	2	28490	2	29550	2	29894	2	31237	2
27400	2	27556	2	27725	2	28102	2	28495	2	29580	2	29895	2	31238	2
27403	2	27557	2	27727	2	28103	2	28496	2	29590	2	29897	2	31239	2

© 2008 Ingenix

CPT	MUE	CPT	MUE	CPT	MUE	CPT	MUE	CPT	MUE	CPT	MUE	CPT	MUE	CPT	MUE
31240	2	31610	1	32488	1	33223	1	33507	2	33788	1	34808	1	35501	2
31254	2	31611	1	32500	2	33224	1	33508	1	33800	1	34813	1	35506	2
31255	2	31612	1	32540	1	33225	1	33510	1	33802	1	34825	2	35508	2
31256	2	31613	1	32601	1	33226	1	33511	1	33803	1	34830	1	35509	1
31267	2	31614	1	32602	1	33233	1	33512	1	33813	1	34831	1	35510	2
31276	2	31615	1	32603	1	33234	1	33513	1	33814	1	34832	1	35511	1
31287	2	31620	1	32604	1	33235	1	33514	1	33820	1	35001	2	35512	2
31288	2	31622	1	32605	1	33236	1	33516	1	33822	1	35002	2	35515	2
31290	2	31623	1	32606	1	33237	1	33517	1	33824	1	35005	2	35516	2
31291	2	31624	1	32650	2	33238	1	33518	1	33840	1	35011	2	35518	1
31292	2	31625	1	32651	2	33240	1	33519	1	33845	1	35013	2	35521	2
31293	2	31628	1	32652	2	33241	1	33521	1	33851	1	35021	2	35522	2
31294	2	31629	1	32653	1	33243	1	33522	1	33852	1	35022	2	35525	2
31300	1	31630	2	32654	2	33244	1	33523	1	33853	1	35081	1	35526	3
31320	1	31631	1	32655	2	33249	1	33530	1	33860	1	35082	1	35533	1
31360	1	31635	1	32656	2	33250	1	33533	1	33861	1	35091	1	35536	1
31365	1	31636	1	32657	2	33251	1	33534	1	33863	1	35092	1	35548	1
31367	1	31637	2	32658	1	33261	1	33535	1	33870	1	35102	1	35549	1
31368	1	31638	2	32659	1	33282	1	33536	1	33875	1	35103	1	35551	2
31370	1	31640	1	32660	1	33284	1	33542	1	33877	1	35111	1	35556	2
31375	1	31641	1	32661	1	33300	1	33545	1	33880	1	35112	1	35558	1
31380	1	31643	1	32662	1	33305	1	33548	1	33881	1	35131	2	35560	2
31382	1	31645	1	32663	2	33310	1	33572	3	33883	1	35132	2	35563	2
31390	1	31656	1	32664	2	33315	1	33606	1	33886	1	35141	2	35565	2
31395	1	31715	1	32665	1	33320	1	33608	1	33889	1	35142	2	35566	2
31400	1	31717	1	32800	1	33321	1	33610	1	33891	1	35151	2	35571	2
31420	1	31720	1	32810	1	33322	1	33611	1	33910	1	35152	2	35583	2
31500	2	31725	1	32815	1	33330	1	33612	1	33915	1	35180	2	35585	2
31502	1	31730	1	32820	1	33332	1	33615	1	33916	1	35182	2	35587	2
31505	1	31750	1	32850	1	33335	1	33617	1	33917	1	35184	2	35601	2
31510	1	31755	1	32851	1	33400	1	33619	1	33920	1	35188	2	35606	2
31511	1	31760	1	32852	1	33401	1	33641	1	33922	1	35190	2	35612	1
31512	1	31766	1	32853	1	33403	1	33645	1	33924	1	35201	2	35616	2
31513	1	31770	2	32854	1	33404	1	33647	1	33925	1	35206	2	35621	2
31515	1	31775	1	32855	1	33405	1	33660	1	33926	1	35211	3	35626	3
31520	1	31780	1	32856	1	33406	1	33681	1	33930	1	35216	3	35636	1
31525	1	31781	1	32900	1	33410	1	33684	1	33933	1	35221	3	35642	2
31526	1	31785	1	32905	1	33411	1	33688	1	33935	1	35226	3	35645	2
31527	1	31786	1	32906	1	33412	1	33690	1	33940	1	35231	2	35646	1
31528	1	31800	1	32940	1	33413	1	33692	1	33944	1	35236	2	35650	1
31529	1	31805	1	32960	1	33414	1	33694	1	33945	1	35251	3	35651	2
31530	1	31820	1	32997	2	33415	1	33697	1	33960	1	35256	2	35654	1
31531	1	31825	1	33010	1	33416	1	33702	1	33961	1	35266	2	35656	2
31535	1	31830	1	33011	1	33417	1	33710	1	33967	1	35286	2	35661	1
31536	1	32035	2	33015	1	33420	1	33720	1	33968	1	35311	2	35663	2
31540	1	32036	2	33020	1	33422	1	33722	1	33970	1	35321	2	35665	2
31541	1	32095	2	33025	1	33425	1	33730	1	33971	1	35331	1	35671	2
31545	2	32100	1	33030	1	33426	1	33732	1	33973	1	35351	2	35681	2
31546	2	32110	2	33031	1	33427	1	33735	1	33974	1	35355	2	35682	1
31560	1	32120	1	33050	1	33430	1	33736	1	33975	1	35361	2	35683	1
31561	1	32124	2	33120	1	33460	1	33737	1	33976	1	35363	2	35685	2
31570	1	32140	1	33130	1	33463	1	33750	1	33977	1	35371	2	35686	1
31571	1	32141	1	33140	1	33464	1	33755	1	33978	1	35372	2	35691	2
31575	1	32150	1	33141	1	33465	1	33762	1	33979	1	35390	2	35693	2
31576	1	32151	1	33202	1	33468	1	33764	1	33980	1	35400	1	35694	2
31577	1	32160	1	33206	1	33470	1	33766	1	34101	2	35452	1	35695	2
31578	1	32215	2	33207	1	33471	1	33767	1	34111	2	35456	2	35697	2
31579	1	32220	2	33208	1	33472	1	33768	1	34201	2	35459	2	35700	2
31580	1	32225	2	33210	1	33474	1	33770	1	34203	2	35471	3	35701	2
31582	1	32400	2	33211	1	33475	1	33771	1	34421	2	35472	1	35721	2
31584	1	32402	2	33212	1	33476	1	33774	1	34490	2	35474	2	35741	2
31587	1	32405	2	33213	1	33478	1	33775	1	34501	2	35481	1	35761	2
31588	1	32420	2	33214	1	33500	1	33776	1	34520	1	35483	2	35820	2
31590	1	32440	1	33215	2	33501	1	33777	1	34530	2	35485	2	35840	2
31595	2	32442	1	33216	1	33502	1	33778	1	34800	1	35491	1	35860	2
31600	1	32445	1	33217	1	33503	1	33779	1	34802	1	35492	2	35870	1
31601	1	32480	2	33218	1	33504	1	33780	1	34803	1	35493	1	35875	2
31603	1	32482	1	33220	1	33505	1	33781	1	34804	1	35495	1	35876	2
31605	1	32484	2	33222	1	33506	1	33786	1	34805	1	35500	2	35879	2

CPT	MUE	CPT	MUE	CPT	MUE	CPT	MUE	CPT	MUE	CPT	MUE	CPT	MUE	CPT	MUE
35881	2	36640	1	38241	1	40819	2	42310	2	43118	1	43340	1	43880	1
35901	1	36660	1	38242	1	40820	2	42320	2	43121	1	43341	1	43886	1
35903	2	36680	1	38300	2	40830	2	42330	3	43122	1	43350	1	43887	1
35905	1	36800	1	38305	2	40831	2	42335	2	43123	1	43351	1	43888	1
35907	1	36810	1	38308	1	40840	1	42340	2	43124	1	43352	1	44005	1
36002	2	36815	1	38380	1	40842	1	42405	2	43130	1	43360	1	44010	1
36005	2	36820	2	38381	1	40843	1	42408	1	43135	1	43361	1	44015	1
36010	2	36821	2	38382	1	40844	1	42409	1	43200	1	43400	1	44020	2
36013	2	36822	1	38500	2	40845	1	42410	2	43201	1	43401	1	44021	1
36014	2	36823	1	38505	3	41000	2	42415	2	43202	1	43405	1	44025	1
36120	2	36825	1	38510	2	41005	2	42420	2	43204	1	43410	1	44050	1
36145	1	36830	2	38520	2	41008	2	42425	2	43205	1	43415	1	44055	1
36160	1	36831	1	38525	2	41009	2	42426	2	43215	1	43420	1	44100	1
36200	2	36832	2	38530	2	41010	2	42440	2	43216	1	43425	1	44110	1
36260	1	36833	1	38542	2	41015	2	42507	1	43217	1	43450	1	44111	1
36261	1	36834	1	38550	1	41016	1	42508	1	43219	1	43453	1	44120	1
36262	1	36835	1	38555	1	41017	2	42509	1	43220	1	43456	1	44125	1
36410	3	36838	2	38562	1	41018	2	42510	1	43226	1	43458	1	44126	1
36420	2	36860	2	38564	1	41100	3	42550	2	43227	2	43460	1	44127	1
36425	1	36861	2	38570	1	41105	3	42600	1	43228	1	43496	1	44128	2
36430	1	36870	2	38571	1	41108	2	42650	2	43231	1	43500	1	44132	1
36450	1	37140	1	38572	1	41110	2	42660	2	43232	1	43501	1	44133	1
36455	1	37145	1	38700	1	41114	2	42665	2	43234	1	43502	1	44135	1
36468	1	37160	1	38724	2	41115	1	42700	2	43235	1	43510	1	44136	1
36469	1	37180	1	38740	2	41116	3	42725	2	43236	1	43520	1	44137	1
36470	2	37181	1	38745	2	41120	1	42800	3	43237	1	43600	1	44139	1
36471	2	37182	1	38746	1	41130	1	42802	2	43238	1	43605	1	44140	2
36475	1	37183	1	38747	1	41135	1	42806	1	43239	1	43610	1	44141	1
36478	2	37184	2	38765	1	41140	1	42808	2	43240	1	43611	1	44143	1
36479	2	37188	1	38770	1	41145	1	42809	1	43241	1	43620	1	44144	1
36481	1	37195	1	38780	1	41150	1	42810	2	43242	1	43621	1	44145	1
36510	1	37200	2	38790	1	41153	1	42815	2	43243	1	43622	1	44146	1
36511	1	37201	1	38792	2	41155	1	42820	1	43244	1	43631	1	44147	1
36512	1	37203	2	38794	1	41251	2	42821	1	43245	1	43632	1	44150	1
36513	1	37205	1	39000	1	41252	2	42825	1	43246	1	43633	1	44151	1
36514	1	37207	1	39010	1	41500	1	42826	1	43247	1	43634	1	44155	1
36515	1	37209	2	39200	1	41510	1	42830	1	43248	1	43635	1	44156	1
36516	1	37215	2	39220	1	41520	1	42831	1	43249	1	43640	1	44160	1
36522	1	37250	1	39400	1	41800	2	42835	1	43250	1	43641	1	44180	1
36555	2	37500	2	39501	1	41822	1	42836	1	43251	1	43644	1	44186	1
36556	2	37565	2	39502	1	41823	1	42842	1	43255	2	43645	1	44187	1
36557	2	37600	1	39503	1	41825	2	42844	1	43256	1	43651	1	44188	1
36558	2	37605	2	39520	1	41826	2	42845	1	43257	1	43652	1	44202	1
36560	2	37606	2	39530	1	41827	2	42860	1	43258	1	43653	1	44203	2
36561	2	37607	1	39531	1	41850	2	42870	1	43259	1	43752	2	44204	2
36563	2	37609	2	39540	1	42000	1	42890	1	43260	1	43760	2	44205	1
36565	2	37615	2	39541	1	42100	3	42892	1	43261	1	43761	2	44206	1
36566	2	37616	1	39545	1	42104	3	42894	1	43262	2	43770	1	44207	1
36568	2	37617	3	39560	1	42106	2	42900	1	43263	2	43771	1	44208	1
36569	2	37618	2	39561	1	42107	2	42950	1	43264	1	43772	1	44210	1
36570	2	37620	1	40500	2	42120	1	42953	1	43265	1	43773	1	44211	1
36571	2	37660	2	40510	2	42140	1	42955	1	43267	1	43774	1	44212	1
36575	2	37760	2	40520	2	42145	1	42960	1	43268	2	43800	1	44213	1
36576	2	37765	2	40525	2	42180	1	42961	1	43269	2	43810	1	44227	1
36578	2	37766	2	40527	2	42182	1	42962	1	43271	1	43820	1	44300	1
36580	2	37788	1	40530	2	42200	1	42970	2	43272	1	43825	1	44310	2
36581	2	37790	1	40650	2	42205	1	42971	1	43280	1	43830	1	44312	1
36582	2	38100	1	40652	2	42210	1	42972	1	43300	1	43831	1	44314	1
36583	2	38101	1	40654	2	42215	1	43020	1	43305	1	43832	1	44316	1
36584	2	38102	1	40700	1	42220	1	43030	1	43310	1	43843	1	44320	1
36585	2	38115	1	40701	1	42225	1	43045	1	43312	1	43845	1	44322	1
36589	2	38120	1	40702	1	42226	1	43100	1	43313	1	43846	1	44340	1
36590	2	38200	1	40720	1	42227	1	43101	1	43314	1	43847	1	44345	1
36595	2	38205	1	40761	1	42235	1	43107	1	43320	1	43848	1	44346	1
36596	2	38206	1	40800	1	42260	1	43108	1	43324	1	43850	1	44360	1
36597	2	38220	2	40801	1	42280	1	43112	1	43325	1	43855	1	44361	1
36598	2	38221	1	40806	2	42281	1	43113	1	43326	1	43860	1	44363	1
36620	3	38230	1	40816	2	42300	2	43116	1	43330	1	43865	1	44364	1
36625	2	38240	1	40818	2	42305	2	43117	1	43331	1	43870	1	44365	1

© 2008 Ingenix

CPT	MUE	CPT	MUE	CPT	MUE	CPT	MUE	CPT	MUE	CPT	MUE	CPT	MUE	CPT	MUE
44366	1	45300	1	46211	1	47015	1	48001	1	49580	1	50543	2	51530	1
44369	1	45303	1	46220	2	47100	3	48020	1	49582	1	50544	2	51550	1
44370	1	45305	1	46221	1	47120	1	48100	1	49585	1	50545	2	51555	1
44372	1	45307	1	46230	1	47122	1	48102	2	49587	1	50546	2	51565	1
44373	1	45308	1	46250	1	47125	1	48120	1	49600	1	50547	1	51570	1
44376	1	45309	1	46255	1	47130	1	48140	1	49605	1	50548	2	51575	1
44377	1	45315	1	46257	1	47133	1	48145	1	49606	1	50551	2	51580	1
44378	1	45320	1	46258	1	47135	1	48146	1	49610	1	50553	2	51585	1
44379	1	45321	1	46260	1	47136	1	48148	1	49611	1	50557	2	51590	1
44380	1	45327	1	46261	1	47140	1	48150	1	49900	1	50561	2	51595	1
44382	1	45330	1	46262	1	47141	1	48152	1	49904	1	50570	2	51596	1
44383	1	45331	1	46270	1	47142	1	48153	1	49905	1	50572	2	51597	1
44385	1	45332	1	46275	1	47143	1	48154	1	49906	1	50575	2	51600	1
44386	1	45333	1	46280	1	47144	1	48155	1	50010	2	50576	2	51605	1
44388	1	45334	1	46285	1	47145	1	48400	1	50020	1	50590	1	51610	1
44389	1	45335	1	46288	1	47147	3	48500	1	50021	2	50600	2	51700	1
44390	1	45337	1	46320	2	47370	1	48510	1	50040	2	50605	2	51701	2
44392	1	45338	1	46500	1	47371	1	48511	1	50045	2	50610	2	51702	2
44393	1	45339	1	46505	1	47380	1	48520	1	50060	2	50620	2	51703	2
44394	1	45340	1	46600	1	47381	1	48540	1	50065	2	50630	2	51705	1
44397	1	45341	1	46604	1	47382	1	48545	1	50070	2	50650	2	51710	1
44500	1	45342	1	46606	1	47400	1	48547	1	50075	2	50660	2	51715	1
44602	1	45345	1	46608	1	47420	1	48550	1	50080	2	50684	2	51720	1
44603	1	45355	1	46610	1	47425	1	48551	1	50081	2	50686	2	51725	1
44604	1	45378	1	46611	1	47460	1	48552	2	50100	2	50688	2	51726	1
44605	1	45379	1	46612	1	47480	1	48554	1	50120	2	50690	2	51736	1
44620	2	45380	1	46614	1	47490	1	48556	1	50125	2	50700	2	51741	1
44625	1	45381	1	46615	1	47500	2	49000	1	50130	2	50722	2	51772	1
44626	1	45382	2	46700	1	47505	2	49002	1	50135	2	50725	1	51784	1
44660	1	45383	1	46705	1	47510	2	49010	1	50200	2	50727	1	51785	1
44661	1	45384	1	46706	2	47511	2	49020	2	50205	2	50728	1	51792	1
44680	1	45385	1	46710	1	47525	3	49021	3	50220	2	50740	2	51795	1
44700	1	45386	1	46712	1	47530	3	49040	2	50225	2	50750	2	51797	1
44701	1	45387	1	46715	1	47550	1	49041	3	50230	2	50760	2	51798	1
44715	1	45391	1	46716	1	47552	1	49060	2	50234	2	50770	1	51800	1
44720	2	45392	1	46730	1	47553	1	49061	3	50236	2	50782	2	51820	1
44721	2	45395	1	46735	1	47554	1	49062	1	50240	2	50783	2	51840	1
44800	1	45397	1	46740	1	47555	1	49080	1	50250	1	50810	1	51841	1
44820	2	45400	1	46742	1	47556	1	49081	2	50280	2	50825	1	51845	1
44850	1	45402	1	46744	1	47560	1	49180	3	50290	1	50830	1	51860	1
44900	1	45500	1	46746	1	47561	1	49215	1	50300	1	50845	1	51865	1
44901	1	45505	1	46748	1	47562	1	49220	1	50320	1	50900	2	51880	1
44950	1	45520	1	46751	1	47563	1	49250	1	50323	1	50920	2	51900	1
44955	1	45540	1	46753	1	47564	1	49255	1	50325	1	50930	2	51920	1
44960	1	45541	1	46754	1	47570	1	49320	1	50327	3	50940	2	51925	1
44970	1	45550	1	46760	1	47600	1	49321	1	50328	3	50945	2	51940	1
45000	1	45560	1	46761	1	47605	1	49322	1	50329	2	50947	2	51960	1
45005	1	45562	1	46762	1	47610	1	49323	1	50360	1	50948	2	51980	1
45020	1	45563	1	46900	1	47612	1	49324	1	50365	1	50951	2	51990	1
45100	1	45800	1	46910	1	47620	1	49400	1	50370	1	50953	2	51992	1
45108	1	45805	1	46916	1	47630	1	49402	1	50380	1	50955	2	52000	1
45110	1	45820	1	46917	1	47700	1	49419	1	50389	2	50957	2	52001	1
45111	1	45825	1	46922	1	47701	1	49421	1	50390	2	50961	2	52005	2
45112	1	45900	1	46924	1	47711	1	49422	1	50391	2	50970	2	52007	2
45113	1	45905	1	46934	1	47712	1	49423	3	50392	2	50972	2	52010	1
45114	1	45910	1	46935	1	47715	1	49424	3	50393	2	50974	2	52204	1
45116	1	45915	1	46936	1	47720	1	49425	1	50394	2	50976	2	52214	1
45119	1	45990	1	46937	1	47721	1	49426	1	50395	2	50980	2	52224	1
45120	1	46020	1	46938	1	47740	1	49427	1	50396	2	51020	1	52234	1
45121	1	46030	1	46940	1	47741	1	49428	1	50398	2	51030	1	52235	1
45123	1	46040	2	46942	1	47760	1	49429	1	50400	2	51040	1	52240	1
45126	1	46045	2	46945	1	47765	1	49525	2	50405	2	51045	2	52250	1
45130	1	46050	2	46946	1	47780	1	49540	1	50500	1	51050	1	52260	1
45135	1	46060	2	46947	1	47785	1	49550	1	50520	1	51060	2	52265	1
45136	1	46070	1	47000	3	47800	1	49553	2	50525	1	51065	1	52270	1
45150	1	46080	1	47001	3	47801	1	49555	2	50526	1	51080	2	52275	1
45160	1	46083	2	47010	3	47802	1	49557	2	50540	1	51500	1	52276	1
45170	1	46200	1	47011	3	47900	1	49570	1	50541	2	51520	1	52277	1
45190	1	46210	1	47011	3	48000	1	49572	1	50542	2	51525	1	52281	1

CPT	MUE	CPT	MUE	CPT	MUE	CPT	MUE	CPT	MUE	CPT	MUE	CPT	MUE	CPT	MUE
52282	1	53440	1	54328	1	55700	1	57220	1	58240	1	58943	1	60270	1
52283	1	53442	1	54332	1	55705	1	57230	1	58260	1	58950	1	60271	1
52285	1	53444	1	54336	1	55720	1	57240	1	58262	1	58951	1	60280	1
52290	1	53445	1	54340	1	55725	1	57250	1	58263	1	58952	1	60281	1
52300	1	53446	1	54344	1	55801	1	57260	1	58267	1	58953	1	60500	1
52301	1	53447	1	54348	1	55810	1	57265	1	58270	1	58954	1	60502	1
52305	1	53448	1	54352	1	55812	1	57267	3	58275	1	58956	1	60505	1
52310	1	53449	1	54360	1	55815	1	57268	1	58280	1	58960	1	60512	1
52315	2	53450	1	54380	1	55821	1	57270	1	58285	1	58970	1	60520	1
52317	1	53460	1	54385	1	55831	1	57280	1	58290	1	58974	1	60521	1
52318	1	53500	1	54390	1	55840	1	57282	1	58291	1	58976	2	60522	1
52320	2	53502	1	54400	1	55842	1	57283	1	58292	1	59025	1	60545	2
52325	2	53505	1	54401	1	55845	1	57284	1	58293	1	59050	1	60600	1
52327	2	53510	1	54405	1	55860	1	57287	1	58294	1	59051	1	60605	1
52330	2	53515	1	54406	1	55862	1	57288	1	58301	1	59100	1	60650	2
52334	2	53520	1	54408	1	55865	1	57289	1	58321	1	59120	1	61000	1
52341	2	53600	1	54410	1	55866	1	57291	1	58322	1	59121	1	61001	1
52342	2	53601	1	54411	1	55870	1	57292	1	58323	1	59130	1	61020	2
52343	2	53605	1	54415	1	55873	1	57295	1	58340	1	59135	1	61026	2
52344	2	53620	1	54416	1	55876	1	57300	1	58345	2	59136	1	61050	1
52345	2	53621	1	54417	1	56405	2	57305	1	58346	1	59140	1	61055	1
52346	2	53660	1	54420	1	56420	1	57307	1	58350	2	59150	1	61070	2
52351	1	53661	1	54430	1	56440	1	57308	1	58353	1	59151	1	61105	2
52352	2	53665	1	54435	1	56441	1	57310	1	58356	1	59160	1	61107	2
52353	2	53850	1	54440	1	56442	1	57311	1	58400	1	59300	1	61108	2
52354	2	53852	1	54450	1	56501	1	57320	1	58410	1	59320	1	61120	1
52355	2	53853	1	54500	2	56515	1	57330	1	58520	1	59325	1	61140	2
52400	1	54000	1	54512	2	56605	1	57335	1	58540	1	59350	1	61150	2
52402	1	54001	1	54522	2	56620	1	57400	1	58541	1	59400	1	61151	2
52450	1	54015	1	54530	2	56625	1	57410	1	58542	1	59410	1	61156	2
52500	1	54050	1	54535	1	56630	1	57415	1	58545	1	59412	2	61210	1
52601	1	54055	1	54600	2	56631	1	57420	1	58546	1	59414	1	61215	1
52606	1	54056	1	54620	1	56632	1	57421	1	58550	1	59425	1	61253	1
52612	1	54057	1	54650	2	56633	1	57425	1	58552	1	59426	1	61305	1
52614	1	54060	1	54670	2	56634	1	57452	1	58553	1	59430	1	61312	2
52620	1	54065	1	54680	1	56637	1	57454	1	58554	1	59510	1	61313	2
52630	1	54100	3	54690	2	56640	1	57455	1	58555	1	59514	1	61314	2
52640	1	54105	2	54692	2	56700	1	57456	1	58558	1	59515	1	61315	1
52647	1	54110	1	54700	2	56740	2	57460	1	58559	1	59525	1	61316	1
52648	1	54111	1	54800	1	56800	1	57461	1	58560	1	59610	1	61320	2
52700	1	54112	1	54830	2	56805	1	57500	1	58561	1	59614	1	61321	2
53000	1	54115	1	54840	2	56810	1	57505	1	58562	1	59618	1	61322	1
53010	1	54120	1	54860	1	56820	1	57510	1	58563	1	59620	1	61323	1
53020	1	54125	1	54861	1	56821	1	57511	1	58565	1	59622	1	61332	2
53025	1	54130	1	54865	1	57000	1	57513	1	58600	1	59812	1	61333	2
53040	1	54135	1	54900	1	57010	1	57520	1	58605	1	59820	1	61334	2
53060	1	54150	1	54901	1	57020	1	57522	1	58611	1	59821	1	61343	1
53080	1	54160	1	55000	2	57022	2	57530	1	58615	1	59830	1	61345	1
53085	1	54161	1	55040	1	57023	2	57531	1	58660	1	59840	1	61440	1
53200	1	54162	1	55041	1	57061	1	57540	1	58661	1	59841	1	61450	1
53210	1	54163	1	55060	2	57065	1	57545	1	58662	1	59850	1	61458	1
53215	1	54164	1	55100	2	57100	3	57550	1	58670	1	59851	1	61460	1
53220	1	54200	1	55110	1	57105	2	57555	1	58671	1	59852	1	61470	1
53230	1	54205	1	55120	1	57106	1	57556	1	58700	1	59855	1	61480	1
53235	1	54220	1	55150	1	57107	1	57558	1	58720	1	59856	1	61500	3
53240	1	54230	1	55175	1	57109	1	57700	1	58740	1	59857	1	61501	1
53250	1	54231	1	55180	1	57110	1	57720	1	58750	2	59866	1	61512	3
53260	1	54235	1	55200	1	57111	1	57800	1	58752	2	59870	1	61516	2
53265	1	54240	1	55250	1	57112	1	58100	1	58760	2	59871	1	61517	1
53270	1	54250	1	55300	1	57120	1	58110	1	58770	2	60000	1	61518	2
53275	1	54300	1	55450	1	57130	1	58120	1	58800	1	60200	2	61519	2
53400	1	54304	1	55500	2	57135	2	58140	1	58805	1	60210	1	61520	1
53405	1	54308	1	55520	2	57150	1	58145	1	58820	2	60212	1	61521	1
53410	1	54312	1	55530	2	57155	1	58146	1	58822	2	60220	1	61522	2
53415	1	54316	1	55535	2	57160	1	58150	1	58825	1	60225	1	61524	2
53420	1	54318	1	55540	2	57170	1	58152	1	58900	1	60240	1	61526	1
53425	1	54322	1	55550	2	57180	1	58180	1	58920	1	60252	1	61530	1
53430	1	54324	1	55605	2	57200	1	58200	1	58925	1	60254	1	61534	1
53431	1	54326	1	55680	2	57210	1	58210	1	58940	1	60260	1	61536	1

© 2008 Ingenix

Appendix J — Medically Unlikely Edits (MUEs) — Professional

CPT	MUE	CPT	MUE	CPT	MUE	CPT	MUE	CPT	MUE	CPT	MUE	CPT	MUE	CPT	MUE
61537	1	61770	1	62360	1	63300	1	64595	1	64895	2	66020	2	67208	2
61538	1	61790	2	62361	1	63301	1	64600	2	64898	2	66030	2	67210	2
61539	1	61791	2	62362	1	63302	1	64605	2	64901	2	66130	2	67218	2
61540	1	61795	2	62365	1	63303	1	64610	2	64905	1	66150	2	67220	2
61541	1	61850	1	62367	1	63304	1	64612	2	64907	1	66155	2	67221	1
61542	1	61860	1	62368	1	63305	1	64630	1	65091	2	66160	2	67225	1
61543	1	61863	2	63001	1	63306	1	64650	1	65093	2	66165	2	67227	2
61544	2	61864	1	63003	1	63307	1	64653	1	65101	2	66170	2	67250	2
61545	1	61867	2	63005	1	63600	2	64680	1	65103	2	66172	2	67255	2
61546	1	61868	2	63011	1	63610	1	64681	1	65105	2	66180	2	67311	2
61548	1	61870	1	63012	1	63615	1	64702	2	65110	2	66185	2	67312	2
61550	1	61875	1	63015	1	63650	2	64712	2	65112	2	66220	2	67314	2
61552	1	61880	1	63016	1	63655	1	64713	2	65114	2	66225	2	67316	2
61556	1	61885	2	63017	1	63660	1	64714	2	65125	2	66250	2	67318	2
61557	1	61886	1	63045	1	63685	2	64718	2	65130	2	66500	2	67320	2
61558	1	61888	2	63046	1	63688	2	64719	2	65135	2	66505	2	67331	2
61559	1	62100	1	63047	1	63700	1	64721	2	65140	2	66600	2	67332	2
61563	2	62115	1	63050	1	63702	1	64726	2	65150	2	66605	2	67334	2
61564	2	62116	1	63051	1	63704	1	64727	3	65155	2	66625	2	67335	2
61566	1	62117	1	63055	1	63706	1	64732	2	65175	2	66630	2	67340	2
61567	1	62120	1	63056	1	63707	1	64734	2	65205	2	66635	2	67343	2
61570	2	62121	1	63064	1	63709	1	64736	2	65210	2	66680	2	67345	2
61571	2	62140	1	63066	3	63710	1	64738	2	65220	2	66682	2	67400	2
61575	1	62141	1	63075	1	63740	1	64740	2	65222	2	66700	2	67405	2
61576	1	62142	2	63077	1	63741	1	64742	2	65235	2	66710	2	67412	2
61580	1	62143	2	63081	1	63744	1	64744	2	65260	2	66711	2	67413	2
61581	1	62145	2	63085	1	63746	1	64746	2	65265	2	66720	2	67414	2
61582	1	62146	2	63087	1	64402	2	64752	1	65270	2	66740	2	67415	2
61583	1	62147	2	63090	1	64405	2	64755	1	65272	2	66761	2	67420	2
61584	1	62148	2	63101	1	64408	2	64760	1	65273	2	66762	2	67430	2
61585	1	62160	1	63102	1	64410	2	64761	1	65275	2	66770	2	67440	2
61586	1	62161	1	63170	1	64412	2	64771	2	65280	2	66820	2	67445	2
61590	1	62162	1	63172	1	64413	2	64772	2	65285	2	66821	2	67450	2
61591	1	62163	1	63173	1	64415	2	64774	3	65286	2	66825	2	67500	2
61592	1	62164	1	63180	1	64416	2	64776	1	65290	2	66830	2	67505	2
61595	1	62165	1	63182	1	64417	2	64778	3	65400	2	66840	2	67515	2
61596	1	62180	1	63185	1	64418	2	64782	2	65410	2	66850	2	67550	2
61597	1	62190	1	63190	1	64420	3	64783	2	65420	2	66852	2	67560	2
61598	1	62192	1	63194	1	64421	3	64786	2	65426	2	66920	2	67570	2
61600	1	62194	2	63195	1	64425	2	64790	1	65430	2	66930	2	67710	2
61605	1	62200	1	63196	1	64430	2	64792	2	65435	2	66940	2	67715	2
61607	1	62201	1	63197	1	64435	2	64795	2	65436	2	66982	2	67800	1
61609	1	62220	1	63198	1	64445	2	64821	2	65450	2	66983	2	67801	1
61610	1	62223	1	63199	1	64446	2	64822	2	65600	2	66984	2	67805	1
61611	1	62225	2	63200	1	64447	2	64823	2	65710	2	66985	2	67808	1
61612	1	62230	2	63250	1	64448	2	64831	2	65730	2	66986	2	67820	2
61613	1	62252	2	63251	1	64449	2	64834	2	65750	2	66990	2	67825	2
61615	1	62256	1	63252	1	64470	2	64835	2	65755	2	67005	2	67830	3
61618	1	62258	1	63265	1	64475	2	64836	2	65770	2	67010	2	67835	2
61619	2	62263	1	63266	1	64479	2	64837	3	65772	2	67015	2	67875	2
61623	2	62264	1	63267	1	64483	2	64840	2	65775	2	67025	2	67880	2
61624	2	62268	1	63268	1	64505	2	64856	2	65780	2	67027	2	67882	2
61626	2	62269	2	63270	1	64508	2	64857	3	65781	2	67028	2	67900	2
61680	1	62270	2	63271	1	64510	2	64858	2	65782	2	67030	2	67901	2
61682	1	62272	1	63272	1	64517	1	64859	2	65800	2	67031	2	67902	2
61684	1	62273	2	63273	1	64520	2	64861	2	65805	2	67036	2	67903	2
61686	1	62280	1	63275	1	64530	2	64862	2	65810	2	67039	2	67904	2
61690	1	62281	1	63276	1	64553	1	64864	2	65815	2	67040	2	67906	2
61692	1	62282	1	63277	1	64555	2	64865	1	65820	2	67101	2	67908	2
61697	3	62284	1	63278	1	64560	1	64866	1	65850	2	67105	2	67909	2
61698	2	62287	1	63280	1	64561	2	64868	1	65855	2	67107	2	67912	2
61700	3	62292	1	63281	1	64565	2	64870	1	65860	2	67108	2	67938	2
61702	2	62310	2	63282	1	64573	1	64872	3	65865	2	67110	2	67950	2
61703	1	62311	2	63283	1	64575	2	64874	1	65870	2	67112	2	67971	2
61705	1	62318	2	63285	1	64577	1	64876	1	65875	2	67115	2	67973	2
61720	2	62319	2	63286	1	64580	2	64885	1	65880	2	67120	2	67974	2
61735	2	62350	1	63287	1	64581	2	64886	1	65900	2	67121	2	67975	2
61751	3	62351	1	63290	1	64585	2	64890	3	65920	2	67141	2	68020	2
61760	1	62355	1	63295	1	64590	1	64891	2	65930	2	67145	2	68040	2

CPT	MUE	CPT	MUE	CPT	MUE	CPT	MUE	CPT	MUE	CPT	MUE	CPT	MUE	CPT	MUE
68100	2	69602	1	70300	1	72010	1	73200	2	74283	1	75827	1	76805	1
68110	2	69603	1	70310	1	72040	3	73201	2	74290	1	75831	1	76810	3
68115	2	69604	1	70320	1	72050	1	73202	2	74291	1	75833	1	76811	1
68130	2	69605	1	70328	1	72052	1	73206	2	74300	1	75840	1	76812	3
68135	2	69610	2	70330	1	72069	1	73218	2	74301	2	75842	1	76814	3
68200	2	69620	2	70332	2	72070	1	73219	2	74305	1	75860	2	76815	1
68320	2	69631	2	70336	1	72072	1	73220	2	74320	1	75870	1	76817	1
68325	2	69632	1	70350	1	72074	1	73221	2	74327	1	75872	1	76830	1
68326	2	69633	1	70355	1	72080	1	73222	2	74328	1	75880	2	76831	1
68328	2	69635	1	70360	1	72090	1	73223	2	74329	1	75885	1	76856	1
68330	2	69636	1	70370	1	72100	1	73500	2	74330	1	75887	1	76857	1
68335	2	69637	1	70371	1	72110	1	73510	1	74340	1	75889	1	76870	1
68340	2	69641	1	70373	1	72114	1	73520	1	74355	1	75891	1	76872	1
68360	2	69642	1	70380	2	72120	1	73525	2	74360	1	75900	3	76873	1
68362	2	69643	1	70390	2	72125	1	73530	2	74363	2	75901	1	76880	2
68371	1	69644	1	70450	3	72126	1	73540	1	74400	1	75902	2	76885	1
68400	2	69645	1	70460	1	72127	1	73542	2	74410	1	75940	1	76886	1
68420	2	69646	1	70470	2	72128	1	73550	2	74415	1	75945	1	76930	1
68440	2	69650	1	70480	1	72129	1	73560	2	74420	2	75952	1	76932	1
68500	2	69660	1	70481	1	72130	1	73562	2	74425	1	75954	2	76936	2
68505	2	69661	1	70482	1	72131	1	73564	2	74430	1	75956	1	76937	2
68510	2	69662	2	70486	1	72132	1	73565	1	74440	2	75957	1	76940	1
68520	2	69666	2	70487	1	72133	1	73580	2	74445	1	75958	2	76942	1
68525	2	69667	2	70488	1	72141	1	73590	2	74450	1	75959	1	76945	1
68530	2	69670	1	70490	1	72142	1	73592	2	74455	1	75962	1	76946	1
68540	1	69700	2	70491	1	72146	1	73600	2	74470	2	75964	3	76948	1
68550	1	69711	2	70492	1	72147	1	73610	2	74475	2	75966	1	76950	2
68700	2	69714	2	70496	1	72148	1	73615	2	74480	2	75970	2	76965	2
68705	2	69715	1	70498	1	72149	1	73620	2	74485	2	75980	1	76970	1
68720	2	69717	1	70540	1	72156	1	73630	2	74710	1	75982	2	76975	1
68745	2	69718	1	70542	1	72157	1	73650	2	74740	1	75984	2	76977	1
68750	2	69720	2	70543	1	72158	1	73660	2	74742	2	75989	2	76998	1
68770	2	69725	2	70544	1	72170	1	73700	2	74775	1	75992	1	77002	1
68840	2	69740	2	70545	1	72190	1	73701	2	75600	1	75994	2	77003	1
68850	2	69745	2	70546	1	72191	1	73702	2	75605	1	75995	1	77011	1
69000	2	69801	1	70547	1	72192	1	73706	2	75625	1	75996	2	77012	1
69005	2	69802	1	70548	1	72193	1	73718	2	75630	1	76000	3	77013	1
69020	2	69805	1	70549	1	72194	1	73719	2	75635	1	76001	2	77014	2
69100	3	69806	1	70551	1	72195	1	73720	2	75650	2	76010	2	77021	1
69105	2	69820	1	70552	1	72196	1	73722	2	75658	2	76080	2	77022	1
69110	2	69840	1	70553	1	72197	1	73725	2	75660	1	76100	1	77053	2
69120	1	69905	1	70554	1	72198	1	74000	3	75662	1	76101	1	77054	2
69140	2	69910	1	70557	1	72200	1	74010	2	75665	1	76102	1	77071	1
69145	2	69915	1	70558	1	72202	1	74020	2	75671	1	76120	1	77261	1
69150	1	69930	2	70559	1	72220	1	74022	2	75676	1	76125	1	77262	1
69155	1	69950	2	71015	2	72240	1	74150	1	75680	1	76350	1	77263	1
69200	2	69955	2	71021	1	72255	1	74160	1	75685	2	76376	2	77280	2
69205	2	69960	2	71022	1	72265	1	74170	1	75710	1	76377	2	77285	1
69210	1	69970	1	71023	2	72270	1	74175	1	75716	1	76380	1	77290	1
69310	2	69990	1	71030	2	72275	3	74181	1	75722	1	76506	1	77295	1
69320	2	70010	1	71034	1	72292	3	74182	1	75724	1	76510	2	77301	1
69400	2	70015	1	71035	2	73000	2	74183	1	75726	1	76511	2	77305	2
69401	2	70030	2	71040	1	73010	2	74185	1	75731	1	76512	2	77310	2
69405	2	70100	1	71060	1	73020	2	74190	1	75733	1	76513	2	77315	2
69420	2	70110	1	71090	1	73030	2	74210	1	75736	1	76514	1	77321	1
69421	2	70120	2	71100	1	73040	2	74220	1	75741	1	76516	1	77326	1
69440	2	70130	2	71101	1	73050	1	74230	1	75743	1	76519	2	77327	1
69450	2	70134	1	71110	1	73060	2	74235	1	75746	1	76529	2	77328	1
69501	1	70140	1	71111	1	73070	2	74240	1	75756	2	76536	1	77336	1
69502	1	70150	1	71120	1	73080	2	74241	1	75790	2	76604	1	77370	1
69505	1	70160	1	71130	1	73085	2	74245	1	75801	1	76645	1	77373	1
69511	1	70170	2	71250	1	73090	2	74246	1	75803	1	76700	1	77401	2
69530	1	70190	1	71260	1	73092	2	74247	1	75805	1	76705	2	77402	2
69535	1	70200	1	71270	1	73100	2	74249	1	75807	1	76770	1	77403	2
69540	2	70210	1	71275	1	73110	2	74250	1	75809	1	76775	2	77404	2
69550	1	70220	1	71550	1	73115	2	74251	1	75810	1	76776	1	77406	2
69552	1	70240	1	71551	1	73120	2	74260	1	75820	1	76800	1	77407	2
69554	1	70250	1	71552	1	73130	2	74270	1	75822	1	76801	1	77408	2
69601	1	70260	1	71555	1	73140	2	74280	1	75825	1	76802	3	77409	2

CPT	MUE	CPT	MUE	CPT	MUE	CPT	MUE	CPT	MUE	CPT	MUE	CPT	MUE	CPT	MUE
77411	2	78215	1	78700	1	80412	1	82247	2	82657	3	83071	1	84061	1
77412	2	78216	1	78701	2	80414	1	82248	2	82666	1	83080	2	84066	1
77413	2	78220	1	78707	1	80415	1	82252	1	82668	1	83088	1	84075	2
77414	2	78223	1	78708	1	80416	1	82261	1	82670	2	83090	2	84078	1
77416	2	78230	1	78709	1	80417	1	82270	1	82671	1	83150	1	84080	1
77417	1	78231	1	78725	1	80418	1	82271	1	82672	1	83491	1	84081	1
77418	2	78232	1	78730	1	80420	1	82272	1	82677	1	83497	1	84085	1
77421	2	78258	1	78740	1	80422	1	82274	1	82679	1	83498	2	84087	1
77422	1	78261	1	78761	1	80424	1	82286	1	82690	1	83499	1	84100	3
77423	1	78262	1	78800	1	80426	1	82300	1	82693	2	83500	1	84105	1
77427	1	78264	1	78801	1	80428	1	82306	1	82696	1	83505	1	84106	1
77431	1	78267	1	78802	1	80430	1	82307	1	82705	1	83527	1	84110	1
77432	1	78268	1	78803	1	80432	1	82308	3	82710	1	83528	1	84119	1
77435	1	78270	1	78804	1	80434	1	82331	1	82715	1	83540	2	84120	1
77470	1	78271	1	78805	1	80435	1	82340	1	82725	1	83550	1	84126	1
77520	1	78272	1	78806	1	80436	1	82355	3	82726	1	83570	1	84127	1
77522	1	78278	2	78807	1	80438	1	82360	3	82728	1	83582	1	84133	2
77523	1	78282	1	78811	1	80439	1	82365	3	82731	1	83586	1	84134	1
77525	1	78290	1	78812	1	80440	1	82370	3	82735	1	83593	1	84135	1
77600	1	78291	1	78813	1	80500	1	82373	1	82742	1	83605	3	84138	1
77605	1	78300	1	78814	1	80502	1	82374	2	82746	1	83615	2	84140	1
77610	1	78305	1	78815	1	81000	2	82378	2	82747	1	83625	1	84143	2
77615	1	78306	1	78816	1	81001	2	82379	1	82757	1	83630	1	84144	1
77620	1	78315	1	79005	1	81002	2	82380	1	82759	1	83631	1	84146	3
77750	1	78320	1	79101	1	81003	2	82382	1	82760	1	83632	1	84150	2
77761	1	78414	1	79200	1	81005	2	82383	1	82775	1	83633	1	84152	1
77762	1	78428	1	79403	1	81007	1	82384	2	82776	1	83634	1	84153	1
77763	1	78445	1	79445	1	81015	1	82387	1	82785	1	83655	2	84154	1
77776	1	78456	1	80048	2	81020	1	82390	1	82820	1	83670	1	84155	1
77777	1	78457	1	80053	1	81025	1	82415	1	82928	1	83690	2	84156	1
77778	1	78458	1	80061	1	81050	2	82435	2	82941	1	83695	1	84157	3
77781	3	78459	1	80069	1	82000	1	82436	1	82943	1	83700	1	84160	2
77782	3	78460	1	80074	1	82003	2	82438	1	82946	1	83701	1	84163	1
77783	3	78461	1	80076	1	82009	1	82441	1	82950	3	83704	1	84165	1
77784	3	78464	1	80150	2	82013	1	82465	1	82951	1	83718	1	84166	2
77789	2	78465	1	80152	2	82016	1	82480	2	82952	3	83719	1	84202	1
77790	2	78466	1	80154	2	82017	1	82482	1	82953	1	83721	1	84203	1
70000	1	78468	1	80156	2	82030	1	82485	1	82955	1	83727	1	84206	1
78001	1	78469	1	80157	2	82040	1	82495	1	82960	1	83775	1	84207	1
78003	1	78472	1	80158	2	82042	2	82507	1	82963	1	83785	1	84210	2
78006	1	78473	1	80160	2	82043	1	82520	2	82965	1	83805	1	84220	1
78007	1	78478	1	80162	2	82044	1	82523	1	82975	1	83825	2	84228	1
78010	1	78480	1	80164	2	82045	1	82525	1	82977	1	83835	2	84233	2
78011	1	78481	1	80166	2	82055	2	82528	1	82978	1	83840	2	84234	2
78015	1	78483	1	80170	2	82085	1	82530	2	82979	1	83857	1	84235	1
78016	1	78491	1	80172	2	82101	1	82540	1	82980	1	83858	1	84238	3
78018	1	78492	1	80173	2	82103	1	82550	3	82985	1	83864	1	84262	1
78020	1	78494	1	80174	2	82104	1	82552	3	83008	1	83866	1	84255	2
78070	1	78496	1	80176	1	82105	1	82553	3	83009	1	83872	2	84260	1
78075	1	78580	1	80178	2	82108	1	82565	2	83010	1	83873	1	84270	1
78102	1	78584	2	80182	2	82120	1	82570	3	83012	1	83880	1	84275	1
78103	1	78585	2	80184	2	82131	3	82575	1	83013	1	83885	2	84285	1
78104	1	78586	1	80185	2	82135	1	82585	1	83014	1	83887	2	84300	2
78110	1	78587	1	80186	2	82136	3	82595	1	83015	1	83915	1	84305	1
78111	1	78588	1	80188	2	82139	3	82600	1	83020	2	83916	2	84307	1
78120	1	78591	1	80190	2	82140	2	82607	1	83021	2	83918	2	84315	2
78121	1	78593	1	80192	2	82143	2	82608	1	83026	1	83919	1	84375	1
78122	1	78594	1	80194	2	82145	1	82615	1	83030	1	83921	2	84376	1
78130	1	78596	1	80195	2	82154	1	82626	1	83033	1	83930	2	84377	1
78135	1	78601	1	80197	2	82157	1	82627	1	83036	1	83935	2	84378	2
78140	1	78607	1	80198	2	82160	1	82633	1	83037	1	83937	1	84379	1
78185	1	78608	1	80200	2	82163	1	82634	2	83045	1	83945	2	84392	1
78190	1	78610	1	80201	2	82164	1	82638	1	83051	1	83950	1	84402	1
78191	1	78630	2	80202	2	82172	3	82646	1	83055	1	83986	2	84403	2
78195	1	78635	1	80400	1	82175	2	82649	1	83060	1	83992	2	84425	1
78201	1	78645	1	80402	1	82180	1	82651	1	83065	1	84022	2	84432	1
78202	1	78647	1	80406	1	82232	2	82652	1	83068	1	84030	1	84436	1
78205	1	78650	1	80408	1	82239	1	82654	1	83069	1	84035	1	84437	1
78206	1	78660	1	80410	1	82240	1	82656	1	83070	1	84060	1	84439	1

CPT	MUE	CPT	MUE	CPT	MUE	CPT	MUE	CPT	MUE	CPT	MUE	CPT	MUE	CPT	MUE
84442	1	85280	2	86146	3	86663	2	87073	3	87485	2	88140	1	89344	1
84445	1	85290	2	86148	1	86664	2	87084	2	87486	2	88141	1	89346	1
84446	1	85291	2	86155	1	86665	2	87086	3	87487	2	88142	1	89352	1
84449	1	85292	2	86156	1	86668	2	87103	3	87490	2	88143	1	89353	1
84450	1	85293	2	86157	1	86674	3	87109	3	87491	2	88147	1	89354	1
84460	1	85300	2	86161	3	86677	3	87110	2	87492	2	88148	1	89356	2
84466	1	85301	2	86162	1	86684	2	87118	3	87495	2	88150	1	90465	1
84478	1	85302	2	86171	2	86687	2	87143	2	87496	2	88152	1	90467	1
84479	1	85303	2	86200	1	86688	2	87164	2	87497	2	88153	1	90468	3
84480	1	85305	2	86215	1	86689	2	87166	2	87510	2	88154	1	90471	1
84481	1	85306	2	86225	1	86692	2	87168	2	87511	2	88155	1	90473	1
84482	1	85307	2	86226	1	86694	2	87169	2	87512	2	88164	1	90474	1
84484	2	85335	2	86243	1	86695	2	87172	2	87515	2	88165	1	90760	2
84485	1	85337	1	86277	1	86696	2	87177	3	87516	2	88166	1	90768	2
84488	1	85345	2	86280	1	86698	3	87197	1	87517	2	88167	1	90773	2
84490	1	85348	1	86294	1	86701	2	87207	3	87520	2	88174	1	90774	2
84510	1	85360	1	86301	1	86702	2	87220	3	87521	2	88175	1	90801	1
84512	1	85362	2	86304	1	86703	2	87230	3	87522	2	88184	1	90802	1
84525	1	85366	2	86308	1	86704	1	87250	3	87525	2	88321	1	90804	1
84540	2	85370	2	86309	1	86705	1	87255	2	87526	2	88323	1	90805	1
84545	1	85378	2	86310	1	86706	2	87260	2	87527	2	88325	1	90806	1
84550	1	85379	2	86316	3	86707	2	87265	2	87528	2	88400	1	90807	1
84560	2	85380	2	86320	1	86708	1	87267	2	87529	2	89049	1	90808	1
84577	1	85384	2	86325	2	86709	1	87269	3	87530	2	89050	2	90809	1
84578	1	85385	1	86327	1	86713	3	87270	2	87531	2	89051	2	90810	1
84580	1	85390	3	86332	1	86720	2	87271	2	87532	2	89055	2	90811	1
84583	1	85396	1	86334	1	86723	2	87272	3	87533	2	89060	2	90812	1
84585	1	85400	2	86335	2	86727	2	87273	2	87534	2	89100	1	90813	1
84586	1	85410	2	86336	1	86732	2	87274	2	87535	2	89105	1	90814	1
84588	2	85415	2	86337	1	86738	2	87275	2	87536	2	89125	2	90815	1
84590	1	85420	2	86340	1	86741	2	87276	2	87537	2	89130	1	90816	1
84597	1	85421	2	86341	1	86744	2	87277	2	87538	2	89132	1	90817	1
84600	2	85441	1	86343	1	86747	2	87278	3	87539	2	89135	1	90818	1
84620	1	85445	1	86344	1	86756	2	87280	2	87540	2	89136	1	90819	1
84630	2	85460	1	86355	1	86759	2	87283	2	87541	2	89140	1	90821	1
84702	2	85461	1	86357	1	86762	2	87285	2	87542	2	89141	1	90822	1
84703	1	85475	1	86359	1	86774	2	87290	2	87550	2	89160	1	90823	1
84830	1	85525	2	86360	1	86777	2	87301	2	87551	2	89190	1	90824	1
85002	1	85530	1	86361	1	86778	2	87320	2	87552	2	89220	1	90826	1
85004	2	85536	1	86367	1	86781	2	87324	3	87557	2	89225	1	90827	1
85007	1	85540	1	86376	2	86784	2	87327	2	87560	2	89230	1	90828	1
85008	1	85547	1	86378	1	86787	2	87328	3	87561	2	89235	1	90829	1
85009	1	85549	1	86382	3	86793	2	87329	3	87562	2	89250	1	90845	1
85013	2	85555	1	86384	1	86800	1	87332	2	87580	2	89251	1	90846	1
85025	2	85557	1	86406	2	86803	2	87335	2	87581	2	89253	1	90847	1
85032	3	85597	2	86430	2	86804	1	87336	3	87582	2	89254	1	90849	1
85041	2	85611	2	86431	2	86807	1	87337	3	87590	3	89255	1	90853	1
85044	1	85612	1	86480	1	86808	1	87338	1	87591	3	89257	1	90857	1
85045	1	85613	1	86485	1	86812	1	87339	1	87592	2	89258	1	90862	1
85046	1	85635	1	86490	1	86816	1	87340	1	87620	2	89259	1	90865	1
85048	2	85651	1	86510	1	86817	1	87341	1	87621	3	89260	1	90870	1
85049	2	85652	1	86580	1	86821	3	87350	1	87622	2	89261	1	90880	1
85055	1	85660	1	86590	1	86822	3	87380	1	87650	1	89264	1	90911	1
85060	1	85670	2	86592	2	86850	3	87385	2	87651	1	89268	1	90935	1
85097	2	85675	1	86593	2	86860	2	87390	2	87652	1	89272	1	90937	1
85130	2	85705	1	86602	3	86885	3	87391	2	87660	1	89280	1	90940	2
85170	1	85810	2	86603	2	86906	1	87400	2	87802	2	89281	1	90945	1
85175	1	86021	1	86612	1	86930	2	87420	2	87803	3	89290	1	90947	1
85210	2	86022	1	86617	2	86940	1	87425	2	87804	2	89291	1	90989	1
85220	2	86023	2	86618	2	86941	1	87427	3	87807	2	89300	1	90993	1
85230	2	86038	1	86619	2	86945	3	87430	2	87810	2	89310	1	90997	1
85240	2	86039	1	86625	2	86950	1	87470	2	87850	1	89320	1	91000	1
85244	2	86060	1	86628	3	86960	3	87471	2	87880	2	89321	1	91010	1
85245	2	86063	1	86632	3	86975	2	87472	2	87900	1	89325	1	91011	1
85246	2	86077	1	86641	2	86976	2	87475	2	87901	1	89329	1	91012	1
85247	2	86078	1	86645	1	86977	2	87476	2	87902	1	89330	1	91020	1
85250	2	86079	1	86648	2	87001	1	87477	2	87903	1	89335	1	91022	1
85260	2	86140	1	86651	2	87003	1	87480	2	88125	1	89342	1	91030	1
85270	2	86141	1	86654	2	87045	3	87482	2	88130	1	89343	1	91034	1

CPT	MUE	CPT	MUE	CPT	MUE	CPT	MUE	CPT	MUE	CPT	MUE	CPT	MUE	CPT	MUE
91035	1	92553	1	93017	2	93562	3	93930	1	95812	1	96416	1	99244	1
91037	1	92555	1	93018	2	93571	1	93931	1	95813	1	96420	2	99245	1
91038	1	92556	1	93024	1	93572	2	93965	1	95816	1	96425	1	99251	1
91040	1	92557	1	93025	1	93580	1	93970	1	95819	1	96440	1	99252	1
91052	1	92561	1	93040	3	93581	1	93971	1	95822	1	96445	1	99253	1
91055	1	92562	1	93041	2	93600	1	93975	1	95824	1	96450	1	99254	1
91065	1	92563	1	93042	3	93602	1	93976	1	95827	1	96521	2	99255	1
91100	1	92564	1	93224	1	93603	1	93978	1	95829	1	96522	1	99281	1
91105	2	92565	1	93225	1	93609	1	93979	1	95830	1	96523	1	99282	1
91110	1	92567	1	93226	1	93610	1	93980	1	95857	1	96542	1	99283	1
91111	1	92568	1	93227	1	93612	1	93981	1	95860	1	96567	1	99284	1
91120	1	92569	1	93230	1	93613	1	93990	2	95861	1	96570	1	99285	1
91122	1	92571	1	93231	1	93615	1	94010	1	95863	1	96900	1	99289	1
91132	1	92572	1	93232	1	93616	1	94014	1	95864	1	96910	1	99291	1
91133	1	92575	1	93233	1	93618	1	94015	1	95865	1	96912	1	99293	1
92002	1	92576	1	93235	1	93619	1	94016	1	95866	2	96913	1	99294	1
92004	1	92577	1	93236	1	93620	1	94060	1	95867	1	96920	1	99295	1
92012	1	92579	1	93237	1	93621	1	94070	1	95868	1	96921	1	99296	1
92014	1	92582	1	93268	1	93622	1	94200	1	95869	1	96922	1	99298	1
92018	1	92583	1	93270	1	93623	1	94240	1	95873	1	97545	1	99299	1
92019	1	92584	1	93271	1	93624	1	94250	1	95874	1	97546	2	99300	1
92020	1	92585	1	93272	1	93631	1	94260	1	95875	2	98925	1	99304	1
92060	1	92586	1	93278	1	93640	1	94350	1	95921	1	98926	1	99305	1
92065	1	92587	1	93303	1	93641	1	94360	1	95922	1	98927	1	99306	1
92070	2	92588	1	93304	1	93642	1	94370	1	95923	1	98928	1	99307	1
92081	1	92596	1	93307	1	93650	1	94375	1	95925	1	98929	1	99308	1
92082	1	92601	1	93308	2	93651	1	94400	1	95926	1	98940	1	99309	1
92083	1	92602	1	93312	2	93652	1	94450	1	95927	1	98941	1	99310	1
92100	1	92603	1	93313	2	93660	1	94452	1	95928	1	98942	1	99315	1
92120	1	92604	1	93314	2	93662	1	94453	1	95929	1	99082	1	99316	1
92130	1	92613	1	93315	2	93701	1	94620	1	95930	1	99143	1	99318	1
92135	2	92615	1	93316	2	93720	2	94621	1	95933	1	99144	1	99324	1
92140	1	92617	1	93317	2	93721	2	94642	1	95950	1	99148	1	99325	1
92225	2	92620	1	93318	2	93722	1	94660	1	95951	1	99149	1	99326	1
92226	2	92625	1	93320	1	93724	2	94662	1	95953	1	99170	1	99327	1
92230	2	92626	1	93321	1	93727	2	94664	2	95954	1	99175	1	99328	1
92235	2	92628	1	93325	1	93731	2	94667	1	95955	1	99183	2	99334	1
92240	2	92953	2	93350	1	93732	2	94680	1	95956	1	99185	1	99335	1
92250	1	92960	2	93501	2	93733	2	94681	1	95957	1	99186	1	99336	1
92260	1	92961	1	93503	2	93734	2	94690	1	95958	1	99195	2	99337	1
92270	1	92970	1	93505	1	93735	2	94720	1	95961	1	99201	1	99341	1
92275	1	92971	1	93508	2	93736	2	94725	1	95965	1	99202	1	99342	1
92283	1	92975	1	93510	2	93741	2	94750	1	95966	1	99203	1	99343	1
92284	1	92977	1	93511	1	93742	2	94760	1	95967	3	99204	1	99344	1
92285	1	92978	1	93514	1	93743	2	94761	1	95970	1	99205	1	99345	1
92286	1	92979	2	93524	1	93744	2	94762	1	95971	1	99211	1	99347	1
92287	1	92980	1	93526	2	93745	1	94770	1	95972	1	99217	1	99348	1
92311	1	92981	2	93527	1	93784	1	94772	1	95974	1	99218	1	99349	1
92312	1	92982	1	93528	1	93786	1	95056	1	95975	2	99219	1	99350	1
92315	1	92984	2	93529	1	93788	1	95060	1	95978	1	99220	1	99354	1
92316	1	92986	1	93530	1	93790	1	95065	1	95990	2	99221	1	99356	1
92502	1	92987	1	93531	1	93875	1	95070	1	95991	2	99222	1	99431	1
92504	1	92990	1	93532	1	93880	1	95071	1	96000	1	99223	1	99432	1
92511	1	92992	1	93533	1	93882	1	95075	1	96001	1	99231	1	99433	1
92512	1	92993	1	93539	2	93886	1	95115	1	96002	1	99232	1	99435	1
92516	1	92995	1	93540	2	93888	1	95117	1	96003	1	99233	1	99436	1
92520	1	92996	2	93541	1	93890	1	95250	1	96004	1	99234	1	99440	1
92541	1	92997	1	93542	1	93892	1	95251	1	96103	1	99235	1	99455	1
92542	1	92998	2	93543	1	93893	1	95805	1	96120	1	99236	1	99456	1
92544	1	93000	3	93544	1	93922	2	95806	1	96402	2	99238	1	99477	1
92545	1	93005	3	93545	2	93923	1	95807	1	96405	1	99239	1		
92546	1	93012	1	93555	2	93924	1	95808	1	96406	1	99241	1		
92548	1	93014	1	93556	2	93925	1	95810	1	96409	2	99242	1		
92552	1	93015	2	93561	1	93926	1	95811	1	96413	2	99243	1		
		93016	2												

OPPS

CPT	MUE	CPT	MUE	CPT	MUE	CPT	MUE	CPT	MUE	CPT	MUE	CPT	MUE	CPT	MUE
0016T	2	11720	1	14300	3	15851	1	19396	2	21243	2	22103	3	23515	2
0017T	2	11721	1	15002	1	15852	2	20150	2	21244	1	22222	1	23520	2
0026T	1	11730	1	15004	1	15860	1	20526	2	21245	2	22305	1	23525	2
0027T	1	11770	1	15040	1	15876	1	20552	1	21246	2	22310	1	23530	2
0041T	1	11771	1	15050	1	15877	1	20553	1	21260	1	22315	1	23532	2
0043T	1	11772	1	15100	1	15878	2	20662	1	21261	1	22505	1	23540	2
0046T	2	11900	1	15110	1	15879	2	20663	2	21263	1	22520	1	23545	2
0047T	2	11901	1	15115	1	15920	1	20665	1	21267	2	22521	1	23550	2
0058T	1	11920	1	15120	1	15922	1	20900	2	21270	2	22523	1	23552	2
0059T	1	11921	1	15130	1	15931	1	20912	1	21275	1	22524	1	23570	2
0062T	1	11922	1	15135	1	15933	1	20920	2	21280	2	22612	1	23575	2
0063T	1	11950	1	15150	1	15934	1	20922	2	21282	2	22900	3	23585	2
0064T	1	11951	1	15151	1	15935	1	20926	2	21295	2	23000	2	23600	2
0067T	1	11952	1	15155	1	15936	1	20972	2	21296	2	23020	2	23605	2
0071T	1	11954	1	15156	1	15937	1	20973	2	21310	1	23030	2	23615	2
0072T	1	11960	3	15170	1	15940	2	20974	1	21315	1	23031	2	23616	2
0073T	2	11970	2	15175	1	15941	2	20975	2	21320	1	23035	2	23620	2
0084T	1	11971	2	15200	1	15944	2	20979	1	21325	1	23040	2	23625	2
0085T	1	11976	1	15220	1	15945	2	20982	1	21330	1	23044	2	23630	2
0087T	1	11980	1	15240	1	15946	2	21015	2	21335	1	23065	2	23650	2
0088T	1	11981	1	15260	1	15950	2	21025	2	21336	1	23066	2	23655	2
0089T	1	11982	1	15300	1	15951	2	21026	2	21337	1	23076	2	23660	2
0099T	2	11983	1	15320	1	15952	2	21029	2	21338	1	23100	2	23665	2
0100T	2	12001	1	15330	1	15953	2	21030	2	21339	1	23101	2	23670	2
0101T	1	12002	1	15335	1	15956	2	21031	2	21340	1	23105	2	23675	2
0102T	2	12004	1	15340	1	15958	2	21032	1	21345	1	23106	2	23680	2
0103T	1	12005	1	15360	1	16000	1	21034	1	21355	2	23107	2	23700	2
0104T	1	12006	1	15365	1	16020	1	21040	2	21356	2	23120	2	23800	2
0105T	1	12007	1	15400	1	16025	1	21044	1	21390	2	23125	2	23802	2
0111T	1	12011	1	15420	1	16030	1	21046	2	21400	2	23130	2	23921	2
0123T	2	12013	1	15430	1	17000	1	21047	2	21401	2	23150	1	23930	2
0124T	2	12014	1	15570	3	17004	1	21048	2	21406	2	23155	1	23931	2
0137T	1	12015	1	15572	2	17106	1	21049	2	21407	2	23156	1	23935	2
0140T	1	12016	1	15574	2	17107	1	21076	1	21408	2	23170	1	24000	2
0144T	1	12017	1	15576	2	17108	1	21077	2	21421	1	23172	1	24006	2
0145T	1	12018	1	15600	2	17110	1	21079	1	21440	2	23174	1	24065	2
0146T	1	12020	3	15610	2	17111	1	21080	1	21445	2	23180	1	24066	2
0147T	1	12021	3	15620	2	17276	3	21081	1	21450	1	23182	1	24077	2
0148T	1	12031	1	15630	2	17286	3	21082	1	21451	1	23184	1	24100	2
0149T	1	12032	1	15650	1	17340	1	21083	1	21452	1	23190	1	24101	2
0150T	1	12034	1	15740	3	17360	1	21084	1	21453	1	23195	1	24102	2
0151T	1	12035	1	15750	2	19000	2	21085	2	21454	1	23330	2	24105	2
0177T	2	12036	1	15760	2	19020	2	21086	2	21461	1	23331	2	24115	2
10040	1	12037	1	15770	2	19296	2	21087	1	21462	1	23395	1	24120	2
10060	1	12041	1	15775	1	19297	2	21088	1	21465	2	23397	1	24130	2
10061	1	12042	1	15776	1	19298	2	21100	1	21470	1	23400	1	24138	2
10080	1	12044	1	15780	1	19300	2	21110	2	21480	2	23405	2	24140	2
10081	1	12045	1	15786	1	19301	2	21120	1	21485	2	23406	2	24145	2
10180	3	12046	1	15787	3	19302	2	21121	1	21490	2	23410	2	24147	2
11000	1	12047	1	15788	1	19303	2	21122	1	21495	1	23412	2	24149	2
11010	1	12051	1	15789	1	19304	2	21123	1	21497	1	23415	2	24150	1
11011	1	12052	1	15819	1	19307	2	21125	2	21501	3	23420	2	24152	1
11012	1	12053	1	15824	1	19316	2	21127	2	21557	1	23430	2	24153	1
11055	1	12054	1	15825	1	19318	2	21137	1	21685	1	23440	2	24155	2
11056	1	12055	1	15826	1	19324	2	21138	1	21700	2	23450	2	24160	2
11057	1	12056	1	15828	1	19325	2	21139	1	21720	1	23455	2	24164	2
11100	1	12057	1	15830	1	19328	2	21150	1	21725	1	23460	2	24200	3
11200	1	13100	1	15832	2	19330	2	21175	1	21742	1	23462	2	24201	3
11201	1	13101	1	15833	2	19340	2	21181	1	21743	1	23465	2	24300	2
11446	3	13120	1	15834	2	19342	2	21195	1	21805	3	23466	2	24301	2
11450	2	13121	1	15835	1	19350	2	21198	1	21820	1	23470	2	24320	2
11451	2	13131	1	15836	2	19355	1	21199	1	21920	3	23480	2	24330	2
11462	2	13132	1	15838	1	19357	2	21206	1	21925	3	23485	2	24331	2
11463	2	13150	1	15841	2	19366	2	21215	2	21935	1	23490	2	24332	2
11646	3	13151	1	15842	2	19370	2	21235	2	22100	1	23491	2	24340	2
11719	1	13152	1	15845	2	19371	2	21240	2	22101	1	23500	2	24342	2
		13160	3	15850	1	19380	2	21242	2	22102	1	23505	2	24343	2

CPT	MUE	CPT	MUE	CPT	MUE	CPT	MUE	CPT	MUE	CPT	MUE	CPT	MUE	CPT	MUE
24344	2	25130	2	25624	2	26550	2	27332	2	27560	2	27792	2	28238	2
24345	2	25135	2	25628	2	26555	2	27333	2	27562	2	27808	2	28240	2
24346	2	25136	2	25630	2	26560	2	27334	2	27566	2	27810	2	28250	2
24360	2	25210	2	25635	2	26561	2	27335	2	27570	2	27814	2	28260	2
24361	2	25215	2	25650	2	26562	2	27340	2	27594	2	27816	2	28261	2
24362	2	25230	2	25651	2	26580	2	27345	2	27600	2	27818	2	28262	2
24363	2	25240	2	25652	2	26641	2	27347	2	27601	2	27822	2	28264	2
24365	2	25250	2	25660	2	26645	2	27350	2	27602	2	27823	2	28280	2
24366	2	25251	2	25670	2	26650	2	27355	2	27604	2	27824	2	28286	2
24400	2	25259	2	25671	2	26665	2	27356	2	27605	2	27825	2	28289	2
24410	2	25300	2	25675	2	26740	3	27357	2	27606	2	27826	2	28290	2
24420	2	25301	2	25676	2	26742	3	27358	2	27607	2	27827	2	28292	2
24430	2	25315	2	25680	2	26746	3	27380	2	27610	2	27828	2	28293	2
24435	2	25316	2	25685	2	26820	2	27381	2	27612	2	27829	2	28294	2
24470	2	25320	2	25690	2	26841	2	27385	2	27615	2	27830	2	28296	2
24495	2	25332	2	25695	2	26842	2	27386	2	27620	2	27831	2	28297	2
24498	2	25335	2	25800	2	26860	1	27390	2	27625	2	27832	2	28298	2
24500	2	25337	2	25805	2	26862	1	27391	1	27626	2	27840	2	28299	2
24505	2	25350	2	25810	2	26990	2	27392	1	27630	2	27842	2	28300	2
24515	2	25355	2	25020	2	26991	2	27393	2	27635	2	27846	2	28302	2
24516	2	25360	2	25825	2	27000	2	27394	1	27637	2	27848	2	28304	2
24530	2	25365	2	25830	2	27033	2	27395	1	27638	2	27860	2	28305	2
24535	2	25370	2	25907	2	27035	2	27396	2	27640	2	27870	2	28306	2
24538	2	25375	2	25922	2	27040	2	27397	2	27641	2	27871	2	28307	2
24545	2	25390	2	25929	2	27041	3	27400	2	27647	2	27884	2	28309	2
24546	2	25391	2	26010	3	27048	2	27403	2	27650	2	27889	2	28310	2
24560	2	25392	2	26011	3	27049	2	27405	2	27652	2	27892	2	28315	2
24565	2	25393	2	26025	2	27050	2	27407	2	27654	2	27893	2	28320	2
24576	2	25394	2	26030	2	27052	2	27409	2	27656	2	27894	2	28322	2
24577	2	25400	2	26034	2	27060	2	27412	2	27658	2	28001	2	28340	2
24586	2	25405	2	26035	3	27062	2	27415	2	27659	2	28002	3	28341	2
24587	2	25415	2	20037	2	27005	2	27410	2	27664	2	28003	2	28344	2
24600	2	25420	2	26040	2	27066	2	27420	2	27665	2	28005	3	28360	2
24605	2	25425	2	26045	2	27067	2	27422	2	27675	2	28035	2	28400	2
24615	2	25426	2	26070	3	27080	1	27424	2	27676	2	28052	2	28405	2
24620	2	25430	2	26100	2	27086	2	27425	2	27680	3	28054	2	28406	2
24635	2	25440	2	26105	2	27087	2	27427	2	27681	2	28060	2	28415	2
24640	2	25441	2	26110	3	27097	2	27428	2	27685	2	28062	2	28420	2
24650	2	25442	2	20117	2	27090	2	27429	2	27686	2	28086	2	28430	2
24655	2	25443	2	26121	2	27100	2	27430	2	27687	2	28088	2	28435	2
24665	2	25444	2	26123	2	27105	2	27435	2	27690	2	28090	2	28436	2
24666	2	25445	2	26185	1	27110	2	27437	2	27691	2	28092	2	28445	2
24670	2	25446	2	26205	2	27111	2	27438	2	27695	2	28100	2	28490	2
24675	2	25449	2	26215	2	27193	1	27440	2	27696	2	28102	2	28495	2
24685	2	25450	2	26230	3	27194	1	27441	2	27698	2	28103	2	28496	2
24800	2	25455	2	26236	3	27200	1	27442	2	27700	2	28106	2	28505	2
24802	2	25490	2	26250	2	27202	1	27443	2	27704	2	28107	2	28530	2
24925	2	25491	2	26255	2	27216	1	27446	2	27705	2	28108	2	28531	2
24935	2	25492	2	26260	2	27220	2	27475	2	27707	2	28110	2	28540	2
25000	2	25500	2	26261	2	27230	2	27496	2	27709	2	28111	2	28545	2
25001	2	25505	2	26262	2	27235	2	27497	2	27730	2	28113	2	28546	2
25020	2	25515	2	26357	3	27238	2	27498	2	27732	2	28114	2	28555	2
25023	2	25520	2	26358	3	27246	2	27499	2	27734	2	28116	2	28570	2
25024	2	25525	2	26390	3	27250	2	27500	2	27740	2	28118	2	28575	2
25025	2	25526	2	26392	3	27252	3	27501	2	27742	2	28119	2	28576	2
25035	2	25530	2	26416	2	27256	2	27502	2	27745	2	28120	2	28585	2
25040	2	25535	2	26428	2	27257	2	27503	2	27750	2	28130	2	28600	3
25077	2	25545	2	26432	2	27265	2	27508	2	27752	2	28171	2	28605	3
25085	2	25560	2	26433	2	27266	2	27509	2	27756	2	28173	2	28630	3
25100	2	25565	2	26434	3	27275	2	27510	2	27758	2	28175	2	28705	2
25101	2	25574	2	26494	2	27305	2	27516	2	27759	2	28192	2	28715	2
25105	2	25575	2	26496	2	27306	2	27517	2	27760	2	28193	2	28725	2
25107	2	25600	2	26497	2	27307	2	27520	2	27762	2	28202	2	28730	2
25111	2	25605	2	26498	2	27310	2	27524	2	27766	2	28210	2	28735	2
25112	2	25606	2	26508	2	27325	1	27530	2	27780	2	28220	2	28737	2
25115	2	25607	2	26516	2	27326	1	27532	2	27781	2	28222	2	28750	2
25116	2	25608	2	26517	2	27329	2	27538	2	27784	2	28225	2	28755	2
25119	2	25609	2	26518	2	27330	2	27550	2	27786	2	28226	2	28760	2
25120	2	25622	2	26548	3	27331	2	27552	2	27700	2	28230	2	28890	2

CPT	MUE	CPT	MUE	CPT	MUE	CPT	MUE	CPT	MUE	CPT	MUE	CPT	MUE	CPT	MUE
29000	1	29838	2	30430	1	31529	1	32960	1	35879	2	36860	2	40761	1
29010	1	29840	2	30435	1	31530	1	33010	1	35881	2	36861	2	40800	1
29015	1	29843	2	30450	1	31531	1	33011	1	35903	2	36870	2	40801	1
29020	1	29844	2	30460	1	31535	1	33206	1	36002	2	37183	1	40806	2
29025	1	29845	2	30462	1	31536	1	33207	1	36260	1	37184	2	40816	2
29035	1	29846	2	30520	1	31540	1	33208	1	36261	1	37188	2	40818	2
29040	1	29847	2	30540	1	31541	1	33210	1	36262	1	37195	1	40819	2
29044	1	29848	2	30545	1	31545	2	33211	1	36420	2	37200	2	40820	2
29046	1	29850	2	30560	1	31546	2	33212	1	36425	3	37201	1	40830	1
29049	1	29851	2	30580	2	31560	1	33213	1	36430	1	37203	2	40831	2
29055	1	29855	2	30600	1	31561	1	33214	1	36450	1	37205	2	40840	1
29065	2	29856	2	30620	1	31570	1	33215	2	36455	1	37207	1	40842	1
29075	2	29860	2	30630	1	31571	1	33216	1	36468	1	37209	2	40843	1
29085	2	29861	2	30801	1	31575	1	33217	1	36469	1	37250	1	40844	1
29086	2	29862	2	30802	1	31576	1	33218	1	36470	2	37500	2	40845	1
29105	2	29863	2	30905	1	31577	1	33220	1	36471	2	37565	2	41000	1
29125	2	29866	2	30906	1	31578	1	33222	1	36475	2	37600	1	41005	1
29126	2	29867	2	30915	1	31579	1	33223	1	36478	2	37605	2	41008	2
29200	1	29868	2	30920	1	31580	1	33224	1	36479	2	37606	2	41009	2
29220	1	29870	2	31002	2	31582	1	33225	1	36511	1	37607	1	41010	1
29240	2	29871	2	31040	2	31588	1	33226	1	36512	1	37609	2	41015	2
29260	2	29873	2	31050	2	31590	1	33233	1	36513	1	37615	2	41016	1
29280	2	29874	2	31051	2	31595	2	33234	1	36514	1	37620	1	41017	2
29305	1	29875	2	31070	2	31600	1	33235	1	36515	1	37760	2	41018	2
29325	1	29876	2	31075	2	31601	1	33240	1	36516	1	37765	2	41100	3
29345	2	29877	2	31080	2	31603	1	33241	1	36522	1	37766	2	41105	3
29355	2	29879	2	31081	2	31605	1	33244	1	36555	2	37790	1	41108	2
29358	2	29880	2	31084	2	31610	1	33249	1	36556	2	38120	1	41110	2
29365	2	29881	2	31085	2	31611	1	33282	1	36557	2	38205	1	41114	2
29405	2	29882	2	31086	2	31612	1	33284	1	36558	2	38206	1	41115	1
29425	2	29883	2	31087	2	31613	1	34101	2	36560	2	38220	2	41116	3
29435	2	29884	2	31090	2	31614	1	34111	2	36561	2	38221	2	41120	1
29440	2	29885	2	31200	2	31615	1	34201	2	36563	2	38230	1	41251	2
29445	2	29886	2	31201	2	31620	1	34203	2	36565	2	38240	1	41252	2
29450	2	29887	2	31205	2	31622	1	34421	2	36566	2	38241	1	41500	1
29505	2	29888	2	31231	1	31623	1	34490	2	36568	2	38242	1	41510	1
29515	2	29889	2	31233	2	31624	1	34501	2	36569	3	38300	2	41520	1
29520	2	29891	2	31235	2	31625	1	34520	1	36570	2	38305	2	41800	2
29530	2	29892	2	31237	2	31628	1	34530	2	36571	2	38308	1	41822	1
29540	2	29893	2	31238	2	31629	1	35011	2	36575	2	38500	2	41823	1
29550	2	29894	2	31239	2	31630	2	35180	2	36576	2	38505	3	41825	2
29580	2	29895	2	31240	2	31631	1	35184	2	36578	2	38510	2	41826	2
29590	2	29897	2	31254	2	31635	1	35188	2	36580	2	38520	2	41827	2
29700	2	29898	2	31255	2	31636	1	35190	2	36581	2	38525	2	41850	2
29705	2	29899	2	31256	2	31637	2	35201	2	36582	2	38530	2	42000	1
29710	2	29900	2	31267	2	31638	2	35206	2	36583	2	38542	2	42100	3
29715	1	29901	2	31276	2	31640	1	35226	3	36584	2	38550	1	42104	3
29720	1	29902	2	31287	2	31641	1	35231	2	36585	2	38555	1	42106	2
29730	2	30000	1	31288	2	31643	1	35236	2	36589	2	38570	1	42107	2
29740	1	30020	1	31292	2	31645	1	35256	2	36590	2	38571	1	42120	1
29800	2	30100	3	31293	2	31656	1	35266	2	36595	2	38572	1	42140	1
29804	2	30117	2	31294	2	31717	1	35286	2	36596	2	38700	1	42145	1
29805	2	30118	2	31300	1	31720	2	35321	2	36597	2	38740	2	42180	1
29806	2	30120	1	31320	1	31730	1	35459	2	36598	2	38745	2	42182	1
29807	2	30124	2	31400	1	31750	1	35471	3	36640	1	38792	2	42200	1
29819	2	30125	1	31420	1	31755	1	35472	1	36680	1	39400	1	42205	1
29820	2	30130	2	31500	2	31785	1	35474	2	36800	1	40500	2	42210	1
29821	2	30140	2	31502	1	31820	1	35485	2	36810	1	40510	2	42215	1
29822	2	30150	1	31505	1	31825	1	35491	1	36815	1	40520	2	42220	1
29823	2	30160	1	31510	1	31830	1	35492	2	36820	2	40525	2	42225	1
29824	2	30200	1	31511	1	32400	2	35493	2	36821	2	40527	2	42226	1
29825	2	30210	1	31512	1	32405	2	35495	2	36825	1	40530	2	42227	1
29826	2	30220	1	31513	1	32420	2	35500	2	36830	2	40650	2	42235	1
29827	2	30300	1	31515	1	32601	1	35685	2	36831	1	40652	2	42260	1
29830	2	30310	1	31520	1	32602	1	35686	1	36832	2	40654	2	42280	1
29834	2	30320	1	31525	1	32603	1	35761	2	36833	1	40700	1	42281	1
29835	2	30400	1	31526	1	32604	1	35860	2	36834	1	40701	1	42300	2
29836	2	30410	1	31527	1	32605	1	35875	2	36835	1	40702	1	42305	2
29837	2	30420	1	31528	1	32606	1	35876	2	36838	2	40720	1	42310	2

© 2008 Ingenix

Appendix J — Medically unlikely Edits (MUEs) — OPPS

CPT	MUE	CPT	MUE	CPT	MUE	CPT	MUE	CPT	MUE	CPT	MUE	CPT	MUE	CPT	MUE
42320	2	43235	1	44372	1	45541	1	46947	1	50541	2	52240	1	53275	1
42330	3	43236	1	44373	1	45560	1	47000	3	50542	2	52250	1	53400	1
42335	2	43237	1	44376	1	45900	1	47011	3	50543	2	52260	1	53405	1
42340	2	43238	1	44377	1	45905	1	47370	1	50544	2	52265	1	53410	1
42405	2	43239	1	44378	1	45910	1	47371	1	50551	2	52270	1	53420	1
42408	1	43240	1	44379	1	45915	1	47382	1	50553	2	52275	1	53425	1
42409	1	43241	1	44380	1	45990	1	47490	1	50557	2	52276	1	53430	1
42410	2	43242	1	44382	1	46020	1	47510	2	50561	2	52277	1	53431	1
42415	1	43243	1	44383	1	46030	1	47511	2	50570	2	52281	1	53440	1
42420	2	43244	1	44385	1	46040	2	47525	3	50572	2	52282	1	53442	1
42425	2	43245	1	44386	1	46045	2	47530	3	50575	2	52283	1	53444	1
42440	2	43246	1	44388	1	46050	2	47552	1	50576	2	52285	1	53445	1
42507	1	43247	1	44389	1	46060	2	47553	1	50590	1	52290	1	53446	1
42508	1	43248	1	44390	1	46070	1	47554	1	50686	2	52300	1	53447	1
42509	1	43249	1	44392	1	46080	1	47555	1	50688	2	52301	1	53449	1
42510	1	43250	1	44393	1	46083	2	47556	1	50945	2	52305	1	53450	1
42600	1	43251	1	44394	1	46200	1	47560	1	50947	2	52310	1	53460	1
42650	2	43255	2	44397	1	46210	1	47561	1	50948	2	52315	2	53500	1
42660	2	43256	1	44500	1	46211	1	47562	1	50951	2	52317	1	53502	1
42665	2	43257	1	44901	1	46220	2	47563	1	50953	2	52318	1	53505	1
42700	2	43258	1	44970	1	46221	1	47564	1	50955	2	52320	2	53510	1
42725	2	43259	1	45000	1	46230	1	47630	1	50957	2	52325	2	53515	1
42800	3	43260	1	45005	1	46250	1	48102	2	50961	2	52327	2	53520	1
42802	2	43261	1	45020	1	46255	1	48511	1	50970	2	52330	2	53600	1
42806	1	43262	2	45100	1	46257	1	49021	3	50972	2	52334	2	53601	1
42808	2	43263	2	45100	1	46258	1	49041	3	50974	2	52341	2	53605	1
42809	1	43264	1	45150	1	46260	1	49061	3	50976	2	52342	2	53620	1
42810	2	43265	1	45160	1	46261	1	49080	1	50980	2	52343	2	53621	1
42815	2	43267	1	45170	1	46262	1	49081	2	51020	1	52344	2	53660	1
42820	1	43268	2	45190	1	46270	1	49180	3	51030	1	52345	2	53661	1
42821	1	43269	2	45300	1	46275	1	49250	1	51040	1	52346	2	53665	1
42825	1	43271	1	45303	1	46280	1	49320	1	51045	2	52351	1	53850	1
42826	1	43272	1	45305	1	46285	1	49321	1	51050	1	52352	2	53852	1
42830	1	43280	1	45307	1	46288	1	49322	1	51065	1	52353	2	53853	1
42831	1	43450	1	45308	1	46320	2	49323	1	51080	2	52354	2	54000	1
42835	1	43453	1	45309	1	46500	1	49324	1	51500	1	52355	2	54001	1
42836	1	43456	1	45315	1	46505	1	49402	1	51520	1	52400	1	54015	1
42842	1	43458	1	45320	1	46600	1	49419	1	51700	1	52402	1	54050	1
42844	1	43510	1	45321	1	46604	1	49421	1	51701	2	52450	1	54055	1
42860	1	43600	1	45327	1	46606	1	49422	1	51702	2	52500	1	54056	1
42870	1	43651	1	45330	1	46608	1	49423	3	51703	2	52601	1	54057	1
42890	1	43652	1	45331	1	46610	1	49426	1	51705	2	52606	1	54060	1
42892	1	43653	1	45332	1	46611	1	49429	1	51710	1	52612	1	54065	1
42900	1	43752	2	45333	1	46612	1	49525	2	51715	1	52614	1	54100	3
42950	1	43760	2	45334	1	46614	1	49540	1	51720	1	52620	1	54105	2
42955	1	43761	2	45335	1	46615	1	49550	2	51725	1	52630	1	54110	1
42960	1	43830	1	45337	1	46700	1	49553	2	51726	1	52640	1	54111	1
42962	1	43831	1	45338	1	46706	2	49555	2	51736	1	52647	1	54112	1
42970	2	43870	1	45339	1	46750	1	49557	2	51741	1	52648	1	54115	1
42972	1	43886	1	45340	1	46753	1	49570	1	51772	1	52700	1	54120	1
43020	1	43887	1	45341	1	46754	1	49572	1	51784	1	53000	1	54150	1
43030	1	43888	1	45342	1	46760	1	49580	1	51785	1	53010	1	54160	1
43130	1	44100	1	45345	1	46761	1	49582	1	51792	1	53020	1	54161	1
43200	1	44180	1	45355	1	46762	1	49585	1	51795	1	53025	1	54162	1
43201	1	44186	1	45378	1	46900	1	49587	1	51797	1	53040	1	54163	1
43202	1	44206	1	45379	1	46910	1	49600	1	51798	1	53060	1	54164	1
43204	1	44207	1	45380	1	46916	1	50020	1	51880	1	53080	1	54200	1
43205	1	44208	1	45381	1	46917	1	50021	2	51990	1	53085	1	54205	1
43215	1	44213	1	45382	2	46922	1	50080	2	51992	1	53200	1	54220	1
43216	1	44312	1	45383	1	46924	1	50081	2	52000	1	53210	1	54231	1
43217	1	44340	1	45384	1	46934	1	50200	2	52001	1	53215	1	54235	1
43219	1	44360	1	45385	1	46935	1	50389	2	52005	2	53220	1	54240	1
43220	1	44361	1	45386	1	46936	1	50390	2	52007	2	53230	1	54250	1
43226	1	44363	1	45387	1	46937	1	50391	2	52010	1	53235	1	54300	1
43227	2	44364	1	45391	1	46938	1	50392	2	52204	1	53240	1	54304	1
43228	1	44365	1	45392	1	46940	1	50393	2	52214	1	53250	1	54308	1
43231	1	44366	1	45500	1	46942	1	50395	2	52224	1	53260	1	54312	1
43232	1	44369	1	45505	1	46945	1	50396	2	52234	1	53265	1	54316	1
43234	1	44370	1	45520	1	46946	1	50398	2	52235	1	53270	1	54318	1

Appendix J — Medically unlikely Edits (MUEs) — OPPS

CPT	MUE	CPT	MUE	CPT	MUE	CPT	MUE	CPT	MUE	CPT	MUE	CPT	MUE	CPT	MUE
54322	1	55876	1	57454	1	58925	1	62281	1	64508	2	64861	2	65820	2
54324	1	56405	2	57455	1	58970	1	62282	1	64510	2	64862	2	65850	2
54326	1	56420	1	57456	1	58974	1	62287	1	64517	1	64864	2	65855	2
54328	1	56440	1	57460	1	58976	2	62292	1	64520	2	64865	1	65860	2
54340	1	56441	1	57461	1	59025	1	62310	2	64530	2	64870	1	65865	2
54344	1	56442	1	57500	1	59051	1	62311	2	64553	1	64872	3	65870	2
54348	1	56501	1	57505	1	59100	1	62318	1	64555	2	64874	1	65875	2
54352	1	56515	1	57510	1	59150	1	62319	1	64560	1	64876	1	65880	2
54360	1	56605	1	57511	1	59151	1	62350	1	64561	2	64885	1	65900	2
54380	1	56620	1	57513	1	59160	1	62351	1	64565	2	64886	1	65920	2
54385	1	56625	1	57520	1	59300	1	62355	1	64573	1	64890	3	65930	2
54400	1	56700	1	57522	1	59320	1	62360	1	64575	2	64891	2	66020	2
54401	1	56740	2	57530	1	59412	2	62361	1	64577	1	64895	2	66030	2
54405	1	56800	1	57550	1	59414	1	62362	1	64580	2	64898	2	66130	2
54406	1	56805	1	57555	1	59812	1	62365	1	64581	2	64901	2	66150	2
54408	1	56810	1	57556	1	59820	1	62367	1	64585	2	64905	1	66155	2
54410	1	56820	1	57558	1	59821	1	62368	1	64590	1	64907	1	66160	2
54415	1	56821	1	57700	1	59840	1	63001	1	64595	1	65091	2	66165	2
54416	1	57000	1	57720	1	59841	1	63003	1	64600	2	65093	2	66170	2
54420	1	57010	1	57800	1	59866	1	63005	1	64605	2	65101	2	66172	2
54435	1	57020	1	58100	1	59870	1	63011	1	64610	2	65103	2	66180	2
54440	1	57022	2	58110	1	59871	1	63012	1	64612	2	65105	2	66185	2
54450	1	57023	2	58120	1	60000	1	63015	1	64630	1	65110	2	66220	2
54500	2	57061	1	58145	1	60200	2	63016	1	64650	1	65112	2	66225	2
54512	2	57065	1	58260	1	60210	1	63017	1	64653	1	65114	2	66250	2
54522	2	57100	3	58262	1	60212	1	63045	1	64680	1	65125	2	66500	2
54530	2	57105	2	58263	1	60220	1	63046	1	64681	1	65130	2	66505	2
54600	2	57106	1	58270	1	60225	1	63047	1	64702	2	65135	2	66600	2
54620	1	57107	1	58290	1	60240	1	63055	1	64712	2	65140	2	66605	2
54670	2	57109	1	58291	1	60252	1	63056	1	64713	2	65150	2	66625	2
54680	1	57120	1	58292	1	60260	1	63064	1	64714	2	65155	2	66630	2
54690	2	57130	1	58294	1	60280	1	63066	3	64718	2	65175	2	66635	2
54692	2	57135	2	58301	1	60281	1	63075	1	64719	2	65205	2	66680	2
54700	2	57150	1	58321	1	60500	1	63600	2	64721	2	65210	2	66682	2
54800	2	57155	1	58322	1	60502	1	63610	1	64726	2	65220	2	66700	2
54830	2	57160	1	58323	1	60512	1	63615	1	64727	3	65222	2	66710	2
54840	2	57170	1	58345	2	60520	1	63650	2	64732	2	65235	2	66711	2
54860	1	57180	1	58346	1	61000	1	63655	1	64734	2	65260	2	66720	2
54861	1	57200	1	58350	2	61001	1	63660	1	64736	2	65265	2	66740	2
54865	1	57210	1	58353	1	61020	2	63685	2	64738	2	65270	2	66761	2
54900	1	57220	1	58356	1	61026	2	63688	2	64740	2	65272	2	66762	2
54901	1	57230	1	58541	1	61050	1	63741	1	64742	2	65275	2	66770	2
55000	2	57240	1	58542	1	61055	1	63744	1	64744	2	65280	2	66820	2
55040	1	57250	1	58545	1	61070	2	63746	1	64746	2	65285	2	66821	2
55041	1	57260	1	58546	1	61215	1	64402	2	64761	1	65286	2	66825	2
55060	2	57265	1	58550	1	61334	2	64405	2	64771	2	65290	2	66830	2
55100	2	57267	3	58552	1	61623	2	64408	2	64772	2	65400	2	66840	2
55110	1	57268	1	58553	1	61626	2	64410	2	64774	3	65410	2	66850	2
55120	1	57282	1	58554	1	61720	2	64412	2	64776	1	65420	2	66852	2
55150	1	57283	1	58555	1	61790	2	64413	2	64778	3	65426	2	66920	2
55175	1	57284	1	58558	1	61791	2	64415	2	64782	2	65430	2	66930	2
55180	1	57287	1	58559	1	61795	2	64416	2	64783	2	65435	2	66940	2
55200	1	57288	1	58560	1	61880	1	64417	2	64786	2	65436	2	66982	2
55250	1	57289	1	58561	1	61885	2	64418	2	64790	1	65450	2	66983	2
55450	1	57291	1	58562	1	61886	1	64420	3	64792	2	65600	2	66984	2
55500	2	57292	1	58563	1	61888	2	64421	3	64795	2	65710	2	66985	2
55520	2	57295	1	58565	1	62160	1	64425	2	64821	2	65730	2	66986	2
55530	2	57300	1	58600	1	62194	2	64430	2	64822	2	65750	2	67005	2
55535	2	57310	1	58615	1	62225	2	64435	2	64823	2	65755	2	67010	2
55540	2	57320	1	58660	1	62230	2	64445	2	64831	2	65770	2	67015	2
55550	2	57330	1	58661	1	62252	2	64446	2	64834	2	65772	2	67025	2
55680	2	57335	1	58662	1	62263	1	64447	2	64835	2	65775	2	67027	2
55700	1	57400	1	58670	1	62264	1	64448	2	64836	2	65780	2	67028	2
55705	1	57410	1	58671	1	62268	1	64449	2	64837	3	65781	2	67030	2
55720	1	57415	1	58770	2	62269	2	64470	2	64840	2	65782	2	67031	2
55725	1	57420	1	58800	1	62270	2	64475	2	64856	2	65800	2	67036	2
55860	1	57421	1	58820	2	62272	2	64479	2	64857	3	65805	2	67039	2
55870	1	57425	1	58900	1	62273	2	64483	2	64858	2	65810	2	67040	2
55873	1	57452	1	58920	1	62280	1	64505	2	64859	2	65815	2	67101	2

© 2008 Ingenix

CPT	MUE	CPT	MUE	CPT	MUE	CPT	MUE	CPT	MUE	CPT	MUE	CPT	MUE	CPT	MUE
67105	2	67909	2	69511	1	70240	1	71551	1	73200	2	74291	1	75860	2
67107	2	67912	2	69530	1	70250	1	71552	1	73201	2	74300	1	75870	1
67108	2	67938	2	69540	2	70260	1	72010	1	73202	2	74301	2	75872	1
67110	2	67950	2	69550	1	70300	1	72040	3	73206	2	74305	1	75880	2
67112	2	67971	2	69552	1	70310	1	72050	1	73218	2	74320	1	75885	1
67115	2	67973	2	69601	1	70320	1	72052	1	73219	2	74327	1	75887	1
67120	2	67974	2	69602	1	70328	1	72069	1	73220	2	74340	1	75889	1
67121	2	67975	2	69603	1	70330	1	72070	1	73221	2	74355	1	75891	1
67141	2	68020	2	69604	1	70332	2	72072	1	73222	2	74360	1	75901	1
67145	2	68040	2	69605	1	70336	1	72074	1	73223	2	74363	2	75902	2
67208	2	68100	2	69610	2	70350	1	72080	1	73500	2	74400	1	75940	1
67210	2	68110	2	69620	2	70355	1	72090	1	73510	1	74410	1	75945	1
67218	2	68115	2	69631	2	70360	1	72100	1	73520	1	74415	1	75962	1
67220	2	68130	2	69632	1	70370	1	72110	1	73525	2	74420	2	75966	1
67221	1	68135	2	69633	1	70371	1	72114	1	73530	2	74425	1	75970	2
67225	1	68200	2	69635	1	70373	1	72120	1	73540	1	74430	1	75980	1
67227	2	68320	2	69636	1	70380	2	72125	1	73542	2	74440	2	75982	2
67250	2	68325	2	69637	1	70390	2	72126	1	73550	2	74445	1	75984	2
67255	2	68326	2	69641	1	70450	3	72127	1	73560	2	74450	1	75992	1
67311	2	68328	2	69642	1	70460	1	72128	1	73562	2	74455	1	75994	2
67312	2	68330	2	69643	1	70470	2	72129	1	73564	2	74470	2	75995	1
67314	2	68335	2	69644	1	70480	1	72130	1	73565	1	74475	2	75996	2
67316	2	68340	2	69645	1	70481	1	72131	1	73580	2	74480	2	76000	3
67318	2	68360	2	69646	1	70482	1	72132	1	73590	2	74485	2	76010	1
67320	2	68362	2	69650	1	70486	1	72133	1	73592	2	74710	1	76080	2
67331	2	68371	1	69660	1	70487	1	72141	1	73600	2	74740	1	76100	2
67332	2	68400	2	69661	1	70488	1	72142	1	73610	2	74742	2	76101	1
67334	2	68420	2	69662	2	70490	1	72146	1	73615	2	74775	1	76102	1
67335	2	68440	2	69666	2	70491	1	72147	1	73620	2	75600	1	76120	1
67340	2	68500	2	69667	2	70492	1	72148	1	73630	2	75605	1	76125	1
67343	2	68505	2	69670	1	70496	1	72149	1	73650	2	75625	1	76376	2
67345	2	68510	2	69700	2	70498	1	72156	1	73660	2	75630	1	76377	2
67400	2	68520	2	69711	2	70540	1	72157	1	73700	2	75635	1	76380	2
67405	2	68525	2	69714	2	70542	1	72158	1	73701	2	75650	2	76506	1
67412	2	68530	2	69715	1	70543	1	72170	1	73702	2	75658	2	76510	2
67413	2	68540	1	69717	1	70544	1	72190	1	73706	2	75660	1	76511	2
67414	2	68550	1	69718	1	70545	1	72191	1	73718	2	75662	1	76512	2
67415	2	68700	2	69720	2	70546	1	72192	1	73719	2	75665	1	76513	2
67420	2	68705	2	69725	2	70547	1	72193	1	73720	2	75671	1	76514	1
67430	2	68720	2	69740	2	70548	1	72194	1	73722	2	75676	1	76516	1
67440	2	68745	2	69745	2	70549	1	72195	1	74000	3	75680	1	76519	1
67445	2	68750	2	69801	1	70551	1	72196	1	74010	2	75685	2	76529	2
67450	2	68770	2	69802	1	70552	1	72197	1	74020	2	75710	1	76536	1
67500	2	68840	2	69805	1	70553	1	72200	1	74022	2	75716	1	76604	1
67505	2	69000	2	69806	1	70554	1	72202	1	74150	1	75722	1	76645	1
67515	2	69005	2	69820	1	70557	1	72220	1	74160	1	75724	1	76700	1
67550	2	69020	2	69840	1	70558	1	72240	1	74170	1	75726	1	76705	1
67560	2	69100	3	69905	1	70559	1	72255	1	74175	1	75731	1	76770	1
67570	2	69105	2	69910	1	71015	2	72265	1	74181	1	75733	1	76775	2
67710	2	69110	2	69915	1	71021	1	72270	1	74182	1	75736	1	76776	1
67715	2	69120	1	69930	2	71022	1	72292	3	74183	1	75741	1	76800	1
67800	1	69140	2	69955	2	71023	2	73000	2	74190	1	75743	1	76801	1
67801	1	69145	2	69960	2	71030	2	73010	2	74210	1	75746	1	76802	3
67805	1	69150	1	70010	1	71034	1	73020	2	74220	1	75756	2	76805	1
67808	1	69200	2	70015	1	71035	2	73030	2	74230	1	75790	2	76810	3
67820	2	69205	2	70030	2	71040	1	73040	2	74235	1	75801	1	76811	1
67825	2	69210	1	70100	1	71060	1	73050	1	74240	1	75803	1	76812	3
67830	3	69310	2	70110	1	71090	1	73060	2	74241	1	75805	1	76814	3
67835	2	69320	2	70120	2	71100	1	73070	2	74245	1	75807	1	76815	1
67875	2	69400	2	70130	2	71101	1	73080	2	74246	1	75809	1	76817	1
67880	2	69401	2	70134	1	71110	1	73085	2	74247	1	75810	1	76830	1
67882	2	69405	2	70140	1	71111	1	73090	2	74249	1	75820	1	76831	1
67900	2	69420	2	70150	1	71120	1	73092	2	74250	1	75822	1	76856	1
67901	2	69421	2	70160	1	71130	1	73100	2	74251	1	75825	1	76857	1
67902	2	69440	2	70170	2	71250	1	73110	2	74260	1	75827	1	76870	1
67903	2	69450	2	70190	1	71260	1	73115	2	74270	1	75831	1	76872	1
67904	2	69501	1	70200	1	71270	1	73120	2	74280	1	75833	1	76873	1
67906	2	69502	1	70210	1	71275	1	73130	2	74283	1	75840	1	76880	2
67908	2	69505	1	70220	1	71550	1	73140	2	74290	1	75842	1	76885	1

Appendix J — Medically unlikely Edits (MUEs) — OPPS

CPT	MUE	CPT	MUE	CPT	MUE	CPT	MUE	CPT	MUE	CPT	MUE	CPT	MUE	CPT	MUE
76886	1	77778	1	78459	1	80069	1	82000	1	82436	1	82943	1	83700	1
76930	1	77781	3	78460	1	80074	1	82003	3	82438	1	82946	1	83701	1
76932	1	77782	3	78461	1	80076	1	82009	3	82441	1	82950	3	83704	1
76936	2	77783	3	78464	1	80150	2	82013	1	82465	1	82951	1	83718	1
76940	1	77784	3	78465	1	80152	2	82016	1	82480	2	82952	3	83719	1
76942	1	77789	2	78466	1	80154	2	82017	1	82482	1	82953	1	83721	1
76945	1	78000	1	78468	1	80156	2	82030	1	82485	1	82955	1	83727	1
76946	1	78001	1	78469	1	80157	2	82040	1	82495	1	82960	1	83775	1
76948	1	78003	1	78472	1	80158	3	82042	2	82507	1	82963	1	83785	1
76950	2	78006	1	78473	1	80160	2	82043	1	82520	2	82965	1	83805	1
76965	2	78007	1	78478	1	80162	2	82044	1	82523	1	82975	1	83825	2
76970	1	78010	1	78480	1	80164	2	82045	2	82525	2	82977	1	83835	2
76975	1	78011	1	78481	1	80166	2	82055	3	82528	1	82978	1	83840	2
76977	1	78015	1	78483	1	80170	2	82085	1	82530	2	82979	1	83857	1
76998	1	78016	1	78491	1	80172	2	82101	1	82540	1	82980	1	83858	1
77011	1	78018	1	78492	1	80173	2	82103	1	82550	3	82985	1	83864	1
77014	2	78020	1	78494	1	80174	2	82104	1	82552	3	83008	1	83866	1
77022	1	78070	1	78496	1	80176	1	82105	1	82553	3	83009	1	83872	2
77053	2	78075	1	78580	1	80178	2	82108	1	82565	3	83010	1	83873	1
77054	2	78102	1	78584	2	80182	2	82120	1	82570	3	83012	1	83880	1
77071	1	78103	1	78585	2	80184	2	82131	3	82575	3	83013	1	83885	2
77280	2	78104	1	78586	1	80185	2	82135	1	82585	1	83014	1	83887	2
77285	1	78110	1	78587	1	80186	2	82136	3	82595	1	83015	1	83915	1
77290	1	78111	1	78588	1	80188	2	82139	3	82600	1	83020	2	83916	2
77295	1	78120	1	78591	1	80190	2	82140	2	82607	1	83021	2	83918	2
77301	1	78121	1	78593	1	80192	2	82143	2	82608	1	83026	1	83919	1
77305	2	78122	1	78594	1	80194	2	82145	1	82615	1	83030	1	83921	2
77310	2	78130	1	78596	1	80195	2	82154	1	82626	1	83033	1	83930	1
77315	2	78135	1	78601	1	80197	2	82157	1	82627	1	83036	1	83935	2
77321	1	78140	1	78607	1	80198	2	82160	1	82633	1	83037	1	83937	1
77326	1	78185	1	78608	1	80200	2	82163	1	82634	2	83045	1	83945	2
77327	1	78190	1	78610	1	80201	2	82164	1	82638	1	83051	1	83950	1
77328	1	78191	1	78630	2	80202	2	82172	3	82646	1	83055	1	83986	2
77336	1	78195	1	78635	1	80400	1	82175	2	82649	1	83060	1	83992	2
77370	1	78201	1	78645	1	80402	1	82180	1	82651	1	83065	1	84022	2
77401	2	78202	1	78647	1	80406	1	82232	2	82652	1	83068	1	84030	1
77402	2	78205	1	78650	1	80408	1	82239	1	82654	1	83069	1	84035	1
77403	2	78206	1	78660	1	80410	1	82240	1	82656	1	83070	1	84060	1
77404	2	78215	1	78700	1	80412	1	82247	2	82657	3	83071	1	84061	1
77406	2	78216	1	78701	2	80414	1	82248	2	82666	1	83080	2	84066	1
77407	2	78220	1	78707	1	80415	1	82252	1	82668	1	83088	1	84075	2
77408	2	78223	1	78708	1	80416	1	82261	1	82670	2	83090	2	84078	1
77409	2	78230	1	78709	1	80417	1	82270	1	82671	1	83150	1	84080	1
77411	2	78231	1	78725	1	80418	1	82271	3	82672	1	83491	1	84081	1
77412	2	78232	1	78730	1	80420	1	82272	1	82677	1	83497	1	84085	1
77413	2	78258	1	78740	1	80422	1	82274	1	82679	1	83498	2	84087	1
77414	2	78261	1	78761	1	80424	1	82286	1	82690	1	83499	1	84100	3
77416	2	78262	1	78800	1	80426	1	82300	1	82693	2	83500	1	84105	1
77417	1	78264	1	78801	1	80428	1	82306	1	82696	1	83505	1	84106	1
77418	2	78267	1	78802	1	80430	1	82307	1	82705	1	83527	1	84110	1
77421	2	78268	1	78803	1	80432	1	82308	3	82710	1	83528	1	84119	1
77422	1	78270	1	78804	1	80434	1	82331	1	82715	1	83540	2	84120	1
77423	1	78271	1	78805	1	80435	1	82340	1	82725	1	83550	1	84126	1
77470	1	78272	1	78806	1	80436	1	82355	3	82726	1	83570	1	84127	1
77520	1	78278	2	78807	1	80438	1	82360	3	82728	1	83582	1	84133	2
77522	1	78282	1	78811	1	80439	1	82365	3	82731	1	83586	1	84134	1
77523	1	78290	1	78812	1	80440	1	82370	3	82735	1	83593	1	84135	1
77525	1	78291	1	78813	1	80500	1	82373	1	82742	1	83605	3	84138	1
77600	1	78300	1	78814	1	80502	1	82374	3	82746	1	83615	3	84140	1
77605	1	78305	1	78815	1	81000	2	82378	2	82747	1	83625	1	84143	2
77610	1	78306	1	78816	1	81001	2	82379	1	82757	1	83630	1	84144	1
77615	1	78315	1	79005	1	81002	2	82380	1	82759	1	83631	1	84146	3
77620	1	78320	1	79101	1	81003	2	82382	1	82760	1	83632	1	84150	2
77750	1	78414	1	79200	1	81005	2	82383	1	82775	1	83633	1	84152	1
77761	1	78428	1	79403	1	81007	1	82384	2	82776	1	83634	1	84153	1
77762	1	78445	1	79445	1	81015	1	82387	1	82785	1	83655	2	84154	1
77763	1	78456	1	80048	2	81020	1	82390	1	82820	1	83670	1	84155	1
77776	1	78457	1	80053	1	81025	1	82415	1	82928	1	83690	2	84156	1
77777	1	78458	1	80061	1	81050	2	82435	3	82941	1	83695	1	84157	3

© 2008 Ingenix

CPT	MUE	CPT	MUE	CPT	MUE	CPT	MUE	CPT	MUE	CPT	MUE	CPT	MUE	CPT	MUE
84160	2	84597	1	85445	1	86344	1	86756	2	87280	2	87540	2	89140	1
84163	1	84600	2	85460	1	86355	1	86759	2	87283	2	87541	2	89141	1
84165	1	84620	1	85461	1	86357	1	86762	2	87285	2	87542	2	89160	1
84166	2	84630	2	85475	1	86359	1	86774	2	87290	2	87550	2	89190	1
84202	1	84702	2	85525	2	86360	1	86777	2	87301	2	87551	2	89220	2
84203	1	84703	1	85530	1	86361	1	86778	2	87320	2	87552	2	89225	1
84206	1	84830	1	85536	1	86367	2	86781	2	87324	3	87557	2	89230	1
84207	1	85002	2	85540	1	86376	2	86784	2	87327	2	87560	2	89235	1
84210	2	85004	2	85547	1	86378	1	86787	2	87328	3	87561	2	89250	1
84220	1	85007	1	85549	1	86382	3	86793	2	87329	3	87562	2	89251	1
84228	1	85008	2	85555	1	86384	1	86800	1	87332	2	87580	2	89253	1
84233	2	85009	1	85557	1	86406	2	86803	2	87335	2	87581	2	89254	1
84234	2	85013	2	85597	2	86430	2	86804	1	87336	3	87582	2	89255	1
84235	1	85025	2	85611	2	86431	2	86807	2	87337	3	87590	3	89257	1
84238	3	85032	3	85612	1	86480	1	86808	1	87338	2	87591	3	89258	1
84252	1	85041	2	85613	1	86485	1	86812	1	87339	1	87592	2	89259	1
84255	2	85044	1	85635	1	86490	1	86816	1	87340	1	87620	2	89260	1
84260	1	85045	1	85651	1	86510	1	86817	1	87341	1	87621	3	89261	1
84270	1	85046	1	85652	1	86580	1	86821	3	87350	1	87622	2	89264	1
84275	1	85048	2	85660	1	86590	1	86822	3	87380	1	87650	1	89268	1
84285	1	85049	2	85670	2	86592	2	86850	3	87385	2	87651	1	89272	1
84300	2	85055	1	85675	1	86593	2	86860	2	87390	2	87652	1	89280	1
84305	1	85097	2	85705	1	86602	3	86885	3	87391	2	87660	1	89281	1
84307	1	85130	2	85810	2	86603	2	86906	1	87400	2	87802	2	89290	1
84315	2	85170	1	86021	1	86612	2	86930	3	87420	2	87803	3	89291	1
84375	1	85175	1	86022	1	86617	2	86940	3	87425	2	87804	2	89300	1
84376	1	85210	2	86023	2	86618	2	86941	3	87427	3	87807	2	89310	1
84377	1	85220	2	86038	1	86619	2	86945	3	87430	2	87810	2	89320	1
84378	2	85230	2	86039	1	86625	2	86950	1	87470	2	87850	1	89321	1
84379	1	85240	3	86060	1	86628	3	86960	3	87471	2	87880	2	89325	1
84392	1	85244	2	86063	1	86632	3	86975	2	87472	2	87900	1	89329	1
84402	1	85245	2	86077	1	86641	2	86976	2	87475	2	87901	1	89330	1
84403	2	85246	2	86078	1	86645	1	86977	2	87476	2	87902	1	89335	1
84425	1	85247	2	86079	1	86648	2	87001	1	87477	2	87903	1	89342	1
84432	1	85250	2	86140	1	86651	2	87003	1	87480	2	88125	1	89343	1
84436	1	85260	2	86141	1	86654	2	87045	3	87482	2	88130	1	89344	1
84437	1	85270	2	86146	3	86663	2	87073	3	87485	2	88140	1	89346	1
84439	1	85280	2	86148	1	86664	2	87084	2	87486	2	88142	1	89352	1
84442	1	85290	2	86155	1	86665	2	87086	3	87487	2	88143	1	89353	1
84445	1	85291	2	86156	1	86668	2	87103	3	87490	2	88147	1	89354	1
84446	1	85292	2	86157	1	86674	3	87109	3	87491	2	88148	1	89356	2
84449	1	85293	2	86160	3	86677	3	87110	2	87492	2	88150	1	90471	1
84450	1	85300	2	86162	1	86684	2	87118	3	87495	2	88152	1	90473	1
84460	1	85301	2	86171	3	86687	2	87143	2	87496	2	88153	1	90474	1
84466	1	85302	2	86200	1	86688	2	87164	2	87497	2	88154	1	90760	2
84478	1	85303	2	86215	1	86689	2	87166	2	87510	2	88155	1	90773	3
84479	1	85305	2	86225	1	86692	2	87168	2	87511	2	88164	1	90774	2
84480	1	85306	2	86226	1	86694	2	87169	2	87512	2	88165	1	90801	2
84481	1	85307	2	86243	1	86695	2	87172	2	87515	2	88166	1	90802	2
84482	1	85335	2	86277	1	86696	2	87177	3	87516	2	88167	1	90804	2
84484	3	85337	1	86280	1	86698	3	87197	1	87517	2	88174	1	90805	2
84485	1	85345	2	86294	1	86701	2	87207	3	87520	2	88175	1	90806	2
84488	1	85348	2	86301	1	86702	2	87220	3	87521	2	88184	1	90807	2
84490	1	85360	1	86304	1	86703	2	87230	3	87522	2	88321	1	90808	2
84510	1	85362	2	86308	1	86704	1	87250	3	87525	2	88323	1	90809	2
84512	3	85366	2	86309	1	86705	1	87255	2	87526	2	88325	1	90810	2
84525	1	85370	2	86310	1	86706	1	87260	2	87527	2	88400	1	90811	2
84540	2	85378	2	86316	3	86707	2	87265	2	87528	2	89049	1	90812	2
84545	1	85379	2	86320	1	86708	1	87267	2	87529	2	89050	2	90813	2
84550	1	85380	2	86325	2	86709	1	87269	3	87530	2	89051	2	90814	2
84560	2	85384	2	86327	1	86713	3	87270	2	87531	2	89055	2	90815	2
84577	1	85385	1	86332	1	86720	2	87271	2	87532	2	89060	2	90816	2
84578	1	85390	3	86334	1	86723	2	87272	3	87533	2	89100	1	90817	2
84580	1	85400	2	86335	2	86727	2	87273	2	87534	2	89105	1	90818	2
84583	1	85410	2	86336	1	86732	2	87274	2	87535	2	89125	2	90819	2
84585	1	85415	2	86337	1	86738	2	87275	2	87536	2	89130	1	90821	2
84586	1	85420	2	86340	1	86741	2	87276	2	87537	2	89132	1	90822	2
84588	2	85421	2	86341	1	86744	2	87277	2	87538	2	89135	1	90823	2
84590	1	85441	1	86343	1	86747	2	87278	3	87539	2	89136	1	90824	2

CPT	MUE	CPT	MUE	CPT	MUE	CPT	MUE	CPT	MUE	CPT	MUE	CPT	MUE	CPT	MUE
90826	2	92083	1	92577	1	93308	2	93660	1	94150	2	95829	1	96405	1
90827	2	92120	1	92579	1	93312	2	93662	1	94200	1	95857	1	96406	1
90828	2	92130	1	92582	1	93313	2	93701	1	94240	1	95860	1	96409	2
90829	2	92135	2	92583	1	93315	2	93721	2	94250	1	95861	1	96413	2
90845	1	92140	1	92584	1	93316	2	93724	2	94260	1	95863	1	96416	1
90846	1	92225	2	92585	1	93318	2	93727	2	94350	1	95864	1	96420	2
90847	1	92226	2	92586	1	93320	1	93731	2	94360	1	95865	1	96425	1
90849	1	92230	2	92587	1	93321	1	93732	2	94370	1	95866	2	96440	1
90853	3	92235	2	92588	1	93325	1	93733	2	94375	1	95867	1	96445	1
90857	3	92240	2	92596	1	93350	1	93734	2	94400	1	95868	1	96450	1
90862	1	92250	1	92601	1	93501	2	93735	2	94450	1	95869	1	96521	2
90865	1	92260	1	92602	1	93503	2	93736	2	94452	1	95873	1	96522	1
90870	1	92270	1	92603	1	93505	1	93740	1	94453	1	95874	1	96523	1
90880	1	92275	1	92604	1	93508	2	93741	2	94620	1	95875	2	96542	1
90911	1	92283	1	92613	1	93510	2	93742	2	94621	1	95921	1	96567	1
90935	1	92284	1	92620	1	93511	1	93743	2	94642	1	95922	1	96570	1
90945	1	92285	1	92625	1	93514	1	93744	2	94660	1	95923	1	96900	1
91000	1	92286	1	92626	1	93524	1	93745	1	94662	1	95925	1	96910	1
91010	1	92287	1	92953	2	93526	2	93786	1	94664	2	95926	1	96912	1
91011	1	92311	1	92960	2	93527	1	93788	1	94667	1	95927	1	96913	1
91012	1	92312	1	92961	1	93528	1	93875	1	94680	1	95928	1	96920	1
91020	1	92315	1	92977	1	93529	1	93880	1	94681	1	95929	1	96921	1
91022	1	92316	1	92978	1	93530	1	93882	1	94690	1	95930	1	96922	1
91030	1	92502	1	92979	2	93531	1	93886	1	94720	1	95933	1	97545	1
91034	1	92511	1	92980	1	93532	1	93888	1	94725	1	95950	1	97546	2
91035	1	92512	1	92981	2	93533	1	93890	1	94750	1	95951	1	98925	1
91037	1	92516	1	92982	1	93571	1	93892	1	94762	1	95953	1	98926	1
91038	1	92520	1	92984	2	93572	2	93893	1	94770	1	95954	1	98927	1
91040	1	92541	1	92986	1	93580	1	93922	2	94772	1	95955	1	98928	1
91052	1	92542	1	92987	1	93581	1	93923	1	95056	1	95956	1	98929	1
91055	1	92544	1	92990	1	93600	1	93924	1	95060	1	95957	1	98940	1
91065	1	92545	1	92995	1	93602	1	93925	1	95065	1	95958	1	98941	1
91100	1	92546	1	92996	2	93603	1	93926	1	95070	1	95961	1	98942	1
91105	2	92548	1	92997	1	93609	1	93930	1	95071	1	95965	1	99170	1
91110	1	92552	1	92998	2	93610	1	93931	1	95075	1	95966	1	99195	2
91111	1	92553	1	93005	3	93612	1	93965	1	95115	1	95967	3	99201	1
91120	1	92555	1	93017	2	93613	1	93970	1	95117	1	95970	1	99202	1
91122	1	92556	1	93024	1	93615	1	93971	1	95250	1	95971	1	99203	1
91132	1	92557	1	93025	1	93616	1	93975	1	95805	1	95972	1	99204	1
91133	1	92561	1	93041	3	93618	1	93976	1	95806	1	95974	1	99205	1
92002	1	92562	1	93225	1	93619	1	93978	1	95807	1	95975	2	99211	3
92004	1	92563	1	93226	1	93620	1	93979	1	95808	1	95978	1	99281	2
92012	1	92564	1	93231	1	93621	1	93980	1	95810	1	95990	2	99282	2
92014	1	92565	1	93232	1	93622	1	93981	1	95811	1	95991	2	99283	2
92018	1	92567	1	93236	1	93623	1	93990	2	95812	1	96000	1	99284	2
92019	1	92568	1	93270	1	93624	1	94010	1	95813	1	96001	1	99285	2
92020	1	92569	1	93271	1	93631	1	94014	1	95816	1	96002	1	99291	1
92060	1	92571	1	93278	1	93642	1	94015	1	95819	1	96003	1	99431	1
92065	1	92572	1	93303	1	93650	1	94016	1	95822	1	96103	1	99440	1
92081	1	92575	1	93304	1	93651	1	94060	1	95824	1	96120	1		
92082	1	92576	1	93307	1	93652	1	94070	1	95827	1	96402	2		